CONTENTS

Name Index on page 1119

Contents

Contents

110th Congress*

THE VICE PRESIDENT

RICHARD B. CHENEY, Republican, of Wyoming, born in Lincoln, NE, January 30, 1941; education: B.A., and M.A., degrees from the University of Wyoming; public service: served on the Cost of Living Council and Office of Economic Opportunity in the Nixon Administration; served as Assistant to the President and White House Chief of Staff for President Gerald R. Ford; elected to the U.S. House of Representatives in 1978, and re-elected 5 times, through 1988; in the House he served as Chairman of the House Republican Conference and House Minority Whip; in 1989 he was nominated to the Secretary of Defense by President George H.W. Bush, and was confirmed by the U.S. Senate; he served from 1989 to 1993; on July 3, 1991, President Bush awarded Secretary Cheney the Presidential Medal of Freedom; after leaving the Department of Defense, he joined the Halliburton Company serving as Chairman of the Board and Chief Executive Officer; religion: Methodist; family: married to Lynne Cheney, 1964; two daughters; elected Vice President of the United States on November 7, 2000; took the oath of office on January 20, 2001; reelected November 2, 2004.

The Ceremonial Office of the Vice President is S–212 in the Capitol. The Vice President has offices in the Dirksen Senate Office Building, the Eisenhower Executive Office Building (EEOB) and the White House (West Wing).

Chief of Staff to the Vice President and Counsel.—David Addington, EEOB, room 276, 456–9000.
Deputy Chief of Staff.—Claire O'Donnell, EEOB, room 272, 456–6770.
Counsel to the Vice President.—Shannen Coffin, EEOB, room 282, 456–9089.
Assistant to the Vice President for—
Communications/Press Secretary.—Lea Anne McBride, EEOB, room 293, 456–0373.
Domestic Policy.—Neil Patel, EEOB, room 286, 456–2728.
Legislative Affairs.—Brenda Becker, EEOB, room 285, 456–6774.
National Security Affairs.—John Hannah, EEOB, room 298, 456–9501.
Political Affairs.—Mel Raines, EEOB, room 272, 456–9033.
Executive Assistant to the Vice President.—Debra Heiden, West Wing, 456–7549.
Chief of Staff to Mrs. Cheney.—Cecelia Boyer, EEOB, room 200, 456–7458.
Deputy Assistant to the Vice President and Director of Scheduling.—Elizabeth Kleppe, EEOB, room 279, 456–6773.
Director of Correspondence.—Rose Folsom, EEOB, room 200, 456–9002.

*Biographies are based on information furnished or authorized by the respective Senators and Representatives.

ALABAMA

(Population 2000, 4,447,100)

SENATORS

RICHARD C. SHELBY, Republican, of Tuscaloosa, AL; born in Birmingham, AL, May 6, 1934; education: attended the public schools; A.B., University of Alabama, 1957; LL.B., University of Alabama School of Law, 1963; professional: attorney; admitted to the Alabama bar in 1961 and commenced practice in Tuscaloosa; member, Alabama State Senate, 1970–78; law clerk, Supreme Court of Alabama, 1961–62; city prosecutor, Tuscaloosa, 1963–71; U.S. Commissioner, Northern District of Alabama, 1966–70; special assistant Attorney General, State of Alabama, 1968–70; chairman, legislative council of the Alabama Legislature, 1977–78; former president, Tuscaloosa County Mental Health Association; member of Alabama Code Revision Committee, 1971–75; member: Phi Alpha Delta legal fraternity, Tuscaloosa County; Alabama and American bar associations; First Presbyterian Church of Tuscaloosa; Exchange Club; American Judicature Society; Alabama Law Institute; married: the former Annette Nevin in 1960; children: Richard C., Jr. and Claude Nevin; committees: ranking member, Appropriations; ranking member, Banking, Housing, and Urban Affairs; Special Committee on Aging; elected to the 96th Congress on November 7, 1978; reelected to the three succeeding Congresses; elected to the U.S. Senate on November 4, 1986; reelected to each succeeding Senate term.

Office Listings

http://shelby.senate.gov

110 Hart Senate Office Building, Washington, DC 20510 .... (202) 224–5744
Chief of Staff.—Shannon Hines. FAX: 224–3416
Personal Secretary / Appointments.—Anne Caldwell.
Press Secretary.—Katie Boyd.
1118 Greensboro Avenue #240, Tuscaloosa, AL 35403 .... (205) 759–5047
Federal Building, Room 321, 1800 5th Avenue North, Birmingham, AL 35203 ...... (205) 731–1384
308 U.S. Court House, 113 St. Joseph Street, Mobile, AL 36602 .... (251) 694–4164
Frank M. Johnson Federal Court House, Suite 208, 15 Lee Street, Montgomery, AL 36104 .... (334) 223–7303
Huntsville International Airport, 1000 Glenn Hearn Boulevard, Box 20127, Huntsville, AL 35824 .... (256) 772–0460

* * *

JEFF SESSIONS, Republican, of Mobile, AL; born in Hybart, AL, December 24, 1946; education: graduated Wilcox County High School, Camden, AL; B.A., Huntingdon College, Montgomery, AL, 1969; J.D., University of Alabama, Tuscaloosa, 1973; professional: U.S. Army Reserves, captain, 1973–86; attorney; admitted to the Alabama bar in 1973 and commenced practice for Guin, Bouldin and Porch in Russellville, 1973–75; Assistant U.S. Attorney, South District of Alabama, 1975–77; attorney for Stockman & Bedsole, 1977–81; U.S. Attorney, South District of Alabama, 1981–93; attorney for Stockman, Bedsole and Sessions, 1993–94; Attorney General, State of Alabama, 1994–96; member: Huntingdon College Board of Trustees; Samford University, Board of Overseers; delegate, General Conference, United Methodist Church; Montgomery Lions Club; Mobile United Methodist Inner City Mission; American Bar Association; Ashland Place United Methodist Church; married: the former Mary Blackshear, 1969; children: Ruth, Mary Abigail and Samuel; International Narcotics Control Caucus; committees: Armed Services; Budget; Energy and Natural Resources; Judiciary; elected to the U.S. Senate on November 5, 1996; reelected to each succeeding Senate term.

Office Listings

http://sessions.senate.gov

335 Russell Senate Office Building, Washington, DC 20510 .... (202) 224–4124
Chief of Staff.—Rick Dearborn. FAX: 224–3149
Scheduler.—Kate Hollis.
Executive Assistant.—Peggi Hanrahan.
Communications Director.—Mike Brumas.
341 Vance Federal Bldg., 1800 Fifth Avenue North, Birmingham, AL 35203 .... (205) 731–1500
Field Representative.—Lindsay Davis.
Colonial Bank Cntr., Suite 2300-A, 41 W. I–65 Service Rd. N., Mobile, AL 36608 (251) 414–3083
Field Representative.—Valerie Day.
200 Clinton Avenue, NW, Suite 802, Huntsville, AL 35801 .... (256) 533–0979
Field Representative.—Lisa Montgomery.
7550 Halcyon Summit Drive, Suite 150, Montgomery, AL 36117 .... (334) 244–7017

State Director.—Chuck Spurlock.

REPRESENTATIVES

FIRST DISTRICT

JO BONNER, Republican, of Mobile, AL; born in Selma, AL, November 19, 1959; education: B.A., in Journalism, University of Alabama, 1982; organizations: Rotary Club; Mobile Area Chamber of Commerce; University of Alabama Alumni Association; Leadership Mobile; Junior League of Mobile; International Committee for the Mobile Tricentennial; professional: congressional aide to Representative Sonny Callahan, serving as Press Secretary, 1985–89, and Chief of Staff, 1989–2002; married: Janee; children: Jennifer Lee and Josiah Robins, III; committees: Agriculture; Budget; Science and Technology; Standards of Official Conduct; elected to the 108th Congress on November 5, 2002; reelected to each succeeding Congress.

Office Listings

http://bonner.house.gov

315 Cannon House Office Building, Washington, DC 20515 .... (202) 225–4931
Chief of Staff.—Alan Spencer. FAX: 225–0562
Legislative Director.—Kelle Strickland.
Scheduler.—Suzanna Weeks.
1141 Montlimar Drive, Suite 3010, Mobile, AL 36609 .... (251) 690–2811
(800) 288–8721
1302 North McKenzie Street, Foley, AL 36535 .... (251) 943–2073

Counties: BALDWIN, CLARKE (part), ESCAMBIA, MOBILE, MONROE, WASHINGTON. Population (2000), 635,300.

ZIP Codes: 36420, 36425–27, 36432, 36436, 36439, 36441, 36444–46, 36451, 36456–58, 36460–62, 36470–71, 36475, 36480–83, 36502–05, 36507, 36509, 36511–13, 36515, 36518, 36521–30, 36532–33, 36535–36, 36538–39, 36541–45, 36547–51, 36553, 36555–56, 36558–62, 36564, 36567–69, 36571–72, 36575–85, 36587, 36590, 36601–13, 36615–19, 36621–22, 36628, 36633, 36640, 36652, 36660, 36663, 36670–71, 36685, 36688–89, 36691, 36693, 36695, 36720–23, 36726, 36728, 36741, 36751, 36762, 36768–69, 36784

* * *

SECOND DISTRICT

TERRY EVERETT, Republican, of Enterprise, AL; born in Dothan, AL, February 15, 1937; education: attended Enterprise State Junior College; professional: journalist; newspaper publisher; Premium Home Builders; Everett Land Development Company; Union Springs Newspapers, Inc.; owner and operator, Hickory Ridge Farms; Alabama Press Association; chairman of the board, Union Springs Newspapers, Inc.; married: Barbara Pitts Everett; committees: Agriculture; Armed Services; Permanent Select Committee on Intelligence; elected on November 3, 1992 to the 103rd Congress; reelected to each succeeding Congress.

Office Listings

http://www.house.gov/everett

2312 Rayburn House Office Building, Washington, DC 20515 .... (202) 225–2901
Chief of Staff.—Wade Heck. FAX: 225–8913
Legislative Director.—Forrest Allen.
Press Secretary.—Mike Lewis.
Scheduler.—Nancy Pack.
3500 Eastern Boulevard, No. 250, Montgomery, AL 36116 .... (334) 277–9113
256 Honeysuckle Road, Suite #15, Dothan, AL 36305 .... (334) 794–9680
101 North Main Street, Opp, AL 36467 .... (334) 493–9253

Counties: AUTAUGA, BARBOUR, BULLOCK, BUTLER, COFFEE, CONECUH, COVINGTON, CRENSHAW, DALE, ELMORE, GENEVA, HENRY, HOUSTON, LOWNDES, MONTGOMERY (part), PIKE. Population (2000), 635,300.

ZIP Codes: 35010, 36003, 36005–06, 36008–10, 36015–17, 36020, 36022, 36024–43, 36046–49, 36051–54, 36061–62, 36064–69, 36071–72, 36078–82, 36089, 36091–93, 36101–18, 36120–21, 36123–25, 36130, 36132, 36135, 36140–42, 36177, 36191, 36301–05, 36310–14, 36316–23, 36330–31, 36340, 36343–46, 36349–53, 36360–62, 36370–71, 36373–76, 36401, 36420, 36426, 36429, 36432, 36442, 36449, 36453–56, 36467, 36471, 36473–77, 36483, 36502, 36524, 36703, 36749, 36752, 36758, 36761, 36775, 36785

* * *

THIRD DISTRICT

MIKE ROGERS, Republican, of Saks, AL; born in Hammond, IN, July 16, 1958; education: B.A., Jacksonville State University, 1981; M.P.A., Jacksonville State University, 1984; J.D.,

Birmingham School of Law, 1991; professional: attorney; awards: Anniston Star Citizen of the Year, 1998; public service: Calhoun County Commissioner, 1987–91; Alabama House of Representatives, 1994–2002; family: married to Beth; children: Emily, Evan, and Elliot; committees: Agriculture; Armed Services; Homeland Security; elected to the 108th Congress on November 5, 2002; reelected to each succeeding Congress.

Office Listings

http://www/house.gov/mike-rogers

324 Cannon House Office Building, Washington, DC 20515 .... (202) 225–3261
Chief of Staff.—Marshall Macomber. FAX: 226–8485
Deputy Chief of Staff.—Chris Brinson.
Press Secretary.—Shea Snider.
Scheduler.—Laura Hooper.
1129 Noble Street, 104 Federal Building, Anniston, AL 36201 .... (256) 236–5655
District Director.—Sheri Rollins.
1819 Pepperell Parkway, Suite 203, Opelika, AL 36801 .... (334) 745–6222
Field Representative.—Cheryl Cunningham.
7550 Halcyon Summit Drive, Montgomery, AL 36117 .... (334) 277–4210
Field Representative.—Alvin Lewis.

Counties: CALHOUN, CHAMBERS, CHEROKEE, CLAY, CLEBURNE, COOSA (part), LEE, MACON, MONTGOMERY (part), RANDOLPH, RUSSELL, TALLADEGA, TALLAPOOSA. Population (2000), 635,300.

ZIP Codes: 35010, 35014, 35032, 35044, 35078, 35082, 35089, 35096, 35136, 35160, 35183, 35960, 35973, 35983, 36013, 36023, 36026, 36036, 36039, 36043, 36046–47, 36052, 36057–58, 36064–65, 36069–70, 36075, 36088, 36101–21, 36123–25, 36201, 36215, 36252–63, 36265–76, 36278–80, 36766, 36801–04, 36825, 36830, 36850, 36853–55, 36858–65, 36867–79, 36959

* * *

FOURTH DISTRICT

ROBERT B. ADERHOLT, Republican, of Haleyville, AL; born in Haleyville, July 22, 1965; education: graduate, Birmingham Southern University; J.D., Cumberland School of Law, Samford University; professional: attorney; assistant legal advisor to Governor Fob James, 1995–96; Haleyville municipal judge, 1992–96; George Bush delegate, Republican National Convention, 1992; Republican nominee for the 17th District, Alabama House of Representatives, 1990; married: Caroline McDonald; children: Mary Elliott, Robert Hayes; committees: Appropriations; elected to the 105th Congress; reelected to each succeeding Congress.

Office Listings

1433 Longworth House Office Building, Washington, DC 20515 .... (202) 225–4876
Chief of Staff.—Hood Harris. FAX: 225–5587
Legislative Director.—Mark Dawson.
Press Secretary.—Michael Lowry.
Executive Assistant.—Tiffany Noel.
247 Carl Elliott Building, 1710 Alabama Avenue, Room 247, Jasper, AL 35501 .... (205) 221–2310
District Field Director.—Paul Housel.
205 Fourth Avenue, NE., Suite 104, Cullman, AL 35055 .... (256) 734–6043
Director of Constituent Services.—Jennifer Taylor.
107 Federal Building, 600 Broad Street, Gadsden, AL 35901 .... (256) 546–0201
Field Representative.—Jason Harper.
Morgan County Courthouse, P.O. Box 668, Decatur, AL 35602 .... (256) 350–4093
Field Representative.—John Ross.

Counties: BLOUNT, CULLMAN, DEKALB, ETOWAH, FAYETTE, FRANKLIN, LAMAR, MARION, MARSHALL, MORGAN (part), PICKENS (part), ST. CLAIR (part), WALKER, WINSTON. Population (2000), 635,300.

ZIP Codes: 35006, 35013, 35016, 35019, 35031, 35033, 35038, 35049, 35053, 35055–58, 35062–63, 35070, 35077, 35079, 35083, 35087, 35097–98, 35121, 35126, 35130–31, 35133, 35146, 35148, 35172, 35175, 35179–80, 35205–07, 35212–13, 35215, 35441, 35447, 35461, 35466, 35481, 35501–04, 35540–46, 35548–55, 35559–60, 35563–65, 35570–82, 35584–87, 35592–94, 35601, 35603, 35619, 35621–22, 35640, 35651, 35653–54, 35670, 35672–73, 35747, 35754–55, 35760, 35765, 35769, 35771, 35775–76, 35901–07, 35950–54, 35956–57, 35959–64, 35966–68, 35971–76, 35978–81, 35983–84, 35986–90, 36064, 36117, 36271–72, 36275

* * *

FIFTH DISTRICT

ROBERT E. ''BUD'' CRAMER, JR., Democrat, of Huntsville, AL; born in Huntsville, August 22, 1947; education: graduated, Huntsville High School, 1965; B.A., University of Alabama, Tuscaloosa, 1969, ROTC; J.D., University of Alabama School of Law, Tuscaloosa, 1972; professional: U.S. Army, 1972; captain, U.S. Army Reserves, 1976–78; attorney; instructor, University of Alabama School of Law, Tuscaloosa; director of clinical studies program, 1972–73; assistant district attorney, Madison County, AL, 1973–75; private law practice, Huntsville, AL, 1975–80; district attorney, Madison County, 1981–90; member: Alabama District Attorneys Association; National District Attorneys Association; founder, National Children's Advocacy Center, Huntsville; National Center for Missing and Exploited Children Advisory Council; American Bar Association, 1975–present; State of Alabama Bar Association, 1972–present; American Bar Association's National Legal Resource Center for Child Advocacy and Protection; awards and honors: received certificate of appreciation, presented by President Ronald Reagan, for outstanding dedication and commitment in promoting safety and well-being of children from the President's Child Safety Partnership, 1987; 1986 recipient of the Vincent De Francis Award, presented by the American Humane Association; selected as National Public Citizen of the Year, 1984; Alabama District Attorneys Investigators Association, ''District Attorney of the Year, 1986''; Methodist; widower; one daughter: Hollan C. Gaines; committees: Appropriations; Permanent Select Committee on Intelligence; elected to the 102nd Congress, November 6, 1990; reelected to each succeeding Congress.

Office Listings

http://www.house.gov/cramer

2184 Rayburn House Office Building, Washington, DC 20515 .... (202) 225–4801
Administrative Assistant.—Carter Wells. FAX: 225–4392
Legislative Director.—Denise Edwards.
Scheduler.—Alex Igou.
200 Pratt Avenue, NE., Suite A, Huntsville, AL 35801 .... (256) 551–0190
District Coordinator.—Jim McCamy.
Morgan County Courthouse, Box 668, Decatur, AL 35602 .... (256) 355–9400
1011 George Wallace Boulevard, Tuscumbia, AL 35674 .... (256) 381–3450

Counties: COLBERT, JACKSON, LAUDERDALE, LAWRENCE, LIMESTONE, MADISON, MORGAN (part). Population (2000), 635,300.

ZIP Codes: 35016, 35205–06, 35209–10, 35212, 35215, 35540, 35582, 35601–03, 35609–20, 35630–34, 35640, 35643, 35645–54, 35660–62, 35671–74, 35677, 35699, 35739–42, 35744–46, 35748–52, 35755–69, 35771–74, 35776, 35801–16, 35824, 35893–96, 35898–99, 35958, 35966, 35978–79, 36104

* * *

SIXTH DISTRICT

SPENCER BACHUS, Republican, of Vestavia Hills, AL; born in Birmingham, AL, December 28, 1947; education: B.A., Auburn University, 1969; J.D., University of Alabama, 1972; professional: law firm, Bachus, Dempsey, Carson, and Steed, senior partner; member: Hunter Street Baptist Church; Alabama State Representative and Senator; school board; Republican Party Chair; children: Warren, Stuart, Elliott, Candace, and Lisa; committees: ranking member, Financial Services; elected to the 103rd Congress, November 3, 1992; reelected to each succeeding Congress.

Office Listings

http://www.house.gov/bachus

2246 Rayburn House Office Building, Washington, DC 20515 .... (202) 225–4921
Chief of Staff.—Larry Lavender. FAX: 225–2082
Press Secretary.—Tim Johnson.
Legislative Director.—Jason Reese.
1900 International Park Drive, Suite 107, Birmingham, AL 35243 .... (205) 969–2296
Northport Civic Center, P.O. Box 569, 3500 McFarland Boulevard, Northport, AL 35476 .... (205) 333–9894
703 Second Avenue, North, P.O. Box 502, Clanton, AL 35046 .... (205) 280–0704

Counties: BIBB, CHILTON, COOSA (part), JEFFERSON (part), SHELBY, ST. CLAIR (part), TUSCALOOSA (part). CITIES AND TOWNSHIPS: Adamsville, Alabaster, Argo, Brookside, Brookwood, Calera, Cardiff, Clanton, Columbiana, County Line, Fultondale, Gardendale, Graysville, Harpersville, Helena, Homewood, Hoover, Hueytown, Irondale, Jemison, Kimberly, Leeds, Maytown, Montevallo, Morris, Mountain Brook, Mulga, North Johns, Northport, Pelham, Pell City, Pleasant Grove, Ragland, Sumiton, Sylvan Springs, Thorsby, Trafford, Trussville, Vestavia Hills, Vincent, Warrior, West Jefferson, Wilsonville, Wilton, and portions of Bessemer, Birmingham, Tarrant, Tuscaloosa, and West Blocton. Population (2000), 635,300.

ZIP Codes: 35004–07, 35015, 35022–23, 35035, 35040, 35043, 35046, 35048, 35051–52, 35054, 35060, 35062–63, 35068, 35071, 35073–74, 35078–80, 35085, 35091, 35094, 35096, 35111–12, 35114–20, 35123–28, 35130–31, 35133, 35135, 35137, 35139, 35142–44, 35146–48, 35151, 35171–73, 35175–76, 35178, 35180–88, 35201–03, 35205–07, 35209–

10, 35212–17, 35219, 35222–26, 35230, 35233, 35235–37, 35240, 35242–46, 35249, 35253–55, 35259–61, 35266, 35277–83, 35285, 35287–99, 35402–03, 35406–07, 35444, 35446, 35452, 35456–58, 35466, 35468, 35473, 35475–76, 35480, 35482, 35490, 35546, 35579, 35953, 35987, 36006, 36051, 36064, 36091, 36750, 36758, 36790, 36792–93

* * *

SEVENTH DISTRICT

ARTUR DAVIS, Democrat, of Birmingham, AL; born in Montgomery, AL, October 9, 1967; education: Harvard University, graduated *magna cum laude;* Harvard Law School, graduated *cum laude;* professional: Attorney; public service: interned with U.S. Senator Howell Heflin (D–AL); interned with the Southern Poverty Law Center; clerked for Federal Judge Myron Thompson; served as an Assistant U.S. Attorney for the Middle District of Alabama, 1994–98; attorney in private practice, 1998–2002; memberships and boards: Board of Trustees, Tuskegee University; Board of Advisors, Harvard Law and Policy Review; Board of Directors, Alabama Center for Law and Civic Government; Board of Directors, The Salvation Army, Jefferson County Alabama; religion: Lutheran; committees: House Administration; Judiciary; Ways and Means; elected to the 108th Congress on November 5, 2002; reelected to each succeeding Congress.

Office Listings

http://www.house.gov/arturdavis

208 Cannon House Office Building, Washington, DC 20515 .... (202) 225–2665
Chief of Staff.—Dana Gresham. FAX: 226–9567
Deputy Chief of Staff / Communications Director.—Corey Ealons.
1728 3rd Avenue North, Birmingham, AL 35203 .... (205) 254–1960
District Director.—Daryl Perkins.
908 Alabama Avenue, Federal Building, Suite 112, Selma, AL 36701 .... (334) 877–4414
102 East Washington Street, Suite F, Demopolis, AL 36732 .... (334) 287–0860
205 North Washington Street, UWA Station 40, Suites 236–237, Livingston, AL 35470 .... (205) 652–5834
1118 Greensboro Avenue, Suite 336, Tuscaloosa, AL 35401 .... (205) 752–5380

Counties: CHOCTAW, CLARKE (part), DALLAS, GREENE, HALE, JEFFERSON (part), MARENGO, PERRY, PICKENS (part), SUMTER, TUSCALOOSA (part), WILCOX. Population (2000), 635,300.

ZIP Codes: 35005–06, 35020–23, 35034, 35036, 35041–42, 35061, 35064, 35068, 35071, 35073–74, 35079, 35111, 35117, 35126–27, 35173, 35175, 35184, 35188, 35203–15, 35217–18, 35221–22, 35224, 35228–29, 35233–35, 35238, 35243, 35401, 35404–06, 35440–44, 35446–49, 35452–53, 35456, 35459–60, 35462–64, 35466, 35469–71, 35473–78, 35480–81, 35485–87, 35490–91, 35546, 35601, 35603, 35640, 35754, 36030, 36032, 36040, 36064, 36105, 36435–36, 36451, 36482, 36524, 36540, 36545, 36558, 36701–03, 36720, 36722–23, 36726–28, 36732, 36736, 36738, 36740–42, 36744–45, 36748–54, 36756, 36758–59, 36761–69, 36773, 36775–76, 36782–86, 36790, 36792–93, 36901, 36904, 36906–08, 36910, 36912–13, 36915–16, 36919, 36921–22, 36925

ALASKA

(Population 2000, 626,932)

SENATORS

TED STEVENS, Republican, of Girdwood, AK; born in Indianapolis, IN, November 18, 1923; education: graduated, UCLA, 1947; Harvard Law School, 1950; military service: served as a first lieutenant (pilot), 1943–46; 14th Air Force in China, 1944–45; professional: practiced law in Washington, DC, and Fairbanks, AK, 1950–53; U.S. Attorney, Fairbanks, AK, 1953–56; legislative counsel, U.S. Department of the Interior, 1956–57; assistant to the Secretary of the Interior (Fred Seaton), 1958–59; appointed solicitor of the Department of the Interior by President Eisenhower, 1960; opened law office, Anchorage, AK, 1961; Alaska House of Representatives, 1964–68; assistant Republican leader, 1977–85; member: Rotary, American Legion, Veterans of Foreign Wars, Igloo No. 4 Pioneers of Alaska; American, Federal, California, Alaska, and District of Columbia bar associations; married: Catherine Chandler of Anchorage, AK; one daughter; five children with first wife, Ann Cherrington (deceased, 1978); committees: Appropriations; ranking member, Commerce, Science, and Transportation; Homeland Security and Governmental Affairs; Rules and Administration; Joint Committee on the Library; appointed by the governor December 24, 1968 to fill a vacancy; elected November 3, 1970 for a term ending January 2, 1973; reelected to each succeeding Senate term.

Office Listings

http://stevens.senate.gov

522 Hart Senate Office Building, Washington, DC 20510 .... (202) 224–3004
Chief of Staff.—George Lowe. FAX: 224–2354
Legislative Director.—Karina Waller.
Administrative Director.—Mark Davis.
Scheduling Director.—DeLynn Henry.
222 West Seventh Avenue, No. 2, Anchorage, AK 99513 .... (907) 271–5915
Federal Building, Room 206, Box 4, 101 12th Avenue, Fairbanks, AK 99701 .... (907) 456–0261
Federal Building, Room 971, Box 20149, Juneau, AK 99802 .... (907) 586–7400
130 Trading Bay Road, Suite 350, Kenai, AK 99611 .... (907) 283–5808
540 Water Street, Suite 101, Ketchikan, AK 99901 .... (907) 225–6880

* * *

LISA MURKOWSKI, Republican, of Anchorage, AK; born in Ketchikan, AK, May 22, 1957; education: Willamette University, 1975–77; Georgetown University, 1978–80, B.A., Economics; Willamette College of Law, 1982–85, J.D.; professional: attorney; private law practice; Alaska and Anchorage Bar Associations: First Bank Board of Directors; organizations: Catholic Social Services; YWCA; Alaskans for Drug-Free Youth; Alaska Federation of Republican Women; Arctic Power; public service: Anchorage Equal Rights Commission; Anchorage District Court Attorney, 1987–89; Task Force on the Homeless, 1990–91; Alaska State Representative, 1998–2002; family: married to Verne Martell; children: Nicholas and Matthew; committees: Energy and Natural Resources; Foreign Relations; Health, Education, Labor and Pensions; Indian Affairs; appointed to the U.S. Senate on December 20, 2002; elected to the 109th Congress for a full Senate term on November 2, 2004.

Office Listings

http://murkowski.senate.gov

709 Hart Senate Office Building, Washington, DC 20510 .... (202) 224–6665
Chief of Staff.—Donna Murray. FAX: 224–5301
Legislative Director.—Isaac Edwards.
Scheduler.—Kristen Nothdurft.
Communications Director.—Danielle Holland.
510 L Street, #550, Anchorage, AK 99501 .... (907) 271–3735
101 12th Avenue, Room 216, Fairbanks, AK 99701 .... (907) 456–0233
709 W. 9th, Room 971, Juneau, AK 99802 .... (907) 586–7400

REPRESENTATIVE

AT LARGE

DON YOUNG, Republican, of Fort Yukon, AK; born in Meridian, CA, June 9, 1933; education: A.A., Yuba Junior College; B.A., Chico State College, Chico, CA; Honorary Doctorate of Laws, University of Alaska, Fairbanks; State House of Representatives, 1966–70; U.S. Army, 41st Tank Battalion, 1955–57; elected member of the State Senate, 1970–73; served on the Fort Yukon City Council for six years, serving four years as mayor; educator for nine years; river boat captain; member: National Education Association, Elks, Lions, Jaycees; married: Lula Fredson of Fort Yukon; children: Joni and Dawn; committees: ranking member, Natural Resources; Transportation and Infrastructure; elected to the 93rd Congress in a special election, March 6, 1973, to fill the vacancy created by the death of Congressman Nick Begich; reelected to each succeeding Congress.

Office Listings

http://www.house.gov/donyoung

2111 Rayburn House Office Building, Washington, DC 20515 .... (202) 225–5765
Administrative Assistant.—Michael Anderson. FAX: 225–0425
Press Secretary.—Meredith Kenny.
Executive Assistant / Office Manager.—Sara Parsons.
Legislative Director.—Pamela Day.
510 L Street, Suite 580, Anchorage, AK 99501 .... (907) 271–5978
101 12th Avenue, Box 10, Fairbanks, AK 99701 .... (907) 456–0210
971 Federal Building, Box 21247, Juneau, AK 99802 .... (907) 586–7400
540 Water Street, Ketchikan, AK 99901 .... (907) 225–6880
130 Trading Bay Road, Suite 350, Kenai, AK 99611 .... (907) 283–5808
851 East Westpoint Drive, #307, Wasilla, AK 99654 .... (907) 376–7665

Population (2000), 626,932.

ZIP Codes: 99501–24, 99540, 99546–59, 99561, 99563–69, 99571–81, 99583–91, 99599, 99602–15, 99619–22, 99624–41, 99643–45, 99647–72, 99674–95, 99697, 99701–12, 99714, 99716, 99720–27, 99729–30, 99732–34, 99736–86, 99788–89, 99791, 99801–03, 99811, 99820–21, 99824–27, 99829–30, 99832–33, 99835–36, 99840–41, 99850, 99901, 99903, 99918–19, 99921–23, 99925–29, 99950

ARIZONA

(Population 2000, 5,140,683)

SENATORS

JOHN McCAIN, Republican, of Phoenix, AZ; born in the Panama Canal Zone, August 29, 1936; education: graduated Episcopal High School, Alexandria, VA, 1954; graduated, U.S. Naval Academy, Annapolis, MD, 1958; National War College, Washington, DC, 1973; retired captain (pilot), U.S. Navy, 1958–81; military awards: Silver Star, Bronze Star, Legion of Merit, Purple Heart, and Distinguished Flying Cross; chair, International Republican Institute; married to the former Cindy Hensley; seven children: Doug, Andy, Sidney, Meghan, Jack, Jim, and Bridget; committees: ranking member, Armed Services; Commerce, Science, and Transportation; Indian Affairs; elected to the 98th Congress in November, 1982; reelected to the 99th Congress in November, 1984; elected to the U.S. Senate in November, 1986; reelected to each succeeding Senate term.

Office Listings

http://mccain.senate.gov

241 Russell Senate Office Building, Washington, DC 20510 .... (202) 224–2235
TDD: 224–7132
Administrative Assistant.—Mark Salter.
Legislative Director.—Ann Begeman.
Communications Director.—Eileen McMenamin.
Scheduler.—Ellen Cahill.
5353 N. 16th Street, Suite 105, Phoenix, AZ 85016 .... (602) 952–2410
TDD: 952–0170
4703 S. Lakeshore Drive, Suite 1, Tempe, AZ 85282 .... (480) 897–6289
407 West Congress Street, Suite 301, Tucson, AZ 85701 .... (602) 670–6334

* * *

JON KYL, Republican, of Phoenix, AZ; born in Oakland, NE, April 25, 1942; education: graduated Bloomfield High School, Bloomfield, IA, 1960; B.A., University of Arizona, Tucson, 1964 (Phi Beta Kappa, Phi Kappa Phi); LL.B., University of Arizona, 1966; professional: editor-in-chief, *Arizona Law Review*; attorney, admitted to the Arizona State bar, 1966; former partner in Phoenix law firm of Jennings, Strouss and Salmon, 1966–86; chairman, Phoenix Chamber of Commerce (1984–85); married: the former Caryll Louise Collins; children: Kristine and John; committees: Finance; Judiciary; elected to the 100th Congress on November 4, 1986; reelected to each succeeding Congress; elected to the U.S. Senate in November, 1994; reelected to each succeeding Senate term.

Office Listings

http://kyl.senate.gov

730 Hart Senate Office Building, Washington, DC 20515 .... (202) 224–4521
FAX: 224–2207
Chief of Staff.—Tim Glazewski.
Legislative Director.—Elizabeth Maier.
Office Director.—Celeste Gold.
Scheduler.—Jill Larrabee.
Suite 120, 2200 East Camelback Road, Phoenix, AZ 85016 .... (602) 840–1891
Suite 220, 7315 North Oracle, Tucson, AZ 85704 .... (520) 575–8633

REPRESENTATIVES

FIRST DISTRICT

RICK RENZI, Republican, of Flagstaff, AZ; born in Sierra Vista, AZ, June 11, 1958; education: B.S., Northern Arizona University, 1980; J.D., Catholic University, 2002; professional: businessman; founded Renzi and Co., an insurance company designed to help non-profit organizations; while working on his law degree, he served as a legal extern for members of Arizona's congressional delegation; researched legal issues on religious freedoms, Federal land policies, and private property rights; married: Roberta; twelve children; committees: Financial Services; Natural Resources; Permanent Select Committee on Intelligence; elected to the 108th Congress on November 5, 2002; reelected to each succeeding Congress.

Office Listings

http://www.house.gov/renzi

418 Cannon House Office Building, Washington, DC 20515 .... (202) 225–2315
Chief of Staff.—Patty Roe. FAX: 226–9739
Chief of Staff, Arizona.—Brian Murray.
Legislative Director.—Jim Lester.
Communications Director.—Vartan Djihanian.
501 N. Florence Street, Suite 102, Casa Grande, AZ 85222 .... (520) 876–0929
Congressional Liaison.—Teresa Martinez.
123 North San Francisco Street, Suite 105, Flagstaff, AZ 86001 .... (866) 537–2800
Congressional Liaison.—Chelsea Lett.
107 North Cortez, Suite 208, Prescott, AZ 86301 .... (928) 708–9120
Congressional Liaison.—Don Packard.
1420 First Avenue, Suite 100, Safford, AZ 85546 .... (928) 428–8194
Congressional Liaison.—Keith Alexander.
EPA Building, 10 West Tonto, P.O. Box 0, San Carlos, AZ 85550 .... (928) 475–3733
Congressional Liaison.—Keith Alexander.
1151 East Duce of Clubs, Suite A, Show Low, AZ 85901 .... (928) 537–2800
Congressional Liaisons: Jack Latham, Penny Pew.
Apache Veteran's Center, 201 East Walnut, Whiteriver, AZ 85941 .... (928) 607–0792
Congressional Liaison.—Dayrl Begay.
DNA Legal Services Building, Highway 254 and Route 12, P.O. Box 4673, Window Rock, AZ 86515 .... (928) 607–0792
Congressional Liaison.—Dayrl Begay.

Counties: APACHE, COCONINO, GILA, GRAHAM, GREENLEE, NAVAJO (part), PINAL (part), YAVAPAI. CITIES AND TOWNSHIPS: Flagstaff, Prescott, Payson, Show Low, and Casa Grande. Population (2000), 641,329.

ZIP Codes: 85218, 85221–23, 85228, 85230–32, 85235, 85237, 85241, 85245, 85247, 85272–73, 85291–92, 85324, 85332, 85362, 85501–02, 85530–36, 85539–48, 85550–54, 85618, 85623, 85631, 85653, 85901–02, 85911–12, 85920, 85922–42, 86001–04, 86011, 86015–18, 86020, 86022–25, 86028–29, 86031–33, 86035–36, 86038, 86040, 86044–47, 86052–54, 86301–05, 86312–14, 86320–27, 86329–43, 86351, 86503, 86505, 86514–15, 86520, 86535, 86538, 86540, 86544–45, 86547, 86549, 86556

* * *

SECOND DISTRICT

TRENT FRANKS, Republican, of Phoenix, AZ; born in Uravan, CO, June 19, 1957; education: attended Ottawa University; graduate of the Center for Constitutional Studies; professional: small business owner; oil field and drilling engineer; Executive Director, Arizona Family Research Institute; conservative writer, and former radio commentator, with Family Life Radio and NBC affiliate KTKP 1280 AM; public service: Arizona House of Representatives, 1985–87; appointed in 1987 to head the Arizona Governor's Office for Children; awards: True Blue award, Family Research Council; Spirit of Enterprise award, U.S. Chamber of Commerce; Taxpayer Hero, Council for Citizens Against Government Waste; Friend of Education award, Education Freedom Coalition; religion: Baptist; member, North Phoenix Baptist Church; married: Josephine; committees: Armed Services; Judiciary; elected to the 108th Congress on November 5, 2002; reelected to each succeeding Congress.

Office Listings

http://www.house.gov/franks

1237 Longworth House Office Building, Washington, DC 20515 .... (202) 225–4576
Chief of Staff.—Tom Stallings. FAX: 225–6328
Deputy Chief of Staff.—Doyle Scott.
Legislative Director.—Jeff Choudhry.
Scheduler.—Lisa Teschler.
7121 W. Bell Road, Suite 200, Glendale, AZ 85308 .... (623) 776–7911

Counties: COCONINO (part), LAPAZ (part), MARICOPA (part), MOHAVE, NAVAJO (part), YAVAPAI (part). Population (2000), 641,329.

ZIP Codes: 85029, 85037, 85051, 85098, 85301–10, 85312, 85318, 85320, 85326, 85335, 85338, 85340, 85342, 85345, 85351, 85355, 85358, 85360–61, 85363, 85372–76, 85378–83, 85385, 85387, 85390, 86021, 86030, 86034, 86039, 86042–43, 86401–06, 86411–13, 86426–27, 86429–46

* * *

THIRD DISTRICT

JOHN B. SHADEGG, Republican, of Phoenix, AZ; born in Phoenix, October 22, 1949; education: graduated Camelback High School; B.A., University of Arizona, Tucson, 1972; J.D.,

University of Arizona, 1975; professional: Air National Guard, 1969–75; admitted to the Arizona bar, 1976; law offices of John Shadegg; special counsel, Arizona House Republican Caucus, 1991–92; special assistant attorney general, 1983–90; advisor, U.S. Sentencing Commission; founding director/executive committee member, Goldwater Institute for Public Policy; member/former president, Crime Victim Foundation; chairman, Arizona Juvenile Justice Advisory Council; advisory board, Salvation Army; vestry, Christ Church of the Ascension Episcopal, 1989–91; member, Law Society, ASU College of Law; chairman, Arizona Republican Caucus, 1985–87; chairman, Proposition 108—Two-Thirds Tax Limitation Initiative, 1992; member, Fiscal Accountability and Reform Efforts (FARE) Committee, 1991–92; counsel, Arizonans for Wildlife Conservation (no on Proposition 200), 1992; Victims Bill of Rights Task Force, 1989–90; member, Growing Smarter Committee, (yes on Proposition 303), 1998; married: Shirley; children: Courtney and Stephen; assistant whip; committees: Energy and Commerce; Select Committee on Energy Independence and Global Warming; elected to the 104th Congress; reelected to each succeeding Congress.

Office Listings

http://johnshadegg.house.gov

306 Cannon House Office Building, Washington, DC 20515 .... (202) 225–3361
Chief of Staff.—Sean Noble. FAX: 225–3462
Deputy Chief of Staff.—Kristin Thompson.
Scheduler.—Courtney Johnson.
Press Secretary.—Ken Spain.
301 East Bethany Home Road, Suite C–178, Phoenix, AZ 85012 .... (602) 263–5300
District Chief of Staff.—Sean Noble.

Counties: MARICOPA (part). CITIES AND TOWNSHIPS: Carefree, Cave Creek, Paradise Valley, and Phoenix (part). Population (2000), 641,329.

ZIP Codes: 85012–24, 85027–29, 85032, 85046, 85050–51, 85053–54, 85060, 85071, 85075, 85078–80, 85082, 85098–99, 85250–51, 85253–54, 85262, 85308, 85310, 85327, 85331, 85377

* * *

FOURTH DISTRICT

ED PASTOR, Democrat, of Phoenix, AZ; born in Claypool, AZ, June 28, 1943; education: attended public schools in Miami, AZ; graduate of Arizona State University; B.A., chemistry, 1966; J.D., Arizona University, 1974; professional: member, Governor Raul Castro's staff; taught chemistry, North High School; former deputy director of Guadalupe Organization, Inc.; elected supervisor, board of supervisors, Maricopa County; served board of directors for the National Association of Counties; vice chairman, Employment Steering Committee; president, Arizona County Supervisors Association; member, executive committee of the Arizona Association of Counties; resigned, May, 1991; board of directors, Neighborhood Housing Services of America; National Association of Latino Elected Officials; served as director at large, ASU Alumni Association; founding board member, ASU Los Diablos Alumni Association; served on board of directors of the National Council of La Raza; Arizona Joint Partnership Training Council; National Conference of Christians and Jews; Friendly House; Chicanos Por La Causa; Phoenix Economic Growth Corporation; Sun Angel Foundation; vice president, Valley of the Sun United Way; advisory member, Boys Club of Metropolitan Phoenix; married: Verma; two daughters: Yvonne and Laura; appointed a Chief Deputy Minority Whip; committees: Appropriations; elected by special election on September 24, 1991, to fill the vacancy caused by the resignation of Morris K. Udall; elected in November, 1992, to the 103rd Congress; reelected to each succeeding Congress.

Office Listings

http://www.house.gov/pastor

2465 Rayburn House Office Building, Washington, DC 20515 .... (202) 225–4065
Executive Assistant.—Laura Campos. FAX: 225–1655
411 N. Central Avenue, Suite 150, Phoenix, AZ 85004 .... (602) 256–0551
District Director.—Ron Piceno.

Counties: MARICOPA (part). Population (2000), 641,329.

ZIP Codes: 85001–09, 85012–19, 85025–26, 85030–31, 85033–36, 85038, 85040–44, 85051, 85061–64, 85066–69, 85072–74, 85076, 85082, 85099, 85283, 85301, 85303, 85309, 85311, 85339, 86045, 86329, 86337

* * *

FIFTH DISTRICT

HARRY E. MITCHELL, Democrat, of Tempe, AZ; born in Phoenix, AZ, July 18, 1940; education: graduated from Tempe High School, Tempe, AZ; B.S. in political science, Arizona State University, 1962; master's degree in public administration, Arizona State University, 1980; professional: taught American government and economics, Tempe High School, 1964–92; former Mayor and Councilman, Tempe, AZ; former member, Arizona State Senate; former chairman, Arizona Democratic Party; to honor his success as Mayor, the City of Tempe erected a 35-foot statute of Harry in downtown Tempe and renamed the city's government center the Harry E. Mitchell Government Complex; served as an adjunct professor at his alma mater, ASU; family: married to Marianne; two children; five grandchildren; committees: Science and Technology; Transportation and Infrastructure; Veterans' Affairs; elected to the 110th Congress on November 7, 2006.

Office Listings

http://mitchell.house.gov

2434 Rayburn House Office Building, Washington, DC 20515 .... (202) 225–2190
Chief of Staff.—Gene Fisher. FAX: 225–3263
Executive Assistant.—Phyllis Khaing.
Legislative Assistants: Chris Quigley, Katy Quinn, Matthew Weisman.
Staff Assistant / Tour Coordinator.—Alyssa Miller.
7201 East Camelback Road, Suite 335, Scottsdale, AZ 85251 .... (480) 946–2411

Counties: MARICOPA (part). CITIES AND TOWNSHIPS: Chandler, Fountain Hills, Mesa, Phoenix, Rio Verde, Scottsdale, Tempe. Ahwatukee, the Salt River Pima Indian Reservation, and the Fort McDowell Yavapai Apache Indian Reservation. Population (2000), 641,329.

ZIP Codes: 85008, 85018, 85044–45, 05048, 85070, 85076, 85201–03, 85210, 85215, 85224–26, 85250–64, 85267–69, 85274, 85287, 85331, 85281, 85283

* * *

SIXTH DISTRICT

JEFF FLAKE, Republican, of Mesa, AZ; born in Snowflake, AZ, December 31, 1962; education: Brigham Young University; B.A., International Relations; M.A., Political Science; religion: Mormon; served a mission in South Africa and Zimbabwe; professional: businessman; Shipley, Smoak & Henry (public affairs firm); Executive Director, Foundation for Democracy; Executive Director, Goldwater Institute; married: Cheryl; children: Ryan, Alexis, Austin, Tanner, and Dallin; committees: Foreign Affairs; Natural Resources; elected to the 107th Congress on November 7, 2000; reelected to each succeeding Congress.

Office Listings

http://www.house.gov/flake

240 Cannon House Office Building, Washington, DC 20515 .... (202) 225–2635
Chief of Staff.—Margaret Klessig. FAX: 226–4386
Scheduler.—Noelle Lecheminant.
Press Secretary.—Matthew Specht.
1640 South Stapley, Suite 215, Mesa, AZ 85204 .... (480) 833–0092

Counties: MARICOPA (part), PINAL (part). CITIES AND TOWNSHIPS: Apache Junction, Chandler, Gilbert, Mesa, and Queen Creek. Population (2000), 641,329.

ZIP Codes: 85201, 85203–08, 85210–20, 85224–25, 85227, 85233–34, 85236, 85242, 85244, 85246, 85248–49, 85254, 85275, 85277–78, 85290, 85296–97, 85299

* * *

SEVENTH DISTRICT

RAÚL M. GRIJALVA, Democrat, of Tucson, AZ; born in Tucson, February 19, 1948; education: Sunnyside High School, Tucson, AZ; B.A., University of Arizona; professional: former Assistant Dean for Hispanic Student Affairs, University of Arizona; former Director of the El Pueblo Neighborhood Center; public service: Tucson Unified School District Governing Board, 1974–86; Pima County Board of Supervisors, 1989–2002; family: married to Ramona; three daughters; committees: Education and Labor; Natural Resources; Small Business; elected to the 108th Congress on November 5, 2002; reelected to each succeeding Congress.

Office Listings

http://www.house.gov/grijalva

1440 Longworth House Office Building, Washington, DC 20515 .... (202) 225–2435
Chief of Staff.—Gloria Montaño. FAX: 225–1541
Legislative Director.—Chris Kaumo.
Press Liaison / Scheduler.—Natalie Luna.
Scheduler.—Ana Ma.
810 East 22nd Street, Suite 102, Tucson, AZ 85713 .... (520) 622–6788
1455 South 4th Avenue, Suite 4, Yuma, AZ 85364 .... (928) 343–7933

Counties: LA PAZ (part), MARICOPA (part), PIMA (part), PINAL (part), SANTA CRUZ (part), YUMA. Population (2000), 641,329.

ZIP Codes: 85033, 85035, 85037, 85043, 85221–22, 85226, 85228, 85232, 85239, 85242, 85248–49, 85273, 85321–23, 85325–26, 85328–29, 85333–34, 85336–37, 85339–41, 85343–44, 85346–50, 85352–54, 85356–57, 85359, 85364–67, 85369, 85371, 85601, 85621, 85628, 85631, 85633–34, 85639–40, 85648, 85653, 85662, 85701–03, 85705–06, 85711, 85713–14, 85716–17, 85719, 85721–26, 85733–36, 85743, 85745–46, 85754

* * *

EIGHTH DISTRICT

GABRIELLE GIFFORDS, Democrat, of Tucson, AZ; born in Tucson, June 8, 1970; education: B.A., Scripps College, Claremont, CA, 1993; William Fulbright Scholarship, study abroad Chihuahua, Mexico; M.A. in regional planning, Cornell University, NY, 1996; president, Atlantic Association of Young Political Leaders; represents the National Committee on China–U.S. Relations as a Young Leader's Forum Fellow; German Marshall Fund Manfred-Worner Fellow; selected for the inaugural two-year class of the Aspen-Rodel Fellowships in Public Leadership, 2005; Arizona State House of Representatives, 2002–02; Arizona State Senator, 2003–06; committees: Armed Services; Foreign Affairs; Science and Technology; elected to the 110th Congress on November 7, 2006.

Office Listings

http://giffords.house.gov/

502 Cannon House Office Building, Washington, DC 20515 .... (202) 225–2542
Chief of Staff.—Maura Policelli. FAX: 225–0378
Office Manager/Scheduler.—Kim Hiller.
1661 North Swan, Suite 112, Tucson, AZ 85712 .... (520) 881–3588
District Director.—Ron Barber.
77 Calle Portal, Suite B–160, Sierra Vista, AZ 85635 .... (520) 459–3115

Counties: COCHISE, PIMA (part), PINAL (part), SANTA CRUZ (part). Population (2000), 641,329.

ZIP Codes: 85602–03, 85605–11, 85613–17, 85619–20, 85622, 85624–27, 85629–30, 85632, 85635–38, 85641, 85643–46, 85650, 85652–55, 85670, 85704–16, 85718–19, 85728, 85730–32, 85736–45, 85747–52

ARKANSAS

(Population 2000, 2,673,400)

SENATORS

BLANCHE L. LINCOLN, Democrat, of Helena, AR; born in Helena, September 30, 1960; education: graduate of Helena Central High School; daughter of the late Jordan Bennett Lambert, Jr., and Martha Kelly Lambert; B.S., in biology, at Randolph Macon Woman's College, Lynchburg, VA, 1982; also attended the University of Arkansas, Fayetteville; member, Chi Omega sorority; American Red Cross volunteer; married to Dr. Stephen R. Lincoln; mother of twin boys, Bennett and Reece; committees: Agriculture, Nutrition, and Foresty; Energy and Natural Resources; Finance; Special Committee on Aging; elected to the U.S. House of Representatives for the 103rd and 104th Congresses; elected to the U.S. Senate on November 3, 1998; reelected to each succeeding Senate term.

Office Listings

http://lincoln.senate.gov

355 Dirksen Senate Office Building, Washington, DC 20510 .... (202) 224–4843
Chief of Staff.—Elizabeth Burks. FAX: 228–1371
Legislative Director.—Jim Stowers.
Press Secretary.—Katie Laning.
Scheduler.—Megan Robertson.
912 West Fourth Street, Little Rock, AR 72201 .... (501) 375–2993
4 South College Ave. #205, Fayetteville, AR 72701 .... (479) 251–1224
Federal Building, Suite 315, 615 South Main, Jonesboro, AR 72401 .... (870) 910–6896
101 E. Waterman, Dumas, AR 71693 .... (870) 382–1023
Miller County Courthouse, 400 Laurel Street, #101, Texarkana, AR 71854 .... (870) 774–3106

* * *

MARK L. PRYOR, Democrat, of Little Rock, AR; born in Fayetteville, AR, January 10, 1963; education: B.A., University of Arkansas, 1985; J.D., University of Arkansas, 1988; professional: attorney; Wright, Lindsey & Jennings (law firm); public service: elected, Arkansas House of Representatives, 1990; elected, Arkansas Attorney General, 1998; family: married to Jill; children: Adams and Porter; his father, David Pryor, was a former Governor and U.S. Senator from Arkansas; committees: Armed Services; Commerce, Science, and Transportation; Homeland Security and Governmental Affairs; Rules and Administration; Small Business and Entrepreneurship; Select Committee on Ethics; elected to the U.S. Senate on November 5, 2002.

Office Listings

http://pryor.senate.gov

257 Dirksen Senate Office Building, Washington, DC 20510 .... (202) 224–2353
Chief of Staff.—Bob Russell. FAX: 228–0908
Legislative Director.—Andy York.
Communications Director.—Michael Teague.
Office Manager.—Patrice Bolling.
500 Clinton Avenue, Suite 401, Little Rock, AR 72201 .... (501) 324–6336

REPRESENTATIVES

FIRST DISTRICT

MARION BERRY, Democrat, of Gillett, AR; born in Stuttgart, AR, August 27, 1942; education: graduated, DeWitt High School; B.S., pharmacy, University of Arkansas, 1965; professional: Gillett, Arkansas city council, 1976–80; Arkansas Soil and Water Conservation Commission, 1964–86; White House Domestic Policy Council, 1993–96; special assistant to President William Clinton for Agricultural Trade and Food Assistance, 1993; member, Domestic Policy Council, The White House, 1993–96; member, Arkansas Soil and Water Conservation Commission, 1986–94, serving as chairman in 1992; Gillett City Councilman, 1976–80; married: the former Carolyn Lowe in 1962; children: Ann Coggin and Mitchell; co-chairman, Democratic Blue Dog Coalition's Health Care Task Force; co-chair, House Affordable Medicines Task Force; Congressional Methamphetamine Caucus; Congressional Missing and Exploited Children's Caucus; Congressional Rural Caucus; Congressional Silk Road Caucus; co-chair, Congressional Soybean Caucus; Congressional Steel Caucus; House Renewable Energy and Energy Efficiency Caucus; New Democrat Coalition; Rural Health Care Coalition; Brain Injury Caucus; Rural Working Group; committees: Appropriations; Budget; elected to the 105th Congress; reelected to each succeeding Congress.

Office Listings

http://www.house.gov/berry

2305 Rayburn House Office Building, Washington, DC 20515 .... (202) 225–4076
FAX: 225–5602
Chief of Staff.—Chad Causey.
Press Secretary.—Angela Guyadeen.
Legislative Director.—Chris Wallace.
116 North First Street, Suite C–1, Cabot, AR 72023 .... (501) 843–3043
108 East Huntington Avenue, Jonesboro, AR 72401 .... (800) 866–2701
1 East 7th Street, Suite 200, Mountain Home, AR 72653 .... (870) 425–3511

Counties: ARKANSAS, BAXTER, CLAY, CLEBURNE, CRAIGHEAD, CRITTENDEN, CROSS, FULTON, GREENE, INDEPENDENCE, IZARD, JACKSON, LAWRENCE, LEE, LONOKE, MISSISSIPPI, MONROE, PHILLIPS, POINSETT, PRAIRIE, RANDOLPH, ST. FRANCIS, SEARCY, SHARP, STONE, WOODRUFF. Population (2000), 668,360.

ZIP Codes: 72003, 72005–07, 72014, 72017, 72020–21, 72023–24, 72026, 72029, 72031, 72036–38, 72040–44, 72046, 72048, 72051, 72055, 72059–60, 72064, 72067, 72069, 72072–76, 72083, 72086, 72101–02, 72108, 72112, 72121, 72123, 72130–31, 72134, 72137, 72139–40, 72142–43, 72153, 72160, 72165–66, 72169–70, 72175–76, 72179, 72189, 72301, 72303, 72310–13, 72315–16, 72319–22, 72324–33, 72335–36, 72338–42, 72346–48, 72350–55, 72358–60, 72364–70, 72372–74, 72376–77, 72383–84, 72386–87, 72389–92, 72394–96, 72401–04, 72410–17, 72419, 72421–22, 72424–45, 72447, 72449–51, 72453–62, 72464–67, 72469–76, 72478–79, 72482, 72501, 72503, 72512–13, 72515, 72517, 72519–34, 72536–40, 72542–46, 72550, 72553–56, 72560–62, 72564–69, 72571–73, 72575–79, 72581, 72583–85, 72587, 72610, 72613, 72617, 72623, 72626, 72629, 72631, 72633, 72635–36, 72639, 72642, 72645, 72650–51, 72653–54, 72658, 72663, 72669, 72675, 72679–80, 72685–86

* * *

SECOND DISTRICT

VIC SNYDER, Democrat, of Little Rock, AR; born in Medford, OR, September 27, 1947; education: graduated from Medford High School, 1965; corporal, U.S. Marine Corps, 1967–69, including one year in Vietnam with Headquarters Company, First Marine Division; B.A., chemistry, 1975, Willamette University, Salem, OR; M.D., 1979, University of Oregon Health Sciences Center, Portland; family practice residency, 1979–82, University of Arkansas for Medical Sciences; family practice physician in central Arkansas, 1982–96; medical missions to Cambodian refugee camps in Thailand, El Salvadoran refugee camps in Honduras, a West African mission hospital in Sierra Leone, and an Ethiopian refugee camp in Sudan; J.D., 1988, University of Arkansas at Little Rock School of Law; Arkansas State Senator, 1991–96; committees: Armed Services; Veterans' Affairs; elected to the 105th Congress; reelected to each succeeding Congress.

Office Listings

http://www.house.gov/snyder

1330 Longworth House Office Building, Washington, DC 20515 .... (202) 225–2506
FAX: 225–5903
Chief of Staff.—Ed Fry.
Press Secretary.—Jennifer Oglesby Holman.
Legislative Director.—Mike Casey.
1501 N. University, Suite 150, Little Rock, AR 72207 .... (501) 324–5941
District Director.—Amanda Nixon White.

Counties: CONWAY, FAULKNER, PERRY, PULASKI, SALINE, VAN BUREN, WHITE, YELL. Population (2000), 668,176.

ZIP Codes: 71772, 71909, 72001–02, 72010–13, 72015–18, 72020, 72022–23, 72025, 72027–28, 72030–35, 72039, 72045–47, 72052–53, 72057–61, 72063, 72065–68, 72070, 72076, 72078–82, 72085, 72087–89, 72099, 72102–04, 72106–08, 72110–11, 72113–22, 72124–27, 72131, 72135–37, 72139, 72141–43, 72145, 72149, 72153, 72156–57, 72164, 72167, 72173, 72178, 72180–81, 72183, 72190, 72199, 72201–07, 72209–12, 72214–17, 72219, 72221–23, 72225, 72227, 72231, 72260, 72295, 72419, 72568, 72629, 72645, 72679, 72823–24, 72827–29, 72833–34, 72838, 72841–42, 72853, 72857, 72860, 72943

* * *

THIRD DISTRICT

JOHN BOOZMAN, Republican, of Rogers, AR; born in Shreveport, LA, December 10, 1950; education: Northside High School, Fort Smith, AR; University of Arkansas, completing his pre-optometry requirements; graduated, Southern College of Optometry, 1977; professional: optometrist; entered private practice as a co-founder of the Boozman-Hof Eye Clinic; community service: volunteer optometrist at the Arkansas School for the Blind, and at area clinics;

public service: Rogers School Board, serving two terms; member: state and local cattlemen's associations; Benton County Fair Board; Fellowship of Christian Athletes; Arkansas Athletes Outreach Board; religion: Baptist; married: the former Cathy Marley; three daughters; committees: Foreign Affairs; Transportation and Infrastructure; Veterans' Affairs; elected to the 107th Congress, by special election, on November 20, 2001; reelected to each succeeding Congress.

Office Listings

http://www.house.gov/boozman

1519 Longworth House Office Building, Washington, DC 20515 .... (202) 225–4301
Chief of Staff.—Matthew Sagely. FAX: 225–5713
Communications Director.—Ryan James.
Scheduler.—Lesley Parker.
4943 Old Greenwood, Suite 1, Fort Smith, AR 72903 .... (479) 782–7787
303 N. Main, Suite 102, Harrison, AR 72601 .... (870) 741–6900
213 W. Monroe, Suite K, Lowell, AR 72745 .... (479) 725–0400
Deputy Chief of Staff.—Stacey McClure.

Counties: BENTON, BOONE, CARROLL, CRAWFORD, FRANKLIN, JOHNSON, MADISON, MARION, NEWTON, POPE, SEBASTIAN, WASHINGTON. Population (2000), 668,479.

ZIP Codes: 71937, 71944–45, 71953, 71972–73, 72063, 72080, 72601–02, 72611, 72613, 72615–16, 72619, 72624, 72628, 72630–34, 72638–41, 72644–45, 72648, 72653, 72655, 72660–63, 72666, 72668, 72670, 72672, 72675, 72677, 72679, 72682–83, 72685–87, 72701–04, 72711–12, 72714–19, 72721–22, 72727–30, 72732–42, 72744–45, 72747, 72749, 72751–53, 72756–58, 72760–62, 72764–66, 72768–70, 72773–74, 72776, 72801–02, 72811–12, 72820–21, 72823, 72830, 72832, 72837–43, 72845–47, 72852, 72854, 72856–58, 72860, 72901–06, 72908, 72913–14, 72916–19, 72921, 72923, 72927–28, 72930, 72932–38, 72940–41, 72944–49, 72951–52, 72955–57, 72959

* * *

FOURTH DISTRICT

MIKE ROSS, Democrat, of Prescott, AR; born in Texarkana, AR, August 2, 1961; education: Hope High School; B.A., University of Arkansas at Little Rock, 1987; professional: small businessman; owner of Ross Pharmacy, Inc., in Prescott, AR; public service: Chief of Staff to Arkansas Lt. Governor Winston Bryant, 1985–89; three term State Senator, 1991–2000; organizations: Executive Director, Arkansas Youth Suicide Prevention Commission, 1985–89; First United Methodist Church in Prescott, AR; awards: National Association of Social Workers Public Citizen of the Year, 1999; Arkansas State Police Association Distinguished Service Award; Arkansas Kids Count Coalition Achievement Award; married: Holly; children: Alex and Sydney Beth; committees: Energy and Commerce; Science and Technology; elected to the 107th Congress on November 7, 2000; reelected to each succeeding Congress.

Office Listings

http://www.house.gov/ross

314 Cannon House Office Building, Washington, DC 20515 .... (202) 225–3772
Chief of Staff.—Drew Goesl. FAX: 225–1314
Senior Legislative Assistant.—Kate Callanan.
Communications Director.—Jon Niven.
District Director.—Jeff Weaver.
221 West Main Street, Prescott, AR 71857 .... (870) 887–6787
2300 West 29th, Suite 1A, Pine Bluff, AR 71603 .... (870) 536–3376
300 Exchange Street, Suite A, Hot Springs, AR 71901 .... (501) 520–5892
Union County Courthouse, Suite 406, 101 North Washington Street, El Dorado, AR 71730 .... (870) 881–0681

Counties: ASHLEY, BRADLEY, CALHOUN, CHICOT, CLARK, CLEVELAND, COLUMBIA, DALLAS, DESHA, DREW, GARLAND, GRANT, HEMPSTEAD, HOT SPRING, HOWARD, JEFFERSON, LAFAYETTE, LINCOLN, LITTLE RIVER, LOGAN, MILLER, MONTGOMERY, NEVADA, OUACHITA, PIKE, POLK, SCOTT, SEVIER, UNION. Population (2000), 668,385.

ZIP Codes: 71601–03, 71611–13, 71630–31, 71635, 71638–40, 71642–44, 71646–47, 71651–63, 71665–67, 71670–71, 71674–78, 71701, 71711, 71720–22, 71724–26, 71728, 71730–31, 71740, 71742–45, 71747–54, 71758–59, 71762–66, 71768, 71770, 71772, 71801–02, 71820, 71822–23, 71825–28, 71831–42, 71844–47, 71851–55, 71857–62, 71864–66, 71901–03, 71909–10, 71913–14, 71920–23, 71929, 71932–33, 71935, 71937, 71940–45, 71949–50, 71952–53, 71956–62, 71964–65, 71968–73, 71998–99, 72004, 72015, 72046, 72055, 72057, 72065, 72072–73, 72079, 72084, 72087, 72104–05, 72128–29, 72132–33, 72150, 72152, 72160, 72167–68, 72175, 72182, 72379, 72826–27, 72833–35, 72838, 72841–42, 72851, 72855, 72863, 72865, 72924, 72926–28, 72933, 72943–44, 72949–51, 72958

CALIFORNIA

(Population 2000, 33,871,648)

SENATORS

DIANNE FEINSTEIN, Democrat, of San Francisco, CA; born in San Francisco, June 22, 1933; education: B.A., Stanford University, 1955; elected to San Francisco Board of Supervisors, 1970–78; president of Board of Supervisors: 1970–71, 1974–75, 1978; mayor of San Francisco, 1978–88; candidate for governor of California, 1990; recipient: Distinguished Woman Award, *San Francisco Examiner;* Achievement Award, Business and Professional Women's Club, 1970; Golden Gate University, California, LL.D. (hon.), 1979; SCOPUS Award for Outstanding Public Service, American Friends of the Hebrew University of Jerusalem; University of Santa Clara, D.P.S. (hon.); University of Manila, D.P.A. (hon.), 1981; Antioch University, LL.D. (hon.), 1983; Los Angeles Anti-Defamation League of B'nai B'rith's Distinguished Service Award, 1984; French Legion d'Honneur from President Mitterand, 1984; Mills College, LL.D. (hon.), 1985; U.S. Army's Commander's Award for Public Service, 1986; Brotherhood/Sisterhood Award, National Conference of Christians and Jews, 1986; Paulist Fathers Award, 1987; Episcopal Church Award for Service, 1987; U.S. Navy Distinguished Civilian Award, 1987; Silver Spur Award for Outstanding Public Service, San Francisco Planning and Urban Renewal Association, 1987; All Pro Management Team Award for No. 1 Mayor, *City and State* Magazine, 1987; Community Service Award Honoree for Public Service, 1987; American Jewish Congress, 1987; President's Award, St. Ignatius High School, San Francisco, 1988; Coro Investment in Leadership Award, 1988; President's Medal, University of California at San Francisco, 1988; University of San Francisco, D.H.L. (hon.), 1988; member: Coro Foundation, Fellowship, 1955–56; California Women's Board of Terms and Parole, 1960–66, executive committee; U.S. Conference of Mayors, 1983–88; Mayor's Commission on Crime, San Francisco; Bank of California, director, 1988–89; San Francisco Education Fund's Permanent Fund, 1988–89; Japan Society of Northern California, 1988–89; Inter-American Dialogue, 1988–present; married: Dr. Bertram Feinstein (dec.); married on January 20, 1980, to Richard C. Blum; children: one child; three stepchildren; religion: Jewish; committees: chair, Rules and Administration; chair, Joint Committee on the Library; vice chair, Joint Committee on Printing; Appropriations; Judiciary; Select Committee on Intelligence; elected to the U.S. Senate, by special election, on November 3, 1992, to fill the vacancy caused by the resignation of Senator Pete Wilson; reelected to each succeeding Senate term.

Office Listings

http://feinstein.senate.gov

331 Hart Senate Office Building, Washington, DC 20510 .... (202) 224–3841
FAX: 228–3954
Chief of Staff.—Peter Cleveland.
Legislative Director.—Chris Thompson.
Director of Communications.—Scott Gerber.
750 B Street, Suite 1030, San Diego, CA 92101 .... (619) 231–9712
2500 Tulare Street, Suite 4290, Fresno, CA 93721 .... (559) 485–7430
One Post Street, Suite 2450, San Francisco, CA 94104 .... (415) 393–0707
11111 San Monica Boulevard, Suite 915, Los Angles, CA 90025 .... (310) 914–7300

* * *

BARBARA BOXER, Democrat, of Palm Springs, CA; born in Brooklyn, NY, November 11, 1940; education: B.A. in economics, Brooklyn College, 1962; professional: stockbroker and economic researcher with securities firms on Wall Street, 1962–65; journalist and associate editor, *Pacific Sun* newspaper, 1972–74; congressional aide, Fifth Congressional District, California, 1974–76; elected Marin County Board of Supervisors, 1976–82; first woman president, Marin County Board of Supervisors; Edgar Wayburn award, Sierra Club, 1997; Policy Leadership award, Family Violence Prevention Fund, 2000; Circle of Courage award, Afghan Women Association International and the Women's Intercultural Network, 2003; Children's Champion award, California Head Start Association, 2003; married: Stewart Boxer, 1962; children: Doug and Nicole; committees: chair, Environment and Public Works; Commerce, Science, and Transportation; Foreign Relations; Select Committee on Ethics; elected November 2, 1982 to 98th Congress; reelected to the 99th–102nd Congresses; elected to the U.S. Senate on November 3, 1992; reelected to each succeeding Senate term.

Office Listings

http://boxer.senate.gov

112 Hart Senate Office Building, Washington, DC 20510 .... (202) 224–3553

Chief of Staff.—Laura Schiller. FAX: 228–2382
Legislative Director.—Polly Trottenberg.
Communications Director.—Natalie Ravitz.
1700 Montgomery Street, Suite 240, San Francisco, CA 94111 .... (415) 403–0100
312 North Spring Street, Suite 1748, Los Angeles, CA 90012 .... (213) 894–5000
501 I Street, Suite 7–600, Sacramento, CA 95814 .... (916) 448–2787
201North E Street, Suite 210, San Bernadino, CA 92401 .... (909) 888–8525
600 B Street, Suite 2240, San Diego, CA 92101 .... (619) 239–3884
2500 Tulare Street, Suite 5290, Fresno, CA 93721 .... (209) 497–5109

REPRESENTATIVES

FIRST DISTRICT

MIKE THOMPSON, Democrat, of Napa Valley, CA; born in St. Helena, CA, January 24, 1951; education: graduated, St. Helena High School, St. Helena, CA; U.S. Army, 1969–72; Purple Heart; B.A., Chico State University, 1982; M.A., Chico State University, 1996; teacher at San Francisco State University, and Chico State University; elected to the California State Senate, 2nd District, 1990–98; former chairman of the California State Senate Budget Committee; married to Janet; two children: Christopher and Jon; committees: Ways and Means; Permanent Select Committee on Intelligence; elected to the 106th Congress; reelected to each succeeding Congress.

Office Listings

http://mikethompson.house.gov http://www.house.gov/writerep

231 Cannon House Office Building, Washington, DC 20515 .... (202) 225–3311
Chief of Staff.—Charles Jefferson. FAX: 225–4335
Legislative Director.—Jonathan Birdsong.
Communication Director.—Anne Warden.
1040 Main Street, Suite 101, Napa, CA 94559 .... (707) 226–9898
Chief of Staff/Press Secretary.—Ed Matovcik.
317 Third Street, Suite 1, Eureka, CA 95501 .... (707) 269–9595
Post Office Box 2208, Fort Bragg, CA 95437 .... (707) 962–0933
712 Main Street, Suite 1, Woodland, CA 95695 .... (530) 662–5272

Counties: Del Norte County. Cities and townships: Crescent City, Fortdeck, Gasquet, Klamath, Prison, Smith River. Humboldt County. Cities and townships: Alderpoint, Areata, Bayside, Blocksburg, Blue Lake, Burcka, Carlotta, Eureka, Ferndale, Fortuna, Garberville, Hoopa, Hydseville, Kneeland, Korbel, Loleta, McKinlayville, Myers Flat, Orick, Petrolia, Redcrest, Redway, Rio Del, Scotia, Trinidad, Whitehorn, Willow Creek. Lake County. Cities and townships: Clearlake, Clearlake Oaks, Clearlake Park, Cobb, Glenhaven, Kelseyville, Lakeport, Lower Lake, Lucerne, Middletown, Nice, Upper Lake. Mendocino County. Cities and townships: Albion, Boonville, Calpella, Compiche, Covelo, Elk, Finley, Fort Bragg, Gualala, Hopland, Laytonville, Little River, Manchester, Mendocino, Philo, Piercy, Point Arena, Potter Valley, Redwood Valley, Talmage, Ukiah, Willits, Yorkville. Napa County. Cities and townships: American Canyon, Angwin, Aetna Springs, Calistoga, Deer Park, Oakville, Pope Valley, Rutherford, St. Helena. Sonoma County (part). Cities and townships: Alexander Valley, Cloverdale, Geyserville, Healdsburg, Mark West, Santa Rosa, Sonoma, Windsor. Yolo County (part). Cities and townships: Davis, West Sacramento, Winters, and Woodland. Population (2000), 639,087.

ZIP Codes: 94503, 94508, 94515, 94558–59, 94562, 94567, 94573–74, 94576, 94581, 94589–90, 94599, 95403–04, 95409–10, 95415–18, 95420, 95422–29, 95432–33, 95435, 95437, 95441–43, 95445, 95448–49, 95451–54, 95456–61, 95463–64, 95466, 95468–70, 95476, 95481–82, 95485, 95487–88, 95490, 95492–94, 95501–03, 95511, 95514, 95518–19, 95521, 95524–26, 95528, 95531–32, 95534, 95536–38, 95540, 95542–43, 95545–51, 95553–56, 95558–60, 95562, 95564–65, 95567, 95569–71, 95573, 95585, 95587, 95589, 95605, 95612, 95615–16, 95618, 95691, 95694–95, 95776, 95798–99, 95899

* * *

SECOND DISTRICT

WALLY HERGER, Republican, of Marysville, CA; born in Sutter County, CA, May 20, 1945; education: graduated East Nicolaus High School; attended California State University, Sacramento, CA; professional: cattle rancher; small businessman; East Nicolaus High School Board of Trustees, 1977–80; California State Assemblyman, 1980–86; member: National Federation of Independent Business; Sutter County Taxpayers Association; Yuba-Sutter Farm Bureau; California Cattlemen's Association; California Chamber of Commerce; Big Brothers/ Big Sisters Board of Directors; South Yuba Rotary Club; married: the former Pamela Sargent; children: eight; committees: Ways and Means; elected to the 100th Congress, November 4, 1986; reelected to each succeeding Congress.

Office Listings

2268 Rayburn House Office Building, Washington, DC 20515 .... (202) 225–3076

Administrative Assistant.—Derek Harley. FAX: 226–0852
Legislative Director.—Daniel MacLean.
Press Secretary.—Darin Thacker.
Executive Assistant / Scheduler.—Laura Cannon.
Suite 104, 55 Independence Circle, Chico, CA 95973 .... (530) 893–8363
District Director.—Fran Peace.
410 Hemsted Drive, Suite 115, Redding, CA 96002 .... (530) 223–5898

Counties: BUTTE (part), COLUSA, GLENN, SHASTA, SISKIYOU, SUTTER, TEHAMA, TRINITY, YOLO (part), YUBA. Population (2000), 639,087.

ZIP Codes: 95526–27, 95552, 95563, 95568, 95595, 95606–07, 95627, 95637, 95645, 95653, 95659, 95668, 95674, 95676, 95679, 95692, 95697–98, 95837, 95901, 95903, 95912–14, 95917–20, 95922, 95925–29, 95932, 95935–39, 95941–43, 95947–48, 95950–51, 95953–55, 95957–58, 95960–63, 95967, 95969–74, 95976–79, 95981–82, 95987–88, 95991–93, 96001–03, 96007–08, 96010–11, 96013–14, 96016–17, 96019, 96021–25, 96027–29, 96031–35, 96037–41, 96044, 96046–52, 96055–59, 96061–65, 96067, 96069–71, 96073–76, 96078–80, 96084–97, 96099, 96101, 96103–04, 96114, 96118, 96122, 96124, 96134, 96137, 96161

* * *

THIRD DISTRICT

DANIEL E. LUNGREN, Republican, of Gold River, CA; born in Long Beach, CA, September 22, 1946; education: St. Anthony's High School, Long Beach, CA, 1964; B.A., English, University of Notre Dame, 1968 (with honors); attended University of Southern California Law Center, 1968–69; J.D., Georgetown University Law Center, 1971; professional: attorney, associate and partner, Ball, Hunt, Brown & Baerwitz (law firm), 1973–78; U.S. House of Representatives, 1979–89; elected California Attorney General, 1990, served two terms; Republican nominee for Governor of California, 1998; radio talk show host; consultant; private law practice, 1999–2004; religion: Catholic; married: the former Barbara (Bobbi) Knolls, 1969; children: Jeff, Kelly, and Kathleen; committees: Budget; Homeland Security; House Administration; Judiciary; elected to the 109th Congress on November 2, 2004; reelected to each succeeding Congress.

Office Listings

http://www.house.gov/lungren

2448 Rayburn House Office Building, Washington, DC 20515 .... (202) 225–5716
FAX: 226–1298
Chief of Staff.—Victor Arnold-Bik.
Communications Director.—Brian Kaveney.
Scheduler.—Samantha Dravis.
2339 Gold Medal Way, Suite 220, Gold River, CA 95670 .... (916) 859–9906

Counties: ALPINE, AMADOR, CALAVERAS, SACRAMENTO (part), SOLANO (part). CITIES AND TOWNSHIPS: Amador, Arden-Arcade, Carmichael, Citrus Heights, Elk Grove, Fair Oaks, Folsom, Foothill Farms, Galt, Gold River, Ione, Jackson, Laguna, Laguna West, LaRiviera, North Highland, Rancho Cordova, Rancho Murieta, Rio Linda, Rio Vista, Roseville, Sacramento, Vineyard, and Wilton. Population (2000), 639,088.

ZIP Codes: 94571, 94585, 95221–26, 95228–30, 95232–33, 95236, 95245–52, 95254–55, 95257, 95601, 95608, 95610–11, 95615, 95620–21, 95624, 95626, 95628–30, 95632, 95638–40, 95642, 95646, 95652, 95654–55, 95660, 95662, 95665–66, 95668–71, 95673, 95675, 95683, 95685, 95688–90, 95693–94, 95699, 95742, 95758–59, 95763, 95821, 95825–30, 95832, 95835–37, 95841–43, 95864, 96021–22, 96029, 96035, 96055, 96061, 96080, 96120

* * *

FOURTH DISTRICT

JOHN T. DOOLITTLE, Republican, of Rocklin, CA; born in Glendale, CA, October 30, 1950; education: graduated Cupertino High School, Cupertino, CA, 1968; University of California at Santa Cruz, 1972; University of the Pacific, McGeorge School of Law, 1978; professional: lawyer; member: California bar; elected to the California State Senate, 1980; reelected 1984 and 1988; served as chairman of the Senate Republican Caucus, May 1987–April 1990; married: the former Julia Harlow, 1979; children: John, Jr. and Courtney Doolittle; committees: Appropriations; elected to the 102nd Congress, November 6, 1990; reelected to each succeeding Congress.

Office Listings

http://www.house.gov/doolittle

2410 Rayburn House Office Building, Washington, DC 20515 .... (202) 225–2511
FAX: 225–5444
Chief of Staff.—Richard Robinson.
Executive Assistant.—Alisha Perkins.
Legislative Director.—Evan Goitein.
4230 Douglas Boulevard, Suite 200, Granite Bay, CA 95746 .... (916) 786–5560

Deputy Chief of Staff.—Dan Blankenburg.

Counties: BUTTE (part), EL DORADO, LASSEN, MODOC, NEVADA, PLACER, PLUMAS, SACRAMENTO (part), SIERRA. Population (2000), 639,088.

ZIP Codes: 95602–04, 95609, 95613–14, 95617, 95619, 95623, 95626, 95628–31, 95633–36, 95648, 95650–51, 95656, 95658, 95661–64, 95667–68, 95672, 95677–78, 95681–82, 95684, 95701, 95703, 95709, 95712–15, 95717, 95720–22, 95724, 95726, 95728, 95735–36, 95741, 95746–47, 95762, 95765, 95816, 95910, 95915–16, 95922–24, 95930, 95934, 95940–41, 95944–47, 95949, 95956, 95959–60, 95965–66, 95968, 95971, 95975, 95977, 95980, 95983–84, 95986, 96006, 96009, 96015, 96020, 96054, 96056, 96068, 96101, 96103–30, 96132–33, 96135–37, 96140–43, 96145–46, 96148, 96150–52, 96154–56, 96158, 96160–62

* * *

FIFTH DISTRICT

DORIS OKADA MATSUI, Democrat, of Sacramento, CA; born in Posten, AZ, September 25, 1944; education: B.A., University of California, Berkeley, CA, 1966; professional: staff, White House, 1992–98; private advocate; organizations: Meridian International Center Board of Trustees; Woodrow Wilson Center Board of Trustees; California Institute Board of Directors; married: Robert Matsui, 1966; children: Brian Robert; committees: Rules; Transportation and Infrastructure; elected by special election on March 8, 2005 to the 109th Congress, to fill the vacancy caused by the death of her husband, Representative Robert Matsui; reelected to each succeeding Congress.

Office Listings

http://www.house.gov/matsui

222 Cannon House Office Building, Washington, DC 20515 .... (202) 225–7163
Chief of Staff.—Joe Trahern. FAX: 225–0566
Executive Assistant.—Deborah Chusmir.
Legislative Director.—John Young.
Press Secretary.—Adriana Surfas.
501 I Street, 12–600, Sacramento, CA 95814 .... (916) 498–5600
District Director.—Chris Norem.

County: SACRAMENTO COUNTY (part). CITY: Sacramento. Population (2000), 639,088.

ZIP Codes: 94204–09, 94211, 94229–30, 94232, 94234–37, 94239–40, 94244, 94246–49, 94252, 94254, 94256–59, 94261–63, 94267–69, 94271, 94273–74, 94277–80, 94282, 94284–91, 94293–99, 95660, 95670, 95758, 95812–20, 95822–29, 95831–35, 95838, 95840–43, 95851–53, 95860, 95864–67, 95887, 95894

* * *

SIXTH DISTRICT

LYNN C. WOOLSEY, Democrat, of Petaluma, CA; born in Seattle, WA, November 3, 1937; education: graduated from Lincoln High School, Seattle; B.S., University of San Francisco, 1981; president and founder, Woolsey Personnel Service, 1980–92; human resources manager, Harris Digital Telephone Systems, 1969–80; elected member, Petaluma City Council, 1984–92; vice mayor, 1989 and 1992; member and chair, Sonoma County National Women's Political Caucus; chair, Sonoma County Commission on the Status of Women; Business and Professional Women; National Organization for Women; Sierra Club; chair, Sonoma County Hazardous Materials Management Commission; Association of Bay Area Governments, Regional Hazardous Materials Representative; advisory committee, CAL Energy Commission; co-chair, Education Task Force of the California Delegation Bipartisan Caucus; the Renewable Energy Caucus; the Congressional Human Rights Caucus; the Missing and Exploited Children's Caucus (founding member); the Congressional Task Force on Health and Tobacco; the Internet Caucus; the Congressional Task Force on International HIV/AIDS; the Congressional Friends of Animals; and the Livable Communities Task Force; chair of the Children's Task Force; co-chair of the Democratic Caucus Task Force on Welfare Reform; co-chair of the Progressive Caucus; member of the House Democratic leadership as a Regional Whip; four children: Joseph Critchett, Michael Woolsey, Ed Critchett, and Amy Critchett; four grandchildren; committees: Education and Labor; Foreign Affairs; Science and Technology; elected on November 3, 1992 to the 103rd Congress; reelected to each succeeding Congress.

Office Listings

http://www.house.gov/woolsey

2263 Rayburn House Office Building, Washington, DC 20515 .... (202) 225–5161

Chief of Staff.—Nora Matus. FAX: 225–5163
Press Secretary.—Christopher Shields.
1101 College Avenue, Suite 200, Santa Rosa, CA 95404 .... (707) 542–7182
District Director.—Wendy Friefeld.
1050 Northgate Drive, Suite 140, San Rafael, CA 94903 .... (415) 507–9554

Counties: MARIN, SONOMA (part). CITIES AND TOWNSHIPS: Santa Rosa, Sebastapol, Cotati, Petaluma, and Sonoma to Golden Gate Bridge. Population (2000), 639,087.

ZIP Codes: 94901, 94903–04, 94912–15, 94920, 94922–31, 94933, 94937–42, 94945–57, 94960, 94963–66, 94970–79, 94998–99, 95401–07, 95409, 95412, 95419, 95421, 95430–31, 95436, 95439, 95441–42, 95444, 95446, 95448, 95450, 95452, 95462, 95465, 95471–73, 95476, 95480, 95486, 95492, 95497

* * *

SEVENTH DISTRICT

GEORGE MILLER, Democrat, of Martinez, CA; born in Richmond, CA, May 17, 1945; education: attended Martinez public schools; Diablo Valley College; graduated, San Francisco State College, 1968; J.D., University of California at Davis School of Law, 1972; member: California State bar; Davis Law School Alumni Association; served five years as legislative aide to Senate majority leader, California State Legislature; past chairman and member of Contra Costa County Democratic Central Committee; past president of Martinez Democratic Club; married: the former Cynthia Caccavo; children: George and Stephen; four grandchildren; committees: chair, Education and Labor; Natural Resources; elected to the 94th Congress, November 5, 1974; reelected to each succeeding Congress.

Office Listings

http://www.house.gov/georgemiller george.miller@mail.house.gov

2205 Rayburn House Office Building, Washington, DC 20515 .... (202) 225–2095
FAX: 225–5609
Chief of Staff/Press Secretary.—Daniel Weiss.
Personal Secretary.—Sylvia Arthur.
1333 Willow Pass Road, Suite 203, Concord, CA 94520 .... (925) 602–1880
District Director.—Barbara Johnson.
Room 281, 3220 Blume Drive, Richmond, CA 94806 .... (510) 262–6500
Field Representative.—Latressa Alford.
375 G Street, Suite 1, Vallejo, CA 94592 .... (707) 645–1888
Field Representative.—Kathy Hoffman.

Counties: CONTRA COSTA (part), SOLANO (part). CITIES AND TOWNSHIPS: Benicia, Clayton, Concord, Crockett, El Sobrante, Green Valley, Hercules, Martinez, Pinole, Pittsburg, Port Costa, Richmond, Rodeo, San Pablo, Sulsun Valley, Vacaville, and Vallejo. Population (2000), 639,088.

ZIP Codes: 94503, 94510, 94517, 94519–25, 94527, 94529, 94533–34, 94547, 94553, 94564–65, 94569, 94572, 94585, 94589–92, 94801–08, 94820, 94875, 95687–88, 95696

* * *

EIGHTH DISTRICT

NANCY PELOSI, Democrat, of San Francisco, CA; born in Baltimore, MD, March 26, 1940; daughter of the late Representative Thomas D'Alesandro, Jr., of MD; education: graduated, Institute of Notre Dame High School, 1958; B.A., Trinity College, Washington, DC (major, political science; minor, history), 1962; northern chair, California Democratic Party, 1977–81; state chair, California Democratic Party, 1981–83; chair, 1984 Democratic National Convention Host Committee; finance chair, Democratic Senatorial Campaign Committee, 1985–86; member: Democratic National Committee; California Democratic Party Executive Committee; San Francisco Library Commission; Board of Trustees, LSB Leakey Foundation; married: Paul F. Pelosi, 1963; children: Nancy Corinne, Christine, Jacqueline, Paul, Jr., and Alexandra; elected by special election, June 2, 1987, to the 100th Congress to fill the vacancy caused by the death of Sala Burton; elected Minority Leader for the 108th and 109th Congress; elected Speaker of the House for the 110th Congress.

Office Listings

http://www.house.gov/pelosi sf.nancy@mail.house.gov

235 Cannon House Office Building, Washington, DC 20515 .... (202) 225–4965

Chief of Staff.—Terri McCullough. FAX: 225–8259
Office Manager.—Paula Short.
450 Golden Gate Avenue, Room 14370, San Francisco, CA 94102 .... (415) 556–4862
District Director.—Dan Bernal.

County: SAN FRANCISCO COUNTY (part). CITY: San Francisco. Population (2000), 639,088.

ZIP Codes: 94101–12, 94114–15, 94117–26, 94128–47, 94150–52, 94155–56, 94158–66, 94168, 94170, 94172, 94175, 94177, 94188, 94199

* * *

NINTH DISTRICT

BARBARA LEE, Democrat, of Oakland, CA; born in El Paso, TX, July 16, 1946; education: graduated, San Fernando High School; B.A., Mills College, 1973; MSW, University of California, Berkeley, 1975; congressional aide and public servant; senior advisor and chief of staff to Congressman Ronald V. Dellums in Washington, DC, and Oakland, CA, 1975–87; California State Assembly, 1990–96; California State Senate, 1996–98; Assembly committees: Housing and Land Use; Appropriations; Business and Professions; Industrial Relations; Judiciary; Revenue and Taxation; board member, California State Coastal Conservancy, District Export Council, and California Defense Conversion Council; committees: Appropriations; elected to the 105th Congress on April 7, 1998, by special election, to fill the remaining term of retiring Representative Ronald V. Dellums; reelected to each succeeding Congress.

Office Listings

http://www.house.gov/lee

2444 Rayburn House Office Building, Washington, DC 20515 .... (202) 225–2661
Administrative Assistant.—Julie Nickson. FAX: 225–9817
Scheduler.—Tatyana Kalinga.
Communications Director.—Nathan Britton.
Legislative Director.—Ven Neralla.
1301 Clay Street, Suite 1000–N, Oakland, CA 94612 .... (510) 763–0370

Counties: ALAMEDA COUNTY. CITIES: Alameda, Albany, Berkeley, Emeryville, Kensington, Piedmont. OAKLAND COUNTY (part). Population (2000), 639,088.

ZIP Codes: 94541–42, 94546, 94552, 94577–80, 94588, 94601–13, 94615, 94617–26, 94643, 94649, 94659–62, 94666, 94701–10, 94712, 94720

* * *

TENTH DISTRICT

ELLEN O. TAUSCHER, Democrat, of Alamo, CA; born in East Newark, NJ, November 15, 1951; education: graduated, Harrison High School, Harrison, NJ, 1969; B.S. in early childhood education, Seton Hall University, NJ; founder and CEO, The Registry Companies, the first national child care provider pre-employment screening service, 1992–present; one of the first women to hold a seat on the New York Stock Exchange (1977–79); Wall Street trader and investment banker, 1979–88; author of *The Child Care Source Book*; created the Tauscher Foundation, which has provided $150,000 to California and Texas elementary schools for purchase of computer equipment; member: NARAL, CARAL, Planned Parenthood, Seton Hall University Board of Regents; endorsed by Emily's List; co-chair, Dianne Feinstein's 1992, and 1994, U.S. Senatorial campaigns; married William Y. Tauscher in 1989; one child: Katherine; committees: Armed Services; Transportation and Infrastructure; elected to the 105th Congress; reelected to each succeeding Congress.

Office Listings

http://www.house.gov/tauscher

2459 Rayburn House Office Building, Washington, DC 20515 .... (202) 225–1880
Chief of Staff.—April Boyd. FAX: 225–5914
Legislative Director.—Simon Limage.
2121 North California Boulevard, Suite 555, Walnut Creek, CA 94596 .... (925) 932–8899
District Director.—Jennifer Barton.
2000 Cadenasso Drive, Suite A, Fairfield, CA 94533 .... (707) 428–7792
420 West Third Street, Antioch, CA 94509 .... (925) 757–7187

Counties: CONTRA COSTA (part), ALAMEDA (part), SACRAMENTO (part), SOLANO (part). CITIES AND TOWNSHIPS: Alamo, Antioch, Blackhawk, Bethel Island, Brentwood, Byron, Clayton, Concord, Danville, Diablo, Dublin, Fairfield, Lafayette, Livermore, Moraga, Oakley, Orinda, Pleasant Hill, and Walnut Creek. Population (2000), 639,088.

ZIP Codes: 94507, 94509–12, 94516, 94518, 94520–21, 94523, 94530–31, 94533–35, 94548–51, 94556, 94561, 94563, 94570–71, 94575, 94585, 94588, 94595–98, 94706–08, 94803, 95377, 95391, 95620, 95625, 95641, 95680, 95690

* * *

ELEVENTH DISTRICT

JERRY MCNERNEY, Democrat, of Pleasanton, CA; born in Albuquerque, NM, June 18, 1951; attended the U.S. Military Academy, West Point, NY, 1969–71; A.S., University of New Mexico, Albuquerque, NM, 1973; M.S., University of New Mexico, NM, 1975; Ph.D. in Mathematics, University on New Mexico, 1981; professional: wind engineer; entrepreneur; business owner; married: Mary; children: Michael, Windy and Greg; committees: Science and Technology; Transporation and Infrastructure; elected to the 110th Congress on November 7, 2006.

Office Listings

http://www.house.gov

312 Cannon House Office Building, Washington, DC 20515 .... (202) 225–1947
FAX: 225–4060
Chief of Staff.—Angela Louters.
Executive Assistant.—Teresa Frison.
Communications Director.—Nicole Philbin.
Legislative Director.—Nick Holder.
Press Secretary.—Andy Stone.
2495 West March Lane, Suite 104, Stockton, CA 95207 .... (209) 951–3091
District Director.—Nicole Goehring.
3000 Executive Parkway, Suite 104, San Ramon, CA 94583 .... (925) 866–7040
Bay Area Director.—Cindy Chin.

Counties: ALAMEDA (part), CONTRA COSTA (part), SAN JOAQUIN (part), SANTA CLARA (part). CITIES AND TOWNSHIPS: Blackhawk, Brentwood, Byron, Clements, Danville, Diablo, Discovery Bay, Dublin, Escalon, Farmington, Linden, Lockeford, Lodi, Manteca, Morada, Morgan Hill, Pleasanton, Ripon, San Ramon, Stockton, Sunol, Tracy, and Woodbridge. Population (2000), 639,088.

ZIP Codes: 94506–07, 94509, 94513–14, 94526, 94528, 94539, 94550, 94566, 94568, 94583, 94586, 94588, 95020, 95023, 95037–38, 95046, 95127, 95132, 95135, 95138, 95140, 95204, 95207, 95209–12, 95215, 95219–20, 95227, 95230, 95234, 95236–37, 95240–42, 95253, 95258, 95267, 95297, 95304, 95320, 95336–37, 95361, 95366, 95376–77, 95391, 95686

* * *

TWELFTH DISTRICT

TOM LANTOS, Democrat, of San Mateo, CA; born in Budapest, February 1, 1928; during World War II active in anti-Nazi underground; came to the United States in 1947 on academic scholarship; education: B.A., University of Washington, 1949; M.A., University of Washington, 1950; Ph.D., University of California, 1953, Phi Beta Kappa; professor of economics; consultant, TV news analyst and commentator; member, Millbrae Board of Education, 1950–66; administrative assistant, economic and foreign policy adviser, U.S. Senate; married: Annette Tillemann; two married daughters: Annette Tillemann-Dick and Katrina Swett; 17 grandchildren; co-chairman, Congressional Human Rights Caucus; member, U.S. Holocaust Memorial Council; committees: chair, Foreign Affairs; Oversight and Government Reform; elected to the 97th Congress on November 4, 1980; reelected to each succeeding Congress.

Office Listings

http://www.house.gov/lantos

2413 Rayburn House Office Building, Washington, DC 20515 .... (202) 225–3531
FAX: 226–4183
Administrative Assistant.—Robert R. King.
Legislative Director.—Ron Grimes.
400 South El Camino Real, Suite 410, San Mateo, CA 94402 .... (650) 342–0300
District Representative.—Evelyn Szelenyi.

Counties: SAN MATEO COUNTY (part). CITIES: Brisbane, Burlingame, Colma, Daly City, Foster City, Hillsborough, Millbrae, Montara, Moss Beach, Pacifica, Redwood City, San Bruno, San Carlos, San Mateo, South San Francisco. SAN FRANCISCO COUNTY (part). CITIES: San Francisco. Population (2000), 639,088.

ZIP Codes: 94005, 94010–11, 94013–17, 94021, 94030, 94037–38, 94044, 94061–63, 94065–66, 94070, 94080, 94083, 94099, 94112, 94116–17, 94122, 94127–28, 94131–32, 94143, 94401–09, 94497

* * *

THIRTEENTH DISTRICT

FORTNEY PETE STARK, Democrat, of Fremont, CA; born in Milwaukee, WI, November 11, 1931; education: graduated, Wauwatosa, WI, High School, 1949; B.S., Massachusetts Institute of Technology, 1953; M.B.A., University of California, Berkeley, 1960; G.E.D., East Bay Skills Center, Oakland, 1972 (honorary); served in U.S. Air Force, 1955–57, first lieutenant; banker, founder, and president, Security National Bank, Walnut Creek, CA, 1963–72; trustee, California Democratic Council; chairman, board of trustees, Starr King School of Ministry, Berkeley; trustee, Graduate Theological Union, Berkeley; sponsor, Northern California American Civil Liberties Union; board member, Housing Development Corporation and Council for Civic Unity; director, Common Cause, 1971–72; married: Deborah Roderick; children: Jeffrey Peter, Beatrice Stark Winslow, Thekla Stark Wainwright, Sarah Stark Ramirez, Fortney Stark III, Hannah and Andrew; committees: Ways and Means; elected to the 93rd Congress, November 7, 1972; reelected to each succeeding Congress.

Office Listings

239 Cannon House Office Building, Washington, DC 20515 .... (202) 225–5065
Chief of Staff.—Debbie Curtis. FAX: 226–3805
Personal Assistant.—Krista Lamoreaux.
39300 Civic Center Drive, Fremont, CA 94538 .... (510) 494–1388
District Administrator.—Jo Cazenave.

Counties: ALAMEDA COUNTY (part). CITIES AND TOWNSHIPS: Alameda, Castro Valley, Fremont, Hayward, Milpitas, Newark, Oakland, San Leandro, San Lorenzo, Sunnyvale, Sunol, and Union City. Population (2000), 639,088.

ZIP Codes: 94501–02, 94536–46, 94552, 94555, 94557, 94560, 94566, 94577–80, 94586–88, 94603, 94605, 94621, 94622

* * *

FOURTEENTH DISTRICT

ANNA G. ESHOO, Democrat, of Menlo Park, CA; born in New Britain, CT, December 13, 1942; education: attended Canada College; San Mateo supervisor, 1983–92; served on the House Committees on Science, Space, and Technology, and Merchant Marine and Fisheries; Democratic Regional Whip since 1993; selected to co-chair the House Medical Technology Caucus, 1994; committees: Energy and Commerce; Permanent Select Committee on Intelligence; elected on November 3, 1992, to the 103rd Congress; reelected to each succeeding Congress.

Office Listings

http://www-eshoo.house.gov

205 Cannon House Office Building, Washington, DC 20515 .... (202) 225–8104
Chief of Staff.—Jason Mahler. FAX: 225–8890
Executive Assistant.—Dana Sandman.
Legislative Director.—Steven Keenan.
698 Emerson Street, Palo Alto, CA 94301 .... (650) 323–2984
Chief of Staff.—Karen Chapman.

Counties: SAN MATEO (part), SANTA CLARA (part), SANTA CRUZ (part). CITIES AND TOWNSHIPS: Amesti, Aptos, Atherton, Belmont, Ben Lomond, Bonny Doon, Boulder Creek, Brookdale, Corralitos, Davenport, East Palo Alto, Felton, Half Moon Bay, Interlaken, La Honda, Los Altos, Los Altos Hills, Menlo Park, Monte Sereno, Mountain View, Palo Alto, Portola Valley, Redwood City, San Carlos, Scotts Valley, Stanford, Sunnyvale, and Woodside. Population (2000), 639,088.

ZIP Codes: 94002, 94018–28, 94035, 94039–43, 94060–64, 94074, 94085–89, 94301–06, 94309, 95003, 95005–08, 95014, 95017–18, 95030, 95033, 95041, 95051, 95060, 95065–67, 95070–71, 95073, 95076, 95130

* * *

FIFTEENTH DISTRICT

MICHAEL M. HONDA, Democrat, of San Jose, CA; born in Walnut Creek, CA, June 27, 1941; education: San Jose State University, received degrees in Biological Sciences and Spanish, and a Masters Degree in Education; awards: California Federation of Teachers Legislator of the Year; Outreach Paratransit Services Humanitarian Award; AEA Legislator of the Year; Service Employees International Union Home Care Champion Award; Asian Law Alliance Community Impact Award; AFL–CIO Distinguished Friend of Labor Award; chair, Congressional Asian Pacific American Caucus; chair, Ethiopia and Ethiopian American Caucus; public service: Peace Corps; San Jose Planning Commission; San Jose Unified School Board; Santa Clara County Board of Supervisors; California State Assemblyman; married: Jeanne; children: Mark and Michelle; committees: Appropriations; Science and Technology; vice chair, Democratic National Committee; senior Majority Whip; elected to the 107th Congress on November 7, 2000; reelected to each succeeding Congress.

Office Listings

http://www.house.gov/honda

1713 Longworth House Office Building, Washington, DC 20515 .... (202) 225–2631
Chief of Staff.—Jennifer Van der Heide Escobar. FAX: 225–2699
Legislative Director.—Eric Werwa.
Senior Legislative Counsel.—Bob Sakaniwa.
Communications Director.—Daniel Kohns.
1999 South Bascom Avenue, Suite 815, Campbell, CA 95008 .... (408) 558–8085
District Director.—Meri Maben.

Counties: SANTA CLARA COUNTY (part). CITIES AND TOWNSHIPS: Campbell, Cambrian Park, Cupertino, Fruitdale, Gilroy, Lexington Hill, Los Gatos, Milpitas, San Jose, and Santa Clara. Population (2000), 639,088.

ZIP Codes: 94024, 94087, 95002, 95008–09, 95011, 95014–15, 95020–21, 95026, 95030–33, 95035–37, 95044, 95050–56, 95070, 95101, 95112, 95117–18, 95120, 95123–34, 95150, 95153–55, 95157, 95160–61, 95170

* * *

SIXTEENTH DISTRICT

ZOE LOFGREN, Democrat, of San Jose, CA; born in San Mateo, CA, December 21, 1947; education: graduated Gunn High School, 1966; B.A., Stanford University, Stanford, CA, 1970; J.D., Santa Clara Law School, Santa Clara, CA, 1975; admitted to the California bar, 1975; District of Columbia bar, 1981; Supreme Court, 1986; member: board of trustees, San Jose Evergreen Community College District, 1979–81; board of supervisors, Santa Clara County, CA, 1981–94; married: John Marshall Collins, 1978; children: Sheila and John; committees: Homeland Security; House Administration; Judiciary; elected to the 104th Congress; reelected to each succeeding Congress.

Office Listings

http://www.house.gov/lofgren

102 Cannon House Office Building, Washington, DC 20515 .... (202) 225–3072
Chief of Staff.—Stacey Leavandosky. FAX: 225–3336
Communications Director.—Kyra Jennings.
Executive Assistant / Scheduler.—Haley Smith.
635 North First Street, Suite B, San Jose, CA 95112 .... (408) 271–8700
Chief of Staff.—Sandra Soto.

Counties: SANTA CLARA COUNTY (part). CITIES AND TOWNSHIPS: San Jose, San Martin, and unincorporated portions of southern Santa Clara County. Population (2000), 639,088.

ZIP Codes: 95008, 95013, 95020, 95035, 95037, 95042, 95046, 95103, 95106, 95108–13, 95115–16, 95118–28, 95131–36, 95138–40, 95148, 95151–52, 95156, 95158–59, 95164, 95172–73, 95190–94, 95196

* * *

SEVENTEENTH DISTRICT

SAM FARR, Democrat, of Carmel, CA; born in San Francisco, CA, July 4, 1941; education: attended Carmel, CA, public schools; B.S., biology, Willamette University, Salem, OR; studied at the Monterey Institute of International Studies; served in the Peace Corps for two years in Colombia, South America; worked as a consultant and employee of the California Assembly; elected to the California Assembly, 1980–93; former member of California Assembly's Committees on Education, Insurance, and Natural Resources; married to Shary Baldwin; one daughter: Jessica; committees: Appropriations; elected on June 8, 1993, by special election, to fill the vacancy caused by the resignation of Representative Leon Panetta; reelected to each succeeding Congress.

Office Listings

http://www.farr.house.gov

1221 Longworth House Office Building, Washington, DC 20515 .... (202) 225–2861
Administrative Assistant.—Rochelle Dornatt.
Legislative Director.—Debbie Merrill.
Press Secretary.—Jessica Schafer.
701 Ocean Avenue, Santa Cruz, CA 95060 .... (831) 429–1976
100 West Alisal Street, Salinas, CA 93901 .... (831) 424–2229

Counties: MONTEREY, SAN BENITO, SANTA CRUZ (southern half). Population (2000), 639,088.

ZIP Codes: 93426, 93450–51, 93901–02, 93905–08, 93912, 93915, 93920–28, 93930, 93932–33, 93940, 93942–44, 93950, 93953–55, 93960, 93962, 95001, 95003–04, 95010, 95012, 95019, 95023–24, 95039, 95043, 95045, 95060–65, 95073, 95075–77

* * *

EIGHTEENTH DISTRICT

DENNIS A. CARDOZA, Democrat, of Atwater, CA; born in Merced, CA, March 31, 1959; education: B.A., University of Maryland, 1982; professional: businessman; public service: Atwater City Council, 1984–87; California State Assembly, 1996–2002; awards: California State Sheriff's Association Legislator of the Year; Small Business Roundtable Legislator of the Year; Small Business Association Legislator of the Year; and University of California Legislator of the Year, for his work on behalf of U.C. Merced; religion: Catholic; family: married to Dr. Kathleen McLoughlin; children: Joey, Brittany, and Elaina; committees: Agriculture; Rules; elected to the 108th Congress on November 5, 2002; reelected to each succeeding Congress.

Office Listings

http://www.house.gov/cardoza

435 Cannon House Office Building, Washington, DC 20515 .... (202) 225–6131
FAX: 225–0819
Deputy Chief of Staff.—Jennifer Walsh.
Senior Policy Advisor.—Robin Adam.
Legislative Director.—Gary Palmquist.
1010 10th Street, Suite 5800, Modesto, CA 95354 .... (209) 527–1914
District Director.—Lisa Mantarro Moore.

Counties: FRESNO (part), MADERA (part), MERCED, SAN JOAQUIN (part), STANISLAUS (part). CITIES AND TOWNSHIPS: Atwater, Ceres, Dos Palos, Gustine, Lathrop, Livingston, Los Banos, Modesto, Newman, Patterson, and Stockton. Population (2000), 639,088.

ZIP Codes: 93606, 93610, 93620, 93622, 93630, 93635, 93637, 93661, 93665, 93706, 93722, 95201–08, 95210, 95213, 95215, 95231, 95269, 95296, 95301, 95303–04, 95307, 95312–13, 95315, 95317, 95319, 95322, 95324, 95326, 95330, 95333–34, 95336–37, 95340–41, 95344, 95348, 95350–54, 95357–58, 95360, 95363, 95365, 95369, 95374, 95380, 95385, 95387–88, 95397

* * *

NINETEENTH DISTRICT

GEORGE RADANOVICH, Republican, of Mariposa, CA; born in Mariposa, June 20, 1955; education: graduated, Mariposa County High School; B.A., California State Polytechnic University, 1978; assistant manager, Yosemite Bank, 1980–83; opened Mariposa County's first winery, 1986; charter member and president of the Mariposa Wine Grape Growers Association; founder, Mariposa Creek Parkway, 1985; treasurer, Mariposa Historical Society, 1982–83; member: Wine Institute; California Farm Bureau; California Association of Wine Grape Growers; Chambers of Commerce; California Ag Leadership, class XXI; chairman: Mariposa County Board of Supervisors; Mariposa County Planning Commission; executive director of the California State Mining and Mineral Museum Association; former chairman, Western Caucus, 106th Congress; founding member of the Wine Caucus; committees: Energy and Commerce; elected to the 104th Congress; reelected to each succeeding Congress.

Office Listings

http://www.radanovich.house.gov

2367 Rayburn House Office Building, Washington, DC 20515 .... (202) 225–4540
FAX: 225–3402
Chief of Staff.—Ted Maness.
Scheduler.—Alisa Sisemore.
1040 East Herndon, Suite 201, Fresno, CA 93720 .... (559) 449–2490

District Director.—Darren Rose.

Counties: FRESNO (part), MADERA (part), MARIPOSA (part), STANISLAUS (part), TUOLUMNE. CITIES AND TOWNSHIPS: Ahwahnee, Auberry, Bass Lake, Big Oak Flat, Cathey's Valley, Ceres, Chinese Camp, Chowchilla, Coarsegold, Columbia, Coleville, Coulterville, Crows Landing, Dardanelle, Denair, El Portal, Farmington, Firebaugh, Fish Camp, Fresno, Groveland, Hickman, Hornitos, Hughson, Kerman, Keyes, La Grange, Long Barn, Madera, Mariposa, Mendota, Midpines, Mi Wuk Village, Moccasin, Modesto, North Fork, Oakdale, Oakhurst, O'Neals, Pinecrest, Raymond, Riverbank, Salida, San Joaquin, Snelling, Sonora, Soulsbyville, Standard, Strawberry, Tranquillity, Tuolumne, Turlock, Twain Harte, Vernalis, Waterford, Wishon, and Yosemite National Park. Population (2000), 639,088.

ZIP Codes: 93601–02, 93604, 93610–11, 93614, 93622–23, 93626, 93630, 93637–40, 93643–45, 93650, 93653, 93660, 93668–69, 93704–06, 93710–11, 93720, 93722, 93726, 93728–29, 93741, 93755, 93765, 93780, 93784, 93790–94, 95230, 95305–07, 95309–11, 95313–14, 95316, 95318, 95321, 95323, 95325–29, 95335, 95338, 95345–47, 95350–51, 95355–57, 95360–61, 95364, 95367–68, 95370, 95372–73, 95375, 95379–80, 95382–83, 95386, 95389

* * *

TWENTIETH DISTRICT

JIM COSTA, Democrat, of Fresno, CA; born in Fresno, April 13, 1952; education: B.A., California State University, Fresno, CA, 1974; professional: Chief Executive Officer Costa Group, 2002–present; employee, Costa Brothers Dairy, 1959–74; Senator California State Senate, 1994–2002; assembly member, California State Assembly, 1978–94; administrative assistant, California Assemblyman Richard Lehman, 1976–78; special assistant, Congressman John Krebs, 1975–76; member of the California State Assembly, 1978–94; member of the California State Senate, 1994–2002; private advocate; member: Fact Steering Committee, Fresno County Farm Board; religion: Catholic; committees: Agriculture; Foreign Affairs; Natural Resources; elected to the 109th Congress on November 2, 2004; reelected to each succeeding Congress.

Office Listings

http://www.house.gov/costa

1314 Longworth House Office Building, Washington, DC 20515 .... (202) 225–3341
FAX: 225–9308
Chief of Staff.—Scott Nishioki.
Scheduler.—Juan Lopez.
2300 Tulare Street, #315, Fresno, CA 93721 .... (559) 495–1620
District Director.—Bob Sanders.

Counties: FRESNO (part), KERN (part), KINGS. Population (2000), 639,088.

ZIP Codes: 93202–04, 93206, 93210, 93212, 93215–16, 93220, 93230, 93232, 93234, 93239, 93241–42, 93245–46, 93249–50, 93263, 93266, 93280, 93282, 93301, 93305, 93307, 93383, 93387, 93518, 93607–09, 93616, 93620, 93622, 93624–25, 93627, 93631, 93640, 93648, 93652, 93656–57, 93660, 93662, 93668, 93701–09, 93712, 93714–18, 93721–22, 93724–25, 93727–28, 93744–45, 93750, 93760–62, 93764, 93771–79, 93786, 93844, 93888

* * *

TWENTY-FIRST DISTRICT

DEVIN NUNES, Republican, of Visalia, CA; born in Tulare County, CA, October 1, 1973; education: A.A., College of the Sequoias; B.S., Agricultural Business, and a Masters Degree in Agriculture, from California Polytechnic State University, San Luis Obispo; graduate, California Agriculture Leadership Fellowship Program; professional: farmer and businessman; elected, College of the Sequoias Board of Trustees, 1996; reelected, 2000; appointed by President George W. Bush to serve as California State Director of the U.S. Department of Agriculture Rural Development Office, 2001; religion: Catholic; married: the former Elizabeth Tamariz, 2003; committees: Ways and Means; elected to the 108th Congress on November 5, 2002; reelected to each succeeding Congress.

Office Listings

http://www.nunes.house.gov

1013 Longworth House Office Building, Washington, DC 20515 .... (202) 225–2523
FAX: 225–3404
Chief of Staff.—Johnny Amaral.
Legislative Director.—Damon Nelson.
Communications Director.—Andrew House.
Executive Assistant.—Jennifer Buckley.
113 North Church Street, Suite 208, Visalia, CA 93291 .... (559) 733–3861
264 Clovis Avenue, Suite 206, Clovis, CA 93612 .... (559) 323–5235

Counties: TULARE, FRESNO (part). Population (2000), 639,088.

ZIP Codes: 93201, 93207–08, 93212, 93215, 93218–19, 93221, 93223, 93227, 93235, 93237, 93242, 93244, 93247, 93256–58, 93260–62, 93265, 93267, 93270–72, 93274–75, 93277–79, 93286, 93290–92, 93602–03, 93605, 93609, 93611–13, 93615–16, 93618, 93621, 93625–26, 93628, 93631, 93633–34, 93641–42, 93646–49, 93651, 93654, 93656–57, 93662, 93664, 93666–67, 93670, 93673, 93675, 93703, 93710, 93720, 93726–27, 93740, 93747

* * *

TWENTY-SECOND DISTRICT

KEVIN McCARTHY, Republican, of Bakersfield, CA; born in Bakersfield, January 26, 1965; education: graduated, Bakersfield High School, 1983; B.S., Business Administration, CSU–Bakersfield, 1989; M.B.A., CSU–Bakersfield, 1994; professional: intern, worked up to District Director for U.S. Congressman Bill Thomas, 1987–2002; served as Trustee, Kern Community College District, 2000–02; served in the California State Assembly, 2002–06; elected, California Assembly Republican Leader, 2003–06; married to the former Judy Wages, 1992; two children: Connor and Meghan; committees: Agriculture; Homeland Security; House Administration; elected to the 110th Congress on November 7, 2006.

Office Listings

http://www.kevinmccarthy.house.gov

1523 Longworth House Office Building, Washington, DC 20515 .... (202) 225–2915
Chief of Staff.—James Min. FAX: 225–2908
Scheduler.—Courtney Mayo.
Legislative Director.—Shelby Hagenauer.
Press Secretary.—Nick Bouknight.
4100 Empire Drive, Suite 150, Bakersfield, CA 93309 .... (661) 327–3611
District Administrator.—Robin Lake Foster.
5805 Capistrano Avenue, Suite C, Atascadero, CA 93422 .... (805) 461–1034

Counties: KERN COUNTY (part). CITIES AND TOWNSHIPS: Arvin, Bakersfield, Bodfish, Boron, Caliente, California City, Cantil, China Lake, Edison, Edwards, Fellows, Frazier Park, Glennville, Havilah, Inyokern, Keene, Kernville, Lake Isabella, Lebec, Maricopa, McKittrick, Mojave, Monolith, North Edwards, Onyx, Randsberg, Ridgecrest, Rosamond, Taft, Tehachapi, Tupman, Weldon, Willow Springs, Wofford Heights, Woody. SAN LUIS OBISPO COUNTY (part). CITIES AND TOWNSHIPS: Arroyo Grande, Paso Robles, San Miguel, Atascadero, Shandon, Templeton, San Luis Obispo, Nipomo. LOS ANGELES COUNTY (part). CITIES AND TOWNSHIPS: Lancaster. Population (2000) 639,088.

ZIP Codes: 91390, 92832, 92834, 93203, 93205–06, 93215, 93222, 93224–26, 93238, 93240–41, 93243, 93249–52, 93255, 93263, 93268, 93276, 93283, 93285, 93287, 93301–09, 93311–14, 93380, 93384–86, 93388–90, 93401–02, 93405, 93407, 93409–10, 93420, 93422–23, 93426, 93428, 93430, 93432, 93442, 93444, 93446–47, 93451, 93453–54, 93461, 93465, 93501–02, 93504–05, 93516, 93518–19, 93522–24, 93527–28, 93531–32, 93534–36, 93539, 93554–56, 93558, 93560–61, 93581, 93584, 93596

* * *

TWENTY-THIRD DISTRICT

LOIS CAPPS, Democrat, of Santa Barbara, CA; born in Ladysmith, WI, January 10, 1938; education: graduated Flathead County High School, Kalispell, MT, 1955; B.S. in Nursing, Pacific Lutheran University, 1959; M.A. in Religion, Yale University, 1964; M.A. in Education, University of California at Santa Barbara, 1990; professional: head nurse, Yale New Haven Hospital; staff nurse, Visiting Nurses Association, Hamden, CT; elementary district nurse, Santa Barbara School District; director, Teenage Pregnancy and Parenting Project, Santa Barbara County; director, Santa Barbara School District Parent and Child Education Center; instructor of early childhood education, Santa Barbara City College; board member: American Red Cross, American Heart Association, Family Service Agency, Santa Barbara Women's Political Committee; married: Walter Capps, 1960; children: Lisa, Todd, and Laura; committees: Energy and Commerce; Natural Resources; elected by special election on March 10, 1998, to the 105th Congress, to fill the vacancy caused by the death of her husband Rep. Walter Capps; reelected to each succeeding Congress.

Office Listings

http://www.house.gov/capps

1110 Longworth House Office Building, Washington, DC 20515 .... (202) 225–3601
Chief of Staff.—Randolph Harrison. FAX: 225–5632
Legislative Director.—Jonathan Levenshus.
Press Secretary.—Emily Kryder.
Executive Assistant.—Sarah Ethington.
1411 Marsh Street, Suite 205, San Luis Obispo, CA 93401 .... (805) 546–8348
District Representatives: Betsy Umhofer, Greg Haas.
101 West Anapamu Street, Suite C, Santa Barbara, CA 93101 .... (805) 730–1710

District Director.—Sharon Siegel.
2675 North Ventura Road, Suite 104, Port Hueneme, CA 93041 .... (805) 985–6807
District Representative.—Vanessa Hernandez.

Counties: SAN LUIS OBISPO COUNTY (part). CITIES AND TOWNSHIPS: Baywood-Los Osos, Cambria, Cayucos, Grover Beach, Morro Bay, Nipomo, Oceano, Pismo Beach, San Luis Obispo. SANTA BARBARA COUNTY (part). CITIES AND TOWNSHIPS: Carpinteria, Goleta, Guadalupe, Isla Vista, Mission Canyon, Montecito, Santa Barbara, Santa Maria, Summerland, Toro Canyon. VENTURA COUNTY (part). CITIES AND TOWNSHIPS: Channel Island, El Rio, Oxnard, Port Hueneme, and San Buenaventura. Population (2000), 639,088.

ZIP Codes: 92832, 93001, 93003, 93013–14, 93030–36, 93041, 93043–44, 93067, 93101–03, 93105–11, 93116–18, 93120–21, 93130, 93140, 93150, 93160, 93190, 93199, 93401–03, 93405–06, 93408, 93412, 93420–21, 93424, 93428, 93430, 93433–35, 93442–45, 93448–49, 93452, 93454–56, 93458, 93483

* * *

TWENTY-FOURTH DISTRICT

ELTON GALLEGLY, Republican, of Simi Valley, CA; born in Huntington Park, CA, March 7, 1944; education: graduated Huntington Park High School, 1962; attended Los Angeles State College; businessman; member, Simi Valley City Council, 1979; mayor, city of Simi Valley, 1980–86; former vice-chairman and chairman, Ventura County Association of Governments; former member, board of directors, Moorpark College Foundation; delegate to 1988 Republican National Convention; married: the former Janice L. Shrader, 1974; children: Shawn G., Shawn P., Kevin, and Shannon; committees: Foreign Affairs; Judiciary; Natural Resources; elected to the 100th Congress on November 4, 1986; reelected to each succeeding Congress.

Office Listings

2309 Rayburn House Office Building, Washington, DC 20515 .... (202) 225–5811
Chief of Staff.—Patrick Murphy. FAX: 225–1100
Executive Assistant.—Pamela Roller.
Press Secretary.—Tom Pfeifer.
2829 Townsgate Road, Suite 315, Thousand Oaks, CA 91361 .... (805) 497–2224
District Chief of Staff.—Brian Miller. (800) 423–0023

Counties: VENTURA COUNTY (part). CITIES AND TOWNSHIPS: Bell Canyon, Camarillo, Fillmore, Moorpark, Newbury Park, Oak Park, Oak View, Ojai, Piru, Santa Paula, Simi Valley, Somis, Thousand Oaks, Ventura, Westlake Village. SANTA BARBARA COUNTY (part). CITIES AND TOWNSHIPS: Buellton, Lompoc, Los Alamos, Los Olivos, Orcutt, Santa Barbara, Santa Ynez, and Solvang. Population (2000), 639,088.

ZIP Codes: 91301, 91304, 91307, 91311, 91319–20, 91358–62, 91377, 91406, 91413, 93001, 93003–07, 93009–13, 93015–16, 93020–24, 93030, 93033, 93036, 93040–42, 93060–66, 93094, 93099, 93105, 93111, 93117, 93225, 93252, 93254, 93427, 93429, 93436–38, 93440–41, 93454–55, 93457–58, 93460, 93463–64

* * *

TWENTY-FIFTH DISTRICT

HOWARD P. ''BUCK'' MCKEON, Republican, of Santa Clarita, CA; born in Los Angeles, CA, September 9, 1938; education: graduated, Verdugo Hills High School, Tujunga, CA; B.S., Brigham Young University; owner, Howard and Phil's Western Wear; mayor and city councilman, Santa Clarita, 1987–92; member: board of directors, Canyon Country Chamber of Commerce; California Republican State Central Committee; advisory council, Boy Scouts of America; president and trustee, William S. Hart School District, 1979–87; chairman and director, Henry Mayo Newhall Memorial Hospital, 1983–87; chairman and founding director, Valencia National Bank, 1987–92; honorary chairman, Red Cross Community Support Campaign, 1992; honorary chairman, Leukemia Society Celebrity Program, 1990 and 1994; president, Republican Freshman Class of the 103rd Congress; married: to the former Patricia Kunz, 1962; children: Tamara, Howard D., John Matthew, Kimberly, David Owen, and Tricia; committees: Armed Services; Education and Labor; elected on November 3, 1992, to the 103rd Congress; reelected to each succeeding Congress.

Office Listings

http://www.house.gov/mckeon

2351 Rayburn House Office Building, Washington, DC 20515 .... (202) 225–1956
Chief of Staff.—Bob Cochran. FAX: 226–0683
Executive Assistant/Appointments.—Michelle A. Baker.
District Director.—Scott Wilk.
26650 The Old Road, Suite 203, Santa Clarita, CA 91355 .... (661) 254–2111

1008 West Avenue, M–14, Suite E1, Palmdale, CA 93551 .... (661) 274–9688

Counties: INYO, LOS ANGELES (part), MONO, SAN BERNARDINO (part). CITIES AND TOWNSHIPS: Acton, Adelanto, Baker, Barstow, Benton, Big Pine, Bishop, Bridgeport, Castaic, Canyon Country, Coleville, Death Valley, Edwards, Ft. Irwin, Helendale, Hesperia, Hinkley, Independence, Inyokern, June Lake, Keeler, La Crescenta, Lancaster, Littlerock, Little Lake, Little Vinning, Llano, Lone Pine, Mammoth Lakes, Newberry Springs, Newhall, Nipton, Olancha, Oro Grande, Palmdale, Pearblossom, Phelan, Pinon Hills, Ridgecrest, Santa Clarita, Shoshone, Stevenson Ranch, Sunland, Sylmar, Tecopa, Topaz, Trona, Tujunga, Valencia, Valyerno, Victorville, and Yermo. Population (2000), 639,087.

ZIP Codes: 91042, 91214, 91310, 91321–22, 91350–51, 91354–55, 91380–81, 91383–87, 91390, 92301, 92309–12, 92328, 92342, 92345, 92347, 92364–65, 92368, 92371–72, 92384, 92389, 92392–94, 92398, 92832, 93510, 93512–17, 93524, 93526–27, 93529–30, 93534–35, 93541–46, 93549–53, 93560, 93562, 93586, 93590–92, 93599, 96107, 96133

* * *

TWENTY-SIXTH DISTRICT

DAVID DREIER, Republican, of San Dimas, CA; born in Kansas City, MO, July 5, 1952; education: B.A. (*cum laude*) in political science, Claremont McKenna College, 1975; M.A., American Government, Claremont Graduate School, 1976; Winston S. Churchill Fellow; Phi Sigma Alpha; professional: director, corporate relations, Claremont McKenna College, 1975–78; member: board of governors, James Madison Society; Republican State Central Committee of California; Los Angeles Town Hall; named Outstanding Young Man of America and Outstanding Young Californian, 1976 and 1978; director, marketing and government affairs, Industrial Hydrocarbons, 1979–80; vice president, Dreier Development, 1985–present; author of congressional reform package incorporated into the House Rules; committees: Rules; elected to the 97th Congress on November 4, 1980; reelected to each succeeding Congress.

Office Listings

http://www.house.gov/dreier

233 Cannon House Office Building, Washington, DC 20515 .... (202) 225–2305
Chief of Staff.—Bradley W. Smith. FAX: 225–7018
Administrative Assistant.—Ryan Maxson.
Legislative Director.—Alisa Do.
2220 East Route 66, Suite 225, Glendora, CA 91740 .... (626) 852–2626

Counties: LOS ANGELES (part). CITIES: Altadena, Arcadia, Bradbury, Claremont, Covina, El Monte, Glendora, La Canada Flintridge, La Crescenta, La Verne, Monrovia, Montrose, Pasadena, San Antonio Heights, San Dimas, San Gabriel, San Marino, Sierra Madre, Walnut. SAN BERNARDINO (part). CITIES: Montclair, Rancho Cucamonga, Upland, and Wrightwood. Population (2000), 639,088.

ZIP Codes: 91001, 91006–07, 91010–12, 91016–17, 91020–21, 91023–25, 91066, 91077, 91104, 91107–08, 91118, 91131, 91185, 91187, 91191, 91214, 91390, 91410, 91701, 91711, 91730, 91737, 91739–41, 91750, 91759, 91763, 91773, 91775, 91784, 91786, 91789, 92329, 92336, 92345, 92358, 92371–72, 92397, 92407

* * *

TWENTY-SEVENTH DISTRICT

BRAD SHERMAN, Democrat, of Sherman Oaks, CA; born in Los Angeles, CA, October 24, 1954; education: B.A., *summa cum laude,* UCLA, 1974; J.D., *magna cum laude,* Harvard Law School, 1979; professional: admitted to the California bar in 1979 and began practice in Los Angeles; attorney, CPA, certified tax law specialist; elected to the California State Board of Equalization, 1990, serving as chairman, 1991–95; committees: Financial Services; Foreign Affairs; Judiciary; elected to the 105th Congress; reelected to each succeeding Congress.

Office Listings

2242 Rayburn House Office Building, Washington, DC 20515 .... (202) 225–5911
Chief of Staff.—Andrew S. Wright. FAX: 225–5879
Legislative Director.—Gary Goldberg.
Communications Director.—Michael Briggs.
Legislative Correspondent.—India McKinney.
5000 Van Nuys Boulevard, Suite 420, Sherman Oaks, CA 91403 .... (818) 501–9200
District Director.—Erin Prangley.

Counties: LOS ANGELES COUNTY (part). Population (2000), 639,088.

ZIP Codes: 91040–41, 91043, 91303–06, 91309, 91311–12, 91316, 91324–30, 91335, 91337, 91342–46, 91352, 91356–57, 91364, 91367, 91371, 91394–96, 91401, 91403, 91405–06, 91409, 91411, 91416, 91423, 91426, 91436, 91470, 91482, 91495–96, 91504–07, 91510, 91601, 91605–06

* * *

TWENTY-EIGHTH DISTRICT

HOWARD L. BERMAN, Democrat, of Van Nuys, CA; born in Los Angeles, CA, April 15, 1941; education: B.A. in international relations, UCLA, 1962; LL.B., UCLA School of Law, 1965; California Assembly Fellowship Program, 1965–70; Vista volunteer, 1966–67; admitted to the California bar, 1966; practiced law until election to California Assembly in 1972; named assembly majority leader in first term; served as chair of the Assembly Democratic Caucus and policy research management committee; member: regional board of the Anti-Defamation League; past president, California Federation of Young Democrats; married: Janis; children: Brinley and Lindsey; committees: Foreign Affairs; Judiciary; elected to the 98th Congress on November 2, 1982; reelected to each succeeding Congress.

Office Listings

http://www.house.gov/berman

2221 Rayburn House Office Building, Washington, DC 20515 .... (202) 225–4695
Chief of Staff.—Gene Smith. FAX: 225–3196
Legislative Director.—Doug Campbell.
Executive Assistant/Appointments.—Deanne Samuels.
14546 Hamlin Street, Suite 202, Van Nuys, CA 91411 .... (818) 994–7200
District Director.—Bob Blumenfield.

Counties: LOS ANGELES COUNTY (part). Portions of the city of Los Angeles, including all or part of the communities of Arleta, Encino, North Hollywood, North Hills, Pacoima, Panorama City, San Fernando, Sherman Oaks, Studio City, Valley Village, and Van Nuys. Population (2000), 639,087.

ZIP Codes: 90028, 90046, 90049, 90068, 91316, 91331, 91333–34, 91340–43, 91345, 91352–53, 91356, 91388, 91392–93, 91401–08, 91411–12, 91423, 91436, 91497, 91499, 91505, 91601–12, 91614–18

* * *

TWENTY-NINTH DISTRICT

ADAM B. SCHIFF, Democrat, of Burbank, CA; born in Framingham, MA, June 20, 1960; education: B.A., Stanford University, 1982; J.D., Harvard University, 1985; professional: Attorney; U.S. Attorney's Office, served as a criminal prosecutor; chosen by the Dept. of Justice to assist the Czechoslovakian government in reforming their criminal justice system; public service: elected to the California State Senate, 1996; involved in numerous community service activities; awards: Dept. of Justice Special Achievement Award; Council of State Governments Toll Fellowship; California League of High Schools Legislator of the Year; family: married: Eve; children: Alexa and Elijah; committees: Appropriations; Judiciary; elected to the 107th Congress on November 7, 2000; reelected to each succeeding Congress.

Office Listings

http://www.house.gov/schiff

326 Cannon House Office Building, Washington, DC 20515 .... (202) 225–4176
Chief of Staff.—Timothy Bergreen. FAX: 225–5828
Press Secretary.—Sean Oblack.
Executive Assistant.—Christopher Hoven.
87 North Raymond Avenue, Suite 800, Pasadena, CA 91103 .... (626) 304–2727
District Director.—Ann Peifer.

Counties: LOS ANGELES COUNTY (part). CITIES: Alhambra, Altadena, Burbank, Glendale, Griffith Park, Monterey Park, Pasadena, San Gabriel, South Pasadena, and Temple City. Population (2000), 639,088.

ZIP Codes: 90004–06, 90010, 90020, 90026–27, 90029, 90035–36, 90038–39, 90046, 90048, 90064, 90068, 91001, 91003, 91007, 91011, 91030–31, 91046, 91101–10, 91114–17, 91121, 91123–26, 91129, 91175, 91182, 91184, 91186, 91188–89, 91201–10, 91214, 91221–22, 91224–26, 91501–06, 91508, 91521–23, 91775–76, 91780, 91801, 91803–04

* * *

THIRTIETH DISTRICT

HENRY A. WAXMAN, Democrat, of Los Angeles, CA; born in Los Angeles, September 12, 1939; education: B.A., political science, UCLA, 1961; J.D., School of Law; admitted to the California State bar, 1965; served three terms as California State Assemblyman; former chairman, California Assembly Health Committee; Select Committee on Medical Malpractice; and Committee on Elections and Reapportionment; president, California Federation of Young Democrats, 1965–67; member: Guardians of the Jewish Home for the Aged; American Jewish Congress; Sierra Club; married: the former Janet Kessler, 1971; children: Carol Lynn and Michael David; committees: chair, Oversight and Government Reform; Energy and Commerce; elected to the 94th Congress on November 5, 1974; reelected to each succeeding Congress.

Office Listings

http://www.house.gov/waxman

2204 Rayburn House Office Building, Washington, DC 20515 .... (202) 225–3976
Chief of Staff.—Philip M. Schiliro. FAX: 225–4099
Administrative Assistant.—Patricia Delgado.
8436 West Third Street, Suite 600, Los Angeles, CA 90048 .... (323) 651–1040
District Director.—Lisa Pinto.

Counties: LOS ANGELES COUNTY (part). CITIES AND TOWNSHIPS: Agoura Hills, Bel-Air, Beverly Hills, Brentwood, Calabasas, Canoga Park, Century City, Chatsworth, Hidden Hills, Malibu, Northridge, Pacific Palisades, Pico-Robertson, Santa Monica, Tarzana, Topanga, West Hills, West Hollywood, Westlake Village, West Los Angeles, Westwood, and Woodland Hills. Population (2000), 639,088.

ZIP Codes: 90024–25, 90027–29, 90032, 90034–36, 90038–39, 90046, 90048–49, 90057, 90063–64, 90067–69, 90072–73, 90075–77, 90095, 90209–13, 90263–65, 90272, 90290–91, 90401–11, 91301–04, 91307–08, 91311, 91313, 91324, 91356, 91361–65, 91367, 91372, 91376, 91399

* * *

THIRTY-FIRST DISTRICT

XAVIER BECERRA, Democrat, of Los Angeles, CA; born in Sacramento, CA, January 26, 1958; education: graduated, McClatchy High School, Sacramento, 1976; B.A., Stanford University, 1980; J.D., Stanford Law School, 1984; admitted to California bar, 1985; attended Universidad de Salamanca, 1978–79; staff attorney, ''Reggie Fellow,'' Legal Assistance Corporation of Central Massachusetts, 1984–85; administrative assistant for State Senator Art Torres, California State Legislature, 1986; Deputy Attorney General, Office of the Attorney General, State of California, 1987–90; Assemblyman, California State Legislature, 1990–92; member: Mexican American State Legislators Policy Institute; Mexican American Bar Association; chairperson: Hispanic Employee Advisory Committee to the State Attorney General, 1989; honorary member: Association of California State Attorneys and Administrative Law Judges; former member: steering committee, Greater Eastside Voter Registration Project; Construction and General Laborers Union, Local 185 (Sacramento); Pitzer College Board of Trustees; National Association of Latino's Electoral and appointed to the Official Board of Directors; married to Dr. Carolina Reyes; children: Clarisa, Olivia, Natalia; committees: Budget; Ways and Means; appointed Assistant to the Speaker of the House for the 110th Congress; elected on November 3, 1992, to the 103rd Congress; reelected to each succeeding Congress.

Office Listings

http://www.house.gov/becerra

1119 Longworth House Office Building, Washington, DC 20515 .... (202) 225–6235
Chief of Staff.—Debra Dixon. FAX: 225–2202
Legislative / Communications Director.—Steve Haro.
Scheduler.—Henry Truong.
1910 Sunset Boulevard, Suite 560, Los Angeles, CA 90026 .... (213) 483–1425
District Director.—Laura Arciniega.

Counties: LOS ANGELES COUNTY (part). CITIES: Los Angeles. Population (2000), 639,088.

ZIP Codes: 90004–07, 90011–12, 90015, 90018, 90020–22, 90026, 90028–29, 90031–32, 90037–39, 90041–42, 90048, 90057–58, 90065, 90072

* * *

THIRTY-SECOND DISTRICT

HILDA L. SOLIS, Democrat, of El Monte, CA; born in Los Angeles, CA, October 20, 1957; education: B.A., California Polytechnic University, Pomona; M.S., University of Southern California; professional: White House Office of Hispanic Affairs during the Carter Administration; management analyst, U.S. Office of Management and Budget; Rio Hondo Community College Board of Trustees; Los Angeles County Insurance Commission; public service: California State Assembly, 1992–94; California State Senate, 1994–2000; first Latina to serve in the State Senate; recognized and honored by numerous community and civic organizations; co-chair, Congressional Caucus on Women's Issues; member, Congressional Hispanic Caucus; committees: Energy and Commerce; Natural Resources; Select Committee on Energy Independence and Global Warming; elected to the 107th Congress on November 7, 2000; reelected to each succeeding Congress.

Office Listings

http://www.house.gov/solis

1414 Longworth House Office Building, Washington, DC 20515 .... (202) 225–5464
Chief of Staff.—Don Lyster. FAX: 225–5467
Legislative Director.—Megan Uzzell.
Press Secretary.—Sonia Melendez.
Scheduler.—April Elliott.
4401 Santa Anita Avenue, Suite 211, El Monte, CA 91731 .... (626) 448–1271
4716 Cesar Chavez Avenue, Building A, East Los Angeles, CA 90022 .... (323) 307–9904
Deputy District Director.—Benita Duran.

Counties: LOS ANGELES COUNTY (part). CITIES: Azusa, Baldwin Park, Covina, Duarte, El Monte, South El Monte, Irwindale, Monterey Park, Rosemead, San Gabriel, South San Gabriel, and portions of East Los Angeles, Citrus CDP, Glendora, Industry City, Los Angeles, Temple City, Vincent CDP, and West Covina. Population (2000), 639,087.

ZIP Codes: 90022, 90032, 90034–36, 90044–45, 90047–48, 90063–64, 90066–67, 90089, 91009–10, 91016, 91702, 91706, 91722–24, 91731–33, 91740, 91754–55, 91770, 91790–93

* * *

THIRTY-THIRD DISTRICT

DIANE E. WATSON, Democrat, of Los Angeles, CA; born in Los Angeles, November 12, 1933; education: B.A. in Education, University of California, Los Angeles; M.S. in School Psychology, California State University, Los Angeles; attended the John F. Kennedy School of Government at Harvard University and earned a Ph.D., in Educational Administration from the Claremont Graduate University; professional: served as an elementary school teacher, acting principal, assistant superintendent of child welfare and attendance, and school psychologist; served on the faculty at both California State University, Los Angeles, and Long Beach; Health Occupations Specialist, California Department of Education; awards: named Legislator of the Year by numerous California universities, associations, and organizations; public service: Los Angeles Unified School District Board Member; served as California State Senator, 1979–99; served as U.S. Ambassador to the Federated States of Micronesia, 1999–2001; committees: Foreign Affairs; Oversight and Government Reform; elected to the 107th Congress, by special election, on June 5, 2001; reelected to each succeeding Congress.

Office Listings

125 Cannon House Office Building, Washington, DC 20515 .... (202) 225–7084
Chief of Staff.—Jim B. Clarke. FAX: 225–2422
Legislative Director.—Gregory Adams.
Scheduler / Special Assistant.—Alice Holmes-McKoy.
Communications Director.—Bert Hammond.
4322 Wilshire Boulevard, Suite 302, Los Angeles, CA 90010 .... (323) 965–1422
District Director.—Paullette Starks.

Counties: LOS ANGELES COUNTY (part). CITIES: Culver City, Los Angeles City, communities of Ladera Heights and View Park-Windsor Hills. Population (2000), 639,088.

ZIP Codes: 90004–08, 90010–11, 90016, 90018–20, 90022, 90026–29, 90033–39, 90043–45, 90047–48, 90053, 90056–58, 90062–64, 90066, 90068, 90070, 90078, 90083, 90093, 90099, 90103, 90230–33

* * *

THIRTY-FOURTH DISTRICT

LUCILLE ROYBAL-ALLARD, Democrat, of Los Angeles, CA; born in Los Angeles, June 12, 1941; education: B.A., California State University, Los Angeles, 1965; served in the California State Assembly, 1987–92; married: Edward T. Allard III; two children: Lisa Marie and Ricardo; two stepchildren: Angela and Guy Mark; the first woman to serve as the chair of the California Democratic Congressional Delegation in the 105th Congress; in the 106th Congress, she became the first woman to chair the Congressional Hispanic Caucus, and the first Latina in history to be appointed to the House Appropriations Committee; committees: Appropriations; Standards of Official Conduct; the first Mexican-American woman elected to Congress on November 3, 1992 to the 103rd Congress; reelected to each succeeding Congress.

Office Listings

http://www.house.gov/roybal-allard

2330 Rayburn House Office Building, Washington, DC 20515–0534 .... (202) 225–1766
Chief of Staff.—Paul Cunningham. FAX: 226–0350
Legislative Director.—Victor G. Castillo.
Executive Assistant.—Christine C. Ochoa.
255 East Temple Street, Suite 1860, Los Angeles, CA 90012–3334 .... (213) 628–9230
District Director.—Ana Figueroa.

Counties: LOS ANGELES COUNTY (part). CITIES: Bell, Belflower, Bell Gardens, Boyle Heights, Chinatown, Commerce, Cudahy, Downey, Downtown Los Angeles, East Los Angeles, Florence, Huntington Park, Little Tokyo, Maywood, Pico Union, South Park, Vernon, and Westlake. Population (2000), 639,088.

ZIP Codes: 90001, 90011–15, 90017, 90021–23, 90026, 90033, 90040, 90057–58, 90063, 90071, 90081, 90086–87, 90091, 90201, 90239, 90241–42, 90255, 90270, 90280, 90703, 90706, 90712–13, 90723

* * *

THIRTY-FIFTH DISTRICT

MAXINE WATERS, Democrat, of Los Angeles, CA; born in St. Louis, MO, August 15, 1938; education: B.A., California State University; honorary degrees: Harris-Stowe State College, St. Louis, MO, and Central State University, Wilberforce, OH, Spelman College, Atlanta, GA, North Carolina A&T State University, Howard University, Central State University, Bishop College, Morgan State University; elected to California State Assembly, 1976; reelected every two years thereafter; member: Assembly Democratic Caucus, Board of TransAfrica Foundation, National Women's Political Caucus; chair, Democratic Caucus Special Committee on Election Reform; chair, Ways and Means Subcommittee on State Administration; chair, Joint Committee on Public Pension Fund Investments; founding member, National Commission for Economic Conversion and Disarmament; member of the board, Center for National Policy; Clara Elizabeth Jackson Carter Foundation (Spelman College); Minority AIDS Project; married to Sidney Williams, former U.S. Ambassador to the Commonwealth of the Bahamas; two children: Karen and Edward; committees: Financial Services; Judiciary; Chief Deputy Minority Whip; elected to the 102nd Congress on November 6, 1990; reelected to each succeeding Congress.

Office Listings

2344 Rayburn House Office Building, Washington, DC 20515 .... (202) 225–2201
Chief of Staff.—Mikael Moore. FAX: 225–7854
Legislative Director.—Dana Thompson.
10124 South Broadway, Suite 1, Los Angeles, CA 90003 .... (323) 757–8900
District Director.—Derrick Mims.

Counties: LOS ANGELES COUNTY (part). CITIES: Gardena, Hawthorne, Inglewood, Lawndale, Los Angeles, Playa Del Ray, and Torrance. Population (2000), 639,088.

ZIP Codes: 90001–03, 90007, 90009, 90037, 90044–45, 90047, 90052, 90056, 90059, 90061, 90066, 90082, 90094, 90189, 90247–51, 90260–61, 90293, 90301–13, 90397–98, 90504, 90506

* * *

THIRTY-SIXTH DISTRICT

JANE HARMAN, Democrat, of Venice, CA; born in New York, NY, June 28, 1945; education: University High School, Los Angeles, CA, 1962; B.A., Smith College, Northampton, MA, 1966; J.D., Harvard University Law School, Cambridge, MA, 1969; professional: attorney; admitted to the District of Columbia Bar, 1969; counsel for Jones, Day, Reavis and Pogue (law firm); Director and General Counsel for Harman International Industries; Special Counsel, Department of Defense, 1979; Regents' Professor at UCLA, 1999; organizations: L.A. County High Technology Committee; South Bay Alliance for Choice; Center for National Policy; International Human Rights Law Group; member of the Visiting Committee of the John F. Kennedy School of Government, Harvard University; National Commission on Terrorism; family: married to Sidney Harman, 1980; children: Brian Lakes Frank, Hilary Lakes Frank, Daniel Geier Harman, and Justine Leigh Harman; committees: Energy and Commerce; Homeland Security; elected to the 103rd, 104th, and 105th Congresses; candidate for Governor of California, 1998; elected to the 107th Congress on November 7, 2000; reelected to each succeeding Congress.

Office Listings
http://www.house.gov/harman

2400 Rayburn House Office Building, Washington, DC 20515 .... (202) 225–8220
Chief of Staff.—John Hess. FAX: 226–7290
Legislative Director.—Jay Hulings.
Scheduler.—Janaki Dighe.
2321 East Rosecrans Boulevard, Suite 3270, El Segundo, CA 90245 .... (310) 643–3636
544 North Avalon Boulevard, Suite 307, Wilmington, CA 90744 .... (310) 549–8282

Counties: LOS ANGELES COUNTY (part). CITIES: El Segundo, Harbor City, Hermosa Beach, Lawndale, Lennox, Los Angeles, Manhattan Beach, Marina Del Rey, Playa Del Rey, Redondo Beach, San Pedro, Torrance, Venice, Westchester, West Carson, and Wilmington. Population (2000), 639,087.

ZIP Codes: 90009, 90025, 90034, 90039, 90045, 90064, 90066, 90080, 90245, 90248, 90254, 90266–67, 90277–78, 90291–92, 90294–96, 90304, 90404–05, 90501–10, 90710, 90717, 90731–34, 90744, 90748

* * *

THIRTY-SEVENTH DISTRICT

VACANT

Counties: LOS ANGELES COUNTY (part). CITIES: Carson, Compton, and Long Beach. Population (2000), 639,088.

ZIP Codes: 90002–03, 90044, 90059, 90061, 90220–24, 90247, 90501–02, 90713, 90723, 90745–47, 90749, 90755, 90801–10, 90813–15, 90822, 90842, 90844–48, 90888, 90899

* * *

THIRTY-EIGHTH DISTRICT

GRACE F. NAPOLITANO, Democrat, of Los Angeles, CA; born in Brownsville, TX, December 4, 1936; maiden name: Flores; education: Brownsville High School, Brownsville, TX; Cerritos College; Southmost College; professional: Transportation Coordinator, Ford Motor Company; elected to Norwalk, CA, City Council, 1986; became mayor of Norwalk, CA, 1989; elected to the California Assembly, 58th District, 1992–98; married: Frank Napolitano; children: Yolanda Dyer, Fred Musquiz, Edward Musquiz, Michael Musquiz, and Cynthia Dowling; organizations: Norwalk Lions Club; Veterans of Foreign Wars (auxiliary); American Legion (auxiliary); Soroptimist International; past director, Cerritos College Foundation; director, Community Family Guidance Center; League of United Latin American Citizens; director, Los Angeles County Sanitation District; director, Los Angeles County Vector Control (Southeast District); director, Southeast Los Angeles Private Industry Council; director, Los Angeles County Sheriff's Authority; National Women's Political Caucus; past national board secretary, United States-Mexico Sister Cities Association; member, Hispanic Caucus; co-chair, Mental Health Caucus; committees: Natural Resources; Transportation and Infrastructure; elected to the 106th Congress; reelected to each succeeding Congress.

Office Listings
http://www.house.gov/napolitano

1610 Longworth House Office Building, Washington, DC 20515 .... (202) 225–5256
Chief of Staff.—Daniel Choa. FAX: 225–0027
Legislative Director.—Joe Sheehy.
Press Secretary.—Jeremy Cogan.
Scheduler.—Corinne Hart.
11627 East Telegraph Road, Suite 100, Santa Fe Springs, CA 90670 .... (562) 801–2134
District Director.—Amelia Wang.

Counties: LOS ANGELES COUNTY (part). Population (2000), 639,088.

ZIP Codes: 90601, 90605–06, 90640, 90650–52, 90659–62, 90665, 90670, 90703, 90731, 90806, 91715–16, 91744–47, 91766–70, 91789–90, 91792, 91795

* * *

THIRTY-NINTH DISTRICT

LINDA T. SÁNCHEZ, Democrat, of Lakewood, CA; born in Orange, CA, January 28, 1969; education: B.A., University of California, Berkeley; J.D., U.C.L.A. Law School; passed bar exam in 1995; professional: attorney; has practiced in the areas of appellate, civil rights, and employment law; International Brotherhood of Electrical Workers Local 441; National Electrical Contractors Association; and Orange County Central Labor Council Executive Secretary, AFL–CIO; organizations: National Women's Political Caucus; Women in Leadership; religion: Catholic; committees: Education and Labor; Foreign Affairs; Judiciary; elected to the 108th Congress on November 5, 2002; reelected to each succeeding Congress.

Office Listings

http://www.house.gov/lindasanchez

1222 Longworth House Office Building, Washington, DC 20515 .... (202) 225–6676
Chief of Staff.—Michael Torra. FAX: 226–1012
Legislative Director.—Celeste Drake.
Communications Director.—James Dau.
Scheduler.—Ruth Carnegie.
17906 Crusader Avenue, Suite 100, Cerritos, CA 90703 .... (562) 860–5050
District Director.—Bill Grady.

Counties: LOS ANGELES COUNTY (part). Population (2000), 639,088.

ZIP Codes: 90001–02, 90059, 90255, 90262, 90280, 90601–06, 90608–10, 90637–39, 90670, 90701–03, 90706, 90711–16, 90723, 90805, 90807–08

* * *

FORTIETH DISTRICT

EDWARD R. ROYCE, Republican, of Fullerton, CA; born in Los Angeles, CA, October 12, 1951; education: B.A., California State University, Fullerton, 1977; professional: small business owner; controller; corporate tax manager; California State Senate, 1982–92; member: Fullerton Chamber of Commerce; board member, Literacy Volunteers of America; California Interscholastic Athletic Foundation board of advisers; married: Marie Therese Porter, 1985; committees: Financial Services; Foreign Affairs; elected on November 3, 1992 to the 103rd Congress; reelected to each succeeding Congress.

Office Listings

http://www.royce.house.gov

2185 Rayburn House Office Building, Washington, DC 20515 .... (202) 225–4111
Chief of Staff / Legislative Director.—Amy Porter. FAX: 226–0335
Press Secretary.—Gregory Keeley.
305 North Harbor Boulevard, Suite 300, Fullerton, CA 92832 .... (714) 992–8081
District Director.—Sara Carmack.

Counties: ORANGE COUNTY. The north and west part including the cities of Anaheim, Buena Park, Cypress, Fullerton, Garden Grove, La Palma, Los Alamitos, Orange, Placentia, Rossmoor, Stanton, Villa Park, and Westminster. Population (2000), 639,088.

ZIP Codes: 90620–24, 90630–31, 90638, 90680, 90720–21, 90740, 90808, 92647, 92683–84, 92705–06, 92801–02, 92804–07, 92821, 92831–38, 92840–41, 92844–46, 92856–57, 92859, 92861, 92863, 92865–71

* * *

FORTY-FIRST DISTRICT

JERRY LEWIS, Republican, of Redlands, CA; born in Seattle, WA, October 21, 1934; education: graduated, San Bernardino High School, 1952; B.A., UCLA, 1956; graduate intern in public affairs, Coro Foundation; life underwriter; former member, San Bernardino School Board; served in California State Assembly, 1968–78; insurance executive, 1959–78; married to Arlene Willis; seven children; committees: Appropriations; elected to the 96th Congress, November 7, 1978; reelected to each succeeding Congress.

Office Listings

http://www.house.gov/jerrylewis

2112 Rayburn House Office Building, Washington, DC 20515 .... (202) 225–5861
Administrative Assistant.—Arlene Willis. FAX: 225–6498
Deputy Chief of Staff / Communications Director.—Jim Specht.
1150 Brookside Avenue, No. J5, Redlands, CA 92373 .... (909) 862–6030
District Representative.—Tara Clarke.

Counties: RIVERSIDE (part), SAN BERNARDINO (part). CITIES AND TOWNSHIPS: Adelanto, Amboy, Angelus Oaks, Apple Valley, Argus, Arrowbear Lake, Banning, Beaumont, Big Bear City, Big Bear Lake, Blue Jay, Bryn Mawr, Big River, Cabazon, Cadiz, Calimesa, Cedar Glen, Cedar Pines Park, Cherry Valley, Cima, Colton, Crestline, Crest Park, Daggett, Desert Hot Springs, Earp, East Highlands, Essex, Fawnskin, Forest Falls, Grand Terrace, Green Valley Lake, Havasu Lake, Hesperia, Highland, Joshua Tree, Kelso, Lake Arrowhead, Landers, Loma Linda, Lucerne Valley, Ludlow, Mentone, Morongo Valley, Mountain Pass, Needles, Newberry Springs, Nipton, Oro Grande, Parker Dam, Redlands, Rim Forest, Running Springs, San Bernardino, San Jacinto, Sky Forest, Spring Valley Lake, Sugarloaf, Twentynine Palms, Twin Peaks, Valle Vista, Vidal, Yucaipa, and Yucca Valley. Population (2000), 639,088.

ZIP Codes: 92220, 92223, 92230, 92240–42, 92252, 92256, 92258, 92267–68, 92277–78, 92280, 92282, 92284–86, 92304–05, 92307–08, 92311, 92313–15, 92317–18, 92320–27, 92332–33, 92338–42, 92345–46, 92350, 92352, 92354, 92356–57, 92359, 92363–66, 92368–69, 92371, 92373–75, 92378, 92382, 92385–86, 92391–92, 92399, 92404–05, 92407–08, 92410, 92424, 92427, 92544, 92555, 92557, 92581–83

* * *

FORTY-SECOND DISTRICT

GARY G. MILLER, Republican, of Diamond Bar, CA; born in Huntsville, AR, October 16, 1948; education: Loma Vista Elementary School, Whittier, CA; California High School, Whittier, CA; Lowell High School, LaHabra, CA; Mount San Antonio College, Walnut, CA; military service: private, U.S. Army, 1967; professional: developer; owner, G. Miller Development Company; public service: Diamond Bar, CA, City Council, 1989–95; Mayor, 1992; California State Assembly, 1995–98; married: Cathy Miller; children: Brian, Elizabeth, Loren, and Matthew; committees: Financial Services; Transportation and Infrastructure; elected to the 106th Congress; reelected to each succeeding Congress.

Office Listings

http://www.house.gov/garymiller

2438 Rayburn House Office Building, Washington, DC 20515 .... (202) 225–3201
Chief of Staff.—John Rothrock. FAX: 226–6962
Legislative Director / Senior Policy Advisor.—Lesli McCollum Gooch, Ph.D.
Executive Director.—Kevin McKee.
1800 East Lambert Road, Suite 150, Brea, CA 92821 .... (714) 257–1142
District Director.—Steven Thornton.

Counties: LOS ANGELES (part), ORANGE (part), and SAN BERNARDINO (part). CITIES AND TOWNSHIPS: Anaheim, Brea, Chino, Chino Hills, Diamond Bar, La Habra, La Habra Heights, Las Flores, Mission Viejo, Placentia, Rancho Santa Margarita, Rowland Heights, Yorba Linda and Whittier. Population (2000), 639,088.

ZIP Codes: 90601–05, 90607, 90631–33, 91708–10, 91729, 91743, 91748, 91758, 91765, 92676, 92679, 92688, 92691–92, 92807–08, 92821–23, 92833, 92885–87

* * *

FORTY-THIRD DISTRICT

JOE BACA, Democrat, of San Bernardino County, CA; born in Belen, NM, January 23, 1947; education: graduated from California State University, Los Angeles, with a bachelor's degree in Sociology; professional: GTE Corp. (community relations); Interstate World Travel (owner); military service: Army; public service: elected to the California State Assembly, 1992, and served as Assistant Speaker Pro Tempore, and the Speaker's Federal Government Liaison, 1997–98; elected to the California State Senate, 1998; awards: American Legion California Legislator of the Year; VFW Outstanding Legislator; League of Women Voters Citizen of

Distinction; San Bernardino Kiwanis Club Kiwanian of the Year; Boy Scouts of America Distinguished Citizen; 2004 National Farmers Union Presidential Award; U.S. Department of Agriculture Coalition of Minority Employees Award of Excellence; U.S. Hispanic Chamber of Commerce President's Achievement Award; Democratic Caucus Task Force on Homeland Security; vice chair, Democratic Caucus Task Force on Immigration; chair, Congressional Hispanic Caucus; co-chair, Congressional Sex and Violence in the Media Caucus; House Army Caucus; Congressional Diabetes Caucus; Cancer Caucus; Military/Veterans Caucus; U.S.-Mexico Caucus; Blue Dog Coalition, the Nursing Caucus, Native American Caucus; Armenian Caucus; Good Movement Caucus and Out of Poverty Caucus; married: Barbara; four children: Joe Jr., Jeremy, Natalie, and Jennifer; committees: Agriculture; Financial Services; Natural Resources; elected to the 106th Congress on November 16, 1999, by special election; reelected to each succeeding Congress.

Office Listings

328 Cannon House Office Building, Washington, DC 20515 .... (202) 225–6161
Chief of Staff.—Linda Macias. FAX: 225–8671
Executive Assistant.—Erica Woodward.
Press Secretary.—Joanne Peters.
201 North E Street, Suite 102, San Bernardino, CA 92401 .... (909) 885–2222
District Director.—Mike Trujillo.

Counties: SAN BERNARDINO COUNTY (part). CITIES: Colton, Fontana, Ontario, Redlands, Rialto, and San Bernardino. Population (2000), 639,087.

ZIP Codes: 91758, 91761–62, 91764, 92316, 92324, 92334–37, 92346, 92376–77, 92401–08, 92410–13, 92415, 92418, 92423

* * *

FORTY-FOURTH DISTRICT

KEN CALVERT, Republican, of Corona, CA; born in Corona, June 8, 1953; education: A.A., Chaffey College (CA), 1973; B.A. in economics, San Diego State University, 1975; professional: congressional aide to Rep. Victor V. Veysey, CA; general manager, Jolly Fox Restaurant, Corona, 1975–79; Marcus W. Meairs Co., Corona, 1979–81; president and general manager, Ken Calvert Real Properties, 1981–92; County Youth Chairman, Rep. Veysey's District, 1970, then 43rd District, 1972; Corona/Norco Youth Chairman for Nixon, 1968 and 1972; Reagan-Bush campaign worker, 1980; co-chair, Wilson for Senate Campaign, 1982; chairman Riverside Republican Party, 1984–88; co-chairman, George Deukmejian election, 1978, 1982 and 1986; co-chairman, George Bush election, 1988; co-chairman, Pete Wilson Senate elections, 1982 and 1988; co-chairman, Pete Wilson for Governor election, 1990; charter member, Riverside County Republican Winners Circle; former vice president, Corona/Norco Republican Assembly; chairman and charter member, Lincoln Club of Riverside County, 1986–90; president, Corona Rotary Club, 1991; past president, Corona Elks; Navy League of Corona/Norco; Corona Chamber of Commerce, 1990; past chairman, Norco Chamber of Commerce; County of Riverside Asset Leasing; past chairman, Corona/Norco Board of Realtors; Monday Morning Group; Corona Group; executive board, Economic Development Partnership; charter member, Corona Community Hospital Corporate 200 Club; Silver Eagles (March AFB Support Group); co-chair, Corona Airport Advisory Commission; Generic Drug Equity Caucus; co-chair, Caucus to Fight and Control Methamphetamine; co-chair, Manufactured Housing Caucus; Defense Study Group; Hellenic Caucus; Fire Caucus; National Guard & Reserve Caucus; Human Rights Caucus; Baltic Caucus; Travel and Tourism Caucus; Coalition for Autism Research and Education; Diabetes Caucus; Missing and Exploited Children's Caucus; Zero Capital Gains Tax Caucus; Medical Technology Caucus; Law Enforcement Caucus; Correctional Officers Caucus; Western Caucus; Sportsman's Caucus; Native American Caucus; Coastal Caucus; committees: Armed Services; Natural Resources; Science and Technology; elected on November 3, 1992 to the 103rd Congress; reelected to each succeeding Congress.

Office Listings

http://www.house.gov/calvert

2201 Rayburn House Office Building, Washington, DC 20515 .... (202) 225–1986
Chief of Staff.—Dave Ramey. FAX: 225–2004
Legislative Director.—Maria Bowie.
Press Secretary.—Rebecca Rudman.
3400 Central Avenue, Suite 200, Riverside, CA 92506 .... (951) 784–4300
District Manager.—Jolyn Murphy.

Counties: ORANGE COUNTY (part). CITIES AND TOWNSHIPS: Coto d'Casa, Ledera Ranch, Margarita, Rancho Santa, San Clemente, San Juan Capistrano. RIVERSIDE COUNTY (part). CITIES AND TOWNSHIPS: Corona, March AFB, Mira Loma, Norco, Perris, and Riverside. Population (2000), 639,088.

ZIP Codes: 92501–09, 92513–18, 92521–22, 92532, 92557, 92570, 92596, 92672–75, 92679, 92694, 92860, 92879–83

* * *

FORTY-FIFTH DISTRICT

MARY BONO, Republican, of Palm Springs, CA; born in Cleveland, OH, October 24, 1961; daughter of Clay Whitaker, retired physician and surgeon, and Karen, retired chemist; Bachelor of Fine Arts in Art History, University of Southern California, 1984; Woman of the Year, 1993, San Gorgonio Chapter of the Girl Scouts of America for her assistance to victims of a tragic Girl Scout bus crash in Palm Springs; board member: Palm Springs International Film Festival; first lady of Palm Springs and active in a wide range of community charities and service organizations; leadership role in support of the D.A.R.E. program, Olive Crest Home for Abused Children, Tiempos de Los Ninos; certified personal fitness instructor in martial arts (Karate, Tae Kwan Do); accomplished gymnast with Gymnastics Olympica; appointed chair, Congressional Salton Sea Task Force; married Sonny Bono, 1986; two children: Chesare Elan and Chianna Maria; committees: Energy and Commerce; elected by special election on April 7, 1998 to the 105th Congress, to fill the vacancy caused by the death of her husband Rep. Sonny Bono; reelected to each succeeding Congress.

Office Listings

http://www.house.gov/bono

104 Cannon House Office Building, Washington, DC 20515 .... (202) 225–5330
Chief of Staff.—Frank Cullen. FAX: 225–2961
Legislative Director.—Chris Foster.
Communications Director.—Jason Vasquez.
Scheduler / Executive Assistant.—Krissy Rodriguez.
707 East Tahquitz Canyon Way, Suite 9, Palm Springs, CA 92262 .... (760) 320–1076
District Director.—Marc Troast.
1600 E. Florida Avenue, Suite 301, Hemet, CA 92544 .... (951) 658–2312

Counties: RIVERSIDE COUNTY (part). CITIES AND TOWNSHIPS: Bermuda Dunes, Blythe, Cathedral City, Coachella, East Blythe, East Hemet, Hemet, Idyllwild-Pine, Indian Wells, Indio, La Quinta, Mecca, Moreno Valley, Murrieta, Palm Desert, Palm Springs, Rancho Mirage, Thousand Palms, and Winchester. Population (2000), 639,088.

ZIP Codes: 92201, 92203, 92210–11, 92220, 92225–26, 92234–36, 92239–41, 92253–55, 92260–64, 92270, 92274, 92276, 92282, 92536, 92539, 92543–46, 92548–49, 92551–57, 92561–64, 92567, 92571, 92584–86, 92590–92, 92595–96

* * *

FORTY-SIXTH DISTRICT

DANA ROHRABACHER, Republican, of Huntington Beach, CA; born in Coronado, CA, June 21, 1947; education: graduated Palos Verdes High School, CA, 1965; attended Los Angeles Harbor College, Wilmington, CA, 1965–67; B.A., Long Beach State College, CA, 1969; M.A., University of Southern California, Los Angeles, 1975; writer/journalist; speechwriter and special assistant to the President, The White House, Washington, D.C., 1981–88; assistant press secretary, Reagan/Bush Committee, 1980; reporter, City News Service/Radio News West, and editorial writer, *Orange County Register*, 1972–80; committees: Foreign Affairs; Science and Technology; elected on November 8, 1988, to the 101st Congress; reelected to each succeeding Congress.

Office Listings

http://www.house.gov/rohrabacher

2300 Rayburn House Office Building, Washington, DC 20515 .... (202) 225–2415
Chief of Staff/Legislative Director.—Richard T. "Rick" Dykema. FAX: 225–0145
Communications Director.—Tara Setmayer.
101 Main Street, Suite 380, Huntington Beach, CA 92648 .... (714) 960–6483
District Director.—Kathleen M. Hollingsworth.

Counties: ORANGE COUNTY (part). Communities of Fountain Valley, Huntington Beach, Costa Mesa, Westminster, Seal Beach, Santa Ana, Midway City, Garden Grove, Newport Beach, Sunset Beach, Surfside. LOS ANGELES COUNTY (part). COMMUNITIES OF: Avalon, Long Beach, Palos Verdes, Palos Verdes Estates, Rancho Palos Verdes, Rolling Hills, Rolling Hills Estates, and San Pedro. Population (2000), 639,088.

ZIP Codes: 90274–75, 90704, 90731–32, 90740, 90742–44, 90802–04, 90808, 90813–15, 90822, 90831–35, 90840, 90853, 92626–28, 92646–49, 92655, 92683, 92702, 92708, 92711–12, 92725, 92735, 92799, 92841, 92843–44

* * *

FORTY-SEVENTH DISTRICT

LORETTA SANCHEZ, Democrat, of Anaheim, CA; born in Lynwood, CA, January 7, 1960; education: graduate of Chapman University; M.B.A., American University; specializes in assisting public agencies with finance matters; member, Blue Dog Coalition; Law Enforcement Caucus; Congressional Women's Caucus; committees: Armed Services; Homeland Security; elected to the 105th Congress; reelected to each succeeding Congress.

Office Listings

http://www.house.gov/sanchez

1230 Longworth House Office Building, Washington, DC 20515 .... (202) 225–2965
Chief of Staff.—Susan Horsfall. FAX: 225–5859
Legislative Director.—Edward Steiner.
Legislative Assistants: Kate Riley, Andrew Stephenson, Marisa Sturza.
Communications Director.—Paula Negrete.
12397 Lewis Street, Suite 101, Garden Grove, CA 92840 .... (714) 621–0102
District Director.—Raul Luna.

Counties: ORANGE COUNTY (part). CITIES: Anaheim (west and north-south of the Anaheim Stadium-Disneyland corridor), Fullerton, Garden Grove, Orange, and Santa Ana. Population (2000), 639,087.

ZIP Codes: 90680, 92609, 92616, 92619, 92623, 92650, 92652, 92654, 92658, 92679, 92697–98, 92701–04, 92706–07, 92735, 92781, 92801–02, 92804–05, 92812, 92815–17, 92825, 92832–33, 92840–41, 92843–44, 92850, 92868

* * *

FORTY-EIGHTH DISTRICT

JOHN CAMPBELL, Republican, of Irvine, CA; born in Los Angeles, CA, July 19, 1955; education: B.A., University of California, Los Angeles, CA; M.A., University of Southern California, Los Angeles, CA; professional: certified public accountant; member of the California state senate; married: Catherine; children: two sons; committees: Budget; Financial Services; elected to the 109th Congress by special election to fill the vacancy caused by the resignation of United States Representative Christopher Cox and reelected to the 110th Congress.

Office Listings

http://www.house.gov/campbell

1728 Longworth House Office Building, Washington, DC 20515 .... (202) 225–5611
Chief of Staff.—David Bowser. FAX: 225–9177
Executive Assistant.—Rosemary Müller.
Legislative Director.—David Malech.
Press Secretary.—Vartan Djihanian.
610 Newport Center Drive, Suite 330, Newport Beach, CA 92660 .... (949) 756–2244

Counties: ORANGE COUNTY (part). CITIES: Aliso Viejo, Corona del Mar, Dana Point, Foothill Ranch, Irvine, Laguna Beach, Laguna Hills, Laguna Niguel, Laguna Woods, Lake Forest, Newport Beach, Orange, San Juan Capistrano, Santa Ana, and Tustin. Population (2000), 639,089.

ZIP Codes: 92602–04, 92606–07, 92610, 92612, 92614, 92618, 92620, 92624–25, 92629–30, 92651, 92653, 92656–57, 92660–63, 92674–75, 92677–79, 92690, 92693, 92705, 92780, 92782

* * *

FORTY-NINTH DISTRICT

DARRELL E. ISSA, Republican, of Vista, CA; born in Cleveland, OH, November 1, 1953; education: Siena Heights College; military service: U.S. Army; attended college on an ROTC scholarship; professional: Businessman; founder and CEO of Directed Electronics, Inc.; past Chairman, Consumer Electronics Association; Board of Directors, Electronics Industry Association; public service: Co-Chairman of the campaign to pass the California Civil Rights Initiative (Proposition 209); Chairman of the Volunteer Committee for the 1996 Republican National Convention; Chairman of the San Diego County Lincoln Club; candidate for the U.S. Senate in 1998; architect of 2003 California recall campaign of former Governor Gray Davis; married: Kathy; children: William; committees: Judiciary; elected to the 107th Congress on November 7, 2000; reelected to each succeeding Congress.

Office Listings

http://www.house.gov/issa

211 Cannon House Office Building, Washington, DC 20515 .... (202) 225–3906
Chief of Staff.—Dale Neugebauer. FAX: 225–3303
Legislative Director.—Paige Anderson.
Press Secretary.—Frederick Hill.
Scheduler.—Mary Pritschau.
1800 Thibodo Road, #310, Vista, CA 92081 .... (760) 599–5000

Counties: RIVERSIDE (part), SAN DIEGO (part). Population (2000), 639,087

ZIP Codes: 92003, 92025–28, 92036, 92049, 92051–52, 92054–61, 92065–66, 92068–70, 92081–86, 92088, 92128, 92530, 92532, 92548, 92562–63, 92567, 92570–72, 92584–87, 92589–93, 92595–96, 92599

* * *

FIFTIETH DISTRICT

BRIAN P. BILBRAY, Republican, of San Diego, CA; born in Coronado, CA, January 28, 1951; education: graduated Mar Vista High School; attended South Western College; professional: tax consultant; city council; Imperial Beach, CA; 1976–78; mayor, Imperial Beach, CA, 1978–85; San Diego County Board of Supervisors, 1985–95; married: Karen; five children; committees: Oversight and Government Reform; Science and Technology; Veterans' Affairs; elected to the 104th Congress and to the two succeeding Congresses (January 3, 1995–2001); unsuccessful candidate for reelection to the 107th Congress; elected by special election, to fill the vacancy caused by the resignation of United States Representative Randall ''Duke'' Cunningham and reelected to each succeeding Congress.

Office Listings

http://www.house.gov/bilbray

227 Cannon House Office Building, Washington, DC 20515 .... (202) 225–0508
Chief of Staff.—Steve Danon. FAX: 225–2558
Legislative Director.—Amy Smith.
Scheduler.—Jenny Hauser.
Press Secretary.—Kurt Bardella.
462 Stevens Avenue, Suite 107, Solana Beach, CA 92075 .... (858) 350–1150

Counties: SAN DIEGO COUNTY (part). Population (2000), 639,087.

ZIP Codes: 92007–09, 92013–14, 92018, 92023–27, 92029–30, 92033, 92037, 92046, 92067, 92069, 92075, 92078–79, 92081–84, 92091, 92096, 92109–11, 92117, 92121–22, 92126–30, 92145, 92172, 92177, 92191, 92196, 92198

* * *

FIFTY-FIRST DISTRICT

BOB FILNER, Democrat, of San Diego, CA; born in Pittsburgh, PA, September 4, 1942; education: B.A., Cornell University, Ithaca, NY, 1963; M.A., University of Delaware, 1969; Ph.D., Cornell University, 1973; professor, San Diego State University, 1970–92; San Diego Board of Education, 1979–83 (president, 1982); San Diego City Council, 1987–92 (deputy mayor, 1990); member: Sierra Club, NAACP, Navy League, Gray Panthers, Economic Conversion Council, Common Cause, ACLU, ADL, NWPC, MAPA; married: Jane Merrill Filner, 1985; children: Erin and Adam; committees: chair, Veterans' Affairs; Transportation and Infrastructure; elected on November 3, 1992 to the 103rd Congress; reelected to each succeeding Congress.

Office Listings

http://www.house.gov/filner

2428 Rayburn House Office Building, Washington, DC 20515 .... (202) 225–8045
Chief of Staff.—Tony Buckles. FAX: 225–9073
Executive Assistant.—Kim Messineo.
Legislative Director.—Sharon Wagener.
Senior Legislative Assistant.—Sharon Schultze.
333 F Street, Suite A, Chula Vista, CA 91910 .... (619) 422–5963
1101 Airport Road, Suite D, Imperial, CA 92251 .... (760) 355–8800

Counties: SAN DIEGO COUNTY (part), IMPERIAL COUNTY. CITIES: Brawley, Calexico, Calipatria, Chula Vista, El Centro, Holtville, Imperial, National City, San Diego, San Ysidro, and Westmorland. Population (2000), 639,087.

ZIP Codes: 91902, 91905–06, 91908–15, 91917, 91921, 91934, 91945, 91947, 91950, 91963, 91977, 91980, 92102, 92105, 92113–15, 92136, 92139, 92143, 92149, 92153–54, 92173, 92179, 92222, 92227, 92231–33, 92243–44, 92249–51, 92257, 92259, 92266, 92273–75, 92281, 92283

* * *

FIFTY-SECOND DISTRICT

DUNCAN HUNTER, Republican, of Alpine, CA; born in Riverside, CA, May 31, 1948; education: graduated, Rubidoux High School, 1966; J.D., Western State University, 1976; first lieutenant, U.S. Army Airborne, 1969–71; professional: trial lawyer; admitted to the California bar, 1976; commenced practice in San Diego; member: Baptist Church, Navy League; married: the former Lynne Layh, 1973; children: Duncan Duane and Robert Samuel; committees: Armed Services; elected to the 97th Congress, November 4, 1980; reelected to each succeeding Congress.

Office Listings

http://www.house.gov/hunter

2265 Rayburn House Office Building, Washington, DC 20515 .... (202) 225–5672
Administrative Assistant.—Victoria Middleton. FAX: 225–0235
Office Manager / Appointment Secretary.—Valerie Snesko.
Press Secretary.—Joe Kasper.
1870 Cordell Court, Suite 206, El Cajon, CA 92020 .... (619) 579–3001

Counties: SAN DIEGO COUNTY (part). CITIES AND TOWNSHIPS: Alpine, Barona I.R., Borrego Springs, Boulder Park, Boulevard, Campo, Descanso, Dulzura, El Cajon, Guatay, Indian Res., Jacumba, Jamul, Lakeside, La Mesa, Lemon Grove, Mount Laguna, Pine Valley, Potrero, Poway, Ramona, San Diego, Santee, Spring Valley, Tecate, and Palo Verde. Population (2000), 639,087.

ZIP Codes: 91901, 91903, 91905–06, 91915–17, 91931, 91935, 91941–45, 91948, 91962, 91976–79, 92004, 92019–22, 92025, 92036, 92040, 92064–66, 92071–72, 92074, 92090, 92108, 92111, 92115, 92119–20, 92123–24, 92126, 92128–29, 92131, 92142, 92145, 92150, 92158–60, 92190, 92193–94, 92199

* * *

FIFTY-THIRD DISTRICT

SUSAN A. DAVIS, Democrat, of San Diego, CA; born in Cambridge, MA, April 13, 1944; education: B.S., University of California at Berkeley; M.A., University of North Carolina; public service: served three terms in the California State Assembly; served nine years on the San Diego City School Board; former President of the League of Women Voters of San Diego; awards: California School Boards Association Legislator of the Year; League of Middle Schools Legislator of the Year; family: married to Steve; children: Jeffrey and Benjamin; grandson: Henry; granddaughter: Jane; committees: Armed Services; Education and Labor; House Administration; elected to the 107th Congress on November 7, 2000; reelected to each succeeding Congress.

Office Listings

http://www.house.gov/susandavis

1526 Longworth House Office Building, Washington DC 20515 .... (202) 225–2040
Chief of Staff.—Lisa Sherman. FAX: 225–2948
Press Secretary.—Aaron Hunter.
Scheduler.—Cynthia Patton.
4305 University Avenue, Suite 515, San Diego, CA 92105 .... (619) 280–5353
District Director.—Todd Gloria.

Counties: SAN DIEGO COUNTY (part). Population (2000), 639,087.

ZIP Codes: 91932–33, 91945–46, 91977, 92037–39, 92092–93, 92101–18, 92120–23, 92132–38, 92140, 92147, 92152, 92155, 92161, 92163–71, 92175–76, 92178, 92182, 92184, 92186–87, 92192, 92195

COLORADO

(Population 2000, 4,301,261)

SENATORS

WAYNE ALLARD, Republican, of Loveland, CO; born in Fort Collins, CO, December 2, 1943; education: graduated, Fort Collins High School, 1963; preveterinary studies, Colorado State University, 1964; Doctor of Veterinary Medicine, Colorado State University, 1968; received veterinarian license in Colorado; Chief Health Officer, Loveland, CO, 1970–78; Larimer County Board of Health, 1978–82; Colorado State Senate, 1982–90; chair, Health and Human Services Committee and majority caucus; member: American Veterinary Medical Association, National Federation of Independent Business, Chamber of Commerce, Loveland Rotary, American Animal Hospital Association, American Board of Veterinary Practitioners, Companion Animal; married: the former Joan Elizabeth Malcolm; children: Christi and Cheryl; Deputy Majority Whip; in February 2001, appointed by Senate Majority Leader Trent Lott to serve on the High Tech Task Force and the National Security Working Group; chairman, Senate Renewable Energy and Energy Efficiency Caucus, and the Veterinary Caucus; elected to the 102nd Congress, November 6, 1990; reelected to each succeeding Congress; committees: Appropriations; Banking, Housing, and Urban Affairs; Budget; Health, Education, Labor, and Pensions; elected to the U.S. Senate on November 6, 1996; reelected to each succeeding Senate term.

Office Listings

http://allard.senate.gov

521 Dirksen Senate Office Building, Washington, DC 20510 .... (202) 224–5941
Chief of Staff.—Sean Conway. FAX: 224–6471
Scheduler.—Ali Monroe.
Communications Director.—Laura Condeluci.
7340 East Caley, Suite 215, Englewood, CO 80111 .... (303) 220–7414
5401 Stone Creek Circle, Suite 203, Loveland, CO 80538 .... (970) 461–3530
111 S. Tejon Street, Suite 300, Colorado Springs, CO 80903 .... (719) 634–6071
411 Thatcher Building, Fifth and Main Streets, Pueblo, CO 81003 .... (719) 545–9751
215 Federal Building, 400 Rood Avenue, Grand Junction, CO 81501 .... (970) 245–9553
954 East Second Avenue, #107, Durango, CO 81301 .... (970) 375–6311

* * *

KEN SALAZAR, Democrat, of Denver, CO; born in Alamosa, CO, March 2, 1955; education: B.A., Colorado College, Political Science, 1977; J.D., University of Michigan School of Law, 1981; professional: attorney; Sherman & Howard (law firm), 1981–86; Parcel, Mauro, Hultin & Spaanstra (law firm), 1994–98; public service: chief legal counsel to Colorado Governor Roy Romer, 1986–90; executive director, Colorado Department of Natural Resources, 1990–94; Colorado Attorney General, 1999–2004; married: Hope; children: Melinda and Andrea; committees: Agriculture, Nutrition, and Forestry; Energy and Natural Resources; Finance; Select Committee on Ethics; Special Committee on Aging; elected to the U.S. Senate on November 2, 2004.

Office Listings

http://salazar.senate.gov

702 Hart Senate Office Building, Washington, DC 20510 .... (202) 224–5852
Chief of Staff.—Jeff Lane. FAX: 228–5036
Communications Director.—Cody Wertz.
Executive Assistant.—Joan Padilla.
2300 15th Street, 4th Floor, Denver, CO 80202 .... (303) 455–4600
State Director.—Renny Fagan.

REPRESENTATIVES

FIRST DISTRICT

DIANA DEGETTE, Democrat, of Denver, CO; born in Tachikowa, Japan, July 29, 1957; education: B.A., political science, *magna cum laude*, The Colorado College, 1979; J.D., New York University School of Law, 1982 (Root Tilden Scholar); professional: attorney with McDermott, Hansen, and Reilly; Colorado Deputy State Public Defender, Appellate Division, 1982–84; Colorado House of Representatives, 1992–96; board of directors, Planned Parenthood,

Rocky Mountain Chapter; member and formerly on board of governors, Colorado Bar Association; member, Colorado Women's Bar Association; past memberships: board of trustees, The Colorado College; Denver Women's Commission; board of directors, Colorado Trial Lawyers Association; former editor, *Trial Talk* magazine; listed in 1994–96 edition of *Who's Who in America*; chief deputy whip; committees: vice chair, Energy and Commerce; elected to the 105th Congress; reelected to each succeeding Congress.

Office Listings

2421 Rayburn House Office Building, Washington, DC 20515 .... (202) 225–4431
Chief of Staff.—Lisa B. Cohen. FAX: 225–5657
Scheduler.—Eric Blackwell.
Communications Director.—Brandon MacGillis.
600 Grant Street, Suite 202, Denver, CO 80203 .... (303) 844–4988
District Administrator.—Greg Diamond.

Counties: ADAMS (part), ARAPAHOE (part), DENVER, JEFFERSON (part). Population (2000), 614,465.

ZIP Codes: 80110–11, 80113, 80121, 80123, 80127, 80150–51, 80155, 80201–12, 80214–24, 80226–32, 80235–39, 80243–44, 80246–52, 80255–57, 80259, 80261–62, 80264–66, 80270–71, 80273–75, 80279, 80281, 80285, 80290–95, 80299

* * *

SECOND DISTRICT

MARK UDALL, Democrat, of Boulder, CO; born in Tucson, AR, July 18, 1950; son of Morris ''Mo'' Udall, U.S. Representative, 1961–91, and candidate for President of the United States, 1976; education: B.A., Williams College, 1972; professional: course director, educator, and executive director, Outward Bound, 1985–95; Colorado State House of Representatives, District 13, 1997–98; married: Maggie Fox; two children; committees: Armed Services; Natural Resources; Science and Technology; elected to the 106th Congress; reelected to each succeeding Congress.

Office Listings

http://www.house.gov/markudall

100 Cannon House Office Building, Washington, DC 20515 .... (202) 225–2161
Chief of Staff.—Alan Salazar. FAX: 226–7840
Legislative Director/Senior Legislative Counsel.—Stan Sloss.
Press Secretary/Legislative Assistant.—Lawrence Pacheco.
Scheduler.—Valerie Nosler.
8601 Turnpike Drive, Suite 206, Westminster, CO 80031 .... (303) 650–7820
291 Main Street, P.O. Box 325, Minturn, CO 81645 .... (970) 827–4154

Counties: ADAMS (part), BOULDER (part), BROOMFIELD, CLEAR CREEK, EAGLE, GILPIN, GRAND, JEFFERSON (part), SUMMIT, WELD (part). Population (2000), 614,465.

ZIP Codes: 80003, 80005, 80007, 80020–21, 80025–28, 80030–31, 80035–36, 80038, 80212, 80221, 80229, 80233–34, 80241, 80260, 80263, 80301–10, 80314, 80321–23, 80328–29, 80403, 80422–24, 80426–28, 80435–36, 80438–39, 80442–44, 80446–47, 80451–52, 80455, 80459, 80463, 80466, 80468, 80471, 80474, 80476–78, 80481–82, 80497–98, 80503–04, 80510, 80514, 80516, 80520, 80530, 80540, 80544, 80602, 80614, 80640, 81620–21, 81623, 81631–32, 81637, 81645, 81649, 81655, 81657–58

* * *

THIRD DISTRICT

JOHN T. SALAZAR, Democrat, of Manassas, CO; born in Alamosa, CO, July 21, 1953; education: B.S., Adams State College, Alamosa, CO, 1981; graduated from the Colorado Agricultural Leadership Forum, 1992; professional: served in the U.S. Army, 1973–76; farmer; rancher; business owner; public service: Governor's Economic Development Advisory Board; the state Agricultural Commission; board of directors of the Rio Grande Water Conservation District; board of directors of the Colorado Agricultural Leadership Forum; Colorado Agricultural Commission, 1999–2002; Colorado State House of Representatives, 2003–04; married: Mary Lou Salazar; children: Jesus, Esteban, and Miguel; committees: Agriculture; Transportation and Infrastructure; Veterans' Affairs; elected to the 109th Congress on November 2, 2004; reelected to each succeeding Congress.

Office Listings

http://www.house.gov/salazar

1531 Longworth House Office Building, Washington, DC 20515 .... (202) 225–4761
Chief of Staff.—Ronnie Carleton. FAX: 226–9669
Legislative Director.—Eric Wortman.
Scheduler.—Jennifer Barela.
134 West B Street, Pueblo, CO 81003 .... (719) 543–8200
225 North 5th Street, Suite 702, Grand Junction, CO 81501 .... (970) 245–7107

Counties: ALAMOSA, ARCHULETA, CONEJOS, COSTILLA, CUSTER, DELTA, DOLORES, GARFIELD, GUNNISON, HINSDALE, HUERFANO, JACKSON, LA PLATA, LAS ANIMAS, MESA, MINERAL, MOFFAT, MONTEZUMA, MONTROSE, OTERO (part), OURAY, PITKIN, PUEBLO, RIO BLANCO, RIO GRANDE, ROUTT, SAGUACHE, SAN JUAN, SAN MIGUEL. Population (2000), 614,467.

ZIP Codes: 80423–24, 80428, 80430, 80434–35, 80443, 80446–47, 80456, 80459, 80463, 80467, 80469, 80473, 80479–80, 80483, 80487–88, 80498, 81001–12, 81019–20, 81022–25, 81027, 81029, 81033, 81039–41, 81043–44, 81046, 81049–50, 81054–55, 81058–59, 81062, 81064, 81067, 81069, 81077, 81081–82, 81089, 81091, 81101–02, 81120–38, 81140–41, 81143–44, 81146–49, 81151–55, 81157, 81201, 81210–12, 81215, 81220–26, 81228, 81230–33, 81235–37, 81239–41, 81243, 81248, 81251–53, 81301–03, 81320–21, 81323–32, 81334–35, 81401–02, 81410–11, 81413–16, 81418–20, 81422–35, 81501–06, 81520–27, 81601–02, 81610–12, 81615, 81621, 81623–26, 81630, 81633, 81635–36, 81638–43, 81646–48, 81650, 81652–56

* * *

FOURTH DISTRICT

MARILYN N. MUSGRAVE, Republican, of Fort Morgan, CO; born, January 27, 1949; raised in Weld County, CO; education: graduated, Eaton High School, and Colorado State University; professional: school teacher; businesswoman (agricultural business); public service: Fort Morgan School Board; State House of Representatives, and State Senate; elected State Senate Republican Caucus Chairman; religion: First Assembly of God Church; married: Steve Musgrave; four children; committees: Agriculture; Small Business; elected to the 108th Congress on November 5, 2002; reelected to each succeeding Congress.

Office Listings

http://www.house.gov/musgrave

1507 Longworth House Office Building, Washington, DC 20515 .... (202) 225–4676
Chief of Staff.—Guy Short. FAX: 225–5870
Senior Legislative Analyst.—Nina Schmidgall.
Press Secretary.—Aaron Johnson.
Office Manager / Executive Assistant.—Jessica Rager.
3553 Clydesdale Parkway, Loveland, CO 80538 .... (970) 663–3536
705 South Division Avenue, Sterling, CO 80751 .... (970) 522–1788
109½ South 3rd Street, Sterling, CO 81054 .... (970) 522–1788

Counties: BACA, BOULDER (part), CHEYENNE, CROWLEY, KENT, KIOWA, KIT CARSON, LARIMER, LINCOLN, LOGAN, MORGAN, PHILLIPS, PROWERS, OTERO (part), SEDGEWICK, WASHINGTON, WELD (part), YUMA. Population (2000), 614,466.

ZIP Codes: 80501–04, 80510–13, 80515, 80517, 80521–28, 80530, 80532–43, 80545–47, 80549–51, 80553, 80603, 80610–12, 80615, 80620–24, 80631–34, 80638–39, 80642–46, 80648–54, 80701, 80705, 80720–23, 80726–29, 80731–37, 80740–47, 80749–51, 80754–55, 80757–59, 80801–02, 80804–05, 80807, 80810, 80812, 80815, 80818, 80821–26, 80828, 80830, 80832–34, 80836, 80861–62, 81021, 81024, 81027, 81029–30, 81033–34, 81036, 81038, 81041, 81043–47, 81049–50, 81052, 81054, 81057, 81059, 81062–64, 81071, 81073, 81076, 81084, 81087, 81090, 81092

* * *

FIFTH DISTRICT

DOUG LAMBORN, Republican, of Colorado Springs, CO; born in Leavenworth, KS, May 24, 1954; education: B.S., University of Kansas Lawrence, 1978; J.D., University of Kansas Lawrence, 1985; lawyer, private practice (business and real estate); Colorado State House of Representatives 1995–98; Colorado State Senate, 1998–2006; married: Jeanie; five children; committees: Natural Resources; Veterans' Affairs; elected to the 110th Congress on November 7, 2006.

Office Listings

http://www.house.gov/lamborn

437 Cannon House Office Building, Washington, DC 20515 .... (202) 225–4422

Chief of Staff.—Robert McCreary. FAX: 226–2638
Deputy Chief of Staff / Legislative Director.—Melissa Carlson.
Director of Communications.—Christopher Harvin.
Scheduler / Executive Assistant.—Allison Hines.
3730 Sinton Road, Suite 150, Colorado Springs, CO 80907 .... (719) 520–0055

Counties: CHAFFEE, EL PASO, FREMONT, LAKE, PARK (part), TELLER. Population (2000), 614,467.

ZIP Codes: 80104, 80106, 80132–33, 80135, 80420, 80432, 80438, 80440, 80443, 80448–49, 80456, 80461, 80475, 80808–09, 80813–14, 80816–17, 80819–20, 80827, 80829–33, 80835, 80840–41, 80860, 80863–64, 80866, 80901, 80903–22, 80925–26, 80928–37, 80940–47, 80949–50, 80960, 80962, 80970, 80977, 80995, 80997, 81008, 81154, 81201, 81211–12, 81221, 81223, 81226–28, 81233, 81236, 81240–42, 81244, 81251, 81253

* * *

SIXTH DISTRICT

THOMAS G. TANCREDO, Republican, of Littleton, CO; born in North Denver, CO, December 20, 1945; education: graduated, Holy Family High School, 1964; B.A., University of North Colorado, 1968; elected to the Colorado State Legislature in 1976, and served until 1982; appointed, Secretary of Education's Regional Representative, served from 1982 to 1992, during the Reagan and Bush administrations; in 1993, accepted presidency of the Independence Institute, a public policy research organization in Golden, CO; Christian; married: Jackie; children: Ray and Randy; committees: Foreign Affairs; Natural Resources; elected to the 106th Congress; reelected to each succeeding Congress.

Office Listings

http://www.house.gov/tancredo

1131 Longworth House Office Building, Washington, DC 20515 .... (202) 225–7882
Chief of Staff / Legislative Director.—Mac Zimmerman. FAX: 226–4623
Scheduler.—Ashling Thurmond.
6099 S. Quebec Street, #200, Centennial, CO 80111 .... (720) 283–9772
1800 West Littleton Boulevard, Littleton, CO 80120 .... (720) 283–7575
240 Wilcox Street, Suite 111, Castle Rock, CO 80104 .... (303) 688–3430

Counties: ARAPAHOE (part), DOUGLAS, ELBERT, JEFFERSON (part), PARK (part). Population (2000), 614,466.

ZIP Codes: 80013–16, 80018, 80046, 80101–09, 80111–12, 80116–18, 80120–31, 80134–38, 80160–63, 80165–66, 80225, 80231, 80235–36, 80247, 80401, 80403, 80421, 80425, 80433, 80437, 80439, 80453–54, 80457, 80465, 80470, 80808, 80828, 80830–33, 80835

* * *

SEVENTH DISTRICT

ED PERLMUTTER, Democrat, of Golden, CO; born in Denver, CO, May 1, 1953; education: B.A., University of Colorado, 1975; J.D., University of Colorado, 1978; professional: served as a member of the Board of Governors of the Colorado Bar Association; served on the Board of Trustees and Judicial Performance Commission for the First Judicial District; Trustee, Midwest Research Institute, the primary operator of the National Renewable Energy Laboratory; board member, National Jewish Medical and Research Center; elected to two four-year terms to represent central Jefferson County as a Colorado State Senator, 1995–2003; served on numerous committees in the State Senate, including Water, Finance, Judiciary, Child Welfare, Telecommunication, Transportation, Legal Services, and Oil and Gas; also served as chair of the Public Policy and Planning Committee, chair of the Bi-Partisan Renewable Energy Caucus, and President Pro Tem (2001–02 session); married: Deana; three children; committees: Financial Services; Homeland Security; elected to the 110th Congress on November 7, 2006.

Office Listings

http://perlmutter.house.gov/

415 Cannon House Office Building, Washington, DC 20515 .... (202) 225–2645
Chief of Staff.—Danielle Radovich Piper. FAX: 225–5278
Legislative Director.—Michael Spira.
Scheduler / Executive Assistant.—Alison Inderforth.
Staff Assistant.—Jose Rodriguez.
12600 West Colfax Avenue, Suite B400, Lakewood, CO 80215 .... (303) 274–7944

Counties: ADAMS (part), ARAPAHOE (part), JEFFERSON (part). CITIES AND TOWNSHIPS: Arvada, Aurora, Bennett, Brighton, Commerce City, Edgewater, Golden, Lakewood, and Wheat Ridge. Population (2000), 614,465.

ZIP Codes: 80001–07, 80010–14, 80017–19, 80021–22, 80030, 80033–34, 80040–42, 80044–45, 80047, 80102–03, 80105, 80123, 80127, 80136–37, 80212, 80214–16, 80221, 80226–35, 80241, 80247, 80401–03, 80419, 80465, 80601–03, 80640, 80642–43, 80654

CONNECTICUT

(Population 2000, 3,405,565)

SENATORS

CHRISTOPHER J. DODD, Democrat, of East Haddam, CT; born in Willimantic, CT, May 27, 1944; son of Thomas J. and Grace Murphy Dodd; education: graduated, Georgetown Preparatory School, 1962; B.A., English Literature, Providence College, 1966; J.D., University of Louisville School of Law, 1972; admitted to Connecticut bar, 1973; served in U.S. Army Reserves, 1969–75; Peace Corps volunteer, Dominican Republic, 1966–68; married to Jackie Clegg; one child, Grace; founded the Senate Children's Caucus; House committees: served on the Rules Committee, Judiciary Committee, and Science and Technology Committee; appointed to the Select Committee on the Outer Continental Shelf and the Select Committee on Assassinations; appointed to the Commission on Security and Cooperation in Europe; elected to the 94th Congress, November 5, 1974; reelected to the 95th and 96th Congresses; committees: chair, Banking, Housing, and Urban Affairs; Foreign Relations; Health, Education, Labor, and Pensions; Rules and Administration; Joint Committee on the Library; elected to the U.S. Senate, November 4, 1980; reelected to each succeeding Senate term.

Office Listings

http://dodd.senate.gov

448 Russell Senate Office Building, Washington, DC 20510 .... (202) 224–2823
Chief of Staff.—Lori McGrogan (acting). FAX: 224–1083
Legislative Director.—Jim Fenton.
Putnam Park, 100 Great Meadow Road, Wethersfield, CT 06109 .... (860) 258–6940
State Director.—Ed Mann.

* * *

JOSEPH I. LIEBERMAN, Independent Democrat, of New Haven, CT; born in Stamford, CT, February 24, 1942; education: attended Stamford public schools; B.A., Yale University, 1964; law degree, Yale Law School, 1967; Connecticut State Senate, 1970–80; majority leader, 1974–80; honorary degrees: Yeshiva University, University of Hartford; Connecticut's 21st attorney general, 1983; reelected in 1986; author of ''The Power-Broker'' (Houghton Mifflin Company, 1966), a biography of late Democratic Party chairman John M. Bailey; ''The Scorpion and the Tarantula'' (Houghton Mifflin Company, 1970), a study of early efforts to control nuclear proliferation; ''The Legacy'' (Spoonwood Press, 1981), a history of Connecticut politics from 1930–80; ''Child Support in America'' (Yale University Press, 1986); ''In Praise of Public Life'' (Simon and Schuster, 2000); and ''An Amazing Adventure'' (Simon and Schuster, 2003); married: Hadassah Lieberman; children: Matthew, Rebecca, Ethan, and Hana; member, Democratic Leadership Council; Democratic candidate for Vice President, 2000; committees: chair, Homeland Security and Governmental Affairs; Armed Services; Environment and Public Works; Small Business and Entrepreneurship; elected on November 8, 1988, to the U.S. Senate; reelected to each succeeding Senate term.

Office Listings

http://lieberman.senate.gov

706 Hart Senate Office Building, Washington, DC 20510 .... (202) 224–4041
Chief of Staff.—Clarine Nardi Riddle. FAX: 224–9750
Executive Assistant.—Melissa Winter.
Legislative Director.—Joseph Goffman.
One Constitution Plaza, 7th Floor, Hartford, CT 06103 .... (860) 549–8463
State Director.—Sherry Brown.

REPRESENTATIVES

FIRST DISTRICT

JOHN B. LARSON, Democrat, of East Hartford, CT; born in Hartford, July 22, 1948; education: Mayberry Elementary School, East Hartford, CT; East Hartford High School; B.A., Central Connecticut State University; Senior Fellow, Yale University, Bush Center for Child Development and Social Policy; professional: high school teacher, 1972–77; insurance broker, 1978–98; president, Larson and Lyork; public service: Connecticut State Senate, 12 years,

President Pro Tempore, 8 years; married: Leslie Larson; children: Carolyn, Laura, and Raymond; committees: Ways and Means; Select Committee on Energy Independence and Global Warming; elected to the 106th Congress; reelected to each succeeding Congress.

Office Listings

http://www.house.gov/larson

1005 Longworth House Office Building, Washington, DC 20515 .... (202) 225–2265
Chief of Staff.—Jonathan Renfrew. FAX: 225–1031
Press Secretary.—Stephanie Valencia.
Scheduler.—Caroline Rose.
221 Main Street, Hartford, CT 06106–1864 .... (860) 278–8888

Counties: HARTFORD (part), LITCHFIELD (part), MIDDLESEX (part). Population (2000), 681,113.

ZIP Codes: 06002, 06006, 06010–11, 06016, 06021, 06023, 06025–28, 06033, 06035, 06037, 06040–41, 06045, 06057, 06060–61, 06063–65, 06067, 06073–74, 06088, 06090–91, 06094–96, 06098, 06101–12, 06114–15, 06117–20, 06123, 06126–29, 06131–34, 06137–38, 06140–47, 06150–56, 06160–61, 06176, 06180, 06183, 06199, 06416, 06422, 06444, 06457, 06467, 06479–80, 06489, 06759, 06790

* * *

SECOND DISTRICT

JOE COURTNEY, Democrat, of Vernon, CT; born in Hartford, CT, April 6, 1953; education: B.A., Tufts University, 1971–75; University of Connecticut Law School, 1975–78; public service: Connecticut State Representative, 1987–94; Vernon Town Attorney, 2003–06; professional: attorney, Courtney, Boyan, and Foran, LLC, 1978–2006; religion: Roman Catholic; married: Audrey Courtney; children: Robert and Elizabeth; committees: Armed Services; Education and Labor; Transportation and Infrastructure; elected to the 110th Congress on November 7, 2006.

Office Listings

http://www.house.gov/courtney

215 Cannon House Office Building, Washington, DC 20515 .... (202) 225–2076
Chief of Staff.—Jason Gross. FAX: 225–4977
Communications Director.—Brian Farber.
Scheduler.—Irena Vidulovich.
Legislative Director.—Sheila Duffy.
2 Courthouse Square, Norwich, CT 06360 .... (860) 886–0139
District Director.—Jenny Contois.

Counties: HARTFORD (part), MIDDLESEX (part), NEW LONDON, TOLLAND, WINDHAM. Population (2000), 681,113.

ZIP Codes: 06029, 06033, 06040, 06043, 06066, 06071–73, 06075–78, 06080, 06082–84, 06093, 06226, 06230–35, 06237–39, 06241–51, 06254–56, 06258–60, 06262–69, 06277–82, 06320, 06330–40, 06349–51, 06353–55, 06357, 06359–60, 06365, 06370–80, 06382–85, 06387–89, 06409, 06412–15, 06417, 06419–20, 06422–24, 06426, 06438–39, 06441–43, 06447, 06456–57, 06459, 06469, 06474–75, 06498

* * *

THIRD DISTRICT

ROSA L. DELAURO, Democrat, of New Haven, CT; born in New Haven, March 2, 1943; education: graduated, Laurelton Hall High School; attended London School of Economics, Queen Mary College, London, 1962–63; B.A., *cum laude*, history and political science, Marymount College, NY, 1964; M.A., international politics, Columbia University, NY, 1966; professional: executive assistant to Mayor Frank Logue, city of New Haven, 1976–77; executive assistant/development administrator, city of New Haven, 1977–78; chief of staff, Senator Christopher Dodd, 1980–87; executive director, Countdown '87, 1987–88; executive director, Emily's List, 1989–90; married: Stanley Greenberg; children: Anna, Kathryn, and Jonathan; committees: Appropriations; Budget; elected to the 102nd Congress on November 6, 1990; reelected to each succeeding Congress.

Office Listings

2262 Rayburn House Office Building, Washington, DC 20515 .... (202) 225–3661
Chief of Staff.—Ashley Turton. FAX: 225–4890
Legislative Director.—Leticia Mederos.
Executive Assistant.—Tiavalya Jefferson.
59 Elm Street, New Haven, CT 06510 .... (203) 562–3718

District Director.—Jennifer Lamb.

Counties: FAIRFIELD (part), MIDDLESEX (part), NEW HAVEN (part). CITIES AND TOWNSHIPS: Ansonia, Beacon Falls, Bethany, Branford, Derby, Durham, East Haven, Guilford, Hamden, Middlefield, Middletown, Milford, Naugatuck, New Haven, North Branford, North Haven, Orange, Prospect, Seymour, Shelton, Stratford, Wallingford, Waterbury, West Haven, and Woodbridge. Population (2000), 681,113.

ZIP Codes: 06401, 06403, 06405, 06410, 06418, 06422, 06437, 06450, 06455, 06457, 06460, 06471–73, 06477, 06481, 06483–84, 06492–94, 06501–21, 06524–25, 06530–38, 06540, 06607, 06614–15, 06706, 06708, 06712, 06762, 06770

* * *

FOURTH DISTRICT

CHRISTOPHER SHAYS, Republican, of Bridgeport, CT; born in Stamford, CT, October 18, 1945; education: graduated, Darien High School, Darien, CT, 1964; B.A., Principia College, Elsah, IL, 1968; M.B.A., New York University Graduate School of Business, 1974; M.P.A., New York University Graduate School of Public Administration, 1978; member, Peace Corps, Fiji Islands, 1968–70; professional: business consultant; college instructor, realtor; executive aide, Trumbull First Selectman, 1971–72; Connecticut House of Representatives, 1974–87; married: Betsi Shays, 1968; children: Jeramy; committees: Financial Services; Homeland Security; Oversight and Government Reform; elected by special election, August 18, 1987, to the 100th Congress to fill the vacancy caused by the death of Stewart B. McKinney; reelected to each succeeding Congress.

Office Listings

http://www.house.gov/shays rep.shays@mail.house.gov

1126 Longworth House Office Building, Washington, DC 20515 .... (202) 225–5541
FAX: 225–9629
Chief of Staff.—Betsy Wright Hawkings.
Legislative Director.—Matt Meyer.
Executive Assistant.—Diana White.
888 Washington Boulevard, Stamford, CT 06901–2927 .... (203) 357–8277
10 Middle Street, Bridgeport, CT 06604–4223 .... (203) 579–5870
District Director.—Paul Pimentel.

Counties: FAIRFIELD (part), NEW HAVEN (part). CITIES AND TOWNSHIPS: Bridgeport, Darien, Easton, Fairfield, Greenwich, Monroe, New Canaan, Norwalk, Oxford, Redding, Ridgefield, Shelton, Stamford, Trumbull Weston, Westport, and Wilton. Population (2000), 681,113.

ZIP Codes: 06468, 06478, 06483–84, 06491, 06601–02, 06604–08, 06610–12, 06673, 06699, 06807, 06820, 06824–25, 06828–31, 06836, 06838, 06840, 06850–58, 06860, 06870, 06875–81, 06883, 06888–90, 06896–97, 06901–07, 06910–14, 06920–22, 06925–28

* * *

FIFTH DISTRICT

CHRISTOPHER S. MURPHY, Democrat, of Cheshire, CT; born August 3, 1973; grew up in Connecticut; graduated with honors, double major in history and political science, Williams College, MA; graduated, University of Connecticut Law School, Hartford, CT, 2002; former member, Southington Planning and Zoning Commission; served for eight years in the Connecticut General Assembly; in 2005, succeeding in passing Connecticut's landmark stem cell investment act; committees: Financial Services; Oversight and Government Reform; elected to the 110th Congress on November 7, 2006.

Office Listings

http://www.chrismurphy.house.gov

501 Cannon House Office Building, Washington, DC 20515 .... (202) 225–4476
FAX: 225–5933
Chief of Staff.—Joshua Raymond.
Communications Director.—Kristen Bossi.
Scheduler/Executive Assistant.—Jessica Elledge.
1 Grove Street, Suite 225, New Britain, CT 06053 .... (860) 223–8412
District Director.—Robert Michalik.

Counties: FAIRFIELD (part), HARTFORD (part), LITCHFIELD, NEW HAVEN (part). CITIES: Danbury, Meriden, New Britain, Torrington, and Waterbury. Population (2000), 681,113.

ZIP Codes: 06001, 06013, 06018–20, 06022, 06024, 06030–32, 06034, 06039, 06050–53, 06058–59, 06062, 06068–70, 06079, 06081, 06085, 06087, 06089, 06092, 06107, 06404, 06408, 06410–11, 06440, 06450–51, 06454, 06470, 06482,

06487–88, 06701–06, 06708, 06710, 06716, 06720–26, 06749–59, 06762–63, 06776–79, 06781–87, 06790–91, 06793–96, 06798, 06801, 06804, 06810–14, 06816–17

DELAWARE

(Population 2000, 783,600)

SENATORS

JOSEPH R. BIDEN, JR., Democrat, of Wilmington, DE; born in Scranton, PA, November 20, 1942; education: St. Helena's School, Wilmington, DE; Archmere Academy, Claymont, DE; A.B., history and political science, University of Delaware; J.D., Syracuse University College of Law; married: Jill Tracy Biden; children: Joseph R. Biden III, Robert Hunter Biden, and Ashley Blazer Biden; admitted to the bar, December 1968, Wilmington, DE; engaged in private practice until 1972; served on New Castle County Council, 1970–72; committees: chair, Foreign Relations; Judiciary; elected to the U.S. Senate on November 7, 1972; reelected to each succeeding Senate term.

Office Listings

http://biden.senate.gov senator@biden.senate.gov

201 Russell Senate Office Building, Washington, DC 20510 .... (202) 224–5042
Chief of Staff.—Alan Hoffmann. FAX: 224–0139
Legislative Director.—Jane Woodfin. TDD: 224–4048
Communications Director.—Greg Haas.
Office Manager.—Bill Clapp.
1105 North Market Street, Suite 2000, Wilmington, DE 19801–1233 .... (302) 573–6345
State Director.—John DiEleuterio.
24 NW Front Street, Windsor Building, Suite 101, Milford, DE 19963 .... (302) 424–8090

* * *

THOMAS R. CARPER, Democrat, of Wilmington, DE; born in Beckley, WV, January 23, 1947; education: B.A., Ohio State University, 1968; M.B.A., University of Delaware, 1975; military service: U.S. Navy, served during Vietnam War; public service: Delaware State Treasurer, 1977–83; U.S. House of Representatives, 1983–93; Governor of Delaware, 1993–2001; organizations: National Governors' Association; Democratic Leadership Council; religion: Presbyterian; family: married to the former Martha Ann Stacy; children: Ben and Christopher; committees: Banking, Housing, and Urban Affairs; Commerce, Science, and Transportation; Environment and Public Works; Homeland Security and Governmental Affairs; Special Committee on Aging; elected to the U.S. Senate on November 7, 2000; reelected to each succeeding Senate term.

Office Listings

http://carper.senate.gov

513 Hart Senate Office Building, Washington, DC 20510 .... (202) 224–2441
Chief of Staff.—Jim Reilly. FAX: 228–2190
Legislative Director.—Bill Ghent.
Office Manager.—Ann Berry.
2215 Federal Building, 300 South New Street, Dover, DE 19904 .... (302) 674–3308
301 North Walnut Street, Suite 102 L–1, Wilmington, DE 19801 .... (302) 573–6291
12 The Circle, Georgetown, DE 19947 .... (302) 856–7690

REPRESENTATIVE

AT LARGE

MICHAEL N. CASTLE, Republican, of Wilmington, DE; born in Wilmington, July 2, 1939; education: graduate of Tower Hill School, 1957; B.S. in economics, Hamilton College, Clinton, NY, 1961; J.D., Georgetown University Law School, 1964; professional: attorney; admitted to the District of Columbia and Delaware bars, 1964; commenced practice in Wilmington; Delaware House of Representatives, 1966–67; Delaware Senate, 1968–76; Lieutenant Governor of Delaware, 1981–85; Governor, 1985–92; awarded honorary degrees: Wesley College, 1986; Widener College, 1986; Delaware State University, 1986; Hamilton College, 1991; Jefferson Medical College, Philadelphia, PA, 1992; active in the National Governors Association, serving three years as chairman of the Human Resources Committee; co-vice chairman for NGA's Task Force on Health Care with President Clinton; past president of the Council of State Governments; past chairman of the Southern Governors Association; chaired the Republican Governors

Association, 1988; American Diabetes Association's C. Everett Koop Award for Health Promotion and Awareness, 1992; member: Delaware Bar Association, American Bar Association; former member: National Governors Association, Republican Governors Association, National Assessment Governing Board, Council of State Governors, Southern Governors Association; honorary board of directors, Delaware Greenways; task forces: co-chairman, Congressional Task Force to the National Campaign to Reduce Teen Pregnancy; House Tobacco Task Force; co-chair, House Diabetes Caucus; co-chair, Biomedical Research Caucus; co-chair, Passenger Rail Caucus; co-chair, Community College Caucus; married: Jane DiSabatino, 1992; committees: Education and Labor; Financial Services; elected to the 103rd Congress on November 3, 1992; reelected to each succeeding Congress.

Office Listings

http://www.house.gov/castle

1233 Longworth House Office Building, Washington, DC 20515 .... (202) 225–4165
Chief of Staff.—Mike Quaranta. FAX: 225–2291
Deputy Chief of Staff / Press Secretary.—Elizabeth Brealey Wenk.
Legislative Director.—Kate Dickens.
Scheduler.—Kristy Huxhold.
201 North Walnut Street, Suite 107, Wilmington, DE 19801 .... (302) 428–1902
Office Director.—Jeff Dayton. FAX: 428–1905
J. Allen Frear Federal Building, 300 South New Street, Dover, DE 19904 .... (302) 736–1666

Counties: KENT, NEW CASTLE, SUSSEX. CITIES AND TOWNSHIPS: Brookside, Camden, Claymont, Delaware City, Dover, Edgemoor, Elsmere, Georgetown, Harrington, Highland, Acres, Kent Acres, Laurel, Lewes, Middletown, Milford, Millsboro, New Castle, Newark, Pike Creek, Rising Sun-Lebanon, Rodney Village, Seaford, Smyrna, Stanton, Talleyville, Wilmington, Wilmington Minor, and Woodside East. Population (2000), 783,600.

ZIP Codes: 19701–03, 19706–18, 19720–21, 19725–26, 19730–36, 19801–10, 19850, 19880, 19884–87, 19890–99, 19901–06, 19930–31, 19933–34, 19936, 19938–41, 19943–47, 19950–56, 19958, 19960–64, 19966–71, 19973, 19975, 19977, 19979–80

FLORIDA

(Population 2000, 15,982,378)

SENATORS

BILL NELSON, Democrat, of Orlando, FL, born in Miami, FL, September 29, 1942; education: Melbourne High School, 1960; B.A., Yale University, 1965; J.D. University of Virginia School of Law, 1968; professional: attorney; admitted to the Florida Bar, 1968; captain, U.S. Army Reserve, 1965–71; active duty, 1968–70; public service: Florida State House of Representatives, 1973–79; U.S. House of Representatives, 1979–91; Florida Treasurer, Insurance Commissioner, and State Fire Marshal, 1995–2001; Astronaut: payload specialist on the space shuttle *Columbia*, January, 1986; married: the former Grace Cavert; children: Bill Jr. and Nan Ellen; committees: Armed Services; Budget; Commerce, Science, and Transportation; Foreign Relations; Select Committee on Intelligence; Special Committee on Aging; elected to the U.S. Senate on November 7, 2000; reelected to each succeeding Senate term.

Office Listings

http://billnelson.senate.gov

716 Hart Senate Office Building, Washington, DC 20510 .... (202) 224–5274
Chief of Staff.—Pete Mitchell. FAX: 228–2183
Deputy Chief of Staff, Communications.—Dan McLaughlin.
Deputy Chief of Staff, Administration.—Brenda Strickland.
Legislative Director.—Dan Shapiro.
U.S. Courthouse Annex, 111 North Adams Street, Tallahassee, FL 32301 .... (850) 942–8415
Chief of Staff.—Pete Mitchell.
801 North Florida Avenue, 4th Floor, Tampa, FL 33602 .... (813) 225–7040
2925 Salzedo Street, Coral Gables, FL 33134 .... (305) 536–5999
3416 University Drive, Ft. Lauderdale, FL 33328 .... (954) 693–4851
500 Australian Avenue, Suite 125, West Palm Beach, FL 33401 .... (561) 514–0189
225 East Robinson Street, Suite 410, Orlando, FL 32801 .... (407) 872–7161
1301 Riverplace Boulevard, Suite 2281, Jacksonville, FL 32207 .... (904) 346–4500
2000 Main Street, Suite 801, Ft. Myers, FL 33901 .... (239) 334–7760

* * *

MELQUIADES ''MEL'' R. MARTINEZ, Republican, of Orlando, FL; born in Sagua La Grande, Cuba, October 23, 1946; immigrated to the United States in 1962; lived with foster families until reunited with his family in Orlando, FL, in 1966; education: B.A., Florida State University, 1969; J.D., Florida State University School of Law, 1973; professional: admitted to Florida Bar, 1973; U.S. District Court for Middle District of FL, 1973; U.S. Supreme Court, 1979; U.S. District Court for Southern District of FL, 1986; attorney and partner, Martinez, Dalton, Dellecker and Wilson, Orlando, FL, 1973–85 and Martinez, Dalton, Dellecker, Wilson and King, 1985–98; Florida co-chair, Presidential campaigns of Robert J. Dole, 1996 and George W. Bush, 2000; delegate to Republican National Convention, 2000; Orange County Chairman; secretary, Department of Housing and Urban Development, 2001–04; married: Kitty; children: Lauren Shea, John, Andrew; committees: Armed Services; Banking, Housing, and Urban Affairs; Energy and Natural Resources; Special Committee on Aging; elected to the U.S. Senate on November 2, 2004.

Office Listings

http://martinez.senate.gov

317 Hart Senate Office Building, Washington, DC 20510 .... (202) 224–3041
Chief of Staff.—John Little. FAX: 228–5171
Legislative Director.—Michael Zehr.
315 East Robinson Street, Landmark Center 1, Suite 475, Orlando, FL 32801 .... (407) 254–2573
1650 Prudential Drive, Suite 220, Jacksonville, FL 32207 .... (904) 398–8586
800 Douglas Road, Suite 148, Coral Gables, FL 33134 .... (305) 444–8332
3301 Tamiami Trail East, Building F, Suite 223, Naples, FL 34112 .... (239) 774–3367
1 North Palafox Street, Suite 159, Pensacola, FL 32502 .... (850) 433–2603
5100 West Kennedy Boulevard, Suite 190, Tampa, FL 33609 .... (813) 207–0509

REPRESENTATIVES

FIRST DISTRICT

JEFF MILLER, Republican, of Chumuckla, FL; born in St. Petersburg, FL, June 27, 1959; education: B.S., University of Florida, 1984; professional: real estate broker; public service: Executive Assistant to the Commissioner of Agriculture, 1984–88; Environmental Land Management Study Commission, 1992; Santa Rosa County Planning Board Vice Chairman, 1996–98; elected to the Florida House of Representatives in 1998; reelected in 2000; served as House Majority Whip: organizations: Kiwanis Club of Milton; Florida Historical Society; Santa Rosa County United Way; Milton Pregnancy Resource Center Advisory Board; Gulf Coast Council of Boy Scouts; Florida FFA Foundation; religion: Methodist; married: Vicki Griswold; children: Scott and Clint; committees: Armed Services; Veterans' Affairs; elected to the 107th Congress, by special election, on October 16, 2001; reelected to each succeeding Congress.

Office Listings

1535 Longworth House Office Building, Washington, DC 20515 .... (202) 225–4136
Chief of Staff.—Dan McFaul. FAX: 225–3414
Legislative Director.—Anne Pizzato.
Scheduler.—Diane Cihota.
4300 Bayou Boulevard, Suite 17–C, Pensacola, FL 32503 .... (850) 479–1183
District Director.—Sheilah Bowman.
348 SW Miracle Strip Parkway, Unit 21, Ft. Walton Beach, FL 32548 .... (850) 664–1266

Counties: ESCAMBIA, HOLMES, OKALOOSA (part), SANTA ROSA, WALTON (part), WASHINGTON. CITIES AND TOWNSHIPS: Bonifay, Carryville, Crestview, DeFuniak Springs, Destin, Fountain, Freeport, Ft. Walton Beach, Gulf Breeze, Jay, Laurel Hill, Lynn Haven, Milton, Noma, Pace, Paxton, Pensacola, Sunnyside, Westville, and Youngstown. Population (2000), 639,295.

ZIP Codes: 32501–09, 32511–14, 32516, 32520–24, 32526, 32530–31, 32533–42, 32544, 32547–49, 32559–72, 32577–79, 32580, 32583, 32588, 32591, 32598

* * *

SECOND DISTRICT

ALLEN BOYD, Democrat, of Monticello, FL; born in Valdosta, GA, June 6, 1945; education: graduated, Jefferson County High School, Monticello, 1963; B.S., Florida State University, 1969; professional: partner and general manager, F.A. Boyd and Sons, Inc., family farm corporation; first lieutenant, U.S. Army 101st Airborne Division, Vietnam, 1969–71, receiving the CIB and other decorations; Florida House of Representatives, 1989–96; elected majority whip; chaired Governmental Operations Committee (1992–94) and House Democratic Conservative Caucus (Blue Dogs); member: Peanut Producers Association; Farm Bureau; Cattlemen's Association; local historical association; Chamber of Commerce; and Kiwanis; board member, National Cotton Council; member, First United Methodist Church; married: the former Stephannie Ann Roush, 1970; children: Fred Allen Boyd III (d), Suzanne, John, and David; committees: Appropriations; Budget; elected to the 105th Congress; reelected to each succeeding Congress.

Office Listings

http:/www.house.gov/boyd

1227 Longworth House Office Building, Washington, DC 20515 .... (202) 225–5235
Chief of Staff.—Libby Greer. FAX: 225–5615
Legislative Director.—Jason Quaranto.
Legislative Assistants: Josh Gifford, Megan Murphy.
Executive Assistant/Scheduler.—Robin Nichols.
1650 Summit Lake Drive, Suite 103, Tallahassee, FL 32317 .... (850) 561–3979
District Director.—Jerry Smithwick.
30 W. Government Street, Panama City, FL 32401 .... (850) 785–0812
District Representative.—Bobby Pickels.

Counties: BAY, CALHOUN, DIXIE, FRANKLIN, GADSDEN, GULF, JACKSON, JEFFERSON (part), LAFEYETTE, LEON (part), LIBERTY, OKALOOSA (part), SUWANNE, TAYLOR, WALKULLA, WALTON (part). Population (2000), 639,295.

ZIP Codes: 32008, 32013, 32024, 32038, 32055, 32060, 32062, 32064, 32066, 32071, 32094, 32096, 32126, 32140, 32170, 32175, 32267, 32301–18, 32320–24, 32326–34, 32336, 32343–44, 32346–48, 32351–53, 32355–62, 32395, 32399,

32401–13, 32417, 32420–21, 32423–24, 32426, 32428, 32430–32, 32437–38, 32440, 32442–49, 32454, 32456–57, 32459–61, 32465–66, 32541, 32550, 32578, 32628, 32648, 32680, 32692

* * *

THIRD DISTRICT

CORRINE BROWN, Democrat, of Jacksonville, FL; born in Jacksonville, November 11, 1946; education: B.S., Florida A&M University, 1969; master's degree, Florida A&M University, 1971; education specialist degree, University of Florida; honorary doctor of law, Edward Waters College; faculty member: Florida Community College in Jacksonville; University of Florida; and Edward Waters College; served in the Florida House of Representatives for 10 years; first woman elected chairperson of the Duval County Legislative Delegation; served as a consultant to the Governor's Committee on Aging; member: Congressional Black Caucus; Women's Caucus; and Progressive Caucus; one child: Shantrel; committees: Transportation and Infrastructure; Veterans' Affairs; elected on November 3, 1992, to the 103rd Congress; reelected to each succeeding Congress.

Office Listings

http://www.house.gov/corrinebrown

2336 Rayburn House Office Building, Washington, DC 20515 .... (202) 225–0123
FAX: 225–2256
Chief of Staff.—E. Ronnie Simmons.
Executive Assistant/Scheduler.—Darla E. Smallwood.
Legislative Director.—Nick Martinelli.
Communications Director.—David Simon.
101 East Union Street, Suite 202, Jacksonville, FL 32202 .... (904) 354–1652
219 Lime Avenue, Orlando, FL 32802 .... (407) 872–0656

Counties: ALACHUA (part), CLAY (part), DUVAL (part), LAKE (part), MARION (part), ORANGE (part), PUTNAM (part), SEMINOLE (part), VOLUSIA (part). Population (2000), 639,295.

ZIP Codes: 32003, 32007, 32043, 32066, 32073, 32102, 32105, 32112–13, 32130–31, 32134, 32138, 32140, 32147–49, 32160, 32177, 32179–80, 32182, 32185, 32190, 32201–11, 32215–16, 32218–19, 32231–32, 32234, 32236, 32238–39, 32244, 32247, 32254, 32277, 32601–04, 32627, 32631, 32640–41, 32653–54, 32662, 32666–67, 32681, 32702–03, 32712–13, 32720–24, 32736, 32751, 32757, 32763, 32767–68, 32771–73, 32776, 32789, 32798, 32801, 32804–05, 32808–11, 32818–19, 32835, 32839, 32855, 32858, 32861, 32868, 33142, 33160–61, 33179, 34488, 34761

* * *

FOURTH DISTRICT

ANDER CRENSHAW, Republican, of Jacksonville, FL; born in Jacksonville, September 1, 1944; education: B.A., University of Georgia, 1966; J.D., University of Florida, 1969; professional: investment banker; religion: Episcopal; public service: former member of the Florida House of Representatives and the Florida State Senate; served as President of the Florida State Senate; married: Kitty; children: Sarah and Alex; committees: Appropriations; elected to the 107th Congress on November 7, 2000; reelected to each succeeding Congress.

Office Listings

http://www.house.gov/crenshaw

127 Cannon House Office Building, Washington, DC 20515 .... (202) 225–2501
FAX: 225–2504
Chief of Staff.—John Ariale.
Legislative Director.—Erica Striebel.
Communications Director.—David Taft.
1061 Riverside Avenue, Suite 100, Jacksonville, FL 32204 .... (904) 598–0481
District Director.—Jacqueline Smith.
212 North Marion Avenue, Suite 209, Lake City, FL 32055 .... (386) 365–3316

Counties: BAKER, COLUMBIA, DUVAL (part), HAMILTON, JEFFERSON (part), LEON (part), MADISON, NASSAU, UNION. CITIES AND TOWNSHIPS: Greenville, Hilliard, Jacksonville, Jacksonville Beach, Jasper, Jennings, Lake Butler, Lake City, Lee, Macclenny, Madison, Monticello, Nassau Village-Ratliff, Palm Valley, Tallahassee, White Springs, and Yulee. Population (2000), 639,295.

ZIP Codes: 32009, 32011, 32024–26, 32034–35, 32038, 32040–41, 32046, 32052–56, 32058–59, 32061, 32063, 32072, 32083, 32087, 32094, 32096–97, 32204–05, 32207, 32210–12, 32214, 32216–18, 32223–29, 32233–35, 32237, 32240–41, 32244–46, 32250, 32255–58, 32266, 32277, 32301, 32311, 32317, 32331, 32336–37, 32340–41, 32344–45, 32350, 32643, 32697, 33142

* * *

FIFTH DISTRICT

GINNY BROWN-WAITE, Republican, of Brooksville, FL; born in Albany, NY, October 5, 1943; education: B.S., State University of New York, 1976; Russell Sage College, 1984; Labor Studies Program Certification, Cornell University; professional: served as a Legislative Director in the New York State Senate for almost 18 years; public service: Hernando County, FL, Commissioner; Florida State Senate, 1992–2002; served as Senate Majority Whip, and President Pro Tempore; recipient of numerous awards for community service; married: Harvey; children: three daughters; committees: Financial Services; Homeland Security; Veterans' Affairs; elected to the 108th Congress on November 5, 2002; reelected to each succeeding Congress.

Office Listings

http://www.house.gov/brown-waite

414 Cannon House Office Building, Washington, DC 20515 .... (202) 225–1002
Chief of Staff.—Pete Meachum. FAX: 226–6559
Scheduler.—Kathleen Smoak.
Senior Legislative Assistant.—Amie Woeber.
Press Secretary.—Charlie Keller.
20 North Main Street, Room 200, Brooksville, FL 34601 .... (352) 799–8354
15000 Citrus County Drive, Unit 100, Dade City Business Center, Dade City, FL 33523 .... (352) 567–6707

Counties: CITRUS, HERNANDO, LAKE (part), LEVY (part), MARION (part), PASCO (part), POLK (part), SUMTER. CITIES AND TOWNSHIPS: Brooksville, Dade City, and Clermont. Population (2000), 639,295.

ZIP Codes: 32159, 32162, 32621, 32625–26, 32635, 32639, 32644, 32658, 32668, 32683, 32696, 32778, 32825, 33513–14, 33521, 33523–26, 33537–38, 33540–44, 33548–49, 33556, 33558–59, 33574, 33576, 33585, 33593, 33597, 33809–10, 33849, 33868, 34218, 34220, 34423, 34428–34, 34436, 34442, 34445–53, 34460–61, 34464–65, 34481–82, 34484, 34487, 34498, 34601–11, 34613–14, 34636, 34639, 34653–55, 34661, 34667, 34669, 34711–13, 34731, 34736–37, 34748, 34753, 34755, 34762, 34785, 34787–89, 34797

* * *

SIXTH DISTRICT

CLIFF STEARNS, Republican, of Ocala, FL; born in Washington, DC, April 16, 1941; education: graduated, Woodrow Wilson High, Washington, DC, 1959; B.S., electrical engineering, George Washington University, Washington, DC, 1963; Air Force ROTC Distinguished Military Graduate; graduate work, University of California, Los Angeles, 1965; served, U.S. Air Force (captain), 1963–67; businessman; past president: Silver Springs Kiwanis; member: Marion County/Ocala Energy Task Force, Tourist Development Council, Ocala Board of Realtors, American Hotel/Motel Association in Florida, American Hotel/Motel Association of the United States, Grace Presbyterian Church; board of directors, Boys Club of Ocala; trustee: Munroe Regional Hospital; married: the former Joan Moore; children: Douglas, Bundy, and Scott; committees: Energy and Commerce; Veterans' Affairs; elected November 8, 1988, to the 101st Congress; reelected to each succeeding Congress.

Office Listings

http://www.house.gov/stearns

2370 Rayburn House Office Building, Washington, DC 20515 .... (202) 225–5744
Chief of Staff.—Jack Seum. FAX: 225–3973
Legislative Director.—Lauren Semeniuk.
Scheduler / Office Manager.—Joan Smutko.
115 Southeast 25th Avenue, Ocala, FL 34471 .... (352) 351–8777
District Manager.—John Konkus.
5700 S.W. 34th Street, #425, Gainesville, FL 32608 .... (352) 337–0003
1726 Kinglsey Avenue S.E., Suite 8, Orange Park, FL 32073 .... (904) 269–3203

Counties: ALACHUA (part), BRADFORD, CLAY (part), DUVAL (part), GILCHREST, LAKE (part), LEVY (part), MARION (part). CITIES AND TOWNSHIPS: Ocala, Gainesville, Leesburg, Orange Park, Middleburg, and Jacksonville. Population (2000), 639,295.

ZIP Codes: 32003, 32006, 32008, 32030, 32042–44, 32050, 32054, 32058, 32065, 32067–68, 32073, 32079, 32083, 32091, 32099, 32111, 32113, 32133, 32140, 32158–59, 32162, 32179, 32183, 32195, 32205, 32210, 32215, 32219–22, 32234, 32244, 32254, 32276, 32601, 32603, 32605–12, 32614–16, 32618–19, 32621–22, 32631, 32633–34, 32643, 32653, 32655–56, 32658, 32663–64, 32666–69, 32681, 32686, 32693–94, 32696, 33142, 33160–61, 34420–21, 34432, 34436, 34470–76, 34478, 34480–83, 34491–92, 34731, 34748–49

* * *

SEVENTH DISTRICT

JOHN L. MICA, Republican, of Winter Park, FL; born in Binghamton, NY, January 27, 1943; education: graduated, Miami-Edison High School, Miami, FL; B.A., University of Florida, 1967; professional: president, MK Development; managing general partner, Cellular Communications; former government affairs consultant, Mica, Dudinsky and Associates; executive director, Local Government Study Commissions, Palm Beach County, 1970–72; executive director, Orange County Local Government Study Commission, 1972–74; Florida State House of Representatives, 1976–80; administrative assistant, U.S. Senator Paula Hawkins, 1980–85; Florida State Good Government Award, 1973; one of five Florida Jaycees Outstanding Young Men of America, 1978; member: Kiwanis, U.S. Capitol Preservation Commission, Tiger Bay Club, co-chairman, Speaker's Task Force for a Drug Free America, Florida Blue Key; U.S. Capitol Preservation Commission; brother of former Congressman Daniel A. Mica; married: the former Patricia Szymanek, 1972; children: D'Anne Leigh and John Clark; committees: Oversight and Government Reform; Transportation and Infrastructure; elected on November 3, 1992 to the 103rd Congress; reelected to each succeeding Congress.

Office Listings

http://www.house.gov/mica

2313 Rayburn House Office Building, Washington, DC 20515 .... (202) 225–4035
Chief of Staff.—Russell L. Roberts. FAX: 226–0821
Executive Assistant / Scheduler.—Mike Matousek.
Legislative Director / Press Secretary.—Gary Burns.
100 East Sybelia Avenue, #340, Maitland, FL 32751 .... (407) 657–8080
840 Deltona Boulevard, Suite G, Deltona, FL 32725 .... (386) 860–1499
770 W. Granada Boulevard, Suite 315, Ormond Beach, FL 32174 .... (386) 676–7750
3000 N. Ponce de Leon Boulevard, Suite 1, St. Augustine, FL 32084 .... (904) 810–5048
613 St. Johns Avenue, Suite 107, Palatka, FL 32177 .... (386) 328–1622
1 Florida Park Drive South, Suite 100, Palm Coast, FL 32137 .... (386) 246–6042

Counties: ORANGE COUNTY (part). CITIES AND TOWNSHIPS: Maitland, Winter Park. SEMINOLE COUNTY. CITIES AND TOWNSHIPS: Altamonte Springs, Casselberry, Heathrow, Lake Mary, Longwood, Sanford, Winter Springs. VOLUSIA COUNTY (part). CITIES AND TOWNSHIPS: Daytona Beach, Debary, Deland, Deltona, Holly Hill, Lake Helen, Orange City, Ormond Beach, Pierson. FLAGLER COUNTY. CITIES AND TOWNSHIPS: Beverly Beach, Bunnell, Flagler Beach, Marineland, Palm Coast. ST. JOHNS COUNTY. CITIES AND TOWNSHIPS: Hastings, Ponte Vedra Beach, St. Augustine, St. Augustine Beach. PUTNAM COUNTY (part). CITIES AND TOWNSHIPS: Crescent City, Palatka, Pomona Park, and Welaka. Population, (2000), 639,295.

ZIP Codes: 32004, 32033, 32080, 32082, 32084–86, 32092, 32095, 32110, 32112, 32114–22, 32125, 32130–31, 32135–37, 32139, 32142, 32145, 32151, 32157, 32164, 32173–78, 32180–81, 32187, 32189, 32193, 32198, 32259–60, 32701, 32706–08, 32713–15, 32718, 32720, 32724–25, 32728, 32730, 32738, 32744, 32746–47, 32750–53, 32763–64, 32771, 32773–74, 32779, 32789, 32791–92, 32795, 32799

* * *

EIGHTH DISTRICT

RIC KELLER, Republican, of Orlando, FL; born in Johnson City, TN, September 5, 1964; education: Boone High School, 1982; B.S., East Tennessee State University, 1986; J.D., Vanderbilt University, 1992; professional: attorney; partner in the law firm of Rumberger, Kirk & Caldwell; community service: Chairman of the Board of Directors of the Orlando/Orange County COMPACT Program; co-author of two amendments to Florida's Constitution (the Everglades Polluter Pays amendment, and the Everglades Trust Fund amendment); religion: United Methodist; remarried; children: Nick, Christy and Kaylee; committees: Education and Labor; Judiciary; elected to the 107th Congress on November 7, 2000; reelected to each succeeding Congress.

Office Listings

http://www.house.gov/keller

419 Cannon House Office Building, Washington, DC 20515 .... (202) 225–2176
Chief of Staff.—Bryan Malenius. FAX: 225–0999
Deputy Chief of Staff.—Brian Crawford.
Scheduler.—Elizabeth Davis.
605 East Robinson Street, Suite 650, Orlando, FL 32801 .... (407) 872–1962
District Director.—Cheryl Mills.

Counties: ORANGE (part), OSCEOLA (part), MARION (part), LAKE (part). CITIES AND TOWNSHIPS: Astatula, Azalea, Bay Hill, Bay Lake, Belle Isle, Belleview, Celebration, Conway, Doctor Phillips, Edgewood, Eustis, Fairview Shores, Howeyin-the-Hills, Holden Heights, Leesburg, Meadow Wood, Mid Florida Lakes, Montverde, Oakland, Ocala Part, Ocoee, Orlando, Silver Springs Shores, Sky Lakes, Tavares, Umatilla, Union Park, Williamsburg, Windermere, Winter Garden, and Winter Park. Population (2000), 639,295.

ZIP Codes: 32113, 32179, 32192, 32617, 32702–03, 32710, 32726–27, 32735–36, 32756–57, 32777–78, 32784, 32789, 32792, 32801–07, 32809–12, 32814, 32817–19, 32821–22, 32824–25, 32827, 32829–30, 32835–37, 32839, 32853–54, 32856–57, 32859–60, 32862, 32867, 32869, 32872, 32877, 32885–87, 32890–91, 32893, 32896–98, 33030, 33032–33, 33161, 33186, 34470–72, 34475, 34479–80, 34488–89, 34705, 34711, 34729, 34734, 34740, 34746–47, 34756, 34760–61, 34777–78, 34786–88

* * *

NINTH DISTRICT

GUS M. BILIRAKIS, Republican, of Palm Harbor, FL; born in Gainesville, FL, February 8, 1963; raised in Tarpon Springs, FL; education: B.A., University of Florida, 1986; J.D., Stetson University, 1989; son of former Representative Michael Bilirakis (1983–2006); volunteered on his father's congressional campaigns; interned for President Ronald Reagan and the National Republican Congressional Committee; worked for former Representative Don Sundquist (R–TN); ran the Bilirakis Law Group, specializing in wills, trusts, and estate planning, Holiday, FL; taught government classes, St. Petersburg College; member of the Florida House of Representatives, 1998–2006; chaired several prominent panels in the State House, including Crime Prevention, Public Safety Appropriations, and the Economic Development, Trade, and Banking Committee; married: Eva; children: Michael, Teddy, Manuel, and Nicholas; Senior Republican Freshman Whip; committees: Homeland Security; Veterans' Affairs; elected to the 110th Congress on November 7, 2006.

Office Listings

http://bilirakis.house.gov

1630 Longworth House Office Building, Washington, DC 20515 .... (202) 225–5755
Chief of Staff.—Rebecca Hyder. FAX: 225–4085
Legislative Director.—Jerry White.
Press Secretary.—John Randall.
Executive Assistant.—David Peluso.
Palm Harbor Professional Center, 35111 U.S. Highway 19 North, Suite 301, Palm Harbor, FL 34684 .... (727) 773–2871
District Director.—Shawn Foster.
10941 North 56th Street, Temple Terrace, FL 33617 .... (813) 985–8541

Counties: HILLSBOROUGH (part), PASCO (part), PINELLAS (part). CITIES AND TOWNSHIPS: Bearss, Bloomingdale, Brandon, Carrollwood Village, Citrus Park, Clearwater, Countryside, Crystal Springs, Dale Mabry, Eastlake Woodlands, Elfers, Fishhawk, Holiday, Hudson, Hunters Green, Lutz, New Port Richey, Odessa, Oldsmar, Palm Harbor, Plant City, Safety Harbor, Seffner, Seven Springs, Tarpon Springs, Temple Terrace, Thonotosassa, Trinity, Valrico, and Veterans Village. Population (2000), 639,296.

ZIP Codes: 33511, 33527, 33530, 33539–40, 33542, 33547–49, 33556, 33558–59, 33563, 33565–67, 33569, 33583–84, 33587, 33592, 33594–95, 33598, 33612–13, 33617–18, 33624–26, 33637, 33647, 33688, 33755–59, 33761, 33763–66, 33769, 33810, 34652–56, 34667–69, 34673–74, 34677, 34679–80, 34683–85, 34688–91, 34695

* * *

TENTH DISTRICT

C.W. BILL YOUNG, Republican, of Indian Shores, FL; born in Harmarville, PA, December 16, 1930; elected Florida's only Republican State Senator in 1960; reelected 1964, 1966, 1967 (special election), and 1968, serving as minority leader from 1963 to 1970; national committeeman, Florida Young Republicans, 1957–59; state chairman, Florida Young Republicans, 1959–61; member, Florida Constitution Revision Commission, 1965–67; dean of the Florida Republican delegation; the senior Republican in the House; married: Beverly; children: three sons; committees: Appropriations; elected to the 92nd Congress, November 3, 1970; reelected to each succeeding Congress.

Office Listings

2407 Rayburn House Office Building, Washington, DC 20515 .... (202) 225–5961
Chief of Staff.—Harry Glenn. FAX: 225–9764
Legislative Director.—Brad Stine.
Defense Appropriations.—Tom Rice.
360 Central Avenue, Suite 1480, St. Petersburg, FL 33701 .... (727) 893–3191
Administrative Assistant.—George N. Cretekos.
801 West Bay Drive, Suite 606, Largo, FL 33770 .... (727) 581–0980

9210 113th Street, Seminole, FL 33772 .... (727) 391–6030

Counties: PINELLAS COUNTY (part). Population (2000), 639,295.

ZIP Codes: 33701–16, 33729, 33731–32, 33734, 33736–38, 33740–44, 33755–56, 33760–65, 33767, 33770–82, 33784–86, 34660, 34681–84, 34697–98

* * *

ELEVENTH DISTRICT

KATHY CASTOR, Democrat, of Tampa, FL; born in Miami, FL, August 20, 1966; education: B.A., Political Science, Emory University, 1988; J.D., Florida State University, 1991; professional: Assistant General Counsel, State of Florida, Department of Community Affairs, 1991–94; attorney, Icard Merrill, 1994–95; partner, Broad and Cassel, 1995–2000; ran for Florida State Senate, 2000; Hillsborough County Commissioner, 2002–06; religion: member of Palma Ceia Presbyterian Church; married: William Lewis; children: two; committees: Armed Services; Rules; elected to the 110th Congress on November 7, 2006.

Office Listings

http://castor.house.gov

317 Cannon House Office Building, Washington, DC 20515 .... (202) 225–3376
Chief of Staff.—Clay Phillips. FAX: 225–5652
Legislative Director.—Carol Forthman.
Scheduler.—Lara Hopkins.
Press Secretary.—Agustina Guerrero.
4144 North Armenia Avenue, Suite 300, Tampa, FL 33607 .... (813) 871–2817
District Director.—Chloe Coney.

Counties: HILLSBOROUGH (part), MANATEE, PINELLAS. CITIES: Apollo Beach, Bradenton, Carrollwood, Carrollwood Village, Citrus Park, Ellenton, Gibsonton, Gulfport, Lutz, Northdale, Oldsmar, Palmetto, Riverview, Ruskin, St. Petersburg, Tampa, Temple Terrace, and Town 'N' Country, Ybor City. Population (2000), 639,295.

ZIP Codes: 33534, 33549, 33559, 33569–70, 33572, 33586, 33601–19, 33621–26, 33629–31, 33634–35, 33637, 33647, 33650–51, 33655, 33663–64, 33672–75, 33677, 33679–82, 33684–87, 33690, 33694, 33697, 33701, 33705, 33707, 33710–13, 33730, 33733, 33747, 33784, 34205, 34208, 34221–22, 34677

* * *

TWELFTH DISTRICT

ADAM H. PUTNAM, Republican, of Bartow, FL; born in Bartow, FL, July 31, 1974; education: Bartow High School; University of Florida, B.S., Food and Resource Economics; professional: farmer; rancher; awards: Outstanding Male Graduate of the University of Florida; Who's Who in American Politics; organizations: Florida 4–H Foundation; Sheriff's Youth Villa Board of Associates; Chamber of Commerce; Polk County Farm Bureau; married: Melissa; public service: Florida House of Representatives, 1996–2000; committees: Financial Services; elected to the 107th Congress on November 7, 2000; reelected to each succeeding Congress.

Office Listings

http://www.house.gov/putnam

1725 Longworth House Office Building, Washington, DC 20515 .... (202) 225–1252
Chief of Staff / Director of Communications.—John Hambel. FAX: 226–0585
Executive Assistant.—Andrea Becker.
Legislative Director.—Karen Williams.
650 East Davidson Street, Bartow, FL 33830 .... (863) 534–3530
District Director.—Cheryl Fulford.

Counties: HILLSBOROUGH (part), OSCEOLA (part), POLK (part). CITIES AND TOWNSHIPS: Apollo Beach, Auburndale, Babson Park, Bartow, Brandon, Davenport, Dundee, Eagle Lake, Fort Meade, Frostproof, Gibsonton, Haines City, Highland City, Hillcrest Heights, Indian Lake Estates, Lakeland, Lake Alfred, Lake Hamilton, Lake Wales, Mulberry, Plant City, Poinciana, Polk City, Riverview, Ruskin, Seffner, Sun City Center, Tampa, Temple Terrace, Thonotosassa, Wimauma, and Winter Haven. Population (2000), 639,296.

ZIP Codes: 33030, 33033, 33170, 33183, 33186, 33503, 33508–11, 33527, 33534, 33547, 33550, 33563–64, 33566–73, 33575, 33584, 33592, 33594, 33598, 33610, 33617, 33619, 33637, 33689, 33801–07, 33809–11, 33813, 33815, 33820, 33823, 33825, 33827, 33830–31, 33834–41, 33843–47, 33850–51, 33853–56, 33859–60, 33863, 33867–68, 33877, 33880–85, 33888, 33896–98, 34758–59

* * *

THIRTEENTH DISTRICT

VERN BUCHANAN, Republican, of Longboat Key, FL; born in Detroit, MI, May 8, 1951; education: B.B.A., Business Administration, Cleary University; M.B.A., University of Detroit; honorary degree: Doctorate of Science in Business Administration, Cleary University; professional: founder and chairman, Buchanan Enterprises; founder and chairman, Buchanan Automotive Group, 1992; operations include Sarasota Ford and 18 auto franchises in the southeastern United States; experience in real estate including home building and property development and management; awards: One of America's Ten Outstanding Young Men, U.S. Jaycees; Entrepreneur of the Year, Inc Magazine and Arthur Young; Entrepreneur of the Year, Harvard Business School, Club of Detroit; One of Michigan's Five Outstanding Young Men, Michigan Jaycees; President's Award, Ford Motor Company; Certified Retailer Award, J.D. Power and Associates; Outstanding Citizen Award, United Negro College Fund; Outstanding Philanthropic Corporation Award, National Society of Fund Raising Executives; Freedom Award for Business and Industry, NAACP; The American Jewish Committee Civic Achievement Award; Tampa Bay Business Hall of Fame Award; married: Sandy Buchanan; children: James and Matt; committees: Small Business; Transportation and Infrastructure; Veterans' Affairs; elected to the 110th Congress on November 7, 2006.

Office Listings

http://www.buchanan.house.gov

1516 Longworth House Office Building, Washington, DC 20515 .... (202) 225–5015
Chief of Staff.—Dave Karvelas. FAX: 226–0828
Legislative Director.—Todd Mitchell.
Scheduler.—Andrew Fasoli.
235 North Orange Avenue, Suite 201, Sarasota, FL 34236 .... (941) 951–6643
District Director.—Ron Turner.
1001 Third Avenue West, Suite 380, Bradenton, FL 34205 .... (941) 749–5310

Counties: CHARLOTTE (part), DESOTO, HARDEE, MANATEE (part), SARASOTA. Population (2000), 639,295.

ZIP Codes: 33138, 33160–61, 33598, 33834, 33865, 33873, 33890, 33946–47, 34201–12, 34215–19, 34221–24, 34228–43, 34250–51, 34260, 34264–70, 34272, 34274–78, 34280–82, 34284–89, 34292–93, 34295

* * *

FOURTEENTH DISTRICT

CONNIE MACK, Republican, of Fort Myers, FL; born in Fort Myers, August 12, 1967; education: B.S., University of Florida, Gainesville, FL, 1993; professional: marketing executive; member, Florida state House of Representatives, 2000–03; son of U.S. Senator Connie Mack III, step-great-grandson of Senator Tom Connally, great-grandson of Senator Morris Sheppard, and great-great-grandson of Congressman John Levi Sheppard; children: Addison and Connie; committees: Budget; Foreign Affairs; Transportation and Infrastructure; elected to the 109th Congress on November 2, 2004; reelected to the 110th Congress.

Office Listings

http://www.house.gov/mack

115 Cannon House Office Building, Washington, DC 20515 .... (202) 225–2536
Chief of Staff.—Jeff Cohen. FAX: 226–0439
Legislative Director.—Francis Gibbs.
Executive Assistant.—Betsy Kampas.
804 Nicholas Parkway East, Suite 1, Cape Coral, FL 33990 .... (239) 573–5837
3301 Tamiami Trail E, Bldg. F, First Floor, Naples, FL 34112 .... (239) 774–8035

Counties: CHARLOTTE (part), COLLIER (part), LEE. Population (2000), 639,295.

ZIP Codes: 33030, 33033, 33160, 33186, 33189, 33901–22, 33924, 33927–28, 33931–32, 33936, 33945–46, 33948, 33953–57, 33965, 33970–72, 33981, 33990–91, 33993–94, 34101–10, 34112–14, 34116, 34119, 34133–36, 34140, 34142, 34145–46, 34224

* * *

FIFTEENTH DISTRICT

DAVE WELDON, Republican, of India Lantic, FL; born in Long Island, NY, August 31, 1953; education: graduated Farmingdale High School, Farmingdale, NY, 1971; B.S., biochemistry, State University of New York, Stony Brook, 1978; M.D., State University of New York, Buffalo, 1981; U.S. Army Major, 1981–87; physician, internal medicine; member: American College of Physicians, Florida Medical Association, Brevard County Medical Society, Retired Officers Association, Good Samaritan Club, Brevard Veterans Council, Vietnam Veterans of Brevard, American Legion; founder, Space Coast Family Forum; married: Nancy Weldon, 1979; children: Katherine and David; committees: Appropriations; Select Committee on Energy Independence and Global Warming; elected to the 104th Congress; reelected to each succeeding Congress.

Office Listings

http://www.house.gov/weldon

2347 Rayburn House Office Building, Washington, DC 20515 .... (202) 225–3671
Chief of Staff.—Dana Gartzke. FAX: 225–3516
Deputy Chief of Staff.—Stuart Burns.
Scheduler / Office Manager.—Cathy Graham.
Legislative Director.—Ryan Fierst.
Building C, 2725 Judge Fran Jamieson Way, Melbourne, FL 32940 .... (321) 632–1776
District Director.—J.B. Kump.
2000 16th Avenue, Indian River County Courthouse, Room 157, Vero Beach, FL 32960 .... (772) 778–3534

Counties: BREVARD (part), INDIAN RIVER, OSCEOLA (part), POLK (part). Population (2000), 639,295.

ZIP Codes: 32815, 32899, 32901–12, 32919–20, 32922–26, 32931–32, 32934–37, 32940–41, 32948–53, 32955–58, 32960–71, 32976, 32978, 33837, 33848, 33858, 33868, 33896–98, 34739, 34741–47, 34758–59, 34769–73, 34972

* * *

SIXTEENTH DISTRICT

TIM MAHONEY, Democrat, of Venus, FL; born in Aurora, IL, August 16, 1956; education: B.A. in Computer Science and Business, West Virginia University; M.B.A., George Washington University; professional: Chairman, COO, and co-founder of vFinance, Inc.; founder and President of the Center for Innovative Entrepreneurship; rancher; member: Florida Cattleman's Association; Blue Dog Coalition; New Democrat Coalition; member, Venus United Methodist Church; married: Terry; child: Bailey; committees: Agriculture; Financial Services; elected to the 110th Congress on November 7, 2006.

Office Listings

http://www.mahoney.house.gov

1541 Longworth House Office Building, Washington, DC 20515 .... (202) 225–5792
Chief of Staff.—Charles Halloran. FAX: 225–3132
Deputy Chief of Staff.—Tricia Barrentine.
Communications Director.—Jessica Santillo.
18500 Murdock Circle, Suite 536, Port Charlotte, FL 33948 .... (941) 627–9100
9 Southeast Osceola Street, Stuart, FL 34994 .... (772) 878–3181
368 South Commercial Avenue, Sebring, FL 33870 .... (863) 471–1813

Counties: CHARLOTTE (part), GLADES, HENDRY (part), HIGHLANDS, MARTIN (part), OKEECHOBEE, PALM BEACH (part), ST. LUCIE (part). Population (2000), 639,295.

ZIP Codes: 33138, 33160–61, 33170, 33186, 33410–12, 33414, 33418, 33421, 33440, 33455, 33458, 33467, 33469–71, 33475, 33477–78, 33825–26, 33852, 33857, 33862, 33870–72, 33875–76, 33917, 33920, 33930, 33935, 33938, 33944, 33948–55, 33960, 33972, 33975, 33980, 33982–83, 34142, 34945–47, 34949–53, 34956–58, 34972–74, 34981–88, 34990–92, 34994–97

* * *

SEVENTEENTH DISTRICT

KENDRICK B. MEEK, Democrat, of Miami, FL; born in Miami, September 6, 1966; education: B.S., Florida A&M University, 1989; organizations: NAACP; 100 Black Men of

America, Inc.; Greater Miami Service Corps; Omega Psi Phi Fraternity; awards: Mothers Against Drunk Driving Outstanding Service Award; Ebony Magazine's 50 Leaders of Tomorrow; Adams-Powell Civil Rights Award; public service: Florida House of Representatives, 1994–98; Florida State Senate, 1998–2002; married: Leslie Dixon; children: Lauren and Kendrick B., Jr.; son of former Florida U.S. Representative Carrie P. Meek; committees: Armed Services; Ways and Means; elected to the 108th Congress on November 5, 2002; reelected to each succeeding Congress.

Office Listings

http://www.house.gov/kenmeek

1039 Longworth House Office Building, Washington, DC 20515 .... (202) 225–4506
Chief of Staff.—John Schelble. FAX: 226–0777
Senior Advisor.—Tasha Cole.
Legislative Director.—Clarence Williams.
Scheduler.—Portia Hickson.
111 N.W. 183rd Street, Suite 315, Miami Gardens, FL 33169 .... (305) 690–5905
District Office Director.—Joyce Postell.
10100 Pines Boulevard, 3rd Floor, Building B, Pembroke Pines, FL 33026 .... (954) 450–6767

Counties: DADE (part), BROWARD (part). Population (2000), 639,296.

ZIP Codes: 33008–09, 33013, 33020–25, 33054–56, 33081, 33083, 33090, 33092, 33101, 33110, 33127, 33136–38, 33142, 33147, 33150–51, 33156, 33160–62, 33164, 33167–69, 33179–81, 33197, 33238, 33242, 33247, 33256, 33261

* * *

EIGHTEENTH DISTRICT

ILEANA ROS-LEHTINEN, Republican, of Miami, FL; born in Havana, Cuba, July 15, 1952; education: B.A., English, Florida International University; M.S., educational leadership, Florida International University; Ed.D, University of Miami, 2004; certified Florida school teacher; founder and former owner, Eastern Academy; elected to Florida House of Representatives, 1982; elected to Florida State Senate, 1986; former president, Bilingual Private School Association; regular contributor to leading Spanish-language newspaper; during House tenure, married then-State Representative Dexter Lehtinen; children: Amanda Michelle and Patricia Marie; committees: Foreign Affairs; elected on August 29, 1989 to the 101st Congress; reelected to each succeeding Congress.

Office Listings

2160 Rayburn House Office Building, Washington, DC 20515 .... (202) 225–3931
Chief of Staff.—Arthur Estopinan. FAX: 225–5620
Deputy Administrative Assistant.—Christine del Portillo.
Legislative Director.—Fred Ratliff.
Press Secretary.—Alex Cruz.
Suite 100, 9210 Sunset Drive, Miami, FL 33173 .... (305) 275–1800

Counties: DADE (part), MONROE (part). CITIES AND TOWNSHIPS: Coral Gables, Florida City, Homestead, Key Biscayne, Miami, Miami Beach, South Miami, and West Miami. Population (2000), 639,295.

ZIP Codes: 33001, 33030, 33032–34, 33036–37, 33039–45, 33050–52, 33070, 33109, 33111–12, 33114, 33119, 33121, 33124–36, 33139–46, 33149, 33154–59, 33165, 33170, 33174, 33176, 33186, 33189–90, 33195, 33197, 33199, 33231, 33233–34, 33239, 33243, 33245, 33255, 33257, 33265, 33296, 33299

* * *

NINETEENTH DISTRICT

ROBERT WEXLER, Democrat, of Boca Raton, FL; born in Queens, NY, January 2, 1961; education: graduate of Hollywood Hills High School; University of Florida, 1982; George Washington University Law School, 1985; admitted to the Florida bar in 1985; attorney; Florida State Senator, 1990–96; member: Palm Beach Planning and Zoning Commission, 1989–90, Palm Beach County Democratic Executive Committee, 1989–92, Palm Beach County Affordable Housing Committee, 1990–91, Florida Bar Association, South Palm Beach County Jewish Federation, Palm Beach County Anti-Defamation League; married to the former Laurie Cohen; three children; committees: Financial Services; Foreign Affairs; Judiciary; elected to the 105th Congress; reelected to each succeeding Congress.

Office Listings

2241 Rayburn House Office Building, Washington, DC 20515 .... (202) 225–3001
Chief of Staff.—Eric Johnson. FAX: 225–5974
Deputy Chief of Staff/Communications Director.—Joshua Rugin.
2500 North Military Trail, Suite 100, Boca Raton, FL 33431 .... (561) 988–6302
District Director.—Wendy Lipsich.
5790 Margate Boulevard, Margate, FL 33063 .... (954) 972–6454

Counties: BROWARD (part), PALM BEACH (part). CITIES AND TOWNSHIPS: Boca Raton, Boynton Beach, Coconut Creek, Coral Springs, Deerfield Beach, Delray Beach, Lauderhill, Lake Worth, Margate, North Lauderdale, Parkland, Pompano Beach, Sunrise and Tamarac. Population (2000) 639,295.

ZIP Codes: 33063–66, 33068–69, 33071, 33073, 33075–77, 33093, 33140, 33155, 33309, 33321, 33401, 33406, 33409, 33411, 33413–15, 33417, 33422, 33426, 33428, 33431, 33433–34, 33436–37, 33441–42, 33445–46, 33448, 33454, 33461–63, 33466–67, 33474, 33481–82, 33484, 33486–88, 33496–99

* * *

TWENTIETH DISTRICT

DEBBIE WASSERMAN SCHULTZ, Democrat, of Weston, FL; born in Forest Hills, Queens County, NY, September 27, 1966; education: B.A., University of Florida, Gainesville, FL, 1988; M.A., University of Florida, FL, 1990; professional: Public Policy Curriculum Specialist, Nova Southeastern University; Adjunct Instructor, Political Science, Broward Community College; aide to United States Representative Peter Deutsch, 1989–92; member, Florida State House of Representatives, 1992–2000; member, Florida State Senate, 2000–04; organizations: Board of Trustees, Westside Regional Medical Center; Outstanding Freshman Legislator, Florida Women's Political Caucus; Secretary; Board of Directors, American Jewish Congress; Member, Broward National Organization for Women; Board of Directors, National Safety Council, South Florida Chapter; religion: Jewish; married: Steve; children: Rebecca, Jake, Shelby; Senior Democratic Whip; committees: Appropriations; Judiciary; elected to the 109th Congress on November 2, 2004; reelected to the 110th Congress.

Office Listings

http://www.house.gov/wasserman-schultz

118 Cannon House Office Building, Washington, DC 20515 .... (202) 225–7931
Chief of Staff.—Tracie Pough. FAX: 226–2052
Communications Director.—Jonathon Beeton.
Legislative Director.—Emily Coyle.
Office Manager.—Teri Viers.
10100 Pines Boulevard, Pembroke Pines, FL 33026 .... (954) 437–3936
19200 West Country Club Drive, Third Floor, Aventura, FL 33180 .... (305) 936–5724

Counties: BROWARD COUNTY (PART). CITIES: Dania Beach, Davie, Lazy Lake, Plantation, Wilton Manors, Weston. DADE COUNTY (part). CITIES: Bay Harbor Island, North Bay Village, and Sunny Isles. MIAMI-DADE COUNTY (part). CITIES: Davie, Fort Lauderdale, Hollywood, Miami Beach, North Miami, Sunrise. Population (2000), 639,295.

ZIP Codes: 33004, 33009, 33019–21, 33024, 33026, 33030, 33033, 33084, 33137, 33139–41, 33147, 33154, 33156, 33160–61, 33170, 33180–81, 33301, 33304–05, 33309, 33311–15, 33317–19, 33321–32, 33334, 33336, 33338, 33345, 33351, 33355, 33394

* * *

TWENTY-FIRST DISTRICT

LINCOLN DIAZ-BALART, Republican, of Miami, FL; born in Havana, Cuba, August 13, 1954; education: graduated, American School of Madrid, Spain, 1972; B.A., New College of the University of South Florida, Sarasota, 1976; J.D., Case Western Reserve University Law School, 1979; professional: attorney; admitted to the Florida bar, 1979; partner, Fowler, White, Burnett, Hurley, Banick and Strickroot, P.A., Miami; Florida State House, 1986–89; Florida State Senate, 1989–92; founding member, Miami-Westchester Lions Club; member, Organization for Retarded Citizens; married the former Cristina Fernandez, 1976; two children: Lincoln Gabriel and Daniel; Assistant Republican Whip; Congressional Human Rights Caucus; committees: Rules; elected on November 3, 1992 to the 103rd Congress; reelected to each succeeding Congress.

Office Listings

http://diaz-balart.house.gov

2244 Rayburn House Office Building, Washington, DC 20515 .... (202) 225–4211
Chief of Staff.—Ana M. Carbonell. FAX: 225–8576
Administrative Assistant.—Towner French.
Legislative Director.—Cesar Gonzalez.
Press Secretary.—Victoria Martinez.
8525 NW 53 Terrace, Suite 102, Miami, FL 33166 .... (305) 470–8555
District Director.—Ana M. Carbonell.

Counties: BROWARD COUNTY (part), DADE COUNTY (part). CITIES AND TOWNSHIPS: Central Kendall, Doral, Fontainebleau, Hialeah, Miami Lakes, Miami Springs, Miramar, Pembroke Pines, Richmond Heights, Sweetwater, Virginia Gardens, and Westchester. Population (2000), 639,295.

ZIP Codes: 33002, 33010–17, 33027–29, 33054–55, 33082, 33102, 33107, 33116, 33122, 33126, 33143, 33148, 33152, 33155–58, 33165–66, 33172–74, 33176, 33178, 33186, 33188, 33266, 33283

* * *

TWENTY-SECOND DISTRICT

RON KLEIN, Democrat, of Boca Raton, FL; born in Cleveland, OH, July 7, 1957; education: graduated, Cleveland Heights High School, 1975; B.A., The Ohio State University, 1979; J.D., Case Western Reserve University Law School, 1982; professional: attorney; admitted to the Florida State Bar, 1986; former partner, Sachs, Sax & Klein, P.A.; elected to the Florida House of Representatives, District 90, 1992; reelected, 1994; elected to the Florida Senate, District 30, 1996; reelected in 2000, 2004; married to the former Dori Dragin, 1982; children: Brian and Lauren; committees: Financial Services; Foreign Affairs; elected to the 110th Congress on November 7, 2006.

Office Listings

http://www.klein.house.gov

313 Cannon House Office Building, Washington, DC 20515 .... (202) 225–3026
Chief of Staff.—Brain Smoot. FAX: 225–8398
Deputy Chief of Staff / Media Coordinator.—Adrienne Elrod.
Scheduler.—Jeff Champagne.
800 East Broward Boulevard, Suite 300, Fort Lauderdale, FL 33301 .... (954) 522–4579
District Director.—Felicia Goldstein.
625 North Flagler Drive, Suite 402, West Palm Beach, FL 33401 .... (561) 651–7594

Counties: BROWARD (part), PALM BEACH (part). CITIES: Aventura, Bal Harbour, Bay Harbor Islands, Biscayne Park, Boca Raton, Boynton Beach, Bring Breezes, Cloud Lake, Dania, Deerfield Beach, Delray Beach, Fort Lauderdale, Glen Ridge, Golden Beach, Gulf Stream, Hallandale, Highland Beach, Hillsboro Beach, Hollywood, Hypoluxo, Indian Creek, Juno Beach, Lake Park, Lake Worth, Lantana, Lauderdale by the Sea, Lazy Lake, Lighthouse Point, Manalapan, North Bay Village, North Palm Beach, Oakland Park, Ocean Ridge, Palm Beach, Palm Beach Gardens, Palm Beach Shores, Pembroke Park, Pompano Beach, Rivera Beach, Sea Ranch Lakes, South Palm Beach, Surfside, West Palm Beach, and Wilton Manors. Population (2000), 639,295.

ZIP Codes: 33004, 33009, 33015, 33033, 33060–62, 33064–65, 33067, 33071–74, 33076, 33097, 33128, 33153, 33155–56, 33161, 33163, 33165, 33179, 33186, 33189, 33280, 33301, 33303–09, 33312, 33314–17, 33324, 33328, 33334–35, 33339, 33346, 33348, 33401, 33403–08, 33410–12, 33415, 33418–20, 33424, 33426–27, 33429, 33431–36, 33441–45, 33458, 33460–64, 33468, 33477–78, 33480, 33483, 33486–87

* * *

TWENTY-THIRD DISTRICT

ALCEE L. HASTINGS, Democrat, of Miramar, FL; born in Altamonte Springs, FL, September 5, 1936; education: graduated, Crooms Academy, Sanford, FL, 1954; B.A., Fisk University, Nashville, TN, 1958; Howard University, Washington, DC; J.D., Florida A&M University, Tallahassee, 1963; attorney; admitted to the Florida bar, 1963; circuit judge, U.S. District Court for the Southern District of Florida; member: African Methodist Episcopal Church, NAACP, Miami-Dade Chamber of Commerce, Family Christian Association, ACLU, Southern Poverty Law Center, National Organization for Women, Planned Parenthood, Women and Children First, Inc., Sierra Club, Cousteau Society, Broward County Democratic Executive Committee, Dade County Democratic Executive Committee, Lauderhill Democratic Club, Hollywood Hills Democratic Club, Pembroke Pines Democratic Club, Urban League, National Bar Association, Florida Chapter of the National Bar Association, T.J. Reddick Bar Association, National Conference of Black Lawyers, Simon Wiesenthal Center, The Furtivist Society; Progressive Black Police Officers Club, International Black Firefighters Association; chairman, Helsinki Commission; three children: Alcee Lamar II, Chelsea, and Leigh; committees: Rules; Permanent Select Committee on Intelligence; elected on November 3, 1992, to the 103rd Congress; reelected to each succeeding Congress.

Office Listings

http://www.house.gov/alceehastings

2353 Rayburn House Office Building, Washington, DC 20515 .... (202) 225–1313
Chief of Staff.—David Goldenberg. FAX: 225–1171
Legislative Assistants: Eve Lieberman, Audrey Nicoleau.
Office Manager / Scheduler.—Barbara Harper.
2701 West Oakland Park Boulevard, Suite 200, Ft. Lauderdale, FL 33311 .... (954) 733–2800
Chief of Staff.—Arthur W. Kennedy.
5725 Corporate Way, Suite 208, West Palm Beach, FL 33407 .... (561) 684–0565

Counties: BROWARD (part), HENDRY (part), MARTIN (part), PALM BEACH (part), ST. LUCIE (part). Population (2000), 639,295.

ZIP Codes: 33025, 33027–28, 33033, 33060, 33064, 33066, 33068–69, 33142, 33155–56, 33158, 33160–61, 33179, 33269, 33301–02, 33304–05, 33309–13, 33315, 33317, 33319–22, 33330–32, 33334, 33340, 33349, 33351, 33359, 33401–09, 33411, 33413–17, 33425, 33430, 33435, 33437–41, 33444–45, 33447, 33459–62, 33465, 33467, 33470, 33476, 33483, 33493, 34945–48, 34950–51, 34954, 34956, 34972, 34974, 34979, 34981, 34986–87

* * *

TWENTY-FOURTH DISTRICT

TOM FEENEY, Republican, of Oviedo, FL; born in Abington, PA, May 21, 1958; education: B.A., Pennsylvania State University, 1980; J.D., University of Pittsburgh, 1983; professional: attorney; business interests: Real Estate; religion: Presbyterian; organizations: Cornerstone, Inc., Distribution Center Board of Directors; City of Light Business Leadership Council; Mosley's High-Tech Tutoring Board of Directors; East Orange, Southwest Volusia, Sanford, and Oviedo Chambers of Commerce; James Madison Institute Board of Directors; OIA Kidsway, Inc., Board of Directors; Orange and Seminole County Republican Executive Committees; The Empowerment Network; American Legislative Exchange Council National Education Task Force; public service: Florida House of Representatives, 1990–94, and 1996–2002; Republican nominee for Lieutenant Governor, 1994; Florida Speaker of the House of Representatives, 2000–02; family: married to Ellen Stewart; children: Tommy and Sean; committees: Financial Services; Judiciary; Science and Technology; elected to the 108th Congress on November 5, 2002; reelected to each succeeding Congress.

Office Listings

http://www.house.gov/feeney

323 Cannon House Office Building, Washington, DC 20515 .... (202) 225–2706
Chief of Staff.—Jason Roe. FAX: 226–6299
Legislative Director.—Erin Kanoy.
Executive Assistant.—Erin Houg.
12424 Research Parkway, Suite 135, Orlando, FL 32826 .... (407) 208–1106
1000 City Center Circle, Second Floor, Port Orange, FL 32129 .... (386) 756–9798
400 South Street, Suite 4–A, Titusville, FL 32780 .... (321) 264–6113

Counties: BREVARD (part), ORANGE (part), SEMINOLE (part), VOLUSIA (part). Population (2000), 639,295.

ZIP Codes: 32114, 32118–19, 32123–24, 32127–29, 32132, 32141, 32168–70, 32701, 32703–04, 32707–09, 32712, 32714, 32716, 32719, 32732–33, 32738–39, 32751, 32754, 32757, 32759, 32762, 32764–66, 32775, 32779–83, 32789–90, 32792–94, 32796, 32798, 32810, 32816–17, 32820, 32824–29, 32831–33, 32878, 32922, 32926–27, 32953–54, 32959, 33313, 33319, 33337, 33388

* * *

TWENTY-FIFTH DISTRICT

MARIO DIAZ-BALART, Republican, of Miami, FL; born in Ft. Lauderdale, FL, September 25, 1961; education: University of South Florida; professional: President, Gordon Diaz-Balart and Partners (public relations and marketing business); religion: Catholic; public service: Administrative Assistant to the Mayor of Miami, 1985–88; Florida House of Representatives, 1988–92, and 2000–02; Florida State Senate, 1992–2000; committees: Budget; Science and Technology; Transportation and Infrastructure; elected to the 108th Congress on November 5, 2002; reelected to each succeeding Congress.

Office Listings

http://www.house.gov/mariodiaz-balart

313 Cannon House Office Building, Washington, DC 20515 .... (202) 225–2778
Chief of Staff.—Thomas Bean. FAX: 226–0346
Legislative Director.—Lauren Robitaille.
12851 SW 42nd Street, Suite 131, Miami, FL 33175 .... (305) 225–6866
District Director.—Miguel Otero.
4715 Golden Gate Parkway, Suite 1, Naples, FL 34116 .... (239) 348–1620
District Representative.—Stephen Hart.

Counties: COLLIER (part), DADE (part). Population (2000), 639,295.

ZIP Codes: 33015–16, 33018, 33030–35, 33157, 33166, 33170, 33175–78, 33182–87, 33189–90, 33193–94, 33196, 34113–14, 34116–17, 34120, 34137–39, 34141–43

GEORGIA

(Population 2000, 8,186,453)

SENATORS

SAXBY CHAMBLISS, Republican, of Moultrie, GA; born in Warrenton, NC, November 10, 1943; education: graduated, C.E. Byrd High School, Shreveport, LA, 1962; B.A., University of Georgia, 1966; J.D., University of Tennessee College of Law, 1968; professional: served on the state bar of Georgia's Disciplinary Review Panel, 1969; member: Moultrie-Colquitt County Economic Development Authority; Colquitt County Economic Development Corporation; married: the former Julianne Frohbert, 1966; children: Lia Chambliss Baker, and C. Saxby (Bo), Jr.; committees: Agriculture, Nutrition, and Forestry; Armed Services; Rules and Administration; Joint Committee on Printing; Select Committee on Intelligence; elected to the 104th Congress; reelected to each succeeding Congress; elected to the U.S. Senate on November 5, 2002.

Office Listings

http://chambliss.senate.gov

416 Russell Senate Office Building, Washington, DC 20510 .... (202) 224–3521
Chief of Staff.—Charlie Harman. FAX: 224–0103
Office Manager.—Kate Vickers.
Executive Assistant.—Teresa Ervin.
100 Galleria, Suite 1340, Atlanta, GA 30339 .... (770) 763–9090
State Director.—Steven Meeks.
950 Plantation Centre, Macon, GA 31210 .... (478) 741–1417
Field Representative.—Bill Stembridge.
419–A South Main Street, Moultrie, GA 31768 .... (229) 985–2112
Field Representative.—Debbie Cannon.
2 East Bryan Street, Suite 620, Savannah, GA 31401 .... (912) 232–3657
Field Representative.—Kathryn Murph.
1058 Claussen Road, Suite 105, Augusta, GA 30907 .... (706) 738–0302
Field Representative.—Jim Hussey.

* * *

JOHNNY ISAKSON, Republican, of Marietta GA; born in Fulton County, GA, December 28, 1944; education: University of Georgia; professional: real estate executive; president, Northside Realty; public service: Georgia State House of Representatives, 1976–90; Georgia State Senate, 1992–96; appointed chairman of the Georgia Board of Election, 1996; awards: Republican National Committee ''Best Legislator in America,'' 1989; organizations: chairman of the board, Georgian Club; trustee, Kennesaw State University; board of directors, Metro Atlanta and Georgia Chambers of Commerce; past president, Cobb Chamber of Commerce; executive committee, National Association of Realtors; president, Realty Alliance; advisory board, Federal National Mortgage Association; married: Dianne; children: John, Kevin, and Julie; religion: Methodist; election to the 106th Congress on February 23, 1999, by special election; reelected to each succeeding Congress; committees: Environment and Public Works; Foreign Relations; Health, Education, Labor, and Pensions; Small Business and Entrepreneurship; Veterans' Affairs; elected to the U.S. Senate on November 2, 2004.

Office Listings

http://isakson.senate.gov

120 Russell Senate Office Building, Washington, DC 20510 .... (202) 224–3643
Chief of Staff.—Heath Garrett. FAX: 228–0724
Deputy Chief of Staff.—Chris Carr.
Communications Director.—Joan Kirchner.
Scheduler.—Molly Manning.
One Overton Park, 3625 Cumberland Boulevard, Suite 970, Atlanta, GA 30339 ..... (770) 661–0999

REPRESENTATIVES

FIRST DISTRICT

JACK KINGSTON, Republican, of Savannah, GA; born in Bryan, TX, April, 24, 1955; education: Michigan State University, 1973–74; University of Georgia, 1974–78; insurance salesman; vice president, Palmer and Cay/Carswell; Georgia State Legislature, 1984–92;

member: Savannah Health Mission, Isle of Hope Community Association, Christ Church; married: Elizabeth Morris Kingston, 1979; children: Betsy, John, Ann, and Jim; committees: Appropriations; vice-chair, Republican Conference; elected on November 3, 1992 to the 103rd Congress; reelected to each succeeding Congress.

Office Listings

http://www.house.gov/kingston

2368 Rayburn House Office Building, Washington, DC 20515 .... (202) 225–5831
Chief of Staff.—Heather McNatt. FAX: 226–2269
Legislative Director.—Merritt Myers.
Legislative Assistant.—Norah Bel.
Press Secretary.—Krista Cole.
One Diamond Causeway, Suite 7, Savannah, GA 31406 .... (912) 352–0101
Casework Manager.—Trish DePriest.
P.O. Box 40, Baxley, GA 31515 .... (912) 367–7403
District Director.—Shiela Elliott.
Brunswick Federal Building, 805 Gloucester Street, Room 304, Brunswick, GA 31520 .... (912) 265–9010
Deputy District Director.—Rob Asbell.
P.O. Box 5264, Valdosta, GA 31603 .... (229) 247–9188
Field Representative / Ag Liaison.—Emily Watson

Counties: Appling, Atkinson, Bacon, Berrien, Brantley, Bryan, Camden, Charlton, Chatham (part), Clinch, Coffee, Cook, Echols, Glynn, Jeff Davis, Lanier, Liberty, Long, Lowndes (part), McIntosh, Pierce, Telfair, Ware, Wayne, Wheeler. Population (2005), 629,727.

ZIP Codes: 30411, 30427–28, 31037, 31055, 31060, 31077, 31083, 31300–01, 31305, 31308–09, 31313–16, 31319–21, 31323–24, 31327–28, 31331–33, 31404, 31406, 31410–11, 31419, 31500–31602, 31605–24, 31627, 31630–32, 31634–36, 31637, 31639–42, 31645–99, 31749, 31794, 31798

* * *

SECOND DISTRICT

SANFORD D. BISHOP, Jr., Democrat, of Albany, GA; born in Mobile, AL, February 4, 1947; education: attended Mobile County public schools; B.A., Morehouse College, 1968; J.D., Emory University, 1971; professional: attorney; admitted to the Georgia and Alabama bars; Georgia House of Representatives, 1977–91; Georgia Senate, 1991–93; former member: Executive Board, Boy Scouts of America; YMCA; Sigma Pi Phi Fraternity; Kappa Alpha Psi Fraternity; 32nd Degree Mason, Shriner; member: Mt. Zion Baptist Church, Albany, GA; married: Vivian Creighton Bishop; child: Aeysha Reese; committees: Appropriations; elected to the 103rd Congress; reelected to each succeeding Congress.

Office Listings

http://www.house.gov/bishop

2429 Rayburn House Office Building, Washington, DC 20515 .... (202) 225–3631
Chief of Staff.—Phyllis Hallmon. FAX: 225–2203
Communications Director.—Caroline Burns.
Office Manager / Scheduler.—Martina Morgan.
Albany Towers, 235 W. Roosevelt Avenue, Suite 114, Albany, GA 31701 .... (229) 439–8067
District Director.—Kenneth Cutts.
325 East Jackson Street, Suite A, Thomasville, GA 31792 .... (229) 226–7789
Field Representative.—Michael Bryant.
18 Ninth Street, Suite 201, Columbus, GA 31901 .... (706) 320–9477
Field Representatives: Elaine Gillespie, Wallace Sholar.

Counties: Baker, Brooks, Calhoun, Chattahoochee, Clay, Crawford, Crisp, Decatur, Dooly, Dougherty, Early, Grady, Lee, Lowndes, Macon, Marion, Miller, Mitchell, Muscogee, Peach, Quitman, Randolph, Schley, Seminole, Stewart, Sumter, Talbot, Taylor, Terrell, Thomas, Webster, Worth. Population (2000), 629,735.

ZIP Codes: 30150, 30290, 31010, 31015, 31039, 31068–69, 31072, 31092, 31201, 31204, 31211, 31217, 31328, 31601–03, 31605–06, 31625–26, 31629, 31636–38, 31641, 31643, 31698, 31701–12, 31714, 31716, 31719–22, 31727, 31730, 31733, 31735, 31738–39, 31743–44, 31747, 31749, 31753, 31756–58, 31763–65, 31768, 31771–72, 31775–76, 31778–84, 31787–96, 31799, 31803, 31805, 31814–15, 31821, 31824–25, 31832, 31901–07, 31914, 31995, 31997–99, 39813, 39815, 39817–19, 39823–29, 39832, 39834, 39836–37, 39840–42, 39845–46, 39851–52, 39854, 39859, 39861–62, 39866–67, 39870, 39877, 39885–86, 39897

* * *

THIRD DISTRICT

LYNN A. WESTMORELAND, Republican, of Sharpsburg, GA; born in Atlanta, GA, April 2, 1950; education: graduated from Therrell High School, Atlanta, GA; attended Georgia State University, Atlanta, GA, 1969–71; member of the Georgia State University, 1993–2004; professional: real estate developer; public service: Minority Leader, Georgia State House, 2000–04; Representative, Georgia State House, 1992–2004; religion: Baptist; organizations: Fayette Board of Realtors; Fayette County Safe Kids Council; Georgia Homebuilders; National Board of Realtors; National Rifle Association; married: Joan; children: Heather, Marcy, and Trae; committees: Oversight and Government Reform; Small Business; Transportation and Infrastructure; elected to the 109th Congress on November 2, 2004; reelected to the 110th Congress.

Office Listings

http://www.house.gov/westmoreland

1118 Longworth House Office Building, Washington, DC 20515 .... (202) 225–5901
Chief of Staff.—Chip Lake. FAX: 225–2515
Deputy Chief of Staff / Communications Director.—Brian Robinson.
Legislative Director.—Joe Lillis.
Office Manager.—Alice James.
2753 East Highway 34, Suite 3, Newnan, GA 30265 .... (770) 683–2033

Counties: BIBB COUNTY (part). CITIES AND TOWNSHIPS: Macon, Payne. BUTTS COUNTY (part). CITIES AND TOWNSHIPS: Flovilla, Jackson, Jenkinsburg. CARROLL COUNTY (part). CITIES AND TOWNSHIPS: Bowdon, Carrollton, Mount Zion, Roopville, Temple, Villa Rica, Whitesburg. COWETA COUNTY (part). CITIES AND TOWNSHIPS: Grantville, Haralson, Lone Oak (also Meriwether), Luthersville, Moreland, Newnan, Palmetto, Senoia, Sharpsburg, Turin. DOUGLAS COUNTY (part). CITIES AND TOWNSHIPS: Austell, Douglasville, Lithia Springs, Winston. FAYETTE COUNTY. CITIES AND TOWNSHIPS: Brooks, Fayetteville, Peachtree City, Tyrone, Woolsey. HARRIS COUNTY (part). CITIES AND TOWNSHIPS: Cataula, Ellerslie, Fortson, Hamilton, Midland, Pine Mountain, Pine Mountain Valley, Shiloh, Waverly Hall, West Point. HENRY COUNTY (part). CITIES AND TOWNSHIPS: Hampton, Locust Grove, McDonough, Stockbridge. JASPER COUNTY (part). CITIES AND TOWNSHIPS: Monticello, Shady Dale. JONES COUNTY (part). CITIES AND TOWNSHIPS: Gray, Haddcock. LAMAR COUNTY. CITIES AND TOWNSHIPS: Aldora, Barnesville, Milner. MUSCOGEE COUNTY (part). CITIES AND TOWNSHIPS: Bibb City, Columbus. NEWTON COUNTY (part). CITIES AND TOWNSHIPS: Covington, Mansfield, Newborn, Oxford, Porterdale. PIKE COUNTY. CITIES AND TOWNSHIPS: Concord, Meansville, Molena, Williamson, Zebulon. ROCKDALE COUNTY (part). CITIES AND TOWNSHIPS: Conyers. SPALDING COUNTY (part). CITIES AND TOWNSHIPS: Griffin, Orchard Hill, Sunny Side. TROUP COUNTY (part). CITIES AND TOWNSHIPS: Hogansville, LaGrange. UPSON COUNTY (part). CITIES AND TOWNSHIPS: Thomaston, and Yatesville. Population (2000), 629,700.

ZIP Codes: 30013–14, 30016, 30055–56, 30094, 30108, 30110, 30116–17, 30122, 30133–35, 30154, 30170, 30179–80, 30185, 30187, 30204–06, 30213–17, 30220, 30223–24, 30228–30, 30233–34, 30236, 30238, 30240–41, 30248, 30252–53, 30256–59, 30263–66, 30268–69, 30271, 30273, 30275–77, 30281, 30284–86, 30289–90, 30292, 30295, 30904, 31002, 31004, 31016, 31024, 31029, 31032, 31038, 31046, 31064, 31066, 31085, 31097, 31204, 31210–11, 31220–21, 31602, 31632, 31801, 31804, 31807–08, 31811, 31820, 31822–23, 31826, 31829–31, 31833, 31904, 31907–09, 31993

* * *

FOURTH DISTRICT

HENRY C. "HANK" JOHNSON, JR., Democrat, of Lithonia, GA; born in Washington, DC, October 2, 1954; B.A., Clark College (Clark Atlanta University), Atlanta, GA, 1976; J.D., Thurgood Marshall School of Law, Texas Southern University, Houston, TX, 1979; professional: partner, Johnson & Johnson Law Group LLC, 1980–2007; judge, Magistrate Court, 1989–2001; associate, Dekalb County Commissioner, 2001–06; married: Mereda, 1979; two children: Randi and Alex; committees: Armed Services; Judiciary; Small Business; elected to the 110th Congress on November 7, 2006.

Office Listings

http://www.hankjohnson.house.gov

1133 Longworth House Office Building, Washington, DC 20515 .... (202) 225–1605
Chief of Staff.—Daraka Satcher. FAX: 226–0691
Legislative Director.—Sean Foertsch.
Communications Director.—Deb McGhee Speights.
Operations Director / Deputy Press Assistant.—Kiona Daniels.
5700 Hillandale Drive, Suite 110, Lithonia, GA 30058 .... (770) 987–2291
District Director.—Kathy Register.
3469 Lawrenceville Highway, Suite 205, Tucker, GA 30084 .... (770) 939–2016
Office Manager / Constituent Services Representative.—Katie Dailey.

Counties: DEKALB (part), GWINNETT (part). CITIES: Avondale Estates, Chamblee, Conyers, Clarkston, Decatur, Doraville, Lilburn, Lithonia, Pine Lake, Norcross and Stone Mountain. Population (2000), 629,726.

ZIP Codes: 30002–03, 30012–13, 30021, 30030–38, 30039, 30047, 30052, 30058, 30071, 30079, 30083–88, 30093–94, 30096, 30316–17, 30319, 30329, 30340–41, 30345

* * *

FIFTH DISTRICT

JOHN LEWIS, Democrat, of Atlanta, GA; born in Pike County, AL, February 21, 1940; education: graduated Pike County Training School, Brundidge, AL, 1957; B.A., American Baptist Theological Seminary, Nashville, TN, 1961; B.A., Fisk University, Nashville, TN, 1963; civil rights leader; Atlanta City Council, 1982–86; member: Martin Luther King Center for Social Change, African American Institute, Robert F. Kennedy Memorial; married the former Lillian Miles in 1968; one child, John Miles Lewis; committees: Ways and Means; appointed senior chief deputy Democratic whip for the 109th Congress; elected to the 100th Congress on November 4, 1986; reelected to each succeeding Congress.

Office Listings

http://www.house.gov/johnlewis

343 Cannon House Office Building, Washington, DC 20515 .... (202) 225–3801
Chief of Staff.—Michael Collins. FAX: 225–0351
Officer Manager / Scheduler.—Jacob Gillison.
Director of Communications.—Brenda Jones.
Legislative Director.—Michaeleen Crowell.
100 Peachtree Street NW., Suite 1920, Atlanta, GA 30303 .... (404) 659–0116
District Director.—Tharon Johnson.

Counties: CLAYTON (part), COBB (part), DEKALB (part), FULTON (part). Population (2000), 629,727.

ZIP Codes: 30030, 30032–34, 30297, 30303–19, 30322, 30324, 30326–29, 30331, 30336–39, 30342, 30344–45, 30349, 30354

* * *

SIXTH DISTRICT

TOM PRICE, Republican, of Roswell, GA; born in Lansing, MI, October 8, 1954; education: B.A., University of Michigan, 1976; M.D., University of Michigan, 1979; professional: physician; member of the Georgia state senate, 1997–2004; member: Cobb Chamber of Commerce; Civil Air Patrol; Advisory Board, Georgia Partnership for Excellence in Education; religion: Presbyterian; married: Elizabeth; one child, Robert; committees: Education and Labor; Financial Services; elected to the 109th Congress on November 2, 2004; reelected to the 110th Congress.

Office Listings

http://www.house.gov/tomprice

424 Cannon House Office Building, Washington, DC 20515 .... (202) 225–4501
Chief of Staff.—Matt McGinley. FAX: 225–4656
District Director.—Jeff Hamling.
3730 Roswell Road, Suite 50, Marietta, GA 30062 .... (770) 565–4990

Counties: CHEROKEE (part), COBB (part), FULTON (part). CITIES AND TOWNSHIPS: Dunwoody, Marietta, Roswell, Sandy Springs, and Smyrna. Population (2000), 629,725.

ZIP Codes: 30004–07, 30009–10, 30022–24, 30041, 30060, 30062, 30064–68, 30075–77, 30092, 30096–97, 30101–02, 30106, 30115, 30127, 30141, 30144, 30152, 30156, 30160, 30168, 30188–89, 30327–28, 30339, 30342, 30350, 31032, 31146, 31150, 31156, 31602, 31632

* * *

SEVENTH DISTRICT

JOHN LINDER, Republican, of Duluth, GA; born in Deer River, MN, September 9, 1942; education: graduate, Deer River High School, 1957; B.S., 1963, and D.D.S., University of Minnesota, 1967; captain, U.S. Air Force, 1967–69; former dentist; president, Linder Financial Corporation; Georgia State Representative, 1975–80, 1983–90; member: Georgia GOP, Rotary Club, American Legion; married: Lynne Peterson Linder, 1963; children: Matt and Kristine; committees: Ways and Means; elected on November 3, 1992, to the 103rd Congress; reelected to each succeeding Congress.

Office Listings

http://linder.house.gov

1026 Longworth House Office Building, Washington, DC 20515 .... (202) 225–4272
Chief of Staff.—Rob Woodall. FAX: 225–4696
Legislative Director.—Don Green.
Deputy Chief of Staff.—Joy Burch.
District Offices .... (770) 232–3005

Counties: BARROW, FORSYTH (part), GWINNETT (part), NEWTON, WALTON. Population (2000), 629,725.

ZIP Codes: 30004–05, 30012, 30017, 30019, 30024, 30039–47, 30049, 30052, 30071, 30078, 30087, 30092, 30095–97, 30101–03, 30107, 30114–15, 30120–21, 30123, 30127, 30132, 30134, 30137, 30141–43, 30145–46, 30153, 30157, 30168–69, 30178–80, 30183–84, 30188–89, 30515, 30518–19, 31139

* * *

EIGHTH DISTRICT

JIM MARSHALL, Democrat, of Macon, GA; born in Ithaca, NY, March 31, 1948; education: graduated high school, Mobile, AL, 1966; graduated, Princeton University, 1972 (National Merit Scholarship); graduated, Boston University Law School, 1977; military service: U.S. Army; infantry combat in Vietnam; served as an Airborne-Ranger reconnaissance platoon sergeant; decorated for heroism; received Purple Heart and two Bronze Stars; professional: joined the Mercer University Law School faculty in 1979; public service: participates in numerous community service activities; elected Mayor of Macon, GA, 1995; married: Camille; children: Mary and Robert; committees: Agriculture; Armed Services; Financial Services; elected to the 108th Congress on November 5, 2002; reelected to each succeeding Congress.

Office Listings

http://jimmarshall.house.gov

515 Cannon House Office Building, Washington, DC 20515 .... (202) 225–6531
Chief of Staff.—John Kirincich. FAX: 225–3013
Communications Director.—Doug Moore.
682 Cherry Street, Suite 300, Macon, GA 31201 .... (478) 464–0255
District Director.—Hobby Stripling.
503 Bellevue Avenue, Suite C, Dublin, GA 31021 .... (478) 296–2023
130 East First Street, Tifton, GA 31794 .... (229) 556–7418

Counties: BALDWIN (part), BEN HILL, BIBB, BLECKLEY, BUTTS, COLQUITT, DODGE, HOUSTON, JASPER, JONES, IRWIN, LAURENS, MONROE, NEWTON (part), PULASKI, TIFT, TURNER, TWIGGS, WILCOX, WILKINSON, WORTH (part). Population (2000), 629,748.

ZIP Codes: 30013–16, 30025, 30052, 30054–56, 30070, 30094, 30204, 30216, 30223–24, 30233–34, 30248, 30252, 30411, 30428, 30454, 30457, 31001–05, 31008–09, 31011–15, 31017, 31019–25, 31027–34, 31036–38, 31040, 31042, 31044, 31046–47, 31052, 31054, 31059–62, 31064–66, 31069, 31071–72, 31075, 31077, 31079, 31084–88, 31090–93, 31095–99, 31201–13, 31216–17, 31220–21, 31295–97, 31622, 31637, 31705, 31712, 31714, 31722, 31727, 31733–34, 31738, 31744, 31747, 31753, 31756, 31765, 31768–69, 31771–73, 31775–76, 31778, 31781, 31783–84, 31788–91, 31793–96, 31798

* * *

NINTH DISTRICT

NATHAN DEAL, Republican, of Clermont, GA; born in Millen, GA, August 25, 1942; education: graduated, Washington County High School, Sandersville, 1960; B.A., Mercer University, Macon, GA, 1964; J.D., Mercer University, Walter F. George School of Law, Macon, GA, 1966; admitted to the Georgia bar, 1966; captain, U.S. Army, 1966–68; Georgia State Senate, 1981–92; president pro tempore, 1991–92; married: the former Emilie Sandra Dunagan, 1966; children: Jason, Mary Emily, Carrie, and Katie; committees: Energy and Commerce; elected on November 3, 1992, to the 103rd Congress; reelected to each succeeding Congress.

Office Listings

http://www.house.gov/deal

2133 Rayburn House Office Building, Washington, DC 20515 .... (202) 225–5211

Chief of Staff.—Chris Riley. FAX: 225–8272
Press Secretaries: Chris Riley, Todd Smith.
108 West Lafayette Square, Suite 102, Lafayette, GA 30728 .... (706) 638–7042
P.O. Box 1015, Gainesville, GA 30503 .... (770) 535–2592
415 East Walnut Avenue, Suite 108, Dalton, GA 30721 .... (706) 226–5320

Counties: CATOOSA, DADE, DAWSON, FANNIN, FORSYTH (part), GILMER, GORDON, HALL, LUMPKIN, MURRAY, PICKENS, UNION, WALKER, WHITE, AND WHITFIELD. CITIES AND TOWNSHIPS: Blairsville, Blue Ridge, Calhoun, Chatsworth, Chickamauga, Cisco, Clermont, Cleveland, Cohutta, Conyers, Cumming, Dacula, Dahlonega, Dalton, Dawsonville, East Ellijay, Ellijay, Eton, Fairmount, Flowery Branch, Fort Oglethorpe, Gainesville, Gillsville, Grayson, Helen, Jasper, LaFayette, Lawrenceville, Loganville, Lookout Mountain, Lula, McCaysville, Morgantown, Oakwood, Plainville, Ranger, Rest Haven, Resaca, Ringgold, Rossville, Sautee Nacoochee, Talking Rock, Trenton, Tunnel Hill, and Varnell. Population (2000), 629,702.

ZIP Codes: 30004–05, 30024, 30028, 30040–41, 30097, 30103, 30107, 30139, 30143, 30148, 30171, 30175, 30177, 30501–07, 30510, 30512–14, 30517–19, 30522, 30527–28, 30533–34, 30536, 30539, 30541–43, 30545, 30548, 30554–55, 30559–60, 30564, 30566–67, 30571–72, 30575, 30582, 30597, 30635, 30641, 30701, 30703, 30707–08, 30710–11, 30719–22, 30724–28, 30731–42, 30747, 30750–51, 30753, 30755–57

* * *

TENTH DISTRICT

PAUL C. BROUN, Republican, of Fulton, GA; born in Clarke County, GA, May 14, 1946; education: B.S. in Chemistry, University of Georgia, Athens, GA, 1967; M.D., Medical College of Georgia, Augusta, GA, 1971; professional: physician; served, U.S. Marine Corps Reserves, 1964–67; member: Rotary Club; Athens-Clarke County Chamber of Commerce; Prince Avenue Baptist Church; religion: Southern Baptist; married: Nancy ''Niki'' Bronson Broun; children: Carly, Collins, Lucy; grandchildren: Lucile, Tillman; committees: Homeland Security; Science and Technology; elected by special election to the 110th Congress on July 17, 2007.

Office Listings

http://www.house.gov/broun

2104 Rayburn House Office Building, Washington, DC 20515 .... (202) 225–4101
Chief of Staff.—Aloysius Hogan. FAX: 226–0776
Office Manager / Scheduler.—Teddie Norton.

Counties: BANKS, COLUMBIA, CLARKE, ELBERT, FRANKLIN, GREENE, HABERSHAM, HART, JACKSON, LINCOLN, MCDUFFIE, MADISON, MORGAN, OCONEE, OGLETHORPE, PUTNAM, RABUN, RICHMOND (part), STEPHENS, TOWNS, WILKES. Population (2000), 629,762.

ZIP Codes: 30025, 30055–56, 30510–11, 30516–17, 30520–21, 30523, 30525, 30529–31, 30535, 30537–38, 30543–44, 30546–49, 30552–54, 30557–58, 30562–63, 30565, 30567–68, 30571, 30573, 30575–77, 30580–82, 30596, 30598–99, 30601–09, 30612, 30619, 30621–31, 30633–35, 30638–39, 30641–43, 30645–50, 30660, 30662–69, 30671, 30673, 30677–78, 30683, 30802, 30805–06, 30808–09, 30813–14, 30817, 30824, 30901, 30903–07, 30909, 30911–14, 30916–17, 30919, 31024, 31026, 31061

* * *

ELEVENTH DISTRICT

PHIL GINGREY, Republican, of Marietta, GA; born in Augusta, GA, July 10, 1942; education: B.S., Georgia Tech, 1965; M.D., Medical College of Georgia, 1969; professional: Physician; set up a pro-life OB-GYN practice; organizations: Cobb County Medical Society; Medical Association of Georgia; American Medical Association; Georgia OB-GYN Society; public service: Marietta School Board, 1993–97; Georgia State Senate, 1999–2002; House Policy Committee; married: Billie Ayers; children: Billy, Gannon, Phyllis, and Laura; committees: Armed Services; Science and Technology; elected to the 108th Congress on November 5, 2002; reelected to each succeeding Congress.

Office Listings

http://www.house.gov/gingrey

119 Cannon House Office Building, Washington, DC 20515 .... (202) 225–2931
Chief of Staff / Legislative Director.—Sean Dalton. FAX: 225–2944
Executive Assistant / Director of Operations.—Catherine Gabrysh.
219 Roswell Street, Marietta, GA 30060 .... (770) 429–1776
600 East 1st Street, Suite 301, Rome, GA 30161 .... (706) 290–1776

Counties: BARTOW, CARROLL (part), CHATTOOGA, COBB (part), DOUGLAS, FLOYD, HARALSON, GORDON (part), PAULDING, POLK. Population (2000) 629,730.

ZIP Codes: 30008, 30060–64, 30066–67, 30069, 30080–81, 30090, 30101–05, 30108–13, 30116–27, 30129, 30132, 30134, 30137–41, 30144–45, 30147, 30149–50, 30152–53, 30161–65, 30176, 30178–80, 30182

* * *

TWELFTH DISTRICT

JOHN BARROW, Democrat, of Athens, GA; born in Athens, October 31, 1955; education: graduated from Clarke Central High School, Athens-Clarke County, GA, 1973; B.A., University of Georgia, Athens, GA, 1976; J.D., Harvard University, Cambridge, MA, 1979; professional: law clerk for Judge, Savannah, GA; law clerk for Judge, Fiftieth Circuit Court of Appeals; founding member, Wilburn, Lewis, Barrow and Stotz, PC.; county commissioner; lawyer, private practice; Athens-Clarke, GA, city-county commissioner, 1990–2004; volunteer, Athens-Clarke Heritage Foundation; volunteer, Parkview Playschool; charter member, Second Consolidated City-County Government; religion: Baptist; children: James and Ruth; committees: Agriculture; Energy and Commerce; elected to the 109th Congress on November 2, 2004; reelected to the 110th Congress.

Office Listings

http://www.barrow.house.gov

213 Cannon House Office Building, Washington, DC 20515 .... (202) 225–2823
Chief of Staff.—Roman Levit. FAX: 225–3377
Deputy Chief of Staff.—Ashley Jones.
Legislative Director.—Christopher Schepis.
Communications Director.—Harper Lawson.
699 Broad Street, Suite 1200, Augusta, GA 30901 .... (706) 722–4494
450 Mall Boulevard, Suite A, Savannah, GA 31406 .... (912) 354–7282
City Hall, 141 West Haynes Street, P.O. Box 1017, Sandersville, GA 31082 .... (478) 553–1923
Vidalia Community Center, 107 Old Airport Road, Suite A, Vidalia, GA .... (912) 537–9301

Counties: Baldwin (part), Bulloch, Burke, Candler, Chatham (part), Effingham, Emanuel, Evans, Glascock, Hancock, Jefferson, Jenkins, Johnson, Montgomery, Richmond (part), Screven, Taliaferro, Tattnall, Toombs, Treutlen, Warren, Washington. Cities and townships: Augusta, Milledgeville, Savannah, Statesboro, Vidalia. Population (2000) 629,727.

ZIP Codes: 30400–01, 30410, 30412–15, 30417, 30420–21, 30423, 30425–27, 30429, 30436, 30438–39, 30441–42, 30445–48, 30456, 30452–53, 30455–58, 30461, 30464, 30467, 30470–71, 30473–74, 30477, 30631, 30664, 30669, 30678, 30803, 30805, 30807, 30810, 30815–16, 30818, 30820–24, 30828, 30830, 30833, 30901, 30904, 30906, 30909, 30934, 31002, 31018, 31033–35, 31045, 31049, 31061, 31067, 31082, 31087, 31089, 31094, 31096, 31302–03, 31307–08, 31312, 31318, 31321–22, 31326, 31329, 31401, 31404–08, 31410, 31415, 31419

* * *

THIRTEENTH DISTRICT

DAVID SCOTT, Democrat, of Atlanta, GA; born in Aynor, SC, June 27, 1945; education: Florida A&M University, graduated with honors, 1967; M.B.A., graduated with honors, University of Pennsylvania Wharton School of Finance, 1969; professional: businessman; owner and CEO, Dayn-Mark Advertising; public service: Georgia House of Representatives, 1974–82; Georgia State Senate, 1983–2002; married: Alfredia Aaron, 1969; children: Dayna and Marcye; committees: Agriculture; Financial Services; Foreign Affairs; elected to the 108th Congress on November 5, 2002; reelected to each succeeding Congress.

Office Listings

http://davidscott.house.gov

417 Cannon House Office Building, Washington, DC 20515 .... (202) 225–2939
Chief of Staff.—Michael Andel. FAX: 225–4628
Deputy Chief of Staff for Administration.—Angie Borja.
Legislative Director.—Gary Woodward.
173 North Main Street, Jonesboro, GA 30236 .... (770) 210–5073
888 Concord Road, Suite 100, Smyra, GA 30080 .... (770) 432–5405

Counties: Clayton, Cobb, DeKalb, Douglas, Fulton, Henry. Population (2000) 629,732.

ZIP Codes: 30008, 30034, 30060, 30064, 30067, 30080, 30081–82, 30106, 30111, 30122, 30126–27, 30133–35, 30141, 30154, 30168, 30187, 30213, 30215, 30228, 30236–38, 30250, 30253, 30260, 30268, 30272–74, 30281, 30287–88, 30291, 30294, 30296–97, 30331, 30337, 30339, 30344, 30349, 31192

HAWAII

(Population 2000, 1,211,537)

SENATORS

DANIEL K. INOUYE, Democrat, of Honolulu, HI; born in Honolulu, September 7, 1924; education: A.B., government and economics, University of Hawaii, 1950; J.D., George Washington University Law School, 1952; majority leader, Territorial House of Representatives, 1954–58; Territorial Senate, 1958–59; enlisted as private, 442nd Infantry Regimental Combat Team, 1943; second lieutenant, battlefield commission, 1944; served in France and Italy; retired captain, U.S. Army; religion: Methodist; married: the former Margaret Shinobu Awamura of Honolulu; one son: Daniel Ken Inouye, Jr.; committees: chair, Commerce, Science and Transportation; Appropriations; Indian Affairs; Rules and Administration; Joint Committee on Printing; Senate Democratic Steering and Coordination; elected on July 28, 1959, to the 86th Congress; reelected to the 87th Congress; elected to the U.S. Senate on November 6, 1962; reelected to each succeeding Senate term.

Office Listings

http://inouye.senate.gov

722 Hart Senate Office Building, Washington, DC 20510 .... (202) 224–3934
Administrative Assistant.—Patrick H. DeLeon. FAX: 224–6747
Office Manager.—Beverly MacDonald. TDD: 224–1233
Personal Secretary.—Jessica Lee.
Legislative Director.—Marie Blanco.
300 Ala Moana Boulevard, Suite 7–212, Honolulu, HI 96850 .... (808) 541–2542
Hilo Auxiliary Office, 101 Aupuni Street, No. 205, Hilo, HI 96720 .... (808) 935–0844

* * *

DANIEL K. AKAKA, Democrat, of Honolulu, HI; born in Honolulu, September 11, 1924; education: graduated, Kamehameha High School, 1942; University of Hawaii, 1948–66, bachelor of education, professional certificate, master of education; served in the U.S. Army, 1945–47; teacher, 1953–60; vice principal, 1960; principal, 1963–71; program specialist, 1968–71; director, 1971–74; director and special assistant in human resources, 1975–76; board of directors, Hanahauoli School; Act 4 Educational Advisory Commission; Library Advisory Council; Na Hookama O Pauahi Scholarship Committee, Kamehameha Schools; commissioner, Manpower and Full Employment Commission; member and Minister of Music, Kawaiahao Church; married: the former Mary Mildred Chong (deceased, 2006); children: Millannie, Daniel, Jr., Gerard, Alan, and Nicholas; committees: chair, Veterans' Affairs; Armed Services; Banking, Housing, and Urban Affairs; Energy and Natural Resources; Homeland Security and Governmental Affairs; Indian Affairs; elected to the 95th Congress in November, 1976; reelected to each succeeding Congress; appointed to the U.S. Senate in April, 1990, to fill the vacancy caused by the death of Senator Spark Matsunaga; elected to complete the unexpired term in November, 1990; reelected to each succeeding Senate term.

Office Listings

http://akaka.senate.gov

141 Hart Senate Office Building, Washington, DC 20510 .... (202) 224–6361
Administrative Assistant.—James Sakai. FAX: 224–6747
Legislative Director.—Melissa U. Hampe.
Fiscal Office Secretary.—Patricia L. Hill.
Prince Kuhio Federal Building, 300 Ala Moana Boulevard, Room 3–106, P.O. Box 50144, Honolulu, HI 96850 .... (808) 522–8970
Chief of Staff.—Joan Ohashi Akai.
101 Aupuni Street, Suite 213, Hilo, HI 96720 .... (808) 935–1114

REPRESENTATIVES

FIRST DISTRICT

NEIL ABERCROMBIE, Democrat, of Honolulu, HI; born in Buffalo, NY, June 26, 1938; education: graduated from Williamsville High School, Williamsville, NY; B.A., Union College, 1959; Ph.D., University of Hawaii, 1974; professional: candidate for election to the U.S. Senate,

1970; Hawaii House of Representatives, 1974–78; Hawaii State Senate, 1978–86; Honolulu City Council, 1988–90; married: Nancie Caraway; committees: Armed Services; Natural Resources; elected to the U.S. House of Representatives on September 20, 1986, to fill the vacancy caused by the resignation of Cecil Heftel; elected to the 102nd Congress, November 6, 1990; reelected to each succeeding Congress.

Office Listings

http://www.house.gov/abercrombie

1502 Longworth House Office Building, Washington, DC 20515 .... (202) 225–2726
Legislative Director.—Wendy Clerinx. FAX: 225–4580
Deputy Chief of Staff.—Kathleen Chapman.
Press Secretary.—Dave Helfert.
300 Ala Moana Boulevard, Room 4–104, Honolulu, HI 96850 .... (808) 541–2570
Chief of Staff.—Amy Asselbaye.

Counties: HONOLULU COUNTY (part). CITIES AND TOWNSHIPS: Aiea Pearl City, Ewa Beach, Honolulu, Mililani, and Waipahu. Population (2000), 606,718.

ZIP Codes: 96701, 96706, 96782, 96789, 96797, 96801–28, 96830, 96835–44, 96846–50, 96853, 96858–61

* * *

SECOND DISTRICT

MAZIE K. HIRONO, Democrat, of Hawaii; born in Fukushima, Japan, November 3, 1947; naturalized U.S. citizen in 1959; education: Kaimuki High School, 1966; Phi Beta Kappa, University of Hawaii at Manoa, 1970; Georgetown University Law Center, 1978; Deputy Attorney General, Anti-Trust Division, State of Hawaii, 1978–80; Shim, Tam, Kirimitsu, Kitamura and Chang (law firm), 1984–88; State Representative, Hawaii State Legislature, 1980–94; Lt. Governor, State of Hawaii, 1994–2002; candidate for Governor, State of Hawaii, 2002; married to Leighton Kim Oshima; committees: Education and Labor; Transportation and Infrastructure; elected to the 110th Congress on November 7, 2006.

Office Listings

http://hirono.house.gov/ mazie.hirono@mail.house.gov

1229 Longworth House Office Building, Washington, DC 20515 .... (202) 225–4906
Chief of Staff (Honolulu).—Carl Takamura. FAX: 225–4987
Director.—Francis Nakamoto.
Deputy Chief of Staff.—Susan Kodani.
Prince Kuhio Federal Building, Room 5104, Honolulu, HI 96850 .... (808) 541–1986
District Director.—Yvonne Lau.

Counties: HAWAI'I COUNTY. CITIES: Hawi, Hilo, Honoka'a, Kailua-Kona, Na'alehu, Kealakekua, Pahoa, Ocean View, Volcano, Waimea, Waikoloa. MAUI COUNTY. CITIES: Hana, Kahului, Kaunakakai, Lahaina, Lana'i City, Makawao, Wailuku. KALAWAO COUNTY. CITY: Kalaupapa. HONOLULU COUNTY (part). CITIES: Hale'iwa, Honolulu, Kailua, Kane'ohe, Kapolei, La'ie, Makakilo, Nanakuli, Wahiawa, Waialua, Wai'anae, Waimanalo. KAUA'I COUNTY. CITIES: Hanalei, Hanapepe, Kalaheo, Kapa'a, Kekaha, Kilauea, Koloa, Lihue, Waimea. NORTHWESTERN HAWAIIAN ISLANDS. ISLANDS OF: Becker, French Frigate Shoals, Gardener Pinnacles, Hermes and Kure Atolls, Laysan, Lisianski, Maro Reef, Nihoa, and Pearl. Population (2000), 604,819.

ZIP Codes: 96703–05, 96707–10, 96712–22, 96725–34, 96737–57, 96759–74, 96776–81, 96783–86, 96788–93, 96795–97, 96854, 96857, 96862–63

IDAHO

(Population 2000, 1,293,953)

SENATORS

LARRY E. CRAIG, Republican, of Payette, ID; born in Council, ID, July 20, 1945; education: attended Midvale public schools; graduated, University of Idaho; student body president, University of Idaho, 1968–69; USANG, 1970–72; graduate work in economics and the politics of developing nations, George Washington University, 1970; Idaho State president and national vice president, Future Farmers of America, 1966–67; Idaho State Senate (three terms); chairman, Senate Commerce and Labor Committee; member: National Foundation for Defense Analysis; Idaho State Republican Executive Committee, 1976–78; president, Young Republican League of Idaho, 1976–77; chairman, Republican Central Committee, Washington County, 1971–72; board of directors, National Rifle Association; policy chairman, Republican Study Committee, 1990; farmer-rancher, Midvale area, for 10 years; married to the former Suzanne Thompson; three children: Mike, Shae, and Jay; Senate co-chairman, Congressional Coalition on Adoption; co-founder and co-chair, Senate Private Property Rights Caucus; co-chairman, Congressional Leaders United for a Balanced Budget (CLUBB); committees: Appropriations; Energy and Natural Resources; Environment and Public Works; Veterans' Affairs; Special Committee on Aging; elected to the 97th Congress on November 4, 1980; reelected to each succeeding Congress; elected to the U.S. Senate on November 6, 1990; reelected to each succeeding Senate term.

Office Listings

http://craig.senate.gov

520 Hart Senate Office Building, Washington, DC 20510 .... (202) 224–2752
Chief of Staff.—Michael O. Ware. FAX: 228–1067
Executive Assistant/Scheduler.—Katie Palmer.
Legislative Director/Counsel.—Brooke M. Roberts.
Press Secretary.—Dan Whiting.
225 North Ninth Street, Suite 530, Boise, ID 83702 .... (208) 342–7985
610 Hubbard, Suite 121, Coeur d'Alene, ID 83814 .... (208) 667–6130
313 D Street, Suite 106, Lewiston, ID 83501 .... (208) 743–0792
275 South Fifth Avenue, Suite 290, Pocatello, ID 83201 .... (208) 236–6817
560 Filer Avenue, Suite A, Twin Falls, ID 83301 .... (208) 734–6780
490 Memorial Drive, Suite 101, Idaho Falls, ID 83402 .... (208) 523–5541

* * *

MIKE CRAPO, Republican, of Idaho Falls, ID; born in Idaho Falls, May 20, 1951; education: graduated, Idaho Falls High School, 1969; B.A., Brigham Young University, Provo, UT, 1973; J.D., Harvard University Law School, Cambridge, MA, 1977; professional: attorney; admitted to the California bar, 1977; admitted to the Idaho bar, 1979; law clerk, Hon. James M. Carter, Judge of the U.S. Court of Appeals for the Ninth Circuit, San Diego, CA, 1977–78; associate attorney, Gibson, Dunn, and Crutcher, San Diego, 1978–79; attorney, Holden, Kidwell, Hahn and Crapo, 1979–92; partner, 1983–92; Idaho State Senate, 1984–92, assistant majority leader, 1987–89, president pro tempore, 1989–92; member: American Bar Association, Boy Scouts of America, Idaho Falls Rotary Club, 1984–88; married: the former Susan Diane Hasleton, 1974; children: Michelle, Brian, Stephanie, Lara, and Paul; co-chair, Western Water Caucus; co-chair, Sportsman Caucus; co-chair, COPD Caucus; committees: Agriculture, Nutrition, and Forestry; Banking, Housing, and Urban Affairs; Budget; Finance; elected on November 3, 1992, to the 103rd Congress; reelected to each succeeding Congress; elected to the U.S. Senate on November 3, 1998; reelected to each succeeding Senate term.

Office Listings

http://crapo.senate.gov

239 Dirksen Senate Office Building, Washington, DC 20510 .... (202) 224–6142
Chief of Staff.—Peter Fischer. FAX: 228–1375
Communications Director.—Susan Wheeler.
Legislative Director.—Ken Flanz.
251 E Front Street, Suite 205, Boise, ID 83702 .... (208) 334–1776
Chief of Staff.—John Hoehne.
610 Hubbard Street, Suite 209, Coeur d'Alene, ID 83814 .... (208) 664–5490
Director.—Karen Roetter.
313 D Street, Suite 105, Lewiston, ID 83501 .... (208) 743–1492

Director.—Mitch Silvers.
275 South 5th Avenue, Suite 225, Pocatello, ID 83201 .... (208) 236–6775
Director.—Farhanna Hibbert.
524 E. Cleveland, Suite 220, Caldwell, ID 83605 .... (208) 455–0360
Director.—Ryan White.
490 Memorial Drive, Suite 102, Idaho Falls, ID 83402 .... (208) 522–9779
Director.—Leslie Huddleston.
202 Falls Avenue, Suite 2, Twin Falls, ID 83301 .... (208) 734–2515
Director.—Jimmi Sommer.

REPRESENTATIVES

FIRST DISTRICT

BILL SALI, Republican, of Kuna, ID; born in Portsmouth, OH, February 17, 1954; education: Boise State University, 1981; University of Idaho law school, 1984; professional: attorney, professional musician, a farmer and a Caterpillar machinery salesman; member of the Idaho State House of Representatives, 1990–2006; committees: Natural Resources; Oversight and Government Reform; elected to 110th Congress on November 7, 2006.

Office Listings

http://sali.house.gov/

508 Cannon House Office Building, Washington, DC 20515 .... (202) 225–6611
Chief of Staff.—Rob Schwarzwalder. FAX: 225–3029
Legislative Director.—Lisa Tanner.
Scheduler.—Kathleen Wilber.
802 West Bannock Street, Suite 101, Boise, ID 83702 .... (208) 336–9831
District Director.—Gerry Sweet.
610 West Hubbard, Suite 206, Coeur d'Alene, ID 83814 .... (208) 667–0127
704 Blaine Street, Suite 1, Caldwell, ID 83605 .... (208) 454–5602
313 D Street, Suite 104, Lewiston, ID 83501 .... (208) 743–1388

Counties: ADA (part), ADAMS, BENEWAH, BOISE, BONNER, BOUNDARY, CANYON, CLEARWATER, GEM, IDAHO, KOOTENAI, LATAH, LEWIS, NEZ PERCE, OWYHEE, PAYETTE, SHOSHONE, VALLEY, WASHINGTON. Population (2000), 648,774.

ZIP Codes: 83501, 83520, 83522–26, 83530–31, 83533, 83535–37, 83539–49, 83552–55, 83602, 83604–07, 83610–12, 83615–17, 83619, 83622, 83624, 83626–32, 83634–39, 83641–45, 83647, 83650–57, 83660–61, 83666, 83669–72, 83676–77, 83680, 83686–87, 83702, 83704–06, 83708–09, 83711, 83713–14, 83716, 83719, 83799, 83801–06, 83808–16, 83821–27, 83830, 83832–37, 83839–58, 83860–61, 83864–74, 83876–77

* * *

SECOND DISTRICT

MICHAEL K. SIMPSON, Republican, of Blackfoot, ID; born in Burley, ID, September 8, 1950; education: graduated, Blackfoot High School, 1968; Utah State University, 1972; Washington University School of Dental Medicine, 1977; professional: dentist, private practice; Blackfoot, ID, City Council, 1981–85; Idaho State Legislature, 1985–98; Idaho Speaker of the House 1992–98; married: Kathy Simpson; committees: Appropriations; Budget; elected to the 106th Congress; reelected to each succeeding Congress.

Office Listings

http://www.house.gov/simpson mike.simpson@mail.house.gov

1339 Longworth House Office Building, Washington, DC 20515 .... (202) 225–5531
Chief of Staff.—Lindsay Slater. FAX: 225–8216
Scheduler.—Kaylyn Peterson.
Legislative Director.—Malisah Small.
Press Secretary.—Nikki Watts.
802 West Bannock, Suite 600, Boise, ID 83702 .... (208) 334–1953
1201 Falls Avenue East, #25, Twin Falls, ID 83301 .... (208) 734–7219
490 Memorial Drive, Suite 103, Idaho Falls, ID 83402 .... (208) 523–6701
801 E. Sherman, Suite 194, Pocatello, ID 83201 .... (208) 478–4160

Counties: ADA (part), BANNOCK, BEAR LAKE, BINGHAM, BLAINE, BONNEVILLE, BUTTE, CAMAS, CARIBOU, CASSIA, CLARK, CUSTER, ELMORE, FRANKLIN, FREMONT, GOODING, JEFFERSON, JEROME, LEMHI, LINCOLN, MADISON, MINIDOKA, ONEIDA, POWER, TETON, TWIN FALLS. Population (2000), 645,179.

ZIP Codes: 83201–06, 83209–15, 83217–18, 83220–21, 83223, 83226–30, 83232–39, 83241, 83243–46, 83250–56, 83261–63, 83271–72, 83274, 83276–78, 83281, 83283, 83285–87, 83301–03, 83311–14, 83316, 83318, 83320–25, 83327–

28, 83330, 83332–38, 83340–44, 83346–50, 83352–55, 83401–06, 83415, 83420–25, 83427–29, 83431, 83433–36, 83438, 83440–46, 83448–52, 83454–55, 83460, 83462–69, 83601–02, 83604, 83623–24, 83627, 83633–34, 83647–48, 83701–09, 83712, 83714–17, 83720–33, 83735, 83744, 83756

ILLINOIS

(Population, 2000 12,419,293)

SENATORS

RICHARD DURBIN, Democrat, of Springfield, IL; born in East St. Louis, IL, November 21, 1944; son of William and Ann Durbin; education: graduated, Assumption High School, East St. Louis; B.S., foreign service and economics, Georgetown University, Washington, DC, 1966; J.D., Georgetown University Law Center, 1969; professional: attorney, admitted to the Illinois bar in 1969; began practice in Springfield; legal counsel to Lieutenant Governor Paul Simon, 1969–72; legal counsel to Illinois Senate Judiciary Committee, 1972–82; parliamentarian, Illinois Senate, 1969–82; president, New Members Democratic Caucus, 98th Congress; associate professor of medical humanities, Southern Illinois University School of Medicine; married: the former Loretta Schaefer, 1967; children: Christine, Paul, and Jennifer; committees: Appropriations; Judiciary; Rules and Administration; appointed as Assistant Democratic Leader in 2001; elected to the 98th Congress, November 2, 1982; reelected to each succeeding Congress; elected to the U.S. Senate on November 5, 1996; reelected to each succeeding Senate term.

Office Listings

http://durbin.senate.gov

309 Hart Senate Office Building, Washington, DC 20510 .... (202) 224–2152
Chief of Staff.—Patrick Souders. FAX: 228–0400
Legislative Director.—Dena Morris. TTY: 224–8180
Director of Scheduling.—Andrea Del'Aguila.
230 South Dearborn, Kluczynski Building 38th Floor, Chicago, IL 60604 .... (312) 353–4952
Chief of Staff.—Mike Daly.
525 South Eighth Street, Springfield, IL 62703 .... (217) 492–4062
Director.—Bill Houlihan.
701 N. Court Street, Marion, IL 62959 .... (618) 998–8812

* * *

BARACK OBAMA, Democrat, of Chicago, IL; born in Hawaii, August 4, 1961; education: B.A., Political Science, Columbia University, 1983; J.D., Harvard Law School, *magna cum laude,* 1991; professional: attorney; civil rights lawyer; University of Chicago Law School lecturer in constitutional law; public service: Illinois State Senator, 1997–2004; organizations: chair, Chicago Annenberg Challenge; Cook County Bar Association; Community Law Project; Joyce Foundation; Center for Neighborhood Technology; religion: Church of Christ; married: Michelle; children: Malia and Sasha; committees: Foreign Relations; Health, Education, Labor, and Pensions; Homeland Security and Governmental Affairs; Veterans' Affairs; elected to the U.S. Senate on November 2, 2004.

Office Listings

http://obama.senate.gov

713 Hart Senate Office Building, Washington, DC 20510 .... (202) 224–2854
Chief of Staff.—Peter Rouse. FAX: 228–4260
Legislative Director.—Chris Lu. TDD: 228–1404
Press Secretary.—Ben LaBolt.
Scheduler.—Molly Buford.
230 South Dearborn Street, Suite 3900, Chicago, IL 60604 .... (312) 886–3506
607 East Adams Street, Suite 1520, Springfield, IL 62701 .... (217) 492–5089
701 North Court Street, Marion, IL 62959 .... (618) 997–2402
1911 Fifty-Second Avenue, Moline, IL 61265 .... (309) 736–1217

REPRESENTATIVES

FIRST DISTRICT

BOBBY L. RUSH, Democrat, of Chicago, IL; born in Albany, GA; November 23, 1946; education: attended Marshall High School, Marshall, IL; B.A., Roosevelt University, Chicago, IL, 1974; M.A., University of Illinois, Chicago, IL, 1994; M.A., McCormick Theological Seminary, Chicago, IL, 1998; professional: United States Army, 1963–68; insurance agent; alderman, Chicago, Illinois, city council, 1983–93; deputy chairman, Illinois Democratic Party, 1990; unsuccessful candidate for mayor of Chicago, IL, 1999; minister; married: Carolyn; five children; committees: Energy and Commerce; elected on Novmeber 3, 1992 to the 103rd Congress; reelected to each succeeding Congress.

Office Listings

http://www.house.gov/rush

2416 Rayburn House Office Building, Washington, DC 20515 .... (202) 225–4372
Chief of Staff.—Kimberly Parker. FAX: 226–0333
Legislative Director.—Aysha Moshi.
Executive Assistant/Scheduler.—N. Lenette Myers.
Press Secretary.—Toure Muhammad.
700–706 East 79th Street, Chicago, IL 60619 .... (773) 224–6500
District Director.—Rev. Stanley Watkins.
3235 West 147th Street, Midlothian, IL 60445 .... (708) 385–9550
Suburban Director.—Younus Suleman.

Counties: COOK COUNTY (part). CITIES AND TOWNSHIPS: Alsip, Blue Island, Chicago, Country Club Hills, Evergreen Park, Homewood, Midlothian, Oak Forest, Orland Hills, Orland Park, Palos Heights, Posen, Robbins, and Tinley Park. Population (2000), 653,647.

ZIP Codes: 60406, 60445, 60452, 60456, 60462–63, 60469, 60472, 60477–78, 60482, 60615–16, 60619–21, 60636–37, 60643, 60652–53, 60803, 60805

* * *

SECOND DISTRICT

JESSE L. JACKSON, JR., Democrat, of Chicago, IL; born in Greenville, SC, March 11, 1965; education: B.S. in business management, *magna cum laude,* North Carolina A&T State University, 1987; M.A., Chicago Theological Seminary, 1989; J.D., University of Illinois College of Law, 1993; member, Congressional Black Caucus, Congressional Progressive Caucus; elected Secretary of the Democratic National Committee's Black Caucus; national field director, National Rainbow Coalition, 1993–95; member, Rainbow/Push Action Network; married: Sandi; two children; committees: Appropriations; elected to the 104th Congress (special election); reelected to each succeeding Congress.

Office Listings

http://www.house.gov/jackson

2419 Rayburn House Office Building, Washington, DC 20515 .... (202) 225–0773
Chief of Staff.—Kenneth Edmonds. FAX: 225–0899
Legislative Director.—Charles Dujon.
Legislative Assistant.—Megan Moore.
Executive Assistant/Scheduler.—DeBorah Posey.
17926 South Halsted, Homewood, IL 60430 .... (708) 798–6000
District Director.—Rick Bryant.
2120 East 71st Street, Chicago, IL 60649 .... (773) 241–6500

Counties: COOK (part), WILL (part). CITIES AND TOWNSHIPS: Blue Island, Burnham, Calumet City, Calumet Park, Chicago, Chicago Heights, Country Club Hills Crestwood, Dixmoor, Dolton, East Hazel Crest, Flossmoor, Ford Heights, Glenwood, Harvey, Hazel Crest, Homewood, Lansing, Lynwood, Markham, Matteson, Midlothian, Monee, Oak Forest, Olympia Fields, Park Forest, Phoenix, Posen, Richton Park, Riverdale, Robbins, Sauk Village, South Chicago Heights, South Holland, Steger, Tinley Park, Thornton, and University Park. Population (2000), 653,647.

ZIP Codes: 60406, 60409, 60411–12, 60417, 60419, 60422–23, 60425–26, 60429–30, 60438, 60443, 60445, 60449, 60452, 60461, 60466, 60471, 60473, 60475–78, 60615, 60617, 60620, 60628, 60633, 60636–37, 60643, 60649, 60827

* * *

THIRD DISTRICT

DANIEL W. LIPINSKI, Democrat, of Chicago, IL; born in Chicago, July 15, 1966; son of former Congressman William Lipinski, 1983–2004; education: B.S., Mechanical Engineering, *magna cum laude,* Northwestern University, 1988; M.S., Engineering-Economic Systems, Stanford University, 1989; Ph.D., Political Science, Duke University, 1998; professional: aide to United States Representative George Sangmeister, 1993–94; aide to United States Representative Jerry Costello, 1995–96; aide to United States Representative Rod Blagojevich, 1999–2000; professor, James Madison University Washington Program, Washington, DC, 2000; professor, University of Notre Dame, South Bend, IN, 2000–01; professor, University of Tennessee, Knoxville, TN, 2001–04; married: Judy; committees: Science and Technology; Small Business; Transportation and Infrastructure; elected to the 109th Congress on November 2, 2004; reelected to the 110th Congress.

Office Listings

http://www.lipinski.house.gov

1717 Longworth House Office Building, Washington, DC 20515 .... (202) 225–5701
Chief of Staff.—Jason Tai. FAX: 225–1012
Office Administrative.—Jennifer Sypolt.
Legislative Director.—Ryan Quinn.
Senior Legislative Assistant.—Ashley Musselman.
6245 South Archer Avenue, Chicago, IL 60638 .... (312) 886–0481
Chief of Staff.—Jerry Hurckes.
19 West Hillgrove Avenue, LaGrange, IL 60525 .... (708) 352–0524
5309 West 95th Street, Oak Law, IL 60453 .... (708) 424–0853

Counties: COOK COUNTY (part). CITIES AND TOWNSHIPS: Alsip, Argo, Bedford Park, Berwyn, Bridgeview, Burr Ridge, Chicago, Chicago Ridge, Cicero, Countryside, Hickory Hills, Hinsdale, Hometown, Hodgkins, Indian Head Park, Justice Burbank, LaGrange, Lyons, McCook, North Riverside, Oak Lawn, Oak Park, Palos Hills, Palos Park, Proviso, Riverside, Stickney, Summit Brookfield, Western Springs, Willow Springs, and Worth. Population (2000), 653,647

ZIP Codes: 60126, 60130, 60154, 60162, 60402, 60415, 60426, 60430, 60453–59, 60463–65, 60477, 60480, 60482, 60499, 60501, 60513, 60521, 60525–27, 60534, 60546, 60558, 60570, 60608–09, 60616, 60620, 60623, 60629, 60632, 60636, 60638, 60643, 60652, 60655, 60803–05

* * *

FOURTH DISTRICT

LUIS V. GUTIERREZ, Democrat, of Chicago, IL; born in Chicago, December 10, 1953; education: B.A., Northeastern Illinois University, DeKalb, Ill., 1974; professional: teacher; social worker, llinois; state department of children and family services; administrative assistant, Chicago, Ill., mayor's office subcommittee on infrastructure, 1984–85; co-founder, West Town-26th Ward Independent Political Organization, 1985; alderman, Chicago, Ill., city council, 1986–93, president pro tem, 1989–92; Democratic National Committee, 1984; married: Soraida Arocho; children: Omaira and Jessica; committees: Financial Services; Judiciary; elected on November 3, 1992, to the 103rd Congress; reelected to each succeeding Congress.

Office Listings

http://www.house.gov/gutierrez

2266 Rayburn House Office Building, Washington, DC 20515 .... (202) 225–8203
Chief of Staff.—Jennice Fuentes. FAX: 225–7810
Legislative Director.—Susan Collins.
Communications Director.—Scott Frotman.
3455 West North Avenue, Chicago, IL 60647 .... (773) 384–1655
1310 West 18th Street, Chicago, IL 60608 .... (312) 666–3882

Counties: COOK COUNTY (part). CITIES: Berkeley, Brookfield, Chicago, Ciero, Elmwood Park, Forest Park, Hillside, Maywood, Melrose Park, Northlake, Oak Park, Stickney, Stone Park, and Westchester. Population (2000), 653,647.

ZIP Codes: 60130, 60141, 60153–55, 60160, 60162–65, 60304–05, 60402, 60443, 60446, 60473, 60513, 60526, 60542, 60546, 60608–09, 60612, 60614, 60616, 60618, 60622–23, 60625, 60629, 60632, 60639, 60641, 60644, 60647, 60651, 60707, 60804

* * *

FIFTH DISTRICT

RAHM EMANUEL, Democrat, of Chicago, IL; born in Chicago, November 29, 1959; education: B.A., liberal arts, Sarah Lawrence College, 1981; M.A., speech and communication, Northwestern University, 1985; professional: Illinois Public Action (consumer rights organization); managing director, Dresdner Kleinwort Wasserstein (global investment bank); Democratic Party activities: worked on Paul Simon's successful U.S. Senate campaign, 1984; national campaign director, Democratic Congressional Campaign Committee, 1988; senior advisor and chief fundraiser for Richard M. Daley's successful Mayoral campaign, 1989; Assistant to the President under President Bill Clinton, 1993–2000; married: Amy; children: Zachariah, Ilana, and Leah; chair, Democratic Caucus; committees: Ways and Means; elected to the 108th Congress on November 8, 2002; reelected to each succeeding Congress.

Office Listings

http://www.house.gov/emanuel

1319 Longworth House Office Building, Washington, DC 20515 .... (202) 225–4061

Chief of Staff.—Elizabeth Sears Smith. FAX: 225–5603
Communications Director.—Kathleen Connery.
Executive Assistant / Scheduler.—Jen Waller.
Legislative Director.—Luis Jimenez.
3742 West Irving Park Road, Chicago, IL 60618 .... (773) 267–5926

Counties: COOK COUNTY (part). Population (2000), 653,647.

ZIP Codes: 60018, 60106, 60131, 60153, 60160–61, 60164–65, 60171, 60176, 60504, 60525, 60613–14, 60618, 60625, 60630–31, 60634, 60639–41, 60646, 60656–57, 60659–60, 60677, 60706–07, 60712, 60714

* * *

SIXTH DISTRICT

PETER J. ROSKAM, Republican, of Wheaton, IL; born in Hinsdale, IL, September 13, 1961; education: B.A., University of Illinois, Urbana-Champaign, IL, 1983; J.D., Illinois Institute of Technology Chicago-Kent College of Law, Chicago, IL, 1989; professional: lawyer, private practice; staff, United States Representative Tom DeLay of Texas, 1985–86; United States Representative Henry Hyde of Illinois, 1986–87; teacher; businessman; member, Illinois house of representatives, 1993–99; member, Illinois senate, 2000–06; married: Elizabeth; children: four; committees: Financial Services; elected to the 110th Congress on November 7, 2006.

Office Listings

http://www.house.gov/roskam

507 Cannon House Office Building, Washington, DC 20515 .... (202) 225–4561
Chief of Staff.—Steven Moore. FAX: 225–1166
Scheduler.—Brigitta Johnson.
Legislative Director.—Victoria Sanville.
Press Secretary.—Matt Vriesema.
150 South Bloomingdale Road, Suite 200, Bloomingdale, IL 60108 .... (630) 893–9670

Counties: COOK (part), DUPAGE (part). CITIES AND TOWNSHIPS: Addison, Arlington Heights, Bensenville, Bloomingdale, Carol Stream, Des Plaines, Elk Grove, Elk Grove Village, Elmhurst, Glen Ellyn, Glendale Heights, Hanover Park Streamwood, Itasca, Leyden Proviso, Lombard, Maine, Milton, Oak Brook, Oak Brook Terrace, Roselle, Villa Park, Wayne, Westchester, Westmont, Wheaton, Winfield, and York. Population (2000), 615,419.

ZIP Codes: 60005, 60007–09, 60016–18, 60056, 60067, 60101, 60103, 60105–08, 60116–17, 60120, 60125–26, 60128, 60131–33, 60137–39, 60143, 60148, 60157, 60172–73, 60176, 60181, 60185, 60187–95, 60197, 60199, 60399, 60515, 60523, 60532, 60559, 60563, 60666, 60688, 60701

* * *

SEVENTH DISTRICT

DANNY K. DAVIS, Democrat, of Chicago, IL; born in Parkdale, AR, September 6, 1941; education: B.A., Arkansas A.M. & N. College, 1961; M.A., Chicago State University; Ph.D., Union Institute, Cincinnati, OH; educator and health planner-administrator; board of directors, National Housing Partnership; Cook County Board of Commissioners, 1990–96; former alderman of the Chicago City Council's 29th ward, receiving the Independent Voters of Illinois ''Best Alderman Award'' for 1980–81, 1981–82, and 1989–90; co-chair, Clinton-Gore-Braun '92; founder and past president, Westside Association for Community Action; past president, National Association of Community Health Centers; 1987 recipient of the Leon M. Despres Award; married to Vera G. Davis; two sons: Jonathan and Stacey; committees: Education and Labor; Oversight and Government Reform; elected to the 105th Congress; reelected to each succeeding Congress.

Office Listings

http://www.house.gov/dannydavis

2159 Rayburn House Office Building, Washington, DC 20515 .... (202) 225–5006
Chief of Staff.—Courtni Pugh. FAX: 225–5641
Legislative Director.—Caleb Gilchrist.
Director of Issues and Communications.—Ira Cohen.
3333 West Arthington Street, Suite 130, Chicago, IL 60624 .... (773) 533–7520
2301 Roosevelt Road, Broadview, IL 60155 .... (708) 345–6857

Counties: COOK COUNTY (part). CITIES AND TOWNSHIPS: Bellwood, Berkley, Broadview, Chicago, Forest Park, Hillside, Maywood, Oak Park, River Forest, and Westchester. Population (2000), 653,647.

ZIP Codes: 60104, 60130, 60141, 60153–55, 60160, 60162–63, 60301–05, 60546, 60601–12, 60614–16, 60621–24, 60636–37, 60639, 60644, 60651, 60653–54, 60661, 60663–65, 60667–75, 60678–81, 60683–88, 60690–91, 60693–97, 60707, 60804

* * *

EIGHTH DISTRICT

MELISSA L. BEAN, Democrat, of Chicago, IL; born in Chicago, January 22, 1962; education: graduated, Maine East High School, Park Ridge, IL, 1980; A.A., Oakton Community College, Des Plaines, IL, 1982; B.A., Roosevelt University, Chicago, IL, 2002; professional: president, sales; Resources Incorporated, 1995–present; vice president, sales, Dataflex Corporation, 1994–95; area manager, UDS/Motorola, 1989–91; branch manager, MTI Systems Incorporated/Arrow Electronics, 1985–89; district sales manager, DJC Corporation 1982–85; Palatine Chamber of Commerce; Barrington area Professional Women; National Association of Women Business Owners; president of Deer Lake Homeowners Association; boards of Barrington Children's Choir and the Lines Elementary parent-teacher organization; religion: Serbian Orthodox; married: Alan; children: Victoria, Michelle; committees: Financial Services; Small Business; elected to the 109th Congress on November 2, 2004; reelected to the 110th Congress.

Office Listings

http://www.house.gov/bean

318 Cannon House Office Building, Washington, DC 20515 .... (202) 225–3711
Chief of Staff.—John Michael Gonzalez. FAX: 225–7830
Legislative Director.—Elizabeth Hart.
1430 North Meatham Road, Schaumburg, IL 60173 .... (847) 519–3434
District Director.—Gideon Bluestein.

Counties: COOK COUNTY (part). TOWNSHIPS: Barrington, Hanover, Palatine, and Schaumburg. LAKE COUNTY (part). TOWNSHIPS: Antioch, Avon, Bentor, Cuba, Ela, Fremont, Grant, Lake Villa, Libertyville, Newport, Warren, Wauconda, and Zion. MCHENRY COUNTY (part). CITIES: Burton, Dorr, Greenwood, Hebron, McHenry, Nunda, and Richmond. Population (2000), 653,647.

ZIP Codes: 60002, 60004–05, 60007–08, 60010–14, 60020–21, 60030–31, 60033–34, 60038, 60041–42, 60046–51, 60060–61, 60067, 60071–75, 60081, 60083–85, 60087, 60095–99, 60103, 60107, 60120, 60133, 60159, 60168, 60172–73, 60179, 60192–96

* * *

NINTH DISTRICT

JANICE D. SCHAKOWSKY, Democrat, of Evanston, IL; born in Chicago, IL, May 26, 1944; education: B.A., University of Illinois, 1965; consumer advocate; program director, Illinois Public Action; executive director, Illinois State Council of Senior Citizens, 1985–90; State Representative, 18th District, Illinois General Assembly, 1991–99; served on Labor and Commerce, Human Service Appropriations, Health Care, and Electric Deregulation Committees; religion: Jewish; married: Robert Creamer; children: Ian, Mary, and Lauren; committees: Energy and Commerce; Permanent Select Committee on Intelligence; elected to the 106th Congress; reelected to each succeeding Congress.

Office Listings

http://www.house.gov/schakowsky

1027 Longworth House Office Building, Washington, DC 20515 .... (202) 225–2111
Chief of Staff.—Cathy Hurwit. FAX: 226–6890
Deputy Chief of Staff / Communications Director.—Peter Karafotas.
Legislative Director.—Diane Beedle.
Appointments Secretary.—Kim Muzeroll.
5533 Broadway, Chicago, IL 60640 .... (773) 506–7100
District Director.—Leslie Combs.

Counties: COOK COUNTY (part). CITIES: Chicago, Evanston, Glenview, Golf, Lincolnwood, Morton Grove, Niles, and Skokie. Population (2000), 653,647.

ZIP Codes: 60016, 60018–19, 60025, 60029, 60053, 60056, 60068, 60076–77, 60091, 60176, 60201–04, 60208, 60611, 60613, 60626, 60630–31, 60640, 60645–46, 60656–57, 60659–60, 60706, 60712, 60714

* * *

TENTH DISTRICT

MARK STEVEN KIRK, Republican, of Highland Park, IL; born in Champaign, IL, September 15, 1959; education: New Trier East High School, Winnetka, IL, 1977; B.A., Cornell University, 1981; J.D., Georgetown University, 1992; professional: attorney; military service: Lt. Commander, U.S. Navy Reserve; Administrative Assistant to Rep. John Porter (R–IL), 1984–90; World Bank, served as an International Finance Corp. officer; Dept. of State, served as Special Assistant to the Assistant Secretary for Inter-American Affairs; Baker & McKenzie (law firm); served as Counsel on the House Committee on International Relations; married: Kimberly Vertolli; committees: Appropriations; elected to the 107th Congress on November 7, 2000; reelected to each succeeding Congress.

Office Listings

http://www.house.gov/kirk

1030 Longworth House Office Building, Washington, DC 20515 .... (202) 225–4835
Chief of Staff.—Liesl Hickey. FAX: 225–0837
Legislative Director.—Patrick Magnuson.
707 Skokie Boulevard, Suite 350, Northbrook, IL 60062 .... (847) 940–0202
Press Secretary.—Eric Elk.

Counties: COOK (part), LAKE (part). Population (2000), 653,647.

ZIP Codes: 60004–06, 60008, 60010, 60015–16, 60022, 60025–26, 60030–31, 60035, 60037, 60040, 60043–45, 60047–48, 60056, 60060–62, 60064–65, 60067, 60069–70, 60074, 60078–79, 60082–83, 60085–93, 60173, 60195, 60201

* * *

ELEVENTH DISTRICT

JERRY WELLER, Republican, of Morris, IL; born in Streator, IL, July 7, 1957; education: graduated, Dwight High School, 1975; B.A., agriculture, University of Illinois, 1979; aide to Congressman Tom Corcoran, 1980–81; aide to John R. Block (U.S. Secretary of Agriculture), 1981–85; former State Representative, 1988–94; National Republican Legislative Association Legislator of the Year; listed in the 1990 *Almanac of Illinois Politics*; committees: Ways and Means; assistant minority whip; House Republican Steering Committee; elected to the 104th Congress; reelected to each succeeding Congress.

Office Listings

http://www.house.gov/weller

108 Cannon House Office Building, Washington, DC 20515 .... (202) 225–3635
Chief of Staff.—Jeanette Forcash. FAX: 225–3521
Executive Assistant.—Lisa Randogno.
Deputy Chief of Staff / Legislative Director.—Alan Tennille.
Press Secretary.—Andy Fuller.
2701 Black Road, Suite 201, Joliet, IL 60435 .... (815) 740–2028
District Manager.—Reed Wilson.

Counties: BUREAU (part), GRUNDY, KANKAKEE, LA SALLE, LIVINGSTON (part), MCLEAN (part), WILL (part), and WOODFORD (part). Population (2000), 653,658.

ZIP Codes: 60401, 60407–11, 60416–17, 60420–21, 60423–24, 60430–37, 60442, 60444–45, 60447–51, 60466, 60468, 60470, 60474–75, 60477, 60479, 60481, 60504, 60518, 60531, 60541, 60544, 60548–49, 60551–52, 60557, 60625, 60640, 60646, 60660, 60901–02, 60910, 60912–15, 60917, 60919, 60922, 60935, 60940–41, 60944, 60950, 60954, 60961, 60964, 61238, 61240–41, 61254, 61262, 61273, 61301, 61312, 61314–17, 61320–23, 61325–26, 61328–30, 61332, 61334, 61337–38, 61341–42, 61344–45, 61348–50, 61354, 61356, 61358–62, 61364, 61368, 61370–74, 61376–77, 61379, 61701–02, 61704, 61725, 61732, 61736, 61744–45, 61748, 61752, 61754, 61760–61, 61772, 61774, 61790

* * *

TWELFTH DISTRICT

JERRY F. COSTELLO, Democrat, of Belleville, IL; born in East St. Louis, IL, September 25, 1949; education: graduated, Assumption High, East St. Louis, IL, 1968; A.A.,

Belleville Area College, IL, 1970; B.A., Maryville College of the Sacred Heart, St. Louis, MO, 1973; professional: county bailiff, Illinois 20th judicial circuit; deputy sheriff, St. Clair County, IL; director of court services and probation, Illinois 20th judicial district; chief investigator, Illinois state attorney's office, St. Clair County, IL; elected board chair, St. Clair County, IL, 1980–88; married: the former Georgia Jean Cockrum, 1968; children: Jerry II, Gina Keen, and John; committees: Science and Technology; Transportation and Infrastructure; elected to the 100th Congress by special election to fill the vacancy caused by the death of United States Representative Charles Melvin Price; reelected to each succeeding Congress.

Office Listings

http://www.house.gov/costello

2408 Rayburn House Office Building, Washington, DC 20515 .... (202) 225–5661
FAX: 225–0285
Chief of Staff.—David Gillies.
Scheduler.—Karl Britton.
Legislative Director.—Christa Fornarotto.
Press Secretary.—David Gillies.
2060 Delmar Avenue, Suite B, Granite City, IL 62040 .... (618) 451–7065
8787 State Street, Suite 102, East Saint Louis, IL 62203 .... (618) 397–8833
144 Lincoln Place Court, Suite 4, Belleville, IL 62221 .... (618) 233–8026
201 East Nolen Street, West Frankfort, IL 62896 .... (618) 937–6402
250 West Cherry Street, Carbondale, IL 62901 .... (618) 529–3791
1330 Swanwick Street, Chester, IL 62233 .... (618) 826–3043

Counties: ALEXANDER, FRANKLIN, JACKSON, MADISON (part), MONROE, PERRY, PULASKI, RANDOLPH, ST. CLAIR, UNION, WILLIAMSON (part). Population (2000), 653,647.

ZIP Codes: 62002, 62010, 62018, 62024–25, 62035, 62040, 62048, 62059–60, 62071, 62084, 62087, 62090, 62095, 62201–08, 62217, 62220–26, 62232–34, 62236–44, 62246, 62248, 62254–61, 62263–65, 62268–69, 62272, 62274, 62277–80, 62282, 62284–86, 62288–89, 62292–95, 62297–98, 62812, 62819, 62822, 62831–32, 62836, 62840, 62846, 62859–60, 62865, 62883–84, 62888, 62890, 62896–97, 62901–03, 62905–07, 62912, 62914–18, 62920, 62922–24, 62926–27, 62932–33, 62939–42, 62948–52, 62956–59, 62961–64, 62966, 62969–71, 62973–76, 62983, 62987–88, 62990, 62992–94, 62996–99

* * *

THIRTEENTH DISTRICT

JUDY BIGGERT, Republican, of Hinsdale, IL; born in Chicago, IL, August 15, 1937; education: graduated from New Trier High School, 1955; B.A., Stanford University, 1959; J.D., Northwestern University School of Law, 1963; professional: attorney, 1975–99; Illinois House of Representatives (81st District), 1993–98; Assistant House Republican Leader, 1995–99; has served on numerous local civic and community organizations and groups; religion: Episcopalian; married: Rody P. Biggert; children: Courtney, Alison, Rody, and Adrienne; committees: Education and Labor; Financial Services; Science and Technology; elected to the 106th Congress; reelected to each succeeding Congress.

Office Listings

1034 Longworth House Office Building, Washington, DC 20515 .... (202) 225–3515
FAX: 225–9420
Chief of Staff.—Kathy Lydon.
Press Secretary.—Shauna Riley.
Legislative Director.—Paul Doucette.
Scheduler.—Jackie Abba.
6262 South Route 83, Suite 305, Willowbrook, IL 60527 .... (630) 655–2052

Counties: COOK (part), DUPAGE (part), WILL (part). Population (2000), 653,647.

ZIP Codes: 60181, 60403, 60432, 60435, 60439, 60440–41, 60446, 60448, 60462–64, 60467, 60477, 60483, 60487, 60490–91, 60502–04, 60514–17, 60519, 60521–23, 60527, 60532, 60540, 60543–44, 60555, 60559, 60561, 60563–67, 60572, 60585–86, 60597, 60599

* * *

FOURTEENTH DISTRICT

J. DENNIS HASTERT, Republican, of Yorkville, IL; born in Aurora, IL, January 2, 1942; education: graduated, Oswego High School, 1960; B.A., Wheaton College, IL, 1964; M.S., Northern Illinois University, DeKalb, 1967; teacher/coach, Yorkville High School; partner, family restaurant business; member, Illinois General Assembly House of Representatives, 1980–86; Republican spokesman for the Appropriations II Committee; chair, Joint Committee on Public

Utility Regulation; member, Legislative Audit Commission; named one of Illinois' 20 top legislators in 1985 by *Chicago Sun-Times*; member, Yorkville Lions Club; board of directors, Aurora Family Support Center; married the former Jean Kahl in 1973; two children: Joshua and Ethan; committees: Energy and Commerce; elected Speaker of the House for the 106th–109th Congresses; elected to the 100th Congress on November 4, 1986; reelected to each succeeding Congress.

Office Listings

http://www.house.gov/hastert

2304 Rayburn House Office Building, Washington, DC 20515 .... (202) 225–2976
Chief of Staff.—Mike Stokke. FAX: 225–0697
Scheduler.—Sam Lancaster.
Legislative Director.—Anthony Reed.
27 North River Street, Batavia, IL 60510 .... (630) 406–1114
Office Manager.—Lisa Post.
119 West First Street, Dixon, IL 61021 .... (815) 288–0680

Counties: BUREAU (part), DEKALB (part), DUPAGE (part), HENRY (part), KANE, KENDALL, LEE, WHITESIDE (part). CITIES AND TOWNSHIPS: Amboy, Ashton, Aurora, Barrington Hills, Bartlett, Batavia, Big Rock, Bristol, Burlington, Carol Stream, Carpentersville, Clare, Compton, Cornell, Cortland, DeKalb, Dixon, Dundee, East and West, Earlville, Elburn, Elgin, Esmond, Forreston, Franklin Grove, Geneva, Genoa, Gilberts, Hampshire, Harmon, Hinckley, Kaneville, Kingston, Kirkland, Lee, Leland, Malta, Maple Park, Mendota, Millbrook, Millington, Minooka, Montgomery, Mooseheart, Nelson, Newark, North Aurora, Oswego, Paw Paw, Plano, Plato Center, St. Charles, Sandwich, Shabbona, Sleepy Hollow, Somonauk, South Elgin, Steward, Sublette, Sugar Grove, Sycamore, Virgil, Warrenville, Wasco, Waterman, Wayne, West Brooklyn, West Chicago, Wheaton, Winfield, and Yorkville. Population (2000), 653,647.

ZIP Codes: 60010, 60102–03, 60109–10, 60112, 60115, 60118–23, 60134, 60136, 60140, 60142, 60144, 60147, 60150–52, 60170, 60174–75, 60177–78, 60183–87, 60190, 60431, 60447, 60450, 60504–06, 60510–12, 60518, 60520, 60530–31, 60536–39, 60541–45, 60548, 60550, 60552–56, 60560, 60563, 60568, 60640, 60660, 61006, 61021, 61031, 61042, 61057–58, 61068, 61071, 61081, 61234–35, 61238, 61240–41, 61243, 61250, 61254, 61258, 61270, 61273–74, 61277, 61283, 61310, 61318, 61324, 61330–31, 61342, 61344, 61346, 61349, 61353, 61367, 61376, 61378, 61434, 61443

* * *

FIFTEENTH DISTRICT

TIMOTHY V. JOHNSON, Republican, of Sidney, IL; born in Champaign, IL, July 23, 1946; education: B.A., University of Illinois, Phi Beta Kappa; J.D., University of Illinois College of Law, graduated with high honors; professional: attorney; public service: Urbana, IL, City Council, 1971–75; Illinois House of Representatives, 1976–2000; Deputy Majority Leader; Champaign County, IL, Republican Party Chair, 1990–96; committees: Agriculture; Transportation and Infrastructure; elected to the 107th Congress on November 7, 2000; reelected to each succeeding Congress.

Office Listings

http://www.house.gov/timjohnson

1207 Longworth House Office Building, Washington, DC 20515 .... (202) 225–2371
Chief of Staff.—Jerome T. Clarke. FAX: 226–0791
Legislative Director.—Stephen Borg.
2004 Fox Drive, Champaign, IL 61820 .... (217) 403–4690

Counties: CHAMPAIGN, CLARK, COLES, CRAWFORD, CUMBERLAND, DEWITT, DOUGLAS, EDGAR, EDWARDS (part), FORD, GALLATIN (part), IROQUOIS, LAWRENCE (part), LIVINGSTON (part), MACON (part), MCLEAN (part), MOULTRIE, PIATT, SALINE (part), VERMILION, WABASH (part), WHITE (part). CITIES AND TOWNSHIPS: Bloomington-Normal, Champaign-Urbana, Charleston-Mattoon, Danville, Decatur, Mount Carmel, and Pontiac. Population (2000), 653,647.

ZIP Codes: 60420, 60423, 60437, 60449, 60460, 60518, 60531, 60551–52, 60901–02, 60911–14, 60917–22, 60924, 60926–34, 60936, 60938–42, 60945–46, 60948–49, 60951–53, 60955–57, 60959–64, 60966–70, 60973–74, 61252, 61270, 61311, 61313, 61319, 61321, 61333, 61364, 61401, 61434, 61448–49, 61530, 61701–02, 61704, 61709–10, 61720, 61722, 61724, 61726–28, 61730–31, 61735, 61737, 61739–41, 61743, 61748–50, 61752–53, 61758, 61761, 61764, 61769–70, 61772–73, 61775–78, 61791, 61799, 61801–03, 61810–18, 61820–22, 61824–26, 61830–34, 61839–59, 61862–66, 61870–78, 61880, 61882–84, 61910–14, 61917, 61919–20, 61924–25, 61928–33, 61936–38, 61940–44, 61949, 61951, 61953, 61955–56, 62401, 62410, 62413, 62420–21, 62423, 62427–28, 62432–33, 62435–36, 62439–42, 62445, 62447, 62449, 62451, 62454, 62460, 62462, 62466–69, 62474, 62477–78, 62481, 62521–22, 62526, 62532, 62544, 62549–50, 62701–03, 62821, 62827, 62844, 62863, 62867, 62869, 62871, 62930, 62934, 62946, 62984

* * *

SIXTEENTH DISTRICT

DONALD A. MANZULLO, Republican, of Egan, IL; born in Rockford, IL, March 24, 1944; education: B.A., American University, Washington, DC, 1987; J.D., Marquette University Law

School, Milwaukee, WI, 1970; admitted to Illinois bar, 1970; president, Ogle County Bar Association, 1971, 1973; advisor, Oregon Ambulance Corporation; founder, Oregon Youth, Inc.; member: State of Illinois and City of Oregon chambers of commerce; Friends of Severson Dells; Natural Land Institute; Ogle County Historic Society; Northern Illinois Alliance for the Arts; Aircraft Owners and Pilots Association; Ogle County Pilots Association; Kiwanis International; Illinois Farm Bureau; Ogle County Farm Bureau; National Federation of Independent Business; Citizens Against Government Waste; married: Freda Teslik, 1982; children: Niel, Noel, and Katherine; committees: Financial Services; Foreign Affairs; elected on November 3, 1992, to the 103rd Congress; reelected to each succeeding Congress.

Office Listings

2228 Rayburn House Office Building, Washington, DC 20515 .... (202) 225–5676
Chief of Staff.—Adam Magary FAX: 225–5284
Legislative Director.—John Westmoreland.
Scheduler.—Erin Davis.
Communications Director (Rockford).—Rich Carter.
415 South Mulford Road, Rockford, IL 61108 .... (815) 394–1231
District Director.—Pam Sexton.
5186 Northwest Highway, Suite 130, Crystal Lake, IL 60014 .... (815) 356–9800
Caseworker.—Bridget Johnson.

Counties: BOONE, CARROLL, DEKALB (part), JO DAVIESS, MCHENRY (part), OGLE, STEPHENSON, WHITESIDE (part), WINNEBAGO. Population (2000), 653,647.

ZIP Codes: 60001, 60010, 60012–14, 60021, 60033–34, 60039, 60042, 60050–51, 60098, 60102, 60111, 60113, 60115, 60129, 60135, 60140, 60142, 60145–46, 60150, 60152, 60156, 60178, 60180, 60530, 61001, 61006–08, 61010–16, 61018–21, 61024–25, 61027–28, 61030–32, 61036, 61038–39, 61041, 61043–44, 61046–54, 61059–65, 61067–68, 61070–75, 61077–81, 61084–85, 61087–89, 61091, 61101–12, 61114–15, 61125–26, 61130–32, 61230, 61250–52, 61261, 61266, 61270, 61285

* * *

SEVENTEENTH DISTRICT

PHILIP G. ''PHIL'' HARE, Democrat, of Rock Island, IL; born in Galesburg, IL, February 21, 1949; education: graduated, Alleman High School, 1969; attended Blackhawk College, Moline, IL; tailor of men's suits for 13 years at Seaford Clothing Factory; served as union leader and as president of UNITE HERE, Local 617; served in the U.S. Army Reserves for six years; District Director for Illinois Representative Lane Evans, 1982–2006; married: Beckie; children: Lou and Amy; committees: Education and Labor; Veterans' Affairs; assistant whip; elected on November 7, 2006 to the 110th Congress.

Office Listings

1118 Longworth House Office Building, Washington, DC 20515 .... (202) 225–5905
Administrative Assistant.—Dennis King. FAX: 225–5396
Office Manager.—Eda Robinson.
Press Secretary.—Tim Schlittner.
1535 47th Avenue, Room 5, Moline, IL 61265 .... (309) 793–5760
District Representative.—Pat O'Brien.
261 North Broad, Suite 5, Galesburg, IL 61401 .... (309) 342–4411
236 North Water, Suite 765, Decatur, IL 62523 .... (217) 422–9150

Counties: ADAMS (part), CALHOUN, CHRISTIAN (part), FAYETTE (part), FULTON, GREENE (part), HANCOCK, HENDERSON, HENRY (part), JERSEY (part), KNOX (part), MACON (part), MACOUPIN, MADISON (part), MCDONOUGH, MERCER, MONTGOMERY (part), PIKE (part), ROCK ISLAND, SANGAMON (part), SHELBY (part), WARREN, WHITESIDE (part). Population (2000), 653,647.

ZIP Codes: 61037, 61071, 61081, 61201, 61204, 61230–33, 61236–37, 61239–42, 61244, 61251, 61256–57, 61259–65, 61272, 61275–76, 61278–79, 61281–82, 61284, 61299, 61318, 61342, 61364, 61401–02, 61410–20, 61422–23, 61425, 61427, 61430–43, 61447–48, 61450, 61452–55, 61458–60, 61462, 61465–78, 61480, 61482, 61484, 61486, 61488–90, 61501, 61519–20, 61524, 61531, 61533, 61542–44, 61553, 61560, 61563, 61569, 61572, 61611, 61701, 61761, 62001–02, 62006, 62009, 62011–14, 62017, 62019, 62021, 62023, 62027, 62031–33, 62036–37, 62044–45, 62047, 62049–53, 62056, 62058, 62063, 62065, 62069–70, 62074–75, 62077–79, 62082, 62085–86, 62088–89, 62091–94, 62097–98, 62262, 62301, 62305–06, 62311, 62313, 62316, 62320–21, 62326, 62329–30, 62334, 62336, 62338, 62341, 62343, 62345, 62348, 62351, 62354–56, 62358, 62360–61, 62366–67, 62370, 62373–74, 62376, 62379–80, 62431, 62513–15, 62520–23, 62525–26, 62537, 62539, 62544, 62549–51, 62557, 62560–61, 62572, 62615, 62624, 62626, 62629–30, 62640, 62644, 62649, 62661, 62667, 62670, 62672, 62674, 62683, 62685, 62690, 62692, 62701–05, 62707–08, 62713, 62781, 62794, 62796

* * *

EIGHTEENTH DISTRICT

RAY LAHOOD, Republican, of Peoria, IL; born in Peoria, December 6, 1945; education: graduate of Spalding High School; Canton Junior College, Canton, IL; B.S. in education and sociology, Bradley University, Peoria, IL, 1971; honorary degrees: Doctorate in Political Science, Lincoln College; Doctorate in Public Service, Eureka College; Doctorate in Humane Letters, Tri-State University; Doctorate in Public Service, MacMurray College; professional: junior high school teacher; director of Rock Island County Youth Services Bureau; chief planner for Bi-State Metropolitan Planning Commission; administrative assistant to Congressman Tom Railsback and chief of staff for Congressman Bob Michel; member, Illinois House of Representatives, 1982; awards: named Ray A. Neumann Tri-County Citizen of the Year by the Downtown Kiwanis Club of Peoria, 2001; received Peoria Notre Dame High School's Distinguished Alumnus Award, 1999; Eillis Island Medal of Honor; the Chamber of Commerce's Spirit of Enterprise Award; the Friend of Agriculture Award; the Guardian of Small Business Award; the Guardian of Medicare Award; the Tax Fighter Award; the Manufacturing Legislative Excellence Award; member, Holy Family Church; married: Kathy Dunk LaHood, 1967; children: Darin (wife, Kristin); Amy (husband, Kevin); Sam; Sara (husband, Brian); grandchildren: Ella, McKay, Henry, Luke, Oliver, Theodore; committees: Appropriations; elected on November 8, 1994, to the 104th Congress; reelected to each succeeding Congress.

Office Listings

http://www.house.gov/lahood

1424 Longworth House Office Building, Washington, DC 20515 .... (202) 225–6201
Chief of Staff.—Diane Liesman. FAX: 225–9249
Deputy Chief of Staff.—Joan DeBoer.
100 Monroe Street, NE., Room 100, Peoria, IL 61602 .... (309) 671–7027
District Deputy Chief of Staff.—Carol Merna.
209 West State Street, Jacksonville, IL 62650 .... (217) 245–1431
Office Manager.—Barb Baker.
3050 Montvale Drive, Suite D, Springfield, IL 62704 .... (217) 793–0808
District Chief of Staff.—Tim Butler.

Counties: ADAMS (part), BROWN, BUREAU (part), CASS, KNOX (part), LOGAN, MACON (part), MARSHALL, MASON, MCLEAN, MENARD, MORGAN, PEORIA, PIKE (part), PUTNAM, SANGAMON (part), SCHUYLER, SCOTT, STARK, TAZEWELL, WOODFORD (part). Population (2000), 653,647.

ZIP Codes: 61314, 61320–21, 61326–27, 61330, 61334–36, 61340, 61345, 61349, 61362–63, 61369–70, 61375, 61377, 61401, 61410, 61414, 61421, 61424, 61426, 61428, 61434, 61436, 61440, 61443, 61448–49, 61451–52, 61455, 61458, 61467, 61472, 61479, 61483–85, 61488–89, 61491, 61501, 61516–17, 61523, 61525–26, 61528–37, 61539–42, 61545–48, 61550, 61552, 61554–55, 61558–62, 61564–65, 61567–72, 61601–07, 61610–12, 61614–16, 61625, 61628–30, 61632–41, 61643–44, 61650–56, 61704, 61721, 61723, 61729, 61733–34, 61738, 61742, 61747, 61749, 61751, 61755–56, 61759–61, 61771, 61774, 61778, 61830, 62305, 62311–12, 62314, 62319–20, 62323–25, 62338–40, 62344, 62346–47, 62349, 62352–53, 62357, 62359–60, 62362–63, 62365, 62367, 62375, 62378, 62501, 62512, 62515, 62518–22, 62524, 62526, 62535, 62539, 62541, 62543, 62548, 62551, 62554, 62561, 62573, 62601, 62610–13, 62615, 62617–18, 62621–22, 62624–25, 62627–29, 62631, 62633–35, 62638–39, 62642–44, 62650–51, 62655–56, 62660–68, 62670–71, 62673, 62675, 62677, 62681–82, 62684, 62688, 62690–95, 62701–07, 62713, 62715, 62719, 62721–22, 62726, 62736, 62739, 62746, 62756–57, 62761, 62765, 62767, 62769, 62776–77, 62781, 62786, 62791, 62796

* * *

NINETEENTH DISTRICT

JOHN SHIMKUS, Republican, of Collinsville, IL; born in Collinsville, February 21, 1958; education: graduated from Collinsville High School; B.S., West Point Military Academy, West Point, NY, 1980; teaching certificate, Christ College, Irvine, CA, 1990; M.B.A., Southern Illinois University, Edwardsville, 1997; U.S. Army Reserves, 1980–85; government and history teacher, Metro East Lutheran High School, Edwardsville, IL; Collinsville township trustee, 1989; Madison county treasurer, 1990–96; married: the former Karen Muth, 1987; children: David, Daniel, and Joshua; committees: Energy and Commerce; elected to the 105th Congress; reelected to each succeeding Congress.

Office Listings

http://www.house.gov/shimkus

2452 Rayburn House Office Building, Washington, DC 20515 .... (202) 225–5271
Chief of Staff.—Craig Roberts. FAX: 225–5880
Legislative Director.—Mo Zilly.
240 Regency Centre, Collinsville, IL 62234 .... (618) 344–3065

3130 Chatham Road, Suite C, Springfield, IL 62704 .... (217) 492–5090
District Director.—Deb Detmeys.
221 East Broadway, Suite 102, Centralia, IL 62801 .... (618) 532–9676
120 South Fair, Olney, IL 62450 .... (618) 392–7737
110 East Locust Street, Room 12, Harrisburg, IL 62946 .... (618) 252–8271

Counties: Bond, Christian (part), Clay, Clinton, Edwards (part), Effingham, Fayette (part), Gallatin (part), Greene (part), Hamilton, Hardin, Jasper, Jefferson, Jersey (part), Johnson, Lawrence (part), Madison (part), Marion, Massac, Montgomery (part), Pope, Richland, Saline (part), Sangamon (part), Shelby (part), Wabash (part), Washington, Wayne, White (part), Williamson (part). Population (2000), 653,647.

ZIP Codes: 61957, 62001–02, 62010, 62012, 62015–17, 62019, 62021–22, 62024–26, 62028, 62030, 62034–35, 62040, 62044, 62046, 62049, 62051–52, 62054, 62056, 62061–62, 62067, 62074–76, 62080–81, 62083, 62086, 62088, 62094, 62097, 62214–16, 62218–19, 62230–31, 62234, 62237, 62245–47, 62249–50, 62252–55, 62257–58, 62262–63, 62265–66, 62268–69, 62271, 62273, 62275, 62281, 62284, 62293–94, 62338, 62401, 62410–11, 62413–14, 62417–28, 62431–36, 62438–52, 62454, 62458–69, 62471, 62473–81, 62510, 62513, 62515, 62517, 62520–22, 62526, 62530–31, 62533–34, 62536, 62538–40, 62545–48, 62550, 62553, 62555–58, 62560, 62563, 62565, 62567–68, 62570–72, 62615, 62629, 62689–90, 62703–04, 62707, 62716, 62723, 62762–64, 62766, 62791, 62801, 62803, 62805–12, 62814–25, 62827–31, 62833–44, 62846, 62848–72, 62874–87, 62889–99, 62908–10, 62912, 62917, 62919, 62921–23, 62926, 62928, 62930–31, 62934–35, 62938–39, 62941, 62943, 62946–47, 62953–56, 62959–60, 62965, 62967, 62972, 62977, 62979, 62982–85, 62987, 62991, 62995

INDIANA

(Population 2000, 6,080,485)

SENATORS

RICHARD G. LUGAR, Republican, of Indianapolis, IN; born in Indianapolis, April 4, 1932; education: graduated, Shortridge High School, 1950; B.A., Denison University, Granville, OH; Rhodes Scholar, B.A., M.A., Pembroke College, Oxford, England, 1956; served in the U.S. Navy, 1957–60; businessman; treasurer, Lugar Stock Farms, Inc., a livestock and grain operation; vice president and treasurer, Thomas L. Green and Co., manufacturers of food production machinery, 1960–67; member, Indianapolis Board of School Commissioners, 1964–67; mayor of Indianapolis, 1968–75; member, advisory board, U.S. Conference of Mayors, 1969–75; National League of Cities, advisory council, 1972–75, president, 1971; Advisory Commission on Intergovernmental Relations, 1969–75, vice chairman, 1971–75; board of trustees, Denison University and the University at Indianapolis; advisory board, Indiana University-Purdue University at Indianapolis; visiting professor of political science, director of public affairs, Indiana Central University; 31 honorary doctorates; recipient of Fiorello LaGuardia Award, 1975; GOP National Convention Keynote Speaker, 1972; SFRC chairman, 1985–86; NRSC chairman, 1983–84; member, St. Luke's Methodist Church; married the former Charlene Smeltzer, 1956; four children; committees: Agriculture, Nutrition, and Forestry; Foreign Relations; elected to the U.S. Senate on November 2, 1976; reelected to each succeeding Senate term.

Office Listings

http://lugar.senate.gov

306 Hart Senate Office Building, Washington, DC 20510 .... (202) 224–4814
    FAX: 228–0360
    Administrative Assistant.—Martin W. Morris.
    Legislative Director.—Chris Geeslin.
    Press Secretary.—Andy Fisher.
    Scheduler.—Justin Ailes.
10 West Market Street, Room 1180, Indianapolis, IN 46204 .... (317) 226–5555
Federal Building, Room 122, 101 Northwest Martin Luther King Boulevard, Evansville, IN 47708 .... (812) 465–6313
Federal Building, Room 3158, 1300 South Harrison Street, Fort Wayne, IN 46802 (260) 422–1505
175 West Lincolnway, Suite G–1, Valparaiso, IN 46383 .... (219) 548–8035
Federal Center, Room 103, 1201 East 10th Street, Jeffersonville, IN 47132 .... (812) 288–3377

* * *

EVAN BAYH, Democrat, of Indianapolis, IN; born in Shirkieville, IN, December 26, 1955; education: graduated St. Albans School, Washington, DC, 1974; B.A. with honors in business economics, Indiana University, 1978; J.D., University of Virginia Law School, 1982; professional: admitted to the District of Columbia and Indiana bars, 1984; law clerk for the Southern District of Indiana court, 1982–83; attorney with Hogan and Hartson, Washington, 1983–84; attorney for Bayh, Tabbert and Capehart, Washington, 1985; attorney for Bingham Summers, Welsh and Spilman, Indianapolis, 1986; elected as Secretary of State of Indiana, 1986–89; elected Governor of Indiana, 1988; reelected, 1992; chairman, Democratic Governors' Association, 1994; chairman, National Education Goals Panel, 1995; chairman, Education Commission of the States, 1995; Above and Beyond Award, Indiana Black Expo, 1995; Breaking the Glass Ceiling Award Women Executives in State Government, 1996; keynote speaker, National Democratic Convention, 1996; member of the executive committee on the National Governors' Association, 1996; Red Poling Chair, business economics at Indiana University, 1997; chairman, Democratic Leadership Council; married: Susan Breshears, April 13, 1985; twin sons, Birch Evans IV, and Nicholas Harrison; committees: Armed Services; Banking, Housing and Urban Affairs; Small Business and Entrepreneurship; Special Committee on Aging; Select Committee on Intelligence; elected to the U.S. Senate on November 3, 1998; reelected to each succeeding Senate term.

Office Listings

http://bayh.senate.gov

131 Russell Senate Office Building, Washington, DC 20510 .... (202) 224–5623
    FAX: 228–1377
    Chief of Staff.—Tom Sugar.
    Executive Assistant.—Elizabeth Breckenridge.
    Legislative Director.—Charlie Salem.
    Scheduler.—Sarah Rozensky.
130 South Main Street, Suite 110, South Bend, IN 44601 .... (574) 236–8302
1650 Market Tower, 10 W. Market Street, Indianapolis, IN 46204 .... (317) 554–0750
101 Martin Luther King, Jr. Boulevard, Evansville, IN 47708 .... (812) 465–6500

1300 South Harrison Street, Room 3161, Ft. Wayne, IL 36802 .... (260) 426–3151
1201 East 10th Street, Suite 106, Jeffersonville, IN 47130 .... (812) 218–2317
Hammond Courthouse, 5400 Federal Plaza, Suite 3200, Hammond, IL 46320 .... (219) 852–2763

REPRESENTATIVES

FIRST DISTRICT

PETER J. VISCLOSKY, Democrat, of Merrillville, IN; born in Gary, IN, August 13, 1949; education: graduated, Andrean High School, Merrillville, 1967; B.S., accounting, Indiana University Northwest, Gary, 1970; J.D., University of Notre Dame Law School, Notre Dame, IN, 1973; LL.M., international and comparative law, Georgetown University Law Center, Washington, DC, 1982; professional: attorney; admitted to the Indiana state bar, 1974, the District of Columbia bar, 1978, and the U.S. Supreme Court bar, 1980; associate staff, U.S. House of Representatives, Committee on Appropriations, 1977–80, Committee on the Budget, 1980–82; practicing attorney, Merrillville law firm, 1983–84; two children: John Daniel and Timothy Patrick; committees: Appropriations; elected to the 99th Congress on November 6, 1984; reelected to each succeeding Congress.

Office Listings

http://www.house.gov/visclosky

2256 Rayburn House Office Building, Washington, DC 20515 .... (202) 225–2461
Administrative Assistant.—Charles Brimmer. FAX: 225–2493
Appropriations Director.—Shari Davenport.
Executive Assistant/Scheduler.—Korry Baack.
Press Assistant.—Justin Kitsch.
701 East 83rd Avenue, Suite 9, Merrillville, IN 46410 .... (219) 795–1844
District Director.—Mark Lopez. (888) 423–7383

Counties: BENTON, JASPER, LAKE, NEWTON, PORTER (part). Population (2000), 675,767.

ZIP Codes: 46301–04, 46307–08, 46310–12, 46319–25, 46327, 46341–42, 46345, 46347–49, 46355–56, 46360, 46366, 46368, 46372–73, 46375–77, 46379–85, 46390, 46392–94, 46401–11, 47917, 47921–22, 47942–44, 47948, 47951, 47963–64, 47970–71, 47977–78, 47984, 47986, 47995

* * *

SECOND DISTRICT

JOE DONNELLY, Democrat, of Granger, IN; born in Massapequa, NY, September 29, 1955; education: B.A., major: government, the University of Notre Dame, 1977; J.D., the University of Notre Dame, 1981; member: Law Firm of Nemeth, Feeny and Masters, in South Bend, IN; small business owner in Mishawaka; served on Indiana State Election Board, 1988–89; member of the Mishawaka Marian High School Board, 1997–2001, served as president; 2000–01; married to Jill; children: Molly and Joseph Jr.; committees: Agriculture; Financial Services; Veterans' Affairs; elected to the 110th Congress on November 7, 2006.

Office Listings

http://donnelly.house.gov

1218 Longworth House Office Building, Washington, DC 20515 .... (202) 225–3915
Chief of Staff.—Joel Elliott. FAX: 225–6798
Legislative Director.—Nathan Fenstermacher.
Scheduler.—Jessica McEwen.
Press Secretary.—Betsy Hart.
207 West Colfax Avenue, South Bend, IN 46601–1601 .... (574) 288–2780

Counties: CARROLL, CASS, ELKHART (part), FULTON, LAPORTE, MARSHALL, PORTER (part), PULASKI, ST. JOSEPH, STARKE, WHITE (part). CITIES: Elkhart, Kokomo, LaPorte, Logansport, Monticello, Mishawaka, Plymouth, Rochester, South Bend, and Westville. Population (2000), 675,767.

ZIP Codes: 46041, 46051, 46056, 46065, 46143, 46301, 46304, 46340–42, 46345–46, 46348, 46350, 46352, 46360–61, 46365–66, 46371, 46374, 46382–83, 46390–91, 46501, 46504, 46506, 46511, 46513–17, 46524, 46526, 46528, 46530–32, 46534, 46536–37, 46539, 46544–46, 46550, 46552, 46554, 46556, 46561, 46563, 46570, 46572, 46574, 46595, 46601, 46604, 46613–17, 46619–20, 46624, 46626, 46628–29, 46634–35, 46637, 46660, 46680, 46699, 46901–02, 46910, 46912–13, 46915–17, 46920, 46922–23, 46926, 46929, 46931–32, 46939, 46942, 46945, 46947, 46950–51, 46960–61, 46967–68, 46970, 46975, 46977–79, 46982, 46985, 46988, 46994, 46996, 46998, 47920, 47923, 47925–26, 47946, 47950, 47957, 47959, 47960, 47997

* * *

THIRD DISTRICT

MARK E. SOUDER, Republican, of Fort Wayne, IN; born in Grabill, IN, July 18, 1950; education: graduated from Leo High School, 1968; B.S., Indiana University, Fort Wayne, 1972; M.B.A., University of Notre Dame Graduate School of Business, 1974; professional: partner, Historic Souder's of Grabill; majority owner of Souder's General Store; vice president, Our Country Home, fixture manufacturing business; attends Emmanuel Community Church; served as economic development liaison for then-Representative Dan Coats (IN–4th District); appointed Republican staff director of the House Select Committee on Children, Youth and Families, 1984; legislative director and deputy chief of staff for former Senator Coats; member: Grabill Chamber of Commerce; former head of Congressional Action Committee of Ft. Wayne Chamber of Commerce; married: the former Diane Zimmer, 1974; children: Brooke, Nathan, and Zachary; committees: Education and Labor; Homeland Security; Oversight and Government Reform; elected to the 104th Congress; reelected to each succeeding Congress.

Office Listings

http://www.house.gov/souder

2231 Rayburn House Office Building, Washington, DC 20515 .... (202) 225–4436
Chief of Staff.—Renee Howell. FAX: 225–3479
Scheduler.—Kari Amstutz.
1300 South Harrison, Room 3105, Fort Wayne, IN 46802 .... (260) 424–3041
District Director.—Derek Pillie.
320 North Chicago Avenue, Suite 9B, Goshen, IN 46528 .... (574) 533–5802
700 Park Avenue, The Boathouse, Suite D, Winona Lake, IN 46590 .... (574) 269–1940

Counties: ALLEN (part), DEKALB, ELKHART (part), KOSCIUSKO, LAGRANGE, NOBLE, STEUBEN, WHITLEY. Population (2000), 675,617.

ZIP Codes: 46502, 46504, 46506–08, 46510, 46516, 46524, 46526–28, 46538–40, 46542–43, 46550, 46553, 46555, 46562, 46565–67, 46571, 46573, 46580–82, 46590, 46701, 46703–06, 46710, 46721, 46723, 46725, 46730, 46732, 46737–38, 46741–43, 46746–48, 46750, 46755, 46760–61, 46763–65, 46767, 46771, 46773–74, 46776–77, 46779, 46783–89, 46793–99, 46801–09, 46814–16, 46818–19, 46825, 46835, 46845, 46850–69, 46885, 46895–99, 46910, 46962, 46975, 46982

* * *

FOURTH DISTRICT

STEVE BUYER, Republican, of Monticello, IN; born in Rensselaer, IN, November 26, 1958; education: graduated, North White High School, 1976; B.S., business administration, The Citadel, 1980; J.D., Valparaiso University School of Law, 1984; admitted to the Virginia and Indiana bars; professional: U.S. Army Judge Advocate General Corps, 1984–87; assigned Deputy to the Attorney General of Indiana, 1987–88; family law practice, 1988–92; U.S. Army Reserves, 1980–present (major); legal counsel, 22nd Theatre Army in Operations Desert Shield and Desert Storm; married: to the former Joni Lynn Geyer; children: Colleen and Ryan; co-chair, National Guard and Reserve Components Caucus; committees: Energy and Commerce; Veterans' Affairs; Assistant Whip; elected to the 103rd Congress, November 3, 1992; reelected to each succeeding Congress.

Office Listings

http://www.house.gov/buyer

2230 Rayburn House Office Building, Washington, DC 20515 .... (202) 225–5037
Chief of Staff.—Mike Copher.
Executive Assistant.—Anjulen Anderson.
Legislative Director.—Myrna Dugan.
Press Secretary.—Laura Zuckerman.
148 North Perry Road, Plainfield, IN 46168 .... (317) 838–0404
District Director.—Jim Huston.
100 South Main Street, Monticello, IN 47960 .... (574) 583–9819
1801 I Street, Bedford, IN 47421 .... (812) 277–9590

Counties: BOONE, CLINTON, FOUNTAIN (part), HENDRICKS, JOHNSON (part), LAWRENCE (part), MARION (part), MONROE (part), MONTGOMERY, MORGAN, TIPPECANOE, WHITE (part). Population (2000), 675,617.

ZIP Codes: 46035, 46039, 46041, 46049–50, 46052, 46057–58, 46060, 46065, 46067, 46069, 46071, 46075, 46077, 46102–03, 46106, 46111–13, 46118, 46120–23, 46125, 46131, 46142–43, 46147, 46149, 46151, 46157–58, 46160, 46165–

68, 46172, 46175, 46180–81, 46183–84, 46214, 46221, 46224, 46231, 46234, 46241, 46254, 46268, 46278, 46920, 46923, 46979, 47108, 47260, 47264, 47403–04, 47420–21, 47429–30, 47433, 47436–37, 47446, 47451, 47456, 47460, 47462–64, 47467, 47470, 47901–07, 47909, 47916, 47918, 47920, 47923–24, 47929–30, 47932–41, 47944, 47949, 47952, 47954–55, 47958–60, 47962, 47965, 47967–68, 47970–71, 47978, 47980–81, 47983, 47987–90, 47992, 47994–96

* * *

FIFTH DISTRICT

DAN BURTON, Republican, of Indianapolis, IN; born in Indianapolis, June 21, 1938; education: graduated, Shortridge High School, 1956; Indiana University, 1956–57; Cincinnati Bible Seminary, 1958–60; served in the U.S. Army, 1957–58; U.S. Army Reserves, 1958–64; businessman, insurance and real estate firm owner since 1968; served, Indiana House of Representatives, 1967–68 and 1977–80; Indiana State Senate, 1969–70 and 1981–82; president: Volunteers of America, Indiana Christian Benevolent Association, Committee for Constitutional Government, and Family Support Center; member, Jaycees; 33rd degree Mason, Scottish rite division; married the former Barbara Jean Logan, 1959 (deceased, 2002); three children: Kelly, Danielle Lee, and Danny Lee II; remarried: Dr. Samia Tawii, 2006; committees: Foreign Affairs; Oversight and Government Reform; elected on November 2, 1982, to the 98th Congress; reelected to each succeeding Congress.

Office Listings

http://www.house.gov/burton

2308 Rayburn House Office Building, Washington, DC 20515 .... (202) 225–2276
Chief of Staff.—Mark Walker. FAX: 225–0016
Scheduler / Office Manager.—Diane Menorca.
Press Secretary.—Clark G. Rehme.
8900 Keystone at the Crossing, Suite 1050, Indianapolis, IN 46240 .... (317) 848–0201
District Director.—Rick Wilson.
209 South Washington Street, Marion, IN 46952 .... (765) 662–6770

Counties: GRANT, HAMILTON, HANCOCK, HOWARD (part), HUNTINGTON, JOHNSON (part), MARION (part), MIAMI, SHELBY, TIPTON, WABASH. Population (2000), 675,794.

ZIP Codes: 46030–34, 46036, 46038, 46040, 46045, 46047, 46049, 46055, 46060–61, 46064, 46068–70, 46072, 46074, 46076–77, 46082, 46110, 46115, 46117, 46124, 46126, 46129–31, 46140, 46143, 46148, 46150, 46154, 46161–63, 46176, 46182, 46184, 46186, 46217, 46220, 46226–27, 46229, 46236–37, 46239–40, 46250, 46256, 46259–60, 46280, 46290, 46307, 46347, 46355, 46379–80, 46702, 46713–14, 46725, 46750, 46766, 46770, 46783, 46787, 46792, 46901–04, 46910–11, 46914, 46919, 46921, 46926, 46928–30, 46932–33, 46936–38, 46940–41, 46943, 46946, 46951–53, 46957–59, 46962, 46965, 46970–71, 46974–75, 46979–80, 46982, 46984, 46986–87, 46989–92, 46995, 47234, 47246, 47272, 47342, 47384

* * *

SIXTH DISTRICT

MIKE PENCE, Republican, of Columbus, IN; born in Columbus, June 7, 1959; education: Hanover College, 1981; J.D., Indiana University School of Law, 1986; professional: former Republican nominee for the U.S. House of Representatives in the 2nd District in 1988 and 1990; President, Indiana Policy Review Foundation, 1991–93; radio broadcaster: the Mike Pence Show, syndicated statewide in Indiana; married: Karen; children: Michael, Charlotte, and Audrey; committees: Foreign Affairs; Judiciary; elected to the 107th Congress on November 7, 2000; reelected to each succeeding Congress.

Office Listings

http://mikepence.house.gov

426 Cannon House Office Building, Washington, DC 20515 .... (202) 225–3021
Chief of Staff.—Bill Smith. FAX: 225–3382
Legislative Director.—LeAnne Holdman.
Press Secretary.—Matt Lloyd.
Executive Assistant.—Jennifer Pavlik.
1134 Meridian Street, Anderson, IN 46016 .... (765) 640–2919
District Director.—Lani Czarniecki.

Counties: ALLEN (part), ADAMS, BARTHOLOMEW (part), BLACKFORD, DEARBORN (part), DECATUR, DELAWARE, FAYETTE, FRANKLIN, HENRY, JAY, JOHNSON (part), MADISON, RANDOLPH, RUSH, SHELBY (part), UNION, WAYNE, WELLS. Population (2000), 675,669.

ZIP Codes: 46001, 46011–18, 46036, 46040, 46044, 46048, 46051, 46056, 46063–64, 46070, 46104, 46110, 46115, 46124, 46126–27, 46131, 46133, 46140, 46142, 46144, 46146, 46148, 46150–51, 46155–56, 46160–62, 46164, 46173, 46176,

46181–82, 46186, 46711, 46714, 46731, 46733, 46740, 46745, 46750, 46759, 46766, 46769–70, 46772–73, 46777–78, 46780–83, 46791–92, 46797–98, 46809, 46816, 46819, 46928, 46952–53, 46989, 46991, 47003, 47006, 47010, 47012, 47016, 47022, 47024–25, 47030, 47035–37, 47060, 47201, 47203, 47225–26, 47234, 47240, 47244, 47246, 47261, 47263, 47265, 47272, 47280, 47283, 47302–08, 47320, 47322, 47324–27, 47330–31, 47334–42, 47344–46, 47348, 47351–62, 47366–71, 47373–75, 47380–88, 47390, 47392–94, 47396, 47448

* * *

SEVENTH DISTRICT

JULIA CARSON, Democrat, of Indianapolis, IN; born in Louisville, KY, July 8, 1938; education: graduated, Crispus Attucks High School, Indianapolis, IN, 1955; attended: Martin University, Indianapolis, IN; Indiana University-Purdue University at Indianapolis; professional: manager and businesswoman; Indiana House of Representatives, 1972–76; Indiana State Senate, 1976–90; as Indianapolis center township trustee, 1990–96, she targeted fraud and waste to eliminate the city's $20-million debt; twice named Woman of the Year by the *Indianapolis Star*; children: two; committees: Financial Services; Transportation and Infrastructure; elected on November 5, 1996, to the 105th Congress; reelected to each succeeding Congress.

Office Listings

http://www.juliacarson.house.gov

2455 Rayburn House Office Building, Washington, DC 20515 .... (202) 225–4011
Deputy Chief of Staff.—Deron Roberson. FAX: 225–5633
Legislative Director.—Marti Thomas.
Legislative Assistants: Mia Clarkson, Hilary Swab, Sara Williams.
Executive Assistant.—Aarti Nayak.
300 East Fall Creek Parkway, Suite 300, Indianapolis, IN 46205 .... (317) 283–6516
Chief of Staff.—S. Sargent ''Sarge'' Visher.

Counties: MARION COUNTY. City of Indianapolis, township of Center, parts of the townships of Decatur, Lawrence, Perry, Pike, Warren, Washington, and Wayne, included are the cities of Beech Grove and Lawrence. Population (2000), 675,456.

ZIP Codes: 46107, 46160, 46201–09, 46211, 46214, 46216–22, 46224–31, 46234–35, 46237, 46239–42, 46244, 46247, 46249, 46251, 46253–55, 46260, 46266, 46268, 46274–75, 46277–78, 46282–83, 46285, 46291, 46295–96, 46298

* * *

EIGHTH DISTRICT

BRAD ELLSWORTH, Democrat, of Evansville, IN; born in Jasper, IN, September 11, 1958; graduated from William Henry Harrison High School, Evansville, IN, 1979; bachelor's degree in Sociology, Indiana State University–Evansville, 1981; M.B.A. in Criminology, Indiana State University, 1993; sheriff, Vanderburgh County Sheriff's Department, 1999–2006; married the former Beth Wannamueller; one daughter: Andrea; committees: Agriculture; Armed Services; Small Business; elected to the 110th Congress on November 7, 2006.

Office Listings

http://www.house.gov/ellsworth

513 Cannon House Office Building, Washington, DC 20515 .... (202) 225–4636
Chief of Staff.—Cori Smith. FAX: 225–3284
Press Secretary.—Liz Farrar.
Legislative Director.—Jed D'Ercole.
Executive Assistant.—Laura Kirtley.
101 Northwest Martin Luther King, Jr. Boulevard, Room 124, Evansville, IN 47708 .... (812) 465–6484
Deputy Chief of Staff.—Jay Howser.
901 Wabash Avenue, Suite 140, Terre Haute, IN 47807 .... (812) 232–0523

Counties: CLAY, DAVIESS, FOUNTAIN (part), GIBSON, GREENE, PARKE, PIKE, POSEY, PUTNAM, SULLIVAN, VANDERBURGH, VERMILLION, VIGO, WARREN, WARRICK. Population (2000), 675,564.

ZIP Codes: 46105, 46120–21, 46128, 46135, 46165–66, 46170–72, 46175, 47403–04, 47424, 47427, 47429, 47431–33, 47438–39, 47441, 47443, 47445–46, 47449, 47453, 47455–57, 47459–60, 47462, 47465, 47469–71, 47501, 47512, 47516, 47519, 47522–24, 47527–29, 47535, 47537, 47541–42, 47553, 47557–58, 47561–62, 47564, 47567–68, 47573, 47578, 47581, 47584–85, 47590–91, 47596–98, 47601, 47610–14, 47616, 47618–20, 47629–31, 47633, 47637–40, 47647–49, 47654, 47660, 47665–66, 47670, 47683, 47701–06, 47708, 47710–16, 47719–22, 47724–25, 47727–28, 47730–37, 47739–41, 47744, 47747, 47750, 47801–05, 47807–09, 47811–12, 47830–34, 47836–38, 47840–42, 47845–66, 47868–72, 47874–76, 47878–82, 47884–85, 47917–18, 47921, 47928, 47932, 47952, 47966, 47969–70, 47974–75, 47982, 47987, 47989, 47991–93

* * *

NINTH DISTRICT

BARON P. HILL, Democrat, of Seymour, IN; born in Seymour, June 23, 1953; education: graduated, Seymour High School; B.A. in history, Furman University, Greenville, SC, 1975; professional: ran an insurance and real estate business in Seymour; Indiana House of Representatives, 1982–90; Executive Director to the Indiana Student Assistance Commission, 1992; financial analyst with Merrill Lynch; named to the Indiana Basketball Hall of Fame, 2000; participated in the Elks Club, American Red Cross, and Seymour Chamber of Commerce; former president, Seymour Jaycees; former Communications Co-Chair, Blue Dog Coalition; former member, New Democrat Coalition; named Chief Deputy Whip, 108th Congress; member: First United Methodist Church, Seymour, IN; married: Betty Schepman Hill; children: Jennifer, Cara and Elizabeth; committees: Energy and Commerce; Science and Technology; elected to the 106th Congress in November, 1998; reelected to the 107th and 108th Congresses; elected to the 110th Congress on November 7, 2006.

Office Listings

http://www.baronhill.house.gov

223 Cannon House Office Building, Washington, DC 20515 .... (202) 225–5315
Chief of Staff.—Ryan Guthrie. FAX: 226–6866
Scheduler.—Joel Riethmiller.
Press Secretary.—Katie Moreau.
Legislative Director.—Lori Pepper.
279 Quartermaster Drive, Jeffersonville, IN 47130 .... (812) 288–1321
District Director.—John Zody.
320 West 8th Street, Suite 114, Bloomington, IN 47404 .... (812) 336–3000

Counties: BARTHOLOMEW (part), BROWN, CLARK, CRAWFORD, DEARBORN (part), DUBOIS, FLOYD, HARRISON, JACKSON, JEFFERSON, MONROE (part), OHIO, ORANGE, PERRY, RIPLEY, SCOTT, SPENCER, SWITZERLAND, WASHINGTON. Population (2000), 675,599.

ZIP Codes: 46151, 46160, 46164, 46181, 47001, 47006, 47011, 47017–23, 47025, 47031–34, 47037–43, 47102, 47104, 47106–08, 47110–12, 47114–20, 47122–26, 47129–47, 47150–51, 47160–67, 47170, 47172, 47174, 47177, 47199, 47201–03, 47220, 47223–24, 47227–32, 47235–36, 47240, 47243–45, 47247, 47249–50, 47260, 47264–65, 47270, 47273–74, 47281–83, 47401–08, 47426, 47432, 47434–36, 47448, 47452, 47454, 47458, 47462, 47468–69, 47513–15, 47520–21, 47523, 47525, 47527, 47531–32, 47536–37, 47541–42, 47545–47, 47549–52, 47556, 47564, 47574–77, 47579–81, 47586, 47588, 47590, 47601, 47611, 47615, 47617, 47634–35, 47637

IOWA

(Population 2000, 2,926,324)

SENATORS

CHARLES E. GRASSLEY, Republican, of Cedar Falls, IA; born in New Hartford, IA, September 17, 1933; education: graduated, New Hartford Community High School, 1951; B.A., University of Northern Iowa, 1955; M.A., University of Northern Iowa, 1956; doctoral studies, University of Iowa, 1957–58; professional: farmer; member: Iowa State Legislature, 1959–74; Farm Bureau; State and County Historical Society; Masons; Baptist Church; and International Association of Machinists, 1962–71; co-chair, International Narcotics Control Caucus; married: the former Barbara Ann Speicher, 1954; children: Lee, Wendy, Robin Lynn, Michele Marie; committees: Agriculture, Nutrition, and Forestry; Budget; Finance; Judiciary; Joint Committee on Taxation; elected to the 94th Congress, November 5, 1974; reelected to the 95th and 96th Congresses; elected to the U.S. Senate, November 4, 1980; reelected to each succeeding Senate term.

Office Listings

http://grassley.senate.gov

135 Hart Senate Office Building, Washington, DC 20510 .... (202) 224–3744
Chief of Staff.—David Young. FAX: 224–6020
Director of Communications.—Jill Kozeny.
Legislative Director.—Kolan Davis.
721 Federal Building, 210 Walnut Street, Des Moines, IA 50309 .... (515) 288–1145
State Administrator.—Robert Renaud.
206 Federal Building, 101 First Street, SE., Cedar Rapids, IA 52401 .... (319) 363–6832
120 Federal Courthouse Building, 320 Sixth Street, Sioux City, IA 51101 .... (712) 233–1860
210 Waterloo Building, 531 Commercial Street, Waterloo, IA 50701 .... (319) 232–6657
131 West 3rd Street, Suite 180, Davenport, IA 52801 .... (319) 322–4331
307 Federal Building, 8 South Sixth Street, Council Bluffs, IA 51501 .... (712) 322–7103

* * *

TOM HARKIN, Democrat, of Cumming, IA; born in Cumming, November 19, 1939; education: graduated, Dowling Catholic High School, Des Moines, IA; B.S., Iowa State University, Ames, 1962; U.S. Navy, 1962–67; military service: LCDR, U.S. Naval Reserves; LL.B., Catholic University of America, Washington, DC, 1972; admitted to the bar, Des Moines, IA, 1972; married: the former Ruth Raduenz, 1968; children: Amy and Jenny; committees: chair, Agriculture, Nutrition, and Forestry; Appropriations; Health, Education, Labor, and Pensions; Small Business and Entrepreneurship; elected to the 94th Congress on November 5, 1974; reelected to four succeeding Congresses; elected to the U.S. Senate on November 6, 1984; reelected to each succeeding Senate term.

Office Listings

http://harkin.senate.gov

731 Hart Senate Office Building, Washington, DC 20510 .... (202) 224–3254
Chief of Staff.—Brian Ahlberg. FAX: 224–9369
Communications Director.—Jennifer Mullin.
Federal Building, 210 Walnut Street, Room 733, Des Moines, IA 50309 .... (515) 284–4574
150 First Avenue, NE., Suite 370, Cedar Rapids, IA 52401 .... (319) 365–4504
1606 Brady Street, Suite 323, Davenport, IA 52801 .... (563) 322–1338
Federal Building, 320 Sixth Street, Room 110, Sioux City, IA 51101 .... (712) 252–1550
Federal Building, 350 West Sixth Street, Room 315, Dubuque, IA 52001 .... (563) 582–2130

REPRESENTATIVES

FIRST DISTRICT

BRUCE L. BRALEY, Democrat, of Waterloo, IA; born in Grinnell, IA, October 30, 1957; education: B.A., Iowa State University, Ames, IA, 1980; J.D., University of Iowa Law School, Iowa City, IA, 1983; professional: attorney, Dulton, Braun, Staack & Hellman, 1983–2006; married: Carolyn; children: Lisa, David and Paul; committees: Oversight and Government Reform; Small Business; Transportation and Infrastructure; elected to the 110th Congress on November 7, 2006.

Office Listings

http://www.house.gov/braley

1408 Longworth House Office Building, Washington, DC 20515 .... (202) 225–2911

Chief of Staff.—Sarah Benzing. FAX: 226–0757
501 Sycamore Street, Suite 623, Waterloo, IA 50703 .... (319) 287–3233
District Director.—Karen Erickson.
350 West Sixth Street, Suite 222, Dubuque, IA 52001 .... (563) 557–7789
209 West Fourth Street, Davenport, IA 52801 .... (563) 323–5988
District Director.—Pete DeKock.

Counties: BLACK HAWK, BREMER, BUCHANAN, BUTLER, CLAYTON, CLINTON, DELAWARE, DUBUQUE, FAYETTE, JACKSON, JONES, SCOTT. Population (2000), 585,302.

ZIP Codes: 50601–02, 50604–08, 50611, 50613–14, 50619, 50622–23, 50625–26, 50629, 50631, 50634, 50636, 50641, 50643–44, 50647–51, 50654–55, 50660, 50662, 50664–68, 50670–71, 50674, 50676–77, 50681–82, 50701–04, 50706–07, 50799, 52001–04, 52030–33, 52035–50, 52052–54, 52056–57, 52060, 52064–66, 52068–79, 52099, 52135, 52141–42, 52147, 52156–59, 52164, 52166, 52169, 52171, 52175, 52205, 52207, 52210, 52212, 52223, 52226, 52237, 52252, 52254, 52305, 52309–10, 52312, 52320–21, 52323, 52326, 52329–30, 52362, 52701, 52722, 52726–33, 52736, 52742, 52745–48, 52750–51, 52753, 52756–58, 52765, 52767–68, 52771, 52773–74, 52777, 52801–09

* * *

SECOND DISTRICT

DAVID LOEBSACK, Democrat, of Mt. Vernon, IA; born in Sioux City, IA, December 23, 1952; education: graduated, East High School, 1970; B.A., Iowa State University, 1974; M.A., Iowa State University, 1976; PhD., Political Science, University of California, Davis, 1985; professional: professor, Political Science, Cornell College, 1982–2006; married: Teresa Loebsack; four children; committees: Armed Services; Education and Labor; elected to the 110th Congress on November 7, 2006.

Office Listings

http://www.loebsack.house.gov

1513 Longworth House Office Building, Washington, DC 20515 .... (202) 225–6576
Legislative Director.—Kara Marchione FAX: 226–0757
Office Manager.—Jessica Woolley.
150 First Avenue, NE., Suite 375, Cedar Rapids, IA 52401 .... (319) 364–2288
125 South Dubuque Street, Iowa City, IA 52240–4003 .... (319) 351–0789

Counties: APPANOOSE, CEDAR, DAVIS, DES MOINES, HENRY, JEFFERSON, JOHNSON, LEE, LINN, LOUISA, MUSCATINE, VAN BUREN, WAPELLO, WASHINGTON, WAYNE. Population (2000), 585,241.

ZIP Codes: 50008, 50052, 50060, 50123, 50147, 50165, 50238, 52201–02, 52213–14, 52216, 52218–19, 52227–28, 52233, 52235, 52240–48, 52253, 52255, 52302, 52305–06, 52314, 52317, 52319–20, 52322–24, 52327–28, 52333, 52336–38, 52340–41, 52344, 52350, 52352–53, 52356, 52358–59, 52401–11, 52497–99, 52501, 52530–31, 52533, 52535–38, 52540, 52542, 52544, 52548–49, 52551, 52553–57, 52560, 52565–67, 52570–74, 52580–81, 52583–84, 52588, 52590, 52593–94, 52601, 52619–21, 52623–27, 52630–32, 52635, 52637–42, 52644–56, 52658–60, 52720–21, 52731, 52737–39, 52747, 52749, 52752, 52754–55, 52759–61, 52766, 52769, 52772, 52776, 52778

* * *

THIRD DISTRICT

LEONARD L. BOSWELL, Democrat, of Des Moines, IA; born in Harrison County, MO, January 10, 1934; education: graduated, Lamoni High School, 1952; B.A., Graceland College, Lamoni, IA, 1969; military service: lieutenant colonel, U.S. Army, 1956–76; awards: two Distinguished Flying Crosses, two Bronze Stars, Soldier's Medal; Iowa State Senate, 1984–96; Iowa State Senate President, 1992–96; lay minister, RLDS Church; member: American Legion, Disabled American Veterans of Foreign Wars, Iowa Farm Bureau, Iowa Cattlemen's Association, Graceland College Board of Trustees; Farmer's Co-op Grain and Seed Board of Directors, 1979–93 (president for 13 years); The Coalition (Blue Dogs); co-chair and member emeritus, Mississippi River Caucus; co-chair, Methamphetamine Caucus; married Darlene (Dody) Votava Boswell, 1955; three children: Cindy, Diana and Joe; committees: Agriculture; Transportation and Infrastructure; Permanent Select Committee on Intelligence; elected to the 105th Congress; reelected to each succeeding Congress.

Office Listings

http://boswell.house.gov

1427 Longworth House Office Building, Washington, DC 20515 .... (202) 225–3806
Chief of Staff.—E.H. "Ned" Michalek. FAX: 225–5608
Legislative Director/Communications Director.—Susan McAvoy.
Executive Assistant.—Sandy Carter.
300 East Locust Street, Suite 320, Des Moines, IA 50309 .... (515) 282–1909

District Director.—Sally Bowzer.

Counties: BENTON, GRUNDY, IOWA, JASPER, KEOKUK, LUCAS, MAHASKA, MARION, MONROE, POLK, POWESHIEK, TAMA. Population (2000), 585,305.

ZIP Codes: 50007, 50009, 50015, 50021, 50027–28, 50032, 50035, 50044, 50047, 50049, 50054, 50057, 50061–62, 50068, 50073, 50104, 50109, 50111–12, 50116, 50119, 50127, 50131, 50135–39, 50143, 50148, 50150–51, 50153, 50156–58, 50163, 50168–71, 50173, 50206–08, 50214, 50219, 50222, 50225–26, 50228, 50232, 50237–38, 50240, 50242–43, 50251–52, 50255–58, 50265–66, 50268, 50272, 50301–23, 50325, 50327–36, 50338–40, 50347, 50350, 50359–64, 50367–69, 50380–81, 50391–96, 50398, 50601, 50604, 50609, 50612–13, 50621, 50624, 50627, 50632, 50635, 50638, 50642–43, 50651–52, 50657, 50660, 50665, 50669, 50672–73, 50675, 50680, 50936, 50940, 50947, 50950, 50980–81, 52203–04, 52206, 52208–09, 52211, 52213, 52215, 52217, 52220–22, 52224–25, 52228–29, 52231–32, 52236, 52248–49, 52251, 52257, 52301, 52307–08, 52313, 52315–16, 52318, 52322, 52324–25, 52332, 52334–35, 52339, 52342, 52345–49, 52351, 52354–55, 52361, 52404, 52531, 52534, 52543, 52550, 52552, 52561–63, 52568–69, 52576–77, 52585–86, 52591, 52595

* * *

FOURTH DISTRICT

TOM LATHAM, Republican, of Alexander, IA; born in Hampton, IA, July 14, 1948; education: attended Alexander Community School; graduated Cal (Latimer) Community College, 1966; attended Wartburg College, 1966–67; Iowa State University, 1976–70; agriculture business major; professional: marketing representative, independent insurance agent, bank teller and bookkeeper; member and past president, Nazareth Lutheran Church; past chairman, Franklin County Extension Council; secretary, Republican Party of Iowa; 5th District representative, Republican State Central Committee; co-chairman, Franklin County Republican Central Committee; Iowa delegation whip; member: 1992 Republican National Convention, Iowa Farm Bureau Federation, Iowa Soybean Association, American Seed Trade Association, Iowa Corn Growers Association, Iowa Seed Association, Agribusiness Association of Iowa, I.S.U. Extension Citizens Advisory Council; married: Mary Katherine (Kathy), 1975; children: Justin, Jennifer, and Jill; committees: Appropriations; elected to the 104th Congress; reelected to each succeeding Congress.

Office Listings

http://www.house.gov/latham

2447 Rayburn House Office Building, Washington, DC 20515 .... (202) 225–5476
Chief of Staff.—Michael R. Gruber. FAX: 225–3301
Press Secretary.—James D. Carstensen.
Scheduler.—Amanda McDonnell.
1421 South Bell Avenue, Ames, IA 50010 .... (515) 232–2885
District Director.—Clarke Scanlon.
812 Highway 18 East, P.O. Box 532, Clear Lake, IA 50428 .... (641) 357–5225
Regional Representative.—Lois Clark.
1426 Central Avenue, Suite A, Fort Dodge, IA 50501 .... (515) 573–2738
Regional Representative.—Jim Oberhelman.

Counties: ALLAMAKEE, BOONE, CALHOUN, CERRO GORDO, CHICKASAW, DALLAS, EMMET, FLOYD, FRANKLIN, GREENE, HAMILTON, HANCOCK, HARDIN, HOWARD, HUMBOLDT, KOSSUTH, MADISON, MARSHALL, MITCHELL, PALO ALTO, POCAHONTAS, STORY, WARREN, WEBSTER, WINNEBAGO, WINNESHIEK, WORTH, WRIGHT. Population (2000), 585,305.

ZIP Codes: 50001, 50003, 50005–06, 50010–14, 50028, 50031, 50033–34, 50036–41, 50046–47, 50050–51, 50055–56, 50058–59, 50061, 50063–64, 50066, 50069–72, 50075, 50078, 50101–02, 50105–07, 50109, 50118, 50120, 50122, 50124–26, 50129–30, 50132, 50134, 50139, 50141–42, 50145–46, 50148–49, 50151–52, 50154–56, 50158, 50160–62, 50166–67, 50201, 50206, 50210–13, 50217–18, 50220, 50222–23, 50225, 50227, 50229–31, 50233–36, 50239–41, 50244, 50246–49, 50252, 50257–59, 50261, 50263, 50266, 50269, 50271, 50273, 50276, 50278, 50320, 50323, 50325, 50401–02, 50420–21, 50423–24, 50426–28, 50430–36, 50438–41, 50444, 50446–61, 50464–73, 50475–84, 50501, 50510–11, 50514–33, 50536, 50538–46, 50548, 50551–52, 50554, 50556–63, 50566, 50568–71, 50573–75, 50577–79, 50581–83, 50586, 50590–91, 50593–95, 50597–99, 50601, 50603, 50605, 50609, 50616, 50619–21, 50625, 50627–28, 50630, 50632–33, 50635–36, 50645, 50653, 50658–59, 50661, 50672, 50674, 50680, 51334, 51342, 51344, 51358, 51364–65, 51433, 51443, 51449, 51453, 51462, 51510, 52101, 52132–34, 52136, 52140, 52144, 52146, 52149, 52151, 52154–56, 52159–63, 52165, 52168, 52170–72

* * *

FIFTH DISTRICT

STEVE KING, Republican, of Odebolt, IA; born in Storm Lake, IA, May 28, 1949; education: graduated, Denison Community High School; attended Northwest Missouri State University, Maryville, MO, 1967–70; professional: agri-businessman; owner and operator of King Construction Company; public service: Iowa State Senate, 1996–2002; religion: Catholic; family: married to Marilyn; children: David, Michael, and Jeff; committees: Agriculture; Judiciary;

Small Business; elected to the 108th Congress on November 5, 2002; reelected to each succeeding Congress.

Office Listings

http://www.house.gov/steveking

1609 Longworth House Office Building, Washington, DC 20515 .... (202) 225–4426
Chief of Staff.—Brenna Findley. FAX: 225–3193
Legislative Director.—Paula Steiner.
Scheduler / Executive Assistant.—Sarah Stewart.
Communications Director.—Brandon Lerch.
526 Nebraska Street, Sioux City, IA 51101 .... (712) 224–4692
40 Pearl Street, Council Bluffs, IA 51503 .... (712) 325–1404
208 West Taylor Street, Creston, IA 50801 .... (641) 782–2495
306 North Grand Avenue, Spencer, IA 51301 .... (712) 580–7754
800 Oneida Street, Suite A, Storm Lake, IA 50588 .... (712) 732–4197

Counties: ADAIR, ADAMS, AUDUBON, BUENA VISTA, CARROLL, CASS, CHEROKEE, CLARKE, CLAY, CRAWFORD, DECATUR, DICKINSON, FREMONT, GUTHRIE, HARRISON, IDA, LYON, MILLS, MONONA, MONTGOMERY, O'BRIEN, OSCEOLA, PAGE, PLYMOUTH, POTTAWATTAMIE, RINGGOLD, SAC, SHELBY, SIOUX, TAYLOR, UNION, WOODBURY. Population (2000), 584,967.

ZIP Codes: 50002, 50020, 50022, 50025–26, 50029, 50042, 50048, 50058, 50065, 50067, 50070, 50074, 50076, 50103, 50108, 50110, 50115, 50117, 50119, 50123, 50128, 50133, 50140, 50144, 50146, 50149, 50151, 50155, 50164, 50174, 50210, 50213, 50216, 50222, 50233, 50250, 50254, 50257, 50262, 50264, 50273–77, 50510, 50535, 50565, 50567–68, 50576, 50583, 50585, 50588, 50592, 50801, 50830–31, 50833, 50835–37, 50839–43, 50845–49, 50851, 50853–54, 50857–64, 51001–12, 51014–16, 51018–20, 51022–31, 51033–41, 51044–56, 51058–63, 51101–06, 51108–09, 51111, 51201, 51230–32, 51234–35, 51237–50, 51301, 51331, 51333, 51338, 51340–41, 51343, 51345–47, 51350–51, 51354–55, 51357, 51360, 51363–64, 51366, 51401, 51430–33, 51436, 51439–52, 51454–55, 51458–61, 51463, 51465–67, 51501–03, 51510, 51520–21, 51523, 51525–37, 51540–46, 51548–49, 51551–66, 51570–73, 51575–79, 51591, 51593, 51601–03, 51630–32, 51636–40, 51645–54, 51656

KANSAS

(Population 2000, 2,688,418)

SENATORS

SAM BROWNBACK, Republican, of Topeka, KS; born in Garrett, KS, September 12, 1956; education: graduated from Prairie View High School, 1974; B.S., with honors, Kansas State University, Manhattan, KS, 1978; J.D., University of Kansas, Lawrence, 1982; professional: Kansas Bar; attorney, broadcaster, teacher; U.S. House of Representatives, 1994–96; State Secretary of Agriculture, 1986–93; White House Fellow, Office of the U.S. Trade Representative, 1990–91; member: Topeka Fellowship Council, Kansas Bar Association, Kansas State University and Kansas University alumni associations; married: the former Mary Stauffer, 1982; children: Abby, Andy, Liz, Mark and Jenna; committees: Appropriations; Judiciary; Joint Economic Committee; elected to the U.S. Senate in November, 1996, to fill the remainder of the vacancy caused by the resignation of Senator Bob Dole; reelected to each succeeding Senate term.

Office Listings

http://brownback.senate.gov

303 Hart Senate Office Building, Washington, DC 20510 .... (202) 224–6521
Chief of Staff / Legislative Director.—Glen Chambers. FAX: 228–1265
Scheduler.—Sally Berwick.
Communications Director.—Brian Hart.
612 South Kansas, Topeka, KS 66603 .... (785) 233–2503
Kansas Scheduler.—Denise Coatney.
1001–C North Broadway, Pittsburg, KS 66762 .... (316) 231–6040
Grant Director.—Anne Emerson.
245 North Waco, Suite 240, Wichita, KS 67202 .... (620) 264–8066
State Director.—Chuck Alderson.
11111 West 95th, Suite 245, Overland Park, KS 66214 .... (913) 492–6378
Deputy Chief of Staff.—George Stafford.
811 North Main, Suite A, Garden City, KS 67846 .... (620) 275–1124
Regional Director.—Dennis Mesa.

* * *

PAT ROBERTS, Republican, of Dodge City, KS; born in Topeka, KS, April 20, 1936; education: graduated, Holton High School, Holton, KS, 1954; B.S., journalism, Kansas State University, Manhattan, KS, 1958; professional: captain, U.S. Marine Corps, 1958–62; editor and reporter, Arizona newspapers, 1962–67; aide to Senator Frank Carlson, 1967–68; aide to Representative Keith Sebelius, 1969–80; U.S. House of Representatives, 1980–96; founding member: bipartisan Caucus on Unfunded Mandates, House Rural Health Care Coalition; shepherded the 1996 Freedom to Farm Act through the House and Senate; awards: honorary American Farmer, Future Farmers of America; 1993 Wheat Man of the Year, Kansas Association of Wheat Growers; Golden Carrot Award, Public Voice; Golden Bulldog Award, Watchdogs of the Treasury; numerous Guardian of Small Business awards, National Federation of Independent Business; 1995 Dwight D. Eisenhower Medal, Eisenhower Exchange Fellowship; 2001 U.S. Marine Corps Semper Fidelis Award; married: the former Franki Fann, 1969; children: David, Ashleigh, and Anne-Wesley; committees: Agriculture, Nutrition, and Forestry; Finance; Health Education, Labor, and Pensions; Select Committee on Ethics; elected to the U.S. Senate in November, 1996; reelected to each succeeding Senate term.

Office Listings

http://roberts.senate.gov

109 Hart Senate Office Building, Washington, DC 20510 .... (202) 224–4774
Chief of Staff.—Jackie Cottrell. FAX: 224–3514
Legislative Director.—Mike Seyfert.
Scheduler.—Maggie Ward.
Communications Director.—Sarah Little.
100 Military Plaza, P.O. Box 550, Dodge City, KS 67801 .... (620) 227–2244
District Director.—Debbie Pugh.
155 North Market Street, Suite 120, Wichita, KS 67202 .... (316) 263–0416
District Director.—Karin Wisdom.
Frank Carlson Federal Building, 444 SE Quincy, Room 392, Topeka, KS 66683 .... (785) 295–2745
District Director.—Gilda Lintz.
11900 College Boulevard, Suite 203, Overland Park, KS 66210 .... (913) 451–9343
State Director.—Chad Tenpenny.

REPRESENTATIVES

FIRST DISTRICT

JERRY MORAN, Republican, of Hays, KS; born in Great Bend, KS, May 29, 1954; education: B.S., economics, 1976, and J.D., 1981, University of Kansas; M.B.A. candidate, Fort Hays State University; partner, Jeter and Moran, Attorneys at Law, Hays, KS; former bank officer and university instructor; represented 37th District in Kansas Senate, 1989–97, serving as vice president in 1993–95 and majority leader in 1995–97; Special Assistant Attorney General, State of Kansas, 1982–85; Deputy Attorney, Rooks County, 1987–95; governor, board of governors, University of Kansas School of Law, 1990 (vice president, 1993–94; president, 1994–95); member: board of directors, Kansas Chamber of Commerce and Industry, 1996–97; Hays Chamber of Commerce; Northwest Kansas and Ellis County bar associations; Phi Alpha Delta legal fraternity; Rotary Club; Lions International; board of trustees, Fort Hays State University Endowment Association; founding co-chair, Congressional Rural Caucus; co-chair, Dwight D. Eisenhower Memorial Commission; married: Robba Moran; children: Kelsey and Alex; committees: Agriculture; Transportation and Infrastructure; Veterans' Affairs; elected to the 105th Congress; reelected to each succeeding Congress.

Office Listings

http://www.house.gov/moranks01

2443 Rayburn House Office Building, Washington, DC 20515 .... (202) 225–2715
Chief of Staff.—Todd Novascore. FAX: 225–5124
Legislative Director.—Alex Richard.
Press Secretary.—Nicole Young.
Office Manager—Crystal Emel.
1200 Main Street, Suite 402, P.O. Box 249, Hays KS 67601–0249 .... (785) 628–6401
1 North Main, Suite 525, Hutchinson, KS 67504–1128 .... (620) 665–6138
119 West Iron Avenue, Salina, KS 67401 .... (785) 309–0572

Counties: Barber, Barton, Chase, Cheyenne, Clark, Clay, Cloud, Comanche, Decatur, Dickinson, Edwards, Ellis, Ellsworth, Finney, Ford, Geary (part), Gove, Graham, Grant, Gray, Greeley, Greenwood (part), Hamilton, Haskell, Hodgeman, Jewell, Kearny, Kiowa, Lane, Lincoln, Logan, Lyon, McPherson, Marion (part), Marshall, Meade, Mitchell, Morris, Morton, Nemaha (part), Ness, Norton, Osborne, Ottawa, Pawnee, Phillips, Pratt, Rawlins, Reno, Republic, Rice, Rooks, Rush, Russell, Saline, Scott, Seward, Sheridan, Sherman, Smith, Stafford, Stanton, Stevens, Thomas, Trego, Wabaunsee, Wallace, Washington, Wichita. Population (2000), 672,105.

ZIP Codes: 66401, 66403–04, 66406–08, 66411–13, 66423, 66427, 66431, 66438, 66441, 66501–02, 66507–08, 66514, 66518, 66523, 66526, 66534, 66536, 66538, 66541, 66544, 66547–48, 66610, 66614–15, 66801, 66830, 66833–35, 66838, 66840, 66843, 66845–46, 66849–51, 66853–54, 66858–62, 66864–66, 66868–70, 66872–73, 66901, 66930, 66932–33, 66935–46, 66948–49, 66951–53, 66955–56, 66958–64, 66966–68, 66970, 67009, 67020–21, 67028–29, 67035, 67053–54, 67057, 67059, 67061–63, 67065–66, 67068, 67070, 67073, 67104, 67107–09, 67112, 67114, 67124, 67127, 67134, 67138, 67143, 67151, 67155, 67335, 67401–02, 67410, 67416–18, 67420, 67422–23, 67425, 67427–28, 67430–32, 67436–39, 67441–52, 67454–60, 67464, 67466–68, 67470, 67473–76, 67478, 67480–85, 67487, 67490–92, 67501–02, 67504–05, 67510–16, 67518–26, 67529–30, 67543–48, 67550, 67552–54, 67556–57, 67559–61, 67563–68, 67570, 67572–76, 67578–79, 67581, 67583–85, 67601, 67621–23, 67625–29, 67631–32, 67634–35, 67637–40, 67642–51, 67653–61, 67663–65, 67667, 67669, 67671–75, 67701, 67730–41, 67743–45, 67748–49, 67751–53, 67756–58, 67761–62, 67764, 67801, 67831, 67834–42, 67844, 67846, 67849–51, 67853–55, 67857, 67859–65, 67867, 67869–71, 67876–80, 67882, 67901, 67905, 67950–54

* * *

SECOND DISTRICT

NANCY E. BOYDA, Democrat, of Topeka, KS; born in Clayton, MO, August 2, 1955; education: B.A., education and chemistry, William Jewell College, Liberty, MO, 1977; professional: analytical chemist and field inspector, Environmental Protection Agency; held management positions in several pharmaceutical companies, including Marion Laboratories; married: Steve Boyda; children: Leah Thrutchley, Ben Thrutchley, Steve Boyda, Brian Boyda, Andre Boyda, Renee Boyda, Jamie Boyda; committees: Agriculture; Armed Services; elected to the 110th Congress on November 7, 2006.

Office Listings

http://boyda.house.gov

1110 Longworth House Office Building, Washington, DC 20515 .... (202) 225–6601
Chief of Staff.—Shanan Guinn. FAX: 225–7986
Legislative Director.—Doug Matties.
Scheduler.—Allison Harvey.
Press Aide.—Thomas Seay.
510 SW 10th Avenue, Topeka, KS 66612 .... (785) 234–8111

District Director.—Jason Fizell.
The Stilwell Hotel, 701 North Broadway, Pittsburg, KS 66762 .... (620) 231–3011
Regional Representative.—Beth Bradrick.

Counties: ALLEN, ANDERSON, ATCHISON, BOURBON, BROWN, CHEROKEE, COFFEY, CRAWFORD, DONIPHAN, DOUGLAS (part), FRANKLIN, GEARY, JACKSON, JEFFERSON, LABETE, LEAVENWORTH, LINN, MIAMI, NEMAHA (part), NEOSHO, OSAGE, POTTAWATOMIE, RILEY, SHAWNEE, WILSON, WOODSON. Population (2000), 672,102.

ZIP Codes: 66002, 66006–08, 66010, 66012–17, 66020–21, 66023–27, 66032–33, 66035–36, 66039–50, 66052–54, 66056, 66058, 66060, 66064, 66066–67, 66070–73, 66075–80, 66083, 66086–88, 66090–91, 66093–95, 66097, 66109, 66112, 66401–04, 66407, 66409, 66413–20, 66422, 66424–29, 66431–32, 66434, 66436, 66439–40, 66442, 66449, 66451, 66502–03, 66505–06, 66509–10, 66512, 66515–17, 66520–24, 66527–28, 66531–40, 66542–44, 66546–50, 66552, 66554, 66601, 66603–12, 66614–22, 66624–26, 66628–29, 66636–37, 66642, 66647, 66652–53, 66667, 66675, 66683, 66692, 66699, 66701, 66710–14, 66716–17, 66720, 66724–25, 66728, 66732–36, 66738–43, 66746, 66748–49, 66751, 66753–63, 66767, 66769–73, 66775–83, 66834, 66839, 66849, 66852, 66854, 66856–57, 66864, 66868, 66870–71, 66933, 67047, 67330, 67332, 67335–37, 67341–42, 67351, 67354, 67356–57

* * *

THIRD DISTRICT

DENNIS MOORE, Democrat, of Lenexa, KS; born in Anthony, KS, November 8, 1945; education: Jefferson Elementary School, and Charles Curtis Intermediate School, Wichita, KS; B.A., University of Kansas, 1967; J.D., Washburn University of Law, 1970; professional: attorney; admitted to Kansas Bar, 1970, first practiced in Topeka, KS; Assistant Attorney General of Kansas, 1971–73; Johnson County District Attorney, 1977–89; Johnson County Community College Board of Trustees, 1993–99; member, American Legion; married: Stephene Moore; seven children: Todd, Scott, Andrew, Felicia Barge, Valerie Swearingen, Nathan Hansen, and Adam Hansen; military: U.S. Army, 2nd Lieutenant, 1970; U.S. Army Reserves, Captain, 1970–73; committees: Budget; Financial Services; elected to the 106th Congress; reelected to each succeeding Congress.

Office Listings

http://www.house.gov/moore

1727 Longworth House Office Building, Washington, DC 20515 .... (202) 225–2865
Chief of Staff.—Howard Bauleke. FAX: 225–2807
Scheduler.—Brandon Naylor.
Communications Director.—Rebecca Black.
8417 Santa Fe Drive, Room 101, Overland Park, KS 66212 .... (913) 383–2013
District Director.—Julie Merz.
500 State Avenue, Room 176, Kansas City, KS 66101 .... (913) 621–0832
901 Kentucky Street, #205, Lawrence, KS 66044 .... (785) 842–9313
Constituent Services Director.—Becky Fast.

Counties: DOUGLAS (part), JOHNSON, WYANDOTTE. Population (2000), 672,124.

ZIP Codes: 66006–07, 66012–13, 66018–19, 66026, 66030–31, 66035–36, 66044–47, 66049–51, 66053, 66061–64, 66071, 66077, 66083, 66085, 66092, 66101–06, 66109–13, 66115, 66117–19, 66160, 66201–27, 66250–51, 66276, 66282–83, 66285–86

* * *

FOURTH DISTRICT

TODD TIAHRT, Republican, of Goddard, KS; born in Vermillion, SD, June 15, 1951; education: attended South Dakota School of Mines and Technology; B.A., Evangel College, Springfield, MO, 1975; M.B.A., Southwest Missouri State, 1989; professional: proposal manager, The Boeing Company; married: the former Vicki Holland, 1976; children: Jessica, John, and Luke; committees: Appropriations; Permanent Select Committee on Intelligence; elected to the 104th Congress; reelected to each succeeding Congress.

Office Listings

http://www.house.gov/tiahrt

2441 Rayburn House Office Building, Washington, DC 20515 .... (202) 225–6216
Administrative Assistant.—Jeff Kahrs. FAX: 225–3489
Legislative Director.—Amy Claire Brusch.
Scheduler.—Melissa James.
Communications Director.—Chuck Knapp.
155 North Market Street, Suite 400, Wichita, KS 67202 .... (316) 262–8992

District Director.—Robert Noland.

Counties: BUTLER, CHAUTAUQUA, COWLEY, ELK, GREENWOOD (part), HARPER, HARVEY, KINGMAN, MONTGOMERY, SEDGWICK, SUMNER. Population (2000), 672,101.

ZIP Codes: 66840, 66842, 66853, 66863, 66866, 66870, 67001–05, 67008–10, 67012–13, 67016–20, 67022–26, 67030–31, 67035–39, 67041–42, 67045, 67047, 67049–52, 67055–56, 67058, 67060–62, 67067–68, 67070, 67072, 67074, 67101, 67103, 67105–08, 67110–12, 67114, 67117–20, 67122–23, 67131–33, 67135, 67137–38, 67140, 67142, 67144, 67146–47, 67149–52, 67154, 67156, 67159, 67201–21, 67226, 67230, 67235, 67260, 67275–78, 67301, 67333–35, 67337, 67340, 67344–47, 67349, 67351–53, 67355, 67360–61, 67363–64, 67522, 67543

KENTUCKY

(Population 2000, 4,041,769)

SENATORS

MITCH McCONNELL, Republican, of Louisville, KY; born in Colbert County, AL, February 20, 1942; education: graduated Manual High School, Louisville, 1960, president of the student body; B.A. with honors, University of Louisville, 1964, president of the student council, president of the student body of the College of Arts and Sciences; J.D., University of Kentucky Law School, 1967, president of student bar association, outstanding oral advocate; professional: attorney, admitted to the Kentucky bar, 1967; chief legislative assistant to U.S. Senator Marlow Cook, 1968–70; Deputy Assistant U.S. Attorney General, 1974–75; Judge/Executive of Jefferson County, KY, 1978–84; chairman, National Republican Senatorial Committee, 1997–2000; chairman, Joint Congressional Committee on Inaugural Ceremonies, 1999–2001; Senate Majority Whip, 2002–06; Senate Republican Leader, 2007-present; married to Elaine Chao on February 6, 1993; children: Elly, Claire and Porter; committees: Agriculture, Nutrition, and Forestry; Appropriations; Rules and Administration; Select Committee on Intelligence; elected to the U.S. Senate on November 6, 1984; reelected to each succeeding Senate term.

Office Listings

http://mcconnell.senate.gov

361A Russell Senate Office Building, Washington, DC 20510 .... (202) 224–2541
Chief of Staff.—William H. Piper. FAX: 224–2499
Scheduler.—Stefanie Hagar.
Legislative Director.—Scott Raab.
Press Secretary.—Robert Steurer.
601 West Broadway, Suite 630, Louisville, KY 40202 .... (502) 582–6304
State Director.—Larry Cox.
1885 Dixie Highway, Suite 345, Fort Wright, KY 41011 .... (606) 578–0188
300 South Main Street, Suite 310, London, KY 40741 .... (606) 864–2026
Professional Arts Building, Suite 100, 2320 Broadway, Paducah, KY 42001 .... (270) 442–4554
771 Corporate Drive, Suite 108, Lexington, KY 40503 .... (606) 224–8286
Federal Building, Room 102, 241 Main Street, Bowling Green, KY 42101 .... (270) 781–1673

* * *

JIM BUNNING, Republican, of Southgate, KY; born in Southgate, October 23, 1931; education: graduated, St. Xavier High School, Cincinnati, OH, 1949; B.S., Xavier University, Cincinnati, OH, 1953; professional: baseball player, Hall of Fame; investment broker and agent; president, Jim Bunning Agency, Inc.; member of Kentucky State Senate (minority floor leader), 1979–83; member: Ft. Thomas City Council, 1977–79; appointed member, Ohio, Kentucky, and Indiana Regional Council of Governments, Cincinnati, OH; National Committeeman, Republican National Committee, 1983–92; appointed member, President's National Advisory Board on International Education Programs, 1984–88; member: board of directors of Kentucky Special Olympics, Ft. Thomas (KY) Lions Club, Brighton Street Center Community Action Group; married: the former Mary Catherine Theis, 1952; children: Barbara, Jim, Joan, Cathy, Bill, Bridgett, Mark, David and Amy; committees: Banking, Housing, and Urban Affairs; Budget; Energy and Natural Resources; Finance; elected to the 100th Congress, November 4, 1986; reelected to each succeeding Congress; elected to the U.S. Senate in November, 1998; reelected to each succeeding Senate term.

Office Listings

http://bunning.senate.gov

316 Hart Senate Office Building, Washington, DC 20515 .... (202) 224–4343
Personnel Assistant / Scheduler.—Kara Kirtley. FAX: 228–1373
Chief of Staff.—Blake Brickman.
Legislative Director.—Kim Taylor.
Press Secretary.—Michael Reynard.
1717 Dixie Highway, Suite 220, Fort Wright, KY 41011 .... (859) 341–2602
State Director.—Debbie McKinney.
The Federal Building, 423 Frederica Street, Room 305, Owensboro, KY 42301 ..... (270) 689–9085
717 Corporate Drive, Lexington, KY 40503 .... (606) 219–2239
1100 South Main Street, Suite 12, Hopkinsville, KY 42240 .... (270) 885–1212

REPRESENTATIVES

FIRST DISTRICT

ED WHITFIELD, Republican, of Hopkinsville, KY; born in Hopkinsville, May 25, 1943; education: graduated, Madisonville High School, Madisonville, KY; B.S., University of Kentucky, Lexington, 1965; J.D., University of Kentucky, 1969; attended American University's Wesley Theological Seminary, Washington, DC; military service: first lieutenant, U.S. Army Reserves, 1967–73; professional: attorney, private practice, 1970–79; vice president, CSX Corporation, 1979–90; admitted to bar: Kentucky, 1970, and Florida, 1993; began practice in 1970 in Hopkinsville, KY; member, Kentucky House, 1973, one term; married: Constance Harriman Whitfield; children: Kate; committees: Energy and Commerce; elected to the 104th Congress; reelected to each succeeding Congress.

Office Listings

2411 Rayburn House Office Building, Washington, DC 20515 .... (202) 225–3115
FAX: 225–3547
Chief of Staff.—John Halliwell.
Scheduler / Office Manager.—Jennifer Sutherland.
Legislative Director.—Lesley Stout.
1403 South Main Street, Hopkinsville, KY 42240 .... (270) 885–8079
District Director.—Michael Pape.
200 North Main, Suite F, Tompkinsville, KY 42167 .... (270) 487–9509
Field Representative.—Sandy Simpson.
222 First Street, Suite 206A, Henderson, KY 42420 .... (270) 826–4180
Field Representative.—Ed West.
100 Fountain Avenue, Room 104, Paducah, KY 42001 .... (270) 442–6901
Field Representative.—David Mast.

Counties: Adair, Allen, Ballard, Butler, Caldwell, Calloway, Carlisle, Casey, Christian, Clinton, Crittenden, Cumberland, Fulton, Graves, Henderson, Hickman, Hopkins, Lincoln (part), Livingston, Logan, Lyon, Marshall, McCracken, McLean, Metcalf, Monroe, Muhlenberg, Ohio (part), Russell, Simpson, Todd, Trigg, Union, Webster. Population (2000), 673,629.

ZIP Codes: 40009, 40328, 40437, 40442, 40448, 40464, 40484, 40489, 42001–03, 42020–25, 42027–29, 42031–33, 42035–41, 42044–45, 42047–51, 42053–56, 42058, 42060–61, 42063–64, 42066, 42069–71, 42076, 42078–79, 42081–88, 42101, 42104, 42120, 42122–24, 42129, 42133–35, 42140–41, 42150–51, 42153–54, 42164, 42166–67, 42170, 42201–04, 42206, 42209–211, 42214–17, 42219–21, 42223, 42232, 42234, 42236, 42240–41, 42251–52, 42254, 42256, 42261–62, 42265–67, 42273–74, 42276, 42280, 42283, 42286–88, 42301, 42320–28, 42330, 42332–34, 42337, 42339, 42344–45, 42347, 42349–50, 42352, 42354, 42356, 42367–69, 42371–72, 42374–76, 42402–04, 42406, 42408–11, 42413, 42419–20, 42431, 42436–37, 42440–42, 42444–45, 42450–53, 42455–64, 42516, 42528, 42539, 42541, 42544, 42565–67, 42602–03, 42629, 42642, 42711, 42715, 42717, 42720–21, 42728, 42731, 42733, 42735, 42740–43, 42746, 42749, 42753, 42759, 42786

* * *

SECOND DISTRICT

RON LEWIS, Republican, of Cecilia, KY; born in South Shore, KY, September 14, 1946; education: graduated, McKell High School, 1964; B.A., University of Kentucky, 1969; M.A., higher education, Morehead State University, 1981; U.S. Navy Officer Candidate School, 1972; laborer, Morehead State, Armco Steel Corporation; Kentucky Highway Department, Eastern State Hospital; sales for Ashland Oil; teacher, Watterson College, 1980; minister, White Mills Baptist Church; member, Elizabethtown Chamber of Commerce; past president, Hardin and Larue County jail ministry; member, Serverus Valley Ministerial Association; honored for his voting record by League of Private Property Rights, Council for Citizens Against Government Waste, National Federation of Independent Business; married: the former Kayi Gambill, 1966; children: Ronald Brent and Allison Faye; committees: Ways and Means; elected to the 104th Congress; reelected to each succeeding Congress.

Office Listings

http://www.house.gov/ronlewis

2418 Rayburn House Office Building, Washington, DC 20515 .... (202) 225–3501
Chief of Staff.—Daniel London.
Legislative Director.—Eric Bergren.
Press Secretary.—Mike Dodge.
Scheduler.—Lindy Salem.
1690 Ring Road, Suite 260, Elizabethtown, KY 42701 .... (270) 765–4360
District Administrator.—Daniel London.
Warren Co. Justice Ctr, 1001 Center St., Suite 300, Bowling Green, KY 42101 ..... (270) 842–9896
Owensboro, KY 42301 .... (270) 688–8858

Counties: BARREN, BRECKINRIDGE, BULLITT, DAVIESS, EDMONSON, GRAYSON, GREEN, HANCOCK, HARDIN, HART, JEFFERSON (part), LARUE, MARION, MEADE, NELSON, OHIO (part), SHELBY, SPENCER, TAYLOR, WARREN, WASHINGTON. Population (2000), 673,244.

ZIP Codes: 40003–04, 40008–09, 40012–13, 40018–20, 40022–23, 40033, 40037, 40040, 40046–49, 40051–52, 40057, 40060–63, 40065–69, 40071, 40076, 40078, 40104, 40107–11, 40115, 40117–19, 40121, 40129, 40140, 40142–46, 40150, 40152–53, 40155, 40157, 40159–62, 40164–65, 40170–71, 40175–78, 40219, 40229, 40245, 40272, 40291, 40299, 40328, 40330, 40342, 40448, 40468, 40601, 42101–04, 42122–23, 42127–31, 42133, 42141–42, 42152, 42156–57, 42159–60, 42163, 42166, 42170–71, 42201, 42206–07, 42210, 42251, 42257, 42259, 42270, 42274–75, 42283, 42285, 42301–04, 42320, 42327, 42333–34, 42338, 42343, 42347–49, 42351–52, 42355–56, 42361, 42364, 42366, 42368, 42370, 42375–78, 42701–02, 42712–13, 42716, 42718–19, 42721–22, 42724, 42726, 42728–29, 42732–33, 42740, 42743, 42746, 42748–49, 42754–55, 42757–58, 42762, 42764–65, 42776, 42782–84, 42788

* * *

THIRD DISTRICT

JOHN A. YARMUTH, Democrat, of Louisville, KY; born in Louisville, November 4, 1947; education: graduated, Atherton High School, Louisville, 1965; graduated, Yale University, New Haven, CT, 1969; professional: Legislative Aide for Kentucky Senator Marlow Cook 1971–74; publisher, *Louisville Today Magazine*, 1976–82; Associate Vice President of University Relations at the University of Louisville, 1983–86; Vice President of a local healthcare firm 1986–90; founder, editor and writer *LEO Newsweekly*, 1990–2005; Television host and commentator, 2003–05; awards: 2007 Spirit of Enterprise Award; Louisville Alzheimer's Association Person of the Year; World Dainty Champion; 16 Metro Louisville Journalism Awards for editorial and column writing; married: Cathy Yarmuth, 1981; child: Aaron; committees: Education and Labor; Oversight and Reform; elected to the 110th Congress on November 7, 2006.

Office Listings

http://www.house.gov/yarmuth

319 Cannon House Office Building, Washington, DC 20515 .... (202) 225–5401
Chief of Staff.—Julie Carr. FAX: 225–5776
Legislative Director.—Lillian Pace.
Press Secretary.—Stuart Perelmuter.
Scheduler.—Keidra King.
600 Martin Luther King, Jr. Place, Suite 216, Louisville, KY 40202 .... (502) 582–5129
District Director.—Carolyn Tandy.

Counties: JEFFERSON COUNTY. Population (2000), 674,032.

ZIP Codes: 40018, 40023, 40025, 40027, 40041, 40059, 40109, 40118, 40201–25, 40228–29, 40231–33, 40241–43, 40245, 40250–53, 40255–59, 40261, 40266, 40268–70, 40272, 40280–83, 40285, 40287, 40289–99

* * *

FOURTH DISTRICT

GEOFF DAVIS, Republican, of Hebron, KY; born October 26, 1958; education: attended public schools, West Pittsburgh, PA; B.S., U.S. Military Academy, West Point, NY, 1981; professional: U.S. Army, 1976–87; Assault Helicopter Flight Commander, 82nd Airborne Division; Army Ranger and Senior Parachutist; manufacturing consultant; founder, Republic Consulting, formerly known as Capstone, Incorporated, 1992–present; organizations: 82nd Airborne Association; American Legion volunteer chaplain; National Rifle Association; Northern Kentucky Chamber of Commerce; married: Pat; six children; committees: Armed Services; Financial Services; elected to the 109th Congress on November 2, 2004; reelected to the 110th Congress.

Office Listings

http://www.house.gov/geoffdavis

1108 Longworth House Office Building, Washington, DC 20515 .... (202) 225–3465
Chief of Staff / Legislative Director.—Justin Brasell. FAX: 225–0003
Scheduler / Office Manager.—Roberta Quis.
Communications Director.—Amanda Keating.
277 Buttermilk Pike, Fort Mitchell, KY 41017 .... (859) 426–0080
1405 Greenup Avenue, Suite 236, Ashland, KY 41101 .... (606) 324–9898
108 West Jefferson Street, La Grange, KY 40031 .... (502) 222–2233
201 Government Street, Kenton Commonwealth Center, Suite 102, Maysville, KY 41056 .... (606) 564–6004

400 North Main Street, City Building, Suite 145, Williamstown, KY 41097 .... (859) 824–3320

Counties: BATH (part), BOONE, BOYD, BRACKEN, CAMPBELL, CARROLL, CARTER, ELLIOTT, FLEMING, GALLATIN, GRANT, GREENUP, HARRISON, HENRY, KENTON, LEWIS, MASON, NICHOLAS, OLDHAM, OWEN, PENDLETON, ROBERTSON, SCOTT (part), TRIMBLE. Population (2000), 673,588.

ZIP Codes: 40006–07, 40010–11, 40014, 40019, 40026, 40031–32, 40036, 40045, 40050, 40055–59, 40068, 40070, 40075, 40077, 40241, 40245, 40311, 40324, 40346, 40350–51, 40353, 40355, 40358–61, 40363, 40366, 40370–71, 40374, 40379, 40601, 41001–08, 41010–12, 41014–19, 41022, 41030–31, 41033–35, 41037, 41039–46, 41048–49, 41051–56, 41059, 41061–65, 41071–76, 41080–81, 41083, 41085–86, 41091–99, 41101–02, 41105, 41121, 41128–29, 41132, 41135, 41139, 41141–44, 41146, 41149, 41164, 41166, 41168–69, 41171, 41173–75, 41179–81, 41183, 41189, 41472, 45275, 45277, 45298, 45999

* * *

FIFTH DISTRICT

HAROLD ROGERS, Republican, of Somerset, KY; born in Barrier, KY, December 31, 1937; education: graduated, Wayne County High School, 1955; attended Western Kentucky University, 1956–57; A.B., University of Kentucky, 1962; LL.B., University of Kentucky Law School, 1964; professional: lawyer, admitted to the Kentucky State bar, 1964; commenced practice in Somerset; member, North Carolina and Kentucky National Guard, 1957–64; associate, Smith and Blackburn, 1964–67; private practice, 1967–69; Commonwealth Attorney, Pulaski and Rockcastle Counties, KY, 1969–80; delegate, Republican National Convention, 1972, 1976, 1980, 1984, and 1988; Republican nominee for Lieutenant Governor, KY, 1979; past president, Kentucky Commonwealth Attorneys Association; member and past president, Somerset-Pulaski County Chamber of Commerce and Pulaski County Industrial Foundation; founder, Southern Kentucky Economic Development Council, 1986; member, Chowder and Marching Society, 1981–present; married the former Shirley McDowell, 1957; three children: Anthony, Allison, and John Marshall; committees: Appropriations; member, Republican Steering Committee; elected to the 97th Congress, November 4, 1980; reelected to each succeeding Congress.

Office Listings

http://www.house.gov/rogers

2406 Rayburn House Office Building, Washington, DC 20515 .... (202) 225–4601
Administrative Assistant.—Will Smith. FAX: 225–0940
Office Manager.—Julia Casey.
Communications Director.—Leslie Cupp.
551 Clifty Street, Somerset, KY 42501 .... (606) 679–8346
District Administrator.—Robert L. Mitchell.
601 Main Street, Hazard, KY 41701 .... (606) 439–0794
100 Resource Drive, Suite A, Prestonsburg, KY 41653 .... (606) 886–0844

Counties: BATH (part), BELL, BREATHITT, CLAY, FLOYD, HARLAN, JACKSON, JOHNSON, KNOTT, KNOX, LAUREL, LAWRENCE, LEE, LESLIE, LETCHER, MAGOFFIN, MARTIN, MCCREARY, MENIFEE, MORGAN, OWSLEY, PERRY, PIKE, PULASKI, ROCKCASTLE, ROWAN, WAYNE, WHITLEY, WOLFE. Population (2000), 673,670.

ZIP Codes: 40313, 40316–17, 40319, 40322, 40329, 40336–37, 40346, 40351, 40358, 40360, 40371, 40387, 40402–03, 40409, 40419, 40421, 40434, 40445, 40447, 40456, 40460, 40467, 40481, 40486, 40488, 40492, 40701–02, 40724, 40729–30, 40734, 40737, 40740–45, 40751, 40754–55, 40759, 40763, 40769, 40771, 40801, 40803, 40806–08, 40810, 40813, 40815–16, 40818–20, 40823–24, 40826–31, 40840, 40843–45, 40847, 40849, 40854–56, 40858, 40862–63, 40865, 40868, 40870, 40873–74, 40902–03, 40906, 40913–15, 40921, 40923, 40927, 40930, 40932, 40935, 40939–41, 40943–44, 40946, 40949, 40951, 40953, 40955, 40958, 40962, 40964–65, 40972, 40977, 40979, 40981–83, 40988, 40995, 40997, 40999, 41124, 41129, 41132, 41159–60, 41164, 41168, 41180, 41201, 41203–04, 41214, 41216, 41219, 41222, 41224, 41226, 41230–32, 41234, 41238, 41240, 41250, 41254–57, 41260, 41262–65, 41267–68, 41271, 41274, 41301, 41307, 41310–11, 41313–14, 41317, 41332–33, 41338–39, 41342, 41344, 41347–48, 41351–52, 41360, 41362, 41364–68, 41385–86, 41390, 41397, 41408, 41410, 41413, 41419, 41421–22, 41425–26, 41433, 41451, 41459, 41464–65, 41472, 41477, 41501–03, 41512–14, 41517, 41519–20, 41522, 41524, 41526–28, 41531, 41534–35, 41537–40, 41542–44, 41546–49, 41553–55, 41557–64, 41566–68, 41571–72, 41601–07, 41612, 41615–16, 41619, 41621–22, 41630–32, 41635–36, 41640, 41642–43, 41645, 41647, 41649–51, 41653, 41655, 41659–60, 41663, 41666–67, 41669, 41701–02, 41712–14, 41719, 41721–23, 41725, 41727, 41729, 41731, 41735–36, 41739–40, 41743, 41745–47, 41749, 41751, 41754, 41759–60, 41762–64, 41766, 41772–78, 41804, 41810, 41812, 41815, 41817, 41819, 41821–22, 41824–26, 41828, 41831–40, 41843–45, 41847–49, 41855, 41858–59, 41861–62, 42501–03, 42518–19, 42533, 42544, 42553, 42558, 42564, 42567, 42603, 42631, 42633–35, 42638, 42642, 42647, 42649, 42653

* * *

SIXTH DISTRICT

BEN CHANDLER, Democrat, of Woodford County, KY; born in Versailles, KY, September 12, 1959; education: B.A., History, University of Kentucky; J.D., University of Kentucky

College of Law; public service: elected Kentucky State Auditor, 1991; elected Kentucky Attorney General, 1995; reelected in 1999; Democratic nominee for Governor, 2003; religion: member of Pisgah Presbyterian Church; family: married to Jennifer; children: Lucie, Albert IV, and Branham; committees: Appropriations; Science and Technology; elected to the 108th Congress, by special election, on February 17, 2004; reelected to each succeeding Congress.

Office Listings

1504 Longworth House Office Building, Washington, DC 20515 .... (202) 225–4706
Chief of Staff.—Dennis Fleming, Jr. FAX: 225–2122
Legislative Director.—Jim Creevy.
Communications Director.—Jennifer Spalding.
1021 Majestic Street, Suite 280, Lexington, KY 40503 .... (859) 219–1366

Counties: ANDERSON, BOURBON, BOYLE, CLARK, ESTILL, FAYETTE, FRANKLIN, GARRARD, JESSAMINE, LINCOLN (part), MADISON, MERCER, MONTGOMERY, POWELL, SCOTT (part), WOODFORD. Population (2000), 673,626.

ZIP Codes: 40003, 40046, 40076, 40078, 40310–12, 40320, 40324, 40328, 40330, 40334, 40336–37, 40339–40, 40342, 40346–48, 40353, 40355–57, 40361–62, 40370, 40372, 40374, 40376, 40379–80, 40383–86, 40390–92, 40403–05, 40409–10, 40419, 40422–23, 40437, 40440, 40444–47, 40452, 40461, 40464, 40468, 40472–73, 40475–76, 40484, 40489, 40495, 40502–17, 40522–24, 40526, 40533, 40536, 40544, 40546, 40550, 40555, 40574–83, 40588, 40591, 40598, 40601–04, 40618–22, 41031, 41901–06, 42567

LOUISIANA

(Population 2000, 4,468,976)

SENATORS

MARY L. LANDRIEU, Democrat, of New Orleans, LA; born in Alexandria, VA, November 23, 1955; education: B.A., Louisiana State University, 1977; real estate broker, specializing in townhouse development; represented New Orleans House District 90 in Louisiana Legislature, 1979–87; State Treasurer, 1987–95; vice chair, Louisiana Council on Child Abuse; member, Business and Professional Women; majority council member, Emily's List; past national president, Women's Legislative Network; past vice president, Women Executives in State Government; delegate to every Democratic National Convention since 1980; married: E. Frank Snellings; children: Connor, and Mary Shannon; committees: Appropriations; Energy and Natural Resources; Homeland Security and Governmental Affairs; Small Business and Entrepreneurship; elected to the U.S. Senate on November 5, 1996; reelected to each succeeding Senate term.

Office Listings

http://landrieu.senate.gov

724 Hart Senate Office Building, Washington, DC 20510 .... (202) 224–5824
Chief of Staff.—Ron Faucheux. FAX: 224–9735
Scheduler.—Mufyn Lynn.
Communications Director.—Adam Sharp.
Legislative Director.—Janet Woodka.
Hale Boggs Federal Building, 500 Poydras Street, Room 1005, New Orleans, LA 70130 .... (504) 589–2427
U.S. Courthouse, 300 Fannin Street, Room 2240, Shreveport, LA 71101–3086 .... (318) 676–3085
U.S. Federal Court House, 707 Florida Street, Room 326, Baton Rouge, LA 70801 .. (225) 389–0395
Hibernia Tower, One Lakeshore Drive, Suite 1260, Lake Charles, LA 70629 .... (337) 436–6650

* * *

DAVID VITTER, Republican, of Metairie, LA; born in Metairie, May 3, 1961; education: Harvard University; Oxford University Rhodes Scholar; Tulane University School of Law; professional: attorney; adjunct law professor, Tulane and Loyola Universities; religion: Catholic; public service: Louisiana House of Representatives, 1992–99; U.S. House of Representatives, 1999–2005; awards: Alliance for Good Government ''Legislator of the Year''; Victims and Citizens Against Crime ''Outstanding Legislator'' and ''Lifetime Achievement Award''; married: Wendy Baldwin Vitter; children: Sophie, Lise, Airey, and Jack; committees: Commerce, Science, and Transportation; Environment and Public Works; Foreign Relations; Small Business and Entrepreneurship; Special Committee on Aging; elected to the U.S. Senate on November 2, 2004.

Office Listings

http://vitter.senate.gov

516 Hart Senate Office Building, Washington, DC 20510 .... (202) 224–4623
Chief of Staff.—Kyle Ruckert. FAX: 228–5061
Deputy Chief of Staff.—Tonya Newman.
2800 Veterans Boulevard, Suite 201, Metairie, LA 70002 .... (504) 589–2753
858 Convention Street, Baton Rouge, LA 70801 .... (225) 383–0331
1217 North 19th Street, Monroe, LA 71201 .... (318) 325–8120
2230 South MacArthur Street, Suite 4, Alexandria, LA 7130 .... (318) 448–0169
920 Pierremont Road, Suite 113, Shreveport, LA 71106 .... (318) 861–0437
3221 Ryan Street, Suite E, Lake Charles, LA 70601 .... (337) 436–0453
800 Lafayette Street, Suite 1200, Lafayette, LA 70501 .... (337) 262–6898

REPRESENTATIVES

FIRST DISTRICT

BOBBY JINDAL, Republican, of Baton Rouge, LA; born in Baton Rouge, June 10, 1971; education: B.S., Brown University, with honors, 1991; M. Litt, Oxford University, 1994; professional: secretary, Louisiana Department of Health and Hospitals, 1996–98; appointed executive director of the National Bipartisan Commission on the Future of Medicare, 1998; president, University of Louisiana system, 1999; appointed Assistant Secretary for Planning and Evaluation, Department of Health and Human Services by President George W. Bush on March 7,

2001; consultant for McKinsey & Company; religion: Catholic; married: the former Supriya Jolly; children: Selia Elizabeth, Shaan Robert and Slade Ryan; committees: Homeland Security; Natural Resources; elected to the 109th Congress on November 2, 2004; reelected to the 110th Congress.

Office Listings

http://www.house.gov/jindal

1205 Longworth House Office Building, Washington, DC 20515 .... (202) 225–3015
Chief of Staff.—Timmy Teepell. FAX: 226–0386
Legislative Director.—Sapna Delacourt.
Scheduler.—Whitney Hunt.
Deputy Communications Director.—Kim Allen.
3525 North Causeway Blvd., Suite 1020, Metairie, LA 70002 .... (504) 837–1259
District Director.—Luke Letlow.

Parishes: JEFFERSON (part), ORLEANS (part), ST. CHARLES (part), ST. TAMMANY, TANGIPAHOA, WASHINGTON. Population (2000), 638,355.

ZIP Codes: 70001–06, 70009–11, 70033, 70047, 70053, 70055–56, 70058, 70060, 70062, 70064–65, 70072, 70087, 70094, 70115, 70118–19, 70121–24, 70160, 70181, 70183–84, 70401–04, 70420, 70422, 70426–27, 70429, 70431, 70433–38, 70442–48, 70450–52, 70454–67, 70469–71

* * *

SECOND DISTRICT

WILLIAM J. JEFFERSON, Democrat, of New Orleans, LA; born in Lake Providence, LA, March 14, 1947; education: graduated, G.W. Griffin High School, Lake Providence, LA, 1965; B.A., Political Science and English, Southern University and A&M College, Baton Rouge, LA, 1969; J.D., Harvard Law School, Cambridge, MA, 1972; LL.M., Georgetown University, 1996; professional: admitted to the bar, New Orleans, LA, 1972; attorney, Jefferson, Bryan, Jupiter, Lewis and Blanson, New Orleans, LA; first lieutenant, U.S. Army, J.A.G. Corps, 1975; member, board of trustees, Greater St. Stephen's Baptist Church; Urban League of Greater New Orleans; Southern University Foundation Board; Louisiana State Senate, March, 1980 to January, 1991; family: married: the former Andrea Green in 1970; children: Jamila, Jalila, Jelani, Nailah, and Akilah; elected to the 102nd Congress; reelected to each succeeding Congress.

Office Listings

2113 Rayburn House Office Building, Washington, DC 20515 .... (202) 225–6636
Chief of Staff.—Eugene Green. FAX: 225–1988
Deputy Chief of Staff.—Roberta Hopkins.
Communications Director.—Remi Braden-Cooper.
1012 Hale Boggs Federal Building, 500 Poydras Street, New Orleans, LA 70130 .. (504) 589–2274
District Office Manager.—Stephanie Butler.
200 Derbigny Street, Suite 3200, Gretna, LA 70053 .... (504) 368–7019
Congressional Aide.—Ericka Edwards.

Parishes: JEFFERSON (part), ORLEANS (part). Population (2000), 638,562.

ZIP Codes: 70001, 70003, 70053–54, 70056, 70058, 70062–63, 70065, 70067, 70072–73, 70094, 70096, 70112–19, 70121–31, 70139–43, 70145–46, 70148–54, 70156–67, 70170, 70172, 70174–79, 70182, 70185–87, 70189–90, 70195

* * *

THIRD DISTRICT

CHARLIE MELANCON, Democrat, of Lafayette, LA; born in Napoleonville, LA, October 3, 1947; education: B.S., University of Southwestern Louisiana, Lafayette, LA, 1971; professional: businessman; chairman, Louisiana State University Agricultural Development Council; member, Louisiana State House of Representatives, 1987–93; awards: named Outstanding Legislator by the Louisiana Municipal Association; received the Distinguished Service Award from the Louisiana Restaurant Association; member: UL–Lafayette Alumni Association; Ducks Unlimited; Kappa Sigma Alumni Association; married: Peachy; children: Charles Joseph, Claire; committees: Energy and Commerce; Science and Technology; elected to the 109th Congress on November 2, 2004; reelected to the 110th Congress.

Office Listings

http://www.house.gov/melancon

404 Cannon House Office Building, Washington, DC 20515 .... (202) 225–4031

Chief of Staff.—Casey O'Shea. FAX: 226–3944
Legislative Director.—Jacob Roche.
Scheduler.—Jody Comeaux.
828 S. Irma Boulevard, 212A, Gonzales, LA 70737 .... (225) 621–8490
District Director.—Barney Arceneaux.
423 Lafayette Street, Suite 107, Houma, LA 70360 .... (985) 876–3033
210 East Main Street, New Iberia, LA 70560 .... (337) 367–8231
8201 West Judge Perez Drive, Chalmette, LA 70043 .... (504) 271–1707

Parishes: ASCENSION (part), ASSUMPTION, IBERIA, JEFFERSON (part), LAFOURCHE, PLAQUEMINES, ST. BERNARD, ST. CHARLES (part), ST. JAMES, ST. JOHN THE BAPTIST, ST. MARTIN, ST. MARY, TERREBONNE. Population (2000), 638,322.

ZIP Codes: 70030–32, 70036–41, 70043–44, 70047, 70049–52, 70056–58, 70067–72, 70075–76, 70078–87, 70090–92, 70301–02, 70310, 70339–46, 70353–54, 70356–61, 70363–64, 70371–75, 70377, 70380–81, 70390–95, 70397, 70512–14, 70517–19, 70521–23, 70528, 70538, 70540, 70544, 70552, 70560, 70562–63, 70569, 70582, 70592, 70723, 70725, 70734, 70737, 70743, 70763, 70778, 70792

* * *

FOURTH DISTRICT

JIM MCCRERY, Republican, of Shreveport, LA; born in Shreveport, September 18, 1949; education: graduated Leesville High, Louisiana, 1967; B.A., Louisiana Tech University, Ruston, 1971; J.D., Louisiana State University, Baton Rouge, 1975; attorney; admitted to the Louisiana bar in 1975 and commenced practice in Leesville, LA; Jackson, Smith, and Ford (Leesville), 1975–78; assistant city attorney, Shreveport, 1979–80; district manager, U.S. Representative Buddy Roemer, 1981–82; legislative director, U.S. Representative Buddy Roemer, 1982–84; board of directors, Louisiana Association of Business and Industry, 1986–87; chairman, Regulatory Affairs Committee, Louisiana Forestry Association, 1987; regional manager for Government Affairs, Georgia-Pacific Corporation, 1984–88; committees: Ways and Means; elected by special election to the 100th Congress, April 16, 1988, to fill the vacancy caused by the resignation of Charles E. (Buddy) Roemer; reelected to each succeeding Congress.

Office Listings

http://www.house.gov/mccrery

242 Cannon House Office Building, Washington, DC 20515 .... (202) 225–2777
Chief of Staff.—Clayton Hall. FAX: 225–8039
6425 Youree Drive, Suite 350, Shreveport, LA 71105 .... (318) 798–2254
District Manager.—Linda Wright.
Southgate Plaza Shopping Center, 1606 South Fifth Street, Leesville, LA 71446 .... (337) 238–0778

Parishes: ALLEN (part), BEAUREGARD, BIENVILLE, BOSSIER, CADDO, CLAIBORNE, DESOTO, GRANT, NATCHITOCHES, RED RIVER, SABINE, VERNON, WEBSTER. Population (2000), 638,466.

ZIP Codes: 70633–34, 70637–39, 70644, 70648, 70651–57, 70659–60, 70662, 71001–04, 71006–09, 71016, 71018–19, 71021, 71023–25, 71027–34, 71036–40, 71043–52, 71055, 71058, 71060–61, 71063–73, 71075, 71078–80, 71082, 71101–13, 71115, 71118–20, 71129–30, 71133–38, 71148–49, 71151–54, 71156, 71161–66, 71171–72, 71222, 71235, 71251, 71256, 71268, 71275, 71360, 71403–04, 71406–07, 71411, 71414, 71416–17, 71419, 71423, 71426–29, 71432, 71434, 71438–39, 71443, 71446–47, 71449–50, 71452, 71454–63, 71467–69, 71474–75, 71486, 71496–97

* * *

FIFTH DISTRICT

RODNEY ALEXANDER, Republican, of Quitman, LA; born in Bienville, LA, December 5, 1946; education: attended Louisiana Tech University; professional: businessman, with a background in the insurance and construction industries; organizations: member, Louisiana Farm Bureau and the National Rifle Association; public service: Jackson Parish Police Jury, 1970–85; served as President during the last seven years of his tenure; Louisiana House of Representatives, 1987–2002; religion: Baptist; married: Nancy; three children; committees: Appropriations; Budget; elected to the 108th Congress on December 7, 2002; reelected to each succeeding Congress.

Office Listings

http://www.house.gov/alexander

316 Cannon House Office Building, Washington, DC 20515 .... (202) 225–8490
Chief of Staff.—Royal Alexander. FAX: 225–5639
Press Secretary.—Jenni Terry.
Scheduler.—Meyer Seligman.
1900 Stubbs Avenue, Suite B, Monroe, LA 71201 .... (318) 322–3500

1412 Centre Court, Suite 402, Alexandria, LA 71301 .... (318) 445–0818

Parishes: ALLEN (part), AVOYELLES, CALDWELL, CATAHOULA, CONCORDIA, EVANGELINE (part), EAST CARROLL, FRANKLIN, IBERVILLE (part), JACKSON, LASALLE, LINCOLN, MADISON, MOREHOUSE, OUACHITA, POINT COUPEE (part), RAPIDES, RICHLAND, TENSAS, UNION, WEST CARROLL, WIN. Population (2000), 638,517.

ZIP Codes: 70532, 70554, 70576, 70585–86, 70655–57, 70759–60, 70764–65, 70772, 70781, 70783, 71001, 71031, 71201–03, 71207–13, 71218–23, 71225–27, 71229–30, 71232–35, 71237–38, 71240–43, 71245, 71247, 71249–51, 71253–54, 71256, 71259–61, 71263–64, 71266, 71268–70, 71272–73, 71275–77, 71279–82, 71284, 71286, 71291–92, 71294–95, 71301–03, 71306–07, 71309, 71315–16, 71320, 71322–31, 71333–34, 71336, 71339–43, 71346, 71348, 71350–51, 71354–57, 71360–63, 71365–69, 71371, 71373, 71375, 71377–78, 71401, 71404–05, 71407, 71409–10, 71415, 71417–18, 71422–25, 71427, 71430–33, 71435, 71438, 71440–41, 71447–48, 71454–55, 71457, 71463, 71465–67, 71471–73, 71477, 71479–80, 71483, 71485

* * *

SIXTH DISTRICT

RICHARD H. BAKER, Republican, of Baton Rouge, LA; born in New Orleans, LA, May 22, 1948; education: graduated, University High School; Louisiana State University, Baton Rouge; professional: real estate broker; Louisiana House of Representatives, 1972–86; chairman, Committee on Transportation, Highways, and Public Works, 1980–86; member: Southern Legislative Conference, ALEC, Central Area Homebuilders, East Baton Rouge Airport Commission, Baton Rouge Lodge No. 372 Central Region Planning Commission; married: the former Kay Carpenter in 1969; children: Brandon and Julie; committees: Financial Services; Transportation and Infrastructure; Veterans' Affairs; elected to the 100th Congress on November 4, 1986; reelected to each succeeding Congress.

Office Listings

341 Cannon House Office Building, Washington, DC 20515 .... (202) 225–3901
Administrative Assistant.—Paul Sawyer. FAX: 225–7313
Office Manager / Executive Assistant.—Lynn Kirk.
5555 Hilton Avenue, Suite 100, Baton Rouge, LA 70808 .... (225) 929–7711
Chief of Staff.—Christina Kyle Casteel.

Parishes: ASCENSION (part), EAST BATON ROUGE, EAST FELICIANA, IBERVILLE (part), LIVINGSTON, POINTE COUPEE (part), ST. HELENA, WEST BATON ROUGE (part), WEST FELICIANA. CITIES: Addis, Albany, Angola, Baker, Batchelor, Baton Rouge, Bayou Goula, Blanks, Brittany, Brusly, Bueche, Carville, Clinton, Denham Springs, Duplessis, Erwinville, Ethel, Fordoche, French Settlement, Geismar, Glynn, Gonzales, Greenburg, Greenwell Springs, Grosse Tete, Hardwood, Holden, Innis, Jackson, Jarreau, Labarre, Lakeland, Lettsworth, Livingston, Livonia, Lottie, Maringouin, Maurepas, Morganza, New Roads, Norwood, Oscar, Pine Grove, Plaquemine, Port Allen, Prairieville, Pride, Rosedale, Rougon, Slaughter, Sorrento, Springfield, St. Amant, St. Francisville, St. Gabriel, Sunshine, Torbert, Tunica, Ventress, Wakefield, Walker, Watson, Weyanoke, White Castle, Wilson, and Zachary. Population (2000), 638,324.

ZIP Codes: 70403, 70422, 70436, 70441, 70443–44, 70449, 70453, 70462, 70466, 70586, 70704, 70706–07, 70710–12, 70714–15, 70718–19, 70721–22, 70726–30, 70732–34, 70736–40, 70744, 70747–49, 70752–57, 70759–62, 70764, 70767, 70769–70, 70772–78, 70780, 70782–89, 70791, 70801–23, 70826, 70831, 70833, 70835–37, 70874, 70879, 70883–84, 70892–96, 70898

* * *

SEVENTH DISTRICT

CHARLES W. BOUSTANY, JR., Republican, of Lafayette, LA; born in New Orleans, LA, February 21, 1956; education: graduated Cathedral Carmel High School, Lafayette, LA; B.S., University of Southwestern Louisiana, Lafayette, LA, 1978; M.D., Louisiana State University School of Medicine, New Orleans, LA, 1982; professional: surgeon; public service: served on the Louisiana Organ Procurement Agency Tissue Advisory Board; board of directors for the Greater Lafayette Chamber of Commerce, 2001; Chamber of Commerce as Vice President for Government Affairs, 2002; president of the Lafayette Parish Medical Society; chaired the American Heart Association's Gala; Healthcare Division of the UL-Lafayette Centennial Fundraiser, which provided $75 million of university endowed chairs, professorships and scholarships; member of Leadership Lafayette Class IIIXX, 2002; member, Lafayette Parish Republican Executive Committee, 1996–2001; vice-chairman of the Bush/Cheney Victory 2000 Campaign for Lafayette Parish; board of directors for Lafayette General Medical Center; married: the former Bridget Edwards; children: Erik and Ashley; committees: Agriculture; Education and Labor; Transportation and Infrastructure; Republican Policy Committee; elected to the 109th Congress on December 4, 2004; reelected to the 110th Congress.

Office Listings

http://www.house.gov/boustany

1117 Longworth House Office Building, Washington, DC 20515 .... (202) 225–2031
Chief of Staff.—Jeff Dobrozsi. FAX: 225–5724
Legislative Director.—Terry Fish.
Scheduler.—Hunter Pickels.
800 Lafayette Street, Suite 1400, Lafayette, LA 70501 .... (337) 235–6322
700 Ryan Street, Lake Charles, LA 70601 .... (337) 433–1747

Parishes: ACADIA, CALCASIEU, CAMERON, EVANGELINE, JEFFERSON DAVIS, LAFAYETTE, ST. LANDRY, VERMILION. Population (2000), 638,430.

ZIP Codes: 70501–12, 70515–18, 70520, 70524–29, 70531–35, 70537, 70541–43, 70546, 70548–51, 70554–56, 70558–59, 70570–71, 70575, 70577–78, 70580–81, 70583–84, 70586, 70589, 70591–92, 70596, 70598, 70601–02, 70605–07, 70609, 70611–12, 70615–16, 70630–33, 70640, 70643, 70645–48, 70650, 70655, 70658, 70661, 70663–65, 70668–69, 70750, 71322, 71345, 71353, 71356, 71358, 71362

MAINE

(Population, 2000 1,274,923)

SENATORS

OLYMPIA J. SNOWE, Republican, of Auburn, ME; born in Augusta, ME, February 21, 1947; education: graduated from Edward Little High School, Auburn, ME, 1965; B.A., University of Maine, Orono, 1969; member, Holy Trinity Greek Orthodox Church of Lewiston-Auburn; active member of civic and community organizations; elected to the Maine House of Representatives, 1973, to the seat vacated by the death of her first husband, the late Peter Snowe; reelected for a full two-year term in 1974; elected to the Maine Senate, 1976; chaired the Joint Standing Committee on Health and Institutional Services; elected to the 96th Congress on November 7, 1978—the youngest Republican woman, and first Greek-American woman elected; reelected to the 97th through 103rd Congresses; past member: House Budget Committee; House Foreign Affairs Committee; leading member of the former House Select Committee on Aging, ranking Republican on its Subcommittee on Human Services; married to former Maine Governor John R. McKernan, Jr.; committees: Commerce, Science, and Transportation; Finance; Small Business and Entrepreneurship; Select Committee on Intelligence; elected to the U.S. Senate on November 8, 1994; reelected to each succeeding Senate term.

Office Listings

http://snowe.senate.gov

154 Russell Senate Office Building, Washington, DC 20510 .... (202) 224–5344
Chief of Staff.—John Richter. FAX: 224–1946
Executive Assistant.—Anna Levin.
Communications Director.—David Snepp.
2 Great Falls Plaza, Suite 7B, Auburn, ME 04210 .... (207) 786–2451
Regional Representative.—Diane Jackson.
40 Western Avenue, Suite 408C, Augusta, ME 04330 .... (207) 622–8292
Regional Representative.—Deb McNeil.
One Cumberland Place, Suite 306, Bangor, ME 04401 .... (207) 945–0432
State Director.—Gail Kelly.
231 Main Street, P.O. Box 215, Biddeford, ME 04005 .... (207) 282–4144
Regional Representative.—Peter Morin.
3 Canal Plaza, Suite 601, P.O. Box 188, Portland, ME 04112 .... (207) 874–0883
Regional Representative.—Cheryl Leeman.
169 Academy Street, Suite 3, Presque Isle, ME 04769 .... (207) 764–5124
Regional Representative.—Sharon Campbell.

* * *

SUSAN M. COLLINS, Republican, of Bangor, ME; born in Caribou, ME, December 7, 1952; education: graduated, Caribou High School, 1971; B.A., *magna cum laude,* Phi Beta Kappa, St. Lawrence University, Canton, NY; Outstanding Alumni Award, St. Lawrence University, 1992; staff director, Senate Subcommittee on the Oversight of Government Management, 1981–87; for 12 years, principal advisor on business issues to former Senator William S. Cohen; Commissioner of Professional and Financial Regulation for Maine Governor John R. McKernan, Jr., 1987; New England administrator, Small Business Administration, 1992–93; appointed Deputy Treasurer of Massachusetts, 1993; executive director, Husson College Center for Family Business, 1994–96; committees: Armed Services; Homeland Security and Governmental Affairs; Special Committee on Aging; elected to the U.S. Senate on November 5, 1996; reelected to each succeeding Senate term.

Office Listings

http://collins.senate.gov

413 Dirksen Senate Office Building, Washington, DC 20510 .... (202) 224–2523
Chief of Staff.—Steven Abbott. FAX: 224–2693
Communications Director.—Jen Burita.
Legislative Director.—Jane Alonso.
P.O. Box 655, 202 Harlow Street, Room 204, Bangor, ME 04402 .... (207) 945–0417
State Representative.—Carol Woodcock.
68 Sewall Street, Room 507, Augusta, ME 04330 .... (207) 622–8414
State Representative.—William Card.
160 Main Street, Biddeford, ME 04005 .... (207) 283–1101
State Representative.—William Vail.
11 Lisbon Street, Lewiston, ME 04240 .... (207) 784–6969
State Representative.—Peter Rogers.
25 Sweden Street, Suite A, Caribou, ME 04736 .... (207) 493–5873

State Representative.—Philip Bosse.
One City Center, Stop 23, Portland, ME 04101 .... (207) 780–3575
State Representative.—Jennifer Duddy.

REPRESENTATIVES

FIRST DISTRICT

THOMAS H. ALLEN, Democrat, of Portland, ME; born in Portland, April 16, 1945; education: graduated, Deering High School, Portland; Bowdoin College, Phi Beta Kappa; Oxford University, Rhodes scholar; J.D., Harvard University; Bowdin College Board of Trustees; board of directors of Shalom House and the United Way of Greater Portland; president, Portland Stage Company; Executive and Legislative Policy committees; Maine Municipal Association; chair, Governor's Task Force on Foster Care; Portland City Council and Mayor; married: Diana Allen; children: Gwen and Kate; committees: Budget; Energy and Commerce; elected to the 105th Congress; reelected to each succeeding Congress.

Office Listings

http://tomallen.house.gov

1127 Longworth House Office Building, Washington, DC 20515 .... (202) 225–6116
Chief of Staff.—Mark Ouellette. FAX: 225–5590
Executive Assistant.—Jolene Chonko.
Legislative Director.—James Bradley.
Legislative Assistants: Molly Jacobs, Susan Lexer, Megan Shannon-Winterson, Todd Stein.
57 Exchange Street, Suite 302, Portland, ME 04101 .... (207) 774–5019
Office Manager / Scheduler.—Stephanie Betzold.

Counties: CUMBERLAND, KENNEBEC (part), KNOX, LINCOLN, SAGADAHOC, YORK. Population (2000), 637,461.

ZIP Codes: 03901–11, 04001–11, 04013–15, 04017, 04019–21, 04024, 04027–30, 04032–34, 04038–40, 04042–43, 04046–50, 04053–57, 04061–64, 04066, 04069–79, 04082–87, 04090–98, 04101–10, 04112, 04116, 04122–24, 04259–60, 04265, 04284, 04287, 04330, 04332–33, 04336, 04338, 04341–55, 04357–60, 04363–64, 04530, 04535–39, 04541, 04543–44, 04547–48, 04551, 04553–56, 04558, 04562–65, 04567–68, 04570–76, 04578–79, 04841, 04843, 04846–56, 04858–65, 04901, 04910, 04917–18, 04922, 04926–27, 04935, 04937, 04941, 04949, 04952, 04962–63, 04973, 04987–89, 04992

* * *

SECOND DISTRICT

MICHAEL H. MICHAUD, Democrat, of East Millinocket, ME; born on January 18, 1955; grew up in Medway, ME; education: graduate, Harvard University John F. Kennedy School of Government Program for Senior Executives in State and Local Government; professional: mill worker; community service: actively involved in a variety of local, regional, and statewide civic and economic development organizations; public service: Maine House of Representatives, 1980–94; Maine State Senate, 1994–2002; religion: Catholic; committees: Small Business; Transportation and Infrastructure; Veterans' Affairs; elected to the 108th Congress on November 5, 2002; reelected to each succeeding Congress.

Office Listings

http://www.house.gov/michaud

1724 Longworth Office Building, Washington, DC 20515 .... (202) 225–6306
Chief of Staff.—Peter Chandler. FAX: 225–2943
Legislative Director.—Matt Robison.
Scheduler.—Diane Smith.
23 Water Street, Bangor, ME 04401 .... (207) 942–6935
179 Lisbon Street, Ground Floor, Lewiston, ME 04240 .... (207) 782–3704
445 Main Street, Presque Isle, ME 04769 .... (207) 764–1036
16 Common Street, Waterville, ME 04901 .... (207) 873–5713

Counties: ANDROSCOGGIN, AROOSTOOK, FRANKLIN, HANCOCK, KENNEBEC (part), OXFORD, PENOBSCOT, PISCATAQUIS, SOMERSET, WALDO, WASHINGTON. Population (2000), 637,461.

ZIP Codes: 04010, 04016, 04022, 04037, 04041, 04051, 04068, 04088, 04210–12, 04216–17, 04219–28, 04230–31, 04234, 04236–41, 04243, 04250, 04252–58, 04261–63, 04266–68, 04270–71, 04274–76, 04278, 04280–83, 04285–86, 04288–

92, 04294, 04354, 04401–02, 04406, 04408, 04410–24, 04426–31, 04434–35, 04438, 04441–44, 04448–51, 04453–57, 04459–64, 04467–69, 04471–76, 04478–79, 04481, 04485, 04487–93, 04495–97, 04549, 04605–07, 04609, 04611–17, 04619, 04622–31, 04634–35, 04637, 04640, 04642–46, 04648–50, 04652–58, 04660, 04662, 04664, 04666–69, 04671–77, 04679–81, 04683–86, 04691, 04693–94, 04730, 04732–47, 04750–51, 04756–66, 04768–70, 04772–77, 04779–81, 04783, 04785–88, 04848–51, 04857, 04903, 04911–12, 04915, 04920–25, 04928–30, 04932–33, 04936–45, 04947, 04949–58, 04961, 04964–67, 04969–76, 04978–79, 04981–88, 04992

MARYLAND

(Population 2000, 5,296,486)

SENATORS

BARBARA A. MIKULSKI, Democrat, of Baltimore, MD; born in Baltimore, July 20, 1936; education: B.A., Mount St. Agnes College, 1958; M.S.W., University of Maryland School of Social Work, 1965; former social worker for Catholic Charities and city of Baltimore; served as an adjunct professor, Department of Sociology, Loyola College; elected to the Baltimore City Council, 1971; Democratic nominee for the U.S. Senate in 1974, winning 43 percent of vote; elected to the U.S. House of Representatives in November, 1976; first woman appointed to the Energy and Commerce Committee; also served on the Merchant Marine and Fisheries Committee; became the first woman representing the Democratic Party to be elected to a Senate seat not previously held by her husband, and the first Democratic woman ever to serve in both houses of Congress; Secretary, Democratic Conference; first woman to be elected to a leadership post; committees: Appropriations; Health, Education, Labor, and Pensions; Select Committee on Intelligence; elected to the U.S. Senate in November, 1986; reelected to each succeeding Senate term.

Office Listings

http://mikulski.senate.gov

503 Hart Senate Office Building, Washington, DC 20510 .... (202) 224–4654
Chief of Staff.—Julia Frifield. FAX: 224–8858
Legislative Director.—Dvora Lovinger.
1629 Thames Street, Suite 400, Baltimore, MD 2123 .... (410) 962–4510
State Director.—Ellen Jones.
32 West Street, Suite 202, Annapolis, MD 21401 .... (410) 263–1805
6404 Ivy Lane, Suite 406, Greenbelt, MD 20770 .... (301) 345–5517
94 West Washington Street, Hagerstown, MD 21740 .... (301) 797–2826
1201 Pemberton Drive, Suite 1E, Building B, Salisbury, MD 21801 .... (410) 546–7711

* * *

BENJAMIN L. CARDIN, Democrat, of Baltimore, MD; born in Baltimore, October 5, 1943; education: graduated, City College High School, 1961; B.A., *cum laude*, University of Pittsburgh, 1964; L.L.B., 1st in class, University of Maryland School of Law, 1967; professional: attorney in the law firm of Rosen and Esterson, 1967–78; elected to Maryland House of Delegates in November 1966, serving from 1967–86; Speaker of the House of Delegates, 1979–86, the youngest Speaker at the time; elected to U.S. House of Representatives in November 1986, representing the 3rd Congressional District in Maryland, serving from 1987–2006; Senior Democratic Whip, 2003–06; Assistant Democrat Whip, 1987–2003; Commissioner, Commission for Security and Cooperation in Europe (CSCE), 1997–2006; Ranking Member, CSCE, 2003–06; co-chairman, CSCE, 2007; Vice President, Organization for Security and Cooperation in Europe Parliamentary Assembly; member: Associated Jewish Charities and Welfare Fund, 1985–89; Trustee, St. Mary's College, 1988–99; Lifetime Member, NAACP, since 1990; Board of Visitors, University of Maryland Law School, 1991–2007; married: Myrna Edelman of Baltimore, 1964; two children, two grandchildren; committees: Budget; Environment and Public Works; Foreign Relations; Judiciary; Small Business and Entrepreneurship; elected to U.S. Senate on November 7, 2006.

Office Listings

http://cardin.senate.gov

509 Hart Senate Office Building, Washington, DC 20510 .... (202) 224–4524
Chief of Staff.—Chris Lynch. FAX: 224–1651
Policy Director.—Priscilla Ross. TDD: 224–3452
Appointments Secretary.—Debbie Yamada.
100 South Charles Street, Tower I, Suite 1710, Baltimore, MD 21201 .... (410) 962–4436

REPRESENTATIVES

FIRST DISTRICT

WAYNE T. GILCHREST, Republican, of Kennedyville, MD; born in Rahway, NJ, April 15, 1946; education: graduated from Rahway High School, 1964; attended Wesley College, Dover,

DE; B.A. in History, Delaware State College, Dover, 1973; graduate studies, Loyola University, Baltimore, MD, 1984–present; military service: served in the U.S. Marine Corps, 1964–68; awarded the Purple Heart, Bronze Star, Navy Commendation Medal, Navy Unit Citation, and others; professional: government and history teacher, Kent County High School, 1973–present; member: Kent County Teachers Association, American Legion, Veterans of Foreign Wars, Order of the Purple Heart; religion: Kennedyville Methodist Church; married: the former Barbara Rawley; children: Kevin, Joel, and Katie; committees: Natural Resources; Transportation and Infrastructure; elected to the 102nd Congress; reelected to each succeeding Congress.

Office Listings

2245 Rayburn House Office Building, Washington, DC 20515 .... (202) 225–5311
Chief of Staff.—Tony Caligiuri. FAX: 225–0254
Office Manager / Scheduler.—Kathy Hicks.
Legislative Director.—Tammy Fisher.
Press Secretary / District Director.—Cathy Bassett.
315 High Street, Suite 105, Chestertown, MD 21620 .... (410) 778–9407
District Office Manager.—Karen Willis.
One Plaza East, Salisbury, MD 21801 .... (410) 749–3184
District Office Manager.—Monica Bell.
112 W. Pennsylvania Avenue, Suite 102, Bel Air, MD 21014 .... (410) 838–2517
District Office Manager.—Virginia Sanders.

Counties: ANNE ARUNDEL (part), BALTIMORE (part), CAROLINE, CECIL, DORCHESTER, HARFORD (part), KENT, QUEEN ANNE'S, SOMERSET, TALBOT, WICOMICO, WORCESTER. Population (2000), 662,062.

ZIP Codes: 21001, 21009, 21012–15, 21018, 21023, 21028, 21030–32, 21034, 21047, 21050–51, 21054, 21057, 21078, 21082, 21084–85, 21087, 21092–93, 21108, 21111, 21113, 21122, 21128, 21131, 21136, 21144, 21146, 21156, 21162, 21206, 21225–26, 21234, 21236, 21240, 21286, 21401–05, 21411–12, 21601, 21606–07, 21609–10, 21612–13, 21617, 21619–20, 21622–29, 21631–32, 21634–36, 21638–41, 21643–45, 21647–73, 21675–79, 21681–85, 21687, 21690, 21801–04, 21810–11, 21813–14, 21817, 21821–22, 21824, 21826, 21829–30, 21835–38, 21840–43, 21849–53, 21856–57, 21861–67, 21869, 21871–72, 21874–75, 21890, 21901–04, 21911–22, 21930

* * *

SECOND DISTRICT

C.A. DUTCH RUPPERSBERGER, Democrat, of Cockeysville, MD; born in Baltimore, MD, January 31, 1946; education: Baltimore City College; University of Maryland, College Park; J.D., University of Baltimore Law School, 1970; professional: attorney; partner, Ruppersberger, Clark, and Mister (law firm); public service: Baltimore County Assistant State's Attorney; Baltimore County Council; Baltimore County Executive, 1994–2002; married: the former Kay Murphy; children: Cory and Jill; committees: Appropriations; Permanent Select Committee on Intelligence; elected to the 108th Congress on November 5, 2002; reelected to each succeeding Congress.

Office Listings

http://dutch.house.gov

1730 Longworth House Office Building, Washington, DC 20515 .... (202) 225–3061
Chief of Staff.—Tara Oursler. FAX: 225–3094
Deputy Chief of Staff / Press Secretary.—Heather Molino.
Senior Policy Advisor.—Walter Gonzales.
Legislative Director.—Steve Jost.
The Atrium, 375 West Padonia Road, Suite 200, Timonium, MD 21093 .... (410) 628–2701
District Office Manager / Scheduler.—Carol Merkel.

Counties: ANNE ARUNDEL (part), BALTIMORE CITY (part), BALTIMORE COUNTY (part), HARFORD (part). Population (2000), 662,060.

ZIP Codes: 20755, 21001, 21005, 21009–10, 21017, 21022, 21027, 21030–31, 21034, 21040, 21047, 21050–52, 21056–57, 21060–62, 21065, 21071, 21076–78, 21085, 21087, 21090, 21093–94, 21104, 21111, 21113, 21117, 21122–23, 21130, 21133, 21136, 21144, 21162–63, 21204, 21206, 21208, 21212–14, 21219–22, 21224–27, 21230, 21234, 21236–37, 21239, 21244, 21252, 21284–86

* * *

THIRD DISTRICT

JOHN P. SARBANES, Democrat, of Baltimore, MD; born in Baltimore, May 22, 1962; education: A.B., *cum laude*, Woodrow Wilson School of Public and International Affairs, Princeton

University, 1984; Fulbright Scholar, Greece, 1985; J.D., Harvard University School of Law, 1988; professional: law clerk to Judge J. Frederick Motz, U.S. District Court for the District of Maryland, 1988–89; admitted to Maryland Bar, 1988; member: American Bar Association; Maryland State Bar Association; attorney, Venable, LLP, 1989–2006 (chair, health care practice); founding member, Board of Trustees, Dunbar Project, 1990–94; Board of Directors, Public Justice Center, 1991–2006 (president, 1994–97); Institute for Christian and Jewish Studies, 1991-present (past chair, membership committee); Special Assistant to State Superintendent of Schools, State Department of Education, 1998–2005; awards: Unsung Hero Award, Maryland Chapter of the Association of Fundraising Professionals, 2006; Arthur W. Machen, Jr., Award, Maryland Legal Services Corp., 2006; married to Dina Sarbanes; three children; committees: Education and Labor; Natural Resources; Oversight and Government Reform; elected to the 110th Congress on November 7, 2006.

Office Listings

http://www.sarbanes.house.gov

426 Cannon House Office Building, Washington, DC 20510 .... (202) 225–4016
Chief of Staff.—Jonathan Davidson. FAX: 225–9219
Press Secretary.—Pia Carusone.
600 Baltimore Avenue, Suite 303, Towson, MD 21204 .... (410) 832–8890

Counties: ANNE ARUNDEL (part), BALTIMORE (part), HOWARD (part), BALTIMORE CITY (part). TOWNS: Arbutus, Crofton, Ellicott City, Elkridge, Glen Burnie, Halethrope, Lansdowne, Linthicum, Maryland City, Odenton, Owings Mills, Parkville, Pikesville, Reisterstown, Russett City, Severn, and Towson. Population (2000), 662,062.

ZIP Codes: 20701, 20723–24, 20755, 20759, 20794, 21022, 21029, 21032, 21035, 21037, 21043–46, 21054–55, 21060–61, 21071, 21075–77, 21090, 21093, 21098, 21108, 21113–14, 21117, 21122, 21136, 21139, 21144, 21146, 21150, 21153, 21201–02, 21204–06, 21208–15, 21218, 21222–25, 21227–31, 21234, 21236–37, 21239, 21281–82, 21285–86, 21401–05, 21411–12

* * *

FOURTH DISTRICT

ALBERT RUSSELL WYNN, Democrat, of Largo, MD; born in Philadelphia, PA, September 10, 1951; education: graduated DuVal High School, Lanham, 1969; B.S., University of Pittsburgh, PA, 1973; attended Howard University Graduate School of Political Science, 1974; J.D., Georgetown University Law School, Washington, DC, 1977; professional: attorney; admitted to the Maryland bar, 1979; Maryland House of Delegates, 1983–86; Maryland State Senate, 1987–92; executive director, Prince George's County Consumer Protection Commission, 1979–82; member: Kappa Alpha Psi Fraternity; J. Franklyn Bourne Bar Association; board of directors, Consumer Credit Counseling Service; Prince George's County Economic Development Corporation; Ploughman and Fisherman; committees: Energy and Commerce; elected to the 103rd Congress, November 3, 1992; reelected to each succeeding Congress.

Office Listings

http://www.wynn.house.gov

2470 Rayburn Office Building, Washington, DC 20515 .... (202) 225–8699
Chief of Staff.—Curt Clifton. FAX: 225–8714
Legislative Director.—Alon Kupferman.
Press Secretary.—Sarah Misailidis.
9200 Basil Court, Suite 221, Largo, MD 20774 .... (301) 773–4094
18401 Woodfield Road, Suite D, Gaithersburg, MD 20879 .... (301) 987–2054

Counties: MONTGOMERY (part), PRINCE GEORGE'S (part). CITIES AND TOWNSHIPS: Bladensburg, Brentwood, Brookeville, Capitol Heights, Cheverly, Colmar Manor, Cottage City, District Heights, Edmonston, Fairmount Heights, Glenarden, Landover Hills, Largo, Laytonsville, Morningside, Mount Rainier, New Carrollton, North Brentwood, Olney, Riverdale, Rockville, Seat Pleasant, University Park, and Upper Marlboro. Population (2000), 662,062.

ZIP Codes: 20703, 20706–07, 20710, 20720–21, 20731, 20735, 20737, 20743–48, 20750, 20752–53, 20757, 20762, 20769, 20772, 20774–75, 20777, 20781–85, 20788, 20790–92, 20797, 20799, 20830, 20832–33, 20841, 20853, 20855, 20860–62, 20866, 20868, 20871–72, 20874, 20876–77, 20879, 20882, 20886, 20901, 20903–06, 20910–12, 21771, 21797

* * *

FIFTH DISTRICT

STENY H. HOYER, Democrat, of Mechanicsville, MD; born in New York, NY, June 14, 1939; education: graduated Suitland High School; B.S., University of Maryland, 1963; J.D.,

Georgetown University Law Center, 1966; Honorary Doctor of Public Service, University of Maryland, 1988; admitted to the Maryland Bar Association, 1966; professional: practicing attorney, 1966–90; Maryland State Senate, 1967–79; vice chairman, Prince George's County, MD, Senate delegation, 1967–69; chairman, Prince George's County, MD, Senate delegation, 1969–75; president, Maryland State Senate, 1975–79; member, State Board for Higher Education, 1978–81; married: Judith Pickett, deceased, February 6, 1997; children: Susan, Stefany, and Anne; Democratic Steering Committee; House Majority Leader, 110th Congress; elected to the 97th Congress on May 19, 1981, by special election; reelected to each succeeding Congress.

Office Listings

http://www.hoyer.house.gov

1705 Longworth House Office Building, Washington, DC 20515 .... (202) 225–4131
Chief of Staff.—Terry Lierman. FAX: 226–0663
Administrative Assistant.—Jim Wood.
U.S. Federal Courthouse, Suite 310, 6500 Cherrywood Lane, Greenbelt, MD 20770 .... (301) 474–0119
401 Post Office Road, Suite 202, Waldorf, MD 20602 .... (301) 843–1577

Counties: ANNE ARUNDEL (part), CALVERT, CHARLES, PRINCE GEORGE'S (part), ST. MARY'S. Population (2000), 662,060.

ZIP Codes: 20601–04, 20606–13, 20615–30, 20632, 20634–37, 20639–40, 20643, 20645–46, 20650, 20653, 20656–62, 20664, 20667, 20670, 20674–78, 20680, 20682, 20684–90, 20692–93, 20695, 20697, 20704–09, 20711, 20714–21, 20725–26, 20732–33, 20735–38, 20740–42, 20744, 20748–49, 20751, 20754, 20758, 20764–65, 20768–74, 20776, 20778–79, 20781–84, 20904, 21035, 21037, 21054, 21106, 21113, 21140

* * *

SIXTH DISTRICT

ROSCOE G. BARTLETT, Republican, of Frederick, MD; born in Moreland, KY, June 3, 1926; education: B.A., Columbia Union College, 1947; M.A., 1948, and Ph.D., University of Maryland, 1952; still an active farmer, prior to his election to Congress, he had retired after owning and operating a small business for ten years; awarded 20 patents for inventions during his scientific career as a professor and research engineer; held positions at Loma Linda University, the Navy's School of Aviation Medicine, John Hopkins Applied Physics Laboratory, and at IBM; married to Ellen; 10 children; committees: Armed Services; elected to the 103rd Congress; reelected to each succeeding Congress.

Office Listings

http://www.bartlett.house.gov

2412 Rayburn House Office Building, Washington, DC 20515 .... (202) 225–2721
Chief of Staff / Legislative Director.—Bud Otis. FAX: 225–2193
Office Manager / Scheduler.—Barb Calligan.
11377 Robinwood Drive, Hagerstown, MD 21742 .... (301) 797–6043
7360 Guilford Drive, Suite 101, Frederick, MD 21704 .... (301) 694–3030
15 Main Street, Suite 110, Westminster, MD 21157 .... (410) 857–1115
1 Frederick Street, Cumberland, MD 21502 .... (301) 724–3105

Counties: ALLEGANY, BALTIMORE (part), CARROLL, FREDERICK, GARRETT, HARFORD (part), MONTGOMERY (part), WASHINGTON. CITIES AND TOWNSHIPS: Baltimore, Boonsboro, Cumberland, Emmitsburg, Frederick, Frostburg, Funkstown, Hagerstown, Hancock, Middletown, Mount Airy, Oakland, Reisterstown, Sharpsburg, Smithburg, Thurmont, Timonium, Walkersville, Westminster, Williamsport, Woodsboro. Also includes Antietam National Battlefield and Camp David. Population (2000), 662,060.

ZIP Codes: 20842, 20871–72, 20876, 20882, 21014, 21020, 21029–30, 21034, 21036, 21041–43, 21047–48, 21050, 21053, 21074–75, 21084, 21088, 21102, 21104–05, 21111, 21120, 21131–32, 21136, 21152, 21154–55, 21157–58, 21160–61, 21163, 21501–05, 21520–24, 21528–32, 21536, 21538–43, 21545, 21550, 21555–57, 21560–62, 21701–05, 21709–11, 21713–23, 21727, 21733–34, 21740–42, 21746–50, 21754–59, 21762, 21766–67, 21769–71, 21773–84, 21787–88, 21790–91, 21793, 21795, 21797–98

* * *

SEVENTH DISTRICT

ELIJAH E. CUMMINGS, Democrat, of Baltimore, MD; born in Baltimore, January 18, 1951; education: graduated, Baltimore City College High School, 1969; B.S., political science, Phi Beta Kappa, Howard University, Washington, DC, 1973; J.D., University of Maryland Law School, 1976; professional: attorney; admitted to the Maryland bar in 1976; delegate, Maryland State Legislature, 1982–96; chairman, Maryland Legislative Black Caucus, 1984; speaker pro tempore, Maryland General Assembly, 1995–96; vice chairman, Constitutional and Administrative Law Committee; vice chairman, Economic Matters Committee; president, sophomore class, student government treasurer and student government president at Howard University; member: Governor's Commission on Black Males; New Psalmist Baptist Church, Baltimore, MD; active in civic affairs, and recipient of numerous community awards; co-chair of the House AIDS Working Group; Task Force on Health Care Reform; one child: Jennifer; committees: Armed Services; Oversight and Government Reform; Transportation and Infrastructure; elected to the 104th Congress by special election in April, 1996; reelected to each succeeding Congress.

Office Listings

http://www.house.gov/cummings

2235 Rayburn House Office Building, Washington, DC 20515 .... (202) 225–4741
Chief of Staff.—Vernon Simms. FAX: 225–3178
Legislative Director.—Kimberly Ross.
Legislative Assistants.—Danielle Grote, Lucinda Lessley.
Press Secretary.—Devika Koppikar.
1010 Park Avenue, Suite 105, Baltimore, MD 21201 .... (410) 685–9199
754 Frederick Road, Catonsville, MD 21228 .... (410) 719–8777
8267 Main Street, Room 102, Ellicott City, MD 21043 .... (410) 465–8259

Counties: BALTIMORE (part), HOWARD (part), BALTIMORE CITY (part). Population (2000), 662,060.

ZIP Codes: 20701, 20723, 20759, 20763, 20777, 20794, 20833, 21029, 21036, 21042–45, 21075, 21104, 21117, 21133, 21163, 21201–03, 21205–18, 21223–24, 21227–31, 21233, 21235, 21239, 21241, 21244, 21250–51, 21263–65, 21268, 21270, 21273–75, 21278–80, 21283, 21287–90, 21297–98, 21723, 21737–38, 21765, 21771, 21784, 21794, 21797

* * *

EIGHTH DISTRICT

CHRIS VAN HOLLEN, Democrat, of Kensington, MD; born in Karachi, Pakistan, January 10, 1959; education: B.A., Swarthmore College, 1982; Masters in Public Policy, Harvard University, 1985; J.D., Georgetown University, 1990; professional: attorney; legislative assistant to former Maryland U.S. Senator Charles McC. Mathias, Jr.; staff member, U.S. Senate Committee on Foreign Relations; senior legislative advisor to former Maryland Governor William Donald Schaefer; public service: elected, Maryland House of Delegates, 1990; elected, Maryland State Senate, 1994; married: Katherine; children: Anna, Nicholas, and Alexander; elected to the 108th Congress on November 5, 2002; reelected to each succeeding Congress.

Office Listings

http://www.house.gov/vanhollen

1707 Longworth House Office Building, Washington, DC 20515 .... (202) 225–5341
Chief of Staff.—Karen Robb. FAX: 225–0375
Legislative Director.—Bill Parsons.
Press Secretary.—Marilyn Campbell.
51 Monroe Street, Suite 507, Rockville, MD 20850 .... (301) 424–3501
District Director.—Joan Kleinman.

Counties: MONTGOMERY (part), PRINCE GEORGES (part). Population (2000), 662,060.

ZIP Codes: 20712, 20722, 20782–83, 20787, 20810–18, 20824–25, 20827, 20837–39, 20841–42, 20847–55, 20857, 20859, 20871, 20874–80, 20883–86, 20889, 20891–92, 20894–99, 20901–08, 20910, 20912–16, 20918, 20997

MASSACHUSETTS

(Population 2000, 6,349,097)

SENATORS

EDWARD M. KENNEDY, Democrat, of Barnstable, MA; born in Boston, MA, February 22, 1932; son of Joseph P. and Rose F. Kennedy; education: graduated, Milton Academy, 1950; A.B., Harvard College, 1956; professional: International Law School, The Hague, the Netherlands, 1958; LL.B., University of Virginia Law School, 1959; enlisted in the U.S. Army as a private and served in France and Germany, 1951–53; married: Victoria Reggie Kennedy; children: Kara, Edward M., Jr., Patrick J., Curran, and Caroline; committees: chair, Health, Education, Labor, and Pensions; Armed Services; Judiciary; Joint Economic Committee; elected to the U.S. Senate on November 7, 1962, to fill the unexpired term of his brother John F. Kennedy; reelected to each succeeding Senate term.

Office Listings

http://kennedy.senate.gov

315 Russell Senate Office Building, Washington, DC 20510 .... (202) 224–4543
Chief of Staff.—Eric Mogilnicki. FAX: 224–2417
Legislative Director.—Carey Parker. TDD: 224–1819
Administrative Manager.—John Dutton.
2400 John F. Kennedy Federal Building, Boston, MA 02203 .... (617) 565–3170
State Administrative Director.—Barbara Souliotis.

* * *

JOHN F. KERRY, Democrat, of Boston, MA; born in Denver, CO, December 11, 1943; education: graduated, St. Paul's School, Concord, NH, 1962; B.A., Yale University, New Haven, CT, 1966; J.D., Boston College Law School, Boston, MA, 1976; served, U.S. Navy, discharged with rank of lieutenant; decorations: Silver Star, Bronze Star with Combat ''V'', three Purple Hearts, various theatre campaign decorations; attorney, admitted to Massachusetts bar, 1976; appointed first assistant district attorney, Middlesex County, 1977; elected lieutenant governor, Massachusetts, 1982; married: Teresa Heinz; committees: chair, Small Business and Entrepreneurship; Commerce, Science, and Transportation; Finance; Foreign Relations; appointed to Democratic Leadership for 104th and 105th Congresses; elected to the U.S. Senate on November 6, 1984; reelected to each succeeding Senate term.

Office Listings

http://kerry.senate.gov

304 Russell Senate Office Building, Washington, DC 20510 .... (202) 224–2742
Administrative Assistant.—David McKean. FAX: 224–8525
Legislative Director.—Heather Zichal.
Personal Secretary.—Patricia Ferrone.
One Bowdoin Square, 10th Floor, Boston, MA 02114 .... (617) 565–8519
Suite 311, 222 Milliken Place, Fall River, MA 02722 .... (508) 677–0522
One Financial Plaza, Springfield, MA 01103 .... (413) 747–3942

REPRESENTATIVES

FIRST DISTRICT

JOHN W. OLVER, Democrat, of Amherst, MA; born in Honesdale, PA, September 3, 1936; education: B.S., Rensselaer Polytechnic Institute, 1955; M.A., Tufts University, 1956; taught for two years at Franklin Technical Institute, Boston, MA; Ph.D., Massachusetts Institute of Technology, 1961; professional: chemistry professor, University of Massachusetts-Amherst; Massachusetts House, 1968–72; Massachusetts Senate, 1972–91; became first Democrat since the Spanish-American War to represent the First Congressional District, 1991; elected by special election on June 4, 1991, to fill the vacancy caused by the death of Silvio Conte; married: Rose Olver; children: Martha; committees: Appropriations; elected on June 4, 1991, by special election, to the 102nd Congress; reelected to each succeeding Congress.

Office Listings

http://www.house.gov/olver

1111 Longworth House Office Building, Washington, DC 20515 .... (202) 225–5335
Chief of Staff.—Hunter Ridgway. FAX: 226–1224
Press Secretary.—Sara Burch.
Scheduler.—Saranah Holmes.
Legislative Director.—Abbie Meador.
463 Main Street, Fitchburg, MA 01420 .... (978) 342–8722
Office Manager.—Peggy Kane.
57 Suffolk Street, Suite 310, Holyoke, MA 01040 .... (413) 532–7010
District Director.—Jon Niedzielski.
78 Center Street, Pittsfield, MA 01201 .... (413) 442–0946
Office Manager.—Cindy Clark.

Counties: BERKSHIRE, FRANKLIN, HAMPDEN (part), HAMPSHIRE (part), MIDDLESEX (part), WORCESTER (part). Population (2000), 634,479.

ZIP Codes: 01002–05, 01007–08, 01011–12, 01026–27, 01029, 01031–34, 01037–41, 01050, 01054, 01059, 01066, 01068–75, 01077, 01080–82, 01084–86, 01088–90, 01093–94, 01096–98, 01102, 01107, 01201–03, 01220, 01222–27, 01229–30, 01235–38, 01240, 01242–45, 01247, 01252–60, 01262–64, 01266–67, 01270, 01301–02, 01330–31, 01337–44, 01346–47, 01349–51, 01355, 01360, 01364, 01366–68, 01370, 01373, 01375–76, 01378–80, 01420, 01430–31, 01436, 01438, 01440–41, 01452–53, 01462–63, 01468–69, 01473–75, 01477, 01531, 01564, 01585

* * *

SECOND DISTRICT

RICHARD E. NEAL, Democrat, of Springfield, MA; born in Springfield, February 14, 1949; education: graduated, Springfield Technical High School, 1968; B.A., American International College, Springfield, 1972; M.A., University of Hartford Barney School of Business and Public Administration, CT, 1976; instructor and lecturer; assistant to mayor of Springfield, 1973–78; Springfield City Council, 1978–84; mayor, city of Springfield, 1983–89; member: Massachusetts Mayors Association; Adult Education Council; American International College Alumni Association; Boys Club Alumni Association; Emily Bill Athletic Association; Cancer Crusade; John Boyle O'Reilly Club; United States Conference of Mayors; Valley Press Club; Solid Waste Advisory Committee for the State of Massachusetts; Committee on Leadership and Government; Mass Jobs Council; trustee: Springfield Libraries and Museums Association, Springfield Red Cross, Springfield YMCA; married: Maureen; four children: Rory Christopher, Brendan Conway, Maura Katherine, and Sean Richard; committees: Ways and Means; elected on November 8, 1988, to the 101st Congress; reelected to each succeeding Congress.

Office Listings

http://www.house.gov/neal

2208 Rayburn House Office Building, Washington, DC 20515 .... (202) 225–5601
Administrative Assistant.—Ann Jablon. FAX: 225–8112
Executive Assistant.—Sarah Bontempo.
Press Secretary.—Bill Tranghese.
Federal Building, Room 309, 1550 Main Street, Springfield, MA 01103 .... (413) 785–0325
District Manager.—James Leydon.
4 Congress Street, Milford, MA 01757 .... (508) 634–8198
Office Manager.—Virginia Purcell.

Counties: HAMPDEN (part), HAMPSHIRE (part), NORFOLK (part), WORCESTER (part). Population (2000), 634,444.

ZIP Codes: 01001, 01009–10, 01013–14, 01020–22, 01027–28, 01030, 01035–36, 01053, 01056–57, 01060–63, 01069, 01075, 01079–81, 01083, 01092, 01095, 01101–09, 01111, 01115–16, 01118–19, 01128–29, 01133, 01138–39, 01144, 01151–52, 01199, 01504, 01506–09, 01515–16, 01518–19, 01521, 01524–27, 01529, 01534–38, 01540, 01542, 01550, 01560, 01562, 01566, 01568–71, 01585–86, 01588, 01590, 01607, 01611, 01747, 01756–57

* * *

THIRD DISTRICT

JAMES P. MCGOVERN, Democrat, of Worcester, MA; born in Worcester, November 20, 1959; education: B.A., M.P.A., American University; legislative director and senior aide to Congressman Joe Moakley (D–South Boston); led the 1989 investigation into the murders of six Jesuit priests and two lay women in El Salvador; managed George McGovern's (D–SD) 1984 presidential campaign in Massachusetts and delivered his nomination speech at the Democratic

National Convention; board of directors, Jesuit International Volunteers; former volunteer, Mt. Carmel House, an emergency shelter for battered and abused women; married: Lisa Murray McGovern; committees: Budget; Rules; elected to the 105th Congress; reelected to each succeeding Congress.

Office Listings

http://www.house.gov/mcgovern

438 Cannon House Office Building, Washington, DC 20515 .... (202) 225–6101
Chief of Staff.—Christopher Philbin. FAX: 225–5759
Legislative Director.—Cindy Buhl.
Press Secretary.—Michael Mershon.
34 Mechanic Street, Worcester, MA 01608 .... (508) 831–7356
District Director.—Matthew Pacheco.
8 North Main Street, Room 200, Attleboro, MA 02703 .... (508) 431–8025
District Representative.—Lisa Nelson.
218 South Main Street, Room 204, Fall River, MA 02721 .... (508) 677–0140
District Representative.—Patrick Norton.
255 Main Street, Room 104, Marlborough, MA 01752 .... (508) 460–9292
District Representative.—Sean Navin.

Counties: BRISTOL (part), MIDDLESEX (part), NORFOLK (part), WORCESTER (part). CITIES AND TOWNSHIPS: Ashland, Attleborough, Auburn, Boylston, Clinton, Fall River, Franklin, Holden, Holliston, Hopkinton, Marlborough, Medway, North Attleborough, Northborough, Paxton, Plainville, Princeton, Rehoboth, Rutland, Seekonk, Shrewsbury, Somerset, Southborough, Swansea, West Boylston, Westborough, Worcester, and Wrentham. Population (2000), 634,585.

ZIP Codes: 01501, 01505, 01510, 01517, 01520, 01522, 01527, 01532, 01541, 01543, 01545–46, 01580–83, 01601–15, 01653–55, 01721, 01745–46, 01748–49, 01752, 01772, 01784, 02038, 02053, 02070, 02093, 02703, 02720–21, 02723–26, 02760–63, 02769, 02771, 02777

* * *

FOURTH DISTRICT

BARNEY FRANK, Democrat, of Newton, MA; born in Bayonne, NJ, March 31, 1940; education: graduated, Bayonne High School, 1957; B.A., Harvard College, 1962; graduate student in political science, Harvard University, 1962–67; teaching fellow in government, Harvard College, 1963–66; J.D., Harvard University, 1977; admitted to the Massachusetts bar, 1979; executive assistant to Mayor Kevin White of Boston, 1968–71; administrative assistant to U.S. Congressman Michael F. Harrington, 1971–72; member, Massachusetts Legislature, 1973–80; Senior Whip; co-chair, Democratic Parliamentary Group; committees: chair, Financial Services; elected to the 97th Congress, November 4, 1980; reelected to each succeeding Congress.

Office Listings

http://www.house.gov/frank

2252 Rayburn House Office Building, Washington, DC 20515 .... (202) 225–5931
Chief of Staff.—Peter Kovar. FAX: 225–0182
Deputy Chief of Staff / Scheduler.—Maria Giesta.
Assistant to the Chief of Staff.—Marisa Greenwald.
29 Crafts Street, Suite 375, Newton, MA 02458 .... (617) 332–3920
District Director.—Dorothy Reichard.
558 Pleasant Street, Room 309, New Bedford, MA 02740 .... (508) 999–6462
Office Manager.—Lisa Lowney.
The Jones Building, Suite 310, 29 Broadway, Taunton, MA 02780 .... (508) 822–4796
Office Manager.—Garth Patterson.

Counties: BRISTOL (part), MIDDLESEX (part), NORFOLK (part), PLYMOUTH (part). CITIES AND TOWNSHIPS: Acushnet, Berkley, Brookline, Dartmouth, Dighton, Dover, Fairhaven, Fall River, Foxboro, Freetown, Halifax, Lakeville, Mansfield, Marion, Mattapoisett, Middleborough, Millis, New Bedford, Newton, Norfolk, Norton, Raynham, Rochester, Sharon, Sherborn, Taunton, Wareham, Wellesley, and Westport. Population (2000), 634,624.

ZIP Codes: 02021, 02030, 02032, 02035, 02048, 02053–54, 02056, 02067, 02130, 02135, 02215, 02330, 02333, 02338, 02344, 02346–47, 02349, 02360, 02367, 02445–47, 02456–62, 02464–68, 02472, 02476, 02481–82, 02492–93, 02495, 02532, 02538, 02558, 02571, 02576, 02702, 02712, 02714–15, 02717–23, 02738–48, 02764, 02766–70, 02779–80, 02783, 02790–91

* * *

FIFTH DISTRICT

VACANT

Counties: ESSEX (part), MIDDLESEX (part), WORCESTER (part). CITIES AND TOWNSHIPS: Acton, Andover, Ayer, Berlin, Bolton, Boxborough, Carlisle, Chelmsford, Concord, Dillerjca, Drocut, Dunstable, Groton, Harvard, Haverhill, Hudson, Lawrence, Lancaster, Littleton, Lowell, Maynard, Methuen, Shirley, Stow, Sudbury, Tewksbury, Tyngsborough, Wayland, and Westford. Population (2000), 635,326.

ZIP Codes: 01432, 01450–51, 01453, 01460, 01464, 01467, 01470–72, 01503, 01523, 01561, 01718–20, 01740–42, 01749, 01754, 01775–76, 01778, 01810, 01812, 01821–22, 01824, 01826–27, 01830, 01832, 01835, 01840–44, 01850–54, 01862–63, 01865–66, 01876, 01879, 01886, 01899, 02493, 05501, 05544

* * *

SIXTH DISTRICT

JOHN F. TIERNEY, Democrat, of Salem, MA; born in Salem, September 18, 1951; education: graduated, Salem High School; B.A., political science, Salem State College, 1973; J.D., Suffolk University, 1976; professional: attorney, admitted to the Massachusetts bar in 1976; sole practitioner, 1976–80; partner, Tierney, Kalis and Lucas, 1981–96; member: Salem Chamber of Commerce, 1976–96 (president, 1995); trustee, Salem State College, 1992–97; married: Patrice M., 1997; committees: Education and Labor; Oversight and Government Reform; Permanent Select Committee on Intelligence; elected to the 105th Congress; reelected to each succeeding Congress.

Office Listings

http://www.house.gov/tierney

2238 Rayburn House Office Building, Washington, DC 20515 .... (202) 225–8020
Chief of Staff.—Betsy Arnold. FAX: 225–5915
Legislative Director.—Kevin McDermott.
Executive Assistant.—Bambi Yingst.
17 Peabody Square, Peabody, MA 01960 .... (978) 531–1669
District Director.—Gary Barrett.
Room 105, Lynn City Hall, Lynn, MA 01902 .... (781) 595–7375

Counties: ESSEX, MIDDLESEX. CITIES AND TOWNSHIPS: Amesbury, Bedford, Beverly, Boxford, Burlington, Danvers, Essex, Georgetown, Gloucester, Groveland, Hamilton, Ipswich, Lynn, Lynnfield, Manchester by the Sea, Marblehead, Merrimac, Middletown, Nahant, Newbury, Newburyport, North Andover, North Reading, Peabody, Reading, Rockport, Rowley, Salem, Salisbury, Saugus, Swampscott, Topsfield, Wenham, West Newbury, Wakefield, and Wilmington. Population (2000), 636,554.

ZIP Codes: 01730–31, 01801, 01803, 01805, 01810, 01821, 01833–34, 01845, 01860, 01864, 01867, 01880, 01885, 01887, 01889, 01901–08, 01910, 01913, 01915, 01921–23, 01929–31, 01936–38, 01940, 01944–45, 01949–52, 01960–61, 01965–66, 01969–71, 01982–85

* * *

SEVENTH DISTRICT

EDWARD J. MARKEY, Democrat, of Malden, MA; born in Malden, July 11, 1946; graduated from Malden Catholic High School, Malden, MA, 1964; B.A., Boston College, Chestnut Hill, MA, 1968; J.D., Boston College Law School, Chestnut Hill, MA, 1972; professional: lawyer, private practice; member, Massachusetts State house of representatives, 1973–76; military: United States Army Reserve, 1968–73; married: Dr. Susan Blumenthal; committees: chair, Select Committee on Energy Independence and Global Warming; Energy and Commerce; Homeland Security; Natural Resources; elected to the 94th Congress, November 2, 1976, to fill the vacancy caused by the death of Representative Torbert H. Macdonald; at the same time elected to the 95th Congress; reelected to each succeeding Congress.

Office Listings

http://www.house.gov/markey

2108 Rayburn House Office Building, Washington, DC 20515 .... (202) 225–2836
Chief of Staff.—Jeff Duncan. FAX: 226–0092
Scheduler.—Nancy Morrissey.
5 High Street, Suite 101, Medford, MA 02155 .... (781) 396–2900

188 Concord Street, Suite 102, Framingham, MA 01701 .... (508) 875–2900

Counties: MIDDLESEX (part), SUFFOLK (part). CITIES AND TOWNSHIPS: Arlington, Belmont, Everett, Framingham, Lexington, Lincoln, Malden, Medford, Melrose, Natick, Revere, Stoneham, Waltham, Watertown, Wayland, Weston, Winchester, Winthrop, and Woburn. Population (2000), 634,287.

ZIP Codes: 01701–02, 01760, 01773, 01778, 01801, 01890, 02148–49, 02151–52, 02155, 02176, 02180, 02420–21, 02451–54, 02472, 02474–76, 02478, 02493

* * *

EIGHTH DISTRICT

MICHAEL E. CAPUANO, Democrat, of Somerville, MA; born in Somerville, January 9, 1952; education: graduated, Somerville High School, 1969; B.A., Dartmouth College, 1973; J.D., Boston College Law School, 1977; professional: admitted to the Massachusetts Bar, 1977; Alderman in Somerville, MA, 1977–79; Alderman-at-Large, 1985–89; elected Mayor for five terms, 1990 to January, 1999, when he resigned to be sworn in as a U.S. Representative; Democratic Regional Whip; married: Barbara Teebagy of Somerville, MA, in 1974; children: Michael and Joseph; committees: Financial Services; House Administration; Transportation and Infrastructure; elected to the 106th Congress; reelected to each succeeding Congress.

Office Listings

http://www.house.gov/capuano

1530 Longworth House Office Building, Washington, DC 20515 .... (202) 225–5111
Chief of Staff.—Robert Primus. FAX: 225–9322
Legislative Director.—Jon Skarin.
Office Manager / Scheduler.—Mary Doherty.
Senior Legislative Assistants: Kaitlin McColgan, Noelle Melton.
110 First Street, Cambridge, MA 02141 .... (617) 621–6208
District Director.—Jon Lenicheck.

Counties: MIDDLESEX (part), SUFFOLK (part). CITIES AND TOWNSHIPS: Boston, Cambridge, Chelsea, and Somerville. Population (2000), 634,835.

ZIP Codes: 02108–11, 02113–22, 02124–26, 02128–31, 02133–36, 02138–45, 02150–51, 02155, 02163, 02199, 02215–17, 02228, 02238–39, 02295, 02297, 02446, 02458, 02467, 02472, 02478

* * *

NINTH DISTRICT

STEPHEN F. LYNCH, Democrat, of South Boston, MA; born in South Boston, March 31, 1955; education: South Boston High School, 1973; B.S., Wentworth Institute of Technology; J.D., Boston College Law School; Master in Public Administration, JFK School of Government, Harvard University; professional: attorney; former President of Ironworkers Local #7; organizations: South Boston Boys and Girls Club; Boston Children's Museum; Colonel Daniel Marr Boys and Girls Club; Chinatown Trust Fund; South Boston Harbor Academy Charter School; Friends for Children; public service: elected to the Massachusetts House of Representatives in 1994, and the State Senate in 1996; family: married to Margaret; one child: Victoria; committees: Financial Services; Oversight and Government Reform; elected to the 107th Congress, by special election, on October 16, 2001; reelected to each succeeding Congress.

Office Listings

221 Cannon House Office Building, Washington, DC 20515 .... (202) 225–8273
Chief of Staff.—Kevin Ryan. FAX: 225–3984
Legislative Director.—Caroline Powers.
Executive Assistant.—Greta Hebert.
88 Black Falcon Avenue, Suite 340, Boston, MA 02210 .... (617) 428–2000
166 Main Street, Brockton, MA 02401 .... (508) 586–5555

Counties: BRISTOL (part), NORFOLK (part), PLYMOUTH (part), SUFFOLK (part). Population (2000), 634,062.

ZIP Codes: 02021, 02026–27, 02032, 02052, 02062, 02071–72, 02081, 02090, 02101–10, 02112, 02114, 02116, 02122, 02124–27, 02130–32, 02136–37, 02151, 02169–71, 02184–87, 02196, 02201–12, 02222, 02241, 02266, 02283–84, 02293, 02297, 02301–05, 02322, 02324–25, 02333–34, 02337, 02341, 02343, 02350, 02356–57, 02368, 02375, 02379, 02382, 02467, 02481, 02492, 02494

* * *

TENTH DISTRICT

WILLIAM D. DELAHUNT, Democrat, of Quincy, MA; born in Boston, MA, July 18, 1941; education: B.A., political science, Middlebury College, VT; M.A., J.D., Boston College Law School, 1967; U.S. Coast Guard Reserves, 1963–71; professional: admitted to the Massachusetts Bar in 1967 and began practice in Boston; assistant majority leader, Massachusetts House of Representatives, 1973–75; Norfolk County District Attorney, 1975–96; president, Massachusetts District Attorneys Association, 1985; member, Council of Young American Political Leaders fact-finding mission to Poland, 1979; named citizen of the Year by South Shore Coalition for Human Rights, 1983; delegate, Human Rights Project fact-finding mission to Cuba, 1988; member, Anti-Defamation League of B'nai B'rith fact-finding mission to Israel, 1990; chairman, Development Committee, South Shore Association for Retarded Citizens; Democratic State Committeeman, Norfolk District; advisory board member, Jane Doe Safety Fund; honoree of the Boston Area Rape Crisis Center for contribution to preventing sexual assault, 1993; New England Region honoree, Anti-Defamation League, 1994; Massachusetts Bar Association Public Service Award, 1994; member, Board of Directors, RYKA Rose Foundation; co-chair, Coast Guard Caucus; Older Americans Caucus; Democratic Task Force on Crime; Law Enforcement Caucus; Congressional Human Rights Caucus; Democratic Steering Committee; two daughters: Kirsten and Kara; committees: Foreign Affairs; Judiciary; Standards of Official Conduct; elected to the 105th Congress; reelected to each succeeding Congress.

Office Listings

http://www.house.gov/delahunt

2454 Rayburn House Office Building, Washington, DC 20515 .... (202) 225–3111
Chief of Staff.—Mark Forest. FAX: 225–5658
146 Main Street, Hyannis, MA 02601 .... (508) 771–0666
Regional Representative.—Mark Forest.
1250 Hancock Street, Suite 802N, Quincy, MA 02169 .... (617) 770–3700
Regional Representative.—Corinne Young.

Counties: BARNSTABLE, DUKES, NANTUCKET, NORFOLK (part), PLYMOUTH (part). Population (2000), 635,901.

ZIP Codes: 02018, 02020, 02025, 02035, 02040–41, 02043–45, 02047, 02050–51, 02055, 02059–61, 02065–66, 02169–71, 02184, 02186, 02188–91, 02269, 02327, 02330–32, 02339–41, 02345, 02351, 02355, 02358–62, 02364, 02366–67, 02370, 02381, 02532, 02534–37, 02539–43, 02552–54, 02556–57, 02559, 02561–65, 02568, 02573–75, 02584, 02601, 02630–35, 02637–39, 02641–53, 02655, 02657, 02659–64, 02666–73, 02675, 02713

MICHIGAN

(Population 2000, 9,938,444)

SENATORS

CARL LEVIN, Democrat, of Detroit, MI; born in Detroit, June 28, 1934; education: graduated, Central High School, Detroit, 1952; Swarthmore College, Swarthmore, PA, 1956; Harvard Law School, Boston, MA, 1959; admitted to the Michigan bar in 1959; professional: lawyer; Grossman, Hyman and Grossman, Detroit, 1959–64; assistant attorney general and general counsel for Michigan Civil Rights Commission, 1964–67; chief appellate defender for city of Detroit, 1968–69; counsel, Schlussel, Lifton, Simon, Rands and Kaufman, 1971–73; counsel, Jaffe, Snider, Raitt, Garratt and Heuer, 1978–79; member, City Council of Detroit, 1969–77 (president, 1974–77); member: Congregation T'Chiyah; American, Michigan and Detroit bar associations; former instructor at Wayne State University and the University of Detroit; married: the former Barbara Halpern, 1961; children: Kate, Laura, and Erica; committees: chair, Armed Services; Homeland Security and Governmental Affairs; Small Business and Entrepreneurship; Select Committee on Intelligence; elected to the U.S. Senate on November 7, 1978; reelected to each succeeding Senate term.

Office Listings

http://levin.senate.gov

269 Russell Senate Office Building, Washington, DC 20510 .... (202) 224–6221
Chief of Staff.—David Lyles. FAX: 224–1388
Legislative Director.—Rich Arenberg.
Scheduler.—Alison Warner.
Press Secretary.—Tara Andringa.
477 Michigan Avenue, McNamara Building, Room 1860, Detroit, MI 48226 .... (313) 226–6020
Federal Building, Room 720, 110 Michigan Street, NW, Grand Rapids, MI 49503.. (616) 456–2531
1810 Michigan National Tower, 124 West Allegan Street, Suite 1810, Lansing, MI 48933 .... (517) 377–1508
524 Ludington Street, Suite LL103, Escanaba, MI 49829 .... (906) 789–0052
515 North Washington, Suite 402, Saginaw, MI 48607 .... (989) 754–2494
30500 VanDyke, Suite 206, Warren, MI 48093 .... (810) 573–9145
107 Cass Street, Suite E, Traverse City, MI 49684 .... (616) 947–9569

* * *

DEBBIE STABENOW, Democrat, of Lansing, MI; born in Gladwin, MI, April 29, 1950; education: Clare High School; B.A., Michigan State University, 1972; M.S.W., Michigan State University, 1975; public service: Ingham County, MI, Commissioner, 1975–78, chairperson for two years; Michigan State House of Representatives, 1979–90; Michigan State Senate, 1991–94; religion: Methodist; married to Thomas Athans; children: Todd and Michelle; committees: Agriculture, Nutrition, and Forestry; Budget; Finance; elected to the U.S. House of Representatives in 1996 and 1998; elected to the U.S. Senate on November 7, 2000; reelected to each succeeding Senate term.

Office Listings

http://stabenow.senate.gov

133 Hart Senate Office Building, Washington, DC 20510 .... (202) 224–4822
Chief of Staff.—Sander Lurie. FAX: 228–0325
Legislative Director.—Amanda Renteria.
Deputy Chief of Staff.—Brent Colburn.
Scheduler.—Anne Stanski.
221 West Lake Lansing Road, Suite 100, East Lansing, MI 48823 .... (517) 203–1760
Marquette Building, 243 West Congress, Suite 550, Detroit, MI 48226 .... (313) 961–4330
2503 South Linden Road, Flint, MI 48532 .... (810) 720–4172
3335 South Airport Road West, Suite 6B, Traverse City, MI 49684 .... (231) 929–1031
3280 Beltline Court, Suite 400, Grand Rapids, MI 49525 .... (616) 975–0052
1901 West Ridge, Suite 7, Marquette, MI 49855 .... (906) 228–8756

REPRESENTATIVES

FIRST DISTRICT

BART STUPAK, Democrat, of Menominee, MI; born in Milwaukee, WI, February 29, 1952; education: graduated, Gladstone High School, Gladstone, MI, 1970; B.S., Saginaw Valley State

College, 1977; J.D., Thomas Cooley Law School, 1981; professional: attorney; admitted to the Michigan bar, 1981; Michigan State House of Representatives, 1989–90; member: Elks Club; State Employees Retirement Association; Sons of the American Legion; Wildlife Unlimited; National Rifle Association; Knights of Columbus; national committeeman, Boy Scouts of America; married: the former Laurie Ann Olsen; children: Ken and Bart, Jr. (deceased); committees: Energy and Commerce; elected on November 3, 1992, to the 103rd Congress; reelected to each succeeding Congress.

Office Listings

http://www.house.gov/stupak

2352 Rayburn House Office Building, Washington, DC 20515 .... (202) 225–4735
Chief of Staff.—Scott Schloegel. FAX: 225–4744
Press Secretary.—Alex Haurek.
District Administrator.—Tom Baldini.
575 Court Street, West Branch, MI 48661 .... (989) 345–2258
902 Ludington Street, Escanaba, MI 49829 .... (906) 786–4504
1229 West Washington, Marquette, MI 49855 .... (906) 228–3700
111 East Chisholm, Alpena, MI 49707 .... (989) 356–0690
2 South 6th Street, Suite 3, Crystal Falls, MI 49920 .... (906) 875–3751
616 Sheldon Avenue, Room 213, Houghton, MI 49931 .... (906) 482–1371
200 Division Street, Petoskey, MI 49770 .... (231) 348–0657

Counties: ALCONA, ALGER, ALPENA, ANTRIM, ARENAC, BARAGA, BAY (part), CHARLEVOIX, CHEBOYGAN, CHIPPEWA, CRAWFORD, DELTA, DICKINSON, EMMET, GOGEBIC, HOUGHTON, IRON, KEWEENAW, LUCE, MACKINAC, MARQUETTE, MENOMINEE, MONTMORENCY, OGEMAW, ONTONAGON, OSCODA, OTSEGO, PRESQUE ISLE, SCHOOLCRAFT. Population (2000), 662,563.

ZIP Codes: 48610–13, 48618–19, 48621, 48623–24, 48628, 48631, 48634–36, 48642, 48647, 48650, 48652–54, 48658–59, 48661, 48703, 48705–06, 48721, 48728, 48730, 48737–40, 48742–43, 48745, 48748–50, 48756, 48761–66, 48770, 49611–12, 49615, 49622, 49627, 49629, 49648, 49659, 49676, 49701, 49705–07, 49709–13, 49715–30, 49733–40, 49743–49, 49751–53, 49755–57, 49759–62, 49764–66, 49768–70, 49774–77, 49779–85, 49788, 49790–93, 49795–97, 49799, 49801–02, 49805–08, 49812, 49814–22, 49825–27, 49829, 49831, 49833–41, 49845, 49847–49, 49852–55, 49858, 49861–64, 49866, 49868, 49870–74, 49876–81, 49883–87, 49891–96, 49901–03, 49905, 49908, 49910–13, 49915–22, 49925, 49927, 49929–31, 49934–35, 49938, 49945–48, 49950, 49952–53, 49955, 49958–65, 49967–71

* * *

SECOND DISTRICT

PETER HOEKSTRA, Republican, of Holland, MI; born in Groningen, the Netherlands, October 30, 1953; education: graduated, Holland Christian High School; B.A., Hope College, Holland, 1975; M.B.A., University of Michigan, 1977; professional: vice president for product management, Herman Miller, Inc.; married: the former Diane Johnson; children: Erin, Allison, and Bryan; committees: Education and Labor; Permanent Select Committee on Intelligence; elected on November 3, 1992, to the 103rd Congress; reelected to each succeeding Congress.

Office Listings

http://hoekstra.house.gov

2234 Rayburn House Office Building, Washington, DC 20515 .... (202) 225–4401
Chief of Staff.—Amy Plaster. FAX: 226–0779
Legislative Director.—Justin Wormmeester.
Scheduler / Executive Assistant.—Leah Scott.
District Director of Policy.—Jon DeWitte.
184 South River, Holland, MI 49423 .... (616) 395–0030
900 Third Street, Suite 203, Muskegon, MI 49440 .... (231) 722–8386
210½ North Mitchell Street, Cadillac, MI 49601 .... (231) 775–0050

Counties: ALLEGAN (part), BENZIE, KENT (part), LAKE, MANISTEE, MASON, MUSKEGON, NEWAYGO, OCEANA, OTTAWA, WEXFORD. Population (2000), 662,563.

ZIP Codes: 49010, 49078, 49080, 49303–04, 49307, 49309, 49312, 49314–15, 49318–19, 49321, 49323, 49327–30, 49333, 49336–38, 49343, 49345–46, 49348–49, 49401–06, 49408–13, 49415, 49417–31, 49434–37, 49440–46, 49448–49, 49451–61, 49463–64, 49544, 49601, 49613–14, 49616–20, 49623, 49625–26, 49628, 49630, 49633–35, 49638, 49640, 49642–45, 49649–50, 49655–56, 49660, 49663, 49668, 49675, 49677, 49683, 49688–89

* * *

THIRD DISTRICT

VERNON J. EHLERS, Republican, of Grand Rapids, MI; born in Pipestone, MN, February 6, 1934; educated at home by his parents; attended Calvin College; undergraduate degree in physics and Ph.D. in nuclear physics, University of California at Berkeley; taught and did research at Berkeley for 6 years; returned to Calvin College; taught physics and became chairman, Physics Department; served on various boards and commissions; member, Michigan House and Senate; first research physicist in Congress; while on Science Committee in 1997–98, was selected to rewrite the nation's science policy; introduced National Science Education Acts aimed at reforming K–12 science, mathematics, engineering, and technology education; as member of House Administration Committee, guided the program to revamp the House computer system, connect it to the Internet, and allow all citizens to access House documents; member and former elder, Eastern Avenue Christian Reformed Church, Grand Rapids, MI; married: the former Johanna Meulink; four adult children: Heidi, Brian, Marla, and Todd; three grandchildren; one great-grandchild; committees: Education and Labor; House Administration; Science and Technology; Transportation and Infrastructure; elected to the 103rd Congress, by special election, on December 7, 1993; reelected to each succeeding Congress.

Office Listings

http://www.house.gov/ehlers

2182 Rayburn House Office Building, Washington, DC 20515 .... (202) 225–3831
Chief of Staff.—Bill McBride. FAX: 225–5144
Legislative Director.—Matt Reiffer.
Executive Assistant / Scheduler.—Kelli Scholten.
Press Secretary.—Jon Brandt.
110 Michigan Street, NW., Suite 166, Grand Rapids, MI 49503 .... (616) 451–8383
Community Services Director.—Rick Treur.

Counties: BARRY, IONIA, KENT (part). CITIES: Belding, Cedar Springs, East Grand Rapids, Grand Rapids, Grandville, Hastings, Ionia, Kentwood, Lowell, Portland, Rockford, Walker, and Wyoming. Population (2000), 662,563.

ZIP Codes: 48809, 48815, 48834, 48837–38, 48845–46, 48849, 48851, 48860–61, 48865, 48870–71, 48873, 48875, 48881, 48887, 48890, 48897, 49017, 49021, 49035, 49046, 49050, 49058, 49060, 49073, 49080, 49083, 49301–02, 49306, 49315–17, 49319, 49321, 49325–26, 49331, 49333, 49341, 49343–45, 49347–48, 49351, 49355–57, 49418, 49468, 49501–10, 49512, 49514–16, 49518, 49523, 49525, 49530, 49544, 49546, 49548, 49550, 49555, 49560, 49588, 49599

* * *

FOURTH DISTRICT

DAVE CAMP, Republican, of Midland, MI; born in Midland, July 9, 1953; education: graduated, H.H. Dow High School, Midland, 1971; B.A., *magna cum laude*, Albion College, Albion, MI, 1975; J.D., University of San Diego, 1978; attorney; member: State Bar of Michigan; State Bar of California; District of Columbia bar, U.S. Supreme Court; U.S. District Court, Eastern District of Michigan and Southern District of California; Midland County Bar Association; law practice, Midland, 1979–91; Special Assistant Attorney General, 1980–84; administrative assistant to Congressman Bill Schuette, Michigan's 10th Congressional District, 1985–87; State Representative, Michigan's 102nd district, 1989–91; chairman, Corrections Day Advisory Group; deputy minority whip; Executive Committee, National Republican Congressional Committee; Rural Health Care Coalition; 1998 Adoption Hall of Fame Inductee; American Farm Bureau Federation 1998 Golden Plow award recipient; married: attorney Nancy Keil of Midland, 1994; three children; committees: Ways and Means; elected to Congress on November 6, 1990; reelected to each succeeding Congress.

Office Listings

http://www.house.gov/camp

137 Cannon House Office Building, Washington, DC 20515 .... (202) 225–3561
Chief of Staff.—Jim Brandell. FAX: 225–9679
Communications Director.—Sage Eastman.
Legislative Director.—Joanna Foust.
Scheduler.—Julie Donovan.
135 Ashman Street, Midland, MI, 48640 .... (989) 631–2552
121 East Front Street, Suite 202, Traverse City, MI 49684 .... (231) 929–4711

Counties: CLARE COUNTY. CITIES: Clare, Farwell, Harrison, Lake, Lake George. CLINTON COUNTY. CITY: Carland. GRAND TRAVERSE COUNTY. CITIES: Acme, Fife Lake, Grawn, Interlochen, Kingsley, Mayfield, Old Mission, Traverse City, Williamsburg. GRATIOT COUNTY. CITIES: Alma, Ashley, Bannister, Breckenridge, Elm Hall, Elwell, Ithaca, Middleton, North Star, Perrinton, Pompeii, Riverdale, Sumner, St. Louis, Wheeler. ISABELLA COUNTY. CITIES: Blanchard, Millbrook, Mt. Pleasant, Rosebush, Shepherd, Weidman, Winn. KALKASKA COUNTY. CITIES: Kalkaska, Rapid City, South Boardman. LEELANAU COUNTY. CITIES: Cedar, Empire, Glen Arbor, Lake Leelanau, Leland, Maple City, Northport, Omena, Suttons Bay. MECOSTA COUNTY. CITIES: Barryton, Big Rapids, Canadian Lakes, Chippewa Lakes, Mecosta, Morley, Paris, Remus, Stanwood. MIDLAND COUNTY. CITIES: Coleman, Edenville, Hope, Laporte, Midland, North Bradley, Poseyville, Sanford. MISSAUKEE COUNTY. CITIES: Falmouth, Lake City, McBain, Merritt, Moorestown. MONTCALM COUNTY. CITIES: Alger, Butternut, Carson City, Cedar Lake, Coral, Crystal, Edmore, Entrican, Fenwick, Gowen, Greenville, Howard City, Lakeview, Langston, Maple Hill, McBride, Pierson, Sand Lake, Sheridan, Sidney, Six Lakes, Stanton, Trufant,

Vestaburg, Vickeryville. OSCEOLA COUNTY. CITIES: Evart, Hersey, LeRoy, Marion, Reed City, Sears, Tustin. ROSCOMMON COUNTY. CITIES: Higgins Lake, Houghton Lake, Houghton Lake Heights, Prudenville, Roscommon, St. Helen. SAGINAW COUNTY (part). CITIES: Birch Run, Brant, Bridgeport, Burt, Carrolton, Chesaning, Fosters, Freeland, Fremont, Hemlock, Merrill, Oakley, Richland, Saginaw, Shields, Spalding, St. Charles, University Center. SHIAWASSEE COUNTY (part). CITIES: Bancroft, Caledonia, Chapin, Corunna, Henderson, Laingsburg, Morrice, New Haven, New Lothrup, Owosso, Perry, Shaftsburg, Venice, and Vernon. Population (2000), 662,563.

ZIP Codes: 48415, 48417, 48429, 48433, 48436, 48449, 48457, 48460, 48476, 48601–04, 48608–09, 48614–18, 48620, 48622–30, 48632–33, 48637, 48640–42, 48649, 48651–53, 48655–57, 48662, 48667, 48670, 48674, 48686, 48706, 48722, 48724, 48801–02, 48804, 48806–07, 48809, 48811–12, 48817–18, 48829–32, 48834, 48837–38, 48841, 48845, 48847, 48850, 48852–53, 48856, 48858–59, 48862, 48866–67, 48874–75, 48877–80, 48883–86, 48888–89, 48891, 48893, 48896, 49305, 49307, 49310, 49320, 49322–23, 49326, 49328–29, 49332, 49336–40, 49342–43, 49346–47, 49601, 49610, 49612, 49620–21, 49630–33, 49636–37, 49639–40, 49643, 49646, 49649, 49651, 49653–55, 49657, 49659, 49663–67, 49670, 49673–74, 49676–77, 49679–80, 49682–86, 49688, 49690, 49696, 49738

* * *

FIFTH DISTRICT

DALE E. KILDEE, Democrat, of Flint, MI; born in Flint, September 16, 1929; education: graduated, St. Mary High School, 1947; B.A., Sacred Heart Seminary, Detroit, 1952; M.A., University of Michigan, Ann Arbor, 1961; graduate studies in history and political science, University of Peshawar, Pakistan, under Rotary Foundation Fellowship; professional: teacher, University of Detroit High School, 1954–56; Flint Central High School, 1956–64; served as State Representative, 1965–74; State Senator, 1975–77; member: Optimists, Urban League, Knights of Columbus, Phi Delta Kappa national honorary fraternity, American Federation of Teachers; life member, National Association for the Advancement of Colored People; married: the former Gayle Heyn, 1965; children: David, Laura, and Paul; six grandchildren; committees: Education and Labor; Natural Resources; elected to the 95th Congress, November 2, 1976; reelected to each succeeding Congress.

Office Listings

2107 Rayburn House Office Building, Washington, DC 20515 .... (202) 225–3611
Administrative Assistant.—Christopher J. Mansour. FAX: 225–6393
Legislative Director.—Callie Coffman.
Personal Secretary.—Greta Moore.
432 North Saginaw, Suite 410, Flint, MI 48502 .... (810) 239–1437
District Director, all Districts.—Tiffany Anderson-Flynn. (800) 662–2685
515 North Washington Avenue, Suite 401, Saginaw, MI 48607 .... (989) 755–8904
916 Washington Avenue, Suite 205, Bay City, MI 48708 .... (989) 891–0990

Counties: BAY (part), GENESEE, SAGINAW (part), TUSCOLA. Population (2000), 662,563.

ZIP Codes: 48411, 48415, 48417–18, 48420–21, 48423, 48426, 48429–30, 48433, 48435–39, 48449, 48451, 48453, 48457–58, 48460, 48462–64, 48473, 48501–07, 48509, 48519, 48529, 48531–32, 48550–57, 48601–07, 48623, 48631, 48663, 48701, 48706–08, 48710, 48722–23, 48726–27, 48729, 48732–36, 48741, 48744, 48746–47, 48757–60, 48767–69, 48787

* * *

SIXTH DISTRICT

FRED UPTON, Republican, of St. Joseph, MI; born in St. Joseph, April 23, 1953; education: graduated, Shattuck School, Fairbault, MN, 1971; B.A., journalism, University of Michigan, Ann Arbor, 1975; professional: field manager, Dave Stockman Campaign, 1976; staff member, Congressman Dave Stockman, 1976–80; legislative assistant, Office of Management and Budget, 1981–83; deputy director of Legislative Affairs, 1983–84; director of Legislative Affairs, 1984–85; member: First Congregational Church, Emil Verbin Society; married: the former Amey Rulon-Miller; committees: Energy and Commerce; elected to the 100th Congress on November 4, 1986; reelected to each succeeding Congress.

Office Listings

2183 Rayburn House Office Building, Washington, DC 20515 .... (202) 225–3761
Administrative Assistant.—Joan Hillebrands. FAX: 225–4986
Executive Assistant.—Ryan Hollowell.
800 Centre, Suite 106, 800 Ship Street, St. Joseph, MI 49085 .... (269) 982–1986
157 South Kalamazoo Mall, Suite 180, Kalamazoo, MI 49006 .... (269) 385–0039

Counties: ALLEGAN (part), BERRIEN, CALHOUN (part), CASS, KALAMAZOO, ST. JOSEPH, VAN BUREN. CITIES AND TOWNSHIPS: Allegan, Augusta, Bangor, Baroda, Benton Harbor, Berrien Springs, Berrien Center, Bloomingdale, Breedsville, Bridgman,

Buchanan, Burr Oak, Cassopolis, Centreville, Climax, Coloma, Colon, Comstock, Constantine, Covert, Decatur, Delton, Dowagiac, Eau Claire, Edwardsburg, Fulton, Galesburg, Galien, Gobles, Grand Junction, Hagar Shores, Harbert, Hartford, Hickory Corners, Jones, Kalamazoo, Kendall, Lacota, Lakeside, Lawrence, Lawton, Leonidas, Marcellus, Mattawan, Mendon, Nazareth, New Troy, New Buffalo, Niles, Nottawa, Oshtemo, Otsego, Paw Paw, Plainwell, Portage, Pullman, Richland, Riverside, Sawyer, Schoolcraft, Scotts, Sodus, South Haven, St. Joseph, Stevensville, Sturgis, Three Oaks, Three Rivers, Union Pier, Union, Vandalia, Vicksburg, Watervliet, and White Pigeon. Population (2000), 662,563.

ZIP Codes: 48867, 49001–15, 49017, 49019, 49022–24, 49026–27, 49030–32, 49034, 49038–43, 49045, 49047–48, 49051–53, 49055–57, 49060–67, 49070–72, 49074–75, 49077–81, 49083–85, 49087–88, 49090–91, 49093, 49095, 49097–99, 49101–04, 49106–07, 49111–13, 49115–17, 49119–21, 49125–30, 49311, 49315–16, 49323, 49328, 49333, 49335, 49344, 49348, 49408, 49416, 49450

* * *

SEVENTH DISTRICT

TIMOTHY ''TIM'' L. WALBERG, Republican, of Tipton, MI; born in Chicago, Illinois, April 12, 1951; education: attended Thornton Fractional North High School; attended Western Illinois University, Moody Bible Institute; B.S., Taylor University in Fort Wayne, IN (formerly Fort Wayne Bible College); M.A., Wheaton College Graduate School; served as a pastor for almost 10 years; served in the Michigan State House of Representatives, 1983–99; served as president, Warren Reuther Center for Education and Community Impact; worked as a division manager for the Moody Bible Institute of Chicago, before retiring in January 2006; married to Sue; three children: Caleb, Matthew, and Heidi; committees: Agriculture; Education and Labor; elected to the 110th Congress on November 7, 2006.

Office Listings

http://www.walberg.house.gov

325 Cannon House Office Building, Washington, DC 20515 .... (202) 225–6276
Chief of Staff.—Joe Wicks. FAX: 225–6281
Legislative Director.—Aric Nesbitt.
Press Secretary.—Matt Lahr.
Executive Assistant.—Tony Reinhard.
800 West Ganson Avenue, Jackson, MI 49202 .... (517) 780–9075
District Director.—Rick Baxter.
77 East Michigan Avenue, Suite 201, Battle Creek, MI 49017 .... (877) 846–6407

Counties: BRANCH, CALHOUN (part), EATON, HILLSDALE, JACKSON, LENAWEE, WASHTENAW (part). Population (2000), 662,563.

ZIP Codes: 48103, 48105, 48115, 48118, 48130, 48158, 48160, 48167, 48170, 48175–76, 48178, 48189, 48601, 48813, 48821, 48827, 48837, 48849, 48861, 48876, 48890, 48906, 48908, 48911, 48917, 49011, 49014–18, 49020–21, 49028–30, 49033, 49036, 49040, 49051–52, 49058, 49068–69, 49073, 49076, 49082, 49089, 49092, 49094, 49096, 49201–04, 49220–21, 49224, 49227–30, 49232–42, 49245–59, 49261–69, 49271–72, 49274–77, 49279, 49281–89

* * *

EIGHTH DISTRICT

MIKE ROGERS, Republican, of Brighton, MI; born in Livingston County, MI, June 2, 1963; education: B.S., Adrian College; also attended the University of Michigan as an Army ROTC member; military service: U.S. Army, 1st Lieutenant, served in a rapid deployment unit as a Company Commander; professional: FBI Special Agent, assigned to public corruption and organized crime units; businessman; co-founder of E.B.I. Builders, Inc.; organizations: American Heart Association; Women's Resource Center; Brighton Rotary Club; Society of Former Special Agents of the FBI; religion: Methodist; married: Diane; children: Erin and Jonathan; committees: Energy and Commerce; Permanent Select Committee on Intelligence; elected to the 107th Congress on November 7, 2000; reelected to each succeeding Congress.

Office Listings

http://www.house.gov/mikerogers

133 Cannon House Office Building, Washington, DC 20515 .... (202) 225–4872
Chief of Staff.—Matt Strawn. FAX: 225–5820
Legislative Director.—Andrew Keiser.
Press Secretary.—Sylvia Warner.
1327 East Michigan Avenue, Lansing, MI 48912 .... (517) 702–8000

Counties: CLINTON, INGHAM, LIVINGSTON, OAKLAND (part), SHIAWASSE (part). Population (2000), 662,563.

ZIP Codes: 48114, 48116, 48137, 48139, 48143, 48169, 48178, 48189, 48329, 48346–48, 48350, 48353, 48356–57, 48359–62, 48366–67, 48370–71, 48380, 48386, 48414, 48418, 48428–30, 48436, 48438–39, 48442, 48451, 48455, 48462,

48504, 48507, 48805, 48807–08, 48816–17, 48819–27, 48831, 48833, 48835–37, 48840, 48842–45, 48848, 48854–55, 48857, 48863–64, 48866–67, 48872–73, 48875, 48879, 48882, 48892, 48894–95, 48901, 48906, 48909–13, 48915–19, 48921–22, 48924, 48929–30, 48933, 48937, 48950–51, 48956, 48980, 49078, 49080, 49251, 49264, 49285

* * *

NINTH DISTRICT

JOE KNOLLENBERG, Republican, of Bloomfield Hills, MI; born in Mattoon, IL, November 28, 1933; education: B.S., Eastern Illinois University; professional: operated family insurance agency; past vice chairman, Troy Chamber of Commerce; past member, Birmingham Cable TV Community Advisory Board; past president and board member, St. Bede's Parish Council; past president, Evergreen School PTA; past president, Bloomfield Glens Homeowners Association; past president, Cranbrook Homeowners Association; past coordinator, Southfield Ad Hoc Park and Recreational Development Committee; past member, Southfield Mayor's Wage and Salary Committee; elected to the Freshman Class Leadership, liaison to the National Republican Congressional Committee; married to the former Sandra Moco; two sons, Martin and Stephen; committees: Appropriations; elected on November 3, 1992, to the 103rd Congress; reelected to each succeeding Congress.

Office Listings

http://www.house.gov/knollenberg

2349 Rayburn House Office Building, Washington, DC 20515 .... (202) 225–5802
Chief of Staff.—Jeff Onizuk. FAX: 226–2356
Legislative Director.—Craig Albright.
Press Secretary.—Christopher Close.
30833 Northwestern Highway, Suite 100, Farmington Hills, MI 48334 .... (248) 851–1366

Counties: OAKLAND (part). CITIES AND TOWNSHIPS: Auburn Hills, Berkley, Beverly Hills, Bingham Farms, Birmingham, Birmingham Farms, Bloomfield Hills, Bloomfield, Clawson, Farmington, Farmington Hills, Franklin, Keego Harbo, Lake Angelus, Oakland, Orchard Lake Village, Orion, Pontiac, Rochester, Rochester Hills, Royal Oak, Sylvan Lake, Troy, Waterford, and West Bloomfield. Population (2000), 662,563.

ZIP Codes: 48007, 48009, 48012, 48017, 48025, 48067–68, 48072–73, 48083–85, 48098–99, 48167, 48301–04, 48306–09, 48320–36, 48340–43, 48346, 48359–60, 48362–63, 48367, 48370, 48382, 48387, 48390, 48398

* * *

TENTH DISTRICT

CANDICE S. MILLER, Republican, of Harrison Township, MI; born in St. Clair Shores, MI, May 7, 1954; education: attended Macomb Community College and Northwood University; public service: Harrison Township Board of Trustees, 1979; Harrison Township Supervisor, 1980–92; Macomb County Treasurer, 1992–94; Michigan Secretary of State, 1994–2002; professional: worked in a family-owned marina business before she became involved in public service; religion: Presbyterian; married: Macomb County Circuit Court Judge Donald Miller; children: Wendy; committees: Armed Services; Transportation and Infrastructure; Select Committee on Energy Independence and Global Warming; elected to the 108th Congress on November 5, 2002; reelected to each succeeding Congress.

Office Listings

http://candicemiller.house.gov

228 Cannon House Office Building, Washington, DC 20515 .... (202) 225–2106
Chief of Staff.—Jamie Roe. FAX: 226–1169
Legislative Director.—Sean Moran.
Senior Legislative Assistant.—Caleb Overdorff.
48653 Van Dyke Avenue, Shelby Township, MI 48317 .... (586) 997–5010

Counties: HURON, LAPEER, MACOMB (part), SAINT CLAIR, SANILAC. Population (2000), 662,562.

ZIP Codes: 48001–06, 48014, 48022–23, 48027–28, 48032, 48039–42, 48044–45, 48047–51, 48054, 48059–65, 48074, 48079, 48094–97, 48306, 48310–18, 48371, 48401, 48410, 48412–13, 48416, 48419, 48421–23, 48426–28, 48432, 48434–35, 48438, 48440–41, 48444–46, 48450, 48453–56, 48461–72, 48475, 48720, 48725–27, 48729, 48731, 48735, 48741, 48744, 48754–55, 48759–60, 48767

* * *

ELEVENTH DISTRICT

THADDEUS G. McCOTTER, Republican, of Livonia, MI; born in Detroit, MI, August 22, 1965; education: B.A., University of Detroit, 1987; J.D., University of Detroit Law School, 1990; professional: attorney; public service: elected to the Schoolcraft Community College Trustees, 1989; elected to the Wayne County Commission, 1992; elected to the Michigan State Senate, 1998; awards: Michigan Jaycees Outstanding Michigander, 2001; Police Officers Association of Michigan Legislator of the Year, 2002; religion: Catholic; married: Rita; children: George, Timothy, and Emilia; committees: Budget; Foreign Affairs; elected to the 108th Congress on November 5, 2002; reelected to each succeeding Congress.

Office Listings

http://www.house.gov/mccotter

1632 Longworth House Office Building, Washington, DC 20515 .... (202) 225–8171
Chief of Staff.—Martin Van Valkenburg. FAX: 225–2667
Legislative Director.—Caroline Elting.
17197 North Laurel Park Drive, Suite 216, Livonia, MI 48152 .... (734) 632–0314
213 West Huron, Milford, MI 48381 .... (248) 685–9495

Counties: WAYNE COUNTY. CITIES: Livonia, Canton Township, Plymouth City, Plymouth Township, Northville City, Northville Township, Belleville, Van Buren Township, Wayne, Westland, Garden City, Redford Township, Dearborn Heights. OAKLAND COUNTY. CITIES: Novi, South Lyon, Lyon Township, Milford, Wixom, Walled Lake, Commerce Township, White Lake, Highland, and Waterford. Population (2000), 662,563.

ZIP Codes: 48111–12, 48127, 48135–36, 48141, 48150–54, 48165, 48167, 48170, 48174, 48178, 48184–88, 48239–40, 48327, 48329, 48346, 48356–57, 48374–77, 48380–83, 48386–87, 48390–91, 48393

* * *

TWELFTH DISTRICT

SANDER M. LEVIN, Democrat, of Royal Oak, MI; born in Detroit, MI, September 6, 1931; education: graduated, Central High School, Detroit, 1949; B.A., University of Chicago, 1952; M.A., Columbia University, New York, NY, 1954; LL.B., Harvard University, Cambridge, MA, 1957; professional: attorney, admitted to the Michigan bar in 1958 and commenced practice in Detroit, MI; member: Oakland Board of Supervisors, 1961–64; Michigan Senate, 1965–70; Democratic floor leader in State Senate; served on the Advisory Committee on the Education of Handicapped Children in the Department of Health, Education, and Welfare, 1965–68; chairman, Michigan Democratic Party, 1968–69; Democratic candidate for governor, 1970 and 1974; fellow, Kennedy School of Government, Institute of Politics, Harvard University, 1975; assistant administrator, Agency for International Development, 1977–81; married: the former Victoria Schlafer, 1957; children: Jennifer, Andrew, Madeleine, and Matthew; committees: Ways and Means; elected on November 2, 1982, to the 98th Congress; reelected to each succeeding Congress.

Office Listings

http://www.house.gov/levin

1236 Longworth Office House Building, Washington, DC 20515 .... (202) 225–4961
Administrative Assistant.—Hilarie Chambers. FAX: 226–1033
Scheduler.—Monica Chrzaszcz.
27085 Gratiot Avenue, Roseville, MI 48066 .... (586) 498–7122
District Administrator.—Judy Hartwell.

Counties: MACOMB (part), OAKLAND (part). CITIES: Center Line, Clinton Township, Eastpointe, Ferndale, Fraser, Hazel Park, Huntington Woods, Lake Township, Lathrup Village, Madison Heights, Mt. Clemens, Oak Park, Pleasant Ridge, Roseville, Royal Oak, Royal Oak Township, Southfield, St. Clair Shores, Sterling Heights, and Warren. Population (2000), 662,563.

ZIP Codes: 48015, 48021, 48025–26, 48030, 48034–38, 48043, 48046, 48066–67, 48069–71, 48075–76, 48080–82, 48086, 48088–93, 48220, 48236–37, 48310, 48312, 48397

* * *

THIRTEENTH DISTRICT

CAROLYN C. KILPATRICK, Democrat, of Detroit, MI; born in Detroit, June 25, 1945; education: attended Ferris State University; graduate, Western Michigan University, 1972; M.S.,

Education Administration, University of Michigan, 1977; teacher; served in Michigan House of Representatives, 1979–96; member, Detroit Substance Abuse Advisory Council; former chair, Michigan Legislative Black Caucus; participated in first-of-its-kind African Trade Mission; delegate, U.N. International Women's Conference; led Michigan Department of Agriculture delegation to the International Agriculture Show, Nairobi, Kenya; awards: Anthony Wayne Award for leadership, Wayne State University; Burton-Abercrombie Award, 13th Congressional District; Distinguished Legislator Award, University of Michigan; named Woman of the Year by Gentlemen of Wall Street, Inc.; listed in *Who's Who in Black America* and *Who's Who in American Politics*; Women of Achievement and Courage Award; U.S. Air Force Academy Board; chair, Congressional Black Caucus; two children: Kwame and Ayanna; committees: Appropriations; elected to the 105th Congress; reelected to each succeeding Congress.

Office Listings

http://www.house.gov/kilpatrick

1610 Longworth House Office Building, Washington, DC 20515 .... (202) 225–2261
Chief of Staff.—Kimberly Rudolph. FAX: 225–5730
Executive Assistant.—Gerri Houston.
Legislative Director.—James Williams.
Press Secretary.—Tracy Walker.
1274 Library Street, Suite 1B, Detroit, MI 48226 .... (313) 965–9004

Counties: WAYNE COUNTY (part). Population (2000), 628,363.

ZIP Codes: 48146, 48178, 48192, 48195, 48201–18, 48220, 48222, 48224–26, 48229–34, 48236, 48238, 48242–44, 48255, 48260, 48264–69, 48272, 48275, 48277–79

* * *

FOURTEENTH DISTRICT

JOHN CONYERS, JR., Democrat, of Detroit, MI; born in Detroit, May 16, 1929; son of John and Lucille Conyers; education: B.A., Wayne State University, 1957; LL.B., Wayne State Law School, June 1958; served as officer in the U.S. Army Corps of Engineers, one year in Korea; awarded combat and merit citations; engaged in many civil rights and labor activities; legislative assistant to Congressman John D. Dingell, December 1958 to May 1961; appointed Referee for the Workmen's Compensation Department, State of Michigan, by Governor John B. Swainson in October 1961; former vice chairman of Americans for Democratic Action; vice chairman of the National Advisory Council of the ACLU; member: Kappa Alpha Psi; Wolverine Bar; NAACP; Tuskegee Airmen, Inc.; organizations: Congressional Black Caucus; Congressional Urban Caucus; Progressive Caucus; married: Monica Conyers; children: John III, and Carl; committees: chair, Judiciary; elected to the 89th Congress on November 3, 1964; reelected to each succeeding Congress.

Office Listings

http://www.house.gov/conyers

2426 Rayburn House Office Building, Washington, DC 20515 .... (202) 225–5126
Administrative Assistant.—Cynthia Martin. FAX: 225–0072
Scheduler.—Rinia Shelby.
Federal Courthouse, Suite 669, 231 West Lafayette, Detroit, MI 48226 .... (313) 961–5670
District Director.—Patricia Hartig.

Counties: WAYNE COUNTY (part). CITIES AND TOWNSHIPS: Allen Park, Detroit, Dearborn, Gibraltar, Grosse Ile, Hamtramack, Highland Park, Melvindale, Riverview, Southgate, and Trenton. Population (2000), 662,563.

ZIP Codes: 48101–02, 48120–22, 48124, 48126–27, 48138, 48173, 48180, 48183, 48192, 48195, 48203–04, 48206, 48210–12, 48219, 48221, 48223, 48227–28, 48235, 48238–40

* * *

FIFTEENTH DISTRICT

JOHN D. DINGELL, Democrat, of Dearborn, MI; born in Colorado Springs, CO, July 8, 1926; education: B.S., Georgetown University, 1949; J.D., Georgetown University Law School, 1952; professional: World War II veteran; assistant Wayne County prosecutor, 1953–55; member: Migratory Bird Conservation Commission; married: the former Deborah Insley; committees: chair, Energy and Commerce; elected to the 84th Congress in a special election to fill

the vacant seat of his late father, the Honorable John D. Dingell, December 13, 1955; reelected to the 85th and each succeeding Congress.

Office Listings

http://www.house.gov/dingell

2328 Rayburn House Office Building, Washington, DC 20515 .... (202) 225–4071
Chief of Staff.—Michael Robbins.
Press Secretary.—Adam Benson.
19855 West Outer Drive, Suite 103–E, Dearborn, MI 48124 .... (313) 278–2936
District Administrator.—Jeff Donofrio.
23 East Front Street, Suite 103, Monroe, MI 48161 .... (734) 243–1849
301 West Michigan Avenue, Ypsilanti, MI 48197 .... (734) 481–1100

Counties: WAYNE COUNTY (part). CITIES AND TOWNSHIPS: Brownstown Township, Dearborn, Dearborn Heights, Flat Rock, Gibraltar, Rockwood, Romulus, Taylor, Woodhaven. MONROE COUNTY. CITIES AND TOWNSHIPS: Azalia, Carleton, Dundee, Erie, Ida, Lambertville, LaSalle, Luna Pier, Maybee, Milan, Monroe, Newport, Ottawa Lake, Petersburg, Samaria, S. Rockwood, Temperance. WASHTENAW COUNTY (part). CITIES AND TOWNSHIPS: Ann Arbor, Pittsfield Township, York Township, Superior Township, Ypsilanti, and Ypsilanti Township. Population (2000), 662,563.

ZIP Codes: 48103–11, 48113, 48117, 48123–28, 48131, 48133–34, 48140–41, 48144–45, 48157, 48159–62, 48164, 48166, 48170, 48173–74, 48176–77, 48179–80, 48182–84, 48186, 48190–92, 48197–98, 48228, 48239, 49228–29, 49238, 49267, 49270, 49276

MINNESOTA

(Population 2000, 4,919,479)

SENATORS

NORM COLEMAN, Republican, of St. Paul, MN; born in Brooklyn, NY, August 17, 1949; education: B.A., Hofstra University; J.D., University of Iowa; professional: attorney; public service: served for 17 years in the Minnesota Attorney General's office, holding the positions of Chief Prosecutor and Solicitor General of Minnesota; Mayor of St. Paul, MN, 1993–2001; Republican candidate for Governor of Minnesota, 1998; married: Laurie; children: Jacob and Sarah; committees: Agriculture, Nutrition, and Forestry; Foreign Relations; Homeland Security and Governmental Affairs; Small Business and Entrepreneurship; Special Committee on Aging; elected to the U.S. Senate on November 5, 2002.

Office Listings

http://coleman.senate.gov

320 Hart Senate Office Building, Washington, DC 20510 .... (202) 224–5641
Chief of Staff.—Jennifer Lowe. FAX: 224–1152
Legislative Director.—Lorraine Moss.
Administrative Director.—Lucia Lebens.
Communications Director.—Tom Steward.
2550 University Avenue West, Suite 100N, St. Paul, MN 55114 .... (651) 645–0323
State Director.—Vicki Tigwell.
12 Civic Center Plaza, Suite 2167, Mankato, MN 56001 .... (507) 625–6800
200 Northbank Center 206 B, Northeast 3rd Street, Grand Rapids, MN 55744 .... (218) 327–9333
810 4th Avenue South, Suite 203, MooreHead, MN 56560 .... (218) 477–3106

* * *

AMY KLOBUCHAR, Democrat, of Minneapolis, MN; born in Plymouth, MN, May 25, 1960; education: B.A., *magna cum laude*, Yale University, 1982; J.D., *magna cum laude*, University of Chicago Law School, 1985; professional: Attorney at law firm Dorsey & Whitney, 1985–93, Partner in 1993; Partner at law firm Gray, Plant, Mooty, Mooty & Bennett, 1993–98; religion: Congregationalist; public service: City of Minneapolis prosecutor, 1988; elected Hennepin County Attorney, 1998, reelected, 2002; married: John; child: Abigail; committees: Agriculture, Nutrition, and Forestry; Commerce, Science, and Transportation, Environment and Public Works; Joint Economic Committee; elected to the U.S. Senate on November 7, 2006.

Office Listings

http://klobuchar.senate.gov

302 Hart Senate Office Building, Washington, DC 20510 .... (202) 224–3244
Chief of Staff.—Sean Richardson.
Deputy Chief of Staff.—Jeffrey Levensaler.
Legislative Director.—Sheila Murphy.
Scheduler.—Sally Cluthe.
Federal Building, Suite 298, Fort Snelling, MN 55111 .... (612) 727–5220
State Director.—Sara Grewing.

REPRESENTATIVES

FIRST DISTRICT

TIMOTHY J. WALZ, Democrat, of Mankato, MN; born in West Point, NE, April 6, 1964; education: B.S., Chadron State College, Chadron, NE; M.S., St. Mary's University, Winona, MN; professional: high school teacher; military: Command Sergeant Major, Minnesota's 1st/34th Division of the Army National Guard, 1981–2005; awards: 2002 Minnesota Ethics in Education award winner, 2003 Mankato Teacher of the Year, and the 2003 Minnesota Teacher of Excellence; married: Gwen Whipple Walz, 1994; children: Hope and Gus; committees: Agriculture; Transportation and Infrastructure; Veterans' Affairs; elected to the 110th Congress on November 7, 2006.

Office Listings

http://www.house.gov/walz

1529 Longworth House Office Building, Washington, DC 20515 .... (202) 225–2472

Chief of Staff.—Peg McGlinch. FAX: 225–3133
Legislative Director.—Jeremy Bratt.
Legislative Assistant.—Chris Schmitter.
Scheduler.—Craig McDonnell.
227 East Main Street, Suite 220, Mankato, MN 56001 .... (507) 388–2149
1134 Seventh Street NW., Rochester, MN 55901 .... (507) 206–0643

Counties: BLUE EARTH COUNTY. CITIES: Amboy, Eagle Lake, Garden City, Good Thunder, Lake Crystal, Madison Lake, Mankato, Mapleton, Pemberton, St. Clair, Vernon Center. BROWN COUNTY. CITIES: Comfrey, Hanska, New Ulm, Sleepy Eye, Springfield. COTTONWOOD COUNTY. CITIES: Mountain Lake, Storedon, Westbrook. DODGE COUNTY. CITIES: Claremont, Dodge Center, Hayfield, Kasson, Mantorville, West Concord, Windom. FARIBAULT COUNTY. CITIES: Blue Earth, Bricelyn, Delavan, Easton, Elmore, Frost, Huntley, Kiester, Minnesota Lake, Walters, Wells, Winnebago. FILLMORE COUNTY. CITIES: Canton, Chatfield, Fountain, Harmony, Lanesboro, Mabel, Ostrander, Peterson, Preston, Rushford, Spring Valley, Whalan, Wykoff. FREEBORN COUNTY. CITIES: Albert Lea, Alden, Clarks Grove, Conger, Emmons, Freeborn, Geneva, Glenville, Hartland, Hayward, Hollandale, London, Manchester, Myrtle, Oakland, Twin Lakes. HOUSTON COUNTY. CITIES: Brownsville, Caledonia, Eitzen, Hokah, Houston, La Crescent, Spring Grove. JACKSON COUNTY. CITIES: Heron, Jackson, Lake Field. MARTIN COUNTY. CITY: Fairmont. MOWER COUNTY. CITIES: Adams, Austin, Brownsdale, Dexter, Elkton, Grand Meadow, Lansing, LeRoy, Lyle, Rose Creek, Sargeant, Taopi, Waltham. MURRAY COUNTY. CITIES: Fulda, Slayton. NICOLLET COUNTY. CITIES: North Mankato, St. Peter. NOBLES COUNTY. CITIES: Adrian, Worthington. OLMSTED COUNTY. CITIES: Byron, Dover, Eyota, Oronoco, Rochester, Stewartville, Viola. PIPESTONE COUNTY. CITIES: Edgerton, Jasper, Pipestone Ruthton. ROCK COUNTY. CITY: Lurverne. STEELE COUNTY. CITIES: Blooming Prairie, Ellendale, Hope, Medford, Meriden, Owatonna. WABASHA COUNTY. CITIES: Elgin, Hammond, Kellogg, Lake City, Mazeppa, Milleville, Plainview, Reads Landing, Theilman, Wabasha. WASECA COUNTY. CITIES: Janesville, New Richland, Otisco, Waldorf, Waseca. WATONWAN COUNTY. CITIES: Madelia, St. James. WINONA COUNTY. CITIES: Altura, Dakota, Goodview, Homer, Lewiston, Minnesota City, Rollingstone, St. Charles, Stockton, Utica, and Winona. Population (2000), 614,935.

ZIP Codes: 55021, 55027, 55041, 55049, 55052, 55060, 55901–06, 55909–10, 55912, 55917–27, 55929, 55931–36, 55939–47, 55949–57, 55959–65, 55967–77, 55979, 55981–83, 55985, 55987–88, 55990–92, 56001–03, 56006–07, 56009–11, 56013–14, 56016, 56019–21, 56023–29, 56031, 56033–34, 56036–37, 56039, 56041–43, 56045–48, 56050–51, 56054–55, 56058, 56060, 56062–63, 56065, 56068, 56072–74, 56078, 56080–83, 56085, 56087–91, 56093, 56096–98, 56101, 56110–11, 56114–23, 56125, 56127–29, 56131, 56134, 56136–41, 56143–47, 56149–53, 56155–56, 56158–62, 56164–68, 56170–74, 56176–77, 56180–81, 56183, 56185–87, 56266

* * *

SECOND DISTRICT

JOHN KLINE, Republican, of Lakeville, MN; born in Allentown, PA, September 6, 1947; education: B.A., Rice University, 1969; M.P.A., Shippensburg University, 1988; military service: U.S. Marine Corps, 1969–94; retired at the rank of Colonel; organizations: Boy Scouts of America; Marine Corps League; Veterans of Foreign Wars; Marine Corps Association; American Legion; Retired Officers Association; past president, Marine Corps Coordinating Council of Minnesota; religion: Methodist; family: married to Vicky; children: Kathy and Dan; committees: Armed Services; Education and Labor; Standards of Official Conduct; elected to the 108th Congress on November 5, 2002; reelected to each succeeding Congress.

Office Listings

http://www.house.gov/kline

1429 Longworth House Office Building, Washington, DC 20515 .... (202) 225–2271
Chief of Staff.—Jean Hinz. FAX: 225–2595
Legislative Director.—Jeff McNichols.
Executive Assistant.—Brooke Dorobiala.
Press Secretary.—Troy Young.
101 West Burnsville Parkway, Suite 201, Burnsville, MN 55337 .... (952) 808–1213

Counties: CARVER COUNTY. CITIES: Chanhassen, Chaska, Waconia, Victoria. DAKOTA COUNTY (part). CITIES: Apple Valley, Burnsville, Eagan, Farmington, Hastings, Inver Grove Heights. GOODHUE COUNTY. CITIES: Cannon Falls, Pine Island, Red Wing, Zumbrota. LE SUEUR COUNTY. CITIES: Le Sueur, Le Center, Montgomery. RICE COUNTY. CITIES: Faribault, Northfield. SCOTT COUNTY. CITIES: Shakopee, Savage, Prior Lake, New Prague, Jordan, Belle Plaine. WASHINGTON COUNTY (part). CITIES: Woodbury, and Cottage Grove. Population (2000), 614,934.

ZIP Codes: 55001, 55009–10, 55016, 55018–21, 55024, 55026–27, 55031, 55033, 55041, 55044, 55046, 55049, 55052–55, 55057, 55065–66, 55068, 55071, 55075–77, 55085, 55087–89, 55118, 55120–25, 55129, 55306, 55315, 55317–18, 55322, 55328, 55331, 55337, 55339, 55346–47, 55352, 55360, 55367–68, 55372, 55375, 55378–79, 55386–88, 55397, 55946, 55956, 55963, 55983, 55985, 55992, 56011, 56017, 56028, 56050, 56052, 56057–58, 56063, 56069, 56071, 56082, 56096

* * *

THIRD DISTRICT

JIM RAMSTAD, Republican, of Minnetonka, MN; born in Jamestown, ND, May 6, 1946; education: B.A., Phi Beta Kappa, University of Minnesota, 1968; J.D. with honors, George

Washington University, 1973; military service: first lieutenant, U.S. Army Reserve, 1968–74; elected to the Minnesota Senate, 1980; reelected 1982, 1986; assistant minority leader; attorney; adjunct professor; awards: Representative of the Year, National Association of Police Organizations, 1997, 2000; Legislator of the Year, National Association of Alcoholism and Drug Addiction Counselors, 1998; Legislator of the Year, National Mental Health Association, 1999; Legislator of the Year, Arc Minnesota, 2003; Betty Ford National Leadership Award, National Association for Children of Alcoholics, 2003; Legislator of the Year, National Association for the Mentally Ill of Minnesota, 2004; Unsung Hero of America's Veterans, American Legion, 2004; Congressional Partner of the Year, United Way, 2004; Justice for All Disability Rights Award, American Association of People with Disabilities, 2006; Representative of the Year, National MS Society, 2006; Lifetime Achievement Award, Johnson Institute, 2006; Fulbright Distinguished Public Service award; co-chair, Medical Technology Caucus; co-chair, Law Enforcement Caucus; co-chair, Addiction, Treatment and Recovery Caucus; committees: Ways and Means; elected to the 102nd Congress, November 6, 1990; reelected to each succeeding Congress.

Office Listings

103 Cannon House Office Building, Washington, DC 20515 .... (202) 225–2871
FAX: 225–6351
Administrative Assistant.—Dean Peterson.
Legislative Director.—Karin Hope.
Executive Assistant / Scheduler.—Margeaux Plaisted.

1809 Plymouth Road South, Suite 300, Minnetonka, MN 55305 .... (952) 738–8200
District Director.—Lance Olson.

Counties: ANOKA (part), HENNEPIN (part). CITIES AND TOWNSHIPS: Bloomington, Brooklyn Center, Brooklyn Park, Champlin, Coon Rapids, Corcoran, Dayton, Deephaven, Eden Prarie, Edina, Excelsior, Greenwood, Hassan, Hopkins, Independence, Long Lake, Loretto, Maple Grove, Maple Plain, Medicine Lake, Medina, Minnetonka Beach, Minnetonka, Minnetrista, Mound, Orono, Osseo, Plymouth, Rogers, Saint Bonifacius, Shorewood, Spring Park, Tonka Bay, Wayzata, and Woodland. Population (2000), 614,935.

ZIP Codes: 55304–05, 55311, 55316, 55323, 55327, 55331, 55340–41, 55343–48, 55356–57, 55359, 55361, 55364, 55369, 55373–75, 55378, 55384, 55387–88, 55391–92, 55410, 55416, 55420, 55422–26, 55428–31, 55433, 55435–39, 55441–48, 55569–72, 55574, 55576–79, 55592–93, 55595–99

* * *

FOURTH DISTRICT

BETTY McCOLLUM, Democrat-Farmer-Labor, of St. Paul, MN; born in Minneapolis, MN, July 12, 1954; education: A.A., Inver Hills Community College; B.S., College of St. Catherine; professional: teacher and sales manager; single; children: Sean and Katie; public service: North St. Paul City Council, 1986–92; Minnesota House of Representatives, 1992–2000; organizations: Girl Scouts of America; VFW Ladies' Auxiliary; and American Legion Ladies' Auxiliary; awards: Friend of the National Parks Award, National Parks Conservation Association, 2005; Friend of College Access Award, National Association for College Admission Counseling, 2006; Congressional Leadership Award, InterAction, 2006; Congressional Arts Leadership Award, Americans for the Arts, 2007; founder, Congressional Global Health Caucus; appointments: National Council on the Arts; committees: Appropriations; Oversight and Government Reform; Senior Democratic Whip; elected to the 107th Congress on November 7, 2000; reelected to each succeeding Congress.

Office Listings

http://www.house.gov/mccollum

1714 Longworth House Office Building, Washington, DC 20515 .... (202) 225–6631
FAX: 225–1968
Chief of Staff.—Bill Harper.
Legislative Director.—Emily Lawrence.
Office Director.—Shelly Schafer.

165 Western Avenue North, Suite 17, St. Paul, MN 55102 .... (651) 224–9191
Communications / District Director.—Joshua Straka.

Counties: DAKOTA (part), RAMSEY, WASHINGTON (part). Population (2000), 614,935.

ZIP Codes: 55016, 55042, 55055, 55071, 55075–77, 55090, 55101–10, 55112–20, 55125–29, 55133, 55144, 55146, 55150, 55155, 55161, 55164–66, 55168–70, 55172, 55175, 55177, 55182, 55187–88, 55190–91, 55199, 55421, 55432, 55449

* * *

FIFTH DISTRICT

KEITH ELLISON, Democrat-Farmer-Labor, of Minneapolis, MN; born in Detroit, MI, August 4, 1963; education: University of Detroit Jesuit High School and Academy, 1981; Wayne State University, 1987; University of Minnesota Law School, 1990; professional: The Law Office of Lindquist & Vennum, 1990–93; Executive Director of the nonprofit Legal Rights Center in Minneapolis, 1993–98; Hassan & Reed Ltd., 1998–2001; Ellison Law Offices, 2003–06; served in Minnesota State Legislature District 58B, January 2003–December 2006; married: Kim; children: Isaiah, Jeremiah, Elijah, Amirah; committees: Financial Services; Judiciary; elected to the 110th Congress on November 7, 2006.

Office Listings

http://ellison.house.gov/

1130 Longworth House Office Building, Washington, DC 20515 .... (202) 225–4755
Chief of Staff.—Kari Moe. FAX: 225–4886
Legislative Director.—Minh Ta.
Communications Director.—Rick Jauert.
2100 Plymouth Avenue, Minneapolis, MN 55411 .... (612) 522–1212
District Director.—Brian Elliott.

Counties: ANOKA (part), HENNEPIN (part), RAMSEY (part). CITIES: Columbia Heights, Crystal, Ft. Snelling, Fridley, Golden Valley, Hilltop, Hopkins, Minneapolis, New Hope, Richfield, Robbinsdale, St. Anthony, St. Louis Park, and Spring Lake Park, Population (2000), 614,935.

ZIP Codes: 55111–12, 55305, 55343, 55401–30, 55432–33, 55440–41, 55450, 55454–55, 55458–60, 55470, 55472, 55474, 55479–80, 55483–88

* * *

SIXTH DISTRICT

MICHELE BACHMANN, Republican, of Stillwater, MN; born in Waterloo, IA, April 6, 1956; education: B.A., Winona State University, Winona, MN, 1978; J.D., Oral Roberts University, Tulsa, OK; Post Doctorate in Tax Law at the College of William and Mary, Williamsburg, VA; professional: federal tax litigation attorney; served six years in the Minnesota State Senate; organizations: New Heights Charter School; married: Marcus; children: Lucas, Harrison, Elisa, Caroline, and Sophia; committees: Financial Services; elected to the 110th Congress on November 7, 2006.

Office Listings

http://www.bachmann.house.gov

412 Cannon House Office Building, Washington, DC 20515 .... (202) 225–2331
Chief of Staff.—Brooks Kochvar. FAX: 225–6475
Legislative Director.—Rich Dunn.
Scheduler.—Kim Rubin.
Press Secretary.—Heidi Frederickson.
6043 Hudson Road, Suite 330, Woodbury, MN 55125 .... (651) 731–5400

Counties: ANOKA (part), BENTON, SHERBURNE, STEARNS (part), WASHINGTON (part), WRIGHT. CITIES: Andover, Anoka, Blaine, Elk River, Forest Lake, Lino Lakes, St. Cloud, Stillwater, Ramsey, and Woodbury. Population (2000), 614,935.

ZIP Codes: 55001, 55003, 55005–06, 55011, 55014, 55025, 55031, 55038, 55042–43, 55047, 55070, 55073, 55079, 55082–83, 55092, 55110, 55112, 55115, 55125, 55128–29, 55301–04, 55308–09, 55313, 55319–21, 55328–30, 55341, 55349, 55353, 55358–59, 55362–63, 55365, 55371, 55373–74, 55376, 55380–82, 55388–90, 55395, 55398, 55412–13, 55417–18, 55429–30, 55432, 55434, 55448–49, 56301, 56303–04, 56307, 56310, 56314, 56320, 56329–31, 56340, 56352, 56357, 56362, 56367–68, 56373–75, 56377, 56379, 56387–88, 56393, 56395–99

* * *

SEVENTH DISTRICT

COLLIN C. PETERSON, Democrat, of Detroit Lakes, MN; born in Fargo, ND, June 29, 1944; education: graduated from Glyndon (MN) High School, 1962; B.A. in business administration and accounting, Moorhead State University, 1966; U.S. Army National Guard, 1963–69; CPA, owner and partner; Minnesota State Senator, 1976–86; member: AOPA, Safari Club,

Ducks Unlimited, American Legion, Sea Plane Pilots Association, Pheasants Forever, Benevolent Protective Order of Elks, Cormorant Lakes Sportsmen Club; three children: Sean, Jason, and Elliott; committees: chair, Agriculture; elected to the 102nd Congress, November 6, 1990; reelected to each succeeding Congress.

Office Listings

http://collinpeterson.house.gov

2211 Rayburn House Office Building, Washington, DC 20515 .... (202) 225–2165
Chief of Staff.—Mark Brownell.
Legislative Director.—Robin Goracke.
Executive Assistant.—Cherie Slayton.
Assistants: Chris Iacaruso, Sara Kloek, Andrew Martin.
Lake Avenue Plaza Building, Suite 107, 714 Lake Avenue, Detroit Lakes, MN 56501 .... (218) 847–5056
Minnesota Wheat Growers Building, 2603 Wheat Drive, Red Lake, MN 56750 ..... (218) 253–4356
320 Southwest Fourth Street, Centre Point Mall, Willmar, MN 56201 .... (320) 235–1061

Counties: Becker, Beltrami (part), Big Stone, Chippewa, Clay, Clearwater, Douglas, Grant, Kandiyohi, Kittson, Lac qui Parle, Lake of the Woods, Lincoln, Lyon, Mahnomen, Marshall, McLeod, Meeker, Norman, Otter Tail, Pennington, Polk, Pope, Red Lake, Redwood, Renville, Roseau, Sibley, Stearns (part), Stevens, Swift, Todd, Traverse, Wilkin, Yellow Medicine. Population (2000) 614,935.

ZIP Codes: 55307, 55310, 55312, 55314, 55321, 55324–25, 55329, 55332–36, 55338–39, 55342, 55350, 55353–55, 55366, 55368, 55370, 55381–82, 55385, 55389, 55395–96, 55409, 55970, 56011, 56044, 56054, 56058, 56083, 56085, 56087, 56113, 56115, 56129, 56132, 56136, 56142, 56149, 56152, 56157, 56164, 56166, 56169–70, 56175, 56178, 56180, 56201, 56207–12, 56214–16, 56218–32, 56235–37, 56239–41, 56243–45, 56248–49, 56251–53, 56255–58, 56260, 56262–67, 56270–71, 56273–74, 56276–85, 56287–89, 56291–97, 56301–04, 56307–12, 56314–16, 56318–21, 56323–24, 56326–27, 56329, 56331–32, 56334, 56336, 56339–40, 56343, 56345, 56347, 56349, 56352, 56354–55, 56360–62, 56368, 56372–74, 56377–79, 56381–82, 56385, 56387, 56393, 56395–99, 56433–34, 56436–38, 56440, 56443, 56446, 56453, 56458, 56461, 56464, 56466–67, 56470, 56475, 56477–79, 56481–82, 56501–02, 56510–11, 56514–25, 56527–29, 56531, 56533–38, 56540–54, 56556–57, 56560–63, 56565–81, 56583–94, 56601, 56619, 56621, 56623, 56633–34, 56644, 56646–47, 56650–52, 56661, 56663, 56666–67, 56670–71, 56673, 56676, 56678, 56682–87, 56701, 56710–11, 56713–16, 56720–29, 56731–38, 56740–42, 56744, 56748, 56750–51, 56754–63

* * *

EIGHTH DISTRICT

JAMES L. OBERSTAR, Democrat, of Chisholm, MN; born in Chisholm, September 10, 1934; education: graduated, Chisholm High School, 1952; B.A., *summa cum laude*, French and political science, College of St. Thomas, St. Paul, MN, 1956; M.A., European area studies, College of Europe, Bruges, Belgium, 1957; Laval University, Canada; Georgetown University, former teacher of English, French, and Creole; served as administrative assistant to the late Congressman John A. Blatnik, 1963–74; administrator of the House Public Works Committee, 1971–74; co-chair, Congressional Travel and Tourism Caucus; Democratic Study Group; Great Lakes Task Force; National Water Alliance; Northeast Midwest Congressional Coalition; Steel Caucus; chairman, Conference of Great Lakes Congressmen; married: Jean Kurth, 1993; children: Thomas Edward, Katherine Noelle, Anne-Therese, Monica Rose, Charlie, and Lindy; committees: chair, Transportation and Infrastructure; elected to the 94th Congress, November 5, 1974; reelected to each succeeding Congress.

Office Listings

http://www.house.gov/oberstar

2365 Rayburn House Office Building, Washington, DC 20515 .... (202) 225–6211
Administrative Assistant.—William Richard.
Office Manager.—Marianne Buckley.
Legislative Director.—Chip Gardiner.
Communications Director.—John Schadl.
231 Federal Building, Duluth, MN 55802 .... (218) 727–7474
District Manager.—Jackie Morris.
Chisholm City Hall, 316 West Lake Street, Chisholm, MN 55719 .... (218) 254–5761
District Representative.—Peter Makowski.
Brainerd City Hall, 501 Laurel Street, Brainerd, MN 56401 .... (218) 828–4400
District Representative.—Ken Hasskamp.
38625 14th Avenue, Suite 300B, North Branch, MN 55056 .... (651) 277–1234
District Representative.—Alana Petersen.

Counties: Aitkin, Beltrami (part), Carlton, Cass, Chisago, Cook, Crow Wing, Hubbard, Isanti, Itasca, Kanabec, Koochiching, Lake, Mille Lacs, Morrison, Pine, St. Louis, Wadena. Cities: Brainerd, Chisholm, Cloquet, Duluth, Grand Rapids, Hibbing, International Falls, and Little Falls. Population (2000), 614,935.

ZIP Codes: 55002, 55005–08, 55012–13, 55017, 55025, 55029–30, 55032, 55036–37, 55040, 55045, 55051, 55056, 55063, 55067, 55069–70, 55072–74, 55078–80, 55084, 55092, 55330–31, 55362, 55371, 55377, 55398, 55408, 55601–07,

55609, 55612–16, 55701–13, 55716–26, 55730–36, 55738, 55741–42, 55744–46, 55748–53, 55756–58, 55760, 55763–69, 55771–72, 55775, 55777, 55779–87, 55790–93, 55795–98, 55801–08, 55810–12, 55814–16, 56028, 56058, 56304, 56307, 56309–11, 56313–15, 56317–19, 56323, 56325–33, 56335–36, 56338–45, 56347, 56350, 56353–61, 56363–64, 56367–69, 56371, 56373, 56376–77, 56381–82, 56384, 56386, 56389, 56401, 56425, 56430–31, 56433–35, 56437, 56441–44, 56446–50, 56452–53, 56455–56, 56458–59, 56461, 56464–70, 56472–75, 56477, 56479, 56481–82, 56484, 56601, 56623, 56626–31, 56633, 56636–37, 56639, 56641, 56647, 56649, 56653–55, 56657–63, 56668–69, 56672, 56678–81, 56683, 56688

MISSISSIPPI

(Population 2000, 2,844,658)

SENATORS

THAD COCHRAN, Republican, of Jackson, MS; born in Pontotoc, MS, December 7, 1937; education: B.A., University of Mississippi, 1959; J.D., University of Mississippi Law School, 1965; received a Rotary Foundation Fellowship and studied international law and jurisprudence at Trinity College, University of Dublin, Ireland, 1963–64; military service: served in U.S. Navy, 1959–61; professional: admitted to Mississippi bar in 1965; board of directors, Jackson Rotary Club, 1970–71; Outstanding Young Man of the Year Award, Junior Chamber of Commerce in Mississippi, 1971; president, young lawyers section of Mississippi State bar, 1972–73; married: the former Rose Clayton of New Albany, MS, 1964; two children and three grandchildren; committees: Agriculture, Nutrition, and Forestry; Appropriations; Rules and Administration; elected to the 93rd Congress, November 7, 1972; reelected to 94th and 95th Congresses; chairman of the Senate Republican Conference, 1990–96; elected to the U.S. Senate, November 7, 1978, for the six-year term beginning January 3, 1979; subsequently appointed by the governor, December 27, 1978, to fill the vacancy caused by the resignation of Senator James O. Eastland; reelected to each succeeding Senate term.

Office Listings

http://cochran.senate.gov

113 Dirksen Senate Office Building, Washington, DC 20510 .... (202) 224–5054
Chief of Staff.—Jenny Manley.
Legislative Director.—T.A. Hawks.
Press Secretary.—Margaret Wicker.
Scheduler.—Doris Wagley.
188 East Capitol Street, Suite 614, Jackson, MS 39201 .... (601) 965–4459
P.O. Box 1434, Oxford, MS 38655 .... (662) 236–1018
14094 Customs Boulevard, Suite 201, Gulfport, MS 39503 .... (228) 867–9710

* * *

TRENT LOTT, Republican, of Pascagoula, MS; born in Grenada, MS, October 9, 1941; son of Chester P. and Iona (Watson) Lott; education: B.P.A., 1963, J.D., 1967, University of Mississippi; served as field representative for the University of Mississippi, 1963–65; acting Law Alumni Secretary of the Ole Miss Alumni Association, 1966–67; practiced law in Pascagoula in 1967 with Bryan and Gordon law firm; administrative assistant to Congressman William M. Colmer, 1968–72; member: Sigma Nu social fraternity, Phi Alpha Delta legal fraternity, Jackson County Bar Association, American Bar Association, the Masons, First Baptist Church of Pascagoula; married Patricia E. Thompson of Pascagoula, 1964; two children: Chester T., Jr. and Tyler Elizabeth; committees: Commerce, Science, and Transportation; Finance; Rules and Administration; elected to the 93rd Congress, November 7, 1972; reelected to each succeeding Congress; Republican Whip, 1995–96; Senate Republican Leader, 1996–2003; committees: Republican Whip; Commerce, Science and Transportation; Finance; Rules and Administration; elected to the U.S. Senate on November 8, 1988; reelected to each succeeding Senate term.

Office Listings

http://lott.senate.gov

487 Russell Senate Office Building, Washington, DC 20510 .... (202) 224–6253
Chief of Staff.—Bret Boyles. FAX: 224–2262
Scheduler.—Hardy Lott.
Press Secretary.—Lee Youngblood.
Legislative Director.—Jim Sartucci.
245 East Capitol Street, Suite 226, Jackson, MS 39201 .... (601) 965–4644
3118 South Pascagoula Street, Pascagoula, MS 39567 .... (228) 762–5400
2012 15th Street, Suite 451, Gulfport, MS 39501 .... (228) 863–1988
911 Jackson Avenue, Suite 127, Oxford, MS 38655 .... (662) 234–3774

REPRESENTATIVES

FIRST DISTRICT

ROGER F. WICKER, Republican, of Tupelo, MS; born in Pontotoc, MS, July 5, 1951; education: graduated, Pontotoc High School; University of Mississippi: B.A., 1973, J.D., 1975;

president, Associated Student Body, 1972–73; Mississippi Law Journal, 1973–75; Air Force ROTC; U.S. Air Force, 1976–80; lieutenant colonel, U.S. Air Force Reserve, 1980–2004; U.S. House of Representatives Rules Committee staff for Representative Trent Lott, 1980–82; private law practice, 1982–94; Lee County Public Defender, 1984–87; Tupelo City Judge pro tempore, 1986–87; Mississippi State Senate, 1988–94, chairman: Elections Committee (1992), Public Health and Welfare Committee (1993–94); member: Lions Club; University of Mississippi Hall of Fame; Sigma Nu Fraternity Hall of Fame; Omicron Delta Kappa; Phi Delta Phi; religion: Southern Baptist, deacon, adult choir, First Baptist Church, Tupelo, MS; married: Gayle Long Wicker; children: Margaret, Caroline and McDaniel; committees: Appropriations; Republican Policy Committee; Deputy Republican Whip; elected to the 104th Congress, November 8, 1994; president, Republican freshman class, 1995; reelected to each succeeding Congress.

Office Listings

http://www.house.gov/wicker

2350 Rayburn House Office Building, Washington, DC 20515 .... (202) 225–4306
Chief of Staff.—Michelle Barlow. FAX: 225–3549
Legislative Director.—Susan Sweat.
Press Secretary.—Kyle Steward.
Scheduler.—Ariel Owens.
500 West Main Street, Suite 210, P.O. Box 1482, Tupelo, MS 38802 .... (662) 844–5437
Administrative Assistant / Press Secretary.—Kyle Steward.
8700 Northwest Drive, Suite 102, P.O. Box 70, Southaven, MS 38671 .... (662) 342–3942
1360 Sunset Drive, Suite 2, Grenada, MS 38901 .... (662) 294–1321
523 Main Street, Columbus, MS 39701 .... (662) 327–0748

Counties: Alcorn, Benton, Calhoun, Chickasaw, Choctaw, Clay, DeSoto, Grenada, Ittawamba, Lafayette, Lee, Lowndes, Marshall, Monroe, Panola, Pontotoc, Prentiss, Tate, Tippah, Tishomingo, Union, Webster (part), Winston (part), Yalobusha. Population (2000), 711,160.

ZIP Codes: 38601–03, 38606, 38610–11, 38618–21, 38625, 38627, 38629, 38632–35, 38637–38, 38641–42, 38647, 38649–52, 38654–55, 38658–59, 38661, 38663, 38665–66, 38668, 38670–74, 38677, 38679–80, 38683, 38685–86, 38801–04, 38820–21, 38824–29, 38833–35, 38838–39, 38841, 38843–44, 38846–52, 38854–60, 38862–66, 38868–71, 38873–80, 38901–02, 38913–16, 38920, 38922, 38925–27, 38929, 38940, 38948–49, 38951, 38953, 38955, 38960–61, 38965, 39108, 39339, 39701–05, 39710, 39730, 39735–37, 39740–41, 39743–46, 39750–56, 39759, 39766–67, 39769, 39771–73, 39776

* * *

SECOND DISTRICT

BENNIE G. THOMPSON, Democrat, of Bolton, MS; born in Bolton, January 28, 1948; education: graduated, Hinds County Agriculture High School; B.A., Tougaloo College, 1968; M.S., Jackson State University, 1972; professional: teacher; Bolton Board of Aldermen, 1969–73; mayor of Bolton, 1973–79; Hinds County Board of Supervisors, 1980–93; Congressional Black Caucus; Sunbelt Caucus; Rural Caucus; Progressive Caucus; Housing Assistance Council; NAACP 100 Black Men of Jackson, MS; Southern Regional Council; Kappa Alpha Psi Fraternity; married to the former London Johnson, Ph.D.; one daughter: BendaLonne; committees: chair, Homeland Security; elected to the 103rd Congress in a special election; reelected to each succeeding Congress.

Office Listings

http://www.house.gov/thompson

2432 Rayburn House Office Building, Washington, DC 20515 .... (202) 225–5876
Administrative Assistant.—Marsha G. McCraven. FAX: 225–5898
Communications Director.—Lanier Avant.
Legislative Director.—Karis Gutter.
107 West Madison Street, P.O. Box 610, Bolton, MS 39041–0610 .... (601) 866–9003
District Director.—Charlie Horhn.
3607 Medgar Evers Boulevard, Jackson, MS 39213 .... (601) 982–8582
263 East Main Street, Marks, MS 38646 .... (662) 326–9003
Mound Bayou City Hall, Room 134, 106 West Green Street, Mound Bayou, MS 38762 .... (662) 741–9003
509 Highway 82 West, Greenwood, MS 38930 .... (662) 455–9003
910 Courthouse Lane, Greenville, MS 38701 .... (662) 335–9003

Counties: Attala, Bolivar, Carroll, Claiborne, Coahoma, Copiah, Hinds (part), Holmes, Humphreys, Issaquena, Jefferson, Leake (part), Leflore, Madison (part), Montgomery, Quitman, Sharkey, Sunflower, Tallahatchie, Tunica, Warren, Washington, Yazoo. Population (2000), 711,164.

ZIP Codes: 38606, 38609, 38614, 38617, 38621–23, 38626, 38628, 38630–31, 38639, 38643–46, 38664–65, 38669–70, 38676, 38701–04, 38720–23, 38725–26, 38730–33, 38736–40, 38744–46, 38748–49, 38751, 38753–54, 38756, 38758–

62, 38764–65, 38767–69, 38771–74, 38776, 38778, 38780–82, 38901, 38912, 38917, 38920–21, 38923–25, 38927–28, 38930, 38935, 38940–41, 38943–48, 38950, 38952–54, 38957–59, 38961–64, 38966–67, 39038–41, 39045–46, 39051, 39054, 39056, 39058–61, 39063, 39066–67, 39069, 39071–72, 39077–79, 39083, 39086, 39088, 39090, 39095–97, 39107–08, 39110, 39113, 39115, 39120, 39144, 39146, 39150, 39154, 39156–57, 39159–60, 39162–63, 39166, 39169–71, 39173–77, 39179–83, 39191–92, 39194, 39201–07, 39209–10, 39212–13, 39215–17, 39225, 39235, 39269, 39271–72, 39282–84, 39286, 39289, 39296, 39653, 39661, 39668, 39745, 39747, 39767

* * *

THIRD DISTRICT

CHARLES W. ''CHIP'' PICKERING, JR., Republican, of Laurel, MS; born in Laurel, August 10, 1963; education: B.A., Business Administration, University of Mississippi, 1986; M.B.A., Baylor University; professional: farmer; legislative aide to Senate Majority Leader Trent Lott, 1992–96; Bush administration appointee, U.S. Department of Agriculture, 1989–91; Southern Baptist missionary to Budapest, Hungary, 1986–87; Congressional Wireless Caucus; married: the former Leisha Jane Prather; children: Will, Ross, Jackson, Asher, and Harper; committees: Energy and Commerce; elected to the 105th Congress; reelected to each succeeding Congress.

Office Listings

http://www.house.gov/pickering

229 Cannon House Office Building, Washington, DC 20515 .... (202) 225–5031
Chief of Staff.—Susan Butler. FAX: 225–5797
Press Secretary.—Brian Perry.
Legislative Director.—Mike Lipski.
Scheduler.—Marcy Scoggins.
110–D Airport Road, Pearl, MS 39208 .... (601) 932–2410
District Director.—Stanley Shows.
823 22nd Avenue, Meridian, MS 39301 .... (601) 693–6681
Staff Assistants: Lynne Compton, Carol Mabry.
1 Research Boulevard, Suite 206, Starkville, MS 39759 .... (662) 324–0007
District Representative.—Henry Moseley.
230 South Whitworth Street, Brookhaven, MS 39601 .... (601) 823–3400
Staff Assistant.—Mary Martha Dixon.
308 Franklin Street, Natchez, MS 39120 .... (601) 442–2515

Counties: ADANS, AMITE, COVINGTON, FRANKLIN, HINDS (part), JASPER (part), JEFF DAVIS, JONES (part), KEMPER, LAUDERDALE, LAWRENCE, LEAKE (part), LINCOLN, MADISON (part), MARION (part), NESHOBA, NEWTON, NOXUBEE, OKTIBBEHA, PIKE, RANKIN, SCOTT, SIMPSON, SMITH, WALTHALL, WEBSTER (part), WILKINSON, WINSTON. Population (2000), 711,164.

ZIP Codes: 39041–44, 39046–47, 39051, 39057, 39062, 39069, 39071, 39073–74, 39078, 39080, 39082–83, 39087, 39090, 39092, 39094, 39098, 39108–12, 39114, 39116–17, 39119–22, 39130, 39140, 39145, 39148–49, 39151–53, 39157–58, 39161, 39165, 39167–68, 39189–91, 39193, 39202, 39206, 39208–09, 39211, 39213, 39216, 39218, 39232, 39236, 39288, 39298, 39301–05, 39307, 39309, 39320, 39323, 39325–28, 39332, 39335–39, 39341–42, 39345–46, 39350, 39352, 39354, 39358–59, 39361, 39364–65, 39402, 39421–22, 39427–29, 39439, 39443, 39460, 39474, 39478–80, 39482–83, 39601–03, 39629–33, 39635, 39638, 39641, 39643, 39645, 39647–49, 39652–54, 39656–57, 39661–69, 39701, 39735, 39739, 39743, 39750, 39755, 39759–60, 39762, 39769

* * *

FOURTH DISTRICT

GENE TAYLOR, Democrat, of Bay St. Louis, MS; born in New Orleans, LA, September 17, 1953; education: graduated from De LaSalle High School, New Orleans, LA, 1971; B.A., Tulane University, New Orleans, LA, 1974; graduate studies in business and economics, University of Southern Mississippi, August 1978–April 1980; U.S. Coast Guard Reserves, 1971–84, first class petty officer, search and rescue boat skipper; sales representative, Stone Container Corporation, 1977–89; city councilman, Bay St. Louis, 1981–83; State Senator, 1983–89; member: American Legion; Rotary; Boys and Girls Club of the Gulf Coast; married the former Margaret Gordon, 1978; children: Sarah, Emily, Gary; committees: Armed Services; Transportation and Infrastructure; elected to the 101st Congress, by special election, on October 17, 1989, to fill the vacancy caused by the death of Larkin Smith; reelected to each succeeding Congress.

Office Listings

http://www.house.gov/genetaylor

2269 Rayburn House Office Building, Washington, DC 20515 .... (202) 225–5772

Chief of Staff.—Stephen Peranich. FAX: 225–7074
Legislative Director.—Courtney Littig.
Executive Assistant.—Elizabeth Harris.
2424 Fourteenth Street, Gulfport, MS 39501 .... (228) 864–7670
District Manager.—Beau Gex.
215 Federal Building, 701 Main Street, Hattiesburg, MS 39401 .... (601) 582–3246
1314 Government Street, Ocean Springs, MS 39564 .... (228) 872–7950
527 Central Avenue, Laurel, MS 39440 .... (601) 425–3905

Counties: CLARKE, FORREST, GEORGE, GREENE, HANCOCK, HARRISON, JACKSON, JASPER (part), JONES, LAMAR, MARION (part), PEARL RIVER, PERRY, STONE, WAYNE. CITIES AND TOWNSHIPS: Biloxi, Gulfport, Hattiesburg, Laurel, and Pascagoula. Population (2000), 711,170.

ZIP Codes: 39301, 39307, 39322, 39324, 39330, 39332, 39347–48, 39355–56, 39360, 39362–63, 39366–67, 39401–04, 39406, 39422–23, 39425–26, 39429, 39436–37, 39439–43, 39451–52, 39455–57, 39459, 39461–66, 39470, 39475–78, 39480–82, 39501–03, 39505–07, 39520–22, 39525, 39529–35, 39540, 39552–53, 39555–56, 39558, 39560–69, 39571–74, 39576–77, 39581, 39595

MISSOURI

(Population 2000, 5,595,211)

SENATORS

CHRISTOPHER S. ''KIT'' BOND, Republican, of Mexico, MO; born in St. Louis, MO, March 6, 1939; education: B.A., *cum laude*, Woodrow Wilson School of Public and International Affairs of Princeton University, 1960; J.D., valedictorian, University of Virginia, 1963; held a clerkship with the U.S. Court of Appeals for the Fifth Circuit, 1964; practiced law in Washington, DC, and returned to Missouri, 1967; assistant attorney general of Missouri, 1969; state auditor, 1970; Governor of Missouri, 1973–77, 1981–85; married: the former Linda Holwick; children: Samuel Reid Bond; committees: Appropriations; Environment and Public Works; Small Business and Entrepreneurship; Select Committee on Intelligence; elected to the U.S. Senate on November 4, 1986; reelected to each succeeding Senate term.

Office Listings

http://bond.senate.gov

274 Russell Senate Office Building, Washington, DC 20510 .... (202) 224–5721
Chief of Staff.—Brian Klippenstein. FAX: 224–8149
Legislative Director.—Kara Smith.
Legal Counsel.—John Stoody.
Scheduling Secretary.—Annie O'Toole.
1001 Cherry Street, Suite 204, Columbia, MO 65201 .... (573) 442–8151
911 Main Street, Suite 2224, Kansas City, MO 64105 .... (816) 471–7141
7700 Bonhomme, Suite 615, Clayton, MO 63105 .... (314) 725–4484
300 South Jefferson, Suite 401, Springfield, MO 65806 .... (417) 864–8258
Federal Building, Room 140, 339 Broadway, Cape Girardeau, MO 63701 .... (573) 334–7044
308 East High, Suite 202, Jefferson City, MO 65101 .... (573) 634–2488

* * *

CLAIRE MCCASKILL, Democrat of Kirkwood, MO; born in Rolla, MO, July 25, 1953; raised in Lebanon, MO and Columbia, MO; education: B.A., University of Missouri-Columbia, 1975; J.D., University of Missouri-Columbia School of Law, 1978; professional: clerk with the Missouri Court of Appeals, Western District in Kansas City, 1978; assistant prosecutor, Jackson County prosecutor's office, 1979–83; Missouri state representative, 1983–88; practiced law in Kansas City, MO, 1983–92; Jackson County Prosecutor, 1993–99; Missouri state auditor, 1999–2006; member: St. Gerard Majella Catholic Church in St. Louis; married: Joseph Shephard, 2002; together, they have seven children: Benjamin, Carl, Marilyn, Michael, Austin, Maddie, Lily; appointed deputy whip for the majority, 2007; committees: Armed Services; Commerce, Science, and Transportation; Homeland Security and Governmental Affairs; Indian Affairs; Special Committee on Aging; elected to the U.S. Senate of the 110th Congress on November 7, 2006.

Office Listings

http://mccaskill.senate.gov

717 Hart Senate Office Building, Washington, DC 20510 .... (202) 224–6154
Chief of Staff.—Sean Kennedy. FAX: 228–6326
Deputy Chief of Staff.—Tod Martin.
Legislative Director.—Chani Wiggins.
Communications Director.—Adrianne Marsh.
5856 Delmar Boulevard, Suite A, St. Louis, MO 631112 .... (314) 621–8227
Regional Director.—Michelle Sherod.
Federal Office Building, 400 East 9th Street, Suite 40 Plaza Level, Kansas City, MO 64106 .... (816) 421–1639
Regional Director.—Corey Dillon.
H&H Building, 400 Broadway, Suite 520, Cape Girardeau, MO 63701 .... (573) 651–0964
Regional Director.—Cindy Hall.

REPRESENTATIVES

FIRST DISTRICT

WM. LACY CLAY, Democrat, of St. Louis, MO; born in St. Louis, July 27, 1956; education: Springbrook High School, Silver Spring, MD, 1974; B.S., University of Maryland, 1983, with a degree in government and politics, and a certificate in paralegal studies; public service: Missouri House of Representatives, 1983–91; Missouri State Senate, 1991–2000; nonprofit organizations: St. Louis Gateway Classic Sports Foundation; Mary Ryder Homes; William L. Clay Scholarship and Research Fund; married: Ivie Lewellen Clay; children: Carol, and William III; committees: Financial Services; Oversight and Government Reform; elected to the 107th Congress on November 7, 2000; reelected to each succeeding Congress.

Office Listings

http://www.house.gov/clay

434 Cannon House Office Building, Washington, DC 20515 .... (202) 225–2406
Legislative Director.—Michele Bogdanovich.
Scheduler.—Karyn Long.
Senior Policy Advisor.—Frank Davis.
Legislative Assistant.—Michelle Mitchell.
625 North Euclid Avenue, Suite 326, St. Louis, MO 63108 .... (314) 367–1970
8021 West Florissant, St. Louis, MO 63136 .... (314) 890–0349
Press Secretary.—Steven Engelhardt.

Counties: ST. LOUIS (part). Population (2000), 621,690.

ZIP Codes: 63031–34, 63042–44, 63074, 63101–08, 63110, 63112–15, 63117, 63119–22, 63124, 63130–38, 63141, 63145–47, 63150, 63155–56, 63160, 63164, 63166–67, 63169, 63171, 63177–80, 63182, 63188, 63190, 63195–99

* * *

SECOND DISTRICT

W. TODD AKIN, Republican, of St. Louis, MO; born in New York, NY, July 5, 1947; education: B.S., Worcester Polytechnic Institute, 1971; military service: Officer, U.S. Army Engineers; professional: engineer and businessman; IBM; Laclede Steel; taught International Marketing, undergraduate level; public service: appointed to the Bicentennial Commission of the U.S. Constitution, 1987; Missouri House of Representatives, 1988–2000; organizations: Boy Scouts of America; Missouri Right to Life; Mission Gate Prison Ministry; family: married to Lulli; children: Wynn, Perry, Micah, Ezra, Hannah and Abigail; committees: Armed Services; Science and Technology; Small Business; elected to the 107th Congress on November 7, 2000; reelected to each succeeding Congress.

Office Listings

http://www.house.gov/akin

117 Cannon House Office Building, Washington, DC 20515 .... (202) 225–2561
Chief of Staff.—Paul Protic. FAX: 225–2563
Scheduler.—Tressa Merola.
301 Sovereign Court, Suite 201, St. Louis, MO 63011 .... (314) 590–0029
District Director.—Patrick Werner.

Counties: LINCOLN, ST. CHARLES (part), ST. LOUIS (part). Population (2000), 621,690.

ZIP Codes: 63001, 63005–06, 63011, 63017, 63021–22, 63024–26, 63038, 63040, 63043, 63049, 63069, 63088, 63099, 63110, 63114, 63117, 63119, 63122–29, 63131, 63134, 63141, 63144–46, 63301–04, 63333–34, 63338, 63343–44, 63346–49, 63359, 63362, 63366–67, 63369–70, 63373, 63376–77, 63379, 63381, 63383, 63385–87, 63389–90

* * *

THIRD DISTRICT

RUSS CARNAHAN, Democrat, of St. Louis, MO; born in Columbia, MO, July 10, 1958; education: B.S., Public Administration, University of Missouri-Columbia, 1979; J.D., University of Missouri-Columbia School of Law, 1983; professional: Missouri State Representative, 2001–04; BJC Healthcare, 1995–2004; private law practice; organizations: United Way of Greater St. Louis; Louis Regional Commerce and Growth Association; FOCUS Leadership St. Louis, Class of 1997–98; State Historical Society of Missouri; Landmarks Association of St. Louis; Compton Heights Neighborhood Association; Missouri Bar Association; Bar Association of Metropolitan St. Louis; Boy Scouts, Eagle Scout recipient; Friends of Tower Grove Park, Missouri Botanical Gardens and DeMenil Mansion; awards: St. Louis Regional Chamber of Commerce and Growth Association Lewis and Clark Statesman Award; St. Louis Business Journal 2002 Legislative

Award and the Missouri Bar 2002 Legislative Award; married: Debra Carnahan; children: Austin and Andrew; committees: Foreign Affairs; Science and Technology; Transportation and Infrastructure; elected to the 109th Congress on November 2, 2004; reelected to the 110th Congress.

Office Listings

http://russcarnahan.house.gov

1710 Longworth House Office Building, Washington, DC 20515 .... (202) 225–2671
FAX: 225–7452
Administrative Director.—Allen Todd.
Legislative Director.—Jeremy Haldeman.
Communications Director.—Glenn Campbell.
8764 Manchester Road, Suite 203, St. Louis, MO 63144 .... (314) 962–1523

Counties: JEFFERSON, SAINTE GENEVIEVE, ST. LOUIS, ST. LOUIS CITY. CITIES: St. Louis. Population (2000), 621,690.

ZIP Codes: 63010, 63012, 63015–16, 63019–20, 63023, 63025–26, 63028, 63030, 63036, 63041, 63047–53, 63057, 63060, 63065–66, 63069–72, 63087, 63102, 63104–05, 63109–11, 63116–19, 63122–30, 63132, 63139, 63143–44, 63151, 63157–58, 63163, 63627–28, 63640, 63645, 63661, 63670, 63673

* * *

FOURTH DISTRICT

IKE SKELTON, Democrat, of Lexington, MO; born in Lexington, December 20, 1931; education: graduated, Lexington High School, 1949; attended Wentworth Military Academy, Lexington; A.B., 1953, LL.B., 1956, University of Missouri; attended University of Edinburgh (Scotland), 1953; professional: lawyer; admitted to the Missouri bar in 1956 and commenced practice in Lexington; prosecuting attorney, Lafayette County, 1957–60; special assistant attorney general, 1961–63; elected, State Senate, 1970; reelected, 1974; member: Phi Beta Kappa honor society, Missouri Bar Association, Lions, Elks, Masons, Boy Scouts, First Christian Church; married the former Susan B. Anding, 1961; three children: Ike, James, and Page; committees: chair, Armed Services; elected to the 95th Congress on November 2, 1976; reelected to each succeeding Congress.

Office Listings

http://www.house.gov/skelton

2206 Rayburn House Office Building, Washington, DC 20515 .... (202) 225–2876
Chief of Staff.—Robert Hagedorn.
Administrative Assistant.—Whitney Frost.
Legislative Director.—Dana O'Brien.
Press Secretary.—Anne Hucker.
514–B Northwest 7 Highway, Blue Springs, MO 64014 .... (816) 228–4242
Chief of Staff.—Robert Hagedorn.
908 Thompson Boulevard, Sedalia, MO 65301 .... (660) 826–2675
1401 Southwest Boulevard, Jefferson City, MO 65109 .... (573) 635–3499
219 North Adams, Lebanon, MO 65536 .... (417) 532–7964

Counties: BARTON, BATES, BENTON, CAMDEN (part), CASS (part), CEDAR, COLE, DADE, DALLAS, HENRY, HICKORY, JACKSON (part), JOHNSON, LACLEDE, LAFAYETTE, MONITEAU, MORGAN, PETTIS, POLK (part), PULASKI, RAY, SALINE, ST. CLAIR, VERNON, WEBSTER. Population (2000), 621,690.

ZIP Codes: 64001, 64011, 64013–14, 64016–17, 64019–22, 64024, 64029, 64034–37, 64040, 64058, 64061–62, 64067, 64071, 64074–77, 64080, 64082, 64084–86, 64088, 64090, 64093, 64096–97, 64624, 64637, 64668, 64670–71, 64701, 64720, 64722–26, 64728, 64730, 64733, 64735, 64738–48, 64750, 64752, 64755–56, 64759, 64761–63, 64765, 64767, 64769–72, 64776, 64778–81, 64783–84, 64788, 64790, 64832, 64855, 65011, 65018, 65020, 65023, 65025–26, 65032, 65034, 65037–38, 65040, 65042, 65046, 65049–50, 65052–53, 65055, 65065, 65072, 65074, 65076, 65078–79, 65081, 65084, 65101–11, 65287, 65301–02, 65305, 65320–21, 65323–27, 65329–30, 65332–40, 65344–45, 65347–51, 65354–55, 65360, 65452, 65457, 65459, 65461, 65463, 65470, 65473, 65534, 65536, 65543, 65550, 65552, 65556–67, 65572, 65583–84, 65590–91, 65601, 65603–04, 65607, 65632, 65634–36, 65640, 65644, 65646, 65648–50, 65652, 65661–62, 65668, 65674, 65682, 65685, 65706, 65713, 65722, 65724, 65727, 65732, 65735, 65742, 65746, 65752, 65757, 65764, 65767, 65774, 65779, 65783, 65785–87

* * *

FIFTH DISTRICT

EMANUEL CLEAVER II, Democrat, of Kansas City, MO; born in Waxahachie, TX, October 27, 1944; education: MDiv, Saint Paul School of Theology, MO, 1974; B.S., Prairie View A&M University, TX, 1972; professional: Senior Pastor, St. James United Methodist Church;

City Councilman, Kansas City, MO, 5th District, 1979–91; founder, Harmony in a World of Difference, 1991; founder, Southern Christian Leadership Conference, Kansas City Chapter; Mayor of Kansas City, MO, 1991–99; member, President-elect Bill Clinton's Transitional Team, 1992; host, Under the Clock, KCUR radio, 1999–2004; married: Dianne; four children; three grandchildren; committees: Financial Services; Select Committee on Energy Independence and Global Warming; elected to the 109th Congress on November 2, 2004; reelected to the 110th Congress.

Office Listings

http://www.house.gov/cleaver

1641 Longworth House Office Building, Washington, DC 20515 .... (202) 225–4535
Chief of Staff.—Phil Scaglia. FAX: 225–4403
Scheduler.—Joyce Elkins.
400 East 9th Street, Suite 9350, Kansas City, MO 64106 .... (816) 842–4545
District Director.—Geoff Jolley.

Counties: CASS COUNTY (part), JACKSON COUNTY (part). CITIES AND TOWNSHIPS: Belton, Grandview, Greenwood, Independence, Kansas City, Lee's Summit, Peculiar, Raymore, Raytown, and Sugar Creek. Population (2000), 621,691.

ZIP Codes: 64012, 64014–15, 64029–30, 64034, 64050–58, 64061, 64063–65, 64070, 64075, 64078, 64080–83, 64086, 64101–02, 64105–06, 64108–14, 64120–21, 64123–34, 64136–39, 64141, 64145–49, 64170–71, 64179–80, 64184–85, 64187–88, 64191–94, 64196–99, 64701, 64734, 64944, 64999

* * *

SIXTH DISTRICT

SAM GRAVES, Republican, of Tarkio, MO; born in Fairfax, MO, November 7, 1963; education: B.S., University of Missouri-Columbia, 1986; professional: farmer; organizations: Missouri Farm Bureau; Northwest Missouri State University Agriculture Advisory Committee; University Extension Council; Rotary Club; awards: Associated Industries Voice of Missouri Business Award; Tom Henderson Award; Tarkio Community Betterment Award; Missouri Physical Therapy Association Award; Outstanding Young Farmer Award, 1997; Hero of the Taxpayer Award; NFIB Guardian of Small Business Award; public service: elected to the Missouri House of Representatives, 1992; and the Missouri State Senate, 1994; religion: Baptist; married: Lesley; children: Megan, Emily, and Sam III; committees: Agriculture; Small Business; Transportation and Infrastructure; elected to the 107th Congress on November 7, 2000; reelected to each succeeding Congress.

Office Listings

http://www.house.gov/graves

1415 Longworth House Office Building, Washington, DC 20515 .... (202) 225–7041
Chief of Staff.—Tom Brown. FAX: 225–8221
Press Secretary.—Melissa Goss.
201 S. Eighth Street, Room 330, St. Joseph, MO 64501 .... (816) 233–9818
113 Blue Jay Drive, Suite 100, Liberty, MO 64068 .... (816) 792–3976

Counties: ANDREW, ATCHISON, BUCHANAN, CALDWELL, CARROLL, CHARITON, CLAY, CLINTON, COOPER, DAVIESS, DEKALB, GENTRY, GRUNDY, HARRISON, HOLT, HOWARD, JACKSON (part), LINN, LIVINGSTON, MERCER, NODAWAY, PLATTE, PUTNAM, SCHUYLER, SULLIVAN, WORTH. Population (2000), 621,690.

ZIP Codes: 63535–36, 63541, 63544–46, 63548, 63551, 63556–57, 63560–61, 63565–67, 64013–16, 64018, 64024, 64028–29, 64048, 64056–58, 64060, 64062, 64064, 64066, 64068–69, 64072–75, 64077, 64079, 64085–88, 64092, 64098, 64116–19, 64144, 64150–58, 64161, 64163–68, 64188, 64190, 64193, 64195, 64243, 64401–02, 64420–24, 64426–34, 64436–49, 64451, 64453–59, 64461, 64463, 64465–71, 64473–77, 64479–94, 64496–99, 64501–08, 64601, 64620, 64622–25, 64628, 64630–33, 64635–61, 64664, 64667–68, 64670–74, 64676, 64679, 64681–83, 64686, 64688–89, 65018, 65025, 65046, 65068, 65081, 65230, 65233, 65236–37, 65246, 65248, 65250, 65254, 65256–57, 65261, 65274, 65276, 65279, 65281, 65286–87, 65301, 65322, 65347–48, 65354

* * *

SEVENTH DISTRICT

ROY BLUNT, Republican, of Branson, MO; born in Niangua, MO, January 10, 1950; education: B.A. in history, Southwest Baptist University, 1970; M.A. in history, Missouri State University (then Southwest Missouri State University), 1972; professional: president of Southwest Baptist University, 1993–96; author; two-term Missouri Secretary of State; clerk and chief election officer, Greene County, MO; past chair: Missouri Housing Development Commission, Governor's Council on Literacy; past co-chairman, Missouri Opportunity 2000 Commission; past member, Project Democracy Commission for Voter Participation in the United States; board member, American Council of Young Political Leaders; served as first chairman of the Missouri Prison Fellowship; named one of the Ten Outstanding Young Americans, 1986; member, the Travel-Tourism Caucus; married to Abigail Blunt; children: Matt, Governor of the state of Missouri and Naval reserve officer; Amy, a lawyer in the Kansas City area; Andy, an attorney in Jefferson City; and Charlie, who lives at home with his parents; committees: Republican Leadership Steering Committee; Republican Whip; elected to the 105th Congress; reelected to each succeeding Congress.

Office Listings

http://www.gopwhip.gov http://www.blunt.house.gov

H–307, U.S. Capitol Building (Office of the Republican Whip), Washington, DC 20515 .... (202) 225–0197
Chief of Staff.—Brian Gaston.
Communications Director.—Burson Snyder.
Director of Scheduling.—Richard Eddings.
217 Cannon House Office Building, Washington, DC 20515 .... (202) 225–6536
Chief of Staff.—Amy Poe. FAX: 225–5604
Legislative Assistants: Jennifer Douris, Matt Haase.
Legislative Correspondent.—Peter Henry.
2740–B East Sunshine, Springfield, MO 65804 .... (417) 889–1800
Chief of Staff.—Amy Field.
Northpark Mall, 101 Range Line Road, Box 20, Joplin, MO 64801 .... (417) 781–1041
District Director.—Sharon Nahon.

Counties: BARRY, CHRISTIAN, GREENE, JASPER, LAWRENCE, MCDONALD, NEWTON, POLK (part), STONE, TANEY (part). Population (2000), 621,690.

ZIP Codes: 64748, 64755–56, 64766, 64769, 64801–04, 64830–36, 64840–44, 64847–50, 64853–59, 64861–70, 64873–74, 65603–05, 65608–20, 65622–27, 65629–31, 65633, 65635, 65637–38, 65640–41, 65645–50, 65652–58, 65661, 65663–64, 65666, 65669, 65672–76, 65680–82, 65686, 65702, 65705, 65707–08, 65710, 65712, 65714–15, 65720–21, 65723, 65725–30, 65733–34, 65737–42, 65744–45, 65747, 65752–57, 65759–62, 65765–73, 65781, 65784–85, 65801–10, 65814, 65817, 65890, 65898–99

* * *

EIGHTH DISTRICT

JO ANN EMERSON, Republican, of Cape Girardeau, MO; born in Washington, DC, September 16, 1950; education: B.A., political science, Ohio Wesleyan University, Delaware, OH, 1972; Senior Vice President of Public Affairs, American Insurance Association; director, State Relations and Grassroots Programs, National Restaurant Association; deputy communications director, National Republican Congressional Committee; member: board of directors, Bread for the World; co-chair, board of directors, Congressional Hunger Caucus; PEO Women's Service Group, Cape Girardeau, MO; Copper Dome Society, Southeast Missouri State University; advisory committee, Children's Inn, National Institutes of Health; advisory board, Arneson Institute for Practical Politics and Public Affairs, Ohio Weslyan University; married: Ron Gladney, 2000; children: Victoria and Katharine; six stepchildren: Elizabeth, Abigail, Victoria, Stephanie, Alison, Jessica, and Sam; committees: Appropriations; elected on November 5, 1996, by special election, to the 104th Congress: reelected to each succeeding Congress.

Office Listings

http://www.house.gov/emerson

2440 Rayburn House Office Building, Washington, DC 20515 .... (202) 225–4404
Administrative Assistant / Communications Director.—Jeffrey Connor. FAX: 226–0326
Executive Assistant / Scheduler.—Atalie Ebersole.
339 Broadway, Cape Girardeau, MO 63701 .... (573) 335–0101
Chief of Staff.—Lloyd Smith.
612 Pine Street, Rolla, MO 65401 .... (573) 364–2455
22 East Columbia, Farmington, MO 63640 .... (573) 756–9755

Counties: BOLLINGER, BUTLER, CAPE GIRARDEAU, CARTER, CRAWFORD, DENT, DOUGLAS, DUNKLIN, HOWELL, IRON, MADISON, MISSISSIPPI, NEW MADRID, OREGON, OZARK, PEMISCOT, PERRY, PHELPS, REYNOLDS, RIPLEY, ST. FRANCOIS, SCOTT, SHANNON, STODDARD, TANEY (part), TEXAS, WASHINGTON, WAYNE, WRIGHT. Population (2000), 621,690.

ZIP Codes: 63028, 63030, 63036, 63071, 63080, 63087, 63601, 63620–26, 63628–33, 63636–38, 63640, 63648, 63650–51, 63653–56, 63660, 63662–66, 63674–75, 63701–03, 63730, 63732, 63735–40, 63742–48, 63750–52, 63755, 63758, 63760, 63763–64, 63766–67, 63769–72, 63774–76, 63779–85, 63787, 63801, 63820–30, 63833–34, 63837, 63839–41, 63845–53, 63855, 63857, 63860, 63862–63, 63866–70, 63873–82, 63901–02, 63931–45, 63950–57, 63960–67, 65401–

02, 65409, 65436, 65438–41, 65444, 65446, 65449, 65453, 65456, 65459, 65461–62, 65464, 65466, 65468, 65479, 65483–84, 65501, 65529, 65532, 65541–42, 65546, 65548, 65550, 65552, 65555, 65557, 65564–66, 65570–71, 65586, 65588–89, 65606, 65608–09, 65614, 65616, 65618, 65620, 65626–27, 65629, 65637–38, 65652–53, 65655, 65660, 65662, 65666–67, 65676, 65679–80, 65688–90, 65692, 65701–02, 65704, 65711, 65713, 65715, 65717, 65720, 65729, 65731, 65733, 65740–41, 65744, 65746, 65753, 65755, 65759–62, 65766, 65768, 65773, 65775, 65777–78, 65784, 65788–91, 65793

* * *

NINTH DISTRICT

KENNY C. HULSHOF, Republican, of Columbia, MO; born in Sikeston, MO, May 22, 1958; education: graduated from Thomas W. Kelly High School, Benton, MO; agriculture economics degree, University of Missouri School of Agriculture, 1980; J.D., University of Mississippi Law School, 1983; attorney, admitted to Missouri and Mississippi bars in 1983; Assistant Public Defender, 32nd judicial circuit, 1983–86; Assistant Prosecuting Attorney, Cape Girardeau, MO, 1986–89; Assistant Attorney General, State of Missouri, 1989–96; member: Newman Center Catholic Church, Boone County Farm Bureau, FarmHouse Foundation, Ducks Unlimited; married: Renee Howell Hulshof, 1994; committees: Ways and Means; House Republican Policy Committee; elected to the 105th Congress; reelected to each succeeding Congress.

Office Listings

http://hulshof.house.gov

409 Cannon House Office Building, Washington, DC 20515 .... (202) 225–2956
Chief of Staff.—Manning Feraci. FAX: 225–5712
Executive Assistant / Scheduler.—Mary Stundeback.
33 Broadway, Suite 280, Columbia, MO 65203 .... (573) 449–5111
201 N. 3rd Street, Hannibal, MO 63401 .... (573) 221–1200
516 Jefferson Street, Washington, MO 63090 .... (636) 239–4001

Counties: ADAIR, AUDRAIN, BOONE, CALLAWAY, CAMDEN (part), CLARK, CRAWFORD, FRANKLIN, GASCONADE, KNOX, LEWIS, MACON, MARIES, MARION, MILLER, MONROE, MONTGOMERY, OSAGE, PIKE, RALLS, RANDOLPH, ST. CHARLES (part), SCOTLAND, SHELBY, WARREN. Population (2000), 621,690.

ZIP Codes: 63005, 63013–15, 63037, 63039, 63041, 63055–56, 63060, 63068–69, 63072–73, 63077, 63079–80, 63084, 63089–91, 63303–04, 63330, 63332–34, 63336, 63339, 63341–42, 63344–45, 63348–53, 63357, 63359, 63361, 63363, 63365–67, 63376, 63378, 63381–85, 63388, 63390, 63401, 63430–43, 63445–48, 63450–54, 63456–69, 63471–74, 63501, 63530–34, 63536–40, 63543–44, 63546–47, 63549, 63552, 63555, 63557–59, 63563, 64631, 64658, 64856, 65001, 65010, 65013–14, 65016–17, 65024, 65026, 65031–32, 65035–36, 65039–41, 65043, 65047–49, 65051, 65054, 65058–59, 65061–67, 65069, 65072, 65074–77, 65080, 65082–83, 65085, 65101, 65201–03, 65205, 65211–12, 65215–18, 65230–32, 65239–40, 65243–44, 65247, 65251, 65255–60, 65262–65, 65270, 65275, 65278–85, 65299, 65337, 65441, 65443, 65446, 65449, 65452–53, 65456, 65459, 65486, 65535, 65559–60, 65565, 65580, 65582, 65586, 65591

MONTANA

(Population 2000, 902,195)

SENATORS

MAX BAUCUS, Democrat, of Helena, MT; born in Helena, December 11, 1941; education: graduated, Helena High School, 1959; B.A. in economics, Stanford University, 1964; LL.B., Stanford University Law School, 1967; attorney, Civil Aeronautics Board, 1967–71; attorney, George and Baucus law firm, Missoula, MT; married to the former Wanda Minge; one child, Zeno; member, Montana and District of Columbia bar associations; served in Montana House of Representatives, 1973–74; committees: chair, Finance; Agriculture, Nutrition, and Forestry; Environment and Public Works; Joint Committee on Taxation; elected to the 94th Congress, November 5, 1974; reelected to the 95th Congress; elected to the U.S. Senate, November 7, 1978, for the six-year term beginning January 3, 1979; subsequently appointed on December 15, 1978, to fill the vacancy caused by the resignation of Senator Paul Hatfield; reelected to each succeeding Senate term.

Office Listings

http://baucus.senate.gov

511 Hart Senate Office Building, Washington, DC 20510 .... (202) 224–2651
Chief of Staff.—Jim Messina. FAX: 224–0515
Legislative Director.—Jon Selib.
Press Secretary.—Barrett Kaiser.
DC Scheduler.—Brianne Rogers.
222 North 32nd Street, Suite 100, Billings, MT 59101 .... (406) 657–6790
32 East Babcock, Room 114, Bozeman, MT 59715 .... (406) 586–6104
125 West Granite, Butte, MT 59701 .... (406) 782–8700
113 3rd Street North, Great Falls, MT 59401 .... (406) 761–1574
30 West 14th Street, Helena, MT 59601 .... (406) 449–5480
8 Third Street East, Kalispell, MT 59901 .... (406) 756–1150
1821 South Avenue West, Suite 203, Missoula, MT 59801 .... (406) 329–3123
State Chief of Staff.—Melodee Hanes. (800) 332–6106

* * *

JON TESTER, Democrat, of Big Sandy, MT; born in Havre, MT, August 21, 1956; education: graduated, Big Sandy High School, 1974; B.S. in Music, University of Great Falls, 1978; professional: farmer, T-Bone Farms, Big Sandy, 1978–present; teacher, Big Sandy School District, 1978–80; member, Big Sandy Soil Conservation Service Committee, 1980–83; chairman, Big Sandy School Board of Trustees, 1983–92; Past Master, Treasure Lodge #95 of the Masons; member, Chouteau County Agricultural Stabilization and Conservation Service Committee, 1990–95; member, Organic Crop Improvement Association, 1996–97; served in Montana Senate, 1999–2007; Montana Senate Democratic Whip, 2001–03; Montana Senate Democratic Leader, 2003–05; Montana Senate President, 2005–07; married: the former Sharla Bitz; two children: Christine and Shon; committees: Banking, Housing, and Urban Affairs; Energy and Natural Resources; Homeland Security and Governmental Affairs; Indian Affairs; Small Business and Entrepreneurship; Veterans' Affairs; elected to the U.S. Senate on November 7, 2006.

Office Listings

http://tester.senate.gov

204 Russell Senate Office Building, Washington, DC 20510 .... (202) 224–2644
Chief of Staff.—Stephanie Schriock. FAX: 224–8594
Legislative Director.—Bridget Walsh.
Communications Director.—Matt McKenna.
Director of Scheduling.—Gina Ormand.
Granite Tower, 222 North 32nd Street, Suite 101, Billings, MT 59101 .... (406) 252–0550
211 Haggerty Lane, Bozeman, MT 59715 .... (406) 586–4450
Silver Bow Center, 125 West Granite, Suite 200, Butte, MT 59701 .... (406) 723–3277
122 West Towne, Glendine, MT 59330 .... (406) 365–2391
321 First Avenue North, Great Falls, MT 59401 .... (406) 452–9585
Capital One Center, 208 North Montana Avenue, Suite 202, Helena, MT 59601 .... (406) 449–5401
State Director.—Bill Lombardi.
1845 Highway 93 South, Suite 210, Kalispell, MT 59901 .... (406) 257–3360
116 West Front Street, Missoula, MT 59801 .... (406) 728–3003
Deputy State Director.—Dayna Swanson.

REPRESENTATIVE

AT LARGE

DENNIS R. REHBERG, Republican, of Billings, MT; born in Billings, October 5, 1955; education: B.A., Washington State University, 1977; professional: rancher; manages the Rehberg Ranch; public service: interned in the Montana State Senate, 1977–79; legislative assistant to Rep. Ron Marlenee (R–MT), 1979–82; elected to the Montana House of Representatives, 1984; appointed Lt. Governor of Montana in 1991; elected Lt. Governor in 1992; chairman, Drought Advisory Committee; Worker's Compensation Task Force; and the Montana Rural Development Council; Republican nominee for the U.S. Senate, 1996; married: Janice; children: A.J., Katie, and Elsie; committees: Appropriations; elected to the 107th Congress on November 7, 2000; reelected to each succeeding Congress.

Office Listings

http://www.house.gov/rehberg

516 Cannon House Office Building, Washington, DC 20515 .... (202) 225–3211
Chief of Staff.—Erik Iverson. FAX: 225–5687
Communications Director.—Bridger Pierce.
1201 Grand Avenue, Suite 1, Billings, MT 59102 .... (406) 256–1019
District Director.—Randy Vogel.

Counties: BEAVERHEAD, BIG HORN, BLAINE, BROADWATER, CARBON, CARTER, CASCADE, CHOUTEAU, CUSTER, DANIELS, DAWSON, DEER LODGE, FALLON, FERGUS, FLATHEAD, GALLATIN, GARFIELD, GLACIER, GOLDEN VALLEY, GRANITE, HILL, JEFFERSON, JUDITH BASIN, LAKE, LEWIS AND CLARK, LIBERTY, LINCOLN, MADISON, MCCONE, MEAGHER, MINERAL, MISSOULA, MUSSELLSHELL PARK, PETROLEUM, PHILLIPS, PONDERA, POWDER RIVER, POWELL, PRAIRIE, RAVALLI, RICHLAND, ROOSEVELT, ROSEBUD, SANDERS, SHERIDAN, SILVER BOW, STILLWATER, SWEET GRASS, TETON, TOOLE, TREASURE, VALLEY, WHEATLAND, WIBAUX, YELLOWSTONE. Population (2000), 902,195.

ZIP Codes: 59001–04, 59006–08, 59010–16, 59018–20, 59022, 59024–39, 59041, 59043–44, 59046–47, 59050, 59052–55, 59057–59, 59061–72, 59074–79, 59081–89, 59101–08, 59201, 59211–15, 59217–19, 59221–23, 59225–26, 59230–31, 59240–44, 59247–48, 59250, 59252–63, 59270, 59273–76, 59301, 59311–19, 59322–24, 59326–27, 59330, 59332–33, 59336–39, 59341, 59343–45, 59347, 59349, 59351, 59353–54, 59401–06, 59410–12, 59414, 59416–22, 59424–25, 59427, 59430, 59432–36, 59440–48, 59450–54, 59456–57, 59460–69, 59471–72, 59474, 59477, 59479–80, 59482–87, 59489, 59501, 59520–32, 59535, 59537–38, 59540, 59542, 59544–47, 59601–02, 59604, 59620, 59623–24, 59626, 59631–36, 59638–45, 59647–48, 59701–03, 59710–11, 59713–22, 59724–25, 59727–33, 59735–36, 59739–41, 59743, 59745–52, 59754–56, 59758–62, 59771–73, 59801–04, 59806–08, 59812, 59820–21, 59823–35, 59837, 59840–48, 59851, 59853–56, 59858–60, 59863–68, 59870–75, 59901, 59903–04, 59910–23, 59925–37

NEBRASKA

(Population 2000, 1,711,263)

SENATORS

CHUCK HAGEL, Republican, of Omaha, NE; born in North Platte, NE, October 4, 1946; education: graduated, St. Bonaventure High School, Columbus, NE, 1964; Brown Institute for Radio and Television, Minneapolis, MN; University of Nebraska, Omaha; military service: served with U.S. Army in Vietnam, 1968, receiving two Purple Hearts, other decorations; professional: president, McCarthy and Company, Omaha, NE; president and CEO, Private Sector Council (PSC), Washington, DC; deputy director and CEO, Economic Summit of Industrialized Nations (G–7 Summit), 1990; president and CEO, World USO; cofounder, director, and executive vice president, VANGUARD Cellular Systems, Inc.; cofounder and chairman of VANGUARD subsidiary, Communications Corporation International, Ltd.; president, Collins, Hagel and Clarke, Inc.; former deputy administrator, Veterans' Administration; former administrative assistant to Congressman John Y. McCollister (R–NE); former newscaster and talk show host, Omaha radio stations KBON and KLNG; member: American Legion; Veterans of Foreign Wars; Disabled American Veterans; Military Order of the Purple Heart; Business-Government Relations Council, Washington, DC; Council for Excellence in Government; University of Nebraska Chancellors Club; board of directors, Omaha Chamber of Commerce; board of trustees: Bellevue University, Hastings College, Heartland Chapter of the American Red Cross; chairman: Building Campaign, Great Plains Chapter of Paralyzed Veterans of America; 10th Anniversary Vietnam Veterans' Memorial; board of directors and national advisory committee, Friends of the Vietnam Veterans' Memorial; board of directors, Arlington National Cemetery Historical Society; chairman of the board, No Greater Love, Inc.; awards: first-ever World USO Leadership Award; International Men of Achievement; Outstanding Young Men of America; Distinguished Alumni Award, University of Nebraska, Omaha, 1988; Freedom Foundation (Omaha Chapter) 1993 Recognition Award; married: the former Lilibet Ziller, 1985; children: Allyn and Ziller; committees: Banking, Housing, and Urban Affairs; Foreign Relations; Rules and Administration; Select Committee on Intelligence; elected to the U.S. Senate on November 5, 1996; reelected to each succeeding Senate term.

Office Listings

http://hagel.senate.gov

248 Russell Senate Office Building, Washington, DC 20510 .... (202) 224–4224
Legislative Director.—Paul Kong. FAX: 224–5213
Office Manager.—Margaret Cook.
Communications Director.—Michael Buttry.
9900 Nicholas Street, Suite 325, Omaha, NE 68114 .... (402) 758–8981
Deputy Chief of Staff.—Tom Janssen.
294 Federal Building, 100 Centennial Mall North, Lincoln, NE 68508 .... (402) 476–1400
State Director.—Todd Wilgen.
4111 Fourth Avenue, Suite 26, Kearney, NE 68845 .... (308) 236–7473
Constituent Services Representative.—Julie Brooker.
115 Railway Street, C102, Scottsbluff, NE 69361 .... (308) 632–6032
Constituent Services Representative.—Pam Cooper Hebbert.

* * *

E. BENJAMIN NELSON, Democrat, of Omaha, NE; born in McCook, NE, May 17, 1941; education: received a bachelor's degree in 1963, a master's degree in 1965, and a law degree in 1970, University of Nebraska at Lincoln; professional: attorney; Director, Nebraska Department of Insurance; President and CEO of the Central National Insurance Group; Executive Vice President and Chief of Staff of the National Association of Insurance Commissioners; Kennedy, Holland, DeLacy, and Svoboda (law firm); Governor of Nebraska, 1991–99; awards: Thomas Jefferson Freedom Award; George W. Norris Award; National Eagle Scout Association Distinguished Eagle Award; family: married to Diane; four children; committees: Agriculture, Nutrition, and Forestry; Appropriations; Armed Services; Rules and Administration; elected to the U.S. Senate on November 7, 2000; reelected to each succeeding Senate term.

Office Listings

http://bennelson.senate.gov

720 Hart Senate Office Building, Washington, DC 20510 .... (202) 224–6551
Chief of Staff.—Tim Becker. FAX: 228–0012
Communications Director.—David DiMartino.
Federal Building, Room 287, Centennial Mall North, Lincoln, NE 68508 .... (402) 441–4600

State Director.—W. Don Nelson.
7602 Pacific Street, Suite 205, Omaha, NE 68154 .... (402) 391–3411
P.O. Box 1472, Scottsbluff, NE 69361 .... (308) 631–7614
P.O. Box 1033, Chadron, NE 69337 .... (308) 430–0587
P.O. Box 2105, Kearney, NE 68848 .... (308) 293–5818

REPRESENTATIVES

FIRST DISTRICT

JEFF FORTENBERRY, Republican, of Lincoln, NE; born in Baton Rouge, LA, December 27, 1960; education: B.A., Louisiana State University, 1978; M.P.P., Georgetown University, Washington, DC, 1986; M. Div., Franciscan University, Steubenville, Ohio, 1996; professional: Lincoln City Council, 1997–2001; publishing executive; worked as economist; managed a public relations firm; congressional aide for the Senate Subcommittee on Intergovernmental Relations; family: married to Celeste Gregory; children: five; committees: Agriculture; Foreign Affairs; Small Business; elected to the 109th Congress on November 2, 2004; reelected to the 110th Congress.

Office Listings

http://www.house.gov/fortenberry

1517 Longworth House Office Building, Washington, DC 20515 .... (202) 225–4806
Chief of Staff.—Kelly Lungren-McCollum. FAX: 225–5686
Legislative Director.—Alan Feyerherm.
Press Secretary.—Audra Miller.
Scheduler.—Katie Parsley.
301 South 13th Street, Suite 100, Lincoln, NE 68508 .... (402) 438–1598
629 North Broad Street, P.O. Box 377, Fremont, NE 68025 .... (402) 727–0888
125 South 4th Street, Suite 101, Norfolk, NE 68701 .... (402) 379–2064

Counties: BURT, BUTLER, CASS, CEDAR (part), COLFAX, CUMING, DAKOTA, DIXON, DODGE, GAGE, JOHNSON, LANCASTER, MADISON, NEMAHA, OTOE, PAWNEE, RICHARDSON, SARPY (part), THURSTON, WASHINGTON, WAYNE. Population (2000), 570,421.

ZIP Codes: 68001–04, 68007–09, 68014–20, 68023, 68025–26, 68028–31, 68033–34, 68036–42, 68044–48, 68050, 68055, 68057–59, 68061–68, 68070–73, 68112, 68122–23, 68133, 68136, 68138, 68142, 68144, 68152, 68301, 68304–05, 68307, 68309–10, 68313–14, 68316–21, 68323–24, 68328–33, 68336–37, 68339, 68341–49, 68351, 68355, 68357–60, 68364, 68366–68, 68371–72, 68376, 68378, 68380–82, 68401–05, 68407, 68409–10, 68413–15, 68417–24, 68428, 68430–31, 68433–34, 68437–39, 68441–43, 68445–48, 68450, 68452–58, 68460–67, 68501–10, 68512, 68514, 68516, 68520–24, 68526, 68528–29, 68532, 68542, 68583, 68588, 68601, 68621, 68624, 68626, 68629, 68631–33, 68635, 68641–44, 68648–49, 68658–59, 68661–62, 68666–67, 68669, 68701–02, 68710, 68715–17, 68723–24, 68727–28, 68731–33, 68739–41, 68743, 68745, 68747–49, 68751–52, 68757–58, 68767–68, 68770–71, 68776, 68779, 68781, 68784–85, 68787–88, 68790–92

* * *

SECOND DISTRICT

LEE TERRY, Republican, of Omaha, NE; born in Omaha, January 29, 1962; education: B.A., University of Nebraska, 1984; J.D., Creighton Law School, 1987; attorney; elected to the Omaha, NE, City Council, 1990–98; served as vice president and president, and on the audit, legislative, and cable television committees; religion: Methodist; married: Robyn; children: Nolan, Ryan, and Jack; committees: Energy and Commerce; elected to the 106th Congress; reelected to each succeeding Congress.

Office Listings

http://www.house.gov/terry

1524 Longworth House Office Building, Washington, DC 20515 .... (202) 225–4155
Chief of Staff.—Eric Hultman. FAX: 226–5452
Legislative Director.—Scott Shiller.
Appointment Secretary.—Lindsey Witt.
Press Secretary.—Jen Rae Hein.
11717 Burt Street, Suite 106, Omaha, NE 68144 .... (402) 397–9944
District Director.—Molly Koozer-Lloyd.

Counties: DOUGLAS, SARPY (part). CITIES: Bellevue, Bennington, Boys Town, Elkhorn, Gretna, La Vista, Omaha, Offutt AFB, Papillion, Plattsmouth, Ralston, Springfield, Valley, and Waterloo. Population (2000), 570,421.

ZIP Codes: 68005, 68007, 68010, 68022, 68028, 68046, 68056, 68064, 68069, 68101–14, 68116–20, 68122–24, 68127–28, 68130–39, 68142, 68144–45, 68147, 68152, 68154–55, 68157, 68164, 68172, 68175–76, 68178–83, 68197–98

* * *

THIRD DISTRICT

ADRIAN SMITH, Republican, of Gering, NE; born in Scotts Bluff, NE, December 19, 1970; education: graduated from Gering High School, Gering, NE, 1989; attended Liberty University, Lynchburg, VA; 1989–90; B.S., University of Nebraska, 1993; professional: business owner; teacher; Gering, NE, city council, 1994–98; member of the Nebraska state legislature, 1999–2007; committees: Agriculture; Budget; Science and Technology; elected to the 110th Congress on November 7, 2006.

Office Listings

http://adriansmith.house.gov

503 Cannon House Office Building, Washington, DC 20515 .... (202) 225–6435
Chief of Staff.—Jeff Shapiro. FAX: 225–0207
Legislative Director.—Monica Jirik.
Press Secretary.—Charles Isom.
Scheduler.—Jena Hoehne.
416 Valley View Drive, Suite 600, Scottsbluff, NE 69361 .... (308) 633–6333
1811 West Second Street, Suite 105, Grand Island, NE 68803 .... (308) 384–3900

Counties: ADAMS, ANTELOPE, ARTHUR, BANNER, BLAINE, BOONE, BOX BUTTE, BOYD, BROWN, BUFFALO, CEDAR (part), CHASE, CHERRY, CHEYENNE, CLAY, CUSTER, DAWES, DAWSON, DEUEL, DUNDY, FILLMORE, FRANKLIN, FRONTIER, FURNAS, GARDEN, GARFIELD, GOSPER, GRANT, GREELEY, HALL, HAMILTON, HARLAN, HAYES, HITCHCOCK, HOLT, HOOKER, HOWARD, JEFFERSON, KEARNEY, KEITH, KEYA PAHA, KIMBALL, KNOX, LINCOLN, LOGAN, LOUP, MCPHERSON, MERRICK, MORRILL, NANCE, NUCKOLLS, PERKINS, PHELPS, PIERCE, PLATTE, POLK, RED WILLOW, ROCK, SALINE, SCOTTS BLUFF, SHERIDAN, SHERMAN, SIOUX, THAYER, THOMAS, VALLEY, WEBSTER, WHEELER, YORK. Population (2000), 570,421.

ZIP Codes: 68303, 68310, 68313, 68315–16, 68319, 68322, 68325–27, 68333, 68335, 68338–43, 68350–52, 68354, 68359, 68361–62, 68365, 68367, 68370–71, 68375, 68377, 68401, 68405–06, 68416, 68423–24, 68429, 68436, 68440, 68444–45, 68452–53, 68460, 68464–65, 68467, 68601–02, 68620–23, 68627–28, 68631, 68634, 68636–38, 68640, 68642–44, 68647, 68651–55, 68658, 68660, 68662–66, 68701, 68711, 68713–14, 68717–20, 68722–27, 68729–30, 68734–36, 68738–39, 68742, 68746–48, 68752–53, 68755–56, 68758–61, 68763–67, 68769, 68771, 68773–74, 68777–78, 68780–81, 68783, 68786, 68789, 68792, 68801–03, 68810, 68812–18, 68820–28, 68831–38, 68840–50, 68852–56, 68858–66, 68869–76, 68878–79, 68881–83, 68901–02, 68920, 68922–30, 68932–50, 68952, 68954–61, 68964, 68966–67, 68969–82, 69001, 69020–30, 69032–34, 69036–46, 69101, 69103, 69120–23, 69125, 69127–35, 69138, 69140–57, 69160–63, 69165–71, 69190, 69201, 69210–12, 69214, 69216–21, 69301, 69331, 69333–37, 69339–41, 69343, 69345–48, 69350–58, 69360–61, 69363, 69365–67

NEVADA

(Population 2000, 1,998,257)

SENATORS

HARRY REID, Democrat, of Searchlight, NV; born in Searchlight, December 2, 1939; education: graduated, Basic High School, Henderson, NV, 1957; associate degree in science, Southern Utah State College, 1959; B.S., Utah State University, Phi Kappa Phi, 1961; J.D., George Washington School of Law, Washington, DC, 1964; admitted to the Nevada State bar in 1963, a year before graduating from law school; while attending law school, worked as a U.S. Capitol police officer; city attorney, Henderson, 1964–66; member and chairman, South Nevada Memorial Hospital Board of Trustees, 1967–69; elected: Nevada State Assembly, 1969–70; Lieutenant Governor, State of Nevada, 1970–74; served, executive committee, National Conference of Lieutenant Governors; chairman, Nevada Gaming Commission, 1977–81; member: Nevada State, Clark County and American bar associations; married the former Landra Gould in 1959; five children: Lana, Rory, Leif, Josh, and Key; committees: Rules and Administration; Select Committee on Intelligence; elected to the 98th Congress on November 2, 1982, and reelected to the 99th Congress; Assistant Democratic Leader, 1998–2004; elected Democratic leader for the 109th Congress, and Majority leader for the 110th Congress; elected to the U.S. Senate on November 4, 1986; reelected to each succeeding Senate term.

Office Listings

http://reid.senate.gov

528 Hart Senate Office Building, Washington, DC 20510 .... (202) 224–3542
Chief of Staff.—Gary Myrick. FAX: 224–7327
Deputy Chief of Staff: David McCallum.
Executive Assistant.—Janice Shelton.
Legislative Director.—Dayle Cristinzo.
600 East Williams Street, Room 302, Carson City, NV 89701 .... (775) 882–7343
Office Director.—Yolanda Garcia.
333 Las Vegas Boulevard South, Suite 8016, Las Vegas, NV 89101 .... (702) 388–5020
Office Director.—Rebecca Lambe.
400 S. Virginia Street, Suite 902, Reno, NV 89501 .... (775) 686–5750
District Manager.—Mary Conelly.

* * *

JOHN ENSIGN, Republican, of Las Vegas, NV; born in Roseville, CA, March 25, 1958; education: E.W. Clark High School, Las Vegas, NV, 1976; B.S., University of Nevada at Las Vegas, 1976–79; Oregon State University, 1981; Colorado State University, 1985; professional: veterinarian; organizations: Las Vegas Southwest Rotary; Las Vegas Chamber of Commerce; Sigma Chi (fraternal organization); Meadows Christian Fellowship; married: Darlene Ensign, 1987; children: Trevor, Siena, and Michael; committees: Armed Services; Budget; Commerce, Science, and Transportation; Veterans' Affairs; elected to the U.S. House of Representatives in 1994; reelected in 1996; elected to the U.S. Senate on November 7, 2000; reelected to each succeeding Senate term.

Office Listings

http://ensign.senate.gov

119 Russell Senate Office Building, Washington, DC 20510 .... (202) 224–6244
Chief of Staff.—John Lopez. FAX: 228–2193
Scheduler.—Tinna Jackson.
Legislative Director.—Pam Thiessen.
Communications Director.—Tory Mazzola.
333 Las Vegas Boulevard South, Suite 8203, Las Vegas, NV 89101 .... (702) 388–6605
State Director.—Sonja Joya.
600 East William Street, Suite 304, Carson City, NV 89701 .... (775) 885–9111
Rural Coordinator.—Kevin Kirkeby.
400 S. Virginia Street, Suite 738, Reno, NV 89501 .... (775) 686–5770

REPRESENTATIVES

FIRST DISTRICT

SHELLEY BERKLEY, Democrat, of Las Vegas, NV; born in New York, NY, January 20, 1951; education: graduate of Clark County, NV, public school system; B.A., University of Nevada at Las Vegas, 1972; J.D., University of San Diego School of Law, 1976; professional:

attorney; Nevada State Assembly, 1982–84; former deputy director, Nevada State Commerce Department; hotel executive; vice-chair, Nevada University and Community College System Board of Regents, 1990–98; has served on numerous civic, business, and professional organizations; married: Larry Lehrner; children: Max Berkley and Sam Berkley; committees: Veterans' Affairs; Ways and Means; elected to the 106h Congress; reelected to each succeeding Congress.

Office Listings

http://www.house.gov/berkley

405 Cannon House Office Building, Washington, DC 20515 .... (202) 225–5965
Chief of Staff.—Richard Urey. FAX: 225–3119
Legislative Director.—Bryan George.
Communications Director.—David Cherry.
Scheduler.—Joanne Jensen.
2340 Paseo Del Prado, Suite D–106, Las Vegas, NV 89102 .... (702) 220–9823
District Director.—Tod Story.

Counties: CLARK COUNTY (part). CITIES: Las Vegas, and North Las Vegas. Population (2000), 666,088.

ZIP Codes: 89030–33, 89036, 89084, 89086, 89101–04, 89106–10, 89114–17, 89119, 89121–22, 89125–35, 89137, 89142–46, 89149–56, 89160, 89170, 89177, 89185, 89193

* * *

SECOND DISTRICT

DEAN HELLER, Republican, of Carson City, NV; born in Castro Valley, CA, May 10, 1960; education: B.B.A., specializing in finance and securities analysis, University of Southern California, 1985; institutional stockbroker and broker/trader on the Pacific Stock Exchange; Chief Deputy State Treasurer, Public Funds Representative; Nevada State Assemblyman, 1990–94; Secretary of State, 1994–2002; Founding Board Member of the Boys and Girls Club of Western Nevada and the Western Nevada Community College Foundation; Advisory Board Member for Nevada's Foster Grandparent program; married: Lynne Heller; children: Hilary, Harris, Drew and Emmy; committees: Education and labor; Natural Resources; Small Business; elected to the 110th Congress on November 7, 2006.

Office Listings

100 Cannon House Office Building, Washington, DC 20515 .... (202) 225–6155
Chief of Staff.—Mac Abrams. FAX: 225–5679
Legislative Director.—Greg Facchiano.
Press Secretary.—Stewart Bybee.
Scheduler.—Stefanie Beverly.
400 South Virginia Street, Suite 502, Reno, NV 89501 .... (775) 686–5760
District Director.—Verita Black Prothro.
600 Las Vegas Boulevard South, Suite 680, Las Vegas, NV 89101 .... (702) 255–1651
491 Fourth Street, Elko, NV 89801 .... (775) 777–7920

Counties: CARSON CITY, CHURCHILL, CLARK (part), DOUGLAS, ELKO, ESMERALDA, EUREKA, HUMBOLDT, LANDER, LINCOLN, LYON, MINERAL, NYE, PERSHING, STOREY, WASHOE, WHITE PINE. Population (2000), 666,087.

ZIP Codes: 89001, 89003, 89008, 89010, 89013, 89017, 89019–24, 89026–27, 89030–31, 89041–43, 89045, 89047–49, 89052, 89060–61, 89115, 89124, 89137, 89139, 89141, 89156, 89191, 89301, 89310–11, 89314–19, 89402–15, 89418–36, 89438–40, 89442, 89444–52, 89460, 89496, 89501–07, 89509–13, 89515, 89520–21, 89523, 89533, 89557, 89570, 89701–06, 89711–14, 89721, 89801–03, 89815, 89820–26, 89828, 89830–32, 89834–35, 89883

* * *

THIRD DISTRICT

JON C. PORTER, Republican, of Boulder City, NV; born in Fort Dodge, IA, May 16, 1955; education: attended Briar Cliff College in Sioux City, IA; professional: insurance business; worked with the Farmers Insurance Group; public service: former Mayor (1987–91), and City Councilman (1983–93), in Boulder City; elected to the Nevada State Senate, 1994; awards: Nevada League of Cities' Elected Official of the Year; Clark County School District's Crystal Apple Award; religion: Catholic; married: Laurie; children: J. Chris and Nicole; committees: Budget; Ways and Means; elected to the 108th Congress on November 5, 2002; reelected to each succeeding Congress.

Office Listings

http://www.house.gov/porter

218 Cannon House Office Building, Washington, DC 20515 .... (202) 225–3252
Chief of Staff.—Mike Hesse. FAX: 225–2185
Legislative Director.—Trevor Kolego.
Administrative Assistant.—Sara Rogers.
Press Secretary.—Matt Leffingwell.
2470 Saint Rose Parkway, Suite 204, Henderson, NV 89014 .... (702) 387–4941
District Director.—Kay Finfrock.

Counties: CLARK COUNTY (part). Population (2000), 666,082.

ZIP Codes: 89004–05, 89007, 89009, 89011–12, 89014–16, 89018, 89025, 89028–30, 89039–40, 89046, 89052–53, 89070, 89074, 89077, 89101–4, 89108–11, 89113, 89117–24, 89128–29, 89134–36, 89138–39, 89141–42, 89146–49, 89156, 89159, 89162–63, 89170, 89173, 89177, 89180, 89185, 89191, 89193, 89195, 89199

NEW HAMPSHIRE

(Population 2000, 1,235,786)

SENATORS

JUDD GREGG, Republican, of Rye, NH; born in Nashua, NH, February 14, 1947; education: graduated Phillips Exeter Academy, 1965; A.B., Columbia University, New York City, 1969; J.D., 1972, and LL.M., 1975, Boston University; professional: attorney; admitted to the New Hampshire bar, 1972; commenced practice in Nashua, NH; practiced law, 1975–80; member, Governor's Executive Council, 1978–80; elected Governor of New Hampshire, 1988–92; married to the former Kathleen MacLellan, 1973; three children: Molly, Sarah, and Joshua; committees: Appropriations; ranking member, Budget; Health, Education, Labor, and Pensions; elected to the 97th Congress, November 4, 1980, and reelected to the 98th–100th Congresses; elected to the U.S. Senate on November 3, 1992; reelected to each succeeding Senate term.

Office Listings

http://gregg.senate.gov

393 Russell Senate Office Building, Washington, DC 20510 .... (202) 224–3324
Chief of Staff.—Joel Maiola. FAX: 224–4952
Administrative Assistant.—Vasiliki Christopoulos.
Communications Director.—Erin Rath.
125 North Main Street, Concord, NH 03301 .... (603) 225–7115
41 Hooksett Road, Unit #2, Manchester, NH 03104 .... (603) 622–7979
16 Pease Boulevard, Portsmouth, NH 03801 .... (603) 431–2171
60 Pleasant Street, Berlin, NH 03570 .... (603) 752–2604
170 Main Street, Nashua, NH 03060 .... (603) 577–3823

* * *

JOHN E. SUNUNU, Republican, of Waterville Valley, NH; born in Boston, MA, September 10, 1964; education: graduated, Salem High School, Salem, NH, 1982; B.S., mechanical engineering, Massachusetts Institute of Technology, 1986; M.S., mechanical engineering, Massachusetts Institute of Technology, 1987; M.B.A., Harvard University Business School, Boston, MA, 1991; professional: Chief Financial Officer and Director of Operations, Teletrol Systems, Inc.; married to Catherine Halloran Sununu, 1988; three children: John Hayes, Grace, and Charlotte; committees: Banking, Housing and Urban Affairs; Commerce, Science, and Transportation; Foreign Relations; Homeland Security and Governmental Affairs; Joint Economic Committee; elected to the 105th Congress; reelected to each succeeding Congress; elected to the U.S. Senate on November 5, 2002.

Office Listings

http://sununu.senate.gov

111 Russell Senate Office Building, Washington, DC 20510 .... (202) 224–2841
Chief of Staff.—Paul Collins. FAX: 228–4131
Legislative Director.—Mike O'Rielly.
Communications Director.—Barbara Riley.
One New Hampshire Avenue, Suite 120, Portsmouth, NH 03801 .... (603) 430–9560
1589 Elm Street, Suite 3, Manchester, NH 03101 .... (603) 647–7500
60 Pleasant Street, Berlin, NH 03570 .... (603) 752–6074
50 Opera House Square, Claremont, NH 03743 .... (603) 542–4872
170 Main Street, Nashua, NH 03060 .... (603) 577–8960

REPRESENTATIVES

FIRST DISTRICT

CAROL SHEA-PORTER, Democrat, of Rochester, NH; born in New York City, NY; December, 1952; education: graduated from Oyster River High School, Durham, NH, 1971; B.A., University of New Hampshire, Durham, NH, 1975; M.P.A., University of New Hampshire, Durham, NH, 1979; professional: social worker; professor; married: Gene; two children; committees: Armed Services; Education and Labor; elected to the 110th Congress on November 7, 2006.

Office Listings

http://www.house.gov/shea-porter

1508 Longworth House Office Building, Washington, DC 20515 .... (202) 225–5456

Chief of Staff.—Harry Gural. FAX: 225–5822
Legislative Director.—Susan Mayer.
Press Secretary.—Harry Gural.
Scheduler.—Naomi Andrews.
33 Lowell Street, Manchester, NH, 03101 .... (603) 641–9536
104 Washington Street, Dover, NH, 03820 .... (603) 743–4813

Counties: BELKNAP (part), CARROLL, HILLSBOROUGH (part), ROCKINGHAM, STAFFORD. CITIES: Bedford, Conway, Derry, Dover, Exeter, Goffstown, Laconia, Londonderry, Manchester, Merrimack, Portsmouth, and Rochester. Population (2000), 617,575.

ZIP Codes: 03032, 03034, 03036–38, 03040–42, 03044–45, 03053–54, 03077, 03101–06, 03108–11, 03218, 03220, 03225–27, 03237, 03246–47, 03249, 03253–54, 03256, 03259, 03261, 03263, 03269, 03290–91, 03298–99, 03307, 03801–05, 03809–10, 03812–22, 03824–27, 03830, 03832–33, 03835–60, 03862, 03864–75, 03878, 03882–87, 03890, 03894, 03896–97

* * *

SECOND DISTRICT

PAUL W. HODES, Democrat, of Concord, NH; born in New York City, NY, on March 21, 1951; education: B.A., Dartmouth College, Hanover, NH, 1972; J.D., Boston College, Chestnut Hill, MA, 1978; professional: assistant attorney general of New Hampshire, 1979–82; special prosecutor for the state of New Hampshire, 1992; lawyer, private practice; professional entertainer; married: Peggo Horstmann Hodes; children: Max and Ariana; committees: Financial Services; Oversight and Government Reform; unsuccessful candidate for election to 109th Congress in 2004; elected to the 110th Congress on November 7, 2006.

Office Listings

http://www.house.gov/hodes

506 Cannon House Office Building, Washington, DC 20515 .... (202) 225–5206
Chief of Staff.—Dana Houle. FAX: 225–2946
Scheduler.—Luke Watson.
Legislative Director.—Lisette Morton.
Press Secretary.—Bergen Kenny.
114 North Main Street, Second Floor, Concord, NH 03301 .... (603) 223–9814

Counties: BELKNAP (part), CHESHIRE, COOS, GRAFTON, HILLSBOROUGH (part), MERRIMACK (part), ROCKINGHAM (part), SULLIVAN. Population (2000), 618,211.

ZIP Codes: 03031, 03033, 03037, 03043, 03045–49, 03051–52, 03055, 03057, 03060–64, 03070–71, 03073, 03076, 03079, 03082, 03084, 03086–87, 03215–17, 03220–24, 03226, 03229–31, 03233–35, 03238, 03240–45, 03251–52, 03255, 03257–58, 03260–64, 03266, 03268–69, 03272–76, 03278–82, 03284, 03287, 03289, 03293, 03301–05, 03307, 03431, 03435, 03440–52, 03455–58, 03461–62, 03464–70, 03561, 03570, 03574–76, 03579–85, 03587–90, 03592–93, 03595, 03597–98, 03601–05, 03607–09, 03740–41, 03743, 03745–46, 03748–56, 03765–66, 03768–71, 03773–74, 03777, 03779–82, 03784–85, 03811

NEW JERSEY

(Population 2000 8,414,350)

SENATORS

FRANK LAUTENBERG, Democrat, of Cliffside Park, NJ; born in Paterson, NJ, January 23, 1924; education: Nutley High School, Nutley, NJ, 1941; B.S., Economics, Columbia University School of Business, New York, NY, 1949; professional: U.S. Army Signal Corps, 1942–46; data processing firm founder, and CEO, 1952–82; commissioner, Port Authority of New York and New Jersey, 1978–82; commissioner, New Jersey Economic Development Authority; member: U.S. Holocaust Memorial Council; Advisory Council of the Graduate School of Business, Columbia University; appointed by the Governor on December 27, 1982, to complete the unexpired term of Senator Nicholas F. Brady; elected to the U.S. Senate on November 2, 1982; reelected in 1988 and 1994; not a candidate for reelection in 2000; replaced Senator Robert Torricelli as the Democratic candidate for the U.S. Senate in October 2002; four children: Ellen, Nan, Lisa and Joshua; committees: Appropriations; Budget; Commerce, Science, and Transportation; Environment and Public Works; Homeland Security and Governmental Affairs; elected to the U.S. Senate on November 5, 2002.

Office Listings

http://lautenberg.senate.gov

324 Hart Senate Office Building, Washington, DC 20510 .... (202) 224–3224
Chief of Staff.—Dan Katz. FAX: 228–4054
Chief Counsel.—Scott Mulhauser.
Legislative Director.—Doug Mehan.
Press Secretary.—Michael Pagan.
One Gateway Center, Suite 102, Newark, NJ 07102 .... (973) 639–8700

* * *

ROBERT MENENDEZ, Democrat, of Hoboken, NJ; born in New York City, NY, January 1, 1954; education: graduated, Union Hill High School, 1972; B.A., St. Peter's College, Jersey City, NJ, 1976; J.D., Rutgers Law School, Newark, NJ, 1979; professional: attorney; elected to the Union City Board of Education, 1974–78; admitted to the New Jersey bar, 1980; mayor of Union City, 1986–92; member: New Jersey Assembly, 1987–91; New Jersey State Senate, 1991–92; chair, New Jersey Hispanic Leadership Program; New Jersey Hispanic Elected Officials Organization; New Jersey Majors Coalition; president and co-founder, Alliance Civic Association; U.S. House of Representatives 1993–2006; vice chair, Democratic Caucus, 1998–2002; chair, Democratic Caucus, 2002–06; children: Alicia and Robert; committees: vice chair, Democratic Senatorial Campaign Committee; Banking, Housing and Urban Affairs; Budget; Energy and Natural Resources; Foreign Relations; elected on November 3, 1992 to the 103rd Congress; reelected to each succeeding Congress; appointed to the U.S. Senate on January 17, 2006 by Governor Jon S. Corzine; elected to the U.S. Senate on November 7, 2006.

Office Listings

http://menendez.senate.gov

317 Hart Senate Office Building, Washington, DC 20510 .... (202) 224–4744
Chief of Staff.—Ivan Zapien. FAX: 228–2197
Press Secretary.—Afshin Mohamadi.
Office Manager.—Margaret Wetherald.
One Gateway Center, 11th Floor, Newark, NJ 07102 .... (973) 645–3030
208 Whitehorse Pike, Suite 18, Barrington, NJ 08007–1322 .... (856) 757–5353

REPRESENTATIVES

FIRST DISTRICT

ROBERT E. ANDREWS, Democrat, of Haddon Heights, NJ; born in Camden, NJ, August 4, 1957; education: graduated, Triton High School, Runnemede, NJ, 1975; B.S., political science, Bucknell University, *summa cum laude*, Phi Beta Kappa, Lewisburg, PA, 1979; J.D., *magna cum laude*, Cornell Law School, Cornell Law Review, Ithaca, NY, 1982; Camden County Freeholder, 1986–90; Camden County Freeholder Director, 1988–90; married: Camille Spinello; children: Jacquelyn and Josi; committees: Armed Services; Budget; Education and Labor; election on November 6, 1990, to the 101st Congress, to fill the vacancy caused by the resignation of James Florio; elected at the same time to the 102nd Congress; reelected to each succeeding Congress.

Office Listings

http://www.house.gov/andrews

2439 Rayburn House Office Building, Washington, DC 20515 .... (202) 225–6501
Chief of Staff.—Bill Caruso. FAX: 225–6583
Scheduler.—Fran Tagmire.
Legislative Director.—Reisha Phills.
Press Secretary.—Bill Caruso.
506A White Horse Pike, Haddon Heights, NJ 08035 .... (856) 546–5100
District Director.—Amanda Caruso.
63 North Broad Street, Woodbury, NJ 08096 .... (856) 848–3900

Counties: BURLINGTON COUNTY. CITIES AND TOWNSHIPS: Maple Shade, Palmyra, Riverton. CAMDEN COUNTY. CITIES AND TOWNSHIPS: Audubon, Audubon Park, Barrington, Bellmawr, Berlin, Berlin Township, Brooklawn, Camden, Chesilhurst, Clementon, Collingswood, Gibbsboro, Gloucester City, Gloucester Township, Haddon Heights, Haddon Township, Hi-Nella, Laurel Springs, Lawnside, Lindenwold, Magnolia, Mt. Ephraim, Oaklyn, Pennsauken, Pine Hill, Pine Valley, Runnemede, Somerdale, Stratford, Tavistock, Voorhees, Winslow, Woodlynne. GLOUCESTER COUNTY. CITIES AND TOWNSHIPS: Deptford, E. Greenwich, Greenwich, Logan Township, Mantua, Monroe, National Park, Paulsboro, Washington Township, and Wenonah. Population (2000), 647,258.

ZIP Codes: 08002–04, 08007, 08009, 08012, 08014, 08018, 08020–21, 08026–33, 08035, 08037, 08043, 08045, 08049, 08051–52, 08056, 08059, 08061–63, 08065–66, 08071, 08076–80, 08081, 08083–86, 08089–91, 08093–97, 08099, 08101–10

* * *

SECOND DISTRICT

FRANK A. LOBIONDO, Republican, of Ventnor, NJ; born in Bridgeton, NJ, May 12, 1946; education: graduated, St. Joseph's University, Philadelphia, PA, 1968; professional: operations manager, LoBiondo Brothers Motor Express, 1968–94; Cumberland County Freeholder, 1985–87; New Jersey General Assembly, 1988–94; awards and honors: honorary Coast Guard Chief Petty Officer; Board of Directors, Young Mens Christian Association; Honorary Rotarian; Taxpayer Hero award; Watchdog of the Treasury award; Super Friend of Seniors award; two-time winner of the Friend of the National Parks award; March of Dimes FDR award for community service; 2001 President's award, Literacy Volunteers of America, NJ, Inc.; committees: Armed Services; Transportation and Infrastructure; elected to the 104th Congress; reelected to each succeeding Congress.

Office Listings

http://www.house.gov/lobiondo

2427 Rayburn House Office Building, Washington, DC 20515 .... (202) 225–6572
Chief of Staff.—Mary Annie Harper. FAX: 225–3318
Executive Assistant.—Alicia Melvin.
5914 Main Street, Mays Landing, NJ 08330 .... (609) 625–5008
District Director.—Linda Hinckley.

Counties: BURLINGTON (part). CITIES AND TOWNSHIPS: Shamong, Washington, Waterford. CAMDEN COUNTY (part). ATLANTIC COUNTY. CITIES AND TOWNSHIPS: Absecon, Atlantic City, Brigantine, Buena, Cardiff, Collings Lake, Cologne, Corbin City, Dorothy, Egg Harbor, Estell Manor, Galloway, Hammonton, Landisville, Leeds Point, Linwood, Longport, Margate, Mays Landing, Milmay, Minotola, Mizpah, Newtonville, Northfield, Oceanville, Pleasantville, Pomona, Port Republic, Richland, Somers Point, Ventnor. CAPE MAY COUNTY. CITIES AND TOWNSHIPS: Avalon, Bargaintown, Beesley's, Belleplain, Burleigh, Cape May, Cape May C.H., Cape May Point, Cold Springs, Del Haven, Dennisville, Dias Creek, Eldora, Erma, Fishing Creek, Goshen, Green Creek, Greenfield, Marmora, Ocean City, Ocean View, Rio Grande, Sea Isle, South Dennis, South Seaville, Stone Harbor, Strathmere, Tuckahoe, Villas, Whitesboro, Wildwood, Woodbine. CUMBERLAND COUNTY. CITIES AND TOWNSHIPS: Bridgeton, Cedarville, Centerton, Deerfield, Delmont, Dividing Creek, Dorchester, Elwood, Fairton, Fortescue, Greenwich, Heislerville, Hopewell, Leesburg, Mauricetown, Millville, Newport, Port Elizabeth, Port Norris, Rosenhayn, Shiloh, Vineland. GLOUCESTER COUNTY (part). CITIES AND TOWNSHIPS: Clayton, Ewan, Franklinville, Glassboro, Harrisonville, Malaga, Mantua, Mickleton, Mullica Hill, Newfield, Pitman, Richwood, Sewell, Swedesboro, Williamstown, Woodbury. SALEM COUNTY. CITIES AND TOWNSHIPS: Alloway, Carney's Point, Daretown, Deepwater, Elmer, Elsinboro, Hancocks Bridge, Monroeville, Norma, Pedricktown, Penns Grove, Pennsville, Quinton, Salem, and Woodstown. Population (2000), 647,258.

ZIP Codes: 08001, 08004, 08009, 08019–20, 08023, 08025, 08028, 08037–39, 08051, 08056, 08061–62, 08067, 08069–72, 08074, 08079–80, 08085, 08088–89, 08094, 08098, 08201–05, 08210, 08212–15, 08217–21, 08223, 08225–26, 08230–32, 08234, 08240–48, 08250–52, 08260, 08270, 08302, 08310–24, 08326–30, 08332, 08340–50, 08352–53, 08360–62, 08401–04, 08406

* * *

THIRD DISTRICT

JIM SAXTON, Republican, of Mt. Holly, NJ; born in Nicholson, PA, January 22, 1943; education: graduated, Lackawanna Trail High School, Factoryville, PA, 1961; B.A., Education, East Stroudsburg State College, PA, 1965; graduate courses, Elementary Education, Temple University, Philadelphia, PA, 1968; professional: public school teacher, 1965–68; realtor, owner of Jim Saxton Realty Company, 1968–85; New Jersey General Assembly, 1976–82; State Senate, 1982–84; chairman, State Republican Platform Committee, 1983; former member: Chamber of Commerce; Association of the U.S. Air Force; Leadership Foundation of New Jersey; Boy Scouts of America; Rotary International; former chairman, American Cancer Committee; children: Jennifer and Martin; committees: Armed Services; Natural Resources; elected to the 98th Congress, by special election, on November 6, 1984; reelected to each succeeding Congress.

Office Listings

2217 Rayburn House Office Building, Washington, DC 20515 .... (202) 225–4765
Chief of Staff.—Elise Kenderian Aronson. FAX: 225–0778
Executive Assistant.—Derek Walker.
100 High Street, Mount Holly, NJ 08060 .... (609) 261–5800
District Representative / Business Manager.—Sandra Condit.
247 Main Street, Toms River, NJ 08753 .... (732) 914–2020

Counties: BURLINGTON (part), CAMDEN (part), OCEAN (part). Population (2000), 647,257.

ZIP Codes: 08002–06, 08008–11, 08015–16, 08019, 08034, 08036, 08043, 08046, 08048, 08050, 08053–55, 08057, 08060, 08064–65, 08068, 08073, 08075, 08077, 08087–88, 08092, 08109, 08215, 08224, 08352, 08501, 08511, 08562, 08618, 08640–41, 08690, 08721–23, 08731–32, 08734–35, 08739–41, 08751–59

* * *

FOURTH DISTRICT

CHRISTOPHER H. SMITH, Republican, of Robbinsville, NJ; born in Rahway, NJ, March 4, 1953; attended Worcester College, England, 1974; B.A., Trenton State College, 1975; businessman; executive director, New Jersey Right to Life Committee, Inc., 1976–78; religion: Catholic; married to the former Marie Hahn, 1976; children: Melissa Elyse, Christopher, and Michael; co-chair, Commission on Security and Cooperation in Europe; co-chair, Congressional Pro-Life Caucus; committees: Foreign Affairs; elected to the 97th Congress, November 4, 1980; reelected to each succeeding Congress.

Office Listings

http://www.house.gov/chrissmith

2373 Rayburn House Office Building, Washington, DC 20515 .... (202) 225–3765
Chief of Staff.—Mary Noonan. FAX: 225–7768
1540 Kuser Road, Suite A9, Hamilton, NJ 08619 .... (609) 585–7878
108 Lacey Road, Suite 38A, Whiting, NJ 08759 .... (732) 350–2300

Counties: BURLINGTON COUNTY. MUNICIPALITIES: Bordentown City, Bordentown Township, Burlington City, Burlington Township, Chesterfield, Fieldsboro, Florence, Mansfield, Springfield. MERCER COUNTY. MUNICIPALITIES: East Windsor, Hamilton, Highstown, Trenton, Washington Township. MONMOUTH COUNTY. MUNICIPALITIES: Allentown, Brielle, Colts Neck, Farmingdale, Freehold, Freehold Borough, Howell, Manasquan, Millstone Township, Roosevelt, Sea Girt, Spring Lake Heights, Upper Freehold, Wall. OCEAN COUNTY. MUNICIPALITIES: Bay Head, Brick, Jackson, Lakehurst, Lakewood, Manchester, Mantoloking, Plumstead, Pt. Pleasant, and Pt. Pleasant Beach. Population (2000), 647,258.

ZIP Codes: 07710, 07715, 07719, 07722, 07726–28, 07731, 07753, 07762, 08010, 08016, 08022, 08041–42, 08060, 08068, 08075, 08501, 08505, 08510, 08512, 08514–15, 08518, 08520, 08526–27, 08533, 08535, 08554–55, 08561, 08601–07, 08609–11, 08619–20, 08625, 08629, 08638, 08645–48, 08650, 08666, 08690–91, 08695, 08701, 08720, 08723–24, 08730, 08733, 08736, 08738, 08742, 08750, 08753, 08757, 08759

* * *

FIFTH DISTRICT

SCOTT GARRETT, Republican, of Wantage Township, NJ; born in Englewood, NJ, July 7, 1959; education: High Point Regional High School, 1977; B.A., Montclair State University,

1981; J.D., Rutgers University Law School, 1984; professional: attorney; counsel attorney with law firm of Sellar Richardson; organizations: Big Brothers, Big Sisters; Sussex County Chamber of Commerce; Sussex County Board of Agriculture; New Jersey State Assemblyman, 1990–2002; family: married to Mary Ellen; children: Jennifer and Brittany; committees: Budget; Financial Services; elected to the 108th Congress on November 5, 2002; reelected to each succeeding Congress.

Office Listings

http://www.house.gov/garrett

1318 Longworth House Office Building, Washington, DC 20515 .... (202) 225–4465
Chief of Staff.—Michelle Presson. FAX: 225–9048
Legislative Director.—Chris Russell.
Press Secretary.—Will Holley.
210 Route 4 East, Suite 206, Paramus, NJ 07652 .... (201) 712–0330
District Director.—Tatiana Glavan.
93 Main Street, Newton, NJ 07860 .... (973) 300–2000

Counties: BERGEN (part), PASSAIC (part), SUSSEX, WARREN. Population (2000), 647,257.

ZIP Codes: 07401, 07403, 07416–23, 07428, 07430, 07432, 07435–36, 07438–39, 07446, 07450–52, 07456, 07458, 07460–63, 07465, 07480–81, 07495, 07498, 07620–21, 07624, 07626–28, 07630, 07640–42, 07645–49, 07652–53, 07656, 07661–62, 07670, 07675–77, 07820–23, 07825–27, 07829, 07831–33, 07838–40, 07844, 07846, 07848, 07851, 07855, 07860, 07863, 07865, 07871, 07875, 07877, 07879–82, 07890, 08802, 08804, 08808, 08865–86

* * *

SIXTH DISTRICT

FRANK PALLONE, JR., Democrat, of Long Branch, NJ; born in Long Branch, October 30, 1951; education: B.A., Middlebury College, Middlebury, VT, 1973; M.A., Fletcher School of Law and Diplomacy, 1974; J.D., Rutgers University School of Law, 1978; member of the bar: Florida, New York, Pennsylvania, and New Jersey; attorney, Marine Advisory Service; assistant professor, Cook College, Rutgers University Sea Grant Extension Program; counsel, Monmouth County, NJ, Protective Services for the Elderly; instructor, Monmouth College; Long Branch City Council, 1982–88; New Jersey State Senate, 1983–88; married the former Sarah Hospodor, 1992; committees: Energy and Commerce; Natural Resources; elected to the 100th Congress, by special election, on November 8, 1988, to fill the vacancy caused by the death of James J. Howard; reelected to each succeeding Congress.

Office Listings

237 Cannon House Office Building, Washington, DC 20515 .... (202) 225–4671
Chief of Staff.—Jeff Carroll. FAX: 225–9665
Legislative Director.—Eric Gordon.
Communications Director.—Andrew Souvall.
District Director.—Shawn Brennan.
504 Broadway, Long Branch, NJ 07740 .... (732) 571–1140
67/69 Church Street, Kilmer Square, New Brunswick, NJ 08901–1242 .... (732) 249–8892

Counties: MONMOUTH COUNTY. CITIES AND TOWNSHIPS: Aberdeen, Allenhurst, Asbury Park, Atlantic Highlands, Avon-by-the-Sea, Belmar, Bradley Beach, Deal, Hazlet, Highlands, Interlaken, Keansburg, Keyport, Loch Arbour, Long Branch, Manalapan, Marlboro, Matawan, Middletown, Monmouth Beach, Neptune City, Neptune Twp., Ocean, Red Bank, Sea Birght, South Belmar, Union Beach, West Long Branch. MIDDLESEX COUNTY. CITIES AND TOWNSHIPS: Dunellen, Edison, Highland Park, Metuchen, Middlesex, New Brunswick, Old Bridge, Piscataway, Sayerville, South Amboy. SOMERSET COUNTY. CITIES: Franklin. UNION COUNTY. CITIES: Plainfield. Population (2000), 647,257.

ZIP Codes: 07060–63, 07080, 07701–02, 07704, 07709–12, 07715–21, 07723–24, 07726, 07730, 07732, 07734–35, 07737, 07740, 07746–48, 07750–56, 07758, 07760, 07764, 08812, 08816–18, 08820, 08830–31, 08837, 08840, 08846, 08854–55, 08857, 08859, 08871–73, 08877–79, 08899, 08901, 08903–04, 08906, 08922, 08933, 08988–89

* * *

SEVENTH DISTRICT

MIKE FERGUSON, Republican, of Warren, NJ; born in Ridgewood, NJ, July 2, 1970; education: Delbarton School, Morristown, NJ; B.A., University of Notre Dame; M.P.P., Georgetown University; professional: educator and small businessman; Executive Director, Better Schools Foundation; Executive Director, Catholic Campaign of America; Director, Save Our Schoolchildren; President, Strategic Education Initiatives, Inc.; organizations: National Federation of Independent Business; Knights of Columbus; Epilepsy Foundation of New Jersey; Sierra

Club; Friendly Sons of St. Patrick; National Italian American Association; religion: Roman Catholic; family: married to Maureen; four children; committees: Energy and Commerce; elected to the 107th Congress on November 7, 2000; reelected to each succeeding Congress.

Office Listings

http://www.house.gov/ferguson

214 Cannon House Office Building, Washington, DC 20515 .... (202) 225–5361
FAX: 225–9460
Chief of Staff.—Chris Jones.
Legislative Director.—Greg Orlando.
Scheduler.—Erin Connolly.
Communications Director.—Angie Lundberg.

45 Mountain Boulevard, Building D, Suite 1, Warren, NJ 07059 .... (908) 757–7835
District Director.—Marcus Rayner.

Counties: Middlesex County. Municipalities: Edison, South Plainfield, Woodbridge. Union County. Municipalities: Berkeley Heights, Clark, Cranford, Fanwood, Garwood, Kenilworth, Linden, Mountainside, New Providence, Roselle Park, Scotch Plains, Springfield, Summit, Union, Westfield, Winfield. Hunterdon County. Municipalities: Alexandria, Bethlehem, Bloomsbury, Califon, Clinton Township, Clinton, Flemington, Glen Gardner, Hampton, High Bridge, Holland, Lebanon, Lebanon Township, Milford, Oldwick, Raritan, Readington, Tewksbury, Union. Somerset County. Municipalities: Bedminster, Bernardsville, Bound Brook, Branchburg, Bridgewater, Far Hills, Green Brook, Hillsborough, Manville, Montgomery Township, Millstone, North Plainfield, Peapack-Gladstone, Rocky Hill, South Bound Brook, Warren, and Watchung. Population (2000), 647,257.

ZIP Codes: 07001, 07008, 07016, 07023, 07027, 07033, 07036, 07040, 07059–60, 07062–64, 07066–67, 07069, 07076, 07080–81, 07083, 07090–92, 07095, 07204, 07830, 07901–02, 07921–22, 07924, 07931, 07934, 07974, 07977–79, 08502, 08504, 08540, 08551, 08553, 08558, 08801–02, 08804–05, 08807, 08809, 08812, 08820–22, 08825–27, 08829–30, 08832–37, 08840, 08844, 08848, 08853, 08858, 08863, 08867, 08870, 08876, 08880, 08885, 08887–89

* * *

EIGHTH DISTRICT

BILL PASCRELL, Jr., Democrat, of Paterson, NJ; born in Paterson, January 25, 1937; education: B.A., journalism, and M.A., philosophy, Fordham University; veteran, U.S. Army and Army Reserves; professional: educator; elected Minority Leader Pro Tempore, New Jersey General Assembly, 1988–96; mayor of Paterson, 1990–96; named Mayor of the Year by bipartisan NJ Conference of Mayors, 1996; started Paterson's first Economic Development Corporation; married the former Elsie Marie Botto; three children: William III, Glenn, and David; committees: Ways and Means; elected to the 105th Congress; reelected to each succeeding Congress.

Office Listings

http://www.pascrell.house.gov

2464 Rayburn House Office Building, Washington, DC 20515 .... (202) 225–5751
FAX: 225–5782
Chief of Staff.—Ben Rich.
Legislative Director.—Rich Thomas.
Scheduler.—Hope Mandel.

200 Federal Plaza, Suite 500, Paterson, NJ 07505 .... (201) 523–5152
District Director.—Jacky Grindrod.

Counties: Essex County. Cities: Belleville, Bloomfield, Cedar Grove. Glen Ridge, Livingston, Montclair, Nutley, South Orange, Verona, West Orange. Passaic County. Cities: Clifton, Haledon, Little Falls, North Haledon, Passaic, Paterson, Pompton Lakes, Prospect Park, Totowa, Wayne, and West Paterson. Population (2000), 647,258

ZIP Codes: 07003–04, 07009, 07011–15, 07028, 07039, 07042–44, 07052, 07055, 07079, 07107, 07109–10, 07424, 07442, 07470, 07474, 07477, 07501–14, 07522, 07524, 07533, 07538, 07543–44

* * *

NINTH DISTRICT

STEVEN R. ROTHMAN, Democrat, of Fair Lawn, NJ; born in Englewood, NJ, October 14, 1952; education: graduate, Tenafly High School, 1970; B.A., Syracuse University, Syracuse, NY, 1974; LL.B., Washington University School of Law, St. Louis, MO, 1977; professional: attorney; two-term mayor of Englewood, NJ, spearheaded business growth and installed a fiscally conservative management team, transforming Englewood's bond rating from one of the worst to the best in Bergen County; Judge, Bergen County Surrogate Court, 1993–96; founding member, New Democratic Coalition; authored the Secure Our Schools Act; married to Jennifer; two children and three step children; committees: Appropriations; Science and Technology; elected to the 105th Congress; reelected to each succeeding Congress.

Office Listings

http://www.house.gov/rothman

2303 Rayburn House Office Building, Washington, DC 20515 .... (202) 225–5061
Chief of Staff.—Bob Decheine. FAX: 225–5851
Executive Assistant / Scheduler.—Mary Flanagan.
Legislative Director.—Shelly Stoneman.
25 Main Street, Court Plaza, Hackensack, NJ 07601–7089 .... (201) 646–0808
District Director.—Michael Soliman.
130 Central Avenue, Jersey City, NJ 07306–2118 .... (201) 798–1366
Office Director.—Al Zampella.

Counties: BERGEN COUNTY. CITIES AND TOWNS: Bogota, Carlstadt, Cliffside Park, East Rutherford, Edgewater, Elmwood Park, Englewood, Englewood Cliffs, Fair Lawn, Fairview, Fort Lee, Garfield, Hackensack, Hasbrouck Heights, Leonia, Little Ferry, Lodi, Lyndhurst, Maywood, Moonachie, New Milford, North Arlington, Palisades Park, Ridgefield, Ridgefield Park, Rutherford, Saddle Brook, South Hackensack, Teaneck, Teterboro, Wallington, Wood Ridge. HUDSON COUNTY. CITIES AND TOWNS: Kearny (ward 1: districts 1, 2, and 6; ward 3; and ward 4: districts 5–7), Secaucus, North Bergen, Jersey City. PASSAIC COUNTY (part). BOROUGH: Hawthorne. Population (2000), 647,258.

ZIP Codes: 07010, 07020, 07022, 07024, 07026, 07031–32, 07042, 07047, 07057, 07070–75, 07094, 07096–97, 07099, 07306–08, 07407, 07410, 07601–08, 07631–32, 07643–44, 07646, 07650, 07657, 07660, 07663, 07666, 07670

* * *

TENTH DISTRICT

DONALD M. PAYNE, Democrat, of Newark, NJ; born in Newark, July 16, 1934; education: graduated, Barringer High School, Newark, 1952; B.A., Seton Hall University, South Orange, NJ, 1957; professional: businessman; president, YMCA of the USA, 1970–73; elected to the Essex County Board of Chosen Freeholders, 1972–78; elected to the Newark Municipal Council, 1982–88; member: NAACP; Council on Foreign Relations; serves on the advisory council of the U.S. Committee for UNICEF; Advisory Commission on Intergovernmental Relations; former chairman, Congressional Black Caucus; board of directors: Congressional Black Caucus Foundation, National Endowment for Democracy; Bethlehem Baptist Church; family: widower; three children; committees: Education and Labor; Foreign Affairs; elected on November 8, 1988, to the 101st Congress; reelected to each succeeding Congress.

Office Listings

2209 Rayburn House Office Building, Washington, DC 20515 .... (202) 225–3436
Chief of Staff.—Maxine James. FAX: 225–4160
Legislative Director / Press Secretary.—Kerry McKenney.
50 Walnut Street, Room 1016, Newark, NJ 07102 .... (973) 645–3213
333 North Broad Street, Elizabeth, NJ 07202 .... (908) 629–0222
253 Martin Luther King Drive, Jersey City, NJ 07305 .... (201) 369–0392

Counties: ESSEX, HUDSON, SHORT HILLS, UNION. CITIES AND TOWNSHIPS: Bayonne, East Orange, Elizabeth, Hillside, Irvington, Jersey City, Linden, Maplewood Millburn, Montclair, Newark, Orange, Rahway, Roselle, South Orange, Union, and West Orange. Population (2000), 647,258.

ZIP Codes: 07002, 07017–19, 07028, 07036, 07040–42, 07044, 07050–52, 07065, 07078–79, 07083, 07088, 07101–03, 07105–08, 07111–12, 07114–75, 07184, 07188–89, 07191–95, 07197–99, 07201–03, 07205–08, 07304–05

* * *

ELEVENTH DISTRICT

RODNEY P. FRELINGHUYSEN, Republican, of Morristown, NJ; born in New York, NY, April 29, 1946; education: graduated Hobart College, NY, 1969; attended graduate school in Connecticut; served, U.S. Army, 93rd Engineer Battalion; honorably discharged, 1971; Morris County state and federal aid coordinator and administrative assistant, 1972; member, Morris County Board of Chosen Freeholders, 1974–83 (director, 1980); served on: Welfare and Mental Health boards; Human Services and Private Industry councils; New Jersey General Assembly, 1983–94; chairman, Assembly Appropriations Committee, 1988–89 and 1992–94; member: American Legion, and Veterans of Foreign Wars; named Legislator of the Year by the Veterans of Foreign Wars, the New Jersey Association of Mental Health Agencies, and the New Jersey Association of Retarded Citizens; honored by numerous organizations; married: Virginia Frelinghuysen; children: Louisine and Sarah; committees: Appropriations; elected to the 104th Congress in November, 1994; reelected to each succeeding Congress.

Office Listings

http://www.house.gov/frelinghuysen

2442 Rayburn House Office Building, Washington, DC 20515 .... (202) 225–5034
Chief of Staff.—Nancy Fox. FAX: 225–3186
Press Secretary.—Erin Hennessy.
Legislative Director.—Steve Wilson.
Scheduler.—Meghan McBride.
30 Schuyler Place, 2nd Floor, Morristown, NJ 07960 .... (973) 984–0711

Counties: ESSEX COUNTY. CITIES AND TOWNSHIPS: Caldwell, Essex Fells, Fairfield Township, Livingston, Millburn, North Caldwell, Roseland, West Caldwell. MORRIS COUNTY. CITIES AND TOWNSHIPS: Bernardsville, municipalities of Boonton Town, Boonton Township, Brookside, Budd Lake, Butler, Califon, Cedar Knolls, Chatham Borough, Chatham Township, Chester Borough, Chester Township, Convent Station, Denville, Dover Town, East Hanover, Flanders, Florham Park, Gillette, Green Pond, Green Village, Hanover, Harding, Hibernia, Ironia, Jefferson, Kenvill, Kinnelon, Lake Hiawatha, Lake Hopatcong, Landing, Ledgewood, Lincoln Park, Long Valley, Madison, Mendham Borough, Mendham Township, Millington, Mine Hill, Montville, Morris Plains, Morris Township, Morristown, Mount Arlington, Mountain Lakes, Mount Olive, Mount Tabor, Netcong, Newfoundland, New Vernon, Oak Ridge, Parsippany-Troy Hills, Passaic Township, Pequannock, Picatinny, Pine Brook, Randolph, Riverdale, Rockaway Borough, Rockaway Township, Roxbury, Schooley's Mountain, Stanhope, Stirling, Succasunna, Towaco, Victory Gardens, Washington Township, Wharton, and Whippany. PASSAIC COUNTY. CITIES: Bloomingdale. SOMERSET COUNTY. CITIES AND TOWNSHIPS: Bernards Township, Bridgewater, Raritan Borough, and Somerville. SUSSEX COUNTY. CITIES AND TOWNSHIPS: Byram, Hopatcong, Sparta, and Stanhope. Population (2000), 647,258.

ZIP Codes: 07004–07, 07021, 07034–35, 07039, 07041, 07045–46, 07054, 07058, 07068, 07078, 07082, 07405, 07438, 07440, 07444, 07457, 07801–03, 07806, 07821, 07828, 07830, 07834, 07836–37, 07840, 07842–43, 07845, 07847, 07849–50, 07852–53, 07856–57, 07866, 07869–71, 07874, 07876, 07878, 07885, 07920, 07926–28, 07930, 07932–36, 07938–40, 07945–46, 07950, 07960–63, 07970, 07976, 07980–81, 07983, 07999, 08807, 08869, 08876, 08896

* * *

TWELFTH DISTRICT

RUSH D. HOLT, Democrat, of Hopewell Township, NJ; born in Weston, WV, October 15, 1948; son of the youngest person ever to be elected to the U.S. Senate; education: B.A., Carleton College, 1970; M.S. and Ph.D., physics, New York University, 1981; physicist; New York City Environmental Protection Administration, 1972–74; teaching fellow, New York University, 1974–80; Congressional Science Fellow, U.S. House of Representatives, Office of Representative Bob Edgar, 1982–83; professor, Swarthmore College, 1980–88; acting chief, Nuclear & Scientific Division, Office of Strategic Forces, U.S. Department of State, 1987–89; assistant director, Princeton Plasma Physics Laboratory, Princeton, NJ, 1989–97; Protestant; married: Margaret Lancefield; children: Michael, Dejan, and Rachel; committees: Education and Labor; Natural Resources; Permanent Select Committee on Intelligence; elected to the 106th Congress; reelected to each succeeding Congress.

Office Listings

http://holt.house.gov

1019 Longworth House Office Building, Washington, DC 20515 .... (202) 225–5801
Chief of Staff.—Tom O'Donnell. FAX: 225–6025
Legislative Director.—Christopher Hartmann.
Press Secretary.—Matthew Dennis.
Executive Assistant.—Sarah Steward.
50 Washington Road, West Windsor, NJ 08550 .... (609) 750–9365
District Director.—Leslie Potter.

Counties: HUNTERDON COUNTY. CITIES AND TOWNSHIPS: Delaware, East Amwell, Franklin, Frenchtown, Kingwood, Lambertville, Stockton, West Amwell. MERCER COUNTY. CITIES AND TOWNSHIPS: Ewing, Hopewell Borough, Hopewell Township, Lawrence, Pennington, Princeton Borough, Princeton Township, West Windsor. MIDDLESEX COUNTY. CITIES AND TOWNSHIPS: Cranbury, East Brunswick, Helmetta, Jamesburg, Monroe, North Brunswick, Old Bridge, Plainsboro Township, South River, Spotswood, South Brunswick. MONMOUTH COUNTY. CITIES AND TOWNSHIPS: Eatontown, Englishtown, Fair Haven, Freehold Township, Holmdel, Little Silver, Manalapan, Marlboro, Middletown, Oceanport, Rumson, Shrewsbury Borough, Shrewsbury Township, Tinton Falls. SOMERSET COUNTY. CITIES AND TOWNSHIPS: Franklin Township. Population (2000), 647,258.

ZIP Codes: 07701–04, 07712, 07724, 07726, 07728, 07733, 07738–39, 07746, 07748, 07751, 07753, 07757, 07760, 07763, 07765, 07777, 07799, 08512, 08525, 08528, 08530, 08534, 08536, 08540–44, 08550–51, 08556–57, 08559–60, 08570, 08608–09, 08611, 08618–19, 08628, 08638, 08648, 08690, 08801, 08803, 08809–10, 08816, 08822–25, 08828, 08831, 08844, 08850, 08852, 08857, 08859, 08867–68, 08873, 08875, 08882, 08884, 08890, 08901–02, 08905, 08922

* * *

THIRTEENTH DISTRICT

ALBIO SIRES, Democrat, of West New York, NJ; born in Bejucal, Provincia de la Habana, Cuba, January 26, 1951; education: graduated, Memorial High School; B.A., St. Peter's College, 1974; M.A., Middlebury College, Middlebury, VT, 1985; studied Spanish in Madrid, Spain; professional: businessman, teacher; part-owner, A.M. Title Agency, Union Township; mayor, West New York, NJ, 1995–2006; member: New Jersey House, 1999–2006; speaker, New Jersey House, 2002–2005; family: wife, Adrienne; stepdaughter, Tara Kole; committees: Financial Services; Foreign Affairs; elected to the 109th Congress by special election to fill the vacancy caused by the resignation of Robert Menendez; reelected to the 110th Congress.

Office Listings

http://www.house.gov/sires

1024 Longworth House Office Building, Washington, DC 20515 .... (202) 225–7919
Chief of Staff.—Gene Martorony. FAX: 226–0792
Administrative Director / Scheduler.—Judi Wolford.
Legislative Director.—Annie Russo.
Communications Director.—Olga Alvarez.
35 Journal Square, Suite 906, Jersey City, NJ 07306 .... (201) 222–2828
Bayonne City Hall, 630 Avenue C, Room 4, Bayonne, NJ 07002 .... (201) 823–2900
5500 Palisades Avenue, Suite A, West New York, NJ 07093 .... (201) 558–0800
100 Cooke Avenue, Second Floor, Carteret, NJ 07008 .... (732) 969–9160

Counties: ESSEX (part), HUDSON (part), MIDDLESEX (part), UNION (part). CITIES AND TOWNSHIPS: Bayonne, Carteret, East Newark, Elizabeth, Guttenberg, Harrison Township, Hoboken, Jersey City, Kearny, Linden, Newark, North Bergen, Port Reading, Perth Amboy, Sewaren, Union City, Weehawken, West New York, and Woodbridge. Population (2000), 647,258.

ZIP Codes: 07002–03, 07008, 07029–30, 07036, 07047, 07064, 07077, 07086–87, 07093, 07095, 07102–05, 07107, 07114, 07201–02, 07206, 07302–11, 08861–62

NEW MEXICO

(Population 2000, 1,819,046)

SENATORS

PETE V. DOMENICI, Republican, of Albuquerque, NM; born in Albuquerque, May 7, 1932; education: graduate of St. Mary's High School, 1954; B.S., University of New Mexico, 1966; LL.D., Denver University, 1958; professional: admitted to New Mexico bar, 1958; elected to Albuquerque City Commission, 1966; chairman (ex officio mayor), 1967; married: Nancy Burk, 1958; children: Lisa, Peter, Nella, Clare, David, Nanette, Helen, and Paula; committees: Appropriations; Budget; Energy and Natural Resources; Homeland Security and Governmental Affairs; Indian Affairs; elected to the U.S. Senate on November 7, 1972; reelected to each succeeding Senate term.

Office Listings

http://domenici.senate.gov

328 Hart Senate Office Building, Washington, DC 20510 .... (202) 224–6621
FAX: 228–3261
Chief of Staff.—Steve Bell.
Deputy Chief of Staff for Administration.—Lynden Armstrong.
Deputy Chief of Staff for Legislation.—Edward Hild.
Press Secretary.—Chris Gallegos.
201 3rd Street NW, Suite 710, Albuquerque, NM 87102 .... (505) 346–6791
Loretto Town Centre, 505 South Main, Suite 118, Las Cruces, NM 88001 .... (505) 526–5475
120 South Federal Place, Suite 302, Santa Fe, NM 87501 .... (505) 988–6511
Federal Building, 500 North Richardson, Suite 227, Roswell, NM 88201 .... (505) 623–6170

* * *

JEFF BINGAMAN, Democrat, of Santa Fe, NM; born in El Paso, TX, October 3, 1943; raised in Silver City, NM; graduate of Western High (now Silver High), 1961; B.A., government, Harvard University, 1965; J.D., Stanford Law School, 1968; U.S. Army Reserves, 1968–74; Assistant New Mexico Attorney General, 1969, as counsel to the State constitutional convention; private practice, 1970–78; New Mexico Attorney General, 1979–83; member: Methodist Church; married: the former Anne Kovacovich; one son, John; committees: chair, Energy and Natural Resources; Finance; Health, Labor, and Pensions; Joint Economic Committee; elected to the U.S. Senate on November 2, 1982; reelected to each succeeding Senate term.

Office Listings

http://bingaman.senate.gov

703 Hart Senate Office Building, Washington, DC 20510 .... (202) 224–5521
TDD: 224–1792
Administrative Assistant.—Stephen Ward.
Legislative Director.—Trudy Vincent.
Press Secretary.—Jude McCartin.
Personal Assistant.—Virginia White.
Loretto Town Centre, Suite 148, 505 South Main, Las Cruces, NM 88001 .... (505) 523–6561
625 Silver Avenue SW, Suite 130, Albuquerque, NM 87102 .... (505) 346–6601
105 West Third Street, Suite 409, Roswell, NM 88201 .... (505) 622–7113
119 East Marcy, Suite 101, Santa Fe, NM 87501 .... (505) 988–6647
118 Bridge Street, Suite 3, Las Vegas, NM 87701 .... (505) 454–8824

REPRESENTATIVES

FIRST DISTRICT

HEATHER WILSON, Republican, of Albuquerque, NM; born in Keene, NH, December 30, 1960; George S. Emerson Elementary School, Fitzwilliam, NH; Keene High School, NH; B.S., United States Air Force Academy; Rhodes Scholar, Oxford University, England; Masters and Doctoral degrees in Philosophy (international relations); United States Air Force, Captain, 1978–89; President, Keystone International, Inc., 1991–95; New Mexico Secretary of Children, Youth, and Families; 1995–98; married: Jay R. Hone, 1991; children: Scott, Joshua, and Caitlin Hone; committees: Energy and Commerce; Permanent Select Committee on Intelligence; elected to the 105th Congress on June 23, 1998, by special election; reelected to each succeeding Congress.

Office Listings

http://www.house.gov/wilson

442 Cannon House Office Building, Washington, DC 20515 .... (202) 225–6316

Chief of Staff.—Bryce Dustman. FAX: 225–4975
Legislative Director.—Joe Moser.
Executive Assistant.—Barbara Cohen.
20 First Plaza, NW., Suite 603, Albuquerque, NM 87102 .... (505) 346–6781
Scheduler.—Jan Duffield.

Counties: BERNALILLO (part), SANDOVAL (part), SANTA FE (part), TORRANCE, VALENCIA (part). CITIES AND TOWNSHIPS: Albuquerque, Belen, Estancia, Los Lunas, Moriarty, Mountainair, and Rio Rancho. Population (2000), 606,391.

ZIP Codes: 87001–02, 87004, 87008–09, 87015–16, 87031–32, 87035–36, 87042–43, 87047–48, 87059–61, 87063, 87068, 87070, 87101–25, 87131, 87151, 87153–54, 87158, 87176, 87181, 87184–85, 87187, 87190–99, 88301, 88321

* * *

SECOND DISTRICT

STEVAN PEARCE, Republican, of Hobbs, NM; born in Lamesa, TX, August 24, 1947; education: B.B.A., New Mexico State University; M.B.A., Eastern New Mexico University; professional: businessman; owner, Trinity Industries; military service: U.S. Air Force pilot, 1970–76; attained the rank of Captain; awarded the Distinguished Flying Cross; public service: New Mexico House of Representatives, 1996–2000; religion: Baptist; married: Cynthia; children: Lori; committees: Financial Services; Natural Resources; elected to the 108th Congress on November 5, 2002; reelected to each succeeding Congress.

Office Listings

http://www.house.gov/pearce

1607 Longworth House Office Building, Washington, DC 20515 .... (202) 225–2365
Chief of Staff.—Bob Carter. FAX: 225–9599
Press Secretary.—David Host.
Scheduler.—Kathleen Amacio.
1717 West 2nd Street, Suite 100, Roswell, NM 88201 .... (505) 622–0055
400 North Telshor, Suite E, Las Cruces, NM 88011 .... (505) 522–2219
1923 North Dal Paso, Hobbs, NM 88240 .... (505) 392–8325
District Director.—Bob Carter.
111 School of Mines Road, Socorro, NM 87801 .... (505) 838–7516

Counties: BERNALILLO (part), CATRON, CHAVES, CIBOLA, DEBACA, DONA ANA, EDDY, GRANT, GUADALUPE, HIDALGO, LEA, LINCOLN, LUNA, MCKINLEY (part), OTERO, SIERRA, SOCORRO, VALENCIA (part). Population (2000), 606,406.

ZIP Codes: 87002, 87005–07, 87011, 87014, 87020–23, 87026, 87028, 87031, 87034, 87038, 87040, 87045, 87049, 87051, 87062, 87068, 87105, 87121, 87315, 87321, 87327, 87357, 87711, 87724, 87801, 87820–21, 87823–25, 87827–32, 87901, 87930–31, 87933, 87935–37, 87939–43, 88001–09, 88011–12, 88020–21, 88023–34, 88036, 88038–49, 88051–56, 88058, 88061–63, 88065, 88072, 88081, 88114, 88116, 88119, 88134, 88136, 88201–03, 88210–11, 88220–21, 88230–32, 88240–42, 88244, 88250, 88252–56, 88260, 88262–65, 88267–68, 88301, 88310–12, 88314, 88316–18, 88323–25, 88330, 88336–55, 88417, 88431, 88435

* * *

THIRD DISTRICT

TOM UDALL, Democrat, of Santa Fe, NM; born in Tucson, AZ, May 18, 1948; son of U.S. Representative (1955–61), and Secretary of the Interior (1961–69), Stewart Udall; education: McLean, VA, High School; B.A., Prescott College, 1970; Cambridge (England) University, 1975; J.D., University of New Mexico, 1977; professional: law clerk for Chief Justice Oliver Seth of the Tenth Circuit Court of Appeals, Santa Fe, NM; assistant U.S. Attorney, 1977–81; private attorney, 1981; chief counsel, New Mexico Health and Environment Department, 1983–84; New Mexico Attorney General, 1990–98; married: Jill Z. Cooper; one child; committees: Appropriations; elected to the 106th Congress; reelected to each succeeding Congress.

Office Listings

http://www.house.gov/tomudall

1414 Longworth House Office Building, Washington, DC 20515 .... (202) 225–6190
Chief of Staff.—Tom Nagle. FAX: 226–1331
Legislative Director.—Mike Collins.
Press Secretary.—Marissa Padilla.
Appointment Secretary.—Donda Morgan.
811 St. Michaels Drive, Suite 104, Santa Fe, NM 87505 .... (505) 984–8950
District Director.—Michele Jacquez-Ortiz.
701 North Main, Clovis, NM 88101 .... (505) 763–7616

800 Municipal Drive, Farmington, NM 87401 .... (505) 324–1005
Constituent Services Representative / Veterans Liaison.—Pete Valencia.
110 West Aztec, Suite 102, Gallup, NM 87301 .... (505) 863–0582
100 Luna Drive, Administration Building 106, Las Vegas, NM 87701 .... (505) 454–4080
3900 Southern Boulevard, SE, Room 105–A, Rio Rancho, NM 87124 .... (505) 994–0499
Field Representative.—Sarah Cobb.

Counties: BERNALILLO (part), COLFAX, CURRY, HARDING, LOS ALAMOS, MCKINLEY (part), MORA, QUAY, RIO ARRIBA, ROOSEVELT, SANDOVAL (part), SAN JUAN, SAN MIGUEL, SANTA FE (part), TAOS, UNION. Population (2000), 606,249.

ZIP Codes: 87001, 87004, 87010, 87012–13, 87015, 87017–18, 87024–25, 87027, 87029, 87037, 87041, 87044–48, 87052–53, 87056, 87064, 87072, 87083, 87114, 87120, 87123–24, 87144, 87174, 87301–02, 87305, 87310–13, 87316–17, 87319–23, 87325–26, 87328, 87347, 87364–65, 87375, 87401–02, 87410, 87412–13, 87415–21, 87455, 87461, 87499, 87501–25, 87527–33, 87535, 87537–40, 87543–45, 87548–49, 87551–54, 87556–58, 87560, 87562, 87564–67, 87569, 87571, 87573–83, 87592, 87594, 87701, 87710, 87712–15, 87718, 87722–23, 87728–36, 87740, 87742–43, 87745–47, 87749–50, 87752–53, 88101–03, 88112–13, 88115–16, 88118, 88120–26, 88130, 88132–35, 88401, 88410–11, 88414–16, 88418–19, 88421–22, 88424, 88426–27, 88430, 88433–34, 88436–37, 88439

NEW YORK

(Population 2000, 18,976,457)

SENATORS

CHARLES E. SCHUMER, Democrat, of Brooklyn and Queens, NY; born in Brooklyn, November 23, 1950; education: graduated valedictorian, Madison High School; Harvard University, *magna cum laude*, 1971; J.D. with honors, Harvard Law School, 1974; professional: admitted to the New York State bar in 1975; elected to the New York State Assembly, 1974; served on Judiciary, Health, Education, and Cities committees; chairman, subcommittee on City Management and Governance, 1977; chairman, Committee on Oversight and Investigation, 1979; reelected to each succeeding legislative session until December 1980; married: Iris Weinshall, 1980; children: Jessica Emily and Alison Emma; committees: chair, Democratic Senatorial Campaign Committee; chair, Joint Economic Committee; Banking, Housing, and Urban Affairs; Finance; Judiciary; Rules and Administration; Joint Committee on the Library; elected to the 97th Congress on November 4, 1980; reelected to each succeeding Congress; elected to the U.S. Senate on November 3, 1998; reelected to each succeeding Senate term.

Office Listings

http://schumer.senate.gov

313 Hart Senate Office Building, Washington, DC 20510 .... (202) 224–6542
Chief of Staff.—Mike Lynch. FAX: 228–3027
Communications Director.—Eric Schultz.
Executive Assistant.—Kim Magee.
757 Third Avenue, Suite 1702, New York, NY 10017 .... (212) 486–4430
Leo O'Brien Building, Room 420, Albany, NY 12207 .... (518) 431–4070
130 South Elmwood Avenue, #660, Buffalo, NY 14202 .... (716) 846–4111
100 State Street, Room 3040, Rochester, NY 14614 .... (585) 263–5866
100 South Clinton, Room 841, Syracuse, NY 13261–7318 .... (315) 423–5471
Federal Office Building, 15 Henry Street, #B6, Binghamton, NY 13901 .... (607) 772–8109
Two Greenway Plaza, 145 Pine Lawn Road, #300, Melville, NY 11747 .... (631) 753–0978
One Park Place, Suite 100, Peekskill, NY 10566 .... (914) 734–1532

* * *

HILLARY RODHAM CLINTON, Democrat, of Chappaqua, NY; born in Chicago, IL, October 26, 1947; education: B.A., Wellesley College, 1969; J.D., Yale University, 1973; professional: attorney; advised the Children's Defense Fund and the U.S. House of Representatives' Judiciary Committee; faculty, University of Arkansas Law School at Fayetteville, 1975; private legal practice; family: married to former Arkansas Governor and President William Jefferson Clinton, 1975; one daughter: Chelsea, 1980; First Lady of Arkansas, 1979–1981, and 1983–1993; First Lady of the United States, 1993–2001; author: *It Takes a Village and Other Lessons Children Teach Us; Dear Socks, Dear Buddy: Kids' Letters to the First Pets; An Invitation to the White House*; *Living History*; religion: Methodist; recipient of numerous awards; committees: Armed Services; Environment and Public Works; Health, Education, Labor, and Pensions; Special Committee on Aging; elected to the U.S. Senate on November 7, 2000; reelected to each succeeding Senate term.

Office Listings

http://clinton.senate.gov

476 Russell Senate Office Building, Washington, DC 20510 .... (202) 224–4451
Chief of Staff.—Tamera Luzzatto. FAX: 228–0282
Press Secretary.—Philippe Reines.
Communications Director.—Lorraine Voles.
Scheduler.—Lona Valmoro.
Federal Office Building, 1 Clinton Square, Room 821, Albany, NY 12207 .... (518) 431–0120
Larkin at Exchange, 726 Exchange Street, Suite 511, Buffalo, NY 14210 .... (716) 854–9725
Federal Office Building, 100 State Street, Room 3280, Rochester, NY 14614 .... (585) 263–6250
Federal Office Building, 100 South Clinton Street, P.O. Box 7378, Syracuse, NY 13261 .... (315) 448–0470
P.O. Box 273, Lowville, NY 13367 .... (315) 376–6118
P.O. Box 617, Hartsdale, NY 10530 .... (914) 725–9294
Three Greenway Plaza, 155 Pinclawn Road, Suite 250 North, Melville, NY 11747 .... (631) 249–2825

REPRESENTATIVES

FIRST DISTRICT

TIMOTHY H. BISHOP, Democrat, of Southampton, NY; born in Southampton, June 1, 1950; education: Southampton High School, 1968; A.B., in History, from Holy Cross College; M.P.A., Long Island University, 1981; professional: educator; Provost of Southampton College, 1986–2002; community service: Southampton Rotary Club Scholarship Committee; Southampton Town Board of Ethics; Eastern Long Island Coastal Conservation Alliance; Bridgehampton Childcare and Recreation Center; religion: Catholic; married: Kathryn; children: Molly and Meghan; committees: Budget; Education and Labor; Transportation and Infrastructure; elected to the 108th Congress on November 5, 2002; reelected to each succeeding Congress.

Office Listings

http:/www.house.gov/timbishop

225 Cannon House Office Building, Washington, DC 20515 .... (202) 225–3826
FAX: 225–3143
Chief of Staff.—Pete Spiro.
Legislative Director.—Kate Ryan.
Scheduler / Staff Assistant.—Eddie Shimkus.
District Director / Communications Director.—Jon Schneider.
3680 Route 112, Suite C, Coram, NY 11727 .... (631) 696–6500

Counties: SUFFOLK COUNTY (part). CITIES: Brookhaven, Smithtown, Southampton, and Montauk. Population (2000), 654,360.

ZIP Codes: 00501, 00544, 11713, 11715, 11719–20, 11727, 11733, 11738, 11741–42, 11745, 11754–55, 11763–64, 11766–68, 11772, 11776–80, 11784, 11786–90, 11792, 11794, 11901, 11930–35, 11937, 11939–42, 11944, 11946–65, 11967–73, 11975–78, 11980

* * *

SECOND DISTRICT

STEVE ISRAEL, Democrat, of Huntington, NY; born in Brooklyn, NY, May 30, 1958; education: B.A., George Washington University, 1982; professional: public relations and marketing executive; public service: Legislative Assistant for Rep. Richard Ottinger (D–NY), 1980–83; Suffolk County Executive for Intergovernmental Relations, 1988–91; elected to the Huntington Town Board, 1993; reelected two times; organizations: Institute on the Holocaust; Touro Law Center; Nature Conservancy; Audubon Society; awards: Child Care Council of Suffolk Leadership Award; Anti-Defamation League and Sons of Italy Purple Aster Award; committees: Appropriations; elected to the 107th Congress on November 7, 2000; reelected to each succeeding Congress.

Office Listings

http://www.house.gov/israel

432 Cannon House Office Building, Washington, DC 20515 .... (202) 225–3335
FAX: 225–4669
Chief of Staff.—Jack Pratt.
Communications Director.—Meghan Dubyak.
Legislative Director.—Heather McHugh.
150 Motor Parkway, Suite 108, Hauppauge, NY 11788 .... (631) 951–2210
(516) 505–1448
District Director.—Holli Dunayer.

Counties: NASSAU COUNTY (part), SUFFOLK COUNTY (part). CITIES: Asharoken, Bay Shore, Bayport, Bohemia, Brentwood, Brightwaters, Centerport, Central Islip, Cold Springs Harbor, Commack, Copiague, Deer Park, Dix Hills, East Farmingdale, East Northport, Eaton's Neck, Elwood, Fort Salonga, Great River, Greenlawn, Halesite, Hauppauge, Holbrook, Huntington, Huntington Station, Islandia, Islip, Islip Terrace, Jericho, King's Park, Lindenhurst, Lloyd Harbor, Melville, North Amityville, Northport, Oakdale, Ocean Beach, Old Bethpage, Plainview, Ronkonkoma, Sayville, Smithtown, South Huntington, Syosset, West Babylon, West Hills, West Islip, West Sayville, Wheatley Heights, Woodbury and Wyandanch. Population (2000), 654,360.

ZIP Codes: 11701, 11703–06, 11714–18, 11721–22, 11724–26, 11729–31, 11735, 11737, 11739–43, 11746–47, 11749–54, 11757, 11760, 11767–70, 11772, 11775, 11779, 11782, 11787–88, 11791, 11796–98, 11801, 11803–04

* * *

THIRD DISTRICT

PETER T. KING, Republican, of Seaford, NY; born in Manhattan, NY, April 5, 1944; education: B.A., St. Francis College, NY, 1965; J.D., University of Notre Dame Law School,

IN, 1968; military service: served, U.S. Army Reserve National Guard, specialist 5, 1968–73; admitted to New York bar, 1968; professional: attorney; Deputy Nassau County Attorney, 1972–74, executive assistant to the Nassau County Executive, 1974–76; general counsel, Nassau Off-Track Betting Corporation, 1977; Hempstead Town Councilman, 1978–81; Nassau County Comptroller, 1981–92; member: Ancient Order of Hiberians, Long Island Committee for Soviet Jewry, Sons of Italy, Knights of Columbus, 69th Infantry Veterans Corps, American Legion; married: Rosemary Wiedl King, 1967; children: Sean and Erin; grandson, Jack; committees: Financial Services; Homeland Security; elected on November 3, 1992 to the 103rd Congress; reelected to each succeeding Congress.

Office Listings

http://www.house.gov/king

339 Cannon House Office Building, Washington, DC 20515 .... (202) 225–7896
Chief of Staff / Press Secretary.—Kevin Fogarty. FAX: 226–2279
Legislative Director.—Kerryann Watkins.
1003 Park Boulevard, Massapequa Park, NY 11762 .... (516) 541–4225
District Director.—Anne Rosenfeld.
Suffolk County .... (631) 541–4225

Counties: NASSAU (part), SUFFOLK (part). CITIES AND TOWNSHIPS: Amityville, Babylon, Baldwin, Bayshore, Bayville, Bellmore, Bethpage, Brightwaters, Brookville, Cedar Beach, Centre Island, Copiague, Cove Neck, East Islip, East Norwich, Farmingdale, Freeport, Gilgo Beach, Glen Cove, Glen Head, Glenwood Landing, Greenvale, Harbor Isle, Hicksville, Island Park, Islip, Jericho, Lattingtown, Laurel Hollow, Levittown, Lido Beach, Lindenhurst, Locust Grove, Locust Valley, Long Beach, Massapequa, Massapequa Park, Matinecock, Merrick, Mill Neck, Muttontown, North Babylon, North Bellmore, North Lindenhurst, Oak Beach, Oceanside, Old Bethpage, Old Brookville, Old Westbury, Oyster Bay, Oyster Bay Cove, Plainview, Point Lookout, Sea Cliff, Seaford, Syosset, Wantagh, West Babylon, West Bayshore, Westbury, West Islip, and Woodbury. Population (2000), 654,361.

ZIP Codes: 11510, 11520, 11542, 11545, 11547–48, 11558, 11560–61, 11566, 11568–69, 11572, 11576, 11579, 11590, 11599, 11701–04, 11706, 11709–10, 11714, 11718, 11724, 11726, 11730, 11732, 11735–37, 11751, 11753, 11756–58, 11762, 11765, 11771, 11773–74, 11783, 11791, 11793, 11795, 11797, 11801–04, 11815, 11819, 11854–55

* * *

FOURTH DISTRICT

CAROLYN MCCARTHY, Democrat, of Mineola, NY; born in Brooklyn, NY, January 5, 1944; education: graduated, Mineola High School, 1962; graduated, nursing school, 1964; professonal: licensed practical nurse in ICU Section, Glen Cove Hospital; married: Dennis McCarthy, 1967; widowed on December 7, 1993, when her husband was killed and her only son, Kevin, severely wounded in the Long Island Railroad Massacre; turned personal nightmare into a crusade against violence—speaking out with other families of the Long Island tragedy, not just to the victims of the shooting but to crime victims across the country; board of directors, New Yorkers Against Gun Violence; board of directors, New York City "Stop the Violence" campaign; committees: Education and Labor; Financial Services; elected to the 105th Congress; reelected to each succeeding Congress.

Office Listings

http://www.house.gov/carolynmccarthy

106 Cannon House Office Building, Washington, DC 20515 .... (202) 225–5516
Chief of Staff.—Robert Recklaus. FAX: 225–5758
District Director.—Christopher Chaffee.
Executive Assistant.—Shannon Carlin.
Communications Director.—George Burke.
200 Garden City Plaza, Suite 320, Garden City, NY 11530 .... (516) 739–3008

Counties: NASSAU (part). CITIES AND TOWNSHIPS: Atlantic Beach, Baldwin, Bellerose, Carle Place, Cedarhurst, East Meadow, East Rockaway, East Williston, Elmont, Floral Park, Franklin Square, Freeport, Garden City, Garden City Park, Hempstead, Hewlett, Inwood, Lakeview, Lawrence, Lynbrook, Malverne, Merrick, Mineola, New Cassel, New Hyde Park, North Bellmore, North New Hyde Park, Oceanside, Rockville Centre, Roosevelt, Salisbury, Stewart Manor, South Floral Park, South Valley Stream, Uniondale, Valley Stream, West Hempstead, Westbury, Williston Park, Woodmere, and Woodsburgh. Population (2000) 654,360.

ZIP Codes: 11001–03, 11010, 11040, 11042, 11096, 11501, 11509–10, 11514, 11516, 11518, 11520, 11530–31, 11535–36, 11549–57, 11559, 11561, 11563–66, 11568, 11570–72, 11575, 11577, 11580–83, 11588, 11590, 11592–99, 11710, 11793

* * *

FIFTH DISTRICT

GARY L. ACKERMAN, Democrat, of Queens, NY; born in Brooklyn, NY, November 19, 1942; education: graduate, Queens College, Flushing, NY; attended St. John's University, Jamaica, NY; professional: public school teacher; newspaper editor; businessman; New York State Senate, 1979–83; married: the former Rita Tewel; children: Lauren, Corey, and Ari; committees: Financial Services; Foreign Affairs; elected by special election on March 1, 1983, to the 98th Congress, to fill the vacancy caused by the death of Representative Benjamin Rosenthal; reelected to each succeeding Congress.

Office Listings

http://www.house.gov/ackerman

2243 Rayburn House Office Building, Washington, DC 20515 .... (202) 225–2601
FAX: 225–1589
Chief of Staff.—Jedd Moskowitz.
Scheduler.—Brenda Connolly.
Legislative Director.—Howard Diamond.
Press Secretary.—Jordan Goldes.
218–14 Northern Boulevard, Bayside, NY 11361 .... (718) 423–2154
District Office Administrator.—Moya Berry.

Counties: NASSAU (part), QUEENS (part). CITIES AND TOWNSHIPS: Auburndale, Bay Terrace, Bayside, Bell Park Gardens, Bell Park Manor, Centre Island, Clearview, Corona, Deepdale, Douglaston, Douglaston Manor, East Elmhurst, East Hills, Flushing, Fresh Meadows, Glen Oaks, Great Neck, Great Neck Estates, Great Neck Gardens, Great Neck Plaza, Greenvale, Herricks, Hillcrest, Hollis Court Gardens, Hollis Hills, Jackson Heights, Jamaica Estates, Kensington, Kew Gardens Hills, Kings Point, Lake Success, Lefrak City, Linden Hill, Little Neck, Malba, Manor Haven, North Shore Towers, Oakland Gardens, Pomonok, Port Washington, Port Washington North, Queensboro Hill, Roslyn, Roslyn Estates, Roslyn Harbor, Roslyn Heights, Russell Gardens, Saddle Rock, Saddle Rock Estates, Sands Point, Searington, Thomaston, University Gardens, West Neck, and Windsor Park. Population (2000), 654,361.

ZIP Codes: 11004–05, 11020–24, 11030, 11040, 11042, 11050–55, 11351–52, 11354–58, 11360–66, 11368–69, 11372–73, 11375, 11379, 11423, 11426–27, 11432, 11507, 11542, 11548, 11560, 11568, 11576–77, 11596

* * *

SIXTH DISTRICT

GREGORY W. MEEKS, Democrat, of Far Rockaway, NY; born in Harlem, NY, September 25, 1953; education: P.S. 183; Robert F. Wagner Junior High School; Julia Richman High School, New York, NY; bachelor degree, Adelphi University, 1971–75; J.D., Howard University School of Law, 1975–78; professional: lawyer, admitted to bar, 1979; Queens District Attorney's Office, 1978–83, serving as Assistant District Attorney; Judge, New York State Workers' Compensation Board; public service: New York State Assemblyman, 1992–97; organizations: Alpha Phi Alpha Fraternity; Council of Black-Elected Democrats; National Bar Association; Task Force on Financial Services; active member of the Congressional Black Caucus; married: Simone-Marie Meeks, 1997; children: Aja, Ebony, and Nia-Ayana; committees: Financial Services; Foreign Affairs; elected to the 105th Congress on February 3, 1998; reelected to each succeeding Congress.

Office Listings

http://www.house.gov/meeks

2342 Rayburn House Office Building, Washington, DC 20515 .... (202) 225–3461
FAX: 226–4169
Chief of Staff.—Jameel Aalim-Johnson.
Legislative Director.—Sophia King.
Office Manager / Scheduler.—Patricia Fisher.
153–01 Jamaica Avenue, Jamaica, NY 11432 .... (718) 725–6000
Chief of Staff.—Robert Simmons.
1931 Mott Avenue, Room 305, Far Rockaway, NY 11691 .... (718) 327–9791
Community Liaison.—Edward Williams.

Counties: QUEENS COUNTY (part). CITIES AND TOWNSHIPS: Arverne, Cambria Heights, Edgemere, Far Rockaway, Floral Park, Glen Oaks, Hammels, Hollis, Howard Beach, Jamaica, Jamaica Estates, Kew Gardens, Laurelton, New Hyde Park, Ozone Park, Queens Village, Richmond Hill, Rosedale, St. Albans, South Jamaica, South Ozone Park, Springfield Gardens, and Woodhaven. Population (2000), 654,361.

ZIP Codes: 11001, 11004, 11040, 11405, 11411–20, 11422–23, 11425–36, 11439, 11451, 11484, 11690–93

* * *

SEVENTH DISTRICT

JOSEPH CROWLEY, Democrat, of Elmhurst, Queens, NY; born in New York, NY, March 16, 1962; education: graduated, Power Memorial High School, 1981; B.A., Queens College, 1985; professional: elected to the New York State Assembly, 1986–98; Assembly Committees: Racing and Wagering; Banking, Consumer Affairs, and Protection; Election Law; Labor and Housing; religion: Roman Catholic; married: Kasey Nilson; committees: Ways and Means; elected to the 106th Congress; reelected to each succeeding Congress.

Office Listings

http://house.gov/crowley

2404 Rayburn House Office Building, Washington, DC 20510 .... (202) 225–3965
Chief of Staff.—Christopher McCannell. FAX: 225–1909
Office Manager.—Sylvia Stanojev.
Legislative Director.—Kevin Casey.
2800 Bruckner Boulevard, Suite 301, Bronx, NY 10465 .... (718) 931–1400
82–11 37th Avenue, Suite 705, Jackson Heights, NY 11372 .... (718) 779–1400
177 Dreiser Loop, Room 3, Bronx, NY 10475 .... (718) 320–2314

Counties: BRONX (part), QUEENS (part). Population (2000), 654,360.

ZIP Codes: 10458, 10460–62, 10464–67, 10469, 10472–75, 10805, 11103–04, 11354, 11356, 11368–73, 11377–78, 11380

* * *

EIGHTH DISTRICT

JERROLD NADLER, Democrat, of New York, NY; born in Brooklyn, NY, June 13, 1947; education: graduated from Stuyvesant High School, 1965; B.A., Columbia University, 1970; J.D., Fordham University, 1978; professional: New York State Assembly, 1977–92; member: American Jewish Congress; ACLU; National Abortion Rights Action League; AIPAC; National Organization for Women; Assistant Whip; married: 1976; one child; committees: Judiciary; Transportation and Infrastructure; elected to the 102nd Congress on November 3, 1992, to fill the vacancy caused by the death of Representative Ted Weiss; at the same time elected to the 103rd Congress; reelected to each succeeding Congress.

Office Listings

http://www.house.gov/nadler

2334 Rayburn House Office Building, Washington, DC 20515 .... (202) 225–5635
Director.—John Doty. FAX: 225–6923
201 Varick Street, Suite 669, New York, NY 10014 .... (212) 367–7350
Chief of Staff.—Amy Rutkin.
445 Neptune Avenue, Brooklyn, NY 11224 .... (718) 373–3198
Community Representative.—Ilan Kayatsky.

Counties: KINGS (part), NEW YORK (part). Population (2000), 654,360.

ZIP Codes: 10001–08, 10010–14, 10016, 10018–20, 10023–24, 10036, 10038, 10041, 10043, 10047–48, 10069, 10072, 10080–81, 10101–02, 10108–09, 10113–14, 10116–17, 10119–24, 10129, 10132–33, 10149, 10199, 10209, 10213, 10242, 10249, 10256, 10260, 10265, 10268–70, 10272–82, 10285–86, 10292, 11204, 11214–15, 11218–20, 11223–24, 11228, 11230–32, 11235

* * *

NINTH DISTRICT

ANTHONY D. WEINER, Democrat, of Brooklyn, NY; born in Brooklyn, September 4, 1964; education: graduated, Brooklyn Tech High School; B.A., State University of New York at Plattsburgh, 1985; professional: served in the New York City Council, 1992–98; selected to serve as Freshman Whip, 106th Congress; committees: Energy and Commerce; Judiciary; elected to the 106th Congress; reelected to each succeeding Congress.

Office Listings

http://www.house.gov/weiner

1122 Longworth House Office Building, Washington, DC 20515 .... (202) 225–6616

Chief of Staff / Legislative Director.—Marc Dunkelman. FAX: 226–7253
Executive Assistant.—Michael Marcy.
Special Assistant.—Emily Berman.
80–02 Kew Gardens Road, Suite 5000, Kew Gardens, NY 11415 .... (718) 520–9001
90–16 Rockaway Beach Boulevard, Rockaway, NY 11693 .... (718) 318–9255
1800 Sheepshead Bay Road, Brooklyn, NY 11235 .... (718) 743–0441
District Director.—Glen Caplin.

Counties: KINGS COUNTY (part). CITIES AND TOWNSHIPS: Bergen Beach, Brighton Beach, Canasie, Flatbush, Flatlands, Gerritsen Beach, Georgetowne, Kensington, Manhattan Beach, Marine Park, Midwood, Mill Basin, Park Slope, Parkville, Sheepshead Bay, Windsor Terrace. QUEENS COUNTY (part). CITIES AND TOWNSHIPS: Belle Harbor, Breezy Point, Briarwood, Broad Channel, Corona, Elmhurst, Far Rockaway, Forest Hills, Glendale, Hamilton Beach, Howard Beach, Kew Gardens, Lindenwood, Middle Village, Neponsit, Ozone Park, Rego Park, Richmond Hill, Ridgewood, Rockway Point, Roxbury, West Lawrence, and Woodhaven. Population (2000), 654,360.

ZIP Codes: 11204, 11208, 11210, 11218, 11223, 11229–30, 11234–36, 11358, 11361, 11364–67, 11373–75, 11378–79, 11381, 11385, 11414–18, 11421, 11424, 11427, 11432, 11435, 11693–95, 11697

* * *

TENTH DISTRICT

EDOLPHUS TOWNS, Democrat, of Brooklyn, NY; born in Chadbourn, NC, July 21, 1934; graduated, West Side High School, Chadbourn, 1952; B.S., North Carolina A&T State University, Greensboro, 1956; master's degree in social work, Adelphi University, Garden City, NY, 1973; U.S. Army, 1956–58; teacher, Medgar Evers College, Brooklyn, NY, and for the New York City public school system; deputy hospital administrator, 1965–71; deputy president, Borough of Brooklyn, 1976–82; member: Kiwanis, Boy Scouts Advisory Council, Salvation Army, Phi Beta Sigma Fraternity; married the former Gwendolyn Forbes in 1960; two children: Darryl and Deidra; committees: Energy and Commerce; Oversight and Government Reform; elected on November 2, 1982, to the 98th Congress; reelected to each succeeding Congress.

Office Listings

http://www.house.gov/towns

2232 Rayburn House Office Building, Washington, DC 20515 .... (202) 225–5936
Senior Political and Policy Advisor.—Alex Beckles. FAX: 225–1018
Office Manager / Scheduler.—Gerri Taylor.
26 Court Street, Suite 1510, Brookyln, NY 11241 .... (718) 255–2018
District Director.—Karen Johnson.
1670 Fulton Street, Brooklyn, NY 11213 .... (718) 774–5682
Chief of Staff.—Val Henry.
104–08 Flatlands Avenue, Brooklyn, NY 11236 .... (718) 272–1175
District Director.—Tony Foreman.

Counties: KINGS COUNTY (part). Population (2000), 654,361.

ZIP Codes: 11201–03, 11205–08, 11210–13, 11216–17, 11221, 11230, 11233–34, 11236, 11238–39, 11245, 11247–48, 11251, 11256

* * *

ELEVENTH DISTRICT

YVETTE D. CLARKE, Democrat, of Brooklyn, NY; born in Brooklyn, November 21, 1964; education: attended Edward R. Murrow High School; attended Oberlin College; professional: Legislative Aide to New York State Senator Velmanette Montgomery; Executive Assistant to NY Assemblywoman Barbara Clark; Staff Assistant, NY Compensation Board Chair Barbara Patton; Director of Youth Programs, Hospital League; Director of Business Development for the Bronx Empowerment Zone (BOEDC); member of City Council of New York, 2001–06; committees: Education and Labor; Homeland Security; Small Business; elected to the 110th Congress on November 7, 2006.

Office Listings

http://clarke.house.gov

1029 Longworth House Office Building, Washington, DC 20515 .... (202) 225–6231
Chief of Staff.—Terrill North. FAX: 226–0112
Legislative Director.—Ian Campbell.
123 Linden Boulevard, 4th Floor, Brooklyn, NY 11226 .... (718) 287–1142

Counties: KINGS COUNTY (part). Population (2000), 654,361.

ZIP Codes: 11201, 11203, 11210, 11212–13, 11215–18, 11225–26, 11230–31, 11233–34, 11236, 11238, 11241–42

* * *

TWELFTH DISTRICT

NYDIA M. VELÁZQUEZ, Democrat, of New York, NY; born in Yabucoa, Puerto Rico, March 28, 1953; education: B.A. in political science, University of Puerto Rico, 1974; M.A. in political science, New York University, 1976; professional: faculty member, University of Puerto Rico, 1976–81; adjunct professor, Hunter College of the City University of New York, 1981–83; special assistant to Congressman Ed Towns, 1983; member, City Council of New York, 1984–86; national director of Migration Division Office, Department of Labor and Human Resources of Puerto Rico, 1986–89; director, Department of Puerto Rican Community Affairs in the United States, 1989–92; committees: chair, Small Business; Financial Services; elected on November 3, 1992, to the 103rd Congress; reelected to each succeeding Congress.

Office Listings

http://www.house.gov/velazquez

2466 Rayburn House Office Building, Washington, DC 20515 .... (202) 225–2361
Chief of Staff.—Michael Day. FAX: 226–0327
Press Secretary.—Melissa DeRosa.
268 Broadway, 2nd Floor, Brooklyn, NY 11211 .... (718) 599–3658
16 Court Street, Suite 1006, Brooklyn, NY 11241 .... (718) 222–5819
173 Avenue B, New York, NY 10009 .... (212) 673–3997

Counties: KINGS (part), NEW YORK (part), QUEENS (part). Population (2000), 654,360.

ZIP Codes: 10002, 10009, 10012–13, 10038, 11104, 11201, 11205–08, 11211, 11215, 11219–22, 11231–32, 11237, 11251, 11377–78, 11385, 11416, 11421

* * *

THIRTEENTH DISTRICT

VITO FOSSELLA, Republican, of Staten Island, NY; born in Staten Island, March 9, 1965; education: Public School 39, South Beach; Intermediate School 2, Midland Beach; Monsignor Farrell High School; B.S., University of Pennsylvania Wharton School; Fordham University School of Law; professional: lawyer, admitted to New York bar, 1994; New York City Council, 1994–97; married: Mary Pat Fossella, 1990; children: Dylan, Griffin, and Rowan; organizations: Ancient Order of Hibernians; South Shore Rotary; Staten Island Bucks; committees: Energy and Commerce; elected to the 105th Congress, by special election, on November 4, 1997; reelected to each succeeding Congress.

Office Listings

http://www.house.gov/fossella

2453 Rayburn House Office Building, Washington, DC 20515 .... (202) 225–3371
Chief of Staff.—Tom Quaadman. FAX: 226–1272
Office Manager.—Vicki J. Hook.
Legislative Director.—Brendan Williams.
4434 Amboy Road, Second Floor, Staten Island, NY 10312 .... (718) 356–8400
District Director.—Sherry Diamond.
8505 4th Avenue, Brooklyn, NY 11209 .... (718) 630–5277
Office Manager.—Bob Capano.

Counties: KINGS (part), RICHMOND. Population (2000), 654,361.

ZIP Codes: 10301–10, 10312–14, 11204, 11209, 11214, 11219–20, 11223, 11228, 11252

* * *

FOURTEENTH DISTRICT

CAROLYN B. MALONEY, Democrat, of New York City, NY; born in Greensboro, NC, February 19, 1948; education: B.A., Greensboro College, Greensboro, NC, 1968; professional:

various positions, New York City Board of Education, 1970–77; legislative aide, New York State Assembly, senior program analyst, 1977–79; executive director of advisory council, 1979–82; director of special projects, New York State Senate Office of the Minority Leader; New York City council member, 1982–93; chairperson, New York City Council Committee on Contracts; member: Council Committee on Aging, National Organization of Women, Common Cause, Sierra Club, Americans for Democratic Action, New York City Council Committee on Housing and Buildings, Citizens Union, Grand Central Business Improvement District, Harlem Urban Development Corporation (1982–91), Commission on Early Childhood Development Programs, Council of Senior Citizen Centers of New York City (1982–87); married: Clifton H.W. Maloney, 1976; children: Virginia Marshall Maloney and Christina Paul Maloney; committees: Financial Services; Oversight and Government Reform; elected on November 3, 1992, to the 103rd Congress; reelected to each succeeding Congress.

Office Listings

http://www.house.gov/maloney

2331 Rayburn House Office Building, Washington, DC 20515 .... (202) 225–7944
Administrative Assistant.—Ben Chevat. FAX: 225–4709
Legislative Director.—Orly Isaacson.
1651 Third Avenue, Suite 311, New York, NY 10128 .... (212) 860–0606
28–11 Astoria Boulevard, Long Island City, NY 11102 .... (718) 932–1804

Counties: NEW YORK (part), QUEENS (part). CITIES AND TOWNSHIPS: Astoria, Manhattan, Queens, Long Island City, Roosevelt Island, Sunnyside, and Woodside. Population (2000), 654,361.

ZIP Codes: 10012, 10016–24, 10026, 10028–29, 10036, 10044, 10055, 10103–07, 10110–12, 10126, 10128, 10138, 10150–60, 10162–79, 11101–06, 11375, 11377

* * *

FIFTEENTH DISTRICT

CHARLES B. RANGEL, Democrat-Liberal, of New York, NY; born in Harlem, NY, June 11, 1930; attended DeWitt Clinton High School; served in U.S. Army, 1948–52; awarded the Purple Heart, Bronze Star for Valor, U.S. and Korean presidential citations, and three battle stars while serving in combat with the Second Infantry Division in Korea; honorably discharged with rank of staff sergeant; after military duty, completed high school, 1953; graduated from New York University School of Commerce, student under the G.I. bill; 1957 dean's list; graduated from St. John's University School of Law, dean's list student under a full three-year scholarship, 1960; lawyer; admitted to practice in the courts of the State of New York, U.S. Federal Court, Southern District of New York, and U.S. Customs Court; appointed assistant U.S. attorney, Southern District of New York, 1961; legal counsel, New York City Housing and Redevelopment Board, Neighborhood Conservation Bureau; general counsel, National Advisory Commission on Selective Service, 1966; served two terms in the New York State Assembly, 1966–70; active in 369th Veterans Association; Community Education Program; and Martin Luther King, Jr., Democratic Club; married: Alma Carter; two children: Steven and Alicia; committees: chair, Ways and Means; chair, Joint Committee on Taxation; elected to the 92nd Congress, November 3, 1970; reelected to each succeeding Congress.

Office Listings

http://www.house.gov/rangel

2354 Rayburn House Office Building, Washington, DC 20515 .... (202) 225–4365
Counsel / Chief of Staff.—George A. Dalley, Esq. FAX: 225–0816
163 West 125th Street, Room 737, New York, NY 10027 .... (212) 663–3900
District Administrator.—Vivian E. Jones.

Counties: BRONX (part), NEW YORK (part), QUEENS (part). Population (2000), 654,361.

ZIP Codes: 10023–27, 10029–35, 10037, 10039–40, 10115–16, 10169, 10463, 11105

* * *

SIXTEENTH DISTRICT

JOSÉ E. SERRANO, Democrat, of Bronx, NY; born in Mayagüez, PR, October 24, 1943; education: Dodge Vocational High School, Bronx, NY; attended Lehman College, City University of New York, NY; served with the U.S. Army Medical Corps, 1964–66; employed by the Manufacturers Hanover Bank, 1961–69; Community School District 7, 1969–74; New York State Assemblyman, 1974–90; chairman, Consumer Affairs Committee, 1979–83; chairman, Education Committee, 1983–90; married to the former Mary Staucet, 1987; five children: Lisa, Jose Marco, Justine, Jonathan and Benjamin; committees: Appropriations; elected to the 101st Congress, by special election, March 28, 1990, to fill the vacancy caused by the resignation of Robert Garcia; reelected to each succeeding Congress.

Office Listings

http://serrano.house.gov

2227 Rayburn House Office Building, Washington, DC 20515 .... (202) 225–4361
Executive Assistant.—Pichy Marty. FAX: 225–6001
Legislative Director.—Nadine Berg.
Scheduler.—Elisa Howie.
788 Southern Boulevard, Bronx, NY 10455 .... (718) 620–0084
Chief of Staff.—Paul Lipson.

Counties: BRONX COUNTY (part). CITIES AND TOWNSHIPS: Bronx. Population (2000), 654,360.

ZIP Codes: 10451–60, 10463, 10468, 10472–74

* * *

SEVENTEENTH DISTRICT

ELIOT L. ENGEL, Democrat, of Bronx, NY; born in Bronx, February 18, 1947; education: B.A., Hunter-Lehman College, 1969; M.A., City University of New York, 1973; New York Law School, 1987; professional: teacher and counselor in the New York City public school system, 1969–77; elected to the New York legislature, 1977–88; chaired the Assembly Committee on Alcoholism and Substance Abuse and subcommittee on Mitchell-Lama Housing (twelve years prior to his election to Congress); member: Congressional Human Rights Caucus; Democratic Study Group on Health; Long Island Sound Caucus; co-chairman, Albanian Issues Caucus; board member, Congressional Ad Hoc Committee on Irish Affairs; married: Patricia Ennis, 1980; children: Julia, Jonathan, and Philip; committees: Energy and Commerce; Foreign Affairs; elected on November 8, 1988, to the 101st Congress; reelected to each succeeding Congress.

Office Listings

http://www.house.gov/engel

2161 Rayburn House Office Building, Washington, DC 20515 .... (202) 225–2464
Administrative Assistant.—E.H. ''Ned'' Michalek. FAX: 225–5513
Office Manager.—Michelle Shwimer.
3655 Johnson Avenue, Bronx, NY 10463 .... (718) 796–9700
Chief of Staff.—William Weitz.
6 Gramatan Avenue, Mt. Vernon, NY 10550 .... (914) 699–4100
261 West Nyack Road, West Nyack, NY 10994 .... (845) 358–7800

Counties: BRONX (part), WESTCHESTER (part). CITIES AND TOWNSHIPS: Parts of Bronx, Yonkers, Mount Vernon, New Rochelle and Pelham. Population (2000), 654,360.

ZIP Codes: 10458, 10463, 10466–71, 10475, 10522, 10533, 10550–53, 10557–58, 10591, 10701, 10704–06, 10708, 10901, 10913, 10920, 10931, 10952, 10954, 10956, 10960, 10962, 10964–65, 10968, 10970, 10974, 10976–77, 10983, 10989, 10994

* * *

EIGHTEENTH DISTRICT

NITA M. LOWEY, Democrat, of Harrison, NY; born in New York, NY, July 5, 1937; education: graduated, Bronx High School of Science, 1955; B.S., Mount Holyoke College, 1959; assistant to Secretary of State for Economic Development and Neighborhood Preservation, and deputy director, Division of Economic Opportunity, 1975–85; Assistant Secretary of State, 1985–87; member: boards of directors, Close-Up Foundation; Effective Parenting Information for Children; Windward School, Downstate (New York Region); Westchester Jewish Conference; Westchester Opportunity Program; National Committee of the Police Corps; Women's Network of the YWCA; Legal Awareness for Women; National Women's Political Caucus of Westchester; American Jewish Committee of Westchester; married: Stephen Lowey,

1961; children: Dana, Jacqueline, and Douglas; committees: Appropriations; Homeland Security; elected on November 8, 1988, to the 101st Congress; reelected to each succeeding Congress.

Office Listings

http://www.house.gov/lowey

2329 Rayburn House Office Building, Washington, DC 20515 .... (202) 225–6506
Chief of Staff.—Clare Coleman. FAX: 225–0546
Executive Assistant.—Katie Papa.
Suite 310, 222 Mamaroneck Avenue, White Plains, NY 10605 .... (914) 428–1707
District Administrator.—Patricia Keegan.

Counties: ROCKLAND (part), WESTCHESTER (part). CITIES AND TOWNSHIPS: Ardsley, Ardsley on the Hundson, Briarcliff Manor; Bronxville, Chappaqua, Congers, Crestwood, Dobbs Ferry, Eastchester, Elmsford, Harrison, Hartsdale, Hasting-on-Hudson, Haverstraw, Hawthorne, Irvington, Larchmont, Mamaroneck, Maryknoll, Millwood, Mt. Kisco, New City, New Rochelle, North Castle, Ossining, Pelham, Pleasantville, Port Chester, Purchase, Rye, Rye Brook, Scarsdale, Sleepy Hollow, Tarrytown, Thornwood, Tuckahoe, Valhalla, Valley Cottage, West Harrison, West Haverstraw, White Plains, and Yonkers. Population (2000), 654,360.

ZIP Codes: 10502, 10504, 10506, 10510, 10514, 10522–23, 10528, 10530, 10532–33, 10538, 10543, 10546, 10549, 10562, 10570, 10573, 10577, 10580, 10583, 10591, 10594–95, 10601–07, 10610, 10650, 10701–10, 10801–05, 10920, 10923, 10927, 10956, 10989, 10993–94

* * *

NINETEENTH DISTRICT

JOHN J. HALL, Democrat, of Dover Plains, NY; born in Baltimore, MD, July 23, 1948; a three-time National Science Foundation scholar in High School; studied physics at Notre Dame University and transferred to Loyola College; professional: musician and co-founder of the band Orleans; served one term on Ulster County Legislature; served two terms on the Saugerties School Board; married: Pamela Bingham Hall; one daughter; committees: Transportation and Infrastructure; Veterans' Affairs; Select Committee on Energy Independence and Global Warming; elected to the 110th Congress on November 7, 2006.

Office Listings

http://www.johnhall.house.gov

1217 Longworth House Office Building, Washington, DC 20515 .... (202) 225–5441
Chief of Staff.—Jean Bordewich. FAX: 225–3289
Legislative Director.—Ryan McConaghy.
Orange County Government Center, 255 Main Street, Room 3232G, Goshen, NY 10924 .... (845) 291–4100
Putnam County Office Building, 40 Gleneida Avenue, 3rd Floor, Carmel, NY 10512 .... (845) 225–3641
District Director.—Susan Spear.

Counties: DUTCHESS COUNTY (part). CITIES AND TOWNSHIPS: Beacon, Castle Point, Chelsea, Dover Plains, Fishkill, Glenham, Holmes, Hopewell Junction, Hughsonville, Pawling, Poughkeepsie, Poughquag, Stormville, Wappingers Falls, Wingdale. ORANGE COUNTY (part). CITIES AND TOWNSHIPS: Amity, Arden, Bear Mountain, Bellvale, Blooming Grove, Burnside, Campbell Hall, Central Valley, Chester, Cornwall, Cornwall-on-Hudson, Craigville, Cuddebackville, Durlandville, Eagle Valley, Edenville, Finchville, Finnegan's Corner, Firthcliff, Florida, Fort Montgomery, Gardnerville, Goddefroy, Goshen, Greenwood Lake, Guymard, Harriman, Highland Falls, Highland Mills, Huguenot, Johnson, Kiryas Joel, Little Britain, Little York, Maybrook, Middletown, Monroe, Montgomery, Mountainville, New Hampton, New Milford, New Vernon, New Windsor, Newburgh, Otisville, Oxford Depot, Phillipsburg, Pine Island, Port Jervis, Ridgebury, Rock Tavern, Salisbury Mills, Slate Hill, Sloatsburg, Southfields, Sparrowbush, Sterling Forest, Stony Ford, Suffern, Sugarloaf, Tuxedo, Tuxedo Park, Unionville, Vails Gate, Wallkill, Warwick, Washingtonville, West Point, Westbrookville, Westtown, Wickham Village. PUTNAM COUNTY. CITIES AND TOWNSHIPS: Baldwin Place, Brewster, Carmel, Cold Spring, Garrison, Kent, Lake Peekskill, Mahopac, Mahopac Falls, Patterson, Putnam Valley. ROCKLAND COUNTY. CITIES AND TOWNSHIPS: Garnerville, Haverstraw, Pomona, Stony Point, Thiells, Tomkins Cove. WESTCHESTER COUNTY. CITIES AND TOWNSHIPS: Amawalk, Baldwin Place, Bedford, Bedford Hills, Buchanan, Cortlandt Manor, Crompound, Cross River, Croton Falls, Croton-on-Hudson, Golden's Bridge, Jefferson Valley, Katonah, Lincolndale, Mohegan Lake, Montrose, Mt. Kisco, North Salem, Peekskill, Pound Ridge, Purdys, Shenorock, Shrub Oak, Somers, South Salem, Verplanck, Waccabuc, and Yorktown Heights. Population (2000), 654,361.

ZIP Codes: 10501, 10504–07, 10509, 10511–12, 10516–21, 10524, 10526–27, 10530, 10535–37, 10540–42, 10545, 10547–49, 10551, 10558, 10560, 10562, 10566–67, 10571–72, 10576, 10578–79, 10587–90, 10596–98, 10602, 10911, 10916–18, 10921–26, 10928, 10930, 10940–41, 10943, 10950, 10953, 10958, 10963, 10969–70, 10973, 10975, 10979–80, 10984, 10986–87, 10990, 10992, 10996–98, 11518, 11542, 11568, 11572, 11701–02, 11704, 11706–09, 11721, 11724, 11730–31, 11740, 11757, 11768, 11797, 12508, 12510–12, 12518, 12520, 12522, 12524, 12527, 12531, 12533, 12537–38, 12540, 12543, 12549, 12552–53, 12555, 12563–64, 12570, 12575, 12577–78, 12582, 12584, 12590, 12592, 12594, 12601–04, 12729, 12746, 12771, 12780, 12785

* * *

TWENTIETH DISTRICT

KIRSTEN E. GILLIBRAND, Democrat, of Hudson, NY; born in Albany, NY, December 9, 1966; education: attended Academy of Holy Names grade school; graduated, Emma Willard High School, 1984; bachelor's degree, Dartmouth College, 1988; law degree, UCLA School of Law, 1991; professional: worked for law firm of Davis Polk; served as Special Counsel to the U.S. Secretary of Housing and Urban Development, Andrew Cuomo; was a partner at the law firm of Boies Schiller & Flexner; married to Jonathan; one child, Theo; committees: Agriculture; Armed Services; elected to the 110th Congress on November 7, 2006.

Office Listings

http://www.gillibrand.house.gov

120 Cannon House Office Building, Washington, DC 20515 .... (202) 225–5614
Chief of Staff.—Jess Fassler. FAX: 225–1168
Deputy Chief of Staff.—Anne Bradley.
Legislative Director.—Brooke Jamison.
Press Secretary.—Rachel McEneny.
446 Warren Street, Hudson, NY 12534 .... (518) 828–3109
333 Glen Street, Suite 302, Glens Falls, NY 12886 .... (518) 743–0964
487 Broadway, Saratoga Springs, NY 12866 .... (518) 581–8247
District Director.—Mike Russo.

Counties: COLUMBIA, DELAWARE (part), DUTCHESS (part), ESSEX (part), GREENE, RENSSELAER (part), SARATOGA (part), OTSEGO (part), WARREN, and WASHINGTON. Population (2000), 654,360.

ZIP Codes: 12010, 12015, 12017–20, 12022, 12024–25, 12027–29, 12033, 12037, 12040, 12042, 12046, 12050–52, 12057–60, 12062, 12065, 12074–76, 12083, 12086–87, 12089–90, 12093–94, 12106, 12115, 12118, 12123–25, 12130, 12132–34, 12136, 12138, 12140, 12143, 12148, 12151, 12153–56, 12165, 12167–70, 12172–74, 12176, 12180, 12182, 12184–85, 12192, 12195–96, 12198, 12405–07, 12413–14, 12418, 12421–24, 12427, 12430–31, 12434, 12438–39, 12442, 12444, 12450–51, 12454–55, 12459–60, 12463, 12468–70, 12473–74, 12480, 12482, 12485, 12492, 12496, 12501–03, 12507, 12513–14, 12516–17, 12521–23, 12526, 12529, 12533–34, 12538, 12540, 12545–46, 12565, 12567, 12569–72, 12578, 12580–81, 12583, 12585, 12590, 12592, 12594, 12601, 12603, 12776, 12801, 12803–04, 12808–11, 12814–17, 12819–24, 12827–28, 12831–39, 12841, 12843–46, 12848–50, 12853–56, 12859–63, 12865–66, 12870–74, 12878, 12883–87, 12942–43, 12946, 12977, 12983, 13326, 13450, 13488, 13731, 13739–40, 13750, 13752–53, 13755, 13757, 13775, 13782, 13786, 13788, 13804, 13806–07, 13820, 13838, 13842, 13846, 13849, 13856, 13860

* * *

TWENTY-FIRST DISTRICT

MICHAEL R. MCNULTY, Democrat, of Green Island, NY; born in Troy, Rensselaer County, NY, September 16, 1947; education: graduated St. Joseph's Institute, Barrytown, NY, 1965; attended Loyola University, Rome Center, Rome, Italy, 1967–68; B.A., Holy Cross College, Worcester, MA, 1969; attended Hill School of Insurance, New York City, 1970; professional: insurance broker; town supervisor, Green Island, NY, 1969–77; Mayor, village of Green Island, 1977–83; New York State Assembly, 1983–88; member: Albany County Democratic Executive Committee; Green Island Democratic Committee; New York State Democratic Committee; board of directors, Capital Region Technology Development Council; delegate, Democratic National Convention, 1972; married: the former Nancy Ann Lazzaro, 1971; children: Michele, Angela, Nancy, and Maria; committees: Ways and Means; elected on November 8, 1988, to the 101st Congress; reelected to each succeeding Congress.

Office Listings

http://www.house.gov/mcnulty

2210 Rayburn House Office Building, Washington, DC 20515 .... (202) 225–5076
Chief of Staff.—David Torian. FAX: 225–5077
Press Secretary.—Lisa Blumenstock.
Legislative Director.—Jim Glenn.
Leo W. O'Brien Federal Building, Albany, NY 12207 .... (518) 465–0700
U.S. Office, Schenectady, NY 12305 .... (518) 374–4547
33 Second Street, Troy, NY 12180 .... (518) 271–0822
2490 Riverfront Center, Amsterdam, NY 12010 .... (518) 843–3400
233 West Main Street, Room 10, Johnstown, NY 12095 .... (518) 762–3568

Counties: ALBANY, FULTON (part), MONTGOMERY, RENSSELAER (part), SARATOGA (part), SCHOHARIE, and SCHENECTADY. Population (2000), 654,361.

ZIP Codes: 12007–10, 12016, 12019, 12027, 12031, 12033, 12035–36, 12041, 12043, 12045–47, 12053–54, 12056, 12061, 12063–64, 12066–73, 12077–78, 12082–87, 12092–93, 12095, 12107, 12110, 12116, 12120–23, 12128, 12131, 12137,

12141, 12143–44, 12147, 12149–50, 12157–61, 12166–67, 12175, 12177, 12179–83, 12186–89, 12193–94, 12197–98, 12201–12, 12214, 12220, 12222–40, 12242–50, 12252, 12255–57, 12260–61, 12288, 12301–09, 12325, 12345, 12434, 12469, 13317, 13320, 13339, 13410, 13428, 13452, 13459

* * *

TWENTY-SECOND DISTRICT

MAURICE D. HINCHEY, Democrat, of Hurley, NY; born in New York, NY, October 27, 1938; education: graduated, Saugerties High School, 1956; B.S., State College, New Paltz, NY, 1968; M.A., State College, New Paltz, 1969; professional: Seaman First Class, U.S. Navy, 1956–59; teacher; public administrator; elected to the New York State Assembly, 1975–92; member: New York Council of State Governments; National Conference of State Legislatures; married: Allison Lee Hinchey, 2006; three children: Maurice Scott, Josef, and Michelle Rebecca; committees: Appropriations; Natural Resources; elected on November 3, 1992 to the 103rd Congress; reelected to each succeeding Congress.

Office Listings

http://www.house.gov/hinchey

2431 Rayburn House Office Building, Washington, DC 20515 .... (202) 225–6335
Chief of Staff.—Wendy Darwell. FAX: 226–0774
Legislative Director.—Moria Campion.
Communications Director.—Jeff Lieberson.
291 Wall Street, Kingston, NY 12401 .... (845) 331–4466
100A Federal Building, Binghamton, NY 13901 .... (607) 773–2768
123 S. Cayuga Street, Suite 201, Ithaca, NY 14850 .... (607) 273–1388
16 James Street, Middletown, NY 10940 .... (845) 344–3211

Counties: BROOME COUNTY (part); CITIES AND TOWNS OF: Binghamton, Conklin, Kirkwood, Sanford, Union (includes villages of Endicott and Johnson City), Vestal, and Windsor. DELAWARE COUNTY (part); TOWNS OF: Deposit, Hancock, and Tompkins. DUTCHESS COUNTY (part). CITIES: Poughkeepsie. ORANGE COUNTY (part); CITIES AND TOWNS OF: Crawford, Middletown, Montgomery (includes village of Walden), Newburgh, and Wallkill. SULLIVAN COUNTY; CITIES AND TOWNS OF: Bethel, Callicoon, Cochecton, Delaware, Fallsburg, Forestburgh, Fremont, Highland, Liberty, Lumberland, Mamakating, Neversink, Rockland, Thompson, and Tusten. TIOGA COUNTY (part). CITIES AND TOWNS: Barton, Nichols, Owego, and Spencer. TOMPKINS COUNTY (part). CITIES AND TOWNS: Danby, and Ithaca. ULSTER COUNTY. CITIES AND TOWNS: Denning, Esopus, Gardiner, Hardenburgh, Hurley, Kingston, Lloyd, Marbletown, Marlborough, New Paltz, Olive, Plattekill, Rochester, Rosendale, Saugerties, Shandaken, Shawangunk, Ulster, Wawarsing (includes village of Ellenville), and Woodstock. Population (2000), 654,361.

ZIP Codes: 10915, 10919, 10932, 10940–41, 10985, 12401–02, 12404, 12406, 12409–12, 12416, 12419–20, 12428–29, 12432–33, 12435–36, 12440–41, 12443, 12446, 12448–49, 12451–53, 12455–58, 12461, 12464–66, 12469, 12471–72, 12475, 12477, 12480–81, 12483–84, 12486–87, 12489–91, 12493–95, 12498, 12504, 12506, 12515, 12525, 12528, 12530, 12541–44, 12547–51, 12561, 12566, 12568, 12574–75, 12583, 12586, 12588–89, 12601, 12603, 12701, 12719–27, 12729, 12732–34, 12736–38, 12740–43, 12745, 12747–52, 12754, 12758–60, 12762–70, 12775–84, 12786–92, 12814, 12853, 12857–58, 12879, 12883, 12928, 12983, 13068, 13501, 13730, 13732, 13734, 13737, 13743, 13748–49, 13754, 13756, 13760, 13774, 13783, 13790, 13795, 13811–13, 13820, 13826, 13850, 13856, 13864–65, 13901–05, 14817, 14850–51, 14853, 14859, 14867, 14883, 14889, 14892

* * *

TWENTY-THIRD DISTRICT

JOHN M. MCHUGH, Republican, of Pierrepoint Manor, NY; born in Watertown, NY, September 29, 1948; education: graduated from Watertown High School, 1966; B.A., Utica College of Syracuse University; M.A., Nelson A. Rockefeller Graduate School of Public Affairs; professional: assistant to the city manager, Watertown; liaison with local governments for New York State Senator H. Douglas Barclay; New York State Senate, 1984–92; co-chair, Army Caucus; committees: Armed Services; Oversight and Government Reform; Permanent Select Committee on Intelligence; elected on November 3, 1992, to the 103rd Congress; reelected to each succeeding Congress.

Office Listings

http://www.house.gov/mchugh

2366 Rayburn House Office Building, Washington, DC 20515 .... (202) 225–4611
Chief of Staff.—Robert Taub. FAX: 226–0621
Administrative Secretary.—Donna M. Bell.
205 South Peterboro Street, Canastota, NY 13032 .... (315) 697–2063
28 North School Street, P.O. Box 800, Mayfield, NY 12117 .... (518) 661–6486
104 Federal Building, Plattsburgh, NY 12901 .... (518) 563–1406
120 Washington Street, Suite 200, Watertown, NY 13601 .... (315) 782–3150

Counties: CLINTON, ESSEX (part), FRANKLIN, FULTON (part), HAMILTON, JEFFERSON, LEWIS, MADISON, ONEIDA (part), OSWEGO, ST. LAWRENCE. Population (2000), 654,361.

ZIP Codes: 12010, 12023, 12025, 12032, 12036, 12070, 12078, 12086, 12095, 12108, 12117, 12134, 12139, 12164, 12167, 12190, 12812, 12842, 12847, 12851–52, 12857, 12864, 12883, 12901, 12903, 12910–24, 12926–30, 12932–37, 12939, 12941, 12944–46, 12949–50, 12952–53, 12955–62, 12964–67, 12969–70, 12972–76, 12978–81, 12983, 12985–87, 12989, 12992–93, 12996–98, 13028, 13030, 13032–33, 13035–37, 13042–44, 13052, 13061, 13064, 13069, 13072, 13074, 13076, 13082–83, 13093, 13103–04, 13107, 13111, 13114–15, 13121–23, 13126, 13131–32, 13134–36, 13142, 13144–45, 13156, 13158, 13163, 13167, 13301–04, 13308–10, 13313–16, 13318–19, 13321–23, 13325–29, 13332–35, 13337–43, 13345–46, 13348, 13350, 13352, 13354–55, 13357, 13360–65, 13367–68, 13401–03, 13406–11, 13413, 13415, 13417–18, 13421, 13424–25, 13428, 13431, 13433, 13435–41, 13449–50, 13452, 13455–57, 13460–61, 13465, 13468–69, 13471, 13473, 13475, 13477–80, 13482–86, 13488–95, 13501–05, 13599, 13601–03, 13605–08, 13611–28, 13630–43, 13645–52, 13654–62, 13664–85, 13687–88, 13690–97, 13699

* * *

TWENTY-FOURTH DISTRICT

MICHAEL A. ARCURI, Democrat, of Utica, NY; born in Utica, June 11, 1959; education: graduated, Proctor High School; B.A., SUNY Albany, 1981; J.D., New York Law School, 1984; professional: private practice attorney, 1988–94; counsel, New Hartford Central School District Board of Education; elected Oneida County District Attorney, 1993; President, New York District Attorney's Association, 2003; two children; committees: Rules; Transportation and Infrastructure; elected to the 110th Congress on November 7, 2006.

Office Listings

http://arcuri.house.gov/

327 Cannon House Office Building, Washington, DC 20515 .... (202) 225–3665
Chief of Staff.—Hayley Rumback. FAX: 225–1891
Executive Assistant.—Mark Cornell.
Alexander Pirnie Federal Office Building, 10 Broad Street, Room 200, Utica, NY 13501 .... (313) 793–8146
District Director.—Joe Johnson.

Counties: BROOME (part), CAYUGA (part), CHENANGO, CORTLAND, HERKIMER (part), ONEIDA (part), ONTARIO (part), OTSEGO (part), SENECA, TIOGA (part), TOMPKINS (part). Population (2000), 654,361.

ZIP Codes: 13021–22, 13024, 13026, 13032–34, 13040, 13042, 13045, 13052–54, 13056, 13062, 13065, 13068, 13071–74, 13077, 13080–81, 13083, 13087, 13092, 13101–02, 13117–18, 13124, 13136, 13139–41, 13147–48, 13152, 13155, 13157–60, 13162, 13165–66, 13302–05, 13308–09, 13312, 13315, 13317–20, 13322–29, 13331–33, 13335, 13337–40, 13342–43, 13345, 13348, 13350, 13353–54, 13357, 13360–61, 13363, 13365, 13367–68, 13403–04, 13406–07, 13411, 13413, 13415–17, 13420–21, 13424–26, 13431, 13433, 13436–42, 13452, 13454, 13456, 13460–61, 13464, 13468–73, 13475–78, 13480, 13485–86, 13489–93, 13495, 13501–02, 13601, 13603, 13605–08, 13611–26, 13628, 13630, 13632–43, 13645–52, 13654–56, 13658–62, 13664–69, 13672–85, 13687, 13690–97, 13699, 13730, 13733–34, 13736, 13738, 13743–47, 13752–54, 13758, 13760, 13776–78, 13780, 13784, 13787, 13790, 13794, 13796–97, 13801–03, 13807–11, 13813–15, 13820, 13825–27, 13830, 13832–33, 13835, 13838, 13840–41, 13843–45, 13848–49, 13856, 13859, 13861–64, 14433, 14443, 14456, 14468–69, 14489, 14504, 14521, 14532, 14541, 14548, 14571, 14588, 14817, 14841, 14847, 14850–52, 14854, 14860, 14867, 14881–83, 14886

* * *

TWENTY-FIFTH DISTRICT

JAMES T. WALSH, Republican, of Syracuse, NY; born in Syracuse, June 19, 1947; son of former U.S. Representative William F. Walsh; education: B.A., St. Bonaventure University, Olean, NY, 1970; professional: marketing executive; president, Syracuse Common Council; member: Syracuse Board of Estimates; board of trustees of Erie Canal Museum; advisory council of the Catholic Schools Drug-Free Schools and Communities Consortium; Valley Men's Club; South Side Businessmen's Club; Nine Mile Republican Club; Onondaga Anglers Association; Oneida Lake Association; Otisco Lake Association; married: the former Diane Elizabeth Ryan, 1974; children: James (Jed), Benjamin, and Maureen; committees: Appropriations; elected on November 8, 1988, to the 101st Congress; reelected to each succeeding Congress.

Office Listings

http://www.house.gov/walsh

2372 Rayburn House Office Building, Washington, DC 20515 .... (202) 225–3701
Chief of Staff.—Dan Gage. FAX: 225–4042
Executive Assistant.—Blaire Bartlett.
Appropriations Associate.—Ron Anderson.
P.O. Box 7306, Syracuse, NY 13261 .... (315) 423–5657
District Representative.—Virginia Carmody.
1180 Canandaigua Road, Palmyra, NY 14522 .... (315) 597–6138

Counties: CAYUGA (part), MONROE (part), ONONDAGA, and WAYNE. CITIES AND TOWNSHIPS: Arcadia, Butler, Camillus, Cato, Cicero, Clay, Conquest, DeWitt, Elbridge, Fabius, Galen, Geddes, Huron, Ira, Irondequoit, LaFayette, Lyons,

Lysander, Macedon, Manlius, Marcellus, Marion, Onondaga, Ontario, Otisco, Palmyra, Penfield, Pompey, Rose, Salina, Savannah, Skaneateles, Sodus, Spafford, Sterling, Syracuse, Tully, Van Buren, Victory, Walworth, Webster, Williamson, and Wolcott. Population (2000), 654,361.

ZIP Codes: 13020–21, 13027, 13029–31, 13033, 13035, 13037, 13039–41, 13051–53, 13057, 13060, 13063–64, 13066, 13068–69, 13077–78, 13080, 13082, 13084, 13088, 13090, 13104, 13108, 13110–13, 13116–17, 13119–20, 13122, 13126, 13135, 13137–38, 13140–41, 13143, 13146, 13148, 13152–54, 13156, 13159, 13164–66, 13201–12, 13214–15, 13217–21, 13224–25, 13235, 13244, 13250–52, 13261, 13290, 14413, 14432–33, 14449–50, 14489, 14502, 14505, 14513, 14516, 14519–20, 14522, 14526, 14537–38, 14542, 14551, 14555, 14563–64, 14568, 14580, 14589–90, 14609, 14617, 14621–22, 14625

* * *

TWENTY-SIXTH DISTRICT

THOMAS M. REYNOLDS, Republican, of Springville, NY; born in Springville, September 3, 1950; education: attended Kent State University; professional: Erie County legislator, 1982–88; New York State Assembly, 1988–98; former director, Better Business Bureau; Cooperative Extension and Central Referral Service; married: Donna; children: four; committees: Ways and Means; chair, National Republican Congressional Committee; Deputy Republican Whip; elected to the 106th Congress; reelected to each succeeding Congress.

Office Listings

http://www.house.gov/reynolds

332 Cannon House Office Building, Washington, DC 20515 .... (202) 225–5265
Chief of Staff.—Sally Vastola. FAX: 225–5910
Executive Assistant.—Katie Roth.
Legislative Director.—Tina Mufford.
500 Essjay Road, Suite 260, Williamsville, NY 14221 .... (716) 634–2324
1577 Ridge Road West, Rochester, NY 14615 .... (585) 663–5570

Counties: ERIE (part), GENESEE, LIVINGSTON, MONROE (part), NIAGARA (part), ORLEANS (part), WYOMING. Population (2000), 654,361.

ZIP Codes: 14001, 14004–05, 14008–09, 14011–13, 14020–21, 14024, 14026, 14030–32, 14036, 14038–39, 14043, 14051, 14054, 14056, 14058–59, 14066–68, 14082–83, 14086, 14094–95, 14098, 14103, 14105, 14113, 14120, 14125, 14130–32, 14139, 14143, 14145, 14167, 14215, 14221, 14224–26, 14228, 14231, 14260, 14304, 14410–11, 14414, 14416, 14420, 14422–23, 14427–30, 14435, 14437, 14452, 14454, 14462, 14464, 14466, 14468, 14470–72, 14476–77, 14479–82, 14485–88, 14510–12, 14514–15, 14517, 14525, 14530, 14533, 14536, 14539, 14545–46, 14549–50, 14556–60, 14569, 14571–72, 14591–92, 14606, 14612, 14615–16, 14624, 14626, 14822, 14836, 14846

* * *

TWENTY-SEVENTH DISTRICT

BRIAN HIGGINS, Democrat, of Buffalo, NY; born in Buffalo, October 6, 1959; education: B.A., Buffalo State College, NY, 1984; M.A., Buffalo State College, 1985; M.P.A., Harvard University, Cambridge, MA, 1996; professional: lecturer, Buffalo State College; member of the Buffalo Common Council, 1988–94; member of the New York state assembly, 1999–2004; married: Mary Jane Hannon; two children: John and Maeve; committees: Oversight and Government Reform; Transportation and Infrastructure; elected to the 109th Congress on November 2, 2004; reelected to the 110th Congress.

Office Listings

http://www.house.gov/higgins

431 Cannon House Office Building, Washington, DC 20515 .... (202) 225–3306
Chief of Staff.—Charles Eaton. FAX: 226–0347
Administrative Assistant / Communications Director.—Suzanne Anziska.
Legislative Director.—Brooke Sharkey.
Larkin Building, 726 Exchange Street, Suite 601, Buffalo, NY 14210 .... (716) 852–3501
Fenton Building, 2 East 2nd Street, Suite 300, Jamestown, NY 14701 .... (716) 484–0729

Counties: CHAUTAUQUA, ERIE (part). CITIES AND TOWNSHIPS: Boston, Brant, Buffalo, Cheektowaga, Colden, Concord, Collins, East Aurora, Eden, Elma, Evans, Hamburg, Holland, Lackawanna, North Boston, North Collins, Orchard Park, Sardinia, and Seneca. Population (2000), 654,361.

ZIP Codes: 14004, 14006, 14010, 14025–27, 14030, 14033–35, 14037, 14040, 14043, 14047–48, 14052, 14055, 14057, 14059, 14061–63, 14069–70, 14075, 14080–81, 14085–86, 14091, 14102, 14110–12, 14127, 14134–36, 14138–41, 14145, 14166, 14169–70, 14201–03, 14206–16, 14218–22, 14224–27, 14233, 14240–41, 14264–65, 14267, 14269, 14272, 14276, 14280, 14504, 14701–04, 14710, 14712, 14716, 14718, 14720, 14722–24, 14726, 14728, 14732–33, 14736, 14738, 14740, 14742, 14747, 14750, 14752, 14756–58, 14767, 14769, 14775, 14781–82, 14784–85, 14787

* * *

TWENTY-EIGHTH DISTRICT

LOUISE McINTOSH SLAUGHTER, Democrat, of Fairport, NY; born in Harlan County, KY, August 14, 1929; education: B.S. in microbiology (1951) and M.S. in public health (1953), University of Kentucky; elected to Monroe County legislature, two terms, 1976–79; elected to New York State Assembly, two terms, 1982–86; Distinguished Public Health Legislation Award, American Public Health Association, 1998; married: Robert Slaughter; three daughters; four grandchildren; committees: chair, Rules; elected to the 100th Congress on November 4, 1986; reelected to each succeeding Congress.

Office Listings

http://www.house.gov/slaughter

2469 Rayburn House Office Building, Washington, DC 20515 .... (202) 225–3615
Chief of Staff.—Crystal King. FAX: 225–7822
Legislative Director.—Michelle Adams.
Communications Director.—Frank Benenati.
3120 Federal Building, 100 State Street, Rochester, NY 14614 .... (716) 232–4850
465 Main Street, Suite 105, Buffalo, NY 14203 .... (716) 853–5813
1910 Pine Avenue, Niagara Falls, NY 14301 .... (716) 282–1274

Counties: Erie (part), Monroe (part), Niagara (part), Orleans (part). CITIES AND TOWNSHIPS: Appleton, Barker, Brighton, Buffalo, Burt, East Rochester, Fairport, Grand Island, Greece, Hamlin, Hilton, Irondequoit, Kendall, Kent, Lewiston, Lyndonville, Model City, Morton, Newfane, Niagara Falls, Olcott, Penfield, Perinton, Ransomville, Rochester, Sanborn, Stella Niagara, Tonawanda, Waterport, Wilson and Youngstown. Population (2000), 654,361.

ZIP Codes: 14008, 14012, 14028, 14067, 14072, 14092, 14094, 14098, 14107–09, 14126, 14131–32, 14144, 14150–51, 14172, 14174, 14202–03, 14205–12, 14214–15, 14217, 14222–23, 14225–26, 14263, 14270, 14273, 14301–05, 14411, 14420, 14445, 14450, 14464, 14468, 14470, 14476–77, 14508, 14526, 14534, 14571, 14602–25, 14627, 14638–39, 14642–47, 14649–53, 14660, 14664, 14673

* * *

TWENTY-NINTH DISTRICT

JOHN R. ''RANDY'' KUHL, JR., Republican, of Hammondsport, NY; born in Bath, NY, April 19, 1943; education: graduated, Hammondsport Central School; B.S., Civil Engineering, Union College; J.D., Syracuse University College of Law; professional: lawyer; member, New York Assembly, 1981–87; member, New York Senate, 1987–2004; former State Chairman of the American Legislative Exchange Council (ALEC); former vice chairman, National Conference of State Legislatures' (NCSL) Wine Industry Task Force; Hammondsport Rotary Club; BPOE 1547; Advisory Committee of the Steuben Area Council of the Boy Souts of America; Branchport Rod and Gun Club; Executive Committee of the Steuben County Republican Committee; President of the Board of Directors of the Reginald Wood Scouting Memorial; member, Board of Directors, Alliance for Manufacturing and Technology; communicant, St. James Episcopal; family: three children; committees: Agriculture; Education and Labor; Transportation and Infrastructure; elected to the 109th Congress on November 2, 2004; reelected to the 110th Congress.

Office Listings

http://www.house.gov/kuhl

1505 Longworth House Office Building, Washington, DC 20515 .... (202) 225–3161
Chief of Staff.—Brian Fitzpatrick. FAX: 226–6599
Deputy Chief of Staff / Press Secretary / Legislative Director.—
Bob Van Wicklin.
Scheduling Coordinator.—Meredith Bicher.
Legislative Assistants: Lauryn Bernier, John Bressler, Karen Livingston.
P.O. Box 153, Bath, NY 14810 .... (607) 937–3333

Counties: ALLEGANY, CATTARAUGUS, CHEMUNG, MONROE (part), ONTARIO (part), SCHUYLER, STEUBEN, YATES. Population (2000), 654,361.

ZIP Codes: 14009, 14024, 14029–30, 14041–42, 14060, 14065, 14070, 14081, 14101, 14129, 14133, 14138, 14141, 14168, 14171, 14173, 14414–15, 14418, 14423–25, 14428, 14432, 14437, 14441, 14445, 14450, 14453, 14456, 14461, 14463, 14466–67, 14469, 14471–72, 14475, 14478, 14482, 14485, 14487, 14489, 14502, 14504, 14506–07, 14512–14, 14518, 14522, 14526–27, 14529, 14532, 14534, 14536, 14543–44, 14546–48, 14559–61, 14564, 14572, 14585–86, 14606, 14610, 14618, 14620, 14623–25, 14706–09, 14711, 14714–15, 14717, 14719, 14721, 14726–27, 14729–31, 14735, 14737–39, 14741, 14743–45, 14747–48, 14751, 14753–55, 14760, 14766, 14770, 14772, 14774, 14777–79, 14783, 14786, 14788, 14801–10, 14812–16, 14818–27, 14830–31, 14836–46, 14855–59, 14861, 14863–65, 14867, 14869–74, 14876–80, 14884–87, 14889, 14891–95, 14897–98, 14901–05, 14925

NORTH CAROLINA

(Population 2000, 8,049,313)

SENATORS

ELIZABETH DOLE, Republican, of Salisbury, NC; born in Salisbury, NC, July 29, 1936; education: B.A., Duke University, 1958; M.A., Harvard University, 1960; J.D., Harvard University, 1965; Phi Beta Kappa; public service: Deputy Assistant to President Nixon for Consumer Affairs, 1971–73; member, Federal Trade Commission, 1973–79; Assistant to President Reagan for Public Liaison, 1981–83; Secretary of Transportation, 1983–87, under President Reagan; Secretary of Labor, 1989–91, under President George H.W. Bush; President, American Red Cross, 1991–99; awards: National Safety Council's Distinguished Service Award; National Commission Against Drunk Driving Humanitarian Award; Women Executives in State Government Lifetime Achievement Award; North Carolina Award; National Religious Broadcasters' Board of Directors Award; League of Women Voters Leadership Award; organizations: Duke University Board of Trustees, 1974–85; Harvard University Board of Overseers, 1990–96; married to former Senator Bob Dole (R–KS); committees: Armed Services; Banking, Housing, and Urban Affairs; Small Business and Entrepreneurship; Special Committee on Aging; elected to the U.S. Senate on November 5, 2002.

Office Listings

http://dole.senate.gov

555 Dirksen Senate Office Building, Washington, DC 20510 .... (202) 224–6342
Chief of Staff.—Greg Gross. FAX: 224–1100
Legislative Counsel / Policy Director.—Scott Quesenberry.
Scheduler.—Camille Griffin.
Press Secretary.—Katie Norman.
310 New Bern Avenue, Suite 122, Raleigh NC 27601 .... (919) 856–4630
225 North Main Street, Suite 404, Salisbury, NC 28144 .... (704) 633–5011
State Director.—Margaret Klutta.
401 N. Main Street, Suite 200, Hendersonville, NC 28792, ... (828) 698–3747
306 South Evans Street, Greenville, NC 27835 .... (252) 329–1093

* * *

RICHARD BURR, Republican, of Winston-Salem, NC; born in Charlottesville, VA, November 30, 1955; education: R.J. Reynolds High School, Winston-Salem, NC, 1974; B.A., Communications, Wake Forest University, Winston-Salem, NC, 1978; professional: sales manager, Carswell Distributing; member: Reynolds Rotary Club; board member, Brenner Children's Hospital; public service: U.S. House of Representatives, 1995–2005; served as vice-chairman of the Energy and Commerce Committee; married: Brooke Fauth, 1984; children: two sons; committees: Energy and Natural Resources; Health, Education, Labor, and Pensions; Indian Affairs; Veterans' Affairs; Select Committee on Intelligence; elected to the U.S. Senate on November 2, 2004.

Office Listings

http://burr.senate.gov

217 Russell Senate Office Building, Washington, DC 20510 .... (202) 224–3154
Chief of Staff.—Alicia Peterson Clark. FAX: 228–2981
Legislative Director.—Natasha Hickman.
2000 West First Street, Suite 508, Winston-Salem, NC 27104 .... (336) 631–5125
State Director.—Dean Myers.

REPRESENTATIVES

FIRST DISTRICT

G.K. BUTTERFIELD, Democrat, of Wilson County, NC; born, April 27, 1947; education: North Carolina Central University, graduated in 1971, with degrees in Sociology and Political Science; North Carolina Central University School of Law, graduated in 1974, with a Juris Doctor degree; military service: U.S. Army, 1968–1970; served as a Personnel Specialist; discharged with the rank of Specialist E–4; professional: attorney; private practice, 1974–1988; public service: elected to the North Carolina Superior Court bench in November, 1988; appointed on February 8, 2001, by Governor Michael F. Easley to the North Carolina Supreme Court; after leaving the Supreme Court, following the 2002 election, Governor Easley appointed Justice

Butterfield as a Special Superior Court Judge; served until his retirement on May 7, 2004; organizations: North Carolina Bar Association; North Carolina Association of Black Lawyers; Wilson Opportunities Industrialization Center; religion: Baptist; appointed Chief Deputy Whip, 110th Congress; committees: Energy and Commerce; elected to the 108th Congress, by special election, on July 20, 2004; elected to the 109th Congress on November 2, 2004; reelected to the 110th Congress.

Office Listings

413 Cannon House Office Building, Washington, DC 20515 .... (202) 225–3101
Chief of Staff.—Corliss Clemonts-James. FAX: 225–3354
Communications Director.—Ken Willis.
Senior Legislative Assistant.—Robert Harris.
Executive Assistant.—Darnise Nelson.
415 East Boulevard, Suite 100, Williamston, NC 27892 .... (252) 789–4939

Counties: BEAUFORT (part), BERTIE, CHOWAN, CRAVEN (part), EDGECOMBE, GATES, GRANVILLE VANCE (part), GREENE, HALIFAX, HARTFORD, JONES (part), MARTIN, NORTHAMPTON, PASQUOTANK, PERQUIMANS, PITT (part), WARREN, WASHINGTON, WAYNE (part), WILSON (part). Population (2000), 619,178.

ZIP Codes: 27507, 27530–31, 27533–34, 27536–37, 27551, 27553, 27556, 27563, 27565, 27570, 27584, 27586, 27589, 27594, 27801, 27803–06, 27809, 27811–14, 27817–23, 27825, 27827–29, 27831–35, 27837, 27839–47, 27849–50, 27852–55, 27857–58, 27860–64, 27866–67, 27869–74, 27876–77, 27879, 27881, 27883–84, 27886–95, 27897, 27906–07, 27909–10, 27919, 27922, 27924, 27926, 27928, 27930, 27932, 27935, 27937–38, 27942, 27944, 27946, 27957, 27962, 27967, 27969–70, 27979–80, 27983, 27985–86, 28216, 28226, 28502–04, 28513, 28523, 28526, 28530, 28538, 28551, 28554–55, 28560–63, 28573, 28580, 28585–86, 28590, 28645

* * *

SECOND DISTRICT

BOB ETHERIDGE, Democrat, of Lillington, NC; born in Sampson County, NC, August 7, 1941; B.S., business administration, Campbell University, NC, 1965; graduate studies in economics, North Carolina State University, 1967; U.S. Army, 1965–67; businessman, bank director, licensed realtor; North Carolina General Assembly, 1978–88; North Carolina Superintendent of Public Instruction, 1988–96; Harnett County commissioner, 1972–76, serving as chairman of the board in 1974–76; past member: National Council of Chief State School Officers; Governor's Executive Cabinet; advisory board, Mathematics / Science Education Network; Board of the North Carolina Council on Economic Education; board of trustees, North Carolina Symphony; board of trustees, University of North Carolina Center for Public Television; Harnett County Mental Health Board; North Carolina Law and Order Commission; member and past president, Occoneechee Boy Scout Council; received Lillington Jaycees Distinguished Service Award and Lillington Community Service Award; elder, Presbyterian Church; married the former Faye Cameron in 1965; three children: Brian, Catherine, and David; committees: Agriculture; elected to the 105th Congress; reelected to each succeeding Congress.

Office Listings

http://www.house.gov/etheridge

1533 Longworth House Office Building, Washington, DC 20515 .... (202) 225–4531
Chief of Staff.—Julie Dwyer. FAX: 225–5662
Legislative Director.—Pat Devlin.
Press Secretary.—Joanne Peters.
Scheduler / Executive Assistant.—Latanza McCoy.
225 Hillsborough Street, Suite 490, Raleigh, NC 27603 .... (919) 829–9122
609 North First Street, Lillington, NC 27564 .... (910) 814–0335

Counties: CHATHAM, CUMBERLAND, FRANKLIN, HARNETT, JOHNSTON, LEE, NASH, SAMPSON (part), VANCE, and WAKE (part). Population (2000), 619,178.

ZIP Codes: 27207–08, 27213, 27237, 27252, 27256, 27298, 27312, 27325, 27330–32, 27344, 27349, 27355, 27405, 27501, 27504–06, 27508, 27520–21, 27524–26, 27529, 27536–37, 27540, 27542–44, 27546, 27549, 27552, 27555, 27557, 27559, 27562, 27564, 27568–70, 27576–77, 27589, 27591–93, 27596–97, 27601–03, 27605–07, 27610, 27614, 27625, 27698, 27801–04, 27807, 27809, 27816, 27822, 27829, 27850, 27856, 27863, 27878, 27880, 27882, 27891, 27893–94, 27896, 28301, 28303, 28307–08, 28310–11, 28314, 28323, 28326, 28328, 28334–35, 28339, 28341, 28355–56, 28365–66, 28368, 28382, 28385, 28390, 28393, 28441, 28444, 28447, 28453, 28458, 28466, 28478

* * *

THIRD DISTRICT

WALTER B. JONES, Republican, of Farmville, NC; born in Farmville, February 10, 1943; education: graduated Hargrave Military Academy, Chatham, VA, 1961; B.A., Atlantic Christian College, Wilson, NC, 1966; served in North Carolina National Guard; self-employed, sales; member: North Carolina House of Representatives, 1983–92; married: Joe Anne Whitehurst Jones; one child, Ashley Elizabeth Jones Scarborough; committees: Armed Services; Financial Services; elected to the 104th Congress; reelected to each succeeding Congress.

Office Listings

2333 Rayburn House Office Building, Washington, DC 20515 .... (202) 225–3415
FAX: 225–3286
Chief of Staff.—Glen Downs.
Office Manager.—Molly Norton.
Press Secretary.—Kathleen Joyce.
1105 C Corporate Drive, Greenville, NC 27858 .... (252) 931–1003
District Office Manager.—Millicent A. Lilley.

Counties: BEAUFORT (part), CAMDEN, CARTERET, CRAVEN (part), CURRITUCK, DARE, DUPLIN (part), HYDE, JONES (part), LENOIR (part), MARTIN (part), ONSLOW (part), PAMLICO, PENDER (part), PITT (part), SAMPSON, TYRRELL and WAYNE (part). CITIES: Atlantic Beach, Ayden, Beaufort, Belhaven, Burgaw, Clinton, Emerald Isle, Fremont, Goldsboro, Greenville, Havelock, Jacksonville, Kill Devil Hills, Kinston, Kitty Hawk, Morehead City, Mount Olive, Nags Head, New Bern, Newport, River Bend, Trent Woods, Wallace, Washington, and Winterville. Population (2000), 619,178.

ZIP Codes: 27530–32, 27534, 27542, 27557, 27569, 27803–04, 27807–10, 27814, 27817, 27822, 27824, 27826, 27828–30, 27834, 27836–37, 27851–52, 27856, 27858, 27860, 27863, 27865, 27868, 27871, 27875, 27879, 27880, 27882–83, 27885, 27888–89, 27892–93, 27896, 27909, 27915–17, 27920–21, 27923, 27925, 27927–29, 27936, 27939, 27941, 27943, 27947–50, 27953–54, 27956, 27958–60, 27962, 27964–66, 27968, 27972–74, 27976, 27978, 27981–82, 28333, 28341, 28445, 28454, 28460, 28501, 28504, 28508–13, 28515–16, 28518–22, 28524–29, 28531–33, 28537, 28539–47, 28551–53, 28555–57, 28560, 28562, 28564, 28570–72, 28574–75, 28577–87, 28589–90, 28594

* * *

FOURTH DISTRICT

DAVID E. PRICE, Democrat, of Chapel Hill, NC; born in Erwin, TN, August 17, 1940; education: B.A., Morehead Scholar, University of North Carolina; Bachelor of Divinity, 1964, and Ph.D., political science, 1969, Yale University; professional: professor of political science and public policy, Duke University; author of four books on Congress and the American political system; served North Carolina's Fourth District in the U.S. House of Representatives, 1987–94; in the 102nd Congress, wrote and pushed to passage the Scientific and Advanced Technology Bill and sponsored the Home Ownership Assistance Act; past chairman and executive director, North Carolina Democratic Party; Hubert Humphrey Public Service Award, American Political Science Association, 1990; member, North Carolina's Transit 2001 Commission; past chairman of the board and Sunday School teacher, Binkley Memorial Baptist Church; married: Lisa Price; children: Karen and Michael; committees: Appropriations; elected to the 100th–103rd Congresses; elected to the 105th Congress; reelected to each succeeding Congress.

Office Listings

http://www.house.gov/price

2162 Rayburn House Office Building, Washington, DC 20515 .... (202) 225–1784
FAX: 225–2014
Chief of Staff.—Jean-Louise Beard.
Legislative Director / Deputy Chief of Staff.—Darek Newby.
Executive Assistant.—Teresa Saunders.
Systems Manager.—Kate Roetzer.
5400 Trinity Place, Suite 205, Raleigh, NC 27607 .... (919) 859–5999
District Director.—Rose Auman.
88 Vilcom Circle, Suite 140, Chapel Hill, NC 27514 .... (919) 967–7924
411 W. Chapel Hill Street, Durham, NC 27701 .... (919) 688–3004

Counties: CHATHAM (part), DURHAM, ORANGE, WAKE (part). Population (2000), 619,178.

ZIP Codes: 27228, 27231, 27243, 27278, 27302, 27312, 27330, 27501–03, 27510–17, 27519, 27523, 27526, 27529, 27539–41, 27560, 27562, 27572, 27583, 27592, 27599, 27603, 27606–07, 27610, 27612–15, 27617, 27623–24, 27656, 27675–76, 27690, 27695, 27699, 27701–05, 27707–13, 27715, 27717, 27722

* * *

FIFTH DISTRICT

VIRGINIA FOXX, Republican, of Banner Elk, NC; born in New York, NY, June 29, 1943; education: B.A., University of North Carolina, Chapel Hill, NC, 1968; M.A.C.T., University of North Carolina, Chapel Hill, NC, 1972; Ed.D., University of North Carolina, Greensboro, NC, 1985; professional: professor, Caldwell Community College, Hudson, NC; professor, Appalachian State University, Boone, NC; Assistant Dean, Appalachian State University, Boone, NC; president, Mayland Community College, Spruce Pine, NC, 1987–94; nursery operator; deputy secretary for management, North Carolina Department of Administration; organizations: member, Watauga County board of education, 1967–88; member, North Carolina State Senate, 1994–2004; Executive Committee of North Carolina Citizens for Business and Industry; Z. Smith Reynolds Foundation Advisory Panel; National Advisory Council for Women's Educational Programs; Board of Directors of the NC Center for Public Research; UNC–Chapel Hill Board of Visitors; National Conference of State Legislatures' Blue Ribbon Advisory Panel on Child Care; Foscoe-Grandfather Community Center Board; family: married to Tom Foxx; one daughter; committees: Agriculture; Education and Labor; Oversight and Government Reform; elected to the 109th Congress on November 2, 2004; reelected to the 110th Congress.

Office Listings

http://www.house.gov/foxx

430 Cannon House Office Building, Washington, DC 20515 .... (202) 225–2071
Chief of Staff.—Todd Poole. FAX: 225–2995
Legislative Director.—Brandon Renz.
Press Secretary.—Aaron Groen.
6000 Meadowbrook Mall, Suite 3, Clemmons, NC 27012 .... (336) 778–0211
240 Highway 105 Extension, Suite 200, Boone, NC 28607 .... (828) 265–0240

Counties: ALEXANDER COUNTY. CITIES: Bethlehem, Hiddenite, Stony Point, Taylorsville. ALLEGANY COUNTY. CITIES: Ennice, Glade Valley, Laurel Springs, Sparta. ASHE COUNTY. CITIES: Crumpler, Glendale Springs, Grassy Creek, Jefferson, Lansing, Scottville, Todd, Warrensville, West Jefferson. DAVIE COUNTY. CITIES: Advance, Cooleemee, Mocksville. FORSYTH COUNTY (part). CITIES: Bethania, Clemmons, Kernersville, King, Lewisville, Pfafftown, Rural Hall, Tobaccoville, Walkertown, Winston-Salem. IREDELL COUNTY (part). CITIES: Harmony, Love Valley, Mooresville, Olin, Statesville, Turnersburg, Troutman. ROCKINGHAM COUNTY (part). CITIES: Madison, Stokesdale. STOKES COUNTY. CITIES: Danbury, Germanton, Lawsonville, King, Pine Hall, Pinnacle, Sandy Ridge, and Walnut Cove. SURRY COUNTY. CITIES: Ararat, Dobson, Elkin, Flat Rock, Mount Airy, Pilot Mountain, Siloam, Toast, Westfield, White Plains. WATAUGA COUNTY. CITIES: Beech Mountain, Blowing Rock, Boone, Deep Gap, Seven Devils, Sugar Grove, Triplett, Vilas, Zionville. WILKES COUNTY. CITIES: Boomer, Cricket, Hays, Fairplains, Ferguson, Millers Creek, Moravian Falls, Mulberry, N. Wilkesboro, Olin, Pleasant Hill, Roaring River, Ronda, Thurmond, Traphill, Wilkesboro. YADKIN COUNTY. CITIES: Arlington, Booneville, East Bend, Hamptonville, Jonesville, Turnersburg, and Yadkinville. Population (2000), 619,178.

ZIP Codes: 27006–07, 27009–14, 27016–25, 27028, 27030, 27040–43, 27045–47, 27049–53, 27055, 27094, 27098–99, 27101–09, 27111, 27113–17, 27120, 27127, 27130, 27150–51, 27155–57, 27199, 27201–02, 27235, 27244, 27265, 27284–85, 27305, 27314–15, 27320, 27326, 27343, 27357–58, 27360, 27379, 27565, 27582, 27893, 28115, 28125, 28166, 28601, 28604–08, 28615, 28617–18, 28621–27, 28629–31, 28634–36, 28640, 28642–45, 28649, 28651, 28654, 28656, 28659–60, 28663, 28665, 28668–70, 28672, 28675–79, 28681, 28683–85, 28688–89, 28691–94, 28697–99

* * *

SIXTH DISTRICT

HOWARD COBLE, Republican, of Greensboro, NC; born in Greensboro, March 18, 1931; education: Appalachian State University, Boone, NC, 1949–50; A.B., history, Guilford College, Greensboro, NC, 1958; J.D., University of North Carolina School of Law, Chapel Hill, 1962; military service: U.S. Coast Guard as a seaman recruit, 1952; active duty, 1952–56 and 1977–78; reserve duty, 1960–82; presently holds rank of captain; last reserve duty assignment, commanding officer, U.S. Coast Guard Reserve Unit, Wilmington, NC; professional: attorney; admitted to North Carolina bar, 1966; field claim representative and superintendent, auto insurance, 1961–67; elected to North Carolina House of Representives, 1969; assistant U.S. attorney, Middle District of North Carolina, 1969–73; commissioner (secretary), North Carolina Department of Revenue, 1973–77; North Carolina House of Representatives, 1979–83; practiced law with law firm of Turner, Enochs and Sparrow, Greensboro, NC, 1979–84; member: Alamance Presbyterian Church, American Legion, Veterans of Foreign Wars of the United States, Lions Club, Greensboro Bar Association, North Carolina Bar Association, North Carolina State Bar; North Carolina State co-chairman, American Legislative Exchange Council, 1983–84; committees: Judiciary; Transportation and Infrastructure; elected to the 99th Congress on November 6, 1984; reelected to each succeeding Congress.

Office Listings

http://www.house.gov/coble

2468 Rayburn House Office Building, Washington, DC 20515 .... (202) 225–3065
Chief of Staff / Press Secretary.—Ed McDonald. FAX: 225–8611
Executive Assistant.—Jennifer Brooks.
2102 North Elm Street, Suite B, Greensboro, NC 27408–5100 .... (336) 333–5005
Office Manager.—Chris Beaman.
155 Northpoint Avenue, Suite 200B, High Point, NC 27262–7723 .... (336) 886–5106
District Representative.—Nancy Mazza.
241 Sunset Avenue, Suite 101, Asheboro, NC 27203–5658 .... (336) 626–3060
District Representative.—Rebecca Redding.
P.O. Box 807, Granite Quarry, NC 28027–0807 .... (704) 209–0426
District Representative.—Terri Welch.
124 West Elm Street, P.O. Box 812, Graham, NC 27253–0812 .... (336) 229–0159
District Representative.—Janine Osborne.

Counties: ALAMANCE (part), DAVIDSON (part), GUILFORD (part), MOORE, RANDOLPH, ROWAN (part). Population (2000), 620,590.

ZIP Codes: 27201–05, 27208–09, 27214–17, 27220, 27230, 27233, 27235, 27239, 27242, 27244, 27248–49, 27252–53, 27258–65, 27281–84, 27288–89, 27292, 27295, 27298–99, 27301–02, 27310, 27312–13, 27316–17, 27325, 27330, 27340–42, 27344, 27349–50, 27355–61, 27370–71, 27373–74, 27376–77, 27401–10, 27415–17, 27419–20, 27425, 27427, 27429, 27435, 27438, 27455, 27495, 27498–99, 27607, 27612–13, 27640, 27803–04, 28023, 28041, 28071–72, 28081, 28083, 28088, 28125, 28127, 28137–38, 28144, 28146–47, 28315, 28326–27, 28347, 28350, 28370, 28373–74, 28387–88, 28394

* * *

SEVENTH DISTRICT

MIKE McINTYRE, Democrat, of Lumberton, NC; born in Robeson County, August 6, 1956; education: B.A., Phi Beta Kappa Morehead Scholar, 1978, and J.D., 1981, University of North Carolina; upon graduation, received the Algernon Sydney Sullivan Award for ''unselfish interest in the welfare of his fellow man''; professional: attorney; past president, Lumberton Economic Advancement for Dowtown; formerly on board of directors of Lumberton Rotary Club, Chamber of Commerce and a local group home for the mentally handicapped; active in the Boy Scouts of America, and Lumberton PTA; married: the former Dee Strickland; two children; committees: Agriculture; Armed Services; elected to the 105th Congress; reelected to each succeeding Congress.

Office Listings

http://www.house.gov/mcintyre

2437 Rayburn House Office Building, Washington, DC 20515 .... (202) 225–2731
Chief of Staff / Press Secretary.—Dean Mitchell. FAX: 225–5773
Deputy Chief of Staff.—Audrey Lesesne.
Chief of Constituent Services.—Vivian Lipford.
Legislative Director.—Blair Miligan.
Federal Building, 301 Green Street, Room 218, Fayetteville, NC 28401 .... (910) 323–0260
201 North Front Street, Suite 440, Wilmington, NC 28401 .... (910) 815–4959
701 Elm Street, Lumberton, NC 28358 .... (910) 671–6223
District Chief of Staff.—Marie Thompson.

Counties: BLADEN, BRUNSWICK, COLUMBUS, CUMBERLAND (part), DUPLIN (part), NEW HANOVER, PENDER, ROBESON, SAMPSON (part). Population (2000), 619,178.

ZIP Codes: 28301–06, 28309, 28311–12, 28318–20, 28325, 28328, 28331–32, 28334, 28337, 28340–42, 28344, 28348–49, 28356–60, 28362, 28364–66, 28369, 28371–72, 28375, 28377–78, 28383–86, 28390–93, 28395, 28398–99, 28401–12, 28420–25, 28428–36, 28438–39, 28441–59, 28461–70, 28472, 28478–80, 28513, 28518, 28521, 28572, 28574

* * *

EIGHTH DISTRICT

ROBIN HAYES, Republican, of Concord, NC; born in Concord, August 14, 1945; education: B.A., history, Duke University, 1967; professional: owner and operator, Mt. Pleasant Hosiery Mill; member, North Carolina House of Representatives, 1992–96; married: Barbara Weiland, 1968; children: Winslow and Bob; appointed to the Armed Services Committee Panel on Morale, Welfare, and Recreation for the 106th Congress; appointed to Special Oversight Panel on Terrorism for the 107th Congress; committees: Agriculture; Armed Services; Transportation and Infrastructure; elected to the 106th Congress; reelected to each succeeding Congress.

Office Listings

http://www.hayes.house.gov

130 Cannon House Office Building, Washington, DC 20515 .... (202) 225–3715
Administrative Assistant.—Andrew Duke. FAX: 225–4036
Legislative Director.—Jennifer Thompson.
Scheduler.—Andy Munn.
137 Union Street South, Concord, NC 28025 .... (704) 786–1612
District Director.—Gary Mitchell.
230 East Franklin Street, Rockingham, NC 28379 .... (910) 997–2070

Counties: ANSON, CABARRUS (part), CUMBERLAND (part), HOKE, MECKLENBURG (part), MONTGOMERY, RICHMOND, SCOTLAND (part), STANLY, UNION (part). Population (2000), 619,178.

ZIP Codes: 27209, 27215, 27229, 27247, 27253, 27281, 27284, 27306, 27312, 27320, 27341, 27356, 27358, 27371, 27405, 27534, 27803–04, 27893, 28001–02, 28007, 28009, 28025–27, 28036, 28071, 28075, 28081–83, 28091, 28097, 28102–04, 28107–12, 28119, 28124, 28127–29, 28133, 28135, 28137–38, 28159, 28163, 28167, 28170, 28174, 28204–05, 28209–13, 28215, 28217–18, 28220, 28223, 28227, 28229, 28262, 28270, 28278, 28301, 28303–06, 28308, 28311, 28314–15, 28325, 28329–30, 28338, 28343, 28345, 28347, 28349, 28351–53, 28357, 28361, 28363–64, 28367, 28371, 28376–77, 28379–80, 28382, 28386, 28396

* * *

NINTH DISTRICT

SUE WILKINS MYRICK, Republican, of Charlotte, NC; born in Tiffin, OH, August 1, 1941; education: graduated Port Clinton High School, Port Clinton, OH; attended Heidelberg College; professional: former president and CEO, Myrick Advertising and Myrick Enterprises; mayor of Charlotte, NC, 1987–91; Charlotte City Council, 1983–85; active with the National League of Cities and the U.S. Conference of Mayors; served on former President Bush's Affordable Housing Commission; member: Charlotte Chamber of Commerce; Muscular Dystrophy Association; March of Dimes; Elks Auxiliary; PTA; Cub Scout den mother; United Methodist Church; founder, Charitable Outreach Society; married Ed Myrick, 1977; five children; committees: Energy and Commerce; elected to the 104th Congress; reelected to each succeeding Congress.

Office Listings

http://www.myrick.house.gov

230 Cannon House Office Building, Washington, DC 20515 .... (202) 225–1976
Administrative Assistant.—Ashley Hoy. FAX: 225–3389
Executive Assistant.—Hollie Arnold.
6525 Morrison Boulevard, Suite 402, Charlotte, NC 28211 .... (704) 362–1060
197 W. Main Avenue, Gastonia, NC 28052 .... (704) 861–1976

Counties: GASTON (part), MECKLENBURG (part), UNION. Population (2000), 619,178.

ZIP Codes: 28006, 28012, 28016–17, 28031–34, 28036, 28042, 28052–56, 28070, 28077–80, 28086, 28092–93, 28098, 28101, 28103–07, 28110, 28112, 28114, 28120, 28126, 28130, 28134, 28136, 28150–52, 28164, 28169, 28173–74, 28201, 28203–04, 28206–11, 28213–17, 28222, 28226–27, 28241, 28247, 28250, 28253, 28261–62, 28269–71, 28273–74, 28277–78, 28287

* * *

TENTH DISTRICT

PATRICK T. McHENRY, Republican, of Cherryville, NC; born in Charlotte, NC, October 22, 1975; education: graduated Ashbrook High School, Gastonia, NC; attended North Carolina State University, Raleigh, NC; B.A., Belmont Abbey College, Belmont, NC, 1999; professional: realtor; media executive; appointed special assistant to the U.S. Secretary of Labor by President George W. Bush in 2001; member, North Carolina House of Representatives, 2002–04; organizations: Gaston Chamber of Commerce, Gastonia Rotary Club, the National Rifle Association, Saint Michael Church; board of directors, United Way's Success by Six Youth Program; committees: Budget; Financial Services; Oversight and Government Reform; elected to the 109th Congress on November 2, 2004; reelected to the 110th Congress.

Office Listings

http://www.house.gov/mchenry

224 Cannon House Office Building, Washington, DC 20515 .... (202) 225–2576

Chief of Staff.—Jon Causey. FAX: 225–0316
Legislative Director.—Jennifer Mundy.
Communications Director.—Aaron Latham.
Scheduler.—Sara Causey.
87 Fourth Street, NW., Suite A, P.O. Box 1830, Hickory, NC 28603 .... (828) 327–6100

Counties: AVERY, BURKE, CALDWELL, CATAWBA, CLEVELAND, GASTON (part), IREDELL (part), LINCOLN, MITCHELL, and RUTHERFORD (part). CITIES AND TOWNSHIPS: Hickory, Lenoir, Morganton, Shelby, and Mooresville. Population (2000), 619,178.

ZIP Codes: 28006, 28010, 28016–21, 28024, 28033, 28036–38, 28040, 28042–43, 28052, 28073–74, 28076, 28080, 28086, 28089–90, 28092, 28114–15, 28117, 28139, 28150, 28152, 28164, 28166–69, 28601–07, 28609–13, 28616, 28619, 28621–22, 28624–25, 28628–30, 28633, 28635–38, 28641, 28645–47, 28650, 28652–55, 28657–58, 28661–62, 28664, 28666–67, 28671, 28673, 28676–78, 28680–82, 28687, 28690, 28699, 28705, 28720, 28740, 28746, 28752, 28761, 28765, 28777

* * *

ELEVENTH DISTRICT

HEATH SHULER, Democrat, of Waynesville, NC; born in Bryson City, NC, December 31, 1971; graduated from Swain County High School; B.A., University of Tennessee, 2001; entrepreneur; married to the former Nikol Davis; two children: Navy and Island; committees: Natural Resources; Small Business; Transportation and Infrastructure; elected to the 110th Congress on November 7, 2006.

Office Listings

512 Cannon House Office Building, Washington, DC 20515 .... (202) 225–6401
Chief of Staff.—Hayden Rogers. FAX: 226–6422
Legislative Director.—Sean O'Brien.
Communications Director.—Andrew Whalen.
Scheduler.—Blakely Whilden.
356 Biltmore Avenue, Suite 400, Asheville, NC 28801 .... (828) 252–1651
District Director.—Bruce Peterson.

Counties: BUNCOMBE, CHEROKEE, CLAY, GRAHAM, HAYWOOD, HENDERSON, JACKSON, MCDOWELL, MACON, MADISON, POLK, RUTHERFORD (part), SWAIN, TRANSYLVANIA, YANCEY. Population (2000), 619,177.

ZIP Codes: 28043, 28074, 28114, 28139, 28160, 28647, 28655, 28701–02, 28704, 28707–19, 28721–45, 28747–58, 28760–63, 28766, 28768, 28770–79, 28781–93, 28801–06, 28810, 28813–16, 28901–06, 28909

* * *

TWELFTH DISTRICT

MELVIN L. WATT, Democrat, of Charlotte, NC; born in Charlotte, August 26, 1945; education: graduated, York Road High School, Charlotte, 1963; B.S., business adminisration, University of North Carolina, Chapel Hill, 1967; J.D., Yale University Law School, New Haven, CT, 1970; professional: attorney; admitted to the District of Columbia bar, 1970, admitted to the North Carolina bar, 1971; began practice with Chambers, Stein, Ferguson and Becton, 1971–92; North Carolina State Senate, 1985–86; life member, NAACP; member, Mount Olive Presbyterian Church; past president, Mecklenburg County Bar Association, Johnston C. Smith University Board of Visitors; Central Piedmont Community College Foundation; North Carolina Association of Black Lawyers; North Carolina Association of Trial Lawyers; Legal Aid of Southern Piedmont; NationsBank Community Development Corporation; Charlotte Chamber of Commerce; Sports Action Council; Auditorium-Coliseum-Civic Center Authority; United Way; Mint Museum; Inroads, Inc.; Family Housing Services; Public Education Forum; Dilworth Community Development Association; Cities in Schools; West Charlotte Business Incubator; Housing Authority Scholarship Board; Morehead Scholarship Selection Committee, Forsyth Region; married: the former Eulada Paysour, 1968; children: Brian and Jason; committees: Financial Services; Judiciary; elected on November 3, 1992, to the 103rd Congress; reelected to each succeeding Congress.

Office Listings

http://www.house.gov/watt

2236 Rayburn House Office Building, Washington, DC 20515 .... (202) 225–1510
Chief of Staff.—Joyce Brayboy. FAX: 225–1512
1230 West Morehead Street, Suite 306, Charlotte, NC 28208 .... (704) 344–9950

301 South Greene Street, Suite 210, Greensboro, NC 27401 .... (336) 275–9950
District Director.—Pam Stubbs.

Counties: CABARRUS COUNTY (part). DAVIDSON COUNTY (part). CITIES AND TOWNSHIPS: Lexington, and Thomasville. FORSYTH COUNTY (part). CITIES AND TOWNSHIPS: Winston-Salem. GUILFORD COUNTY (part). CITIES AND TOWNSHIPS: High Point, Greensboro. MECKLENBURG COUNTY. CITIES AND TOWNSHIPS: Charlotte. ROWAN COUNTY. CITIES: Salisbury. Population (2000), 619,178.

ZIP Codes: 27010, 27012–13, 27019, 27040, 27045, 27051, 27054, 27101, 27103–07, 27110, 27127, 27214, 27260, 27262–63, 27265, 27282, 27284, 27292–95, 27299, 27310, 27320, 27351, 27360, 27401, 27403, 27405–11, 27534, 27803–04, 27893, 28023, 28027, 28035–36, 28039, 28078, 28081, 28115, 28123, 28125, 28134, 28144–47, 28159, 28202–17, 28219, 28221, 28224, 28226–28, 28230–37, 28240, 28242–43, 28254–56, 28258, 28260, 28262, 28265–66, 28269–70, 28272–73, 28275, 28278, 28280–82, 28284–85, 28289–90, 28296–97

* * *

THIRTEENTH DISTRICT

BRAD MILLER, Democrat, of Raleigh, NC; born in Fayetteville, NC, May 19, 1953; education: B.A., Political Science, University of North Carolina, 1975; Master's Degree, Political Science, London School of Economics, 1978; J.D., Columbia University Law School, 1979; professional: attorney; law clerk to Circuit Court of Appeals Judge J. Dickson Phillips, Jr., 1979–80; has practiced law in Raleigh since 1980, and has been in private practice since 1991; public service: North Carolina House of Representatives, 1992–94; North Carolina State Senate, 1996–2002; religion: Episcopal; family: married to Esther Hall; committees: Financial Services; Foreign Affairs; Science and Technology; elected to the 108th Congress on November 5, 2002; reelected to each succeeding Congress.

Office Listings

http://www.house.gov/bradmiller

1722 Longworth House Office Building, Washington, DC 20515 .... (202) 225–3032
Chief of Staff.—Mark Harkins. FAX: 225–0181
Deputy Chief of Staff / Legislative Director.—Ryan Hedgepeth.
Communications Director.—LuAnn Canipe.
Scheduler.—Anna Rose.
1300 St. Mary's Street, Suite 504, Raleigh, NC 27605 .... (919) 836–1313
125 South Elm Street, Suite 504, Greensboro, NC 27401 .... (336) 574–2909

Counties: ALAMANCE (part), CASWELL, GRANVILLE (part), GUILFORD (part), PERSON, ROCKINGHAM (part), WAKE (part). Population (2000), 619,178.

ZIP Codes: 27025, 27027, 27048, 27212, 27214–17, 27231, 27244, 27249, 27253, 27258, 27288–89, 27291, 27301–02, 27305, 27311, 27320, 27323, 27326, 27343, 27375, 27379, 27401, 27403, 27403–10, 27412–13, 27415, 27419, 27455, 27495, 27497, 27507, 27509, 27511–12, 27522, 27525, 27541, 27544–45, 27564–65, 27571–74, 27581–83, 27587–88, 27591, 27596–97, 27601, 27603–10, 27612–17, 27619–20, 27622, 27625, 27627–29, 27635–36, 27640, 27658, 27661, 27668, 27690, 27698

NORTH DAKOTA

(Population 2000, 642,200)

SENATORS

KENT CONRAD, Democrat, of Bismarck, ND; born in Bismarck, March 12, 1948; education: graduated from Wheelus High School, Tripoli, Libya, 1966; attended the University of Missouri, Columbia, 1967; B.A., Stanford University, CA, 1971; M.B.A., George Washington University, Washington, DC, 1975; professional: assistant to the Tax Commissioner, Bismarck, 1974–80; director, Management Planning and Personnel, North Dakota Tax Department, March–December 1980; Tax Commissioner, State of North Dakota, 1981–86; married Lucy Calautti, February 1987; one child by former marriage: Jessamyn Abigail; committees: chair, Budget; Agriculture, Nutrition, and Forestry; Finance; Indian Affairs; Joint Committee on Taxation; elected to the U.S. Senate on November 4, 1986; was not a candidate for a second term to Senate seat he had won in 1986; subsequently elected by special election on December 4, 1992, to fill the vacancy caused by the death of Senator Quentin Burdick, whose term would have expired on January 3, 1995; took the oath of office on December 14, 1992; reelected to each succeeding Senate term.

Office Listings

http://conrad.senate.gov

530 Hart Senate Office Building, Washington, DC 20510 .... (202) 224–2043
Chief of Staff.—Bob Van Heuvelen. FAX: 224–7776
Legislative Director.—Tom Mahr.
220 East Rosser Avenue, Room 228, Bismarck, ND 58501 .... (701) 258–4648
State Director (West Region).—Marty Boeckel.
657 Second Avenue North, Room 306, Fargo, ND 58102 .... (701) 232–8030
State Director (East Region).—Scott Stofferahn. TDD: 232–2139
102 North Fourth Street, Suite 104, Grand Forks, ND 58203 .... (701) 775–9601
100 First Street, SW, Room 105, Minot, ND 58701 .... (701) 852–0703

* * *

BYRON L. DORGAN, Democrat, of Bismarck, ND; born in Dickinson, ND, May 14, 1942; education: graduated, Regent High School, 1961; B.S., University of North Dakota, 1965; M.B.A., University of Denver, 1966; professional: North Dakota State Tax Commissioner, 1969–80, the only elected state tax commissioner in the nation; received 80 percent of the vote in 1976 tax commissioner reelection bid; chairman, Multi-State Tax Commission, 1972–74; executive committee member, National Association of Tax Administrators, 1972–75; selected by the *Washington Monthly* as one of the outstanding state officials in the United States, 1975; chosen by one of North Dakota's leading newspapers as the individual with the greatest influence on State government, 1977; elected to Congress, 1980; elected president of Democratic freshman class during first term; reelected, 1982, with 72 percent of the vote; reelected to Congress in 1984 with 78.5 percent of the vote, setting three election records in North Dakota—largest vote ever received by a statewide candidate, largest vote by a U.S. House candidate, and largest majority by a U.S. House candidate; his 242,000 votes in 1984 were the most received anywhere in the nation by an opposed House candidate; reelected to each succeeding Congress; served on three congressional committees during first term in Congress: Agriculture, Small Business, and Veterans' Affairs; named to the Ways and Means Committee, January 1983; called the real successor to Bill Langer and the State's most exciting office holder in generations, by the 1983 *Book of America*; 1990 *New York Times* editorial said, ''Mr. Dorgan sets an example for political statesmanship''; named to Select Committee on Hunger in 1985; chairman, International Task Force on Select Committee on Hunger; chairman, Democratic Policy Committee, 106th thru 109th Congresses; assistant Democratic Leader for Policy, 106th and 107th Congresses; assistant Democratic Floor Leader, 104th and 105th Congresses; assistant Democratic Floor Leader, ex officio, 106th and 107th Congresses; married: Kim Dorgan; children: Scott, Shelly (deceased), Brendon, and Haley; committees: chair, Indian Affairs; Appropriations; Commerce, Science, and Transportation; Energy and Natural Resources; elected to the U.S. Senate on November 3, 1992; first sworn in on December 15, 1992, to fill the remainder of the term in North Dakota's open Senate seat, then sworn in January 5, 1993, for six-year term; reelected to each succeeding Senate term.

Office Listings

http://dorgan.senate.gov

322 Hart Senate Office Building, Washington, DC 20510 .... (202) 224–2551

Chief of Staff.—Elizabeth Gore. FAX: 224–1193
Communications Director.—Barry E. Piatt.
Office Manager.—Dana McCallum.
State Director.—Bob Valeu.

220 East Rosser Avenue, Room 312, Bismarck, ND 58502 .... (701) 250–4618
1802 32nd Avenue South, Suite B, P.O. Box 9060, Fargo, ND 58106 .... (701) 239–5389
102 North Fourth Street, Room 108, Grand Forks, ND 58201 .... (701) 746–8972
100 First Street SW, Suite 105, Minot, ND 58701 .... (701) 852–0703

REPRESENTATIVE

AT LARGE

EARL POMEROY, Democrat-NPL, of Valley City, ND; born in Valley City, September 2, 1952; education: B.A. and J.D., University of North Dakota, Grand Forks, 1974, 1979; graduate research in legal history, University of Durham, England, 1975–76; professional: attorney; admitted to North Dakota bar, 1979; North Dakota House of Representatives, 1980–84; Insurance Commissioner of North Dakota, 1985–92; president, National Association of Insurance Commissioners, 1990; children: Kathryn and Scott; committees: Agriculture; Ways and Means; elected to the 103rd Congress on November 3, 1992; reelected to each succeeding Congress.

Office Listings

http://www.house.gov/pomeroy

1501 Longworth House Office Building, Washington, DC 20515 .... (202) 225–2611
Chief of Staff.—Bob Siggins. FAX: 226–0893
Legislative Director.—Melanie Rhinehart.
Press Secretary.—Sandra Salstrom.

Federal Building, 220 East Rosser Avenue, Room 328, Bismarck, ND 58501 .... (701) 224–0355
3003 32nd Avenue South, Suite 6, Fargo, ND 58103 .... (701) 235–9760
State Director.—Gail Skaley.

Population (2000), 642,200.

ZIP Codes: 58001–02, 58004–09, 58011–13, 58015–18, 58021, 58027, 58029, 58030–33, 58035–36, 58038, 58040–43, 58045–49, 58051–54, 58056–65, 58067–69, 58071–72, 58074–79, 58081, 58102–09, 58121–22, 58124–26, 58201–06, 58208, 58210, 58212, 58214, 58216, 58218–20, 58222–25, 58227–31, 58233, 58235–41, 58243–44, 58249–51, 58254–62, 58265–67, 58269–78, 58281–82, 58301, 58310–11, 58313, 58316–19, 58321, 58323–25, 58327, 58329–32, 58335, 58338–39, 58341, 58343–46, 58348, 58351–53, 58355–57, 58359, 58361–63, 58365–70, 58372, 58374, 58377, 58379–82, 58384–86, 58401–02, 58405, 58413, 58415–16, 58418, 58420–26, 58428–31, 58433, 58436, 58438–45, 58448, 58451–52, 58454–56, 58458, 58460–61, 58463–64, 58466–67, 58472, 58474–84, 58486–88, 58490, 58492, 58494–97, 58501–07, 58520–21, 58523–24, 58528–33, 58535, 58538, 58540–42, 58544–45, 58549, 58552, 58554, 58558–66, 58568–73, 58575–77, 58579–81, 58601–02, 58620–23, 58625–27, 58630–32, 58634, 58636, 58638–47, 58649–56, 58701–05, 58707, 58710–13, 58716, 58718, 58721–23, 58725, 58727, 58730–31, 58733–37, 58740–41, 58744, 58746–48, 58750, 58752, 58755–63, 58765, 58768–73, 58775–76, 58778–79, 58781–85, 58787–90, 58792–95, 58801–02, 58830–31, 58833, 58835, 58838, 58843–45, 58847, 58849, 58852–54, 58856

OHIO

(Population 2000, 11,353,140)

SENATORS

GEORGE V. VOINOVICH, Republican, of Cleveland, OH; born in Cleveland, July 15, 1936; B.A., Ohio University, 1958; J.D., College of Law, Ohio State University, 1961; Honorary Doctorate of Law, Ohio University, 1981; Honorary Doctorate of Public Administration, Findlay University, 1993; public service: Assistant Attorney General, Ohio, 1963; member, Ohio House of Representatives, 1967–71; Cuyahoga County Auditor, 1971–76; Cuyahoga County Commissioner, 1977–78; Lieutenant Governor, Ohio, 1979; Mayor, Cleveland, OH, 1979–86; 65th Governor of Ohio, 1990–98; President, National League of Cities, 1985; chairman, National Governor's Association, 1997–98; Catholic; married: Janet Voinovich; three children: George, Betsy, and Peter; committees: Environment and Public Works; Foreign Relations; Homeland Security and Governmental Affairs; elected to the U.S. Senate on November 3, 1998; reelected to each succeeding Senate term.

Office Listings

http://voinovich.senate.gov

524 Hart Senate Office Building, Washington, DC 20510 .... (202) 224–3353
FAX: 228–1382
Chief of Staff.—Phil Park.
Communication Director.—Chris Paulitz.
Director of Operations.—Christi Mayer.
1240 East Ninth Street, Suite 2955, Cleveland, OH 44199 .... (216) 522–7095
Regional Representative.—Dora Pruce.
37 West Broad Street, Suite 300, Columbus, OH 43215 .... (614) 469–6697
37 West Broad Street, Suite 300, Columbus, OH 43215 .... (614) 469–6774
State Director.—Beth Hansen.
36 East 7th Street, Room 2615, Cincinnati, OH 45202 .... (513) 684–3265
District Representative.—Tony Condia.
420 Madison Avenue, Room 1210, Toledo, OH 43604 .... (419) 259–3895
District Representative.—Dennis Fligor.
Constituent Services Director.—Michael Dustman.
417 Second Avenue, Gallipolis, OH 45631 .... (740) 441–6410
District Representative.—Cara Dingus.

* * *

SHERROD BROWN, Democrat, of Avon Lake, OH; born in Mansfield, OH, November 9, 1952; education: B.A., Yale University, New Haven, CT, 1974; M.A., Education, Ohio State University, Columbus, OH, 1979; M.A., Public Administration, Ohio State University, Columbus, OH, 1981; professional: Ohio House of Representatives, 1975–83; Ohio secretary of State, 1983–91; U.S. House of Representatives, 1992–2006; member: Eagle Scouts of America; married: Connie Schultz; children: Emily, Elizabeth, Andrew and Caitlin; committees: Agriculture, Nutrition, and Forestry; Banking, Housing, and Urban Affairs; Health, Education, Labor, and Pensions; Veterans' Affairs; elected to the 103rd Congress on November 3, 1992; reelected to each succeeding Congress; elected to the U.S. Senate on November 7, 2006.

Office Listings

http://brown.senate.gov

455 Russell Senate Office Building, Washington, DC 20510 .... (202) 224–2315
FAX: 228–6321
Chief of Staff.—James Heimbach.
Legislative Director.—Eleanor Dehoney.
Communications Director.—Joanna Kuebler.
Press Secretary.—Bethany Lesser.
600 East Superior Avenue, Room 2450, Cleveland, OH 44114 .... (216) 522–7272
Deputy State Director.—Beth Thames.
200 North High Street, Room 2450, Columbus, OH 43215 .... (614) 469–2083
205 West Twentieth Street, Suite M280, Lorain, OH 44052 .... (440) 242–4100

REPRESENTATIVES

FIRST DISTRICT

STEVE CHABOT, Republican, of Cincinnati, OH; born in Cincinnati, January 22, 1953; attended LaSalle High School, Cincinnati; B.A., College of William and Mary, Williamsburg,

VA, 1975; J.D., Salmon P. Chase College of Law, 1978; former school teacher; private practice lawyer, 1978–94; Hamilton County commissioner, 1990–94; member, Cincinnati City Council, 1985–90; chairman, County Council's Urban Development and Law and Public Safety committees; married: Donna Chabot, 1973; children: Randy and Erica; committees: Foreign Affairs; Judiciary; Small Business; elected to the 104th Congress; reelected to each succeeding Congress.

Office Listings

129 Cannon House Office Building, Washington, DC 20515 .... (202) 225–2216
Chief of Staff.—Gary Lindgren. FAX: 225–3012
Legislative Director.—Mike Smullen.
Office Manager.—Angela Weaver.
Carew Tower, 441 Vine Street, Room 3003, Cincinnati, OH 45202 .... (513) 684–2723
District Director.—Mike Cantwell.

Counties: BUTLER (part), HAMILTON (part). Population (2000), 630,730.

ZIP Codes: 45001–02, 45013–14, 45030, 45033, 45040–41, 45051–54, 45056, 45070, 45201–21, 45223–25, 45229, 45231–34, 45236–41, 45246–48, 45250–53, 45258, 45262–64, 45267–71, 45273–74, 45277, 45280, 45296, 45298–99

* * *

SECOND DISTRICT

JEAN SCHMIDT, Republican, of Miami Township; born in Cincinnati, OH, November 29th; education: B.A., University of Cincinnati, 1974; professional: Miami Township Trustee, 1989–2000; Ohio House of Representatives, 2000–04; president, Right to Life of Greater Cincinnati, 2004–05; religion: Catholic; married: Peter; children: Emilie; committees: Agriculture; Transportation and Infrastructure; elected to the 109th Congress by special election on August 5, 2005; reelected to each succeeding Congress.

Office Listings

http://www.house.gov/schmidt

238 Cannon House Office Building, Washington, DC 20515 .... (202) 225–3164
Chief of Staff.—Barry Bennett. FAX: 225–1992
Legislative Director.—Joe Jansen.
Scheduler.—James Langenderfer.
Press Secretary.—Ben LaRocco.
8044 Montgomery Road, Suite 540, Cincinnati, OH 45236 .... (513) 791–0381
601 Chillicothe Street, Portsmouth, OH 45662 .... (740) 354–1440

Counties: ADAMS, BROWN, CLERMONT, HAMILTON (part), PIKE, SCIOTO (part), WARREN (part). Population (2000), 630,730.

ZIP Codes: 45034, 45036, 45039–40, 45054, 45065, 45068, 45101–03, 45105–07, 45111–13, 45115, 45118–22, 45130–31, 45133, 45140, 45142, 45144–45, 45147–48, 45150, 45152–54, 45156–58, 45160, 45162, 45167–68, 45171, 45174, 45176, 45202, 45206–09, 45212–13, 45222, 45226–27, 45230, 45235–37, 45241–46, 45249, 45254–55, 45601, 45612–13, 45616, 45618, 45624, 45630, 45642, 45646, 45648, 45650, 45652, 45657, 45660–63, 45671, 45679, 45683–84, 45687, 45690, 45693, 45697

* * *

THIRD DISTRICT

MICHAEL R. TURNER, Republican, of Dayton, OH; born in Dayton, January 11, 1960; education: B.A., Ohio Northern University, 1982; J.D., Case Western Reserve University Law School, 1985; M.B.A., University of Dayton, 1992; professional: attorney; president, JMD Development (real estate company); corporate counsel, MTC International (holding company); organizations: Ohio Bar Association; California Bar Association; public service: Mayor of Dayton, 1994–2002; married to Lori; children: Jessica and Carolyn; committees: Armed Services; Oversight and Government Reform; Veterans' Affairs; elected to the 108th Congress on November 5, 2002; reelected to each succeeding Congress.

Office Listings

http://www.house.gov/miketurner

1740 Longworth House Office Building, Washington, DC 20515 .... (202) 225–6465
Chief of Staff.—Stacy Palmer-Barton. FAX: 225–6754
Legislative Director.—Mike Wiehe.
120 West Third Street, Suite 305, Dayton, OH 45402 .... (937) 225–2843

Counties: CLINTON, HIGHLAND, MONTGOMERY (part), WARREN (part). Population (2000), 630,730.

ZIP Codes: 45005, 45032, 45036, 45040, 45042, 45044, 45054, 45066, 45068, 45107, 45110, 45113–14, 45118, 45123, 45132–33, 45135, 45138, 45140, 45142, 45146, 45148, 45155, 45159, 45164, 45166, 45169, 45177, 45206, 45240–41, 45309, 45315, 45322, 45325, 45327, 45335, 45338, 45342–45, 45354, 45371, 45377, 45381, 45401–10, 45412–20, 45422, 45426–29, 45431–32, 45437, 45439–41, 45448–49, 45454, 45458–59, 45463, 45469–70, 45475, 45479, 45481–82, 45490, 45612, 45660, 45679, 45697

* * *

FOURTH DISTRICT

JAMES D. ''JIM'' JORDAN, Republican, of Urbana, OH; born in Troy, OH, February 17, 1964; education: graduated, Graham High School, St. Paris, OH, 1982; B.S. in economics, University of Wisconsin, Madison, WI, 1986; M.A. in education, The Ohio State University, Columbus, OH, 1991; J.D., Capital University School of Law, Columbus, OH, 2001; professional: assistant wrestling coach, The Ohio State University, 1987–95; State Representative, Ohio House of Representatives, 85th District, 1995–2001; State Senator, Ohio State Senate, 12th District, 2001–07; awards: four-time high school wrestling champion (Ohio), 1979–82; two-time NCAA Division 1 National Wrestling Champion, 1985–86; three-time All American, 1984–86; Wisconsin Badger's Hall of Fame; third place, Olympic Trials in Wrestling, 1988; Friend of the Taxpayer, Americans for the Tax Reform, 1997; Leadership in Government Award from the Ohio Roundtable and Freedom forum, 2001; awards from the United States Conservatives of Ohio: Outstanding Freshman Legislator Award, 1996; Watchdog of the Treasury, 1996, 2000, 2004; Pro-Life Legislator of the Year, 1998; Outstanding Legislator Award, 2004; activities: Grace Bible Church, West Liberty; Local and National Right to Life organizations; Champaign County Republican Executive Committee; married: Polly (Stickley) Jordan; parents: John and Shirley Jordan; children: Rachel, Benjamin, Jessie, and Issac; committees: Judiciary; Small Business; elected to the 110th Congress on November 7, 2006.

Office Listings

http://jordan.house.gov

515 Cannon House Office Building, Washington, DC 20515 .... (202) 225–2676
FAX: 226–0577
Chief of Staff.—Ray Yonkura.
Legislative Director.—George Poulios.
Executive Assistant / Scheduler.—Melissa Evans.
Office Manager / Staff Assistant.—Wesley Goodman.
3121 West Elm Plaza, Lima, OH 45805–2516 .... (419) 999–6455
100 East Main Cross Street, Suite 201, Findlay, OH 45840–3311 .... (419) 423–3210
24 West Third Street, Room 314, Mansfield, OH 44902–1299 .... (419) 522–5757
District Director.—Fred Shimp.

Counties: ALLEN, AUGLAIZE, CHAMPAIGN, HANCOCK, HARDIN, LOGAN, MARION, MORROW, RICHLAND, SHELBY, WYANDOT (part). Population (2000), 630,730.

ZIP Codes: 43003, 43009, 43011, 43019, 43044–45, 43047, 43050, 43060, 43067, 43070, 43072, 43074, 43078, 43083–84, 43301–02, 43306, 43310–11, 43314–26, 43330–38, 43340–51, 43356–60, 43516, 44802, 44804–05, 44813, 44817, 44822, 44827, 44830, 44833, 44837, 44843, 44849, 44862, 44864–65, 44875, 44878, 44901–07, 44999, 45013, 45302, 45306, 45312, 45317, 45326, 45333–34, 45336, 45340, 45344, 45353, 45356, 45360, 45363, 45365, 45380, 45388–89, 45404, 45414, 45420, 45424, 45431–32, 45502, 45801–02, 45804–10, 45812, 45814, 45816–17, 45819–20, 45822, 45830, 45833, 45835–36, 45839–41, 45843–45, 45850, 45854, 45856, 45858–59, 45862, 45865, 45867–72, 45877, 45881, 45884–85, 45887–90, 45894–97

* * *

FIFTH DISTRICT

PAUL E. GILLMOR, Republican, of Tiffin, OH; born in Tiffin, OH, February 1, 1939; education: graduated, Old Fort High School, Old Fort, OH, 1957; B.A., Ohio Wesleyan University, Delaware, 1961; J.D., University of Michigan Law School, Ann Arbor, 1964; military service: served in the U.S. Air Force, captain, 1965–66; professional: attorney; admitted to the Ohio bar, 1965; commenced practice in Tiffin, OH; Ohio State Senate, 1967–88; minority leader and president, Ohio State Senate; married the former Karen Lako, 1983; five children: Linda, Julie, Paul Michael, Adam, and Connor; committees: Financial Services; elected to the 101st Congress on November 8, 1988; reelected to each succeeding Congress.

Office Listings

http://gillmor.house.gov

1203 Longworth House Office Building, Washington, DC 20515 .... (202) 225–6405

Chief of Staff.—Mark Wellman. FAX: 225–1985
Scheduler.—Kelley Kurtz.
Legislative Director.—Ryan Walker.
Communications Director.—Brad Mascho.
96 South Washington Street, Suite 400, Tiffin, OH 44883 .... (419) 448–9016
613 West Third Street, Defiance, OH 43512 .... (419) 782–1996
130 Shady Lane Drive, Norwalk, OH 44857 .... (419) 668–0206

Counties: ASHLAND (part), CRAWFORD, DEFIANCE, FULTON, HENRY, HURON, LUCAS (part), MERCER (part), PAULDING, PUTNAM, SANDUSKY, SENECA, VAN WERT, WILLIAMS, WOOD, WYANDOT (part). Population (2000), 630,730.

ZIP Codes: 43302, 43314, 43316, 43323, 43337, 43351, 43402–03, 43406–07, 43410, 43413–14, 43416, 43420, 43430–31, 43435, 43437, 43441–43, 43447, 43449–51, 43457, 43460, 43462–67, 43469, 43501–02, 43504–06, 4351012, 43515–27, 43529–36, 43540–43, 43545, 43547–58, 43565–67, 43569–71, 43605, 43619, 43654, 44035, 44235, 44287, 44802, 44805, 44807, 44809, 44811, 44815, 44817–18, 44820, 44825–28, 44830, 44833, 44836–37, 44841, 44844–51, 44853–57, 44859–61, 44865–67, 44874–75, 44878, 44880–83, 44887–90, 45813, 45815, 45817, 45821–22, 45827–28, 45830–33, 45837–38, 45844, 45846, 45848–49, 45851, 45853, 45855–56, 45858, 45861–64, 45868, 45872–77, 45879–80, 45882, 45886–87, 45889, 45891, 45893–94, 45898–99

* * *

SIXTH DISTRICT

CHARLES A. WILSON, Democrat, of St. Clairsville, OH; born in Martins Ferry, OH, January 18, 1943; raised in Dillonvale, OH; education: B.A., Ohio University; degree from the Cincinnati College of Mortuary Science; professional: director, Wilson Furniture and Funeral Company; served in the Ohio Legislative; 1997–2003, and Ohio Senate, 2004–05; family: four sons and eight grandchildren; committees: Financial Services; Science and Technology; elected to the 110th Congress on November 7, 2006.

Office Listings

226 Cannon House Office Building, Washington, DC 20515 .... (202) 225–5705
Chief of Staff.—Michelle Dallafior. FAX: 225–5907
Legislative Director.—Dan Craig.
Press Secretary.—Jason Friedman.
Legislative Assistant.—Joan Gregory.
258 Front Street, Marietta, OH 45750 .... (740) 376–0868
District Director.—Jess Goode.
800 Main Street, Bridgeport, OH 43912 .... (740) 633–5705
4137 Boardman-Canfield Road, Canfield, OH 44406 .... (330) 533–7136

Counties: ATHENS (part), BELMONT, COLUMBIANA, GALLIA, JEFFERSON, LAWRENCE, MAHONING (part), MEIGS, MONROE, NOBLE, SCIOTO (part), WASHINGTON. Population (2000), 630,730.

ZIP Codes: 43711, 43713, 4371619, 43724, 43728, 43732, 43747, 43752, 43754, 43757, 43759, 43772–73, 43778–80, 43786–89, 43793, 43901–03, 43905–10, 43912–17, 43920, 43925–26, 43930–35, 43937–48, 43950–53, 43961–64, 43967–68, 43970–71, 43973, 43977, 43983, 43985, 44401, 44406, 44408, 44412–13, 44415–16, 44422–23, 44427, 44429, 44431–32, 44441–45, 44449, 44451–52, 44454–55, 44460, 44481, 44490, 44492–93, 44502, 44507, 44511–15, 44601, 44609, 44619, 44625, 44634, 44657, 44665, 44672, 45014, 45040, 45054, 45065, 45067–68, 45107, 45110, 45113–14, 45123, 45132–33, 45135, 45138, 45140, 45142, 45146, 45148, 45155, 45159, 45162, 45164, 45166, 45172, 45177, 45419, 45614, 45619–20, 45623, 45629, 45631, 45636, 45638, 45643, 45645, 45648, 45653, 45656, 45658–59, 45662, 45669, 45674–75, 45677–78, 45680, 45682, 45685–86, 45688, 45694, 45696, 45699, 45701, 45710–15, 45720–21, 45723–24, 45727, 45729, 45732, 45734–35, 45739, 45741–46, 45750, 45760–61, 45764, 45766–73, 45775–80, 45783–84, 45786–89

* * *

SEVENTH DISTRICT

DAVID L. HOBSON, Republican, of Springfield, OH; born in Cincinnati, OH, October 17, 1936; education: graduated from Withrow High School, Cincinnati, 1954; B.A., Ohio Wesleyan University, Delaware, OH, 1958; J.D., Ohio State College of Law, Columbus, 1963; admitted to the Kentucky bar, 1965; airman, Ohio Air National Guard, 1958–63; businessman; member: VFW Post No. 1031, Springfield Rotary, Shrine Club No. 5121, Moose No. 536, Elks No. 51; member: board of Ohio Wesleyan University; appointed to Ohio State Senate, 1982; Ohio State Senator, 1982–90; majority whip, 1986–88; president pro tempore, 1988–90; married: the former Carolyn Alexander, 1958; children: Susan Marie, Lynn Martha, Douglas Lee; six grandchildren; assistant minority whip; committees: Appropriations; elected to the 102nd Congress on November 6, 1990; reelected to each succeeding Congress.

Office Listings

http://www.house.gov/hobson

2346 Rayburn House Office Building, Washington, DC 20515 .... (202) 225–4324
Chief of Staff.—Wayne Struble. FAX: 225–1984
Legislative Director.—Kenny Kraft.
Scheduler.—Rhiannon Burruss.
Press Secretary.—Sara Perkins.
5 West North Street, Suite 200, P.O. Box 269, Springfield, OH 45501–0269 .... (937) 325–0474
212 South Broad Street, Room 55, Lancaster, OH 43130–4389 .... (740) 654–5149

Counties: CLARK, FAIRFIELD, FAYETTE, FRANKLIN (part), GREENE, PERRY, PICKAWAY, ROSS (part). Population (2000), 630,730.

ZIP Codes: 43009–10, 43044, 43046, 43062, 43068, 43076, 43078, 43102–03, 43105–07, 43109–10, 43112–13, 43115–17, 43125, 43128, 43130, 43135–38, 43140, 43142–43, 43145–48, 43150, 43153–57, 43160, 43163–64, 43199, 43207, 43213, 43217, 43227, 43232, 43314, 43730–31, 43739, 43748, 43758, 43760–61, 43764, 43766, 43777, 43782–83, 45123, 45135, 45169, 45301, 45305, 45307, 45314, 45316, 45319, 45323–24, 45335, 45341, 45344, 45349, 45368–70, 45372, 45384–85, 45387, 45424, 45430–35, 45440, 45458–59, 45501–06, 45601, 45628, 45644, 45671, 45732

* * *

EIGHTH DISTRICT

JOHN A. BOEHNER, Republican, of West Chester, OH; born in Reading, OH, November 17, 1949; education: graduated, Moeller High School, Cincinnati, OH, 1968; B.S., Xavier University, 1977; president, Nucite Sales, Inc.; Ohio House of Representatives, 1984–90; ranking Republican member, Commerce and Labor Committee; Energy and Environment Committee; Judiciary and Criminal Justice; elected, Union Township Trustees, 1981; elected, president, Union Township Board of Trustees, 1984; member: St. John Catholic Church; Ohio Farm Bureau; Lakota Hills Homeowners Association; Knights of Columbus, Pope John XXIII; Union Chamber of Commerce; American Heart Association Board; Butler County Mental Health Association; YMCA Capital Campaign; Union Elementary School PTA; Middletown Chamber of Commerce; American Legion Post 218 of Middletown Butler County Trustees and Clerks Association; married the former Deborah Gunlack, 1973; two children: Lindsay, Tricia; committees: Republican Leader; elected to the 102nd Congress; reelected to each succeeding Congress.

Office Listings

http://johnboehner.house.gov

1011 Longworth House Office Building, Washington, DC 20515 .... (202) 225–6205
Chief of Staff.—Mick Krieger. FAX: 225–5117
Press Secretary.—Jessica R. Towhey.
7969 Cincinnati-Dayton road, Suite B, West Chester, OH 45069 .... (513) 779–5400
12 South Plum Street, Troy, Ohio 45373 .... (937) 339–1524

Counties: BUTLER (part), DARKE, MERCER (part), MIAMI, MONTGOMERY (part), PREBLE. Population (2000), 630,730.

ZIP Codes: 45003–05, 45011–15, 45018, 45025–26, 45036, 45042–44, 45050, 45055–56, 45061–64, 45067, 45069, 45071, 45073, 45099, 45241, 45246, 45303–04, 45308–12, 45317–18, 45320–22, 45325–28, 45330–32, 45337–39, 45344, 45346–48, 45350–52, 45356, 45358–59, 45361–62, 45365, 45371, 45373–74, 45378, 45380–83, 45388, 45390, 45402–04, 45406, 45414, 45424, 45431–32, 45822, 45826, 45828, 45845–46, 45860, 45865–66, 45869, 45883, 45885

* * *

NINTH DISTRICT

MARCY KAPTUR, Democrat, of Toledo, OH; born in Toledo, June 17, 1946; education: graduated, St. Ursula Academy, Toledo, 1964; B.A., University of Wisconsin, Madison, 1968; Master of Urban Planning, University of Michigan, Ann Arbor, 1974; attended University of Manchester, England, 1974; professional: urban planner; assistant director for urban affairs, domestic policy staff, White House, 1977–79; American Planning Association and American Institute of Certified Planners Fellow; member: National Center for Urban Ethnic Affairs advisory committee; University of Michigan Urban Planning Alumni Association; NAACP Urban League; Polish Museum; Polish American Historical Association; Lucas County Democratic Party Executive Committee; Democratic Women's Campaign Association; Little Flower Parish Church; House Auto Parts Task Force; co-chair, Congressional Competitiveness Caucus; co-chair, Ukrainian and 4–H Caucuses; religion: Roman Catholic; committees: Appropriations; Budget; elected on November 2, 1982, to the 98th Congress; reelected to each succeeding Congress.

Office Listings

http://www.house.gov/kaptur

2186 Rayburn House Office Building, Washington, DC 20515 .... (202) 225–4146
Chief of Staff.—Roger Szemraj. FAX: 225–7711
Office Manager / Scheduler.—Norma Olsen.
One Maritime Plaza, Suite 600, Toledo, OH 43604 .... (419) 259–7500
Administrative Assistant.—Steve Katich.

Counties: ERIE COUNTY. CITIES AND TOWNSHIPS: Bellevue, Berlin Heights, Berlinville, Birmingham, Bloomingville, Bronson, Castalia, Chatham, Clarksfield, Collins, East Townsend, Fitchville, Hartland, Huron, Kimball, Litchfield, Milan, Mitiwanga, Monroeville, New London, Norwalk, Nova, Olena, Ridgefield, River Corners, Ruggles, Ruggles Beach, Sandusky, Shinrock, Spencer, Steuben, Sullivan, Wakeman, West Clarksfield. LORAIN COUNTY. CITIES AND TOWNSHIPS: Amherst, Beaver Park, Belden, Beulah Beach, Brownhelm, Columbia Station, Elyria, Grafton, Henrietta, Kipton, Lagrange, Linwood Park, Lorain, North Eaton, Oberlin, Ridgeville, Rochester, South Amherst, Vermilion, Wellington. LUCAS COUNTY (part). CITIES AND TOWNSHIPS: Berkey, Curtice, Gypsum, Harbor View, Holland, Maumee, Monclova, Northwood, Oregon, Swanton, Sylvania, Toledo, Waterville, Whitehouse, Woodville. OTTAWA COUNTY. CITIES AND TOWNSHIPS: Bay Shore, Bono, Catawba Island, Clay Center, Danbury, Eagle Beach, Elliston, Elmore, Gem Beach, Genoa, Graytown, Hessville, Isle St. George, Kelleys Island, Lacarne, Lakeside, Lindsey, Marblehead, Martin, Oak Harbor, Port Clinton, Portage, Put-in-Bay, Rocky Ridge, Springbrook, Vickery, Washington, Wayne, Whites Landing, and Williston. Population (2000), 630,730.

ZIP Codes: 43408, 43412, 43416, 43430, 43432–34, 43436, 43438–40, 43442, 43445–47, 43449, 43452, 43456, 43458, 43464, 43468–69, 43504, 43528, 43537, 43542, 43558, 43560, 43566, 43571, 43601–18, 43620, 43623–24, 43635, 43652, 43656–57, 43659–61, 43666–67, 43681–82, 43697, 43699, 44001, 44028, 44035, 44044, 44049–50, 44053, 44074, 44089–90, 44253, 44256, 44275, 44280, 44811, 44814, 44816, 44824, 44826, 44839, 44846–47, 44851, 44857, 44859, 44870–71, 44880, 44889

* * *

TENTH DISTRICT

DENNIS J. KUCINICH, Democrat, of Cleveland, OH; born in Cleveland, October 8, 1946; B.A., and M.A. in speech and communications, Case Western Reserve University, 1974; editor, professor; Cleveland City Councilman, 1969–75; Clerk of the Municipal Court, 1975–77; Mayor of Cleveland, 1977–79; Ohio Senate, 1994–96; named outstanding Ohio Senator by National Association of Social Workers for his work on health and social welfare issues; one child, Jackie; committees: Education and Labor; Oversight and Government Reform; elected to the 105th Congress; reelected to each succeeding Congress.

Office Listings

http://kucinich.house.gov

2445 Rayburn House Office Building, Washington, DC 20515 .... (202) 225–5871
Chief of Staff.—Jaron Bourke. FAX: 225–5745
Legislative Director.—Auke Mahar-Piersma.
14400 Detroit Avenue, Lakewood, OH 44107 .... (216) 228–8850

Counties: CUYAHOGA COUNTY (part). CITIES AND TOWNSHIPS: Bay Village, Berea, Brooklyn, Brooklyn Heights, Cleveland, Cuyahaga Heights, Fairview Park, Lakewood, Newberg Heights, North Olmsted, Olmsted Falls, Olmsted Township, Parma, Rocky River, Seven Hills, Strongsville, and Westlake. Population (2000), 630,730.

ZIP Codes: 44017, 44070, 44102, 44105, 44107, 44109, 44111, 44113, 44115–16, 44125–27, 44129–31, 44134–42, 44144–46, 44149, 44181

* * *

ELEVENTH DISTRICT

STEPHANIE TUBBS JONES, Democrat, of Cleveland, OH; born in Cleveland, September 10, 1949; B.A., Case Western Reserve University, 1971; J.D., Case Western Reserve University, 1974; Prosecutor, Cuyahoga County, OH; Judge of Common Pleas and Municipal Courts; Baptist; married: Mervyn, deceased; one son: Mervyn II; committees: chair, Standards of Official Conduct; Ways and Means; elected to the 106th Congress; reelected to each succeeding Congress.

Office Listings

http://www.house.gov/tubbsjones

1009 Longworth House Office Building, Washington, DC 20515 .... (202) 225–7032
Chief of Staff.—Patrice Willoughby. FAX: 225–1339
Legislative Director.—Melvenia Gueye.
Communications Director.—Nicole Williams.
Scheduler.—Lalla King.
3645 Warrensville Center Road, Suite 204, Shaker Heights, OH 44122 .... (216) 522–4900

Counties: CUYAHOGA COUNTY (part). CITIES: Beachwood, Bedford, Bedford Heights, Bratenahl Village, Cleveland, Cleveland Heights, East Cleveland, Euclid, Garfield Heights, Highland Hills, Linndale, Lyndhurst, Maple Heights, Mayfield Heights, North Randall, Oakwood, Oakwood Village, Orange, Orange Village, Pepper Pike, Richmond Heights, Shaker Heights, South Euclid, University Heights, Warrensville Heights, and Woodmere, Woodmere Village. Population (2000), 630,730.

ZIP Codes: 44022, 44101–06, 44108–10, 44112–15, 44117–25, 44127–28, 44132, 44137, 44143, 44146, 44178, 44185, 44188–95, 44197–99

* * *

TWELFTH DISTRICT

PATRICK J. TIBERI, Republican, of Columbus, OH; born in Columbus, October 21, 1962; education: B.A., Ohio State University, 1985; professional: real estate agent; assistant to U.S. Representative John Kasich (R–OH); public service: served as Majority Leader, Ohio House of Representatives, 1992–2000; organizations: American Red Cross Columbus Chapter Advisory Board; Westerville Chamber of Commerce; Columbus Board of Realtors; Military Veterans and Community Service Commission; Sons of Italy; awards: Fraternal Order of Police Outstanding Legislator; Watchdog of the Treasury Award; American Red Cross Volunteer Service Award; married: Denice; committees: Budget; Ways and Means; elected to the 107th Congress on November 7, 2000; reelected to each succeeding Congress.

Office Listings

http://www.house.gov/tiberi

113 Cannon House Office Building, Washington, DC 20515 .... (202) 225–5355
FAX: 226–4523
Chief of Staff.—Chris Zeigler.
Legislative Director.—Adam Francis.
Communications Director.—Breann Gonzalez.
3000 Corporate Drive, Suite 310, Columbus, OH 43231 .... (614) 523–2555
District Director.—Mark Bell.

Counties: DELAWARE, FRANKLIN (part), LICKING (part). Population (2000), 630,730.

ZIP Codes: 43001–04, 43011, 43013, 43015–18, 43021, 43023, 43025–27, 43031–33, 43035, 43040, 43046, 43054–56, 43061–62, 43064–66, 43068, 43071, 43073–74, 43080–82, 43085–86, 43105, 43147, 43201, 43203, 43205–07, 43209, 43211, 43213–15, 43218–19, 43224, 43226–27, 43229–32, 43235–36, 43240, 43334, 43342, 43344, 43356

* * *

THIRTEENTH DISTRICT

BETTY SUTTON, Democrat, of Copley, OH; born in Barberton, OH, July 31, 1963; education: B.A., Kent State University, Kent, OH, 1985; J.D., University of Akron, Akron, OH, 1990; professional: lawyer, private practice; city council, Barberton, OH, 1991–92; member, Ohio House of Representatives, state of Ohio, 1993–2000; married: Doug Corwon; committees: Budget; Rules; elected to the 110th Congress on November 7, 2006.

Office Listings

http://www.sutton.house.gov

1721 Longworth House Office Building, Washington, DC 20515 .... (202) 225–3401
FAX: 225–2266
205 West Twentieth Street, M–230, Lorain, OH 44052 .... (440) 245–5350
1655 West Market Street, Room 435, Akron, OH 44313 .... (330) 865–8450

Counties: CUYAHOGA (part), LORAIN (part), MEDINA (part), SUMMIT (part). CITIES AND TOWNSHIPS: Akron, Lorain, Elyria, N. Ridgeville, Brunswick, Strongsville, and N. Royalton. Population (2000), 630,730.

ZIP Codes: 44001, 44011–12, 44028, 44035–36, 44039, 44044, 44052–55, 44133, 44136, 44141, 44147, 44149, 44203, 44210, 44212, 44216, 44221–24, 44230, 44233, 44253, 44256, 44264, 44280–81, 44286, 44301–04, 44306–14, 44317, 44319–22, 44325–26, 44328, 44333–34, 44372, 44393, 44398–99, 44614, 44645, 44685, 44720

* * *

FOURTEENTH DISTRICT

STEVEN C. LATOURETTE, Republican, of Concord, OH; born in Cleveland, OH, July 22, 1954; education: graduated, Cleveland Heights High School, 1972; B.A., University of Michigan, 1976; J.D., Cleveland State University, 1979; professional: assistant public defender, Lake County, OH, Public Defender's Office, 1980–83; associated with Painesville firm of Cannon, Stern, Aveni and Krivok, 1983–86; Baker, Hackenberg and Collins, 1986–88; prosecuting attorney, Lake County, OH, 1988–94; served on the Lake County Budget Commission; executive board of the Lake County Narcotics Agency; chairman, County Task Force on Domestic Violence; trustee, Cleveland Policy Historical Society; director, Regional Forensic Laboratory; member: Lake County Association of Police Chiefs, Ohio Prosecuting Attorneys Association, and National District Attorneys Association; appointed to serve as a fellow of the American College of Prosecuting Attorneys; married: Jennifer; children: Sarah, Sam, Clare, Amy, and Emma; committees: Financial Services; Transportation and Infrastructure; elected to the 104th Congress; reelected to each succeeding Congress.

Office Listings

http://www.house.gov/latourette

2371 Rayburn House Office Building, Washington, DC 20515 .... (202) 225–5731
Chief of Staff.—Matt Wallen. FAX: 225–3307
Communications Director.—Deborah Setliff.
Executive Assistant / Scheduler.—Kathy Kato.
1 Victoria Place, Room 320, Painesville, OH 44077 .... (440) 352–3939

Counties: ASHTABULA, CUYAHOGA (part), GEAUGA, LAKE, PORTAGE (part), SUMMIT (part), TRUMBULL (part). Population (2000), 630,730.

ZIP Codes: 44003–05, 44010, 44021–24, 44026, 44030, 44032–33, 44040–41, 44045–48, 44056–57, 44060–62, 44064–65, 44067–68, 44072–73, 44076–77, 44080–82, 44084–88, 44092–97, 44099, 44124, 44139, 44141, 44143, 44202, 44221, 44223–24, 44231, 44234, 44236–37, 44240, 44255, 44262, 44264, 44278, 44404, 44410, 44417–18, 44428, 44439, 44450, 44470, 44491

* * *

FIFTEENTH DISTRICT

DEBORAH PRYCE, Republican, of Columbus, OH; born in Warren, OH, July 29, 1951; education: B.A., *cum laude,* Ohio State University, Columbus, 1973; J.D., Capital University Law School, Columbus, OH, 1976; professional: attorney; admitted to the Ohio bar in 1976; administrative law judge, Ohio Department of Insurance, 1976–78; first assistant city prosecutor, senior assistant city attorney, and assistant city attorney, Columbus City Attorney's Office, 1978–85; judge, Franklin County Municipal Court, presiding judge for two terms; awards: Ohio Supreme Court Victims of Crime Award, 1986–92; YWCA Woman of the Year Award, 1995; Ohio Women's Hall of Fame Inductee, 2001; member: Ohio Supreme Court Committee on Dispute Resolution; chair, Municipal Court Subcommittee; board member, National Fund for the U.S. Botanic Garden; Board member, John F. Kennedy Center for the Performing Arts; delegate to Australia, American Council of Young Political Leaders, 1986; session member, former deacon and stewardship chair, Indianola Presbyterian Church; 103rd Congress freshman class policy director; 104th Congress transition team; elected Republican Conference Secretary for the 105th Congress; elected Republican Conference vice-chair, 107th Congress; elected Republican Conference chair, 108th and 109th Congresses; children: Caroline (deceased), and Mia; committees: Financial Services; National Republican Congressional Committee; Executive Committee; Deputy Whip; elected to the 103rd Congress; reelected to each succeeding Congress.

Office Listings

http://www.house.gov/pryce

320 Cannon House Office Building, Washington, DC 20515 .... (202) 225–2015
Chief of Staff.—Lori Salley. FAX: 225–3529
Legislative Director.—Peter Freeman.
Executive Assistant.—Natasha Prolago.
500 South Front Street, Room1130, Columbus, OH 43215 .... (614) 469–5614
District Director.—Marcee McCreary.

Counties: FRANKLIN (part), MADISON, UNION. Population (2000), 630,730.

ZIP Codes: 43007, 43015–17, 43026, 43029, 43036, 43040–41, 43044–45, 43060–61, 43064–67, 43077, 43084–85, 43110, 43119, 43123, 43125–26, 43137, 43140, 43143, 43146, 43151, 43153, 43162, 43196, 43198, 43201–04, 43206–07, 43210–12, 43214–16, 43220–24, 43228–29, 43231–32, 43234–35, 43251, 43260, 43265–66, 43268, 43270–72, 43279, 43287, 43291, 43299, 43302, 43319, 43340, 43342, 43344, 43358, 45368–69

* * *

SIXTEENTH DISTRICT

RALPH REGULA, Republican, of Navarre, OH; born in Beach City, OH, December 3, 1924; education: B.A., Mount Union College, Alliance, OH, 1948; LL.B., William McKinley School of Law, Canton, OH, 1952; military service: U.S. Navy, 1944–46; professional: attorney at law; admitted to Ohio bar and began practice in Navarre, OH, 1952; Ohio House of Representatives, 1965–66, and Ohio Senate, 1967–72; member: Ohio State Board of Education, 1960–64; Saint Timothy Episcopal Church, Massillon, OH; board of trustees, Mount Union College; honorary member, board of advisors, Walsh College; Kiwanis; Grange; trustee, Stark County Historical Society; married: Mary Ann Rogusky, 1950; children: Martha, David, and Richard; committees: Appropriations; elected to the 93rd Congress, November 7, 1972; reelected to each succeeding Congress.

Office Listings

http://www.house.gov/regula

2306 Rayburn House Office Building, Washington, DC 20515 .... (202) 225–3876
Chief of Staff / Press Secretary.—Lori Rowley. FAX: 225–3059
Executive Assistant.—Sylvia Snyder.
Legislative Director.—Rick Limardo.
Assistant.—Viquar Ahmad.
4150 Belden Village Street NW, Suite 408, Canton, OH 44718 .... (330) 489–4414
District Staff Director.—Robert Mullen.
124 West Washington Street, Suite 1A, Medina, OH 44256 .... (330) 722–3793

Counties: ASHLAND (part), MEDINA (part), STARK, WAYNE. Population (2000), 630,730.

ZIP Codes: 44090, 44201, 44203, 44214–17, 44230, 44233, 44235, 44251, 44253–54, 44256, 44258, 44260, 44270, 44273–76, 44280–82, 44287, 44321, 44333, 44601, 44606, 44608, 44611–14, 44618, 44624, 44626–27, 44630, 44632, 44634, 44636, 44638, 44640–41, 44643, 44645–48, 44650, 44652, 44657, 44659, 44662, 44666–67, 44669–70, 44676–77, 44680, 44685, 44688–89, 44691, 44701–12, 44714, 44718, 44720–21, 44730, 44735, 44750, 44760, 44767, 44799, 44805, 44822, 44838, 44840, 44842–43, 44864, 44866, 44878, 44880, 44903

* * *

SEVENTEENTH DISTRICT

TIM RYAN, Democrat, of Niles, OH; born in Niles, July 16, 1973; education: B.S., Bowling Green University, 1995; J.D., Franklin Pierce Law Center, 2000; awarded a National Italian American Foundation Scholarship; professional: attorney; internship, Trumbull County Prosecutor's Office; also worked as a congressional legislative aide in Washington, DC; organizations: former president, Trumbull County Young Democrats; former chairman, Earning by Learning Program in Warren, OH; public service: Ohio State Senate, 2000–02; religion: Catholic; committees: Appropriations; elected to the 108th Congress on November 5, 2002; reelected to each succeeding Congress.

Office Listings

http://timryan.house.gov

1421 Longworth House Office Building, Washington, DC 20515 .... (202) 225–5261
Chief of Staff.—Mary Anne Walsh. FAX: 225–3719
Scheduler.—Erin Isenberg.
Legislative Director.—Ryan Keating.
197 West Market Street, Warren, OH 44481 .... (330) 373–0074
241 Federal Plaza West, Youngstown, OH 44503 .... (330) 740–0193

Counties: MAHONING (part), PORTAGE (part), SUMMIT (part), TRUMBULL (part). Population (2000), 630,730.

ZIP Codes: 44201, 44211, 44221, 44223–24, 44231–32, 44236, 44240–43, 44250, 44255, 44260, 44265–66, 44272, 44278, 44285, 44288, 44302–06, 44308, 44310–13, 44315–16, 44319, 44402–06, 44410–12, 44417–18, 44420, 44424–25, 44429–30, 44436–38, 44440, 44444, 44446, 44449–50, 44453, 44470–71, 44473, 44481–86, 44488, 44491, 44501–07, 44509–12, 44514–15, 44555, 44599, 44632, 44685, 44720

* * *

EIGHTEENTH DISTRICT

ZACHARY T. SPACE, Democrat, of Dover, OH; born in Dover, OH, January 27, 1961; education: graduated from Dover High School, Dover, OH, 1979; B.A., Kenyon College, Gambier,

OH, 1983; J.D., The Ohio State University, 1986; professional: lawyer, private practice; Dover, Law Director, 2000–06; married: Mary Space; children: Gina and Nicholas; committees: Agriculture; Transportation and Infrastructure; Veterans' Affairs; elected to the 110th Congress on November 7, 2006.

Office Listings

http://www.house.gov/space

315 Cannon House Office Building, Washington, DC 20515 .... (202) 225–6265
FAX: 225–3394
Chief of Staff.—Stuart Chapman.
Scheduler.—Julie Ross.
Legislative Director.—Aaron Schmidt.
Communications Director.—Stuart Chapman.

137 East Iron Avenue, Dover, OH 44622 .... (330) 364–4300
Toll-free (866) 910–7577
District Director.—Ken Engstrom.

17 North Fourth Street, Zanesville, OH 43701 .... (740) 452–6338

14 South Paint Street, Suite 6, Chillicothe, OH 45601 .... (740) 779–1636

Counties: ATHENS (part), BELMONT (PART), CARROLL, COSHOCTON, GUERNSEY, HARRISON, HOCKING, HOLMES, JACKSON, KNOX, LICKING (part), MORGAN, MUSKINGUM, ROSS (part), TUSCARAWAS, VINTON. Population (2000), 630,730.

ZIP Codes: 43005–06, 43008, 43011, 43014, 43019, 43022–23, 43025, 43028, 43030, 43037, 43048, 43050, 43055–56, 43058, 43071, 43076, 43080, 43093, 43098, 43101–02, 43107, 43111, 43127, 43130, 43135, 43138, 43144, 43149, 43152, 43155, 43158, 43160, 43701–02, 43718, 43720–25, 43727–28, 43730–36, 43738–40, 43746, 43749–50, 43755–56, 43758, 43760, 43762, 43766–68, 43771–73, 43777–78, 43780, 43787, 43791, 43802–05, 43811–12, 43821–22, 43824, 43828, 43830, 43832, 43836–37, 43840, 43842–45, 43901, 43903, 43906–08, 43910, 43927–28, 43933, 43945, 43950, 43972–74, 43976–77, 43981, 43983–84, 43986, 43988, 44427, 44607–08, 44610–12, 44615, 44617, 44620–22, 44624–29, 44631, 44633, 44637–39, 44643–44, 44651, 44653–54, 44656–57, 44660–61, 44663, 44671, 44675–76, 44678–83, 44687–90, 44693, 44695, 44697, 44699, 44730, 44813, 44822, 44842, 45123, 45601, 45612–13, 45617, 45621–22, 45628, 45633–34, 45640, 45644, 45647, 45651, 45653–54, 45656, 45672–73, 45681–82, 45685, 45690, 45692, 45695, 45698, 45701, 45710–11, 45715–16, 45719, 45732, 45740–41, 45761, 45764, 45766, 45780, 45782, 45786

OKLAHOMA

(Population 2000, 3,450,654)

SENATORS

JAMES M. INHOFE, Republican, of Tulsa, OK; born in Des Moines, IA, November 17, 1934; education: graduated Central High School, Tulsa, OK, 1953; B.A., University of Tulsa, OK, 1959; military service: served in the U.S. Army, private first class, 1957–58; professional: businessman; active pilot; president, Quaker Life Insurance Company; Oklahoma House of Representatives, 1967–69; Oklahoma State Senate, 1969–77; Mayor of Tulsa, OK, 1978–84; religion: member, First Presbyterian Church of Tulsa; married: the former Kay Kirkpatrick; children: Jim, Perry, Molly, and Katy; eleven grandchildren; committees: ranking member, Environment and Public Works; Armed Services; elected to the 100th Congress on November 4, 1986; reelected to each succeeding Congress; elected to the U.S. Senate on November 8, 1994, finishing the unexpired term of Senator David Boren; reelected to each succeeding Senate term.

Office Listings

http://inhofe.senate.gov

453 Russell Senate Office Building, Washington, DC 20510 .... (202) 224–4721
FAX: 228–0380
Chief of Staff.—Glenn Powell.
Legislative Director.—Aloysius Hogan.
Press Secretary.—Ryan Thompson.
Scheduler.—Wendi Price.
1924 South Utica, Suite 530, Tulsa, OK 74104–6511 .... (918) 748–5111
1900 Northwest Expressway, Suite 1210, Oklahoma City, OK 73118 .... (405) 608–4381
302 North Independence, Suite 104, Enid, OK 73701 .... (580) 234–5101
215 East Choctaw, Suite 106, McAlester, OK 74501 .... (918) 426–0933

* * *

TOM COBURN, Republican, of Muskogee, OK; born in Casper, WY, March 14, 1948; education: Central High School, Muskogee, OK, 1955; B.S., Oklahoma State University, 1970; Oklahoma University Medical School, 1983; professional: manufacturing manager, Coburn Ophthalmic Division, Coburn Optical Industries, 1970–78; family physician, 1983–present; member, American Medical Association, Oklahoma State Medical Association, East Central County Medical Society, American Academy of Family Practice; religion: First Baptist Church, ordained deacon; member, Promise Keepers; public service: U.S. House of Representatives, 1995–2001; married: Carolyn Denton Coburn, 1968; children: Callie, Katie, and Sarah; committees: Health, Education, Labor, and Pensions; Homeland Security and Government Affairs; Indian Affairs; Judiciary; elected to the U.S. Senate on November 2, 2004.

Office Listings

http://coburn.senate.gov

172 Russell Hart Senate Office Building, Washington, DC 20510 .... (202) 224–5754
FAX: 224–6008
Chief of Staff.—Michael Schwartz.
Legislative Director.—Roland Foster.
Communications Director.—John Hart.
Scheduler.—Courtney Shadegg.
1800 South Baltimore, Suite 800, Tulsa, OK 74119 .... (918) 581–7651
100 North Broadway, Suite 1820, Oklahoma City, OK 73102 .... (405) 231–4941

REPRESENTATIVES

FIRST DISTRICT

JOHN SULLIVAN, Republican, of Tulsa, OK; born in Tulsa, January 1, 1965; education: B.B.A., Northeastern State University, 1992; professional: fuel sales, Love's Country Stores; Real Estate, McGraw, Davison, Stewart; public service: Oklahoma House of Representatives, 1995–2002; organizations: member, St. Mary's Church; member, National Rifle Association; member, Tulsa County Republican Men's Club; U.S. House of Representatives Assistant Majority Whip; family: married to Judy; children: Thomas, Meredith, Sydney, Daniel; committees: Energy and Commerce; Select Committee on Energy Independence and Global Warming; elected to the 107th Congress, by special election, on January 8, 2002; reelected to each succeeding Congress.

Office Listings

http://sullivan.house.gov

114 Cannon House Office Building, Washington, DC 20510 .... (202) 225–2211
Chief of Staff.—Elizabeth Bartheld. FAX: 225–9187
Scheduler.—Morgan Levy.
5727 S. Lewis, Suite 520, Tulsa, OK 74105 .... (918) 749–0014
Chief of Staff.—Richard Hedgecock.

Counties: CREEK (part), ROGERS (part), TULSA, WAGONER, WASHINGTON. Population (2000), 690,131.

ZIP Codes: 74003–06, 74008, 74011–14, 74021–22, 74029, 74033, 74037, 74039, 74041, 74043, 74047–48, 74050–51, 74053, 74055, 74061, 74063, 74066, 74070, 74073, 74080, 74082–83, 74101–08, 74110, 74112, 74114–17, 74119–21, 74126–30, 74132–37, 74141, 74145–50, 74152–53, 74155–59, 74169–72, 74182–84, 74186–87, 74189, 74192–94, 74337, 74352, 74403, 74429, 74434, 74436, 74446, 74454, 74458, 74467, 74477

* * *

SECOND DISTRICT

DAN BOREN, Democrat, of Muskogee, OK; born in Shawnee, OK, August 2, 1973; education: B.S., Texas Christian University, Fort Worth, TX, 1997; M.B.A., University of Oklahoma, 2001; professional: president, Seminole State College Educational Foundation; vice-president, Robbins Energy Corporation; loan processor, Banc First Corporation; staff for United States Representative Wesley Watkins; education administrator; bank teller; aide, Oklahoma Corporation Commission; member of the Oklahoma State House of Representatives, 2002–04; organizations: Big Brothers Big Sisters Board; The Jasmine Moran Children's Museum Board; KIPP Foundation Board Member; married: Andrea; committees: Armed Services; Financial Services; Natural Resources; elected to the 109th Congress on November 2, 2004; reelected to the 110th Congress.

Office Listings

http://www.house.gov/boren

216 Cannon House Office Building, Washington, DC 20515 .... (202) 225–2701
Chief of Staff.—Bill Blumenthal. FAX: 225–3038
Legislative Director.—Jason Buckner.
Press Secretary.—Nick Choate.
Scheduler.—Erica Giers.
431 West Broadway, Muskogee, OK 74401 .... (918) 687–2533
District Coordinator.—Ward Curtin.
309 West 1st Street, Claremore, OK 74017 .... (918) 341–9336
Field Representative.—Marguerite McKinney.
321 South Third, Suite 4, McAlester, OK 74501 .... (918) 423–5951
Case Worker.—Janice Beatty.

Counties: ADAIR, ATOKA, BRYAN, CANADIAN, CHEROKEE, CHOCTAW, COAL, CRAIG, CREEK, DELAWARE, HASKELL, HUGHES, JOHNSTON, LATIMER, LEFLORE, MAYES, MCCURTAIN, MCINTOSH, MUSKOGEE, NOWATA, OKFUSKEE, OTTAWA, PAWNEE, PITTSBURG, PUSHMATAHA, ROGERS, SEMINOLE, SEQUOYAH. Population (2000), 690,130.

ZIP Codes: 73014, 73036, 73064, 73078, 73085, 73090, 73447, 73449–50, 73455, 73460–62, 74010, 74015–16, 74018, 74020, 74027–28, 74030–31, 74034, 74036, 74038–39, 74041–42, 74044–45, 74047–49, 74052–53, 74058, 74067–68, 74071–72, 74080–81, 74083, 74085, 74101, 74103, 74301, 74330–33, 74335, 74337–40, 74343–44, 74346–47, 74349–50, 74352, 74355, 74358–63, 74365–67, 74369–70, 74401–02, 74421–23, 74425–26, 74428, 74430–32, 74434–38, 74441–42, 74445, 74447, 74450, 74455, 74459, 74461–64, 74468–70, 74472, 74502, 74521–23, 74525, 74530–31, 74533–34, 74536, 74538, 74546–47, 74552–54, 74556, 74560–63, 74565, 74569–72, 74576, 74578, 74650, 74701, 74720, 74723, 74726–30, 74733, 74735–36, 74740–41, 74743, 74745, 74747–48, 74750, 74756, 74759, 74764, 74766, 74829–30, 74833, 74837, 74839, 74845, 74848–50, 74856, 74859–60, 74867–68, 74880, 74883–85, 74901–02, 74930, 74932, 74935–37, 74940–42, 74944–46, 74948, 74951, 74953–56, 74959–60, 74962, 74964–66

* * *

THIRD DISTRICT

FRANK D. LUCAS, Republican, of Cheyenne, OK; born in Cheyenne, January 6, 1960; education: B.S., Agricultural Economics, Oklahoma State University, 1982; professional: rancher and farmer; served in Oklahoma State House of Representatives, 1989–94; secretary, Oklahoma House Republican Caucus, 1991–94; member: Oklahoma Farm Bureau, Oklahoma Cattlemen's Association, and Oklahoma Shorthorn Association; married: Lynda Bradshaw Lucas; children: Jessica, Ashlea, and Grant; committees: Agriculture; Financial Services; Science and Technology; elected to the 103rd Congress, by special election, in May 1994; reelected to each succeeding Congress.

Office Listings

http://www.house.gov/lucas

2311 Rayburn House Office Building, Washington, DC 20515 .... (202) 225–5565 FAX: 225–8698
Deputy Chief of Staff.—Nicole Scott.
Communications Director.—Jim Luetkemeyer.
Scheduler / Office Manager.—Tonia Batts.
Legislative Assistants: Courtney Box, Craig Perry, Jordan Russell.
10952 Northwest Expressway, Suite B, Yukon, OK 73099 .... (405) 373–1958
Chief of Staff.—Stacey Glasscock.
720 South Husband, Suite 7, Stillwater, OK 74075 .... (405) 624–6407
Field Representative.—Lauren Detten.
2728 Williams Avenue, Suite F, Woodward, OK 73801 .... (580) 256–5752
Field Representative.—Troy White.

Counties: ALFALFA, BEAVER, BECKHAM, BLAINE, CADDO, CANADIAN (part), CIMARRON, CREEK (part), CUSTER, DEWEY, ELLIS, GARFIELD, GRANT, GREER, HARMON, HARPER, JACKSON, KINGFISHER, KAY, KIOWA, LINCOLN, LOGAN, MAJOR, NOBLE, OSAGE, PAWNEE, PAYNE, ROGER MILLS, TEXAS, WASHITA, WOODS, AND WOODWARD. CITIES: Altus, Clinton, El Reno, Elk City, Enid, Guthrie, Guymon, Oklahoma City, Perry, Ponce City, Sapulpa, Stillwater, Tulsa, Weatherford, Woodward and Yukon. Population (2000), 690,131.

ZIP Codes: 73001, 73003, 73005–07, 73009, 73014–17, 73021–22, 73024, 73027–29, 73033–34, 73036, 73038, 73040–45, 73047–48, 73050, 73053–54, 73056, 73058–59, 73061–64, 73073, 73077–79, 73085, 73090, 73092, 73094, 73096–97, 73099, 73127, 73437, 73501, 73521–23, 73526, 73532, 73537, 73539, 73544, 73547, 73549–50, 73554, 73556, 73559–60, 73564, 73566, 73571, 73601, 73620, 73622, 73624–28, 73632, 73638–39, 73641–42, 73644–48, 73650–51, 73654–55, 73658–64, 73666–69, 73673, 73701–03, 73705–06, 73716–20, 73722, 73724, 73726–31, 73733–39, 73741–44, 73746–47, 73749–50, 73753–64, 73766, 73768, 73770–73, 73801–02, 73832, 73834–35, 73838, 73840–44, 73847–48, 73851–53, 73855, 73857–60, 73901, 73931–33, 73937–39, 73942, 73944–47, 73949–51, 74001–03, 74010, 74020, 74022–23, 74026, 74028, 74030, 74032, 74034–35, 74038–39, 74044–47, 74051–52, 74054, 74056, 74058–60, 74062–63, 74066–68, 74070–71, 74073–79, 74081, 74084–85, 74106, 74126–27, 74131–32, 74601–02, 74604, 74630–33, 74636–37, 74640–41, 74643–44, 74646–47, 74650–53, 74824, 74832, 74834, 74851, 74855, 74859, 74864, 74869, 74875, 74881

* * *

FOURTH DISTRICT

TOM COLE, Republican, of Moore, OK; born in Shreveport, LA, April 28, 1949; education: B.A., Grinnell College, 1971; M.A. Yale University, 1974; Ph.D., University of Oklahoma, 1984; Watson Fellow, 1971–72; and a Fulbright Fellow, 1977–78; professional: former college professor of history and politics; President, Cole Hargrave Snodgrass & Associates (political consulting firm); public service: Oklahoma State Senate, 1988–91; Oklahoma Secretary of State, 1995–99; has served as Chairman, and Executive Director, of the Oklahoma Republican Party; currenty serving as Chairman of the National Republican Congressional Committee; and Chief of Staff of the Republican National Committee; family: married to Ellen; one child: Mason; religion: United Methodist; committees: Armed Services; Natural Resources; elected to the 108th Congress on November 5, 2002; reelected to each succeeding Congress.

Office Listings

http://www.house.gov/cole

236 Cannon House Office Building, Washington, DC 20515 .... (202) 225–6165 FAX: 225–3512
Chief of Staff.—Sean Murphy.
Legislative Director / Rules Associate.—Chris Caron.
Press Secretary.—Carmen Terry.
2420 Springer Drive, Suite 120, Norman, OK 73069 .... (405) 329–6500
711 SW., D Avenue, Suite 201, Lawton, OK 73501 .... (580) 357–2131
104 East 12th, Ada, OK 74820 .... (580) 436–5375

Counties: CANADIAN (part), CARTER, CLEVELAND, COMANCHE, COTTON, GARVIN, GRADY, JEFFERSON, LOVE, MARSHALL, MCCLAIN, MURRAY, OKLAHOMA (part), PONTOTOC, STEPHENS, TILLMAN. Population (2000), 690,131.

ZIP Codes: 73002, 73004, 73006, 73010–11, 73017–20, 73023, 73026, 73030–32, 73036, 73051–52, 73055, 73057, 73059, 73064–65, 73067–72, 73074–75, 73079–80, 73082, 73086, 73089, 73092–93, 73095, 73098–99, 73110, 73115, 73127–30, 73135, 73139–40, 73145, 73149–50, 73153, 73159–60, 73165, 73169–70, 73173, 73179, 73189, 73401–03, 73425, 73430, 73433–44, 73446, 73448, 73453, 73456, 73458–59, 73463, 73476, 73481, 73487–88, 73491, 73501–03, 73505–07, 73520, 73527–31, 73533–34, 73536, 73538, 73540–43, 73546, 73548, 73551–53, 73555, 73557, 73559, 73561–62, 73564–70, 73572–73, 74820–21, 74825, 74831, 74842–44, 74851, 74857, 74865, 74871–72

* * *

FIFTH DISTRICT

MARY FALLIN, Republican, of Oklahoma City, OK; born in Warrensburg, MO, December 9, 1954; education: attended Oklahoma Baptist University, Shawnee, OK, 1973–75; B.S., Oklahoma State University, Stillwater, OK, 1977; attended, University of Central Oklahoma, Edmond, OK, 1979–81; professional: hotel management; member of the Oklahoma State House of Representatives, 1990–94; Oklahoma Lieutenant Governor, 1995–2007; children: Christina and Price; committees: Small Business; Transportation and Infrastructure; elected to the 110th Congress on November 7, 2006.

Office Listings

http://www.house.gov/fallin

1432 Longworth House Office Building, Washington, DC 20515 .... (202) 225–2132
Chief of Staff.—Nate Webb. FAX: 226–1463
Scheduler.—Hannah Barton.
Legislative Director.—Jeff Ringer.
Communications Director.—Alex Weintz.
120 North Robinson Avenue, Suite 100, Oklahoma City, OK 73102 .... (405) 234–9900
District Director.—Devery Youngblood.
20 East 9th Street, Suite 137, Shawnee, OK 74801 .... (405) 273–1733

Counties: OKLAHOMA (part), POTTAWATOMIE, and SEMINOLE. CITIES: Arcadia, Asher, Aydelotte, Bethany, Bethel Acres, Bowlegs, Brooksville, Choctaw, Cromwell, Del City, Earlsboro, Edmond, Forrest Park, Harrah, Johnson, Jones, Konawa, Lake Aluma, Lima, Luther, Macomb, Maud, McLoud, Midwest City, Newalla, Nichols Hills, Nicoma Park, Oklahoma City, Pink, Sasakwa, Seminole, Shawnee, Smith Village, Spencer, St. Louis, Tecumesh, The Village, Tribbey, Valley Brook, Wanette, Warr Acres, Wewoka, and Woodlawn Park. Population (2000), 690,131.

ZIP Codes: 73003, 73007–08, 73013, 73020, 73034, 73045, 73049, 73054, 73066, 73078, 73083–84, 73097, 73099, 73101–32, 73134–37, 73139, 73141–49, 73151–52, 73154–57, 73159–60, 73162, 73164, 73169, 73172–73, 73178–79, 73184–85, 73190, 73194–96, 73198, 74587, 74801–02, 74804, 74818, 74826, 74830, 74837, 74840, 74849, 74851–52, 74854–55, 74857, 74859, 74866–68, 74873, 74878, 74884

OREGON

(Population 2000, 3,421,399)

SENATORS

RON WYDEN, Democrat, of Portland, OR; born in Wichita, KS, May 3, 1949; education: graduated from Palo Alto High School, 1967; B.A. in political science, with distinction, Stanford University, 1971; J.D., University of Oregon Law School, 1974; professional: attorney; member, American Bar Association; former director, Oregon Legal Services for the Elderly; former public member, Oregon State Board of Examiners of Nursing Home Administrators; co-founder and codirector, Oregon Gray Panthers, 1974–80; married: Nancy Bass Wyden; children: Adam David and Lilly Anne; committees: Budget; Energy and Natural Resources; Finance; Special Committee on Aging; Select Committee on Intelligence; elected to the 97th Congress, November 4, 1980; reelected to each succeeding Congress; elected to the U.S. Senate on February 6, 1996, to fill the unexpired term of Senator Bob Packwood; reelected to each succeeding Senate term.

Office Listings

http://wyden.senate.gov

223 Dirksen Senate Office Building, Washington, DC 20510 .... (202) 224–5244
FAX: 228–2717
Chief of Staff.—Josh Kardon.
Legislative Aides: Jeff Michels, Joshua Sheinkman.
Communications Director.—Melissa Merz.
Schedulers: Sallie Derr, Nancy Hadley.
1220 Southwest Third Avenue, Suite 585, Portland, OR 97204 .... (503) 326–7525
405 East Eighth Avenue, Suite 2020, Eugene, OR 97401 .... (541) 431–0229
The Federal Courthouse, 310 West Sixth Street, Room 118, Medford, OR 97501 ... (541) 858–5122
The Jamison Building, 131 Northwest Hawthorne Avenue, Suite 107, Bend, OR 97701 .... (541) 330–9142
SAC Annex Building, 105 Fir Street, Suite 201, LaGrande, OR 97850 .... (541) 962–7691
777 Thirteenth Street, SE, Suite 110, Salem, OR 97310 .... (503) 589–4555

* * *

GORDON HAROLD SMITH, Republican, of Pendleton, OR; born in Pendleton, May 25, 1952; B.A., Brigham Young University, 1976; LL.B, Southwestern University, 1979; served as law clerk to Justice H. Vernon Payne of the New Mexico Supreme Court and practiced law in Arizona; elected to State of Oregon Senate, 1993; elected Oregon Senate President, 1994; president/owner of Smith Frozen Foods, Inc., since 1981; married: Sharon Lankford Smith, 1975; three children: Brittany, Garrett, and Morgan; committees: Commerce, Science, and Transportation; Energy and Natural Resources; Finance; Indian Affairs; Special Committee on Aging; elected to the U.S. Senate on November 5, 1996; reelected to each succeeding Senate term.

Office Listings

http://gsmith.senate.gov

404 Russell Senate Office Building, Washington, DC 20510 .... (202) 224–3753
FAX: 228–3997
Chief of Staff.—John Easton.
Legislative Director.—Rob Epplin.
Director of Administration.—Sue Keenom.
Communications Director.—R.C. Hammond.
121 SW Salmon, Suite 1250, Portland, OR 97204 .... (503) 326–3386
Jager Building, 116 South Main Street, Suite 3, Pendleton, OR 97801 .... (541) 278–1129
Wayne Morse Federal Courthouse, 405 East 8th Avenue, Suite 2010, Eugene, OR 97401 .... (541) 465–6750
Security Plaza, 1175 East Main Street, Suite 2D, Medford, OR 97504 .... (541) 608–9102
Jamison Building, 131 NW Hawthorne Avenue, Suite 208, Bend, OR 97701 .... (541) 318–1298

REPRESENTATIVES

FIRST DISTRICT

DAVID WU, Democrat, of Portland, OR; born in Taiwan, April 8, 1955; moved to the United States, with his family, in October, 1961; education: B.S., Stanford University, 1977; attended, Harvard University Medical School; law degree, Yale University, 1982; professional:

lawyer; co-founder of Cohen & Wu (law firm), 1988; first Chinese American member of the U.S. House of Representatives; past chair, Congressional Asian Pacific American Caucus; member, New Democrat Coalition; married: Michelle; two children: Matthew and Sarah; committees: Education and Labor; Foreign Affairs; Science and Technology; elected to the 106th Congress; reelected to each succeeding Congress.

Office Listings

http://www.house.gov/wu

2338 Rayburn House Office Building, Washington, DC 20515 .... (202) 225–0855
Chief of Staff.—Julie Tippens. FAX: 225–9497
Executive Assistant.—Lisa Bianco.
Press Secretary.—Jillian Schoene.
620 Southwest Main Street, Suite 606, Portland, OR 97205 .... (503) 326–2901

Counties: CLATSOP, COLUMBIA, MULTNOMAH (part), WASHINGTON, YAMHILL. Population (2000), 684,277.

ZIP Codes: 97005–08, 97016, 97018, 97035, 97048, 97051, 97053–54, 97056, 97062, 97064, 97070, 97075–78, 97101–03, 97106, 97109–11, 97113–17, 97119, 97121, 97123–25, 97127–28, 97132–33, 97138, 97140, 97144–46, 97148, 97201, 97204–05, 97207–10, 97219, 97221, 97223–25, 97228–29, 97231, 97239–40, 97251, 97253–55, 97258, 97272, 97280–81, 97291, 97296, 97298, 97378, 97396, 97498

* * *

SECOND DISTRICT

GREG WALDEN, Republican, of Hood River, OR; born in The Dalles, OR, January 10, 1957; education: B.S., Journalism, University of Oregon, 1981; member: Associated Oregon Industries; Oregon Health Sciences Foundation; Hood River Rotary Club; Hood River Elk's Club; National Federation of Independent Business; Hood River Chamber of Commerce; Hood River Memorial Hospital; Columbia Bancorp; Oregon State House of Representatives, 1989–95, and Majority Leader, 1991–93; Assistant Majority Leader, Oregon State Senate, 1995–97; awards: Oregon Jaycees Outstanding Young Oregonian, 1991; National Republican Legislators Association Legislator of the Year, 1993; married: Mylene Walden; one child: Anthony David Walden; committees: Energy and Commerce; Select Committee on Energy Independence and Global Warming; elected to the 106th Congress; reelected to each succeeding Congress.

Office Listings

http://www.walden.house.gov

1210 Longworth House Office Building, Washington, DC 20515 .... (202) 225–6730
Chief of Staff.—Brian MacDonald. FAX: 225–5774
Senior Policy Advisors: Valerie Henry, Colby Marshall.
Executive Assistant.—Blair Larkens.
843 East Main, Suite 400, Medford, OR 97504 .... (541) 776–4646
District Director.—John Snider. (800) 533–3303
131 Northwest Hawthorne Street, Suite 201, Bend, OR 97701 .... (541) 389–4408

Counties: BAKER, CROOK, DESCHUTES, GILLIAM, GRANT, HARNEY, HOOD RIVER, JACKSON, JEFFERSON, JOSEPHINE (part), KLAMATH, LAKE, MALHEUR, MORROW, SHERMAN, UMATILLA, UNION, WALLOWA, WASCO, WHEELER. Population (2000), 684,280.

ZIP Codes: 97001, 97014, 97021, 97029, 97031, 97033, 97037, 97039–41, 97044, 97050, 97057–58, 97063, 97065, 97116, 97425, 97501–04, 97520, 97522, 97524–28, 97530, 97533, 97535–37, 97539–41, 97544, 97601–04, 97620–27, 97630, 97632–41, 97701–02, 97707–12, 97720–22, 97730–39, 97741, 97750–54, 97756, 97758–61, 97801, 97810, 97812–14, 97817–20, 97823–28, 97830, 97833–46, 97848, 97850, 97856–57, 97859, 97861–62, 97864–65, 97867–70, 97873–77, 97880, 97882–86, 97901–11, 97913–14, 97917–18, 97920

* * *

THIRD DISTRICT

EARL BLUMENAUER, Democrat, of Portland, OR; born in Portland, August 16, 1948; education: graduated from Centennial High School; Lewis and Clark College; J.D., Northwestern School of Law; professional: assistant to the president, Portland State University; served in Oregon State Legislature 1973–78; chaired Revenue and School Finance Committee; Multnomah County Commissioner, 1978–85; Portland City Commissioner 1986–96; served on Governor's Commission on Higher Education; National League of Cities Transportation Committee; National Civic League Board of Directors; Oregon Environmental Council; Oregon

Public Broadcasting; married: Margaret Kirkpatrick; children: Jon and Anne; committees: Budget; Ways and Means; Select Committee on Energy Independence and Global Warming; elected to the U.S. House of Representatives on May 21, 1996, to fill the vacancy created by Representative Ron Wyden's election to the U.S. Senate; reelected to each succeeding Congress.

Office Listings

http://blumenauer.house.gov

2267 Rayburn House Office Building, Washington, DC 20515 .... (202) 225–4811
Deputy Chief of Staff.—James Koski. FAX: 225–8941
Communications Director.—Erin Allweiss.
Legislative Director.—Janine Benner.
729 Northeast Oregon Street, Suite 115, Portland, OR 97232 .... (503) 231–2300
District Director.—Julia Pomeroy.

Counties: MULTNOMAH (part), CLAKAMUS (part). Population (2000), 684,279.

ZIP Codes: 97004, 97009, 97011, 97014–15, 97017, 97019, 97022–24, 97028, 97030, 97035, 97045, 97049, 97055, 97060, 97067, 97080, 97124, 97133, 97202–03, 97206, 97210–18, 97220, 97222, 97227, 97229–33, 97236, 97238, 97242, 97256, 97266–67, 97269, 97282–83, 97286, 97290, 97292–94, 97299

* * *

FOURTH DISTRICT

PETER A. DEFAZIO, Democrat, of Springfield, OR; born in Needham, MA, May 27, 1947; B.A., Tufts University, 1969; M.S., University of Oregon, 1977; professional: aide to Representative Jim Weaver, 1977–82; commissioner, Lane County, 1983–86; married: Myrnie Daut; committees: Homeland Security; Natural Resources; Transportation and Infrastructure; elected to the 100th Congress, November 4, 1986; reelected to each succeeding Congress.

Office Listings

http://www.house.gov/defazio

2134 Rayburn House Office Building, Washington, DC 20515 .... (202) 225–6416
Chief of Staff.—Penny Dodge. FAX: 225–0032
Legislative Director.—Tom Vinson.
Scheduler.—Jamie Harrell.
405 East Eighth Avenue, Suite 2030, Eugene, OR 97401 .... (541) 465–6732
District Director.—Karmen Fore.
125 Central Avenue, Room 350, Coos Bay, OR 97420 .... (541) 269–2609
612 Southeast Jackson Street, Room 9, Roseburg, OR 97470 .... (541) 440–3523

Counties: BENTON (part), COOS, CURRY, DOUGLAS, JOSEPHINE (part), LANE, LINN. CITIES: Eugene, Roseburg, and Coos Bay. Population (2000), 684,280.

ZIP Codes: 97321–22, 97324, 97326–27, 97329–30, 97333, 97335–36, 97345–46, 97348, 97350, 97352, 97355, 97358, 97360–61, 97370, 97374, 97377, 97383, 97386, 97389, 97401–17, 97419–20, 97423–24, 97426–32, 97434–44, 97446–59, 97461–67, 97469–70, 97472–73, 97476–82, 97484, 97486–99, 97523, 97526–27, 97530–34, 97537–38, 97543–44

* * *

FIFTH DISTRICT

DARLENE HOOLEY, Democrat, of West Linn, OR; born in Williston, ND, April 4, 1939; education: B.S., Oregon State University; professional: teacher; past member: Oregon House of Representatives, West Linn City Council, Clackamas County Board of Commissioners; children: Chad and Erin; committees: Budget; Energy and Commerce; Science and Technology; elected to the 105th Congress; reelected to each succeeding Congress.

Office Listings

http://house.gov/hooley

2430 Rayburn House Office Building, Washington, DC 20515 .... (202) 225–5711
Chief of Staff / Press.—Joan Mooney-Evans. FAX: 225–5699
Executive Assistant / Scheduler.—Anne Marie Feeney.
Legislative Director.—Chris Huckleberry.

315 Mission Street, Suite 101, Salem, OR 97302 .... (503) 588–9100

21570 Williamette Drive West, Linn, OR 97068 .... (503) 557–1324
District Director.—Suzanne Kunse.

Counties: BENTON (part); CLACKAMAS (part); LINCOLN; MARION; MULTNOMAH (part); POLK; TILLAMOOK. CITIES: Corvallis, Portland, Salem, and Tillamook. Population (2000), 684,333.

ZIP Codes: 97002, 97004, 97010, 97013, 97015, 97017, 97020, 97023, 97026–27, 97032, 97034–36, 97038, 97042, 97045, 97062, 97068, 97070–71, 97101, 97107–08, 97112, 97118, 97122, 97130–31, 97134–37, 97140–41, 97143, 97147, 97149, 97201, 97219, 97222, 97239, 97267–68, 97301–14, 97321, 97324–25, 97330–31, 97333, 97338–39, 97341–44, 97346–47, 97350–52, 97357–62, 97364–73, 97375–76, 97380–81, 97383–85, 97388, 97390–92, 97394, 97396, 97498

PENNSYLVANIA

(Population 2000, 12,281,054)

SENATORS

ARLEN SPECTER, Republican, of Philadelphia, PA; born in Wichita, KS, February 12, 1930; education: graduated, Russell High School, Russell, KS, 1947; B.A., international relations, Phi Beta Kappa, University of Pennsylvania, 1951; LL.B., Yale Law School, 1956; board of editors, *Law Journal*; military service: served in U.S. Air Force, 1951–53, attaining rank of first lieutenant; professional: member, law firm of Dechert, Price and Rhoads before and after serving two terms as district attorney of Philadelphia, 1966–74; married: former Joan Levy, who was elected to the city council of Philadelphia in 1979; children: Shanin and Stephen; served as assistant counsel to the Warren Commission, 1964; served on Pennsylvania's State Planning Board, The White House Conference on Youth, The National Commission on Criminal Justice, and the Peace Corps National Advisory Council; committees: Appropriations; Judiciary; Veterans' Affairs; Special Committee on Aging; elected to the U.S. Senate on November 4, 1980; reelected to each succeeding Senate term.

Office Listings

http://specter.senate.gov

711 Hart Senate Office Building, Washington, DC 20510 .... (202) 224–4254
Chief of Staff.—Scott Hoeflich. FAX: 228–1229
Legislative Director.—Tom Dower.
Administrative Director.—Reagan Blewett.
600 Arch Street, Suite 9400, Philadelphia, PA 19106 .... (215) 597–7200
Regional Enterprise Tower, 425 Sixth Avenue, Suite 1450, Pittsburgh, PA 15219–1837 .... (412) 644–3400
Federal Building, 17 South Park Row, Suite B–120, Erie, PA 16501 .... (814) 453–3010
Federal Building, 228 Walnut Street, Room 1104, Harrisburg, PA 17101 .... (717) 782–3951
Federal Building, 504 West Hamilton Street, Suite 3814, Allentown, PA 18101 .... (610) 434–1444
310 Spruce Street, Suite 201, Scranton, PA 18503 .... (570) 346–2006
7 North Wilkes Barre Boulevard, Stegmaier Building, Room 377M, Wilkes Barre, PA 18702 .... (570) 826–6265

* * *

ROBERT P. CASEY, JR., Democrat, of Scranton, PA; born in Scranton, April 13, 1960; education: A.B., English, College of the Holy Cross, 1982; J.D., Catholic University of America, 1988; professional: lawyer; Pennsylvania State Auditor General, 1997–2005; Pennsylvania State Treasurer, 2005–07; married: Terese; four daughters: Elyse, Caroline, Julia, and Marena; committees: Agriculture, Nutrition, and Forestry; Banking, Housing, and Urban Affairs; Foreign Relations; Joint Economic Committee; Special Committee on Aging; elected to the 110th Congress on November 7, 2006.

Office Listings

http://casey.senate.gov

383 Russell Senate Office Building, Washington, DC 20510 .... (202) 224–6324
Chief of Staff.—James W. Brown. FAX: 228–0604
Legislative Director.—Richard D. Spiegelman.
Communications Director.—Larry Smar.
555 Walnut Street, First Floor, Harrisburg, PA 17101 .... (717) 231–7540

REPRESENTATIVES

FIRST DISTRICT

ROBERT A. BRADY, Democrat, of Philadelphia, PA; born in Philadelphia, April 7, 1945; education: graduated from St. Thomas More High School; professional: carpenter; union official; assistant Sergeant-At-Arms, Philadelphia City Council, 1975–83; Deputy Mayor for Labor, W. Wilson Goode Administration; consultant to Pennsylvania State Senate; Pennsylvania Turnpike Commissioner; board of directors, Philadelphia Redevelopment Authority; Democratic Party Executive; ward leader; chairman, Philadelphia Democratic Party; member of Pennsylvania Democratic State Committee, and Democratic National Committee; religion: Catholic; married: Debra Brady; children: Robert and Kimberly; committees: chair, House Administration; Armed Services; elected to the 105th Congress on May 21, 1998, to fill the unexpired term of Representative Tom Foglietta; reelected to each succeeding Congress.

Office Listings

http://www.house.gov/robertbrady

206 Cannon House Office Building, Washington, DC 20515 .... (202) 225–4731
Chief of Staff.—Stan White. FAX: 225–0088
Legislative Director.—Nicole Barcliff.
Appointments Secretary.—Katherine Bissell.
Press Secretary.—Karen Warrington.
1907 South Broad Street, Philadelphia, PA 19148 .... (215) 389–4627
The Colony Building, 511–13 Welsh Street, 1st Floor, Chester, PA 19103 .... (610) 874–7094

Counties: PHILADELPHIA (part). CITIES AND TOWNSHIPS: Chester City, Chester Township, Eddystone Borough, Colwyn Borough, Ridley Township, Tinicum Township, Darby Township, and Yeadon Borough. Population (2000), 630,730.

ZIP Codes: 19012–16, 19018, 19022–23, 19029, 19032, 19036, 19050, 19078–79, 19086, 19092–93, 19101, 19105–09, 19111–13, 19120, 19122–26, 19130–34, 19137–51, 19153–54, 19160–62, 19170–73, 19175, 19177–78, 19181–82, 19185, 19187–88

* * *

SECOND DISTRICT

CHAKA FATTAH, Democrat, of Philadelphia, PA; born in Philadelphia, November 21, 1956; education: attended Overbrook High School, Community College of Philadelphia, University of Pennsylvania's Wharton School; M.A., University of Pennsylvania's Fels School of State and Local Government, 1986; Harvard University's John F. Kennedy School of Government; State House of Representatives, 1982–88; Pennsylvania State Senate, 1988–94; created the Jobs Project; in Pennsylvania House of Representatives, sponsored 1987 Employment Opportunities Act; supported Ben Franklin Technology Center, a conduit for securing government contracts for African-American and women-owned businesses; founded Graduate Opportunities Conference; chairman of the executive committee of the Pennsylvania Higher Education Assistance Agency; convened and led a task force, Child Development Initiative; supported measures to reform the Philadelphia Housing Authority; formed the Drug-Free Program; founded the American Cities Foundation; trustee, Lincoln University and Community College of Philadelphia; recognized for outstanding leadership in *Time* magazine, and in *Ebony* magazine as one of 50 Future Leaders; recipient, Pennsylvania Public Interest Coalition's State Legislator of the Year Award; member, Mt. Carmel Baptist Church; married: the former Renée Chenault; four children; committees: Appropriations; elected to the 104th Congress; reelected to each succeeding Congress.

Office Listings

http://www.house.gov/fattah

2301 Rayburn House Office Building, Washington, DC 20515 .... (202) 225–4001
Chief of Staff.—Michelle Anderson Lee. FAX: 225–5392
Legislative Director.—Noko Ofori.
Communications Director.—Debra Anderson.
4104 Walnut Street, Philadelphia, PA 19104 .... (215) 387–6404
6632 Germantown Avenue, Philadelphia, PA 19119 .... (215) 848–9386

Counties: MONTGOMERY (part), PHILADELPHIA. Population (2000), 630,730.

ZIP Codes: 19004, 19012, 19027, 19038, 19046, 19093, 19095, 19101–04, 19107, 19109–11, 19118–24, 19126–32, 19138–41, 19143–48, 19150, 19161–62, 19170–71, 19173, 19178, 19184, 19187, 19191–93, 19196–97

* * *

THIRD DISTRICT

PHIL ENGLISH, Republican, of Erie, PA; born in Erie, June 20, 1956; education: B.A., political science, University of Pennsylvania; professional: chief of staff, State Senator Melissa Hart; minority executive director, State Senate Finance Committee; executive director, State Senate Transportation Committee; research director, State Senate Labor and Industry Committee; City Controller, Erie, 1985; married Christiane Weschler-English, 1992; committees: Ways and Means; elected to the 104th Congress; reelected to each succeeding Congress.

Office Listings

http://www.house.gov/english

2332 Rayburn House Office Building, Washington, DC 20515 .... (202) 225–5406

Chief of Staff.—Bob Holste. FAX: 225–3103
Office Manager.—Nancy Billet.
Press Secretary.—Julia Wanzco.
Legislative Director.—David Stewart.
208 East Bayfront Parkway, Suite 102, Erie, PA 16507 .... (814) 456–2038
City Annex Building, 900 North Hermitage Road, Suite 6, Hermitage, PA 16148 .. (724) 342–6132
101 East Dramond Street, Suite 213, Butler PA 16001 .... (724) 285–7005
325 Penn Avenue, West, Warren, PA 16365 .... (814) 723–7282

Counties: ARMSTRONG (part), BUTLER (part), CRAWFORD (part), ERIE, MERCER (part), VENANGO (part), WARREN (part). Population (2000), 630,730.

ZIP Codes: 16001–03, 16016–18, 16020, 16022–23, 16025, 16027–30, 16033–35, 16037–41, 16045–46, 16048–53, 16055–57, 16059, 16061, 16110–11, 16113–14, 16124–25, 16127, 16130–31, 16133–34, 16137, 16142–43, 16145–46, 16148, 16150–51, 16153–54, 16156, 16159, 16201, 16210, 16218, 16222–24, 16226, 16229, 16232, 16242, 16244–45, 16249–50, 16253, 16259, 16261–63, 16311–12, 16314, 16316–17, 16319, 16323, 16327, 16329, 16335, 16340, 16342, 16345, 16350–51, 16354, 16360, 16362, 16365–69, 16371–74, 16388, 16401–07, 16410–13, 16415, 16417, 16420–24, 16426–28, 16430, 16432–36, 16438, 16440–44, 16475, 16501–12, 16514–15, 16522, 16530–34, 16538, 16541, 16544, 16546, 16550, 16553–54, 16563, 16565

* * *

FOURTH DISTRICT

JASON ALTMIRE, Democrat, of McCandless, PA; born in Lower Burrell, PA, March 7, 1968; B.S., Florida State University, Tallahassee, FL, 1990; M.H.S.A., George Washington University, Washington, D.C., 1998; professional: Acting Vice President for Government Relations and Community Health Services for University of Pittsburg Medical Center; Director of Federal Government Relations, Federation of American Hospitals; Legislative Assistant to Congressman Pete Peterson (D-FL); married: Kelly Altmire; two children; committees: Education and Labor; Small Business; Transportation and Infrastructure; elected to the 110th Congress on November 7, 2006.

Office Listings

1419 Longworth House Office Building, Washington, DC 20515 .... (202) 225–2565
Chief of Staff.—Sharon Werner. FAX: 226–2274
Legislative Director.—Erik Komendant.
Scheduler.—Carolyn Kahler.
2110 McLean Street, Aliquippa, PA 15001 .... (724) 378–0928
District Director.—Mike Butler.
2124 Freeport Road, Natrona Heights, PA 15065 .... (724) 226–1304

Counties: ALLEGHENY (part), BEAVER, BUTLER (part), LAWRENCE, MERCER (part), WESTMORELAND (part). Population (2000), 630,730.

ZIP Codes: 15001, 15003, 15005–07, 15009–10, 15014–15, 15024, 15026–27, 15030, 15032, 15042–44, 15046, 15049–52, 15056, 15059, 15061, 15065–66, 15068–69, 15074, 15076–77, 15081, 15084–86, 15090–91, 15095–96, 15101, 15108, 15116, 15127, 15139, 15143–44, 15146, 15202, 15209, 15212, 15214–15, 15223, 15229, 15235, 15237–39, 15601, 15626, 15632, 15650, 15668, 16002, 16024–25, 16033, 16037, 16040, 16046, 16051–52, 16055–57, 16059, 16061, 16063, 16066, 16101–03, 16105, 16107–08, 16112, 16115–17, 16120–21, 16123, 16127, 16132, 16136, 16140–43, 16148, 16155–57, 16159–61, 16172, 16229

* * *

FIFTH DISTRICT

JOHN E. PETERSON, Republican, of Pleasantville, PA; born in Titusville, PA, December 25, 1938; education: attended Pennsylvania State University; military service: served in U.S. Army, 1958–64; professional: past owner of supermarket; served in Pennsylvania House of Representatives, 1977–84, and in Pennsylvania Senate, 1985–96; Pleasantville Borough Councilman, 1968–77; past president: Pleasantville Lions Club, Titusville Chamber of Commerce, Pleasantville PTA, and Pleasantville Borough Council; formerly served on: board of directors of Titusville Hospital; and University of Pittsburgh's Titusville and Bradford campuses; advisory board of Pennsylvania State University School of Forest Resources; and advisory committee of the University of Pittsburgh Graduate School of Public Health; married: Saundra J. Watson in 1966; children: Richard; committees: Appropriations; elected to the 105th Congress; reelected to each succeeding Congress.

Office Listings

123 Cannon House Office Building, Washington, DC 20515 .... (202) 225–5121
Chief of Staff.—Jordan Clark. FAX: 225–5796
Legislative Director.—Jeff Vorberger.
Scheduler.—Patrick Creighton.
Communications Director.—Travis Windle.
127 West Spring Street, Suite C, Titusville, PA 16354 .... (814) 827–3985

1524 West College Avenue, State College, PA 16801 .... (814) 238–1776

Counties: CAMERON, CENTRE, CLARION, CLEARFIELD (part), CLINTON, CRAWFORD (part), ELK, FOREST, JEFFERSON, LYCOMING (part), MCKEAN, MIFFLIN (part), POTTER, TIOGA, VENANGO (part), WARREN (part). Population (2000), 630,730.

ZIP Codes: 15711, 15715, 15730, 15733, 15744, 15753, 15757, 15764, 15767, 15770, 15772, 15776, 15778, 15780–81, 15784, 15801, 15821, 15823–25, 15827–29, 15831–32, 15834, 15840–41, 15845–49, 15851, 15853, 15856–57, 15860–61, 15863–66, 15868, 15870, 16028, 16036, 16049, 16054, 16058, 16153, 16213–14, 16217, 16220–22, 16224–26, 16230, 16232–35, 16239–40, 16242, 16248, 16254–58, 16260, 16301, 16311, 16313–14, 16317, 16319, 16321–23, 16326–29, 16331–34, 16340–47, 16351–54, 16361–62, 16364–65, 16370–71, 16373–75, 16404, 16416, 16434, 16620, 16627, 16645, 16651, 16661, 16663, 16666–77, 16681, 16686, 16701, 16720, 16724–35, 16738, 16740, 16743–46, 16748–50, 16801–05, 16820–23, 16825–30, 16832–41, 16843–45, 16847–56, 16858–61, 16863–66, 16868, 16870–79, 16881–82, 16901, 16911–12, 16914–15, 16917–18, 16920–23, 16927–30, 16932–33, 16935–40, 16942–43, 16946–48, 16950, 17004, 17009, 17029, 17044, 17051, 17063, 17084, 17099, 17701–02, 17720–21, 17723–24, 17726–27, 17729, 17738–40, 17744–45, 17747–48, 17750–52, 17754, 17759–60, 17764–65, 17767, 17769, 17773, 17776–79, 17810, 17841

* * *

SIXTH DISTRICT

JIM GERLACH, Republican, of West Whiteland Township, PA; born in Ellwood City, PA, February 25, 1955; education: B.A., Dickinson College, 1977; J.D., Dickinson School of Law, 1980; professional: attorney; former special counsel to the regional law firm of Fox, Rothschild, O'Brien & Frankel; community service: board of directors, Brandywine Hospital and Trauma Center; board of directors, MECA (Mission for Educating Children with Autism); Dickinson College Board of Trustees; Chester County Agricultural Development Council; West Brandywine Township Zoning Hearing Board; public service: Pennsylvania House of Representatives, 1991–94; Pennsylvania State Senate, 1995–2002; children: Katie, Jimmy, and Robby; committees: Financial Services; Transportation and Infrastructure; elected to the 108th Congress on November 5, 2002; reelected to each succeeding Congress.

Office Listings

http://www.house.gov/gerlach

308 Cannon House Office Building, Washington, DC 20515 .... (202) 225–4315
Chief of Staff.—Guy Ciarrocchi. FAX: 225–8440
Legislative Director.—Bill Tighe.
Communications Director.—John Gentzel.
111 East Uwchlan Avenue, Exton, PA 19341 .... (610) 594–1415
501 North Park Road, Wyomissing, PA 19610 .... (610) 376–7630
580 Main Street, Suite #4, Trappe, PA 19426 .... (610) 409–2780

Counties: BERKS (part), CHESTER (part), LEHIGH (part), MONTGOMERY (part). Population (2000), 630,730.

ZIP Codes: 17527, 17555, 17569, 18011, 18031, 18041, 18056, 18062, 18070, 18092, 19003–04, 19010, 19025, 19031, 19034–35, 19041, 19066, 19072, 19085, 19087, 19096, 19131, 19151, 19301, 19310, 19312, 19316, 19320, 19333, 19335, 19341, 19343–45, 19353–55, 19358, 19365–67, 19369, 19371–72, 19376, 19380, 19382, 19401, 19403–04, 19409, 19421, 19423, 19425–26, 19428, 19430, 19432, 19438, 19442, 19444, 19446, 19457, 19460, 19462, 19464–65, 19468, 19470, 19473–75, 19480–85, 19490, 19493–96, 19503–05, 19508, 19511–12, 19518–20, 19522–23, 19525, 19530, 19535, 19538–40, 19542–43, 19545, 19547–48, 19562, 19565, 19601–02, 19604–12

* * *

SEVENTH DISTRICT

JOE SESTAK, Democrat, of Edgmont, PA; born in Secane, PA, December 12, 1951; education: B.S., United States Naval Academy, Annapolis, MD, 1974; Masters of Public Administration, Harvard University, Cambridge, MA, 1980; Ph.D., Political Economy and Government, Harvard University, Cambridge, MA, 1984; professional: Director for Defense Policy, National Security Council, 1994–97; Director of Deep Blue, the Navy's anti-terrorism group, United States Navy, 2001–02; Deputy Chief of Naval Operations, Warfare Requirements and Programs, United States Navy, 2005; military: Commander of the USS George Washington aircraft carrier battle group in combat in Afghanistan and Iraq, 2002–03; awards: Vice Admiral, United States Navy, 2005; married to Susan Leslie Clark-Sestak; father of Alexandra Megan Sestak; committees: Armed Services; Education and Labor; Small Business; elected to the 110th Congress on November 7, 2006.

Office Listings

http://sestak.house.gov

1022 Longworth House Office Building, Washington, DC 20515 .... (202) 225–2011

Chief of Staff.—Brian Branton. FAX: 226–0280
600 North Jackson Street, Suite 203, Media, PA 19063 .... (610) 892–8623
District Director.—Bill Walsh.

Counties: CHESTER (part), DELAWARE (part), MONTGOMERY (part). Population (2000), 630,730.

ZIP Codes: 19008, 19010, 19014–15, 19017–18, 19022–23, 19026, 19028–29, 19032–33, 19036–37, 19039, 19041, 19043, 19050, 19052, 19061, 19063–65, 19070, 19073–74, 19076, 19078–79, 19081–83, 19085–87, 19094, 19312, 19317, 19319, 19331, 19333, 19339–40, 19342, 19355, 19373, 19380, 19382, 19395, 19403, 19405–06, 19426, 19428, 19468

* * *

EIGHTH DISTRICT

PATRICK MURPHY, Democrat, of Bristol, PA; born in Philadelphia, PA, October 19, 1973; education: attended Bucks County Community College, 1991–92; B.S., psychology and human resources, King's College, Wilkes-Barre, PA, 1996; J.D., Widener University School of Law, Harrisburg, PA, 1999; military service: Army, 1996–2004; Army Reserve, deployed to Bosnia, 2002, and as a paratrooper with the 82nd Airborne Division, Baghdad, Iraq, 2003–04; military awards: Bronze Star; Presidential Unit citation; professional: Harrisburg Civil Law Clinic; practiced law at Cozen O'Connor; religion: Roman Catholic; married: Jenni (Safford) Murphy; one daughter, Margaret (Maggie); committees: Armed Services; Financial Services; Small Business; Permanent Select Committee on Intelligence; elected to the 110th Congress on November 7, 2006.

Office Listings

http://patrickmurphy.house.gov/

1007 Longworth House Office Building, Washington, DC 20515 .... (202) 225–4276
Chief of Staff.—Scott Fairchild. FAX: 225–9511
Legislative Director.—Seth Frotman.
414 Mill Street, Bristol, PA 19007 .... (215) 826–1963
District Director.—Phil Lorenzon.
60 North Main Street, Doylestown, PA 18901 .... (215) 348–1194
Deputy District Director.—Doug Platz.

Counties: BUCKS, MONTGOMERY (part), PHILADELPHIA (part). Population (2000), 630,730.

ZIP Codes: 18036, 18039, 18041–42, 18054–55, 18073, 18077, 18081, 18901, 18910–17, 18920–23, 18925–35, 18938, 18940, 18942–44, 18946–47, 18949–51, 18953–56, 18960, 18962–64, 18966, 18968–70, 18972, 18974, 18976–77, 18980–81, 18991, 19001–02, 19006–08, 19020–21, 19025, 19030, 19034, 19038, 19040, 19044, 19047–49, 19053–59, 19067, 19075, 19090, 19114, 19116, 19154–55, 19440, 19454

* * *

NINTH DISTRICT

BILL SHUSTER, Republican, of Hollidaysburg, PA; born in McKeesport, PA, January 10, 1961; education: Everett High School, Bedford County, PA; B.A., Dickinson College; M.B.A., American University; professional: businessman; Goodyear Tire & Rubber Corp.; Bandag, Inc.; President and General Manager, Shuster Chrysler; organizations: member, Zion Lutheran Church; National Federation of Independent Business; National Rifle Association; Y.M.C.A.; Precious Life, Inc.; Rotary Club; Director, Pennsylvania Automotive Association; Board of Trustees, Homewood Home Retirement Community; Sigma Chi Fraternity; family: married to Rebecca; two children: Ali and Garrett; committees: Natural Resources; Small Business; Transportation and Infrastructure; elected to the 107th Congress, by special election, on May 15, 2001; reelected to each succeeding Congress.

Office Listings

http://www.house.gov/shuster

204 Cannon House Office Building, Washington, DC 20515 .... (202) 225–2431
Chief of Staff.—Jeff Loveng. FAX: 225–2486
Legislative Director.—Joel Brubaker.
Scheduler.—Robbe Bendick.
310 Penn Street, Suite 200, Hollidaysburg, PA 16648 .... (814) 696–6318
100 Lincoln Way East, Suite B, Chambersburg, PA 17201 .... (717) 264–8308
645 Philadelphia Street, Suite 304, Indiana, PA 15701 .... (724) 463–0516
118 West Main Street, Suite 302, Somerset, PA 15501 .... (814) 443–3918

Counties: BEDFORD, BLAIR, CAMBRIA (part), CLEARFIELD (part), CUMBERLAND (part), FAYETTE (part), FRANKLIN, FULTON, HUNTINGDON, INDIANA (part), JUNIATA, MIFFLIN, PERRY (part), SOMERSET (part), WESTMORELAND (part). Population (2000), 630,730.

ZIP Codes: 15411, 15416, 15421, 15424–25, 15431, 15436–37, 15440, 15445, 15451, 15459, 15462, 15464–65, 15469–70, 15478–79, 15501, 15510, 15521–22, 15530, 15532–42, 15545, 15549–54, 15557–60, 15562–65, 15681, 15701, 15712–14, 15716–17, 15720–25, 15727–29, 15731–32, 15734, 15738–39, 15741–42, 15746–48, 15750, 15752–54, 15756–59, 15763, 15765, 15767, 15771–72, 15774–75, 15777, 15783, 15840, 15920, 15924, 15926, 15929, 15931, 15936, 15940, 15944, 15946, 15949, 15954, 15961, 15963, 16211, 16222, 16246, 16256, 16601–03, 16611, 16613, 16616–17, 16619, 16621–25, 16627, 16629–31, 16633–41, 16644, 16646–48, 16650–52, 16654–57, 16659–62, 16664–65, 16667–75, 16678–80, 16682–86, 16689, 16691–95, 16823, 16833, 16844, 16861, 16865, 16871, 16877, 17002, 17004, 17006, 17013–14, 17021, 17024, 17035, 17037, 17040, 17044–45, 17047, 17049, 17051–54, 17056, 17058–60, 17062, 17065–66, 17068, 17071, 17074–76, 17081–82, 17086, 17090, 17094, 17201, 17210–15, 17217, 17219–25, 17228–29, 17231–33, 17235–41, 17243–44, 17246–47, 17249–57, 17260–68, 17270–72, 17307, 17324

* * *

TENTH DISTRICT

CHRISTOPHER P. CARNEY, Democrat, of Dimock, PA, born in Cedar Rapids, IA, March 2, 1959; education: B.S.S., Cornell College, 1981; M.A., University of Wyoming, 1983; Ph.D., University of Nebraska, 1993; professional: Associate Professor of Political Science, Penn State University, Scranton; United States Navy Reserves; Senior Counterterrorism Advisor (Civilian); Special Advisor on Counterterrorism to Deputy Secretary of Defense; married: Jennifer, 1987; five children: Ryne, Sean, Seth, Keeley, and Brett; committees: Homeland Security; Transportation and Infrastructure; elected to the 110th Congress on November 7, 2006.

Office Listings

416 Cannon House Office Building, Washington, DC 20515 .... (202) 225–3731
Chief of Staff.—April Metwalli. FAX: 225–9594
Legislative Director.—Jeffrey Gabriel.
Communications Director.—Rebecca Gale.
Scheduler.—Joseph Toth.
233 Northern Boulevard, Suite 4, Lackawanna County, PA 18411 .... (570) 585–9988
District Director.—Paul Macknosky.
175 Pine Street, Suite 103, Lycoming County, PA 17701 .... (570) 327–1902

Counties: BRADFORD, LACKAWANNA (part), LUZERNE (part), LYCOMING (part), MONTOUR, NORTHUMBERLAND, PIKE, SNYDER, SULLIVAN, SUSQUEHANNA, TIOGA (part), UNION, WAYNE, WYOMING. Population (2000), 630,730.

ZIP Codes: 16910, 16914, 16925–26, 16930, 16932, 16936, 16945, 16947, 17017, 17045, 17063, 17086, 17701, 17703, 17705, 17724, 17728, 17730, 17731, 17735, 17737, 17742, 17749, 17756, 17758, 17762–63, 17765, 17768, 17771–72, 17774, 17777, 17801, 17810, 17812–15, 17820–24, 17827, 17829–37, 17840–42, 17844–45, 17847, 17850–51, 17853, 17855–57, 17860–62, 17864–68, 17870, 17872, 17876–77, 17880–87, 17889, 18301, 18324–26, 18328, 18336–37, 18340, 18371, 18403, 18405, 18407, 18410–11, 18413–17, 18419–21, 18424–28, 18430–31, 18433–41, 18443–49, 18451–65, 18469–73, 18512, 18612, 18614–16, 18618–19, 18622–23, 18625–30, 18632, 18636, 18640–41, 18653–54, 18656–57, 18704, 18708, 18801, 18810, 18812–18, 18820–34, 18837, 18840, 18842–48, 18850–51, 18853–54

* * *

ELEVENTH DISTRICT

PAUL E. KANJORSKI, Democrat, of Nanticoke, PA; born in Nanticoke, April 2, 1937; U.S. Capitol Page School, Washington, DC, 1954; attended: Wyoming Seminary, Kingston, PA; Temple University, Philadelphia, PA; Dickinson School of Law, Carlisle, PA; served in U.S. Army, private, 1960–61; attorney, admitted to Pennsylvania State bar, 1966; began practice in Wilkes Barre, PA, November 7, 1966; married to the former Nancy Marie Hickerson; one daughter, Nancy; committees: Financial Services; Oversight and Government Reform; Science and Technology; elected to the 99th Congress on November 6, 1984; reelected to each succeeding Congress.

Office Listings

http://kanjorski.house.gov

2188 Rayburn House Office Building, Washington, DC 20515 .... (202) 225–6511
Chief of Staff.—Karen Feather. FAX: 225–0764
Legislative Director.—Kate McMahon.
Executive Assistant.—Donna Giobbi.
Press Secretary.—Gretchen M. Wintermantel.
The Stegmaier Building, 7 North Wilkes Barre Boulevard, Suite 400–M, Wilkes Barre, PA 18702–5283 .... (570) 825–2200
546 Spruce Street, Scranton, PA 18503 .... (570) 496–1011

Counties: CARBON, COLUMBIA, LACKAWANNA (part), LUZERNE (part), MONROE. Population (2000), 630,730.

ZIP Codes: 17814–15, 17820–21, 17824, 17839, 17846, 17858–59, 17878, 17888, 17920, 17985, 18012, 18030, 18058, 18071, 18201–02, 18210–12, 18216, 18219, 18221–25, 18229–30, 18232, 18234–35, 18237, 18239–41, 18244, 18246–47, 18249–51, 18254–56, 18301, 18320–23, 18325–27, 18330–35, 18341–42, 18344, 18346–50, 18352–57, 18360, 18370, 18372, 18424, 18434, 18445, 18447, 18466, 18501–05, 18507–10, 18512, 18514–15, 18517–19, 18522, 18540, 18577, 18601–03, 18610–12, 18617, 18621–22, 18624, 18631, 18634–35, 18640–44, 18651, 18655, 18660–61, 18690, 18701–11, 18761–67, 18769, 18773–74

* * *

TWELFTH DISTRICT

JOHN P. MURTHA, Democrat, of Johnstown, PA; born in New Martinsville, WV, June 17, 1932; graduated, Ramsey High School, Mount Pleasant, PA; Kiskiminetas Spring School; B.A. in economics, University of Pittsburgh; graduate study at Indiana University of Pennsylvania; served in Marine Corps as an enlisted Marine commissioned as an officer; discharged as a first lieutenant; maintained active reserve officer status; volunteered for one year of active duty in Vietnam as a major; served with 1st Marines, a Marine infantry regiment, 1966–67, south of Danang; awarded Bronze Star Medal with combat ''V'', two Purple Heart medals, Vietnamese Cross of Gallantry, and service medals; retired colonel, U.S. Marine Corps Reserves; elected to Pennsylvania House of Representatives in 1969, served continuously until elected to U.S. House of Representatives; recipient of Pennsylvania Distinguished Service Medal and Pennsylvania Meritorious Service Medal (the commonwealth's two highest honors); first Vietnam veteran to be elected to Congress; received 9 honorary doctorate degrees from colleges and universities; married Joyce Bell; three children: Donna Sue and twin sons, John and Patrick; committees: Appropriations; elected to the 93rd Congress, February 5, 1974; reelected to each succeeding Congress.

Office Listings

http://www.house.gov/murtha

2423 Rayburn House Office Building, Washington, DC 20515 .... (202) 225–2065
Administrator / Director.—Winifred Frederick.
Legislative Director.—Debra Tekavac.
Schedule Coordinator.—Jane Phipps.
Appropriations Staff.—Gabrielle Carruth.
647 Main Street, Suite 401, Johnstown, PA 15901 .... (814) 535–2642
Chief of Staff.—John Hugya.
District Director.—Brad Clemenson.

Counties: ALLEGHENY COUNTY (part). CITIES AND TOWNSHIPS: East Deer, and Tarentum; ARMSTRONG COUNTY (part). CITIES AND TOWNSHIPS: Apollo, Bethel, Burrell, Elderton, Ford City, Ford Cliff, Freeport, Gilpin, Kiskiminetas, Kittanning, Leechburg, Manor, Manorville, North Apollo, North Buffalo, Parks, Plumcreek, South Bend, and South Buffalo; CAMBRIA COUNTY (part). CITIES AND TOWNSHIPS: Adams, Barr, Blacklick, Brownstown, Cambria, Carrolltown, Cassandra, Conemaugh, Cresson, Croyle, Daisytown, Dale, East Carroll, East Conemaugh, East Taylor, Ebensburg, Ehrenfeld, Ferndale, Franklin, Geistown, Jackson, Johnstown, Lilly, Lorain, Lower Yoder, Middle Taylor, Munster, Nanty Glo, Portage, Richland, Sankertown, Scalp Level, South Fork, Southmonth, Stonycreek, Summerhill, Susquehanna, Upper Yoder, Vintondale, Washington, Westmont, West Carroll, West Taylor, Wilmore. FAYETTE COUNTY (part). CITIES AND TOWNSHIPS: Belle Vernon, Brownsville, Bullskin, Connellsville, Dawson, Dunbar, Everson, Fayette City, Franklin, Georges, German, Jefferson, Lower Tyrone, Luzerne, Masontown, Menallen, Newell, Nicholson, North Union, Perry, Perryopolis, Point Marion, Redstone, Saltlick, South Union, Springhill, Upper Tyrone, Uniontown, Vanderbilt, Washington. GREENE COUNTY, INDIANA COUNTY (part). CITIES AND TOWNSHIPS: Cherryhill, Clymer, Indiana, Pine, White. SOMERSET COUNTY (part). CITIES AND TOWNSHIPS: Benson, Boswell, Conemaugh, Hooversville, Jefferson, Jenner, Jennerstown, Lincoln, Middlecreek, Paint, Quemahoning, Seven Springs, Stoystown, Windber. WASHINGTON COUNTY (part). CITIES AND TOWNSHIPS: Allenport, Beallsville, Bentleyville, California, Canonsburg, Canton, Carroll, Centerville, Charleroi, Chartier, Coal Center, Cokeburg, Deemston, Donora, Dunlevy, East Bethlehem, East Washington, Elco, Ellsworth, Fallowfield, Finleyville, Houston, Long Branch, Marianna, Monongahela, New Eagle, North Bethlehem, North Charleroi, North Strabane, Roscoe, Somerset, South Strabane, Speers, Stockdale, Twilight, Union, Washington, West Bethlehem, West Brownsville, West Pike Run. WESTMORELAND COUNTY (part). CITIES AND TOWNSHIPS: Allegheny, Arnold, Avonmore, Bell, Bessemer, Bolivar, Bovard, Bridgeport, Crabtree, Derry, Dorothy, Duncan, East Herminie, East Huntingdon, East Vandergrift, Fairfield, Hannastown, Heccla, Hempfield, Hugus, Hyde Park, Jacobs Creek, Latrobe, Laurel Run, Lloydsville, Lowber, Lower Burrell, Loyalhanna, Luxor, Mammoth, Mechlings, Mineral, Monessen, Mount Pleasant, New Alexandria, New Florence, New Kensington, North Belle Vernon, North Washington, Oklahoma, Paulton, Port Royal, Rillton, Rostraver, Salem, Scottdale, Seward, Sewickley, Smithton, South Huntingdon, Spring Garden, St. Clair, United, Unity, Upper Burrell, Vandergrift, Washington, Wayne, Westmoreland, West Herminie, West Leechburg, West Newton, Wyano, and Yukon. Population (2000), 630,730.

ZIP Codes: 15012, 15022, 15030, 15033, 15038, 15062–63, 15067–68, 15072, 15083, 15087, 15089, 15301, 15310, 15313–17, 15320, 15322, 15324–25, 15327, 15329–34, 15336–38, 15341–42, 15344–49, 15351–54, 15357–60, 15362–64, 15366, 15368, 15370, 15377, 15380, 15401, 15410–13, 15415, 15417, 15419–20, 15422–25, 15427–36, 15438, 15442–44, 15446–47, 15449–51, 15454–56, 15458, 15460, 15463, 15466–68, 15472–77, 15479–80, 15482–86, 15488–90, 15492, 15501–02, 15520, 15531, 15541, 15544, 15547–48, 15551, 15555, 15557, 15561, 15563, 15601, 15610, 15613, 15618, 15620–22, 15624–25, 15627, 15629, 15631, 15633, 15635, 15637, 15641–42, 15644, 15646, 15650, 15655–56, 15660–62, 15664, 15666, 15670–71, 15673–74, 15677–78, 15680–90, 15701, 15705, 15710, 15714, 15717, 15722, 15724, 15728, 15732, 15736–37, 15745, 15748, 15760–62, 15765, 15773–74, 15779, 15901–02, 15904–07, 15909, 15921–23, 15925, 15927–28, 15930–31, 15934–38, 15940, 15942–46, 15948, 15951–63, 16055, 16201, 16215, 16226, 16228–29, 16236, 16238, 16240, 16249, 16630, 16641, 16646, 16668–69

* * *

THIRTEENTH DISTRICT

ALLYSON Y. SCHWARTZ, Democrat, of Rydal, PA; born in Queens County, NY, October 3, 1948; education: graduated from the Calhoun School, New York, NY, 1966; B.A., Simmons College, Boston, MA, 1970; M.S.W., Bryn Mawr College, Bryn Mawr, PA, 1972; professional: executive director of the Elizabeth Blackwell Center, 1977–88; Deputy Commissioner of the Philadelphia Department of Human Services, 1988–90; elected to the Pennsylvania state Senate, 1991–2004; member: Pennsylvania State Board of Education; Pennsylvania Council on Higher Education; Education Commission of the States; married: Dr. David Schwartz; children: Daniel and Jordan; committees: Budget; Ways and Means; elected to the 109th Congress on November 2, 2004; reelected to the 110th Congress.

Office Listings

http://www.house.gov/schwartz

423 Cannon House Office Building, Washington, DC 20515 .... (202) 225–6111
Chief of Staff.—Daniel McElhatton. FAX: 226–0611
Legislative Director.—Kate Winkler.
Communications Director.—Rachel Magnuson.
706 West Avenue, Jenkintown, PA 19046 .... (215) 517–6572
District Director.—Julie Slavet.
7219 Frankford Avenue, Philadelphia, PA 19135 .... (215) 335–3355

County: MONTGOMERY COUNTY; CITIES AND TOWNSHIPS: Abington Wards, Hatfield, Horsham, Lower Frederick, Lower Gwynedd, Lower Moreland, Lower Salford, Malborough, Montgomery, New Hanover, Plymouth, Springfield, Towamencin, Upper Dublin, Upper Frederick, Upper Gwynedd, Upper Moreland, Upper Salford, Whitemarsh, Whitpain. Boroughs of Ambler, Bryn Athyn, Green Lane, Hatboro, Hatfield, Jenkintown, Lansdale, North Wales, Rockledge, Schwenksville. PHILADELPHIA COUNTY; CITY OF: Philadelphia. Population (2000), 630,730.

ZIP Codes: 18054, 18074, 18914–15, 18932, 18936, 18957–58, 18964, 18969, 18979, 19001–02, 19006, 19009, 19019, 19025, 19027, 19038, 19040, 19044, 19046, 19075, 19090, 19096, 19111, 19114–16, 19118, 19120, 19124, 19128, 19134–37, 19149, 19152, 19154–55, 19244, 19255, 19422, 19424, 19428, 19435–38, 19440–41, 19443–44, 19446, 19450–51, 19454–55, 19462, 19464, 19473, 19477–78, 19486–87, 19489, 19492, 19504, 19512, 19525

* * *

FOURTEENTH DISTRICT

MICHAEL F. DOYLE, Democrat, of Forest Hills, PA; born in Swissvale, PA, August 5, 1953; graduated, Swissvale Area High School, 1971; B.S., Pennsylvania State University, 1975; co-owner, Eastgate Insurance Agency, Inc., 1983; elected and served as finance and recreation chairman, Swissvale Borough Council, 1977–81; member: Leadership Pittsburgh Alumni Association, Lions Club, Ancient Order of the Hibernians, Italian Sons and Daughters of America, and Penn State Alumni Association; member: Democratic Caucus, Democratic Study Group, Pennsylvania Democratic Delegation, Congressional Steel Caucus, Travel and Tourism CMO, Ad Hoc Committee on Irish Affairs, and National Italian-American Foundation; married Susan Beth Doyle, 1975; four children: Michael, David, Kevin, and Alexandra; committees: Energy and Commerce; Standards of Official Conduct; Veterans' Affairs; elected to the 104th Congress, November 8, 1994; reelected to each succeeding Congress.

Office Listings

http://www.house.gov/doyle

401 Cannon House Office Building, Washington, DC 20515 .... (202) 225–2135
Administrative Assistant.—David Lucas. FAX: 225–3084
Legislative Director.—Pat Cavanagh.
Office Manager / Scheduler.—Ellen Young.
225 Ross Street, Pittsburgh, PA 15219 .... (412) 261–5091
District Director.—Paul D'Alesandro.
11 Duff Road, Penn Hills, PA 15235 .... (412) 241–6055
627 Lysle Boulevard, McKeesport, PA 15132 .... (412) 664–4049

County: ALLEGHENY COUNTY (part); CITIES AND TOWNSHIPS OF: Avalon, Baldwin Borough, Baldwin Township, Blawnox, Braddock, Braddock Hills, Chalfant, Clairton, Coraopolis, Dravosburg, Duquesne, E. McKeesport, E. Pittsburgh, Edgewood, Elizabeth Borough, Elizabeth Township, Etna, Forest Hills, Glassport, Ingram, Kennedy, Liberty, Lincoln, McKees Rocks, McKeesport, Millvale, Monroeville, Mt. Oliver, Munhall, Neville, North Braddock, North Versailles, O'Hara Township, Penn Hills, Pitcairn, Pittsburgh, Port Vue, Rankin, Reserve, Robinson, Stowe, Swissvale, Sharpsburg, Turtle Creek, Verona, Versailles, Wall, West Homestead, West Mifflin, Whitaker, Wilkins, Wilkinsburg, and Wilmerding. Population (2000), 630,730.

ZIP Codes: 15025, 15034–35, 15037, 15044–45, 15063, 15104, 15106, 15108, 15110, 15112, 15116, 15120, 15122, 15132–37, 15140, 15145–48, 15201–19, 15221–27, 15230, 15232–36, 15238–40, 15242, 15244, 15250–51, 15253, 15255, 15257–62, 15264–65, 15267–68, 15272, 15274, 15278–79, 15281–83, 15285–86, 15290, 15295

* * *

FIFTEENTH DISTRICT

CHARLES W. DENT, Republican, of Allentown, PA, born in Allentown, May 24, 1960; education: B.A., Foreign Service and International Politics, Pennsylvania State University, 1982; M.A., Public Administration, Lehigh University, 1993; professional: Legislator Development Officer, Lehigh University, 1986–90; sales representative, P.A. Peters, Inc.; Pennsylvania State House, District 132, 1991–98; Representative, Pennsylvania State Senate, 1998–2004; religion: First Presbyterian Church; married: Pamela Jane Serfass; children: Kathryn Elizabeth, William Reed, and Charles John (Jack); committees: Homeland Security; Transportation and Infrastructure; elected to the 109th Congress on November 2, 2004; reelected to the 110th Congress.

Office Listings

http://www.house.gov/dent

116 Cannon House Office Building, Washington, DC 20515 .... (202) 225–6411
Chief of Staff.—George McElwee. FAX: 226–0778
Legislative Director.—Peter Richards.
701 West Broad Street, Suite 200, Bethlehem, PA 18018 .... (610) 861–9734
206 Main Street, East Greenville, PA 18041 .... (215) 541–4106

Counties: BERKS (part), LEHIGH, MONTGOMERY (part), NORTHAMPTON. POPULATION (2000), 630,730.

ZIP Codes: 18001–03, 18010–11, 18013–18, 18020, 18025, 18031–32, 18034–38, 18040–46, 18049–55, 18059–60, 18062–70, 18072–74, 18076–80, 18083–88, 18091–92, 18098–99, 18101–06, 18109, 18175, 18195, 18343, 18351, 18918, 18924, 18951, 18960, 18964, 18969, 18971, 19438, 19440, 19464, 19472, 19504–05, 19512, 19525, 19529–30, 19539

* * *

SIXTEENTH DISTRICT

JOSEPH R. PITTS, Republican, of Kennett Square, PA; born in Lexington, KY, October 10, 1939; education: B.A., philosophy and religion, Asbury College, KY; military service: served in U.S. Air Force, 1963–69, rising from second lieutenant to captain; professional: nursery business owner and operator; math and science teacher, Great Valley High School, Malvern, PA, 1969–72; teacher, Mortonsville Elementary School, Versailles, KY; member: Pennsylvania House of Representatives, 1972–96, serving as chairman of Appropriations Committee, 1989–96, and of Labor Relations Committee, 1981–88; married: the former Virginia M. Pratt in 1961; children: Karen, Carol, and Daniel; committees: Energy and Commerce; elected to the 105th Congress; reelected to each succeeding Congress.

Office Listings

http://www.house.gov/pitts

221 Cannon House Office Building, Washington, DC 20515 .... (202) 225–2411
Chief of Staff.—Gabe Neville. FAX: 225–2013
Legislative Director.—Monica Volante.
Press Secretary.—Skip Brown.
P.O. Box 837, Unionville, PA 19375 .... (610) 444–4581
50 North Duke Street, Lancaster, PA 17602 .... (717) 393–0667

Counties: LANCASTER, BERK (part). CITIES AND TOWNSHIPS: Reading, Bern, Lower Heidelberg, South Heidelberg, Spring. BOROUGH OF: Wernersville. CHESTER COUNTY (part). CITIES AND TOWNSHIPS: Birmingham, East Bradford, East Fallowfield, East Marlborough, East Nottingham, Elk, Franklin, Highland, Kennett, London Britain, London Grove, Londonderry, Lower Oxford, New Garden, New London, Newlin, Penn, Pennsbury, Upper Oxford, West Fallowfield, West Marlborough, West Nottingham. BOROUGHS OF: Avondale, Kennett Square, Oxford, Parkesburg, West Chester, and West Grove. Population (2000), 630,730.

ZIP Codes: 17501–09, 17512, 17516–22, 17527–29, 17532–38, 17540, 17543, 17545, 17547, 17549–52, 17554–55, 17557, 17560, 17562–70, 17572–73, 17575–76, 17578–85, 17601–08, 19106, 19310–11, 19317–20, 19330, 19342, 19346–48, 19350–52, 19357, 19360, 19362–63, 19365, 19374–75, 19380–83, 19390, 19395, 19464, 19501, 19540, 19543, 19565, 19601–02, 19604–05, 19608–11

* * *

SEVENTEENTH DISTRICT

TIM HOLDEN, Democrat, of St. Clair, PA; born in Pottsville, PA, March 5, 1957; education: attended St. Clair High School, St. Clair; Fork Union Military Academy; University of Richmond, Richmond, VA; B.A., Bloomsburg State College, 1980; professional: sheriff of Schuylkill County, PA, 1985–93; licensed insurance broker and real estate agent, John J. Holden Insurance Agency and Holden Realty Company, St. Clair; member: Pennsylvania Sheriffs Association; Fraternal Order of Police; St. Clair Fish and Game Association; Benevolent and Protective Order of the Elks Lodge 1533; co-chair, Correctional Officers Caucus; co-chair, House Mining Caucus; co-chair, Northeast Agriculture Caucus; Ad-Hoc Committee for Irish Affairs; Alzheimer's Caucus; Appalachian Region Commission Caucus; Arts Caucus; Autism Caucus; Blue Dog Coalition; Congressional 4–H Caucus; Congressional Beef Caucus; Congressional Caucus on Armenian Issues; Congressional Cement Caucus; Congressional Hellenic Caucus; Diabetes Caucus; Firefighter's Caucus; Friends of Ireland; Home Health Care Working Group; Homeland Security Caucus; House Auto Caucus; House Baltic Caucus; House Commuter Caucus; House Nursing Caucus; Iraq Fallen Heroes Caucus; Law Enforcement Caucus; Mental Health Caucus; National Guard and Reserve Components Caucus; Rural Caucus; Rural Health Care Caucus; Special Operations Forces Caucus; Sportsmens Causus; Steel Caucus; Water Infrastructure Caucus; Wine Caucus; committees: Agriculture; Transportation and Infrastructure; elected to the 103rd Congress; reelected to each succeeding Congress.

Office Listings

2417 Rayburn House Office Building, Washington, DC 20515 .... (202) 225–5546
Chief of Staff.—Trish Reilly-Hudock. FAX: 226–0996
Legislative Director.—Ari Strauss.
Projects Director.—Bill Hanley.
Scheduler.—Rebecca Spangler.
1721 North Front Street, Suite 105, Harrisburg, PA 17102 .... (717) 234–5904
4918 Kutztown Road, Temple, PA 19560 .... (610) 921–3502
47 South 8th Street, Lebanon, PA 17042 .... (717) 270–1395
101 North Centre Street, Suite 303, Pottsville, PA 17901 .... (570) 622–4212

Counties: BERKS (part), DAUPHIN, LEBANON, PERRY (part), SCHUYLKILL. Population (2000), 630,730.

ZIP Codes: 17003, 17005, 17010, 17016–18, 17020, 17022–24, 17026, 17028, 17030, 17032–34, 17036, 17038–39, 17041–42, 17045–46, 17048, 17053, 17057, 17061–62, 17064, 17067–69, 17073–74, 17077–78, 17080, 17083, 17085, 17087–88, 17097–98, 17101–13, 17120–30, 17140, 17177, 17502, 17830, 17836, 17901, 17921–23, 17925, 17929–36, 17938, 17941–46, 17948–49, 17951–54, 17957, 17959–61, 17963–68, 17970, 17972, 17974, 17976, 17978–83, 17985, 18211, 18214, 18218, 18220, 18231, 18237, 18240–42, 18245, 18248, 18250, 18252, 18255, 19506–07, 19510, 19512, 19516, 19518, 19522, 19526, 19529–30, 19533–34, 19536, 19541, 19544, 19547, 19549–51, 19554–55, 19559–60, 19564–65, 19567, 19601, 19604–06

* * *

EIGHTEENTH DISTRICT

TIM MURPHY, Republican, of Upper St. Clair, PA; born in Cleveland, OH, September 11, 1952; education: B.S., Wheeling Jesuit University, 1974; M.A., Cleveland State University, 1976; Ph.D., University of Pittsburgh, 1979; professional: Psychologist; holds two adjunct faculty positions at the University of Pittsburgh; Associate Professor in the Department of Public Health, and in the Department of Pediatrics; public service: Pennsylvania State Senate, 1996–2002; religion: Catholic; family: married to Nan Missig; children: Bevin; committees: Energy and Commerce; elected to the 108th Congress on November 5, 2002; reelected to each succeeding Congress.

Office Listings

http://murphy.house.gov

322 Cannon House Office Building, Washington, DC 20515 .... (202) 225–2301
Chief of Staff.—Susan Mosychuk.
Legislative Director.—Michael Baxter.
Executive Assistant / Scheduler.—Morgan Jones.
Press Secretary.—Mark Carpen.
504 Washington Road, Pittsburgh, PA 15228 .... (412) 344–5583

Counties: ALLEGHENY (part), WASHINGTON (part), WESTMORELAND (part). CITIES AND TOWNSHIPS: Pittsburgh (part), Greensburg, and Jeannette. Population (2000), 630,730.

ZIP Codes: 15001, 15004, 15017–22, 15025–26, 15028, 15031, 15033, 15036–37, 15044, 15046–47, 15053–55, 15057, 15060, 15063–64, 15071, 15075, 15078, 15082–83, 15085, 15088–89, 15102, 15106, 15108, 15126, 15129, 15131,

15136, 15142, 15146, 15205, 15209, 15212, 15215–16, 15220–21, 15226–28, 15231, 15234–36, 15238, 15241, 15243, 15270, 15277, 15301, 15311–12, 15314, 15317, 15321, 15323, 15329–30, 15332, 15339–40, 15342, 15345, 15350, 15361, 15363, 15365, 15367, 15376–79, 15448, 15501, 15601, 15605–06, 15611–12, 15615–17, 15619, 15622–23, 15626, 15628, 15632, 15634, 15636–40, 15642, 15644, 15647, 15650, 15655, 15658, 15663, 15665, 15668, 15672, 15675–76, 15679, 15683, 15687–88, 15691–93, 15695–97

* * *

NINETEENTH DISTRICT

TODD RUSSELL PLATTS, Republican, of York County, PA; born in York County, March 5, 1962; education: York Suburban High School, 1980; B.S. in Public Administration, Shippensburg University of Pennsylvania, 1984; J.D., Pepperdine University School of Law, 1991; professional: Attorney; organizations: York County Transportation Coalition; Statewide Children's Health Insurance Program Advisory Council; York Metropolitan Planning Organization; public service: Pennsylvania House of Representatives, 1992–2000; married: Leslie; children: T.J. and Kelsey; committees: Education and Labor; Oversight and Government Reform; Transportation and Infrastructure; elected to the 107th Congress on November 7, 2000; reelected to each succeeding Congress.

Office Listings

http://www.house.gov/platts

1032 Longworth House Office Building, Washington, DC 20515 .... (202) 225–5836
Chief of Staff.—Scott E. Miller. FAX: 226–1000
2209 East Market Street, York, PA 17402 .... (717) 600–1919
Deputy Chief of Staff.—Bob Reilly.
22 Chambersburg Street, Gettysburg, PA 17325 .... (717) 338–1919
59 West Louther Street, Carlisle, PA 17013 .... (717) 249–0190

Counties: ADAMS COUNTY. CITIES OF: Abbottstown, Arendtsville, Aspers, Bendersville, Biglerville, East Berlin, Fairfield, Gardners, Gettysburg, Littlestown, McKnightstown, McSherrystown, New Oxford, Orrtanna. CUMBERLAND COUNTY. CITIES OF: Boiling Springs, Carlisle, Camp Hill, East Pennsboro, Enola, Grantham, Lemoyne, Mechanicsburg, Mt. Holly Springs, Newburg, New Cumberland, Newville, Shippensburg, Shiremanstown, Summerdale, Walnut Bottom, West Fairview, Wormleysburg; TOWNSHIPS OF Hampden, Lower Allen, Middlesex, Monroe, Shippensburg, Silver Spring, South Newton, Southampton, Upper Allen, the boroughs of Camp Hill, Carlisle, Lemoyne, Mt. Holly Springs, New Cumberland, Shippensburg, Shiremanstown, Wormleysburg. YORK COUNTY. CITIES AND TOWNSHIPS: Airville, Brodbecks, Brogue, Dallastown, Delta, Dillsburg, Dover, Emigsville, East Prospect, Etters, Felton, Fawn Grove, Glen Rock, Hanover, Hellam, Jacobus, Lewisberry, Loganville, Manchester, Mount Wolf, New Freedom, New Park, Red Lion, Spring Grove, Shrewsbury, Stewartstown, Seven Valleys, Thomasville, Wellsville, Windsor, Wrightsville, York, York Haven, York New Salem, Yoe, and York Springs. Population (2000), 647,065.

ZIP Codes: 17001, 17007–08, 17011–13, 17019, 17025, 17027, 17043, 17050, 17053, 17055, 17065, 17070, 17072, 17089–90, 17093, 17222, 17257, 17301–04, 17306–07, 17309–27, 17329, 17331–33, 17337, 17339–40, 17342–45, 17347, 17349–50, 17352–56, 17358, 17360–66, 17368, 17370–72, 17401–07, 17415

RHODE ISLAND

(Population 2000, 1,048,319)

SENATORS

JACK REED, Democrat, of Jamestown, RI; born in Providence, RI, November 12, 1949; graduated, La Salle Academy, Providence, RI, 1967; B.S., U.S. Military Academy, West Point, NY, 1971; M.P.P., Kennedy School of Government, Harvard University, 1973; J.D., Harvard Law School, 1982; professional: served in the U.S. Army, 1967–79; platoon leader, company commander, battalion staff officer, 1973–77; associate professor, Department of Social Sciences, U.S. Military Academy, West Point, NY, 1978–79; 2nd BN (Abn) 504th Infantry, 82nd Airborne Division, Fort Bragg, NC; lawyer, admitted to the Washington, DC bar, 1983; military awards: Army commendation medal with Oak Leaf Cluster, ranger, senior parachutist, jumpmaster, expert infantryman's badge; elected to the Rhode Island State Senate, 1985–90; committees: Appropriations; Armed Services; Banking, Housing, and Urban Affairs; Health, Education, Labor, and Pensions; elected to the 102nd Congress on November 6, 1990; served three terms in the U.S. House of Representatives; elected to the U.S. Senate, November 5, 1996; reelected to each succeeding Senate term.

Office Listings

http://reed.senate.gov

728 Hart Senate Office Building, Washington, DC 20510 .... (202) 224–4642
Chief of Staff.—Neil Campbell. FAX: 224–4680
Deputy Chief of Staff.—Cathy Nagle.
Press Secretary.—Chip Unruh.
201 Hillside Road, Suite 200, Cranston, RI 02920 .... (401) 943–3100
Chief of Staff.—Raymond Simone.
U.S. District Courthouse, One Exchange Terrace, Suite 408, Providence, RI 02903 (401) 528–5200

* * *

SHELDON WHITEHOUSE, Democrat, of Providence, RI; born in New York City, NY, October 20, 1955; education: B.A., Yale University, New Haven, CT, 1978; J.D., University of Virginia, Charlottesville, VA, 1982; director, Rhode Island Department of Business Regulation, 1992–94; United States Attorney, 1994–98; Attorney General, Rhode Island state, 1999–2003; committees: Budget; Environment and Public Works; Judiciary; Select Committee on Intelligence; Special Committee on Aging; elected to the U.S. Senate on November 7, 2006.

Office Listings

http://whitehouse.senate.gov

502 Hart Senate Office Building, Washington, DC 20510 .... (202) 224–2921
Chief of Staff.—Mindy Myers. FAX: 228–6362
Senior Advisory.—Laura Petrou.
Legislative Director.—Natacha Blain.
Communications Director.—Alex Swartsel.
170 Westminster Street, Suite 1100, Providence, RI 02903 .... (401) 453–5294
State Director.—George Carvahlo.

REPRESENTATIVES

FIRST DISTRICT

PATRICK J. KENNEDY, Democrat, of Providence, RI; born in Brighton, MA, July 14, 1967; education: graduated, Phillips Academy, Andover, MA; B.A., Providence College, Providence, RI, 1991; public service: Rhode Island State Legislature, 1988–94; member: Rhode Island Special Olympics (board of directors), Rhode Island March of Dimes, Rhode Island Lung Association, Rhode Island Mental Health Association, Rhode Island Chapter of National Committee for the Prevention of Child Abuse; committees: Appropriations; Natural Resources; elected to the 104th Congress; reelected to each succeeding Congress.

Office Listings

http://www.house.gov/patrickkennedy

407 Cannon House Office Building, Washington, DC 20515 .... (202) 225–4911

Chief of Staff.—Adam Brand. FAX: 225–3290
Legislative Director.—Kimber Colton.
Executive Assistant.—Terri Alford.
Press Secretary.—Robin Costello.
249 Roosevelt Avenue, Suite 200, Pawtucket, RI 02860 .... (401) 729–5600
District Director.—George Zainyeh.

Counties: BRISTOL, NEWPORT, PROVIDENCE (part). CITIES AND TOWNSHIPS: Barrington, Bristol, Burrillville, Central Falls, Cumberland, East Providence, Jamestown, Lincoln, Little Compton, Middleton, Newport, North Providence, North Smithfield, Providence, Pawtucket, Portsmouth, Smithfield, Tiverton, Warren, and Woonsocket. Population (2000), 524,157.

ZIP Codes: 02801, 02802, 02806, 02809, 02824, 02826, 02828, 02830, 02835, 02837, 02838, 02839, 02840, 02841, 02842, 02858, 02859, 02860, 02861, 02862, 02863, 02864, 02865, 02871, 02872, 02876, 02878, 02885, 02895, 02896, 02903, 02904, 02906, 02908, 02909, 02911, 02912, 02914, 02915, 02916, 02917, 02918, 02940

* * *

SECOND DISTRICT

JAMES R. LANGEVIN, Democrat, of Warwick, RI; born in Providence, RI, April 22, 1964; education: B.A., Political Science / Public Administration, Rhode Island College, 1990; Masters of Public Administration, Harvard University, 1994; community service: American Red Cross; March of Dimes; Lions Club of Warwick; PARI Independent Living Center; Knights of Columbus; public service: secretary, Rhode Island Constitutional Convention, 1986; Rhode Island State Representative, 1989–95; Rhode Island Secretary of State, 1995–2000; committees: Homeland Security; Permanent Select Committee on Intelligence; elected to the 107th Congress; reelected to each succeeding Congress.

Office Listings

http://www.house.gov/langevin

109 Cannon House Office Building, Washington, DC 20515 .... (202) 225–2735
Chief of Staff.—Kristin Nicholson. FAX: 225–5976
Legislative Director.—Brian Daniels.
Office Manager.—Stu Rose.
The Summit South, 300 Centerville Road, Suite 200, Warwick, RI 02886 .... (401) 732–9400
District Director.—Ken Wild.

Counties: KENT, PROVIDENCE (part), WASHINGTON. CITIES AND TOWNSHIPS: Charleston, Coventry, Cranston, Exeter, Foster, Glocester, Greenwich (East and West), Hopkinton, Johnston, Kingstown (North and South), Narragansett, New Shoreham, Providence, Richmond, Warwick, West Warwick, Westerly, and Sctuate. Population (2000), 538,032.

ZIP Codes: 02804, 02807–08, 02812–18, 02822–23, 02825, 02827–29, 02831–33, 02836, 02852, 02857, 02873–75, 02877, 02879–83, 02886–89, 02891–94, 02898, 02901–05, 02907–11, 02917, 02919–21

SOUTH CAROLINA

(Population 2000, 4,012,012)

SENATORS

LINDSEY GRAHAM, Republican, of Seneca, SC; born in Seneca, July 9, 1955; education: graduated, Daniel High School, Central, SC; B.A., University of South Carolina, 1977; awarded J.D., 1981; military service: joined the U.S. Air Force, 1982; Base Legal Office and Area Defense Counsel, Rhein Main Air Force Base, Germany, 1984; circuit trial counsel, U.S. Air Forces; Base Staff Judge Advocate, McEntire Air National Guard Base, SC, 1989–1994; presently a Colonel, Air Force Reserves; award: Meritorious Service Medal for Active Duty Tour in Europe; professional: established private law practice, 1988; former member, South Carolina House of Representatives; Assistant County Attorney for Oconee County, 1988–92; City Attorney for Central, SC, 1990–94; member: Walhalla Rotary; American Legion Post 120; appointed to the Judicial Arbitration Commission by the Chief Justice of the Supreme Court; religion: attends Corinth Baptist Church; committees: Agriculture, Nutrition, and Forestry; Armed Services; Budget; Judiciary; Veterans' Affairs; elected to the 104th Congress on November 8, 1994; reelected to each succeeding Congress; elected to the U.S. Senate on November 5, 2002.

Office Listings

http://lgraham.senate.gov

290 Russell Senate Office Building, Washington, DC 20510 .... (202) 224–5972
Chief of Staff.—Richard Perry. FAX: 224–3808
Legislative Director.—Jen Olson.
Press Secretary.—Wes Hickman.
Scheduler.—Lauren Edwards.
101 East Washington Street, Suite 220, Greenville, SC 29601 .... (864) 250–1417
State Director.—Jane Goolsby.
530 Johnnie Dodds Boulevard, Suite 202, Mt. Pleasant, SC 29464 .... (843) 849–3887
Low Country Regional Director.—Bill Tuten.
508 Hampton Street, Suite 202, Columbia, SC 29201 .... (803) 933–0112
Midlands Regional Director.—Rene Ann Tewkesbury.
John L. McMillan Federal Building, 401 West Evans Street, Suite 111, Florence, SC 29501 .... (843) 669–1505
140 East Main Street, Suite 110, Rock Hill, SC 29730 .... (803) 366–2828
135 Eagles Nest Drive, Suite B, Seneca, SC 29678 .... (864) 888–3330
State Outreach Manager, Medical and Business Sector.—Denise Bauld.

* * *

JIM DEMINT, Republican, of Greenville, SC; born in Greenville, September 2, 1951; education: West Hampton High School, Greenville, SC, 1969; B.S., University of Tennessee, 1973; M.B.A., Clemson University, 1981; certified management consultant and certified quality trainer; advertising and marketing businessman; started his own company, DeMint Marketing; active in Greenville, SC, business and educational organizations; U.S. House of Representatives, 1999–2005; religion: Presbyterian; family: married to Debbie; four children; committees: Commerce, Science, and Transportation; Energy and Natural Resources; Foreign Relations; Joint Economic Committee; elected to the U.S. Senate on November 2, 2004.

Office Listings

http://demint.senate.gov

340 Russell Senate Office Building, Washington, DC 20510 .... (202) 224–6121
Chief of Staff.—Bret Bernhardt. FAX: 228–5143
Policy Director.—Matt Hoskins.
Senior Administrative Advisor.—Ellen Weaver.
Communications Director.—Wesley Denton.
105 North Spring Street, Suite 109, Greenville, SC 29601 .... (864) 233–5366
112 Custom House, 200 East Bay Street, Charleston, SC 29401 .... (843) 727–4525
1901 Main Street, Suite 1475, Columbia, SC 29201 .... (803) 771–6112

REPRESENTATIVES

FIRST DISTRICT

HENRY E. BROWN, JR., Republican, of Hanahan, SC; born in Lee County, SC, December 20, 1935; education: Berkeley High School; Baptist College; and The Citadel; professional:

Businessman; Piggly Wiggly Carolina Co., Inc.; helped develop the Lowcountry Investment Corp.; awards: National Republican Legislator of the Year; South Carolina Taxpayers Watchdog Award; South Carolina Association of Realtors Legislator of the Year; honorary degree, Doctor of Business Administration, The Citadel; married: Billye; three children; public service: Hanahan City Council, 1981–85; South Carolina House of Representatives, 1985–2000; committees: Natural Resources; Transportation and Infrastructure; Veterans' Affairs; elected to the 107th Congress on November 7, 2000; reelected to each succeeding Congress.

Office Listings

http://www.house.gov/henrybrown

1124 Longworth House Office Building, Washington, DC 20515 .... (202) 225–3176
Chief of Staff.—Delores Dacosta. FAX: 225–3407
Legislative Director.—Chris Berardini.
Press Secretary.—Sharon Axson.
5900 Core Avenue, Suite 401, North Charleston, SC 29406 .... (843) 747–4175
District Director.—Kathy Crawford.
1800 North Oak Street, Suite C, Myrtle Beach, SC 29577 .... (843) 445–6459

Counties: BERKELEY (part), CHARLESTON (part), DORCHESTER (part), GEORGETOWN (part), HORRY. Population (2000), 668,668.

ZIP Codes: 29401–07, 29410, 29412–14, 29416–20, 29422–25, 29429, 29436, 29439–40, 29442, 29445, 29449, 29451, 29455–58, 29461, 29464–66, 29469–70, 29472, 29474–75, 29482–85, 29487, 29511, 29526–28, 29544–45, 29566, 29568–69, 29572, 29575–79, 29581–82, 29585, 29587–88, 29597–98

* * *

SECOND DISTRICT

JOE WILSON, Republican, of Springdale, SC; born in Charleston, SC, July 31, 1947; education: graduated, Washington & Lee University, Lexington, VA; University of South Carolina School of Law; professional: attorney; Kirkland, Wilson, Moore, Taylor & Thomas (law firm); served on the staff of Senator Strom Thurmond and Congressman Floyd Spence; former Deputy General Counsel, U.S. Department of Energy; former Judge of the town of Springdale, SC; military service: U.S. Army Reserves, 1972–75; currently a Colonel in the South Carolina Army National Guard as a Staff Judge Advocate for the 218th Mechanized Infantry Brigade; organizations: Cayce-West Columbia Rotary Club; Sheriff's Department Law Enforcement Advisory Council; Reserve Officers Association; Lexington County Historical Society; Columbia Home Builders Association; County Community and Resource Development Committee; American Heart Association; Mid-Carolina Mental Health Association; Cayce-West Columbia Jaycees; Kidney Foundation; South Carolina Lung Association; Alston-Wilkes Society; Cayce-West Metro Chamber of Commerce; Columbia World Affairs Council; Fellowship of Christian Athletes, Sinclair Lodge 154; Jamil Temple; Woodmen of the World; Sons of Confederate Veterans; Military Order of the World Wars; Lexington, Greater Irmo, Chapin, Columbia, West Metro, and Batesburg-Leesville Chambers of Commerce; West Metro and Dutch Fork Women's Republican Clubs; and Executive Council of the Indian Waters Council, Boy Scouts of America; awards: U.S. Chamber of Commerce Spirit of Enterprise Award, 2001; Americans for Tax Reform Friend of the Taxpayer Award, 2001; public service: South Carolina State Senate, 1984–2001; family: married to Roxanne Dusenbury McCrory; four sons; committees: Armed Services; Education and Labor; Foreign Affairs; Assistant GOP Whip; member, Republican Policy Committee; elected to the 107th Congress, by special election, on December 18, 2001; reelected to each succeeding Congress.

Office Listings

http://joewilson.house.gov

212 Cannon House Office Building, Washington, DC 20515 .... (202) 225–2452
Chief of Staff.—Eric Dell. FAX: 225–2455
Press Secretary.—Kim Olive.
Legislative Director.—Micki Work.
903 Port Republic Street, P.O. Box 1538, Beaufort, SC 29901 .... (843) 521–2530
1700 Sunset Boulevard (U.S. 378), Suite 1, West Columbia, SC 29169 .... (803) 939–0041

Counties: AIKEN (part), ALLENDALE, BARNWELL, BEAUFORT, CALHOUN (part), HAMPTON, JASPER, LEXINGTON, ORANGEBURG (part), RICHLAND (part). CITIES AND TOWNSHIPS: Aiken, Allendale, Ballentine, Barnwell, Batesburg, Beaufort, Blackville, Bluffton, Blythewood, Brunson, Cayce, Chapin, Columbia, Coosawhatchie, Cope, Cordova, Crocketville, Daufuskie Island, Early Branch, Elko, Estill, Fairfax, Furman, Garnett, Gaston, Gifford, Gilbert, Hampton, Hardeeville, Hilda, Hilton Head Island, Irmo, Islandston, Kline, Leesville, Lexington, Livingston, Luray, Martin, Miley, Montmorenci, Neeses, North, Norway, Orangeburg, Pelion, Pineland, Port Royal, Ridgeland, Ruffin, Scotia, Springfield, St. Helena Island, St. Matthews, State Park, Swansea, Sycamore, Tillman, Ulmer, Varnville, West Columbia, White Rock, Williams, Williston, Windsor, and Yemassee. Population (2000), 668,668.

ZIP Codes: 29002, 29006, 29016, 29033, 29036, 29045, 29053–54, 29063, 29070–73, 29075, 29078, 29107, 29112–13, 29115–16, 29118, 29123, 29128, 29130, 29135, 29137, 29142, 29146–47, 29160, 29164, 29169–72, 29177, 29180, 29203–07, 29209–10, 29212, 29219, 29221, 29223–24, 29226–27, 29229, 29260, 29290, 29292, 29405, 29412–13, 29436, 29470, 29472, 29801, 29803, 29805, 29810, 29812–13, 29817, 29826–27, 29836, 29839, 29843, 29846, 29849, 29853, 29901–07, 29909–11, 29913–16, 29918, 29920–28, 29932–36, 29938–41, 29943–45

* * *

THIRD DISTRICT

J. GRESHAM BARRETT, Republican, of Westminster, SC; born in Oconee County, SC, February 14, 1961; education: B.S., Business Administration, The Citadel, 1983; military service: U.S. Army, 1983–87; professional: small businessman; organizations: Westminster Rotary Club; Oconee County Boy Scouts; Westminster Chamber of Commerce; Oconee County Red Cross; public service: South Carolina House of Representatives, 1987–2002; religion: Baptist; attends Westminster Baptist Church; married to Natalie; children: Madison, Jeb, and Ross; committees: Budget; Financial Services; Foreign Affairs; Standard of Official Conduct; elected to the 108th Congress on November 5, 2002; reelected to each succeeding Congress.

Office Listings

http://www.house.gov/barrett

439 Cannon House Office Building, Washington, DC 20515 .... (202) 225–5301
Chief of Staff.—William ''Lance'' Williams. FAX: 225–3216
Legislative Director.—Sandra Campbell.
303 West Beltline Boulevard, Anderson, SC 29625 .... (864) 224–7401
115 Enterprise Court, Suite B, Greenwood, SC 29649 .... (864) 223–8251
233 Pendleton Street, NW., Aiken, SC 29801 .... (803) 649–5571

Counties: ABBEVILLE, AIKEN (part), ANDERSON, EDGEFIELD, GREENWOOD, LAURENS (part), MCCORMICK, OCONEE, PICKENS, SALUDA. Population (2000), 668,669.

ZIP Codes: 29006, 29037, 29070, 29105, 29127–29, 29138, 29166, 29178, 29325, 29332, 29334–35, 29351, 29355, 29360, 29370, 29384, 29388, 29406, 29611, 29620–28, 29630–33, 29635, 29638–49, 29653–59, 29661, 29664–67, 29669–73, 29675–79, 29682, 29684–86, 29689, 29691–93, 29695–97, 29801–05, 29808–09, 29816, 29819, 29821–22, 29824, 29828–29, 29831–32, 29834–35, 29838, 29840–42, 29844–45, 29847–48, 29850–51, 29853, 29856, 29860–61

* * *

FOURTH DISTRICT

BOB INGLIS, Republican, of Travelers Rest, SC; born in Savannah, GA, October 11, 1959; native of Bluffton, SC; education: May River Academy, Bluffton, SC, 1977; Duke University, Durham, NC, 1981; University of Virginia Law School, Charlottesville, VA, 1984; professional: attorney; admitted to the South Carolina Bar, 1984; Hunger, Maclean, Exley & Dunn (law firm), 1984–86; Leatherwood, Walker, Todd & Mann (law firm), 1986–92 and 1999–2004; religion: Presbyterian; member, Redeemer Presbyterian Church; married: the former Mary Anne Williams, 1982; five children; U.S. House of Representatives, 1993–98; committees: Foreign Affairs; Science and Technology; elected to the 109th Congress on November 2, 2004; reelected to the 110th Congress.

Office Listings

http://www.house.gov/inglis

330 Cannon House Office Building, Washington, DC 20515 .... (202) 225–6030
Chief of Staff.—Wayne Roper. FAX: 226–1177
Legislative Director.—Garth Van Meter.
Legislative Assistants: Lucie Burford, Ryan Hamilton, Philip Van Steenburgh.
Executive Assistant.—Marcus Huskey.
105 North Spring Street, Suite 111, Greenville, SC 29601 .... (864) 232–1141
Communications Director.—Price Atkinson.
145 North Church Street, BTC #56, Spartanburg, SC 29306 .... (864) 582–6422
Constituent Liaison.—Dwayne Hatchett.

Counties: GREENVILLE, LAURENS (part), SPARTANBURG, UNION. Population (2000), 668,669.

ZIP Codes: 29031, 29178, 29301–07, 29316, 29318–24, 29329–31, 29333–36, 29338, 29346, 29348–49, 29353, 29356, 29364–65, 29368–69, 29372–79, 29385–86, 29388, 29390–91, 29395, 29564, 29601–17, 29627, 29635–36, 29644–45, 29650–52, 29654, 29661–62, 29669, 29673, 29680–81, 29683, 29687–88, 29690, 29698

* * *

FIFTH DISTRICT

JOHN M. SPRATT, JR., Democrat, of York, SC; born in Charlotte, NC, November 1, 1942; education: graduated, York High School, 1960; A.B., Davidson College, 1964; president of student body and Phi Beta Kappa, Davidson College; M.A., economics, Oxford University, Corpus Christi College (Marshall Scholar), 1966; LL.B., Yale Law School, 1969; admitted to the South Carolina Bar in 1969; military service: active duty, U.S. Army, 1969–71, discharged as captain; member: Operations Analysis Group, Office of the Assistant Secretary of Defense (Comptroller), received Meritorious Service Medal; professional: private practice of law, Spratt, McKeown and Spratt, York, SC, 1971–82; attorney, York County, 1973–82; president, Bank of Fort Mill, 1973–82; president, Spratt Insurance Agency, Inc.; president, York Chamber of Commerce; chairman, Winthrop College Board of Visitors; chairman, Divine Saviour Hospital Board; board of visitors, Davidson and Coker Colleges; president, Western York County United Fund; board of directors, Piedmont Legal Services; House of Delegates, South Carolina bar; religion: elder, First Presbyterian Church, York; married: Jane Stacy Spratt, 1968; children: Susan, Sarah, and Catherine; committees: chair, Budget; Armed Services; elected to the 98th Congress, November 2, 1982; reelected to each succeeding Congress.

Office Listings

http://www.house.gov/spratt

1401 Longworth House Office Building, Washington, DC 20515 .... (202) 225–5501
  Chief of Staff.—Dawn O'Connell. FAX: 225–0464
  Deputy Chief of Staff / Press Secretary.—Chuck Fant.
P.O. Box 350, Rock Hill, SC 29731 .... (803) 327–1114
  District Administrator.—Robert Hopkins.
707 Bultman Drive, Sumter, SC 29150 .... (803) 773–3362
88 Public Square, Darlington, SC 29532–0025 .... (843) 393–3998

Counties: CHEROKEE, CHESTER, CHESTERFIELD, DARLINGTON, DILLON, FAIRFIELD, FLORENCE (part), KERSHAW, LANCASTER, LEE, MARLBORO, NEWBERRY, SUMTER (part), YORK. Population (2000), 668,668.

ZIP Codes: 29009–10, 29014–16, 29020, 29031–32, 29036–37, 29040, 29045, 29055, 29058, 29065, 29067, 29069, 29074–75, 29078–79, 29101–02, 29104, 29106, 29108, 29122, 29126–28, 29130, 29132, 29145, 29150–54, 29161, 29163, 29175–76, 29178, 29180, 29203, 29218, 29307, 29323, 29330, 29332, 29340–42, 29355, 29372, 29501, 29506, 29512, 29516, 29520, 29525, 29532, 29536, 29540, 29543, 29547, 29550–51, 29563, 29565, 29567, 29570, 29573–74, 29581, 29584, 29592–94, 29596, 29654, 29702–04, 29706, 29708–10, 29712, 29714–18, 29720–22, 29724, 29726–32, 29734, 29741–45

* * *

SIXTH DISTRICT

JAMES E. CLYBURN, Democrat, of Columbia, SC; born in Sumter, SC, July 21, 1940; education: graduated, Mather Academy, Camden, SC, 1957; B.S., South Carolina State University, Orangeburg, 1962; attended University of South Carolina Law School, Columbia, 1972–74; professional: South Carolina State Human Affairs Commissioner; assistant to the Governor for Human Resource Development; executive director, South Carolina Commission for Farm Workers, Inc.; director, Neighborhood Youth Corps and New Careers; counselor, South Carolina Employment Security Commission; member; lifetime member, NAACP; Southern Regional Council; Omega Psi Phi Fraternity, Inc.; Arabian Temple, No. 139; Nemiah Lodge No. 51 F&AM; married: the former Emily England; children: Mignon, Jennifer and Angela; elected vice chair, Democratic Caucus, 2002; chair, Democratic Caucus 2006; Majority Whip; elected on November 3, 1992, to the 103rd Congress; reelected to each succeeding Congress.

Office Listings

http://www.house.gov/clyburn

2135 Rayburn House Office Building, Washington, DC 20515 .... (202) 225–3315
  Chief of Staff.—Yelberton Watkins. FAX: 225–2313
  Deputy Chief of Staff.—Barvetta Singletary.
  Legislative Director.—Danny Cromer.
  Scheduler.—Jennie Chaplin.
1703 Gervais Street, Columbia, SC 29201 .... (803) 799–1100
  District Director.—Robert Nance.
181 East Evans Street, Suite 314, Post Office Box 6286, Florence, SC 29502 .... (803) 662–1212
8833 Old Number Six Highway, Santee, SC 29142 .... (803) 854–4700

Counties: BAMBERG COUNTY. CITIES AND TOWNSHIPS: Bamberg, Denmark, Erhardt, Olar. BERKELEY COUNTY (part). CITIES AND TOWNSHIPS: Bethera, Cross, Daniel Island, Huger, Jamestown, Pineville, Russellville, Saint Stephen, Wando. CALHOUN COUNTY (part). CITY OF: Cameron, Creston, Fort Motte, St. Matthews. CHARLESTON COUNTY (part). CITIES AND TOWNSHIPS: Adams Run, Charleston, Edisto Island, Hollywood, Johns Island, Ravenel, Wadmalaw Island. CLARENDON COUNTY. CITIES AND TOWNSHIPS: Alcolu, Davis Station, Gable, Manning, New Zion, Rimini, Summerton, Turbeville. COLLETON COUNTY. CITIES AND TOWNSHIPS: Ashton, Cottageville, Green Pond, Hendersonville, Islandton, Jacksonboro, Lodge, Ritter, Round O, Smoaks, Walterboro, Williams. DORCHESTER COUNTY (part). CITIES AND TOWNSHIPS: Dorchester, Harleyville, Reevesville, Ridgeville, Rosinville, Saint George. FLORENCE COUNTY (part). CITIES AND TOWNSHIPS: Coward, Effingham, Florence, Johnsonville, Lake City, Olanta, Pamplico, Quinby, Scranton, Timmonsville. GEORGETOWN COUNTY (part). CITIES AND TOWNSHIPS: Andrews, Outland, Sampit. MARION COUNTY. CITIES AND TOWNSHIPS: Centenary, Gresham, Marion, Mullins, Nichols, Rains, Sellers. LEE COUNTY (part). CITIES AND TOWNSHIPS: Elliott, Lynchburg. ORANGEBURG COUNTY (part). CITIES AND TOWNSHIPS: Bowman, Branchville, Cardova, Cope, Elloree, Eutawville, Holly Hill, Norway, Orangeburg, Rowesville, Santee, Vance. RICHLAND COUNTY (part). CITIES AND TOWNSHIPS: Blythewood, Columbia, Eastover, Gadsden, Hopkins. SUMTER COUNTY (part). CITIES AND TOWNSHIPS: Mayesville, Oswego, Pinewood, Sumter. WILLIAMSBURG COUNTY. CITIES AND TOWNSHIPS: Cades, Greeleyville, Hemingway, Kingstree, Lane, Nesmith, Salters, and Trio. Population (2000), 668,670.

ZIP Codes: 29001, 29003, 29006, 29010, 29018, 29030, 29038–42, 29044–48, 29051–52, 29056, 29059, 29061–62, 29078, 29080–82, 29102, 29104, 29107, 29111, 29113–15, 29117–18, 29125, 29128, 29130, 29133, 29135, 29142–43, 29146, 29148, 29150, 29153–54, 29161–63, 29168, 29201–05, 29208–09, 29211, 29214–17, 29220, 29223, 29225, 29228, 29230, 29240, 29250, 29403, 29405–06, 29409, 29415, 29418, 29426, 29430–38, 29440, 29446–50, 29452–53, 29461, 29466, 29468, 29470–72, 29474–77, 29479, 29481, 29488, 29492–93, 29501–06, 29510, 29518–19, 29530, 29541, 29546, 29554–56, 29560, 29565, 29571, 29574, 29580–81, 29583, 29589–92, 29817, 29843, 29929, 29931, 29945

SOUTH DAKOTA

(Population 2000, 754,844)

SENATORS

TIM JOHNSON, Democrat, of Vermillion, SD, born in Canton, SD, December 28, 1946; education: B.A., Phi Beta Kappa, University of South Dakota, 1969; M.A., political science, University of South Dakota, 1970; post-graduate study in political science, Michigan State University, 1970–71; J.D., University of South Dakota, 1975; budget advisor to the Michigan State Senate Appropriations Committee, 1971–72; admitted to the South Dakota bar in 1975 and began private law practice in Vermillion; elected to the South Dakota House of Representatives, 1978; reelected, 1980; elected to the South Dakota State Senate, 1982; reelected, 1984; served on the Joint Appropriations Committee and the Senate Judiciary Committee; served as Clay County Deputy State's Attorney, 1985; awards: named Outstanding Citizen of Vermillion, 1983; received South Dakota Education Association's ''Friend of Education'' Award, 1983; Billy Sutton Award for Legislative Achievement, 1984; elected to the U.S. House of Representatives, 1986; reelected to each succeeding Congress; delegate, Democratic National Convention, 1988–92; member: President's Export Council, 1999; religion Lutheran; married: Barbara Brooks, 1969; children: Brooks, Brendan and Kelsey Marie; committees: chair, Select Committee on Ethics; Appropriations; Banking, Housing, and Urban Affairs; Energy and Natural Resources; Indian Affairs; elected to the U.S. Senate on November 5, 1996; reelected to each succeeding Senate term.

Office Listings

http://johnson.senate.gov

136 Hart Senate Office Building, Washington, DC 20510 .... (202) 224–5842
Chief of Staff.—Drey Samuelson. FAX: 228–5765
Legislative Director.—Todd Stubbendieck.
Communications Director.—Julianne Fisher.
715 S. Minnesota Avenue, Sioux Falls, SD 57104 .... (605) 332–8896
State Director.—Sharon Boysen.
320 S. First Street, Suite 103, Aberdeen, SD 57401 .... (605) 226–3440
405 E. Omaha Street, Suite B, Rapid City, SD 57701 .... (605) 341–3990

* * *

JOHN THUNE, Republican, of Sioux Falls, SD; born in Pierre, SD, January 7, 1961; education: Jones County High School, 1979; B.S., business administration, Biola University, CA; M.B.A., University of South Dakota, 1984; professional: executive director, South Dakota Municipal League; board of directors, National League of Cities; executive director, South Dakota Republican Party, 1989–91; appointed, State Railroad Director, 1991; former congressional legislative assistant, and deputy staff director; elected, U.S. House of Representatives, 1997–2003; married: Kimberly Weems, 1984; children: Brittany and Larissa; committees: Agriculture, Nutrition, and Forestry; Armed Services; Commerce, Science, and Transportation; Small Business and Entrepreneurship; elected to the U.S. Senate on November 2, 2004.

Office Listings

http://thune.senate.gov

383 Russell Senate Office Building, Washington, DC 20510 .... (202) 224–2321
Chief of Staff.—Matt Zabel. FAX: 228–5429
Executive Director.—Summer Pitlick.
Legislative Director.—Dave Schwietert.
Communications Director.—Kyle Downey.
320 North Main Avenue, Suite B, Sioux Falls, SD 57104 .... (605) 334–9596
1312 West Main Street, Rapid City, SD 57701 .... (605) 348–7551
320 South First Street, Suite 101, Aberdeen, SD 57401 .... (605) 225–8823

REPRESENTATIVE

AT LARGE

STEPHANIE HERSETH SANDLIN, Democrat, of Brookings, SD; born in Groton, SD, December 3, 1970; education: graduated, Valedictorian, Groton High School; B.A. in Government, Georgetown University, *summa cum laude* and Phi Beta Kappa; J.D., with honors from the Georgetown University Law Center, and was a senior editor of the law review; professional: attorney; member, South Dakota Bar; served on the faculty of Georgetown University Law Center; worked on telecommunications and energy issues for the South Dakota Public Utilities Commission; organized commission meetings with Indian tribal leaders regarding utility regulation on Indian reservations; worked with U.S. District Court Judge Charles B. Kornmann; also served as a law clerk on the U.S. Court of Appeals for the Fourth Circuit; Executive Director, South Dakota Farmers Union Foundation; committees: Agriculture; Natural Resources; Veterans' Affairs; Select Committee on Energy Independence and Global Warming; elected to the 108th Congress by special election, on June 1, 2004; reelected to each succeeding Congress.

Office Listings

331 Cannon House Office Building, Washington, DC 20515 .... (202) 225–2801
Chief of Staff.—Tessa Gould. FAX: 225–5823
Communications Director.—Russ Levsen.
Legislative Director.—Ryan Stroschein.
Scheduler.—Magaret Sampson.
326 East 8th Street, Suite 108, Sioux Falls, SD 57103 .... (605) 367–8371
Southeast Director.—Mark Gerhardt.
1823 West Main Street, Rapid City, SD 57702 .... (605) 394–5280
Western Director.—Lesley Kandaras.
10 Sixth Avenue, SW., Aberdeen, SD 57401 .... (605) 626–3440
District Director.—Maeve King.

Population (2000), 754,844.

ZIP Codes: 57001–07, 57010, 57012–18, 57020–22, 57024–59, 57061–73, 57075–79, 57101, 57103–10, 57117–18, 57186, 57188–89, 57192–98, 57201, 57212–14, 57216–21, 57223–27, 57231–39, 57241–43, 57245–49, 57251–53, 57255–66, 57268–74, 57276, 57278–79, 57301, 57311–15, 57317, 57319, 57321–26, 57328–32, 57334–35, 57337, 57339–42, 57344–46, 57348–50, 57353–56, 57358–59, 57361–71, 57373–76, 57379–86, 57399, 57401–02, 57420–22, 57424, 57426–30, 57432–42, 57445–46, 57448–52, 57454–57, 57460–61, 57465–77, 57479, 57481, 57501, 57520–23, 57528–29, 57531–34, 57536–38, 57540–44, 57547–48, 57551–53, 57555, 57559–60, 57562–64, 57566–72, 57574, 57576–77, 57579–80, 57584–85, 57601, 57620–23, 57625–26, 57630–34, 57636, 57638–42, 57644–46, 57648–52, 57656–61, 57701–03, 57706, 57709, 57714, 57716–20, 57722, 57724–25, 57730, 57732, 57735, 57737–38, 57741, 57744–45, 57747–48, 57750–52, 57754–56, 57758–64, 57766–67, 57769–70, 57772–73, 57775–77, 57779–80, 57782–83, 57785, 57787–88, 57790–94, 57799

TENNESSEE

(Population 2000, 5,689,283)

SENATORS

LAMAR ALEXANDER, Republican, of Nashville, TN; born in Maryville, TN, July 3, 1940; education: graduated with honors in Latin American history, Phi Beta Kappa, Vanderbilt University; New York University Law School; served as Law Review editor; professional: clerk to Judge John Minor Wisdom, U.S. Court of Appeals in New Orleans; legislative assistant to Senator Howard Baker (R–TN), 1967; executive assistant to Bryce Harlow, counselor to President Nixon, 1969; President, University of Tennessee, 1988–91; co-director, Empower America, 1994–95; helped found a company that is now the nation's largest provider of worksite day care, Bright Horizons; public service: Republican nominee for Governor of Tennessee, 1974; Governor of Tennessee, 1979–87; U.S. Secretary of Education, 1991–93; community service: chairman, Salvation Army Red Shield Family Initiative; and the Museum of Appalachia in Norris, TN; received Tennessee Conservation League Conservationist of the Year Award; family: married to Honey Alexander; four children; committees: Appropriations; Budget; elected to the U.S. Senate on November 5, 2002.

Office Listings

http://alexander.senate.gov

455 Dirksen Senate Office Building, Washington, DC 20510 .... (202) 224–4944
Chief of Staff.—Tom Ingram. FAX: 228–3398
Legislative Director.—David Morgenstern.
Press Secretary.—Scot Montrey.
Executive Assistant / Scheduler.—Bonnie Sansonetti.
3322 West End Avenue, Suite 120, Nashville, TN 37203 .... (615) 736–5129
Howard H. Baker, Jr. U.S. Courthouse; 800 Market Street, Suite 112, Knoxville, TN 37902 .... (865) 545–4253
Federal Building, 167 North Main Street, Suite 1068, Memphis, TN 38103 .... (901) 544–4224
Federal Building, 109 South Highland Street, Suite B–9, Jackson, TN 38301 .... (731) 423–9344
Joel E. Solomon Federal Building, 900 Georgia Avenue, Suite 260, Chattanooga, TN 37402 .... (423) 752–5337
Tri-Cities Regional Airport, Terminal Building, Suite 101, Blountville, TN 37617 .... (423) 325–6240

* * *

BOB CORKER, Republican, of Chattanooga, TN; born in Orangeburg, SC, August 24, 1952; education: B.S., Industrial Management, University of Tennessee, Knoxville, TN, 1974; professional: founder of Bencor Corporation, a construction company specializing in retail properties which operated in 18 states, 1978–90; founder of the Corker Group, acquisition, development, and operation of commercial real estate, 1982–2006; honors: named to the University of Tennessee at Chattanooga's ''Entrepreneurial Hall of Fame,'' 2005; community service: founding chair, Chattanooga Neighborhood Enterprise, Inc., a non-profit organization that has helped over 10,000 families secure decent, fit and affordable housing, 1986–92; public service: commissioner, State of Tennessee Department of Finance and Administration, 1995–96; mayor, City of Chattanooga, 2001–05; married: Elizabeth Corker, 1987; two children: Julia and Emily; committees: Energy and Natural Resources; Foreign Relations; Small Business and Entrepreneurship; Special Committee on Aging; elected to the U.S. Senate on November 7, 2006.

Office Listings

http://corker.senate.gov

185 Dirksen Senate Office Building, Washington, DC 20510 .... (202) 224–3344
Chief of Staff.—Todd Womack. FAX: 228–0566
Legislative Director.—Paul Palagyi.
Executive Assistant / Scheduler.—Ramona Lessen.
Press Secretary.—Laura Lefler.
3322 West End Avenue, Suite 610, Nashville, TN 37203 .... (615) 279–8125
100 Peabody Place, Suite 1335, Memphis, TN 38103 .... (901) 683–1910
Howard Baker Federal Building, 800 Market Street, Suite 121, Knoxville, TN 37902 .... (865) 637–4180
Tri-Cities Regional Airport 2525, Highway 75, Suite 126, Blountville, TN 37617 .. (423) 323–1252
10 West Martin Luther King Boulevard, Sixth Floor, Chattanooga, TN 37402 .... (423) 756–2757
Ed Jones Federal Building, 109 South Highland Avenue, Suite B8, Jackson, TN 38301 .... (731) 424–9655

REPRESENTATIVES

FIRST DISTRICT

DAVID DAVIS, Republican, of Johnson City, TN; born in Johnson City, November 6, 1959; raised in Limestone Cove, TN; education: Respiratory Therapy Certification, East Tennessee State University, 1979; A.A.S., Respiratory Therapy, California College, 1983; B.S., Organizational Management, Milligan College, 1991; professional: respiratory therapist; President and founder, Advanced Homecare; President and founder, Shared Health Services, Inc.; Tennessee State Legislature, 1998–2006; member: American Association for Respiratory Care; Coalition for Kids; Conservative Round Table; Farm Bureau; Johnson City Chamber of Commerce; Johnson City Rotary Club; President's Council of Milligan College; Northeast Caucus; Sportsman Legislative Caucus; Tourism Caucus; chairman, Medicare Part B, Tennessee Association for Home Care; former chairman, Unicoi County Republican Party; delegate, White House Conference on Small Business; Washington County Republican Party; awards: Home Medical Equipment Supplier of the Year; John W. Hines Award, Tennessee Association for Home Care; Respiratory Care Practitioner of the Year, 1994; Health Care Hero Award, 2004; Legislator of the Year, Tennessee Podiatric Association, 2005; member: Central Baptist Church, Johnson City; married to the former Joyce Engle, 1980; children: Matthew and Rachel; committees: Education and Labor; Homeland Security; Small Business; member, Republican House Policy Committee; elected to the 110th Congress on November 7, 2006.

Office Listings

514 Cannon House Office Building, Washington, DC 20515 .... (202) 225–6356
Chief of Staff.—Brenda J. Otterson. FAX: 225–5714
Executive Assistant / Scheduler.—Karen Kaumeier.
Legislative Director.—Richard Vaughn.
320 West Center Street, Kingsport, TN 37662 .... (423) 247–8161
District Director.—Paul Chapman.

Counties: CARTER, COCKE, GREENE, HAMBLEN, HANCOCK, HAWKINS, JEFFERSON, JOHNSON, SEVIER, SULLIVAN, UNICOI, WASHINGTON. Population (2000), 632,143.

ZIP Codes: 37601–02, 37604–05, 37614–18, 37620–21, 37625, 37640–45, 37650, 37656–60, 37662–65, 37680–84, 37686–88, 37690–92, 37694, 37699, 37711, 37713, 37722, 37725, 37727, 37731, 37738, 37743–45, 37752–53, 37760, 37764–65, 37778, 37809–11, 37813–16, 37818, 37821–22, 37843, 37857, 37860, 37862–65, 37868–69, 37873, 37876–77, 37879, 37881, 37890–91

* * *

SECOND DISTRICT

JOHN J. DUNCAN, JR., Republican, of Knoxville, TN; born in Lebanon, TN, July 21, 1947; education: B.S. in journalism, University of Tennessee, 1969; J.D., National Law Center, George Washington University, 1973; served in both the Army National Guard and the U.S. Army Reserves, retiring with the rank of captain; private law practice, Knoxville, 1973–81; appointed State Trial Judge by Governor Lamar Alexander in 1981 and elected to a full eight-year term in 1982 without opposition, receiving the highest number of votes of any candidate on the ballot that year; member: American Legion 40 and 8, Elks, Sertoma Club, Masons, Scottish Rite and Shrine; present or past board member: Red Cross, Girl's Club, YWCA, Sunshine Center for the Mentally Retarded, Beck Black Heritage Center, Knoxville Union Rescue Mission, Senior Citizens Home Aid Service; religion: active elder at Eastminster Presbyterian Church; married: the former Lynn Hawkins; children: Tara, Whitney, John J. III and Zane; committees: Natural Resources; Oversight and Government Reform; Transportation and Infrastructure; elected to both the 100th Congress (special election) and the 101st Congress in separate elections held on November 8, 1988; reelected to each succeeding Congress.

Office Listings

http://www.house.gov/duncan

2207 Rayburn House Office Building, Washington, DC 20515 .... (202) 225–5435
Chief of Staff.—Bob Griffitts. FAX: 225–6440
Deputy Chief of Staff.—Don Walker.
Press Secretary.—Amy Westmoreland.
6 East Madison Avenue, Athens, TN 37303 .... (423) 745–4671
800 Market Street, Suite 100, Knoxville, TN 37902 .... (423) 523–3772
District Director.—Bob Griffitts.
200 East Broadway Avenue, Suite 414, Maryville, TN 37804 .... (423) 984–5464

Counties: BLOUNT, KNOX (part), LOUDON, MCMINN, MONROE. CITIES AND TOWNSHIPS: Alcoa, Athens, Englewood, Etowah, Farragut, Halls (Knox Co.), Knoxville, Lenoir City, Loudon, Madisonville, Maryville, Powell, Seymour, and Sweetwater. Population (2000), 632,144.

ZIP Codes: 37303, 37309, 37311–12, 37314, 37322–23, 37325, 37329, 37331, 37353–54, 37369–71, 37385, 37701, 37709, 37721, 37725, 37737, 37742, 37754, 37764, 37771–72, 37774, 37777, 37779, 37801–04, 37806–07, 37820, 37826, 37830, 37846, 37849, 37853, 37865, 37871, 37874, 37876, 37878, 37880, 37882, 37885–86, 37901–02, 37909, 37912, 37914–24, 37927–33, 37938–40, 37950, 37990, 37995–98

* * *

THIRD DISTRICT

ZACH WAMP, Republican, of Chattanooga, TN; born in Fort Benning, GA, October 28, 1957; graduated, McCallie School, Chattanooga, 1976; attended University of North Carolina at Chapel Hill and University of Tennessee; commercial and industrial real estate broker; named Chattanooga Business Leader of the Year; chairman, Hamilton County Republican Party; regional director, Tennessee Republican Party; awards: received Tennessee Jaycees' Outstanding Young Tennessean Award, 1996; U.S. Chamber of Commerce Spirit of Enterprise Award; Citizens Against Government Waste ''A'' Rating; National Taxpayers Union Friend of the Taxpayers Award; recognized by the Citizens Taxpayers Association of Hamilton County, the National Federation of Independent Business and the Concord Coalition for casting tough votes to reduce spending; member, Red Bank Baptist Church; married: Kimberly Watts Wamp, 1985; two children: Weston and Coty; committees: Appropriations; elected to the 104th Congress; reelected to each succeeding Congress.

Office Listings

http://www.house.gov/wamp

1436 Longworth House Office Building, Washington, DC 20515 .... (202) 225–3271
FAX: 225–3494
Chief of Staff.—Helen Hardin.
Legislative Director.—Melissa Chapman.
Scheduler.—Emily Hall.
900 Georgia Avenue, Suite 126, Chattanooga, TN 37402 .... (423) 756–2342
District Staff Coordinator.—Trish Mullins.
Federal Building, 200 Administration Road, Suite 100, Oak Ridge, TN 37830 .... (865) 576–1976
District Representative.—Gina Boom.

Counties: ANDERSON, BRADLEY, CLAIBORNE, GRAINGER, HAMILTON, JEFFERSON (part), MEIGS, POLK, RHEA, ROANE (part), UNION. Population (2000), 632,143.

ZIP Codes: 37302, 37304, 37307–12, 37315–17, 37320–23, 37325–26, 37332–33, 37336–38, 37341, 37343, 37350–51, 37353, 37361–64, 37369, 37373, 37375, 37377, 37379, 37381, 37384, 37391, 37397, 37401–12, 37414–16, 37419, 37421–22, 37424, 37450, 37705, 37707–10, 37715–17, 37719, 37721, 37724–26, 37730, 37752, 37754, 37760, 37763–64, 37769, 37771, 37774, 37779, 37806–07, 37811, 37820–21, 37824–26, 37828, 37830–31, 37840, 37846, 37848–49, 37851, 37861, 37866, 37869–71, 37874, 37876–77, 37879–81, 37888, 37890, 37931, 37938

* * *

FOURTH DISTRICT

LINCOLN DAVIS, Democrat, of Pall Mall, TN; born in Pall Mall, September 13, 1943; education: Alvin C. York Agricultural Institute, 1962; B.S., Agronomy, Tennessee Technological University, 1966; professional: farmer and general contractor; civic organizations: Tennessee State Jaycees; Pickett County Chamber of Commerce; Upper Cumberland Developmental District; Boy Scouts; public service: Mayor of Byrdstown, TN, 1978–82; Tennessee State Representative, 1980–84; Tennessee State Senator, 1996–2002; religion: Baptist; married: Lynda; children: Larissa, Lynn and Libby; committees: Agriculture; Financial Services; elected to the 108th Congress on November 5, 2002; reelected to each succeeding Congress.

Office Listings

http://www.house.gov/lincolndavis

410 Cannon House Office Building, Washington, DC 20515 .... (202) 225–6831
FAX: 226–5172
Chief of Staff.—Beecher Frasier.
Legislative Director.—Brandi Lowell.
Press Secretary.—Tom Hayden.
1064 North Gateway Avenue, Rockwood, TN 37854 .... (865) 354–3323
629 North Main Street, Jamestown, TN 38556 .... (931) 879–2361
1804 Carmack Boulevard, Suite A, Columbia, TN 38401 .... (931) 490–8699
477 North Chancery Street, Suite A–1, McMinnville, TN 37110 .... (931) 473–7251

Counties: BLEDSOE, CAMPBELL, COFFEE, CUMBERLAND, FENTRESS, FRANKLIN, GILES, GRUNDY, HICKMAN (part), LAWRENCE, LEWIS, LINCOLN, MARION, MAURY, MOORE, MORGAN, PICKETT, ROANE (part), SCOTT, SEQUATCHIE, VAN BUREN, WARREN, WHITE, WILLIAMSON (part). Population (2000), 632,143.

ZIP Codes: 37018, 37025–26, 37033, 37037, 37047, 37062, 37064, 37078, 37091, 37096, 37098, 37110–11, 37129–33, 37137, 37144, 37160, 37166, 37171, 37174, 37179, 37183, 37190, 37301, 37305–06, 37313, 37318, 37324, 37327–28, 37330, 37334–35, 37337, 37339–40, 37342, 37345, 37347–49, 37352, 37355–57, 37359–60, 37365–67, 37374–83, 37387–89, 37394, 37396–98, 37419, 37714–15, 37719, 37721, 37723, 37726, 37729, 37732–33, 37748, 37755–57, 37762–63, 37766, 37769–71, 37773, 37778, 37819, 37829, 37840–41, 37845, 37847, 37852, 37854, 37867, 37869–70, 37872, 37880, 37887, 37892, 38370, 38401–02, 38449, 38451, 38453–57, 38459–64, 38468–69, 38472–78, 38481–83, 38486–88, 38504, 38506, 38549–50, 38553, 38555–59, 38565, 38571–72, 38574, 38577–79, 38581, 38583, 38585, 38587, 38589

* * *

FIFTH DISTRICT

JIM COOPER, Democrat, of Nashville, TN; born in Nashville, June 19, 1954; education: B.A., history and economics, University of North Carolina at Chapel Hill, 1975; Rhodes Scholar, Oxford University, 1977; J.D., Harvard Law School, 1980; admitted to Tennessee bar, 1980; professional: attorney; Waller, Lansden, Dortch, and Davis (law firm), 1980–82; Managing Director, Equitable Securities, 1995–99; Adjunct Professor, Vanderbilt University Owen School of Management, 1995–2002; partner, Brentwood Capital Advisors LLC, 1999–2002; married: Martha Hays; children: Mary, Jamie, and Hayes; committees: Armed Services; Budget; Oversight and Government Reform; elected to the U.S. House of Representatives, 1982–95; elected to the 108th Congress on November 5, 2002; reelected to each succeeding Congress.

Office Listings

http://www.cooper.house.gov

1536 Longworth House Office Building, Washington, DC 20515 .... (202) 225–4311
Chief of Staff.—Greg Hinote. FAX: 226–1035
Legislative Director.—Thomas Fields.
605 Church Street, Nashville, TN 37219 .... (615) 736–5295

Counties: CHEATHAM (part), DAVIDSON, WILSON (part). Population (2000), 632,143.

ZIP Codes: 37011, 37013, 37015, 37027, 37032, 37034–35, 37064, 37070–72, 37076, 37080, 37082, 37086–88, 37090, 37115–16, 37121–22, 37135, 37138, 37143, 37146, 37189, 37201–22, 37224, 37227–30, 37232, 37234–36, 37238–50

* * *

SIXTH DISTRICT

BART GORDON, Democrat, of Murfreesboro, TN; born in Murfreesboro, January 24, 1949; graduated, Central High School, Murfreesboro, 1967; B.S., *cum laude*, Middle Tennessee State University, Murfreesboro, 1971; J.D., University of Tennessee College of Law, Knoxville, 1973; admitted to the Tennessee State bar, 1974; opened private law practice in Murfreesboro, 1974; elected to the Tennessee Democratic Party's executive committee, 1974; appointed executive director of the Tennessee Democratic Party, 1979; elected the first full-time chairman of the Tennessee Democratic Party, 1981; resigned chairmanship, 1983, to successfully seek congressional seat; past chairman: Rutherford County United Givers Fund and Rutherford County Cancer Crusade; board member: Rutherford County Chamber of Commerce, MTSU Foundation; member, St. Mark's Methodist Church, Murfreesboro; married: Leslie Peyton Gordon; child: Peyton Margaret; committees: chair, Science and Technology; Energy and Commerce; elected to the 99th Congress on November 6, 1984; reelected to each succeeding Congress.

Office Listings

http://www.house.gov/gordon

2310 Rayburn House Office Building, Washington, DC 20515 .... (202) 225–4231
Chief of Staff.—Donna Pignatelli. FAX: 225–6887
Scheduler.—Amy Taylor.
P.O. Box 1986, 305 West Main Street, Murfreesboro, TN 37133 .... (615) 896–1986
District Chief of Staff.—Kent Syler.
P.O. Box 1140, 15 South Jefferson, Cookeville, TN 38501 .... (931) 528–5907
Sumner County Courthouse, Room B–100, Gallatin, TN 37066 .... (615) 451–5174

Counties: BEDFORD, CANNON, CLAY, DEKALB, JACKSON, MACON, MARSHALL, OVERTON, PUTNAM, ROBERTSON, RUTHERFORD, SMITH, SUMNER, TROUSDALE, WILSON (part). CITIES AND TOWNSHIPS: Cookeville, Gallatin, Hendersonville, Lafayette, Lebanon, Lewisburg, Livingston, Murfreesboro, Shelbyville, and Springfield. Population (2000), 632,143.

ZIP Codes: 37010, 37012, 37014, 37016, 37018–20, 37022, 37026, 37030–32, 37034, 37037, 37046–49, 37057, 37059–60, 37063, 37066, 37072–75, 37077, 37080, 37083, 37085–87, 37090–91, 37095, 37110, 37118–19, 37122, 37127–28, 37135–36, 37141, 37144–46, 37148–53, 37160–62, 37166–67, 37172, 37174, 37180, 37183–84, 37186, 37188, 37190, 37357, 37360, 37388, 38451, 38472, 38501–03, 38505–06, 38541–45, 38547–48, 38551–52, 38554, 38560, 38562–64, 38567–70, 38573–75, 38580–83, 38588–89

* * *

SEVENTH DISTRICT

MARSHA BLACKBURN, Republican, of Franklin, TN; born in Laurel, MS, June 6, 1952; education: B.S., Mississippi State University, 1973; professional: retail marketing; public service: American Council of Young Political Leaders; executive director, Tennessee Film, Entertainment, and Music Commission; chairman, Governor's Prayer Breakfast; Tennessee State Senate, 1998–2002; minority whip; community service: Rotary Club; Chamber of Commerce; Arthritis Foundation; Nashville Symphony Guild Board; Tennessee Biotechnology Association; March of Dimes; American Lung Association; awards: Chi Omega Alumnae Greek Woman of the Year, 1999; Middle Tennessee 100 Most Powerful People, 1999–2002; married: Chuck; children: Mary Morgan Ketchel and Chad; committees: Energy and Commerce; Select Committee on Energy Independence and Global Warming; elected to the 108th Congress on November 5, 2002; reelected to each succeeding Congress.

Office Listings

http://www.house.gov/blackburn

509 Cannon House Office Building, Washington, DC 20515 .... (202) 225–2811
Chief of Staff.—Steve Brophy. FAX: 225–3004
Executive Assistant.—Meredith Simpson.
7975 Stage Hill Boulevard, Suite 1, Memphis, TN 38133 .... (901) 382–5811
City Hall Mall, 201 3rd Avenue South, Suite 117, Franklin, TN 37064 .... (615) 591–5161
1850 Memorial Drive, Clarksville, TN 37043 .... (931) 503–0391

Counties: CHEATHAM (part), CHESTER, DAVIDSON (part), DECATUR, FAYETTE, HARDEMAN, HARDIN, HENDERSON, HICKMAN (part), MCNAIRY, MONTGOMERY (part), PERRY, SHELBY (part), WAYNE, WILLIAMSON (part). Population (2000), 632,139.

ZIP Codes: 37010, 37014–15, 37024–25, 37027, 37032–33, 37035–36, 37040–43, 37046, 37052, 37055, 37060, 37062, 37064–65, 37067–69, 37079, 37082, 37096–98, 37101, 37135, 37137, 37140, 37155, 37174, 37179, 37187, 37191, 37211, 37215, 37220–21, 38002, 38004, 38008, 38010–11, 38014, 38016–18, 38027–29, 38036, 38039, 38042, 38044–46, 38048–49, 38052–53, 38057, 38060–61, 38066–69, 38075–76, 38088, 38128, 38133–34, 38138–39, 38141, 38163, 38183–84, 38310–11, 38313, 38315, 38321, 38326–29, 38332, 38334, 38339–41, 38345, 38347, 38351–52, 38356–57, 38359, 38361, 38363, 38365–68, 38370–72, 38374–76, 38379–81, 38388, 38390, 38392–93, 38425, 38450, 38452, 38463, 38471, 38475, 38485–86

* * *

EIGHTH DISTRICT

JOHN S. TANNER, Democrat, of Union City, TN; born at Dyersburg Army Air Base, Halls, TN, September 22, 1944; attended elementary and high school in Union City; B.S., University of Tennessee at Knoxville, 1966; J.D., University of Tennessee at Knoxville, 1968; professional: attorney; admitted to the Tennessee bar, 1968; commenced practice in Union City; served, U.S. Navy, lieutenant, 1968–72; colonel, Tennessee Army National Guard, 1974–2000; member, Elam, Glasgow, Tanner and Acree law firm until 1988; businessman; elected to Tennessee House of Representatives, 1976–88; chairman, House Committee on Commerce, 1987–88; member: Obion County Chamber of Commerce; Obion County Cancer Society; Union City Rotary Club, Paul Harris Fellow; Obion County Bar Association; American Legion; Masons; religion: First Christian Church (Disciples of Christ) of Union City; married: the former Betty Ann Portis; children: Elizabeth Tanner Atkins and John Portis; three grandchildren; member: chair, delegation to NATO Parlimentary Assembly; Blue Dog Coalition; Congressional Sportsmen's Caucus; committees: Foreign Affairs; Ways and Means; elected to the 101st Congress on November 8, 1988; reelected to each succeeding Congress.

Office Listings

http://www.house.gov/tanner

1226 Longworth House Office Building, Washington, DC 20515 .... (202) 225–4714
Administrative Assistant.—Vickie Walling. FAX: 225–1765
Communications Director.—Randy Ford.
Executive Assistant.—Kathy Becker.
203 West Church Street, Union City, TN 38261 .... (731) 885–7070

District Director.—Joe Hill.
Federal Building, Room B–7, Jackson, TN 38301 .... (731) 423–4848
8120 Highway 51 North, Suite 3, Millington, TN 38053 .... (901) 873–5690

Counties: BENTON, CARROLL, CROCKETT, DICKSON, DYER, GIBSON, HAYWOOD, HENRY, HOUSTON, HUMPHREYS, LAKE, LAUDERDALE, MADISON, MONTGOMERY (part), OBION, SHELBY (part), STEWART, TIPTON, WEAKLEY. Population (2000), 632,142.

ZIP Codes: 37015, 37023, 37025, 37028–29, 37036, 37040, 37043–44, 37050–52, 37055–56, 37058, 37061–62, 37078–79, 37097, 37101, 37134, 37142, 37165, 37171, 37175, 37178, 37181, 37185, 37187, 38001, 38004, 38006–07, 38011–12, 38015, 38019, 38021, 38023–25, 38030, 38034, 38037, 38040–41, 38047, 38049–50, 38053–55, 38058–59, 38063, 38069–71, 38075, 38077, 38079–80, 38083, 38127–29, 38135, 38201, 38220–26, 38229–33, 38235–38, 38240–42, 38251, 38253–61, 38271, 38281, 38301–03, 38305, 38308, 38313–14, 38316–18, 38320–21, 38324, 38330–31, 38333, 38336–38, 38341–44, 38346, 38348, 38355–56, 38358, 38362, 38366, 38369, 38378, 38380, 38382, 38387, 38389–92

* * *

NINTH DISTRICT

STEPHEN IRA ''STEVE'' COHEN, Democrat, of Memphis, TN; born in Memphis, May 24, 1949 of Dr. Morris D. Cohen and Genevieve Cohen; B.A., Vanderbilt University in Nashville, TN, 1971; J.D., Cecil C. Humphreys School of Law of Memphis State University (renamed University of Memphis), 1973; Legal Advisor for the Memphis Police Department, 1974–77; Delegate to and Vice President of Tennessee Constitutional Convention, 1977; Commissioner on the Shelby County Commission, 1978–80; Tennessee State Senator for District 30, 1982–2006; committees: Judiciary; Transportation and Infrastructure; elected to the 110th Congress on November 7, 2006.

Office Listings

http://www.cohen.house.gov

1004 Longworth House Office Building, Washington, DC 20515 .... (202) 225–3265
Chief of Staff.—Shirley Cooks. FAX: 225–5663
Scheduler.—Craig Dulniak.
Legislative Director.—Marilyn Dillihay.
Communications Director.—Marilyn Dillihay.
167 North Main Street, Suite 369, Memphis, TN 38103 .... (901) 544–4131

County: SHELBY COUNTY (part). CITY OF: Memphis. Population (2000), 632,143.

ZIP Codes: 37501, 38016–18, 38101, 38103–09, 38111–20, 38122, 38124–28, 38130–37, 38139, 38141–42, 38145–48, 38151–52, 38157, 38159, 38161, 38165–68, 38173–75, 38177, 38181–82, 38186–88, 38190, 38193–95, 38197

TEXAS

(Population 2000, 20,851,820)

SENATORS

KAY BAILEY HUTCHISON, Republican, of Dallas, TX; born in Galveston, TX, July 22, 1943; raised in La Marque, TX; education: graduated, The University of Texas at Austin and The University of Texas School of Law; professional: Texas House of Representatives, 1972–76; appointed vice chair, National Transportation Safety Board, 1976; senior vice president and general counsel, RepublicBank Corporation; co-founded, Fidelity National Bank of Dallas; owned, McCraw Candies, Inc.; political and legal correspondent, KPRC–TV, Houston; member: development boards of SMU and Texas A&M schools of business; trustee, The University of Texas Law School Foundation; elected Texas State Treasurer, 1990; religion: Episcopalian; married: Ray Hutchison; committees: chair, Republican Policy Committee; Appropriations; Commerce, Science and Transportation; Rules and Administration; Veterans' Affairs; elected to the U.S. Senate, by special election, on June 5, 1993, to fill the vacancy caused by the resignation of Senator Lloyd Bentsen; reelected to each succeeding Senate term.

Office Listings

http://hutchison.senate.gov

284 Russell Senate Office Building, Washington, DC 20510 .... (202) 224–5922
Chief of Staff.—Marc Short. FAX: 224–0776
Deputy Chief of Staff.—James Christoferson.
Legislative Director.—Matthew Acock.
Press Secretary.—Matt Mackowiak.
961 Federal Building, 300 East Eighth Street, Austin, TX 78701 .... (512) 916–5834
10440 North Central Expressway, Suite 1160, LB 606, Dallas, TX 75231 .... (214) 361–3500
1919 Smith Street, Suite 800, Houston, TX 77002 .... (713) 653–3456
1906–G Tyler Street, Harlingen, TX 78550 .... (956) 425–2253
500 Chestnut Street, Suite 1570, Abilene, TX 79602 .... (325) 676–2839
145 Duncan Drive, Suite 120, San Antonio, TX 78226 .... (210) 340–2885

* * *

JOHN CORNYN, Republican, of San Antonio, TX; born in Houston, TX, February 2, 1952; education: graduated, Trinity University, and St. Mary's School of Law, San Antonio, TX; Masters of Law, University of Virginia, Charlottesville, VA; professional: attorney; Bexar County District Court Judge; Presiding Judge, Fourth Administrative Judicial Region; Texas Supreme Court, 1990–97; Texas Attorney General, 1999–2002; community service: Salvation Army Adult Rehabilitation Council; World Affairs Council of San Antonio; Lutheran General Hospital Board; awards: Outstanding Texas Leader Award, 2000; James Madison Award, 2001; committees: Armed Services; Budget; Judiciary; Special Committee on Aging; vice-chair, Senate Republican Conference; elected to the U.S. Senate on November 5, 2002, for the term beginning January 3, 2003; appointed to the Senate on December 2, 2002, to fill the vacancy caused by the resignation of Senator Phil Gramm.

Office Listings

http://cornyn.senate.gov

517 Hart Senate Office Building, Washington, DC 20510 .... (202) 224–2934
Chief of Staff.—Beth Jafari. FAX: 228–2856
Legislative Director.—Jeff Thomasson.
5300 Memorial Drive, Houston, TX 77007 .... (713) 572–3337
Occidental Tower, 5005 LBJ Freeway, Suite 1150, Dallas, TX 75244 .... (972) 239–1310
100 East Ferguson Street, Suite 1004, Tyler, TX 75702 .... (903) 593–0902
221 West Sixth Street, Suite 1530, Austin, TX 78701 .... (512) 469–6034
3405 Twenty-Second Street, Suite 203, Lubbock, TX 79410 .... (806) 472–7533
222 East Van Buren, Suite 404, Harlingen, TX 78550 .... (956) 423–0162

REPRESENTATIVES

FIRST DISTRICT

LOUIE GOHMERT, Republican, of Tyler, TX; born in Pittsburg, TX, August 18, 1953; education: B.A., Texas A&M University, 1975; J.D., Baylor University, Waco, TX, 1977; professional: United States Army, 1978–82; district judge, Smith County, 1992–2002; appointed by Governor Rick Perry to complete an unexpired term as Chief Justice of the 12th Court of Appeals, 2002–03; Brigade Commander of the Corps of Cadets, Texas A&M; organizations: President of the South Tyler Rotary Club; Boy Scout District Board of Directors; religion: deacon at Green Acres Baptist Church; director of Leadership Tyler; director of Centrepoint Ministries; married: Kathy; children: Katy, Caroline, Sarah; committees: Judiciary; Natural Resources; Small Business; elected to the 109th Congress on November 2, 2004; reelected to the 110th Congress.

Office Listings

http://www.house.gov/gohmert

510 Cannon House Office Building, Washington, DC 20515 .... (202) 225–3035
Chief of Staff.—Michael Tomberlin. FAX: 226–1230
Legislative Director.—Ashley Callen.
Communications Director.—Lauren Huly.
1121 E. Southeast Loop 323, Suite 206, Tyler, TX 75701 .... (903) 561–6349

Counties: Angelina, Cass (part), Gregg, Harrison, Marion, Nacogdoches, Panola, Rusk, Sabine, San Augustine, Shelby, Smith, Upshur. Population (2000), 651,619.

ZIP Codes: 75551, 75555, 75562, 75564–65, 75601–08, 75615, 75631, 75633, 75637, 75639–45, 75647, 75650–54, 75657–63, 75666–67, 75669–72, 75680, 75682–85, 75687–89, 75691–94, 75701–13, 75750, 75755, 75757, 75760, 75762, 75771, 75788–89, 75791–92, 75797–99, 75901–04, 75915, 75929–31, 75935, 75937, 75941, 75943–44, 75946–49, 75954, 75958–59, 75961–65, 75968–69, 75972–75, 75978, 75980

* * *

SECOND DISTRICT

TED POE, Republican, of Humble, TX; born in Temple, TX, October 13, 1948; education: B.A., Political Science, Abilene Christian University, Abilene, TX, 1970; J.D., University of Houston, TX, 1973; professional: United States Air Force, 1970–1976; Felony Court Judge, 1981–2004; Trainer, Federal Bureau of Investigations National Academy; Chief Felony Prosecutor, District Attorney, Harris County, TX; United States Air Force Reserves Instructor, University of Houston; organizations: Board of the National Children's Alliance; Child Abuse Prevention Council; family: married to Carol; children: Kim, Kara, Kurt, and Kellee; committees: Foreign Affairs; Transportation and Infrastructure; elected to the 109th Congress on November 2, 2004; reelected to the 110th Congress.

Office Listings

http://www.house.gov/poe

1605 Longworth House Office Building, Washington, DC 20515 .... (202) 225–6565
Chief of Staff.—Heather Ramsey. FAX: 225–5547
Legislative Director.—Alan Knapp.
Press Secretary.—DeeAnn Thigpen.
Scheduler.—Megan Moore.
20202 US Highway 59 North, Suite 105, Humble, TX 77338–2400 .... (281) 446–0242
505 Orleans, Suite 100, Beaumont, TX 77701 .... (409) 212–1997

Counties: Angelina, Cherokee, Grimes, Hardin, Houston, Jasper, Liberty, Montgomery (part), Nacogdoches (part), Newton, Orange, Polk, Sabine, San Augustine, San Jacinto, Trinity, Tyler, Walker. Population (2000), 651,619.

ZIP Codes: 75757, 75759, 75764, 75766, 75772, 75780, 75784–85, 75789, 75834–35, 75839, 75844–45, 75847, 75849, 75851–52, 75856, 75858, 75862, 75865, 75901–04, 75915, 75925–26, 75928–34, 75936–39, 75941–42, 75944, 75947–49, 75951, 75956, 75959–61, 75965–66, 75968–69, 75972, 75976–80, 77301–03, 77306, 77320, 77326–28, 77331–32, 77334–35, 77340–42, 77350–51, 77354, 77356–60, 77363–64, 77367–69, 77371–72, 77374, 77376, 77378, 77399, 77519, 77533, 77535, 77538, 77561, 77564, 77574–75, 77582, 77585, 77611–12, 77614–17, 77624–26, 77630–32, 77639, 77656–57, 77659, 77660, 77662–64, 77670, 77830–31, 77861, 77868, 77872, 77875–76

* * *

THIRD DISTRICT

SAM JOHNSON, Republican, of Dallas, TX; born in San Antonio, TX, October 11, 1930; education: B.S., business administration, Southern Methodist University, Dallas, TX, 1951; M.A., international affairs, George Washington University, Washington, DC, 1974; military service: served in Air Force, 29 years; Korea and Vietnam (POW in Vietnam, six years, ten months); director, Air Force Fighter Weapons School; flew with Air Force Thunderbirds Precision Flying Demonstration Team; graduate of Armed Services Staff College and National War

College; military awards: two Silver Stars, two Legions of Merit, Distinguished Flying Cross, one Bronze Star with Valor, two Purple Hearts, four Air Medals, and three Outstanding Unit awards; ended career with rank of colonel and Air Division commander; retired, 1979; professional: opened homebuilding company, 1979; served seven years in Texas House of Representatives; Smithsonian Board of Regents; U.S. / Russian Joint Commission on POW / MIA; member: Executive Board of Dedman College; Southern Methodist University; Associated Texans Against Crime; Texas State Society; elected to Texas State House of Representatives, 1984; married the former Shirley L. Melton, 1950; three children: Dr. James Robert Johnson, Shirley Virginia (Gini) Mulligan and Beverly Briney; committees: Ways and Means; elected to the 102nd Congress by special election on May 18, 1991, to fill the vacancy caused by the resignation of Steve Bartlett; reelected to each succeeding Congress.

Office Listings

http://www.house.gov/samjohnson

1211 Longworth House Office Building, Washington, DC 20515 .... (202) 225–4201
Chief of Staff.—Dave Heil. FAX: 225–1485
Legislative Director.—Layton Griffin.
Executive Assistant.—Ellie Mae Harrison.
2929 North Central Expressway, Suite 240, Richardson, TX 75080 .... (972) 470–0892

Counties: COLLIN (part), DALLAS, (part). CITIES AND TOWNSHIPS: Allen, Dallas, Frisno, Garland, McKinney, Plano, Richardson, Rowlett, and Sachse. Population (2000), 651,620.

ZIP Codes: 75002, 75007, 75009, 75013, 75023–26, 75030, 75034–35, 75040–42, 75044–48, 75069–71, 75074–75, 75078, 75080–82, 75085–86, 75088–89, 75093–94, 75098, 75228, 75238, 75245, 75248, 75252, 75287, 75355, 75367, 75370, 75378, 75382, 75409, 75424, 75442, 75454, 78243

* * *

FOURTH DISTRICT

RALPH M. HALL, Republican, of Rockwall, TX; born in Fate, TX, May 3, 1923; education: graduated, Rockwall High School, 1941; attended, Texas Christian University and the University of Texas; LL.B., Southern Methodist University, 1951; professional: lieutenant, carrier pilot (senior grade), U.S. Navy, 1942–45; lawyer; admitted to the Texas bar, 1951; practiced law in Rockwall; county judge, Rockwall County, 1950–62; former president and chief executive officer, Texas Aluminum Corporation; past general counsel, Texas Extrusion Company, Inc.; past organizer, chairman, board of directors, now chairman of board, Lakeside National Bank of Rockwall (now Lakeside Bancshares, Inc.); past chairman, board of directors, Lakeside News, Inc.; past vice chairman, board of directors, Bank of Crowley; president, North and East Trading Company; vice president, Crowley Holding Co.; member: Texas State Senate, 1962–72; American Legion Post 117; VFW Post 6796; Rockwall Rotary Club; Rotary Clubs International; member: First Methodist Church; married: the former Mary Ellen Murphy, 1944; three sons: Hampton, Brett and Blakeley; committees: Energy and Commerce; Science and Technology; elected to the 97th Congress, November 4, 1980; reelected to each succeeding Congress.

Office Listings

http://www.house.gov/ralphhall

2405 Rayburn House Office Building, Washington, DC 20515 .... (202) 225–6673
Chief of Staff.—Janet Perry Poppleton. FAX: 225–3332
Legislative Director.—Amy Dyer.
104 North San Jacinto Street, Rockwall, TX 75087–2508 .... (972) 771–9118
District Assistant.—Tom Hughes.
101 East Pecan Street, Suite 114, Sherman, TX 75090–5989 .... (903) 892–1112
District Assistant.—Judy Rowton.
U.S. P.O., 320 Church Street, Suite 132, Sulphur Springs, TX 75482–2606 .... (903) 885–8138
District Assistant.—Martha Glover.
Bowie County Courthouse, 700 James Bowie Dr., New Boston, TX 75570–2328 ... (903) 628–8309
District Assistant.—Eric Cain.
4303 Texas Boulevard, Suite 2, Texarkana, TX 75503–3094 .... (903) 794–4445
District Assistant.—Marjorie Chandler.
Collin County Courts Facility, 1800 North Graves Street, Suite 101, McKinney, TX 75069–3322 .... (214) 726–9949
District Assistant.—Linda Schenck.

Counties: BOWIE COUNTY. CITIES AND TOWNSHIPS: De Kalb, Hooks, Leary, Maud, Nash, New Boston, Red Lick, Redwater, Texarkana, Wake Village. CAMP COUNTY, CITIES AND TOWNSHIPS: Pittsburg, Rocky Mound. CASS COUNTY. CITIES AND TOWNSHIPS: Atlanta, Avinger, Bloomburg, Domino, Douglassville, Hughes Springs, Linden, Marietta, Queen City. COLLIN COUNTY. CITIES AND TOWNSHIPS: Allen, Anna, Blue Ridge, Celina, Fairview, Farmersville, Frisco, Josephine,

Lavon, Lowry Crossing, Lucas, McKinney, Melissa, Nevada, New Hope, Parker, Princeton, Prosper, Royse City, Sachse, St. Paul, Van Alstyne, Westminster, Weston, Wylie, Winfield. DELTA COUNTY. CITIES AND TOWNSHIPS: Cooper, Pecan Gap. FANNIN COUNTY. CITIES AND TOWNSHIPS: Bailey, Bonham, Dodd City, Ector, Honey Grove, Ladonia, Leonard, Pecan Gap, Ravenna, Savoy, Trenton, Whitewright, Windom. FRANKLIN COUNTY. CITIES AND TOWNSHIPS: Mount Vernon, Winnsboro. GRAYSON COUNTY. CITIES AND TOWNSHIPS: Bells, Collinsville, Denison, Dorchester, Gunter, Howe, Knollwood, Pottsboro, Sadler, Sherman, Southmayd, Tioga, Tom Bean, Van Alstyne, Whitesboro, Whitewright. HOPKINS COUNTY. CITIES AND TOWNSHIPS: Como, Cumby, Sulphur Springs, Tira. HUNT COUNTY. CITIES AND TOWNSHIPS: Caddo Mills, Campbell, Celeste, Commerce, Greenville, Hawk Cove, Josephine, Lone Oak, Neylandville, Quinlan, West Tawakoni, Wolfe City. LAMAR COUNTY. CITIES AND TOWNSHIPS: Blossom, Deport, Paris, Reno, Roxton, Sun Valley, Toco. MORRIS COUNTY. CITIES AND TOWNSHIPS: Daingerfield, Hughes Springs, Lone Star, Naples, Omaha. RAINS COUNTY. CITIES AND TOWNSHIPS: Alba, East Tawakoni, Emory, Point. RED RIVER COUNTY. CITIES AND TOWNSHIPS: Annona, Avery, Bogata, Clarksville, Deport, Detroit. ROCKWALL COUNTY. CITIES AND TOWNSHIPS: Fate, Garland, Heath, McLendon-Chisholm, Mobile City, Rockwall, Rowlett, Royse City, Wylie. TITUS COUNTY. CITIES AND TOWNSHIPS: Miller's Cove, Mount Pleasant, Talco.

ZIP Codes: 75002, 75009, 75013, 75019, 75030, 75032, 75034–35, 75040–41, 75058, 75069, 75071, 75074, 75076, 75078, 75087–88, 75090, 75094, 75097–98, 75132, 75135, 75164, 75166, 75173, 75189, 75407, 75409, 75413–14, 75416–18, 75422–24, 75426, 75428–29, 75431–33, 75435–36, 75438–40, 75442, 75446, 75449, 75452–55, 75457, 75459, 75460, 75462, 75469, 75472–73, 75474, 75476, 75477, 75479, 75482, 75486–87, 75489, 75490–95, 75501, 75550–51, 75554, 75556, 75559–61, 75563, 75566–73, 75572, 75630, 75638, 75656, 75668, 75686, 75855, 76233, 76264, 76268, 76271, 76273

* * *

FIFTH DISTRICT

JEB HENSARLING, Republican, of Dallas, TX; born in Stephenville, TX, May 29, 1957; education: B.A., economics, Texas A&M University, 1979; J.D., University of Texas School of Law, 1982; professional: businessman; vice president, Maverick Capital, 1993–96; owner, San Jacinto Ventures, 1996–2002; vice president, Green Mountain Energy Co., 1999–2001; community service: American Cancer Society for the Dallas Metro Area; Children's Education Fund; Habitat for Humanity; religion: Christian; married: Melissa; children: Claire and Travis; committees: Budget; Financial Services; elected to the 108th Congress on November 5, 2002; reelected to each succeeding Congress.

Office Listings

http://www.house.gov/hensarling

132 Cannon House Office Building, Washington, DC 20515 .... (202) 225–3484
Chief of Staff.—Dee Buchanan. FAX: 226–4888
Legislative Director.—Gerry O'Shea.
Press Secretary.—Mike Walz.
10675 East Northwest Highway, Suite 1685, Dallas, TX 75238 .... (214) 349–9996
100 East Corsicana Street, Suite 208, Athens, TX 77571 .... (903) 675–8288

Counties: ANDERSON, CHEROKEE, DALLAS (part), HENDERSON, KAUFMAN, VAN ZANDT, WOOD. Population (2000), 651,620.

ZIP Codes: 75030, 75032, 75041, 75043, 75047, 75049, 75088, 75103, 75114, 75117–18, 75124, 75126–27, 75140, 75142–43, 75147–50, 75156–61, 75163, 75169, 75180–82, 75185, 75187, 75214, 75218, 75227–28, 75231, 75238, 75243, 75253, 75336, 75355, 75357, 75359, 75374, 75382, 75390, 75393–94, 75410, 75444, 75474, 75480, 75494, 75497, 75751–52, 75754, 75756–59, 75763–66, 75770, 75772–73, 75778–80, 75782–85, 75789–90, 75801–03, 75832, 75839, 75844, 75853, 75861, 75880, 75882, 75884, 75886, 75925, 75976

* * *

SIXTH DISTRICT

JOE BARTON, Republican, of Ennis, TX; born in Waco, TX, September 15, 1949; education: graduated Waco High School, 1968; B.S., industrial engineering, Texas A&M University, College Station, 1972; M.S., industrial administration, Purdue University, West Lafayette, IN, 1973; professional: plant manager, and assistant to the vice president, Ennis Business Forms, Inc., 1973–81; awarded White House Fellowship, 1981–82; served as aide to James B. Edwards, Secretary, Department of Energy; member, Natural Gas Decontrol Task Force in the Office of Planning, Policy and Analysis; worked with the Department of Energy task force in support of the President's Private Sector Survey on Cost Control; natural gas decontrol and project cost control consultant, Atlantic Richfield Company; cofounder, Houston County Volunteer Ambulance Service, 1976; vice president, Houston County Industrial Development Authority, 1980; chairman, Crockett Parks and Recreation Board, 1979–80; vice president, Houston County Chamber of Commerce, 1977–80; member, Dallas Energy Forum; religion: Methodist; married: Terri, son, Jack; children: Brad, Alison and Kristin, from a previous marriage; stepchildren: Lindsay, and Cullen; committees: Energy and Commerce; elected to the 99th Congress on November 6, 1984; reelected to each succeeding Congress.

Office Listings

http://www.joebarton.house.gov

2109 Rayburn House Office Building, Washington, DC 20515 .... (202) 225–2002
Chief of Staff.—Heather Couri. FAX: 225–3052
Legislative Director.—Theresa Lavery.
Press Secretary.—Karen Modlin.
Scheduler.—Linda Gillespie.
6001 West I–20, Suite 200, Arlington, TX 76017 .... (817) 543–1000
2106A West Ennis Avenue, Ennis, TX 75119 .... (972) 875–8488

Counties: ELLIS, FREESTONE, HOUSTON, LEON, LIMESTONE, NAVARRO, TARRANT, TRINITY. CITIES AND TOWNSHIPS: Arlington, Bardwell, Buffalo, Centerville, Corsicana, Crockett, Crowley, Dawson, Ennis, Fairfield, Ferris, Fort Worth, Frost, Grapeland, Groveton, Italy, Kerens, Lovelady, Mansfield, Maypearl, Mexia, Midlothian, Milford, Oak Leaf, Palmer, Pecan Hill, Red Oak, Rice, Richland, and Waxahachie. Population (2000), 651,620.

ZIP Codes: 75050, 75052, 75054, 75101–02, 75104–06, 75109–10, 75119–20, 75125, 75144, 75146, 75151–55, 75165, 75167–68, 75831, 75833–35, 75838, 75840, 75844–52, 75855–56, 75858–60, 75862, 75865, 75926, 76001–07, 76010–19, 76028, 76036, 76040–41, 76050, 76055, 76060, 76063–65, 76084, 76094, 76096–97, 76119–20, 76123, 76126, 76132–34, 76140, 76155, 76162–63, 76623, 76626, 76635, 76639, 76641–42, 76651, 76667, 76670, 76679, 76681, 76686, 76693, 77850, 77855, 77865, 77871

* * *

SEVENTH DISTRICT

JOHN ABNEY CULBERSON, Republican, of Harris County, TX; born in Houston, TX, August 24, 1956; education: B.A., Southern Methodist University; J.D., South Texas College of Law; professional: attorney; awards: Citizens for a Sound Economy Friend of the Taxpayer Award; Texas Eagle Forum Freedom and Family Award; Houston Jaycees Outstanding Young Houstonian Award; public service: Texas House of Representatives, 1987–2000; married: Belinda Burney, 1989; child: Caroline; committees: Appropriations; elected to the 107th Congress on November 7, 2000; reelected to each succeeding Congress.

Office Listings

http://www.house.gov/culberson

438 Cannon House Office Building, Washington, DC 20515 .... (202) 225–2571
Chief of Staff.—Tony Essalih. FAX: 225–4381
Legislative Director.—Ellie Essalih.
Office Manager.—Jamie Gahun.
10000 Memorial Drive, Suite 620, Houston, TX 77024–3490 .... (713) 682–8828
District Director.—Nick Swyka.

County: HARRIS COUNTY (part). Population (2000), 651,620.

ZIP Codes: 77002, 77004–08, 77019, 77024–25, 77027, 77030, 77035–36, 77040–43, 77046, 77055–57, 77063–65, 77070, 77074, 77077, 77079–81, 77084, 77086, 77094–96, 77098, 77215, 77218–19, 77224–25, 77227, 77241–44, 77255–57, 77265–66, 77269, 77277, 77279–82, 77284, 77401–02, 77429, 77433

* * *

EIGHTH DISTRICT

KEVIN BRADY, Republican, of The Woodlands, TX; born in Vermillion, SD, April 11, 1955; education: B.S., business, University of South Dakota; professional: served in Texas House of Representatives, 1991–96, the first Republican to capture the 15th District seat since the 1800s; chair, Council of Chambers of Greater Houston; president, East Texas Chamber Executive Association; president, South Montgomery County Woodlands Chamber of Commerce, 1985–present; director, Texas Chamber of Commerce Executives; Rotarian; awards: Achievement Award, Texas Conservative Coalition; Outstanding Young Texan (one of five), Texas Jaycees; Ten Best Legislators for Families and Children, State Bar of Texas; Legislative Standout, Dallas Morning News; Scholars Achievement Award for Excellence in Public Service, North Harris Montgomery Community College District; Victims Rights Equalizer Award, Texans for Equal Justice Center; Support for Family Issues Award, Texas Extension Homemakers Association; religion: attends Saints Simon and Jude Catholic Church; married: Cathy Brady; committees: Ways and Means; elected to the 105th Congress; reelected to each succeeding Congress.

Office Listings

http://www.house.gov/brady

428 Cannon House Office Building, Washington, DC 20515 .... (202) 225–4901
Chief of Staff.—Doug Centilli. FAX: 225–5524
Press Secretary.—Jessica Peetoom.
Legislative Director.—Kimberly Thompson.
200 River Pointe Drive, Suite 304, Conroe, TX 77304 .... (936) 441–5700
District Director.—Sarah Stephens.
1202 Sam Houston Avenue, Suite 7, Huntsville, TX 77340 .... (936) 439–9542
420 Green Avenue, Orange, TX 77630 .... (409) 883–4197

COUNTIES: HARDIN, JASPER, LIBERTY (part), MONTGOMERY, NEWTON, ORANGE, POLK, SAN JACINTO, TRINTY (part), TYLER, WALKER. CITIES AND TOWNSHIPS: Bevil Oaks, Bridge City, Browndell, Buna, Chester, Coldspring, Conroe, Colmesneil, Corrigan, Cut and Shoot, Dayton Lakes, Deweyville, Evadale, Goodrich, Hardin, Huntsville, Jasper, Kenefick, Kirbyville, Kountze, Lake Livingston, Lumberton, Magnolia, Mauriceville, Montgomery, New Waverly, Newton, Oak Ridge North, Oakhurst, Onalaska, Orange, Palton Village, Panorama Village, Pine Forest, Pinehurst, Pinewood Estates, Point Blank, Porter Heights, Roman Fores, Rose City, Rose Hill Acres, Seven Oaks, Shenandoah, Shepherd, Silshee, Sour Lake, South Toledo Bend, Splendora, Stagecoach, The Woodlands, Trinity, Vidor, West Livingston, West Orange, Willis, Woodbranch, and Woodville. Population (2000), 651,619.

ZIP Codes: 75931, 75951, 75956, 75966, 77318, 77320, 77340–44, 77348–49, 77350–51, 77355, 77359–60, 77364, 77367, 77371, 77378, 77399, 77561, 77611, 77614, 77630–32, 77656, 77659, 77862, 77939

* * *

NINTH DISTRICT

AL GREEN, Democrat, of Houston, TX; born in New Orleans, LA, September 1, 1947; raised in Florida; education: A&M University, 1966–71; attended Tuskegee University, Tuskegee, AL; J.D., Texas Southern University, Houston, TX, 1974; professional: co-founded and co-managed the law firm of Green, Wilson, Dewberry and Fitch; Justice of the Peace, Precinct 7, Position 2, 1977–2004; organizations: former president of the Houston NAACP; Houston Citizens Chamber of Commerce; awards: Distinguished Service Award, 1978; Black Heritage Society, Outstanding Leadership Award, 1981; American Federation of Teachers, Citation for Service as a ''Courageous Defender of Due Process for Educators,'' 1983; committees: Financial Services; Homeland Security; elected to the 109th Congress on November 2, 2004; reelected to the 110th Congress.

Office Listings

http://www.house.gov/algreen

425 Cannon House Office Building, Washington, DC 20515 .... (202) 225–7508
Chief of Staff.—Jacqueline Ellis. FAX: 225–2947
Legislative Director.—Oscar Ramirez.
Senior Legislative Assistant.—John H. Jones.
Communications Director.—Sahar Wali.
3003 South Loop West, Suite 460, Houston, TX 77054 .... (713) 383–9234
District Director.—Lucinda Daniels.

Counties: FORT BEND, HARRIS. Population (2000), 651,619.

ZIP Codes: 77004–05, 77021, 77025, 77030–31, 77033, 77035–36, 77042, 77045, 77047–48, 77051, 77053–54, 77056–57, 77061, 77063, 77071–72, 77074, 77077, 77081–83, 77085, 77087, 77096, 77099, 77230–31, 77233, 77235–37, 77251, 77254, 77263, 77271–72, 77274, 77401, 77411, 77469, 77477–78, 77489

* * *

TENTH DISTRICT

MICHAEL T. McCAUL, Republican, of Austin, TX; born in Dallas, TX, January 14, 1962; education: B.S., Trinity University, San Antonio, TX, 1984; J.D., St. Mary's University, San Antonio, TX, 1987; professional: lawyer, private practice; deputy attorney general, office of Texas state attorney general; committees: Foreign Affairs; Homeland Security; Science and Technology; Standards of Official Conduct; elected to the 109th Congress on November 2, 2004; reelected to the 110th Congress.

Office Listings

http://www.house.gov/mccaul

131 Cannon House Office Builiding, Washington, DC 20515 .... (202) 225–2401

Chief of Staff.—Greg Hill. FAX: 225–5955
Deputy Chief of Staff.—Gene Irisari.
Legislative Director.—Alex Manning.
Scheduler / Office Manager.—Mary Elen Williams.
903 San Jacinto, Suite 320, Austin, TX 78701 .... (512) 473–2357
Communications Director.—Jack Hirschfield.
Rosewood Professional Building, 990 Village Square, Suite B, Tomball, TX 77375 (281) 255–8372
1550 Fox Lake, Suite 120, Houston, TX 77084 .... (281) 398–1247
2000 South Market Street, Suite 303, Brenham, TX 77833 .... (979) 830–8497

Counties: AUSTIN, BASTROP, BURLESON, HARRIS, LEE, TRAVIS, WALLER, WASHINGTON. Population (2000), 651,619.

ZIP Codes: 77070, 77084, 77094–95, 77218, 77269, 77284, 77375, 77377, 77379, 77383, 77388–89, 77391, 77410, 77413, 77418, 77423, 77426, 77429, 77433, 77445–47, 77449–50, 77452, 77466, 77473–74, 77476, 77484–85, 77491–94, 77833–36, 77838, 77852–53, 77863, 77868, 77878–80, 78602, 78615, 78621, 78650–51, 78653, 78659–60, 78664, 78682–83, 78691, 78703, 78705, 78708, 78710, 78713, 78716, 78718, 78720, 78724, 78727–31, 78733, 78746, 78751–59, 78761, 78763, 78765–66, 78779–80, 78785, 78788–89, 78931–33, 78940, 78942, 78944, 78946–48, 78950

* * *

ELEVENTH DISTRICT

K. MICHAEL CONAWAY, Republican, of Midland, TX; born in Borger, TX, June 11, 1948; education: B.B.A., Texas A&M–Commerce, 1970; professional: Spec 5 United States Army, 1970–72; tax manager, Price Waterhouse & Company, 1972–80; Chief Financial Officer, Keith D. Graham & Lantern Petroleum Company, 1980–81; Chief Financial Officer, Bush Exploration Company, 1982–84; Chief Financial Officer, Spectrum 7 Energy Corporation, 1984–86; Senior Vice President / Chief Financial Officer, United Bank, 1987–90; Senior Vice President, Texas Commerce Bank, 1990–92; owner, K. Conaway CPA, 1993–present; religion: Baptist; married: Suzanne; children: Brian, Erin, Kara, and Stephanie; committees: Agriculture; Armed Services; Budget; Assistant Minority Whip; elected to the 109th Congress on November 2, 2004; reelected to the 110th Congress.

Office Listings

http://www.house.gov/conaway

511 Cannon House Office Building, Washington, DC 20515 .... (202) 225–3605
Chief of Staff.—Jeff Burton. FAX: 225–1783
Legislative Director.—Michael Beckerman.
Scheduler.—Cassandra Harrison.
6 Desta Drive, Suite 2000, Midland, TX 79705 .... (432) 687–2390
District Scheduler.—Patsy Bain.
33 East Twohig, Room 307, San Angelo, TX 76903 .... (325) 659–4010
Regional Director.—Joanne Powell.

Counties: ANDREWS, BROWN, BURNET, COKE, COLEMAN, COMANCHE, CONCHO, CRANE, DAWSON, ECTOR, GILLESPIE, MENARD, MIDLAND, MILLS, GLASSCOCK, IRION, KIMBLE, LAMPASAS, LLANO, LOVING, MARTIN, MASON, MCCULLOCH, SUTTON (part), TOM GREEN, UPTON, MITCHELL, NOLAN (part), REAGAN, RUNNELS, SAN SABA, SCHLEICHER, SCURRY, STERLING, WARD, WINKLER. POPULATION (2000), 651,620.

ZIP Codes: 76246, 76432, 76442, 76444, 76455, 76550, 76801–04, 76821, 76823, 76825, 76834, 76837, 76844, 76853, 76856, 76859, 76861, 76864, 76866, 76872–73, 76877, 76901–04, 76932–33, 76935–36, 76941, 76945, 76950–51, 76957, 77381–82, 77393, 78611, 78624, 78643, 78654–69, 79331, 79512, 79532, 79545, 79549–50, 79556, 79565, 79567, 79605–09, 79714, 79760–69, 79701–13, 79739, 79742, 79745, 79756, 79778, 79789

* * *

TWELFTH DISTRICT

KAY GRANGER, Republican, of Fort Worth, TX; born in Greenville, TX, January 18, 1943; education: B.S., *magna cum laude*, 1965, and Honorary Doctorate of Humane Letters, 1992, Texas Wesleyan University; professional: owner, Kay Granger Insurance Agency, Inc.; former public school teacher; elected Mayor of Fort Worth, 1991, serving three terms; during her tenure, Fort Worth received All-America City Award from the National Civic League; former Fort Worth Councilwoman; past chair, Fort Worth Zoning Commission; past board member: Dallas-Fort Worth International Airport; North Texas Commission; Fort Worth Convention and Visitors Bureau; U.S. Conference of Mayors Advisory Board; Business and Professional Women's Woman of the Year, 1989; three grown children: J.D., Brandon and Chelsea; first woman Republican to represent Texas in the U.S. House; committees: Appropriations; vice chair, Republican Conference; Deputy Republican Whip; elected to the 105th Congress; reelected to each succeeding Congress.

Office Listings

http://www.house.gov/granger

440 Cannon House Office Building, Washington, DC 20515 .... (202) 225–5071
Chief of Staff.—Robert Head. FAX: 225–5683
Legislative Director.—Amy Tenhouse.
Administrative Assistant.—Stacey Kounelias.
Staff Assistant.—Melody Parlett.
1701 River Run Road, Suite 407, Fort Worth, TX 76107 .... (817) 338–0909
District Director.—Barbara Ragland. (817) 335–5852

Counties: PARKER, TARRANT (part), WISE. Population (2000), 651,619.

ZIP Codes: 76008, 76020, 76023, 76035–36, 76049, 76052, 76066–68, 76071, 76073, 76078, 76082, 76085–88, 76098, 76101–02, 76104, 76106–11, 76113–18, 76121–23, 76126–27, 76129–37, 76147–48, 76161–64, 76177, 76179–82, 76185, 76191–93, 76195–99, 76225, 76234, 76244, 76246, 76248, 76262, 76267, 76270, 76299, 76426, 76431, 76439, 76462, 76485–87, 76490

* * *

THIRTEENTH DISTRICT

MAC THORNBERRY, Republican, of Clarendon, TX; born in Clarendon, July 15, 1958; education: graduate, Clarendon High School; B.A., Texas Tech University; law degree, University of Texas; professional: rancher; attorney; admitted to the Texas bar, 1983; member: Texas and Southwestern Cattle Raisers; co-chair, Congressional Oil and Gas Forum; Rural Health Care Coalition; co-founder/co-chair, Defense Study Group; married: Sarah Adams, 1986; children: Will and Mary Kemp; committees: Armed Services; Permanent Select Committee on Intelligence; elected to the 104th Congress; reelected to each succeeding Congress.

Office Listings

http://www.house.gov/thornberry

2457 Rayburn House Office Building, Washington, DC 20515 .... (202) 225–3706
Administrative Assistant.—Kim Kotlar. FAX: 225–3486
Office Manager.—Kala Weller.
905 South Filmore, Suite 520, Amarillo, TX 79101 .... (806) 371–8844
Chief of Staff.—Bill Harris.
4245 Kemp, Suite 506, Wichita Falls, TX 76308 .... (940) 692–1700

Counties: ARCHER (part), ARMSTRONG, BAYLOR, BRISCOE, CARSON, CHILDRESS, CLAY, COLLINGSWORTH, COOKE (part), COTTLE, CROSBY, DALLAM, DICKENS, DONLEY, FOARD, GRAY, HALL, HANSFORD, HARDEMAN, HARTLEY, HASKELL, HEMPHILL, HUTCHINSON, JACK, JONES, KING, KNOX, LIPSCOMB, MONTAGUE, MOORE, MOTLEY, OCHILTREE, OLDHAM, PALO PINTO, POTTER, RANDALL, ROBERTS, SHERMAN, STONEWALL, SWISHER, THROCKMORTON, WHEELER, WICHITA, WILBARGER. Population (2000), 651,619.

ZIP Codes: 76066, 76067–68, 76228, 76230, 76234, 76238–40, 76250–53, 76255, 76261, 76263, 76265–66, 76270, 76272, 76301–02, 76305–11, 76352, 76354, 76357, 76360, 76363–67, 76369, 76371–73, 76377, 76379–80, 76384–85, 76388–89, 76427, 76430, 76449–50, 76453, 76458–59, 76462–63, 76472, 76475, 76483–84, 76486–87, 76491, 79001–03, 79005, 79007–08, 79010–16, 79018–19, 79022, 79024, 79029, 79033–34, 79036, 79039–40, 79042, 79044, 79046, 79051–52, 79054, 79056–59, 79061–62, 79065–66, 79068, 79070, 79077–81, 79083–84, 79086–88, 79091–97, 79101–11, 79114, 79116–21, 79124, 79159, 79166, 79168, 79172, 79174, 79178, 79185, 79187, 79189, 79201, 79220, 79223, 79225–27, 79229–30, 79233–34, 79236–37, 79239, 79243–45, 79247–48, 79251–52, 79255–57, 79259, 79261, 79322, 79343, 79357, 79370, 79501–03, 79505, 79520–21, 79525, 79529, 79533, 79536, 79539–40, 79544, 79547–48, 79553, 79560, 79601

* * *

FOURTEENTH DISTRICT

RON PAUL, Republican, of Surfside Beach, TX; born in Pittsburgh, PA, August 20, 1935; education: B.A., Gettysburg College, 1957; M.D., Duke College of Medicine, North Carolina, 1961; professional: captain, U.S. Air Force, 1963–68; obstetrician and gynecologist; represented Texas' 22nd District in the U.S. House of Representatives, 1976–77, and 1979–85; married: the former Carol Wells, 1957; children: Ronnie, Lori, Pyeatt, Rand, Robert and Joy LeBlanc; committees: Financial Services; Foreign Affairs; elected to the 105th Congress; reelected to each succeeding Congress.

Office Listings

http://www.house.gov/paul

203 Cannon House Office Building, Washington, DC 20515 .... (202) 225–2831

Chief of Staff.—Tom Lizardo. FAX: 226–6553
Legislative Director.—Norman Singleton.
Press Secretary.—Jeff Deist.
1501 East Mockingbird Lane, Suite 229, Victoria, TX 77904 .... (361) 576–1231
122 West Way Street, Suite 301, Lake Jackson, TX 77566 .... (979) 285–0231
601 Twenty-Fifth Street, Suite 216, Galveston, TX 77550 .... (409) 766–7013

Counties: ARANSAS, BRAZORIA (part), CALHOUN, CHAMBERS, FORT BEND (part), GALVESTON (part), JACKSON, MATAGORDA, VICTORIA, WHARTON. Population (2000), 651,619.

ZIP Codes: 77082, 77404, 77414–15, 77417, 77419–20, 77422–23, 77428, 77430–32, 77435–37, 77440–41, 77443–44, 77448, 77450–51, 77453–58, 77461, 77463–65, 77467–69, 77471, 77476, 77480, 77482–83, 77485–86, 77488, 77493–94, 77510–12, 77514–18, 77520–21, 77531, 77534–35, 77539, 77541–42, 77546, 77549–55, 77560, 77563, 77565–66, 77568, 77571, 77573–74, 77577–78, 77580–81, 77583–84, 77590–92, 77597, 77617, 77623, 77650, 77661, 77665, 77901–05, 77951, 77957, 77961–62, 77968–71, 77973, 77976–79, 77982–83, 77988, 77991, 77995, 78336, 78358, 78381–82

* * *

FIFTEENTH DISTRICT

RUBÉN HINOJOSA, Democrat, of Mercedes, TX; born in Mercedes, August 20, 1940; education: B.B.A., 1962, and M.B.A., 1980, University of Texas; professional: president and chief financial officer, H&H Foods, Inc.; elected member, Texas State Board of Education, 1975–84; board of directors, National Livestock and Meat Board and Texas Beef Industry Council, 1989–93; past president and chair of the board of directors, Southwestern Meat Packers Association; chair and member, board of trustees, South Texas Community College, 1993–96; past public member, Texas State Bar Board of Directors; former adjunct professor, Pan American University School of Business; past director, Rio Grande Valley Chamber of Commerce; Knapp Memorial Hospital Board of Trustees; Our Lady of Mercy Church Board of Catholic Advisors; past member, board of trustees, Mercedes Independent School District; former U.S. Jaycee Ambassador to Colombia and Ecuador; married: Martha; children: Ruben, Jr., Laura, Iliana, Kaitlin, and Karen; committees: Education and Labor; Financial Services; Foreign Affairs; elected to the 105th Congress; reelected to each succeeding Congress.

Office Listings

http://www.house.gov/hinojosa

2463 Rayburn House Office Building, Washington, DC 20515 .... (202) 225–2531
Chief of Staff.—Connie Humphrey. FAX: 225–5688
Policy Advisor.—Greg Davis.
Communications Director.—Elizabeth Esfahani.
2864 West Trenton Road, Edinburg, TX 78539 .... (956) 682–5545
District Director.—Salomon Torres.
107 South St. Mary's Street, Beeville, TX 78102 .... (361) 358–8400
District Director.—Judy McAda.

Counties: BEE, BROOKS, GOLIAD, HIDALGO (part), KLEGERG (part), LIVE OAK, NUECES (part), SAN PATRICIO. CITIES AND TOWNSHIPS: Agua Dulce, Alamo, Beeville, Bishop, Donna, Driscoll, Edcouch, Edinburg, Elroy, Elsa, Goliad, Gregory, Kingsville, LaVilla, Mathis, McAllen, Mercedes, Mission, Odem, Pharr, Portland, Robstown, San Juan, Sinton, Taft, Three Rivers, and Weslaco. Population: (2000) 651,619.

ZIP Codes: 77905, 77954, 77960, 77963, 77967, 77974, 77989, 77993–94, 78022, 78060, 78071, 78075, 78102, 78104, 78107, 78119, 78125, 78142, 78145–46, 78151, 78162, 78330, 78332, 78335–36, 78343, 78350, 78352–53, 78355, 78359, 78362–64, 78368, 78370, 78372, 78374, 78380, 78383, 78387, 78389–91, 78501–05, 78516, 78537–41, 78543, 78549, 78557–58, 78561–63, 78565, 78569–70, 78572–74, 78577, 78579–80, 78589, 78595–96, 78599

* * *

SIXTEENTH DISTRICT

SILVESTRE REYES, Democrat, of El Paso, TX; born in Canutillo, TX, November 10, 1944; education: graduated, Canutillo High School, 1964; associate degree, El Paso Community College, 1976; attended University of Texas, Austin, 1964–65, and El Paso, 1965–66; served in U.S. Army, 1966–68, Vietnam combat veteran; U.S. Border Patrol, chief patrol agent, 26½ years, retired December 1, 1995; member: Canutillo School Board, 1968–69, 21st Century Democrats, El Paso County Democrats, and Unite El Paso; married: the former Carolina Gaytan, 1968; children: Monica, Rebecca and Silvestre Reyes, Jr.; committees: chair, Intelligence; Armed Services; elected on November 5, 1996, to the 105th Congress; reelected to each succeeding Congress.

Office Listings

http://www.house.gov/reyes

2433 Rayburn House Office Building, Washington, DC 20515 .... (202) 225–4831
Chief of Staff.—Perry Finney Brody. FAX: 225–2016
Press Secretary.—Kira Maas.
Scheduler / Office Manager.—Liza Lynch.
Legislative Director.—Philip LoPiccolo.
310 North Mesa, Suite 400, El Paso, TX 79901 .... (915) 534–4400
Deputy Chief of Staff.—Sal Payan. FAX: 534–7426

Counties: El Paso (part). Cities and townships: Anthony, Canutillo, El Paso, Fabens, Horizon City, San Elizario, Socorro, Vinton, and Westway. Population (2000), 651,619.

ZIP Codes: 79821, 79835–36, 79838–39, 79849, 79901–08, 79910, 79912–18, 79920, 79922–27, 79929–32, 79934–38, 79940–55, 79958, 79960–61, 79968, 79976, 79978, 79980, 79995–99, 88510–21, 88523–36, 88538–50, 88553–63, 88565–90, 88595

* * *

SEVENTEENTH DISTRICT

CHET EDWARDS, Democrat, of Waco, TX; born in Corpus Christi, TX, November 24, 1951; education: graduated Memorial High School, Houston, TX, 1970; B.A., Texas A&M University, College Station, 1974; M.B.A., Harvard Business School, Boston, MA, 1981; professional: legislative assistant to Texas Congressman Olin "Tiger" Teague, 1974–77; marketing representative, Trammell Crow Company, 1981–85; president, Edwards Communications, Inc.; member, Texas State Senate, 1983–90; married: the former Lea Ann Wood; children: John Thomas and Garrison Alexander; committees: Appropriations; Budget; elected to the 102nd Congress, November 6, 1990; reelected to each succeeding Congress.

Office Listings

http://edwards.house.gov

2369 Rayburn House Office Building, Washington, DC 20515 .... (202) 225–6105
Administrative Assistant.—Chris Chwastyk. FAX: 225–0350
Press Secretary.—Joshua Taylor.
600 Austin Avenue, Suite 29, Waco, TX 76710 .... (254) 752–9600
District Director.—Sam Murphey.
Wright Plaza, 115 South Main Street, Suite 202, Cleburne, TX 76033 .... (817) 645–4743
Deputy District Director.—Chris Turner.
111 University Drive East, Suite 216, College Station, TX 77840 .... (979) 691–8797

Counties: Bosque, Brazos, Burleson (part), Grimes (part), Hill, Hood, Johnson, Limestone (part), Madison, McLennan, Robertson (part), Sommervell. Cities of: Anderson, Bryan, Cleburne, College Station, Glen Rose, Granbury, Groesbeck, Hillsboro, Madisonville, Miami, Valley Mills, and Waco. Population (2005), 651,786.

ZIP Codes: 75846, 75852, 76009, 76028, 76031, 76033, 76035–36, 76043–44, 76048–50, 76055, 76058–59, 76061, 76063, 76070, 76077, 76084, 76087, 76093, 76097, 76433, 76439, 76462, 76465, 76467, 76476, 76524, 76557, 76561, 76596, 76621–22, 76624, 76627–31, 76633–38, 76640, 76642–45, 76648–50, 76652–55, 76657, 76660, 76664–66, 76670–71, 76673, 76676, 76678, 76682, 76684, 76687, 76689–92, 76701–08, 76710–12, 76714–16, 76795, 76797–99, 77333, 77356, 77363, 77801–03, 77805–08, 77830–31, 77836–38, 77840–45, 77852, 77856, 77859, 77861–64, 77866–68, 77870, 77872–73, 77875–76, 77878–79, 77881–82

* * *

EIGHTEENTH DISTRICT

SHEILA JACKSON LEE, Democrat, of Houston, TX; born in Queens, NY, January 12, 1950; education: graduated, Jamaica High School; B.A., Yale University, New Haven, CT, 1972; J.D., University of Virginia Law School, 1975; professional: practicing attorney for 12 years; AKA Sorority; Houston Area Urban League; American Bar Association; staff counsel, U.S. House Select Committee on Assassinations, 1977–78; admitted to the Texas bar, 1975; city council (at large), Houston, 1990–94; Houston Municipal Judge, 1987–90; married Dr. Elwyn Cornelius Lee, 1973; two children: Erica Shelwyn and Jason Cornelius Bennett; committees: Foreign Affairs; Homeland Security; Judiciary; elected to the 104th Congress; reelected to each succeeding Congress.

Office Listings

http://www.jacksonlee.house.gov

2435 Rayburn Cannon House Office Building, Washington, DC 20515 .... (202) 225–3816

Chief of Staff.—Yohannes Tsehai (acting). FAX: 225–3317
Scheduler.—Vanessa Griddine.
Staff Assistant/Legislative Correspondent.—Matthew Mason.
Senior Legislative Counsel.—Yohannes Tsehai.
Scheduler.—Jeanette Lenoir.
1919 Smith Street, Suite 1180, Mickey Leland Building, Houston, TX 77002 .... (713) 655–0050
District Director.—Cynthia Buggage.
420 West 19th Street, Houston, TX 77008 .... (713) 861–4070

Counties: HARRIS COUNTY (part). CITY OF: Houston. Population (2000), 651,620.

ZIP Codes: 77001–10, 77013, 77016, 77018–24, 77026, 77028–30, 77033, 77035, 77038, 77040–41, 77045, 77047–48, 77051–52, 77054–55, 77064, 77066–67, 77076, 77078, 77080, 77086–88, 77091–93, 77097–98, 77201–06, 77208, 77210, 77212, 77216, 77219, 77221, 77226, 77230, 77233, 77238, 77240–41, 77251–53, 77255, 77265–66, 77277, 77288, 77291–93, 77297–99

* * *

NINETEENTH DISTRICT

RANDY NEUGEBAUER, Republican, of Lubbock, TX; born in St. Louis, MO, December 24, 1949; education: Texas Tech University, 1972; professional: small businessman (home building industry); organizations: West Texas Home Builders Association; Land Use and Developers Council; Texas Association of Builders; National Association of Home Builders; Campus Crusade for Christ; public service: Lubbock City Council, 1992–98; served as Mayor Pro Tempore, 1994–96; leader, coalition to create the Ports-to-Plains Trade Corridor; awards: Lubbock Chamber of Commerce Distinguished Service Award; Reese Air Force Base Friend of Reese Award; religion: Baptist; married: Dana; two children; committees: Agriculture; Financial Services; Science and Technology; elected to the 108th Congress, by special election, on June 3, 2003; reelected to each succeeding Congress.

Office Listings

429 Cannon House Office Building, Washington, DC 20515 .... (202) 225–4005
Chief of Staff.—Gayland Barksdale. FAX: 225–9615
Communications Director.—Josh Noland.
Federal Building, 1205 Texas Avenue, Room 810, Lubbock, TX 79401 .... (806) 763–1611
District Director.—Jimmy Clark.

Counties: ARCHER, BAILEY, BORDEN, CALLAHAN, CASTRO, COCHRAN, DEAF SMITH, EASTLAND, FISHER, FLOYD, GAINES, GARZA, HALE, HOCKLEY, HOWARD, KENT, LAMB, LUBBOCK, LYNN, NOLAN, PARMER, SHACKELFORD, STEPHENS, TAYLOR, TERRY, YOAKUM, YOUNG. Population (2000), 651,619.

ZIP Codes: 76302, 76305, 76308, 76310, 76351, 76360, 76366, 76370, 76372, 76374, 76379, 76389, 76424, 76427, 76429–30, 76435, 76437, 76442–43, 76445, 76448, 76450, 76454, 76459–60, 76462–64, 76466, 76469–70, 76475, 76481, 76491, 79009, 79021, 79025, 79027, 79031–32, 79035, 79041, 79043, 79045, 79053, 79063–64, 79072–73, 79082, 79085, 79221, 79231, 79235, 79241, 79250, 79258, 79311–14, 79316, 79320, 79323–26, 79329–30, 79336, 79338–39, 79342, 79344–47, 79350–51, 79353, 79355–56, 79358–60, 79363–64, 79366–67, 79369–73, 79376, 79378–83, 79401–16, 79423–24, 79430, 79452–53, 79457, 79464, 79490–91, 79493, 79499, 79504, 79506, 79508, 79510–11, 79518–20, 79526, 79528, 79530, 79532–37, 79541, 79543, 79545–46, 79549, 79556, 79560–63, 79566–67, 79601–05, 79720–21, 79733, 79738, 79748

* * *

TWENTIETH DISTRICT

CHARLES A. GONZALEZ, Democrat, of San Antonio, TX; born in San Antonio, May 5, 1945; son of former Representative Henry Gonzalez, who served the 20th district from 1961–99; education: Thomas A. Edison High School, 1965; B.A., University of Texas at Austin, 1969; J.D., St. Mary's School of Law, 1972; professional: elementary school teacher; private attorney, 1972–82; Municipal Court Judge; County Court at Law Judge, 1983–87; District Judge, 1989–97; chair, Congressional Hispanic Caucus Civil Rights Task Force; committees: Energy and Commerce; House Administration; Small Business; Democratic Senior Whip; elected to the 106th Congress; reelected to each succeeding Congress.

Office Listings

303 Cannon House Office Building, Washington, DC 20515 .... (202) 225–3236
Chief of Staff.—Kevin Kimble. FAX: 225–1915
Executive Assistant.—Rose Ann Maldonado.
Legislative Director.—Leo Munoz.
Press Secretary.—Shripal Shah.
Federal Building, B–124, 727 East Durango Boulevard, San Antonio, TX 78206 ... (210) 472–6195

Counties: BEXAR COUNTY (part). CITIES OF: Alamo Heights, Balcones Heights, Converse, Kirby, Lackland AFB, Leon Valley, and San Antonio. Population (2000), 651,619.

ZIP Codes: 78073, 78109, 78201–19, 78225–31, 78233, 78236–46, 78250, 78252, 78254

* * *

TWENTY-FIRST DISTRICT

LAMAR S. SMITH, Republican, of San Antonio, TX; born in San Antonio, November 19, 1947; education: graduated, Texas Military Institute, San Antonio, 1965; B.A., Yale University, New Haven, CT, 1969; management intern, Small Business Administration, Washington, DC, 1969–70; business and financial writer, *The Christian Science Monitor*, Boston, MA, 1970–72; J.D., Southern Methodist University School of Law, Dallas, TX, 1975; admitted to the State bar of Texas, 1975, and commenced practice in San Antonio with the firm of Maebius and Duncan, Inc.; elected chairman of the Republican Party of Bexar County, TX, 1978 and 1980; elected District 57–F State Representative, 1981; elected Precinct 3 Commissioner of Bexar County, 1982 and 1984; partner, Lamar Seeligson Ranch, Jim Wells County, TX; married: Beth Schaefer; children: Nell Seeligson and Tobin Wells; committees: Homeland Security; Judiciary; Science and Technology; elected to the 100th Congress on November 4, 1986; reelected to each succeeding Congress.

Office Listings

http://lamarsmith.house.gov

2409 Rayburn House Office Building, Washington, DC 20515 .... (202) 225–4236
Chief of Staff / Assistant to the Chairman.—Jennifer Brown. FAX: 225–8628
Administrative Assistant / Scheduler.—Kristina Harris.
Guaranty Federal Building, 1100 North East Loop 410, Suite 640, San Antonio, TX 78209 .... (210) 821–5024
District Director.—O'Lene Stone.
3536 Bee Cave Road, Suite 212, Austin, TX 78746 .... (512) 306–0439
301 Junction Highway, Suite 346C, Kerrville, TX 78028 .... (830) 896–0154

Counties: BEXAR (part), BLANCO, COMAL, HAYS (part), KERR, REAL, TRAVIS (part). Population (2000), 651,619.

ZIP Codes: 78006, 78015, 78070, 78135, 78148, 78150, 78154, 78163, 78209, 78213, 78216–18, 78239, 78247, 78258–61, 78266, 78270, 78280, 78606, 78610–11, 78613, 78618–20, 78623, 78630–31, 78635–36, 78641, 78645–46, 78652, 78654, 78663, 78666, 78669, 78676, 78726, 78730, 78732–39, 78746, 78749–50, 78759, 78780

* * *

TWENTY-SECOND DISTRICT

NICK LAMPSON, Democrat, of Stafford, TX; born in Beaumont, February 14, 1945; education: graduated, South Park High School, Beaumont, TX, 1964; B.S., biology, Lamar University Beaumont, 1968; M.Ed., Lamar University, 1971; teacher; elected Jefferson County Tax Assessor-Collector; member: Young Men's Business League; Clean Air and Water; Sierra International; Knights of Columbus; married: the former Susan Floyd; children: Hillary and Stephanie; committees: Agriculture; Education and Labor; Science and Technology; Transportation and Infrastructure; elected to the 105th Congress; reelected to the 106th–108th Congress; elected to the 110th Congress on November 7, 2006.

Office Listings

http://house.gov/lampson

436 Cannon House Office Building, Washington, DC 20515 .... (202) 225–5951
Chief of Staff.—Dan Easley. FAX: 225–5241
Scheduler.—Suzanne Jordan.
Legislative Director.—Bobby Zafarnia.
10701 Corporate Drive, Suite 118, Stafford, TX 77477 .... (281) 240–3700
1020 Bay Area Boulevard, Suite 224, Houston, TX 77058 .... (281) 461–6300

Counties: BRAZORIA, FORT BEND, GALVESTON, HARRIS (part), JEFFERSON. CITIES OF: Baytown, Beaumont, Galveston, La Marque, Missouri City, Port Arthur, Pearland, Rosenberg, Stafford, Sugar Land and Texas City. Population (2000), 651,619.

ZIP Codes: 77044, 77049, 77058, 77062, 77089, 77258, 77346, 77362, 77364, 77369, 77435, 77510–11, 77514, 77517–18, 77520–22, 77532, 77535, 77539, 77546, 77549–55, 77560, 77562–63, 77565, 77568, 77573–75, 77580–82, 77590–

92, 77597–98, 77613, 77617, 77619, 77622–23, 77625–27, 77629, 77631, 77640–43, 77650–51, 77655, 77659–61, 77663–65, 77701–08, 77710, 77713, 77720, 77725–26

* * *

TWENTY-THIRD DISTRICT

CIRO D. RODRIGUEZ, Democrat, of San Antonio, TX; born in Piedras Negras, Mexico; education: attended San Antonio College; B.A., Political Science, St. Mary's University; M.S.W., Our Lady of the Lake University; professional: Harlandale Independent School District School Board; served, Texas State House of Representatives, 1987–97; taught undergraduate and graduate courses at Worden School of Social Work; caseworker, Texas Department of Mental Health and Mental Retardation; faculty associate, Our Lady of the Lake University; consultant, Intercultural Development Research Association; married: Carolina Pena; children: one daughter, Xochil Daria; member: Congressional Hispanic Caucus; chair, Congressional Hispanic Caucus Veterans' Taskforce; U.S.-Mexico Inter-Parliamentary Group; committees: Appropriations; Veterans' Affairs; elected to the 105th Congress in a special election, reelected to the 106th–108th Congress; elected to the 110th Congress on November 7, 2006.

Office Listings

http://www.rodriguez.house.gov

2458 Rayburn House Office Building, Washington, DC 20515 .... (202) 225–4511
FAX: 225–2237
Chief of Staff.—Adrian Saenz.
Legislative Director.—Rene Munoz.
Press Secretary.—Angela Barranco.
Scheduler / Executive Assistant.—Natalie Thorpe.
1950 Southwest Military Drive, San Antonio, TX 78221 .... (210) 922–1874
District Director.—Tomas Larralde.
1995 Williams Street, Suite B, Eagle Pass, TX 78852 .... (830) 757–8398
103 West Callaghan, Fort Stockton, TX 79735 .... (432) 336–3975

Counties: BEXAR (part), BREWSTER, CROCKETT, CULBERSON, DIMMIT, EDWARDS, EL PASO (part), HUDSPETH, JEFF DAVIS, KINNEY, MAVERICK, MEDINA, PECOS, PRESIDIO, REEVES, SUTTON (part), TERRELL, UVALDE, VAL VERDE, ZAVALA. POPULATION (2000) 651,619.

ZIP Codes: 76943, 76950, 78002, 78006, 78009, 78015–16, 78023, 78039, 78052, 78054, 78056, 78059, 78066, 78069, 78073, 78112, 78163, 78202–03, 78205, 78210–11, 78214, 78216, 78220–26, 78230–32, 78235, 78240, 78242, 78245, 78248–58, 78260, 78263–64, 78269, 78801–02, 78827–30, 78832, 78834, 78836–43, 78847, 78850–53, 78860–61, 78870–72, 78877, 78880–81, 78884, 78886, 79718, 79730, 79734–35, 79740, 79743–44, 79770, 79772, 79780–81, 79785–86, 79830–32, 79834, 79836–37, 79839, 79842–43, 79845–48, 79851–55, 79927–28, 79938

* * *

TWENTY-FOURTH DISTRICT

KENNY MARCHANT, Republican, of Coppell, TX; born in Bonham, TX, February 23, 1951; education: B.A., Southern Nazarene University, Bethany, OK, 1974; attended Nazarene Theological Seminary, Kansas City, MO, 1975–76; professional: real estate developer; member of the Carrollton, TX, city council, 1980–84; mayor of Carrollton, TX, 1984–87; member of the Texas state House of Representatives, 1987–2004; member, Advisory Board of Children's Medical Center; married: Donna; four children; committees: Education and Labor; Financial Services; Oversight and Government Reform; elected to the 109th Congress on November 2, 2004; reelected to the 110th Congress.

Office Listings

http://www.house.gov/marchant

1037 Longworth House Office Building, Washington, DC 20515 .... (202) 225–6605
FAX: 225–0074
Chief of Staff.—Brian Thomas.
Scheduler.—Neal Carlton.
9901 East Valley Ranch Parkway, Suite 3035, Irving, TX 75063 .... (972) 556–0162

Counties: DALLAS (part), TARRANT (part). CITIES AND TOWNSHIPS: Bedford, Carrollton, Cedar Hill, Colleyville, Coppell, Dallas, Duncanville, Euless, Farmer's Branch, Fort Worth, Grand Prairie, Irving, and Southlake. Population (2000), 651,619.

ZIP Codes: 75006–07, 75010–11, 75014–17, 75019, 75024, 75027, 75029, 75037, 75038, 75050–54, 75056–57, 75060–63, 75067, 75093, 75099, 75104, 75106, 75116, 75137–38, 75211, 75234, 75236, 75244, 75249, 75261, 75287, 75368, 75370, 75379, 75381, 75387, 75396, 75398, 76005–06, 76011, 76021–22, 76034, 76039, 76040, 76051, 76054, 76092, 76095, 76099, 76155, 76262, 76299

* * *

TWENTY-FIFTH DISTRICT

LLOYD DOGGETT, Democrat, of Austin, TX; born in Austin, October 6, 1946; education: graduated, Austin High School; B.B.A., University of Texas, Austin, 1967; J.D., University of Texas, 1970; president, University of Texas Student Body; associate editor, *Texas Law Review*; Outstanding Young Lawyer, Austin Association of Young Lawyers; president, Texas Consumer Association; religion: member, First United Methodist Church; admitted to the Texas State bar, 1971; Texas State Senate, 1973–85, elected at age 26; Senate author of 124 state laws and Senate sponsor of 63 House bills enacted into law; elected president pro tempore of Texas Senate; served as acting governor; named Outstanding Young Texan by Texas Jaycees; Arthur B. DeWitty Award for outstanding achievement in human rights, Austin NAACP; honored for work by Austin Rape Crisis Center, Planned Parenthood of Austin; Austin Chapter, American Institute of Architects; Austin Council on Alcoholism; Disabled American Veterans; justice on Texas Supreme Court, 1989–94; chairman, Supreme Court Task Force on Judicial Ethics, 1992–94; Outstanding Judge (Mexican-American Bar of Texas), 1993; adjunct professor, University of Texas School of Law, 1989–94; James Madison Award, Texas Freedom of Information Foundation, 1990; First Amendment Award, National Society of Professional Journalists, 1990; member: co-founder, House Information Technology Roundtable; Democratic Caucus Task Force on Education; Congressional Task Force on Tobacco and Health; Democratic Caucus Task Force on Child Care; married: Libby Belk Doggett, 1969; children: Lisa and Cathy; committees: Budget; Ways and Means; elected to the 104th Congress; reelected to each succeeding Congress.

Office Listings

http://www.house.gov/doggett

201 Cannon House Office Building, Washington, DC 20515 .... (202) 225–4865
Chief of Staff.—Michael J. Mucchetti. FAX: 225–3073
Systems Administrator.—Luke George.
Press Secretary.—Wyeth Ruthven.
Staff Assistant.—Juan Garcia.
300 East 8th Street, Suite 763, Austin, TX 78701 .... (512) 916–5921
District Director.—Melissa Abel
311 North 15th Street, McAllen, TX 78501 .... (956) 687–5921
District Director.—Olga Gabriel.

Counties: CALDWELL, DUVAL, GONZALES, HIDALGO (part), JIM HOGG, KARNES, LIKE OAK, STARR, TRAVIS (part). Population (2000), 651,619.

ZIP Codes: 73301, 73344, 78008, 78022, 78060, 78071, 78075, 78102, 78111, 78113, 78116–19, 78122, 78125, 78140, 78144, 78151, 78159, 78341, 78349–50, 78357, 78360–61, 78368, 78376, 78383–84, 78501–05, 78536, 78545, 78547–48, 78557, 78560, 78565, 78572–74, 78576–77, 78582, 78584–85, 78588, 78591, 78595, 78604, 78610, 78612, 78614, 78616–17, 78621–22, 78629, 78632, 78640, 78644, 78648, 78653, 78655–56, 78658, 78661, 78666, 78677, 78702, 78704–05, 78713, 78715, 78719, 78721–25, 78741–42, 78744–45, 78747–48, 78751–52, 78760–62, 78764–65, 78772, 78781, 78783, 78785, 78799, 78953, 78959

* * *

TWENTY-SIXTH DISTRICT

MICHAEL C. BURGESS, Republican, of Denton County, TX; born, December 23, 1950; education: Bachelor and Masters degrees in Physiology, North Texas State University, M.D., University of Texas Medical School in Houston; Masters degree in Medical Management, University of Texas in Dallas; completed medical residency programs, Parkland Hospital in Dallas; professional: founder, Private Practice Specialty Group for Obstetrics and Gynecology; former Chief of Staff and Chief of Obstetrics, Lewisville Medical Center; organizations: former president, Denton County Medical Society; Denton County delegate, Texas Medical Association; alternate delegate, American Medical Association; married: Laura; three children; committees: Energy and Commerce; vice chair, House Republican Policy Committee; elected to the 108th Congress on November 5, 2002; reelected to each succeeding Congress.

Office Listings

http://www.house.gov/burgess

1224 Longworth House Office Building, Washington, DC 20515 .... (202) 225–7772
Chief of Staff.—Barry Brown. FAX: 225–2919
Legislative Director.—Josh Martin.
Press Secretary.—Michelle Stein.
1660 South Stemmons Freeway, Suite 230, Lewisville, TX 75067 .... (972) 434–9700
1100 Circle Drive, Suite 200, Fort Worth, TX 76119 .... (817) 531–8454

Counties: COOKE (part), DALLAS (part), DENTON (part), TARRANT (part). Population (2000) 651,619.

ZIP Codes: 75009, 75019, 75022, 75028, 75034, 75056–57, 75063, 75067–68, 75077–78, 75261, 76012–13, 76021–22, 76034, 76040, 76051–54, 76092, 76102–05, 7610–12, 76115, 76117–20, 76134, 76140, 76148, 76177, 76180, 76201, 76205, 76207–10, 76226–27, 76233–34, 76240, 76247–49, 76258–59, 76262, 76266, 76272, 76273

* * *

TWENTY-SEVENTH DISTRICT

SOLOMON P. ORTIZ, Democrat, of Corpus Christi, TX; born in Robstown, TX, June 3, 1937; education: attended Robstown High School; attended Del Mar College, Corpus Christi; officers certificate, Institute of Applied Science, Chicago, IL, 1962; officers certificate, National Sheriffs Training Institute, Los Angeles, CA, 1977; served in U.S. Army, Sp4c. 1960–62; professional: insurance agent; Nueces County constable, 1965–68; Nueces County commissioner, 1969–76; Nueces County sheriff, 1977–82; member: Congressional Hispanic Caucus (chairman, 102nd Congress); Congressional Hispanic Caucus Institute (chairman of the board, 102nd Congress); Army Caucus; Depot Caucus; Sheriffs' Association of Texas; National Sheriffs' Association; Corpus Christi Rotary Club; American Red Cross; United Way; honors: *Who's Who Among Hispanic Americans;* Man of the Year, International Order of Foresters (1981); Conservation Legislator of the Year for the Sportsman Clubs of Texas (1986); Boss of the Year by the American Businesswomen Association (1980); National Government Hispanic Business Advocate, U.S. Hispanic Chamber of Commerce (1992); Leadership Award, Latin American Management Association (1991); National Security Leadership Award, American Security Council (1992); Tree of Life Award, Jewish National Fund (1987); Quality of Life Award (USO) 2001; children: Yvette and Solomon, Jr.; committees: Armed Services; Natural Resources; elected on November 2, 1982, to the 98th Congress; reelected to each succeeding Congress.

Office Listings

2470 Rayburn House Office Building, Washington, DC 20515 .... (202) 225–7742
FAX: 226–1134
Chief of Staff.—Florencio H. Rendon.
Executive Assistant / Scheduling.—Rhiannon Burruss.
Legislative Director.—Nando Gomez.
Press Secretary.—Cathy Travis.
3649 Leopard, Suite 510, Corpus Christi, TX 78408 .... (361) 883–5868
3505 Boca Chica Boulevard, Suite 200, Brownsville, TX 78521 .... (956) 541–1242

Counties: CAMERON (part), KENNEDY, KLEBERG, NUECES, SAN PATRICO, (part), WILLACY. Population (2000), 651,619.

ZIP Codes: 78330, 78335–36, 78338–39, 78343, 78347, 78351, 78359, 78362–64, 78373–74, 78379–80, 78383, 78385, 78390, 78401–19, 78426–27, 78460, 78463, 78465–78, 78480, 78520–23, 78526, 78550, 78552, 78559, 78561, 78566–67, 78569, 78575, 78578, 78580, 78583, 78586, 78590, 78592, 78594, 78597–98

* * *

TWENTY-EIGHTH DISTRICT

HENRY CUELLAR, Democrat, of Laredo, TX; born in Laredo, September 19, 1955; education: A.A., political science, Laredo Community College, Laredo, TX, 1976; B.S., foreign service, Georgetown University, Washington, DC, 1978; J.D., University of Texas, 1981; M.B.A., international trade, Texas A&M University, Laredo, TX, 1982; PhD., government, University of Texas, Austin, TX, 1998; professional: lawyer, private practice; attorney, Law Office of Henry Cuellar, 1981–present; instructor, Department of Government, Laredo Community College, Laredo, TX, 1982–86; Licensed United States Customs Broker, 1983–present; adjunct professor, International Commercial Law, Texas A&M International, 1984–86; Representative, Texas State House of Representatives, 1986–2001; Secretary of State, State of Texas, 2001; public and civic organizations: board of directors, Kiwanis Club of Laredo, TX, 1982–83; co-founder/president, Laredo Volunteers Lawyers Program, Inc., 1982–83; board of directors, United Way, 1982–83; co-founder/treasurer, Stop Child Abuse and Neglect, 1982–83, and advisory board member, 1984; president, board of directors, Laredo Legal Aid Society, Inc., 1982–84; president, board of directors, Laredo Young Lawyers Association, 1983–84; sustaining member, Texas Democratic Party, 1984; legal advisor, American GI, local chapter, 1986–87; International Trade Association, Laredo State University, 1988; Texas Delegate, National Democratic Convention, 1992; president, board of directors, International Good Neighbor Council; member, The College of the State Bar of Texas, 1994; Texas Lyceum, 1997; policy board of advisors, Texas Hispanic Journal of Law, University of Texas Law School, 2002; member: American Bar Association; Inter-American Bar Association; Texas Bar Association; Webb/Laredo Bar Association; recipient of various awards; religion: Catholic; married: Imelda; children: Christina Alexandra and Catherine Ann; committees: Agriculture; Homeland Security; Small Business; elected to the 109th Congress on November 2, 2004; reelected to the 110th Congress.

Office Listings

http://www.house.gov/cuellar

336 Cannon House Office Building, Washington, DC 20515 .... (202) 225–1640
Chief of Staff.—Terry Stinson. FAX: 225–1641
Legislative Director.—Jordan Haas.
Scheduler.—Lauren Smith.
615 East Houston Street, Suite 451, San Antonio, TX 78205 .... (210) 271–2851
320 North Main, Suite 221, McAllen, TX 78501 .... (956) 631–4826
602 Calton Road, Suite 2, Laredo, TX 78041 .... (956) 725–0639
100 South Austin, Suite 1, Seguin, TX 78155 .... (830) 401–0457

Counties: ATASCOSA, BEXAR, FRIO, GUADALUPE, HIDALGO, IM HOGG, LA SALLE, MCMULLEN, STARR, WEBB, WILSON, ZAPATA. Population (2000), 651,627.

ZIP Codes: 76272, 78005–08, 78011–12, 78014, 78017, 78019, 78021, 78026, 78040–41, 78043, 78045–46, 78050, 78052, 78057, 78061–62, 78064–65, 78067, 78072, 78076, 78108, 78112–14, 78121, 78123–24, 78143, 78147, 78150, 78152, 78154–55, 78160–61, 78263, 78344, 78360–61, 78369, 78371, 78501, 78503–04, 78536, 78545, 78548, 78557, 78560, 78565, 78572–74, 78576–77, 78582, 78584–85, 78588, 78591, 78595, 78638, 78670

* * *

TWENTY-NINTH DISTRICT

GENE GREEN, Democrat, of Houston, TX; born in Houston, October 17, 1947; education: B.A., University of Houston, 1971; admitted, Texas bar, 1977; professional: business manager; attorney; Texas State Representative, 1973–85; Texas State Senator, 1985–92; member: Houston Bar Association; Texas Bar Association; American Bar Association; Communications Workers of America; Aldine Optimist Club; Gulf Coast Conservation Association; Lindale Lions Club; Texas Historical Society; Texas State Society; co-chair, Democratic Israel Working Group; Traumatic Brain Injury Task Force; Bi-Cameral Congressional Caucus on Parkinson's Disease; Community College Caucus; Congressional Steel Caucus; co-chair, Congressional Urban Healthcare Caucus; Missing and Exploited Children's Caucus; National Marine Sanctuary Caucus; National Wildlife Refuge Caucus; Pell Grant Caucus; Recycling Caucus; Sportsmen's Caucus; Urban Caucus; Victim's Rights Caucus; co-chair, Vision Caucus; Democratic Deputy Whip; married: Helen Albers, January 23, 1970; children: Angela and Christopher; committees: Energy and Commerce; Standards of Official Conduct; elected on November 3, 1992, to the 103rd Congress; reelected to each succeeding Congress.

Office Listings

http://www.house.gov/green

2335 Rayburn House Office Building, Washington, DC 20515 .... (202) 225–1688
Legislative Director.—Andrew Wallace. FAX: 225–9903
Press Secretary.—Jesse Christopherson.
Legislative Assistants: Vince Jesaitis, Abigail Pinkele, Lantie Slenzak.
Scheduler.—Lindsay Mosshart.
256 North Sam Houston Parkway East, Suite 29, Houston, TX 77060 .... (281) 999–5879
Chief of Staff / Administrative Assistant.—Rhonda Jackson.
11811 Interstate–10 East, Suite 430, Houston, TX 77029 .... (713) 330–0761
10 North Gaillard, Baytown, TX 77520 .... (281) 420–0502

Counties: HARRIS COUNTY (part). CITIES AND TOWNSHIPS: Baytown, Channelview, Galena Park, Houston, Humble, Jacinto City, La Porte, Pasadena, and South Houston. Population (2000), 651,620.

ZIP Codes: 77003, 77009, 77011–13, 77015–18, 77020–23, 77026, 77029, 77032, 77034, 77037, 77039, 77044, 77049–50, 77060–61, 77075–76, 77087, 77091, 77093, 77205–07, 77213, 77216–17, 77220–23, 77226, 77229, 77234, 77249, 77261–62, 77275, 77287, 77291–93, 77315, 77396, 77501–04, 77506, 77520–22, 77530, 77536, 77547, 77562, 77571–72, 77580, 77587

* * *

THIRTIETH DISTRICT

EDDIE BERNICE JOHNSON, Democrat, of Dallas, TX; born in Waco, TX, December, 3, 1935; education: nursing diploma, St. Mary's at Notre Dame, 1955; B.S., nursing, Texas Christian, 1967; M.P.A, Southern Methodist, 1976; proprietor, Eddie Bernice Johnson and Associates consulting and airport concession management; Texas House of Representatives, 1972–77; Carter administration appointee, 1977–81; Texas State Senate, 1986–92; NABTP Mickey Leland Award for Excellence in Diversity, 2000; National Association of School Nurses, Inc., Legislative Award, 2000; The State of Texas Honorary Texan issued by the Governor of Texas, 2000; Links, Inc., Co-Founders Award, 2000; 100 Black Men of America, Inc., Woman of the Year, 2001; National Black Caucus of State Legislators Image Award, 2001; National Conference of Black Mayors, Inc. President's Award, 2001; Alpha Kappa Alpha Trailblazer, 2002; Thurgood Marshall Scholarship Community Leader, 2002; Phi Beta Sigma Fraternity Woman of the Year, 2002; CBCF Outstanding Leadership, 2002; congressional caucuses: Asian-Pacific; Airpower; Army; Arts; Biomedical Research; chair (107th Congress), Congressional Black Caucus; Children's Working Group; co-chair, Task Force on International HIV / AIDS; Fire Services; Human Rights Caucus; Korean Caucus; Livable Communities Task Force; Medical Technology; Oil & Gas Educational Forum; Singapore Caucus; Study Group on Japan; Tex-21 Transportation Caucus; Urban; Womens' Caucus; Women's Issues; member: St. John Baptist Church, Dallas; children: Dawrence Kirk; committees: Science and Technology; Transportation and Infrastructure; elected on November 3, 1992, to the 103rd Congress; reelected to each succeeding Congress.

Office Listings

http://www.house.gov/ebjohnson

1511 Longworth House Office Building, Washington, DC 20515 .... (202) 225–8885
Chief of Staff / Legislative Director.—Murat Gokcigdem. FAX: 226–1477
Scheduler / Executive Assistant.—Barbara Hamlett.
Communications Director.—Beth Glenn.
Legislative Assistants: Ron Hall, Joye Purser, Jennifer Stiddard.
3102 Maple Avenue, Suite 600, Dallas, TX 75201 .... (214) 922–8885
District Director.—Rod Givens.

Counties: DALLAS (part). CITIES AND TOWNSHIPS: Cedar Hill, Dallas, De Soto, Duncanville, Glenn Heights, Hutchins, Lancaster, Ovilla, and Wilmer. Population (2000), 651,620.

ZIP Codes: 75104, 75115–16, 75125, 75134, 75137, 75141, 75146, 75149, 75154, 75159, 75172, 75201–04, 75206–10, 75212, 75214–20, 75223–24, 75226–28, 75232–33, 75235–37, 75239, 75241, 75246–47, 75253

* * *

THIRTY-FIRST DISTRICT

JOHN R. CARTER, Republican, of Round Rock, TX; born in Houston, TX, November 6, 1941; education: Texas Tech University, 1964; University of Texas Law School, 1969; professional: attorney; private law practice; public service: appointed and elected a Texas District Court Judge, 1981–2001; awards: recipient and namesake of the Williamson County ''John R. Carter Lifetime Achievement Award''; family: married to Erika Carter; children: Gilianne, John, Theodore, and Erika Danielle; committees: Appropriations; elected to 108th Congress on November 5, 2002; reelected to each succeeding Congress.

Office Listings

http://www.house.gov/carter

408 Cannon House Office Building, Washington, DC 20515 .... (202) 225–3864
Chief of Staff.—Richard Hudson. FAX: 225–5886
Administrative Assistant.—Elizabeth Hoffman.
Press Secretary.—Lindsey Willis.
Scheduler.—Mary Randolph Carpenter.
1717 North IH 35, Round Rock, TX 78664 .... (512) 246–1600
Deputy Chief of Staff.—Jonas Miller.
6544 B South General Bruce Drive, Temple, TX 76502 .... (254) 933–1392
Regional Director.—Greg Schannep.

Counties: BELL, CORYELL, ERATH, FALLS, HAMILTON, MILIAM, SOUTHERN ROBERTSON, WILLIAMSON. POPULATION (2000), 651,209.

ZIP Codes: 76401, 76436, 76446, 76457, 76501–05, 76508, 76511, 76513, 76518–20, 76522–28, 76530–31, 76533–34, 76537–38, 76540–44, 76547–49, 76554, 76557–59, 76561, 76564–67, 76569–71, 76573–74, 76577–79, 76596–99, 76632, 76656, 76680, 76685, 76689, 77410, 77426, 77466, 77473, 77492, 77805–07, 77834, 77836, 77838, 77841, 77852, 77857, 77862, 77866, 77878–79, 77881, 78363, 78602, 78613, 78615, 78626, 78628, 78634, 78641–42, 78646, 78673–74, 78664, 78681, 78717, 78729, 78931, 78933, 78940, 78942, 78944, 78948, 78950

* * *

THIRTY-SECOND DISTRICT

PETE SESSIONS, Republican, of Dallas, TX; born, March 22, 1955; education: graduate, Southwestern University, 1978; worked for Southwestern Bell, and Bell Communications Research (formerly Bell Labs), 1978–94, rising to the position of district manager; past vice president for public policy, National Center for Policy Analysis, 1994–95; board member, East Dallas YMCA; past chairman, East Dallas Chamber of Commerce; past district chairman, White Rock Council of the Boy Scouts of America; member, East Dallas Rotary Club; chairman, Results Caucus; married: Juanita Sessions; two children, Bill and Alex; committees: Rules; elected on November 5, 1996, to the 105th Congress; reelected to each succeeding Congress.

Office Listings

http://www.house.gov/sessions

1514 Longworth House Office Building, Washington, DC 20515 .... (202) 225–2231
Chief of Staff.—Guy Harrison. FAX: 225–5878
Communications Director.—Gina Vaughn.
Legislative Director.—Robert ''Bobby'' Hillert.
Park Central VII, 12750 Merit Drive, Suite 1434, Dallas, TX 75251 .... (972) 392–0505

County: DALLAS (part). CITIES AND TOWNSHIPS: Addison, Cockrell Hill, Dallas, Grand Prairie, Highland Park, Irving, Richardson, and University Park. Population (2000), 651,619.

ZIP Codes: 75001, 75038–39, 75050–51, 75060–63, 75080–81, 75203–06, 75208–09, 75211–12, 75214, 75219–20, 75222, 75224–25, 75229–31, 75233, 75240, 75244, 75248, 75251, 75254, 75262

UTAH

(Population 2000, 2,233,169)

SENATORS

ORRIN G. HATCH, Republican, of Salt Lake City, UT; born in Pittsburgh, PA, March 22, 1934; education: B.S., Brigham Young University, Provo, UT, 1959; LL.B., University of Pittsburgh, 1962; practiced law in Salt Lake City, UT, and Pittsburgh, PA; senior partner, Hatch and Plumb law firm, Salt Lake City; worked his way through high school, college, and law school at the metal lathing building trade; holds ''AV'' rating in Martindale-Hubbell Law Directory; member: AFL-CIO, Salt Lake County Bar Association, Utah Bar Association, American Bar Association, Pennsylvania Bar Association, Allegheny County Bar Association, Help Eliminate Litter and Pollution (HELP) Association, and numerous other professional and fraternal organizations; honorary doctorate, University of Maryland; honorary doctor of laws: Pepperdine University and Southern Utah State University; honorary national ski patroller; author of numerous national publications; member, Church of Jesus Christ of Latter-Day Saints; married: Elaine Hansen of Newton, UT; children: Brent, Marcia, Scott, Kimberly, Alysa and Jess; committees: Finance; Health, Education, Labor, and Pensions; Judiciary; Joint Committee on Taxation; Select Committee on Intelligence; elected to the U.S. Senate on November 2, 1976; reelected to each succeeding Senate term.

Office Listings

http://hatch.senate.gov

104 Hart Senate Office Building, Washington, DC 20510 .... (202) 224–5251
FAX: 224–6331
Chief of Staff.—Patricia Knight.
Legislative Director.—Jace Johnson.
Communications Director.—Peter Carr.
Scheduler.—Ruth Montoya.
Federal Building, Suite 8402, Salt Lake City, UT 84138 .... (801) 524–4380
State Director.—Melanie Bowen.
Federal Building, 324 25th Street, Suite 1006, Ogden, UT 84401 .... (801) 625–5672
51 South University Avenue, Suite 320, Provo, UT 84606 .... (801) 375–7881
197 East Tabernacle, Room 2, St. George, UT 84770 .... (435) 634–1795
2390 West Highway 56, P.O. Box 99, Cedar City, UT 84720 .... (435) 586–8435

* * *

ROBERT F. BENNETT, Republican, of Salt Lake City, UT; born in Salt Lake City, September 18, 1933; education: B.S., University of Utah, 1957; professional: chief executive officer of Franklin Quest, Salt Lake City; chief congressional liaison, U.S. Department of Transportation; awards: ''Entrepreneur of the Year,'' *Inc.* magazine, 1989; High-Tech Legislator of the Year, 2001; Emerging Congressional Leader, 2002; author, *Gaining Control*; member, The Church of Jesus Christ of Latter-Day Saints; honorary doctorates: University of Utah, Utah Valley State College, Snow College, Westminster College, Salt Lake Community College; married: Joyce McKay; children: James, Julie, Robert, Wendy, Heather, and Heidi; committees: Appropriations; Banking, Housing, and Urban Affairs; Rules and Administration; Joint Economic Committee; Joint Committee on the Library; Joint Committee on Printing; elected to the U.S. Senate on November 3, 1992; reelected to each succeeding Senate term.

Office Listings

http://bennett.senate.gov

431 Dirksen Senate Office Building, Washington, DC 20510 .... (202) 224–5444
FAX: 228–1168
Chief of Staff.—Mary Jane Collipriest.
Deputy Chief of Staff/Legislative Director.—Mark Morrison.
Office Manager.—Sandy Knickman.
Press Secretary.—Emily Christensen.
Wallace F. Bennett Federal Building, Suite 4225, Salt Lake City, UT 84138 .... (801) 524–5933
State Director.—Tim Sheehan.
Federal Building, 324 25th Street, Suite 1410, Ogden, UT 84401 .... (801) 625–5675
51 South University Avenue, Suite 310, Provo, UT 84601–4424 .... (801) 379–2525
Federal Building, 196 East Tabernacle Street, Room 21, St. George, UT 84770–3474 .... (435) 628–5514
2390 West Highway 56, Suite 4B, Cedar City, UT 84720 .... (435) 865–1335

REPRESENTATIVES

FIRST DISTRICT

ROB BISHOP, Republican, of Brigham City, UT; born in Kaysville, UT, July 13, 1951; education: B.A., Political Science, *magna cum laude,* University of Utah, 1974; professional:

high-school teacher; public service: Utah House of Representatives, 1979–94, Speaker of the House his last two years; elected, chair, Utah Republican Party, 1997 (served two terms); religion: Church of Jesus Christ of Latter-day Saints; family: married to Jeralynn Hansen; children: Shule, Jarom, Zenock, Maren and Jashon; committees: Armed Services; Education and Labor; Natural Resources; elected to the 108th Congress on November 5, 2002; reelected to each succeeding Congress.

Office Listings

http://www.house.gov/robbishop

124 Cannon House Office Building, Washington, DC 20515 .... (202) 225–0453
Chief of Staff.—Scott Parker. FAX: 225–5857
Legislative Assistants: Justin Harding, Gordon Larsen, Steve Petersen.
Scheduler / Office Manager.—Jennifer Griffith.
1017 Federal Building, 324 Twenty-Fifth Street, Ogden, UT 84401 .... (801) 625–0107

Counties: BOX ELDER, CACHE, DAVIS, JUAB (part), MORGAN, RICH, SALT LAKE (part), SUMMIT, TOOELE, WEBER. Population (2000), 744,389.

ZIP Codes: 84010–11, 84014–18, 84022, 84024–25, 84028–29, 84033–34, 84036–38, 84040–41, 84044, 84050, 84054–56, 84060–61, 84064, 84067–69, 84071, 84074–75, 84080, 84083, 84086–87, 84089, 84098, 84101–06, 84110–11, 84114–16, 84119–20, 84122, 84125–28, 84130–31, 84133–34, 84136, 84138–39, 84141, 84144–45, 84147, 84150–51, 84180, 84189–90, 84199, 84201, 84244, 84301–02, 84304–41, 84401–05, 84407–09, 84412, 84414–15, 84628

* * *

SECOND DISTRICT

JIM MATHESON, Democrat, of Salt Lake City, UT; born in Salt Lake City, March 21, 1960; education: B.A., Harvard University; M.B.A., University of California at Los Angeles (UCLA); professional: energy consultant; Bonneville Pacific; Energy Strategies, Inc.; The Matheson Group; organizations: Environmental Policy Institute; Salt Lake Public Utilities Board; Scott M. Matheson Leadership Forum; religion: Mormon; married: Amy; children: Will and Harris; committees: Energy and Commerce; Science and Technology; elected to the 107th Congress on November 7, 2000; reelected to each succeeding Congress.

Office Listings

http://www.house.gov/matheson

1323 Longworth House Office Building, Washington, DC 20515 .... (202) 225–3011
Chief of Staff.—Stacey Alexander. FAX: 225–5638
Executive Assistant.—Kendall Murphy.
240 E. Morris Avenue, #235, Salt Lake City, UT 84115 .... (801) 486–1236
District Director.—Mike Reberg.
321 North Mall Drive, #E101B, St. George, UT 84790 .... (435) 627–0880

Counties: CARBON, DAGGETT, DUCHENSNE, EMERY, GARFIELD, GRAND, IRON, KANE, PIUTE, SALT LAKE (part), SAN JUAN, UNITAH, UTAH (part), WASATCH, WASHINGTON, WAYNE. Population (2000), 744,390.

ZIP Codes: 84001–04, 84007–08, 84020–21, 84023, 84026–27, 84031–32, 84035, 84039, 84043, 84046–47, 84049, 84051–53, 84062–63, 84066, 84070, 84072–73, 84076, 84078–79, 84082, 84085, 84090–94, 84102–03, 84105–09, 84112–13, 84115–17, 84119, 84121, 84123–24, 84132, 84143, 84148, 84152, 84157–58, 84165, 84171, 84501, 84510–13, 84515–16, 84518, 84520–23, 84525–26, 84528–37, 84539, 84540, 84542, 84604, 84710, 84712, 84714–23, 84725–26, 84729, 84732–38, 84740–43, 84745–47, 84749–50, 84753, 84755–65, 84767, 84770–76, 84779–84, 84790–91

* * *

THIRD DISTRICT

CHRIS CANNON, Republican, of Mapleton, UT; born in Salt Lake City, UT, October 20, 1950; education: B.S., University Studies, Brigham Young University, 1974; graduate work at Harvard School of Business, 1974–75; J.D., Brigham Young University, 1977–80; professional: admitted to the Utah bar in 1980 and began practice in Provo, UT; attorney, Robinson, Seiler and Glazier; former associate and deputy associate solicitor, Department of the Interior; co-founder, Geneva Steel, Provo; founder, president, and chairman, Cannon Industries, Salt Lake City; member, Utah Republican Party Elephant Club and Finance Committee; Utah Chairman, Lamar Alexander for President; Utah Finance Chairman, Bush-Quayle '92; married: the former Claudia Ann Fox in 1978; religion: Church of Jesus Christ of Latter-day Saints; children: Rachel, Jane, Laura, Emily, Elizabeth, Jonathan, Matthew, Katherine; committees: Judiciary; Natural Resources; Oversight and Government Reform; elected to the 105th Congress; reelected to each succeeding Congress.

Office Listings

http://chriscannon.house.gov

2436 Cannon House Office Building, Washington, DC 20515 .... (202) 225–7751
FAX: 225–5629
Chief of Staff.—Joe Hunter.
Legislative Director.—Matt Iandoli.
Press Secretary.—Fred Piccolo.
Scheduler.—Alia Cardwell.
51 South University Avenue, Suite 319, Provo, UT 84606 .... (801) 851–2500
Chief of Staff.—Joe Hunter.

Counties: BEAVER, JUAB (part), MILLARD, SALT LAKE (part), SANPETE, SEVIER, UTAH (part). Population (2000), 744,390.

ZIP Codes: 84003, 84006, 84013, 84042–44, 84047, 84057–59, 84062, 84065, 84070, 84084, 84088, 84095, 84097, 84107, 84118–20, 84123, 84128, 84170, 84184, 84199, 84601–06, 84620–24, 84626–27, 84629–40, 84642–57, 84660, 84662–65, 84667, 84701, 84711, 84713, 84724, 84728, 84730–31, 84739, 84744, 84751–52, 84754, 84766

VERMONT

(Population 2000, 608,827)

SENATORS

PATRICK J. LEAHY, Democrat, of Middlesex, VT; born in Montpelier, VT, March 31, 1940, son of Howard and Alba Leahy; education: graduate of St. Michael's High School, Montpelier, 1957; B.A., St. Michael's College, 1961; J.D., Georgetown University, 1964; professional: attorney, admitted to the Vermont bar, 1964; admitted to the District of Columbia bar, 1979; admitted to practice before: the Vermont Supreme Court, 1964; the Federal District Court of Vermont, 1965; the Second Circuit Court of Appeals in New York, 1966; and the U.S. Supreme Court, 1968; State's Attorney, Chittenden County, 1966–74; vice president, National District Attorneys Association, 1971–74; married: the former Marcelle Pomerleau, 1962; children: Kevin, Alicia and Mark; first Democrat and youngest person in Vermont to be elected to the U.S. Senate; committees: chair, Judiciary; Agriculture, Nutrition, and Forestry; Appropriations; elected to the Senate on November 5, 1974; reelected to each succeeding Senate term.

Office Listings

http://leahy.senate.gov

433 Russell Senate Office Building, Washington, DC 20515 .... (202) 224–4242
Chief of Staff.—Ed Pagano. FAX: 224–3479
Deputy Chief of Staff.—Clara Kircher.
Legislative Director.—John P. Dowd.
Press Secretary.—David Carle.
Federal Building, Room 338, Montpelier, VT 05602 .... (802) 229–0569
Office Director.—Robert G. Paquin.
199 Main Street, Courthouse Plaza, Burlington, VT 05401 .... (802) 863–2525
State Director.—Chuck Ross.

* * *

BERNARD SANDERS, Independent, of Burlington, VT; born in Brooklyn, NY, September 8, 1941; education: graduated, Madison High School, Brooklyn; B.S., Political Science, University of Chicago, 1964; professional: carpenter; writer; college professor; Mayor of Burlington, VT, 1981–89; married: the former Jane O'Meara, 1988; children: Levi, Heather, Carina and David; committees: Budget; Energy and Natural Resources; Environment and Public Works; Health, Education, Labor, and Pensions; Veterans' Affairs; elected to the 102nd Congress on November 6, 1990; reelected to each succeeding Congress; elected to the U.S. Senate on November 7, 2006.

Office Listings

http://sanders.senate.gov

332 Dirksen Senate Office Building, Washington, DC 20510 .... (202) 224–5141
Chief of Staff.—Jeff Weaver. FAX: 228–0776
Legislative Director.—Peter Tyler.
Communications Director.—Michael Briggs.
1 Church Street, Second Floor, Burlington, VT 05401 .... (802) 862–0697

REPRESENTATIVE

AT LARGE

PETER WELCH, Democrat, of Hartland, VT; born in Springfield, MA, May 2, 1947; education: Cathedral High School, Springfield, MA, 1969; B.A., *magna cum laude*, College of the Holy Cross, 1969; J.D., University of California at Berkley, 1973; professional: attorney, admitted to VT Bar, 1974; founding partner, Welch, Graham & Manby; served in Vermont State Senate, 1981–89, 2001–07; Minority Leader, 1983–85; President pro tempore, 1985–89, 2003–07; family: wife, Joan Smith (deceased); five children: Beth, Mary, Bill, John and Michael; committees: Oversight and Government Reform; Rules; elected to the 110th Congress on November 7, 2006.

Office Listings

1404 Longworth House Office Building, Washington, DC 20515 .... (202) 225–4115
Chief of Staff.—Bob Rogan. FAX: 225–6790
Scheduler/Executive Assistant.—Molly Gray.
Legislative Director.—Constance Dougherty.
Communications Director.—Andrew Savage.
30 Main Street, Third Floor, Suite 350, VT 05401 .... (802) 652–2450

State Director.—Patricia Coates.

Population (2000), 608,827.

ZIP Codes: 05001, 05009, 05030–43, 05045–56, 05058–62, 05065, 05067–77, 05079, 05081, 05083–86, 05088–89, 05091, 05101, 05141–43, 05146, 05148–56, 05158–59, 05161, 05201, 05250–55, 05257, 05260–62, 05301–04, 05340–46, 05350–63, 05401–07, 05439–66, 05468–74, 05476–79, 05481–83, 05485–92, 05494–95, 05601–04, 05609, 05620, 05633, 05640–41, 05647–58, 05660–67, 05669–82, 05701–02, 05730–48, 05750–51, 05753, 05757–70, 05772–78, 05819–30, 05832–33, 05836–43, 05845–51, 05853, 05855, 05857–63, 05866–68, 05871–75, 05901–07

VIRGINIA

(Population 2000, 7,078,515)

SENATORS

JOHN W. WARNER, Republican, of Alexandria, VA; born in Washington, DC, February 18, 1927; grandson of John W. and Mary Tinsley Warner of Amherst County, VA; son of the late Dr. John W. Warner and Martha Budd Warner; education: left high school in 1944 to serve in the U.S. Navy, released from active duty, third class electronics technician, July 1946; graduated Washington and Lee University (engineering), 1949; entered University of Virginia Law School, 1949; U.S. Marine Corps, second tour of active military duty as a first lieutenant, September, 1950 to May, 1952, with service in Korea, October, 1951 to May, 1952 as a ground communications officer with Marine Air Group 33, 1st Marine Air Wing; received LL.B. from University of Virginia, 1953; former owner and operator of Atoka, a cattle and crops farm, 1961–94; law clerk to E. Barrett Prettyman, late chief judge for the U.S. Court of Appeals for D.C. Circuit, 1953–54; private law practice, 1954–56; assistant U.S. attorney, 1956–60; private law practice, 1960–69; trustee, Protestant Episcopal Cathedral, Mount St. Albans, 1967–72; member, board of trustees, Washington and Lee University, 1968–79; presidential appointments: Under Secretary, U.S. Navy, February 1969–April 1972; Secretary, U.S. Navy, May 1972–April 1974; Department of Defense delegate to Law of Sea Conferences, 1969–72, head of U.S. delegation for Incidents at Sea Conference, treaty signed in Moscow, May 1972; administrator, American Revolution Bicentennial Administration, April 1974–October 1976; National Security Working Group; Commission on Roles and Capabilities of U.S. Intelligence; U.S. Delegate to the 12th special session of the U.N. General Assembly devoted to disarmament, 1982; appointed in 1985 as a Senate observer to the Geneva arms control talks with the Soviet Union; committees: Armed Services; Environment and Public Works; Homeland Security and Governmental Affairs; Select Committee on Intelligence; elected to the U.S. Senate on November 7, 1978, and took the oath of office in Richmond, VA, on January 2, 1979; reelected to each succeeding Senate term.

Office Listings

http//warner.senate.gov

225 Russell Senate Office Building, Washington, DC 20510 .... (202) 224–2023
Chief of Staff.—Ann Loomis. FAX: 228–4515
Executive Assistant / Scheduler.—Anna Reilly.
Communications Director.—John Ullyot.
Office Manager.—Kristin White.
235 Federal Building, 180 West Main Street, Abingdon, VA 24210 .... (276) 628–8158
5309 Commonwealth Centre Parkway, Midlothian, VA 23112 .... (804) 739–0247
4900 World Trade Center, Norfolk, VA 23510 .... (757) 441–3079
1003 First Union Bank Building, 213 South Jefferson Street, Roanoke, VA 24011.. (540) 857–2676

* * *

JIM WEBB, Democrat, of Arlington County, VA; born in St. Joseph, MO, February 9, 1946; education: B.S., engineering, U.S. Naval Academy, 1968; J.D., Georgetown University Law Center, 1975; professional: Infantry officer, U.S. Marine Corps, 1968–72 (combat service in Vietnam); counsel, House Committee on Veterans' Affairs, 1977–81; Assistant Secretary of Defense, Reserve Affairs, 1984–87; Secretary of the Navy, 1987–88; broad career as a writer and journalist; literature professor, U.S. Naval Academy; Emmy-Award winning TV journalist; author, six best-selling novels, two non-fiction works, including a history of the Scots-Irish people; screenwriter and producer; business consultant; awards: Military awards: Navy Cross; Silver Star Medal; two Bronze Star Medals with combat ''V''; two Purple Heart Medals; campaign and unit citations; numerous civilian awards: Department of Defense Distinguished Public Service Medal; Medal of Honor Society's Patriot Award; American Legion National Commander's Public Service Award; Veterans of Foreign Wars Media Service Award; Marine Corps League's Military Order of the Iron Mike Award; John H. Russell Leadership Award; Marine Corps Correspondent Association's Robert L. Denig Distinguished Service Award; married: Hong: Hong Le; children: Amy, James Robert, Sarah, Julia, and Georgia; committees: Armed Services; Foreign Relations; Veterans' Affairs; Joint Economic Committee; elected to the U.S. Senate on November 7, 2006.

Office Listings

http://webb.senate.gov

144 Russell Senate Office Building, Washington, DC 20510 .... (202) 224–4024

Chief of Staff.—Paul Reagan. FAX: 228–6363
Communications Director.—Jessica Smith.
Legislative Director.—Michael Sozan.
Scheduler.—Lisa Stark.
507 East Franklin Street, Richmond, VA 23219 .... (804) 771–2221
State Director.—Louise Ware.
3140 Chaparral Drive, Building C, Suite 101, Roanoke, VA 24018 .... (540) 772–4236
756 Park Avenue, Norton, VA 24273 ....
222 Central Park Avenue, Suite 120, Virginia Beach, VA 23462 .... (757) 518–1674

REPRESENTATIVES

FIRST DISTRICT

JO ANN DAVIS, Republican, of Yorktown, VA; born in Rowan County, NC, June 29, 1950; education: Kecoughtan High School, Hampton, VA; Hampton Roads Business College; professional: Real Estate Broker; established Davis Management Co., 1988; and Jo Ann Davis Realty, 1990; organizations: Peninsula Chamber of Commerce; Better Business Bureau; National Association of Realtors; Mothers Against Drunk Driving; York County Business Association; public service: Virginia House of Delegates, 1997–2000; married: Chuck Davis; children: Charlie and Chris; committees: Armed Services; Foreign Affairs; elected to the 107th Congress on November 7, 2000; reelected to each succeeding Congress.

Office Listings

http://www.house.gov/joanndavis

1123 Longworth House Office Building, Washington, DC 20515 .... (202) 225–4261
Chief of Staff.—Chris Connelly. FAX: 225–4382
Legislative Director.—Mary Springer.
Scheduler / Office Manager.—Jessica Walton.
4904–B George Washington Memorial Highway, Yorktown, VA 23692 .... (757) 874–6687
District Director.—Joe Schumacher.
4500 Plank Road, Suite 105, Fredericksburg, VA 22407 .... (540) 548–1086
508 Church Lane, Tappahannock, VA 22560 .... (804) 443–0668

Counties: Caroline (part), Essex, Fauquier (part), Gloucester, James City, King and Queen, King George, King William, Lancaster, Mathews, Middlesex, Northumberland, Prince William (part), Richmond, Spotsylvania (part), Stafford, Westmoreland, York. Cities and townships: Bowling Green, Chancellorsville, Cobbs Creek, Colonial Beach, Dumfries, Falmouth, Fredericksburg, Hampton, Kilmarnock, Lightfoot, Montross, Newport News, Poquoson, Quantico, Saluda, Seaford, Tappahannock, Toano, Triangle, Warsaw, West Point, White Stone, Williamsburg, and Yorktown. Population (2000), 643,514.

ZIP Codes: 20106, 20112, 20115, 20119, 20128, 20138–39, 20181, 20186–87, 22026, 22134–35, 22172, 22191, 22193, 22401–08, 22412, 22427, 22430, 22432, 22435–38, 22442–43, 22446, 22448, 22451, 22454, 22456, 22460, 22463, 22469, 22471–73, 22476, 22480–82, 22485, 22488, 22501, 22503–04, 22507–09, 22511, 22513–14, 22517, 22520, 22523–24, 22526, 22528–30, 22535, 22538–39, 22544–48, 22552–56, 22558, 22560, 22570, 22572, 22576–81, 22639, 22712, 22720, 22728, 22734, 22739, 22742, 23001, 23003, 23009, 23011, 23017–18, 23021, 23023–25, 23031–32, 23035, 23043, 23045, 23050, 23056, 23061–62, 23064, 23066, 23068–72, 23076, 23079, 23081, 23085–86, 23089–92, 23106–10, 23115, 23117, 23119, 23125–28, 23130–31, 23138, 23148–49, 2315356, 23161, 23163, 23168–69, 23175–78, 23180–81, 23183–88, 23190–91, 23354, 23601–03, 23605–06, 23608–09, 23612, 23662–63, 23665–67, 23669–70, 23681, 23690–94, 23696

* * *

SECOND DISTRICT

THELMA D. DRAKE, Republican, of Norfolk, VA; born in Elyria, OH, November 20, 1949; education: graduated, Elyria High School; professional: realtor; Delegate, Virginia House of Delegates, 1995–2004; Concerned Citizens for Effective Government; Lee's Friends Bay View PTA; board member, East Ocean View Civic League; Northside Civic League; Bay View Civic League; Norfolk Republican Women; Housing and Community Development Board; awards: Crime Prevention Association Award; Tidewater Association of Realtors Circle of Excellence Award; Coldwell Banker's Presidents Circle, Sales and Marketing Executives Award; religion: United Church of Christ; married: Thomas E. (Ted); children: Lynn Sorey and J. Mark Sawyers; committees: Armed Services; Transportation and Infrastructure; elected to the 109th Congress on November 2, 2004; reelected to the 110th Congress.

Office Listings

http://www.house.gov/drake

1208 Longworth House Office Building, Washington, DC 20515 .... (202) 225–4215

Chief of Staff.—Carrie Melvin. FAX: 225–4218
Communications Director.—J. Tyler Brown.
Executive Assistant.—Kelly Williams.
Counsel.—Dena Kozanas.
4772 Euclid Road, Suite E, Virginia Beach, VA 23462 .... (757) 497–6859
District Chief of Staff.—Mary Lou Stone.
23386 Front Street, Accomac, VA 23301 .... (757) 787–7836

Counties: ACCOMACK, NORTHAMPTON. CITIES: Hampton, Norfolk, and Virginia Beach. Population (2000), 643,510.

ZIP Codes: 23301–03, 23306–08, 23310, 23313, 23316, 23336–37, 23341, 23345, 23347, 23350, 23354, 23356–59, 23389, 23395, 23398–99, 23401, 23404–05, 23407–10, 23412–23, 23426–27, 23429, 23440–43, 23450–67, 23471, 23479–80, 23482–83, 23486, 23488, 23502–03, 23505–08, 23511–13, 23515, 23518–19, 23521, 23529, 23541, 23551, 23605, 23651, 23661, 23663–66, 23669

* * *

THIRD DISTRICT

ROBERT C. ''BOBBY'' SCOTT, Democrat, of Newport News, VA; born in Washington, DC, April 30, 1947; education: graduated, Groton High School; B.A., Harvard University; J.D., Boston College Law School; professional: served in the Massachusetts National Guard; attorney; admitted to the Virginia bar; Virginia House of Representatives, 1978–83; Virginia State Senate, 1983–92; member: Alpha Phi Alpha Fraternity; March of Dimes Board of Directors; NAACP; Peninsula Chamber of Commerce; Peninsula Legal Aid Center Board of Directors; Sigma Pi Phi Fraternity; committees: Budget; Education and Labor; Judiciary; elected on November 3, 1992 to the 103rd Congress; reelected to each succeeding Congress.

Office Listings

wttp://www.house.gov/scott

1201 Longworth House Office Building, Washington, DC 20515 .... (202) 225–8351
Chief of Staff.—Joni L. Ivey. FAX: 225–8354
Special Assistant.—Randi Estes.
Legislative Counsels: Ilana Fisher, LaQuita Honeysucker.
2600 Washington Avenue, Suite 1010, Newport News, VA 23607 .... (757) 380–1000
501 North Second Street, Suite 401, Richmond, VA 23219–1321 .... (804) 644–4845

Counties: CHARLES CITY, HENRICO (part), NEW KENT, SURRY. CITIES: Hampton, Norfolk, Portsmouth and Richmond. Population (2000), 643,476.

ZIP Codes: 23011, 23030, 23059–60, 23075, 23089, 23111, 23124, 23140–41, 23147, 23150, 23181, 23185, 23218–25, 23227–28, 23230–32, 23234, 23240–41, 23249–50, 23260–61, 23269–70, 23272, 23274–76, 23278–79, 23282, 23284–86, 23290–93, 23295, 23298, 23501–02, 23504–05, 23507–10, 23513–14, 23517–18, 23520, 23523, 23530, 23601–09, 23628, 23630–31, 23653, 23661, 23663–64, 23666–70, 23701–05, 23707–09, 23839, 23842, 23846, 23860, 23875, 23881, 23883, 23888, 23898–99

* * *

FOURTH DISTRICT

J. RANDY FORBES, Republican, of Chesapeake, VA; born in Chesapeake, February 17, 1952; education: B.A., Randolph-Macon College; J.D., University of Virginia School of Law; professional: attorney; religion: Baptist; public service: Virginia House of Delegates, 1990–97; Virginia State Senate, 1997–2001; Republican House Floor Leader, 1994–97; Republican Senate Floor Leader, 1998–2001; Chairman of the Republican Party of Virginia, 1996–2000; married: Shirley; children: Neil, Jamie, Jordan, and Justin; committees: Armed Services; Judiciary; elected to the 107th Congress, by special election, on June 19, 2001; reelected to each succeeding Congress.

Office Listings

307 Cannon House Office Building, Washington, DC 20515 .... (202) 225–6365
Chief of Staff.—Dee Gilmore. FAX: 226–1170
Press Secretary.—Christy Boardman.
Legislative Director.—Christy Grubbs.
636 Cedar Road, Suite 200, Chesapeake, VA 23322 .... (757) 382–0080
2903 Boulevard, Suite B, Colonial Heights, VA 23834 .... (804) 526–4969
District Representative.—Jason Gray.
425 H. South Main Street, Emporia, VA 23847 .... (434) 634–5575
District Field Representative.—Rick Franklin.

Counties: AMELIA, BRUNSWICK (part), CHESTERFIELD (part), DINWIDDIE, GREENSVILLE, ISLE OF WIGHT (part), NOTTOWAY, POWHATAN, PRINCE GEORGE (part), SOUTHAMPTON, SUSSEX. Population (2000), 643,477.

ZIP Codes: 23002, 23083, 23101, 23105, 23112–14, 23120, 23139, 23234, 23236–37, 23304, 23314–15, 23320–28, 23397, 23424, 23430–39, 23487, 23501, 23801, 23803–06, 23821, 23824, 23827–34, 23836–38, 23840–42, 23844–45, 23847, 23850–51, 23856–57, 23860, 23866–67, 23872–76, 23878–79, 23882, 23884–85, 23887–91, 23894, 23897–98, 23920, 23922, 23930, 23938, 23950, 23955

* * *

FIFTH DISTRICT

VIRGIL H. GOODE, JR., Republican, of Rocky Mount, VA; born in Richmond, VA, October 17, 1946; education: B.A., University of Richmond, 1969; J.D., University of Virginia Law School, 1973; served in Virginia Army National Guard; professional: attorney; admitted to the Virginia bar in 1973; member, Virginia State Senate, 1973–97; former member: Ruritan Chamber of Commerce; Jaycees; married: Lucy Dodson Goode, 1991; children: Catherine; committees: Appropriations; elected to the 105th Congress; reelected to each succeeding Congress.

Office Listings

http://www.house.gov/goode

1520 Longworth House Office Building, Washington, DC 20515 .... (202) 225–4711
FAX: 225–5681
Chief of Staff.—Jerr Rosenbaum.
70 East Court Street, Suite 215, Rocky Mount, VA 24151 .... (540) 484–1254
437 Main Street, Danville, VA 24541 .... (434) 792–1280
Scheduler.—Judy Mattox.
104 South First Street, Charlottesville, VA 22902 .... (434) 295–6372
P.O. Box 366, Farmville, VA 23901 .... (434) 392–8331

Counties: ALBEMARLE COUNTY. CITIES AND TOWNSHIPS: Charlotteville, Batesville, Covesville, Esmont, Greenwood, Hatton, Ivy, Keene, Keswick, North Garden, Scottsville. APPOMATTOX COUNTY. CITIES AND TOWNSHIPS: Appomattox, Evergreen, Pamplin, Spout Spring. BEDFORD COUNTY. CITIES AND TOWNSHIPS: Bedford, Big Island, Goodview, Coleman Falls, Forest, Goode, Huddleston, Lowry, Thaxton. BRUNSWICK COUNTY. BUCKINGHAM COUNTY. CITIES AND TOWNSHIPS: Andersonville, Arvonia, Buckingham, Dillwyn, Buckingham, New Canton. CAMPBELL COUNTY. CITIES AND TOWNSHIPS: Altavista, Brookneal, Concord, Evington, Gladys, Long Island, Lynch Station, Naruna, Rustburg. CHARLOTTE COUNTY. CITIES AND TOWNSHIPS: Barnesville, Charlotte Court House, Cullen, Drakes Branch, Keysville, Phenix, Randolph, Red House, Red Oak, Saxe, Wylliesburg. CUMBERLAND COUNTY. CITIES AND TOWNSHIPS: Carterville, Cumberland. DANVILLE COUNTY. CITY: Danville. FLUVANNA COUNTY. CITIES AND TOWNSHIPS: Bremo Bluff, Bybee, Carysbrook, Columbia, Fort Union, Kents Store, Palmyra, Troy. FRANKLIN COUNTY. CITIES AND TOWNSHIPS: Boones Mill, Callaway, Ferrum, Glade Hill, Henry, Redwood, Penhook, Rocky Mount, Union Hall, Waidsboro, Wirtz. GREENE COUNTY. HALIFAX COUNTY. CITIES AND TOWNSHIPS: Alton, Clover, Cluster Springs, Crystal Hall, Denniston, Halifax, Ingram, Lennig, Mayo, Nathalie, Republican Grove, Scottsburg, Turbeville, Vernon Hill, Virgilina. HENRY COUNTY. CITIES AND TOWNSHIPS: Axton, Bassett, Collinsville, Fieldale, Ridgeway, Spencer, Stanleytown. LUNENBURG COUNTY. CITIES AND TOWNSHIPS: Tamworth, Dundas, Fort Mitchell, Kenbridge, Lunenburg, Rehoboth, Victoria. MARTINSVILLE COUNTY. CITY: Martinsville. MECKLENBURG COUNTY. CITIES AND TOWNSHIPS: Baskerville, Blackridge, Boydton, Bracey, Chase City, Clarksville, Forksville, LaCross, Palmer Springs, Skipwith, South Hill, Union Level Buffalo Junction, Nelson. NELSON COUNTY. CITIES AND TOWNSHIPS: Afton, Arrington, Faber, Lovingston, Massies Mill, Nellysford, Montebello, Gladstone, Norwood, Piney River, Roseland, Schuyler, Shipman, Tye River, Tyro, Wingina. PITTSYLVANIA COUNTY. CITIES AND TOWNSHIPS: Blairs, Callands, Cascade, Chatham, Pittsville, Sandy Level, Dry Fork, Gretna, Hurt, Java, Keeling, Ringgold, Sutherlin. PRINCE EDWARD COUNTY. CITIES AND TOWNSHIPS: Green Bay, Farmville, Darlington, Heights, Green Bay, Hampden-Sydney, Meherrin, Prospect, Rice, and South Boston. Population (2000), 643,497.

ZIP Codes: 22901–11, 22920, 22922–24, 22931–32, 22935–38, 22940, 22942–43, 22945–47, 22949, 22952, 22954, 22958–59, 22963–65, 22967–69, 22971, 22973–74, 22976, 22987, 23004, 23022, 23027, 23038, 23040, 23055, 23084, 23093, 23123, 23139, 23821, 23824, 23843, 23845, 23856–57, 23868, 23887, 23889, 23893, 23901, 23909, 23915, 23917, 23919–24, 23927, 23934, 23936–39, 23941–44, 23947, 23950, 23952, 23954, 23958–60, 23962–64, 23966–68, 23970, 23974, 23976, 24012, 24053–55, 24059, 24064–65, 24067, 24069, 24076, 24078–79, 24082, 24088–89, 24091–92, 24095, 24101–02, 24104, 24112–15, 24120–22, 24133, 24137, 24139, 24146, 24148, 24151, 24153, 24161, 24168, 24171, 24174, 24176–77, 24179, 24184–85, 24312, 24464, 24483, 24501–02, 24504, 24517, 24520, 24522–23, 24527–31, 24534–35, 24538–41, 24543–44, 24549–51, 24553–54, 24556–58, 24562–63, 24565–66, 24569–71, 24574, 24576–77, 24580–81, 24585–86, 24588–90, 24592–94, 24597–99

* * *

SIXTH DISTRICT

BOB GOODLATTE, Republican, of Roanoke, VA; born in Holyoke, MA, September 22, 1952; education: B.A., Bates College, Lewiston, ME, 1974; J.D., Washington and Lee University, 1977; Massachusetts bar, 1977; Virginia bar, 1978; professional: began practice in Roanoke, VA, 1979; district director for Congressman M. Caldwell Butler, 1977–79; attorney, sole practitioner, 1979–81; partner, 1981–92; chairman of the sixth district Virginia Republican Committee, 1983–88; member: Civitan Club of Roanoke (president, 1989–90); former member, Building Better Boards Advisory Council; married: Maryellen Flaherty, 1974; children: Jennifer and Robert; deputy Republican whip; committees: ranking member, Agriculture; Judiciary; elected on November 3, 1992, to the 103rd Congress; reelected to each succeeding Congress.

Office Listings

http://www.house.gov/goodlatte

2240 Rayburn House Office Building, Washington, DC 20515 .... (202) 225–5431
Chief of Staff.—Shelley Husband. FAX: 225–9681
Legislative Counsel.—Branden Ritchie.
Press Secretary.—Kathryn Rexrode.
10 Franklin Road, SE, Suite 540, Roanoke, VA 24011 .... (540) 857–2672
District Director.—Pete Larkin.
916 Main Street, Suite 300, Lynchburg, VA 24504 .... (804) 845–8306
7 Court Square, Staunton, VA 24401 .... (540) 885–3861
2 South Main Street, First Floor, Suite A, Harrisonburg, VA 22801 .... (540) 432–2391

Counties: ALLEGHANY (part), AMHERST, AUGUSTA, BATH, BEDFORD (part), BOTETOURT, HIGHLAND, ROANOKE (part), ROCKBRIDGE, ROCKINGHAM , SHENANDOAH. CITIES: Buena Vista, Covington, Harrisonburg, Lexington, Lynchburg, Roanoke, Salem, Staunton, and Waynesboro. Population (2000), 643,504.

ZIP Codes: 22626, 22641, 22644–45, 22652, 22654, 22657, 22660, 22664, 22801–03, 22807, 22810–12, 22815, 22820–21, 22824, 22827, 22830–34, 22840–48, 22850, 22853, 22920, 22922, 22939, 22952, 22967, 22980, 24001–20, 24022–38, 24040, 24042–44, 24048, 24053, 24059, 24064–66, 24070, 24077, 24079, 24083, 24085, 24087, 24090, 24101, 24121–22, 24130, 24153, 24156, 24174–75, 24178–79, 24401–02, 24411–13, 24415–16, 24421–22, 24426, 24430–33, 24435, 24437–42, 24445, 24450, 24458–60, 24463, 24465, 24467–69, 24471–73, 24476–77, 24479, 24482–87, 24501–06, 24512–15, 24521, 24523, 24526, 24533, 24536, 24550–51, 24553, 24555–56, 24572, 24574, 24578–79, 24595

* * *

SEVENTH DISTRICT

ERIC CANTOR, Republican, of Henrico County, VA; born in Henrico County, June 6, 1963; education: Bachelor's Degree, George Washington University, 1985; Law Degree, College of William and Mary, 1988; Masters Degree, Columbia University, 1989; professional: attorney; organizations: Western Henrico Rotary; Henrico County Republican Committee; President, Virginia-Israel Foundation; Virginia Holocaust Museum Board of Trustees; Elk Hill Farm Board of Trustees; elected to the Virginia House of Delegates, 1991; appointed Chief Deputy Majority Whip, December, 2002; married: Diana; three children; committees: Ways and Means; elected to the 107th Congress on November 7, 2000; reelected to each succeeding Congress.

Office Listings

http://www.house.gov/cantor

329 Cannon House Office Building, Washington, DC 20515 .... (202) 225–2815
Chief of Staff.—Rob Collins. FAX: 225–0011
Legislative Director.—Shimmy Stein.
4201 Dominion Boulevard, Suite 110, Glen Allen, VA 23060 .... (804) 747–4073
763 Madison Road, Suite 207, Culpeper, VA 22701 .... (540) 825–8960

Counties: CAROLINE (part), CHESTERFIELD (part), CULPEPER, GOOCHLAND, HANOVER, HENRICO (part), LOUISIA, MADISON, ORANGE, PAGE, RAPPAHANNOCK, SPOTSYLVANIA (part). CITIES: Richmond. Population (2000), 643,499.

ZIP Codes: 20106, 20119, 20186, 22407, 22433, 22508, 22534, 22542, 22546, 22553, 22565, 22567, 22580, 22610, 22623, 22627, 22630, 22640, 22650, 22701, 22709, 22711, 22713–16, 22718–19, 22721–27, 22729–38, 22740–41, 22743, 22746–49, 22827, 22835, 22849, 22851, 22903, 22923, 22942, 22947–48, 22957, 22960, 22972, 22974, 22989, 23005, 23015, 23024, 23038–39, 23047, 23058–60, 23063, 23065, 23067, 23069, 23084, 23093, 23102–03, 23111–14, 23116–17, 23120, 23124, 23129, 23146, 23153, 23160, 23162, 23170, 23173, 23192, 23221–30, 23233–36, 23242, 23255, 23273, 23280, 23288–89, 23294–95

* * *

EIGHTH DISTRICT

JAMES P. MORAN, Democrat, of Alexandria, VA; born in Buffalo, NY, May 16, 1945; education: B.A., College of Holy Cross; Bernard Baruch Graduate School of Finance—City University of New York; M.P.A., University of Pittsburgh Graduate School of Public and International Affairs; served on City Council of Alexandria, 1979–82; Vice Mayor, 1982–84; Mayor, 1985–90; founding member of the New Democrat Coalition, a group of more than 75 centrist House Democrats committed to fiscal responsibility, improvements to education, and maintaining America's economic competitiveness; co-chair of the Congressional Prevention Coalition; named as one of two ''High Technology Legislators of the Year'' by the Information Technology Industry Council; in 2000 named to the ''Legislative Hall of Fame'' by the American Electronics Association for his work on technology issues; married: LuAnn; children: James,

Patrick, Mary, and Dorothy; committees: Appropriations; elected to the 102nd Congress on November 6, 1990; reelected to each succeeding Congress.

Office Listings

http://www.house.gov/moran

2239 Rayburn House Office Building, Washington, DC 20515 .... (202) 225–4376
Chief of Staff.—Phil Sunderland. FAX: 225–0017
Legislative Director.—Tim Aiken.
333 North Fairfax Street, Suite 201, Alexandria, VA 22314 .... (703) 971–4700
District Director.—Susie Warner.
1900 Campus Commons Drive, Suite 102, VA 20191 .... (703) 971–4700

Counties: ARLINGTON, FAIRFAX (part). CITIES: Alexandria, and Falls Church. Population (2000), 643,503.

ZIP Codes: 20170–71, 20190–91, 20194–96, 20206, 20231, 20301, 20310, 20330, 20350, 20406, 20453, 22003, 22027, 22031, 22037, 22040–44, 22046–47, 22060, 22079, 22101–03, 22107–09, 22122, 22124, 22150–51, 22159, 22180–82, 22201–07, 22209–17, 22219, 22222, 22225–27, 22229–30, 22234, 22240–45, 22301–07, 22310–15, 22320–21, 22331–34, 22336

* * *

NINTH DISTRICT

RICK BOUCHER, Democrat, of Abingdon, VA; born in Washington County, VA, August 1, 1946; education: graduated, Abingdon High School, 1964; B.A., Roanoke College, 1968; J.D., University of Virginia School of Law, 1971; professional: associate, Milbank, Tweed, Hadley and McCloy, New York, NY; partner, Boucher and Boucher, Abingdon, VA; elected to the Virginia State Senate in 1975 and reelected in 1979; former chairman of the Oil and Gas Subcommittee of the Virginia Coal and Energy Commission; former member: Virginia State Crime Commission; Virginia Commission on Interstate Cooperation; Law and Justice Committee of the National Conference of State Legislatures; member: board of directors, First Virginia Bank, Damascus; Abingdon United Methodist Church; Kappa Alpha order; Phi Alpha Delta legal fraternity; American Bar Association; Virginia Bar Association; Association of the Bar of the City of New York; recipient of the Abingdon Jaycees Outstanding Young Businessman Award, 1975; assistant whip; committees: Energy and Commerce; Judiciary; elected to the 98th Congress on November 2, 1982; reelected to each succeeding Congress.

Office Listings

http://www.house.gov/boucher

2187 Rayburn House Office Building, Washington, DC 20515 .... (202) 225–3861
Chief of Staff.—Becky Coleman. FAX: 225–0442
Deputy Chief of Staff/Comunications Director.—Sharon Ringley.
188 East Main Street, Abingdon, VA 24210 .... (540) 628–1145
District Administrator.—Linda Di Yorio.
1 Cloverleaf Square, Suite C–1, Big Stone Gap, VA 24219 .... (540) 523–5450
112 North Washington Avenue, P.O. Box 1268, Pulaski, VA 24301 .... (540) 980–4310

Counties: ALLEGHANY (part), BLAND, BUCHANAN, CARROLL, CRAIG, DICKENSON, FLOYD, GILES, GRAYSON, HENRY (part), LEE, MONTGOMERY, PATRICK, PULASKI, ROANOKE (part), RUSSELL, SCOTT, SMYTH, TAZEWELL, WASHINGTON, WISE, WYTHE. CITIES: Bristol, Covington, Galax, Norton, and Radford. Population (2000), 643,514.

ZIP Codes: 24018–19, 24053, 24055, 24058–64, 24068, 24070, 24072–73, 24076, 24079, 24082, 24084, 24086–87, 24089, 24091, 24093–94, 24104–05, 24111–12, 24120–22, 24124, 24126–29, 24131–34, 24136, 24138, 24141–43, 24147–50, 24153, 24162, 24165, 24167, 24171, 24175, 24177, 24185, 24201–03, 24209–12, 24215–21, 24224–26, 24228, 24230, 24236–37, 24239, 24243–46, 24248, 24250–51, 24256, 24258, 24260, 24263, 24265–66, 24269–73, 24277, 24279–83, 24290, 24292–93, 24301, 24311–19, 24322–28, 24330, 24333, 24340, 24343, 24347–48, 24350–52, 24354, 24360–61, 24363, 24366, 24368, 24370, 24374–75, 24377–78, 24380–82, 24422, 24426, 24448, 24457, 24474, 24502, 24526, 24550–51, 24556, 24601–09, 24612–14, 24618–20, 24622, 24624, 24627–28, 24630–31, 24634–35, 24637, 24639–41, 24646–47, 24649, 24651, 24656–58

* * *

TENTH DISTRICT

FRANK R. WOLF, Republican, of Vienna, VA; born in Philadelphia, PA, January 30, 1939; education: B.A., Pennsylvania State University, 1961; LL.B., Georgetown University Law School, 1965; served in the U.S. Army Signal Corps (Reserves); professional: lawyer, admitted to the Virginia State bar; legislative assistant for former U.S. Congressman Edward G. Biester, Jr., 1968–71; assistant to Secretary of the Interior Rogers C.B. Morton, 1971–74; Deputy Assistant Secretary for Congressional and Legislative Affairs, Department of the Interior, 1974–75;

member, Vienna Presbyterian Church; married: the former Carolyn Stover; children: Frank, Jr., Virginia, Anne, Brenda, and Rebecca; committees: Appropriations; elected to the 97th Congress, November 4, 1980; reelected to each succeeding Congress.

Office Listings

http://www.house.gov/wolf

241 Cannon House Office Building, Washington, DC 20515 .... (202) 225–5136
Chief of Staff/Press Secretary.—Dan Scandling. FAX: 225–0437
Legislative Director.—Janet Shaffron.
13873 Park Center Road, Suite 130, Herndon, VA 20171 .... (703) 709–5800
Director of Constituent Services.—Judy McCary.
110 North Cameron Street, Winchester, VA 22601 .... (540) 667–0900

Counties: CLARKE, FAIRFAX (part), FAUQUIER (part), FREDERICK, LOUDOUN, PRINCE WILLIAM (part), WARREN. CITIES: Manassas, Manassas Park, and Winchester. Population (2000), 643,512.

ZIP Codes: 20101–05, 20107–13, 20115–18, 20120–22, 20129–32, 20134–35, 20137, 20140–44, 20146–49, 20151–53, 20158–60, 20163–67, 20170–72, 20175–78, 20180, 20184–90, 20194, 20197–98, 22026, 22033, 22043–44, 22046, 22066–67, 22101, 22106, 22184–85, 22193, 22207, 22556, 22601–04, 22610–11, 22620, 22622, 22624–25, 22630, 22637, 22639, 22642–43, 22645–46, 22649, 22654–57, 22663

* * *

ELEVENTH DISTRICT

TOM DAVIS, Republican, of Falls Church, VA; born in Minot, ND, January 5, 1949; education: graduated, U.S. Capitol Page School; graduated, Amherst College with honors in political science; law degree, University of Virginia; attended officer candidate school; served in the U.S. Army Reserves; member: Fairfax County Board of Supervisors, 1980–94, Chairman, 1992–94; vice president and general counsel of PRC, Inc., McLean, VA; past president, Washington Metropolitan Council of Governments; founding member and past president, Bailey's Crossroads Rotary Club; married Jeannemarie Devolites, 2004; three children: Carlton, Pamela, and Shelley; committees: Homeland Security; Oversight and Government Reform; elected to the 104th Congress; reelected to each succeeding Congress.

Office Listings

http://www.house.gov/tomdavis

2348 Rayburn House Office Building, Washington, DC 20515 .... (202) 225–1492
Chief of Staff.—David Thomas. FAX: 225–3071
Legislative Director.—Bill Womack.
Communications Director.—David Martin.
4115 Annandale Road, Annandale, VA 22003 .... (703) 916–9610
District Director.—Dave Foreman.
Telecommuting District Office .... (703) 437–1726
Constituent Service Director.—Ann Rust.
Dominion Center, 13546 Minnieville Road, Woodbridge, VA 22192 .... (703) 590–4599
Constituent Service Director.—Ryan Kelly.

Counties: FAIRFAX (part), PRINCE WILLIAM (part). CITIES: Alexandria, Annandale, Burke, Centreville, Clifton, Fairfax, Fairfax Station, Herndon, Lorton, Manassas, Oakton, Occoquan, Springfield, Vienna, and Woodbridge. Population (2000), 643,509.

ZIP Codes: 20069–70, 20109–10, 20112, 20119–22, 20124, 20136–37, 20155–56, 20168–69, 20171, 20181–82, 22003, 22009, 22015, 22027, 22030–33, 22035, 22038–39, 22044, 22060, 22079, 22081–82, 22102, 22116, 22118–21, 22124–25, 22150–53, 22156, 22158–61, 22180–83, 22185, 22191–95, 22199, 22308–09, 22312

WASHINGTON

(Population 2000, 5,894,121)

SENATORS

PATTY MURRAY, Democrat, of Seattle, WA; born in Seattle, October 11, 1950; education: B.A., Washington State University, 1972; professional: teacher; lobbyist; Shoreline Community College; citizen lobbyist for environmental and educational issues, 1983–88; parent education instructor for Crystal Springs, 1984–87; school board member, 1985–89; elected Board of Directors, Shoreline School District, 1985–89; Washington State Senate, 1988–92; Democratic Whip, 1990–92; State Senate committees: Education; Ways and Means; Commerce and Labor; Domestic Timber Processing Select Committee; Open Government Select Committee; chair, School Transportation Safety Task Force; award: Washington State Legislator of the Year, 1990; married: Rob Murray; children: Randy and Sara; committees: Appropriations; Budget; Health, Education, Labor and Pensions; Rules and Administration; Veterans' Affairs; Joint Committee on Printing; elected to the U.S. Senate on November 3, 1992; reelected to each succeeding Senate term.

Office Listings

http://murray.senate.gov

173 Russell Senate Office Building, Washington, DC 20510 .... (202) 224–2621
Chief of Staff.—Jeff Bjornstad. FAX: 224–0238
Legislative Director.—Evan Schatz. TDD: 224–4430
Communications Director.—Alex Glass.
2988 Jackson Federal Building, 915 Second Avenue, Seattle, WA 98174 .... (206) 553–5545
State Director.—John Engber.
The Marshall House, 1323 Officer's Row, Vancouver, WA 98661 .... (360) 696–7797
District Director.—Mindi Linquist.
601 West Main Avenue, Suite 1213, Spokane, WA 99201 .... (509) 624–9515
District Director.—Judy Olson.
2930 Wetmore Avenue, Suite 903, Everett, WA 98201 .... (425) 259–6515
District Director.—Christy Guillon.
402 East Yakima Avenue, Suite 390, Yakima, WA 98901 .... (509) 453–7462
District Director.—Rebecca Thornton.
1611 116th Avenue, NW., Suite 214, Bellevue, WA 98004 .... (425) 462–4460
District Director.—Kimberley Panicek.
950 Pacific Avenue, Room 650, Tacoma, WA 98402 .... (253) 572–3636
District Director.—Mary McBride.

* * *

MARIA CANTWELL, Democrat, of Edmonds, WA; born in Indianapolis, IN, October 13, 1958; education: B.A., Miami University, Miami, OH, 1980; professional: businesswoman; RealNetworks, Inc.; organizations: South Snohomish County Chamber of Commerce; Alderwood Rotary; Mountlake Terrace Friends of the Library; public service: Washington State House of Representatives, 1987–92; U.S. House of Representatives, 1992–94; religion: Roman Catholic; committees: Commerce, Science, and Transportation; Energy and Natural Resources; Finance; Indian Affairs; Small Business and Entrepreneurship; elected to the U.S. Senate on November 7, 2000; reelected to each succeeding Senate term.

Office Listings

http://cantwell.senate.gov

511 Dirksen Senate Office Building, Washington, DC 20510 .... (202) 224–3441
Chief of Staff.—Kurt Beckett. FAX: 228–0514
Deputy Chief of Staff.—Katharine Lister.
Legislative Director.—Courtney Gregoire.
Office Manager.—Michael Hill.
915 Second Avenue, Suite 3206, Seattle, WA 98174 .... (206) 220–6400
The Marshall House, 1313 Officers Row, Vancouver, WA 98661 .... (360) 696–7838
950 Pacific Avenue, Suite 615, Tacoma, WA 98402 .... (253) 572–2281
U.S. Federal Courthouse, West 920 Riverside, Suite 697, Spokane, WA 99201 ...... (509) 353–2507
825 Jadwin Avenue, 204/204A, Richland, WA 99352 .... (509) 946–8106
2930 Wetmore Avenue, Suite 9B, Everett, WA 98201 .... (425) 303–0114

REPRESENTATIVES

FIRST DISTRICT

JAY INSLEE, Democrat, of Bainbridge Island, WA; born in Seattle, WA, February 9, 1951; education: graduated, Ingraham High School, 1969; B.A., University of Washington, 1973; J.D., Willamette School of Law, 1976; professional: attorney, 1976–92; Washington State House of Representatives, 14th Legislative District, 1988–92; served on Appropriations; Housing; Judiciary; and Financial Institutions and Insurance Committees; attorney, 1995–96; Regional Director, U.S. Department of Health and Human Services, 1997–98; married: Trudi; three children: Jack, Connor, and Joe; committees: Energy and Commerce; Natural Resources; Select Committee on Energy Independence and Global Warming; elected to the 103rd Congress to represent the 4th District, November 3, 1992; elected to the 106th Congress to represent the 1st District on November 3, 1998; reelected to each succeeding Congress.

Office Listings

http://www.house.gov/inslee

403 Cannon House Office Building, Washington, DC 20515 .... (202) 225–6311
Chief of Staff.—Brain Bonlender. FAX: 226–1606
Legislative Director.—Nick Shipley.
Press Secretary.—Christine Hanson.
Executive Assistant.—Chandini Bachman.
Shoreline Center, 18560 First Avenue NE, Suite E–800, Shoreline, WA 98155–2150 .... (206) 361–0233
17701 Fjord Drive NE, Suite A–112, Liberty Bay Marina, Poulsbo, WA 98370 ..... (360) 598–2342
District Director.—Sharmila K. Swenson.

Counties: KING (part), KITSAP (part), SNOHOMISH (part). CITIES AND TOWNSHIPS: Bainbridge Island, Bothell, Bremerton, Brier, Duvall, Edmonds, Everett, Hansville, Indianola, Kenmore, Keyport, Kingston, Kirkland, Lake Forest, Lynnwood, Mill Creek, Monroe, Mountlake Terrace, Mukilteo, Port Gamble, Poulsbo, Redmond, Rollingbay, Seabeck, Seattle, Shoreline, Silverdale, Snohomish, Suquamish, and Woodinville. Population (2000), 654,904.

ZIP Codes: 98011–12, 98019–20, 98021, 98026, 98028, 98033–34, 98036–37, 98041, 98043, 98046, 98052, 98061, 98072–74, 98077, 98082–83, 98110, 98133, 98155, 98160, 98177, 98204, 98208, 98272, 98275, 98290, 98296, 98311–12, 98315, 98340, 98342, 98345–46, 98364, 98370, 98380, 98383, 98392–93

* * *

SECOND DISTRICT

RICK LARSEN, Democrat, of Lake Stevens, WA; born in Arlington, WA, June 15, 1965; education: B.A., Pacific Lutheran University; M.P.A., University of Minnesota; professional: economic development official at the Port of Everett; Director of Public Affairs for a health provider association; public service: Snohomish County Council; religion: Methodist; married: Tiia Karlen; children: Robert and Per; committees: Armed Services; Small Business; Transportation and Infrastructure; elected to the 107th Congress on November 7, 2000; reelected to each succeeding Congress.

Office Listings

http:/www.house.gov/larsen

107 Cannon House Office Building, Washington, DC 20515 .... (202) 225–2605
Chief of Staff.—Kimberly Johnston. FAX: 225–4420
Legislative Director.—Michael Dabbs.
Press Secretary.—Amanda Mahnke.
2930 Wetmore Avenue, Suite 9F, Everett, WA 98201 .... (425) 252–3188
104 West Magnolia, Room 206, Bellingham, WA 98225 .... (360) 733–4500

Counties: ISLAND, KING (part), SAN JUAN, SKAGIT, SNOHOMISH (part), WHATCOM. CITIES AND TOWNSHIPS: Bellingham, Everett, and Mount Vernon. Population (2000), 654,903.

ZIP Codes: 98201, 98203–08, 98213, 98220–33, 98235–41, 98243–45, 98247–53, 98255–64, 98266–67, 98270–84, 98286–88, 98290–97

* * *

THIRD DISTRICT

BRIAN BAIRD, Democrat, of Vancouver, WA; born in Chauma, NM, March 7, 1956; education: B.S., University of Utah, 1977; M.S., University of Wyoming, 1980; Ph.D., University of Wyoming, 1984; professional: licensed clinical psychologist; practiced in Washington P & CState and Oregon; professor and former chair, Department of Psychology at Pacific Lutheran University; has worked in a variety of medical environments prior to election to the U.S. Congress; elected President of the Democratic Freshman Class for the 106th Congress; committees: Budget; Science and Transportation and Infrastructure; Democratic Regional Whip; elected to the 106th Congress; reelected to each succeeding Congress.

Office Listings

http://www.house.gov/baird

1421 Longworth House Office Building, Washington, DC 20515 .... (202) 225–3536
Chief of Staff.—Lisa Boyd. FAX: 225–3478
Press Secretary.—Meghan O'Shaughnessy.
Executive Assistant.—Rachel Brehm.
750 Anderson Street, Suite B, Vancouver, WA 98661 .... (360) 695–6292
District Director.—Pam Browkaw.
120 Union Avenue, Suite 105, Olympia, WA 98501 .... (360) 352–9768

Counties: CLARK COUNTY. CITIES AND TOWNSHIPS: Amboy, Ariel, Battle Ground, Brush Prairie, Camas, Heisson, La Center, Ridgefield, Vancouver, Washougal, Woodland, Yacolt. COWLITZ COUNTY. CITIES AND TOWNSHIPS: Carrolls, Castle Rock, Cougar, Kalama, Kelso, Longview, Ryderwood, Silverlake, Toutle. LEWIS COUNTY. CITIES AND TOWNSHIPS: Adna, Centralia, Chehalis, Cinebar, Curtis, Doty, Ethel, Galvin, Glenoma, Mineral, Morton, Mossyrock, Napavine, Onalaska, Packwood, Pe Ell, Randle, Salkum, Silver Creek, Toledo, Vader, Winlock. PACIFIC COUNTY. CITIES AND TOWNSHIPS: Bay Center, Chinook, Ilwaco, Lebam, Long Beach, Menlo, Nahcotta, Naselle, Ocean Park, Oysterville, Raymond, Seaview, South Bend, Tokeland. PIERCE COUNTY. CITIES AND TOWNSHIPS: Elbe. SKAMANIA COUNTY (part). CITIES AND TOWNSHIPS: Carson, North Bonneville, Stevenson, Underwood. THURSTON COUNTY (part). CITIES AND TOWNSHIPS: Buroda, Littlerock, Olympia, Tenino, and Rochester. WAHKIAKUM COUNTY. CITIES AND TOWNSHIPS: Cathlamet, Grays River, Rosburg, and Skamokawa. Population (2000), 654,898.

ZIP Codes: 98304, 98328, 98330, 98336, 98355–56, 98361, 98377, 98501–09, 98511–13, 98522, 98527, 98531–33, 98537–39, 98541–42, 98544, 98547, 98554, 98556–57, 98559, 98561, 98564–65, 98568, 98570, 98572, 98576–77, 98579, 98581–83, 98585–86, 98589–91, 98593, 98595–97, 98601–04, 98606–07, 98609–12, 98614, 98616, 98621–22, 98624–26, 98628–29, 98631–32, 98635, 98637–45, 98647–51, 98660–66, 98668, 98671–72, 98674–75, 98682–87

* * *

FOURTH DISTRICT

DOC HASTINGS, Republican, of Pasco, WA; born in Spokane, WA, February 7, 1941; education: graduated, Pasco High School, 1959; attended Columbia Basin College and Central Washington State University, Ellensburg, WA; military service: U.S. Army Reserves, 1963–69; professional: president, Columbia Basin Paper and Supply; board of directors, Yakima Federal Savings and Loan; member: Washington State House of Representatives, 1979–87; Republican Caucus chairman, assistant majority leader, and National Platform Committee, 1984; president: Pasco Chamber of Commerce; Pasco Downtown Development Association; Pasco Jaycees (chamber president); chairman, Franklin County Republican Central Committee, 1974–78; delegate, Republican National Convention, 1976–84; married: Claire Hastings, 1967; children: Kirsten, Petrina and Colin; committees: Rules; Standards of Official Conduct; elected to the 104th Congress; reelected to each succeeding Congress.

Office Listings

http://www.house.gov/hastings

1214 Longworth House Office Building, Washington, DC 20515 .... (202) 225–5816
Administrative Assistant.—Todd Young. FAX: 225–3251
Scheduler / Office Manager.—Ilene Clauson.
Press Secretary.—Jessica Gleason.
2715 Saint Andrews Loop, Suite D, Pasco, WA 99302 .... (509) 543–9396
302 East Chestnut, Yakima, WA 98901 .... (509) 452–3243

Counties: ADAMS COUNTY (part). CITIES: Othello. BENTON COUNTY. CITIES AND TOWNSHIPS: Benton City, Kennewick, Paterson, Plymouth, Prosser, Richland, West Richland. CHELAN COUNTY. CITIES AND TOWNSHIPS: Ardenvoir, Cashmere, Chelan, Chelan Falls, Dryden, Entiat, Leavenworth, Malaga, Manson, Monitor, Peshastin, Stehekin, Wenatchee. DOUGLAS COUNTY. CITIES AND TOWNSHIPS: Bridgeport, East Wenatchee, Leahy, Mansfield, Orondo, Palisades, Rock Island, Waterville. FRANKLIN COUNTY. CITIES AND TOWNSHIPS: Basin City, Connell, Eltopia, Kahlotus, Mesa, Pasco, Windust. GRANT COUNTY. CITIES AND TOWNSHIPS: Beverly, Coulee City, Desert Aire, Electric City, Ephrata, George, Grand Coulee, Hartline, Marlin, Mattawa, Moses Lake, Quincy, Royal City, Soap Lake, Stratford, Warden, Wilson Creek. KITTITAS COUNTY. CITIES AND TOWNSHIPS: Cle Elum, Easton, Ellensburg, Hyak, Kittitas, Ronald, Roslyn, Snoqualmic Pass, South Cle Elum, Thorp, Vantage. KLICKITAT COUNTY. CITIES AND TOWNSHIPS: Alderdale, Appleton, Bickleton, Bingen, Centerville, Cook, Dallesport, Glenwood, Goldendale, Husum, Klickitat, Lyle, Roosevelt, Trout Lake, Wahkiacus, White Salmon, Wishram, Wishram Heights. SKAMANIA COUNTY (part), YAKIMA COUNTY. CITIES AND TOWNSHIPS: Brownstown, Buena, Carson, Cowiche, Grandview, Granger, Harrah, Mabton, Moxee, Naches, Outlook, Parker, Selah, Sunnyside, Tieton, Toppenish, Underwood, Wapato, White Swan, Yakima, and Zillah. Population (2000), 654,901.

ZIP Codes: 98068, 98602, 98605, 98610, 98613, 98617, 98619–20, 98623, 98628, 98635, 98648, 98650–51, 98670, 98672–73, 98801–02, 98807, 98811–13, 98815–17, 98819, 98821–24, 98826, 98828–32, 98834, 98836–37, 98843, 98845,

98847–48, 98850–53, 98857–58, 98860, 98901–04, 98907–09, 98920–23, 98925–26, 98929–30, 98932–44, 98946–48, 98950–53, 99103, 99115–16, 99123–24, 99133, 99135, 99155, 99301–02, 99320–22, 99326, 99330, 99335–38, 99343–46, 99349–50, 99352–54, 99356–57

* * *

FIFTH DISTRICT

CATHY McMORRIS RODGERS, Republican, of Colville, WA; born in Salem, OR, May 22, 1969; education: B.A., Pensacola Christian College, Pensacola, FL, 1990; M.B.A., University of Washington, Seattle, WA, 2002; professional: fruit orchard worker; member, Washington State House of Representatives, 1994–2004; minority leader, 2002–03; organizations: member, Grace Evangelical Free Church; married: Brian Rodgers; committees: Armed Services; Education and Labor; Natural Resources; elected to the 109th Congress on November 2, 2004; reelected to each succeeding Congress.

Office Listings

http://www.house.gov/mcmorris

1708 Longworth House Office Building, Washington, DC 20515 .... (202) 225–2006
Chief of Staff.—Connie Partoyan. FAX: 225–3392
Legislative Director.—Ryan Work.
Scheduler.—Brian Frankovic.
Press Secretary.—Jill Strait.
10 North Post Street, 6th floor, Spokane, WA 99210 .... (509) 353–2374
District Director.—David Condon.
555 South Main Street, Colville, WA 99114 .... (509) 684–3481
29 South Palouse Street, Walla Walla, WA 99362 .... (509) 529–9358

Counties: ADAMS (part), ASOTIN, COLUMBIA, FERRY, GARFIELD, LINCOLN, PEND OREILLE, OKANAGAN, SPOKANE, STEVENS, WALLA WALLA, WHITMAN. Population (2000), 654,901.

ZIP Codes: 98812, 98814, 98819, 98827, 98829, 98832–34, 98840–41, 98844, 98846, 98849, 98855–57, 98859, 98862, 99001, 99003–06, 99008–09, 99011–14, 99016–23, 99025–27, 99029–34, 99036–37, 99039–40, 99101–05, 99107, 99109–11, 99113–14, 99116–19, 99121–22, 99125–26, 99128–31, 99133–41, 99143–44, 99146–61, 99163–67, 99169–71, 99173–74, 99176, 99179–81, 99185, 99201–20, 99223–24, 99228, 99251–52, 99256, 99258, 99260, 99302, 99323–24, 99326, 99328–29, 99333, 99335, 99341, 99344, 99347–48, 99356, 99359–63, 99371, 99401–03

* * *

SIXTH DISTRICT

NORMAN D. DICKS, Democrat, of Bremerton, WA; born in Bremerton, December 16, 1940; education: graduated, West Bremerton High School, 1959; B.A., political science, University of Washington, 1963; J.D., University of Washington School of Law, 1968; admitted to Washington bar, 1968; joined the staff of Senator Warren G. Magnuson in 1968 as legislative assistant and appropriations assistant, named administrative assistant in 1973, and held that post until he resigned to campaign for Congress in February 1976; member: Democratic Caucus; Washington, DC, and Washington State Bars; Puget Sound Naval Bases Association; Navy League of the United States; married: the former Suzanne Callison, 1967; children: David and Ryan; committees: Appropriations; Homeland Security; elected to the 95th Congress; reelected to each succeeding Congress.

Office Listings

2467 Rayburn House Office Building, Washington, DC 20515 .... (202) 225–5916
Chief of Staff / Press Secretary.—George Behan. FAX: 226–1176
Legislative Director.—Pete Modaff.
Scheduler.—Jessica Boegel.
1717 Pacific Avenue, Suite 2244, Tacoma, WA 98402 .... (253) 593–6536
District Director.—Clark Mather.
Norm Dicks Government Center, 345 Sixth Street, Suite 500, Bremerton, WA 98337 .... (360) 479–4011
Deputy District Director.—Cheri Williams.
322 East Fifth Street, Port Angeles, WA 98362 .... (360) 452–3370
District Representative.—Mary Schuneman.

Counties: CLALLAM COUNTY. CITIES AND TOWNSHIPS: Forks, Port Angeles, La Push, Sequim, Sekiu, Neah Bay. GRAYS HARBOR COUNTY. CITIES AND TOWNSHIPS: Aberdeen, Hoquiam, Montesano, Ocean City, Ocean Shores, Moclips, Westport. JEFFERSON COUNTY. CITIES AND TOWNSHIPS: Port Townsend, Quilcene. KITSAP COUNTY (part). CITIES AND TOWNSHIPS: Bremerton, Port Orchard, Gorst. MASON COUNTY. CITIES AND TOWNSHIPS: Shelton, Belfair, Allyn, Union. PIERCE COUNTY (part). CITIES AND TOWNSHIPS: Tacoma, Gig Harbor, Lakebay, and Lakewood. Population (2000), 654,902.

ZIP Codes: 98305, 98310–12, 98314, 98320, 98322, 98324–26, 98329, 98331–33, 98335, 98337, 98339, 98343, 98349–51, 98353, 98357–59, 98362–63, 98365–68, 98373, 98376, 98378, 98380–82, 98384, 98386, 98394–95, 98401–09, 98411–13, 98415–16, 98418, 98442, 98444–45, 98464–67, 98471, 98477, 98481, 98492, 98497–99, 98502, 98520, 98524, 98526, 98528, 98535–37, 98541, 98546–48, 98550, 98552, 98555, 98557, 98560, 98562–63, 98566, 98568–69, 98571, 98575, 98584, 98587–88, 98592, 98595

* * *

SEVENTH DISTRICT

JIM McDERMOTT, Democrat, of Seattle, WA; born in Chicago, IL, December 28, 1936; education: B.S., Wheaton College, Wheaton, IL, 1958; M.D., University of Illinois Medical School, Chicago, 1963; residency in adult psychiatry, University of Illinois Hospitals, 1964–66; residency in child psychiatry, University of Washington Hospitals, Seattle, 1966–68; served, U.S. Navy Medical Corps, lieutenant commander, 1968–70; psychiatrist; Washington State House of Representatives, 1971–72; Washington State Senate, 1975–87; Democratic nominee for governor, 1980; regional medical officer, Sub-Saharan Africa, U.S. Foreign Service, 1987–88; practicing psychiatrist and assistant clinical professor of psychiatry, University of Washington, Seattle, 1970–83; member: Washington State Medical Association; King County Medical Society; American Psychiatric Association; religion: St. Mark's Episcopal Church, Seattle; married: Therese Hanson; grown children: Katherine and James; committees: Ways and Means; elected on November 8, 1988, to the 101st Congress; reelected to each succeeding Congress.

Office Listings

1035 Longworth House Office Building, Washington, DC 20515 .... (202) 225–3106
Chief of Staff.—Jan Shinpoch. FAX: 225–6197
Legislative Director.—Jayme White.
Executive Assistant.—Beverly Swain.
1809 Seventh Avenue, Suite 1212, Seattle, WA 98101–1313 .... (206) 553–7170
District Administrator.—James Allen.

Counties: KING COUNTY (part). CITIES AND TOWNSHIPS: Vashon, Burton, Dockton, and Seattle. Population (2000), 654,902.

ZIP Codes: 98013, 98055, 98070, 98101–09, 98111–19, 98121–22, 98124–27, 98129, 98131, 98133–34, 98136, 98139, 98141, 98144–46, 98151, 98154–55, 98161, 98164–66, 98168, 98171, 98174–75, 98177–78, 98181, 98184–85, 98190–91, 98194–95, 98199

* * *

EIGHTH DISTRICT

DAVID G. REICHERT, Republican, of Auburn, WA; born in Detroit Lakes, MI, August 29, 1950; education: graduated, Kent Meridian High School, Renton, WA, 1968; B.A., Concordia Lutheran College, Portland, OR, 1970; professional: U.S. Air Force Reserve, 1971–76; U.S. Air Force, 1976; police officer, King County, WA, 1972–97; sheriff, King County, WA, 1997–2004; member: president, Washington State Sheriff's Association; executive board member, Washington Association of Sheriffs and Police Chiefs; co-chair, Washington State Partners in Crisis; awards: recipient of the 2004 National Sheriff's Association's "Sheriff of the Year"; two-time Medal of Valor Award Recipient from the King County sheriff's office; Washington Policy Center's Champion of Freedom Award; Families Northwest Public Policy Award; married: Julie; children: Angela, Tabitha, and Daniel; committees: Homeland Security; Science and Technology; Transportation and Infrastructure; elected to the 109th Congress on November 2, 2004; reelected to the 110th Congress.

Office Listings

http://www.house.gov/reichert

1223 Longworth House Office Building, Washington, DC 20515 .... (202) 225–7761
Chief of Staff.—Mike Shields. FAX: 225–4282
Legislative Director.—Chris Miller.
Executive Assistant / Scheduler.—Nichole Robison.
2737 Seventh-Eighth Avenue, SE, Suite 202, Mercer Island, WA 98040 .... (206) 275–3438
District Director.—Mariana Parks.

Counties: KING COUNTY (part). CITIES AND TOWNSHIPS: Auburn, Baring, Beaux Arts Village, Bellevue, Black Diamond, Carnation, Duvall, Enumclaw, Fall City, Issaquah, Kent, Mercer Island, Maple Valley, New Castle, North Bend, Preston, Redmond, Renton, Skykomish, Snoqualmie, Summit, Woodinville. PIERCE COUNTY. CITIES AND TOWNSHIPS: Ashford, Bonney Lake, Buckley, Carbonado, Eatonville, Elbe, Graham, Orting, Roy, South Prairie, Spanaway, and Wilkeson. Population (2000), 654,905.

ZIP Codes: 98002, 98004–10, 98014–15, 98019, 98022, 98024–25, 98027, 98029–31, 98033, 98035, 98038–40, 98042, 98045, 98050–53, 98055–56, 98058–59, 98064–65, 98068, 98074–75, 98077, 98092, 98304, 98321, 98323, 98328, 98330, 98338, 98344, 98348, 98352, 98360, 98372–75, 98385, 98387, 98390, 98396–98, 98446

* * *

NINTH DISTRICT

ADAM SMITH, Democrat, of Tacoma, WA; born in Washington, DC, June 15, 1965; education: graduated, Tyee High School, 1983; graduated, Fordham University, NY, 1987; law degree, University of Washington, 1990; admitted to the Washington bar in 1991; professional: prosecutor for the city of Seattle; Washington State Senate, 1990–96; member: Kent Drinking Driver Task Force; board member, Judson Park Retirement Home; married: Sara Smith, 1993; committees: Armed Services; Foreign Affairs; elected to the 105th Congress; reelected to each succeeding Congress.

Office Listings

2402 Rayburn House Office Building, Washington, DC 20515 .... (202) 225–8901
Chief of Staff.—John Mulligan. FAX: 225–5893
Office Manager.—Kathren Coleman.
Communications Director.—Derrick Crowe.
3600 Port of Tacoma Road, Suite 106, Tacoma, WA 98424 .... (253) 896–3789
District Director.—Linda Danforth.

Counties: KING (part), PIERCE (part), THURSTON (part). CITIES: Algona, Auburn, Des Moines, Dupont, Edgewood, Federal Way, Fife, Kent, Lacey, Lakewood, Milton, Muckleshoot Indian Reservation, Nisqually Indian Reservation, Normandy Park, Pacific, Puyallup, Puyallup Indian Reservation, Renton, Roy, SeaTac, Spanaway, Tacoma, and Yelm. Population (2000), 654,902.

ZIP Codes: 98001–03, 98023, 98030–32, 98047, 98054–58, 98062–63, 98071, 98089, 98092–93, 98131–32, 98138, 98148, 98158, 98166, 98168, 98171, 98178, 98188, 98198, 98303, 98327–28, 98338, 98354, 98371–75, 98387–88, 98390, 98402, 98404, 98421–22, 98424, 98430–31, 98433, 98438–39, 98443–46, 98467, 98493, 98497–99, 98501, 98503, 98506, 98509, 98513, 98516, 98558, 98576, 98580, 98597

WEST VIRGINIA

(Population 2000, 1,808,344)

SENATORS

ROBERT C. BYRD, Democrat, of Sophia, WV; born in North Wilkesboro, NC, November 20, 1917; Baptist; married Erma Ora James; two daughters: Mrs. Mohammad (Mona Byrd) Fatemi and Mrs. Jon (Marjorie Byrd) Moore; six grandchildren: Erik, Darius and Fredrik Fatemi, and Michael (deceased), Mona and Mary Anne Moore; and six great-grandchildren; committees: chair, Appropriations; Armed Services; Budget; Rules and Administration; sworn in to the U.S. Senate on January 3, 1959; reelected to each succeeding Senate term.

Office Listings

http://byrd.senate.gov

311 Hart Senate Office Building, Washington, DC 20510 .... (202) 224–3954
FAX: 228–0002
Chief of Staff.—Barbara Videnieks.
Administrative Assistant.—Gail John.
Press Secretary.—Tom Gavin.
300 Virginia Street East, Suite 2630, Charleston, WV 25301 .... (304) 342–5855
State Director.—Anne Barth.

* * *

JOHN D. ROCKEFELLER IV, Democrat, of Charleston, WV; born in New York City, NY, June 18, 1937; education: graduated, Phillips Exeter Academy, Exeter, NH, 1954; A.B., Harvard University, Cambridge, MA, 1961; honorary degrees: J.D., West Virginia University; Marshall University; Davis and Elkins College; Dickinson College; University of Alabama; University of Cincinnati; doctor of humanities, West Virginia Institute of Technology; doctor of public service, Salem College; professional service: Vista volunteer, Emmons, WV, 1964; West Virginia House of Delegates, 1966–68; elected Secretary of State of West Virginia, 1968; president, West Virginia Wesleyan College, 1973–76; Governor of West Virginia, 1976–84; married: the former Sharon Percy; children: John, Valerie, Charles and Justin; committees: chair, Select Committee on Intelligence; Commerce, Science, and Transportation, Finance; Veterans' Affairs; Joint Committee on Taxation; elected to the U.S. Senate on November 6, 1984; reelected to each succeeding Senate term.

Office Listings

http://rockefeller.senate.gov

531 Hart Senate Office Building, Washington, DC 20510 .... (202) 224–6472
FAX: 224–7665
Chief of Staff.—Kerry Ates.
Legislative Director.—Ellen Doneski.
Communications Director.—Wendy Morigi.
405 Capitol Street, Suite 308, Charleston, WV 25301 .... (304) 347–5372
220 North Kanawha Street, Suite 1, Beckley, WV 25801 .... (304) 253–9704
118 Adams Street, Suite 301, Fairmont, WV 26554 .... (304) 367–0122
225 West King Street, Suite 307, Martinsburg, WV 25401 .... (304) 262–9285

REPRESENTATIVES

FIRST DISTRICT

ALAN B. MOLLOHAN, Democrat, of Fairmont, WV; born in Fairmont, May 14, 1943; son of former Congressman Robert H. Mollohan and Helen Holt Mollohan; education: graduated, Greenbrier Military School, Lewisburg, WV, 1962; A.B., College of William and Mary, Williamsburg, VA, 1966; J.D., West Virginia University College of Law, Morgantown, 1970; professional: captain, U.S. Army Reserves, 1970–83; attorney; admitted to the West Virginia bar, 1970 (commenced practice in Fairmont); admitted to the District of Columbia bar, 1975; religion: member, First Baptist Church, Fairmont; married: the former Barbara Whiting, 1976; children: Alan, Robert, Andrew, Karl and Mary Kathryn; committees: Appropriations; elected to the 98th Congress on November 2, 1982; reelected to each succeeding Congress.

Office Listings

2302 Rayburn House Office Building, Washington, DC 20515 .... (202) 225–4172

Chief of Staff.—Colleen McCarty. FAX: 225–7564
Scheduler.—Jill Butash.
Legislative Director.—Julie Aaronson.
Press Secretary.—Gerry Griffith.

209 Post Office Building, P.O. Box 1400, Clarksburg, WV 26302–1400 .... (304) 623–4422
Federal Building, Room 232, P.O. Box 720, Morgantown, WV 26507–0720 .... (304) 292–3019
Federal Building, Room 2040, 425 Juliana Street, Parkersburg, WV 26101–0145 ... (304) 428–0493
Federal Building, 1125 Chapline Street, Wheeling, WV 26003–2900 .... (304) 232–5390

Counties: BARBOUR, BROOKE, DODDRIDGE, GILMER, GRANT, HANCOCK, HARRISON, MARION, MARSHALL, MINERAL, MONONGALIA, OHIO, PLEASANTS, PRESTON, RITCHIE, TAYLOR, TUCKER, TYLER, WETZEL, WOOD. CITIES AND TOWNSHIPS: Albright, Alma, Alvy, Anmoore, Arthur, Arthurdate, Auburn, Aurora, Baldwin, Barrackville, Baxter, Bayard, Beech Bottom, Belington, Belleville, Belleville, Bellview, Belmont, Bens Run, Benwood, Berea, Bethany, Big Run, Blacksville, Blandville, Booth, Brandonville, Bretz, Bridgeport, Bristol, Brownton, Bruceton Mills, Burlington, Burnt House, Burton, Cabins, Cairo, Cameron, Carolina, Cassville, Cedarville, Center Point, Central Station, Century, Chester, Clarksburg, Coburn, Colfax, Colliers, Core, Corinth, Cove, Coxs Mills, Cuzzart, Dallas, Davis, Davisville, Dawmont, Dellslow, Dorcas, Eglon, Elk Garden, Ellenboro, Elm Grove, Enterprise, Eureka, Everettville, Fairmont, Fairview, Farmington, Flemington, Flower, Follansbee, Folsom, Fort Ashby, Fort Neal, Four States, Friendly, Galloway, Gilmer, Glen Dale, Glen Easton, Glenville, Goffs, Gormania, Grafton, Grant Town, Granville, Greenwood, Gypsy, Hambleton, Harrisville, Hastings, Haywood, Hazelton, Hebron, Hendricks, Hepzibah, Highland, Hundred, Idamay, Independence, Industrial, Jacksonburg, Jere, Jordan, Junior, Keyser, Kingmont, Kingwood, Knob Fork, Lahmansville, Letter Gap, Lima, Linn, Littleton, Lockney, Lost Creek, Lumberport, MacFarlan, Mahone, Maidsville, Mannington, Masontown, Maysville, McMechen, McWhorter, Meadowbrook, Medley, Metz, Middlebourne, Mineralwells, Moatsville, Monongah, Montana Mines, Morgantown, Moundsville, Mount Clare, Mount Storm, Mountain, New Creek, New Cumberland, New England, New Manchester, New Martinsville, New Milton, Newberne, Newburg, Newell, Normantown, North Parkersburg, Nutter Fort, Osage, Owings, Paden City, Parkersburg, Parsons, Pennsboro, Pentress, Perkins, Petersburg, Petroleum, Philippi, Piedmont, Pine Grove, Porters Falls, Proctor, Pullman, Pursglove, Rachel, Reader, Red Creek, Reedsville, Reynoldsville, Riegeley, Rivesville, Rocket Center, Rockport, Rosedale, Rosemont, Rowlesburg, Saint George, Saint Marys, Salem, Sand Fork, Shinnston, Shirley, Shocks, Short Creek, Simpson, Sistersville, Smithburg, Smithfield, Smithville, Spelter, Stonewood, Stouts Mill, Stumptown, Tanner, Terra Alta, Thomas, Thornton, Toll Gate, Troy, Triadelphia, Tunnelton, Valley Grove, Vienna, Volga, Wadestown, Walker, Wallace, Wana, Warwood, Washington, Watson, Waverly Weirton, Wellsburg, Wendel, West Liberty, West Milford, West Union, Westover, Wheeling Wick, Wilbur, Wiley Ford, Wileyville, Williamstown, Wilson, Wilsonburg, Windsor Heights, Wolf Summit, Worthington, and Wyatt. Population (2000), 602,543.

ZIP Codes: 25258, 25267, 26003, 26030–41, 26047, 26050, 26055–56, 26058–60, 26062, 26070, 26074–75, 26101–06, 26120–21, 26133–34, 26142–43, 26146–50, 26155, 26159, 26161–62, 26164, 26167, 26169–70, 26175, 26178, 26180–81, 26184, 26186–87, 26201, 26238, 26250, 26254, 26260, 26263, 26269, 26271, 26275–76, 26283, 26287, 26289, 26292, 26301–02, 26306, 26320–21, 26323, 26325, 26327, 26330, 26332, 26334–35, 26337, 26339, 26342, 26346–49, 26351, 26354, 26361–62, 26366, 26369, 26374, 26377–78, 26384–86, 26404–05, 26408, 26410–12, 26415–16, 26419, 26421–22, 26424–26, 26430–31, 26434–38, 26440, 26443–44, 26448, 26451, 26456, 26463, 26501–02, 26504–08, 26519–21, 26524–25, 26527, 26529, 26531, 26534, 26537, 26541–44, 26546–47, 26554–55, 26559–63, 26566, 26568, 26570–72, 26574–76, 26578, 26581–82, 26585–88, 26590–91, 26611, 26623, 26636, 26638, 26705, 26710, 26716–17, 26719–20, 26726, 26731, 26734, 26739, 26743, 26750, 26753, 26764, 26767, 26833, 26847, 26852, 26855

* * *

SECOND DISTRICT

SHELLEY MOORE CAPITO, Republican, of Charleston, WV; born in Glen Dale, WV, November 26, 1953; education: B.S., Duke University; M.Ed., University of Virginia; professional: career counselor; West Virginia State College; West Virginia Board of Regents; organizations: Community Council of Kanawha Valley; YWCA; West Virginia Interagency Council for Early Intervention; Habitat for Humanity; public service: elected to the West Virginia House of Delegates, 1996; reelected in 1998; awards: Coalition for a Tobacco-Free West Virginia Legislator of the Year; religion: Presbyterian; married: to Charles L., Jr.; three children; committees: Financial Services; Transportation and Infrastructure; elected to the 107th Congress on November 7, 2000; reelected to each succeeding Congress.

Office Listings

http://www.house.gov/capito

1431 Longworth House Office Building, Washington, DC 20515 .... (202) 225–2711
Chief of Staff.—Joel Brubaker. FAX: 225–7856
Office Manager.—Alison Bibbee.
Legislative Director.—Aaron Sporck.

4815 MacCorkle Avenue, Southeast, Charleston, WV 25304 .... (304) 925–5964
300 Foxcroft Avenue, Suite 102, Martinsburg, WV 25401 .... (304) 264–8810

Counties: BERKELEY, BRAXTON, CALHOUN, CLAY, HAMPSHIRE, HARDY, JACKSON, JEFFERSON, KANAWHA, LEWIS, MASON, MORGAN, PENDLETON, PUTNAM, RANDOLPH, ROANE, UPSHUR, WIRT. Population (2000), 602,245.

ZIP Codes: 25002–03, 25005, 25011, 25015, 25019, 25025–26, 25030, 25033, 25035, 25039, 25043, 25045–46, 25054, 25059, 25061, 25063–64, 25067, 25070–71, 25075, 25079, 25081–83, 25085–86, 25088, 25102–03, 25106–07, 25109–13, 25123–26, 25132–34, 25136, 25139, 25141, 25143, 25147, 25150, 25156, 25159–60, 25162, 25164, 25168, 25177, 25187, 25201–02, 25211, 25213–14, 25231, 25234–35, 25239, 25241, 25243–45, 25247–48, 25251–53, 25259–62, 25264–68, 25270–71, 25275–76, 25279, 25281, 25285–87, 25301–06, 25309, 25311–15, 25317, 25320–39, 25350, 25356–58, 25360–62, 25364–65, 25375, 25392, 25396, 25401–02, 25410–11, 25413–14, 25419–23, 25425, 25427–32, 25434,

25437–38, 25440–44, 25446, 25502–03, 25510, 25515, 25520, 25523, 25526, 25541, 25550, 25560, 25569, 26133, 26136–38, 26141, 26143, 26147, 26151–52, 26160–61, 26164, 26173, 26180, 26201–02, 26205, 26210, 26215, 26218, 26224, 26228–30, 26234, 26236–38, 26241, 26253–54, 26257, 26259, 26261, 26263, 26267–68, 26270, 26273, 26276, 26278, 26280, 26282–83, 26285, 26293–94, 26296, 26321, 26335, 26338, 26342–43, 26351, 26372, 26376, 26378, 26384–85, 26412, 26430, 26443, 26447, 26452, 26546, 26590, 26601, 26610–11, 26615, 26617, 26619, 26621, 26623–24, 26627, 26629, 26631, 26636, 26638–39, 26641, 26651, 26656, 26660, 26662, 26667, 26671, 26675–76, 26678–79, 26681, 26684, 26690–91, 26704–05, 26707, 26710–11, 26714, 26717, 26722, 26731, 26739, 26743, 26750, 26755, 26757, 26761, 26763–64, 26801–02, 26804, 26807–08, 26810, 26812, 26814–15, 26817–18, 26823–24, 26836, 26838, 26845, 26847, 26851–52, 26865–66, 26884, 26886

* * *

THIRD DISTRICT

NICK J. RAHALL II, Democrat, of Beckley, WV; born in Beckley, May 20, 1949; education: graduated, Woodrow Wilson High School, Beckley, 1967; A.B., Duke University, Durham, NC, 1971; graduate work, George Washington University, Washington, DC; colonel, U.S. Air Force Civil Air Patrol; president, West Virginia Society of Washington, DC; business executive; sales representative, WWNR radio station; president, Mountaineer Tour and Travel Agency, 1974; president, West Virginia Broadcasting; awards: Coal Man of the Year, *Coal Industry News,* 1979; Young Democrat of the Year, Young Democrats, 1980; recipient, West Virginia American Legion Distingushed Service Award, 1984; delegate, Democratic National Conventions, 1972, 1976, 1980, 1984; member: Rotary; Elks; Moose; Eagles; NAACP; National Rifle Association; AF & AM; RAM; Mount Hope Commandery; Shrine Club; Benie Kedeem Temple in Charleston; Beckley Presbyterian Church; chairman and founder, Congressional Coal Group; Democratic Leadership Council; Congressional Arts Caucus; Congressional Black Caucus; Congressional Fitness Caucus; International Workers' Rights Caucus; ITS Caucus; Qatar Caucus; Congressional Rural Caucus; Congressional Steel Caucus; Congressional Textile Caucus; Congressional Travel and Tourism Caucus; Congressional Truck Caucus; Wine Caucus; Automobile Task Force; Democratic Congressional Campaign Committee; Democratic Study Group; Energy and Environment Study Conference; married: the former Melinda Ross; children: Rebecca Ashley, Nick Joe III, and Suzanne Nicole; committees: chair, Natural Resources; Transportation and Infrastructure; elected to the 95th Congress, November 2, 1976; reelected to each succeeding Congress.

Office Listings

http://www.house.gov/rahall

2307 Rayburn House Office Building, Washington, DC 20515 .... (202) 225–3452
FAX: 225–9061
Administrative Assistant.—Kent Keyser.
Executive Assistant.—Vickie Bandy.
Legislative Director.—Erika Young.
Press Secretary.—Tonya Allen.
815 Fifth Avenue, Huntington, WV 25701 .... (304) 522–6425
301 Prince Street, Beckley, WV 25801 .... (304) 252–5000
220 Dingess Street, Logan, WV 25601 .... (304) 752–4934
1005 Federal Building, Bluefield, WV 24701 .... (304) 325–6222

Counties: BOONE, CABELL, FAYETTE, GREENBRIER, LINCOLN, LOGAN, MCDOWELL, MERCER, MINGO, MONROE, NICHOLAS, POCAHONTAS, RALEIGH, SUMMERS, WAYNE, WEBSTER, WYOMING. Population (2000), 603,556.

ZIP Codes: 24701, 24712, 24714–16, 24719, 24724, 24726, 24729, 24731–33, 24736–40, 24747, 24751, 24801, 24808, 24811, 24813, 24815–18, 24820–31, 24834, 24836, 24839, 24842–57, 24859–62, 24866–74, 24878–82, 24884, 24887–88, 24892, 24894–99, 24901–02, 24910, 24915–18, 24920, 24924–25, 24927, 24931, 24934–36, 24938, 24941, 24943–46, 24950–51, 24954, 24957, 24961–63, 24966, 24970, 24974, 24976–77, 24981, 24983–86, 24991, 24993, 25002–04, 25007–10, 25021–22, 25024, 25028, 25031, 25036, 25040, 25043–44, 25047–49, 25051, 25053, 25057, 25059–60, 25062, 25076, 25081, 25083, 25085, 25090, 25093, 25108, 25114–15, 25118–19, 25121, 25130, 25136, 25139–40, 25142, 25148–49, 25152, 25154, 25161, 25165, 25169, 25173–74, 25180–81, 25183, 25185–86, 25193, 25202–06, 25208–09, 25213, 25501, 25504–08, 25510–12, 25514, 25517, 25520–21, 25523–24, 25526, 25529–30, 25534–35, 25537, 25540–41, 25544–45, 25547, 25555, 25557, 25559, 25562, 25564–65, 25567, 25570–73, 25601, 25606–08, 25611–12, 25614, 25617, 25621, 25624–25, 25628, 25630, 25632, 25634–39, 25644, 25646–47, 25649–54, 25661, 25665–67, 25669–72, 25674, 25676, 25678, 25682, 25685–88, 25690–92, 25694, 25696, 25699, 25701–29, 25755, 25770–79, 25801–02, 25810–13, 25816–18, 25820, 25823, 25825–27, 25831–33, 25836–37, 25839–41, 25843–49, 25851, 25853–57, 25859–60, 25862, 25864–66, 25868, 25870–71, 25873, 25875–76, 25878–80, 25882, 25901–02, 25904, 25906–09, 25911, 25913–22, 25927–28, 25931–32, 25934, 25936, 25938, 25942–43, 25951, 25958, 25961–62, 25965–67, 25969, 25971–72, 25976–79, 25981, 25984–86, 25989, 26202–03, 26205–06, 26208–09, 26217, 26222, 26230, 26234, 26261, 26264, 26266, 26288, 26291, 26294, 26298, 26610, 26617, 26639, 26651, 26656, 26660, 26662, 26674, 26676, 26678–81, 26684, 26690–91

WISCONSIN

(Population 2000, 5,363,675)

SENATORS

HERB KOHL, Democrat, of Milwaukee, WI; born in Milwaukee, February 7, 1935; education: graduated, Washington High School, Milwaukee, 1952; B.A., University of Wisconsin, Madison, 1956; M.B.A., Harvard Graduate School of Business Administration, Cambridge, MA, 1958; LL.D., Cardinal Stritch College, Milwaukee, WI, 1986 (honorary); served, U.S. Army Reserves, 1958–64; businessman; president, Herbert Kohl Investments; owner, Milwaukee Bucks NBA basketball team; past chairman, Milwaukee's United Way Campaign; State Chairman, Democratic Party of Wisconsin, 1975–77; honors and awards: Pen and Mike Club Wisconsin Sports Personality of the Year, 1985; Wisconsin Broadcasters Association Joe Killeen Memorial Sportsman of the Year, 1985; Greater Milwaukee Convention and Visitors Bureau Lamplighter Award, 1986; Wisconsin Parkinson's Association Humanitarian of the Year, 1986; Kiwanis Milwaukee Award, 1987; committees: chair, Special Committee on Aging; Appropriations; Judiciary; elected to the U.S. Senate on November 8, 1988; reelected to each succeeding Senate term.

Office Listings

http://kohl.senate.gov

330 Hart Senate Office Building, Washington, DC 20510 .... (202) 224–5653
Chief of Staff.—Paul Bock. FAX: 224–9787
Legislative Director.—Chad Metzler.
Communications Director.—Lynn Becker.
Executive Assistant.—Arlene Branca.
310 West Wisconsin Avenue, Suite 950, Milwaukee, WI 53203 .... (414) 297–4451
14 West Muffin Street, Suite 207, Madison, WI 53703 .... (608) 264–5338
402 Graham Avenue, Suite 206, Eau Claire, WI 54701 .... (715) 832–8424
4321 West College Avenue, Suite 235, Appleton, WI 54914 .... (920) 738–1640
425 State Street, Suite 202, LaCrosse, WI 54601 .... (608) 796–0045

* * *

RUSSELL D. FEINGOLD, Democrat, of Middleton, WI; born in Janesville, WI, March 2, 1953; education: graduated, Craig High School, Janesville, WI, 1971; B.A., University of Wisconsin-Madison, 1975; Rhodes Scholar, Oxford University, 1977; J.D., Harvard Law School, 1979; professional: practicing attorney, Foley & Lardner and LaFollette & Sinykin, Madison, WI, 1979–85; Wisconsin State Senate, 1983–93; four children: daughters, Jessica and Ellen; stepsons, Sam Speerschneider and Ted Speerschneider; committees: Budget; Foreign Relations; Judiciary; Select Committee on Intelligence; Democratic Policy Committee; elected to the U.S. Senate on November 3, 1992; reelected to each succeeding Senate term.

Office Listings

http://feingold.senate.gov

506 Hart Senate Office Building, Washington, DC 20510 .... (202) 224–5323
Chief of Staff.—Mary Irvine. FAX: 224–2725
Legislative Director.—Paul Weinberger.
Press Secretary.—Zach Lowe.
517 East Wisconsin Avenue, Room 408, Milwaukee, WI 53202 .... (414) 276–7282
1600 Aspen Commons, Room 100, Middleton, WI 53562 .... (608) 828–1200
State Coordinator.—Jay Robaidek.
401 Fifth Street, Room 410, Wausau, WI 54401 .... (715) 848–5660
425 State Street, Room 225, LaCrosse, WI 54603 .... (608) 782–5585
1640 Main Street, Green Bay, WI 54302 .... (920) 465–7508

REPRESENTATIVES

FIRST DISTRICT

PAUL RYAN, Republican, of Janesville, WI; born in Janesville, January 29, 1970; education: Joseph A. Craig High School; economic and political science degrees, Miami University, Ohio; professional: marketing consultant, Ryan Inc., Central (construction firm); aide to former U.S. Senator Bob Kasten (R–WI); advisor to former Vice Presidential candidate Jack Kemp, and U.S. Drug Czar Bill Bennett; legislative director, U.S. Senate; organizations: Janesville Bowmen,

Inc.; Ducks Unlimited; married: Janna Ryan; three children: daughter, Liza; sons, Charlie and Sam; committees: ranking member, Budget; Ways and Means; elected to the 106th Congress; reelected to each succeeding Congress.

Office Listings

http://www.house.gov/ryan

1113 Longworth House Office Building, Washington, DC 20515 .... (202) 225–3031
FAX: 225–3393
Administrative Assistant.—Joyce Meyer.
Senior Legislative Assistant.—Matt Hoffmann.
Scheduler.—Maureen Mitchell.
20 South Main Street, Suite 10, Janesville, WI 53545 .... (608) 752–4050
5712 Seventh Avenue, Kenosha, WI 53140 .... (262) 654–1901
216 Sixth Street, Racine, WI 53403 .... (262) 637–0510

Counties: KENOSHA, MILWAUKEE (part), RACINE, ROCK (part), WALWORTH (part), WAUKESHA (part). Population (2000), 670,458.

ZIP Codes: 53101–05, 53108–09, 53114–15, 53119–21, 53125–26, 53128–30, 53132, 53138–44, 53146–54, 53156–59, 53167–68, 53170–72, 53176–77, 53179, 53181–82, 53184–85, 53189–92, 53194–95, 53207, 53219–21, 53228, 53401–08, 53501, 53505, 53511, 53525, 53534, 53538, 53545–48, 53563, 53585

* * *

SECOND DISTRICT

TAMMY BALDWIN, Democrat, of Madison, WI; born in Madison, February 11, 1962; education: graduated from Madison West High School, 1980; A.B., mathematics and government, Smith College, 1984; J.D., University of Wisconsin Law School, 1989; professional: attorney, 1989–92; elected to the Dane County Board of Supervisors, 1986–94; elected to the State Assembly from the 78th district, 1993–99; committees: Energy and Commerce; Judiciary; elected to the 106th Congress; reelected to each succeeding Congress.

Office Listings

http://tammybaldwin.house.gov

2446 Rayburn House Office Building, Washington, DC 20515 .... (202) 225–2906
FAX: 225–6942
Chief of Staff.—Bill Murat.
Legislative Director.—Elizabeth Pika.
Appointment Secretary.—Maureen Hekmat.
Press Secretary.—Jerilyn Goodman. (608) 258–9800
10 East Doty Street, Suite 405, Madison, WI 53703 .... (608) 258–9800
District Director.—Curt Finkelmeyer.
400 East Grand Avenue, Suite 402, Beloit, WI 53511 .... (608) 362–2800

Counties: COLUMBIA, DANE, GREEN, JEFFERSON (part), ROCK (part), SAUK (part), WALWORTH (part). Population (2000), 670,457.

ZIP Codes: 53038, 53094, 53098, 53190, 53501–02, 53504, 53508, 53511–12, 53515–17, 53520–23, 53527–29, 53531–32, 53534, 53536–38, 53542, 53544–46, 53548–51, 53555, 53558–63, 53566, 53570–72, 53574–76, 53578, 53581–83, 53589–91, 53593–94, 53596–98, 53701–08, 53711, 53713–19, 53725–26, 53744, 53777–79, 53782–94, 53901, 53911, 53913, 53916, 53923, 53925–26, 53928, 53932–33, 53935, 53951, 53954–57, 53959–60, 53965, 53968–69

* * *

THIRD DISTRICT

RON KIND, Democrat, of La Crosse, WI; born in La Crosse, March 16, 1963; education: B.A., Harvard University, 1985; M.A., London School of Economics, 1986; J.D., University of Minnesota Law School, 1990; admitted to the Wisconsin bar, 1990; state prosecutor, La Crosse County District Attorney's Office; board of directors, La Crosse Boys and Girls Club; Coulee Council on Alcohol and Drug Abuse; Wisconsin Harvard Club; Wisconsin Bar Association; La Crosse County Bar Association; married: Tawni Zappa in 1994; two sons: Jonathan and Matthew; committees: Natural Resources; Ways and Means; elected to the 105th Congress; reelected to each succeeding Congress.

Office Listings

1406 Longworth House Office Building, Washington, DC 20515 .... (202) 225–5506

Chief of Staff.—Cindy Brown. FAX: 225–5739
Press Secretary.—Anne Lupardus.
Legislative Director.—Kate Spaziani.
Scheduler.—Cody Lundquist.
205 Fifth Avenue South, Suite 400, La Crosse, WI 54601 .... (608) 782–2558
District Director.—Loren Kannenberg.
131 South Barstow Street, Suite 301, Eau Claire, WI 54701 .... (715) 831–9214
Staff Assistant / Case Worker.—Mark Aumann.

Counties: BUFFALO, CLARK (part), CRAWFORD, DUNN, EAU CLAIRE, GRANT, IOWA, JACKSON, JUNEAU, LA CROSSE, LAFAYETTE, MONROE, PEPIN, PIERCE, RICHLAND, SAUK (part), ST. CROIX, TREMPEALEAU, VERNON. Population (2000), 670,462.

ZIP Codes: 53503–04, 53506–07, 53510, 53516–18, 53522, 53526, 53530, 53533, 53535, 53540–41, 53543–44, 53553–54, 53556, 53560, 53565, 53569, 53573, 53577–78, 53580–84, 53586–88, 53595, 53599, 53801–13, 53816–18, 53820–21, 53824–27, 53913, 53924, 53929, 53937, 53940–44, 53948, 53950–51, 53958–59, 53961–62, 53965, 53968, 54001–05, 54007, 54009–11, 54013–17, 54020–28, 54082, 54420, 54436–37, 54446, 54449, 54456–57, 54460, 54466, 54479, 54488, 54493, 54601–03, 54610–12, 54614–16, 54618–32, 54634–46, 54648–62, 54664–67, 54669–70, 54701–03, 54720–30, 54733–43, 54746–47, 54749–51, 54754–65, 54767–73

* * *

FOURTH DISTRICT

GWEN MOORE, Democrat, of Milwaukee, WI; born in Racine, WI, April 18, 1951; education: graduated North Division High School, Milwaukee; B.A., Political Science, Marquette University, Milwaukee, WI, 1978; professional: Program and Planning Analyst for the State of Wisconsin Services; housing officer, Wisconsin Housing and Development Authority; member: Wisconsin state assembly, 1989–92; Wisconsin state senate, 1993–2004; president pro tempore, 1997–98; three children; committees: Budget; Financial Services; Small Business; elected to the 109th Congress on November 2, 2004; reelected to the 110th Congress.

Office Listings

http://www.house.gov/moore

1239 Longworth House Office Building, Washington, DC 20515 .... (202) 225–4572
Legislative Director.—Andrew Stevens. FAX: 225–8135
219 North Milwaukee Street, Suite 3A, Milwaukee, WI 53202 .... (414) 297–1140
Chief of Staff.—Shirley Elllis.

Counties: MILWAUKEE (part). CITIES AND TOWNSHIPS: Milwaukee, Cudahy, South Milwaukee, St. Francis, West Allis, and West Milwaukee. Population (2000), 670,458.

ZIP Codes: 53110, 53154, 53172, 53201–28, 53233–35, 53237, 53268, 53270, 53277–78, 53280–81, 53284–85, 53288, 53290, 53293, 53295

* * *

FIFTH DISTRICT

F. JAMES SENSENBRENNER, JR., Republican, of Menomonee Falls, WI; born in Chicago, IL, June 14, 1943; education: graduated, Milwaukee Country Day School, 1961; A.B., Stanford University, 1965; J.D., University of Wisconsin Law School, 1968; admitted to the Wisconsin bar, 1968; commenced practice in Cedarburg, WI; admitted to practice before the U.S. Supreme Court in 1972; professional: attorney; staff member of former U.S. Congressman J. Arthur Younger of California, 1965; elected to the Wisconsin Assembly, 1968, reelected in 1970, 1972, and 1974; elected to Wisconsin Senate in a special election, 1975, reelected in 1976 (assistant minority leader); member: Waukesha County Republican Party; Wisconsin Bar Association; Riveredge Nature Center; Friends of Museums; American Philatelic Society; married: the former Cheryl Warren, 1977; children: Frank James III and Robert Alan; committees: ranking member, Select Committee on Energy Independence and Global Warming; Judiciary; Science and Technology; elected to the 96th Congress, November 7, 1978; reelected to each succeeding Congress.

Office Listings

http://www.house.gov/sensenbrenner

2449 Rayburn House Office Building, Washington, DC 20515 .... (202) 225–5101
Chief of Staff.—Tom Schreibel.
Deputy Chief of Staff / Press Secretary.—Raj Bharwani.
Scheduler / Office Manager.—Rachael Seidenschnur.
120 Bishops Way, Room 154, Brookfield, WI 53005 .... (262) 784–1111

Chief of Staff.—Tom Schreibel.

Counties: JEFFERSON (part), MILWAUKEE (part), OZAUKEE, WASHINGTON, WAUKESHA (part). Population (2000), 670,458.

ZIP Codes: 53002, 53004–05, 53007–08, 53012–13, 53017–18, 53021–22, 53024, 53027, 53029, 53033, 53037–38, 53040, 53045–46, 53051–52, 53056, 53058, 53060, 53064, 53066, 53069, 53072, 53074, 53076, 53080, 53085–86, 53089–90, 53092, 53095, 53097–98, 53118, 53122, 53127, 53137, 53146, 53151, 53156, 53178, 53183, 53186–90, 53208–14, 53217, 53219, 53222–23, 53225–28, 53263, 53538, 53549

* * *

SIXTH DISTRICT

THOMAS E. PETRI, Republican, of Fond du Lac, WI; born in Marinette, WI, May 28, 1940; education: graduated, Lowell P. Goodrich High School, 1958; B.A., Harvard University, Cambridge, MA, 1962; J.D., Harvard Law School, 1965; professional: admitted to the Wisconsin state and Fond du Lac county bar associations, 1965; lawyer; law clerk to Federal Judge James Doyle, 1965; Peace Corps volunteer, 1966–67; White House aide, 1969; commenced law practice in Fond du Lac, 1970; elected to the Wisconsin State Senate in 1972; reelected in 1976, and served until April, 1979; married; one daughter; committees: Education and Labor; Transportation and Infrastructure; elected to the 96th Congress, by special election, on April 3, 1979, to fill the vacancy caused by the death of William A. Steiger; reelected to each succeeding Congress.

Office Listings

http://www.house.gov/petri

2462 Rayburn House Office Building, Washington, DC 20515 .... (202) 225–2476
Administrative Assistant / Legislative Director.—Debra Gebhardt. FAX: 225–2356
Communications Director.—Niel Wright.
Office Manager.—Linda Towse.
490 West Rolling Meadows Drive, Suite B, Fond du Lac, WI 54937 .... (920) 922–1180
District Director.—David G. Anderson.
2390 State Road, Suite B, Oshkosh, WI 54904 .... (920) 231–6333

Counties: ADAMS, CALUMET (part), DODGE, FOND DU LAC, GREEN LAKE, JEFFERSON (part), MANITOWOC, MARQUETTE, OUTAGAMIE (part), SHEBOYGAN, WAUSHARA, WINNEBAGO. Population (2000), 670,459.

ZIP Codes: 53001, 53003, 53006, 53010–11, 53013–16, 53019–21, 53023, 53026–27, 53031–32, 53034–36, 53039, 53042, 53044, 53047–50, 53057, 53059, 53061–63, 53065–66, 53070, 53073, 53075, 53078–79, 53081–83, 53085, 53088, 53091, 53093–94, 53098–99, 53137, 53205, 53207, 53215, 53221, 53557, 53579, 53594, 53901, 53910, 53916–17, 53919–20, 53922–23, 53925–27, 53930–34, 53936, 53939, 53946–47, 53949–50, 53952–54, 53956, 53963–65, 53968, 54110, 54115, 54123, 54126, 54129–30, 54136, 54140, 54160, 54169, 54207–08, 54214–16, 54220–21, 54227–28, 54230, 54232, 54240–41, 54245, 54247, 54413, 54457, 54486, 54494, 54499, 54613, 54619, 54638, 54648, 54660, 54755, 54901–04, 54906, 54909, 54911, 54913–15, 54921–23, 54927, 54930, 54932–37, 54941, 54943–44, 54947, 54950, 54952, 54956–57, 54960, 54963–68, 54970–71, 54974, 54976, 54979–86

* * *

SEVENTH DISTRICT

DAVID R. OBEY, Democrat, of Wausau, WI; born in Okmulgee, OK, October 3, 1938; education: graduated Wausau High School, 1956; M.A. in political science, University of Wisconsin, 1960 (graduate work in Russian government and foreign policy); elected to the Wisconsin Legislature from Marathon County's 2nd District at the age of 24; reelected three times; assistant Democratic floor leader; married: Joan Lepinski of Wausau, WI, 1962; children: Craig David and Douglas David; committees: chair, Appropriations; elected to the 91st Congress, by special election, on April 1, 1969, to fill the vacancy created by the resignation of Melvin R. Laird; reelected to each succeeding Congress.

Office Listings

http://www.house.gov/obey

2314 Rayburn House Office Building, Washington, DC 20515 .... (202) 225–3365
Chief of Staff.—Christina Hamilton.
Scheduler.—Carly M. Burns.
Press Secretary.—Ellis Brachman.
401 Fifth Street, Suite 406A, Wausau, WI 54403 .... (715) 842–5606
District Representative.—Doug Hill.
1401 Tower Avenue, Suite 307, Superior, WI 54880 .... (715) 398–4426

Counties: Ashland, Barron, Bayfield, Burnett, Chippewa, Clark (part), Douglas, Iron, Langlade (part), Lincoln, Marathon, Oneida (part), Polk, Portage, Price, Rusk, Sawyer, Taylor, Washburn, Wood. Population (2000), 670,462.

ZIP Codes: 54001, 54004–07, 54009, 54017, 54020, 54024, 54026, 54401–12, 54414–15, 54417–18, 54420–29, 54432–35, 54437, 54439–43, 54447–49, 54451–52, 54454–55, 54457–60, 54462–63, 54466–67, 54469–76, 54479–81, 54484–85, 54487–90, 54492, 54494–95, 54498–99, 54501, 54513–15, 54517, 54524–27, 54529–32, 54534, 54536–38, 54545–47, 54550, 54552, 54555–56, 54559, 54563–65, 54703, 54724, 54726–33, 54739, 54745, 54748, 54757, 54762–63, 54766, 54768, 54771, 54774, 54801, 54805–06, 54810, 54812–14, 54816–22, 54824, 54826–30, 54832, 54834–50, 54853–59, 54861–62, 54864–65, 54867–68, 54870–76, 54880, 54888–91, 54893, 54895–96, 54909, 54921, 54945, 54966, 54977, 54981

* * *

EIGHTH DISTRICT

STEVEN KAGEN, Democrat, of Appleton, WI; born in Appleton, WI, December 12, 1949; education: B.S., University of Wisconsin, Madison, WI, 1972; M.D., University of Wisconsin, Madison, WI, 1976; professional: physician; married: Gayle; committees: Agriculture; Transportation and Infrastructure; elected to the 110th Congress on November 7, 2006.

Office Listings

http://www.house.gov/kagen

1232 Longworth House Office Building, Washington, DC 20515 .... (202) 225–5665
Chief of Staff.—David Williams. FAX: 225–5729
Legislative Director.—Rob Mosher.
Scheduler.—Katie Tilley.
Communications Director.—Curtis Ellis.
700 East Walnut Street, Green Bay, WI 54301 .... (920) 437–1954
District Director.—Carl Carmichael.
333 West College Avenue, Appleton, WI 54911 .... (920) 380–0061
Director of Constituent Services.—Craig Moser.

Counties: Brown, Calumet (part), Door, Florence, Forest, Kewaunee, Langlade (part), Marinette, Menominee, Oconto, Oneida (part), Outagamie (part), Shawano, Vilas, Waupaca. Population (2000), 670,461.

ZIP Codes: 54101–04, 54106–07, 54110–15, 54119–21, 54124–28, 54130–31, 54135, 54137–41, 54143, 54149–57, 54159, 54161–62, 54165–66, 54169–71, 54173–75, 54177, 54180, 54182, 54201–02, 54204–05, 54208–13, 54216–17, 54226–27, 54229–30, 54234–35, 54241, 54246, 54301–08, 54311, 54313, 54324, 54344, 54408–09, 54414, 54416, 54418, 54424, 54427–28, 54430, 54435, 54450, 54452, 54462–65, 54485–87, 54491, 54499, 54501, 54511–12, 54519–21, 54529, 54531, 54538–43, 54545, 54548, 54554, 54557–58, 54560–62, 54564, 54566, 54568, 54911–15, 54919, 54922, 54926, 54928–29, 54931, 54933, 54940, 54942, 54944–50, 54952, 54956, 54961–62, 54965, 54969, 54975, 54977–78, 54981, 54983, 54990

WYOMING

(Population 2000, 493,782)

SENATORS

MICHAEL B. ENZI, Republican, of Gillette, WY; born in Bremerton, WA, February 1, 1944; education: B.S., accounting, George Washington University, 1966; M.B.A., Denver University, 1968; professional: served in Wyoming National Guard, 1967–73; accounting manager and computer programmer, Dunbar Well Service, 1985–97; director, Black Hills Corporation, a New York Stock Exchange company, 1992–96; member, founding board of directors, First Wyoming Bank of Gillette, 1978–88; owner, with wife, of NZ Shoes; served in Wyoming House of Representatives, 1987–91, and in Wyoming State Senate, 1991–96; Mayor of Gillette, 1975–82; commissioner, Western Interstate Commission for Higher Education, 1995–96; served on the Education Commission of the States, 1989–93; president, Wyoming Association of Municipalities, 1980–82; president, Wyoming Jaycees, 1973–74; member: Lions Club; elder, Presbyterian Church; Eagle Scout; married: Diana Buckley, 1969; children: Amy, Brad, and Emily; committees: Banking, Housing, and Urban Affairs; Budget; ranking member, Health, Education, Labor and Pensions; Small Business and Entrepreneurship; elected to the U.S. Senate in November, 1996; reelected to each succeeding Senate term.

Office Listings

http://enzi.senate.gov

379–A Russell Senate Office Building, Washington, DC 20510 .... (202) 224–3424
Chief of Staff.—Flip McConnaughey. FAX: 228–0359
Legislative Director.—Randi Reid.
Press Secretary.—Coy Knobel.
Office Manager.—Christen Petersen.
Federal Center, Suite 2007, 2120 Capitol Avenue, Cheyenne, WY 82001 .... (307) 772–2477
400 S. Kendrick, Suite 303, Gillette, WY 82716 .... (307) 682–6268
100 East B Street, Room 3201, P.O. Box 33201, Casper, WY 82602 .... (307) 261–6572
1285 Sheridan Avenue, Suite 210, Cody, WY 82414 .... (307) 527–9444
P.O. Box 12470, Jackson, WY 83002 .... (307) 739–9507

* * *

JOHN BARRASSO, Republican, of Casper, WY; born in Reading, PA, July 21, 1952; education: B.S., Georgetown University, Washington, DC, 1974; M.D., Georgetown University, Washington, DC, 1978; professional: Casper Orthopaedic Associates, 1983–2007; Chief of Staff, Wyoming Medical Center, 2003–05; President, Wyoming Medical Society; President, National Association of Physician Broadcasters, 1988–89; member, Wyoming State Senate, 2002–06; children: Peter and Emma; appointed on June 22, 2007 to the 110th Congress to fill the vacancy caused by the death of Senator Craig Thomas.

Office Listings

http://barrasso.senate.gov

307 Dirksen Senate Office Building, Washington, DC 20510 .... (202) 224–6441
Chief of Staff.—Shawn Whitman. FAX: 224–1724
Legislative Director.—Bryn Stewart.
Press Secretary.—Cameron Hardy.
Office Manger.—Amber Moyerman.
2201 Federal Building, Casper, WY 82601 .... (307) 261–6413
2120 Capitol Avenue, Suite 2013, Cheyenne, WY 82001 .... (307) 772–2451
2632 Foothills Boulevard, Suite 101, Rock Springs, WY 82901 .... (307) 362–5012
325 West Main, Suite F, Riverton, WY 82501 .... (307) 856–6642
2 North Main Street, Suite 206, Sheridan, WY 82801 .... (307) 672–6456

REPRESENTATIVE

AT LARGE

BARBARA CUBIN, Republican, of Casper, WY; born in Salinas, CA, November 30, 1946; education: graduated, Natrona County High School; B.S., Creighton University, 1969; professional: manager; substitute teacher; social worker; chemist; founding member of the Casper Suicide Prevention League; Casper Service League; president, Southridge Elementary School Parent/Teacher Organization; Mercer House, president and executive member; Casper Self Help

Center, board member; Seton House, board member; Central Wyoming Rescue Mission, volunteer cook and server; Wyoming State Choir; Casper Civic Chorale; Cub Scout leader; Sunday School teacher at Saint Stephen's Episcopal Church; past memberships: executive committee of the Energy Council; chair, Center for Legislators Energy and Environment Research (CLEER); National Council of State Legislatures; vice chair, Energy Committee; 1994 Edison Electric Institutes' Wyoming Legislator of the Year and Toll Fellowship from the Council of State Governments, 1990; Wyoming House of Representatives committees, 1987–92: Minerals, Business and Economic Development; Revenue; Transportation; chair, Joint Interim Economic Development Subcommittee; Wyoming Senate committees, 1993–94: Travel, Recreation, Wildlife, and Cultural Resources; Revenue; Republican activities: chair, Wyoming Senate Conference, 1992–94; precinct committeewoman, 1988–94; legislative liaison and member, Natrona County Republican Women; 1992 Wyoming State Convention Parliamentarian; delegate, Wyoming State Convention, 1990, 1992, and 1994; State Legislative Candidate Recruitment Committee for the Wyoming Republican Party in 1988, 1990, and 1992; married: Frederick W. (Fritz) Cubin; children: William ''Bill'' and Frederick III (Eric); committees: Energy and Commerce; elected to the 104th Congress; reelected to each succeeding Congress.

Office Listings

http://www.house.gov/cubin

1114 Longworth House Office Building, Washington, DC 20515 .... (202) 225–2311
Chief of Staff.—Tom Wiblemo. FAX: 225–3057
Legislative Director.—Rick Axthelm.
Senior Legislative Assistant.—Landon Stropko.
Press Secretary.—Alison McGuire.
100 East B Street, Suite 4003, Casper, WY 82601 .... (307) 261–6595
State Director.—Jackie King.
2120 Capitol Avenue, Suite 2015, Cheyenne, WY 82001 .... (307) 772–2595
District Representative.—Erin Begeman.
2515 Foothill Boulevard, Suite 204, Rock Springs, WY 82901 .... (307) 362–4095
District Representative.—Bonnie Cannon.

Population (2000), 493,782.

ZIP Codes: 82001, 82003, 82005–10, 82050–55, 82058–61, 82063, 82070–73, 82081–84, 82190, 82201, 82210, 82212–15, 82217–19, 82221–25, 82227, 82229, 82240, 82242–44, 82301, 82310, 82321–25, 82327, 82329, 82331–32, 82334–36, 82401, 82410–12, 82414, 82420–23, 82426, 82428, 82430–35, 82440–43, 82450, 82501, 82510, 82512–16, 82520, 82523–24, 82601–02, 82604–05, 82609, 82615, 82620, 82630, 82633, 82635–40, 82642–44, 82646, 82648–49, 82701, 82710–12, 82714–18, 82720–21, 82723, 82725, 82727, 82729–32, 82801, 82831–40, 82842, 82844–45, 82901–02, 82922–23, 82925, 82929–39, 82941–45, 83001–02, 83011–14, 83025, 83101, 83110–16, 83118–24, 83126–28

AMERICAN SAMOA

(Population 2000, 57,291)

DELEGATE

ENI F.H. FALEOMAVAEGA, Democrat, of Vailoatai, AS; born in Vailoatai, August 15, 1943; education: graduate of Kahuku High School, Hawaii, 1962; B.A., Brigham Young University, 1966; J.D., University of Houston Law School, 1972; LL.M., University of California, Berkeley, 1973; admitted to U.S. Supreme Court and American Samoa bars; military service: enlisted, U.S. Army, 1966–69; Vietnam veteran; captain, USAR, Judge Advocate General Corps, 1982–92; professional: administrative assistant to American Samoa's Delegate to Washington, 1973–75; staff counsel, Committee on Interior and Insular Affairs, 1975–81; deputy attorney general, American Samoa, 1981–84; elected Lieutenant Governor, American Samoa, 1984–89; member: Democratic Study Group; National American Indian Prayer Breakfast Group; National Association of Secretaries of State; National Conference of Lieutenant Governors; Navy League of the United States; Pago Pago Lions Club; Veterans of Foreign Wars; Congressional Arts Caucus; Congressional Hispanic Caucus; Congressional Human Rights Caucus; Congressional Travel and Tourism Caucus; married: Hinanui Bambridge Cave of Tahiti; five children; committees: Foreign Affairs; Natural Resources; elected to the 101st Congress on November 8, 1988; reelected to each succeeding Congress.

Office Listings

http://www.house.gov/faleomavaega

2422 Rayburn House Office Building, Washington, DC 20515 .... (202) 225–8577
Deputy Chief of Staff.—Lisa Williams. FAX: 225–8757
Office Manager.—Hana Atuatasi.
Legislative Director.—David Richmond.
P.O. Drawer X, Pago Pago, AS 96799 .... (684) 633–1372

ZIP Codes: 96799

* * *

DISTRICT OF COLUMBIA

(Population 2000, 572,059)

DELEGATE

ELEANOR HOLMES NORTON, Democrat, of Washington, DC; born in Washington, DC, June 13, 1937; education: graduated, Dunbar High School, 1955; B.A., Antioch College, 1960; M.A., Yale Graduate School, 1963; J.D., Yale Law School, 1964; honorary degrees: Cedar Crest College, 1969; Bard College, 1971; Princeton University, 1973; Marymount College, 1974; City College of New York, 1975; Georgetown University, 1977; New York University, 1978; Howard University, 1978; Brown University, 1978; Wilberforce University, 1978; Wayne State University, 1980; Gallaudet College, 1980; Denison University, 1980; Syracuse University, 1981; Yeshiva University, 1981; Lawrence University, 1981; Emanuel College, 1981; Spelman College, 1982; University of Massachusetts, 1983; Smith College, 1983; Medical College of Pennsylvania, 1983; Tufts University, 1984; Bowdoin College, 1985; Antioch College, 1985; Haverford College, 1986; Lesley College, 1986; New Haven University, 1986; University of San Diego, 1986; Sojourner-Douglas College, 1987; Salem State College, 1987; Rutgers University, 1988; St. Joseph's College, 1988; University of Lowell, 1988; Colgate University, 1989; Drury College, 1989; Florida International University, 1989; St. Lawrence University, 1989; University of Wisconsin, 1989; University of Hartford, 1990; Ohio Wesleyan University, 1990; Wake Forest University, 1990; Fisk University, 1991; Tougalvo University, 1992; University of Southern Connecticut, 1992; professional: professor of law, Georgetown University, 1982–90; past/present member: chair, New York Commission on Human Rights, 1970–76; chair, Equal Employment Opportunity Commission, 1977–81; Community Foundation of Greater Washington, board; Yale Corporation, 1982–88; trustee, Rockefeller Foundation, 1982–90; executive assistant to the mayor of New York City (concurrent appointment); law clerk, Judge A. Leon Higginbotham, Federal District Court, 3rd Circuit; attorney, admitted to practice by examination in the District of Columbia, Pennsylvania and in the U.S. Supreme Court; Council on Foreign Relations; Overseas Development Council; U.S. Committee to Monitor the Helsinki accords; Carter Center, Atlanta, Georgia; boards of Martin Luther King, Jr. Center for Social Change and Environmental Law Institute; Workplace Health Fund; honors awards: Harper Fellow, Yale Law School, 1976, (for ''a person . . . who has made a distinguished contribution to the public life of the nation . . .''); Yale Law School Association Citation of Merit Medal to the Outstanding Alumnus of the Law School, 1980; Chancellor's Distinguished Lecturer, University of California Law School (Boalt Hall), Berkeley, 1981; Visiting Fellow, Harvard University, John F. Kennedy School of Government, spring 1984; Visiting Phi Beta Kappa Scholar, 1985; Distinguished Public Service Award, Center for National Policy, 1985; Ralph E. Shikes Bicentennial Fellow, Harvard Law School, 1987; One Hundred Most Important Women (*Ladies Home Journal*, 1988); One Hundred Most Powerful Women in Washington (The *Washingtonian* magazine, September 1989); divorced; two children: John and Katherine; committees: Homeland Security; Oversight and Government Reform; Transportation and Infrastructure; elected to the 102nd Congress on November 6, 1990; reelected to each succeeding Congress.

Office Listings

http://www.house.gov/norton

2136 Rayburn House Office Building, Washington, DC 20515 .... (202) 225–8050
Chief of Staff.—Julia Hudson. FAX: 225–3002
Legislative Director.—David Grosso.
Executive Assistant.—Raven Roddey.
Communications Director.—Doxie McCoy.

ZIP Codes: 20001–13, 20015–20, 20024, 20026–27, 20029–30, 20032–33, 20035–45, 20047, 20049–53, 20055–71, 20073–77, 20080, 20088, 20090–91, 20099, 20201–04, 20206–08, 20210–13, 20215–24, 20226–33, 20235, 20237, 20239–42, 20244–45, 20250, 20254, 20260, 20268, 20270, 20277, 20289, 20301, 20303, 20306–07, 20310, 20314–15, 20317–19, 20330, 20340, 20350, 20370, 20372–76, 20380, 20388–95, 20398, 20401–16, 20418–29, 20431, 20433–37, 20439–42, 20444, 20447, 20451, 20453, 20456, 20460, 20463, 20469, 20472, 20500, 20503–10, 20515, 20520–27, 20530–36, 20538–44, 20546–49, 20551–55, 20557, 20559–60, 20565–66, 20570–73, 20575–77, 20579–81, 20585–86, 20590–91, 20593–94, 20597, 20599

* * *

GUAM

(Population 2000, 154,805)

DELEGATE

MADELEINE Z. BORDALLO, Democrat, of Tamuning, Guam, born on, May 31, 1933; education: Associate Degree in Music, St. Catherine's College, St. Paul, MN, 1953; professional: First Lady of Guam, 1975–78, and 1983–86; Guam Senator, 1981–82, and 1987–94 (five terms); Lt. Governor of Guam, 1995–2002 (two terms); National Committee Chair for the National Democratic Party, 1964–2004; family: Ricardo J. Bordallo (deceased); daughter, Deborah; granddaughter, Nicole; committees: Armed Services; Natural Resources; elected to the 108th Congress on November 5, 2002; reelected to each succeeding Congress.

Office Listings

http://www.house.gov/bordallo

427 Cannon House Office Building, Washington, DC 20515 .... (202) 225–1188
Chief of Staff.—John Whitt. FAX: 226–0341
Legislative Director.—Jed Bullock.
Press Secretary.—Joseph E. Duenas.
Scheduler.—Rosanne Meno.
120 Father Duenas Avenue, Suite 107, Hagåtña, GU 96910 .... (671) 477–4272

ZIP Codes: 96910, 96912–13, 96915–17, 96919, 96921, 96923, 96926, 96928–29, 96931–32

* * *

PUERTO RICO

(Population 2000, 3,808,610)

RESIDENT COMMISSIONER

LUIS G. FORTUÑO, Republican, of Guaynabo, PR; born in San Juan, PR, October 31, 1960; education: B.S., Georgetown University, School of Foreign Service; J.D., University of Virginia Law School; professional: attorney; public service: Secretary of Economic Development and

Commerce for Puerto Rico, 1994–97; member, New Progressive Party; religion: Catholic; family: married to Lucé; three children: Luis, Guillermo, and Maria; committees: Education and Labor; Foreign Affairs; Natural Resources; elected November 2, 2004, to serve a four year term in the 109th and 110th Congresses.

Office Listings

http://www.house.gov/fortuno

126 Cannon House Office Building, Washington, DC 20515 .... (202) 225–2615
Chief of Staff.—Luis A. Bacó. FAX: 225–2154
Deputy Chief of Staff.—Javier de la Luz.
Senior Legislative Counsel.—Carmen Feliciano.
Executive Assistant / Scheduler.—Mary Taronji.
250 Calle Fortaleza, Old San Juan, PR 00901 .... (787) 723–6333
Deputy District Director.—Tere Nolla.

ZIP Codes: 00601–06, 00610–14, 00616–17, 00622–25, 00627, 00631, 00636–38, 00641, 00646–48, 00650, 00652–62, 00664, 00667, 00669–70, 00674, 00676–78, 00680–83, 00685, 00687–88, 00690, 00692–94, 00698, 00701, 00703–05, 00707, 00714–21, 00723, 00725–42, 00744–45, 00751, 00754, 00757, 00765–69, 00771–73, 00775, 00777–78, 00780, 00782–86, 00791–92, 00794–95, 00901–36, 00938, 00940, 00949–63, 00965–66, 00968–71, 00975–79, 00981–88

* * *

VIRGIN ISLANDS

(Population 2000, 108,612)

DELEGATE

DONNA M. CHRISTENSEN, Democrat, of St. Croix, VI; born in Teaneck, NJ, September 19, 1945; B.S., St. Mary's College, Notre Dame, IN, 1966; M.D., George Washington University School of Medicine, 1970; physician, family medicine; Acting Commissioner of Health, 1994–95; medical director, St. Croix Hospital, 1987–88; founding member and vice president, Virgin Islands Medical Institute; trustee, National Medical Association; past secretary and two-time past president, Virgin Islands Medical Society; founding member and trustee, Caribbean Youth Organization; member: Democratic National Committee; Virgin Islands Democratic Territorial Committee (past vice chair); Substance Abuse Coalition; St. Dunstan's Episcopal School Board of Directors; Caribbean Studies Association; Women's Coalition of St. Croix; St. Croix Environmental Association; past chair, Christian Education Committee; Friedensthal Moravian Church; past member: Virgin Islands Board of Education; Democratic Platform Committee; cohost, Straight Up TV interview program, 1993; married: Chris Christensen; children: two daughters: Rabiah Layla and Karida Yasmeen; member: Congressional Black Caucus; Congressional Women's Caucus; committees: Homeland Security; Natural Resources; elected to the 105th Congress; reelected to each succeeding Congress.

Office Listings

1510 Longworth House Office Building, Washington, DC 20515 .... (202) 225–1790
Chief of Staff.—Monique Clendinen Watson. FAX: 225–5517
Legislative Director.—Brian Modeste.
District Director / Administrative Director.—Steven Steele.
Executive Assistant / Scheduler.—Shelley Thomas.
Nisky Center, 2nd Floor, Suite 207, St. Thomas, VI 00802 .... (340) 774–4408
Office Assistant.—Joyce Jackson.
Sunny Isle Shopping Center, Space No. 25, P.O. Box 5980, St. Croix, VI 00823 ... (340) 778–5900

ZIP Codes: 00801–05, 00820–24, 00830–31, 00840–41, 00850–51

STATE DELEGATIONS

Number before names designates Congressional district. Democrats in roman; Republicans in *italic*; Independent in SMALL CAPS; Independent Democrat in *SMALL CAPS ITALIC;* Resident Commissioner and Delegates in **boldface**.

ALABAMA

SENATORS
Richard C. Shelby
Jeff Sessions

REPRESENTATIVES
[Democrats 2, Republicans 5]

1. *Jo Bonner*
2. *Terry Everett*
3. *Mike Rogers*
4. *Robert B. Aderholt*
5. Robert E. ''Bud'' Cramer, Jr.
6. *Spencer Bachus*
7. Artur Davis

ALASKA

SENATORS
Ted Stevens
Lisa Murkowski

REPRESENTATIVE
[Republican 1]
At Large - *Don Young*

ARIZONA

SENATORS
John McCain
Jon Kyl

REPRESENTATIVES
[Democrats 4, Republicans 4]

1. *Rick Renzi*
2. *Trent Franks*
3. *John B. Shadegg*
4. Ed Pastor
5. Harry E. Mitchell
6. *Jeff Flake*
7. Raúl M. Grijalva
8. Gabrielle Giffords

ARKANSAS

SENATORS
Blanche L. Lincoln
Mark L. Pryor

REPRESENTATIVES
[Democrats 3, Republicans 1]

1. Marion Berry
2. Vic Snyder
3. *John Boozman*
4. Mike Ross

CALIFORNIA

SENATORS
Dianne Feinstein
Barbara Boxer

REPRESENTATIVES
[Democrats 33, Republicans 19]

1. Mike Thompson
2. *Wally Herger*
3. *Daniel E. Lungren*
4. *John T. Doolittle*
5. Doris O. Matsui
6. Lynn C. Woolsey
7. George Miller
8. Nancy Pelosi

9. Barbara Lee
10. Ellen O. Tauscher
11. Jerry McNerney
12. Tom Lantos
13. Fortney Pete Stark
14. Anna G. Eshoo
15. Michael M. Honda
16. Zoe Lofgren
17. Sam Farr
18. Dennis A. Cardoza
19. *George Radanovich*
20. Jim Costa
21. *Devin Nunes*
22. *Kevin McCarthy*
23. Lois Capps
24. *Elton Gallegly*
25. *Howard P. "Buck" McKeon*
26. *David Dreier*
27. Brad Sherman
28. Howard L. Berman
29. Adam B. Schiff
30. Henry A. Waxman
31. Xavier Becerra
32. Hilda L. Solis
33. Diane E. Watson
34. Lucille Roybal-Allard
35. Maxine Waters
36. Jane Harman
37. ——[1]
38. Grace F. Napolitano
39. Linda T. Sánchez
40. *Edward R. Royce*
41. *Jerry Lewis*
42. *Gary G. Miller*
43. Joe Baca
44. *Ken Calvert*
45. *Mary Bono*
46. *Dana Rohrabacher*
47. Loretta Sanchez
48. *John Campbell*
49. *Darrell E. Issa*
50. *Brian P. Bilbray*
51. Bob Filner
52. *Duncan Hunter*
53. Susan A. Davis

COLORADO

SENATORS
Wayne Allard
Ken Salazar

REPRESENTATIVES
[Democrats 4, Republicans 3]

1. Diana DeGette
2. Mark Udall
3. John T. Salazar
4. *Marilyn N. Musgrave*
5. *Doug Lamborn*
6. *Thomas G. Tancredo*
7. Ed Perlmutter

CONNECTICUT

SENATORS
Christopher J. Dodd
*Joseph I. Lieberman***

REPRESENTATIVES
[Democrats 4, Republicans 1]

1. John B. Larson
2. Joe Courtney
3. Rosa L. DeLauro
4. *Christopher Shays*
5. Christopher S. Murphy

DELAWARE

SENATORS
Joseph R. Biden, Jr.
Thomas R. Carper

REPRESENTATIVE
[Republican 1]
At Large - *Michael N. Castle*

FLORIDA

SENATORS
Bill Nelson
Mel Martinez

REPRESENTATIVES
[Democrats 9, Republicans 16]

1. *Jeff Miller*
2. Allen Boyd
3. Corrine Brown
4. *Ander Crenshaw*
5. *Ginny Brown-Waite*
6. *Cliff Stearns*
7. *John L. Mica*
8. *Ric Keller*
9. *Gus M. Bilirakis*
10. *C.W. Bill Young*
11. Kathy Castor
12. *Adam H. Putnam*

13. *Vern Buchanan*
14. *Connie Mack*
15. *Dave Weldon*
16. Tim Mahoney
17. Kendrick B. Meek
18. *Ileana Ros-Lehtinen*
19. Robert Wexler
20. Debbie Wasserman Schultz
21. *Lincoln Diaz-Balart*
22. Ron Klein
23. Alcee L. Hastings
24. *Tom Feeney*
25. *Mario Diaz-Balart*

GEORGIA

SENATORS
Saxby Chambliss
Johnny Isakson

REPRESENTATIVES
[Democrats 6, Republicans 7]

1. *Jack Kingston*
2. Sanford D. Bishop, Jr.
3. *Lynn A. Westmoreland*
4. Henry C. ''Hank'' Johnson, Jr.
5. John Lewis
6. *Tom Price*
7. *John Linder*
8. Jim Marshall
9. *Nathan Deal*
10. *Paul C. Broun*
11. *Phil Gingrey*
12. John Barrow
13. David Scott

HAWAII

SENATORS
Daniel K. Inouye
Daniel K. Akaka

REPRESENTATIVES
[Democrats 2]

1. Neil Abercrombie
2. Mazie K. Hirono

IDAHO

SENATORS
Larry E. Craig
Mike Crapo

REPRESENTATIVES
[Republicans 2]

1. *Bill Sali*
2. *Michael K. Simpson*

ILLINOIS

SENATORS
Richard Durbin
Barack Obama

REPRESENTATIVES
[Democrats 10, Republicans 9]

1. Bobby L. Rush
2. Jesse L. Jackson, Jr.
3. Daniel Lipinski
4. Luis V. Gutierrez
5. Rahm Emanuel
6. *Peter J. Roskam*
7. Danny K. Davis
8. Melissa L. Bean
9. Janice D. Schakowsky
10. *Mark Steven Kirk*
11. *Jerry Weller*
12. Jerry F. Costello
13. *Judy Biggert*
14. *J. Dennis Hastert*
15. *Timothy V. Johnson*
16. *Donald A. Manzullo*
17. Phil Hare
18. *Ray LaHood*
19. *John Shimkus*

INDIANA

SENATORS
Richard G. Lugar
Evan Bayh

REPRESENTATIVES
[Democrats 5, Republicans 4]

1. Peter J. Visclosky
2. Joe Donnelly
3. *Mark E. Souder*
4. *Steve Buyer*
5. *Dan Burton*
6. *Mike Pence*
7. Julia Carson
8. Brad Ellsworth
9. Baron P. Hill

IOWA

SENATORS
Chuck Grassley
Tom Harkin

REPRESENTATIVES
[Democrats 3, Republicans 2]
1. Bruce L. Braley
2. David Loebsack
3. Leonard L. Boswell
4. *Tom Latham*
5. *Steve King*

KANSAS

SENATORS
Sam Brownback
Pat Roberts

REPRESENTATIVES
[Democrats 2, Republicans 2]
1. *Jerry Moran*
2. Nancy E. Boyda
3. Dennis Moore
4. *Todd Tiahrt*

KENTUCKY

SENATORS
Mitch McConnell
Jim Bunning

REPRESENTATIVES
[Democrats 2, Republicans 4]
1. *Ed Whitfield*
2. *Ron Lewis*
3. John A. Yarmuth
4. *Geoff Davis*
5. *Harold Rogers*
6. Ben Chandler

LOUISIANA

SENATORS
Mary L. Landrieu
David Vitter

REPRESENTATIVES
[Democrats 2, Republicans 5]
1. *Bobby Jindal*
2. William J. Jefferson
3. Charlie Melancon
4. *Jim McCrery*
5. *Rodney Alexander*
6. *Richard H. Baker*
7. *Charles W. Boustany, Jr.*

MAINE

SENATORS
Olympia J. Snowe
Susan M. Collins

REPRESENTATIVES
[Democrats 2]
1. Thomas H. Allen
2. Michael H. Michaud

MARYLAND

SENATORS
Barbara A. Mikulski
Benjamin L. Cardin

REPRESENTATIVES
[Democrats 6, Republicans 2]
1. *Wayne T. Gilchrest*
2. C.A. Dutch Ruppersberger
3. John P. Sarbanes
4. Albert Russell Wynn
5. Steny H. Hoyer
6. *Roscoe G. Bartlett*
7. Elijah E. Cummings
8. Chris Van Hollen

MASSACHUSETTS

SENATORS
Edward M. Kennedy
John F. Kerry

REPRESENTATIVES
[Democrats 9]

1. John W. Olver
2. Richard E. Neal
3. James P. McGovern
4. Barney Frank
5. ——[2]
6. John F. Tierney
7. Edward J. Markey
8. Michael E. Capuano
9. Stephen F. Lynch
10. William D. Delahunt

MICHIGAN

SENATORS
Carl Levin
Debbie Stabenow

REPRESENTATIVES
[Democrats 6, Republicans 9]

1. Bart Stupak
2. *Peter Hoekstra*
3. *Vernon J. Ehlers*
4. *Dave Camp*
5. Dale E. Kildee
6. *Fred Upton*
7. *Timothy Walberg*
8. *Mike Rogers*
9. *Joe Knollenberg*
10. *Candice S. Miller*
11. *Thaddeus G. McCotter*
12. Sander M. Levin
13. Carolyn C. Kilpatrick
14. John Conyers, Jr.
15. John D. Dingell

MINNESOTA

SENATORS
Norm Coleman
Amy Klobuchar

REPRESENTATIVES
[Democrats 5, Republicans 3]

1. Timothy J. Walz
2. *John Kline*
3. *Jim Ramstad*
4. Betty McCollum
5. Keith Ellison
6. *Michele Bachmann*
7. Collin C. Peterson
8. James L. Oberstar

MISSISSIPPI

SENATORS
Thad Cochran
Trent Lott

REPRESENTATIVES
[Democrats 2, Republicans 2]

1. *Roger F. Wicker*
2. Bennie G. Thompson
3. *Charles W. "Chip" Pickering*
4. Gene Taylor

MISSOURI

SENATORS
Christopher S. Bond
Claire McCaskill

REPRESENTATIVES
[Democrats 4, Republicans 5]

1. Wm. Lacy Clay
2. *W. Todd Akin*
3. Russ Carnahan
4. Ike Skelton
5. Emanuel Cleaver
6. *Sam Graves*
7. *Roy Blunt*
8. *Jo Ann Emerson*
9. *Kenny C. Hulshof*

MONTANA

SENATORS
Max Baucus
Jon Tester

REPRESENTATIVE
[Republican 1]

At Large - *Dennis R. Rehberg*

NEBRASKA

SENATORS
Chuck Hagel
E. Benjamin Nelson

REPRESENTATIVES
[Republicans 3]
1. *Jeff Fortenberry*
2. *Lee Terry*
3. *Adrian Smith*

NEVADA

SENATORS
Harry Reid
John Ensign

REPRESENTATIVES
[Democrats 1, Republicans 2]
1. Shelley Berkley
2. *Dean Heller*
3. *Jon C. Porter*

NEW HAMPSHIRE

SENATORS
Judd Gregg
John E. Sununu

REPRESENTATIVES
[Democrats 2]
1. Carol Shea-Porter
2. Paul W. Hodes

NEW JERSEY

SENATORS
Frank R. Lautenberg
Robert Menendez

REPRESENTATIVES
[Democrats 7, Republicans 6]
1. Robert E. Andrews
2. *Frank A. LoBiondo*
3. *Jim Saxton*
4. *Christopher H. Smith*
5. *Scott Garrett*
6. Frank Pallone, Jr.
7. *Mike Ferguson*
8. Bill Pascrell, Jr.
9. Steven R. Rothman
10. Donald M. Payne
11. *Rodney P. Frelinghuysen*
12. Rush D. Holt
13. Albio Sires

NEW MEXICO

SENATORS
Pete V. Domenici
Jeff Bingaman

REPRESENTATIVES
[Democrats 1, Republicans 2]
1. *Heather Wilson*
2. *Stevan Pearce*
3. Tom Udall

NEW YORK

SENATORS
Charles E. Schumer
Hillary Rodham Clinton

REPRESENTATIVES
[Democrats 23, Republicans 6]
1. Timothy H. Bishop
2. Steve Israel
3. *Peter T. King*
4. Carolyn McCarthy
5. Gary L. Ackerman
6. Gregory W. Meeks
7. Joseph Crowley
8. Jerrold Nadler
9. Anthony D. Weiner
10. Edolphus Towns
11. Yvette D. Clarke
12. Nydia M. Velázquez
13. *Vito Fossella*
14. Carolyn B. Maloney

15. Charles B. Rangel
16. José E. Serrano
17. Eliot L. Engel
18. Nita M. Lowey
19. John J. Hall
20. Kirsten E. Gillibrand
21. Michael R. McNulty
22. Maurice D. Hinchey
23. *John M. McHugh*
24. Michael A. Arcuri
25. *James T. Walsh*
26. *Thomas M. Reynolds*
27. Brian Higgins
28. Louise McIntosh Slaughter
29. *John R. ''Randy'' Kuhl, Jr.*

NORTH CAROLINA

SENATORS
Elizabeth Dole
Richard Burr

REPRESENTATIVES
[Democrats 7, Republicans 6]

1. G.K. Butterfield
2. Bob Etheridge
3. *Walter B. Jones*
4. David E. Price
5. *Virginia Foxx*
6. *Howard Coble*
7. Mike McIntyre
8. *Robin Hayes*
9. *Sue Wilkins Myrick*
10. *Patrick T. McHenry*
11. Heath Shuler
12. Melvin L. Watt
13. Brad Miller

NORTH DAKOTA

SENATORS
Kent Conrad
Byron L. Dorgan

REPRESENTATIVE
[Democrat 1]

At Large - Earl Pomeroy

OHIO

SENATORS
George V. Voinovich
Sherrod Brown

REPRESENTATIVES
[Democrats 7, Republicans 11]

1. *Steve Chabot*
2. *Jean Schmidt*
3. *Michael R. Turner*
4. *Jim Jordan*
5. *Paul E. Gillmor*
6. Charles A. Wilson
7. *David L. Hobson*
8. *John A. Boehner*
9. Marcy Kaptur
10. Dennis J. Kucinich
11. Stephanie Tubbs Jones
12. *Patrick J. Tiberi*
13. Betty Sutton
14. *Steven C. LaTourette*
15. *Deborah Pryce*
16. *Ralph Regula*
17. Tim Ryan
18. Zachary T. Space

OKLAHOMA

SENATORS
James M. Inhofe
Tom Coburn

REPRESENTATIVES
[Democrats 1, Republicans 4]

1. *John Sullivan*
2. Dan Boren
3. *Frank D. Lucas*
4. *Tom Cole*
5. *Mary Fallin*

OREGON

SENATORS
Ron Wyden
Gordon H. Smith

REPRESENTATIVES
[Democrats 4, Republicans 1]

1. David Wu

2. *Greg Walden*
3. Earl Blumenauer
4. Peter A. DeFazio
5. Darlene Hooley

PENNSYLVANIA

SENATORS
Arlen Specter
Robert P. Casey, Jr.

REPRESENTATIVES
[Democrats 11, Republicans 8]

1. Robert A. Brady
2. Chaka Fattah
3. *Phil English*
4. Jason Altmire
5. *John E. Peterson*
6. *Jim Gerlach*
7. Joe Sestak
8. Patrick J. Murphy
9. *Bill Shuster*
10. Christopher P. Carney
11. Paul E. Kanjorski
12. John P. Murtha
13. Allyson Y. Schwartz
14. Michael F. Doyle
15. *Charles W. Dent*
16. *Joseph R. Pitts*
17. Tim Holden
18. *Tim Murphy*
19. *Todd Russell Platts*

RHODE ISLAND

SENATORS
Jack Reed
Sheldon Whitehouse

REPRESENTATIVES
[Democrats 2]

1. Patrick J. Kennedy
2. James R. Langevin

SOUTH CAROLINA

SENATORS
Lindsey Graham
Jim DeMint

REPRESENTATIVES
[Democrats 2, Republicans 4]

1. *Henry E. Brown, Jr.*
2. *Joe Wilson*
3. *J. Gresham Barrett*
4. *Bob Inglis*
5. John M. Spratt, Jr.
6. James E. Clyburn

SOUTH DAKOTA

SENATORS
Tim Johnson
John Thune

REPRESENTATIVE
[Democrat 1]
At Large - Stephanie Herseth Sandlin

TENNESSEE

SENATORS
Lamar Alexander
Bob Corker

REPRESENTATIVES
[Democrats 5, Republicans 4]

1. *David Davis*
2. *John J. Duncan, Jr.*
3. *Zach Wamp*
4. Lincoln Davis
5. Jim Cooper
6. Bart Gordon
7. *Marsha Blackburn*
8. John S. Tanner
9. Steve Cohen

TEXAS

SENATORS
Kay Bailey Hutchison
John Cornyn

REPRESENTATIVES
[Democrats 13, Republicans 19]

1. *Louie Gohmert*
2. *Ted Poe*
3. *Sam Johnson*
4. *Ralph M. Hall*
5. *Jeb Hensarling*
6. *Joe Barton*
7. *John Abney Culberson*
8. *Kevin Brady*
9. Al Green
10. *Michael T. McCaul*
11. *K. Michael Conaway*
12. *Kay Granger*
13. *Mac Thornberry*
14. *Ron Paul*
15. Rubén Hinojosa
16. Silvestre Reyes
17. Chet Edwards
18. Sheila Jackson Lee
19. *Randy Neugebauer*
20. Charles A. Gonzalez
21. *Lamar Smith*
22. Nick Lampson
23. Ciro D. Rodriguez
24. *Kenny Marchant*
25. Lloyd Doggett
26. *Michael C. Burgess*
27. Solomon P. Ortiz
28. Henry Cuellar
29. Gene Green
30. Eddie Bernice Johnson
31. *John R. Carter*
32. *Pete Sessions*

UTAH

SENATORS
Orrin G. Hatch
Robert F. Bennett

REPRESENTATIVES
[Democrats 1, Republicans 2]

1. *Rob Bishop*
2. Jim Matheson
3. *Chris Cannon*

VERMONT

SENATORS
Patrick J. Leahy
BERNARD SANDERS*

REPRESENTATIVE
[Democrat 1]

At Large - Peter Welch

VIRGINIA

SENATORS
John Warner
Jim Webb

REPRESENTATIVES
[Democrats 3, Republicans 8]

1. *Jo Ann Davis*
2. *Thelma D. Drake*
3. Robert C. ''Bobby'' Scott
4. *J. Randy Forbes*
5. *Virgil H. Goode, Jr.*
6. *Bob Goodlatte*
7. *Eric Cantor*
8. James P. Moran
9. Rick Boucher
10. *Frank R. Wolf*
11. *Tom Davis*

WASHINGTON

SENATORS
Patty Murray
Maria Cantwell

REPRESENTATIVES
[Democrats 6, Republicans 3]

1. Jay Inslee
2. Rick Larsen
3. Brian Baird
4. *Doc Hastings*
5. *Cathy McMorris Rodgers*
6. Norman D. Dicks
7. Jim McDermott
8. *David G. Reichert*
9. Adam Smith

WEST VIRGINIA

SENATORS
Robert C. Byrd
John D. Rockefeller IV

REPRESENTATIVES
[Democrats 2, Republicans 1]
1. Alan B. Mollohan
2. *Shelley Moore Capito*
3. Nick J. Rahall II

WISCONSIN

SENATORS
Herb Kohl
Russell D. Feingold

REPRESENTATIVES
[Democrats 5, Republicans 3]
1. *Paul Ryan*
2. Tammy Baldwin
3. Ron Kind
4. Gwen Moore
5. *F. James Sensenbrenner, Jr.*
6. *Thomas E. Petri*
7. David R. Obey
8. Steve Kagen

WYOMING

SENATORS
Michael B. Enzi
John Barrasso

REPRESENTATIVE
[Republican 1]
At Large - *Barbara Cubin*

AMERICAN SAMOA

DELEGATE
[Democrat 1]

Eni F.H. Faleomavaega

DISTRICT OF COLUMBIA

DELEGATE
[Democrat 1]

Eleanor Holmes Norton

GUAM

DELEGATE
[Democrat 1]

Madeleine Z. Bordallo

PUERTO RICO

RESIDENT COMMISSIONER
[Republican 1]

Luis G. Fortuño

VIRGIN ISLANDS

DELEGATE
[Democrat 1]

Donna M. Christensen

*Independent
**Independent Democrat
[1] Vacancy due to the death of Juanita Millender-McDonald, April 22, 2007.
[2] Vacancy due to the resignation of *Martin T. Meehan* effective July 1, 2007.

ALPHABETICAL LIST

SENATORS

Alphabetical list of Senators, Representatives, Delegates, and Resident Commissioner. Democrats in roman (49); Republicans in *italic* (49); Independent in SMALL CAPS (1); Independent Democrat in *SMALL CAPS ITALIC* (1).

Akaka, Daniel K., HI
Alexander, Lamar, TN
Allard, Wayne, CO
Barrasso, John, WY
Baucus, Max, MT
Bayh, Evan, IN
Bennett, Robert F., UT
Biden, Joseph R., Jr., DE
Bingaman, Jeff, NM
Bond, Christopher S., MO
Boxer, Barbara, CA
Brown, Sherrod, OH
Brownback, Sam, KS
Bunning, Jim, KY
Burr, Richard, NC
Byrd, Robert C., WV
Cantwell, Maria, WA
Cardin, Benjamin L., MD
Carper, Thomas R., DE
Casey, Robert P., Jr. PA
Chambliss, Saxby, GA
Clinton, Hillary Rodham, NY
Coburn, Tom, OK
Cochran, Thad, MS
Coleman, Norm, MN
Collins, Susan M., ME
Conrad, Kent, ND
Corker, Bob, TN
Cornyn, John, TX
Craig, Larry E., ID
Crapo, Mike, ID
DeMint, Jim, SC
Dodd, Christopher J., CT
Dole, Elizabeth, NC
Domenici, Pete V., NM
Dorgan, Byron L., ND
Durbin, Richard, IL
Ensign, John, NV
Enzi, Michael B., WY
Feingold, Russell D., WI
Feinstein, Dianne, CA
Graham, Lindsey, SC
Grassley, Chuck, IA
Gregg, Judd, NH
Hagel, Chuck, NE
Harkin, Tom, IA
Hatch, Orrin G., UT
Hutchison, Kay Bailey, TX
Inhofe, James M., OK
Inouye, Daniel K., HI
Isakson, Johnny, GA
Johnson, Tim, SD
Kennedy, Edward M., MA
Kerry, John F., MA
Klobuchar, Amy, MN
Kohl, Herb, WI
Kyl, Jon, AZ
Landrieu, Mary L., LA
Lautenberg, Frank R., NJ
Leahy, Patrick J., VT
Levin, Carl, MI
LIEBERMAN, JOSEPH I., CT
Lincoln, Blanche L., AR
Lott, Trent, MS
Lugar, Richard G., IN
McCain, John, AZ
McCaskill, Claire, MO
McConnell, Mitch, KY
Martinez, Mel, FL
Menendez, Robert, NJ
Mikulski, Barbara A., MD
Murkowski, Lisa, AK
Murray, Patty, WA
Nelson, Bill, FL
Nelson, E. Benjamin, NE
Obama, Barack, IL
Pryor, Mark L., AR
Reed, Jack, RI
Reid, Harry, NV
Roberts, Pat, KS
Rockefeller, John D., IV, WV
Salazar, Ken, CO
SANDERS, BERNARD, VT
Schumer, Charles E., NY
Sessions, Jeff, AL
Shelby, Richard C., AL
Smith, Gordon H., OR
Snowe, Olympia J., ME
Specter, Arlen, PA
Stabenow, Debbie, MI
Stevens, Ted, AK
Sununu, John E., NH
Tester, Jon, MT
Thune, John, SD
Vitter, David, LA
Voinovich, George V., OH
Warner, John, VA
Webb, Jim, VA
Whitehouse, Sheldon, RI
Wyden, Ron, OR

REPRESENTATIVES

Democrats in roman (231); Republicans in *italic* (202); Vacancies (2); Resident Commissioner and Delegates in **boldface** (5); total, 440.

Abercrombie, Neil, HI (1st)
Ackerman, Gary L., NY (5th)
Aderholt, Robert B., AL (4th)
Akin, W. Todd, MO (2nd)
Alexander, Rodney, LA (5th)
Allen, Thomas H., ME (1st)
Altmire, Jason, PA (4th)
Andrews, Robert E., NJ (1st)
Arcuri, Michael A., NY (24th)
Baca, Joe, CA (43rd)
Bachmann, Michele, MN (6th)
Bachus, Spencer, AL (6th)
Baird, Brian, WA (3rd)
Baker, Richard H., LA (6th)
Baldwin, Tammy, WI (2nd)
Barrett, J. Gresham, SC (3rd)
Barrow, John, GA (12th)
Bartlett, Roscoe G., MD (6th)
Barton, Joe, TX (6th)
Bean, Melissa L., IL (8th)
Becerra, Xavier, CA (31st)
Berkley, Shelley, NV (1st)
Berman, Howard L., CA (28th)
Berry, Marion, AR (1st)
Biggert, Judy, IL (13th)
Bilbray, Brian P., CA (50th)
Bilirakis, Gus M., FL (9th)
Bishop, Rob, UT (1st)
Bishop, Sanford D., Jr., GA (2nd)
Bishop, Timothy H., NY (1st)
Blackburn, Marsha, TN (7th)
Blumenauer, Earl, OR (3rd)
Blunt, Roy, MO (7th)
Boehner, John A., OH (8th)
Bonner, Jo, AL (1st)
Bono, Mary, CA (45th)
Boozman, John, AR (3rd)
Boren, Dan, OK (2nd)
Boswell, Leonard L., IA (3rd)
Boucher, Rick, VA (9th)
Boustany, Charles W., Jr., LA (7th)
Boyd, Allen, FL (2nd)
Boyda, Nancy E., KS (2nd)
Brady, Kevin, TX (8th)
Brady, Robert A., PA (1st)
Braley, Bruce L., IA (1st)
Broun, Paul C., GA (10th)
Brown, Corrine, FL (3rd)
Brown, Henry E., Jr., SC (1st)
Brown-Waite, Ginny, FL (5th)
Buchanan, Vern, FL (13th)
Burgess, Michael C., TX (26th)
Burton, Dan, IN (5th)
Butterfield, G.K., NC (1st)
Buyer, Steve, IN (4th)
Calvert, Ken, CA (44th)
Camp, Dave, MI (4th)
Campbell, John, CA (48th)
Cannon, Chris, UT (3rd)
Cantor, Eric, VA (7th)
Capito, Shelley Moore, WV (2nd)
Capps, Lois, CA (23rd)
Capuano, Michael E., MA (8th)
Cardoza, Dennis A., CA (18th)
Carnahan, Russ, MO (3rd)
Carney, Christopher P., PA (10th)
Carson, Julia, IN (7th)
Carter, John R., TX (31st)
Castle, Michael N., DE (At Large)
Castor, Kathy, FL (11th)
Chabot, Steve, OH (1st)
Chandler, Ben, KY (6th)
Clarke, Yvette D., NY (11th)
Clay, Wm. Lacy, MO (1st)
Cleaver, Emanuel, MO (5th)
Clyburn, James E., SC (6th)
Coble, Howard, NC (6th)
Cohen, Steve, TN (9th)
Cole, Tom, OK (4th)
Conaway, K. Michael, TX (11th)
Conyers, John, Jr., MI (14th)
Cooper, Jim, TN (5th)
Costa, Jim, CA (20th)
Costello, Jerry F., IL (12th)
Courtney, Joe, CT (2nd)
Cramer, Robert E. ''Bud'', Jr., AL (5th)
Crenshaw, Ander, FL (4th)
Crowley, Joseph, NY (7th)
Cubin, Barbara, WY (At Large)
Cuellar, Henry, TX (28th)
Culberson, John Abney, TX (7th)
Cummings, Elijah E., MD (7th)
Davis, Artur, AL (7th)
Davis, Danny K., IL (7th)
Davis, David, TN (1st)
Davis, Geoff, KY (4th)
Davis, Jo Ann, VA (1st)
Davis, Lincoln, TN (4th)
Davis, Susan A., CA (53rd)
Davis, Tom, VA (11th)
Deal, Nathan, GA (9th)
DeFazio, Peter A., OR (4th)
DeGette, Diana, CO (1st)
Delahunt, William D., MA (10th)
DeLauro, Rosa L., CT (3rd)
Dent, Charles W., PA (15th)
Diaz-Balart, Lincoln, FL (21st)
Diaz-Balart, Mario, FL (25th)
Dicks, Norman D., WA (6th)
Dingell, John D., MI (15th)
Doggett, Lloyd, TX (25th)
Donnelly, Joe, IN (2nd)
Doolittle, John T., CA (4th)
Doyle, Michael F., PA (14th)
Drake, Thelma D., VA (2nd)
Dreier, David, CA (26th)
Duncan, John J., Jr., TN (2nd)
Edwards, Chet, TX (17th)
Ehlers, Vernon J., MI (3rd)
Ellison, Keith, MN (5th)

Ellsworth, Brad, IN (8th)
Emanuel, Rahm, IL (5th)
Emerson, Jo Ann, MO (8th)
Engel, Eliot L., NY (17th)
English, Phil, PA (3rd)
Eshoo, Anna G., CA (14th)
Etheridge, Bob, NC (2nd)
Everett, Terry, AL (2nd)
Fallin, Mary, OK (5th)
Farr, Sam, CA (17th)
Fattah, Chaka, PA (2nd)
Feeney, Tom, FL (24th)
Ferguson, Mike, NJ (7th)
Filner, Bob, CA (51st)
Flake, Jeff, AZ (6th)
Forbes, J. Randy, VA (4th)
Fortenberry, Jeff, NE (1st)
Fossella, Vito, NY (13th)
Foxx, Virginia, NC (5th)
Frank, Barney, MA (4th)
Franks, Trent, AZ (2nd)
Frelinghuysen, Rodney P., NJ (11th)
Gallegly, Elton, CA (24th)
Garrett, Scott, NJ (5th)
Gerlach, Jim, PA (6th)
Giffords, Gabrielle, AZ (8th)
Gilchrest, Wayne T., MD (1st)
Gillibrand, Kirsten E., NY (20th)
Gillmor, Paul E., OH (5th)
Gingrey, Phil, GA (11th)
Gohmert, Louie, TX (1st)
Gonzalez, Charles A., TX (20th)
Goode, Virgil H., Jr., VA (5th)
Goodlatte, Bob, VA (6th)
Gordon, Bart, TN (6th)
Granger, Kay, TX (12th)
Graves, Sam, MO (6th)
Green, Al, TX (9th)
Green, Gene, TX (29th)
Grijalva, Raúl M., AZ (7th)
Gutierrez, Luis V., IL (4th)
Hall, John J., NY (19th)
Hall, Ralph M., TX (4th)
Hare, Phil, IL (17th)
Harman, Jane, CA (36th)
Hastert, J. Dennis, IL (14th)
Hastings, Alcee L., FL (23rd)
Hastings, Doc, WA (4th)
Hayes, Robin, NC (8th)
Heller, Dean, NV (2nd)
Hensarling, Jeb, TX (5th)
Herger, Wally, CA (2nd)
Herseth Sandlin, Stephanie, SD (At Large)
Higgins, Brian, NY (27th)
Hill, Baron P., IN (9th)
Hinchey, Maurice D., NY (22nd)
Hinojosa, Rubén, TX (15th)
Hirono, Mazie K., HI (2nd)
Hobson, David L., OH (7th)
Hodes, Paul W., NH (2nd)
Hoekstra, Peter, MI (2nd)
Holden, Tim, PA (17th)
Holt, Rush D., NJ (12th)
Honda, Michael M., CA (15th)
Hooley, Darlene, OR (5th)
Hoyer, Steny H., MD (5th)
Hulshof, Kenny C., MO (9th)
Hunter, Duncan, CA (52nd)
Inglis, Bob, SC (4th)
Inslee, Jay, WA (1st)
Israel, Steve, NY (2nd)
Issa, Darrell E., CA (49th)
Jackson, Jesse L., Jr., IL (2nd)
Jackson Lee, Sheila, TX (18th)
Jefferson, William J., LA (2nd)
Jindal, Bobby, LA (1st)
Johnson, Eddie Bernice, TX (30th)
Johnson, Henry C. "Hank", Jr., GA (4th)
Johnson, Sam, TX (3rd)
Johnson, Timothy V., IL (15th)
Jones, Stephanie Tubbs, OH (11th)
Jones, Walter B., NC (3rd)
Jordan, Jim, OH (4th)
Kagen, Steve, WI (8th)
Kanjorski, Paul E., PA (11th)
Kaptur, Marcy, OH (9th)
Keller, Ric, FL (8th)
Kennedy, Patrick J., RI (1st)
Kildee, Dale E., MI (5th)
Kilpatrick, Carolyn C., MI (13th)
Kind, Ron, WI (3rd)
King, Peter T., NY (3rd)
King, Steve, IA (5th)
Kingston, Jack, GA (1st)
Kirk, Mark Steven, IL (10th)
Klein, Ron, FL (22nd)
Kline, John, MN (2nd)
Knollenberg, Joe, MI (9th)
Kucinich, Dennis J., OH (10th)
Kuhl, John R. "Randy", Jr., NY (29th)
LaHood, Ray, IL (18th)
Lamborn, Doug, CO (5th)
Lampson, Nick, TX (22nd)
Langevin, James R., RI (2nd)
Lantos, Tom, CA (12th)
Larsen, Rick, WA (2nd)
Larson, John B., CT (1st)
Latham, Tom, IA (4th)
LaTourette, Steven C., OH (14th)
Lee, Barbara, CA (9th)
Levin, Sander M., MI (12th)
Lewis, Jerry, CA (41st)
Lewis, John, GA (5th)
Lewis, Ron, KY (2nd)
Linder, John, GA (7th)
Lipinski, Daniel, IL (3rd)
LoBiondo, Frank A., NJ (2nd)
Loebsack, David, IA (2nd)
Lofgren, Zoe, CA (16th)
Lowey, Nita M., NY (18th)
Lucas, Frank D., OK (3rd)
Lungren, Daniel E., CA (3rd)
Lynch, Stephen F., MA (9th)
McCarthy, Carolyn, NY (4th)
McCarthy, Kevin, CA (22nd)
McCaul, Michael, T., TX (10th)
McCollum, Betty, MN (4th)
McCotter, Thaddeus G., MI (11th)
McCrery, Jim, LA (4th)
McDermott, Jim, WA (7th)
McGovern, James P., MA (3rd)
McHenry, Patrick T., NC (10th)

McHugh, John M., NY (23rd)
McIntyre, Mike, NC (7th)
McKeon, Howard P. ''Buck'', CA (25th)
McMorris Rodgers, Cathy, WA (5th)
McNerney, Jerry, CA (11th)
McNulty, Michael R., NY (21st)
Mack, Connie, FL (14th)
Mahoney, Tim, FL (16th)
Maloney, Carolyn B., NY (14th)
Manzullo, Donald A., IL (16th)
Marchant, Kenny, TX (24th)
Markey, Edward J., MA (7th)
Marshall, Jim, GA (8th)
Matheson, Jim, UT (2nd)
Matsui, Doris O., CA (5th)
Meek, Kendrick B., FL (17th)
Meeks, Gregory W., NY (6th)
Melancon, Charlie, LA (3rd)
Mica, John L., FL (7th)
Michaud, Michael H., ME (2nd)
Miller, Brad, NC (13th)
Miller, Candice S., MI (10th)
Miller, Gary G., CA (42nd)
Miller, George, CA (7th)
Miller, Jeff, FL (1st)
Mitchell, Harry E., AZ (5th)
Mollohan, Alan B., WV (1st)
Moore, Dennis, KS (3rd)
Moore, Gwen, WI (4th)
Moran, James P., VA (8th)
Moran, Jerry, KS (1st)
Murphy, Christopher S., CT (5th)
Murphy, Patrick J., PA (8th)
Murphy, Tim, PA (18th)
Murtha, John P., PA (12th)
Musgrave, Marilyn N., CO (4th)
Myrick, Sue Wilkins, NC (9th)
Nadler, Jerrold, NY (8th)
Napolitano, Grace F., CA (38th)
Neal, Richard E., MA (2nd)
Neugebauer, Randy, TX (19th)
Nunes, Devin, CA (21st)
Oberstar, James L., MN (8th)
Obey, David R., WI (7th)
Olver, John W., MA (1st)
Ortiz, Solomon P., TX (27th)
Pallone, Frank, Jr., NJ (6th)
Pascrell, Bill, Jr., NJ (8th)
Pastor, Ed, AZ (4th)
Paul, Ron, TX (14th)
Payne, Donald M., NJ (10th)
Pearce, Stevan, NM (2nd)
Pelosi, Nancy, CA (8th)
Pence, Mike, IN (6th)
Perlmutter, Ed, CO (7th)
Peterson, Collin C., MN (7th)
Peterson, John E., PA (5th)
Petri, Thomas E., WI (6th)
Pickering, Charles W. ''Chip'', MS (3rd)
Pitts, Joseph R., PA (16th)
Platts, Todd Russell, PA (19th)
Poe, Ted, TX (2nd)
Pomeroy, Earl, ND (At Large)
Porter, Jon C., NV (3rd)
Price, David E., NC (4th)
Price, Tom, GA (6th)
Pryce, Deborah, OH (15th)
Putnam, Adam H., FL (12th)
Radanovich, George, CA (19th)
Rahall, Nick J. II, WV (3rd)
Ramstad, Jim, MN (3rd)
Rangel, Charles B., NY (15th)
Regula, Ralph, OH (16th)
Rehberg, Dennis, MT (At Large)
Reichert, David G., WA (8th)
Renzi, Rick, AZ (1st)
Reyes, Silvestre, TX (16th)
Reynolds, Thomas M., NY (26th)
Rodriguez, Ciro D., TX (23rd)
Rogers, Harold, KY (5th)
Rogers, Mike, AL (3rd)
Rogers, Mike, MI (8th)
Rohrabacher, Dana, CA (46th)
Roskam, Peter J., IL (6th)
Ros-Lehtinen, Ileana, FL (18th)
Ross, Mike, AR (4th)
Rothman, Steven R., NJ (9th)
Roybal-Allard, Lucille, CA (34th)
Royce, Edward R., CA (40th)
Ruppersberger, C.A. Dutch, MD (2nd)
Rush, Bobby L., IL (1st)
Ryan, Paul, WI (1st)
Ryan, Tim, OH (17th)
Salazar, John T., CO (3rd)
Sali, Bill, ID (1st)
Sánchez, Linda T., CA (39th)
Sanchez, Loretta, CA (47th)
Sarbanes, John P., MD (3rd)
Saxton, Jim, NJ (3rd)
Schakowsky, Janice D., IL (9th)
Schiff, Adam B., CA (29th)
Schmidt, Jean, OH (2nd)
Schwartz, Allyson Y., PA (13th)
Scott, David, GA (13th)
Scott, Robert C. ''Bobby'', VA (3rd)
Sensenbrenner, F. James, Jr., WI (5th)
Serrano, José E., NY (16th)
Sessions, Pete, TX (32nd)
Sestak, Joe, PA (7th)
Shadegg, John B., AZ (3rd)
Shays, Christopher, CT (4th)
Shea-Porter, Carol, NH (1st)
Sherman, Brad, CA (27th)
Shimkus, John, IL (19th)
Shuler, Heath, NC (11th)
Shuster, Bill, PA (9th)
Simpson, Michael K., ID (2nd)
Sires, Albio, NJ (13th)
Skelton, Ike, MO (4th)
Slaughter, Louise McIntosh, NY (28th)
Smith, Adam, WA (9th)
Smith, Adrian, NE (3rd)
Smith, Christopher H., NJ (4th)
Smith, Lamar, TX (21st)
Snyder, Vic, AR (2nd)
Solis, Hilda L., CA (32nd)
Souder, Mark E., IN (3rd)
Space, Zachary T., OH (18th)
Spratt, John M., Jr., SC (5th)
Stark, Fortney Pete, CA (13th)
Stearns, Cliff, FL (6th)
Stupak, Bart, MI (1st)

Sullivan, John, OK (1st)
Sutton, Betty, OH (13th)
Tancredo, Thomas G., CO (6th)
Tanner, John S., TN (8th)
Tauscher, Ellen O., CA (10th)
Taylor, Gene, MS (4th)
Terry, Lee, NE (2nd)
Thompson, Bennie G., MS (2nd)
Thompson, Mike, CA (1st)
Thornberry, Mac, TX (13th)
Tiahrt, Todd, KS (4th)
Tiberi, Patrick J., OH (12th)
Tierney, John F., MA (6th)
Towns, Edolphus, NY (10th)
Turner, Michael R., OH (3rd)
Udall, Mark, CO (2nd)
Udall, Tom, NM (3rd)
Upton, Fred, MI (6th)
Van Hollen, Chris, MD (8th)
Velázquez, Nydia M., NY (12th)
Visclosky, Peter J., IN (1st)
Walberg, Tim, MI (7th)
Walden, Greg, OR (2nd)
Walsh, James T., NY (25th)
Walz, Timothy J., MN (1st)
Wamp, Zach, TN (3rd)
Wasserman Schultz, Debbie, FL (20th)
Waters, Maxine, CA (35th)
Watson, Diane E., CA (33rd)
Watt, Melvin L., NC (12th)
Waxman, Henry A., CA (30th)
Weiner, Anthony D., NY (9th)
Welch, Peter, VT (At Large)
Weldon, Dave, FL (15th)
Weller, Jerry, IL (11th)
Westmoreland, Lynn A., GA (3rd)
Wexler, Robert, FL (19th)
Whitfield, Ed, KY (1st)
Wicker, Roger F., MS (1st)
Wilson, Charles A., OH (6th)
Wilson, Heather, NM (1st)
Wilson, Joe, SC (2nd)
Wolf, Frank R., VA (10th)
Woolsey, Lynn C., CA (6th)
Wu, David, OR (1st)
Wynn, Albert Russell, MD (4th)
Yarmuth, John A., KY (3rd)
Young, C.W. Bill, FL (10th)
Young, Don, AK (At Large)

DELEGATES
Bordallo, Madeleine Z., GU
Christensen, Donna M., VI
Faleomavaega, Eni F.H., AS
Norton, Eleanor Holmes, DC

RESIDENT COMISSIONER
Fortuño, Luis G., PR

110th Congress
Nine-Digit Postal ZIP Codes

Senate Post Office (20510): The four-digit numbers in these tables were assigned by the Senate Committee on Rules and Administration. Mail to all Senate offices is delivered by the main Post Office in the Dirksen Senate Office Building.

Senate Committees

Committee on Agriculture, Nutrition, and Forestry	–6000
Committee on Appropriations	–6025
Committee on Armed Services	–6050
Committee on Banking, Housing, and Urban Affairs	–6075
Committee on the Budget	–6100
Committee on Commerce, Science, and Transportation	–6125
Committee on Energy and Natural Resources	–6150
Committee on Environment and Public Works	–6175
Committee on Finance	–6200
Committee on Foreign Relations	–6225
Committee on Homeland Security and Governmental Affairs	–6250
Committee on Health, Education, Labor and Pensions	–6300
Committee on Indian Affairs	–6450
Committee on the Judiciary	–6275
Committee on Rules and Administration	–6325
Committee on Small Business and Entrepreneurship	–6350
Committee on Veterans' Affairs	–6375
Committee on Aging (Special)	–6400
Committee on Ethics (Select)	–6425
Committee on Intelligence (Select)	–6475

Joint Committee Offices, Senate Side

Joint Economic Committee	–6602
Joint Committee on the Library	–6625
Joint Committee on Printing	–6650
Joint Committee on Taxation	–6675

Senate Leadership Offices

President Pro Tempore	–7000
Chaplain	–7002
Majority Leader	–7010
Assistant Majority Leader	–7012
Secretary for the Majority	–7014
Minority Leader	–7020
Assistant Minority Leader	–7022
Secretary for the Minority	–7024
Democratic Policy Committee	–7050
Republican Conference	–7060
Secretary to the Republican Conference	–7062
Republican Policy Committee	–7064
Republican Steering Committee	–7066
Arms Control Observer Group	–7070

Senate Officers

Secretary of the Senate	–7100
Curator of Art and Antiquities	–7102
Disbursing Office	–7104
Document Room	–7106
Historian	–7108
Interparliamentary Services	–7110
Senate Library	–7112
Office of Senate Security	–7114
Office of Public Records	–7116
Office of Official Recorders of Debates	–7117
Stationery Room	–7118
Office of Printing Services	–7120
U.S. Capitol Preservation Commission	–7122
Office of Conservation and Preservation	–7124
Senate Gift Shop	–7128
Legal Counsel, Employment Management Relations	–7130
Senate Sergeant at Arms	–7200
General Counsel	–7201
Facilities	–7204
Finance Division	–7205
Hair Care Services	–7206
Procurement	–7207
Capitol Guides	–7209
Parking	–7210
Employee Assistance Program Office	–7211
Human Resources	–7212
Health Promotion Seminars	–7213
Placement	–7214
Senate Office of Education and Training	–7215
Photographic Studio	–7261
Capitol Police	–7218
Senate Post Office	–7263
Senate Recording Studio	–7222
Congressional Special Services Office	–7228
Customer Relations	–7230
CR-Customer Support	–7231

Other Offices on the Senate Side

Senate Legal Counsel	–7250
Central Operations (CO)—Administration	–7260
CO-Photo Studio	–7261
CO-Parking/ID	–7262
CO-Post Office	–7263
CO-Printing Graphics & Direct Mail—Production	–7264
CO-Recording	–7265
CO-Printing Graphics & Direct Mail—Reprographics	–7266
Chief of Operations	–7270
Deputy Chief of Operations	–7271
Senate Legislative Counsel	–7275
Program Management	–7276
Systems Architecture	–7277
Office Operations (OO)—Administration	–7280
OO-IT/Telecom Support	–7281
OO-Equipment Services	–7282
OO-Communication Installation & Support	–7283
OO-Desktop/LAN Support	–7284
OO-State Office Liasion	–7285
Technical Operations (TO)—Administration	–7290
TO-Applications Development	–7291
TO-Web & Technology Assessment	–7292
TO-Network Engineering & Management	–7293
TO-Enterprise It Systems	–7294
TO-Voice & RF Systems	–7295
TO-Inter/Intranet Services	–7296
Architect of the Capitol	–8000
Superintendent of Senate Buildings	–8002

Restaurant –8050
Amtrak Ticket Office –9010
Airlines Ticket Office (CATO) –9014
Child Care Center –9022
Credit Union –9026
Periodical Press Gallery –7234
Press Gallery –7238
Press Photo Gallery –7242
Radio and TV Gallery –7246
Webster Hall –7248
Office of Compliance –9061
Social Security Liaison –9064
Veterans Liaison –9054
Western Union –9058
Office of Senate Fair Employment Practices –9060
Frank Delano Roosevelt Memorial Commission –9066
Caucus on International Narcotics Control –9070
Army Liaison –9082
Air Force Liaison –9083
Coast Guard Liaison –9084
Navy Liaison –9085
Marine Liaison –9087

House Post Office (20515): Mail to all House offices is delivered by the main Post Office in the Longworth House Office Building.

House Committees, Leadership and Officers

U.S. House of Representatives –0001
Cannon House Office Building –0002
Rayburn House Office Building –0003
Longworth House Office Building –0004
O'Neill House Office Building –0005
Ford House Office Building –0006
The Capitol –0007
Office of the Chaplain –6655
Committee on Agriculture –6001
Committee on Appropriations –6015
Committee on Armed Services –6035
Committee on the Budget –6065
Committee on Education and Labor –6100
Committee on Energy and Commerce –6115
Committee on Financial Services –6050
Committee on Foreign Affairs –6128
Committee on Homeland Security –6480
Committee on House Administration –6157
Committee on the Judiciary –6216
Committee on Natural Resources –6201
Committee on Oversight and Government Reform –6143
Committee on Rules –6269
Committee on Science and Technology –6301
Committee on Small Business –6315
Committee on Standards of Official Conduct –6328
Committee on Transportation and Infrastructure –6256
Committee on Veterans' Affairs –6335
Committee on Ways and Means –6348
Select Committee on Energy Independence and Global Warming –6482
Select Committee on Intelligence –6415

Joint Committee Offices, House Side

Joint Economic Committee –6432
Joint Committee on the Library –6439
Joint Committee on Printing –6445
Joint Committee on Taxation –6453

House Leadership Offices

Office of the Speaker –6501
Office of the Majority Leader –6502
Office of the Majority Whip –6503
Office of the Deputy Majority Whip –6504
Democratic Caucus –6524
Democratic Congressional Campaign Committee –6525
Democratic Personnel Committee –6526
Democratic Steering and Policy Committee –6527
Democratic Cloakroom –6528
Office of the Republican Leader –6537
Office of the Republican Whip –6538
House Republican Conference –6544
House Republican Research Committee –6545
Legislative Digest (Republican Conference) –6546
Republican Congressional Committee, National –6547
Republican Policy Committee –6549
Republican Cloakroom –6650

House Officers

Office of the Clerk –6601
- Office of History and Preservation –6612
- Office of Employment and Counsel –6622
- House Page School –9996
- House Page Dorm –6606
- Legislative Computer Systems –6618
- Office of Legislative Operations –6602
- Legislative Resource Center –6612
- Official Reporters –6615
- Office of Publication Services –6611

Office of Interparliamentary Affairs –6579
Office of the House Historian –6701
Office of the Parliamentarian –6731
Chief Administrative Officer –6861
- First Call –6660
- Administrative Counsel –6660
- Periodical Press Gallery –6624
- Press Gallery –6625
- Radio/TV Correspondents' Gallery –6627
- HIR Call Center –6165
- HIR Information Systems Security –6165
- Outplacement Services –9920
- Office of Employee Assistance –6619
- ADA Services –6860
- Personnel and Benefits –9980
- Child Care Center –0001
- Payroll –9920
- Members' Services –9970
- Office Supply Service –6860
- House Gift Shop –6860
- Mail List/Processing –6860
- Mailing Services –6860
- Contractor Management –6860
- Photography –6623
- House Recording Studio –6613
- Furniture Support Services –6610
- House Office Service Center –6860
- Budget –6604
- Financial Counseling –6604
- Procurement Desktop Help –9940

Office of the Sergeant at Arms –6611

House Commissions and Offices

Congressional Executive Commission on China	–0001
Commission on Security and Cooperation in Europe	–6460
Commission on Congressional Mailing Standards	–6461
Office of the Law Revision Counsel	–6711
Office of Emergency Planning, Preparedness and Operations	–6462
Office of the Legislative Counsel	–6721
General Counsel	–6532
Architect of the Capitol	–6906
Attending Physician	–6907
Congressional Budget Office	–6925

Liaison Offices

Air Force	–6854
Army	–6855
Coast Guard	–6856
Navy	–6857
Office of Personnel Management	–6858
Veterans' Administration	–6859

TERMS OF SERVICE

EXPIRATION OF THE TERMS OF SENATORS

CLASS I.—SENATORS WHOSE TERMS OF SERVICE EXPIRE IN 2013

[32 Senators in this group: Democrats, 22; Republicans, 9; Independent, 1; Independent Democrat, 1]

Name	Party	Residence
Akaka, Daniel K.[1]	D.	Honolulu, HI.
Barraso, John[2]	R.	Casper, WY.
Bingaman, Jeff	D.	Santa Fe, NM.
Brown, Sherrod	D.	Avon, OH.
Byrd, Robert C.	D.	Sophia, WV.
Cantwell, Maria	D.	Edmonds, WA.
Cardin, Benjamin L.	D.	Baltimore, MD.
Carper, Thomas R.	D.	Wilmington, DE.
Casey, Robert P., Jr.	D.	Scranton, PA.
Clinton, Hillary Rodham	D.	Chappaqua, NY.
Conrad, Kent[3]	D.	Bismarck, ND.
Corker, Bob	R.	Chattanooga, TN.
Ensign, John	R.	Las Vegas, NV.
Feinstein, Dianne[4]	D.	San Francisco, CA.
Hatch, Orrin G.	R.	Salt Lake City, UT.
Hutchison, Kay Bailey[5]	R.	Dallas, TX.
Kennedy, Edward M.	D.	Barnstable, MA.
Klobuchar, Amy	D.	Minneapolis, MN.
Kohl, Herb	D.	Milwaukee, WI.
Kyl, Jon	R.	Phoenix, AZ.
Lieberman, Joseph I.	I.D.	New Haven, CT.
Lott, Trent	R.	Pascagoula, MS.
Lugar, Richard G.	R.	Indianapolis, IN.
McCaskill, Claire	D.	Kirkwood, MO.
Menendez, Robert[6]	D.	Hoboken, NJ.
Nelson, Bill	D.	Orlando, FL.
Nelson, E. Benjamin	D.	Omaha, NE.
Sanders, Bernard	I.	Burlington, VT.
Snowe, Olympia J.	R.	Auburn, ME.
Stabenow, Debbie	D.	Lansing, MI.
Tester, Jon	D.	Big Sandy, MT.
Webb, Jim	D.	Arlington, VA.
Whitehouse, Sheldon	D.	Providence, RI.

[1] Senator Akaka was appointed April 28, 1990, to fill the vacancy caused by the death of Senator Spark M. Matsunaga, and took the oath of office on May 16, 1990; subsequently elected in a special election on November 6, 1990, for the remainder of the unexpired term.

[2] Senator Barrasso was appointed on June 22, 2007, to fill the vacancy caused by the death of Senator Craig Thomas, and took the oath of office on June 25, 2007.

[3] Senator Conrad resigned his term from Class III after winning a special election on December 4, 1992, to fill the vacancy caused by the death of Senator Quentin Burdick. Senator Conrad's seniority in the Senate continues without a break in service. He took the oath of office on December 15, 1992.

[4] Senator Feinstein won the special election held on November 3, 1992, to fill the vacancy caused by the resignation of Senator Pete Wilson. She took the oath of office on November 10, 1992. This seat was filled, pending the election, by Senator John Seymour who was appointed on January 7, 1991.

[5] Senator Hutchison won the special election held on June 5, 1993, to fill remainder of the term of Senator Lloyd Bentsen. She took the oath of office on June 14, 1993. She won the seat from Senator Bob Krueger, who had been appointed on January 21, 1993.

[6] Senator Menendez was appointed on January 17, 2006, to fill the vacancy caused by the resignation of Senator Jon S. Corzine; subsequently elected to a full term in November 2006.

Class II.—SENATORS WHOSE TERMS OF SERVICE EXPIRE IN 2009

[33 Senators in this group: Democrats, 12; Republicans, 21]

Name	Party	Residence
Alexander, Lamar	R.	Nashville, TN.
Allard, Wayne	R.	Loveland, CO.
Baucus, Max	D.	Helena, MT.
Biden, Joseph R., Jr.	D.	Wilmington, DE.
Chambliss, Saxby	R.	Moultrie, GA.
Cochran, Thad	R.	Jackson, MS.
Coleman, Norm	R.	St. Paul, MN.
Collins, Susan M.	R.	Bangor, ME.
Cornyn, John	R.	San Antonio, TX.
Craig, Larry E.	R.	Payette, ID.
Dole, Elizabeth	R.	Salisbury, NC.
Domenici, Pete V.	R.	Albuquerque, NM.
Durbin, Richard	D.	Springfield, IL.
Enzi, Michael B.	R.	Gillette, WY.
Graham, Lindsey	R.	Seneca, SC.
Hagel, Chuck	R.	Omaha, NE.
Harkin, Tom	D.	Cumming, IA.
Inhofe, James M.[1]	R.	Tulsa, OK.
Johnson, Tim	D.	Vermillion, SD.
Kerry, John F.	D.	Boston, MA.
Landrieu, Mary L.	D.	New Orleans, LA.
Lautenberg, Frank R.[2]	D.	Cliffside Park, NJ.
Levin, Carl	D.	Detroit, MI.
McConnell, Mitch	R.	Louisville, KY.
Pryor, Mark L.	D.	Little Rock, AR.
Reed, Jack	D.	Jamestown, RI.
Roberts, Pat	R.	Dodge City, KS.
Rockefeller, John D., IV	D.	Charleston, WV.
Sessions, Jeff	R.	Mobile, AL.
Smith, Gordon H.	R.	Pendleton, OR.
Stevens, Ted[3]	R.	Girdwood, AK.
Sununu, John E.	R.	Bedford, NH.
Warner, John	R.	Alexandria, VA.

[1] Senator Inhofe won the special election held on November 8, 1994, to fill the remainder of the term of Senator David Boren, and took the oath of office on November 17, 1994. He was elected to a full term in 1996.

[2] Senator Lautenberg replaced Senator Robert Torricelli as the Democratic candidate for the U.S. Senate in October 2002.

[3] Senator Stevens was appointed on December 24, 1968, to fill the vacancy caused by the death of Senator E.L. Bartlett, and was elected in a special election on November 3, 1970, to complete the unexpired term ending January 3, 1973.

CLASS III.—SENATORS WHOSE TERMS OF SERVICE EXPIRE IN 2011

[34 Senators in this group: Democrats, 15; Republicans, 19]

Name	Party	Residence
Bayh, Evan	D.	Indianapolis, IN.
Bennett, Robert F.	R.	Salt Lake City, UT.
Bond, Christopher S.	R.	Mexico, MO.
Boxer, Barbara	D.	Palm Springs, CA.
Brownback, Sam [1]	R.	Topeka, KS.
Bunning, Jim	R.	Southgate, KY.
Burr, Richard	R,	Winston-Salem, NC.
Coburn, Tom	R.	Muskogee, OK.
Crapo, Mike	R.	Idaho Falls, ID.
DeMint, Jim	R.	Greenville, SC.
Dodd, Christopher J.	D.	East Haddam, CT.
Dorgan, Byron L.[2]	D.	Bismarck, ND.
Feingold, Russell D.	D.	Middleton, WI.
Grassley, Chuck	R.	Cedar Falls, IA.
Gregg, Judd	R.	Greenfield, NH.
Inouye, Daniel K.	D.	Honolulu, HI.
Isakson, Johnny	R.	Marietta, GA.
Leahy, Patrick J.	D.	Middlesex, VT.
Lincoln, Blanche L.	D.	Helena, AR.
Martinez, Mel	R.	Orlando, FL.
McCain, John	R.	Phoenix, AZ.
Mikulski, Barbara A.	D.	Baltimore, MD.
Murkowski, Lisa [3]	R.	Anchorage, AK.
Murray, Patty	D.	Seattle, WA.
Obama, Barack	D.	Chicago, IL.
Reid, Harry	D.	Searchlight, NV.
Salazar, Ken	D.	Denver, CO.
Schumer, Charles E.	D.	Brooklyn, NY.
Shelby, Richard C.[4]	R.	Tuscaloosa, AL.
Specter, Arlen	R.	Philadelphia, PA.
Thune, John	R.	Sioux Falls, SD.
Vitter, David	R	Metairie, LA.
Voinovich, George V.	R.	Cleveland, OH.
Wyden, Ron [5]	D.	Portland, OR.

[1] Senator Brownback was elected on November 5, 1996, to fill the remainder of the term of Senator Bob Dole. He took the oath of office on November 27, 1996. This seat was filled by Senator Sheila Frahm, who had been appointed, ad interim, on June 11, 1996.

[2] Senator Dorgan was elected to a 6-year term on November 3, 1992, and subsequently was appointed December 14, 1992 to fill the vacancy caused by the resignation of Senator Kent Conrad.

[3] Senator Murkowski was appointed on December 20, 2002, to fill the vacancy caused by the resignation of her father, Senator Frank Murkowski. She was elected to a full term in 2004.

[4] Senator Shelby changed parties on November 5, 1994.

[5] Senator Wyden won a special election on January 30, 1996, to fill the vacancy caused by the resignation of Senator Bob Packwood. He was reelected to a full term in 1998.

CONTINUOUS SERVICE OF SENATORS

[Democrats in roman (49); Republicans in *italic* (49); Independent in SMALL CAPS (1); Independent Democrat in *SMALL CAPS ITALIC* (1); total, 100]

Rank	Name	State	Beginning of present service
1	Byrd, Robert C.†	West Virginia	Jan. 3, 1959.
2	Kennedy, Edward M.[1]	Massachusetts	Nov. 7, 1962. ‡
3	Inouye, Daniel K.†	Hawaii	Jan. 3, 1963.
4	*Stevens, Ted*[2]	Alaska	Dec. 24, 1968.
5	Biden, Joseph R., Jr.	Delaware	Jan. 3, 1973.
	Domenici, Pete V.	New Mexico	
6	Leahy, Patrick J.	Vermont	Jan. 3, 1975.
7	*Hatch, Orrin G.*	Utah	Jan. 3, 1977.
	Lugar, Richard G.	Indiana	
8	Baucus, Max †[3]	Montana	Dec. 15, 1978.
9	*Cochran, Thad* †[4]	Mississippi	Dec. 27, 1978.
10	*Warner, John*[5]	Virginia	Jan. 2, 1979.
11	Levin, Carl	Michigan	Jan. 3, 1979.
12	Dodd, Christopher J.†	Connecticut	Jan. 3, 1981.
	Grassley, Chuck†	Iowa	
	Specter, Arlen	Pennsylvania	
13	Bingaman, Jeff	New Mexico	Jan. 3, 1983.
14	Kerry, John F.[6]	Massachusetts	Jan. 2, 1985.
15	Harkin, Tom †	Iowa	Jan. 3, 1985
	McConnell, Mitch	Kentucky	
16	Rockefeller, John D., IV[7]	West Virginia	Jan. 15, 1985.
17	*Bond, Christopher S.*	Missouri	Jan. 3, 1987.
	Conrad, Kent	North Dakota	
	McCain, John †	Arizona	
	Mikulski, Barbara A.†	Maryland	
	Reid, Harry †	Nevada	
	Shelby, Richard C.†	Alabama	
18	Kohl, Herb	Wisconsin	Jan. 3, 1989.
	LIEBERMAN, JOSEPH I.	Connecticut	
	Lott, Trent †	Mississippi	
19	Akaka, Daniel K.†[8]	Hawaii	May 16, 1990.
20	*Craig, Larry E.*†	Idaho	Jan. 3, 1991.
21	Feinstein, Dianne[9]	California	Nov. 3, 1992.‡
22	Dorgan, Byron L.†[10]	North Dakota	Dec. 14, 1992.
23	*Bennett, Robert F.*	Utah	Jan. 3, 1993.
	Boxer, Barbara †	California	
	Feingold, Russell D.	Wisconsin	
	Gregg, Judd †	New Hampshire	
	Murray, Patty	Washington	
24	*Hutchison, Kay Bailey*[11]	Texas	June 14, 1993.
25	*Inhofe, James M.* †[12]	Oklahoma	Nov. 17, 1994. ‡
26	*Kyl, Jon* †	Arizona	Jan. 3, 1995.
	Snowe, Olympia J.†	Maine	
27	Wyden, Ron †[13]	Oregon	Feb. 5, 1996. ‡
28	*Brownback, Sam* †[14]	Kansas	Nov. 7, 1996. ‡
29	*Hagel, Chuck*	Nebraska	Jan. 3, 1997.
	Allard, Wayne †	Colorado	
	Collins, Susan M.	Maine	
	Durbin, Richard †	Illinois	
	Enzi, Michael B.	Wyoming	
	Johnson, Tim †	South Dakota	
	Landrieu, Mary L.	Louisiana	
	Reed, Jack †	Rhode Island	

CONTINUOUS SERVICE OF SENATORS—CONTINUED

[Democrats in roman (49); Republicans in *italic* (49); Independent in SMALL CAPS (1); Independent Democrat in *SMALL CAPS ITALIC* (1); total, 100]

Rank	Name	State	Beginning of present service
	Roberts, Pat †	Kansas	Jan. 3, 1997.
	Sessions, Jeff	Alabama	
	Smith, Gordon H.	Oregon	
30	Bayh, Evan	Indiana	Jan. 3, 1999.
	Bunning, Jim †	Kentucky	
	Crapo, Mike †	Idaho	
	Lincoln, Blanche L. †	Arkansas	
	Schumer, Charles E. †	New York	
	Voinovich, George V.	Ohio	
31	Cantwell, Maria †	Washington	Jan. 3, 2001.
	Carper, Thomas R.†	Delaware	
	Clinton, Hillary Rodham	New York	
	Ensign, John †	Nevada	
	Nelson, Bill †	Florida	
	Nelson, E. Benjamin	Nebraska	
	Stabenow, Debbie †	Michigan	
32	*Cornyn, John* [15]	Texas	Dec. 2, 2002.
33	*Murkowski, Lisa* [16]	Alaska	Dec. 20, 2002.
34	*Alexander, Lamar*	Tennessee	Jan. 3, 2003.
	Chambliss, Saxby †	Georgia	
	Coleman, Norm	Minnesota	
	Dole, Elizabeth	North Carolina	
	Graham, Lindsey †	South Carolina	
	Lautenberg, Frank R. [17]	New Jersey	
	Pryor, Mark L.	Arkansas	
	Sununu, John †	New Hampshire	
35	*Burr, Richard* †	North Carolina	Jan. 3, 2005.
	Coburn, Tom †	Oklahoma	
	DeMint, Jim †	South Carolina	
	Isakson, Johnny †	Georgia	
	Martinez, Mel	Florida	
	Obama, Barack	Illinois	
	Salazar, Ken	Colorado	
	Thune, John †	South Dakota	
	Vitter, David †	Louisiana	
36	Menendez, Robert †[18]	New Jersey	Jan. 18, 2006.
37	Brown, Sherrod †	Ohio	Jan. 3, 2007.
	Cardin, Benjamin L. †	Maryland	
	Casey, Robert P., Jr.	Pennsylvania	
	Corker, Bob	Tennessee	
	Klobuchar, Amy	Minnesota	
	McCaskill, Claire	Missouri	
	SANDERS, BERNARD †	Vermont	
	Tester, Jon	Montana	
	Webb, Jim	Vermont	
	Whitehouse, Sheldon	Rhode Island	
38	Barrasso, John [19]	Wyoming	June 22, 2007.

† Served in the House of Representatives previous to service in the Senate.

‡ Senators elected to complete unexpired terms begin their terms on the day following the election.

1 Senator Kennedy was elected November 6, 1962, to complete the unexpired term caused by the resignation of Senator John F. Kennedy.

2 Senator Stevens was appointed December 24, 1968, to fill the vacancy caused by the death of Senator Edward L. Bartlett.

3 Senator Baucus was elected November 7, 1978, for the 6-year term commencing January 3, 1979; subsequently appointed December 15, 1978, to fill the vacancy caused by the resignation of Senator Paul Hatfield.

[4] Senator Cochran was elected November 6, 1978, for the 6-year term commencing January 3, 1979; subsequently appointed December 27, 1978, to fill the vacancy caused by the resignation of Senator James Eastland.

[5] Senator Warner was elected November 6, 1978, for the 6-year term commencing January 3, 1979; subsequently appointed January 2, 1979, to fill the vacancy caused by the resignation of Senator William Scott.

[6] Senator Kerry was elected November 6, 1984, for the 6-year term commencing January 3, 1985; subsequently appointed January 2, 1985, to fill the vacancy caused by the resignation of Senator Paul E. Tsongas.

[7] Senator Rockefeller was elected November 6, 1984, for the 6-year term commencing January 3, 1985; did not take his seat until January 15, 1985.

[8] Senator Akaka was appointed April 28, 1990, to fill the vacancy caused by the death of Senator Spark M. Matsunaga, and took the oath of office on May 16, 1990; subsequently elected in a special election on November 6, 1990, for the remainder of the unexpired term.

[9] Senator Feinstein was elected on November 3, 1992, to fill the vacancy caused by the resignation of Senator Pete Wilson. She replaced appointed Senator John Seymour when she took the oath of office on November 10, 1992.

[10] Senator Dorgan was elected to a 6-year term on November 3, 1992, and subsequently was appointed December 14, 1992 to complete the unexpired term of Senator Kent Conrad.

[11] Senator Hutchison won a special election on June 5, 1993, to fill the vacancy caused by the resignation of Senator Lloyd Bentsen. She won the seat from Senator Bob Krueger, who had been appointed on January 21, 1993.

[12] Senator Inhofe won the special election held on November 8, 1994, to fill the remainder of the term of Senator David Boren, and took the oath of office on November 17, 1994. He was elected to a full term in 1996.

[13] Senator Wyden won a special election on January 30, 1996, to fill the vacancy caused by the resignation of Senator Bob Packwood. He was reelected to a full term in 1998.

[14] Senator Brownback was elected on November 5, 1996, to fill the vacancy caused by the resignation of Senator Bob Dole. He replaced appointed Senator Sheila Frahm when he took the oath of office on November 27, 1996.

[15] Senator Cornyn was elected on November 5, 2002, for a 6-year term commencing January 3, 2003; subsequently appointed on December 2, 2002, to fill the vacancy caused by the resignation of Senator Phil Gramm.

[16] Senator Murkowski was appointed on December 20, 2002, to fill the vacancy caused by the resignation of her father, Senator Frank Murkowski. She was elected to a full term in 2004.

[17] Senator Lautenberg previously served in the Senate from December 27, 1982, until January 3, 2001.

[18] Senator Menendez was appointed on January 17, 2006, to fill the vacancy caused by the resignation of Senator Jon S. Corzine; subsequently elected to a full term in November 2006.

[19] Senator Barrasso was appointed on June 22, 2007, to fill the vacancy caused by the death of Senator Craig Thomas, and took the oath of office on June 25, 2007.

CONGRESSES IN WHICH REPRESENTATIVES HAVE SERVED, WITH BEGINNING OF PRESENT SERVICE

[* Elected to fill a vacancy; Democrats in roman (231); Republicans in *italic* (202); Vacancies (2); Resident Commissioner and Delegates in **boldface** (5); total, 440]

Name	State	Congresses (inclusive)	Beginning of present service
27 terms, consecutive			
Dingell, John D.	MI	*84th to 110th	Dec. 13, 1955
22 terms, consecutive			
Conyers, John, Jr.	MI	89th to 110th	Jan. 3, 1965
20 terms, consecutive			
Obey, David R.	WI	*91st to 110th	Apr. 1, 1969
19 terms, consecutive			
Rangel, Charles B.	NY	92d to 110th	Jan. 3, 1971
Young, C.W. Bill	FL	92d to 110th	Jan. 3, 1971
18 terms, consecutive			
Murtha, John P.	PA	*93d to 110th	Feb. 5, 1974
Regula, Ralph	OH	93d to 110th	Jan. 3, 1973
Stark, Fortney Pete	CA	93d to 110th	Jan. 3, 1973
Young, Don	AK	*93d to 110th	Mar. 6, 1973
17 terms, consecutive			
Markey, Edward J.	MA	*94th to 110th	Nov. 2, 1976
Miller, George	CA	94th to 110th	Jan. 3, 1975
Oberstar, James L.	MN	94th to 110th	Jan. 3, 1975
Waxman, Henry A.	CA	94th to 110th	Jan. 3, 1975
16 terms, consecutive			
Dicks, Norman D.	WA	95th to 110th	Jan. 3, 1977
Kildee, Dale E.	MI	95th to 110th	Jan. 3, 1977
Rahall, Nick J. II	WV	95th to 110th	Jan. 3, 1977
Skelton, Ike	MO	95th to 110th	Jan. 3, 1977
15 terms, consecutive			
Lewis, Jerry	CA	96th to 110th	Jan. 3, 1979
Petri, Thomas E.	WI	*96th to 110th	Apr. 3, 1979
Sensenbrenner, F. James, Jr.	WI	96th to 110th	Jan. 3, 1979
14 terms, consecutive			
Dreier, David	CA	97th to 110th	Jan. 3, 1981
Frank, Barney	MA	97th to 110th	Jan. 3, 1981
Hall, Ralph M.	TX	97th to 110th	Jan. 3, 1981
Hoyer, Steny H.	MD	*97th to 110th	May 19, 1981
Hunter, Duncan	CA	97th to 110th	Jan. 3, 1981
Lantos, Tom	CA	97th to 110th	Jan. 3, 1981
Rogers, Harold	KY	97th to 110th	Jan. 3, 1981
Smith, Christopher H.	NJ	97th to 110th	Jan. 3, 1981
Wolf, Frank R.	VA	97th to 110th	Jan. 3, 1981
13 terms, consecutive			
Ackerman, Gary L.	NY	*98th to 110th	Mar. 1, 1983

CONGRESSES IN WHICH REPRESENTATIVES HAVE SERVED, WITH BEGINNING OF PRESENT SERVICE—CONTINUED

[* Elected to fill a vacancy; Democrats in roman (231); Republicans in *italic* (202); Vacancies (2); Resident Commissioner and Delegates in **boldface** (5); total, 440]

Name	State	Congresses (inclusive)	Beginning of present service
Berman, Howard L.	CA	98th to 110th	Jan. 3, 1983
Boucher, Rick	VA	98th to 110th	Jan. 3, 1983
Burton, Dan	IN	98th to 110th	Jan. 3, 1983
Kaptur, Marcy	OH	98th to 110th	Jan. 3, 1983
Levin, Sander M.	MI	98th to 110th	Jan. 3, 1983
Mollohan, Alan B.	WV	98th to 110th	Jan. 3, 1983
Ortiz, Solomon P.	TX	98th to 110th	Jan. 3, 1983
Saxton, Jim	NJ	*98th to 110th	Nov. 6, 1984
Spratt, John M., Jr.	SC	98th to 110th	Jan. 3, 1983
Towns, Edolphus	NY	98th to 110th	Jan. 3, 1983
12 terms, consecutive			
Barton, Joe	TX	99th to 110th	Jan. 3, 1985
Coble, Howard	NC	99th to 110th	Jan. 3, 1985
Gordon, Bart	TN	99th to 110th	Jan. 3, 1985
Kanjorski, Paul E.	PA	99th to 110th	Jan. 3, 1985
Visclosky, Peter J.	IN	99th to 110th	Jan. 3, 1985
11 terms, consecutive			
Baker, Richard H.	LA	100th to 110th	Jan. 3, 1987
Costello, Jerry F.	IL	*100th to 110th	Aug. 9, 1988
DeFazio, Peter A.	OR	100th to 110th	Jan. 3, 1987
Duncan, John J., Jr.	TN	*100th to 110th	Nov. 8, 1988
Gallegly, Elton	CA	100th to 110th	Jan. 3, 1987
Hastert, J. Dennis	IL	100th to 110th	Jan. 3, 1987
Herger, Wally	CA	100th to 110th	Jan. 3, 1987
Lewis, John	GA	100th to 110th	Jan. 3, 1987
McCrery, Jim	LA	*100th to 110th	Apr. 16, 1988
Pallone, Frank, Jr.	NJ	*100th to 110th	Nov. 8, 1988
Pelosi, Nancy	CA	*100th to 110th	June 2, 1987
Shays, Christopher	CT	*100th to 110th	Aug. 18, 1987
Slaughter, Louise McIntosh	NY	100th to 110th	Jan. 3, 1987
Smith, Lamar	TX	100th to 110th	Jan. 3, 1987
Upton, Fred	MI	100th to 110th	Jan. 3, 1987
10 terms, consecutive			
Andrews, Robert E.	NJ	*101st to 110th	Nov. 6, 1990
Engel, Eliot L.	NY	101st to 110th	Jan. 3, 1989
Gillmor, Paul E.	OH	101st to 110th	Jan. 3, 1989
Lowey, Nita M.	NY	101st to 110th	Jan. 3, 1989
McDermott, Jim	WA	101st to 110th	Jan. 3, 1989
McNulty, Michael R.	NY	101st to 110th	Jan. 3, 1989
Neal, Richard E.	MA	101st to 110th	Jan. 3, 1989
Payne, Donald M.	NJ	101st to 110th	Jan. 3, 1989
Rohrabacher, Dana	CA	101st to 110th	Jan. 3, 1989
Ros-Lehtinen, Ileana	FL	*101st to 110th	Aug. 29, 1989
Serrano, José E.	NY	*101st to 110th	Mar. 20, 1990
Stearns, Cliff	FL	101st to 110th	Jan. 3, 1989
Tanner, John S.	TN	101st to 110th	Jan. 3, 1989
Taylor, Gene	MS	*101st to 110th	Oct. 17, 1989
Walsh, James T.	NY	101st to 110th	Jan. 3, 1989

CONGRESSES IN WHICH REPRESENTATIVES HAVE SERVED, WITH BEGINNING OF PRESENT SERVICE—CONTINUED

[* Elected to fill a vacancy; Democrats in roman (231); Republicans in *italic* (202); Vacancies (2); Resident Commissioner and Delegates in **boldface** (5); total, 440]

Name	State	Congresses (inclusive)	Beginning of present service
10 terms, not consecutive			
Abercrombie, Neil	HI	*99th, 102d to 110th.	Jan. 3, 1991
Paul, Ron	TX	94th, 96th to 98th, 105th to 110th.	Jan. 3, 1997
Price, David E.	NC	100th to 103d, 105th to 110th.	Jan 3. 1997
9 terms, consecutive			
Boehner, John A.	OH	102d to 110th	Jan. 3, 1991
Camp, Dave	MI	102d to 110th	Jan. 3, 1991
Cramer, Robert E. ''Bud'', Jr.	AL	102d to 110th	Jan. 3, 1991
DeLauro, Rosa L.	CT	102d to 110th	Jan. 3, 1991
Doolittle, John T.	CA	102d to 110th	Jan. 3, 1991
Edwards, Chet	TX	102d to 110th	Jan. 3, 1991
Gilchrest, Wayne T.	MD	102d to 110th	Jan. 3, 1991
Hobson, David L.	OH	102d to 110th	Jan. 3, 1991
Jefferson, William J.	LA	102d to 110th	Jan. 3, 1991
Johnson, Sam	TX	*102d to 110th	May 18, 1991
Moran, James P.	VA	102d to 110th	Jan. 3, 1991
Nadler, Jerrold	NY	*102d to 110th	Nov. 4, 1992
Olver, John W.	MA	*102d to 110th	June 4, 1991
Pastor, Ed	AZ	*102d to 110th	Sep. 24, 1991
Peterson, Collin C.	MN	102d to 110th	Jan. 3, 1991
Ramstad, Jim	MN	102d to 110th	Jan. 3, 1991
Waters, Maxine	CA	102d to 110th	Jan. 3, 1991
9 terms, not consecutive			
Cooper, Jim	TN	98th to 103d and 108th to 110th.	Jan. 3, 2003
8 terms, consecutive			
Bachus, Spencer	AL	103d to 110th	Jan. 3, 1993
Bartlett, Roscoe G.	MD	103d to 110th	Jan. 3, 1993
Becerra, Xavier	CA	103d to 110th	Jan. 3, 1993
Bishop, Sanford D., Jr.	GA	103d to 110th	Jan. 3, 1993
Brown, Corrine	FL	103d to 110th	Jan. 3, 1993
Buyer, Steve	IN	103d to 110th	Jan. 3, 1993
Calvert, Ken	CA	103d to 110th	Jan. 3, 1993
Castle, Michael N.	DE	103d to 110th	Jan. 3, 1993
Clyburn, James E.	SC	103d to 110th	Jan. 3, 1993
Deal, Nathan	GA	103d to 110th	Jan. 3, 1993
Diaz-Balart, Lincoln	FL	103d to 110th	Jan. 3, 1993
Ehlers, Vernon J.	MI	103d to 110th	Dec. 7, 1993
Eshoo, Anna G.	CA	103d to 110th	Jan. 3, 1993
Everett, Terry	AL	103d to 110th	Jan. 3, 1993
Farr, Sam	CA	*103d to 110th	June 8, 1993
Filner, Bob	CA	103d to 110th	Jan. 3, 1993
Goodlatte, Bob	VA	103d to 110th	Jan. 3, 1993
Green, Gene	TX	103d to 110th	Jan. 3, 1993
Gutierrez, Luis V.	IL	103d to 110th	Jan. 3, 1993
Hastings, Alcee L.	FL	103d to 110th	Jan. 3, 1993

CONGRESSES IN WHICH REPRESENTATIVES HAVE SERVED, WITH BEGINNING OF PRESENT SERVICE—CONTINUED

[* Elected to fill a vacancy; Democrats in roman (231); Republicans in *italic* (202); Vacancies (2); Resident Commissioner and Delegates in **boldface** (5); total, 440]

Name	State	Congresses (inclusive)	Beginning of present service
Hinchey, Maurice D.	NY	103d to 110th	Jan. 3, 1993
Hoekstra, Peter	MI	103d to 110th	Jan. 3, 1993
Holden, Tim	PA	103d to 110th	Jan. 3, 1993
Johnson, Eddie Bernice	TX	103d to 110th	Jan. 3, 1993
King, Peter T.	NY	103d to 110th	Jan. 3, 1993
Kingston, Jack	GA	103d to 110th	Jan. 3, 1993
Knollenberg, Joe	MI	103d to 110th	Jan. 3, 1993
Lewis, Ron	KY	*103d to 110th	May 17, 1994
Linder, John	GA	103d to 110th	Jan. 3, 1993
Lucas, Frank D.	OK	*103d to 110th	May 10, 1994
McHugh, John M.	NY	103d to 110th	Jan. 3, 1993
McKeon, Howard P. ''Buck''	CA	103d to 110th	Jan. 3, 1993
Maloney, Carolyn B.	NY	103d to 110th	Jan. 3, 1993
Manzullo, Donald A.	IL	103d to 110th	Jan. 3, 1993
Mica, John L.	FL	103d to 110th	Jan. 3, 1993
Pomeroy, Earl	ND	103d to 110th	Jan. 3, 1993
Pryce, Deborah	OH	103d to 110th	Jan. 3, 1993
Roybal-Allard, Lucille	CA	103d to 110th	Jan. 3, 1993
Royce, Edward R.	CA	103d to 110th	Jan. 3, 1993
Rush, Bobby L.	IL	103d to 110th	Jan. 3, 1993
Scott, Robert C. ''Bobby''	VA	103d to 110th	Jan. 3, 1993
Stupak, Bart	MI	103d to 110th	Jan. 3, 1993
Thompson, Bennie G.	MS	*103d to 110th	Apr. 13, 1993
Velázquez, Nydia M.	NY	103d to 110th	Jan. 3, 1993
Watt, Melvin L.	NC	103d to 110th	Jan. 3, 1993
Woolsey, Lynn C.	CA	103d to 110th	Jan. 3, 1993
Wynn, Albert Russell	MD	103d to 110th	Jan. 3, 1993
7 terms, consecutive			
Blumenauer, Earl	OR	*104th to 110th	May 21, 1996
Chabot, Steve	OH	104th to 110th	Jan. 3, 1995
Cubin, Barbara	WY	104th to 110th	Jan. 3, 1995
Cummings, Elijah E.	MD	*104th to 110th	Apr. 16, 1996
Davis, Tom	VA	104th to 110th	Jan. 3, 1995
Doggett, Lloyd	TX	104th to 110th	Jan. 3, 1995
Doyle, Michael F.	PA	104th to 110th	Jan. 3, 1995
Emerson, Jo Ann	MO	*104th to 110th	Nov. 5, 1996
English, Phil	PA	104th to 110th	Jan. 3, 1995
Fattah, Chaka	PA	104th to 110th	Jan. 3, 1995
Frelinghuysen, Rodney P.	NJ	104th to 110th	Jan. 3, 1995
Hastings, Doc	WA	104th to 110th	Jan. 3, 1995
Jackson Lee, Sheila	TX	104th to 110th	Jan. 3, 1995
Jackson, Jesse L., Jr.	IL	*104th to 110th	Dec. 12, 1995
Jones, Walter B.	NC	104th to 110th	Jan. 3, 1995
Kennedy, Patrick J.	RI	104th to 110th	Jan. 3, 1995
LaHood, Ray	IL	104th to 110th	Jan. 3, 1995
Latham, Tom	IA	104th to 110th	Jan. 3, 1995
LaTourette, Steven C.	OH	104th to 110th	Jan. 3, 1995
LoBiondo, Frank A.	NJ	104th to 110th	Jan. 3, 1995
Lofgren, Zoe	CA	104th to 110th	Jan. 3, 1995
Myrick, Sue Wilkins	NC	104th to 110th	Jan. 3, 1995

CONGRESSES IN WHICH REPRESENTATIVES HAVE SERVED, WITH BEGINNING OF PRESENT SERVICE—CONTINUED

[* Elected to fill a vacancy; Democrats in roman (231); Republicans in *italic* (202); Vacancies (2); Resident Commissioner and Delegates in **boldface** (5); total, 440]

Name	State	Congresses (inclusive)	Beginning of present service
Radanovich, George	CA	104th to 110th	Jan. 3, 1995
Shadegg, John B.	AZ	104th to 110th	Jan. 3, 1995
Souder, Mark E.	IN	104th to 110th	Jan. 3, 1995
Thornberry, Mac	TX	104th to 110th	Jan. 3, 1995
Tiahrt, Todd	KS	104th to 110th	Jan. 3, 1995
Wamp, Zach	TN	104th to 110th	Jan. 3, 1995
Weldon, Dave	FL	104th to 110th	Jan. 3, 1995
Weller, Jerry	IL	104th to 110th	Jan. 3, 1995
Whitfield, Ed	KY	104th to 110th	Jan. 3, 1995
Wicker, Roger F.	MS	104th to 110th	Jan. 3, 1995
7 terms, not consecutive			
Harman, Jane	CA	103d to 105th and 107th to 110th.	Jan. 3, 2001
Lungren, Daniel E.	CA	96th to 100th and 109th to 110th.	Jan. 3, 2005
6 terms			
Aderholt, Robert B.	AL	105th to 110th	Jan. 3, 1997
Allen, Thomas H.	ME	105th to 110th	Jan. 3, 1997
Berry, Marion	AR	105th to 110th	Jan. 3, 1997
Blunt, Roy	MO	105th to 110th	Jan. 3, 1997
Bono, Mary	CA	*105th to 110th	Apr. 7, 1998
Boswell, Leonard L.	IA	105th to 110th	Jan. 3, 1997
Boyd, Allen	FL	105th to 110th	Jan. 3, 1997
Brady, Kevin	TX	105th to 110th	Jan. 3, 1997
Brady, Robert A.	PA	*105th to 110th	May 19, 1998
Cannon, Chris	UT	105th to 110th	Jan. 3, 1997
Capps, Lois	CA	*105th to 110th	Mar. 10, 1998
Carson, Julia	IN	105th to 110th	Jan. 3, 1997
Davis, Danny K.	IL	105th to 110th	Jan. 3, 1997
DeGette, Diana	CO	105th to 110th	Jan. 3, 1997
Delahunt, William D.	MA	105th to 110th	Jan. 3, 1997
Etheridge, Bob	NC	105th to 110th	Jan. 3, 1997
Fossella, Vito	NY	*105th to 110th	Nov. 4, 1997
Goode, Virgil H., Jr.	VA	105th to 110th	Jan. 3, 1997
Granger, Kay	TX	105th to 110th	Jan. 3, 1997
Hinojosa, Rubén	TX	105th to 110th	Jan. 3, 1997
Hooley, Darlene	OR	105th to 110th	Jan. 3, 1997
Hulfshof, Kenny C.	MO	105th to 110th	Jan. 3, 1997
Kilpatrick, Carolyn C.	MI	105th to 110th	Jan. 3, 1997
Kind, Ron	WI	105th to 110th	Jan. 3, 1997
Kucinich, Dennis J.	OH	105th to 110th	Jan. 3, 1997
Lee, Barbara	CA	*105th to 110th	Apr. 7, 1998
McCarthy, Carolyn	NY	105th to 110th	Jan. 3, 1997
McGovern, James P.	MA	105th to 110th	Jan. 3, 1997
McIntyre, Mike	NC	105th to 110th	Jan. 3, 1997
Meeks, Gregory W.	NY	*105th to 110th	Feb. 3, 1998
Moran, Jerry	KS	105th to 110th	Jan. 3, 1997
Pascrell, Bill, Jr.	NJ	105th to 110th	Jan. 3, 1997
Peterson, John E.	PA	105th to 110th	Jan. 3, 1997
Pickering, Charles W. "Chip"	MS	105th to 110th	Jan. 3, 1997

CONGRESSES IN WHICH REPRESENTATIVES HAVE SERVED, WITH BEGINNING OF PRESENT SERVICE—CONTINUED

[* Elected to fill a vacancy; Democrats in roman (231); Republicans in *italic* (202); Vacancies (2); Resident Commissioner and Delegates in **boldface** (5); total, 440]

Name	State	Congresses (inclusive)	Beginning of present service
Pitts, Joseph R.	PA	105th to 110th	Jan. 3, 1997
Reyes, Silvestre	TX	105th to 110th	Jan. 3, 1997
Rothman, Steven R.	NJ	105th to 110th	Jan. 3, 1997
Sanchez, Loretta	CA	105th to 110th	Jan. 3, 1997
Sessions, Pete	TX	105th to 110th	Jan. 3, 1997
Sherman, Brad	CA	105th to 110th	Jan. 3, 1997
Shimkus, John	IL	105th to 110th	Jan. 3, 1997
Smith, Adam	WA	105th to 110th	Jan. 3, 1997
Snyder, Vic	AR	105th to 110th	Jan. 3, 1997
Tauscher, Ellen O.	CA	105th to 110th	Jan. 3, 1997
Tierney, John F.	MA	105th to 110th	Jan. 3, 1997
Wexler, Robert	FL	105th to 110th	Jan. 3, 1997
Wilson, Heather	NM	*105th to 110th	June 23, 1998
6 terms, not consecutive			
Inslee, Jay	WA	*103d, 106th to 110th.	Jan. 3, 1999
5 terms			
Baca, Joe	CA	*106th to 110th	Nov. 17, 1999
Baird, Brian	WA	106th to 110th	Jan. 3, 1999
Baldwin, Tammy	WI	106th to 110th	Jan. 3, 1999
Berkley, Shelley	NV	106th to 110th	Jan. 3, 1999
Biggert, Judy	IL	106th to 110th	Jan. 3, 1999
Capuano, Michael E.	MA	106th to 110th	Jan. 3, 1999
Crowley, Joseph	NY	106th to 110th	Jan. 3, 1999
Gonzalez, Charles A.	TX	106th to 110th	Jan. 3, 1999
Hayes, Robin	NC	106th to 110th	Jan. 3, 1999
Holt, Rush D.	NJ	106th to 110th	Jan. 3, 1999
Jones, Stephanie Tubbs	OH	106th to 110th	Jan. 3, 1999
Larson, John B.	CT	106th to 110th	Jan. 3, 1999
Miller, Gary G.	CA	106th to 110th	Jan. 3, 1999
Moore, Dennis	KS	106th to 110th	Jan. 3, 1999
Napolitano, Grace F.	CA	106th to 110th	Jan. 3, 1999
Reynolds, Thomas M.	NY	106th to 110th	Jan. 3, 1999
Ryan, Paul	WI	106th to 110th	Jan. 3, 1999
Schakowsky, Janice D.	IL	106th to 110th	Jan. 3, 1999
Simpson, Michael K.	ID	106th to 110th	Jan. 3, 1999
Tancredo, Thomas G.	CO	106th to 110th	Jan. 3, 1999
Terry, Lee	NE	106th to 110th	Jan. 3, 1999
Thompson, Mike	CA	106th to 110th	Jan. 3, 1999
Udall, Mark	CO	106th to 110th	Jan. 3, 1999
Udall, Tom	NM	106th to 110th	Jan. 3, 1999
Walden, Greg	OR	106th to 110th	Jan. 3, 1999
Weiner, Anthony D.	NY	106th to 110th	Jan. 3, 1999
Wu, David	OR	106th to 110th	Jan. 3, 1999
5 terms, not consecutive			
Bilbray, Brian P.	CA	104th to 106th and 109th to 110th.	June 13, 2006

CONGRESSES IN WHICH REPRESENTATIVES HAVE SERVED, WITH BEGINNING OF PRESENT SERVICE—CONTINUED

[* Elected to fill a vacancy; Democrats in roman (231); Republicans in *italic* (202); Vacancies (2); Resident Commissioner and Delegates in **boldface** (5); total, 440]

Name	State	Congresses (inclusive)	Beginning of present service
Inglis, Bob	SC	103d to 105th and 109th to 110th.	Jan. 3, 2005
Lampson, Nick	TX	105th to 108th and 110th.	Jan. 3, 2007
Rodriguez, Ciro D.	TX	105th to 108th and 110th.	Jan. 3, 2007
4 terms			
Akin, W. Todd	MO	107th to 110th	Jan. 3, 2001
Boozman, John	AR	*107th to 110th	Nov. 20, 2001
Brown, Henry E., Jr.	SC	107th to 110th	Jan. 3, 2001
Cantor, Eric	VA	107th to 110th	Jan. 3, 2001
Capito, Shelley Moore	WV	107th to 110th	Jan. 3, 2001
Clay, Wm. Lacy	MO	107th to 110th	Jan. 3, 2001
Crenshaw, Ander	FL	107th to 110th	Jan. 3, 2001
Culberson, John Abney	TX	107th to 110th	Jan. 3, 2001
Davis, Jo Ann	VA	107th to 110th	Jan. 3, 2001
Davis, Susan A.	CA	107th to 110th	Jan. 3, 2001
Ferguson, Mike	NJ	107th to 110th	Jan. 3, 2001
Flake, Jeff	AZ	107th to 110th	Jan. 3, 2001
Forbes, J. Randy	VA	*107th to 110th	June 19, 2001
Graves, Sam	MO	107th to 110th	Jan. 3, 2001
Honda, Michael M.	CA	107th to 110th	Jan. 3, 2001
Israel, Steve	NY	107th to 110th	Jan. 3, 2001
Issa, Darrell E.	CA	107th to 110th	Jan. 3, 2001
Johnson, Timothy V.	IL	107th to 110th	Jan. 3, 2001
Keller, Ric	FL	107th to 110th	Jan. 3, 2001
Kirk, Mark Steven	IL	107th to 110th	Jan. 3, 2001
Langevin, James R.	RI	107th to 110th	Jan. 3, 2001
Larsen, Rick	WA	107th to 110th	Jan. 3, 2001
Lynch, Stephen F.	MA	*107th to 110th	Oct. 16, 2001
McCollum, Betty	MN	107th to 110th	Jan. 3, 2001
Matheson, Jim	UT	107th to 110th	Jan. 3, 2001
Miller, Jeff	FL	*107th to 110th	Oct. 16, 2001
Pence, Mike	IN	107th to 110th	Jan. 3, 2001
Platts, Todd Russell	ID	107th to 110th	Jan. 3, 2001
Putnam, Adam H.	FL	107th to 110th	Jan. 3, 2001
Rehberg, Dennis R.	MT	107th to 110th	Jan. 3, 2001
Rogers, Mike	MI	107th to 110th	Jan. 3, 2001
Ross, Mike	AR	107th to 110th	Jan. 3, 2001
Schiff, Adam B.	CA	107th to 110th	Jan. 3, 2001
Shuster, Bill	PA	*107th to 110th	May 15, 2001
Solis, Hilda L.	CA	107th to 110th	Jan. 3, 2001
Sullivan, John	OK	*107th to 110th	Feb. 27, 2002
Tiberi, Patrick J.	OH	107th to 110th	Jan. 3, 2001
Watson, Diane E.	CA	*107th to 110th	June 5, 2001
Wilson, Joe	SC	*107th to 110th	Dec. 18, 2001
4 terms, not consecutive			
Hill, Baron P.	IN	106th to 108th and 110th.	Jan. 3, 2007

CONGRESSES IN WHICH REPRESENTATIVES HAVE SERVED, WITH BEGINNING OF PRESENT SERVICE—CONTINUED

[* Elected to fill a vacancy; Democrats in roman (231); Republicans in *italic* (202); Vacancies (2); Resident Commissioner and Delegates in **boldface** (5); total, 440]

Name	State	Congresses (inclusive)	Beginning of present service
3 terms			
Alexander, Rodney	LA	108th to 110th	Jan. 3, 2003
Barrett, J. Gresham	SC	108th to 110th	Jan. 3, 2003
Bishop, Rob	UT	108th to 110th	Jan. 3, 2003
Bishop, Timothy H.	NY	108th to 110th	Jan. 3, 2003
Blackburn, Marsha	TN	108th to 110th	Jan. 3, 2003
Bonner, Jo	AL	108th to 110th	Jan. 3, 2003
Brown-Waite, Ginny	FL	108th to 110th	Jan. 3, 2003
Burgess, Michael C.	TX	108th to 110th	Jan. 3, 2003
Butterfield, G.K.	NC	* 108th to 110th	July 20, 2004
Cardoza, Dennis A.	CA	108th to 110th	Jan. 3, 2003
Carter, John R.	TX	108th to 110th	Jan. 3, 2003
Chandler, Ben	KY	* 108th to 110th	Feb. 17, 2004
Cole, Tom	OK	108th to 110th	Jan. 3, 2003
Davis, Artur	AL	108th to 110th	Jan. 3, 2003
Davis, Lincoln	TN	108th to 110th	Jan. 3, 2003
Diaz-Balart, Mario	FL	108th to 110th	Jan. 3, 2003
Emanuel, Rahm	IL	108th to 110th	Jan. 3, 2003
Feeney, Tom	FL	108th to 110th	Jan. 3, 2003
Franks, Trent	AZ	108th to 110th	Jan. 3, 2003
Garrett, Scott	NJ	108th to 110th	Jan. 3, 2003
Gerlach, Jim	PA	108th to 110th	Jan. 3, 2003
Gingrey, Phil	GA	108th to 110th	Jan. 3, 2003
Grijalva, Raúl M.	AZ	108th to 110th	Jan. 3, 2003
Hensarling, Jeb	TX	108th to 110th	Jan. 3, 2003
Herseth Sandlin, Stephanie	SD	* 108th to 110th	June 1, 2004
King, Steve	IA	108th to 110th	Jan. 3, 2003
Kline, John	MN	108th to 110th	Jan. 3, 2003
Marshall, Jim	GA	108th to 110th	Jan. 3, 2003
McCotter, Thaddeus G.	MI	108th to 110th	Jan. 3, 2003
Meek, Kendrick B.	FL	108th to 110th	Jan. 3, 2003
Michaud, Michael H.	ME	108th to 110th	Jan. 3, 2003
Miller, Brad	NC	108th to 110th	Jan. 3, 2003
Miller, Candice S.	MI	108th to 110th	Jan. 3, 2003
Murphy, Tim	PA	108th to 110th	Jan. 3, 2003
Musgrave, Marilyn N.	CO	108th to 110th	Jan. 3, 2003
Neugebauer, Randy	TX	*108th to 110th	June 3, 2003
Nunes, Devin	CA	108th to 110th	Jan. 3, 2003
Pearce, Stevan	NM	108th to 110th	Jan. 3, 2003
Porter, Jon C.	NV	108th to 110th	Jan. 3, 2003
Renzi, Rick	AZ	108th to 110th	Jan. 3, 2003
Rogers, Mike	AL	108th to 110th	Jan. 3, 2003
Ruppersberger, C.A. Dutch	MD	108th to 110th	Jan. 3, 2003
Ryan, Tim	OH	108th to 110th	Jan. 3, 2003
Sánchez, Linda T.	CA	108th to 110th	Jan. 3, 2003
Scott, David	GA	108th to 110th	Jan. 3, 2003
Turner, Michael R.	OH	108th to 110th	Jan. 3, 2003
Van Hollen, Chris	MD	108th to 110th	Jan. 3, 2003
2 terms			
Barrow, John	GA	109th and 110th	Jan. 3, 2005

CONGRESSES IN WHICH REPRESENTATIVES HAVE SERVED, WITH BEGINNING OF PRESENT SERVICE—CONTINUED

[* Elected to fill a vacancy; Democrats in roman (231); Republicans in *italic* (202); Vacancies (2); Resident Commissioner and Delegates in **boldface** (5); total, 440]

Name	State	Congresses (inclusive)	Beginning of present service
Bean, Melissa L.	IL	109th and 110th	Jan. 3, 2005
Boren, Dan	OK	109th and 110th	Jan. 3, 2005
Boustany, Charles W., Jr.	LA	109th and 110th	Jan. 3, 2005
Campbell, John	CA	109th and 110th	Dec. 7, 2005
Carnahan, Russ	MO	109th and 110th	Jan. 3, 2005
Cleaver, Emanuel	MO	109th and 110th	Jan. 3, 2005
Conaway, K. Michael	TX	109th and 110th	Jan. 3, 2005
Costa, Jim	CA	109th and 110th	Jan. 3, 2005
Cuellar, Henry	TX	109th and 110th	Jan. 3, 2005
Davis, Geoff	KY	109th and 110th	Jan. 3, 2005
Dent, Charles W.	PA	109th and 110th	Jan. 3, 2005
Drake, Thelma D.	VA	109th and 110th	Jan. 3, 2005
Fortenberry, Jeff	NE	109th and 110th	Jan. 3, 2005
Foxx, Virginia	NC	109th and 110th	Jan. 3, 2005
Gohmert, Louie	TX	109th and 110th	Jan. 3, 2005
Green, Al	TX	109th and 110th	Jan. 3, 2005
Higgins, Brian	NY	109th and 110th	Jan. 3, 2005
Jindal, Bobby	LA	109th and 110th	Jan. 3, 2005
Kuhl, John R. ''Randy'', Jr.	NY	109th and 110th	Jan. 3, 2005
Lipinski, Daniel	IL	109th and 110th	Jan. 3, 2005
McCaul, Michael T.	TX	109th and 110th	Jan. 3, 2005
McHenry, Patrick T.	NC	109th and 110th	Jan. 3, 2005
McMorris Rodgers, Cathy	WA	109th and 110th	Jan. 3, 2005
Mack, Connie	FL	109th and 110th	Jan. 3, 2005
Marchant, Kenny	TX	109th and 110th	Jan. 3, 2005
Matsui, Doris O.	CA	109th and 110th	Mar. 10, 2005
Melancon, Charlie	LA	109th and 110th	Jan. 3, 2005
Moore, Gwen	WI	109th and 110th	Jan. 3, 2005
Poe, Ted	TX	109th and 110th	Jan. 3, 2005
Price, Tom	GA	109th and 110th	Jan. 3, 2005
Reichert, David G.	WA	109th and 110th	Jan. 3, 2005
Salazar, John T.	CO	109th and 110th	Jan. 3, 2005
Schwartz, Allyson Y.	PA	109th and 110th	Jan. 3, 2005
Schmidt, Jean	OH	109th and 110th	Sept. 6, 2005
Sires, Albio	NJ	109th and 110th	Nov. 13, 2006
Wasserman Schultz, Debbie	FL	109th and 110th	Jan. 3, 2005
Westmoreland, Lynn A.	GA	109th and 110th	Jan. 3, 2005
1 term			
Altmire, Jason	PA	110th	Jan. 3, 2007
Arcuri, Michael A.	NY	110th	Jan. 3, 2007
Bachmann, Michele	MN	110th	Jan. 3, 2007
Bilirakis, Gus M.	FL	110th	Jan. 3, 2007
Boyda, Nancy E.	KS	110th	Jan. 3, 2007
Braley, Bruce L.	IA	110th	Jan. 3, 2007
Broun, Paul C.	GA	110th	July 17, 2007
Buchanan, Vern	FL	110th	Jan. 3, 2007
Carney, Christopher P.	PA	110th	Jan. 3, 2007
Castor, Kathy	FL	110th	Jan. 3, 2007
Clarke, Yvette D.	NY	110th	Jan. 3, 2007
Cohen, Steve	TN	110th	Jan. 3, 2007
Courtney, Joe	CT	110th	Jan. 3, 2007

CONGRESSES IN WHICH REPRESENTATIVES HAVE SERVED, WITH BEGINNING OF PRESENT SERVICE—CONTINUED

[* Elected to fill a vacancy; Democrats in roman (231); Republicans in *italic* (202); Vacancies (2); Resident Commissioner and Delegates in **boldface** (5); total, 440]

Name	State	Congresses (inclusive)	Beginning of present service
Davis, David	TN	110th	Jan. 3, 2007
Donnelly, Joe	IN	110th	Jan. 3, 2007
Ellison, Keith	MN	110th	Jan. 3, 2007
Ellsworth, Brad	OK	110th	Jan. 3, 2007
Fallin, Mary	OK	110th	Jan. 3, 2007
Giffords, Gabrielle	AZ	110th	Jan. 3, 2007
Gillibrand, Kirsten E.	NY	110th	Jan. 3, 2007
Hall, John J.	NY	110th	Jan. 3, 2007
Hare, Phil	IL	110th	Jan. 3, 2007
Heller, Dean	NV	110th	Jan. 3, 2007
Hill, Baron P.	IN	110th	Jan. 3, 2007
Hirono, Mazie K.	HI	110th	Jan. 3, 2007
Hodes, Paul W.	NH	110th	Jan. 3, 2007
Johnson, Henry C. ''Hank'', Jr.	GA	110th	Jan. 3, 2007
Jordan, Jim	OH	110th	Jan. 3, 2007
Kagen, Steve	WI	110th	Jan. 3, 2007
Klein, Ron	FL	110th	Jan. 3, 2007
Lamborn, Doug	CO	110th	Jan. 3, 2007
Lampson, Nick	TX	110th	Jan. 3, 2007
Loebsack, David	IA	110th	Jan. 3, 2007
Mahoney, Tim	FL	110th	Jan. 3, 2007
McCarthy, Kevin	CA	110th	Jan. 3, 2007
McNerney, Jerry	CA	110th	Jan. 3, 2007
Mitchell, Harry E.	AZ	110th	Jan. 3, 2007
Murphy, Christopher S.	CT	110th	Jan. 3, 2007
Murphy, Patrick J.	PA	110th	Jan. 3, 2007
Perlmutter, Ed	CO	110th	Jan. 3, 2007
Roskam, Peter J.	IL	110th	Jan. 3, 2007
Sali, Bill	ID	110th	Jan. 3, 2007
Sarbanes, John P.	MD	110th	Jan. 3, 2007
Sestak, Joe	PA	110th	Jan. 3, 2007
Shea-Porter, Carol	NH	110th	Jan. 3, 2007
Shuler, Heath	NC	110th	Jan. 3, 2007
Smith, Adrian	NE	110th	Jan. 3, 2007
Space, Zackary T.	OH	110th	Jan. 3, 2007
Sutton, Betty	OH	110th	Jan. 3, 2007
Walberg, Timothy	MI	110th	Jan. 3, 2007
Walz, Timothy J.	MN	110th	Jan. 3, 2007
Welch, Peter	VT	110th	Jan. 3, 2007
Wilson, Charles A.	OH	110th	Jan. 3, 2007
Yarmuth, John A.	KY	110th	Jan. 3, 2007
RESIDENT COMMISSIONER			
Fortuño, Luis G.	PR	109th and 110th	Jan. 3, 2005
DELEGATES			
Faleomavaega, Eni F.H.	AS	101st to 110th	Jan. 3, 1989
Norton, Eleanor Holmes	DC	102d to 110th	Jan. 3, 1991
Christensen, Donna M.	VI	105th to 110th	Jan. 3, 1997

CONGRESSES IN WHICH REPRESENTATIVES HAVE SERVED, WITH BEGINNING OF PRESENT SERVICE—CONTINUED

[*Elected to fill a vacancy; Democrats in roman (231); Republicans in *italic* (202); Vacancies (2); Resident Commissioner and Delegates in **boldface** (5); total, 440]

Name	State	Congresses (inclusive)	Beginning of present service
Bordallo, Madeleine Z.	GU	108th to 110th	Jan. 3, 2003

NOTE: Members elected by special election are considered to begin service on the date of the election, except for those elected after a sine die adjournment. If elected after the Congress has adjourned for the session, Members are considered to begin their service on the day after the election.

STANDING COMMITTEES OF THE SENATE

[Democrats in roman; Republicans in *italic*; Independent in SMALL CAPS; Independent Democrat in *SMALL CAPS ITALIC*]

[Room numbers beginning with SD are in the Dirksen Building, SH in the Hart Building, SR in the Russell Building, and S in The Capitol]

Agriculture, Nutrition, and Forestry

328A Russell Senate Office Building 20510–6000

phone 224–2035, fax 224–1725, TTY / TDD 224–2587

http://agriculture.senate.gov

meets first and third Wednesdays of each month

Tom Harkin, of Iowa, *Chair*

Patrick J. Leahy, of Vermont.
Kent Conrad, of North Dakota.
Max Baucus, of Montana.
Blanche L. Lincoln, of Arkansas.
Debbie Stabenow, of Michigan.
E. Benjamin Nelson, of Nebraska.
Ken Salazar, of Colorado.
Sherrod Brown, of Ohio.
Robert P. Casey, Jr., of Pennsylvania.
Amy Klobuchar, of Minnesota.

Saxby Chambliss, of Georgia.
Richard G. Lugar, of Indiana.
Thad Cochran, of Mississippi.
Mitch McConnell, of Kentucky.
Pat Roberts, of Kansas.
Lindsey Graham, of South Carolina.
Norm Coleman, of Minnesota.
Mike Crapo, of Idaho.
John Thune, of South Dakota.
Chuck Grassley, of Iowa.

SUBCOMMITTEES

[The chairman and ranking minority member are ex officio (non-voting) members of all subcommittees on which they do not serve.]

Domestic and Foreign Marketing, Inspection, and Plant and Animal Health

Max Baucus, of Montana, *Chair*

Kent Conrad, of North Dakota.
Debbie Stabenow, of Michigan.
E. Benjamin Nelson, of Nebraska.
Ken Salazar, of Colorado.
Robert P. Casey, Jr., of Pennsylvania.

Lindsey Graham, of South Carolina.
Mitch McConnell, of Kentucky.
Pat Roberts, of Kansas.
Mike Crapo, of Idaho.
John Thune, of South Dakota.

Energy, Science and Technology

Kent Conrad, of North Dakota, *Chair*

E. Benjamin Nelson, of Nebraska.
Ken Salazar, of Colorado.
Sherrod Brown, of Ohio.
Robert P. Casey, Jr., of Pennsylvania.
Amy Klobuchar, of Minnesota.

John Thune, of South Dakota.
Richard G. Lugar, of Indiana.
Lindsey Graham, of South Carolina.
Norm Coleman, of Minnesota.
Chuck Grassley, of Iowa.

Nutrition and Food Assistance, Sustainable and Organic Agriculture, and General Legislation

Patrick J. Leahy, of Vermont, *Chair*

Blanche L. Lincoln, of Arkansas.
Debbie Stabenow, of Michigan.
Sherrod Brown, of Ohio.
Robert P. Casey, Jr., of Pennsylvania.
Amy Klobuchar, of Minnesota.

Norm Coleman, of Minnesota.
Richard G. Lugar, of Indiana.
Thad Cochran, of Mississippi.
Mitch McConnell, of Kentucky.
Mike Crapo, of Idaho.

Production, Income Protection and Price Support

Blanche L. Lincoln, of Arkansas, *Chair*

Patrick J. Leahy, of Vermont.
Kent Conrad, of North Dakota.
Max Baucus, of Montana.
Sherrod Brown, of Ohio.
Amy Klobuchar, of Minnesota.

Pat Roberts, of Kansas.
Thad Cochran, of Mississippi.
Norm Coleman, of Minnesota.
John Thune, of South Dakota.
Chuck Grassley, of Iowa.

Rural Revitalization, Conservation, Forestry and Credit Jurisdiction

Debbie Stabenow, of Michigan, *Chair*

Patrick J. Leahy, of Vermont.
Max Baucus, of Montana.
Blanche L. Lincoln, of Arkansas.
E. Benjamin Nelson, of Nebraska.
Ken Salazar, of Colorado.

Mike Crapo, of Idaho.
Richard G. Lugar, of Indiana.
Thad Cochran, of Mississippi.
Mitch McConnell, of Kentucky.
Lindsey Graham, of South Carolina.

STAFF

Committee on Agriculture, Nutrition, and Forestry (SR–328A), 224–2035, fax 224–1725.
Majority Staff Director.—Mark Halverson.
Senior Professional Staff: Richard Bender, Ellen King-Huntoon.
Senior Counsel.—Susan Keith.
Counsels: Phil Buchan, Derek Miller.
Professional Staff: Todd Batta, Dan Christenson, Katharine Ferguson, John Ferrell, Katherine Johannson, Jenelle Krishnamoorthy, Adela Ramos, Shakti.
Chief Economist.—Stephanie Mercier.
Communications Director.—Kate Cyrul.
Chief Clerk/System Administrator.—Robert Sturm.
Systems Administrator.—Jacob Chaney.
Staff Assistant.—Peter Kelley.
Legislative Correspondent.—Jonathan Urban.
Minority Staff Director.—Martha Scott Poindexter.
General Counsel.—Vernie Hubert.
Senior Policy Director.—Kate Coler.
Communications Director.—Erin Hamm.
Senior Economist.—Haydon Milberg.
Senior Professional Staff: Elizabeth Crocker, Christy Seyfert.
Professional Staff: Cameron Bruett, Matt Coley, Jane Anna Harris, Eric Steiner.

Appropriations

S–128 The Capitol 20510–6025, phone 224–7363

http://appropriations.senate.gov

meets upon call of the chair

Robert C. Byrd, of West Virginia, *Chair*

Daniel K. Inouye, of Hawaii.
Patrick J. Leahy, of Vermont.
Tom Harkin, of Iowa.
Barbara A. Mikulski, of Maryland.
Herb Kohl, of Wisconsin.
Patty Murray, of Washington.
Byron L. Dorgan, of North Dakota.
Dianne Feinstein, of California.
Richard Durbin, of Illinois.
Tim Johnson, of South Dakota.
Mary L. Landrieu, of Louisiana.
Jack Reed, of Rhode Island.
Frank R. Lautenberg, of New Jersey.
E. Benjamin Nelson, of Nebraska.

Thad Cochran, of Mississippi.
Ted Stevens, of Alaska.
Arlen Specter, of Pennsylvania.
Pete V. Domenici, of New Mexico.
Christopher S. Bond, of Missouri.
Mitch McConnell, of Kentucky.
Richard C. Shelby, of Alabama.
Judd Gregg, of New Hampshire.
Robert F. Bennett, of Utah.
Larry E. Craig, of Idaho.
Kay Bailey Hutchison, of Texas.
Sam Brownback, of Kansas.
Wayne Allard, of Colorado.
Lamar Alexander, of Tennessee.

SUBCOMMITTEES

[The chairman and ranking minority member are ex officio members of all subcommittees on which they do not serve.]

Agriculture, Rural Development, Food and Drug Administration, and Related Agencies

Herb Kohl, of Wisconsin, *Chair*

Tom Harkin, of Iowa.
Byron L. Dorgan, of North Dakota.
Dianne Feinstein, of California.
Richard Durbin, of Illinois.
Tim Johnson, of South Dakota.
E. Benjamin Nelson, of Nebraska.
Jack Reed, of Rhode Island.

Robert F. Bennett, of Utah.
Thad Cochran, of Mississippi.
Arlen Specter, of Pennsylvania.
Christopher S. Bond, of Missouri.
Mitch McConnell, of Kentucky.
Larry E. Craig, of Idaho.
Sam Brownback, of Kansas.

Commerce, Justice, Science, and Related Agencies

Barbara A. Mikulski, of Maryland, *Chair*

Daniel K. Inouye, of Hawaii.
Patrick J. Leahy, of Vermont.
Herb Kohl, of Wisconsin.
Tom Harkin, of Iowa.
Byron L. Dorgan, of North Dakota.
Dianne Feinstein, of California.
Jack Reed, of Rhode Island.
Frank R. Lautenberg, of New Jersey.

Richard C. Shelby, of Alabama.
Judd Gregg, of New Hampshire.
Ted Stevens, of Alaska.
Pete V. Domenici, of New Mexico.
Mitch McConnell, of Kentucky.
Kay Bailey Hutchison, of Texas.
Sam Brownback, of Kansas.
Lamar Alexander, of Tennessee.

Defense

Daniel K. Inouye, of Hawaii, *Chair*

Robert C. Byrd, of West Virginia.
Patrick J. Leahy, of Vermont.
Tom Harkin, of Iowa.
Byron L. Dorgan, of North Dakota.
Richard Durbin, of Illinois.
Dianne Feinstein, of California.
Barbara A. Mikulski, of Maryland.
Herb Kohl, of Wisconsin.
Patty Murray, of Washington.

Ted Stevens, of Alaska.
Thad Cochran, of Mississippi.
Arlen Specter, of Pennsylvania.
Pete V. Domenici, of New Mexico.
Christopher S. Bond, of Missouri.
Mitch McConnell, of Kentucky.
Richard C. Shelby, of Alabama.
Judd Gregg, of New Hampshire.
Kay Bailey Hutchison, of Texas.

Energy and Water Development

Byron L. Dorgan, of North Dakota, *Chair*

Robert C. Byrd, of West Virginia.
Patty Murray, of Washington.
Dianne Feinstein, of California.
Tim Johnson, of South Dakota.
Mary L. Landrieu, of Louisiana.
Daniel K. Inouye, of Hawaii.
Jack Reed, of Rhode Island.
Frank R. Lautenberg, of New Jersey.

Pete V. Domenici, of New Mexico.
Thad Cochran, of Mississippi.
Mitch McConnell, of Kentucky.
Robert F. Bennett, of Utah.
Larry E. Craig, of Idaho.
Christopher S. Bond, of Missouri.
Kay Bailey Hutchison, of Texas.
Wayne Allard, of Colorado.

Financial Services and General Government

Richard Durbin, of Illinois, *Chair*

Patty Murray, of Washington.
Mary L. Landrieu, of Louisiana.
Frank R. Lautenberg, of New Jersey.
E. Benjamin Nelson, of Nebraska.

Sam Brownback, of Kansas.
Christopher S. Bond, of Missouri.
Richard C. Shelby, of Alabama.
Wayne Allard, of Colorado.

Homeland Security

Robert C. Byrd, of West Virginia, *Chair*

Daniel K. Inouye, of Hawaii.
Patrick J. Leahy, of Vermont.
Barbara A. Mikulski, of Maryland.
Herb Kohl, of Wisconsin.
Patty Murray, of Washington.
Mary L. Landrieu, of Louisiana.
Frank R. Lautenberg, of New Jersey.
E. Benjamin Nelson, of Nebraska.

Thad Cochran, of Mississippi.
Judd Gregg, of New Hampshire.
Ted Stevens, of Alaska.
Arlen Specter, of Pennsylvania.
Pete V. Domenici, of New Mexico.
Richard C. Shelby, of Alabama.
Larry E. Craig, of Idaho.
Lamar Alexander, of Tennessee.

Interior, Environment, and Related Agencies

Dianne Feinstein, of California, *Chair*

Robert C. Byrd, of West Virginia.
Patrick J. Leahy, of Vermont.
Byron L. Dorgan, of North Dakota.
Barbara A. Mikulski, of Maryland.
Herb Kohl, of Wisconsin.
Tim Johnson, of South Dakota.
Jack Reed, of Rhode Island.
E. Benjamin Nelson, of Nebraska.

Larry E. Craig, of Idaho.
Ted Stevens, of Alaska.
Thad Cochran, of Mississippi.
Pete V. Domenici, of New Mexico.
Robert F. Bennett, of Utah.
Judd Gregg, of New Hampshire.
Wayne Allard, of Colorado.
Lamar Alexander, of Tennessee.

Labor, Health and Human Services, Education, and Related Agencies

Tom Harkin, of Iowa, *Chair*

Daniel K. Inouye, of Hawaii.
Herb Kohl, of Wisconsin.
Patty Murray, of Washington.
Mary L. Landrieu, of Louisiana.
Richard Durbin, of Illinois.
Jack Reed, of Rhode Island.
Frank R. Lautenberg, of New Jersey.

Arlen Specter, of Pennsylvania.
Thad Cochran, of Mississippi.
Judd Gregg, of New Hampshire.
Larry E. Craig, of Idaho.
Kay Bailey Hutchison, of Texas.
Ted Stevens, of Alaska.
Richard C. Shelby, of Alabama.

Legislative Branch

Mary L. Landrieu, of Louisiana, *Chair*

Richard Durbin, of Illinois.
E. Benjamin Nelson, of Nebraska.

Wayne Allard, of Colorado.
Lamar Alexander, of Tennessee.

Military Construction and Veterans Affairs, and Related Agencies

Tim Johnson, of South Dakota, *Chair*

Daniel K. Inouye, of Hawaii.
Mary L. Landrieu, of Louisiana.
Robert C. Byrd, of West Virginia.
Patty Murray, of Washington.
Jack Reed, of Rhode Island.
E. Benjamin Nelson, of Nebraska.

Kay Bailey Hutchison, of Texas.
Larry E. Craig, of Idaho.
Sam Brownback, of Kansas.
Wayne Allard, of Colorado.
Mitch McConnell, of Kentucky.
Robert F. Bennett, of Utah.

State, Foreign Operations, and Related Programs

Patrick J. Leahy, of Vermont, *Chair*

Daniel K. Inouye, of Hawaii.
Tom Harkin, of Iowa.
Barbara A. Mikulski, of Maryland.
Richard Durbin, of Illinois.
Tim Johnson, of South Dakota.
Mary L. Landrieu, of Louisiana.
Jack Reed, of Rhode Island.

Judd Gregg, of New Hampshire.
Mitch McConnell, of Kentucky.
Arlen Specter, of Pennsylvania.
Robert F. Bennett, of Utah.
Christopher S. Bond, of Missouri.
Sam Brownback, of Kansas.
Lamar Alexander, of Tennessee.

Transportation and Housing and Urban Development, and Related Agencies

Patty Murray, of Washington, *Chair*

Robert C. Byrd, of West Virginia.
Barbara A. Mikulski, of Maryland.
Herb Kohl, of Wisconsin.
Richard Durbin, of Illinois.
Byron L. Dorgan, of North Dakota.
Patrick J. Leahy, of Vermont.
Tom Harkin, of Iowa.
Dianne Feinstein, of California.
Tim Johnson, of South Dakota.
Frank R. Lautenberg, of New Jersey.

Christopher S. Bond, of Missouri.
Richard C. Shelby, of Alabama.
Arlen Specter, of Pennsylvania.
Robert F. Bennett, of Utah.
Kay Bailey Hutchison, of Texas.
Sam Brownback, of Kansas.
Ted Stevens, of Alaska.
Pete V. Domenici, of New Mexico.
Lamar Alexander, of Tennessee.
Wayne Allard, of Colorado.

STAFF

Committee on Appropriations (S–131), 224–7363.
Majority Staff Director.—Terrence E. Sauvain (S–131).
Deputy Staff Director.—Charles Kieffer (S–131).

Chief Clerk.—Robert W. Putnam (SD–114).
Deputy Chief Clerk.—Elnora Harvey (S–131).
Communications Director.—Tom Gavin (S–126).
Professional Staff: John J. Conway (SD–114); Suzanne Bentzel (S–125); Leslie Staples (S–125); Nora Martin; Robert Knisely (SD–184); Tom Gonzales (S–125A); Fernanda Motta (SD–114).
Technical Systems Manager.—Hong Nguyen (SD–114).
Security Manager.—Megan McCray (SD–118).
Staff Assistant.—Colleen Gaydos (S–131).
Minority Staff Director.—Bruce Evans (S–146A), 4–7257.
Deputy Staff Director.—Blake Thompson (S–146A).
Professional Staff: Margaret Wicker (SD–113); Carolyn E. Apostolou (S–146A); Josh Manley (S–146A); Mimi Braniff (SD–120).
Staff Assistant.—Sarah Wilson (S–146A).

Subcommittee on Agriculture, Rural Development, Food and Drug Administration and Related Agencies (SD–129), 4–8090.
Majority Clerk.—Galen Fountain (SD–129).
Professional Staff: Jessica Arden Frederick; Dianne Preece (SD–129).
Staff Assistant.—Renan Snowden (SD–119).
Minority Clerk.—Fitz Elder (SD–190), 4–5270.
Professional Staff: Stacy McBride (SD–190); Graham Harper (SD–190); Brad Fuller (SD–188).

Subcommittee on Commerce, Justice, Science, and Related Agencies (SD–144), 4–5202.
Majority Clerk.—Paul Carliner (SD–144).
Professional Staff: Gabrielle Batkin (SD–144); Erin Corcoran (SD–144); Kevin Kimball (SD–144).
Staff Assistant.—Robert Rich (SD–131).
Minority Clerk.—Art Cameron (SH–123), 4–7277.
Professional Staff: Allen Cutler (SH–123); Rachelle Schroeder (SH–123); Goodloe Sutton (SH–123).
Staff Assistant.—Augusta Wilson (SH–123).

Subcommittee on Defense (SD–119), 4–6688.
Majority Clerk.—Charles J. Houy (SD–119).
Professional Staff: Nicole Di Resta (SD–119); Kate Fitzpatrick (SD–119); Katy Hagan (SD–119); Kate Kaufer (SD–119), Ellen Maldonado (SD–119); Erik Raven (SD–119); Betsy Schmid (SD–119); Bridget Zarate (SD–119).
Staff Assistant.—Renan Snowden (SD–119).
Minority Clerk.—Sid Ashworth (SD–117), 4–7255.
Professional Staff: Alycia Farrell (SD–115); Brian Potts (SD–115); Brian Wilson (SD–115).

Subcommittee on Energy and Water, and Development (SD–186), 4–8119.
Majority Clerk.—Doug Clapp (SD–186).
Professional Staff: Roger Cockrell (SD–186); Fanz Wuerfmannsdobler (SD–186).
Staff Assistant.—Robert Rich (SD–131)
Minority Clerk.—Scott O'Malia (SD–188), 4–7260.
Professional Staff.—Brad Fuller (SD–188).

Subcommittee on Financial Services and General Government (SD–184), 4–1133.
Majority Clerk.—Marianne Upton (SD–184).
Professional Staff: Diana Gourlay Hamilton (SD–184); Robert Knisely (SD–184).
Staff Assistant.—Robert Rich (SD–131).
Minority Clerk.—Mary Dietrich (SD–142), 4–2104.
Professional Staff.—Rachel Jones (SD–142).
Staff Assistant.—LaShawnda Smith (SD–142)

Subcommittee on Homeland Security (S–131), 4–8244.
Majority Clerk.—Charles Kieffer (S–131).
Professional Staff: Chip Walgren (SD–135); Scott Nance (SD–135); Drenan E. Dudley (SD–135); Tad Gallion (SD–135); Christa Thompson (SD–135).
Minority Clerk.—Rebecca Davies (SH–123), 4–4319.
Professional Staff: Carol Cribbs (SH–123); Mark Van de Water (SH–123).

Subcommittee on Interior, Environment, and Related Agencies (SD–131), 8–0774.
Majority Clerk.—Peter Keifhaber (SD–131).
Professional Staff: Ginny James (SD–131); Rachael Taylor (SD–131); Scott Dalzell (SD–131); Chris Watkins (SD–131).
Minority Clerk.—Leif Fonnesbeck (SH–123), 4–7233.
Professional Staff: Rebecca Benn (SH–124); Christine Heggem (SH–123); Calli Daly (SH–123).

Subcommittee on Departments of Labor, Health and Human Services, and Education, and Related Agencies (SD–131), 4–9145.

Majority Clerk.—Ellen Murray (SD–131).

Professional Staff: Erik Fatemi (SD–131); Jim Sourwine (SD–131); Mark Laisch (SD–131); Adrienne Hallett (SD–131); Lisa Bernhardt (SD–131).

Staff Assistant.—Teri Curtin (SD–131).

Minority Clerk.—Bettilou Taylor (SD–156), 4–7230.

Professional Staff: Sudip Shrikant Parikh (SD–156); Candice Ngo (SH–123).

Staff Assistant.—Jeff Kratz (SD–156).

Subcommittee on Legislative Branch (SD–135) 4–3477.

Majority Clerk.—Nancy Oklewicz (SD–135).

Staff Assistant.—Teri Curtin (SD–131).

Minority Clerk.—Carolyn E. Apostolou (S–146A), 4–7238.

Staff Assistant.—Sarah Wilson (S–146A).

Subcommittee on Military Construction and Veterans Affairs, and Related Agencies (SD–125), 4–8224.

Majority Clerk.—Christina Evans (SD–125).

Professional Staff: B.G. Wright (SD–125); Chad Schulken (SD–125).

Staff Assistant.—Renan Snowden (SD–119).

Minority Clerk.—Dennis Balkham (SH–123), 4–5245.

Professional Staff.—Sean Knowles (SH–123).

Subcommittee on State, Foreign Operations, and Related Programs (SD–127), 4–7284.

Majority Clerk.—Tim Rieser (SD–127).

Professional Staff: Kate Eltrich (SD–127); Jennifer Park (SD–127).

Staff Assistant.—Renan Snowden (SD–119).

Minority Clerk.—Paul Grove (SD–142), 4–2104.

Professional Staff.—Michele Gordon (SD–142).

Staff Assistant.—LaShawnda Smith, (SD–142).

Subcommittee on Transportation and Housing and Urban Development, and Related Agencies (SD–133), 4–7281.

Majority Clerk.—Peter Rogoff (SD–133).

Professional Staff: William Simpson (SD–133); Meaghan L. McCarthy (SD–133); Rachel Milberg (SD–133).

Staff Assistant.—Teri Curtin (SD–131).

Minority Clerk.—Jon Kamarck (SD–128), 4–5310.

Professional Staff: Cheh Kim (SD–128); Matthew McCardle (SD–128); Ellen Beares (SD–128).

Editorial and Printing (SD–126): Richard L. Larson, 4–7265; Wayne W. Hosier (GPO), 4–7267; Doris Jackson (GPO), 4–7217; Heather Crowell (GPO), 4–7266.

Clerical Assistant.—George Castro (SDB–120), 4–5433.

Armed Services

228 Russell Senate Office Building 20510–6050

phone 224–3871, http://www.senate.gov/~armed_services

meets every Tuesday and Thursday

Carl Levin, of Michigan, *Chair*

Edward M. Kennedy, of Massachusetts.
Robert C. Byrd, of West Virginia.
JOSEPH I. LIEBERMAN, of Connecticut.
Jack Reed, of Rhode Island.
Daniel K. Akaka, of Hawaii.
Bill Nelson, of Florida.
E. Benjamin Nelson, of Nebraska.
Evan Bayh, of Indiana.
Hillary Rodham Clinton, of New York.
Mark L. Pryor, of Arkansas.
Jim Webb, of Virginia.
Claire McCaskill, of Missouri.

John McCain, of Arizona.
John Warner, of Virginia.
James M. Inhofe, of Oklahoma.
Jeff Sessions, of Alabama.
Susan M. Collins, of Maine.
John Ensign, of Nevada.
Saxby Chambliss, of Georgia.
Lindsey Graham, of South Carolina.
Elizabeth Dole, of North Carolina.
John Cornyn, of Texas.
John Thune, of South Dakota.
Mel Martinez, of Florida.

SUBCOMMITTEES

[The chairman and the ranking minority member are ex officio (non-voting) members of all subcommittees on which they do not serve.]

Airland

JOSEPH I. LIEBERMAN, of Connecticut, *Chair*

Daniel K. Akaka, of Hawaii.
Evan Bayh, of Indiana.
Hillary Rodham Clinton, of New York.
Mark L. Pryor, of Arkansas.
Jim Webb, of Virginia.
Claire McCaskill, of Missouri.

John Cornyn, of Texas.
John Warner, of Virginia.
James M. Inhofe, of Oklahoma.
Jeff Sessions, of Alabama.
John Ensign, of Nevada.
Saxby Chambliss, of Georgia.

Emerging Threats and Capabilities

Jack Reed, of Rhode Island, *Chair*

Edward M. Kennedy, of Massachusetts.
Robert C. Byrd, of West Virginia.
Bill Nelson, of Florida.
E. Benjamin Nelson, of Nebraska.
Evan Bayh, of Indiana.
Hillary Rodham Clinton, of New York.

Elizabeth Dole, of North Carolina.
John Warner, of Virginia.
Susan M. Collins, of Maine.
Lindsey Graham, of South Carolina.
John Cornyn, of Texas.
Mel Martinez, of Florida.

Personnel

E. Benjamin Nelson, of Nebraska, *Chair*

Edward M. Kennedy, of Massachusetts.
JOSEPH I. LIEBERMAN, of Connecticut.
Jim Webb, of Virginia.
Claire McCaskill, of Missouri.

Lindsey Graham, of South Carolina.
Susan M. Collins, of Maine.
Saxby Chambliss, of Georgia.
Elizabeth Dole, of North Carolina.

Readiness and Management Support

Daniel K. Akaka, of Hawaii, *Chair*

Robert C. Byrd, of West Virginia.
Evan Bayh, of Indiana.
Hillary Rodham Clinton, of New York.
Mark L. Pryor, of Arkansas.
Claire McCaskill, of Missouri.

John Ensign, of Nevada.
James M. Inhofe, of Oklahoma.
Jeff Sessions, of Alabama.
Saxby Chambliss, of Georgia.
Elizabeth Dole, of North Carolina.

Seapower

Edward M. Kennedy, of Massachusetts, *Chair*

JOSEPH I. LIEBERMAN, of Connecticut.
Jack Reed, of Rhode Island.
Daniel K. Akaka, of Hawaii.
Bill Nelson, of Florida.
Jim Webb, of Virginia.

John Thune, of South Dakota.
John Warner, of Virginia.
Susan M. Collins, of Maine.
John Ensign, of Nevada.
Mel Martinez, of Florida.

Strategic Forces

Bill Nelson, of Florida, *Chair*

Robert C. Byrd, of West Virginia.
Jack Reed, of Rhode Island.
E. Benjamin Nelson, of Nebraska.
Mark L. Pryor, of Arkansas.

Jeff Sessions, of Alabama.
James M. Inhofe, of Oklahoma.
Lindsey Graham, of South Carolina.
John Thune, of South Dakota.

STAFF

Committee on Armed Services (SR–228), 224–3871.
Majority Staff Director.—Richard D. DeBobes.
Chief Clerk.—Christine E. Cowart.
General Counsel.—Peter K. Levine.
Counsels: Madelyn R. Creedon, Gerald J. Leeling, William G.P. Monahan, Jonathan D. Clark.
Professional Staff: Joseph M. Bryan, Daniel J. Cox, Jr., Gabriella Eisen, Evelyn N. Farkas, Richard W. Fieldhouse, Creighton Greene, Mark R. Jacobson, Michael J. Kuiken, Thomas K. McConnell, Michael J. McCord, Arun A. Seraphin, William K. Sutey.
Research Assistant.—Michael J. Noblet.
Assistant Chief Clerk and Security Manager.—Cindy Pearson.
Nominations and Hearings Clerk.—Leah C. Brewer.
Systems Administrator.—Gary J. Howard.
Printing and Documents Clerk.—June M. Borawski.
Security Clerk.—John H. Quirk V.
Special Assistant.—Catherine E. Sendak.
Staff Assistants: David G. Collins, Fletcher L. Cork, Kevin A. Cronin, Micah H. Harris, Jessica L. Kingston, Benjamin L. Rubin.
Receptionist.—Brian F. Sebold.
Republican Staff Director.—Michael V. Kostiw.
Administrative Assistant for the Minority.—Marie Fabrizio Dickinson.
Minority Counsels: Derek J. Maurer, David M. Morriss, Richard F. Walsh.
Professional Staff Members: William M. Caniano, Gregory T. Kiley, Lucian L. Niemeyer, Christopher J. Paul, Lynn F. Rusten, Robert M. Soofer, Sean G. Stackley, Kristine L. Svinicki, Diana G. Tabler.
Minority Investigative Counsels: Pablo E. Carrillo, Bryan D. Parker.
Research Assistants: Paul C. Hutton, Jill L. Simodejka.
Subcommittee on Airland:
Majority Professional Staff: Daniel J. Cox, Jr., Creighton Greene, Michael J. Kuiken, William K. Sutey.
Minority Professional Staff: William M. Caniano, Gregory T. Kiley.
Subcommittee on Emerging Threats and Capabilities:

Majority Professional Staff: Madelyn R. Creedon, Richard W. Fieldhouse, Evelyn N. Farkas, Arun A. Seraphin.

Minority Professional Staff: William M. Caniano, Lynn F. Rusten, Robert M. Soofer, Kristine L. Svinicki.

Subcommittee on Personnel:

Majority Professional Staff: Jonathan D. Clark, Gabriella Eisen, Gerald J. Leeling.

Minority Professional Staff: Diana G. Tabler, Richard F. Walsh.

Subcommittee on Readiness and Management Support:

Majority Professional Staff: Peter K. Levine, Michael J. McCord, William K. Sutey.

Minority Professional Staff: Derek J. Maurer, Lucian L. Niemeyer, Bryan D. Parker.

Subcommittee on Seapower:

Majority Professional Staff: Creighton Greene, Thomas K. McConnell.

Minority Professional Staff: Gregory T. Kiley, Sean G. Stackley.

Subcommittee on Strategic Forces:

Majority Professional Staff: Madelyn R. Creedon, Richard W. Fieldhouse, Creighton Greene, Thomas K. McConnell.

Minority Professional Staff: Gregory T. Kiley, Derek J. Maurer, Robert M. Soofer, Kristine L. Svinicki.

Majority Professional Staff for—

Acquisition Policy.—Peter K. Levine.

Acquisition Workforce.—Peter K. Levine.

Ammunition.—William K. Sutey.

Arms Control/Non-proliferation: Madelyn R. Creedon, Richard W. Fieldhouse.

Aviation Systems: Daniel J. Cox, Jr., Madelyn R. Creedon, Creighton Greene.

Base Realignment and Closure (BRAC).—Michael J. McCord.

Buy America.—Peter K. Levine.

Chemical-Biological Defense.—Richard W. Fieldhouse.

Chemical Demilitarization.—Richard W. Fieldhouse.

Civilian Nominations.—Peter K. Levine.

Civilian Personnel Policy: Gabriella Eisen, Gerald J. Leeling.

Combatant Commands.—

AFRICOM.—Michael J. Kuiken.

CENTCOM.—Daniel J. Cox, Jr., Gabriella Eisen, Michael J. Kuiken, William G.P. Monohan.

EUCOM.—William G.P. Monohan.

JFCOM.—Arun A. Seraphin, William K. Sutey.

NORTHCOM.—Richard W. Fieldhouse.

PACOM.—Evelyn N. Farkas.

SOCOM.—Evelyn N. Farkas.

SOUTHCOM.—Evelyn N. Farkas.

STRATCOM.—Madelyn R. Creedon.

TRANSCOM.—Creighton Greene.

Combating Terrorism.—Evelyn N. Farkas.

Competition Policy/Mergers and Acquisitions.—Peter K. Levine.

Competitive Sourcing/A-76.—Peter K. Levine.

Contracting (including service contracts).—Peter K. Levine.

Construction, Housing, Global Basing, and Land Use.—Michael J. McCord.

Cooperative Threat Reduction Programs.—Madelyn R. Creedon.

Counterdrug Programs.—Evelyn N. Farkas.

Defense Laboratory Management: Peter K. Levine, Arun A. Seraphin.

Defense Security Assistance: Evelyn N. Farkas, William G.P. Monahan.

Defense Spending and Supplementals.—Michael J. McCord.

Department of Defense Schools: Gabriella Eisen, Gerald J. Leeling.

Department of Energy Issues.—Madelyn R. Creedon.

Depot Maintenance.—William K. Sutey.

Detainee Policy: Peter K. Levine, William G.P. Monahan.

Domestic Preparedness.—Richard W. Fieldhouse.

Environmental Issues.—Peter K. Levine.

Export Controls: Evelyn N. Farkas, Peter K. Levine.

Financial Management.—Peter K. Levine.

Force Readiness/Training.—William K. Sutey.

Foreign Language Policy: Evelyn N. Farkas, Creighton Greene.

Foreign Policy/Geographical Region.—

Afghanistan: Daniel J. Cox, Jr., Evelyn N. Farkas, William G.P. Monahan.

Africa: Gabriella Eisen, Michael J. Kuiken, William G.P. Monahan.

Asia/Pacific Region.—Evelyn N. Farkas.

Europe/Russia: Madelyn R. Creedon, William G.P. Monahan.

Iraq: Daniel J. Cox, Jr., William K. Sutey.
Middle East: Gabriella Eisen, Michael J. Kuiken.
South America.—Evelyn N. Farkas.
Ground Systems.—
Army: Daniel J. Cox, Jr., Michael J. Kuiken, William K. Sutey.
Marine Corps.—Thomas K. McConnell.
Homeland Defense/Security: Richard W. Fieldhouse, Gary Leeling.
Humanitarian and Civic Assistance: Evelyn N. Farkas, William G.P. Monahan.
Information Assurance/Cyber Security: Creighton Greene, Thomas K. McConnell, Arun A. Seraphin.
Information Management: Creighton Greene, Peter K. Levine.
Information Technology Systems.—
Business Systems.—Peter K. Levine.
Tactical Systems: Creighton Greene, Arun A. Seraphin.
Intelligence Issues: Creighton Greene, Thomas K. McConnell.
Interagency Reform/Goldwater-Nichols II: Evelyn N. Farkas, Thomas K. McConnell.
International Defense Cooperation: Evelyn N. Farkas, Peter K. Levine, William G.P. Monahan.
Inventory Management: Peter K. Levine, William K. Sutey.
Investigations: Joseph M. Bryan, Mark R. Jacobson.
Military Personnel Issues: Jonathan D. Clark, Gerald J. Leeling.
End Strength: Jonathan D. Clark, Gerald J. Leeling.
Health Care: Gabriella Eisen, Gerald J. Leeling.
Military Family Policy: Gabriella Eisen, Gerald J. Leeling.
Military Personnel Policy: Jonathan D. Clark, Gerald J. Leeling.
Pay and Benefits: Jonathan D. Clark, Gerald J. Leeling.
Military Nominations.—Gerald J. Leeling.
Military Space.—Madelyn R. Creedon.
Military Strategy.—Daniel J. Cox, Jr.
Missile Defense.—Richard W. Fieldhouse.
Morale, Welfare and Recreation/Commissaries/Exchanges: Gabriella Eisen, Gerald J. Leeling.
National Defense Stockpile.—William K. Sutey.
Nuclear Weapons Stockpile.—Madelyn R. Creedon.
POW/MIA Issues.—Jonathan D. Clark.
Personnel Protective Items.—William K. Sutey.
Quadrennial Defense Review (QDR).—Michael J. McCord.
Readiness/O&M.—William K. Sutey.
Reprogramming.—Michael J. McCord.
Science and Technology.—Arun A. Seraphin.
Sexual Harassment/Sexual Assault Policy: Gabriella Eisen, Gerald J. Leeling.
Shipbuilding Programs.—Creighton Greene.
Small Business.—Peter K. Levine.
Special Operations Forces.—Evelyn N. Farkas.
Stability Operations: Evelyn N. Farkas, William G.P. Monahan.
Strategic Programs.—Madelyn R. Creedon.
Test and Evaluation: Peter K. Levine, Arun A. Seraphin.
Transportation and Logistics Policy.—Creighton Greene.
Unmanned Aircraft Systems: Daniel J. Cox, Jr., Creighton Greene.
Women in Combat: Jonathan D. Clark, Gerald J. Leeling.
Working Capital Fund: Michael J. McCord, William K. Sutey.

Minority Professional Staff for—
Acquisition and Contracting Policy: Pablo E. Carrillo, Bryan D. Parker, Christopher J. Paul.
Arms Control and Non-proliferation.—Lynn F. Rusten.
Army Programs.—William M. Caniano.
Budget and Reprogramming.—Gregory T. Kiley.
Chemical-Biological Defense.—Robert M. Soofer.
Chemical-Demilitarization.—Lynn F. Rusten.
Civilian Personnel.—Diana G. Tabler.
Combatant Commands.—
AFRICOM.—Lynn F. Rusten.
CENTCOM.—William M. Caniano.
EUCOM.—Lynn F. Rusten.
JFCOM.—Kristine L. Svinicki.
NORTHCOM.—Robert M. Soofer.
PACOM.—Lynn F. Rusten.

SOCOM.—William M. Caniano.
SOUTHCOM.—William M. Caniano.
STRATCOM.—Robert M. Soofer.
TRANSCOM: Gregory T. Kiley, Sean G. Stackley.

Counterdrug Programs.—Lynn F. Rusten.
Defense Security Assistance.—Lynn F. Rusten.
Depot Maintenance.—Derek J. Maurer.
Detainees and Military Commissions: William M. Caniano, Pablo E. Carrillo, David M. Morriss, Christopher J. Paul.
Department of Energy National Security Programs.—Kristine L. Svinicki.
Environmental Issues.—David M. Morriss.
Export Controls.—Lynn F. Rusten.
Health Care.—Diana G. Tabler.
Homeland Security.—Robert M. Soofer.
Information Assurance and Cyber Security.—Gregory T. Kiley.
Information Technology: William M. Caniano, Gregory T. Kiley.
Intelligence Programs: William M. Caniano, Derek J. Maurer.
Laboratories.—Kristine L. Svinicki.
Military Construction and BRAC.—Lucian L. Niemeyer.
Military Personnel and Family Benefits: Diana G. Tabler, Richard F. Walsh.
National Military Strategy.—William M. Caniano.
Missile Defense.—Robert M. Soofer.
Navy and Marine Corps Programs.—Sean G. Stackley.
Nominations.—Richard F. Walsh.
Oversight Investigations: Pablo E. Carrillo, Bryan D. Parker, Christopher J. Paul,
Readiness/Operations and Maintenance.—Derek J. Maurer.
Science and Technology.—Kristine L. Svinicki.
Space Programs.—Robert M. Soofer.
Special Operations Forces.—William M. Caniano.
Strategic and Tactical Aviation Programs.—Gregory T. Kiley.
Test and Evaluation.—Kristine L. Svinicki.

Banking, Housing, and Urban Affairs

534 Dirksen Senate Office Building 20510

phone 224–7391, http://banking.senate.gov

Christopher J. Dodd, of Connecticut, *Chair*

Tim Johnson, of South Dakota.
Jack Reed, of Rhode Island.
Charles E. Schumer, of New York.
Evan Bayh, of Indiana.
Thomas R. Carper, of Delaware.
Robert Menendez, of New Jersey.
Daniel K. Akaka, of Hawaii.
Sherrod Brown, of Ohio.
Robert P. Casey, Jr., of Pennsylvania.
Jon Tester, of Montana.

Richard C. Shelby, of Alabama.
Robert F. Bennett, of Utah.
Wayne Allard, of Colorado.
Michael B. Enzi, of Wyoming.
Chuck Hagel, of Nebraska.
Jim Bunning, of Kentucky.
Mike Crapo, of Idaho.
John E. Sununu, of New Hampshire.
Elizabeth Dole, of North Carolina.
Mel Martinez, of Florida.

SUBCOMMITTEES

[The chairman and ranking minority member are ex officio members of all subcommittees.]

Economic Policy

Thomas R. Carper, of Delaware, *Chair*

Sherrod Brown, of Ohio.

Jim Bunning, of Kentucky.

Financial Institutions

Tim Johnson, of South Dakota, *Chair*

Jon Tester, of Montana.
Robert Menendez, of New Jersey.
Daniel K. Akaka, of Hawaii.
Jack Reed, of Rhode Island.
Charles E. Schumer, of New York.
Evan Bayh, of Indiana.
Thomas R. Carper, of Delaware.

Chuck Hagel, of Nebraska.
Robert F. Bennett, of Utah.
Wayne Allard, of Colorado.
John E. Sununu, of New Hampshire.
Jim Bunning, of Kentucky.
Mike Crapo, of Idaho.
Elizabeth Dole, of North Carolina.

Housing, Transportation, and Community Development

Charles E. Schumer, of New York, *Chair*

Daniel K. Akaka, of Hawaii.
Robert P. Casey, Jr., of Pennsylvania.
Jack Reed, of Rhode Island.
Thomas R. Carper, of Delaware.
Sherrod Brown, of Ohio.
Jon Tester, of Montana.
Robert Menendez, of New Jersey.

Mike Crapo, of Idaho.
Elizabeth Dole, of North Carolina.
Mel Martinez, of Florida.
Wayne Allard, of Colorado.
Michael B. Enzi, of Wyoming.
Chuck Hagel, of Nebraska.
John E. Sununu, of New Hampshire.

Securities, Insurance, and Investment

Jack Reed, of Rhode Island, *Chair*

Robert Menendez, of New Jersey.
Tim Johnson, of South Dakota.
Charles E. Schumer, of New York.
Evan Bayh, of Indiana.
Robert P. Casey, Jr., of Pennsylvania.
Daniel K. Akaka, of Hawaii.
Jon Tester, of Montana.

Wayne Allard, of Colorado.
Michael B. Enzi, of Wyoming.
John E. Sununu, of New Hampshire.
Robert F. Bennett, of Utah.
Chuck Hagel, of Nebraska.
Jim Bunning, of Kentucky.
Mike Crapo, of Idaho.

Security and International Trade and Finance

Evan Bayh, of Indiana, *Chair*

Sherrod Brown, of Ohio.
Tim Johnson, of South Dakota.
Robert P. Casey, Jr., of Pennsylvania.
Christopher J. Dodd, of Connecticut.
Mel Martinez, of Florida.
Michael B. Enzi, of Wyoming.
Elizabeth Dole, of North Carolina.
Robert F. Bennett, of Utah.

STAFF

Committee on Banking, Housing, and Urban Affairs (SD–534), 224–7391.
Majority Staff Director and Chief Counsel.—Shawn Maher.
Deputy Staff Director.—Alex Sternhell.
Senior Counsel.—Dean Shahinian.
Senior Adviser.—Roger Hollingsworth.
Senior Policy Adviser.—Colin McGinnis.
Counsels: Jennifer Fogel-Bublick, Lynsey Graham Rea, Sarah Kline.
Professional Staff: Joseph Hepp, Jonathan Miller, Neil Orringer.
Chief Economist.—Aaron Klein.
International Economic Adviser.—Julie Chon.
Legislative Assistants: Gretchen Adelson, Alexandra Cawthorne.
Communications Director.—Marvin Fast.
Subcommittee Staff Directors:
Economic Policy.—Chuck Jones.
Financial Institutions.—Laura Swanson.
Housing, Transportation and Community Development.—Carmencita Whonder.
Securities, Insurance, and Investment.—Didem Nisanci.
Security and International Trade and Finance.—Jayme Roth.
Minority Staff Director and General Counsel.—William Duhnke.
Minority Deputy Staff Director and Chief Counsel.—Mark Oesterle.
Senior Counsel.—Justin Daly.
Senior Financial Economist.—Peggy Kuhn.
Senior Professional Staff: Mark Calabria, Skip Fischer, Shannon Hines.
Senior Investigative Counsel.—John O'Hara.
Counsels: Jonathan Gould, Jim Johnson, Andrew Olmem.
Professional Staff.—Brandon Barford, Genevieve de Sanctis.
Communications Director.—Jonathan Graffeo.
Chief Clerk/Systems Administrator.—Joseph Kolinski.
Deputy Chief Clerk.—Liz Hackett.
Editor.—George Whittle.
Editorial Assistant.—Jim Crowell.

Budget

624 Dirksen Senate Office Building 20510–6100

phone 224–0642, http://budget.senate.gov

meets first Thursday of each month

Kent Conrad, of North Dakota, *Chair*

Patty Murray, of Washington.
Ron Wyden, of Oregon.
Russell D. Feingold, of Wisconsin.
Robert C. Byrd, of West Virginia.
Bill Nelson, of Florida.
Debbie Stabenow, of Michigan.
Robert Menendez, of New Jersey.
Frank R. Lautenberg, of New Jersey.
Benjamin L. Cardin, of Maryland.
BERNARD SANDERS, of Vermont.
Sheldon Whitehouse, of Rhode Island.

Judd Gregg, of New Hampshire.
Pete V. Domenici, of New Mexico.
Chuck Grassley, of Iowa.
Wayne Allard, of Colorado.
Michael B. Enzi, of Wyoming.
Jeff Sessions, of Alabama.
Jim Bunning, of Kentucky.
Mike Crapo, of Idaho.
John Ensign, of Nevada.
John Cornyn, of Texas.
Lindsey Graham, of South Carolina.

(No Subcommittees)

STAFF

Committee on Budget (SD–624), 224–0642.
Majority Staff Director.—Mary Naylor, 4–0862.
Deputy Staff Directors: Joel Friedman, 4–0538; John Righter, 4–0544.
Counsel.—Lisa Konwinski, 4–2757.
Senior Analyst for—
Agriculture and Trade.—Jim Miller, 4–8463.
Education and Appropriations.—Joan Huffer, 4–7216.
Revenues.—Steve Bailey, 4–2835.
Analyst for—
Budget.—Robyn Hiestand, 4–9731.
Energy, Environment, and General Government.—Cliff Isenberg, 4–0835.
Income Security, Medicaid.—Jim Esquea, 4–5811.
Justice, Homeland Security, Community, and Regional Development.—Mike Jones, 4–0833.
National Security and International Affairs, National Security.—Jamie Morin, 4–0872.
Social Security and Medicare.—Sarah Kuehl, 4–0559.
Transportation, Veterans' Affairs, Commerce and Housing Credit.—Brodi Fontenot, 4–0560.
Director of Strategic Planning and Outreach.—David Vandivier, 4–8604.
Executive Assistant.—Anne Page, 4–0533.
Communications Director.—Stu Nagurka, 4–7436.
Deputy Communications Director.—Steve Posner, 4–7925.
Graphics Production Coordinator.—Kobye Noel, 4–3728.
Chief Economist.—Jim Klumpner, 4–6588.
Staff Assistants: Tyler Haskell, 4–0547; Matthew Havlik, 4–0581.
Fellow.—Susan Reeves, 4–0571.
Intern.—Kevin Burch, 4–0061.
Minority Staff Director.—Scott Gudes, 4–0856.
Deputy Staff Director.—Denzel McGuire, 8–5846.
Counsel.—Allison Parent, 4–0857.
Communications Director.—Betsy Holahan, 4–6011.
Economist.—Dan Brandt, 4–0797.
Director for—
Federal Programs and Budget Process.—Jim Hearn, 4–2370.
Health Policy.—David Fisher, 2–6988.
Revenues and Budget Review.—Cheri Reidy, 4–0557.
Professional Staff: Kevin Bargo, 4–8695; Winnie Chang, 4–1602; Jason Delisle, 4–0865; Don Dempsey, 4–0543; Vanessa Green, 4–4999; Jay Khosla, 4–4471; Mike Lofgren, 4–9373; Seema Mittal, 4–0838; David Myers, 4–0843; David Pappone, 4–0564; Jennifer

Pollom, 4–3023; Conwell Smith, 4–0543; Richard Weiblinger, 4–1107; Elizabeth Wore, 4–6744.

Press Secretary.—Jeff Turcotte, 4–2574.

Staff Assistant.—Matt Giroux, 4–5831.

Non-designated:

Chief Clerk.—Lynne Seymour, 4–0191.

Computer Systems Administrator.—George Woodall, 4–6576.

Publications Department.—Letitia Fletcher, 4–0855.

Staff Assistants: Sarah Eyster, 4–0565; Andrew Kermick, 4–0796.

Commerce, Science, and Transportation

508 Dirksen Senate Office Building 20510–6125

phone 224–5115, TTY / TDD 224–8418 http://commerce.senate.gov

meets first and third Tuesdays of each month

Daniel K. Inouye, of Hawaii, *Chair*

Ted Stevens, of Alaska, *Vice Chair*

John D. Rockefeller IV, of West Virginia.
John F. Kerry, of Massachusetts.
Byron L. Dorgan, of North Dakota.
Barbara Boxer, of California.
Bill Nelson, of Florida.
Maria Cantwell, of Washington.
Frank R. Lautenberg, of New Jersey.
Mark L. Pryor, of Arkansas.
Thomas R. Carper, of Delaware.
Claire McCaskill, of Missouri.
Amy Klobuchar, of Minnesota.

John McCain, of Arizona.
Trent Lott, of Mississippi.
Kay Bailey Hutchison, of Texas.
Olympia J. Snowe, of Maine.
Gordon H. Smith, of Oregon.
John Ensign, of Nevada.
John E. Sununu, of New Hampshire.
Jim DeMint, of South Carolina.
David Vitter, of Louisiana.
John Thune, of South Dakota.

SUBCOMMITTEES

[The chair and the vice chair are ex officio members of all subcommittees.]

Aviation Operations, Safety, and Security

John D. Rockefeller IV, of West Virginia, *Chair*

John F. Kerry, of Massachusetts.
Byron L. Dorgan, of North Dakota.
Barbara Boxer, of California.
Bill Nelson, of Florida.
Maria Cantwell, of Washington.
Frank R. Lautenberg, of New Jersey.
Mark L. Pryor, of Arkansas.
Thomas R. Carper, of Delaware.
Claire McCaskill, of Missouri.
Amy Klobuchar, of Minnesota.

Trent Lott, of Mississippi.
John McCain, of Arizona.
Kay Bailey Hutchison, of Texas.
Olympia J. Snowe, of Maine.
Gordon H. Smith, of Oregon.
John Ensign, of Nevada.
John E. Sununu, of New Hampshire.
Jim DeMint, of South Carolina.
David Vitter, of Louisiana.
John Thune, of South Dakota.

Consumer Affairs, Insurance, and Automotive Safety

Mark L. Pryor, of Arkansas, *Chair*

John D. Rockefeller IV, of West Virginia.
Bill Nelson, of Florida.
Maria Cantwell, of Washington.
Frank R. Lautenberg, of New Jersey.
Thomas R. Carper, of Delaware.
Claire McCaskill, of Missouri.
Amy Klobuchar, of Minnesota.

John E. Sununu, of New Hampshire.
John McCain, of Arizona.
Trent Lott, of Mississippi.
Olympia J. Snowe, of Maine.
Gordon H. Smith, of Oregon.
David Vitter, of Louisiana.
John Thune, of South Dakota.

Interstate Commerce, Trade, and Tourism

Byron L. Dorgan, of North Dakota, *Chair*

John D. Rockefeller IV, of West Virginia.
John F. Kerry, of Massachusetts.
Barbara Boxer, of California.
Maria Cantwell, of Washington.
Mark L. Pryor, of Arkansas.
Claire McCaskill, of Missouri.

Jim DeMint, of South Carolina.
John McCain, of Arizona.
Olympia J. Snowe, of Maine.
Gordon H. Smith, of Oregon.
John Ensign, of Nevada.
John E. Sununu, of New Hampshire.

Oceans, Atmosphere, Fisheries, and Coast Guard

Maria Cantwell, of Washington, *Chair*

John F. Kerry, of Massachusetts.
Barbara Boxer, of California.
Bill Nelson, of Florida.
Frank R. Lautenberg, of New Jersey.
Thomas R. Carper, of Delaware.
Amy Klobuchar, of Minnesota.
Olympia J. Snowe, of Maine.
Trent Lott, of Mississippi.
Gordon H. Smith, of Oregon.
John E. Sununu, of New Hampshire.
Jim DeMint, of South Carolina.
David Vitter, of Louisiana.

Science, Technology, and Innovation

John F. Kerry, of Massachusetts, *Chair*

John D. Rockefeller IV, of West Virginia.
Byron L. Dorgan, of North Dakota.
Barbara Boxer, of California.
Maria Cantwell, of Washington.
Mark L. Pryor, of Arkansas.
Claire McCaskill, of Missouri.
Amy Klobuchar, of Minnesota.
John Ensign, of Nevada.
John McCain, of Arizona.
Kay Bailey Hutchison, of Texas.
Gordon H. Smith, of Oregon.
John E. Sununu, of New Hampshire.
Jim DeMint, of South Carolina.
John Thune, of South Dakota.

Space, Aeronautics, and Related Sciences

Bill Nelson, of Florida, *Chair*

John F. Kerry, of Massachusetts.
Byron L. Dorgan, of North Dakota.
Mark L. Pryor, of Arkansas.
Kay Bailey Hutchison, of Texas.
Trent Lott, of Mississippi.
John E. Sununu, of New Hampshire.

Surface Transportation and Merchant Marine Infrastructure, Safety, and Security

Frank R. Lautenberg, of New Jersey, *Chair*

John D. Rockefeller IV, of West Virginia.
John F. Kerry, of Massachusetts.
Byron L. Dorgan, of North Dakota.
Maria Cantwell, of Washington.
Mark L. Pryor, of Arkansas.
Thomas R. Carper, of Delaware.
Claire McCaskill, of Missouri.
Amy Klobuchar, of Minnesota.
Gordon H. Smith, of Oregon.
John McCain, of Arizona.
Trent Lott, of Mississippi.
Kay Bailey Hutchison, of Texas.
Olympia J. Snowe, of Maine.
Jim DeMint, of South Carolina.
David Vitter, of Louisiana.
John Thune, of South Dakota.

STAFF

Committee on Commerce, Science, and Transportation (SD–508), 224–5115.
Majority Staff Director / Chief Counsel.—Margaret Cummisky.
Deputy Staff Director / Policy Director.—Lila Helms.
Professional Staff.—Jean Toal-Eisen.
Press Aide.—Jenilee Keefe.
Executive Assistant, Director of Operations.—Vanessa Jones.
Staff Assistants: Jason Bradshaw, Emily Deimel.
Telecom Senior Counsel.—James Assey.
Senior Communications Counsel.—Jessica Rosenworcel.
Legislative Assistant.—Helen Colosimo.
Minority Staff Director / General Counsel.—Christine Kurth.
Deputy Staff Director.—Ken Nahigian.
Senior Counsel.—Paul Nagle.
Communications Director.—Joe Brenckle.
Press Secretary.—Brian Eaton.
Professional Staff.—Megan Beechener.
Oceans Counsel.—Todd Bertoson.
Climate Change (PSM).—Garret Graves.
Senior Advisor.—Floyd DesChamps.
Staff Assistant.—Sara Gibson.

Nominations Clerk.—Becky Hooks.
TSA Detailee.—Pamela Friedman.
Telecom Senior Counsel.—Paul Nagle.

Aviation Operations, Safety, and Security Staff
Majority Senior Professional Staff.—Gael Sullivan.
Legislative Assistant.—Channon Hanna.
GAO Detailee.—Rich Swayze.
Minority Senior Professional Staff.—Chris Bertram.
Professional Staff: Mike Blank, Jarrod Thompson.
FAA Detailee.—John Hennigan.

Consumer Affairs, Insurance, and Automotive Safety Staff
Majority Senior Counsel.—David Strickland.
Counsel.—Alex Hoehn-Saric.
Staff Assistants: Jared Bomberg, Maria Petrini.
Minority Professional Staff: Megan Beechener, Peter Phipps.
Staff Assistant.—Sara Gibson.

Interstate Commerce, Trade, and Tourism Staff
Majority Senior Counsel.—David Strickland.
Counsel.—Alex Hoehn-Saric.
Staff Assistants: Jared Bomberg, Maria Petrini.
Minority Professional Staff: Mark Delich, Tom Jones.

Oceans, Atmosphere, Fisheries, and Coast Guard Staff
Majority Senior Counsel.—Amy Fraenkel.
Professional Staff.—Amanda Hallberg.
Staff Assistant.—Julie Hrdlicka.
Sea Grant Fellow.—Ann Zulkosky.
Minority Professional Staff: Mike Conathan, Kris Lynch.
Staff Assistant.—Theresa Eugene.
Coast Guard Fellow.—Harl Romine.
Sea Grant Fellow.—Stuart Levenbach.
Detailee.—Kevin Simpson.

Science, Technology, and Innovation Staff
Majority Professional Staff.—Chan Lieu.
Staff Assistant.—Elizabeth Bacon.
AAAS Fellow.—Kevin Eckerle.
Minority Counsel.—Jason Mulvihill.
Professional Staff.—H.J. Derr.

Space, Aeronautics, and Related Sciences Staff
Majority Professional Staff.—Chan Lieu.
Staff Assistant.—Elizabeth Bacon.
AAAS Fellow.—Kevin Eckerle.
Minority Senior Advisor.—Jeff Bingham.

Surface, Transportation, and Merchant Marine Infrastructure, Safety, and Security Staff
Majority Professional Staff: Stephen Gardner, Dabney Hegg.
Legislative Assistant.—Channon Hanna.
Federal Railroad Administration Detailee.—Melissa Porter.
Minority Professional Staff: Elizabeth McDonnell, David Wonnenberg.
Staff Assistant.—Dan Neumann.

Bipartisan Staff:
Financial Clerk.—Barbara Flanders.
Hearing Clerk.—Jane Swensen.
Director, Information Technology.—Jonathan Bowen ''JJ''.
Editor.—Becky Kojm.
GPO Detailees: Brian Martin-Haynes, Jacqueline Washington.

Bipartisan Staff, Legislative Counsel's Office:
Legislative Counsel.—Lloyd Ator.
Staff Assistant.—Gayle Aikens.

Bipartisan Staff, Public Information Office:
Professional Staff.—Robert Foster.
Public Information Staff.—Yvonne Gowdy.
Staff Assistant.—Stephanie Lieu.

Energy and Natural Resources

304 Dirksen Senate Office Building 20510

phone 224–4971, fax 224–6163, http://energy.senate.gov

meets upon call of the chair

Jeff Bingaman, of New Mexico, *Chair*

Daniel K. Akaka, of Hawaii.
Byron L. Dorgan, of North Dakota.
Ron Wyden, of Oregon.
Tim Johnson, of South Dakota.
Mary L. Landrieu, of Louisiana.
Maria Cantwell, of Washington.
Ken Salazar, of Colorado.
Robert Menendez, of New Jersey.
Blanche L. Lincoln, of Arkansas.
BERNARD SANDERS, of Vermont.
Jon Tester, of Montana.

Pete V. Domenici, of New Mexico.
Larry E. Craig, of Idaho.
Lisa Murkowski, of Alaska.
Richard Burr, of North Carolina.
Jim DeMint, of South Carolina.
Bob Corker, of Tennessee.
Jeff Sessions, of Alabama.
Jim Bunning, of Kentucky.
Gordon H. Smith, of Oregon.
Mel Martinez, of Florida.

SUBCOMMITTEES

[The chairman and the ranking minority member are ex officio members of all subcommittees.]

Energy

Byron L. Dorgan, of North Dakota, *Chair*

Daniel K. Akaka, of Hawaii.
Ron Wyden, of Oregon.
Tim Johnson, of South Dakota.
Mary L. Landrieu, of Louisiana.
Maria Cantwell, of Washington.
Robert Menendez, of New Jersey.
BERNARD SANDERS, of Vermont.
Jon Tester, of Montana.

Lisa Murkowski, of Alaska.
Larry E. Craig, of Idaho.
Richard Burr, of North Carolina.
Jim DeMint, of South Carolina.
Bob Corker, of Tennessee.
Jeff Sessions, of Alabama.
Jim Bunning, of Kentucky.
Mel Martinez, of Florida.

National Parks

Daniel K. Akaka, of Hawaii, *Chair*

Byron L. Dorgan, of North Dakota.
Mary L. Landrieu, of Louisiana.
Ken Salazar, of Colorado.
Robert Menendez, of New Jersey.
Blanche L. Lincoln, of Arkansas.
BERNARD SANDERS, of Vermont.
Jon Tester, of Montana.

Lisa Murkowski, of Alaska.
Richard Burr, of North Carolina.
Bob Corker, of Tennessee.
Jeff Sessions, of Alabama.
Gordon H. Smith, of Oregon.
Mel Martinez, of Florida.

Public Lands and Forests

Ron Wyden, of Oregon, *Chair*

Daniel K. Akaka, of Hawaii.
Tim Johnson, of South Dakota.
Mary L. Landrieu, of Louisiana.
Maria Cantwell, of Washington.
Ken Salazar, of Colorado.
Robert Menendez, of New Jersey.
Blanche L. Lincoln, of Arkansas.
BERNARD SANDERS, of Vermont.

Richard Burr, of North Carolina.
Larry E. Craig, of Idaho.
Lisa Murkowski, of Alaska.
Jim DeMint, of South Carolina.
Jeff Sessions, of Alabama.
Gordon H. Smith, of Oregon.
Jim Bunning, of Kentucky.

Water and Power

Tim Johnson, of South Dakota, *Chair*

Byron L. Dorgan, of North Dakota.
Ron Wyden, of Oregon.
Maria Cantwell, of Washington.
Ken Salazar, of Colorado.
Blanche L. Lincoln, of Arkansas.
Jon Tester, of Montana.

Bob Corker, of Tennessee.
Larry E. Craig, of Idaho.
Jim DeMint, of South Carolina.
Gordon H. Smith, of Oregon.
Jim Bunning, of Kentucky.

STAFF

Committee on Energy and Natural Resources (SD–304), 224–4971, fax 224–6163.

Majority Staff Director.—Bob Simon.
Administrator Director.—Nancy Hall.
Chief Counsel.—Sam Fowler.
Senior Counsels: Patty Beneke, David Brooks.
Counsels: Michael Carr, Mike Connor, Deborah Estes, Leon Lowery, Scott Miller.
Chief Clerk.—Mia Bennett.
Executive Assistant.—Amanda Kelly.
Computer Systems Administrator.—Dawson Foard.
Communications Director.—Bill Wicker.
Press Assistant.—David Marks.
Professional Staff: Angela Becker-Dippmann, Tara Billingsley, Jonathan Black, Jonathan Epstein, Al Stayman.
Legislative Assistant.—Jorge Silva-Banuelos.
Staff Assistants: Mike Misurek, Rachel Pasternack, Britni Rillera.
Calendar Clerk.—Christie Sharp.
Printer/Editor.—Richard Smith.
Fellows: Allyson Anderson, Paul Augustine, KP Lau.

Minority Staff Director.—Frank Macchiarola.
Chief Counsel.—Judy Pensabene.
Counsels: Kellie Donnelly, Nate Gentry.
Deputy Chief Counsel.—Karen Billups.
Communications Director.—Matt Letorneau.
Professional Staff: Elizabeth Abrams, Kathryn Clay, Frank Gladics, Josh Johnson, Thomas Lillie.
Press Secretary.—Charles Chamberlayne.
Executive Assistant.—Kara Gleason.
Staff Assistants: Sara Decker, Shannon Ewan.

Environment and Public Works

410 Dirksen Senate Office Building 20510–6175

phone 224–6176, www.senate.gov/~epw

meets first and third Thursdays of each month

Barbara Boxer, of California, *Chair*

Max Baucus, of Montana.
JOSEPH I. LIEBERMAN, of Connecticut.
Thomas R. Carper, of Delaware.
Hillary Rodham Clinton, of New York.
Frank R. Lautenberg, of New Jersey.
Benjamin L. Cardin, of Maryland.
BERNARD SANDERS, of Vermont.
Amy Klobuchar, of Minnesota.
Sheldon Whitehouse, of Rhode Island.

James M. Inhofe, of Oklahoma.
John Warner, of Virginia.
George V. Voinovich, of Ohio.
Johnny Isakson, of Georgia.
David Vitter, of Louisiana.
Larry E. Craig, of Idaho.
Lamar Alexander, of Tennessee.
Christopher S. Bond, of Missouri.

SUBCOMMITTEES

[The chairman and the ranking minority member are ex officio (non-voting) members of all subcommittees on which they do not serve.]

Clean Air and Nuclear Safety

Thomas R. Carper, of Delaware, *Chair*

JOSEPH I. LIEBERMAN, of Connecticut.
Hillary Rodham Clinton, of New York.
BERNARD SANDERS, of Vermont.

George V. Voinovich, of Ohio.
Johnny Isakson, of Georgia.
Lamar Alexander, of Tennessee.

Private Sector and Consumer Solutions to Global Warming and Wildlife Protection

JOSEPH I. LIEBERMAN, of Connecticut, *Chair*

Max Baucus, of Montana.
Frank R. Lautenberg, of New Jersey.
BERNARD SANDERS, of Vermont.

John Warner, of Virginia.
Johnny Isakson, of Georgia.

Public Sector Solutions to Global Warming, Oversight, and Children's Health Protection

Barbara Boxer, of California, *Chair*

JOSEPH I. LIEBERMAN, of Connecticut.
Thomas R. Carper, of Delaware.
Amy Klobuchar, of Minnesota.
Sheldon Whitehouse, of Rhode Island.

Lamar Alexander, of Tennessee.
Larry E. Craig, of Idaho.
Christopher S. Bond, of Missouri.

Superfund and Environmental Health

Hillary Rodham Clinton, of New York, *Chair*

Max Baucus, of Montana.
Frank R. Lautenberg, of New Jersey.
Benjamin L. Cardin, of Maryland.

Larry E. Craig, of Idaho.
David Vitter, of Louisiana.
Christopher S. Bond, of Missouri.

Transportation and Infrastructure

Max Baucus, of Montana, *Chair*

Thomas R. Carper, of Delaware.	*Johnny Isakson,* of Georgia.
Hillary Rodham Clinton, of New York.	*John Warner,* of Virginia.
Benjamin L. Cardin, of Maryland.	*George V. Voinovich,* of Ohio.
BERNARD SANDERS, of Vermont.	*David Vitter,* of Louisiana.

Transportation Safety, Infrastructure Security, and Water Quality

Frank R. Lautenberg, of New Jersey, *Chair*

Benjamin L. Cardin, of Maryland.	*David Vitter,* of Louisiana.
Amy Klobuchar, of Minnesota.	*Christopher S. Bond,* of Missouri.
Sheldon Whitehouse, of Rhode Island.	*George V. Voinovich,* of Ohio.

STAFF

Committee on Environment and Public Works (SD–410), phone 224–8832; Majority fax (SD–410), 224–1273; (SH–508), 228–0574.

Majority Staff Director/Chief Counsel.—Bettina Poirier.
Deputy Staff Director/General Counsel.—Erik D. Olson.
Deputy Staff Director for Infrastructure.—Ken Kopocis.
Majority Senior Counsel.—Michael Goo.
Counsels: Alyson Cooke, Grant Cope, Tyler Rushforth.
Senior Policy Advisors/Counsel.—Jeff Rosato.
Office Manager.—Carolyn Dupree.
Chief Clerk.—Alicia Gordon.
Systems Administrator.—Rae Ann Phipps.
Communications Director.—Peter Rafle.
Professional Staff.—Mary Frances Repko.
Editorial Director.—Stephen Chapman.
GPO Detailees: LaVern Finks, Brenda Samuels.
Staff Assistants: Amanda Fox, Nicole Parisi-Smith.
Research Assistants: Eric Thu, Rachel Winnik.
Interns: Rachel Black, Lewis Taylor.

Minority fax (SD–456), 224–1273; (SH–508), 228–0574.

Minority Staff Director/Chief Counsel.—Andrew Wheeler.
Deputy Staff Director for Transportation.—Ruth Van Mark.
Executive Assistant/Office Manager.—Nancy Kate Ryder.
Senior Professional Staff.—Michele Nellenbach.
Counsels: Katherine English, Frank Fannon, Ryan Jackson, John Shanahan.
Senior Economist.—James O'Keeffe.
Professional Staff: Angelina Giancarlo, Maryanne Dunlap.
Research Assistant.—Alex Herrgott.
Fellow.—T.J. Kim.
Correspondence Manager.—Steve Higley.
Minority Press Secretary.—Matt Dempsey.
Staff Assistants: Elizabeth Fox, David Lundgreen, Mandy McNally.
Communications Director.—Marc Morano.

Finance

219 Dirksen Senate Office Building 20510

phone 224–4515, fax 224–0554, http://finance.senate.gov

meets second and fourth Tuesdays of each month

Max Baucus, of Montana, *Chair*

John D. Rockefeller IV, of West Virginia.
Kent Conrad, of North Dakota.
Jeff Bingaman, of New Mexico.
John F. Kerry, of Massachusetts.
Blanche L. Lincoln, of Arkansas.
Ron Wyden, of Oregon.
Charles E. Schumer, of New York.
Debbie Stabenow, of Michigan.
Maria Cantwell, of Washington.
Ken Salazar, of Colorado.

Chuck Grassley, of Iowa.
Orrin G. Hatch, of Utah.
Trent Lott, of Mississippi.
Olympia J. Snowe, of Maine.
Jon Kyl, of Arizona.
Gordon H. Smith, of Oregon.
Jim Bunning, of Kentucky.
Mike Crapo, of Idaho.
Pat Roberts, of Kansas.

SUBCOMMITTEES

[The chairman and the ranking minority member are ex officio (non-voting) members of all subcommittees on which they do not serve.]

Energy, Natural Resources, and Infrastructure

Jeff Bingaman, of New Mexico, *Chair*

Kent Conrad, of North Dakota.
John F. Kerry, of Massachusetts.
Blanche L. Lincoln, of Arkansas.
Ron Wyden, of Oregon.
Maria Cantwell, of Washington.
Ken Salazar, of Colorado.

Gordon H. Smith, of Oregon.
Orrin G. Hatch, of Utah.
Jim Bunning, of Kentucky.
Trent Lott, of Mississippi.
Mike Crapo, of Idaho.

Health Care

John D. Rockefeller IV, of West Virginia, *Chair*

John F. Kerry, of Massachusetts.
Jeff Bingaman, of New Mexico.
Blanche L. Lincoln, of Arkansas.
Ron Wyden, of Oregon.
Debbie Stabenow, of Michigan.
Maria Cantwell, of Washington.
Ken Salazar, of Colorado.

Orrin G. Hatch, of Utah.
Chuck Grassley, of Iowa.
Olympia J. Snowe, of Maine.
Jon Kyl, of Arizona.
Pat Roberts, of Kansas.
Jim Bunning, of Kentucky.

International Trade, and Global Competitiveness

Blanche L. Lincoln, of Arkansas, *Chair*

Max Baucus, of Montana.
John D. Rockefeller IV, of West Virginia.
Jeff Bingaman, of New Mexico.
Debbie Stabenow, of Michigan.
Charles E. Schumer, of New York.

Gordon H. Smith, of Oregon.
Mike Crapo, of Idaho.
Olympia J. Snowe, of Maine.
Pat Roberts, of Kansas.

Social Security, Pensions, and Family Policy

John F. Kerry, of Massachusetts, *Chair*

John D. Rockefeller IV, of West Virginia.
Kent Conrad, of North Dakota.
Charles E. Schumer, of New York.

Jim Bunning, of Kentucky.
Trent Lott, of Mississippi.
Jon Kyl, of Arizona.

Taxation and IRS Oversight and Long-Term Growth

Kent Conrad, of North Dakota, *Chair*

Max Baucus, of Montana.
Ron Wyden, of Oregon.
Maria Cantwell, of Washington.
Charles E. Schumer, of New York.
Debbie Stabenow, of Michigan.
Ken Salazar, of Colorado.

Jon Kyl, of Arizona.
Trent Lott, of Mississippi.
Pat Roberts, of Kansas.
Olympia J. Snowe, of Maine.
Mike Crapo, of Idaho.
Orrin G. Hatch, of Utah.

STAFF

Committee on Finance (SD–219), 224–4515, fax 228–0554.

Majority Staff Director.—Russ Sullivan.
Chief Counsel.—Bill Dauster.
Senior Advisor.—John Angell.
Counsel and Senior Advisor for Indian Affairs.—Richard Litsey.
Chief Tax Counsel.—Pat Heck.
Tax Counsels: Rebecca Baxter, Judy Miller, Joshua Odintz, Tiffany Smith.
Policy Advisors: Kristin Bailey, Pat Bousliman.
Tax Research Assistant.—Ryan Abraham.
Tax Detailee.—Mary Baker.
Chief Health and Welfare Counsel.—Michelle Easton.
Health Policy Advisors: Shawn Bishop, David Schwartz, Alice Weiss, William Wynne.
Health Research Assistant.—Catherine Dratz.
Health Policy Detailee.—Deidra Henry-Spires.
Chief Trade Counsel.—Demetrios Marantis.
Trade Counsels: Amber Cottle, Anya Landau, Janis Lazda.
International Trade Analyst.—Chelsea Thomas.
Trade Detailee.—Russell Ugone.
Senior Budget Analyst.—Alan Cohen.
Professional Staff Social Security.—Tom Klouda.
Senior Environmental Advisor.—Jo-Ellen Darcy.
Detailees: Tom Kornfield, Neil Ohlenkamp, Suzanne Payne, Sara Shepherd, Jennifer Smith.
Fellows: Leona Cuttler, Susan Douglas, Avi Salzman, Howard Tuch.
Legislative Fellow.—Tom Louthan.
Assistant to the Staff Director.—Jon Samson.
Communications Director.—Carol Guthrie.
Press Assistant.—Erin Shields.
Chief Editor.—Robert Merulla.
Editor.—Tim Danowski.
Chief Clerk.—Carla Martin.
Deputy Clerk.—Mark Blair.
Hearing Clerk.—Jewel Harper.
Staff Assistants: Brian Downey, Shaun Freiman, Jesse Schoolnik.
System Administrator.—Geoffrey Burrell.
Archivist.—Josh Levasseur.

Minority Staff Director/Chief Counsel.—Kolan Davis.
Deputy Staff Director/Chief Tax Counsel.—Mark Prater.
Senior Advisor/Tax Counsel.—Dean Zerbe.
Tax Counsels: Cathy Barre, Chris Javens, Elizabeth Paris.
Tax Assistant.—Nick Wyatt.
Special Counsel/Chief Investigator.—Emilia DiSanto.
Investigative Counsel.—Jason Foster.
Investigative Health Counsel.—Angela Choy.
Oversight Staff Assistant.—Tom Novelli.
Chief Health Counsel.—Mark Hayes.
Health Policy Advisors: Colette Desmarais, Michael Park, Becky Shipp, Susan Walden, Rodney Whitlock.
Health Assistant.—Sean McGuire.
Health Legislative Correspondent.—Ann McEniry.
Chief International Trade Counsel.—Stephen Schaefer.
International Trade Counsel.—David Johanson.
International Trade Policy Advisor.—Claudia Bridgeford.

Chief Social Security Analyst.—Steve Robinson.
Communications Director.—Jill Kozeny.
Press Secretary.—Jill Gerber.
Detailees: Anne Freeman, John Kalitka, Douglas Lund, Lynda Simmons, Julie Taitsman.
Fellow.—Martin Sobel.

Foreign Relations

450 Dirksen Senate Office Building 20510–6225

phone 224–4651, http://foreign.senate.gov

meets each Tuesday

Joseph R. Biden, Jr., of Delaware, *Chair*

Christopher J. Dodd, of Connecticut.
John F. Kerry, of Massachusetts.
Russell D. Feingold, of Wisconsin.
Barbara Boxer, of California.
Bill Nelson, of Florida.
Barack Obama, of Illinois.
Robert Menendez, of New Jersey.
Benjamin L. Cardin, of Maryland.
Robert P. Casey, Jr., of Pennsylvania.
Jim Webb, of Virginia.

Richard G. Lugar, of Indiana.
Chuck Hagel, of Nebraska.
Norm Coleman, of Minnesota.
Bob Corker, of Tennessee.
John E. Sununu, of New Hampshire.
George V. Voinovich, of Ohio.
Lisa Murkowski, of Alaska.
Jim DeMint, of South Carolina.
Johnny Isakson, of Georgia.
David Vitter, of Louisiana.

SUBCOMMITTEES

[The chairman and ranking minority member are ex officio (non-voting) members of all subcommittees on which they do not serve.]

African Affairs

Russell D. Feingold, of Wisconsin, *Chair*

Bill Nelson, of Florida.
Barack Obama, of Illinois.
Benjamin L. Cardin, of Maryland.
Jim Webb, of Virginia.

John E. Sununu, of New Hampshire.
Norm Coleman, of Minnesota.
David Vitter, of Louisiana.
Chuck Hagel, of Nebraska.

East Asian and Pacific Affairs

Barbara Boxer, of California, *Chair*

John F. Kerry, of Massachusetts.
Russell D. Feingold, of Wisconsin.
Barack Obama, of Illinois.
Jim Webb, of Virginia.

Lisa Murkowski, of Alaska.
Johnny Isakson, of Georgia.
David Vitter, of Louisiana.
Chuck Hagel, of Nebraska.

European Affairs

Barack Obama, of Illinois, *Chair*

Christopher J. Dodd, of Connecticut.
Robert Menendez, of New Jersey.
Benjamin L. Cardin, of Maryland.
Robert P. Casey, Jr., of Pennsylvania.

Jim DeMint, of South Carolina.
George V. Voinovich, of Ohio.
Bob Corker, of Tennessee.
Lisa Murkowski, of Alaska.

Near Eastern and South and Central Asian Affairs

John F. Kerry, of Massachusetts, *Chair*

Christopher J. Dodd, of Connecticut.
Russell D. Feingold, of Wisconsin.
Barbara Boxer, of California.
Benjamin L. Cardin, of Maryland.

Norm Coleman, of Minnesota.
Chuck Hagel, of Nebraska.
John E. Sununu, of New Hampshire.
George V. Voinovich, of Ohio.

International Development and Foreign Assistance, Economic Affairs and International Environmental Protection

Robert Menendez, of New Jersey, *Chair*

John F. Kerry, of Massachusetts.
Barbara Boxer, of California.
Barack Obama, of Illinois.
Robert P. Casey, Jr., of Pennsylvania.
Chuck Hagel, of Nebraska.
Bob Corker, of Tennessee.
Lisa Murkowski, of Alaska.
Jim DeMint, of South Carolina.

International Operations and Organizations, Democracy and Human Rights

Bill Nelson, of Florida, *Chair*

Russell D. Feingold, of Wisconsin.
Robert Menendez, of New Jersey.
Robert P. Casey, Jr., of Pennsylvania.
Jim Webb, of Virginia.
David Vitter, of Louisiana.
George V. Voinovich, of Ohio.
Jim DeMint, of South Carolina.
Johnny Isakson, of Georgia.

Western Hemisphere, Peace Corps, and Narcotics Affairs

Christopher J. Dodd, of Connecticut, *Chair*

John F. Kerry, of Massachusetts.
Bill Nelson, of Florida.
Robert Menendez, of New Jersey.
Jim Webb, of Virginia.
Bob Corker, of Tennessee.
Johnny Isakson, of Georgia.
Norm Coleman, of Minnesota.
John E. Sununu, of New Hampshire.

STAFF

Committee on Foreign Relations (SD–439), 224–4651.
Majority Staff Director.—Antony J. Blinken.
Special Assistant to the Staff Director.—Gabriel J. Bitol.
Deputy Staff Director / Chief Counsel.—Brian P. McKeon.
Professional Staff: Jeffrey Baron, Jonah B. Blank, Jennifer J. Simon Butler, Perry Cammack, Edward P. Levine, Erin M. Logan, Janice M. O'Connell, Sherman Patrick, Puneet Talwar, Tomicah Tillermann, Anthony Wier.
Legislative Research Assistants: Iris Ferguson, Sherman Patrick.
Minority Staff.—Kenneth A. Myers, Jr. (SD–450), 224–6797
Deputy Staff Director.—Daniel C. Diller.
Administrative Director.—Kristen C. Armitage.
Press Secretary.—Andrew J. Fisher.
Chief Counsel.—Paul F. Clayman.
Deputy Chief Counsels: Chris Ann Keehner, Manisha Singh.
Professional Staff: Jay Branegan, Neil Brown, Paul S. Foldi, Patrick Garvey, Mark Helmke, Mary Locke, W. Keith Luse, Carl E. Meacham, Thomas C. Moore, Kenneth A. Myers III, Michael V. Phelan, Nilmini G. Rubin, Bernard R. Toon II.
Staff Assistants: Brooke Daley, Marik String.
Non-Designated Committee Staff (SD–439), 224–4651.
Office Manager.—Gail Coppage.
Chief Clerk.—Susan Oursler.
Deputy Chief Clerk.—Megan Moyerman.
Executive / Legislative Clerk.—Angie Evans.
Director for Protocol / Foreign Travel.—Sandra S. Mason.
Hearing Coordinator.—Bertie H. Bowman.
Systems Administrator.—Alan Browne.
Staff Assistants: Matt Dixson, Matthew McMillan, Brittany Opacak.
Archivist Research Assistant.—Deborah M. Johnson.
Printing Clerks: Betty Acton, Michael W. Bennett.

Health, Education, Labor, and Pensions

428 Dirksen Senate Office Building 20510–6300

phone 224–5375, http://help.senate.gov

meets second and fourth Wednesdays of each month

Edward M. Kennedy, of Massachusetts, *Chair*

Christopher J. Dodd, of Connecticut.
Tom Harkin, of Iowa.
Barbara A. Mikulski, of Maryland.
Jeff Bingaman, of New Mexico.
Patty Murray, of Washington.
Jack Reed, of Rhode Island.
Hillary Rodham Clinton, of New York.
Barack Obama, of Illinois.
BERNARD SANDERS, of Vermont.
Sherrod Brown, of Ohio.

Michael B. Enzi, of Wyoming.
Judd Gregg, of New Hampshire.
Lamar Alexander, of Tennessee.
Richard Burr, of North Carolina.
Johnny Isakson, of Georgia.
Lisa Murkowski, of Alaska.
Orrin G. Hatch, of Utah.
Pat Roberts, of Kansas.
Wayne Allard, of Colorado.
Tom Coburn, of Oklahoma.

SUBCOMMITTEES

[The chairman and ranking minority member are ex officio members of all subcommittees on which they do not serve.]

* Children and Families [1]

Christopher J. Dodd, of Connecticut, *Chair*

Jeff Bingaman, of New Mexico.
Patty Murray, of Washington.
Jack Reed, of Rhode Island.
Hillary Rodham Clinton, of New York.
Barack Obama, of Illinois.
BERNARD SANDERS, of Vermont.

Lamar Alexander, of Tennessee.
Judd Gregg, of New Hampshire.
Lisa Murkowski, of Alaska.
Orrin G. Hatch, of Utah.
Pat Roberts, of Kansas.
Wayne Allard, of Colorado.

Employment and Workplace Safety

Patty Murray, of Washington, *Chair*

Christopher J. Dodd, of Connecticut.
Tom Harkin, of Iowa.
Barbara A. Mikulski, of Maryland.
Hillary Rodham Clinton, of New York.
Barack Obama, of Illinois.
Sherrod Brown, of Ohio.

Johnny Isakson, of Georgia.
Richard Burr, of North Carolina.
Lisa Murkowski, of Alaska.
Pat Roberts, of Kansas.
Wayne Allard, of Colorado.
Tom Coburn, of Oklahoma.

Retirement and Aging [1]

Barbara A. Mikulski, of Maryland, *Chair*

Tom Harkin, of Iowa.
Jeff Bingaman, of New Mexico.
Jack Reed, of Rhode Island.
BERNARD SANDERS, of Vermont.
Sherrod Brown, of Ohio.

Richard Burr, of North Carolina.
Judd Gregg, of New Hampshire.
Lamar Alexander, of Tennessee.
Johnny Isakson, of Georgia.
Orrin G. Hatch, of Utah.

STAFF

Committee on Health, Education, Labor, and Pensions (SH–644), 224–0767, fax 224–6510, TDD 224–1975.

Majority Staff Director/Chief Counsel.—Michael J. Myers.
Chief Counsel/Chief Education Adviser.—Carmel M. Martin.

Chief Counsel on Policy.—Jeffrey J. Teitz.
Policy Advisor.—Kelsey Phipps.
Policy Director for Disability and Special.—Constance M. Garner.
Senior Staff Assistant.—Benjamin M. Gruenbaum.
Staff Assistant.—Charles Garrison.
Professional Staff Member.—Ronny A. Carlton.
Staff Director for Health.—David C. Bowen (SH–527), 4–0767.
Deputy Staff Director for Health.—Caya B. Lewis.
Staff Assistant.—Molly C. Nicholson.
Detailees: David H. Dorsey, Stacey Sachs.
Education Counsel.—Melissa A. Rohrbach (SH–615), 4–5501.
Senior Counsels for Education: Jean-Daniel G. LaRock, Roberto J. Rodriguez.
Staff Assistant.—Nora C. Crowley.
Chief Labor Counsel.—Portia Wu (SH–632), 4–5441.
Labor and Economic Advisor.—Benjamin C. Olinsky.
Labor Counsel.—Lauren J. McGarity.
Counsel for Oversight and Investigations: Nicolas Bath, Sandra M. Gallardo (SH–615), 4–3112.
Staff Assistant.—Sarah Whitton.
Disability Counsel.—Lee A. Perselay (SH–113), 4–3254.
Legislative Assistant.—Michele Evermore.
Professional Staff Member.—Michael P. Woody.
Minority Staff Director.—Katherine B. McGuire (SH–835), 4–6770.
Chief Counsel.—Ilyse W. Schuman.
General Counsel/Pensions Director.—Gregory J. Dean.
Senior Policy Advisor.—Amy Shank.
Office Administrator.—Christina E. Sink.
Senior Communications Advisor.—Ron Hindle.
Health Policy Director.—Shana M. Christrup (SH–727), 4–0623.
Health Counsel.—Keith J. Flanagan.
Deputy Health Policy Director/Senior Counsel.—Andrew D. Patzman.
Professional Staff Members: Kathryn N. Barr, Aaron Bishop, Amy Muhlberg.
Research Assistants: Brittany K. Moore, Todd S. Spangler.
Detailee.—David Schmickel.
Education Policy Director.—Beth B. Buehlmann (SH–833), 4–8484.
Research Assistant.—Kelly B. Hastings.
Professional Staff Member.—Adam L. Briddell.
Senior Education Policy Advisor.—Lindsay Hunsicker.
Detailee.—Ann Clough.
Labor Policy Director.—Brian Hayes (SH–622B), 4–6770.
Labor Counsel.—Kyle K. Hicks.
Pension Policy Director.—Diann Howland.
Investigations Associate.—Koren P. Forster (SH–639), 4–6770.
Chief Investigative Counsel.—Lauren L. Fuller.
Investigative Associate.—Kristyn R. Vermeesch.
Communications/Director.—James Craig Orfield (SH–440), 4–6770.
Deputy Communications Director.—Michael T. Mahaffey.
Non-Designated Staff.—(SD–428), 4–5375.
Chief Clerk.—Denis P. O'Donovan.
Deputy Chief Clerk.—Jessie Lin Williams.
Editor.—Denise Lowery.
Senior Staff Assistant/Hearing Clerk.—Mary M. Smith.
Director, Information Technology.—Jizhi Zhang.
Detailee.—Carolyn E. Golden.

Subcommittee on Children and Families (SH–404B), 4–5630.
Majority Subcommittee Staff Director.—Mary Ellen C. McGuire.
Professional Staff Members: Catherine D. Graham-Hildum, Sherry F. Kaiman, Tamar Magarik.
Minority Subcommittee Staff Director (SH–607), 4–5800.
Professional Staff: Mary Sumpter, Sarah T. Rittling.
Subcommittee on Employment and Workplace Safety (SH–113), 4–2621.
Majority Subcommittee Staff Director (E,S&T).—William C. Kamela.
Research Assistant.—Michael J. Waske.
Minority Subcommittee Staff Director.—Glee Smith.
Professional Staff Member.—Edwin W. Egee.
Suubcommittee on Retirement and Aging (SD–424), 4–9243.
Majority Subcommittee Staff Director.—Ellen-Marie Whelan.
Professional Staff.—Okeysha Y. Brooks-Coley.
Minority Public Health Preparedness Policy Director.—Jennifer Bryning (SH–132), 4–0121.
Health Policy Director.—Jennifer L. Ware.
Retirement Policy Director.—Stephen Perrotta.
Staff Assistant.—Elizabeth Kendall Byrum.

---

[1] On January 31, 2007, the Committee was polled and agreed that the name of the Subcommittee on Education and Early Childhood Development would be changed to the Subcommittee on Children and Families, the Subcommittee on Retirement Security and Aging would be changed to the Subcommittee on Retirement and Aging, and that the Committee would discontinue the Subcommittee on Bioterrorism and Public Health Preparedness.

* Minority Subcommittee Member order corrected March 2007.

Homeland Security and Governmental Affairs

340 Dirksen Senate Office Building 20510

phone 224–2627, fax 228–3792, http://hsgac.senate.gov

Hearing Room—SD–342 Dirksen Senate Office Building

meets first Thursday of each month

JOSEPH I. LIEBERMAN, of Connecticut, *Chair*

Carl Levin, of Michigan.
Daniel K. Akaka, of Hawaii.
Thomas R. Carper, of Delaware.
Mark L. Pryor, of Arkansas.
Mary L. Landrieu, of Louisiana.
Barack Obama, of Illinois.
Claire McCaskill, of Missouri.
Jon Tester, of Montana.

Susan M. Collins, of Maine.
Ted Stevens, of Alaska.
George V. Voinovich, of Ohio.
Norm Coleman, of Minnesota.
Tom Coburn, of Oklahoma.
Pete V. Domenici, of New Mexico.
John Warner, of Virginia.
John E. Sununu, of New Hampshire.

SUBCOMMITTEES

[The chairman and the ranking minority member are ex officio members of all subcommittees.]

Federal Financial Management, Government Information, Federal Services, and International Security (FFM)

Thomas R. Carper, of Delaware, *Chair*

Carl Levin, of Michigan.
Daniel K. Akaka, of Hawaii.
Barack Obama, of Illinois.
Claire McCaskill, of Missouri.
Jon Tester, of Montana.

Tom Coburn, of Oklahoma.
Ted Stevens, of Alaska.
George V. Voinovich, of Ohio.
Pete V. Domenici, of New Mexico.
John E. Sununu, of New Hampshire.

Oversight of Government Management, the Federal Workforce, and the District of Columbia (OGM)

Daniel K. Akaka, of Hawaii, *Chair*

Carl Levin, of Michigan.
Thomas R. Carper, of Delaware.
Mark L. Pryor, of Arkansas.
Mary L. Landrieu, of Louisiana.

George V. Voinovich, of Ohio.
Ted Stevens, of Alaska.
Tom Coburn, of Oklahoma.
John Warner, of Virginia.

Permanent Subcommittee on Investigations (PSI)

Carl Levin, of Michigan, *Chair*

Thomas R. Carper, of Delaware.
Mark L. Pryor, of Arkansas.
Barack Obama, of Illinois.
Claire McCaskill, of Missouri.
Jon Tester, of Montana.

Norm Coleman, of Minnesota.
Tom Coburn, of Oklahoma.
Pete V. Domenici, of New Mexico.
John Warner, of Virginia.
John E. Sununu, of New Hampshire.

Ad Hoc Subcommittee on State, Local, and Private Sector Preparedness and Integration (SLPSPI)

Mark L. Pryor, of Arkansas, *Chair*

Daniel K. Akaka, of Hawaii.
Mary L. Landrieu, of Louisiana.
Barack Obama, of Illinois.
Claire McCaskill, of Missouri.
Jon Tester, of Montana.
John E. Sununu, of New Hampshire.
George V. Voinovich, of Ohio.
Norm Coleman, of Minnesota.
Pete V. Domenici, of New Mexico.
John Warner, of Virginia.

Ad Hoc Subcommittee on Disaster Recovery (SDR)

Mary L. Landrieu, of Louisiana, *Chair*

Thomas R. Carper, of Delaware.
Mark L. Pryor, of Arkansas.
Ted Stevens, of Alaska.
Pete V. Domenici, of New Mexico.

STAFF

Committee on Homeland Security and Governmental Affairs (SD–340), 224–2627
Majority Staff Director.—Michael Alexander.
Chief Counsel.—Kevin Landy.
Chief Clerk.—Trina Driessnack Tyrer.
Senior Counsels: Beth Grossman, Larry Novey.
Counsels: Troy Cribb, Holly Idelson, Mary Beth Schultz, Todd Stein.
Professional Staff: Eric Andersen, Christian Beckner, Jim McGee, Deborah Parkinson, Patricia Rojas, Adam Sedgewick, Jason Yanussi.
Communications Director.—Leslie Phillips.
Communications Advisor.—Scott Campbell.
Deputy Press Secretary.—Sheila Menz.
Executive Assistant/Office Manager.—Janet Burrell.
Legislative Assistant.—Alistair Reader.
Research Assistants: Elyse Greenwald, Kristine Lam.
Staff Assistants: Caroline Bolton, Seamus Hughes, Wesley Young.
Detailees: Nathan Lesser, Tracey Silberling.
Fellow.—Aaron Firoved.
Systems Administrator/Web Master.—Dan Muchow.
Financial Clerk.—John Gleason.
Publications Clerk.—Pat Hogan.
Archivist/Librarian.—Elisabeth Butler.
Minority Staff Director/Chief Counsel.—Brandon Milhorn (SD–344), 224–4751.
General Counsel.—Andy Weis.
Director of Homeland Security Affairs.—Rob Strayer.
Director of Governmental Affairs.—Amy Hall.
Counsels: Melvin Albritton, Mark LeDuc, Asha Mathew, Mark Winter, Amanda Wood.
Professional Staff: John Grant, Priscilla Hanley, Brooke Hayes, David Hunter, Clark Irwin.
Associate Counsels: Kate Alford, Jen Tarr.
Communications Director.—Jen Burita.
Press Secretary.—Elissa Davidson.
Executive Assistant.—Emily Meeks.
Staff Assistants: Tom Bishop, Doug Campbell.
Detailees: Steve Midas, Mike Moncibaiz, Leah Nash.

Subcommittee on Federal Financial Management, Government Information, Federal Services, and International Security (FFM) (SH–432), 224–7155.
Majority Staff Director.—John Kilvington.
Clerk.—Liz Scranton.
Professional Staff.—Mischa Thompson.
Staff Assistant.—Claudette David.
Minority Staff Director.—Katy French (SH–439), 224–2254.
Professional Staff: Chris Barkley, Drew Berky, Emily Cochran, Trey Hicks, Anna Shopen.

Subcommittee on Oversight of Government Management, the Federal Workforce, and the District of Columbia (OGM) (SH–605), 224–4551.
Majority Staff Director.—Richard J. Kessler.
Clerk.—Emily Marthaler.

Counsel.—Jennifer Tyree.
Professional Staff.—Jodi Lieberman.
Fellow.—Nicole Dyson.
Minority Staff Director.—Jennifer Hemingway (SH–604) 224–3862.
Counsel.—Doug Dziak.
Professional Staff: Tara Baird, David Cole, Theresa Prych.

Permanent Subcommittee on Investigations (PSI) (SR–199), 224–9505.
Majority Staff Director/Chief Counsel.—Elise Bean.
Clerk.—Mary Robertson.
Counsel/Chief Investigator.—Robert Roach.
Counsels: Dan Berkovitz, Zachary Schram, Laura Stuber.
Law Clerk.—Leslie Garthwaite.
Detailees: Kate Bittinger, John McDougal.
Fellow.—Guy Ficco.
Minority Staff Director/Chief Counsel.—Mark Greenblatt (SR–199), 224–3721.
Deputy Chief Counsel.—Mark Nelson.
Counsels: Michael Flowers, Sharon Beth Kristal, Clifford Stoddard, Timothy Terry.
Senior Investigator.—Jay Jennings.
Staff Assistant.—Emily Germain.
Detailee.—Ruth Perez.

Ad Hoc Subcommittee on State, Local, and Private Sector Preparedness and Integration (SLPSPI) (SH–613B).
Majority Staff Director.—Kristin Sharp.
Professional Staff.—Lauren Henry.

Ad Hoc Subcommittee on Disaster Recovery (SDR) (SH–605).
Majority Staff Director.—Donny Williams.
Minority Staff Director.—Charles Abernathy (SH–6091).

Judiciary

224 Dirksen Senate Office Building 20510–6275

phone 224–7703, fax 224–9516, http://www.senate.gov/~judiciary

meets upon call of the chair

Patrick J. Leahy, of Vermont, *Chair*

Edward M. Kennedy, of Massachusetts.
Joseph R. Biden, Jr., of Delaware.
Herb Kohl, of Wisconsin.
Dianne Feinstein, of California.
Russell D. Feingold, of Wisconsin.
Charles E. Schumer, of New York.
Richard Durbin, of Illinois.
Benjamin L. Cardin, of Maryland.
Sheldon Whitehouse, of Rhode Island.

Arlen Specter, of Pennsylvania.
Orrin G. Hatch, of Utah.
Chuck Grassley, of Iowa.
Jon Kyl, of Arizona.
Jeff Sessions, of Alabama.
Lindsey Graham, of South Carolina.
John Cornyn, of Texas.
Sam Brownback, of Kansas.
Tom Coburn, of Oklahoma.

SUBCOMMITTEES

Administrative Oversight and the Courts

Charles E. Schumer, of New York, *Chair*

Dianne Feinstein, of California.
Russell D. Feingold, of Wisconsin.
Sheldon Whitehouse, of Rhode Island.

Jeff Sessions, of Alabama.
Chuck Grassley, of Iowa.
Lindsey Graham, of South Carolina.

Antitrust, Competition Policy and Consumer Rights

Herb Kohl, of Wisconsin, *Chair*

Patrick J. Leahy, of Vermont.
Joseph R. Biden, Jr., of Delaware.
Russell D. Feingold, of Wisconsin.
Charles E. Schumer, of New York.
Benjamin L. Cardin, of Maryland.

Orrin G. Hatch, of Utah.
Arlen Specter, of Pennsylvania.
Chuck Grassley, of Iowa.
Sam Brownback, of Kansas.
Tom Coburn, of Oklahoma.

Crime and Drugs

Joseph R. Biden, Jr., of Delaware, *Chair*

Edward M. Kennedy, of Massachusetts.
Herb Kohl, of Wisconsin.
Dianne Feinstein, of California.
Russell D. Feingold, of Wisconsin.
Charles E. Schumer, of New York.
Richard Durbin, of Illinois.

Lindsey Graham, of South Carolina.
Arlen Specter, of Pennsylvania.
Orrin G. Hatch, of Utah.
Chuck Grassley, of Iowa.
Jeff Sessions, of Alabama.
Tom Coburn, of Oklahoma.

Human Rights and the Law

Edward M. Kennedy, of Massachusetts.
Joseph R. Biden, Jr., of Delaware.
Russell D. Feingold, of Wisconsin.
Benjamin L. Cardin, of Maryland.
Sheldon Whitehouse, of Rhode Island.

Tom Coburn, of Oklahoma.
Jon Kyl, of Arizona.
Lindsey Graham, of South Carolina.
John Cornyn, of Texas.
Sam Brownback, of Kansas.

Immigration, Refugees and Border Security

Edward M. Kennedy, of Massachusetts, *Chair*

Joseph R. Biden, Jr., of Delaware.
Dianne Feinstein, of California.
Charles E. Schumer, of New York.
Richard Durbin, of Illinois.

John Cornyn, of Texas.
Chuck Grassley, of Iowa.
Jon Kyl, of Arizona.
Jeff Sessions, of Alabama.

Terrorism, Technology and Homeland Security

Dianne Feinstein, of California, *Chair*

Edward M. Kennedy, of Massachusetts.
Joseph R. Biden, Jr., of Delaware.
Herb Kohl, of Wisconsin.
Charles E. Schumer, of New York.
Richard Durbin, of Illinois.
Benjamin L. Cardin, of Maryland.
Jon Kyl, of Arizona.
Orrin G. Hatch, of Utah.
Jeff Sessions, of Alabama.
John Cornyn, of Texas.
Sam Brownback, of Kansas.
Tom Coburn, of Oklahoma.

The Constitution

Russell D. Feingold, of Wisconsin, *Chair*

Edward M. Kennedy, of Massachusetts.
Dianne Feinstein, of California.
Richard Durbin, of Illinois.
Benjamin L. Cardin, of Maryland.
Sam Brownback, of Kansas.
Arlen Specter, of Pennsylvania.
Lindsey Graham, of South Carolina.
John Cornyn, of Texas.

STAFF

Committee on the Judiciary (SD–224), 224–77703, fax 224–9516.
Majority Staff Director/Chief Counsel.—Bruce Cohen (SD–226), 224–7703, fax 224–9516.
Legislative Staff Assistant to the Chief Counsel.—Leila George Wheeler.
Chief Counsel for Civil Justice.—Kristine Lucius.
Chief Counsel for Intellectual Property.—Susan Davies.
Chief Counsel for National Security.—Mary DeRosa.
Chief Counsel for Privacy.—Lydia Griggsby.
Senior Counsel.—Noah Bookbinder.
Counsels: Jeremy Paris, Zulima Espinel, Roscoe Jones, Aaron Cooper, Matthew Virkstis.
Professional Staff Members: Brian Baening, Adrienne Wojeciechowski, Kathryn Neal.
Detailees: Stephen Kelly, Matthew Solomon, Ellen Gallagher, John Whealan.
Communications Director.—Tracy Schmaler.
Press Assistant.—Matthew Smith.
Nominations Clerk.—William Bittinger.
Legislative Correspondent.—Kyra Harris.
Legislataive Staff Assistant.—Susan Audet, Kathryn Hutchinson.
Chief Clerk.—Jane Butterfield, 4–1444.
Deputy Chief Clerk.—Roslyne Turner, 4–6928.
Hearings Clerk.—Jennifer Leathers, 4–9376.
Librarian.—Charles Papirmeister.
Archivist.—Stuart Paine.
Court Reporter.—Lisa Dennis.
GPO Printers: Preble Marmion, Cecilia Morcombe.
Staff Assistants: Scott Wilson, Justin Pentenrieder.
Minority Staff Director/Chief Counsel.—Mike O'Neil.
Assistant to the Chief Counsel.—Ashlee Cutler.
Deputy Staff Director/Chief Counsel.—Nick Rossi.
Crime and Oversight Chief Counsel.—Matt Miner.
Crime and Oversight Counsels: Lisa Owings, Adam Turner, Jack Daly, Stephanie Hessler, Christine Fahrenback.
Crime and Oversight Legislative Assistant.—Damion Nielsen.
Nominations Chief Counsel.—Gregg Nunziata.
Naminations Counsels: Elizabeth Hays, Gabe Bell, Frank Scaturo.
Nominations Clerks: Chris Mills, Carrie DeLone.
Courts and Immigration Chief Counsel.—Juria Jones.
Courts and Immigration Counsels: Michelle Grossman, Lauren Petron, Gavin Young.
Courts and Immigration Detailee.—Lynn Quan Feldman.
Courts and Immigration Staff Assistant.—Lauren Pastarnack.
Civil Unit Chief Counsel.—Stephane Middleton.
Civil Unit Counsels: Ivy Johnson, Tim Streehan, Danny Fisher, Ryan Triplette, Hannibal Kemerer.
Civil Unit Professional Staff Member.—Nathan Morris.
Press Secretary.—Courtney Boone.
Press Assistant.—Blair Latoff.
Staff Assistants: Joe Lambert, Catherine Boudreaux.

Subcommittee on Administrative Oversight and the Courts (SD–161) 224–8352.
Majority Chief Counsel.—Preet Bharara.
Counsels: Julia Kernochan, Elliot Williams.
Legislative Correspondent.—Marco DeLeon.
Minority Chief Counsel.—Cindy Hayden (SDG–66), 224–7572.
Deputy Chief Counsel.—Charles Campbell.
Legislative Counsels: Maggie Harrell, Bradley Hays, Tenley Garvich.
Subcommittee on Antitrust, Competition Policy and Consumer Rights (SD–308) 224–3406.
Majority Chief Counsel.—Jeffrey Miller.
Senior Counsel.—Seth Bloom.
Counsel.—Caroline Holland, Nate Jones.
Legislative Aide.—Margaret Horn.
Minority Chief Counsel.—David Jones (SD–161), 224–5251.
Counsel.—Tom Tipping.
Professional Staff Member.—Brendan Dunn.
Detailee.—Jesse Baker.
Subcommittee on the Constitution (SH–807) 224–5573.
Majority Chief Counsel.—Bob Schiff.
Counsel.—Lara Flint.
Fellow.—Katherine Kimpel.
Legislative Clerks: Matt Robinson, Margaret Whiting.
Minority Legislative Assistants: Galen Roehl, Amy Blankenship, (SD–162), 224–6521.
Subcommittee on Crime and Drugs (SH–305), 224–0558.
Majority Chief Counsel.—Todd Hinnen.
Counsels: Nancy Libin, Nelson Peacock, Paul Rosen.
Staff Assistant.—Kristen Adams.
Minority Chief Counsel.—James Galyean (SD–524), 224–5972.
Clerk.—Walt Kuhn.
Subcommittee on Human Rights and the Law (SD–524), 224–1158.
Majority Chief Counsel.—Joseph Zogby.
Senior Counsel.—Michael Zubrensky.
Counsel.—Daniel Swanson.
Legislative Aide.—Reema Dodin.
Minority Legal Assistant.—Jane Treat (SD–155), 224–4280.
Counsel.—Tim Tardibono.
Legislative Assistant.—Matt Blackburn.
Subcommittee on Immigration, Border Security and Refugees (SD–520), 224–7878.
Majority Chief Counsel.—Bill Yeomans.
Counsels: Charlotte Burrows, Janice Kaguyutan, Christine Leonard, Esther Olavarria, Melissa Crow.
Immigration Fellow.—Todd Kushner.
Immigration Detailee.—Mary Giovagnoli.
Fellow.—Michelle Van Brakle.
Staff Assistant.—Gaurav Laroia.
Minority Chief Counsel.—Reed O'Conner (SD–139), 4–7840.
Legislative Director.—Beth Jafari.
Legal Assistant.—Anne Idsal.
Counsels: Chip Roy, Matt Johnson, Ramona McGee.
Subcommittee on Terrorism, Technology and Homeland Security (SH–815), 224–4933.
Majority Chief Counsel.—Jennifer Duck.
Counsels: Amy Pope, Greg Smith, Dave Stetson.
Legislative Aide.—Jason Knapp.
Legislative Correspondent.—Caitlin Doyle.
Staff Assistant.—Diana Bowen.
Minority Chief Counsel.—Stephen Higgins (SH–325), 224–6791.
Counsels: Mike Dougherty, Joe Matal.
Legislative Correspondent/Clerk.—Tom Humphrey.
Senator Cardin Judiciary Staff (SH–509), 224–4524.
Counsel.—Bill Van Horne.
Senator Whitehouse Judiciary Staff (SD–B40 (D)), 224–2921.
Chief Counsel.—Sam Goodstein.
Senator Grassley Judiciary Staff (SD–159), 224–5564.
Chief Counsel.—Rita Lari Jochum.
Counsel.—Nick Podsiadly.
Detailees: Nick Steen, Beth Gibble.
Staff Assistant.—David Bleich.

Rules and Administration

305 Russell Senate Office Building 20510–6325

phone 224–6352, http://rules.senate.gov

[Legislative Reorganization Act of 1946]

meets second and fourth Wednesday of each month

Dianne Feinstein, of California, *Chair*

Robert C. Byrd, of West Virginia.
Daniel K. Inouye, of Hawaii.
Christopher J. Dodd, of Connecticut.
Charles E. Schumer, of New York.
Richard Durbin, of Illinois.
E. Benjamin Nelson, of Nebraska.
Harry Reid, of Nevada.
Patty Murray, of Washington.
Mark L. Pryor, of Arkansas.

Robert F. Bennett, of Utah.
Ted Stevens, of Alaska.
Mitch McConnell, of Kentucky.
Thad Cochran, of Mississippi.
Trent Lott, of Mississippi.
Kay Bailey Hutchison, of Texas.
Saxby Chambliss, of Georgia.
Chuck Hagel, of Nebraska.
Lamar Alexander, of Tennessee.

(No Subcommittees)

STAFF

Committee on Rules and Administration (SR–305), 224–6352.
Majority Staff Director.—Howard Gantman.
Deputy Staff Director.—Jennifer Griffith.
Counsel.—Adam Ambrogi.
Elections Counsel.—Veronica Gillespie, 4–5648.
Administrative Assistant to Democratic Staff Director.—Carole Blessington, 4–0278.
Professional Staff: Erin Crowder, Natalie Price.
Minority Staff Director.—Mary Suit Jones.
Deputy Staff Director.—Shaun Parkin.
Chief Counsel.—Matthew Petersen.
Counsel.—Michael Merrell.
Professional Staff: Rachel Creviston, Trish Kent, Abbie Platt.
Non-Designated Staff:
Director for Administration and Policy.—Chris Shunk, 4–9528.
Chief Clerk.—Sue Wright, 4–2536.
Professional Staff: Leann Alwood, 4–7569; Matthew McGowan, 4–0281.
Staff Assistants: Katherine Rea, Travis Smith.

Small Business and Entrepreneurship

428A Russell Senate Office Building 20510

phone 224–5175, fax 224–5619, http://sbc.senate.gov/

[Created pursuant to S. Res. 58, 81st Congress]

meets first Wednesday of each month

John F. Kerry, of Massachusetts, *Chair*

Carl Levin, of Michigan.
Tom Harkin, of Iowa.
Joseph I. Lieberman, of Connecticut.
Mary L. Landrieu, of Louisiana.
Maria Cantwell, of Washington.
Evan Bayh, of Indiana.
Mark L. Pryor, of Arkansas.
Benjamin L. Cardin, of Maryland.
Jon Tester, of Montana.

Olympia J. Snowe, of Maine.
Christopher S. Bond, of Missouri.
Norm Coleman, of Minnesota.
David Vitter, of Louisiana.
Elizabeth Dole, of North Carolina.
John Thune, of South Dakota.
Bob Corker, of Tennessee.
Michael B. Enzi, of Wyoming.
Johnny Isakson, of Georgia.

(No Subcommittees)

STAFF

Committee on Small Business and Entrepreneurship (SR–428A), 224–5175, fax 224–6619.
Majority Staff Director.—Naomi Baum.
Deputy Staff Director.—Kevin Wheeler.
Assistant to the Staff Director.—Amber Gorman.
Social Security and Tax Counsel.—Kathy Kerrigan.
Counsels: Barry La Sala, Greg Willis.
Legislative Correspondent.—Oriel Feldman Hall.
Legislative Assistant.—Brian Rice.
Professional Staff Member.—John Phillips.
Press Secretary.—Kathryn Seck.
Research Analyst.—Karen Radermacher.
Chief Clerk.—Lena Postanowicz.
Staff Assistant.—Kelly Aschliman.
Minority Staff Director.—Wally Hsueh.
Executive Assistant.—Jennifer Rybicki.
Counsel.—Max Kidalov.
Regulatory Counsel.—Alex Hecht.
Tax and Finance Counsel.—Tucker Shumack.
Professional Staff Members: Jason Bassett, Matthew Berger, Jackie Ferko.
Research Analysts: Linda Le, Sean Philbin, Dan Westlake.
Staff Assistant.—Chris Averill.

Veterans' Affairs

SR–412 Russell Senate Office Building

phone 224–9126, http://veterans.senate.gov

meets first Wednesday of each month

Daniel K. Akaka, of Hawaii, *Chair*

John D. Rockefeller IV, of West Virginia.
Patty Murray, of Washington.
Barack Obama, of Illinois.
BERNARD SANDERS, of Vermont.
Sherrod Brown, of Ohio.
Jim Webb, of Virginia.
Jon Tester, of Montana.

Larry E. Craig, of Idaho.
Arlen Specter, of Pennsylvania.
Richard Burr, of North Carolina.
Johnny Isakson, of Georgia.
Lindsey Graham, of South Carolina.
Kay Bailey Hutchison, of Texas.
John Ensign, of Nevada.

(No Subcommittees)

STAFF

Committee on Veterans' Affairs (SR–412), 224–9126, fax 224–9575.
Majority Staff Director.—William E. Brew.
Deputy Staff Director.—Kim Lipsky.
Benefits Counsel.—Dahlia Melendrez.
Professional Staff Member for Health.—Alexandra Sardegna.
Professional Staff Member.—Edward B. Pusey.
Director of Special Projects/Investigations.—Mary Ellen McCarthy.
Legislative Assistants: Jacob Dreizin, Patrick McGreevey, Babette Polzer, Aaron Sheldon, Ginny Tucker.
Legislative Correspondent.—Jenny McCarthy.
Deputy Chief Clerk/Press Secretary.—Jessica Scheufele.
Director of Constituent Relations.—Michelle Moreno.
Staff Assistant.—Kawika Riley.
Minority Staff Director.—Lupe Wissel (825–A Hart), 224–2074, fax 224–8908.
Chief Counsel.—William T. Cahill.
Professional Staff Member.—Jonathan Towers.
Counsel.—Helen Walker.
Special Legislative Assistant.—Theresa Vawter.
Communications Director.—Jeffrey A. Schrade.
Republican Office Coordinator.—Kendra Waitley.
Non-Designated:
Chief Clerk.—Kelly Fado.
Hearing Clerk/Systems Administrator.—Matt Lawrence.

SELECT AND SPECIAL COMMITTEES OF THE SENATE

Committee on Indian Affairs

838 Hart Senate Office Building 20510–6450

phone 224–2251, http://indian.senate.gov

[Created pursuant to S. Res. 4, 95th Congress; amended by S. Res. 71, 103d Congress]

meets every Thursday of each month

Byron L. Dorgan, of North Dakota, *Chair*

Lisa Murkowski, of Alaska, *Vice Chair*

Daniel K. Inouye, of Hawaii.
Kent Conrad, of North Dakota.
Daniel K. Akaka, of Hawaii.
Tim Johnson, of South Dakota.
Maria Cantwell, of Washington.
Claire McCaskill, of Missouri.
Jon Tester, of Montana.

John McCain, of Arizona.
John Barrasso, of Wyoming.
Tom Coburn, of Oklahoma.
Pete V. Domenici, of New Mexico.
Gordon H. Smith, of Oregon.
Richard Burr, of North Carolina.

(No Subcommittees)

STAFF

Majority Staff Director.—Sara G. Garland.
Deputy Staff Director.—Cindy Darcy.
General Counsel.—Allison Binney.
Counsels: Heidi Frechette, Tracy Hartzler-Toon.
Policy Director.—John Harte.
Research Director.—Eamon Walsh.
Minority Staff Director/Chief Counsel.—David A. Mullon, Jr.
Deputy Chief Counsel.—Rhonda Harjo.
Senior Counsel.—James Hall.
Professional Staff.—Patrick McMullen.
Staff Assistant.—Jon Murphy.

Select Committee on Ethics

220 Hart Senate Office Building 20510, phone 224–2981, fax 224–7416

[Created pursuant to S. Res. 338, 88th Congress; amended by S. Res. 110, 95th Congress]

Barbara Boxer, of California, *Chair*

John Cornyn, of Texas, *Vice Chair*

Mark L. Pryor, of Arkansas.
Ken Salazar, of Colorado.

Pat Roberts, of Kansas.

STAFF

Staff Director/Chief Counsel.—Robert L. Walker.

Deputy Staff Director.—Annette Gillis.
Senior Counsel/Director of Education and Training.—Kenyen Brown.
Counsels: Tremayne Bunaugh, William Corcoran, Katja Eichinger, Elizabeth Horton, Matthew Mesmer.
Professional Staff.—John Lewter.
Systems Administrator.—Danny Remington.
Staff Assistants: Shannon Noble, Patricia Parker, Dawne Vernon.

Select Committee on Intelligence

211 Hart Senate Office Building 20510–6475, phone 224–1700

http://www.senate.gov/~intelligence

[Created pursuant to S. Res. 400, 94th Congress]

John D. Rockefeller IV, of West Virginia, *Chair*

Christopher S. Bond, of Missouri, *Vice Chair*

Dianne Feinstein, of California.
Ron Wyden, of Oregon.
Evan Bayh, of Indiana.
Barbara A. Mikulski, of Maryland.
Russell D. Feingold, of Wisconsin.
Bill Nelson, of Florida.
Sheldon Whitehouse, of Rhode Island.

John Warner, of Virginia.
Chuck Hagel, of Nebraska.
Saxby Chambliss, of Georgia.
Orrin G. Hatch, of Utah.
Olympia J. Snowe, of Maine.
Richard Burr, of North Carolina.

Ex Officio

Harry Reid, of Nevada.
Carl Levin, of Michigan.

Mitch McConnell, of Kentucky.
John McCain, of Arizona.

STAFF

Majority Staff Director.—Andrew W. Johnson.
Minority Staff Director.—Louis B. Tucker.
Chief Clerk.—Kathleen P. McGhee.

Special Committee on Aging

G–31 Dirksen Senate Office Building 20510, phone 224–5364

http://aging.senate.gov

[Reauthorized pursuant to S. Res. 4, 95th Congress]

Herb Kohl, of Wisconsin, *Chair*

Ron Wyden, of Oregon.
Blanche L. Lincoln, of Arkansas.
Evan Bayh, of Indiana.
Thomas R. Carper, of Delaware.
Bill Nelson, of Florida.
Hillary Rodham Clinton, of New York.
Ken Salazar, of Colorado.
Robert P. Casey, Jr., of Pennsylvania.
Claire McCaskill, of Missouri.
Sheldon Whitehouse, of Rhode Island.

Gordon H. Smith, of Oregon.
Richard C. Shelby, of Alabama.
Susan M. Collins, of Maine.
Mel Martinez, of Florida.
Larry E. Craig, of Idaho.
Elizabeth Dole, of North Carolina.
Norm Coleman, of Minnesota.
David Vitter, of Louisiana.
Bob Corker, of Tennessee.
Arlen Specter, of Pennsylvania.

STAFF

Majority Staff Director.—Julie Cohen.

Policy Advisor.—Nicole Brown.
Press Secretary.—Ashley Glacel.
Research Assistant.—Will Kramer.
Chief of Investigations.—Jack Mitchell.
Senior Policy Advisors: Anne Montgomery, Stacy Stordahl, Cherie Wilson.
Senior Counsel.—Cecil Swamidoss.
Staff Assistants: Barry Landy, Meredith Symonds.

Minority Staff (SH–628), 224–5364, fax 224–9926.
Staff Director.—Catherine Finley.
Legislative Assistant.—Jill Canino.
Communications Director.—Kimberly Collins.
Investigative Assistant.—Danny Fernendez.
Senior Investigative Counsel.—Chris Hinkle.
Legislative Correspondent.—Chris Holt.
Investigative Counsel.—Brandi Kupchella.
Staff Assistants: Elizabeth Canja, Sarah Cody
Professional Staff Members: Matt Canedy, Kara Getz, Lindsay Morris, Mike Smith.

National Republican Senatorial Committee

425 Second Street, NE., 20002, phone 675–6000, fax 675–6058

John Ensign, of Nevada, *Chair*

STAFF

Executive Director.—Scott Bensing.
Director of:
Administration.—Doug Robinson.
Communications.—Rebecca Fisher.
Finance.—Lindsey Slanker.
Legal Counsel.—Chris Gober.
Political Director.—Mike Slanker.
Research.—Bill Wykpisz.

Senate Republican Policy Committee

347 Russell Senate Office Building, phone 224–2946
fax 224–1235, http://rpc.senate.gov

Kay Bailey Hutchison, of Texas, *Chair*

STAFF

Staff Director.—Bill Hughes.
Deputy Staff Director.—Gay Westbrook.
Administrative Director.—Craig Cheney.
Analysts:
Commerce, Agriculture, and Trade.—Patrick Lehman.
Defense Policy.—Michael Stransky.
Health Care Policy.—Kishan Kumar Putta.
Immigration/DHS.—Luke Bellocchi.
Labor, Education, Welfare Policy.—Dana Barbieri.
Professional Staff:
Editor.—Judy Gorman Prinkey.
Associate Editor.—Molly Giammarco.
Economic Policy.—Derek Kan.
Tax Counsel.—Sarah Novascone.
Staff Assistant.—Anna-Claire Whitehead.
Station Manager/Special Projects.—Carolyn Laird.
Station Operators/Project Assistant.—Scott Strain.
System Administrator/RVA Analyst.—Tom Pulju.

Senate Republican Conference

405 Hart Senate Office Building, phone 224–2764
http://src.senate.gov

Chair.—Jon Kyl, of Arizona.
Vice Chair.—John Cornyn, of Texas.

STAFF

Conference of the Majority (SH–405), 224–2764.
Staff Director.—Ron Bonjean.
Policy Director/Chief Counsel.—Steven Duffield.
Communications Director.—Ryan Loskarn.
Senior Writer.—Mary Katherine Ascik.
Deputy Policy Director.—Brooke Bacak.
Press Secretary.—Andy Chasin.
Director of Operations.—Leigh Hightower.
Hispanic Outreach.—Carlos Gonzalez.
Radio Services Director.—Dave Hodgdon.
Assistant Radio Services Director.—Curtis Swager.
Television Services Director.—Henry Peterson, Jr.
Production Manager.—Cyrus Pearson.
Videographer.—Lane Marshall.
Art Director.—Chris Angrisani.
Senior Graphics Designer.—Laura Gill.
Graphics Designer.—Nick Schweich.
Director of Information Technology.—Aaron Broughton.
Deputy Director of Information Resources.—Nate Green.
Press Assistant.—Sharon Warren.

Democratic Policy Committee

419 Hart Senate Office Building, phone 224–3232

Byron L. Dorgan, of North Dakota, *Chair*

Ken Salazar, of Colorado, Regional Chair.
Evan Bayh, of Indiana, Regional Chair.
Jack Reed, of Rhode Island, Regional Chair.
Mary L. Landrieu, of Louisiana, Regional Chair.
Harry Reid, of Nevada.
John D. Rockefeller IV, of West Virginia.
Daniel K. Akaka, of Hawaii.
Russell D. Feingold, of Wisconsin.
JOSEPH I. LIEBERMAN, of Connecticut.
Dianne Feinstein, of California.
Ron Wyden, of Oregon.
Tim Johnson, of South Dakota.
Charles E. Schumer, of New York.
Blanche L. Lincoln, of Arkansas.
Bill Nelson, of Florida.
Thomas R. Carper, of Delaware.
Barbara A. Mikulski, of Maryland.
Frank R. Lautenberg, of New Jersey.
Sherrod Brown, of Ohio.
Richard Durbin, of Illinois, ex officio, (as Assistant Democratic Leader).
Patty Murray, of Washington, ex officio, (as Secretary of the Conference).

STAFF

Staff Director.—Chuck Cooper.
Assistant to the Staff Director.—Casey Gillece.
Research Director.—Tim Gaffaney.
Policy Advisors: Joi Chaney, Kristin Devine, Liz Engel, Sara Mills, Erika Moritsugu.
New Policy Director.—Doug Steiger.
New Policy Outreach.—Brad Weltman.
Deputy Staff Director and Chief Counsel.—Neal Higgins.
Publications Director.—Doug Connolly.
Votes Analyst.—Michael Mozden.
Congressional Fellow.—Brendan Doherty.

Steering and Outreach Committee

712 Hart Senate Office Building, phone 224–9048

Debbie Stabenow, of Michigan *Chair*

John F. Kerry, of Massachusetts.
Daniel K. Inouye, of Hawaii.
Robert C. Byrd, of West Virginia.
Edward M. Kennedy, of Massachusetts.
Joseph R. Biden, Jr., of Delaware.
Patrick J. Leahy, of Vermont.
Christopher J. Dodd, of Connecticut.
Tom Harkin, of Iowa.
Max Baucus, of Montana.
Kent Conrad, of North Dakota.
Carl Levin, of Michigan.
Herb Kohl, of Wisconsin.
Barbara Boxer, of California.
Jeff Bingaman, of New Mexico.
Harry Reid, of Nevada.
Richard Durbin, of Illinois.
Hillary Rodham Clinton, of New York.
Mark L. Pryor, of Arkansas.

STAFF

Staff Director.—Tom Russell.
Deputy Director.—Kriston Alford McIntosh.
Associate Directors: Kory Vargas Caro, Robert Holifield, Josh King.
Staff Assistant.—Marcus Fleming.

Senate Democratic Communications Center

619 Hart Senate Office Building, phone 224–1430

Harry Reid, of Nevada, *Chair*

STAFF

Communications Director.—Rodell Mollineau.
Administrator.—Mary Helen Fuller.
Editors: Ike Blake, Toby Hayman, Alice Liu.
Engineer.—Rick Singer.
Graphic Design Specialist.—Perisha Gates.
Internet Technology Adviser.—Jordan Higgins.
Press Assistant.—Kim Rymsha.
Radio Producer.—Ian Shifrin.
Videographers: Clare Flood, Brian Jones, Kevin Kelleher.

Senate Democratic Conference

37A Russell Senate Office Building, Basement, phone 224–4822, fax 228–0325

Secretary.—Patty Murray, of Washington State.
Leadership Staff Director.—Mike Spahn.
Floor and Communication Adie.—Nathan Blumenthal.

Democratic Senatorial Campaign Committee

120 Maryland Avenue, NE., 20002, phone 224–2447

Charles E. Schumer, of New York, *Chair*

Robert Menendez, of New Jersey, *Vice Chair*

Harry Reid, of Nevada, *Democratic Leader*

Amy Klobuchar, of Minnesota, *Outreach and Policy Chair*

STAFF

Executive Director.—J.B. Poersch.
Communications Director.—Matthew Miller.
Political Director.—Guy Cecil.
Finance Director.—Tom Lopach.
Comptroller.—Darlene Setter.
Assistant to the Executive Director.—Nicki Sacco.
Legal Counsel.—Mark Elias.

OFFICERS AND OFFICIALS OF THE SENATE

Capitol Telephone Directory, 224–3121
Senate room prefixes:
Capitol—S, Russell Senate Office Building—SR
Dirksen Senate Office Building—SD, Hart Senate Office Building—SH

PRESIDENT OF THE SENATE

Vice President of the United States and President of the Senate.—Richard B. Cheney.

The Ceremonial Office of the Vice President is S–212 in the Capitol. The Vice President has offices in the Dirksen Senate Office Building, the Eisenhower Executive Office Building (EEOB) and the White House (West Wing).

Chief of Staff to the Vice President and Counsel.—David Addington, EEOB, room 276, 456–9000.
Deputy Chief of Staff.—Claire O'Donnell, EEOB, room 272, 456–6770.
Counsel to the Vice President.—Shannen Coffin, EEOB, room 282, 456–9089.
Assistant to the Vice President for—
Communications / Press Secretary.—Lea Anne McBride, EEOB, room 293, 456–0373.
Domestic Policy.—Neil Patel, EEOB, room 286, 456–2728.
Legislative Affairs.—Brenda Becker, EEOB, room 285, 456–6774.
National Security Affairs.—John Hannah, EEOB, room 298, 456–9501.
Political Affairs.—Mel Raines, EEOB, room 272, 456–9033.
Executive Assistant to the Vice President.—Debra Heiden, West Wing, 456–7549.
Chief of Staff to Mrs. Cheney.—Cecelia Boyer, EEOB, room 200, 456–7458.
Deputy Assistant to the Vice President and Director of Scheduling.—Elizabeth Kleppe, EEOB, room 279, 456–6773.
Director of Correspondence.—Rose Folsom, EEOB, room 200, 456–9002.

PRESIDENT PRO TEMPORE

S–131 The Capitol, phone 224–2848

President Pro Tempore of the Senate.—Robert C. Byrd.
Executive Assistant.—Betsy Dietz, 224–2848.

MAJORITY LEADER

S–221 The Capitol, phone 224–2158, fax 224–7362

Majority Leader.—Harry Reid.
Chief of Staff.—Gary Myrick.
Deputy Chief of Staff.—David McCallum.
Executive Assistant.—Janice Shelton.
Scheduler.—Robin McCain.
Assistant to the Chief of Staff.—Sarah Ferguson.
Chief Counsel.—Ron Weich.
Policy Director.—Randy Devalk.
Senior Advisor for Communications and Outreach.—Penny Lee.

ASSISTANT MAJORITY LEADER

S–321 The Capitol, phone 224–9447

Assistant Democratic Leader.—Richard Durbin.

Chief of Staff.—Pat Souders.
Director of Operations.—Sally Brown-Shaklee.
Director of Scheduling.—Michael Kolenc.
Communications Director.—Joe Shoemaker.
Deputy Communications Director.—Sandra Abrevaya.
Press Secretary.—Christina Mulka.
Democratic Media Coordinator.—Max Gleischman.
Speechwriter.—Molly Rowley.
Director of Floor Operations.—Chris Kang.
Floor Counsel.—Nicole Isaac.
Special Assistant.—Michael Delich.
Staff Assistant.—Claire Dickhut.

REPUBLICAN LEADER

S–230 The Capitol, phone 224–3135, fax 228–1264

Republican Leader.—Mitch McConnell.
Chief of Staff.—Kyle Simmons.
Deputy Chief of Staff.—Sharon Soderstrom.
Personal Assistant.—Will Dorton.
Scheduler.—Stefanie Hagar.
Assistant Scheduler.—Rebecca Winnett.
Director of Administration.—Laura Sequeira.
Policy Advisor and Counsel.—Brandi White.
Domestic Policy Director.—Rohit Kumar.
Policy Advisors: Megan Hauck, Libby Jarvis, Malloy McDaniel, Lanier Swann.
Legal Counsels: John Abegg, Brian Lewis.
National Security Advisor.—Tom Hawkins.
Communications Director.—Don Stewart.
Speechwriter.—Brian McGuire.
Press Secretary.—Jennifer Morris.
Deputy Press Secretary.—Ashley Rogers.
Systems Administrator.—Elmamoun Sulfab.
Staff Assistants: Kristen Forcht, Allison Moore, Janie Romaine.

OFFICE OF THE REPUBLICAN WHIP

S–208 The Capitol, phone 224–2708, fax 228–1507

Republican Whip.—Trent Lott.
Chief of Staff.—Manny Rossman.
Staff Director.—Susan Wells.
Policy Director.—John O'Neill.
Floor Counsel.—Alexander Polinsky.
Whip Liaisons: Ryan Peebles, Amy Swonger.
Floor Assistant.—Conner Collins.
Staff Assistants: Lauren Bellman, Annie Estrada.

OFFICE OF THE SECRETARY

S–312 The Capitol, phone 224–3622

NANCY ERICKSON, Secretary of the Senate; elected and sworn in as the 32nd Secretary of the Senate on January 4, 2007; native of South Dakota; B.A. in Government and History from Augustana College, Sioux Falls, SD; M.A. in public policy from American University, Washington, DC; Democratic Representative, Senate Sergeant at Arms (SAA); Deputy Chief of Staff, Senator Tom Daschle; General Accounting Office.

Secretary of the Senate.—Nancy Erickson (S–312), 224–3622.
Chief of Staff.—Robert W. Paxton (S–333), 224–5636.
Deputy Chief of Staff.—Beth Provenzano (S–312), 224–6254.
Capitol Offices Liaison.—Gerald Thompson (SB–36), 224–1483.

Assistant Secretary of the Senate.—Sheila M. Dwyer (S–414C), 224–2114.
General Counsel.—Adam Bramwell (S–333), 224–8789.
Executive Accounts Administrator.—Zoraida Torres (S–414B), 224–7099.
Director (LIS Project Office).—Marsha Misenhimer (SD–B44A), 224–2500.
Bill Clerk.—Mary Anne Clarkson (S–123), 224–2120.
Director of:
Captioning Services.—JoEllen R. Dicken (ST–54), 224–4321.
Conservation and Preservation.—Carl Fritter, (S–416), 224–4550.
Curator.—Diane Skvarla (S–411), 224–2955.
Daily Digest, Editor.—Ken Dean (S–421 and S–421A), 224–2658.
Assistant Editor.—Elizabeth Brown, 224–2658.
Disbursing Office, Financial Clerk.—Chris J. Doby (SH–127), 224–3205.
Assistant Financial Clerk.—Ileana Garcia, 224–3208.
Enrolling Clerk.—Margarida Curtis (S–139), 224–8427.
Assistant Enrolling Clerk.—Cassandra Byrd, 224–7108.
Executive Clerk.—Michelle Haynes (S–138), 224–4341.
Assistant Executive Clerk.—Brian Malloy, 224–1918.
Historian.—Richard A. Baker (SH–201), 224–6900.
Associate Historian.—Donald A. Ritchie, 224–6816.
Assistant Historian.—Betty K. Koed, 224–0753.
Human Resources, Director.—Vacant (SH–231B), 224–3625.
Information Systems, Systems Administrator.—Dan Kulnis (S–422), 224–4883.
Webmaster.—Cheri Allen, 224–2020.
Interparliamentary Services, Director.—Sally Walsh (SH–808), 224–3047.
Journal Clerk.—Scott Sanborn (S–135), 224–4650.
Legislative Clerk.—David J. Tinsley (S–134), 224–4350.
Assistant Legislative Clerk.—Kathleen Alvarez, 224–3630.
Librarian.—Gregory C. Harness (SR–B15), 224–3313.
Official Reporters of Debates, Chief Reporter.—Jerald D. Linell (S–410A), 224–7525.
Coordinator of the Record.—Petie Gallacher, 224–1238.
Morning Business Editor.—Jack Hickman (S–123), 224–3079.
Parliamentarian.—Alan S. Frumin (S–133), 224–6128.
Senior Assistant Parliamentarians: Elizabeth MacDonough, 224–6128; Peter Robinson, 224–5133.
Printing and Document Services, Director.—Karen Moore (SH–B04), 224–0205.
Assistant to the Director.—Bud Johnson, 224–2555.
Public Records, Superintendent.—Pamela B. Gavin (SH–232), 224–0762.
Assistant Superintendent.—Dana McCallum, 224–0329.
Information Specialist for—
Campaign Finance.—Raymond Davis, 224–0761.
Ethics and Disclosure.—April Judd, 224–0763.
Lobbying and Foreign Travel.—Erica Omorogieva, 224–0758.
Senate Chief Counsel for Employment.—Jean Manning (SH–103), 224–5424.
Senate Gift Shop, Director.—Ernie LePire (SDG–42), 224–7308.
Senate Page School, Principal.—Kathryn S. Weeden, 224–3926.
Senate Security, Director.—Michael P. DiSilvestro (S–407), 224–5632.
Deputy Director.—Margaret Garland, 224–5632.
Stationery, Keeper of the Stationery.—Michael V. McNeal, 224–3381.
Assistant Keeper of the Stationery.—Tony Super, 224–4846.
Joint Office of Education and Training, Director.—Peggy Greenberg (SH–121), 224–5969.

OFFICE OF THE CHAPLAIN

S–332 The Capitol, phone 224–2510, fax 224–9686

BARRY C. BLACK, Chaplain, U.S. Senate; born in Baltimore, MD, on November 1, 1948; education: Bachelor of Arts, Theology, Oakwood College, 1970; Master of Divinity, Andrews Theological Seminary, 1973; Master of Arts, Counseling, North Carolina Central University, 1978; Doctor of Ministry, Theology, Eastern Baptist Seminary, 1982; Master of Arts, Management, Salve Regina University, 1989; Doctor of Philosophy, Psychology, United States International University, 1996; military service: U.S. Navy, 1976–2003; rising to the rank of Rear Admiral; Chief of Navy Chaplains, 2000–2003; awards: Navy Distingusihed Service Medal; Legion of Merit Medal; Defense Meritorious Service Medal; Meritorious Service Medals (two awards); Navy and Marine Corps Commendation Medals (two awards); 1995 NAACP Renowned Service Award; family: married to Brenda; three children: Barry II, Brendan, and Bradford.

Chaplain of the Senate.—Barry C. Black.
Chief of Staff.—Alan N. Keiran, 224–7456.
Communications Director.—Meg Saunders, 224–3894.
Staff Scheduler/Executive Assistant.—Jody Spraggins-Scott, 224–2048.

OFFICE OF THE SERGEANT AT ARMS

S–151 The Capitol, phone 224–2341, fax 224–7690

TERRANCE W. GAINER, Sergeant at Arms, U.S. Senate; elected and sworn in as 38th Sergeant at Arms on January 4, 2007; education: B.A., Sociology from St. Benedict's College; M.S., Management and Public Service; J.D. from DePaul University of Chicago; Military service: Decorated veteran who served in the Vietnam War and as a Captain in the U.S. Naval Reserve until 2000; professional: Law enforcement career began in Chicago, IL, 1968; rose through the ranks serving as Deputy IG of Illinois, Deputy Director of Illinois State Police and U.S. Department of Transportation; Appointed Director of Illinois State Police in March, 1991; Gainer went on to serve as second in command of the Metropolitan Police Department of the District of Columbia beginning in May, 1998 and Chief of the U.S. Capitol Police from 2002–06; Until his appointment as Sergeant at Arms; Gainer served the private sector focusing on emergency preparedness issues and law enforcement programs supporting Army and Marine operations in Iraq and Afghanistan; family: married, with 6 children and 12 grandchildren.

Sergeant at Arms.—Terrance W. Gainer.
Deputy Sergeant at Arms.—Drew Willison.
Administrative Assistant.—Rick Edwards, SB–8.
Executive Assistant.—Lynne Halbrooks, ST–39, 224–6355.
Assistant Sergeant at Arms for Police Operations.—Bret Swanson, SDG–10, 224–7052.
Assistant Sergeant at Arms for Operations.—Esther L. Gordon, SD–150, 224–7747.
Assistant Sergeant at Arms and Chief Information Officer.—J. Greg Hanson, Ph.D., (Postal Square), 224–9430.
Assistant Sergeant at Arms for Security and Emergency Prepardness.—Chuck Kaylor (Postal Square), 224–1404.

EXECUTIVE OFFICE

Appointment Desk Manager.—Joy Ogden, North Door Capitol Building, 1st Floor, 224–6304.
Capitol Information Officer.—Laura Parker, S–151, 224–2341.
Doorkeeper Supervisor.—Myron J. Fleming, SB–6, 224–1879.
Employee Assistance Program Administrator.—Christy Prietsch, Hart Senate Office Building, 228–3902.
Protocol Officer.—Becky Daugherty, S–151, 224–2341.

CAPITOL FACILITIES

Capitol Facilities Manager.—Skip Rouse, ST–62, 224–4171.

CENTRAL OPERATIONS

Director of Central Operations.—Juanita Rilling, SD–G61A, 224–8587.
Administrative Services Manager.—Joann Soults, SD–G84, 224–4716.
Hair Care Manager.—Kimberly Johnson, SR–B70, 224–4560.
Parking Manager.—Vacant, SD–G58, 224–8888.

Photo Studio Manager.—Bill Allen, SD–G85, 224–6000.
Printing, Graphics and Direct Mail Manager.—Hazel Getty, SD–G82, 224–5981.

FINANCIAL MANAGEMENT

Chief Financial Officer.—Christopher Dey (Postal Square), 224–6292.
Accounting and Budget Manager.—Peter DuBois, 224–1499.
Accounts Payable Manager.—Roy McElwee, 224–6074.
Financial Analysis Manager.—David Salem, 224–8844.
Procurement Manager.—David Baker, 224–2547.

HUMAN RESOURCES

Director of Human Resources.—Patrick Murphy, SH–142, 224–2889.
SAA Safety Office Officer.—Irvin Queja, 228–0823.
Senate Placement Officer Manager.—Brian Bean, 224–9167.
Workers' Compensation Office Manager.—Catherine Modeste Brooks, 224–3796.

IT SUPPORT SERVICES

Director of IT Support Services.—Kimball Winn (Postal Square), 224–0459.
Desktop/LAN Support Manager.—Tim Dean, 224–3564.
Office Equipment Services Manager.—Vicki Jinnett, 224–6779.
Telecom Services Manager.—Rick Kauffman, 224–9293.

MEDIA GALLERIES

Director of the Daily Press Gallery.—S. Joseph Keenan, S–316, 224–0241.
Director of the Periodical Press Gallery.—Edward V. Pesce, S–320, 224–0265.
Director of the Press Photographers Gallery.—Jeff Kent, S–317, 224–6548.
Director of the Radio and Television Gallery.—Michael Mastrian, S–325, 224–7610.

OFFICE OF EDUCATION AND TRAINING

Director of the Office of Education and Training.—Peggy Greenberg, SH–121, 224–5969.

OFFICE OF SECURITY AND EMERGENCY PREPARDNESS

Deputy Assistant Sergeant at Arms for Security and Emergency Preparedness.—Michael Johnson (Postal Square), 224–1969.
Continuity Programs Executive Manager.—Dick Attridge, 224–3691.
Security Planning and Operations Executive Manager.—Vacant, 228–6737.

OFFICE SUPPORT SERVICES

Administrative Services Executive Manager.—Barbara Graybill (Postal Square), 224–5402.
Customer Support Manager.—Dave Cape, SD–180, 224–0310.
State Office Liaison.—Jeanne Tessieri (Postal Square), 224–5409.

PAGE PROGRAM

Director of the Page Program.—Elizabeth Roach (Webster Hall), 228–1291.

POLICE OPERATIONS

Deputy Assistant Sergeant at Arms for Police Operations.—Kristan Trugman, SDG–10, 224–8997.

PROCESS MANAGEMENT & INNOVATION

Director of Process Management & Innovation.—Ed Jankus (Postal Square), 224–7780.
IT Research & Deployment Manager.—Steve Walker, 224–1768.
Program Management Manager.—Joe Eckert, 224–2982.

RECORDING STUDIO

Recording Studio Manager.—Dave Bass, ST–29, 224–4979.

SENATE POST OFFICE

Senate Postmaster.—Joe Collins, SD–B23, 224–5675.
Superintendent of Mails.—Alan Stone, SD–B28, 224–1060.

TECHNOLOGY DEVELOPMENT

Director of Technology Development.—Tracy Williams (Postal Square), 224–8157.
Enterprise IT Operations Manager.—Karlos Davis, 224–3322.
Information Technology Security Manager.—Paul Grabow, 224–4966.
Research Services Branch.—Tom Meenan, 224–8620.
Network Engineering and Management Manager.—Wes Gardner, 224–9269.
Systems Development Services Manager.—Jay Moore, 224–0092.

OFFICE OF THE MAJORITY SECRETARY

S–309 The Capitol, phone 224–3735

Secretary for the Majority.—Martin P. Paone.
Assistant Secretary for the Majority.—Lula J. Davis (S–118), 224–5551.
Administrative Assistant to the Secretary.—Nancy Iacomini.
Executive Assistant to the Secretary.—Amber Huus.

S–225 Majority Cloakroom, phone 224–4691

Cloakroom Assistants: Joe Lapia, Meredith Mellody, Jacques Purvis, Ben Vaughn.

OFFICE OF THE MINORITY SECRETARY

S–337 The Capitol, phone 224–3835, fax 224–2860

Secretary for the Minority.—David Schiappa (S–337).
Assistant Secretary for the Minority.—Laura Dove (S–335).
Administrative Assistant.—Noelle Ringel (S–337).
Floor Assistant.—Jody Hernandez (S–335), phone 224–6191.

S–226 Minority Cloakroom, phone 224–6191

Cloakroom Assistants: Robert Duncan, Ashley Messictz, Loren Streit, Robert White.

S–335 Republican Legislative Scheduling, phone 224–5456

OFFICE OF THE LEGISLATIVE COUNSEL

668 Dirksen Senate Office Building, phone 224–6461, fax 224–0567

Legislative Counsel.—James W. Fransen.
Deputy Legislative Counsel.—William F. Jensen III.
Senior Counsels: Anthony C. Coe, Polly W. Craighill, Gary L. Endicott, Mark J. Mathiesen.
Assistant Counsels: Charles E. Armstrong, Heather A. Arpin, Laura M. Ayoud, William R. Baird, Heather L. Burnham, Darcie E. Chan, Kevin M. Davis, Stephanie Easley,

Ruth A. Ernst, Amy E. Gaynor, John A. Goetcheus, Robert A. Grant, John A. Henderson, Michelle L. Johnson-Weider, Stacy E. Kern-Scheerer, Elizabeth Aldridge King, Mark S. Koster, Kelly J. Malone, Matthew D. McGhie, Mark M. McGunagle, Kristin K. Romero.

Staff Attorneys: John W. Baggaley, Colin D. Campbell, Allison M. Otto, Margaret A. Roth.

Systems Integrator.—Thomas E. Cole.

Office Manager.—Donna L. Pasqualino.

Staff Assistants: Kimberly Bourne-Goldring, Lauren M. DeLaCruz, Daniela A. Gonzalez, Patricia E. Harris, Rebekah J. Musgrove, Diane E. Nesmeyer.

OFFICE OF SENATE LEGAL COUNSEL

642 Hart Senate Office Building, phone 224–4435, fax 224–3391

Senate Legal Counsel.—Morgan J. Frankel.

Deputy Senate Legal Counsel.—Patricia Mack Bryan.

Assistant Senate Legal Counsels: Thomas E. Caballero, Grant R. Vinik.

Systems Administrator/Legal Assistant.—Sara Fox Jones.

Administrative Assistant.—Kathleen M. Parker.

STANDING COMMITTEES OF THE HOUSE

[Democrats in roman; Republicans in *italic*; Resident Commissioner and Delegates in **boldface**]

[Room numbers beginning with H are in the Capitol, with CHOB in the Cannon House Office Building, with LHOB in the Longworth House Office Building, with RHOB in the Rayburn House Office Building, with H1 in O'Neill House Office Building, and with H2 in the Ford House Office Building]

Agriculture

1301 Longworth House Office Building, phone 225–2171, fax 225–8510

http://agriculture.house.gov

meets first Wednesday of each month

Collin C. Peterson, of Minnesota, *Chair*

Tim Holden, of Pennsylvania.
Mike McIntyre, of North Carolina.
Bob Etheridge, of North Carolina.
Leonard L. Boswell, of Iowa.
Joe Baca, of California.
Dennis A. Cardoza, of California.
David Scott, of Georgia.
Jim Marshall, of Georgia.
Stephanie Herseth Sandlin, of South Dakota.
Henry Cuellar, of Texas.
Jim Costa, of California.
John T. Salazar, of Colorado.
Brad Ellsworth, of Indiana.
Nancy E. Boyda, of Kansas.
Zachary T. Space, of Ohio.
Timothy J. Walz, of Minnesota.
Kirsten E. Gillibrand, of New York.
Steve Kagen, of Wisconsin.
Earl Pomeroy, of North Dakota.
Lincoln Davis, of Tennessee.
John Barrow, of Georgia.
Nick Lampson, of Texas.
Joe Donnelly, of Indiana.
Tim Mahoney, of Florida.

Bob Goodlatte, of Virginia.
Terry Everett, of Alabama.
Frank D. Lucas, of Oklahoma.
Jerry Moran, of Kansas.
Robin Hayes, of North Carolina.
Timothy V. Johnson, of Illinois.
Sam Graves, of Missouri.
Jo Bonner, of Alabama.
Mike Rogers, of Alabama.
Steve King, of Iowa.
Marilyn N. Musgrave, of Colorado.
Randy Neugebauer, of Texas.
Charles W. Boustany, Jr., of Louisiana.
John R. ''Randy'' Kuhl, Jr., of New York.
Virginia Foxx, of North Carolina.
K. Michael Conaway, of Texas.
Jeff Fortenberry, of Nebraska.
Jean Schmidt, of Ohio.
Adrian Smith, of Nebraska.
Kevin McCarthy, of California.
Timothy Walberg, of Michigan.

SUBCOMMITTEES

[The chairman and ranking minority member are ex officio (voting) members of all subcommittees on which they do not serve.]

Conservation, Credit, Energy, and Research

Tim Holden, of Pennsylvania, *Chair*

Stephanie Herseth Sandlin, of South Dakota.
Henry Cuellar, of Texas.
Jim Costa, of California.
Brad Ellsworth, of Indiana.
Zachary T. Space, of Ohio.
Timothy J. Walz, of Minnesota.
David Scott, of Georgia.
John T. Salazar, of Colorado.
Nancy E. Boyda, of Kansas.
Kirsten E. Gillibrand, of New York.
Dennis A. Cardoza, of California.
Leonard L. Boswell, of Iowa.
Steve Kagen, of Wisconsin.

Frank D. Lucas, of Oklahoma.
Mike Rogers, of Alabama.
Steve King, of Iowa.
Jeff Fortenberry, of Nebraska.
Jean Schmidt, of Ohio.
Timothy Walberg, of Michigan.
Terry Everett, of Alabama.
Jerry Moran, of Kansas.
Robin Hayes, of North Carolina.
Jo Bonner, of Alabama.
Marilyn N. Musgrave, of Colorado.

Department Operations, Oversight, Nutrition, and Forestry

Joe Baca, of California, *Chair*

Earl Pomeroy, of North Dakota.
Lincoln Davis, of Tennessee.
Nick Lampson, of Texas.
Steve Kagen, of Wisconsin.
Nancy E. Boyda, of Kansas.

Jo Bonner, of Alabama.
Jerry Moran, of Kansas.
Steve King, of Iowa.
Randy Neugebauer, of Texas.
Charles W. Boustany, Jr., of Louisiana.

General Farm Commodities and Risk Management

Bob Etheridge, of North Carolina, *Chair*

David Scott, of Georgia.
Jim Marshall, of Georgia.
John T. Salazar, of Colorado.
Nancy E. Boyda, of Kansas.
Stephanie Herseth Sandlin, of South Dakota.
Brad Ellsworth, of Indiana.
Zachary T. Space, of Ohio.
Timothy J. Walz, of Minnesota.
Earl Pomeroy, of North Dakota.

Jerry Moran, of Kansas.
Timothy V. Johnson, of Illinois.
Sam Graves, of Missouri.
Charles W. Boustany, Jr., of Louisiana.
K. Michael Conaway, of Texas.
Frank D. Lucas, of Oklahoma.
Randy Neugebauer, of Texas.
Kevin McCarthy, of California.

Horticulture and Organic Agriculture

Dennis A. Cardoza, of California, *Chair*

Bob Etheridge, of North Carolina.
Lincoln Davis, of Tennessee.
Tim Mahoney, of Florida.
John Barrow, of Georgia.
Kirsten E. Gillibrand, of New York.

Randy Neugebauer, of Texas.
John R. ''Randy'' Kuhl, Jr., of New York.
Virginia Foxx, of North Carolina.
Kevin McCarthy, of California.
K. Michael Conaway, of Texas.

Livestock, Dairy, and Poultry

Leonard L. Boswell, of Iowa, *Chair*

Kirsten E. Gillibrand, of New York.
Steve Kagen, of Wisconsin.
Tim Holden, of Pennsylvania.
Joe Baca, of California.
Dennis A. Cardoza, of California.
Nick Lampson, of Texas.
Joe Donnelly, of Indiana.
Jim Costa, of California.
Tim Mahoney, of Florida.
Robin Hayes, of North Carolina.
Mike Rogers, of Alabama.
Steve King, of Iowa.
Virginia Foxx, of North Carolina.
K. Michael Conaway, of Texas.
Jean Schmidt, of Ohio.
Adrian Smith, of Nebraska.
Timothy Walberg, of Michigan.

Specialty Crops, Rural Development, and Foreign Agriculture

Mike McIntyre, of North Carolina, *Chair*

Jim Marshall, of Georgia.
Henry Cuellar, of Texas.
John T. Salazar, of Colorado.
John Barrow, of Georgia.
Earl Pomeroy, of North Dakota.
Marilyn N. Musgrave, of Colorado.
Terry Everett, of Alabama.
Adrian Smith, of Nebraska.
Jeff Fortenberry, of Nebraska.
Robin Hayes, of North Carolina.

STAFF

Committee on Agriculture (1301 LHOB), 225–2171, fax 225–0917.
Majority Staff Director.—Rob Larew.
Deputy Chief of Staff.—John Riley, 5–7987.
Chief Administrative Officer.—Sharon Rusnak, 5–6878.
Financial Administrator.—Wynn Bott (1340–A LHOB), 5–4963.
Director, Information Systems.—Merrick Munday.
Outreach Director.—Jack Danielson, 5–1564.
Chief Counsel.—Andy Baker (1304 LHOB), 5–3069.
Counsel.—Christy Birdsong (1304 LHOB), 5–4453.
Communications Director.—April Demert Slayton (1301–A LHOB), 5–6872.
Chief Economist.—Craig Jagger (1407–A LHOB), 5–1130.
Executive Assistant.—Cherie Slayton.
Hearing Clerk.—Jamie Weyer (1303 LHOB), 5–3329.
Senior Professional Staff.—Anne Simmons (1534 LHOB), 5–1494.
Professional Staff.—Scott Kuschmider (1301–A LHOB), 5–1496.
Legislative Assistant.—Martha Josephson, 5–4982.
Legislative Clerk.—Debbie Smith (1304 LHOB), 5–9384.
Staff Assistants: Adam Durand, Tyler Jameson, Kristin Sosanie.
Subcommittee Staff Directors:
Conservation, Credit, Rural Development and Research.—Nona Darrell (1336 LHOB), 5–0420.
Department Operations, Oversight, Nutrition and Forestry.—Lisa Shelton (1407 LHOB), 5–6395.
General Farm Commodities and Risk Management.—Clark Ogilvie (1407 LHOB), 5–0720.
Horticulture and Organic Agriculture.—Keith Jones (1336 LHOB), 5–6238.
Livestock, Dairy, and Poultry.—Chandler Goule (1336 LHOB), 5–8407.
Specialty Crops, Rural Development, and Foreign Agriculture Programs.—Aleta Botts (1407 LHOB), 5–8248.
Minority Chief of Staff.—Bill O'Conner (1305 LHOB), 5–0029.
Chief Counsel/Deputy Chief of Staff.—Kevin Kramp.
Legislative Assistants: Lindsey Correa, Mike Dunlap.
Deputy Chief Counsel.—Stephanie Myers.
Associate Counsel.—Brian Knipling.
Communications Director.—Alise Kowalski.
Office Manager.—Scott Martin.
Senior Professional Staff: Bryan Dierlam, John Goldberg, Pam Miller, Pelham Straughn, Pete Thomson.
Professional Staff: Josh Maxwell, Rita Neznek, Matt Schertz.

Appropriations

H–218 The Capitol, phone 225–2771

http://www.house.gov/appropriations

David R. Obey, of Wisconsin, *Chair*

John P. Murtha, of Pennsylvania.
Norman D. Dicks, of Washington.
Alan B. Mollohan, of West Virginia.
Marcy Kaptur, of Ohio.
Peter J. Visclosky, of Indiana.
Nita M. Lowey, of New York.
José E. Serrano, of New York.
Rosa L. DeLauro, of Connecticut.
James P. Moran, of Virginia.
John W. Olver, of Massachusetts.
Ed Pastor, of Arizona.
David E. Price, of North Carolina.
Chet Edwards, of Texas.
Robert E. ''Bud'' Cramer, Jr., of Alabama.
Patrick J. Kennedy, of Rhode Island.
Maurice D. Hinchey, of New York.
Lucille Roybal-Allard, of California.
Sam Farr, of California.
Jesse L. Jackson, Jr., of Illinois.
Carolyn C. Kilpatrick, of Michigan.
Allen Boyd, of Florida.
Chaka Fattah, of Pennsylvania.
Steven R. Rothman, of New Jersey.
Sanford D. Bishop, Jr., of Georgia.
Marion Berry, of Arkansas.
Barbara Lee, of California.
Tom Udall, of New Mexico.
Adam B. Schiff, of California.
Michael M. Honda, of California.
Betty McCollum, of Minnesota.
Steve Israel, of New York.
Tim Ryan, of Ohio.
C.A. Dutch Ruppersberger, of Maryland.
Ben Chandler, of Kentucky.
Debbie Wasserman Schultz, of Florida.
Ciro D. Rodriguez, of Texas.

Jerry Lewis, of California.
C.W. Bill Young, of Florida.
Ralph Regula, of Ohio.
Harold Rogers, of Kentucky.
Frank R. Wolf, of Virginia.
James T. Walsh, of New York.
David L. Hobson, of Ohio.
Joe Knollenberg, of Michigan.
Jack Kingston, of Georgia.
Rodney P. Frelinghuysen, of New Jersey.
Roger F. Wicker, of Mississippi.
Todd Tiahrt, of Kansas.
Zach Wamp, of Tennessee.
Tom Latham, of Iowa.
Robert B. Aderholt, of Alabama.
Jo Ann Emerson, of Missouri.
Kay Granger, of Texas.
John E. Peterson, of Pennsylvania.
Virgil H. Goode, Jr., of Virginia.
John T. Doolittle, of California.
Ray LaHood, of Illinois.
Dave Weldon, of Florida.
Michael K. Simpson, of Idaho.
John Abney Culberson, of Texas.
Mark Steven Kirk, of Illinois.
Ander Crenshaw, of Florida.
Dennis R. Rehberg, of Montana.
John R. Carter, of Texas.
Rodney Alexander, of Louisiana.

SUBCOMMITTEES

[The chairman and ranking minority member are ex officio (voting) members of all subcommittees on which they do not serve.]

Agriculture, Rural Development, Food and Drug Administration, and Related Agencies

Rosa L. DeLauro, of Connecticut, *Chair*

Maurice D. Hinchey, of New York.
Sam Farr, of California.
Allen Boyd, of Florida.
Sanford D. Bishop, Jr., of Georgia.
Marcy Kaptur, of Ohio.
Jesse L. Jackson, Jr., of Illinois.
Steven R. Rothman, of New Jersey.

Jack Kingston, of Georgia.
Tom Latham, of Iowa.
Jo Ann Emerson, of Missouri.
Ray LaHood, of Illinois.
Rodney Alexander, of Louisiana.

Commerce, Justice, Science, and Related Agencies

Alan B. Mollohan, of West Virginia, *Chair*

Patrick J. Kennedy, of Rhode Island.
Chaka Fattah, of Pennsylvania.
C.A. Dutch Ruppersberger, of Maryland.
Adam B. Schiff, of California.
Michael M. Honda, of California.
Rosa L. DeLauro, of Connecticut.
David E. Price, of North Carolina.

Rodney P. Frelinghuysen, of New Jersey.
John Abney Culberson, of Texas.
Harold Rogers, of Kentucky.
Tom Latham, of Iowa.
Robert B. Aderholt, of Alabama.

Defense

John P. Murtha, of Pennsylvania, *Chair*

Norman D. Dicks, of Washington.
Peter J. Visclosky, of Indiana.
James P. Moran, of Virginia.
Marcy Kaptur, of Ohio.
Robert E. ''Bud'' Cramer, Jr., of Alabama.
Allen Boyd, of Florida.
Steven R. Rothman, of New Jersey.
Sanford D. Bishop, Jr., of Georgia.

C.W. Bill Young, of Florida.
David L. Hobson, of Ohio.
Rodney P. Frelinghuysen, of New Jersey.
Todd Tiahrt, of Kansas.
Roger F. Wicker, of Mississippi.
Jack Kingston, of Georgia.

Energy and Water Development, and Related Agencies

Peter J. Visclosky, of Indiana, *Chair*

Chet Edwards, of Texas.
Ed Pastor, of Arizona.
Marion Berry, of Arkansas.
Chaka Fattah, of Pennsylvania.
Steve Israel, of New York.
Tim Ryan, of Ohio.
José E. Serrano, of New York.
John W. Olver, of Massachusetts.

David L. Hobson, of Ohio.
Zach Wamp, of Tennessee.
Jo Ann Emerson, of Missouri.
John T. Doolittle, of California.
Michael K. Simpson, of Idaho.
Kay Granger, of Texas.

Financial Services and General Government

José E. Serrano, of New York, *Chair*

Carolyn C. Kilpatrick, of Michigan.
C.A. Dutch Ruppersberger, of Maryland.
Debbie Wasserman Schultz, of Florida.
Peter J. Visclosky, of Indiana.
James P. Moran, of Virginia.
Robert E. ''Bud'' Cramer, Jr., of Alabama.
Maurice D. Hinchey, of New York.

Ralph Regula, of Ohio.
Tom Latham, of Iowa.
Mark Steven Kirk, of Illinois.
Dennis R. Rehberg, of Montana.
Rodney Alexander, of Louisiana.

Homeland Security

David E. Price, of North Carolina, *Chair*

José E. Serrano, of New York.
Carolyn C. Kilpatrick, of Michigan.
Ciro D. Rodriguez, of Texas.
Nita M. Lowey, of New York.
Chet Edwards, of Texas.
Lucille Roybal-Allard, of California.
Sam Farr, of California.
Chaka Fattah, of Pennsylvania.

Harold Rogers, of Kentucky.
John R. Carter, of Texas.
Robert B. Aderholt, of Alabama.
Kay Granger, of Texas.
John E. Peterson, of Pennsylvania.
John Abney Culberson, of Texas.

Interior, Environment, and Related Agencies

Norman D. Dicks, of Washington, *Chair*

James P. Moran, of Virginia.
Maurice D. Hinchey, of New York.
John W. Olver, of Massachusetts.
Alan B. Mollohan, of West Virginia.
Tom Udall, of New Mexico.
Ben Chandler, of Kentucky.
Ed Pastor, of Arizona.

Todd Tiahrt, of Kansas.
John E. Peterson, of Pennsylvania.
John T. Doolittle, of California.
Jo Ann Emerson, of Missouri.
Virgil H. Goode, Jr., of Virginia.

Labor, Health and Human Services, Education, and Related Agencies

David R. Obey, of Wisconsin, *Chair*

Nita M. Lowey, of New York.
Rosa L. DeLauro, of Connecticut.
Jesse L. Jackson, Jr., of Illinois.
Patrick J. Kennedy, of Rhode Island.
Lucille Roybal-Allard, of California.
Barbara Lee, of California.
Tom Udall, of New Mexico.
Michael M. Honda, of California.
Betty McCollum, of Minnesota.
Tim Ryan, of Ohio.

James T. Walsh, of New York.
Ralph Regula, of Ohio.
John E. Peterson, of Pennsylvania.
Dave Weldon, of Florida.
Michael K. Simpson, of Idaho.
Dennis R. Rehberg, of Montana.

Legislative Branch

Debbie Wasserman Schultz, of Florida, *Chair*

Barbara Lee, of California.
Tom Udall, of New Mexico.
Michael M. Honda, of California.
Betty McCollum, of Minnesota.
C.A. Dutch Ruppersberger, of Maryland.

Zach Wamp, of Tennessee.
Ray LaHood, of Illinois.
John T. Doolittle, of California.

Military Construction, Veterans' Affairs, and Related Agencies

Chet Edwards, of Texas, *Chair*

Sam Farr, of California.
Norman D. Dicks, of Washington.
Alan B. Mollohan, of West Virginia.
Patrick J. Kennedy, of Rhode Island.
Allen Boyd, of Florida.
Sanford D. Bishop, Jr., of Georgia.
Marion Berry, of Arkansas.

Roger F. Wicker, of Mississippi.
Ander Crenshaw, of Florida.
C.W. Bill Young, of Florida.
John R. Carter, of Texas.
Kay Granger, of Texas.

State, Foreign Operations, and Related Programs

Nita M. Lowey, of New York, *Chair*

Jesse L. Jackson, Jr., of Illinois.
Adam B. Schiff, of California.
Steve Israel, of New York.
Ben Chandler, of Kentucky.
Steven R. Rothman, of New Jersey.
Barbara Lee, of California.
Betty McCollum, of Minnesota.

Frank R. Wolf, of Virginia.
Joe Knollenberg, of Michigan.
Mark Steven Kirk, of Illinois.
Ander Crenshaw, of Florida.
Dave Weldon, of Florida.

Transportation, Housing and Urban Development, and Related Agencies

John W. Olver, of Massachusetts, *Chair*

Ed Pastor, of Arizona.
Ciro D. Rodriguez, of Texas.
Marcy Kaptur, of Ohio.
David E. Price, of North Carolina.
Robert E. "Bud" Cramer, Jr., of Alabama.
Lucille Roybal-Allard, of California.
Marion Berry, of Arkansas.

Joe Knollenberg, of Michigan.
Frank R. Wolf, of Virginia.
Robert B. Aderholt, of Alabama.
James T. Walsh, of New York.
Virgil H. Goode, Jr., of Virginia.

STAFF

Committee on Appropriations (H–218), 225–2771.
Majority Clerk and Staff Director.—Rob Nabors.
Administrative Assistant.—Di Kane.
Office Assistant.—Theodore Powell.
Staff Assistants: David Reich, David Pomerantz, Jennifer Miller, Dale Oak.
Administrative Aide.—Sandy Farrow.
Spokesperson.—Kirstin Brost.
Editors: Larry Boarman, Cathy Edwards (B–301A RHOB), 5–2851.
Computer Operations: Carrie Campbell, Vernon Hammett, Cathy Little, Linda Muir, Chauncey Powell, Jay Sivulich (B–305 RHOB), 5–2718.
Minority Staff Director.—Frank Cushing (1016 LHOB), 5–3481.
Minority Deputy Staff Directors: Dave LesStrang, Jeff Shockey.
Administrative Aides: Jenny Mummert, Kelly Shea.
Subcommittee on Agriculture, Rural Development, Food and Drug Administration, and Related Agencies (2362–A RHOB), 5–2638.
Staff Assistants: Leslie Barrack, Martha Foley, Maureen Holohan.
Administrative Aide.—Kelly Wade.
Minority Staff Assistant.—Martin Delgado (1016 LHOB), 5–3481.
Minority Administrative Aide.—Jamie Swafford.
Subcommittee on Commerce, Justice, Science and Related Agencies (H–309), 5–3351.
Staff Assistants: Michelle Burkett, Doug Disrud, Marjorie Duske, Meg Thompson.
Administrative Aide.—Tracy LaTurner.
Minority Staff Assistant.—Mike Ringler (1016 LHOB), 5–3481.
Subcommittee on Defense (H–149), 5–2847.
Staff Assistants: Leslie Albright, John Blazey, Brooke Boyer, Adam Harris, Kevin Jones, Paul Juola, Greg Lankler, Kris Mallard, David Morrison, Linda Pagelsen, Tim Prince, Ann Reese, Paul Terry, Sarah Young.
Administrative Aide.—Sherry Young.
Minority Staff Assistants: Josh Hartman, Jennifer Miller, John Shank (1016 LHOB), 5–3481.
Subcommittee on Energy and Water Development, and Related Agencies (2362–B RHOB), 5–3421.
Staff Assistants: Taunja Berquam, Scott Burnison, Dixon Butler, Terry Tyborowski.
Administrative Aide.—Lori Maes.
Minority Staff Assistants: Rob Blair, Kevin Cook, Ben Nicholson (1016 LHOB), 5–3481.
Subcommittee on Financial Services (1040A LHOB), 5–7245.
Staff Assistants: Bob Bonner, Dale Oak, Karen Kendall.
Administrative Aide.—Frank Carillo.
Minority Staff Assistants: Anne Marie Goldsmith, Alice Hogans, John Martens (1016 LHOB), 5–3481.
Subcommittee on Homeland Security (B–307 RHOB), 5–5834.
Staff Assistants: Jeff Ashford, Stephanie Gupta, Jim Holm, Shalanda Young.
Administrative Aide.—Tammy Hughes.
Minority Staff Assistants: Christine Kojac, Tom McLemore, Beth Nicholson (1016 LHOB), 5–3481.
Subcommittee on Interior, Environment, and Related Agencies (B–308 RHOB), 5–3081.
Staff Assistants: Greg Knadle, Delia Scott, Christopher Topik.
Administrative Aide.—Beth Houser.
Minority Staff Assistants: Steve Crain, Dave LesStrang, Debbie Weatherly (1016 LHOB), 5–3481.
Subcommittee on Labor, Health and Human Services, Education, and Related Agencies (2358 RHOB), 5–3508.

Staff Assistants: Teri Bergman, Nicole Kunko, Sue Quantius, Cheryl Smith, Meg Thompson.

Administrative Aide.—Andria Oliver.

Minority Staff Assistants: Steve Crain, Anne Marie Goldsmith (1016 LHOB), 5–3481.

Subcommittee on Legislative Branch (H–147), 6–7252.

Staff Assistants: Tom Forhan, Chuck Turner.

Minority Staff Assistants: Liz Dawson, Jeff Shockey.

Subcommittee on Military Construction, Veterans' Affairs, and Related Agencies (H–143), 5–3047.

Staff Assistants: Walter Hearne, Carol Murphy, Tim Peterson, Donna Shahbaz.

Administrative Aide.—Mary Arnold.

Minority Administrative Aide.—Jamie Swafford.

Minority Staff Assistant.—Liz Dawson (1016 LHOB), 5–3481.

Subcommittee on State and Foreign Operations (HB–26), 5–2401.

Staff Assistants: Nisha Desai, Craig Higgins, Steve Marchese, Michele Sumilas.

Administrative Aide.—Clelia Alvarado.

Minority Staff Assistants: Rob Blair, Alice Hogans, Christine Kojac, Mike Ringler (1016 LHOB), 5–3481.

Subcommittee on Transportation, HUD, and Independent Agencies (2358 RHOB), 5–2141.

Staff Assistants: Kate Hallahan, Laura Hogshead, David Napoliello, Cheryle Tucker.

Administrative Aide.—Alex Gillen.

Minority Staff Assistants: Dena Baron, Dave Gibbons (1016 LHOB), 5–3481.

Armed Services

2120 Rayburn House Office Building, phone 225–4151, fax 225–9077

http://www.house.gov/hasc

Ike Skelton, of Missouri, *Chair*

John M. Spratt, Jr., of South Carolina.
Solomon P. Ortiz, of Texas.
Gene Taylor, of Mississippi.
Neil Abercrombie, of Hawaii.
Silvestre Reyes, of Texas.
Vic Snyder, of Arkansas.
Adam Smith, of Washington.
Loretta Sanchez, of California.
Mike McIntyre, of North Carolina.
Ellen O. Tauscher, of California.
Robert A. Brady, of Pennsylvania.
Robert E. Andrews, of New Jersey.
Susan A. Davis, of California.
Rick Larsen, of Washington.
Jim Cooper, of Tennessee.
Jim Marshall, of Georgia.
Madeleine Z. Bordallo, of Guam.
Mark Udall, of Colorado.
Dan Boren, of Oklahoma.
Brad Ellsworth, of Indiana.
Nancy E. Boyda, of Kansas.
Patrick J. Murphy, of Pennsylvania.
Henry C. ''Hank'' Johnson, Jr., of Georgia.
Carol Shea-Porter, of New Hampshire.
Joe Courtney, of Connecticut.
David Loebsack, of Iowa.
Kirsten E. Gillibrand, of New York.
Joe Sestak, of Pennsylvania.
Gabrielle Giffords, of Arizona.
Elijah E. Cummings, of Maryland.
Kendrick B. Meek, of Florida.
Kathy Castor, of Florida.

Duncan Hunter, of California.
Jim Saxton, of New Jersey.
John M. McHugh, of New York.
Terry Everett, of Alabama.
Roscoe G. Bartlett, of Maryland.
Howard P. ''Buck'' McKeon, of California.
Mac Thornberry, of Texas.
Walter B. Jones, of North Carolina.
Robin Hayes, of North Carolina.
Ken Calvert, of California.
Jo Ann Davis, of Virginia.
W. Todd Akin, of Missouri.
J. Randy Forbes, of Virginia.
Jeff Miller, of Florida.
Joe Wilson, of South Carolina.
Frank A. LoBiondo, of New Jersey.
Tom Cole, of Oklahoma.
Rob Bishop, of Utah.
Michael R. Turner, of Ohio.
John Kline, of Minnesota.
Candice S. Miller, of Michigan.
Phil Gingrey, of Georgia.
Mike Rogers, of Alabama.
Trent Franks, of Arizona.
Thelma D. Drake, of Virginia.
Cathy McMorris Rodgers, of Washington.
K. Michael Conaway, of Texas.
Geoff Davis, of Kentucky.

SUBCOMMITTEES

Air and Land Forces

Neil Abercrombie, of Hawaii, *Chair*

John M. Spratt, Jr., of South Carolina.
Solomon P. Ortiz, of Texas.
Silvestre Reyes, of Texas.
Mike McIntyre, of North Carolina.
Ellen O. Tauscher, of California.
Robert A. Brady, of Pennsylvania.
Jim Marshall, of Georgia.
Dan Boren, of Oklahoma.
Henry C. ''Hank'' Johnson, Jr., of Georgia.
Joe Sestak, of Pennsylvania.
Gabrielle Giffords, of Arizona.
Kendrick B. Meek, of Florida.
Kathy Castor, of Florida.

Jim Saxton, of New Jersey.
Howard P. ''Buck'' McKeon, of California.
Jeff Miller, of Florida.
Phil Gingrey, of Georgia.
Cathy McMorris Rodgers, of Washington.
Geoff Davis, of Kentucky.
W. Todd Akin, of Missouri.

Military Personnel

Vic Snyder, of Arkansas, *Chair*

Loretta Sanchez, of California.
Susan A. Davis, of California.
Nancy E. Boyda, of Kansas.
Patrick J. Murphy, of Pennsylvania.
Carol Shea-Porter, of New Hampshire.
John M. McHugh, of New York.
John Kline, of Minnesota.
Thelma D. Drake, of Virginia.
Walter B. Jones, of North Carolina.
Joe Wilson, of South Carolina.

Oversight and Investigations

Vic Snyder, of Arkansas, *Chair*

John M. Spratt, Jr., of South Carolina.
Loretta Sanchez, of California.
Ellen O. Tauscher, of California.
Robert E. Andrews, of New Jersey.
Susan A. Davis, of California.
Jim Cooper, of Tennessee.
Joe Sestak, of Pennsylvania.
W. Todd Akin, of Missouri.
Roscoe G. Bartlett, of Maryland.
Walter B. Jones, of North Carolina.
Jeff Miller, of Florida.
Phil Gingrey, of Georgia.
K. Michael Conaway, of Texas.
Geoff Davis, of Kentucky.

Readiness

Solomon P. Ortiz, of Texas, *Chair*

Gene Taylor, of Mississippi.
Silvestre Reyes, of Texas.
Loretta Sanchez, of California.
Robert A. Brady, of Pennsylvania.
Jim Marshall, of Georgia.
Madeleine Z. Bordallo, of Guam.
Mark Udall, of Colorado.
Dan Boren, of Oklahoma.
Nancy E. Boyda, of Kansas.
Carol Shea-Porter, of New Hampshire.
Joe Courtney, of Connecticut.
David Loebsack, of Iowa.
Gabrielle Giffords, of Arizona.
Elijah E. Cummings, of Maryland.
Jo Ann Davis, of Virginia.
Walter B. Jones, of North Carolina.
J. Randy Forbes, of Virginia.
John M. McHugh, of New York.
Robin Hayes, of North Carolina.
Frank A. LoBiondo, of New Jersey.
Tom Cole, of Oklahoma.
Rob Bishop, of Utah.
Candice S. Miller, of Michigan.
Trent Franks, of Arizona.
Cathy McMorris Rodgers, of Washington.

Seapower and Expeditionary Forces

Gene Taylor, of Mississippi, *Chair*

Neil Abercrombie, of Hawaii.
Rick Larsen, of Washington.
Madeleine Z. Bordallo, of Guam.
Brad Ellsworth, of Indiana.
Joe Courtney, of Connecticut.
Kirsten E. Gillibrand, of New York.
Joe Sestak, of Pennsylvania.
Roscoe G. Bartlett, of Maryland.
Ken Calvert, of California.
Terry Everett, of Alabama.
Jo Ann Davis, of Virginia.
J. Randy Forbes, of Virginia.
Joe Wilson, of South Carolina.

Strategic Forces

Ellen O. Tauscher, of California, *Chair*

John M. Spratt, Jr., of South Carolina.
Silvestre Reyes, of Texas.
Rick Larsen, of Washington.
Jim Cooper, of Tennessee.
Henry C. ''Hank'' Johnson, Jr., of Georgia.
David Loebsack, of Iowa.
Terry Everett, of Alabama.
Trent Franks, of Arizona.
Mac Thornberry, of Texas.
Michael R. Turner, of Ohio.
Mike Rogers, of Alabama.

Terrorism, Unconventional Threats and Capabilities

Adam Smith, of Washington, *Chair*

Mike McIntyre, of North Carolina.
Robert E. Andrews, of New Jersey.
Jim Cooper, of Tennessee.
Jim Marshall, of Georgia.
Mark Udall, of Colorado.
Brad Ellsworth, of Indiana.
Kirsten E. Gillibrand, of New York.
Kathy Castor, of Florida.
Mac Thornberry, of Texas.
Robin Hayes, of North Carolina.
Ken Calvert, of California.
John Kline, of Minnesota.
Thelma D. Drake, of Virginia.
K. Michael Conaway, of Texas.
Jim Saxton, of New Jersey.

STAFF

Committee on Armed Services (2120 RHOB), 225–4151; fax 225–9077.
Staff Director.—Erin C. Conaton.
Deputy Staff Director.—Bob DeGrasse.
General Counsel.—Paul Oostburg Sanz.
Counsels: Kevin Coughlin, Suzanne McKenna, Julie Unmacht, Roger Zakheim.
Professional Staff: Aileen Alexander, Paul Arcangeli, Rudy Barnes, John D. Chapla, Kari Bingen, Heath Bope, Douglas Bush, Michael Casey, William Ebbs, Lorry Fenner, Cathy Garman, Kevin Gates, Thomas E. Hawley, Michael R. Higgins, Joshua Holly, Andrew Hunter, Jeanette S. James, Dave Kildee, John Kruse, Alex Kugajevsky, Mark R. Lewis, Timothy McClees, William H. Natter, Roy Phillips, Vickie Plunkett, Adrienne Ramsey, Douglas C. Roach, Eryn Robinson, Frank Rose, Rebecca Ross, Stephanie Sanok, Robert L. Simmons, Jenness Simter, John F. Sullivan, Jesse Tolleson, Debra S. Wada, Nancy M. Warner, John Wason, Lynn Williams.
Press Secretaries: Lara Battles, Loren L. Dealy.
Legislative Operations Director.—W. Holly Graning.
Staff Assistants: Kristine Ellison, Betty B. Gray, Jason Hagadern, Joe Hicken, Cyndi Howard, Ben Kohr, Christine Lamb, Margee Meckstroth, Sasha Rogers, Christine Roushdy, Derek Scott, Andrew Tabler, Ernest B. Warrington, Jr., Lindsay D. Young.
Printing Clerk.—Linda M. Burnette.

Budget

309 Cannon House Office Building 20515–6065, phone 226–7270, fax 226–7174

http://www.budget.house.gov

John M. Spratt, Jr., of South Carolina, *Chair*

Rosa L. DeLauro, of Connecticut.
Chet Edwards, of Texas.
Jim Cooper, of Tennessee.
Thomas H. Allen, of Maine.
Allyson Y. Schwartz, of Pennsylvania.
Marcy Kaptur, of Ohio.
Xavier Becerra, of California.
Lloyd Doggett, of Texas.
Earl Blumenauer, of Oregon.
Marion Berry, of Arkansas.
Allen Boyd, of Florida.
James P. McGovern, of Massachusetts.
Betty Sutton, of Ohio.
Robert E. Andrews, of New Jersey.
Robert C. ''Bobby'' Scott, of Virginia.
Bob Etheridge, of North Carolina.
Darlene Hooley, of Oregon.
Brian Baird, of Washington.
Dennis Moore, of Kansas.
Timothy H. Bishop, of New York.
Gwen Moore, of Wisconsin.

Paul Ryan, of Wisconsin.
J. Gresham Barrett, of South Carolina.
Jo Bonner, of Alabama.
Scott Garrett, of New Jersey.
Thaddeus G. McCotter, of Michigan.
Mario Diaz-Balart, of Florida.
Jeb Hensarling, of Texas.
Daniel E. Lungren, of California.
Michael K. Simpson, of Idaho.
Patrick T. McHenry, of North Carolina.
Connie Mack, of Florida.
K. Michael Conaway, of Texas.
John Campbell, of California.
Patrick J. Tiberi, of Ohio.
Jon C. Porter, of Nevada.
Rodney Alexander, of Louisiana.
Adrian Smith, of Nebraska.

(No Subcommittees)

Committee on Budget (207 CHOB), 226–7200; fax 225–9905.
Majority Staff Director/Chief Counsel.—Tom Kahn.
Deputy Staff Director.—Arthur Burris.
General Counsel.—Gail Millar.
Parliamentary Counsel.—Lisa Venus.
Counsel.—Naomi S. Stern.
Chief Economist.—Diane Lim Rogers.
Director of Policy.—Barbara Chow.
Policy Assistant.—Kitty Richards.
Senior Policy Coordinator.—Sarah Abernathy.
Budget Review Director.—Kimberly Overbeek.
Senior Budget Review Specialist.—Ellen J. Balis.
Analysts: Stephen Elmore, Jennifer Hanson-Kilbride, Diana Meredith, Morna Miller, Ifie Okwuje, Scott Russell, Greg Waring, Andrea Weathers, Jason Weller.
Chief Administrator.—Marsha Douglas.
Office Manager.—Shelia McDowell.
Senior Staff Assistant.—Linda Bywaters.
Systems Administrator.—Jose Guillen.
Communications Assistant.—Chris Long.
Staff Assistants: Namrata Mujumdar, Mark Middaugh.
Minority Chief of Staff.—Jim Bates, (B71 Cannon), 226–7270, fax 226–7174.
Executive Assistant.—Jonathan Romito.
Policy Director.—Pat Knudsen.
Director of Communications.—Angela Kuck.
Special Assistant.—John Gray.
Director of Budget Review.—Chauncey Goss.
Appropriations/Budget Analyst.—Stephen Sepp.
Budget Analysts: Jimmy Christopoulos, Andy Morton.
Chief Counsel/Budget Analyst.—Paul Restuccia.
Counsels/Budget Analysts: Charlene Crawford, Charlotte Ivancic, Clete Willems.
Economist.—Timothy Flynn.

Education and Labor

2181 Rayburn House Office Building, phone 225–3725, fax 226–5398

http://edlabor.house.gov

George Miller, of California, *Chair*

Dale E. Kildee, of Michigan.
Donald M. Payne, of New Jersey.
Robert E. Andrews, of New Jersey.
Robert C. "Bobby" Scott, of Virginia.
Lynn C. Woolsey, of California.
Rubén Hinojosa, of Texas.
Carolyn McCarthy, of New York.
John F. Tierney, of Massachusetts.
Dennis J. Kucinich, of Ohio.
David Wu, of Oregon.
Rush D. Holt, of New Jersey.
Susan A. Davis, of California.
Danny K. Davis, of Illinois.
Raúl M. Grijalva, of Arizona.
Timothy H. Bishop, of New York.
Linda T. Sánchez, of California.
John P. Sarbanes, of Maryland.
Joe Sestak, of Pennsylvania.
David Loebsack, of Iowa.
Mazie K. Hirono, of Hawaii.
Jason Altmire, of Pennsylvania.
John A. Yarmuth, of Kentucky.
Phil Hare, of Illinois.
Yvette D. Clarke, of New York.
Joe Courtney, of Connecticut.
Carol Shea-Porter, of New Hampshire.

Howard P. "Buck" McKeon, of California.
Thomas E. Petri, of Wisconsin.
Peter Hoekstra, of Michigan.
Michael N. Castle, of Delaware.
Mark E. Souder, of Indiana.
Vernon J. Ehlers, of Michigan.
Judy Biggert, of Illinois.
Todd Russell Platts, of Pennsylvania.
Ric Keller, of Florida.
Joe Wilson, of South Carolina.
John Kline, of Minnesota.
Cathy McMorris Rodgers, of Washington.
Kenny Marchant, of Texas.
Tom Price, of Georgia.
Luis G. Fortuño, of Puerto Rico.
Charles W. Boustany, Jr., of Louisiana.
Virginia Foxx, of North Carolina.
John R. "Randy" Kuhl, Jr., of New York.
Rob Bishop, of Utah.
David Davis, of Tennessee.
Timothy Walberg, of Michigan.
Dean Heller, of Nevada.

SUBCOMMITTEES

[The chairman and ranking minority member are ex officio (non-voting) members of all subcommittees on which they do not serve.]

Early Childhood, Elementary and Secondary Education

Dale E. Kildee, of Michigan, *Chair*

Robert C. "Bobby" Scott, of Virginia.
Dennis J. Kucinich, of Ohio.
Susan A. Davis, of California.
Danny K. Davis, of Illinois.
Raúl M. Grijalva, of Arizona.
Donald M. Payne, of New Jersey.
Rush D. Holt, of New Jersey.
Linda T. Sánchez, of California.
John P. Sarbanes, of Maryland.
Joe Sestak, of Pennsylvania.
David Loebsack, of Iowa.
Mazie K. Hirono, of Hawaii.
Phil Hare, of Illinois.
Lynn C. Woolsey, of California.
Rubén Hinojosa, of Texas.

Michael N. Castle, of Delaware.
Peter Hoekstra, of Michigan.
Mark E. Souder, of Indiana.
Vernon J. Ehlers, of Michigan.
Judy Biggert, of Illinois.
Luis G. Fortuño, of Puerto Rico.
Rob Bishop, of Utah.
Todd Russell Platts, of Pennsylvania.
Ric Keller, of Florida.
Joe Wilson, of South Carolina.
Charles W. Boustany, Jr., of Louisiana.
John R. "Randy" Kuhl, Jr., of New York.
Dean Heller, of Nevada.

Healthy Families and Communities

Carolyn McCarthy, of New York, *Chair*

Yvette D. Clarke, of New York.
Carol Shea-Porter, of New Hampshire.
Dennis J. Kucinich, of Ohio.
Raúl M. Grijalva, of Arizona.
John P. Sarbanes, of Maryland.
Jason Altmire, of Pennsylvania.
John A. Yarmuth, of Kentucky.
Todd Russell Platts, of Pennsylvania.
Howard P. "Buck" McKeon, of California.
Bob Inglis, of South Carolina
Kenny Marchant, of Texas.
Luis G. Fortuño, of Puerto Rico.
David Davis, of Tennessee.

Higher Education, Lifelong Learning, and Competitiveness

Rubén Hinojosa, of Texas, of Ohio, *Chair*

George Miller, of California.
John F. Tierney, of Massachusetts.
David Wu, of Oregon.
Timothy H. Bishop, of New York.
Jason Altmire, of Pennsylvania.
John A. Yarmuth, of Kentucky.
Joe Courtney, of Connecticut.
Robert E. Andrews, of New Jersey.
Robert C. "Bobby" Scott, of Virginia.
Susan A. Davis, of California.
Danny K. Davis, of Illinois.
Mazie K. Hirono, of Hawaii.
Ric Keller, of Florida.
Thomas E. Petri, of Wisconsin.
Cathy McMorris Rodgers, of Washington.
Virginia Foxx, of North Carolina.
John R. "Randy" Kuhl, Jr., of New York.
Timothy Walberg, of Michigan.
Michael N. Castle, of Delaware.
Mark E. Souder, of Indiana.
Vernon J. Ehlers, of Michigan.
Judy Biggert, of Illinois.

Health, Employment, Labor, and Pensions

Robert E. Andrews, of New Jersey, *Chair*

George Miller, of California.
Dale E. Kildee, of Michigan.
Carolyn McCarthy, of New York.
John F. Tierney, of Massachusetts.
David Wu, of Oregon.
Rush D. Holt, of New Jersey.
Linda T. Sánchez, of California.
Joe Sestak, of Pennsylvania.
David Loebsack, of Iowa.
Phil Hare, of Illinois.
Yvette D. Clarke, of New York.
John Kline, of Minnesota.
Howard P. "Buck" McKeon, of California.
Kenny Marchant, of Texas.
Charles W. Boustany, Jr., of Louisiana.
David Davis, of Tennessee.
Peter Hoekstra, of Michigan.
Cathy McMorris Rodgers, of Washington.
Tom Price, of Georgia.
Virginia Foxx, of North Carolina.
Timothy Walberg, of Michigan.

Workforce Protections

Lynn C. Woolsey, of California, *Chair*

Donald M. Payne, of New Jersey.
Timothy H. Bishop, of New York.
Carol Shea-Porter, of New Hampshire.
Phil Hare, of Illinois.
Joe Wilson, of South Carolina.
Tom Price, of Georgia.
John Kline, of Minnesota.

STAFF

Committee on Education and Labor (2181 RHOB), 225–3725.
Majority Staff Director.—Mark Zuckerman.
Administrative Assistant to Staff Director.—Liz Hollis.
Special Assistant to the Chair.—Daniel Weiss.
General Counsels: Brian Kennedy, Stephanie Moore.
Education Policy Director.—Denise Forte.
Administrative Assistant.—Ann-Frances Lambert.
Senior Education Policy Advisors:
Early Childhood.—Ruth Friedman.
K–12.—Alice Johnson Cain.

Higher Education.—Gabriella Gomez.
Senior Disability Policy Advisor.—Theda Zawaiza.
Education Policy Advisors: Jill Morningstar, Julie Radocchia.
Policy Advisors for Subcommittee on:
Early Childhood.—Lloyd Horwich.
Higher Education.—Ricardo Martinez.
Legislative Associate, Education.—Lauren Gibbs.
Legislative Fellow, Education.—Amy Elverum.
Staff Assistants, Education: Lamont Ivey, Lisette Partelow.
Labor Policy Director.—Michele Varnhagen.
Senior Labor Policy Advisors: Jordan Barab, Peter Galvin.
Labor Policy Advisors: Carlos Fenwick, Megan O'Reilly.
Staff Assistant, Labor.—Michael Gaffin.
Senior Budget/Appropriations Advisor.—Alejandra Ceja.
Financial Administrators: Daisy Minter, Dianna Ruskowsky.
Senior Systems Administrator.—Dray Thorne.
Systems Administrator.—David Hartzler.
Communications Director.—Thomas Kiley.
Research and Outreach Director.—Betsy Miller Kittredge.
Press/Outreach Assistant.—Danielle Lee.
Senior Investigator.—Ryan Holden.
Chief Investigative Counsel.—Michael Zola.
Hearing Clerk.—Tylease Fitzgerald-Alli.
Administrative Assistant.—Sarah Dyson.
Receptionist.—Sara Lonardo.
Minority Staff Director.—Vic Klatt, (2101 RHOB), 5–4527.
Executive Assistant.—Nancy DeLuca.
Director of:
Education and HR Policy.—Susan Ross.
Labor Policy.—Ed Gilroy.
Executive Assistant/Education/Labor.—Angela Jones.
Legislative Assistants/Education: Katie Bruns, Taylor Hansen.
Legislative Assistant/Labor.—Robert Gregg.
Office Manager/Education.—Lisa Paschal.
Professional Staff/Education: Amy Raff Jones, Chad Miller, Brad Thomas.
Proffessional Staff/Labor: Jim Paretti, Ken Serafin, Loren Sweatt.
Systems Administrator.—Thomas Benjamin.
Financial Assistant.—Rita Marchegiani.
General Counsel.—Rob Borden (2174 RHOB).
Chief Clerk/Assistant to the General Counsel.—Linda Stevens.
Communications Director.—Steve Forde.
Director of Outreach.—Lindsey Mask.

Energy and Commerce

2125 Rayburn House Office Building, phone 225–2927

http://www.house.gov/commerce

meets fourth Tuesday of each month

John D. Dingell, of Michigan, *Chair*

Diana DeGette, of Colorado.
Henry A. Waxman, of California.
Edward J. Markey, of Massachusetts.
Rick Boucher, of Virginia.
Edolphus Towns, of New York.
Frank Pallone, Jr., of New Jersey.
Bart Gordon, of Tennessee.
Bobby L. Rush, of Illinois.
Anna G. Eshoo, of California.
Bart Stupak, of Michigan.
Eliot L. Engel, of New York.
Albert Russell Wynn, of Maryland.
Gene Green, of Texas.
Lois Capps, of California.
Michael F. Doyle, of Pennsylvania.
Jane Harman, of California.
Thomas H. Allen, of Maine.
Janice D. Schakowsky, of Illinois.
Hilda L. Solis, of California.
Charles A. Gonzalez, of Texas.
Jay Inslee, of Washington.
Tammy Baldwin, of Wisconsin.
Mike Ross, of Arkansas.
Darlene Hooley, of Oregon.
Anthony D. Weiner, of New York.
Jim Matheson, of Utah.
G.K. Butterfield, of North Carolina.
Charlie Melancon, of Louisiana.
John Barrow, of Georgia.
Baron P. Hill, of Indiana.

Joe Barton, of Texas.
Ralph M. Hall, of Texas.
J. Dennis Hastert, of Illinois.
Fred Upton, of Michigan.
Cliff Stearns, of Florida.
Nathan Deal, of Georgia.
Ed Whitfield, of Kentucky.
Barbara Cubin, of Wyoming.
John Shimkus, of Illinois.
Heather Wilson, of New Mexico.
John B. Shadegg, of Arizona.
Charles W. ''Chip'' Pickering, of Mississippi.
Vito Fossella, of New York.
Steve Buyer, of Indiana.
George Radanovich, of California.
Joseph R. Pitts, of Pennsylvania.
Mary Bono, of California.
Greg Walden, of Oregon.
Lee Terry, of Nebraska.
Mike Ferguson, of New Jersey.
Mike Rogers, of Michigan.
Sue Wilkins Myrick, of North Carolina.
John Sullivan, of Oklahoma.
Tim Murphy, of Pennsylvania.
Michael C. Burgess, of Texas.
Marsha Blackburn, of Tennessee.

SUBCOMMITTEES

[The chairman and ranking minority member are ex officio (voting) members of all subcommittees on which they do not serve.]

Commerce, Trade, and Consumer Protection

Bobby L. Rush, of Illinois, *Chair*

Janice D. Schakowsky, of Illinois.
G.K. Butterfield, of North Carolina.
John Barrow, of Georgia.
Baron P. Hill, of Indiana.
Edward J. Markey, of Massachusetts.
Rick Boucher, of Virginia.
Edolphus Towns, of New York.
Diana DeGette, of Colorado.
Charles A. Gonzalez, of Texas.
Mike Ross, of Arkansas.
Darlene Hooley, of Oregon.
Anthony D. Weiner, of New York.
Jim Matheson, of Utah.
Charlie Melancon, of Louisiana.

Cliff Stearns, of Florida.
J. Dennis Hastert, of Illinois.
Ed Whitfield, of Kentucky.
Charles W. ''Chip'' Pickering, of Mississippi.
Vito Fossella, of New York.
George Radanovich, of California.
Joseph R. Pitts, of Pennsylvania.
Mary Bono, of California.
Lee Terry, of Nebraska.
Sue Wilkins Myrick, of North Carolina.
Michael C. Burgess, of Texas.
Marsha Blackburn, of Tennessee.

Energy and Air Quality

Rick Boucher, of Virginia, *Chair*

G.K. Butterfield, of North Carolina.
Charlie Melancon, of Louisiana.
John Barrow, of Georgia.
Henry A. Waxman, of California.
Edward J. Markey, of Massachusetts.
Albert Russell Wynn, of Maryland.
Michael F. Doyle, of Pennsylvania.
Jane Harman, of California.
Thomas H. Allen, of Maine.
Charles A. Gonzalez, of Texas.
Jay Inslee, of Washington.
Tammy Baldwin, of Wisconsin.
Mike Ross, of Arkansas.
Darlene Hooley, of Oregon.
Anthony D. Weiner, of New York.
Jim Matheson, of Utah.

J. Dennis Hastert, of Illinois.
Ralph M. Hall, of Texas.
Fred Upton, of Michigan.
Ed Whitfield, of Kentucky.
John Shimkus, of Illinois.
John B. Shadegg, of Arizona.
Charles W. "Chip" Pickering, of Mississippi.
Steve Buyer, of Indiana.
Mary Bono, of California.
Greg Walden, of Oregon.
Mike Rogers, of Michigan.
Sue Wilkins Myrick, of North Carolina.
John Sullivan, of Oklahoma.
Michael C. Burgess, of Texas.

Environment and Hazardous Materials

Albert Russell Wynn, of Maryland, *Chair*

Hilda L. Solis, of California.
Frank Pallone, Jr., of New Jersey.
Bart Stupak, of Michigan.
Lois Capps, of California.
Thomas H. Allen, of Maine.
Tammy Baldwin, of Wisconsin.
G.K. Butterfield, of North Carolina.
John Barrow, of Georgia.
Baron P. Hill, of Indiana.
Diana DeGette, of Colorado.
Anthony D. Weiner, of New York.
Henry A. Waxman, of California.
Gene Green, of Texas.
Janice D. Schakowsky, of Illinois.

John Shimkus, of Illinois.
Cliff Stearns, of Florida.
Nathan Deal, of Georgia.
Heather Wilson, of New Mexico.
John B. Shadegg, of Arizona.
Vito Fossella, of New York.
George Radanovich, of California.
Joseph R. Pitts, of Pennsylvania.
Lee Terry, of Nebraska.
Mike Rogers, of Michigan.
John Sullivan, of Oklahoma.
Tim Murphy, of Pennsylvania.

Health

Frank Pallone, Jr., of New Jersey, *Chair*

Gene Green, of Texas.
Henry A. Waxman, of California.
Edolphus Towns, of New York.
Bart Gordon, of Tennessee.
Anna G. Eshoo, of California.
Diana DeGette, of Colorado.
Lois Capps, of California.
Thomas H. Allen, of Maine.
Tammy Baldwin, of Wisconsin.
Eliot L. Engel, of New York.
Janice D. Schakowsky, of Illinois.
Hilda L. Solis, of California.
Mike Ross, of Arkansas.
Darlene Hooley, of Oregon.
Anthony D. Weiner, of New York.
Jim Matheson, of Utah.

Nathan Deal, of Georgia.
Ralph M. Hall, of Texas.
Barbara Cubin, of Wyoming.
Heather Wilson, of New Mexico.
John B. Shadegg, of Arizona.
Steve Buyer, of Indiana.
Joseph R. Pitts, of Pennsylvania.
Mike Ferguson, of New Jersey.
Mike Rogers, of Michigan.
Sue Wilkins Myrick, of North Carolina.
John Sullivan, of Oklahoma.
Tim Murphy, of Pennsylvania.
Michael C. Burgess, of Texas.
Marsha Blackburn, of Tennessee.

Oversight and Investigations

Bart Stupak, of Michigan, *Chair*

Charlie Melancon, of Louisiana.
Diana DeGette, of Colorado.
Henry A. Waxman, of California.
Gene Green, of Texas.
Michael F. Doyle, of Pennsylvania.
Janice D. Schakowsky, of Illinois.
Jay Inslee, of Washington.
Ed Whitfield, of Kentucky.
Greg Walden, of Oregon.
Mike Ferguson, of New Jersey.
Tim Murphy, of Pennsylvania.
Michael C. Burgess, of Texas.
Marsha Blackburn, of Tennessee.

Telecommunications and the Internet

Edward J. Markey, of Massachusetts, *Chair*

Michael F. Doyle, of Pennsylvania.
Jane Harman, of California.
Charles A. Gonzalez, of Texas.
Jay Inslee, of Washington.
Baron P. Hill, of Indiana.
Rick Boucher, of Virginia.
Edolphus Towns, of New York.
Frank Pallone, Jr., of New Jersey.
Bart Gordon, of Tennessee.
Bobby L. Rush, of Illinois.
Anna G. Eshoo, of California.
Bart Stupak, of Michigan.
Eliot L. Engel, of New York.
Gene Green, of Texas.
Lois Capps, of California.
Hilda L. Solis, of California.
Fred Upton, of Michigan.
J. Dennis Hastert, of Illinois.
Cliff Stearns, of Florida.
Nathan Deal, of Georgia.
Barbara Cubin, of Wyoming.
John Shimkus, of Illinois.
Heather Wilson, of New Mexico.
Charles W. ''Chip'' Pickering, of Mississippi.
Vito Fossella, of New York.
George Radanovich, of California.
Mary Bono, of California.
Greg Walden, of Oregon.
Lee Terry, of Nebraska.
Mike Ferguson, of New Jersey.

STAFF

Committee on Energy and Commerce (2125 RHOB), 225–2927; fax 225–2525.
Majority Chief of Staff.—Dennis B. Fitzgibbons.
Chief Counsel.—Gregg A. Rothschild.
Chief Clerk.—Sharon E. Davis.
Communications Director.—Jodi B. Seth.
Legislative Counsel.—Peter M. Goodloe.
Deputy Chief Counsel.—Jonathan J. Cordone.
Chief Counsel for:
Oversight.—John F. Sopko.
Enviroment.—Richard A. Frandsen.
Commerce, Trade, and Consumer Protection.—Consuela M. Washington.
Energy and Air Quality.—Sue D. Sheridan.
Chief Health Finance Policy Advisor.—Bridgett Taylor.
Senior Counsel (Public Health Policy).—John Ford.
Senior Counsel for Telecommunications and the Internet.—Johanna Mikes Shelton.
Senior Advisor, Energy Policy.—Burce C. Harris.
Counsels: Caroline C. Ahearn, Judith Bailey, Kevin S. Barstow, Maureen Flood, John W. Jimison, Purvee Parekh Kempf, Jack A. Maniko, Timothy E. Powderly, Lorie J. Schmidt, Mark Seifert, Karen E. Torrent.
Professional Staff Members: Colin E. Crowell, Yvette E. Fontenot, William Garner, Amy B. Hall, Scott P. Schloegel, Andrew J. Woelfing.
Senior Investigator/Professional Staff Member.—Christopher H. Knauer.
Senior Investigator.—David W. Nelson.
Investigator.—Richard Miller.
Assistant Investigator.—Voncille Trotter Hines.
Senior Investigative Counsel.—John G. Arlington.
Investigative Counsels: Kristine Blackwood, Kevin S. Barstow, Steven C. Rangel, Joanne Royce.
Policy Coordinators: Robert L. Clark, Christian Tamotsu Fjeld, Laura E. Vaught.
Deputy Clerk for Technology and Administration.—Carla R. Hultberg.
Deputy Clerk for Finance and Administration.—Raymond R. Kent, Jr.
Network Engineer.—Eddie Walker.

Assistant Clerk for Records and Legislative Calendar.—Sean Corcoran.
Printing Editor.—James Cahill.
Technology Support Specialist.—Walter J. Cross.
Assistant Clerks: Lisa E. Cody, Angela E. Davis, Elizabeth B. Ertel, Linda A. Good, Sarah Guerrieri, Tom Papageorge.
Legislative Clerks:
Health Finance.—Christie Houlihan.
Public Health.—Melissa R. Sidman.
Energy and Environment.—Rachel Bleshman.
Oversight and Investigations.—Kyle Chapman.
Legislative Analysts for:
Public Health.—Jessica Armao McNiece.
Telecommunications and the Internet.—David A. Vogel.
Legislative Analyst.—Jonathan P. Brater.
Policy Analyst for Energy and Environment.—Christopher Treanor.
Deputy Communications Director.—Brin Frazier.
Deputy Press Secretary.—Carrie Annand.
Deputy Press Secretary.—John Alexander ''Alec'' Gerlach.
Press Assistant.—Lauren Bloomberg.
Special Assistant: Erin R. Bzymek, Luke Entelis.
Staff Assistants: Valerie Baron, Matthew D. Eisenberg, Jesse E. Levine.

Minority Staff Director.—Clarence ''Bud'' Albright (2332A RHOB), 225–3641.
General Counsel/Chief Counsel, CTCP.—David L. Cavicke.
Deputy General Counsel.—Michael D. Bloomquist.
Deputy Staff Director, Communications.—Lawrence A. Neal.
Chief Counsel, Oversight.—Alan M. Slobodin.
Chief Counsel, Health.—Ryan Long.
Chief Counsel, Energy and Environment.—David J. McCarthy.
Senior Counsel: Nandan Kenkeremath, Neil Fried.
Counsels: Melissa Bartlett, Kurt W. Bilas, Krista L. Carpenter, Karen E. Christian, Thomas Hassenboehler, William Koetzle, E. Courtney Reinhard, Shannon M. Weinberg.
Professional Staff: William R.D. Carty, Brandon J. Clark, Gerald S. Couri II, Katherine M. Martin, Brian McCullough, Peter Spencer.
Deputy Communications Director.—Lisa Miller.
Administrative and Human Resources Coordinator.—Linda L. Walker.
Senior Legislative Clerk.—Peter E. Kielty.
Legislative Clerk.—Chad R. Grant.
Legislative Clerk/Financial Assistant.—Matthew P. Johnson.
Director, Information Technology.—Jean M. McGinley.
Special Assistant.—Whitney E. Drew.
Staff Assistant.—Garrett J. Golding.

Financial Services

2129 Rayburn House Office Building, phone 225–4247

http://www.house.gov/financialservices

meets first Tuesday of each month

Barney Frank, of Massachusetts, *Chair*

Paul E. Kanjorski, of Pennsylvania.
Maxine Waters, of California.
Carolyn B. Maloney, of New York.
Luis V. Gutierrez, of Illinois.
Nydia M. Velázquez, of New York.
Melvin L. Watt, of North Carolina.
Gary L. Ackerman, of New York.
Julia Carson, of Indiana.
Brad Sherman, of California.
Gregory W. Meeks, of New York.
Dennis Moore, of Kansas.
Michael E. Capuano, of Massachusetts.
Rubén Hinojosa, of Texas.
Wm. Lacy Clay, of Missouri.
Carolyn McCarthy, of New York.
Joe Baca, of California.
Stephen F. Lynch, of Massachusetts.
Brad Miller, of North Carolina.
David Scott, of Georgia.
Al Green, of Texas.
Emanuel Cleaver, of Missouri.
Melissa L. Bean, of Illinois.
Gwen Moore, of Wisconsin.
Lincoln Davis, of Tennessee.
Albio Sires, of New Jersey.
Paul W. Hodes, of New Hampshire.
Keith Ellison, of Minnesota.
Ron Klein, of Florida.
Tim Mahoney, of Florida.
Charles A. Wilson, of Ohio.
Ed Perlmutter, of Colorado.
Christopher S. Murphy, of Connecticut.
Joe Donnelly, of Indiana.
Robert Wexler, of Florida.
Jim Marshall, of Georgia.
Dan Boren, of Oklahoma.

Spencer Bachus, of Alabama.
Richard H. Baker, of Louisiana.
Deborah Pryce, of Ohio.
Michael N. Castle, of Delaware.
Peter T. King, of New York.
Edward R. Royce, of California.
Frank D. Lucas, of Oklahoma.
Ron Paul, of Texas.
Paul E. Gillmor, of Ohio.
Steven C. LaTourette, of Ohio.
Donald A. Manzullo, of Illinois.
Walter B. Jones, of North Carolina.
Judy Biggert, of Illinois.
Christopher Shays, of Connecticut.
Gary G. Miller, of California.
Shelley Moore Capito, of West Virginia.
Tom Feeney, of Florida.
Jeb Hensarling, of Texas.
Scott Garrett, of New Jersey.
Ginny Brown-Waite, of Florida.
J. Gresham Barrett, of South Carolina.
Jim Gerlach, of Pennsylvania.
Stevan Pearce, of New Mexico.
Randy Neugebauer, of Texas.
Tom Price, of Georgia.
Geoff Davis, of Kentucky.
Patrick T. McHenry, of North Carolina.
John Campbell, of California.
Adam H. Putnam, of Florida.
Michele Bachmann, of Minnesota.
Peter J. Roskam, of Illinois.
Kenny Marchant, of Texas.
Thaddeus G. McCotter, of Michigan.

SUBCOMMITTEES

[The chairman and ranking minority member are ex officio (voting) members of all subcommittees on which they do not serve.]

Capital Markets, Insurance, and Government-Sponsored Enterprises

Paul E. Kanjorski, of Pennsylvania, *Chair*

Gary L. Ackerman, of New York.
Brad Sherman, of California.
Dennis Moore, of Kansas.
Michael E. Capuano, of Massachusetts.
Rubén Hinojosa, of Texas.
Carolyn McCarthy, of New York.
Joe Baca, of California.
Stephen F. Lynch, of Massachusetts.
Brad Miller, of North Carolina.
David Scott, of Georgia.
Nydia M. Velázquez, of New York.
Melissa L. Bean, of Illinois.
Gwen Moore, of Wisconsin.
Lincoln Davis, of Tennessee.
Albio Sires, of New Jersey.
Paul W. Hodes, of New Hampshire.
Ron Klein, of Florida.
Tim Mahoney, of Florida.
Ed Perlmutter, of Colorado.
Christopher S. Murphy, of Connecticut.
Joe Donnelly, of Indiana.
Robert Wexler, of Florida.
Jim Marshall, of Georgia.
Dan Boren, of Oklahoma.

Deborah Pryce, of Ohio.
Richard H. Baker, of Louisiana.
Christopher Shays, of Connecticut.
Paul E. Gillmor, of Ohio.
Michael N. Castle, of Delaware.
Peter T. King, of New York.
Frank D. Lucas, of Oklahoma.
Donald A. Manzullo, of Illinois.
Edward R. Royce, of California.
Shelley Moore Capito, of West Virginia.
Adam H. Putnam, of Florida.
J. Gresham Barrett, of South Carolina.
Ginny Brown-Waite, of Florida.
Tom Feeney, of Florida.
Scott Garrett, of New Jersey.
Jim Gerlach, of Pennsylvania.
Jeb Hensarling, of Texas.
Geoff Davis, of Kentucky.
John Campbell, of California.
Michele Bachmann, of Minnesota.
Peter J. Roskam, of Illinois.
Kenny Marchant, of Texas.
Thaddeus G. McCotter, of Michigan.

Domestic and International Monetary Policy, Trade and Technology

Luis V. Gutierrez, of Illinois, *Chair*

Carolyn B. Maloney, of New York.
Maxine Waters, of California.
Paul E. Kanjorski, of Pennsylvania.
Brad Sherman, of California.
Gwen Moore, of Wisconsin.
Gregory W. Meeks, of New York.
Dennis Moore, of Kansas.
Wm. Lacy Clay, of Missouri.
Keith Ellison, of Minnesota.
Charles A. Wilson, of Ohio.
Robert Wexler, of Florida.
Jim Marshall, of Georgia.
Dan Boren, of Oklahoma.

Ron Paul, of Texas.
Michael N. Castle, of Delaware.
Frank D. Lucas, of Oklahoma.
Steven C. LaTourette, of Ohio.
Donald A. Manzullo, of Illinois.
Walter B. Jones, of North Carolina.
Jeb Hensarling, of Texas.
Tom Price, of Georgia.
Patrick T. McHenry, of North Carolina.
Michele Bachmann, of Minnesota.
Peter J. Roskam, of Illinois.
Kenny Marchant, of Texas.

Financial Institutions and Consumer Credit

Carolyn B. Maloney, of New York, *Chair*

Melvin L. Watt, of North Carolina.
Gary L. Ackerman, of New York.
Brad Sherman, of California.
Luis V. Gutierrez, of Illinois.
Dennis Moore, of Kansas.
Paul E. Kanjorski, of Pennsylvania.
Maxine Waters, of California.
Julia Carson, of Indiana.
Rubén Hinojosa, of Texas.
Carolyn McCarthy, of New York.
Joe Baca, of California.
Al Green, of Texas.
Wm. Lacy Clay, of Missouri.
Brad Miller, of North Carolina.
David Scott, of Georgia.
Emanuel Cleaver, of Missouri.
Melissa L. Bean, of Illinois.
Lincoln Davis, of Tennessee.
Paul W. Hodes, of New Hampshire.
Keith Ellison, of Minnesota.
Ron Klein, of Florida.
Tim Mahoney, of Florida.
Charles A. Wilson, of Ohio.
Ed Perlmutter, of Colorado.

Paul E. Gillmor, of Ohio.
Tom Price, of Georgia.
Richard H. Baker, of Louisiana.
Deborah Pryce, of Ohio.
Michael N. Castle, of Delaware.
Peter T. King, of New York.
Edward R. Royce, of California.
Steven C. LaTourette, of Ohio.
Walter B. Jones, of North Carolina.
Judy Biggert, of Illinois.
Shelley Moore Capito, of West Virginia.
Tom Feeney, of Florida.
Jeb Hensarling, of Texas.
Scott Garrett, of New Jersey.
Ginny Brown-Waite, of Florida.
J. Gresham Barrett, of South Carolina.
Jim Gerlach, of Pennsylvania.
Stevan Pearce, of New Mexico.
Randy Neugebauer, of Texas.
Geoff Davis, of Kentucky.
Patrick T. McHenry, of North Carolina.
John Campbell, of California.

Housing and Community Opportunity

Maxine Waters, of California, *Chair*

Nydia M. Velázquez, of New York.
Julia Carson, of Indiana.
Stephen F. Lynch, of Massachusetts.
Emanuel Cleaver, of Missouri.
Al Green, of Texas.
Wm. Lacy Clay, of Missouri.
Carolyn B. Maloney, of New York.
Gwen Moore, of Wisconsin.
Albio Sires, of New Jersey.
Keith Ellison, of Minnesota.
Charles A. Wilson, of Ohio.
Christopher S. Murphy, of Connecticut.
Joe Donnelly, of Indiana.

Judy Biggert, of Illinois.
Stevan Pearce, of New Mexico.
Peter T. King, of New York.
Paul E. Gillmor, of Ohio.
Christopher Shays, of Connecticut.
Gary G. Miller, of California.
Shelley Moore Capito, of West Virginia.
Scott Garrett, of New Jersey.
Randy Neugebauer, of Texas.
Geoff Davis, of Kentucky.
John Campbell, of California.
Thaddeus G. McCotter, of Michigan.

Oversight and Investigations

Melvin L. Watt, of North Carolina, *Chair*

Luis V. Gutierrez, of Illinois.
Maxine Waters, of California.
Stephen F. Lynch, of Massachusetts.
Nydia M. Velázquez, of New York.
Michael E. Capuano, of Massachusetts.
Carolyn McCarthy, of New York.
Ron Klein, of Florida.
Tim Mahoney, of Florida.
Robert Wexler, of Florida.
[Vacancy]

Gary G. Miller, of California.
Patrick T. McHenry, of North Carolina.
Edward R. Royce, of California.
Ron Paul, of Texas.
Steven C. LaTourette, of Ohio.
J. Gresham Barrett, of South Carolina.
Tom Price, of Georgia.
Michele Bachmann, of Minnesota.
Peter J. Roskam, of Illinois.

STAFF

Committee on Financial Services (2129 RHOB), 225–4247.
Majority Staff Director / Chief Counsel.—Jeanne Roslanowick.
Deputy Staff Director.—Michael Paese.

General Counsel.—Tom Duncan.
Deputy Chief Counsels: Gail Laster, Lawranne Stewart.
Chief Economist.—David A. Smith.
Senior Policy Director.—Michael Beresik.
Senior Counsels: Ricardo Delfin, Jeffrey Riley, Deborah Silberman.
Counsels: Sanders Adu, Eleni Constantine, Eric Edwards, Jonathan Harwitz, Erika Jeffers, Kellie Larkin, Dominique McCoy, Kathleen Mellody, Patience Singleton, Charles Yi.
Director of Legislative Affairs.—Jaime Lizarrage.
Senior Professional Staff: Todd Harper, Daniel McGlinchey, Scott Morris, Peter Roberson, Dennis Shaul.
Professional Staff Members: Meredith Connelly, Patricia Lord, Edward Mills, Jonathan Obee, Charla Ouertatani, Nathaniel Thomas.
Policy Director, Housing.—Scott Olson.
Communications Director.—Steven Adamske.
Press Secretary.—Heather Wong.
Clerk.—Lois Richerson.
Staff Associates: Jean Carroll, Gabriel Goldwasser, Brian Kelly, Garrett Rose.
Systems Administrator.—Alfred Forman.
Assistant Systems Administrator.—Steve Arauz.
Editor.—Terisa Allison.

Minority Chief of Staff.—Larry Lavender, B–371A Rayburn, 5–7502.
Deputy Chief of Staff.—Warren Tryon.
Senior Counsels: James Clinger, Kevin Edgar, Dina Ellis, Robert Gordon.
Counsels: Michael Borden, Rashmi Puri.
Senior Professional Staff: Cindy Chetti, Danielle English, Tallman Johnson.
Professional Staff: Nicole Austin, Paul Martin Foss, Peter Freeman, Lesli McCollum-Gooch, David Oxner, Joe Pinder, James Sims, Jr.
Communications Director.—Richard Cross III.
Assistant Communications Director.—Marisol Garibay.
Administrative Assistant.—Angela Gambo.
Executive Staff Assistant.—Rosemary Keech.
System Administrator.—Kim Trimble.
Staff Assistant.—Anthony Cimino.

Foreign Affairs

2170 Rayburn House Office Building, phone 225–5021

http://www.foreignaffairs.house.gov

meets first Tuesday of each month

Tom Lantos, of California, *Chair*

Howard L. Berman, of California.
Gary L. Ackerman, of New York.
Eni F.H. Faleomavaega, of American Samoa.
Donald M. Payne, of New Jersey.
Brad Sherman, of California.
Robert Wexler, of Florida.
Eliot L. Engel, of New York.
William D. Delahunt, of Massachusetts.
Gregory W. Meeks, of New York.
Diane E. Watson, of California.
Adam Smith, of Washington.
Russ Carnahan, of Missouri.
John S. Tanner, of Tennessee.
Gene Green, of Texas.
Lynn C. Woolsey, of California.
Sheila Jackson Lee, of Texas.
Rubén Hinojosa, of Texas.
Joseph Crowley, of New York.
David Wu, of Oregon.
Brad Miller, of North Carolina.
Linda T. Sánchez, of California.
David Scott, of Georgia.
Jim Costa, of California.
Albio Sires, of New Jersey.
Gabrielle Giffords, of Arizona.
Ron Klein, of Florida.

Ileana Ros-Lehtinen, of Florida.
Christopher H. Smith, of New Jersey.
Dan Burton, of Indiana.
Elton Gallegly, of California.
Dana Rohrabacher, of California.
Donald A. Manzullo, of Illinois.
Edward R. Royce, of California.
Steve Chabot, of Ohio.
Thomas G. Tancredo, of Colorado.
Ron Paul, of Texas.
Jeff Flake, of Arizona.
Jo Ann Davis, of Virginia.
Mike Pence, of Indiana.
Thaddeus G. McCotter, of Michigan.
Joe Wilson, of South Carolina.
John Boozman, of Arkansas.
J. Gresham Barrett, of South Carolina.
Connie Mack, of Florida.
Jeff Fortenberry, of Nebraska.
Michael T. McCaul, of Texas.
Ted Poe, of Texas.
Bob Inglis, of South Carolina.
Louis G. Fortuño, of Puerto Rico.

SUBCOMMITTEES

[The chairman and ranking minority member are ex officio (non-voting) members of all subcommittees on which they do not serve.]

Africa and Global Health

Donald M. Payne, of New Jersey, *Chair*

Diane E. Watson, of California.
Lynn C. Woolsey, of California.
Sheila Jackson Lee, of Texas.
Adam Smith, of Washington.
Brad Miller, of North Carolina.

Christopher H. Smith, of New Jersey.
Thomas G. Tancredo, of Colorado.
John Boozman, of Arkansas.
Jeff Fortenberry, of Nebraska.
Michael T. McCaul, of Texas.

Asia, the Pacific, and the Global Environment

Eni F.H. Faleomavaega, of American Samoa, *Chair*

Adam Smith, of Washington.
Gary L. Ackerman, of New York.
Gregory W. Meeks, of New York.
Diane E. Watson, of California.
Rubén Hinojosa, of Texas.
Albio Sires, of New Jersey.

Donald A. Manzullo, of Illinois.
Dan Burton, of Indiana.
Dana Rohrabacher, of California.
Edward R. Royce, of California.
Steve Chabot, of Ohio.
Jeff Flake, of Arizona.

Europe

Robert Wexler, of Florida, *Chair*

John S. Tanner, of Tennessee.
Rubén Hinojosa, of Texas.
Brad Miller, of North Carolina.
Linda T. Sánchez, of California.
Eliot L. Engel, of New York.
Jim Costa, of California.
Albio Sires, of New Jersey.

Elton Gallegly, of California.
Thaddeus G. McCotter, of Michigan.
Joe Wilson, of South Carolina.
Ted Poe, of Texas.
Bob Inglis, of South Carolina.
Louis G. Fortuño, of Puerto Rico.

International Organizations, Human Rights, and Oversight

William D. Delahunt, of Massachusetts, *Chair*

Russ Carnahan, of Missouri.
Donald M. Payne, of New Jersey.
Gregory W. Meeks, of New York.
Joseph Crowley, of New York.

Dana Rohrabacher, of California.
Ron Paul, of Texas.
Jeff Flake, of Arizona.

Middle East and South Asia

Gary L. Ackerman, of New York, *Chair*

Howard L. Berman, of California.
David Scott, of Georgia.
Jim Costa, of California.
Ron Klein, of Florida.
Brad Sherman, of California.
Robert Wexler, of Florida.
Eliot L. Engel, of New York.
Russ Carnahan, of Missouri.
Sheila Jackson Lee, of Texas.

Mike Pence, of Indiana.
Steve Chabot, of Ohio.
Jo Ann Davis, of Virginia.
Thaddeus G. McCotter, of Michigan.
Joe Wilson, of South Carolina.
J. Gresham Barrett, of South Carolina.
Jeff Fortenberry, of Nebraska.
Bob Inglis, of South Carolina.
Connie Mack, of Florida.

Terrorism, Nonproliferation, and Trade

Brad Sherman, of California, *Chair*

David Wu, of Oregon.
David Scott, of Georgia.
Ron Klein, of Florida.
Gene Green, of Texas.
Joseph Crowley, of New York.

Edward R. Royce, of California.
John Boozman, of Arkansas.
Ted Poe, of Texas.
Donald A. Manzullo, of Illinois.
Thomas G. Tancredo, of Colorado.

The Western Hemisphere

Eliot L. Engel, of New York, *Chair*

Gregory W. Meeks, of New York.
Linda T. Sánchez, of California.
Albio Sires, of New Jersey.
Gabrielle Giffords, of Arizona.
Eni F.H. Faleomavaega, of American Samoa.
Donald M. Payne, of New Jersey.
William D. Delahunt, of Massachusetts.
Ron Klein, of Florida.
Gene Green, of Texas.

Dan Burton, of Indiana.
Connie Mack, of Florida.
Michael T. McCaul, of Texas.
Louis G. Fortuño, of Puerto Rico.
Ron Paul, of Texas.
Jo Ann Davis, of Virginia.

STAFF

Committee on Foreign Affairs (2170 RHOB), 225–5021.
Majority Staff Director.—Robert R. King.
Deputy Staff Director.—Peter M. Yeo.
Chief Counsel.—David S. Abramowitz.
Deputy Chief Counsel.—Kristen Wells.

Senior Professional Staff: David Fite, Hans Hogrefe, David Killion, Pearl Alice Marsh, Alan Makovsky.
Professional Staff: Manpreet Anand, Peter Ford, Cobb Mixter, Robin Roizman, Peter Quilter, Jed Seltzer, Amanda Sloat, Patrick Stephenson, David Weinberg.
Security Officer/Clerk.—Laura Rush.
Administrative Director/Assistant to Staff Director.—Melissa Adamson.
Financial Administrator.—Jim Farr.
Travel Coordinator.—David Beraka.
Information Resource Manager.—Vlad Cerga.
Senior Staff Associate.—Marilyn Owen.
Staff Associates: Riley Moore, Don Phan, Marin Stein.
Printing Manager/Web Assistant.—Shirley Alexander.
Full Committee Hearing Coordinator.—Genell Brown.
Assistant Systems Administrator.—Denis Munoz.
Minority Staff Director.—Yleem Poblete (B–360 RHOB), 226–8467.
Senior Policy Advisor.—Mark Gage.
Chief Counsel.—Kirsti Garlock.
Senior Professional Staff: Doug Anderson, Cassie Bevan.
Professional Staff: Lee Cohen, Joan Condon, Gene Gurevich, Dennis Halpin, Jamie McCormick, Matt Zweig.
Communications Director/Professional Staff.—Sam Stratman.
Policy Analyst.—Alan Goldsmith.
Administrative Director.—Sarah Kiko.
Special Assistant.—Alexandra Zweig.

Subcommittee on Africa and Global Health (259A FHOB), 6–7812.
Staff Director.—Noelle Lusane.
Professional Staff.—Heather Flynn.
Minority Professional Staff.—Sheri Rickert.
Staff Associate.—Fay Johnson.

Subcommittee on Asia, the Pacific, and Global Environment (2401A RHOB), 6–7825.
Staff Director.—Lisa Williams.
Professional Staff.—David Richmond.
Minority Professional Staff.—Nien Su.
Staff Associate.—Vili Lei.

Subcommittee on Europe (257 FHOB B), 6–7820.
Staff Director.—Jonathan Katz.
Professional Staff.—Eric Johnson.
Minority Professional Staff.—Richard Mereu.
Staff Associate.—Beverly Razon.

Subcommittee on International Organizations, Human Rights, and Oversight (256 FHOB), 6–6434.
Staff Director.—Clifford A. Stammerman.
Professional Staff: Natalie Coburn, Caleb Rossitier.
Minority Professional Staff.—Phaedra Dugan.
Staff Associate.—Elisa Perry.

Subcommittee on the Middle East and South Asia (B358 RHOB), 5–3345.
Staff Director.—David S. Adams.
Professional Staff.—Howard Diamond.
Minority Professional Staff.—Greg McCarthy.
Staff Associate.—Dalis Blumenfeld.

Subcommittee on Terrorism, Nonproliferation, and Trade (253 FHOB), 6–1500.
Staff Director.—Don MacDonald.
Professional Staff.—John Brodtke.
Minority Professional Staff.—Thom Sheehy.
Staff Associate.—Kinsey Kiriakos.

Subcommittee on the Western Hemisphere (255 FHOB), 6–9980.
Staff Director.—Jason Steinbaum.
Professional Staff.—Eric Jacobstein.
Minority Professional Staff.—Mark Walker.
Staff Associate.—Erin Diamond.

Homeland Security

phone 226–8417, fax 226–3399

Bennie G. Thompson, of Mississippi, *Chair*

Loretta Sanchez, of California, *Vice Chair.*
Edward J. Markey, of Massachusetts.
Norman D. Dicks, of Washington.
Jane Harman, of California.
Peter A. DeFazio, of Oregon.
Nita M. Lowey, of New York.
Eleanor Holmes Norton, of the District of Columbia.
Zoe Lofgren, of California.
Sheila Jackson Lee, of Texas.
Donna M. Christensen, of the Virgin Islands.
Bob Etheridge, of North Carolina.
James R. Langevin, of Rhode Island.
Henry Cuellar, of Texas.
Christopher P. Carney, of Pennsylvania.
Yvette D. Clarke, of New York.
Al Green, of Texas.
Ed Perlmutter, of Colorado.

Peter T. King, of New York.
Lamar Smith, of Texas.
Christopher Shays, of Connecticut.
Mark E. Souder, of Indiana.
Tom Davis, of Virginia.
Daniel E. Lungren, of California.
Mike Rogers, of Alabama.
Bobby Jindal, of Louisiana.
David G. Reichert, of Washington.
Michael T. McCaul, of Texas.
Charles W. Dent, of Pennsylvania.
Ginny Brown-Waite, of Florida.
Gus M. Bilirakis, of Florida.
David Davis, of Tennessee.
Kevin McCarthy, of California.

SUBCOMMITTEES

[The chairman and ranking minority member are ex officio (voting) members of all subcommittees on which they do not serve.]

Border, Maritime, and Global Counterterrorism

Loretta Sanchez, of California, *Chair*

Jane Harman, of California.
Zoe Lofgren, of California.
Sheila Jackson Lee, of Texas.
James R. Langevin, of Rhode Island.
Henry Cuellar, of Texas.
Al Green, of Texas.

Mark E. Souder, of Indiana.
Bobby Jindal, of Louisiana.
David G. Reichert, of Washington.
Michael T. McCaul, of Texas.
Gus M. Bilirakis, of Florida.

Emergency Communications, Preparedness, and Response

Henry Cuellar, of Texas, *Chair*

Loretta Sanchez, of California.
Norman D. Dicks, of Washington.
Nita M. Lowey, of New York.
Eleanor Holmes Norton, of the District of Columbia.
Donna M. Christensen, of the Virgin Islands.
Bob Etheridge, of North Carolina.

Charles W. Dent, of Pennsylvania.
Mark E. Souder, of Indiana.
Mike Rogers, of Alabama.
Bobby Jindal, of Louisiana.
David Davis, of Tennessee.

Emerging Threats, Cybersecurity, and Science and Technology

James R. Langevin, of Rhode Island, *Chair*

Zoe Lofgren, of California.
Donna M. Christensen, of the Virgin Islands.
Bob Etheridge, of North Carolina.
Al Green, of Texas.

Michael T. McCaul, of Texas.
Daniel E. Lungren, of California.
Ginny Brown-Waite, of Florida.
Kevin McCarthy, of California.

Intelligence, Information Sharing, and Terrorism Risk Assessment

Jane Harman, of California, *Chair*

Norman D. Dicks, of Washington.
James R. Langevin, of Rhode Island.
Christopher P. Carney, of Pennsylvania.
Ed Perlmutter, of Colorado.
David G. Reichert, of Washington.
Christopher Shays, of Connecticut.
Charles W. Dent, of Pennsylvania.

Management, Investigations and Oversight

Christopher P. Carney, of Pennsylvania, *Chair*

Peter A. DeFazio, of Oregon.
Yvette D. Clarke, of New York.
Ed Perlmutter, of Colorado.
Mike Rogers, of Alabama.
Tom Davis, of Virginia.
Michael T. McCaul, of Texas.

Transportation Security and Infrastructure Protection

Sheila Jackson Lee, of Texas, *Chair*

Edward J. Markey, of Massachusetts.
Peter A. DeFazio, of Oregon.
Eleanor Holmes Norton, of the District of Columbia.
Yvette D. Clarke, of New York.
Ed Perlmutter, of Colorado.
Daniel E. Lungren, of California.
Ginny Brown-Waite, of Florida.
Gus M. Bilirakis, of Florida.
Kevin McCarthy, of California.

STAFF

Committee on Homeland Security (H2–176 Ford House Office Building) phone 226–2616, fax 226–4499.

Majority Staff Director / General Counsel.—Jessica Herrera-Flanigan.
Deputy Staff Director.—Lanier Avant.
Clerk of the Committee.—Michael Twinchek.
Deputy Chief Clerk.—Natalie Nixon.
Deputy Clerks: Brian Turbyfill, Carla Zamudio-Dolan.
Chief Financial Officer.—Dawn M. Criste.
Office Manager.—Nikki Johnson.
Security Officer.—Etienne Singleton.
Communications Director.—Dena Graziano.
Advisory for Policy and Outreach.—Todd Levett.
Press Staff.—Adam Comis.
Policy Director.—Veronique Pulviose-Fenton.
Chief Counsel.—Todd Gee.
Deputy Chief Counsel.—Rosaline Cohen.
Legislative Assistant.—Erin Murphy.
Law Clerk.—Kandis Gibson.
Chief Oversight Counsel.—Cherri Branson.
Investigator.—Denton Herring.
Investigative Counsels: Areto Imoukhuede, Kathryn Minor.

Minority Staff Director.—Rob O'Connor (H2–117 Ford House Office Building), 226–8417, fax 226–3399.
Chief Counsel.—Mike Power.
Deputy Chief Counsel.—Sue Ramanathan.
General Counsel.—Mark Klaassen.
Senior Counsels: Coley O'Brien, Mike Russell.
Counsels: Jennifer Arangio, Kevin Gronberg, Kerry Kinirons, Matthew McCabe, Colleen O'Keefe, Will Rubens.
Communications Director.—Chad Scarborough.
Senior Professional Staff: Diane Berry, Mandy Bowers, Heather Hogg, Deron McElroy.
Professional Staff Member.—Sterling Marchand.
Press / Staff Assistant.—Janice Tolley.
Staff Assistant.—Adam Hepburn.
Legislative Assistant.—Amanda Halpern.

Subcommittee Directors:
Border, Maritime, and Global Counterterrorism.—Alison Rosso.

Emergency Communications, Preparedness, and Response.—Craig Sharman.
Emerging Threats, Cybersecurity, and Science and Technology.—Jacob Olcott.
Intelligence, Information Sharing, and Terrorism Risk Assessment.—Tom Finan.
Management, Investigations, and Oversight.—Jeff Greene.
Transportation Security and Infrastructure Protection.—Michael Stroud.
Professional Staff: Aneda Arriaga, Diane Bean, Chris Beck, Erin Daste, Brendan Declet, Bill Ellis, Nicole Francis, Karis Gutter, Denise Krepp, Jeanne Lin, Erin Murphy, Marisela Salayandia, Tamla Scott, Scott Springer, Stephen Viña, Matthew Washington.

House Administration

1309 Longworth House Office Building, phone 225–2061, fax 225–2774

http://cha.house.gov/

meets second Wednesday of each month

Robert A. Brady, of Pennsylvania, *Chair*

Zoe Lofgren, of California, *Vice Chair*

Michael E. Capuano, of Massachusetts.
Charles A. Gonzalez, of Texas.
Susan A. Davis, of California.
Artur Davis, of Alabama.

Vernon J. Ehlers, of Michigan.
Daniel E. Lungren, of California.
Kevin McCarthy, of California.

SUBCOMMITTEES

Capitol Security

Robert A. Brady, of Pennsylvania, *Chair*

Michael E. Capuano, of Massachusetts.

Daniel E. Lungren, of California.

Elections

Zoe Lofgren, of California, *Chair*

Charles A. Gonzalez, of Texas.
Susan A. Davis, of California.
Artur Davis, of Alabama.

Kevin McCarthy, of California.
Vernon J. Ehlers, of Michigan.

STAFF

Committee on House Administration (1309 LHOB), 5–2061.
Majority Staff Director.—S. Elizabeth Birnbaum.
Deputy Staff Director.—Jamie P.D. Fleet II.
Chief Counsel.—Charles T. Howell.
Deputy Chief Counsel.—Teri A. Morgan.
Senior Elections Counsel.—Thomas Hicks.
Elections Counsel: Jennifer Daehn, Janelle Hu.
Staff Assistant / Elections.—Daniel D. Favarulo.
Technology Director.—Sterling D. Spriggs.
IT Director.—Mike Lowell.
Chief Legislative Clerk.—Kristin N. McCowan.
Communications Director.—Janice K. Crump.
Press Director.—Kyle Anderson.
Operations Director.—Eddie Flaherty.
Financial Director.—Kim Stevens.
Professional Staff: Khalil Abbuod, Michael L. Harrison, Ellen A. McCarthy, Kristie Muchnok, Kevin F. Peterson, Matthew Pinkus, Diana Rodriguez.
Staff Assistants: Matthew DeFreitas, Robert Henline.
Minority Staff Director.—William Plaster (1313 LHOB), 5–8281.
General Counsel.—Fred Hay.
Counsel.—Gineen Beach.
Professional Staff: Bryan Dorsey, Alec Hoppes, Katie Ryan, Robert Wehagen.
Director, Member and Committee Services.—George Hadijski.
Administrative Director.—Darren Feist.
Communications Director.—Sunita Ray.
Press Secretary / Senior Communications Specialist.—Salley Collins.

Commission on Congressional Mailing Standards (1216 LHOB), 5–9337.
Majority Staff Director.—Ellen A. McCarthy.
Professional Staff: Connie D. Goode, Brian M. McCue, Mary E. McHugh.
Minority Staff Director.—Jack Dail (1216A LHOB), 6–0647.
Professional Staff.—Lauren Sholley.

Judiciary

2138 Rayburn House Office Building, phone 225–3951

http://www.house.gov/judiciary

meets every Tuesday

John Conyers, Jr., of Michigan, *Chair*

Howard L. Berman, of California.
Rick Boucher, of Virginia.
Jerrold Nadler, of New York.
Robert C. ''Bobby'' Scott, of Virginia.
Melvin L. Watt, of North Carolina.
Zoe Lofgren, of California.
Sheila Jackson Lee, of Texas.
Maxine Waters, of California.
William D. Delahunt, of Massachusetts.
Robert Wexler, of Florida.
Linda T. Sánchez, of California.
Steve Cohen, of Tennessee.
Henry C. ''Hank'' Johnson, Jr., of Georgia.
Luis V. Gutierrez, of Illinois.
Brad Sherman, of California.
Anthony D. Weiner, of New York.
Adam B. Schiff, of California.
Artur Davis, of Alabama.
Debbie Wasserman Schultz, of Florida.
Keith Ellison, of Minnesota.

Lamar Smith, of Texas.
F. James Sensenbrenner, Jr., of Wisconsin.
Howard Coble, of North Carolina.
Elton Gallegly, of California.
Bob Goodlatte, of Virginia.
Steve Chabot, of Ohio.
Daniel E. Lungren, of California.
Chris Cannon, of Utah.
Ric Keller, of Florida.
Darrell E. Issa, of California.
Mike Pence, of Indiana.
J. Randy Forbes, of Virginia.
Steve King, of Iowa.
Tom Feeney, of Florida.
Trent Franks, of Arizona.
Louie Gohmert, of Texas.
Jim Jordan, of Ohio.

SUBCOMMITTEES

[The chairman and the ranking minority member are ex officio (non-voting) members of all subcommittees on which they do not serve.]

Commercial and Administrative Law

Linda T. Sánchez, of California, *Chair*

John Conyers, Jr., of Michigan.
Henry C. ''Hank'' Johnson, Jr., of Georgia.
Zoe Lofgren, of California.
William D. Delahunt, of Massachusetts.
Melvin L. Watt, of North Carolina.
Steve Cohen, of Tennessee.

Chris Cannon, of Utah.
Jim Jordan, of Ohio.
Ric Keller, of Florida.
Tom Feeney, of Florida.
Trent Franks, of Arizona.

The Constitution, Civil Rights, and Civil Liberties

Jerrold Nadler, of New York, *Chair*

Artur Davis, of Alabama.
Debbie Wasserman Schultz, of Florida.
Keith Ellison, of Minnesota.
John Conyers, Jr., of Michigan.
Robert C. ''Bobby'' Scott, of Virginia.
Melvin L. Watt, of North Carolina.
Steve Cohen, of Tennessee.

Trent Franks, of Arizona.
Mike Pence, of Indiana.
Darrell E. Issa, of California.
Steve King, of Iowa.
Jim Jordan, of Ohio.

Courts, the Internet, and Intellectual Property

Howard L. Berman, of California, *Chair*

John Conyers, Jr., of Michigan.
Rick Boucher, of Virginia.
Robert Wexler, of Florida.
Melvin L. Watt, of North Carolina.
Sheila Jackson Lee, of Texas.
Steve Cohen, of Tennessee.
Henry C. "Hank" Johnson, Jr., of Georgia.
Brad Sherman, of California.
Anthony D. Weiner, of New York.
Adam B. Schiff, of California.
Zoe Lofgren, of California.

Howard Coble, of North Carolina.
Tom Feeney, of Florida.
F. James Sensenbrenner, Jr., of Wisconsin.
Lamar Smith, of Texas.
Elton Gallegly, of California.
Bob Goodlatte, of Virginia.
Steve Chabot, of Ohio.
Chris Cannon, of Utah.
Ric Keller, of Florida.
Darrell E. Issa, of California.
Mike Pence, of Indiana.

Crime, Terrorism, and Homeland Security

Robert C. "Bobby" Scott, of Virginia, *Chair*

Maxine Waters, of California.
William D. Delahunt, of Massachusetts.
Jerrold Nadler, of New York.
Henry C. "Hank" Johnson, Jr., of Georgia.
Anthony D. Weiner, of New York.
Sheila Jackson Lee, of Texas.
Artur Davis, of Alabama.

J. Randy Forbes, of Virginia.
Louie Gohmert, of Texas.
F. James Sensenbrenner, Jr., of Wisconsin.
Howard Coble, of North Carolina.
Steve Chabot, of Ohio.
Daniel E. Lungren, of California.

Immigration, Citizenship, Refugees, Border Security, and International Law

Zoe Lofgren, of California, *Chair*

Luis V. Gutierrez, of Illinois.
Howard L. Berman, of California.
Sheila Jackson Lee, of Texas.
Maxine Waters, of California.
William D. Delahunt, of Massachusetts.
Linda T. Sánchez, of California.
Artur Davis, of Alabama.
Keith Ellison, of Minnesota.

Steve King, of Iowa.
Elton Gallegly, of California.
Bob Goodlatte, of Virginia.
Daniel E. Lungren, of California.
J. Randy Forbes, of Virginia.
Louie Gohmert, of Texas.

STAFF

Committee on the Judiciary (2138 RHOB), 225–3951.
Majority Chief Counsel / Staff Director.—Perry H. Apelbaum.
Assistant to the Deputy Staff Director.—Andrea Culebras.
General Counsel / Deputy Staff Director.—Ted Kalo.
Legislative Counsel / Parliamentarian.—George Slover.
Chief Oversight Investigative Counsel.—Elliot Mincberg.
Chief Administrative Officer.—Anita L. Johnson.
Antitrust Counsel.—Stacey Dansky.
Oversight Counsels: Lillian German, Robert Reed, LaShawn Warren.
Counsels: Sam Broderick-Sokol, Michelle Persaud.
Press Secretary / Spokesperson.—Melanie Roussell.
Communications Director.—Jonathan Godfrey.
Information Systems Manager.—Kerli Philippe.
Information Systems Specialist: Seth Ciango, Dwight Sullivan.
Chief Clerk / Office Manager.—Teresa Vest.
Calendar Clerk.—Jennifer Noll.
Publications Clerk.—Timothy Pearson.
Staff Assistants: Brandon Johns, Matthew Morgan, Renata Strause.
Minority Chief Counsel.—Joseph Gibson (2142 RHOB), 6–0002.
Staff Assistant.—Eunice Goldring.

Communications Director.—Elizabeth Frigola.
Deputy Chief Counsel/Staff Director.—Sean McLaughlin (B–351 RHOB), 5–6906.
Chief Oversight Counsel.—Crystal Roberts Jezierski.
Senior Legislative Assistant/Deputy Parliamentarian.—Christopher Cylke.
Legislative Counsel/Parliamentarian.—Allison Beach.
Legislative Assistant/Legislative Clerk.—Bryan Blom.
Antitrust Counsel.—Stewart Jeffries (B–336 RHOB), 5–2022.
Administrative Assistant.—Jennifer Burba.
Finance Clerk/Office Manager.—Diane Hill.
Staff Assistants: Benton Keatley, Kelsey Whitlock.

Subcommittee on Commercial and Administrative Law (H2–362 FHOB), 6–7680.
Majority Chief Counsel.—Michone Johnson.
Counsels: Susan Jensen, Norberto Salinas, Eric Tamarkin.
Professional Staff.—Elias Wolfberg.
Minority Chief Counsel.—Daniel Flores (B–351 RHOB), 5–6906.

Subcommittee on the Constitution, Civil Rights, and Civil Liberties (B–353 RHOB), 5–2825.
Majority Chief of Staff.—David Lachmann.
Senior Counsel.—Burt Wides.
Counsels: Kanya Bennett, Lou deBaca, Keenan Keller.
Professional Staff.—Susana Gutierrez.
Minority Chief Counsel.—Paul Taylor (H2–347 FHOB), 5–7157.

Subcommittee on Courts, the Internet, and Intellectual Property (B–352 RHOB), 5–5741.
Majority Chief Counsel.—Shanna Winters.
Counsels: Eric Garduno, Julia Massimino.
Professional Staff.—Rosalind Jackson.
Minority Chief Counsel.—Blaine Merritt (B–336 RHOB), 5–2022.
Counsel.—David Whitney.

Subcommittee on Crime, Terrorism, and Homeland Security (B–370 RHOB), 5–5727.
Majority Chief Counsel.—Bobby Vassar.
Counsels: Gregory Barnes, Ameer Gopalani, Rachel King.
Professional Staff.—Veronica Eligan.
Minority Chief Counsel.—Michael Volkov (B–351 RHOB), 5–6906.
Counsel.—Caroline Lynch.

Subcommittee on Immigration, Citizenship, Refugees, Border Security, and International Law (517 CHOB), 5–3926.
Majority Chief Counsel.—Ur Jaddou (105 CHOB).
Counsels: Blake Chisam, Traci Hong, David Shahoulian.
Printing Clerk.—Douglas Alexander.
Professional Staff.—Benjamin Staub.
Minority Chief Counsel.—George Fishman (B–351 RHOB), 5–6906.
Counsel.—Andrea Loving.

Natural Resources

1324 Longworth House Office Building, phone 225–6065

http://www.house.gov/resources

meets each Wednesday

Nick J. Rahall II, of West Virginia, *Chair*

Dale E. Kildee, of Michigan.
Eni F.H. Faleomavaega, of American Samoa.
Neil Abercrombie, of Hawaii.
Solomon P. Ortiz, of Texas.
Frank Pallone, Jr., of New Jersey.
Donna M. Christensen, of the Virgin Islands.
Grace F. Napolitano, of California.
Rush D. Holt, of New Jersey.
Raúl M. Grijalva, of Arizona.
Madeleine Z. Bordallo, of Guam.
Jim Costa, of California.
Dan Boren, of Oklahoma.
John P. Sarbanes, of Maryland.
George Miller, of California.
Edward J. Markey, of Massachusetts.
Peter A. DeFazio, of Oregon.
Maurice D. Hinchey, of New York.
Patrick J. Kennedy, of Rhode Island.
Ron Kind, of Wisconsin.
Lois Capps, of California.
Jay Inslee, of Washington.
Mark Udall, of Colorado.
Joe Baca, of California.
Hilda L. Solis, of California.
Stephanie Herseth Sandlin, of South Dakota.
Heath Shuler, of North Carolina.

Don Young, of Alaska.
Jim Saxton, of New Jersey.
Elton Gallegly, of California.
John J. Duncan, Jr., of Tennessee.
Wayne T. Gilchrest, of Maryland.
Ken Calvert, of California.
Chris Cannon, of Utah.
Thomas G. Tancredo, of Colorado.
Jeff Flake, of Arizona.
Rick Renzi, of Arizona.
Stevan Pearce, of New Mexico.
Henry E. Brown, Jr., of South Carolina.
Luis G. Fortuño, of Puerto Rico.
Cathy McMorris Rodgers, of Washington.
Bobby Jindal, of Louisiana.
Louie Gohmert, of Texas.
Tom Cole, of Oklahoma.
Rob Bishop, of Utah.
Bill Shuster, of Pennsylvania.
Dean Heller, of Nevada.
Bill Sali, of Idaho.
Doug Lamborn, of Colorado.

SUBCOMMITTEES

[The chairman and ranking minority member are ex officio (non-voting) members of all subcommittees on which they do not serve.]

Energy and Mineral Resources

Jim Costa, of California, *Chair*

Eni F.H. Faleomavaega, of American Samoa.
Solomon P. Ortiz, of Texas.
Rush D. Holt, of New Jersey.
Dan Boren, of Oklahoma.
Maurice D. Hinchey, of New York.
Patrick J. Kennedy, of Rhode Island.
Hilda L. Solis, of California.

Stevan Pearce, of New Mexico.
Bobby Jindal, of Louisiana.
Louie Gohmert, of Texas.
Bill Shuster, of Pennsylvania.
Dean Heller, of Nevada.
Bill Sali, of Idaho.

Fisheries, Wildlife, and Oceans

Madeleine Z. Bordallo, of Guam, *Chair*

Dale E. Kildee, of Michigan.
Eni F.H. Faleomavaega, of American Samoa.
Neil Abercrombie, of Hawaii.
Solomon P. Ortiz, of Texas.
Frank Pallone, Jr., of New Jersey.
Patrick J. Kennedy, of Rhode Island.
Ron Kind, of Wisconsin.
Lois Capps, of California.

Henry E. Brown, Jr., of South Carolina.
Jim Saxton, of New Jersey.
Wayne T. Gilchrest, of Maryland.
Cathy McMorris Rodgers, of Washington.
Bobby Jindal, of Louisiana.
Tom Cole, of Oklahoma.
Bill Sali, of Idaho.

Insular Affairs

Donna M. Christensen, of the Virgin Islands, *Chair*

Eni F.H. Faleomavaega, of American Samoa.
Raúl M. Grijalva, of Arizona.
Madeleine Z. Bordallo, of Guam.
Luis G. Fortuño, of Puerto Rico.
Elton Gallegly, of California.
Jeff Flake, of Arizona.

National Parks, Forests, and Public Lands

Raúl M. Grijalva, of Arizona, *Chair*

Dale E. Kildee, of Michigan.
Neil Abercrombie, of Hawaii.
Donna M. Christensen, of the Virgin Islands.
Rush D. Holt, of New Jersey.
Dan Boren, of Oklahoma.
John P. Sarbanes, of Maryland.
Peter A. DeFazio, of Oregon.
Maurice D. Hinchey, of New York.
Ron Kind, of Wisconsin.
Lois Capps, of California.
Jay Inslee, of Washington.
Mark Udall, of Colorado.
Stephanie Herseth Sandlin, of South Dakota.
Heath Shuler, of North Carolina.
Rob Bishop, of Utah.
John J. Duncan, Jr., of Tennessee.
Chris Cannon, of Utah.
Thomas G. Tancredo, of Colorado.
Jeff Flake, of Arizona.
Rick Renzi, of Arizona.
Stevan Pearce, of New Mexico.
Henry E. Brown, Jr., of South Carolina.
Louie Gohmert, of Texas.
Tom Cole, of Oklahoma.
Dean Heller, of Nevada.
Bill Sali, of Idaho.
Doug Lamborn, of Colorado.

Water and Power

Grace F. Napolitano, of California, *Chair*

Jim Costa, of California.
George Miller, of California.
Mark Udall, of Colorado.
Joe Baca, of California.
Hilda L. Solis, of California.
Cathy McMorris Rodgers, of Washington.
Ken Calvert, of California.
Dean Heller, of Nevada.
Doug Lamborn, of Colorado.

STAFF

Committee on Natural Resources (1324 LHOB), 225–6065.
Majority Chief of Staff.—Jim Zoia
Executive Assistant.—Lisa James.
Chief Counsel.—Jeff Petrich.
Legislative Assistant to the Chief Counsel.—Amy Haskell.
Chief Financial Officer.—Linda Booth.
Communications Director.—Allyson Groff.
Deputy Press Secretary.—Jessica Gillman.
Press Assistant.—Heather Warren.
Chief Administrator.—Linda Livingston.
Administrative Assistant.—Megan Maassen.
Chief Clerk.—Nancy Locke.
Calendar Clerk.—Joycelyn Coleman.
Information Technology: Ed Van Scoyoc, Matt Vaccaro.
Editor/Printer.—Kathy Miller.
Senior Policy Advisor.—Ann Adler.
Policy Advisors: Laurel Angell, Amelia Jenkins.
Minority Chief of Staff.—Lloyd Jones (1329 LHOB), 5–2761.
Chief Counsel.—Lisa Pittman.
General Counsel to the Ranking Member.—Jack Coleman (H2–186), 6–2311.
Senior Advisor to the Ranking Member.—Dan Kish.
Administrator.—Debbie Callis.
Communications Director.—Steve Hansen.
Legislative Assistant.—Sophia Varnasidis.
Office of Indian Affairs (140 CHOB), 6–9725.
Majority Staff Director.—Marie Howard.

Counsel.—Janet Erickson.
Legislative Staff.—Tracey Parker.
Clerk.—Cynthia Freeman.
Minority Staff Director.—Chris Fluhr.
Counsel.—Rich Stanton.
Legislative Staff.—Cynthia Ahwinona.
Subcommittee on Energy and Mineral Resources (1626 LHOB), 225–9297.
Majority Staff Director.—Deborah Lanzone.
Legislative Staff.—Wendy Van Asselt.
Clerk.—Holly Wagenet.
Minority Staff Director.—Maryam Sabbaghian (H2–186), 6–2311.
Legislative Staff.—Kathy Benedetto.
Subcommittee on Fisheries, Wildlife, and Oceans (187 FHOB), 6–0200.
Majority Staff Director.—Lori Sonken.
Legislative Staff: Jean Flemma, Dave Jansen.
Clerk.—Charlotte Stevenson.
Minority Staff Director.—Harry Burroughs (H2–269), 6–2311.
Legislative Staff: Bonnie Bruce, Dave Whaley.
Subcommittee on Insular Affairs (1337 LHOB), 5–0691.
Majority Staff Director.—Tony Babauta.
Counsel.—Brian Modeste.
Clerk.—Allison Cowan.
Minority Staff Director.—Chris Fluhr.
Counsel.—Rich Stanton.
Legislative Staff.—Cynthia Ahwinona.
Subcommittee on National Parks, Forests, and Public Lands (1333 LHOB), 226–7736.
Majority Staff Director.—Rick Healy.
Counsel.—David Watkins.
Legislative Staff: Meghan Conklin, Leslie Duncan.
Minority Staff Director.—Kurt Christensen.
Legislative Staff: Casey Hammond, Jason Knox.
Subcommittee on Water and Power (1522 LHOB), 225–8331.
Majority Staff Director.—Steve Lanich.
Legislative Staff: Camille Calimlim, David Zacher.
Clerk.—Emily Knight.
Minority Staff Director.—Kiel Weaver.

Oversight and Government Reform

2157 Rayburn House Office Building, phone 225–5051, fax 225–3974, TTY 225–6852

http://reform.house.gov

Henry A. Waxman, of California, *Chair*

Tom Lantos, of California.
Edolphus Towns, of New York.
Paul E. Kanjorski, of Pennsylvania.
Carolyn B. Maloney, of New York.
Elijah E. Cummings, of Maryland.
Dennis J. Kucinich, of Ohio.
Danny K. Davis, of Illinois.
John F. Tierney, of Massachusetts.
Wm. Lacy Clay, of Missouri.
Diane E. Watson, of California.
Stephen F. Lynch, of Massachusetts.
Brian Higgins, of New York.
John A. Yarmuth, of Kentucky.
Bruce L. Braley, of Iowa.
Eleanor Holmes Norton, of the District of Columbia.
Betty McCollum, of Minnesota.
Jim Cooper, of Tennessee.
Chris Van Hollen, of Maryland.
Paul W. Hodes, of New Hampshire.
Christopher S. Murphy, of Connecticut.
John P. Sarbanes, of Maryland.
Peter Welch, of Vermont.

Tom Davis, of Virginia.
Dan Burton, of Indiana.
Christopher Shays, of Connecticut.
John M. McHugh, of New York.
John L. Mica, of Florida.
Mark E. Souder, of Indiana.
Todd Russell Platts, of Pennsylvania.
Chris Cannon, of Utah.
John J. Duncan, Jr., of Tennessee.
Michael R. Turner, of Ohio.
Darrell E. Issa, of California.
Kenny Marchant, of Texas.
Lynn A. Westmoreland, of Georgia.
Patrick T. McHenry, of North Carolina.
Virginia Foxx, of North Carolina.
Brian P. Bilbray, of California.
Bill Sali, of Idaho.
Jim Jordan, of Ohio.

SUBCOMMITTEES

[The chairman and ranking minority member are ex officio (voting) members of all subcommittees]

Domestic Policy

Dennis J. Kucinich, of Ohio, *Chair*

Tom Lantos, of California.
Elijah E. Cummings, of Maryland.
Diane E. Watson, of California.
Christopher S. Murphy, of Connecticut.
Danny K. Davis, of Illinois.
John F. Tierney, of Massachusetts.
Brian Higgins, of New York.
Bruce L. Braley, of Iowa.

Darrell E. Issa, of California.
Dan Burton, of Indiana.
Christopher Shays, of Connecticut.
John L. Mica, of Florida.
Mark E. Souder, of Indiana.
Chris Cannon, of Utah.
Brian P. Bilbray, of California.

Federal Workforce, Postal Service, and the District of Columbia

Danny K. Davis, of Illinois, *Chair*

Eleanor Holmes Norton, of the District of Columbia.
John P. Sarbanes, of Maryland.
Elijah E. Cummings, of Maryland.
Dennis J. Kucinich, of Ohio.
Wm. Lacy Clay, of Missouri.
Stephen F. Lynch, of Massachusetts.

Kenny Marchant, of Texas.
John M. McHugh, of New York.
John L. Mica, of Florida.
Darrell E. Issa, of California.
Jim Jordan, of Ohio.

Government Management, Organization, and Procurement

Edolphus Towns, of New York, *Chair*

Paul E. Kanjorski, of Pennsylvania.
Christopher S. Murphy, of Connecticut.
Peter Welch, of Vermont.
Carolyn B. Maloney, of New York.

Brian P. Bilbray, of California.
Todd Russell Platts, of Pennsylvania.
John J. Duncan, Jr., of Tennessee.

Information Policy, Census, and National Archives

Wm. Lacy Clay, of Missouri, *Chair*

Paul E. Kanjorski, of Pennsylvania.
Carolyn B. Maloney, of New York.
John A. Yarmuth, of Kentucky.
Paul W. Hodes, of New Hampshire.

Michael R. Turner, of Ohio.
Chris Cannon, of Utah.
Bill Sali, of Idaho.

National Security and Foreign Affairs

John F. Tierney, of Massachusetts, *Chair*

Carolyn B. Maloney, of New York.
Stephen F. Lynch, of Massachusetts.
Brian Higgins, of New York.
John A. Yarmuth, of Kentucky.
Bruce L. Braley, of Iowa.
Betty McCollum, of Minnesota.
Jim Cooper, of Tennessee.
Chris Van Hollen, of Maryland.
Paul W. Hodes, of New Hampshire.
Peter Welch, of Vermont.
Tom Lantos, of California.

Christopher Shays, of Connecticut.
Dan Burton, of Indiana.
John M. McHugh, of New York.
Todd Russell Platts, of Pennsylvania.
John J. Duncan, Jr., of Tennessee.
Michael R. Turner, of Ohio.
Kenny Marchant, of Texas.
Lynn A. Westmoreland, of Georgia.
Patrick T. McHenry, of North Carolina.
Virginia Foxx, of North Carolina.

STAFF

Oversight and Government Reform (2157 RHOB), 225–5051.

Majority Staff Director.—Phil Barnett.
Chief of Staff.—Phil Schiliro.
Chief Counsel.—Kristin Amerling.
Chief Legislative Counsel.—Michelle Ash.
Deputy Chief Counsel.—Roger Sherman.
Communications Director/Senior Policy Advisor.—Karen Lighfoot.
Press Assistant.—Caren Auchman.
Online Communications Director.—John Palmer.
Chief Investigative Counsel.—David Rapallo.
Senior Investigator/Policy Advisor.—Brian Cohen.
Deputy Chief Investigative Counsels: Theordore Chuang, John Williams.
Senior Investigative Counsels: Michael Gordon, David Leviss.
Health Policy Director.—Karen Nelson.
Chief Health Counsel.—Andy Schneider.
Senior Health Counsel.—Sarah Despres.
Health Counsel.—Ann Witt.
Chief Environment Counsel.—Greg Dotson.
Senior Environment Counsel.—Alexandra Teitz.
Chief Clerk.—Earley Green.
Deputy Clerk.—Teresa Coufal.
Financial Administrator.—Robin Butler.
Office Manager/Executive Assistant to Staff Director.—Sheila Klein.
Counsels: Robin Appleberry, Jeff Baran, Krista Boyd, Margaret Daum, Steve Glickman, Erik Jones, Suzanne Renaud, Susanne Sachsman, Naomi Seiler.
Professional Staff: Stephen Cha, Christopher Davis, Daniel Davis, Anna Laitin, Mark Stephenson, Denise Wilson.
Special Assistants: Jesseca Boyer, Matt Siegler, Gilad Wilkenfeld.

Staff Assistants: Lauren Belive, Sam Buffone, Robb Cobbs, Miriam Edelman, Kerry Gutknecht, LaKeshia Myers, William Ragland, Nidia Salazar, Bret Schothorst.
Chief Information Officer.—J.R. Deng.
Information Officer.—Leneal Scott.
Minority Staff Director.—David Marin (2157 RHOB), 225–5074.
Deputy Staff Director.—Larry Halloran.
Communications Director.—Brian McNicoll.
General Counsel.—Keith Ausbrook.
Legislative Director/Senior Policy Counsel.—Ellen Brown.
Deputy Legislative Director.—Mason Alinger.
Chief Counsel/Oversight and Investigations.—Jennifer Safavian.
Parliamentarian/Member SVC Coordinator.—Patrick Lyden.
Senior Procurement Counsel.—John Brosnan.
Counsels: Brooke Bennett, Jack Callender, Steve Castor, Jim Moore, Chas Phillips, Ann Marie Turner.
Senior Professional Staff Members: Howie Denis, Victoria Proctor, Susie Schulte, Grace Washbourne.
Professional Staff: Allyson Blandford, Christopher Bright, Alex Cooper, Kristinia Husar, Teddy Kidd, Jay O'Callaghan, Ed Puccerella.
Senior Investigators/Policy Advisors: Larry Brady, John Cuaderes, Nick Palarino.
Clerk.—Benjamin Chance.
Office Manager/Staff Assistant.—Kay Lauren Miller.
Staff Assistant/Online Communication Coordinator.—Ali Ahmad.
Staff Assistant/Correspondence Coordinator.—Meredith Liberty.

Subcommittee on Federal Workforce, Postal Service, and the District of Columbia (B–349A RHOB), 5–5147.
Staff Director.—Tania Shand.
Counsel.—Lori Hayman.
Professional Staff.—Caleb Gilchrest.
Clerk.—Cecelia Morton.
Editor/Staff Assistant.—LaKeshia Myers.

Subcommittee on Government Management, Organization, and Procurement (B–349A RHOB), 5–3741.
Staff Director/Chief Counsel.—Mike McCarthy.
Counsel.—Velvet Johnson.
Professional Staff.—Rick Blake.
Clerk.—Cecelia Morton.

Subcommittee on Domestic Policy (B–349B RHOB), 5–6427.
Staff Director.—Jaron Bourke.
Counsels: Noura Erakat, Charles Honig.
Clerk.—Jean Gosa.

Subcommittee on Information Policy, Census, and National Archives (B–349C RHOB), 5–6751.
Staff Director/Counsel.—Tony Haywood.
Professional Staff: Adam Bordes, Alissa Bonner.
Clerk.—Jean Gosa.
Staff Assistant.—Nidia Salazar.

Subcommittee on National Security and Foreign Affairs (B–371C RHOB), 5–2548.
Staff Director.—Dave Turk.
Professional Staff: Andrew Su, Andrew Wright.
Clerk.—Davis Hake.

Rules

H–312 The Capitol, phone 225–9191

http://www.house.gov/rules

meets every Tuesday

Louise McIntosh Slaughter, of New York, *Chair*

James P. McGovern, of Massachusetts.
Alcee L. Hastings, of Florida.
Doris O. Matsui, of California.
Dennis A. Cardoza, of California.
Peter Welch, of Vermont.
Kathy Castor, of Florida.
Michael A. Arcuri, of New York.
Betty Sutton, of Ohio.

David Dreier, of California.
Lincoln Diaz-Balart, of Florida.
Doc Hastings, of Washington.
Pete Sessions, of Texas.

SUBCOMMITTEES

Legislative and Budget Process

Alcee L. Hastings, of Florida, *Chair*

Dennis A. Cardoza, of California.
Peter Welch, of Vermont.
Betty Sutton, of Ohio.

Lincoln Diaz-Balart, of Florida.
David Dreier, of California.

Rules and Organization of the House

James P. McGovern, of Massachusetts, *Chair*

Doris O. Matsui, of California.
Kathy Castor, of Florida.
Michael A. Arcuri, of New York.

Doc Hastings, of Washington.
Pete Sessions, of Texas.

STAFF

Committee on Rules (H–312 The Capitol), 225–9191.
Majority Staff Director.—Dan Turton.
Deputy Staff Director.—Muftiah McCartin.
Counsels: Sampak Garg, Sophie Hayford.
Professional Staff (HC–4 The Capitol): Rebecca Motley, Liz Pardue.
Communications Director.—John Santore (2460 RHOB).
Office Manager/Hearing Coordinator.—Tim Sheehan.
Legislative Clerk.—Don Sisson.
Technology Director.—Sonny Sinha (HC–4 The Capitol).
Staff Assistant.—Adam Berg.
Associate Staff: David Goldenberg (Alcee L. Hastings, 5–1313), Adri Jayaratne (Sutton, 5–3401), Rob Leonard (Matsui, 5–7163), Jason Lumia (Cardoza, 5–6131), Sam Marchio (Arcuri, 5–3665), Clay Phillips (Cator, 5–3376), Phil Putter (Welch, 5–4115).
Minority Staff Director.—Hugh Halpern.
Press Secretary.—Jo Maney.
Professional Staff: Shane Chambers, Adam Jarvis, Celeste West, Kathy White.
Staff Assistant.—Alison Orologio.
Associate Staff: Keith Stern (430 CHOB), Fred Turner (2235 RHOB).
Subcommittee on Legislative and Budget Process (1627 LHOB), 5–4211.
Majority Staff Director.—David Goldenberg (Alcee L. Hastings).
Minority Staff Director.—Cesar Gonzalez (Diaz-Balart).
Subcommittee on Rules and Organization of the House (1627 LHOB), 5–5816.
Majority Staff Director.—Keith Stern (McGovern).
Minority Staff Director.—E.J. Cassidy (Doc Hastings).

Science and Technology

2320 Rayburn House Office Building, phone 225–6375, fax 225–3895

http://www.house.gov/science

meets second and fourth Wednesdays of each month

Bart Gordon, of Tennessee, *Chair*

Jerry F. Costello, of Illinois.
Eddie Bernice Johnson, of Texas.
Lynn C. Woolsey, of California.
Mark Udall, of Colorado.
David Wu, of Oregon.
Brian Baird, of Washington.
Brad Miller, of North Carolina.
Daniel Lipinski, of Illinois.
Nick Lampson, of Texas.
Gabrielle Giffords, of Arizona.
Jerry McNerney, of California.
Paul E. Kanjorski, of Pennsylvania.
Darlene Hooley, of Oregon.
Steven R. Rothman, of New Jersey.
Michael M. Honda, of California.
Jim Matheson, of Utah.
Mike Ross, of Arkansas.
Ben Chandler, of Kentucky.
Russ Carnahan, of Missouri.
Charlie Melancon, of Louisiana.
Baron P. Hill, of Indiana.
Harry E. Mitchell, of Arizona.
Charles A. Wilson, of Ohio.

Ralph M. Hall, of Texas.
F. James Sensenbrenner, Jr., of Wisconsin.
Lamar Smith, of Texas.
Dana Rohrabacher, of California.
Ken Calvert, of California.
Roscoe G. Bartlett, of Maryland.
Vernon J. Ehlers, of Michigan.
Frank D. Lucas, of Oklahoma.
Judy Biggert, of Illinois.
W. Todd Akin, of Missouri.
Jo Bonner, of Alabama.
Tom Feeney, of Florida.
Randy Neugebauer, of Texas.
Bob Inglis, of South Carolina.
David G. Reichert, of Washington.
Michael T. McCaul, of Texas.
Mario Diaz-Balart, of Florida.
Phil Gingrey, of Georgia.
Brian P. Bilbray, of California.
Adrian Smith, of Nebraska.

SUBCOMMITTEES

[The chairman and ranking minority member are ex officio (voting) members of all subcommittees on which they do not serve.]

Energy and Environment

Nick Lampson, of Texas, *Chair*

Jerry F. Costello, of Illinois.
Lynn C. Woolsey, of California.
Daniel Lipinski, of Illinois.
Gabrielle Giffords, of Arizona.
Jerry McNerney, of California.
Mark Udall, of Colorado.
Brian Baird, of Washington.
Paul E. Kanjorski, of Pennsylvania.

Bob Inglis, of South Carolina.
Roscoe G. Bartlett, of Maryland.
Judy Biggert, of Illinois.
W. Todd Akin, of Missouri.
Randy Neugebauer, of Texas.
Michael T. McCaul, of Texas.
Mario Diaz-Balart, of Florida.

Investigations and Oversight

Brad Miller, of North Carolina, *Chair*

Jerry F. Costello, of Illinois.
Eddie Bernice Johnson, of Texas.
Darlene Hooley, of Oregon.
Steven R. Rothman, of New Jersey.
Brian Baird, of Washington.

F. James Sensenbrenner, Jr., of Wisconsin.
Dana Rohrabacher, of California.
Tom Feeney, of Florida.
Michael T. McCaul, of Texas.

Research and Science Education

Brian Baird, of Washington, *Chair*

Eddie Bernice Johnson, of Texas.
Daniel Lipinski, of Illinois.
Charlie Melancon, of Louisiana.
Jerry McNerney, of California.
Darlene Hooley, of Oregon.
Russ Carnahan, of Missouri.
Baron P. Hill, of Indiana.

Vernon J. Ehlers, of Michigan.
Roscoe G. Bartlett, of Maryland.
Frank D. Lucas, of Oklahoma.
Randy Neugebauer, of Texas.
Brian P. Bilbray, of California.

Space and Aeronautics

Mark Udall, of Colorado, *Chair*

David Wu, of Oregon.
Nick Lampson, of Texas.
Steven R. Rothman, of New Jersey.
Mike Ross, of Arkansas.
Ben Chandler, of Kentucky.
Charlie Melancon, of Louisiana.

Ken Calvert, of California.
Dana Rohrabacher, of California.
Frank D. Lucas, of Oklahoma.
Jo Bonner, of Alabama.
Tom Feeney, of Florida.

Technology and Innovation

David Wu, of Oregon, *Chair*

Jim Matheson, of Utah.
Harry E. Mitchell, of Arizona.
Charles A. Wilson, of Ohio.
Ben Chandler, of Kentucky.
Mike Ross, of Arkansas.
Michael M. Honda, of California.

Phil Gingrey, of Georgia.
Vernon J. Ehlers, of Michigan.
Judy Biggert, of Illinois.
Adrian Smith, of Nebraska.

STAFF

Committee on Science (2320 RHOB), 225–6375, fax 225–3895.
Majority Chief of Staff.—Chuck Atkins, 6–5275.
Director of Policy and Outreach.—Louis Finkel, 5–7950.
Legislative Director.—Alisa Ferguson, 5–0278.
Chief Counsel.—Jim Turner, 5–0125.
Counsel.—John Piazza, 6–8668.
Communications Director.—Alisha Prather, 6–8670.
Deputy Communications Director.—Brandis Griffith, 6–1430.
Financial Administrator.—Dave Laughter, 5–5977.
Legislative Director.—Alisa Ferguson, 5–0278.
Legislative Clerk.—Deborah Samantar, 5–8121.
Director of Information Technology.—Larry Whittaker, 5–4414.
Administrative Assistant.—Leigh Ann Brown, 6–8669.
Printer.—Jude Ruckel, 5–6371.
Staff Assistant.—Bess Caughran, 5–5848.
Shared Research Assistants: Stacey Steep, 5–7567; Meghan Housewright, 5–8115.
Research Assistant.—Devin Bryant, 5–9011.
Minority Staff Director.—Janet Poppleton 5–6675.
Deputy Staff Director.—Leslee Gilbert, 5–9816.
Counsel.—Margaret Caravelli, 6–0584.
Press Secretary.—Zachary Kurz, 6–4955.
Staff Assistant.—Clark Trimmer, 5–7567.
Subcommittee on Energy and Environment (2319 RHOB) 5–8844, fax 5–4438.
Majority Staff Director.—Jean Fruci, 6–0697.
Staff Assistant.—Stacey Steep, 5–7567.
Professional Staff: Chris King, 5–7255; Elaine Paulionis, 6–4851; Shimere Williams, 5–2070; Michelle Dallafior, 6–2179; Wyatt King, 6–3614.
Minority Professional Staff: Amy Carroll, 6–5342; Elizabeth Stack, 6–2943.
Subcommittee on Technology and Innovation (2320 RHOB), 5–9662, fax 5–6983.

Majority Staff Director.—Mike Quear, 5–6917.
Professional Staff: Rachel Jagoda-Brunette, 5–8123; Colin McCormick, 5–0585.
Staff Assistant.—Meghan Housewright, 5–8115.
Minority Professional Staff: Piper Largent, 5–8896; Shep Ryen, 5–2656.
Subcommittee on Research (2324 RHOB), 5–9662, fax 5–6983.
Majority Staff Director.—Jim Wilson, 5–2634.
Professional Staff.—Dahlia Sokolov, 5–2157.
Staff Assistant.—Meghan Housewright, 5–9011.
Minority Professional Staff.—Mele Williams, 6–9557.
Subcommittee on Space and Aeronautics (B–374 RHOB), 5–7858, fax 5–6415.
Majority Staff Director.—Dick Obermann, 5–7223.
Professional Staff.—Pam Whitney, 5–0581.
Staff Assistant.—Devin Bryant, 5–9011.
Minority Professional Staff.—Ken Monroe, 6–3660; Ed Feddeman, 5–0587.
Subcommittee on Investigations and Oversight (B–374 RHOB), 5–8772, fax 5–7815.
Majority Staff Director.—Dan Pearson, 5–4494.
Professional Staff.—James Paul, 6–3639; Doug Pasternak, 6–8892; Edith Holleman, 5–8459; Ken Jacobson, 6–3096.
Staff Assistant.—Stacey Steep, 5–7567.

Small Business

2361 Rayburn House Office Building, phone 225–4038, fax 225–7209

http://www.house.gov/smbiz

meets second Thursday of each month

Nydia M. Velázquez, of New York, *Chair*

Heath Shuler, of North Carolina.
Charles A. Gonzalez, of Texas.
Rick Larsen, of Washington.
Daniel Lipinski, of Illinois.
Raúl M. Grijalva, of Arizona.
Michael H. Michaud, of Maine.
Melissa L. Bean, of Illinois.
Henry Cuellar, of Texas.
Daniel Lipinski, of Illinois.
Gwen Moore, of Wisconsin.
Jason Altmire, of Pennsylvania.
Bruce L. Braley, of Iowa.
Yvette D. Clarke, of New York.
Brad Ellsworth, of Indiana.
Henry C. ''Hank'' Johnson, Jr., of Georgia.
Joe Sestak, of Pennsylvania.

Steve Chabot, of Ohio.
Roscoe G. Bartlett, of Maryland.
Sam Graves, of Missouri.
W. Todd Akin, of Missouri.
Bill Shuster, of Pennsylvania.
Marilyn N. Musgrave, of Colorado.
Steve King, of Iowa.
Jeff Fortenberry, of Nebraska.
Lynn A. Westmoreland, of Georgia.
Louie Gohmert, of Texas.
Dean Heller, of Nevada.
David Davis, of Tennessee.
Mary Fallin, of Oklahoma.
Vern Buchanan, of Florida.
Jim Jordan, of Ohio.

SUBCOMMITTEES

[The chairman and ranking minority member are ex officio (non-voting) members of all subcommittees on which they do not serve.]

Contracting and Technology

Bruce L. Braley, of Iowa, *Chair*

Henry Cuellar, of Texas.
Gwen Moore, of Wisconsin.
Yvette D. Clarke, of New York.
Joe Sestak, of Pennsylvania.

Roscoe G. Bartlett, of Maryland.
Sam Graves, of Missouri.
W. Todd Akin, of Missouri.
Mary Fallin, of Oklahoma.

Finance and Tax

Melissa L. Bean, of Illinois.

Raúl M. Grijalva, of Arizona.
Michael H. Michaud, of Maine.
Henry C. ''Hank'' Johnson, Jr., of Georgia.
Joe Sestak, of Pennsylvania.
Brad Ellsworth, of Indiana.

Dean Heller, of Nevada.
Vern Buchanan, of Florida.
Jim Jordan, of Ohio.
Bill Shuster, of Pennsylvania.
Steve King, of Iowa.

Investigations and Oversight

Jason Altmire, of Pennsylvania, *Chair*

Charles A. Gonzalez, of Texas.
Raúl M. Grijalva, of Arizona.

Louie Gohmert, of Texas.
Lynn A. Westmoreland, of Georgia.

Regulations, Healthcare and Trade

Charles A. Gonzalez, of Texas, *Chair*

Daniel Lipinski, of Illinois.
Rick Larsen, of Washington.
Jason Altmire, of Pennsylvania.
Melissa L. Bean, of Illinois, *Chair*
Gwen Moore, of Wisconsin.
Joe Sestak, of Pennsylvania.

Lynn A. Westmoreland, of Georgia.
Steve King, of Iowa.
Mary Fallin, of Oklahoma.
Marilyn N. Musgrave, of Colorado.
Vern Buchanan, of Florida.
Jim Jordan, of Ohio.

Rural and Urban Entrepreneurship

Heath Shuler, of North Carolina, *Chair*

Rick Larsen, of Washington.
Brad Ellsworth, of Indiana.
Michael H. Michaud, of Maine.
Gwen Moore, of Wisconsin.
Yvette D. Clarke, of New York.
Henry C. ''Hank'' Johnson, Jr., of Georgia.

Jeff Fortenberry, of Nebraska.
Marilyn N. Musgrave, of Colorado.
Roscoe G. Bartlett, of Maryland.
Dean Heller, of Nevada.
David Davis, of Tennessee.

STAFF

Committee on Small Business (2361 RHOB), 225–7209.
Majority Staff Director.—Michael Day.
Deputy Staff Director.—Adam Minehardt.
Chief Counsel.—Timothy Slattery.
Press Secretary.—Kate Davis.
Deputy Press Secretary.—Austin Bonner.
Senior Procurement Counsel.—LeAnn Delaney.
Banking Counsel.—Andy Jiminez.
General Counsel.—Russell Orban.
Trade Counsel.—Nicole Witenstein.
Office Manager.—Mory Garcia.
Clerk.—Zuraya Tapia.
Health Counsel.—Tom Dawson.
Procurement Staff Member.—Melody Reis.
Technology Counsel.—Bill Maguire.
Regulations Counsel.—Erik Lieberman.
Agriculture Counsel.—Mark Palmer.
Scheduler.—Clarinda Landeros.
Staff Assistant.—Eduardo Lerma.
Minority Staff Director.—Kevin Fitzpatrick (B–363 RHOB) 225–5821.
Deputy Staff Director.—Mike Smullen.
Chief Counsel.—Barry Pineles.
Chief of Staff to the Member.—Gary Lindgren.
Counsel.—Jan Oliver.
Press Secretary.—Katie Fox.
Professional Staff: Lisa Christian, Ralph DeStefano, Joe Hartz.

Standards of Official Conduct

HT–2 The Capitol, phone 225–7103, fax 225–7392

Stephanie Tubbs Jones, of Ohio, *Chair*

Gene Green, of Texas.
Lucille Roybal-Allard, of California.
Michael F. Doyle, of Pennsylvania.
William D. Delahunt, of Massachusetts.

Doc Hastings, of Washington.
Jo Bonner, of Alabama.
J. Gresham Barrett, of South Carolina.
John Kline, of Minnesota.
Michael T. McCaul, of Texas.

(No Subcommittees)

STAFF

Chief Counsel/Staff Director.—William V. O'Reilly.
Counsel to the Chair.—Dawn Kelly Mobley.
Counsel to the Ranking Republican Member.—Todd Ungerecht.
Senior Counsels: Kenneth E. Kellner, John C. Sassaman.
Counsels: Carol E. Dixon, Morgan Kim, Susan Olson, Stan Simpson, Peter Van Hartesveldt.
Staff Assistant.—Hilary B. Smith.
System Administrator.—Pete Johnson.
Administrative Assistant.—Joanne White.

Transportation and Infrastructure

2165 Rayburn House Office Building, phone 225–4472, fax 225–6782

http://www.house.gov/transportation

meets first Wednesday of each month

James L. Oberstar, of Minnesota, *Chair*

Nick J. Rahall II, of West Virginia.
Peter A. DeFazio, of Oregon.
Jerry F. Costello, of Illinois.
Eleanor Holmes Norton, of the District of Columbia.
Jerrold Nadler, of New York.
Corrine Brown, of Florida.
Bob Filner, of California.
Eddie Bernice Johnson, of Texas.
Gene Taylor, of Mississippi.
Elijah E. Cummings, of Maryland.
Ellen O. Tauscher, of California.
Leonard L. Boswell, of Iowa.
Tim Holden, of Pennsylvania.
Brian Baird, of Washington.
Rick Larsen, of Washington.
Michael E. Capuano, of Massachusetts.
Julia Carson, of Indiana.
Timothy H. Bishop, of New York.
Michael H. Michaud, of Maine.
Brian Higgins, of New York.
Russ Carnahan, of Missouri.
John T. Salazar, of Colorado.
Grace F. Napolitano, of California.
Daniel Lipinski, of Illinois.
Doris O. Matsui, of California.
Nick Lampson, of Texas.
Zachary T. Space, of Ohio.
Mazie K. Hirono, of Hawaii.
Bruce L. Braley, of Iowa.
Jason Altmire, of Pennsylvania.
Timothy J. Walz, of Minnesota.
Heath Shuler, of North Carolina.
Michael A. Arcuri, of New York.
Harry E. Mitchell, of Arizona.
Christopher P. Carney, of Pennsylvania.
John J. Hall, of New York.
Steve Kagen, of Wisconsin.
Steve Cohen, of Tennessee.
Jerry McNerney, of California.

John L. Mica, of Florida.
Don Young, of Alaska.
Thomas E. Petri, of Wisconsin.
Howard Coble, of North Carolina.
John J. Duncan, Jr., of Tennessee.
Wayne T. Gilchrest, of Maryland.
Vernon J. Ehlers, of Michigan.
Steven C. LaTourette, of Ohio.
Richard H. Baker, of Louisiana.
Frank A. LoBiondo, of New Jersey.
Jerry Moran, of Kansas.
Gary G. Miller, of California.
Robin Hayes, of North Carolina.
Henry E. Brown, Jr., of South Carolina.
Timothy V. Johnson, of Illinois.
Todd Russell Platts, of Pennsylvania.
Sam Graves, of Missouri.
Bill Shuster, of Pennsylvania.
John Boozman, of Arkansas.
Shelley Moore Capito, of West Virginia.
Jim Gerlach, of Pennsylvania.
Mario Diaz-Balart, of Florida.
Charles W. Dent, of Pennsylvania.
Ted Poe, of Texas.
David G. Reichert, of Washington.
Connie Mack, of Florida.
John R. ''Randy'' Kuhl, Jr., of New York.
Lynn A. Westmoreland, of Georgia.
Charles W. Boustany, Jr., of Louisiana.
Jean Schmidt, of Ohio.
Candice S. Miller, of Michigan.
Thelma D. Drake, of Virginia.
Mary Fallin, of Oklahoma.
Vern Buchanan, of Florida.

SUBCOMMITTEES

[The chairman and ranking minority member are ex officio (voting) members of all subcommittees on which they do not serve.]

Aviation

Jerry F. Costello, of Illinois, *Chair*

Bob Filner, of California.
Leonard L. Boswell, of Iowa.
Rick Larsen, of Washington.
Russ Carnahan, of Missouri.
John T. Salazar, of Colorado.
Daniel Lipinski, of Illinois.
Nick Lampson, of Texas.
Zachary T. Space, of Ohio.
Bruce L. Braley, of Iowa.
Harry E. Mitchell, of Arizona.
John J. Hall, of New York.
Steve Kagen, of Wisconsin.
Steve Cohen, of Tennessee.
Nick J. Rahall II, of West Virginia.
Peter A. DeFazio, of Oregon.
Eleanor Holmes Norton, of the District of Columbia.
Corrine Brown, of Florida.
Eddie Bernice Johnson, of Texas.
Ellen O. Tauscher, of California.
Tim Holden, of Pennsylvania.
Michael E. Capuano, of Massachusetts.
Doris O. Matsui, of California.
Mazie K. Hirono, of Hawaii.

Thomas E. Petri, of Wisconsin.
Howard Coble, of North Carolina.
John J. Duncan, Jr., of Tennessee.
Vernon J. Ehlers, of Michigan.
Steven C. LaTourette, of Ohio.
Frank A. LoBiondo, of New Jersey.
Jerry Moran, of Kansas.
Robin Hayes, of North Carolina.
Sam Graves, of Missouri.
John Boozman, of Arkansas.
Shelley Moore Capito, of West Virginia.
Jim Gerlach, of Pennsylvania.
Mario Diaz-Balart, of Florida.
Charles W. Dent, of Pennsylvania.
Ted Poe, of Texas.
David G. Reichert, of Washington.
Connie Mack, of Florida.
John R. ''Randy'' Kuhl, Jr., of New York.
Lynn A. Westmoreland, of Georgia.
Mary Fallin, of Oklahoma.
Vern Buchanan, of Florida.

Coast Guard and Maritime Transportation

Elijah E. Cummings, of Maryland, *Chair*

Gene Taylor, of Mississippi.
Rick Larsen, of Washington.
Corrine Brown, of Florida.
Brian Higgins, of New York.
Brian Baird, of Washington.
Timothy H. Bishop, of New York.

Steven C. LaTourette, of Ohio.
Don Young, of Alaska.
Howard Coble, of North Carolina.
Wayne T. Gilchrest, of Maryland.
Frank A. LoBiondo, of New Jersey.
Ted Poe, of Texas.

Economic Development, Public Buildings, and Emergency Management

Eleanor Holmes Norton, of the District of Columbia, *Chair*

Michael H. Michaud, of Maine.
Jason Altmire, of Pennsylvania.
Michael A. Arcuri, of New York.
Christopher P. Carney, of Pennsylvania.
Timothy J. Walz, of Minnesota.
Steve Cohen, of Tennessee

Sam Graves, of Missouri.
Bill Shuster, of Pennsylvania.
Shelley Moore Capito, of West Virginia.
Charles W. Dent, of Pennsylvania.
John R. ''Randy'' Kuhl, Jr., of New York.

Highways and Transit

Peter A. DeFazio, of Oregon, *Chair*

Nick J. Rahall II, of West Virginia.
Jerrold Nadler, of New York.
Ellen O. Tauscher, of California.
Tim Holden, of Pennsylvania.
Michael E. Capuano, of Massachusetts.
Julia Carson, of Indiana.
Timothy H. Bishop, of New York.
Michael H. Michaud, of Maine.
Brian Higgins, of New York.
Grace F. Napolitano, of California.
Mazie K. Hirono, of Hawaii.
Jason Altmire, of Pennsylvania.
Timothy J. Walz, of Minnesota.
Heath Shuler, of North Carolina.
Michael A. Arcuri, of New York.
Christopher P. Carney, of Pennsylvania.
Jerry McNerney, of California.
Bob Filner, of California.
Elijah E. Cummings, of Maryland.
Brian Baird, of Washington.
Daniel Lipinski, of Illinois.
Doris O. Matsui, of California.
Steve Cohen, of Tennessee.
Zachary T. Space, of Ohio.
Bruce L. Braley, of Iowa.
Harry E. Mitchell, of Arizona.

John J. Duncan, Jr., of Tennessee.
Don Young, of Alaska.
Thomas E. Petri, of Wisconsin.
Howard Coble, of North Carolina.
Richard H. Baker, of Louisiana.
Gary G. Miller, of California.
Robin Hayes, of North Carolina.
Henry E. Brown, Jr., of South Carolina.
Timothy V. Johnson, of Illinois.
Todd Russell Platts, of Pennsylvania.
John Boozman, of Arkansas.
Shelley Moore Capito, of West Virginia.
Jim Gerlach, of Pennsylvania.
Mario Diaz-Balart, of Florida.
Charles W. Dent, of Pennsylvania.
Ted Poe, of Texas.
David G. Reichert, of Washington.
Charles W. Boustany, Jr., of Louisiana.
Jean Schmidt, of Ohio.
Candice S. Miller, of Michigan.
Thelma D. Drake, of Virginia.
Mary Fallin, of Oklahoma.
Vern Buchanan, of Florida.

Railroads, Pipelines, and Hazardous Materials

Corrine Brown, of Florida, *Chair*

Jerrold Nadler, of New York.
Leonard L. Boswell, of Iowa.
Julia Carson, of Indiana.
Grace F. Napolitano, of California.
Nick Lampson, of Texas.
Zachary T. Space, of Ohio.
Bruce L. Braley, of Iowa.
Timothy J. Walz, of Minnesota.
Nick J. Rahall II, of West Virginia.
Peter A. DeFazio, of Oregon.
Jerry F. Costello, of Illinois.
Eddie Bernice Johnson, of Texas.
Elijah E. Cummings, of Maryland.
Michael H. Michaud, of Maine.
Daniel Lipinski, of Illinois.

Bill Shuster, of Pennsylvania.
Thomas E. Petri, of Wisconsin.
Wayne T. Gilchrest, of Maryland.
Steven C. LaTourette, of Ohio.
Jerry Moran, of Kansas.
Gary G. Miller, of California.
Henry E. Brown, Jr., of South Carolina.
Timothy V. Johnson, of Illinois.
Todd Russell Platts, of Pennsylvania.
Sam Graves, of Missouri.
Jim Gerlach, of Pennsylvania.
Mario Diaz-Balart, of Florida.
Lynn A. Westmoreland, of Georgia.

Water Resources and Environment

Eddie Bernice Johnson, of Texas, *Chair*

Gene Taylor, of Mississippi.
Brian Baird, of Washington.
Doris O. Matsui, of California.
Jerry F. Costello, of Illinois.
Timothy H. Bishop, of New York.
Brian Higgins, of New York.
Russ Carnahan, of Missouri.
John T. Salazar, of Colorado.
Mazie K. Hirono, of Hawaii.
Heath Shuler, of North Carolina.
Harry E. Mitchell, of Arizona.
John J. Hall, of New York.
Steve Kagen, of Wisconsin.
Jerry McNerney, of California.
Eleanor Holmes Norton, of the District of Columbia.
Bob Filner, of California.
Ellen O. Tauscher, of California.
Michael E. Capuano, of Massachusetts.
Grace F. Napolitano, of California.
Michael A. Arcuri, of New York.

Richard H. Baker, of Louisiana.
John J. Duncan, Jr., of Tennessee.
Wayne T. Gilchrest, of Maryland.
Vernon J. Ehlers, of Michigan.
Frank A. LoBiondo, of New Jersey.
Gary G. Miller, of California.
Robin Hayes, of North Carolina.
Henry E. Brown, Jr., of South Carolina.
Todd Russell Platts, of Pennsylvania.
Bill Shuster, of Pennsylvania.
John Boozman, of Arkansas.
Connie Mack, of Florida.
John R. ''Randy'' Kuhl, Jr., of New York.
Charles W. Boustany, Jr., of Louisiana.
Jean Schmidt, of Ohio.
Candice S. Miller, of Michigan.
Thelma D. Drake, of Virginia.

STAFF

Committee on Transportation and Infrastructure (2165 RHOB), 225–9446, fax 225–6782.
Majority Chief of Staff.—David A. Heymsfeld.
Administrator.—Dara Schlieker.
Chief Counsel.—Ward W. McCarragher.
Director of Committee Facilities/Travel.—Jimmy Miller.
Communications Director.—Jim Berard.
Communications Assistant.—Julie Carpenter Lotz.
Information Systems Manager.—Keven Sard.
Assistant Systems Administrator.—Scott Putz.
Senior Professional Staff: Sharon Barkeloo, Helena Zyblikewycz.
Staff Assistants: Keelin Haddix, Erik Hansen, Michael O'Brock, Elisa Yi.
Senior Counsel, Investigations.—Trinita E. Brown (586 FHOB), 6–4697.
Senior Professional Staff, Investigations: Stephanie Manning, H. Clay Foushee, Leila Khan.
Staff Assistant, Investigations.—Laurie Bertenthal.
Press Secretary.—Mary Kerr.
Editor.—Gilda Shirley.
Clerk.—Tracy Mosebey.
Minority Chief of Staff.—Jim Coon (2163 RHOB), 5–9446.
Special Assistant to the Chief of Staff.—Tom Corcoran.
Counsel.—Charles Ziegler.
Policy Director.—Fraser Verrusio.
Deputy Press Secretary.—Justin Harclerode (2167A RHOB), 6–8767.
Legislative Staff Assistant.—Phillip Maxwell (592 FHOB), 5–5504.
Professional Staff.—Justin Sprinzen.
Subcommittee on Aviation (2251 RHOB), 6–3220, fax 5–4629.
Majority Staff Director.—Stacie Soumbeniotis.
Senior Counsel.—Giles Giovinazzi.
Professional Staff: Jana Denning, Christa Formarotto.
Senior Administrative Staff Assistant.—Pamela Keller.
Minority Staff Director.—Holly E. Woodruff Lyons, 6–3220, fax 5–4629.
Legislative Staff Assistant.—Russell Kline.
Professional Staff.—Bailey Edwards.

Subcommittee on Coast Guard and Maritime Transportation (507 FHOB), 6–3587, fax 6–0922.

Majority Staff Director.—John Cullather.

Senior Professional Staff.—Richard Hiscock.

Professional Staff.—Lucinda Lessley.

Staff Assistant.—Ianta Summers.

Minority Staff Director.—John Rayfield (505 FHOB), 6–3552, fax 6–2524.

Professional Staff.—Eric Nagel.

Senior Legislative Staff Assistant.—Marsha Canter.

Subcommittee on Economic Development, Public Buildings, and Emergency Management (585 FHOB), 5–9961, fax 6–0922.

Majority Staff Director.—Susan Brita.

Senior Counsel.—Michael Herman.

Counsel.—Elliot Doomes.

Staff Assistant.—Alexis Barrios.

Minority Staff Director.—Dan Mathews (592 FHOB), 5–3014, fax 6–1898.

Counsel.—Jennifer Hall.

Legislative Staff Assistant.—Phillip Maxwell.

Subcommittee on Highways and Transit (B–370A RHOB), 5–9989, fax 5–4627.

Majority Staff Director.—Jim Kolb.

Counsel.—Amy Scarton.

Highway Policy Director.—Art Chan.

Legislative Assistant.—Jackie Schmitz.

Staff Assistant.—Peter Gould.

Minority Staff Director.—James Tymon (B–375 RHOB), 5–6715, fax 5–4623.

Counsel.—Suzanne Newhouse.

Professional Staff.—Joyce Rose.

Legislative Staff Assistant.—Tim Lundquist.

Subcommittee on Railroads, Pipelines, and Hazardous Materials (589 FHOB), 5–3274, fax 6–3475.

Majority Staff Director.—Jennifer Esposito.

Professional Staff: John Drake, Nick Martinelli.

Senior Staff Assistant.—Rose Hamlin.

Legislative Assistant.—Niels Knutsen.

Minority Staff Director.—John Brennan (592 RHOB), 6–0727, fax 6–1898.

Legislative Staff Assistant.—Phillip Maxwell.

Subcommittee on Water Resources and Environment (B–376 RHOB), 5–0060, fax 5–4627.

Majority Staff Director.—Ryan Seiger.

Counsel.—Ted Illston.

Professional Staff: Rod Hall, Ben Webster.

Legislative Assistant.—Beth Goldstein.

Staff Assistant.—Michael Brain.

Minority Staff Director.—John Anderson (B–375 RHOB), 5–4360, fax 5–5435.

Counsel.—Jonathan Pawlow.

Professional Staff.—Geoff Bowman.

Legislative Staff Assistant.—Tim Lundquist.

Veterans' Affairs

335 Cannon House Office Building, phone 225–9756, fax 225–2034

http://www.veterans.house.gov

meets second Wednesday of each month

Bob Filner, of California, *Chair*

Corrine Brown, of Florida.
Vic Snyder, of Arkansas.
Michael H. Michaud, of Maine.
Stephanie Herseth Sandlin, of South Dakota.
Harry E. Mitchell, of Arizona.
John J. Hall, of New York.
Phil Hare, of Illinois.
Michael F. Doyle, of Pennsylvania.
Shelley Berkley, of Nevada.
John T. Salazar, of Colorado.
Ciro D. Rodriguez, of Texas.
Joe Donnelly, of Indiana.
Jerry McNerney, of California.
Zachary T. Space, of Ohio.
Timothy J. Walz, of Minnesota.

Steve Buyer, of Indiana.
Cliff Stearns, of Florida.
Jerry Moran, of Kansas.
Richard H. Baker, of Louisiana.
Henry E. Brown, Jr., of South Carolina.
Jeff Miller, of Florida.
John Boozman, of Arkansas.
Ginny Brown-Waite, of Florida.
Michael R. Turner, of Ohio.
Brian P. Bilbray, of California.
Doug Lamborn, of Colorado.
Gus M. Bilirakis, of Florida.
Vern Buchanan, of Florida.

SUBCOMMITTEES

Disability Assistance and Memorial Affairs

John J. Hall, of New York, *Chair*

Ciro D. Rodriguez, of Texas.
Phil Hare, of Illinois.
Shelley Berkley, of Nevada.

Doug Lamborn, of Colorado.
Michael R. Turner, of Ohio.
Gus M. Bilirakis, of Florida.

Economic Opportunity

Stephanie Herseth Sandlin, of South Dakota, *Chair*

Joe Donnelly, of Indiana.
Jerry McNerney, of California.
John J. Hall, of New York.

John Boozman, of Arkansas.
Richard H. Baker, of Louisiana.
Jerry Moran, of Kansas.

Health

Michael H. Michaud, of Maine, *Chair*

Corrine Brown, of Florida.
Vic Snyder, of Arkansas.
Phil Hare, of Illinois.
Michael F. Doyle, of Pennsylvania.
Shelley Berkley, of Nevada.
John T. Salazar, of Colorado.

Jeff Miller, of Florida.
Cliff Stearns, of Florida.
Jerry Moran, of Kansas.
Richard H. Baker, of Louisiana.
Henry E. Brown, Jr., of South Carolina.

Oversight and Investigations

Harry E. Mitchell, of Arizona, *Chair*

Zachary T. Space, of Ohio.
Timothy J. Walz, of Minnesota.
Ciro D. Rodriguez, of Texas.

Ginny Brown-Waite, of Florida.
Cliff Stearns, of Florida.
Brian P. Bilbray, of California.

STAFF

Committee on Veterans' Affairs (335 CHOB), 225–9756, fax 225–2034.

Majority Staff Director.—Malcom Shorter.
Chief of Staff.—Tony Buckles.
Chief Counsel.—David Tucker.
Legislative Coordinator.—Debbie Smith.
Communications Director.—Kristal DeKleer.
Financial Manager.—Bernie Dotson.
Office Manager.—Carol Murray.
Committee Clerk.—Shannon Taylor.
Printing Clerk.—Diane Kirkland.
Executive Assistant.—Jian Zapata.
Minority Staff Director.—Jim Lariviere (333 CHOB), 225–3527.
Chief Counsel.—Kingston Smith.
Executive Assistant.—Sheriè Grove.
Legislative Director.—Deborah Collier.
Subcommittee on Disability Assistance and Memorial Affairs (337 CHOB), 225–9164.
Majority Staff Director.—Thaddeus Hoffmeister.
Professional Staff Member.—Kimberly Ross.
Executive Assistant.—Orfa Torres.
Minority Staff and Communications Director.—Jeff Phillips.
Executive Assistant.—Sheriè Grove.
Subcommittee on Economic Opportunity (335 CHOB), 226–5491.
Majority Staff Director.—Juan Lara.
Professional Staff Member.—Javier Martinez.
Executive Assistant.—Orfa Torres.
Minority Staff Director.—Mike Brinck.
Legislative Assistant.—Jon Clark.
Subcommittee on Health (338 CHOB), 225–9154.
Majority Staff Director.—Cathy Wiblemo.
Professional Staff Member.—Sharon Schultze.
Executive Assistant.—Chris Austin.
Minority Staff Director.—Dolores Dunn.
Professional Staff Member.—Risa Salsburg.
Legislative Assistant.—Jon Clark.
Subcommittee on Oversight and Investigations (337A CHOB), 225–3569.
Majority Staff Director.—Geoffrey Bestor.
Professional Staff Member.—Dion Trahan.
Executive Assistant.—Caitlin Ostomel.
Minority Staff Director.—Art Wu.
Legislative Director.—Deborah Collier.

Ways and Means

1102 Longworth House Office Building, phone 225–3625

http://waysandmeans.house.gov

Charles B. Rangel, of New York, *Chair*

Fortney Pete Stark, of California.
Sander M. Levin, of Michigan.
Jim McDermott, of Washington.
John Lewis, of Georgia.
Richard E. Neal, of Massachusetts.
Michael R. McNulty, of New York.
John S. Tanner, of Tennessee.
Xavier Becerra, of California.
Lloyd Doggett, of Texas.
Earl Pomeroy, of North Dakota.
Stephanie Tubbs Jones, of Ohio.
Mike Thompson, of California.
John B. Larson, of Connecticut.
Rahm Emanuel, of Illinois.
Earl Blumenauer, of Oregon.
Ron Kind, of Wisconsin.
Bill Pascrell, Jr., of New Jersey.
Shelley Berkley, of Nevada.
Joseph Crowley, of New York.
Chris Van Hollen, of Maryland.
Kendrick B. Meek, of Florida.
Allyson Y. Schwartz, of Pennsylvania.
Artur Davis, of Alabama.

Jim McCrery, of Louisiana.
Wally Herger, of California.
Dave Camp, of Michigan.
Jim Ramstad, of Minnesota.
Sam Johnson, of Texas.
Phil English, of Pennsylvania.
Jerry Weller, of Illinois.
Kenny C. Hulshof, of Missouri.
Ron Lewis, of Kentucky.
Kevin Brady, of Texas.
Thomas M. Reynolds, of New York.
Paul Ryan, of Wisconsin.
Eric Cantor, of Virginia.
John Linder, of Georgia.
Devin Nunes, of California.
Patrick J. Tiberi, of Ohio.
Jon C. Porter, of Nevada.

SUBCOMMITTEES

[The chairman and ranking minority member are ex officio (non-voting) members of all subcommittees.]

Health

Fortney Pete Stark, of California, *Chair*

Lloyd Doggett, of Texas.
Mike Thompson, of California.
Rahm Emanuel, of Illinois.
Xavier Becerra, of California.
Earl Pomeroy, of North Dakota.
Stephanie Tubbs Jones, of Ohio.
Ron Kind, of Wisconsin.

Dave Camp, of Michigan.
Sam Johnson, of Texas.
Jim Ramstad, of Minnesota.
Phil English, of Pennsylvania.
Kenny C. Hulshof, of Missouri.

Income Security and Family Support

Jim McDermott, of Washington, *Chair*

Fortney Pete Stark, of California.
Artur Davis, of Alabama.
John Lewis, of Georgia.
Michael R. McNulty, of New York.
Shelley Berkley, of Nevada.
Chris Van Hollen, of Maryland.
Kendrick B. Meek, of Florida.

Jerry Weller, of Illinois.
Wally Herger, of California.
Dave Camp, of Michigan.
Jon C. Porter, of Nevada.
Phil English, of Pennsylvania.

Oversight

John Lewis, of Georgia, *Chair*

John S. Tanner, of Tennessee.
Richard E. Neal, of Massachusetts.
Xavier Becerra, of California.
Stephanie Tubbs Jones, of Ohio.
Ron Kind, of Wisconsin.
Bill Pascrell, Jr., of New Jersey.
Joseph Crowley, of New York.
Jim Ramstad, of Minnesota.
Eric Cantor, of Virginia.
John Linder, of Georgia.
Devin Nunes, of California.
Patrick J. Tiberi, of Ohio.

Select Revenue Measures

Richard E. Neal, of Massachusetts, *Chair*

Lloyd Doggett, of Texas.
Mike Thompson, of California.
John B. Larson, of Connecticut.
Allyson Y. Schwartz, of Pennsylvania.
Jim McDermott, of Washington.
Rahm Emanuel, of Illinois.
Earl Blumenauer, of Oregon.
Phil English, of Pennsylvania.
Thomas M. Reynolds, of New York.
Eric Cantor, of Virginia.
John Linder, of Georgia.
Paul Ryan, of Wisconsin.

Social Security

Michael R. McNulty, of New York, *Chair*

Sander M. Levin, of Michigan.
Earl Pomeroy, of North Dakota.
Allyson Y. Schwartz, of Pennsylvania.
Artur Davis, of Alabama.
Xavier Becerra, of California.
Lloyd Doggett, of Texas.
Stephanie Tubbs Jones, of Ohio.
Sam Johnson, of Texas.
Ron Lewis, of Kentucky.
Kevin Brady, of Texas.
Paul Ryan, of Wisconsin.
Devin Nunes, of California.

Trade

Sander M. Levin, of Michigan, *Chair*

John S. Tanner, of Tennessee.
John B. Larson, of Connecticut.
Earl Blumenauer, of Oregon.
Bill Pascrell, Jr., of New Jersey.
Shelley Berkley, of Nevada.
Joseph Crowley, of New York.
Chris Van Hollen, of Maryland.
Kendrick B. Meek, of Florida.
Wally Herger, of California.
Jerry Weller, of Illinois.
Ron Lewis, of Kentucky.
Kevin Brady, of Texas.
Thomas M. Reynolds, of New York.
Kenny C. Hulshof, of Missouri.

STAFF

Committee on Ways and Means (1102 LHOB), 225–3625, fax 225–2610.
Majority Chief of Staff.—Janice Mays.
Assistant to Chief of Staff.—Kristin Eagan.
Deputy Staff Director.—Askia Suruma.
Assistant to the Chairman (CBR).—Jon Sheiner.
Professional Staff (CBR).—Grant Cedric.
Assistant of Staff Director.—Kristin Eagan.
Committee Administrator.—Jennifer Gould.
Office Manger.—Anthony Tait.
Hearing Clerk.—Cooper Smith.
Calendar Clerk.—Carren Turko.
Documents Clerk.—Reggie Greene.
Finance Manger.—Kendra Murray.
Staff Assistant.—Bonnie Allen.
Communications Director.—Matthew Beck.
Press Secretary.—Jioni Palmer.
IT Manger.—Antoine Walker.

Systems Administrator.—Wuan Perkins.
Web Administrator.—Carrie Breinbach.
Chief Tax Counsel.—John Buckley (1336 LHOB), 225–5522, fax 225–0787.
Oversight Director.—Beth Vance.
Select Revenue Measures Staff Director.—Worrell Mildeen.
Tax Counsels: Kase Juffer, Karen McAfee, Melissa Mueller.
Tax Professional Staff.—Aruna Kayanam.
Professional Staff on Budget and Economy.—Ted Zegers.
Senior Staff Assistant.—Pam Murray.
Clerk.—Chris Strader.
Minority Director of Operations.—Andrew Barber (1139E LHOB), 225–4021.
Chief Trade Counsel.—Angela Ellard.
Deputy Communications Director.—Betsy Andres.
Staff Director.—Brett Loper.
Legislative Staff Assistants: Ken Barbic, Brian Newell, Jean-Rene.
Chief Economist/Tax Advisor.—Chris Giosa.
Chief Health Counsel.—Chuck Clapton.
Professional Staff: Laura Bozell, Dan Elling, Joelle Oishi, Margo Smith.
Trade Counsels.—Evan Alexander, David Thomas.
Senior Tax Counsel.—John Gimigliano.
Chief Tax Counsel.—Jon Traub.
Staff Assistant.—Kevin Kuhlman.
Chief Social Security Advisor.—Kim Hildred.
Tax Counsel.—Libby Coffin.
Human Resources Staff Director.—Matt Weindinger.
Communications Director.—Mike Steel.
Subcommittee on Health (1135 LHOB), 225–3943, fax 226–1765.
Majority Staff Director.—Cybele Bjorklund.
Professional Staff: Debbie Curtis, Jennifer Friedman, Deb Mizeur.
Senior Staff Assistant/Clerk.—Drew Dawson.
Subcommittee on Income Security (B–317 RHOB), 225–1025, fax 225–9480.
Majority Staff Director.—Nick Gwyn.
Professional Staff: Sonja Nesbitt, Indi Dutta-Gupta.
Clerk.—Joe Budd.
Subcommittee on Social Security (1129 LHOB), 225–9263, fax 225–5286.
Majority Staff Director.—Kathryn Olson.
Professional Staff.—Joel Najar, Alaine Perry.
Staff Assistant/Clerk.—Jennifer Beeler.
Subcommittee on Trade (1104 LHOB), 225–6649, fax 225–0518.
Majority Staff Director.—Tim Reif.
Deputy Staff Director.—Viji Rangaswami.
Trade Counsels: Jason Kearns, Jennifer McCadney.
Senior Staff Assistant/Clerk.—Gwen McFadden.
Clerk.—Katherine Wang.

SELECT AND SPECIAL COMMITTEES OF THE HOUSE

Select Committee on Energy Independence and Global Warming

H2–250 Ford House Office Building, 20515, phone 225–4012, fax 225–4092

[Created pursuant to H. Res. 202, 110th Congress]

Edward J. Markey, of Massachusetts, *Chair*

Earl Blumenauer, of Oregon.
Jay Inslee, of Washington.
John B. Larson, of Connecticut.
Hilda L. Solis, of California.
Stephanie Herseth Sandlin, of South Dakota.
Emanuel Cleaver, of Missouri.
John J. Hall, of New York.
Jerry McNerney, of California.

F. James Sensenbrenner, Jr., of Wisconsin.
John B. Shadegg, of Arizona.
Greg Walden, of Oregon.
John Sullivan, of Oklahoma.
Marsha Blackburn, of Tennessee.
Candice S. Miller, of Michigan.

STAFF

Majority Staff Director and Chief Counsel.—David Moulton.
Counsels: Danielle Baussan, Joel Beauvais.
Chief Clerk.—Ali Brodsky.
Communications Director.—Eben Burnham-Snyder.
Senior Policy Advisor.—Ana Unruh Cohen.
Professional Staff: Jeff Duncan, Michal Freedhoff, Morgan Gray, Jonathan Phillips.
Hearings Coordinator.—Mitchell Robinson.
Minority Staff Director.—Tom Weimer.
Communications Director.—Terry Lane.
Senior Policy Advisor.—Debbie Marshall.
Research Director and Communications Assistant.—Ray Robbins.
Special Assistant.—Andy Zach.

Permanent Select Committee on Intelligence

H–405 The Capitol, phone 225–7690

[Created pursuant to H. Res. 658, 95th Congress]

Silvestre Reyes, of Texas, *Chair*

Alcee L. Hastings, of Florida, *Vice Chair*

Leonard L. Boswell, of Iowa.
Robert E. ''Bud'' Cramer, Jr., of Alabama.
Anna G. Eshoo, of California.
Rush D. Holt, of New Jersey.
C.A. Dutch Ruppersberger, of Maryland.
John F. Tierney, of Massachusetts.
Mike Thompson, of California.
Janice D. Schakowsky, of Illinois.
James R. Langevin, of Rhode Island.
Patrick J. Murphy, of Pennsylvania.

Peter Hoekstra, of Michigan.
Terry Everett, of Alabama.
Heather Wilson, of New Mexico.
Mac Thornberry, of Texas.
John M. McHugh, of New York.
Todd Tiahrt, of Kansas.
Mike Rogers, of Michigan.
Darrell E. Issa, of California.

SUBCOMMITTEES

[The Speaker and Minority Leader are ex officio (non-voting) members of the committee.]

Intelligence Community Management

Anna G. Eshoo, of California, *Chair*

Rush D. Holt, of New Jersey, *Vice Chair*

C.A. Dutch Ruppersberger, of Maryland.
Mike Thompson, of California.
Patrick J. Murphy, of Pennsylvania.
Darrell E. Issa, of California.
Mac Thornberry, of Texas.
Todd Tiahrt, of Kansas.

Oversight and Investigations

Robert E. ''Bud'' Cramer, Jr., of Alabama, *Chair*

Alcee L. Hastings, of Florida, *Vice Chair*

John F. Tierney, of Massachusetts.
Janice D. Schakowsky, of Illinois.
C.A. Dutch Ruppersberger, of Maryland.
Peter Hoekstra, of Michigan.
Heather Wilson, of New Mexico.
John M. McHugh, of New York.

Technical and Tactical Intelligence

C.A. Dutch Ruppersberger, of Maryland, *Chair*

Robert E. ''Bud'' Cramer, Jr., of Alabama, *Vice Chair*

James R. Langevin, of Rhode Island.
Rush D. Holt, of New Jersey.
Patrick J. Murphy, of Pennsylvania.
Heather Wilson, of New Mexico.
Terry Everett, of Alabama.
Mac Thornberry, of Texas.

Terrorism, Human Intelligence, Analysis and Counterintelligence

Mike Thompson, of California, *Chair*

Leonard L. Boswell, of Iowa, *Vice Chair*

James R. Langevin, of Rhode Island.
Patrick J. Murphy, of Pennsylvania.
Alcee L. Hastings, of Florida, *Vice Chair.*
Mike Rogers, of Michigan.
Terry Everett, of Alabama.
John M. McHugh, of New York.

STAFF

Majority Staff Director.—Michael Delaney.
Deputy Staff Director/General Counsel.—Wyndee Parker.
Chief Counsel.—Jeremy Bash.
Chief Clerk.—Curtis Flood.
Executive Assistant.—Stephanie Leaman.
Security Director.—Kristin R. Jepson.
Deputy Security Director.—Ashley Lowry.
Systems Administrator.—Brandon Smith.
Budget Director.—Caryn Wagener.
Receptionist.—Katrina Gammon.
Staff Assistants: Chandler Lockhart, Josh Resnick.
Professional Staff: Iram Ali, Don Campbell, Stacey Dixon, Mieke Eoyang, Eric Greenwald, Larry Hanauer, Jody Houck, Carolyn Lyons, Robert Minehart, Brian Morrison, Don Vieira, Mark Young.
Minority Staff Director.—Michael Meermans.
Deputy Minority Staff Director/Chief Counsel.—Chris Donesa.
Minority Staff Assistant.—Meghann Courtner.

Professional Staff: David Abruzzino, Fred Fleitz, Frank Garcia, John W. Heath, James Lewis, George Pappas, Kathleen Reilly.
Minority Press Secretary.—Jamal Ware.

House Republican Policy Committee

B–58 Cannon House Office Building, phone, 225–6168

http://policy.house.gov

meets at the call of the Chair or the Speaker

Thaddeus G. McCotter, of Michigan, *Chair*

Michael C. Burgess, of Texas, *Vice Chair*

Republican Leadership:
Minority Leader.—John A. Boehner, of Ohio.
Minority Whip.—Roy Blunt, of Missouri.
Conference Chair.—Adam H. Putnam, of Florida.
Conference Vice Chair.—Kay Granger, of Texas.
Conference Secretary.—John R. Carter, of Texas.
NRCC Chair.—Tom Cole, of Oklahoma.

Policy Committee Staff.—B–58 Cannon HOB, 225–6168.
Chief of Staff.—Patrick Rothwell.
Policy Analyst: Paul Blocher, Eric Wilson.
Policy Research Assistant.—Nicole Alexander, Sarah Barfield.

Democratic Congressional Campaign Committee

430 South Capitol Street, SE., 20003, phone (202) 863–1500

Executive Committee:
Nancy Pelosi, of California, *Speaker.*
Chris Van Hollen, of Maryland, *Chair.*
Rahm Emanuel, of Illinois, *Chair Emeritus.*
Nita M. Lowey, of New York, *Chair Emeritus.*
Patrick J. Kennedy, of Rhode Island, *Chair Emeritus.*
John D. Dingell, of Michigan, *Chair Council.*
Charles B. Rangel, of New York, *Chair of the Board.*
Joseph Crowley, of New York, *Business Council Chair.*
Debbie Wasserman Schultz, of Florida, *Frontline Democrats Chair.*
George Miller, of California, *Labor Council Chair.*
Artur Davis, of Alabama, *Recruitment Chair.*
Allyson Y. Schwartz, of Pennsylvania, *Women LEAD Chair.*

STAFF

Executive Director.—Brian Wolff, 485–3419.
Chief Operating Officer.—Kristie Mark, 485–3435.
Political Director.—Jon Vogel, 485–3533.
Political Outreach Director.—Leticia Martinez, 485–3507.
Communications Director.—Jennifer Crider, 485–3442.
Chief Financial Officer.—Jackie Forte-Mackay, 485–3401.
Managing Director/Finance and Marketing.—Nicole Runge, 485–3526.
Direct Marketing Director.—Katie Dowd, 485–3441.
Online Marketing Director.—Taryn Rosenkranz, 485–3527.
Candidate Services Director.—Renee Schaffer, 485–3452.
Member Services Director.—Beverly Gilyard, 485–3516.
Research Director.—Brian Walsworth, 485–3428.
Press Secretary.—Doug Thornell, 485–3411.

Democratic Steering and Policy Committee

H–204 The Capitol, phone 225–0100

Chair.—Nancy Pelosi, Speaker of the House from California.
Co-Chairs:
Steering.—Rosa L. DeLauro, Representative from Connecticut.
Policy.—George Miller, Representative from California.

STAFF

Democratic Steering Committee 225–0100, fax 225–4188.
Steering Advisors: George Kundanis, Jonathan Stivers, Ashley Turton.

Democratic Policy Committee (H–130), 225–0100, fax 226–0938.
Policy Advisors: George Kundanis, John Lawrence, Amy Rosenbaum.

Democratic Caucus

202A Cannon House Office Building, phone 225–1400, fax 226–4412

democratic.caucus@mail.house.gov

Rahm Emanuel, of Illinois, *Chair*

John B. Larson, of Connecticut, *Vice Chair*

STAFF

Executive Director.—Sean Sweeney.
Communications Director.—Sarah Feinberg.
Press Secretary.—Nick Papas.
Policy Director.—Jon Hoganson.
Deputy Policy Director.—Eric Feldman.
Director of Member Services.—Jim Papa.
Deputy Director of Member Services.—Adria Crutchfield.
Director of Special Projects.—Amanda Anderson.
Staff Assistant.—Christy Lombardi.
Parliamentarian.—Matt Pinkus.
Staff Director to the Vice Chair.—George Shevlin.
Communications Director to the Vice Chair.—Brian Mahar.
Assistants to the Vice Chair: Adwoadh Ansah ''A.J.'', Kim Jaworski, Yana Miles.

National Republican Congressional Committee

320 First Street, SE., 20003, phone 479–7000

Tom Cole, of Oklahoma, *Chair*

Chair, Executive Committee.—Tom Davis, of Virginia.
Chair of:
Management.—John Kline, of Minnesota.
Fundraising.—Eric Cantor, of Virgina.
Communications.—Marsha Blackburn, of Tennessee.
Audit.—K. Michael Conaway, of Texas.
Candidate Recruitment.—Candice S. Miller, of Michigan.
IE Task Force.—Patrick T. McHenry, of North Carolina.
Incumbent Retention.—Bob Goodlatte, of Virginia.

EXECUTIVE COMMITTEE MEMBERS

Marsha Blackburn, of Tennessee.
J. Gresham Barrett, South Carolina.
Roy Blunt, of Missouri.
John A. Boehner, of Ohio.
Ginny Brown-Waite, of Florida.
Eric Cantor, of Virginia.
John R. Carter, of Texas.
Michael N. Castle, of Delaware.
K. Michael Conaway, of Texas.
Tom Davis, of Virginia.
Phil English, of Pennsylvania.
Mary Fallin, of Oklahoma.
Luis G. Fortuño, of Puerto Rico.
Virginia Foxx, of North Carolina.
Phil Gingrey, of Georgia.
Bob Goodlatte, of Virginia.
Kay Granger, of Texas.
J. Dennis Hastert, of Illinois.
Jeb Hensarling, of Texas.
Darrell E. Issa, of California.
John Kline, of Minnesota.
John Linder, of Georgia.
Kevin McCarthy, of California.
Thaddeus G. McCotter, of Michigan.
Patrick T. McHenry, of North Carolina.
Howard P. ''Buck'' McKeon, of California.
Cathy McMorris Rodgers, of Washington.
Candice S. Miller, of Michigan.
Jeff Miller, of Florida.
Devin Nunes, of California.
Jon C. Porter, of Nevada.
Adam H. Putnam, of Florida.
Thomas M. Reynolds, of New York.
Pete Sessions, of Texas.
Bill Shuster, of Pennsylvania.
Patrick J. Tiberi, of Ohio.
Lynn A. Westmoreland, of Georgia.
Jerry Weller, of Illinois.
Roger F. Wicker, of Mississippi.

STAFF

Executive Director.—Pete Kirkham.
Political Director.—Terry Carmack.
Director of:
Communications.—Jessica Boulanger.
Finance.—Janice Knopp.
Research.—Ed Mullen.
Counsel.—Beth Beacham.

House Republican Conference

1420 Longworth House Office Building, phone 225–5107, fax 226–0154

Adam H. Putman, of Florida, *Chair*

Kay Granger, of Texas, *Vice Chair*

John R. Carter, of Texas, *Secretary*

STAFF

Chief of Staff.—Seth Webb.
Executive Director.—Karen Haas.
Director of Operations.—Emily Seidel.
Policy/Operations.—Luke Hatzis.
Staff Assistants: Katherine Bentley, Kristene Henkelman.
Director of Member Relations.—Rachel Hodges.
Policy Director.—Charles Cooper.
Senior Policy Analyst.—Matt Lakin.
Policy Analysts: Shea Loper, Chris Vieson.
Communications Director.—Ed Patru.
Deputy Director of External Media.—Brian Schubert.
Deputy Director of Internal Media.—Katie Strand.
Media Coordinator.—Courtney Kolb.
Director of Visual Media.—Nathan Imperiale.
Deputy Director of Visual Media.—Ryan Howell.

OFFICERS AND OFFICIALS OF THE HOUSE

OFFICE OF THE SPEAKER

H–232 The Capitol, phone 225–0100, fax 225–4188

http://speaker.house.gov

The Speaker.—Nancy Pelosi.
Chief of Staff.—John Lawrence, H–232, The Capitol, 225–0100.
Chief of Staff (District).—Terri McCullough, 235 CHOB, 225–0100.
Deputy Chief of Staff.—George Kundanis, H–232, The Capitol, 225–0100.
Counsels to the Speaker: Bernie Raimo, Joe Onek.
Special Assistant to the Speaker.—Kate Knudson, H–232, The Capitol, 225–0100.
Staff Assistants: Hera Abbasi, Stephanie Adika, Yuri Beckelman, Matthew Jorgenson, Robyn Lee.
Staff Assistant/Scheduling Assistant.—Michael Long.
Staff Researcher.—April Greener.
Director, New Media.—Karina Newton.
Senior New Media Advisor.—Jesse Lee.
Production Advisor.—Carey Lane.
Online Writer.—Erica Sagrans.
Office Manager.—Paula Short, 235 CHOB, 225–4965.
Legislative Correspondents: Meghna Raj, Alex Volberding.
Director of Scheduling.—Bridget Fallon, H–232, The Capitol, 225–0100.
Scheduler.—Gabby Riggio.
Policy Director.—Amy Rosenbaum, H–232, The Capitol, 225–0100.
Senior Policy Advisor to the Speaker.—Mike Sheehy, H–419, The Capitol, 225–0100.
Senior Policy Advisor.—Wendell Primus.
Policy Advisors: Scott Boule, Margie Capron, Amy Fuerstenau, Kit Judge, Lara Levison, Reva Price, Melissa Shannon, Arshi Siddiqui, Michael Tecklenburg.
Policy Assistant.—Michael Bloom.
Senior Advisor to the Speaker.—Diane Dewhirst, H–232, The Capitol, 225–0100.
Advisors to the Speaker: Micaela Fernandez, Stacy Kerr, Jonathan Stivers.
Senior Advisor, Strategic Planning.—Ellen Qualls.
Director, Member Services Program.—Dean Aguillen.
Advisor, Member Services.—Sydney Jones.
Director, Information Technology.—Wil Haynes, HB 13, 225–0100.
Director, Intergovernmental Affairs.—Cheryl Parker Rose.

SPEAKER'S PRESS OFFICE

H–326 The Capitol, phone 225–0100

Communications Director.—Brendan Daly.
Deputy Communications Director.—Nadeam Elshami.
Press Secretary.—Drew Hammill.
Press Assistants: Crystal Chui, Andrew Stoddard.
Director, Hispanic Media Outreach.—Marcela Salazar.
Outreach Assistant.—Samantha Smith.
Director of Advance, Advisor.—Tom Manatos, H–327, The Capitol, 225–0100.
Advance, Outreach.—Carmela Clendening, H–419, The Capitol, 225–0100.
Speechwriters: Chris Fitzgerald, Alexandra Veitch.

SPEAKER'S FLOOR OFFICE

H–210 The Capitol, phone 225–0100

Floor Director.—Jerry Hartz.
Deputy Floor Director.—Catlin O'Neill.
Floor Assistant.—Marisa Harrilchak.

OFFICE OF THE MAJORITY LEADER

H–107 The Capitol, phone 225–3130, fax 226–0663

Majority Leader.—Steny H. Hoyer.
Chief of Staff.—Terry Lierman.
Scheduler.—Simone LiTrenta.
Office Manager/Executive Assistant.—Austin Burnes.
Floor Director.—Rob Cogorno.
Deputy Floor Director.—Alejandro Perez.
Member Services Director.—Brian Romick.
Deputy Director of Member Services/Floor Assistant.—Alexis Covey-Brandt.
Senior Communications/Policy Advisor.—David Ransom.
Communications Director.—Stacey Farnen-Bernards.
Press and Research Assistant.—Katie Grant.
Speechwriter.—Mike Kerwin.
Policy Director.—Michele Stockwell.
Senior Policy Advisors: Keith Abouchar, Ed Lorenzen, Gina Mahony.
Policy Advisor.—Mariah Sixkiller.
Director of External Relations.—Marta David.
Deputy Director of External Relations.—Sudafi Henry.
Special Assistant.—Troy Clair.
Technology Director.—Stephen Dwyer.

OFFICE OF THE MAJORITY WHIP

H–329 The Capitol, phone 226–3210

http://democraticwhip.house.gov

Majority Whip.—James E. Clyburn.
Chief of Staff.—Yelberton R. Watkins.
Director of:
Coalitions.—Michael Hacker.
Floor Operations and Counsel.—Jaime R. Harrison.
Member Services.—Wendy Hartman.
Outreach.—Tony Harrison.
Policy and Research.—Aranthan S. Jones II.
Special Events.—Lindy Birch.
Communications Director.—Kristie Greco.
Deputy Floor Directors: J. Todd Metcalf, Allie Neill, Jonathan Samuels.
Senior Policy Advisor.—Alex Silbey.
Policy Advisor.—Margaret M. Cantrell.

CHIEF DEPUTY MAJORITY WHIPS

Senior Chief Deputy Whip.—John Lewis.
Chief of Staff.—Michael Collins.

Chief Deputy Whips:
Ed Pastor.
John S. Tanner.
Janice D. Schakowsky.
G.K. Butterfield.
Maxine Waters.
Joseph Crowley.
Diana DeGette.
Debbie Wasserman Schultz.

OFFICE OF THE REPUBLICAN LEADER

H–204 The Capitol, phone 225–4000, fax 225–5117

Republican Leader.—John A. Boehner.
Chief of Staff.—Paula Nowakowski.
Deputy Chief of Staff.—Dave Schnittger.
Deputy to the Chief of Staff.—Amy Lozupone.
Executive Assistant.—Kristen Frahler.
Senior Advisor/Floor Assistant.—Ed Cassidy.
Press Secretary.—Brian Kennedy.
Press Assistant.—Kimberly Ketchel.
Communications Director.—Kevin Smith.
Deputy Communications Director.—Don Seymour.
Director, Member Services.—Greg Maurer.
Member Services Manager.—Ed Mullen.
Outreach Director.—Bill Greene.
Director, Information Technology.—Billy Benjamin.
Director, Planning and Policy Development.—George Canty.
General Counsel/Director of Floor Operations.—Jo-Marie St. Martin.
Deputy Director of Floor Operations.—Anne Thorsen.
Policy Director.—Mike Sommers.
Counsel/Policy Advisor.—George Rogers.
Policy Advisors: Jay Cranford, Stacey Dion, Erika Heikkila, Cindy Herrle, Emily Porter.
Policy Analyst.—Jen Stewart.
Financial Assistant.—Karen Paulson.
Special Assistant.—Meredith Sawyer.
Floor Assistants: Pete Eskew, Jay Pierson, Adrian Sferle.
Staff Assistants: Jared Eichhorn, Elizabeth Kim.

OFFICE OF THE REPUBLICAN WHIP

H–307 The Capitol, phone 225–0197, fax 226–1115

Republican Whip.—Roy Blunt.
Chief of Staff.—Brian Gaston.
Director of Policy.—Neil Bradley.
Director of Floor Operations.—Amy Steinmann.
Chief Floor Assistant.—Kyle Nevins.
Floor Assistant.—John Stipicevic.
Communications Director.—Burson Synder.
Press Secretary.—Amos Snead.
Communications Advisor.—Chris Tucker.
Press Assistant.—Sarah Little.
Director of Scheduling.—Richard Eddings.
Assistant Scheduler.—Kathleen O'Connor.
Policy Advisor.—Brian Diffell.
Policy Advisor/Counsel.—Melanie Looney.
Senior Policy Advisors: Mike Ference, Johnnie Kaberle, Cheryl Jaeger.
Director of Information Technology.—Shannon Mulhern.
Assistant to the Chief of Staff.—Kristina Merrick.
Staff Assistants: Tad Bardenwerper, Justin Hanson.

OFFICE OF THE CHIEF DEPUTY REPUBLICAN WHIP

H–305 The Capitol, phone 225–0197

Chief Deputy Republican Whip.—Eric Cantor.
Chief of Staff.—Steve Stombres.
Special Assistant.—John Hand.

OFFICE OF THE CLERK

H–154 The Capitol, phone 225–7000

LORRAINE C. MILLER, Clerk of the House of Representatives; native of Fort Worth, TX; holds an executive master's degree from the Georgetown School of Business; previously served as a senior advisor to Speaker Nancy Pelosi and has nearly two decades of experience working for the House; in addition, has worked for two other Speakers, Jim Wright and Tom Foley, as well as Congressman John Lewis (D–GA); elected president of the Washington, DC Branch NAACP, 2004; member of the historic Shiloh Baptist Church of Washington, DC; member of Shiloh's Henry C. Gregory Family Life Center Foundation Board of Directors; the first African American to serve as an official of the House of Representatives; sworn in as the 35th Clerk of the House of Representatives on February 15, 2007.

Clerk.—Lorraine C. Miller.
Deputy Clerk.—Jorge E. Sorensen.
Chief of—
Legislative Computer Systems.—Goldey Vansant, 2401 RHOB, 225–1182.
Legislative Operations.—Frances Chiappardi, HT–13, 225–7925.
Legislative Resource Center.—Deborah Turner, B–106 CHOB, 226–5200.
Office of History and Preservation.—Farar Elliott, B–53 CHOB, 226–1300.
Office of House Employment Counsel.—Gloria Lett, 1036 LHOB, 225–7075.
Office of Publication Services.—Janice Wallace-Robinson, B–28 CHOB, 225–1908.
Official Reporter.—Joe Strickland, 1718 LHOB, 225–2627.
Service Groups—
Majority Chief of Pages.—225–7350.
Minority Chief of Pages.—Peggy Sampson, 225–7350.
Congresswoman's Suite.—225–4196.
Members and Family Committee.—225–0622.
Prayer Room.—225–8070.

CHIEF ADMINISTRATIVE OFFICER

HB–30 The Capitol, phone 225–6969

[Authorized by House Resolution 423, 102nd Congress, enacted April 9, 1992]

DANIEL P. BEARD, Chief Administrative Officer of the House of Representatives; native of Bellingham, WA; B.A., Western Washington University, 1965; M.A. (1969) and Ph.D. (1973), University of Washington; worked for the Domestic Policy Staff at the White House; Deputy Assistant Secretary for Water and Science, Interior Department; conducted research for the Congressional Research Service at the Library of Congress; Special Assistant to Congressman Sidney R. Yates (D–IL); Administrative Assistant to Senator Max Baucus (D–MT); former Chief Operating Officer and Senior Vice President for Public Policy, National Audubon Society; Staff Director, Committee on Natural Resources, U.S. House of Representatives; Commissioner of the Bureau of Reclamation, Interior Department; senior advisor for the consulting firm Booz Allen Hamilton, Inc.; elected February 15, 2007, as Chief Administrative Officer of the House of Representatives.

Chief Administrative Officer.—Daniel P. Beard.
Deputy Chief Administrative Officer for—
Customer Solutions.—Helene Flanagan, H2–217 FHOB.
Operations.—Dan Doody, H2–217 FHOB.
Strategy.—Philip Flewallen, H2–217 FHOB.
Administrative Counsel.—Tim Blodgett, H2–217 FHOB.
Financial Officer.—Barbara Burkhalter, H2–217 FHOB.
Human Capital Officer.—Kathy Wyszynski, H2–217 FHOB.
Executive Assistant.—Jordana Zubkoff.

CHAPLAIN

HB–25 The Capitol, phone 225–2509, fax 226–4928

DANIEL P. COUGHLIN, Chaplain, House of Representatives; residence: St. Clement Parish, Chicago, IL; attended St. Mary of the Lake University, Mundelein, IL, and received a Licentiate Degree in Sacred Theology; ordained a Roman Catholic priest on May 3, 1960; also attended Loyola University, Chicago, IL, and received a degree in Pastoral Studies; Director of the Office for Divine Worship, Archdiocese of Chicago, under John Cardinal Cody, 1969–84; appointed pastor of St. Francis Xavier Parish by Joseph Cardinal Bernardin and Director of the Cardinal Stritch Retreat House, Mundelein, IL, 1990–95; Vicar for Priests under Francis Cardinal George, Archbishop of Chicago, 1995–2000; appointed House Chaplain on March 23, 2000.

Chaplain of the House.—Daniel P. Coughlin.
Assistant to the Chaplain.—Don Myhill.
Liaison to Staff.—Karen Bronson.

OFFICE OF THE HOUSE HISTORIAN

B–56 Cannon House Office Building, phone 226–5525

House Historian.—Dr. Robert Remini.
Deputy House Historian.—Dr. Fred L. Beuttler.
Office Manager.—Michael J. Cronin.
Research Assistant.—Anthony A. Wallis.

OFFICE OF INTERPARLIAMENTARY AFFAIRS

HB–28 Capitol, phone 226–1766

Director.—Dr. Kay King.
Assistant Director.—Janice McKinney.

HOUSE INFORMATION RESOURCES

H2–63 Ford House Office Building, 20515, phone 225–9276, fax 226–6150

Associate Administrator.—Dan Doody.

OFFICE OF THE ATTENDING PHYSICIAN

H–166 The Capitol, phone 225–5421

(After office hours, call Capitol Operator 224–2145)

Attending Physician.—Dr. John F. Eisold.
Chief of Staff.—Christopher R. Picaut.
Deputy Chief of Staff.—Keith Pray.

OFFICE OF INSPECTOR GENERAL

H2–386 Ford House Office Building, phone 226–1250

Inspector General.—James J. Cornell.
Deputy Inspector General.—Dave Smith.
Special Assistant.—Jaima List.
Director of Administration.—Susan M. Kozubski.
Director, Computer Assisted Audit Techniques.—Mike Benner.
Director, Performance and Financial Audits.—G. Kenneth Eichelman.
Assistant Directors: Marie Hughes, Gary A. Muller.

Auditor.—Julie A. Poole.
Director, Information Systems Audits.—Debbie Hunter.
Assistant Director.—Steven Johnson.
Auditors: Doug Carney, Stephen Lockhart, Walter McClean.
Director, Management Advisory Services.—Theresa M. Grafenstine.
Assistant Directors: Michael Bowman, Keith Sullenberger.
Auditors: Steve Connard, Terry Upshur, Donna Wolfgang.

OFFICE OF THE LAW REVISION COUNSEL

H2–304 Ford House Office Building, 20515–6711, phone 226–2411, fax 225–0010

Law Revision Counsel.—Peter G. LeFevre.
Deputy Counsel.—Richard B. Simpson.
Senior Counsel.—Kenneth I. Paretzky.
Assistant Counsels: Ray Kaselonis, Katherine L. Lane, Brian Lindsey, Sally-Anne Moringello, Edward T. Mulligan, Ralph V. Seep, Robert M. Sukol, Timothy D. Trushel, John F. Wagner, Jr.
Staff Assistants: Debra L. Johnson, Monica Thompson.
Printing Editors: Robert E. Belcher, Lawrence J. Foster.
Senior Systems Engineer.—Eric Loach.

OFFICE OF THE LEGISLATIVE COUNSEL

136 Cannon House Office Building, phone 225–6060

Legislative Counsel.—Pope Barrow.
Deputy Legislative Counsel.—Douglass Bellis.
Senior Counsels: Wade Ballou, Timothy Brown, Sherry Criss, Steven Cope, Ira Forstater, Edward Grossman, James Grossman, Jean Harmann, Gregory M. Kostka, Lawrence Johnston, Edward Leong, David Mendelsohn, Hank Savage, Sandra Strokoff, Robert Weinhagen, James Wert, Noah L. Wofsy.
Assistant Counsels: Philip Bayer, Warren Burke, Paul C. Callen, Henry Christrup, Lisa M. Daly, Tobias A. Dorsey, Matthew Eckstein, Susan Fleishman, Rosemary Gallagher, Curt C. Haensel, Molly Lothamer, Hadley Ross, Kate Sawyer, Jessica Shapiro, Ellen J. Sutherland, Mark A. Synnes, Brady Young.
Office Administrator.—Renate Stehr.
Assistant Office Administrator.—Nancy McNeillie.
Front Office Manager/Assistant Systems Administrator.—David Topper.
Senior Systems Analyst.—Peter Szwec.
Director, Information Systems.—Willie Blount.
Publications Coordinator.—Craig Sterkx.
Staff Assistants: Ashley Anderson, Debra Birch, Elonda Blount, Pamela Griffiths, Kelly Meryweather, Tom Meryweather, Melissa Weiss.

OFFICE OF THE PARLIAMENTARIAN

H–209 The Capitol, phone 225–7373

Parliamentarian.—John V. Sullivan.
Deputy Parliamentarian.—Thomas J. Wickham.
Assistant Parliamentarians: Ethan B. Lauer, Max A. Spitzer, Carrie E. Wolf, M. Elizabeth Woodworth.
Chief Clerk.—Gay S. Topper.
Assistant Clerk.—Brian C. Cooper.
Precedent Consultant.—Charles W. Johnson III.
Precedent Editor.—Deborah W. Khalili.
Counsel.—Robert W. Cover.
Information Technology Manager.—Bryan J. Feldblum.

OFFICE OF THE SERGEANT AT ARMS

H–124 The Capitol, phone 225–2456

WILSON ''BILL'' LIVINGOOD, Sergeant at Arms of the U.S. House of Representatives; born on October 1, 1936 in Philadelphia, PA; B.S., Police Administration, Michigan State

University; career record: special agent, U.S. Secret Service's Dallas Field Office, 1961–69; assistant to the special agent in charge of the Presidential Protective Division, 1969; special agent in charge of the Office of Protective Forces, 1970; inspector, Office of Inspection, 1978–82; special agent in charge, Houston Field Office, 1982–86; deputy assistant director, Office of Training, 1986–89; executive assistant to the Director of Secret Service, 1989–95; elected 36th Sergeant at Arms of the U.S. House of Representatives on January 4, 1995, for the 104th Congress; reelected for each succeeding Congress.

Sergeant at Arms.—Wilson "Bill" Livingood.
Deputy Sergeant at Arms.—Kerri Hanley.
Assistant Sergeant at Arms.—Don Kellaher.
Executive Assistant.—Kathleen Joyce.
Directors:
Chamber Security.—Bill Sims.
Assistant Director.—Richard Wilson.
House Garages and Parking Security.—Rod Myers.
Assistant Directors: Bill Lomax, Jeanne Mershon.
House Security.—William McFarland.
Identification Services.—Melissa Franger.
Information Services.—Jim Kaelin.
Special Events.—Ted Daniel.
Assistants to the Sergeant at Arms: Stefan Bieret, Kevin Brennan, Kara Carlson, David Cohen, KaSandra Greenhow, Teresa Johnson, Jack Kelliher.
Appointments/Public Information Center: Kati Magaw, Tripp Jones, Robin Pegues, Alissa Strawcutter, Vivian Dixon-Tymus.
Assistants to Identification Services: Doris Boyd, Karen Forriest, Tanya Hughes, Susan Lowe, Patricia Thomas-Wright, Anthony Titus.
Assistants to House Security: Sheri Bohs, Alexander Storino.

OFFICE OF EMERGENCY PLANNING, PREPAREDNESS, AND OPERATIONS

H2–192 Ford House Office Building, phone 226–0950

Director.—Curt Coughlin.
Deputy Director.—Lawrence Himmelsbach.
Assistant Director for—
Operations.—Michael P. Susalla.
Planning.—Eric M. Kruse.
Preparedness.—John E. Veatch.
Special Projects.—W. Lee Trolan.
Executive Assistant.—Linda R. Shealy.
Senior Program Manager.—Traci L. Brasher.
Senior Systems Engineer.—Eddie X. Tutivene.
Emergency Planning Analyst.—Amy R. Rhodes.
Emergency Preparedness Analyst.—Kate Hansen.
Program Analyst.—Joseph P. Lowry.

JOINT COMMITTEES

Joint Economic Committee

G01 Dirksen Senate Office Building 20510–6432, phone 224–5171

[Created pursuant to sec. 5(a) of Public Law 304, 79th Congress]

Charles E. Schumer, Senator from New York, *Chair*

Carolyn B. Maloney, Representative from New York, *Vice Chair*

HOUSE

Maurice D. Hinchey, of New York.
Baron P. Hill, of Indiana.
Loretta Sanchez, of California.
Elijah E. Cummings, of Maryland.
Lloyd Doggett, of Texas.

Jim Saxton, of New Jersey.
Kevin Brady, of Texas.
Phil English, of Pennsylvania.
Ron Paul, of Texas.

SENATE

Edward M. Kennedy, of Massachusetts.
Jeff Bingaman, of New Mexico.
Amy Klobuchar, of Minnesota.
Robert P. Casey, Jr., of Pennsylvania.
Jim Webb, of Virginia.

Sam Brownback, of Kansas.
John E. Sununu, of New Hampshire.
Jim DeMint, of South Carolina.
Robert F. Bennett, of Utah.

STAFF

Joint Economic Committee (SDG–01), 224–5171, fax 224–0240.
Majority Staff:
Deputy Staff Director for Policy.—Katie Beirne (SDG–07), 4–7943.
Staff Assistant.—Christina Baumgardner (SDG–01), 4–5171.
System Administrator.—Barry Dexter (SDG–01), 4–0374.
Senior Policy Analysts: Christina FitzPatrick (804 Hart), 4–7683; Kasia Murray.
Deputy Staff Director for Planning.—Nan Gibson (SDG–05), 4–0377.
Financial Director.—Colleen Healy (SDG–01), 4–0370.
Policy Analysts: Aaron Kabaker (SDG–07), 4–2978; Zachary Luck (SDG–07), 4–0376; Adam Wilson (SDG–05), 4–9065.
Deputy Staff Director for Communications.—Israel Klein (SDG–07), 4–0368.
Senior Policy Advisor.—Michael Laskawy (SDG–05), 4–0379.
Deputy Press Secretary.—Kimberly Magee (SDG–09), 8–6512.
Deputy Communications Directory.—Siobhan Oat-Judge (SDG–09), 4–5334.
Principal Economist.—Matthew Salomon (804 Hart), 4–0373.
Managing Analyst.—Almas Sayeed (SDG–01), 4–8757.
Policy Associate.—Annabelle Tamerjan (SDG–01), 4–5436.
Press Intern.—Stephanie Formas (SDG–09), 4–5171.
Minority Staff:
Senior Economists: Ted Boll (246 FHOB), 6–3511; Ike Brannon (244 FHOB), 6–7108; Jason Fichtner (433 CHOB), 5–0371; Dan Miller (433 CHOB), 5–2223; Robert O'Quinn (246 Ford), 6–4065.
Staff Director.—Chris Frenze (433A CHOB), 5–3923.
Assistant to Staff Director.—Connie Foster (433 CHOB), 6–3231.
Chief Macroeconomist.—Bob Keleher (368 Ford), 6–3227.
Senate Legislative Policy Director.—Doug Branch (805 Hart), 4–9091.

Senate Economist.—Rachel Greszler (805 Hart), 4–2944.
Senate Staff Director.—Jeff Schlagenhauf (805 Hart), 4–3922.
Senate Research Assistants: Justin Underwood (805 Hart), 4–0367; Robert Weingart (805 Hart), 4–3915.
Senate Chief Economist.—Jeff Wrase (805 Hart), 4–2335.

Joint Committee on the Library of Congress

SR–305 Russell Senate Office Building, 20515, phone 224–6352

Dianne Feinstein, Senator from California, *Chair*

Robert A. Brady, Representative from Pennsylvania, *Vice Chair*

SENATE

Christopher J. Dodd, of Connecticut.
Charles E. Schumer, of New York.
Robert F. Bennett, of Utah.
Ted Stevens, of Alaska.

HOUSE

Zoe Lofgren, of California.
Debbie Wasserman Schultz, of Florida.
Vernon J. Ehlers, of Michigan.
Daniel E. Lungren, of California.

STAFF

Matthew McGowan
Abbie Platt
Matthew Pinkus
Bryan Dorsey

Joint Committee on Printing

1309 Longworth Building, 20515, phone 225–2061

[Created by act of August 3, 1846 (9 Stat. 114); U.S. Code 44, Section 101]

Robert A. Brady, Representative from Pennsylvania, *Chair*

Dianne Feinstein, Senator from California, *Vice Chair*

SENATE

Daniel K. Inouye, of Hawaii.
Patty Murray, of Washington.
Robert F. Bennett, of Utah.
Saxby Chambliss, of Georgia.

HOUSE

Michael E. Capuano, of Massachusetts.
Susan A. Davis, of California.
Vernon J. Ehlers, of Michigan.
Kevin McCarthy, of California.

STAFF

Michael Harrison, *Staff Director.*
Bryan Dorsey
Matthew McGowan
Abbie Platt

Joint Committee on Taxation

1015 Longworth House Office Building 20515–6453, phone 225–3621

http://www.house.gov/jct

[Created by Public Law 20, 69th Congress]

Charles B. Rangel, Representative from New York, *Chair*

Max Baucus, Senator from Montana, *Vice Chair*

HOUSE

Fortney Pete Stark, of California.
Sander M. Levin, of Michigan.
Jim McCrery, of Louisiana.
Wally Herger, of California.

SENATE

John D. Rockefeller IV, of West Virginia.
Kent Conrad, of North Dakota.
Chuck Grassley, of Iowa.
Orrin G. Hatch, of Utah.

STAFF

Joint Committee on Taxation (1015 LHOB), 225–3621.
Chief of Staff.—Thomas A. Barthold (acting).
Deputy Chief of Staff.—Bernard A. Schmitt (594 FHOB), 6–7575.
Associate Deputy Chief of Staff.—Carolyn E. Smith (1620 LHOB), 5–7377.
Administrative Specialist.—Frank J. Shima (1015 LHOB), 5–3621.
Chief Clerk.—John H. Bloyer (1620 LHOB), 5–7377.
Senior Legislation Counsels: Laurie A. Coady (1620 LHOB), 5–7377; Harold E. Hirsch (1620 LHOB), 5–7377; Cecily W. Rock (1620 LHOB), 5–7377; Melvin C. Thomas, Jr. (1620 LHOB), 5–7377.
Legislation Counsels: Gary W. Bornholdt (1620 LHOB), 5–7377; Gordon M. Clay (SD–204), 4–5561; Roger Colinvaux (SD–204), 4–5561; Christopher A. ''Drew'' Crouch (1620 LHOB), 5–7377; Nikole C. Flax (1620 LHOB), 5–7377; Christopher A. ''Chris'' Gerke (1620 LHOB), 5–7377; Brion D. Graber (1620 LHOB), 5–7377; Deirdre James (1620 LHOB), 5–7377; David Lenter (1620 LHOB), 5–7377; Allen J. Littman (SD–204), 4–5561; Joseph W. Nega (1620 LHOB), 5–7377; Kashi Way (1620 LHOB), 5–7377.
Senior Economists: Patrick A. Driessen (560A FHOB), 6–7575; Ronald A. Jeremias (593 FHOB), 6–7575; Pamela H. Moomau (593 FHOB), 6–7575; ''Ned'' D.E. Newland (561 FHOB), 6–7575; William T. Sutton (560B FHOB).
Economists: Nicholas Bull (560 FHOB), 6–7575; James Cilke (560 FHOB), 6–7575; Timothy Dowd (578 FHOB), 6–7575; Robert P. Harvey (561 FHOB), 6–7575; Thomas Holtman (578 FHOB), 6–7575; Gary Koenig (575 FHOB), 6–7575; John F. Navratil (1620 LHOB), 5–7377; Christopher J. Overend (574B FHOB), 6–7575; Karl E. Russo (FHOB), 6–7575; Lori Stuntz (FHOB), 6–7575; Brent Trigg (561 FHOB), 6–7575; Michael Udell (574A FHOB), 6–7575; James Williamson (FHOB), 6–7575.
Accountant.—Darrell Poplock (1620 LHOB), 5–7377.
Chief Statistical Analyst.—Melani M. Houser (596 FHOB), 6–7575.
Statistical Analyst.—Tanya Butler (596 FHOB), 6–7575.
Senior Refund Counsel.—Norman J. Brand (3565 IRS), 622–3580.
Refund Counsels: Chase Gibson (3565 IRS) 622–3580; Robert C. Gotwald (3565 IRS), 622–3580.
Document Production Specialist.—Christine J. Simmons (1620 LHOB), 5–7377.
Tax Resource Specialist.—Melissa A. O'Brien (SD–462), 4–0494.
Fellow.—Brittany Harrison (1620 LHOB), 5–7377.
Executive Assistants: B. Jean Best (596 FHOB), 6–7575; Jayne Northern (SD–204), 4–5561; Lucia J. Rogers (596 FHOB), 6–7575; Patricia C. Smith (1620 LHOB), 5–7377; Sharon Watts (3565 IRS), 622–3580.
Senior Computer Specialist.—Hal G. Norman (577 FHOB), 6–7575.
Computer Specialists: Mark High (577 FHOB), 6–7575; Sandeep Yadav (577 FHOB), 6–7575.

Senior Staff Assistant.—Debra L. McMullen (1620 LHOB), 5–2647.
Staff Assistants: Neval E. McMullen (1620 LHOB), 5–2647; Kris Means (1620 LHOB), 5–2647.

ASSIGNMENTS OF SENATORS TO COMMITTEES

[Democrats in roman (49); Republicans in *italic* (49); Independent in SMALL CAPS (1); Independent Democrat in *SMALL CAPS ITALIC* (1); total, 100]

Senator	Committees (Standing, Joint, Special, Select)
Akaka	Veterans' Affairs, *chair.* Armed Services. Banking, Housing, and Urban Affairs. Energy and Natural Resources. Homeland Security and Governmental Affairs. Indian Affairs.
Alexander	Appropriations. Environment and Public Works. Health, Education, Labor, and Pensions. Rules and Administration.
Allard	Appropriations. Banking, Housing, and Urban Affairs. Budget. Health, Education, Labor, and Pensions.
Barrasso	Energy and Natural Resources. Environment and Public Works. Indian Affairs.
Baucus	Finance, *chair.* Joint Committee on Taxation, *vice chair.* Agriculture, Nutrition, and Forestry. Environment and Public Works.
Bayh	Armed Services. Banking, Housing, and Urban Affairs. Small Business and Entrepreneurship. Select Committee on Intelligence. Special Committee on Aging.
Bennett	Appropriations. Banking, Housing, and Urban Affairs. Rules and Administration. Joint Economic Committee. Joint Committee on the Library of Congress. Joint Committee on the Printing.
Biden	Foreign Relations, *chair.* Judiciary.
Bingaman	Energy and Natural Resources, *chair.* Finance. Health, Education, Labor, and Pensions. Joint Economic Committee.
Bond	Select Committee on Intelligence, *vice chair.* Appropriations. Environment and Public Works. Small Business and Entrepreneurship.
Boxer	Environment and Public Works, *chair.* Commerce, Science, and Transportation. Foreign Relations.

Senator	Committees (Standing, Joint, Special, Select)
	Select Committee on Ethics.
Brown	Agriculture, Nutrition, and Forestry.
	Banking, Housing, and Urban Affairs.
	Health, Education, Labor, and Pensions.
	Veterans' Affairs.
Brownback	Appropriations.
	Judiciary.
	Joint Economic Committee.
Bunning	Banking, Housing, and Urban Affairs.
	Budget.
	Energy and Natural Resources.
	Finance.
Burr	Energy and Natural Resources.
	Health, Education, Labor, and Pensions.
	Veterans' Affairs.
	Indian Affairs.
	Select Committee on Intelligence.
Byrd	Appropriations, *chair.*
	Armed Services.
	Budget.
	Rules and Administration.
Cantwell	Commerce, Science, and Transportation.
	Energy and Natural Resources.
	Finance.
	Small Business and Entrepreneurship.
	Indian Affairs.
Cardin	Budget.
	Environment and Public Works.
	Foreign Relations.
	Judiciary.
	Small Business and Entrepreneurship.
Carper	Banking, Housing, and Urban Affairs.
	Commerce, Science, and Transportation.
	Environment and Public Works.
	Homeland Security and Governmental Affairs.
	Special Committee on Aging.
Casey	Agriculture, Nutrition, and Forestry
	Banking, Housing, and Urban Affairs.
	Foreign Relations.
	Joint Economic Committee.
	Special Committee on Aging.
Chambliss	Agriculture, Nutrition, and Forestry.
	Armed Services.
	Rules and Administration.
	Joint Committee on Printing.
	Select Committee on Intelligence.
Clinton	Armed Services.
	Environment and Public Works.
	Health, Education, Labor, and Pensions.
	Special Committee on Aging.
Coburn	Health, Education, Labor, and Pensions.
	Homeland Security and Governmental Affairs.
	Judiciary.
	Indian Affairs.
Cochran	Agriculture, Nutrition, and Forestry.

Senator	Committees (Standing, Joint, Special, Select)
	Appropriations. Rules and Administration.
Coleman	Agriculture, Nutrition, and Forestry. Foreign Relations. Homeland Security and Governmental Affairs. Small Business and Entrepreneurship. Special Committee on Aging.
Collins	Armed Services. Homeland Security and Governmental Affairs. Special Committee on Aging.
Conrad	Budget, *chair.* Agriculture, Nutrition, and Forestry. Finance. Joint Committee on Taxation. Indian Affairs.
Corker	Energy and Natural Resources. Foreign Relations. Small Business and Entrepreneurship. Special Committee on Aging.
Cornyn	Armed Services. Budget. Judiciary. Special Committee on Ethics.
Craig	Appropriations. Energy and Natural Resources. Environment and Public Works. Veterans' Affairs. Special Committee on Aging.
Crapo	Agriculture, Nutrition, and Forestry. Banking, Housing, and Urban Affairs. Budget. Finance.
DeMint	Commerce, Science, and Transportation. Energy and Natural Resources. Foreign Relations. Joint Economic Committee.
Dodd	Banking, Housing, and Urban Affairs, *chair.* Foreign Relations. Health, Education, Labor, and Pensions. Rules and Administration. Joint Committee on the Library of Congress.
Dole	Armed Services. Banking, Housing, and Urban Affairs. Small Business and Entrepreneurship. Special Committee on Aging.
Domenici	Appropriations. Budget. Energy and Natural Resources. Homeland Security and Governmental Affairs. Indian Affairs.
Dorgan	Indian Affairs, *chair.* Appropriations. Commerce, Science, and Transportation. Energy and Natural Resources.
Durbin	Appropriations.

Senator	Committees (Standing, Joint, Special, Select)
	Judiciary. Rules and Administration.
Ensign	Armed Services. Budget. Commerce, Science, and Transportation. Veterans' Affairs.
Enzi	Banking, Housing, and Urban Affairs. Budget. Health, Education, Labor, and Pensions. Small Business and Entrepreneurship.
Feingold	Budget. Foreign Relations. Judiciary. Select Committee on Intelligence.
Feinstein	Rules and Administration, *chair.* Joint Committee on the Library of Congress, *chair.* Joint Committee on Printing, *vice chair.* Appropriations. Judiciary. Select Committee on Intelligence.
Graham	Agriculture, Nutrition, and Forestry. Armed Services. Budget. Judiciary. Veterans' Affairs.
Grassley	Agriculture, Nutrition, and Forestry. Budget. Finance. Judiciary. Joint Committee on Taxation.
Gregg	Appropriations. Budget. Health, Education, Labor, and Pensions.
Hagel	Banking, Housing, and Urban Affairs. Foreign Relations. Rules and Administration. Select Committee on Intelligence.
Harkin	Agriculture, Nutrition, and Forestry, *chair.* Appropriations. Health, Education, Labor, and Pensions. Small Business and Entrepreneurship.
Hatch	Finance. Health, Education, Labor, and Pensions. Judiciary. Joint Committee on Taxation. Select Committee on Intelligence.
Hutchison	Appropriations. Commerce, Science, and Transportation. Rules and Administration. Veterans' Affairs.
Inhofe	Environment and Public Works, *ranking member.* Armed Services.
Inouye	Commerce, Science, and Transportation, *chair.* Appropriations. Rules and Administration. Joint Committee on Printing.

Senator	Committees (Standing, Joint, Special, Select)
	Indian Affairs.
Isakson	Environment and Public Works. Foreign Relations. Health, Education, Labor, and Pensions. Small Business and Entrepreneurship. Veterans' Affairs.
Johnson	Select Committee on Ethics, *chair.* Appropriations. Banking, Housing, and Urban Affairs. Energy and Natural Resources. Indian Affairs.
Kennedy	Health, Education, Labor, and Pensions, *chair.* Armed Services. Judiciary. Joint Economic Committee.
Kerry	Small Business and Entrepreneurship, *chair.* Commerce, Science, and Transportation. Finance. Foreign Relations.
Klobuchar	Agriculture, Nutrition, and Foresty. Commerce, Science, and Transportation. Environment and Public Works. Joint Economic Committee.
Kohl	Special Committee on Aging, *chair.* Appropriations. Judiciary.
Kyl	Finance. Judiciary.
Landrieu	Appropriations. Energy and Natural Resources. Homeland Security and Governmental Affairs. Small Business and Entrepreneurship.
Lautenberg	Appropriations. Budget. Commerce, Science, and Transportation. Environment and Public Works. Homeland Security and Governmental Affairs.
Leahy	Judiciary, *chair.* Agriculture, Nutrition, and Forestry. Appropriations.
Levin	Armed Services, *chair.* Homeland Security and Governmental Affairs. Small Business and Entrepreneurship. Select Committee on Intelligence.
LIEBERMAN	Homeland Security and Governmental Affairs, *chair.* Armed Services. Environment and Public Works. Small Business and Entrepreneurship.
Lincoln	Agriculture, Nutrition, and Forestry. Energy and Natural Resources. Finance. Special Committee on Aging.
Lott	Commerce, Science, and Transportation. Finance.

Senator	Committees (Standing, Joint, Special, Select)
	Rules and Administration.
Lugar	Agriculture, Nutrition, and Forestry. Foreign Relations.
Martinez	Armed Services. Banking, Housing, and Urban Affairs. Energy and Natural Resources. Special Committee on Aging.
McCain	Armed Services. Commerce, Science, and Transportation. Indian Affairs.
McCaskill	Armed Services. Commerce, Science, and Transportation. Homeland Security and Governmental Affairs. Indian Affairs. Special Committee on Aging.
McConnell	Agriculture, Nutrition, and Forestry. Appropriations. Rules and Administration. Select Committee on Intelligence.
Menendez	Banking, Housing, and Urban Affairs. Budget. Energy and Natural Resources. Foreign Relations.
Mikulski	Appropriations. Health, Education, Labor, and Pensions. Select Committee on Intelligence.
Murkowski	Energy and Natural Resources. Foreign Relations. Health, Education, Labor, and Pensions. Indian Affairs.
Murray	Appropriations. Budget. Health, Education, Labor, and Pensions. Rules and Administration. Veterans' Affairs. Joint Committee on Printing.
Nelson, Bill, of Florida	Armed Services. Budget. Commerce, Science, and Transportation. Foreign Relations. Select Committee on Intelligence. Special Committee on Aging.
Nelson, E. Benjamin, of Nebraska	Agriculture, Nutrition, and Forestry. Appropriations. Armed Services. Rules and Administration.
Obama	Foreign Relations. Health, Education, Labor, and Pensions. Homeland Security and Governmental Affairs. Veterans' Affairs.
Pryor	Armed Services. Commerce, Science and Transportation. Homeland Security and Governmental Affairs. Rules and Administration.

Senator	Committees (Standing, Joint, Special, Select)
	Small Business and Entrepreneurship. Select Committee on Ethics.
Reed, of Rhode Island	Appropriations. Armed Services. Banking, Housing, and Urban Affairs. Health, Education, Labor, and Pensions.
Reid, of Nevada	Rules and Administration. Select Committee on Intelligence.
Roberts	Agriculture, Nutrition, and Forestry. Finance. Health, Education, Labor, and Pensions. Select Committee on Ethics.
Rockefeller	Select Committee on Intelligence, *chair.* Commerce, Science, and Transportation. Finance. Veterans' Affairs. Joint Committee on Taxation.
Salazar	Agriculture, Nutrition, and Forestry. Energy and Natural Resources. Finance. Select Committee on Ethics. Special Committee on Aging.
SANDERS	Budget. Energy and Natural Resources. Environment and Public Works. Health, Education, Labor, and Pensions. Veterans' Affairs.
Schumer	Joint Economic Committee, *chair.* Banking, Housing, and Urban Affairs. Finance. Judiciary. Rules and Administration. Joint Committee on the Library of Congress.
Sessions	Armed Services. Budget. Energy and Natural Resources. Judiciary.
Shelby	Appropriations. Banking, Housing, and Urban Affairs. Special Committee on Aging.
Smith	Commerce, Science, and Transportation. Energy and Natural Resources. Finance. Indian Affairs. Special Committee on Aging.
Snowe	Commerce, Science, and Transportation. Finance. Small Business and Entrepreneurship. Select Committee on Intelligence.
Specter	Appropriations. Judiciary. Veterans' Affairs. Special Committee on Aging.
Stabenow	Agriculture, Nutrition, and Forestry.

Senator	Committees (Standing, Joint, Special, Select)
	Budget. Finance.
Stevens	Appropriations. Commerce, Science, and Transportation. Homeland Security and Governmental Affairs. Rules and Administration. Joint Committee on the Library of Congress.
Sununu	Banking, Housing, and Urban Affairs. Commerce, Science, and Transportation. Foreign Relations. Homeland Security and Governmental Affairs. Joint Economic Committee.
Tester	Banking, Housing, and Urban Affairs. Energy and Natural Resources. Homeland Security and Governmental Affairs. Small Business and Entrepreneurship. Veterans' Affairs. Indian Affairs.
Thune	Agriculture, Nutrition, and Forestry. Armed Services. Commerce, Science, and Transportation. Small Business and Entrepreneurship.
Vitter	Commerce, Science, and Transportation. Environment and Public Works. Foreign Relations. Small Business and Entrepreneurship. Special Committee on Aging.
Voinovich	Environment and Public Works. Foreign Relations. Homeland Security and Governmental Affairs.
Warner	Armed Services. Environment and Public Works. Homeland Security and Governmental Affairs. Select Committee on Intelligence.
Webb	Armed Services. Foreign Relations. Veterans' Affairs. Joint Economic Committee.
Whitehouse	Budget. Environment and Public Works. Judiciary. Select Committee on Intelligence. Special Committee on Aging.
Wyden	Budget. Energy and Natural Resources. Finance. Select Committee on Intelligence. Special Committee on Aging.

ASSIGNMENTS OF REPRESENTATIVES TO COMMITTEES

[Democrats in roman (231); Republicans in *italic* (202); Vacancy (2); Resident Commissioner and Delegates in **boldface** (5); total, 440]

Representative	Committees (Standing, Joint, Special, and Select)
Abercrombie	Armed Services. Natural Resources.
Ackerman	Financial Services. Foreign Affairs.
Aderholt	Appropriations.
Akin	Armed Services. Science and Technology. Small Business.
Alexander	Appropriations. Budget.
Allen	Budget. Energy and Commerce.
Altmire	Education and Labor. Small Business. Transportation and Infrastructure.
Andrews	Armed Services. Budget. Education and Labor.
Arcuri	Rules. Transportation and Infrastructure.
Baca	Agriculture. Financial Services. Natural Resources.
Bachmann	Financial Services.
Bachus	Financial Services.
Baird	Budget. Science and Technology. Transportation and Infrastructure.
Baker	Financial Services. Transportation and Infrastructure. Veterans' Affairs.
Baldwin	Energy and Commerce. Judiciary.
Barrett, J. Gresham, of South Carolina	Budget. Financial Services. Foreign Affairs. Standards of Official Conduct.
Barrow	Agriculture. Energy and Commerce.

Representative	Committees (Standing, Joint, Special, and Select)
Bartlett, Roscoe G., of Maryland	Armed Services.
	Science and Technology.
	Small Business.
Barton, Joe, of Texas	Energy and Commerce.
Bean	Financial Services.
	Small Business.
Becerra	Budget.
	Ways and Means.
Berkley	Veterans' Affairs.
	Ways and Means.
Berman	Foreign Affairs.
	Judiciary.
Berry	Appropriations.
	Budget.
Biggert	Education and Labor.
	Financial Services.
	Science and Technology.
Bilbray	Oversight and Government Reform.
	Science and Technology.
	Veterans' Affairs.
Bilirakis	Homeland Security.
	Veterans' Affairs.
Bishop, Rob, of Utah	Armed Services.
	Education and Labor.
	Natural Resources.
Bishop, Sanford D., Jr., of Georgia	Appropriations.
Bishop, Timothy H., of New York	Budget.
	Education and Labor.
	Transportation and Infrastructure.
Blackburn	Energy and Commerce.
	Select Committee on Energy Independence and Global Warming.
Blumenauer	Budget.
	Ways and Means.
	Select Committee on Energy Independence and Global Warming.
Blunt	Republican Whip.
Boehner	Republican Leader.
Bonner	Agriculture.
	Budget.
	Science and Technology.
	Standards of Official Conduct.
Bono	Energy and Commerce.
Boozman	Foreign Affairs.
	Transportation and Infrastructure.
	Veterans' Affairs.
Bordallo	Armed Services.
	Natural Resources.

Representative	Committees (Standing, Joint, Special, and Select)
Boren	Armed Services. Financial Services. Natural Resources.
Boswell	Agriculture. Transportation and Infrastructure. Permanent Select Committee on Intelligence.
Boucher	Energy and Commerce. Judiciary.
Boustany	Agriculture. Education and Labor. Transportation and Infrastructure.
Boyd, Allen, of Florida	Appropriations. Budget.
Boyda, Nancy E., of Kansas	Agriculture. Armed Services.
Brady, Kevin, of Texas	Ways and Means. Joint Economic Committee.
Brady, Robert A., of Pennsylvania	Armed Services. House Administration. Joint Committee on Printing, *chair.* Joint Committee on Library of Congress, *vice-chair.*
Braley, Bruce L., of Iowa	Oversight and Government Reform. Small Business. Transportation and Infrastructure.
Brown, Corrine, of Florida	Transportation and Infrastructure. Veterans' Affairs.
Brown, Henry E., Jr., of South Carolina	Natural Resources. Transportation and Infrastructure. Veterans' Affairs.
Brown-Waite, Ginny, of Florida	Financial Services. Homeland Security. Veterans' Affairs.
Buchanan	Small Business. Transportation and Infrastructure. Veterans' Affairs.
Burgess	Energy and Commerce.
Burton, Dan, of Indiana	Foreign Affairs. Oversight and Government Reform.
Butterfield	Energy and Commerce.
Buyer	Energy and Commerce. Veterans' Affairs.
Calvert	Armed Services. Natural Resources. Science and Technology.
Camp, Dave, of Michigan	Ways and Means.
Campbell, John, of California	Budget. Financial Services.
Cannon	Judiciary.

Representative	Committees (Standing, Joint, Special, and Select)
	Natural Resources. Oversight and Government Reform.
Cantor	Ways and Means.
Capito	Financial Services. Transportation and Infrastructure.
Capps	Energy and Commerce. Natural Resources.
Capuano	Financial Services. House Administration. Transportation and Infrastructure. Joint Committee on Printing.
Cardoza	Agriculture. Rules.
Carnahan	Foreign Affairs. Science and Technology. Transportation and Infrastructure.
Carney	Homeland Security. Transportation and Infrastructure.
Carson	Financial Services. Transportation and Infrastructure.
Carter	Appropriations.
Castle	Education and Labor. Financial Services.
Castor	Armed Services. Rules.
Chabot	Foreign Affairs. Judiciary. Small Business.
Chandler	Appropriations. Science and Technology.
Christensen	Homeland Security. Natural Resources.
Clarke	Education and Labor. Homeland Security. Small Business.
Clay	Financial Services. Oversight and Government Reform.
Cleaver	Financial Services. Select Committee on Energy Independence and Global Warming.
Clyburn	Majority Whip.
Coble	Judiciary. Transportation and Infrastructure.
Cohen	Judiciary. Transportation and Infrastructure.
Cole, Tom, of Oklahoma	Armed Services. Natural Resources.
Conaway	Agriculture. Armed Services.

Representative	Committees (Standing, Joint, Special, and Select)
	Budget.
Conyers	Judiciary, *chair.*
Cooper	Armed Services. Budget. Oversight and Government Reform.
Costa	Agriculture. Foreign Affairs. Natural Resources.
Costello	Science and Technology. Transportation and Infrastructure.
Courtney	Armed Services. Education and Labor. Transportation and Infrastructure.
Cramer	Appropriations. Permanent Select Committee on Intelligence.
Crenshaw	Appropriations.
Crowley	Ways and Means.
Cubin	Energy and Commerce.
Cuellar	Agriculture. Homeland Security. Small Business.
Culberson	Appropriations.
Cummings	Armed Services. Oversight and Government Reform. Transportation and Infrastructure. Joint Economic Committee.
Davis, Artur, of Alabama	House Administration. Judiciary. Ways and Means.
Davis, Danny K., of Illinois	Education and Labor. Oversight and Government Reform.
Davis, David, of Tennessee	Education and Labor. Homeland Security. Small Business.
Davis, Geoff, of Kentucky	Armed Services. Financial Services.
Davis, Jo Ann, of Virginia	Armed Services. Foreign Affairs.
Davis, Lincoln, of Tennessee	Agriculture. Financial Services.
Davis, Susan A., of California	Armed Services. Education and Labor. House Administration. Joint Committee on Printing.
Davis, Tom, of Virginia	Homeland Security. Oversight and Government Reform.
Deal, Nathan, of Georgia	Energy and Commerce.
DeFazio	Homeland Security. Natural Resources.

Representative	Committees (Standing, Joint, Special, and Select)
	Transportation and Infrastructure.
DeGette	Energy and Commerce.
Delahunt	Foreign Affairs. Judiciary. Standards of Official Conduct.
DeLauro	Appropriations. Budget.
Dent	Homeland Security. Transportation and Infrastructure.
Diaz-Balart, Lincoln, of Florida	Rules.
Diaz-Balart, Mario, of Florida	Budget. Science and Technology. Transportation and Infrastructure.
Dicks	Appropriations. Homeland Security.
Dingell	Energy and Commerce, *chair.*
Doggett	Budget. Ways and Means. Joint Economic Committee.
Donnelly	Agriculture. Financial Services. Veterans' Affairs.
Doolittle	Appropriations.
Doyle	Energy and Commerce. Standards of Official Conduct. Veterans' Affairs.
Drake	Armed Services. Transportation and Infrastructure.
Dreier	Rules.
Duncan	Natural Resources. Oversight and Government Reform. Transportation and Infrastructure.
Edwards	Appropriations. Budget.
Ehlers	Education and Labor. House Administration. Science and Technology. Transportation and Infrastructure. Joint Committee on Printing. Joint Committee on Library of Congress.
Ellison	Financial Services. Judiciary.
Ellsworth	Agriculture. Armed Services. Small Business.
Emanuel	Ways and Means.
Emerson	Appropriations.
Engel	Energy and Commerce.

Representative	Committees (Standing, Joint, Special, and Select)
	Foreign Affairs.
English, Phil, of Pennsylvania	Ways and Means. Joint Economic Committee.
Eshoo	Energy and Commerce. Permanent Select Committee on Intelligence.
Etheridge	Agriculture. Budget. Homeland Security.
Everett	Agriculture. Armed Services. Permanent Select Committee on Intelligence.
Faleomavaega	Foreign Affairs. Natural Resources.
Fallin	Small Business. Transportation and Infrastructure.
Farr	Appropriations.
Fattah	Appropriations.
Feeney	Financial Services. Judiciary. Science and Technology.
Ferguson	Energy and Commerce.
Filner	Veterans' Affairs, *chair.* Transportation and Infrastructure.
Flake	Foreign Affairs. Natural Resources.
Forbes	Armed Services. Judiciary.
Fortenberry	Agriculture. Foreign Affairs. Small Business.
Fortuño	Education and Labor. Foreign Affairs. Natural Resources.
Fossella	Energy and Commerce.
Foxx	Agriculture. Education and Labor. Oversight and Government Reform.
Frank, Barney, of Massachusetts	Financial Services, *chair.*
Franks, Trent, of Arizona	Armed Services. Judiciary.
Frelinghuysen	Appropriations.
Gallegly	Foreign Affairs. Judiciary. Natural Resources.
Garrett, Scott, of New Jersey	Budget. Financial Services.
Gerlach	Financial Services. Transportation and Infrastructure.

Representative	Committees (Standing, Joint, Special, and Select)
Giffords	Armed Services. Foreign Affairs. Science and Technology.
Gilchrest	Natural Resources. Transportation and Infrastructure.
Gillibrand	Agriculture. Armed Services.
Gillmor	Financial Services.
Gingrey	Armed Services. Science and Technology.
Gohmert	Judiciary. Natural Resources. Small Business.
Gonzalez	Energy and Commerce. House Administration. Small Business.
Goode	Appropriations.
Goodlatte	Agriculture. Judiciary.
Gordon, Bart, of Tennessee	Science and Technology, *chair.* Energy and Commerce.
Granger	Appropriations.
Graves	Agriculture. Small Business. Transportation and Infrastructure.
Green, Al, of Texas	Financial Services. Homeland Security.
Green, Gene, of Texas	Energy and Commerce. Standards of Official Conduct.
Grijalva	Education and Labor. Natural Resources. Small Business.
Gutierrez	Financial Services. Judiciary.
Hall, John J., of New York	Transportation and Infrastructure. Veterans' Affairs. Select Committee on Energy Independence and Global Warming.
Hall, Ralph M., of Texas	Energy and Commerce. Science and Technology.
Hare	Education and Labor. Veterans' Affairs.
Harman	Energy and Commerce. Homeland Security.
Hastert	Energy and Commerce.
Hastings, Alcee L., of Florida	Rules. Permanent Select Committee on Intelligence.
Hastings, Doc, of Washington	Rules. Standards of Official Conduct.

Representative	Committees (Standing, Joint, Special, and Select)
Hayes	Agriculture. Armed Services. Transportation and Infrastructure.
Heller, Dean, of Nevada	Education and Labor. Natural Resources. Small Business.
Hensarling	Budget. Financial Services.
Herger	Ways and Means. Joint Committee on Taxation.
Herseth	Agriculture. Natural Resources. Veterans' Affairs. Select Committee on Energy Independence and Global Warming.
Higgins	Oversight and Government Reform. Transportation and Infrastructure.
Hill	Energy and Commerce. Science and Technology. Joint Economic Committee.
Hinchey	Appropriations. Natural Resources. Joint Economic Committee.
Hinojosa	Education and Labor. Financial Services. Foreign Affairs.
Hirono	Education and Labor. Transportation and Infrastructure.
Hobson	Appropriations.
Hodes	Financial Services. Oversight and Government Reform.
Hoekstra	Education and Labor. Permanent Select Committee on Intelligence.
Holden	Agriculture. Transportation and Infrastructure.
Holt	Education and Labor. Natural Resources. Permanent Select Committee on Intelligence.
Honda	Appropriations. Science and Technology.
Hooley	Budget. Energy and Commerce. Science and Technology.
Hoyer	Majority Leader.
Hulshof	Ways and Means.
Hunter	Armed Services.
Inglis, Bob, of South Carolina	Foreign Affairs. Science and Technology.
Inslee	Energy and Commerce. Natural Resources.

Representative	Committees (Standing, Joint, Special, and Select)
	Select Committee on Energy Independence and Global Warming.
Israel	Appropriations.
Issa	Judiciary. Oversight and Government Reform. Permanent Select Committee on Intelligence.
Jackson, Jesse L., of Illinois	Appropriations.
Jackson Lee, Sheila of Texas	Foreign Affairs. Homeland Security. Judiciary.
Jefferson	Small Business.
Jindal, Bobby, of Louisiana	Homeland Security. Natural Resources.
Johnson, Eddie Bernice, of Texas	Science and Technology. Transportation and Infrastructure.
Johnson, Henry C. ''Hank'', Jr., of Georgia	Armed Services. Judiciary. Small Business.
Johnson, Sam, of Texas	Ways and Means.
Johnson, Timothy V., of Illinois	Agriculture. Transportation and Infrastructure.
Jones, Stephanie Tubbs, of Ohio	Standards of Official Conduct, *chair.* Ways and Means.
Jones, Walter B., of North Carolina	Armed Services. Financial Services.
Jordan	Judiciary. Small Business.
Kagen	Agriculture. Transportation and Infrastructure.
Kanjorski	Financial Services. Oversight and Government Reform. Science and Technology.
Kaptur	Appropriations. Budget.
Keller, Ric, of Florida	Education and Labor. Judiciary.
Kennedy	Appropriations. Natural Resources.
Kildee	Education and Labor. Natural Resources.
Kilpatrick	Appropriations.
Kind, Ron, of Wisconsin	Natural Resources. Ways and Means.
King, Peter T., of New York	Financial Services.

Representative	Committees (Standing, Joint, Special, and Select)
	Homeland Security.
King, Steve, of Iowa	Agriculture. Judiciary. Small Business.
Kingston	Appropriations.
Kirk	Appropriations.
Klein, Ron, of Florida	Financial Services. Foreign Affairs.
Kline, John, of Minnesota	Armed Services. Education and Labor. Standards of Official Conduct.
Knollenberg	Appropriations.
Kucinich	Education and Labor. Oversight and Government Reform.
Kuhl, John R. ''Randy'', Jr., of New York	Agriculture. Education and Labor. Transportation and Infrastructure.
LaHood	Appropriations.
Lamborn	Natural Resources. Veterans' Affairs.
Lampson	Agriculture. Education and Labor. Science and Technology. Transportation and Infrastructure.
Langevin	Homeland Security. Permanent Select Committee on Intelligence.
Lantos	Foreign Affairs, *chair.* Oversight and Government Reform.
Larsen, Rick, of Washington	Armed Services. Small Business. Transportation and Infrastructure.
Larson, John B., of Connecticut	Ways and Means. Select Committee on Energy Independence and Global Warming.
Latham	Appropriations.
LaTourette	Financial Services. Transportation and Infrastructure.
Lee	Appropriations.
Levin	Ways and Means. Joint Committee on Taxation.
Lewis, Jerry, of California	Appropriations.
Lewis, John, of Georgia	Ways and Means.
Lewis, Ron, of Kentucky	Ways and Means.
Linder	Ways and Means.
Lipinski	Science and Technology. Small Business.

Representative	Committees (Standing, Joint, Special, and Select)
	Transportation and Infrastructure.
LoBiondo	Armed Services. Transportation and Infrastructure.
Loebsack	Armed Services. Education and Labor.
Lofgren, Zoe, of California	Homeland Security. House Administration. Judiciary. Joint Committee on Library of Congress.
Lowey	Appropriations. Homeland Security.
Lucas	Agriculture. Financial Services. Science and Technology.
Lungren, Daniel E., of California	Budget. Homeland Security. House Administration. Judiciary. Joint Committee on Library of Congress.
Lynch	Financial Services. Oversight and Government Reform.
McCarthy, Carolyn, of New York	Education and Labor. Financial Services.
McCarthy, Kevin, of California	Agriculture. House Administration. Homeland Security. Joint Committee on Printing.
McCaul, Michael T., of Texas	Foreign Affairs. Homeland Security. Science and Technology. Standards of Official Conduct.
McCollum, Betty, of Minnesota	Appropriations. Oversight and Government Reform.
McCotter	Budget. Foreign Affairs.
McCrery	Ways and Means. Joint Committee on Taxation.
McDermott	Ways and Means.
McGovern	Budget. Rules.
McHenry	Budget. Financial Services. Oversight and Government Reform.
McHugh	Armed Services. Oversight and Government Reform. Permanent Select Committee on Intelligence.
McIntyre	Agriculture. Armed Services.
McKeon	Armed Services.

Representative	Committees (Standing, Joint, Special, and Select)
	Education and Labor.
McMorris Rodgers	Armed Services. Education and Labor. Natural Resources.
McNerney	Science and Technology. Transportation and Infrastructure. Veterans' Affairs. Select Committee on Energy Independence and Global Warming.
McNulty	Ways and Means.
Mack	Budget. Foreign Affairs. Transportation and Infrastructure.
Mahoney, Tim, of Florida	Agriculture. Financial Services.
Maloney, Carolyn B., of New York	Financial Services. Oversight and Government Reform. Joint Economic Committee, *vice-chair.*
Manzullo	Financial Services. Foreign Affairs.
Marchant	Education and Labor. Financial Services. Oversight and Government Reform.
Markey	Select Committee on Energy Independence and Global Warming, *chair.* Energy and Commerce. Homeland Security. Natural Resources.
Marshall	Agriculture. Armed Services. Financial Services.
Matheson	Energy and Commerce. Science and Technology.
Matsui	Rules. Transportation and Infrastructure.
Meek, Kendrick B., Florida	Armed Services. Ways and Means.
Meeks, Gregory W., of New York	Financial Services. Foreign Affairs.
Melancon	Energy and Commerce. Science and Technology.
Mica	Oversight and Government Reform. Transportation and Infrastructure.
Michaud	Small Business. Transportation and Infrastructure. Veterans' Affairs.
Miller, Brad, of North Carolina	Financial Services. Foreign Affairs. Science and Technology.

Representative	Committees (Standing, Joint, Special, and Select)
Miller, Candice S., of Michigan	Armed Services. Transportation and Infrastructure. Select Committee on Energy Independence and Global Warming.
Miller, Gary G., of California	Financial Services. Transportation and Infrastructure.
Miller, George, of California	Education and Labor, *chair*. Natural Resources.
Miller, Jeff, of Florida	Armed Services. Veterans' Affairs.
Mitchell	Science and Technology. Transportation and Infrastructure. Veterans' Affairs.
Mollohan	Appropriations.
Moore, Dennis, of Kansas	Budget. Financial Services.
Moore, Gwen, of Wisconsin	Budget. Financial Services. Small Business.
Moran, James P., of Virginia	Appropriations.
Moran, Jerry, of Kansas	Agriculture. Transportation and Infrastructure. Veterans' Affairs.
Murphy, Christopher S., of Connecticut	Financial Services. Oversight and Government Reform.
Murphy, Patrick J., of Pennsylvania	Armed Services. Financial Services. Small Business. Permanent Select Committee on Intelligence.
Murphy, Tim, of Pennsylvania	Energy and Commerce.
Murtha	Appropriations.
Musgrave	Agriculture. Small Business.
Myrick	Energy and Commerce.
Nadler	Judiciary. Transportation and Infrastructure.
Napolitano	Natural Resources. Transportation and Infrastructure.
Neal, Richard E., of Massachusetts	Ways and Means.
Neugebauer	Agriculture. Financial Services. Science and Technology.
Norton	Homeland Security. Oversight and Government Reform. Transportation and Infrastructure.
Nunes	Ways and Means.

Representative	Committees (Standing, Joint, Special, and Select)
Oberstar	Transportation and Infrastructure, *chair.*
Obey	Appropriations, *chair.*
Olver	Appropriations.
Ortiz	Armed Services. Natural Resources.
Pallone	Energy and Commerce. Natural Resources.
Pascrell	Ways and Means.
Pastor	Appropriations.
Paul	Financial Services. Foreign Affairs. Joint Economic Committee.
Payne	Education and Labor. Foreign Affairs.
Pearce	Financial Services. Natural Resources.
Pelosi	The Speaker.
Pence	Foreign Affairs. Judiciary.
Perlmutter	Financial Services. Homeland Security.
Peterson, Collin C., of Minnesota	Agriculture, *chair.*
Peterson, John E., of Pennsylvania	Appropriations.
Petri	Education and Labor. Transportation and Infrastructure.
Pickering	Energy and Commerce.
Pitts	Energy and Commerce.
Platts	Education and Labor. Oversight and Government Reform. Transportation and Infrastructure.
Poe	Foreign Affairs. Transportation and Infrastructure.
Pomeroy	Agriculture. Ways and Means.
Porter	Budget. Ways and Means.
Price, David E., of North Carolina	Appropriations.
Price, Tom, of Georgia	Education and Labor. Financial Services.
Pryce, Deborah, of Ohio	Financial Services.
Putnam	Financial Services.
Radanovich	Energy and Commerce.
Rahall	Natural Resources, *chair.* Transportation and Infrastructure.

Representative	Committees (Standing, Joint, Special, and Select)
Ramstad	Ways and Means.
Rangel	Ways and Means, *chair.* Joint Committee on Taxation, *chair.*
Regula	Appropriations.
Rehberg	Appropriations.
Reichert	Homeland Security. Science and Technology. Transportation and Infrastructure.
Renzi	Financial Services. Natural Resources. Permanent Select Committee on Intelligence.
Reyes	Intelligence, *chair.* Armed Services.
Reynolds	Ways and Means.
Rodriguez	Appropriations. Veterans' Affairs.
Rogers, Harold, of Kentucky	Appropriations.
Rogers, Mike, of Alabama	Agriculture. Armed Services. Homeland Security.
Rogers, Mike, of Michigan	Energy and Commerce. Permanent Select Committee on Intelligence.
Rohrabacher	Foreign Affairs. Science and Technology.
Roskam	Financial Services.
Ros-Lehtinen	Foreign Affairs.
Ross	Energy and Commerce. Science and Technology.
Rothman	Appropriations. Science and Technology.
Roybal-Allard	Appropriations. Standards of Official Conduct.
Royce	Financial Services. Foreign Affairs.
Ruppersberger	Appropriations. Permanent Select Committee on Intelligence.
Rush	Energy and Commerce.
Ryan, Paul, of Wisconsin	Budget. Ways and Means.
Ryan, Tim, of Ohio	Appropriations.
Salazar	Agriculture. Transportation and Infrastructure. Veterans' Affairs.
Sali	Natural Resources. Oversight and Government Reform.
Sánchez, Linda T., of California	Education and Labor. Foreign Affairs. Judiciary.

Representative	Committees (Standing, Joint, Special, and Select)
Sanchez, Loretta, of California	Armed Services. Homeland Security. Joint Economic Committee.
Sarbanes	Education and Labor. Natural Resources. Oversight and Government Reform.
Saxton	Armed Services. Natural Resources. Joint Economic Committee.
Schakowsky	Energy and Commerce. Permanent Select Committee on Intelligence.
Schiff	Appropriations. Judiciary.
Schmidt	Agriculture. Transportation and Infrastructure.
Schwartz	Budget. Ways and Means.
Scott, David, of Georgia	Agriculture. Financial Services. Foreign Affairs.
Scott, Robert C. "Bobby", of Virginia	Budget. Education and Labor. Judiciary.
Sensenbrenner	Judiciary. Science and Technology. Select Committee on Energy Independence and Global Warming.
Serrano	Appropriations.
Sessions	Rules.
Sestak	Armed Services. Education and Labor. Small Business.
Shadegg	Energy and Commerce. Select Committee on Energy Independence and Global Warming.
Shays	Financial Services. Homeland Security. Oversight and Government Reform.
Shea-Porter	Armed Services. Education and Labor.
Sherman	Financial Services. Foreign Affairs. Judiciary.
Shimkus	Energy and Commerce.
Shuler	Natural Resources. Small Business. Transportation and Infrastructure.
Shuster	Natural Resources. Small Business. Transportation and Infrastructure.
Simpson	Appropriations.

Representative	Committees (Standing, Joint, Special, and Select)
	Budget.
Sires	Financial Services. Foreign Affairs.
Skelton	Armed Services, *chair.*
Slaughter	Rules, *chair.*
Smith, Adam, of Washington	Armed Services. Foreign Affairs.
Smith, Adrian, of Nebraska	Agriculture. Budget. Science and Technology.
Smith, Christopher H., of New Jersey	Foreign Affairs.
Smith, Lamar, of Texas	Homeland Security. Judiciary. Science and Technology.
Snyder	Armed Services. Veterans' Affairs.
Solis	Energy and Commerce. Natural Resources. Select Committee on Energy Independence and Global Warming.
Souder	Education and Labor. Homeland Security. Oversight and Government Reform.
Space	Agriculture. Transportation and Infrastructure. Veterans' Affairs.
Spratt	Budget, *chair.* Armed Services.
Stark	Ways and Means. Joint Committee on Taxation.
Stearns	Energy and Commerce. Veterans' Affairs.
Stupak	Energy and Commerce.
Sullivan	Energy and Commerce. Select Committee on Energy Independence and Global Warming.
Sutton	Budget. Rules.
Tancredo	Foreign Affairs. Natural Resources.
Tanner	Foreign Affairs. Ways and Means.
Tauscher	Armed Services. Transportation and Infrastructure.
Taylor	Armed Services. Transportation and Infrastructure.
Terry	Energy and Commerce.
Thompson, Bennie G., of Mississippi	Homeland Security, *chair.*

Representative	Committees (Standing, Joint, Special, and Select)
Thompson, Mike, of California	Ways and Means. Permanent Select Committee on Intelligence.
Thornberry	Armed Services. Permanent Select Committee on Intelligence.
Tiahrt	Appropriations. Permanent Select Committee on Intelligence.
Tiberi	Budget. Ways and Means.
Tierney	Education and Labor. Oversight and Government Reform. Permanent Select Committee on Intelligence.
Towns	Energy and Commerce. Oversight and Government Reform.
Turner	Armed Services. Oversight and Government Reform. Veterans' Affairs.
Udall, Mark, of Colorado	Armed Services. Natural Resources. Science and Technology.
Udall, Tom, of New Mexico	Appropriations.
Upton	Energy and Commerce.
Van Hollen	Oversight and Government Reform. Ways and Means.
Velázquez	Small Business, *chair.* Financial Services.
Visclosky	Appropriations.
Walberg	Agriculture. Education and Labor.
Walden, Greg, of Oregon	Energy and Commerce. Select Committee on Energy Independence and Global Warming.
Walsh, James T., of New York	Appropriations.
Walz, Timothy J., of Minnesota	Agriculture. Transportation and Infrastructure. Veterans' Affairs.
Wamp	Appropriations.
Wasserman Schultz	Appropriations. Judiciary. Joint Committee on Library of Congress.
Waters	Financial Services. Judiciary.
Watson	Foreign Affairs. Oversight and Government Reform.
Watt	Financial Services. Judiciary.
Waxman	Oversight and Government Reform, *chair.* Energy and Commerce.
Weiner	Energy and Commerce. Judiciary.

Representative	Committees (Standing, Joint, Special, and Select)
Welch, Peter, of Vermont	Oversight and Government Reform. Rules.
Weldon, Dave, of Florida	Appropriations.
Weller, Jerry, of Illinois	Ways and Means.
Westmoreland	Oversight and Government Reform. Small Business. Transportation and Infrastructure.
Wexler	Financial Services. Foreign Affairs. Judiciary.
Whitfield	Energy and Commerce.
Wicker	Appropriations.
Wilson, Charles A., of Ohio	Financial Services. Science and Technology.
Wilson, Heather, of New Mexico	Energy and Commerce. Permanent Select Committee on Intelligence.
Wilson, Joe, of South Carolina..	Armed Services. Education and Labor. Foreign Affairs.
Wolf	Appropriations.
Woolsey	Education and Labor. Foreign Affairs. Science and Technology.
Wu	Education and Labor. Foreign Affairs. Science and Technology.
Wynn	Energy and Commerce.
Yarmuth	Education and Labor. Oversight and Government Reform.
Young, C.W. Bill, of Florida	Appropriations.
Young, Don, of Alaska	Natural Resources. Transportation and Infrastructure.

CONGRESSIONAL ADVISORY BOARDS, COMMISSIONS, AND GROUPS

BOARD OF VISITORS TO THE AIR FORCE ACADEMY

[Title 10, U.S.C., Section 9355(a)]

Wayne Allard, of Colorado.
Larry E. Craig, of Idaho.
Tim Johnson, of South Dakota.
Mark L. Pryor, of Arkansas.

Doug Lamborn, of Colorado.
Kay Granger, of Texas.
Carolyn C. Kilpatrick, of Michigan.
Mark Udall, of Colorado.
Peter A. DeFazio, of Oregon.
Loretta Sanchez, of California.

BOARD OF VISITORS TO THE MILITARY ACADEMY

[Title 10, U.S.C., Section 4355(a)]

Jack Reed, of Rhode Island.
Mary L. Landrieu, of Louisiana.
Kay Bailey Hutchison, of Texas.
Susan M. Collins, of Maine.

John M. McHugh, of New York.
Maurice D. Hinchey, of New York.
Jim Marshall, of Georgia.
Todd Tiahrt, of Kansas.
John J. Hall, of New York.

BOARD OF VISITORS TO THE NAVAL ACADEMY

[Title 10, U.S.C., Section 6968(a)]

Barbara A. Mikulski, of Maryland.
John P. Sarbanes, of Maryland.
Thad Cochran, of Mississippi.
Roger F. Wicker, of Mississippi.

Steny H. Hoyer, of Maryland.
Elijah E. Cummings, of Maryland.
John Kline, of Minnesota.
C.A. Dutch Ruppersberger, of Maryland.

BOARD OF VISITORS TO THE COAST GUARD ACADEMY

[Title 14 U.S.C., Section 194(a)]

Joe Courtney, of Connecticut.
Christopher Shays, of Connecticut.
Mazie K. Hirono, of Hawaii.
John McCain, of Arizona.
Patty Murray, of Washington.

James L. Oberstar, of Minnesota.
Michael H. Michaud, of Maine.
John L. Mica, of Florida.
Don Young, of Alaska.
Howard Coble, of North Carolina.
Bob Filner, of California.

BRITISH–AMERICAN PARLIAMENTARY GROUP

Senate Hart Building, Room 808, phone 224–3047

[Created by Public Law 98–164]

Senate Delegation:
Chair.—Patrick J. Leahy, Senator from Vermont.
Vice Chair.—Thad Cochran, Senator from Mississippi.

House Delegation:
Chair.—Ben Chandler, of Kentucky.
Vice Chair.—John Boozman of Arkansas.

CANADA–UNITED STATES INTERPARLIAMENTARY GROUP

Senate Hart Building, Room 808, 224–3047

[Created by Public Law 86–42, 22 U.S.C., 1928a–1928d, 276d–276g]

Senate Delegation:
Chair.—Amy Klobuchar, Senator from Minnesota.
Vice Chair.—Mike Crapo, Senator from Idaho.
Director, Interparliamentary Services.—Sally Walsh.

House Delegation:
Paul W. Hodes, of New Hampshire.
James L. Oberstar, of Minnesota.
Michael R. McNulty, of New York.
Peter Welch, of Vermont.

CHINA–UNITED STATES INTERPARLIAMENTARY GROUP

Senate Hart Building, Room 808, phone 224–3047

[Created by Public Law 108–199, Section 153]

Senate Delegation:
Chair.—Daniel K. Inouye, Senator from Hawaii.
Vice Chair.—Ted Stevens, Senator from Alaska.

COMMISSION ON CONGRESSIONAL MAILING STANDARDS

1216 Longworth House Office Building, phone 225–9337

[Created by Public Law 93–191]

Chair.—Michael E. Capuano, of Massachusetts.
Brad Sherman, of California.
Artur Davis, of Alabama.
Vernon J. Ehlers, of Michigan.
Tom Price, of Georgia.
Kevin McCarthy, of California.

STAFF

Majority Staff Director.—Ellen McCarthy, 225–9337.
Professional Staff: Connie Goode, Brian McCue, Mary McHugh.
Counsel.—Charles T. Howell.
Minority Staff Director.—Jack Dail, 226–6044.
Professional Staff: George Hadjiski, Matthew Skipper.

COMMISSION ON SECURITY AND COOPERATION IN EUROPE

234 Ford House Office Building, phone 225–1901, fax 226–4199

http://www.csce.gov

Alcee L. Hastings, Representative from Florida, *Chair*

Benjamin L. Cardin, Senator from Maryland, *Co-Chair*

LEGISLATIVE BRANCH COMMISSIONERS

Senate

Christopher J. Dodd, of Connecticut.
Russell D. Feingold, of Wisconsin.
Hillary Rodham Clinton, of New York.
John F. Kerry, of Massachusetts.
Sam Brownback, of Kansas.
Gordon H. Smith, of Oregon.
Saxby Chambliss, of Georgia.
Richard Burr, of North Carolina.

House

Louise McIntosh Slaughter, of New York.
Mike McIntyre, of North Carolina.
Hilda L. Solis, of California.
G.K. Butterfield, of North Carolina.
Christopher H. Smith, of New Jersey.
Robert B. Aderholt, of Alabama.
Mike Pence, of Indiana.
Joseph R. Pitts, of Pennsylvania.

EXECUTIVE BRANCH COMMISSIONER

Department of Commerce.—Vacant.

COMMISSION STAFF

Chief of Staff.—Fred L. Turner.
Office Manager.—Daniel Redfield.
Senior Advisors: Cliff Bond, Shelly Han.
Staff Advisors: Orest Deychakiwsky, John Finerty, Robert Hand, Janice Helwig, Michael Ochs, Winsome Packer, Kyle Parker, Mischa E. Thompson.
Counsel for International Law.—Erika B. Schlager.
General Counsel.—Marlene Kauffmann.
International Policy Director.—Ronald J. McNamara.
Communications Director.—Lale Mamaux.

CONGRESSIONAL AWARD FOUNDATION

379 Ford House Office Building, phone (202) 226–0130, fax 226–0131

[Created by Public Law 96–114]

Chair.—John M. Falk, Esq., (202) 215–9511.
Vice Chairs:
Linda Mitchell, Mississippi State University Extension Service (662) 534–7776.
Paxton Baker, BET (202) 608–2052.
Secretary.—Michael Cohen, Esq., Heller Ehrman White & McAuliffe LLP (202) 912–2515.
Treasurer.—Dan Scherder, Compressus, Inc. (202) 742–4296.
National Director.—Erica Wheelan Heyse (202) 226–0130.

Members:
Paxton Baker, BET (202) 608–2052.
Bridget Barrus (208) 375–3628.

Max Baucus, Senator from Montana (202) 224–2651.
Michael Carozza, Bristol-Myers Squibb Company (202) 783–8659.
Michael Cohen, Heller Ehrman White & McAuliffe LLP (202) 912–2515.
Larry E. Craig, Senator from Idaho (202) 224–2752.
Kathy Didawick, Blue Cross Blue Shield (202) 626–4804.
Brad Enzi, South Park Development (307) 778–0400.
John M. Falk, Esq.
George B. Gould.
J. Steven Hart, Esq., Williams & Jensen, P.C. (202) 659–8201.
David W. Hunt, Esq., White & Case, L.L.P. (202) 626–3604.
Sheila Jackson Lee, Representative from Texas (202) 225–3816.
Reynaldo L. Martinez, Strategic Dimensions (703) 941–4420.
Linda Mitchell, Mississippi State University Extension Service (662) 534–7776.
Marc Monyek, McDonald's Corporation (630) 623–3795.
Sir James Murray K.C.M.G., New York, NY (718) 852–3320.
Andrew F. Ortiz, J.D., M.P.A., Arizona Cleaning the Air (602) 224–0524 ext. 2055.
Altagracia Ramos, Hispanic Youth Foundation, (937) 427–3565.
Felix R. Sanchez, TerraCom, Inc. (202) 965–5151.
Daniel B. Scherder, The Willard Group (703) 893–8409.
Debbie Snyder, Kintera (972) 342–8429.
Kimberly Talley Norman, Affiliated Computer Systems, Inc. (214) 584–5403.
Greg Walker, Foundation Coal (410) 689–7602.

CONGRESSIONAL CLUB

2001 New Hampshire Avenue, NW., 20009, phone (202) 332–1155, fax 797–0698

President.—Vivian Bishop.
Vice Presidents:
(1st) Vicki Miller.
(2d) Joyce Murtha.
(3d) Julie Reichert.
(4th) Cissy Marshall.
(5th) Jackie Tancredo.
(6th) Betty Ann Tanner.
Treasurer.—Peachy Melancon.
Corresponding Secretary.—Suzanne Conaway.
Recording Secretary.—Cathryn Greigg.
Administrative Assistant.—Lydia de La Vina de Foley.

CONGRESSIONAL EXECUTIVE COMMISSION ON CHINA

242 Ford House Office Building, phone 226–3766, fax 226–3804

[Created by Public Law 106–286]

Sander M. Levin, Representative from Michigan, *Chair.*

Byron L. Dorgan, Senator from North Dakota, Co-Chair.

LEGISLATIVE BRANCH COMMISSIONERS

House

Marcy Kaptur, of Ohio.
Tom Udall, of New Mexico.
Michael M. Honda, of California.
Timothy J. Walz, of Minnesota.
Christopher H. Smith, of New Jersey.
Edward R. Royce, of California.
Donald A. Manzullo, of Illinois.
Joseph R. Pitts, of Pennsylvania.

Senate

Max Baucus, of Montana.
Carl Levin, of Michigan.
Dianne Feinstein, of California.
Chuck Hagel, of Nebraska.
Sam Brownback, of Kansas.
Gordon H. Smith, of Oregon.
Mel Martinez, of Florida.

EXECUTIVE BRANCH COMMISSIONERS

Department of Commerce.—Franklin L. Lavin.
Department of State: Paula J. Dobriansky, Christopher R. Hill.

COMMISSION STAFF

Staff Director.—Douglas Grob.
Deputy Staff Director.—Scot Tanner.
Director of Administration.—Judy Wright.
Senior Advisor.—Steve Marshall.
Senior Counsels: Kara Abramson, Patricia Dyson, Pamela Phan.
Counsel.—Lawrence Liu.
Senior Research Associates: Diana Wang, Katherine Zhao.
Printing Clerk.—Deidre Jackson.

HOUSE DEMOCRACY ASSISTANCE COMMISSION

341 Ford House Office Building, phone 226–1641, fax 226–6062

[Created by H. Res. 24, 110th Congress]

Chair.—David E. Price, of North Carolina.
Ranking Member.—*David Dreier*, of California.

COMMISSIONERS

Lois Capps, of California.
Rush D. Holt, of New Jersey.
Adam B. Schiff, of California.
Allyson Y. Schwartz, of Pennsylvania.
Donald M. Payne, of New Jersey.
Earl Pomeroy, of North Dakota.
Sam Farr, of California.
John T. Salazar, of Colorado.
Keith Ellison, of Minnesota.
Mazie K. Hirono, of Hawaii.

John Boozman, of Arkansas.
Jeff Fortenberry, of Nebraska.
Joe Wilson, of South Carolina.
Judy Biggert, of Illinois.
Jerry Weller, of Illinois.
Jeff Miller, of Florida.
Wayne T. Gilchrest, of Maryland.
Bill Shuster, of Pennsylvania.

Staff Director.—John J. Lis.

HOUSE OFFICE BUILDING COMMISSION

H–232 The Capitol, phone 225–0100

[Title 40, U.S.C. 175–176]

Chair.—Nancy Pelosi, Speaker of the House of Representatives.
Steny H. Hoyer, House Majority Leader.
John A. Boehner, House Minority Leader.

HOUSE OF REPRESENTATIVES PAGE BOARD

H–154 The Capitol, phone 225–7000

[Established by House Resolution 611, 97th Congress]

Chair.—Dale E. Kildee, Representative from Michigan.
Members:
Diana DeGette, Representative from Colorado.
Shelley Moore Capito, Representative from West Virginia.
Ginny Brown-Waite, Representative from Florida.
Lorraine C. Miller, Clerk of the House.

Wilson ''Bill'' Livingood, Sergeant at Arms of the House.

Staff Contact:

Ellen McNamara, Office of the Clerk, Page Program Coordinator.

JAPAN–UNITED STATES FRIENDSHIP COMMISSION

1201 15th Street, NW., Suite 330, phone (202) 653–9800, fax 653–9802

[Created by Public Law 94–118]

Chairman.—Dr. Richard J. Samuels, Massachusetts Institute of Technology.
Executive Director.—Dr. Eric J. Gangloff.
Assistant Executive Director.—Margaret P. Mihori.
Assistant Executive Director, CULCON.—Pamela L. Fields.
Staff Assistant.—Sylvia L. Dandridge.

Members:

The Honorable Dana Gioia, Chairman, National Endowment for the Arts.
Bruce Cole, Chairman, National Endowment for the Humanities.
The Honorable Thomas Petri, U.S. House of Representatives.
The Honorable John D. Rockefeller IV, U.S. Senate.
The Honorable Jim McDermott, U.S. House of Representatives.
Dr. Richard E. Dyck, President, TCS Japan, KK
The Honorable Patricia De Stacy Harrison, Assistant Secretary of State for Educational and Cultural Affairs.
Frank P. Stanek, President, International Business Development, Universal Studios Recreation Group, Universal Studios.
The Honorable Sally Stroup, Assistant Secretary of Education for Post-Secondary Education.
The Honorable Christopher R. Hill, Assistant Secretary of State for East Asian and Pacific Affairs, U.S. Department of State.
The Honorable Lisa Murkowski, U.S. Senate.
Willard G. Clark, Founder, Center for Japanese Art and Culture.

MEXICO–UNITED STATES INTERPARLIAMENTARY GROUP

Senate Hart Building, Room 808, phone 224–3047

[Created by Public Law 82–420, 22 U.S.C. 276h–276k]

Senate Delegation:

Chair.—Christopher J. Dodd, of Connecticut.
Vice Chair.—John Cornyn, of Texas.

House Delegation:

Chair.—Ciro D. Rodriguez, of Texas.

MIGRATORY BIRD CONSERVATION COMMISSION

4401 North Fairfax Drive, Room 622, Arlington, VA 22203
phone (703) 358–1716 fax (703) 358–2223

[Created by act of February 18, 1929, 16 U.S.C. 715a]

Chair.—Dirk Kempthorne, Secretary of the Interior.
Blanche L. Lincoln, Senator from Arkansas.
Thad Cochran, Senator from Mississippi.
John D. Dingell, Representative from Michigan.
Mike Johanns, Secretary of Agriculture.
Stephen L. Johnson, Administrator of Environmental Protection Agency.
Secretary.—A. Eric Alvarez.

NATO PARLIAMENTARY ASSEMBLY

Headquarters: Place du Petit Sablon 3, B–1000 Brussels, Belgium

[Created by Public Law 84–689, 22 U.S.C., 1928z]

Senate Delegation:

Chair.—Joseph R. Biden, Jr., Senator from Delaware.
Vice Chair.—Gordon H. Smith, Senator from Oregon.

House Delegation:
Chair.—Kendrick B. Meek, Representative from Florida.

STAFF

Secretary, Senate Delegation.—Julia Hart Reed, Interparliamentary Services, SH–808, 224–3047.
Secretary, House Delegation.—Susan Olsen, 226–8806.

PERMANENT COMMITTEE FOR THE OLIVER WENDELL HOLMES DEVISE FUND

Library of Congress, 20540, phone 707–1082

[Created by act of Congress approved Aug. 5, 1955 (Public Law 246, 84th Congress), to administer Oliver Wendell Holmes Devise Fund, established by same act]

Chairman ex officio.—James H. Billington.
Administrative Officer for the Devise.—James H. Hutson.

UNITED STATES–CHINA ECONOMIC AND SECURITY REVIEW COMMISSION

444 North Capitol Street, NW., phone 624–1407, fax 624–1406

[Created by Public Law 106–398, 114 STAT]

COMMISSIONERS

Chair.—Carolyn Bartholomew.
Vice Chair.—Daniel A. Blumenthal.

Members:
Peter Brookes, Senior Fellow, National Security Affairs.
Hon. C. Richard D'Amato, Maryland Attorney.
Jeffrey L. Fiedler, President, Research Associates of America.
Kerri Houston, Senior Fellow, Institute for Liberty.
Hon. Dennis C. Shea, Attorney, Government and Public Policy.
Hon. William A. Reinsch, President, National Foreign Trade Council.
Peter Videnieks, Advisor, Foreign Affairs and Energy.
Michael R. Wessel, President, The Wessel Group Inc.
Larry M. Wortzel, Ph.D., Asian Studies and Foreign Policy / Strategic Studies.

COMMISISON STAFF

Executive Director.—T. Scott Bunton.
Associate Director.—Kathleen J. Michels.
Senior Policy Analyst, Trade and Economics.—Paul Magnusson.
Policy Analyst, Trade and Economics.—C. Erick Lundh.
Policy Analyst, Military and Security Issues.—Shannon Knight.
Policy Analyst, Foreign Affairs and Energy.—Marta McLellan.
Congressoinal Liaison.—Erick Pederson.
Research Assistant.—Nargiza Salidjanova.
Management Analyst.—Kathleen Wilson.
Program-IT Specialist.—Omar Aslam.
Program Assistant.—M.L. Faunce.
Office Manager.—Carmela Bradshaw.
Executive / Administrative Assistant.—Teresa Garcia.

RUSSIA–UNITED STATES INTERPARLIAMENTARY GROUP

Senate Hart Building, Room 808, phone 224–3047

[Created by Public Law 108–199, Section 154]

Senate Delegation:

Chair.—E. Benjamin Nelson, Senator from Nebraska.
Vice Chair.—*Trent Lott,* Senator from Mississippi.

SENATE NATIONAL SECURITY WORKING GROUP

113 Dirksen Senate Office Building, 20510, phone 224–3941

Administrative Co-Chair.—Robert C. Byrd, Senator from West Virginia.
Administrative Co-Chair.—*Jon Kyl,* Senator from Arizona.
Democratic Leader.—Harry Reid, Senator from Nevada.
Co-Chair.—Carl Levin, Senator from Michigan.
Co-Chair.—Joseph R. Biden, Jr., Senator from Delaware.
Co-Chair.—Frank R. Lautenberg, Senator from New Jersey.
Republican Leader.—*Mitch McConnell,* Senator from Kentucky.
Co-Chair.—*Thad Cochran,* Senator from Mississippi.
Co-Chair.—*Trent Lott,* Senator from Mississippi.

Members:
Edward M. Kennedy, Senator from Massachusetts.
Richard Durbin, Senator from Illinois.
Bryon L. Dorgan, Senator from North Dakota.
Bill Nelson, Senator from Florida.
JOSEPH I. LIEBERMAN, Senator from Connecticut.
Richard G. Lugar, Senator from Indiana.
John Warner, Senator from Virginia.
Jeff Sessions, Senator from Alabama.
Pete V. Domenici, Senator from New Mexico.
Bob Corker, Senator from Tennessee.
Norm Coleman, Senator from Minnesota.

STAFF

Democratic Staff Director.—David Bonine, 224–5190.
Republican Staff Director.—Tim Morrison, 224–8175.

U.S. ASSOCIATION OF FORMER MEMBERS OF CONGRESS

1401 K Street, NW., Suite 503, 20005
phone (202) 222–0972, fax 222–0977

The nonpartisan United States Association of Former Members of Congress was founded in 1970 as a nonprofit, educational, research and social organization. It has been chartered by the United States Congress and has approximately 600 members who represented American citizens in both the U.S. Senate and House of Representatives. The Association promotes improved public understanding of the role of Congress as a unique institution as well as the crucial importance of representative democracy as a system of government, both domestically and internationally.

President.—Jim Slattery, of Kansas.
Vice President.—John J. Rhodes III, of Arizona.
Treasurer.—Dennis Hertel, of Michigan.
Secretary.—Mike Parker, of Mississippi.
Immediate Past President.—Jack Buechner, of Missouri.
Honorary Chair.—Walter F. Mondale, of Minnesota.
Executive Director.—Peter M. Weichlein.
Counselors: Mark Andrews, of North Dakota; Robert Kastenmeier, of Wisconsin; Matthew F. McHugh, of New York; James W. Symington, of Missouri.

U.S. CAPITOL HISTORICAL SOCIETY

200 Maryland Avenue, NE., 20002, phone (202) 543–8919, fax 544–8244

[Congressional Charter, October 20, 1978, Public Law 95–493, 95th Congress, 92 Stat. 1643]

Chairman of the Board.—Hon. E. Thomas Coleman.
President.—Hon. Ron Sarasin.
Treasurer.—L. Neale Cosby.

General Secretary.—Suzanne C. Dicks.
Vice Presidents of:
Finance and Administration.—Paul E. McGuire.
Membership and Development.—Rebecca A. Evans.
Merchandising.—Diana E. Wailes.
Scholarship and Education.—Donald R. Kennon, Ph.D.

EXECUTIVE COMMITTEE

Steve Chaudet
Hon. E. Thomas Coleman
L. Neale Cosby
Curtis C. Deane
Suzanne C. Dicks
Hon. Thomas S. Foley
Susan Fritschler
Robert W. Lively
Hon. Robert H. Michel
Hon. Ron Sarasin

STAFF

Director of:
Education and Outreach.—Felicia Bell.
Marketing.—Mary Hughes.
Retail Sales.—Chuck Keyton.
Manager of:
Accounting Department.—Sheri Williams.
Corporate Committee.—Marilyn Green.
Historical Programs.—Chris Leibundguth.
Member Programs.—Diana Friedman Chiu.
Public Programs and Chief Guide.—Steve Livengood.
Associate Historian.—Lauren Borchard
Operations Manager.—Randy Groves.
Receiving Supervisor.—Vince Scott.
Receptionist.—Ann McNeil.

U.S. CAPITOL PRESERVATION COMMISSION

[Created pursuant to Public Law 100–696]

Co-Chairs:
Nancy Pelosi, Speaker of the House.
Robert C. Byrd, Senate President Pro Tempore.

House Members:
Steny H. Hoyer, Majority Leader.
John A. Boehner, Republican Leader.
David R. Obey.
Robert A. Brady.
Vernon J. Ehlers.
Zach Wamp.
Marcy Kaptur.
Michael E. Capuano.

Senate Members:
Harry Reid, Majority Leader.
Mitch McConnell, Republican Leader.
Mary L. Landrieu.
Dianne Feinstein.
Robert F. Bennett.
Richard Durbin.
Wayne Allard.

Acting Architect of the Capitol.—Stephen T. Ayers.

U.S. HOUSE OF REPRESENTATIVES FINE ARTS BOARD

1309 Longworth House Office Building, phone 225–2061

[Created by Public Law 101–696]

Chair.—Robert A. Brady, of Pennsylvania.

Members:
Zoe Lofgren, of California.
Debbie Wasserman Schultz, of Florida.
Vernon J. Ehlers, of Michigan.
Daniel E. Lungren, of California.

U.S. SENATE COMMISSION ON ART

S–411 The Capitol, phone 224–2955

[Created by Public Law 100–696]

Chair.—Harry Reid, of Nevada.
Vice Chair.—Mitch McConnell, of Kentucky.

Members:
Robert C. Byrd, of West Virginia.
Dianne Feinstein, of California.
Robert F. Bennett, of Utah.

STAFF

Executive Secretary.—Nancy Erickson.
Curator.—Diane K. Skvarla.
Administrator.—Scott M. Strong.
Associate Curator.—Melinda K. Smith.
Collections Manager.—Deborah Wood.
Museum Specialist.—Richard L. Doerner.
Registrar.—Courtney Morfeld.
Collections Specialist.—Theresa Malanum.
Curatorial Assistant.—Amy Burton.
Historical Preservation Officer.—Kelly Steele.
Staff Assistant.—Amy Camilleri.

OTHER CONGRESSIONAL OFFICIALS AND SERVICES

ARCHITECT OF THE CAPITOL

ARCHITECT'S OFFICE

SB–15, U.S. Capitol, phone 228–1793, fax 228–1893, http://www.aoc.gov

Acting Architect of the Capitol.—Stephen T. Ayers, AIA.
Special Assistant to the Architect of the Capitol.—Michael G. Turnbull, 228–1221.
Director of:
Congressional and External Relations.—Cynthia Snyder, 228–1701.
Safety, Fire and Environmental Programs.—Susan Adams, 226–0630.
Chief Administrative Officer.—David Ferguson, 228–1205.
Chief Financial Officer.—Paula Lettice, 228–1819.
Budget Officer.—Lauri Smith, 228–1793.
Communications Officer.—Eva Malecki, 228–1793.
General Counsel.—Peter Kushner, 228–1793.
Executive Officer, U.S. Botanic Garden.—Holly Shimizu, 225–6670.
Curator.—Barbara Wolanin, 228–1222.

U.S. CAPITOL

HT–42, Capitol Superintendent's Service Center, phone 228–8800, fax 225–7351

Superintendent.—Carlos Elias, 226–4859.
Assistant Superintendents: Larry Brown, 228–1793; Don White, 228–1875.

SENATE OFFICE BUILDINGS

G–45 Dirksen Senate Office Building, phone 224–3141, fax 224–0652

Superintendent.—Robin Morey, 224–6951.
Deputy Superintendent.—Takis Tzamaras, 224–2021.
Assistant Superintendent.—Marvin Simpson, 224–7686.

HOUSE OFFICE BUILDINGS

B–341 Rayburn House Office Building, phone 225–4141, fax 225–3003

Superintendent.—Frank Tiscione, 225–7012.
Deputy Superintendent.—Robert Gleich, 225–4142.
Assistant Superintendents: Sterling Thomas, Bill Wood, 225–4142.

CAPITOL TELEPHONE EXCHANGE

6110 Postal Square Building, phone 224–3121

Supervisor.—Joan Sartori.

CHILD CARE CENTERS

HOUSE OF REPRESENTATIVES CHILD CARE CENTER

147 Ford House Office Building
Virginia Avenue and 3rd Street, SW., 20515
phone 226–9321, fax 225–6908

Administrative Director.—Monica Barnabae.
Program Director.—Paige Beatty.

SENATE EMPLOYEES' CHILD CARE CENTER

United States Senate, 20510
phone 224–1461, fax 228–3686

Director.—Christine Wauls.

COMBINED AIRLINES TICKET OFFICES (CATO)

1800 N. Kent Street, Suite 950, Arlington, VA 22209
phone (703) 522–8664, fax 522–0616

General Manager.—Charles A. Dinardo.
Administrative Assistant.—Susan Willis.

B–222 Longworth House Office Building
phone (703) 522–2286, fax (202) 226–5992

Supervisor.—Misty Conner.

B–24 Russell Senate Office Building
phone (703) 522–2286, fax (202) 393–1981

Supervisor.—Sandra Hishmeh.

CONGRESSIONAL RECORD DAILY DIGEST

HOUSE SECTION

HT–13 The Capitol, phone 225–2868 (committees), 225–1501 (chamber)

Editors for—
Committee Meetings.—Maura Patricia Kelly.
Chamber Action.—Jenelle Pulis.

SENATE SECTION

S–421 The Capitol, phone 224–2658, fax 224–1220

Editor.—Ken Dean.
Assistant Editor.—Elizabeth Brown.

CONGRESSIONAL RECORD INDEX OFFICE

U.S. Government Printing Office, Room C–738

North Capitol and H Streets, NW., 20401, phone 512–0275

Director.—Marcia Thompson, 512–2010, ext. 3–1975.

Deputy Director.—Philip C. Hart, 512–2010, ext. 3–1973.
Historian of Bills.—Barbre A. Brunson, 512–2010, ext. 3–1957.
Editors: Grafton J. Daniels, Jason Parsons.
Indexers: Ytta B. Carr, Joel K. Church, Jennifer E. Jones, Jane M. Wallace.

CAPITOL GUIDE SERVICE AND CONGRESSIONAL SPECIAL SERVICES OFFICE

ST–13 The Capitol 20510, phone 224–3235, Recorded Information 225–6827
Special Services 224–4048, TTY 224–4049

Director.—Tom Stevens.
Administration.—Sharon Nevitt.
Special Services Office.—David Hauck, Crypt, 224–4048.
Tours.—Jeff Aaron, 224–3235.
Training.—Tina Pearson.

LIAISON OFFICES

AIR FORCE

B–322 Rayburn House Office Building, phone 225–6656, fax 685–2592

Chief.—COL Lori Robinson.
Deputy Chief.—MAJ David Kincaid.
Action Officers: MAJ Eric Hummel, MAJ Elena Thompson.
Appropriations Liaison Officer.—MAJ Craig Harding.
Legislative Liaison Specialist.—Alice Geishecker.
Legislative Liaison Assistant.—MSGT Lloyd Jenkins.

182 Russell Senate Office Building, phone 224–2481, fax 685–2575

Chief.—COL Tony Lazarski.
Deputy Chief.—LTC Vince Smith.
Liaison Officers: LTC Carlos Hill, Dolores Toni, LTC Scott Fisher.

ARMY

B–325 Rayburn House Office Building, phone 225–3853, fax 685–2674

Chief.—COL Raymond Bingham.
Deputy Chief.—Dr. Dale Jones.
Liaison Officers: MAJ Matt Allison, LTC Jim Garrison, LTC Carl Grunow, MAJ Pat Lewis, MAJ Marne Sutten, LTC Carolyn Walford.
Congressional Caseworkers: Bob Nelson, Jr, Gail Warren.

183 Russell Senate Office Building, phone 224–2881, fax 685–2570

Chief.—COL Mike Barbero.
Deputy Chief.—LTC Jean McGinnis.
Liaison Officer.—MAJ William McKnight.
Chief, Casework Liaison.—Margaret T. Tyler.
Casework Liaison Officers: Cynthia Gray, MAJ Bill Moore, MAJ Mark Sherkey.

COAST GUARD

B–320 Rayburn House Office Building, phone 225–4775, fax 426–6081

Liaison Officer.—CDR Mark Meservy.
Assistant Liaison Officers: LT Sara Moser, LT Andy Pate.

183 Russell Senate Office Building, phone 224–2913, fax 755–1695

Liaison Officer.—CDR Anthony Popiel.
Liaison Assistants: LCDR Cynthia Lederer, Lee Williams.

NAVY/MARINE CORPS

B–324 Rayburn House Office Building, phone Navy 225–7126; Marine Corps 225–7124

Director.—CAPT Earl Gay, USN.
Deputy Director.—CDR Jerry Miranda, USN.
USN Liaison Officers: LT Laura Eifler, USN; LT Andrew Hill, USN; LT Phil MacNaughton, USN; LT Kelechi Ndukwe, USN; LCDR Kristin Piotrowski, USN (contracts); LT William Wellman, USN.
Director USMC.—COL Paul Kennedy, USMC.
USMC Liaison Officers: CAPT Brian Sharp, USMC; MAJ Gerald Thomas, USMC.
Office Manager/Administrative Clerk.—CORP Jennifer Evitts, USMC.
House Staff NCO.—GSGT Ramses Cypress.

182 Russell Senate Office Building, phone: Navy 224–4682; Marine Corps 224–4681

Director.—CAPT Gene Moran, USN.
Deputy Director.—CAPT Steve Vahsen, USN.
USN Liaison Officers: LT Meghan Latcovitch, LT Matthew Shaffer.
Assistant Liaison Officer.—YNC(SQ) Floyd Logan.
Director, USMC.—COL Gregg Olson.
Deputy Director, USMC.—MAJ Benjamin Venning.
Assistant Liaison Officers: SSGT Juan Carrasco, USMC; SGT Shane Cooley, USMC.

GOVERNMENT ACCOUNTABILITY OFFICE

Room 7125, 441 G Street, 20548, phone 512–4400, fax 512–4641

Congressional Relations Director.—Gloria L. Jarmon.
Executive Assistant.—Delore Watley, 512–6278.
Legislative Advisers: Doris Cannon, 512–4507; Ralph Dawn, 512–4544; Rosa Harris, 512–9492; Elizabeth Johnston, 512–6345; Larry Malenich, 512–9399; Elizabeth Sirois, 512–8989; Mary Frances Widner, 512–3804.
Associate Legislative Adviser.—Carolyn McCowan, 512–3503.
Congressional Information Systems Specialist.—Ellen A. Smith, 512–6817.
Congressional Correspondence Assistant.—Eileen Figgins, 512–5466.
Engagement and Administrative Operations Assistant.—Theodora Guardado-Gallegos, 512–6224.

OFFICE OF PERSONNEL MANAGEMENT

B–332 Rayburn House Office Building, phone 225–4955

Chief.—Charlene E. Luskey.
Senior Civil Service Representative.—Carlos Tingle.
Administrative Assistant.—Kirk H. Brightman.

SOCIAL SECURITY ADMINISTRATION

G3, L1, Rayburn House Office Building, phone 225–3133, fax 225–3144

Director.—Sharon Wilson.
Congressional Relations Liaison.—LaQuitta Moultrie.

STATE DEPARTMENT LIAISON OFFICE

B–330 Rayburn House Office Building, phone 226–4640, fax 226–4643

Office Director.—Scott Thayer.
Consular Officer.—Peter VanBuren.
Congressional Relations Specialist.—Janette Brockenborough.

VETERANS' AFFAIRS

B–328 Rayburn House Office Building, phone 225–2280, fax 453–5225

Director.—Patricia Covington.
Assistant Director.—Paul Downs.
Liaison Assistant.—Jewell Knight.
Representatives: Richard Armstrong Jr., Pamela Mugg.

189 Russell Senate Office Building, phone 224–5351, fax 453–5218

Director.—Patricia Covington.
Assistant Director.—Paul Downs.
Representatives: Erica Jones, Stuart Weiner.

PAGE SCHOOLS

SENATE

Daniel Webster Senate Page Residence 20510, fax 224–1838

Principal.—Kathryn S. Weeden, 224–3926.
English.—Frances Owens, 228–1024.
Mathematics.—Raymond Cwalina, 228–1018.
Science.—John Malek, 228–1025.
Social Studies.—Michael Bowers, 228–1012.
Administrative Assistant.—Lorraine Foreman, 224–3927.

HOUSE OF REPRESENTATIVES

LJ–A11 Library of Congress 20540–9996, phone 225–9000, fax 225–9001

Principal.—Linda G. Miranda.
English.—Lona Carwile-Klein.
Guidance.—Thomas Savannah.
Languages: Sebastian Hobson, French; Linda G. Miranda, Spanish.
Mathematics.—Barbara R. Bowen.
Science.—Walter Cuirle.
Social Studies.—Thomas Faith.
Technology.—Darryl Gonzalez.
Administrative Assistant.—Robin Bridges.

U.S. CAPITOL POLICE

119 D Street, NE., 20510–7218

Office of the Chief 224–9806, Command Center 224–0908
Communications 224–5151, Emergency 224–0911

U.S. CAPITOL POLICE BOARD

Sergeant at Arms, U.S. Senate.—Terrance W. "Terry" Gainer.

Sergeant at Arms, U.S. House of Representatives.—Wilson ''Bill'' Livingood.
Acting Architect of the Capitol.—Stephen T. Ayers, AIA.

OFFICE OF THE CHIEF

Chief of Police.—Phillip D. Morse, Sr.
Administrative Assistant.—Carol A. Absher.
Acting General Counsel.—Gretchen DeMar.
Acting Deputy Counsel.—James W. Joyce.
Office of:
Directives and Accreditation Division.—Jan E. Jones.
Internal Affairs.—LT David Wells.
Public Information.—SGT Kimberly A. Schneider.
Chief of Staff.—Richard M. Majauskas.

CHIEF OF OPERATIONS

Assistant Chief.—Daniel R. Nichols.
Administration Assistant.—LT David E. Pasierb.
Command Center: Insp. Gregory Parman, CAPT Mark Sullivan, CAPT William Uber.
Special Events.—LT Kathryn Stillman.

OPERATIONAL SERVICES BUREAU

Bureau Commander.—Deputy Chief Larry D. Thompson.
Hazardous Incident Response Division.—CAPT Shirley Johnson.
Patrol/Mobile Response Division.—Insp. Thomas M. Loyd (acting).

PROTECTIVE SERVICES BUREAU

Bureau Commander.—Deputy Chief Michael A. Jarboe.
Investigations Division.—CAPT Sandra D. Coffman.
Dignitary Protection Division.—Insp. David Calloway.

SECURITY SERVICES BUREAU

Bureau Commander.—Robert M. Greeley.
Physical Security Division.—Robert F. Ford.
Technical Countermeasures Division.—Michael Marinucci.
Construction Security Division.—CAPT Lawrence Loughery.

UNIFORM SERVICES BUREAU

Acting Bureau Commander.—Deputy Chief Thomas P. Reynolds.
Acting Executive Assistant.—LT Rhonda Parken.
Capitol Division Commander.—Insp. Yancey H. Garner.
House Division Commander.—Insp. Matthew R. Verderosa.
Senate Division Commander.—Insp. Alan D. Morris.

CHIEF ADMINISTRATIVE OFFICER

Chief Administrative Officer.—Anthony J. Stamilio.
Deputy Chief Administrative Officer.—Richard Braddock.

Director, Office of:
Financial Management.—Mary Jean Buhler.
Human Resources.—Rosanna Tucker (acting).
Information Systems.—Michael V. Valivullah.
Logistics.—Dana S. Bouley.
Commander, Training Services Bureau.—Deputy Chief Michael A. Jarboe.

WESTERN UNION TELEGRAPH CO.

B–244 Longworth House Office Building, phone 225–4553/4554, fax 226–1212

Manager.—Donald Lawson.

STATISTICAL INFORMATION

VOTES CAST FOR SENATORS IN 2002, 2004, and 2006

[Compiled from official statistics obtained by the Clerk of the House. Figures in the last column, for the 2006 election, may include totals for more candidates than the ones shown.]

State	Vote						Total vote cast in 2006
	2002		2004		2006		
	Republican	Democrat	Republican	Democrat	Democrat	Republican	
Alabama	792,561	538,878	1,242,200	595,018			
Alaska	179,438	24,133	149,773	140,424			
Arizona			1,505,372	404,507	664,141	814,398	1,526,782
Arkansas	370,735	433,386	458,036	580,973			
California			4,555,922	6,955,728	5,076,289	2,990,822	8,541,476
Colorado	717,893	648,130	980,668	1,081,188			
Connecticut			457,749	945,347	450,844 [1]	109,198	1,134,777
Delaware	94,793	135,253			170,567	69,734	242,972
Florida			3,672,864	3,590,201	2,890,548	1,826,127	4,793,534
Georgia	1,071,352	932,422	1,864,202	1,287,690			
Hawaii			87,172	313,629	210,330	126,097	342,842
Idaho	266,215	132,975	499,796				
Illinois	1,325,703	2,103,766	1,390,690	3,597,456			
Indiana			903,913	1,496,976		1,171,553	1,341,111
Iowa	447,892	554,278	1,038,175	412,365			
Kansas	641,075		780,863	310,337			
Kentucky	731,679	399,634	873,507	850,855			
Louisiana	596,642	638,654 [2]	943,014	877,482			
Maine	295,041	209,858			113,131	405,596	545,128
Maryland			783,055	1,504,691	965,477	787,182	1,781,139
Massachusetts		1,605,976			1,500,738	661,532	2,243,835
Michigan	1,185,545	1,896,614			2,151,278	1,559,597	3,780,142
Minnesota	1,116,697	1,078,627			1,278,849	835,653	2,202,772
Mississippi	533,269				213,000	388,399	610,921
Missouri	935,032	913,778	1,518,089	1,158,261	1,055,255	1,006,941	2,128,459
Montana	103,611	204,853			199,845	196,283	406,505
Nebraska	397,438	70,290			378,388	213,928	592,316
Nevada			284,640	494,805	238,796	322,501	582,572
New Hampshire	227,229	207,478	434,847	221,549			
New Jersey	928,439	1,138,193			58,333	41,998	101,973
New Mexico	314,193	168,863			394,365	163,826	558,550
New York			1,625,069	4,384,907	2,698,931	1,212,902	4,700,632
North Carolina	1,248,664	1,047,983	1,791,450	1,632,527			
North Dakota			98,553	212,143	150,146	64,417	218,152
Ohio			3,464,356	1,961,171	2,257,369	1,761,037	4,019,236
Oklahoma	583,579	369,789	763,433	596,750			
Oregon	712,287	501,898	565,254	1,128,728			
Pennsylvania			2,925,080	2,334,126	2,392,984	1,684,778	4,081,043
Rhode Island	69,808	253,774			206,043	178,950	384,993
South Carolina	600,010	487,359	857,167	704,384			
South Dakota	166,949	167,481	197,848	193,340			
Tennessee	891,498	728,232			879,976	929,911	1,833,695
Texas	2,496,243	1,955,758			1,555,202	2,661,789	4,314,663
Utah			626,640	258,955	177,459	356,238	571,252
Vermont			75,398	216,972	(3)	84,924	262,419
Virginia	1,229,894				1,175,606	1,166,277	2,370,445
Washington			1,204,584	1,549,708	1,184,659	832,106	2,083,734
West Virginia	160,902	275,281			159,154	47,408	206,562
Wisconsin			1,301,183	1,632,697	1,439,214	630,299	2,138,297
Wyoming	133,710	49,570			57,671	135,174	196,215

[1] Independent Democrat Joseph I. Lieberman was elected on November 7, 2006 with 564,095 votes.

[2] Louisiana law requires a runoff election between the top two candidates in the general election if none of the candidates receives 50 percent of the total votes cast. The runoff election was held on December 7, 2002.

[3] The Independent Bernard Sanders was elected on November 7, 2006 with 171,638 votes.

VOTES CAST FOR REPRESENTATIVES, RESIDENT COMMISSIONER, AND DELEGATES IN 2002, 2004, and 2006

[The figures, compiled from official statistics obtained by the Clerk of the House, show the votes for the Democratic and Republican nominees, except as otherwise indicated. Figures in the last column, for the 2006 election, may include totals for more candidates than the ones shown. The 2002 congressional districts reflect changes in apportionments resulting from the 2000 census.]

State and district	Vote cast in 2002		State and district	Vote cast in 2004		State and district	Vote cast in 2006		Total vote cast in 2006
	Republican	Democrat		Republican	Democrat		Democrat	Republican	
AL:			AL:			AL:			
1st	108,102	67,507	1st	161,067	93,938	1st	52,770	112,944	165,841
2d	129,233	55,495	2d	70,562	177,086	2d	54,450	124,302	178,919
3d	91,169	87,351	3d	150,411	95,240	3d	63,559	98,257	165,301
4th	139,705	....	4th	191,110	64,278	4th	54,382	128,484	183,072
5th	48,226	143,029	5th	74,145	200,999	5th	143,015	....	145,555
6th	178,171	....	6th	264,819	....	6th	....	163,514	166,300
7th	....	153,735	7th	61,019	183,408	7th	133,870	....	135,164
AK:			AK:			AK:			
At large	169,685	39,357	At large	213,216	67,074	At large	93,879	132,743	234,645
AZ:			AZ:			AZ:			
1st	85,967	79,730	1st	148,315	91,776	1st	88,691	105,646	204,139
2d	100,359	61,217	2d	165,260	107,406	2d	89,671	135,150	230,560
3d	104,847	47,173	3d	181,012	....	3d	72,586	112,519	189,849
4th	18,381	44,517	4th	28,238	77,150	4th	56,464	18,627	77,861
5th	103,870	61,559	5th	159,455	102,363	5th	101,838	93,815	202,010
6th	103,094	49,355	6th	202,882	....	6th	....	152,201	203,486
7th	38,474	61,256	7th	59,066	108,868	7th	80,354	46,498	131,525
8th	126,930	67,328	8th	183,363	109,963	8th	137,655	106,790	253,720
AR:			AR:			AR:			
1st	64,357	129,701	1st	81,556	162,388	1st	127,577	56,611	184,188
2d	....	142,752	2d	115,655	160,834	2d	124,871	81,432	206,303
3d	141,478	....	3d	160,629	103,158	3d	75,885	125,039	200,924
4th	77,904	119,633	4th	....	(1)	4th	128,236	43,360	171,596
CA:			CA:			CA:			
1st	60,013	118,669	1st	79,970	189,366	1st	144,409	63,194	218,044
2d	117,747	52,455	2d	182,119	90,310	2d	68,234	134,911	210,202
3d	121,732	67,136	3d	177,738	100,025	3d	86,318	135,709	228,169
4th	147,997	72,860	4th	221,926	117,443	4th	126,999	135,818	276,893
5th	34,749	92,726	5th	45,120	138,004	5th	105,676	35,106	149,266
6th	62,052	139,750	6th	85,244	226,423	6th	173,190	64,405	246,628
7th	36,584	97,849	7th	52,446	166,831	7th	118,000	....	140,486
8th	20,063	127,684	8th	31,074	224,017	8th	148,435	19,800	184,639
9th	25,333	135,893	9th	31,278	215,630	9th	167,245	20,786	193,686
10th	....	126,390	10th	95,349	182,750	10th	130,859	66,069	196,978
11th	104,921	69,035	11th	163,582	103,587	11th	109,868	96,396	206,264
12th	38,381	105,597	12th	52,593	171,852	12th	138,650	43,674	182,324
13th	26,852	86,495	13th	48,439	144,605	13th	110,756	37,141	147,897
14th	48,346	117,055	14th	69,564	182,712	14th	141,153	48,097	198,575
15th	41,251	87,482	15th	59,953	154,385	15th	115,532	44,186	159,718
16th	32,182	72,370	16th	47,992	129,222	16th	98,929	37,130	136,059
17th	40,334	101,632	17th	65,117	148,958	17th	120,750	35,932	156,293
18th	47,528	56,181	18th	49,973	103,732	18th	71,182	37,531	108,713
19th	106,209	47,403	19th	155,354	64,047	19th	71,748	110,246	181,994
20th	25,628	47,627	20th	53,231	61,005	20th	61,120	....	61,120
21st	87,544	32,584	21st	140,721	51,594	21st	42,718	95,214	142,661
22d	120,473	38,988	22d	209,384	....	22d	55,226	133,278	188,504
23d	62,604	95,752	23d	83,926	153,980	23d	114,661	61,272	175,933
24th	120,585	58,755	24th	178,660	96,397	24th	79,461	129,812	209,292
25th	80,775	38,674	25th	145,575	80,395	25th	55,913	93,987	156,773
26th	95,360	50,081	26th	134,596	107,522	26th	67,878	102,028	179,144
27th	48,996	79,815	27th	66,946	125,296	27th	92,650	42,074	134,724
28th	23,926	73,771	28th	37,868	115,303	28th	79,866	20,629	108,042
29th	40,616	76,036	29th	62,871	133,670	29th	91,014	39,321	143,389
30th	54,989	130,604	30th	87,465	216,682	30th	151,284	55,904	211,734
31st	12,674	54,569	31st	22,048	89,363	31st	64,952	....	64,952
32d	23,366	58,530	32d	....	119,144	32d	76,059	....	91,686
33d	16,699	97,779	33d	....	166,801	33d	113,715	....	113,715
34th	17,090	48,734	34th	28,175	82,282	34th	57,459	17,359	74,819
35th	18,094	72,401	35th	23,591	125,949	35th	82,498	....	98,506
36th	50,328	88,198	36th	81,666	151,208	36th	105,323	53,068	166,153
37th	20,154	63,445	37th	31,960	118,823	37th	80,716	....	97,962
38th	23,126	62,600	38th	....	116,851	38th	75,181	24,620	99,801
39th	38,925	52,256	39th	64,832	100,132	39th	72,149	37,384	109,533
40th	92,422	40,265	40th	147,617	69,684	40th	46,418	100,995	151,289
41st	91,326	40,155	41st	181,605	....	41st	54,235	109,761	164,044
42d	98,476	42,090	42d	167,632	78,393	42d	....	129,720	129,720
43d	20,821	45,374	43d	44,004	86,830	43d	52,791	29,069	81,860
44th	76,686	38,021	44th	138,768	78,796	44th	55,275	89,555	149,316
45th	87,101	43,692	45th	153,523	76,967	45th	64,613	99,638	164,251
46th	108,807	60,890	46th	171,318	90,129	46th	71,573	116,176	195,052
47th	24,346	42,501	47th	43,099	65,684	47th	47,134	28,485	75,619
48th	122,884	51,058	48th	189,004	93,525	48th	74,647	120,130	200,527
49th	94,594	....	49th	141,658	79,057	49th	52,227	98,831	156,137
50th	111,095	55,855	50th	169,025	105,590	50th	96,612	118,018	222,102

VOTES CAST FOR REPRESENTATIVES, RESIDENT COMMISSIONER, AND DELEGATES IN 2002, 2004, and 2006—CONTINUED

[The figures, compiled from official statistics obtained by the Clerk of the House, show the votes for the Democratic and Republican nominees, except as otherwise indicated. Figures in the last column, for the 2006 election, may include totals for more candidates than the ones shown. The 2002 congressional districts reflect changes in apportionments resulting from the 2000 census.]

State and district	Vote cast in 2002		State and district	Vote cast in 2004		State and district	Vote cast in 2006		Total vote cast in 2006
	Repub-lican	Demo-crat		Repub-lican	Demo-crat		Demo-crat	Repub-lican	
51st	40,430	59,541	51st	63,526	111,441	51st	78,114	34,931	115,839
52d	118,561	43,526	52d	187,799	74,857	52d	61,208	123,696	191,369
53d	43,891	72,252	53d	63,897	146,449	53d	97,541	43,312	144,387
CO:			CO:			CO:			
1st	49,884	111,718	1st	58,659	177,077	1st	129,446	....	162,271
2d	75,564	123,504	2d	94,160	207,900	2d	157,850	65,481	231,307
3d	143,433	68,160	3d	141,376	153,500	3d	146,488	86,930	237,858
4th	115,359	87,499	4th	155,958	136,812	4th	103,748	109,732	240,613
5th	128,118	45,587	5th	193,333	74,098	5th	83,431	123,264	206,756
6th	158,851	71,327	6th	212,778	139,870	6th	108,007	158,806	270,931
7th	81,789	81,668	7th	135,571	106,026	7th	103,918	79,571	189,172
CT:			CT:			CT:			
1st	66,968	134,698	1st	73,601	198,802	1st	154,539	53,010	207,592
2d	117,434	99,674	2d	166,412	140,536	2d	121,248	121,165	242,413
3d	54,757	121,557	3d	69,160	200,638	3d	150,436	44,386	197,911
4th	113,197	62,491	4th	152,493	138,333	4th	99,450	106,510	209,019
5th	113,626	90,616	5th	168,268	107,438	5th	....	94,824	217,804
DE:			DE:			DE:			
At large	164,605	61,011	At large	245,978	105,716	At large	97,565	143,897	251,694
FL:			FL:			FL:			
1st	152,635	51,972	1st	236,604	72,506	1st	62,340	135,786	198,126
2d	75,275	152,164	2d	125,399	201,577	2d	(2)	....	(2)
3d	60,747	88,462	3d	....	172,833	3d	(2)	....	(2)
4th	171,152	....	4th	256,157	....	4th	61,704	141,759	203,479
5th	121,998	117,758	5th	240,315	124,140	5th	108,959	162,421	271,380
6th	141,570	75,046	6th	211,137	116,680	6th	91,528	136,601	228,129
7th	142,147	96,444	7th	(2)	....	7th	87,584	149,656	237,240
8th	123,497	66,099	8th	172,232	112,343	8th	82,526	95,258	180,444
9th	169,369	67,623	9th	284,035	....	9th	96,978	123,016	220,013
10th	(2)	....	10th	207,175	91,658	10th	67,950	131,488	199,445
11th	....	(2)	11th	....	191,780	11th	97,470	42,454	139,942
12th	(2)	....	12th	179,204	96,965	12th	....	124,452	180,064
13th	139,048	114,739	13th	190,477	153,961	13th	118,940	119,309	238,249
14th	(2)	....	14th	226,662	108,672	14th	83,920	151,615	235,539
15th	146,414	85,433	15th	210,388	111,538	15th	97,834	125,965	223,799
16th	176,171	....	16th	215,563	101,247	16th	115,832	111,415	233,773
17th	....	113,749	17th	....	178,690	17th	90,663	....	90,686
18th	103,512	42,852	18th	143,647	78,281	18th	48,499	79,631	128,132
19th	60,477	156,747	19th	....	(2)	19th	(2)	....	(2)
20th	....	(2)	20th	81,213	191,195	20th	(2)	....	(2)
21st	(2)	....	21st	146,507	....	21st	45,522	66,784	112,306
22d	131,930	83,265	22d	192,581	108,258	22d	108,688	100,663	213,605
23d	27,986	96,347	23d	....	(2)	23d	....	....	(2)
24th	135,576	83,667	24th	(2)	....	24th	89,863	123,795	213,658
25th	81,845	44,757	25th	(2)	....	25th	43,168	60,765	103,933
GA:			GA:			GA:			
1st	103,661	40,026	1st	188,347	....	1st	43,668	94,961	138,629
2d	....	102,925	2d	64,645	129,984	2d	88,662	41,967	130,629
3d	73,866	75,394	3d	80,435	136,273	3d	62,371	130,428	192,799
4th	35,202	118,045	4th	89,509	157,461	4th	106,352	34,778	141,130
5th	....	116,259	5th	....	201,773	5th	122,380	....	122,380
6th	163,525	41,204	6th	267,542	....	6th	55,294	144,958	200,252
7th	138,997	37,124	7th	258,982	....	7th	53,553	130,561	184,114
8th	142,505	39,422	8th	227,524	73,632	8th	80,660	78,908	159,568
9th	123,313	45,974	9th	197,869	68,462	9th	39,240	128,685	167,925
10th	129,242	....	10th	219,136	....	10th	57,032	117,721	174,753
11th	69,427	65,007	11th	120,696	89,591	11th	48,261	118,524	166,785
12th	77,479	62,904	12th	105,132	113,036	12th	71,651	70,787	142,438
13th	47,405	70,011	13th	....	170,657	13th	103,019	45,770	148,789
HI:			HI:			HI:			
1st	45,032	131,673	1st	69,371	128,567	1st	112,904	49,890	162,794
2d	71,661	100,671	2d	79,072	133,317	2d	106,906	68,244	175,150
ID:			ID:			ID:			
1st	120,743	80,269	1st	207,662	90,927	1st	103,935	115,843	231,974
2d	135,605	57,769	2d	193,704	80,133	2d	73,441	132,262	213,332
IL:			IL:			IL:			
1st	29,776	149,068	1st	37,840	212,109	1st	146,623	27,804	174,427
2d	32,567	151,443	2d	....	207,535	2d	146,347	20,395	172,490
3d	....	156,042	3d	57,845	167,034	3d	127,768	37,954	165,722
4th	12,778	67,339	4th	15,536	104,761	4th	69,910	11,532	81,442
5th	46,008	106,514	5th	49,530	158,400	5th	114,319	32,250	146,581
6th	113,174	60,698	6th	139,627	110,470	6th	86,572	91,382	177,957
7th	25,280	137,933	7th	35,603	221,133	7th	143,071	21,939	165,011
8th	95,275	70,626	8th	130,601	139,792	8th	93,355	80,720	183,394
9th	45,307	118,642	9th	56,135	175,282	9th	122,852	41,858	164,713

VOTES CAST FOR REPRESENTATIVES, RESIDENT COMMISSIONER, AND DELEGATES IN 2002, 2004, and 2006—CONTINUED

[The figures, compiled from official statistics obtained by the Clerk of the House, show the votes for the Democratic and Republican nominees, except as otherwise indicated. Figures in the last column, for the 2006 election, may include totals for more candidates than the ones shown. The 2002 congressional districts reflect changes in apportionments resulting from the 2000 census.]

State and district	Vote cast in 2002		State and district	Vote cast in 2004		State and district	Vote cast in 2006		Total vote cast in 2006
	Republican	Democrat		Republican	Democrat		Democrat	Republican	
10th	128,611	58,300	10th	177,493	99,218	10th	94,278	107,929	202,208
11th	124,192	68,893	11th	173,057	121,903	11th	88,846	109,009	197,855
12th	58,440	131,580	12th	82,677	198,962	12th	157,284	....	157,291
13th	139,546	59,069	13th	200,472	107,836	13th	85,507	119,720	205,234
14th	135,198	47,165	14th	191,618	87,590	14th	79,274	117,870	197,144
15th	134,650	64,131	15th	178,114	113,625	15th	86,025	116,810	202,835
16th	133,339	55,488	16th	204,350	91,452	16th	63,462	125,508	197,493
17th	76,519	127,093	17th	111,680	172,320	17th	115,025	86,161	201,186
18th	192,567	....	18th	216,047	91,548	18th	73,052	150,194	223,246
19th	133,956	110,517	19th	213,451	94,303	19th	92,861	143,491	236,352
IN:			IN:			IN:			
1st	41,909	90,443	1st	82,858	178,406	1st	104,195	40,146	149,607
2d	95,081	86,253	2d	140,496	115,513	2d	103,561	88,300	191,861
3d	92,566	50,509	3d	171,389	76,232	3d	80,357	95,421	175,778
4th	112,760	41,314	4th	190,445	77,574	4th	66,986	111,057	178,043
5th	129,442	45,283	5th	228,718	82,637	5th	64,362	133,118	204,929
6th	118,436	63,871	6th	182,529	85,123	6th	76,812	115,266	192,078
7th	64,379	77,478	7th	97,491	121,303	7th	74,750	64,304	139,054
8th	98,952	88,763	8th	145,576	121,522	8th	131,019	83,704	214,723
9th	87,169	96,654	9th	142,197	140,772	9th	110,454	100,469	220,849
IA:			IA:			IA:			
1st	112,280	83,779	1st	159,993	125,490	1st	114,322	89,729	207,478
2d	108,130	94,767	2d	176,684	117,405	2d	107,683	101,707	209,390
3d	97,285	115,367	3d	136,099	168,007	3d	115,769	103,722	223,082
4th	115,430	90,784	4th	181,294	116,121	4th	90,982	121,650	212,632
5th	113,257	68,853	5th	168,583	97,597	5th	64,181	105,580	180,399
KS:			KS:			KS:			
1st	189,976	....	1st	239,776	....	1st	39,781	156,728	199,378
2d	127,477	79,160	2d	165,325	121,532	2d	114,139	106,329	225,562
3d	102,882	110,095	3d	145,542	184,050	3d	153,105	79,824	236,980
4th	115,691	70,656	4th	173,151	81,388	4th	62,166	116,386	183,207
KY:			KY:			KY:			
1st	117,600	62,617	1st	175,972	85,229	1st	83,865	123,618	207,483
2d	122,773	51,431	2d	185,394	87,585	2d	95,415	118,548	213,963
3d	118,228	110,846	3d	197,736	124,040	3d	122,489	116,568	241,965
4th	81,651	87,776	4th	160,982	129,876	4th	88,822	105,845	204,767
5th	137,986	38,254	5th	177,579	....	5th	52,367	147,201	199,568
6th	115,622	....	6th	119,716	175,355	6th	158,765	....	185,780
LA:			LA:			LA:			
1st	174,614	....	1st	233,683	54,214	1st	15,944	130,508	148,128
2d	15,440	122,927	2d	46,097	173,510	2d	93,211	13,928	107,543
3d	130,323	....	3d	57,042	57,611	3d	79,213	54,950	136,331
4th	114,649	42,340	4th	(3)	....	4th	40,545	93,727	134,272
5th	85,744	86,718	5th	179,466	58,591	5th	33,233	78,211	114,582
6th	146,932	....	6th	189,106	72,763	6th	....	94,658	114,306
7th	....	138,659	7th	75,039	61,493	7th	47,133	113,720	160,853
ME:			ME:			ME:			
1st	97,931	172,646	1st	147,663	219,077	1st	170,949	88,009	280,987
2d	107,849	116,868	2d	135,547	199,303	2d	179,772	75,156	254,928
MD:			MD:			MD:			
1st	192,004	57,986	1st	245,149	77,872	1st	83,738	185,177	269,147
2d	88,954	105,718	2d	75,812	164,751	2d	135,818	60,195	196,228
3d	75,721	145,589	3d	97,008	182,066	3d	150,142	79,174	234,486
4th	34,890	131,644	4th	52,907	196,809	4th	141,897	32,792	175,903
5th	60,758	137,903	5th	87,189	204,867	5th	168,114	....	203,323
6th	147,825	75,575	6th	206,076	90,108	6th	92,030	141,200	239,453
7th	49,172	137,047	7th	60,102	179,189	7th	158,830	....	161,977
8th	103,587	112,788	8th	71,989	215,129	8th	168,872	48,324	220,685
MA:			MA:			MA:			
1st	66,061	137,841	1st	....	229,465	1st	158,057	....	219,932
2d	....	153,387	2d	....	217,682	2d	164,939	....	214,939
3d	....	155,697	3d	80,197	192,036	3d	166,973	....	215,101
4th	....	166,125	4th	....	219,260	4th	176,513	....	226,914
5th	69,337	122,562	5th	88,232	179,652	5th	159,120	....	216,832
6th	75,462	162,900	6th	91,597	213,458	6th	168,056	72,997	253,284
7th	....	170,968	7th	60,334	202,399	7th	171,902	....	226,130
8th	....	111,861	8th	....	165,852	8th	125,515	....	159,425
9th	....	168,055	9th	....	218,167	9th	169,420	47,114	234,505
10th	79,624	179,238	10th	114,879	222,013	10th	171,812	78,439	276,773
MI:			MI:			MI:			
1st	69,254	150,701	1st	105,706	211,571	1st	180,448	72,753	259,927
2d	156,937	61,749	2d	225,343	94,040	2d	86,950	183,006	275,394
3d	153,131	61,987	3d	214,465	101,395	3d	93,846	171,212	271,352
4th	149,090	65,950	4th	205,274	110,885	4th	100,260	160,041	264,245
5th	....	158,709	5th	96,934	208,163	5th	176,171	60,967	241,691

VOTES CAST FOR REPRESENTATIVES, RESIDENT COMMISSIONER, AND DELEGATES IN 2002, 2004, and 2006—CONTINUED

[The figures, compiled from official statistics obtained by the Clerk of the House, show the votes for the Democratic and Republican nominees, except as otherwise indicated. Figures in the last column, for the 2006 election, may include totals for more candidates than the ones shown. The 2002 congressional districts reflect changes in apportionments resulting from the 2000 census.]

State and district	Vote cast in 2002		State and district	Vote cast in 2004		State and district	Vote cast in 2006		Total vote cast in 2006
	Repub-lican	Demo-crat		Repub-lican	Demo-crat		Demo-crat	Repub-lican	
6th	126,936	53,793	6th	197,425	97,978	6th	88,978	142,125	234,583
7th	121,142	78,412	7th	176,053	109,527	7th	112,665	122,348	245,026
8th	156,525	70,920	8th	207,925	125,619	8th	122,107	157,237	284,471
9th	141,102	96,856	9th	199,210	134,764	9th	127,620	142,390	276,180
10th	137,339	77,053	10th	227,720	98,029	10th	84,689	179,072	270,421
11th	126,050	87,402	11th	186,431	134,301	11th	114,248	143,658	265,784
12th	61,502	140,970	12th	88,256	210,827	12th	168,494	62,689	238,039
13th	....	120,859	13th	40,935	173,246	13th	126,308	....	126,323
14th	26,544	145,285	14th	35,089	213,681	14th	158,755	27,367	186,122
15th	48,626	136,518	15th	81,828	218,409	15th	181,946	....	206,868
MN:			MN:			MN:			
1st	163,570	92,165	1st	193,132	115,088	1st	141,556	126,486	268,421
2d	152,970	121,121	2d	206,313	147,527	2d	116,343	163,269	290,540
3d	213,334	82,575	3d	231,871	126,665	3d	99,588	184,333	284,244
4th	89,705	164,597	4th	105,467	182,387	4th	172,096	74,797	247,466
5th	66,271	171,572	5th	76,600	218,434	5th	136,060	52,263	244,905
6th	164,747	100,738	6th	203,669	173,309	6th	127,144	151,248	302,188
7th	90,342	170,234	7th	106,349	207,628	7th	179,164	74,557	257,194
8th	88,673	194,909	8th	112,693	228,586	8th	180,670	97,683	284,016
MS:			MS:			MS:			
1st	95,404	32,318	1st	219,328	....	1st	49,174	95,098	144,272
2d	69,711	89,913	2d	107,647	154,626	2d	100,160	55,672	155,832
3d	139,329	76,184	3d	234,874	....	3d	....	125,421	161,480
4th	34,373	121,742	4th	96,740	179,979	4th	110,996	28,117	139,113
MO:			MO:			MO:			
1st	51,755	133,946	1st	64,791	213,658	1st	141,574	47,893	194,235
2d	167,057	77,223	2d	228,725	115,366	2d	105,242	176,452	287,617
3d	80,551	122,181	3d	125,422	146,894	3d	145,219	70,189	221,448
4th	64,451	142,204	4th	93,334	190,800	4th	159,303	69,254	235,525
5th	60,245	122,645	5th	123,431	161,727	5th	136,149	68,456	211,919
6th	131,151	73,202	6th	196,516	106,987	6th	87,477	150,882	244,795
7th	149,519	45,964	7th	210,080	84,356	7th	72,592	160,942	241,123
8th	135,144	50,686	8th	194,039	71,543	8th	57,557	156,164	217,989
9th	146,032	61,126	9th	193,429	101,343	9th	87,145	149,114	242,671
MT:			MT:			MT:			
At large ..	214,100	108,233	At large ..	286,076	145,606	At large ..	158,916	239,124	406,125
NE:			NE:			NE:			
1st	133,013	....	1st	143,756	113,971	1st	86,360	121,015	207,375
2d	89,917	46,843	2d	152,608	90,292	2d	82,504	99,475	181,979
3d	163,939	....	3d	218,751	26,434	3d	93,046	113,687	206,733
NV:			NV:			NV:			
1st	51,148	64,312	1st	63,005	133,569	1st	85,025	40,917	131,124
2d	149,574	40,189	2d	195,466	79,978	2d	104,593	117,168	232,724
3d	100,378	66,659	3d	162,240	120,365	3d	98,261	102,232	210,979
NH:			NH:			NH:			
1st	128,993	85,426	1st	204,836	118,226	1st	100,691	95,527	196,377
2d	125,804	90,479	2d	191,188	125,280	2d	108,743	94,088	206,292
NJ:			NJ:			NJ:			
1st	....	121,846	1st	66,109	201,163	1st	140,110	....	140,110
2d	116,834	47,735	2d	172,779	86,792	2d	64,277	111,245	180,573
3d	123,375	64,364	3d	195,938	107,034	3d	86,113	122,559	209,851
4th	115,293	55,967	4th	192,671	92,826	4th	62,905	124,482	189,540
5th	118,881	76,504	5th	171,220	122,259	5th	89,503	112,142	204,242
6th	42,479	91,379	6th	70,942	153,981	6th	98,615	43,539	143,773
7th	106,055	74,879	7th	162,597	119,081	7th	95,454	98,399	199,075
8th	40,318	88,101	8th	62,747	152,001	8th	97,568	39,053	137,639
9th	42,088	97,108	9th	68,564	146,038	9th	105,853	40,879	148,095
10th	15,913	86,433	10th	....	155,697	10th	90,264	....	90,264
11th	132,938	48,477	11th	200,915	91,811	11th	74,414	126,085	203,071
12th	62,938	104,806	12th	115,014	171,691	12th	125,468	65,509	190,977
13th	16,852	72,605	13th	35,288	121,018	13th	77,238	19,284	99,630
NM:			NM:			NM:			
1st	95,711	77,234	1st	147,372	123,339	1st	105,125	105,986	211,111
2d	79,631	61,916	2d	130,498	86,292	2d	63,119	92,620	155,874
3d	....	122,921	3d	79,935	175,269	3d	144,880	49,219	194,099
NY:			NY:			NY:			
1st	64,999	81,325	1st	110,786	140,878	1st	92,546	54,044	179,113
2d	48,239	75,845	2d	72,953	147,197	2d	94,100	37,671	163,589
3d	98,874	46,022	3d	151,323	100,737	3d	76,169	86,918	192,919
4th	61,473	85,496	4th	85,505	148,615	4th	93,041	48,121	170,640
5th	....	68,773	5th	43,002	114,132	5th	70,033	....	118,527
6th	....	68,718	6th	....	125,127	6th	69,405	....	99,110
7th	16,460	48,983	7th	21,843	100,382	7th	60,266	10,402	99,290
8th	18,623	71,996	8th	35,177	154,098	8th	96,115	17,413	142,528
9th	27,882	57,104	9th	39,648	108,577	9th	67,040	....	108,063

VOTES CAST FOR REPRESENTATIVES, RESIDENT COMMISSIONER, AND DELEGATES IN 2002, 2004, and 2006—CONTINUED

[The figures, compiled from official statistics obtained by the Clerk of the House, show the votes for the Democratic and Republican nominees, except as otherwise indicated. Figures in the last column, for the 2006 election, may include totals for more candidates than the ones shown. The 2002 congressional districts reflect changes in apportionments resulting from the 2000 census.]

State and district	Vote cast in 2002		State and district	Vote cast in 2004		State and district	Vote cast in 2006		Total vote cast in 2006
	Republican	Democrat		Republican	Democrat		Democrat	Republican	
10th	....	72,313	10th	11,099	130,265	10th	72,171	4,666	103,030
11th	9,250	67,967	11th	....	134,175	11th	75,520	6,776	113,812
12th	....	43,809	12th	15,697	100,402	12th	55,674	6,143	84,346
13th	62,520	27,304	13th	102,713	72,180	13th	42,229	49,818	116,051
14th	30,053	85,029	14th	41,936	175,886	14th	107,095	....	153,883
15th	8,790	77,036	15th	12,355	153,099	15th	93,857	6,592	129,189
16th	3,916	48,411	16th	4,917	106,739	16th	53,179	2,045	73,362
17th	35,389	73,569	17th	40,524	135,344	17th	88,714	22,608	141,955
18th	....	95,396	18th	73,975	159,072	18th	119,041	45,472	199,273
19th	102,848	44,967	19th	152,051	87,429	19th	100,119	79,545	209,491
20th	125,335	45,878	20th	163,343	96,630	20th	116,416	94,093	250,301
21st	53,525	128,584	21st	80,121	167,247	21st	139,997	46,752	231,910
22d	52,499	92,336	22d	81,881	148,588	22d	104,423	....	195,645
23d	110,042	....	23d	136,222	66,448	23d	58,859	89,482	184,944
24th	108,017	....	24th	128,493	85,140	24th	96,093	83,228	214,965
25th	113,914	53,290	25th	155,163	....	25th	100,605	[4]91,187	227,311
26th	105,807	41,140	26th	137,425	116,484	26th	85,145	94,157	223,964
27th	105,946	45,060	27th	125,275	127,267	27th	116,935	36,614	176,641
28th	45,125	94,209	28th	48,981	150,431	28th	98,382	33,361	166,565
29th	116,245	37,128	29th	136,883	104,555	29th	94,609	[4]91,383	216,780
NC:			NC:			NC:			
1st	50,907	93,157	1st	77,508	137,667	1st	82,510	....	82,510
2d	50,965	100,121	2d	87,811	145,079	2d	85,993	43,271	129,264
3d	131,448	....	3d	171,863	71,227	3d	45,458	99,519	144,977
4th	78,095	132,185	4th	121,717	217,441	4th	127,340	68,599	195,939
5th	137,879	58,558	5th	167,546	117,271	5th	72,061	96,138	168,199
6th	151,430	....	6th	207,470	76,153	6th	44,661	108,433	153,094
7th	45,537	118,543	7th	66,084	180,382	7th	101,787	38,033	139,820
8th	80,298	66,819	8th	125,070	100,101	8th	60,597	60,926	121,523
9th	140,095	49,974	9th	210,783	89,318	9th	53,437	106,206	159,643
10th	102,768	65,587	10th	157,884	88,233	10th	58,214	94,179	152,393
11th	112,335	86,664	11th	159,709	131,188	11th	124,972	107,342	232,314
12th	49,588	98,821	12th	76,898	154,908	12th	71,345	35,127	106,472
13th	77,688	100,287	13th	112,788	160,896	13th	98,540	56,120	154,660
ND:			ND:			ND:			
At large	109,957	121,073	At large	125,684	185,130	At large	142,934	74,687	217,621
OH:			OH:			OH:			
1st	110,760	60,168	1st	173,430	116,235	1st	96,584	105,680	202,264
2d	139,218	48,785	2d	227,102	89,598	2d	117,595	120,112	238,081
3d	111,630	78,307	3d	197,290	119,448	3d	90,650	127,978	218,628
4th	120,001	57,726	4th	167,807	118,538	4th	86,678	129,958	216,636
5th	126,286	51,872	5th	196,649	96,656	5th	98,544	129,813	228,357
6th	77,643	113,972	6th	....	223,842	6th	135,628	82,848	218,476
7th	113,252	45,568	7th	186,534	100,617	7th	89,579	137,899	227,478
8th	119,947	49,444	8th	201,675	90,574	8th	77,640	136,863	214,503
9th	46,481	132,236	9th	95,983	205,149	9th	153,880	55,119	208,999
10th	41,778	129,997	10th	96,463	172,406	10th	138,393	69,996	208,389
11th	36,146	116,590	11th	....	222,371	11th	146,799	29,125	175,924
12th	116,982	64,707	12th	198,912	122,109	12th	108,746	145,943	254,689
13th	55,357	123,025	13th	97,090	201,004	13th	135,639	85,922	221,561
14th	134,413	51,846	14th	201,652	119,714	14th	97,753	144,069	250,322
15th	108,193	54,286	15th	166,520	110,915	15th	109,659	110,714	220,567
16th	129,734	58,644	16th	202,544	101,817	16th	97,955	137,167	235,122
17th	62,188	94,441	17th	62,871	212,800	17th	170,369	41,925	212,294
18th	125,546	....	18th	177,600	90,820	18th	129,646	79,259	208,905
OK:			OK:			OK:			
1st	119,566	90,649	1st	187,145	116,731	1st	56,724	116,920	183,729
2d	51,234	146,748	2d	92,963	179,579	2d	122,347	45,861	168,208
3d	148,206	....	3d	215,510	....	3d	61,749	128,042	189,791
4th	106,452	91,322	4th	198,985	....	4th	64,775	118,266	183,041
5th	121,374	63,208	5th	180,430	92,719	5th	67,293	108,936	180,425
OR:			OR:			OR:			
1st	80,917	149,215	1st	135,164	203,771	1st	169,409	90,904	269,627
2d	181,295	64,991	2d	248,461	88,914	2d	82,484	181,529	271,719
3d	62,821	156,851	3d	82,045	245,559	3d	186,380	59,529	253,610
4th	90,523	168,150	4th	140,882	228,611	4th	180,607	109,105	290,244
5th	113,441	137,713	5th	154,993	184,833	5th	146,973	116,424	272,234
PA:			PA:			PA:			
1st	17,444	121,076	1st	33,266	214,462	1st	137,987	....	137,999
2d	20,988	150,623	2d	34,411	253,226	2d	165,867	17,291	187,283
3d	116,763	....	3d	166,580	110,684	3d	85,110	108,525	202,518
4th	130,534	71,674	4th	204,329	116,303	4th	131,847	122,049	254,084
5th	124,942	....	5th	192,852	....	5th	76,456	115,126	191,727
6th	103,648	98,128	6th	160,348	153,977	6th	117,892	121,047	238,939

VOTES CAST FOR REPRESENTATIVES, RESIDENT COMMISSIONER, AND DELEGATES IN 2002, 2004, and 2006—CONTINUED

[The figures, compiled from official statistics obtained by the Clerk of the House, show the votes for the Democratic and Republican nominees, except as otherwise indicated. Figures in the last column, for the 2006 election, may include totals for more candidates than the ones shown. The 2002 congressional districts reflect changes in apportionments resulting from the 2000 census.]

State and district	Vote cast in 2002		State and district	Vote cast in 2004		State and district	Vote cast in 2006		Total vote cast in 2006
	Republican	Democrat		Republican	Democrat		Democrat	Republican	
7th	146,296	75,055	7th	196,556	134,932	7th	147,898	114,426	262,434
8th	127,475	76,178	8th	183,229	143,427	8th	125,656	124,138	249,817
9th	124,184	50,558	9th	184,320	80,787	9th	79,610	121,069	200,820
10th	152,017	....	10th	191,967	....	10th	110,115	97,862	208,173
11th	71,543	93,758	11th	....	171,147	11th	134,340	51,033	185,413
12th	44,818	124,201	12th	....	204,504	12th	123,472	79,612	203,163
13th	100,295	107,945	13th	127,205	171,763	13th	147,368	75,492	222,860
14th	....	123,323	14th	....	220,139	14th	161,075	....	179,401
15th	98,493	73,212	15th	170,634	114,646	15th	86,186	106,153	198,173
16th	119,046	....	16th	183,620	98,410	16th	80,915	115,741	204,669
17th	97,802	103,483	17th	113,592	172,412	17th	137,253	75,455	212,777
18th	119,885	79,451	18th	197,894	117,420	18th	105,419	144,632	250,240
19th	143,097	....	19th	224,274	....	19th	74,625	142,512	222,898
RI:			RI:			RI:			
1st	59,370	95,286	1st	69,819	124,923	1st	124,634	41,836	180,104
2d	37,767	129,390	2d	43,139	154,392	2d	140,315	....	193,044
SC:			SC:			SC:			
1st	127,562	....	1st	186,448	....	1st	....	115,766	193,375
2d	144,149	....	2d	181,862	93,249	2d	76,090	127,811	204,052
3d	119,644	55,743	3d	191,052	....	3d	....	111,882	177,988
4th	122,422	51,462	4th	188,795	78,376	4th	57,490	115,553	179,931
5th	....	121,912	5th	89,568	152,867	5th	99,669	75,422	175,154
6th	55,760	116,586	6th	75,443	161,987	6th	100,213	53,181	155,706
SD:			SD:			SD:			
At large	180,023	153,551	At large	178,823	207,837	At large	230,468	97,864	333,562
TN:			TN:			TN:			
1st	127,300	....	1st	172,543	56,361	1st	65,538	108,336	177,278
2d	146,887	37,035	2d	215,795	52,155	2d	45,025	157,095	202,120
3d	112,254	58,824	3d	166,154	84,295	3d	68,324	130,791	199,115
4th	85,680	95,989	4th	109,993	138,459	4th	123,666	62,449	186,115
5th	56,825	108,903	5th	74,978	168,970	5th	122,919	49,702	178,142
6th	57,397	117,119	6th	87,523	167,448	6th	129,069	60,392	192,380
7th	138,314	51,790	7th	232,404	....	7th	73,369	152,288	230,582
8th	45,853	117,811	8th	59,853	173,623	8th	129,610	47,492	177,108
9th	....	120,904	9th	41,578	190,648	9th	103,341	31,002	172,586
TX:			TX:			TX:			
1st	66,654	86,384	1st	157,068	96,281	1st	46,303	104,099	153,070
2d	53,656	85,492	2d	139,951	108,156	2d	45,080	90,490	137,865
3d	113,974	37,503	3d	180,099	....	3d	49,529	88,690	141,881
4th	67,939	97,304	4th	182,866	81,585	4th	55,278	106,495	165,269
5th	81,439	56,330	5th	148,816	75,911	5th	50,983	88,478	143,252
6th	115,396	45,404	6th	168,767	83,609	6th	56,369	91,927	152,036
7th	96,795	....	7th	175,440	91,126	7th	64,514	99,318	167,785
8th	140,575	....	8th	179,599	77,324	8th	51,393	105,665	157,058
9th	59,635	86,710	9th	42,132	114,462	9th	60,253	....	60,253
10th	....	114,428	10th	182,113	....	10th	71,415	97,726	176,755
11th	68,236	74,678	11th	177,291	50,339	11th	....	107,268	107,268
12th	121,208	....	12th	173,222	66,316	12th	45,676	98,371	146,935
13th	119,401	31,218	13th	189,448	....	13th	33,460	10,107	145,396
14th	102,905	48,224	14th	173,668	....	14th	62,429	94,380	156,809
15th	....	66,311	15th	67,917	96,089	15th	43,236	26,751	69,987
16th	....	72,383	16th	49,972	108,577	16th	61,116	....	77,688
17th	77,622	84,136	17th	116,049	125,309	17th	92,478	64,142	159,124
18th	27,980	99,161	18th	....	136,018	18th	65,936	16,448	86,051
19th	117,092	....	19th	136,459	93,531	19th	41,676	94,785	140,007
20th	....	68,685	20th	54,976	112,480	20th	68,348	....	78,245
21st	161,836	56,206	21st	209,774	121,129	21st	68,312	122,486	203,782
22d	100,499	55,716	22d	150,386	112,034	22d	76,775	....	148,239
23d	77,573	71,067	23d	170,716	72,480	23d	38,256	32,217	70,473
24th	38,332	73,002	24th	154,435	82,599	24th	52,075	83,835	140,138
25th	50,041	63,590	25th	49,252	108,309	25th	109,911	42,975	163,424
26th	123,195	37,485	26th	180,519	89,809	26th	58,271	94,219	156,483
27th	41,004	68,559	27th	61,955	112,081	27th	62,058	42,538	109,314
28th	26,973	71,393	28th	69,538	106,323	28th	68,372	....	68,372
29th	....	55,760	29th	....	78,256	29th	37,174	12,347	50,550
30th	28,981	88,980	30th	....	144,513	30th	81,348	17,850	101,448
31st	111,556	44,183	31st	160,247	80,292	31st	60,293	90,869	155,383
32d	100,226	44,886	32d	109,859	89,030	32d	52,269	71,461	126,652
UT:			UT:			UT:			
1st	109,265	66,104	1st	199,615	85,630	1st	57,922	112,546	178,474
2d	109,123	110,764	2d	147,778	187,250	2d	133,231	84,234	225,818
3d	103,598	44,533	3d	173,010	88,748	3d	53,330	95,455	165,398
VT:			VT:			VT:			
At large	[5] 72,813	....	At large	[6] 74,271	21,684	At large	139,815	117,023	262,726
VA:			VA:			VA:			
1st	113,168	....	1st	225,071	....	1st	81,083	143,889	228,534

VOTES CAST FOR REPRESENTATIVES, RESIDENT COMMISSIONER, AND DELEGATES IN 2002, 2004, and 2006—CONTINUED

[The figures, compiled from official statistics obtained by the Clerk of the House, show the votes for the Democratic and Republican nominees, except as otherwise indicated. Figures in the last column, for the 2006 election, may include totals for more candidates than the ones shown. The 2002 congressional districts reflect changes in apportionments resulting from the 2000 census.]

State and district	Vote cast in 2002		State and district	Vote cast in 2004		State and district	Vote cast in 2006		Total vote cast in 2006
	Repub-lican	Demo-crat		Repub-lican	Demo-crat		Demo-crat	Repub-lican	
2d	104,081	....	2d	132,946	108,180	2d	83,901	88,777	173,159
3d	....	87,521	3d	70,194	159,373	3d	133,546	....	138,994
4th	108,733	....	4th	182,444	100,413	4th	....	150,967	198,340
5th	95,360	54,805	5th	172,431	98,237	5th	84,682	125,370	212,079
6th	105,530	....	6th	206,560	....	6th	....	153,187	203,995
7th	113,658	49,854	7th	230,765		7th	88,206	163,706	256,397
8th	64,121	102,759	8th	106,231	171,986	8th	144,700	66,639	217,909
9th	....	100,075	9th	98,499	150,039	9th	129,705	61,574	191,415
10th	115,917	45,464	10th	205,982	116,654	10th	98,769	138,213	241,134
11th	135,379	....	11th	186,299	118,305	11th	102,511	130,468	235,280
WA:			WA:			WA:			
1st	84,696	114,087	1st	117,850	204,121	1st	163,832	78,105	241,937
2d	92,528	101,219	2d	106,333	202,383	2d	157,064	87,730	244,794
3d	74,065	119,264	3d	119,027	193,626	3d	147,065	85,915	232,980
4th	108,257	53,572	4th	154,627	92,486	4th	77,054	115,246	192,300
5th	126,757	65,146	5th	179,600	121,333	5th	104,357	134,967	239,324
6th	61,584	126,116	6th	91,228	202,919	6th	158,202	65,883	224,085
7th	46,256	156,300	7th	65,226	272,302	7th	195,462	38,715	246,133
8th	121,633	75,931	8th	173,298	157,148	8th	122,021	129,362	251,383
9th	63,146	95,805	9th	88,304	162,433	9th	119,038	62,082	181,120
WV:			WV:			WV:			
1st	....	110,941	1st	79,196	166,583	1st	100,939	55,963	157,000
2d	98,276	65,400	2d	147,676	106,131	2d	70,470	94,110	164,580
3d	37,229	87,783	3d	76,170	142,682	3d	92,413	40,820	133,233
WI:			WI:			WI:			
1st	140,176	63,895	1st	233,372	116,250	1st	95,761	161,320	257,596
2d	83,694	163,313	2d	145,810	251,637	2d	191,414	113,015	304,688
3d	69,955	131,038	3d	157,866	204,856	3d	163,322	88,523	252,087
4th	....	122,031	4th	85,928	212,382	4th	136,735	54,486	191,742
5th	191,224	....	5th	271,153	129,384	5th	112,451	194,669	315,180
6th	169,834	....	6th	238,620	107,209	6th	....	201,367	203,557
7th	81,518	146,364	7th	....	241,306	7th	161,903	91,069	260,428
8th	152,745	50,284	8th	248,070	105,513	8th	141,570	135,622	278,135
WY:			WY:			WY:			
At large	110,229	65,961	At large	132,107	99,989	At large	92,324	93,336	196,215

[Table continues on next page]

VOTES CAST FOR REPRESENTATIVES, RESIDENT COMMISSIONER, AND DELEGATES IN 2002, 2004, and 2006—CONTINUED

[The figures, compiled from official statistics obtained by the Clerk of the House, show the votes for the Democratic and Republican nominees, except as otherwise indicated. Figures in the last column, for the 2006 election, may include totals for more candidates than the ones shown.]

Commonwealth of Puerto Rico	Vote 2002		2004		2006		Total vote cast in 2006
	New Progressive	Popular Democrat	New Progressive	Popular Democrat	Popular Democrat	New Progressive	
Resident Commissioner (4-year term)	....	....	956,828	945,691	....	....	....

District of Columbia	Vote 2002		2004		2006		Total vote cast in 2006
	Republican	Democrat	Republican	Democrat	Democrat	Republican	
Delegate	....	119,268	18,296	202,027	111,726	....	114,777

Guam	Vote 2002		2004		2006		Total vote cast in 2006
	Republican	Democrat	Republican	Democrat	Democrat	Republican	
Delegate	14,836	27,081	....	31,051	32,677	....	33,878

Virgin Islands	Vote 2002		2004		2006		Total vote cast in 2006
	Independent	Democrat	Republican	Democrat	Democrat	Independent	
Delegate	20,414	4,286	1,512	17,379	19,593	4,447	24,047

American Samoa	Vote 2002		2004		2006		Total vote cast in 2006
	Republican	Democrat	Republican	Democrat	Democrat	Republican	
Delegate	....	[7] 4,959	5,472	6,656	5,195	4,493	11,033

[1] According to Arkansas law, it is not required to tabulate votes for unopposed candidates.
[2] Under Florida law, the names of those with no opposition are not printed on the ballot.
[3] Under Louisiana law, the names of those with no opposition are not printed on the ballot.
[4] Numbers do not include votes cast for Republican candidate as nominee of other political parties.
[5] The Independent candidate was elected with 144,880 votes.
[6] The Independent candidate was elected with 186,540 votes.
[7] A runoff election was held on November 19, 2002.

SESSIONS OF CONGRESS, 1st–110th CONGRESSES, 1789–2007

[Closing date for this table was July 25, 2007.]

MEETING DATES OF CONGRESS: Pursuant to a resolution of the Confederation Congress in 1788, the Constitution went into effect on March 4, 1789. From then until the 20th amendment took effect in January 1934, the term of each Congress began on March 4th of each odd-numbered year; however, Article I, section 4, of the Constitution provided that "The Congress shall assemble at least once in every Year, and such Meeting shall be on the first Monday in December, unless they shall by law appoint a different day." The Congress therefore convened regularly on the first Monday in December until the 20th amendment became effective, which changed the beginning of Congress's term as well as its convening date to January 3rd. So prior to 1934, a new Congress typically would not convene for regular business until 13 months after being elected. One effect of this was that the last session of each Congress was a "lame duck" session. After the 20th amendment, the time from the election to the beginning of Congress's term as well as when it convened was reduced to two months. Recognizing that the need might exist for Congress to meet at times other than the regularly scheduled convening date, Article II, section 3 of the Constitution provides that the President "may, on extraordinary occasions, convene both Houses, or either of them"; hence these sessions occur only if convened by Presidential proclamation. Except as noted, these are separately numbered sessions of a Congress, and are marked by an E in the session column of the table. Until the 20th amendment was adopted, there were also times when special sessions of the Senate were convened, principally for confirming Cabinet and other executive nominations, and occasionally for the ratification of treaties or other executive business. These Senate sessions were also called by Presidential proclamation (typically by the outgoing President, although on occasion by incumbents as well) and are marked by an S in the session column. MEETING PLACES OF CONGRESS: Congress met for the first and second sessions of the First Congress (1789 and 1790) in New York City. From the third session of the First Congress through the first session of the Sixth Congress (1790 to 1800), Philadelphia was the meeting place. Congress has convened in Washington since the second session of the Sixth Congress (1800).

Congress	Session	Convening Date	Adjournment Date	Length in days [1]	Recesses [2]		President pro tempore of the Senate [3]	Speaker of the House of Representatives
					Senate	House of Representatives		
1st	1	Mar. 4, 1789	Sept. 29, 1789	210			John Langdon, of New Hampshire	Frederick A.C. Muhlenberg, of Pennsylvania.
	2	Jan. 4, 1790	Aug. 12, 1790	221			......do.	
	3	Dec. 6, 1790	Mar. 3, 1791	88			......do.	
2d	S	Mar. 4, 1791	Mar. 4, 1791	1			......do.	
	1	Oct. 24, 1791	May 8, 1792	197			Richard Henry Lee, of Virginia	Jonathan Trumbull, of Connecticut.
	2	Nov. 5, 1792	Mar. 2, 1793	119			John Langdon, of New Hampshire.	
3d	S	Mar. 4, 1793	Mar. 4, 1793	1			......do.	
	1	Dec. 2, 1793	June 9, 1794	190			John Langdon, of New Hampshire; Ralph Izard, of South Carolina.	Frederick A.C. Muhlenberg, of Pennsylvania.
	2	Nov. 3, 1794	Mar. 3, 1795	121			Henry Tazewell, of Virginia.	
4th	S	June 8, 1795	June 26, 1795	19			......do.	
	1	Dec. 7, 1795	June 1, 1796	177			Henry Tazewell, of Virginia; Samuel Livermore, of New Hampshire.	Jonathan Dayton, of New Jersey.
	2	Dec. 5, 1796	Mar. 3, 1797	89			William Bingham, of Pennsylvania.	
5th	S	Mar. 4, 1797	Mar. 4, 1797	1				
	1–E	May 15, 1797	July 10, 1797	57			William Bradford, of Rhode Island	Do.
	S	July 17, 1798	July 19, 1798	3				
	2	Nov. 13, 1797	July 16, 1798	246			Jacob Read, of South Carolina; Theodore Sedgwick, of Massachusetts.	
	3	Dec. 3, 1798	Mar. 3, 1799	91			John Laurance, of New York; James Ross, of Pennsylvania.	
6th	1	Dec. 2, 1799	May 14, 1800	164			Samuel Livermore, of New Hampshire; Uriah Tracy, of Connecticut.	Theodore Sedgwick, of Massachusetts.
	2	Nov. 17, 1800	Mar. 3, 1801	107	Dec. 23–Dec. 30, 1800	Dec. 23–Dec. 30, 1800	John E. Howard, of Maryland; James Hillhouse, of Connecticut.	
7th	S	Mar. 4, 1801	Mar. 5, 1801	2				
	1	Dec. 7, 1801	May 3, 1802	148			Abraham Baldwin, of Georgia	Nathaniel Macon, of North Carolina.

	2	Dec. 6, 1802	Mar. 3, 1803	88			Stephen R. Bradley, of Vermont.	
8th	1–E	Oct. 17, 1803	Mar. 27, 1804	163			John Brown, of Kentucky; Jesse Franklin, of North Carolina.	Do.
	2	Nov. 5, 1804	Mar. 3, 1805	119			Joseph Anderson, of Tennessee.	
9th	1	Dec. 2, 1805	Apr. 21, 1806	141			Samuel Smith, of Maryland	Do.
	2	Dec. 1, 1806	Mar. 3, 1807	93			do.	
10th	1–E	Oct. 26, 1807	Apr. 25, 1808	182			do	Joseph B. Varnum, of Massachusetts.
	2	Nov. 7, 1808	Mar. 3, 1809	117			Stephen R. Bradley, of Vermont; John Milledge, of Georgia.	
11th	S	Mar. 4, 1809	Mar. 7, 1809	4				
	1	May 22, 1809	June 28, 1809	38			Andrew Gregg, of Pennsylvania	Do.
	2	Nov. 27, 1809	May 1, 1810	156			John Gaillard, of South Carolina.	
	3	Dec. 3, 1810	Mar. 3, 1811	91			John Pope, of Kentucky.	
12th	1–E	Nov. 4, 1811	July 6, 1812	245			William H. Crawford, of Georgia	Henry Clay, of Kentucky.
	2	Nov. 2, 1812	Mar. 3, 1813	122			do.	
13th	1	May 24, 1813	Aug. 2, 1813	71			do	Do.[4]
	2	Dec. 6, 1813	Apr. 18, 1814	134			Joseph B. Varnum, of Massachusetts; John Gaillard, of South Carolina.	Langdon Cheves, of South Carolina.[4]
	3–E	Sept. 19, 1814	Mar. 3, 1815	166			John Gaillard, of South Carolina.	
14th	1	Dec. 4, 1815	Apr. 30, 1816	148			do	Henry Clay, of Kentucky.
	2	Dec. 2, 1816	Mar. 3, 1817	92			do.	
15th	S	Mar. 4, 1817	Mar. 6, 1817	3			do.	
	1	Dec. 1, 1817	Apr. 20, 1818	141	Dec. 24–Dec. 29, 1817	Dec. 24–Dec. 29, 1817	do	Do.
	2	Nov. 16, 1818	Mar. 3, 1819	108			James Barbour, of Virginia.	
16th	1	Dec. 6, 1819	May 15, 1820	162			James Barbour, of Virginia; John Gaillard, of South Carolina.	Do.[5]
	2	Nov. 13, 1820	Mar. 3, 1821	111			John Gaillard, of South Carolina	John W. Taylor, of New York.[5]
17th	1	Dec. 3, 1821	May 8, 1822	157			do	Philip P. Barbour, of Virginia.
	2	Dec. 2, 1822	Mar. 3, 1823	92			do.	
18th	1	Dec. 1, 1823	May 27, 1824	178			do	Henry Clay, of Kentucky.
	2	Dec. 6, 1824	Mar. 3, 1825	88			do.	
19th	S	Mar. 4, 1825	Mar, 9, 1825	6			do.	
	1	Dec. 5, 1825	May 22, 1826	169			Nathaniel Macon, of North Carolina	John W. Taylor, of New York.
	2	Dec. 4, 1826	Mar. 3, 1827	90			do.	
20th	1	Dec. 3, 1827	May 26, 1828	175			Samuel Smith, of Maryland	Andrew Stevenson, of Virginia.
	2	Dec. 1, 1828	Mar. 3, 1829	93	Dec. 24–Dec. 29, 1828	Dec. 24–Dec. 29, 1828	do.	
21st	S	Mar. 4, 1829	Mar. 17, 1829	14			do.	
	1	Dec. 7, 1829	May 31, 1830	176			do	Do.
	2	Dec. 6, 1830	Mar. 3, 1831	88			do.	
22d	1	Dec. 5, 1831	July 16, 1832	225			Littleton Waller Tazewell, of Virginia	Do.
	2	Dec. 3, 1832	Mar. 2, 1833	91			Hugh Lawson White, of Tennessee.	
23d	1	Dec. 2, 1833	June 30, 1834	211			Hugh Lawson White, of Tennessee; George Poindexter, of Mississippi.	Do.[6]
	2	Dec. 1, 1834	Mar. 3, 1835	93			John Tyler, of Virginia	John Bell, of Tennessee.[6]
24th	1	Dec. 7, 1835	July 4, 1836	211			William R. King, of Alabama	James K. Polk, of Tennessee.
	2	Dec. 5, 1836	Mar. 3, 1837	89			do.	
25th	S	Mar. 4, 1837	Mar. 10, 1837	7			do.	
	1–E	Sept. 4, 1837	Oct. 16, 1837	43			do	Do.
	2	Dec. 4, 1837	July 9, 1838	218			do.	
	3	Dec. 3, 1838	Mar. 3, 1839	91			do.	
26th	1	Dec. 2, 1839	July 21, 1840	233			do	Robert M.T. Hunter, of Virginia.
	2	Dec. 7, 1840	Mar. 3, 1841	87			do.	
27th	S	Mar. 4, 1841	Mar. 15, 1841	12			William R. King, of Alabama; Samuel L. Southard, of New Jersey.	

SESSIONS OF CONGRESS, 1st–110th CONGRESSES, 1789–2007—CONTINUED

[Closing date for this table was July 25, 2007.]

MEETING DATES OF CONGRESS: Pursuant to a resolution of the Confederation Congress in 1788, the Constitution went into effect on March 4, 1789. From then until the 20th amendment took effect in January 1934, the term of each Congress began on March 4th of each odd-numbered year; however, Article I, section 4, of the Constitution provided that ''The Congress shall assemble at least once in every Year, and such Meeting shall be on the first Monday in December, unless they shall by law appoint a different day.'' The Congress therefore convened regularly on the first Monday in December until the 20th amendment became effective, which changed the beginning of Congress's term as well as its convening date to January 3rd. So prior to 1934, a new Congress typically would not convene for regular business until 13 months after being elected. One effect of this was that the last session of each Congress was a ''lame duck'' session. After the 20th amendment, the time from the election to the beginning of Congress's term as well as when it convened was reduced to two months. Recognizing that the need might exist for Congress to meet at times other than the regularly scheduled convening date, Article II, section 3 of the Constitution provides that the President ''may, on extraordinary occasions, convene both Houses, or either of them''; hence these sessions occur only if convened by Presidential proclamation. Except as noted, these are separately numbered sessions of a Congress, and are marked by an E in the session column of the table. Until the 20th amendment was adopted, there were also times when special sessions of the Senate were convened, principally for confirming Cabinet and other executive nominations, and occasionally for the ratification of treaties or other executive business. These Senate sessions were also called by Presidential proclamation (typically by the outgoing President, although on occasion by incumbents as well) and are marked by an S in the session column. MEETING PLACES OF CONGRESS: Congress met for the first and second sessions of the First Congress (1789 and 1790) in New York City. From the third session of the First Congress through the first session of the Sixth Congress (1790 to 1800), Philadelphia was the meeting place. Congress has convened in Washington since the second session of the Sixth Congress (1800).

Congress	Session	Convening Date	Adjournment Date	Length in days [1]	Recesses [2] Senate	Recesses [2] House of Representatives	President pro tempore of the Senate [3]	Speaker of the House of Representatives
	1–E	May 31, 1841	Sept. 13, 1841	106			Samuel L. Southard, of New Jersey	John White, of Kentucky.
	2	Dec. 6, 1841	Aug. 31, 1842	269			Willie P. Mangum, of North Carolina.	
	3	Dec. 5, 1842	Mar. 3, 1843	89			do.	
28th	1	Dec. 4, 1843	June 17, 1844	196			do	John W. Jones, of Virginia.
	2	Dec. 2, 1844	Mar. 3, 1845	92			do.	
29th	S	Mar. 4, 1845	Mar. 20, 1845	17				
	1	Dec. 1, 1845	Aug. 10, 1846	253			Ambrose H. Sevier; David R. Atchison, of Missouri.	John W. Davis, of Indiana.
	2	Dec. 7, 1846	Mar. 3, 1847	87			David R. Atchison, of Missouri.	
30th	1	Dec. 6, 1847	Aug. 14, 1848	254			do	Robert C. Winthrop, of Massachusetts.
	2	Dec. 4, 1848	Mar. 3, 1849	90			do.	
31st	S	Mar. 5, 1849	Mar. 23, 1849	19			do.	
	1	Dec. 3, 1849	Sept. 30, 1850	302			William R. King, of Alabama	Howell Cobb, of Georgia.
	2	Dec. 2, 1850	Mar. 3, 1851	92			do.	
32d	S	Mar. 4, 1851	Mar. 13, 1851	10				
	1	Dec. 1, 1851	Aug. 31, 1852	275			do	Linn Boyd, of Kentucky.
	2	Dec. 6, 1852	Mar. 3, 1853	88			David R. Atchison, of Missouri.	
33d	S	Mar. 4, 1853	Apr. 11, 1853	39			do.	
	1	Dec. 5, 1853	Aug. 7, 1854	246			do	Do.
	2	Dec. 4, 1854	Mar. 3, 1855	90			Lewis Cass, of Michigan; Jesse D. Bright, of Indiana.	
34th	1	Dec. 3, 1855	Aug. 18, 1856	260			Charles E. Stuart, of Michigan; Jesse D. Bright, of Indiana.	Nathaniel P. Banks, of Massachusetts.
	2–E	Aug. 21, 1856	Aug. 30, 1856	10			Jesse D. Bright, of Indiana.	
	3	Dec. 1, 1856	Mar. 3, 1857	93			James M. Mason, of Virginia.	
35th	S	Mar. 4, 1857	Mar. 14, 1857	11			James M. Mason, of Virginia; Thomas J. Rusk, of Texas.	
	1	Dec. 7, 1857	June 14, 1858	189	Dec. 23, 1857–Jan. 4, 1858	Dec. 23, 1857–Jan. 4, 1858	Benjamin Fitzpatrick, of Alabama	James L. Orr, of South Carolina.

	S	June 15, 1858	June 16, 1858	2				
	2	Dec. 6, 1858	Mar. 3, 1859	88	Dec. 23, 1858–Jan. 4, 1859	Dec. 23, 1858–Jan. 4, 1859	......do.	
36th	S	Mar. 4, 1859	Mar. 10, 1859	7			......do.	
	1	Dec. 5, 1859	June 25, 1860	202			Benjamin Fitzpatrick, of Alabama; Jesse D. Bright, of Indiana.	William Pennington, of New Jersey.
	S	June 26, 1860	June 28, 1860	3			Benjamin Fitzpatrick, of Alabama.	
	2	Dec. 3, 1860	Mar. 3, 1861	93			Solomon Foot, of Vermont.	
37th	S	Mar. 4, 1861	Mar. 28, 1861	25			......do.	
	1–E	July 4, 1861	Aug. 6, 1861	34			......do	Galusha A. Grow, of Pennsylvania.
	2	Dec. 2, 1861	July 17, 1862	228			......do.	
	3	Dec. 1, 1862	Mar. 3, 1863	93	Dec. 23, 1862–Jan. 5, 1863	Dec. 23, 1862–Jan. 5, 1863	......do.	
38th	S	Mar. 4, 1863	Mar. 14, 1863	11			......do.	
	1	Dec. 7, 1863	July 4, 1864	209	Dec. 23, 1863–Jan. 5, 1864	Dec. 23, 1863–Jan. 5, 1864	Solomon Foot, of Vermont; Daniel Clark, of New Hampshire.	Schuyler Colfax, of Indiana.
	2	Dec. 5, 1864	Mar. 3, 1865	89	Dec. 22, 1864–Jan. 5, 1865	Dec. 22, 1864–Jan. 5, 1865	Daniel Clark, of New Hampshire.	
39th	S	Mar. 4, 1865	Mar. 11, 1865	8			Lafayette S. Foster, of Connecticut.	
	1	Dec. 4, 1865	July 28, 1866	237	Dec. 6–Dec. 11, 1865 Dec. 21, 1865–Jan. 5, 1866	Dec. 6–Dec. 11, 1865 Dec. 21, 1865–Jan. 5, 1866	......do	Do.
	2	Dec. 3, 1866	Mar. 3, 1867	91	Dec. 20, 1866–Jan. 3, 1867	Dec. 20, 1866–Jan. 3, 1867	Benjamin F. Wade, of Ohio.	
40th	1	Mar. 4, 1867	Dec. 1, 1867	273	Mar. 30–July 3, 1867 July 20–Nov. 21, 1867	Mar. 30–July 3, 1867 July 20–Nov. 21, 1867	......do	Do.[7]
	S	Apr. 1, 1867	Apr. 20, 1867	20				
	2	Dec. 2, 1867	Nov. 10, 1868	345	Dec. 20, 1867–Jan. 6, 1868 July 27–Sept. 21, 1868 Sept. 21–Oct. 16, 1868 Oct. 16–Nov. 10, 1868	Dec. 20, 1867–Jan. 6, 1868 July 27–Sept. 21, 1868 Sept. 21–Oct. 16, 1868 Oct. 16–Nov. 10, 1868		
	3	Dec. 7, 1868	Mar. 3, 1869	87	Dec. 21, 1868–Jan. 5, 1869	Dec. 21, 1868–Jan. 5, 1869	......do	Theodore M. Pomeroy, of New York.[7]
41st	1	Mar. 4, 1869	Apr. 10, 1869	38			Henry B. Anthony, of Rhode Island	James G. Blaine, of Maine.
	S	Apr. 12, 1869	Apr. 22, 1869	11				
	2	Dec. 6, 1869	July 15, 1870	222	Dec. 22, 1869–Jan. 10, 1870	Dec. 22, 1869–Jan. 10, 1870	......do.	
	3	Dec. 5, 1870	Mar. 3, 1871	89	Dec. 23, 1870–Jan. 4, 1871	Dec. 22, 1870–Jan. 4, 1871	......do.	
42d	1	Mar. 4, 1871	Apr. 20, 1871	48			......do	Do.
	S	May 10, 1871	May 27, 1871	18			......do.	
	2	Dec. 4, 1871	June 10, 1872	190	Dec. 21, 1871–Jan. 8, 1872	Dec. 21, 1871–Jan. 8, 1872	......do.	
	3	Dec. 2, 1872	Mar. 3, 1873	92	Dec. 20, 1872–Jan. 6, 1873	Dec. 20, 1872–Jan. 6, 1873	......do.	
43d	S	Mar. 4, 1873	Mar. 26, 1873	23			Matthew H. Carpenter, of Wisconsin.	
	1	Dec. 1, 1873	June 23, 1874	204	Dec. 19, 1873–Jan. 5, 1874	Dec. 19, 1873–Jan. 5, 1874	......do	Do.
	2	Dec. 7, 1874	Mar. 3, 1875	87	Dec. 23, 1874–Jan. 5, 1875	Dec. 23, 1874–Jan. 5, 1875	Matthew H. Carpenter, of Wisconsin; Henry B. Anthony, of Rhode Island.	
44th	S	Mar. 5, 1875	Mar. 24, 1875	20			Thomas W. Ferry, of Michigan.	
	1	Dec. 6, 1875	Aug. 15, 1876	254	Dec. 20, 1875–Jan. 5, 1876	Dec. 21, 1875–Jan. 5, 1876	......do	Michael C. Kerr, of Indiana.[8]
	2	Dec. 4, 1876	Mar. 3, 1877	90			......do	Samuel J. Randall, of Pennsylvania.[8]
45th	S	Mar. 5, 1877	Mar. 17, 1877	13			......do.	
	1–E	Oct. 15, 1877	Dec. 3, 1877	50			......do	Do.
	2	Dec. 3, 1877	June 20, 1878	200	Dec. 15, 1877–Jan. 10, 1878	Dec. 15, 1877–Jan. 10, 1878	......do.	
	3	Dec. 2, 1878	Mar. 3, 1879	92	Dec. 20, 1878–Jan. 7, 1879	Dec. 20, 1878–Jan. 7, 1879	......do.	
46th	1–E	Mar. 18, 1879	July 1, 1879	106			Allen G. Thurman, of Ohio	Do.
	2	Dec. 1, 1879	June 16, 1880	199	Dec. 19, 1879–Jan. 6, 1880	Dec. 19, 1879–Jan. 6, 1880	......do.	
	3	Dec. 6, 1880	Mar. 3, 1881	88	Dec. 23, 1880–Jan. 5, 1881	Dec. 23, 1880–Jan. 5, 1881	......do.	
47th	S	Mar. 4, 1881	May. 20, 1881	78				
	S	Oct. 10, 1881	Oct. 29, 1881	20			Thomas F. Bayard, of Delaware; David Davis, of Illinois.	
	1	Dec. 5, 1881	Aug. 8, 1882	247	Dec. 22, 1881–Jan. 5, 1882	Dec. 22, 1881–Jan. 5, 1882	David Davis, of Illinois	J. Warren Keifer, of Ohio.

SESSIONS OF CONGRESS, 1st–110th CONGRESSES, 1789–2007—CONTINUED

[Closing date for this table was July 25, 2007.]

MEETING DATES OF CONGRESS: Pursuant to a resolution of the Confederation Congress in 1788, the Constitution went into effect on March 4, 1789. From then until the 20th amendment took effect in January 1934, the term of each Congress began on March 4th of each odd-numbered year; however, Article I, section 4, of the Constitution provided that ''The Congress shall assemble at least once in every Year, and such Meeting shall be on the first Monday in December, unless they shall by law appoint a different day.'' The Congress therefore convened regularly on the first Monday in December until the 20th amendment became effective, which changed the beginning of Congress's term as well as its convening date to January 3rd. So prior to 1934, a new Congress typically would not convene for regular business until 13 months after being elected. One effect of this was that the last session of each Congress was a ''lame duck'' session. After the 20th amendment, the time from the election to the beginning of Congress's term as well as when it convened was reduced to two months. Recognizing that the need might exist for Congress to meet at times other than the regularly scheduled convening date, Article II, section 3 of the Constitution provides that the President ''may, on extraordinary occasions, convene both Houses, or either of them''; hence these sessions occur only if convened by Presidential proclamation. Except as noted, these are separately numbered sessions of a Congress, and are marked by an E in the session column of the table. Until the 20th amendment was adopted, there were also times when special sessions of the Senate were convened, principally for confirming Cabinet and other executive nominations, and occasionally for the ratification of treaties or other executive business. These Senate sessions were also called by Presidential proclamation (typically by the outgoing President, although on occasion by incumbents as well) and are marked by an S in the session column. MEETING PLACES OF CONGRESS: Congress met for the first and second sessions of the First Congress (1789 and 1790) in New York City. From the third session of the First Congress through the first session of the Sixth Congress (1790 to 1800), Philadelphia was the meeting place. Congress has convened in Washington since the second session of the Sixth Congress (1800).

Congress	Session	Convening Date	Adjournment Date	Length in days[1]	Recesses[2]		President pro tempore of the Senate[3]	Speaker of the House of Representatives
					Senate	House of Representatives		
	2	Dec. 4, 1882	Mar. 3, 1883	90			George F. Edmunds, of Vermont.	J. Warren Keifer, of Ohio.
48th	1	Dec. 3, 1883	July 7, 1884	218	Dec. 24, 1883–Jan. 7, 1884	Dec. 24, 1883–Jan. 7, 1884	......do	John G. Carlisle, of Kentucky.
	2	Dec. 1, 1884	Mar. 3, 1885	93	Dec. 24, 1884–Jan. 5, 1885	Dec. 24, 1884–Jan. 5, 1885	......do.	
49th	S	Mar. 4, 1885	Apr. 2, 1885	30				
	1	Dec. 7, 1885	Aug. 5, 1886	242	Dec. 21, 1885–Jan. 5, 1886	Dec. 21, 1885–Jan. 5, 1886	John Sherman, of Ohio	Do.
	2	Dec. 6, 1886	Mar. 3, 1887	88	Dec. 22, 1886–Jan. 4, 1887	Dec. 22, 1886–Jan. 4, 1887	John J. Ingalls, of Kansas.	
50th	1	Dec. 5, 1887	Oct. 20, 1888	321	Dec. 22, 1887–Jan. 4, 1888	Dec. 22, 1887–Jan. 4, 1888	......do	Do.
	2	Dec. 3, 1888	Mar. 3, 1889	91	Dec. 21, 1888–Jan. 2, 1889	Dec. 21, 1888–Jan. 2, 1889	......do.	
51st	S	Mar. 4, 1889	Apr. 2, 1889	30			......do.	
	1	Dec. 2, 1889	Oct. 1, 1890	304	Dec. 21, 1889–Jan. 6, 1890	Dec. 21, 1889–Jan. 6, 1890	......do	Thomas B. Reed, of Maine.
	2	Dec. 1, 1890	Mar. 3, 1891	93			Charles F. Manderson, of Nebraska.	
52d	1	Dec. 7, 1891	Aug. 5, 1892	251			......do	Charles F. Crisp, of Georgia.
	2	Dec. 5, 1892	Mar. 3, 1893	89	Dec. 22, 1892–Jan. 4, 1893	Dec. 22, 1892–Jan. 4, 1893	......do.	
53d	S	Mar. 4, 1893	Apr. 15, 1893	43			Charles F. Manderson, of Nebraska; Isham G. Harris, of Tennessee.	
	1–E	Aug. 7, 1893	Nov. 3, 1893	89			Isham G. Harris, of Tennessee	Do.
	2	Dec. 4, 1893	Aug. 28, 1894	268		Dec. 21, 1893–Jan. 3, 1894	......do.	
	3	Dec. 3, 1894	Mar. 3, 1895	97		Dec. 23, 1894–Jan. 3, 1895	Matt W. Ransom, of North Carolina; Isham G. Harris, of Tennessee.	
54th	1	Dec. 2, 1895	June 11, 1896	193			William P. Frye, of Maine	Thomas B. Reed, of Maine.
	2	Dec. 7, 1896	Mar. 3, 1897	87	Dec. 22, 1896–Jan. 5, 1897	Dec. 22, 1896–Jan. 5, 1897	......do.	
55th	S	Mar. 4, 1897	Mar. 10, 1897	11			......do.	
	1–E	Mar. 15, 1897	July 24, 1897	131			......do	Do.
	2	Dec. 6, 1897	July 8, 1898	215	Dec. 18, 1897–Jan. 5, 1898	Dec. 18, 1897–Jan. 5, 1898	......do.	
	3	Dec. 5, 1898	Mar. 3, 1899	89	Dec. 21, 1898–Jan. 4, 1899	Dec. 21, 1898–Jan. 4, 1899	......do.	
56th	1	Dec. 4, 1899	June 7, 1900	186	Dec. 20, 1899–Jan. 3, 1900	Dec. 20, 1899–Jan. 3, 1900	......do	David B. Henderson, of Iowa.
	2	Dec. 3, 1900	Mar. 3, 1901	91	Dec. 20, 1900–Jan. 3, 1901	Dec. 21, 1900–Jan. 3, 1901	......do.	
57th	S	Mar. 4, 1901	Mar. 9, 1901	6			......do.	

	1	Dec. 2, 1901	July 1, 1902	212	Dec. 19, 1901–Jan. 6, 1902	Dec. 19, 1901–Jan. 6, 1902	......do	Do.
	2	Dec. 1, 1902	Mar. 3, 1903	93	Dec. 20, 1902–Jan. 5, 1903	Dec. 20, 1902–Jan. 5, 1903	......do.	
58th ...	S	Mar. 5, 1903	Mar. 19, 1903	15			......do.	
	1–E	Nov. 9, 1903	Dec. 7, 1903	29			......do	Joseph G. Cannon, of Illinois.
	2	Dec. 7, 1903	Apr. 28, 1904	144	Dec. 19, 1903–Jan. 4, 1904	Dec. 19, 1903–Jan. 4, 1904	......do.	
	3	Dec. 5, 1904	Mar. 3, 1905	89	Dec. 21, 1904–Jan. 4, 1905	Dec. 21, 1904–Jan. 4, 1905	......do.	
59th ...	S	Mar. 4, 1905	Mar. 18, 1905	15			......do.	
	1	Dec. 4, 1905	June 30, 1906	209	Dec. 21, 1905–Jan. 4, 1906	Dec. 21, 1905–Jan. 4, 1906	......do	Do.
	2	Dec. 3, 1906	Mar. 3, 1907	91	Dec. 20, 1906–Jan. 3, 1907	Dec. 20, 1906–Jan. 3, 1907	......do.	
60th ...	1	Dec. 2, 1907	May 30, 1908	181	Dec. 21, 1907–Jan. 6, 1908	Dec. 21, 1907–Jan. 6, 1908	......do	Do.
	2	Dec. 7, 1908	Mar. 3, 1909	87	Dec. 19, 1908–Jan. 4, 1909	Dec. 19, 1908–Jan. 4, 1909	......do.	
61st	S	Mar. 4, 1909	Mar. 6, 1909	3			......do.	
	1–E	Mar. 15, 1909	Aug. 5, 1909	144			......do	Do.
	2	Dec. 6, 1909	June 25, 1910	202	Dec. 21, 1909–Jan. 4, 1910	Dec. 21, 1909–Jan. 4, 1910	......do.	
	3	Dec. 5, 1910	Mar. 3, 1911	89	Dec. 21, 1910–Jan. 5, 1911	Dec. 21, 1910–Jan. 5, 1911	......do.	
62d	1–E	Apr. 4, 1911	Aug. 22, 1911	141			......do.[9]	Champ Clark, of Missouri.
	2	Dec. 4, 1911	Aug. 26, 1912	267	Dec. 21, 1911–Jan. 3, 1912	Dec. 21, 1911–Jan. 3, 1912	Charles Curtis, of Kansas; Augustus O. Bacon, of Georgia; Jacob H. Gallinger, of New Hampshire; Henry Cabot Lodge, of Massachusetts; Frank B. Brandegee, of Connecticut.	
	3	Dec. 2, 1912	Mar. 3, 1913	92	Dec. 19, 1912–Jan. 2, 1913	Dec. 19, 1912–Jan. 2, 1913	Augustus O. Bacon, of Georgia; Jacob H. Gallinger, of New Hampshire.	
63d	S	Mar. 4, 1913	Mar. 17, 1913	14			James P. Clarke, of Arkansas.	
	1–E	Apr. 7, 1913	Dec. 1, 1913	239			......do	Do.
	2	Dec. 1, 1913	Oct. 24, 1914	328	Dec. 23, 1913–Jan. 12, 1914	Dec. 23, 1913–Jan. 12, 1914	......do.	
	3	Dec. 7, 1914	Mar. 3, 1915	87	Dec. 23–Dec. 28, 1914	Dec. 23–Dec. 28, 1914	......do.	
64th ...	1	Dec. 6, 1915	Sept. 8, 1916	278	Dec. 17, 1915–Jan. 4, 1916	Dec. 17, 1915–Jan. 4, 1916	......do[10]	Do.
	2	Dec. 4, 1916	Mar. 3, 1917	90	Dec. 22, 1916–Jan. 2, 1917	Dec. 22, 1916–Jan. 2, 1917	Willard Saulsbury, of Delaware[10]	
65th ...	S	Mar. 5, 1917	Mar. 16, 1917	12			......do.	
	1–E	Apr. 2, 1917	Oct. 6, 1917	188			......do	Do.
	2	Dec. 3, 1917	Nov. 21, 1918	354	Dec. 18, 1917–Jan. 3, 1918	Dec. 18, 1917–Jan. 3, 1918	......do.	
	3	Dec. 2, 1918	Mar. 3, 1919	92			......do.	
66th ...	1–E	May 19, 1919	Nov. 19, 1919	185	July 1–July 8, 1919	July 1–July 8, 1919	Albert B. Cummins, of Iowa	Frederick H. Gillett, of Massachusetts.
	2	Dec. 1, 1919	June 5, 1920	188	Dec. 20, 1919–Jan. 5, 1920	Dec. 20, 1919–Jan. 5, 1920	......do.	
	3	Dec. 6, 1920	Mar. 3, 1921	88			......do.	
67th ...	S	Mar. 4, 1921	Mar. 15, 1921	12			......do.	
	1–E	Apr. 11, 1921	Nov. 23, 1921	227	Aug. 24–Sept. 21, 1921	Aug. 24–Sept. 21, 1921	......do	Do.
	2	Dec. 5, 1921	Sept. 22, 1922	292	Dec. 22, 1921–Jan. 3, 1922	Dec. 22, 1921–Jan. 3, 1922	......do.	
	3–E	Nov. 20, 1922	Dec. 4, 1922	15			......do.	
	4	Dec. 4, 1922	Mar. 3, 1923	90			......do.	
68th ...	1	Dec. 3, 1923	June 7, 1924	188	Dec. 20, 1923–Jan. 3, 1924	Dec. 20, 1923–Jan. 3, 1924	......do	Do.
	2	Dec. 1, 1924	Mar. 3, 1925	93	Dec. 20–Dec. 29, 1924	Dec. 20–Dec. 29, 1924	......do.	
69th ...	S	Mar. 4, 1925	Mar. 18, 1925	15			Albert B. Cummins, of Iowa; George H. Moses, of New Hampshire.	
	1	Dec. 7, 1925	July 3, 1926	209	Dec. 22, 1925–Jan. 4, 1926	Dec. 22, 1925–Jan. 4, 1926	......do	Nicholas Longworth, of Ohio.
	2	Dec. 6, 1926	Mar. 4, 1927	88	Dec. 22, 1926–Jan. 3, 1927	Dec. 22, 1926–Jan. 3, 1927	......do.	
70th ...	1	Dec. 5, 1927	May 29, 1928	177	Dec. 21, 1927–Jan. 4, 1928	Dec. 21, 1927–Jan. 4, 1928	......do	Do.
	2	Dec. 3, 1928	Mar. 3, 1929	91	Dec. 22, 1928–Jan. 3, 1929	Dec. 22, 1928–Jan. 3, 1929	......do.	
71st	S	Mar. 4, 1929	Mar. 5, 1929	2			......do.	
	1–E	Apr. 15, 1929	Nov. 22, 1929	222	June 19–Aug. 19, 1929	June 19–Sept. 23, 1929	......do	Do.
	2	Dec. 2, 1929	July 3, 1930	214	Dec. 21, 1929–Jan. 6, 1930	Dec. 21, 1929–Jan. 6, 1930	......do.	
	S	July 7, 1930	July 21, 1930	15			......do.	

SESSIONS OF CONGRESS, 1st–110th CONGRESSES, 1789–2007—CONTINUED

[Closing date for this table was July 25, 2007.]

MEETING DATES OF CONGRESS: Pursuant to a resolution of the Confederation Congress in 1788, the Constitution went into effect on March 4, 1789. From then until the 20th amendment took effect in January 1934, the term of each Congress began on March 4th of each odd-numbered year; however, Article I, section 4, of the Constitution provided that ''The Congress shall assemble at least once in every Year, and such Meeting shall be on the first Monday in December, unless they shall by law appoint a different day.'' The Congress therefore convened regularly on the first Monday in December until the 20th amendment became effective, which changed the beginning of Congress's term as well as its convening date to January 3rd. So prior to 1934, a new Congress typically would not convene for regular business until 13 months after being elected. One effect of this was that the last session of each Congress was a ''lame duck'' session. After the 20th amendment, the time from the election to the beginning of Congress's term as well as when it convened was reduced to two months. Recognizing that the need might exist for Congress to meet at times other than the regularly scheduled convening date, Article II, section 3 of the Constitution provides that the President ''may, on extraordinary occasions, convene both Houses, or either of them''; hence these sessions occur only if convened by Presidential proclamation. Except as noted, these are separately numbered sessions of a Congress, and are marked by an E in the session column of the table. Until the 20th amendment was adopted, there were also times when special sessions of the Senate were convened, principally for confirming Cabinet and other executive nominations, and occasionally for the ratification of treaties or other executive business. These Senate sessions were also called by Presidential proclamation (typically by the outgoing President, although on occasion by incumbents as well) and are marked by an S in the session column. MEETING PLACES OF CONGRESS: Congress met for the first and second sessions of the First Congress (1789 and 1790) in New York City. From the third session of the First Congress through the first session of the Sixth Congress (1790 to 1800), Philadelphia was the meeting place. Congress has convened in Washington since the second session of the Sixth Congress (1800).

Congress	Session	Convening Date	Adjournment Date	Length in days [1]	Recesses [2] Senate	Recesses [2] House of Representatives	President pro tempore of the Senate [3]	Speaker of the House of Representatives
	3	Dec. 1, 1930	Mar. 3, 1931	93	Dec. 20, 1930–Jan. 5, 1931	Dec. 20, 1930–Jan. 5, 1931	George H. Moses, of New Hampshire	Nicholas Longworth, of Ohio.
72d	1	Dec. 7, 1931	July 16, 1932	223	Dec. 22, 1931–Jan. 4, 1932	Dec. 22, 1931–Jan. 4, 1932	do	John N. Garner, of Texas.
	2	Dec. 5, 1932	Mar. 3, 1933	89			do.	
73d	S	Mar. 4, 1933	Mar. 6, 1933	3			do.	
	1–E	Mar. 9, 1933	June 15, 1933	99			Key Pittman, of Nevada	Henry T. Rainey, of Illinois.
	2	Jan. 3, 1934	June 18, 1934	167			do.	
74th	1	Jan. 3, 1935	Aug. 26, 1935	236			do	Joseph W. Byrns, of Tennessee.[11]
	2	Jan. 3, 1936	June 20, 1936	170	June 8–June 15, 1936	June 8–June 15, 1936	do	William B. Bankhead, of Alabama.[11]
75th	1	Jan. 5, 1937	Aug. 21, 1937	229			do	Do.
	2–E	Nov. 15, 1937	Dec. 21, 1937	37			do.	
	3	Jan. 3, 1938	June 16, 1938	165			do.	
76th	1	Jan. 3, 1939	Aug. 5, 1939	215			do	Do.[12]
	2–E	Sept. 21, 1939	Nov. 3, 1939	44			do.	
	3	Jan. 3, 1940	Jan. 3, 1941	366	July 11–July 22, 1940	July 11–July 22, 1940	Key Pittman, of Nevada; [13] William H. King, of Utah.[13]	Sam Rayburn, of Texas.[12]
77th	1	Jan. 3, 1941	Jan. 2, 1942	365			Pat Harrison, of Mississippi;[14] Carter Glass, of Virginia.[14]	Do.
	2	Jan. 5, 1942	Dec. 16, 1942	346			Carter Glass, of Virginia.	
78th	1	Jan. 6, 1943	Dec. 21, 1943	350	July 8–Sept. 14, 1943	July 8–Sept. 14, 1943	do	Do.
	2	Jan. 10, 1944	Dec. 19, 1944	345	Apr. 1–Apr. 12, 1944 June 23–Aug. 1, 1944 Sept. 21–Nov. 14, 1944	Apr. 1–Apr. 12, 1944 June 23–Aug. 1, 1944 Sept. 21–Nov. 14, 1944	do.	
79th	1	Jan. 3, 1945	Dec. 21, 1945	353	Aug. 1–Sept. 5, 1945	July 21–Sept. 5, 1945	Kenneth McKellar, of Tennessee	Do.
	2	Jan. 14, 1946	Aug. 2, 1946	201		Apr. 18–Apr. 30, 1946	do.	
80th	[15] 1	Jan. 3, 1947	Dec. 19, 1947	351	July 27–Nov. 17, 1947	July 27–Nov. 17, 1947	Arthur H. Vandenberg, of Michigan	Joseph W. Martin, Jr., of Massachusetts.
	[15] 2	Jan. 6, 1948	Dec. 31, 1948	361	June 20–July 26, 1948 Aug. 7–Dec. 31, 1948	June 20–July 26, 1948 Aug. 7–Dec. 31, 1948	do.	

81st	1	Jan. 3, 1949	Oct. 19, 1949	290			Kenneth McKellar, of Tennessee	Sam Rayburn, of Texas.
	2	Jan. 3, 1950	Jan. 2, 1951	365	Sept. 23–Nov. 27–1950	Apr. 6–Apr. 18, 1950 Sept. 23–Nov. 27, 1950	......do.	
82d	1	Jan. 3, 1951	Oct. 20, 1951	291		Mar. 22–Apr. 2, 1951 Aug. 23–Sept. 12, 1951	......do	Do.
	2	Jan. 8, 1952	July 7, 1952	182		Apr. 10–Apr. 22, 1952	......do.	
83d	1	Jan. 3, 1953	Aug. 3, 1953	213		Apr. 2–Apr. 13, 1953	Styles Bridges, of New Hampshire	Joseph W. Martin, Jr., of Massachusetts.
	2	Jan. 6, 1954	Dec. 2, 1954	331	Aug. 20–Nov. 8, 1954 Nov. 18–Nov. 29, 1954	Apr. 15–Apr. 22, 1954 Adjourned sine die Aug. 20, 1954	......do.	
84th	1	Jan. 5, 1955	Aug. 2, 1955	210	Apr. 4–Apr. 13, 1955	Apr. 4–Apr. 13, 1955	Walter F. George, of Georgia	Sam Rayburn, of Texas.
	2	Jan. 3, 1956	July 27, 1956	207	Mar. 29–Apr. 9, 1956	Mar. 29–Apr. 9, 1956	......do.	
85th	1	Jan. 3, 1957	Aug. 30, 1957	239	Apr. 18–Apr. 29, 1957	Apr. 18–Apr. 29, 1957	Carl Hayden, of Arizona	Do.
	2	Jan. 7, 1958	Aug. 24, 1958	230	Apr. 3–Apr. 14, 1958	Apr. 3–Apr. 14, 1958	......do.	
86th	1	Jan. 7, 1959	Sept. 15, 1959	252	Mar. 26–Apr. 7, 1959	Mar. 26–Apr. 7, 1959	......do	Do.
	2	Jan. 6, 1960	Sept. 1, 1960	240	Apr. 14–Apr. 18, 1960 May 27–May 31, 1960 July 3–Aug. 8, 1960	Apr. 14–Apr. 18, 1960 May 27–May 31, 1960 July 3–Aug. 15, 1960	......do.	
87th	1	Jan. 3, 1961	Sept. 27, 1961	268		Mar. 30–Apr. 10, 1961	......do	Do.[16]
	2	Jan. 10, 1962	Oct. 13, 1962	277		Apr. 19–Apr. 30, 1962	......do	John W. McCormack, of Massachusetts.[16]
88th	1	Jan. 9, 1963	Dec. 30, 1963	356		Apr. 11–Apr. 22, 1963	......do	Do.
	2	Jan. 7, 1964	Oct. 3, 1964	270	July 10–July 20, 1964 Aug. 21–Aug. 31, 1964	Mar. 26–Apr. 6, 1964 July 2–July 20, 1964 Aug. 21–Aug. 31, 1964	......do.	
89th	1	Jan. 4, 1965	Oct. 23, 1965	293			......do	Do.
	2	Jan. 10, 1966	Oct. 22, 1966	286	Apr. 7–Apr. 13, 1966 June 30–July 11, 1966	Apr. 7–Apr. 18, 1966 June 30–July 11, 1966	......do.	
90th	1	Jan. 10, 1967	Dec. 15, 1967	340	Mar. 23–Apr. 3, 1967 June 29–July 10, 1967 Aug. 31–Sept. 11, 1967 Nov. 22–Nov. 27, 1967	Mar. 23–Apr. 3, 1967 June 29–July 10, 1967 Aug. 31–Sept. 11, 1967 Nov. 22–Nov. 27, 1967	......do	Do.
	2	Jan. 15, 1968	Oct. 14, 1968	274	Apr. 11–Apr. 17, 1968 May 29–June 3, 1968 June 3–July 8, 1968 Aug. 2–Sept. 4, 1968	Apr. 11–Apr. 22, 1968 May 29–June 3, 1968 June 3–July 8, 1968 Aug. 2–Sept. 4, 1968	......do.	
91st	1	Jan. 3, 1969	Dec. 23, 1969	355	Feb. 7–Feb. 17, 1969 Apr. 3–Apr. 14, 1969 July 2–July 7, 1969 Aug. 13–Sept. 3, 1969 Nov. 26–Dec. 1, 1969	Feb. 7–Feb. 17, 1969 Apr. 3–Apr. 14, 1969 May 28–June 2, 1969 July 2–July 7, 1969 Aug. 13–Sept. 3, 1969 Nov. 6–Nov. 12, 1969 Nov. 26–Dec. 1, 1969	Richard B. Russell, of Georgia	Do.
	2	Jan. 19, 1970	Jan. 2, 1971	349	Feb. 10–Feb. 16, 1970 Mar. 26–Mar. 31, 1970 Sept. 2–Sept. 8, 1970 Oct. 14–Nov. 16, 1970 Nov. 25–Nov. 30, 1970 Dec. 22–Dec. 28, 1970	Feb. 10–Feb. 16, 1970 Mar. 26–Mar. 31, 1970 May 27–June 1, 1970 July 1–July 6, 1970 Aug. 14–Sept. 9, 1970 Oct. 14–Nov. 16, 1970 Nov. 25–Nov. 30, 1970 Dec. 22–Dec. 29, 1970	......do.	

SESSIONS OF CONGRESS, 1st–110th CONGRESSES, 1789–2007—CONTINUED

[Closing date for this table was July 25, 2007.]

MEETING DATES OF CONGRESS: Pursuant to a resolution of the Confederation Congress in 1788, the Constitution went into effect on March 4, 1789. From then until the 20th amendment took effect in January 1934, the term of each Congress began on March 4th of each odd-numbered year; however, Article I, section 4, of the Constitution provided that ''The Congress shall assemble at least once in every Year, and such Meeting shall be on the first Monday in December, unless they shall by law appoint a different day.'' The Congress therefore convened regularly on the first Monday in December until the 20th amendment became effective, which changed the beginning of Congress's term as well as its convening date to January 3rd. So prior to 1934, a new Congress typically would not convene for regular business until 13 months after being elected. One effect of this was that the last session of each Congress was a ''lame duck'' session. After the 20th amendment, the time from the election to the beginning of Congress's term as well as when it convened was reduced to two months. Recognizing that the need might exist for Congress to meet at times other than the regularly scheduled convening date, Article II, section 3 of the Constitution provides that the President ''may, on extraordinary occasions, convene both Houses, or either of them''; hence these sessions occur only if convened by Presidential proclamation. Except as noted, these are separately numbered sessions of a Congress, and are marked by an E in the session column of the table. Until the 20th amendment was adopted, there were also times when special sessions of the Senate were convened, principally for confirming Cabinet and other executive nominations, and occasionally for the ratification of treaties or other executive business. These Senate sessions were also called by Presidential proclamation (typically by the outgoing President, although on occasion by incumbents as well) and are marked by an S in the session column. MEETING PLACES OF CONGRESS: Congress met for the first and second sessions of the First Congress (1789 and 1790) in New York City. From the third session of the First Congress through the first session of the Sixth Congress (1790 to 1800), Philadelphia was the meeting place. Congress has convened in Washington since the second session of the Sixth Congress (1800).

Congress	Session	Convening Date	Adjournment Date	Length in days [1]	Recesses [2]		President pro tempore of the Senate [3]	Speaker of the House of Representatives
					Senate	House of Representatives		
92d	1	Jan. 21, 1971	Dec. 17, 1971 ...	331	Feb. 11–Feb. 17, 1971 .... Apr. 7–Apr. 14, 1971 May 26–June 1, 1971 June 30–July 6, 1971 Aug. 6–Sept. 8, 1971 Oct. 21–Oct. 26, 1971 Nov. 24–Nov. 29, 1971	Feb. 10–Feb. 17, 1971 .... Apr. 7–Apr. 19, 1971 May 27–June 1, 1971 July 1–July 6, 1971 Aug. 6–Sept. 8, 1971 Oct. 7–Oct. 12, 1971 Oct. 21–Oct. 26, 1971 Nov. 19–Nov. 29, 1971	Richard B. Russell, of Georgia;[17] Allen J. Ellender, of Louisiana.[17]	Carl B. Albert, of Oklahoma.
	2	Jan. 18, 1972	Oct. 18, 1972 ...	275	Feb. 9–Feb. 14, 1972 .... Mar. 30–Apr. 4, 1972 May 25–May 30, 1972 June 30–July 17, 1972 Aug. 18–Sept. 5, 1972	Feb. 9–Feb. 16, 1972 .... Mar. 29–Apr. 10, 1972 May 24–May 30, 1972 June 30–July 17, 1972 Aug. 18–Sept. 5, 1972	Allen J. Ellender, of Louisiana;[18] James O. Eastland, of Mississippi.[18]	
93d	1	Jan. 3, 1973	Dec. 22, 1973 ...	354	Feb. 8–Feb. 15, 1973 .... Apr. 18–Apr. 30, 1973 May 23–May 29, 1973 June 30–July 9, 1973 Aug. 3–Sept. 5, 1973 Oct. 18–Oct. 23, 1973 Nov. 21–Nov. 26, 1973	Feb. 8–Feb. 19, 1973 .... Apr. 19–Apr. 30, 1973 May 24–May 29, 1973 June 30–July 10, 1973 Aug. 3–Sept. 5, 1973 Oct. 4–Oct. 9, 1973 Oct. 18–Oct. 23, 1973 Nov. 15–Nov. 26, 1973	James O. Eastland, of Mississippi	Do.
	2	Jan. 21, 1974	Dec. 20, 1974 ...	334	Feb. 8–Feb. 18, 1974 .... Mar. 13–Mar. 19, 1974 Apr. 11–Apr. 22, 1974 May 23–May 28, 1974 Aug. 22–Sept. 4, 1974 Oct. 17–Nov. 18, 1974 Nov. 26–Dec. 2, 1974	Feb. 7–Feb. 13, 1974 .... Apr. 11–Apr. 22, 1974 May 23–May 28, 1974 Aug. 22–Sept. 11, 1974 Oct. 17–Nov. 18, 1974 Nov. 26–Dec. 3, 1974	......do.	

94th ...	1	Jan. 14, 1975	Dec. 19, 1975 ...	340	Mar. 26–Apr. 7, 1975 .... May 22–June 2, 1975 June 27–July 7, 1975 Aug. 1–Sept. 3, 1975 Oct. 9–Oct. 20, 1975 Oct. 23–Oct. 28, 1975 Nov. 20–Dec. 1, 1975	Mar. 26–Apr. 7, 1975 .... May 22–June 2, 1975 June 26–July 8, 1975 Aug. 1–Sept. 3, 1975 Oct. 9–Oct. 20, 1975 Oct. 23–Oct. 28, 1975 Nov. 20–Dec. 1, 1975	......do	Do.
	2	Jan. 19, 1976	Oct. 1, 1976	257	Feb. 6–Feb. 16, 1976 .... Apr. 14–Apr. 26, 1976 May 28–June 2, 1976 July 2–July 19, 1976 Aug. 10–Aug. 23, 1976 Sept. 1–Sept. 7, 1976	Feb. 11–Feb. 16, 1976 .... Apr. 14–Apr. 26, 1976 May 27–June 1, 1976 July 2–July 19, 1976 Aug. 10–Aug. 23, 1976 Sept. 2–Sept. 8, 1976	......do.	
95th ...	1	Jan. 4, 1977	Dec. 15, 1977 ...	346	Feb. 11–Feb. 21, 1977 .... Apr. 7–Apr. 18, 1977 May 27–June 6, 1977 July 1–July 11, 1977 Aug. 6–Sept. 7, 1977	Feb. 9–Feb. 16, 1977 .... Apr. 6–Apr. 18, 1977 May 26–June 1, 1977 June 30–July 11, 1977 Aug. 5–Sept. 7, 1977 Oct. 6–Oct. 11, 1977	......do	Thomas P. O'Neill, Jr., of Massachusetts.
	2	Jan. 19, 1978	Oct. 15, 1978 ...	270	Feb. 10–Feb. 20, 1978 .... Mar. 23–Apr. 3, 1978 May 26–June 5, 1978 June 29–July 10, 1978 Aug. 25–Sept. 6, 1978	Feb. 9–Feb. 14, 1978 .... Mar. 22–Apr. 3, 1978 May 25–May 31, 1978 June 29–July 10, 1978 Aug. 17–Sept. 6, 1978	......do.	
96th ...	1	Jan. 15, 1979	Jan. 3, 1980	354	Feb. 9–Feb. 19, 1979 .... Apr. 10–Apr. 23, 1979 May 24–June 4, 1979 June 27–July 9, 1979 Aug. 3–Sept. 5, 1979 Nov. 20–Nov. 26, 1979 Adjourned sine die, Dec. 20, 1979	Feb. 8–Feb. 13, 1979 .... Apr. 10–Apr. 23, 1979 May 24–May 30, 1979 June 29–July 9, 1979 Aug. 2–Sept. 5, 1979 Nov. 20–Nov. 26, 1979	Warren G. Magnuson, of Washington ...	Do.
	2	Jan. 3, 1980	Dec. 16, 1980 ...	349	Apr. 3–Apr. 15, 1980 .... May 22–May 28, 1980 July 2–July 21, 1980 Aug. 6–Aug. 18, 1980 Aug. 27–Sept. 3, 1980 Oct. 1–Nov. 12, 1980 Nov. 25–Dec. 1, 1980	Feb. 13–Feb. 19, 1980 .... Apr. 2–Apr. 15, 1980 May 22–May 28, 1980 July 2–July 21, 1980 Aug. 1–Aug. 18, 1980 Aug. 28–Sept. 3, 1980 Oct. 2–Nov. 12, 1980 Nov. 21–Dec. 1, 1980	Warren G. Magnuson, of Washington; Milton Young, of North Dakota;[19] Warren G. Magnuson, of Washington.[19]	
97th ...	1	Jan. 5, 1981	Dec. 16, 1981 ...	347	Feb. 6–Feb. 16, 1981 .... Apr. 10–Apr. 27, 1981 June 25–July 8, 1981 Aug. 3–Sept. 9, 1981 Oct. 7–Oct. 14, 1981 Nov. 24–Nov. 30, 1981	Feb. 6–Feb. 17, 1981 .... Apr. 10–Apr. 27, 1981 June 26–July 8, 1981 Aug. 4–Sept. 9, 1981 Oct. 7–Oct. 13, 1981 Nov. 23–Nov. 30, 1981	Strom Thurmond, of South Carolina	Do.
	2	Jan. 25, 1982	Dec. 23, 1982 ...	333	Feb. 11–Feb. 22, 1982 .... Apr. 1–Apr. 13, 1982 May 27–June 8, 1982 July 1–July 12, 1982 Aug. 20–Sept. 8, 1982 Oct. 1–Nov. 29, 1982	Feb. 10–Feb. 22, 1982 .... Apr. 6–Apr. 20, 1982 May 27–June 2, 1982 July 1–July 12, 1982 Aug. 20–Sept. 8, 1982 Oct. 1–Nov. 29, 1982	......do	

SESSIONS OF CONGRESS, 1st–110th CONGRESSES, 1789–2007—CONTINUED

[Closing date for this table was July 25, 2007.]

MEETING DATES OF CONGRESS: Pursuant to a resolution of the Confederation Congress in 1788, the Constitution went into effect on March 4, 1789. From then until the 20th amendment took effect in January 1934, the term of each Congress began on March 4th of each odd-numbered year; however, Article I, section 4, of the Constitution provided that ''The Congress shall assemble at least once in every Year, and such Meeting shall be on the first Monday in December, unless they shall by law appoint a different day.'' The Congress therefore convened regularly on the first Monday in December until the 20th amendment became effective, which changed the beginning of Congress's term as well as its convening date to January 3rd. So prior to 1934, a new Congress typically would not convene for regular business until 13 months after being elected. One effect of this was that the last session of each Congress was a ''lame duck'' session. After the 20th amendment, the time from the election to the beginning of Congress's term as well as when it convened was reduced to two months. Recognizing that the need might exist for Congress to meet at times other than the regularly scheduled convening date, Article II, section 3 of the Constitution provides that the President ''may, on extraordinary occasions, convene both Houses, or either of them''; hence these sessions occur only if convened by Presidential proclamation. Except as noted, these are separately numbered sessions of a Congress, and are marked by an E in the session column of the table. Until the 20th amendment was adopted, there were also times when special sessions of the Senate were convened, principally for confirming Cabinet and other executive nominations, and occasionally for the ratification of treaties or other executive business. These Senate sessions were also called by Presidential proclamation (typically by the outgoing President, although on occasion by incumbents as well) and are marked by an S in the session column. MEETING PLACES OF CONGRESS: Congress met for the first and second sessions of the First Congress (1789 and 1790) in New York City. From the third session of the First Congress through the first session of the Sixth Congress (1790 to 1800), Philadelphia was the meeting place. Congress has convened in Washington since the second session of the Sixth Congress (1800).

Congress	Session	Convening Date	Adjournment Date	Length in days[1]	Recesses[2]		President pro tempore of the Senate[3]	Speaker of the House of Representatives
					Senate	House of Representatives		
98th ...	1	Jan. 3, 1983	Nov. 18, 1983 ..	320	Jan. 3–Jan. 25, 1983	Jan. 6–Jan. 25, 1983	Strom Thurmond, of South Carolina	Thomas P. O'Neill, Jr., of Massachusetts.
					Feb. 3–Feb. 14, 1983	Feb. 17–Feb. 22, 1983		
					Mar. 24–Apr. 5, 1983	Mar. 24–Apr. 5, 1983		
					May 26–June 6, 1983	May 26–June 1, 1983		
					June 29–July 11, 1983	June 30–July 11, 1983		
					Aug. 4–Sept. 12, 1983	Aug. 4–Sept. 12, 1983		
					Oct. 7–Oct. 17, 1983	Oct. 6–Oct. 17, 1983		
	2	Jan. 23, 1984	Oct. 12, 1984 ...	264	Feb. 9–Feb. 20, 1984	Feb. 9–Feb. 21, 1984	......do.	
					Apr. 12–Apr. 24, 1984	Apr. 12–Apr. 24, 1984		
					May 24–May 31, 1984	May 24–May 30, 1984		
					June 29–July 23, 1984	June 29–July 23, 1984		
					Aug. 10–Sept. 5, 1984	Aug. 10–Sept. 5, 1984		
99th ...	1	Jan. 3, 1985	Dec. 20, 1985 ...	352	Jan. 7–Jan. 21, 1985	Jan. 3–Jan. 21, 1985	......do	Do.
					Feb. 7–Feb. 18, 1985	Feb. 7–Feb. 19, 1985		
					Apr. 4–Apr. 15, 1985	Mar. 7–Mar. 19, 1985		
					May 9–May 14, 1985	Apr. 4–Apr. 15, 1985		
					May 24–June 3, 1985	May 23–June 3, 1985		
					June 27–July 8, 1985	June 27–July 8, 1985		
					Aug. 1–Sept. 9, 1985	Aug. 1–Sept. 4, 1985		
					Nov. 23–Dec. 2, 1985	Nov. 21–Dec. 2, 1985		
	2	Jan. 21, 1986	Oct. 18, 1986 ...	278	Feb. 7–Feb. 17, 1986	Feb. 6–Feb. 18, 1986	......do.	
					Mar. 27–Apr. 8, 1986	Mar. 25–Apr. 8, 1986		
					May 21–June 2, 1986	May 22–June 3, 1986		
					June 26–July 7, 1986	June 26–July 14, 1986		
					Aug. 15–Sept. 8, 1986	Aug. 16–Sept. 8, 1986		

100th ..	1	Jan. 6, 1987	Dec. 22, 1987 ...	351	Jan. 6–Jan. 12, 1987 .... Feb. 5–Feb. 16, 1987 Apr. 10–Apr. 21, 1987 May 21–May 27, 1987 July 1–July 7, 1987 Aug. 7–Sept. 9, 1987 Nov. 20–Nov. 30, 1987	Jan. 8–Jan. 20, 1987 .... Feb. 11–Feb. 18, 1987 Apr. 9–Apr. 21, 1987 May 21–May 27, 1987 July 1–July 7, 1987 July 15–July 20, 1987 Aug. 7–Sept. 9, 1987 Nov. 10–Nov. 16, 1987 Nov. 20–Nov. 30, 1987	John C. Stennis, of Mississippi	James C. Wright, Jr., of Texas.
	2	Jan. 25, 1988	Oct. 22, 1988 ...	272	Feb. 4–Feb. 15, 1988 .... Mar. 4– Mar. 14, 1988 Mar. 31–Apr. 11, 1988 Apr. 29–May 9, 1988 May 27–June 6, 1988 June 29–July 6, 1988 July 14–July 25, 1988 Aug. 11–Sept. 7, 1988	Feb. 9–Feb. 16, 1988 .... Mar. 31–Apr. 11, 1988 May 26–June 1, 1988 June 30–July 7, 1988 July 14–July 26, 1988 Aug. 11–Sept. 7,1988	......do.	
101st ..	1	Jan. 3, 1989	Nov. 22, 1989 ..	324	Jan. 4–Jan. 20, 1989 .... Jan. 20–Jan. 25, 1989 Feb. 9–Feb. 21, 1989 Mar. 17–Apr. 4, 1989 Apr. 19–May 1, 1989 May 18–May 31, 1989 June 23–July 11, 1989 Aug. 4–Sept. 6, 1989	Jan. 4–Jan. 19, 1989 .... Feb. 9–Feb. 21, 1989 Mar. 23–Apr. 3, 1989 Apr. 18–Apr. 25, 1989 May 25–May 31, 1989 June 29–July 10, 1989 Aug. 5–Sept. 6, 1989	Robert C. Byrd, of West Virginia	James C. Wright, Jr., of Texas;[20] Thomas S. Foley, of Washington.[20]
	2	Jan. 23, 1990	Oct. 28, 1990 ...	260	Feb. 8–Feb. 20, 1990 .... Mar. 9–Mar. 20, 1990 Apr. 5–Apr. 18, 1990 May 24–June 5, 1990 June 28–July 10, 1990 Aug. 4–Sept. 10, 1990	Feb. 7–Feb. 20, 1990 .... Apr. 4–Apr. 18, 1990 May 25–June 5, 1990 June 28–July 10, 1990 Aug. 4–Sept. 5, 1990	......do.	
102d ...	1	Jan. 3, 1991	Jan. 3, 1992	366	Feb. 7–Feb. 19, 1991 .... Mar. 22–Apr. 9, 1991 Apr. 25–May 6, 1991 May 24–June 3, 1991 June 28–July 8, 1991 Aug. 2–Sept. 10, 1991 Nov. 27, 1991–Jan. 3, 1992	Feb. 6–Feb. 19, 1991 .... Mar. 22–Apr. 9, 1991 May 23–May 29, 1991 June 27–July 9, 1991 Aug. 2–Sept. 11, 1991 Nov. 27, 1991–Jan. 3, 1992	......do	Thomas S. Foley, of Washington.
	2	Jan. 3, 1992	Oct. 9, 1992	281	Jan. 3–Jan. 21, 1992 .... Feb. 7–Feb. 18, 1992 Apr. 10–Apr. 28, 1992 May 21–June 1, 1992 July 2–July 20, 1992 Aug. 12–Sept. 8, 1992	Jan. 3–Jan. 22, 1992 .... Apr. 10–Apr. 28, 1992 May 21–May 26, 1992 July 2–July 7, 1992 July 9–July 21, 1992 Aug. 12–Sept. 9, 1992	......do.	

SESSIONS OF CONGRESS, 1st–110th CONGRESSES, 1789–2007—CONTINUED

[Closing date for this table was July 25, 2007.]

MEETING DATES OF CONGRESS: Pursuant to a resolution of the Confederation Congress in 1788, the Constitution went into effect on March 4, 1789. From then until the 20th amendment took effect in January 1934, the term of each Congress began on March 4th of each odd-numbered year; however, Article I, section 4, of the Constitution provided that ''The Congress shall assemble at least once in every Year, and such Meeting shall be on the first Monday in December, unless they shall by law appoint a different day.'' The Congress therefore convened regularly on the first Monday in December until the 20th amendment became effective, which changed the beginning of Congress's term as well as its convening date to January 3rd. So prior to 1934, a new Congress typically would not convene for regular business until 13 months after being elected. One effect of this was that the last session of each Congress was a ''lame duck'' session. After the 20th amendment, the time from the election to the beginning of Congress's term as well as when it convened was reduced to two months. Recognizing that the need might exist for Congress to meet at times other than the regularly scheduled convening date, Article II, section 3 of the Constitution provides that the President ''may, on extraordinary occasions, convene both Houses, or either of them''; hence these sessions occur only if convened by Presidential proclamation. Except as noted, these are separately numbered sessions of a Congress, and are marked by an E in the session column of the table. Until the 20th amendment was adopted, there were also times when special sessions of the Senate were convened, principally for confirming Cabinet and other executive nominations, and occasionally for the ratification of treaties or other executive business. These Senate sessions were also called by Presidential proclamation (typically by the outgoing President, although on occasion by incumbents as well) and are marked by an S in the session column. MEETING PLACES OF CONGRESS: Congress met for the first and second sessions of the First Congress (1789 and 1790) in New York City. From the third session of the First Congress through the first session of the Sixth Congress (1790 to 1800), Philadelphia was the meeting place. Congress has convened in Washington since the second session of the Sixth Congress (1800).

Congress	Session	Convening Date	Adjournment Date	Length in days [1]	Recesses [2]		President pro tempore of the Senate [3]	Speaker of the House of Representatives
					Senate	House of Representatives		
103d ...	1	Jan. 5, 1993	Nov. 26, 1993 ..	326	Jan. 7–Jan. 20, 1993 .... Feb. 4–Feb. 16, 1993 Apr. 7–Apr. 19, 1993 May 28–June 7, 1993 July 1–July 13, 1993 Aug. 7–Sept. 7, 1993 Oct. 7–Oct. 13, 1993 Nov. 11–Nov. 16, 1993	Jan. 6–Jan. 20, 1993 .... Jan. 27–Feb. 2, 1993 Feb. 4–Feb. 16, 1993 Apr. 7–Apr. 19, 1993 May 27–June 8, 1993 July 1–July 13, 1993 Aug. 6–Sept. 8, 1993 Sept. 15–Sept. 21, 1993 Oct. 7–Oct. 12, 1993 Nov. 10–Nov. 15, 1993	Robert C. Byrd, of West Virginia	Thomas S. Foley, of Washington.
	2	Jan. 25, 1994	Dec. 1, 1994	311	Feb. 11–Feb. 22, 1994 .... Mar. 26–Apr. 11, 1994 May 25–June 7, 1994 July 1–July 11, 1994 Aug. 25–Sept. 12, 1994 Oct. 8–Nov. 30, 1994	Jan. 26–Feb. 1, 1994 .... Feb. 11–Feb. 22, 1994 Mar. 24–Apr. 12, 1994 May 26–June 8, 1994 June 30–July 12, 1994 Aug. 26–Sept. 12, 1994 Oct. 8–Nov. 29, 1994	......do.	
104th ..	1	Jan. 4, 1995	Jan. 3, 1996	365	Feb. 16–Feb. 22, 1995 .... Apr. 7–Apr. 24, 1995 May 26–June 5, 1995 June 30–July 10, 1995 Aug. 11–Sept. 5, 1995 Sept. 29–Oct. 10, 1995 Nov. 20–Nov. 27, 1995	Feb. 16–Feb. 21, 1995 .... Mar. 16–Mar. 21, 1995 Apr. 7–May 1, 1995 May 3–May 9, 1995 May 25–June 6, 1995 June 30–July 10, 1995 Aug. 4–Sept. 6, 1995 Sept. 29–Oct. 6, 1995 Nov. 20–Nov. 28, 1995	Strom Thurmond, of South Carolina	Newt Gingrich, of Georgia.

	2	Jan. 3, 1996	Oct. 4, 1996	276	Jan. 10–Jan. 22, 1996 .... Mar. 29–Apr. 15, 1996 May 24–June 3, 1996 June 28–July 8, 1996 Aug. 2–Sept. 3, 1996	Jan. 9–Jan. 22, 1996 .... Mar. 29–Apr. 15, 1996 May 23–May 29, 1996 June 28–July 8, 1996 Aug. 2–Sept. 4, 1996	......do.	
105th ..	1	Jan. 7, 1997	Nov. 13, 1997 ..	311	Jan. 9–Jan. 21, 1997 .... Feb. 13–Feb. 24, 1997 Mar. 21–Apr. 7, 1997 June 27–July 7, 1997 July 31–Sept. 2, 1997 Oct. 9–Oct. 20, 1997	Jan. 9–Jan. 20, 1997 .... Jan. 21–Feb. 4, 1997 Feb. 13–Feb. 25, 1997 Mar. 21–Apr. 8, 1997 June 26–July 8, 1997 Aug. 1–Sept. 3, 1997 Oct. 9–Oct. 21, 1997	......do	Do.
	2	Jan. 27, 1998	Dec. 19, 1998 ...	327	Feb. 13–Feb. 23, 1998 .... Apr. 3–Apr. 20, 1998 May 22–June 1, 1998 June 26–July 6, 1998 July 31–Aug. 31, 1998 Adjourned sine die, Oct. 21, 1998.	Jan. 28–Feb. 3, 1998 .... Feb. 5–Feb. 11, 1998 Feb. 12–Feb. 24, 1998 Apr. 1–Apr. 21, 1998 May 22–June 3, 1998 June 25–July 14, 1998 Aug. 7–Sept. 9, 1998 Oct. 21–Dec. 17, 1998	......do.	
106th ..	1	Jan. 6, 1999	Nov. 22, 1999 ..	321	Feb. 12–Feb. 22, 1999 .... Mar. 25–Apr. 12, 1999 May 27–June 7, 1999 July 1–July 12, 1999 Aug. 5–Sept. 8, 1999	Jan. 6–Jan. 19, 1999 .... Jan. 19–Feb. 2, 1999 Feb. 12–Feb. 23, 1999 Mar. 25–Apr. 12, 1999 May 27–June 7, 1999 July 1–July 12, 1999 Aug. 6–Sept. 8, 1999	......do	J. Dennis Hastert, of Illinois.
	2	Jan. 24, 2000	Dec. 15, 2000 ...	326	Feb. 10–Feb. 22, 2000 .... Mar. 9–Mar. 20, 2000 Apr. 13–Apr. 25, 2000 May 25–June 6, 2000 June 30–July 10, 2000 July 27–Sept. 5, 2000 Nov. 2–Nov. 14, 2000 Nov. 14–Dec. 5, 2000	Feb. 16–Feb. 29, 2000 .... Apr. 13–May 2, 2000 May 25–June 6, 2000 June 30–July 10, 2000 July 27–Sept. 6, 2000 Nov. 3–Nov. 13, 2000 Nov. 14–Dec. 4, 2000	......do.	
107th ..	1	Jan. 3, 2001	Dec. 20, 2001 ...	352	Jan. 8–Jan. 20, 2001 .... Feb. 15–Feb. 26, 2001 Apr. 6–Apr. 23, 2001 May 26–June 5, 2001 June 29–July 9, 2001 Aug. 3–Sept. 4, 2001 Oct. 18–Oct. 23, 2001 Nov. 16–Nov. 27, 2001	Jan. 6–Jan. 20, 2001 .... Jan. 20–Jan 30, 2001 Jan. 31–Feb. 6, 2001 Feb. 14–Feb. 26, 2001 Apr. 4–Apr. 24, 2001 May 26–June 5, 2001 June 28–July 10, 2001 Aug. 2–Sept. 5, 2001 Oct. 17–Oct. 23, 2001 Nov. 19–Nov. 27, 2001	Robert C. Byrd, of West Virginia;[21] Strom Thurmond, of South Carolina;[21] Robert C. Byrd, of West Virginia.[21]	Do.
	2	Jan. 23, 2002	Nov. 22, 2002 ..	304	Jan. 29–Feb. 4, 2002 .... Feb. 15–Feb. 25, 2002 Mar. 22–Apr. 8, 2002 May 23–June 3, 2002 June 28–July 8, 202 Aug. 1–Sept. 3, 2002	Jan. 29–Feb. 4, 2002 .... Feb. 14–Feb. 26, 2002 Mar. 20–Apr. 9, 2002 May 24–June 4, 2002 June 28–July 8, 2002 July 27–Sept. 4, 2002	Robert C. Byrd, of West Virginia.	

SESSIONS OF CONGRESS, 1st–110th CONGRESSES, 1789–2007—CONTINUED

[Closing date for this table was July 25, 2007.]

MEETING DATES OF CONGRESS: Pursuant to a resolution of the Confederation Congress in 1788, the Constitution went into effect on March 4, 1789. From then until the 20th amendment took effect in January 1934, the term of each Congress began on March 4th of each odd-numbered year; however, Article I, section 4, of the Constitution provided that ''The Congress shall assemble at least once in every Year, and such Meeting shall be on the first Monday in December, unless they shall by law appoint a different day.'' The Congress therefore convened regularly on the first Monday in December until the 20th amendment became effective, which changed the beginning of Congress's term as well as its convening date to January 3rd. So prior to 1934, a new Congress typically would not convene for regular business until 13 months after being elected. One effect of this was that the last session of each Congress was a ''lame duck'' session. After the 20th amendment, the time from the election to the beginning of Congress's term as well as when it convened was reduced to two months. Recognizing that the need might exist for Congress to meet at times other than the regularly scheduled convening date, Article II, section 3 of the Constitution provides that the President ''may, on extraordinary occasions, convene both Houses, or either of them''; hence these sessions occur only if convened by Presidential proclamation. Except as noted, these are separately numbered sessions of a Congress, and are marked by an E in the session column of the table. Until the 20th amendment was adopted, there were also times when special sessions of the Senate were convened, principally for confirming Cabinet and other executive nominations, and occasionally for the ratification of treaties or other executive business. These Senate sessions were also called by Presidential proclamation (typically by the outgoing President, although on occasion by incumbents as well) and are marked by an S in the session column. MEETING PLACES OF CONGRESS: Congress met for the first and second sessions of the First Congress (1789 and 1790) in New York City. From the third session of the First Congress through the first session of the Sixth Congress (1790 to 1800), Philadelphia was the meeting place. Congress has convened in Washington since the second session of the Sixth Congress (1800).

Congress	Session	Convening Date	Adjournment Date	Length in days [1]	Recesses [2]		President pro tempore of the Senate [3]	Speaker of the House of Representatives
					Senate	House of Representatives		
108th..	1	Jan. 7, 2003	Dec. 9, 2003	337	Feb. 14–Feb. 24, 2003 .... Apr. 11–Apr. 28, 2003 May 23–June 2, 2003 June 27–July 7, 2003 Aug. 1–Sept 2, 2003 Oct. 3–Oct. 14, 2003 Nov. 25–Dec. 9, 2003	Jan. 8–Jan. 27, 2003 .... Feb. 13–Feb. 25, 2003 Apr. 12–Apr. 29, 2003 May 23–June 2, 2003 June 27–July 7, 2003 July 29–Sept. 3, 2003 Nov. 25–Dec. 8, 2003	Ted Stevens, of Alaska	J. Dennis Hastert, of Illinois.
	2	Jan. 20, 2004	Dec. 8, 2004	324	Feb. 12–Feb. 23, 2004 .... Mar. 12–Mar. 22, 2004 Apr. 8–Apr. 19, 2004 May 21–June 1, 2004 June 9–June 14, 2004 June 25–July 6, 2004 July 22–Sept. 7, 2004 Oct. 11–Nov. 16, 2004 Nov. 24–Dec. 7, 2004	Feb. 11–Feb. 24, 2004 .... Apr. 2–Apr. 20, 2004 May 20–June 1, 2004 June 9–June 14, 2004 June 25–July 6, 2004 July 22–Sept. 7, 2004 Oct. 9–Nov. 16, 2004 Nov. 24–Dec. 6, 2004	......do.	
109th..	1	Jan. 4, 2005	Dec. 22, 2005 ...	353	Jan. 6–Jan. 20, 2005 .... Jan. 26–Jan. 31, 2005 Feb. 18–Feb. 28, 2005 Mar. 20–Apr. 4, 2005 Apr. 29–May 9, 2005 May 26–June 6, 2005 July 1–July 11, 2005 July 29–Sept. 1, 2005 Sept. 1–Sept. 6, 2005 Oct. 7–Oct. 17, 2005 Nov. 18–Dec. 12, 2005	Jan. 6–Jan. 20, 2005 .... Jan. 20–Jan. 25, 2005 Jan. 26–Feb. 1, 2005 Feb. 2–Feb. 8, 2005 Feb. 17–Mar. 1, 2005 Mar. 21–Apr. 5, 2005 May 26–June 7, 2005 July 1–July 11, 2005 July 29–Sept. 2, 2005 Oct. 7–Oct. 17, 2005 Nov. 18–Dec. 6, 2005	......do	Do.

	2	Jan. 3, 2006	Dec. 9, 2006	341	Jan. 3–Jan. 18, 2006 Feb. 17–Feb. 27, 2006 Mar. 16–Mar. 27, 2006 Apr. 7–Apr. 24, 2006 May 26–June 5, 2006 June 29–July 10, 2006 Aug. 4–Sept. 5, 2006 Sept. 30–Nov. 9, 2006 Nov. 16–Dec. 4, 2006	Jan. 3–Jan. 31, 2006 Feb. 1–Feb. 7, 2006 Feb. 8–Feb. 14, 2006 Feb. 16–Feb. 28, 2006 Mar. 16–Mar. 28, 2006 Apr. 6–Apr. 25, 2006 May 25–June 6, 2006 June 29–July 10, 2006 Aug. 2–Sept. 6, 2006 Sept. 30–Nov. 9, 2006 Nov. 15–Dec. 5, 2006	......do.	
110th..	1	Jan. 4, 2007	....	....	Feb. 17–Feb. 26, 2007 Mar. 29–Apr. 10, 2007 May 25–June 4, 2007 June 29–July 9, 2007	Jan. 24–Jan. 29, 2007 Jan. 31–Feb. 5, 2007 Feb. 16–Feb. 27, 2007 Mar. 30–Apr. 16, 2007 May 24–June 5, 2007 June 28–July 10, 2007	Robert C. Byrd, of West Virginia	Nancy Pelosi, of California.

[1] For the purposes of this table, a session's ''length in days'' is defined as the total number of calendar days from the convening date to the adjournment date, inclusive. It does not mean the actual number of days that Congress met during that session.

[2] For the purposes of this table, a ''recess'' is defined as any period of three or more complete days—excluding Sundays—when either the House of Representatives or the Senate is not in session; however, as listed, the recess periods also are inclusive of days only partially in the recess, i.e., the day (or days) when the House and Senate each adjourn to begin the recess, as well as the day (or days) when each body reconvenes at the end of the recess.

[3] The election and role of the President pro tempore has evolved considerably over the Senate's history. ''*Pro tempore* is Latin for 'for the time being'; thus, the post was conceived as a temporary presiding officer. In the eighteenth and nineteenth centuries, the Senate frequently elected several Presidents pro tempore during a single session. Since Vice Presidents presided routinely, the Senate thought it necessary to choose a President pro tempore only for the limited periods when the Vice President might be ill or otherwise absent.'' Since no provision was in place (until the 25th amendment was adopted in 1967) for replacing the Vice President if he died or resigned from office, or if he assumed the Presidency, the President pro tempore would continue under such circumstances to fill the duties of the chair until the next Vice President was elected. Since Mar. 12, 1890, however, Presidents pro tempore have served until ''the Senate otherwise ordered.'' Since 1949, while still elected, the position has gone to the most senior member of the majority party (see footnote 19 for a minority party exception). To gain a more complete understanding of this position, see Robert C. Byrd's *The Senate 1789–1989: Addresses on the History of the United States Senate*, vol. 2, ch. 6 ''The President Pro Tempore,'' pp. 167–183, from which the quotes in this footnote are taken. Also, a complete listing of the dates of election of the Presidents pro tempore is in vol. 4 of the Byrd series (*The Senate 1789–1989: Historical Statistics, 1789–1992*), table 6–2, pp. 647–653.

[4] Henry Clay resigned as Speaker on Jan. 19, 1814. He was succeeded by Langdon Cheves who was elected on that same day.

[5] Henry Clay resigned as Speaker on Oct. 28, 1820, after the sine die adjournment of the first session of the 16th Congress. He was succeeded by John W. Taylor who was elected at the beginning of the second session.

[6] Andrew Stevenson resigned as Speaker on June 2, 1834. He was succeeded by John Bell who was elected on that same day.

[7] Speaker Schuyler Colfax resigned as Speaker on the last day of the 40th Congress, Mar. 3, 1869, in preparation for becoming Vice President of the United States on the following day. Theodore M. Pomeroy was elected Speaker on Mar. 3, and served for only that one day.

[8] Speaker Michael C. Kerr died on Aug. 19, 1876, after the sine die adjournment of the first session of the 44th Congress. Samuel J. Randall was elected Speaker at the beginning of the second session.

[9] William P. Frye resigned as President pro tempore on Apr. 27, 1911.

[10] President pro tempore James P. Clarke died on Oct. 1, 1916, after the sine die adjournment of the first session of the 64th Congress. Willard Saulsbury was elected President pro tempore during the second session.

[11] Speaker Joseph W. Byrns died on June 4, 1936. He was succeeded by William B. Bankhead who was elected Speaker on that same day.

[12] Speaker William B. Bankhead died on Sept. 15, 1940. He was succeeded by Sam Rayburn who was elected Speaker on that same day.

[13] President pro tempore Key Pittman died on Nov. 10, 1940. He was succeeded by William H. King who was elected President pro tempore on Nov. 19, 1940.

[14] President pro tempore Pat Harrison died on June 22, 1941. He was succeeded by Carter Glass who was elected President pro tempore on July 10, 1941.

[15] President Harry S. Truman called the Congress into extraordinary session twice, both times during the 80th Congress. Each time Congress had essentially wrapped up its business for the year, but for technical reasons had not adjourned sine die, so in each case the extraordinary session is considered an extension of the regularly numbered session rather than a separately numbered one. The dates of these extraordinary sessions were Nov. 17 to Dec. 19, 1947, and July 26 to Aug. 7, 1948.

[16] Speaker Sam Rayburn died on Nov. 16, 1961, after the sine die adjournment of the first session of the 87th Congress. John W. McCormack was elected Speaker at the beginning of the second session.

[17] President pro tempore Richard B. Russell died on Jan. 21, 1971. He was succeeded by Allen J. Ellender who was elected to that position on Jan. 22, 1971.

[18] President pro tempore Allen J. Ellender died on July 27, 1972. He was succeeded by James O. Eastland who was elected President pro tempore on July 28, 1972.

[19] Milton Young was elected President pro tempore for one day, Dec. 5, 1980, which was at the end of his 36-year career in the Senate. He was Republican, which was the minority party at that time. Warren G. Magnuson resumed the position of President pro tempore on Dec. 6, 1980.

[20] James C. Wright, Jr., resigned as Speaker on June 6, 1989. He was succeeded by Thomas S. Foley who was elected on that same day.

[21] The 2000 election resulted in an even split in the Senate between Republicans and Democrats. From the date the 107th Congress convened on Jan. 3, 2001, until Inauguration Day on Jan. 20, 2001, Vice President Albert Gore tipped the scale to a Democratic majority, hence Robert C. Byrd served as President pro tempore during this brief period. When Vice President Richard B. Cheney took office on Jan. 20, the Republicans became the majority party, and Strom Thurmond was elected President pro tempore. On June 6, 2001, Republican Senator James Jeffords became an Independent, creating a Democratic majority, and Robert C. Byrd was elected President pro tempore on that day.

CEREMONIAL MEETINGS OF CONGRESS

The following ceremonial meetings of Congress occurred on the following dates, at the designated locations, and for the reasons indicated. Please note that Congress was not in session on these occasions.

–999July 16, 1987, 100th Congress, Philadelphia, Pennsylvania, Independence Hall and Congress Hall—In honor of the bicentennial of the Constitution, and in commemoration of the Great Compromise of the Constitutional Convention which was agreed to on July 16, 1787.

–999September 6, 2002, 107th Congress, New York City, New York, Federal Hall—In remembrance of the victims and heroes of September 11, 2001, and in recognition of the courage and spirit of the City of New York.

JOINT SESSIONS AND MEETINGS, ADDRESSES TO THE SENATE OR THE HOUSE, AND INAUGURATIONS

1st–110th CONGRESSES, 1789–2007 [1]

The parliamentary difference between a joint session and a joint meeting has evolved over time. In recent years the distinctions have become clearer: a joint session is more formal, and occurs upon the adoption of a concurrent resolution; a joint meeting occurs when each body adopts a unanimous consent agreement to recess to meet with the other legislative body. Joint sessions typically are held to hear an address from the President of the United States or to count electoral votes. Joint meetings typically are held to hear an address from a foreign dignitary or visitors other than the President.

The Speaker of the House of Representatives usually presides over joint sessions and joint meetings; however, the President of the Senate does preside over joint sessions where the electoral votes are counted, as required by the Constitution.

In the earliest years of the Republic, 1789 and 1790, when the national legislature met in New York City, joint gatherings were held in the Senate Chamber in Federal Hall. In Philadelphia, when the legislature met in Congress Hall, such meetings were held in the Senate Chamber, 1790–1793, and in the Hall of the House of Representatives, 1794–1799. Once the Congress moved to the Capitol in Washington in 1800, the Senate Chamber again was used for joint gatherings through 1805. Since 1809, with few exceptions, joint sessions and joint meetings have occurred in the Hall of the House.

Presidential messages on the state of the Union were originally known as the ''Annual Message,'' but since the 80th Congress, in 1947, have been called the ''State of the Union Address.'' After President John Adams's Annual Message on November 22, 1800, these addresses were read by clerks to the individual bodies until President Woodrow Wilson resumed the practice of delivering them to joint sessions on December 2, 1913.

In some instances more than one joint gathering has occurred on the same day. For example, on January 6, 1941, Congress met in joint session to count electoral votes for President and Vice President, and then met again in joint session to receive President Franklin Delano Roosevelt's Annual Message.

Whereas in more recent decades, foreign dignitaries invited to speak before Congress have typically done so at joint meetings, in earlier times (and with several notable exceptions), such visitors were received by the Senate and the House separately, or by one or the other singly, a tradition begun with the visit of General Lafayette of France in 1824. At that time a joint committee decided that each body would honor Lafayette separately, establishing the precedent. (See fotnote 7 for more details.) Not all such occasions included formal addresses by such dignitaries (e.g., Lafayette's reception by the Senate in their chamber, at which he did not speak before they adjourned to greet him), hence the ''occasions'' listed in the third column of the table include not only addresses, but also remarks (defined as brief greetings or off-the-cuff comments often requested of the visitor at the last minute) and receptions. Relatively few foreign dignitaries were received by Congress before World War I.

Congress has hosted inaugurations since the first occasion in 1789. They always have been formal joint gatherings, and sometimes they also were joint sessions. Inaugurations were joint sessions when both houses of Congress were in session, and they processed to the ceremony as part of the business of the day. In many cases, however, one or both houses were not in session or were in recess at the time of the ceremony. In this table, inaugurations that were not joint sessions are listed in the second column. Those that were joint sessions are so identified and described in the third column.

JOINT SESSIONS AND MEETINGS, ADDRESSES TO THE SENATE OR THE HOUSE, AND INAUGURATIONS

[See notes at end of table]

Congress & Date	Type	Occasion, topic, or inaugural location	Name and position of dignitary (where applicable)
		NEW YORK CITY	
1st CONGRESS			
Apr. 6, 1789	Joint session	Counting electoral votes	N.A.
Apr. 30, 1789	......do	Inauguration and church service [2]	President George Washington; Right Reverend Samuel Provoost, Senate-appointed Chaplain.
Jan. 8, 1790	......do	Annual Message	President George Washington.
		PHILADELPHIA	
Dec. 8, 1790	......do	......do	Do.
2d CONGRESS			
Oct. 25, 1791	......do	......do	Do.
Nov. 6, 1792	......do	......do	Do.
Feb. 13, 1793	......do	Counting electoral votes	N.A.
3d CONGRESS			
Mar. 4, 1793	Inauguration	Senate Chamber	President George Washington.
Dec. 3, 1793	Joint session	Annual Message	Do.
Nov. 19, 1794	......do	......do	Do.
4th CONGRESS			
Dec. 8, 1795	......do	......do	Do.
Dec. 7, 1796	......do	......do	Do.
Feb. 8, 1797	......do	Counting electoral votes	N.A.
5th CONGRESS			
Mar. 4, 1797	Inauguration	Hall of the House	President John Adams.
May 16, 1797	Joint session	Relations with France	Do.
Nov. 23, 1797	......do	Annual Message	Do.
Dec. 8, 1798	......do	......do	Do.
6th CONGRESS			
Dec. 3, 1799	......do	......do	Do.
Dec. 26, 1799	......do	Funeral procession and oration in memory of George Washington.[3]	Representative Henry Lee.
		WASHINGTON	
Nov. 22, 1800	......do	Annual Message	President John Adams.
Feb. 11, 1801	......do	Counting electoral votes [4]	N.A.
7th CONGRESS			
Mar. 4, 1801	Inauguration	Senate Chamber	President Thomas Jefferson.
8th CONGRESS			
Feb. 13, 1805	Joint session	Counting electoral votes	N.A.
9th CONGRESS			
Mar. 4, 1805	Inauguration	Senate Chamber	President Thomas Jefferson.
10th CONGRESS			
Feb. 8, 1809	Joint session	Counting electoral votes	N.A.
11th CONGRESS			
Mar. 4, 1809	Inauguration	Hall of the House	President James Madison.
12th CONGRESS			
Feb. 10, 1813	Joint session	Counting electoral votes	N.A.
13th CONGRESS			
Mar. 4, 1813	Inauguration	Hall of the House	President James Madison.
14th CONGRESS			
Feb. 12, 1817	Joint session	Counting electoral votes [5]	N.A.
15th CONGRESS			
Mar. 4, 1817	Inauguration	In front of Brick Capitol	President James Monroe.
16th CONGRESS			
Feb. 14, 1821	Joint session	Counting electoral votes [6]	N.A.
17th CONGRESS			
Mar. 5, 1821	Inauguration	Hall of the House	President James Monroe.
18th CONGRESS			
Dec. 9, 1824	Senate	Reception	General Gilbert du Motier, Marquis de Lafayette, of France.

JOINT SESSIONS AND MEETINGS, ADDRESSES TO THE SENATE OR THE HOUSE, AND INAUGURATIONS—CONTINUED

[See notes at end of table]

Congress & Date	Type	Occasion, topic, or inaugural location	Name and position of dignitary (where applicable)
Dec. 10, 1824	House[7]	Address	Speaker Henry Clay; General Gilbert du Motier, Marquis de Lafayette, of France.
Feb. 9, 1825	Joint session	Counting electoral votes[8]	N.A.
19th CONGRESS			
Mar. 4, 1825	Inauguration	Hall of the House	President John Quincy Adams.
20th CONGRESS			
Feb. 11, 1829	Joint session	Counting electoral votes	N.A.
21st CONGRESS			
Mar. 4, 1829	Inauguration	East Portico[9]	President Andrew Jackson.
22d CONGRESS			
Feb. 13, 1833	Joint session	Counting electoral votes	N.A.
23d CONGRESS			
Mar. 4, 1833	Inauguration	Hall of the House[10]	President Andrew Jackson.
Dec. 31, 1834	Joint session	Lafayette eulogy	Representative and former President John Quincy Adams; ceremony attended by President Andrew Jackson.
24th CONGRESS			
Feb. 8, 1837	......do	Counting electoral votes	N.A.
25th CONGRESS			
Mar. 4, 1837	Inauguration	East Portico	President Martin Van Buren.
26th CONGRESS			
Feb. 10, 1841	Joint session	Counting electoral votes	N.A.
27th CONGRESS			
Mar. 4, 1841	Inauguration	East Portico	President William Henry Harrison.
28th CONGRESS			
Feb. 12, 1845	Joint session	Counting electoral votes	N.A.
29th CONGRESS			
Mar. 4, 1845	Inauguration	East Portico	President James Knox Polk.
30th CONGRESS			
Feb. 14, 1849	Joint session	Counting electoral votes	N.A.
31st CONGRESS			
Mar. 5, 1849	Inauguration	East Portico	President Zachary Taylor.
July 10, 1850	Joint session	Oath of office to President Millard Fillmore.[11]	N.A.
32d CONGRESS			
Jan. 5, 1852	Senate	Reception	Louis Kossuth, exiled Governor of Hungary.
Jan. 7, 1852	House	Remarks and Reception	Do.
Feb. 9, 1853	Joint session	Counting electoral votes	N.A.
33d CONGRESS			
Mar. 4, 1853	Inauguration	East Portico	President Franklin Pierce.
34th CONGRESS			
Feb. 11, 1857	Joint session	Counting electoral votes	N.A.
35th CONGRESS			
Mar. 4, 1857	Inauguration	East Portico	President James Buchanan.
36th CONGRESS			
Feb. 13, 1861	Joint session	Counting electoral votes	N.A.
37th CONGRESS			
Mar. 4, 1861	Inauguration	East Portico	President Abraham Lincoln.
Feb. 22, 1862	Joint session	Reading of Washington's farewell address.	John W. Forney, Secretary of the Senate.
38th CONGRESS			
Feb. 8, 1865	......do	Counting electoral votes	N.A.
39th CONGRESS			
Mar. 4, 1865	Inauguration	East Portico	President Abraham Lincoln.
Feb. 12, 1866	Joint session	Memorial to Abraham Lincoln	George Bancroft, historian; ceremony attended by President Andrew Johnson.

JOINT SESSIONS AND MEETINGS, ADDRESSES TO THE SENATE OR THE HOUSE, AND INAUGURATIONS—CONTINUED

[See notes at end of table]

Congress & Date	Type	Occasion, topic, or inaugural location	Name and position of dignitary (where applicable)
40th CONGRESS			
June 9, 1868	House	Address	Anson Burlingame, Envoy to the U.S. from China, and former Representative.
Feb. 10, 1869	Joint session	Counting electoral votes	N.A.
41st CONGRESS			
Mar. 4, 1869	Inauguration	East Portico	President Ulysses S. Grant.
42d CONGRESS			
Mar. 6, 1872	House	Address	Tomomi Iwakura, Ambassador from Japan.
Feb. 12, 1873	Joint session	Counting electoral votes [12]	N.A.
43d CONGRESS			
Mar. 4, 1873	Inauguration	East Portico	President Ulysses S. Grant.
Dec. 18, 1874	Joint meeting	Reception and Remarks	Speaker James G. Blaine; David Kalakaua, King of the Hawaiian Islands.[13]
44th CONGRESS			
Feb. 1, 1877 Feb. 10, 1877 Feb. 12, 1877 Feb. 19, 1877 Feb. 20, 1877 Feb. 21, 1877 Feb. 24, 1877 Feb. 26, 1877 Feb. 28, 1877 Mar. 1, 1877 Mar. 2, 1877	Joint session	Counting electoral votes [14]	N.A.
45th CONGRESS			
Mar. 5, 1877	Inauguration	East Portico	President Rutherford B. Hayes.
46th CONGRESS			
Feb. 2, 1880	House	Address	Charles Stewart Parnell, member of Parliament from Ireland.
Feb. 9, 1881	Joint session	Counting electoral votes	N.A.
47th CONGRESS			
Mar. 4, 1881	Inauguration	East Portico	President James A. Garfield.
Feb. 27, 1882	Joint session	Memorial to James A. Garfield	James G. Blaine, former Speaker, Senator, and Secretary of State; ceremony attended by President Chester A. Arthur.
48th CONGRESS			
Feb. 11, 1885	......do	Counting electoral votes	N.A.
Feb. 21, 1885	......do	Completion of Washington Monument	Representative John D. Long; Representative-elect John W. Daniel,[15] ceremony attended by President Chester A. Arthur.
49th CONGRESS			
Mar. 4, 1885	Inauguration	East Portico	President Grover Cleveland.
50th CONGRESS			
Feb. 13, 1889	Joint session	Counting electoral votes	N.A.
51st CONGRESS			
Mar. 4, 1889	Inauguration	East Portico	President Benjamin Harrison.
Dec. 11, 1889	Joint session	Centennial of George Washington's first inauguration.	Melville W. Fuller, Chief Justice of the United States; ceremony attended by President Benjamin Harrison.
52d CONGRESS			
Feb. 8, 1893	......do	Counting electoral votes	N.A.
53d CONGRESS			
Mar. 4, 1893	Inauguration	East Portico	President Grover Cleveland.
54th CONGRESS			
Feb. 10, 1897	Joint session	Counting electoral votes	N.A.
55th CONGRESS			
Mar. 4, 1897	Inauguration	In front of original Senate Wing of Capitol.	President William McKinley.

JOINT SESSIONS AND MEETINGS, ADDRESSES TO THE SENATE OR THE HOUSE, AND INAUGURATIONS—CONTINUED

[See notes at end of table]

Congress & Date	Type	Occasion, topic, or inaugural location	Name and position of dignitary (where applicable)
56th CONGRESS			
Dec. 12, 1900	Joint meeting	Centennial of the Capital City	Representatives James D. Richardson and Sereno E. Payne, and Senator George F. Hoar; ceremony attended by President William McKinley.
Feb. 13, 1901	Joint session	Counting electoral votes	N.A.
57th CONGRESS			
Mar. 4, 1901	Inauguration	East Portico	President William McKinley.
Feb. 27, 1902	Joint session	Memorial to William McKinley	John Hay, Secretary of State; ceremony attended by President Theodore Roosevelt and Prince Henry of Prussia.
58th CONGRESS			
Feb. 8, 1905	......do	Counting electoral votes	N.A.
59th CONGRESS			
Mar. 4, 1905	Inauguration	East Portico	President Theodore Roosevelt.
60th CONGRESS			
Feb. 10, 1909	Joint session	Counting electoral votes	N.A.
61st CONGRESS			
Mar. 4, 1909	Inauguration	Senate Chamber [16]	President William Howard Taft.
Feb. 9, 1911	House	Address	Count Albert Apponyi, Minister of Education from Hungary.
62d CONGRESS			
Feb. 12, 1913	Joint session	Counting electoral votes	N.A.
Feb. 15, 1913	......do	Memorial for Vice President James S. Sherman.[17]	Senators Elihu Root, Thomas S. Martin, Jacob H. Gallinger, John R. Thornton, Henry Cabot Lodge, John W. Kern, Robert M. LaFollette, John Sharp Williams, Charles Curtis, Albert B. Cummins, George T. Oliver, James A. O'Gorman; Speaker Champ Clark; President William Howard Taft.
63d CONGRESS			
Mar. 4, 1913	Inauguration	East Portico	President Woodrow Wilson.
Apr. 8, 1913	Joint session	Tariff message	Do.
June 23, 1913	......do	Currency and bank reform message	Do.
Aug. 27, 1913	......do	Mexican affairs message	Do.
Dec. 2, 1913	......do	Annual Message	Do.
Jan. 20, 1914	......do	Trusts message	Do.
Mar. 5, 1914	......do	Panama Canal tolls	Do.
Apr. 20, 1914	......do	Mexico message	Do.
Sept. 4, 1914	......do	War tax message	Do.
Dec. 8, 1914	......do	Annual Message	Do.
64th CONGRESS			
Dec. 7, 1915	......do	......do	Do.
Aug. 29, 1916	......do	Railroad message (labor-management dispute).	Do.
Dec. 5, 1916	......do	Annual Message	Do.
Jan. 22, 1917	Senate	Planning ahead for peace	Do.
Feb. 3, 1917	Joint session	Severing diplomatic relations with Germany.	Do.
Feb. 14, 1917	......do	Counting electoral votes	N.A.
Feb. 26, 1917	......do	Arming of merchant ships	President Woodrow Wilson.
65th CONGRESS			
Mar. 5, 1917	Inauguration	East Portico	Do.
Apr. 2, 1917	Joint session	War with Germany	Do.
May 1, 1917	Senate	Address	René Raphaël Viviani, Minister of Justice from France; Jules Jusserand, Ambassador from France; address attended by Marshal Joseph Jacques Césaire Joffre, member of French Commission to U.S.
May 3, 1917	House	......do	Do.
May 5, 1917	......do	......do	Arthur James Balfour, British Secretary of State for Foreign Affairs.
May 8, 1917	Senate	......do	Do.
May 31, 1917	......do	......do	Ferdinando di'Savoia, Prince of Udine, Head of Italian Mission to U.S.
June 2, 1917	House	......do	Ferdinando di'Savoia, Prince of Udine, Head of Italian Mission to U.S.; Guglielmo Marconi, member of Italian Mission to U.S.

JOINT SESSIONS AND MEETINGS, ADDRESSES TO THE SENATE OR THE HOUSE, AND INAUGURATIONS—CONTINUED

[See notes at end of table]

Congress & Date	Type	Occasion, topic, or inaugural location	Name and position of dignitary (where applicable)
June 22, 1917	Senate	Address	Baron Moncheur, Chief of Political Bureau of Belgian Foreign Office at Havre.
June 23, 1917	House	......do	Boris Bakhmetieff, Ambassador from Russia.[18]
June 26, 1917	Senate	......do	Do.
June 27, 1917	House	......do	Baron Moncheur, Chief of Political Bureau of Belgian Foreign Office at Havre.
Aug. 30, 1917	Senate	......do	Kikujirō Ishii, Ambassador from Japan.
Sept. 5, 1917	House	......do	Do.
Dec. 4, 1917	Joint session	Annual Message/War with Austria-Hungary.	President Woodrow Wilson.
Jan. 4, 1918	......do	Federal operation of transportation systems.	Do.
Jan. 5, 1918	Senate	Address	Milenko Vesnic, Head of Serbian War Mission.
Jan. 8, 1918	House	Address	Milenko Vesnic, Head of Serbian War Mission.
Do	Joint session	Program for world's peace	President Woodrow Wilson.
Feb. 11, 1918	......do	Peace message	Do.
May 27, 1918	......do	War finance message	Do.
Sept. 24, 1918	Senate	Address and Reception[19]	Jules Jusserand, Ambassador from France; Vice President Thomas R. Marshall.
Sept. 30 1918	......do	Support of woman suffrage	President Woodrow Wilson.
Nov. 11, 1918	Joint session	Terms of armistice signed by Germany	Do.
Dec. 2, 1918	......do	Annual Message	Do.
Feb. 9, 1919	......do	Memorial to Theodore Roosevelt	Senator Henry Cabot Lodge, Sr.; ceremony attended by former President William Howard Taft.
66th CONGRESS			
June 23, 1919	Senate	Address	Epitácio da Silva Pessoa, President-elect of Brazil.
July 10, 1919	......do	Versailles Treaty	President Woodrow Wilson.
Aug. 8, 1919	Joint session	Cost of living message	Do.
Sept. 18, 1919	......do	Address	President pro tempore Albert B. Cummins; Speaker Frederick H. Gillett; Representative and former Speaker Champ Clark; General John J. Pershing.
Oct. 28, 1919	Senate	......do	Albert I, King of the Belgians.
Do	House	......do	Do.
Feb. 9, 1921	Joint session	Counting electoral votes	N.A.
67th CONGRESS			
Mar. 4, 1921	Inauguration	East Portico	President Warren G. Harding.
Apr. 12, 1921	Joint session	Federal problem message	Do.
July 12, 1921	Senate	Adjusted compensation for veterans of the World War[20].	Do.
Dec. 6, 1921	Joint session	Annual Message	Do.
Feb. 28, 1922	......do	Maintenance of the merchant marine	Do.
Aug. 18, 1922	......do	Coal and railroad message	Do.
Nov. 21, 1922	......do	Promotion of the American merchant marine.	Do.
Dec. 8, 1922	......do	Annual Message[21]	Do.
Feb. 7, 1923	......do	British debt due to the United States	Do.
68th CONGRESS			
Dec. 6, 1923	......do	Annual Message	President Calvin Coolidge.
Feb. 27, 1924	......do	Memorial to Warren G. Harding	Charles Evans Hughes, Secretary of State; ceremony attended by President Calvin Coolidge.
Dec. 15, 1924	......do	Memorial to Woodrow Wilson	Dr. Edwin Anderson Alderman, President of the University of Virginia; ceremony attended by President Calvin Coolidge.
Feb. 11, 1925	......do	Counting electoral votes	N.A.
69th CONGRESS			
Mar. 4, 1925	Inauguration	East Portico	President Calvin Coolidge.
Feb. 22, 1927	Joint session	George Washington birthday message	Do.
70th CONGRESS			
Jan. 25, 1928	House	Reception and Address	William Thomas Cosgrave, President of Executive Council of Ireland.
Feb. 13, 1929	Joint session	Counting electoral votes	N.A.

JOINT SESSIONS AND MEETINGS, ADDRESSES TO THE SENATE OR THE HOUSE, AND INAUGURATIONS—CONTINUED

[See notes at end of table]

Congress & Date	Type	Occasion, topic, or inaugural location	Name and position of dignitary (where applicable)
71st CONGRESS			
Mar. 4, 1929	Inauguration	East Portico	President Herbert Hoover.
Oct. 7, 1929	Senate	Address	James Ramsay MacDonald, Prime Minister of the United Kingdom.
Jan. 13, 1930	......do	Reception	Jan Christiaan Smuts, former Prime Minister of South Africa.
72d CONGRESS			
Feb. 22, 1932	Joint session	Bicentennial of George Washington's birth.	President Herbert Hoover.
May 31, 1932	Senate	Emergency character of economic situation in U.S.	Do.
Feb. 6, 1933	Joint meeting	Memorial to Calvin Coolidge	Arthur Prentice Rugg, Chief Justice of the Supreme Judicial Court of Massachusetts; ceremony attended by President Herbert Hoover.
Feb. 8, 1933	Joint session	Counting electoral votes	N.A.
73d CONGRESS			
Mar. 4, 1933	Inauguration	East Portico	President Franklin Delano Roosevelt.
Jan. 3, 1934	Joint session	Annual Message	President Franklin Delano Roosevelt.
May 20, 1934	......do	100th anniversary, death of Lafayette	André de Laboulaye, Ambassador of France; President Franklin Delano Roosevelt; ceremony attended by Count de Chambrun, great-grandson of Lafayette.
74th CONGRESS			
Jan. 4, 1935	......do	Annual Message	President Franklin Delano Roosevelt.
May 22, 1935	......do	Veto message	Do.
Jan. 3, 1936	......do	Annual Message	Do.
75th CONGRESS			
Jan. 6, 1937	......do	Counting electoral votes	N.A.
Do	......do	Annual Message	President Franklin Delano Roosevelt.
Jan. 20, 1937	Inauguration	East Portico	President Franklin Delano Roosevelt; Vice President John Nance Garner.[22]
Apr. 1, 1937	Senate	Address	John Buchan, Lord Tweedsmuir, Governor General of Canada.
Do	House	......do	Do.
Jan. 3, 1938	Joint session	Annual Message	President Franklin Delano Roosevelt.
76th CONGRESS			
Jan. 4, 1939	......do	......do	Do.
Mar. 4, 1939	......do	Sesquicentennial of the 1st Congress	Do.
May 8, 1939	Senate	Address	Anastasio Somoza Garcia, President of Nicaragua.
Do	House	......do	Do.
June 9, 1939	Joint meeting	Reception[23]	George VI and Elizabeth, King and Queen of the United Kingdom.
Sept. 21, 1939	Joint session	Neutrality address	President Franklin Delano Roosevelt.
Jan. 3, 1940	......do	Annual Message	Do.
May 16, 1940	......do	National defense message	Do.
77th CONGRESS			
Jan. 6, 1941	......do	Counting electoral votes	N.A.
Do	......do	Annual Message	President Franklin Delano Roosevelt.
Jan. 20, 1941	......do	Inauguration, East Portico	President Franklin Delano Roosevelt; Vice President Henry A. Wallace.
Dec. 8, 1941	......do	War with Japan	President Franklin Delano Roosevelt.
Dec. 26, 1941	Joint meeting[24]	Address	Winston Churchill, Prime Minister of the United Kingdom.
Jan. 6, 1942	Joint session	Annual Message	President Franklin Delano Roosevelt.
May 11, 1942	Senate	Address	Manuel Prado, President of Peru.
Do	House	......do	Do.
June 2, 1942	......do	......do	Manuel Luis Quezon, President of the Philippines.[25]
June 4, 1942	Senate	......do	Do.
June 15, 1942	......do	......do	George II, King of Greece.[26]
Do	House	......do	Do.
June 25, 1942	Senate	......do	Peter II, King of Yugoslavia.[26]
Do	House	......do	Do.
Aug. 6, 1942	Senate[27]	......do	Wilhelmina, Queen of the Netherlands.[26]
Nov. 24, 1942	House	......do	Carlos Arroyo del Río, President of Ecuador.
Nov. 25, 1942	Senate	......do	Do.
Dec. 10, 1942	House	......do	Fulgencio Batista, President of Cuba.
78th CONGRESS			
Jan. 7, 1943	Joint session	Annual Message	President Franklin Delano Roosevelt.

JOINT SESSIONS AND MEETINGS, ADDRESSES TO THE SENATE OR THE HOUSE, AND INAUGURATIONS—CONTINUED

[See notes at end of table]

Congress & Date	Type	Occasion, topic, or inaugural location	Name and position of dignitary (where applicable)
Feb. 18, 1943	Senate	Remarks	Madame Chiang Kai-shek, of China.
Do	House	Address	Do.
May 6, 1943	Senate	......do	Enrique Peñaranda, President of Bolivia.
Do	House	......do	Do.
May 13, 1943	Senate	......do	Edvard Beneš, President of Czechoslovakia.[26]
Do	House	......do	Do.
May 19, 1943	Joint meeting	Address	Winston Churchill, Prime Minister of the United Kingdom.
May 27, 1943	Senate	Remarks	Edwin Barclay, President of Liberia.
Do	House	Address	Do.
June 10, 1943	Senate	......do	President Higinio Moriñigo M., President of Paraguay.
Do	House	......do	Do.
Oct. 15, 1943	Senate	......do	Elie Lescot, President of Haiti.
Nov. 18, 1943	Joint meeting	Moscow Conference	Cordell Hull, Secretary of State.
Jan. 20, 1944	Senate	Address	Isaías Medina Angarita, President of Venezuela.
Do	House	......do	Do.
79th CONGRESS			
Jan. 6, 1945	Joint session	Counting electoral votes	N.A.
Jan. 6, 1945	......do	Annual Message	President Roosevelt was not present. His message was read before the Joint Session of Congress.
Jan. 20, 1945	Inauguration	South Portico, The White House[28]	President Franklin Delano Roosevelt; Vice President Harry S. Truman.
Mar. 1, 1945	Joint session	Yalta Conference	President Franklin Delano Roosevelt.
Apr. 16, 1945	......do	Prosecution of the War	President Harry S. Truman.
May 21, 1945	......do	Bestowal of Congressional Medal of Honor on Tech. Sgt. Jake William Lindsey.	General George C. Marshall, Chief of Staff, U.S. Army; President Harry S. Truman.
June 18, 1945	Joint meeting	Address	General Dwight D. Eisenhower, Supreme Commander, Allied Expeditionary Force.
July 2, 1945	Senate	United Nations Charter	President Harry S. Truman.
Oct. 5, 1945	Joint meeting	Address	Admiral Chester W. Nimitz, Commander-in-Chief, Pacific Fleet.
Oct. 23, 1945	Joint session	Universal military training message	President Harry S. Truman.
Nov. 13, 1945	Joint meeting	Address	Clement R. Attlee, Prime Minister of the United Kingdom.
May 25, 1946	Joint session	Railroad strike message	President Harry S. Truman.
July 1, 1946	......do	Memorial to Franklin Delano Roosevelt	John Winant, U.S. Representative on the Economic and Social Council of the United Nations; ceremony attended by President Harry S. Truman and Mrs. Franklin Delano Roosevelt.
80th CONGRESS			
Jan. 6, 1947	......do	State of the Union Address[29]	President Harry S. Truman.
Mar. 12, 1947	......do	Greek-Turkish aid policy	Do.
May 1, 1947	Joint meeting	Address	Miguel Alemán, President of Mexico.
Nov. 17, 1947	Joint session	Aid to Europe message	President Harry S. Truman.
Jan. 7, 1948	......do	State of the Union Address	Do.
Mar. 17, 1948	......do	National security and conditions in Europe.	Do.
Apr. 19, 1948	......do	50th anniversary, liberation of Cuba	President Harry S. Truman; Guillermo Belt, Ambassador of Cuba.
July 27, 1948	......do	Inflation, housing, and civil rights	President Harry S. Truman.
81st CONGRESS			
Jan. 5, 1949	......do	State of the Union Address	Do.
Jan. 6, 1949	......do	Counting electoral votes	N.A.
Jan. 20, 1949	......do	Inauguration, East Portico	President Harry S. Truman; Vice President Alben W. Barkley.
May 19, 1949	Joint meeting	Address	Eurico Gaspar Dutra, President of Brazil.
Aug. 9, 1949	House	......do	Elpidio Quirino, President of the Philippines.
Do	Senate	......do	Do.
Oct. 13, 1949	......do	......do	Jawaharlal Nehru, Prime Minister of India.
Do	House	......do	Do.
Jan. 4, 1950	Joint session	State of the Union Address	President Harry S. Truman.
Apr. 13, 1950	Senate	Address	Gabriel González-Videla, President of Chile.
May 4, 1950	......do	......do	Liaquat Ali Khan, Prime Minister of Pakistan.
Do	House	......do	Do.

JOINT SESSIONS AND MEETINGS, ADDRESSES TO THE SENATE OR THE HOUSE, AND INAUGURATIONS—CONTINUED

[See notes at end of table]

Congress & Date	Type	Occasion, topic, or inaugural location	Name and position of dignitary (where applicable)
May 31, 1950	Joint meeting	Address	Dean Acheson, Secretary of State.
July 28, 1950	Senate	do	Chōjirō Kuriyama, member of Japanese Diet.
July 31, 1950	House	do	Tokutarō Kitamura, member of Japanese Diet.
Aug. 1, 1950	do	do	Robert Gordon Menzies, Prime Minister of Australia.
Do	Senate	do	Do.
82d CONGRESS			
Jan. 8, 1951	Joint session	State of the Union Address	President Harry S. Truman.
Feb. 1, 1951	Joint meeting [30]	North Atlantic Treaty Organization	General Dwight D. Eisenhower.
Apr. 2, 1951	Joint meeting	Address	Vincent Auriol, President of France.
Apr. 19, 1951	do	Return from Pacific Command	General Douglas MacArthur.
June 21, 1951	do	Address	Galo Plaza, President of Ecuador.
July 2, 1951	Senate	Addresses	Tadao Kuraishi, and Aisuke Okamoto, members of Japanese Diet.
Aug. 23, 1951	do	Address	Zentarō Kosaka, member of Japanese Diet.
Sept. 24, 1951	Joint meeting	do	Alcide de Gasperi, Prime Minister of Italy.
Jan. 9, 1952	Joint session	State of the Union Address	President Harry S. Truman.
Jan. 17, 1952	Joint meeting	Address	Winston Churchill, Prime Minister of the United Kingdom.
Apr. 3, 1952	do	do	Juliana, Queen of the Netherlands.
May 22, 1952	do	Korea	General Matthew B. Ridgway.
June 10, 1952	Joint session	Steel industry dispute	President Harry S. Truman.
83d CONGRESS			
Jan. 6, 1953	do	Counting electoral votes	N.A.
Jan. 20, 1953	do	Inauguration, East Portico	President Dwight D. Eisenhower; Vice President Richard M. Nixon.
Feb. 2, 1953	do	State of the Union Address	President Dwight D. Eisenhower.
Jan. 7, 1954	do	do	Do.
Jan. 29, 1954	Joint meeting	Address	Celal Bayar, President of Turkey.
May 4, 1954	do	do	Vincent Massey, Governor General of Canada.
May 28, 1954	do	do	Haile Selassie I, Emperor of Ethiopia.
July 28, 1954	do	do	Syngman Rhee, President of South Korea.
Nov. 12, 1954	Senate	Remarks	Shigeru Yoshida, Prime Minister of Japan.
Nov. 17, 1954	do	Address [31]	Sarvepalli Radhakrishnan, Vice President of India.
Nov. 18, 1954	do	Remarks	Pierre Mendès-France, Premier of France.
84th CONGRESS			
Jan. 6, 1955	Joint session	State of the Union Address	President Dwight D. Eisenhower.
Jan. 27, 1955	Joint meeting	Address	Paul E. Magliore, President of Haiti.
Mar. 16, 1955	Senate	do	Robert Gordon Menzies, Prime Minister of Australia.
Do	House	do	Do.
Mar. 30, 1955	Senate	do	Mario Scelba, Prime Minister of Italy.
Do	House	do	Do.
May 4, 1955	Senate	do	P. Phibunsongkhram, Prime Minister of Thailand.
Do	House	do	Do.
June 30, 1955	Senate	do	U Nu, Prime Minister of Burma.
Do	House	do	Do.
Jan. 5, 1956	Senate	do	Juscelino Kubitschek de Oliverira, President-elect of Brazil.
Feb. 2, 1956	do	do	Anthony Eden, Prime Minister of the United Kingdom.
Do	House	do	Do.
Feb. 29, 1956	Joint meeting	do	Giovanni Gronchi, President of Italy.
Mar. 15, 1956	Senate	do	John Aloysius Costello, Prime Minister of Ireland.
Do	House	do	Do.
Apr. 30, 1956	Senate	do	João Goulart, Vice President of Brazil.
May 17, 1956	Joint meeting	do	Sukarno, President of Indonesia.
85th CONGRESS			
Jan. 5, 1957	Joint session	Middle East message	President Dwight D. Eisenhower.
Jan. 7, 1957	do	Counting electoral votes	N.A.
Jan. 10, 1957	do	State of the Union Address	President Dwight D. Eisenhower.
Jan. 21, 1957	do	Inauguration, East Portico	President Dwight D. Eisenhower; Vice President Richard M. Nixon.
Feb. 27, 1957	House	Address	Guy Mollet, Premier of France.
Do	Senate	do	Do.

JOINT SESSIONS AND MEETINGS, ADDRESSES TO THE SENATE OR THE HOUSE, AND INAUGURATIONS—CONTINUED

[See notes at end of table]

Congress & Date	Type	Occasion, topic, or inaugural location	Name and position of dignitary (where applicable)
May 9, 1957	Joint meeting	Address	Ngo Dinh Diem, President of Vietnam.
May 28, 1957	House	......do	Konrad Adenauer, Chancellor of West Germany.
Do	Senate	......do	Do.
June 20, 1957	......do	......do	Nobusuke Kishi, Prime Minister of Japan.
Do	House	......do	Do.
July 11, 1957	Senate	......do	Husseyn Shaheed Suhrawardy, Prime Minister of Pakistan.
Jan. 9, 1958	Joint session	State of the Union Address	President Dwight D. Eisenhower.
June 5, 1958	Joint meeting	Address	Theodor Heuss, President of West Germany.
June 10, 1958	Senate	......do	Harold Macmillan, Prime Minister of the United Kingdom.
June 18, 1958	Joint meeting	......do	Carlos F. Garcia, President of the Philippines.
June 25, 1958	House	......do	Muhammad Daoud Khan, Prime Minister of Afghanistan.
Do	Senate	......do	Do.
July 24, 1958	......do	......do	Kwame Nkrumah, Prime Minister of Ghana.
July 25, 1958	House	......do	Do.
July 29, 1958	Senate	......do	Amintore Fanfani, Prime Minister of Italy.
Do	House	......do	Do.
86th CONGRESS			
Jan. 9, 1959	Joint session	State of the Union Address	President Dwight D. Eisenhower.
Jan. 21, 1959	Joint meeting	Address	Arturo Frondizi, President of Argentina.
Feb. 12, 1959	Joint session	Sesquicentennial of Abraham Lincoln's birth.	Fredric March, actor; Carl Sandburg, poet.
Mar. 11, 1959	Joint meeting	Address	Jose Maria Lemus, President of El Salvador.
Mar. 18, 1959	......do	......do	Sean T. O'Kelly, President of Ireland.
May 12, 1959	......do	......do	Baudouin, King of the Belgians.
Jan. 7, 1960	Joint session	State of the Union Address	President Dwight D. Eisenhower.
Mar. 30, 1960	Senate	Address	Harold Macmillan, Prime Minister of the United Kingdom.
Apr. 6, 1960	Joint meeting	......do	Alberto Lleras-Camargo, President of Colombia.
Apr. 25, 1960	......do	......do	Charles de Gaulle, President of France.
Apr. 28, 1960	......do	......do	Mahendra, King of Nepal.
June 29, 1960	......do	......do	Bhumibol Adulyadej, King of Thailand.
87th CONGRESS			
Jan. 6, 1961	Joint session	Counting electoral votes	N.A.
Jan. 20, 1961	......do	Inauguration, East Portico	President John F. Kennedy; Vice President Lyndon B. Johnson.
Jan. 30, 1961	......do	State of the Union Address	President John F. Kennedy.
Apr. 13, 1961	Senate	Remarks	Konrad Adenauer, Chancellor of West Germany.
Apr. 18, 1961	House	Address	Constantine Karamanlis, Prime Minister of Greece.
May 4, 1961	Joint meeting	......do	Habib Bourguiba, President of Tunisia.
May 25, 1961	Joint session	Urgent national needs: foreign aid, defense, civil defense, and outer space.	President John F. Kennedy.
June 22, 1961	Senate	Remarks	Hayato Ikeda, Prime Minister of Japan.
Do	House	Address	Do.
July 12, 1961	Joint meeting	......do	Mohammad Ayub Khan, President of Pakistan.
July 26, 1961	House	......do	Abubakar Tafawa Balewa, Prime Minister of Nigeria.
Sept. 21, 1961	Joint meeting	......do	Manuel Prado, President of Peru.
Jan. 11, 1962	Joint session	State of the Union Address	President John F. Kennedy.
Feb. 26, 1962	Joint meeting	Friendship 7: 1st United States orbital space flight.	Lt. Col. John H. Glenn, Jr., USMC; Friendship 7 astronaut.
Apr. 4, 1962	......do	Address	João Goulart, President of Brazil.
Apr. 12, 1962	......do	......do	Mohammad Reza Shah Pahlavi, Shahanshah of Iran.
88th CONGRESS			
Jan. 14, 1963	Joint session	State of the Union Address	President John F. Kennedy.
May 21, 1963	Joint meeting	Flight of Faith 7 Spacecraft	Maj. Gordon L. Cooper, Jr., USAF, Faith 7 astronaut.
Oct. 2, 1963	Senate	Address	Haile Selassie I, Emperor of Ethiopia.
Nov. 27, 1963	Joint session	Assumption of office	President Lyndon B. Johnson.
Jan. 8, 1964	......do	State of the Union Address	Do.
Jan. 15, 1964	Joint meeting	Address	Antonio Segni, President of Italy.
May 28, 1964	......do	......do	Eamon de Valera, President of Ireland.

JOINT SESSIONS AND MEETINGS, ADDRESSES TO THE SENATE OR THE HOUSE, AND INAUGURATIONS—CONTINUED

[See notes at end of table]

Congress & Date	Type	Occasion, topic, or inaugural location	Name and position of dignitary (where applicable)
89th CONGRESS			
Jan. 4, 1965	Joint session	State of the Union Address	President Lyndon B. Johnson.
Jan. 6, 1965	......do	Counting electoral votes	N.A.
Jan. 20, 1965	Joint session [32]	Inauguration, East Portico	President Lyndon B. Johnson; Vice President Hubert H. Humphrey.
Mar. 15, 1965	Joint session	Voting rights	President Lyndon B. Johnson.
Sept. 14, 1965	Joint meeting	Flight of Gemini 5 Spacecraft	Lt. Col. Gordon L. Cooper, Jr., USAF; and Charles Conrad, Jr., USN; Gemini 5 astronauts.
Jan. 12, 1966	Joint session	State of the Union Address	President Lyndon B. Johnson.
Sept. 15, 1966	Joint meeting	Address	Ferdinand E. Marcos, President of the Philippines.
90th CONGRESS			
Jan. 10, 1967	Joint session	State of the Union Address	President Lyndon B. Johnson.
Apr. 28, 1967	Joint meeting	Vietnam policy	General William C. Westmoreland.
Aug. 16, 1967	Senate	Address	Kurt George Kiesinger, Chancellor of West Germany.
Oct. 27, 1967	Joint meeting	......do	Gustavo Diaz Ordaz, President of Mexico.
Jan. 17, 1968	Joint session	State of the Union Address	President Lyndon B. Johnson.
91st CONGRESS			
Jan. 6, 1969	......do	Counting electoral votes [33]	N.A.
Jan. 9, 1969	Joint meeting	Apollo 8: 1st flight around the moon	Col. Frank Borman, USAF; Capt. James A. Lowell, Jr., USN; Lt. Col. William A. Anders, USAF; Apollo 8 astronauts.
Jan. 14, 1969	Joint session	State of the Union Address	President Lyndon B. Johnson.
Jan. 20, 1969	Joint session [32]	Inauguration, East Portico	President Richard M. Nixon; Vice President Spiro T. Agnew.
Sept. 16, 1969	Joint meeting	Apollo 11: 1st lunar landing	Neil A. Armstrong; Col. Edwin E. Aldrin, Jr., USAF; and Lt. Col. Michael Collins, USAF; Apollo 11 astronauts.
Nov. 13, 1969	House	Executive-Legislative branch relations and Vietnam policy.	President Richard M. Nixon.
Do	Senate	......do	Do.
Jan. 22, 1970	Joint session	State of the Union Address	Do.
Feb. 25, 1970	Joint meeting	Address	Georges Pompidou, President of France.
June 3, 1970	......do	......do	Rafael Caldera, President of Venezuela.
Sept. 22, 1970	......do	Report on prisoners of war	Col. Frank Borman, Representative to the President on Prisoners of War.
92d CONGRESS			
Jan. 22, 1971	Joint session	State of the Union Address	President Richard M. Nixon.
Sept. 9, 1971	......do	Economic policy	Do.
Do	Joint meeting	Apollo 15: lunar mission	Col. David R. Scott, USAF; Col. James B. Irwin, USAF; and Lt. Col. Alfred M. Worden, USAF; Apollo 15 astronauts.
Jan. 20, 1972	Joint session	State of the Union Address	President Richard M. Nixon.
June 1, 1972	......do	European trip report	Do.
June 15, 1972	Joint meeting	Address	Luis Echeverria Alvarez, President of Mexico.
93d CONGRESS			
Jan. 6, 1973	Joint session	Counting electoral votes	N.A.
Jan. 20, 1973	Inauguration	East Portico	President Richard M. Nixon; Vice President Spiro T. Agnew.
Dec. 6, 1973	Joint meeting	Oath of office to, and Address by Vice President Gerald R. Ford.	Vice President Gerald R. Ford; ceremony attended by President Richard M. Nixon.
Do	Senate	Remarks and Reception	Vice President Gerald R. Ford.
Jan. 30 1974	Joint session	State of the Union Address	President Richard M. Nixon.
Aug. 12, 1974	......do	Assumption of office	President Gerald R. Ford.
Oct. 8, 1974	......do	Economy	Do.
Dec. 19, 1974	Senate	Address [34]	Vice President Nelson A. Rockefeller.
94th CONGRESS			
Jan. 15, 1975	Joint session	State of the Union Address	President Gerald R. Ford.
Apr. 10, 1975	......do	State of the World message	Do.
June 17, 1975	Joint meeting	Address	Walter Scheel, President of West Germany.
Nov. 5, 1975	......do	......do	Anwar El Sadat, President of Egypt.
Jan. 19, 1976	Joint session	State of the Union Address	President Gerald R. Ford.
Jan. 28, 1976	Joint meeting	Address	Yitzhak Rabin, Prime Minister of Israel.
Mar. 17, 1976	......do	......do	Liam Cosgrave, Prime Minister of Ireland.

JOINT SESSIONS AND MEETINGS, ADDRESSES TO THE SENATE OR THE HOUSE, AND INAUGURATIONS—CONTINUED

[See notes at end of table]

Congress & Date	Type	Occasion, topic, or inaugural location	Name and position of dignitary (where applicable)
May 18, 1976	Joint meeting	Address	Valery Giscard d'Estaing, President of France.
June 2, 1976	......do	......do	Juan Carlos I, King of Spain.
Sept. 23, 1976	......do	......do	William R. Tolbert, Jr., President of Liberia.
95th CONGRESS			
Jan. 6, 1977	Joint session	Counting electoral votes	N.A.
Jan. 12, 1977	......do	State of the Union Address	President Gerald R. Ford.
Jan. 20, 1977	Inauguration	East Portico	President Jimmy Carter; Vice President Walter F. Mondale.
Feb. 17, 1977	House	Address	José López Portillo, President of Mexico.
Feb. 22, 1977	Joint meeting	Address	Pierre Elliot Trudeau, Prime Minister of Canada.
Apr. 20, 1977	Joint session	Energy	President Jimmy Carter.
Jan. 19, 1978	......do	State of the Union Address	Do.
Sept. 18, 1978	......do	Middle East Peace agreements	President Jimmy Carter; joint session attended by Anwar El Sadat, President of Egypt, and by Menachem Begin, Prime Minister of Israel.
96th CONGRESS			
Jan. 23, 1979	......do	State of the Union Address	Do.
June 18, 1979	......do	Salt II agreements	Do.
Jan. 23, 1980	......do	State of the Union Address	Do.
97th CONGRESS			
Jan. 6, 1981	......do	Counting electoral votes	N.A.
Jan. 20, 1981	Joint session[32]	Inauguration, West Front	President Ronald Reagan; Vice President George Bush.
Feb. 18, 1981	Joint session	Economic recovery	President Ronald Reagan.
Apr. 28, 1981	......do	Economic recovery—inflation	Do.
Jan. 26, 1982	......do	State of the Union Address	Do.
Jan. 28, 1982	Joint meeting	Centennial of birth of Franklin Delano Roosevelt.	Dr. Arthur Schlesinger, historian; Senator Jennings Randolph; Representative Claude Pepper; Averell Harriman, former Governor of New York[35]; former Representative James Roosevelt, son of President Roosevelt.
Apr. 21, 1982	......do	Address	Beatrix, Queen of the Netherlands.
98th CONGRESS			
Jan. 25, 1983	Joint session	State of the Union Address	President Ronald Reagan.
Apr. 27, 1983	......do	Central America	Do.
Oct. 5, 1983	Joint meeting	Address	Karl Carstens, President of West Germany.
Jan. 25, 1984	Joint session	State of the Union Address	President Ronald Reagan.
Mar. 15, 1984	Joint meeting	Address	Dr. Garett FitzGerald, Prime Minister of Ireland.
Mar. 22, 1984	......do	......do	François Mitterand, President of France.
May 8, 1984	......do	Centennial of birth of Harry S. Truman	Representatives Ike Skelton and Alan Wheat; former Senator Stuart Symington; Margaret Truman-Daniel, daughter of President Truman; and Senator Mark Hatfield.
May 16, 1984	......do	Address	Miguel de la Madrid, President of Mexico.
99th CONGRESS			
Jan. 7, 1985	Joint session	Counting electoral votes	N.A.
Jan. 21, 1985	Inauguration	Rotunda[36]	President Ronald Reagan; Vice President George Bush.
Feb. 6, 1985	Joint session	State of the Union Address	President Ronald Reagan.
Feb. 20, 1985	Joint meeting	Address	Margaret Thatcher, Prime Minister of the United Kingdom.
Mar. 6, 1985	......do	......do	Bettino Craxi, President of the Council of Ministers of Italy.
Mar. 20, 1985	......do	......do	Raul Alfonsin, President of Argentina.
June 13, 1985	......do	......do	Rajiv Gandhi, Prime Minister of India.
Oct. 9, 1985	......do	......do	Lee Kuan Yew, Prime Minister of Singapore.
Nov. 21, 1985	Joint session	Geneva Summit	President Ronald Reagan.
Feb. 4, 1986	......do	State of the Union Address	Do.
Sept. 11, 1986	Joint meeting	Address	Jose Sarney, President of Brazil.
Sept. 18, 1986	......do	......do	Corazon C. Aquino, President of the Philippines.
100th CONGRESS			
Jan. 27, 1987	Joint session	State of the Union Address	President Ronald Reagan.

JOINT SESSIONS AND MEETINGS, ADDRESSES TO THE SENATE OR THE HOUSE, AND INAUGURATIONS—CONTINUED

[See notes at end of table]

Congress & Date	Type	Occasion, topic, or inaugural location	Name and position of dignitary (where applicable)
Nov. 10, 1987	Joint meeting	Address	Chaim Herzog, President of Israel.
Jan. 25, 1988	Joint session	State of the Union Address	President Ronald Reagan.
Apr. 27, 1988	Joint meeting	Address	Brian Mulroney, Prime Minister of Canada.
June 23, 1988	......do	......do	Robert Hawke, Prime Minister of Australia.
101st CONGRESS			
Jan. 4, 1989	Joint session	Counting electoral votes	N.A.
Jan. 20, 1989	Inauguration	West Front	President George Bush; Vice President Dan Quayle.
Feb. 9, 1989	Joint session	Building a Better America	President George Bush.
Mar. 2, 1989	Joint meeting	Bicentennial of the 1st Congress	President Pro Tempore Robert C. Byrd; Speaker James C. Wright, Jr.; Representatives Lindy Boggs, Thomas S. Foley, and Robert H. Michel; Senators George Mitchell and Robert Dole; Howard Nemerov, Poet Laureate of the United States; David McCullough, historian; Anthony M. Frank, Postmaster General; former Senator Nicholas Brady, Secretary of the Treasury.
Apr. 6, 1989	Senate [37]	Addresses on the 200th anniversary commemoration of Senate's first legislative session.	Former Senators Thomas F. Eagleton and Howard H. Baker, Jr..
June 7, 1989	Joint meeting	Address	Benazir Bhutto, Prime Minister of Pakistan.
Oct. 4, 1989	......do	......do	Carlos Salinas de Gortari, President of Mexico.
Oct. 18, 1989	......do	......do	Roh Tae Woo, President of South Korea.
Nov. 15, 1989	......do	......do	Lech Walesa, chairman of Solidarność labor union, Poland.
Jan. 31, 1990	Joint session	State of the Union Address	President George Bush.
Feb. 21, 1990	Joint meeting	Address	Vaclav Hável, President of Czechoslovakia.
Mar. 7, 1990	......do	......do	Giulio Andreotti, President of the Council of Ministers of Italy.
Mar. 27, 1990	......do	Centennial of birth of Dwight D. Eisenhower.	Senator Robert Dole; Walter Cronkite, television journalist; Winston S. Churchill, member of British Parliament and grandson of Prime Minister Churchill; Clark M. Clifford, former Secretary of Defense; James D. Robinson III, chairman of Eisenhower Centennial Foundation; Arnold Palmer, professional golfer; John S.D. Eisenhower, former Ambassador to Belgium and son of President Eisenhower; Representatives Beverly Byron, William F. Goodling, and Pat Roberts.
June 26, 1990	......do	Address	Nelson Mandela, Deputy President of the African National Congress, South Africa.
Sept. 11, 1990	Joint session	Invasion of Kuwait by Iraq	President George Bush.
102d CONGRESS			
Jan. 29, 1991	......do	State of the Union Address	Do.
Mar. 6, 1991	......do	Conclusion of Persian Gulf War	Do.
Apr. 16, 1991	Joint meeting	Address	Violeta B. de Chamorro, President of Nicaragua.
May 8, 1991	House [38]	......do	General H. Norman Schwarzkopf.
May 16, 1991	Joint meeting	Address	Elizabeth II, Queen of the United Kingdom; joint meeting also attended by Prince Philip.
Nov. 14, 1991	......do	......do	Carlos Saul Menem, President of Argentina.
Jan. 28, 1992	Joint session	State of the Union Address	President George Bush.
Apr. 30, 1992	Joint meeting	Address	Richard von Weizsäcker, President of Germany.
June 17, 1992	......do	......do	Boris Yeltsin, President of Russia.
103d CONGRESS			
Jan. 6, 1993	Joint session	Counting electoral votes	N.A.
Jan. 20, 1993	Inauguration	West Front	President William J. Clinton; Vice President Albert Gore.
Feb. 17, 1993	Joint session	Economic Address [39]	President William J. Clinton.
Sept. 22, 1993	......do	Health care reform	Do.
Jan. 25, 1994	......do	State of the Union Address	Do.

JOINT SESSIONS AND MEETINGS, ADDRESSES TO THE SENATE OR THE HOUSE, AND INAUGURATIONS—CONTINUED

[See notes at end of table]

Congress & Date	Type	Occasion, topic, or inaugural location	Name and position of dignitary (where applicable)
May 18, 1994	Joint meeting	Address	Narasimha Rao, Prime Minister of India.
July 26, 1994	......do	Addresses	Hussein I, King of Jordan; Yitzhak Rabin, Prime Minister of Israel.
Oct. 6, 1994	......do	Address	Nelson Mandela, President of South Africa.
104th CONGRESS			
Jan. 24, 1995	Joint session	State of the Union Address	President William J. Clinton.
July 26, 1995	Joint meeting	Address	Kim Yong-sam, President of South Korea.[40]
Oct. 11, 1995	......do	Close of the Commemoration of the 50th Anniversary of World War II.	Speaker Newt Gingrich; Vice President Albert Gore; President Pro Tempore Strom Thurmond; Representatives Henry J. Hyde and G.V. ''Sonny'' Montgomery; Senators Daniel K. Inouye and Robert Dole; former Representative Robert H. Michel; General Louis H. Wilson (ret.), former Commandant of the Marine Corps.
Dec. 12, 1995	......do	Address	Shimon Peres, Prime Minister of Israel.
Jan. 30, 1996	Joint session	State of the Union Address	President William J. Clinton.
Feb. 1, 1996	Joint meeting	Address	Jacques Chirac, President of France.
July 10, 1996	......do	......do	Benyamin Netanyahu, Prime Minister of Israel.
Sept. 11, 1996	......do	......do	John Bruton, Prime Minister of Ireland.
105th CONGRESS			
Jan. 9, 1997	Joint session	Counting electoral votes	N.A.
Jan. 20, 1997	Inauguration	West Front	President William J. Clinton; Vice President Albert Gore.
Feb. 4, 1997	Joint session	State of the Union Address[41]	President William J. Clinton.
Feb. 27, 1997	Joint meeting	Address	Eduardo Frei, President of Chile.
Jan. 27, 1998	Joint session	State of the Union Address	President William J. Clinton.
June 10, 1998	Joint meeting	Address	Kim Dae-jung, President of South Korea.
July 15, 1998	......do	......do	Emil Constantinescu, President of Romania.
106th CONGRESS			
Jan. 19, 1999	Joint session	State of the Union Address	President William J. Clinton.
Jan. 27, 2000	......do	......do	Do.
Sept. 14, 2000	Joint meeting	Address	Atal Bihari Vajpayee, Prime Minister of India.
107th CONGRESS			
Jan. 6, 2001	Joint session	Counting electoral votes	N.A.
Jan. 20, 2001	Inauguration	West Front	President George W. Bush; Vice President Richard B. Cheney.
Feb. 27, 2001	Joint session	Budget message[39]	President George W. Bush.
Sept. 6, 2001	Joint meeting	Address	Vicente Fox, President of Mexico.
Sept. 20, 2001	Joint session	War on terrorism	President George W. Bush; joint session attended by Tony Blair, Prime Minister of the United Kingdom, by Tom Ridge, Governor of Pennsylvania, by George Pataki, Governor of New York, and by Rudolph Giuliani, Mayor of New York City.
Jan. 29, 2002	......do	State of the Union Address	President George W. Bush; joint session attended by Hamid Karzai, Chairman of the Interim Authority of Afghanistan.
108th CONGRESS			
Jan. 28, 2003	......do	......do	President George W. Bush.
July 17, 2003	Joint meeting	Address	Tony Blair, Prime Minister of the United Kingdom; joint meeting attended by Mrs. George W. Bush.
Jan. 20, 2004	Joint session	State of the Union Address	President George W. Bush.
Feb. 4, 2004	Joint meeting	Address	Jose Maria Aznar, President of the Government of Spain.
June 15, 2004	......do	......do	Hamid Karzai, President of Afghanistan.
Sept. 23, 2004	......do	......do	Ayad Allawi, Interim Prime Minister of Iraq.
109th CONGRESS			
Jan. 6, 2005	Joint session	Counting electoral votes[42]	N.A.
Jan. 20, 2005	Inauguration	West Front	President George W. Bush; Vice President Richard B. Cheney.
Feb. 2, 2005	Joint session	State of the Union Address	President George W. Bush.
Apr. 6, 2005	Joint meeting	Address	Viktor Yushchenko, President of Ukraine.
July 19, 2005	......do	......do	Dr. Manmohan Singh, Prime Minister of India.
Jan. 31, 2006	Joint session	State of the Union Address	President George W. Bush.
Mar. 1, 2006	Joint meeting	Address	Silvio Berlusconi, Prime Minister of Italy.

JOINT SESSIONS AND MEETINGS, ADDRESSES TO THE SENATE OR THE HOUSE, AND INAUGURATIONS—CONTINUED

[See notes at end of table]

Congress & Date	Type	Occasion, topic, or inaugural location	Name and position of dignitary (where applicable)
Mar. 15, 2006	Joint meeting	Address	Ellen Johnson Sirleaf, President of Liberia.
May 24, 2006	......do	......do	Ehud Olmert, Prime Minister of Israel.
June 7, 2006	......do	......do	Dr. Vaira Vike-Freiberga, President of Latvia.
July 26, 2006	......do	......do	Nouri Al-Maliki, Prime Minister of Iraq.
110th CONGRESS			
Jan. 23, 2007	Joint session	State of the Union Address	President George W. Bush.
Mar. 7, 2007	Joint meeting	Address	Abdullah II Ibn Al Hussein, King of Jordan.

[1] Closing date for this table was May 21, 2007.

[2] The oath of office was administered to George Washington outside on the gallery in front of the Senate Chamber, after which the Congress and the President returned to the chamber to hear the inaugural address. They then proceeded to St. Paul's Chapel for the "divine service" performed by the Chaplain of the Congress. Adjournment of the ceremony did not occur until the Congress returned to Federal Hall.

[3] Funeral oration was delivered at the German Lutheran Church in Philadelphia.

[4] Because of a tie in the electoral vote between Thomas Jefferson and Aaron Burr, the House of Representatives had to decide the election. Thirty-six ballots were required to break the deadlock, with Jefferson's election as President and Burr's as Vice President on February 17. The Twelfth Amendment was added to the Constitution to prevent the 1800 problem from recurring.

[5] During most of the period while the Capitol was being reconstructed following the fire of 1814, the Congress met in the "Brick Capitol," constructed on the site of the present Supreme Court building. This joint session took place in the Representatives' chamber on the 2d floor of the building.

[6] The joint session to count electoral votes was dissolved because the House and Senate disagreed on Missouri's status regarding statehood. The joint session was reconvened the same day and Missouri's votes were counted.

[7] While this occasion has historically been referred to as the first joint meeting of Congress, the Journals of the House and Senate indicate that Lafayette actually addressed the House of Representatives, with some of the Senators present as guests of the House (having been invited at the last minute to attend). Similar occasions, when members of the one body were invited as guests of the other, include the Senate address by Queen Wilhelmina of the Netherlands on Aug. 6, 1942, and the House address by General H. Norman Schwarzkopf on May 8, 1991.

[8] Although Andrew Jackson won the popular vote by a substantial amount and had the highest number of electoral votes from among the several candidates, he did not receive the required majority of the electoral votes. The responsibility for choosing the new President therefore devolved upon the House of Representatives. As soon as the Senators left the chamber, the balloting proceeded, and John Quincy Adams was elected on the first ballot.

[9] The ceremony was moved outside to accommodate the extraordinarily large crowd of people who had come to Washington to see the inauguration.

[10] The ceremony was moved inside because of cold weather.

[11] Following the death of President Zachary Taylor, Vice President Millard Fillmore took the Presidential oath of office in a special joint session in the Hall of the House.

[12] The joint session to count electoral votes was dissolved three times so that the House and Senate could resolve several electoral disputes.

[13] Because of a severe cold and hoarseness, the King could not deliver his speech, which was read by former Representative Elisha Hunt Allen, then serving as Chancellor and Chief Justice of the Hawaiian Islands.

[14] The contested election between Rutherford B. Hayes and Samuel J. Tilden created a constitutional crisis. Tilden won the popular vote by a close margin, but disputes concerning the electoral vote returns from four states deadlocked the proceedings of the joint session. Anticipating this development, the Congress had created a special commission of five Senators, five Representatives, and five Supreme Court Justices to resolve such disputes. The Commission met in the Supreme Court Chamber (the present Old Senate Chamber) as each problem arose. In each case, the Commission accepted the Hayes electors, securing his election by one electoral vote. The joint session was convened on 15 occasions, with the last on March 2, just three days before the inauguration.

[15] The speech was written by former Speaker and Senator Robert C. Winthrop, who could not attend the ceremony because of ill health.

[16] Because of a blizzard, the ceremony was moved inside, where it was held as part of the Senate's special session. President William Howard Taft took the oath of office and gave his inaugural address after Vice President James S. Sherman's inaugural address and the swearing-in of the new senators.

[17] Held in the Senate Chamber.

[18] Bakhmetieff represented the provisional government of Russia set up after the overthrow of the monarchy in March 1917 and recognized by the United States. The Bolsheviks took over in November 1917.

[19] The address and reception were in conjunction with the presentation to the Senate by France of two Sèvres vases in appreciation of the United States' involvement in World War I. The vases are today in the Senate lobby, just off the Senate floor. Two additional Sèvres vases were given without ceremony to the House of Representatives, which today are in the Rayburn Room, not far from the floor of the House.

[20] Senators later objected to President Harding's speech (given with no advance notice to most of the Senators) as an unconstitutional effort to interfere with the deliberations of the Senate, and Harding did not repeat visits of this kind.

[21] This was the first Annual Message broadcast live on radio.

[22] This was the first inauguration held pursuant to the Twentieth Amendment, which changed the date from March 4 to January 20. The Vice Presidential oath, which previously had been given earlier on the same day in the Senate Chamber, was added to the inaugural ceremony as well, but the Vice Presidential inaugural address was discontinued.

[23] A joint reception for the King and Queen of the United Kingdom was held in the Rotunda, authorized by Senate Concurrent Resolution 17, 76th Congress. Although the concurrent resolution was structured to establish a joint meeting, the Senate, in fact, adjourned rather than recessed as called for by the resolution.

[24] Held in the Senate Chamber.

[25] At this time, the Philippines was still a possession of the United States, although it had been made a self-governing commonwealth in 1935, in preparation for full independence in 1946. From 1909 to 1916, Quezon had served in the U.S. House of Representatives as the resident commissioner from the Philippines.

[26] In exile.

[27] For this Senate Address by Queen Wilhelmina, the members of the House of Representatives were invited as guests. This occasion has sometimes been mistakenly referred to as a joint meeting.

[28] The oaths of office were taken in simple ceremonies at the White House because the expense and festivity of a Capitol ceremony were thought inappropriate because of the war. The Joint Committee on Arrangements of the Congress was in charge, however, and both the Senate and the House of Representatives were present.

[29] This was the first time the term ''State of the Union Address'' was used for the President's Annual Message. Also, it was the first time the address was shown live on television.

[30] This was an informal meeting in the Coolidge Auditorium of the Library of Congress.

[31] Presentation of new ivory gavel to the Senate.

[32] According to the Congressional Record, the Senate adjourned prior to the inaugural ceremonies, even though the previously adopted resolution had stated the adjournment would come immediately following the inauguration. The Senate Journal records the adjournment as called for in the resolution, hence this listing as a joint session.

[33] The joint session to count electoral votes was dissolved so that the House and Senate could each resolve the dispute regarding a ballot from North Carolina. The joint session was reconvened the same day and the North Carolina vote was counted.

[34] Rockefeller was sworn in as Vice President by Chief Justice Warren E. Burger, after which, by unanimous consent, he was allowed to address the Senate.

[35] Because the Governor had laryngitis, his speech was read by his wife, Pamela.

[36] The ceremony was moved inside because of extremely cold weather.

[37] These commemorative addresses were given in the Old Senate Chamber during a regular legislative session.

[38] For this House Address by General Schwarzkopf, the members of the Senate were invited as guests.

[39] This speech was mislabeled in many sources as a State of the Union Address.

[40] President Kim Yong-sam was in Washington for the dedication of the Korean Veterans' Memorial, held the day after this joint meeting.

[41] This was the first State of the Union Address carried live on the Internet.

[42] The joint session to count electoral votes was dissolved so that the House and Senate could each discuss the dispute regarding the ballots from Ohio. The joint session was reconvened the same day and the Ohio votes were counted.

REPRESENTATIVES UNDER EACH APPORTIONMENT

The original apportionment of Representatives was assigned in 1787 in the Constitution and remained in effect for the 1st and 2d Congresses. Subsequent apportionments based on the censuses over the years have been figured using several different methods approved by Congress, all with the goal of dividing representation among the states as equally as possible. After each census up to and including the thirteenth in 1910, Congress would enact a law designating the specific changese in the actual number of Representatives as well as the increase in the ratio of persons-per-Representative. After having made no apportionment after the Fourteenth census in 1920, Congress by statute in 1929 fixed the total number of Representatives at 435 (the number attained with the apportionment after the 1910 census), and since that time, only the ratio of persons-per-Representative has continued to increase, in fact, significantly so. Since the total is now fixed, the specific number of Representatives per state is adjusted after each census to reflect its percentage of the entire population. Since the Sixteenth Census in 1940, the "equal proportions" method of apportioning Representatives within the 435 total has been employed. A detailed explanation of the entire apportionment process can be found in *The Historical Atlas of United States Congressional Districts, 1989–1983.* Kenneth C. Martis, The Free Press, New York, 1982.

State	Constitutional apportionment	First Census, 1790	Second Census, 1800	Third Census, 1810	Fourth Census, 1820	Fifth Census, 1830	Sixth Census, 1840	Seventh Census, 1850	Eighth Census, 1860	Ninth Census, 1870	Tenth Census, 1880	Eleventh Census, 1890	Twelfth Census, 1900	Thirteenth Census, 1910	Fifteenth Census, 1930[1]	Sixteenth Census, 1940	Seventeenth Census, 1950	Eighteenth Census, 1960	Nineteenth Census, 1970	Twentieth Census, 1980	Twenty-First Census, 1990	Twenty-Second Census, 2000
AL				[2]	3	5	7	7	6	8	8	9	9	10	9	9	9	8	7	7	7	7
AK																	[2,3]	1	1	1	1	1
AZ													[2]	[4]1	1	2	2	3	4	5	6	8
AR						[2]	1	2	3	4	5	6	7	7	7	7	6	4	4	4	4	4
CA							[2]	[4]2	3	4	6	7	8	11	20	23	30	38	43	45	52	53
CO										[2]	1	2	3	4	4	4	4	4	5	6	6	7
CT	5	7	7	7	6	6	4	4	4	4	4	4	5	5	6	6	6	6	6	6	6	5
DE	1	1	1	2	1	1	1	1	1	1	1	1	1	1	1	1	1	1	1	1	1	1
FL							[2]	1	1	2	2	2	3	4	5	6	8	12	15	19	23	25
GA	3	2	4	6	7	9	8	8	7	9	10	11	11	12	10	10	10	10	10	10	11	13
HI																	[2,3]	2	2	2	2	2
ID											[2]	1	1	2	2	2	2	2	2	2	2	2
IL				[2]	1	3	7	9	14	19	20	22	25	27	27	26	25	24	24	22	20	19
IN				[2]	3	7	10	11	11	13	13	13	13	13	12	11	11	11	11	10	10	9
IA							[2]	2	6	9	11	11	11	11	9	8	8	7	6	6	5	5
KS								[2]	[4]1	3	7	8	8	8	7	6	6	5	5	5	4	4
KY	[2]	[4]2	6	10	12	13	10	10	9	10	11	11	11	11	9	9	8	7	7	7	6	6
LA				[2]	3	3	4	4	5	6	6	6	7	8	8	8	8	8	8	8	7	7
ME				[5]	7	8	7	6	5	5	4	4	4	4	3	3	3	2	2	2	2	2
MD	6	8	9	9	9	8	6	6	5	6	6	6	6	6	6	6	7	8	8	8	8	8
MA	8	14	17	[5]20	13	12	10	11	10	11	12	13	14	16	15	14	14	12	12	11	10	10
MI						[2]	3	4	6	9	11	12	12	13	17	17	18	19	19	18	16	15
MN								[2]	2	3	5	7	9	10	9	9	9	8	8	8	8	8
MS				[2]	1	2	4	5	5	6	7	7	8	8	7	7	6	5	5	5	5	4
MO				[2]	[4]1	2	5	7	9	13	14	15	16	16	13	13	11	10	10	9	9	9
MT											[2]	1	1	2	2	2	2	2	2	2	1	1
NE									[2]	1	3	6	6	6	5	4	4	3	3	3	3	3
NV									[2]	1	1	1	1	1	1	1	1	1	1	2	2	3
NH	3	4	5	6	6	5	4	3	3	3	2	2	2	2	2	2	2	2	2	2	2	2
NJ	4	5	6	6	6	6	5	5	5	7	7	8	10	12	14	14	14	15	15	14	13	13
NM													[2]	[4]1	1	2	2	2	2	3	3	3
NY	6	10	17	27	34	40	34	33	31	33	34	34	37	43	45	45	43	41	39	34	31	29
NC	5	10	12	13	13	13	9	8	7	8	9	9	10	10	11	12	12	11	11	11	12	13
ND											[2]	1	2	3	2	2	2	2	1	1	1	1
OH			[2]	6	14	19	21	21	19	20	21	21	21	22	24	23	23	24	23	21	19	18
OK													[2]	8	9	8	6	6	6	6	6	5
OR								[2]	1	1	1	2	2	3	3	4	4	4	4	5	5	5
PA	8	13	18	23	26	28	24	25	24	27	28	30	32	36	34	33	30	27	25	23	21	19
RI	1	2	2	2	2	2	2	2	2	2	2	2	2	3	2	2	2	2	2	2	2	2
SC	5	6	8	9	9	9	7	6	4	5	7	7	7	7	6	6	6	6	6	6	6	6
SD											[2]	2	2	3	2	2	2	2	2	1	1	1
TN		[2]	3	6	9	13	11	10	8	10	10	10	10	10	9	10	9	9	8	9	9	9
TX							[2]	2	4	6	11	13	16	18	21	21	22	23	24	27	30	32
UT												[2]	1	2	2	2	2	2	2	3	3	3
VT	[2]	[4]2	4	6	5	5	4	3	3	3	2	2	2	2	1	1	1	1	1	1	1	1
VA	10	19	22	23	22	21	15	13	[6]11	9	10	10	10	10	9	9	10	10	10	10	11	11
WA											[2]	2	3	5	6	6	7	7	7	8	9	9
WV									[6]	3	4	4	5	6	6	6	6	5	4	4	3	3
WI							[2]	3	6	8	9	10	11	11	10	10	10	10	9	9	9	8
WY											[2]	1	1	1	1	1	1	1	1	1	1	1
Total	65	105	141	181	213	240	223	234	241	292	325	356	386	435	435	435	435	435	435	435	435	435

[1] No apportionment was made after the 1920 census.

[2] The following Representatives were added after the indicated apportionments when these states were admitted in the years listed. The number of these additonal Representatives for each state remained in effect until the next census's apportionment (with the exceptions of California and New Mexico, as explained in footnote 4). They are not included in the total for each column. In reading this table, please remember that the apportionments made after each census took effect with the election two years after the census date. As a result, in the table footnote 2 is placed for several states under the decade preceding the one in which it entered the Union, since the previous decade's apportionment was still in effect at the time of statehood. *Constitutional:* Vermont (1791), 2; Kentucky (1792), 2; *First:* Tennessee (1796), 1; *Second:* Ohio (1803), 1; *Third:* Louisiana (1812), 1; Indiana (1816), 1; Mississippi (1817), 1; Illinois (1818), 1; Alabama (1819), 1; Missouri (1821), 1; *Fifth:* Arkansas (1836), 1; Michigan (1837), 1; *Sixth:* Florida (1845), 1; Texas (1845), 2; Iowa (1846), 2; Wisconsin (1848), 2; California (1850), 2; *Seventh:* Minnesota (1858), 2; Oregon (1859), 1; Kansas (1861), 1; *Eighth:* Nevada (1864), 1; Nebraska (1867), 1; *Ninth:* Colorado (1876), 1; *Tenth:* North Dakota (1889), 1; South Dakota (1889), 2; Montana (1889), 1; Washington (1889), 1; Idaho (1890), 1; Wyoming (1890), 1; *Eleventh:* Utah (1896), 1; *Twelth:* Oklahoma (1907), 5; New Mexico (1912), 2; Arizona (1912), 1; *Seventeenth:* Alaska (1959), 1; Hawaii (1959), 1.

[3] When Alaska and then Hawaii joined the Union in 1959, the law was changed to allow the total membership of the House of Representatives to increase to 436 and then to 437, apportioning one new Representative for each of those states. The total returned to 435 in 1963, when the 1960 census apportionment took effect.

[4] Even though the respective censuses were taken before the following states joined the Union, Representatives for them were apportioned either because of anticipation of statehood or because they had become states in the period between the census and the apportionment, hence they are included in the totals of the respective columns. *First:* Vermont (1791); Kentucky (1792); *Fourth:* Missouri (1821); *Seventh:* California (1850); *Eighth:* Kansas (1861); *Thirteenth:* New Mexico (1912); Arizona (1912). (Please note: These seven states are also included in footnote 2 because they became states while the previous decade's apportionment was still in effect for the House of Representatives.) California's situation was unusual. It was scheduled for inclusion in the figures for the 1850 census apportionment; however, when the apportionment law was passed in 1852, California's census returns were still incomplete so Congress made special provision that the state would retain ''the number of Representatives [two] prescribed by the act of admission * * * into the Union until a new apportionment [i.e., after the 1860 census]'' would be made. The number of Representatives from California actually increased before the next apportionment to three when Congress gave the state an extra Representative during part of the 37th Congress, from 1862 to 1863. Regarding New Mexico, the 1911 apportionment law, passed by the 62d Congress in response to the 1910 census and effective with the 63d Congress in 1913, stated that ''if the Territor[y] of * * * New Mexico shall become [a State] in the Union before the apportionment of Representatives under the next decennial census [it] shall have one Representative * * *.'' When New Mexico became a state in 1912 during the 62d Congress, it was given two Representatives. The number was decreased to one beginning the next year in the 63d.

[5] The ''Maine District'' of Massachusetts became a separate state during the term of the 16th Congress, in 1820. For the remainder of that Congress, Maine was assigned one ''at large'' Representative while Massachusetts continued to have 20 Representatives, the number apportioned to it after the 1810 census. For the 17th Congress (the last before the 1820 census apportionment took effect), seven of Massachusetts's Representatives were reassigned to Maine, leaving Massachusetts with 13.

[6] Of the 11 Representatives apportioned to Virginia after the 1860 census, three were reassigned to West Virginia when that part of Virginia became a separate state in 1863. Since the Virginia seats in the House were vacant at that time because of the Civil War, all of the new Representatives from West Virginia were able to take their seats at once. When Representatives from Virginia reentered the House in 1870, only eight members represented it.

IMPEACHMENT PROCEEDINGS

The provisions of the United States Constitution which apply specifically to impeachments are as follows: Article I, section 2, clause 5; Article I, section 3, clauses 6 and 7; Article II, section 2, clause 1; Article II, section 4; and Article III, section 2, clause 3.

For the officials listed below, the date of impeachment by the House of Representatives is followed by the dates of the Senate trial, with the result of each listed at the end of the entry.

WILLIAM BLOUNT, a Senator of the United States from Tennessee; impeached July 7, 1797; tried Monday, December 17, 1798, to Monday, January 14, 1799; charges dismissed for want of jurisdiction.

JOHN PICKERING, judge of the United States district court for the district of New Hampshire; impeached March 2, 1803; tried Thursday, March 3, 1803, to Monday, March 12, 1804; removed from office.

SAMUEL CHASE, Associate Justice of the Supreme Court of the United States; impeached March 12, 1804; tried Friday, November 30, 1804, to Friday, March 1, 1805; acquitted.

JAMES H. PECK, judge of the United States district court for the district of Missouri; impeached April 24, 1830; tried Monday, April 26, 1830, to Monday, January 31, 1831; acquitted.

WEST H. HUMPHREYS, judge of the United States district court for the middle, eastern, and western districts of Tennessee; impeached May 6, 1862; tried Wednesday, May 7, 1862, to Thursday, June 26, 1862; removed from office and disqualified from future office.

ANDREW JOHNSON, President of the United States; impeached February 24, 1868; tried Tuesday, February 25, 1868, to Tuesday, May 26, 1868; acquitted.

WILLIAM W. BELKNAP, Secretary of War; impeached March 2, 1876; tried Friday, March 3, 1876, to Tuesday, August 1, 1876; acquitted.

CHARLES SWAYNE, judge of the United States district court for the northern district of Florida; impeached December 13, 1904; tried Wednesday, December 14, 1904, to Monday, February 27, 1905; acquitted.

ROBERT W. ARCHBALD, associate judge, United States Commerce Court; impeached July 11, 1912; tried Saturday, July 13, 1912, to Monday, January 13, 1913; removed from office and disqualified from future office.

GEORGE W. ENGLISH, judge of the United States district court for the eastern district of Illinois; impeached April 1, 1926; tried Friday, April 23, 1926, to Monday, December 13, 1926; resigned office Thursday, November 4, 1926; Court of Impeachment adjourned to December 13, 1926, when, on request of House managers, the proceedings were dismissed.

HAROLD LOUDERBACK, judge of the United States district court for the northern district of California; impeached February 24, 1933; tried Monday, May 15, 1933, to Wednesday, May 24, 1933; acquitted.

HALSTED L. RITTER, judge of the United States district court for the southern district of Florida; impeached March 2, 1936; tried Monday, April 6, 1936, to Friday, April 17, 1936; removed from office.

HARRY E. CLAIBORNE, judge of the United States district court of Nevada; impeached July 22, 1986; tried Tuesday, October 7, 1986, to Thursday, October 9, 1986; removed from office.

ALCEE L. HASTINGS, judge of the United States district court for the southern district of Florida; impeached August 3, 1988; tried Wednesday, October 18, 1989, to Friday, October 20, 1989; removed from office.

WALTER L. NIXON, judge of the United States district court for the southern district of Mississippi; impeached May 10, 1989; tried Wednesday, November 1, 1989, to Friday, November 3, 1989; removed from office.

WILLIAM JEFFERSON CLINTON, President of the United States; impeached December 19, 1998; tried Thursday, January 7, 1999, to Friday, February 12, 1999; acquitted.

DELEGATES, REPRESENTATIVES, AND SENATORS SERVING IN THE 1st–110th CONGRESSES [1]

As of February 14, 2007, 11,814 individuals have served: 9,920 only in the House of Representatives, 1,250 only in the Senate, and 645 in both Houses. Total serving in the House of Representatives (including individuals serving in both bodies) is 10,564. Total for the Senate (including individuals serving in both bodies) is 1,895.[2]

State	Date Became Territory	Date Entered Union	Delegates	Representatives Only	Senators Only	Both Houses	Total, Not Including Delegates
Alabama	Mar. 3, 1817	Dec. 14, 1819 (22d)	1	166	24	15	205
Alaska	Aug. 24, 1912	Jan. 3, 1959 (49th)	9	4	6	0	10
Arizona	Feb. 24, 1863	Feb. 14, 1912 (48th)	11	27	7	4	38
Arkansas	Mar. 2, 1819	June 15, 1836 (25th)	3	83	23	9	115
California		Sept. 9, 1850 (31st)		328	32	11	370
Colorado	Feb. 28, 1861	Aug. 1, 1876 (38th)	3	56	24	9	88
Connecticut		Jan. 9, 1788 (5th)		190	28	25	243
Delaware		Dec. 7, 1787 (1st)		47	35	14	96
Florida	Mar. 30, 1822	Mar. 3, 1845 (27th)	5	107	26	6	139
Georgia		Jan. 2, 1788 (4th)		249	37	22	308
Hawaii	June 14, 1900	Aug. 21, 1959 (50th)	10	7	2	3	12
Idaho	Mar. 3, 1863	July 3, 1890 (43d)	9	26	19	6	51
Illinois	Feb. 3, 1809	Dec. 3, 1818 (21st)	3	433	29	22	484
Indiana	May 7, 1800	Dec. 11, 1816 (19th)	3	297	27	17	341
Iowa	June 12, 1838	Dec. 28, 1846 (29th)	2	170	22	11	203
Kansas	May 30, 1854	Jan. 29, 1861 (34th)	2	105	22	9	136
Kentucky		June 1, 1792 (15th)		310	36	29	375
Louisiana	Mar. 24, 1804	Apr. 30, 1812 (18th)	2	144	34	14	192
Maine		Mar. 15, 1820 (23d)		141	18	18	177
Maryland		Apr. 28, 1788 (7th)		252	28	28	308
Massachusetts		Feb. 6, 1788 (6th)		383	20	28	431
Michigan	Jan. 11, 1805	Jan. 26, 1837 (26th)	7	247	24	14	286
Minnesota	Mar. 3, 1849	May 11, 1858 (32d)	3	122	26	11	159
Mississippi	Apr. 17, 1798	Dec. 10, 1817 (20th)	5	109	27	16	152
Missouri	June 4, 1812	Aug. 10, 1821 (24th)	3	291	35	9	335
Montana	May 26, 1864	Nov. 8, 1889 (41st)	5	26	14	6	46
Nebraska	May 30, 1854	Mar. 1, 1867 (37th)	6	87	28	7	122
Nevada	Mar. 2, 1861	Oct. 31, 1864 (36th)	2	26	19	6	51
New Hampshire		June 21, 1788 (9th)		119	35	26	180
New Jersey		Dec. 18, 1787 (3d)		297	48	15	360
New Mexico	Sept. 9, 1850	Jan. 6, 1912 (47th)	13	21	12	3	36
New York		July 26, 1788 (11th)		1,402	36	23	1,461
North Carolina		Nov. 21, 1789 (12th)		306	35	18	359
North Dakota [3]	Mar. 2, 1861	Nov. 2, 1889 (39th)	11	21	15	6	42
Ohio [4]		Mar. 1, 1803 (17th)	2	620	36	19	675
Oklahoma	May 2, 1890	Nov. 16, 1907 (46th)	4	72	11	6	89
Oregon	Aug. 14, 1848	Feb. 14, 1859 (33d)	2	56	31	5	92
Pennsylvania		Dec. 12, 1787 (2d)		999	33	21	1,052
Rhode Island		May 29, 1790 (13th)		61	37	10	108
South Carolina		May 23, 1788 (8th)		195	39	16	250
South Dakota [3]	Mar. 2, 1861	Nov. 2, 1889 (40th)	11	25	16	10	51
Tennessee		June 1, 1796 (16th)	2	244	40	18	302
Texas		Dec. 29, 1845 (28th)		237	21	10	268
Utah	Sept. 9, 1850	Jan. 4, 1896 (45th)	7	33	12	3	48
Vermont		Mar. 4, 1791 (14th)		80	24	16	120
Virginia		June 25, 1788 (10th)		380	26	26	432
Washington	Mar. 2, 1853	Nov. 11, 1889 (42d)	10	68	13	10	91
West Virginia		June 20, 1863 (35th)		91	22	8	121
Wisconsin	Apr. 20, 1836	May 29, 1848 (30th)	6	171	19	7	197
Wyoming	July 25, 1868	July 10, 1890 (44th)	4	14	17	3	34

[1] March 4, 1789 until February 14, 2007.

[2] Some of the larger states split into smaller states as the country grew westward (e.g., part of Virginia became West Virginia); hence, some individuals represented more than one state in the Congress.

[3] North and South Dakota were formed from a single territory on the same date, and they shared the same delegates before statehood.

[4] The Territory Northwest of the Ohio River was established as a district for purposes of temporary government by the Act of July 13, 1787. Virginia ceded the land beyond the Ohio River, and delegates representing the district first came to the 6th Congress on March 4, 1799.

NOTE: Information was supplied by the Congressional Research Service.

POLITICAL DIVISIONS OF THE SENATE AND HOUSE FROM 1855 TO 2007

[All Figures Reflect Immediate Result of Elections. Figures Supplied by the Clerk of the House]

Congress	Years	SENATE					HOUSE OF REPRESENTATIVES				
		No. of Senators	Democrats	Republicans	Other parties	Vacancies	No. of Representatives	Democrats	Republicans	Other parties	Vacancies
34th	1855–1857	62	42	15	5	....	234	83	108	43	....
35th	1857–1859	64	39	20	5	....	237	131	92	14	....
36th	1859–1861	66	38	26	2	....	237	101	113	23	....
37th	1861–1863	50	11	31	7	1	178	42	106	28	2
38th	1863–1865	51	12	39	....	....	183	80	103	....	....
39th	1865–1867	52	10	42	....	....	191	46	145	....	....
40th	1867–1869	53	11	42	....	....	193	49	143	....	1
41st	1869–1871	74	11	61	....	2	243	73	170	....	....
42d	1871–1873	74	17	57	....	....	243	104	139	....	....
43d	1873–1875	74	19	54	....	1	293	88	203	....	2
44th	1875–1877	76	29	46	....	1	293	181	107	3	2
45th	1877–1879	76	36	39	1	....	293	156	137	....	....
46th	1879–1881	76	43	33	....	....	293	150	128	14	1
47th	1881–1883	76	37	37	2	....	293	130	152	11	....
48th	1883–1885	76	36	40	....	....	325	200	119	6	....
49th	1885–1887	76	34	41	....	1	325	182	140	2	1
50th	1887–1889	76	37	39	....	....	325	170	151	4	....
51st	1889–1891	84	37	47	....	....	330	156	173	1	....
52d	1891–1893	88	39	47	2	....	333	231	88	14	....
53d	1893–1895	88	44	38	3	3	356	220	126	10	....
54th	1895–1897	88	39	44	5	....	357	104	246	7	....
55th	1897–1899	90	34	46	10	....	357	134	206	16	1
56th	1899–1901	90	26	53	11	....	357	163	185	9	....
57th	1901–1903	90	29	56	3	2	357	153	198	5	1
58th	1903–1905	90	32	58	....	....	386	178	207	....	1
59th	1905–1907	90	32	58	....	....	386	136	250	....	....
60th	1907–1909	92	29	61	....	2	386	164	222	....	....
61st	1909–1911	92	32	59	....	1	391	172	219	....	....
62d	1911–1913	92	42	49	....	1	391	228	162	1	....
63d	1913–1915	96	51	44	1	....	435	290	127	18	....
64th	1915–1917	96	56	39	1	....	435	231	193	8	3
65th	1917–1919	96	42	53	1	....	435	[1]210	216	9	....
66th	1919–1921	96	47	48	1	....	435	191	237	7	....
67th	1921–1923	96	37	59	....	....	435	132	300	1	2
68th	1923–1925	96	43	51	2	....	435	207	225	3	....
69th	1925–1927	96	40	54	1	1	435	183	247	5	....
70th	1927–1929	96	47	48	1	....	435	195	237	3	....
71st	1929–1931	96	39	56	1	....	435	163	267	1	4
72d	1931–1933	96	47	48	1	....	435	[2]216	218	1	....
73d	1933–1935	96	59	36	1	....	435	313	117	5	....
74th	1935–1937	96	69	25	2	....	435	322	103	10	....
75th	1937–1939	96	75	17	4	....	435	333	89	13	....
76th	1939–1941	96	69	23	4	....	435	262	169	4	....
77th	1941–1943	96	66	28	2	....	435	267	162	6	....
78th	1943–1945	96	57	38	1	....	435	222	209	4	....
79th	1945–1947	96	57	38	1	....	435	243	190	2	....
80th	1947–1949	96	45	51	....	....	435	188	246	1	....
81st	1949–1951	96	54	42	....	....	435	263	171	1	....
82d	1951–1953	96	48	47	1	....	435	234	199	2	....
83d	1953–1955	96	46	48	2	....	435	213	221	1	....
84th	1955–1957	96	48	47	1	....	435	232	203	....	....
85th	1957–1959	96	49	47	....	....	435	234	201	....	....
86th	1959–1961	98	64	34	....	....	[3]436	283	153	....	....
87th	1961–1963	100	64	36	....	....	[4]437	262	175	....	....
88th	1963–1965	100	67	33	....	....	435	258	176	....	1
89th	1965–1967	100	68	32	....	....	435	295	140	....	....
90th	1967–1969	100	64	36	....	....	435	248	187	....	....
91st	1969–1971	100	58	42	....	....	435	243	192	....	....
92d	1971–1973	100	54	44	2	....	435	255	180	....	....
93d	1973–1975	100	56	42	2	....	435	242	192	1	....
94th	1975–1977	100	60	37	2	....	435	291	144	1	....
95th	1977–1979	100	61	38	1	....	435	292	143	....	....
96th	1979–1981	100	58	41	1	....	435	277	158	....	....
97th	1981–1983	100	46	53	1	....	435	242	192	1	....
98th	1983–1985	100	46	54	....	....	435	269	166	....	....
99th	1985–1987	100	47	53	....	....	435	253	182	....	....
100th	1987–1989	100	55	45	....	....	435	258	177	....	....
101st	1989–1991	100	55	45	....	....	435	260	175	....	....
102d	1991–1993	100	56	44	....	....	435	267	167	1	....
103d	1993–1995	100	57	43	....	....	435	258	176	1	....
104th	1995–1997	100	48	52	....	....	435	204	230	1	....
105th	1997–1999	100	45	55	....	....	435	207	226	2	....
106th	1999–2001	100	45	55	....	....	435	211	223	1	....
107th	2001–2003	100	50	50	....	....	435	212	221	2	....
108th	2003–2005	100	48	51	1	....	435	204	229	1	1
109th	2005–2007	100	44	55	1	....	435	202	232	1	....
110th	2007–2009	100	49	49	2	....	435	233	202	....	....

[1] Democrats organized House with help of other parties.

[2] Democrats organized House because of Republican deaths.
[3] Proclamation declaring Alaska a State issued January 3, 1959.
[4] Proclamation declaring Hawaii a State issued August 21, 1959.

GOVERNORS OF THE STATES, COMMONWEALTH, AND TERRITORIES—2007

State, Commonwealth, or Territory	Capital	Governor	Party	Term of service	Expiration of term
STATE				*Years*	
Alabama	Montgomery	Bob Riley	Republican	[c] 4	Jan. 2011
Alaska	Juneau	Sarah Palin	Republican	[f] 4	Dec. 2010
Arizona	Phoenix	Janet Napolitano	Democrat	[f] 4	Jan. 2011
Arkansas	Little Rock	Mike Beebe	Democrat	[c] 4	Jan. 2011
California	Sacramento	Arnold Schwarzenegger	Republican	[c] 4	Jan. 2011
Colorado	Denver	Bill Ritter	Democratic	[c] 4	Jan. 2011
Connecticut	Hartford	M. Jodi Rell	Republican	[b] 4	Jan. 2011
Delaware	Dover	Ruth Ann Minner	Democrat	[c] 4	Jan. 2009
Florida	Tallahassee	Charlie Crist	Republican	[f] 4	Jan. 2011
Georgia	Atlanta	Sonny Perdue	Republican	[f] 4	Jan. 2011
Hawaii	Honolulu	Linda Lingle	Republican	[c] 4	Dec. 2010
Idaho	Boise	Butch Otter	Republican	[b] 4	Jan. 2011
Illinois	Springfield	Rod R. Blagojevich	Democrat	[b] 4	Jan. 2011
Indiana	Indianapolis	Mitch Daniels	Republican	[f] 4	Jan. 2009
Iowa	Des Moines	Chet Culver	Democrat	[b] 4	Jan. 2011
Kansas	Topeka	Kathleen Sebelius	Democrat	[c] 4	Jan. 2011
Kentucky	Frankfort	Ernie Fletcher	Republican	[c] 4	Dec. 2007
Louisiana	Baton Rouge	Kathleen Blanco	Democrat	[f] 4	Jan. 2008
Maine	Augusta	John Baldacci	Democrat	[f] 4	Jan. 2011
Maryland	Annapolis	Martin O'Malley	Democrat	[f] 4	Jan. 2011
Massachusetts	Boston	Deval Patrick	Democrat	[b] 4	Jan. 2011
Michigan	Lansing	Jennifer Granholm	Democrat	[b] 4	Jan. 2011
Minnesota	St. Paul	Tim Pawlenty	Republican	[b] 4	Jan. 2011
Mississippi	Jackson	Haley Barbour	Republican	[c] 4	Jan. 2008
Missouri	Jefferson City	Matt Blunt	Republican	[c] 4	Jan. 2009
Montana	Helena	Brian Schweitzer	Democrat	[g] 4	Jan. 2009
Nebraska	Lincoln	Dave Heineman	Republican	[c] 4	Jan. 2011
Nevada	Carson City	Jim Gibbons	Republican	[c] 4	Jan. 2011
New Hampshire	Concord	John Lynch	Democrat	[b] 2	Jan. 2009
New Jersey	Trenton	Jon Corzine	Democrat	[c] 4	Jan. 2010
New Mexico	Santa Fe	Bill Richardson	Democrat	[c] 4	Jan. 2011
New York	Albany	Eliot Spitzer	Democratic	[b] 4	Jan. 2011
North Carolina	Raleigh	Mike Easley	Democrat	[c] 4	Jan. 2009
North Dakota	Bismarck	John Hoeven	Republican	[b] 4	Dec. 2008
Ohio	Columbus	Ted Strickland	Democrat	[c] 4	Jan. 2011
Oklahoma	Oklahoma City	Brad Henry	Democrat	[c] 4	Jan. 2011
Oregon	Salem	Ted Kulongoski	Democrat	[f] 4	Jan. 2011
Pennsylvania	Harrisburg	Ed Rendell	Democrat	[c] 4	Jan. 2011
Rhode Island	Providence	Donald Carcieri	Republican	[c] 4	Jan. 2011
South Carolina	Columbia	Mark Sanford	Republican	[c] 4	Jan. 2011
South Dakota	Pierre	Mike Rounds	Republican	[c] 4	Jan. 2011
Tennessee	Nashville	Phil Bredesen	Democrat	[c] 4	Jan. 2011
Texas	Austin	Rick Perry	Republican	[b] 4	Jan. 2011
Utah	Salt Lake City	Jon Huntsman, Jr.	Republican	[b] 4	Jan. 2009
Vermont	Montpelier	Jim Douglas	Republican	[b] 2	Jan. 2009
Virginia	Richmond	Tim Kaine	Democrat	[a] 4	Jan. 2010
Washington	Olympia	Christine Gregoire	Democrat	[d] 4	Jan. 2009
West Virginia	Charleston	Joe Manchin III	Democrat	[c] 4	Jan. 2009
Wisconsin	Madison	Jim Doyle	Democrat	[b] 4	Jan. 2011
Wyoming	Cheyenne	Dave Freudenthal	Democrat	[c] 4	Jan. 2011
COMMONWEALTH OF					
Puerto Rico	San Juan	Anibal Acevedo-Vilá	[1] P.D.P.	[b] 4	Jan. 2009
TERRITORIES					
Guam	Agana	Felix Perez Camacho	Republican	[c] 4	Jan. 2011
Virgin Islands	Charlotte Amalie	John de Jongh, Jr.	Democrat	[c] 4	Jan. 2011
American Samoa	Pago Pago	Togiola Tulafono	Democrat	[c] 4	Jan. 2009
Northern Mariana Islands.	Saipan	Benigno R. Fitial	Covenant	[c] 4	Jan. 2010

[a] Cannot succeed himself. [b] No limit. [c] Can serve 2 consecutive terms. [d] Can serve 3 consecutive terms. [e] Can serve 4 consecutive terms. [f] Can serve no more than 8 years in a 12-year period. [g] Can serve no more than 8 years in a 16-year period.

[1] Popular Democratic Party.

PRESIDENTS AND VICE PRESIDENTS AND THE CONGRESSES COINCIDENT WITH THEIR TERMS[1]

President	Vice President	Service	Congresses
George Washington	John Adams	Apr. 30, 1789–Mar. 3, 1797	1, 2, 3, 4.
John Adams	Thomas Jefferson	Mar. 4, 1797–Mar. 3, 1801	5, 6.
Thomas Jefferson	Aaron Burr	Mar. 4, 1801–Mar. 3, 1805	7, 8.
Do	George Clinton	Mar. 4, 1805–Mar. 3, 1809	9, 10.
James Madison	......do.[2]	Mar. 4, 1809–Mar. 3, 1813	11, 12.
Do	Elbridge Gerry[3]	Mar. 4, 1813–Mar. 3, 1817	13, 14.
James Monroe	Daniel D. Tompkins	Mar. 4, 1817–Mar. 3, 1825	15, 16, 17, 18, 19
John Quincy Adams	John C. Calhoun	Mar. 4, 1825–Mar. 3, 1829	19, 20.
Andrew Jackson	......do.[4]	Mar. 4, 1829–Mar. 3, 1833	21, 22.
Do	Martin Van Buren	Mar. 4, 1833–Mar. 3, 1837	23, 24.
Martin Van Buren	Richard M. Johnson	Mar. 4, 1837–Mar. 3, 1841	25, 26.
William Henry Harrison[5]	John Tyler	Mar. 4, 1841–Apr. 4, 1841	27.
John Tyler		Apr. 6, 1841–Mar. 3, 1845	27, 28.
James K. Polk	George M. Dallas	Mar. 4, 1845–Mar. 3, 1849	29, 30.
Zachary Taylor[5]	Millard Fillmore	Mar. 5, 1849–July 9, 1850	31.
Millard Fillmore		July 10, 1850–Mar. 3, 1853	31, 32.
Franklin Pierce	William R. King[6]	Mar. 4, 1853–Mar. 3, 1857	33, 34.
James Buchanan	John C. Breckinridge	Mar. 4, 1857–Mar. 3, 1861	35, 36.
Abraham Lincoln	Hannibal Hamlin	Mar. 4, 1861–Mar. 3, 1865	37, 38.
Do.[5]	Andrew Johnson	Mar. 4, 1865–Apr. 15, 1865	39.
Andrew Johnson		Apr. 15, 1865–Mar. 3, 1869	39, 40.
Ulysses S. Grant	Schuyler Colfax	Mar. 4, 1869–Mar. 3, 1873	41, 42.
Do	Henry Wilson[7]	Mar. 4, 1873–Mar. 3, 1877	43, 44.
Rutherford B. Hayes	William A. Wheeler	Mar. 4, 1877–Mar. 3, 1881	45, 46.
James A. Garfield[5]	Chester A. Arthur	Mar. 4, 1881–Sept. 19, 1881	47.
Chester A. Arthur		Sept. 20, 1881–Mar. 3, 1885	47, 48.
Grover Cleveland	Thomas A. Hendricks[8]	Mar. 4, 1885–Mar. 3, 1889	49, 50.
Benjamin Harrison	Levi P. Morton	Mar. 4, 1889–Mar. 3, 1893	51, 52.
Grover Cleveland	Adlai E. Stevenson	Mar. 4, 1893–Mar. 3, 1897	53, 54.
William McKinley	Garret A. Hobart[9]	Mar. 4, 1897–Mar. 3, 1901	55, 56.
Do.[5]	Theodore Roosevelt	Mar. 4, 1901–Sept. 14, 1901	57.
Theodore Roosevelt		Sept. 14, 1901–Mar. 3, 1905	57, 58.
Do	Charles W. Fairbanks	Mar. 4, 1905–Mar. 3, 1909	59, 60.
William H. Taft	James S. Sherman[10]	Mar. 4, 1909–Mar. 3, 1913	61, 62.
Woodrow Wilson	Thomas R. Marshall	Mar. 4, 1913–Mar. 3, 1921	63, 64, 65, 66, 67.
Warren G. Harding[5]	Calvin Coolidge	Mar. 4, 1921–Aug. 2, 1923	67.
Calvin Coolidge		Aug. 3, 1923–Mar. 3, 1925	68.
Do	Charles G. Dawes	Mar. 4, 1925–Mar. 3, 1929	69, 70.
Herbert C. Hoover	Charles Curtis	Mar. 4, 1929–Mar. 3, 1933	71, 72.
Franklin D. Roosevelt	John N. Garner	Mar. 4, 1933–Jan. 20, 1941	73, 74, 75, 76, 77.
Do	Henry A. Wallace	Jan. 20, 1941–Jan. 20, 1945	77, 78, 79.
Do.[5]	Harry S. Truman	Jan. 20, 1945–Apr. 12, 1945	79.
Harry S. Truman		Apr. 12, 1945–Jan. 20, 1949	79, 80, 81.
Do	Alben W. Barkley	Jan. 20, 1949–Jan. 20, 1953	81, 82, 83.
Dwight D. Eisenhower	Richard M. Nixon	Jan. 20, 1953–Jan. 20, 1961	83, 84, 85, 86, 87.
John F. Kennedy[5]	Lyndon B. Johnson	Jan. 20, 1961–Nov. 22, 1963	87, 88, 89.
Lyndon B. Johnson		Nov. 22, 1963–Jan. 20, 1965	88, 89.
Do	Hubert H. Humphrey	Jan. 20, 1965–Jan. 20, 1969	89, 90, 91.
Richard M. Nixon	Spiro T. Agnew[11]	Jan. 20, 1969–Dec. 6, 1973	91, 92, 93.
Do.[13]	Gerald R. Ford[12]	Dec. 6, 1973–Aug. 9, 1974	93.
Gerald R. Ford		Aug. 9, 1974–Dec. 19, 1974	93.
Do	Nelson A. Rockefeller[14]	Dec. 19, 1974–Jan. 20, 1977	93, 94, 95.
James Earl "Jimmy" Carter	Walter F. Mondale	Jan. 20, 1977–Jan. 20, 1981	95, 96, 97.
Ronald Reagan	George Bush	Jan. 20, 1981–Jan. 20, 1989	97, 98, 99, 100, 101.
George Bush	Dan Quayle	Jan. 20, 1989–Jan. 20, 1993	101, 102, 103.
William J. Clinton	Albert Gore	Jan. 20, 1993–Jan. 20, 2001	103, 104, 105, 106, 107.
George W. Bush	Richard B. Cheney	Jan. 20, 2001–	107, 108, 109, 110.

[1] From 1789 until 1933, the terms of the President and Vice President and the term of the Congress coincided, beginning on March 4 and ending on March 3. This changed when the 20th amendment to the Constitution was adopted in 1933. Beginning in 1934 the convening date for Congress became January 3, and beginning in 1937 the starting date for the Presidential term became January 20. Because of this change, the number of Congresses overlapping with a Presidential term increased from two to three, although the third only overlaps by a few weeks.

[2] Died Apr. 20, 1812.

[3] Died Nov. 23, 1814.

[4] Resigned Dec. 28, 1832, to become a United States Senator from South Carolina.

[5] Died in office.

[6] Died Apr. 18, 1853.

[7] Died Nov. 22, 1875.

[8] Died Nov. 25, 1885.

[9] Died Nov. 21, 1899.

[10] Died Oct. 30, 1912.

[11] Resigned Oct. 10, 1973.

[12] Nominated to be Vice President by President Richard M. Nixon on Oct. 12, 1973; confirmed by the Senate on Nov. 27, 1973; confirmed by the House of Representatives on Dec. 6, 1973; took the oath of office on Dec. 6, 1973 in the Hall of the House of Representatives. This was the first time a Vice President was nominated by the President and confirmed by the Congress pursuant to the 25th amendment to the Constitution.

[13] Resigned from office.

[14] Nominated to be Vice President by President Gerald R. Ford on Aug. 20, 1974; confirmed by the Senate on Dec. 10, 1974; confirmed by the House of Representatives on Dec. 19, 1974; took the oath of office on Dec. 19, 1974, in the Senate Chamber.

CAPITOL BUILDINGS AND GROUNDS

UNITED STATES CAPITOL

Overview of the Building and its Function

The United States Capitol is among the most architecturally impressive and symbolically important buildings in the world. It has housed the chambers of the Senate and the House of Representatives for more than two centuries. Begun in 1793, the Capitol has been built, burnt, rebuilt, extended, and restored; today, it stands as a monument not only to its builders but also to the American people and their government.

As the focal point of the government's legislative branch, the Capitol is the centerpiece of the Capitol complex, which includes the six principal congressional office buildings and three Library of Congress buildings constructed on Capitol Hill in the 19th and 20th centuries.

In addition to its active use by Congress, the Capitol is a museum of American art and history. Each year, it is visited by millions of people from around the world.

A fine example of 19th-century neoclassical architecture, the Capitol combines function with aesthetics. Its design was derived from ancient Greece and Rome and evokes the ideals that guided the nation's founders as they framed their new republic. As the building was expanded from its original design, harmony with the existing portions was carefully maintained.

Today, the Capitol covers a ground area of 175,170 square feet, or about 4 acres, and has a floor area of approximately 16½ acres. Its length, from north to south, is 751 feet 4 inches; its greatest width, including approaches, is 350 feet. Its height above the base line on the east front to the top of the Statue of Freedom is 288 feet; from the basement floor to the top of the dome is an ascent of 365 steps. The building contains approximately 540 rooms and has 658 windows (108 in the dome alone) and approximately 850 doorways.

The building is divided into five levels. The first, or ground, floor is occupied chiefly by committee rooms and the spaces allocated to various congressional officers. The areas accessible to visitors on this level include the Hall of Columns, the Brumidi Corridor, the restored Old Supreme Court Chamber, and the Crypt beneath the Rotunda, where historical exhibits are presented.

The second floor holds the chambers of the House of Representatives (in the south wing) and the Senate (in the north wing). This floor also contains three major public areas. In the center under the dome is the rotunda, a circular ceremonial space that also serves as a gallery of paintings and sculpture depicting significant people and events in the nation's history. The rotunda is 96 feet in diameter and rises 180 feet 3 inches to the canopy. The semicircular chamber south of the rotunda served as the Hall of the House until 1857; now designated National Statuary Hall, it houses part of the Capitol's collection of statues donated by the states in commemoration of notable citizens. The Old Senate Chamber northeast of the rotunda, which was used by the Senate until 1859, has been returned to its mid-19th-century appearance.

The third floor allows access to the galleries from which visitors to the Capitol may watch the proceedings of the House and the Senate when Congress is in session. The rest of this floor is occupied by offices, committee rooms, and press galleries.

The fourth floor and the basement/terrace level of the Capitol are occupied by offices, machinery rooms, workshops, and other support areas.

Location of the Capitol

The Capitol is located at the eastern end of the Mall on a plateau 88 feet above the level of the Potomac River, commanding a westward view across the Capitol Reflecting Pool to the Washington Monument 1.4 miles away and the Lincoln Memorial 2.2 miles away.

Before 1791, the Federal Government had no permanent site. The early Congresses met in eight different cities: Philadelphia, Baltimore, Lancaster, York, Princeton, Annapolis, Trenton, and New York City. The subject of a permanent capital for the government of the United

States was first raised by Congress in 1783; it was ultimately addressed in Article I, Section 8 of the Constitution (1787), which gave the Congress legislative authority over ''such District (not exceeding ten Miles square) as may, by Cession of Particular States, and the Acceptance of Congress, become the Seat of the Government of the United States. . . .''

In 1788, the state of Maryland ceded to Congress ''any district in this State, not exceeding ten miles square,'' and in 1789 the State of Virginia ceded an equivalent amount of land. In accordance with the ''Residence Act'' passed by Congress in 1790, President Washington in 1791 selected the area that is now the District of Columbia from the land ceded by Maryland (private landowners whose property fell within this area were compensated by a payment of £25 per acre); that ceded by Virginia was not used for the capital and was returned to Virginia in 1846. Also under the provisions of that Act, he selected three commissioners to survey the site and oversee the design and construction of the capital city and its government buildings. The commissioners, in turn, selected the French-American engineer Peter Charles L'Enfant to plan the new city of Washington. L'Enfant's plan, which was influenced by the gardens at Versailles, arranged the city's streets and avenues in a grid overlaid with baroque diagonals; the result is a functional and aesthetic whole in which government buildings are balanced against public lawns, gardens, squares, and paths. The Capitol itself was located at the elevated east end of the Mall, on the brow of what was then called Jenkins' Hill. The site was, in L'Enfant's words, ''a pedestal waiting for a monument.''

Selection of a Plan

L'Enfant was expected to design the Capitol and to supervise its construction. However, he refused to produce any drawings for the building, claiming that he carried the design ''in his head''; this fact and his refusal to consider himself subject to the commissioners' authority led to his dismissal in 1792. In March of that year the commissioners announced a competition, suggested by Secretary of State Thomas Jefferson, that would award $500 and a city lot to whoever produced ''the most approved plan'' for the Capitol by mid-July. None of the 17 plans submitted, however, was wholly satisfactory. In October, a letter arrived from Dr. William Thornton, a Scottish-trained physician living in Tortola, British West Indies, requesting an opportunity to present a plan even though the competition had closed. The commissioners granted this request.

Thornton's plan depicted a building composed of three sections. The central section, which was topped by a low dome, was to be flanked on the north and south by two rectangular wings (one for the Senate and one for the House of Representatives). President Washington commended the plan for its ''grandeur, simplicity and convenience,'' and on April 5, 1793, it was accepted by the commissioners; Washington gave his formal approval on July 25.

Brief Construction History
1793–1829

The cornerstone was laid by President Washington in the building's southeast corner on September 18, 1793, with Masonic ceremonies. Work progressed under the direction of three architects in succession. Stephen H. Hallet (an entrant in the earlier competition) and George Hadfield were eventually dismissed by the commissioners because of inappropriate design changes that they tried to impose; James Hoban, the architect of the White House, saw the first phase of the project through to completion.

Construction was a laborious and time-consuming process: the sandstone used for the building had to be ferried on boats from the quarries at Aquia, Virginia; workers had to be induced to leave their homes to come to the relative wilderness of Capitol Hill; and funding was inadequate. By August 1796 the commissioners were forced to focus the entire work effort on the building's north wing so that it at least could be ready for government occupancy as scheduled. Even so, some third-floor rooms were still unfinished when the Congress, the Supreme Court, the Library of Congress, and the courts of the District of Columbia occupied the Capitol in late 1800.

In 1803, Congress allocated funds to resume construction. A year earlier, the office of the Commissioners had been abolished and replaced by a superintendent of the city of Washington. To oversee the renewed construction effort, B. Henry Latrobe was appointed surveyor of public buildings. The first professional architect and engineer to work in America, Latrobe modified Thornton's plan for the south wing to include space for offices and committee rooms; he also introduced alterations to simplify the construction work. Latrobe began work by removing a squat, oval, temporary building known as ''the Oven,'' which had been erected in 1801 as a meeting place for the House of Representatives. By 1807 construction on the south wing was sufficiently advanced that the House was able to occupy its new legislative chamber, and the wing was completed in 1811.

In 1808, as work on the south wing progressed, Latrobe began the rebuilding of the north wing, which had fallen into disrepair. Rather than simply repair the wing, he redesigned the interior of the building to increase its usefulness and durability; among his changes was the addition of a chamber for the Supreme Court. By 1811, he had completed the eastern half of this wing, but funding was being increasingly diverted to preparations for a second war with Great Britain. By 1813, Latrobe had no further work in Washington and so he departed, leaving the north and south wings of the Capitol connected only by a temporary wooden passageway.

The War of 1812 left the Capitol, in Latrobe's later words, "a most magnificent ruin": on August 24, 1814, British troops set fire to the building, and only a sudden rainstorm prevented its complete destruction. Immediately after the fire, Congress met for one session in Blodget's Hotel, which was at Seventh and E Streets, NW. From 1815 to 1819, Congress occupied a building erected for it on First Street, NE, on part of the site now occupied by the Supreme Court Building. This building later came to be known as the Old Brick Capitol.

Latrobe returned to Washington in 1815, when he was rehired to restore the Capitol. In addition to making repairs, he took advantage of this opportunity to make further changes in the building's interior design (for example, an enlargement of the Senate Chamber) and introduce new materials (for example, marble discovered along the upper Potomac). However, he came under increasing pressure because of construction delays (most of which were beyond his control) and cost overruns; finally, he resigned his post in November 1817.

On January 8, 1818, Charles Bulfinch, a prominent Boston architect, was appointed Latrobe's successor. Continuing the restoration of the north and south wings, he was able to make the chambers for the Supreme Court, the House, and the Senate ready for use by 1819. Bulfinch also redesigned and supervised the construction of the Capitol's central section. The copper-covered wooden dome that topped this section was made higher than Bulfinch considered appropriate to the building's size (at the direction of President James Monroe and Secretary of State John Quincy Adams). After completing the last part of the building in 1826, Bulfinch spent the next few years on the Capitol's decoration and landscaping. In 1829, his work was done and his position with the government was terminated. In the 38 years following Bulfinch's tenure, the Capitol was entrusted to the care of the commissioner of public buildings.

1830–1868

The Capitol was by this point already an impressive structure. At ground level, its length was 351 feet 7½ inches and its width was 282 feet 10½ inches. Up to the year 1827—records from later years being incomplete—the project cost was $2,432,851.34. Improvements to the building continued in the years to come (running water in 1832, gas lighting in the 1840s), but by 1850 its size could no longer accommodate the increasing numbers of senators and representatives from newly admitted states. The Senate therefore voted to hold another competition, offering a prize of $500 for the best plan to extend the Capitol. Several suitable plans were submitted, some proposing an eastward extension of the building and others proposing the addition of large north and south wings. However, Congress was unable to decide between these two approaches, and the prize money was divided among five architects. Thus, the tasks of selecting a plan and appointing an architect fell to President Millard Fillmore.

Fillmore's choice was Thomas U. Walter, a Philadelphia architect who had entered the competition. On July 4, 1851, in a ceremony whose principal oration was delivered by Secretary of State Daniel Webster, the president laid the cornerstone in the northeast corner of the House wing. Over the next 14 years, Walter supervised the construction of the extension, ensuring their compatibility with the architectural style of the existing building. However, because the Aquia Creek sandstone used earlier had deteriorated noticeably, he chose to use marble for the exterior. For the veneer, Walter selected marble quarried at Lee, MA, and for the columns he used marble from Cockeysville, MD.

Walter faced several significant challenges during the course of construction. Chief among these was the steady imposition by the government of additional tasks without additional pay. Aside from his work on the Capitol extension, Walter designed the wings of the Patent Office building, extensions to the Treasury and Post Office buildings, and the Marine barracks in Pensacola and Brooklyn. When the Library of Congress in the Capitol's west central section was gutted by a fire in 1851, Walter was commissioned to restore it. He also encountered obstacles in his work on the Capitol extensions. His location of the legislative chambers was changed in 1853 at the direction of President Franklin Pierce, based on the suggestions of the newly appointed supervising engineer, Captain Montgomery C. Meigs. In general, however, the project progressed rapidly: the House of Representatives was able to meet in its new chamber on December 16, 1857, and the Senate first met in its present chamber on January 4, 1859. The old House chamber was later designated National Statuary Hall. In 1861 most construction was suspended because of the Civil War, and the Capitol was used briefly as a military barracks, hospital, and bakery. In 1862 work on the entire building was resumed.

As the new wings were constructed, more than doubling the length of the Capitol, it became apparent that the dome erected by Bulfinch no longer suited the building's proportions. In 1855 Congress voted for its replacement based on Walter's design for a new, fireproof cast-iron dome. The old dome was removed in 1856–56, and 5,000,000 pounds of new masonry was placed on the existing rotunda walls. Iron used in the dome construction had an aggregate weight of 8,909,200 pounds and was lifted into place by steam-powered derricks.

In 1859, Thomas Crawford's plaster model for the Statue of Freedom, designed for the top of the dome, arrived from the sculptor's studio in Rome. With a height of 19 feet 6 inches, the statue was almost 3 feet taller than specified, and Walter was compelled to make revisions to his design for the dome. When cast in bronze by Clark Mills at his foundry on the outskirts of Washington, it weighed 14,985 pounds. The statue was lifted into place atop the dome in 1863, its final section being installed on December 2 to the accompaniment of gun salutes from the forts around the city.

The work on the dome and the extension was completed under the direction of Edward Clark, who had served as Walter's assistant and was appointed Architect of the Capitol in 1865 after Walter's resignation. In 1866, the Italian-born artist Constantino Brumidi finished the canopy fresco, a monumental painting entitled *The Apotheosis of George Washington.* The Capitol extension was completed in 1868.

1869–1902

Clark continued to hold the post of Architect of the Capitol until his death in 1902. During his tenure, the Capitol underwent considerable modernization. Steam heat was gradually installed in the old Capitol. In 1874 the first elevator was installed, and in the 1880s electric lighting began to replace gas lights.

Between 1884 and 1891, the marble terraces on the north, west, and south sides of the Capitol were constructed. As part of the landscape plan devised by Frederick Law Olmsted, these terraces not only added over 100 rooms to the Capitol but also provided a broader, more substantial visual base for the building.

On November 6, 1898, a gas explosion and fire in the original north wing dramatically illustrated the need for fireproofing. The roofs over the Statuary Hall wing and the original north wing were reconstructed and fireproofed, the work being completed in 1902 by Clark's successor, Elliott Woods. In 1901 the space in the west central front vacated by the Library of Congress was converted to committee rooms.

1903–1970

During the remainder of Woods's service, which ended with his death in 1923, no major structural work was required on the Capitol. The activities performed in the building were limited chiefly to cleaning and refurbishing the interior. David Lynn, the Architect of the Capitol from 1923 until his retirement in 1954, continued these tasks. Between July 1949 and January 1951, the corroded roofs and skylights of both wings and the connecting corridors were replaced with new roofs of concrete and steel, covered with copper. The cast-iron and glass ceilings of the House and Senate chambers were replaced with ceilings of stainless steel and plaster, with a laylight of carved glass and bronze in the middle of each. The House and Senate chambers were completely redecorated, modern lighting was added, and acoustical problems were solved. During this renovation program, the House and Senate vacated their chambers on several occasions so that the work could progress.

The next significant modification made to the Capitol was the east front extension. This project was carried out under the supervision of Architect of the Capitol J. George Stewart, who served from 1954 until his death in 1970. Begun in 1958, it involved the construction of a new east front 32 feet 6 inches east of the old front, faithfully reproducing the sandstone structure in marble. The old sandstone walls were not destroyed; rather, they were left in place to become a part of the interior wall and are now buttressed by the addition. The marble columns of the connecting corridors were also moved and reused. Other elements of this project included repairing the dome, constructing a subway terminal under the Senate steps, reconstructing those steps, cleaning both wings, birdproofing the building, providing furniture and furnishings for 90 new rooms created by the extension, and improving the lighting throughout the building. The project was completed in 1962.

1971–PRESENT

During the nearly 25-year tenure (1971–1995) of Architect of the Capitol George M. White, FAIA, the building was both modernized and restored. Electronic voting equipment was installed in the House chamber in 1973; facilities were added to allow television coverage of the House and Senate debates in 1979 and 1986, respectively; and improved climate control, electronic surveillance systems, and new computer and communications facilities have been added to bring the Capitol up-to-date. The Old Senate Chamber, National Statuary Hall, and the Old Supreme Court Chamber, on the other hand, were restored to their mid-19th-century appearance in the 1970s.

In 1983, work began on the strengthening, renovation, and preservation of the west front of the Capitol. Structural problems had developed over the years because of defects in the original foundations, deterioration of the sandstone facing material, alterations to the basic building fabric (a fourth-floor addition and channeling of the walls to install interior utilities), and damage from the fires of 1814 and 1851 and the 1898 gas explosion

To strengthen the structure, over one thousand stainless steel tie rods were set into the building's masonry. More than 30 layers of paint were removed, and damaged stonework was repaired or replicated. Ultimately, 40 percent of the sandstone blocks were replaced with limestone. The walls were treated with a special consolidant and then painted to match the marble wings. The entire project was completed in 1987.

A related project, completed in January 1993, effected the repair of the Olmsted terraces, which had been subject to damage from settling, and converted the terrace courtyards into several thousand square feet of meeting space.

As the Capitol enters its third century, restoration and modernization work continues. Major projects completed in recent years include; repair and restoration of the House monumental stairs; conservation of the Statue of Freedom atop the Capitol dome; completion of the murals in the first-floor House corridors; preparation and publication of a book on the artist Constantino Brumidi, whose paintings decorate much of the Capitol; installation of an improved Senate subway system; construction of the Thurgood Marshall Federal Judiciary Building; construction of new House and Senate child care facilities and a new Senate Page school; and renovation, restoration, and modification of the interiors and exteriors of the Thomas Jefferson and John Adams Buildings of the Library of Congress.

The most recent Architect of the Capitol, Alan M. Hantman, FAIA, was appointed in February 1997. New and ongoing projects under his direction included rehabilitation of the Capitol dome; conservation of murals; improvement of speech-reinforcement, electrical, and fire-protection systems in the Capitol and the Congressional office buildings; work on security improvements within the Capitol complex; restoration of the U.S. Botanic Garden Conservatory; the design and construction of the National Garden adjacent to the Botanic Garden Conservatory; renovation of the building systems in the Dirksen Senate Office Building; preparation and publication of the first comprehensive history of the Capitol to appear in a century; and construction of a new Capitol Visitor Center. At the end of Mr. Hantman's term in February 2007, Mr. Stephen T. Ayers, AIA, assumed the position of Acting Architect of the Capitol.

Work is now under way on the Capitol Visitor Center, which will make the U.S. Capitol more accessible, comfortable, secure, and informative for all visitors. Preparatory construction activities began in summer 2002, including relocation of utilities and visitor screening facilities, and implementation of a comprehensive tree preservation program. It is scheduled to be completed in 2008.

The CVC will be located underground on the East Front of the Capitol, so as to enhance rather than detract from the appearance of the Capitol and its historic Frederick Law Olmsted landscape. When completed, the CVC will contain 580,000 square feet on three levels, requiring a 196,000-square-foot excavation, or ''footprint,'' on the East Front of the Capitol. (For purposes of comparison, the Capitol itself encompasses 775,000 square feet.)

The project will include space for exhibits, visitor comfort, food service, two orientation theaters, an auditorium, gift shops, security, a service tunnel for truck loading and deliveries, mechanical facilities, storage, and much needed space for the House and Senate. When completed, the CVC will preserve and maximize public access to the Capitol while greatly enhancing the experience for the millions who walks its historic corridors and experience its monumental spaces every year.

All activities related to the Capitol Visitor Center take place under the direction of the Capitol Preservation Commission.

HOUSE OFFICE BUILDINGS

Cannon House Office Building

An increased membership of the Senate and House resulted in a demand for additional rooms for the accommodations of the Senators and Representatives. On March 3, 1903, the Congress authorized the erection of a fireproofed office building for the use of the House. It was designed by the firm of Carrere & Hastings of New York City in the Beaux Arts style. The first brick was laid July 5, 1905, in square No. 690, and formal exercises were held at the laying of the cornerstone on April 14, 1906, in which President Theodore Roosevelt participated. The building was completed and occupied January 10, 1908. A subsequent change in the basis of congressional representation made necessary the building of an additional story in 1913–14. The total cost of the building, including site, furnishings, equipment, and the subway connecting it with the U.S. Capitol, amounted to $4,860,155. This office building contains about 500 rooms, and was considered at the time of its completion fully equipped for all the needs of a modern building for office purposes. A garage was added in the building's courtyard in the 1960s.

Pursuant to authority in the Second Supplemental Appropriations Act, 1955, and subsequent action of the House Office Building Commission, remodeling of the Cannon Building began in 1966. The estimated cost of this work was $5,200,000. Pursuant to the provisions of Public Law 87–453, approved May 21, 1962, the building was named in honor of Joseph G. Cannon of Illinois, who was Speaker at the time the building was constructed.

Longworth House Office Building

Under legislation contained in the authorization act of January 10, 1929, and in the urgent deficiency bill of March 4, 1929, provisions were made for an additional House office building, to be located on the west side of New Jersey Avenue (opposite the first House office building). The building was designed by the Allied Architects of Washington in the Neoclassical Revival style.

The cornerstone was laid June 24, 1932, and the building was completed on April 20, 1933. It contains 251 two-room suites and 16 committee rooms. Each suite and committee room is provided with a storeroom. Eight floors are occupied by members. The basement and subbasement contain shops and mechanical areas needed for the maintenance of the building. A cafeteria was added in the building's courtyard in the 1960s. The cost of this building, including site, furnishings, and equipment, was $7,805,705. Pursuant to the provisions of Public Law 87–453, approved May 21, 1962, the building was named in honor of Nicholas Longworth of Ohio, who was Speaker when the second House office building was constructed.

Rayburn House Office Building and Other Related Changes and Improvements

Under legislation contained in the Second Supplemental Appropriations Act, 1955, provision was made for construction of a fireproof office building for the House of Representatives.

All work was carried forward by the Architect of the Capitol under the direction of the House Office Building Commission at a cost totaling $135,279,000.

The Rayburn Building is connected to the Capitol by a subway. Designs for the building were prepared by the firm of Harbeson, Hough, Livingston & Larson of Philadelphia, Associate Architects. The building contains 169 congressional suites; full-committee hearing rooms for 9 standing committees, 16 subcommittee hearing rooms, committee staff rooms and other committee facilities; a large cafeteria and other restaurant facilities; an underground garage; and a variety of liaison offices, press and television facilities, maintenance and equipment shops or rooms, and storage areas. This building has nine stories and a penthouse for machinery.

The cornerstone was laid May 24, 1962, by John W. McCormack, Speaker of the House of Representatives. President John F. Kennedy participated in the cornerstone laying and delivered the address.

A portion of the basement floor was occupied beginning March 12, 1964, by House of Representatives personnel moved from the George Washington Inn property. Full occupancy of the Rayburn Building, under the room-filing regulations, was begun February 23, 1965, and completed April 2, 1965. Pursuant to the provisions of Public Law 87–453, approved May 21, 1962, the building was named in honor of Sam Rayburn of Texas.

House Office Building Annex No. 2, named the ''Gerald R. Ford House of Representatives Office Building'', was acquired in 1975 from the General Services Administration. The structure, located at Second and D Streets SW., was built in 1939 for the Federal Bureau of Investigation as a fingerprint file archives. This building has approximately 432,000 square feet of space.

SENATE OFFICE BUILDINGS

Richard Brevard Russell Senate Office Building

In 1891 the Senate provided itself with office space by the purchase of the Maltby Building, then located on the northwest corner of B Street (now Constitution Avenue) and New Jersey Avenue, NW. When it was condemned as an unsafe structure, senators needed safer and more commodious office space. Under authorization of the Act of April 28, 1904, square 686 on the northeast corner of Delaware Avenue and B Street NE. was purchased as a site for the Senate Office Building. The plans for the House Office Building were adapted for the Senate Office Building by the firm of Carrere & Hastings, with the exception that the side of the building fronting on First Street NE. was temporarily omitted. The cornerstone was laid without special exercises on July 31, 1906, and the building was occupied March 5, 1909. In 1931, the completion of the fourth side of the building was commenced. In 1933 it was completed, together with alterations to the C Street facade, and the construction of terraces, balustrades, and approaches. The cost of the completed building, including the site, furnishings, equipment and the subway connecting it with the United States Capitol, was $8,390,892.

The building was named the ''Richard Brevard Russell Senate Office Building'' by Senate Resolution 296, 92nd Congress, agreed to October 11, 1972, as amended by Senate Resolution 295, 96th Congress, agreed to December 3, 1979.

Everett McKinley Dirksen Senate Office Building

Under legislation contained in the Second Deficiency Appropriations Act, 1948, Public Law 80–785, provision was made for an additional office building for the United States Senate with limits of cost of $1,100,000 for acquisition of the site and $20,600,000 for constructing and equipping the building.

The construction cost limit was subsequently increased to $24,196. All work was carried forward by the Architect of the Capitol under the direction of the Senate Office Building Commission. The New York firm of Eggers & Higgins served as the consulting architect. The site was acquired and cleared in 1948–49 at a total cost of $1,011,492.

A contract for excavation, concrete footings and mats for the new building was awarded in January 1955, in the amount of $747,200. Groundbreaking ceremonies were held January 26, 1955.

A contract for the superstructure of the new building was awarded September 9, 1955, in the amount of $17,200,000. The cornerstone was laid July 13, 1956.

As a part of this project, a new underground subway system was installed from the Capitol to both the Old and New Senate Office Buildings.

An appropriation of $1,000,000 for furniture and furnishings for the new building was provided in 1958. The building was accepted for beneficial occupancy October 15, 1958.

The building was named the ''Everett McKinley Dirksen Senate Office Building'' by Senate Resolution 296, 92nd Congress, agreed to October 11, 1972, and Senate Resolution 295, 96th Congress, agreed to December 3, 1979.

Philip A. Hart Senate Office Building

Construction as an extension to the Dirksen Senate Office Building was authorized on October 31, 1972; legislation enacted in subsequent years increased the scope of the project and established a total cost ceiling of $137,700,400. The firm of John Carl Warnecke & Associates served as Associate Architect for the project.

Senate Resolution 525, passed August 30, 1976, amended by Senate Resolution 295, 96th Congress, agreed to December 3, 1979, provided that upon completion of the extension it would be named the ''Philip A. Hart Senate Office Building'' to honor the senator from Michigan.

The contract for clearing of the site, piping for utilities, excavation, and construction of foundation was awarded in December 1975. Groundbreaking took place January 5, 1976. The contract for furnishing and delivery of the exterior stone was awarded in February 1977, and the contract for the superstructure, which included wall and roof systems and the erection of all exterior stonework, was awarded in October 1977. The contract for the first portion of the interior and related work was awarded in December 1978. A contract for interior finishing was awarded in July 1980. The first suite was occupied on November 22, 1982. Alexander Calder's mobile / stabile *Mountains and Clouds* was installed in the building's atrium in November 1986.

CAPITOL POWER PLANT

During the development of the plans for the Cannon and Russell Buildings, the question of heat, light, and power was considered. The Senate and House wings of the Capitol were heated by separate heating plants. The Library of Congress also had a heating plant for that building. It was determined that needs for heating and lighting and electrical power could be met by a central power plant.

A site was selected in Garfield Park. Since this park was a Government reservation, an appropriation was not required to secure title. The determining factors leading to the selection of this site were its proximity to the tracks of what is now the Penn Central Railroad and to the buildings to be served.

The dimensions of the Capitol Power Plant, which was authorized on April 28, 1904, and completed in 1910, were 244 feet 8 inches by 117 feet. There are two radial brick chimneys 174 feet in height (reduced from 212 feet to 174 feet in 1951–52) and 11 feet in diameter at the top.

The buildings originally served by the Capitol Power Plant were connected to it by a reinforced-concrete steam tunnel.

In September 1951, when the demand for electrical energy was reaching the maximum capacity of the Capitol Power Plant, arrangements were made to purchase electrical service from the local public utility company and to discontinue electrical generation. The heating and cooling functions of the Capitol Power Plant were expanded in 1935, 1939, 1958, 1973, and 1980. A new modernization and expansion project is now underway.

U.S. CAPITOL GROUNDS

A Description of the Grounds

Originally a wooded wilderness, the U.S. Capitol Grounds today provide a parklike setting for the Nation's Capitol, offering a picturesque counterpoint to the building's formal architecture. The grounds immediately surrounding the Capitol are bordered by a stone wall and cover an area of 58.8 acres. Their boundaries are Independence Avenue on the south, Constitution Avenue on the north, First Street NE. / SE. on the east, and First Street NW. / SW. on the west. Over 100 varieties of trees and bushes are planted around the Capitol, and thousands of flowers are used in seasonal displays. In contrast to the building's straight, neoclassical lines, most of the walkways in the grounds are curved. Benches along the paths offer pleasant spots for visitors to appreciate the building, its landscape, and the surrounding areas, most notably the Mall to the west.

The grounds were designed by Frederick Law Olmsted (1822–1903), who planned the landscaping of the area that was performed from 1874 to 1892. Olmsted, who also designed New York's Central Park, is considered the greatest American landscape architect of his day. He was a pioneer in the development of public parks in America, and many of his designs were influenced by his studies of European parks, gardens, and estates. In describing his plan for the Capitol grounds, Olmsted noted that "The ground is in design part of the Capitol, but in all respects subsidiary to the central structure." Therefore, he was careful not to group trees or other landscape features in any way that would distract the viewer from the Capitol. The use of sculpture and other ornamentation has also been kept to a minimum.

Many of the trees on the Capitol grounds have historic or memorial associations. Over 30 states have made symbolic gifts of their state trees to the Capitol grounds. Many of the trees on the grounds bear plaques that identify their species and their historic significance.

At the East Capitol Street entrance to the Capitol plaza are two large rectangular stone fountains. The bottom levels now contain plantings, but at times in the past they have been used to catch the spillover from the fountains. At other times, both levels have held plantings. Six massive red granite lamp piers topped with light fixtures in wrought-iron cages, and 16 smaller bronze light fixtures, line the paved plaza. Seats are placed at intervals along the sidewalks. Three sets of benches are enclosed with wrought-iron railings and grilles; the roofed bench was originally a shelter for streetcar passengers. This area was closed to the public for the construction of the Capitol Visitor Center.

The northern part of the grounds offers a shaded walk among trees, flowers, and shrubbery. A small, hexagonal brick structure named the Summer House may be found in the northwest corner of the grounds. This structure contains shaded benches, a central ornamental fountain, and three public drinking fountains. In a small grotto on the eastern side of the Summer House, a stream of water flows and splashes over rocks to create a pleasing sound and cool the summer breezes.

A Brief History of the Grounds Before Olmsted

The land on which the Capitol stands was first occupied by the Manahoacs and the Monacans, who were subtribes of the Algonquin Indians. Early settlers reported that these tribes occasionally held councils not far from the foot of the hill. This land eventually became a part of Cerne Abbey Manor, and at the time of its acquisition by the Federal Government it was owned by Daniel Carroll of Duddington.

The "Residence Act" of 1790 provided that the federal government should be established in a permanent location by the year 1800. In early March 1791 the commissioners of the city of Washington, who had been appointed by President George Washington, selected the French engineer Peter Charles L'Enfant to plan the new federal city. L'Enfant decided to locate the Capitol at the elevated east end of the Mall (on what was then called Jenkins' Hill); he described the site as "a pedestal waiting for a monument."

At this time the site of the Capitol was a relative wilderness partly overgrown with scrub oak. Oliver Wolcott, a signer of the Declaration of Independence, described the soil as an "*exceedingly stiff* clay, becoming dust in dry and mortar in rainy weather."

In 1825, a plan was devised for imposing order on the Capitol grounds, and it was carried out for almost 15 years. The plan divided the area into flat, rectangular grassy areas bordered by trees, flower beds, and gravel walks. The growth of the trees, however, soon deprived the other plantings of nourishment, and the design became increasingly difficult to maintain in light of sporadic and small appropriations. John Foy, who had charge of the grounds during most of this period, was "superseded for political reasons," and the area was then maintained with little care or forethought. Many rapidly growing but short-lived trees were introduced and soon depleted the soil; a lack of proper pruning and thinning left the majority of the area's vegetation ill-grown, feeble, or dead. Virtually all was removed by the early 1870's, either to make way for building operations during Thomas U. Walter's enlargement of the Capitol or as required by changes in grading to accommodate the new work on the building or the alterations to surrounding streets.

The Olmsted Plan

The mid-19th-century extension of the Capitol, in which the House and Senate wings and the new dome were added, required also that the Capitol grounds be enlarged, and in 1874 Frederick Law Olmsted was commissioned to plan and oversee the project. As noted above, Olmsted was determined that the grounds should complement the building. In addition, he addressed an architectural problem that had persisted for some years: from the west (the growth of the city had nothing to do with the terraces)—the earthen terraces at the building's base made it seem inadequately supported at the top of the hill. The solution, Olmsted believed, was to construct marble terraces on the north, west, and south sides of the building, thereby causing it to "gain greatly in the supreme qualities of stability, endurance, and repose." He submitted his design for these features in 1875, and after extensive study it was approved.

Work on the grounds began in 1874, concentrating first on the east side and then progressing to the west, north, and south sides. First, the ground was reduced in elevation. Almost 300,000 cubic yards of earth and other material were eventually removed, and over 200 trees were removed. New sewer, gas, and water lines were installed. The soil was then enriched with fertilizers to provide a suitable growth medium for new plantings. Paths and roadways were graded and laid.

By 1876, gas and water service was completed for the entire grounds, and electrical lamp-lighting apparatuses had been installed. Stables and workshops had been removed from the northwest and southwest corners. A streetcar system north and south of the west grounds had been relocated farther from the Capitol, and ornamental shelters were in place at the north and south car-track termini. The granite and bronze lamp piers and ornamental bronze lamps for the east plaza area were completed.

Work accelerated in 1877. By this time, according to Olmsted's report, "altogether 7,837 plants and trees [had] been set out." However, not all had survived: hundreds were stolen or destroyed by vandals, and, as Olmsted explained, "a large number of cattle [had] been caught trespassing." Other work met with less difficulty. Foot-walks were laid with artificial stone, a mixture of cement and sand, and approaches were paved with concrete. An ornamental iron trellis had been installed on the northern east-side walk, and another was under way on the southern walk.

The 1878 appointment of watchmen to patrol the grounds was quite effective in preventing further vandalism, allowing the lawns to be completed and much shrubbery to be added. Also in that year, the roads throughout the grounds were paved.

Most of the work required on the east side of the grounds was completed by 1879, and effort thus shifted largely to the west side. The Pennsylvania Avenue approach was virtually finished, and work on the Maryland Avenue approach had begun. The stone walls on the west side of the grounds were almost finished, and the red granite lamp piers were placed at the eastward entrance from Pennsylvania Avenue.

In the years 1880–82, many features of the grounds were completed. These included the walls and coping around the entire perimeter, the approaches and entrances, and the Summer House. Work on the terraces began in 1882, and most work from this point until 1892 was concentrated on these structures.

In 1885, Olmsted retired from superintendency of the terrace project; he continued to direct the work on the grounds until 1889. Landscaping work was performed to adapt the surrounding areas to the new construction, grading the ground and planting shrubs at the bases of the walls, as the progress of the masonry work allowed. Some trees and other types of vegetation were removed, either because they had decayed or as part of a careful thinning-out process.

In 1888, the wrought-iron lamp frames and railings were placed at the Maryland Avenue entrance, making it the last to be completed. In 1892, the streetcar track that had extended into grounds from Independence Avenue was removed.

The Grounds After Olmsted

In the last years of the 19th century, work on the grounds consisted chiefly of maintenance and repairs as needed. Trees, lawns, and plantings were tended, pruned, and thinned to allow their best growth. This work was quite successful: by 1894, the grounds were so deeply shaded by trees and shrubs that Architect of the Capitol Edward Clark recommended an all-night patrol by watchmen to ensure public safety. A hurricane in September 1896 damaged or destroyed a number of trees, requiring extensive removals in the following year. Also in 1897, electric lighting replaced gas lighting in the grounds.

Between 1910 and 1935, 61.4 acres north of Constitution Avenue were added to the grounds. Approximately 100 acres was added in subsequent years, bringing the total area to 274 acres.

Since 1983, increased security measures have been put into effect, including the installation of barriers at vehicular entrances. However, the area still functions in many ways as a public park, and visitors are welcome to use the walks to tour the grounds. Demonstrations and ceremonies are often held on the grounds. In the summer, a series of evening concerts by the bands of the Armed Forces is offered free of charge on the west front plaza. On various holidays, concerts by the National Symphony Orchestra are held on the west front lawn.

LEGISLATIVE BRANCH AGENCIES

CONGRESSIONAL BUDGET OFFICE

H2–405 Ford House Office Building, Second and D Streets, SW., 20515
phone (202) 226–2600, http://www.cbo.gov

[Created by Public Law 93–344]

Director.—Peter R. Orszag, 6–2700.
Deputy Director.—Robert A. Sunshine, 6–2702.
General Counsel.—Robert P. Murphy, 5–1971.
Assistant Director for—
Budget Analysis.—Peter H. Fontaine, 6–2800.
Health and Human Resources.—Bruce Vavrichek, 6–2666.
Macroeconomic Analysis.—Robert A. Dennis, 6–2784.
Management, Business and Information Services.—Stephen A. Weigler, 6–2600.
Microeconomic and Financial Studies.—Joe Kile, 6–2940.
National Security.—J. Michael Gilmore, 6–2900.
Tax Analysis.—G. Thomas Woodward, 6–2687.

GOVERNMENT ACCOUNTABILITY OFFICE

441 G Street, NW., 20548, phone (202) 512–3000
http://www.gao.gov

Comptroller General of the United States.—David M. Walker, 512–5500, fax 512–5500.
Chief Operating Officer.—Gene Dodaro, 512–5600.
Chief Administrative Officer.—Sallyanne Harper, 512–5800.
General Counsel.—Gary Kepplinger, 512–5400.
Deputy General Counsel and Ethics Counselor.—Dan Gordon, 512–5400.

TEAMS

Acquisition and Sourcing Management.—Katherine Schinasi, 512–4841.
Applied Research and Methods.—Nancy Kingsbury, 512–2700.
Defense Capabilities and Management.—Butch Hinton, 512–4300.
Education Workforce and Income Security.—Cindy Fagnoni, 512–7215.
Financial Management and Assurance.—Jeff Steinhoff, 512–2600.
Financial Markets and Community Investments.—Rick Hillman, 512–9073.
Health Care.—Marjorie Kanof, 512–7114.
Homeland Security and Justice / National Preparedness.—Norm Rabkin, 512–9110.
Information Technology.—Joel Willemssen, 512–6408.
International Affairs and Trade.—Jacquie Williams-Bridgers, 512–3101.
Natural Resources and Environment.—Bob Robinson, 512–3841.
Physical Infrastructure.—Pat Dalton, 512–6737.
Strategic Issues.—J. Christophe Mihm, 512–6806.

SUPPORT FUNCTIONS

Congressional Relations.—Gloria Jarmon, 512–4400.
Legislative Advisers: Doris Cannon, 512–4507; Ralph Dawn, 512–4544; Rosa Harris, 512–9492; Elizabeth Johnston, 512–6345; Larry Malenich, 512–9399; Elizabeth Sirois, 512–8989; Mary Frances Widner, 512–3804.
Associate Legislative Adviser.—Carolyn McCowan, 512–3503.
Field Offices.—John Anderson, 512–8024.

Inspector General.—Frances Garcia, 512–5748.
Opportunity and Inclusiveness.—Ron Stroman, 512–6388.
Personnel Appeals Board.—Anne Wagner, 512–6137.
Public Affairs.—Paul L. Anderson, 512–3823.
Quality and Continuous Improvement.—Tim Bowling, 512–6100.
Strategic Planning and External Liaison.—Helen Hsing, 512–2639.

MISSION SUPPORT OFFICES

Deputy Chief Administrative Officer/Chief Information Officer.—Joseph Kraus, 512–2898.
Controller.—Stan Czerwinski, 512–6520.
Human Capital Officer.—Jesse Hoskins, 512–5533.
Knowledge Services Officer.—Catherine Teti, 512–9255.
Professional Development Program.—Dave Clark, 512–9484.

U.S. GOVERNMENT PRINTING OFFICE

732 North Capitol Street, NW., 20401

phone (202) 512–0000, http://www.gpo.gov

OFFICE OF THE PUBLIC PRINTER

Public Printer of the United States.—William H. Turri (acting), 512–1000.
Deputy Public Printer.—William H. Turri, 512–2036.
Chief of Staff.—Robert C. Tapella, 512–1100.
Deputy Chief of Staff.—Maria Lefevre.
Inspector General.—J. Anthony Ogden, 512–0039.
General Counsel.—Gregory A. Brower, 512–0033.
Deputy General Counsel.—Drew Spalding.
Director for—
Congressional Relations.—Andrew M. Sherman, 512–1991, fax 512–1293.
Equal Employment Opportunity.—Nadine L. Elzy, 512–2014.
Public Relations.—Caroline Scullin, 512–1957.
Chief Technology Officer, Office of Innovation and New Technology.—Reynold Schweickhardt, 512–1913.

CUSTOMER SERVICES

Managing Director.—Jim Bradley, 512–0111.
Deputy Managing Director.—Davita Vance-Cooks, 512–0014.
Director for—
Acquisition Policy and Planning Staff.—Jeffrey Dulberg, 512–0376.
Agency Publishing Services: Jon Carr, 512–0238; Sandra MacAfee, 512–0320; Raymond T. Sullivan, 512–0528; David Thomas, 512–1239.
Congressional Publishing Services.—Lyle Green, 512–0224, fax 512–1101.
Creative Services.—Janice Sterling, 512–0212.
Digital Media Services.—Sung ''Jeannie'' Lee, 512–1295.
Institute for Federal Printing and Electronic Publishing.—Patricia Hammond, 512–1116.
Office of Development and Program Support.—Sandy Zanko, 512–0559.
Printing Support Operations.—Larry Vines, 512–0458.
Program Analysis and Research Office.—Paul Giannini, 512–2270.
Program and Operations Management Office.—Ginger Thomas, 512–0327.
Sales and Marketing Office.—Stuart M. Spence, 512–1904.

GPO OFFICES NATIONWIDE

Atlanta.—Gary C. Bush, Manager, 1888 Emery Street, Suite 110, Atlanta, GA 30318–2542, (404) 605–9160, fax 605–9185.
Boston.—Ira Fishkin, Manager, 28 Court Square, Boston, MA 02108–2504, (617) 720–3680, fax 720–0281.
Charleston Satellite Office.—Robert Mann, Manager, 2825 Noisette Boulevard, Charleston, SC 29405–1819, (843) 743–2036, fax 743–2068.

Chicago.—Rebecca Coale, Manager, 200 North La Salle Street, Suite 810, Chicago, IL 60601–1055, (312) 353–3916, fax 886–3163.

Columbus.—Steven A. Boortz, Assistant Manager, 1335 Dublin Road, Suite 112–B, Columbus, OH 43215–7034, (614) 488–4616, fax 488–4577.

Dallas.—Kelle J. Chatham, Assistant Manager, Federal Office Building, 1100 Commerce Street, Room 731, Dallas, TX 75242–1027, (214) 767–0451, fax 767–4101.

Denver.—Barbara Lessans, Manager, 12345 W. Alameda Parkway, Suite 208, Lakewood, CO 80228, (303) 236–5292, fax 236–5304.

Hampton, VA.—Robert Mann, Manager, 11836 Canon Boulevard, Suite 400, Newport News, VA 23606–2555, (757) 873–2800, fax 873–2805.

New York.—Ira Fishkin, Manager, 26 Federal Plaza Room 2930, New York, NY 10278, (212) 264–2252, fax 264–2413.

Oklahoma City Satellite Office.—Timothy J. Ashcraft, Manager, 3420 D Avenue, Suite 100, Tinker AFB, OK 73145–9188, (405) 610–4146, fax 610–4125.

Philadelphia.—Ira Fishkin, Manager, 928 Jaymore Road, Suite A190, Southampton, PA 8966–3820, (215) 364–6465, fax 364–6479.

San Antonio Satellite Office.—Kelle J. Chatham, Assistant Manager, 1531 Connally Street, Suite 2, Lackland AFB, TX 78236–5514, (210) 675–1480, fax 675–2429.

San Diego Satellite Office.—John J. O'Connor, Manager, 8880 Rio San Diego Drive, 18th Floor, San Diego, CA 92108–3609, (619) 209–6178, fax 209–6179.

San Francisco.—John J. O'Connor, Manager, 536 Stone Road, Suite 1, Benicia, CA 94510–1170, (707) 748–1970, fax 748–1980.

Seattle.—David Goldberg, Manager, Federal Center South, 4735 East Marginal Way S., Seattle, WA 98134–2397, (206) 764–3726, fax 764–3301.

INFORMATION DISSEMINATION

Superintendent of Documents.—Richard G. Davis (acting), 512–1622.
Director for—
Library Services and Content Management.—Richard G. Davis, 512–1622.

GPO BOOKSTORE

Washington, DC, Metropolitan Area: GPO Bookstore, 710 North Capitol Street, NW., Washington, DC 20401, 512–0132.

TO ORDER PUBLICATIONS:

Phone toll free (866) 512–1800 [DC area: (202) 512–1800], fax (202) 512–2104. Mail orders to Superintendent of Documents, P.O. Box 371954, Pittsburgh, PA 15250–7954, or order online from http://bookstore.gpo.gov. *GPO Access* technical support: contactcenter@gpo.gov, or toll free (888) 293–6498 [DC area (202) 512–1530].

PLANT OPERATIONS

Managing Director.—Robert E. Schwenk, 512–0707.
Deputy Managing Director of Plant Operations.—Olivier Girod, 512–1097.
Production Manager.—Stephen LeBlanc, 512–0707.
Assistant Production Manager (days).—Marvin Verter, 512–0589.
Assistant Production Manager (night).—Katherine Taylor, 512–0688.
Assistant to the Production Manager (night).—David N. Boddie, 512–0688.
Superintendent of:
Binding Division.—John W. Crawford, 512–0593.
Digital Pre-Press.—Dannie E. Young, 512–0625.
Press Division.—Barry McMahon, 512–0673.
Production Planning Division.—Philip J. Markett, Jr., 512–0233.
Manager, Quality Control and Technical Department.—Sylvia S.Y. Subt, 512–0766.
Director, Engineering Service.—Dennis J. Carey (acting), 512–1018.

INFORMATION TECHNOLOGY AND SYSTEMS

Chief Information Officer.—Michael Wash, 512–1037.
Deputy Chief Information Officer.—Bruce C. O'Dell, 512–1956.

Director of:
Business Systems Support Division.—Layton F. Clay, 512–2001.
End User Support Division.—Melvin C. Eley, 512–0737.
Information Security.—John Hannan, 512–1020.
Enterprise Projects.—Richard G. Leeds, Jr., 512–0029.
Systems Architecture Division.—Ida Milner, 512–1313.
Systems Integration Division.—Bartholomew G. Hill, 512–2299.
Technology.—Scott Stovall, 512–1080.
Program Management: Ernest Baldwin, Selene Dalecky, Kirk Knoll, 512–1080.

HUMAN CAPITAL

Chief Human Capital Officer.—William T. Harris, 512–1111.
Deputy Chief Human Capital Officer.—Rafael E. Landrau, 512–2077.
Director, Strategic Human Capital Policy Staff.—James L. Curran, 512–1182.
Director of Labor Relations.—Mendelssohn V. McLean, 512–0201.

FINANCE AND ADMINISTRATION

Chief Financial Officer.—Steven T. Shedd, 512–2073.
Comptroller.—William L. Boesch, Jr., 512–2073.
Director, Financial Planning and Control.—William M. Guy, 512–0832.
Controller of:
Customer Service.—Akiko Ward, 512–1197.
Information Dissemination.—Allison Brown, 512–1195.
Plant Operations.—David Ford, 512–1194.
Systems.—Emily Dean, 512–2073.

LIBRARY OF CONGRESS

101 Independence Avenue, SE., 20540, phone (202) 707–5000, fax 707–5844

http://www.loc.gov

OFFICE OF THE LIBRARIAN, LM 608

Librarian of Congress.—James H. Billington, 707–5205.
Confidential Assistant to the Librarian.—Timothy L. Robbins, 707–8174.
Chief Operating Officer.—Jo Ann C. Jenkins, 707–0351.
Director, Office of:
Communications.—Matt Raymond, LM 105, 707–2905.
Editor for—
Calendar of Events.—Erin Allen, 707–2905.
Library of Congress Information Bulletin.—Audrey Fischer, 707–0022.
The Gazette.—Gail Fineberg, 707–9194.
Congressional Relations.—Geraldine Otremba, LM 611, 707–6577.
Development.—Susan Siegel, LM 605, 707–1447.
Special Events Officer.—Larry Stafford, LM 612, 707–1523.
General Counsel.—Elizabeth Pugh, LM 601, 707–6316.
Inspector General.—Karl W. Schornagel, LM 630, 707–6314.
Chief of Contracts and Grants Management.—Nydia Coleman, LA 325, 707–6109.

OFFICE OF SECURITY AND EMERGENCY PREPAREDNESS, LM G03

Director.—Kenneth Lopez, 707–8708.

OFFICE OF WORKFORCE DIVERSITY, LM 624

Director.—Debra Hayes, 707–0348.
Affirmative Action and Special Programs Office (LM 623), 707–5479.
Dispute Resolution Center (LM 624), 707–4170.
Equal Employment Opportunity Complaints Office (LM 626), 707–6024.

OFFICE OF THE DIRECTOR FOR HUMAN RESOURCES SERVICES, LM 645

Director.—Dennis Hanratty, LM 645, 707–5659.
Special Assistants: William Ayers, 707–0289; Timothy W. Cannon, 707–6544.
Director, Office of:
Strategic Planning and Automation.—Belinda Harris, 707–6648.
Workforce Acquisitions.—Sheila Williamson, 707–8072.
Workforce Management.—Charles Carron, LM 653, 707–6637.
Worklife Services Center.—Tim Cannon (acting), 707–6544.

OFFICE OF THE CHIEF FINANCIAL OFFICER, LM 613

Chief Financial Officer.—Jeffrey Page, LM 617, 707–7350.
Budget Officer.—Kathryn B. Murphy, 707–5186.
Disbursing Officer.—Nicholas Roseto, 707–5202.
Financial Systems Officer.—Jamie L. McCullough, LM 617, 707–4160.

OFFICE OF THE DIRECTOR FOR INTEGRATED SUPPORT SERVICES, LM 327

Director.—Mary Berghaus Levering, 707–1393.
Facility Services Officer.—Neal Graham, 707–7512.
Health Services Officer.—Sandra Charles, LM G40, 707–8035.
Safety Services Officer.—Robert Browne, LM B28, 707–6204.

OFFICE OF STRATEGIC INITIATIVES, LM 637

Associate Librarian for Strategic Initiatives/Chief Information Officer.—Laura E. Campbell, 707–3300.
Confidential Assistant to the Associate Librarian.—George Coulbourne, 707–7856.
Director, Digital Resource Management and Planning.—Molly H. Johnson, 707–0809.
Senior Advisor, Integration Management.—Elizabeth S. Dulabahn, 707–2369.
Director for Information Technology Services.—James M. Gallagher, LM G51, 707–5114.
Special Assistant to the Director.—Karen Caldwell, 707–3797.

LAW LIBRARY, OFFICE OF THE LAW LIBRARIAN, LM 240

Law Librarian.—Rubens Medina, 707–5065.
Director, Directorate of Law Library Services.—Donna Scheeder, 707–8939.
Chief, Public Services.—Robert N. Gee, LM 201, 707–0638.
Chief, Eastern Law Division.—Tao-tai Hsia, LM 235, 707–5085.
Chief, Western Law Division.—Kersi B. Shroff, LM 235, 707–7850.

LIBRARY SERVICES, OFFICE OF THE ASSOCIATE LIBRARIAN FOR LIBRARY SERVICES, LM 642

Associate Librarian.—Deanna Marcum, 707–5325.
Deputy Associate Librarian.—Robert Dizard, Jr., 707–7085.
Director of:
American Folklife Center.—Peggy Bulger, LJ G59, 707–1745.
Veterans History Project.—Robert W. Patrick, LA 143, 707–7308.
Director for Acquisitions and Bibliographic Access.—Beacher Wiggins, 707–5137.
Chief, Cataloging Distribution Service.—Barbara Tillett, LA 206, 707–6120.
Director, Office for Collections and Services.—Jeremy Adamson, LM 642, 707–7789.
Chief of:
African and Middle Eastern Division.—Mary-Jane Deeb, LJ 220, 707–7937.
Asian Division.—Hwa-Wei Lee, LJ 149, 707–5240.
Children's Literature Center.—Sybille A. Jagusch, LJ 100, 707–5535.
Collections Access, Loan and Management.—Steven J. Herman, LJ G02, 707–7400.
European Division.—Georgette M. Dorn (acting), LJ 250, 707–5414.
Federal Research Division.—Robert L. Worden, LA 5282, 707–3900.
Geography and Map Division.—John R. Hebert, LM B02, 707–8530.
Hispanic Division.—Georgette M. Dorn, LJ 205, 707–5400.

Manuscript Division.—James H. Hutson, LM 102, 707–5383.
Motion Picture, Broadcasting and Recorded Sound Division.—Gregory A. Lukow, LM 338, 707–5840.
Music Division.—Susan H. Vita, LM 113, 707–5503.
Prints and Photographs Division.—Helena Zinkham (acting), LM 339, 707–5836.
Rare Book and Special Collections Division.—Mark G. Dimunation, LJ Dk B, 707–5434.
Science Technology and Business Division.—William J. Sittig, LA 5203, 707–5664.
Director, Partnerships and Outreach Programs.—Kathryn Mendenhall, LM 642, 707–5325.
Director, Center for the Book.—John Y. Cole, Jr., LM 650, 707–5221.
Executive Director, Federal Library and Information Center Committee.—Roberta I. Shaffer, LA 217, 707–4800.
Interpretive Programs Officer.—Irene U. Chambers, LA G25, 707–5223.
Director, Office of National Library Service for the Blind and Physically Handicapped, TSA.—Frank K. Cylke, 707–5104.
Director, Office of Scholarly Programs.—Carolyn Brown, LJ 120, 707–3302.
Co-Chiefs, Photoduplication Service: Myron Chace (acting); Virginia Sorkin (acting), LA 130, 707–5650.
Director, Publishing Office.—W. Ralph Eubanks, LM 602, 707–3892.
Retail Marketing Officer.—Anna S. Lee, LM 225Q, 707–7715.
Visitor Services Officer.—Guilia Adelfio, 707–9779.
Director for Preservation.—Dianne Van Der Reyden, 707–7423.

CONGRESSIONAL RESEARCH SERVICE, LM 203

Director.—Daniel P. Mulhollan, 707–5775.
Deputy Director.—Angela Evans, 707–7375.
Chief Technology Officer.—Arthur M. Graham, LM 413, 707–4228.
Associate Director, Office of:
Congressional Affairs and Counselor to the Director.—Kent M. Ronhovde, 707–7090.
Finance and Administration.—Edward Jablonski (acting), LM 209, 707–8397.
Legislative Information.—Martha M. Dexter, LM 223, 707–6817.
Research.—Roger S. White, LM–203, 707–7844.
Workforce Development.—Bessie E.H. Alkisswani, LM 208, 707–8835.
Assistant Director of:
American Law Division.—Ellen Lazarus (acting), LM 227, 707–2945.
Domestic Social Policy Division.—Margot Schenet (acting), LM 323, 707–7378.
Foreign Affairs, Defense and Trade Division.—Charlotte P. Preece, LM 315, 707–7654.
Government and Finance Division.—Robert J. Dilger, LM 303, 707–3110.
Knowledge Services Group.—Stephanie V. Williams, LM 215, 707–6818.
Resources, Science and Industry Division.—John L. Moore, LM 423, 707–7232.

U.S. COPYRIGHT OFFICE, LM 403

Register of Copyrights and Associate Librarian for Copyright Services.—Marybeth Peters, 707–8350.
General Counsel.—Tanya Sandros (acting), 707–8380.
Deputy General Counsel.—Maria Pallante.
Chief Operating Officer.—Julia B. Huff, 707–8350.
Special Legal Advisor for Reengineering.—Nanette Petruzzelli, 707–8350.
Chief of:
Cataloging Division.—Joanna Roussis (acting), LM 513, 707–8040.
Information and Reference Division.—James P. Cole, LM 453, 707–6800.
Receiving and Processing Division.—Melissa Dadant, LM 435, 707–7700.
Copyright Acquisitions Division.—Jewel Player, LM 438C, 707–7125.

UNITED STATES BOTANIC GARDEN

245 First Street, SW., Washington, DC 20024

(202) 225–8333 (information); (202) 226–8333 (receptionist)

http://www.usbg.gov

Director.—Stephen T. Ayers (acting), Architect of the Capitol, 228–1204.

Executive Director.—Holly H. Shimizu, 225–6670.
Administrative Officer.—Elizabeth A. Spar, 225–5002.
Public Programs Manager.—Christine A. Flanagan, 225–1269.
Horticulture Division Manager.—Robert Pennington, 225–6647.
Operations Division Manager.—John M. Gallagher, 225–6646.

THE CABINET

Vice President of the United States	RICHARD B. CHENEY.
Secretary of State	CONDOLEEZZA RICE.
Secretary of the Treasury	HENRY M. PAULSON, JR.
Secretary of Defense	ROBERT M. GATES.
Attorney General	ALBERTO R. GONZALES.
Secretary of the Interior	DIRK KEMPTHORNE.
Secretary of Agriculture	MICHAEL JOHANNS.
Secretary of Commerce	CARLOS GUTIERREZ.
Secretary of Labor	ELAINE L. CHAO.
Secretary of Health and Human Services	MICHAEL O. LEAVITT.
Secretary of Housing and Urban Development	ALPHONSO JACKSON.
Secretary of Transportation	MARY E. PETERS.
Secretary of Energy	SAMUEL W. BODMAN.
Secretary of Education	MARGARET SPELLINGS.
Secretary of Veterans Affairs	JAMES NICHOLSON.
Secretary of Homeland Security	MICHAEL CHERTOFF.
Chief of Staff	JOSHUA B. BOLTEN.
Director, Office of Management and Budget	[Vacant.]
U.S. Trade Representative	SUSAN SCHWAB.
Administrator, Environmental Protection Agency	STEPHEN L. JOHNSON.
Director, Office of National Drug Control Policy	JOHN P. WALTERS.

EXECUTIVE BRANCH

THE PRESIDENT

GEORGE W. BUSH, Republican, of Texas; born on July 6, 1946; raised in Midland and Houston, TX; education: Yale University (Bachelor's Degree); Harvard University (M.B.A.); military service: Texas Air National Guard; occupations: businessman (energy industry); Managing General Partner of the Texas Rangers (Major League Baseball team); public service: elected Governor of Texas on November 8, 1994; reelected as Governor on November 3, 1998; became the first Governor in Texas history to be elected to consecutive four-year terms; religion: Methodist; family: married to Laura; two children, Barbara and Jenna; elected President of the United States on November 7, 2000; took the oath of office on January 20, 2001; reelected November 2, 2004.

EXECUTIVE OFFICE OF THE PRESIDENT

1600 Pennsylvania Avenue, NW., 20500

Eisenhower Executive Office Building (EEOB), 17th Street and Pennsylvania Avenue, NW., 20500, phone (202) 456–1414, http://www.whitehouse.gov

The President of the United States.—George W. Bush.
Personal Secretary to the President.—Karen Keller.
Personal Aide to the President.—Jared Weinstein.

OFFICE OF THE VICE PRESIDENT

phone (202) 456–1414

The Vice President.—Richard B. Cheney.
Chief of Staff to the Vice President and Counsel.—David Addington, EEOB, room 276, 456–9000.
Deputy Chief of Staff.—Claire O'Donnell, EEOB, room 272, 456–6770.
Counsel to the Vice President.—Shannen Coffin, EEOB, room 282, 456–9089.
Assistant to the Vice President for—
Communications/Press Secretary.—Lea Anne McBride, EEOB, room 293, 456–0373.
Domestic Policy.—Neil Patel, EEOB, room 286, 456–2728.
Legislative Affairs.—Brenda Becker, EEOB, room 285, 456–6774.
National Security Affairs.—John Hannah, EEOB, room 298, 456–9501.
Political Affairs.—Mel Raines, EEOB, room 272, 456–9033.
Executive Assistant to the Vice President.—Debra Heiden, West Wing, 456–7549.
Chief of Staff to Mrs. Cheney.—Cecelia Boyer, EEOB, room 200, 456–7458.
Deputy Assistant to the Vice President and Director of Scheduling.—Elizabeth Kleppe, EEOB, room 279, 456–6773.
Director of Correspondence.—Rose Folsom, EEOB, room 200, 456–9002.

COUNCIL OF ECONOMIC ADVISERS

1800 G Street, NW., 8th floor, 20006, phone (202) 395–5084
http://www.whitehouse.gov/cea

Chair.—Edward P. Lazear.
Chief of Staff.—Gary Blank.
Members: Katherine Baicker, Matthew J. Slaughter.

COUNCIL ON ENVIRONMENTAL QUALITY

730 Jackson Place, NW., 20503, phone (202) 456–6224
http://www.whitehouse.gov/ceq

Chair.—James Connaughton.
Chief of Staff.—Martin Hall.
Special Assistant to the Chair.—Alexander Berger.
Executive Assistant to the Chair.—Ludmilla Savelieff.
Associate Director for—
Agriculture, Lands and Wildlife.—Gregory Schildwachter.
Communications.—Kristen Hellmer.
Congressional Affairs.—Ashley Cohen.
Cooperative Conservation.—Mitchell Butler.
Energy and Transportation.—Robert Rainey.
International Affairs and Climate Change.—George Banks.
Natural Resources.—Kathy Copeland.
NEPA Oversight.—Horst Greczmiel.
General Counsel.—Dinah Bear.
Deputy General Counsel.—Edward ''Ted'' Boling.
Administrative Officer.—Angela Stewart.
Administrative Assistant.—Essence Washington.
Records Clerk.—Elizabeth Moss.

CENTRAL INTELLIGENCE AGENCY

phone (703) 482–1100

Director.—GEN Michael V. Hayden.
Deputy Director.—Stephen R. Kappes.
Associate Deputy Director.—Michael J. Morell.
General Counsel.—John Rizzo (acting).
Director of:
Intelligence.—John A. Kringen.
Public Affairs.—Mark Mansfield.
Science and Technology.—Stephanie L. O'Sullivan.
Support.—Scott White.

FOREIGN INTELLIGENCE ADVISORY BOARD

phone (202) 456–2352

Executive Director.—Stefanie Osburn.

NATIONAL SECURITY COUNCIL

phone (202) 456–9491

MEMBERS

The President.—George W. Bush.
The Vice President.—Richard B. Cheney.
The Secretary of State.—Condoleezza Rice.
The Secretary of Defense.—Robert M. Gates.
The Secretary of Treasury.—Henry M. Paulson, Jr.
Assistant to the President for National Security Affairs.—Stephen J. Hadley.

STATUTORY ADVISERS

Director of National Intelligence.—John M. ''Mike'' McConnell.
Chairman, Joint Chiefs of Staff.—GEN Peter Pace, USMC.
Assistant to the President and Deputy National Security Advisor.—J.D. Crouch II.

OFFICE OF ADMINISTRATION

Eisenhower Executive Office Building, phone (202) 456–2861

Special Assistant to the President/Director of Administration.—Alan R. Swendiman.
Deputy Director.—Larrilyn Bertocchio.
Chief, Office of:
Equal Employment Opportunity.—Clara Patterson.
Finance.—Edgar Bennett.
General Counsel.—Alan R. Swendiman (acting).
Information.—Theresa Payton.
Operations.—Sandy Evans.
Security.—Jim Knodell.

OFFICE OF MANAGEMENT AND BUDGET

Eisenhower Executive Office Building, phone (202) 395–4840

Director.—Robert J. Portman.
Deputy Director.—Stephen S. McMillin.
Deputy Director for Management.—Clay Johnson III.
Executive Associate Director.—Austin Smythe.
Administrator, Office of:
Federal Procurement Policy.—Paul Denett.
Information and Regulatory Affairs.—Steve Aitken (acting).
Assistant Director for—
Budget.—Elizabeth Robinson.
Legislative Reference.—James J. Jukes.
Associate Director for—
Communications.—Christin Baker.
Economic Policy.—J.D. Foster.
Human Resources Programs.—Donald Dempsey.
General Government Programs.—Michael Bopp.
Legislative Affairs.—Margaret Stewart.
National Security Programs.—Joseph Bowab.
Natural Resources, Energy and Science Programs.—David Anderson.
General Counsel.—Jeffrey Rosen.

OFFICE OF NATIONAL DRUG CONTROL POLICY

750 17th Street, NW., phone (202) 395–6738 or 6695, fax 395–7251

Director.—John P. Walters, room 805, 395–6700.
Chief of Staff.—Stephen A. Katsurinis, room 809, 395–6732.
Deputy Director, Office of:
Demand Reduction.—Dr. Bertha Madras, room 609, 395–3036.
State and Local Affairs.—Scott M. Burns, room 661, 395–7252.
Supply Reduction.—James F.X. O'Gara, room 713, 395–7225.
Assistant Deputy Director, Office of:
Demand Reduction.—Martha M. Gagné, room 610, 395–4622.
State and Local Affairs.—Joseph D. Keefe, room 659, 395–6755.
Supply Reduction.—Patrick M. Ward, room 712, 395–5535.
General Counsel.—Edward H. Jurith, room 518, 395–6709.
Director, Counterdrug Technology Assessment Center.—David W. Murray, room 804, 395–6788.
Associate Director, National Youth Anti-drug Media Campaign.—Robert W. Denniston, room 560, 395–4653.
Associate Director, Office of:
Legislative Affairs.—Keith B. Nelson, room 825, 395–5594.
Management and Administration.—Michele C. Marx, room 326, 395–6883.
Planning and Budget.—David J. Rivait, room 846, 395–5505.
Public Affairs.—Thomas A. Riley, room 842, 395–6627.

OFFICE OF SCIENCE AND TECHNOLOGY POLICY

Eisenhower Executive Office Building, phone (202) 456–7116, fax 456–6021
http://www.ostp.gov

Director.—John H. Marburger III.
Associate Director and Deputy Director for—
Science.—Sharon L. Hays.
Technology.—Richard Russell.
Chief of Staff and General Counsel.—Stanley S. Sokul.
Executive Secretary for National Science and Technology Council.—Ted Wackler.
Executive Director for President's Committee of Advisors on Science and Technology.—Celia Merzbacher.

OFFICE OF THE UNITED STATES TRADE REPRESENTATIVE

600 17th Street, NW., 20508, phone (202) 395–6890
http://www.ustr.gov

United States Trade Representative.—Susan Schwab.
Deputy United States Trade Representative.—Peter F. Allgeier.
Deputy U.S. Trade Representative, Geneva.—Linnett F. Deily.
Associate U.S. Trade Representative.—Sheeran Shiner.
Special Textile Negotiator.—Scott Qusenberry.
Chief Agricultural Negotiator.—Richard Crowder.
General Counsel.—James Mendenhall (acting).
Assistant U.S. Trade Representative for—
Administration.—Fred Ames.
Africa.—Florie Liser.
Agricultural Affairs.—James Murphy.
China Affairs.—Tim Stratford.
Congressional Affairs.—Justin McCarthy.
Economic Affairs.—David Walters.
Environment and Natural Resources.—Mark Linscott.
Europe and the Mediterranean.—Shaun Donnelly.
Industry.—Meredith Broadbent.
Intergovernmental Affairs and Public Liaison.—Tiffany Moore.
Japan, Korea and APEC Affairs.—Wendy Cutler.
Monitoring and Enforcement.—Dan Brinza.
Office of the Americas.—Everett Eissnstat.
Policy Coordination.—Carmen Suro-Bredie.
Public/Media Affairs.—Sean Spicer.
Services, Investment and Intellectual Property.—Christine Bliss.
South Asian Affairs.—Douglas Hartwick.
Southeast Asia, Pacific and Pharmaceutical Policy.—Barbara Weisel.
Trade and Labor.—Lewis Karesh.
World Trade Organization (WTO) and Multilateral Affairs.—Dorothy Dwoskin.

THE WHITE HOUSE OFFICE

ADVANCE

phone (202) 456–5309

Deputy Assistant to the President and Director of Advance.—Todd Beyer.
Special Assistants to the President and Deputy Directors of Advance for Press: John Meyers, Christian Edwards.

CABINET LIAISON

phone (202) 456–2572

Special Assistant to the President for Cabinet Liaison.—Ross Kyle.

CHIEF OF STAFF

phone (202) 456–6798

Assistant to the President and Chief of Staff—Joshua B. Bolten.

COMMUNICATIONS AND SPEECHWRITING

phone (202) 456–9271

Assistant to the President for Communications.—Kevin Sullivan.
Assistant to the President for Speechwriting.—William McGurn.
Counselor to the President.—Dan Bartlett.

CORRESPONDENCE

phone (202) 456–9002

Director of Presidential Correspondence.—Duke Hipp.
Deputy Director of Presidential Correspondence.—Kerri Speight Watson, 456–6779.
Editor/Quality Control.—Nathaniel Kraft, 456–5867.
Director of:
Agency Liaison.—Richard Henry, 456–5485.
Gift Unit.—Brian Eppes, 456–5457.
Mail Analysis.—Gertrude Roddick, 456–5490.

DOMESTIC POLICY COUNCIL

phone (202) 456–5594

Assistant to the President for Domestic Policy.—Karl Zinsmeister.

OFFICE OF FAITH-BASED AND COMMUNITY INITIATIVES

phone (202) 456–6708

Deputy Assistant to the President and Director.—Jay Hein.

OFFICE OF THE FIRST LADY

phone (202) 456–7064

The First Lady.—Laura Bush.
Assistant to the President and Chief of Staff to the First Lady.—Anita McBride.
Special Assistant to the President and White House Social Secretary.—Lea Berman.

HOMELAND SECURITY COUNCIL

phone (202) 456–6317

Assistant to the President for Homeland Security and Counterterrorism.—Frances Fragos Townsend.

INTERGOVERNMENTAL AFFAIRS

phone (202) 456–2896

Deputy Assistant to the President and Director for Intergovernmental Affairs.—Maggie Grant.
Special Assistants to the President for Intergovernmental Affairs: John Burke, Rudy Fernandez.

LEGISLATIVE AFFAIRS
phone (202) 456–2230

Assistant to the President for Legislative Affairs.—Candida Wolff.
Deputy Assistant to the President for Legislative Affairs.—Debbie Fiddelke.
Special Assistant to the Assistant to the President for Legislative Affairs.—Lindley Kratovil.
Deputy Assistant to the President for—
Legislative Affairs (House).—Brian Conklin.
Legislative Affairs (Senate).—Sean O'Hollaren.
Director of Legislative Correspondence.—Erica Crocker.

MANAGEMENT AND ADMINISTRATION
phone (202) 456–5400

Deputy Assistant to the President for Management and Administration.—Linda Gambatesa.
Special Assistant to the President for Management.—Neal Burnham.
Director of:
Visitors Office.—Sara Armstrong.
White House Management.—Jacquie Hayes-Byrd.
White House Personnel.—Caroline Swan.

NATIONAL ECONOMIC COUNCIL
phone (202) 456–2800

Assistant to the President for Economic Policy and Director, National Economic Council.—Allan B. Hubbard.
Deputy Assistant to the President for Economic Policy and Deputy Director, National Economic Council.—Keith Hennessey.
Executive Assistant to the Director.—Dougie Simmons.
Special Assistants to the President for Economic Policy: Charles Blahous, Bryan Corbett, Lisa Epifani, Julie Goon, Hunter Moorhead.

POLICY AND STRATEGIC PLANNING
phone (202) 456–0170

Assistant to the President for Policy and Strategic Planning.—Mike Gerson.
Special Assistant to the Director.—Emily Kropp.

POLITICAL AFFAIRS
phone (202) 456–6257

Deputy Assistant to the President and Director of Political Affairs.—Sara Taylor.
Executive Assistant.—Jessica ''Swinehart'' Thorpe.
Special Assistant to the President and Deputy Director of Political Affairs.—Scott Jennings.
Associate Political Directors: Jane Cherry, Jonathan Felts, Jonathan Seaton, Steven Soper.

PRESIDENT'S COMMISSION ON WHITE HOUSE FELLOWSHIPS
phone (202) 395–4522

Director.—Janet Eissenstat.
Associate Director.—Lindsey Drouin.
Administrative Officer.—Pandoria Nobles-Jones.

PRESIDENTIAL PERSONNEL
phone (202) 456–9713

Assistant to the President for Presidential Personnel.—Liza Wright.

Executive Assistant to the President for Presidential Personnel.—Christopher Byrne.
Special Assistants to the President and Associate Directors.—Katja Bullock, Jennifer Christie, David Clark, Martha Miller, Luis Reyes.

OFFICE OF THE PRESS SECRETARY

Upper Press Office phone (202) 456–2673, Lower Press Office phone (202) 456–2580

Assistant to the President and White House Press Secretary.—Tony Snow.

OFFICE OF PUBLIC LIAISON

phone (202) 456–2380

Deputy Assistant to the President and Director of Public Liaison.—Rhonda Keenum.

SCHEDULING

phone (202) 456–5325

Deputy Assistant to the President for Appointments and Scheduling.—Melissa Bennett.
Deputy Director of Appointments and Scheduling.—Rhonda Houston.
Assistant Director of:
Scheduling.—Mindy McLaughlin.
Scheduling-Research.—Daniel Aires.
Research Assistant.—Kimberly Krebs.
Schedulers: Ashley Anderson, Rebecca Maescher, Kyle Maxwell.
Deputy Associate Director of Scheduling for Invitations and Correspondence.—Jeremy Carl.
Presidential Diarist.—Ellen McCathran.

STAFF SECRETARY

phone (202) 456–2702

Assistant to the President and Staff Secretary.—Raul Yanes.
Deputy Assistant to the President and Deputy Staff Secretary.—Bill Burck.
Assistant Staff Secretaries: Thomas Bowman, Michael Drummond, Melissa Price.
Special Assistants to the Staff Secretary: Amanda DeVuonno, David Meyers.

STRATEGIC INITIATIVES

phone (202) 456–2108

Assistant to the President, Deputy Chief of Staff and Senior Advisor to the President.—Karl Rove.
Executive Assistant to the Senior Advisor.—Taylor Hughes.

WHITE HOUSE COUNSEL

phone (202) 456–2632

Assistant to the President and White House Counsel.—Fred F. Fielding.
Executive Assistant to the Counsel.—Heather Roebke.
Deputy Assistant to the President and Deputy Counsel to the President.—William Kelley.
Special Assistants to the President and Associate Counsels to the President: Rene Augustine, Jennifer Brosnahan, Paul Eckert, Leslie Fahrenkopf, Kenneth Lee, Ann Loughlin, Brent McIntosh, John Mitnick, John Smith, Richard Painter, Cheryl Stanton.

WHITE HOUSE MILITARY OFFICE

phone (202) 757–2151

Director.—RADM Raymond Spicer, USN.

Deputy Director.—George Mulligan.
Air Force Aide to the President.—LTC Thomas D. McCarthy.
Army Aide to the President.—LTC Samuel A. Floyd.
Coast Guard Aide to the President.—CDR Geoffrey P. Gagnier.
Marine Corps Aide to the President.—MAJ Mark Thompson.
Naval Aide to the President.—LCDR Robert Roncska.
Director of:
Administration/Senior Enlisted Officer.—MGySgt Richard W. Dunnuck, USMC.
Counsel.—LTC Paul H. Turney, USA.
Financial Management and Comptroller.—LTC David R. Zorzi, USAF.
Information and Technology Management.—Karin E. Appel.
Operations.—COL Dana J. Hourihan, USAF.
Policy, Plans and Requirements.—Paul J. Jackson.
Presidential Food Service.—LCDR Michael E. Chapman, USN.
Security.—LTC Jeffrey H. Hurlbert, USAF.
White House Transportation Agency.—MAJ Ryan M. Werling, USA.
White House Medical Unit.—COL William Lang, USA.
Commander for—
Presidential Airlift Group.—COL Mark Tillman, USAF.
White House Communications Agency.—COL James Lien, USA.

USA FREEDOM CORPS

phone 1–877–USA–CORPS, http://www.usafreedomcorps.gov

Deputy Assistant to the President and Director of USA Freedom Corps.—Desiree Sayle.

DEPARTMENT OF STATE

2201 C Street, NW., 20520, phone (202) 647–4000

CONDOLEEZZA RICE, Secretary of State; born in Birmingham, AL, November 14, 1954; education: B.A., *cum laude,* Phi Beta Kappa, University of Denver, 1974; M.A., University of Notre Dame, 1975; Ph.D., Graduate School of International Studies, University of Denver, 1981; professional: professor of political science; Provost, Stanford University, 1993–99; National Security Advisor for President George W. Bush, 2001–04; founding board member, Center for a New Generation; senior fellow, American Academy of Arts and Sciences; member, Center for International Security and Arms Control; senior fellow, Institute for International Studies; fellow, Hoover Institution; awards: Walter J. Gores Award for Excellence in Teaching, 1984; School of Humanities and Sciences Dean's Award for Distinguished Teaching, 1993; author, *Germany Unified and Europe Transformed,* 1995 (with Philip Zelikow); *The Gorbachev Era,* 1986 (with Alexander Dallin); *Uncertain Allegiance: The Soviet Union and the Czechoslovak Army,* 1984; nominated by President George W. Bush to become the 66th Secretary of State, and was confirmed by the U.S. Senate on January 26, 2005.

OFFICE OF THE SECRETARY

Secretary of State.—Condoleezza Rice, room 7226, 647–9572.
Deputy Secretary.—John D. Negroponte.
Executive Assistant.—Steve Beecroft.
Chief of Staff.—Brian Gunderson, 647–5548.

AMBASSADOR-AT-LARGE FOR WAR CRIMES ISSUES

Ambassador-at-Large.—John C. ''Clint'' Williamson, room 7419A, 647–5072.
Deputy.—Sandra Hodgkinson, 647–5543.

OFFICE OF THE CHIEF OF PROTOCOL

Chief of Protocol.—Donald Ensenat, room 1232, 647–4543.
Deputy Chief.—Raymond P. Martinez, 647–4120.

OFFICE OF CIVIL RIGHTS

Director.—Barry L. Wells, room 7428, 647–9294.
Deputy Director.—Gregory B. Smith.

OFFICE OF COORDINATOR FOR COUNTERTERRORISM

Coordinator/Ambassador-at-Large.—Henry A. Crumpton, room 2509, 647–9892.
Principal Deputy Coordinator.—Frank C. Urbancic, 647–8949.

COORDINATOR FOR RECONSTRUCTION AND STABILIZATION

Coordinator.—Amb. John Herbst, 663–0307.
Deputy Coordinator.—Mark Asquino, 663–0803.

EXECUTIVE SECRETARIAT

Special Assistant and Executive Secretary.—Harry Thomas, Jr., room 7224, 647–5301.
Deputy Executive Secretaries: Arnold Chacon, 647–5302; Susan Elliott, 647–5302; Kenneth H. Merten, 647–8448.

OFFICE OF THE INSPECTOR GENERAL

2121 Virginia Avenue, NW., 20037

Inspector General.—Howard J. Krongard, room 8100, 663–0361.
Deputy Inspector General.—William E. Todd, 663–0362.

BUREAU OF INTELLIGENCE AND RESEARCH

Assistant Secretary.—Randall M. Fort, room 6531, 647–9177.
Deputy Assistant Secretaries: James Buchanan, 647–9633; Paula Causey, 647–7754.

OFFICE OF LEGAL ADVISER

The Legal Advisor.—John B. Bellinger III, room 6423, 647–9598.
Principal Deputy Legal Adviser.—James H. Thessin, 647–8460.
Deputy Legal Advisers: Ronald J. Bettauer, 647–7942; Jonathan B. Schwartz, 647–5036; Samuel M. Witten, 647–7942.

BUREAU OF LEGISLATIVE AFFAIRS

Assistant Secretary.—Jeffrey T. Bergner, room 7325, 647–4204.
Deputy Assistant Secretary (Global, Regional and Functional).—Joseph E. Macmanus, 647–2233.
Deputy Assistant Secretary (Senate).—Bruce A. Brown (acting), 647–1890.
Deputy Assistant Secretary (House).—Thomas Callahan, 647–2623.

POLICY PLANNING STAFF

Director.—Dr. Stephen Krasner, room 7311, 647–2972.
Principal Deputy Director.—Matthew C. Waxman, 647–3599.

BUREAU OF RESOURCE MANAGEMENT

Assistant Secretary/Chief Financial Officer.—Bradford R. Higgins, room 7427, 647–7490.
Deputy Chief Financial Officer.—Christopher Flaggs, 261–8620.

OFFICE OF THE U.S. GLOBAL AIDS COORDINATOR

Coordinator.—Amb. Mark R. Dybul, room SA–29, 663–2304.
Principal Deputy Coordinator/Chief Medical Officer.—Dr. Thomas A. Kenyon, 663–3189.
Deputy Coordinator/Director of Diplomatic Outreach.—Amb. Jimmy J. Kolker, 663–2706.

UNDER SECRETARY FOR POLITICAL AFFAIRS

Under Secretary.—Amb. Nicholas Burns, room 7240, 647–2471.
Executive Assistant.—Erin Rubin, 647–1598.

AFRICAN AFFAIRS

Assistant Secretary.—Jendayi Frazier, room 6234, 647–4440.
Principal Deputy Assistant Secretary.—Linda Thomas-Greenfield, 647–4493.

EAST ASIAN AND PACIFIC AFFAIRS

Assistant Secretary.—Amb. Christopher Hill, 647–9596.
Principal Deputy Assistant Secretary.—Kathleen Stephens, 736–4393.
Deputy Assistant Secretaries: Tom Christensen, 647–6910; Glyn Davies, 647–8929; Eric John, 647–6904.

EUROPEAN AND EURASIAN AFFAIRS

Assistant Secretary.—Daniel Fried, room 6226, 647–9626.
Principal Deputy Assistant Secretary.—Kurt Volker, 647–5146.
Deputy Assistant Secretaries: Matthew Bryza, 647–5547; Rosemary DiCarlo, 647–6415; Colleen Graffy, 647–6402; David Kramer, 647–5174; Mark Pekala, 647–6238.

NEAR EASTERN AFFAIRS

Assistant Secretary.—C. David Welch, room 6242, 647–7209.
Principal Deputy Assistant Secretary.—Jim Jeffrey, 647–7207.
Deputy Assistant Secretaries: J. Scott Carpenter, 647–7168; Robert M. Danin, 647–4246; Gordon Gray, 647–7166; Victor Hurtado, 647–0554.

SOUTH AND CENTRAL ASIAN AFFAIRS

Assistant Secretary.—Richard Boucher, room 6254, 736–4325.
Principal Deputy Assistant Secretary.—Donald A. Camp, 736–5497.
Deputy Assistant Secretaries: Evan A. Feigenbaum, 736–4331; John A. Gastright, 736–4331.

WESTERN HEMISPHERE AFFAIRS

Assistant Secretary.—Thomas Shannon, room 6262, 647–8386.
Principal Deputy Assistant Secretary.—Charles S. Shapiro, 647–6754.
Deputy Assistant Secretaries: Patrick Duddy, 647–8563; Kirsten Madison, 647–7337; Elizabeth Whitaker, 647–8386.

INTERNATIONAL NARCOTICS AND LAW ENFORCEMENT AFFAIRS

Assistant Secretary.—Anne Patterson, room 7333, 647–8464.
Principal Deputy Assistant Secretary.—Thomas A. Schweich, 647–6642.
Deputy Assistant Secretaries: Christy McCampbell, 647–9822; Elizabeth Verville (acting), 647–9822.

INTERNATIONAL ORGANIZATION AFFAIRS

Assistant Secretary.—Kristen L. Sliverberg, room 6323, 647–9600.
Principal Deputy Assistant Secretary.—James B. Warlick, 647–9602.
Deputy Assistant Secretary.—Gerald C. Anderson, 647–9604.

UNDER SECRETARY FOR ECONOMIC, BUSINESS, AND AGRICULTURAL AFFAIRS

Under Secretary.—Josette Sheeran, room 7256, 647–7575.
Executive Assistant.—Douglas Hengel, 647–7674.

ECONOMIC AND BUSINESS AFFAIRS

Assistant Secretary.—Daniel S. Sullivan, room 4932/4934, 647–7971.
Principal Deputy Assistant Secretary.—Elizabeth L. Dibble, 647–9496.
Deputy Assistant Secretaries: John Byerly, 647–4045; David Gross, 647–5858; Christopher Moore, 647–5991; Paul Simons, 647–5152.

UNDER SECRETARY FOR ARMS CONTROL AND INTERNATIONAL SECURITY

Under Secretary.—Robert Joseph, room 7208, 647–1049.
Executive Assistant.—Stephen A. Elliott, 647–1749.

INTERNATIONAL SECURITY AND NONPROLIFERATION

Head.—John Rood, room 7531, 647–9610.

Principal Deputy Assistant Secretary.—Patricia McNerney, 647–6977.

POLITICAL–MILITARY AFFAIRS

Assistant Secretary.—John Hillen, room 6212, 647–9022.
Principal Deputy Assistant Secretary.—Stephen Mull.

VERIFICATION, COMPLIANCE, AND IMPLEMENTATION

Assistant Secretary.—Paula DeSutter, room 5950, 647–5315.
Principal Deputy Assistant Secretary.—Stephen Elliott, 736–7981.
Deputy Assistant Secretary.—Karin Look, 647–5553.

UNDER SECRETARY FOR PUBLIC DIPLOMACY AND PUBLIC AFFAIRS

Under Secretary.—Karen Hughes, room 7261, 647–9199.
Deputy Under Secretary.—Dina Habib Powell.
Executive Assistant.—Daniel B. Smith.

EDUCATIONAL AND CULTURAL AFFAIRS

Assistant Secretary.—Dina Habib Powell, 203–5118.
Principal Deputy Assistant Secretary.—C. Miller Crouch, 203–5112.
Deputy Assistant Secretaries: Tom Farrell, 453–8111; Alina Romanowski, 203–8687.

INTERNATIONAL INFORMATION PROGRAMS

Coordinator.—Jeremy Curtin, 736–4405.

PUBLIC AFFAIRS

Assistant Secretary.—Sean McCormack, room 6800, 647–6607.
Deputy Assistant Secretary.—Theresa Dean, 647–6088.
Director, Office of Press Relations.—Tom Casey, 647–6088.

UNDER SECRETARY FOR MANAGEMENT

Under Secretary.—Henrietta H. Fore, room 7207, 647–1500.
Executive Assistant.—Frank Coulter, 647–1501.

ADMINISTRATION

Assistant Secretary.—Rajkumar Chellaraj, room 6330, 647–1492.
Deputy Assistant Secretaries: Lee R. Lohman, 663–2217; Will Moser (703) 875–6956; Steve Rodriguez, 647–3427.

CONSULAR AFFAIRS

Assistant Secretary.—Maura Harty, room 6811, 647–9576.
Principal Deputy Assistant Secretary.—Wanda Nesbitt, 647–9577.

DIPLOMATIC SECURITY AND OFFICE OF FOREIGN MISSIONS

Assistant Secretary.—Richard J. Griffin, room 6316, 647–6290.
Principal Deputy Assistant Secretary.—Joe Morton (571) 345–3815.
Deputy Assistant Secretary.—John T. Sheely (acting), 647–3417.

DIRECTOR GENERAL OF THE FOREIGN SERVICE AND DIRECTOR OF HUMAN RESOURCES

Director General.—George M. Staples, room 6218, 647–9898.
Principal Deputy Assistant Secretary.—Heather Hodges, 647–9438.
Deputy Assistant Secretaries: Linda Taglialatela, 647–5152; Teddy Taylor, 647–5942.

FOREIGN SERVICE INSTITUTE

Director.—Ruth Whiteside, room F2102 (703) 302–6703.
Deputy Director.—John O'Keefe (703) 302–6707.

INFORMATION RESOURCE MANAGEMENT

Assistant Secretary.—James VanDerhoff, 647–2889.
Deputy Chief Information Officers: Susan Swart, 647–3184; Charles Wisecarver, 647–2863.

MEDICAL SERVICES

Assistant Secretary.—Larry Brown, 663–1611.
Deputy Assistant Secretary.—Thomas W. Yun, 663–1641.

OVERSEAS BUILDING OPERATIONS

Assistant Secretary.—Charles Williams (703) 875–4144.
Managing Director.—Jay Hicks, 875–6357.
Chief of Staff.—Robert Castro, 875–4053.

UNDER SECRETARY FOR DEMOCRACY AND GLOBAL AFFAIRS

Under Secretary.—Paula Dobriansky, room 7250, 647–6240.
Executive Assistant.—Jeffrey DeLaurentis, 647–7609.

DEMOCRACY, HUMAN RIGHTS AND LABOR

Assistant Secretary.—Barry Lowenkron, room 7802, 647–2126.
Principal Deputy Assistant Secretary.—Jonathan Farrar, 647–3315.

OCEANS AND INTERNATIONAL ENVIRONMENTAL AND SCIENTIFIC AFFAIRS

Assistant Secretary.—Claudia A. McMurray, room 7831, 647–1554.
Principal Deputy Assistant Secretary.—Reno Harnish, 647–3004.
Deputy Assistant Secretaries: David A. Balton, 647–2396; Daniel Reifsnyder, 647–2232.

POPULATION, REFUGEES AND MIGRATION

Assistant Secretary.—Ellen Sauerbrey, room 5824, 647–5767.
Principal Deputy Assistant Secretary.—Richard L. Greene, 647–5982.
Deputy Assistant Secretaries: William Fitzgerald, 647–5822; Kelly Ryan, 647–5767.

UNITED STATES PERMANENT REPRESENTATIVE TO THE UNITED NATIONS

U.S. Permanent Representative.—Alejandro Daniel Wolff (acting), room 6317, 736–7555.
Deputy to the Ambassador/Director.—Sarah Tinsley Demarest.
Deputy to the Ambassador.—Matthew C. Freedman.

DIRECTOR OF FOREIGN ASSISTANCE

Director of U.S. Foreign Assistance/Administrator of USAID.—Amb. Randall L. Tobias, room 5932, 647–2527.

Chief of Staff.—Nazanin Ash, 647–2604.

UNITED STATES DIPLOMATIC OFFICES—FOREIGN SERVICE

(C= Consular Office, N= No Embassy or Consular Office)

http://usembassy.state.gov

LIST OF CHIEFS OF MISSION

AFGHANISTAN, ISLAMIC REPUBLIC OF (Kabul).
Hon. William B. Wood.
ALBANIA, REPUBLIC OF (Tirana).
Hon. Marcie B. Ries.
ALGERIA, DEMOCRATIC AND POPULAR REPUBLIC OF (Algiers).
Hon. Robert S. Ford.
ANDORRA (Andorra La Vella) (N)
Hon. Eduardo Aguirre, Jr.
ANGOLA, REPUBLIC OF (Luanda).
Hon. Cynthia G. Efird.
ANTIGUA AND BARBUDA (St. John's) (N).
Hon. Mary Martin Ourisman.
ARGENTINA (Buenos Aires).
Hon. Earl Anthony Wayne.
ARMENIA, REPUBLIC OF (Yerevan).
Vacant.
AUSTRALIA (Canberra).
Hon. Robert M. McCallum.
AUSTRIA, REPUBLIC OF (Vienna).
Hon. Susan Rasinski McCaw.
AZERBAIJAN, REPUBLIC OF (Baku).
Hon. Anne E. Derse.
BAHAMAS, THE COMMONWEALTH OF THE (Nassau).
Vacant.
BAHRAIN, STATE OF (Manama).
Hon. William T. Monroe.
BANGLADESH, PEOPLE'S REPUBLIC OF (Dhaka).
Hon. Patricia A. Butenis.
BARBADOS (Bridgetown).
Hon. Mary Martin Ourisman.
BELARUS, REPUBLIC OF (Minsk).
Hon. Karen B. Stewart.
BELGIUM (Brussels).
Hon. Sam Fox.
BELIZE (Belize City).
Hon. Robert Johann Dieter.
BENIN, REPUBLIC OF (Cotonou).
Hon. Gayleatha Beatrice Brown.
BOLIVIA, REPUBLIC OF (La Paz).
Hon. Philip S. Goldberg.
BOSNIA-HERZEGOVINA (Sarajevo).
Hon. Douglas L. McElhaney.
BOTSWANA, REPUBLIC OF (Gaborone).
Hon. Katherine Canavan.
BRAZIL, FEDERATIVE REPUBLIC OF (Brasilia).
Hon. Clifford M. Sobel.
BRUNEI DARUSSALAM (Bandar Seri Begawan).
Hon. Emil M. Skodon.
BULGARIA, REPUBLIC OF (Sofia).
Hon. John Ross Beyrle.
BURKINA FASO (Ouagadougou).
Hon. Jeanine E. Jackson.
BURMA, UNION OF (Rangoon).
Ms. Sharon E. Villarosa.
BURUNDI, REPUBLIC OF (Bujumbura).
Hon. Patricia Newton Moller.
CAMBODIA, KINGDOM OF (Phnom Penh).
Hon. Joseph A. Mussomeli.
CAMEROON, REPUBLIC OF (Yaounde).
Hon. R. Niels Marquardt.
CANADA (Ottawa).
Hon. David Horton Wilkins.
CAPE VERDE, REPUBLIC OF (Praia).
Hon. Roger Dwayne Pierce.
CENTRAL AFRICAN REPUBLIC (Bangui).
Vacant.
CHAD, REPUBLIC OF (N'Djamena).
Hon. Marc McGowan Wall.
CHILE, REPUBLIC OF (Santiago).
Hon. Craig A. Kelly.
CHINA, PEOPLE'S REPUBLIC OF (Beijing).
Hon. Clark T. Randt, Jr.
COLOMBIA, REPUBLIC OF (Bogota).
Vacant.
COMOROS, UNION OF (Moroni) (N).
Hon. James D. McGee.
CONGO, REPUBLIC OF THE (Brazzaville).
Hon. Robert Weisberg.
CONGO, DEMOCRATIC REPUBLIC OF THE (Kinshasa).
Hon. Roger A. Meece.
COSTA RICA, REPUBLIC OF (San Jose).
Hon. Mark Langdale.
COTE D'IVOIRE, REPUBLIC OF (Abidjan).
Hon. Aubrey Hooks.
CROATIA, REPUBLIC OF (Zagreb).
Hon. Robert Anthony Bradtke.
CUBA (Havana).
Mr. Michael E. Parmly.
CURACAO (Willemstad).
Mr. Robert Earl Sorenson.
CYPRUS, REPUBLIC OF (Nicosia).
Hon. Ronald L. Schlicher.
CZECH REPUBLIC (Prague).
Hon. Richard W. Graber.
DENMARK (Copenhagen).
Hon. James Cain.
DJIBOUTI, REPUBLIC OF (Djibouti).
Hon. W. Stuart Symington IV.
DOMINICAN REPUBLIC (Santo Domingo).
Hon. Hans H. Hertell.
EAST TIMOR, DEMOCRATIC REPUBLIC OF (Dili).
Vacant.
ECUADOR, REPUBLIC OF (Quito).

Hon. Linda Jewell.
EGYPT, ARAB REPUBLIC OF (Cairo).
Hon. Francis Joseph Ricciardone, Jr.
EL SALVADOR, REPUBLIC OF (San Salvador).
Hon. Charles L. Glazer.
EQUATORIAL GUINEA, REPUBLIC OF (Malabo) (N).
Hon. Donald C. Johnson.
ERITREA, STATE OF (Asmara).
Hon. Scott H. DeLisi.
ESTONIA, REPUBLIC OF (Tallinn).
Hon. Stanley Davis Phillips.
ETHIOPIA, FEDERAL DEMOCRATIC REPUBLIC OF (Addis Ababa).
Hon. Donald Y. Yamamoto.
FIJI ISLANDS, REPUBLIC OF THE (Suva).
Hon. Larry Miles Dinger.
FINLAND, REPUBLIC OF (Helsinki).
Hon. Marilyn Ware.
FRANCE (Paris).
Hon. Craig Roberts Stapleton.
GABONESE REPUBLIC (Libreville).
Hon. R. Barrie Walkley.
GAMBIA, REPUBLIC OF THE (Banjul).
Hon. Joseph D. Stafford III.
GEORGIA (Tbilisi).
Hon. John F. Tefft.
GERMANY, FEDERAL REPUBLIC OF (Berlin).
Hon. William Robert Timken, Jr.
GHANA, REPUBLIC OF (Accra).
Hon. Pamela E. Bridgewater.
GREECE (Athens).
Hon. Charles P. Ries.
GRENADA (St. George) (N).
Hon. Mary Martin Ourisman.
GUATEMALA, REPUBLIC OF (Guatemala).
Hon. James M. Derham.
GUINEA, REPUBLIC OF (Conakry).
Hon. Jackson McDonald.
GUINEA-BISSAU, REPUBLIC OF (Bissau) (N).
Hon. Janice L. Jacobs.
GUYANA, CO-OPERATIVE REPUBLIC OF (Georgetown).
Hon. David M. Robinson.
HAITI, REPUBLIC OF (Port-au-Prince).
Hon. Janet Ann Sanderson.
HOLY SEE (Vatican City).
Hon. Francis Rooney.
HONDURAS, REPUBLIC OF (Tegucigalpa).
Hon. Charles A. Ford.
HONG KONG (Hong Kong) (C).
Mr. James B. Cunningham.
HUNGARY, REPUBLIC OF (Budapest).
Hon. April H. Foley.
ICELAND, REPUBLIC OF (Reykjavik).
Hon. Carol van Voorst.
INDIA (New Delhi).
Hon. David C. Mulford.
INDONESIA, REPUBLIC OF (Jakarta).
Vacant.
IRAQ, REPUBLIC OF (Baghdad)
Hon. Ryan Crocker.
IRELAND (Dublin).
Hon. Thomas C. Foley.
ISRAEL, STATE OF (Tel Aviv).
Hon. Richard Henry Jones.
ITALY (Rome).
Hon. Ronald Spogli.
JAMAICA (Kingston).
Hon. Brenda LaGrange Johnson.
JAPAN (Tokyo).
Hon. John T. Schieffer.
JERUSALEM (C).
Mr. Jacob Walles.
JORDAN, HASHEMITE KINGDOM OF (Amman).
Hon. David M. Hale.
KAZAKHSTAN, REPUBLIC OF (Almaty).
Hon. John M. Ordway.
KENYA, REPUBLIC OF (Nairobi).
Hon. Michael E. Ranneberger.
KIRIBATI, REPUBLIC OF (Tarawa) (N).
Hon. Larry Miles Dinger.
KOREA, REPUBLIC OF (Seoul).
Hon. Alexander R. Vershbow.
KOSOVO (Pristina).
Ms. Tina S. Kaidanow.
KYRGYZ REPUBLIC (Bishkek).
Hon. Marie L. Yovanovitch.
KUWAIT, STATE OF (Kuwait City).
Hon. Richard LeBaron.
LAO PEOPLE'S DEMOCRATIC REPUBLIC (Vientiane).
Hon. Patricia M. Haslach.
LATVIA, REPUBLIC OF (Riga).
Hon. Catherine Todd Bailey.
LEBANON, REPUBLIC OF (Beirut).
Hon. Jeffrey D. Feltman.
LESOTHO, KINGDOM OF (Maseru).
Hon. June Carter Perry.
LIBERIA, REPUBLIC OF (Monrovia).
Hon. Donald E. Booth.
LIBYA (Tripoli).
Vacant.
LIECHTENSTEIN, PRINCIPALITY OF (Vaduz) (N).
Hon. Peter R. Coneway.
LITHUANIA, REPUBLIC OF (Vilnius).
Hon. John A. Cloud, Jr.
LUXEMBOURG, GRAND DUCHY OF (Luxembourg).
Hon. Ann Louise Wagner.
MACEDONIA, THE FORMER YUGOSLAV REPUBLIC OF (Skopje).
Hon. Gillian Arlette Milovanovic.
MADAGASCAR, REPUBLIC OF (Antananarivo).
Hon. James D. McGee.
MALAWI, REPUBLIC OF (Lilongwe).
Hon. Alan W. Eastham, Jr.
MALAYSIA (Kuala Lumpur).
Hon. Christopher J. LeFleur.
MALDIVES, REPUBLIC OF (Male) (N).
Hon. Robert O. Blake, Jr.
MALI, REPUBLIC OF (Bamako).
Hon. Terence Patrick McCulley.
MALTA, REPUBLIC OF (Valletta).
Hon. Molly Hering Bordonaro.

MARSHALL ISLANDS, REPUBLIC OF THE (Majuro).
Hon. Clyde Bishop.
MAURITANIA, ISLAMIC REPUBLIC OF (Nouakchott).
Vacant.
MAURITIUS, REPUBLIC OF (Port Louis).
Hon. Cesar Benito Cabrera.
MEXICO (Mexico City).
Hon. Antonio O. Garza, Jr.
MICRONESIA, FEDERATED STATES OF (Kolonia).
Hon. Suzanne Hale.
MOLDOVA, REPUBLIC OF (Chisinau).
Hon. Michael D. Kirby.
MONACO (Monaco).
Hon. Craig Roberts Stapleton.
MONGOLIA (Ulaanbaatar).
Hon. Mark C. Minton.
MONTENEGRO, REPUBLIC OF (Podgorica).
Vacant.
MOROCCO, KINGDOM OF (Rabat).
Hon. Thomas Riley.
MOZAMBIQUE, REPUBLIC OF (Maputo).
Vacant.
NAMIBIA, REPUBLIC OF (Windhoek).
Hon. Joyce A. Barr.
NAURU, REPUBLIC OF (Yaren) (N).
Hon. Larry Miles Dinger.
NEPAL, KINGDOM OF (Kathmandu).
Hon. James Francis Moriarty.
NETHERLANDS, KINGDOM OF THE (The Hague).
Hon. Roland Arnall.
NEW ZEALAND (Wellington).
Hon. William Paul McCormick.
NICARAGUA, REPUBLIC OF (Managua).
Hon. Paul A. Trivelli.
NIGER, REPUBLIC OF (Niamey).
Hon. Bernadette Mary Allen.
NIGERIA, FEDERAL REPUBLIC OF (Abuja).
Hon. John Campbell.
NORWAY (Oslo).
Hon. Benson K. Whitney.
OMAN, SULTANATE OF (Muscat).
Hon. Gary A. Grappo.
PAKISTAN, ISLAMIC REPUBLIC OF (Islamabad).
Vacant.
PANAMA, REPUBLIC OF (Panama).
Hon. William A. Eaton.
PAPUA NEW GUINEA (Port Moresby).
Hon. Leslie V. Rowe.
PARAGUAY, REPUBLIC OF (Asunción)
Hon. James Caldwell Cason.
PERU, REPUBLIC OF (Lima).
Hon. James Curtis Struble.
PHILIPPINES, REPUBLIC OF THE (Manila).
Hon. Kristie A. Kenney.
POLAND, REPUBLIC OF (Warsaw).
Hon. Victor Henderson Ashe.
PORTUGAL, REPUBLIC OF (Lisbon).
Hon. Alfred Hoffman.
QATAR, STATE OF (Doha).
Hon. Charles Graves Untermeyer.
ROMANIA (Bucharest).
Hon. Nicholas F. Taubman.
RUSSIAN FEDERATION (Moscow).
Hon. William J. Burns.
RWANDA, REPUBLIC OF (Kigali).
Hon. Michael R. Arietti.
SAINT KITTS AND NEVIS (Basseterre) (N).
Hon. Mary Martin Ourisman.
SAINT LUCIA (Castries) (N).
Hon. Mary Martin Ourisman.
SAINT VINCENT AND THE GRENADINES (Kingstown) (N).
Hon. Mary Martin Ourisman.
SAMOA (Apia) (N).
Hon. William Paul McCormick.
SAN MARINO, REPUBLIC OF (San Marino) (N).
Hon. Ronald Spogli.
SAO TOME AND PRINCIPE, DEMOCRATIC REPUBLIC OF (Sao Tome) (N).
Hon. R. Barrie Walkley.
SAUDI ARABIA, KINGDOM OF (Riyadh).
Hon. Ford M. Fraker.
SENEGAL, REPUBLIC OF (Dakar).
Hon. Janice L. Jacobs.
SERBIA (Belgrade)
Hon. Michael Christian Polt.
SEYCHELLES, REPUBLIC OF (Victoria) (N).
Hon. Cesar Benito Cabrera.
SIERRA LEONE, REPUBLIC OF (Freetown).
Hon. Thomas Neil Hull III.
SINGAPORE, REPUBLIC OF (Singapore).
Hon. Patricia Louise Herbold.
SLOVAK REPUBLIC (Bratislava).
Hon. Rodolphe M. Vallee.
SLOVENIA, REPUBLIC OF (Ljubljana).
Hon. Thomas Bolling Robertson.
SOLOMON ISLANDS (Honiara) (N).
Hon. Leslie V. Rowe.
SOUTH AFRICA, REPUBLIC OF (Pretoria).
Hon. Eric M. Bost.
SPAIN (Madrid).
Hon. Eduardo Aguirre, Jr.
SRI LANKA, DEMOCRATIC SOCIALIST REPUBLIC OF (Colombo).
Hon. Robert O. Blake, Jr.
SUDAN, REPUBLIC OF THE (Khartoum).
Vacant.
SURINAME, REPUBLIC OF (Paramaribo).
Hon. Lisa Bobbie Schreiber Hughes.
SWAZILAND, KINGDOM OF (Mbabane).
Vacant.
SWEDEN (Stockholm).
Hon. Michael Wood.
SWITZERLAND (Bern).
Hon. Peter R. Coneway.
SYRIAN ARAB REPUBLIC (Damascus).
Vacant.
TAJIKISTAN, REPUBLIC OF (Dushanbe).
Hon. Tracey Ann Jacobson.
TANZANIA, UNITED REPUBLIC OF (Dar es Salaam).
Hon. Michael Retzer.

THAILAND, KINGDOM OF (Bangkok).
Hon. Ralph Leo Boyce, Jr.
TOGOLESE REPUBLIC (Lome).
Hon. David B. Dunn.
TONGA, KINGDOM OF (Nuku'alofe) (N).
Hon. Larry Miles Dinger.
TRINIDAD AND TOBAGO, REPUBLIC OF (Port-of-Spain).
Hon. Roy L. Austin.
TUNISIA, REPUBLIC OF (Tunis).
Hon. Robert F. Godec.
TURKEY, REPUBLIC OF (Ankara).
Hon. Ross Wilson.
TURKMENISTAN (Ashgabat).
Hon. George A. Kroll.
TUVALU (Funafuti) (N).
Hon. Larry Miles Dinger.
UGANDA, REPUBLIC OF (Kampala).
Hon. Steven Alan Browning.
UKRAINE (Kyiv).
Hon. William B. Taylor, Jr.
UNITED ARAB EMIRATES (Abu Dhabi).
Hon. Michele J. Sison.
UNITED KINGDOM OF GREAT BRITAIN AND NORTHERN IRELAND (London).
Hon. Robert H. Tuttle.
URUGUAY, ORIENTAL REPUBLIC OF (Montevideo).
Hon. Frank Baxter.
UZBEKISTAN, REPUBLIC OF (Tashkent).
Hon. Jon R. Purnell.
VANUATU, REPUBLIC OF (Port Vila) (N).
Hon. Leslie V. Rowe.
VENEZUELA, BOLIVARIAN REPUBLIC OF (Caracas).
Hon. William R. Brownfield.
VIETNAM, SOCIALIST REPUBLIC OF (Hanoi).
Hon. Michael W. Marine.
YEMEN, REPUBLIC OF (Sanaa).
Hon. Thomas Charles Krajeski.
ZAMBIA, REPUBLIC OF (Lusaka).
Hon. Carmen Maria Martinez.
ZIMBABWE, REPUBLIC OF (Harare).
Hon. Christopher William Dell.

UNITED STATES PERMANENT DIPLOMATIC MISSIONS TO INTERNATIONAL ORGANIZATIONS

AFRICAN UNION (Addis Ababa).
Hon. Cindy Lou Courville.
EUROPEAN UNION (Brussels).
Hon. C. Boyden Gray.
NORTH ATLANTIC TREATY ORGANIZATION (Brussels).
Hon. Victoria Nuland.
ORGANIZATION FOR ECONOMIC COOPERATION AND DEVELOPMENT (Paris).
Hon. Constance Albanese Morella.
ORGANIZATION FOR SECURITY AND COOPERATION IN EUROPE (Vienna).
Hon. Julie Finley.
ORGANIZATION OF AMERICAN STATES (Washington, DC).
Hon. J. Robert Manzanares.
UNITED NATIONS (Geneva).
Hon. Warren W. Tichnor.
UNITED NATIONS (New York).
Hon. Zalmay Khalilzed.
UNITED NATIONS (Vienna).
Hon. Gregory L. Schulte.

DEPARTMENT OF THE TREASURY

15th and Pennsylvania Ave., NW., 20220, phone (202) 622–2000, http://www.ustreas.gov

HENRY M. PAULSON, JR., Secretary of the Treasury; born in Palm Beach, FL, March 28, 1946; education: B.A., Dartmouth College, 1968; M.B.A., Harvard Business School, 1970; professional: Staff Assistant to the Assistant Secretary of Defense, Pentagon, 1970–72; Staff Assistant to the President, White House Council on Domestic Affairs, 1972–73; Goldman Sachs (investment banking group), 1974–82; Partner, Goldman Sachs, 1982; Investment Banking Services–Midwest Region, Goldman Sachs, 1983–88; Managing Partner, Chicago Office, Goldman Sachs, 1988; Co-head of Investment Banking, Goldman Sachs, 1990–94; President and Chief Operating Officer, Goldman Sachs, 1994–98; Co-Senior Partner, Goldman Sachs, 1998; Chairman and CEO, Goldman Sachs, 1999–2006; religion: Christian Scientist; married: Wendy; children: Amanda and Merritt; nominated by President George W. Bush to become the 74th Secretary to the Treasury on June 19, 2006; and was confirmed by the U.S. Senate on June 28, 2006.

OFFICE OF THE SECRETARY

Secretary of the Treasury.—Henry M. Paulson, Jr., room 3330 (202) 622–1100.
Executive Assistants: Lindsay Valdeon, 622–5780; Christal West, 622–2147.
Confidential Assistant.—Cheryl Matera, 622–0190.

OFFICE OF THE DEPUTY SECRETARY

Deputy Secretary.—Robert M. Kimmit, room 3326 (202) 622–1080.
Executive Assistant.—Annabella Mejia.
Confidential Assistant.—Lorraine Marshall.

OFFICE OF THE CHIEF OF STAFF

Chief of Staff.—Jim Wilkinson, room 3408 (202) 622–1906.
Deputy Chief of Staff/Executive Secretary.—Taiya Smith, 622–6096.
Review Analyst.—Shirley Gathers, 622–5377.
Senior Advisors to the Secretary: Neel Kashkari, 622–5800; Kimberly Reed, 622–0520.
White House Liaison.—Janan Grissom, 622–3101.

OFFICE OF THE GENERAL COUNSEL

General Counsel.—Robert Hoyt, room 3000 (202) 622–0283.
Deputy General Counsel.—Lily Fu, 622–6362.
Staff Assistants: Karen M. Hill, Teresa R. Jones, 622–0283.
Senior Advisor to the General Counsel.—Mike Maher, room 3010, 622–3654.
Assistant General Counsel for—
Banking and Finance.—Roberta McInerney, room 2000, 622–1988.
Enforcement and Intelligence.—Mark Monborne, room 2308, 622–1286.
General Law and Ethics.—Bernard Knight, room 2020, 622–1137.
International Affairs.—Russell L. Munk, room 2316, 622–1899.
Legislation and Litigation.—Tom McGivern, room 2312, 622–2317.
Deputy Assistant General Counsel for—
Banking and Finance.—Peter Bieger, room 2000, 622–1975.
Enforcement and Intelligence.—James Freis, room 2306, 622–0264.
General Law and Ethics.—John Schorn, room 2019, 622–1142.
International Affairs.—Marilyn L. Muench, room 2010, 622–1986.
Chief Counsel, Foreign Assets Control.—Sean Thorton, Annex 3123, 622–9880.
Deputy Chief Counsel.—Matthew Tuchband, Annex 3121, 622–1654.

OFFICE OF THE INSPECTOR GENERAL

Inspector General.—Harold Damelin, room 4436 (202) 622–1090.
Deputy Inspector General.—Dennis S. Schindel.
Counsel to the Inspector General.—Richard Delmar, suite 510, 927–0650.
Assistant Inspector General for—
Audit.—Marla Freedman, suite 600, 927–5400.
Investigations.—Nick Swanstrom, suite 500, 927–5260.
Management Services.—Adam Silverman, suite 510, 927–5200.
Deputy Assistant Inspector General for—
Audit.—Robert Taylor, suite 600, 927–5400.
Investigations.—P. Brian Crane, suite 500, 927–5260.
Management.—Debra McGruder, suite 510, 927–5229.

OFFICE OF THE UNDER SECRETARY FOR DOMESTIC FINANCE

Under Secretary.—Robert K. Steel, room 3312 (202) 622–1703.
Review Analyst.—Diana Ridgway.
Senior Advisor to the Under Secretary.—Matthew Scogin, room 3015, 622–2797.

OFFICE OF THE ASSISTANT SECRETARY FOR FINANCIAL INSTITUTIONS

Assistant Secretary.—Emil W. Henry, Jr., room 2326 (202) 622–2610.
Deputy Assistant Secretary, Office of:
Critical Infrastructure Protection and Compliance Policy.—D. Scott Parsons, room 2327 MT, 622–0887.
Financial Education.—Dan Iannicola, Jr., room 1332, 622–5770.
Financial Institutions Policy.—David Nason, room 2328, 622–0430.
Director, Office of:
Community Adjustment and Investment Program (CAIP).—Louisa Quittman, room 1407, 622–8103.
Community Development Financial Institutions Fund.—Arthur A. Garcia, room 601, 622–4203.
Critical Infrastructure Protection and Compliance Policy.—Valerie Abend, room 1321, 622–1677.
Financial Education.—Dubis Correal, room 1332, 622–4848.
Financial Institutions Policy.—Mario Ugoletti, room 1418, 622–0715.
Outreach.—Luz Figuereo, room 1332, 622–8811.
Executive Director, Terrorism Risk Insurance Program.—Jeffrey S. Bragg, 1425 New York Ave., NW., room 2114, 622–6770.

OFFICE OF THE ASSISTANT SECRETARY FOR FINANCIAL MARKETS

Assistant Secretary.—Anthony Ryan, room 2000 (202) 622–2245.
Deputy Assistant Secretary, Office of:
Federal Finance.—Matthew T. Abbott, room 2422, 622–1244.
Government Financial Policy.—Roger Kodat, room 2418, 622–7073.
Director, Office of:
Advanced Counterfeit Deterrence.—Reese Fuller, room 1326, 622–1882.
Debt Management.—Karthik Ramanathan, room 2414, 622–6844.
Financial Market Policy.—Heidilynne Schultheiss, room 1404, 622–2692.
Policy and Legislative Review.—Paula Farrell, 1120 Vermont Avenue, NW., room 934, 622–2450.

OFFICE OF THE FISCAL ASSISTANT SECRETARY

Fiscal Assistant Secretary.—Donald Hammond, room 2112 (202) 622–0560.
Deputy Assistant Secretary for—
Accounting Policy.—Robert Reid, room 2108, 622–0550.
Fiscal Operations and Policy.—Kenneth Carfine, room 2054, 622–0570.
Director, Office of Fiscal Projections.—David Monroe, room 2044, 622–0580.

FINANCIAL MANAGEMENT SERVICE

401 14th Street, SW., 20227, phone (202) 874–6750, fax 874–7016

Commissioner.—Kenneth R. Papaj.
Deputy Commissioner.—Judith R. Tillman.
Assistant Commissioner for—
Debt Management Services.—Rita Bratcher.
Federal Finance.—Gary Grippo.
Financial Operations.—Janice P. Lucas.
Governmentwide Accounting.—D. James Sturgill.
Information Resources (Chief Information Officer).—Chuck Simpson.
Management (Chief Financial Officer).—Scott Johnson.
Regional Operations.—Wanda J. Rogers.
Treasury Agency Services.—Don McKay.
Chief Counsel.—Margaret Marquette.
Director for Legislative and Public Affairs.—Alvina M. McHale.

BUREAU OF THE PUBLIC DEBT

799 9th Street, NW., 20239, phone (202) 504–3500, fax 504–3630

[Codified under U.S.C. 31, section 306]

Commissioner.—Van Zeck.
Deputy Commissioner.—Nancy Fleetwood.
Executive Director for—
Administrative Resource Center.—Cynthia Springer (304) 480–7227.
Government Securities Regulations Staff.—Lori Santamorena, 504–3632.
Public and Legislative Affairs Staff.—Kim B. Treat, 504–3535.
Assistant Commissioner, Office of:
Financing.—Anita Shandor, 504–3697.
Management Services.—Fred Pyatt (acting), (304) 480–8101.
Public Debt Accounting.—Debra Hines (304) 480–5101.
Securities Operations.—John Swales (304) 480–6516.

OFFICE OF THE UNDER SECRETARY FOR INTERNATIONAL AFFAIRS

Under Secretary.—Timothy D. Adams, room 3432 MT (202) 622–0656.
Senior Advisor.—Jonathan Burks, room 3221, 622–6923.
Staff Assistant.—Meghann Jenkins, room 3432, 622–0656.

OFFICE OF THE ASSISTANT SECRETARY FOR INTERNATIONAL AFFAIRS

Assistant Secretary.—Clay Lowery, room 3430 MT (202) 622–1270.
Staff Assistant.—Clara Robinson.
Senior Advisor.—Traci Phillips, room 3217 MT, 622–6959.
Special Assistant for Personnel and Management.—Judy Laufman, room 4122C MT, 622–0105.
Deputy Assistant Secretary for—
Africa and the Middle East.—Ahmed Saeed, room 3218 MT, 622–0659.
Asia.—Robert Dohner, rolom 3218B MT, 622–7222.
Development Finance and Debt.—Kenneth Peel, room 3204A MT, 622–0070.
Europe, Eurasia, and the Western Hemisphere.—Nancy Lee, room 3204 MT, 622–2916.
International Monetary and Financial Policy.—Mark Sobel, room 3034 MT, 622–0168.
Investment Security.—Nova Daly, room 3203 MT, 622–2752.
Research and Analysis.—Marvin Barth, room 3213 MT, 622–1231.
Technical Assistance Policy.—W. Larry McDonald, room 3041 MT, 622–5504.
Trade and Investment Policy.—Charles Schott, room 3205 MT, 622–0237.
Directors for International Affairs:
Africa (INN).—John Ralyea, room 4456B MT, 622–0716.
Business Office.—Theresa Wagoner, room 4138B MT, 622–1196.
Development Policy.—John Hurley, room 5417B MT, 622–9124.
East Asia (ISA).—Matthew Haarsager, room 4462 MT, 622–0138.
Europe and Eurasia (ICN).—Eric Meyer, room 5441J MT, 622–0603.
Global Economics Group (IMG).—John Weeks, room 5422F MT, 622–9885.
International Banking and Securities Markets (IMB).—William Murden, room 5308 MT, 622–2775.

International Debt Policy (IDD).—Stephen Donovan, room 5132H MT, 622–0159.
International Monetary Policy (IMF).—Robert Kaproth, room 5326 MT, 622–4797.
International Trade (ITT).—Whit Warthin, room 5204A MT, 622–1733.
Investment Security (IFI).—Gay Sills, room 5221A MT, 622–9066.
Middle East and North Africa (INM).—Karen Mathiasen, room 5008 MT, 622–7144.
Multilateral Development Banks (IDB).—Mark Jaskowiak, room 5313M MT, 622–5052.
South and Southeast Asia (ISS).—Andrew Baukol, room 4440 MT, 622–2129.
Trade Finance and Investment Negotiations (ITF).—Steven Tvardek, room 5419J MT, 622–1749.
Western Hemisphere (ICL).—Luyen Tran, room 5466C MT, 622–0763.

OVERSEAS

U.S. Executive Director of:
African Development Bank and Fund (AFDB) (Tunisia).—Amb. Cynthia Shepard Perry, 9–011–216–71–102–810.
Asian Development Bank (ADB) (Manila, Philippines).—Paul W. Curry (acting), 9–011–632–632–6050.
European Bank for Reconstruction and Development (EBRD).—Mark Sullivan, 9–011–44–207–338–6459.
Inter-American Development Bank (IADB).—Hector Morales, 9–623–1075.
International Monetary Fund.—Meg Lundsager (acting), 9–623–7759.
World Bank.—Jenna Dorn (acting), 458–0115 / 6.

UNDER SECRETARY FOR TERRORISM AND FINANCIAL INTELLIGENCE

Under Secretary.—Stuart Levey, room 4326 (202) 622–8260.

ASSISTANT SECRETARY FOR TERRORIST FINANCING

Assistant Secretary.—Patrick M. O'Brien, room 4316 (202) 622–2849.
Deputy Assistant Secretary for Terrorist Financing and Financial Crimes.—Daniel Glaser, room 4304, 622–1943.
Director, Office of:
Global Affairs.—Patrick Heffernan, room 4310, 622–0769.
Strategic Policy.—Chip Poncy, room 4308, 622–9761.

ASSISTANT SECRETARY FOR INTELLIGENCE AND ANALYSIS

Assistant Secretary.—Janice B. Gardner, room 4332 (202) 622–1835.
Deputy Assistant Secretary.—Matthew Levitt, room 2441, 622–1841.
Deputy Assistant Secretary for Security.—Ron Bell, Annex 3180, 622–0160.
Director, Emergency Programs.—Kelly Wolslayer, room 1020, 622–2195.

OFFICE OF FOREIGN ASSETS CONTROL

Director.—Adam J. Szubin, room 2240 (202) 622–2510.

EXECUTIVE OFFICE FOR ASSET FORFEITURE

1341 G Street, NW., Suite 900, 20005, phone (202) 622–9600

Director.—Eric Hampl.

FINANCIAL CRIMES ENFORCEMENT NETWORK (FINCEN)

P.O. Box 39, Vienna, VA 22183, phone (703) 905–3591

Director.—William Baity (acting).

OFFICE OF THE ASSISTANT SECRETARY FOR ECONOMIC POLICY

Assistant Secretary.—Phillip L. Swagel, room 3454 (202) 622–2200.
Senior Advisor to the Assistant Secretary.—Natasha Hickman, room 3445D, 622–2734.

Deputy Assistant Secretary for Microeconomics Analysis.—Nada Eissa, room 3449, 622–4995.
Director, Office of Microeconomic Analysis.—John Worth, room 4426, 622–2683.
Director, Office of Macroeconomic Analysis.—Ralph Monaco, room 2449, 622–2293.

OFFICE OF THE ASSISTANT SECRETARY FOR LEGISLATIVE AFFAIRS

Assistant Secretary.—Kevin I. Fromer, room 3134 (202) 622–1900.
Deputy to the Assistant Secretary.—Alex Kaplan, room 3464.
Special Assistant.—Elizabeth Hawkins, room 3134.
Deputy Assistant Secretary for—
Appropriations and Management.—Andy Fishburn, room 2464.
Banking and Finance.—Kevin MacMillan, room 3462.
Special Assistant.—Mary Kertz, room 3124.
International Affairs.—Jack Bartling, room 3128.
Special Assistant.—Sarah Lockart, room 3124.
Tax and Budget.—Mark Warren, room 3132.
Special Assistant.—Carolyn Coda, room 3124.
Administrative Specialist.—Linda L. Powell, room 3111, 622–0535.
Congressional Inquiry Analyst.—Ora D. Starks, room 3453, 622–0576.
Legislative Analyst.—Gail Harris-Berry, room 3453, 622–4401.

OFFICE OF THE ASSISTANT SECRETARY FOR MANAGEMENT / CHIEF FINANCIAL OFFICER

Assistant Secretary for Management.—Wesley T. Foster (acting), room 2438 (202) 622–0410.
Deputy Assistant Secretary for Management and Budget.—Wesley T. Foster, 622–0021.
Deputy Assistant Secretary for Human Resources and Chief Human Capital Officer.—Rochelle Granat, 1500 Pennsylvania Avenue, NW., room 1136, 622–6052.
Deputy Chief Financial Officer.—Richard Holcomb, room 6253, 622–0750.
Director of:
Accounting and Internal Control.—James R. Lingebach, room 6263, 622–0818.
Asset Management.—Carolyn Austin-Diggs, room 6179, 622–0500.
Budget.—Mark Olechowski, room 6118, 622–1479.
Conference Events and Meeting Services.—Lucinda Gooch, room 3094, Annex, 622–2071.
Departmental Budget Execution.—Chantale Wong, room 6123, Met Square, 622–5475.
Disclosure Services.—Dale Underwood, room 6200, Annex, 622–0874.
Environmental Safety and Health.—Gary Adams, room 6001, 622–1712.
Equal Opportunity and Diversity.—Mariam Harvey, room 8139, 622–1160.
Facilities Management.—Polly Dietz, room 1155, 622–7067.
Facilities Support Services.—James Thomas, room 6100, Annex, 622–4080.
Financial Management.—Andy Pavord, room 6069, Met Square, 622–5644.
Human Resource Strategy and Solutions.—Dennis Cannon, room 8121, 622–1109.
Human Resources Operations.—Jim Hyland, room 1458, 622–1577.
Information Services.—Veronica Marco, room 6904, 622–2477.
Printing and Graphics.—Craig Larsen, room 6100, Annex, 622–1409.
Procurement Services.—Ernest Dilworth, room 2154, New York Avenue, 622–1066.
Small and Disadvantaged Business Utilization.—Virginia Bellamy-Graham, room 6099, Met Square, 622–2826.
Strategic Planning and Performance Management.—Martin Malone, room 6133, Met Square, 622–9316.
Treasury Building.—Polly Dietz, room 1041, 622–7067.
Senior Procurement Executive.—Thomas Sharpe, room 6111, Met Square, 622–1039.
Budget Officer.—Carol Bryant, room 6075, Met Square, 622–7346.
Accounting Officer.—David Legge, room 6070, Met Square, 622–1167.
Facilities Support Services DD.—Melissa Hartman, room 6100, Annex, 622–4901.

OFFICE OF THE ASSISTANT SECRETARY FOR PUBLIC AFFAIRS

Assistant Secretary.—Michele Davis, room 3438 MT (202) 622–2910.
Deputy Assistant Secretary, Public Affairs / International Affairs Specialist.—Brookly McLaughlin, room 3446 MT, 622–2910.
Senior Advisor, Public Affairs.—Eileen Gilligan, room 3028A MT, 622–1374.

Deputy Assistant Secretary/Public Liaison.—Kirstie Tucker, room 3127 MT, 622–1330.
Review Analyst and Scheduling Coordinator.—Carmen Alvarado, room 3442 MT, 622–7483.
Director, Public Affairs/Enforcement Specialist.—Molly Millerwise, room 3020 MT, 622–2960.
Public Affairs Specialist, Domestic Finance.—Jennifer Zuccarelli, room 3028B MT, 622–2960.
Speechwriter to the Secretary.—Edmund Walsh, room 3030 MT, 622–0631.
Media Coordinator.—Brittni Aldridge, room 3023A MT, 622–2591.

OFFICE OF THE ASSISTANT SECRETARY FOR TAX POLICY

Assistant Secretary.—Eric Solomon, room 3120 (202) 622–0050.
Deputy Assistant Secretary for—
Tax Analysis.—Robert Carroll, room 3064–A, 622–0120.
Tax, Trade and Tariff Policy.—Tim Skud, room 3045, 622–0220.
Tax Legislative Counsel.—Michael Desmond, room 3040, 622–1981.
Deputy Tax Legislative Counsel.—John Parcell, room 4224, 622–2578.
International Tax Counsel.—Harry J. Hicks III, room 3054, 622–1317.
Deputy International Tax Counsel.—John Harrington, room 5064D, 622–0589.
Deputy International Tax Counsel (Strategic Programs).—Benedetta Kissel, room 3060, 622–9461.
Benefits Tax Counsel.—William Thomas Reeder, room 3050, 622–0155.
Director, Office of Tax Analysis.—Donald Kiefer, room 4116, 622–0269.
Director, Division of:
Business and Informational Taxation.—Geraldine A. Gerardi, room 4221, 622–1782.
Economic Modeling and Computer Applications.—Paul Dobbins, room 4039, 622–0846.
Individual Taxation.—James R. Nunns, room 4043, 622–1328.
International Taxation.—William Randolph, room 5117, 622–0471.
Receipts Forecasting.—Joel Platt, room 4112, 622–0259.
Revenue Estimating.—James Mackie III, room 4064A, 622–1326.

BUREAU OF ENGRAVING AND PRINTING

14th and C Streets, NW., 20228, phone (202) 874–2000

[Created by act of July 11, 1862; codified under U.S.C. 31, section 303]

Director.—Larry R. Felix.
Chief Counsel.—Michael Davidson, 874–5363.
Executive Assistant.—Fannie W. Smith.
Associate Directors:
Chief Financial Officer (CFO).—Leonard Olijar, 874–2020.
Chief Information Officer (CIO).—Peter O. Johnson, 874–3000.
Associate Director for—
Eastern Currency Facility.—Jon J. Cameron, 874–2032.
Western Currency Facility.—Charlene Williams (817) 847–3802.
Management.—Pamela J. Gardiner, 874–2040.
Technology.—Judith Diaz-Myers, 874–2008.

OFFICE OF THE COMPTROLLER OF THE CURRENCY

250 E Street, SW., 20219, phone (202) 874–5000

Comptroller.—John C. Dugan, 874–4900.
Chief of Staff/Senior Deputy Comptroller (Public Affairs).—John G. Walsh, 874–4880.
Chief Counsel.—Julie L. Williams, 874–5200.
Director for Congressional Liaison.—Carolyn Z. McFarlane, 874–4840.
Senior Deputy Comptroller of:
Chief National Bank Examiner.—Emory W. Rushton, 874–2870.
International and Economic Affairs.—Mark Levonian, 874–5010.
Large Bank Supervision.—Douglas W. Roeder, 874–4610.
Management.—Thomas R. Bloom, 874–5080.
Midsize/Community Bank Supervision.—Timothy W. Long, 874–5020.
Executive Officer for Leadership, Learning and Workplace Fairness.—Mark A. Nishan, 874–4050.

Ombudsman.—Samuel P. Golden (713) 336–4350.
Chief Information Officer.—Jackie Fletcher, 874–4480.

INTERNAL REVENUE SERVICE

1111 Constitution Avenue, NW., 20224, phone (202) 622–5000

[Created by act of July 1, 1862; codified under U.S.C. 26, section 7802]

Commissioner.—Mark W. Everson, 622–9511.
Deputy Commissioner, Services and Enforcement.—Kevin Brown, 622–4255.
Commissioner of:
Large and Mid-Size Business.—Deborah Nolan, 283–8710.
Small Business/Self-Employed.—Kathy Petronchak, 622–0600.
Tax Exempt and Government Entities.—Steven T. Miller, 283–2500.
Wage and Investment.—Richard Morgante, 622–6860.
Chief, Criminal Investigation.—John H. Imhoff, Jr. (acting), 622–3200.
Director, Office of Professional Responsibility.—Steve Whitlock (acting), 927–3397.
Deputy Commissioner, Operations Support.—Linda Stiff, 622–6860.
Chief:
Agency-Wide Shared Services.—Carl Froehlich, 622–7500.
Appeals.—Sarah Hall Ingram, 435–5600.
Communications and Liaison.—Frank Keith, 622–5440.
EEO and Diversity.—Diane Crothers, 622–5400.
Financial Officer.—Janice Lambert, 622–6400.
Human Capital Officer.—Robert Buggs (acting), 622–7676.
Information Officer/Modernization & Information Technology Services.—Richard Spires, 622–6800.
Mission Assurance and Security Services.—Daniel Galik, 622–8910.
Office of Privacy.—Barbra E. Symonds.
Chief Counsel.—Donald L. Korb, 622–3300.
National Taxpayer Advocate.—Nina E. Olson, 622–6100.
Director, Research, Analysis and Statistics.—Mark J. Mazur, 874–0100.
Office of Legislative Affairs.—Floyd L. Williams, 622–3720.

OFFICE OF THRIFT SUPERVISION

1700 G Street, NW., 20552, phone (202) 906–6000, fax 906–5660

[Codified in U.S.C. 12, section 1462a]

Director.—John M. Reich, 906–6590.
Deputy Director/Chief Operating Officer.—Scott M. Polakoff, 906–6853.
Chief Counsel.—John Bowman, 906–6372.
Managing Director of:
Examinations, Supervision and Consumer Protection.—Scott M. Albinson, 906–7984.
External Affairs.—Kevin Petrasic, 906–6288.
Chief Financial Officer.—Timothy T. Ward, 906–5666.
Chief Information Officer.—Wayne G. Leiss, 906–6101.

INSPECTOR GENERAL FOR TAX ADMINISTRATION (TIGTA)

1125 15th Street, NW., Room 700A, 20005

phone (202) 622–6500, fax 927–0001

Inspector General.—J. Russell George.
Congressional Liaison.—Bonnie Heald, 927–7037.
Chief Counsel.—Mary Anne Curtin, 622–4068.
Deputy Inspector General for Audit.—Michael R. Phillips, 622–6510.
Assistant Inspector General for Audit of:
Headquarter Operations and Exempt Organization Programs.—Nancy Nakamura, 622–8500.
Information Systems Programs.—Margaret Begg, 622–8510.
Small Business and Corporate Programs.—Daniel Devlin, 622–6510.
Wage and Investment Income Programs.—Michael McKenney, 622–5916.

Deputy Inspector General for Investigations.—Steven M. Jones, 927–7160.
Assistant Inspectors General for Investigations: —Timothy P. Camus, Michael A. Delgado.
Deputy Assistant Inspector General for Investigations.—Gregory L. Holley, Sr.
Assistant Inspector General for—
Information Technology/CIO.—Joseph I. Hungate, 622–5931.
Management Services/CFO/CHCO.—Joseph I. Hungate (acting).

OFFICE OF THE TREASURER OF THE UNITED STATES

Treasurer.—Anna Escobedo Cabral (202) 622–0100.
Senior Advisor.—Sandra Pedroarias.
Senior Writer.—Denise Cardamone.

UNITED STATES MINT

801 9th Street, NW., 20002, phone (202) 354–7200, fax 756–6160

Director.—Edmund C. Moy.
Executive Assistant to the Director.—Arnetta Cain.
Deputy Director.—David A. Lebryk.
Staff Assistant to the Deputy Director.—Pamela Carr.
Chief Counsel.—Dan Shaver.
Director, Legislative and Intergovernmental Affairs.—Clifford Northup.
Director, Public Affairs.—Becky Bailey.
Associate Director for Protection.—William F. Daddio.
Deputy Associate Director.—Bill R. Bailey.
Associate Director/Chief Information Officer.—Jerry Horton.
Deputy Associate Director.—Jay Mahanand.
Associate Director/Chief Financial Officer.—Patricia M. Greiner.
Deputy Associate Director.—David Motl.
Associate Director, Sales and Marketing.—Gloria Eskridge.
Deputy Associate Director.—Kevin Hamer.
Associate Director, Manufacturing.—R. Scott Myers.
Deputy Associate Director.—James Riedford.

DEPARTMENT OF DEFENSE

The Pentagon 20301–1155, phone (703) 545–6700

fax 695–3362/693–2161, http://www.defenselink.mil

ROBERT M. GATES, Secretary of Defense; born in Wichita, KS, September 25, 1943; education: B.A., College of William and Mary, 1965; M.A., Indiana University, 1966; Ph.D., Georgetown University, 1974; military service: U.S. Air Force, 1967–69, served as an officer in the Strategic Air Command; professional: intelligence analyst, Central Intelligence Agency (CIA), 1966–74; staff, National Security Council, 1974–79; Director, DCA/DDCI Executive Staff, CIA, 1981–82; Deputy Director for Intelligence, CIA, 1982–86; Chair, National Intelligence Council, 1983–86; Deputy Director of Central Intelligence, CIA, 1986–89; Deputy Assistant to the President for National Security Affairs, CIA, 1989; Assistant to the President and Deputy for National Security Affairs, CIA, 1989–91; Director, CIA, 1991–93; private consultant; author, *From the Shadows: The Ultimate Insider's Story of Five Presidents and How They Won the Cold War,* 1996; interim Dean of the George Bush School of Government and Public Service, Texas A & M University, 1999–2001; President, Texas A & M University, 2002–07; President, National Eagle Scout Association; awards: National Security Medal; Presidential Citizens Medal; National Intelligence Distinguished Service Medal; Distinguished Intelligence Medal; family: married to Becky; two children; nominated by President George W. Bush to become to 22nd Secretary of Defense, and was confirmed by the U.S. Senate on December 6, 2006.

OFFICE OF THE SECRETARY

Pentagon, Room 3E718, 20301–1000, phone (703) 692–7100, fax 697–8339

Secretary of Defense.—Robert M. Gates.

OFFICE OF THE DEPUTY SECRETARY

1010 Defense Pentagon, Room 3E678, 20301–1010, phone (703) 692–7150

Deputy Secretary of Defense.—Gordon England.

EXECUTIVE SECRETARIAT

Pentagon, Room 3E718, 20301–1000, phone (703) 692–7120, fax 695–2553

Executive Secretary.—SES William P. Marriott.

GENERAL COUNSEL

Pentagon, Room 3E833, 20301–1600, phone (703) 695–3341, fax 693–7278

General Counsel.—William J. Haynes.
Principal Deputy.—Daniel J. Dell'Orto (703) 697–7248.

OPERATIONAL TEST AND EVALUATION

Pentagon, Room 3D1067, 20301–1700, phone (703) 697–4813, fax 614–9103

Director.—Dr. Charles McQueary.

INSPECTOR GENERAL

400 Army Navy Drive, Suite 1000, Arlington VA 22202–4704, phone (703) 604–8300 fax 604–8310, hotline 1–800–424–9098, hotline fax 604–8569

Inspector General.—Thomas F. Gimble (acting).

UNDER SECRETARY OF DEFENSE FOR ACQUISITION, TECHNOLOGY AND LOGISTICS

Pentagon, Room 3E673, 20301, phone (703) 697–7021

Under Secretary.—Kenneth Krieg.
Deputy Under Secretary for—
Advanced Systems and Concepts.—John Kubricky.
Industrial Policy.—William Greenwalt.
Installations and Environment.—Philip W. Grone.
Logistics.—Phillip J. Bell.
Science and Technology.—Alan Haggerty.
Director, Office of Small Business Program.—Linda Oliver (acting).
Director, Defense Research and Engineering.—John Young.
Assistant to the Secretary of Defense for Nuclear and Chemical and Biological Defense Programs.—Tom Hopkins (acting).

JOINT STRIKE FIGHTER PROGRAM OFFICE

200 12th Street South, Suite 600, Arlington, VA 22202–5402, phone (703) 602–7640, fax 602–7649

Program Executive Officer.—BG Charles R. Davis, USAF.

UNDER SECRETARY OF DEFENSE (COMPTROLLER) AND CHIEF FINANCIAL OFFICER

Pentagon, Room 3E620, 20301–1100, phone (703) 695–3237

Under Secretary/Chief Financial Officer.—Tina W. Jonas.
Principal Deputy Under Secretary.—J. David Patterson.

UNDER SECRETARY OF DEFENSE FOR PERSONNEL AND READINESS

Pentagon, Room 3E764, 20301–4000, phone (703) 695–5254

Under Secretary.—David S.C. Chu.
Principal Deputy Under Secretary.—Michael L. Dominquez.
Assistant Secretary for—
Health Affairs.—William Winkenwerder.
Reserve Affairs.—Thomas Hall.
Deputy Under Secretary for—
Personnel and Readiness.—Paul Mayberry.
Program Integration.—Jeanne Fites.

UNDER SECRETARY OF DEFENSE FOR POLICY

Pentagon, Room 3E634, 20301–2000, phone (703) 697–7200

Under Secretary.—Eric Edelman.
Principal Deputy Under Secretary.—Ryan Henry.
Assistant Secretary of Defense for—
Homeland Defense.—Paul McHale.
International Security Affairs.—Peter Rodman.
Special Operations and Low-Intensity Conflict.—Tom O'Connell.
Principal Deputy Assistant Secretary of Defense for Global Security Affairs.—Joseph Benkert (acting).
Deputy Under Secretary of Defense for Asia Pacific Affairs.—Richard Lawless.

ASSISTANT SECRETARY FOR NETWORKS AND INFORMATION INTEGRATION / CHIEF INFORMATION OFFICER

Pentagon, Room 3E172, 20301–6000, phone (703) 695–0348

Assistant Secretary.—John Grimes.
Principal Deputy Assistant Secretary.—Dr. Linton Wells II.

ASSISTANT SECRETARY FOR LEGISLATIVE AFFAIRS

Pentagon, Room 3D844, 20301–1301, phone (703) 697–6210, fax 695–5860

Assistant Secretary.—Robert L. Wilkie.
Principal Deputy.—Lisa Marie Cheney (acting).

ASSISTANT TO THE SECRETARY OF DEFENSE FOR INTELLIGENCE OVERSIGHT

Pentagon, Room 2E253, 20301–7200, phone (703) 275–6550.

Assistant to the Secretary.—William R. Dugan (acting).

ASSISTANT SECRETARY FOR PUBLIC AFFAIRS

Pentagon, Room 2E556, 20301–1400, phone (703) 697–9312, fax 695–4299 public inquiries 697–5737

Assistant Secretary.—John Dorrance Smith.

ADMINISTRATION AND MANAGEMENT

Pentagon, Roon 3A710, 20301–1950, phone (703) 692–7138

Director.—Michael B. Donley.
Deputy Director.—Michael L. Rhodes, room 3A724, 693–7995.

DEPARTMENT OF DEFENSE FIELD ACTIVITIES

AMERICAN FORCES INFORMATION SERVICE

EFC Plaza, 601 North Fairfax Street, Room 300, Alexandria, VA 22314 phone (703) 428–1200

Director.—John Dorrance Smith, 697–9312.
Director for American Forces Radio and Television Services.—Melvin W. Russell, room 360, 428–0617.

DEPARTMENT OF DEFENSE EDUCATION ACTIVITY

4040 North Fairfax Drive, Arlington, VA 22203
School Information (703) 588–3030

Director.—Dr. Joseph Tafoya, 588–3200.
Principal Deputy Director.—Taffy Corrigan (acting), 588–3104.
Associate Director for Management and Business Operations.—Robert Blewi (acting), 588–3300.
General Counsel.—Karen Grosso, 588–3064.

DEPARTMENT OF DEFENSE HUMAN RESOURCES ACTIVITY

4040 Fairfax Drive, Arlington, VA 22209, phone (703) 696–1036

Director.—David S.C. Chu.
Deputy Director.—Jeanne Fites.

Assistant Director.—Sharon Cooper, 696–0909.

TRICARE MANAGEMENT ACTIVITY

5111 Leesburg Pike, Suite 810, Falls Church, VA 22041, phone (703) 681–8707

Director.—Dr. William Winkenwerder, Jr.
Deputy Director.—MG Elder Granger.

DEFENSE PRISONER OF WAR / MISSING PERSONNEL OFFICE

241 18th Street, Suite 800, Arlington, VA 22202, phone (703) 699–1100

Director.—Amb. Charles A. Ray.

OFFICE OF ECONOMIC ADJUSTMENT

400 Army Navy Drive, Suite 200, Arlington, VA 22202, phone (703) 604–6020

Director.—Patrick J. O'Brien.
Director of:
Operations.—Ronald Adkins, 604–5141.
Programs.—Dave Larson, 604–5148.
Assistant to Director.—Martha Sands, 604–5131, fax 604–5843.
Sacramento Regional Manager.—Anthony Gallegos (916) 557–7365.

WASHINGTON HEADQUARTERS SERVICES

Pentagon, phone (703) 693–7995

Director.—Michael L. Rhodes.
Director for—
Acquisitions and Procurement Office.—Frances Sullivan, 696–4030.
Administrative Services.—Larry Barlow, 601–2553 x118.
Defense Facilities.—Ralph Newton, 697–7241.
Executive Services and Communications.—Craig Glassner, 693–7965.
Financial Management Directorate.—Clai Ellett, 699–3350.
Human Resources.—Jan Thompson, 699–1800.
Information Technology.—Mary George, 604–4569.
Pentagon Renovation Program Office.—Sajeel Ahmed, 614–5129.
Planning and Evaluation Office.—Anne O'Connor, 588–8140.
WHS General Counsel.—William ''Bill'' Brazis, 693–7374.

JOINT CHIEFS OF STAFF

OFFICE OF THE CHAIRMAN

Pentagon, Room 2E872, 20318–0001, phone (703) 697–9121

Chairman.—GEN Peter Pace, USMC.
Vice Chairman.—ADM Edmund P. Giambastiani, Jr., USN, room 2E724, 614–8948.
Assistant to Chairman, Joint Chiefs of Staff.—LTG Frasier, USAF, room 2E868, 695–4605.

JOINT STAFF

Director.—LTG Walter L. Sharp, USA, room 2E936, 614–5221.
Vice Director.—MG Goldfein, USAF, room 2E936, 614–5223.
Director for—
Manpower and Personnel, J–1.—RADM Donna L. Crisp, USN, room 1E948, 697–6098.
Intelligence, J–2.—RADM Dorsett, USN, room 1E880, 697–9773.
Operations, J–3.—LTG Douglas Lute, USA, room 2D874, 697–3702.
Logistics, J–4.—LTG Christianson, USA, room 2E828, 697–7000.
Strategic Plans and Policy, J–5.—LTG John F. Sattler, USMC, room 2E996, 695–5618.
Command, Control, Communications and Computer Systems, J–6.—VADM Nancy Brown, USN, room 2D860, 695–6478.

Operational Plans and Interoperability, J–7.—RADM Richard Mauldin, USMC, room 2B865, 697–9031.

Force Structure, Resource, and Assessment, J–8.—VADM Steven Stanley, USN, room 1E962, 697–8853.

DEFENSE AGENCIES

BALLISTIC MISSILE DEFENSE AGENCY

7100 Defense Pentagon, 20301–7100, phone (703) 695–6344

Director.—LTG Henry A. ''Trey'' Obering III, USAF, 695–6330.
Deputy Director.—BG Patrick O'Reilly, USA, 695–6330.
Director, Public Affairs.—Richard Lehner, 697–8997.
Director, Legislative Affairs.—Timothy Coy, 697–8889.

DEFENSE ADVANCED RESEARCH PROJECTS AGENCY

3701 North Fairfax Drive, Arlington, VA 22203, phone (703) 696–2444

Director.—Anthony Tether.
Deputy Director.—Dr. Robert Leheny, 696–2402.

DEFENSE COMMISSARY AGENCY

1300 E Avenue, Fort Lee, VA 23801–1800, phone (804) 734–8718/8330

Director.—Patrick B. Nixon, 734–8720.
Chief Operating Officer.—Scott E. Simpson, 734–8330.

WASHINGTON OFFICE

Pentagon, Room 2E335, 20301–4100, phone (703) 695–3265

Chief.—Daniel W. Sclater.

DEFENSE CONTRACT AUDIT AGENCY

8725 John J. Kingman Road, Suite 2135, Fort Belvoir, VA 22060 phone (703) 767–3200

Director.—William H. Reed.
Deputy Director.—April G. Stephenson, 767–3272.

DEFENSE FINANCE AND ACCOUNTING SERVICE

1851 South Bell Street, Room 920, Arlington, VA 22240 phone (703) 607–2616

Director.—Zack E. Gaddy.
Deputy Director.—Teresa A. McKay.

DEFENSE INFORMATION SYSTEMS AGENCY

P.O. Box 4502, Arlington, VA 22204, phone (703) 607–6020

Director.—LTG Charles E. Croom, Jr., USAF, room 4222, 607–6001.
Vice Director.—MG Marilyn Quagliotti, USA, room 4235, 607–6010.

DEFENSE INTELLIGENCE AGENCY

Pentagon, Room 3E258, 20340–7400, phone (703) 697–5101

Director.—LTG Michael Maples.

Deputy Director.—LeLilia Long.

DEFENSE LEGAL SERVICES AGENCY

Pentagon, Room 3E833, 20301–1600, phone (703) 695–3341, fax 693–7278

Director/General Counsel.—William J. Haynes.
Principal Deputy Director.—Daniel Dell'Orto, 697–7248.

DEFENSE LOGISTICS AGENCY

8725 John J. Kingman Road, Suite 2533, Ft. Belvoir, VA 22060
phone (703) 767–5264

Director.—LTG Robert T. Dail, USA, 767–5200.
Vice Director.—MG Loren M. Reno, USAF, 767–5222.

DEFENSE SECURITY COOPERATION AGENCY

201 12th Street South, Suite 203, Arlington, VA 22202–5408, phone (703) 604–6604

Director.—LTG Jeffrey B. Kohler, USAF.
Deputy Director.—Richard Millies, 604–6606.

DEFENSE SECURITY SERVICE

1340 Braddock Place, Alexandria, VA 22314–1651, phone (703) 325–5364

Director.—Kathleen Watson (acting).
Chief of Staff.—Wendell Warner.
Director, Security Education, Training and Awareness.—Kevin Jones.
Director, Industrial Security Program.—Mary Griggs.
Chief Information Officer.—John Skudlarek (acting).

DEFENSE THREAT REDUCTION AGENCY

8725 John J. Kingman Road, Ft. Belvoir, VA 22060, phone (703) 325–2102

Director.—Dr. James A. Tegnelia.
Deputy Director.—GEN Randall Castro, USAF.

NATIONAL GEOSPATIAL—INTELLIGENCE AGENCY

4600 Sangamore Road, Bethesda, MD 20816, phone (301) 227–7400

Director.—VADM Robert B. Murrett, USN.
Deputy Director.—Lloyd B. Rowland.

NATIONAL SECURITY AGENCY / CENTRAL SECURITY SERVICE

Ft. George G. Meade, MD 20755, phone (301) 688–6524

Director.—Keith B. Alexander, USA.
Deputy Director.—John C. Inglis.

JOINT SERVICE SCHOOLS

9820 Belvoir Road, Ft. Belvoir, VA 22060, phone (800) 845–7606

DEFENSE ACQUISITION UNIVERSITY

President.—Frank J. Anderson, Jr. (703) 805–3360.

Commandant.—COL Mary Kringer, USAF, 805–4811.

NATIONAL DEFENSE INTELLIGENCE COLLEGE

President.—A. Denis Clift (202) 231–3344.

NATIONAL DEFENSE UNIVERSITY

Fort McNair, Building 62, 300 Fifth Avenue, 203319
phone (202) 685–3912

President.—LTG Frances Wilson, USAF, room 308, 685–3922.
Senior Vice President.— Amb. William Bellamy, 685–3923.

INFORMATION RESOURCES MANAGEMENT COLLEGE

Director.— Dr. Robert D. Childs (202) 685–3884.

JOINT FORCES STAFF COLLEGE

7800 Hampton Boulevard, Norfolk, VA 23511–1702, phone (757) 443–6200

Commandant.—MG Byron S. Bagby, USA, room A201.

INDUSTRIAL COLLEGE OF THE ARMED FORCES

Commandant.—RDML Girard Mauer, USN, room 200 (202) 685–4337.

NATIONAL WAR COLLEGE

Commandant.—MG Teresa Marné Peters, USAF, room 124 (202) 685–4312.

UNIFORMED SERVICES UNIVERSITY OF THE HEALTH SCIENCES

4301 Jones Bridge Road, Bethesda, MD 20814

President.—Charles L. Rice, M.D., room A1019 (301) 295–3013.

DEPARTMENT OF THE AIR FORCE

Pentagon, 1670 Air Force, Washington, DC 20330–1670
phone (703) 697–7376, fax 695–8809

SECRETARY OF THE AIR FORCE

Secretary of the Air Force.—Michael W. Wynne, room 4E540.
Confidential Assistant.—Caroline D. Wilson.
Senior Military Assistant.—COL Darryl Bruke.
Deputy Military Assistant.—LTC Scott V. DeThomas, 697–8141.
Military Aid.—MAJ Michele Pearce.
Protocol.—Karen Tibus.

SECAF / CSAF EXECUTIVE ACTION GROUP

Chief.—COL Walter Givhan (703) 697–5540.
Deputy Chief.—LTC Gregory Guillot.

UNDER SECRETARY OF THE AIR FORCE

Pentagon, 1670 Air Force, Room 4E522, 20330, phone (703) 697–1361

Under Secretary.—Dr. Ronald M. Sega.
Confidential Assistant.—Elizabeth Owen.
Senior Military Assistant.—COL Charles Porter.
Military Assistant.—LTC Vernon Lucas.
Executive Assistant.—TSgt Shepis Poisson.

CHIEF OF STAFF

Pentagon, 1670 Air Force, Room 4E562, 20330
phone (703) 697–9225

Chief of Staff.—GEN T. Michael Moseley.
Executive Officer.—COL Thomas Tinsley.
Vice Chief of Staff.—GEN John D.W. Corley, room 4E936, 695–7911.
Assistant Vice Chief of Staff.—LTG Arthur Lichte, room 4E944, 695–7913.
Director, Operations Group.—COL Walter Givhan, room 4E941, 697–5540.
Chief Master Sergeant of the Air Force.—CMSAF Rodney J. McKinley, room 4B948, 695–0498.

DEPUTY UNDER SECRETARY FOR INTERNATIONAL AFFAIRS

Pentagon, 1080 Air Force, Room 4E236, 20330–1080

Rosslyn, 1500 Wilson Boulevard, 8th Floor, Arlington, VA 22209

Deputy Under Secretary.—Bruce S. Lemkin (703) 695–7261.
Senior Executive Officer.—LTC George Risse, 695–7262.
Executive Officer.—MAJ Darren Halford, 693–1941.
Executive Assistant.—Georgia Smothers, 695–7261.
Assistant Deputy.—LMG Eric J. Rosborg, 588–8855.
Executive Officers: MAJ Art Primas; 588–8833; MAJ David Ballew, 588–8828.
Executive Assistant.—Rroxane Porter, 588–8800.
Director of Policy.—Richard A. Genaille, 588–8860.

Director of Regional Affairs.—BG John M. Howlett (acting), 588–8820.

ASSISTANT SECRETARY FOR ACQUISITION

Pentagon, 1060 Air Force, 20330

1500 Wilson Boulevard, Arlington, VA 22209 (Rosslyn)

1745 Jefferson Davis Highway, Suite 307, Arlington, VA 22202

Assistant Secretary.—Sue C. Payton (703) 697–6363.
Military Assistant.—LTC Andrew Ingram, 697–6990.
Executive Officer.—LTC Michael Guetlein, 697–6362.

PRINCIPAL DEPUTY ASSISTANT SECRETARY FOR ACQUISITION

Military Deputy.—LTG Donald Hoffman (703) 697–6363.
Executive Officer.—LTC David Morgan.
Chief Enlisted Manager.—SMSgt Rebecca Dayden, 697–8331.

DEPUTY ASSISTANT SECRETARY FOR ACQUISITION INTEGRATION

1500 Wilson Boulevard, Arlington, VA 22209 (Rosslyn)

Deputy Assistant Secretary.—Blaise J. Durante (703) 588–7211.
Associate Deputy Assistant Secretary.—Richard W. Lombardi, 696–0082.
Division of:
Acquisition Center for Excellence.—Ralph DiCicco, 253–5656.
Acquisition Chief Process Office.—Janet Hassan, 253–5615.
Career Management and Resources.—Pat Hogan, 588–7108.
Information Technology.—Terry Balven, 253–5646.
Management Policy.—Joseph ''Mike'' McWilliams, 588–7110.
Operations Support.—Joe Casso, 588–7124.
Program Integration.—Greg Parker, 588–7232.

DEPUTY ASSISTANT SECRETARY FOR CONTRACTING

Deputy Assistant Secretary.—Charlie E. Williams, Jr., Rosslyn, 7th Floor (703) 588–7070.
Associate Deputy Assistant Secretary.—COL Wendy Masiello, 588–7010.
Chief of:
Business Systems.—William Bishop.
Contingency Contracting.—Steve Zamparelli.
Contracting Mission Support Division.—COL Denean Machis, 588–7029.
Contracting Operations Division.—COL (S) Steve Blizzard, 588–7050.
Procurement Transformation.—Stuart Hazlett.

DEPUTY ASSISTANT SECRETARY FOR
SCIENCE, TECHNOLOGY AND ENGINEERING

Deputy Assistant Secretary.—Terry Jaggers, Rosslyn, 6th Floor (703) 588–7766.
Associate Deputy Assistant Secretary.—COL Jocelyn Seng, 588–7768.

CAPABILITY DIRECTORATE FOR GLOBAL POWER PROGRAMS

Director.—MG David M. Edgington (703) 588–7170.
Deputy Director.—COL Duke Z. Richardson, 588–7170.
Division Chief for—
Air Dominance Division.—COL Steven Kempf, 588–6502.
Combat Support and Joint Counter Air Division.—Charles Fellows, 588–6500.
Power Protection Division.—COL Roy Cleland, 588–1201.
Program Integration Division.—Donna Jonkoff, 588–9657.
Weapons Division.—COL Richard Burns, 588–1260.

CAPABILITY DIRECTORATE FOR GLOBAL REACH PROGRAMS

Director.—BG Wendell L. Griffin, Rosslyn, 14th Floor (703) 588–7752.

Deputy Director.—COL Mark T. Beierle, 14th Floor, 588–7756.
Division Chief for—
Mobility.—COL John Brunderman, 14th Floor, 588–7757.
Program, Budget and Congressional.—COL Rockford Reiners, 15th Floor, 588–8330.
Tactical Airlift, SOF, and Trainer.—COL Bo Tye, 14th Floor, 588–7740.

CAPABILITY DIRECTORATE FOR INFORMATION DOMINANCE

Director.—Martha J. ''Marty'' Evans, Rosslyn, 12th Floor (703) 588–6346.
Deputy.—COL Jon Link, 12th Floor, 588–6350.
Division Chief for—
Airborne Reconnaissance.—COL William Bridges, 15th Floor, 588–2625.
C2 and Combat Support.—John Whitmore, 12th Floor, 588–6461.
C2 Platforms and ATC Systems.—COL William McManus, 12th Floor, 588–6360.
C4ISR Future Capabilities.—COL Craig Bendorf, 12th Floor, 588–6430.
Congressional/Budget and Program Integration.—COL John Hunnell, 12th Floor, 588–6370.

DIRECTORATE FOR AIR FORCE RAPID CAPABILITIES

Director.—David E. Hamilton, Rosslyn, 1st Floor (703) 696–2407.
Deputy and Technical Director.—Randall G. Walden.
Program Integration.—LTC Stephen Uyehata.

DIRECTORATE FOR SPECIAL PROGRAMS

Director.—COL Richard ''Scott'' Stapp, Rosslyn, 15th Floor (703) 588–1631.
Deputy Director.—COL John Gibbons.
Associate Director.—Ryan Dow.
Division Chief for—
Advance Aircraft Survivability.—COL Randy Petyak, 588–2117.
Advanced Sensors and Weapons.—LTC Joseph Cappello, 588–2704.
Operational and Export Policy.—LTC Edward Conant, 588–2083.

AIR FORCE PROGRAM EXECUTIVE OFFICERS

Program Executive Officer for—
Aircraft.—LTG John Hudson (937) 255–5714.
Combat and Mission Support.—Ron Poussard (703) 588–7190.
Command and Control/Combat Support Systems.—LTG Charles Johnson (781) 478–5102.
F–22 Program.—MG Jeff Riemer (703) 588–7300.
Weapons.—MG David Eidsaune (850) 882–5422.

ASSISTANT SECRETARY FOR FINANCIAL MANAGEMENT AND COMPTROLLER OF THE AIR FORCE

Pentagon, 1130 Air Force, 20330

CGN, Air Force Cost Analysis Agency, Crystal Gateway North

1111 Jefferson Davis Highway, Suite 403, Arlington, VA 22202

Assistant Secretary.—John G. Vonglis (acting), room 4E984 (703) 693–6457.
Military Assistant.—LTC Gary J. Nanfito, 695–0837.
Chief, Enlisted Matters.—CMSgt Joseph C. Banks, 614–5437.

PRINCIPAL DEPUTY ASSISTANT SECRETARY FOR FINANCIAL MANAGEMENT

Principal Deputy Assistant Secretary.—John G. Voglis (703) 695–0829.
Military Assistant.—LTC Timothy J. Landvogt, 695–0829.

DEPUTY ASSISTANT SECRETARY FOR BUDGET

Deputy Assistant Secretary.—MG Faykes, room 4D131 (703) 695–1875.
Executive Officer.—LTC Jim O'Brien, 695–1876.
Deputy.—Patricia J. Zarodkiewicz, 695–1877.
Director of:
Budget and Appropriations Liaison.—COL Robert E. Chapman, room 5D911, 614–8110.
Budget Investment.—Marilyn Thomas, room 4D120, 695–1220.
Budget Management and Execution.—BJ White-Olsen, room 4D120, 695–9737.
Budget Operations and Personnel.—BG Larry O. Spencer, room 4D120, 697–0627.
Budget Programs.—COL Anthony Thompson, room 4C239, 614–7883.

DEPUTY ASSISTANT SECRETARY FOR COST AND ECONOMICS

Deputy Assistant Secretary.—Richard K. Hartley, room 4D159 (703) 697–5311.
Associate Deputy Assistant Secretary.—Ranae Woods, 697–5313.
Executive Officer.—LTC Michael Greiner, 697–5312.
Technical Director for Cost and Economics.—Jay Jordan, CGN, room 403, 604–0404.
Director, Economics and Business Management.—Stephen M. Connair, room 4D167, 693–0347.

DEPUTY ASSISTANT SECRETARY FOR FINANCIAL OPERATIONS

Deputy Assistant Secretary.—James E. Short, room 5E989 (703) 697–2905.
Associate Deputy Assistant Secretary.—Richard ''Gus'' Gustafson, 693–7066.
Military Assistant.—CAPT Scott Mathis, 697–3831.
Director for—
AF Accounting and Financial Office.—COL Patrick Coe, DFAS–DE (303) 676–5853.
Financial Accounting and Reporting.—Linda Yansky, room 4D164, 697–0292.
FM Workforce Management.—Glenda Sheiner, room 4D160, 697–2657.

ASSISTANT SECRETARY FOR INSTALLATIONS, ENVIRONMENT AND LOGISTICS

Assistant Secretary.—William C. Anderson, room 4D836 (703) 697–4936.
Executive Officer.—LTC Anthony Ramage, 697–4219.
Special Assistant.—Paul Bollinger, 693–5797.
Confidential Assistant.—Cathy Hudock, 697–4936.
Administrative Support.—MSgt Florence Robinson, 697–6300.

DEPUTY ASSISTANT SECRETARY FOR ENVIRONMENT, SAFETY AND OCCUPATIONAL HEALTH

Deputy Assistant Secretary.—Michael McGhee (acting), (703) 697–1019.
Executive Secretary.—Sheenia Williams, 697–9297.
Compliance.—LTC Christopher Duffy, 697–0997.
ESHO.—Donald Hickman, 697–9297.
Legislation, BRAC and Planning.—Michele Indermark, 614–8458.
Occupational Health.—LTC Wade Weisman, 693–9544.
Restoration.—LTC Thomas Devenoge, 692–9515.
Safety.—Vance Lineberger, 693–7706.

DEPUTY ASSISTANT SECRETARY FOR INSTALLATIONS

Deputy Assistant Secretary.—Fred W. Kuhn, room 4C746 (703) 695–3592.
Assistant for Installation Management.—John E.B. Smith, 593–9327.
Administrative Office Manager.—Pamela L. Coghill, 695–3592.
Director for—
Facility and Energy Management.—LTC Mark Bednar, 697–7003.
Installation Policy.—MAJ Laura Johnson, 695–3592.
Assistant for the Air National Guard Affairs.—COL Ron Sachse, 695–5730.
Assistant for the Reserve Affairs.—COL Joe Morganti, 693–9328.
Chief, BRAC Program Management Office Division.—COL James Holland, room 5C266, 692–9510.

Secretary.—Pamela L. Coghill, room 4C940, 695–3592.

DIRECTORATE OF LOGISTICS

Deputy Assistant Secretary.—Debra K. Walker, room 4C746 (703) 695–3592.
Director of Logistics and Transformation.—Mark Van Gilst, room 4C746, 692–9090.
Chief, Depot Operations and Strategy Planning.—LTC Willie Holt, room 4C746, 693–2185.
Chief, Weapons System Integration.—Candy Jones, room 4C746, 695–6716.

AIR FORCE REAL PROPERTY AGENCY

Director.—Kathryn M. Halvorson (703) 696–5501.
Deputy Director.—Jeffrey Domm, 696–5502.
Executive Officer.—Aubris Pfeiffer, 696–5504.
Secretary.—LaShelle M. Taylor, 696–5503.
Chief—
Financial Officer.—Kathleen O' Sullivan, 696–5250.
Information Officer.—Robert McCann, 696–5534.
Legal Council—Derry Fivehouse, 696–5522.
Operating Officer.—Gerald Johnson, 696–5540.
Branch Chief of—
Central Region.—Gene Aefsky, 696–4012.
Eastern Region.—Elton Wilson, 696–5555.
Western Region.—Steve Matteo, 696–5544.

ASSISTANT SECRETARY FOR MANPOWER AND RESERVE AFFAIRS
1660 Air Force Pentagon, Room 4E1020, 20330

Mobilization Assistant.—MG Peter K. Sullivan (703) 693–9312.
Confidential Assistant.—Ruth N. Thornton, 695–6677.
Military Assistant.—COL Anne Sobota, 697–2303.
Executive Officer.—LTC Joel Morin, 697–1258.
Superintendent.—TSgt Henry Lopez, 697–5828.

DEPUTY ASSISTANT SECRETARY FOR FORCE MANAGEMENT INTEGRATION

Deputy Assistant Secretary.—Robert J. Goodwin (703) 614–4751.
Executive Secretary.—Dottie A. Baltimore.
Special Assistant for Stability Operations.—Lynne M. Schneider, 695–2459.
Assistant Deputy for—
Civilian Personnel.—Charlene M. Bradley, 614–4753.
Family Programs.—Linda Stephens-Jones, 693–9574.
Health Affairs.—Carol J. Thompson, 693–9764.
USAFA Affairs.—David A. French, 693–9333.
Force Support Services.—Edward F. Shock, 693–9765.
Total Force Integration.—Thomas E. Booth, 697–7783.

DEPUTY ASSISTANT SECRETARY FOR RESERVE AFFAIRS

Deputy Assistant Secretary.—John C. Truesdell, room 5C938 (703) 697–6376.
Secretary.—Rosa R. Ramirez, 697–6375.
IMA.—COL Anne Hamilton, 693–9505.
Assistant for—
Air Force Reserve Affairs Matters.—COL Steve Kett, 697–6431.
ANG Matters.—COL Ronald Gionta, 693–9504.
Enlisted Matters.—CMSgt Darise Jackson, 697–6429.
Military Executive for Air Reserve Forces Policy Division Committee.—LTC Laura Hunter, 697–6430.

DEPUTY ASSISTANT SECRETARY FOR STRATEGIC DIVERSITY AND INTEGRATION

Executive Secretary.—Karen Sauls (703) 697–6586.

Chief, Military Research Analyst.—MAJ Richard Cooney, 697–6583.

AIR FORCE REVIEW BOARDS AGENCY

Director.—Joe G. Lineberger, AAFB, Building 1535 (240) 857–3137.
Confidential Assistant.—Donna Atchison.
Chief, Review Boards Management.—CMSgt Susan Ayala, 857–3119.

CHIEF OF WARFIGHTING INTEGRATION AND CHIEF INFORMATION OFFICER

1800 Air Force Pentagon, Room 4E212, 20330

Chief of Warfighting Integration and Chief Information Officer.—LTG Mike W. Peterson (703) 695–6829.
Deputy Chief of Warfighting Integration and Deputy Chief Information Officer.—David Tillotson III, 697–1605.
Director of:
Information, Services and Integration.—MG William T. Lord, room 4B1060, 697–1326.
Operations and Support Integration.—BG James A. Whitmore, room 4C1059, 695–1835.
Policy, Planning and Resources.—Daniel F. McMillin, room 4C1059, 605–1939.

DEPUTY CHIEF OF STAFF FOR INTELLIGENCE, SURVEILLANCE AND RECONNAISSANCE

Deputy Chief of Staff.—LTG David A. Deptula (703) 695–5613.
Assistant Deputy Chief of Staff.—BG Paul Dettmer.
Executive.—LTC Stacee Bako.
Director of:
Analysis.—Steven Cantrell.
Integration.—Dean Yount, 693–5201.
Plans and Requirements.—Kenneth Dumm, 614–2144.
Intelligence, Surveillance and Reconnaissance Programs.—COL Robert Marlin, 695–6240.

DEPUTY CHIEF OF STAFF FOR LOGISTICS, INSTALLATIONS AND MISSION SUPPORT

Pentagon, 1030 Air Force, 20330

Crystal Gateway North, 1111 Jefferson Davis Highway, Arlington, VA 22202 (CGN)

Crystal Gateway 1, 1235 Jefferson Davis Highway, Arlington, VA 22202 (CG1)

Rosslyn, 1500 Wilson Boulevard, Arlington, VA 22209 (ROS)

Deputy Chief of Staff.—LTG Donald J. Wetekam, Pentagon, room 4E260 (703) 695–3153.
Assistant Deputy.—Michael A. Aimone, Pentagon, room 4E260, 695–6236.
Director of:
Transformation.—Grover L. Dunn, Pentagon, room 5D967, 697–6559.
Logistics Readiness.—MG Gary McCoy, Pentagon, room 4B283, 697–1429.
Maintenance.—BG Kathleen Close, Pentagon, room 4E278, 695–4900.
Resources Intregation.—MG Polly Peyerl, Pentagon, room 4A272, 697–2822.
The Civil Engineer.—MG Del Eulberg, CG1, room 1000, 607–0200.
Security Forces.—BG Mary Hertog, room 4C166, 693–5401.

DEPUTY CHIEF OF STAFF FOR MANPOWER AND PERSONNEL

Pentagon, 1040 Air Force, Room 4E194, 20330

Deputy Chief of Staff.—LTG Roger A. Brady (703) 697–6088.
Assistant Deputy.—Roger M. Blanchard.
Chief, Personnel Issues Team.—LTC Mary Boucher, room 4E185, 695–4212.
Director of:
Air Force Senior Leader Management Office.—COL Cathy Clothier, room 5C238, 697–1181.
Airmen Development and Sustainment.—BG Robert Allardice, room 4E144, 695–2144.
Executive Services.—CAPT Angel J. Lugo, room 4E207, 697–1125.

Force Management Policy.—BG K.C. McClain, room 4E228, 695–6770.
Manpower and Organization.—BG (Sel) Tom Smoot, room 5A328, 692–1601.
Plans and Integration.— Timothy Beyland, room 4E178, 697–5222.

DEPUTY CHIEF OF STAFF FOR OPERATIONS, PLANS AND REQUIREMENTS

Pentagon, 1630 Air Force, Room 4C844, 20330

Deputy Chief of Staff.—LTG Howie Chandler (703) 697–9991.
Assistant Deputy.—MG Richard Y. Newton, 697–9881.
Mobility Assistant.—BG Commons, 697–3087.
Director of:
Current Operations and Training.—MG David Clary, room 5D756, 695–9067.
Executive Support.—Eugene Collins, room 5C1072, 697–7823.
Operations Capability Requirements.—BG Marshall Sabol, room 5D756, 695–3018.
Strategic Security.—MG Roger Burg, room 5D756, 693–9747.

DEPUTY CHIEF OF STAFF FOR STRATEGIC PLANS AND PROGRAMS

Pentagon, 1070 Air Force, Room 4E124, 20330–1070

Deputy Chief of Staff.—LTG Raymond Johns, Jr. (703) 697–9472.
Assistant Deputy Chief of Staff.—MG Charles Stenner, Jr.
Directorate of Programs.—MG Timothy Jones, room 5B279, 697–2405.
Directorate of Total Force integration.—BG Allison Hickey.
Director for Strategic Planning.—BG Stanley Clarke, room 5E171, 697–3117.

DIRECTORATE OF STUDIES AND ANALYSIS, ASSESSMENTS AND LESSONS LEARNED

Pentagon, 1570 Air Force, 20330

1500 Wilson Boulevard, 6th Floors, Arlington, VA 22209 (Rossyln)

Director.—Dr. Jacqueline R. Henningsen, Ph.D., SES (703) 588–6995.
Deputy Director.—BG David Fadok.
Senior Advisor.—COL James Brooks.
Technical Director.—Daniel Barker.
Chief Analyst.—COL Roxann A. Oyler.

ADMINISTRATIVE ASSISTANT TO THE SECRETARY

Pentagon, 1720 Air Force, 20330

2221 South Clark Street, Arlington, VA 22202 (CP6)

220 Brookley Avenue, Bolling AFB, Washington, DC 20032 (BAFB1)

200 McChord Street, Box 94, Bolling AFB, Washington, DC 20032 (BAFB2)

Administrative Assistant.—William A. Davidson, Pentagon, room 4D881 (703) 695–9492.
Deputy Administrative Assistant.—Robert E. Corsi, Jr., 695–9492.
Senior Executive Assistant.—LTC Tim Zoerlein, 695–8806.
Executive Assistant.—MAJ Kristine Burnett, 695–8807.
Executive Administrator.—Nancy Beeson.
General Manager, Executive Dining Facility.—Alfonso Sisneros, room 4C854, 697–1112.
Director of:
Art Program Office.—Russell Kirk, room 5E271, 697–2858.
Central Adjudication Facility.—COL Laura Hickman, BAFB1 (202) 767–9236.
Declassification Office.—Linda Smith, CP6, Suite 600,604–4665.
Departmental Publishing Office.—Jessica Spencer-Gallucci, BAFB2 (202) 404–2380.
Facilities Support Division.—Larry Bickel, room 5E1083, 697–8222.
Human Resources and Manpower Division.—Patricia Robey, room 4D570, 697–1806.
Policy, Plans and Resources Division.—Carolyn Lunsford, room 5E117, 695–4007.
Security, Counterintelligence and Special Programs Oversight Division.—Barry Hennessey, room 5D972, 693–2013.

AUDITOR GENERAL

Pentagon, 1120 Air Force, 20330

4170 Hebble Creek Road, Building 280, Room 1,
Wright-Patterson AFB, OH 45433 (WPAFB)

5023 Fourth Street, March ARB, CA 95218 (MARB)

1101 Wilson Boulevard, Suite 1010, Arlington, VA 22201 (Rosslyn)

2509 Kennedy Circle, Building 125, Brooks City-Base, TX 78235

Auditor General.—Robert E. Dawes, room 4E168 (703) 614–5626.

AIR FORCE AUDIT AGENCY

Deputy Auditor General and Director of Operations.—Cathy Novel, room 4E168 (703) 614–5738.
Assistant Deputy Auditor General.—Michael V. Barbino, Rosslyn (703) 696–7764.
Assistant Auditor General for—
Acquisition and Logistics Audits.—Theodore J. Williams, WPAFB (937) 257–6355.
Financial and Systems Audits.—Judith Simon, MAFB (951) 655–7011.
Support and Personnel Audits.—James W. Salter, Jr., Brooks City-Base (210) 536–1999.

CHIEF OF CHAPLAINS

Bolling AFB, 112 Luke Avenue, Building 5683, Washington, DC 20032

Chief.—Chaplain (MG) Charles Baldwin, room 316 (202) 767–4577.
Deputy Chief.—Chaplain (BG) Cecil Richardson, room 313, 767–4599.

CHIEF OF SAFETY

Pentagon, 1400 Air Force, Room 5E161, 20330–1400

Chief of Safety/Commander, Air Force Safety Center.—MG Stanley Gorenc, (703) 693–7281.
Executive.—MAJ Brad Sturgis, 614–3389.
Director, Safety Issues Division.—COL Daniel Stanton, 693–3333.

OFFICE OF COMMUNICATIONS

Pentagon, 1690 Air Force, Room 4C712, 20330

Director.—MG (S) Erv Lessel (703) 697–6061.
Executive Officer.—MAJ Max Despain.

GENERAL COUNSEL

Pentagon, 1740 Air Force, 20330

General Counsel.—Mary L. Walker (703) 697–0941.
Principal Deputy.—Daniel Ramos.
Military Assistant/Special Counsel.—COL Kevin Baron, 697–8418.
Deputy General Counsel for—
Acquisition.—James Hughes, room 4D980, 697–3900.
Contractor Responsibility.—Steven A. Shaw, Ballston, 588–0057.
Dispute Resolution.—Richard Deavel, Rosslyn, 588–2211.
Fiscal and Administrative Law.—Don W. Fox, room 4C916, 693–9291.
Installations and Environment.—J. Steven Rogers, room 4C921, 695–4691.
International Affairs.—Michael W. Zehner, room 4C941, 697–5196.
Military Affairs.—W. Kipling Atlee, room 4C948, 695–5663.

AIR FORCE HISTORIAN

3 Brookley Avenue, Box 94, Bolling Air Force Base, Washington, DC 20032–5000 (BAFB)

Director.—C.R. ''Dick'' Anderegg, room 401 (202) 404–2167.

Executive Officer.—MAJ Rodney Gray (703) 697–2289.
Director, Air Force Historical Research Agency, Maxwell AFB, AL.—Dr. Charles O'Connell (334) 953–5342.

INSPECTOR GENERAL

Pentagon, 1140 Air Force, Room 4E1076, 20330

Inspector General.—LTG Ronald F. Sams (703) 697–6733.
Deputy Inspector General.—MG Jeff M. Musfeldt, 697–4351.
Executive Officer.—MAJ Wayne Blanchette, 697–4787.
Advisor for—
Air National Guard Matters.—COL Thelma Jones, 588–1559.
Reserve Matters.—COL Ray Joinson, room 4E119, 697–0066.
Director of:
Complaints Resolution Directorate.—COL Michael Kaster, room 110, 588–1558.
Inspections.—COL Susanne LeClere, room 110, 588–1531.
Special Investigations.—COL Carl Goodison, room 4E1081, 697–0411.
Senior Officials Inquiries.—COL Ted LePlante, room 4E119, 693–3579.

JUDGE ADVOCATE GENERAL

Pentagon, 1420 Air Force, 20330

1501 Wilson Boulevard, Suite 810, Arlington, VA 22209 (Rosslyn)

112 Luke Avenue, Suite 343, Bolling AFB, Washington, DC 20032 (BAFB)

Judge Advocate General.—MG Jack L. Rives (703) 614–5732.
Director for—
Civil Law and Litigation.—COL Gregory Girard, Rosslyn, room 810, 696–9040.
USAF Judiciary.—COL Roberta Moro, BAFB, room 336 (202) 767–1535.
General Law.—Harlan G. Wilder, room 5E279, 614–4075.
International Law.—COL Barry Youngner, room 5C269, 695–9631.

LEGAL SERVICES

Commander, Air Force Legal Services Agency.—COL Evan Haberman, BAFB, room 336 (202) 404–8758.

DIRECTORATE OF LEGISLATIVE LIAISON

Pentagon, 1160 Air Force, 20330

Rayburn House Office Building, Room B–322, 20515 (RHOB)

Russell Senate Office Building, Room SR–182, 20510 (RSOB)

Director.—MG Daniel Darnell, Pentagon, room 4C654 (703) 697–8153.
Deputy Director.—BG John W. Hesterman III, 697–2650.
Mobilization Assistant to the Director.—BG Christine Turner, 695–2650.
Executive Officer to the Director.—MAJ Tim Goodroe, 697–4142.
Executive Officer to the Deputy Director.—CAPT Maureen Schumann, 697–2650.
Chief of:
Air Operations.—Sandi J. Esty, room 4B654, 697–1500.
Congressional Action.—Daniel Sitterly, room 4C689, 695–0182.
Congressional Inquiries.—COL Darrell Adams, room 4B654, 697–3783.
House Liaison Office.—COL Lori Robinson, RHOB (202) 685–4531.
Programs and Legislation.—COL JR Smith, room 4C689, 697–7950.
Senate Liaison Office.—COL Anthony Lazarski, RSOB (202) 685–2573.
Weapons Systems Liaison.—COL Warren Henderson, room 4B689, 697–3376.

NATIONAL GUARD BUREAU

1411 Jefferson Davis Highway, Arlington, VA 22202

Chief.—LTG H. Steven Blum, JP–1, Pentagon, Washington, DC, 2A514B (703) 614–3117.

Legislative Liaison.—BG Kelly A. McKeague, JP–1, Crystal City, Suite 9200, 607–2770.
Vice Chief, Air National Guard.—LTG Craig McKinley, JP–1, Crystal City, Suite 12200, 607–2790.
Vice Chief, Army National Guard.—LTG Clyde A. Vaughn, Readiness Center, Arlington, VA, 607–1708.
Director Joint Staff.—MG Terry Scherling, JP–1, Crystal City, Suite 12000, 607–2789.

OFFICE OF PUBLIC AFFAIRS

Director.—BG (S) Michelle Johnson (703) 967–6061.
Executive Officer.—MAJ Jim Cunningham.
Chief of:
Current Operations.—Jean Schaefer, room 4C712, 695–0640.
Outreach.—LTC Eric Butterbaugh, room 4A120, 695–2414.
Plans.—LTC Marcella Adams, room 5D227, 697–6715.
Plans Writer.—Nicole VanNatter, room 5D227, 697–8817.
Product Development.—CPT Sharon Kibiloski, room 4C712, 696–9146.
Requirements and Development.—Sherry Medders, room 4A120, 697–6701.
Research and Assessment.—LTC Larry Clavette, room 5C279, 693–3631.

AIR FORCE RESERVE

Pentagon, 1150 Air Force, Room 4E160, 20330

Chief, Air Force Reserve/Commander, Air Force Reserve Command.—LTG John A. Bradley (703) 695–9225.
Deputy to Chief of Air Force Reserve.—BG Charles D. Ethredge, 614–7307.
Deputy Executive Officer.—MAJ Mary Harp, 695–5528.
Executive NCO.—SMSgt Glenn E. Coleman, 614–7307.

SCIENTIFIC ADVISORY BOARD

Pentagon, 1180 Air Force, Room 5D982, 20330

Chair.—Heidi Shyu (703) 697–4811.
Vice Chair.—Ann Karagozian.
Military Director.—LTG Donald J. Hoffman, room 4E964, 697–6363.
Executive Director.—COL Thurmon Deloney II, 697–8288.
Deputy Executive Director.—LTC Kyle Gresham, 697–8652.
Military Assistants: MAJ Aaron Taylor, 697–4648; MAJ Deven Lowman, 697–4808.
Executive Assistants: TSgt Marcus Nash; SSgt Monique Horton, 697–4811.

AIR FORCE SCIENTIST

Pentagon, 1075 Air Force, Room 4E288, 20330

Chief Scientist.—Dr. Mark J. Lewis (703) 697–7842.
Military Assistant.—COL Robert Fredell.

OFFICE OF SMALL BUSINESS PROGRAMS

Pentagon, 1060 Air Force, 20330–1060

Director.—John G. Capora (acting), (703) 696–1103.

SURGEON GENERAL

Pentagon, 1780 Air Force, Room 4E1084, 20330–1780

Bolling AFB, 110 Luke Avenue, Building 5681, Suite 400, Washington, DC 20332–7050

Surgeon General.—LTG James G. Roudebush (703) 692–6800.
Executive Officer.—COL Mike Miller (703) 692–6990.
Deputy Surgeon General.—MG C. Bruce Green (202) 767–4766.
Executive Officer.—MAJ Jody Ocker (202) 767–4759.

Director for—
Congressional and Public Affairs.—Donna Tinsley (202) 767–4774.
Financial Management.—COL Denise Comfort (703) 681–6045.
Medical Operations.—MG Thomas Loftus (202) 767–0020.
Force Development.—MG Melissa Rank (202) 767–4498.
Plans and Programs.—BG Patricia Lewis (202) 767–4915.
Modernization.—BG Theresa Casey (703) 681–7055.
Corps Directors for—
Medical.—COL Arnyce Pock (202) 767–4492.
Biomedical Sciences.—COL Bonnie Johnson (202) 767–4499.
Nursing.—COL Linda Kisner (202) 767–4462.
Medical Services.—COL Brian Acker (202) 767–4432.
Dental Corps.—COL Grant Hartup (202) 767–4385.

DIRECTORATE OF TEST AND EVALUATION

Pentagon, 1650 Air Force, Room 5E839, 20330

Director.—John Manclark (703) 697–4774.
Deputy Director.—David Hamilton.
Executive Officer.—MAJ Waldemar Barnes, 697–5067.

AIR FORCE BOARD FOR CORRECTION OF MILITARY RECORDS (AFBCMR)

Executive Director.—Mack M. Burton, AAFB, Building 1535 (240) 857–3502.
Chief Examiners: Ralph Prete, Phillip Horton, Al Walker, Gregory Johnson.
Superintendent, AFBCMR Information Management.—Eleanor Bain, 857–3502.

AIR FORCE CIVILIAN APPELLATE REVIEW OFFICE

Director.—Rita Looney, AAFB Building 1535 (240) 857–7071.
Assistant Director.—J. Hayward Kight, 857–3168.

AIR FORCE PERSONNEL COUNCIL

Director.—COL Venetia Brown, AAFB Building 1535 (240) 857–3138.
Senior Legal Advisor.—COL Del Grissom, 857–9043.
Senior Medical Advisor.—COL Horace Carson, 857–5353.
Chief, Air Force Discharge Review Board.—Wanda Langley, 857–3504.
Chief, Awards/Decoration/Air Force Reserve Advisor.—COL Loye Eschenbury, 857–5342.
Executive Secretary/Attorney Advisor on Clemency/Parole Board.—James D. Johnston, 857–5329.
Executive Secretary, DOD Civilian/Military Service Review Board.—James D. Johnston, 857–5329.

ARMY AND AIR FORCE EXCHANGE SERVICE

3911 S. Walton Walker Boulevard, Dallas, TX 75236, phone 1–800–527–6790

Commander.—MG Bill Essex, USAF.
Chief Operating Officer.—Michael P. Howard.

WASHINGTON OFFICE/OFFICE OF THE BOARD OF DIRECTORS

National Center 1 (NC1), 2511 Jefferson Davis Highway, Suite 11600

Arlington, VA 22202, phone (703) 604–7523, DSN 664–7523

Director/Executive Secretary.—Gregg Cox.
Deputy Director/Executive Assistant.—Richard W. Harpham, Jr.

DEPARTMENT OF THE ARMY

The Pentagon, Washington, DC 20310, phone (703) 695–2442

OFFICE OF THE SECRETARY

Pentagon, Room 3E560, 20310, phone (703) 695–3211, fax 697–8036

Secretary of the Army.—Dr. Francis J. Harvey.
Executive Officer.—COL Patrick J. Donahue, 695–1717.

OFFICE OF THE UNDER SECRETARY

Pentagon, Room 3E588, 20310–0102, phone (703) 695–4311

Under Secretary of the Army.—Hon. Pete Geren.
Executive Officer.—COL Charles Taylor, 697–6806.

CHIEF OF STAFF

Pentagon, Room 3E528, 20310–0200, phone (703) 695–2077

Chief of Staff.—GEN Peter J. Schoomaker.
Vice Chief of Staff—GEN Richard A. Cody, 695–4371.
Director, CSA's Staff Group.—COL Kim Kadesch, 697–4120.
Director of Army Staff.—LTG James L. Campbell, 695–6636.
Sergeant Major.—SMA Kenneth O. Preston, 695–2150.
Director, Office of:
Army Protocol.—Arlene York, 697–0692.
Executive Commission and Control.—COL Joseph Sartiana, 697–5280.
Program Analysis and Evaluation.—MG William T. Grisoli, room 3E362, 695–4697.
Test and Evaluation Management Agency.—Larry Leiby, 695–8998.

DEPUTY UNDER SECRETARY OF THE ARMY

101 Army Pentagon, Room 3E573, 20310–0001, phone (703) 697–5075

Deputy Under Secretary.—Thomas Kelly III.
Executive Officer.—COL Carlton Reid, 695–4392.
Executive Assistant.—Sarah Martin (703) 697–5075.

DEPUTY UNDER SECRETARY OF THE ARMY (BUSINESS TRANSFORMATION)

Pentagon, Room 5D564, 20310–0101, phone (703) 695–7595

Deputy Under Secretary.—Michael Kirby.
Deputy.—Jeffrey White.
Executive Officer.—LTC David Trybula.
Executive Assistant.—Carol Hopper.

ASSISTANT SECRETARY FOR ACQUISITION, LOGISTICS AND TECHNOLOGY

103 Army Pentagon, Room 2E532, 20310–0103, phone (703) 693–6154

Assistant Secretary.—Hon. Claude M. Bolton, Jr.
Confidential Assistant.—Cassandra Barnes.
Chief of Staff.—COL Ainsworth ''Andy'' Mills, 695–5749.

Executive Officer.—Robert L. Riddick, 695–6742.
Military Deputy.—LTG N. Ross Thompson, 697–0356.
Secretary to the Military Deputy.—LTC Tracey Beaulieu, 693–3927.
Executive Officer to the Military Deputy.—LTC Linda Herbert, 697–0356.
DASA Plans, Programs and Resources.—Tom Mullins, 697–0387.
DASA Science and Technology.—Dr. Thomas H. Killion, 692–1830.
DASA Defense Export and Cooperation.—Keith Webster, 588–8070.

ASSISTANT SECRETARY FOR CIVIL WORKS

Pentagon, Room 3E446, 20310–0108, phone (703) 697–8986, fax 697–7401

Assistant Secretary.—Hon. John Paul Woodley, Jr.
Executive Officer.—COL Michael J. Donovan, 697–9809.
Military Assistant.—MAJ Dwayne Smith, 695–0482.
Deputy Assistant Secretary for—
Management and Budget.—Claudia L. Tornblom, 695–1376.
Policy, Planning and Review.—Douglas Lamont (202) 761–0016.
Policy and Legislation.—George Dunlop, 695–1370.

ASSISTANT SECRETARY FOR FINANCIAL MANAGEMENT AND COMPTROLLER

Pentagon, Room 3E324, 20310–0109, phone (703) 614–4356

Assistant Secretary.—Hon. Nelson Miford.
Executive Officer.—COL Karen Dyson, 614–4337.
Deputy Assistant Secretary for—
Army Budget.—MG Edgar Stanton, room 3A314, 614–4035.
Director for U.S. Cost and Economic Analysis Center.—Steve Bagby, room 3E352.
Financial Operations.—John Argodale, room 3A320A, 693–2741.
Resource Analysis and Business Practices.—Jim Anderholm, room 3A712, 697–7399.

ASSISTANT SECRETARY FOR INSTALLATIONS AND ENVIRONMENT

Pentagon, Room 3E464, 20310–0110, phone (703) 692–9800

Assistant Secretary.—Hon. Keith E. Eastin.
Principal Deputy Assistant Secretary.—Geoffrey G. Prosch, 692–9802.
Executive Officer.—COL Thomas W. Young, 692–9804.
Deputy Assistant Secretary for—
Environment, Safety and Occupational Health.—Addison "Tad" Davis, room 3D453, 697–1913.
Infrastructure and Analysis.—Kathryn T.H. Szymanski, room 3D453, 692–9817.
Installations and Housing.—Joseph Whitaker, 697–8161, room 3E475.
Privatizations and Partnerships.—William Armbruster, room 3D453, 692–9890.

ASSISTANT SECRETARY FOR MANPOWER AND RESERVE AFFAIRS

Pentagon, Room 2E468, 20310–0111, phone (703) 697–9253

Assistant Secretary.—Ronald J. James.
Principal Deputy Assistant Secretary.—Daniel B. Benning, room 2E460, 692–1292.
Executive Officer.—COL Michael Cardanelli, 695–1375.
Deputy Assistant Secretary for—
Force Management, Manpower and Resources.—Mark Manning, room 2E460, 695–9033.
Human Resources.—John P. McLaurin III, room 2E482, 697–2631.
Review Boards.—Bud Shatzer (acting), Crystal City #4, 607–1597.
Training, Readiness, and Mobility.—Daniel B. Denning, room 2E460, 692–1292.
Military Executive, Army Reserve Forces Policy Committee.—COL Dianna Cleven, 695–7785.

ASSISTANT CHIEF OF STAFF FOR INSTALLATION MANAGEMENT

Pentagon, Room 3E474, 20310–0600, phone (703) 693–3233, fax 693–3507

Assistant Chief of Staff.—LTG Robert Wilson.

Deputy Assistant.—Dr. Craig College.

ADMINISTRATIVE ASSISTANT

Pentagon, Room 3E585, 20310–0105, phone (703) 695–2442, fax 697–6194

Administrative Assistant.—Joyce E. Morrow.
Deputy Administrative Assistant.—Larry Stubblefield, Taylor Building, room 13178, 602–5541.
Executive Officer.—COL Linda A. Thomas, Pentagon, room 3E585, 695–7444.
Chief, Resource Operations Center.—Gem A. Loranger, Taylor Building, room 13140, 602–7181.
Executive Director for—
US Army Information Technology Agency.—Edward C. Horton (acting), Taylor Building, room 1316, 602–2027.
US Army Resources and Programs Agency.—Larry Stubblefield, Taylor Building, room 13178, 602–5541.
US Army Services and Operations Agency.—Edward C. Horton, Taylor Building, room 13116, 602–2027.
Army Information Management Support Center.—J. Cunningham, Taylor Building, room 9088, 602–4197.
Army Multimedia and Visual Information.—Edward Jonas, Pentagon, room MG652, 697–1798.
Army Publishing.—Susan Maks, Hoffman 1, room 1010, 325–6801.
Consolidated Customer Service Center.—LTC Stephen Sobotta, 1671 Nelson Street, Ft. Detrick, MD (301) 571–2200.
Data Center Services (Pentagon).—Gerald Reed (acting), Pentagon, room BF849D, 692–0880.
Defense Telecommunications Services (Washington).—Larry Miller, Taylor Building, room 10202, 602–2699.
Equal Employment Opportunity.—Debra Muse, Taylor Building, room 8202, 604–2736.
HQDA Resource Management.—Robert Jaworski, Taylor Building, room 8122, 602–1503.
Human Resources Management.—Lorraine Phillips, Taylor Building, room 8016, 602–2220.
Information Technology Integration (Pentagon).—Paul Beardsley, 1777 N. Kent Street, room 4100, 588–8730.
Logistics (Washington).—Mary Costa, Taylor Building, room 10122, 602–7856.
Network Infrastructure Services and Operations (Pentagon).—Virginia Arreguin, Pentagon, room ME872, 614–5761.
Network Security Services (Pentagon).—David Beltz, 1777 N. Kent Street, room 8200, 588–8050.
Pentagon Chaplain.—COL William Broome, Pentagon, room 1E443, 692–9376.
Real Estate and Facilities.—Lacy Saunders, Taylor Building, room 13038, 602–6157.
Records Management & Declassification Agency.—Steve Raho, 7701 Telegraph Road, room 102, 428–6462.
Security and Safety.—David Beltz, Taylor Building, room 3056, 602–0306.
Support Services (Washington).—I. Washburn (acting), Pentagon, room BF666A, 692–4857.
Telecommunications Center (Pentagon).—George Krenik, Pentagon, room 2C654, 695–1874.
The Institute of Heraldry.—Charles Mugno, Ft. Belvior, Building 1466, room S–103, 806–4969.
Transportation.—Mary Costa, Taylor Building, room 10122, 602–7856.

ARMY RESERVE

Pentagon, Room 2B548, 20310–2400, phone (703) 697–1784

Chief.—LTG Jack C. Stultz.
Deputy Chief.—BG Richard J. Skerlock, 697–1260.
Chief of Staff.—Oscar R. Anderson.

AUDITOR GENERAL

3101 Park Center Drive, Alexandria, VA 22302, phone (703) 681–9809, fax 681–4602

Auditor General.—Patrick J. Fitzgerald.
Principal Deputy Auditor General.—Benjamin J. Piccolo, 681–9819.
Deputy Auditor General for—

Acquisition and Logistics Audits.—Joseph P. Mizzoni, 681–9583.
Forces and Financial Audits.—Anita F. Bales, 681–9585.
Policy and Operations Management.—Belinda A. Tiner, 681–9820.

AIR FORCE AUDIT AGENCY

Deputy Auditor General and Director of Operations.—Cathy Novel, room 4E168 (703) 614–5738.
Assistant Deputy Auditor General.—Michael V. Barbino, Rosslyn (703) 696–7764.
Assistant Auditor General for—
Acquisition and Logistics Audits.—Theodore J. Williams, WPAFB (937) 257–6355.
Financial and Systems Audits.—Judith Simon, MAFB (951) 655–7011.
Support and Personnel Audits.—James W. Salter, Jr., Brooks City-Base (210) 536–1999.

CHIEF INFORMATION OFFICER / G–6

Pentagon, Room 1A271, 20310–0107, phone (703) 695–4366, fax 695–3091

Chief Information Officer.—LTG Steven W. Boutelle.
Deputy Chief Information Officer.—Vernon Bettencourt, 695–6604.
Executive Officer.—COL Alan Lynn, 697–5503.
Director of:
Architecture, Operations, Network and Space.—BG Jeffrey Foley, room 1E148, 602–3842.
Goverance, Acquisition and Chief Knowledge Office.—Gary Winkler, room 7178, Taylor Building, Crystal City, VA, 602–9316.

CHIEF OF CHAPLAINS

Pentagon, Room 2A514A, 20310–2700, phone (703) 695–1133, fax 695–9834

Chief of Chaplains.—Chaplain (MG) David H. Hicks.
Deputy Chief of Chaplains.—Chaplain (BG) Douglas L. Carver, 695–1135.

CHIEF OF ENGINEERS

GAO Building, 441 G Street, NW., 20314, phone (202) 761–0001
fax 761–4463

Chief of Engineers / Commanding General for U.S. Army Corps of Engineers.—LTG Carl A. Strock.
Deputy Commander.—MG Ronald L. Johnson.
Director of Civil Works.—MG Don T. Riley, 761–0099.
Deputy Director for Civil Works.—Steve Stockton, 761–0100.
Director of Military Programs.—BG (P) Bo Temple, 761–0379.
Deputy Director of Military Programs.—Joe Tyler, 761–0382.
Chief of Staff.—COL Yvonne J. Prettyman-Beck, 761–0761.

GENERAL COUNSEL

Pentagon, Room 2E722, 20310–0104, phone (703) 697–9235, fax 697–6553

General Counsel.—Benedict S. Cohen.
Principal Deputy General Counsel.—E. Scott Castle (acting).
Executive Officer / Special Counsel.—COL John B. Hoffman.
Deputy General Counsel for—
Acquisition.—Levator Norsworthy, Jr., room 3D546, 697–5120.
Civil Works and Environment.—Craig R. Schmauder, room 3D546, 695–3024.
Ethics and Fiscal Law.—Matt Reres, room 3D546, 695–5105.
Operations and Personnel.—Stephanie Barna (acting), room 3D456, 695–0562.

INSPECTOR GENERAL

Pentagon, Room 5D561, 20310–1700, phone (703) 695–1500, fax 614–5628

Inspector General.—MG Stanley E. Green.

Executive Officer.—COL Robert C. Faille, Jr., 695–1502.
Chief Integration Office.—MG Conrad Ponder, Taylor Building, room 7154, Crystal City, VA, 602–8002.
Commander, NETCOM.—BG Carroll Pollett, Ft. Huachuca, AZ (502) 538–6161.

INTELLIGENCE / G–2

Pentagon, Room 2E408, 20310–1000, phone (703) 695–3033

Deputy Chief of Staff.—LTG John Kimmons.
Executive Officer.—COL Gerry Turnbow.
Assistant Deputy Chiefs: Termace M. Ford, 697–4644; MG George Fay, 695–3033; BG Margrit Farmer, 695–3329.
Director, Office of:
Counterintelligence / HUMINT.—Thomas Gandy, 695–2374.
Foreign Liaison.—COL William Cosby, 692–1467.
Foreign Intelligence.—Bill Speer, 695–2186.
Information Management.—COL Lynn Schnurr, 693–7019.
Plans and Operations.—COL Scott St. Cyr, 695–1623.
Resource Integration.—Patricia Zitz, 695–1233.

JUDGE ADVOCATE GENERAL

Pentagon, Room 2B514, 20310–2200, phone (703) 697–5151, fax 693–0600

Judge Advocate General.—MG Scott C. Black.
Assistant Judge Advocate General.—MG Daniel V. Wright, 693–5112.
Special Assistant to the Judge Advocate General.—COL (P) Marc L. Warren, Rosslyn, VA, 588–6734.
Commander, United States Army Legal Services Agency.—BG Malinda E. Dunn, Ballston, VA, 588–6269.
Commander / Commandant, USA The Judge Advocate General's Legal Center and School.—BG Clyde J. Tate II, Charlottesville, VA (434) 971–3301.

LEGISLATIVE LIAISON

Pentagon, Room 1E416, 20310–1600, phone (703) 697–6767, fax 614–7599

Chief.—MG Galen B. Jackman.
Deputy Chief.—BG Bernard S. Champoux, 695–1235.
Principal Deputy.—Joseph Guzowski, 695–1374.
Special Assistant for Legislative Affairs for Intelligence.—Robert J. Winchester, 695–3918.
Executive Officer.—COL Charles A. Stafford, room 1E428, 695–3524.
Chief of:
Congressional Activities Division.—COL Steve McHugh, room 1D437, 697–3206.
Congressional Inquiry.—Janet Fagan, room 1E423, 697–8381.
House Liaison Division.—COL Raymond Bingham, room B325, Rayburn House Office Building, Washington DC (202) 225–6818.
Investigations and Legislative Division.—COL Mark Rivest, room 1E433, 697–0276.
Programs Division.—COL Robert Ferrell, room 1E385, 693–8766.
Senate Liaison Division.—COL Michael Barbero, room SR183, Senate Russell Office Building, Washington DC (202) 224–2881.
Support Operations Division.—Debra Billington, room 1E423, 693–9910.

LIAISON OFFICES

Pentagon, Room 2A474, 20310–2200

U.S. Army, Europe (USAREUR): Dr. Bryan T. van Sweringen; David Dull; SFC Ralf S. Vogt (703) 692–6886, fax 614–9714.
U.S. Army Accessions Command.—Howard A. Koretz (703) 603–4034, fax 603–4036.
U.S. Army Forces Command (FORSCOM) / US Army Training and Doctrine Command (TRADOC): LTC Wayne G. Cherry, Jr.; SSgt Gary Stone; Laverne De Sett; Celeste Johnson (703) 697–2552 / 2588, fax 697–5725.
U.S. Army, Pacific (USARPAC).—Robert Ralston (703) 693–4032, fax 693–4036.
U.S. Forces Korea (USFK): Ronald R. Rollison; Cathy Abell; Harrison J. Parker III; Sharon L. Smith (703) 693–4038, fax 695–4576.

LOGISTICS / G–4

Pentagon, Room 1E394, 20310–0500, phone (703) 695–4102, fax 614–6702

Deputy Chief of Staff.—LTG Ann E. Dunwoody.
Assistant Deputy Chief of Staff.—MG Vincent E. Boles.
Director of:
Force Projection.—BG Patricia L. Kelly, room 1E384.
Logistics Integration Agency.—Mark O'Konski.
Operations, and Readiness.—MG Timothy P. McHale, room 1E367.
Resource Integration.—Robert Turzak.
Strategy and Integration.—COL (P) Xavier P. Lobeto.

NATIONAL GUARD BUREAU

1411 Jefferson Davis Highway, Arlington, VA 22202–3231, phone (703) 614–3087

Chief.—LTG H. Steven Blum.
Director, Army National Guard.—LTG Clyde A. Vaughn, 607–7000.
Director, Joint Staff.—MG Terry Scherling, 607–2204.

OPERATIONS AND PLANS / G–3/5/7

Pentagon, Room 2E366, 20310–0400, phone (703) 695–2904

Deputy Chief of Staff.—LTG James J. Lovelace, Jr.
Assistant Deputy Chiefs of Staff: Mark R. Lewis, 692–7883; MG George A. Higgins, 697–5180.

PERSONNEL / G–1

Pentagon, Room 2E446, 20310–0300, phone (703) 697–8060

Deputy Chief of Staff.—LTG Michael D. Rochelle.
Assistant Deputy Chief of Staff.—Karl Schneider, 692–1585.
Assistant Deputy Chief of Staff for Mobilization and Reserve Affairs.—MG John Hawkins, room 1D449, 695–5868.
Director, Office of:
Army Research Institute.—Dr. Michelle Sams, 602–7766.
Civilian Personnel.—Melinda Darby, room 2C453, 695–5701.
Human Resources.—COL Dennis Dingle, room 2C453, 693–1850.
MANPRINT.—Dr. Michael Drillings, room 2C485, 695–6761.
Military Personnel Management.—BG Gina Farrisee, room 1D429, 695–5871.
Plans, Resources and Operations.—Roy Wallace, room 2B453, 697–5263.

PUBLIC AFFAIRS

Pentagon, Room 1E484, 20310–1500, phone (703) 695–5135, fax 693–8362

Chief.—BG Tony Cucolo.
Deputy Chief.—BG Mari K. Eder.
Principal Deputy Chief.—Stephanie Hoehne.
Commander, Soldiers Media Center.—COL Richard Breen.
Executive Officer.—COL Henry Huntley.
Chief of:
Community Relations and Outreach Division.—COL Garrie Dornan.
Media Relations Division.—COL Dan Baggio.
Plans.—COL Hiram Bell.
Resource Management Division.—Tina Kitts.

SMALL BUSINESS PROGRAMS

Pentagon, Room 3B514, 20310–0106, phone (703) 697–2868, fax 693–3898

Director.—Tracey L. Pinson.
Deputy Director.—Paul L. Gardner.

SURGEON GENERAL

Skyline Place 6, Suite 672, 5109 Leesburg Pike, Falls Church, VA 22041–3258

phone (703) 681–3000, fax 681–3167

Surgeon General.—LTG Kevin C. Kiley.
Deputy Surgeon General.—MG Gale S. Pollock, 681–3002.

MAJOR ARMY COMMANDS

U.S. ARMY FORCES COMMAND (FORSCOM)

Fort McPerson, GA 30330–1062, phone (404) 464–5054

Commanding General.—GEN Dan K. McNeill.
Executive Officer.—COL Jeff Bailey.
Deputy Commanding General for—
Army National Guard.—MG William Wofford, 464–7596.
Chief of Staff.—LTG Joseph Peterson, 464–5367.
US Army Reserve.—LTG Jack C. Stultz, Jr., 464–8002.
Command Sergeant Major.—CSM Dennis M. Carey, 464–5055.
Secretary of the General Staff.—COL Scott Hampton, 464–6051.
Operations Center.—COL Frank Barth (800) 974–8480.
Liaison Office (Washington, DC).—LTC Wayne Cherry (703) 697–2591.

U.S. ARMY MATERIEL COMMAND (AMC)

9301 Chapek Road, Fort Belvoir, VA 22060–5527

phone (703) 806–9625

Commanding General.—GEN Benjamin Griffin.
Executive Officer.—COL Paul Wentz.
Deputy Executive to the Commanding General.—Kathryn Condon, 806–9637.
Executive Officer.—Josh Davis, 806–9637.
Deputy Commanding General/Chief of Staff.—LTG William Mortensen, 806–9705.
Executive Officer.—COL Tom Richardson, 806–9701.
Deputy Chief of Staff.—COL Tracy Ellis, 806–9709.
Command Sergeant Major.—CSM Daniel Elder, 806–8257.
Secretary of the General Staff.—LTC Gray Cockerham, 806–8116.

U.S. ARMY TRAINING AND DOCTRINE COMMAND (TRADOC)

Fort Monroe, VA 23651–5000

Commanding General.—GEN William S. Wallace (757) 788–3514.
Executive Officer.—COL Peter Bayer, 788–2922.
Deputy Commanding General/Chief of Staff.—LTG Thomas F. Metz, 788–3126.
Executive Officer.—LTC Catherine Yarberry, 788–3112.
Assistant Chief of Staff.—COL Anthony Crutchfield, 788–3112.
CG USAAC/DCG (IMT).—LTG R.L. Van Antwerp, 788–2207.
Executive Officer.—LTC (P) Robert E. Choppa, 788–4415.
Command Sergeant Major.—CSM John D. Sparks, 788–4133.
Secretary of the General Staff.—Fred Batchelor, 788–3563.
Operations Center.—COL Damian P. Carr, 788–2256.
Liaison Office (Washington, DC).—LTC Wayne Cherry, 697–2588.

DEPARTMENT OF THE NAVY

Pentagon 20350–1000, phone (703) 695–3131

OFFICE OF THE SECRETARY OF THE NAVY

Pentagon, Room 4E686, phone (703) 695–3131

Secretary of the Navy.—Donald C. Winter.
Confidential Assistant.—Laura McAleer.
Executive Assistant and Marine Aide.—COL Doug Wadsworth, USMC.
Special Assistants: Jon Ferko, Michael Griffes.
Administrative Aide.—LCDR Tom Williams, 695–5410.
Personal Aide.—LCDR Keith Williams.
Special Assistant for Public Affairs.—CAPT Beci Brenton, 697–7491.
Senior Military Assistant.—RDML (Sel.) Michelle Howard.

OFFICE OF THE UNDER SECRETARY OF THE NAVY

Pentagon, Room 4E576, phone (703) 695–3141

Executive Assistant and Naval Aide.—CAPT K. Sweeney, USN.
Military Assistant and Marine Aide.—COL G. Hoppe, USMC.
Administrative Assistants: GYSGT L. Dunlap, USMC; YN2 W. Hall, USN.
Confidential Assistant.—L. Isenhour, 697–5799.
Assistant for Administration.—J. La Raia, room 4E610, 697–0047.
Facilities and Support Services Division.—W. O'Donnell, room 5A532, 695–2843.
Director of:
Financial Management Division.—D. Nugent, AA/2507, 693–0321.
OPTI.—G. Wyckoff, room AA/4101, 695–6191.
SADBU.—Paulette Widmann (acting) (202) 685–6485.
SHHRO and Special Programs Division.—W. Mann, room AA/2510, 693–0888.
EEO Manager.—D. McCormick, room AA/2052, 693–0202.

GENERAL COUNSEL

Pentagon, Room 4E635
Washington Navy Yard, Building 36, 720 Kennon Street, SE., 20374
phone (703) 614–1994

General Counsel.—Hon. Frank R. Jimenez.
Principal Deputy General Counsel.—W. Molzahn, 614–8733.
Executive Assistant and Special Counsel.—CAPT B. Wilson, JAGC, USN.
Associate General Counsel for—
Litigation.—T. Ledvina, building 36, 685–6989.
Management.—S. Krasik, room 4D644, 614–5066.
Assistant General Counsel for—
Ethics.—D. Grimord, room NC–1, 604–8211.
Manpower and Reserve Affairs.—R. Cali, room 4D730, 614–5066.
Research, Development and Acquisition.—S. Raps, room 5C546, 614–6985.
Military Assistant.—LTC J. Duncan, USMC, 692–6164.
Administrative Assistant.—LT C. Schuenemann, USNR, room 4D644, 614–4472.

INSPECTOR GENERAL

Washington Navy Yard, 1254 9th Street, SE., Building 172, 20374, phone (202) 433–2000

Inspector General.—VADM Ronald Route.
Deputy Naval Inspector General.—Jill Vines-Loftus.

OFFICE OF INFORMATION

Pentagon, Room 4B463, phone (703) 697–7391

Chief.—RDML Greg Smith.

Deputy Chief.—CAPT Tom Van Leunen.
Executive Assistant.—CDR Cate Mueller.
Assistant Chief for—
Administration and Resource Management.—William Mason, 692–4747.
Media Operations.—CDR Dave Werner, 697–5342.
Naval Media Center.—CAPT Gordon Hume (202) 433–5764.
Requirements and Policy.—CAPT Bruce Cole, 692–4730.
Strategic Plans.—CDR Ron Hill, 692–4728.

JUDGE ADVOCATE GENERAL

Pentagon, Room 5D834

Washington Navy Yard, 1322 Patterson Avenue, Suite 3000, 20374–5066
phone (703) 614–7420, fax (703) 614–4610

Judge Advocate General.—RADM Bruce E. MacDonald.
Executive Assistant.—CAPT Michael I. Quinn.
Deputy Judge Advocate General.—RADM James W. Houck.
Executive Assistant to the Deputy Judge Advocate General.—CDR Lisa O. Sullivan.
Assistant Judge Advocate General for Civil Law.—CAPT Hal H. Dronberger, WNY, Building 33 (202) 685–5198, fax 685–5461.
Deputy Assistant Judge Advocate General for—
Administrative Law.—CDR Richard K. Giroux (703) 604–8200.
Admiralty.—CDR Gregg Cervi (202) 685–5075.
Claims, Investigations and Tort Litigation.—Patricia A. Leonard (202) 685–5996, fax 685–5484.
General Litigation.—CAPT Lawson Almand (202) 685–5396, fax 685–5472.
International and Operational Law.—CAPT Patrick J. Neher (703) 697–9161.
Legal Assistance.—CDR Jeffrey Fischer (202) 685–5393, fax 685–5486.
National Security Litigation and Intelligence Law.—CDR Peter D. Schmid (202) 685–5464, fax 685–5467.
Assistant Judge Advocate General for Military Justice.—COL Edward M. McCue, USMC, Building 111, 1st Floor, Washington Navy Yard, 20374–1111 (202) 685–7050, fax 685–7084.
Deputy Assistant Judge Advocate General for Criminal Law.—CDR Christian L. Reismeir, USMC (202) 685–7060, fax 685–7687.
Assistant Judge Advocate General for Operations and Management.—CAPT Henry R. Molinengo (202) 685–5190, fax 685–5461.
Deputy Assistant Judge Advocate General for—
Management and Plans.—CAPT Thomas L. Copenhawer (202) 685–5218, fax 685–5479.
Military Personnel.—CAPT Richard D. Zeigler (202) 685–7254, fax 685–5489.
Reserve and Retired Personnel Programs.—LCDR Ryan C. Torgrimson (202) 685–5216, fax 685–5489.
Special Assistants to the Judge Advocate General—
Command Master Chief.—LNCM Stephen S. Distefano (202) 685–5194, fax 685–5461.
Comptroller.—Dennis J. Oppman (202) 685–5274, fax 685–5455.
Inspector General.—Joseph Scranton (202) 685–5192, fax 685–5461.

LEGISLATIVE AFFAIRS

Room 4C549, phone (703) 697–7146, fax 697–1009

Chief.—RDML Mark Ferguson.
Deputy Chief.—CAPT Jim Colgary.
Executive Assistant.—Sam Hancock.
Congressional Information and Public Affairs.—CDR Chris Dour, 695–5764.
Congressional Operations.—Dee Wingfield, 693–5764.
Director for—
House Liaison.—CAPT Earl Gay, room B324 (202) 225–7808.
Assistant House Liaison.—CDR Jerry Miranda (202) 225–3075.
Legislation.—CAPT Russ Shaffer, 695–2776.
Naval Programs.—CAPT John Zangardi, 693–2919.
Senate Liaison.—CAPT Gene Moran (202) 685–6006.
Assistant Senate Liaison.—CDR Steve Vahsen (202) 685–6007.

ASSISTANT SECRETARY FOR FINANCIAL MANAGEMENT AND COMPTROLLER

Pentagon, Room 4E569, phone (703) 697–2325

Executive Assistant and Naval Aide.—CAPT B. Nutt.
Military Assistant and Marine Aide.—MAJ G. Brown, USMC.
Director, Office of:
Budget.—RADM S. Bozin, room 4E348, 697–7105.
Financial Operations.—M. Easton, WNY, 685–6701.

ASSISTANT SECRETARY FOR INSTALLATIONS AND ENVIRONMENT

Pentagon, Room 4E523, phone (703) 693–4530

Assistant Secretary.—Hon. B.J. Penn.
Executive Assistant and Naval Aide.—CAPT David Steindl.
Confidential Assistant.—John G. Athon.
Military Aide.—LCDR Matt Motsko.
Assistant General Counsel.—Ronald Borro, 614–1090.
Deputy of:
Environment.—D. Schregardus, 614–5080.
Infrastructure Analysis.—Dennis Biccick, Crystal City, 602–6633.
Installations and Facilities.—Wayne Arny, room 4D573, 693–4527.
Safety.—Tom Rollow, 614–5179.

ASSISTANT SECRETARY FOR MANPOWER AND RESERVE AFFAIRS

Pentagon, Room 4E615, phone (703) 697–2180

Assistant Secretary.—Hon. William A. Navas, Jr.
Executive Assistant and Naval Aide.—CAPT Cindy Covell, USN, 695–4537.
Military Assistant and Marine Aide.—LCOL Jay Huston, USMC, 697–0975.
Special Assistant for Military Law.—CDR Robert O'Neill, USN, room 4C636, 695–4367.
Administrative Assistant.—CAPT Latham Fell, USMC, room 4C640, 614–8288.
Assistant General Counsel.—R. Cali, room 4C648, 692–6162.
Director of Personnel Readiness Community Support.—B. Tate, room 4C637, 614–3553.
Deputy Assistant Secretary of:
Civilian Human Resources.—P. Adams, room 4D648, 695–2633.
Manpower Analysis and Assessment.—R. Beland, room 4D648, 695–4350.
Military Manpower Personnel.—L. Davis, room 4C640, 693–1213.
Reserve Affairs.—H. Barnum, room 4D648, 614–1327.
Total Force Transformation.—A. Blair, room 4E609, 693–7700.
Staff Directors: C. Donovan, room 4C640, 614–3053; CDR T. Berry, USN, room 4D643, 571–9095; CAPT Layne Smith, USN, room 4D643, 695–5302; CAPT K. Vigneron, USN, room 4C640, 693–0592; M. Lepore, room 4D643, 571–9032; CAPT M. Thomas, USN, room 4E609, 614–8480.

SECRETARY OF THE NAVY COUNCIL OF REVIEW BOARDS

Washington Navy Yard, 720 Kennon Street, SE., Room 309, 20374–5023
phone (202) 685–6407, fax 685–6610

Director.—COL Marsha L. Culver, USMC.
Counsel.—Roger R. Claussen.
Special Correspondence Officer.—Frank A. Walker, Jr.
Physical Evaluation Board.—Paul D. Williamson.
Naval Clemency and Parole Board.—LTCOL Paul D'Antonio, USMC.
Naval Discharge Review Board.—COL Jacob Graham, USMC, 685–6408.

BOARD FOR DECORATIONS AND MEDALS

Washington Navy Yard, 720 Kennon Street, SE., Building 36, Room 135, 20374
phone (202) 685–6378

Senior Member.—VADM Ronald Route.

Secretary to the Board.—LCDR Lesley Priest.

ASSISTANT SECRETARY FOR RESEARCH, DEVELOPMENT AND ACQUISITION

Pentagon, Room 4E741, phone (703) 695–6315

Assistant Secretary.—Hon. Delores Etter, room 4E759.
Executive Assistant and Naval Aide.—CAPT David T. Norris.
Military Assistant and Marine Aide.—COL Frank L. Kelley.
Deputy Assistant Secretary of the Navy for—
Acquisition and Career Management.—Carolyn Willis, room BF992, 614–0522.
Acquisition Management.—RDML Martin Brown, room BF999, 614–9445.
Air Programs.—B. Balderson, room 5B546, 614–7794.
C4I/Space Program.—Dr. Gary A. Federici, room BF963, 914–6619.
Integrated Warfare Programs.—Anne Sandel, room 5B546, 614–8806.
International Programs.—RDML Jeff Wieringe, Crystal City, VA, 601–9800.
Littoral and Mine Warfare Programs.—Roger Smith, room 5B546, 614–4794.
Logistics.—Nick Kunesh, room 5B546, 697–1799.
Management and Budget.—John Thackrah, room 5C547, 697–4938.
Manpower and Administration.—Tom Sipe, 614–5516.
RDT&E.—Dr. M. McGrath, room 5B546, 695–2204.
Ship Programs.—Allison Stiller, room 5B546, 697–1710.

CHIEF INFORMATION OFFICER

Chief Information Officer.—R. Carey, room PT1/2100, 602–1800.

CHIEF OF NAVAL OPERATIONS

Pentagon, Room 4E660, phone (703) 695–0532, fax 693–9408

Chief.—ADM M.G. Mullen.
Vice Chief.—ADM R.F. Willard.
Director, Naval Nuclear Propulsion Program.—ADM K.H. Donald.
Naval Inspector General.—VADM R.A. Route.
Legal Services.—RADM Bruce McDonald.
Legislative Support.—RADL I. Houck.
Material Inspections and Surveys.—RADM C.A. Kemp.
Naval Investigative Matters and Security.—D. Brant.
Public Affairs Support.—RAML Smith.
Safety Matters.—RADM R.E. Brooks.
Deputy Chief of Naval Operations for Logistics.—VADM Loose.
Manpower.—VADM John C. Haruft.
Plans, Policy, and Operations.—RADM J.D. Stufflebeam.
Warfare Requirements, and Assessments.—VADM Greenert.
Warfare Requirements and Programs.—VADM D.V. McGinn.
Director, Office of:
Naval Intelligence.—RADM Cothron.
Naval Medicine and Surgery.—VADM D.C. Arthur, Jr.
Naval Network Warfare.—VADM J.D. McArthur, Jr.
Naval Reserve.—VADM J.G. Cotton.
Naval Training.—VADM J.K. Moran.
Test and Evaluation and Technology Requirements.—RADM J.M. Cohen.
Chief of Chaplains.—RADM Burt, USN.
Oceanographer.—RADM S.J. Tomaszeski.

BUREAU OF MEDICINE AND SURGERY

2300 E Street, NW., 20372, phone (202) 762–3701
fax 762–3750

Chief.—VADM D.C. Arthur, MC.

MILITARY SEALIFT COMMAND

Washington Navy Yard, Building No. 210, 9th and M Streets, SE., 20398, phone (202) 685–5001, fax 685–5020

Commander.—RADM Robert Rilley.

NATIONAL NAVAL MEDICAL CENTER

Bethesda, MD 20889, phone (301) 295–5800/5802, fax 295–5336.

Commander.—RADM Adam M. Robinson, Jr.

NAVAL AIR SYSTEMS COMMAND

47123 Buse Road, Building 2272, Patuxent River, MD 20670 phone (301) 757–1487

Commander.—VADM David Venlet.

NAVAL CRIMINAL INVESTIGATIVE SERVICE COMMAND

716 Sicard Street SE., Suite 2000, 20388, phone (202) 433–8800, fax 433–9619

Director.—Thomas A. Bethro.

NAVAL DISTRICT OF WASHINGTON

1343 Dahlgren Avenue, SE., 20374–5001, phone (202) 433–2777, fax 433–2207

Commandant.—RADM Terence McKnight.
Deputy Commandant.—CAPT Thomas McGuire.

NAVAL FACILITIES ENGINEERING COMMAND

Washington Navy Yard, 1322 Patterson Avenue, SE., Suite 1000, 20374 phone (202) 685–9003, fax 685–1463

Commander.—RADM Wayne G. Shear.

OFFICE OF NAVAL INTELLIGENCE

4251 Suitland Road, 20395, phone (301) 669–3001, fax 669–3099

Commander.—CAPT Alexander Butterfield.

NAVAL SEA SYSTEMS COMMAND

Washington Navy Yard, 1333 Isaac Hull Avenue, SE., Stop 1010, 20376–1010, phone (202) 781–0100

Commander.—VADM Phillip M. Balisle.

NAVAL SUPPLY SYSTEMS COMMAND

Mechanicsburg, PA, phone (717) 605–3433

Commander.—RADM D.H. Stone.

SPACE AND NAVAL WARFARE SYSTEMS COMMAND

14675 Lee Road, Chantilly, VA 20151, phone (703) 808–3000
fax 808–2779

Commander.—RADM Victor C. See, Jr.

U.S. NAVAL ACADEMY

Annapolis, MD 21402, phone (410) 293–1000

Superintendent.—RADM Rodney P. Rempt, 293–1500.
Commandant of Midshipmen.—CAPT Margaret Kline, 293–7005.

U.S. MARINE CORPS HEADQUARTERS

Pentagon, Room 4E586, phone (703) 614–2500

Commandant.—GEN J.T. Conway.
Assistant Commandant.—GEN R. Magnus.
Aide-de-Camp.—LTC T.S. Clark.
Chaplain.—RADM R.F. Burt.
Dental Officer.—COL A. Williams, US Army.
Fiscal Director of the Marine Corps.—W.J. Wallhenhorst.
Inspector General of the Marine Corps.—MG David Biu.
Judge Advocate.—BG J.C. Walker.
Legislative Assistant.—BG J.F. Kelly.
Medical Officer.—RADM (LH) R.D. Hufstader.
Military Secretary.—COL F.T. McKenzie.
Sergeant Major of the Marine Corps.—SMAJ J. Estrada.
Deputy Chief of Staff for—
Aviation.—LTG M.A. Hough.
Installations and Logistics.—LTG R.L. Kelly.
Manpower and Reserve Affairs.—LTG H.P. Osman.
Plans, Policies, and Operations.—LTG J.C. Huly.
Public Affairs.—BG M.A. Krusa-Dossin.
Programs and Resources.—LTG R. Mangus (703) 614–3435.
Director of:
Intelligence.—BG M.E. Ennis.
Marine Corps History and Museums.—COL (Ret) J.W. Ripley.

MARINE BARRACKS

Eighth and I Streets, SE., 20390, phone (202) 433–4094

Commanding Officer.—COL T.M. Lockard.

TRAINING AND EDUCATION COMMAND

3300 Russell Road, Quantico, VA 22134, phone (703) 784–3730, fax 784–3724

Commanding General.—MG George J. Finn.

DEPARTMENT OF JUSTICE

Robert F. Kennedy Department of Justice Building

950 Pennsylvania Avenue, NW., 20530, phone (202) 514–2000

http://www.usdoj.gov

ALBERTO R. GONZALES, Attorney General; born in San Antonio, TX, August 4, 1955; education: Rice University, 1979; Harvard Law School, 1982; United States Air Force Academy, 1977; military service: U.S. Air Force, 1973–75; professional: partner with law firm of Vinson & Elkins L.L.P., 1982–94; taught law at University of Houston Law Center; President of the Houston Hispanic Bar Association, 1990–91; Texas General Counsel, 1994–97; Texas Secretary of State, 1997–99; Justice of the Texas Supreme Court, 1999–2001; Counsel to President George W. Bush, 2001–05; married: Rebecca Turner; children: Jared, Graham and Gabriel; nominated by George W. Bush to become the Attorney General of the United States on November 10, 2004, and was confirmed by the U.S. Senate on February 3, 2005.

OFFICE OF THE ATTORNEY GENERAL

RFK Main Justice Building, Room 5111, phone (202) 514–2001

Attorney General.—Alberto R. Gonzales.

Chief of Staff.—D. Kyle Sampson, room 5115, 514–3892.

Deputy Chief of Staff and Counselor.—Courtney Simmons Elwood, room 5110, 514–2267.

Counselor to the Attorney General.—Matthew Friedrich, room 5116, 616–2372.

Director of Scheduling.—Andrew A. Beach, room 5131, 514–4195.

Director of Advance.—Theresa Pagliocca, room 5214, 514–9798.

White House Liaison.—Monica Goodling, room 5119A, 353–4435.

Deputy White House Liaison.—Angela Williamson, room 5121, 514–2927.

Special Assistant to the Attorney General.—Raquel Cabral Sours, room 5111, 514–2001.

OFFICE OF THE DEPUTY ATTORNEY GENERAL

RFK Main Justice Building, Room 4111, phone (202) 514–2101

Deputy Attorney General.—Paul J. McNulty.

Principal Associate Deputy Attorney General.—William E. Moschella, room 4206, 514–2105.

Counselor/Chief of Staff.—Michael J. Elston, room 4210, 307–2090.

Senior Advisor to the Deputy Attorney General.—Frank Shults, room 4119, 305–7848.

Associate Deputy Attorneys General: David Margolis, room 4113, 514–4945; Thomas Monheim, room 4115, 514–8086; Stuart Nash, room 4212, 514–8699; Lee Liberman Otis, room 4116, 305–3481; Ronald J. Tenpas, room 4216, 514–3286.

Senior Counsels to the Deputy Attorney General: Mark D. Epley, room 4121, 305–0091; Mark Grider, room 4213, 514–8500; James A. McAtamney, room 4311, 514–6907; Joan Meyer, room 4214, 307–2510; Michael Purpura, room 4220, 353–1957; Mythili Raman, room 4315, 305–9886; Robyn Thiemann, room 4215, 514–5705.

Counsels to the Deputy Attorney General: Stephen M. Campbell, room 4222, 305–8657; Daniel Fridman, room 4114, 514–5650; Michael Scudder, room 4317, 514–9340.

Chief Privacy/Civil Liberties Officer.—Jane C. Horvath, room 4218, 514–0049.

Deputy Chief Privacy/Civil Liberties Officer/Counsel to the DAG.—Michael G. Adams, room 4129, 514–6753.

Director, Faith Based and Community Initiatives Task Force.—Steven T. McFarland, room 4413, 514–7473.

Special Assistant to the Deputy Attorney General.—Luis Caballero, room 4112, 514–0438.

Confidential Assistant to the Deputy Attorney General.—Linda E. Long, room 4111, 514–1904.

OFFICE OF THE ASSOCIATE ATTORNEY GENERAL

RFK Main Justice Building, Room 5706, phone (202) 514–9500

Associate Attorney General.—William W. ''Bill'' Mercer (acting).

Principal Deputy Associate Attorney General.—Gregory Katsas.

Deputy Associate Attorneys General: John Battaglia, room 5724, 305–1777; John O'Quinn, room 5722, 514–2331.

Counsel to the Associate Attorney General.—Esther Slater McDonald, room 5730, 353–2811.

Confidential Assistant.—Currie Gunn, room 5708, 305–2636.

OFFICE OF THE SOLICITOR GENERAL

RFK Main Justice Building, Room 5143, phone (202) 514–2201
http://www.usdoj.gov/osg

Solicitor General.—Paul D. Clement.

Principal Deputy Solicitor General.—Gregory G. Garre, room 5141, 514–2206.

Deputy Solicitors General: Edwin S. Kneedler, room 5139, 514–3261; Michael R. Dreeben, room 5621, 514–4285; Thomas G. Hungar, room 5135, 514–2211.

Executive Officer.—James F. Bellot, room 5142, 514–3957.

Executive Assistant to the Solicitor General.—Janet Potter, 514–2201.

Supervisory Case Management Specialist.—Emily C. Spadoni, room 5614, 514–2217.

Chief, Research and Publications Section.—G. Shirley Anderson, room 6636, 514–2080.

ANTITRUST DIVISION

RFK Main Justice Building, 950 Pennsylvania Avenue, NW., 20530

City Center Building, 1401 H Street, NW., 20530 (CCB)

Bicentennial Building, 600 E Street, NW., 20530 (BICN)

Liberty Place Building, 325 Seventh Street, NW., 20530 (LPB)

Patrick Henry Building, 601 D Street, NW., 20530 (PHB)

Assistant Attorney General.—Thomas O. Barnett, room 3109 (202) 514–2401.

Deputy Assistant Attorneys General: Dennis Carlton, room 3117, 514–0731; Scott M. Hammond, room 3214, 514–3543; Gerald Masoudi, room 3212, 305–4517; J. Bruce McDonald, room 3210, 514–1157; David Meyer, room 3121, 514–2408.

Director of:

Criminal Enforcement.—Marc Siegel, room 3217, 514–3543.

Economics Enforcement.—Kenneth Heyer, room 3112, 514–6995.

Operations.—Robert J. Kramer, room 3118, 514–3544.

Freedom of Information Act Officer.—SueAnn Slates (LPB), room 200, 514–2692.

Executive Officer.—Thomas D. King (PHB), room 10150, 514–4005.

Section Chiefs:

Appellate.—Catherine G. O'Sullivan (PHB), room 3222, 514–2413.

Competition Policy.—Robert Majure (acting), (BICN), room 10900, 307–6341.

Economic Litigation.—Norman Familant (BICN), room 10800, 307–6323.

Economic Regulatory.—Daniel O'Brien (BICN), room 10100, 307–6591.

Foreign Commerce.—Edward T. Hand, room 3623, 514–2464.

Legal Policy.—Robert A. Potter, room 3236, 514–2512.

Litigation I.—Mark J. Botti (CCB), room 4000, 307–0827.

Litigation II.—Maribeth Petrizzi (CCB), room 3000, 307–0924.

Litigation III.—John R. Read (LPB), room 300, 616–5935.

National Criminal Enforcement.—Lisa M. Phelan (CCB), room 3700, 307–6694.

Networks and Technology.—James Tierney (BICN), room 9300, 514–5634.

Telecommunications and Media.—Nancy M. Goodman (CCB), room 8000, 514–5621.

Transportation, Energy, and Agriculture.—Donna Kooperstein (LPB), room 500, 307–6351.

FIELD OFFICES

California: Phillip H. Warren, 450 Golden Gate Avenue, Room 10–0101, Box 36046, San Francisco, CA 94102 (415) 436–6660.

Georgia: Nezida S. Davis, Richard B. Russell Building, 75 Spring Street, SW., Suite 1176, Atlanta, GA 30303 (404) 331–7100.

Illinois: Marvin N. Price, Jr., Rookery Building, 209 South LaSalle Street, Suite 600, Chicago, IL 60604 (312) 353–7530.

New York: Ralph T. Giordano, 26 Federal Plaza, Room 3630, New York, NY 10278 (212) 264–0391.

Ohio: Scott M. Watson, Plaza 9 Building, 55 Erieview Plaza, Suite 700, Cleveland, OH 44114 (216) 522–4070.

Pennsylvania: Robert E. Connolly, Curtis Center, One Independence Square West, 7th and Walnut Streets, Suite 650, Philadelphia, PA 19106 (215) 597–7405.

Texas: Duncan S. Currie, Thanksgiving Tower, 1601 Elm Street, Suite 4950, Dallas, TX 75201 (214) 880–9401.

CIVIL DIVISION

RFK Main Justice Building, 950 Pennsylvania Avenue, NW., 20530

20 Massachusetts Avenue, NW., 20530 (20MASS)

1100 L Street, NW., 20530 (L ST)

National Place Building, 1331 Pennsylvania Avenue, NW., 20530 (NATP)

1425 New York Avenue, NW., 20530 (NYAV)

Patrick Henry Building, 601 D Street, NW., 20530 (PHB)

Assistant Attorney General.—Peter D. Keisler, room 3141 (202) 514–3301.

Principal Deputy Assistant Attorney General.—Jeffrey Bucholtz, room 3605, 353–2793.

APPELLATE STAFF

Deputy Assistant Attorney General.—Jonathan Cohn, room 3131, 514–1258.

Director.—Robert E. Kopp, room 7519, 514–3311.

Deputy Director.—William Kanter, room 7517, 514–4575.

COMMERCIAL LITIGATION BRANCH

Deputy Assistant Attorney General.—Stuart E. Schiffer, room 3607, 514–3306.

Directors: David M. Cohen (L ST), room 12124, 514–7300; John N. Fargo (L ST), room 11116, 514–7223; Michael F. Hertz (PHB), room 9902, 514–7179; J. Christopher Kohn (L ST), room 10036, 514–7450.

Office of Foreign Litigation.—Robert Hollis (L ST), room 11006, 514–7455.

Deputy Directors: Joyce R. Branda (PHB), room 9904, 307–0231; Jeanne Davidson (L ST), room 12132, 307–0290.

Legal Officer.—Donna C. Maizel, Esq., U.S. Department of Justice, Civil Division European Office, The American Embassy, London, England, PSC 801, Box 42, FPO AE, 09498–4042, 9+011–44–20–7894–0840.

Attorney-in-Charge.—Barbara Williams, Suite 359, 26 Federal Plaza, New York, NY 10278 (212) 264–9240.

CONSUMER LITIGATION

Deputy Assistant Attorney General.—C. Frederick Beckner, room 3127, 514–3045.

Director.—Eugene M. Thirolf (NATP), room 950N, 307–3009.

FEDERAL PROGRAMS BRANCH

Deputy Assistant Attorney General.—Carl J. Nichols, room 3137, 514–3310.

Directors: Felix Baxter (20MASS), room 7100, 514–4651; Joseph H. Hunt, room 7348, 514–1259; Jennifer D. Rivera (20MASS), room 6100, 514–3671.

Deputy Directors: Vincent M. Garvey (20MASS), room 7346, 514–3449; Sheila M. Lieber (20MASS), room 7102, 514–3786.

IMMIGRATION LITIGATION

Deputy Assistant Attorney General.—Jonathan F. Cohn (acting), room 3131, 514–1258.

Director.—Thomas W. Hussey (NATP), room 7026S, 616–4852.

Deputy Directors: Donald E. Keener (NATP), room 7022S, 616–4878; David J. Kline (NATP), room 7006N, 616–4856; David M. McConnell (NATP), room 7260N, 616–4881.

MANAGEMENT PROGRAMS

Director.—Kenneth L. Zwick, room 3140, 514–4552.

Directors, Office of:
Administration.—Shirley Lloyd (L ST), room 9008, 307–0016.
Planning, Budget, and Evaluation.—Linda S. Liner (L ST), room 9042, 307–0034.
Management Information.—Dorothy Bahr (L ST), room 8044, 616–8026.
Litigation Support.—Clarisse Abramidis (L ST), room 9126, 616–5014.
Policy and Management Operations.—Kevin Burket (L ST), room 8128, 616–8073.

TORTS BRANCH

Deputy Assistant Attorney General.—C. Frederick Beckner, room 3127, 514–3045.
Directors: Peter Frost (NYAV), room 10122, 616–4000; Timothy P. Garren (NYAV), room 8122, 616–4171; J. Patrick Glynn (NATP), room 8028S, 616–4200; Phyllis J. Pyles (NATP), room 8098N, 616–4252;
Deputy Directors: JoAnn J. Bordeaux (NATP), room 8024S, 616–4204; Paul F. Figley (NATP), room 8096N, 616–4248.
Attorneys-in-Charge: Robert Underhill, 450 Golden Gate Avenue, 10/6610, Box 36028, San Francisco, CA 94102–3463, FTS: (415) 436–6630; [Vacant], Suite 320, 26 Federal Plaza, New York, NY 10278–0140, FTS: (212) 264–0480.

CIVIL RIGHTS DIVISION

RFK Main Justice Building, 950 Pennsylvania Avenue, NW., 20530

1425 New York Avenue, NW., 20035 (NYAV)

601 D Street, NW., 20004 (PHB)

100 Indiana Avenue, NW., 20004 (NALC)

1800 G Street, NW., 20004 (NWB)

http://www.usdoj.gov/crt

Assistant Attorney General.—Wan J. Kim, room 5643 (202) 514–2151.
Principal Deputy Assistant Attorney General.—Rena J. Comisac, room 5748, 353–9065.
Deputy Assistant Attorneys General: Asheesh Agarwal, room 5646, 353–7957; Grace C. Becker, room 5541, 353–0742; Loretta King, room 5744, 616–1278.
Counsels to the Assistant Attorney General: T. March Bell, room 5529, 616–7920; Matt Dummermuth, room 5639, 514–2337; John Gillies, room 5742, 305–1876; Cynthia McKnight, room 5535, 305–0864; Cameron Quinn, room 5539, 305–9750; Emily Smith, room 5637, 514–3845; Eric Treene, room 5531, 353–8622.
Section Chiefs:
Appellate.—David K. Flynn, room 3647, 514–2195.
Coordination and Review.—Merrily A. Friedlander (NYAV), room 6001, 307–2222.
Criminal.—Mark Kappelhoff (PHB), room 5102, 514–3204.
Disability Rights.—John L. Wodatch (NYAV), room 4055, 307–2227.
Educational Opportunities.—Jeremiah Glassman (PHB), room 4002, 514–4092.
Employment Litigation.—David Palmer (PHB), room 4040, 514–3831.
Housing and Civil Enforcement.—Steven H. Rosenbaum (NWB), room 7002, 514–4713.
Special Litigation.—Shanetta Brown Cutler (PHB), room 5114, 514–6255.
Voting.—Jojn K. Tanner (NWB), room 7254, 307–2767.
Deputy Chief, Special Counsel Office.—Katherine Baldwin, room 9030, 514–3896.
Special Counsel for Immigration Related Unfair Employment Practices.—William Sanchez, room 9032, 616–5528.

OFFICE OF COMMUNITY ORIENTED POLICING SERVICES

1110 Vermont Avenue, NW., 20530

DIRECTOR'S OFFICE

Director.—Carl Peed, 616–2888.
Special Assistant.—Laurel Matthews.
Office Manager.—Sharon Baker.
Chief of Staff.—Timothy Quinn.
Deputy Director for—
Management.—Timothy Quinn.

Operations.—Robert Phillips.

ADMINISTRATIVE DIVISION

Assistant Director.—Diane Hughes, 4th floor, 353–2500.
Human Resources Program Manager.—Debbie Brown, 4th floor, 514–8956.
Management Information Technology Specialist.—Darren Neely, 2nd floor, 307–3971.

AUDIT DIVISION

Assistant Director.—Cynthia Bowie, 4th floor, 616–3645.

COMMUNICATIONS DIVISION

Assistant Director.—David Buchanan, 11th floor, 514–9079.

GRANTS ADMINISTRATION DIVISION

Assistant Director.—Michael Dame, 8th floor, 305–7541.
Grant Regional Supervisors:

Jamie French, 7th floor, 616–9767.
Keesha Thompson, 5th floor, 616–1902.
Andy Dorr, 9th floor, 353–9736.
Linda Gist, 8th floor, 514–8091.

GRANT MONITORING DIVISION

Assistant Director.—Juliette White, 9th floor, 514–9195.
Grant Monitoring Regional Supervisors: David Neely, 514–8553; Marcia Samuels, 514–8507.

LEGAL DIVISION

General Counsel.—Lani Lee, 12th floor, 514–3750.
Deputy General Counsel.—Charlotte C. Grzebien, 616–2899.
Associate General Counsel.—Jenny Wu, 514–9424.

PROGRAM / POLICY SUPPORT AND EVALUATION

Assistant Director.—Matthew Scheider, 7th floor, 514–2301.

TECHNICAL ASSISTANCE AND TRAINING DIVISION

Assistant Director.—Beverly Alford, 7th floor, 514–2301.

COMMUNITY RELATIONS SERVICE

600 E Street, NW., Suite 6000, 20530, phone (202) 305–2935
fax 305–3009 (BICN)

Director.—Sharee M. Freeman.
Deputy Associate Director.—Diane Mitchum.
Attorney Advisor.—George Henderson, 305–2964.
Media Affairs Officer.—Daryl Borgquist, 305–2966.

REGIONAL DIRECTORS

New England.—Frances Amoroso, 408 Atlantic Avenue, Suite 222, Boston, MA 02110–1032 (617) 424–5715.

Northeast Region.—Reinaldo Rivera, 26 Federal Plaza, Suite 36–118, New York, NY 10278 (212) 264–0700.

Mid-Atlantic Region.—Vermont McKinney, Customs House, Second and Chestnut Streets, Suite 208, Philadelphia, PA 19106 (215) 597–2344.

Southeast Region.—Thomas Battles, Citizens Trust Company Bank Building, Suite 900, 75 Piedmont Avenue NE., Atlanta, GA 30303 (404) 331–6883.

Midwest Region.—Jesse Taylor, Xerox Center Building, 55 West Monroe Street, Suite 420, Chicago, IL 60603 (312) 353–4391.

Southwest Region.—Carmelita P. Freeman, 1420 West Mockingbird Lane, Suite 250, Dallas, TX 75247 (214) 655–8175.

Central Region.—Pascual Marquez, 1100 Maine Street, Suite 320, Kansas City, MO 64106 (816) 426–7433.

Rocky Mountain Region.—Philip Arreola, 1244 Speer Boulevard, Suite 650, Denver, CO 80204–3584 (303) 844–2973.

Northwest Region.—Rosa Melendez, Federal Office Building, 915 Second Avenue, Suite 1808, Seattle, WA, 98174 (206) 220–6700.

Western Region.—Ron Wakabayashi, 888 South Figueroa Street, Suite 1880, Los Angeles, CA 90017 (213) 894–2941.

CRIMINAL DIVISION

RFK Main Justice Building, 950 Pennsylvania Avenue, NW., 20530
phone (202) 514–2601

Bond Building, 1400 New York Avenue, NW., 20530 (BB)

1331 F Street, NW., 20530 (F Street)

1301 New York Avenue, NW., 20530 (1301 NY)

Patrick Henry Building, 601 D Street, NW., 20530 (PHB)

Assistant Attorney General.—Alice S. Fisher, room 2107, 514–7200.

Principal Deputy Assistant Attorney General / Chief of Staff.—Benton J. Campbell (acting), room 2206, 514–9351.

Deputy Assistant Attorneys General: John C. Keeney, room 2109, 514–2621; Sigal P. Mandelker, room 2113, 305–8319; Barry M. Sabin, room 2212, 353–3485; Bruce C. Swartz, room 2119, 514–2333; Mary Lee Warren, room 2115, 514–3729.

Deputy Chief of Staff.—Robert E. Coughlin, room 2208, 514–0169.

Counselor to the Assistant Attorney General.—Michael G. Geffroy, room 2220, 514–8275.

Senior Counsels to the Assistant Attorney General: Kevin O. Driscoll, room 2114, 307–6465; Matthew R. Lewis, room 2222, 353–1754; Benjamin S. Longlet, room 2217, 307–0510; Edward E. McNally, room 2117, 514–2601; James S. Reynolds, room 2313, 616–8664; Richard M. Rogers, room 2110, 307–0030; Christopher P. Simkins, room 2311, 305–8761.

Special Assistant to the Assistant Attorney General.—Bryan Sierra, room 2228, 515–4389.

Executive Officer.—Paul R. Johnson (acting), (BB), room 5100, 514–2641.

Section Chiefs / Office Directors:

Appellate.—Patty M. Stemler, room 1264, 514–3521.

Asset Forfeiture and Money Laundering.—Richard Weber (BB), room 10100, 514–1263.

Capital Case Unit.—Margaret P. Griffey (PHB), room 6140, 353–9779.

Child Exploitation and Obscenity.—Andrew G. Oosterbaan (BB), room 6000, 514–5780.

Computer Crime and Intellectual Property.—Martha Stansell-Gramm (1301 NY), suite 600, 514–1026.

Domestic Security.—Teresa McHenry room 7748, 353–3845.

Enforcement Operations.—Maureen Killion (1301 NY), suite 1200, 514–6809.

Fraud.—Steve Tyrell (acting), (BB), room 4100, 514–7023.

International Affairs.—Mary Ellen Warlow (1301 NY), suite 900, 514–0000.

International Criminal Investigative Training Assistance Program.—Car Trevillian IV (acting), (F Street), suite 500, 514–8881.

Narcotics and Dangerous Drugs.—Kenneth A. Blanco (BB), room 11100, 616–3027.

Overseas Prosecutorial Development, Assistance and Training.—Carl Alexandre (F Street), room 400, 514–1323.

Organized Crime and Racketeering.—Bruce Ohr (1301 NY), suite 700, 514–3594.

Policy and Legislation.—Julie E. Samuels, room 7730, 514–4193.

Public Integrity.—Edward C. Nucci (acting), (BB), room 12000, 514–2329.

Special Investigations.—Eli M. Rosenbaum (1301 NY), suite 200, 616–2492.

OFFICE OF DISPUTE RESOLUTION

RFK Main Justice Building, Room 5736, phone (202) 616–9471
http://www.usdoj.gov/odr

Director/Senior Counsel.—Linda Cinciotta, room 5734, 514–8910.
Deputy Director/Deputy Senior Counsel.—Joanna M. Jacobs, room 5738, 305–4439.
Dispute Resolution Support Specialist.—Krista van der Horst, room 5736, 616–0666.

DRUG ENFORCEMENT ADMINISTRATION

Lincoln Place-1 (East), 600 Army-Navy Drive, Arlington, VA 22202 (LP–1)

Lincoln Place-2 (West), 700 Army-Navy Drive, Arlington, VA 22202 (LP–2)

Administrator.—Karen P. Tandy, room W–12060 (202) 307–8000.
Deputy Administrator.—Michele M. Leonhart, room W–12058–F, 307–7345.
Executive Assistant.—Michael J. McManamon, room W–12058–E, 307–8770.
Equal Employment Opportunity Officer.—Oliver C. Allen, room E–11275, 307–8888.
Chief, Office of Congressional and Public Affairs.—Mary Irene Cooper, room W–12228, 307–7363.
Chief, Executive Policy and Strategic Planning.—Douglas N. Biales, room W–11100, 307–7420.
Section Chiefs:
Congressional Affairs.—Eric Akers, room W–12104, 307–7988.
Demand Reduction.—Catherine Harnett, room W–9049–E, 307–7936.
Information Services.—Donald E. Joseph, room W–12232, 307–7967.
Public Affairs.—Garrison K. Courtney (acting), 307–7979.
Chief Counsel.—Wendy H. Goggin, room W–12142–C, 307–7322.
Deputy Chief Counsel.—Robert C. Gleason, room E–12375, 307–8020.
Chief, Office of Administrative Law Judges.—Mary Ellen Bittner, room E–2129, 307–8188.

FINANCIAL MANAGEMENT DIVISION

Chief Financial Officer.—Frank M. Kalder, room W–12138, 307–7330.
Deputy Assistant Administrators for—
Acquisition Management.—Christinia K. Sisk, room W–5100, 307–7888.
Finance.—John Osterday, room E–7397, 307–7002.
Resource Management.—Charlotte A. Saunders, room E–7399, 307–4800.
Section Chiefs:
Acquisition Management.—Angel Perez, room W–5028, 307–7831.
Controls and Coordination.—John Osterday, room E–7395, 307–7080.
Evaluations and Planning.—Donna Wilson, room E–850P, 307–7463.
Financial Integrity.—Bradley J. Honkus, room E–7101, 307–7082.
Financial Operations.—Tammy Balas, room E–7165, 307–9933.
Financial Reports.—Sherri Woodle, room E–7297, 307–7040.
Financial Systems.—Daniel G. Gillette, room E–7205, 307–7031.
Organization and Staffing Management.—Donna Ciccolella, room E–7331, 307–7077.
Policy and Transportation.—Barbara J. Joplin, room W–5018, 307–7808.
Program Liaison and Analysis.—Brain Horn, room E–7225, 305–9149.
Statistical Services.—Patrick R. Gartin, room W–6300, 307–8276.

HUMAN RESOURCES DIVISION

Assistant Administrator.—Catherine J. Kasch, room W–12020, 307–4177.
Section Chiefs:
Administrative Management.—Gienda A. Rollins, room W–3058, 307–4701.
Recruitment and Placement.—Margie Aira, room W–3242, 307–4055.
Career Board Executive Secretary.—Mark Mazzei, room W–2268, 307–7349.
Chairman, Board of Professional Conduct.—Patrick T. Dunn, room E–9333, 307–8980.
Special Agent-in-Charge, Office of Training.—John R. McCarty, 2500 Investigation Parkway, DEA Academy, Quantico, VA 22135 (703) 632–5010.
Assistant Special Agents-in-Charge:
Domestic Training Section 1.—Bill Faiella (703) 632–5110.
Domestic Training Section 2.—Richard Inscore (703) 632–5310.

International Training Section.—Dominick D. Braccio, Jr. (703) 632–5330.

INSPECTIONS DIVISION

Chief Inspector.—Rogelio E. Guevara, room W–12042A, 307–7358.

Deputy Chief Inspector, Office of:

Inspections.—Gary W. Oetjen, room W–4348, 307–8200.

Professional Responsibility.—John J. Bryfonski, room W–4176, 307–8235.

Security Programs.—Edward L. Gilmore, room W–2340, 307–3465.

INTELLIGENCE DIVISION

Assistant Administrator.—Anthony P. Pacido (acting), room W–12020A, 307–3607.

Special Agent in Charge, El Paso Intelligence Center.—Arthur Doty, Building 11339, SSG Sims Street, El Paso, TX 79908–8098 (915) 760–2011.

Deputy Associate Administrator, Office of Intelligence.—Judith E. Bertini, room W–12020C, 307–3607.

Deputy Assistant Administrator, Office of:

Investigative Intelligence.—Lourdes P. Border, room W–10190, 307–8050.

Special Intelligence.—Ava A. Cooper-Davis, Merrifield, VA (703) 561–7111.

Strategic Intelligence.—Linda Crume (acting), room W–8072, 307–8243.

Section Chiefs:

Management and Production Section.—James A. Curtin, room W–7268, 307–7534.

Operational Support.—Benjamin J. Sanborn, room E–5015, 307–3645.

Regional Strategic Section.—Linda Crume, room W–8258, 307–5442.

Special Strategic Intelligence Section A.—Cheryl E. Hooper. room 8066, 307–4358.

Technical Support.—Gisele Gatjanis, room E–5121A, 307–4872.

Worldwide Investigative Intelligence.—Lourdes P. Border, room W–10280, 307–8431.

OPERATIONS DIVISION

Chief of Operations.—Michael A. Braun, room W–12050, 307–7340.

Chiefs of:

Enforcement Operations.—Thomas M. Harrigan, room W–11070, 307–7927.

Financial Operations.—Donald C. Semesky, room W–10190, 353–9574.

International Programs.—Kevin C. Whaley, room W–11024, 307–4233.

Operations Management.—Steven W. Derr, room W–11148, 307–4200.

Deputy Assistant Administrator, Office of Diversion Control.—Joseph T. Rannazzisi, room E–6295, 307–7165.

Special Agent in Charge, Aviation Division.—William C. Brown, Ft. Worth, TX (817) 837–2004.

Special Agent in Charge, Special Operations Division.—Derek S. Maltz, Chantilly, VA (703) 488–4205.

OPERATIONAL SUPPORT DIVISION

Assistant Administrator.—Richard Sanders, room W–12142, 307–4730.

Deputy Assistant Administrator, Office of:

Administration.—Mary E. Colarusso (acting), room W–9088, 307–7708.

Forensic Sciences.—Thomas J. Janovsky, room W–7342, 307–8866.

Information Systems.—Dennis R. McCrary, room E–3105, 307–7454.

Investigative Technology.—Donald Torres, Lorton, VA (703) 495–6500.

Section Chiefs:

Administrative Operations.—Emmett T. Ridley, Jr., room W–5100–A, 307–7766.

Facilities and Finance.—William A. Kopitz, room W–5244, 307–7792.

Hazardous Waste Disposal.—John Patrick, room W–7308, 307–8872.

Integration and Management.—Venita Phillips, room E–3206, 307–9892.

Laboratory Operations.—Bradley Campbell, room W–7310, 307–8880.

Laboratory Support.—Richard P. Meyers, room W–7348, 307–8785.

Operations and Support.—Michelle Bower, room E–4111, 307–9896.

Program Planning and Control Staff.—Maria Hughes, room E–3163, 307–9885.

Software Development.—Ruth Torres, room E–3285, 307–9883.

Surveillance Support.—Michael Todd, Lorton, VA (703) 495–6575.
Technology Officer.—Mark Shafernich, room E–3101, 353–9691.
Telecommunications Intercept Support.—Joel Reece, Lorton, VA (703) 495–6550.
Associate Deputy Assistant Administrator, Office of:
Forsenic Sciences: Nelson A. Santos, room W–7344, 307–8866; Steven M. Sottolano, room W–7346, 307–8868.
Information Systems.—Julie Jones, room E–3005, 307–5269.

FIELD OFFICES

Special Agent-in-Charge:

Atlanta Division.—John S. Comer, Room 800, 75 Spring Street, SW., Atlanta, GA 30303 (404) 893–7000.

Boston Division.—June Stansbury, JFK Federal Building, Room E–400, 15 New Sudsbury Street, Boston, MA 02203–0402 (617) 557–2100.

Caribbean Division.—Jerome M. Harris, P.O. Box 2167, San Juan, PR 00922–2167 (787) 775–1815.

Chicago Division.—Gary G. Olenkiewicz, Suite 1200, John C. Kluczynski Federal Building, 230 South Dearborn Street, Chicago, IL 60604 (312) 353–7875.

Dallas Division.—James L. Capra, 10160 Technology Boulevard East, Dallas, TX 75220 (214) 366–6900.

Denver Division.—Jeffrey D. Sweetin, 115 Inverness Drive, East, Englewood, CO 80112–5116 (303) 705–7300.

Detroit Division.—Robert L. Corso, 431 Howard Street, Detroit, MI 48226 (313) 234–4000.

El Paso Division.—Zoran Yankovich, 660 Mesa Hills Drive, Suite 2000, El Paso, TX 79912 (915) 832–6000.

Houston Division.—James T. Craig, 1433 West Loop South, Suite 600, Houston, TX 77027–9506 (713) 693–3000.

Los Angeles Division.—Ralph W. Partridge (acting), 255 East Temple Street, 20th Floor, Los Angeles, CA 90012 (213) 621–6700.

Miami Division.—Mark Trouville, Phoenix Building, 8400 NW. 53rd Street, Miami, FL 33166 (305) 994–4870.

Newark Division.—Gerald P. McAleer, 80 Mulberry Street, Second Floor, Newark, NJ 07102–4206 (973) 273–5000.

New Orleans Division.—William J. Renton, Jr., Suite 1800, 3838 North Causeway Boulevard, Metaire, LA 70002 (504) 840–1100.

New York Division.—John P. Gilbride, 99 10th Avenue, New York, NY 10011 (212) 337–3900.

Philadelphia Division.—James M. Kasson, William J. Green Federal Building, 600 Arch Street, Room 10224, Philadelphia, PA 19106 (215) 861–3474.

Phoenix Division.—Timothy J. Landrum, Suite 301, 3010 North Second Street, Phoenix, AZ 85012 (602) 664–5600.

San Diego Division.—4560 Viewridge Avenue, San Diego, CA 92123–1672 (858) 616–4100.

San Francisco Division.—Javier F. Pena, 450 Golden Gate Avenue, P.O. Box 36035, San Francisco, CA 94102 (415) 436–7900.

Seattle Division.—Rodney G. Benson, 400 Second Avenue West, Seattle, WA 98119 (206) 553–5443.

St. Louis Division.—Preston Gubbs, 317 South 16th Street, St. Louis, MO 63103 (314) 538–4600.

Washington, DC Division.—Shawn A. Johnson, 800 K Street, NW., Suite 520, Washington, DC 20001 (202) 305–8500.

OTHER DEA OFFICES

Special Agents-in-Charge:

Arthur A. Doty, El Paso Intelligence Center, Building 11339, SSG Sims Street, El Paso, TX 79908 (915) 760–2000.

William C. Brown, Aviation Operations Division, 2300 Horizon Drive, Fort Worth, TX 76177 (817) 837–2000.

Derek S. Maltz, Special Operations Division, 14560 Avion Parkway, Chantilly, VA 20151 (703) 488–4200.

John R. McCarty, Training Office, P.O. Box 1475, Quantico, VA 22134 (703) 632–5000.

FOREIGN OFFICES

Ankara, Turkey: DEA / Justice, American Embassy Ankara, PSC 93, Box 5000, APO AE 09823, 9–011–90–312–468–6136.

Asuncion, Paraguay: DEA / Justice, American Embassy, Unit 4740, APO AA 34036, 9–011–595–21–210–738.

Athens, Greece: DEA / Justice, American Embassy Athens, PSC 108, Box 14, AA/RE/FPO APO AE 09842, 9–011–30–1–643–4328.

Bangkok, Thailand: DEA / Justice, American Embassy Bangkok, APO AP 96546–0001, 9–011–662–205–4987.

Beijing, China: DEA/Justice, American Embassy Beijing, PSC 461, Box 50, FPO AP 96521–0002, 9–011–8610–8529–6880.

Belize, Country Office: DEA / Justice, American Embassy, PSC 120, Unit 7405, APO AA 34025,
9–011–501–233–3857.

Bern, Switzerland: DEA / Justice, American Embassy, Department of State (Bern), Washington, DC 20521, 9–011–41–31–357–7367.

Bogota, Columbia: DEA / Justice, American Embassy, Unit 5116, APO AA 34038, 9–011–571–315–2121.

Brasilia, Brazil: DEA / Justice, American Embassy, Unit 3500, APO AA 34030, 9–011–55–61–3323–6792.

Bridgetown, Barbados: DEA / Justice, American Embassy, CMR 1014, APO AA 34055, 9–1–246–437–6337.

Brussels, Belgium: DEA / Justice, Brussels Country Office, PSC 82, Box 002, APO AE 09710, 9–011–32–2–508–2420.

Buenos Aires, Argentina: DEA / Justice, American Embassy, Unit 4309, APO AA 34034, 9–011–5411–5777–4696.

Cairo, Egypt: DEA / Justice, Cairo Country Office, American Embassy, Unit 64900, Box 25, APO AE 09839–4900, 9–011–20–2–797–2461.

Canberra, Australia: DEA / Justice, American Embassy Canberra, APO AP 96549, 9–011–61–2–6214–5903.

Caracas, Venezuela: DEA / Justice, American Embassy, Unit 4962, APO AA 34037, 9–011–582–12–975–8910.

Cartagena, Resident Office: DEA / Justice, American Consulate, Unit 5141, APO AA 34038, 9–011–575–664–9375.

Chiang-Mai, Resident Office: DEA / Justice, American Consulate, Box C, APO AP 96546, 9–011–66–53–217–285.

Cochabamba, Resident Office: DEA / Justice, American Embassy, Unit 3913 (Cochabamba), APO AA 34032, 9–011–591–428–8896.

Copenhagen, Denmark: DEA / Justice, American Embassy Copenhagen, PSC 73, APO AE 09716, 9–011–45–35–42–26–80.

Curacao, Netherlands Antilles: DEA / Justice, American Consulate, Washington, DC 20521, 9–011–5999–461–6985.

Frankfurt, Resident Office: DEA / Justice, American Consulate General, PSC 115, Frankfurt / DEA, APO AE 09213, 9–011–49–69–7535–3770.

Freeport, Resident Office: DEA Freeport Airport, P.O. Box 9009, Miami, FL 33159, 1–242–352–5353.

Guadalajara, Resident Office: DEA / Justice, Guadalajara Resident Office, P.O. Box 9001, Brownsville, TX 78520–0901, 9–011–52–33–3268–2191.

Guatemala City, Guatemala: DEA / Justice, American Embassy, Unit 3311, APO AA 34024, 9–011–502–331–4389.

Guayaquil, Resident Office: DEA / Justice, American Embassy Quito, Unit 5350, APO AA, 34039, 9–011–593–42–32–3715.

The Hague, Netherlands: DEA / Justice, American Embassy, Unit 6707, Box 8, APO AE 09715, 9–011–31–70–310–9327.

Hanoi, Vietnam: American Embassy Hanoi, DEA / Justice, PSC 461, Box 461, FPO AP 96521, 9–011–772–1500, ext. 2357 / 9.

Hermosillo, Resident Office: DEA / Justice, Hermosillo Resident Office, P.O. Box 1689, Nogales, AZ 85628, 9–011–52–662–217–4715.

Hong Kong: DEA / Justice, American Consulate General, PSC 461, Box 16, FPO AP 96521, 9–852–2521–4536.

Islamabad, Pakistan Country Office.—American Embassy Islamabad, DEA / Justice, Unit 622156, APO AE 09812–2215, 9–011–92–51–282–5258.

Istanbul: DEA / Justice, American Consulate General, PSC 97, Box 0002, APO AE 09327, 9–011–90–212–335–9179.

Juarez, Resident Office: P.O. Box 10545, El Paso, TX 79995, 9–011–521–611–1179.

Kabul, Afghanistan Country Office.—American Embassy Kabul, Afghanistan c/o DEA, 8160 Kabul Place, Dulles, VA 20521–3210, 9–011–93–20–230–0436 ext. 2019.

Kingston, Jamaica: Kingston Country Office, Department of State, 3210 Kingston Place, Washington, DC 20521, 9–1–876–929–4956.

Kuala Lumpur, Malaysia: DEA / Justice, American Embassy Kuala Lumpur, APO AP 96535, 9–011–603–2168–4957.

Lagos, Nigeria: DEA / Justice, American Embassy Lagos, Department of State, Attn: DEA / Justice, Washington, DC 20521, 9–011–234–1–261–9837.

La Paz, Bolivia: DEA / Justice, American Embassy, Unit 3913, APO AA 34032, 9–011–591–2–431481.

Lima, Peru: DEA / Justice, American Embassy, Unit 3810, APO AA 34031, 9–011–511–618–2475.

London, England: DEA / Justice, American Embassy, PSC 801, Box 08, FPO AE 09498, 9–011–44–20–7408–8026.

Lyon (INTERPOL): American Embassy Paris, DEA / Interpol, Lyon, PSC 116, APO AE 09777, 9–011–33–4–7244–7086.

Madrid, Spain: DEA / Justice, American Embassy Madrid, PSC 61, Box 0014, APO AE 09642, 9–011–34–91–587–2280.

Managua, Nicaragua: DEA / Justice, American Embassy Nicaragua, Unit 2701, Box 21, APO AA 34021, 9–011–505–268–2148.

Manila, Philippines: DEA / Justice, American Embassy, PSC 500, Box 11, FPO AP 96515, 9–011–632–523–1219.

Mazatlan, Resident Office: DEA / Justice, Mazatlan Resident Office, P.O. Box 9006, Brownsville, TX 78520, 9–011–669–982–1775.

Merida: DEA / Justice, U.S. Consulate-Merida, P.O. Box 9003, Brownsville, TX 78520, 9–011–52–999–925–5764.

Mexico City, Mexico: DEA / Justice, U.S. Embassy Mexico City, P.O. Box 9000–DEA, Brownsville, TX 78520, 9–011–52–55–5080–2600.

Milan, Resident Office: DEA / Justice, American Consulate Milan, c/o American Embassy Rome, PSC 59, Box 60–M, APO AE 09624, 9–011–39–02–2903–5522.

Monterrey, Resident Office: DEA / Justice, Monterrey Road, P.O. Box 9002, Brownsville, TX 78520–0902, 9–011–528–340–1299.

Moscow, Russia: DEA / Justice, American Embassy Moscow, PSC 77, APO AE 09721, 9–011–7–095–728–5218.

Nassau: Nassau Country Office, 3370 Nassau Place, Washington, DC 20521, 9–1–242–322–1700.

New Delhi, India: DEA / Justice, New Delhi Country Office, Department of State, 9000 New Delhi Place, Attn: DEA / Justice, Washington, DC 20521, 9–011–91–11–419–8495.

Nicosia, Cyprus: DEA / Justice, American Embassy, PSC 815, Box 1, FPO AE 09836, 9–011–357–22–393–302.

Ottawa, Canada: DEA / Justice, American Embassy Ottawa, P.O. Box 13669, Ogdensburg, New York 13669, 9–1–613–238–5633.

Panama City, Panama: DEA / Justice, American Embassy, Unit 0945, APO AA 34002, 9–011–507–225–9685.

Paris, France: Justice, American Embassy Paris, PSC 116, Box D–401, APO AE 09777, 9–011–33–1–4312–7332.

Peshawar: DEA / Justice, American Consulate General Peshawar, Unit 62217, APO AE 09812–2217, 9–011–92–91–584–0425.

Port-Au-Prince, Haiti: U.S. Department of State, DEA Port-au-Prince, 3400 Port-au-Prince Place, Washington, DC 20521, 9–011–509–223–8888.

Port of Spain, Trinidad and Tobago: DEA / Justice, Port of Spain, Department of State, Port of Spain Country Office, 3410 Port of Spain Place, Washington, DC 20537, 9–1–868–628–8136.

Pretoria, South Africa: DEA / Justice, Pretoria Country Office, Department of State, Washington, DC 20521, 9–011–2712–362–5009.

Quito, Ecuador: DEA / Justice, American Embassy, Unit 5338, APO AA 34039, 9–011–593–22–231–547.

Rangoon, Burma: DEA / Justice, American Embassy Rangoon, Box B, APO AP 96546, 9–011–95–1–282055.

Rome, Italy: DEA / Justice, American Embassy Rome, PSC 59, Box 22, APO AE 09624, 9–011–39–06–4674–2319.

San Jose, Costa Rica: DEA / Justice, American Embassy, Unit 2506, APO AA 34020, 9–011–506–220–2433.

San Salvador, El Salvador: American Embassy, Unit 3130, APO AA 34023, 9–011–503–278–6005.

Santa Cruz, Resident Office: DEA / Justice, American Embassy, Unit 3913 (Santa Cruz), APO AA 34032, 9–011–591–332–7153.

Santiago, Chile: DEA / Justice, American Embassy, Unit 4119, APO AA 34033, 9–011–56–2–330–3401.

Santo Domingo, Dominican Republic: DEA / Justice, American Embassy, Unit 5514, APO AA 34041, 809–687–3754.

Sao Paulo, Resident Office: DEA / Justice, American Embassy, Unit 3502, AP0 AA 34030, 9–011–55–11–5106–700 (Main Consulate number).

Seoul, Korea: DEA / Justice, American Embassy Seoul, Unit 15550, APO AP 96205, 9–011–82–2–397–4260.

Singapore: DEA / Justice, American Embassy Singapore, PSC 470 DEA FPO 96507, 9–011–65–476–9021.

Songkhla, Resident Office: DEA / Justice, American Embassy, APO AP 96546, 9–011–66–74–324–236.

Tashkent: Uzbekistan Country Office, DEA / Justice, 7110 Tashkent Place, Washington, DC 20521, 9–011–998–371–120–8924.

Tegucigalpa, Honduras: DEA / Justice, American Embassy, Unit 2912, APO AA 34022, 9–011–504–236–6780.

Tijuana, Resident Office: P.O. 439039, San Diego, CA 92143, 9–011–526–646–22–7452.

Tokyo, Japan: DEA / Justice, American Embassy Tokyo, Unit 45004, Box 224, APO AP 96337, 9–011–81–3–3224–5452.

Trinidad, Resident Office: DEA / Justice, American Embassy, Unit 3913 (Trinidad), TRO, APO AA 34032, 301–985–9368.

Udorn, Resident Office: DEA / Justice, American Embassy (Udorn), Box UD, APO AP 96546, 9–011–66–42–247–636.

Vancouver Resident Office: United States Consulate, DEA / Justice, Vancouver, P.O. Box 5002, Point Roberts, WA 98281, 9–1–604–694–7710.

Vienna, Austria: American Embassy Vienna, Department of State, Attn: DEA / Justice, Washington, DC 20521, 9–011–43–1–31339–7551.

Vientiane, Laos: American Embassy Vientiane, Box V, APO AP 96546, 9–011–856–2121.

Warsaw, Poland Country Office.—U.S. Embassy, Warsaw Place, Washington, DC 20521, 9–011–48–22–504–2043.

ENVIRONMENT AND NATURAL RESOURCES DIVISION

RFK Main Justice Building, 950 Pennsylvania Avenue, NW., 20530

601 Pennsylvania Avenue, NW., 20044 (PENN)

1425 New York Avenue, NW., 20530 (NYAV)

601 D Street, NW., 20004 (PHB)

Assistant Attorney General.—Sue Ellen Wooldridge, room 2143 (202) 514–2701.

Principal Deputy Assistant Attorney General.—Matthew J. McKeown, room 2141, 514–3370.

Deputy Assistant Attorneys General: John Cruden, room 2611, 514–2718; Ryan Nelson, room 2607, 514–0624; Eileen Sobeck, room 2135, 514–0943.

Counsels to the Assistant Attorney General: John Giordano, room 2129, 514–5243; John Irving, room 2133, 514–4700.

Executive Officer.—Robert L. Bruffy (PHB), room 2038, 616–3147.

Section Chiefs:

Appellate.—James C. Kilbourne (PHB), room 8046, 514–2748.

Environmental Crimes.—David M. Uhlmann (PHB), room 2102, 305–0337.

Environmental Defense.—Letitia J. Grishaw (PHB), room 8002, 514–2219.

Environmental Enforcement.—Bruce Gelber (NYAV), room 13063, 514–4624.

General Litigation.—K. Jack Haugrud (PHB), room 3102, 305–0438.

Indian Resources.—Craig Alexander (PHB), room 3016, 514–9080.

Land Acquisition.—Virginia P. Butler (PHB), room 3638, 305–0316.

Policy, Legislation, and Special Litigation.—Pauline M. Milius (PHB), room 8022, 514–2586.

Wildlife and Marine Resources.—Jean E. Williams (PHB), room 3902, 305–0210.

FIELD OFFICES

801 B Street, Suite 504, Anchorage, AK 99501–3657

Trial Attorneys: Regina Belt (907) 271–3456; Dean Dunsmore (907) 271–5452; Bruce Landon (907) 271–5452.

501 I Street, Suite 9–700, Sacramento, CA 95814–2322

Trial Attorneys: Stephen Macfarlane (916) 930–2204; Charles Shockey (916) 930–2203.

301 Howard Street, Suite 1050, San Francisco, CA 94105–2001

Trial Attorneys: Matt Fogelson (415) 744–6470; David Glazer (415) 744–6477; Robert Mullaney (415) 744–6483; Bradley O'Brien (415) 744–6484; Angela O'Connell (415) 744–6485; Judith Rabinowitz (415) 744–6486; Mark Rigau (415) 744–6487.

999 18th Street, Suite 945, North Tower, Denver, CO 80202

Trial Attorneys: David Askman (303) 844–1381; Bruce Bernard (303) 844–1361; Bradley Bridgewater (303) 844–1359; Dave Carson (303) 844–1349; Jerry Ellington (303) 844–1363; Robert Foster (303) 844–1362; Jim Freeman (303) 844–1489; Dave Gehlert (303) 844–1386; Alan Greenberg (303) 844–1366; David Harder (303) 844–1372; Robert Homiak (303) 844–1391; Lee Leininger (303) 844–1364; John Moscato (303) 844–1380; Mark Nitcynski (303) 844–1498; Terry Petrie (303) 844–1369; Daniel Pinkston (303) 844–1804; Susan Schneider (303) 844–1348.

Administrative Officer.—David Jones (303) 844–1807.

161 East Mallard Drive, Suite A, Boise, ID 83706

Trial Attorneys: David Negri (208) 331–5943; Ronald Sutcliffe (208) 334–1211.

One Gateway Center, Suite 6116, Newton Corner, MA 02158

Trial Attorneys: Catherine Fiske (617) 450–0444; Donald Frankel (617) 450–0442.

c/o U.S. Attorney's Office, 105 E. Pine Street, 2nd Floor, Missoula, MT 59802

Trial Attorney.—Robert Anderson (406) 829–3322.

c/o U.S. Attorney's Office, 555 Pleasant Street, Suite 352, Concord, NH 03301

Trial Attorney.— Kristine Tardiff (603) 225–1562, ext. 283.

c/o U.S. Attorney's Office, 201 Third Street, NW., Suite 900, Albuquerque, NM 87102

Trial Attorney.—Andrew Smith (505) 224–1468.

c/o NOAA / DARCNW, 7600 San Point Way, NE., Seattle, WA 98115–0070

Trial Attorneys: Jim Nicholl (206) 526–6616; David Spohr (206) 526–4603; Mike Zevenbergen (206) 526–6607.

483 Doe Run Road, Sequim, WA 98382

Appraiser.—James Eaton (360) 582–0038.

EXECUTIVE OFFICE FOR IMMIGRATION REVIEW (EOIR)

5107 Leesburg Pike, Suite 2600, Falls Church, VA 22041

Director.—Kevin D. Rooney, 2600 SKYT (703) 305–0169.
Deputy Director.—Kevin A. Ohlson.
Associate Director/Chief of Staff.—Paula Nasca.
Executive Secretariat.—Terry Samuels.
Assistant Director/General Counsel.—Mary Beth Keller, 2500 SKYT, 305–1247.
Deputy General Counsel.—Kevin Chapman, 2600 SKYT, 305–0470.
Assistant Director of:
Administration.—Lawrence M. D'Elia, 2300 SKYT, 305–1171.
Management Programs.—Frances A. Mooney, 2600 SKYT, 305–0289.
Planning, Analysis and Technology.—Amy Dale, 2600 SKYT, 605–0445.
Chairman, Board of Immigration Appeals.—Juan Osuna (acting), 2400 SKYT, 305–1194.
Chief, Office of the Chief Administrative Hearing Officer.—Michael J. Creppy, 2500 SKYT, 305–0864.
Chief Judge, Office of the Chief Immigration Judge.—David L. Neal (acting), 2500 SKYT, 305–1247.
Deputy Chief Immigration Judge.—Thomas L. Pullen, 2500 SKYT, 305–1247.
Telephone Directory Coordinator.—Annette Thomas, 2300 SKYT, 605–1336.

EXECUTIVE OFFICE FOR UNITED STATES ATTORNEYS (EOUSA)

RFK Main Justice Building, Room 2621, phone (202) 514–2121

Director.—Mike Battle.
Deputy Directors: John Nowacki, Steve Parent.
Chief of Staff.—John Kelly.
Editor, AGAC Liaison and United States Attorney's Manual.—Judith A. Beeman, room 2335, 514–4633.
Office of Tribal Justice.—Tracy Toulou, room 2229A, 514–8812.
Assistant Director of:
Budget Execution.—Mary Ellen Kline, room 8000, BICN, 616–6886.
Case Management.—Siobhan Sperin, room 7500, BICN, 616–6919.
Data Analysis Staff.—Barbara Tone, room 2000, BICN, 616–6779.
District Assistance Program.—Debora Cottrell, room 8105, BICN, 353–9394.
Equal Employment Opportunity Staff.—Rita Sampson, room 524, NPB, 514–3982.
Evaluation and Review Staff.—Chris Barnes, room 8500, BICN, 616–6776.
Facilities Management and Support Service.—Robert Stafford, room 2400, BICN, 616–6425.
FOIA and Privacy.—William Stewart, room 7300, BICN, 616–6757.
Information Systems Security Staff.—Ted Shelkey, room 2300, BICN, 616–6973.
Office Automation.—Vance Allen, room 9100, BICN, 616–6969.
Personnel Management Staff.—Jean Dunn, room 8017, BICN, 616–6873.
Security Programs Staff.—Tommie Barnes, room 2600, BICN, 616–6878.
Employee Assistance Program Administrator.—Bob Norton, room 6800, BICN, 514–1036.
General Counsel.—Scott Schools, room 2200, BICN, 514–4024.
Counsel, Legal Programs and Policy.—Dan Villegas, room 7600, BICN, 616–6444.
Director, Legal Education.—Michael W. Bailie, National Advocacy Center, 1620 Pendleton Street, Columbia, SC 29201 (803) 544–5100.
Chief Financial Officer.—Lisa Bevels, room 8000, BICN, 616–6886.
Chief Operating Officer.—David Downs, room 8105, BICN, 616–6600.
Associate Director.—Gail Williamson, room 8105, BICN, 616–6600.
Telecommunications and Technology Development.—Danny Ko, room 6012, BICN, 616–6439.
Telephone Directory Coordinator.—Mary Kay Benavente, room 8200, BICN, 616–6900.

EXECUTIVE OFFICE FOR UNITED STATES TRUSTEES

20 Massachusetts Avenue, NW., 20530, phone (202) 307–1391

http://www.usdoj.gov/ust

Director.—Clifford J. White III, room 8000.
Deputy Director.—Donald F. Walton (acting).

Associate Director.—Jeffrey M. Miller.
General Counsel.—Roberta A. DeAngelis (acting), room 8100, 307–1399.
Chief Information Officer.—Monique K. Bourque, 353–3548.
Assistant Director, Office of:
Administration.—Santal Manos, room 8200, 307–2926.
Research and Planning.—Robert D. Miller, Jr. (acting), room 8310, 307–2605.
Review and Oversight.—Robert D. Miller, Jr. (acting), room 8338, 305–0550.
Chief of:
Civil Enforcement Unit.—Mark A. Redmiles, 307–1365.
Credit Counseling and Debtor Education Unit.—Henry G. Hobbs, Jr. (acting), 307–3698.
Criminal Enforcement Unit.—Richard E. Byrne, 305–2715.

U.S. TRUSTEES

Region I:
Room 1184, 10 Causeway Street, Boston, MA 02222–1043 (617) 788–0400.
Suite 303, 537 Congress Street, Portland, ME 04101 (207) 780–3564.
14th Floor, 446 Main Street, Worchester, MA 01608 (508) 793–0555.
Suite 302, 66 Hanover Street, Manchester, NH 03101 (603) 666–7908.
Suite 910, 10 Dorrance Street, Providence, RI 02903 (401) 528–5551.
Region II:
21st floor, 33 Whitehall Street, New York, NY 10004 (212) 510–0500.
Suite 200, 74 Chapel Street, Albany, NY 12207 (518) 434–4553.
Suite 100, 42 Delaware Avenue, Buffalo, NY 14202 (716) 551–5541.
Long Island Federal Courthouse, 560 Federal Plaza, Central Islip, NY 11722–4456 (631) 715–7800.
Suite 1103, 265 Church Street, New Haven, CT 06510 (203) 773–2210.
Room 609, 100 State Street, Rochester, NY 14614 (716) 263–5812.
Room 105, 10 Broad Street, Utica, NY 13501 (315) 793–8191.
Region III:
Suite 500, 833 Chestnut Street, Philadelphia, PA 19107 (215) 597–4411.
Suite 2100, One Newark Center, Newark, NJ 07102 (973) 645–3014.
Suite 970, 1001 Liberty Avenue, Pittsburgh, PA 15222 (412) 644–4756.
Suite 1190, 228 Walnut Street, Harrisburg, PA 17101 or P.O. Box 969, Harrisburg, PA 17108 (717) 221–4515.
Suite 2207, 844 King Street, Wilmington, DE 19801 (302) 573–6491.
Region IV:
Suite 953, 1835 Assembly Street, Columbia, SC 29201 (803) 765–5250.
Room 210, 115 S. Union Street, Alexandria, VA 22314 (703) 557–7176.
Room 625, 200 Granby Street, Norfolk, VA 23510 (757) 441–6012.
Room 2025, 300 Virginia Street East, Charleston, WV 25301 (304) 347–3400.
First Campbell Square Building, 210 First Street, SW., Suite 505, Roanoke, VA 24011 (540) 857–2806.
Suite 301, 600 East Main Street, Richmond, VA 23219 (804) 771–2310.
Suite 600, 6305 Ivy Lane, Greenbelt, MD 20770 (301) 344–6216.
Suite 2625, 101 W. Lombard Street, Baltimore, MD 21201 (410) 962–4300.
Region V:
Suite 2110, 400 Poydras Street, New Orleans, LA 70130 (504) 589–4018.
Suite 3196, 300 Fannin Street, Shreveport, LA 71101–3099 (318) 676–3456.
Suite 706, 100 West Capitol Street, Jackson, MS 39269 (601) 965–5241.
Region VI:
Room 976, 1100 Commerce Street, Dallas, TX 75242 (214) 767–8967.
Room 300, 110 North College Avenue, Tyler, TX 75702 (903) 590–1450.
Region VII:
Suite 3516, 515 Rusk Avenue, Houston, TX 77002 (713) 718–4650.
Room 230, 903 San Jacinto, Austin, TX 78701 (512) 916–5328.
Suite 533, 615 East Houston Street, San Antonio, TX 78205 (210) 472–4640.
Suite 1107, 606 N. Carancahua Street, Corpus Christi, TX 78476 (361) 888–3261.
Region VIII:
Suite 400, 200 Jefferson Avenue, Memphis, TN 38103 (901) 544–3251.
Suite 512, 601 W. Broadway, Louisville, KY 40202 (502) 582–6000.
Fourth floor, 31 East 11th Street, Chattanooga, TN 37402 (423) 752–5153.
Room 318, 701 Broadway, Nashville, TN 37203 (615) 736–2254.
Suite 500, 100 East Vine Street, Lexington, KY 40507 (859) 233–2822.
Region IX:

Suite 441, BP Building, 201 Superior Avenue East, Cleveland, OH 44114 (216) 522–7800.
Suite 200, Schaff Building, 170 North High Street, Columbus, OH 43215–2403 (614) 469–7411.
Suite 2030, 36 East Seventh Street, Cincinnati, OH 45202 (513) 684–6988.
Suite 700, 211 W. Fort Street, Detroit, MI 48226 (313) 226–7999.
Suite 202, 330 Ionia NW. Grand Rapids, MI 49503 (616) 456–2002.

Region X:
Room 1000, 101 West Ohio Street, Indianapolis, IN 46204 (317) 226–6101.
Suite 1100, 401 Main Street, Peoria, IL 61602 (309) 671–7854.
Suite 555, 100 East Wayne Street, South Bend, IN 46601 (574) 236–8105.

Region XI:
Suite 3350, 227 West Monroe Street, Chicago, IL 60606 (312) 886–5785.
Room 430, 517 East Wisconsin Avenue, Milwaukee, WI 53202 (414) 297–4499.
Suite 304, 780 Regent Street, Madison, WI 53715 (608) 264–5522.

Region XII:
Suite 1015, U.S. Courthouse, 300 S. Fourth Street, Minneapolis, MN 55415 (612) 664–5500.
Suite 400, 225 Second Street SE., Cedar Rapids, IA 52401 (319) 364–2211.
Room 793, 210 Walnut Street, Des Moines, IA 50309–2108 (515) 284–4982.
Suite 502, 230 S. Philips Avenue, Sioux Falls, SD 57102–6321 (605) 330–4450.

Region XIII:
Suite 3440, 400 East 9th Street, Kansas City, MO 64106–1910 (816) 512–1940.
Suite 6353, 111 South 10th Street, St. Louis, MO 63102 (314) 539–2976.
Suite 1200, 200 West Capital Avenue, Little Rock, AR 72201–3344 (501) 324–7357.
Suite 1148, 111 South 18th Plaza, Omaha, NE 68102 (402) 221–4300.

Region XIV:
Suite 204, 230 North First Avenue, Phoenix, AZ 85003 or P.O. Box 36170, Phoenix, AZ 85067 (602) 682–2600.

Region XV:
Suite 600, 402 West Broadway Street, San Diego, CA 92101–8511 (619) 557–5013.
Suite 602, 1132 Bishop Street, Honolulu, HI 96813–2836 (808) 522–8150.

Region XVI:
725 South Figueroa, 26th floor, Los Angeles, CA 90017 (213) 894–6811.
Suite 9041, 411 W. Fourth Street, Santa Ana, CA 92701–8000 (714) 338–3401.
Suite 300, 3685 Main Street, Riverside, CA 92501 (909) 276–6990.
Suite 115, 21051 Warner Center Lane, Woodland Hills, CA 91367 (818) 716–8800.

Region XVII:
Suite 700, 235 Pine Street, San Francisco, CA 94104–3401 (415) 705–3300.
Suite 7–500, U.S. Courthouse, 501 I Street, Sacramento, CA 95814–2322 (916) 930–2100.
Suite 1401, 2500 Tulare Street, Fresno, CA 93721 (559) 487–5002.
Suite 690N, 1301 Clay Street, Oakland, CA 94612–5217 (510) 637–3200.
Room 4300, 300 Las Vegas Boulevard South, Las Vegas, NV 89101 (702) 388–6600.
Suite 2129, 300 Booth Street, Reno, NV 89502 (775) 784–5335.
Room 268, 280 South First Street, San Jose, CA 95113 (408) 535–5525.

Region XVIII:
Suite 5103, 700 Stewart Street, Seattle, WA 98101 (206) 553–2000.
Suite 213, 620 S.W. Main Street, Portland, OR 97205 (503) 326–4000.
Suite 220, 720 Park Boulevard, Boise, ID 83712 (208) 334–1300.
Room 593, 920 West Riverside, Spokane, WA 99201 (509) 353–2999.
Suite 204, 301 Central Avenue, Great Falls, MT 59401 (406) 761–8777.
Suite 258, 605 West Fourth Avenue, Anchorage, AK 99501 (907) 271–2600.
Suite 1100, 405 East Eighth Avenue, Eugene, OR 97401 (541) 465–6330.

Region XIX:
Suite 1551, 999 Eighteenth Street, Denver, CO 80202 (303) 312–7230.
Suite 203, 308 West 21st Street, Cheyenne, WY 82001 (307) 772–2790.
Suite 300, 405 South Main Street, Salt Lake City, UT 84111 (801) 524–5734.

Region XX:
Room 500, Epic Center, 301 North Main Street, Wichita, KS 67202 (316) 269–6637.
Suite 112, 421 Gold Street SW., Albuquerque, NM 87102 (505) 248–6544.
Suite 408, 215 Northwest Dean A. McGee Avenue, Oklahoma City, OK 73102 (405) 231–5950.
Suite 225, 224 S. Boulder Avenue, Tulsa, OK 74103 (918) 581–6670.

Region XXI:
Room 362, 75 Spring Street SW., Atlanta, GA 30303 (404) 331–4437.

Suite 301, 500 Tanca Street, San Juan, PR 00901 (787) 729–7444.
Room 1204, 51 Southwest First Avenue, Miami, FL 33130 (305) 536–7285.
Suite 302, 222 West Oglethorpe Avenue, Savannah, GA 31401 (912) 652–4112.
Suite 1200, 501 E. Polk Street, Tampa, FL 33602 (813) 228–2000.
Suite 302, 440 Martin Luther King Boulevard, Macon, GA 31201 (478) 752–3544.
Suite 128, 110 East Park Avenue, Tallahassee, FL 32301 (850) 521–5050.
Suite 620, 135 West Central Boulevard, Orlando, FL 32801 (407) 648–6301.

FEDERAL BUREAU OF ALCOHOL, TOBACCO, FIREARMS, AND EXPLOSIVES (ATF)

650 Massachusetts Avenue, NW., 20226

OFFICE OF THE DIRECTOR

Director.—Michael J. Sullivan (acting), (202) 927–8700.
Deputy Director.—Edgar A. Domenech, 927–8710.
Chief of Staff.—Brian Benczkowski, 927–8572.
Executive Assistant.—Tina Street, 927–8309.

OFFICE OF CHIEF COUNSEL

Chief Counsel.—Stephen R. Rubenstein, 927–8224.
Deputy Chief Counsel.—Eleaner Loos (acting), 927–8237.

OFFICE OF ENFORCEMENT PROGRAMS AND SERVICES

Assistant Director.—Lewis P. Raden, 927–7940.
Deputy Assistant Director.—Audrey Stucko, 927–7420.
Chief of Staff.—Charlayne Armentrout (acting), 927–7940.
Director of NIBIN Program.—Steve Pugmire, 927–5660.
Chief, Division of:
Arson and Explosives.—Joseph Riehl, 927–7930.
FEA Services.—Scott Mendoza (acting), 927–8300.
Firearms Program.—Phillip Awe (acting), 927–7770.
National Tracing Center.—Charles Houser (304) 274–4100.
Deputy Chief, Division of Arson and Explosives.—Mark Jones, 927–7930.

OFFICE OF EQUAL OPPORTUNITY

Executive Assistant.—Anthony Torres, 927–8154.
Deputy Executive Assistant.—Dora Silas, 927–7760.

OFFICE OF FIELD OPERATIONS

Assistant Director.—Michael R. Bouchard, 927–7970.
Deputy Assistant Director for—
Central.—Carson F. Carroll, 927–7980.
West.—Virginia O'Brien, 927–7970.
Industry Operations.—James A. Zamillo, Sr., 927–7953

OFFICE OF MANAGEMENT/CFO

Assistant Director/Chief Financial Officer.—Melanie Stinnett, 927–8400.
Deputy Assistant Director.—Vivian Michalic.

OFFICE OF OMBUDSMAN

Ombudsman.—Marianne Ketels, 927–3538.

OFFICE OF PROFESSIONAL RESPONSIBILITY AND SECURITY OPERATIONS

Assistant Director.—Richard E. Chase, 927–7800.
Deputy Assistant Director.—Kenneth Massey.

OFFICE OF PUBLIC AND GOVERNMENTAL AFFAIRS

Assistant Director.—W. Larry Ford, 927–8500.
Deputy Assistant Director.—Mark Chait.
Executive Assistant for Legislative Affairs.—Dan Kumor, 927–8490.

OFFICE OF SCIENCE AND TECHNOLOGY/CIO

Assistant Director/Chief Information Officer.—Gregg D. Bailey, 927–8390.
Deputy Assistant Director.—Larry Bell.

OFFICE OF STRATEGIC INTELLIGENCE AND INFORMATION

Assistant Director.—James E. McDermond, 927–6500.
Deputy Assistant Director.—Hugo Barrera, 927–6500.

OFFICE OF TRAINING AND PROFESSIONAL DEVELOPMENT

Assistant Director.—Mark Logan, 927–9380.
Deputy Assistant Director.—Theresa Stoop.

FEDERAL BUREAU OF INVESTIGATION

J. Edgar Hoover Building, 935 Pennsylvania Avenue, NW., 20535–0001
phone (202) 324–3000, http://www.fbi.gov

Director.—Robert S. Mueller III, 324–3444.
Deputy Director.—John S. Pistole, 324–3315.
Associate Deputy Director.—Joseph L. Ford, 324–4180.
Chief of Staff.—W. Lee Rawls, 324–3444.

OFFICE OF THE DIRECTOR/DEPUTY DIRECTOR/ASSOCIATE DEPUTY DIRECTOR

Office of the General Counsel.—Valerie E. Caproni, 324–6829.
Office of Public Affairs.—John Miller, 324–5352.
Office of Congressional Affairs.—Eleni P. Kalisch, 324–5051.
Office of Professional Responsiblity.—Candice M. Will, 324–8284.
Office of Equal Employment Opportunity Affairs.—Veronica Venture, 324–4128.
Office of the Ombudsman.—Sarah Zeigler, 324–2156.
Inspection Division.—Kenneth W. Kaiser, 324–2901.
Facilities and Logistics Services Division.—Patrick G. Findlay, 324–2875.
Finance Division.—Kevin L. Perkins, 324–1345.
Records Management Division.—William L. Hooton, 324–7141.
Security Division.—Charles S. Phalen, Jr., 324–7112.

OFFICE OF THE CHIEF INFORMATION OFFICER

Chief Information Officer.—Zalmai Azmi, 324–6165.
Assistant Director of:
Information Technology Operations Division.—Louis J. Blazy III, 324–4507.
IT Policy and Planning Office.—Sanjeev Bhagowalia, 324–1210.
IT Program Management Office.—Dean E. Hall, 324–2307.
Office of the Chief Technology Officer.—Jerome W. Israel, 324–5441.

CRIMINAL INVESTIGATIONS BRANCH

Executive Assistant Director.—Michael A. Mason, 324–4880.
Assistant Director of:
Criminal Investigative Division.—James H. Burrus, Jr., 324–4260.
Critical Incident Response Group.—Michael J. Wolf (703) 632–4100.
Cyber Division.—James E. Finch, 324–6615.
International Operations Office.—Thomas V. Fuentes, 324–5292.
Law Enforcement Coordination Office.—Louis F. Quijas, 324–7126.

HUMAN RESOURCES BRANCH

Executive Assistant Director.—Donald E. Packham, 324–3514.
Assistant Director of:
Human Resources Division.—John Raucci, 324–3000.
Training and Development Division.—Keith Slotter (703) 632–1100.

NATIONAL SECURITY BRANCH

Executive Assistant Director.—Willie Hulon, 324–7045.
Assistant Director of:
Counterintelligence Division.—Timothy D. Bereznay, 324–4614.
Counterterrorism Division.—Joseph Billy, Jr., 324–2770.
Directorate of Intelligence.—Wayne M. Murphy, 324–3000.
Weapons of Mass Destruction Directorate.—Dr. Vahid Majidi, 324–4965.

SCIENCE AND TECHNOLOGY BRANCH

Executive Assistant Director.—Kerry E. Haynes (703) 632–6100.
Assistant Director of:
Criminal Justice Information Services Division.—Thomas E. Bush III (304) 625–2700.
Laboratory Division.—Joseph A. DiZinno (703) 632–7000.
Operational Technology Division.—Marcus C. Thomas (acting), (703) 632–6100.

FIELD DIVISIONS

Albany: 200 McCarty Avenue, Albany, NY 12209 (518) 465–7551.
Albuquerque: 415 Silver Avenue SW., Suite 300, Albuquerque, NM 87102 (505) 224–2000.
Anchorage: 101 East Sixth Avenue, Anchorage, AK 99501 (907) 258–5322.
Atlanta: 2635 Century Center Parkway, NE., Suite 400, Atlanta, GA 30345 (404) 679–9000.
Baltimore: 7142 Ambassador Road, Baltimore, MD 21244 (410) 265–8080.
Birmingham: 2121 Eighth Avenue North, Room 1400, Birmingham, AL 35203 (205) 326–6166.
Boston: One Center Plaza, Suite 600, Boston, MA 02108 (617) 742–5533.
Buffalo: One FBI Plaza, Buffalo, NY 14202 (716) 856–7800.
Charlotte: Wachovia Building, 400 South Tryon Street, Suite 900, Charlotte, NC 28285 (704) 377–9200.
Chicago: E.M. Dirksen Federal Office Building, 219 South Dearborn Street, Room 905, Chicago, IL 60604 (312) 431–1333.
Cincinnati: Federal Office Building, 550 Main Street, Room 9000, Cincinnati, OH 45202 (513) 421–4310.
Cleveland: 1501 Lakeside Avenue, Cleveland, OH 44114 (216) 522–1400.
Columbia: 151 Westpark Boulevard, Columbia, SC 29210 (803) 551–4200.
Dallas: J. Gordon Shanklin Building, One Justice Way, Dallas, TX 75220 (972) 559–5000.
Denver: Federal Office Building, 1961 Stout Street, Room 1823, Denver, CO 80294 (303) 629–7171.
Detroit: P.V. McNamara Federal Office Building, 477 Michigan Avenue, 26th Floor, Detroit, MI 48226 (313) 965–2323.
El Paso: 660 South Mesa Hills Drive, Suite 3000, El Paso, TX 79912 (915) 832–5000.

Honolulu: Kalanianaole Federal Office Building, 300 Ala Moana Boulevard, Room 4–230, Honolulu, HI 96850 (808) 566–4300.
Houston: 2500 East T.C. Jester, Suite 200, Houston, TX 77008 (713) 693–5000.
Indianapolis: Federal Office Building, 575 North Pennsylvania Street, Room 679, Indianapolis, IN 46204 (371) 639–3301.
Jackson: Federal Office Building, 100 West Capitol Street, Suite 1553, Jackson, MS 39269 (601) 948–5000.
Jacksonville: 7820 Arlington Expressway, Suite 200, Jacksonville, FL 32211 (904) 721–1211.
Kansas City: 1300 Summit, Kansas City, MO 64105 (816) 512–8200.
Knoxville: John J. Duncan Federal Office Building, 710 Locust Street, Room 600, Knoxville, TN 37902 (423) 544–0751.
Las Vegas: John Lawrence Bailey Building, 700 East Charleston Boulevard, Las Vegas, NV 89104 (702) 385–1281.
Little Rock: #24 Shackleford West Boulevard, Little Rock, AR 72211 (501) 221–9100.
Los Angeles: Federal Office Building, 11000 Wilshire Boulevard, Suite 1700, Los Angeles, CA 90024 (310) 477–6565.
Louisville: 600 Martin Luther King, Jr. Place, Room 500, Louisville, KY 40202 (502) 583–2941.
Memphis: Eagle Crest Building, 225 North Humphreys Boulevard, Suite 3000, Memphis, TN 38120 (901) 747–4300.
Miami: 16320 Northwest Second Avenue, Miami, FL 33169 (305) 944–9101.
Milwaukee: 330 East Kilbourn Avenue, Suite 600, Milwaukee, WI 53202 (414) 276–4684.
Minneapolis: 111 Washington Avenue South, Suite 100, Minneapolis, MN 55401 (612) 376–3200.
Mobile: 200 North Royal Street, Mobile, AL 36602 (334) 438–3674.
New Haven: 600 State Street, New Haven, CT 06511 (203) 777–6311.
New Orleans: 2901 Leon C. Simon Boulevard, New Orleans, LA 70126 (504) 816–3122.
New York: 26 Federal Plaza, 23rd Floor, New York, NY 10278 (212) 384–1000.
Newark: Claremont Tower Building, 11 Centre Place, Newark, NJ 07102 (973) 792–3000.
Norfolk: 150 Corporate Boulevard, Norfolk, VA 23502 (757) 455–0100.
Oklahoma City: 3301 West Memorial, Oklahoma City, OK 73134 (405) 290–7770.
Omaha: 10755 Burt Street, Omaha, NE 68114 (402) 493–8688.
Philadelphia: William J. Green, Jr., Federal Office Building, 600 Arch Street, Eighth Floor, Philadelphia, PA 19106 (215) 418–4000.
Phoenix: 201 East Indianola Avenue, Suite 400, Phoenix, AZ 85012 (602) 279–5511.
Pittsburgh: Martha Dixon Building, 3311 East Carson Street, Pittsburgh, PA 15203 (412) 432–4000.
Portland: Crown Plaza Building, 1500 Southwest First Avenue, Suite 401, Portland, OR 97201 (503) 224–4181.
Richmond: 1970 East Parham Road, Richmond, VA 23228 (804) 261–1044.
Sacramento: 4500 Orange Grove Avenue, Sacramento, CA 95841 (916) 481–9110.
Salt Lake City: 257 Towers Building, 257 East 200 South, Suite 1200, Salt Lake City, UT 84111 (801) 579–1400.
San Antonio: U.S. Post Office and Courthouse Building, 614 East Houston Street, Room 200, San Antonio, TX 78205 (210) 225–6741.
San Diego: Federal Office Building, 9797 Aero Drive, San Diego, CA 92123 (858) 565–1255.
San Francisco: 450 Golden Gate Avenue, 13th Floor, San Francisco, CA 64102 (415) 553–7400.
San Juan: U.S. Federal Office Building, 150 Chardon Avenue, Room 526, Hato Rey, PR 00918 (787) 754–6000.
Seattle: 1110 Third Avenue, Seattle, WA 98101 (206) 622–0460.
Springfield: 400 West Monroe Street, Suite 400, Springfield, IL 62704 (217) 522–9675.
St. Louis: 2222 Market Street, St. Louis, MO 63103 (314) 241–5357.
Tampa: Federal Office Building, 500 Zack Street, Room 610, Tampa, FL 33602 (813) 273–4566.
Washington, DC: 601 Fourth Street, NW., Washington, DC 20535 (202) 278–3400.

FEDERAL BUREAU OF PRISONS (BOP)

320 First Street, NW., 20534

General Information Number (202) 307–3198

Director.—Harley G. Lappin, room 654, HOLC, 307–3250.
Director, National Institute of Corrections.—Morris L. Thigpen, Sr., 7th floor, 500 FRST, 307–3106 (0).

Assistant Director of:
Administration.—Bruce K. Sasser, 9th floor, 500 FRST, 307–3123.
Correctional Programs.—John M. Vanyur, Ph.D., room 554, HOLC, 307–3226.
General Counsel.—Kathleen M. Kenney, room 958C, HOLC, 307–3062.
Health Services.—Newton Kending, M.D., room 1054, HOLC, 307–3055.
Human Resources Management.—Whitney LeBlanc, room 754, HOLC, 307–3082.
Industries, Education, and Vocational Training.—Steve Schwalb, 8th floor, 400 FRST, 305–3500.
Information, Policy and Public Affairs.—Thomas R. Kane, Ph.D., room 641, HOLC, 514–6537.
Regional Director for—
Mid-Atlantic.—Kim White (301) 317–3100.
North Central.—Michael K. Nalley (913) 621–3939.
Northeast.—Scott Dodrill (215) 521–7300.
South Central.—Gerardo Maldonado (214) 224–3389.
Southeast.—Ray Holt (678) 686–1200.
Western.—Robert McFadden (925) 803–4700.
Telephone Directory Coordinator.—Jerry Vroegh, 307–3250.

OFFICE OF THE FEDERAL DETENTION TRUSTEE

4601 N. Fairfax Drive, Suite 9110, Arlington, VA 22203, phone (202) 353–4601

Trustee.—Stacia A. Hylton.
Deputy Trustee.—David F. Musel.

FOREIGN CLAIMS SETTLEMENT COMMISSION

Bicentennial Building (BICN), 600 E Street, NW., Suite 6002, 20579, phone (202) 616–6975

Chair.—Mauricio J. Tamargo.
Chief Counsel.—David E. Bradley.
Commissioner.—Stephen C. King.
Special Assistant.—Niklas Warren, 616–6983.
Administrative Officer.—Judith H. Lock, 616–6986.

OFFICE OF INFORMATION AND PRIVACY

1425 New York Avenue, NW., 20035, phone (202) 514–3642

Director.—Daniel J. Metcalfe.
Deputy Director.—Melanie Ann Pustay.
Associate Director.—Janice Galli McLeod.
Assistant Directors: Carmen L. Mallon, Tricia S. Wellman.

OFFICE OF THE INSPECTOR GENERAL

RFK Main Justice Building, Room 4322, phone (202) 514–3435
1425 New York Avenue, NW., 20530

Inspector General.—Glenn A. Fine.
Deputy Inspector General.—Paul K. Martin.
Counselor to the Inspector General.—Cynthia A. Schnedar.
Senior Counsel to the Inspector General.—Scott S. Dahl.
General Counsel.—Gail A. Robinson (NYAV), Suite 6000, 616–0646.
Assistant Inspectors General:
Audit.—Guy K. Zimmerman (NYAV), Suite 5000, 616–4633.
Evaluation and Inspections.—Paul A. Price (NYAV), Suite 6100, 616–4620.
Investigations.—Thomas F. McLaughlin (NYAV), Suite 7100, 616–4760.
Management and Planning.—Gregory T. Peters (NYAV), Suite 7000, 616–4550.
Oversight and Review.—Carol F. Ochoa (RFK), Room 4722, 616–0645.

REGIONAL AUDIT OFFICES

Atlanta: Ferris B. Polk, Suite 1130, 75 Spring Street, Atlanta, GA 30303 (404) 331–5928.

Chicago: Carol S. Taraszka, Suite 3510, Citicorp Center, 500 West Madison Street, Chicago, IL 60661 (312) 353–1203.

Dallas: Robert J. Kaufman, Room 575, Box 4, 207 South Houston Street, Dallas, TX 75202–4724 (214) 655–5000.

Denver: David M. Sheeren, Suite 1500, Chancery Building, 1120 Lincoln Street, Denver, CO 80203 (303) 864–2000.

Philadelphia: Richard A. McGeary, Suite 201, 701 Market Street, Philadelphia, PA 19106 (215) 580–2111.

San Francisco: David J. Gaschke, Suite 201, 1200 Bayhill Drive, San Bruno, CA 94066 (650) 876–9220.

Washington: Troy M. Meyer, 1300 N. 17th Street, Suite 3400, Arlington, VA 22209 (202) 616–4688.

Computer Security and Information Technology Audit Office: Norman Hammonds, room 5000 (202) 616–3801.

Financial Statement Audit Office: Marilyn A. Kessinger, 1125 New York Avenue, NW., #13000, Washington, DC 20530 (202) 616–4660.

REGIONAL INVESTIGATIONS OFFICES

Atlanta: Eddie D. Davis, 60 Forsyth Street, SW., Room 8M45, Atlanta, GA 30303 (404) 562–1980.

Boston: Thomas M. Hopkins, U.S. Courthouse, 1 Courthouse Way, Room 9200, Boston, MA 02210 (617) 748–3218.

Chicago: Edward M. Dyner, P.O. Box 1802, Chicago, IL 60690 (312) 886–7050.

Colorado Springs: Craig Trautner, Suite 1501, 1120 Lincoln Street, Denver, CO 80203 (719) 635–2366.

Dallas: James H. Mahon, 2505 State Highway 360, Room 410, Grand Prairie, TX 75050 (817) 385–5200.

Detroit: Nicholas V. Candela, Suite 1402, 211 West Fort Street, Detroit, MI 48226 (313) 226–4005.

El Paso: Stephen P. Beauchamp, Suite 135, 4050 Rio Bravo, El Paso, TX 79902 (915) 577–0102.

Houston: Fred C. Ball, Jr., P.O. Box 53509, Houston, TX 77052 (713) 718–4888.

Los Angeles: Steve F. Turchek, Suite 655, 330 N. Brand Street, Glendale, CA 91203 (818) 543–1172.

McAllen: Wayne D. Beaman, Suite 510, Bentsen Tower, 1701 W. Business Highway 83, McAllen, TX 78501 (956) 618–8145.

Miami: Alan J. Hazen, Suite 200, 510 Shotgun Road, Sunrise, FL 33326 (954) 370–8300.

New York: Ralph F. Paige, One Battery Park, 29th floor, New York, NY 10004 (212) 824–3650.

Philadelphia: Kenneth R. Connaughton, Jr., P.O. Box 43508, Philadelphia, PA 19106 (215) 861–8755.

San Francisco: Norman K. Lau, Suite 220, 1200 Bayhill Drive, San Bruno, CA 94066 (650) 876–9058.

Seattle: Wayne Hawney, Suite 104, 620 Kirkland Way, Kirkland, WA 98033 (425) 828–3998.

Tucson: William L. King, Jr., 405 West Congress, Room 3600, Tucson, AZ 85701 (520) 620–7389.

Washington: Charles T. Huggins, 1425 New York Avenue, NW., Suite 7100, Washington, DC 20530 (202) 616–4760.

Fraud Detection Office.—David R. Glendinning, room 7100 (202) 353–2975.

INTERPOL—U.S. NATIONAL CENTRAL BUREAU
phone (202) 616–9000

Director.—Martin Renkiewicz, 616–9700.

Deputy Director.—Timothy A. Williams.

Information Technology.—Wayne Towson, 616–3855.

General Counsel.—Kevin Smith, 616–4103.

Assistant Director, Division of:

Administrative Services.—Aaron A. BoBo, 616–7983.

Alien/Fugitive.—Esteban Soto, 616–0310.

Drug.—Linda Winn, 616–3379.

Economic Crimes.—Wai Men Leung, 616–5466.

State and Local Liaison.—Michael D. Muth, 616–8272.

Terrorism and Violent Crimes.—Dennis Bolles, 616–7258.

OFFICE OF INTERGOVERNMENTAL AND PUBLIC LIAISON

RFK Main Justice Building, Room 1629, phone (202) 514–3465

Director.—Crystal R. Jezierski.
Deputy Director.—Eric Holland.
Associate Directors: Brian Cohen, Julie Warren.

JUSTICE MANAGEMENT DIVISION

RFK Main Justice Building, 950 Pennsylvania Avenue, NW., 20530

Rockville Building, 1151–D Seven Locks Road, Rockville, MD 20854 (ROC)

Bicentennial Building, 600 E Street, NW., 20004 (BICN)

National Place Building, 1331 Pennsylvania Avenue, NW., 20530 (NPB)

Liberty Place Building, 325 7th Street, NW., 20530 (LPB)

20 Massachusetts Avenue, NW., 20530

Patrick Henry Building, 601 D Street, NW., 20530 (PHB)

Assistant Attorney General for Administration.—Lee J. Lofthus, room 1111 (202) 514–3101.
Deputy Assistant Attorney General/Policy, Management and Planning.—Michael H. Allen.
Staff Directors for—
Department Ethics Office.—Janice Rodgers, 1331 F Street, 514–8196.
General Counsel Office.—Stuart Frisch, General Counsel (NPB), room 520, 514–3452.
Internal Review and Evaluation Office.—Neil Ryder, room 1055 (NPB), 616–5499.
Management and Planning.—David Orr (NPB), room 1400, 307–1800.
Procurement Executive.—Michael H. Allen, room 1111, 514–3101.
Records Management Policy Office.—Jeanette Plante, room 1209 (NPB), 514–3528.
Small and Disadvantaged Business Utilization Office.—David Sutton (NPB), room 1010, 616–0521.
Deputy Assistant Attorney General/Controller.—Jolene Lauria-Sullens (acting), room 1112, 514–1843.
Staff Directors for—
Asset Forfeiture Management.—Michael Perez, room 6400, 20 Massachusetts Avenue, 616–8000.
Budget.—Karin O'Leary (acting), room 7601, 514–4082.
Debt Collection Management.—Kathleen Haggerty (Liberty Place), 2nd Floor, 514–5343.
Finance.—Melinda Morgan (BICN), room 4070, 616–5800.
Procurement Services.—James Johnston (NPB), room 1000, 307–2000.
Unified Financial System Project Management Office.—Kay Clarey, room 10100 (PHB), 305–3651.
Deputy Assistant Attorney General, Human Resources/Administration.—Mari Santangelo, room 1112, 514–5501.
Associate Assistant Attorney General for Federal Law Enforcement Training.—Thomas G. Milburn, Glynco, GA 31524 (912) 267–2914.
Staff Directors for—
Attorney Recruitment and Management Office.—Louis DeFalaise, Suite 5200, 20 Massachusetts Avenue, 514–8900.
Consolidated Executive Office.—Cyntoria Carter, room 7113, 514–5537.
DOJ Executive Secretariat.—Dana Paige, room 4412, 514–2063.
Equal Employment Opportunity.—Blane Dessy (acting), 620 VT2, 616–4800.
Facilities and Administrative Services.—Ronald Deacon, (NPB), room 1050, 616–2995.
Library.—Blaine Dessy, room 7535, 514–2133.
Personnel.—Roy Pagliarini (NPB), room 1110, 514–6788.
Security and Emergency Planning.—James Dunlap, room 6217, 514–2094.
Deputy Assistant Attorney General/Information Resources Management and CIO.—Vance Hitch, room 1310–A, 514–0507.
Staff Directors for—
E-Government Services.—Mike Duffy, room 1314, 514–0507.

Enterprise Solutions.—John Murray (PHB), room 4606, 514–0507.
IT Security.—Dennis Heretick (PHB), room 1600, 514–0507.
Operation Services.—Roger Beasley (acting), room 1315, 514–3404.
Policy and Planning.—Kent Holgrewe, room 1310, 514–4292.

OFFICE OF JUSTICE PROGRAMS (OJP)

810 7th Street, NW., 20531

Assistant Attorney General.—Regina B. Schofield, room 6400 (202) 307–5933.
Deputy Assistant Attorneys General: Cybele Daley, David Hagy, Beth McGarry.
Manager, Equal Employment Opportunity.—Stacie Brockman, room 6109, 307–6013.

OFFICE OF ADMINISTRATION

Director.—Phillip Merkle, room 3424, 307–2534.
Director of:
Acquisition Management.—Eldred Jackson, room 3605, 514–0696.
Building and Support Services.—Bobby J. Railey, room 3418, 305–1549.
Personnel.—Janie Payne, room 3330, 514–0038.

OFFICE OF BUDGET AND MANAGEMENT SERVICES

Director.—Jill R. Meldon, room 6248, 307–5980.

BUREAU OF JUSTICE ASSISTANCE

Director.—Domingo S. Herraiz, room 4427, 353–2720.
Deputy Directors of:
Planning.—Hope D. Janke (acting), room 4429, 514–6094.
Policy.—James H. Burch II, room 4207, 307–5910.
Programs.—Eileen Garry, room 4345, 307–6226.
Associate Deputy Directors of:
Policy.—Pamela Cammarata, room 4428, 514–9193; Elizabeth Griffith, room 4121, 616–2008; James Patrick McCreary, room 4124, 616–0532.

BUREAU OF JUSTICE STATISTICS

Director.—Jeffrey L. Sedgwick, room 2413, 307–0765.
Principal Deputy Director for Statistical Collections and Analysis.—Allen J. Beck, room 2414, 616–3277.
Deputy Director for Statistical Planning, Policy and Operations.—Maureen A. Henneberg, room 2409, 616–3282.
Chief, Office of:
Corrections Statistics.—William Sabol, room 2239, 514–1062.
Criminal Justice Data Improvement Program.—Gerard Ramker, room 2323, 307–0759.
Law Enforcement, Adjudication, and Federal Statistics.—Steven K. Smith, room 2338, 616–3485.
Publication and Dissemination.—Doris Jams, room 2250, 616–3625.
Special Analysis and Methodology.—Patrick A. Langan, room 2326, 616–3490.
Victimization Statistics.—Michael Rand, room 2215, 616–3494.

OFFICE OF CHIEF INFORMATION OFFICER

Chief Information Officer.—Gerald Fralick, room 8411, 305–9071.
Deputy Chief Information Officer.—Kyle Holtzman, room 8425.

OFFICE FOR CIVIL RIGHTS

Director.—Michael Alston, room 8124, 307–0690.

OFFICE OF COMMUNICATIONS

Director.—Cybele Daley (acting), room 6338, 307–5933.

COMMUNITY CAPACITY DEVELOPMENT OFFICE

Director.—Dennis E. Greenhouse, 616–1152.
Deputy Director.—Denise I. Viera.
Associate Director.—Terrance Donahue.

OFFICE OF THE COMPTROLLER

Chief Financial Officer.—Marica K. Paull, room 5248, 353–2820.
Deputy Comptroller for—
Finance and Accounting.—Frank Ramos, room 5252, 514–5579.
Grants Financial Management.—Larry Hailes, room 5254, 514–7925.
Assistant Deputy Comptrollers: Angel ''Jerry'' Conty, room 8234, 514–7934; Joanne Suttington, room 5322, 305–2122.

OFFICE OF GENERAL COUNSEL

General Counsel.—Rafael A. Madan, room 5418, 307–0790.
Principal Deputy General Counsel.—Gregory C. Brady, room 5328, 616–3254.
Deputy General Counsel.—John L. Pensinger, room 5420, 616–2370.

OFFICE OF JUVENILE JUSTICE AND DELINQUENCY PREVENTION

Administrator.—J. Robert Flores, room 3345, TWC, 307–5911.
Deputy Administrator for—
Policy.—Gregory Harris, room 3353, TWC, 353–7105.
Programs.—Marilyn Roberts, room 3349, TWC, 616–9055.
Associate Administrators of:
Child Protection.—Ronald C. Laney, room 3135, TWC, 616–7323.
Communications Policy Advisor.—Catherine Doyle, room 3319, TWC, 514–9208.
Demonstrations Program Division.—Jeffrey Slowikowski, room 3141, TWC, 616–3646.
State Relations and Assistance Division.—Gregory Thompson, room 3411, TWC, 616–3663.

NATIONAL INSTITUTE OF JUSTICE

Principal Deputy Director.—David W. Hagy, room 7422, 307–2942.
Deputy Directors for—
Research and Evaluation.—Thomas Feucht, room 7330, 307–2949.
Science and Technology.—John Morgan, room 7234, 305–0645.
Division Chief, Office of:
Communications.—Jolene Hernon, room 7117, 307–1464.
Crime Control and Prevention.—Winifred Reed (acting), room 7440, 307–2952.
Evaluations.—Patrick Clark (acting), room 7250, 353–9482.
Information and Sensor Technology.—Hyuk Byun, room 7252, 616–1471.
Investigative and Forensic Sciences.—Susan Narveson, room 7123, 305–4884.
Justice Systems Research.—Marlene Beckman (acting), room 7403, 616–3562.
Planning, Budget, Management and Administration.—Rhonda Jones, room 7423, 616–3233.
Operational Technologies.—Marc Caplan, room 7224, 307–2956.
Violence and Victimization Research.—Angela Moore Parmley, room 7355, 307–0145.

OFFICE FOR VICTIMS OF CRIME

Director.—John W. Gillis, room 8322, 307–5983.
Chief of Staff.—Timothy M. Hagle, room 8327, 307–5983.
Principal Deputy Director.—Carolyn A. Hightower, room 8328, 307–5983.
Deputy Director.—Barbara Walker, room 8331, 307–5983.

Directors of:

Program Development and Dissemination.—Joye Frost, room 8338, 307–5983.

State Compensation and Assistance.—Toni Thomas, room 8216, 307–5983.

OFFICE OF LEGAL COUNSEL

RFK Main Justice Building, Room 5218, phone (202) 514–2051

Assistant Attorney General.—Steven G. Bradbury (acting).

Deputy Assistant Attorneys General: Michelle Boardman, room 5229, 514–8469; John Eisenberg, room 5235, 514–3712; John Elwood, room 5218, 514–4132; C. Kevin Marshall, room 5231, 514–3713.

Counsel to the Assistant Attorney General.—Steve Engel, room 5237, 514–9700.

Special Counsels: Paul P. Colborn, room 5240, 514–2048; Rosemary A. Hart, room 5242, 514–2027; Daniel L. Koffsky, room 5268, 514–2030.

Senior Counsels: Caroline Krass, room 5262, 514–0102; George Smith, room 5244, 514–4174.

OFFICE OF LEGAL POLICY

RFK Main Justice Building, Room 4234, phone (202) 514–4601

Assistant Attorney General.—Rachel Brand, 616–0038.

Principal Deputy Assistant Attorney General.—Richard Hertling, room 4226, 514–9114.

Deputy Assistant Attorneys General: Frank Campbell, room 4245, 514–2283; Elisebeth Cook, room 4233, 514–6131; Kevin Jones, room 4250, 514–4604; Kristi Remington, room 4237, 514–8356.

Staff Director/Senior Counsel.—Ryan Bounds, room 4228, 305–4870.

OFFICE OF LEGISLATIVE AFFAIRS

RFK Main Justice Building, Room 1145, phone (202) 514–2141

Assistant Attorney General.—James H. Clinger (acting).

Special Counsel to the Assistant Attorney General.—M. Faith Burton.

Deputy Assistant Attorneys General: James H. Clinger, Rebecca Seidel.

NATIONAL DRUG INTELLIGENCE CENTER (NDIC)

319 Washington Street, Johnstown, PA 15901–1622, phone (814) 532–4601

RFK Main Justice Building, Room 1335, 20530, phone (202) 532–4040

Director.—Irene S. Hernandez (acting), (814) 532–4607.

Deputy Director/Chief Counsel.—Thomas W. Padden (acting), (814) 532–4984.

Chief of Staff.—Steven R. Frank (814) 532–4728.

Assistant Director for—

Intelligence Division.—Joseph E. Donovan (acting), (814) 532–4613.

Intelligence Support Division.—David J. Mrozowski (814) 532–4926.

Policy and Interagency Affairs.—Joseph E. Donovan (202) 532–4040.

Telephone Directory Coordinator.—Pamela Warchola (814) 532–4607.

NATIONAL SECURITY DIVISION

RFK Main Justice Building, Room 2200C, phone (202) 514–1057

Assistant Attorney General.—Kenneth L. Wainstein.

Deputy Assistant Attorneys General: Brett C. Gerry, Matthew G. Olsen (acting), J. Patrick Rowan.

Chief of Staff.—Charles M. Steele.

Deputy Chief of Staff.—Jessie K. Liu.

Senior Counsels to the Assistant Attorney General: John Demers, George Z. Toscas.

Counsel to the Assistant Attorney General.—Kathryn Haun.

Special Assistant to the Assitant Attorney General.—Jeanette R. Smith.

COUNTERESPIONAGE SECTION

Chief.—John Dion, room 9100, 514–1187.
Deputy Chief.—Ronald Roos.

COUNTERTERRORISM SECTION

Chief.—Michael J. Mullaney (acting), room 2643, 514–0849.
Deputy Chief for—
International Terrorism Unit I.—John Vanlonkhuyzen (acting).
International Terrorism Unit II.—Sharon Lever (acting).
Policy, Legislation, and Planning Unit.—Ronnie L. Edelman.
Terrorist Financing Unit.—Jeffrey Breinholt.

OFFICE OF INTELLIGENCE POLICY AND REVIEW

Counsel for Intelligence Policy.—James A. Baker, room 6150, 514–5600.
Deputy Counsel for—
Intelligence Law.—Lionel Kennedy.
Intelligence Operations.—Margaret Skelly-Nolen.
Intelligence Policy.—Mark A. Bradley.

OFFICE OF JUSTICE FOR VICTIMS OF OVERSEAS TERRORISM
1301 New York Avenue, NW., Room 512, 20005

Director.—Gregg Sofer, 532–4100.

OFFICE OF THE PARDON ATTORNEY
1425 New York Avenue, NW., 20530, phone (202) 616–6070

Pardon Attorney.—Roger C. Adams.
Deputy Pardon Attorney.—Susan M. Kuzma.
Executive Officer.—William J. Dziwura.

OFFICE OF PROFESSIONAL RESPONSIBILITY
RFK Main Justice Building, Room 3266, phone (202) 514–3365

Counsel.—H. Marshall Jarrett.
Deputy Counsel.—Judith B. Wish.
Associate Counsels: William J. Birney, Paul L. Colby, James G. Duncan, Mary Anne Hoopes.
Senior Assistant Counsels: Neil C. Hurley, Tamara Kessler.
Assistant Counsels: Kathleen Brandon, Nadira Clarke, Terry Derden, Mark G. Fraase, Lisa Griffin, Lyn A. Hardy, Lisa Howard, Tamara J. Kessler, Frederick C. Leiner, James Meade, Margaret S. McCarty, Simone E. Ross, Robert Thomson, Marlene M. Wahowiak, Barbara L. Ward, Karen A. Wehner.

PROFESSIONAL RESPONSIBILITY ADVISORY OFFICE
1425 New York Avenue, NW., 20530, phone (202) 514–0458

Director.—Barbara Kammerman (acting).
Deputy Director.—Jerri Dunston (acting).

OFFICE OF PUBLIC AFFAIRS
RFK Main Justice Building, Room 1220, phone (202) 514–2007

Director.—Tasia Scolinos.

Deputy Directors: Brian Roehrkasse, Gina M. Talamona.
Senior Counsel.—Kathleen Blomquist.

TAX DIVISION

RFK Main Justice Building, 950 Pennsylvania Avenue, NW., 20530

Judiciary Center Building, 555 Fourth Street, NW., 20001 (JCB)

Maxus Energy Tower, 7717 N. Harwood Street, Suite 400, Dallas, TX 75242 (MAX)

Patrick Henry Building, 601 D Street, NW., 20004 (PHB)

Assistant Attorney General.—Eileen J. O'Connor, room 4141 (202) 514–2901.
Deputy Assistant Attorneys General: John DiCicco, room 4137, 514–5109 (Civil Matters); Richard T. Morrison, room 4613, 514–2901 (Appellate and Review); Dana Boente, room 4603, 514–2915 (Criminal Matters).
Senior Legislative Counsel.—Stephen J. Csontos, room 4134, 307–6419.
Civil Trial Section Chiefs:
Central Region.—Seth Heald (JCB), room 8921–B, 514–6502.
Eastern Region.—David A. Hubbert (JCB) room 6126, 307–6426.
Northern Region.—D. Patrick Mullarkey (JCB), room 7804–A, 307–6533.
Southern Region.—Michael Kearns (JCB), room 6243–A, 514–5905.
Southwestern Region.—Louise P. Hytken (MAX), room 4100 (214) 880–9725.
Western Region.—Robert S. Watkins (JCB), room 7907–B, 307–6413.
Criminal Enforcement Section Chiefs:
Northern Region.—Rosemary E. Paguni (BICN), room 5824, 514–2323.
Northern Region.—Rosemary E. Paguni (BICN), room 5824, 514–2323.
Southern Region.—Bruce Salad (PHB), room 7640, 514–5112.
Western Region.—Ronald Cimino (PHB), room 7038, 514–5072.
Section Chiefs:
Appellate.—Gilbert S. Rothenberg, room 4326, 514–3361.
Court of Federal Claims.—David Gustafson (JCB), room 8804–A, 307–6440.
Criminal Appeals and Tax Enforcement Policy.—Alan Hechtkopf (PHB), room 7002, 514–3011.
Office of Review.—Deborah Meland (acting), (JCB), room 6846, 307–6567.
Executive Officer.—Joseph E. Young (PHB), room 7802, 616–0010.

UNITED STATES MARSHALS SERVICE (USMS)

Washington, DC 20530–1000

[Use (202) for 307 exchange and (703) for 557, 603, 416 and 285 exchanges]

fax (202) 307–5040

Director.—John F. Clark (202) 307–9001.
Deputy Director.—Robert E. Trono, 307–9005.
Special Counsel to the Director.—Lisa Dickinson, 307–9004.
Equal Employment Opportunity Officer.—Joann Grady, 307–9048.
Chief of Staff.—Charles Dudley, 305–9575.
Chief, Office of Inspections.—William Snelson, 307–9155.
Chief, Office of Congressional and Public Affairs.—John J. McNulty III, 307–5410, fax 307–5228.
Congressional Affairs.—Janice E. Conway (acting), 307–9220, fax 307–5228.
Public Affairs.—Michael L. Kulstad (acting), 307–9065, fax 307–8729.

BUSINESS SERVICES DIVISION

Assistant Director.—Michael A. Pearson, 307–9395, fax 307–5026.
Director, Asset Forfeiture.—Katherine Deoudes, 307–9221, fax (703) 557–9751.

OFFICE OF FINANCE

Chief.—William Truitt, 307–9321, fax (703) 603–0386.

OFFICE OF THE GENERAL COUNSEL

Chief.—Gerald M. Auerbach, 307–9054, fax 307–9456.
Deputy General Counsel.—Lucille Roberts, 307–9050.

HUMAN RESOURCES DIVISION

Assistant Director.—Suzanne Smith, 307–9625, fax 307–9461.
Assistant Director for Training.—Brian R. Beckwith, FLETC Building 70, Glynco, GA (912) 267–2731, fax (912) 267–2882.

INVESTIGATIVE SERVICES DIVISION

24 Hour Communications Center, 307–9000, fax 307–9177

Assistant Director.—Arthur D. Roderick, 307–9707, fax 307–9299.
Chief, Investigative Operations.—T. Michael Earp, 307–9195.

JUSTICE PRISONER AND ALIEN TRANSPORTATION SYSTEM (JPATS)

Assistant Director.—Scott Rolstad, Kansas City, MO (816) 374–6060, fax 374–6040.
Air Operations.—Alexandria, LA (318) 473–7536, fax (318) 473–7522.
Air Operations, OIC.—Jerry Hurd, Oklahoma City, OK (405) 680–3404, fax 680–3466.

JUDICIAL SECURITY DIVISION

Court Security, 307–9500, fax 307–5047

Assistant Director.—Robert F. Finan, 307–9860.

MANAGEMENT AND BUDGET DIVISION

Assistant Director.—Broadine M. Brown, 307–9032, fax 307–8340.
Chief Financial Officer.—Edward Dolan, 307–9193, fax 353–8340.
Chief Information Officer.—Diane Litman, 307–9677, fax 307–5130.

OPERATIONAL SUPPORT DIVISION

Chief.—Marc Farmer, 307–9489.

WITNESS SECURITY AND PRISONER OPERATIONS DIVISION

Assistant Director.—Sylvester Jones, 307–5100, fax 305–9434.

U.S. PAROLE COMMISSION

5550 Friendship Boulevard, Suite 420, Chevy Chase, MD 20815, phone (301) 492–5990 fax (301) 492–6694

Chairman.—Edward F. Reilly, Jr.
Vice Chairman.—Cranston J. Mitchell.
Commissioners: Patricia A. Cushwa, Isaac Fulwood, Jr., Deborah A. Spagnoli.
Chief of Staff.—Thomas W. Hutchison.
Case Operations Administrator.—Stephen J. Husk.
Case Service Administrator.—Roslyn F. Davis.
General Counsel.—Rockne J. Chickinell.
Executive Officer.—Judy I. Carter.
Staff Assistant to the Chairman.—Patricia W. Moore.

OFFICE ON VIOLENCE AGAINST WOMEN

800 K Street, NW., Suite 920, 20530

Director.—Mary Beth Buchanan (acting), room 9327, (202) 307–0728.

Deputy Tribal Director.—Lorraine Edmo, room 9319, 514–8804.
Principal Deputy Director.—Kirsten Rowe, room 9309, 305–7560.
Special Assistant to the Director.—Saundra Lonic, room 9306, 514–6975.
Associate Directors: Darlene Johnson, room 9424, 307–6795; Lauren Nassikas, room 9225, 305–1792; Nadine Neufville, room 9425, 305–2590; Susan Williams, room 9212, 616–3851.

DEPARTMENT OF THE INTERIOR

Interior Building, 1849 C Street, NW., 20240, phone (202) 208–3100, http://www.doi.gov

DIRK KEMPTHORNE, Secretary of the Interior; born in San Diego, CA, October 29, 1951; education: B.S., University of Idaho, 1975; professional: Executive Assistant to the Director, Idaho Department of Public Lands, 1976–78; Executive Vice President, Idaho Home Builders Association, 1978–81; campaign manager for gubernatorial candidate Phil Batt, 1982; State Public Affairs Manager, FMC Corporation, 1983–86; Major of Boise, Idaho, 1986–93; Senator, Idaho, 1993–99; Governor, Idaho, 1999–2006; Chairman, National Governors Association, 2003; appointed to the National Assessment Governing Board; appointed to the Homeland Security Task Force; President, Council of State Governments; Chairman, Western Governors Association; served on Executive Committees of the National Governors Association and Republican Governors Association; religion: Methodist; family: married to Patricia; children: Heather and Jeff; nominated by President George W. Bush to become the 49th Secretary of the Interior, and was confirmed by the U.S. Senate on May 26, 2006.

OFFICE OF THE SECRETARY

Secretary of the Interior.—Dirk Kempthorne, room 6156 (202) 208–7351.
Special Executive Assistant.—Margaret Bradley.
Chief of Staff.—Brian Waidmann.
Deputy Chief of Staff.—Doug Domenech, 208–5504.
Director of External and Intergovernmental Affairs.—Gary Smith, 208–1923.
Senior Adviser for Alaska Affairs.—Drue Pearce, 208–4177.
Counselor to the Secretary.—Michael Bogart, 208–4123.
Senior Advisor to the Secretary.—David Lehman, 513–0758.

EXECUTIVE SECRETARIAT

Director.—Fay Iudicello, room 7212 (202) 208–3181.
Deputy Director.—Dick Stephan, 208–5257.

CONGRESSIONAL AND LEGISLATIVE AFFAIRS

Director.—Matthew Eames, room 6256 (202) 208–7693.
Deputy Director.—Jon Hrobsky.
Legislative Counsel.—Jane Lyder, 208–6706.

OFFICE OF COMMUNICATIONS

Director.—Tina Kreisher, room 6213 (202) 208–6416.
Press Secretary.—Shane Wolfe.
Information Officers: Steve Brooks, Joan Moody, Frank Quimby, Hugh Vickery.

OFFICE OF THE DEPUTY SECRETARY

Deputy Secretary.—P. Lynn Scarlett, room 6117 (202) 208–6291.
Associate Deputy Secretary.—James E. Cason.
Assistant Deputy Secretary.—Abraham E. Haspel.
Counselor to the Deputy Secretary.—Daniel Jorjani.

ASSISTANT SECRETARY FOR FISH AND WILDLIFE AND PARKS

Assistant Secretary.—David Verhey (acting), room 3156 (202) 208–5347.

Deputy Assistant Secretaries.—Julie A. MacDonald, room 3144, 208–3928; Todd Willens, room 3154, 208–5378.

U.S. FISH AND WILDLIFE SERVICE

Director.—H. Dale Hall (202) 208–4717.
Deputy Director.—Kenneth P. Stansell (acting).
Chief, Office of Law Enforcement.—Benito Perez (acting), 208–3809.
Assistant Director for External Affairs.—Elizabeth H. Stevens, 208–3809.
Chief, Division of:
Congressional and Legislative Affairs.—Christine Eustis, 208–5403.
Conservative Partnerships.—Phil Million (703) 358–1711.
Public Affairs.—Chris Tollefson, 208–4131.
Assistant Director for Migratory Birds.—Paul Schmidt, 208–1050.
Chief, Office of Federal Aid.—Jim Greer (703) 358–2156.
Assistant Director for—
Budget, Planning, and Human Resources.—Denise Sheehan (703) 358–2333.
Chief, Division of Human Resources.—Peggy Phelps (703) 358–1776.
Business Management and Operations.—Paul Henne (703) 358–1822.
Endangered Species.—Brian Arroyo (acting), 208–4646.
Fisheries and Habitat Conservation.—Mamie Parker, 208–6394.
International Affairs.—Teiko Saito (acting), 208–6393.
National Wildlife Refuge System.—Geoff Haskett, 208–5333.
Wildlife and Sport Fish Restoration Programs.—Rowan Gould, 208–1050.
Regional Directors:
Region 1.—Renne Lohoefner, Eastside Federal Complex, 911 Northeast 11th Avenue, Portland, OR 97232 (503) 231–6118, fax 872–2716.
California/Nevada Operations.—Steve Thompson, 2800 Cottage Way, Suite W2606, Sacramento, CA 95823 (916) 414–6486.
Region 2.—Benjamin Tuggle, PO Box 1306, Room 1306, 500 Gold Avenue SW., Albuquerque, NM 87103 (505) 248–6845.
Region 3.—Robyn Thorson, Federal Building, Fort Snelling, Twin Cities, MN 55111 (612) 713–5301.
Region 4.—Samuel D. Hamilton, 1875 Century Boulevard, Atlanta, GA 30345 (404) 679–4000, fax 679–4006.
Region 5.—Marvin Moriarty, 300 Westgate Center Drive, Hadley, MA 01035 (413) 253–8300, fax 253–8308.
Region 6.—Mitch King, PO Box 25486, Denver Federal Center, Denver, CO 80225 (303) 236–7920, fax 236–8295.
Region 7.—Thomas O. Melius, 1011 East Tudor Road, Anchorage, AK 99503 (907) 786–3542, fax 786–3306.

NATIONAL PARK SERVICE

Director.—Mary A. Bomar, room 3112 (202) 208–4621.
Deputy Director for Operations.—Steve P. Martin, room 3113.
Deputy Director for Support Services.—Karen Taylor-Goodrich (acting), room 3124.
Chief of Staff.—Sue Masica (acting), room 3120.
Associate Director for—
Cultural Resources.—Jan Matthews, room 3128, 208–7625.
Natural Resources, Stewardship and Science.—Mike Soukup, room 3130, 208–3884.
Park Planning, Facilities and Lands.—Dan Wenk (acting), room 3116, 208–3264.
Partnerships, Interpretation, and Education, Volunteers and Outdoor Recreation.—Chris Jarvi, room 3129, 208–4829.
Visitor and Resource Protection.—Karen Taylor-Goodrich, room 3124, 565–1020.
Comptroller.—Bruce Sheaffer, room 2711, 208–4566.
Assistant Director for Legislative and Congressional Affairs.—Tom Wolfe, room 7256, 208–5655.
Chief, Office of Public Affairs.—Dave Barna, room 7012, 208–6843.

ASSISTANT SECRETARY FOR INDIAN AFFAIRS

Assistant Secretary.—Carl J. Artman, room 4160 (202) 208–6291.
Principal Deputy Assistant Secretary.—Michael Olsen, 208–7163.
Deputy Assistant Secretary for—

Economic Development.—George Skibine (acting), 219–4066.
Management.—Debbie Clark, 208–7163.
Director of:
Communications.—Nedra Darling, 219–4150.
Congressional Affairs.—Jackie Cheek, 208–6983.

BUREAU OF INDIAN AFFAIRS

Director.—William ''Pat'' Ragsdale, room 4600 (202) 208–5116.
Deputy Director of:
Field Operations.—Michael Smith.
Law Enforcement.—Chris Chaney, 208–4853.
Tribal Services.—Jerry Gidner, 513–7640.
Trust.—Arch Wells (acting), 208–5831.

BUREAU OF INDIAN EDUCATION

Director.—Thomas Dowd, room 3609 (202) 208–6123.
Chief of Staff.—Athena Brown.

ASSISTANT SECRETARY FOR LAND AND MINERALS MANAGEMENT

Assistant Secretary.—C. Stephen Allred, room 6613 (202) 208–6734.
Principal Deputy Assistant Secretary.—Chad Calvert.
Deputy Assistant Secretary.—Julie Jacobson.

BUREAU OF LAND MANAGEMENT

Director.—James Hughes (acting), room 5662 (202) 208–3801.
Deputy Director of:
Operations.—Henri Bisson.
Programs and Policy.—James Hughes.
Division Chief, Legislative Affairs and Correspondence.—Nancy Smith, 452–5010.
Deputy Division Chief.—Craig Leff.
State Directors:
Alaska.—Tom Lonnie, 222 West Seventh Avenue No. 13, Anchorage, AK 99513 (907) 271–5080, fax 271–4596.
Arizona.—Elaine Y. Zielinski, One North Central Avenue, Phoenix, AZ 85004 (602) 417–9500, fax 417–9398.
California.—Mike Pool, 2800 Cottage Way, Suite W1834, Sacramento, CA 95825 (916) 978–4600, fax 978–4699.
Colorado.—Sally Wisely, 2850 Youngfield Street, Lakewood, CO 80215 (303) 239–3700, fax 239–3934.
Eastern States.—Mike Nedd, 7450 Boston Boulevard, Springfield, VA 22153 (703) 440–1700, fax 440–1701.
Idaho.—Tom Dyer, 1387 South Vinnell Way, Boise, ID 83709 (208) 373–4000, fax 373–3919.
Montana.—Gene Terland, 5001 Southgate Drive, Billings, MT 59101 (406) 896–5012, fax 896–5004.
Nevada.—Ron Wenker, 1340 Financial Boulevard, Reno, NV 89502 (775) 861–6590, fax 861–6601.
New Mexico.—Linda S.C. Rundell, 1474 Rodeo Road, P.O. Box 27115, Sante Fe, NM 87505 (505) 438–7501, fax 438–7452.
Oregon.—Ed Shepard, 333 S.W. 1st Avenue, P.O. Box 2965, Portland, OR 97204 (503) 808–6024, fax 808–6308.
Utah.—Selma Sierra, 440 West 200 South, Suite 500, P.O. Box 45155, Salt Lake City, UT 84101 (801) 539–4010, fax 539–4013.
Wyoming.—Bob Bennett, 5353 Yellowstone Road, PO Box 1828, Cheyenne, WY 82003 (307) 775–6001, fax 775–6028.

MINERALS MANAGEMENT SERVICE

Director.—R.M. ''Johnnie'' Burton (202) 208–3500.

Deputy Director.—Walter D. Cruickshank.
Associate Director for—
Administration and Budget.—Robert E. Brown, 208–3220.
Minerals Revenue Management.—Lucy Querques Denett, 208–3515.
Offshore Minerals Management.—Robert LaBelle (acting), 208–3530.
Policy and Management Improvement.—George Triebsch, 208–3398.
Congressional Affairs:
Director.—M. Lyn Herdt, 208–3502, fax 208–3918.
Minerals Revenue Issues.—Anita Gonzales-Evans.
Offshore Minerals Issues.—Julie Fleming.
Outer Continental Shelf Regional Directors:
Alaska.—John T. Goll, 949 East 36th Avenue, Suite 300, Anchorage, AK 99508 (907) 334–5200.
Gulf of Mexico.—Chris C. Oynes, 1201 Elmwood Park Boulevard, New Orleans, LA 70123 (504) 736–2589.
Pacific.—Ellen Aronson, 770 Paseo Camarillo, Camarillo, CA 93010 (805) 389–7502.

OFFICE OF SURFACE MINING RECLAMATION AND ENFORCEMENT

Director.—Brent Wahlquist (acting), room 233 (202) 208–4006.
Deputy Director.—Glenda Owens, 208–2807.
Assistant Director for Finance and Administration.—Ted Woronka, 208–2546.
Congressional Contact.—Tom Geoghehan, 208–2838.
Regional Director for—
Appalachian Coordinating Center.—Brent T. Wahlquist, Three Parkway Center, Pittsburgh, PA 15220 (412) 937–2828, fax 937–2903.
Mid-Continent Coordinating Center.—Charles Sandberg, 501 Belle Street, Room 216, Alton, IL 62002 (618) 463–6463, fax 463–6470.
Western Coordinating Center.—Allen Klein, 1999 Broadway, Suite 3320, Denver, CO 80202 (303) 844–1401, fax 844–1522.

ASSISTANT SECRETARY FOR POLICY, MANAGEMENT AND BUDGET

Assistant Secretary.—Tom Weimer, room 5110 (202) 208–1927.
Senior Advisor.—Olivia Ferriter.
Director, Office of Budget.—John D. Trezise, room 4100, 208–5308.
Deputy Assistant Secretary for—
Business Management and Wildland Fire.—Nina Hatfield, 208–7966.
Insular Affairs.—David Cohen, room 4328, 208–4736.
Law Enforcement and Security.—Larry Parkinson, room 7352, 208–5773.
Performance, Accountability, and Human Resources.—Paul Hoffman, room 5120, 208–1738.
Policy and International Affairs.—Chris Kearney, room 5124, 208–3219.
Human Capitol Officer.—Kathleen Wheeler, room 5129, 208–4727.

ASSISTANT SECRETARY FOR WATER AND SCIENCE

Assistant Secretary.—Mark A. Limbaugh, room 6657 (202) 208–3186.
Principal Deputy Assistant Secretary.—Jason Peltier, room 6654, 208–3024.
Deputy Assistant Secretary.—Timothy R. Petty, room 6651, 208–3136.
Chief of Staff.—Amy Holley, room 6645, 208–6011.

U.S. GEOLOGICAL SURVEY

The National Center, 12201 Sunrise Valley Drive, Reston, VA 20192
phone (703) 648–7411, fax 648–4454

Director.—Mark D. Myers.
Deputy Director.—Robert E. Doyle, 648–7412.
Office of:
Administrative Policy and Services.—Karen Baker, 648–7200.
Communications and Outreach.—Barbara Wainman, 648–5750.
Congressional Liaison Officer.—Timothy J. West, 648–4300.

Human Capital.—Pam Malam, 648–7414.
Public Affairs Officer.—Scott D. Harris, 648–4054.
Associate Directors for—
Biology.—Susan D. Haseltine, 648–4050.
Geography.—Barbara J. Ryan, 648–7413.
Geology.—P. Patrick Leahy, 648–6600.
Geospatial Information and Chief Information Officer.—Karen Siderels, 648–5747.
Water.—Robert M. Hirsch, 648–5215.
Regional Director for—
Central Region.—Thomas J. Casadevall, P.O. Box 25046, Denver Federal Center, Building 810, Denver, CO 80225 (303) 202–4740.
Eastern Region.—Suzette Kimball, 11649 Leetown Road, Kearneysville, WV 25430 (304) 724–4521.
Western Region.—Anne Kinsinger (acting), 909 First Avenue, Suite 704, Seattle, WA 98104 (206) 220–4578.

BUREAU OF RECLAMATION

Commissioner.—Robert W. Johnson, room 7654 (202) 513–0501.
Deputy Commisssoner for—
External and Intergovernmental Affairs.—Brenda Burman, room 7645, 513–0615.
Policy, Administration, and Budget.—Larry Todd, room 7650, 513–0509.
Chief of Staff.—Kerry Rae, room 7646.
Chief of:
Congressional and Legislative Affairs.—Luke D. Johnson, room 7643, 513–0565.
Public Affairs.—Daniel J. DuBray, room 7644, 513–0574.
Regional Directors:
Great Plains.—Michael J. Ryan, P.O. Box 36900, Billings, MT 59107 (406) 247–7795, fax 247–7793.
Lower Colorado.—Larry Walkoviak (acting), P.O. Box 61470, Boulder City, NV 89006 (702) 293–8000, fax 293–8614.
Mid-Pacific.—Kirk C. Rodgers, 2800 Cottage Way, Sacramento, CA 95825 (916) 978–5580, fax 978–5599.
Pacific Northwest.—Bill McDonald, 1150 North Curtis Road, Suite 100, Boise, ID 83706 (208) 378–5127, fax 378–5129.
Upper Colorado.—Rick Gold, 125 South State Street, room 6107, Salt Lake City, UT 84138 (801) 524–3785, fax 524–5499.

OFFICE OF THE INSPECTOR GENERAL

Inspector General.—Earl Devaney, room 5359 (202) 208–5745.
Deputy Inspector General.—Mary Kendall Adler.
Associate Inspector General for Whistle Blower Protection.—Richard Trinidad.

OFFICE OF THE SOLICITOR

Solicitor.—David Bernhardt, room 6352 (202) 208–4423.
Deputy Solicitor.—Larry Jensen (acting).
Associate Solicitor for—
Administration.—Edward Keable.
General Law.—Art Gary.
Indian Affairs.—Carl Artman.
Land and Water.—Paul Smythe.
Mineral Resources.—Jim Harris.
Designated Agency Ethics Official.—Melinda Loftin, 208–5295.

OFFICE OF THE SPECIAL TRUSTEE FOR AMERICAN INDIANS

Special Trustee.—Ross O. Swimmer, room 5140 (202) 208–4866.

DEPARTMENT OF AGRICULTURE

Jamie L. Whitten Building, 1400 Independence Avenue, SW., 20250

phone (202) 720–3631, http://www.usda.gov

MIKE JOHANNS, Secretary of Agriculture; born in Osage, IA; education: B.A., St. Mary's University, Minnesota; J.D., Creighton University; professional: Governor, Nebraska, 1999–2005; Mayor, Lincoln, Nebraska, 1991–98; Lancaster County Board, 1982–88; Lincoln City Council, 1989–90; Practicing attorney, 1975–91; member: National Governors' Association; Western Governors' Association; married: Stephanie; two children; nominated by President George W. Bush to become the 28th Secretary of Agriculture, and was confirmed by the U.S. Senate on January 20, 2005.

OFFICE OF THE SECRETARY

Secretary of Agriculture.—Mike Johanns, room 200–A (202) 720–3631.
Deputy Secretary.—Charles F. Conner.
Chief of Staff.—Dale Moore.
Deputy Chief of Staff.—Beth Johnson.
Special Assistant to the President/Personnel.—Anthony Hulen.

ASSISTANT SECRETARY FOR ADMINISTRATION

Jamie L. Whitten Building, Room 209–A, phone (202) 720–3291

Assistant Secretary.—Boyd K. Rutherford.
Deputy Assistant Secretary.—Gilbert L. Smith.
Executive Assistant.—Annette Powe.
Confidential Assistant.—Laura Cuthill.

OFFICE OF ADMINISTRATIVE LAW JUDGES

South Agriculture Building, Room 1070–S, phone (202) 720–6383

Chief Administrative Law Judge.—Marc R. Hillson.
Secretary to the Chief Administrative Law Judge.—Diane Green.
Administrative Law Judges: Jill S. Clifton, Peter M. Davenport, Victor W. Palmer, 720–8161.
Hearing Clerk.—Joyce A. Dawson, 720–4443.

OFFICE OF HUMAN CAPITAL MANAGEMENT

Jamie L. Whitten Building, Room 302–W, phone (202) 720–3585

Director.—Roberta D. Purcell.
Deputy Director.—Lynn Heirakuji.
Division Director for—
Departmental Human Resources.—Leslie Violette, 720–2101.
Human Resources Enterprise.—Thomas Bennett, 690–4187.
Human Resources Policy.—Peter Rockx, 720–3327.
Quality of Work Life.—James Stevens, 720–8248.
Special Projects.—Mary Jo Thompson, 720–0822.
Special Assistant for Human Capital Initiative.—Clifton Taylor, 690–2139.

OFFICE OF THE JUDICIAL OFFICER

South Agriculture Building, Room 1449–S, phone (202) 720–4764

Judicial Officer.—William G. Jenson.
Legal Technician.—Gloria Derobertis.

OFFICE OF MANAGEMENT SERVICES

Finance Officer, Office of Planning and Coordination.—Lauren Godby (202) 720–5008.
Staff Assistant.—Magda Angulo, 720–3874.
Special Assistant.—Shana Love, 205–4008.
Director, Information Resources Division.—Judith Dudley, 720–5348.
Management Analyst.—Art Goldman, 720–8468.

OFFICE OF OPERATIONS

South Agriculture Building, Room 1456–S, phone (202) 720–3937

Director.—Priscilla Carey.
Deputy Director.—Morris Tate (acting).
Division Director for—
Analysis and Resource Management.—Morris Tate, 720–4134.
Beltsville Service Center.—James Connor (301) 394–0410.
Design and Construction.—Wally Aughenbaugh, 720–2804.
Mail and Reproduction.—June Bryan, 720–1806.
Washington Area Service Center.—Earl Brittingham, 720–2777.

OFFICE OF PROCUREMENT AND PROPERTY MANAGEMENT

Reporters Building, Room 302, phone (202) 720–9448

Director.—Glenn Haggstrom.
Division Director for—
Energy & Environment.—Sharon Holcombe, 720–3820.
Hazardous Materials Management.—Jeff Goodman, 401–4747.
Procurement Operations.—Michael McFarland, 690–0142.
Procurement Policy.—Todd Repass, 690–1060.
Procurement Systems.—Ruby Harvey, 401–1023.
Property Management.—Denise Hayes, 720–7283.
Radiation Safety.—John Jensen (301) 504–2440.
Resource Management.—Janet Mitchell, 720–4555.

OFFICE OF SECURITY SERVICES

Director.—Russ Ashworth, room S–310 (202) 720–9448.
Security Specialist.—Richard Holman, 720–3901.
Division Chief for—
Continuity of Operations Planning.—Leslie Pozanek, 720–2667.
Personnel and Document Security.—Susan Gulbranson, 720–7373.
Director, Office of:
Emergency Programs.—James Redington, 690–3191.
Protective Operations.—Ken Lescallett, 720–6270.

OFFICE OF SMALL AND DISADVANTAGED BUSINESS UTILIZATION

South Agriculture Building, Room 1085–S, phone (202) 720–7117

Director.—James E. House.
Deputy Director.—Joe Ware.

ASSISTANT SECRETARY FOR CIVIL RIGHTS

Jamie L. Whitten Building, Room 240–W, phone (202) 720–3808

Assistant Secretary.—Margo M. McKay.
  Deputy Assistant Secretary.—Annabelle Romero.
  Associate Assistant Secretary.—Clyde Thompson.

OFFICE OF BUDGET AND PROGRAM ANALYSIS

Jamie L. Whitten Building, Room 101–A, phone (202) 720–3323

Director.—W. Scott Steele.
  Associate Director.—Michael L. Young, 720–5303.
  Deputy Director for—
    Budget, Legislative and Regulatory Systems.—Dennis Kaplan, room 102–E, 720–6667.
    Program Analysis.—Christopher Zehren, room 126–W, 720–3396.

OFFICE OF THE CHIEF ECONOMIST

Jamie L. Whitten Building, Room 112–A, phone (202) 720–4164

Chief Economist.—Keith Collins.
  Deputy Chief Economist.—Joseph Glauber, 720–6185.
  Chairperson, World Agricultural Outlook Board.—Gerald A. Bange, room 4419–S, 720–6030.
  Chief Meteorologist.—Ray Motha, room 4441–S, 720–8651.
  Global Change Program Office.—William Hohenstein, room 4407–S, 720–6698.
  Office of Energy Policy and New Uses.—Roger Conway, room 4059–S, 401–0461.
  Office of Risk Assessment and Cost Benefit Analysis.—James Schaub, room 4032–S, 720–8022.
  Office of Sustainable Development.—Adela Backiel, room 112–A, 720–2456.
  Supervisory Meteorologist, National Weather Service.—David Miskus, room 4443–S, 720–6030.

OFFICE OF THE CHIEF FINANCIAL OFFICER

Jamie L. Whitten Building, Room 143–W, phone (202) 720–5539

Chief Financial Officer.—Charles R. Christopherson.
  Deputy Chief Financial Officer.—Patricia Healy, room 143–W, 720–0727.
  Associate Chief Financial Officers for—
    Financial Operations.—John Brewer, room 3053–S, 720–9427.
    Financial Policy and Planning.—Jon Holladay, room 3056–S, 720–8345.
    Financial Systems.—Wendy Snow, room 3057–S, 619–7636.
  Director, National Finance Center.—Jerry Lohfink, P.O. Box 60000, New Orleans, LA 70160 (504) 426–0120.

OFFICE OF THE CHIEF INFORMATION OFFICER

Jamie L. Whitten Building, Room 414–W, phone (202) 720–8833

Chief Information Officer.—Dave Combs.
  Deputy Chief Information Officer.—Jerry E. Williams.
  Associate Chief Information Officer for—
    Cyber Security.—Lynn Allen, 690–0048.
    Information Technology Managemnt.—Chris Niedermayer, 690–2118.
    Information Technology Services.—Richard Roberts, 720–3482.
    Integrations and Operations.—Robert Suda, 720–5865.
    National Information Technology Center.—Kathleen Rundle, P.O. Box 205, 8930 Ward Parkway, Kansas City, MO 64114 (816) 926–6501.
    Resource Management.—Kate Hickman, 720–0086.
    Telecommunications Services and Operations.—Jan Lilja, 720–8695.

OFFICE OF COMMUNICATIONS

Jamie L. Whitten Building, Room 402–A, phone (202) 720–4623

Director.—Terri Teuber Moore.
Deputy Director.—Nicol Andrews.
Assistant Director.—Larry Quinn.
Press Secretary.—Keith Williams.
Center Director for—
Broadcast Media and Technology.—David Black.
Constituent Affairs.—Patricia Klintberg.
Creative Services.—Carolyn O'Connor.
Information Technology.—Wayne Moore.
Web Services and Distribution.—Kim Taylor.

OFFICE OF CONGRESSIONAL RELATIONS

Jamie L. Whitten Building, Room 212–A, phone (202) 720–7095

Assistant Secretary.—Linda Avery Strachan.
Deputy Assistant Secretary.—Bruce Blanton.
Congressional Liaison for—
Farm and Foreign Agricultural Service.—James Glueck.
Food Safety and Food, Nutrition and Consumer Services.—Kyle R. Kizzier.
Natural Resources and Environment.—Taylor Oldroyd.
Marketing and Regulatory Programs/Rural Development.—Kelly M. Porter.
Research, Economics and Education.—Andrew Vlasaty.

EXTERNAL AND INTERGOVERNMENTAL AFFAIRS

Room 216–A, phone (202) 720–6643

Director.—Christopher Smith.
Deputy Director.—Matt Shilling.

NATIVE AMERICAN PROGRAMS

Room 544–A, phone (202) 690–1615

Director.—Patrick Atagi.

OFFICE OF THE EXECUTIVE SECRETARIAT

Jamie L. Whitten Building, Room 116–A, phone (202) 720–7100

Director.—Bruce Bundick.
Deputy Director.—MaryAnn Swigart.

GENERAL COUNSEL

Jamie L. Whitten Building, Room 107–W, phone (202) 720–3351

General Counsel.—Marc L. Kesselman.
Deputy General Counsel.—James Michael Kelly.
Associate General Counsel for—
Civil Rights.—Arlean Leland, 720–1760.
International Affairs: Commodity Programs and Food Assistance Programs.—Thomas V. Conway, 720–6883.
Legislation, Litigation, General Law.—James Michael Kelly, 720–3351.
Marketing, Regulatory and Food Safety Programs.—John Golden, 720–3155.
Natural Resources.—Jan Poling, 720–9311.
Rural Development.—David P. Grahn, 720–6187.
Assistant General Counsel, Division of:
Civil Rights Litigation.—Inga Bumbary-Langston, 720–3955.

Community Development.—Paul Loizeaux, 720–4591.
Conservation and Environment.—Stuart L. Shelton, 720–7121.
Food and Nutrition.—Ronald W. Hill, 720–6181.
General Law.—L. Benjamin Young, Jr., 720–5565.
International Affairs and Commodity Programs.—Ralph A. Linden, 720–9246.
Legislation.—Michael J. Knipe, 720–5354.
Litigation.—Margaret M. Breinholt, 720–4733.
Marketing.—Kenneth H. Vail, 720–5935.
Natural Resources.—Thomas Millet, 720–7121.
Regulatory.—Thomas M. Walsh, 720–5550.
Rural Utilities.—Terence M. Brady, 720–2764.
Trade Practices.—Mary K. Hobbie, 720–5293.
Director, Administration and Resource Management.—William Perrelli III, 720–6324.
Resource Management Specialist.—Deborah L. Vita, 720–4861.

INSPECTOR GENERAL

Jamie L. Whitten Building, Room 117–W, phone (202) 720–8001, fax 690–1278

Inspector General.—Phyllis K. Fong.
Deputy Inspector General.—Kathleen Tighe, room 117–W, 720–7431.
Assistant Inspector General for—
Audit.—Robert Young, room 403–E, 720–6945.
Inspections and Research.—Rod DeSmet, room 41–W, 720–7431.
Investigations.—Mark Woods, room 507–A, 720–3306.
Management.—Suzanne Murrin, room 5–E, 720–6979.

NATIONAL APPEALS DIVISION

3101 Park Center Drive, Suite 1100, Alexandria, VA 22302

Director.—Roger J. Klurfeld (703) 305–2708.
Deputy Director.—M. Terry Johnson.

UNDER SECRETARY FOR NATURAL RESOURCES AND ENVIRONMENT

Jamie L. Whitten Building, Room 217–E, phone (202) 720–7173

Under Secretary.—Mark E. Rey.
Deputy Under Secretary.—David P. Tenny.

FOREST SERVICE

Sydney R. Yates Building, 201 14th Street, SW., 20250, phone (202) 205–1661

Chief.—Abigail Kimbell.
Associate Chief.—Sally Collins, 205–1491.
Director for—
International Programs.—Valdis E. Mezainis, 205–1650.
Law Enforcement and Investigations.—John Twiss (703) 605–4690.
Legislative Affairs.—Timothy DeCoster, 205–1637.

BUSINESS OPERATIONS

Sydney R. Yates Building, Second Floor, phone (202) 205–1707

Deputy Chief.—Hank Kashdan.
Associate Deputy Chiefs: Jacqueline Myers, Irving Thomas, 205–1709.
Senior Staff Assistant.—Eurial Turner, 205–2961.
Director for—
Acquisition Management.—Ron Hooper (703) 605–4744.
Communications.—Stana Federighi, 205–1470.
Freedom of Information/Privacy Act.—Rita Morgan, 205–0611.

Human Resources Management.—Kathy Burgers (703) 605–4532.
Information Resources Management.—Vaughn Stokes (703) 605–4535.
Program and Budget Analysis.—Lenise Lago, 205–1088.
Regulatory and Management Services.—Thelma Strong, 205–5102.
Safety and Occupational Health.—Allison Good (acting), 205–2934.
Senior, Youth and Volunteer Programs.—Art Bryant (703) 605–4831.
Strategic Planning and Assessment.—Paul Brouha (703) 605–4482.

NATIONAL FOREST SYSTEM

Sydney R. Yates Building, Third Floor, phone (202) 205–1523

Deputy Chief.—Joel Holtrop.
Associate Deputy Chiefs: Gloria Manning, Fred Norbury.
Staff Director of:
Ecosystem Management Coordination.—Rich Stem (acting), 205–0895.
Engineering.—Lou Leibbrand (acting), (703) 605–4646.
Forest Management.—Corbin Newman, 205–0893.
Minerals and Geology Management: Janine Clayton (acting), Tony Ferguson (acting), (703) 605–4545.
National Partnership Office.—Jan Engert, 205–1072.
Range Management.—Janette Kaiser, 205–0893.
Recreation and Heritage Resources.—Jim Bedwell, 205–0900.
Watershed, Fish, Wildlife, Air and Rare Plants.—Anne Zimmermann, 205–1671.
Wilderness, Wild and Scenic Resources.—Chris Brown, 205–0925.

RESEARCH AND DEVELOPMENT

Sydney R. Yates Building, First Floor, phone (202) 205–1665

Deputy Chief.—Ann Bartuska, 205–1665.
Associate Deputy Chief.—Jimmy Reaves, 205–1702.
Staff Assistant.—Daina Apple, 205–1452.
Staff Director of:
Environmental Sciences.—Deanna Stouder (703) 605–5277.
Quantative Sciences.—Richard W. Guldin (703) 605–4177.
Resource Use Sciences.—Sam Foster (703) 605–4880.

STATE AND PRIVATE FORESTRY

Sydney R. Yates Building, Second Floor, phone (202) 205–1657

Deputy Chief.—James E. Hubbard, 205–1331.
Associate Deputy Chiefs: Kent Connaughton, Robin Thompson.
Staff Assistants: Marilyn Chilton, Ruth McWilliams, Debbie Pressman, Denny Truesdale.
Director of:
Conservation Education.—Safiya Samman, 205–5681.
Cooperative Forestry.—Larry Payne, 205–1643.
Fire and Aviation Management.—Tom Harbour, 205–1483.
Forest Health Protection.—Rob Mangold (703) 605–5334.
National Fire Plan.—Rick Prausa, 205–1332.
Office of Tribal Relations.—Fred Clark, 205–1514.
Urban/Community Forestry.—Larry Payne (acting), 205–1054.

NATURAL RESOURCES CONSERVATION SERVICE

South Building, Room 5105–A, phone (202) 720–7246

Chief.—Arlen Lancaster.
Associate Chief.—Dana D. York, 720–4531.
Director, Division of:
Civil Rights.—Joseph Hairston (301) 504–2181.
Legislative and Public Affairs.—Douglas J. McKalip, 720–3210.
Outreach.—Larry S. Holmes (301) 504–2229.

DEPUTY CHIEF OF MANAGEMENT

Deputy Chief.—Kevin J. Brown (202) 720–6297.
Associate Deputy Chief.—Lindavarner Mount.
Ethics Officer.—Caryl Butcher (301) 504–2202.
Director, Division of:
Financial Management.—Patricia Kelly, 720–5904.
Human Resources Management.—John Glover, 720–2227.
Information Technology.—Anita Byrd (acting), (301) 504–2232.
Management Services.—Edward M. Biggers, Jr., 720–4102.
National Employee Development Center.—Chris Tippie (817) 509–3242.

DEPUTY CHIEF OF PROGRAMS

Deputy Chief.—Thomas W. Christensen (202) 720–4527.
Associate Deputy Chief.—Tony Kramer, 702–0134.
Director, Division of:
Conservation Planning and Technical Assistance.—Leonard Jordan, 720–8851.
Easement Programs.—Robin Heard, 720–1854.
Financial Assistance Programs.—Harry Slawter, 720–1845.
Resource Conservation and Community Development and Rural Lands.—Anne Dubey, 720–2847.
Team Leader for—
Business Tools Team.—Jon Vrana, 720–4527.
Initiatives, Special Studies and Management Support.—Michael Gonzalez, 690–0547.

DEPUTY CHIEF OF SCIENCE AND TECHNOLOGY

Deputy Chief.—Lawrence E. Clark (202) 720–4630.
Director, Division of:
Animal Husbandry and Clean Water.—Richard Swenson (301) 504–2196.
Conservation Engineering.—Daniel Meyer (acting), 720–2520.
Ecological Sciences.—Diane E. Gelburd, 720–2587.
Resource Economics and Social Sciences.—Doug Lawrence, 720–2307.

DEPUTY CHIEF OF SOIL SURVEY AND RESOURCE ASSESSMENT

Deputy Chief.—William E. Puckett (202) 690–4616.
Director, Division of:
International Programs.—Melvin Westbrook (301) 504–2271.
Resources Inventory and Assessment.—Wayne Maresch (301) 504–2300.
Soil Survey.—Michael L. Golden, 720–1820.

DEPUTY CHIEF OF STRATEGIC PLANNING AND ACCOUNTABILITY

Deputy Chief.—Katherine C. Gugulis (202) 720–7847.
Director, Division of:
Budget Planning and Analysis.—Steve Probst, 720–4533.
Operations Management and Oversight.—Dan Runnels, 720–8388.
Strategic and Performance Planning—Patty Lawrence, 690–0467.

UNDER SECRETARY FOR FARM AND FOREIGN AGRICULTURAL SERVICES

Under Secretary.—Mark E. Keenum (202) 720–3111.
Deputy Under Secretaries: Floyd Gaibler, 720–2542; A. Ellen Terpstra, 720–7107.

FARM SERVICE AGENCY

South Building, Room 3086–S, phone (202) 720–3467

Administrator.—Teresa C. Lasseter.
Associate Administrator for—

Operations and Management.—Thomas B. Hofellar.
Programs.—Glen L. Keppy.
Civil Rights.—Johnny Toles, 410–7197.
Economic and Policy Analysis Staff.—Ed Rall (acting), room 3741–S, 720–3451.
Legislative Liaison Staff.—Mary Helen Askins, room 3613–S, 720–3865.
Public Affairs Staff.—Kent Poltish, room 3624–S, 720–5237.
Deputy Administrator for Farm Programs.—John Johnson, room 3612–S, 720–3175.
Assistant Deputy Administrator.—Larry Adams, 720–2070.
Conservation and Environmental Programs Division.—Robert Stephenson, room 4714–S, 720–6221.
Price Support Division.—Grady Bilberry, room 4095–S, 720–7901.
Production, Emergencies and Compliance Division.—Diane Sharp, room 4754, 720–7641.
Deputy Administrator for Loan Programs.—Carolyn Cooksie, room 3605–S, 720–4671.
Program Development and Economic Enhancement Division.—Bobby Reynolds, room 4919–S, 720–3647.
Loan Making Division.—James Radintz, room 5438–S, 720–1632.
Loan Servicing and Property Management Division.—Veldon Hall, room 5449–S, 720–4572.
Deputy Administrator for Field Operations.—Steve Connelly, room 3092, 690–2807.
Assistant Deputy Administrator.—John W. Chott, Jr., room 8092, 690–2807.
Operations Review and Analysis Staff.—Thomas McCann, room 2720–S, 690–2532.
Deputy Administrator for Commodity Operations.—Candy Thompson (acting), room 3080–S, 720–3217.
Kansas City Commodity Office.—George Aldaya (816) 926–6301.
Procurement and Donations Division.—Sue King, room 5755, 720–5074.
Warehouse and Inventory Division.—Steve Gill (acting), room 5962–S, 720–2121.
Deputy Administrator for Management.—John Williams, room 3095–S, 720–3438.
Budget Division.—Dennis Taitano, room 4720–S, 720–3674.
Financial Management Division.—Dennis Taitano, room 4747–S, 720–3674.
Human Resources Division.—Patricia Farmer, room 5200 (L-St), 418–8950.
Information Technology Services Division.—Steve Sanders, room 5768–S, 720–5320.
Management Services Division.—Mary Winters, room 520–PRTL, 720–3438.

FOREIGN AGRICULTURAL SERVICE

South Building, Room 5071, phone (202) 720–3935, fax 690–2159

Administrator.—Michael W. Yost.
Special Assistant.—Robert Rosado, 720–4261.
Chief of Staff.—Jaime Adams, 690–8064.
General Sales Manager.—W. Kirk Miller, 720–5173.
Director of:
Civil Rights Staff.—Robert Day, Jr., 720–7233.
Legislative and Public Affairs.—Dana Johnson, 720–6829.
Public Affairs and Executive Correspondence.—Maureen Quinn, 720–7115.

OFFICE OF ADMINISTRATIVE OPERATIONS

Deputy Administrator.—Robin Tilsworth (202) 720–9227.
Senior Advisor.—David Pendlum, 720–1293.
Director, Division of:
Budget.—Scott Redman, 690–4052.
Contracts and Agreements.—Edwin MacLaughlin, 720–0281.
Information Technology.—Eva Ripollone, 690–2936.
Program Management.—William Hawkins, 720–3241.

OFFICE OF CAPACITY BUILDING AND DEVELOPMENT

Deputy Administrator.—Patricia R. Sheikh (202) 720–6887.
Assistant Deputy Administrators: Christian Foster, 690–1791; Ross Kreamer, 690–4056.
Director, Division of:
Development Resources and Disaster Assistance.—Grant Pettrie, 690–1924.
Food Assistance.—Ronald Croushorn, 720–4221.
Monitoring and Evaluation.—Lorie Jacobs, 720–2074.

Trade and Scientific Capacity Building.—Susan Owens, 690–4872.
Trade and Scientific Exchanges.—Lynne Reich, 690–1821.

OFFICE OF COUNTRY AND REGIONAL AFFAIRS

Deputy Administrator.—Charles Alexander (202) 720–3253.
Assistant Deputy Administrators: Jocelyn Brown, 690–1779; Norval Francis, 720–6138.
Director, Division of:
Africa and Middle East/Western Hemisphere.—Merritt Chesley, 690–3737.
Asia.—Cina Radler, 720–3403.
Europe.—Robert Curtis, 720–1330.

OFFICE OF FOREIGN SERVICE OPERATIONS

Deputy Administrator.—Franklin D. Lee (202) 720–4761.
Assistant Deputy Administrator.—Susan Schayes, 690–4062.
Director for—
Africa and Middle East Area.—Randall Hager, 690–4066.
Asia Area.—David Young, 690–4057.
Europe Area.—James Dever, 690–4053.
Planning and Resources Staff.—Margaret Thursland, 690–0685.
Western Hemisphere Area.—Jeanne Bailey, 720–3223.

OFFICE OF GLOBAL ANALYSIS

Deputy Administrator.—Asif Chaudhry (202) 720–6301.
Assistant Deputy Administrators: John Nuttall, 690–1198; Patrick Packnett, 720–1590.
Agricultural Economists: Michael Dwyer, 720–3124; Renee Schwartz, 720–9825.
Director, Industry and Sector Analysis Division.—Larry Deaton, 720–0895.

OFFICE OF NEGOTIATIONS AND AGREEMENTS

Deputy Administrator.—Robert Riemenschneider (202) 720–6219.
Assistant Deputy Administrators: Kathryn Ting, 720–7136; Gregg Young, 720–1324.
Director, Division of:
Monitoring and Enforcement.—David Mergen, 720–9519.
Multilateral Negotiations and Agreements.—Charles Bertsch, 720–6278.
Regional and Bilateral Negotiations and Agreements.—Brian Grunenfelder, 720–2056.

OFFICE OF SCIENTIFIC AND TECHNICAL AFFAIRS

Deputy Administrator.—William L. Brant II (202) 720–2701.
Assistant Deputy Administrators: Robert Macke, 720–4434; Beverly Simmons, 720–1286; Howard Wetzel, 720–8031.
Director, Division of:
International Regulations and Standards.—Daryl Brehm, 690–0929.
Market Access and Bilateral Issues.—Kent Sisson, 720–2579.

OFFICE OF TRADE PROGRAMS

Deputy Administrator.—Larry Blum (acting), (202) 720–9516.
Assistant Deputy Administrators: Jeff Hesse, 720–2705; Denise Huttenlocker, 720–0921.
Director, Division of:
Credit Programs.—Mark Rowse, 720–0624.
Import and Trade Support Programs.—Lana Bennett, 720–0638.
Market Development and Grants Management.—David Salmon, 720–6343.

RISK MANAGEMENT AGENCY

South Building, Room 6092–S, phone (202) 690–2803

Administrator.—Eldon Gould.

Associate Administrator.—James Callan.
Deputy Administrator for—
Compliance.—Michael Hand, room 4619–S, 720–0642.
Insurance Services.—William Murphy, room 6709–S, 690–4494.
Product Management.—Timothy Witt, Kansas City (816) 926–7394/7822.

UNDER SECRETARY FOR RURAL DEVELOPMENT

Jamie L. Whitten Building, phone (202) 720–4581

Under Secretary.—Thomas C. Dorr.
Deputy Under Secretary.—Douglas L. Faulkner.
Chief of Staff.—Jim Fitzgerald.
Confidential Assistant to the Under Secretary.—Susan Stacey.
Director, Legislative and Public Affairs.—Timothy McNeilly (acting), 720–4581.

BUSINESS AND COOPERATIVE PROGRAMS

South Building, Room 5801–S, phone (202) 690–4730

Administrator.—Jackie J. Gleason.
Associate Administrator.—Ben Anderson, 720–6165.
Oversight/Resource Coordination Staff (OCS).—Nannie Hill-Midgett, 690–4100.
Deputy Administrator for Business Programs.—William F. Hagy III, 720–7287.
Director of:
Business and Industry Division.—Carolyn Parker, 690–4103.
Specialty Lenders Division.—Jody Raskind, 720–0410.
Deputy Administrator for Cooperative Programs.—Leann Oliver, 720–7558.
Assistant Deputy Administrator.—David Sears (acting), 720–8460.
Director of:
Cooperative Development Division.—John H. Wells, 720–3350.
Cooperative Marketing Division.—Thomas H. Stafford, 690–0368.
Cooperative Resources Management Division.—John R. Dunn, 690–1374.

RURAL HOUSING SERVICE

South Building, Room 5014–S, phone (202) 690–1533

Administrator.—Russell T. Davis.
Director, Program Support Staff.—Richard A. Davis, 720–9619.
Deputy Administrator for Single Family.—David J. Vilano, 720–5177.
Director of:
Family Housing Direct Loan Division.—Philip Stetson, 720–1474.
Family Housing Guaranteed Loan Division.—Roger Glendenning, 720–1452.
Deputy Administrator for Multi-Family Housing.—Thomas Hannah, 720–3773.
Deputy Director.—Sue Harris-Green, 720–1606.
Director of:
Direct Loan and Grant Processing Division.—Chadwick Parker, 720–1502.
Multi-Family Housing Portfolio Management Division, Direct Housing.—Stephanie White, 720–1600.

RURAL UTILITIES SERVICE

South Building, Room 5135, phone (202) 720–9540

Administrator.—James M. Andrew.
Deputy Administrator.—Curtis M. Anderson, 720–0962.
Assistant Administrator for—
Electric Division.—Jim Newby, room 5165, 720–9545.
Program Accounting and Regulatory Analysis.—Kenneth M. Ackerman, room 5159, 720–9450.
Telecommunications.—Jacqueline Ponti, room 5151, 720–9554.
Water and Environmental Programs.—Gary J. Morgan, room 5145, 690–2670.
Director of:
Advanced Services Division.—Orren E. Cameron, room 2845–S, 690–4493.

Broadband Division.—Kenneth Kuchno, room 2846–S, 690–4673.
Electric Staff Division.—George J. Bagnall, room 1246–S, 720–1900.
Northern Regional Electric Division.—Nivin Elgohary, room 0243–S, 720–1420.
Northern Area, Telecommunications Program.—Jerry H. Brent, room 2835–S, 720–1025.
Power Supply Division.—Victor T. Vu, room 270–S, 720–6436.
Southern Regional Electric Division.—Robert O. Ellinger, room 221–S, 720–0848.
Southern Area, Telecommunications Program.—Ken B. Chandler, room 2808–S, 720–0800.
Telecommunications Standards Division.—John Schnell (acting), room 2868–S, 720–8663.
Chief, Portfolio Management Branch.—Steve Saulnier, room 2231–S, 720–9631.
Engineering and Environmental Staff.—Mark Plank, room 2237, 720–1649.

UNDER SECRETARY FOR FOOD, NUTRITION AND CONSUMER SERVICES

Jamie L. Whitten Building, Room 240–E, phone (202) 720–7711, fax 690–3100

Under Secretary.—Nancy Montanez Johner.
Deputy Under Secretary.—Kate Coler.

CENTER FOR NUTRITION POLICY AND PROMOTION

3101 Park Center Drive, Room 1032, Alexandria, VA 22302
phone (703) 305–7600, fax 305–3300

Executive Director.—Dr. Eric Hentges.
Director for—
Nutrition Policy and Analysis Staff.—Carole Davis (acting).
Nutrition Promotion Staff.—Carole Davis.
Public Information and Governmental Affairs—John Webster.

FOOD AND NUTRITION SERVICE

3101 Park Center Drive, Room 906, Alexandria, VA 22302, phone (703) 305–2062

Director.—Roberto Salazar.
Associate Administrator.—George A. Braley, 305–2060.

ANALYSIS, NUTRITUION AND EVALUATION

Director.—Steven Carlson (acting), (703) 305–2017.
Division Director of:
Family Program Staff.—Carol Olander, 305–2134.
Nutrition Services Staff.—Judy Wilson, 305–2585.
Special Nutrition Staff.—Jay Hirschman, 305–2117.

COMMUNICATIONS AND GOVERNMENTAL AFFAIRS

Deputy Administrator.—Steve Savage, room 920 (703) 305–2281.
Director of:
Consumer and Community Affairs.—Pam Phillips, room 912, 305–2000.
Governmental Affairs.—Robert Beard (acting), room 910, 305–2010.
Public Affairs.—Susan Acker, room 920, 305–2286.

FINANCIAL MANAGEMENT

Deputy Administrator.—Gary Maupin, room 712 (703) 305–2046.
Divisional Director of:
Accounting.—Rose McClyde, room 724, 305–2447.
Budget.—David Burr, room 708, 305–2189.

FOOD STAMP PROGRAM

Deputy Administrator.—Clarence Carter, room 808 (703) 305–2026.

Associate Deputy Administrator.—Jessica Shahin, room 808, 305–2022.
Division Director of:
Benefit Redemption.—Jeff Cohen, room 400, 305–2756.
Program Accountability.—Karen Walker.
Program Development.—Arthur T. Foley, room 814, 305–2490.

MANAGEMENT

Deputy Administrator.—Gloria Gutierrez, room 314 (703) 305–2030.
Associate Deputy Administrator.—Tim O'Connor, room 314, 305–2032.
Director of:
Human Resources Division.—Laura Wilmot, room 614, 305–2326.
Information Technology Division.—Enrique Gomez, room 304, 305–2754.

SPECIAL NUTRITION PROGRAMS

Deputy Administrator.—Kate Houston, room 628 (703) 305–2052.
Associate Administrator.—Ron Vogel, 305–2054.
Division Director of:
Child Nutrition.—Stan Garnets, room 620, 305–2590.
Food Distribution.—Cathie McCullough, room 500, 305–2680.
Supplemental Food Programs.—Patricia Daniels, room 520, 305–2746.

UNDER SECRETARY FOR FOOD SAFETY

Under Secretary.—Dr. Richard Raymond (202) 720–0350.
Deputy Under Secretary.—Dr. Curt J. Mann.
Confidential Assistant to the Under Secretary.—Michael Steele.

FOOD SAFETY AND INSPECTION SERVICE

Jamie L. Whitten Building, Room 331–E, phone (202) 720–7025, fax 690–0550

Administrator.—Dr. David Goldman (acting).
Deputy Administrator.—Bryce Quick, 720–7900.
U.S. Manager for Codex.—Dr. F. Ed. Scarbrough, room 4861–S, 720–2057.

OFFICE OF FIELD OPERATIONS (OFO)

Assistant Administrator.—Dr. Kenneth E. Petersen, room 344–E (202) 720–8803.
Deputy Assistant Administrator.—Judy Riggins, 720–5190.
Executive Associates, Regulatory Operations: Dr. John C. Prucha, room 3161–S, 720–5768; Dr. Armia Tawadrous, room 3154–S, 720–3697.
Director of:
Recall Management Staff.—Dr. Hany Sidrak, room 0008–S, 690–6389.
State Program Liaison Staff.—Dr. Murli M. Prasad, room 329–WEC, 418–8897.

OFFICE OF FOOD DEFENSE AND EMERGENCY RESPONSE (OFDER)

Assistant Administrator.—Dr. Carol A. Maczka, room 3130–S (202) 720–5643.
Deputy Assistant Administrator.—Dr. Perfecto Santiago, 205–0452.
Executive Associate.—Suzanne Rigby, 690–6418.
Director of:
Biosurveillance and Emergency Response Staff.—Mary K. Cutshall, 414 Aero Building, 690–6486.
Scientific and Technical Support Staff.—Dr. Michelle Catlin (acting), room 409 Aero Building, 690–6520.

OFFICE OF INTERNATIONAL AFFAIRS (OIA)

Assistant Administrator.—Karen Stuck, room 3143–S (202) 720–3473.

Deputy Assistant Administrator.—Dr. William James, 720–5362.
Director, Import Inspection Division.—Mary Stanley, room 3843–S, 720–9904.

OFFICE OF MANAGEMENT (OM)

Assistant Administrator.—William P. ''Billy'' Milton, Jr., room 347–E (202) 720–4425.
Deputy Assistant Administrator.—Karen A. Messmore, 720–4744.

OFFICE OF POLICY, PROGRAM AND EMPLOYEE DEVELOPMENT (OPPED)

Assistant Administrator.—Philip Derfler, room 350–E (202) 720–2709.
Deputy Assistant Administrator.—Daniel Engeljohn, 205–0495.
Director of:
Labeling and Consumer Protection Staff.—Robert Post, room 602 Annex, 205–0279.
New Technology Staff.—Dr. Patricia Schwartz, room 405 Cotton Annex, 205–0210.

OFFICE OF PROGRAM EVALUATION, ENFORCEMENT AND REVIEW (OPEER)

Assistant Administrator.—William C. ''Bill'' Smith, room 3133–S (202) 720–8609.
Director of:
Compliance and Investigations Division.—Zygmunt Sala, room 300, WEC, 418–8874.
Program Evaluation and Improvement Staff.—Matthew Michael, room 3835–S, 720–6735.

OFFICE OF PUBLIC AFFAIRS, EDUCATION AND OUTREACH (OPAEO)

Assistant Administrator.—Terri Nintemann, room 339–E (202) 720–8217.
Deputy Assistant Administrator.—Robert Tynan, room 3137–S, 720–3884.
Director of:
Congressional and Public Affairs Staff.—Lisa Wallenda Picard, room 1175–S, 720–3897 or 9113.
Executive Correspondence and Issues Management Staff.—Jonathan Theodule, room 1167–S, 690–3882.

OFFICE OF PUBLIC HEALTH SCIENCE (OPHS)

Assistant Administrator.—Loren Lange (acting), room 341–E (202) 720–2644.
Deputy Assistant Administrator.—Loren Lange, 205–0293.

UNDER SECRETARY FOR RESEARCH, EDUCATION, AND ECONOMICS

Under Secretary.—Gale A. Buchanan (202) 720–5923.
Deputy Under Secretary.—Dr. Merle Pierson.
Executive Assistant.—Janet Sweat.
Director, Legislative and Intergovernmental Affairs.—Lowell Randel.
Budget Coordinator.—Sara Mazie, 720–4110.

AGRICULTURAL RESEARCH SERVICE

Administration Building, Room 303–A, phone (202) 720–3656, fax 720–5427

Administrator.—Edward B. Knipling.
Associate Administrator for—
Research Operations.—Antoinette A. Betschart, 720–3658.
Research Programs.—Caird E. Rexroad (301) 504–5084.
Director of:
Budget and Program Management Staff.—Joseph S. Garbarino, room 358–A, 720–4421.
Legislative Affairs.—Karen Pearce, 720–3173.
Information Staff.—Sandy Miller-Hays (301) 504–1638.
Assistant Administrator, Research Operations and Management, Office of Technology Transfer.—Richard J. Brenner (301) 504–6905.

Deputy Administrator, Administrative and Financial Management.—James H. Bradley, 690–2575.
National Agricultural Library.—Peter Young (301) 504–5248.
U.S. National Arboretum.—Thomas S. Elias, 245–4539.

AREA OFFICES

Director of:
Beltsville Area.—Phyllis E. Johnson, 10300 Baltimore Boulevard, Bldg. 003, Room 223, BARC–West, Beltsville MD 20705 (301) 504–6078.
North Atlantic Area.—Wilda Martinez, 600 East Mermaid Lane, Room 2031, Wyndmoor, PA 19038 (215) 233–6593.
South Atlantic Area.—Darrell Cole, PO Box 5677, College Station Road, Room 201, Athens, GA 30605 (706) 546–3311.
Mid South Area.—Edgar King, Jr., 141 Experiment Station Road, Stoneville, MS 38776 (662) 686–3000.
Midwest Area.—Steven Shafer, 1815 North University Street, Room 2004, Peoria, IL 61604–0000 (309) 681–6602.
Pacific West Area.—Dwayne R. Buxton, 800 Buchanan Street, Room 2030, Albany, CA 94710 (510) 559–6060.
Northern Plains Area.—Wilbert H. Blackburn, 2150 Centre Avenue, Bldg. D, Ft. Collins, CO 80525–8119 (970) 492–7057.
Southern Plains Area.—Dan Upchurch, 1001 Holleman Drive East, College Station, TX 77845 (979) 260–9346.

COOPERATIVE STATE RESEARCH, EDUCATION AND EXTENSION SERVICE

Jamie L. Whitten Building, Room 305–A, phone (202) 720–4423, fax 720–8987

Administrator.—Dr. Colien Heffernan.
Associate Administrator.—Ralph A. Otto, 720–7441.
Deputy Administrator for—
Budget.—Tina Buch, room 332–A, 720–2675.
Communiucations.—Janet Allen, room 4231, 720–2677.
Economic and Community Systems.—Frank Boteler, room 4343, 720–5305.
Equal Opportunity Staff.—Curt DeVille, room 1230, 720–5843.
Extramural Programs.—Andrea Brandon, room 2256, 401–6021.
Families, 4–H and Nutrition.—Mary Gray, room 4329, 720–2326.
Information Systems and Technology Management.—Michel Desbois, room 4122, 720–1766.
Natural Resources and Environment.—Daniel Kugler, room 3231, 720–0740.
Planning and Accountability.—Robert McDonald, room 1315, 690–1297.
Science and Education Resources Development.—George Cooper, room 3310, 401–2855.

ECONOMIC RESEARCH SERVICE

1800 M Street, NW., 20036–5831, phone (202) 694–5000

Administrator.—Katherine R. Smith (acting), room N4150.
Associate Administrator.—Janet Perry, room N4145.
Division Directors:
Food and Rural Economics.—Betsey A. Kuhn, room N2168, 694–5400.
Information Services.—Ron Bianchi, room S2032, 694–5100.
Market and Trade Economics.—Neilson Conklin, room N5119, 694–5200.
Resource Economics.—Mary Bohman, room S4186, 694–5500.

NATIONAL AGRICULTURAL STATISTICS SERVICE

South Agriculture Building, Room 5041A–S, phone (202) 720–2707, fax 720–9013

Administrator.—R. Ronald Bosecker.
Associate Administrator.—Joseph T. Reilly, 720–4333.
Deputy Administrator for—
Field Operations.—Marshall L. Dantzler, room 5053, 720–3638.

Programs and Products.—Carol House, room 5029, 690–8141.
Division Directors for—
Census and Survey.—Robert T. Bass, room 6306, 720–4557.
Information Technology.—John P. Nealon, room 5847, 720–2984.
Research and Development.—James M. Harris, room 305, Fairfax CBG (703) 235–5211.
Statistics.—Steven D. Wiyatt, room 5433, 720–3896.

UNDER SECRETARY FOR MARKETING AND REGULATORY PROGRAMS

Jamie A. Whitten Building, Room 228–W, phone (202) 720–4256, fax 720–5775

Under Secretary.—Bruce I. Knight.
Deputy Under Secretaries: Dr. Chuck Lambert, J. Burton Eller.
Special Assistant to the Under Secretary.—Terry Van Doren.
Confidential Assistant to the Under Secretary.—Rufino Hurtado, 690–2832.

AGRICULTURAL MARKETING SERVICE

South Agriculture Building, Room 3064–S, phone (202) 720–5115, fax 720–8477

Administrator.—Lloyd Day.
Associate Administrator.—Kenneth C. Clayton, 720–4276.
Deputy Associate Administrator.—Charles R. Martin, 720–4024.
Deputy Administrator for—
Compliance and Analysis Programs.—Ellen King, room 302, Cotton Annex (202) 720–6766.
Cotton Programs.—Darryl Earnest, room 2641–S, 720–3193.
Dairy Programs.—Dana Cole, room 2968–S, 720–4392.
Fruit and Vegetable Programs.—Robert C. Keeney, room 2077–S, 720–4722.
Poultry Programs.—Craig Morse, room 3932–S, 720–4476.
Science and Technology.—Robert L. Epstein, room 1090–S, 720–5231.
Tobacco Programs.—William Coats (acting), room 502 Annex, 205–0567.
Transportation and Marketing.—Barbara C. Robinson, room 1098, 690–1300.
Director, Legislative and Review Staff.—Chris Sarcone, 720–3203.

ANIMAL AND PLANT HEALTH INSPECTION SERVICE (APHIS)

Jamie L. Whitten Building, Room 312–E, phone (202) 720–3668, fax 720–3054

OFFICE OF THE ADMINISTRATOR

Administrator.—Dr. W. Ron DeHaven.
Associate Administrator.—Nicholas Gutierrez.
Chief Operating Officer.—Kevin Shea, room 308–E.
Director of Civil Rights Enforcement and Compliance.—Anna P. Grayson, room 1137–S, 720–6312, fax 720–2365.

ANIMAL CARE

4700 River Road, Riverdale, MD 20737, phone (301) 734–4980, fax 734–4328

Deputy Administrator.—Chester Gipson.
Assistant Deputy Administrator.—Allan Hogue.

BIOTECHNOLOGY REGULATORY SERVICES

4700 River Road, Riverdale, MD 20737, phone (301) 734–7324, fax 734–8724

Deputy Administrator.—Cindy Smith.
Associate Deputy Administrator.—Rebecca Bech, 734–5716.
Director, Regulatory Division.—Neil Hoffman, 734–5716.

INTERNATIONAL SERVICES

Jamie L. Whitten Building, Room 324–E, phone (202) 720–7593, fax 690–1484

Deputy Administrator.—Dan Sheesley.
Associate Deputy Administrator.—Eric Hoffman, 720–7021.
Division Directors: Freida Skaggs (301) 734–5214; John Wyss, 734–3779.
Trade Support Team.—John Greifer, room 1128, 720–7677.

LEGISLATIVE AND PUBLIC AFFAIRS

South Building, Room 1147–S, phone (202) 720–2511, fax 720–3982

Deputy Administrator.—Courtney R. Billet.
Associate Deputy Administrator.—Bethany Jones.
Assistant Director of:
Public Affairs.—Ed Curlett (301) 734–7799.
Executive Correspondence.—Christina Myers (301) 734–7776.
Freedom of Information.—Lesia Banks (301) 734–8296.

MARKETING AND REGULATORY PROGRAMS BUSINESS SERVICES

Jamie L. Whitten Building, Room 308–E, phone (202) 720–5213, fax 690–0686

Deputy Administrator.—William Hudnall.
Associate Deputy Administrator.—Joanne Munno.
Division Directors:
Financial Management.—Laura MacKenzie, 720–7865.
Investigative and Enforcement Services.—Alan Christian (301) 734–6491.
Management Services.—Howard Price (301) 734–6502.
MRP Human Resources: Karen Benham, Ellen King, room 1709–S, 720–6377.

PLANT PROTECTION AND QUARANTINE

Jamie L. Whitten Building, Room 302–E, phone (202) 720–5601, fax 690–0472

Deputy Administrator.—Richard L. Dunkle.
Associate Deputy Administrator.—Paul Eggert, 720–4441.
Assistant to the Deputy Administrator.—John H. Payne, 720–5601.
Director of:
Biocontrol.—Dale Meyerdirk (301) 734–5667.
Center for Plant Health Science and Technology.—Gordon Gordh (919) 513–2400.
Phytosanitary Issues Management.—Cathleen Enright (301) 734–5291.
Resource Management Support.—Terri Burrell (301) 734–7764.
Technical Information Systems.—Allison Young (301) 734–5518.

POLICY AND PROGRAM DEVELOPMENT

4700 River Road, Riverdale, MD 20737, phone (301) 734–5136, fax 734–5899

Deputy Administrator.—Michael Gregoire.
Assistant Deputy Administrator.—Shannon Hamm.
Unit Chiefs:
Planning, Evaluation and Monitoring.—Christine Zakarka, 734–8512.
Policy Analysis and Development.—Janet W. Berls, 734–8667.
Regulatory Analysis and Development.—Cynthia Howard, 734–0682.
Risk Analysis.—Richard Fite, 734–3634.

VETERINARY SERVICES

Jamie L. Whitten Building, Room 317–E, phone (202) 720–5193, fax 690–4171

Deputy Administrator.—John Clifford.
Administrative Assistant.—James Newton, 720–5793.
Associate Deputy Administrator for Regional Operations.—Dr. Andrea Morgan, 720–5193.

Assistant Deputy Administrator.—Dr. Valerie Ragan (301) 734–3754.
Director for—
Emergency Programs.—Randall Crom (301) 734–8073.
Inspection and Compliance.—Steven A. ''Ames'' Karli (515) 232–5785.
National Center of Import and Export.—Gary S. Colgrave (301) 734–4356.
Outreach Liaison.—Joseph Annelli (301) 794–8073.
Policy, Evaluation and Licensing.—Richard E. Hill, Jr. (515) 232–5785.
Chief Staff Veterinarian for National Animal Health Programs.—Michael Gilsdorf (301) 734–6954.

WILDLIFE SERVICES

South Building, Room 1624, phone (202) 720–2054, fax 690–0053

Deputy Administrator.—William H. Clay.
Assistant Deputy Administrator.—Martin Mendoza.
Director for Operational Support.—Joanne Garrett (301) 734–7921.

GRAIN INSPECTION, PACKERS AND STOCKYARDS ADMINISTRATION

South Building, Room 2055, phone (202) 720–0219, fax 205–9237

Administrator.—David R. Shipman (acting), room 2063, 720–9170.
Director of:
Civil Rights.—Eugene Bass, room 0623, 720–0216.
Enterprise Architecture Program Management.—Charles E. Smith, room 0009, 205–4366.
Executive Resource Staff.—Patricia Donohue-Galvin, room 2047, 720–0231.
Information Technology Staff.—Gerald Bromley, room 2446, 720–3204.
Deputy Administrator for Federal Grain Inspection Service.—David R. Shipman, room 2063, 720–9170.
Director of:
Compliance.—John Sharpe, room 1647, 720–8262.
Field Management Division.—David Orr, room 2409, 720–0228.
Office of International Affairs.—John Pitchford, room 1629, 720–0226.
Technical Services.—Steven Tanner, Kansas City, MO (816) 891–0401.
Deputy Administrator for Packers and Stockyards Programs.—Alan Christian, room 2055, 720–7051.
Director of:
Field Operations.—William Crutchfield, room 1641, 720–7063.
Industry Analysis Division.—Gary McBryde, room 2430, 720–7455.
Policy and Litigation Division.—Brett Offutt, room 2420, 720–7363.
Regional Supervisors:
Atlanta, GA.—Elkin Parker (404) 562–5840.
Denver, CO.—John Barthel (303) 375–4240.
Des Moines, IA.—Jay Johnson (515) 323–2579.

DEPARTMENT OF COMMERCE

Herbert C. Hoover Building

14th Street between Pennsylvania and Constitution Avenues, NW., 20230

phone (202) 482–2000, http://www.doc.gov

CARLOS M. GUTIERREZ, Secretary of Commerce; born in Havana, Cuba, in 1953; came to the United States in 1960; education: studied business administration, Monterrey Institute of Technology, Queretaro, Mexico; professional: Chairman of the Board, and Chief Executive Officer, Kellogg Company; married: Edilia; children: Carlos, Erika, and Karina; nominated by President George W. Bush to become the 35th Secretary of Commerce, and was confirmed by the U.S. Senate on January 24, 2005.

OFFICE OF THE SECRETARY

Secretary of Commerce.—Carlos M. Gutierrez, room 5858 (202) 482–2112.
Deputy Secretary.—David A. Sampson, room 5838, 482–8376.
Chief of Staff.—Claire Buchan, room 5858, 482–4246.
Protocol Officer.—Marilouise Sibley, room 5847, 482–8011.
Director, Office of:
Business Liaison.—Dan McCardell, room 5062, 482–1360.
Chief Information Officer.—Barry C. West, room 5029B, 482–4797.
Executive Secretariat.—Tracey Rhoades, room 5516, 482–3934.
Policy and Strategic Planning.—John Duncan, room 5865, 482–4127.
Public Affairs.—E. Richard Mills, room 5413, 482–4883.
Scheduling.—Marilyn Abel, room 5883, 482–5880.
White House Liaison.—Christy Simon, room 5835, 482–1684.

GENERAL COUNSEL

General Counsel.—John J. Sullivan, room 5870 (202) 482–4772.
Deputy General Counsel.—David Bearden.

ASSISTANT SECRETARY FOR LEGISLATIVE AND INTERGOVERNMENTAL AFFAIRS

Assistant Secretary.—Nat Wienecke, room 5421 (202) 482–3663.
Director for—
Intergovernmental Affairs.—Elizabeth Dial, room 5422, 482–8017.
Legislative and Intergovernmental Affairs.—Karen A. Swanson-Woolf, room 5414, 482–4556.

CHIEF FINANCIAL OFFICER (CFO) AND ASSISTANT SECRETARY FOR ADMINISTRATION

Chief Financial Officer and Assistant Secretary.—Otto Wolff, room 5830 (202) 482–4951.
Deputy Chief Financial Officer, Financial Management.—Lisa Casias, room 6827, 482–1207.
Deputy Assistant Secretary for Administration.—Jeffery Nulf.
Director for—
Acquisition Management.—Michael S. Sade, room 6422, 482–2773.
Administrative Services.—Fred Fanning (acting), room 6316, 482–1200.
Budget.—Barbara A. Retzlaff, room 5818, 482–4648.
Civil Rights.—Suzan J. Aramaki, room 6012, 482–0625.
Human Resources Management.—Deborah A. Jefferson, room 5001, 482–4807.
Management and Organization.—John J. Phelan III, room 5327, 482–3707.
Security.—Richard Yamamoto, room 1067, 482–4371.

Small and Disadvantaged Business Utilization.—LaJuene Desmukes, room 6411, 482–1472.

INSPECTOR GENERAL

Inspector General.—Johnnie E. Frazier, room 7898–C (202) 482–4661.
Deputy Inspector General.—Edward Blansitt, room 7898C, 482–3516.
Legislative and Intergovernmental Affairs Officer.—Susan Carnohan, room 7898C, 482–2187.
Counsel to Inspector General.—Carey Croak (acting), room 7892, room 482–0038.
Assistant Inspector General, Office of:
Auditing.—John Seeba, room 7721, 482–3606.
Compliance and Administration.—Jessica Rickenbach, room 7099C, 482–3052.
Inspections and Program Evaluations.—Jill A. Gross, room 7886–B, 482–2754.
Investigations.—Elizabeth T. Barlow, room 7087, 482–3860.
Systems Evaluation.—Judith J. Gordon, room 7876, 482–6186.

ECONOMICS AND STATISTICS ADMINISTRATION

Under Secretary for Economic Affairs.—Cynthia A. Glassman, room 4848 (202) 482–3727.
Chief Counsel.—Roxie Jamison Jones, room 4868A, 482–5394.
Chief Economist.—Keith Hall, room 4842, 482–3523.
Associate Under Secretary for—
Communications.—Elizabeth R. Anderson, room 4836, 482–2760.
Congressional and Intergovernmental Affairs Specialist.—Clark L. Reid, room 4842, 482–3331.
Economic Information Officer.—Jane A. Callen, room 4855, 482–2235.
Director, Office of:
Economic Conditions.—Carl E. Cox, room 4861, 482–4871.
Policy Development.—Jane Molloy, room 4858, 482–5926.
Management.—James K. White, room 4834, 482–2405.
Chief Information Officer and Director.—Kenneth S. Taylor, room 4880, 482–2853.
STAT–USA.—Forrest B. Williams, room 4886, 482–3429.
Chief Financial Officer, Finance and Administration.—Stephen Agostini, room 4842, 482–4885.

BUREAU OF ECONOMIC ANALYSIS

1441 L Street, NW., 20230, phone (202) 606–9900

Director.—J. Steven Landefeld, room 6006, 606–9600.
Deputy Director.—Rosemary Marcuss, room 6005, 606–9602.
Chief Economist.—Rosemary Marcuss (acting), room 6063, 606–9603.
Chief Information Officer.—Alan C. Lorish, Jr., room 3050, 606–9910.
Chief Statistician.—Dennis J. Fixler, room 6060, 606–9607.
Associate Director for—
Industry Accounts.—Sumiye Okubo, room 6004, 606–9612.
International Economics.—Ralph H. Kozlow, room 6065, 606–9604.
National Economic Accounts.—Brent R. Moulton, room 6064, 606–9606.
Regional Economics.—Robert L. Brown (acting), room 8066, 606–9246; John R. Kort (acting), room 9018, 606–9221.
Division Chiefs:
Administrative Services.—C. Brian Grove, room 3003, 606–9624.
Balance of Payments.—Christopher L. Bach, room 8024, 606–9545.
Communications.—Delores Barber (acting), room 3030, 606–9694.
Current Industry Analysis.—Ann M. Lawson, room 4006, 606–9462.
Government.—Brooks B. Robinson, room 4067, 606–9778.
Industry Benchmark.—Mary Streitwieser, room 4005, 606–9583.
International Investment.—Obie G. Wichard, room 7006, 606–9890.
National Income and Wealth.—Carol E. Moylan, room 5006, 606–9711.
Regional Economic Analysis.—John R. Kort, room 9018, 606–9221.
Regional Economic Measurement.—Robert L. Brown, room 8066, 606–9246.

THE CENSUS BUREAU

4600 Silver Hill Road, Suitland, MD 20746

Director.—Charles Louis Kincannon, room 8H002 (301) 763–2135.

Deputy Director and Chief Operating Officer.—Hermann Habermann, room 8H006, 763–2138.

Associate Director for—

Administration and Chief Financial Officer.—Theodore A. Johnson, room 8H144, 763–3464.

Communications.—Ruth Cymber, room 8H138, 763–2512.

Comptroller.—Andrew H. Moxam, room 3586, 763–9575.

Decennial Census.—Preston Jay Waite, room 8H122, 763–3968.

Demographic Programs.—Howard Hogan, room 8H134, 763–2160.

Economic Programs.—Thomas L. Mesenbourg, room 8H132, 763–2932.

Field Operations.—Marvin D. Raines, room 8H126, 763–2072.

Information Technology.—Richard W. Swartz, room 8H140, 763–2117.

Strategic Planning and Innovation.—Nancy M. Gorgon, room 8H128, 763–2126.

Assistant Director for—

Decennial Census and American Community Survey.—Teresa Angueira, room 2016–2, 763–1764.

Decennial IT and Geographic Systems.—Arnold A. Jackson, room 2018–2, 763–8626.

Economic Programs.—Thomas L. Mesenbourg, room 2069, 763–2932.

Information Technology.—Douglas Clift, room 1031, 763–5499.

Division and Office Chiefs for—

Acquisition Division.—Michael L. Palensky, room G–314, 763–1818.

Administrative and Customer Services.—Walter C. Odom, Jr., room 2150, 763–2228.

Administrative and Management Systems Division.—James Aikman, room 3102, 763–3149.

American Community Survey Office.—Lawrence S. McGinn, room 1657, 763–8050.

Budget Division.—James Tyler, room 3430, 763–3903.

Center for Economic Studies.—Daniel H. Weinberg, room 206, 763–6460.

Client Support Office.—Ronald R. Swank, room 1373, 763–6846.

Company Statistics Division.—Ewen M. Wilson, room 1182, 763–3388.

Computer Services Division.—Kenneth A. Riccini, Bowie Computer Center, 763–3922.

Congressional Affairs Office.—James Hayes, room 8H166, 763–2171.

Customer Liaison Office.—Jeri Green, room 8H153, 763–1305.

Decennial Management Division.—Edison Gore (acting), room 2012–2, 763–3998.

Decennial Statistical Studies Division.—Rajendra Singh, room 2024, 763–9295.

Decennial Systems and Contract Management Office.—Michael J. Longini, room 2301, 763–2933.

Demographic Statistical Methods Division.—Alan Tupek, room 3705, 763–4287.

Demographic Surveys Division.—Chester E. Bowie, room 3324, 763–3773.

Economic Planning and Coordination Division.—Shirin A. Ahmed, room 2584, 763–2558.

Economic Statistical Methods and Programming Division.—Howard Hogan, room 3015, 763–5870.

Equal Employment Opportunity Office.—Roy P. Castro, room 1229, 763–2853.

Field Division.—Brian Monaghan, room 1111–2, 763–7879.

Finance Division.—Joan P. Johnson, room 3582, 763–6803.

Foreign Trade Division.—C. Harvey Monk, Jr., room 2104, 763–2255.

Geography Division.—Robert A. LaMacchia, WP1, 763–2131.

Governments Division.—Stephanie H. Brown, room 407, 763–1489.

Human Resources Division.—Tyra Dent Smith, room 3260, 763–5863.

Information Systems Support and Review Office.—J. Jerry Bell, room 1023, 763–1881.

Information Technology Security Office.—Timothy P. Ruland, room 1537, 763–2869.

International Relations Office.—Jay Keller, room 2068, 763–2883.

Manufacturing and Construction.—William G. Bostic, Jr., room 2102–4, 763–4593.

Marketing Services Office.—John C. Kavaliunas, room 3023, 763–4090.

Planning Research and Evaluation.—Ruth Ann Killion, room 1107–2, 763–2048.

Population.—John F. Long, room 2011, 763–2071.

Privacy Office.—Gerald W. Gates, room 8H168, 763–2515.

Public Information Office.—Kenneth C. Meyer, room 8H160, 763–3100.

Security Office.—Harold L. Washington, Jr., room 1631, 763–1716.

Service Sector Statistics.—Mark E. Wallace, room 2633, 763–2683.

Statistical Research Division.—Tommy Wright, room 3203–4, 763–1702.

Systems Support.—Robert G. Munsey, room 1342, 763–2999.

Technologies Management Office.—Barbara M. LoPresti, room 1757, 763–7765.

Telecommunications Office.—Kenneth A. Riccini (acting), room 1101, 763–1793.

BUREAU OF INDUSTRY AND SECURITY

Under Secretary.—Mark Foulon (acting), room 3892 (202) 482–1427.
Deputy Under Secretary.—Mark Foulon.
Chief Counsel.—John Masterson, room 3839, 482–2315.
Office of Congressional and Public Affairs.—Scott Kamins, room 3897, 482–0097.
Director, Office of Administration.—Gay Shrum, room 6622, 482–1900.
Chief Information Officer.—Dawn Leaf, room 6092, 482–4848.
Assistant Secretary for Export Administration.—Christopher Padilla, room 3886, 482–5491.
Deputy Assistant Secretary.—Matthew Borman.
Operating Committee Chair.—Brian Nilsson, room 3889, 482–5485.
Office of:
Exporter Services.—Eileen M. Albanese, room 1093, 482–0436.
National Security and Technology Transfer Controls.—Bernard Kritzer, room 2616, 482–4196.
Nonproliferation and Treaty Compliance.—Steven Goldman, room 2093, 482–3825.
Strategic Industries and Economic Security.—Dan Hill, room 3878, 482–4506.
Technology Evaluation.—Kevin Kurland, room 3886, 482–2385.
Assistant Secretary for Export Enforcement.—Darryl Jackson, room 3730, 482–3618.
Deputy Assistant Secretary.—Wendy Wysong, room 3721, 482–5914.
Office of:
Antiboycott Compliance.—Edward Weant, room 6098, 482–5914.
Enforcement Analysis.—Thomas Andrukonis, room 4065, 482–4255.
Export Enforcement.—Michael Turner, room 4525, 482–2252.

ECONOMIC DEVELOPMENT ADMINISTRATION

Assistant Secretary.—Sandy K. Baruah, room 7800 (202) 482–5081.
Deputy Assistant Secretary.—Benjamin Erulkar.
Chief Counsel.—Barry Bird, room 7005, 482–4687.
Chief Information Officer.—Darice Ahrnsbrak, room 7114, 482–2507.
Deputy Assistant Secretary, Office of External Affairs and Communications (OEAC).—Matthew E. Crow, room 7822, 482–2900.
Director, Division of:
Legislative and Intergovernmental Affairs (LIAD).—Dennis Alvord (acting), room 7816, 482–2900.
Public Affairs (PAD).—Brian Borlik (acting), room 7812, 482–4085.
Deputy Assistant Secretary, Office of Management Service (OMS)/Chief Financial Officer.—Mary Pleffner, room 7015, 482–5891.
Director, Office of Administrative and Support Services (ASSD)/Deputy Chief Financial Officer.—Sandra Walters, room 7217, 482–4020.
Director, Office of Budgeting and Performance Evaluation (BPED).—Bob Gay, room 7106, 482–0547.

INTERNATIONAL TRADE ADMINISTRATION

Under Secretary.—Franklin L. Lavin, room 3850 (202) 482–2867.
Deputy Under Secretary.—Michelle O'Neill, room 3842, 482–3917.
Legislative and Intergovernmental Affairs.—Lori Harju, room 3424, 482–1389.
Public Affairs.—Charles Skuba, room 3416, 482–3809.
Trade Promotion Coordinating Committee.—Pat Kirwan, room 3051, 482–5455.

ADMINISTRATION

Director and Chief Financial Officer.—David Robinson, room 3827 (202) 482–5855.
Deputy Chief Financial Officer.—Jim Donahue, room 4112, 482–0210.
Director, Office of:
Human Resources Management.—Ronald Glaser, room 7060, 482–3505.
Organization and Management Support.—Mary Ann McFate, room 4001, 482–5436.

TRADE PROMOTION AND U.S. AND FOREIGN COMMERCIAL SERVICE

Assistant Secretary for Trade Promotion and Director General of the Commercial Service.—Israel Hernandez, room 3802 (202) 482–5777.
Deputy Director General.—Thomas McGinty (acting), room 3802, 482–0725.
Career Development and Assignment.—Rebecca Mann, room 1222, 482–5208.
Deputy Assistant Secretary for—
Domestic Operations.—Coleen Litkenhaus, room 3810, 482–4767.
International Operations.—Daniel Harris, room 3128, 482–6228.
Office of Global Trade Program.—Stacey Silva, room 2810, 482–6220.
Director for—
Africa, Near East and South Asia.—George Litman, room 2013, 482–1209.
East Asia and Pacific.—William M. Zarit, room 3122, 482–0423.
Europe.—John Breidenstine, room 3133, 482–5402.
Western Hemisphere.—Margaret Keshishian, room 2015B, 482–5857.

ASSISTANT SECRETARY FOR IMPORT ADMINISTRATION

Assistant Secretary.—David Spooner, room 3099 (202) 482–1780.
Chief Counsel.—John D. McInerney, room 3622, 482–5589.
Director for—
Office of Accounting.—Neal Halper, room 3087–B, 482–2210.
Office of Policy.—Ronald Lorentzen, room 3713, 482–4412.
Statutory Import Programs Staff.—Faye Robinson, room 4100W, 482–1660.
Deputy Assistant Secretary for—
Antidumping Countervailing Duty Operations.—Stephen Claeys, room 3095, 482–5497.
Antidumping Countervailing Duty Policy and Negotiations.—Joseph Spetrini, room 3075, 482–2104.

ASSISTANT SECRETARY FOR MARKET ACCESS AND COMPLIANCE

Assistant Secretary.—David Bohigian, room 3868A (202) 482–3022.
Deputy Assistant Secretary for—
Trade Agreements Compliance.—Stephen Jacobs, room 3043, 482–5767.
Europe.—Paul Dyck, room 3863, 482–5638.
Middle East and Africa.—Holly Vineyard, room 2329, 482–4651.
Western Hemisphere.—Walter Bastian, room 3826, 482–5324.
Director, Office of:
Africa.—Kevin Boyd, room 2037, 482–4227.
APEC (Asian and Asia-Pacific Economic Cooperation) Affairs.—Brenda Fisher, room 2308, 482–5334.
European Country Affairs.—Jay Burgess, room 3319, 482–4915.
Japan.—Nicole Melcher, room 2322, 482–2515.
Latin America and the Caribbean.—John Anderson, room 3203, 482–2436.
Middle East and North Africa.—Cherie Loustanau, room 2031, 482–4442.
Multilateral Affairs.—Steward L. ''Skip'' Jones, Jr., room 3027, 482–2307.
NAFTA Secretariat.—Caratina Alston, room 2061, 482–5438.
North American Free Trade Agreement and Inter-American Affairs.—Andrew Rudman, room 3024, 482–0507.
Russia, Ukraine, and Eurasia.—Jack Brougher, room 3318, 482–1104.

ASSISTANT SECRETARY FOR MANUFACTURING

Assistant Secretary.—Albert Frink, room 3832 (202) 482–1461.
Chief of Staff.—Rebecca Bernier, room 3832, 482–1112.
Deputy Assistant Secretary for—
Industry Analysis.—Jack McDougle, room 2815, 482–5145.
Manufacturing.—Jamie Estrada, room 2800A, 482–1872.
Services.—Ana Guevara, room 1128, 482–5261.

PRESIDENT'S EXPORT COUNCIL

[Authorized by Executive Orders 12131, 12534, 12551, 12610, 12692, 12774, 12869, and 12974 (May through September 1995)]

Executive Director, Under Secretary of International Trade.—Frank Lavin, room 2015 (202) 482–1124.
Executive Secretary/Staff Director.—Mark Chittum.

MINORITY BUSINESS DEVELOPMENT AGENCY

Director.—Ronald N. Langston, room 5055 (202) 482–5061.
Associate Directors: Edith McCloud, room 5088, 482–6224; Chiling Tong, room 5090, 482–6279.
Chief of:
Budget Division.—Ronald Marin, room 5089, 482–3341.
Business Development.—Anita Wells, room 5069A, 482–3238.
Legislative, Educational and Intergovernmental Affairs.—Bridget Gonzales, room 5095, 482–3774.
Chief Counsel.—Jedd Vertman, room 5069, 482–5045.
Chief Information Officer.—Yolanda Whitley, room 5080, 482–1960.

NATIONAL OCEANIC AND ATMOSPHERIC ADMINISTRATION

Under Secretary for Oceans and Atmosphere.—VADM Conrad C. Lautenbacher, Jr., USN (Ret.), room 5128 (202) 482–3436.
Deputy Under Secretary.—BGEN John ''Jack'' Kelly, Jr., USAF (Ret.), room 6811, 482–4569.
Assistant Secretary/Deputy Administrator.—Dr. William Brennan (acting), room 5804, 482–3567.
Deputy Assistant Secretary for International Affairs.—Dr. William Brennan, room 6228, 482–6196.
Chief Financial Officer.—Maureen Wylie, room 6805, 482–0917.
Chief Administrative Officer.—William ''Bill'' Broglie, SSMC4, room 8431 (301) 713–0836 ext. 105.
General Counsel.—James Walpole, room 5814, 482–4080.
Director, Office of:
Education and Sustainable Development.—Louisa Koch, room 6869, 482–3384.
Legislative Affairs.—Eric Webster, room 5225, 482–4981.
Marine and Aviation Operations Center.—RADM Samuel P. DeBow, Jr., 8403 Colesville Rd., Suite 500, Silver Spring, MD 20910 (301) 713–1045.
Public and Constituent Affairs.—Jordan St. John, room 6217, 482–6090.

NATIONAL MARINE FISHERIES SERVICE

1315 East-West Highway, Silver Spring, MD 20910

Assistant Administrator.—William T. Hogarth, Ph.D., room 14636 (301) 713–2239.
Deputy Assistant Administrator for—
Operations.—John Oliver, room 14743.
Regulatory Programs.—Samuel Rauch, room 14657.
Director, Office of:
Habitat Conservation.—Patricia Montanio, room 14828, 713–2325.
International Affairs.—Rebecca Lent, Ph.D., room 12659, 713–9090.
Law Enforcement.—Dale Jones, room 415, 427–2300.
Management and Budget.—Gary Reisner, room 14450, 713–2259.
Protected Resources.—Jim Lecky, room 13821, 713–2332.
Science and Technology.—John Boreman, Ph.D., room 12450, 713–2367.
Scientific Programs.—Steven Murawski, Ph.D., room 14659, 713–2239.
Seafood Inspection Program.—Tim Hansen, room 10837, 713–2351.
Sustainable Fisheries.—Alan Risenhoover, room 13362, 713–2334.
Chief Information Officer.—Larry Tyminski, room 3657, 713–2372.
Chief Science Advisor.—Steven Murawski, Ph.D., room 14659, 713–2239.

NATIONAL OCEAN SERVICE

Assistant Administrator.—John H. Dunnigan, room 13632 (301) 713–3074.
Deputy Assistant Administrator.—Dr. William Corso, room 13156, 713–3074.
Director, Office of Operational Oceanographic Products and Services.—Michael Szabados, room 6633, 713–2981.
Deputy Director.—Rick Edwing, room 662, 713–2981.
Chief Financial Officer.—Elizabeth Scheffler, room 13430, 713–3056.
Director, Office of:
Coast Survey.—CAPT Steve Barnum, room 6147, 713–2770.
International Programs.—Clement Lewsey, room 10414, 713–3078.
National Centers for Coastal Ocean Science.—Gary C. Matlock, room 8211, 713–3020.
National Geodetic Survey.—David Zilkoski, room 8657, 713–3222.
NOAA Coastal Services.—Margaret A. Davidson (843) 740–1220.
Ocean and Coastal Resource Management.—David Kennety, room 10413, 713–3155.
Response and Restoration.—Ken Barton (acting), room 10102, 713–2989.
Special Projects.—Daniel Farrow, room 9515, 713–3000.

NATIONAL ENVIRONMENTAL SATELLITE, DATA AND INFORMATION SERVICE

Assistant Administrator.—Mary E. Kicza, room 8338 (301) 713–3578.
Chief Information Officer.—Zachary Goldstein, room 8110, 713–9220.
Chief Financial Officer.—Charles S. Baker, room 8338, 713–9476.
International and Interagency Affairs Chief.—D. Brent Smith, room 7315, 713–2024.
Director, Office of:
Coastal Ocean Laboratory.—Wayne Wilmot, room 4651, 713–3272.
Environmental Information Services.—Ida Hakkarinen, room 7232, 713–0813.
Management Operations and Analysis.—Christine Carpino, room 8132, 713–9210.
National Climatic Data.—Thomas R. Karl, room 557–C (828) 271–4476.
National Geophysical Data Center.—Christopher Fox, room 1B148 (303) 497–6215.
National Oceanographic Data Center.—Zdenka Willis, room 4820, 713–3270.
National Polar Orbiting Operational Environmental Satellite System Integrated Program.—Dan Stockton (acting), room 1450, 427–2070.
Research and Applications.—Marie Colton, room 701, 763–8127.
Satellite Data Processing and Distribution.—Michael Matson (acting), room 1069, 457–5120.
Satellite Operations.—Kathleen A. Kelly, room 0135, 817–4000.
Systems Development.—Gary K. Davis, room 3301, 713–0100.

NATIONAL WEATHER SERVICE

Assistant Administrator.—David L. Johnson, room 18150 (301) 713–9095.
Deputy Assistant Administrator.—John E. Jones, Jr., room 18130, 713–0711.
Chief Financial Officer.—Robert J. Byrd, room 18176, 713–0397.
Deputy Chief Financial Officer.—John Potts, room 18212, 713–0718.
Chief Information Officer.—Larry Curran (acting), room 17424, 713–1360.
Director, Office of:
Climate, Water and Weather Services.—Dennis H. McCarthy (acting), room 14348, 713–0700.
Hydrologic Development.—Gary M. Carter, room 8212, 713–1658.
National Centers for Environmental Prediction.—Louis W. Uccellini, room 101, 763–8016.
Operational Systems.—John McNulty, room 16212, 713–0165.
Science and Technology.—Gregory A. Mandt, room 15146, 713–1746.

OCEANIC AND ATMOSPHERIC RESEARCH

Assistant Administrator.—Richard W. Spinrad, Ph.D. (301) 713–2458.
Deputy Assistant Administrator for—
Labs and Cooperative Institutes.—Alexander MacDonald, Ph.D.
Programs and Administration.—Craig McLean.
Director of:
Earth System Research Laboratory.—Alexander MacDonald, Ph.D. (303) 497–6005.
Division of:
Chemical Sciences.—A.R. ''Ravi'' Ravishankara, Ph.D. (303) 497–3134.

Global Monitoring.—David Hofmann, Ph.D. (303) 497–3264.
Global Systems.—Steve Koch, Ph.D. (303) 497–6818.
Physical Science.—William Neff, Ph.D. (303) 497–6457.
Air Resources Laboratory.—Rick Artz (acting), 713–0684.
Atlantic Oceanographic and Meteorological Laboratory.—Robert Atlas (305) 361–4300.
Geophysical Fluid Dynamics Laboratory.—Ants Leetmaa, Ph.D. (609) 452–6503.
Great Lakes Environmental Research Laboratory.—Stephen E. Brandt, Ph.D. (734) 741–2245.
National Sea Grant College Program.—Leon Cammen, room 11716, 713–2448.
National Severe Storms Laboratory.—James Kimpel, Ph.D. (405) 325–6907.
National Undersea Research Program.—Barbara S.P. Moore, Ph.D., room 11359, 713–2427.
Pacific Marine Environmental Laboratory.—Eddie N. Bernard, Ph.D. (206) 526–6810.
Director, Office of:
Arctic Research.—John Calder, 713–2518.
Climate Program.—Chester Koblinsky, 427–2334.
Ocean Exploration.—Stephen Hammond (acting), 713–9444.

PATENT AND TRADEMARK OFFICE

P.O. Box 1450, 600 Dulany Street, Arlington, VA 22313–1450

phone (571) 272–8600

Under Secretary of Commerce for Intellectual Property and Director of U.S. Patent and Trade Office.—Jon W. Dudas.
Deputy Under Secretary of Commerce for Intellectual Property and Deputy Director of the U.S. Patent and Trademark Office.—Stephen M. Pinkos, 272–8700.
Chief of Staff.—Eleanor Meltzer.
Director of Public Affairs.—Richard Maulsby, 272–8400.
Deputy Director.—Brigid Quinn.

COMMISSIONER FOR PATENTS

Commissioner.—John Doll (571) 272–8800.
Deputy Commissioner for Patent Examination Policy.—John Love (acting).
Director, Office of:
Patent Cooperation Treaty Legal Administration.—Charles Pearson, 272–3224.
Patent Legal Administation.—Robert J. Spar, 272–7700.
Deputy Commissioner for Patent Operations.—Margaret A. Focarino, 272–8800.
Patent Examining Group Directors:
Technology Center 1600 (biotechnology and organic chemistry): George Elliott, 272–0600; Bruce Kisliuk, 272–0700; John LeGuyader, 272–0500.
Technology Center 1700/2900 (chemical and materials engineering/design): Gary Jones, 272–1300; Marian Knode, 272–1100; Jacqueline Stone, 272–1200.
Technology Center 2100 (computer architecture, software and information security): James Dwyer, 272–7220; Jack Harvey, 272–0900; Peter Wong, 272–1400.
Technology Center 2600 (telecommunications): Andrew Christensen, 272–4750; Andrew Faile, 272–4650; Jin F. Ng, 272–3050; Mark R. Powell, 272–4550.
Technology Center 2800 (semiconductors, electrical and optical systems and components): Janice A. Falcone, 272–1550; Sharon Gibson, 272–1650; Howard M. Goldberg, 272–1750; Robert Oberleitner, 272–1950; Richard Seidel, 272–1850.
Technology Center 3600 (transportation, construction, electronic commerce, agriculture, national security, and license and review): Wynn Coggins, 272–5350; Donald T. Hajec, 272–5150; John Love, 272–5250.
Technology Center 3700 (mechanical engineering, manufacturing, and products and designs): Fred Schmidt, 272–2975; Karen Young, 272–3750.
Director, Patent Quality Assurance.—George C. Elliott, 272–5018.
Director, Office of:
Initial Patent Examination.—Thomas I. Koontz (703) 308–9210.
Patent Classification.—Harold P. Smith, 272–7850.
Patent Cooperation Treaty Operations.—Donald Levin (acting), (703) 308–9290.
Patent Financial Management.—John Mielcarek, 272–8110.
Patent Publications.—Kimberly Terrell (703) 308–9250.
Administrator, Office of:
Patent Resources Administration.—John Mielcarek, 272–8110.
Search and Information Resources Administration.—Kristin Vajs (acting), 272–3512.

Director, Scientific and Technical Information Center.—Kristin Vajs, 272–3512.

COMMISSIONER FOR TRADEMARKS

Commissioner.—Lynne Beresford (571) 272–8900.
Deputy Commissioner for Trademark Operations.—Deborah Cohn, 272–8901.
Trademark Examination Law Office Managing Attorneys:
Law Office 101.—Ron Susaman, 272–9696.
Law Office 102.—Thomas Shaw, 272–9261.
Law Office 103.—Michael Hamilton, 272–9278.
Law Office 104.—Chris Doninger, 272–9297.
Law Office 105.—Thomas G. Howell, 272–9302.
Law Office 106.—Mary Sparrow, 272–9332.
Law Office 107.—Leslie Bishop, 272–9445.
Law Office 108.—Andrew Lawrence, 272–9342.
Law Office 109.—Dan Vavonese, 272–9288.
Law Office 110.—Chris Pedersen, 272–9371.
Law Office 111.—Craig Taylor, 272–9395.
Law Office 112.—Angela Wilson, 272–9443.
Law Office 113.—Odette Bonnet, 272–9426.
Law Office 114.—Margaret Le, 272–9456.
Law Office 115.—Thomas Vlcek, 272–9485.
Law Office 116.—Michael Baird, 272–9487.
Law Office 117.—Loretta Beck, 272–9245.
Director, Office of Trademark Program Control.—Betty Andrews, 272–9671.
Deputy Commissioner for Trademark Examination Policy.—Sharon Marsh, 272–8901.
Director, Office of Trademark Quality Review.—Kevin Peska, 272–9658.

ADMINISTRATOR FOR EXTERNAL AFFAIRS

Administrator for External Affairs and Director, Office of International Relations.—Lois Boland (571) 272–9300.
Director, Office of:
Congressional Relations.—Jefferson D. Taylor.
Enforcement.—Robert L. Stoll.

CHIEF FINANCIAL OFFICER AND CHIEF ADMINISTRATIVE OFFICER

Chief Financial Officer.—Barry K. Hudson (571) 272–9200.
Chief Administrative Officer.—Vickers B. Meadows.
Senior Advisor, Process Design and Improvement.—Bo Bounkong.
Director of:
Administration.—John Hassett, 282–8183.
Civil Rights.—Patricia Boylan, 272–8095.
Corporate Planning.—Jack Buie, 272–6283.
Finance.—Michele Picard (703) 305–8360.
Human Resources.—Kent Baum, 272–6200.
Procurement.—Kevin McGinn, 272–6550.

OFFICE OF GENERAL COUNSEL

General Counsel.—James A. Toupin (571) 272–7000.
Deputy General Counsel for—
General Law.—Lisa Belasco (acting), 272–3000.
Intellectual Property Law and Solicitor.—John M. Whealan, 272–9035.
Chief Administrative Law Judge for—
Board of Patent Appeals and Interferences.—Michael Fleming, 272–9797.
Trademark Trial and Appeal Board.—J. David Sams, 272–4304.
Director, Office of Enrollment and Discipline.—Harry Moatz, 272–4097.

CHIEF INFORMATION OFFICER

Chief Information Officer.—David J. Freeland (571) 272–9400.

Chief of Staff.—Pam Kitchens (acting), 272–8987.
Deputy Chief Information Officer.—Griffin Macy, 272–9410.
Director, Group of:
Administrative Management.—Francis O'Hearn (acting), 272–6015.
Architecture Engineering and Technical Services.—Holly Higgins, 272–5437.
Business Relationship Management.—Kay Melvin, 272–9025.
Customer Information Services.—Ted Parr, 272–5450.
Manager, Office of:
Electronic Information Products.—Ed Johnson (acting), 272–5471.
Public Information Services.—Martha Sneed, 272–5486.
Public Records.—Amanda Putnam (acting), 272–5756.
Customer Support Services.—Cheryl Newberger (acting), 272–3188.
Enterprise IT and Security Management.—Rod Turk (acting), 272–1975.
Enterprise Systems Services.—Carol Eakins, 272–5426.
Network and Telecommunications Services.—Jay Chalk (acting), 272–5277.
Systems Development and Maintenance.—Ramingio Silva, 272–8386.
Director, Program Management Office.—Jack Donnelly (acting), 272–5522.
Director, Budget and Finance Division.—Francis O'Hearn, 272–6015.

TECHNOLOGY ADMINISTRATION

Under Secretary.—Robert C. Cresanti (202) 482–1575.
Director of:
Congressional Affairs.—Angela Ewell-Madison, 482–4605.
Public Affairs.—Marjorie Weisskohl (acting), 482–0149.
Research.—Connie K.N. Chang, 482–6814.

NATIONAL INSTITUTE OF STANDARDS AND TECHNOLOGY

Director.—Dr. William A. Jeffrey (301) 975–2300.
Deputy Director.—Dr. James E. Hill (acting).
Chief Scientist.—Dr. Hratch G. Semerjian, 975–5555.
Baldrige National Quality Program.—Dr. Harry S. Hertz, 975–2360.
International and Academic Affairs.—Dr. Claire M. Saundry, 975–2386.
NIST/Boulder Laboratories.—Dr. Thomas R. O'Brian (303) 497–7000.
Chief of Staff.—Matthew Heyman, 975–2759.
Congressional and Legislative Affairs.—Kevin A. Kimball, 975–3080.
Program Office.—Eric Steel, 975–3750.
Public and Business Affairs.—Gail J. Porter, 975–3392.
Chief Financial Officer.—Todd Grams, 975–5000.
Budget.—Thomas P. Klausing, 975–2669.
Business Systems.—Thomas P. Klausing (acting), 975–2670.
Finance.—John Quick, 975–2261.
Grants and Agreements Management.—Angela McNerney, 975–8006.
Chief Human Capital Officer.—Robert Kirkner, 975–3002.
Human Resources Management.—Shirley Purcell (303) 497–6576.
Management and Organization.—Catherine S. Fletcher, 975–4054.
Safety, Health and Environment.—Rosamond A. Rutledge-Burns, 975–5818.
Civil Rights and Diversity Office.—Mirta-Marie M. Keys, 975–2042.
Chief Information Officer.—Dr. Simon Szykman, 975–6500.
Applications Systems.—L. Dale Little, 975–8982.
Customer Access and Support.—Tim Halton, 975–8920.
Enterprise Systems.—James E. Fowler, 975–6888.
Information Technology Security and Networking.—Robert Glenn, 975–3667.
Telecommunications and CIO Support.—Bruce Rose, 975–3299.
Chief Facilities Management Officer.—Robert F. Moore, 975–8836.
Administrative Services.—David T. Henry, 975–8994.
Emergency Services.—Dr. Benjamin Overbey, 975–8247.
Engineering, Maintenance and Support Services.—Stephen S. Salber (303) 497–5680.
Plant.—John Bollinger, 975–6900.
Director, Technology Services.—Dr. Belinda L. Collins, 975–4500.
Deputy Director.—Dr. George W. Arnold, 975–4510.
Information Services.—Mary-Deirdre Coraggio, 975–5158.
Measurement Services.—Robert L. Watters, Jr., 975–4122.
Standards Services.—Mary H. Saunders, 975–2396.
Weights and Measures.—Carol Hockert, 975–5507.

Director, Advanced Technology Program.—Marc G. Stanley, 975–2162.
Deputy Director.—Dr. Lorel Wisniewski, 975–5232.
Chemistry and Life Sciences.—Linda Beth Schilling, 975–2887.
Economic Assessment.—Dr. Stephanie Shipp, 975–8978.
Information Technology and Electronics.—Dr. Michael Schen (acting), 975–6741.
Director, Hollings Manufacturing Extension Partnership Program.—Roger D. Kilmer, 975–4676.
Deputy Director.—Aimee Dobrzeniecki, 975–8322.
Program Development Office.—Stephen J. Thompson, 975–5042.
Systems Operation Office.—Michael J. Simpson, 975–6147.
Director, Electronics and Electrical Engineering Laboratory.—Dr. William E. Anderson, 975–2220.
Deputy Director.—Dr. Alan H. Cookson, 975–2220.
Electromagnetics.—Dr. Michael H. Kelley (acting), (303) 497–3131.
Optoelectronics.—Dr. Kent Rochford, 975–5285.
Quantum Electrical Metrology.—Dr. James K. Olthoff, 975–2431.
Semiconductor Electronics.—Dr. David G. Seiler, 975–2054.
Director, Center for Nanoscale Science and Technology.—Dr. Robert Celotta, 975–8001.
Director, Manufacturing Engineering Laboratory.—Dr. Dale E. Hall, 975–3400.
Deputy Director.—Dr. Howard H. Harary, 975–3401.
Fabrication Technology.—Mark E. Luce, 975–2159.
Intelligent Systems.—Albert Wavering, 975–3418.
Manufacturing Metrology.—Kevin K. Jurrens (acting), 975–6600.
Manufacturing Systems Integration.—Dr. Steven R. Ray, 975–3508.
Director, Chemical Science and Technology Laboratory.—Dr. Willie E. May, 975–8300.
Deputy Director.—Dr. William F. Koch, 975–8301.
Analytical Chemistry.—Dr. Stephen A. Wise, 975–3108.
Biochemical Science.—Dr. Laurie E. Locascio, 975–3130.
Physical and Chemical Properties.—Dr. Daniel G. Friend (acting), 975–5424.
Process Measurements.—Dr. James R. Whetstone, 975–2609.
Surface and Microanalysis Science.—Dr. Richard R. Cavanagh, 975–2368.
Director, Physics Laboratory.—Dr. Katharine B. Gebbie, 975–4201.
Deputy Director.—Dr. William R. Ott, 975–4202.
Atomic Physics.—Dr. Carl J. Williams, 975–3531.
Electron and Optical Physics.—Dr. Charles W. Clark, 975–3709.
Ionizing Radiation.—Dr. Lisa R. Karam (acting), 975–5561.
Optical Technology.—Dr. Albert C. Parr, 975–2316.
Quantum Physics.—Dr. Steven T. Cundiff (303) 492–7858.
Time and Frequency.—Dr. Thomas R. O'Brian (303) 497–4570.
Director, Materials Science and Engineering Laboratory.—Dr. Richard F. Kayser, 975–5658.
Deputy Director.—Dr. Eric J. Amis, 975–6681.
Ceramics.—Dr. Debra L. Kaiser, 975–6119.
Materials Reliability.—Dr. Stephanie Hooker (303) 497–4326.
Metallurgy.—Dr. Frank W. Gayle, 975–6161.
Polymers.—Dr. Chad R. Snyder (acting), 975–4526.
Director, NIST Center for Neutron Research.—Dr. Patrick D. Gallagher, 975–6210.
Director, Building and Fire Research Laboratory.—Dr. S. Shyam-Sunder (acting), 975–5900.
Deputy Director.—Dr. S. Shyam-Sunder, 975–6713.
Building Environment.—Dr. George Kelly, 975–5850.
Fire Research.—Dr. William L. Grosshandler, 975–2310.
Materials and Construction Research.—Dr. Jonathan W. Martin, 975–6707.
Director, Information Technology Laboratory.—Cita M. Furlani, 975–2900.
Deputy Director.—James A. St. Pierre, 975–2900.
Advanced Network Technologies.—Dr. David Su, 975–6194.
Computer Security.—William Curt Barker, 975–8443.
Information Access.—Dr. Martin Herman, 975–4495.
Mathematical and Computational Sciences.—Dr. Ronald F. Boisvert, 975–3800.
Software Diagnostics and Conformance Testing.—Mark W. Skall, 975–3262.
Statistical Engineering.—Dr. Antonio Possolo (acting), 975–2853.

NATIONAL TECHNICAL INFORMATION SERVICE

5285 Port Royal Road, Springfield, VA 22161

Director.—Ellen Herbst (703) 605–6400.

Deputy Director.—Bruce Borzino, 605–6405.
Administration.—Vicki Buttram, 605–6133.
Business Operations.—Bruce Borzino, 605–6405.
Chief Information Officer.—Keith Sinner, 605–6310.
Customer Relations.—Jon Birdsall, 605–6102.
Finance.—Mary Houff, 605–6611.
Policy.—Steven Needle, 605–6404.

NATIONAL TELECOMMUNICATIONS AND INFORMATION ADMINISTRATION

Assistant Secretary and Administrator.—John M.R. Kneuer (acting), room 4898 (202) 482–1840.
Senior Policy Advisor.—Meredith Baker.
Senior Advisor.—David Murray.
Chief Counsel.—Kathy Smith.
Communications and Information Infrastructure Assurance.—Daniel Hurley.
Congressional Affairs.—Jim Wasilewski (acting).
Institute for Telecommunications Sciences.—Al Vincent (303) 497–3500.
International Affairs.—Fiona Alexander (acting).
Policy Analysis and Development.—Eric R. Stark.
Public Affairs.—Todd Sedmak.
Spectrum Management.—Frederick R. Wentland.
Telecommunications and Information Applications.—Bernadette McGuire–Rivera.

DEPARTMENT OF LABOR

Frances Perkins Building, Third Street and Constitution Avenue, NW., 20210

phone (202) 693–5000, http://www.dol.gov

ELAINE L. CHAO, Secretary of Labor; education: B.A., Mount Holyoke College, 1975; M.B.A., Harvard University, 1979; she also studied at the Massachusetts Institute of Technology, Dartmouth College, and Columbia University; employment: Citicorp, 1979–83; BankAmerica Capital Markets Group, 1984–86; Distinguished Fellow, Heritage Foundation, 1996–2001; public service: White House Fellow, Office of Policy Development, 1983–84; Deputy Maritime Administrator, Department of Transportation, 1986–88; Chairwoman, Federal Maritime Commission, 1988–89; Deputy Secretary of Transportation, 1989–91; Peace Corps Director, 1991–92; President and Chief Executive Officer of the United Way of America, 1992–96; family: married to U.S. Senator Mitch McConnell (R–KY); recipient of many awards for her community service and professional accomplishments; and recipient of 11 honorary doctorate degrees from numerous colleges and universities; nominated by President George W. Bush to become the 24th Secretary of Labor, and was confirmed by the U.S. Senate on January 29, 2001.

OFFICE OF THE SECRETARY

phone (202) 693–6000

Secretary of Labor.—Elaine L. Chao.
Deputy Secretary.—Steven J. Law.
Associate Deputy Secretary.—Laura Genero.
Executive Secretariat Director.—Ruth D. Knouse, 693–6100.
Chief of Staff.—Paul T. Conway, 693–6007.
Director of Advance and Scheduling.—Amy Barrera, 693–6003.

OFFICE OF THE 21ST CENTURY WORKFORCE

Director.—Karen Czarnecki (202) 693–6490.
Deputy Director.—Bettye Samuels.
Senior Counsel.—Alan Severson.

ADMINISTRATIVE LAW JUDGES

Techworld, 800 K Street, NW., Suite 400–N, 20001–8002

Chief Administrative Law Judge.—John M. Vittone (202) 693–7542.
Associate Chief Judge.—Thomas M. Burke.

ADMINISTRATIVE REVIEW BOARD

Chairman.—M. Cynthia Douglass, room S4309 (202) 693–6200.

ASSISTANT SECRETARY FOR ADMINISTRATION AND MANAGEMENT

Assistant Secretary.—Patrick Pizzella, room S–2203 (202) 693–4040.
Deputy Assistant Secretary for—
Budget and Performance Planning.—Maureen Walsh.
Operations.—Edward C. Hugler.
Security and Emergency Management.—Kenneth McCreless, room S–1229G, 693–7990.
Special Assistants: Cesar de Guzman, John Pallasch, Terrance Wear.

Administrative Officer.—Noelia Fernandez.
Staff Assistant.—Rawnette Murray.

BUSINESS OPERATIONS CENTER

Director.—Al Stewart, room S–1524 (202) 693–4028.
Deputy Director.—John Saracco.
Office of:
Acquisition and Management Support Services.—Karen Nunley, room S–1519B, 693–7272.
Administrative Services.—Leonard Pettiford, room S–1521, 693–6665.
Competitive Sourcing.—Larry Clark, room S–1519A, 693–4020.
Procurement Services.—Valerie Veatch, room N–5416, 693–4570.
Worker Safety and Health Services.—Sheila Baker, room S–1513B, 693–6670.

CENTER FOR PROGRAM PLANNING AND RESULTS

Director.—Richard French, room S–3317 (202) 693–4088.
Office of:
DOL Historian.—Linda Stinson, room N–2445, 693–4085.
Planning.—Mark Davis, 693–7126.
Wirtz Labor Library.—Jean Bowers, room N–2445, 693–6600.

CIVIL RIGHTS CENTER

Director.—Annabelle T. Lockhart, room N–4123 (202) 693–6500.
Staff Assistant.—Danielle White.
Office of:
Compliance Assistance and Planning.—Gregory Shaw, 693–6501.
EEO Coordinator of Counselors.—Lillian Winstead, 693–6504.
Enforcement/External.—Willie Alexander, 693–6502.
Enforcement/Internal.—Naomi Berry Perez, 693–6503.
Reasonable Accommodation Hotline.—Dawn Johnson, room N–4123, 693–6569.

DEPARTMENTAL BUDGET CENTER

Director.—Kimberly Taylor-Locey, room S–4020 (202) 693–4090.
Deputy Director.—Mark P. Wichlin.
Staff Assistant.—Patricia Smith.
Office of:
Agency Budget Programs.—James Martin, 693–4077.
Budget Policy and Systems.—Sandra Mulcahy, 693–4078.
Financial Management Operations.—Geoffrey Kenyon, room S–5526, 693–4490.

EMERGENCY MANAGEMENT CENTER

Director.—Greg Rize, 800 K Street, NW., Suite 450 North, 20001–8002 (202) 693–7555.
Deputy Director.—Pete Podell.

GOVBENEFITS.GOV

Program Manager.—Curtis Turner, room N–4309 (202) 693–4025.

HUMAN RESOURCES CENTER

Director.—Daliza Salas, room C–5526 (202) 693–7600.
Deputy Director.—Jerry Lelchook.
Office of:
Administration and Management Services.—Tracey Schaeffer, C–5515, 693–7773.
Continuous Learning and Career Management.—Kim Green, room N–5464, 693–7630.
Diversity Management.—Violet R. Parker, room N–6432, 693–7795.
Employee and Labor Management Relations.—Sandra Keppley, room N–5464, 693–7670.

Executive Resources and Personnel Security.—Andrea Burckman, room C–5508, 693–7800.
Human Resources Consulting and Operations.—Joanne Broderick, room C–5516, 693–7690.
Human Resources Policy and Accountability.—Susan Barker, room 5464, 693–7720.
Workforce Planning and e-Innovations.—Dennis Sullivan, room C–5516, 693–7740.
Worklife and Benefits Programs.—Brooke Brewer, room N–5454, 693–7610.

INFORMATION TECHNOLOGY CENTER

Director.—Thomas Wiesner, room N–1301 (202) 693–4567.
Deputy Director.—Yann King.
Administrative Officer.—Kathy Fox, 693–4215.
Director, Office of:
Chief Information Officer Programs.—Peter Sullivan, 693–4211.
Systems Development and Integration.—Richard Lewis, 693–4149.
Technical Services.—Hamid Ouyachi, 693–4173.
IT Help Desk.—8 a.m. to 6:30 p.m., room N–1505, 693–4444.

SECURITY CENTER

Director.—Tom Holman, room S–1229G (202) 693–7200.
Deputy Director.—Robert Rouse.

ASSISTANT SECRETARY FOR POLICY

Assistant Secretary.—Leon B. Sequeira, room S–2312 (202) 693–5959.
Deputy Assistant Secretaries: Susan ''Suey'' Howe, Deborah Misir.
Chief of Staff.—John Britton.
Staff Assistant.—Erika Gutierrez.
Senior Policy Advisor.—Porter Montgomery.
Director, Office of:
Compliance Assistance Policy.—Barbara Bingham, 693–5080.
Economic Policy and Analysis.—Ronald Bird, 693–4966.
Regulatory and Programmatic Policy.—Kathleen Franks, 693–5072.

BENEFITS REVIEW BOARD

Chair.—Nancy S. Dolder, room N5101 (202) 693–6300.

BUREAU OF LABOR STATISTICS

Postal Square Building, Suite 4040, 2 Massachusetts Avenue, NE., 20212, phone (202) 691–7800

Deputy Commissioner.—Philip L. Rones, 691–7802.
Associate Commissioner, Office of:
Administration.—Daniel J. Lacey, suite 4060, 691–7777.
Compensation and Working Conditions.—William Wiatrowski, suite 4130, 691–6300.
Employment and Unemployment Statistics.—John M. Galvin, suite 4945, 691–6400.
Field Operations.—Robert A. Gaddie (acting), suite 2935, 691–5800.
Prices and Living Conditions.—John Greenlees, suite 3120, 691–6960.
Productivity and Technology.—Michael Harper, suite 2150, 691–5600.
Publications and Special Studies.—William Parks, suite 4110, 691–5900.
Survey Methods Research.—John Etinge, suite 4080, 691–7372.
Technology and Survey Processing.—Fernando Burbano, suite 5025, 691–7603.
Assistant Commissioner, Office of:
Compensation Levels and Trends.—Mary McCarthy, suite 4130, 691–6302.
Consumer Prices and Price Indexes.—John Layng, suite 3130, 691–6950.
Current Employment Analysis.—Thomas Nadone, suite 4675, 691–6388.
Industrial Prices and Price Indexes.—Michael Horrigan, suite 3840, 691–7700.
Industry Employment Statistics.—Patricia Getz, suite 4840, 691–6528.
Occupational Statistics and Employment Projections.—Dixie Sommers, suite 2135, 691–5701.

Director of:

Survey Processing.—Richard L. Schroeder (acting), suite 5025, 691–7603.

Technology and Computing Services.—Rick Kryger (acting), suite 5025, 691–7606.

BUREAU OF INTERNATIONAL LABOR AFFAIRS

Deputy Under Secretary.—James Carter, room C–4325 (202) 693–4770.

Associate Deputy Under Secretary.—Robert Owen.

Director, Office of:

Child Labor, Forced Labor, and Human Trafficking.—Marcia Eugenio, 693–4849.

International Relations.—Robert Shepard, 693–4887.

Trade and Labor Affairs.—Gregory Schoepfle, 693–4887.

OFFICE OF THE CHIEF FINANCIAL OFFICER

Chief Financial Officer.—Samuel T. Mok, room S–4030 (202) 693–6800.

Deputy Chief Financial Officer.—Yoko Albayrak (acting).

Associate Deputy Chief Financial Officer.—Valerie M. Harris (acting), 693–6900.

Administrative Officer.—Valerie H. Sollers.

Controller.—Robert Balin.

Special Assistants: Wendy Gehring, Virginia Green.

Assistant.—Richard Lim.

Director, Office of:

Accounting.—Miguel Reyes, 693–6840.

Fiscal Integrity.—Stewart Petchenick, 693–6820.

Financial Policy.—Richard Zeutenhorst, 693–6800.

Financial Systems.—Tim Hurr, 693–6900.

Payroll Systems Support Services.—Darlene Edwards, 693–6850.

OFFICE OF CONGRESSIONAL AND INTERGOVERNMENTAL AFFAIRS

Assistant Secretary.—Kristine Iverson, room S–2006 (202) 693–4601.

Staff Assistant.—Glenda Manning.

Deputy Assistant Secretary, Congressional.—Blake Hanlon, room S–2220, 693–4600.

Deputy Assistant Secretary, Intergovernmental.—Karen Czarnecki, room S–2235, 693–6490.

Senior Legislative Officers:

Budget and Appropriations.—Alice Joe, room S–2220, 693–4600.

Employee Benefits.—Alice Joe, room S–2220, 693–4600.

Employment and Training.—Geoff Burr, room S–2220, 693–4600.

Employment Standards.—James Grande, room S–2220, 693–4600.

Legislative Officers: Ann Carmichael, Erin Tario, room S–2220, 693–4600.

Congressional Research Assistants: Kristina Rivas, Drew Setterberg, Eric Snyder, room S–2220, 693–4600.

Senior Intergovernmental Officers: Matthew Lathrop, Andrew Schauder, room S–2220, 693–4600.

Administrative Officer.—Joycelyn Daniels, room S–1318, 693–4600.

REGIONAL OFFICES

Region I, Boston.—Connecticut, Maine, Massachusetts, New Hampshire, Rhode Island, Vermont.

Region II, New York.—New York, New Jersey, Puerto Rico, Virgin Islands.

Regional Representative.—Angelica O. Tang, 201 Varick Street, Suite 605, New York, NY 10014–4811 (212) 337–2387.

Region III, Philadelphia.—Pennsylvania, Delaware, District of Columbia, Maryland, Virginia, West Virginia.

Regional Representative.—Patrick Marano, The Curtis Center, 170 S. Independence Mall West, Suite 637 East, Philadelphia, PA 19106 (215) 861–5027.

Region IV, Atlanta.—Alabama, Georgia, Florida, Kentucky, Mississippi, North Carolina, South Carolina, Tennessee.

Region V, Chicago.—Illinois, Indiana, Michigan, Minnesota, Ohio, Wisconsin.

Regional Representative.—Robert ''Bob'' Athey, 230 South Dearborn Street, Suite 3810, Chicago, IL 60604 (312) 353–4591.

Region VI, Dallas.—Texas, Arkansas, Louisiana, New Mexico, Oklahoma.

Region VII, Des Moines.—Iowa, Kansas, Nebraska, Missouri.

Regional Representative.—Jack Rife, 210 Walnut Street, Room 275, Des Moines, IA 50309 (515) 284–4740.

Region VIII, Denver.—Colorado, Montana, North Dakota, South Dakota, Wyoming.

Regional Representative.—Rick Collins, 1801 California Street, Suite 945, Denver, CO 80202 (303) 844–1256.

Region IX, San Francisco.—California, Hawaii, Nevada, Arizona, Guam.

Regional Representative.—Marina Tse, 350 South Figeroa Street #370, Los Angeles, CA 90071 (213) 894–2543.

Region X, Seattle.—Alaska, Idaho, Oregon, Washington.

Regional Representative.—Walter Liang, 1111 Third Avenue, Suite 920, Seattle, WA 98101-3212 (206) 553–0574.

OFFICE OF DISABILITY EMPLOYMENT POLICY

Assistant Secretary.—W. Roy Grizzard, Jr., Ed.D., room S–1303, (202) 693–7880, TTY 693–7881.

Chief of Staff.—Nancy Skaggs.

Special Assistants: Robert Brostrom, Loretta Herrington.

Director of:

Office of Policy and Research.—Susan Parker.

Office of Operations.—John Davey.

EMPLOYEE BENEFITS SECURITY ADMINISTRATION

Assistant Secretary.—Bradford P. Campbell (acting), room S–2524 (202) 693–8300.

Deputy Assistant Secretary for Policy.—Bradford P. Campbell.

Deputy Assistant Secretary.—Alan D. Lebowitz, room N–5677, 693–8315.

Chief of Staff.—Thomas Alexander, room S–2524, 693–8300.

Executive Assistant to the Deputy Assistant Secretary.—Sue Ugelow, 693–8315.

Confidential Assistant.—Holly Katherine Winthrop.

Special Assistant.—Christine Heatley.

Senior Director for Policy and Legislative Analysis.—Morton Klevan, room N–5677, 693–8315.

Director of:

Program, Planning, Evaluation and Management.—Brian C. McDonnell, room N–5668, 693–8480.

Chief Accountant.—Ian Dingwall, room N–5459, 693–8360.

Enforcement.—Virginia Smith, room N–5702, 693–8440.

Exemption Determinations.—Ivan L. Strasfeld, room N–5649, 693–8540.

Information Management.—John Helms, room N–5459, 693–8600.

Program Services.—Sharon Watson, room N–5625, 693–8630.

Regulations and Interpretations.—Robert Doyle, room N–5669, 693–8500.

Policy and Research.—Joseph Piacentini, room N–5718, 693–8410.

EMPLOYEES COMPENSATION APPEALS BOARD

Chairman.—Alec Koromilas, room N–2613 (202) 693–6420.

EMPLOYMENT AND TRAINING ADMINISTRATION

Assistant Secretary.—Emily Stover DeRocco, room S–2307 (202) 693–2700.

Deputy Assistant Secretaries: Mason M. Bishop, Douglas F. Small.

Administrator, Office of:

Apprenticeship.—Anthony L. Swoope, room N–5306, 693–2796.

Financial and Administrative Management.—Anna W. Goddard, room N–4653, 693–2800.

Foreign Labor Certification.—William B. Carlson, room C–4312, 693–3010.

National Response.—Erica R. Cantor, room N–5422, 693–3500.

Performance and Technology.—John R. Beverly III, room S–5206, 693–3420.

Policy Development and Research.—Maria Kniesler Flynn, room N–5637, 693–3700.

Regional Operations.—Jack H. Rapport, room C–4517, 693–3690.

Workforce Investment.—Gay M. Gilbert, room S–4231, 693–3980.

Workforce Security.—Cheryl Atkinson, room S–4231, 693–3029.

EMPLOYMENT STANDARDS ADMINISTRATION

Assistant Secretary.—Victoria Lipnic, room S–2321 (202) 693–0200.
Deputy Assistant Secretary.—D. Mark Wilson.
Special Assistant.—Nicolee Ambrose.
Administrator, Wage and Hour Program.—Paul DeCamp, 693–0051.
Deputy Administrator.—Alex Passantino.
Deputy Administrator for Operations.—Russell Harris.
Chief of Staff.—Dave Minsky.
Director, Office of:
External Affairs.—Libby Hendrix.
Planning and Analysis.—Carl Smith (acting).
Wage Determinations.—William M. Gross.
Deputy Assistant Secretary, Office of Federal Contract Compliance Programs.—Charles E. James, Sr., 693–0101.
Deputy Director.—David Frank.
Special Assistant.—Robert McCreary.
Director of Workers' Compensation Programs.—Shelby Hallmark, 693–0031.
Director, Division of:
Coal Mine Worker's Compensation.—James DeMarce.
Energy Employees Occupational Illness Compensation Program.—Peter Turcic.
Federal Employees Compensation.—Douglas Fitzgerald.
Longshore and Harber Worker's Compensation.—Michael Niss.
Director, Office of Management, Administration and Planning.—Anne Baird-Bridges, 693–0608.
Deputy Director.—Bruce Bohanon.
Coordinator, Equal Employment Opportunity Unit.—Pamela Gibbs, 693–0300.

OFFICE OF FAITH BASED INITIATIVES

Director.—Jedd Medefind (202) 693–6451.
Deputy Director.—Jacqueline Halbig, 693–4600.

OFFICE OF THE INSPECTOR GENERAL

Inspector General.—Gordon S. Heddell, room S–5502 (202) 693–5100.
Deputy Inspector General.—Daniel R. Petrole.
Chief of Staff.—Dale Wilson.
Assistant Inspector General for—
Audit.—Elliot P. Lewis, room S–5518, 693–5168.
Inspection and Special Investigations.—Asa Cunningham, room S–5021, 693–5211.
Labor Racketeering and Fraud Investigations.—Thomas F. Farrell, room S–5014, 693–7034.
Legal Services.—Howard L. Shapiro, room S–5508, 693–5116.
Management and Policy.—Nancy Ruiz de Gamboa, room S–5028, 693–5191.

MINE SAFETY AND HEALTH ADMINISTRATION

1100 Wilson Boulevard, Arlington, VA 22209–3939, phone (202) 693–9414, fax 693–9401, http://www.msha.gov

Assistant Secretary.—Richard E. Stickler.
Deputy Assistant Secretary.—Robert M. Friend (acting).
Administrator for—
Coal Mine Safety and Health.—Kevin Stricklin (acting), 693–9502.
Metal and Nonmetal Mine Safety and Health.—Felix Quintana (acting), 693–9603.
Director for—
Administration and Management Office.—David L. Meyer, 693–9802.
Assessments Office.—Jay Mattos (acting), 693–9702.
Educational Policy and Development Office.—Jeffrey A. Duncan, 693–9572.
Information and Public Affairs.—Layne Lathram, 693–9422.
Program Evaluation and Information Resources.—George M. Fesak, 693–9752.
Standards, Regulations and Variances.—Patricia Silvey (acting), 693–9442.
Technical Support.—Mark E. Skiles, 693–9472.

OCCUPATIONAL SAFETY AND HEALTH ADMINISTRATION

Assistant Secretary.—Edwin G. Foulke, Jr., room S–2315 (202) 693–2000.
Deputy Assistant Secretaries: Bryan Little, Donald Shalhoub.
Chief of Staff.—Gabe Sierra.
Director, Office of:
Equal Employment Opportunity.—Bill Burke (acting), 693–2150.
Communications.—Kevin Ropp, 693–1999.
Director of:
Administrative Programs.—David Zeigler, 693–1600.
Construction.—Steven Witt, 693–2020.
Cooperative and State Programs.—Paula White, 693–2200.
Enforcement Programs.—Richard Fairfax, 693–2100.
Evaluation and Analysis.—Keith Goddard, 693–2400.
Information Technology.—Cheryle Greenaugh, 693–1818.
Science, Technology and Medicine.—Ruth McCully, 693–2300.
Standards and Guidance.—Dorothy Dougherty, 693–1950.

OFFICE OF PUBLIC AFFAIRS

Assistant Secretary.—C. James Schaefer (acting), room S–2514 (202) 693–4676.
Deputy Assistant Secretary.—C. James Schaefer.

REGIONAL OFFICES

Region I.—Connecticut, Maine, Massachusetts, New Hampshire, Rhode Island, Vermont.
Public Affairs Director.—John Chavez, JFK Federal Building, Government Center, 25 New Sudbury Street, Room 525–A, Boston, MA 02203 (617) 565–2075.

Region IIA.—New York, Puerto Rico, Virgin Islands.
Regional Representative.—John Chavez, JFK Federal Building, Government Center, 25 New Sudbury Street, Room 525–A, Boston, Massachusetts 02203 (617) 565–2075.

Region IIB.—New Jersey.
Regional Representative.—Kate Dugan, Curtis Center, 170 S. Independence Mall West, Suite 633-East, Philadelphia, PA 19106–3306 (215) 596–1147.

Region III.—Delaware, District of Columbia, Maryland, Pennsylvania, Virginia, West Virginia.
Public Affairs Director.—Kate Dugan, Curtis Center, 170 S. Independence Mall West, Suite 633-East, Philadelphia, PA 19106–3306 (215) 596–1147.

Region IV.—Alabama, Florida, Georgia, Kentucky, Mississippi, North Carolina, South Carolina, Tennessee.
Public Affairs Director.—Dan Fuqua, Atlanta Federal Center, 61 Forsyth SW, Suite 6B75, Atlanta, GA 30303 (404) 562–2078.

Region V.—Illinois, Indiana, Michigan, Minnesota, Ohio, Wisconsin.
Public Affairs Director.—Bradley Mitchell, Room 3194, 230 South Dearborn Street, Room 3192, Chicago, IL 60604 (312) 353–6976.

Region VI.—Arkansas, Louisiana, New Mexico, Oklahoma, Texas.
Public Affairs Director.—Diana Petterson, Room 734, 525 Griffin Street, Dallas, TX 75202 (214) 767–4777.

Region VII.—Iowa, Kansas, Missouri, Nebraska.
Public Affairs Specialist.—Rich Kulczewski, 1999 Broadway, Suite 1640, Denver, CO 80202 (303) 844–1303.

Region VIII.—Colorado, Montana, North Dakota, South Dakota, Utah, Wyoming.
Public Affairs Director.—Rich Kulczewski, 1999 Broadway, Suite 1640, Denver, CO 80202 (303) 844–1303.

Region IX.—Arizona, California, Guam, Hawaii, Nevada.
Public Affairs Director.—Deanne Amaden, Suite 1035, 71 Stevenson Street, San Francisco, CA 94119–3766 (415) 975–4742.

Region X.—Alaska, Idaho, Oregon, Washington.
Public Affairs Director.—Mike Shimizu, Building B, Room 930, 1111 Third Avenue, Seattle WA, 98101 (206) 553–7620.

OFFICE OF SMALL BUSINESS PROGRAMS

Director.—José A. ''Joe'' Lira, room C2318 (202) 693–6460.

OFFICE OF THE SOLICITOR

Solicitor.—Howard M. Radzely, room S–2002 (202) 693–5260.
Deputy Solicitor.—Jonathan L. Snare.
Staff Assistant.—Serene E. Williams.
Special Assistants.—Nicholas C. Geale; Amanda Walker.
Deputy Solicitor for—
National Operations.—Carol A. DeDeo, 693–5261.
Regional Operations.—Ronald O. Whiting, 693–5262.
Assistant Deputy Solicitor for Supreme Court Litigation and Appellate Advice.—Nathaniel I. Spiller, 693–5768.

DIVISION OF BLACK LUNG AND LONGSHORE LEGAL SERVICES

Associate Solicitor.—Allen H. Feldman, room N–2605 (202) 693–5660.
Deputy Associate Solicitor.—Rae Ellen James.
Counsel for—
Administrative Litigation and Legal Advice.—Michael J. Rutledge.
Appellate Litigation.—Patricia M. Nece.
Longshore.—Mark A. Reinhalter.

DIVISION OF CIVIL RIGHTS AND LABOR-MANAGEMENT

Associate Solicitor.—Katherine E. Bissell, room N–2474 (202) 693–5740.
Deputy Associate Solicitor.—Peter J. Constantine.
Counsel for—
Advice.—Alexandra A. Tsiros.
Advice and Statutory Programs.—Mark S. Flynn.
Interpretation and Advice.—Suzan Chastain.
Litigation and Regional Coordination.—Beverly I. Dankowitz.
LMRDA Programs.—Sharon E. Hanley.

DIVISION OF EMPLOYMENT AND TRAINING LEGAL SERVICES

Associate Solicitor.—Gary M. Buff, room N–2101 (202) 693–5710.
Deputy Associate Solicitor.—Jonathan H. Waxman, 693–5730.
Counsel for—
Employment and Training Advise.—Robert P. Hines, Michael N. Apfelbaum.
Immigration Programs.—Bruce W. Alter.
International Affairs and USERRA.—Donald D. Carter, Jr.
Litigation.—Harry L. Sheinfeld.

DIVISION OF FAIR LABOR STANDARDS

Associate Solicitor.—Steven J. Mandel, room N–2716 (202) 693–5555.
Deputy Associate Solicitor.—William C. Lesser.
Counsel for—
Appellate Litigation.—Paul L. Frieden.
Legal Advice.—Diane A. Heim.
Trial Litigation.—Jonathan M. Kronheim.
Whistleblower Programs.—Ellen R. Edmond.

DIVISION OF FEDERAL EMPLOYEE AND ENERGY WORKERS COMPENSATION

Associate Solicitor.—Jeffrey L. Nesvet, room S–4325 (202) 693–5320.
Deputy Associate Solicitor.—Neilda C. Lee.
Counsel for—
Claims and Compensation.—Catherine P. Carter.
Energy Employees Compensation.—Sheldon O. Turley, Jr.
Chief, FECA Subrogation Unit.—Gertrude B. Gordon.

DIVISION OF MINE SAFETY AND HEALTH

1100 Wilson Boulevard, 22nd Floor, Arlington, VA 22209

Associate Solicitor.—Edward P. Clair, room 2222 (202) 693–9333.
Deputy Associate Solicitor.—Heidi W. Strassler.
Counsel for—
Appellate Litigation.—W. Christian Schumann, room 2220.
Standards and Legal Advice.—April E. Nelson, room 2224.
Trial Litigation.—Mark K. Malecki, room 2226.

DIVISION OF OCCUPATIONAL SAFETY AND HEALTH

Associate Solicitor.—Joseph M. Woodward, room S–4004 (202) 693–5452.
Deputy Associate Solicitor.—Ann S. Rosenthal.
Counsel for—
Appellate Litigation: Michael P. Doyle, Charles F. James.
Egregious Litigation.—Kenneth A. Hellman.
Health Standards.—Ian J. Moar.
Regional Litigation and Legal Advice.—Daniel J. Mick, Robert W. Swain.
Safety Standards.—Bradford T. Hammock.

DIVISION OF PLAN BENEFITS SECURITY

Associate Solicitor.—Timothy D. Hauser, room N–4611 (202) 693–5600.
Deputy Associate Solicitors.—Theresa S. Gee, William Scott.
Counsel for—
Appellate and Special Litigation.—Karen L. Handorf.
Fiduciary Litigation.—Risa D. Sandler.
General Litigation.—Leslie Canfield Perlman.
Regulation.—William White Taylor.

HONORS PROGRAM

Director.—Nancy M. Rooney, room N–2700 (202) 693–5260.

OFFICE OF LEGAL COUNSEL

Associate Solicitor.—Robert A. Shapiro, room N–2700 (202) 693–5500.
Counsel for—
Ethics.—Robert M. Sadler, 693–5528.
Legislative Affairs.—Jill M. Otte, 693–5525.

MANAGEMENT AND ADMINISTRATIVE LEGAL SERVICES

Associate Solicitor.—William W. Thompson II, room N–2428 (202) 693–5405.
Counsel for—
Administrative Law.—Ray Mitten, Jr., 693–5405.
Appropriations and Contracts.—Dennis A. Adelson, 695–5719; Myron G. Zeitz, 693–5536.
FOIA/FACA.—Joseph J. Plick, 693–5527.
Human Resources.—James V. Blair, 693–5508.
Financial Manager.—Molly Parker, room N–2427, 693–5433.
IT/IRM Manager.—Cheryl C. Hogans, room N–2414, 693–5368.

VETERANS' EMPLOYMENT AND TRAINING SERVICE

Assistant Secretary.—Charles S. Ciccolella, room S–1313 (202) 693–4700.
Deputy Assistant Secretary.—John McWilliam.
Chief of Staff.—Daniel Nichols.
Special Assistants: Chris Grisafe, Kathi Ladner.
Director for—
Agency Management and Budget.—Paul Briggs, 693–4713.

National HireVetsFirst Committee.—William Offutt, 693–4717.
Operations and Programs.—Gordon Burke, 693–4707.
Strategic Planning.—Ronald Drach, 693–4749.
Chief of:
Investigation and Compliance Division.—Robert Wilson, 693–4719.
Employment and Training Programs Division.—Pamela Langley, 693–4708.

REGIONAL OFFICES

Atlanta:
Administrator.—William J. Bolls, Jr. (404) 562–2305.
Boston:
Administrator.—David Houle (617) 565–2080.
Chicago / Kansas City:
Administrator.—Ronald J. Bachman (312) 353–4942.
Dallas / Denver:
Administrator.—Lester L. Williams, Jr. (214) 767–4987.
Philadelphia:
Administrator.—Joseph W. Hortiz, Jr. (215) 861–5390.
Seattle / San Francisco:
Administrator.—Alex Cuevas (316) 654–8178.

WOMEN'S BUREAU

Director.—Shinae Chun, room S–3002 (202) 693–6710.
Chief of Staff.—Beth Gable Hicks.
National Office Manager.—Karen Furia.
Regional Office Manager.—Collis Philips (404) 562–2336.
Chief of:
Information and Support Services.—Catherine Brietenbach.
Policy and Programs.—Collis Phillips.

DEPARTMENT OF HEALTH AND HUMAN SERVICES

200 Independence Avenue, SW., 20201, http://www.hhs.gov

MICHAEL O. LEAVITT, Secretary of Health and Human Services; born in Cedar City, UT, February 11, 1951; education: B.S., Southern Utah University, 1978; professional: served as Administrator of the U.S. Environmental Protection Agency; Governor of Utah for 11 years; organizations: chairman, National Governors Association; Western Governors Association; Republican Governors Association; married: Jacalyn; five children; nominated by President George W. Bush to become the 20th Secretary of Health and Human Services, and was confirmed by the U.S. Senate on January 26, 2005.

OFFICE OF THE SECRETARY

Secretary of Health and Human Services.—Michael O. Leavitt (202) 690–7000.
Executive Assistant to the Secretary.—Denise Schwartz.

OFFICE OF THE DEPUTY SECRETARY

Chief of Staff.—Richard McKeown (202) 690–8157.
Deputy Chief of Staff.—Kerry Weems, 690–5400.
Executive Secretary.—Ann Agnew, 690–5627.
Deputy Executive Secretary.—Ashley Files, 401–4273.
Director, Intergovernmental Affairs.—Jack Kalavritinos, 690–6060.
Chair, Departmental Appeals Board.—Judy Ballard, 565–0220.

ASSISTANT SECRETARY FOR ADMINISTRATION AND MANAGEMENT

Assistant Secretary.—Joe Ellis (202) 690–7431, fax 401–5207.
Principal Deputy Assistant Secretary.—Linda Garvin.
Deputy Assistant Secretary for Human Resources.—Alan Cigich, 690–6191.
Executive Officer, Office of the Secretary Executive Office.—Lynn Simpson (acting), 690–8794.
Director, Office of:
Acquisition Management and Policy.—Segundo Pereira (acting), 205–2821.
Workforce Diversity and Equal Employment Opportunity.—Segundo Pereira, 205–2821.

PROGRAM SUPPORT CENTER

5600 Fishers Lane, Rockville, MD 20857

Deputy Assistant Secretary.—Philip VanLandingham (301) 443–3921.
Business Technology Optimization.—Jack Stoute (acting), 443–2365.
Federal Operational Health.—Lillian Koeig (acting), 594–0250.
Financial Management Service.—Larry Bedker, 443–1478.
Human Resources Service.—Carol Arbogast, 443–1200.

ASSISTANT SECRETARY FOR LEGISLATION

Assistant Secretary.—Vince Ventimiglia (202) 690–7627.
Director, Congressional Liaison.—Matt Hughes, 690–6786.
Deputy Assistant Secretary for—
Discretionary Health Program.—Craig Burton, 690–7627.
Human Services.—Roger Mahan, 690–6311.
Mandatory Health Programs.—Laura Ott, 690–7450.

ASSISTANT SECRETARY FOR PLANNING AND EVALUATION

Principal Deputy Assistant Secretary.—Jerry Regier (202) 690–7858.
Deputy Assistant Secretary for—
Disability, Aging, and Long Term Care Policy.—Marty McGeein, 690–6443.

Health Policy.—Jim Mathews (acting), 690–6870.
Human Services Policy.—Jerry Regier (acting), 690–7858.
Science and Data Policy.—Jim Scanlon, 690–5874.

ASSISTANT SECRETARY FOR PUBLIC AFFAIRS

Assistant Secretary.—Suzy DeFrancis (202) 690–7850.
Deputy Assistant Secretary for Media.—Christina Pearson, 690–6343, fax 690–6247.
Director, Division of Freedom of Information/Privacy.—Robert Eckert, 690–7453.

ASSISTANT SECRETARY FOR PREPAREDNESS AND RESPONSE

Deputy Assistant Secretary.—RADM W. Craig Vanderwagen (202) 205–2882, fax 690–6512.
Principal Deputy Assistant Secretary.—Dr. William Raub.
Director, Office of:
Emergency Operations and Security Programs.—Robert Blitzer, 205–8387.
Mass Casualty Planning.—Dr. Robert Claypool, 260–1198.
Medicine, Science and Public Health.—Dr. Stuart Nightingale, 690–7707.
Research and Development Coordination.—Dr. Noreen Hynes, 260–1160.

ASSISTANT SECRETARY FOR RESOURCES AND TECHNOLOGY

Assistant Secretary.—Charles E. Johnson (202) 690–6396.
Principal Deputy Assistant Secretary.—Thomas M. Reilly, 690–6061.
Deputy Assistant Secretary for—
Budget.—Richard Turman, 690–7393.
Finance.—Shelia Conley, 690–7084.
Grants.—Terry Hurst, 690–6617.
Chief, Information Office.—Charles Havekost, 690–6162.

OFFICE FOR CIVIL RIGHTS

Director.—Winston A. Wilkinson, J.D. (202) 619–0403.
Principal Deputy Director.—Robinsue Frohboese, 619–0403.
Deputy Director for—
Civil Rights Division.—Tamara L. Miller, J.D. 619–0403.
Health Information Privacy.—Susan McAndrew, J.D. 619–0403.
Management Operations.—Joanne Chiedi, 619–0403.
Toll Free Voice Number (Nationwide)—1–800–368–1019.
Toll Free TDD Number (Nationwide)—1–800–527–7697.

OFFICE OF THE GENERAL COUNSEL

fax [Immediate Office] 690–7998, fax [Admin. Office] 690–5452

General Counsel.—Daniel Meron (202) 690–7741.
Deputy General Counsels: David S. Cade, 690–7721; Demetrios Kouzoukas, Paula Stannard, James Stansel, 690–7741.
Associate General Counsel for:
Centers for Medicare and Medicaid Division.—Kathleen H. McGuan, 619–0300.
Children, Family and Aging Division.—Robert Keith, 690–8005.
Civil Rights Division.—Edwin Woo, 619–0900.
Ethics Division/Special Counsel for Ethics.—Edgar Swindell, 690–7258.
Food and Drug Division.—Sheldon T. Bradshaw (301) 827–1137.
General Law Division.—Jeffrey Davis, 619–0150.
Legislation Division.—Sondra Steigen Wallace, 690–7773.
Public Health Division.—David Benor (301) 443–2644.

OFFICE OF GLOBAL HEALTH AFFAIRS

Director.—William Steiger (202) 690–6174.

OFFICE OF THE INSPECTOR GENERAL

330 Independence Avenue, SW., 20201

Inspector General.—Daniel R. Levinson (202) 619–3148.
Principal Deputy Inspector General.—Larry J. Goldberg, 619–3148.
Chief Counsel to the Inspector General.—Lewis Morris, 619–0335.
Deputy Inspector General for:
Audit Services.—Joseph Vengrin, 619–3155.
Evaluation and Inspections.—Stuart Wright, 619–0480.
Investigations.—Michael Little, 619–3208.
Management and Policy.—Sam Shellenberger, 205–5154.
Director, External Affairs.—Judy Holtz (acting), 619–1343.

OFFICE OF MEDICARE HEARINGS AND APPEALS

Chief Administrative Law Judge.—Hon. Perry Rhew (216) 615–4000.
Executive Director.—Maria Price Detherage (703) 235–0689.

OFFICE OF THE NATIONAL COORDINATOR FOR HEALTH INFORMATION TECHNOLOGY

Interim National Coordinator.—Robert M. Kolodner, M.D. (202) 690–7151.

OFFICE OF PUBLIC HEALTH AND SCIENCE

Assistant Secretary for Health.—John O. Agwunobi, M.D. M.P.H., M.B.A. (202) 690–7694.
The Surgeon General.—Kenneth P. Moritsugu, M.D., M.P.H., (acting), (301) 443–4000.
Principal Deputy Assistant Secretary for Health.—Christina V. Beato, M.D. (202) 690–7694.
Deputy Assistant Secretary, Office of:
Disease Prevention and Health Promotion.—Penelope Royall, P.T., M.S.W. (202) 401–6295.
HIV/AIDS Policy.—Christopher Bates (acting), (202) 690–5560.
Minority Health.—Garth Graham, M.D., M.P.H. (301) 443–5084.
Population Affairs.—Eric Keroack, M.D. (301) 594–4001.
President's Council on Physical Fitness and Sports.—Melissa Johnson, M.S. (202) 690–9000.
Research Integrity.—Christopher Pascal, J.D. (301) 443–3400.
Women's Health.—Dr. Wanda Jones, Ph.D. (202) 690–7650.
Director, Office of:
Commissioned Corps: Force Management.—Denise Canton (202) 205–4859.
National Vaccine Programs.—Bruce Gellin, M.D. (202) 205–5294.
Regional Administrators for—
Region I: CT, ME, MA, NH, RI, VT.—Michael Milner, PA–C (617) 565–4999.
Region II: NJ, NY, PR, VI.—Robert L. Davidson, MSW, M.D., M.S. (212) 742–7036.
Region III: DE, DC, MD, PA, VA, WV.—Dalton G. Paxman, Ph.D. (215) 861–4631.
Region IV: AL, FL, GA, KY, MS, NC, SC, TN.—Clara H. Cobb, M.S., R.N. (404) 562–7894.
Region V: IL, IN, MI, MN, OH, WI.—Michael Milner, (acting), (214) 767–3879.
Region VI: AR, LA, NM, OK, TX.—Epi Elizondo, Ph.D., PA–C (214) 767–3879.
Region VII: IA, KS, MO, NE.—Linda Vogel (816) 426–3291.
Region VIII: CO, MT, ND, SD, UT, WY.—John T. Babb, RPH, MPA (303) 844–7859.
Region IX: AZ, CA, HI, NV, Guam, American Samoa, CNMI, FSMI, RMI, Palau.—Ronald Banks, M.D., M.P.H. (415) 437–8096.
Region X: AK, ID, OR, WA.—Patrick O'Carroll, M.D., M.P.H., FACPM (206) 615–2469.

ADMINISTRATION ON AGING

1 Massachusetts Avenue, SW., 20001

Assistant Secretary.—Josefina G. Carbonell (202) 401–4541.
Deputy Assistant Secretary for—

Center for Wellness and Community-Based Services.—Frank Burns, 357–3516.
Management.—John Wren (acting), 357–3430.
Policy and Programs.—Edwin Walker, 401–4634.
Director for:
Center for Communications and Consumer Services.—Carol Crecy, 401–4541.
Center for Planning and Policy Development.—Greg Case (acting), 357–3460.
Executive Secretariat.—Harry Posman, 357–3540.
Office of Evaluation.—Saadia Greenberg, 357–3516.

ADMINISTRATION FOR CHILDREN AND FAMILIES

370 L'Enfant Promenade, SW., 20447

Assistant Secretary.—Wade F. Horn, Ph.D. (202) 401–9200.
Principal Deputy Assistant Secretary.—Daniel Schneider, 401–5180.
Deputy Assistant Secretary for Policy and External Affairs.—Brent Orrell, 401–9200.
Deputy Assistant Secretary for Administration.—Curtis L. Coy, 401–9238.
Senior Advisor to the Assistant Secretary.—Martin Dannefelser, 401–6947.
Director, Regional Operations Staff.—Diann Dawson, 401–4802.
Commissioner for Administration on:
Children, Youth and Families.—Joan E. Ohl, 205–8347.
Developmental Disabilities.—Patricia Morrissey, 690–6590.
Commissioner, Administration for Native Americans.—Quanah Stamps, 401–5590.
Commissioner, Office of Child Support Enforcement.—Margot Bean, 401–9369.
Associate Commissioner for—
Children's Bureau.—Susan Orr, 205–8618.
Family and Youth Services Bureau.—Harry Wilson, 205–8102.
Director, Office of:
Community Services.—Josephine Robinson, 401–9333.
Family Assistance.—Sidonie Squier, 401–9275.
Head Start.—Channell Wilkins, 205–8573.
Legislative Affairs and Budget.—Madeline Mocko, 401–9223.
Planning, Research and Evaluation.—Noami Goldstein, 401–9220.
Public Affairs.—Pamela Carter (acting), 401–9215.
Refugee Resettlement.—Martha Newton, 401–9246.
Regional Operations.—Diann Dawson, 401–4802.

AGENCY FOR HEALTHCARE RESEARCH AND QUALITY (AHRQ)

Director.—Carolyn Clancy, M.D. (301) 427–1200.
Deputy Director.—Kathie Kendrick, R.N., 427–1577.

AGENCY FOR TOXIC SUBSTANCES AND DISEASE REGISTRY

1600 Clifton Road, NE., Atlanta, GA 30333

Administrator.—Julie L. Gerberding (404) 639–7000.
Deputy Administrator.—Dixie E. Snider.
Assistant Administrator.—Thomas Sinks (acting), 498–0004.

CENTER FOR FAITH BASED AND COMMUNITY INITIATIVES

Director.—Greg Morris (202) 358–3595.
Deputy Director.—Mike Costigan.

CENTERS FOR DISEASE CONTROL AND PREVENTION

1600 Clifton Road, NE., Atlanta, GA 30333, phone (404) 639–7000

Director.—Julie L. Gerberding.
Chief of Public Health Practice.—Dr. Stephanie Bailey.
Chief of Science Office.—Dr. Tanja Popovic (acting).
Chief Operating Officer.—William H. Gimson.
Chief of Staff.—Lynn Austin.
Staff Offices—

CDC Washington.—Donald E. Shriber (202) 690–8598.
Enterprise Communication.—Donna Garland, 639–7540.
Office of Dispute Resolution Equal Employment Opportunity.—Murray Kampf (acting), 371–5931.
Strategy and Innovation.—Brad Perkins, 639–7000.
Workforce and Career Development.—Stephen B. Thacker, 498–6010.
Coordinating Office for:
Global Health.—Steven Blount, 639–7420.
Terrorism Preparedness and Response.—Charles Schable, 639–7405.
Coordinating Center for Environmental Health and Injury Prevention.—Henry Falk, 498–0004.
National Center for Environmental Health.—Thomas Sinks (acting), 498–0004.
National Center for Injury Prevention and Control.—Ileana Arias (acting), (770) 488–4696.
Coordinating Center for Health Information and Services.—Edward J. Sondik (301) 458–4500.
National Center for Health Marketing.—Steve Solomon (acting), (770) 488–8320.
National Center for Health Statistics.—Edward J. Sondik (301) 458–4500.
National Center for Public Health Informatics.—John Loonsk (acting), 639–7600.
Coordinating Center for Health Promotion.—Donna Stroup (770) 488–5971.
National Center for Birth Defects and Developmental Disabilities.—Jose Cordero, 498–3800.
National Center for Chronic Disease Prevention and Health Promotion.—George Mensah (acting), (770) 488–5401.
Office of Genomics and Disease Prevention.—Muin J. Khoury (acting), 498–1420.
Coordinating Center for Infectious Diseases.—Mitchell Cohen, 498–2580.
National Center for HIV, STD, and TB Prevention.—Janet Collins (acting), 639–8005.
National Center for Infectious Disease.—Ann Schuachat (acting), 639–3401.
National Institute for Occupational Safety and Health.—John Howard (202) 401–6997.

CENTERS FOR MEDICARE AND MEDICAID SERVICES

200 Independence Avenue, SW., 20201, phone (202) 690–6726

Administrator.—Leslie Norwalk, Esq. (acting).
Deputy Administrator.—Herb Kuhn (acting).
Chief Operating Officer.—John R. Dyer (410) 786–3151.
Chief, Office of Actuary.—Rick Foster (410) 786–6374.
Director, Center for:
Beneficiary Choices.—Abby Block (202) 690–1291.
Medicaid and State Operations.—Dennis Smith (202) 690–7428.
Medicare Management.—Herb Kuhn (202) 205–2505.
Director, Office of:
Acquisitions and Grants Management.—Rodney Benson (410) 786–8853.
Beneficiary Information Services.—Mary Laureno (410) 786–6885.
Clinical Standards and Quality.—Barry Straube, M.D. (410) 786–6841.
E-Health Standard & Services.—Tony Trenkle (410) 786–4160.
Equal Opportunity and Civil Rights.—Arlene Austin (410) 786–5110.
External Affairs.—Kathleen Harrington (202) 401–3135.
Financial Management.—Tim Hill (410) 786–5448.
Information Services.—Tim Love (410) 786–1800.
Legislation.—Donald Johnson (acting) (202) 690–5960.
Operations Management.—Karen Osteen (410) 786–1051.
Policy.—Carol Kelly (202) 690–8257.
Research, Development, and Information.—Stu Guterman (410) 786–0948.
Strategic Operations and Regulatory Support.—Jacqueline White (202) 690–8390.
Regional Administrator for:
Atlanta.—Roger Perez (404) 562–7150.
Boston.—Charlotte Yeh, M.D. (617) 565–1188.
Chicago.—Jackie Garner (312) 886–6432.
Dallas.—James Farris, M.D. (214) 767–6427.
Denver.—George Mills (acting), (303) 844–2111.
Kansas City.—Tom Lenz (816) 426–5925.
New York.—Gilbert Kunken DMD (212) 616–2205.
Philadelphia.—Nancy O'Connor (215) 861–4140.
San Francisco.—Jeffrey Flick (415) 744–3501.

Seattle.—Alan Constantian (206) 615–2306.

FOOD AND DRUG ADMINISTRATION

5600 Fishers Lane, Rockville, MD 20857

Commissioner.—Lester M. Crawford, D.V.M., Ph.D. (acting), (301) 827–2410.
Deputy Commissioner for International and Special Programs.—Murray M. Lumpkin, M.D. (acting), 827–5709.
Deputy Commissioner for Operations.—Janet Woodcock, M.D. (acting), 827–3310.
Chief Counsel.—Gerald Mausodi (acting), 827–1137.
Director of Scientific Policy and Development.—Susan Bond, 827–1622.
Associate Commissioner for—
External Relations.—Sheila Walcoff, 827–3330.
Management.—Kathleen Heuer, 255–6762.
Policy and Planning.—William K. Hubbard, 827–3370.
Regulatory Affairs.—John Taylor, 827–3101.
Assistant Commissioner for—
International Programs.—Melinda Plaisier, 827–4480.
Legislation.—Patrick Ronan, 827–0087.
Planning.—Theresa Mullin, Ph.D., 827–5292.
Policy.—Jeffrey Shuren, M.D., 827–3360.
Public Affairs.—Bradford Stone (acting), 827–6250.
Special Health Issues.—Theresa A. Toigo, 827–4460.
Women's Health.—Susan Wood, Ph.D., 827–0350.
Director, Center for—
Biologics Evaluation and Research.—Jesse Goodman, M.D., 827–0372.
Devices and Radiological Health.—Daniel Schultz, M.D. (240) 276–3939.
Drug Evaluation and Research.—Steven Galson, M.D. (acting), 594–5400.
Food Safety and Applied Nutrition.—Robert E. Brackett, Ph.D., 436–1600.
Veterinary Medicine.—Stephen Sundlof, D.V.M., Ph.D. (204) 276–9000.
National Center for Toxicological Research.—William Slikker, Jr., Ph.D. (870) 543–7517.
Director, Office of:
Executive Secretariat.—LaJuana Caldwell, 827–4450.
Executive Operations.—Linda Brna, 827–3440.
Equal Opportunity and Diversity Management.—Georgia Coffey, 827–4840.
Financial Management.—Helen Horn, 827–5001.
Orphan Products Development.—Marlene Haffner, M.D., M.P.H., 827–3666.

HEALTH RESOURCES AND SERVICES ADMINISTRATION

5600 Fishers Lane, Rockville, MD 20857

Administrator.—Elizabeth M. Duke (301) 443–2216.
Deputy Administrator.—Dennis P. Williams, 443–2194.
Principal Advisor to the Administrator.—Steve Smith, 443–2216.
Chief Medical Officer.—Tayna Pagan Raggio, 443–2964.
Associate Administrator for—
Administration and Financial Management.—Caroline Lewis (acting), 443–2053.
Federal Assistance Management.—Nancy McGinness, 443–6507.
Health Information Technology.—Cheryl Austein-Casnoff, 443–0210.
Health Professions.—Michelle Snyder, 443–5794.
Healthcare Systems.—Joyce Somsak, 443–3300.
HIV/AIDS.—Deborah Parham-Hopson, 443–1993.
Maternal and Child Health.—Peter C. van Dyck, 443–2170.
Primary Health Care.—James Macrae, 594–4110.
Rural Health Policy.—Marcia Brand, 443–0835.
Director, Office of:
Commissioned Corps Affairs.—Kerry Nesseler, 443–2741.
Communications.—Tina Cheatham (acting), 443–3376.
Equal Opportunity and Civil Rights.—Frank Silva, 443–5636.
Information Technology.—Catherine Flickinger, 443–6846.
International Health.—Kerry Nesseler, 443–2741.
Legislation.—Patricia Stroup, 443–1890.
Minority Health and Health Disparities.—Tanya Pagan Raggio, 443–2964.

Planning and Evaluation.—Lyman Van Nostrand, 443–1891.
Quality.—Denise Geolot, 443–0458.

INDIAN HEALTH SERVICE

801 Thompson Avenue, Rockville, MD 20852

Director.—Charles W. Grim, DDS, MHSA (301) 443–1083.
Deputy Director.—Robert McSwain.
Deputy Director of:
Indian Health Policy.—Mary Lou Stanton.
Management Operations.—Phyllis Eddy.
Chief Medical Officer.—Douglas G. Peter, M.D. (acting).
Director of:
Equal Employment Opportunity.—Vernon Mabry (acting), 443–1108.
Legislative Affairs.—Michael Mahsetky, 443–7261.
Public Affairs.—Thomas W. Sweeney, 443–3593.
Tribal Programs.—Douglas P. Black, 443–1104.
Tribal Self-Governance.—Dennis Heffington (acting), 443–7821.
Urban Indian Health Program.—Phyllis Wolfe, DDS (acting), 443–4680.

NATIONAL INSTITUTES OF HEALTH

9000 Rockville Pike, Bethesda, MD 20892

Director.—Elias A. Zerhouni, M.D. (301) 296–7322.
Deputy Director.—Raynard S. Kington, M.D., Ph.D., 496–7322.
Senior Advisor to the Director.—Ruth L. Kirschstein, M.D., 496–1096.
Director/Executive Secretariat.—Ann Brewer, R.N., 496–1461.
Executive Officer, Office of the Director.—LaVerne Y. Stringfield, 594–8231.
Legal Advisor, Office of the General Counsel.—Barbara M. McGarey, J.D., 496–4108.
Deputy Director, Office of:
Extramural Research.—Norka Ruiz Bravo, Ph.D., 496–1096.
Intramural Research.—Michael M. Gottesman, M.D., 496–1921.
Management.—Colleen Barros, 496–3271.
Associate Director for—
Administration.—Diane Frasier (acting) 496–4422.
AIDS Research.—Jack E. Whitescarver, Ph.D., 496–0357.
Behavioral and Social Sciences Research.—David B. Abrams, Ph.D., 402–1146.
Budget.—John Bartrum, 496–4477.
Communications and Public Liaison.—John T. Burklow, 496–4461.
Disease Prevention.—Barnett S. Kramer, M.D., M.P.H., 496–1508.
Legislative Policy and Analysis.—Marc Smolonsky, 496–3471.
Research on Women's Health.—Vivian W. Pinn, M.D., 402–1770.
Research Services.—Alfred C. Johnson, Ph.D., 496–2215.
Science Policy.—Lana R. Skirboll, Ph.D., 496–2122.
Director, Office of:
Community Liaison.—Dennis Coleman, 496–4461.
Ethics.—Holli Beckerman Jaffe, 402–6628.
Equal Opportunity and Diversity Management.—Lawrence N. Self, 496–6301.
Human Resources.—Chris Major, 496–3592.
Technology Transfer.—Mark L. Rohrbaugh, Ph.D., J.D., 594–7700.
Director of:
Fogarty International Center.—Roger I. Glass, M.D., Ph.D., 496–1415.
National Library of Medicine.—Donald A.B. Lindberg, M.D., 496–6221.
Warren Grant Magnuson Clinical Center.—John I. Gallin, M.D., 496–4114.
Director, National Center for—
Complementary and Alternative Medicine.—Stephen E. Straus, M.D., 435–6826.
Minority Health and Health Disparities.—John Ruffin, Ph.D., 402–1366.
Research Resources.—Barbara Alving, M.D. (acting), 496–5793.
Director, Center for—
Information Technology.—Jack F. Jones, Ph.D (acting), 496–5703.
Scientific Review.—Antonio Scarpa, M.D., Ph.D., 435–1114.
Director, National Institute for—
Aging.—Richard J. Hodes, M.D., 496–9265.

Alcohol Abuse and Alcoholism.—Ting-Kai Li, M.D., 443–3885.
Allergy and Infectious Diseases.—Anthony S. Fauci, M.D., 496–2263.
Arthritis, Musculoskeletal and Skin Diseases.—Stephen I. Katz, M.D., Ph.D., 496–4353.
Biomedical Imaging and Bioengineering.—Roderic I. Pettigrew, Ph.D., M.D., 496–8859.
Cancer.—John E. Niederhuber, M.D., 496–5615.
Child Health and Human Development.—Duane F. Alexander, M.D., 496–3454.
Deafness and Other Communication Disorders.—James F. Battey, Jr., M.D., Ph.D., 402–0900.
Dental and Craniofacial Research.—Lawrence Tabak, D.D.S., Ph.D., 496–3571.
Diabetes, Digestive and Kidney Diseases.—Allen M. Spiegel, M.D., 496–5877.
Drug Abuse.—Nora Volkow, M.D., 443–6480.
Environmental Health Sciences.—David A. Schwartz, M.D., M.P.H. (919) 541–3201.
Eye.—Paul A. Sieving, M.D., Ph.D., 496–0844.
General Medical Sciences.—Jeremy M. Berg, Ph.D., 594–2172.
Heart, Lung and Blood.—Elizabeth G. Nabel, M.D., 496–5166.
Human Genome Research.—Francis Collins, M.D., Ph.D., 496–0844.
Mental Health.—Thomas Insel, M.D., 443–3673.
Neurological Disorders and Stroke.—Story C. Landis, M.D., 496–9746.
Nursing Research.—Patricia A. Grady, Ph.D., R.N., 496–9746.

SUBSTANCE ABUSE AND MENTAL HEALTH SERVICES ADMINISTRATION

1 Choke Cherry Road, Rockville, MD 20857

Administrator.—Terry L. Cline (240) 276–2000.
Deputy Administrator.—Eric Broderick (acting).
Associate Administrator for—
Communications.—Mark Weber, 276–2130.
Policy Planning and Budget.—Daryl Kade, 276–2200.
Director, Center for—
Mental Health Services.—A. Kathryn Power, 276–1310.
Substance Abuse Prevention.—Dennis Romero (acting), 276–2420.
Substance Abuse Treatment.—H. Westley Clark, 276–1670.
Director, Office of:
Applied Studies.—Anna Marsh (acting), 276–1241.
Equal Employment Opportunity.—Donald Inniss (301) 443–1976.
Program Services.—Elaine Parry (acting), 276–1110.

DEPARTMENT OF HOUSING AND URBAN DEVELOPMENT

Robert C. Weaver Federal Building, 451 Seventh Street, SW., 20410

phone (202) 708–1112, http://www.hud.gov

ALPHONSO JACKSON, Secretary of Housing and Urban Development; born on September 9, 1945; education: received a Bachelor's Degree in Political Science, and a Master's Degree in Education Administration, from Truman State University; received a Law Degree from Washington University School of Law; professional: Director of Consultant Services for the accounting firm of Laventhol and Horwath-St. Louis; Special Assistant to the Chancellor, and Assistant Professor, at the University of Missouri; President of American Electric Power-Texas, 1996–2001; public service: Director of Public Safety, St. Louis, MO; Executive Director, St. Louis, MO, Housing Authority; Director, Department of Public and Assisted Housing, Washington, DC; Chairperson, District of Columbia Redevelopment Land Agency Board; President and CEO, Dallas, TX, Housing Authority, 1989–1996; Deputy Secretary of Housing and Urban Development, 2001–2004; nominated by President George W. Bush to become the 13th Secretary of Housing and Urban Development, and was confirmed by the U.S. Senate on March 31, 2004.

OFFICE OF THE SECRETARY

Secretary of Housing and Urban Development.—Alphonso Jackson, room 10000 (202) 708–0417.
- *Chief of Staff.*—Camille Pierce, 708–2713.
- *Deputy Chief of Staff.*—Scott Keller, 708–1781.
- *Director, Center for Faith Based and Community Initiatives.*—Robert Bogart, 708–2404.
- *Chief Executive Officer.*—Marcella Belt, 708–3750.
- *Administrative Officer.*—Marianne C. DeConti, 708–3750.

OFFICE OF THE DEPUTY SECRETARY

Deputy Secretary.—Roy A. Bernardi, room 10100 (202) 708–0123.
- *Senior Advisor to the Deputy Secretary.*—Jim Parenti.

ASSISTANT SECRETARY FOR ADMINISTRATION

Assistant Secretary.—Keith A. Nelson, room 6100 (202) 708–0940.
- *General Deputy Assistant Secretary.*—Dawn M. Petchell.
- *Executive Secretariat.*—Cynthia A. O'Connor, 708–3054.
- *Deputy Assistant Secretary for—*
  - *Budget and Management Support.*—Karen S. Jackson, 708–1583.
  - *Human Resource Management.*—Barbara Edwards, 708–3946.
  - *Operations.*—Sherman R. Lancefield, 708–2268.

ASSISTANT SECRETARY FOR COMMUNITY PLANNING AND DEVELOPMENT

Assistant Secretary.—Pamela H. Patenaude, room 7100 (202) 708–2690.
- *General Deputy Assistant Secretary.*—Nelson R. Bregon.
- *Deputy Assistant Secretary for—*
  - *Grant Programs.*—Anna Maria Farias, 708–2111.
  - *Operations.*—William Eargle, Jr., 401–6367.
  - *Special Needs.*—Mark Johnston, 708–1590.

ASSISTANT SECRETARY FOR CONGRESSIONAL AND INTERGOVERNMENTAL RELATIONS

General Deputy Assistant Secretary.—L. Carter Cornick, room 10120 (202) 708–0005.
Deputy Assistant Secretary for—
Congressional Relations.—Mark Studdert, 708–0380.
Intergovernmental Relations.—Loretta Greene, 708–0005.

ASSISTANT SECRETARY FOR FAIR HOUSING AND EQUAL OPPORTUNITY

Assistant Secretary.—Kim Kendrick, room 5100 (202) 708–4252.
General Deputy Assistant Secretary.—Cheryl Ziegler, 708–4211.
Deputy Assistant Secretary for—
Enforcement and Programs.—Bryan Greene, 619–8046.
Operations and Management.—Karen A. Newton, 708–0768.

ASSISTANT SECRETARY FOR HOUSING

Assistant Secretary/Federal Housing Commissioner.—Brian D. Montgomery, room 9100 (202) 708–2601.
General Deputy Assistant Secretary.—Frank L. Davis.
Deputy Assistant Secretary for—
Affordable Housing Preservation.—Ted Toon, 708–0001.
Finance and Budget.—Ronald Y. Spraker, 401–8975.
Housing Operations.—Craig T. Clemmensen, 708–1104.
Multifamily Housing.—Charles H. Williams, 708–2495.
Regulatory Affairs and Manufactured Housing.—Gary M. Cunningham, 708–6401.
Single Family Housing.—Lily A. Lee (acting), 708–3175.

ASSISTANT SECRETARY FOR POLICY DEVELOPMENT AND RESEARCH

Assistant Secretary.—Darlene F. Williams, room 8100 (202) 708–1600.
General Deputy Assistant Secretary.—Jean Lin Pao.
Deputy Assistant Secretary for—
Economic Affairs.—Harold Bunce 708–3080.
International Affairs.—Shannon Sorzano, 708–0770.
Research, Evaluation, and Monitoring.—Paul K. Gatons, 708–4230.

ASSISTANT SECRETARY FOR PUBLIC AFFAIRS

General Deputy Assistant Secretary.—Jim Parenti (acting), room 10130 (202) 708–0980.
Deputy Assistant Secretary.—Jereon Brown.
Press Secretary.—Stephen O'Halloran, 708–0685.

ASSISTANT SECRETARY FOR PUBLIC AND INDIAN HOUSING

Assistant Secretary.—Orlando J. Cabrera, room 4100 (202) 708–0950.
General Deputy Assistant Secretary.—Paula Blunt.
Deputy Assistant Secretary, for—
Field Operations.—Deborah Hernandez, 708–4016.
Native American Programs.—Rodger J. Boyd, 401–7914.
Office of Field Operations.—Deborah Hernandez, 708–4016.
Policy, Programs and Legislative Initiatives.—Bessy Kong, 708–0713.
Public Housing and Voucher Programs.—Milan Ozdinec, 401–8812.
Public Housing Investments.—Dominique Blom, 401–8812.
Real Estate Assessment Center.—Elizabeth A. Hanson, 475–7943.

ASSISTANT DEPUTY SECRETARY FOR FIELD POLICY AND MANAGEMENT

Assistant Deputy Secretary.—A. Jo Baylor, room 7106 (202) 708–2426.

GOVERNMENT NATIONAL MORTGAGE ASSOCIATION

President.—Robert M. Couch (202) 708–0926.
Executive Vice President.—Michael J. Frenz.
Senior Vice President, Office of:
Finance.—Michael J. Najjum, Jr., 401–2064.
Management Operations.—Cheryl W. Owens, 708–2648.
Mortgage-Backed Securities.—Theodore B. Foster, 708–4141.
Program Operations.—Thomas R. Weakland, 708–2884.
Vice President, Office of Capital Markets.—Kirk D. Freeman, 401–8970.

CHIEF FINANCIAL OFFICER

Chief Financial Officer.—John W. Cox, room 10234 (202) 708–1946.
Deputy Chief Financial Officer.—James M. Martin.
Assistant Chief Financial Officer for—
Accounting.—Mary Sally Matiella, 708–3601.
Systems.—Gail B. Dise, 708–1757.

CHIEF INFORMATION OFFICER

Chief Information Officer.—Lisa Schlosser, room 4160 (202) 708–0306.
Deputy Chief Information Officer for:
Business and Information Technology Modernization.—Stan Buch, 708–0220.
IT Operations.—Bajinder Paul, 708–4562.
Chief Information Security Officer.—Patrick Howard, 619–9057.

CHIEF PROCUREMENT OFFICER

Chief Procurement Officer.—Joseph Nerauter, room 5280 (202) 708–0600.
Deputy Chief Procurement Officer.—Annette E. Hancock, 708–1290.
Associate Chief Procurement Officedr.—David R. Williamson, 708–3477.
Assistant Chief Procurement Officer for:
Administration Support.—Kimberly A. Marshall (acting), 708–1772.
Field Operations.—David Kimbro (404) 331–5001.
Policy and Systems.—Gloria Sochon, 708–0294.
Program Support.—Kimberly A. Marshall, 708–1585.

GENERAL COUNSEL

General Deputy General Counsel.—Robert M. Couch (acting), room 10110 (202) 708–2244.
Deputy General Counsel for Operations.—Sam E. Hutchinson, 708–0888.
Associate General Counsel for—
Assisted Housing and Community Development.—Robert S. Kenison, 708–0212.
Fair Housing.—Harry L. Carey, 708–2787.
Finance and Regulatory Compliance.—John P. Opitz, 708–2203.
Human Resources.—Paula Lincoln (acting), 708–2864.
Insured Housing.—John J. Daly, 708–1274.
Legislation and Regulations.—Camille E. Acevedo, 708–1793.
Litigation.—Nancy Christopher, 708–0300.
Director, Departmental Enforcement Center.—Margarita Maisonet, 708–3354.

INSPECTOR GENERAL

Inspector General.—Kenneth M. Donohue, Sr., room 8256 (202) 708–0430.
Deputy Inspector General.—Michael P. Stephens.
Counsel to the Inspector General, Office of Legal Counsel.—Bryan Saddler, 708–1613.
Assistant Inspector General, Office of:
Audit.—James Heist, 708–0364.
Investigation.—R. Joe Haban, 708–0390.
Management and Policy.—Dennis A. Raschka, 708–0006.

OFFICE OF DEPARTMENTAL EQUAL EMPLOYMENT OPPORTUNITY

Deputy Director.—Linda Bradford Washington, room 2134 (202) 708–3362.

OFFICE OF DEPARTMENTAL OPERATIONS AND COORDINATION

Director.—Inez Banks-Dubose, room 2124 (202) 708–2806.
Deputy Director.—Joe Smith.

OFFICE OF FEDERAL HOUSING ENTERPRISE OVERSIGHT

1700 G Street, NW., 4th Floor, 20552

http://www.ofheo.gov

Director.—James B. Lockhart III (202) 414–3801.
Deputy Director.—Edward J. DeMarco.
Director of Supervision.—Leonard F. Reid, Jr., 414–3754.
Executive Director/Chief of Staff.—Mark Laponsky, 414–3832.
General Counsel.—Alfred Pollard, 414–6924.
Associate Director for—
Congressional Affairs.—Joanne Hanley, 414–6922.
External Relations.—Peter Brereton, 414–6922.

OFFICE OF HEALTHY HOMES AND LEAD HAZARD CONTROL

Director.—Jon L. Gant, room 8236 (202) 755–1785.
Deputy Director.—Warren Friedman.

SMALL AND DISADVANTAGED BUSINESS UTILIZATION

Director.—Valerie T. Hayes (acting), room 10156 (202) 708–1428.

HUD REGIONAL DIRECTORS

Region I.—Connecticut, Maine, Massachusetts, New Hampshire, Rhode Island, Vermont.
Regional Director.—Taylor Caswell, Thomas P. O'Neill, Jr. Federal Building, 10 Causeway Street, Room 301, Boston, MA 02222–1092 (617) 994–8200.

Region II.—New Jersey, New York.
Regional Director.—Sean Moss, 26 Federal Plaza, Suite 3541, New York, NY 10278–0068 (212) 264–8000, ext. 7109.

Region III.—Delaware, District of Columbia, Maryland, Pennsylvania, Virginia, West Virginia.
Regional Director.—Guy Ciarrocchi, The Wanamaker Building, 100 Penn Square East, Philadelphia, PA 19107–3380 (215) 656–0600.

Region IV.—Alabama, Florida, Georgia, Kentucky, Mississippi, North Carolina, Puerto Rico, South Carolina, Tennessee.
Regional Director.—Robert Young, Five Points Plaza, 40 Marietta Street, NW., 2nd Floor, Atlanta, GA 30303–2806 (404) 331–5001.

Region V.—Illinois, Indiana, Michigan, Minnesota, Ohio, Wisconsin.
Regional Director.—Joseph Galvan, Ralph Metcalfe Federal Building, 77 West Jackson Boulevard, 77 West Jackson Boulevard, Chicago, IL 60604–3507 (312) 353–5680.

Region VI.—Arkansas, Louisiana, New Mexico, Oklahoma, Texas.
Regional Director.—A. Cynthia Leon, 801 Cherry Street, Fort Worth, TX 76113–2905 (817) 978–5540.

Region VII.—Iowa, Kansas, Missouri, Nebraska.
Regional Director.—Macie Houston, Gateway Tower II, 400 State Avenue, Room 200, Kansas City, KS 66101–2406 (913) 551–5462.

Region VIII.—Colorado, Montana, North Dakota, South Dakota, Utah, Wyoming.
Regional Director.—John Carson, 1670 Broadway, Denver, CO 80202–4801 (303) 672–5440.

Region IX.—Arizona, California, Hawaii, Nevada.
Regional Director.—Richard K. Rainey, 600 Harrison Street, 3rd Floor, San Francisco, CA 94107–1300 (415) 489–6400.

Region X.—Alaska, Idaho, Oregon, Washington.

Regional Director.—John Meyers, Seattle Federal Office Building, 909 First Avenue, Suite 200, Seattle, WA 98104–1000 (206) 220–5101.

DEPARTMENT OF TRANSPORTATION

Nassif Building, 400 Seventh Street, SW., 20590

phone (202) 366–4000, http://www.dot.gov

MARY E. PETERS, Secretary of Transportation; born in Phoenix, AZ, December 4, 1948; education: B.A., University of Phoenix; attended Harvard University's John F. Kennedy School of Government Program for State and Local Government Executives; professional: Contract Administrator, Deputy Director for Administration, Deputy Director, and then Director, Arizona Department of Transportation, 1985–2001; Federal Highway Administrator, 2001–05; Senior Vice President and National Director of Transportation Policy and Consulting, HDR, Inc.; Co-Vice Chairwoman, National Surface Transportation Policy and Revenue Study Commission; awards: Most Influential Person in Arizona Transportation, Arizona Business Journal; 2004 National Woman of the Year Award, Women's Transportation Seminar; family: married to Terry; three children: Tammy, Terry, and Tina; five grandchildren; nominated by President George W. Bush to become the 15th Secretary of Transportation, and was confirmed by the U.S. Senate on September 30, 2006.

OFFICE OF THE SECRETARY

[Created by the act of October 15, 1966; codified under U.S.C. 49]

Secretary of Transportation.—Mary E. Peters, room 10200 (202) 366–1111.
Deputy Secretary.—Maria Cino, 366–2222.
Chief of Staff.—Robert Johnson, 366–1103.
Deputy Chief of Staff.—Simon Gros, 366–6800.
Under Secretary of Transportation for Policy.—Jeffrey N. Shane, 366–1815.
Chairman, Board of Contract Appeals (Chief Administrative Judge).—James L. Stern, room 5101, 366–4305.
Director, Office of:
Civil Rights.—Michael Trujillo, room 10215, 366–4648.
Executive Secretariat.—J. Richard Henry, room 10205, 366–4277.
Intelligence and Security.—Roger Bohnert (acting), room 10401, 366–6525.
Small and Disadvantaged Business Utilization.—Denise Rodriguez-Lopez, room 9414, 366–1930.

ASSISTANT SECRETARY FOR ADMINISTRATION

Assistant Secretary.—Linda J. Washington (acting), room 10320 (202) 366–2332.
Deputy Assistant Secretary.—Linda Washington.
Director, Office of:
Building Management and Space.—George Fields, room 10314, 366–9284.
Financial Management.—Marie Petrosino, room 10320, 366–9427.
Hearings, Chief Administrative Law Judge.—Judge Ronnie A. Yoder, room 5411C, 366–2142.
Human Resource Management.—Patricia Prosperi, room 7411, 366–4088.
Information Services.—Dorothy Beard, room 2317, 366–3944.
Security and Administrative Management.—Lee A. Privett, room 7404H, 366–4676.
Senior Procurement Executive.—David J. Litman, room 7101D, 366–4263.

ASSISTANT SECRETARY FOR AVIATION AND INTERNATIONAL AFFAIRS

Assistant Secretary.—Andrew Steinberg, room 10232 (202) 366–8822.

Deputy Assistant Secretaries: Susan McDermott, Michael Reynolds, room 10232, 366–4551.
Director, Office of:
Aviation Analysis.—Todd Homan (acting), room 6401, 366–5903.
International Aviation.—Paul Gretch, room 6402, 366–2423.
International Transportation and Trade.—Bernestine Allen, room 10300, 366–4398.

ASSISTANT SECRETARY FOR BUDGET AND PROGRAMS

Assistant Secretary/Chief Financial Officer.—Phyllis F. Scheinberg, room 10101 (202) 366–9191.
Deputy Assistant Secretary.—Alexis M. Stefani, 366–9192.
Deputy Chief Financial Officer.—Lawrence I. Neff, 366–9192.
Director, Office of:
Budget and Program Performance.—Lana Hurdle.
Financial Management.—Laurie Howard, room 6101, 366–1306.

ASSISTANT SECRETARY FOR GOVERNMENTAL AFFAIRS

Assistant Secretary.—Shane Karr, room 10408 (202) 366–4573.
Deputy Assistant Secretaries: Joseph Guzzo, Daniel Hickey, Kerry O'Hare.
Associate Directors for—
Amtrak, FRA, Appropriations, OIG, RITA.—Kelly Kolb.
FAA, Security, Bird Flu, Aviation/International Affairs.—Brian Elson.
FHWA, FTA, MARAD, PHMSA, OSDBU, Nominations, Congestion.—Jessie Torres.
FMCSA, NHTSA, SLSDC, CIO, Outreach.—Janae Barker.
Intergovernmental Affairs.—Jack Blaylock.

ASSISTANT SECRETARY FOR TRANSPORTATION POLICY

Assistant Secretary.—Tyler D. Duvall, room 10228 (202) 366–0582.
Deputy Assistant Secretary.—Robert DeHaan, 366–4067.

GENERAL COUNSEL

General Counsel.—Rosalind A. Knapp (acting), room 10428 (202) 366–4702.
Deputy General Counsel.—Rosalind A. Knapp, 366–4713.
Assistant General Counsel for—
Aviation Enforcement and Proceedings.—Samuel Podberesky, room 4116, 366–9342.
Environmental, Civil Rights and General Law.—Roberta D. Gabel, room 10102, 366–4710.
International Law.—Donald H. Horn, room 10105, 366–2972.
Legislation.—Thomas W. Herlihy, room 10100, 366–4687.
Litigation.—Paul M. Geier, room 4102, 366–4731.
Regulation and Enforcement.—Neil R. Eisner, room 10424, 366–4723.

INSPECTOR GENERAL

Inspector General.—Calvin L. Scovel III, room 9210 (202) 366–1959.
Deputy Inspector General.—Todd J. Zinser, 366–6767.
Associate Deputy Inspector General.—Ted Alves, 366–1992.
Principal Assistant Inspector General for Auditing and Evaluation.—David A. Dobbs, room 9217, 366–0500.
Assistant Inspector General for—
Aviation and Special Program Audits.—Robin Hunt (acting), 201 Mission Street, Suite 150, San Francisco, CA 94105 (415) 744–3090.
Competition and Economic Analysis.—David Tornquist, room 9201, 366–9682.
Financial and Information Technology Audits.—Rebecca Leng, room 9228, 366–1496.
Investigations.—Charles Lee, room 9210, 366–1967.
Legal, Legislative and External Affairs.—Brian A. Dettelbach, room 9208, 366–8751.
Surface and Maritime Programs.—Kurt Hyde, room 9126, 366–5630.
Deputy Assistant Inspector General for—

Financial Management Audits.—Mark Zabarsky, room 9228, 366–1496.
Surface and Maritime Program.—Rebecca Batts, room 9126, 366–5630.
Executive Director, Washington Investigative Operations.—Rick Beitel, room 7234, 366–6581.
Director of Human Resources.—Toby Burt, room 7107, 366–1490.
Chief Financial Officer/Chief Information Officer.—Jackie Weber, room 7117, 366–1495.

REGIONAL AUDIT OFFICES

Regional Program Directors:
Lou Dixon, 61 Forsyth Street, SW, Suite 17T60, Atlanta, GA 30303 (404) 562–3854.
Robin Hunt, 201 Mission Street, Suite 1750, San Francisco, CA 94105 (415) 744–3090.
Darren Murphy, 915 Second Avenue, Room 644, Seattle, WA 98174 (206) 220–7754.
Earl Hedges, 10 South Howard Street, Suite 4500, Baltimore, MD 21201 (410) 962–3612.

REGIONAL INVESTIGATIONS OFFICES

Special Agents-In-Charge:
Region I.—Ted Doherty, 55 Broadway, Room 1055, Cambridge, MA 02142 (617) 494–2701.
Region II.—Ned E. Schwartz, 201 Varick Street, Room 1161, New York, NY 10014 (212) 337–1250.
Region III.—Kathryn Jones, 409 3rd Street, SW., Room 301, Washington, DC 20024 (202) 260–8580.
Region IV.—John Long, 61 Forsythe Street, SW, Suite 17T60, Atlanta, GA 30303 (404) 562–3850.
Region V.—Michelle McVicker, 200 W. Adams Street, Suite 300, Chicago, IL 60606 (312) 353–0106.
Region VI.—Max Smith, 819 Taylor Street, Room 13A42, Fort Worth, TX 76102 (817) 978–3236.
Region IX.—Hank W. Smedley, 201 Mission Street, Suite 1750, San Francisco, CA 94105 (415) 744–3090.

OFFICE OF PUBLIC AFFAIRS

Assistant to the Secretary and Director of Public Affairs.—Brian Turmail, room 10414 (202) 366–4570.
Deputy Director.—Sarah Echols, 366–4531.
Assistant Director for—
Media Relations Division.—William Adams, 366–5580.
Speech Writing and Research Division.—Terri Hauser, room 10413, 366–5580.

FEDERAL AVIATION ADMINISTRATION

800 Independence Avenue, SW., 20591 (202) 267–3484

Administrator.—Marion C. Blakey, 267–3111.
Chief of Staff.—Michael O'Malley.
Senior Counsel to the Administrator.—Louise E. Maillett, 267–7417.
Executive Assistant to the Administrator.—Sharon Harrison, 267–3111.
Deputy Administrator.—Bobby Sturgell, 267–8111.
Senior Advisor to the Deputy Administrator.—Howard Swancy.
Assistant Administrator for Financial Services.—Ramesh K. Punwani 267–9105.
Deputy Assistant Administrator.—John F. Hennigan, 267–8928.
Director of:
Budget.—Alex Keenan, 267–8010.
Financial Controls.—Carl Burrus, 267–7140.
Financial Management.—Timothy Lawler, 267–3018.
Assistant Administrator for Civil Rights.—Fanny Rivera, 267–3254.
Deputy Assistant Administrator.—Barbara A. Edwards, 267–3264.
Assistant Administrator for Aviation Policy, Planning and Environment.—Daniel Elwell, 267–3927.

Deputy Assistant Administrator.—Nancy LoBue, 267–7954.
Director of:
Aviation Policy and Plans.—Nan Shellabarger, 267–3274.
Environment and Energy.—Carl Burleson, 267–3576.
Chief Counsel.—Thomas Romig (acting), 267–3222.
Deputy Chief Counsel.—James W. Whitlow, 267–3773.
Assistant Administrator for Government and Industry Affairs.—Megan Rosia, 267–3277.
Deputy Assistant Administrator.—Chris Brown, 267–8211.
Assistant Administrator for Human Resource Management.—Ventris C. Gibson, 267–3456.
Deputy Assistant Administrator.—Mary Ellen Dix, 267–3850.
Deputy Assistant Administrator for Strategic Labor Relations.—Joe Miniace, 267–3456.
Director of:
Accountability Board.—Maria Fernandez-Greczmiel, 267–3065.
Center for Management and Leadership Development.—Jay Weisz (386) 446–7136.
Corporate, Learning and Development.—Darlene Freeman (acting), 267–9041.
Labor and Employee Relations.—Melvin Harns, 267–3979.
Personnel.—Sue Engelhardt, 267–3850.
Assistant Administrator for Information Services.—David Bowen, 493–4570.
Deputy Assistant Administrator.—Walter Iwanow, 493–4570.
Director of Information Systems Security.—Michael F. Brown, 267–7104.
Assistant Administrator for Public Affairs.—Melanie Alvord, 267–3883.
Deputy Assistant Administrator.—Laura J. Brown, 267–3883.
Deputy Assistant Administrator for Corporate Communications.—Gerald Lavey, 267–3883.
Assistant Administrator for International Aviation.—Di Reimold (acting), 267–3033.
Director of:
Asia-Pacific.—Nancy Graham, 65–6540–4114.
Europe, Africa, and Middle East.—Tony Fagio (322) 508–2700.
International Aviation.—John R. Hancock, 267–3213.
Latin America-Caribbean.—Cecilia Capestany (305) 716–3300.
Assistant Administrator for Regions and Center Operations.—Ruth Leverenz, 267–7369
Deputy Assistant Administrator.—Paula Lewis, 267–7369.
Regional Administrator for—
Alaskan.—Bob Lewis (acting) (907) 271–5645.
Central.—Christopher Blum (816) 329–3050.
Eastern.—Manny Weiss (718) 553–3000.
Great Lakes.—Christopher Blum (847) 294–7294.
New England.—Amy Lind Corbett (781) 238–7020.
Northwest Mountain.—Dennis Roberts (425) 227–2001.
Southern.—Douglas Murphy (404) 305–5000.
Southwest.—Ava L. Wilkerson (817) 222–5001.
Western-Pacific.—William C. Withycombe (310) 725–3550.
Director, Mike Monroney Aeronautical Center.—Lindy Ritz (405) 954–4521.
Assistant Administrator for Security and Hazardous Materials.—Lynne A. Osmus, 267–7211.
Deputy Assistant Administrator.—Claudio Manno, 267–7211.
Director of:
Emergency Operations and Communications.—Chris J. Rocheleau, 267–8075.
Hazardous Materials.—William Wilkening, Jr., 267–9864.
Internal Security.—Bruce Hetter, 267–7714.
Operations.—Thomas D. Ryan, 267–7211.
Chief Operating Officer for Air Traffic Services.—Russell G. Chew, 493–5602.
Vice President for—
Acquisition and Business Services.—James Washington, 267–7222.
Communications Services.—Sandra M. Sanchez, 267–8507.
En Route and Oceanic Services.—Richard Day, 385–8501.
Operations Planning Services.—Victoria Cox, 267–7111.
Safety Services.—Tony Mello (acting), 493–5882.
Systems Operations Services.—Michael A. Cirillo, 267–8558.
Technical Operations Services.—Steven B. Zaidman, 267–8181.
Terminal Services.—David B. Johnson, 385–8801.
Senior Vice President for Finance Services.—Eugene D. Juba, 267–3022.
Director, Joint Planning and Development Office.—Charles Leader, 220–3310.
Director, William J. Hughes Technical Center.—Wilson Felder (609) 485–6641.
Associate Administrator for Airports.—D. Kirk Shaffer, 267–9471.
Deputy Associate Administrator.—Catherine Lang, 267–8738.

Director of:
Airport Planning and Programming.—Benito DeLeon, 267–8775.
Airport Safety and Standards.—David L. Bennett, 267–3053.
Associate Administrator for Commercial Space Transportation.—Patricia Grace Smith, 267–7793.
Deputy Associate Administrator.—Dr. George C. Nield, 267–7848.
Associate Administrator for Aviation Safety.—Nicholas A. Sabatini, 267–3131.
Deputy Associate Administrator.—Peggy Gilligan, 267–7804.
Director of:
Accident Investigation.—Steven B. Wallace, 267–9612.
Air Traffic Oversight.—Tony Ferrante, 267–5202.
Aircraft Certification Service.—John J. Hickey, 267–8235.
Flight Standards Service.—James Ballough, 267–8237.
Quality and Integration.—Vi Lipski, 493–5860.
Rulemaking.—Anthony F. Fazio, 267–9677.
Federal Air Surgeon.—Dr. Fred Tilton, 267–3535.

FEDERAL HIGHWAY ADMINISTRATION

Washington Headquarters, Nassif Building, 400 Seventh Street, SW., 20590

Turner-Fairbank Highway Research Center (TFHRC)

6300 Georgetown Pike, McLean, VA 22201

Administrator.—J. Richard Capka (202) 366–0650.
Executive Director.—Frederick G. ''Bud'' Wright, 366–2242.
Chief Counsel.—James D. Ray, room 4213, 366–0740.
Associate Administrator for—
Civil Rights.—Frederick D. Isler, room 4132, 366–0693.
Federal Lands Highway.—Arthur E. Hamilton, room 6311, 366–9494.
Infrastructure.—King W. Gee, room 3212, 366–0371.
Operations.—Jeffrey F. Paniati, room 3401, 366–0408.
Policy.—Mary B. Phillips, room 3317, 366–0585.
Professional and Corporate Development.—Joseph S. Toole, room 4208, 366–9393.
Turner-Fairbank Highway Research Center.—Dennis C. Judycki, room T–306, 493–3999.

FIELD SERVICES

Organizationally report to Executive Director (HOA–3), Washington, DC

Director of:
Eastern Field Office.—Alan K. Steger, 10 S. Howard Street, Suite 4000, Baltimore, MD 21201 (410) 962–5177.
Southern Field Office.—James E. St. John, 61 Forsyth Street, SW., Suite 17T26, Atlanta, GA 30303 (404) 562–3570.
Western Field Office.—Christine M. Johnson, 2520 West 4700 South, Suite 9C, Salt Lake City, UT 84114 (801) 967–5979.

RESOURCE CENTERS

Manager of:
Eastern Resource Center.—Joyce A. Curtis, 10 S. Howard Street, Suite 4000, Baltimore, MD 21201 (410) 962–0093
Midwestern Resource Center.—Gary White, 19900 Governors Drive, Suite 301, Olympia Fields, IL 60461 (708) 283–3510.
Southern Resource Center.—Rob Elliott, 61 Forsyth Street, SW., Suite 17T26, Atlanta, GA 30303 (404) 562–3570.
Western Resource Center.—Gary White, 201 Mission Street, Suite 2100, San Francisco, CA 94105 (415) 744–3102.

FEDERAL MOTOR CARRIER SAFETY ADMINISTRATION

Administrator.—John H. Hill, room 8202 (202) 366–1927.
Deputy Administrator.—David H. Hugel.

Chief Safety Officer.—Rose A. McMurray (acting).
Chief Counsel.—Suzzane Tebeau, 493–0349.
Associate Administrator for Field Operation.—William Paden, 366–2525.
Director, Office of Communications.—Ian Grossman, 366–8810.

FIELD OFFICES

Eastern Service Center (CT, DC, DE, MA, MD, ME, NJ, NH, NY, PA, PR, RI, VA, VT, WV).—802 Cromwell Park Drive, Suite N, Glen Burnie, MD 21061 (443) 703–2240.

Midwestern Service Center (IA, IL, IN, KS, MI, MO, MN, NE, OH, WI).—19900 Governors Drive, Suite 210, Olympia Fields, IL 60461 (708) 283–3577.

Southern Service Center (AL, AR, FL, GA, KY, LA, MS, NC, NM, OK, SC, TN, TX).—1800 Century Boulevard, NE., Suite 1700, Atlanta, GA 30345–3220 (404) 327–7400.

Western Service Center (American Samoa, AK, AZ, CA, CO, Guam, HI, ID, Mariana Islands, MT, ND, NV, OR, SD, UT, WA, WY).—Golden Hills Office Centre, 12600 W. Colfax Avenue, Suite B–300, Lakewood, CO 80215 (303) 407–2350.

FEDERAL RAILROAD ADMINISTRATION

1120 Vermont Avenue, NW., 20590, phone (202) 493–6000

http://www.fra.dot.gov

Administrator.—Joseph H. Boardman, room 7089, 493–6014.
Associate Administrator for—
Administration and Finance.—Margaret Reid, room 6077, 493–6110.
Policy and Program Development.—Jane H. Bachner (acting), room 7074, 493–6400.
Railroad Development.—Mark E. Yachmetz, room 0729, 493–6381.
Safety.—Jo Strang, room 6014, 493–6300.
Chief Counsel.—Mark Lindsey, room 7022, 493–6052.
Director of:
Budget.—D.J. Stadler, room 6124, 493–6150.
Civil Rights.—Carl-Martin Ruiz, room 7096, 493–6010.
Public Affairs.—Steven W. Kulm, room 7086, 493–6024.

REGIONAL OFFICES (RAILROAD SAFETY)

Region 1 (Northeastern).—Connecticut, Maine, Massachusetts, New Hampshire, New Jersey, New York, Rhode Island, Vermont.
Regional Administrator.—Mark H. McKeon, Room 1077, 55 Broadway, Cambridge, MA 02142 (617) 494–2302.

Region 2 (Eastern).—Delaware, District of Columbia, Maryland, Pennsylvania, Virginia, West Virginia, Ohio.
Regional Administrator.—David Myers, International Plaza, Suite 550, Philadelphia, PA 19113 (610) 521–8200.

Region 3 (Southern).—Kentucky, Tennessee, Mississippi, North Carolina, South Carolina, Georgia, Alabama, Florida.
Regional Administrator.—Fred Denin, 61 Forsyth Street, NW., Suite 16T20, Atlanta, GA 30303 (404) 562–3800.

Region 4 (Central).—Minnesota, Illinois, Indiana, Michigan, Wisconsin.
Regional Administrator.—Lawrence Hasvold, 200 W. Adams Street, Chicago, IL 60606 (312) 353–6203.

Region 5 (Southwestern).—Arkansas, Louisiana, New Mexico, Oklahoma, Texas.
Regional Administrator.—Bonnie Murphy, 4100 International Plaza, Suite 450, Ft. Worth, TX 96109 (817) 862–2200.

Region 6 (Midwestern).—Iowa, Missouri, Kansas, Nebraska, Colorado.
Regional Administrator.—Darrell J. Tisor, DOT Building, 901 Locust Street, Suite 464, Kansas City, MO 64106 (816) 329–3840.

Region 7 (Western).—Arizona, California, Nevada, Utah.
Regional Administrator.—Alvin L. Settle, 801 I Street, Suite 466, Sacramento, CA 95814 (916) 498–6540.

Region 8 (Northwestern).—Idaho, Oregon, Wyoming, Montana, North Dakota, South Dakota, Washington, Alaska.
Regional Administrator.—Dave Brooks, 500 Broadway, Murdock Executive Plaza, Suite 240, Vancouver, WA 98660 (360) 696–7536.

FEDERAL TRANSIT ADMINISTRATION

Administrator.—James S. Simpson, room 9328 (202) 366–4040.
Deputy Administrator.—David Horner (acting).
Chief Counsel.—David Horner, 366–4011.
Director, Office of Civil Rights.—Michael Winter, 366–0343.
Associate Administrator for—
Administration.—Ann Linnertz, 366–4018.
Budget and Policy.—Robert Tuccillo, 366–1691.
Communications and Congressional Affairs.—Wes Irvin, 366–4043.
Planning and Environment.—Susan Borinsky, 366–2360.
Program Management.—Susan Schruth, 366–4020.
Research, Demonstration and Innovation.—Ronald Hynes, 366–4052.

MARITIME ADMINISTRATION

Administrator and Chairman, Maritime Subsidy Board.—Sean T. Connaughton, room 7206 (202) 366–5823.
Deputy Administrator.—Julie A. Nelson, room 7208, 366–1719.
Secretary, Maritime Administration and Maritime Subsidy Board.—Joel Richard, room 7210, 366–5746.
Chief Counsel and Member, Maritime Subsidy Board.—Rand Pixa, room 7232, 366–5711.
Director, Office of Congressional and Public Affairs.—Shannon Russell, room 7206, 366–4105.
Public Affairs Officer.—Susan Clark, room 7219, 366–5067.
Associate Administrator for Administration.—Eileen S. Roberson, room 7216, 366–5802.
Director, Office of:
Accounting.—John G. Hoban, room 7325, 366–5852.
Acquisition.—Tim Roark, room 7310, 366–5757.
Budget.—John Portel, room 7217, 366–5778.
Management and Information Services.—Richard A. Weaver, room 7301, 366–5816.
Personnel.—Lisa M. Williams, room 2109, 366–4141.
Associate Administrator for Policy, International Trade.—Bruce J. Carlton, room 7218, 366–5772.
Director of:
International Activities.—Gregory Hall, room 7119, 366–5773.
Policy and Plans.—Janice G. Weaver, room 7123, 366–4468.
Associate Administrator for National Security.—James E. Caponiti, room 7300, 366–5400.
Director, Office of:
National Security Plans.—Thomas M.P. Christensen, room 7130, 366–5900.
Sealift Support.—Taylor E. Jones, II, room 7304, 366–2323.
Ship Operations.—William H. Cahill (acting), room 2122, 366–1875.
Associate Administrator for Marine Asset Development.—Jean E. McKeever, room 8126, 366–5737.
Director, Office of:
Cargo Preference.—Thomas W. Harrelson, room 8118, 366–4610.
Insurance and Shipping Analysis.—Edmond J. Fitzgerald, room 8117, 366–2400.
Ship Financing.—Mitchell D. Lax, room 8122, 366–5744.
Shipbuilding and Marine Technology.—Joseph A. Byrne, room 8101, 366–1931.
Associate Administrator for Port, Intermodal and Environmental Activities.—Margaret D. Blum, room 7214, 366–4721.
Director, Office of:
Environmental Activities.—Michael C. Carter, room 7209, 366–8887.
Intermodal Development.—Richard L. Walker, room 7209, 366–8888.
Ports and Domestic Shipping.—Richard Lolich (acting), room 7201, 366–4357.

NATIONAL HIGHWAY TRAFFIC SAFETY ADMINISTRATION

Administrator.—Nicole R. Nason, room 5220 (202) 366–1836.
Chief of Staff.—David Kelly, 366–2105.
Executive Director, Public Affairs.—Heather Hopkins, 366–2111.
Senior Associate Administrator for—
Policy and Operation.—Gregory Walter, 366–2330.
Traffic Injury Control.—Brian McLaughlin, 366–1755.

Vehicle Safety.—Ronald Medford, 366–9700.
Associate Administrator for—
Communications and Consumer Information.—Susan Gorcowski, 366–9550.
Planning, Administrative and Financial Management.—Rebecca Pennington, 366–2550.
Regional Operations and Program Delivery.—Marlene Markinson, 366–2121.
Research and Program Development.—Marilena Amoni, 366–1755.
Rulemaking.—Stephen R. Kratzke, 366–1810.
Vehicle Safety Research Program.—Joseph Kanathra, 366–4862.
Director, Office of:
Civil Rights.—George B. Quick, 366–0972.
External Affairs.—Michael Harrington, 366–2111.
Legislative Affairs.—Wilfred Otero, 366–2111.
Chief Counsel.—Anthony Cooke, 366–9511.
Director, Executive Correspondence.—Jane S. Tamai, 366–2330.

REGIONAL OFFICES

New England Region.—Connecticut, Maine, Massachusetts, New Hampshire, Rhode Island, Vermont.
Regional Administrator.—Philip J. Weiser, Volpe National Transportation Center, 55 Broadway, Kendall Square, Code 903, Cambridge, MA 02142 (617) 494–3427.
Eastern Region.—New York, New Jersey, Puerto Rico, Virgin Islands.
Regional Administrator.—Thomas M. Louizou, 222 Mamaroneck Avenue, Suite 204, White Plains, NY 10605 (914) 682–6162.
Mid-Atlantic Region.—Delaware, District of Columbia, Maryland, Pennsylvania, Virginia, West Virginia.
Regional Administrator.—Elizabeth Baker, The Cresent Building, 10 South Howard Street, Suite 6700, Baltimore, MD 21201 (410) 962–0090.
Southeast Region.—Alabama, Florida, Georgia, Kentucky, Mississippi, North Carolina, South Carolina, Tennessee.
Regional Administrator.—Terrance D. Schiavone, Atlanta Federal Center, 61 Forsyth Street, SW, Suite 17T30, Atlanta, GA 30303–3106 (404) 562–3739.
Great Lakes Region.—Illinois, Indiana, Michigan, Minnesota, Ohio, Wisconsin.
Regional Administrator.—Donald J. McNamara, 19900 Governors Drive, Suite 201, Olympia Fields, IL 60461 (708) 503–8892.
South Central Region.—Arkansas, Louisiana, New Mexico, Oklahoma, Texas, Indian Nations.
Regional Administrator.—George S. Chakiris, 819 Taylor Street, Room 8A38, Fort Worth, TX 76102–6177 (817) 978–3653.
Central Region.—Iowa, Kansas, Missouri, Nebraska.
Regional Administrator.—Romell Cooks, 901 Locust Street, Room 466, Kansas City, MO 64106 (816) 329–3900.
Rocky Mountain Region.—Colorado, Montana, North Dakota, South Dakota. Utah, Wyoming.
Regional Administrator.—Bill Watada, 12300 West Dakota Avenue, Suite 140, Lakewood, CO 80228–2583 (720) 963–3100.
Western Region.—American Samoa, Arizona, California, Guam, Hawaii, Nevada.
Regional Administrator.—David Manning, 201 Mission Street, Suite 2230, San Francisco, CA 94105 (415) 744–3089.
Pacific Northwest Region.—Alaska, Idaho, Oregon, Washington.
Regional Administrator.—John Moffat, Federal Building, 915 Second Avenue, Suite 3140, Seattle, WA 98174 (206) 220–7640.

REGIONAL OFFICES

Region I.—Connecticut, Maine, Massachusetts, New Hampshire, Rhode Island, Vermont.
Regional Administrator.—Richard J. Doyle, Transportation Systems Center, Kendall Square, 55 Broadway, Suite 920, Cambridge, MA 02142–1093.
Region II.—New Jersey, New York, Virgin Islands.
Regional Administrator.—Brigid Hynes-Cherin, One Bowling Green, Room 429, New York, NY 10004–1415.
Region III.—Delaware, District of Columbia, Maryland, North Carolina, Pennsylvania, Virginia, West Virginia.
Regional Administrator.—Herman Shipman (acting), 1760 Market Street, Suite 500, Philadelphia, PA 19103–4124.
Region IV.—Alabama, Florida, Georgia, Kentucky, Mississippi, North Carolina, Puerto Rico, South Carolina, Tennessee.

Regional Administrator.—Yvette Taylor, Atlanta Federal Center, 61 Forsyth Street, SW, Suite 17T50, Atlanta, GA 30303.

Region V.—Illinois, Indiana, Michigan, Minnesota, Ohio, Wisconsin.

Regional Administrator.—Marisol Simon, 200 West Adams Street, Suite 320, Chicago, IL 60606.

Region VI.—Arkansas, Louisiana, New Mexico, Oklahoma, Texas.

Regional Administrator.—Robert C. Patrick, 819 Taylor Street, Room 8A36, Fort Worth, TX 76102.

Region VII.—Iowa, Kansas, Missouri, Nebraska.

Regional Administrator.—Mohktee Altmad, 901 Locust Street, Suite 404, Kansas City, MO 64106.

Region VIII.—Colorado, Montana, North Dakota, South Dakota, Utah, Wyoming.

Regional Administrator.—Letitia A. Thompson (acting), 12300 West Dakota Avenue, Suite 310, Lakewood, CO 80228–2583.

Region IX.—Arizona, California, Guam, Hawaii, Nevada, American Samoa.

Regional Administrator.—Leslie T. Rogers, 201 Mission Street, Room 1650, San Francisco, CA 94105–1839.

Region X.—Alaska, Idaho, Oregon, Washington.

Regional Administrator.—Rick Krochalis, Jackson Federal Building, 915 Second Avenue, Suite 3142, Seattle, WA 98174–1002.

LMRO.—Lower Manhattan Recovery Office.

Director.—Bernard Cohen, Lower Manhattan Recovery Office, One Bowling Green, Room 436, New York, NY 10004–1415.

FIELD ACTIVITIES

Director for:

North Atlantic Region.—Robert F. McKeon, 1 Bowling Green, room 418, New York, NY 10004 (212) 668–3330.

Great Lakes Region.—Doris J. Bautch, Suite 185, 2860 S. River Road, Des Plaines, IL 60018 (847) 298–4535.

Western Region.—Francis Johnston III, Suite 2200, 201 Mission Street, San Francisco, CA 94105 (415) 744–2580.

South Atlantic Region.—M. Nuns Jain, Building 4D, Room 211, 7737 Hampton Boulevard, Norfolk, VA 23505 (757) 441–6393.

U.S. MERCHANT MARINE ACADEMY

Superintendent.—RADM Joseph D. Stewart, Kings Point, NY 11024 (516) 773–5000.

Assistant Superintendent for Academic Affairs (Academic Dean).—Dr. Warren F. Mazek.

PIPELINE AND HAZARDOUS MATERIALS SAFETY ADMINISTRATION

Administrator.—VADM Thomas J. Barrett, USCG (Ret.), room 8410 (202) 366–4433.

Assistant Administrator/Chief Safety Officer.—Stacey Gerard.

Chief Counsel.—Elaine Joost, room 8407, 366–4400.

Director, Office of Civil Rights.—Helen E. Hagin, room 8417, 366–9638.

Associate Administrator for—

Governmental, International and Public Affairs.—James Wiggins, room 8406, 366–4831.

Management and Administration.—Edward A. Brigham, room 7128, 366–4347.

Pipeline Safety.—Ted Willke (acting), room 2103, 366–4595.

HAZARDOUS MATERIALS SAFETY OFFICES

Chief of:

Eastern Region.—Colleen D. Abbenhaus, 820 Bear Tavern Road, Suite 306, West Trenton, NJ 08628 (609) 989–2256.

Central Region.—Kevin Boehne, Suite 478, 2350 East Devon Avenue, Des Plaines, IL 60018 (847) 294–8580.

Western Region.—Daniel Derwey, 3401 Centre Lake Drive, Suite 550–B, Ontario, CA 91764 (909) 937–3279.

Southern Region.—John Heneghan, 1701 Columbia Avenue, Suite 520, College Park, GA 30337 (404) 305–6120.

Southwest Region.—Billy Hines, 2320 LaBranch Street, room 2100, Houston, TX 77004 (713) 718–3950.

PIPELINE SAFETY OFFICES

Director of:
Eastern Region.—Mark Wendroff (acting), 409 3rd Street, SW., Suite 300, Washington, DC 20024 (202) 260–8500.
Central Region.—Ivan A. Huntoon, 901 Locust Street, Room 462, Kansas City, MO 64106 (816) 329–3800.
Western Region.—Chris Hoidal, 12600 West Colfax Avenue, Suite A250, Lakewood, CO 80215 (303) 231–5701.
Southwest Region.—Rodrick M. Seeley, 2320 LaBranch Street, Suite 2100, Houston, TX 77004 (713) 718–3748.
Southern Region.—Linda Dougherty, 61 Forsyth Street, Suite 6T15, Atlanta, GA 30303 (404) 562–3530.

RESEARCH AND INNOVATIVE TECHNOLOGY ADMINISTRATION (RITA)

http://www.rita.dot.gov

Deputy Administrator.—John Bobo (acting), room 3103 (202) 366–4180.
Chief Counsel.—Victoria Sutton, 366–4412.
Chief Financial Officer.—Katherine Montgomery, room 3117, 366–2577.
Public Affairs Contact, Bureau of Transportation Statistics.—David Smallen, 366–5568.
Director for—
Governmental, International and Public Affairs.—Paul Feenstra, room 3103, 366–4792.
Intelligent Transportation Systems.—Shelly Row, room 3100–36, 366–5719.
Transportation Safety Institute.—Frank B. Tupper, 6500 South MacArthur Boulevard, Oklahoma City, OK 73169 (405) 954–3153.
Volpe National Transportation Systems Center.—Dr. Curtis J. Tompkins, 55 Broadway, Kendall Square, Cambridge, MA 02142 (617) 494–2222.

SAINT LAWRENCE SEAWAY DEVELOPMENT CORPORATION

Administrator.—Collister Johnson, Jr., room 5424 (202) 366–0091, fax 366–7147
Director, Office of:
Budget and Logistics.—Kevin P. O'Malley.
Chief Counsel.—Craig H. Middlebrook (acting).
Trade Development and Public Affairs.—Rebecca McGill.

SEAWAY OPERATIONS

180 Andrews Street, PO Box 520, Massena, NY 13662–0520
phone (315) 764–3200, fax (315) 764–3235

Associate Administrator.—Salvatore L. Pisani.
Deputy Associate Administrator.—Carol A. Fenton.
Assistant.—Mary C. Fregoe.
Chief Financial Officer.—Edward Margosian.
Director, Office of:
Engineering.—Thomas A. Lavigne.
Financial Management and Administration.—Mary Ann Hazel.
Lock Operations and Marine Services.—Lori K. Curran.
Maintenance.—Jesse Hinojosa.

SURFACE TRANSPORTATION BOARD

395 E Street, SW., 20423–0001, phone (202) 245–0245

http://www.stb.dot.gov

Chairman.—Charles D. Nottingham, 245–0200.

Vice Chairman.—W. Douglas Buttrey, 245–0220.
Commissioner.—Francis P. Mulvey, 245–0210.
Office of:
Compliance and Consumer Assistance.—Melvin F. Clemens, 245–0278.
Congressional and Public Services.—Dan G. King, 245–0230.
Economics, Environmental Analysis, and Administration.—Leland L. Gardner, 245–0291.
General Counsel.—Ellen D. Hanson, 245–0260.
Proceedings.—David M. Konschnik, 245–0350.
Secretary.—Vernon A. Williams, 245–0350.

DEPARTMENT OF ENERGY

James Forrestal Building, 1000 Independence Avenue, SW., 20585
phone (202) 586–5000, http://www.doe.gov

SAMUEL WRIGHT BODMAN, Secretary of Energy; born on November 26, 1938, in Chicago, IL; education: BChE., Cornell University, 1961; ScD, Massachusetts Institute of Technology, 1965; professional: Associate Professor of Chemical Engineering at Massachusetts Institute of Technology; Technical Director of the American Research and Development Corporation; President and Chief Operating Officer of Fidelity Investments and Director of the Fidelity Group of Mutual Funds; Chairman, CEO and Director of the Cabot Corporation; public service: Deputy Secretary, Department of Commerce, 2001–04; Deputy Secretary, Department of the Treasury, 2004; organizations: member, American Academy of Arts and Sciences; Former Director of School of Engineering Practice, Executive and Investment Committees at Massachusetts Institute of Technology; Trustee of the Isabella Stewart Gardner Museum and the New England Aquarium; married: M. Diane Bodman; three children, two stepchildren, and eight grandchildren; nominated by President George W. Bush to become the 11th Secretary of Energy, and was confirmed by the U.S. Senate on January 31, 2005.

OFFICE OF THE SECRETARY

Secretary of Energy.—Samuel Wright Bodman (202) 586–6210.
Deputy Secretary.—Clay Sell, 586–5500.
Chief of Staff.—Jeff Kupfer, 586–6210.
Inspector General.—Gregory H. Friedman, 586–4393.
General Counsel.—David Hill, 586–5281.
Chief Information Officer.—Thomas N. Pyke, Jr., 586–0166.
Chief Human Capital Officer.—Jeff T.H. Pon, 586–5610.
Deputy Chief Financial Officer.—James T. Campbell, 586–4171.
Director, Office of:
Economic Impact and Diversity.—Theresa Alvillar-Speake, 586–8383.
Health, Safety and Security.—Glenn S. Podonski, 586–4360.
Hearings and Appeals.—George B. Breznay, 287–1566.
Intelligence and Counterintelligence.—Rolf Mowatt-Larssen, 586–2610.
Management.—Ingrid Kolb, 586–2550.
Public Affairs.—Anne Womack Kolton, 586–4940.
Assistant Secretary for—
Congressional and Intergovernmental Affairs.—Jill Sigal, 586–5450.
Policy and International Affairs.—Karen Harbert, 586–5800.
Administrator for Energy Information Administration.—Guy F. Caruso, 586–4361.

UNDER SECRETARY OF ENERGY

Under Secretary of Energy.—David K. Garman (202) 586–7700.
Assistant Secretary for—
Energy Efficiency and Renewable Energy.—Alexander ''Andy'' Karsner, 586–9220.
Environmental Management.—James A. Rispoli, 586–7709.
Fossil Energy.—Jeffrey D. Jarrett, 586–6660.
Nuclear Energy.—Dennis R. Spurgeon, 586–6630.
Director, Office of:
Civilian Radioactive Waste Management.—Edward ''Ward'' Sproat, 586–6842.
Electricity Delivery and Energy Reliability.—Kevin Kolevar, 586–1411.
Legacy Management.—Michael W. Owen, 586–7550.

UNDER SECRETARY OF SCIENCE

Under Secretary for Science.—Dr. Raymond Orbach (202) 586–5430.

NATIONAL NUCLEAR SECURITY ADMINISTRATION

Administrator/Under Secretary of Energy for Nuclear Security.—Linton F. Brooks (202) 586–5555.
Deputy Administrator for—
Defense Programs.—Thomas D'Agostino, 586–2179.
Defense Nuclear Nonproliferation.—William Tobey, 586–0645.
Naval Reactors.—ADM Kirland Donald, USN, 781–6174.
Deputy Under Secretary for Counter-terrorism.—Dr. Steven Aoki, 586–4308.
Associate Administrator for—
Defense Nuclear Security.—William Desmond, 586–8900.
Emergency Operations.—RADM Joseph Krol, USN (Ret.), 586–9892.
Infrastructure and Environment.—Bruce Scott, 586–7349.

MAJOR FIELD ORGANIZATIONS

OPERATIONS OFFICES

Managers:
Chicago.—Marvin Gunn (708) 972–2110.
Idaho.—Elizabeth D. Sellers (208) 526–5665.
Oak Ridge.—Gerald Boyd (865) 576–4444.
Richland.—Keith Klein (509) 376–7395.
Savannah River.—Jeffrey Allison (803) 725–2405.

SITE OFFICES

Director, Oakland.—Camille Yuan-Soo Hoo (925) 422–2572.
Manager, Nevada.—Kathleen A. Carlson (702) 295–3211.

NNSA SERVICE CENTER

Director, Albuquerque.—Karen Boardman (505) 845–6050.

FIELD OFFICES

Managers:
Golden.—John Kerston (303) 275–4792.
Rocky Flats.—Frazer R. Lockhart (303) 966–2025.

POWER MARKETING ADMINISTRATIONS

Administrator, Power Administration:
Bonneville.—Stephen J. Wright (503) 230–5101.
Southeastern Area.—Jon C. Worthington (706) 213–3805.
Southwestern Area.—Michael A. Diehl (918) 595–6601.
Western Area.—Timothy J. Meeks (720) 962–7077.

OFFICE OF SCIENTIFIC AND TECHNICAL INFORMATION

Director.—Walter L. Warnick (301) 903–7996.
Deputy Director.—R.L. Scott (865) 576–1193.

NAVAL REACTORS OFFICES

Managers:
Pittsburgh.—Henry A. Cardinali (412) 476–7200.
Schenectady.—Phil E. Salm (518) 395–4690.

OFFICE OF CIVILIAN RADIOACTIVE WASTE MANAGEMENT

Las Vegas.—W. John Arthur III (702) 794–1300.
Washington, DC.—Theodore J. Garrish (202) 586–6850.

FOSSIL ENERGY FIELD OFFICES

Directors:
Albany Research Center (Oregon).—George J. Dooley III (541) 967–5893.
National Energy Technology Lab.—Carl O. Bauer (acting), (304) 285–4511.
Project Manager, Strategic Petroleum Reserve Project Office.—William C. Gibson Jr. (504) 734–4201.

NAVAL PETROLEUM RESERVES

Directors:
California.—James Curtis Killen (661) 837–5000.
Colorado, Utah, Wyoming (Oil Shale Reserves).—Clarke D. Turner (307) 261–5161.

FEDERAL ENERGY REGULATORY COMMISSION

888 First Street, NE., 20426

Chair.—Joseph T. Kelliher (202) 502–8000.
Commissioners:
Suedeen G. Kelly, 502–6501.
Philip D. Moeller, 502–8852.
Marc Spitzer, 502–8366.
Jon Wellinghoff, 502–6580.
Chief Administrative Law Judge.—Curtis L. Wagner, Jr., 502–8500.
Executive Director and Chief Financial Officer.—Thomas R. Herlihy, 502–8300.
General Counsel.—John Moot, 502–6000.
Director, Office of:
Administrative Litigation.—Richard Miles, 502–8702.
Energy Markets and Reliability.—Shelton Cannon, 502–8213.
Energy Projects.—J. Mark Robinson, 502–8700.
Enforcement.—Susan Court, 502–8183.
External Affairs.—Andy Black, 502–8004.

DEPARTMENT OF EDUCATION

400 Maryland Avenue, SW., 20202
phone (202) 401–3000, fax 401–0596, http://www.ed.gov

MARGARET SPELLINGS, Secretary of Education; born in Ann Arbor, MI, November 30, 1957; children: Mary and Grace; education: B.A., University of Houston, 1979; professional: education reform commissioner under Texas Governor William P. Clements; associate executive director, Texas Association of School Boards, 1988–94; senior advisor to George W. Bush during his term as Governor of Texas, 1994–2000; as senior adviser, Secretary Spellings created the Texas Reading Initiative, the Student Success Initiative to eliminate social promotion, and the nation's strongest school assessment and accountability system; Domestic Policy Adviser, 2001–05; one of the principal authors of the 2001 No Child Left Behind Act; first mother of school children to serve as Secretary of Education; nominated by President George W. Bush to become the 8th Secretary of Education on November 17, 2004; confirmed on January 20, 2005.

OFFICE OF THE SECRETARY

Room 7W301, phone (202) 401–3000, fax 401–0596

Secretary of Education.—Margaret Spellings.
Chief of Staff.—David Dunn, 205–9694.
Senior Counselor.—Hudson La Force III.
Director, Center for Faith-Based and Community Initiatives.—Shayam K. Menon, 219–1741.

OFFICE OF THE DEPUTY SECRETARY

Room 7W308, phone (202) 401–8450, fax 205–7655

Deputy Secretary.—Raymond J. Simon.
Chief of Staff.—Wendy Tada.

OFFICE OF THE UNDER SECRETARY

Room 7E307, phone (202) 401–8187, fax 205–0063

Under Secretary.—Sara Martinez Tucker.
Chief of Staff.—Cheryl Oldham.
Executive Assistant.—Devon Gallagher.

OFFICE OF THE CHIEF FINANCIAL OFFICER

Room 4E313, phone (202) 401–0085, fax 401–0006

Chief Financial Officer.—Lawrence A. "Larry" Warder, 401–0477.
Deputy Chief Financial Officer.—Danny A. Harris, Ph.D., room 4E314, 401–0896.
Chief of Staff.—William M. McCabe, room 4E329, 205–0707.
Executive Officer.—Michael Holloway, room 4E231, 401–0322.
Director of:
Contracts and Acquisitions Management.—Glenn Perry, room 7153, 550 12th Street, SW., 20202, 245–6289.
Financial Improvement and Post Audit Operations.—Linda Stracke, room 21A5, 830 First Street, NE., 377–3301.

Financial Management Operations.—Gary Wood, room 4W122, 401–0862.
Financial Systems Operations.—Constance Davis, room 4E230, 401–3892.
Grants Policy and Oversight Staff.—Blanca Rodriguez, room 7065, 550 12th Street SW., 20202, 245–6121.

OFFICE OF THE CHIEF INFORMATION OFFICER

phone (202) 245–6400, fax 245–6621

Chief Information Officer.—Bill Vajda, PCP, room 9112, 245–6400.
Deputy Chief Information Officer.—Brian Burns, PCP, room 10057, 245–6642.
Director of:
Information Assurance Services.—Jerry Davis, PCP, room 9009, 245–6441.
Information Technology Operations and Maintenance.—Brian Burns (acting), PCP, room 10057, 260–6642.

OFFICE OF MANAGEMENT

Room 2W301, phone (202) 401–5848, fax 260–3761

Assistant Secretary.—Michell Clark, room 2W311, 260–7337.
Deputy Assistant Secretary.—Chris Marston, room 2W307, 260–5846.
Chief of Staff.—Donna Butler, room 2W309, 401–8530.
Executive Officer.—David Cogdill, room 2W227, 401–0695, fax 401–3513.
Group Director of:
Facility Services.—Scott Taylor, room 2E315, 401–9496, fax 732–1534.
Human Resource Services.—Colleen Lanza (acting), room 2E308, 401–3136, fax 401–0520.
Management Services.—Wanda Davis, room 2E105, 401–5931.
Office of Hearings and Appeals.—Frank J. Furey, L'Enfant Plaza–2134, 619–9701, fax 619–9726.
Security Services.—Winona Varnon, room 2W330, 401–1583, fax 260–3761.

OFFICE FOR CIVIL RIGHTS

550 12th Street, SW., Room 5000, 20202–1100, phone (202) 245–6800, fax 245–6840 or 6844

Assistant Secretary.—Stephanie Monroe.
Deputy Assistant Secretary for Enforcement.—David Black.
Confidential Assistant.—Kim Proctor, room 6093, 245–6700.
Director of:
Enforcement, East/Midwest.—Thomas Hilbino (acting), room 6094, 245–6700.
Enforcement, South/West.—Sandra Battle (acting), room 6125, 245–6700.
Program Legal Group.—Sandra Battle, room 6125, 245–6767.
Resource Management Group.—Lester Slayton, room 6117, 245–6700.

OFFICE OF COMMUNICATIONS AND OUTREACH

Room 5E300, phone (202) 401–0404, fax 401–8607

Assistant Secretary.—Lauren Maddox.
Chief of Staff.—Meridith Beaton, room 5E329, 401–0026.
Deputy Assistant Secretary.—Cynthia Williams, 260–1488.
Director, Intergovernmental Affairs.—Rogers Johnson, 205–0026.
Senior Director for Community Services.—John McGrath, 401–1309.

OFFICE OF ELEMENTARY AND SECONDARY EDUCATION

Room 3W300, phone (202) 401–0113, fax 205–0303

Deputy Assistant Secretary.—Catherine Freeman, 401–3058.
Chief of Staff.—Anne Campbell, 260–7052.

Deputy Assistant Secretary for Policy and Strategic Initiatives.—Amanda Farris, 260–7052.
Executive Director, White House Initiative on Educational Excellence for Hispanic Americans.—Adam Chavarria, room 5E110, 401–1411.
Director of:
Academic Improvement and Teacher Quality Programs.—Joseph Conaty, 260–8230.
Impact Aid Programs.—Catherine Schagh, room 3E105, 260–3858, fax 205–0088.
Office of Indian Education.—Peirce Hammond, 205–0687.
Office of Migrant Education.—Francisco Garcia, room 3E317, 260–1127, fax 205–0089.
Reading First.—Christopher Doherty, 401–4877.
School Support and Technology Programs.—Jenelle Leonard (acting), 401–3641.
Student Achievement and School Accountability Programs.—Jackie Jackson, 401–3404.

OFFICE OF ENGLISH LANGUAGE ACQUISITION

550 12th Street, SW., 10th Floor, 20202, phone (202) 245–7100, fax 245–7168

Assistant Deputy Secretary and Director.—Kathleen Leos.
Deputy of Policy.—Margarita Pinkos.
Chief of Staff.—Richard L. Smith.

OFFICE OF FEDERAL STUDENT AID

830 First Street, NE., 20202, phone (202) 377–3000, fax 275–5000

Chief Operating Officer.—Theresa S. ''Terri'' Shaw.
Chief of Staff.—James Manning.
Ombudsman.—Deb Wiley, room 41I1, 377–3801.
Chief Financial Officer.—Vicki Bateman, room 54E1, 377–3401.
Chief Information Officer.—Katie Blot, room 102E3, 377–3528.
Director, Policy Liaison and Implementation Staff.—Jeff Baker, room 113C1, 377–4009.
General Manager of:
Business Operations.—Sue Szabo, room 83E3, 377–3437.
Communications and Administration.—Marianna O'Brien, room 114F1, 377–3095.
Enterprise Performance Management Services.—John Fare, room 91J1, 377–3707.
Financial Partner Services.—Matteo Fontana, room 111I4, 377–3005.
Program Compliance.—Victoria Edwards, room 81K2, 377–4273.
Student Awareness and Applicant Services.—Jennifer Douglas, room 32E4, 377–3201.

OFFICE OF THE GENERAL COUNSEL

Room 6E301, phone (202) 401–6000, fax 205–2689

General Counsel.—Kent Talbert.
Senior Counsel.—Robert Wexler.
Chief of Staff.—Robert Wexler (acting).
Executive Officer.—J. Carolyn Adams, 401–8340.
Deputy General Counsel for—
Departmental and Legislative Service.—Robert Eitel.
Postsecondary and Regulatory Service.—Jeffrey Taylor.
Program Service.—Philip Rosenfelt.

OFFICE OF INNOVATION AND IMPROVEMENT

phone (202) 205–4500

Assistant Deputy Secretary.—Morgan Brown, 401–0479.
Associate Assistant Deputy Secretary.—Margo Anderson.
Chief of Staff.—Amanda Schaumberg.

OFFICE OF INSPECTOR GENERAL

Potomac Center Plaza (PCP), 8th Floor, 20024, phone (202) 245–6900, fax 245–6993

Inspector General.—John P. Higgins, Jr.

Deputy Inspector General.—Thomas L. Sipes.
Counsel to the Inspector General.—Mary Mitchelson.
Assistant Inspector General for—
Audit Services.—Helen Lew, 245–7050.
Cyber Audit and Computer Crime Investigations.—Charles E. Coe, 245–7034.

INTERNATIONAL AFFAIRS OFFICE

Room 7E222, phone (202) 401–0430, fax 401–2508

Director.—Robin Gilchrist (acting).
Chief of Staff.—Tori Hatada.
Asia/Pacific, International Education Week, International Briefing Series.—JoAnne Livingston.
Classified Documents, International Agreement Depository.—Betty Ward.
International Visitors, Special Education.—Sambia Shivers-Barclay.
Staff Assistant/Official Passports and Visas.—Mone't Peterson-Cox.
USNEI, Visas and Mobility, Higher Education, Trade, OECD, Europe.—E. Stephen Hunt.
Western Hemisphere, Organization of American States (OAS).—Rafael Nevarez.

INSTITUTE OF EDUCATION SCIENCES

555 New Jersey Avenue, NW., Room 600, 20208, phone (202) 219–1385, fax 219–1466

Director.—Grover J. ''Russ'' Whitehurst.
Deputy Director for—
Administration and Policy.—Sue Betka, 219–1385.
Science.—Anne Riccuiti (acting), 219–2247.
National Center for Education Statistics.—Mark Schneider, 502–7393.
National Center for Education Research.—Lynn Okagaki, 219–2006.
National Center for Education Evaluation and Regional Assistance.—Phoebe Cottingham, 219–2484.
National Center for Special Education Research.—Edward Kame'enui, 219–2128.

OFFICE OF LEGISLATION AND CONGRESSIONAL AFFAIRS

Room 6W301, phone (202) 401–0020, fax 401–1438

Assistant Secretary.—Terrell Halaska, 205–0020.
Deputy Assistant Secretary.—Karen C. Quarles.
Chief of Staff.—Tiffany Watkins, 260–1028.
Congressional Affairs Liaisons:
Central Region.—Steven Tisher, 260–7008.
Northeast Region and Territories.—Julia Phillips, 401–8333.
West Region.—Andrew Kempe, 401–0029.

OFFICE OF PLANNING, EVALUATION AND POLICY DEVELOPMENT

Room 5E301, phone (202) 401–0325, fax 260–7741

Assistant Secretary/Principal Deputy Assistant Secretary.—Kerri Briggs (acting), room 5E311, 205–2540.
Chief of Staff.—Charles R. Hokanson, Jr., room 5E327, 401–6699.
Deputy Assistant Secretary for Data and Information.—Ross C. Santy, room 5E309, 401–3554.
Executive Director, National Math Panel.—Tyrrell Flawn, room 5E322, 260–8354.
Executive Officer.—JoAnn Ryan, room 7E103, 401–3082, fax 205–0723.
Director of:
Budget Service.—Thomas Skelly, room 5W313, 401–0281, fax 401–6139.
Educational Technology.—Timothy J. Magner, room 7E216, 401–1444.
Performance Information Management Service.—Ross C. Santy (acting), room 5E309, 401–3554.
Policy and Program Studies Service.—Alan Ginsburg, room 6W230, 401–3132, fax 401–3036.

OFFICE OF POSTSECONDARY EDUCATION

1990 K Street, NW., 20006, phone (202) 502–7750, fax 502–7677

Assistant Secretary.—James Manning (acting).
Chief of Staff.—Thomas Dawson.
Deputy Assistant Secretary for Higher Education Programs.—Susan Beaudoin (acting), 502–7555.
Executive Director for—
White House Initiative on Historically Black Colleges and Universities.—Charles M. Greene, suite 6107, 502–7900.
White House Initiative on Tribal Colleges and Universities.—Deborah J. Cavett, room 7010, 219–7040.

OFFICE OF SAFE AND DRUG-FREE SCHOOLS

Room 1E110, phone (202) 260–3954, fax 205–5005

Assistant Deputy Secretary.—Deborah A. Price, 205–4169.
Associate Assistant Deputy Secretary.—Bill Modzeleski, room 3E314, 260–1856.

OFFICE OF SPECIAL EDUCATION AND REHABILITATIVE SERVICES

Potomac Center Placa (PCP), 550 12th Street, SW., 5th Floor, 20202

phone (202) 245–7468, fax 245–7636

Assistant Secretary.—John Hager.
Executive Administrator.—Andrew J. Pepin, room 3110, 245–7632.
Director of National Institute on Disability and Rehabilitation Research.—Steve Tingus, 245–7640.

OFFICE OF VOCATIONAL AND ADULT EDUCATION

550 12th Street, SW., Room 1100, 20202, phone (202) 245–7700, fax 245–7171

Assistant Secretary.—Dr. Troy Justesen.
Chief of Staff.—William Knudsen.
Deputy Assistant Secretary.—Dr. Patricia Stanley.
Staff Assistant.—Dorothy Suber.

DEPARTMENT OF VETERANS AFFAIRS

Mail should be addressed to 810 Vermont Avenue, NW., Washington, DC 20420
http://www.va.gov

R. JAMES ''JIM'' NICHOLSON, Secretary of Veterans Affairs; education: graduate, U.S. Military Academy, West Point, NY, 1961; M.A., Columbia University; J.D., University of Denver; military service: paratrooper and Ranger-qualified Army officer, U.S. Army; Vietnam War veteran; military awards: Bronze Star Medal, Combat Infantryman Badge, the Meritorious Service Medal, Republic of Vietnam Cross of Gallantry, and two Air Medals; professional: founded Nicholson Enterprises, Inc., 1978; owner, Renaissance Homes, 1987–present; chairman, Republican National Committee, 1997–2000; U.S. Ambassador to the Holy See, 2001–04; married: Suzanne Marie Ferrell; three children; nominated by President George W. Bush to become the 5th Secretary of Veterans Affairs, and was confirmed by the U.S. Senate on January 26, 2005.

OFFICE OF THE SECRETARY

Secretary of Veterans Affairs.—R. James Nicholson (202) 273–4800.
Chief of Staff.—Thomas G. Bowman, 273–4808.
Deputy Chief of Staff.—Sharon K. Barnes.
Special Assistant for Veterans Service Organizations Liaison.—Kevin S. Secor, 273–4835.
General Counsel.—Paul J. Hutter (acting), 273–6660.
Inspector General.—George J. Opfer, 801 I Street, NW., 565–8620.
Chairman, Board of:
Contract Appeals.—Patricia Sheridan, 1800 G Street, NW., 273–6743.
Veterans Appeals.—James P. Terry, 811 Vermont Avenue, NW., 565–5001.

OFFICE OF THE DEPUTY SECRETARY

Deputy Secretary of Veterans Affairs.—Gordon H. Mansfield (202) 273–4817.
Director of:
Center for Minority Veterans.—Lucretia McClenney, 273–6708.
Center for Women Veterans.—Irene Trowell-Harris, 273–6193.
Employment Discrimination Complaint Adjudication.—Charles R. Delobe, 1722 I Street, NW., 254–0065.
Regulation Policy and Management.—Robert C. McFetridge, 273–9515.
Small and Disadvantaged Business Utilization.—Scott Denniston, 801 I Street, NW., 565–8124.

ASSISTANT SECRETARY FOR CONGRESSIONAL AND LEGISLATIVE AFFAIRS

Assistant Secretary.—Thomas E. Harvey (acting), (202) 273–5611.
Executive Assistant.—Harriet Singleton, 273–5611.
Deputy Assistant Secretary.—Christine O. Hill, 273–5615.
Legislative Advisor.—Charles Likel, 273–5615.
Director for—
Congressional and Legislative Affairs.—Gloria Bennett, 273–5628.
Congressional Liaison.—Patricia Covington, 224–5351 or 225–2280.
Congressional Reports and Correspondence.—Judith Sterne, 273–9435.

ASSISTANT SECRETARY FOR PUBLIC AND INTERGOVERNMENTAL AFFAIRS

Assistant Secretary.—Lisette M. Mondello (202) 273–5750.
Deputy Assistant Secretary for Intergovernmental and International Affairs.—William McLemore, 273–5121.

ASSISTANT SECRETARY FOR POLICY, AND PLANNING

Assistant Secretary.—Patrick W. Dunne (202) 273–5033.
Deputy Assistant Secretary for Planning and Evaluation.—Karen Pane, 273–5068.

ASSISTANT SECRETARY FOR OPERATIONS, SECURITY AND PREPAREDNESS

Executive Assistant.—John Hancock (202) 273–9559.
Deputy Assistant Secretary for—
Emergency Management.—Kevin Hanretta, 273–9573.
Security and Law Enforcement.—John Baffa, 273–5500.

ASSISTANT SECRETARY FOR MANAGEMENT

Assistant Secretary/Chief Financial Officer/Chief Acquisition Officer.—Robert J. Henke (202) 273–5589.
Principal Deputy Assistant Secretary.—Rita A. Reed, 273–5583.
Chief of Staff.—Kathleen Eastberg, 273–5583.
Deputy Assistant Secretary for—
Acquisition and Materiel Management.—Jan Frye, 273–6029.
Budget.—Daniel A. Tucker, 273–5289.
Finance.—Edward J. Murray, 273–5504.

ASSISTANT SECRETARY FOR INFORMATION AND TECHNOLOGY

Assistant Secretary.—Robert T. Howard (202) 273–8842.

ASSISTANT SECRETARY FOR HUMAN RESOURCES AND ADMINISTRATION

Assistant Secretary.—R. Allen Pittman (202) 273–4901.
Principal Deputy Assistant Secretary.—Gary A. Steinberg.
Deputy Assistant Secretary for—
Administration.—C.G. "Deno" Verenes, 273–5356.
Diversity Management and EEO.—Susan C. McHugh, 1575 I Street, NW., 501–1970.
Human Resources Management.—Willie L. Hensley, 273–4920.
Labor-Management Relations.—Megan Serwin Flanz, 273–5369.
Resolution Management.—Ralph Torres, 1575 I Street, NW., 501–2800.
Associate Deputy Assistant Secretary for Human Resources Management.—Barbara Panther, 273–4920.

NATIONAL CEMETERY ADMINISTRATION

Under Secretary for Memorial Affairs.—William F. Tuerk (202) 273–5146.
Deputy Under Secretary.—Richard A. Wannemacher, Jr. (acting), 273–5235.
Senior Advisor.—Richard A. Wannemacher, Jr.
Director of:
Communications Management Service.—Dave Schettler, 273–5175.
Construction Management.—Michael Elliott, 565–5892.
Field Programs.—Steve Muro, 273–5226.
Finance and Planning.—Ronald Walters, 273–5155.
Management Support Service.—Regis Massimino, 273–5212.
Memorial Programs Service.—Lindee Lenox, 501–3060.
State Cemetery Grants Service.—Scott Gebhardtsbauer, 565–4084.

VETERANS BENEFITS ADMINISTRATION

Under Secretary.—Daniel L. Cooper, 1800 G Street, NW. (202) 273–6761.
Deputy Under Secretary.—Ronald R. Aument.
Chief of Staff.—Lois Mittelstaedt.
Associate Deputy Under Secretary for—
Field Operations.—Michael Walcoff, 273–7259.

Policy and Program Management.—Jack McCoy, 273–6851.
Chief Financial Officer.—Jimmy Norris, 273–6728.
VA Deputy Chief Information Officer for Benefits.—K. Adair Martinez, 273–7004.
Director of:
Education.—Keith M. Wilson, 273–7132.
Employee Development and Training.—Dorothy Mackay, 273–5446.
Insurance.—Thomas Lastowka, 215–381–3100.
Loan Guaranty.—R. Keith Pedigo, 273–7331.
Vocational Rehabilitation and Employment.—Judith Caden, 273–7419.

VETERANS HEALTH ADMINISTRATION

Under Secretary.—Michael J. Kussman (acting), M.D., MS, MACP (202) 273–5781.
Principal Deputy Under Secretary.—Gerald M. Cross (acting), M.D., FAAFP, 273–5878.
Deputy Under Secretary for Health (DUSH) for Operations and Management.—William Feeley, MSW, FACHE, 273–5826.
Officer for—
Patient Care Services.—Madhulika Agarwal, M.D., MPH, 273–8474.
Public Health and Environmental Hazards.—Lawrence Deyton, MSPH, M.D., 273–8575.
Research and Development.—Joel Kupersmith, M.D., 254–0183.

DEPARTMENT OF HOMELAND SECURITY

U.S. Naval Security Station, 3801 Nebraska Avenue, NW., 20393

phone (202) 282–8000

MICHAEL CHERTOFF, Secretary of Homeland Security; born on November 28, 1953, in Elizabeth, NJ; education: Harvard College, *magna cum laude*, 1975; Harvard Law School, *magna cum laude*, 1978; public service: clerk to Supreme Court Justice William Brennan, Jr., 1979–80; U.S. Attorney for the District of New Jersey; First Assistant U.S. Attorney for the District of New Jersey; Assistant U.S. Attorney for the Southern District of New York; former partner, law firm of Latham & Watkins; Special Counsel, U.S. Senate Whitewater Committee, 1994–96; United States Circuit Judge for the Third Circuit Court of Appeals; confirmed by the President George W. Bush as Assistant Attorney General for the Criminal Division, Department of Justice, March 5, 2003; family: married to Meryl Justin Chertoff; children: two; nominated by President George W. Bush to become the 2nd Secretary of Homeland Security on January 11, 2005, and was confirmed by the U.S. Senate on February 15, 2005.

OFFICE OF THE SECRETARY

Secretary of Homeland Security.—Michael Chertoff.
Deputy Secretary of Homeland Security.—Michael P. Jackson.
Chief of Staff.—Chad Sweet.

CITIZENSHIP AND IMMIGRATION SERVICES OMBUDSMAN

Ombudsman.—Prakash I. Khatri.

CIVIL RIGHTS AND CIVIL LIBERTIES

phone (202) 401–1474, Toll Free: 1–866–644–8360

Officer for Civil Rights and Civil Liberties.—Daniel Sutherland.

OFFICE OF COUNTERNARCOTICS ENFORCEMENT

Director.—Uttam Dhillon.

EXECUTIVE SECRETARIAT

Executive Secretary.—Fred L. Schwien.

OFFICE OF THE FEDERAL COORDINATOR FOR GULF COAST REBUILDING

Federal Coordinator.—Donald E. Powell.

OFFICE OF THE GENERAL COUNSEL

General Counsel.—Philip J. Perry.

OFFICE OF INSPECTOR GENERAL

phone (202) 254–4100

Inspector General.—Richard L. Skinner.

Principal Deputy Inspector General.—James Taylor.
Deputy Inspector General for Disaster Assistance Oversight.—Matthew Jadacki.
General Counsel to the Inspector General.—Richard N. Reback.
Assistant Inspector General for—
Administration.—Edward F. Cincinnati.
Audits.—David Zavada.
Information Technology.—Frank Deffer.
Inspections.—Carlton ''Carl'' I. Mann.
Investigations.—Elizabeth Redman.
Congressional Affairs Liaison and Media and Public Outreach.—Tamara Faulkner.

OFFICE OF INTELLIGENCE AND ANALYSIS

Chief Intelligence Officer.—Charles E. Allen.

OFFICE OF LEGISLATIVE AND INTERGOVERNMENTAL AFFAIRS

phone (202) 447–5890

Assistant Secretary.—Donald H. Kent, Jr.
Deputy Assistant Secretary.—James Norton.

MILITARY ADVISOR'S OFFICE

Senior Military Advisor to the Secretary.—RDML Daniel B. Lloyd.

PRIVACY OFFICE

phone (571) 227–3813

Chief Privacy Officer.—Hugo Teufel III.

OFFICE OF PUBLIC AFFAIRS

Assistant Secretary.—Cynthia Bergman (acting).

DIRECTORATE FOR PREPAREDNESS

phone (202) 282–8399

Under Secretary.—George W. Foresman.
Chief of Staff.—Sharon Hardie.
Assistant Secretary for—
Cyber and Telecommunications.—Gregory Garcia (703) 235–5125.
Grants and Training.—Corey Gruber (acting), 785–9441.
Infrastructure Protection.—Robert B. Stephan, 282–8230.
Director for—
Center for Faith-Based and Community Initiatives.—Keith Rothfus, 447–3342.
National Capital Region Coordination Office.—Thomas Lockwood, 447–3639.
State and Local Government Coordination Office.—Chet Lunner (acting), 282–8482.
U.S. Fire Administration.—Charlie Dickinson (acting), (301) 447–1018.
Chief Medical Officer.—Dr. Jeffrey W. Runge, 254–6492.

SCIENCE AND TECHNOLOGY DIRECTORATE

Under Secretary.—Jay M. Cohen.
Chief of Staff.—Bradley I. Buswell.
Head of:
Border and Maritime Security Division.—Mervyn Leavitt.
Chemical and Biological Division.—Dr. Elizabeth George (acting).
Command, Control, and Interoperability Division.—David Boyd.
Explosives Division.—James Tuttle.

Human Factors Division.—Dr. Sharla Rausch.
Infrastructure/Geophysical Division.—Dr. Caroline Purdy.
Director of:
Interagency and International Programs Division.—Lilia Ramirez (acting).
Test and Evaluation Standards Division.—George Ryan.

MANAGEMENT DIRECTORATE

Under Secretary.—Paul A. Schneider.
Chief Administrative Services Officer.—Donald Bathurst.
Chief Financial Officer.—David Norquist.
Chief Human Capital Officer.—Marta Perez.
Chief Information Officer.—Scott Charbo.
Chief Procurement Officer.—Elaine Duke.
Chief Security Officer.—Dwight Williams.

OFFICE OF POLICY DIRECTORATE

Assistant Secretary.—Stewart A. Baker.
Assistant Secretary, Office of:
International Affairs.—Paul Rosenzweig (acting).
Policy Development.—Richard C. Barth, Ph.D.
Private Sector.—Alfonso Martinez-Fonts, Jr.
Strategic Plans.—Eric Fagerholm (acting).
Director, Office of Immigration Statistics.—Michael Hoefer, 786–9900.
Chair, Homeland Security Advisory Council.—Hon. William Webster.

FEDERAL EMERGENCY MANAGEMENT (FEMA) DIRECTORATE

500 C Street, SW., 20472, phone (202) 646–2500

Director/Under Secretary.—R. David Paulison.
Deputy Director/Chief Operating Officer.—VADM Harvey Johnson.
Deputy Director for Gulf Coast Recovery.—Gil H. Jamieson.
Assistant Deputy Director.—Robert Shea.
Chief Financial Officer.—Margaret A. Young.
Chief Administrative Services Officer.—Thomas R. McQuillan.
Chief Information Officer.—Tony Cira.
Chief Counsel.—David A. Trissell.
Counselor to the Director and Deputy Director.—Nathaniel Fogg.
Superintendent, Emergency Management Institute.—Cortez Lawrence.
Director of:
Communications.—John P. Philbin, Ph.D.
Office of Equal Rights.—Pauline Campbell.
Office of the Executive Secretariat.—Elizabeth Edge.
Human Resources.—Michael Hall.
Intergovernmental Affairs.—Casey Long.
International Affairs.—Casey Long (acting).
Legislative Affairs.—Dan Shulman.
Management/Chief Acquisition Officer.—Deidre Lee.
Mitigation and Federal Insurance Administrator.—David I. Maurstad.
NIMS Integration Center Training.—Albert H. Fluman.
Office of National Security Coordination.—Charles L. Hopkins III, P.E.
Policy and Program Analysis.—Marko Bourne.
Recovery.—John R. ''Jack'' D'Araujo, Jr.
Response.—Glenn Cannon.
Strategic Planning and Evaluation.—Patricia Stahlschmidt.

OFFICE OF OPERATIONS COORDINATION

phone (202) 282–9580

Director.—Roger T. Rufe, Jr., USCG (Ret.).
Deputy Director.—Wayne Parent.
Chief of Staff.—Derek Rieksts.

DOMESTIC NUCLEAR DETECTION OFFICE

phone (202) 254–7320

Director.—Vayl Oxford.
Assistant Director, Office of:
Assessments.—Huban Gowadia.
National Technical Nuclear Forensics Center.—William Daitch.
Operations Support.—Kevin Stafford.
Systems Architecture.—Mark Mullen.
Systems Development and Acquisition.—Howard Reichel.
Systems Engineering.—Julian Hill.
Transformational Research and Development.—William Hagan.

TRANSPORTATION SECURITY ADMINISTRATION (TSA)

601 South 12th Street, Arlington, VA 22202–4220

Assistant Secretary.—Kip Hawley.
Deputy.—Robert Jamison.

UNITED STATES CUSTOMS AND BORDER PROTECTION (CBP)

1300 Pennsylvania Avenue, NW., 20229

Commissioner.—W. Ralph Basham (202) 344–2001.
Deputy Commissioner.—Deborah J. Spero, 344–1010.
Chief of Staff.—Steven A. Atkiss, 344–1080.
Deputy Chief of Staff.—Christopher J. Clark, 344–1080.
Chief Counsel.—Alfonso Robles, 344–2990.
Equal Employment Opportunity/Special Assistant to the Commissioner.—Franklin C. Jones, 344–1610.
Director, Office of:
Anti-Terrorism.—Thomas L. Bush (acting), 344–2230.
Intelligence.— L. Thomas Bortmes, 344–1150.
Policy and Planning.—Will Houston, 344–2700.
Secure Border Initiative.—Gregory Giddens, 344–2450.
Chief, Office of Border Patrol.—David V. Aguilar, 344–2050.
Assistant Commissioner, Office of:
CBP Air and Marine.—Michael C. Kostelnik, 344–3950.
Congressional Affairs.—Thaddeus M. Bingel, 344–1760.
Field Operations.—Jayson P. Ahern, 344–1620.
Finance/Chief Financial Officer.—Eugene H. Schied, 344–2300.
Human Resources Management.—Robert Hosenfeld, 863–6100.
Information and Technology.—John R. ''Rod'' MacDonald, 344–1680.
Internal Affairs.—James F. Tomsheck, 344–1800.
International Affairs and Trade Relations.—Michael C. Mullen, 344–3000.
International Trade.—Daniel Baldwin, 863–6000.
Public Affairs.—William A. Anthony (acting), 344–1700.
Training and Development.—Thomas J. Walters, 344–1130.

UNITED STATES IMMIGRATION AND CUSTOMS ENFORCEMENT (ICE)

Assistant Secretary.—Julie L. Myers (202) 514–1900.
Counselor to the Assistant Secretary.—Wayne L. Baker.
Chief of Staff.—Gary J. Lang.
Principal Legal Advisor.—Bill Howard, 514–2895.
Policy and Planning.—Susan Cullen, (acting), 514–8693.
Professional Responsibility.—Traci Lembke (acting), 514–2373.
Congressional Relations.—Karyn Lang, 514–5232.
Public Affairs.—Jamie Zuieback (acting), 514–2648.
Executive Secretariat.—Anne-Marie Gatons, 514–2829.
Deputy Assistant Secretary for Operations.—John P. Clark, 514–1900.
Federal Protective Service.—Paul R. Durette (acting), 732–8000.
Office of Detention and Removal Operations.—John P. Torres, 305–2734.
Office of Intelligence.—Michael Nostrand (acting), 514–2960.

Office of Investigations.—Marcy Forman, 514–0078.
Deputy Assistant Secretary for Management.—Theresa C. Bertucci, 514–1900.
Chief Financial Officer.—Debra Bond, 305–9863.
Chief Information Officer.—Luke McCormack, 732–2000.
Equal Employment Opportunity Director.—Deborah Kay Lewis, 514–2824.
Human Resources Director.—Christine Greco, 514–3636.
Student Exchange Visitors Program.—Susan Geary, 305–2346.
Training and Development.—Mark Assur (acting), 732–7808.

FEDERAL LAW ENFORCEMENT TRAINING CENTER

1131 Chapel Crossing Road, Glynco, GA 31524

Director.—Connie L. Patrick (912) 267–2070.
Deputy Director.—Ken Keene, 267–2680.
Senior Associate Director, Washington Operations.—John Dooher (202) 233–0260.
Assistant Director / Chief Financial Officer.—Alan Titus, 267–2999.
Assistant Director / Chief Information Officer.—Sandy Peavy, 267–2014.
Assistant Director for—
Adminstration.—Marcus Hill, 267–2231.
Field Training.—Cynthia Atwood, 267–2445.
Training.—Bruce Bowen, 267–3373.
Training Innovation and Management.—Mike Hanneld, 267–2934.

UNITED STATES CITIZENSHIP AND IMMIGRATION SERVICES

20 Massachusetts Avenue, NW., 20529, phone (202) 272–1000

Director.—Dr. Emilio T. Gonzales.
Deputy Director.—Jonathan ''Jock'' Scharfen.
Chief of Staff.—Thomas C. Paar.
Chief Information Officer.—Jeffrey Conklin.
Associate Director for—
Domestic Operations Directorate.—Michael Aytes.
National Security and Records Verification Directorate.—Janis Sposato.
Refugee, Asylum and International Operations Directorate.—Lori Schialabba.
Chief, Office of:
Administration.—Nancy Guilliams.
Administrative Appeals.—Robert Wiemann.
Chief Counsel.—Lynden Melmed.
Citizenship.—Alfonso Aguilar.
Communications.—Jose Montero.
Congressional Relations.—Sarah Taylor.
Planning, Budget, and Finance / Chief Financial Officer.—Rendell Jones.
Policy and Strategy.—Carlos E. Iturregui.

UNITED STATES COAST GUARD

2100 Second Street, SW., 20593

Commandant.—ADM Thad W. Allen (202) 372–4411.
Vice Commandant.—VADM Viven S. Crea, 372–4422.
Chief of Staff.—VADM Robert J. Papp, Jr., 372–4546.
Special Assistant to the Chief of Staff.—RDML Thomas F. Atkin, 372–2553.
Chief Administrative Law Judge.—Hon. Joseph N. Ingolia, 372–4440.
Chief Knowledge Officer.—Dr. Nathaniel Heiner, 475–3503.
Judge Advocate General / Chief Counsel.—RDML William D. Baumgartner, 372–3726.
Deputy Judge Advocate General / Deputy Chief Counsel.—Calvin Lederer.
Director, Office of Governmental and Public Affairs.—RDML J. Scott Burhoe, 372–4600.
Senior Military Advisor to the Secretary of Homeland Security.—RDML Daniel B. Lloyd, 282–8245.

UNITED STATES SECRET SERVICE

245 Murray Drive, SW., Building 410, 20223

Director.—Mark Sullivan.

Deputy Director.—Brain Nageo.

Deputy Assistant Director, Congressional Affairs Program.—John R. Sullivan (202) 406–5676, fax 406–5740.

INDEPENDENT AGENCIES, COMMISSIONS, BOARDS

ADVISORY COUNCIL ON HISTORIC PRESERVATION

1100 Pennsylvania Avenue, NW., Suite 803, 20004

phone (202) 606–8503, http://www.achp.gov

[Created by Public Law 89–665, as amended]

Executive Director.—John M. Fowler.
Chairman.—John L. Nau III, Houston, Texas.
Vice Chairman.—Susan Snell Barnes, Aurora, Illinois.
Directors for:
Office of Preservation Initiatives.—Ronald D. Anzalone.
Office of Communications, Education, and Outreach.—Sharon S. Conway.
Office of Administration.—Ralston Cox.
Office of Federal Agency Programs.—Don L. Klima.
Coordinator, Native American Program.—Valerie Hauser.
Expert Members:
Jack Williams, Seattle, Washington.
Ann Alexander Pritzlaff, Denver, Colorado.
Julia A. King, St. Leonard, Maryland.
Citizen Members:
Rhonda Bentz, Arlington, Virginia.
Mark A. Sadd, Esq., Charleston, West Virginia.
Native American Member.—Pete Jemsion, Victor, New York.
Governor.—Hon. Matt Blutt, Jefferson City, Missouri.
Mayor.—Hon. Alan Autry, Fresno, California.
Architect of the Capitol.—Hon. Alan M. Hantman, FAIA.
Secretary, Department of:
Agriculture.—Hon. Mike Johanns.
Interior.—Hon. Dirk Kempthorne.
Defense.—Dr. Robert Gates.
Transportation.—Hon. Mary Peters.
Administrator for—
Environmental Protection Agency.—Hon. Stephen L. Johnson.
General Services Administration.—Hon. Lurita A. Doan.
National Trust for Historic Preservation.—Jonathan Kemper, Chairman, Kansas City, Missouri.
National Conference of State Historic Preservation Officer.—Jay D. Vogt, President, Pierre, South Dakota.

AFRICAN DEVELOPMENT FOUNDATION

1400 Eye Street, NW., Suite 1000, 20005–2248, phone (202) 673–3916, fax 673–3810

http://www.adf.gov

[Created by Public Law 96–5331]

BOARD OF DIRECTORS

Chair.—Edward W. Brehm.
Private Members: Dr. Ephraim Batambuze, John W. Leslie, Jr.
Public Member.—Amb. Jendayi Frazer.

STAFF

President.—Rodney J. MacAlister.
Vice President and CEO for African Operations.—Nathaniel Fields.
Vice President and COO.—Richard C. Day.
General Counsel.—Doris Mason Martin.
Chief Financial Officer.—Martha C. Edmondson.
Chief Management Officer.—Larry P. Bevan.
Director of:
Human Resources.—M. Catherine Gates.
Legislative and Public Affairs.—Cynthia Phillips.
Regional Program Coordinators, Program and Field Operations: Rama Bah, Christine S. Fowles.

AMERICAN BATTLE MONUMENTS COMMISSION

Courthouse Plaza II, Suite 500, 2300 Clarendon Blvd., Arlington, VA 22201–3367

phone (703) 696–6902

[Created by Public Law 105–225]

Chairman.—GEN Frederick M. Franks, Jr., U.S. Army (Ret.).
Commissioners:
Hon. Leslie Gromis Baker.
Hon. Chester L. Berryhill, Jr.
Hon. Donald T. Bollinger.
Hon. James B. Culbertson.
Hon. James B. Francis, Jr.
BG Jerry L. Laws, U.S. Army (Ret.).
Senator Zell B. Miller.
LTG Carol A. Mutter, U.S. Marine Corps (Ret.).
Hon. James M. Reynolds III.
Secretary.—BG John W. Nicholson, U.S. Army (Ret.).
Executive Director.—BG William J. Leszczynski, Jr., U.S. Army (Ret.).
Director for—
Engineering and Maintenance.—Thomas R. Sole.
Finance.—Guy A. Giancarlo.
Personnel and Administration.—Theodore Gloukoff.
Public Affairs.—Michael G. Conley.

(Note: Public law changed to 105–225, August 1998; H.R. 1085).

AMERICAN NATIONAL RED CROSS

National Headquarters, 2025 E Street, NW., 20006, phone (202) 737–8300

Government Relations and Public Policy, phone (202) 303–4371, fax 303–0050

HONORARY OFFICERS

Honorary Chair.—George W. Bush, President of the United States.

CORPORATE OFFICERS

Chairman.—Bonnie McElveen-Hunter.

President/CEO.—Mark W. Everson.
General Counsel/Secretary.—Mary S. Elcano.
Chief Financial Officer.—Robert P. McDonald.

BOARD OF GOVERNORS

Gina F. Adams
Cesar A. Aristeiguieta
Sanford A. Belden
Steven E. Carr
Wei-Tih Cheng
M. Victoria Cummock
Brian L. Derksen
Richard M. Fountain
Allan I. Goldberg
James Goodwin
Michael W. Hawkins
James F. Holmes
Suzanne Nora Johnson
Ann F. Kaplan
James W. Keyes
R. Bruce LaBoon
Anna Maria L. Larsen
William Lucy
Elaine M. Lyerly
Bonnie McElveen-Hunter
Laurence E. Paul
Joseph B. Pereles
Melanie R. Sabelhaus
H. Marshall Schwarz
Glenn A. Sieber
E. Francine Stokes
Walter E. Thornton
Steven H. Wunning

ADMINISTRATIVE OFFICERS

Chief Operating Officer.—Kevin M. Brown.
Chief of Operations Support.—Sean McLaughlin.
Chief Public Affairs Officer.—Suzanne DeFrancis.
Ombudsman.—Beverly O. Babers.
Chief Audit Executive.—Dale Bateman.
Congressional Affairs—
Vice President for Government Relations and Public Policy.—Neal Denton.
Director, Congressional Affairs.—Larry T. Decker.
Senior Policy Advisor.—Dawn P. Latham.
Legislative Specialist.—Marin Reynes.

APPALACHIAN REGIONAL COMMISSION

1666 Connecticut Avenue, NW., 20009, phone (202) 884–7660, fax 884–7691

Federal Co-Chair.—Anne B. Pope.
Alternate Federal Co-Chair.—Richard J. Peltz.
States' Washington Representative.—Cameron Whitman.
Executive Director.—Thomas M. Hunter.
Congressional Affairs Officer.—Guy Land.

ARMED FORCES RETIREMENT HOME

3700 N. Capitol Street, NW., Box 1303, Washington, DC 20011–8400
phone (202) 730–3077, fax 730–3166

Chief Operating Officer.—Timothy C. Cox.
Chief Financial Officer.—Steven G. McManus.
Chief Support Services.—Maurice Swinton.

ARMED FORCES RETIREMENT HOME—WASHINGTON

phone (202) 730–3229, fax 730–3127

Director.—Ben Laub.

ARMED FORCES RETIREMENT HOME—GULFPORT
1800 Beach Drive, Gulfport, MS 39507

Closed due to Hurricane Katrina.

BOARD OF GOVERNORS OF THE FEDERAL RESERVE SYSTEM

Constitution Avenue and 20th Street, NW., 20551, phone (202) 452–3000

Chairman.—Ben S. Bernanke.
Vice Chair.—Donald L. Kohn.
Members: Susan Schmidt Bies, Randall S. Kroszner, Frederic S. Mishkin, Kevin M. Warsh.
Assistant to the Board and Director.—Michelle A. Smith.
Assistants to the Board: Winthrop P. Hambley, Rosanna Pianalto-Cameron, David W. Skidmore.
Special Assistants to the Board: Laricke D. Blanchard, Brain J. Gross, Robert M. Pribble.

DIVISION OF BANKING SUPERVISION AND REGULATION

Director.—Roger T. Cole.
Deputy Directors: Deborah P. Bailey, Peter J. Purcell, Steven M. Roberts.
Associate Directors: Norah M. Barger, Betsy Cross, Charles H. Holm, Jack P. Jennings, Robin L. Lumsdaine, William G. Spaniel, Molly S. Wassom, David M. Wright.
Deputy Associate Directors: Barbara J. Bouchard, James A. Embersit, Jon D. Greenlee, Arthur W. Lindo, William C. Schneider, Jr.
Assistant Directors: Robert T. Ashman, Kevin M. Bertsch, Stacy Coleman, Lisa Deferrari, Robert T. Maas, Nina A. Nichols, Dana E. Payne, Nancy J. Perkins, Sabeth I. Siddique.
Advisers: William F. Treacy, Sarkis D. Yoghourtdjian.

DIVISION OF CONSUMER AND COMMUNITY AFFAIRS

Director.—Sandra F. Braunstein.
Deputy Director.—Glenn E. Loney.
Associate Counsel and Advisor.—Adrienne D. Hurt.
Associate Directors: Leonard Chanin, Mary T. Johnsen, Tonda E. Price.
Assistant Directors: Timothy R. Burniston, Suzanne Killian, Sheila F. Maith, James A. Michaels.
Adviser.—Maryann F. Hunter.

DIVISION OF FEDERAL RESERVE BANK OPERATIONS AND PAYMENT SYSTEMS

Director.—Louise L. Roseman.
Deputy Directors: Donald V. Hammond, Jeffrey C. Marquardt.
Senior Associate Director.—Paul W. Bettge.
Associate Directors: Kenneth D. Buckley, Dorothy B. LaChapelle, Jack K. Walton II.
Deputy Associate Director.—Jeff J. Stehm.
Assistant Directors: Gregory L. Evans, Lisa Hoskins, Michael J. Lambert.

DIVISION OF INFORMATION TECHNOLOGY

Director.—Marianne M. Emerson.
Deputy Director.—Maureen T. Hannan.
Assistant Directors: Tillena G. Clark, Geary L. Cunningham, Wayne A. Edmondson, Po Kyung Kim, Susan F. Marycz, Sharon L. Mowry, Raymond Romero, Jill Rosen.

DIVISION OF INTERNATIONAL FINANCE

Director.—Karen H. Johnson.
Senior Associate Director.—Thomas A. Conners.
Associate Director.—Richard T. Freeman, Steven B. Kamin.
Deputy Associate Directors: Joseph E. Gagnon, Michael P. Leahy, D. Nathan Sheets, Ralph W. Tryon.
Assistant Directors: Jon W. Faust, Trevor Reeve, John H. Rogers.
Senior Adviser.—Dale W. Henderson.

DIVISION OF MONETARY AFFAIRS

Director.—Vincent Reinhart.
Deputy Director.—Brian F. Madigan.
Assistant Directors: James A. Clouse, Deborah J. Danker, William B. English.
Deputy Associate Director.—Cheryl L. Edwards.
Assistant Directors: Andrew T. Levin, William R. Nelson, Jonathan H. Wright.
Senior Adviser.—Athansios Orphanides.

DIVISION OF RESEARCH AND STATISTICS

Director.—David J. Stockton.
Deputy Directors: Patrick M. Parkinson, David Wilcox.
Senior Associate Director.—Myron L. Kwast.
Associate Directors: J. Nellie Liang, Lawrence Slifman, Charles S. Struckmeyer, Alice Patricia White.
Deputy Assistant Directors: S. Wayne Passmore, David L. Reifschneider, Janice Shack-Marquez, William L. Wascher III, Joyce K. Zickler.
Assistant Directors: Michael S. Cringoli, Douglas Elmendorf, Michael Gibson, Diana Hancock, Robin A. Prager, Daniel Sichel, Mary M. West.
Senior Advisers: Glenn B. Canner, David S. Jones, Stephen D. Oliner.

INSPECTOR GENERAL

Inspector General.—Barry R. Snyder.
Deputy Inspector General.—Donald L. Robinson.

LEGAL DIVISION

General Counsel.—Scott G. Alvarez.
Deputy General Counsels: Richard M. Ashton, Kathleen M. O'Day.
Associate General Counsels: Stephanie Martin, Anne E. Misback, Katherine H. Wheatley.
Assistant General Counsels: Kieran J. Fallon, Stephen H. Meyer, Patricia A. Robinson, Cary K. Williams.

MANAGEMENT DIVISION

Director.—H. Fay Peters.
Deputy Director.—Darrell R. Pauley.
Senior Associate Directors: Todd A. Glissman, Marsha W. Reidhill, Billy J. Sauls, Donald A. Spicer.
Associate Director.—Christine M. Fields.
Deputy Associate Director.—James Riesz.
Assistant Directors: Keith F. Bates, Elaine M. Boutilier, Charles O'Malley, Tara Tinsley-Jones.

OFFICE OF THE SECRETARY

Secretary.—Jennifer J. Johnson.
Deputy Secretary.—Robert deV. Frierson.
Assistant Secretary.—Margaret M. Shanks.

STAFF DIRECTOR FOR MANAGEMENT

Staff Director.—Stephen R. Malphrus.
EEO Programs Director.—Sheila Clark.
Senior Adviser.—Lynn S. Fox.

BROADCASTING BOARD OF GOVERNORS

330 Independence Avenue, SW., Suite 3360, 20237
phone (202) 203–4545, fax 203–4568

The Broadcasting Board of Governors oversees the operation of the IBB and provides yearly funding grants approved by Congress to three non-profit grantee corporations, Radio Free Europe/Radio Liberty, Radio Free Asia, and the Middle East Broadcasting Networks.

Chairman.—Kenneth Y. Tomlinson.

INTERNATIONAL BROADCASTING BUREAU

[Created by Public Law 103–236]

The International Broadcasting Bureau (IBB) is composed of the Voice of America, and Radio and TV Marti.

Deputy Director, International Broadcasting Bureau.—George Moore (202) 203–4515, fax 203–4587.
Director of:
Cuba Broadcasting.—Pedro Roig (305) 437–7010, fax 437–7016.
Voice of America.—Danforth Austin (202) 203–4500, fax 203–4513.
President, Radio Free Asia.—Libby Liu (202) 530–4900, fax 721–7460.
President, Radio Free Europe.—Jeffrey Trimble (acting) (202) 457–6900, fax 457–6992.
President, Middle East Broadcasting Networks.—Brian Conniff (703) 852–9000, fax 991–1250.

GOVERNORS

Edward E. Kaufman
Blanquita Walsh Cullum
D. Jeffrey Hirschberg
Steven J. Simmons
Condoleezza Rice (ex officio)

STAFF

Executive Director.—Janice Brambilla.
Chief Financial Officer.—Janet Stormes.
Congressional Coordinator.—Susan Andross.
Communications Coordinator.—Larry Hart.
Executive Assistant.—Brenda Hardnett.
Legal Counsel.—Carol Booker.
Policy and Program Coordinator.—John Giambalvo.
Program Review and Planning Officer.—Jim Morrow.
Special Assistant.—Humaira Wakili.
Special Projects Officer.—Oanh Tran.

COMMISSION OF FINE ARTS

National Building Museum, 401 F Street, NW., Suite 312, 20001–2728

phone (202) 504–2200, fax 504–2195, http://www.cfa.gov

Commissioners:
Earl A. Powell III, Washington, DC., Chair.
Pamela Nelson, Dallas, TX, Vice-Chair.
Diana Balmori, New York, NY.
John Belle, New York, NY.
N. Michael McKinnell, Boston, MA.
Witold Rybczynski, Philadelphia, PA.
Elyn Zimmerman, New York, NY.

Secretary.—Thomas Luebke, AIA.
Assistant Secretary.—Frederick J. Lindstrom.

BOARD OF ARCHITECTURAL CONSULTANTS FOR THE OLD GEORGETOWN ACT

Mary Oehrlein, FAIA, Chair.
John McCartney, FAIA.
Stephen Vanze, AIA.

COMMITTEE FOR PURCHASE FROM PEOPLE WHO ARE BLIND OR SEVERELY DISABLED

1421 Jefferson Davis Highway, Suite 10800, Jefferson Plaza 2

Arlington, VA 22202–3259, phone (703) 603–7740, fax 603–0655

Chairperson.—Andrew D. Houghton.
Vice Chairperson.—James H. Omvig.
Private Citizens:
Osborne Day.
Robert T. Kelly, Jr.
Members:
James E. House, Department of Agriculture.
Perry E. Anthony, Department of Education.
Steven B. Schwalb, Department of Justice.
W. Roy Grizzard, Jr., Department of Labor.
RADM Daniel H. Stone, Department of the Navy.
Robert J. Henke, Department of Veterans Affairs.
Felipe Mendoza, General Services Administration.
Andrew D. Houghton and Robert T. Kelly, Jr., private citizens (representing nonprofit agency employees with other severe disabilities).
James H. Omvig, private citizen (representing nonprofit agency employees who are blind).

COMMODITY FUTURES TRADING COMMISSION

Three Lafayette Centre, 1155 21st Street, NW., 20581, phone (202) 418–5000

fax 418–5521, http://www.cftc.gov

Chairman.—Reuben Jeffery III, 418–5050.
Chief of Staff.—Charles Cooper, 418–5054.
Commissioners:
Michael V. Dunn, 418–5070.
Walter L. Lukken, 418–5014.
Executive Director.—Madge A. Bolinger, 418–5160.
General Counsel.—Nanette Everson, 418–5152.
Office of the Chief Economist.—James A. Overdahl, 418–5656.
Director, Division of:
Clearing and Intermediary Oversight.—Ananda Radhakrishnan, 418–5188.
Enforcement.—Gregory Mocek, 418–5320.
Market Oversight.—Rick Shilts (acting), 418–5260.

Director, Office of:
External Affairs.—Ianthe Zabel, 418–5091.
Inspector General.—A. Roy Lavik, 418–5110.
International Affairs.—Jacqueline H. Mesa, 418–5386.
Secretary.—Eileen A. Donovan (acting), 418–6096.

REGIONAL OFFICES

Chicago: 525 West Monroe Street, Suite 1100, Chicago, IL 60601 (312) 596–0700, fax 596–0716.
Kansas City: Two Emanuel Cleaver II Boulevard, Suite 300, Kansas City, MO 64112, (816) 960–7700, fax 960–7750.
Minneapolis: 510 Grain Exchange Building, 400 South 4th Street, Minneapolis, MN 55415, (612) 370–3255, fax 370–3257.
New York: 140 Broadway, Nineteenth floor, New York, NY 10005 (646) 746–9700, fax 746–9938.

CONSUMER PRODUCT SAFETY COMMISSION

4330 East West Highway, Bethesda, MD 20814, phone (301) 504–7923

fax 504–0124, http://www.cpsc.gov

[Created by Public Law 92–573]

Chairperson.—Nancy Nord (acting), 504–7901.
Commissioner.—Thomas H. Moore, 504–7902.
Executive Director.—Patricia M. Semple, 504–7907.
Deputy Executive Director.—Lowell Martin, 504–7628.
Director, Office of:
The Secretary.—Todd A. Stevenson, 504–7923.
Congressional Relations.—Jack Horner, 504–7660.
General Counsel.—Page C. Faulk, 504–7922.

CORPORATION FOR NATIONAL AND COMMUNITY SERVICE

1201 New York Avenue, NW., 20525, phone (202) 606–5000

http://www.cns.gov

[Executive Order 11603, June 30, 1971; codified in 42 U.S.C., section 4951]

Chief Executive Officer.—David Eisner.
Chief of Staff.—Nicola Goren, 606–6676.
Chief Financial Officer.—Jerry Bridges, 606–6683.
Inspector General.—Gerald Walpin, 606–9390.
Director of:
AmeriCorps/National Civilian Community Corps.—Merlene Mazyck, 606–6705.
AmeriCorps/State and National.—Kristin McSwain, 606–6926.
AmeriCorps/VISTA.—Jean Whaley, 606–6943.
Learn and Serve America.—Dr. Amy Cohen, 606–6927.
National Senior Service Corps.—Tess Scannell, 606–6925.
Office of Government Relations.—Kathleen Ott, 606–6732.
General Counsel.—Frank Trinity, 606–6677.

DEFENSE NUCLEAR FACILITIES SAFETY BOARD

625 Indiana Avenue, NW., Suite 700, 20004, phone (202) 694–7000

fax 208–6518, http://www.dnfsb.gov

Chairman.—A.J. Eggenberger.
Members: Joseph F. Bader, Larry W. Brown, John E. Mansfield, Peter S. Winokur.
General Counsel.—Richard A. Azzaro.
General Manager.—Brian Grosner.
Technical Director.—Kent Fortenberry.

DELAWARE RIVER BASIN COMMISSION

25 State Police Drive, P.O. Box 7360, West Trenton, NJ 08628–0360

phone (609) 883–9500, fax 883–9522, http://www.drbc.net

[Created by Public Law 87–328]

FEDERAL REPRESENTATIVES

Federal Commissioner.—MG William T. Grisoli (718) 765–7000.
First Alternate.—COL Christopher J. Larsen, Deputy Commander, U.S. Army Corps of Engineers, North Atlantic Division (718) 765–7001.
Second Alternate.—LTC Gwen E. Baker, District Commander, U.S. Army Corps of Engineers, Philadelphia (215) 656–6502.

STAFF

Executive Director.—Carol R. Collier, ext. 200.
Deputy Executive Director.—Robert Tudor, ext. 208.
Commission Secretary/Assistant General Counsel.—Pamela M. Bush, Esq., ext. 203.
Communications Manager.—Clarke Rupert, ext. 260.

DELAWARE REPRESENTATIVES

State Commissioner.—Ruth Ann Minner, Governor (302) 577–3210.
First Alternate.—John A. Hughes, Secretary, DE Department of Natural Resources and Environmental Control (DNREC), (302) 739–9000.
Second Alternate.—Kevin C. Connelly, Director, Division of Water Resources (DNREC), (302) 739–9949.
Third Alternate.—Dr. Harry W. Otto, Senior Science Advisor, Office of the Director, Division of Water Resources (DNREC), (302) 739–9949.

NEW JERSEY REPRESENTATIVES

State Commissioner.—Jon S. Corzine, Governor (609) 292–6000.
First Alternate.—Lisa P. Jackson, Commissioner, New Jersey Department of Environmental Protection (NJDEP), (609) 292–2885.
Second Alternate.—Mark N. Mauriello, Assistant Commissioner, for Land Use Management (NJDEP), (609) 292–2178.
Third Alternate.—Michele Putman, Director, Division of Water Supply (NJDEP), (609) 292–7219.
Fourth Alternate.—Dr. Joseph A. Miri, Chief, Office of Water Policy (NJDEP), (609) 292–7219.

NEW YORK REPRESENTATIVES

State Commissioner.—Eliot Spitzer, Governor (518) 474–8390.

PENNSYLVANIA REPRESENTATIVES

State Commissioner.—Edward G. Rendell, Governor (717) 787–2500.
First Alternate.—Cathy Curran Myers, Esq., Deputy Secretary for Water Management, Office of Water Management, Pennsylvania Department of Environmental Protection (717) 787–4686.
Second Alternate.—William A. Gast, Chief, Division of Water use Planning, Bureau of Watershed Management (PADEP), (717) 772–5671.

ENVIRONMENTAL PROTECTION AGENCY

1200 Pennsylvania Avenue, NW., 20460, phone (202) 564–4700, http://www.epa.gov

Administrator.—Stephen Johnson.
Deputy Administrator.—Marcus Peacock, 564–4711.
Chief of Staff.—Charles Ingebretson, 564–6999.
Deputy Chiefs of Staff: Cece Kremer, 564–7960; Ray Spears, 564–4715.
Agriculture Counsel.—Jon Scholl, 564–7719.
White House Liaison.—Kelly Sinclair, 564–4693.
Environmental Appeals Board: Scott Fulton, Edward Reich, Kathie Stein, Anna Wolgast, 233–0122.
Associate Administrator for—
Congressional and Intergovernmental Relations.—Brent Fewell (acting), 564–5200.
Homeland Security.—Tom Dunne, 564–2844.
Policy, Economics, and Innovation.—Brian Mannix, 564–4332.
Public Affairs.—Lisa Lybbert.
Director, Office of:
Children's Health Protection.—William Sanders (acting), 564–2188.
Civil Rights.—Karen Higginbotham, 564–7272.
Cooperative Environmental Management.—Rafael DeLeon, 233–0090.
Executive Secretariat.—Brian Hope, 564–7311.
Executive Services.—Diane Bazzle, 564–0444.
Science Advisory Board.—Vanessa Vu, 343–9999.
Small and Disadvantaged Business Utilization.—Jeanette L. Brown, 564–4100.
Director of Management, Office of Administrative Law Judges.—James McDonald, 564–6255.

ADMINISTRATION AND RESOURCES MANAGEMENT

Assistant Administrator.—Luis Luna, 564–4600.

Deputy Assistant Administrator.—Sherry A. Kaschak (acting), 564–1861.

AIR AND RADIATION

Assistant Administrator.—Bill Wehrum (acting), 564–7404.
Deputy Assistant Administrators: John Beale, Beth Craig, 564–7400.

ENFORCEMENT AND COMPLIANCE ASSURANCE

Assistant Administrator.—Granta Nakayama, 564–2440.
Principal Deputy Assistant Administrator.—Catherine McCabe.
Deputy Assistant Administrator.—Lynn Buhl.

OFFICE OF ENVIRONMENTAL INFORMATION

Assistant Administrator.—Linda Travers (acting), 564–6665.
Deputy Assistant Administrator.—Craig Hooks (acting).

CHIEF FINANCIAL OFFICER

Chief Financial Officer.—Lyons Gray, 564–1151.
Deputy Chief Financial Officer.—Maryann Froehlich.

GENERAL COUNSEL

General Counsel.—Roger Martella (acting), 564–8064.
Principal Deputy General Counsel.—Pat Hirsch (acting), 564–8064.
Deputy General Counsel.—Mary Ann Poirier, 564–8040.

INSPECTOR GENERAL

Inspector General.—Bill Roderick (acting), 566–0847.
Deputy Inspector General.—Mark Bialek.

INTERNATIONAL AFFAIRS

Assistant Administrator.—Judith E. Ayres, 564–6600.
Deputy Assistant Administrator.—Jerry Clifford.

PREVENTION, PESTICIDES, AND TOXIC SUBSTANCES

Assistant Administrator.—Jim Gulliford, 564–2902.
Principal Deputy Assistant Administrator.—Susan B. Hazen.
Deputy Assistant Administrator.—Margaret Schneider (acting), 564–2910.

RESEARCH AND DEVELOPMENT

Assistant Administrator.—George Gray, 564–6620.
Deputy Assistant Administrator of:
Management.—Lek Kadeli.
Science.—Kevin Teichman (acting).

SOLID WASTE AND EMERGENCY RESPONSE

Assistant Administrator.—Susan Bodine, 566–0200.
Principal Deputy Assistant Administrator.—Barry Breen.

WATER

Assistant Administrator.—Benjamin H. Grumbles, 564–5700.
Deputy Assistant Administrator.—Michael H. Shapiro.

REGIONAL ADMINISTRATION

Region I, Boston.—Connecticut, Maine, New Hampshire, Rhode Island, Vermont.
Regional Administrator.—Robert W. Varney, One Congress Street, Suite 1100, Boston, MA 02114 (617) 918–1010.
Public Affairs.—Nancy Grantham.
Region II, New York City.—New Jersey, New York, Puerto Rico, Virgin Islands.
Regional Administrator.—Alan Steinberg, 290 Broadway, New York, NY 10007 (212) 637–5000.
Public Affairs.—Bonnie Bellow (212) 637–3660.
Region III, Philadelphia.—Delaware, Washington D.C., Maryland, Pennsylvania, Virginia, West Virginia.
Regional Administrator.—Donald S. Welsh, 1650 Arch Street, Philadelphia, PA 19103–2029 (215) 814–2900.
Public Affairs.—Thomas Damm (215) 814–5100.
Region IV, Atlanta.—Alabama, Florida, Georgia, Kentucky, Mississippi, North Carolina, South Carolina, Tennessee.
Regional Administrator.—James I. Palmer, Jr., 61 Forsyth Street, SW., Atlanta, GA 30303–8960 (404) 562–8357.
Public Affairs.—Carl Terry (404) 562–8327.
Region V, Chicago.—Illinois, Indiana, Michigan, Minnesota, Ohio, Wisconsin.
Regional Administrator.—Mary Gade, 77 West Jackson Boulevard, Chicago, IL 60604–3507 (312) 886–3000.
Public Affairs.—Elissa Speizman.
Region VI, Dallas.—Arkansas, Louisiana, New Mexico, Oklahoma, Texas.
Regional Administrator.—Richard Greene, Fountain Place, 1445 Ross Avenue, 12th Floor, Suite 1200, Dallas, TX 75202–2733 (214) 665–2100.
Public Affairs.—David W. Gray.
Region VII, Kansas City.—Iowa, Kansas, Missouri, Nebraska.
Regional Administrator.—John Askew, 901 N. 5th Street, Kansas City, MO 66101 (913) 551–7006.
Public Affairs.—Patrick Bustos (913) 551–7305.
Region VIII, Denver.—Colorado, Montana, North Dakota, South Dakota, Utah, Wyoming.
Regional Administrator.—Robbie Roberts, 999 18th Street, Suite 300, Denver, CO 80202–2466 (303) 312–6308.
Public Affairs.—Nola Yancy (303) 312–6599.
Region IX, San Francisco.—Arizona, California, Hawaii, Nevada, American Samoa, Guam.
Regional Administrator.—Wayne Nastri, 75 Hawthorne Street, San Francisco, CA 94105 (415) 947–8702.
Public Affairs.—Sally Seymour.
Region X, Seattle.—Alaska, Idaho, Oregon, Washington.
Regional Administrator.—Elin Miller, 1200 Sixth Avenue, Seattle, WA 98101 (206) 553–1234.
Public Affairs.—Michelle Pirzadeh (206) 553–1901.

EQUAL EMPLOYMENT OPPORTUNITY COMMISSION

1801 L Street, NW., 20507, phone (202) 663–4900

Chair.—Naomi Churchill Earp, room 10103, 663–4002, fax 663–4110.
Chief Operating Officer.—Anthony Kaminski, room 10008, 663–4033.
Attorney Advisor.—Richard Roscio, room 10010, 663–4655.
Confidential Assistant.—Michele Waldron, Reception Area, 663–4002.
Senior Advisor.—Michael Richards, room 10127, 663–4010.
Special Assistants: Paula Bruner, room 10036, 663–4731; Thais Mootz, room 10028, 663–4583; John Suhre, room 10042, 663–4716; Lisa Schnall, room 10038, 663–4845.
Staff Assistant.—Cynthia Matthews, room 10016, 663–4026.

COMMISSIONERS

Commissioners: Christine Griffin, room 10054, 663–4036, fax 663–7101; Stuart Ishimaru, room 10133, 663–4052, fax 663–4108; Leslie E. Silverman, room 10305, 663–4099, fax 663–7121.
Special Assistants: Elizabeth Bille, room 10313, 663–4099; Jolinda Johnson, room 10060, 663–4585; Naomi Levin, room 10317, 663–4099; Jacinta Ma, room 10125, 663–4970; Sharyn Tejani, room 10123, 663–4022; Mindy Weinstein, room 10315, 663–4099; Steve Zanowic, room 10062, 663–4404.

Administrative Assistants: Melissa Fenwick, room 10129, 663–4036; Crystal Grant, 663–4099; Priscilla Seaborne, room 10056, 663–4047.
Chief of Staff.—Kenneth Morse, room 10064, 663–4091.
General Counsel.—Ronald Cooper, room 7001, 663–7034, fax 663–4196.
Legal Counsel.—Peggy Mastroianni, room 6001, 663–4327, fax 663–4639.
Director, Office of:
Communications and Legislative Affairs.—Karen Pedrick, room 9027, fax 663–4912.
Equal Opportunity.—Jean M. Watson, room 9024, 663–4012, fax 663–7003.
Executive Secretariat.—Stephen Llewellyn, room 10426, 663–4703, fax 663–4114.
Field Programs.—Nicholas Inzeo, room 8002, 663–4801, fax 663–7190.
Inspector General.—Aletha Brown, room 3001, 663–4327, fax 663–7204.

EXPORT–IMPORT BANK OF THE UNITED STATES

811 Vermont Avenue, NW., 20571, phone (800) 565–EXIM, fax 565–3380

President and Chairman.—James Lambright, room 1215, 565–3500.
Vice President and Vice Chairman.—Linda Conlin, room 1229, 565–3540.
Directors: Max Cleland, room 1257, 565–3520; Linda Conlin, room 1209, 565–3535; J. Jospeh Grandmaison, room 1241, 565–3530.
Chief Operating Officer/General Counsel.—Howard Schweitzer, room 947, 565–3229.
Chief Financial Officer.—Michael Discenza, room 1055, 565–3952.
Chief Information Officer.—Fernanda Young, room 1045, 565–3798.
Senior Vice President of:
Credit Risk Management.—Kenneth Tinsley, room 919, 565–3222.
Export Finance.—John McAdams, room 1115, 565–3222.
Policy and Planning.—James C. Cruse, room 1243, 565–3761.
Resource Management.—Michael Cushing, room 1017, 565–3561.
Vice President and Deputy Head of Export Finance.—John Emens, room 1115, 565–3701.
Vice President of:
Congressional Affairs.—William Hellet, room 1261–A, 565–3233.
Country Risk and Economic Analysis.—William Marsteller, room 701, 565–3739.
Credit Underwriting.—David Carter, room 919, 565–3667.
Domestic Business Development.—Wayne L. Gardella, room 1137, 565–3787.
Engineering and Environment.—James Mahoney, room 1169, 565–3573.
International Business Development.—C. Michael Forgione, room 1107, 565–3224.
Operations.—Raymond J. Ellis, room 719, 565–3674.
Policy.—Piper P. Starr, room 1240, 565–3626.
Policy Analysis.—Michael Kuester, room 1243, 565–3766.
Structured Finance.—Barbara A. O'Boyle, room 1005, 565–3694.
Trade Finance and Insurance.—Jeffrey Abramson, room 931, 565–3633.
Transportation.—Robert A. Morin, room 1035, 565–3453.
Directors of:
Human Resources.—Elliot Davis, room 771, 565–3316.
Employee Development and Training.—Greg DaDamio, room 767, 565–3534.

FARM CREDIT ADMINISTRATION

1501 Farm Credit Drive, McLean, VA 22102–5090

phone (703) 883–4000, fax 734–5784

[Reorganization pursuant to Public Law 99–205, December 23, 1985]

Chair.—Nancy C. Pellett.
Board Members:
Leland Storm.
Dallas Tonsager.
Secretary to the Board.—Roland Smith.
Chief of Staff.—Keith Heffernan.
Chief Examiner and Director, Office of Examination.—Thomas G. McKenzie, 883–4160.
Director, Office of:
Communication and Public Affairs.—Martha Schober, 883–4056, fax 790–3260.
Finance.—Stephen Smith, 883–4200.
General Counsel.—Charles R. Rawls, 883–4020, fax 790–0052.
Information.—Doug Valcour, 883–4200.
Inspector General.—Stephen Smith, 883–4030.

Manager, Equal Employment Opportunity.—Jeff McGiboney, 883–4353.
Personnel/Purchasing.—Philip Shebest, 883–4200.
Policy and Analysis.—Ed Harshbarger, 883–4414.
Regulatory Policy.—Andrew Jacob, 883–4414, fax 883–4477.
Secondary Market Oversight.—Robert Coleman, 883–4280.

FEDERAL COMMUNICATIONS COMMISSION

445 12th Street, SW., 20554, phone (202) 418–0200, http://www.fcc.gov
FCC National Consumer Center: 1–888–225–5322/1–888–835–5322 (TTY)

Chairman.—Kevin J. Martin, room 8–B201, 418–1000.
Confidential Assistant.—Lori Alexiou.
Senior Legal Advisor.—Daniel Gonzalez.
Legal Advisors: Fred Campbell, Heather Dixon, Michelle Carey Shearer.
Commissioner.—Jonathan S. Adelstien, room 8–A302, 418–2300.
Senior Legal Advisor.—Barry Ohlson.
Legal Advisors: Scott Bergman, Rudy Brioche.
Commissioner.—Michael Copps, room 8–B115, 418–2000.
Confidential Assistant.—Carolyn Conyers.
Senior Legal Advisor.—Jessica Rosenworcel.
Legal Advisors: Scott Deutchman, Bruce Gottlieb.
Commissioner.—Robert McDowell, room 8–C302, 418–2200.
Confidential Assistant.—Brigid Nealon Calamis.
Senior Legal Advisor/Chief of Staff.—John Hunter.
Legal Advisors: Angela Giancarlo, Cristina Chou Pauze.
Commissioner.—Deborah Taylor Tate, room 8–A204, 418–2500.
Confidential Assistant.—Susan Fisenne.
Legal Advisors: Ian Dillner, Aaron Goldberger, Chris Robbins (acting).

OFFICE OF ADMINISTRATIVE LAW JUDGES

Administrative Law Judges: Richard L. Sippel, room 1–C768, 418–2280; Arthur I. Steinberg, room 1–C861, 418–2255.

OFFICE OF COMMUNICATIONS BUSINESS OPPORTUNITIES

Director.—Carolyn Fleming Williams, room 4–A760, 418–0990.

CONSUMER AND GOVERNMENTAL AFFAIRS BUREAU

Bureau Chief.—Cathy Seidel, room 5–C758, 418–1400.
Chief of Staff.—Pam Slipakoff (acting).
Deputy Bureau Chief of:
Operations.—Stephen Ebner (acting), room 5–C751.
Outreach.—Thomas Wyatt, room 5–C755.
Policy.—Jay Keithley, room 5–C754.
Assistant Chief, Administration and Management.—Patricia Green, room 5–A848.
Chief, Division of:
Consumer Affairs and Outreach.—Louis Segalos, room 4–C763.
Consumer Inquiries and Complaints Division.—Jeffrey Tignor (acting), room 5–A847.
Consumer Policy.—Erica McMahon, room 5–A844.
Chief, Office of:
Disability Rights.—Thomas Chandler, room 3–B431.
Intergovernmental Affairs.—Alice Elder, room 5–A660.
Infomation Resource Management.—Bill Cline, room CY–B533.
Chief, Reference Information Center.—Bill Cline.

ENFORCEMENT BUREAU

Chief.—Kris Monteith, room 3–C252, 418–1098.
Chief, Division of:

Investigations and Hearings.—Hillary DeNigro, room 4–C321, 418–7334.
Market Disputes Resolution.—Alex Starr, room 4–C342, 418–7248.
Spectrum Enforcement.—Kathryn Berthot, room 3–C366, 418–1160.
Telecommunications.—Colleen Heitkamp, room 4–C224, 418–7320.
Director of:
North East Region: Chicago, IL.—Russell D. ''Joe'' Monie (847) 813–4671.
South Central Region: Kansas City, MO.—Dennis P. ''Denny'' Carlton (816) 316–1243.
Western Region: San Diego, CA.—Rebecca L. Dorch (925) 407–8708.

OFFICE OF ENGINEERING AND TECHNOLOGY

Chief.—Julius Knapp, room 7–C155, 418–2470.

OFFICE OF GENERAL COUNSEL

General Counsel.—Samuel Feder, room 8–C723, 418–1700.
Deputy General Counsels: Matthew Berry, P. Michele Ellison, Joseph Palmore.
Associate General Counsel.—Jacob Lewis.

OFFICE OF INSPECTOR GENERAL

Inspector General.—Dr. Kent Nilsson, room 2–C762, 418–0470.
Deputy Inspector General.—Jon Stover.
Assistant Inspector General for Audits.—Curtis Hagan.

INTERNATIONAL BUREAU

Chief.—Helen Domenic, room 6–C750, 418–0437.
Deputy Chiefs: John Guisti, room 6–C475, 418–1407; Roderick K. Porter, room 6–C752, 418–0423.
Chief, Satellite Division.—Robert Nelson, room 6–A665, 418–0719.
Deputy Chiefs: Fern Jarmulnek, room 6–A760; Cassandra Thomas, room 6–A666.

OFFICE OF LEGISLATIVE AFFAIRS

Director.—S. Kevin Washington, room 8–C432, 418–1900.

OFFICE OF MANAGING DIRECTOR

Managing Director.—Anthony J. Dale, room 1–C144, 418–1919.
Deputy Managing Directors: Mindy Ginsburg, Joseph Hall, Mark Stone.
Secretary.—Marlene Dortch, room TW–B204, 418–0300.
Deputy Secretary.—William F. Caton.
Chief Human Capital Officer.—Johseph Hall (acting), room 1–C144, 418–1919; 418–0126 (TTY); 418–0150 (Employment Verification).
Deputy Human Capital Officer.—Bonita Tingley, room 1–A130, 418–0293.

MEDIA BUREAU

Chief.—Monica Desai, room 3–C740, 418–7200.
Senior Deputy Bureau Chief.—Roy J. Stewart, room 2–C347.
Deputy Bureau Chief.—Rosemary C. Harold, room 3–C486.
Chief of Staff.—Thomas Horan, room 3–C478.
Chief, Division of:
Audio Services.—Peter H. Doyle, room 2–A360, 418–2700
Engineering.—John Wong, room 2–A360, 418–7000.
Industry Analysis.—Royce Sherlock, room 2–C360, 418–2330.
Policy.—Mary Beth Murphy, room 4–A766, 418–2120.
Video Services.—Barbara A. Kreisman, room 2–A666, 418–1600.

OFFICE OF MEDIA RELATIONS

Director.—David H. Fiske, room CY–C314, 418–0500.

OFFICE OF STRATEGIC PLANNING AND POLICY ANALYSIS

Chief.—Catherine Bohegian, room 7–C452, 418–2030.
Chief of Staff.—Maureen C. McLaughlin.

WIRELESS TELECOMMUNICATIONS BUREAU

Chief.—Fred Campbell, room 6–6413, 418–0600.
Deputy Bureau Chiefs: Cathy Massey, room 6–6417 (Portal 1), 418–0600; James Schlichting, room 3–C250 (Portal 1), 418–0600.
Chief of Staff/Associate Bureau Chief.—D'Wana Terry, room 6–6413, 418–0643.
ABC for Management.—Lois Jones, room 6–6421, 418–1487.
Chief, Division of:
Action and Spectrum Access.—Margie Wiener, room 6–6419, 418–0660.
Broadband.—Joel Taubenblatt, room 3–C124; Jennifer Tomchin, room 3–C133, 418–BITS.
Mobility.—Roger Noel, room 6–6411, 418–0620.
Spectrum and Competition Policy.—Blaise Scinto (acting), room 6–6402, 418–1380; John Branscombe, room 6–6415, 418–8205.
Spectrum Management Resources and Technologies.—John Chudovan (Gettysburg), (717) 338–2510.

WIRELINE COMPETITION BUREAU

Senior Deputy Chiefs: Thomas Navin, room 5–C356; Julie Veach, room 5–C354, 418–1500.
Associate Bureau Chief.—Donald Stockdale, room 5–C450, 418–1500.

OFFICE OF WORKPLACE DIVERSITY

Director.—P. June Taylor (acting), room 5–C750, 418–1799.
Deputy Director.—Harvey Lee, room 5–C751.

REGIONAL AND FIELD OFFICES

NORTHEAST REGION

Regional Director of:
Chicago: Russell ''Joe'' Monie, Park Ridge Office Center, Room 306, 1550 Northwest Highway, Park Ridge, IL 60068 (847) 813–4671.

FIELD OFFICES—NORTHEAST REGION

Director of:
Boston: Dennis V. Loria, One Batterymarch Park, Quincy, MA 02169 (617) 786–1154.

Columbia: James T. Higgins, 9200 Farm House Lane, Columbia, MD 21046 (301) 725–0019.

Detroit: James A. Bridgewater, 24897 Hathaway Street, Farmington Hills, MI 48335 (248) 471–5661.

New York: Dan Noel, 201 Varick Street, Room 1151, New York, NY 10014 (212) 337–1865.

Philadelphia: Gene J. Stanbro, One Oxford Valley Office Building, Room 404, 2300 East Lincoln Highway, Langhorne, PA 19047 (215) 741–3022.

SOUTH CENTRAL REGION

Regional Director of:

Kansas City: Dennis P. Carlton, 520 NE Colbern Road, Second Floor, Lee's Summit, MO 64086 (816) 316–1243.

FIELD OFFICES—SOUTH CENTRAL REGION

Director of:

Atlanta: Doug Miller, Koger Center, 3575 Koger Boulevard, Suite 320, Duluth, GA 30096 (770) 935–3372.

Dallas: James D. Wells, 9330 LBJ Freeway, Room 1170, Dallas, TX 75243 (214) 575–6361.

Kansas City: Robert C. McKinney, 520 NE Colbern Road, Second Floor, Lee's Summit, MO 64086 (816) 316–1248.

New Orleans: Leroy ''Bud'' Hall, 2424 Edenborn Avenue, Room 460, Metarie, LA 70001 (504) 219–8989.

Tampa: Ralph M. Barlow, 2203 North Lois Avenue, Room 1215, Tampa, FL 33607 (813) 348–1741.

WESTERN REGION

Regional Director of:

Denver: Rebecca Dorch, 215 South Wadsworth Boulevard, Suite 303, Lakewood, CO 80226 (303) 407–8708.

FIELD OFFICES—WESTERN REGION

Director of:

Denver: Nikki Shears, 215 South Wadsworth Boulevard, Suite 303, Lakewood, CO 80226 (303) 231–5212.

Los Angeles: Catherine Deaton, Cerritos Corporate Towers, 18000 Studebaker Road, Room 660, Cerritos, CA 90701 (562) 865–0235.

San Diego: William Zears, Interstate Office Park, 4542 Ruffner Street, Room 370, San Diego, CA 92111 (858) 496–5125.

San Francisco: Thomas N. Van Stavern, 5653 Stoneridge Drive, Suite 105, Pleasanton, CA 94588 (925) 416–9777.

Seattle: Kris McGowan, 11410 Northeast 122nd Way, Room 312, Kirkland, WA 98034 (425) 820–6271.

FEDERAL DEPOSIT INSURANCE CORPORATION

550 17th Street, NW., 20429

phone (877) 275–3342, http://www.fdic.gov

Chairman.—Sheila C. Bair.
Deputy to the Chairman for Policy.—Alice C. Goodman, 898–8730.
Deputy to the Chairman and Chief Operating Officer.—John F. Bovenzi, 898–6949.
Deputy to the Chairman and Chief Financial Officer.—Steve App, 898–8732.
Vice Chairman.—Martin J. Gruenburg, 898–3888.
Deputy.—Barbara Ryan, 898–3841.
Director.—Thomas J. Curry, 898–3957.
Special Assistant to the Director.—Marianne Lloyd (acting), 898–3505.
Director (OCC).—John C. Dugan, 874–4900.
Deputy.—William Rowe, 898–6960.
Director (OTS).—John M. Reich, 906–6590.
Deputy.—Claude Rollin., 898–8741.
Director, Office of Legislative Affairs.—Eric J. Spitler, 898–3837, fax 898–3745.

FEDERAL ELECTION COMMISSION

999 E Street, NW., 20463

phone (202) 694–1000, Toll Free (800) 424–9530, fax 219–3880, http://www.fec.gov

Chairman.—Robert D. Lenhard, 694–1020.
Vice Chairman.—Dave M. Mason, 694–1050.
Commissioners:
Michael E. Toner, 694–1045.
Hans A. von Spakovsky, 694–1011.
Steven T. Walther, 694–1055.
Ellen L. Weintraub, 694–1035.
Inspector General.—Lynne A. McFarland, 694–1015.
Staff Director.—Patrina M. Clark, 694–1007, fax 219–2338.
Deputy Staff Director for—
Compliance/Chief Compliance Officer.—Margarita Maisonet, 694–1181.
Finance/Chief Finance Officer.—Erin D. Singshinsuk, 694–1217.
Information Technology/Chief Information Officer.—Alec Palmer, 694–1250.
Management and Administration.—John W. Sigmon, 694–1098.
Director for Congressional Affairs.—Tina H. VanBrakle, 694–1006.
General Counsel.—Lawrence H. Norton, 694–1650.
Deputy General Counsel.—James A. Kahl.
Associate General Counsel for—
Enforcement.—Rhonda Vosdingh.
General Law and Advice.—Thomasenia P. Duncan.
Litigation.—Richard B. Bader.
Policy.—Rosemary C. Smith.
Administrative Officer.—Sylvia E. Butler, 694–1240.
Accounting Officer.—Brian J. Duffy, 694–1230.
EEO Director.—Carolyn S. Mackey-Bryant, 694–1228.
Library Director (Law).—Leta L. Holley, 694–1600.
Press Officer.—Bob W. Biersack, 694–1220.

FEDERAL HOUSING FINANCE BOARD

1625 Eye Street, NW., 4th Floor, 20006

phone (202) 408–2500, fax 408–1435

[Created by the Financial Institutions Reform, Recovery, and Enforcement Act of August 9, 1989, 103 Stat. 354, 415]

Chairman.—Ronald A. Rosenfeld, 408–2838.
Board of Directors:
Geoffrey S. Bacino, 408–2810.
Alicia Castaneda, 408–2542.
Allan I. Mendelowitz, 408–2601.
Brian Montgomery,* 708–3600.
Inspector General.—Edward Kelley, 408–2570.
General Counsel.—John Kennedy, 408–2983.
Director of Resource Management.—Judith L. Hofmann, 408–2586.
Director of Supervision.—Stephen M. Cross, 408–2980.

FEDERAL LABOR RELATIONS AUTHORITY

1400 K Street, NW., 20424–0001, phone (202) 218–7000, fax 482–6635

FLRA Agency Head.—Dale Cabaniss, 218–7900.
Executive Director.—Jill M. Crumpacker, 218–7945.
Chief Counsel.—Gail Reinhart.
Director, Case Control.—Gail Reinhart (acting), 218–7944.

*The Secretary of Housing and Urban Development is one of the five Directors of the Federal Housing Finance Board. Secretary Jackson has designated the Assistant Secretary for Housing/Federal Housing Commissioner to act for him on the Board of Directors of the Federal Housing Finance Board.

Solicitor.—William Tobey (acting), 218–7908.
Inspector General.—Francine Eichler, 218–7744.
Collaboration and Alternative Dispute Resolution Program.—Andy Pizzi, 218–7933.
Foreign Service Impasse Disputes Panel.—Olden Lee, 218–7945.
Foreign Service Labor Relations Board.—Dale Cabaniss, 218–7945.

AUTHORITY DECISIONAL COMPONENT

Chariman.—Dale Cabaniss, 218–7900.
Member.—Wayne C. Beyer.

GENERAL COUNSEL OF THE AUTHORITY

General Counsel.—Collen Duffy Kiko, 218–7925.
Assistant General Counsel for Appeals.—Richard Zorn.

OFFICE OF ADMINISTRATIVE LAW JUDGES

Chief Judge.—Charles Center, 218–7918.

FEDERAL SERVICE IMPASSES PANEL (FSIP)

FSIP Chairman.—Becky Norton Dunlop, 218–7746.
Special Assistant to the Chairman.—Victoria Dutcher, 218–7746.
Executive Director.—H. Joseph Schimansky, 218–7991.

REGIONAL OFFICES

Regional Directors:
Atlanta.—Nancy A. Speight, Marquis Two Tower, Suite 701, 285 Peachtree Center Avenue, Atlanta, GA 30303 (404) 331–5300, fax (404) 331–5280.
Boston.—Richard D. Zaiger, 10 Causeway Street, Suite 472, Boston, MA 02222 (617) 565–5100, fax 565–6262.
Chicago.—Peter Sutton (acting), Suite 1150, 55 West Monroe, Chicago, IL 60603 (312) 886–3465, fax 886–5977.
Dallas.—James E. Petrucci, Suite 926, LB 107, 525 Griffin Street, Dallas, TX 75202 (214) 767–6266, fax 767–0156.
Denver.—Matthew Jarvinen, Suite 100, 1244 Speer Boulevard, Denver, CO 80204 (303) 844–5224, fax 844–2774.
San Francisco.—Gerald M. Cole, Suite 220, 901 Market Street, San Francisco, CA 94103 (415) 356–5002, fax 356–5017.
Washington, DC.—Robert Hunter, 1400 K Street, NW., Suite 200, Washington, DC 20005 (202) 482–6700, fax (202) 482–6724.

FEDERAL MARITIME COMMISSION

800 North Capitol Street, NW., 20573
phone (202) 523–5725, fax 523–0014

OFFICE OF THE CHAIRMAN

Commissioner.—Harold J. Creel, Jr., room 1044, 523–5712.
Counsel.—David R. Miles.
Commissioner.—Joseph E. Brennan, room 1032, 523–5723.
Counsel.—Steven D. Najarian.
Commissioner.—Rebecca F. Dye, room 1038, 523–5715.
Counsel.—Edward L. Lee, Jr.
Commissioner.—A. Paul Anderson, room 1026, 523–5721.
Counsel.—Lucille A. Streeter.

OFFICE OF THE SECRETARY

Secretary.—Bryant L. VanBrakle, room 1046, 523–5725.

Assistant Secretary.—Karen V. Gregory.
Librarian.—Charlotte C. White, room 1085, 523–5762.
Director, Office of Consumer Affairs and Dispute Resolution.—Ronald D. Murphy, room 972, 523–5807.

OFFICE OF EQUAL EMPLOYMENT OPPORTUNITY

Director.—Stephaine Y. Burwell (acting), room 1052, 523–5859.

OFFICE OF THE GENERAL COUNSEL

General Counsel.—Amy W. Larson, room 1018, 523–5740.
Deputy General Counsel.—Christopher Hughey.

OFFICE OF ADMINISTRATIVE LAW JUDGES

Chief Judge.—Clay G. Guthridge, room 1089, 523–5750.

OFFICE OF THE INSPECTOR GENERAL

Inspector General.—Adam R. Trzeciak, room 1054, 523–5863.
Deputy Inspector General.—Bridgette S. Hicks.

OFFICE OF ADMINISTRATION

Director.—Peter J. King (acting), room 926, 523–5800.
Deputy Director.—Carmen G. Cantor (acting).
Director of:
Financial Management.—Karon E. Douglass, room 916, 523–5770.
Human Resources.—Hatsie H. Charbonneau, room 924, 523–5773.
Information Technology.—Stephanie Y. Burwell, room 904, 523–5835.
Management Services.—Michael H. Kilby, room 924, 523–5900.

OFFICE OF OPERATIONS

Director.—Austin L. Schmitt, room 972, 523–0988.
Deputy Director.—Rachel E. Dickon.
Area Representatives:
Los Angeles.—Oliver E. Clark (310) 514–4905.
New Orleans.—Alvin N. Kellogg (504) 589–6662.
New York.—Emanuel J. Mingione (718) 553–2228.
Seattle.—Michael A. Moneck (206) 553–0221.
South Florida.—Andrew Margolis (954) 963–5362; Eric O. Mintz (954) 963–5284.
Director of:
Agreements.—Jeremiah D. Hospital, room 940, 523–5793.
Certification and Licensing.—Sandra L. Kusumoto, room 970, 523–5787.
Enforcement.—Vern W. Hill, room 900, 523–5783.
Passenger Vessels and Information Processing.—Anne E. Trotter, room 970, 523–5818.
Service Contracts and Tariffs.—Mamie H. Black, room 940, 523–5856.
Trade Analysis.—Florence A. Carr, room 940, 523–5796.
Transportation Intermediaries.—Ralph W. Freibert, room 970, 523–5843.

BUREAU OF CONSUMER COMPLAINTS AND LICENSING

Director.—Sandra L. Kusumoto, room 970, 523–5787.
Deputy Director.—Ronald D. Murphy.
Director of:
Consumer Complaints.—Joseph T. Farrell, 523–5807.
Passenger Vessels and Information Processing.—Anne E. Trotter, 523–5818.
Transportation Intermediaries.—Ralph W. Freibert, 523–5843.

BUREAU OF ENFORCEMENT

Director.—Vern W. Hill, room 900, 523–5783 or 523–5860.

Deputy Director.—Peter J. King.

AREA REPRESENTATIVES

Los Angeles.—Oliver E. Clark (310) 514–4905.
Miami.—Andrew Margolis (305) 536–4316, Eric O. Mintz (305) 536–5529.
New Orleans.—Alvin N. Kellogg (504) 589–6662.
New York.—Emanuel J. Mingione (212) 637–2929.
Seattle.—Michael A. Moneck (206) 553–0221.

FEDERAL MEDIATION AND CONCILIATION SERVICE

2100 K Street, NW., 20427, phone (202) 606–8100, fax 606–4251

[Codified under 29 U.S.C. 172]

Director.—Arthur F. Rosenfeld.
Deputy Director.—Scot L. Beckenbaugh (acting), 606–8100.
Chief of Staff.—Fran L. Leonard (acting), 606–3361.
General Counsel.—Maria Fried, 606–5444.
Director for—
ADR/International/FMCS Institute.—Kimberly Beg, 606–5445.
Arbitration Services.—Vella M. Traynham, 606–5111.
Budget and Finance.—Fran L. Leonard, 606–3661.
Grants.—Linda Stubbs, 606–8181.
Human Resources.—Dan Ellerman, 606–5460.
Information Systems and Administrative Services.—Dan W. Funkhouser, 606–5477.
Regional Director (Eastern).—John F. Buettner (216) 520–4805.
Regional Director (Western).—Dan O'Leary (acting), (630) 887–4750.

FEDERAL MINE SAFETY AND HEALTH REVIEW COMMISSION

601 New Jersey Avenue, NW., Suite 9500, 20001
phone (202) 434–9900, fax 434–9944

[Created by Public Law 95–164]

Chairperson.—Michael F. Duffy, room 9515, 434–9924.
Commissioner: Mary Lu Jordan, room 9527, 434–9926; Michael Young, room 9517, 434–9914.
Executive Director.—Thomas Stock, room 9519, 434–9905.
Deputy Executive Director.—Lisa M. Boyd, room 9509, 434–9905.
Chief Administrative Law Judge.—Robert J. Lesnick, room 8515, 434–9958.
General Counsel.—Michael McCord, room 9547, 434–9935.

FEDERAL RETIREMENT THRIFT INVESTMENT BOARD

1250 H Street, NW., 20005, phone (202) 942–1600, fax 942–1676

[Authorized by 5 U.S.C. 8472]

Executive Director.—Gary A. Amelio, 942–1601.
General Counsel.—Thomas K. Emswiler, 942–1660.
Director, Office of:
Automated Systems.—Mark Hagerty, 942–1610.
External Affairs.—Thomas J. Trabucco, 942–1640.
Finance.—James B. Petrick, 942–1630.
Investments.—Theresa Ray, 942–1630.
Participant Services.—Pamela-Jeanne Moran, 942–1450.
Product Development.—Greg Long, 942–1630.

Chairman.—Andrew M. Saul, 942–1660.
Board Members:
Thomas A. Fink.

Alejandro M. Sanchez.
Gordon J. Whiting.
Terrence A. Duffy.

FEDERAL TRADE COMMISSION

600 Pennsylvania Avenue, NW., 20580

phone (202) 326–2222, http://www.ftc.gov

Chairman.—Deborah Platt Majoras, room 440, 326–2100.
Executive Assistant.—Martha Schoenborn, room 442, 326–2673.
Chief of Staff.—Maryanne Kane, room 444, 326–2450.
Commissioners: Pamela Jones Harbour, room 328, 326–2907; Thomas B. Leary, room 528, 326–2142; Jonathan Leibowitz, room 340, 326–3400; Orson Swindle, room 540, 326–2150.
Director, Office of:
Competition.—Susan A. Creighton, room 374, 326–2946.
Congressional Relations.—Jeanne Bumpus, room 404, 326–3680.
Consumer Protection.—Lydia Parnes (acting), room 472, 326–2676.
Economics.—Michael Salinger, room 268, 326–2827.
Policy Planning.—Maureen Ohlhausen (acting), room 492, 326–2632.
Public Affairs.—Nancy Ness Judy, room 423, 326–2180.
Executive Director.—Sonna L. Stampone, room 426, 326–3609.
General Counsel.—John D. Graubert (acting), room 570, 326–2186.
Secretary.—Donald S. Clark, room 172, 326–2514.
Inspector General.—Adam Trzeciak (acting), room 1117NJ, 326–2435.
Chief Administrative Law Judge.—Stephen J. McGuire, room 112, 326–3637.

REGIONAL DIRECTORS

East Central Region: John Mendenhall, Eaton Center, Suite 200, 1111 Superior Avenue, Cleveland, OH 44114 (216) 263–3455.
Midwest Region: C. Steve Baker, 55 East Monroe Street, Suite 1860, Chicago, IL 60603 (312) 960–5634.
Northeast Region: Barbara Anthony, One Bowling Green, Suite 318, New York, NY 10004 (212) 607–2829.
Northwest Region: Charles A. Harwood, 915 Second Avenue, Suite 2896, Seattle, WA 98174 (206) 220–6350.
Southeast Region: Bradley Elbein, 60 Forsyth Street, Midrise Building, Suite 5M35, Atlanta, GA 30303 (404) 656–1390.
Southwest Region: Deanya T. Kuckelhan, 1999 Bryan Street, Suite 2150, Dallas, TX 75201 (214) 979–9350.
Western Region—Los Angeles: Jeffrey Klurfeld, 18077 Wilshire Boulevard, Suite 700, Los Angeles, CA 90024–3679 (310) 824–4320.
Western Region—San Francisco: Jeffrey Klurfeld, 901 Market Street, Suite 570, San Francisco, CA 94103 (415) 848–5100.

FOREIGN–TRADE ZONES BOARD

1401 Constitution Avenue, NW., Room 2814B, 20005

phone (202) 482–2862, fax 482–0002

Chairman.—Carlos Gutierrez, Secretary of Commerce.
Member.—Henry M. Paulson, Jr., Secretary of the Treasury.
Executive Secretary.—Andrew McGilvray.

GENERAL SERVICES ADMINISTRATION

1800 F Street, NW., 20405, phone (202) 501–0800, http://www.gsa.gov

Administrator.—Lurita Doan.
Deputy Administrator.—David L. Bibb.
Chief of Staff.—John Phelps.
Associate Administrators, Office of:
Citizen Services and Communications.—David Bethel, 501–0705.

Civil Rights.—Madeline Caliendo, 501–0767.
Congressional and Intergovernmental Affairs.—Kevin Messner, 501–0563.
Small Business Utilization.—Felipe Mendoza, 501–1021.
Principal Deputy Associate Administrator.—Linda Emery, 501–0563.
Deputy Associate Administrators: Regina Budd, 502–4571; Karen Kirksey, 208–2028; Brian Mabrey, 501–0563; Susan Peppler, 501–0563; Michael Rigas, 501–1021.
Senior Congressional Liaison Specialist.—Marcia Herzog, 501–0563.
Inspector General.—Brian D. Miller, 501–0450.
Deputy Inspector General.—Andrew Russoniello (acting), 501–1362.
Advisor to the Inspector General.—Robert M. Samuels, 501–1362.
Counsel to the Inspector General.—Kevin A. Buford, 501–1932.
Assistant Inspector General for—
Administration.—Arrie Etheridge, 501–1734.
Auditing.—Andrew Patchan, 501–0374.
Investigations.—Charles J. Augone, 501–1397.
Deputy Assistant Inspector General for Investigations.—Gregory Rowe.
Deputy Counsel.—Virginia S. Grebasch, 501–1932.
Chairman, Board of Contract Appeals.—Stephen M. Daniels, 606–8820.
Vice Chairman.—Robert W. Parker, 606–8819.
Chief Counsel.—Margaret S. Pfunder, 606–8787.
Clerk.—Beatrice Jones, 606–8800.
Board Judges, 606–8820: Anthony S. Borwick, Stephen M. Daniels, Martha H. DeGraff, Jerome Drummond, Eileen Fennessy, Beryl Gilmore, Allan H. Goodman, Catherine B. Hyatt, Harold Kullberg, Robert McCann, Robert W. Parker, Howard Pollack, Patricia Sheridan, Jeri Somers, Candida Steel, James Stern, Joseph Vergilio, Richard Walters.
Chief Human Capital Officer.—Gail T. Lovelace, 501–0398.
Deputy Chief Human Capital Officer, Office of Human Resources Services.—William A. Kelly, 501–0885.
Associate Administrator for Performance Improvement.—Vince Warrick, 501–1143.
General Counsel.—Lennard S. Loewentritt (acting), 501–2200.
Associate General Counsel for—
General Law.—Eugenia D. Ellison, 501–1460.
Personal Property.—Janet Harney (acting), 501–1156.
Real Property.—Samuel J. Morris III, 501–0430.
Chief Financial Officer (B).—Kathleen M. Turco, 501–1721.
Director of:
Budget.—Deborah Schilling, 501–0719.
Finance.—Douglas Glenn, 501–0562.
Financial Management Systems.—Lynne E. Johnson (acting), 501–3429.
Controller.—Faye Basden (acting), 219–3617.
Chief Information Officer.—Michael Carleton, 501–1000.
Director, Office of:
Enterprise Architecture and IT Capital Planning/Chief Technology Officer.—Christopher Fornicker, 219–3393.
Enterprise Infrastructure Operations.—Mike Seckar, 208–5054.
Enterprise IT Investment Portfolio and Policy.—Phil Klokis, 501–3437.
Associate Administrator, Governmentwide Policy.—Kevin Messner (acting), 501–0563.
Deputy Associate Administrator.—Stan Kaczmarczyk (acting), 501–8880.
Executive Officer.—Nancy Wong, 501–8880.
Director, Regulatory Information Service Center.—John C. Thomas, 482–7340.
Director, GSA Administrative Policy and Committee Management Secretariat.—James L. Dean, 273–3563.
Deputy Associate Administrator for—
Real Property Management.—Stan Kaczmarczyk, 501–8880.
Technology Strategy.—Mary Mitchell, 501–0202.
Travel, Transportation and Asset Management.—Rebecca R. Rhodes, 501–1777.
Commissioner, Public Buildings Service.—David Winstead, 501–1100.
Deputy Commissioner.—Anthony Costa, 501–1100.
Chief of Staff.—Cathleen Kronopolous (acting), 501–1100.
Chief Architect.—Leslie Shepherd, 501–1888.
Chief Financial Officer.—William Brady, 501–0658.
Assistant Commissioner for—
Capital Construction.—Robert Fraga, 501–1888.
Organizational Resources.—Diane Herdt (acting), 501–9103.
Real Property Asset Management.—William H. Matthews, 501–0638.
Commissioner, Federal Acquisition Service.—James A. Williams (703) 605–5400.
Deputy Commissioner.—Marty Wagner, 605–5400.

Chief Information Officer.—Casey Coleman, 605–2601.
Controller.—Jon Jordan, 605–5440.
Assistant Commissioner for—
Acquisition Management.—Michael Sade, 605–5533.
Administration.—Karen Hampel, 605–5574.
Assisted Acquisition Services.—Mary Davie, 306–6728.
Customer Accounts and Research.—Gary Feit, 605–5644.
General Supplies and Services.—Joseph Jeu, 605–5511.
Integrated Technology Services.—John C. Johnson, 306–6007.
Strategic Business Planning and Process Improvement.—Edward O'Hare, 605–2750.
Travel, Motor Vehicle and Card Services.—Barney Brasseux, 605–5501.

REGIONAL OFFICES

National Capital Region: 7th and D Streets, SW., Washington, DC 20407 (202) 708–9100.
Regional Administrator.—Ann W. Everett (acting).
Deputy Administrator.—Pamela Riggs (acting).
Assistant Regional Administrator for—
Federal Technology Service.—Paul McDermott, 708–6100.
Public Buildings Service.—Bart Bush, 708–5891.
Regional Counsel.—Sharon A. Roach, 708–5155.

New England Region: Thomas P. O'Neill Federal Building, 10 Causeway Street, Boston, MA 02222 (617) 565–5860.
Regional Administrator.—Dennis R. Smith.
Deputy Regional Administrator.—Marjorie B. Samra.
Assistant Regional Administrator for—
Federal Technology Service.—Sharon Wall, 565–5760.
Public Buildings Service.—Glenn Rotundo (acting), 565–5694.

Northeast and Caribbean Region: 26 Federal Plaza, New York, NY 10278 (212) 264–2600.
Regional Administrator.—Emily Baker.
Deputy Regional Administrator.—Steve Ruggiero.
Assistant Regional Administrator for—
Federal Acquisition Service.—Steve Ruggiero (acting).
Public Buildings Service.—John Scorcia (acting), 264–4282.

Mid-Atlantic Region: The Strawbridge's Building, 20 N. Eighth Street, Philadelphia, PA 19107 (215) 446–5100.
Regional Administrator.—Barbara Shelton, 446–4900.
Deputy Regional Administrator.—Linda C. Chero, 446–4900.
Assistant Regional Administrator for—
Federal Acquisition Service.—Linda C. Chero (acting), 446–4900.
Public Buildings Service.—Rob Hewell, 446–4500.
Regional Counsel.—Robert J. McCall (acting), 446–4946.

Southeast Sunbelt Region: 77 Forsyth Street, Suite 600, Atlanta, GA 30303 (404) 331–3200.
Regional Administrator.—Ed Fielder.
Deputy Regional Administrator.—Jimmy H. Bridgeman.
Assistant Regional Administrator for—
Federal Acquisition Service.—William ''Bill'' Sisk, 331–5114.
Public Buildings Service.—Ron Hertwig, 562–0263.

Great Lakes Region: 230 South Dearborn Street, Chicago, IL 60604 (312) 353–5395.
Regional Administrator.—James C. Handley.
Deputy Regional Administrator.—Michael Gelber.
Assistant Regional Administrator for—
Federal Acquisition Service.—Michael Gelber.
Public Buildings Service.—J. David Hood, 353–5572.

Heartland Region: 1500 East Bannister Road, Kansas City, MO 64131 (816) 926–7201.
Regional Administrator.—Brad Scott.
Deputy Regional Administrator.—Michael T. Brinks (acting), 926–7217.
Assistant Regional Administrator for—
Federal Acquisition Service.—Sharon Henry, 823–1700.
Public Buildings Service.—Mary Ruwwe, 926–7231.

Greater Southwest Region: 819 Taylor Street, Fort Worth, TX 76102 (817) 978–2321.
Regional Administrator.—Scott Armey.
Deputy Regional Administrator.—George Prochaska.
Assistant Regional Administrator for—
Federal Acquisition Service.—Tyree Varnado, 574–2516.

Public Buildings Service.—Jim Weller, 978–2522.

Rocky Mountain Region: Building 41, Denver Federal Center, Denver, CO 80225 (303) 236–7329.

Deputy Regional Administrator.—Benjamin F. Gonzales.

Assistant Regional Administrator for—

Federal Acquisition Service.—Patrick Mulcare, 236–7197.

Public Buildings Service.—Paul F. Prouty, 236–7245.

Pacific Rim Region: 450 Golden Gate Avenue, Room 5–2690, San Francisco, CA 94102 (415) 522–3001.

Regional Administrator.—Peter G. Stamison.

Deputy Regional Administrator.—Peter T. Glading.

Assistant Regional Administrator for—

Federal Acquisition Service.—John Boyan, 522–2777.

Public Buildings Service.—Jeffrey Neely.

Northwest / Arctic Region: GSA Center, 400 15th Street, SW., Auburn, WA 98001 (253) 931–7000.

Regional Administrator.—Jon Kvistad.

Deputy Regional Administrator.—Gary Casteel.

Assistant Regional Administrator for—

Federal Acquisition Service.—Gary G. Casteel, 931–7115.

Public Buildings Service.—Rob Graf, 931–7200.

HARRY S. TRUMAN SCHOLARSHIP FOUNDATION

712 Jackson Place, NW., 20006

phone (202) 395–4831, fax 395–6995

[Created by Public Law 93–642]

BOARD OF TRUSTEES

President.—Madeleine K. Albright.

Chairman Emeritus.—Elmer B. Staats.

Vice Chairman.—Ike Skelton, Representative from Missouri.

Vice President.—Max Sherman.

General Counsel.—C. Westbrook Murphy.

Members:

W. Todd Akin, Representative from Missouri.

Max Baucus, Senator from Montana.

Christopher S. Bond, Senator from Missouri.

Roger Hunt, U.S. District Judge.

John Kidde, Vice President, Ventura Foods.

Margaret Spellings, Secretary of Education.

Sharon ''Nyota'' Tucker, Assistant Professor, Albany State University.

Juanita Vasquez-Gardner, Judge, 399th District Court of Texas.

Executive Secretary.—Frederick G. Slabach.

Associate Executive Secretary.—Tara Yglesias.

Program Officers.—Tonji Wade.

Administrative Officer.—Ruth Keen.

Financial Desk Officer.—Elise Derstine.

INTER-AMERICAN FOUNDATION

901 North Stuart Street, 10th Floor, Arlington, VA 22203, phone (703) 306–4301

Chair, Board of Directors.—Roger W. Wallace.

Vice Chair, Board of Directors.—Jack C. Vaughn, Jr.

President.—Larry L. Palmer.

General Counsel.—Jennifer Hodges.

Vice President of Operations.—Linda Kolko.

Vice President for External Affairs.—Ramón Daubón.

Regional Director for South America and the Caribbean.—Judith Morrison.

Regional Director for Central America and Mexico.—Jill Wheeler.

JOHN F. KENNEDY CENTER FOR THE PERFORMING ARTS

2700 F Street, NW., 20566, phone (202) 416–8000, fax 416–8205

BOARD OF TRUSTEES

Honorary Chairs:

Mrs. Laura Bush
Senator Hillary Rodham Clinton
Mrs. George Bush
Mrs. Ronald Reagan
Mrs. Jimmy Carter
Mrs. Gerald R. Ford
Mrs. Lyndon B. Johnson

Officers:

Chairman.—Stephen A. Schwarzman.
President.—Michael M. Kaiser.
Secretary.—Jean Kennedy Smith.
Assistant Secretary.—Ann Stock.
Treasurer.—Roland Betts.
General Counsel.—Maria Kersten.

Members Appointed by the President of the United States:

Wilma E. Bernstein
Lois Phifer Betts
Elliott B. Broidy
Bo Derek
Betsy DeVos
Edward W. Easton
Stevie Eller
Emilo Estefan, Jr.
Melvyn J. Estrin
George Farias
David F. Girard-diCarlo
Albert B. Glickman
Roy Goodman
James A. Haslam II
Helen Lee Henderson
Anne Sewell Johnson
Sheldon B. Kamins
James V. Kimsey
Nancy G. Kinder
Kathi Koll
Marlene A. Malek
Norman Y. Mineta
Mary V. Mochary
Michael F. Neidorff
Jack L. Oliver III
Catherine B. Reynolds
Gabrielle B. Reynolds
Duane R. Roberts
David M. Rubenstein
Stephen A. Schwarzman
Jean Kennedy Smith
Dean A. Spanos
Catherine A. Stevens
Alexander F. Treadwell
Beatrice W. Welters
Stephen A. Wynn

Ex Officio Members Designated by Act of Congress:
(Note: The names of Senators and Representatives appear in order of their years of service)

Dr. Condoleezza Rice, Secretary of State.
Michael O. Leavitt, Secretary of Health and Human Services.
Margaret Spellings, Secretary of Education.
Edward M. Kennedy, Senator from Massachusetts.
James M. Inhofe, Senator from Oklahoma.
Kay Bailey Hutchison, Senator from Texas.
Harry Reid, Senator from Nevada.
Thad Cochran, Senator from Mississippi.
James L. Oberstar, Representative from Minnesota.
Patrick J. Kennedy, Representative from Rhode Island.
Deborah Pryce, Representative from Ohio.
Nancy Pelosi, Speaker of the U.S. House of Representatives from California.
John A. Boehner, Representative from Ohio.
John L. Mica, Representative from Florida.
Adrian M. Fenty, Mayor, District of Columbia.
Lawrence M. Small, Secretary, Smithsonian Institution.
James H. Billington, Librarian of Congress.
Earl A. Powell III, Chairman, Commission of Fine Arts.
Mary A. Bomar, Director, National Park Service.
Dr. Clifford Janey, Superintendent, DC Public Schools.

Honorary Trustees:

Buffy Cafritz
Kenneth M. Duberstein
James H. Evans
Alma Gildenhorn
Melvin R. Laird
Leonard L. Silverstein
Henry Strong

Senior Counsel.—Robert Barnett.
Founding Chairman.—Roger L. Stevens (deceased).
Chairmen Emeriti: James A. Johnson, James D. Wolfensohn.

LEGAL SERVICES CORPORATION

3333 K Street, NW., 3rd Floor, 20007–3522

phone (202) 295–1500, fax 337–6386

BOARD OF DIRECTORS

Frank B. Strickland, *Chair*
Lillian R. BeVier, *Vice Chair*
Jonann Chiles
Robert J. Dieter
Thomas A. Fuentes
Herbert S. Garten
David Hall
Michael D. McKay
Thomas R. Meites
Bernice Phillips
Sarah Singleton

President.—Helaine M. Barnett.
Vice President for Programs and Compliance.—Karen Sarjeant.
Vice President, Legal Affairs, General Counsel and Corporate Secretary.—Victor M. Fortuno.
Chief Administrative Officer.—Charles Jeffress.
Inspector General.—Kirt West.

NATIONAL AERONAUTICS AND SPACE ADMINISTRATION

300 E Street, SW., 20546, phone (202) 358–0000, http://www.nasa.gov

OFFICE OF THE ADMINISTRATOR

Code AA000, Room 9F44, phone 358–1010

Administrator.—Michael Griffin.
Deputy Administrator.—Shana Dale, 358–1020.
Executive Assistants: Kia Burnette, 358–1827; Kathryn Manuel, 358–1020.
Chief of Staff.—Paul Morrell, 358–1827.
White House Liaison.—J.T. Jezierski, 358–2198.
Chief Health and Medical Officer.—Dr. Richard S. Williams, room 7P13, 358–2390.

AERONAUTICS RESEARCH MISSION DIRECTORATE

Code EA000, Room 6J39–A, phone 358–4600

Associate Administrator.—Lisa J. Porter.
Deputy Associate Administrator.—Dr. Jaiwon Shin.

OFFICE OF THE CHIEF FINANCIAL OFFICER (CFO)

Code 1A000, Room 8E39–A, phone 358–0978

Chief Financial Officer/Chief Acquisition Officer.—Gwendolyn Sykes.
Deputy Chief Financial Officer.—Terry Bowie, 358–1135.

OFFICE OF DIVERSITY AND EQUAL OPPORTUNITY PROGRAMS

Code LF000, Room 4Y23, phone 358–2167

Assistant Administrator for Equal Opportunity Programs.—Brenda R. Manuel.

EXPLORATION SYSTEMS MISSION DIRECTORATE

Code BA000, Room 2U39, phone 358–1523

Associate Administrator.—Dr. Scott Horowitz, 358–7246.
Deputy Associate Administrator.—Douglas Cooke, 358–1523.
Deputy Associate Administrator for Policy and Plans.—Tom Cremins, 358–1747.

OFFICE OF EXTERNAL RELATIONS

Code ND000, Room 7V39, phone 358–0400

Assistant Administrator.—Michael F. O'Brien.
Deputy Assistant Administrator.—Al Condes.

OFFICE OF THE GENERAL COUNSEL

Code MA000, Room 9V39, phone 358–2450

General Counsel.—Michael Wholley.
Deputy General Counsel.—Keith T. Sefton.

OFFICE OF HUMAN CAPITAL MANAGEMENT

Code LE000–A, Room 4V84, phone 358–0520

Assistant Administrator.—Tony Dawsey.

OFFICE OF INFRASTRUCTURE AND ADMINISTRATION

Code LD000, Room 4G74, phone 358–2800

Deputy Assistant Administrator.—Olga Dominguez.
Deputy Assistant Administrator for—
Headquarters Operations.—Christopher Jedrey.
Policy.—Jeffrey Parker.

OFFICE OF INSPECTOR GENERAL

Code W, Room 8U79, phone 358–1220

Inspector General.—Robert W. Cobb.
Deputy Inspector General.—Thomas Howard.

OFFICE OF LEGISLATIVE AFFAIRS

Code NC000, Room 9L39, phone 358–1948

Assistant Administrator.—Brian E. Chase.
Deputy Assistant Administrator.—Mary D. Kerwin.

OFFICE OF PROCUREMENT

Code LH000, Room 5G70, phone 358–2090

Assistant Administrator.—Thomas S. Luedtke.

OFFICE OF PUBLIC AFFAIRS

Code NB000, Room 9P39, phone 358–1400

Assistant Administrator.—David Mould.

SAFETY AND MISSION ASSURANCE

Code GA000, Room 5W21, phone 358–2406

Chief Officer.—Bryan D. O'Connor.
Deputy Chief Officer.—James D. Lloyd.

SCIENCE MISSION DIRECTORATE

Code DA000, room 3C26, phone 358–3889

Associate Administrator.—Mary L. Cleave.
Deputy Associate Administrator.—Colleen Hartman, 358–2165.
Deputy Associate Administrator for—
Programs.—Michael R. Luther, 358–0260.
Technology.—George Komar, 358–3000.
Chief Engineer.—Kenneth Ledbetter, 358–7245.
Chief Scientist.—Paul Hertz, 358–2470.

OFFICE OF SECURITY AND PROGRAM PROTECTION

Code LG000, Room 9U70, phone 358–2010

Associate Administrator.—David Saleeba.

Deputy Associate Administrator.—Clint Herbert.

OFFICE OF SMALL AND DISADVANTAGED BUSINESS UTILIZATION

Code LI000, Room 5C39, phone 358–2088

Assistant Administrator.—Glenn A. Delgado.

SPACE OPERATIONS MISSION DIRECTORATE

Code CA000, Room 7K39, phone 358–2015

Associate Administrator.—William H. Gerstenmayer.
Deputy Associate Administrator.—Lynn F.H. Cline, 358–1200.
Deputy Associate Administrator for—
Program Integration.—Dr. William Michael Hawes, 358–0104.
Space Shuttle.—William C. Hill, 358–0571.

NASA NATIONAL OFFICES

Air Force Space Command/XPX (NASA): Peterson Air Force Base, CO 80914.
NASA Senior Representative.—Jeffrey Ashby (719) 554–4900.
Ames Research Center: Moffett Field, CA 94035.
Director.—Simon P. Worden (650) 604–5000.
Dryden Flight Research Center: P.O. Box 273, Edwards, CA 93523.
Director.—Kevin L. Petersen (661) 276–3311.
Glenn Research Center at Lewisfield: 21000 Brookpark Road, Cleveland, OH 44135.
Director.—Dr. Woodrow Whitlow (216) 433–4000.
Goddard Institute for Space Studies: Goddard Space Flight Center, 2880 Broadway, New York, NY 10025.
Head.—Dr. James E. Hansen (212) 678–5500.
Goddard Space Flight Center: 8800 Greenbelt Road, Greenbelt, MD 20771.
Director.—Dr. Ed Weiler (301) 286–2000.
Jet Propulsion Laboratory: 4800 Oak Grove Drive, Pasadena, CA 91109.
Director.—Dr. Charles Elachi (818) 354–4321.
Lyndon B. Johnson Space Center: Houston, TX 77058–3696.
Director.—Michael L. Coats (281) 483–0123.
John F. Kennedy Space Center: Kennedy Space Center, FL 32899.
Director.—James W. Kennedy (321) 867–5000.
Langley Research Center: Hampton, VA 23681.
Director.—Lesa Roe (757) 864–1000.
George C. Marshall Space Flight Center: Marshall Space Flight Center, AL 35812.
Director.—David A. King (256) 544–2121.
Michoud Assembly Facility: P.O. Box 29300, New Orleans, LA 70189.
Manager.—John K. White (504) 257–3311.
NASA IV & V Facility: NASA Independent Verification and Validation Facility, 100 University Drive, Fairmont, WV 26554.
Director.—Nelson H. Keeler (304) 367–8200.
NASA Management Office: Jet Propulsion Laboratory, 4800 Oak Grove Drive, Pasadena, CA 91109.
Director.—Dr. Robert A. Parker (818) 354–5359.
John C. Stennis Space Center: Stennis Space Center, MS 39529.
Director.—Dr. Richard Gilbrech (228) 688–2211.
Vandenberg AFB: P.O. Box 425, Lompoc, CA 93438.
Manager.—Ted L. Oglesby (805) 866–5859.
Wallops Flight Facility: Goddard Space Flight Center, Wallops Island, VA 23337.
Director.—John Campbell (757) 824–1000.
White Sands Test Facility: Johnson Space Center, P.O. Drawer MM, Las Cruces, NM 88004.
Manager.—Joseph Fries (505) 524–5771.

NASA OVERSEAS REPRESENTATIVES

Australia: APO AP 96549, 011–61–2–6281–8501.
Europe: U.S. Embassy, Paris, PSC 116 APO AE 09777, 011–33–1–4312–2100.
NASA Representative.—Don Miller.

Japan: U.S. Embassy, Tokyo, Unit 45004, Box 235, APO AP, 96337–5004, 011–81–3–3224–5827.
NASA Representative.—William Jordan.
Russia: U.S. Embassy, Moscow, PSC 77/NASA APO AE 09721, (256) 961–6333.
NASA Representative.—Phillip Cleary.
Spain: PSC No. 61, Box 0037, APO AE 09642, 011–34–91–548–9250.

NATIONAL ARCHIVES AND RECORDS ADMINISTRATION

700 Pennsylvania Avenue, NW., 20408–0001

8601 Adelphi Road, College Park, MD 20740–6001
http://www.nara.gov

[Created by Public Law 98–497]

Archivist of the United States.—Dr. Allen Weinstein (202) 357–5900, fax 357–5901.
Deputy Archivist of the United States/Chief of Staff.—Lewis J. Bellardo (301) 837–1600, fax 837–3218.
Assistant Archivist, Office of:
Administration.—Adrienne C. Thomas (301) 837–3050, fax 837–3217.
Federal Register.—Raymond A. Mosely (202) 741–6010, fax 741–6012.
Information Services.—Martha Morphy (301) 837–3670, fax 837–3213.
Presidential Libraries.—Sharon Fawcett (301) 837–3250, fax 837–3199.
Records Services, Washington, DC.—Michael J. Kurtz (301) 837–3110, fax 837–1617.
Regional Records Services.—Thomas Mills (301) 837–2950, fax 837–1617.
Executive Director, National Historical Publications and Records Commission.—Max J. Evans (202) 501–5010, fax 357–5914.
Director for—
Congressional Affairs and Communications Staff.—John A. Constance (202) 357–5100, fax 357–5959.
Equal Employment Opportunity and Diversity Programs.—Robert Jew (301) 837–1849, fax 837–0869.
Information Security Oversight Office.—J. William Leonard (202) 357–5250, fax 357–5907.
Policy and Planning Staff.—Susan Ashtianie (301) 837–1850, fax 837–0319.
General Counsel.—Gary M. Stern (301) 837–1750, fax 837–0293.
Inspector General.—Paul Brachfeld (301) 837–3000, fax 837–3197.

ADMINISTRATIVE COMMITTEE OF THE FEDERAL REGISTER

800 North Capitol Street, NW., Suite 700, 20002, phone (202) 741–6000

Members:
Dr. Allen Weinstein, Archivist of the United States, *Chair.*
Rosemary Hart, Senior Counsel, Department of Justice.
Secretary.—Raymond A. Mosley, Director of the Federal Register, National Archives and Records Administration.

NATIONAL ARCHIVES TRUST FUND BOARD

phone (301) 837–3550, fax 837–3191

Members:
Kenneth Carfine, National Endowment for the Humanities, *Chair.*
Bruce Cole, Chairman, National Endowment for the Humanities.
Donald V. Hammond, Fiscal Assistant Secretary, Department of the Treasury.
Secretary.—Lawrence Post.

NATIONAL HISTORICAL PUBLICATIONS AND RECORDS COMMISSION

700 Pennsylvania Avenue, NW., 20408

phone (202) 357–5010, fax 357–5914

http://www.archives.gov/nhprc

Members:

Dr. Allen Weinstein, Archivist of the United States, Chairman, National Archives and Records Administration.

Barbara Jacobs Rothstein, Director, Federal Judicial Center, Judicial Branch.

Christopher J. Dodd, Senator of Connecticut.

Tom Cole, Representative of Oklahoma.

Daron R. Shaw, Associate Professor, Government Department, University of Texas at Austin, Presidential Appointee.

Nancy Davenport, President, Nancy Davenport & Associates, LLC, Presidential Appointee.

Alfred Goldberg, Historian, Office of the Secretary, Department of Defense.

Deanna Marcum, Associate Librarian for Library Services, Library of Congress.

Margaret P. Grafeld, Director, Office of Information Programs and Services, Department of State.

Charles T. Cullen, President/Librarian Emeritus, Newberry Library, Association for Documentary Editing.

J. Kevin Graffagnino, Executive Director, Vermont Historical Society, American Association for State and Local History.

Stanley N. Katz, Lecturer with the rank of Professor, Director, Center for Arts and Cultural Policy Studies, Woodrow Wilson School, Princeton University, American Historical Association.

Timothy A. Slavin, Director, Delaware Division of Historical and Cultural Affairs, National Association of Government Archives and Records Administrators.

Barbara Fields, Professor of History, Columbia University, Organization of American Historians.

Lee Stout, Head, Public Services and Outreach, Eberly Family Special Collections Library, Penn State University, Society of American Archivists.

Executive Director.—Max J. Evans (202) 501–5610.

REGIONAL OFFICES

Central Plains Region: *Regional Director.*—R. Reed Whitaker (816) 268–8031.

Central Plains Region.—2312 East Bannister Road, Kansas City, MO 64131 (816) 268–8026.

Great Lakes Region: *Regional Director.*—David E. Kuehl (773) 948–9011.

Chicago.—7358 South Pulaski Road, Chicago, IL 60629 (773) 948–9007.

Dayton.—3150 Springboro Road, Dayton, OH 45439 (937) 425–0605.

Mid Atlantic Region: *Regional Director.*—V. Chapman Smith (215) 606–0102.

Center City Philadelphia.—900 Market Street, Philadelphia, PA, 19107 (215) 606–2100.

Northeast Philadelphia.—14700 Townsend Road, Philadelphia, PA 19154 (215) 305–2000.

Northeast Region: *Regional Director.*—Diane LeBlanc (781) 663–0133.

Boston.—380 Trapelo Road, Waltham, MA 02452–6399 (781) 663–0130.

Pittsfield.—10 Conte Drive, Pittsfield, MA 01201–8230 (413) 236–3600.

New York City.—201 Varick St., New York, NY 10014–4811 (212) 401–1620.

Pacific Alaska Region: *Regional Director.*—Steven M. Edwards, (206) 336–5140.

Seattle.—6125 Sand Point Way NE, Seattle, WA 98115 (206) 336–5143.

Anchorage.—654 West Third Avenue, Anchorage, AK 99501 (907) 261–7810.

Pacific Region: *Director.*—Shirley J. Burton (650) 238–3504.

San Francisco.—1000 Commodore Drive, San Bruno, CA 94066 (650) 238–2471.

Rocky Mountain Region: *Regional Director.*—Barbara Voss (303) 407–5701.

Rocky Mountain Region.—Building 48, Denver Federal Center, Denver, CO 80225 (303) 407–5703.

Southeast Region: *Regional Director.*—James McSweeney (707) 968–2505.

Southeast Region.—4712 Southpark Boulevard, Ellenwood, GA 30294.

Southwest Region: *Regional Director.*—Preston Huff (817) 831–5627.

Southwest Region.—501 W. Felix Street, Ft. Worth, TX 76115 (817) 831–5904.

National Personnel Records Center: *Director.*—Ronald L. Hindman (314) 801–0574.

National Personnel Records Center.—9700 Page Avenue, St. Louis, MO 63132 (314) 801–9221.

Presidential Libraries.—Sharon K. Fawcett (301) 837–3250, fax (301) 837–3199.

Director for—

Herbert Hoover Library.—Timothy G. Walch, West Branch, IA 52358–0488 (319) 643–5301.

Franklin D. Roosevelt Library.—Cynthia M. Koch, Hyde Park, NY 12538–1999 (845) 486–7770.

Harry S. Truman Library.—Michael Devine, Independence, MO 64050–1798 (816) 268–8200.

Dwight D. Eisenhower Library.—Daniel D. Holt, Abilene, KS 67410–2900 (785) 263–4751.

John F. Kennedy Library.—Thomas Putnam, Boston, MA 02125–3398 (617) 514–1600.
Lyndon Baines Johnson Library.—Betty Sue Flowers, Austin, TX 78705–5702 (512) 721–0200.
Nixon Presidential Materials Staff.—Timothy Naftali, Yorba Linda, CA 92886 (714) 981–9121.
Gerald R. Ford Library.—Elaine K. Didier, Ann Arbor, MI 48109–2114 (734) 205–0555.
Gerald R. Ford Museum.—Elaine K. Didier, Grand Rapids, MI 49504–5353 (616) 254–0400.
Jimmy Carter Library.—Jay E. Hakes, Atlanta, GA 30307–1498 (404) 865–7100.
Ronald Reagan Library.—R. Duke Blackwood, Simi Valley, CA 93065–0699 (800) 410–8354.
George Bush Library.—Warren Finch, College Station, TX 77845 (979) 691–4000.
William J. Clinton Library.—David E. Alsobrook, Little Rock, AR 72201 (501) 244–2887.

NATIONAL CAPITAL PLANNING COMMISSION

401 9th Street, NW., North Lobby, Suite 500, 20004, phone (202) 482–7200
fax 482–7272

APPOINTIVE MEMBERS

Presidential Appointees:
John V. Cogbill III, *Chair.*
Herbert F. Ames.
José L. Galvez III.
Mayoral Appointees:
Arrington Dixon.
Stacie S. Turner.
Ex Officio Members:
Dr. Robert M. Gates, Secretary of Defense.
First Alternate.—Michael B. Donley.
Second Alternate.—Ralph E. Newton.
Dirk Kempthorne, Secretary of the Interior.
First Alternate.—Mary A. Bomar.
Third Alternate.—Joseph M. Lawler.
Fourth Alternate.—John G. Parsons.
Lurita Alexis Doan, Administrator of General Services.
First Alternate.—Ann W. Everett.
Third Alternate.—William J. Guerin.
Fourth Alternate.—Michael S. McGill.
Joseph I. Lieberman, Chairman, Senate Committee on Homeland Security and Governmental Affairs.
Alternate.—Donny R. Williams.
Henry A. Waxman, Chairman, House Committee on Oversight and Government Reform.
First Alternate.—Mark Stephenson.
Second Alternate.—Michelle Ash.
Third Alternate.—Denise Wilson.
Adrian M. Fenty, Mayor of the District of Columbia.
First Alternate.—Harriet Tregoning.
Second Alternate.—Jennifer Steingasser.
Third Alternate.—Charles Graves.
Vincent C. Gray, Chairman, Council of the District of Columbia.
First Alternate.—Robert E. Miller, Esq.
Second Alternate.—Christopher Murray.

EXECUTIVE STAFF

Executive Director.—Patricia E. Gallagher, 482–7212.
Deputy Executive Director.—Marcel C. Acosta, 482–7221.
Chief Operating Officer.—Barry S. Socks, 482–7209.
Secretariat.—Deborah B. Young, 482–7228.
General Counsel.—Lois Schiffer, 482–7223.
Director, Office of:
Administration.—C. Jody Rieder (acting), 482–7255.

Plan and Project Implementation.—William G. Dowd, 482–7240.
Planning Research and Policy.—Julia A. Koster, 482–7211.
Public Affairs.—Lisa N. MacSpadden, 482–7263.
Technology Development and Applications.—Michael Sherman, 482–7254.
Urban Design and Plan Review.—Christine L. Saum, 482–7245.

NATIONAL COMMISSION ON LIBRARIES AND INFORMATION SCIENCE

1800 M Street, NW., Suite 350, North Tower 20036–5841

phone (202) 606–9200, fax 606–9203, http://www.nclis.gov

[Created by Public Law 91–345]

Chair.—Beth Fitzsimmons, Ph.D., Ann Arbor, MI.
Vice Chair.—Bridget L. Lamont, Springfield, IL.
Members:
José A. Aponte, San Diego, CA.
Sandra F. Ashworth, Bonners Ferry, ID.
Edward L. Bertorelli, Boston, MA.
James H. Billington, Ph.D., Librarian of Congress, Washington, DC. (Ex-officio)
Serves for the Librarian of Congress:
Deanna Marcum, Ph.D., The Library of Congress, Washington, DC.
Jan Cellucci, Hudson, MA.
Carol L. Diehl, Neenah, WI.
Allison Druin, Ph.D., College Park, MD.
Patricia M. Hines, Mayesville, SC.
Colleen E. Huebner, Ph.D., Seattle, WA.
Stephen M. Kennedy, Concord, NH.
Anne-Imelda Radice, Ph.D., Director, Institute of Museum and Library Services, Washington, DC. (Ex-officio)
Mary H. Perdue, Salisbury, MD.
Diane Rivers, Ph.D., Brimingham, AL.
Herman L. Totten, Ph.D., Denton, TX.
Chairpersons Emeritus:
Charles Benton.
Frederick Burkhardt.
Elinor M. Hashim.
Jerald C. Newman.
Charles E. Reid.

EXECUTIVE STAFF

Director of Operations.—Madeleine C. McCain.
Director, Statistics and Surveys.—Neal K. Kaske.
Special Assistant, Technical.—Kim Miller.
Management Operations Analyst.—Joe Dyer.

NATIONAL COUNCIL ON DISABILITY

1331 F Street, NW., Suite 850, 20004, phone (202) 272–2004, fax 272–2022

Chairperson.—John R. Vaughn, Fort Myers, FL.
First Vice Chairperson.—Patricia Pound, Austin, TX.
Second Vice Chairperson.—Glenn Anderson, Ph.D., Little Rock, AR.
Members:
Milton Aponte, J.D., Cooper City, FL.
Victoria Ray Carlson, Naperville, IN.
Chad Colley, New Smyrna Beach, FL.
Robert R. Davila, Ph.D., New Market, MD.
Barbara Gillcrist, Santa Fe, NM.
Graham Hill, Arlington, VA.
Young Woo Kang, Ph.D., Springfield, VA.
Kathleen Martinez, Oakland, CA.
Lisa Mattheiss, East Ridge, TN.
Anne Rader, McLean, VA.
Marco Rodriguez, Elk Grove, CA.
Linda Wetters, Columbus, OH.

NATIONAL CREDIT UNION ADMINISTRATION

1775 Duke Street, Alexandria, VA 22314–3428, phone (703) 518–6300, fax 518–6319

Chairman.—JoAnn Johnson.
Vice Chairman.—Rodney E. Hood.
Board Member.—Christiane Gigi Hyland.
Secretary to the Board.—Mary Rupp.
Executive Director.—J. Leonard Skiles, 518–6320, fax 518–6661.
Deputy Executive Director.—Jane Walters, 518–6322.
Deputy Director Inspector General.—William DeSarno, 518–6350.
Director, Office of:
Capital Markets and Planning.—Owen Cole, 518–6620, fax 518–6663.
Chief Financial Officer.—Dennis Winans, 518–6570, fax 518–6664.
Chief Information Officer.—Doug Verner, 518–6440, fax 518–6669.
Corporate Credit Unions.—Kent Buckham, 518–6640, fax 518–6665.
EEO.—Chrisanthy Loizos, 518–6325.
Examination and Insurance.—David M. Marquis, 518–6360, fax 518–6666.
General Counsel.—Robert M. Fenner, 518–6540, fax 518–6667.
Deputy General Counsel.—Michael McKenna.
Human Resources.—Kathy Sachen-Gute, 518–6510, fax 518–6668.
Public and Congressional Affairs.—John J. McKechnie III, 518–6330.
Small Credit Union Initiatives.—Tawana James, 518–6610.

REGIONAL OFFICES

Director, Office of:
Region I (Albany).—Mark A. Treichel, 9 Washington Square, Washington Avenue Extension, Albany, NY 12205 (518) 862–7400, fax 862–7420.
Region II (National Capital Region).—Edward Dupcak, 1775 Duke Street, Suite 4206, Alexandria, VA 22314 (703) 519–4600, fax 519–4620.
Region III (Atlanta).—Alonzo A. Swann III, 7000 Central Parkway, Suite 1600, Atlanta, GA 30328 (678) 443–3000, fax 443–3020.
Region IV (Austin).—Jane Walters, 4807 Spicewood Springs Road, Suite 5200, Austin, TX 78759–8490 (512) 342–5600, fax 342–5620.
Region V (Tempe).—Melinda Love, 1230 West Washington Street, Suite 301, Tempe, AZ 85281 (602) 302–6000, fax 302–6024.
President, Asset Management and Assistance Center (Austin).—Mike Barton, 4807 Spicewood Springs Road, Suite 5100, Austin, TX 78759–8490 (512) 231–7900, fax 231–7920.

NATIONAL FOUNDATION ON THE ARTS AND THE HUMANITIES

Old Post Office Building, 1100 Pennsylvania Avenue, NW., 20506

NATIONAL ENDOWMENT FOR THE ARTS

http://www.arts.gov

Chairman.—Dana Gioia (202) 682–5414.
Senior Deputy Chairman.—Eileen B. Mason, 682–5415.
Deputy Chairman for—
Grants and Awards.—Tony Chauveaux, 682–5441.
Management and Budget.—Laurence Baden, 682–5408.
Director of:
Communication.—Felicia Knight, 682–5570.
Development.—John Hewett, 682–5681.
Government Affairs (Congressional/White House/Federal and International Partnerships).—Ann Guthrie Hingston, 682–5434.
Research and Analysis.—Sunil Iyengar, 682–5654.
General Counsel.—Karen Elias (acting), 682–5654.
Inspector General.—Daniel Shaw, 682–5402.

THE NATIONAL COUNCIL ON THE ARTS

Chairman.—Dana Gioia.

Council Operations Director.—Michael Faubion (202) 682–5713.

Members:

James K. Ballinger
Ben Donenberg
Makoto Fujimura
David H. Gelernter
Chico Hamilton
Mark Hofflund
Joan Israelite
Charlotte Power Kessler
Bret Lott
Jerry Pinkney
Frank Price
Gerard Schwarz
Terry Teachout
Karen Lias Wolff

Ex Officio Members:
(Not yet appointed for 110th Congress)

NATIONAL ENDOWMENT FOR THE HUMANITIES

phone (202) 606–8400, info@neh.gov, http://www.neh.gov

Chairman.—Bruce Cole, 606–8310.
Deputy Chairman.—Thomas Lindsay, 606–8273.
Communications.—Elissa Pruett, 606–8446.
Congressional Affairs.—Brian Lee, 606–8328.
General Counsel.—Heather Gottry (acting), 606–8322.
Inspector General.—Sheldon L. Bernstein, 606–8350.
Public Affairs.—Noel Milan, 606–8446.
Public Information Officer.—Joy Evans, 606–8446.
Strategic Planning.—Larry Myers, 606–8428.

NATIONAL COUNCIL ON THE HUMANITIES

Members:

Herman Belz
Jewel Spears Brooker
Josiah Bunting III
Celeste Colgan
Jane Marie "Jamie" Doggett
Jean Bethke Elshtain
Dario Fernandez-Morera
Elizabeth Fox-Genovese
Allen Guelzo
Mary Habeck
Craig Haffner
James Davison Hunter
Tamar Jacoby
Harvey Klehr
Iris Cornelia Love
Robert Martin
Wilfred McClay
Lawrence Okamura
Manfredi Piccolomini
Ricardo J. Quinones
Marguerite Sullivan
Stephan Thernstrom
Kenneth R. Weinstein
Jay Winik

FEDERAL COUNCIL ON THE ARTS AND THE HUMANITIES

Federal Council Members:

Dana Gioia, Chairman, National Endowment for the Arts.
Bruce Cole, Chairman, National Endowment for the Humanities.
Arden L. Bement, Jr., Director, National Science Foundation.
David Bibb (acting), Administrator, General Services Administration.
James H. Billington, Librarian of Congress, Library of Congress.
Elaine L. Chao, Secretary, Department of Labor.
Carlos M. Gutierrez, Secretary, Department of Commerce.
Alphonso Jackson, Secretary, Department of Housing and Urban Development.
Dirk Kempthorne, Secretary, Department of the Interior.
Michael Leavitt, Secretary, Department of Health and Human Services.
Thomas Luebke, Chairman, Commission of Fine Arts.
Norman Y. Mineta, Secretary, Department of Transportation.
R. James Nicholson, Secretary, Department of Veterans Affairs.
Earl A. Powell III, Director, National Gallery of Art.
Anne-Imelda M. Radice Ph.D., Director, Institute for Museum and Library Services.
Emily Reynolds, Secretary of the Senate.
Lawrence M. Small, Secretary, Smithsonian Institution.
Margaret Spellings, Secretary, Department of Education.
Fortney Pete Stark, Member, U.S. House of Representatives.
Allen Weinstein, Archivist of the United States, National Archives and Records Administration.
Staff Contact.—Alice M. Whelihan, Indemnity Administrator, National Endowment for the Arts, 682–5574.

INSTITUTE OF MUSEUM AND LIBRARY SERVICES

phone (202) 653–4657, fax 653–4625, http://www.imls.gov

[The Institute of Museum and Library Services was created by the Museum and Library Services Act of 1996, Public Law 104–208]

Director.—Anne-Imelda M. Radice, Ph.D., 653–4746.
Chief of Staff.—Kate Fernstrom, 653–4643.
Deputy Director for—
Library Services.—Mary Chute, 653–4700.
Museum Services.—Marsha Semmel, 653–4789.
Policy, Planning, Research and Communications.—Mamie Bittner, 653–4757.
Associate Deputy Director for—
Library Services.—Joyce Ray, Ph.D., 653–4700.
Museum Services.—Mary Estelle Kennelly, 653–4789.
State Programs.—George Smith, 653–4650.
Counselors to the Director: Schroeder Cherry, Ed.D., 653–4670; Carol Scannelli, 543–4744.
Chief Financial Officer.—Wayne Morlier, 653–4604.
General Counsel.—Nancy Weiss, 653–4787.

NATIONAL MUSEUM AND LIBRARY SERVICES BOARD

Members:
Beverly E. Allen
Katherine M.B. Berger
Karen Brosius
John E. Buchanan, Jr.
Mary Chute
Gail M. Daly
Beth Fitzsimmons, Ph.D.
A. Wilson Greene
Peter Hero
Donald S. Leslie
Ioannis N. Miaoulis
Christina Orr-Cahall
Amy Owen
Sandra Pickett
Anne-Imelda M. Radice, Ph.D.
Judith Ann Rapanos
Edwin Rigaud
Harry Robinson, Jr.
Margaret Webster Scarlett
Marsha Semmel
Kevin Starr
Katina Strauch
Renee Becker Swartz
Kim Wang

NATIONAL GALLERY OF ART

Sixth Street and Constitution Avenue, NW., 20565

phone (202) 737–4215, http://www.nga.gov

[Under the direction of the Board of Trustees of the National Gallery of Art]

BOARD OF TRUSTEES

General Trustees:
John C. Fontaine, Chairman.
Victoria P. Sant, President.
Mitchell P. Rales.
Sharon Percy Rockefeller.
John Wilmerding.
Trustees Emeriti:
Robert F. Erburu.
Julian Ganz, Jr.
Alexander Laughlin.
David O. Maxwell.
Robert H. Smith.
Ruth Carter Stevenson.
Ex Officio Trustees:
John G. Roberts, Jr., Chief Justice of the United States.
Condoleezza Rice, Secretary of State.
Henry M. Paulson, Jr., Secretary of the Treasury.
Lawrence M. Small, Secretary of the Smithsonian Institution.
Director.—Earl A. Powell III.
Deputy Director.—Alan Shestack.
Dean, Center for Advanced Study in the Visual Arts.—Elizabeth Cropper.
Administrator.—Darrell Willson.
Treasurer.—James E. Duff.

Secretary-General Counsel.—Elizabeth A. Croog.
External Affairs Officer.—Joseph J. Krakora.

NATIONAL LABOR RELATIONS BOARD
1099 14th Street, NW., 20570–0001
Personnel Locator (202) 273–1000

Chairman.—Robert J. Battista, 273–1770, fax 273–4270.
Chief Counsel.—Harold Datz.
Deputy Chief Counsel.—Kathleen Nixon.
Members:
Wilma B. Liebman, 273–1700.
Chief Counsel.—John F. Colwell.
Deputy Chief Counsel.—Gary W. Shinners.
Peter C. Schaumber, 273–1790.
Chief Counsel.—Terence Flynn.
Deputy Chief Counsel.—Robert F. Kane.
Peter N. Kirsanow, 273–1070.
Chief Counsel.—Peter Carlton.
Deputy Chief Counsel.—David P. Martin.
Dennis P. Walsh, 273–1740.
Chief Counsel.—Peter Winkler (acting).
Deputy Chief Counsel.—Jonathan Scheinbart.
Executive Secretary.—Lester A. Heltzer, 273–1940, fax 273–4270.
Deputy Executive Secretary.—David B. Parker, 272–2000.
Associate Executive Secretaries: Henry S. Breiteneicher, 273–2917; Richard D. Hardick, 273–1935; Margaret H. Rafferty, 273–1937.
Solicitor.—William B. Cowen, 273–2914, fax 273–1962.
Inspector General.—Jane E. Altenhofen, 273–1960, fax 273–2344.
Director, Representation Appeals.—Lafe E. Solomon, 273–1975, fax 273–1962.
Associate Director, Division of Information.—Patricia M. Gilbert, 273–1991, fax 273–1789.
General Counsel.—Ronald E. Meisburg, 273–3700, fax 273–4483.
Deputy General Counsel.—John E. Higgins, Jr.

DIVISION OF JUDGES

Chief Administrative Law Judge.—Robert A. Giannasi, 501–8800, fax 501–8686.
Deputy Chief Administrative Law Judge.—Richard Miserendino, 501–8800.
Associate Chief Administrative Law Judges:
Joel P. Biblowitz, 120 West 45th Street, 11th Floor, New York, NY 10036–5503 (212) 944–2943, fax 944–4904.
William N. Cates, 401 West Peachtree Street, NW., Atlanta, GA 30308–3510 (404) 331–6654, fax 331–2061.
Mary Miller Cracraft, 901 Market Street, Suite 300, San Francisco, CA 94103–1779 (415) 356–5255, fax 356–5254.
Director, Office of Appeals.—Yvonne T. Dixon, 273–3760, 273–4283.
Deputy Director.—Deborah M.P. Yaffe.
Director, Division of Administration.—Gloria J. Joseph, 273–3890, fax 273–4266.
Deputy Director.—Frank V. Battle.

DIVISION OF OPERATIONS MANAGEMENT

Associate General Counsel.—Richard Siegel, 273–2900, fax 273–4274.
Deputy Associate General Counsel.—Anne Purcell.
Assistant General Counsels: Joseph F. Frankl, 273–2893; Shelley S. Korch, 273–2889; Nelson Levin, 273–2893; James G. Paulsen, 273–2882.
Executive Assistant.—Carole K. Coleman, 273–2901.
Special Counsels: Elizabeth Bach, Joseph M. Davis, Jennifer S. Kovachich, Barry F. Smith, 273–2918, fax 273–0864.

DIVISION OF ADVICE

Associate General Counsel.—Barry J. Kearney, 273–3800, fax 273–4275.

Deputy Associate General Counsel.—Ellen A. Farrell.
Assistant General Counsels:
Injunction Litigation Branch.—Judith I. Katz, 273–3812.
Regional Advice Branch.—David Colangelo, 273–3831.
Research and Policy Planning Branch.—Jacqueline A. Young, 273–3825.

DIVISION OF ENFORCEMENT LITIGATION

Associate General Counsel.—John H. Ferguson, 273–2950, fax 273–4244.
Appellate Court Branch:
Deputy Associate General Counsel.—Margery E. Lieber, 273–2950.
Assistant General Counsel.—Linda J. Dreeben, 273–2977.
Deputy Assistant General Counsels: Fred Cornell, 273–2993; Howard E. Perlstein, 273–2946.
Supreme Court Branch:
Assistant General Counsel.—Linda Dreeben, 273–2977, fax 273–4244.
Special Litigation Branch:
Assistant General Counsel.—Eric G. Moskowitz, 273–2930, fax 273–1799.
Deputy Assistant General Counsel.—Abby P. Simms, 273–2934.
Contempt Litigation and Compliance Branch:
Assistant General Counsel.—Stanley R. Zirkin, 273–3739, fax 273–4244.
Deputy Assistant General Counsels: Daniel F. Collopy, 273–3745; Kenneth J. Shapiro, 273–3741.

NATIONAL MEDIATION BOARD

1301 K Street, NW., Suite 250 East, 20005, phone (202) 692–5000, fax 692–5080

Chairman.—Elizabeth Dougherty, 692–5016.
Board Members: Harry Hoglander, 692–5022; Read Van de Water, 692–5019.
Director, Office of:
Administration.—June D.W. King, 692–5010.
Alternative Dispute Resolution Services.—Daniel Rainey, 692–5051.
Arbitration Services.—Roland Watkins, 692–5055.
Legal Affaris.—Mary L. Johnson, 692–5040.
Mediation Services.—Larry Gibbons, 692–5040.

NATIONAL RESEARCH COUNCIL—NATIONAL ACADEMY OF SCIENCES NATIONAL ACADEMY OF ENGINEERING—INSTITUTE OF MEDICINE

2101 Constitution Avenue, NW., 20418, phone (202) 334–2000

The National Research Council, National Academy of Sciences, National Academy of Engineering, and Institute of Medicine, serves as an independent adviser to the Federal Government on scientific and technical questions of national importance. Although operating under a congressional charter granted the National Academy of Sciences in 1863, the National Research Council and its three parent organizations are private organizations, not agencies of the Federal Government, and receive no appropriations from Congress.

NATIONAL RESEARCH COUNCIL

Chairman.—Ralph Cicerone, President, National Academy of Sciences, 334–2100.
Vice Chairman.—Wm. A. Wulf, President, National Academy of Engineering, 334–3200.
Executive Officer.—E. William Colglazier, 334–3000.
Director, Office of Congressional and Government Affairs.—James E. Jensen, 334–1601.

NATIONAL ACADEMY OF SCIENCES

President.—Ralph Cicerone, 334–2100.
Vice President.—Barbara Schaal, Washington University, St. Louis.
Home Secretary.—John I. Brauman, Stanford University.
Foreign Secretary.—M.T. Clegg, University of California, Irvine.
Treasurer.—Ronald L. Graham, University of California, San Diego.

Executive Officer.—E. William Colglazier, 334–3000.

NATIONAL ACADEMY OF ENGINEERING

President.—Wm. A. Wulf, 334–3200.
Chairman.—Craig R. Barrett (Ret.), Intel Corporation.
Vice President.—Maxine Savitz (Ret.), Honeywell, Inc.
Home Secretary.—W. Dale Compton, Purdue University.
Foreign Secretary.—George Bugliarello (Ret.), Polytechnic University.
Executive Officer.—Lance Davis, 334–3677.
Treasurer.—William L. Friend, National Labs.

INSTITUTE OF MEDICINE

President.—Harvey V. Fineberg, M.D., 334–3300.
Executive Officer.—Susanne Stoiber, 334–2177.

NATIONAL SCIENCE FOUNDATION

4201 Wilson Boulevard, Suite 1245, Arlington, VA 22230
phone (703) 292–8000, http://www.nsf.gov

Director.—Arden L. Bement, Jr.
Deputy Director.—Joseph Bordogna.
Inspector General.—Christine C. Boesz, 292–7100.
Equal Opportunity Coordinator.—Ronald D. Branch, 292–8020.
Director, Office of:
Legislative and Public Affairs.—Curt Suplee, 292–8070.
Integrative Activities.—Nathaniel G. Pitts, 292–8040.
Polar Programs.—Karl Erb, 292–8030.
General Counsel.—Lawrence Rudolph, 292–8060.
Assistant Director for—
Biological Sciences.—James Collins, 292–8400.
Computer and Information Science and Engineering.—Deborah L. Crawford (acting), 292–8900.
Education and Human Resources.—Donald Thompson (acting), 292–8300.
Engineering.—Richard Buckius, 292–8300.
Geosciences.—Jarvis Moyers (acting), 292–8500.
Mathematical and Physical Sciences.—Tony Chan, 292–8800.
Social, Behavorial, and Economic Sciences.—David W. Lightfoot, 292–8700.
Director, Office of:
Budget, Finance, and Award Management.—Thomas N. Cooley, 292–8200.
Information and Resource Management.—Anthony Arnolie, 292–8100.

NATIONAL SCIENCE BOARD

Chairman.—Steven C. Beering (703) 292–7000.
Vice Chairman.—Kathryn D. Sullivan.
Executive Officer.—Michael Crosby.

MEMBERS

Mark Abbott
Dan E. Arvizu
Barry C. Barish
Steven C. Beering
Camilla Bonbow
Ray M. Bowen
John Bruer
G. Wayne Clough
Kelvin K. Droegemier
Kenneth M. Ford
Patricia Galloway
Jose-Marie Griffiths
Daniel Hastings
Elizabeth Hoffman
Louis J. Lanzerotti
Alan I. Leshner
Douglas D. Randall
Arthur K. Reilly
Jon C. Strauss
Kathryn D. Sullivan
Thomas Taylor
Richard Thompson
JoAnne Vasquez

NATIONAL TRANSPORTATION SAFETY BOARD

490 L'Enfant Plaza, SW., 20594, phone (202) 314–6000

Chairman.—Mark V. Rosenker, 314–6035.

Vice Chairman.—Robert L. Sumwalt III, 314–6061.
Members:
Debbie Hersman, 314–6660.
Kathryn Higgins, 314–6145.
Steven Chealander, 314–6024.
Managing Director.—Joseph Osterman, 314–6690.
General Counsel.—Gary Halbert, 314–6616.
Chief Administrative Law Judge.—William W. Fowler, Jr., 314–6150.
Chief Financial Officer.—Steven Goldberg, 314–6212.
Director, Office of:
Aviation Safety.—Tom Haueter, 314–6302.
Government Affairs.—Brenda Yager, 314–6006.
Highway Safety.—Bruce Magladry, 314–6419.
Marine Safety.—Jack Spender, 314–6495.
Public Affairs.—Ted Lopatkiewicz, 314–6100.
Railroad, Pipeline and Hazardous Materials Investigations.—Bob Chipkevich, 314–6461.
Research and Engineering.—Vernon Ellingstad, 314–6501.
Safety Recommendations / Advocacy.—Elaine Weinstein, 314–6171.
Transportation Disaster Assistance.—Sharon Bryson, 314–6185.

NEIGHBORHOOD REINVESTMENT CORPORATION

(Doing business as NeighborWorks America)

1325 G Street, NW., Suite 800, 20005, phone (202) 220–2300, fax 376–2600

BOARD OF DIRECTORS

Chair.—Thomas J. Curry, Federal Deposit Insurance Corporation.
Vice Chair.—Rodney E. Hood, Vice Chairman, National Credit Union Administration.
Members:
John Dugan, Comptroller, Comptroller of the Currency.
Alphonso Jackson, Secretary, U.S. Department of Housing and Urban Development.
Randall S. Kroszner, Member, Board of Governors, Federal Reserve System.
John M. Reich, Director, Office of Thrift Supervision.
Chief Executive Director.—Kenneth D. Wade, 220–2410.
General Counsel / Secretary.—Jeffrey T. Bryson, 220–2372.
Chief Operating Officer.—Eileen Fitzgerald, 220–2452.
Treasurer.—Steven J. Tuminaro, 220–2415.
Director for—
Development and Communications.—Jeffrey Epremian, 220–2312.
Field Operations.—Robert Burns, 220–2313.
Finance and Administration.—Michael Forster, 223–2374.
Internal Audit.—Frederick Udochi, 220–2409.
Public Policy and Legislative Affairs.—Steven J. Tuminaro, 220–2415.
Training.—Paul Kealey, 220–2375.

NUCLEAR REGULATORY COMMISSION

Washington, DC 20555–0001, phone (301) 415–7000, http//www.nrc.gov

[Authorized by 42 U.S.C. 5801 and U.S.C. 1201]

OFFICE OF THE CHAIRMAN

Chairman.—Dale E. Klein, 415–1759.
Executive Assistant.—Paul T. Dickman.
Chief of Staff.—David L. Skeen, 415–1750.
Administration and Communications Assistant.—Robert B. McOsker, 415–1750.
Counsel.—Roger K. Davis, 415–1750.
Administrative Assistant.—Vicki M. Bolling, 415–1759.

COMMISSIONERS

Edward McGaffigan, Jr.—415–1800.
Executive Assistant.—Jeffry Sharkey.

Technical Assistant for Reactors.—James E. Beall.
Technical Assistant for Materials.—David Brown.
Legal Assistant.—David Cummings.
Special Assistant.—Linda D. Lewis.

Jeffrey S. Merrifield—415–1855.
Chief of Staff/Materials.—John Thoma.
Executive Assistant.—Spiros Droggitis.
Technical Assistants for Reactors.—Frank Akstulewicz.
Legal Counsel.—Sara Brock.
Administrative Assistants: Tojuana Fortune Grasty, Lorna Pini Kipfer.

Gregory B. Jaczko—415–1820.
Executive Assistant/Chief of Staff.—Josh Batkin.
Legal Assistant.—Angela Coggins.
Policy Advisor for Reactors.—Tom Hipschman.
Material Assistant.—Greg Hatchett.
Executive Administrative Assistant.—Jackie Raines.
Technical Administrative Assistant.—Carolyn Harves.

Peter B. Lyons—415–8420.
Executive Assistant.—Josie Piccone.
Technical Assistant for Reactors.—Douglas Coe.
Technical Assistant for Materials.—Steven Baggett.
Legal Assistant.—Catherine Marco.
Administrative Assistants: Carrie Crawford, Vicki Ibarra.

STAFF OFFICES OF THE COMMISSION

Secretary.—Annette L. Vietti-Cook, 415–1969, fax 415–1672.
Chief Financial Officer.—Jesse L. Funches, 415–7322, fax 415–4236.
Commission Appellate Adjudication.—John F. Cordes, 415–1600, fax 415–3200.
Congressional Affairs.—Rebecca L. Schmidt, 415–1776, fax 415–8571.
General Counsel.—Karen D. Cyr, 415–1743, fax 415–3086.
Information Services.—Edward T. Baker III, 415–8700, fax 415–4246.
Inspector General.—Hubert Bell, 415–5930, fax 415–5091.
International Programs.—Janice Dunn Lee, 415–1780, fax 415–2400.
Public Affairs.—Eliot B. Brenner, 415–8200, fax 415–2234.

ADVISORY COMMITTEE ON MEDICAL USES OF ISOTOPES

Committee Coordinator.—Ashley Tull, 415–5294.

ADVISORY COMMITTEE ON NUCLEAR WASTE

Chairman.—Michael T. Ryan.
Executive Director.— Frank P. Gillespie, 415–7360, fax 415–5589.

ADVISORY COMMITTEE ON REACTOR SAFEGUARDS

Chairman.—William J. Shack.
Executive Director.—Frank P. Gillespie, 415–7360, fax 415–5589.

ATOMIC SAFETY AND LICENSING BOARD PANEL

Chief Administrative Judge.—Roy E. Hawkens, 415–7454, fax 415–5599.

OFFICE OF THE EXECUTIVE DIRECTOR FOR OPERATIONS

Executive Director for Operations.—Luis A. Reyes, 415–1700, fax 415–2700.
Deputy Executive Director for—
Information Services and Administration/Chief Information Officer.—Jacqueline E. Silber, 415–7443, fax 415–2700.
Materials, Waste, Research, State, Tribal and Compliance Programs.—Martin J. Virgilio, 415–1705, fax 415–2700.

Reactor and Preparedness Programs.—William F. Kane, 415–1713, fax 415–2700.

Director, Office of:

Administration.—Timothy F. Hagan, 415–6222, fax 415–5400.

Enforcement.—Cynthia Carpenter, 415–2741, fax 415–3431.

Federal and State Materials and Environmental Management Programs.—Charles Miller, 415–7197, fax 415–5369.

Human Resources.—James F. McDermott, 415–7516, fax 415–5106.

Information Services.—Edward T. Baker III, 415–8700, fax 415–4246.

Investigations.—Guy P. Caputo, 415–2373, fax 415–2370.

New Reactors.—Richard William Borchardt, 415–1897, fax 415–2700.

Nuclear Material Safety and Safeguards.—Jack R. Strosnider, 415–7800, fax 415–5371.

Nuclear Reactor Regulation.—James E. Dyer, 415–1270, fax 415–8333.

Nuclear Regulatory Research.—Brian W. Sheron, 415–6641, fax 415–5153.

Nuclear Security and Incident Response.—Roy P. Zimmerman, 415–8003, fax 415–6382.

Small Business and Civil Rights.—Corenthis B. Kelley, 415–7380, fax 415–5953.

REGIONAL OFFICES

Region I: Samuel J. Collins, 475 Allendale Road, King of Prussia, PA 19406 (610) 337–5299, fax 337–5241.

Deputy Regional Administrator.—Marc L. Dapas, 337–5359.

Divisional Director for—

Nuclear Materials Safety.—Brain E. Holian, 337–5281.

Reactor Projects.—David C. Lew, 337–5229.

Reactor Safety.—A. Randolph Blough, 337–5126.

Region II: William D. Travers, 61 Forsyth Street SE, Atlanta, GA 30303 (404) 562–4410, fax 562–4766.

Deputy Regional Administrator for—

Construction.—Loren R. Plisco, 562–0540.

Operations.—Victor M. McCree, 562–4411.

Divisional Director for—

Fuel Facility Inspection.—Douglas M. Collins, 562–4700.

Reactor Projects.—Charles A. Casto, 562–4500.

Reactor Safety.—Joseph W. Shea, 562–4600.

Region III: James L. Caldwell, 2443 Warrensville Road, Suite 210, Lisle, IL 60532 (630) 829–9657, fax 515–1096.

Deputy Regional Administrator.—Geoffrey E. Grant, 829–9658.

Divisional Director for—

Nuclear Materials Safety.—Steve Reynolds, 829–9800.

Reactor Projects.—Mark A. Satorius, 829–9634.

Reactor Safety.—Cynthia D. Pederson, 829–9702.

Region IV: Bruce S. Mallett, Suite 400, 611 Ryan Plaza Drive, Arlington, TX 76011 (817) 860–8225, fax 860–8122.

Deputy Regional Administrator.—Thomas P. Gwynn, 860–8226.

Divisional Director for—

Nuclear Materials Safety.—Leonard S. Wert, 860–8106.

Reactor Projects.—Arthur T. Howell, 860–8248.

Reactor Safety.—Dwight D. Chamberlain, 860–8180.

OCCUPATIONAL SAFETY AND HEALTH REVIEW COMMISSION

1120 20th Street, NW., 20036–3457, phone (202) 606–5398

[Created by Public Law 91–596]

Chairman.—W. Scott Railton, 606–2082.

Commissioners: Thomasina V. Rogers, Horace A. Thompson, 606–5374.

Counsel to the Commissioner.—Richard L. Huberman.

Special Assistant and Counsel to the Chairman.—Richard C. Loeb.

Administrative Law Judges:

James Barkley, 1011 S. Valentia Street, Villa 113, Denver, CO 80231.

Marvin G. Bober, 1120 20th Street, NW., 9th Floor, Washington, DC 20036–3457.

Sidney Goldstein, 1880 Arapahoe Street, Number 2608, Denver, CO 80202–1858.

Benjamin Loye, 3810 Marshall Street, Wheat Ridge, CO 80033.

Covette Rooney, 1120 20th Street, NW., 9th Floor, Washington, DC 20036–3457.

John Schumacher, 1120 20th Street, NW., 9th Floor, Washington, DC 20036–3457.

Stephen J. Simko, 100 Alabama Street, SW., Building 1924, Room 2R90, Atlanta, GA 30303–3104.

Irving Sommer, 1951 Hopewood Drive, Falls Church, VA 22043.

Nancy L. Spies, 100 Alabama Street, SW., Building 1924, Room 2R90, Atlanta, GA 30303–3104.

Ken S. Welsch, 100 Alabama Street, SW., Building 1924, Room 2R90, Atlanta, GA 30303–3104.

General Counsel.—Alexander Fernandez.

Executive Secretary.—Ray H. Darling, Jr.

Director, Office of Administration.—Laura M. Marin.

OFFICE OF GOVERNMENT ETHICS

1201 New York Avenue, NW., Suite 500, 20005, phone (202) 482–9300, fax 482–9238

[Created by Act of October 1, 1989; codified in 5 U.S.C. app., section 401]

Director.—Robert I. Cusick.

Confidential Assistant.—Beverly Johnson.

General Counsel.—Marilyn L. Glynn.

Deputy General Counsel.—Susan Propper.

Deputy Director for—

Administration and Information Management (CIO).—Daniel D. Dunning.

Agency Programs.—Joseph Gangloff.

Government Relations and Special Projects.—Jane S. Ley.

Associate Director for—

Education Division.—Carolyn W. Chapman.

Information Resources Management.—James V. Parle.

Program Review Division.—Dale Christopher.

Program Services Division.—Patricia C. Zemple.

OFFICE OF PERSONNEL MANAGEMENT

Theodore Roosevelt Building, 1900 E Street, NW., 20415–0001

phone (202) 606–1800, http://www.opm.gov

OFFICE OF THE DIRECTOR

Director.—Linda M. Springer, 606–1000.

Senior Executive Assistant.—Bolndell Darby-Boone.

Executive Assistant.—Erikka Robinson.

Special Assistant/Scheduler to the Director.—Heather Fitzgerald.

Chief of Staff/Director of External Affairs.—Tricia Hollis.

Deputy Chief of Staff/Executive Secretariat.—Richard B. Lowe.

White House Liaison.—Carrie B. Cabelka.

Executive Director, Chief Human Capital Officers Council.—John C. Salamone.

OFFICE OF THE CHIEF FINANCIAL OFFICER

Chief Financial Officer.—Mark Reger, 606–1918.

Associate Chief Financial Officer, Center for:

Budget and Performance.—Dan Marella, 606–2368.

Internal Control and Risk Management.—David Cushing, 606–4660.

Director, Financial Modernization Project Office.—Gisele D. Jones, 606–4366.

Administrative Officer.—Patrice W. Mendonca, 606–2204.

OFFICE OF COMMUNICATIONS AND PUBLIC LIAISON

Director.—Susan Bryant, 606–2402.

Deputy Director.—Eldon Girdner.

Director, Office of:

Administration.—Ray Theirault.

Marketing.—Debby Pafel.

Public Liaison.—Charles Cowan.
Web Design.—Vivian Mackey.
Speech Writer.—Hans B. Petersen.

OFFICE OF CONGRESSIONAL RELATIONS

Director.—Susan G. Marshall, 606–1300.
Deputy Director.—Dino L. Carluccio.
Administrative Officer.—Catherine A. Ford.
Capitol Hill Liaison.—Charlene E. Luskey, B332 Rayburn House Office Building, 225–4955, fax 225–4974.
Congressional Relations Officers: T. Scott Clever, Bethany J. Pantuck.
Legislative Analysis.—Harry A. Wolf, 606–1424.

FEDERAL INVESTIGATIVE SERVICES DIVISION

Associate Director.—Kathy L. Dillaman (724) 794–5612.
Deputy Associate Director for—
Operations.—Joy S. Fairtile, 606–1042.
Services.—John Czajkowski, 606–1042.

OFFICE OF THE GENERAL COUNSEL

General Counsel.—Kerry B. McTigue, 606–1700.
Secretary.—Althea D. Elam.
Deputy General Counsel.—Kathie Ann Whipple.
Associate General Counsel, Compensation, Benefits, Products, and Services Group.—James S. Green.
Assistant General Counsel, Merit Systems and Accountability Group.—Steve E. Abow.
Administrative Officer for OGC Administration.—Gloria V. Clark.

HUMAN CAPITAL LEADERSHIP AND MERIT SYSTEM ACCOUNTABILITY DIVISION

Associate Director.—Kevin E. Mahoney, 606–1144.
Deputy Assoicate Director, Center for:
General Government.—Jeffrey E. Sumberg, 606–2786.
Human Capital Implementation and Assessment.—Sydney Smith-Heimbrock, 606–2762.
Human Resources.—Diane Cochran, 606–2464.
Merit System Accountability.—Kevin E. Mahoney, 606–1144.
National Security.—Ray Decker, 606–2511.
Natural Resources Management.—Diane Cochran (acting), 606–1959.
Small Agencies.—David M. Amaral, 606–2530.

HUMAN RESOURCES LINE OF BUSINESS PROGRAM MANAGEMENT OFFICE

Director.—Norman Enger, 606–4185.
HRLOB Shared Service Center Coordinator.—Joseph E. Campbell, 606–1534.
Director, Administration and Finance.—Elizabeth Mautner, 606–1121.

HUMAN RESOURCES PRODUCTS AND SERVICES DIVISION

Associate Director.—Robert F. Danbeck, 606–0600.
Staff Assistant.—Shermaine Kenner.
Resource Management Group.—Eileen Kirwan, 606–2871.
Deputy Associate Director, Center for—
Eastern Management Development Group.—John R. O'Shea (304) 879–8000.
Federal Executive Institute.—Thomas J. Towberman (434) 980–6200.
Retirement and Insurance Services Program.—Kathleen M. McGettigan, 606–0462.
Talent Services.—Frank Esquivel, 606–0142.
Western Management Development Group.—Myhre ''Bud'' Paulson (303) 671–1010.
Assistant Director for—
Insurance Services Programs.—Lorraine Dettman (acting), 606–0745.

Retirement Services Programs.—Joseph E. McDonald, Jr., 606–0300.
Retirement Systems Modernization.—Thomas O'Keefe, 606–0607.
RIS Support Services Program.—Marc Flaster, 606–2115.

OFFICE OF THE INSPECTOR GENERAL

Inspector General.—Patrick E. McFarland, 606–1200.
Executive Assistant.—A. Paulette Berry.
Deputy Inspector General.—Norbert E. Vint.
Counsel to the Inspector General.—Timothy C. Watkins, 606–2030.
Assistant Inspector General, Office of:
Audits.—Michael E. Esser.
Investigations.—Norbert E. Vint (acting).
Legal Affairs.—J. David Cope, 606–3807.
Policy, Resources Management, and Oversight.—Terri Hamlin Fazio.

MANAGEMENT SERVICES DIVISION

Associate Director for Human Capital Management Services and Chief Human Capital Officer.—Ronald C. Flom, 606–3207.
Deputy Associate Director, Center for:
Contracting, Facilities, and Administrative Services.—Kay T. Ely, 606–2200.
Human Capital Management Services and Deputy Chief Human Capital Officer.—William A. Jackson, 606–1402.
Information Services and Chief Information Officer.—Janet L. Barnes, 606–2150.
Security and Emergency Actions.—Thomas L. Forman, 606–1806.
Chief, Center for Equal Employment Opportunity.—Steven T. Shih, 606–2460.

STRATEGIC HUMAN RESOURCES POLICY DIVISION

Associate Director.—Nancy H. Kichak, 606–6500.
Executive Assistant.—Mekaela Nelson.
Deputy Associate Director, Center for:
Employee and Family Support Policy.—Dan Green, 606–0770.
HR Systems Requirements and Strategies.—David Anderson, 606–1343.
Leadership and Executive Resources Policy.—Nancy Randa, 606–8046.
Pay and Peformance Policy.—Jerry Mikowicz, 606–2880.
Talent and Capacity Policy.—Mark Doboga, 606–8097.
Workforce Relations and Accountability Policy.—Ana Mazzi, 606–2930.

OFFICE OF THE SPECIAL COUNSEL

1730 M Street, NW., Suite 300, 20036–4505, phone (202) 254–3600

[Authorized by 5 U.S.C. 1101 and 5 U.S.C. 1211]

Special Counsel.—Scott J. Bloch.
Deputy Special Counsel.—James Byrne.
Legal Advisor.—Erin Berry.
Outreach Director and Counsel.—Sean Brewer.
Congressional and Public Affairs Division.—Loren Smith.
Legal Counsel and Policy Division.—Leonard Dribinsky.
Director of Field Operations.—William Reukauf.

PEACE CORPS

1111 20th Street, NW., 20526, phone (202) 692–2000

Toll-Free Number (800) 424–8580, http://www.peacecorps.gov

[Created by Public Law 97–113]

OFFICE OF THE DIRECTOR

fax 692–2101

Director.—Ron Tschetter.

Deputy Director.—Josephine K. Olsen.
Chief of Staff/Chief of Operations.—David Liner.
Deputy Chief os Staff/Deputy Chief of Operations.—A. Courtney Santonicola.
American Diversity Program Manager.—Shirley Everest.
Chief Information Officer.—Edward Anderson.
Communications Director.—Richard Parker.
Congressional Relations Director.—Michelle Brooks.
General Counsel.—Tyler Posey.
Inspector General.—H. David Kotz.
Marketing Strategist.—Linda Isaac.
Press Director.—Amanda Host.
Printing Officer.—Susan Bloomer.
Office of Private Sector Initiatives.—Nanci Brannan.
Overseas Executive Selection and Support Director.—Lou Barnett.
Chief Financial Officer.—George A. Schutter.
Budget Officer.—Thomas N. Bellamy.
Associate Director for Volunteer Support.—Verle Lanier.
Director of:
Medical Services.—Scott Saxman.
Special Services.—Robert L. Kirkhorn, Jr.
Associate Director for Management.—Wilbert Bryant.
Office of Human Resource Management Director.—Walter Kreamer.
Office of Human Resource Management Deputy Director.—Catherine A. Pearson.
Associate Director for Volunteer Recruitment and Selection.—Chuck Brooks.
Office of Domestic Programs Director.—Amy Horton.
Director of:
Center for Field Assistance and Applied Research.—Lee Lacy (acting).
Crisis Corps.—Mary Angelini.
Planning, Policy and Analysis.—Kyo ''Paul'' Jhin.
Regional Director of:
Africa Operations.—Henry McKoy.
Europe, Mediterranean and Asia Operations.—Jay K. Katzen.
Inter-America and Pacific Operations.—Allene Zanger.

REGIONAL OFFICES

Atlanta (FL, GA, TN, MS, AL, SC, PR, VI): 100 Alabama Street, Building 1924, Suite 2R70, Atlanta, GA 30303 (404) 562–3451, fax 562–3455.
Manager.—Kenton Ayers.
Public Affairs Specialist.—David Leavitt.

Boston (MA, VT, NH, RI, ME): Tip O'Neill Federal Building, 10 Causeway Street, Suite 450, Boston, MA 02222–1099 (617) 565–5555, fax 565–5539.
Manager.—James Arena-DeRosa.
Public Affairs Specialist.—Joanna O'Brien.

Chicago (IL, IN, MO, MI, OH, KY): 55 West Monroe Street, Suite 450, Chicago, IL 60603 (312) 353–4990, fax 353–4192.
Manager.—Virginia Koch.
Public Affairs Specialist.—Christine Cedusky-Torres.

Dallas (TX, OK, LA, NM, AR): 207 South Houston Street, Room 527, Dallas, TX 75202 (214) 253–5400, fax 253–5401.
Manager.—Sharon Sugarek.
Public Affairs Specialist.—Shannon Borders.

Denver (CO, KS, NE, UT, WY): 1999 Broadway, Suite 2205, Denver, CO 80202–3050 (303) 844–7020, fax 844–7010.
Manager.—Nancy Curren.
Public Affairs Specialist.—Jill Thiare.

Los Angeles (Southern CA, AZ): 2361 Rosecrans Avenue, Suite 155, El Segundo, CA 90245–0916 (310) 356–1100, fax 356–1125.
Manager.—Jill Andrews.
Public Affairs Specialist.—David Briery.

Minneapolis (MN, WI, SD, ND, IA): 330 Second Avenue South, Suite 420, Minneapolis, MN 55401 (612) 348–1480, fax 348–1474.
Manager.—Allan Gerber.
Public Affairs Specialist.—Gary Lore.

New York (NY, NJ, CT, PA): 201 Varick Street, Suite 1025, New York, NY 10014 (212) 352–5440, fax 352–5442.

Manager.—Vincent Wickes.
Public Affairs Specialist.—Molly Jennings.

Rosslyn (DC, MD, NC, WV, DE, VA): 1525 Wilson Boulevard, Suite 100, Arlington, VA 22209 (703) 235–9191, fax 235–9189.
Manager.—Lynn Kneedler.
Public Affairs Specialist.—Francoise Castro.

San Francisco (Northern CA, NV, HI): 1301 Clay Street, Suite 620N, Oakland, CA 94612; (510) 637–1539, fax 637–1533.
Manager.—Janet E. Allen.
Public Affairs Specialist.—Nathan Sargent.

Seattle (WA, OR, ID, AK, MT): 1601 5th Avenue, Suite 605, Seattle, WA 98101 (206) 553–5490, fax 553–2343.
Manager.—Wayne Blackwelder.
Public Affairs Specialist.—Maria Lee.

PENSION BENEFIT GUARANTY CORPORATION

1200 K Street, 20005–4026, (202) 326–4000

BOARD OF DIRECTORS

Chairman.—Elaine L. Chao, Secretary of Labor.
Members:
Henry Paulson, Secretary of the Treasury.
Carlos M. Gutierrez, Secretary of Commerce.

OFFICIALS

Director.—Vincent Snowbarger (acting), 326–4010.
Deputy Director.—Vincent Snowbarger, 326–4010.
Chief Officer for—
Finance.—Theodore Winter (acting), 326–4060.
Management and Human Capital.—Stephen Barber, 326–4180.
Operations.—Richard Macy, 326–4010.
Technology.—Jon Baake (acting), 326–4010.
Department Director for—
Benefits Administration and Payment.—Bennie Hagans, 326–4050.
Budget.—Henry Thompson, 326–4120.
Communications and Public Affairs.—Jeffrey Speicher (acting), 326–4040.
Contracts and Controls Review.—Martin Boehm, 326–4161.
Facilities and Services.—Patricia Davis, 326–4150.
Financial Operations.—Theodore Winter, 326–4060.
General Counsel.—Judith Starr, 326–4020.
Human Resources.—Michelle Pilipovich, 326–4110.
Insurance Program.—Terrence Deneen, 326–4050.
Legislative and Regulatory Affairs.—John Hanley, 326–4130.
Policy, Research and Analysis.—David Gustafson, 326–4080.
Procurement.—Gregory Smith (acting), 326–4160.
Strategic Planning and Evaluation.—Wilmer Graham, 326–4180.
Chief Counsel.—Israel Goldowitz, 326–4020.
Inspector General.—Robert Emmons, 326–4030.

POSTAL REGULATORY COMMISSION

901 New York Avenue, NW., Suite 200, 20268–0001
phone (202) 789–6800, fax 789–6886

Chairman.—Dan G. Blair, 789–6801.
Vice Chairman.—Dawn A. Tisdale, 789–6813.
Commissioners:
Mark Acton, 789–6866.
Ruth Y. Goldway, 789–6810.
Tony Hammond, 789–6805.
Chief Administrative Officer and Secretary.—Steven W. Williams, 789–6840.

Chief of Staff.—Ann Fisher, 789–6801.
General Counsel.—Stephen L. Sharfman, 789–6820.
Director, Office of:
Consumer Advocate.—Shelley S. Dreifuss, 789–6830.
Rates, Analysis and Planning.—John Waller, 789–6850.

SECURITIES AND EXCHANGE COMMISSION

100 F Street, NE., 20549, phone (202) 551–7500

TTY Relay Service 1–800–877–8339 http://www.sec.gov

THE COMMISSION

Chairman.—Christopher Cox, 551–2100, fax 772–9200.
Chief of Staff.—Peter Uhlmann.
Deputy Chief of Staff/Counselor to the Chairman.—Mike Halloran.
Senior Advisors to the Chairman: Stephen Devine, William Schulz, Pal Wilkinson.
Counsels: David Huntington, Thomas Kim, Michael Loesch, Michael Post.
Commissioners:
Paul Atkins, 551–2700, fax 772–9330.
Counsels to the Commissioner: Daniel Gallagher, Hester Peirce, Mark Uyeda.
Roel Campos, 551–2500, fax 772–9335.
Counsels to the Commissioner: Cathy Ahn, Jonathan Block, Mia Zur.
Kathleen L. Casey, 551–2600, fax 772–9345.
Counsels to the Commissioner: Mark Berman, Mary Head, Matthew Reed.
Annette L. Nazareth, 551–2800, fax 772–9340.
Counsels to the Commissioner: Christian Broadbent, Denise Landers, Dorothy McCuaig.

OFFICE OF THE SECRETARY

Secretary.—Nancy Morris, 551–5400, fax 772–9324.
Deputy Secretary.—Florence Harmon, 551–5604.
Assistant Secretaries: Jill Peterson, 551–5458; J. Lynn Taylor, 551–5420.
Assistant Director, Library.—Cindy Plisch, 551–5458.

OFFICE OF THE EXECUTIVE DIRECTOR

Executive Director.—Diego Ruiz, 551–4300, fax 777–1025.
Chief Management Analyst.—Kenneth Johnson.

OFFICE OF INVESTOR EDUCATION AND ASSISTANCE

Director.—Lori Schock (acting), 551–6500, fax 772–9295.
Deputy Director.—Lori Schock.

OFFICE OF EQUAL EMPLOYMENT OPPORTUNITY

Director.—Deborah K. Balducchi, 551–6040, fax 772–9316.

OFFICE OF FREEDOM OF INFORMATION AND PRIVACY ACT OPERATIONS

FOIA Officer.—M. Celia Winter, 551–7900, fax 703–914–1005.
FOIA/PA Branch Chiefs: Brenda Fuller, Ligia Glass, Frank Henderson.

OFFICE OF THE CHIEF ACCOUNTANT

Chief Accountant.—Conrad Hewitt, 551–5300, fax 772–9253.
Deputy Chief Accountant:
Accounting.—James Kroeker.
International.—Julie Erhardt.
Professional Practice.—Zoe-Vonna Palmrose.
Senior Associate Chief Accountants: John Albert, 551–5337; Edmund Bailey, 551–5339; Susan Koski-Grafer, 551–5349; Shelly Luisi, 551–5350; Jenifer Minke-Girard, 551–5351; Nancy Salisbury.

Chief Counsel.—Robert Burns, 551–5342.

OFFICE OF COMPLIANCE INSPECTIONS AND EXAMINATIONS

Director.—Lisa Richards, 551–6200, fax 772–9179.
Senior Advisor.—Karen Burgess.
Associate Director/Chief Counsel.—John Walsh, 551–6460.
Associate Directors: Mary Ann Gadziala (Broker/Dealer/Self-Regulatory Organization), 551–6400; Gene Gohlke (Investment Adviser/Investment Company), 551–6300.
Assistant Directors: Louis Becka (Investment Adviser/Investment Company), 551–6300; Mark Donohue (Self-Regulatory Organization), 551–6210; Thomas Eidt (Self-Regulatory Organization), 551–6250; Richard Hannibal (Broker/Dealer), 551–6400; Mavis Kelly (Investment Adviser/Investment Company), 551–6300; Helene McGee (Self-Regulatory Organization), 551–6270; A. Duer Meehan (Broker/Dealer), 551–6400.

OFFICE OF ECONOMIC ANALYSIS

Chief Economist.—Chester Spatt, 551–6600, fax 772–9290.
Deputy Chief Economist.—Jonathan Sokobin, 551–6640.
Assistant Chief Economist.—Cindy Alexander, 551–6602.
Office of:
Litigation Support.—Bill Dale, 551–6654.
Markets and Intermediaries.—Stewart Mayhew, 551–6617.

OFFICE OF THE GENERAL COUNSEL

General Counsel.—Brian Cartwright, 551–5100, fax 772–9260.
Deputy General Counsel for:
Legal Policy and Administrative Practice.—Alexander Cohen, 551–5160.
Litigation and Adjudication.—Andrew Vollmer, 551–5110.
Principal Assistant General Counsel for Litigation and Adjudication.—Joan Loizeuax.
Assistant General Counsels for Adjudication: Kermit Kennedy, 551–5164; Joan McCarthy, 551–5150.
Solicitor, Appellate Litigation and Bankruptcy.—Jacob Stillman, 551–5130.
Deputy Solicitor, Appellate Litigation and Bankruptcy.—Eric Summergrad, 551–5022.
Special Counsel to the Solicitor.—Allan Capute, 551–5122.
Assistant General Counsels for Appellate Litigation and Bankruptcy: Katharine Gresham, 551–5148; Mark Pennington, 551–5189; Randall Quinn, 551–5198.
Associate General Counsel for Counseling and Regulatory Policy.—Diane Sanger, 551–5002.
Ethics Counsel.—William Lenox, 551–5170.
Principal Associate General Counsel for Legal Policy.—Meridith Mitchell, 551–5184.
Assistant General Counsels for Legal Policy: David Fredrickson, 551–5144; Richard Levine, 551–5168; Janice Mitnick, 551–5185; Lori Price, 551–5184.
Assistant General Counsel for Legislation and Financial Services.—Stephen Jung, 551–5162.
Associate General Counsel for Litigation and Administrative Practice.—Richard M. Humes, 551–5140.
Assistant General Counsels for Litigation and Administrative Practice: George Brown, 551–5121, Samuel Forstein, 551–5139; Melinda Hardy, 551–5149; Thomas Karr, 551–5163.

DIVISION OF INVESTMENT MANAGEMENT

Director.—Andrew Donahue, 551–6720, fax 772–9288.
Senior Adviser to the Director.—Jennifer B. McHugh, 551–6720.
Associate Director, Chief Counsel.—Douglas J. Scheidt, 551–6701.
Assistant Chief Counsels: Alison M. Fuller (International Issues), 551–6825; Elizabeth G. Osterman (Financial Institutions).
Associate Director, Office of:
Disclosure and Insurance Product Regulation.—Susan Nash, 551–6742.
Legal and Disclosure.—Barry D. Miller, 551–6725.
Regulatory Policy and Investment Adviser Regulation.—Robert E. Plaze, 551–6702.
Assistant Director, Office of:
Disclosure and Review No. 1.—Michael A. Lainoff, 551–6921.
Disclosure and Review No. 2.—Frank J. Donaty, 551–6925.

Disclosure Regulation.—Brent Fields, 551–6784.
Enforcement Liaison.—Barbara Chretien-Dar, 551–6785.
Financial Analysis.—Paul B. Goldman, 551–6715.
Insurance Products.—William J. Kotapish, 551–6795.
Investment Adviser Regulation.—David Blass, 551–6787.
Investment Company Regulation.—Nadya B. Roytblat, 551–6821.
Regulatory Policy.—C. Hunter Jones, 551–6792.
Chief Accountant, Office of Chief Accountant.—Conrad Hewitt, 551–6918.

DIVISION OF CORPORATION FINANCE

Director.—John W. White, 551–3100, fax 772–9213.
Deputy Director of:
Disclosure Operations.—Shelley E. Parratt, 551–3130.
Legal and Regulatory.—Martin Dunn, 551–3120.
Associate Directors:
Legal Office.—Paula Dubberly, 551–3180.
Regulatory Policy.—Mauri L. Osheroff, 551–3190.
Chief Accountant.—Carol Stacey, 551–3400.
Disclosure Operations: Paul Belvin, 551–3150; James Daly, 551–3140; Barry Summer, 551–3160.
Chief, Office of:
Chief Counsel.—David Lynn, 551–3520.
EDGAR, Information and Analysis.—Herbert D. Scholl, 551–3610.
Enforcement Liaison.—Mary Kosterlitz, 551–3420.
International Corporate Finance.—Paul Dudek, 551–3450.
Mergers and Acquisitions.—Brian Breheny, 551–3440.
Rulemaking.—Elizabeth Murphy, 551–3430.
Small Business Policy.—Gerald Laporte, 551–3460.
Assistant Directors: Karen Garnett, 551–3780; Peggy Fisher, 551–3800; Barbara Jacobs, 551–3730; Pamela Long, 551–3760; H. Christopher Owings, 551–3720; Jeffrey Reidler, 551–3710; John Reynolds, 551–3790; Todd Schiffman, 551–3770; H. Roger Schwall, 551–3740; Larry Spirgel, 551–3810; Max Webb, 551–3750.

DIVISION OF ENFORCEMENT

Director.—Linda Chatman Thomsen, 551–4500, fax 772–9279.
Senior Advisors: Pauline Calande, 551–4950; Donna Norman, 551–4878.
Deputy Directors: Peter Bresnan, 551–4597; Walter Ricciardi, 551–4597.
Associate Director.—Cheryl J. Scarboro, 551–4403.
Chief, Office of Internet Enforcement.—John R. Stark, 551–4892.
Assistant Director.—Josh Felker, 551–4960.
Associate Director.—Fredric Firestone, 551–4711.
Assistant Directors: Gregory Faragasso, 551–4734; Kenneth Lench, 551–4938.
Associate Director.—Christopher Conte, 551–4834.
Assitant Directors: Timothy England, 551–4959; Richard Grime, 551–4915; Mark Kreitman, 551–4484.
Associate Director.—Scott Friestad, 551–4962.
Assistant Directors: James Coffman, 551–4953; Laura Josephs, 551–5117; Robert Kaplan, 551–4969.
Chief, Market Surveillance.—Joseph J. Cella, 551–4951.
Associate Director.—Antonia Chion, 551–4842.
Assistant Directors: Kara Brockmeyer, 551–4829; Yuri Zelinsky, 551–4769.
Chief Counsel.—Joan E. McKown, 551–4933.
Assistant Chief Counsels: Nancy A. Doty, 551–4931; Charlotte L. Buford, 551–4843.
Chief Litigation Counsel.—Luis Mejia, 551–4481.
Deputy Chief Litigation Counsel.—Mark A. Adler, 551–4402.
Chief Accountant.—Susan G. Markel, 551–4610.
Associate Chief Accountants: Regina M. Barrett, 551–4615; Dwayne Brown, 551–4616; David M. Estabrook, 551–4621; Jason Flemmon, 551–4617; Pierron Leef, 551–4620.
Director, Regional Office Operations.—James A. Clarkson, 551–4932.

DIVISION OF MARKET REGULATION

Director.—Erik Sirri, 551–5500, fax 772–9273.
Deputy Director.—Robert L.D. Colby, 551–5770.
Chief of Operations.—Herbert Brooks, 551–5671.
Associate Director, Chief Counsel.—Catherine McGuire, 551–5551.
Deputy Chief Counsel.—Paula Jenson, 551–5581.
Associate Directors:
Broker Dealer Finances.—Michael Macchiaroli, 551–5510.
Market Supervision: Elizabeth King, 551–5600; David Shillman, 551–5685.
Trading Practices and Processing.—James Brigagliano, 551–5700.
Assistant Directors: Katherine England, 551–5611; Kelly Riley, 551–5661; John Roeser, 551–5631; Nancy Sanow, 551–5621; Michael Gaw, 551–5602; Martha Haines (Municipal Finance), 551–5681.
Assistant Directors:
Clearance and Settlement.—Jerry Carpenter, 551–5710.
Enforcement Liaison and Institutional Trading.—Jo Anne Swindler, 551–5750.
Market Operations.—Herb Brooks, 551–5670.
Market Watch.—Alton Harvey, 551–5691.
Financial Responsibility.—Thomas McGowan, 551–5520.
Prudential Supervision and Risk Analysis #1.—Matthew Eichner, 551–5530.

OFFICE OF ADMINISTRATIVE LAW JUDGES

Chief Administrative Law Judge.—Brenda Murray, 551–6030, fax 777–1031.
Administrative Law Judges: Carol Fox Foelak, James Kelly, Robert Mahony.

OFFICE OF INTERNATIONAL AFFAIRS

Director.—Ethiopis Tafara, 551–6690, fax 772–9280.
Deputy Director.—Elizabeth Jacobs.
Assistant Directors: Sherman Boone, 551–6686; Robert Fisher, 551–6652; Susan Yashar, 551–6683.

OFFICE OF LEGISLATIVE AND INTERGOVERNMENTAL AFFAIRS

Director.—Jonathan Burks, 551–2010, fax 772–9250.
Deputy Director.—Peter Kiernan.

OFFICE OF THE INSPECTOR GENERAL

Inspector General.—Walter J. Stachnik, 551–6060, fax 772–9265.
Deputy Inspector General.—Nelson N. Egbert, 551–6035.

OFFICE OF FILINGS AND INFORMATION SERVICES

Associate Executive Director.—Jayne Seidman (acting), 551–7200, fax (703) 914–4340.

OFFICE OF PUBLIC AFFAIRS

Director.—John Nester, 551–4120, fax 777–1026.
Deputy Director.—John D. Heine, 551–4123.

OFFICE OF FINANCIAL MANAGEMENT

Associate Executive Director.—Kristine Chadwick, 551–7840, fax (703) 914–0172.
Assistant Director for Finance and Accounting.—Darrell Dockery, 551–7827.
Assistant Director for Planning and Budget.—Diane Galvin, 551–7853.

OFFICE OF INFORMATION TECHNOLOGY

Director/Chief Information Officer.—R. Corey Booth, 551–8800; fax (703) 914–2621.

OFFICE OF ADMINISTRATIVE SERVICES

Associate Executive Director.—Anne O'Donoghue, 551–7400, fax (703) 914–4459.
Assistant Directors:
Procurement, Security, and Publishing.—Beth Blackwood, 551–7408.
Real Property and Facilities Support.—Cathleen Bealle English, 551–7437.

OFFICE OF HUMAN RESOURCES

Associate Executive Director.—Jeffrey Risinger, 551–7500, fax (703) 914–4411.
Assistant Directors: Adam Ramsey (Employee Development and Labor Relations), 551–7401; Carol Smith, 551–7409.

REGIONAL OFFICES

Atlanta Regional Office: 3475 Lenox Road, NE., Suite 1000, Atlanta, GA 30326 (404) 842–7600, fax (404) 842–7633.
Senior Associate Regional Director.—Ronald L. Crawford, 842–7630.
Assistant Regional Directors, Enforcement: Stephen Donahue, 842–7618, Madison Loomis, 842–7622.
Associate Director, Examinations.—James Carley, 842–7645.
Assistant Regional Director, Broker/Dealer Examinations.—Howard Dennis, 842–7643.
Associate Regional Directors, Investment Company/Investment Adviser Examinations: Herbert Campbell, 842–7677; Diane Eckert, 842–7655.

Boston Regional Office: 33 Arch Street, 23rd Floor, Boston, MA 02110 (617) 573–8900, fax (617) 573–4590.
Regional Director.—David Bergers, 573–8927.
Associate District Administrator, Enforcement.—John Dugan, 573–8936.
Assistant District Administrators, Enforcement: Sandra Bailey, 573–8976; Martin Healey, 573–8952; Philip Koski, 573–8964.
Associate Regional Director, Examinations.—Lucile Corkery, 573–8932.
Assistant District Administrators, Investment Adviser/Investment Company Examinations: Andrew Caverly, (Broker/Dealer), 573–8922; Michael Garrity (Investment Adviser/Investment Company), 573–8944; Joseph Mick (Investment Adviser/Investment Company), 573–8975; Elizabeth Salini, 573–8931.

Chicago Regional Office: 175 West Jackson Boulevard, Suite 900, Chicago, IL 60604 (312) 353–7390, fax 353–7398.
Regional Director.—Merri Jo Gillette, 353–9338.
Senior Associate Regional Director, Enforcement.—Robert J. Burson, 353–7428.
Associate Regional Director, Enforcement.—Timothy L. Warren, 353–7394.
Associate Regional Directors, Examinations: John R. Brissman, 353–7436; Jeannette L. Lewis, 353–7410.
Assistant Regional Directors, Enforcement: Peter Chan, 353–7410; Daniel R. Gregus, 353–7423; Scott J. Hlavacek, 353–1679; Jane Jarcho, 353–5479; John R. Lee, 886–2247; Paul A. Montoya, 353–7429; John J. Sikora, 353–7418.
Assistant Regional Directors, Examinations: Doug R. Adams, 353–7402; Maureen Dempsey, 886–1496; Lewis A. Garcia, 353–6888; J. Gary Hopkins, 886–8511; Lawrence Kendra, 886–8508; Thomas Kirk, 886–3956; David J. Mueller, 353–7404; Thomas Murphy, 886–8513; Larry P. Perdue, 353–7219.

Denver Regional Office: 1801 California Street, Suite 1500, Denver, CO 80202 (303) 844–1000, fax (303) 844–1010.
Regional Director.—George Curtis, 844–1042.
Associate Regional Director.—Donald M. Hoerl, 844–1060.
Assistant Regional Directors, Enforcement: Mary S. Brady, 844–1023; Laura Metcalfe, 844–1092; Amy Norwood, 844–1029.
Assistant Regional Director, Regulation.—Edward A. Lewkowski, 844–1050.

Fort Worth Regional Office: 801 Cherry Street, Unit #18, Fort Worth, TX 76102 (817) 978–3821, fax 978–2700.
Regional Director.—Rose Romero, 900–2623.
Associate Regional Director, Enforcement.—Katherine Addleman, 978–6425.
Assistant Regional Directors, Enforcement: Jeffrey Cohen, 978–6480; David Peavler, 978–6459; Stephen Webster, 978–6459.

Associate Regional Director, Examinations.—Kimberly Garber, 900–2622.
Assistant District Administrators, Broker/Dealer Examinations.—Julie Preuitt, 978–6428.
Assistant District Administrator, Investment Company/Investment Adviser Examinations.—Jim Perry 978–6439.

Los Angeles Regional Office: 5670 Wilshire Boulevard, 11th Floor, Los Angeles, CA 90036 (213) 965–3998, fax 965–3816.

Regional Director.—Randall R. Lee, 965–3807.
Associate Regional Director, Enforcement.—Michele Wein Layne, 965–3850.
Senior Assistant Regional Director, Enforcement.—Kelly C. Bowers, 965–3924.
Assistant Regional Directors, Enforcement: Diana Tani, 965–3991; Finola Halloran Manvelian, 965–3980.
Associate Regional Director, Regulation.—Rosalind Tyson, 965–3893.
Assistant Regional Directors, Investment Company/Investment Adviser Examinations: Michael P. Levitt, 525–2684; Andrew Petillon, 525–3214; Kevin Goodman, 525–2653.
Assistant Regional Directors, Broker/Dealer Examinations: Martin Murphy, 965–3859; Cindy S. Wong, 965–3927.

Miami Regional Office: 801 Brickell Avenue, Suite 1800, Miami, FL 33131 (305) 982–6300, fax (305) 536–4120.

Regional Director.—David Nelson, 982–6332.
Associate Regional Directors:
Enforcement.—Glenn Gordon, 536–6360.
Examination.—John C. Mattimore, 982–6357.
Assistant Regional Directors:
Enforcement: Eric Busto, 982–6362; Chedly Dumomay, 982–6377; Teresa Verges, 982–6384.
Examination: Faye Chin, 982–6305; Nicholas Monaco, 982–6310.

New York Regional Office: 3 World Financial Center, Suite 400, New York, NY 10281–1022, (212) 336–1100, fax (212) 336–1323.

Regional Director.—Mark Schonfeld, 336–1020.
Associate Regional Directors, Enforcement: Robert B. Blackburn, 336–1050; Andrew Calamari, 336–0042; Helene T. Glotzer, 336–0078; David Rosenfeld, 336–0153.
Assistant Regional Directors, Enforcement: Doria Bachenheimer, 336–0024; Alistaire Bambach, 336–0027; Robert DeLeonardis (Investigations), 336–0056; Gerald Gross, 336–0085; Bruce Karpati, 336–0104; Leslie Kazon, 336–0107; Kay Lackey, 336–0117; David Markowitz, 336–0128; George Stepaniuk, 336–0173; Scott York, 336–0188; Alex Vasilescu, 336–0178.
Associate Regional Director, Investment Adviser/Investment Company Examinatins.—Thomas Biolsi, 336–6446.
Assistant Regional Directors: Dawn Blankenship, 336–0197; William Delmage, 336–0495; Joseph Dimaria, 336–0497; Dorothy Eschwie, 336–0502.
Associate Regional Directors, Broker/Dealer: Richard D. Lee, 336–1010; Robert A. Sollazzo, 336–1070.
Assistant Regional Directors, Broker/Dealer Examinations: Richard A. Heapy, 336–0464; Linda Lettieri, 336–0474; John M. Nee, 336–0484; Rosanne R. Smith, 336–0928; Steven Vitulano, 336–0936.

Philadelphia Regional Office: Mellon Independence Center, 701 Market Street, Suite 2000, Philadelphia, PA 19106 (215) 597–3100, fax 597–3194.

Regional Director.—Daniel Hawke, 597–3191.
Associate Regional Director, Regulation.—Joy G. Thompson, 597–6135.
Assistant Regional Directors, Enforcement: Elaine C. Greenberg, 597–3107; David Horowitz, 597–2950.
Senior Assistant Regional Director, Investment Company/Investment Adviser Examinations.—William R. Meck, 597–0789.
Assistant Regional Directors, Investment Company/Investment Adviser Examinations: A. Laurence Ehrhart, 597–2983; Paul Hee, 597–8307.

Salt Lake Regional Office: 15 West South Temple Street, Suite 1800, Salt Lake City, UT 84101 (801) 524–5796, fax 524–3558.

Regional Director.—Kenneth D. Israel, 524–6745.

San Francisco Regional Office: 44 Montgomery Street, Suite 2600, San Francisco, CA 94104 (415) 705–2500, fax 705–2501.

Regional Director.—Helane L. Morrison, 705–2450.
Associate Regional Director.—Marc J. Fagel, 705–2449.
Assistant Regional Directors: Edward Haddad (Investment Adviser/Investment Company), 705–2344; Jennet Leong (Broker/Dealer), 705–2452; Matthew O'Toole (Investment Adviser/Investment Company), 705–2466.
Associate Regional Director, Regulation.—Daryl Hagel, 705–2340.

Assistant Regional Directors, Enforcement: Michael S. Dicke 705–2458; Marc J. Fagel, 705–2449; Cary Robnett, 705–2335.

SELECTIVE SERVICE SYSTEM

1515 Wilson Boulevard, 5th Floor, Arlington, VA 22209–2425

phone (703) 605–4100, fax 605–4106, http://www.sss.gov

Director.—William A. Chatfield, 605–4010.
Deputy Director.—Ernest E. Garcia.
Chief of Staff.—COL Richard A. Moore.
Inspector General.—Carlo Verdino, 605–4022.
Director for—
Operations.—Scott Campbell 605–4110.
Resource Management.—Edward A. Blackadar, Jr., 605–4032.
Public and Intergovernmental Affairs.—Richard S. Flahavan, 605–4017, fax 605–4106.
Financial Management.—William Reese, 605–4028.

Registration Information Office, P.O. Box 94638, Palatine, IL 60094–4638, phone (847) 688–6888, fax (847) 688–2860.

SMALL BUSINESS ADMINISTRATION

409 Third Street, SW., 20416

phone (202) 205–6600, fax 205–7064, http://www.sbaonline.sba.gov

Administrator.—Steven C. Preston, 205–6605.
Deputy Administrator.—Jovita Carranza.
Chief of Staff.—Joel Szabat.
Director of Executive Secretariat.—Kim Bradley, 205–6608.
General Counsel.—Frank Borchert, 205–6642.
Chief Counsel for Advocacy.—Thomas M. Sullivan, 205–6533.
Inspector General.—Eric Thorson, 205–6580.
Chief Financial Officer.—Jennifer Main, 205–6449.
Director, National Advisory Council.—Mina Wales, 205–7180.
Associate Administrator for—
Disaster Assistant.—Herb Mitchell, 205–6734.
Field Operations.—Michael Pappas, 205–6808.
Public Communications.—Sean Rushton, 205–6740.
Assistant Administrator for—
Congressional and Legislative Affairs.—C. Edward ''Tee'' Rowe, 205–6700.
Equal Employment Opportunity and Compliance.—Delorice Ford (acting), 205–6750.
Hearings and Appeals.—Delorice Ford, 205–7340.
Associate Deputy Administrator for Management and Administration.—Lewis Andrews, 205–6610.
Assistant Administrator for—
Administration.—Joanie Newhart, 205–6642.
Chief Information Officer.—Christine Liu, 205–6706.
Human Capital Management.—Richard Brechbiel, 205–6784.
Associate Deputy Administrator for Capital Access.—Michael Hager, 205–6557.
Associate Administrator for—
Business and Community Initiatives.—Ellen Thrasher, 205–6665.
Financial Assistance.—Janet Tasker (acting), 205–6490.
Investment.—Jaime Guzman, 205–6510.
Small Business Development Centers.—Antonio Doss, 205–6766.
Surety Guarantees.—Frank Lalumiere, 205–6540.
Assistant Administrator for—
International Trade.—Manuel Rosales, 205–6720.
Veterans' Affairs.—William Elmore, 205–6773.
Women's Business Ownership.—Wilma Goldstein, 205–6673.
Associate Deputy Administrator for Government Contracting and Business Development.—Anthony Martoccia, 205–6459.
Associate Administrator for—
Business Development.—Luz Hopewell, 205–6463.
Government Contracting.—Arthur Collins (acting), 205–6460.
Assistant Administrator for—

Size Standard.—Gary Jackson, 205–6618.
Technology.—Edsel Brown, 205–6450.

SMITHSONIAN INSTITUTION

Smithsonian Institution Building—The Castle (SIB), 1000 Jefferson Drive, SW., 20560
phone (202) 633–1000, http://www.smithsonian.org

The Smithsonian Institution is an independent trust instrumentality created in accordance with the terms of the will of James Smithson of England who in 1826 bequeathed his property to the United States of America "to found at Washington under the name of the Smithsonian Institution an establishment for the increase and diffusion of knowledge among men." Congress pledged the faith of the United States to carry out the trust in 1836 (Act of July 1, 1836, C. 252, 5 Stat. 64), and established the Institution in its present form in 1846 (August 10, 1846, C. 178, 9 Stat. 102), entrusting the management of the institution to its independent Board of Regents.

THE BOARD OF REGENTS

ex officio

Chief Justice of the United States.—John G. Roberts, Chancellor.
Vice President of the United States.—Richard B. Cheney.

Appointed by the President of the Senate	*Appointed by the Speaker of the House*
Hon. Thad Cochran	Hon. Sam Johnson
Hon. Christopher J. Dodd	Hon. Doris O. Matsui
Hon. Patrick J. Leahy	Hon. Xavier Becerra

Appointed by Joint Resolution of Congress

Eli Broad	Shirley Ann Jackson	Alan G. Spoon
Anne d'Harnoncourt	Robert Kogod	Roger Sant
Phillip Frost	Dr. Patty Stonesifer	

OFFICE OF THE SECRETARY

Acting Secretary.—Dr. Cristián Samper, 633–1846.
Inspector General.—Sprightley Ryan, 633–7050.
General Counsel.—John Huerta, 633–5099.
Director of:
External Affairs.—Virginia Clark, 633–5021.
Policy and Analysis.—Carole M.P. Neves, 633–5585.

OFFICE OF THE DEPUTY SECRETARY AND CHIEF OPERATING OFFICER

Deputy Secretary.—Sheila P. Burke, 633–5240.
Director of:
Accessibility Program.—Elizabeth Ziebarth, 633–2946.
Exhibits, The Arts and Industries Building and the International Gallery.—Ellen Dorn, 633–7421.
Communications and Public Affairs.—Evelyn Lieberman, 633–5190.
Government Relations.—Nell Payne, 633–5125.
National Programs.—Richard Kurin (acting), 633–6440.
Quadrangle Building.—Ronald W. Hawkins, 633–4025.
Special Events and Protocol.—Nicole L. Krakora, 633–2020.

MUSEUMS

Director of:
Anacostia Community Museum.—Camille Akeju, 633–4839.
National Museum of American History.—Brent Glass, 633–3435.

National Museum of the American Indian.—W. Richard West, 633–6700.
National Postal Museum.—Allen Kane, 633–5500.
National Museum of African American History and Culture.—Lonnie Bunch, 633–4751.

PAN-INSTITUTIONAL PROGRAMS

Director of:
Asian Pacific American Program.—Franklin Odo, 786–2963.
Center for Folklife Programs and Cultural Heritage.—Richard Kurin, 633–6440.
Smithsonian Latino Center.—Pilar O'Leary, 633–1240.
Smithsonian Institution Archives.—Anne Van Camp, 633–5908.
Smithsonian Institution Libraries.—Nancy Gwinn, 633–2240.

NATIONAL PROGRAMS

Director of:
Smithsonian Affiliations Program.—Harold Closter, 633–5321.
Smithsonian Associates Program.—Barbara Tuceling, 633–8880.
Smithsonian Center for Education and Museum Studies.—Stephanie L. Norby, 633–5297.
Smithsonian Institution Traveling Exhibition Service.—Anna Cohn, 633–3136.

OPERATING UNITS

Director, Office of:
Equal Employment and Minority Affairs.—Era Marshall, 633–6414.
Exhibits Central.—Michael Headley, 633–4514.
Facilities Engineering and Operations.—William Brubaker, 633–1873.
Human Resources.—James Douglas, 633–6301.
Chief, Office of:
Finance.—Alice Maroni, 633–7120.
Information.—Anne Speyer, 633–1688.
Ombudsman.—Chandra Heilman, 633–2010.

OFFICE OF THE UNDER SECRETARY FOR SCIENCE

Acting Under Secretary.—Dr. Ira Rubinoff, 633–5127.
Director of:
International Relations.—Francine Berkowitz, 633–4795.
National Air and Space Museum.—Jack Dailey, 633–2350.
National Museum of Natural History.—Paul Risser (acting), 633–2664.
National Science Resources Center.—Sally Goetz Shuler, 633–2972.
National Zoological Park.—John Berry, 633–4442.
Smithsonian Astrophysical Observatory.—Charles Alcock (617) 495–7100.
Smithsonian Museum Conservation Institute.—Robert Koestler (301) 238–1205.
Smithsonian Environmental Research Center.—Anson Hines (443) 482–2208.
Smithsonian Tropical Research Institute.—Eldredge Bermingham, 011–507–212–8110.

OFFICE OF THE UNDER SECRETARY FOR ART

Under Secretary.—Ned Rifkin, 633–5090.
Director of:
Archives of American Art.—John Smith, 275–1874.
Cooper Hewitt, National Design Museum.—Paul Thompson (212) 849–8370.
Freer and Sackler Galleries.—Julian Raby, 633–0456.
Hirshhorn Museum and Sculpture Garden.—Olga Viso, 633–2824.
National Museum of African Art.—Sharon Patton, 633–4610.
National Portrait Gallery.—Marc Pachter, 275–1740.
Office of Research and Training Services.—Catherine Harris, 633–7070.
Smithsonian American Art Museum.—Elizabeth Broun, 275–1515.
Smithsonian Photography Initiative.—Merry Foresta, 633–2928.

SMITHSONIAN BUSINESS VENTURES

Chief Executive Officer.—Tom Ott (acting), 633–5169.
Publisher, Smithsonian Magazine.—Peter S. Krieger, 633–6090.
Editor, Smithsonian Magazine.—Carey Winfrey, 633–6072.

SOCIAL SECURITY ADMINISTRATION

International Trade Commission Building, 500 E Street SW., Washington, DC 20254 (ITCB)

Altmeyer Building, 6401 Security Boulevard, Baltimore, MD 21235 (ALTMB)

Annex Building, 6401 Security Boulevard, Baltimore, MD 21235 (ANXB)

National Computer Center, 6201 Security Boulevard, Baltimore, MD 21235 (NCC)

West High Rise Building, 6401 Security Boulevard, Baltimore, MD 21235 (WHRB)

East High Rise Building, 6401 Security Boulevard, Baltimore, MD 21235 (EHRB)

Gwynn Oak Building, 1710 Gwynn Oak Avenue, Baltimore, MD 21207 (GWOB)

Operations Building, 6401 Security Boulevard, Baltimore, MD 21235 (OPRB)

Meadows East Building, 6401 Security Boulevard, Baltimore, MD 21235 (ME)

Metro West Tower Building, 300 North Greene Street, Baltimore, MD 21201 (MWTB)

Security West Tower, 1500 Woodlawn Drive, Baltimore, MD 21241 (SWTB)

One Skyline Tower, 5107 Leesburg Pike, Falls Church, VA 22041 (SKY)

http://www.socialsecurity.gov

OFFICE OF THE COMMISSIONER

Commissioner.—Michael J. Astrue, ITCB, room 850 (202) 358–6000 or ALTMB, room 900 (410) 965–3120.
Deputy Commissioner.—Andrew Biggs, ITCB, room 874 (202) 358–6041 or ALTMB, room 960 (410) 965–9000.
Chief of Staff.—David V. Foster, ITCB, room 858 (202) 358–6000 or ALTMB, room 900 (410) 965–8804.
White House Liaison.—Larry W. Dye, ITCB, room 858 (202) 358–6013.
Senior Advisor.—Michael N. Korbey, ITCB, room 857 (202) 358–6134 or ALTMB, room 960 (410) 965–7410.
Counselor to the Commissioner.—Laurence J. Love, ITCB, room 862 (202) 358–6093.
Executive Secretary.—David A. Rust, ALTMB, room 912 (410) 965–8914.
Executive Director, Disability Service Improvement Staff.—Mary B. Chatel, ITCB, room 800 (202) 358–6093, ALTMB, room 939 (410) 597–4305.
Executive Counselor on Interagency Adjudication.—Rita S. Geier, ITCB, room 700 (202) 358–6502, ALTMB, room 939 (410) 965–9669.

OFFICE OF THE CHIEF ACTUARY

Chief Actuary.—Stephen C. Goss, ALTMB, room 700 (410) 965–3000.
Deputy Chief Actuary for—
Long Range.—Alice H. Wade, ALTMB, room 700 (410) 965–3002.
Short Range.—Eli N. Donkar, OPRB, room 4–N–29 (410) 965–3004.

OFFICE OF THE CHIEF INFORMATION OFFICER

Chief Information Officer.—Thomas P. Hughes, ALTMB, room 500 (410) 966–5738.
Deputy Chief Information Officer.—Gregory C. Pace, ALTMB, room 500 (410) 965–3494.
Director, Systems Review.—Lester P. Diamond, ALTMB, room 348 (410) 965–3429.
Officer, Security Policy.—John T. Smith, ALTMB, room 342 (410) 966–1155.

OFFICE OF COMMUNICATIONS

Deputy Commissioner/Press Officer.—James Courtney, ALTMB, room 460 (410) 965–1720, or ITCB, room 866, (202) 358–6131.

Assistant Deputy Commissioner.—Philip A. Gambino, ALTMB, room 460 (410) 965–1720.

Associate Commissioner, Office of:

Communication, Planning, and Technology.—Thomas J. Tobin, ANXB, room 3165 (410) 965–4029.

External Affairs.—Cheri A. Arnott, ANXB, room 3505 (410) 965–1804.

Public Inquiries.—Annie B. White, OPI Windsor Park (410) 965–2739.

Press Officer.—Mark Lassiter, ALTMB, room 440 (410) 965–8904.

OFFICE OF THE DEPUTY COMMISSIONER FOR DISABILITY ADJUDICATION AND REVIEW

Deputy Commissioner.—Lisa de Soto, SKY (703) 605–8200 or ALTMB, room 315 (410) 966–1635.

Assistant Deputy Commissioner.—A. Jacy Thurmond, Jr., SKY (703) 605–8200.

Director, Office of:

Appellate Operations.—William Taylor, SKY (703) 605–7100.

Management.—Eileen C. McDaniel, SKY (703) 605–8928.

Policy, Planning and Evaluation.—Barbara Hunt, SKY (703) 605–8275.

Office of the Federal Reviewing Official, Chief FedRO.—Beth A. McKinnon, SKY (703) 605–8744.

Chief Administrative Law Judge.—Frank A. Cristaudo, SKY (703) 605–8500.

Regional Chief Administrative Law Judges:

Atlanta.—Ollie Garmon, 61 Forsyth Street SW., Suite 20T10, Atlanta, GA 30303–8701 (404) 562–1182.

Boston.—Patrick B. Augustine, One Bowdoin Square, 10th Floor, Boston, MA 02114 (617) 720–0438.

Chicago.—Paul C. Lillios, 200 West Adams Street, Suite 2901, Chicago, IL 60606 (312) 886–5252.

Dallas.—Joan Parks Saunders, 1301 Young Street, Suite 460, Dallas, TX 75202–5433 (214) 767–9401.

Denver.—James R. Rucker, Jr., 1244 North Speer Boulevard, Suite 600, Denver, CO 80204 (303) 844–6100.

Kansas City.—Marsha R. Stroup, 1100 Main Street, Suite 1700, Kansas City, MO 64105 (816) 842–6423 ext. 1021.

New York.—Robert Wright, 74 North Pearl Street, 6th Floor, Albany, NY 12207 (866) 862–7348.

Philadelphia.—Jay Bede, 300 Spring Garden Street, 4th Floor, Philadelphia, PA 19123 (215) 597–4100.

San Francisco.—Stephen Wright, 555 Battery Street, 5th Floor, San Francisco, CA 94111 (415) 705–2000.

Seattle.—David DeLaittre, 701 5th Avenue, Suite 2900 M/S 904, Seattle, WA 98104 (206) 615–3517.

OFFICE OF THE DEPUTY COMMISSIONER FOR DISABILITY AND INCOME SECURITY PROGRAMS

Deputy Commissioner.—Manuel J. Vaz (acting), ALTMB, room 100 (410) 965–0100.

Assistant Deputy Commissioner for—

Disability Operations.—Patricia A. Jonas, ALTMB, room 100 (410) 966–4107.

Program Policy.—Frederick G. Streckewald, ALTMB, room 100 (410) 965–6212.

Associate Commissioner, Office of Income Security Programs.—Nancy Veillon, ALTMB, room 252 (410) 965–5961.

International Programs.—Rogelio Gomez, ALTMB, room 142 (410) 966–1541.

Program Systems and Innovation Management.—Ramona L. Frentz, ANXB, room 2605 (410) 965–3658.

Disability Programs.—Glenn E. Sklar, ANXB, room 4555 (410) 965–6247.

Employment Support Programs.—Sue Suter, OPRB, room 2607 (410) 965–1352.

Program Development and Research.—Pamela Mazerski, ALTMB, room 128 (410) 965–2161.

Medical and Vocational Expertise.—Robert E. Emrich, Jr., SWTB, room 6190 (410) 966–4800.

OFFICE OF BUDGET, FINANCE, AND MANAGEMENT

Deputy Commissioner.—Dale W. Sopper, ALTMB, room 800 (410) 965–2910.
Assistant Deputy Commissioner.—Anthony F. DiNoto, ALTMB, room 800 (410) 965–2914.
Associate Commissioner, Office of:
Acquisition and Grants.—Stanley J. March, 7111 Security Boulevard (rear entrance), room 120 (410) 965–9455.
Budget.—Phil Kelly (acting), WHRB, room 2126 (410) 965–4656.
Facilities Management.—Donna L. Siegel, ALTMB, room 860 (410) 965–6789.
Financial Policy and Operations.—Jeffrey C. Hild, EHRB, room 200 (410) 965–0613.
Publications and Logistics Management.—Gary G. Arnold, ANXB, room 1540 (410) 965–4272.

OFFICE OF THE GENERAL COUNSEL

General Counsel.—Thomas W. Crawley (acting), ALTMB, room 600 (410) 965–0600.
Deputy General Counsel.—Frank V. Smith III, ALTMB, room 600 (410) 965–3414.
Associate General Counsel for—
General Law.—Michael G. Gallagher, ALTMB, room 560 (410) 965–3148.
Program Law.—James A. Winn, ALTMB, room 616 (410) 965–3137.
Public Disclosure.—Jonathan R. Cantor, SWTB (410) 966–6645.
Regional Chief Counsel for—
Atlanta.—Mary Ann Sloan, Atlanta Federal Center, 61 Forsyth Street, SW., Suite 20T45, Atlanta, GA 30303 (404) 562–1010.
Boston.—Robert J. Triba, JFK Federal Building, Room 625, Boston, MA 02203 (617) 565–2380.
Chicago.—Donna L. Calvert, 200 West Adams Street, 30th Floor, Chicago, IL 60606 (312) 353–8201.
Dallas.—Tina M. Waddell, 1301 Young Street, Suite 430, Dallas, TX 75202 (214) 767–4660.
Denver.—Deana R. Erti-Lombardi, Federal Office Building, 1961 Stout Street, Room 120, Denver, CO 80294 (303) 844–0013.
Kansas City.—Frank V. Smith, Federal Office Building, 601 East 12th Street, Room 535, Kansas City, MO 64106 (816) 936–5755.
New York.—Barbara L. Spivak, 26 Federal Plaza, Suite 3904, New York, NY 12078 (212) 264–3650, ext. 222.
Philadelphia.—Michael McGaughran, 300 Spring Garden Street, 6th Floor, Philadelphia, PA 19123 (215) 597–3335.
San Francisco.—Lucille Gonzales-Meis, 333 Market Street, Suite 1500, San Francisco, CA 94105 (415) 977–8971.
Seattle.—Vikash Chhagan, 701 Fifth Avenue, Suite 2900, M/S 901, Seattle, WA 98104 (206) 615–2274.

OFFICE OF HUMAN RESOURCES

Deputy Commissioner.—Dr. Reginald F. Wells, ALTMB, room 200 (410) 965–1900.
Assistant Deputy Commissioner.—Felicita Sola-Carter, ALTMB, room 200 (410) 965–7642.
Associate Commissioner for—
Civil Rights and Equal Opportunity.—Mark A. Anderson, ANXB, room 2571 (410) 965–3318.
Labor Management and Employee Relations.—Milton R. Beever, ANXB, room 2170 (410) 965–0066.
Office of Personnel.—Lew Kaiser, ANXB, room 4170 (410) 965–3324.
Training.—Wayne H. Harmon, EHRB, room 100 (410) 965–7968.
Director of:
Executive and Special Services.—Bonnie L. Doyle, ANXB, room 2510 (410) 965–4463.
Human Capital Planning.—Fred Glueckstein, ALTMB, room 570 (410) 966–4463.

OFFICE OF THE INSPECTOR GENERAL

Inspector General.—Patrick P. O'Carroll, ALTMB, room 300 (410) 965–7427.
Deputy Inspector General.—James A. Kissko, ALTMB, room 300 (410) 965–2850.
Chief Counsel to the Inspector General.—Kathy A. Buller, 3–ME–1 (410) 966–5136.
Assistant Inspector General for—

Audit.—Steven L. Schaeffer, 3–ME–2 (410) 965–9701.
Investigations.—Richard A. Rohde, 3–ME–3 (410) 966–2436.
Resource Management.—Stephanie Hall, 2–ME–4 (410) 965–9704.

OFFICE OF LEGISLATION AND CONGRESSIONAL AFFAIRS

Deputy Commissioner.—Robert M. Wilson, ITCB, room 826 (202) 358–6030, or ALTMB, room 152 (410) 965–2386.

Assistant Deputy Commissioner.—Diane B. Garro, ALTMB, room 152 (410) 965–2386, or ITCB, room 818 (202) 358–6080.

Associate Commissioner for Legislative Development.—Webster P. Phillips, ITCB, room 813 (202) 358–6027 or ALTMB, room 146 (410) 965–3735.

Director for—

Legislative Research and Congressional Constituent Relations.—Sharon A. Wilsin, WHRB, room 3202 (410) 965–3531.

Old Age and Survivors Insurance Benefits.—Timothy J. Kelley, WHRB, room 3210 (410) 965–3293.

Program Administration and Financing.—Sallie B. Whitney, WHRB, room 3210 (410) 965–3288.

Supplemental Security Income Program.—Erik Hansen, WHRB, room 3227 (410) 965–3112.

OFFICE OF OPERATIONS

Deputy Commissioner.—Linda S. McMahon, WHRB, room 1204 (410) 965–3143.

Assistant Deputy Commissioner.—Mary E. Glenn-Croft, WHRB, room 1204 (410) 965–1880.

Associate Commissioner, Office of:

Automation Support.—N. Mark Blatchford, ANXB, room 4705 (410) 965–4844.
Central Operations.—Carolyn L. Simmons, SWTB, room 7000 (410) 966–7000.
Disability Determinations.—Ruby D. Burrell, ANXB, room 3570 (410) 965–1250.
Electronic Services.—Jo M. Armstrong, ANXB, room 3840 (410) 965–7166.
Public Service and Operations Support.—Roger P. McDonnell, WHRB, room 1224 (410) 965–4292.
Telephone Services.—Donnell Adams, ANXB, room 4845 (410) 966–7758.

Regional Commissioner for—

Atlanta.—Paul D. Barnes, 61 Forsyth Street, Suite 23T30, Atlanta, GA 30303 (404) 562–5600.

Boston.—Susan Harding (acting), JFK Federal Building, Room 1900, Boston, MA 02203 (617) 565–2870.

Chicago.—James F. Martin, Harold Washington Social Security Center, 600 West Madison Street, Chicago, IL 60661 (312) 575–4000.

Dallas.—Ramona Schuenemeyer, 1301 Young Street, Suite 130, Dallas, TX 75202–5433 (214) 767–4207.

Denver.—Nancy A. Berryhill, Federal Office Building, 1961 Stout Street, Room 325, Denver, CO 80294 (303) 844–2388.

Kansas City.—Michael Grochowski, Federal Office Building, 601 East 12th Street, Room 436, Kansas City, MO 64106 (816) 936–5700.

New York.—Beatrice Disman, 26 Federal Plaza, Room 40–102, New York, NY 10278 (212) 264–3915.

Philadelphia.—Laurie Watkins, P.O. Box 8788, 300 Spring Garden Street, Philadelphia, PA 19123 (215) 597–5157.

San Francisco.—Peter D. Spencer, 1221 Nevin Avenue, Richmond, CA 94801 (510) 970–8400.

Seattle.—Don Schoening (acting), 701 5th Avenue, Seattle, WA 98104–7075 (206) 615–3762.

OFFICE OF POLICY

Deputy Commissioner.—Andrew G. Biggs, ITCB, room 845 (202) 358–6014.

Assistant Deputy Commissioner.—Linda D. Maxfield, ITCB, room 830 (202) 358–6137.

Associate Commissioner, Office of:

Disability and Income Assistance Policy.—Richard E. Balkus, ITCB, room 908 (202) 358–6012.

Research, Evaluation and Statistics.—Susan Grad (acting), ITCB, room 823 (202) 358–6220.
Retirement Policy.—David Weaver (acting), ITCB, room 822 (202) 358–6252.

OFFICE OF SYSTEMS

Deputy Commissioner.—William E. Gray, ALTMB, room 400 (410) 965–7747.
Assistant Deputy Commissioner.—Jerry L. Berson, ALTMB, room 400 (410) 965–6124.
Associate Commissioner, Office of:
Applications and Supplemental Security Income Systems.—Peter V. Herrera, Jr., WHRB, room 3224 (410) 965–0413.
Disability Systems.—Phillip Dulaney IV, 3200 Lord Baltimore Drive (410) 966–8193.
Earnings, Enumeration and Administrative Systems.—Ronald T. Raborg, WHRB, room 3124 (410) 965–5200.
Enterprise Support, Architecture and Engineering.—Thomas G. Grzymski, WHRB, room 3100 (410) 965–7626.
Retirement and Survivors Insurance Systems.—Peter J. Malinauskas, WHRB, room 4–K–5 (410) 965–7576.
Systems Electronic Services.—Steve A. Kautsch, OPRB, room 3003 (410) 965–3513.
Telecommunications and Systems Operations.—Phillip H. Becker, Jr., NCC, room 550 (410) 965–1500.

OFFICE OF THE CHIEF STRATEGIC OFFICER

Chief.—Dean Landis (acting), WHR, room 4200 (410) 965–7401.
Deputy Chief.—Laraine Williams, WHR, room 4200 (410) 865–7734.
Director, Office of:
Competitive Sourcing.—Dennis B. Wilhite, ALTMB, room 514 (410) 966–6988.
Strategic Management.—Regina Smith, WHR, room 4322 (410) 966–9423.
Workforce Analysis.—Ethel A. Mymbs, ME, room 4500 (410) 965–3350.

OFFICE OF QUALITY PERFORMANCE

Chief.—G. Kelly Croft, EHRB (410) 965–7481.
Deputy Chief.—H. Alan Lane, EHRB (410) 965–4331.
Director of:
Continuous Improvement.—Laura N. Train, EHRB (410) 965–9223.
Quality Control.—Martin Hansen, EHRB (410) 965–5328.
Quality Data Management.—Judith C. Kautsch, EHRB (410) 965–2645.
Regional Directors:
Atlanta.—Robert L. Raines, 61 Forsyth Street, SW., Suite 21T60, Atlanta, GA 30303 (404) 562–5676.
Baltimore.—Stephan B. Burton, SWTB, 6th Floor (410) 966–4554.
Boston.—Christine D. Tebetts, 99 High Street, Suite 400, Boston, MA 02110 (617) 695–6631.
Chicago.—Thomas R. Zimmer, 600 West Madison Street, 5th Floor, Chicago, IL 60661 (312) 575–6054.
Dallas.—Carl L. Cerrato, 1301 Young Street, Room 300, Dallas, TX 75202 (214) 767–3448.
Denver.—Ronald R. Miller, 1961 Stout Street, FOB Room 126, Denver, CO 80294 (303) 844–2601.
Kansas City.—Daryl A. Gray, 601 East 12th Street, Room 1200 South, Kansas City, MO 64106 (816) 936–5151.
New York.—Vera Bostick-Borden, 26 Federal Plaza, Room 39–100, New York, NY 10278 (212) 264–2827.
Philadelphia.—Gail B. Davis, 300 Spring Garden, 2nd Floor East, Philadelphia, PA 19123 (215) 597–2978.
San Francisco.—Grace K. Williams, 1221 Nevin Avenue, 4th Floor, Richmond, CA 94801 (510) 970–4622.
Seattle.—Rubie Toney, 701 5th Avenue, Seattle, WA 98104 (206) 615–2146.

SUSQUEHANNA RIVER BASIN COMMISSION

COMMISSIONERS AND ALTERNATES

Federal Government.—BG Tood T. Semonite (Commissioner); COL Peter W. Mueller (Alternate); COL Christopher J. Larsen (Alternate).

New York.—Kenneth P. Lynch (Chair); Scott J. Foti (Alternate).
Pennsylvania.—Kathleen A. McGinty (Vice-Chair); Cathleen C. Myers (Alternate); William A. Gast (Alternate).
Maryland.—Dr. Robert Summers (Commissioner); Herbert Sachs (Alternate); Matthew G. Pajerowski (Alternate).

STAFF

1721 North Front Street, Harrisburg, PA 17102, phone (717) 238–0423

srbc@srbc.net, http://www.srbc.net

Executive Director.—Paul O. Swartz.
Deputy Director.—Thomas W. Beauduy.
Chief Administrative Officer.—Duane A. Friends.
Secretary to the Commission.—Deborah J. Dickey.
Chief, Watershed Assessment and Protection.—David W. Heicher.
Chief, Water Resources Management.—Michael G. Brownell.
Director of Communications.—Susan S. Obleski.

STATE JUSTICE INSTITUTE

1650 King Street, Suite 600, Alexandria, VA 22314, phone (703) 684–6100

http://www.statejustice.org

BOARD OF DIRECTORS

Chairman.—Robert A. Miller.
Vice Chairman.—Joseph F. Baca.
Secretary.—Sandra A. O'Connor.
Executive Committee Member.—Keith McNamara.

Members:

Terrence B. Adamson
Robert N. Baldwin
Carlos R. Garza
Sophia H. Hall
Tommy Jewell
Arthur A. McGiverin

Officers:

Executive Director.—Janice Munsterman.
Deputy Director.—John Mattiello.

TENNESSEE VALLEY AUTHORITY

One Massachusetts Avenue, NW., Suite 300, 20444, phone (202) 898–2999

Knoxville, TN 37902, phone (865) 632–2101

Chattanooga, TN 37401, phone (423) 751–0011

Muscle Shoals, AL 35660, phone (202) 386–2601

BOARD OF DIRECTORS

Chairman.—William B. Sansom (865) 632–4000 (Knoxville).
Directors: Dennis Bottorff (Knoxville), Don DePriest (Knoxville), Mike Duncan (Knoxville), Willliam Graves (Knoxville), Skila Harris (Knoxville), Howard Thrailkill (Knoxville), Susan Richardson Williams (Knoxville).
President/Chief Operating Officer.—Tom D. Kilgore (865) 632–2366 (Knoxville).
Chief Financial Officer.—John M. Hoskins (865) 632–4049 (Knoxville).
Chief Nuclear Officer.—Karl W. Singer (423) 751–8682 (Chattanooga).
Chief Operating Officer.—William S. Orser (423) 751–6016 (Chattanooga).

CORPORATE VICE PRESIDENTS

Vice Presidents:
Chief Administrative Officer/Executive Vice President.—John E. Long, Jr. (865) 632–6307 (Knoxville).
Communications.—Peyton T. Hairston, Jr. (865) 632–3199 (Knoxville).
Customer Resources.—Kenneth R. Breeden (615) 232–6011 (Nashville).

General Counsel.—Maureen Dunn (865) 632–4131 (Knoxville).
Human Resources.—Phillip L. Reynolds (423) 751–3185 (Chattanooga).
Inspector General.—Richard W. Moore (865) 621–4120 (Knoxville).

CHIEF OPERATING OFFICER ORGANIZATION

Commercial Operations and Fuels.—Van M. Wardlaw (423) 751–3907 (Chattanooga).
Enterprise Performance and Analysis.—Anda A. Ray (423) 751–8511 (Chattanooga).
Fossil Power Group.—Joseph R. Bynum (423) 751–2601 (Chattanooga).
Power System Operations.—W. Terry Boston (423) 751–6000 (Chattanooga).
River System Operations and Environment.—Kathryn J. Jackson (865) 632–3141 (Knoxville).
Support Services.—Bob M. Tanis (423) 751–8878 (Chattanooga).
TVA Nuclear.—Karl W. Singer (423) 751–8682 (Chattanooga).

WASHINGTON OFFICE

phone (202) 898–2995, fax 898–2991

Government Relations Director.—Justin Maierhofer.

U.S. ADVISORY COMMISSION ON PUBLIC DIPLOMACY

301 Fourth Street SW., Room 600, 20547

phone (202) 203–7880, fax 203–7886

[Created by Executive Order 12048 and Public Law 96–60]

Chair.—Barbara M. Barrett.
Members: Maria Sophia Aguirre, Amb. Elizabeth Bagley, Tre Charles Evers III, Harold C. Pachios, Amb. Penne Korth Peacock, Jay T. Snyder.
Executive Director.—Athena Katsoulos.
Administrative Officer.—Jamice Clayton.

U.S. AGENCY FOR INTERNATIONAL DEVELOPMENT

1300 Pennsylvania Avenue, NW., 20523, phone (202) 712–0000

http://www.usaid.gov

Administrator.—Amb. Randall L. Tobias, room 6.09, 712–4040, fax 216–3455.
Deputy Administrator.—James Kunder (acting), room 6.09, 712–4070.
Counselor.—Mosina Jordan, room 6.08, 712–5010.
Executive Secretary.—Dawn Adams (acting), room 6.08, 712–0700.
Assistant Administrator for—
Democracy, Conflict and Humanitarian Assistance.—Mike Hess, room 8.06, 712–0100.
Economic Growth, Agriculture, and Trade.—Jacqueline Schafer, room 3.09, 712–0670.
Global Health.—Kent Hill, room 3.09, 712–1325.
Latin America and the Caribbean.—Adolfo Franco, room 5.09, 712–0500.
Legislative and Public Affairs.—J. Edward Fox, room 6.10, 712–4300.
Management.—Mosina Jordan (acting), room 6.09, 712–1200.
Director, Small and Disadvantaged Business Utilization.—Marilyn Marton, room 7.08, 712–1500.
General Counsel.—Jane Dana, room 6.06, 712–4476.
Inspector General.—Don Gambetesa, room 6.06, 712–1150.

U.S. COMMISSION ON CIVIL RIGHTS

624 Ninth Street, NW., 20425, phone (202) 376–7700, fax 376–7672

(Codified in 42 U.S.C., section 1975)

Chairperson.—Gerald A. Reynolds.
Vice Chairperson.—Abigail Thernstrom.
Commissioners: Jennifer C. Braceras, Peter N. Kirsanow, Arlan D. Melendez, Ashley L. Taylor, Jr., Michael Yaki.
Staff Director.—Kenneth L. Marcus.

U.S. HOLOCAUST MEMORIAL COUNCIL

The United States Holocaust Memorial Museum

100 Raoul Wallenberg Place, SW., 20024, phone (202) 488–0400, fax 488–2690

Officials:

Chair.—Fred S. Zeidman, Houston, TX.

Vice Chair.—Joel M. Geiderman, Los Angeles, CA.

Director.—Sara J. Bloomfield, Washington, DC.

Members:

Debra Abrams, Boca Raton, FL.
James M. Abroms, Birmingham, AL.
Sheldon G. Adelson, Las Vegas, NV.
Ivan E. Becker, Princeton, NJ.
Dottie Bennett, Falls Church, VA.
Frank R. Berman, Edina, MN.
Tom A. Bernstein, New York, NY.
Bruce L. Blalosky, Los Angeles, CA.
Marek J. Chodakiewicz, Washington, DC.
Debra Lerner Cohen, Washington, DC.
William J. Danhof, Lansing, MI.
Sam M. Devinki, Kansas City, MO.
Donald Etra, Los Angeles, CA.
Itchko Ezratti, Sunrise, FL.
David M. Flaum, Rochester, NY.
Marilyn R. Fox, Clayton, MO.
Howard L. Ganek, New York, NY.
Tony B. Gelbart, Boca Raton, FL.
JoAnne T. Ginsberg, Washington, DC.
Constance B. Girard-diCarlo, Philadelphia, PA.
Norman Hascoe, Greenwich, CT.
Phyllis G. Heideman, Bethesda, MD.
Arlene Herson, Boca Raton, FL.
Rebbetzin Esther Jungreis, New York, NY.
Alice A. Kelikian, Cambridge, MA.
Edward I. Koch, New York, NY.
M. Ronald Krongold, Coral Gables, FL.
Michael I. Lebovitz, Chattanooga, TN.
Elena N. Lefkowitz, New York, NY.
Norma Lerner, Hunting Valley, OH.
Steven M. Levy, New York, NY.
Marcia P. McCraw, Seattle, WA.
Mervin G. Morris, Menlo Park, CA.
Michael A. Morris, Atlanta, GA.
Marvin A. Pomerantz, West Des Moines, IA.
Dennis Prager, Tarzana, CA.
Alan N. Rechtschaffen, New York, NY.
Harry Reicher, Philadelphia, PA.
J. Philip Rosen, New York, NY.
Jack Rosen, New York, NY.
Alvin H. Rosenfeld, Bloomington, IN.
Eric F. Ross, South Orange, NJ.
Richard S. Sambol, Toms River, NJ.
Mickey Shapiro, Farmington Hills, MI.
Jay Stein, Jacksonville, FL.
Ronald G. Steinhart, Dallas, TX.
Nechama Tec, Stamford, CT.
Merryl H. Tisch, New York, NY.
Sonia Weitz, Peabody, MA.
William F. Weld, New York, NY.
Elie Wiesel, Boston, MA.
Bradley D. Wine, Bethesda, MD.
Judith Yudof, Austin, TX.

Former Chairs:

Irving Greenberg, 2000–2002.
Miles Lerman, 1993–2000.
Harvey M. Meyerhoff, 1987–1993.
Elie Wiesel, 1980–1986.

Former Vice Chairs:

Ruth B. Mandel, 1993–2005.
William J. Lowenberg, 1986–1993.
Mark E. Talisman, 1980–1986.

Congressional Members:

Senate:

Norm Coleman, from Minnesota.
Susan Collins, from Maine.
Russell D. Feingold, from Wisconsin.
Orrin G. Hatch, from Utah.
Frank R. Lautenberg, from Nevada.

House of Representatives:

Christopher B. Cannon, from Utah.
Eric I. Cantor, from Virginia.
Tom Lantos, from California.
Steven C. LaTourette, from Ohio.
Henry A. Waxman, from California.

Ex Officio Members:

U.S. Department of:

Education.—Philip H. Rosenfelt.

Interior.—Abraham E. Haspel.

Council Staff:

General Counsel.—Gerard Leval.

Secretary of the Council.—Jane M. Rizer.

U.S. INSTITUTE OF PEACE

1200 17th Street NW, Suite 200, 20036

phone (202) 457–1700, fax 429–6063

BOARD OF DIRECTORS

Public Members:

Chairman.—J. Robinson West.

Vice Chairman.—Maria Otero.
Members:
Betty Bumpers
Holly Burkhalter
Chester Crocker
Laurie Fulton
Charles Horner
Mora McLean
Barbara Snelling
Ex Officio:
Assistant Secretary of Defense.—Peter Rodman (Secretary's Designate).
Assistant Secretary of State.—Barry Lowenkron (Secretary's Designate).
National Defense University.—Frances Wilson.
Officials:
President.—Richard H. Solomon.
Executive Vice President.—Patricia Thompson.
Vice President for—
Center for—
Conflict Analysis and Prevention.—Paul Stares.
Mediation and Conflict Resolution.—David Smock.
Post-Conflict Peace and Stability Operations.—Daniel Serwer.
Education.—Pamela Aall.
Grants and Fellows.—Judy Barsalou.
Headquarters Project.—Charles Nelson.
Management.—Mike Graham.
Training.—Mike Lekson.
Associate Vice President for—
Religion and Peacemaking.—David Smock.
Rule of Law.—Neil Kritz.
Director of:
Congressional Relations.—Laurie Schultz Helm.
Public Affairs and Communication.—Ian Larsen.

U.S. INTERNATIONAL TRADE COMMISSION

500 E Street, SW., 20436

phone (202) 205–2000, fax 205–2798, http://www.usitc.gov

COMMISSIONERS

Chairman.—Daniel R. Pearson, Republican, Minnesota.
Vice Chairman.—Shara L. Aranoff, Democrat, Maryland.
Commissioners:
Charlotte R. Lane, Republican, West Virginia.
Deanna Tanner Okun, Republican, Idaho.
Dean A. Pinkert, Democrat, Virginia.
Irving A. Williamson, Democrat, New York.
Congressional Relations Officer.—Nancy M. Carman, 205–3151.
Secretary.—Marilyn R. Abbott, 205–2799.
Administrative Law Judges: Robert L. Barton, Jr., 708–4051; Charles E. Bullock, 205–2681; Sidney Harris, 205–2692; Paul J. Luckern, 205–2694.
General Counsel.—James M. Lyons, 205–3101.
Inspector General.—Jean Smith (acting), 205–3177.
Chief Information Officer.—Stephen A. McLaughlin, 205–3131.
Director, Office of:
Administration.—Stephen A. McLaughlin, 205–3131.
Economics.—Robert B. Koopman, 205–3216.
Equal Employment Opportunity.—Jacqueline A. Waters, 205–2240.
External Relations.—Lyn M. Schlitt, 205–3141.
Facilities Management.—Jonathan Brown, 205–2745.
Finance.—Patricia Katsouros, 205–2682.
Human Resources.—Paula M. Chandler, 205–2651.
Industries.—Karen Laney-Cummings, 205–3296.
Investigations.—Robert Carpenter, 205–3160.
Operations.—Robert A. Rogowsky, 205–2230.
Tariff Affairs and Trade Agreements.—David Beck, 205–2603.
Unfair Import Investigations.—Lynn I. Levine, 205–2561.

U.S. MERIT SYSTEMS PROTECTION BOARD

1615 M Street, NW., 20419

phone (202) 653–7220, toll-free (800) 209–8960, fax 653–7130

[Created by Public Law 95–454]

Chairman.—Neil Anthony Gordon McPhie.
Vice Chairman.—Mary M. Rose.
Member.—Barbara J. Sapin.
Chief of Staff.—Tracey Watkins.
General Counsel.—B. Chad Bungard.
Appeals Counsel.—Lynore Carnes.

REGIONAL OFFICES

Regional Directors:

Atlanta Regional Office: Covering Alabama, Florida, Georgia, Mississippi, South Carolina, Tennessee.—Thomas J. Lamphear, 10th Floor, 401 West Peachtree Street NW, Atlanta, GA 30308 (404) 730–2755, fax 730–2767.

Central Regional Office: Covering Illinois, Iowa, Kanas City, Kansas, Kentucky, Indiana, Michigan, Minnesota, Missouri, Ohio, Wisconsin.—Martin Baumgaertner, 31st Floor, 230 South Dearborn Street, Chicago, IL 60604 (312) 353–2923, fax 886–4231.

Dallas Regional Office: Covering Arkansas, Louisiana, Oklahoma, Texas.—Sharon Jackson, Chief Administrative Judge, Room 620, 1100 Commerce Street, Dallas, TX 75242 (214) 767–0555, fax 767–0102.

Northeastern Regional Office: Covering Connecticut, Delaware, Maryland (except Montgomery and Prince Georges counties), Massachusetts, New Hampshire, New Jersey (except the counties of Bergen, Essex, Hudson, and Union), Pennsylvania, Rhode Island, Vermont, West Virginia.—William L. Boulden, U.S. Customhouse, Room 501, Second and Chestnut Streets, Philadelphia, PA 19106 (215) 597–9960, fax 597–3456.

New York Field Office: Covering New York, Puerto Rico, Virgin Islands, the following counties in New Jersey: Bergen, Essex, Hudson, Union.—Arthur Joseph, Chief Administrative Judge, Room 3137–A, 26 Federal Plaza, New York, NY 10278 (212) 264–9372, fax 264–1417.

Western Regional Office: Covering Alaska, California, Hawaii, Idaho, Nevada, Oregon, Washington, and Pacific Overseas.—Amy Dunning, 250 Montgomery Street, Suite 400, 4th Floor, San Francisco, CA 94104 (415) 705–2935, fax 705–2945.

Denver Field Office: Covering Arizona, Colorado, Kansas (except Kansas City), Montana, Nebraska, New Mexico, North Dakota, South Dakota, Utah, Wyoming.—Maxanne Witkin, Chief Administrative Judge, 165 South Union Boulevard, Suite 318, Lakewood, CO 80228 (303) 969–5101, fax 969–5109.

Washington Regional Office: Covering Washington, DC, Maryland (counties of Montgomery and Prince Georges), North Carolina, Virginia, all overseas areas not otherwise covered.—P.J. Winzer, 1811 Diagonal Road, Suite 205, Alexandria, VA 22314 (703) 756–6250, fax 756–7112.

U.S. OVERSEAS PRIVATE INVESTMENT CORPORATION

1100 New York Avenue, NW., 20527, phone (202) 336–8400

President and Chief Executive Officer.—Robert Mosbacher, Jr.
Executive Vice President and Chief Operating Officer.—John Simon.
Vice President and General Counsel.—Mark Garfinkel.
Vice President and Chief Financial Officer.—Howard Burris.
Vice President for—
External Affairs.—Christopher Coughlin.
Insurance.—Edith Quintrell.
Investment Development and Economic Growth.—Daniel A. Nichols.
Investment Funds.—Cynthia L. Hostetler.
Investment Policy.—Christine Emery.
Small and Medium Enterprise Finance.—James Polan.
Structured Finance.—Robert B. Drumheller.
Director, Congressional Affairs.—Richard C. Horanburg, 336–8417.

BOARD OF DIRECTORS

Government Directors:

Randall L. Tobias, Administrator, U.S. Agency for International Development, U.S. Director of Foreign Assistance.

Amb. Karan K. Bhatia, Deputy U.S. Trade Representative.

Robert Mosbacher, Jr., President and Chief Executive Officer, Overseas Private Investment Corporation.

Dr. David A. Sampson, Deputy Secretary of Commerce, U.S. Department of Commerce.

Timothy D. Adams, Under Secretary for International Affairs, U.S. Department of Treasury.

Private Sector Directors:

Samuel E. Ebbesen (General, USA, Ret.), President and Chief Executive Officer, Virgin Island Telephone Corporation, St. Thomas, Virgin Islands.

Christopher J. Hanley, General Secretary-Treasurer, International Union of Operating Engineers, Washington, DC.

Diane Ingels Moss, President and Owner, Cartera Investment Corporation, Dallas, Texas.

Diane M. Ruebling, President, The Ruebling Group, Scottsdale, Arizona/Longville, Minnesota.

Ned L. Siegel, President, The Siegel Group, Boca Raton, Florida.

C. William Swank, Retired Executive Vice President, Ohio Farm Bureau Federation, Westerville, Ohio.

Sanford L. Gottesman, President, The Gottesman Company, Austin, Texas.

Staff:

Board Counsel.—Mark Garfinkel, 336–8410.
Corporate Secretary.—Connie M. Downs, 336–8438.

U.S. POSTAL SERVICE

475 L'Enfant Plaza, SW., 20260–0010, phone (202) 268–2000

BOARD OF GOVERNORS

Chairman.—James C. Miller III.
Vice Chairman.—Alan Kessler.
Postmaster General/CEO.—John E. Potter.
Deputy Postmaster General/Chief Operating Officer.—Patrick R. Donahoe.

MEMBERS

Mickey D. Barnett
James H. Bilbray
Carolyn Lewis Gallagher
Louis J. Guiliano
Thurgood Marshall, Jr.
Katherine C. Tobin
Ellen C. Williams

OFFICERS OF THE BOARD OF GOVERNORS

Secretary to the Board of Governors.—Wendy A. Hocking.

OFFICERS OF THE POSTAL SERVICE

Postmaster General, Chief Executive Officer.—John E. Potter, 268–2550.
Deputy Postmaster General/Chief Operating Officer.—Patrick R. Donahoe, 268–4842.
Chief Officer/Executive Vice President of:
Financial.—Glen H. Walker, 268–5272.
Human Resources.—Anthony J. Vegliante, 268–7852.
Marketing.—Anita Bizzotto, 268–4400.
Chief Postal Inspector.—Alexander Lazaroff, 268–5615.
Senior Vice President of:
General Counsel.—Mary Anne Gibbons, 268–2950.
Government Relations.—Thomas G. Day, 268–2506.
Intelligent Mail and Address Quality.—Charles E. Bravo, 268–6200.
Operations.—William P. Galligan, 268–5100.
Strategy and Transition.—Linda A. Kingsley, 268–2252.
Senior Vice President/Managing Director of Global Business.—Paul Vogel, 268–7666.
Vice President of:
Consumer Advocate.—Delores J. Killette, 268–2281.

Controller.—Lynn Malcolm, 268–4177.
Customer Service.—Susan M. Plonkey, 268–8800.
Delivery and Retail.—Kathleen Ainsworth, 268–6500.
Employee Development and Diversity.—Susan LaChance, 268–6566.
Employee Resource Management.—Deborah Giannoni-Jackson, 268–3783.
Engineering.—Walter F. O'Tormey (703) 280–7001.
Facilities.—Tom A. Samra (703) 526–2727.
Network Operations.—Anthony M. Pajunas, 268–4948.
Pricing and Classification.—Stephen M. Kearney, 268–2244.
Product Development.—Nicholas F. Barranca, 268–7301.
Public Affairs and Communications.—Joanne B. Giordano, 268–2143.
Sales.—Jerry Whalen (703) 292–3679.
Supply Management.—Susan M. Brownell, 268–4040.

U.S. RAILROAD RETIREMENT BOARD

844 North Rush Street, Chicago, IL 60611, phone (312) 751–4500, fax 751–7136
Office of Legislative Affairs, 1310 G Street, NW., Suite 500, 20005
phone (202) 272–7742, fax 272–7728, e-mail: ola@rrb.gov
http://www.rrb.gov

Chairman—Michael S. Schwartz (312) 751–4900, fax 751–7193.
Assistant to the Chairman.—Nancy S. Pittman.
Counsel to the Chairman.—Stephen W. Seiple.
Labor Member.—V.M. Speakman, Jr., 751–4905, fax 751–7194.
Assistants to the Labor Member: James C. Boehner, Geraldine L. Clark, Michael J. Collins.
Counsel to the Labor Member.—Thomas W. Sadler.
Management Member.—Jerome F. Kever, 751–4910, fax 751–7189.
Assistant to the Management Member.—Joseph M. Waechter.
Counsel to the Management Member.—Robert M. Perbohner.
Attorney-Advisor to the Management Member.—Ann L. Chaney.
Inspector General.—Martin J. Dickman, 751–4690, fax 751–4342.
General Counsel.—Steven A. Bartholow, 751–4935, fax 751–7102.
Assistant General Counsel.—Marguerite P. Dadabo, 751–4945, fax 751–7102.
Secretary to the Board.—Beatrice E. Ezerski, 751–4920, fax 751–4923.
Director of:
Assessment and Training.—Catherine A. Leyser, 751–4757, fax 751–7190.
Equal Opportunity.—Lynn E. Cousins, 751–4925, fax 751–7179.
Field Service.—Martha M. Barringer, 751–4515, fax 751–3360.
Hearings and Appeals.—Arthur A. Arfa, 751–4346, fax 751–7159.
Human Resources.—Keith B. Earley, 751–4392, fax 751–7164.
Legislative Affairs.—Margaret A. Lindsley (202) 272–7742, fax 272–7728.
Operations.—Robert J. Duda, 751–4698, fax 751–7157.
Policy and Systems.—Ronald Russo, 751–4984, fax 751–4650.
Programs.—Dorothy A. Isherwood, 751–4980, fax 751–4333.
Resource Management Center.—Cecilia A. Freeman, 751–4392, fax 751–7161.

Supervisor of:
Acquisition Management.—Paul T. Ahern, 751–7130, fax 751–4923.
Congressional Inquiry.—Richard M. Konopka, 751–4974, fax 751–7154.
Public Affairs.—Anita J. Rogers, 751–4737, fax 751–7154.
Chief of:
Actuary.—Frank J. Buzzi, 751–4915, fax 751–7129.
Benefit and Employment Analysis.—Marla L. Huddleston, 751–4779, fax 751–7129.
Finance.—Kenneth P. Boehne, 751–4930, fax 751–4931.
Information.—Terri S. Morgan, 751–4851, fax 751–7169.
Librarian.—Katherine Tsang, 751–4926, fax 751–4924.
SEO/Director of Administration.—Henry M. Valiulis, 751–4990, fax 751–7197.

REGIONAL OFFICES

Atlanta: Patricia R. Lawson, Suite 1703, 401 West Peachtree Street, Atlanta, GA 30308 (404) 331–2691, fax (404) 331–7234.
Denver: Louis E. Austin, Suite 2260, 1999 Broadway, Box 7, Denver, CO 80202 (303) 844–0800, fax (303) 844–0806.
Philadelphia: Michael L. Bauer, 900 Market Street, Suite 304, Philadelphia, PA 19107 (215) 597–2647, fax (215) 597–2794.

U.S. SENTENCING COMMISSION

One Columbus Circle, NE., Suite 2–500, South Lobby, 20002–8002

phone (202) 502–4500, fax 502–4699

Chair.—Ricardo H. Hinojosa.
Vice Chairs: Ruben Castillo, William K. Sessions III, John R. Steer.
Commissioners: Dabney L. Friedrich, Michael E. Horowitz, Beryl A. Howell.
Commissioners, ex officio: Benton J. Campbell, Edward F. Reilly, Jr.
Staff Director.—Judith W. Sheon, 502–4510.
General Counsel.—Kenneth P. Cohen, 502–4520.
Director of:
Administration.—Susan L. Winarsky, 502–4610.
Research and Data Collection.—Glenn R. Schmitt, 502–4530.
Director and Chief Counsel of Office of Training.—Pamela G. Montgomery, 502–4540.
Public Affairs Officer.—Michael Courlander, 502–4597.
Legislative and Governmental Affairs.—Lisa A. Rich, 502–4519.

U.S. TRADE AND DEVELOPMENT AGENCY

1000 Wilson Boulevard, Suite 1600, Arlington, VA 22209, phone (703) 875–4357

Director.—Thelma J. Askey.
Deputy Director.—Leocadia I. Zak.
Chief of Staff.—Thomas R. Hardy.
Administrative Officer.—Carolyn Hum.
Communications and Policy Advisor.—Donna Thiessen.
Congressional Relations Advisor.—Amy L. Lorenzini.
Contracting Officer.—Richard Sallee.
Economist/Evaluation Officer.—David Denny.
Financial Manager.—Noreen St. Louis.
General Counsel.—James A. Wilderotter.
Grants Administrator.—Pat Daughetee.
Policy and Planning Director.—Geoffrey Jackson.
Resource Advisor.—Micheal Hillier.
Regional Director for—
Asia.—Henry Steingass.
Eastern Europe/Eurasia.—Daniel D. Stein.
Latin America and Caribbean.—Anne McKinney.
North Africa/Middle East/South Asia.—Carl B. Kress.
Sub-Saharan Africa.—Ned Cabot.

WASHINGTON METROPOLITAN AREA TRANSIT AUTHORITY

600 Fifth Street, NW., 20001, phone (202) 637–1234

General Manager.—John B. Catoe.
General Counsel.—Carol B. O'Keeffe.
Chief Financial Officer.—Charles Woodruff.
Chief Operating Officer for—
Bus Service.—Jack Requa.
Rail Service.—Steve Feil.
Assistant General Manager for—
Communications.—Raymond Feldmann.
System Safety and Risk Protection.—Frederick C. Goodine.
Director, Office of:
Policy and Government Relations.—Deborah S. Lipman.
Public Relations.—Lisa Farbstein.
Chief, Transit Police Department.—Polly Hanson.

WASHINGTON NATIONAL MONUMENT SOCIETY

[Organized 1833; chartered 1859; amended by Acts of August 2, 1876, October, 1888]

President Ex Officio.—George W. Bush, President of the United States.
First Vice President.—James W. Symington, 1666 K Street, NW., Suite 500, Washington, DC 20006–2107 (202) 778–2107.
Treasurer.—Henry Ravenel, Jr.
Secretary.—Steve Lorenzetti, Superintendent (acting), National Mall and Memorial Parks, 900 Ohio Drive, SW., Washington, DC 20024–2000, 485–9875.
Members:
Christopher Addison
Vincent C. Burke, Jr.
Robert W. Duemling
Gilbert M. Grosvenor
Potter Stewart
Richard P. Williams
C. Boyden Gray
George B. Hartzog, Jr.
John D.H. Kane
John A. Washington
Member Emeritus:
Harry F. Byrd, Jr.

WOODROW WILSON INTERNATIONAL CENTER FOR SCHOLARS

One Woodrow Wilson Plaza 1300 Pennsylvania Avenue, NW., 20004–3027
phone (202) 691–4000, fax 691–4001

(Under the direction of the Board of Trustees of
Woodrow Wilson International Center for Scholars)

Director/President.—Lee H. Hamilton, 691–4202.
Deputy Director.—Michael Van Dusen, 691–4055.
Executive Assistant to the President.—Nora Coulter.
Director for—
Administrative Management and Human Resources.—Leslie Johnson.
Financial Management.—John Dysland.
Board of Trustees:
Chairman.—Joseph B. Gildenhorn.
Vice Chairman.—David A. Metzner.
Private Members:
Robin Cook
Donald E. Garcia
Bruce S. Gelb
Sander R. Gerber
Charles L. Glazer
Susan Hutchison
Public Members:
Condoleezza Rice, Secretary of State.
Margaret Spellings, Secretary of Education.
Michael O. Leavitt, Secretary of Health and Human Services.
Bruce Cole, Chairman of the National Endowment for the Humanities.
Lawrence M. Small, Secretary of the Smithsonian Institution.
James H. Billington, Librarian of Congress.
Allen Weinstein, Archivist of the United States.

Designated Appointee of the President of the United States from within the Federal Government.—Tami Longaberger.

JUDICIARY

SUPREME COURT OF THE UNITED STATES

One First Street, NE., 20543, phone (202) 479–3000

JOHN GLOVER ROBERTS, Jr., Chief Justice of the United States; born in Buffalo, NY, January 27, 1955; son of John G. Roberts and Rosemary Podrasky; married to Jane Marie Sullivan, July 27, 1996; children: Josephine and John; A.B., Harvard University, 1976; J.D., Harvard Law School, 1979; managing editor, Harvard Law Review; law clerk for Justice Henry J. Friendly, United States Court of Appeals for the Second Circuit, 1979–80; law clerk for then Associate Justice William H. Rehnquist, Supreme Court of the United States, 1980–81; Special Assistant to the Attorney General, U.S. Department of Justice, 1981–82; Associate Counsel to President Ronald Reagan, White House Counsel's Office, 1982–86; Principal Deputy Solicitor General, U.S. Department of Justice, 1989–93; private practice of law, Hogan and Hartson, Washington, DC, 1986–89 and 1993–2003; member: American Academy of Appellate Lawyers; American Law Institute; Edward Coke Appellate American Inn of Court; served on Advisory Committee on Appellate Rules of the Judicial Conference of the United States; nominated to the United States Court of Appeals for the District of Columbia Circuit by President George W. Bush on January 7, 2003; sworn in on June 2, 2003; nominated Chief Justice of the Supreme Court of the United States by President George W. Bush on September 5, 2005; sworn in on September 29, 2005.

JOHN PAUL STEVENS, Associate Justice of the Supreme Court of the United States; born in Chicago, IL, April 20, 1920; son of Ernest James and Elizabeth Street Stevens; A.B., University of Chicago, 1941, Phi Beta Kappa, Psi Upsilon; J.D. (*magna cum laude*), Northwestern University, 1947, Order of the Coif, Phi Delta Phi, co-editor, Illinois Law Review; married to Maryan Mulholland; children: John Joseph, Kathryn Jedlicka, Elizabeth Jane Sesemann, and Susan Roberta Mullen; entered active duty U.S. Navy in 1942, released as Lt. Commander in 1945 after WWII service, Bronze Star; law clerk to U.S. Supreme Court Justice Wiley Rutledge, 1947–48; admitted to Illinois bar, 1949; practiced law in Chicago, Poppenhusen, Johnston, Thompson and Raymond, 1949–52; associate counsel, Subcommittee on the Study of Monopoly Power, Judiciary Committee of the U.S. House of Representatives, 1951–52; partner, Rothschild, Stevens, Barry and Myers, Chicago, 1952–70; member of the Attorney General's National Committee to Study Antitrust Laws, 1953–55; lecturer in Antitrust Law, Northwestern University School of Law, 1950–54, and University of Chicago Law School, 1955–58; chief counsel, Illinois Supreme Court Special Commission to Investigate Integrity of the Judgment of *People* v. *Isaacs*, 1969; appointed U.S. Circuit Judge for the Seventh Circuit, October 14, 1970, entering on duty November 2, 1970, and serving until becoming an Associate Justice of the Supreme Court; nominated to the Supreme Court December 1, 1975, by President Ford; confirmed by the Senate December 17, 1975; sworn in on December 19, 1975.

ANTONIN SCALIA, Associate Justice of the Supreme Court of the United States; born in Trenton, NJ, March 11, 1936; LL.B., Harvard Law School, 1960; note editor, Harvard Law Review; Sheldon fellow, Harvard University, 1960–61; married to Maureen McCarthy, September 10, 1960; children: Ann Forrest; Eugene, John Francis, Catherine Elisabeth, Mary Clare, Paul David, Matthew, Christopher James, and Margaret Jane; admitted to practice in Ohio (1962) and Virginia (1970); in private practice with Jones, Day, Cockley, and Reavis (Cleveland, OH), 1961–67; professor of law, University of Virginia Law School, 1967–74 (on leave 1971–74); general counsel, Office of Telecommunications Policy, Executive Office of the President, 1971–72; chairman, Administrative Conference of the United States, 1972–74; Assistant Attorney General, Office of Legal Counsel, U.S. Department of Justice, 1974–77; scholar in residence, American Enterprise Institute, 1977; professor of law, University of Chicago, 1977–82; appointed by President Reagan as Circuit Judge of the U.S. Court of Appeals for the District of Columbia Circuit; sworn in on August 17, 1982; appointed by President Reagan as Associate Justice of the U.S. Supreme Court; sworn in on September 26, 1986.

ANTHONY M. KENNEDY, Associate Justice of the Supreme Court of the United States; born in Sacramento, CA, July 23, 1936; son of Anthony James and Gladys McLeod Kennedy; married to Mary Davis, June 29, 1963; children: Justin Anthony, Gregory Davis, and Kristin Marie; Stanford University, 1954–57; London School of Economics, 1957–58; B.A., Stanford University, 1958; LL.B., Harvard Law School, 1961; associate, Thelen, Marrin, Johnson and Bridges, San Francisco, 1961–63; sole practitioner, Sacramento, 1963–67; partner, Evans, Jackson and Kennedy, Sacramento, 1967–75; professor of constitutional law, McGeorge School of Law, University of the Pacific, 1965–88; California Army National Guard, 1961; member: the Judicial Conference of the United States' Advisory Panel on Financial Disclosure Reports and Judicial Activities (subsequently renamed the Advisory Committee of Codes of Conduct), 1979–87; Committee on Pacific Territories, 1979–90 (chairman, 1982–90); board of the Federal Judicial Center, 1987–88; nominated by President Ford to U.S. Court of Appeals for the Ninth Circuit; sworn in on May 30, 1975; nominated by President Reagan as Associate Justice of the U.S. Supreme Court; sworn in on February 18, 1988.

DAVID HACKETT SOUTER, Associate Justice of the Supreme Court of the United States; born in Melrose, MA, September 17, 1939; son of Joseph Alexander and Helen Adams Hackett Souter; A.B., Harvard College, 1961, Phi Beta Kappa, selected Rhodes Scholar; A.B. in Jurisprudence (1963) and M.A. (1989), Magdalen College, Oxford University; LL.B., Harvard Law School, 1966; associate, Orr and Reno, Concord, NH, 1966–68; assistant attorney general of New Hampshire, 1968–71; Deputy Attorney General of New Hampshire, 1971–76; Attorney General of New Hampshire, 1976–78; named Associate Justice, New Hampshire Superior Court, 1978–83; appointed Associate Justice, New Hampshire Supreme Court, 1983–90; member: Maine-New Hampshire Interstate Boundary Commission, 1971–75; New Hampshire Police Standards and Training Council, 1976–78; New Hampshire Governor's Commission on Crime and Delinquency, 1976–78; 1979–83; New Hampshire Judicial Council, 1976–78; Concord Hospital Board of Trustees, 1972–85 (president, 1978–84); New Hampshire Historical Society, 1968–present, (vice-president, 1980–85, trustee, 1976–85); Dartmouth Medical School, Board of Overseers, 1981–87; Merrimack County Bar Association, 1966–present; New Hampshire Bar Association, 1966–present; Honorary Fellow, American Bar Foundation; Honorary Fellow, American College of Trial Lawyers; Honorary Master of the Bench, Gray's Inn, London; Honorary Fellow, Magdalen College, Oxford; Associate, Lowell House, Harvard College; nominated by President Bush to U.S. Court of Appeals for the First Circuit; took oath May 25, 1990; nominated by President Bush as Associate Justice of the U.S. Supreme Court; took oath of office October 9, 1990.

CLARENCE THOMAS, Associate Justice of the Supreme Court of the United States; born in Pin Point, GA (near Savannah), June 23, 1948; son of M.C. and Leola Thomas; raised by his grandparents, Myers and Christine Anderson; married to Virginia Lamp, May 30, 1987; son Jamal Adeen by previous marriage; attended Conception Seminary, 1967–68; A.B. (*cum laude*), Holy Cross College, 1971; J.D., Yale Law School, 1974; admitted to practice in Missouri, 1974; assistant attorney general of Missouri, 1974–77; attorney in the law department of Monsanto Company, 1977–79; legislative assistant to Senator John Danforth, 1979–81; Assistant Secretary for Civil Rights, U.S. Department of Education, 1981–82; chairman, U.S. Equal Employment Opportunity Commission, 1982–90; nominated by President Bush to U.S. Court of Appeals for the District of Columbia Circuit; took oath March 12, 1990; nominated by President Bush as Associate Justice of the U.S. Supreme Court; took the constitutional oath on October 18, 1991 and the judicial oath on October 23, 1991.

RUTH BADER GINSBURG, Associate Justice of the Supreme Court of the United States; born in Brooklyn, NY, March 15, 1933; daughter of Nathan and Celia Amster Bader; married Martin Ginsburg, 1954; two children: Jane C. and James S.; B.A., Phi Beta Kappa, Cornell University, 1954; attended Harvard Law School, 1956–58; LL.B., Columbia Law School, 1959; law clerk to Edmund L. Palmieri, U.S. District Court, Southern District of New York, 1959–61; Columbia Law School Project on International Procedure, 1961–62, associate director, 1962–63; professor, Rutgers University School of Law, 1963–72; professor, Columbia Law School, 1972–80; Fellow, Center for Advanced Study in Behavioral Sciences, 1977–78; American Civil Liberties Union, general counsel, 1973–80; National Board of Directors, 1974–80; Women's Rights Project, founder and Counsel, 1972–80; American Bar Foundation Board of Directors, executive committee, secretary, 1979–89; American Bar Association Board of Editors, 1972–78; ABA Section on Individual Rights and Responsibilities, council member, 1975–81; American Law Institute, council member, 1978–93; American Academy of Arts and Sciences, Fellow, 1982–present; Council on Foreign Relations, 1975–present; nominated by President Carter as a Judge, U.S. Court of Appeals for the District of Columbia Circuit, sworn in on June 30, 1980; nominated Associate Justice by President Clinton, June 14, 1993, confirmed by the Senate, August 3, 1993, and sworn in August 10, 1993.

STEPHEN G. BREYER, Associate Justice of the Supreme Court of the United States; born in San Francisco, CA, August 15, 1938; son of Irving G. and Anne R. Breyer; married Joanna Hare, 1967; three children: Chloe, Nell, and Michael; A.B., Stanford University, 1959; B.A., Oxford University, Magdalen College, Marshall Scholar, 1961; LL.B., Harvard Law School, 1964; law clerk to Associate Justice Arthur J. Goldberg of the Supreme Court of the United States, 1964–65; special assistant to the Assistant Attorney General (Antitrust), Department of Justice, 1965–67; Assistant Special Prosecutor of the Watergate Special Prosecution Force, 1973; Special Counsel of the U.S. Senate Judiciary Committee, Subcommittee on Administrative Practices, 1974–75; Chief Counsel of the U.S. Senate Judiciary Committee, 1979–80; Professor of Law, Harvard Law School, 1970–80; (assistant professor, 1967–70; lecturer, 1980–94); professor, Kennedy School of Government, Harvard University, 1977–80; nominated by President Carter as a Judge, U.S. Court of Appeals for the First Circuit, sworn in on December 10, 1980; Chief Judge, 1990–94; member, U.S. Sentencing Commission, 1985–89; member, Judicial Conference of the United States, 1990–94; nominated Associate Justice by President Clinton May 13, 1994, confirmed by the Senate July 29, 1994, and sworn in on August 3, 1994.

SAMUEL ANTHONY ALITO, JR., Associate Justice of the Supreme Court of the United States; born in Trenton, NJ, April 1, 1950; son of Samuel A. Alito, Sr. and Rose Fradusco Alito; married to Martha-Ann Bomgardner, 1985; children: Philip and Laura; J.D., Yale Law School, 1975; law clerk for Justice Leonard I. Garth, United States Court of Appeals for the Third Circuit, 1976–77; Assistant U.S. Attorney, District of New Jersey, 1977–81; Assistant to the Solicitor General, U.S. Department of Justice, 1981–85; Deputy Assistant U.S. Attorney, U.S. Department of Justice, 1985–87; U.S. Attorney, District of New Jersey, 1987–90; nominated to the United States Court of Appeals for the Third Circuit by President George H.W. Bush on February 20, 1990; sworn in on April 30, 1990; nominated Associate Justice of the U.S. Supreme Court by President George W. Bush on October 31, 2005; sworn in on January 31, 2006.

Officers of the Supreme Court

Clerk.—William K. Suter.
Librarian.—Judith Gaskell.
Marshal.—Pamela Talkin.
Reporter of Decisions.—Frank D. Wagner.
Counsel.—Scott Harris.
Curator.—Catherine Fitts.
Budget and Personnel Officer.—Cyril A. Donnelly.
Public Information Officer.—Kathleen L. Arberg.
Director of Data Systems.—Donna Clement.
Administrative Assistant to the Chief Justice.—Sally M. Rider.

UNITED STATES COURTS OF APPEALS

First Judicial Circuit (Districts of Maine, Massachusetts, New Hampshire, Puerto Rico, and Rhode Island).—*Chief Judge:* Michael Boudin. *Circuit Judges:* Juan R. Torruella; Sandra L. Lynch; Kermit V. Lipez; Jeffrey R. Howard. *Senior Circuit Judges:* Levin H. Campbell; Bruce M. Selya; Conrad K. Cyr; Norman H. Stahl. *Circuit Executive:* Gary H. Wente (617) 748–9613. *Clerk:* Richard C. Donovan (617) 748–9057, John Joseph Moakley U.S. Courthouse, One Courthouse Way, Suite 2500, Boston, MA 02210.

Second Judicial Circuit (Districts of Connecticut, New York, and Vermont).—*Chief Judge:* Dennis Jacobs. *Circuit Judges:* John M. Walker, Jr.; Guido Calabresi; José A. Cabranes; Rosemary S. Pooler; Chester J. Straub; Robert D. Sack; Sonia Sotomayor; Robert A. Katzmann; Barrington D. Parker, Jr.; Reena Raggi. *Senior Circuit Judges:* Wilfred Feinberg; James L. Oakes; Thomas J. Meskill; Jon O. Newman; Richard J. Cardamone; Ralph K. Winter; Roger J. Miner; Joseph M. McLaughlin; Amalya L. Kearse; Pierre N. Leval. *Circuit Executive:* Karen Greve Milton (212) 857–8700. *Clerk:* Tom Asreen (acting), (212) 857–8500, Thurgood Marshall United States Courthouse, 40 Foley Square, New York, NY 10007–1581.

Third Judicial Circuit (Districts of Delaware, New Jersey, Pennsylvania, and Virgin Islands).—*Chief Judge:* Anthony J. Scirica. *Circuit Judges:* Dolores K. Sloviter; Theodore A. McKee; Marjorie O. Rendell; Maryanne Trump Barry; Thomas L. Ambro; Julio M. Fuentes; D. Brooks Smith; D. Michael Fisher; Michael A. Chagares; Kent A. Jordan. *Senior Circuit Judges:* Ruggero J. Aldisert; Joseph F. Weis, Jr.; Leonard I. Garth; Walter K. Stapleton; Morton I. Greenberg; Robert E. Cowen; Richard L. Nygaard; Jane R. Roth; Franklin S. Van Antwerpen. *Circuit Executive:* Toby D. Slawsky (215) 597–0718. *Clerk:* Marcia M. Waldron (215) 597–2995, U.S. Courthouse, 601 Market Street, Philadelphia, PA 19106.

Fourth Judicial Circuit (Districts of Maryland, North Carolina, South Carolina, Virginia, and West Virginia).—*Chief Judge:* William W. Wilkins. *Circuit Judges:* H. Emory Widener, Jr.; Paul V. Niemeyer; J. Harvie Wilkinson III; Karen J. Williams; M. Blane Michael; Diana Gribbon Motz; William B. Traxler, Jr.; Robert B. King; Roger L. Gregory; Dennis W. Shedd; Allyson K. Duncan. *Senior Circuit Judge:* Clyde H. Hamilton. *Circuit Executive:* Samuel W. Phillips (804) 916–2184. *Clerk:* Patricia S. Connor (804) 916–2700, Lewis F. Powell, Jr. U.S. Courthouse Annex, 1100 E. Main Street, Richmond, VA 23219.

Fifth Judicial Circuit (Districts of Louisiana, Mississippi, and Texas).—*Chief Judge:* Edith H. Jones. *Circuit Judges:* E. Grady Jolly; W. Eugene Davis; Jerry E. Smith; Jacques L. Wiener, Jr.; Rhesa H. Barksdale; Emilio M. Garza; Harold R. DeMoss, Jr.; Fortunato P. Benavides; Carl E. Stewart; James L. Dennis; Edith Brown Clement; Edward C. Prado; Carolyn Dineen King. *Senior Circuit Judges:* Thomas M. Reavley; Will Garwood; Patrick E. Higginbotham; John M. Duhé, Jr. *Circuit Executive:* Gregory A. Nussel (504) 310–7777. *Clerk:* Charles R. Fulbruge III (504) 310–7700, John Minor Wisdom, U.S. Court of Appeals Building, 600 Camp Street, New Orleans, LA 70130–3425.

Sixth Judicial Circuit (Districts of Kentucky, Michigan, Ohio, and Tennessee).—*Chief Judge:* Danny J. Boggs; *Circuit Judges:* Boyce F. Martin, Jr.; Alice M. Batchelder; Martha Craig Daughtrey; Karen Nelson Moore; R. Guy Cole, Jr.; Eric Lee Clay; Ronald Lee Gilman; Julie Smith Gibbons; John M. Rogers; Jeffrey S. Sutton; Deborah L. Cook; David McKeague; Richard Allen Griffin. *Senior Circuit Judges:* Damon J. Keith; Gilbert S. Merritt; Cornelia G. Kennedy; Ralph B. Guy, Jr.; James L. Ryan; Alan E. Norris; Richard F. Suhrheinrich; Eugene E. Siler, Jr. *Circuit Executive:* James A. Higgins (513) 564–7200. *Clerk:* Leonard Green (513) 564–7000, Potter Stewart U.S. Courthouse, 100 E. Fifth Street, Cincinnati, OH 45202.

Seventh Judicial Circuit (Districts of Illinois, Indiana, and Wisconsin).—*Chief Judge:* Frank H. Easterbrook. *Circuit Judges:* Richard A. Posner; Joel M. Flaum; Kenneth F. Ripple; Daniel A. Manion; Michael S. Kanne; Ilana Diamond Rovner; Diane P. Wood; Terence T. Evans; Ann Claire Williams; Diane S. Sykes. *Senior Circuit Judges:* Thomas E. Fairchild; William J. Bauer; Richard D. Cudahy; John L. Coffey. *Circuit Executive:* Collins T. Fitzpatrick (312) 435–5803. *Clerk:* Gino J. Agnello (312) 435–5850, 2722 U.S. Courthouse, 219 S. Dearborn Street, Chicago, IL 60604.

Eighth Judicial Circuit (Districts of Arkansas, Iowa, Minnesota, Missouri, Nebraska, North Dakota, and South Dakota).—*Chief Judge:* James B. Loken. *Circuit Judges:* Pasco M. Bowman II; Roger L. Wollman; Morris S. Arnold; Diana E. Murphy; Kermit E. Bye; William Jay Riley; Michael J. Melloy; Lavenski R. Smith; Steven M. Colloton; Raymond W. Gruender; Duane Benton; Bobby E. Shepherd. *Senior Circuit Judges:* Donald P. Lay; Myron H. Bright; John R. Gibson; Pasco M. Bowman II; Frank J. Magill; C. Arlen Beam; David R. Hansen; Morris S. Arnold. *Circuit Executive:* Millie Adams (314) 244–2600. *Clerk:* Michael E. Gans (314) 244–2400, 111 S. Tenth Street, Suite 24.327, St. Louis, MO 63102.

Ninth Judicial Circuit (Districts of Alaska, Arizona, Central California, Eastern California, Northern California, Southern California, Guam, Hawaii, Idaho, Montana, Nevada, Northern Mariana Islands, Oregon, Eastern Washington and Western Washington).—*Chief Judge:* Mary M. Schroeder. *Circuit Judges:* Harry Pregerson; Stephen Reinhardt; Alex Kozinski; Diarmuid F. O'Scannlain; Pamela Ann Rymer; Andrew J. Kleinfeld; Michael Daly Hawkins; Sidney R. Thomas; Barry G. Silverman; Susan P. Graber; M. Margaret McKeown; Kim McLane Wardlaw; William A. Fletcher; Raymond C. Fisher; Ronald M. Gould; Richard A. Paez; Marsha S. Berzon; Richard C. Tallman; Johnnie B. Rawlinson; Richard R. Clifton; Jay S. Bybee; Consuelo M. Callahan; Carlos T. Bea. *Senior Circuit Judges:* James R. Browning; Alfred T. Goodwin; J. Clifford Wallace; Joseph Tyree Sneed III; Procter Hug, Jr.; Otto R. Skopil, Jr.; Betty Binns Fletcher; Jerome Farris; Authur L. Alarcon; Warren J. Ferguson; Dorothy W. Nelson; William C. Canby, Jr.; Robert Boochever; Robert R. Beezer; Cynthia Holcomb Hall; Melvin Brunetti; John T. Noonan, Jr.; David R. Thompson; Edward Leavy; Stephen Trott; Ferdinand F. Fernandez; Thomas G. Nelson; A. Wallace Tashima. *Circuit Executive:* Gregory B. Walters (415) 556–2000. *Clerk:* Cathy A. Catterson (415) 556–9800, P.O. Box 193939, San Francisco, CA 94119–3939.

Tenth Judicial Circuit (Districts of Colorado, Kansas, New Mexico, Oklahoma, Utah, and Wyoming).—*Chief Judge:* Deanell Reece Tacha. *Circuit Judges:* Paul J. Kelly, Jr.; Robert H. Henry; Mary Beck Briscoe; Carlos F. Lucero; Michael R. Murphy; Harris L Hartz; Terrence L. O'Brien; Michael W. McConnell; Timothy M. Tymkovich; Neil M. Gorsuch; Jerome A. Holmes. *Senior Circuit Judges:* William J. Holloway, Jr.; Robert H. McWilliams; Monroe G. McKay; Stephanie K. Seymour; John C. Porfilio; Stephen H. Anderson; Bobby R. Baldock; Wade Brorby; David M. Ebel. *Circuit Executive:* David Tighe (303) 844–2067. *Clerk:* Betsy Shumaker (303) 844–3157, Byron White United States Courthouse, 1823 Stout Street, Denver, CO 80257.

Eleventh Judicial Circuit (Districts of Alabama, Florida, and Georgia).—*Chief Judge:* J.L. Edmondson. *Circuit Judges:* Gerald Bard Tjoflat; R. Lanier Anderson III; Stanley F. Birch, Jr.; Joel F. Dubina; Susan Harrell Black; Edward E. Carnes; Rosemary Barkett; Frank Mays Hull; Stanley Marcus; Charles Reginald Wilson; William H. Pryor Jr. *Senior Circuit Judges:* John C. Godbold; James C. Hill; Peter T. Fay; Phyllis A. Kravitch; Emmett Ripley Cox. *Circuit Executive:* Norman E. Zoller (404) 335–6535. *Clerk:* Thomas K. Kahn (404) 335–6100, 56 Forsyth Street, NW., Atlanta, GA 30303.

UNITED STATES COURT OF APPEALS

FOR THE DISTRICT OF COLUMBIA CIRCUIT

333 Constitution Avenue, NW., 20001, phone (202) 216–7300

DOUGLAS HOWARD GINSBURG, chief judge; born in Chicago, IL, May 25, 1946; diploma, Latin School of Chicago, 1963; B.S., Cornell University, 1970 (Phi Kappa Phi, Ives Award); J.D., University of Chicago, 1973 (Mecham Prize Scholarship 1970–73, Casper Platt Award, 1973, Order of Coif, Articles and Book Rev. Ed., 40 U. Chi. L. Rev.); bar admissions: Illinois (1973), Massachusetts (1982), U.S. Supreme Court (1984), U.S. Court of Appeals for the Ninth Circuit (1986); member: Mont Pelerin Society, American Economic Association, American Law and Economics Association, Honor Society of Phi Kappa Phi, American Bar Association, Antitrust Section, Council, 1985–86 (ex officio), 2000–03 (judicial liaison); advisory boards: Competition Policy International; Harvard Journal of Law and Public Policy; Journal of Competition Law and Economics; Law and Economics Center, George Mason University School of Law; Supreme Court Economic Review; University of Chicago Law Review; Board of Directors: Foundation for Research in Economics and the Environment, 1991–2004; Rappahannock County Conservation Alliance, 1998–2004; Rappahannock Association for Arts and Community, 1997–99; Committees: Judicial Conference of the United States, 2002–08, Budget Committee, 1997–2001, Committee on Judicial Resources, 1987–96; Boston University Law School, Visiting Committee, 1994–97; University of Chicago Law School, Visiting Committee, 1985–88; law clerk to: Judge Carl McGowan, U.S. Court of Appeals for the District of Columbia Circuit, 1973–74; Associate Justice Thurgood Marshall, U.S. Supreme Court, 1974–75; previous positions: assistant professor, Harvard University Law School, 1975–81; Professor 1981–83; Deputy Assistant Attorney General, Antitrust Division, U.S. Department of Justice, 1983–84; Administrator for Information and Regulatory Affairs, Executive Office of the President, Office of Management and Budget, 1984–85; Assistant Attorney General, Antitrust Division, U.S. Department of Justice, 1985–86; visiting professor of law, Columbia University, New York City, 1987–88; lecturer on law, Harvard University, Cambridge, MA, 1988–89; distinguished professor of law, George Mason University, Arlington, VA, 1988–present; Charles J. Merriam visiting scholar, senior lecturer, University of Chicago Law School, 1990–present; appointed to U.S. Court of Appeals for the District of Columbia Circuit by President Reagan on October 14, 1986, taking the oath of office on November 10, 1986, becoming Chief Judge on July 16, 2001.

DAVID BRYAN SENTELLE, circuit judge, born in Canton, NC, February 12, 1943; son of Horace and Maude Sentelle; married to Jane LaRue Oldham; daughters: Sharon, Reagan, and Rebecca; B.A., University of North Carolina at Chapel Hill, 1965; J.D. with honors, Uni-versity of North Carolina School of Law, 1968; associate, Uzzell and Dumont, Charlotte, 1968–79; Assistant U.S. Attorney, Charlotte, 1970–74; North Carolina State District Judge, 1974–77; partner, Tucker, Hicks, Sentelle, Moon and Hodge, Charlotte, 1977–85; U.S. District Judge for the Western District of North Carolina, 1985–87; appointed to the U.S. Court of Appeals by President Reagan in October 1987.

KAREN LECRAFT HENDERSON, circuit judge. [Biographical information not supplied, per Judge Henderson's request.]

A. RAYMOND RANDOLPH, circuit judge; born in Riverside, NJ, November 1, 1943; son of Arthur Raymond Randolph, Sr. and Marile (Kelly); two children: John Trevor and Cynthia Lee Randolph; married to Eileen Janette O'Connor, May 18, 1984. B.S., Drexel University, 1966; J.D., University of Pennsylvania Law School, 1969, *summa cum laude;* managing editor, University of Pennsylvania Law Review; Order of the Coif. Admitted to Supreme Court of the United States; Supreme Court of California; District of Columbia Court of Appeals; U.S. Courts of Appeals for the First, Second, Fourth, Fifth, Sixth, Seventh, Ninth, Eleventh, and District of Columbia Circuits. Memberships: American Law Institute. Law clerk to Judge Henry J. Friendly, U.S. Court of Appeals for the Second Circuit, 1969–70; Assistant to the Solicitor General, 1970–73; adjunct professor of law, Georgetown University Law Center, 1974–78; George Mason School of Law, 1992; Deputy Solicitor General, 1975–77; Special Counsel, Committee on Standards of Official Conduct, House of Representatives, 1979–80; special assistant attorney general, State of Montana (honorary), 1983–July 1990; special assistant attorney general, State of New Mexico, 1985–July 1990; special assistant attorney general, State of Utah, 1986–July 1990; advisory panel, Federal Courts Study Committee, 1989–July 1990; partner, Pepper, Hamilton and Scheetz, 1987–July 1990; chairman, Committee on Codes of Conduct, U.S. Judicial Conference, 1995–98; distinguished professor of law, George Mason Law School, 1999–present; recipient, Distinguished Alumnus Award, University of Pennsylvania Law School, 2002; appointed to the U.S. Court of Appeals for the District of Columbia Circuit by President George H.W. Bush on July 16, 1990, and took oath of office on July 20, 1990.

JUDITH W. ROGERS, circuit judge; born in New York, NY; A.B. (with honors), Radcliffe College, 1961; Phi Beta Kappa honors member; LL.B., Harvard Law School, 1964; LL.M., University of Virginia School of Law, 1988; law clerk, D.C. Juvenile Court, 1964–65; assistant U.S. Attorney for the District of Columbia, 1965–68; trial attorney, San Francisco Neighborhood Legal Assistance Foundation, 1968–69; Attorney, U.S. Department of Justice, Office of the Associate Deputy Attorney General and Criminal Division, 1969–71; General Counsel, Congressional Commission on the Organization of the D.C. Government, 1971–72; legislative assistant to D.C. Mayor Walter E. Washington, 1972–79; Corporation Counsel for the District of Columbia, 1979–83; trustee, Radcliffe College, 1982–90; member of Visiting Committee to Harvard Law School, 1984–90; appointed by President Reagan to the District of Columbia Court of Appeals as an Associate Judge on September 15, 1983; served as chief judge, November 1, 1988 to March 18, 1994; member of Executive Committee, Conference of Chief Justices, 1993–94; member, U.S. Judicial Conference Committee on the Codes of Conduct, 1998–2004; appointed by President Clinton to the U.S. Court of Appeals for the District of Columbia Circuit on March 18, 1994, and entered on duty March 18, 1994.

DAVID S. TATEL, circuit judge; born in Washington, DC, March 16, 1942; son of Molly and Dr. Howard Tatel (deceased); married to the former Edith Bassichis, 1965; children: Rebecca, Stephanie, Joshua, and Emily; grandchildren: Olivia, Maya, Olin, Reuben, Rae, and Cameron; B.A., University of Michigan, 1963; J.D., University of Chicago Law School, 1966; instructor, University of Michigan Law School, 1966–67; associate, Sidley and Austin, 1967–69, 1970–72; director, Chicago Lawyers' Committee for Civil Rights Under Law, 1969–70; director, National Lawyers' Committee for Civil Rights Under Law, 1972–74; director, Office for Civil Rights, U.S. Department of Health, Education and Welfare, 1977–79; associate and partner, Hogan and Hartson, 1974–77, 1979–94; lecturer, Stanford University Law School, 1991–92; board of directors, Spencer Foundation, 1987–97 (chair, 1990–97); board of directors, National Board for Professional Teaching Standards, 1997–2000; National Lawyers' Committee for Civil Rights Under Law, co-chair, 1989–91; chair, Carnegie Foundation for the Advancement of Teaching; admitted to practice law in Illinois in 1966 and the District Columbia in 1970; appointed to the U.S. Court of Appeals for the District of Columbia Circuit by President Clinton on October 7, 1994, and entered on duty October 11, 1994.

MERRICK BRIAN GARLAND, circuit judge; born in Chicago, IL, 1952; A.B., Harvard University, 1974, *summa cum laude,* Phi Beta Kappa; J.D., Harvard Law School, 1977, *magna cum laude,* articles editor, Harvard Law Review; law clerk to Judge Henry J. Friendly, U.S. Court of Appeals for the 2d Circuit, 1977–78; law clerk to Justice William J. Brennan, Jr., U.S. Supreme Court, 1978–79; Special Assistant to the Attorney General, 1979–81; associate then partner, Arnold and Porter, Washington, D.C., 1981–89; Assistant U.S. Attorney, Washington, D.C., 1989–92; partner, Arnold and Porter, 1992–93; Deputy Assistant Attorney General, Criminal Division, U.S. Department of Justice, 1993–94; Principal Associate Deputy Attorney General, 1994–97; Lecturer on Law, Harvard Law School, 1985–86; Associate Independent Counsel, 1987–88. Admitted to the bars of the District of Columbia; U.S. District Court; Court of Appeals, District of Columbia Circuit; U.S. Courts of Appeals for the 4th, 9th, and 10th Circuits; and U.S. Supreme Court. Author: *Antitrust and State Action,* 96 Yale Law Journal 486 (1987); *Antitrust and Federalism,* 96 Yale Law Journal 1291 (1987); *Deregulation and Judicial Review,* 98 Harvard Law Review 505 (1985); co-chair, Administrative Law Section, District of Columbia Bar, 1991–94; member, Board of Overseers, Harvard University, 2003–present; American Law Institute; appointed to the U.S. Court of Appeals for the District of Columbia Circuit on April 9, 1997.

JANCE ROGERS BROWN, circuit judge; born in Greenville, AL; B.A., California State University, 1974; J.D., University of California School of Law, 1977; LL.M., University of Virginia School of Law,2004; Deputy Legislative Counsel, Legislative Counsel Bureau, 1977–79; Deputy Attorney General, California Department of Justice, 1979–87; Deputy Secretary and General Counsel, California Business, Transportation, and Housing Agency, 1987–

90; Senior Associate, Nielsen, Merksamer, Parinello, Mueller and Naylor, 1990–91; Legal Affairs Secretary for Governor Pete Wilson, 1991–94; Associate Justice, California Court of Appeals for the Third District, 1994–96; adjunct professor, University of the Pacific McGeorge School of Law, 1998–99; Associate Justice, California Supreme Court, 1996–2005; appointed to the U.S. Court of Appeals for the District of Columbia Circuit by President George W. Bush on February 14, 2005 and sworn in on July 1, 2005.

THOMAS B. GRIFFITH, circuit judge; born in Yokohama, Japan, July 5, 1954; B.A., Brigham Young University, 1978; J.D., University of Virginia School of Law, 1985; editor, Virginia Law Review; associate, Robinson, Bradshaw and Hinson, Charlotte, NC, 1985–89; associate and then a partner, Wiley, Rein and Fielding, Washington, DC, 1989–95 and 1999–2000; Senate Legal Counsel of the United States, 1995–99; Assistant to the President and General Counsel, Brigham Young University, Provo, UT, 2000–05; member, Executive Committee of the American Bar Association's Central European and Eurasian Law Initiative; appointed to the United States Court of Appeals for the District of Columbia Circuit on June 14, 2005 and sworn in on June 29, 2005.

BRETT M. KAVANAUGH, circuit judge; born in Washington, DC, February 12, 1965; son of Edward and Martha Kavanaugh; married to Ashley Estes; one daughter; B.A., *cum laude*, Yale College, 1987; J.D., Yale Law School, 1990; law clerk to Judge Walter Stapleton of the U.S. Court of Appeals for the Third Circuit, 1990–91; law clerk for Judge Alex Kozinski of the U.S. Court of Appeals for the Ninth Circuit, 1991–92; attorney, Office of the Solicitor General of the United States, 1992–93; law clerk to Associate Justice Anthony Kennedy of the U.S. Supreme Court, 1993–94; Associate Counsel, Office of Independent Counsel, 1994–97; partner, Kirkland & Ellis LLP, 1997–98, 1999–2001; Associate Counsel and then Senior Associate Counsel to President George W. Bush, 2001–03; Assistant to the President and Staff Secretary to President Bush, 2003–06; appointed and sworn in to the U.S. Court of Appeals for the District of Columbia Circuit on May 30, 2006.

SENIOR JUDGES

HARRY T. EDWARDS, senior judge; born in New York, NY, November 3, 1940; son of George H. Edwards and Arline (Ross) Lyle; married to Pamela Carrington Edwards; children: Brent and Michelle; B.S., Cornell University, 1962; J.D. (with distinction), University of Michigan Law School, 1965; associate with Seyfarth, Shaw, Fairweather and Geraldson, 1965–70; professor of law, University of Michigan, 1970–75 and 1977–80; professor of law, Harvard University, 1975–77; visiting professor of law, Free University of Brussels, 1974; arbitrator of labor/management disputes, 1970–80; vice president, National Academy of Arbitrators, 1978–80; member (1977–79) and chairman (1979–80), National Railroad Passenger Corporation (Amtrak); Executive Committee of the Association of American Law Schools, 1979–80; public member of the Administrative Conference of the United States, 1976–80; International Women's Year Commission, 1976–77; American Bar Association Commission of Law and the Economy; coauthor of four books: *Labor Relations Law in the Public Sector, The Lawyer as a Negotiator, Higher Education and the Law*, and *Collective Bargaining and Labor Arbitration*; recipient of the Judge William B. Groat Alumni Award, 1978, given by Cornell University; the Society of American Law Teachers Award (for "distinguished contributions to teaching and public service"); the Whitney North Seymour Medal presented by the American Arbitration Association for outstanding contributions to the use of arbitration; Recipient of the 2004 Robert J. Kutak Award, presented by the American Bar Association Selection of Legal Education and Admission to the Bar "to a person who meets the highest standards of professional responsibility and demonstrates substantial achievement toward increased understanding between legal education and the active practice of law", and several Honorary Doctor of Laws degrees; teaches law on a part-time basis; has recently taught at Duke, Georgetown, Michigan, and Harvard Law Schools, and is presently teaching courses at N.Y.U.; A.B.A.; appointed to the U.S. Court of Appeals, February 20, 1980; served as chief judge September 15, 1994 to July 16, 2001.

LAURENCE HIRSCH SILBERMAN, circuit judge; born in York, PA, October 12, 1935; son of William Silberman and Anna (Hirsch); married to Rosalie G. Gaull on April 28, 1957; children: Robert Stephen Silberman, Katherine DeBoer Balaban, and Anne Gaull Otis; B.A., Dartmouth College, 1957; LL.B., Harvard Law School, 1961; admitted to Hawaii bar, 1962; District of Columbia bar, 1973; associate, Moore, Torkildson and Rice, 1961–64; partner (Moore, Silberman and Schulze), Honolulu, 1964–67; attorney, National Labor Relations Board, Office of General Counsel, Appellate Division, 1967–69; Solicitor, Department of Labor, 1969–70; Under Secretary of Labor, 1970–73; partner, Steptoe and Johnson, 1973–74; Deputy

Attorney General of the United States, 1974–75; Ambassador to Yugoslavia, 1975–77; President's Special Envoy on ILO Affairs, 1976; senior fellow, American Enterprise Institute, 1977–78; visiting fellow, 1978–85; managing partner, Morrison and Foerster, 1978–79 and 1983–85; executive vice president, Crocker National Bank, 1979–83; lecturer, University of Hawaii, 1962–63; board of directors, Commission on Present Danger, 1978–85, Institute for Educational Affairs, New York, NY, 1981–85, member: General Advisory Committee on Arms Control and Disarmament, 1981–85; Defense Policy Board, 1981–85; vice chairman, State Department's Commission on Security and Economic Assistance, 1983–84; American Bar Association (Labor Law Committee, 1965–72, Corporations and Banking Committee, 1973, Law and National Security Advisory Committee, 1981–85); Hawaii Bar Association Ethics Committee, 1965–67; Council on Foreign Relations, 1977–present; Judicial Conference Committee on Court Administration and Case Management, 1994; Adjunct Professor of Law (Administrative Law) Georgetown Law Center, 1987–94; 1997, 1999–present; Adjunct Professor of Law (Labor Law), Georgetown Law Center, 2002–present; Adjunct Professor of Law (Administrative Law) New York University Law School, 1995–96; Distinguished Visitor From the Judiciary, Georgetown Law Center, 2002–present; co-chairman, Commission on The Intelligence Capabilities of the United States Regarding Weapons of Mass Destruction, 2004–05; appointed to the U.S. Court of Appeals for the District of Columbia Circuit by President Reagan on October 28, 1985.

STEPHEN F. WILLIAMS, circuit judge; born in New York, NY, September 23, 1936; son of Charles Dickerman Williams and Virginia (Fain); married to Faith Morrow, 1966; children: Susan, Geoffrey, Sarah, Timothy, and Nicholas; B.A., Yale, 1958, J.D., Harvard Law School, 1961; U.S. Army reserves, 1961–62; associate, Debevoise, Plimpton, Lyons and Gates, 1962–66; Assistant U.S. Attorney, Southern District of New York, 1966–69; associate professor and professor of law, University of Colorado School of Law, 1969–86; visiting professor of law, UCLA, 1975–76; visiting professor of law and fellow in law and economics, University Chicago Law School, 1979–80; visiting George W. Hutchison Professor of Energy Law, SMU, 1983–84; consultant to: Administrative Conference of the United States, 1974–76; Federal Trade Commission on energy-related issues, 1983–85; member, American Law Institute; appointed to the U.S. Court of Appeals for the District of Columbia Circuit by President Reagan, June 16, 1986.

OFFICERS OF THE UNITED STATES COURT OF APPEALS FOR THE DISTRICT OF COLUMBIA CIRCUIT

Circuit Executive.—Jill C. Sayenga (202) 216–7340.
Clerk.—Mark J. Langer, 216–7000.
Chief Deputy Clerk.—Marilyn R. Sargent, 216–7000.
Chief, Legal Division.—Martha Tomich, 216–7500.

UNITED STATES COURT OF APPEALS

FEDERAL CIRCUIT

717 Madison Place, NW., 20439, phone (202) 633–6550

PAUL R. MICHEL, chief judge; born in Philadelphia, PA, February 3, 1941; son of Lincoln M. and Dorothy Michel; educated in public schools in Wayne and Radnor, PA; B.A., Williams College, 1963; J.D., University of Virginia Law School, 1966; married Brooke England, 2004; adult children, Sarah Elizabeth and Margaret Kelley; Second Lieutenant, U.S. Army Reserve, 1966–72; admitted to practice: Pennsylvania (1967), U.S. District Court (1968), U.S. Circuit Court (1969), and U.S. Supreme Court (1969); Assistant District Attorney, Philadelphia, PA, 1967–71; Deputy District Attorney for Investigations, 1972–74; Assistant Watergate Special Prosecutor, 1974–75; assistant counsel, Senate Intelligence Committee, 1975–76; deputy chief, Public Integrity Section, Criminal Division, U.S. Department of Justice, 1976–78; "Koreagate" prosecutor, 1976–78; Associate Deputy Attorney General, 1978–81; Acting Deputy Attorney General, Dec. 1979–Feb. 1980; counsel and administrative assistant to Senator Arlen Specter, 1981–88; nominated December 19, 1987 by President Ronald Reagan to be circuit judge, U.S. Court of Appeals for the Federal Circuit, confirmed by Senate on February 29, 1988, and assumed duties of the office on March 8, 1988; member of the Judicial Conference of the United States, 2004–present; elevated to the position of Chief Judge on December 25, 2004.

PAULINE NEWMAN, circuit judge; born in New York, NY, June 20, 1927; daughter of Maxwell H. and Rosella G. Newman; B.A., Vassar College, 1947; M.A. in pure science, Columbia University, 1948; Ph.D. degree in chemistry, Yale University, 1952; LL.B., New York University School of Law, 1958; Doctor of Laws (honorary), Franklin Pierce School of Law, 1991; admitted to the New York bar in 1958 and to the Pennsylvania bar in 1979; worked as research scientist for the American Cyanamid Co. from 1951–54; worked for the FMC Corp. from 1954–84 as patent attorney and house counsel and, since 1969, as director of the Patent, Trademark, and Licensing Department; on leave from FMC Corp. worked for the United Nations Educational, Scientific and Cultural Organization as a science policy specialist in the Department of Natural Sciences, 1961–62; offices in scientific and professional organizations include: member of Council of the Patent, Trademark and Copyright Section of the American Bar Association, 1982–84; board of directors of the American Patent Law Association, 1981–84; vice president of the United States Trademark Association, 1978–79, and member of the board of directors, 1975–76, 1977–79; board of governors of the New York Patent Law Association, 1970–74; president of the Pacific Industrial Property Association, 1978–80; executive committee of the International Patent and Trademark Association, 1982–84; board of directors: the American Chemical Society, 1973–75, 1976–78, 1979–81; American Institute of Chemists, 1960–66, 1970–76; Research Corp., 1982–84; member: board of trustees of Philadelphia College of Pharmacy and Science, 1983–84; patent policy board of State University of New York, 1983–84; national board of Medical College of Pennsylvania, 1975–84; governmental committees include: State Department Advisory Committee on International Intellectual Property, 1974–84; advisory committee to the Domestic Policy Review of Industrial Innovation, 1978–79; special advisory committee on Patent Office Procedure and Practice, 1972–74; member of the U.S. Delegation to the Diplomatic Conference on the Revision of the Paris Convention for the Protection of Industrial Property, 1982–84; awarded Wilbur Cross Medal of Yale University Graduate School, 1989, the Jefferson Medal of the New Jersey Intellectual Property Law Association, 1988, the Award for Outstanding Contributions in the Intellectual Property Field of the Pacific Industrial Property Association, 1987; Vanderbilt Medal of New York University School of Law, 1995; Vasser College Distinguished Achievement Award, 2002; Distinguished Professor of Law, George Mason University School of Law (adjunct faculty); Council on Foreign Relations; appointed judge of the U.S. Court of Appeals for the Federal Circuit by President Reagan and entered upon duties of that office on May 7, 1984.

HALDANE ROBERT MAYER, circuit judge; born in Buffalo, NY, February 21, 1941; son of Haldane and Myrtle Mayer; educated in the public schools of Lockport, NY; B.S., U.S. Military Academy, West Point, NY, 1963; J.D., Marshall-Wythe School of Law, The College of William and Mary in Virginia, 1971; editor-in-chief, *William and Mary Law Review,* Omicron Delta Kappa; married Mary Anne McCurdy, August 13, 1966; two daughters, Anne Christian and Rebecca Paige; admitted to practice in Virginia and the District of Columbia; board of directors, William and Mary Law School Association, 1979–85; served in the U.S. Army, 1963–75, in the Infantry and the Judge Advocate General's Corps; awarded the Bronze Star Medal, Meritorious Service Medal, Army Commendation Medal with Oak Leaf Cluster, Combat Infantryman Badge, Parachutist Badge, Ranger Tab, Ranger Combat Badge, Campaign and Service Ribbons; resigned from Regular Army and was commissioned in the U.S. Army Reserve, currently Lieutenant Colonel, retired; law clerk for Judge John D. Butzner, Jr., U.S. Court of Appeals for the Fourth Circuit, 1971–72; private practice with McGuire, Woods and Battle in Charlottesville, VA, 1975–77; adjunct professor, University of Virginia School of Law, 1975–77, 1992–94, George Washington University National Law Center, 1992–96; Special Assistant to the Chief Justice of the United States, Warren E. Burger, 1977–80; private practice with Baker and McKenzie in Washington, DC, 1980–81; Deputy and Acting Special Counsel (by designation of the President), U.S. Merit Systems Protection Board, 1981–82; appointed by President Reagan to the U.S. Claims Court, 1982; appointed by President Reagan to the U.S. Court of Appeals for the Federal Circuit, June 15, 1987; assumed duties of the office, June 19, 1987; elevated to the position of Chief Judge on December 25, 1997; relinquished that position on December 24, 2004, after having held it for seven years; Judicial Conference of the U.S. Committee on the International Appellate Judges Conference, 1988–91, Committee on Judicial Resources, 1990–97; member of the Judicial Conference of the United States, 1997–2004.

ALAN D. LOURIE, circuit judge; born in Boston, MA, January 13, 1935; son of Joseph Lourie and Rose; educated in public schools in Brookline, MA; A.B., Harvard University, 1956; M.S., University of Wisconsin, 1958; Ph.D., University of Pennsylvania, 1965; J.D., Temple University, 1970; married to the former L. Elizabeth D. Schwartz; children: Deborah L. Rapoport and Linda S. Lourie; employed at Monsanto Company (chemist, 1957–59); Wyeth Laboratories (chemist, literature scientist, patent liaison specialist, 1959–64); SmithKline Beecham Corporation, (Patent Agent, 1964–70; assistant director, Corporate Patents, 1970–76; director, Corporate Patents, 1976–77; vice president, Corporate Patents and Trademarks and Associate General Counsel, 1977–90); vice chairman of the Industry Functional Advisory Committee on Intellectual Property Rights for Trade Policy Matters (IFAC 3) for the Department of Commerce and the Office of the U.S. Trade Representative, 1987–90; Treasurer of the Association of Corporate Patent Counsel, 1987–89; President of the Philadelphia Patent Law Association, 1984–85; member of the board of directors of the American Intellectual Property Law Association (formerly American Patent Law Association), 1982–85; member of the U.S. delegation to the Diplomatic Conference on the Revision of the Paris Convention for the Protection of Industrial Property, October–November 1982, March 1984; chairman of the Patent Committee of the Law Section of the Pharmaceutical Manufacturers Association, 1980–85; member of Judicial Conference Committee on Financial Disclosure, 1990–98; member of the American Bar Association, the American Chemical Society, the Cosmos Club, and the Harvard Club of Washington; recipient of Jefferson Medal of the New Jersey Intellectual Property Law Association for outstanding contributions to intellectual property law, 1998; admitted to: Supreme Court of Pennsylvania, U.S. District Court for the Eastern District of Pennsylvania, U.S. Court of Appeals for the Third Circuit, U.S. Court of Appeals for the Federal Circuit, U.S. Supreme Court; nominated January 25, 1990, by President George H.W. Bush to be circuit judge, U.S. Court of Appeals for the Federal Circuit, confirmed by Senate on April 5, 1990, and assumed duties of the office on April 11, 1990.

RANDALL R. RADER, circuit judge; born in Hastings, NE, April 21, 1949; son of Raymond A. and Gloria R. Rader; B.A., Brigham Young University, 1971–74, (*magna cum laude*), Phi Beta Kappa; J.D., George Washington University Law Center, 1974–78; married the former Victoria Semenyuk; legislative assistant to Representative Virginia Smith; legislative director, counsel, House Committee on Ways and Means to Representative Philip M. Crane, 1978–81; General Counsel, Chief Counsel, Subcommittee on the Constitution, 1981–86; Minority Chief Counsel, Staff Director, Subcommittee on Patents, Trademarks and Copyrights, Senate Committee on Judiciary, 1987–88; Judge, U.S. Claims Court, 1988–90; recipient: Outstanding Young Federal Lawyer Award by Federal Bar Association, 1983; Jefferson Medal Award, 2003; bar member: District of Columbia, 1978; Supreme Court of the United States, 1984; nominated to the U.S Court of Appeals for the Federal Circuit by President George H.W. Bush on June 12, 1990; confirmed by Senate August 3, 1990, sworn in August 14, 1990.

ALVIN A. SCHALL, circuit judge; born in New York City, NY, April 4, 1944; son of Gordon W. Schall and Helen D. Schall; preparatory education: St. Paul's School, Concord, NH, 1956–62, graduated *cum laude*; higher education: B.A., Princeton University, 1962–66; J.D., Tulane Law School, 1966–69; married to the former Sharon Frances LeBlanc, children: Amanda and Anthony; associate with the law firm of Shearman and Sterling in New York City, 1969–73; Assistant United States Attorney, Office of the United States Attorney for the Eastern District of New York, 1973–78; Chief of the Appeals Division, 1977–78; Trial Attorney, Senior Trial Counsel, Civil Division, United States Department of Justice, Washington, DC, 1978–87; member of the Washington, DC law firm of Perlman and Partners, 1987–88; Assistant to the Attorney General of the United States, 1988–92; author, *Federal Contract Disputes and Forums, Chapter 9 in Construction Litigation: Strategies and Techniques,* published by John Wiley and Sons (Wiley Law Publications), 1989; bar memberships: State of New York (1970), U.S. District Courts for the Eastern and Southern Districts of New York (1973), U.S. Court of Appeals for the Second Circuit (1974), U.S. Court of Federal Claims, formerly the U.S. Claims Court (1978), District of Columbia (1980), U.S. Court of Appeals for the Federal Circuit (1982), Supreme Court of the United States (1989), U.S. Court of Appeals for the District of Columbia Circuit (1991), and United States District Court for the District of Columbia (1991); appointed U.S. Court of Appeals for the Federal Circuit by President George H.W. Bush on August 17, 1992, sworn in on August 19, 1992.

WILLIAM CURTIS BRYSON, circuit judge; born in Houston, TX, August 19, 1945; A.B., Harvard University, 1969; J.D., University of Texas School of Law, 1973; married with two children; law clerk to Hon. Henry J. Friendly, circuit judge, U.S. Court of Appeals for the Second Circuit, 1973–74, and Hon. Thurgood Marshall, associate justice, U.S. Supreme Court, 1974–75; associate, Miller, Cassidy, Larroca and Lewin, Washington, DC, 1975–78; Department of Justice, Criminal Division, 1979–86, Office of Solicitor General, 1978–79 and 1986–94; Office of the Associate Attorney General, 1994; nominated in June 1994 by President Clinton to be circuit judge, U.S. Court of Appeals for the Federal Circuit, and assumed duties of the office on October 7, 1994.

ARTHUR J. GAJARSA, circuit judge; born in Norcia (Pro. Perugia), Italy, March 1, 1941; married to Melanie Gajarsa; five children; Rensselaer Polytechnic Institute, Troy, NY, 1958–62, B.S.E.E., Bausch and Lomb Medal, 1958, Benjamin Franklin Award, 1958; Catholic University of America, Washington, DC, 1968; M.A. in economics, graduate studies; J.D., Georgetown University Law Center, Washington, DC, 1967; patent examiner, U.S. Patent Office, Department of Commerce, 1962–63; patent adviser, U.S. Air Force, Department of Defense, 1963–64; patent adviser, Cushman, Darby and Cushman, 1964–67; law clerk to Judge Joseph McGarraghy, U.S. District Court for the District of Columbia, Washington, DC, 1967–68; attorney, Office of General Counsel, Aetna Life and Casualty Co., 1968–69; special counsel and assistant to the Commissioner of Indian Affairs, Bureau of Indian Affairs, Department of Interior, 1969–71; associate, Duncan and Brown, 1971–72; partner, Gajarsa, Liss and Sterenbuch, 1972–78; partner, Garjarsa, Liss and Conroy, 1978–80; partner, Wender, Murase and White, 1980–86; partner and officer, Joseph Gajarsa, McDermott and Reiner, P.C., 1987–97; registered patent agent, registered patent attorney, 1963; admitted to the D.C. Bar, U.S. District Court for the District of Columbia, and U.S. Court of Appeals for the District of Columbia, 1968; Connecticut State Bar, 1969; U.S. Supreme Court, 1971; Superior Court for D.C., Court of Appeals for D.C., 1972; U.S. Courts of Appeals for the Ninth and Federal Circuits, 1974; U.S. District Court for the Northern District of New York, 1980; awards: Sun and Balance Medal, Rensselaer Polytechnic Institute, 1990; Gigi Pieri Award, Camp Hale Association, Boston, MA, 1992; Rensselaer Key Alumni Award, 1992; 125th Anniversary Medal, Georgetown University Law Center, 1995; Order of Commendatore, Republic of Italy, 1995; Alumni Fellow Award, Rensselaer Alumni Association, 1996; Board of Directors, National Italian American Foundation, 1976–97, serving as general counsel, 1976–89, president, 1989–92, and vice chair, 1993–96; Rensselaer Neuman Foundation, trustee, 1973-present; Foundation for Improving Understanding of the Arts, trustee, 1982–96; Outward Bound, U.S.A., trustee, 1987–2002; John Carroll Society, Board of Governors, 1992–96; Rensselaer Polytechnic Institute, trustee, 1994-present; Georgetown University, regent, 1995–2001; Georgetown University Board of Directors, 2001–present; member: Federal, American, Federal Circuit, and D.C. Bar Associations; American Judicature Association; nominated for appointment to the U.S. Court of Appeals for the Federal Circuit on April 18, 1996 by President Clinton; confirmed by the Senate on July 31, 1997; entered service September 12, 1997.

RICHARD LINN, circuit judge; born in Brooklyn, NY, April 13, 1944; son of Marvin and Enid Linn; Polytechnic Preparatory County Day School, Brooklyn, NY, 1961; Bachelor of Electrical Engineering degree, Rensselaer Polytechnic Institute, 1965; J.D., Georgetown University Law Center, 1969; served as patent examiner at the U.S. Patent and Trademark Office, 1965–68; member of the founding Board of Governors of the Virginia State Bar Section on Patent, Trademark and Copyright Law, chairman, 1975; member of the American Bar Association Intellectual Property Law Section; the American Intellectual Property Law Association; the District of Columbia Bar Association Intellectual Property Section; the Virginia Bar Intellectual Property Law Section; and the Federal Circuit Bar Association; admitted to the Virginia Bar in 1969, the District of Columbia Bar in 1970, and the New York Bar in 1994; admitted to practice before the U.S. Supreme Court, the U.S. Courts of Appeals for the Fourth, Sixth, District of Columbia, and Federal Circuits, and the U.S. District Courts for the Eastern District of Virginia and the District of Columbia; partner, Marks and Murase, L.L.P., 1977–97, and member of the Executive Committee, 1987–97; partner, Foley and Lardner, 1997–99, Practice Group Leader, Electronics Practice Group, and Intellectual Property Department, 1997–99; recipient, Rensselaer Alumni Association Fellows Award for 2000; adjunct professor of law, George Washington University Law School, 2001-present; member, Advisory Board of the George Washington University Law School, 2001-present; Master, Giles S. Rich American Inn of Court, 2000-present; nominated to be Circuit Judge by President Clinton on September 28, 1999, and confirmed by the Senate on November 19, 1999; assumed duties of the office on January 1, 2000.

TIMOTHY B. DYK, circuit judge; A.B., Harvard College (*cum laude*), 1958; LL.B. (*magna cum laude*), Harvard Law School, 1961; law clerk to Justices Reed and Burton (retired), 1961–62; law clerk to Chief Justice Warren, 1962–63; special assistant to Assistant Attorney General, Louis F. Oberdorfer, 1963–64; associate and partner, Wilmer, Cutler & Pickering, 1964–90; partner, and chair, of Issues & Appeals Practice area (until nomination) with Jones, Day, Reavis and Pogue, 1990–2000; and Adjunct Professor at Yale, University of Virginia and Georgetown Law Schools; nominated for appointment to the U.S. Court of Appeals for the Federal Circuit on April 1, 1998 by President Clinton; confirmed by the Senate on May 24, 2000; entered on duty June 9, 2000.

SHARON PROST, circuit judge; born in Newburyport, MA; daughter of Zyskind and Ester Prost; two sons, Matthew and Jeffrey; educated in Hartford, CT; B.S., Cornell University, 1973; M.B.A., George Washington University, 1975; J.D., Washington College of Law, American University, 1979; admitted to practice in Washington, DC, 1979; LL.M., George Washington University School of Law, 1984; Labor Relations Specialist, U.S. Civil Service Commission, 1973–76; Labor Relations Specialist / Auditor, U.S. General Accounting Office, 1976–79; Trial Attorney, Federal Labor Relations Authority, 1979–82; Chief Counsel's Office, Department of Treasury, 1982–84; Assistant Solicitor, Associate Solicitor, and then Acting Solicitor, National Labor Relations Board, 1984–89; Adjunct Professor of Labor Law, George Mason University School of Law, 1986–87; Chief Labor Counsel, Senate Labor Committee—minority, 1989–93; Chief Counsel, Senate Judiciary Committee—minority, 1993–95; Deputy Chief Counsel, Senate Judiciary Committee—majority, 1995–2001; Chief Counsel, Senate Judiciary Committee—majority, 2001; appointed by President George W. Bush to the U.S. Court of Appeals for the Federal Circuit, September 21, 2001; assumed duties of the office on October 3, 2001.

KIMBERLY MOORE, circuit judge; born in Baltimore, MD; married to Matthew J. Moore; three children; B.S.E.E., Massachusetts Institute of Technology, 1990; M.S., Massachusetts Institute of Technology, 1991; J.D. (*cum laude*), Georgetown University Law Center, 1994; Electrical Engineer, Naval Surface Warfare Center, 1988–92; Associate, Kirkland & Ellis, 1994–95; Judicial Clerk, Hon. Glenn L. Archer, Jr., Chief Judge, United States Court of Appeals for the Federal Circuit, 1995–97; Assistant Professor of Law, Chicago-Kent College of Law, 1997–99; Associate Director of the Intellectual Property Law Program, Chicago-Kent College of Law, 1998–99; Assistant Professor of Law, University of Maryland School of Law, 1999–2000; Associate Professor of Law, George Mason University School of Law, 2000–04; Professor of Law, George Mason University School of Law, 2004–06; nominated to the United States Court of Appeals for the Federal Circuit by President George W. Bush on May 18, 2006; confirmed by the Senate on September 5, 2006 and assumed the duties of office on September 8, 2006.

SENIOR JUDGES

DANIEL M. FRIEDMAN, senior judge; born in New York, NY, February 8, 1916; son of Henry M. and Julia (Freedman) Friedman; attended the Ethical Culture Schools in New

York City; A.B., Columbia College, 1937; LL.B., Columbia Law School, 1940; married to Leah L. Lipson (deceased), January 16, 1955; married to Elizabeth M. Ellis (deceased), October 18, 1975; admitted to New York bar, 1941; private practice, New York, NY, 1940–42; legal staff, Securities and Exchange Commission, 1942, 1946–51; served in the U.S. Army, 1942–46; Appellate Section, Antitrust Division, U.S. Department of Justice, 1951–59; assistant to the Solicitor General, 1959–62; second assistant to the Solicitor General, 1962–68; First Deputy Solicitor General, 1968–78; Acting Solicitor General, January–March 1977; nominated by President Carter as chief judge of the U.S. Court of Claims, March 22, 1978; confirmed by the Senate, May 17, 1978, and assumed duties of the office on May 24, 1978; as of October 1, 1982, continued in office as judge of the U.S. Court of Appeals for the Federal Circuit, pursuant to section 165, Federal Courts Improvement Act of 1982, Public Law 97–164, 96 Stat. 50.

GLENN LEROY ARCHER, JR., senior judge; born in Densmore, KS, March 21, 1929; son of Glenn L. and Ruth Agnes Archer; educated in Kansas public schools; B.A., Yale University, 1951; J.D., with honors, George Washington University Law School, 1954; married to Carole Joan Thomas; children: Susan, Sharon, Glenn III, and Thomas; First Lieutenant, Judge Advocate General's Office, U.S. Air Force, 1954–56; associate (1956–60) and partner (1960–81), Hamel, Park, McCabe and Saunders, Washington, DC; nominated in 1981 by President Ronald Reagan to be Assistant Attorney General for the Tax Division, U.S. Department of Justice, and served in that position from December 1981 to December 1985; nominated in October 1985 by President Reagan to be circuit judge, U.S. Court of Appeals for the Federal Circuit; took the oath of office as a Circuit Judge in December 1985; elevated to the position of Chief Judge on March 18, 1994, served in that capacity until December 24, 1997; took senior status beginning December 25, 1997.

S. JAY PLAGER, senior judge; born May 16, 1931; son of A.L. and Clara Plager, three children; educated public schools, Long Branch, NJ; A.B., University of North Carolina, 1952; J.D., University of Florida, with high honors, 1958; LL.M., Columbia University, 1961; Phi Beta Kappa, Phi Kappa Phi, Order of the Coif, Holloway fellow, University of North Carolina; Editor-in-Chief, University of Florida Law Review; Charles Evans Hughes Fellow, Columbia University; commissioned, Ensign U.S. Navy, 1952; active duty Korean conflict; honorable discharge as Commander, USNR, 1971; professor, Faculty of Law, University of Florida, 1958–64; University of Illinois, 1964–77; Indiana University School of Law, Bloomington, 1977–89; visiting research professor of law, University of Wisconsin, 1967–68; visiting fellow, Trinity College and visiting professor, Cambridge University, 1980; visiting scholar, Stanford University Law School, 1984–85; dean and professor, Indiana University School of Law, Bloomington, 1977–84; counselor to the Under Secretary, U.S. Department of Health and Human Services, 1986–87; Associate Director, Office of Management and Budget, Executive Office of the President of the United States, 1987–88; Administrator, Office of Information and Regulatory Affairs, Office of Management and Budget, Executive Office of the President of the United States, 1988–89; appointed by President George H.W. Bush to the U.S. Court of Appeals for the Federal Circuit in November 1989.

RAYMOND C. CLEVENGER III, senior judge; born in Topeka, KS, August 27, 1937; son of R. Charles and Mary Margaret Clevenger; educated in the public schools in Topeka, Kansas, and at Phillips Academy, Andover, MA; B.A., Yale University, 1959; LL.B., Yale University, 1966; law clerk to Justice White, October term, 1966; practice of law at Wilmer, Cutler and Pickering, Washington, DC, 1967–90; nominated to the U.S. Court of Appeals for the Federal Circuit by President George H.W. Bush on January 24, 1990, confirmed on April 27, 1990 and assumed duties on May 3, 1990.

OFFICERS OF THE UNITED STATES COURT OF APPEALS FOR THE FEDERAL CIRCUIT

Circuit Executive and Clerk of Court.—Jan Horbaly, (202) 312–5520.
Senior Technical Assistant.—Melvin L. Halpern, 312–3484.
Senior Staff Attorney.—J. Douglas Steere, 312–3490.
Assistant Circuit Executive for Administrative Services.—Ruth A. Butler, 312–3464.
Circuit Librarian.—Patricia M. McDermott, 312–5500.
Assistant Circuit Executive for Automation Technology.—Larry Luallen, 312–3475.
Operations Officer.—Dale Bosley, 312–5517.
Chief Deputy Clerk for Operations.—Pamela Twiford, 312–5522.

UNITED STATES DISTRICT COURT FOR THE DISTRICT OF COLUMBIA

E. Barrett Prettyman U.S. Courthouse, 333 Constitution Avenue, NW., Room 4106, 20001 phone (202) 354–3320, fax 354–3412

THOMAS F. HOGAN, chief judge; born in Washington, DC, May 31, 1938; son of Adm. Bartholomew W. (MC) (USN) Surgeon Gen., USN, 1956–62, and Grace (Gloninger) Hogan; Georgetown Preparatory School, 1956; A.B., Georgetown University (classical), 1960; master's program, American and English literature, George Washington University, 1960–62; J.D., Georgetown University, 1965–66; Honorary Degree, Doctor of Laws, Georgetown University Law Center, May 1999; St. Thomas More Fellow, Georgetown University Law Center, 1965–66; American Jurisprudence Award: Corporation Law; member, bars of the District of Columbia and Maryland; law clerk to Hon. William B. Jones, U.S. District Court for the District of Columbia, 1966–67; counsel, Federal Commission on Reform of Federal Criminal Laws, 1967–68; private practice of law in the District of Columbia and Maryland, 1968–82; adjunct professor of law, Potomac School of Law, 1977–79; adjunct professor of law, Georgetown University Law Center, 1986–88; public member, officer evaluation board, U.S. Foreign Service, 1973; member: American Bar Association, State Chairman, Maryland Drug Abuse Education Program, Young Lawyers Section (1970–73), District of Columbia Bar Association, Bar Association of the District of Columbia, Maryland State Bar Association, Montgomery County Bar Association, National Institute for Trial Advocacy, Defense Research Institute, The Barristers, The Lawyers Club; chairman, board of directors, Christ Child Institute for Emotionally Ill Children, 1971–74; served on many committees; USDC Executive Committee; Conference Committee on Administration of Federal Magistrates System, 1988–91; chairman, Inter-Circuit Assignment Committee, 1990–present; appointed judge of the U.S. District Court for the District of Columbia by President Reagan on October 4, 1982; Chief Judge June 19, 2001; member: Judicial Conference of the United States 2001–present; Executive Committee of the Judicial Conference, July 2001–present.

ROYCE C. LAMBERTH, judge; born in San Antonio, TX, July 16, 1943; son of Nell Elizabeth Synder and Larimore S. Lamberth, Sr.; South San Antonio High School, 1961; B.A., University of Texas at Austin, 1966; LL.B., University of Texas School of Law, 1967; permanent president, class of 1967, University of Texas School of Law; U.S. Army (Captain, Judge Advocate General's Corps, 1968–74; Vietnam Service Medal, Air Medal, Bronze Star with Oak Leaf Cluster, Meritorious Service Medal with Oak Leaf Cluster); assistant U.S. attorney, District of Columbia, 1974–87 (chief, civil division, 1978–87); President's Reorganization Project, Federal Legal Representation Study, 1978–79; honorary faculty, Army Judge Advocate General's School, 1976; Attorney General's Special Commendation Award; Attorney General's John Marshall Award, 1982; vice chairman, Armed Services and Veterans Affairs Committee, Section on Administrative Law, American Bar Association, 1979–82, chairman, 1983–84; chairman, Professional Ethics Committee, 1989–91; co-chairman, Committee of Article III Judges, Judiciary Section 1989–present; chairman, Federal Litigation Section, 1986–87; chairman, Federal Rules Committee, 1985–86; deputy chairman, Council of the Federal Lawyer, 1980–83; chairman, Career Service Committee, Federal Bar Association, 1978–80; appointed judge, U.S. District Court for the District of Columbia by President Reagan, November 16, 1987; appointed by Chief Justice Rehnquist to be Presiding Judge of the United States Foreign Intelligence Surveillance Court, May 1995–2002.

PAUL L. FRIEDMAN, judge; born in Buffalo, NY, February 20, 1944; son of Cecil A. and Charlotte Wagner Friedman; B.A. (political science), Cornell University, 1965; J.D., *cum laude,* School of Law, State University of New York at Buffalo, 1968; admitted to the bars of the District of Columbia, New York, U.S. Supreme Court, and U.S. Courts of Appeals for the D.C., Federal, Fourth, Fifth, Sixth, Seventh, Ninth and Eleventh Circuits; Law Clerk to Judge Aubrey E. Robinson, Jr., U.S. district court for the District of Columbia, 1968–69; Law Clerk to Judge Roger Robb, U.S. Court of Appeals for the District of Columbia Circuit, 1969–70; Assistant U.S. Attorney for the District of Columbia, 1970–74; assistant to the Solicitor General of the United States, 1974–76; associate independent counsel, Iran-Contra investigation, 1987–88, private law practice, White and Case (partner, 1979–94; associate, 1976–79); member: American Bar Association, Commission on Multidisciplinary Practice (1998–2000), District of Columbia bar (president, 1986–87), American Law Institute (1984) and ALI Council, 1998, American Academy of Appellate Lawyers, Bar Association of the District of Columbia, Women's Bar Association of the District of Columbia, Washington Bar Association, Hispanic Bar Association, Assistant United States Attorneys Association of the District of Columbia (president, 1976–77), Civil Justice Reform Act Advisory Group (chair, 1991–94), District of Columbia Judicial Nomination Commission (member, 1990–94; chair, 1992–94), Advisory Committee on Procedures, U.S. Court of Appeals for the D.C. Circuit (1982–88), Grievance Committee; U.S. District Court for the District of Columbia (member, 1981–87; chair, 1983–85); fellow, American College of Trial Lawyers; fellow, American Bar Foundation; board of directors: Frederick B. Abramson Memorial Foundation (president, 1991–94), Washington Area Lawyers for the Arts (1988–92), Washington Legal Clinic for the Homeless (member, 1987–92; vice-president 1988–91), Stuart Stiller Memorial Foundation (1980–94), American Judicature Society (1990–94), District of Columbia Public Defender Service (1989–92); member: Cosmos Club, Lawyers Club of Washington; appointed judge, U.S. District Court for the District of Columbia by President Clinton, June 16, 1994, and took oath of office August 1, 1994; U.S. Judicial Conference Advisory Committee on Federal Criminal Rules.

RICARDO M. URBINA, judge; born of an Honduran father and Puerto Rican mother in Manhattan, NY; B.A., Georgetown University, 1967; J.D., Georgetown Law Center, 1970; staff attorney, D.C. Public Defender Service, 1970–72; after a period of private practice with an emphasis on commercial litigation, joined the faculty of Howard University School of Law, during which time he maintained a private practice; directed the university's criminal justice clinic and taught criminal law, criminal procedure and torts, 1974–81; voted Professor of the Year by the Howard Law School student body, 1978; nominated to the D.C. Superior Court by President Carter, 1980; appointed to the bench as President Reagan's first presidential judicial appointment and the first Hispanic judge in the history of the District of Columbia, 1981; during his thirteen years on the Superior Court, Judge Urbina served as Chief Presiding Judge of the Family Division for three years and chaired the committee that drafted the Child Support Guidelines later adopted as the District of Columbia's child support law; managed a criminal calendar (1989–90) that consisted exclusively of first degree murder, rape and child molestation cases; designated by the Chief Judge to handle a special calendar consisting of complex civil litigation; twice recognized by the United States Department of Health and Human Services for his work with children and families; selected one of the Washingtonians of the Year by *Washington Magazine,* 1986; received Hugh Johnson Memorial Award for his many contributions to ". . . the creation of harmony among diverse elements of the community and the bar by D.C. Hispanic Bar Association;" received the Hispanic National Bar Association's 1993 award for demonstrated commitment to the "Preservation of Civil and Constitutional Rights of All Americans", and the 1995 NBC-Hispanic Magazine National VIDA Award in recognition of lifetime community service; adjunct professor at the George Washington University Law School since 1993; served as a visiting instructor of trial advocacy at the Harvard Law School, 1996–97; Latino Civil Rights Center presented him with the Justice Award in 1999; conferred Distinguished Adjunct Teacher Award by George Washington University Law School in 2001 and in 2005 has been awarded the David Seidlson Chair for Trial Advocacy; appointment by President Clinton to the U.S. District Court for the District of Columbia in 1994 made him the first Latino ever appointed to the federal bench in Washington, D.C.

EMMET G. SULLIVAN, judge; born in Washington, DC; graduated McKinley High School, 1964; B.A., Howard University, 1968; J.D., Howard University Law School, 1971; law clerk to Judge James A. Washington, Jr.; joined the law firm of Houston and Gardner, 1973–80, became a partner; thereafter was a partner with Houston, Sullivan and Gardner; board of directors of the D.C. Law Students in Court Program; D.C. Judicial Conference Voluntary Arbitration Committee; Nominating Committee of the Bar Association of the District of Columbia; U.S. District Court Committee on Grievances; adjunct professor at Howard University School of Law; member: National Bar Association, Washington Bar Association, Bar Association of the District of Columbia; appointed by President Reagan to the Superior Court of the District of Columbia as an associate judge, 1984; deputy presiding judge and presiding judge of the probate and tax division; chairperson of the rules committees for the probate and tax divisions; member: Court Rules Committee and the Jury Plan Committee; appointed by President George H.W. Bush to serve as an associate judge of the District of Columbia Court of Appeals, 1991; chairperson for the nineteenth annual judicial conference of the District of Columbia, 1994 (the Conference theme was "Rejuvenating Juvenile Justice—Responses to the Problems of Juvenile Violence in the District of Columbia"); appointed by chief judge Wagner to chair the "Task Force on Families and Violence for the District of Columbia Courts"; nominated to the U.S. District Court by President Clinton on March 22, 1994; and confirmed by the U.S. Senate on June 15, 1994; appointed by Chief Justice Rehnquist to serve on the Federal Judicial Conference Committee on Criminal Law, 1998;

District of Columbia Judicial Disabilities and Tenure Commission, 1996–2001; presently serving on the District of Columbia Judicial Nomination Commission; first person in the District of Columbia to have been appointed to three judicial positions by three different U.S. Presidents.

JAMES ROBERTSON, judge; born in Cleveland, OH, May 18, 1938; son of Frederick Irving and Doris (Byars) Robertson; educated at Western Reserve Academy, Hudson, OH; A.B., Princeton University, 1959 (Woodrow Wilson School); served as an officer in the U.S. Navy, on destroyers and in the Office of Naval Intelligence, 1959–64; LL.B., George Washington University, 1965 (editor-in-chief, George Washington Law Review); admitted to the bar of the District of Columbia, 1966; associate, Wilmer, Cutler and Pickering, 1965–69; chief counsel, litigation office, Lawyers' Committee for Civil Rights Under Law, Jackson, MS, 1969–70; executive director, Lawyers' Committee for Civil Rights Under Law, Washington, DC, 1971–72; partner, Wilmer, Cutler and Pickering, 1973–94; co-chair, Lawyers' Committee for Civil Rights Under Law, 1985–87; president, Southern Africa Legal Services and Legal Education Project, Inc., 1989–94; president, District of Columbia bar, 1991–92; fellow, American College of Trial Lawyers; fellow, American Bar Foundation; member, American Law Institute; appointed U.S. District Judge for the District of Columbia by President Clinton on October 11, 1994 and took oath of office on December 31, 1994; member, Judicial Conference Committee on Information Technology, 1996–present, chair, 2002–present; member, Foreign Intelligence Surveillance Court, 2001–present.

COLLEEN KOLLAR-KOTELLY, judge; born in New York, NY; daughter of Konstantine and Irene Kollar; attended bilingual schools in Mexico, Ecuador and Venezuela, and Georgetown Visitation Preparatory School in Washington, D.C.; received B.A. degree in English at Catholic University (Delta Epsilon Honor Society); received J.D. at Catholic University's Columbus School of Law (Moot Court Board of Governors); law clerk to Hon. Catherine B. Kelly, District of Columbia Court of Appeals, 1968–69; attorney, United States Department of Justice, Criminal Division, Appellate Section, 1969–72; chief legal counsel, Saint Elizabeths Hospital, Department of Health and Human Services, 1972–84; received Saint Elizabeths Hospital Certificate of Appreciation, 1981; Meritorious Achievement Award from Alcohol, Drug Abuse and Mental Health Administration (ADAMHA), Department of Health and Human Services, 1981; appointed judge, Superior Court of the District of Columbia by President Reagan, October 3, 1984, took oath of office October 21, 1984; served as Deputy Presiding Judge, Criminal Division, January 1996–April 1997; received Achievement Recognition Award, Hispanic Heritage CORO Awards Celebration, 1996; appointed judge, U.S. District Court for the District of Columbia by President Clinton on March 26, 1997, took oath of office May 12, 1997; appointed by Chief Justice Rehnquist to serve on the Financial Disclosure Committee, 2000–2002; Presiding Judge of the United States Foreign Intelligence Surveillance Court, 2002–present.

HENRY H. KENNEDY, Jr., judge; born in Columbia, SC, February 22, 1948; son of Henry and Rachel Kennedy; A.B., Princeton University, 1970; J.D., Harvard University, 1973; admitted to the bar of the District of Columbia, 1973; Reavis, Pogue, Neal and Rose, 1972 and 1973; Assistant United States Attorney for the District of Columbia, 1973–76; United States Magistrate for the District of Columbia, April 1976–79; appointed Judge, Superior Court of the District of Columbia, by President Carter, December 17, 1979; member: American Bar Foundation; District of Columbia Bar; Washington Bar Association; Bar Association of the District of Columbia; American Law Institute; member: The Barristers; Sigma Pi Phi; Epsilon Boule; Trustee, Princeton University; appointed judge, United States District Court for the District of Columbia, by President Clinton on September 18, 1997.

RICHARD W. ROBERTS, judge; born in New York, NY; son of Beverly N. Roberts and Angeline T. Roberts; graduate of the High School of Music and Art, 1970; A.B. Vassar College, 1974; M.I.A. School for International Training, 1978; J.D., Columbia Law School, 1978; Honors Program trial attorney, Criminal Section, Civil Rights Division, U.S. Department of Justice, Washington, D.C., 1978–82; Associate, Covington and Burling, Washington, D.C., 1982–86; Assistant U.S. Attorney, Southern District of NY, 1986–88; Assistant U.S. Attorney, 1988–93, then Principal Assistant U.S. Attorney, District of Columbia, 1993–95; Chief, Criminal Section, Civil Rights Division, U.S. Department of Justice, Washington, DC, 1995–98; adjunct professor of trial practice, Georgetown University Law Center, Washington, DC, 1983–84; Guest faculty, Harvard Law School, Trial Advocacy Workshop, 1984–present; admitted to bars of NY (1979) and DC (1983); U.S. District Court for District of Columbia, 1983; U.S. Court of Appeals for the D.C. Circuit, 1984; U.S. Supreme Court, 1985; U.S. District Court for the Southern District of NY and U.S. Court of Appeals for the Second Circuit, 1986; past or present member or officer of National Black Prosecutors Association; Washington

Bar Association; National Conference of Black Lawyers; Department of Justice Association of Black Attorneys; Department of Justice Association of Hispanic Employees for Advancement and Development; DC Bar, Committee on Professionalism and Public Understanding About the Law; American Bar Association Criminal Justice Section Committees on Continuing Legal Education, and Race and Racism in the Criminal Justice System; ABA Task Force on the Judiciary; DC Circuit Judicial Conference Arrangements Committee; D.C. Judicial Conference Planning Committee; Edward Bennett Williams Inn of Court, Washington, DC, master; board of directors, Alumnae and Alumni of Vassar College; African American Alumni of Vassar College; Vassar Club of Washington, DC; Concerned Black Men, Inc., Washington DC Chapter; Sigma Pi Phi, Epsilon Boule; Council on Foreign Relations; DC Coalition Against Drugs and Violence; Murch Elementary School Restructuring Team; nominated as U.S. District Judge for the District of Columbia by President Clinton on January 27, 1998 and confirmed by the Senate on June 5, 1998; took oath of office on July 31, 1998.

ELLEN SEGAL HUVELLE, judge; born in Boston, MA, June 3, 1948; daughter of Robert M. Segal, Esq. and Sharlee Segal; B.A., Wellesley College, 1970; Masters in City Planning, Yale University, 1972; J.D., *magna cum laude*, Boston College Law School, 1975 (Order of the Coif; Articles Editor of the law review); law clerk to Chief Justice Edward F. Hennessey, Massachusetts Supreme Judicial Court, 1975–76; associate, Williams & Connolly, 1976–84; partner, Williams & Connolly, 1984–90; associate judge, Superior Court of the District of Columbia, 1990–99; member: American Bar Association, District of Columbia Bar, Women's Bar Association; Fellow of the American Bar Foundation; Master in the Edward Bennett Williams Inn of Court and member of the Inn's Executive Committee; instructor of Trial Advocacy at the University of Virginia Law School; member of Visiting Faculty at Harvard Law School's Trial Advocacy Workshop; Boston College Law School Board of Overseers; appointed judge, U.S. District Court for the District of Columbia by President Clinton in October 1999, and took oath of office on February 25, 2000.

REGGIE B. WALTON, judge; born in Donora, PA, February 8, 1949; son of the late Theodore and Ruth (Garard) Walton; B.A., West Virginia State College, 1971; J.D., American University, Washington College of Law, 1974; admitted to the bars of the Supreme Court of Pennsylvania, 1974; United States District Court for the Eastern District of Pennsylvania, 1975; District of Columbia Court of Appeals, 1976; United States Court of Appeals for the District of Columbia Circuit, 1977; Supreme Court of the United States, 1980; United States District Court for the District of Columbia; Staff Attorney, Defender Association of Philadelphia, 1974–76; Assistant United States Attorney for the District of Columbia, 1976–80; Chief, Career Criminal Unit, Assistant United States Attorney for the District of Columbia, 1979–80; Executive Assistant United States Attorney for the District of Columbia, 1980–81; Associate Judge, Superior Court of the District of Columbia, 1981–89; Deputy Presiding Judge of the Criminal Division, Superior Court of the District of Columbia, 1986–89; Associate Director, Office of National Drug Control Policy, Executive Office of the President, 1989–91; Senior White House Advisor for Crime, The White House, 1991; Associate Judge, Superior Court of the District of Columbia, 1991–2001; Presiding Judge of the Domestic Violence Unit, Superior Court of the District of Columbia, 2000; Presiding Judge of the Family Division, Superior Court of the District of Columbia, 2001; Instructor: National Judicial College, Reno, Nevada, 1999–present; Harvard University Law School, Trial Advocacy Workshop, 1994–present; National Institute of Trial Advocacy, Georgetown University Law School, 1983–present; Co-author, Pretrial Drug Testing—an Essential component of the National Drug Control Strategy, Brigham Young University Law Journal of Public Law (1991); Distinguished Alumnus Award, American University, Washington College of Law (1991); The William H. Hastie Award, The Judicial Council of the National Bar Association (1993); Commissioned as a Kentucky Colonel by the Governor (1990, 1991); Governor's Proclamation declaring April 9, 1991, Judge Reggie B. Walton Day in the State of Louisiana; The West Virginia State College National Alumni Association James R. Waddy Meritorious Service Award (1990); Secretary's Award, United States Department of Veterans Affairs (1990); Outstanding Alumnus Award, Ringgold High School (1987); Director's Award for Superior Performance as an Assistant United States Attorney (1980); Profiled in book entitled ''Black Judges on Justice: Prospectives From The Bench'' by Linn Washington (1995); appointed district judge, United States District Court for the District of Columbia by President George W. Bush, September 24, 2001, and took oath of office October 29, 2001; appointed by President Bush in June of 2004 to serve as the Chairperson of the National Prison Rape Reduction Commission, a two-year commission created by the United States Congress that is tasked with the mission of identifying methods to curb the incidents of prison rape.

JOHN D. BATES, judge; born in Elizabeth, NJ, October 11, 1946; son of Richard D. and Sarah (Deacon) Bates; B.A., Wesleyan University, 1968; J.D., University of Maryland

School of Law, 1976; U.S. Army (1968–71, 1st Lt., Vietnam Service Medal, Bronze Star); law clerk to Hon. Roszel Thomsen, U.S. District Court for the District of Maryland, 1976–77; Assistant U.S. Attorney, District of Columbia, 1980–97 (Chief, Civil Division, 1987–97); Director's Award for Superior Performance (1983); Attorney General's Special commendation Award (1986); Deputy Independent Counsel, Whitewater Investigation, 1995–97; private practice of law, Miller & Chevalier (partner, 1998–2001), Chair of Government Contracts Litigation Department and member of Executive Committee), Steptoe & Johnson (associate, 1977–80); District of Columbia Circuit Advisory Committee for Procedures, 1989–93; Civil Justice Reform Committee of the U.S. District Court for the District of Columbia, 1996–2001; Treasurer, D.C. Bar, 1992–93; Publications Committee, D.C. Bar (1991–97, Chair 1994–97); D.C. Bar Special Committee on Government Lawyers, 1990–91; D.C. Bar Task Force on Civility in the Profession, 1994–96; D.C. Bar Committee on Examination of Rule 49, 1995–96; Chairman, Litigation Section, Federal Bar Association, 1986–89; Board of Directors, Washington Lawyers Committee for Civil Rights and Urban Affairs, 1999–2001; appointed to the U.S. District Court for the District of Columbia in December, 2001.

RICHARD J. LEON, judge; born in South Natick, MA, December 3, 1949; son of Silvano B. Leon and Rita (O'Rorke) Leon; A.B., Holy Cross College, 1971, J.D., *cum laude,* Suffolk Law School, 1974; LL.M. Harvard Law School, 1981; Law Clerk to Chief Justice McLaughlin and the Associate Justices, Superior Court of Massachusetts, 1974–75; Law Clerk to Hon. Thomas F. Kelleher, Supreme Court of Rhode Island, 1975–76; admitted to bar, Rhode Island, 1975 and District of Columbia, 1991; Special Assistant U.S. Attorney, Southern District of New York, 1977–78; Assistant Professor of Law, St. John's Law School, New York, 1979–83; Senior Trial Attorney, Criminal Section, Tax Division, U.S. Department of Justice, 1983–87; Deputy Chief Minority Counsel, U.S. House Select ''Iran-Contra'' Committee, 1987–88; Deputy Assistant U.S. Attorney General, Environment Division, 1988–89; Partner, Baker & Hostetler, Washington, DC, 1989–99; Commissioner, The White House Fellows Commission, 1990–92; Chief Minority Counsel, U.S. House Foreign Affairs Committee ''October Suprise'' Task Force, 1992–93; Special Counsel, U.S. House Banking Committee ''Whitewater'' Investigation, 1994; Special Counsel, U.S. House Ethics Reform Task Force, 1997; Adjunct Professor, Georgetown University Law Center, 1997–present; Partner, Vorys, Sater, Seymour and Pease, Washington, DC, 1999–2002; Commissioner, Judicial Review Commission on Foreign Asset Control, 2000–01; Master, Edward Bennett Williams Inn of Court; appointed U.S. District Judge for the District of Columbia by President George W. Bush on February 19, 2002; took oath of office on March 20, 2002.

ROSEMARY M. COLLYER, judge; born in White Plains, NY, November 19, 1945; daughter of Thomas C. and Alice Henry Mayers; educated in parochial and public schools in Stamford, Connecticut; B.A., Trinity College, Washington, DC, 1968; J.D., University of Denver College of Law, 1977; practiced with Sherman & Howard, Denver, Colorado, 1977–81; Chairman, Federal Mine Safety and Health Review Commission, 1981–84 by appointment of President Reagan with Senate confirmation; General Counsel, National Labor Relations Board, 1984–89 by appointment of President Reagan with Senate confirmation; private practice with Crowell & Moring LLP, Washington, DC 1989–2003; member and chairman of the firm's Management Committee; appointed U.S. District Judge for the District of Columbia by President George W. Bush and took oath of office on January 2, 2003.

SENIOR JUDGES

LOUIS FALK OBERDORFER, senior judge; born in Birmingham, AL, February 21, 1919; son of A. Leo and Stella Falk Oberdorfer; A.B., Dartmouth College, 1939; LL.B., Yale Law School, 1946 (editor in chief, Yale Law Journal, 1941); admitted to the bar of Alabama, 1947, District of Columbia, 1949; U.S. Army, rising from private to captain, 1941–45; law clerk to Justice Hugo L. Black, 1946–47; attorney, Paul Weiss, Wharton, Garrison, 1947–51; partner, Wilmer, Cutler and Pickering, and predecessor firms, 1951–61 and 1965–77; Assistant Attorney General, Tax Division, U.S. Department of Justice, 1961–65; president, District of Columbia Bar, 1977; transition chief executive officer, Legal Services Corp., 1975; co-chairman, Lawyers' Committee for Civil Rights Under Law, 1967–69; member, Advisory Committee on Federal Rules of Civil Procedure, 1963–84; visiting lecturer, Yale Law School, 1966, 1971; adjunct professor, Georgetown Law Center, 1993–present; appointed judge of the U.S. District Court for the District of Columbia by President Carter on October 11, 1977, and took oath of office on November 1, 1977; senior status July 31, 1992.

JOHN GARRETT PENN, senior judge; born in Pittsfield, MA, March 19, 1932; son of John and Eugenie Heyliger Penn; A.B., University of Massachusetts (Amherst), 1954; LL.B.,

Boston University School of Law, 1957; admitted to the bars of Massachusetts, 1957 and District of Columbia, 1970; U.S. Army, first lieutenant, Judge Advocate General Corps, 1958–61; attorney, U.S. Department of Justice, Tax Division, 1961–70; trial attorney, 1961–65, reviewer, 1965–68, assistant chief, 1968–70; National Institute of Public Affairs Fellow, Woodrow Wilson School of Public and International Affairs, Princeton University, 1967–68; awarded the Charles Hamilton Houston Medallion of Merit by the Washington Bar Association, May 1996; appointed judge, Superior Court of the District of Columbia by President Nixon, October 1970; appointed judge, U.S. District Court for the District of Columbia by President Carter, March 23, 1979, and took oath of office, May 15, 1979; Chief Judge March 1, 1992—July 21, 1997.

GLADYS KESSLER, senior judge; born in New York, NY, January 22, 1938; B.A., Cornell University, 1959; LL.B. Harvard Law School, 1962; member: American Judicature Society (board of directors, 1985–89); National Center for State Courts (board of directors, 1984–87); National Association of Women Judges (president, 1983–84); Women Judges' Fund for Justice, (president, 1980–82); Fellows of the American Bar Foundation; President's Council of Cornell Women; American Law Institute; American Bar Association—committees: Alternative Dispute Resolution, Bioethics and AIDS; Executive Committee, Conference of Federal Trial Judges; private law practice—partner, Roisman, Kessler and Cashdan, 1969–77; associate judge, Superior Court of the District of Columbia, 1977–94; court administrative activities: District of Columbia Courts Joint Committee on Judicial Administration, 1989–94; Domestic Violence Coordinating Council (chairperson, 1993–94); Multi-Door Dispute Resolution Program (supervising judge, 1985–90); family division, D.C. Superior Court (presiding judge, 1981–85); Einshac Institute Board of Directors; U.S. Judicial Conference Committee on Court Administration and Court Management; Frederick B. Abramson Memorial Foundation Board of Directors; Our Place Board of Directors; Vice Chair, District of Columbia Judicial Disabilities and Tenure Commission; appointed judge, U.S. District Court for the District of Columbia by President Clinton, June 16, 1994, and took oath of office, July 18, 1994.

OFFICERS OF THE UNITED STATES DISTRICT COURT FOR THE DISTRICT OF COLUMBIA

United States Magistrate Judges: Deborah A. Robinson; Alan Kay; John M. Facciola.
Clerk of Court.—Nancy Mayer-Whittington.
Administrative Assistant to the Chief Judge.—Sheldon L. Snook.
Bankruptcy Judge.—S. Martin Teel, Jr.

UNITED STATES COURT OF INTERNATIONAL TRADE

One Federal Plaza, New York, NY 10278–0001, phone (212) 264–2800

JANE A. RESTANI, chief judge; born in San Francisco, CA, February 27, 1948; parents: Emilia C. and Roy J. Restani; husband: Ira Bloom; B.A., University of California at Berkeley, 1969; J.D., University of California at Davis, 1973; law review staff writer, 1971–72; articles editor, 1972–73; member, Order of the Coif; elected to Phi Kappa Phi Honor Society; admitted to the bar of the Supreme Court of the State of California, 1973; joined the civil division of the Department of Justice under the Attorney General's Honor Program in 1973 as a trial attorney; assistant chief commercial litigation section, civil division, 1976–80; director, commercial litigation branch, civil division, 1980–83; recipient of the John Marshall Award of outstanding legal achievement in 1983; Judicial Improvements Committee (now Committee on Court Administration and Case Management) of the Judicial Conference of the United States from 1987–94; Judicial Conference Advisory Committee on the Federal Rules of Bankruptcy Procedure, and liaison to the Advisory Committee on the Federal Rules of Civil Procedure, 1994–96; ABA Standing Committee on Customs Laws, 1990–93; and the Board of Directors, New York State Association of Women Judges, 1992–present; nominated to the United States Court of International Trade on November 2, 1983 by President Reagan; entered upon the duties of that office on November 25, 1983; elevated to Chief Judge on November 1, 2003.

GREGORY W. CARMAN, judge; born in Farmingdale, Long Island, NY, January 31, 1937; son of Nassau County District Court Judge Willis B. and Marjorie Sosa Carman; married to Nancy Endruschat (deceased); children: Gregory Wright, Jr., John Frederick, James Matthew, and Mira Catherine; married to Judith L. Dennehy, 1995; B.A., St. Lawrence University, Canton, NY, 1958; national exchange student, 1956–57, studying at the University of Paris through Sweet Briar College Junior Year in France Program; J.D., St. John's University School of Law (honors program), 1961; member, St. John's Law Review; University of Virginia Law School, JAG (with honors), 1962; Master in Taxation Program, New York University School of Law; Captain, U.S. Army, 1958–64, stationed with the 2d Infantry Division, Fort Benning, GA; awarded Army Commendation Medal for Meritorious Service, 1964; admitted to the New York bar, 1961; practiced law with the firm of Carman, Callahan & Sabino, Farmingdale, NY; admitted to practice in U.S. Court of Military Appeals, 1962; certified by Judge Advocate General to practice at general court-martial trials, 1962; admitted to practice in the U.S. District Courts, Eastern District of New York and Southern District of New York, 1965; Second Circuit Court of Appeals, 1966; Supreme Court of the United States, 1967; U.S. Court of Appeals, District of Columbia, 1982; Councilman for the town of Oyster Bay, 1972–80; member, U.S. House of Representatives, 97th Congress; appointed to Banking, Finance and Urban Affairs Committee and Select Committee on Aging, 1981–82; member, International Trade, Investment and Monetary Policy Subcommittee of House Banking Committee, 1981–82; U.S. congressional delegate, International I.M.F. Conference, 1982; Statutory Member, Judicial Conference of the United States; member, Executive Committee, Judicial Branch Committee, and Subcommittees of the Judicial Conference of the United States on Long Range Planning, Benefits, Civic Education, and Seminars; member, Bicentennial Commission of Nassau County; Rotary International, 1964–present; named a Paul Harris Fellow of The Rotary Foundation of Rotary International; member, Federal Bar Association; American Bar Association; Fellow, American Bar Foundation; member, New York State Bar Association; member and former chair, New York State Bar Association's Committee on Courts and the Community, and recipient of its 1996 Special Recognition Award; director and member, Respect for Law Alliance, Inc.; past president and Executive Committee member, Theodore Roosevelt American Inn of Court; past president, Protestant Lawyers Association of Long Island; member, Vestry, St. Thomas's Episcopal Church, Farmingdale, NY; Phi Delta Phi legal fraternity; member, Holland Society, and recipient of its 1999 Gold Medal for Distinguished Achievement in Jurisprudence; Doctor of Laws, *honoris causa*, Nova Southeastern University, 1999; Distinguished Jurist in Residence, Touro College Law Center, 2000; Doctor of Laws, *honoris causa*, St. John's University, 2002; Inaugural Lecturer, Hon. Dominick L. DiCarlo U.S. Court of International Trade Lecture, John Marshall

Law School, 2003; Distinguished Alumni Citation, St. Lawrence University, 2003; Italian Board of Guardians Public Service Award, 2003; Sigma Chi, social fraternity; nominated by President Reagan, confirmed and appointed Judge of the U.S. Court of International Trade, March 2, 1983; served as Acting Chief Judge, 1991; became Chief Judge, 1996; served as Chief Judge, 1996–2003.

DONALD C. POGUE, judge; graduated *magna cum laude*, Phi Beta Kappa from Dartmouth College; did graduate work at the University of Essex, England; J.D., Yale Law School and a Masters of Philosophy, Yale University; married to Susan, 1971; served as judge in Connecticut's Superior Court; appointed to the bench in 1994; served as chairman of Connecticut's Commission on Hospitals and Health Care; practiced law in Hartford for 15 years; lectured on labor law at the University of Connecticut School of Law; assisted in teaching the Harvard Law School's program on negotiations and dispute resolution for lawyers; chaired the Connecticut Bar Association's Labor and Employment Law Section; appointed a Judge of the United States Court of International Trade in 1995; chair of the Court's Long Range Planning Committee, and of its Budget Committee.

EVAN J. WALLACH, judge; born in Superior, AZ, November 11, 1949; son of Albert A. and Sara F. Wallach; married to Katherine Colleen Tobin, 1992; graduate of Acalanes High School, Lafayette, CA, 1967; attended Diablo Valley Junior College, Pleasant Hill, CA, 1967–68; news editor, Viking Reporter; member Alfa Gamma Sigma, National Junior College Honor Society, member, Junior Varsity Wrestling Team; enlisted United States Army, January, 1969, PVT–SGT, served as Recognizance Sergeant 8th Engineer Bn., 1st Calvary Division (Air Mobile), Republic of Vietnam, 1970–71, Bronze Star Medal, Air Medal, Valorous Unit Citation, Good Conduct Medal; attended University of Arizona, 1971–73, graduated B.A., Journalism (high honors), Phi Beta Kappa, Phi Kappa Phi, Kappa Tau Alfa, Rufenacht French language prize, Douglas Martin Journalism Scholarship; attended University of California, Berkeley, 1973–76, graduated J.D., 1976, research assistant to Prof. Melvin Eisenberg, member of University of California Honor Society; Associate (1976–82) and Partner (1983–95) Lionel Sawyer and Collins, Las Vegas, NV with emphasis on media representation; attended Cambridge University, Cambridge, England, LL.B. (international law) (honors), 1981, member Hughes Hall College Rowing Club, Cambridge University Tennis Club; General Counsel and Public Policy Advisor to U.S. Senator Harry Reid (D) of Nevada, 1987–88; served CAPT–MAJ Nevada Army National Guard, 1989–95; served as Attorney / Advisor, International Affairs Division; Office of the Judge Advocate General of the Army, February–June, 1991–92; Meritorious Service Medal (oak leaf cluster); Nevada Medal of Merit; General Counsel, Nevada Democratic Party, 1978–80, 1982–86; General Counsel, Reid for Congress campaign, 1982, 1984; Reid for Senate campaign, 1986, 1992; General Counsel, Bryan for Senate campaign, 1988; Nevada State Director, Mondale for President campaign, 1984; State Director, Nevada and Arizona Gore for President campaign, 1988; General Counsel Nevada Assembly Democratic Caucus, 1990–95; General Counsel, Society for Professional Journalists, 1988–95; General Counsel, Nevada Press Association, 1989–95; awarded American Bar Association Liberty Bell Award, 1993; Nevada State Press Association President's Award, 1994; Clark County School Librarians Intellectual Freedom Award, 1995; Law of War, Adjunct Professor, New York Law School, 1997–present; Brooklyn Law School 2000–present; member, Nevada Bar, 1977; U.S. District Court, District of Nevada, 1977; District of Columbia, 1988; Ninth Circuit Court of Appeals, 1989; author, *Legal Handbook for Nevada Reporters* (1994); Comparison of British and American Defense Based Prior Restraint, *ICLQ* (1984); Treatment of Crude Oil As A War Munition, *ICLQ* (1992); Three Ways Nevada Unconstitutionally Chills The Media; Nevada Lawyer (1994); Co-Editor, *Nevada Civil Practice Handbook* (1993); Extradition to the Rwandan War Crimes Tribunal: Is Another Treaty Required, *USCLA Journal of International Law and Foreign Affairs* (Spring / Summer, 1998); The Procedural and Evidentiary Rules of the Post World War II War Crimes Trials: Did They Provide An Outline For International Criminal Procedure? *Columbia Journal of Translational Law* (Spring, 1999); Webmaster, International Law of War Association, lawofwar.org; Afghanistan, Yamashita and Uchiyama: Does the Sauce Suit the Gander? *The Army Lawyer* (June 2003); The Logical Nexus Between the Decision to Deny Application of the Third Geneva Convention to the Taliban and Al Queda and the Mistreatment of Prisoners of War in Abu Ghraib, *Case Western Reserve Journal of International Law 541* (2004); Drop by Drop: Forgetting the History of Water Torture in U.S. Courts, *Columbia Journal of Transnational Law* (2007).

JUDITH M. BARZILAY, judge; born in Russell, KS, January 3, 1944; husband, Sal (Doron) Barzilay; children, Ilan and Michael; parents, Arthur and Hilda Morgenstern; B.A., Wichita State University, 1965; M.L.S., Rutgers University School of Library and Information Science, 1971; J.D., Rutgers University School of Law, 1981, Moot Court Board, 1980–81; trial attorney, U.S. Department of Justice (International Trade Field Office), 1983–86; litigation associate, Siegel, Mandell and Davidson, New York, NY, 1986–88; Sony Corporation of America, 1988–98; customs and international trade counsel, 1988–89; vice-president for import and export operations, 1989–96; vice-president for government affairs, 1996–98; executive board of the American Association of Exporters and Importers, 1993–98; appointed by Treasury Secretary Robert Rubin to the Advisory Committee on Commercial Operations of the United States Customs Service, 1995–98; nominated for appointment on January 27, 1998 by President Clinton; sworn-in as judge June 3, 1998.

DELISSA A. RIDGWAY, judge; born in Kirksville, MO, June 28, 1955; B.A. (honors), University of Missouri-Columbia, 1975; graduate work, University of Missouri-Columbia, 1975–76; J.D., Northeastern University School of Law, 1979; Shaw Pittman Potts & Trowbridge (Washington, D.C.), 1979–94; Chair, Foreign Claims Settlement Commission of the U.S., 1994–98; Adjunct Professor of Law, Cornell Law School, 1999–present; Adjunct Professor of Law, Washington College of Law / The American University, 1992–94; District of Columbia Bar, Secretary, 1991–92; Board of Governors, 1992–98; President, Women's Bar Association, 1992–93; American Bar Association, Commission on Women in the Profession, 2002–05; Federal Bar Association, National Council, 1993–2002, 2003–05; Government Relations Committee, 1996–present, Public Relations Committee Chair, 1998–99; Executive, Committee, National Conference of Federal Trial Judges, 2004–present; Founding Member of Board, D.C. Conference on Opportunities for Minorities in the Legal Profession, 1992–93; Chair, D.C. Bar Summit on Women in the Legal Profession, 1995–98; Fellow, American Bar Foundation; Member, American Law Institute; Fellow, Federal Bar Foundation; Earl W. Kintner Award of the Federal Bar Association (2000); Woman Lawyer of the Year, Washington, DC (2001); Distinguished Visiting Scholar-in-Residence, University of Missouri-Columbia (2003); sworn in as a judge to the U.S. Court of International Trade in May 1998.

RICHARD K. EATON, judge; born in Walton, NY; married to Susan Henshaw Jones; two children: Alice and Elizabeth; attended Walton public schools; B.A., Ithaca College, J.D., Union University Albany Law School, 1974; professional experience: Eaton and Eaton, partner; Mudge Rose Guthrie Alexander & Ferdon, New York, NY, associate and partner; Stroock & Stroock & Lavan, partner served on the staff of Senator Daniel Patrick Moynihan; confirmed by the United States Senate to the U.S. Court of International Trade on October 22, 1999.

TIMOTHY C. STANCEU, judge; born in Canton, OH; graduate, Colgate University, 1973; law degree, Georgetown University Law Center, 1979; professional experience: Special Assistant to the Treasury Department's Assistant Secretary for Enforcement; several positions at the U.S. Environmental Protection Agency, where he concentrated on the development and review of regulations on various environmental subjects; Deputy Director, Office of Trade and Tariff Affairs, U.S. Department of the Treasury; thirteen-year career in private practice in Washington, DC with the law firm Hogan & Hartson L.L.P, during which he represented clients in a variety of matters involving customs and international trade law; appointed to the U.S. Court of International Trade by President George W. Bush and began serving on April 15, 2003.

LEO M. GORDON, judge; graduate of Newark Academy in Livingston, NJ; University of North Carolina—Chapel Hill, Phi Beta Kappa, 1973; J.D., Emory University School of Law, 1977; member of the Bars of New Jersey, Georgia and the District of Columbia; Assistant Counsel at the Subcommittee on Monopolies and Commercial Law, Committee on the Judiciary, U.S. House of Representatives, 1977; in that capacity, Judge Gordon was the principal attorney responsible for the Customs Courts Act of 1980 that created the U.S. Court of International Trade; for the past 25 years of his career, Judge Gordon was on the staff at the Court, serving first as Assistant Clerk from 1981–99, and then Clerk of the Court from 1999–2006; appointed to the U.S. Court of International Trade by President George W. Bush in March 2006.

SENIOR JUDGES

THOMAS J. AQUILINO, Jr., senior judge; born in Mount Kisco, NY, December 7, 1939; son of Thomas J. and Virginia B. (Doughty) Aquilino; married to Edith Berndt Aquilino; children: Christopher Thomas, Philip Andrew, Alexander Berndt; attended Cornell University, 1957–59; B.A., Drew University, 1959–60, 1961–62; University of Munich, Germany, 1960–61; Free University of Berlin, Germany, 1965–66; J.D., Rutgers University School of Law, 1966–69; research assistant, Prof. L.F.E. Goldie (Resources for the Future—Ford Foundation), 1967–69; administrator, Northern Region, 1969 Jessup International Law Moot Court Competition; served in the U.S. Army, 1962–65; law clerk, Hon. John M. Cannella, U.S. district court for the Southern District of New York, 1969–71; attorney with Davis Polk & Wardwell, New York, NY, 1971–85; admitted to practice New York, U.S. Supreme Court, U.S. Courts of Appeals for Second and Third Circuits, U.S. Court of International Trade, U.S. Court of Claims, U.S. district courts for Eastern, Southern and Northern Districts of New York, Interstate Commerce Commission; adjunct professor of law, Benjamin N. Cardozo School of Law, 1984–95; Mem., Drew University Board of Visitors, 1997–present; appointed to the U.S. Court of International Trade by President Reagan on February 22, 1985; confirmed by U.S. Senate, April 3, 1985.

NICHOLAS TSOUCALAS, senior judge; born in New York, NY, August 24, 1926; one of five children of George M. and Maria (Monogenis) Tsoucalas; married to Catherine Aravantinos; two daughters: Stephanie (Mrs. Daniel Turriago) and Georgia (Mrs. Christopher Argyrople); five grandchildren; B.S., Kent State University, 1949; LL.B., New York Law School, 1951; attended New York University Law School; entered U.S. Navy, 1944–46; reentered Navy, 1951–52 and served on the carrier, *U.S.S. Wasp;* admitted to New York bar, 1953; appointed Assistant U.S. Attorney for the Southern District of New York, 1955–59; appointed in 1959 as supervisor of 1960 census for the 17th and 18th Congressional Districts; appointed chairman, Board of Commissioners of Appraisal; appointed judge of Criminal Court of the City of New York, 1968; designated acting Supreme Court Justice, Kings and Queens Counties, 1975–82; resumed service as judge of the Criminal Court of the City of New York until June 1986; former chairman: Committee on Juvenile Delinquency, Federal Bar Association, and the Subcommittee on Public Order and Responsibility of the American Citizenship Committee of the New York County Lawyers' Association; member of the American Bar Association, New York State Bar Association; founder of Eastern Orthodox Lawyers' Association; former president: Greek-American Lawyers' Association, and Board of Directors of Greek Orthodox Church of ''Evangelismos'', St. John's Theologos Society, and Parthenon Foundation; member, Order of Ahepa, Parthenon Lodge, F.A.M.; appointed judge of the U.S. Court of International Trade by President Reagan on September 9, 1985, and confirmed by U.S. Senate on June 6, 1986; assumed senior status on September 30, 1996.

R. KENTON MUSGRAVE, senior judge; born in Clearwater, FL, September 7, 1927; married May 7, 1949 to former Ruth Shippen Hoppe, of Atlanta, GA; three children: Laura Marie Musgrave (deceased), Ruth Shippen Musgrave, Esq., and Forest Kenton Musgrave; attended Augusta Academy (Virginia); B.A., University of Washington, 1948; editorial staff, Journal of International Law, Emory University; J.D., with distinction, Emory University, 1953; assistant general counsel, Lockheed Aircraft and Lockheed International, 1953–62; vice president and general counsel, Mattel, Inc., 1963–71; director, Ringling Bros. and Barnum and Bailey Combined Shows, Inc., 1968–72; commissioner, BSA (Atlanta), 1952–55; partner, Musgrave, Welbourn and Fertman, 1972–75; assistant general counsel, Pacific Enterprises, 1975–81; vice president, general counsel and secretary, Vivitar Corporation, 1981–85; vice president and director, Santa Barbara Applied Research Corp., 1982–87; trustee, Morris Animal Foundation, 1981–94; director Emeritus, Pet Protection Society, 1981–present; director, Dolphins of Shark Bay (Australia) Foundation, 1985–present; trustee, The Dian Fossey Gorilla Fund, 1987–present; trustee, The Ocean Conservancy, 2000–present; vice president and director, South Bay Social Services Group, 1963–70; director, Palos Verdes Community Arts Association, 1973–79; member, Governor of Florida's Council of 100, 1970–73; director, Orlando Bank and Trust, 1970–73; counsel, League of Women Voters, 1964–66; member, State Bar of Georgia, 1953–present; State Bar of California, 1962–present; Los Angeles County Bar Association, 1962–87 and chairman, Corporate Law Departments Section, 1965–66; admitted to practice before the U.S. Supreme Court, 1962; Supreme Court of Georgia, 1953; California Supreme Court, 1962; U.S. Customs Court, 1967; U.S. Court of International Trade, 1980; nominated to the U.S. Court of International Trade by President Reagan on July 1, 1987; confirmed by the Senate on November 9, and took oath of office on November 13, 1987.

RICHARD W. GOLDBERG, senior judge; born in Fargo, ND, September 23, 1927; married; two children, a daughter and a son; J.D., University of Miami, 1952; served on active duty as an Air Force Judge Advocate, 1953–56; admitted to Washington, DC bar, Florida bar and North Dakota bar; from 1959 to 1983, owned and operated a regional grain processing firm in North Dakota; served as State Senator from North Dakota for eight years; taught military law for the Army and Air Force ROTC at North Dakota State University; was vice-chairman of the board of Minneapolis Grain Exchange; joined the Reagan administration in 1983 in Washington at the U.S. Department of Agriculture; served as Deputy Under Secretary for International Affairs and Commodity Programs and later as Acting Under Secretary; in 1990 joined the Washington, DC law firm of Anderson, Hibey and Blair; appointed judge of the U.S. Court of International Trade in 1991; assumed senior status in 2001.

OFFICERS OF THE UNITED STATES COURT OF INTERNATIONAL TRADE

Clerk.—Tina Potuto Kimble (212) 264–2814.

UNITED STATES COURT OF FEDERAL CLAIMS

Lafayette Square, 717 Madison Place, NW., 20005, phone (202) 219–9657

EDWARD J. DAMICH, chief judge; born in Pittsburgh, PA, June 19, 1948; son of John and Josephine (Lovrencic) Damich; A.B., St. Stephen's College, 1970; J.D., Catholic University, 1976; professor of law at Delaware School of Law of Widener University, 1976–84; served as a Law and Economics Fellow at Columbia University School of Law, where he earned his L.L.M. in 1983 and his J.S.D. in 1991; professor of law at George Mason University, 1984–98; appointed by President George H.W. Bush to be a Commissioner of the Copyright Royalty Tribunal, 1992–93; Chief Intellectual Property Counsel for the Senate Judiciary Committee, 1995–98; admitted to the Bars of the District of Columbia and Pennsylvania; member of the District of Columbia Bar Association, Pennsylvania Bar Association, American Bar Association, Supreme Court of the United States, the Federal Circuit and *Association litteraire et artistique internationale;* president of the National Federation of Croatian Americans, 1994–95; appointed by President Clinton as judge, U.S. Court of Federal Claims, October 22, 1998; appointed by President George W. Bush as chief judge, U.S. Court of Federal Claims, May 13, 2002; at present Judge Damich is an adjunct professor of law at the Georgetown University Law Center.

LAWRENCE M. BASKIR, judge; born in Brooklyn, NY, January 10, 1938; married to Marna Tucker, two children; A.B., *magna cum laude*, Princeton University; Woodrow Wilson School of Public and International Affairs, 1959; LL.B., Harvard Law School, 1962; Principal Deputy General Counsel, Department of the Army, 1994–98; private practice and Editor-In-Chief, Military Law Reporter, 1981–94; Legislative Director to Senator Bill Bradley, 1979–81; Deputy Assistant Secretary (Legislation), Office of the Secretary, Department of the Treasury, 1977–79; Director, Vietnam Offender Study; Faculty Fellow, University of Notre Dame Law School, 1975–77; Director, Presidential (Ford) Clemancy Board, White House, 1974–75; Chief Counsel, Subcommittees on Constitutional Rights and Separation of Powers, Senate Judiciary Committee, Senator Sam J. Ervin, Chairman, 1967–74; publications include *Chance and Circumstances: The Draft, the War and the Vietnam Generation*; consultant to Information Intelligence Committees, U.S. Congress; Adjunct Professor and Lecturer, Georgetown, Notre Dame, Catholic Law Schools, and American University; appointed judge of the U.S. Court of Federal Claims on October 22, 1998; chief judge, July 11, 2000 to May 10, 2002.

CHRISTINE ODELL COOK ''O.C.'' MILLER, judge; born in Oakland, CA, August 26, 1944; married to Dennis F. Miller; B.A., Stanford University, 1966; J.D., University of Utah College of Law, 1969; Comment Editor, Utah Law Review; member, Utah Chapter Order of the Coif; Clerk to Chief Judge David T. Lewis, U.S. Court of Appeals for the 10th Circuit; trial attorney, Civil Division, U.S. Department of Justice; trial attorney, Federal Trade Commission, Bureau of Consumer Protection; Hogan and Hartson, litigation section; Pension Benefit Guaranty Corporation, Special Counsel; U.S. Railway Association, Assistant General Counsel; Shack and Kimball P.C., litigation; member of the Bars of the State of California and District of Columbia; member of the University Club and the Cosmos Club; appointed to the U.S. Court of Federal Claims by President Reagan on December 10, 1982, and confirmed as Christine Cook Nettsheim; reappointed by President Clinton on February 4, 1998.

MARIAN BLANK HORN, judge; born in New York, NY, 1943; daughter of Werner P. and Mady R. Blank; married to Robert Jack Horn; three daughters; attended Fieldston School, New York, NY, Barnard College, Columbia University and Fordham University School of Law; admitted to practice U.S. Supreme Court, 1973, Federal and State courts in New York, 1970, and Washington, DC, 1973; assistant district attorney, Deputy Chief Appeals Bureau, Bronx County, NY, 1969–72; attorney, Arent, Fox, Kintner, Plotkin and Kahn, 1972–73; adjunct professor of law, Washington College of Law, American University, 1973–76; litigation attorney, Federal Energy Administration, 1975–76; senior attorney, Office of General

Counsel, Strategic Petroleum Reserve Branch, Department of Energy, 1976–79; deputy assistant general counsel for procurement and financial incentives, Department of Energy, 1979–81; deputy associate solicitor, Division of Surface Mining, Department of the Interior, 1981–83; associate solicitor, Division of General Law, Department of the Interior, 1983–85; principal deputy solicitor and acting solicitor, Department of Interior, 1985–86; adjunct professor of law, George Washington University National Law Center, 1991–present; Woodrow Wilson Visiting Fellow, 1994; assumed duties of judge, U.S. Court of Federal Claims in 1986 and confirmed for a second term in 2003.

LYNN J. BUSH, judge; born in Little Rock, AR, December 30, 1948; daughter of John E. Bush III and Alice (Saville) Bush; one son, Brian Bush Ferguson; B.A., Antioch College, 1970, Thomas J. Watson Fellow; J.D., Georgetown University Law Center, 1976; admitted to the Arkansas Bar in 1976 and to the District of Columbia Bar in 1977; trial attorney, Commercial Litigation Branch, Civil Division, U.S. Department of Justice, 1976–87; senior trial attorney, Naval Facilities Engineering Command, Department of the Navy, 1987–89; counsel, Engineering Field Activity Chesapeake, Naval Facilities Engineering Command, Department of the Navy, 1989–96; administrative judge, U.S. Department of Housing and Urban Development Board of Contract Appeals, 1996–98; nominated by President Clinton to the U.S. Court of Federal Claims, June 22, 1998; and assumed duties of the office on October 26, 1998.

NANCY B. FIRESTONE, judge; born in Manchester, NH, October 17, 1951; B.A., Washington University, 1973; J.D., University of Missouri, Kansas City, 1977; one child: Amanda Leigh; attorney, Appellate Section and Environmental Enforcement Section, U.S. Department of Justice, Washington, D.C., 1977–84; Assistant Chief, Policy Legislation and Special Litigation, Environment and Natural Resources Division, Department of Justice, Washington, D.C., 1984–85; Deputy Chief, Environmental Enforcement Section, Department of Justice, Washington, D.C., 1985–89; Associate Deputy Administrator, Environmental Protection Agency, Washington, D.C., 1989–92; Judge, Environmental Appeals Board, Environmental Protection Agency, Washington, D.C., 1992–95; Deputy Assistant Attorney General, Environment and Natural Resources Division, Department of Justice, Washington, D.C., 1995–98; Adjunct Professor, Georgetown University Law Center, 1985–present; appointed to the U.S. Court of Federal Claims by President Clinton on October 22, 1998.

EMILY CLARK HEWITT, judge; born in Baltimore, MD, May 26, 1944; educated at the Roland Park Country School, Baltimore, MD, 1949–62; A.B., Cornell University, 1966; M. Phil., Union Theological Seminary, 1975; J.D. c.l., Harvard Law School, 1978; ordained minister in the Episcopal Church (diaconate, 1972; priesthood, 1974); member, Bar of the Supreme Judicial Court of The Commonwealth of Massachusetts, 1978; administrator, Cornell/Hofstra Upward Bound Program, 1967–69; lecturer, Union Theological Seminary, 1972–73 and 1974–75; assistant professor, Andover Newton Theological School, 1973–75; private practice of law, Hill & Barlow, 1978–93; council member, Real Property Section, Massachusetts Bar Association, 1983–86; member, Executive Committee and chair, Practice Standards Committee, Massachusetts Conveyancers Association, 1990–92; General Counsel, U.S. General Services Administration, 1993–98; member, Administrative Conference of the United States, 1993–95; member, President's Interagency Council on Women, 1995–98; appointed to the U.S. Court of Federal Claims on October 22, 1998; entered duty on November 10, 1998.

FRANCIS M. ALLEGRA, judge; born in Cleveland, OH, October 14, 1957; married to Regina Allegra; one child (Domenic); B.A., Borromeo College of Ohio, 1978; J.D., Cleveland State University, 1981; judicial clerk to Chief Trial Judge Philip R. Miller, U.S. Court of Claims, 1981–82; associate, Squire, Sanders & Dempsey (Cleveland), 1982–84; line attorney, Appellate Section, then 1984–89, Counselor to the Assistant Attorney General, both with Tax Division, U.S. Department of Justice; Counselor to the Associate Attorney General (1994) then Deputy Associate Attorney General (1994–98), U.S. Department of Justice; appointed to the U.S. Court of Federal Claims on October 22, 1998.

LAWRENCE J. BLOCK, judge, born in New York City, March 15, 1951; son of Jerome Block and Eve Silver; B.A., *magna cum laude,* New York University, 1973; J.D., The John Marshall Law School, 1981; law clerk for Hon. Roger J. Miner, United States District Court Judge for Northern District of New York, 1981–83; Associate, New York office of Skadden, Arps, Slate, Meagher and Flom, 1983–86; Attorney, Commercial Litigation Branch, U.S. Department of Justice, 1986; Senior Attorney-Advisor, Office of Legal Policy and Policy Development, U.S. Department of Justice, 1987–90; adjunct professor, George Mason University School of Law, 1990–91; acting general counsel for legal policy and deputy assistant general counsel for legal policy, U.S. Department of Energy, 1990–94; senior counsel, Senate

Judiciary Committee, 1994–02; admitted to the bar of Connecticut; admitted to practice in the U.S. Supreme Court, 1982, the United States District Court for the northern district of New York, 1982, the U.S. Court of Appeals for the Eleventh Circuit, 1985, the United States District Court for the Eastern District of New York, 1985; appointed by President George W. Bush on October 3, 2002, to a 15-years term as judge, U.S. Court of Federal Claims.

SUSAN G. BRADEN, judge, born in Youngstown, OH, November 8, 1948; married to Thomas M. Susman; daughter (Daily); B.A., Case Western Reserve University, 1970; J.D., Case Western Reserve University School of Law, 1973; post graduate study Harvard Law School, Summer, 1979; private practice, 1985–2003 (1997–2003 Baker & McKenzie); Federal Trade Commission: Special Counsel to Chairman, 1984–85, Senior Attorney Advisor to Commissioner and Acting Chairman, 1980–83; U.S. Department of Justice, Antitrust Division, Senior Trial Attorney, Energy Section, 1978–80; Cleveland Field Office, 1973–78; Special Assistant Attorney General for the State of Alabama, 1990; Consultant to the Administrative Conference of the United States, 1984–85; 2000 Co-Chair, Lawyers for Bush-Cheney; General Counsel Presidential Debate for Dole-Kemp Campaign, 1996; Counsel to RNC Platform, 1996; Coordinator for Regulatory Reform and Antitrust Policy, Dole Presidential Campaign, 1995–96; National Steering Committee, Lawyers for Bush-Quayle, 1992; Assistant General Counsel, Republican National Convention, 1988, 1992, 1996, 2000; elected At-Large Member, D.C. Republican National Committee, 2000–02; member of the American Bar Association (Council Member, Section on Administrative Law and Regulatory Practice, 1996–99), Federal Circuit Bar Association, District of Columbia Bar Association, Computer Law Bar Association; admitted to the Supreme Court of Ohio, 1973, U.S. District Court for the District of Columbia, 1980, U.S. Supreme Court, 1980; U.S. Court of Appeals for the District of Columbia, 1992; U.S. Court of Appeals for the Second Circuit, 1993, U.S. Court of Appeals for the Federal Circuit, 2001; appointed to the U.S. Court of Federal Claims by President George W. Bush on July 14, 2003.

CHARLES F. LETTOW, judge, born in Iowa Falls, IA, February 10, 1941; son of Carl F. and Catherine Lettow; B.S.Ch.E., Iowa State University, 1962; LL.B., Stanford University, 1968, Order of the Coif; M.A., Brown University, 2001; Note Editor, Stanford Law Review; married to B. Sue Lettow; children: Renee Burnett, Carl Frederick II, John Stangland, and Paul Vorbeck; served U.S. Army, 1963–65; law clerk to Judge Ben C. Duniway, U.S. Court of Appeals for the Ninth Circuit, 1968–69, and Chief Justice Warren E. Burger, Supreme Court of the United States, 1969–70; counsel, Council on Environmental Quality, Executive Office of the President, 1970–73; associate (1973–76) and partner (1976–2003), Cleary, Gottlieb, Steen & Hamilton, Washington, DC; admitted to practice before the U.S. Supreme Court, the U.S. Courts of Appeals for the D.C., Second, Third, Fourth, Fifth, Sixth, Eighth, Ninth, Tenth, and Federal Circuits, the U.S. District Courts for the District of Columbia, the Northern District of California, and the District of Maryland, and the U.S. Court of Federal Claims; member: American Law Institute, the American Bar Association, the D.C. Bar, the California State Bar, the Iowa State Bar Association, and the Maryland State Bar; nominated by President George W. Bush to the U.S. Court of Federal Claims in 2001 and confirmed and took office in 2003.

MARY ELLEN COSTER WILLIAMS, judge; born in Flushing, NY, April 3, 1953; married to Mark Calhoun Williams; son: Justin; daughter: Jacquelyn; B.A. *summa cum laude* (Greek and Latin); M.A. (Latin), Catholic University, 1974; J.D. Duke University; Editorial Board, *Duke Law Journal,* 1976–77; admitted to the District of Columbia Bar; Associate, Fulbright and Jaworski, 1977–79; Associate, Schnader, Harrison, Segal and Lewis, 1979–83; Assistant U.S. Attorney, Civil Division, District of Columbia, 1983–87; Partner—Janis, Schuelke, and Wechsler, 1987–89; Administrative Judge, General Services Board of Contract Appeals March 1989–July 2003; Secretary, District of Columbia Bar, 1988–89; Fellow, American Bar Foundation, Elected, 1985; Board of Directors, Bar Association of District of Columbia, 1985–88; Chairman, Young Lawyers Section, Bar Association of District of Columbia, 1985–86; Chair, Public Contract Law Section of American Bar Association, 2002–03, Chair-Elect, Vice-Chair, Secretary, Council, 1995–2002; Delegate, Section of Public Contract Law, ABA House of Delegates 2003–04; Lecturer, Government Contract Law, 1989–present; appointed to the U.S. Court of Federal Claims on July 21, 2003.

VICTOR JOHN WOLSKI, judge; born in New Brunswick, NJ, November 14, 1962; son of Vito and Eugenia Wolski; B.A., B.S., University of Pennsylvania, 1984; J.D., University of Virginia School of Law, 1991; married to Lisa Wolski, June 3, 2000; admitted to Supreme Court of the United States, 1995; California Supreme Court, 1992; Washington Supreme Court, 1994; Oregon Supreme Court, 1996; District of Columbia Court of Appeals, 2001;

U.S. Court of Appeals for the Ninth Circuit, 1993; U.S. Court of Appeals for the Federal Circuit, 2001; U.S. District Court for the Eastern District of California, 1993; U.S. District Court for the Northern District of California, 1995; U.S. Court of Federal Claims, 2001; U.S. District Court for the District of Columbia, 2002; research assistant, Center for Strategic and International Studies, 1984–85; research associate, Institute for Political Economy, 1985–88; Confidential Assistant and Speechwriter to the Secretary, U.S. Dept. of Agriculture, 1988; paralegal specialist, Office of the General Counsel, U.S. Dept. of Energy, 1989; law clerk to Judge Vaughn R. Walker, U.S. District Court for the Northern District of California, 1991–92; attorney, Pacific Legal Foundation, 1992–97; General Counsel, Sacramento County Republican Central Committee, 1995–97; Counsel to Senator Connie Mack, Vice-Chairman of the Joint Economic Committee, U.S. Congress, 1997–98; General Counsel and Chief Tax Adviser, Joint Economic Committee, U.S. Congress, 1999–2000; associate, Cooper, Carvin & Rosenthal, 2000–01; associate, Cooper & Kirk, 2001–03; nominated by President George W. Bush to the U.S. Court of Federal Claims on September 12, 2002, renominated January 7, 2003, and confirmed by U.S. Senate on July 9, 2003.

THOMAS C. WHEELER, judge; born in Chicago, IL, March 18, 1948; married; two grown children; B.A., Gettysburg College, 1970; J.D., Georgetown University Law School, 1973; private practice in Washington, DC, 1973–2005; associate and partner, Pettit & Martin until 1995; partner, Piper & Marbury (later Piper Marbury Rudnick & Wolfe, and then DLA Piper Rudnick Gray Cary); member of the District of Columbia Bar; American Bar Association's Public Contracts and Litigation Sections; appointed to the U.S. Court of Federal Claims on October 24, 2005.

MARGARET M. SWEENEY, judge; born in Baltimore, MD; B.A. in history, Notre Dame of Maryland, 1977; J.D., Delaware Law School, 1981; Delaware Family Court Master, 1981–83; litigation associate, Fedorko, Gilbert, & Lanctot, Morrisville, PA, 1983–85; law clerk to Hon. Loren A. Smith, Chief Judge of the U.S. Court of Federal Claims, 1985–87; Trial Attorney in the General Litigation Section of the Environment and Natural Resources Division of the United States Department of Justice, 1987–99; President, U.S. Court of Federal Claims Bar Association, 1999; Attorney Advisor, United States Department of Justice Office of Intelligence Policy and Review, 1999–2003; Special Master, U.S. Court of Federal Claims, 2003–05; member of the bars of the Supreme Court of Pennsylvania and the District of Columbia Court of Appeals; appointed to the U.S. Court of Federal Claims by President George W. Bush on October 24, 2005, and entered duty on December 14, 2005.

SENIOR JUDGES

THOMAS J. LYDON, senior judge; born in Portland, ME, June 3, 1927; educated in the parochial and public schools in Portland; B.A., University of Maine, 1948–52; LL.B. (1952–55) and LL.M. (1956–57), Georgetown University Law Center; trial attorney, Civil Division, Department of Justice, 1955–67; Chief, Court of Claims Section, Civil Division, 1967–72; trial commissioner (trial judge), U.S. Court of Claims, 1972 to September 30, 1982; judge, U.S. Claims Court, October 1, 1982–July 31, 1987; senior judge, August 1, 1987–present.

JAMES F. MEROW, senior judge; born in Salamanca, NY, March 16, 1932; educated in the public schools of Little Valley, NY and Alexandria, VA; A.B. (with distinction), The George Washington University, 1953; J.D. (with distinction), The George Washington University Law School, 1956; member: Phi Beta Kappa, Order of the Coif, Omicron Delta Kappa; married; officer, U.S. Army Judge Advocate General's Corps, 1956–59; trial attorney-branch director, Civil Division, U.S. Department of Justice, 1959–78; trial judge, U.S. Court of Claims, 1978–82; member of Virginia State Bar, District of Columbia Bar, American Bar Association, and Federal Bar Association; judge, U.S. Court of Federal Claims since October 1, 1982 and reappointed by President Reagan to a 15-year term commencing August 5, 1983.

REGINALD W. GIBSON, senior judge; born in Lynchburg, VA, July 31, 1927; son of McCoy and Julia Gibson; son, Reginald S. Gibson, Jr.; educated in the public schools of Washington, DC; served in the U.S. Army, 1946–47; B.S., Virginia Union University, 1952; Wharton Graduate School of Business Administration, University of Pennsylvania, 1952–53; LL.B., Howard University School of Law, 1956; admitted to the District of Columbia Bar in 1957 and to the Illinois Bar in 1972; Internal Revenue agent, Internal Revenue Service, Washington, DC, 1957–61; trial attorney, tax division, criminal section, Department of Justice, Washington, DC, 1961–71; senior and later general tax attorney, International Harvester Co.,

Chicago, IL, 1971–82; judge, U.S. Court of Federal Claims, December 15, 1982–August 15, 1995; senior status, August 15, 1995–present.

JOHN PAUL WIESE, senior judge; born in Brooklyn, NY, April 19, 1934; son of Gustav and Margaret Wiese; B.A., *cum laude*, Hobart College, 1962, Phi Beta Kappa; LL.B., University of Virginia School of Law, 1965; married to Alice Mary Donoghue, June, 1961; one son, John Patrick; served U.S. Army, 1957–59; law clerk: U.S. Court of Claims, trial division, 1965–66, and Judge Linton M. Collins, U.S. Court of Claims, appellate division, 1966–67; private practice in District of Columbia, 1967–74 (specializing in government contract litigation); trial judge, U.S. Court of Claims, 1974–82; admitted to bar of the District of Columbia, 1966; admitted to practice in the U.S. Supreme Court, the U.S. Court of Appeals for the Federal Circuit, the U.S. Court of Federal Claims; member: District of Columbia Bar Association and American Bar Association; designated in Federal Courts Improvement Act of 1982 as judge, U.S. Court of Federal Claims and reappointed by President Reagan to 15-year term on October 14, 1986.

ROBERT J. YOCK, senior judge; born in St. James, MN, January 11, 1938; son of Dr. William J. and Erma Yock; B.A. St. Olaf College, 1959; J.D., University of Michigan Law School, 1962; married to Carla M. Moen, June 13, 1964; children: Signe Kara and Torunn Ingrid; admitted to the Minnesota Supreme Court in 1962; Court of Military Appeals, 1964; U.S. Supreme Court, 1965; U.S. District Court for the District of Minnesota, 1966; U.S. District Court for the District of Columbia, 1972; U.S. Court of Claims, 1979; and U.S. Court of Federal Claims, 1982; member: Minnesota State Bar Association, and District of Columbia Bar Association; served in the U.S. Navy, Judge Advocate General's Corps, 1962–66; private practice, St. Paul, MN, 1966–69; entered Government service as chief counsel to the National Archives and Record Services of the General Services Administration, 1969–70; executive assistant and legal advisor to the Administrator of General Services, 1970–72; assistant general counsel at GSA, 1972–77; trial judge, U.S. Court of Claims, 1977-82; designated by Public Law 97–164 as judge, U.S. Court of Federal Claims, 1982–83; renominated by President Reagan as judge, U.S. Court of Federal Claims, June 20, 1983, confirmed by U.S. Senate, August 4, 1983, reappointed to 15-year term, August 5, 1983.

LAWRENCE S. MARGOLIS, senior judge; born in Philadelphia, PA, March 13, 1935; son of Reuben and Mollie Margolis; B.A., Central High School, Philadelphia, PA; B.S. in mechanical engineering from the Drexel Institute of Technology (now Drexel University), 1957; J.D., George Washington University Law School, 1961; married to Doris May Rosenberg, January 30, 1960; children: Mary Aleta and Paul Oliver; admitted to the District of Columbia Bar; patent examiner, U.S. Patent Office, 1957–62; patent counsel, Naval Ordnance Laboratory, White Oak, MD, 1962–63; assistant corporation counsel for the District of Columbia, 1963–66; attorney, criminal division, U.S. Department of Justice and special assistant U.S. attorney for District of Columbia, 1966–68; assistant U.S. attorney for the District of Columbia, 1968–71; appointed U.S. magistrate for District of Columbia in 1971; reappointed for a second 8-year term in 1979 and served until December, 1982 when appointed a judge, U.S. Court of Federal Claims; chairman, U.S. Court of Federal Claims: Security Committee, Building Committee, and Alternative Dispute Resolution Committee; chairman, American Bar Association, judicial administration division, 1980–81; chairman, National Conference of Special Court Judges, 1977–78; board of directors, Bar Association of the District of Columbia, 1970–72; editor: DC Bar Journal, 1966–73, Young Lawyers Newspaper editor, 1965–66; executive council, Young Lawyers Section, 1968–69; board of editors, The Judges' Journal and The District Lawyer; president, George Washington University National Law Association, 1983–84; president, George Washington Law Association, District of Columbia Chapter, 1975–76; board of governors, George Washington University General Alumni Association, 1978–85; fellow, Institute of Judicial Administration, 1993–present; member, District of Columbia Judicial Conference; former member, board of directors, National Council of U.S. Magistrates; former president, Federal Bar Toastmasters; former technical editor, Federal Bar Journal; faculty, Federal Judicial Center; trustee, Drexel University, 1983–91; member, Rotary Club; Board of Managers, Central High (Philadelphia, PA); president, Washington, D.C. Rotary Club, 1988–89, District governor, 1991–92; American Bar Association Judicial Administration Division Award for distinguished service as chairman for 1980–81; Drexel University and George Washington University Distinguished Alumni Achievement Awards; Drexel University 100 (one of top 100 graduates); Center for Public Resources Alternative Dispute Resolution Achievement Award, 1987; George Washington University Community Service Award; nominated by President Ronald Reagan as a judge on the U.S. Court of Federal Claims on September 27, 1982, confirmed by the Senate and received Commission on December 10, 1982, took oath of office on December 15, 1982.

LOREN ALLAN SMITH, senior judge; born in Chicago, IL, December 22, 1944; son of Alvin D. and Selma (Halpern) Smith; B.A., Northwestern University, 1966; J.D., Northwestern University School of Law, 1969; married; admitted to the Bars of the Illinois Supreme Court; the Court of Military Appeals; the U.S. Court of Appeals, District of Columbia Circuit; the U.S. Court of Appeals for the Federal Circuit; the U.S. Supreme Court; the U.S. Court of Federal Claims; honorary member: The University Club; consultant, Sidley and Austin Chicago, 1972–73; general attorney, Federal Communications Commission, 1973; assistant to the Special Counsel to the President, 1973–74; Special Assistant U.S. Attorney, District of Columbia, 1974–75; chief counsel, Reagan for President campaigns, 1976 and 1980; professor, Delaware Law School, 1976–84; distinguished lecturer at Columbus School of Law, The Catholic University of America and distinguished adjunct professor at George Mason University School of Law; deputy director, Executive Branch Management Office of Presidential Transition, 1980–81; Chairman, Administrative Conference of the Unites States, 1981–85; served as a member of the President's Cabinet Councils on Legal Policy and on Management and Administration; appointed to the U.S. Court of Federal Claims on July 11, 1985; entered on duty September 12, 1985; served as chief judge from January 14, 1986, until July 11, 2000.

ERIC G. BRUGGINK, senior judge; born in Kalidjati, Indonesia, September 11, 1949; naturalized U.S. citizen, 1961; married to Melinda Harris Bruggink; sons: John and David; B.A., *cum laude* (sociology), Auburn University, AL, 1971; M.A. (speech), 1972; J.D., University of Alabama, 1975; Hugo Black Scholar and Note and Comments Editor of Alabama Law Review; member, Alabama State Bar and District of Columbia Bar; served as law clerk to chief judge Frank H. McFadden, Northern District of Alabama, 1975–76; associate, Hardwick, Hause and Segrest, Dothan, AL, 1976–77; assistant director, Alabama Law Institute, 1977–79; director, Office of Energy and Environmental Law, 1977–79; associate, Steiner, Crum and Baker, Montgomery, AL, 1979–82; Director, Office of Appeals Counsel, Merit Systems Protection Board, 1982–86; appointed to the U.S. Court of Federal Claims on April 15, 1986.

BOHDAN A. FUTEY, senior judge; born in Ukraine, June 28, 1939; B.A., Western Reserve University, 1962; M.A., 1964; J.D., Cleveland Marshall Law School, 1968; married to the former Myra Fur; three children: Andrew, Lidia, and Daria; partner, Futey and Rakowsky, 1968–72; chief assistant police prosecutor, city of Cleveland, 1972–74; executive assistant to the mayor of Cleveland, 1974–75; partner, Bazarko, Futey and Oryshkewych, 1975–84; chairman, U.S. Foreign Claims Settlement Commission, May 1984–87; member: District of Columbia Bar Association, the Ukrainian American Bar Association; actively involved with Democratization and Rule of Law programs organized by the Judicial Conference of the United States, the Department of State, and the American Bar Association in Ukraine and Russia; has participated in judicial exchange programs, seminars, and workshops and has been a consultant to the working group on Ukraine's Constitution and Ukrainian Parliament; advisor to the International Foundation for Election Systems (IFES) and the International Republican Institutes (IRI) democracy programs for Ukraine; served as an official observer during the parliamentary and presidential elections in 1994 and 1998 and conducted briefings on Ukraine's election law for international observers; has lectured on Constitutional Law at the Ukrainian Free University in Munich and Passau University, Germany; also at Kyiv State University and Lviv University in Ukraine; nominated judge of the U.S. Court of Federal Claims on January 30, 1987, and entered on duty, May 29, 1987.

ROBERT HAYNE HODGES, Jr., senior judge; born in Columbia, SC, September 11, 1944, son of Robert Hayne and Mary (Lawton) Hodges; educated in the public schools of Columbia, SC; attended Wofford College, Spartanburg, SC; B.S., University of South Carolina, 1966; J.D., University of South Carolina Law School, 1969; married to Ruth Nicholson (Lady) Hodges, August 23, 1963; three children; appointed to the U.S. Court of Federal Claims on March 12, 1990.

UNITED STATES TAX COURT

400 Second Street, NW., 20217, phone (202) 521–0700

JOHN O. COLVIN, chief judge; born in Ohio, 1946; A.B., University of Missouri, 1968; J.D., 1971; LL.M., Taxation, Georgetown University Law Center, 1978; during college and law school, employed by Niedner, Niedner, Nack and Bodeux, St. Charles, MO; Missouri Attorney General John C. Danforth and Missouri State Representative Richard C. Marshall, Jefferson City, MO; and U.S. Senator Mark O. Hatfield and Congressman Thomas B. Curtis, Washington, DC; admitted to practice law in Missouri (1971) and District of Columbia (1974); Office of the Chief Counsel, U.S. Coast Guard, Washington, DC, 1971–75; served as Tax Counsel, Senator Bob Packwood, 1975–84; Chief Counsel (1985–87), and Chief Minority Counsel (1987–88), U.S. Senate Finance Committee; Officer, Tax Section, Federal Bar Association 1978–present; Adjunct Professor of Law, Georgetown University Law Center, 1987–present; numerous civic and community activities; appointed by President Reagan as Judge, United States Tax Court, on September 1, 1988, for a term ending August 31, 2003; reappointed on August 12, 2004, for a term ending August 11, 2019; elected as Chief Judge for a two-year term effective June 1, 2006.

MARY ANN COHEN, judge; born in New Mexico, 1943; attended public schools in Los Angeles, CA; B.S., University of California, at Los Angeles, 1964; J.D., University of Southern California School of Law, 1967; prracticed law in Los Angeles, member in law firm of Abbott & Cohen; American Bar Association, Section of Taxation, and Continuing Legal Education activities; received Dana Latham Memorial Award from Los Angeles County Bar Association Taxation Section, May 30, 1997; Jules Ritholz Memorial Merit Award from ABA Tax Section Committee on Civil and Criminal Tax Penalties, 1999; appointed by President Reagan as Judge, United States Tax Court, on September 24, 1982, for a term ending September 23, 1997; served as Chief Judge from June 1, 1996 to September 23, 1997; reappointed on November 7, 1997, for a term ending November 6, 2012, and served again as Chief Judge from November 7, 1997 to May 31, 2000.

STEPHEN J. SWIFT, judge; born in Utah, 1943; Menlo Atherton High School, Atherton, CA, 1961; B.S., Brigham Young University, Political Science, 1967; J.D., George Washington University Law School, 1970; Attorney, U.S. Department of Justice, Tax Division, 1970–74; Assistant U.S. Attorney, Tax Division, U.S. Attorney's Office, San Francisco, CA, 1974–77; Vice President and Senior Tax Counsel, Tax Department, Bank of America N.T. and S.A., San Francisco, CA, 1977–83; adjunct professor, Graduate Tax Programs, Golden Gate University and University of Baltimore; member of California Bar, District of Columbia Bar, and American Bar Association, Section of Taxation; appointed by President Reagan as Judge, United States Tax Court, on August 16, 1983, for a term ending August 15, 1998; served as Senior Judge on recall performing judicial duties until reappointed by President Clinton on December 1, 2000, for a term ending November 30, 2015.

THOMAS B. WELLS, judge; born in Ohio, 1945; B.S., Miami University, Oxford, OH, 1967; J.D., Emory University Law School, Atlanta, GA, 1973; LL.M., Taxation, New York University Law School, New York, 1978; Supply Corps Officer, U.S. Naval Reserve, active duty 1967–70, Morocco and Vietnam, received Joint Service Commendation Medal; admitted to practice law in Georgia; member of law firm of Graham and Wells, P.C.; County Attorney for Toombs County, GA; City Attorney, Vidalia, GA, until 1977; member of law firm of Hurt, Richardson, Garner, Todd and Cadenhead, Atlanta, until 1981; law firm of Shearer and Wells, P.C. until 1986; member of American Bar Association, Section of Taxation; State Bar of Georgia, member of Board of Governors; Board of Editors, Georgia State Bar Journal; member, Atlanta Bar Association; Editor of the Atlanta Lawyer; active in various tax organizations, such as Atlanta Tax Forum (presently, Honorary Member); Director, Atlanta Estate Planning Council; Director, North Atlanta Tax Council; American College of Tax Counsel, Honorary Fellow; Emory Law Alumni Association's Distinguished Alumnus Award, 2001; Life Member, National Eagle Scout Association, Eagle Scout, 1960; member: Metropolitan Club, Chevy Chase Club, Vidalia Kiwanis Club (President); recipient, Distinguished President Award; appointed by President Reagan as Judge, United States Tax Court, on October 13, 1986, for a term ending October 12, 2001; reappointed by President Bush on October 10, 2001, for a term ending October 9, 2016; served as Chief Judge from September 24, 1997 to November 6, 1997, and from June 1, 2000 to May 31, 2004.

JAMES S. HALPERN, judge; born in New York, 1945; Hackley School, Terrytown, NY, 1963; B.S., Wharton School, University of Pennsylvania, 1967; J.D., University of Pennsylvania Law School, 1972; LL.M., Taxation, New York University Law School, 1975; Associate Attorney, Mudge, Rose, Guthrie and Alexander, New York City, 1972–74; assistant professor of law, Washington and Lee University, 1975–76; assistant professor of law, St. John's University, New York City, 1976–78; visiting professor, Law School, New York University, 1978–79; associate attorney, Roberts and Holland, New York City, 1979–80; Principal Technical Advisor, Assistant Commissioner (Technical) and Associate Chief Counsel (Technical), Internal Revenue Service, Washington, DC, 1980–83; partner, Baker and Hostetler, Washington, DC, 1983–90; Adjunct Professor, Law School, George Washington University, Washington, DC, 1984–present; Colonel, U.S. Army Reserve (retired); appointed by President George H.W. Bush as Judge, United States Tax Court, on July 3, 1990, for a term ending July 2, 2005; reappointed on November 2, 2005, for a term ending November 1, 2020.

CAROLYN P. CHIECHI, judge; born in New Jersey, 1943; B.S. (*magna cum laude,* Class Rank: 1), Georgetown University, 1965; J.D., 1969 (Class Rank: 9); LL.M., Taxation, 1971; Doctor of Laws, Honoris Causa, 2000; practiced with law firm of Sutherland, Asbill & Brennan, Washington, DC and Atlanta, GA (partner, 1976–92; associate, 1971–76); served as attorney-adviser to Judge Leo H. Irwin, United States Tax Court, 1969–71; member, District of Columbia Bar, 1969–present (member, Taxation Section, 1973–99; member, Taxation Section Steering Committee, 1980–82, Chairperson, 1981–82; member, Tax Audits and Litigation Committee, 1986–92, Chairperson, 1987–88); member, American Bar Association, 1969–present (member, Section of Taxation, 1969–present; member, Committee on Court Procedure, 1991–present; member, Litigation Sectiton, 1995–2000; member, Judicial Division, 1997–2000); Federal Bar Association, 1969–present (member, Section of Taxation, 1969–present; member, Judiciary Division, 1992–present); Fellow, American College of Tax Counsel; Fellow, American Bar Foundation; member, Women's Bar Association of the District of Columbia, 1992–present; Board of Governors, Georgetown University Alumni Association, 1994–97, 1997–2000; Board of Regents, Georgetown University, 1988–94, 1995–2001; National Law Alumni Board, Georgetown University, 1986–93; Board of Directors, Stuart Stiller Memorial Foundation, 1986–99; American Judicature Society, 1994–present; one of several recipients of the first Georgetown University Law Alumni Awards (1994); one of several recipients of the first Georgetown University Law Center Alumnae Achievement Awards (1998); admitted to Who's Who in American Law, Who's Who of American Women, and Who's Who in America; appointed by President George H.W. Bush as Judge, United States Tax Court, on October 1, 1992, for a term ending September 30, 2007.

DAVID LARO, judge; born in Michigan, 1942; B.A., University of Michigan, 1964; J.D., University of Illinois Law School, 1967; LL.M., Taxation, New York University Law School, 1970; admitted to Michigan Bar and United States District Court (Eastern District), 1968; former partner of law firm of Winegarden, Booth, Shedd, and Laro, 1970–75; member of law firm of Laro and Borgeson, 1975–86; member, David Laro, Attorney at Law, P.C., 1986–92; counsel to Dykema Gossett, Ann Arbor, MI, 1989–90; president and chief executive officer of Durakon Industries, Inc., 1989–91; Chairman, Board of Durakon Industries, Inc., 1991–92; Chairman, Board of Republic Bank, 1986–92; Vice Chairman and Co-Founder of Republic Bancorp, Inc., 1986–92; Regent, University of Michigan Board of Regents, 1975–81; member, Michigan State Board of Education, 1982–83; Chairman, Michigan State Tenure Commission, 1972–75; Commissioner, Civil Service Commission, Flint, MI, 1984–85; Commissioner of Police, Flint, 1972–74; member, Political Leadership Program, Institute of Public Policy and Social Research; member, Ann Arbor Art Association Board of Directors; member, Holocaust Foundation (Ann Arbor); adjunct professor of law, Georgetown University Law School; instructor, National Institute for Trial Advocacy; visiting professor, University of San Diego Law School; member, National Advisory Committee for New York University Law School; at the request of the American Bar Association and the Central Eastern European Law Initiative, contributed written comments on the Draft Laws of Ukraine and Uzbekistan and on the creation of specialized courts in Eastern Europe; as a consultant for Harvard University (Harvard Institute for International Development), and Georgia State University, lectured in Moscow to Russian judges on the subject of tax reform and litigation procedures in May 1997 and December 1998; commentator for the American Bar Association's Central and East European Law Initiative on the draft laws of Uzbekistan, Kazakhstan, Slovakia, Ukraine, and Republic of Macedonia; lectured to Judges and tax officials in Azerbaijan on tax reform; appointed by President George H.W. Bush as Judge, United States Tax Court, on November 2, 1992, for a term ending November 1, 2007.

MAURICE B. FOLEY, judge; born in Illinois, 1960; B.A., Swarthmore College; J.D., Boalt Hall School of Law at the University of California at Berkeley; LL.M., Georgetown University Law Center; attorney for the Legislation and Regulations Division of the Internal Revenue Service, Tax Counsel for the United States Senate Committee on Finance; Deputy Tax Legislative Counsel in the U.S. Treasury's Office of Tax Policy; appointed by President Clinton as Judge, United States Tax Court, on April 9, 1995, for a term ending April 8, 2010.

JUAN F. VASQUEZ, judge; born in Texas, 1948; attended Fox Tech High School; A.D. (Data Processing), San Antonio Junior College; B.B.A. (Accounting), University of Texas, Austin, 1972; attended State University of New York, Buffalo in 1st year law school, 1975; J.D., University of Houston Law Center, 1977; LL.M., Taxation, New York University Law School, 1978; admitted to Taxas Bar, 1977; certified in Tax Law by Texas Board of Legal Specialization, 1984; Certified Public Acccountant Certificate from Texas (1976) and California (1974); admitted to the United States District Court, Southern District of Texas (1982), Western District of Texas (1985) and U.S. Court of Appeals for the Fifth Circuit (1982); private practice of tax law, in San Antonio, TX, 1987–April 1995; partner, Leighton, Hood and Vasquez, in San Antonio, TX, 1982–87; Trial Attorney, Office of Chief Counsel, Internal Revenue Service, Houston, TX, 1978–82; accountant, Coopers and Lybrand, Los Angeles, CA, 1972–74; member of American Bar Association, Tax Section; Texas State Bar, Tax and Probate Section; Fellow of Texas and San Antonio Bar Foundations, Mexican American Bar Association (MABA) of San Antonio (Treasurer); Houston MABA; Texas MABA (Treasurer); National Association of Hispanic CPA's San Antonio Chapter (founding member); College of State Bar of Texas, National Hispanic Bar Association; member of Greater Austin Tax Litigation Association; served on Austin Internal Revenue Service District Director's Practitioner Liaison Committee, 1990–91 (chairman, 1991); appointed by President Clinton as Judge, United States Tax Court, on May 1, 1995, for a term ending April 30, 2010.

JOSEPH H. GALE, judge; born in Virginia, 1953; A.B., Philosophy, Princeton University, 1976; J.D., University of Virginia School of Law, Dillard Fellow, 1980; practiced law as an Associate Attorney, Dewey Ballantine, Washington, DC, and New York, 1980–83; Dickstein, Shapiro and Morin, Washington, DC, 1983–85; served as Tax Legislative Counsel for Senator Daniel Patrick Moynihan (D–NY), 1985–88; Administrative Assistant and Tax Legislative Counsel, 1989; Chief Counsel, 1990–93; Chief Tax Counsel, Committee on Finance, U.S. Senate, 1993–95; minority Chief Tax Counsel, Senate Finance Committee, January 1995–July 1995; minority Staff Director and Chief Counsel, Senate Finance Committee, July 1995–January 1996; admitted to District of Columbia Bar; member of American Bar Association, Section of Taxation; appointed by President Clinton as Judge, United States Tax Court, February 6, 1996, for a term ending February 5, 2011.

MICHAEL B. THORNTON, judge; born in Mississippi, 1954; B.S. in Accounting, *summa cum laude*, University of Southern Mississippi, 1976; M.S. in Accounting, 1997; M.A. in English Literature, University of Tennessee, 1979; J.D. (with distinction), Duke University School of Law, 1982; Order of the Coif, Duke Law Journal Editorial Board; admitted to District of Columbia Bar, 1982; served as Law Clerk to the Honorable Charles Clark, Chief Judge, U.S. Court of Appeals for the Fifth Circuit, 1983–84; practiced law as an Associate Attorney, Sutherland, Asbill and Brennan, Washington, DC, 1982–83 and summer 1981; Miller and Chevalier, Chartered, Washington, DC, 1985–88; served as Tax Counsel, U.S. House Committee on Ways and Means, 1988–93; Chief Minority Tax Counsel, U.S. House Committee on Ways and Means, January 1995; Attorney-Adviser, U.S. Treasury Department, February–April 1995; Deputy Tax Legislative Counsel in the Office of Tax Policy, United States Treasury Department, April 1995–February 1998; recipient of Treasury Secretary's Annual Award, U.S. Department of the Treasury, 1997; Meritorious Service Award, U.S. Department of the Treasury, 1998; appointed by President Clinton as Judge, United States Tax Court, on March 8, 1998, for a term ending March 7, 2013.

L. PAIGE MARVEL, judge; born in Maryland, 1949; B.A., *magna cum laude,* College of Notre Dame, 1971; J.D. with honors, University of Maryland School of Law, Baltimore, MD, 1974; Order of the Coif; member, Maryland Law Review and Moot Court Board;

Garbis & Schwait, P.A., associate (1974–76) and shareholder (1976–85); shareholder, Garbis, Marvel & Junghans, P.A., 1985–86; shareholder, Melnicove, Kaufman, Weiner, Smouse & Garbis, P.A., 1986–88; partner, Venabel, Baetjer & Howard L.L.P., 1988–98; member, American Bar Association, Section of Taxation, Vice-Chair, Committee Operations, 1993–95; Council Director 1989–92; Chair, Court Procedure Committee, 1985–87; Maryland State Bar Association, Board of Governors, 1988–90, and 1996–98; Chair, Taxation Section 1982–83; Federal Bar Association, Section of Taxation, Section Council, 1984–90; Fellow, American Bar Foundation; Fellow, Maryland Bar Foundation; Fellow and former Regent, American College of Tax Counsel, 1996–98; member, American Law Institute; Advisor, ALI Restatement of Law Third-The Law Governing Lawyers 1988–98; University of Maryland Law School Board of Visitors, 1995–2001; Loyola/Notre Dame Library, Inc. Board of Trustees, 1996–present; Advisory Committee, University of Baltimore Graduate Tax Program, 1986–present; Co-editor, Procedure Department, The Journal of Taxation, 1990–98; member, Commissioner's Review Panel on IRS Integrity, 1989–91; member and Chair, Procedure Subcommittee, Commission to Revise the Annotated Code of Maryland (Tax Provisions), 1981–87; member, Advisory Commission to the Maryland State Department of Economic and Community Development, 1978–81; recipient of First Annual Tax Excellence Award, Maryland State Bar Association; Tax Section, 2002; named one of Maryland's Top 100 Women for 1998; recipient, ABA Tax Section's Distinguished Service Award, 1995; recipient, MSBA Distinguished Service Award, 1982–83; listed in Best Lawyers in America, 1991–98; author of various articles and book chapters on tax and tax litigation topics; appointed by President Clinton as Judge, United States Tax Court, on April 6, 1998, for a term ending April 5, 2013.

HARRY A. HAINES, judge; born in Montana, 1939; B.A., St. Olaf College, 1961; J.D., University of Montana Law School, 1964; LL.M., Taxation, New York University Law School, 1966; admitted to Montana Bar and U.S. District Court, Montana, 1964; practiced law in Missoula, MT, as a partner, Law Firm of Worden, Thane & Haines, 1966–2003; Adjunct Professor, Law School, University of Montana, 1967–91; appointed by President George W. Bush as Judge, United States Tax Court, on April 22, 2003 for a term ending April 21, 2018.

JOSEPH ROBERT GOEKE, judge; born in Kentucky, 1950; B.S., *cum laude*, Xavier University, 1972; J.D., University of Kentucky College of Law, 1975 (Order of the Coif); admitted to Illinois and Kentucky Bar, U.S. District Court for the Northern District of Illinois (Trial Bar), U.S. Court of Federal Claims; Trial Attorney, Chief Counsel's Office, Internal Revenue Service, New Orleans, LA, 1975–80; Senior Trial Attorney, Chief Counsel's Office, Internal Revenue Service, Cincinnati, OH, 1980–85; Special International Trial Attorney, Chief Counsel's Office, Internal Revenue Service, Cincinnati, OH, 1985–88; partner, Law Firm of Mayer, Brown, Rowe and Maw, Chicago, IL, 1988–2003; appointed by President George W. Bush as Judge, United States Tax Court, on April 22, 2003, for a term ending April 21, 2018.

ROBERT A. WHERRY, Jr., judge; born in Virginia, 1944; B.S., and J.D., University of Colorado; LL.M., Taxation, New York University Law School; fellow and former Regent of the American College of Tax Counsel and former chairman of the Taxation Section of the Colorado Bar Association; served as chairman of the Small-Business Tax Committee of the Colorado Association of Commerce and Industry, as president of the Greater Denver Tax Counsel Association, is a past chairman of the Administrative Practice Committee of the American Bar Association Tax Section, a member of the Council, and a member of the Advisory Committee of the American Bar Association Section of Dispute Resolution; listed in The Best Lawyers in America (in tax litigation); his articles have appeared in ALI-ABA publications, The Colorado Lawyer, Tax Notes, and State Tax Notes; former Colorado correspondent for State Tax Notes and has spoken at numerous tax institutes, including the University of Denver Tax Institute, Tulane University Tax Institute, and American Bar Association Tax Section programs; was an instructor in Tax Court litigation for the National Institute for Trial Advocacy; appointed by President George W. Bush as Judge, United States Tax Court, on April 23, 2003, for a term ending April 22, 2018.

DIANE L. KROUPA, judge; born in South Dakota, 1955; B.S.F.S., Georgetown University School of Foreign Service, 1978; J.D., University of South Dakota Law School, 1981; practiced tax law at Faegre & Benson, LLP in Minneapolis, MN; Minnesota Tax Court Judge, 1995–2001 (Chief Judge, 1998–2001); attorney-advisor, Legislation and Regulations Division, Office of Chief Counsel and served as attorney-advisor to Judge Joel Gerber, United States Tax Court, 1984–85; admitted to practice law in South Dakota (1981), District of Columbia

(1985) and Minnesota (1986); member: American Bar Association (Tax Section), Minnesota State Bar Association (Tax Section), National Association of Women Judges (1995–present), American Judicature Society (1995–present); Distinguished Service Award Recipient (2001), Minnesota State Bar Association (Tax Section); Volunteer of the Year Award, Junior League of Minneapolis (1993); Community Volunteer of the Year, Minnesota State Bar Association (1998); appointed by President George W. Bush as Judge, United States Tax Court, on June 13, 2003, for a term ending June 12, 2018.

MARK V. HOLMES, judge; born in New York, 1960; B.A., Harvard College, 1979; J.D., University of Chicago Law School, 1983; admitted to New York and District of Columbia Bars; U.S. Supreme Court; DC, Second, Fifth and Ninth Circuits; Southern and Eastern Districts of New York, Court of Federal Claims; practiced in New York as an Associate, Cahill Gordon & Reindel, 1983–85; Sullivan & Cromwell, 1987–91; served as Clerk to the Hon. Alex Kozinski, Ninth Circuit, 1985–87; and in Washington as Counsel to Commissioners, United States International Trade Commission, 1991–96; Counsel, Miller & Chevalier, 1996–2001; Deputy Assistant Attorney General, Tax Division, 2001–03; member, American Bar Association (Litigation and Tax Sections); appointed by President George W. Bush as Judge, United States Tax Court, on June 30, 2003, for a term ending June 29, 2018.

SENIOR JUDGES

HOWARD A. DAWSON, Jr., senior judge; born in Arkansas, 1922; Woodrow Wilson High School, Washington, DC, 1940; B.S. in Commerce, University of North Carolina, 1946; J.D. with honors, George Washington University School of Law, 1949; President, Case Club; Secretary-Treasurer, Student Bar Association; private practice of law, Washington, DC, 1949–50; served with the United States Treasury Department, Internal Revenue Service, as follows: Attorney, Civil Division, Office of Chief Counsel, 1950–53; Civil Advisory Counsel, Atlanta Region, 1953–57; Regional Counsel, Atlanta Region, 1958; Personal Assistant to Chief Counsel, 1958–59, Assistant Chief Counsel (Administration), 1959–62; U.S. Army Finance Corps, 1943–45; two years in European Theater; Captain, Finance Corps, U.S. Army Reserve (Retired); member of District of Columbia Bar (1949), Georgia Bar (1958), American Bar Association (Section of Taxation), Federal Bar Association, Chi Psi, Delta Theta Phi, George Washington University Law Alumni Association; appointed by President Kennedy as Judge, Tax Court of the United States, on August 21, 1962, for a term ending June 1, 1970; reappointed on June 2, 1970, for a term ending June 1, 1985; served as Chief Judge of the Tax Court from July 1, 1973, to June 30, 1977, and again from July 1, 1983, to June 1, 1985; retired on June 2, 1985; David Brennan Distinguished Professor of Law, University of Akron Law School, Spring Term, 1986; Professor and Director, Graduate Tax Program, University of Baltimore Law School, 1986–89; Distinguished Visiting Professor of Law, University of San Diego, Winter 1991; recalled as Senior Judge to perform judicial duties 1990–present.

ARTHUR L. NIMS III, senior judge; born in Oklahoma, 1923; attended public schools, Macon, GA, and Deerfield Academy, Deerfield, MA; B.A., Williams College; LL.B., University of Georgia Law School; LL.M., Taxation, New York University Law School; served as an officer, lieutenant (jg.), U.S. Naval Reserve, on active duty in the Pacific Theater during World War II; admitted to Georgia Bar, 1949; practiced law in Macon, GA, 1949–51; Special Attorney, Office of the District Counsel, Internal Revenue Service, New York, 1951–54; attorney, Legislation and Regulations Division, Chief Counsel's Office, Washington, DC, 1954–55; admitted to New Jersey Bar, 1955; partner in the law firm of McCarter and English, Newark, NJ, 1961–79; Secretary, Section of Taxation, American Bar Association, 1977–79; Chairman, Section of Taxation, New Jersey State Bar Association, 1969–71; member, American Law Institute; American College of Tax Counsel; received Kellogg Award for Lifetime Achievement from Williams College; received Tax Society of New York University Award for lifetime achievement; appointed by President Carter as Judge, United States Tax Court, on June 29, 1979, for a term ending June 28, 1994; served as Chief Judge of the Tax Court from June 1, 1988 to May 31, 1992; recalled on June 1, 1992, as Senior Judge to perform judicial duties from that date to the present.

JULIAN I. JACOBS, senior judge; born in Maryland, 1937; B.A., University of Maryland, 1958; LL.B., University of Maryland Law School, 1960; LL.M., Taxation, Georgetown Law Center, 1965; admitted to Maryland Bar, 1960; attorney, Internal Revenue Service, Washington, DC, 1961–65, and Buffalo, NY, in Regional Counsel's Office, 1965–67; entered private practice of law in Baltimore, MD, 1967; associate (1972–74) and partner (1974–84) in the Law Firm of Gordon, Feinblatt, Rothman, Hoffberger and Hollander; Chairman, study commission to improve the quality of the Maryland Tax Court, 1978; member, study groups to consider changes in the Maryland tax laws; Commissioner on a commission to reorganize and recodify article of Maryland law dealing with taxation, 1980; Lecturer, Tax Seminars and Professional programs; Chairman, Section of Taxation, Maryland State Bar Association; Adjunct Professor of Law, Graduate Tax Program, University of Baltimore School of Law, 1991–93; Adjunct Professor of Law, Graduate Tax Program, University of San Diego School of Law, 2001; Adjunct Professor of Law, Graduate Tax Program, University of Denver School of Law, 2001–present; appointed by President Reagan as Judge, United States Tax Court, on March 30, 1984, for a term ending March 29, 1999; recalled on March 30, 1999, as Senior Judge to perform judicial duties from that date to the present.

HERBERT L. CHABOT, senior judge; born in New York, 1931; Stuyvesant High School, 1948; B.A., *cum laude*, C.C.N.Y., 1952; LL.B., Columbia University, 1957; LL.M. in Taxation, Georgetown University, 1964; served in United States Army, 2 years, and Army Reserves (civil affairs units), for 8 years; served on Legal Staff, American Jewish Congress, 1957–61; attorney-adviser to Judge Russell E. Train, 1961–65; Congressional Joint Committee on Taxation, 1965–78; elected Delegate, Maryland Constitutional Convention, 1967–68; adjunct professor, National Law Center, George Washington University, 1974–83; member of American Bar Association, Tax Section, and Federal Bar Association; appointed by President Carter as Judge, United States Tax Court, on April 3, 1978, for a term ending April 2, 1993; served as Senior Judge on recall performing judicial duties until reappointed on October 20, 1993, for a term ending October 19, 2008; retired on June 30, 2001, but recalled on July 1, 2001, as Senior Judge to perform judicial duties to the present time.

ROBERT PAUL RUWE, senior judge; born in Ohio, 1941; Roger Bacon High School, St. Bernard, OH, 1959; Xavier University, Cincinnati, OH, 1963; J.D., Salmon P. Chase College of Law (graduated first in class), 1970; admitted to Ohio Bar, 1970; Special Agent, Intelligence Division, Internal Revenue Service, 1963–70; joined Office of Chief Counsel, Internal Revenue Service in 1970, and held the following positions: Trial Attorney (Indianapolis), Director, Criminal Tax Division, Deputy Associate Chief Counsel (Litigation), and Director, Tax Litigation Division; appointed by President Reagan as Judge, United States Tax Court, on November 20, 1987, for a term ending November 19, 2002; recalled on November 20, 2002, as Senior Judge to perform judicial duties from that date to the present.

LAURENCE J. WHALEN, senior judge; born in Pennsylvania, 1944; A.B., Georgetown University, 1967; J.D., Georgetown University Law Center, 1970; LL.M., 1971; admitted to District of Columbia and Oklahoma Bars; Special Assistant to the Assistant Attorney General, Tax Division, Department of Justice, 1971–72; trial attorney, Tax Division, 1971–75; private law practice in Washington, DC, with Hamel and Park (now Hopkins, Sutter, Hamel and Park), 1977–84; also in Oklahoma City, OK, with Crowe and Dunlevy, 1984–87; member of Oklahoma Bar Association, District of Columbia Bar Association, and American Bar Association, appointed by President Reagan as Judge, United States Tax Court, on November 23, 1987, for a term ending November 22, 2002; recalled on November 23, 2002, as Senior Judge to perform judicial duties from that date to the present.

RENATO BEGHE, senior judge; born in Illinois, 1933; A.B., University of Chicago, 1951; J.D., University of Chicago, 1954; Phi Beta Kappa, Order of the Coif, co-managing editor of Law Review, Phi Gamma Delta; admitted New York Bar, 1955; practiced law with Carter, Ledyard and Milburn, New York City (associate 1954–65; partner 1965–83) and Morgan, Lewis and Bockius, New York City, 1983–89; bar associations: Association of the Bar of City of New York, nonresident member, Taxation Committee (1962–65), Art Law Committee (1979–83), Chairman (1980–83), Special Committee on Lawyer's Role in Tax Practice (1981–83), Committee on Taxation of International Transactions (1990); New York State Bar Association, nonresident member, Tax Section Chairman (1977–78), Co-Chairman, Joint Practice Committee of Lawyers and Accountants (1989–90); American Bar Association, Tax Section; International Bar Association, Business Section Committee N (Taxation), Judge's Forum, Human Rights Institute; International Fiscal Association; member, American Law Institute, Income Tax Advisory Group (1981–89), and American College of Tax Counsel (since 1981); former member, America-Italy Society, Inc; member, Honorable Order of Kentucky Colonels; appointed by President George H.W. Bush as Judge, United States Tax Court, on March 26, 1991, for a term ending March 25, 2006; retired on February 28, 2003, but continues to perform judicial duties as a Senior Judge on recall.

JOEL GERBER, senior judge; born in Illinois, 1940; B.S., business administration, Roosevelt University, 1962; J.D., DePaul University, 1965; LL.M., Taxation, Boston University Law School, 1968; admitted to the Illinois Bar, 1965; Georgia Bar, 1974; Tennessee Bar, 1978; served with U.S. Treasury Department, Internal Revenue Service, as trial attorney, Boston, MA, 1965–72; senior trial attorney, Atlanta, GA, 1972–76; District Counsel, Nashville, TN, 1976–80; Deputy Chief Counsel, Washington, DC, 1980–84; Acting Chief Counsel, May 1983–March 1984; recipient of a Presidential Meritorious Rank Award, 1983; Secretary of the Treasury's Exceptional Service Award, 1984; Lecturer in Law, Vanderbilt University, 1976–80; appointed by President Reagan as Judge, United States Tax Court, on June 18, 1984, for a term ending June 17, 1999; served as Senior Judge on recall performing judicial duties until reappointed on December 15, 2000, for a term ending December 14, 2015; served as Chief Judge from June 1, 2004, to May 31, 2006; assumed senior status on June 1, 2006.

SPECIAL TRIAL JUDGES OF THE COURT

Robert N. Armen, Jr.; Lewis R. Carluzzo; D. Irvin Couvillion; John F. Dean; Stanley J. Goldberg; Peter J. Panuthos (chief special trial judge); Carleton D. Powell.

OFFICERS OF THE COURT

Clerk.—Robert R. Di Trolio, 521–4600.
Budget and Accounting Officer.—Kristi Greenslade.
Librarian.—Elsa Silverman.
Reporter.—John T. Fee.

UNITED STATES COURT OF APPEALS FOR THE ARMED FORCES[1]

450 E Street, NW., 20442–0001, phone 761–1448, fax 761–4672

ANDREW S. EFFRON, chief judge; born in Stamford, CT, September 18, 1948; A.B., Harvard College, 1970; J.D., Harvard Law School, 1975; The Judge Advocate General's School, U.S. Army, 1976, 1983; legislative aide to the late Representative William A. Steiger, 1970–76 (two years full-time, the balance between school semesters); judge advocate, Office of the Staff Judge Advocate, Fort McClellan, Alabama, 1976–77; attorney-adviser, Office of the General Counsel, Department of Defense, 1977–87; Counsel, General Counsel, and Minority Counsel, Committee on Armed Services, U.S. Senate, 1987–96; nominated by President Clinton to serve on the U.S. Court of Appeals for the Armed Forces, June 21, 1996; confirmed by the Senate, July 12, 1996; took office on August 1, 1996.

JAMES E. BAKER, associate judge; born in New Haven, CT, March 25, 1960; education: BA., Yale University, 1982; J.D., Yale Law School, 1990; Attorney, Department of State, 1990–93; Counsel, President's Foreign Intelligence Advisory Board / Intelligence Oversight Board, 1993–94; Deputy Legal Advisor, National Security Counsel, 1994–97; Special Assistant to the President and Legal Advisor, National Security Counsel, 1997–2000; military service: U.S. Marine Corps and U.S. Marine Corp Reserve; nominated by President Clinton to serve on the U.S. Court of Appeals for the Armed Forces; began service on September 19, 2000.

CHARLES E. ERDMANN, associate judge; born in Great Falls, MT, June 26, 1946; B.A., Montana State University, 1972; J.D., University of Montana Law School, 1975; Air Force Judge Advocate Staff Officers Course, 1981; Air Command and Staff College, 1992; Air War College, 1994; Military Service: U.S. Marine Corps, 1967–70; Air National Guard, 1981–2002 (retired as a Colonel); Assistant Montana Attorney General, 1975–76; Chief Counsel, Montana State Auditor's Office, 1976–78; Chief Staff Attorney, Montana Attorney General's Office, Antitrust Bureau; Bureau Chief, Montana Medicaid Fraud Bureau, 1980–82; General Counsel, Montana School Boards Association, 1982–86; Private Practice of Law, 1986–95; Associate Justice, Montana Supreme Court, 1995–97; Office of High Representative of Bosnia and Herzegovina, Judicial Reform Coordinator, 1998–99; Office of High Representative of Bosnia and Herzegovina, Head of Human Rights and Rule of Law Department, 1999; Chairman and Chief Judge, Bosnian Election Court, 2000–01; Judicial Reform and International Law Consultant, 2001–2002; appointed by President George W. Bush to serve on the U.S. Court of Appeals for the Armed Forces on October 9, 2002, commenced service on October 15, 2002.

SCOTT W. STUCKY, associate judge; born in Hutchinson, KS, January 11, 1948; B.A. (*summa cum laude*), Wichita State University, 1970; J.D., Harvard Law School, 1973; M.A., Trinity University, 1980; LL.M. with highest honors, George Washington University, 1983; Federal Executive Institute, 1988; Harvard Program for Senior Officials in National Security, 1990; National War College, 1993; admitted to bar, Kansas and District of Columbia; U.S. Air Force, judge advocate, 1973–78; U.S. Air Force Reserve, 1982–2003 (retired as colonel); married to Jean Elsie Seibert of Oxon Hill, MD, August 18, 1973; children: Mary-Clare, Joseph; private law practice, Washington, DC, 1978–82; branch chief, U.S. Nuclear Regulatory Commission, 1982–83; legislative counsel and principal legislative counsel, U.S. Air Force, 1983–96; General Counsel, Committee on Armed Services, U.S. Senate, 1996–2001 and 2003–06; Minority Counsel, 2001–03; National Commander-in-Chief, Military Order of the Loyal Legion of the United States, 1993–95; Board of Directors, Adoption Service Information Agency, 1998–2002 and 2004–07; Board of Directors, Omicron Delta Kappa Society, 2006–present; member, Federal Bar Association (Pentagon Chapter), Judge Advocates Association,

[1] Prior to October 5, 1994, United States Court of Military Appeals.

The District of Columbia Bar; OPM LEGIS Fellow, office of Senator John Warner (R–VA), 1986–87; member and panel chairman, Air Force Board for Correction of Military records, 1989–96; nominated by President George W. Bush to serve on the U.S. Court of Appeals for the Armed Forces on November 15, 2006; confirmed by the Senate, December 9, 2006; began service on December 20, 2006.

MARGARET A. RYAN, associate judge; born in Chicago, IL, May 23, 1964; B.A. (*cum laude*), Knox College; J.D. (*summa cum laude*), University of Notre Dame Law School; recipient of the William T. Kirby Legal Writing Award and the Colonel William J. Hoynes Award for Outstanding Scholarship; active duty in the U.S. Marine Corps, 1986–99, serving as a communications officer, staff officer, company commander, platoon commander and operations officer in units within the II and III Marine Expeditionary Forces and as a judge advocate in Okinawa, Japan, and Quantico, VA; also served as Aide de Camp to General Charles C. Krulak, the 31st Commandant of the Marine Corps; law clerk to the Honorable J. Michael Luttig, U.S. Court of Appeals for the Fourth Circuit, and law clerk to the Honorable Clarence Thomas, Associate Justice of the Supreme Court of the United States; litigation partner at the law firm of Bartlik Beck Herman Palenchar & Scott LLP and partner in litigation and appellate practices at the law firm Wiley Rein Fielding LLP; nominated by President George W. Bush to serve on the U.S. Court of Appeals for the Armed Forces on November 15, 2006; confirmed by the Senate on December 9, 2006; began service on December 20, 2006.

SENIOR JUDGES

WILLIAM HORACE DARDEN, senior judge; born in Union Point, GA, May 16, 1923; son of William W. and Sara (Newsom) Darden; B.B.A., University of Georgia, 1946; LL.B., University of Georgia, 1948; admitted to bar of Georgia and to practice before the Georgia Supreme Court, 1948; active duty in U.S. Navy from July 1, 1943 to July 3, 1946, when released to inactive duty as lieutenant (jg.); married to Mary Parrish Viccellio of Chatham, VA, December 31, 1949; children: Sara Newsom, Martha Hardy, William H., Jr., Daniel Hobson; secretary to U.S. Senator Richard B. Russell, 1948–51; chief clerk of U.S. Senate Committee on Armed Services, 1951–53; professional staff member and later chief of staff, U.S. Senate Committee on Armed Services, February 1953 to November 1968; received recess appointment as judge of the U.S. Court of Military Appeals from President Johnson on November 5, 1968, to succeed the late Judge Paul J. Kilday; took oath of office on November 13, 1968; nominated by President Johnson for the unexpired part of the term of the late Judge Paul J. Kilday ending May 1, 1976; confirmed by Senate on January 14, 1969; designated chief judge by President Nixon on June 23, 1971; resigned December 29, 1973; elected to become senior judge on February 11, 1974.

ROBINSON O. EVERETT, senior judge; born in Durham, NC, March 18, 1928; son of Reuben O. and Kathrine (Robinson) Everett; A.B. (*magna cum laude*), Harvard College, 1947; J.D. (*magna cum laude*), Harvard Law School, 1950; LL.M., Duke University, 1959; active duty in U.S. Air Force, 1951–53; thereafter served in U.S. Air Force Reserve and retired as colonel, 1978; married to Linda McGregor of Greensboro, NC, August 27, 1966; children: Robinson O., Jr., McGregor, and Lewis Moore; commissioner, U.S. Court of Military Appeals, 1953–55; private law practice, Durham, NC, 1955–80; assistant professor of law, 1950–51; adjunct professor of law, 1963–66; professor of law, Duke Law School, 1967–present; chairman Durham Urban Redevelopment Commission, 1958–75; counsel, 1961–64; consultant, 1964–66; Subcommittee on Constitutional Rights, Senate Committee on the Judiciary; chairman, Standing Committee on Military Law, American Bar Association, 1977–79; president, Durham County Bar Association, 1976–77; commissioner, National Conference of Commissioners on Uniform State Laws, 1961–73, 1977–present; member, American Law Institute, 1966–present; councillor, North Carolina State Bar, 1978–83; nominated by President Carter as judge of U.S. Court of Military Appeals, February 14, 1980, for the remainder of the term expiring May 1, 1981; unanimously confirmed by the Senate and designated chief judge by President Carter, March 28, 1980; took oath of office, April 16, 1980; term of office extended until April 15, 1990, by Act of December 23, 1980, Public Law 96–579, section 12, 94 Stat. 3369; term of office further extended until Sep. 30, 1990 by Act of November 29, 1989, Public Law 101–189, section 1301, 103 Stat 1575–76; immediately upon his retirement at the end of his term on September 30, 1990, assumed status of senior judge and returned to full active service until January 1, 1992.

WALTER THOMPSON COX III, senior judge; born in Anderson, SC, August 13, 1942; son of Walter T. Cox and Mary Johnson Cox; married to Vicki Grubbs of Anderson, SC,

February 8, 1963; children: Lisa and Walter; B.S., Clemson University, 1964; J.D. (*cum laude*), University of South Carolina School of Law, 1967; graduated Defense Language Institute (German), 1969; graduated basic course, the Judge Advocate General's School, Charlottesville, VA, 1967; studied procurement law at that same school, 1968; active duty, U.S. Army judge advocate general's corps, 1964–72 (1964–67, excess leave to U.S.C. Law School); private law practice, 1973–78; elected resident judge, 10th Judicial Circuit, South Carolina, 1978–84; also served as acting associate justice of South Carolina supreme court, on the judicial council, on the circuit court advisory committee, and as a hearing officer of the judicial standards commission; member: bar of the Supreme Court of the United States; bar of the U.S. Court of Military Appeals; South Carolina Bar Association; Anderson County Bar Association; the American Bar Association; the South Carolina Trial Lawyers Association; the Federal Bar Association; and the Bar Association of the District of Columbia; has served as a member of the House of Delegates of the South Carolina Bar, and the Board of Commissioners on Grievances and Discipline; nominated by President Reagan, as judge of U.S. Court of Military Appeals, June 28, 1984, for a term of 15 years; confirmed by the Senate, July 26, 1984; sworn-in and officially assumed his duties on September 6, 1984; retired on September 30, 1999 and immediately assumed status of senior judge on October 1, 1999 and returned to full active service until September 19, 2000.

EUGENE R. SULLIVAN, senior judge; born in St. Louis, MO, August 2, 1941; son of Raymond V. and Rosemary K. Sullivan; married to Lis U. Johansen of Ribe, Denmark, June 18, 1966; children: Kim A. and Eugene R. II; B.S., U.S. Military Academy, West Point, 1964; J.D., Georgetown Law Center, Washington, DC, 1971; active duty with the U.S. Army, 1964–69; service included duty with the 3rd Armored Division in Germany, and the 4th Infantry Division in Vietnam; R&D assignments with the Army Aviation Systems Command; one year as an instructor at the Army Ranger School, Ft. Benning, GA; decorations include: Bronze Star, Air Medal, Army Commendation Medal, Ranger and Parachutist Badges, Air Force Exceptional Civilian Service Medal; following graduation from law school, clerked with U.S. Court of Appeals (8th Circuit), St. Louis, 1971–72; private law practice, Washington, DC, 1972–74; assistant special counsel, White House, 1974; trial attorney, U.S. Department of Justice, 1974–82; deputy general counsel, Department of the Air Force, 1982–84; general counsel of the Department of Air Force, 1984–86; Governor of Wake Island, 1984–86; presently serves on the Board of Governors for the West Point Society of the District of Columbia; the American Cancer Society (Montgomery County Chapter); nominated by President Reagan, as judge, U.S. Court of Military Appeals on February 25, 1986, and confirmed by the Senate on May 20, 1986, and assumed his office on May 27, 1986; President George H.W. Bush named him the chief judge of the U.S. Court of Military Appeals, effective October 1, 1990, a position he held for five years; he retired on September 30, 2001 and immediately assumed status of senior judge and returned to full active service until Sept. 30, 2002.

H.F. ''SPARKY'' GIERKE, senior judge; born in Williston, ND, March 13, 1943; son of Herman F. Gierke, Jr., and Mary Kelly Gierke; children: Todd, Scott, Craig, and Michelle; B.A., University of North Dakota, 1964; J.D., University of North Dakota, 1966; graduated basic course, the Judge Advocate General's School, Charlottesville, VA, 1967; graduated military judge course, the Judge Advocate General's School, Charlottesville, VA, 1969; active duty, U.S. Army judge advocate general's corps, 1967–71; private practice of law, 1971–83; served as a justice of the North Dakota supreme court from October 1, 1983 until appointment to U.S. Court of Military Appeals; admitted to the North Dakota Bar, 1966; admitted to practice law before all North Dakota Courts, U.S. District Court for the District of North Dakota, U.S. District Court for the Southern District of Georgia, U.S. Court of Military Appeals, and U.S. Supreme Court; served as president of the State Bar Association of North Dakota in 1982–83; served as president of the North Dakota State's Attorneys Association in 1979–80; served on the board of governors of the North Dakota Trial Lawyers Association from 1977–83; served on the board of governors of the North Dakota State Bar Association from 1977–79 and from 1981–84; served as vice chairman and later chairman of the North Dakota Judicial Conference from June 1989 until November 1991; fellow of the American Bar Foundation and the American College of Probate Counsel; member of the American Bar Association, American Judicature Society, Association of Trial Lawyers of America, Blue Key National Honor Fraternity, Kappa Sigma Social Fraternity, University of North Dakota President's Club; in 1984, received the Governor's Award from Governor Allen I. Olson for outstanding service to the State of North Dakota; in 1988 and again in 1991, awarded the North Dakota National Leadership Award of Excellence by Governor George A. Sinner; in 1989, selected as the Man of the Year by the Delta Mu Chapter of the Kappa Sigma Fraternity and as Outstanding Greek Alumnus of the University of North Dakota; also awarded the University of North Dakota Sioux Award (UND's alumni association's highest honor); in 1983–84, served as the first Vietnam era state commander of the North Dakota American Legion; in 1988–89, served as the first Viet-nam era national commander of the American Legion; nominated by President George H.W. Bush, October 1, 1991; confirmed by the Senate, November 14, 1991; sworn-in and assumed office on the U.S. Court of Military Appeals, November 20, 1991; on October 1, 2004, he became the Chief Judge until his retirement on September 30, 2006.

SUSAN J. CRAWFORD, senior judge; born in Pittsburgh, PA, April 22, 1947; daughter of William E. and Joan B. Crawford; married to Roger W. Higgins of Geneva, NY, September 8, 1979; one child, Kelley S. Higgins; B.A., Bucknell University, Pennsylvania, 1969; J.D. (*cum laude*), Dean's Award, Arthur McClean Founder's Award, New England School of Law, Boston, MA, 1977; history teacher and coach of women's athletics, Radnor High School, Pennsylvania, 1969–74; associate, Burnett and Eiswert, Oakland, MD, 1977–79; Assistant State's Attorney, Garrett County, Maryland, 1978–80; partner, Burnett, Eiswert and Crasford, 1979–81; instructor, Garrett County Community College, 1979–81; deputy general counsel, 1981–83, and general counsel, Department of the Army, 1983–89; special counsel to Secretary of Defense, 1989; inspector general, Department of Defense, 1989–91; member: bar of the Supreme Court of the United States; bar of the U.S. Court of Military Appeals, Maryland Bar Association, District of Columbia Bar Association, American Bar Association, Federal Bar Association, and the Edward Bennett Williams American Inn of Court; member: board of trustees, 1989–present, and Corporation, 1992–present, of New England School of Law; board of trustees, 1988–present, Bucknell University; nominated by President Bush as judge, U.S. Court of Military Appeals, February 19, 1991, for a term of 15 years; confirmed by the Senate on November 14, 1991, sworn in and officially assumed her duties on November 19, 1991; on October 1, 1999, she became the Chief Judge for a term of five years.

OFFICERS OF THE U.S. COURT OF APPEALS FOR THE ARMED FORCES

Clerk of the Court.—William A. DeCicco.
Chief Deputy Clerk of the Court.—David A. Anderson.
Deputy Clerk for Opinions.—Patricia Mariani.
Administrative Officer.—Robert J. Bieber.
Librarian.—Agnes Kiang.

UNITED STATES COURT OF APPEALS FOR VETERANS CLAIMS

625 Indiana Avenue, NW., 20004, phone (202) 501–5970

WILLIAM P. GREENE, JR., chief judge; born in Bluefield, WV, July 27, 1943, to William and Dorothy Greene; married to Madeline Sinkford of Bluefield, WV; two children; B.A., political science, West Virginia State College, 1965; J.D., Howard University, Washington, D.C., 1968; active duty in the United States Army Judge Advocate General's Corps following graduation from law school; as Judge Advocate, completed military education at the Basic, Advanced, and Military Judges' courses at The Judge Advocate General's School, the Army Command and General Staff College, Fort Leavenworth, KS, and the Army War College, Carlisle Barracks, PA; served as the Chief Prosecutor, Fort Knox, KY, 1969–70, and Chief Defense Counsel, Army Command, Hawaii, 1970–73; Army chief recruiter for lawyers 1974–77; Department Chair, Criminal Law Division, the Judge Advocate General's School, Charlottesville, VA, 1981–84; Deputy Staff Judge Advocate, Third Infantry Division, Germany 1977–80; Staff Judge Advocate, Second Infantry Division, Korea 1984–85; following graduation from the United States Army War College, selected to serve as the Staff Judge Advocate of the United States Military Academy at West Point, NY, 1986–90, followed by another selection as Staff Judge Advocate at Fort Leavenworth, KS; retired from the United States Army as Colonel, 1993, receiving several awards during this service, including three Legions of Merit, three Meritorious Service Medals, and two Army Commendation Medals; appointed by the Attorney General of the United States as an Immigration Judge, Department of Justice, presiding over immigration cases in Maryland and Pennsylvania, June 1993—November 1997; nominated for appointment by President Clinton May 16, 1997; confirmed by the U.S. Senate November 7, 1997; sworn in November 24, 1997.

BRUCE E. KASOLD, judge; born in New York, 1951; B.S., United States Military Academy, 1973; J.D., *cum laude*, University of Florida, 1979; LL.M., Georgetown University, 1982; Honors Graduate, the Judge Advocate General's School Graduate Program, 1984; admitted to the bars of the U.S. Supreme Court, the Florida Supreme Court, the District of Columbia Court of Appeals; member: Florida Bar, District of Columbia Bar, the Federal Bar Association, Order of the Coif; retired from the U.S. Army, Lieutenant Colonel, Air Defense Artillery and Judge Advocate General's Corp, 1994; commercial litigation attorney, Holland & Knight Law Firm, 1994–95; Chief Counsel, U.S. Senate Committee on Rules and Administration, 1995–98; Chief Counsel, Secretary of the Senate and Senate Sergeant at Arms, 1998–2003; appointed by President George W. Bush to the U.S. Court of Appeals for Veterans Claims on December 13, 2003; sworn in December 31, 2003.

LAWRENCE B. HAGEL, judge; born in Washington, IN, 1947; B.S., United States Naval Academy, 1969; J.D., University of the Pacific McGeorge School of Law, 1976; LL.M. (Labor Law, with highest honors) The National Law Center, George Washington University, 1983; admitted to the bars of the U.S. Supreme Court, the United States Court of Appeals for the Fourth, Ninth, Tenth, D.C. and Federal Circuits, U.S. Court of Appeals for the Armed Forces, U.S. Court of Appeals for Veterans Claims, Supreme Court of the States of Iowa and California and the District of Columbia; commissioned in the U.S. Marine Corps, second lieutenant, infantry officer 1969–72 service in Vietnam and Puerto Rico; Marine Corps judge advocate 1973–90, assignments concentrated in criminal and civil litigation; Deputy General Counsel and General Counsel, Paralyzed Veterans of America, 1990–2003; confirmed by the U.S. Senate to the Court of Appeals on December 9, 2003; sworn in January 2, 2004.

WILLIAM A. MOORMAN, judge; born in Chicago, IL, January 23, 1945; B.A., University of Illinois at Champaign-Urbana, 1967; J.D., University of Illinois College of Law, 1970; commissioned in the United States Air Force, second lieutenant, Reserve Officers Training Corps, 1970; entered active duty, 1971; Judge Advocate General's Corps, 1972–2002, serving as the senior attorney at every level of command, culminating his active military service with his appointment as the Judge Advocate General of the United States Air Force; military decorations include the Superior Service Medal with oak leaf cluster, the Legion of Merit with oak leaf cluster, the Joint Meritorious Service Medal, and the Meritorious Service Medal with four oak leaf clusters; retired from the Air Force in April 2002, in the grade of Major General; Counselor to the General Counsel, Department of Veterans Affairs, 2002; Assistant to the Secretary for Regulation Policy and Management, Department of Veterans Affairs, 2003; appointed by President George W. Bush as Acting Assistant Secretary of Management for the Department of Veterans Affairs, August 2004; author: ''Executive Privilege and the Freedom of Information Act: Sufficient Protection for Aircraft Mishap Reports?'', 21 Air Force Law Review 581 (1979); ''Cross-Examination Techniques,'' 27 Air Force Law Review 105 (1987); ''Fifty Years of Military Justice: Does the UCMJ Need to be Changed?'', 48 Air Force Law Review 185 (2000); ''Humanitarian Intervention and International Law in the Case of Kosovo,'' 36 New England Law Review 775 (2002); ''Serving our Veterans Through Clearer Rules,'' 56 Administrative Law Review 207 (2004); recipient: Albert M. Kuhfeld Outstanding Young Judge Advocate of the Air Force Award 1979, Stuart R. Reichart Outstanding Senior Attorney of the Air Force Award 1992, University of Illinois College of Law Distinguished Alumnus Award 2001, Department of Veterans Affairs Exceptional Service Award 2004; nominated for appointment to the U.S. Court of Appeals for Veterans Claims on September 21, 2004, by President George W. Bush; confirmed by the U.S. Senate November 20, 2004; sworn in December 16, 2004.

ALAN G. LANCE, Sr., judge; born in McComb, OH, April 27, 1949; B.A. in English and History, distinguished military graduate, South Dakota State University, 1971; commissioned U.S. Army, June 1971; graduated University of Toledo School of Law and Law Review, 1973; admitted to the U.S. Supreme Court, U.S. Court of Military Appeals, State of Ohio, State of Idaho; commissioned U.S. Army, Judge Advocate Generals Corps, 1974 and served as Claims Officer, defense counsel, Chief of Defense Counsel, Legal Assistance Officer, Administrative Law Officer and in the absence of a military Judge, military Magistrate for the 172nd Infantry Brigade (Alaska) 1974–77; Army Commendation Medal 1977; served as the Command Judge Advocate, Corpus Christi Army Depot, 1977–78; engaged in private practice of law, Ada County, Idaho, 1978–94; elected to the Idaho House of Representatives, 1990, and served as Majority Caucus chairman, 1992–94; elected as Idaho Attorney General (31st) in 1994 and 1998; Distinguished Alumnus Award, University of Toledo School of Law, 2002; inducted into the Ohio Veterans Hall of Fame, November 2004; confirmed by the U.S. Senate to the Court of Appeals for Veterans Claims, November 2004 and sworn in on December 17, 2004.

ROBERT N. DAVIS, judge; born in Kewanee, IL, September 20, 1953; graduated from Davenport Central High School, Davenport, IA, 1971; B.A., University of Hartford, 1975; J.D. Georgetown University Law Center, 1978; admitted to the bars of the U.S. Supreme Court, the Ninth Circuit Court of Appeals; the State of Virginia; and the State of Iowa; career record 1978–83 appellate attorney with the Commodity Futures Trading Commission; 1983–88 attorney with the United States Department of Education, Business and Administrative law division of the Office of General Counsel; 1983 Governmental exchange program with the United States Attorneys office, District of Columbia; Special Assistant United States Attorney; 1988–2001 Professor of Law, University of Mississippi School of Law; 2001–05 Professor of Law, Stetson University College of Law; Published extensively in the areas of constitutional law, administrative law, national security law and sports law. Founder and Faculty Editor-in-Chief, Journal of National Security Law, Arbitrator/mediator with the American Arbitration Association and the United States Postal Service. Gubernatorial appointment to the National Conference of Commissioners on Uniform State Laws 1993–2000. Joined the United States Navy Reserve Intelligence Program in 1988. Presidential recall to active duty in 1999, Bosnia and 2001 for the Global War on Terrorism. Military decorations include Joint Service Commendation Medal, Joint Service Achievement Medal, Navy Achievement Medal, NATO Medal, Armed Forces Expeditionary Medal, Armed Forces Reserve Medal with ''M'' device, Overseas Service Ribbon, National Defense Ribbon, Joint Meritorious Unit Award, and Global War on Terrorism Medal. Nominated for appointment by President George W. Bush on March 23, 2003; confirmed by the United States Senate on November 21, 2004; Commissioned on December 4, 2004 as a Judge, United States Court of Appeals for Veterans Claims.

MARY J. SCHOELEN, judge; born in Rota, Spain; B.A., Political Science, University of California at Irvine, 1990; J.D., George Washington University Law School, 1993; admitted to the State Bar of California; law clerk for the National Veterans Legal Services Project, 1992–93; legal intern to the U.S. Senate Committee on Veterans' Affairs, 1994; staff attorney for Vietnam Veterans of America's Veterans Benefits Program, 1994–97; Minority Counsel, U.S. Senate Committee on Veterans' Affairs, 1997–2001; Minority General Counsel, March 2001–June 2001; Deputy Staff Director, Benefits Programs/General Counsel, June 2001–03; Minority Deputy Staff Director, Benefits Programs/General Counsel, 2003–04; confirmed by the U.S. Senate to the United States Court of Appeals for Veterans Claims on November 20, 2004; sworn in December 20, 2004.

OFFICERS OF THE U.S. COURT OF VETERANS APPEALS

Clerk of the Court.—Norman Y. Herring, 501–5980.
Operations Manager.—Anne P. Stygles.
Counsel and Court Reporter of Decisions.—Jack F. Lane.
Senior Staff Attorney (Central Legal Staff).—Cynthia Brandon-Arnold.
Deputy Executive Officer.—Marlene Davis.
Librarian.—Bernard J. Sussman.

JUDICIAL PANEL ON MULTIDISTRICT LITIGATION

Thurgood Marshall Federal Judiciary Building, Room G–255, North Lobby, One Columbus Circle, NE., 20002, phone (202) 502–2800, fax 502–2888

(National jurisdiction to centralize related cases pending in multiple circuits and districts under 28 U.S.C. §§ 1407 & 2112)

Chairman.—Wm. Terrell Hodges, Senior U.S. District Judge, Middle District of Florida.
Judges:
D. Lowell Jensen, Senior U.S. District Judge, Northern District of California.
J. Frederick Motz, U.S. District Judge, Chief Judge, District of Maryland.
Robert L. Miller, Jr., Chief Judge, U.S. District Court, Northern District of Indiana.
Kathryn H. Vratil, U.S. District Judge, District of Kansas.
David R. Hansen, Senior U.S. Court of Appeals Judge, Eighth Circuit.
Anthony J. Scirica, Chief Judge, United States Court of Appeals, Third Circuit.
Executive Attorney.—Robert A. Cahn.
Clerk.—Jeffery N. Lüthi.

ADMINISTRATIVE OFFICE OF THE U.S. COURTS

Thurgood Marshall Federal Judiciary Building

One Columbus Circle, NE., 20544, phone (202) 502–2600

Director.—James C. Duff, 502–3000.
Deputy Director.—Jill C. Sayenga, 502–3015.
Chief, Office of:
Audit.—Jeff Larioni, 502–1000.
Long-Range Planning.—Brian Lynch, 502–1300.
Management, Planning and Assessment.—Cathy A. McCarthy, 502–1300.
Associate Director and General Counsel.—William R. Burchill, Jr., 502–1100.
Deputy General Counsel.—Robert K. Loesche.
Assistant Director, Judicial Conference Executive Secretariat.—Laura C. Minor, 502–2400.
Deputy Assistant Directors: Jeffrey A. Hennemuth, Wendy Jennis.
Assistant Director, Legislative Affairs.—Cordia A. Strom, 502–1700.
Deputy Assistant Director.—Daniel A. Cunningham.
Chief, Judicial Impact Office.—Richard A. Jaffe.
Assistant Director, Public Affairs.—David A. Sellers, 502–2600.
Assistant Director, Office of Court Administration.—Noel J. Augustyn, 502–1500.
Deputy Assistant Director.—Glen K. Palman.
Chief of:
Appellate Court and Circuit Administration Division.—Gary Bowden, 502–1520.
Bankruptcy Court Administration Division.—Glen K. Palman, 502–1540.
Court Administration Policy Staff.—Abel J. Mattos, 502–1560.
District Court Administration Division.—Robert Lowney, 502–1570.
Electronic Public Access Program Office.—Mary Stickney, 502–1500.
Technology Division.—Gary L. Bockweg, 502–2500.
Assistant Director, Office of Defender Services.—Ted Lidz, 502–3030.
Deputy Assistant Director.—Steven G. Asin.
Chief of:
Information Technology Division.—George M. Drakulich.
Legal, Policy and Training Division.—Richard A. Wolff.
Program Budget, Operations and Assessment Division.—Steven G. Asin (acting).
Assistant Director, Office of Facilities and Security.—Ross Eisenman, 502–1200.
Deputy Assistant Director.—William J. Lehman.
Chief of:
Court Security Office.—Edward M. Templeman, 502–1280.
Judiciary Emergency Preparedness Office.—William J. Lehman.
Security and Facilities Policy Staff.—Melanie F. Gilbert.
Space and Facilities Division.—Debra L. Worley.
Assistant Director, Office of Finance and Budget.—George H. Schafer, 502–2000.
Deputy Assistant Director.—Marguerite A. Moccia.
Chief of:
Accounting and Financial Systems Division.—Philip L. McKinney, 502–2200.
Budget Division.—James R. Baugher, 502–2100.
Financial Liaison and Analysis Office.—Penny Jacobs Fleming, 502–2028.
Assistant Director, Office of Human Resources.—Charlotte G. Peddicord, 502–1170.
Deputy Assistant Director.—Nancy E. Ward.
Chief of:
Benefits Division.—Cynthia Roth, 502–1160.
Business Technology Optimization Division.—Christopher D. Mays, 502–3210.
Court Personnel Management Division.—Nancy E. Ward (acting), 502–3100.
Fair Employment Practices Office.—Trudi M. Morrison, 502–1380.
Judges Compensation and Retirement Services Office.—Carol S. Sefren, 502–1380.
Policy and Strategic Initiatives Office.—H. Allen Brown, 502–3185.
Assistant Director for Information Technology.—Melvin J. Bryson, 502–2300.

Deputy Assistant Director.—Barbara C. Macken.
Chief Technology Officer.—Richard D. Fennell.
Chief of:
IT Applications Development Office.—Wendy R. Fite, 502–2730.
IT Infrastructure Management Division.—Craig W. Jenkins, 502–2640.
IT Policy Staff.—Terry A. Cain, 502–3300.
IT Project Coordination Office.—Robert D. Morse, 502–2377.
IT Security Office.—Robert N. Sinsheimer, 502–2350.
IT Systems Deployment and Support Division.—Howard J. Grandier, 502–2700.
Assistant Director for Internal Services.—Doreen Bydume, 502–4200.
Chief of:
AO Administrative Services Division.—Iris Guerra, 502–1220.
AO Information and Technology Services Division.—John C. Chang, 502–2830.
AO Personnel Division.—Cheri Thompson Reid, 502–3800.
AO Procurement Management Division.—William Roeder, 502–1330.
Assistant Director for Judges Programs.—Peter G. McCabe, 502–1800.
Deputy Assistant Director.—R. Townsend Robinson, 502–1800.
Chief of:
Article III Judges Division.—Margaret A. Irving, 502–1860.
Bankruptcy Judges Division.—Francis F. Szczebak, 502–1900.
Magistrate Judges Division.—Thomas C. Hnatowski, 502–1830.
Rules Committee Support Office.—John K. Rabiej, 502–1820.
Statistics Division.—Steven R. Schlesinger, 502–1440.
Assistant Director, Office of Probation and Pretrial Services.—John M. Hughes, 502–1600.
Deputy Assistant Director.—Matthew G. Roland.
Chief of:
Criminal Law Policy Staff.—James C. Oleson.
Programs Administration Division.—Nancy Beatty Gregoire.
Special Projects Office.—Nancy Lee Bradshaw.
Technology Division.—Nicholas B. DiSabatino.

FEDERAL JUDICIAL CENTER

One Columbus Circle, NE., 20002–8003, phone (202) 502–4000

Director.—Judge Barbara J. Rothstein, 502–4061, fax 502–4099.
Deputy Director.—John S. Cooke, 502–4164, fax 502–4099.
Director of:
Communications, Policy and Design Office.—Sylvan A. Sobel, 502–4250, fax 502–4077.
Education Division.—Bruce M. Clarke, 502–4257, fax 502–4299.
Federal Judicial History Office.—Bruce A. Ragsdale, 502–4181, fax 502–4077.
International Judicial Relations Office.—Mira Gur-Arie, 502–4191, fax 502–4099.
Research Division.—James B. Eaglin, 502–4070, fax 502–4199.
Systems Innovations and Development Office.—Ted Coleman, 502–4223, fax 502–4288.

DISTRICT OF COLUMBIA COURTS

H. Carl Moultrie I Courthouse, 500 Indiana Avenue, NW., 20001
phone (202) 879–1010

Executive Officer.—Anne B. Wicks, 879–1700.
Deputy Executive Officer.—Cheryl R. Bailey, 879–1700; fax 879–4829.
Director, Legislative, Intergovernmental and Public Affairs.—Leah Gurowitz, 879–1700.

DISTRICT OF COLUMBIA COURT OF APPEALS

phone (202) 879–1010

Chief Judge.—Eric T. Washington.

Associate Judges:
Michael W. Farrell.
Vanessa Ruiz.
Inez Smith Reid.
Stephen H. Glickman.
Noël Anketell Kramer.
John R. Fisher.
Anna Blackburne-Rigsby.
Phyllis D. Thompson.

Senior Judges:
Theodore R. Newman.
William C. Pryor.
Annice M. Wagner.
John W. Kern III.
James A. Belson.
Warren R. King.
John M. Ferren.
Frank Q. Nebeker.
John M. Steadman.
John A. Terry.
Frank E. Schwelb.

Clerk.—Garland Pinkston, Jr., 879–2725.
Chief Deputy Clerk.—Joy A. Chapper, 879–2722.
Administration Director.—John Dyson, 879–2738.
Admissions Director.—Jacqueline Smith, 879–2714.
Public Office Operations Director.—Jeanette E. Togans, 879–2702.
Senior Staff Attorney.—Rosanna M. Mason, 879–2718.

SUPERIOR COURT OF THE DISTRICT OF COLUMBIA

phone (202) 879–1010

Chief Judge.—Rufus G. King III.
Associate Judges:
Geoffrey M. Alprin.
Jennifer Anderson.
Judith Bartnoff.
John H. Bayly, Jr.
Ronna L. Beck.
James E. Boasberg.
Patricia A. Broderick.
A. Franklin Burgess, Jr.
Zoe Bush.
Jerry S. Byrd.
John M. Campbell.
Russell F. Canan.
Erik P. Christian.
Kaye K. Christian.
Jeanette Clark.
Natalia M. Combs Greene.
Laura A. Cordero.
Harold L. Cushenberry, Jr.
Linda Kay Davis.
Rafael Diaz.
Herbert B. Dixon, Jr.
Stephanie Duncan-Peters.
Gerald I. Fisher.
Wendell P. Gardner, Jr.
Brook Hedge.
Brian Holeman.
Craig Iscoe.
Gregory Jackson.
William M. Jackson.
John Ramsey Johnson.
Anita Josey-Herring.
Ann O'Regan Keary.
Neal E. Kravitz.
Lynn Lebowitz.
Cheryl M. Long.
José M. López.
Judith N. Macaluso.
Juliet McKenna.
Zinora Mitchell-Rankin.
Robert E. Morin.
Thomas J. Motley.
John M. Mott.
Hiram E. Puig-Lugo.
Michael L. Rankin.
Judith E. Retchin.
Robert I. Richter.
Robert R. Rigsby.
Maurice A. Ross.
Michael Ryan.
Fern Flanagan Saddler.
Lee F. Satterfield.
Mary A. Gooden Terrell.
Linda D. Turner.
Odessa F. Vincent.
Frederick H. Weisberg.
Rhonda Reid-Winston.
Melvin R. Wright.
Joan Zeldon.

Magistrate Judges:
Janet Albert.
Diane Brenneman.
Julie Breslow.
Evelyn B. Coburn.
Carol Ann Dalton.
J. Dennis Doyle.
Diana Harris Epps.
Tara Fentress.
Joan Goldfrank.
Ronald A. Goodbread.
S. Pamela Gray.
Andrea L. Harnett.

Karen Howze.
Noel Johnson.
Milton C. Lee.
Michael McCarthy.
John McCabe.
Aida L. Melendez.
William W. Nooter.
Richard H. Ringell.
Mary Grace Rook.
Frederick Sullivan.
Elizabeth Carroll Wingo.

Senior Judges:

Mary Ellen Abrecht.
Bruce D. Beaudin.
Leonard Braman.
Arthur L. Burnett, Sr.
Frederick Dorsey.
Stephen F. Eilperin.
George Herbert Goodrich.
Henry F. Greene.
Eugene N. Hamilton.
John R. Hess.
Richard A. Levie.
Bruce S. Mencher.
Stephen G. Milliken.
J. Gregory Mize.
Truman A. Morrison III.
Tim Murphy.
Nan R. Shuker.
Robert S. Tignor.
Fred B. Ugast.
Paul R. Webber III.
Ronald P. Wertheim.
Susan R. Winfield.
Peter H. Wolf.
Patricia A. Wynn.

Clerk of the Court.—Duane B. Delaney, 879–1400.

GOVERNMENT OF THE DISTRICT OF COLUMBIA

John A. Wilson Building, 1350 Pennsylvania Avenue, NW., 20004

phone (202) 724–8000

[All area codes within this section are (202)]

COUNCIL OF THE DISTRICT OF COLUMBIA

Council Chairman (at Large).—Vincent C. Gray, Suite 506, 724–8068.
Chairman Pro Tempore.—Jack Evans.
Council Members:
Jim Graham, Ward 1, Suite 105, 724–8181.
Jack Evans, Ward 2, Suite 106, 724–8058.
Mary M. Cheh, Ward 3, Suite 108, 724–8062.
Muriel Bowser, Ward 4, Suite 406, 724–8052.
Harry Thomas, Jr., Ward 5, Suite 107, 724–8028.
Thomas Wells, Ward 6, Suite 408, 724–8072.
Yvette M. Alexander, Ward 7, Suite 400, 724–8068.
Marion Barry, Ward 8, Suite 102, 724–8045.
Council Members (at Large):
Carol Schwartz, Suite 404, 724–8105.
David A. Catania, Suite 110, 724–7772.
Phil Mendelson, Suite 402, 724–8064.
Kwame R. Brown, Suite 406, 724–8174.
Secretary to the Council.—Cynthia Brock-Smith, Suite 5, 724–8080.
Budget Director.—Eric Goulet, Suite 508, 724–8139.
General Counsel.—Brian K. Flowers, Suite 4, 724–8026.

EXECUTIVE OFFICE OF THE MAYOR

Suite 327, phone (202) 727–6300, fax 727–8127

Mayor of the District of Columbia.—Adrian M. Fenty.
Executive Assistant to the Mayor.—Glenis Gillis.
Chief of Staff.—Tené Dolphin.
Special Assistant to the Chief of Staff.—Naomi Shelton.
Deputy Mayor for—
Education.—Victor Reinoso.
Planning and Economic Development.—Neil Albert, Suite 317, 727–6365, fax 727–6307.
Secretary of the District of Columbia.—Stephanie D. Scott, Ph.D., Suite 419, 727–6306, fax 727–3582.
Executive Assistant to the Secretary of the District of Columbia.—Arlethia Thompson, Suite 419, 727–6371, fax 727–3582.
General Counsel.—Peter Nickles, Suite 327, 727–1597, fax 727–8127.
Inspector General.—Charles J. Willoughby, Esq., 717 14th Street, NW., 5th Floor, 20020, 727–2540, fax 727–9846.
Director of:
Communications.—Carrie Brooks, Suite 327, 727–5011, fax 727–8127.
Mayor's Office of Community Relations and Services.—Merritt Drucker, Suite 211, 442–8150, fax 727–5931.
Operations.—Sara Lasner, Suite 327, 727–6300, fax 727–8127.
Policy and Legislative Affairs.—JoAnne Ginsburg, Suite 511, 727–6979, fax 727–3765.
Scheduling.—Aliciamarie Johnson, Suite 327, 727–4043, fax 727–8127.

OFFICE OF THE CITY ADMINISTRATOR
Suite 521, phone (202) 727–6053, fax 727–9878

City Administrator/Deputy Mayor.—Dan Tangherlini.
Executive Assistant to City Administrator.—Tonya Daggett.

COMMISSIONS

Arts and Humanities, 410 8th Street, NW., 5th Floor, 20004, 724–5613, fax 727–4135.
Executive Director.—Anthony Gittens.
Chairperson.—Dorothy McSweeny.

Judicial Disabilities and Tenure, 515 5th Street, NW., Suite 312, 20001, 727–1363, fax 727–9718.
Executive Director.—Cathaee Hudgins.
Chairperson.—William P. Lightfoot.

Judicial Nominations, 616 H Street, NW., Suite 623, 20001, 879–0478, fax 737–9126.
Executive Director.—Peggy Smith.

Serve DC, 441 4th Street, NW., Suite 1140 North, 20001, 727–7925, fax 727–9198.
Executive Director.—Millicent Williams.

Washington Metropolitan Area Transit, 1828 L Street, NW., 20036, 331–1671, fax 653–2179.
Executive Director.—Bill Morrow.

DEPARTMENTS

Child and Family Services Agency, 400 6th Street, SW., 5th Floor, 20024, 442–6000, fax 442–6498.
Director.—Sharlynn E. Bobo.

Consumer and Regulatory Affairs, 941 North Capitol Street, NE., 20002, 442–4400, fax 442–9445.
Director.—Linda Argo.

Corrections, 1923 Vermont Avenue, NW., Room 207N, 20001, 673–7316, fax 671–0169.
Director.—Devon Brown.

Environment, 2000 14th Street, NW., 20009, 673–6700, fax 673–6725.
Director.—Corey R. Buffo, Esq.

Employment Services, 609 H Street, NE., 20002, 724–7000, fax 673–6993.
Director.—Summer Spencer.

Fire and Emergency Medical Services, 1923 Vermont Avenue, NW., Suite 201, 20001, 673–3331, fax 673–3188.
Fire Chief.—Dennis L. Rubin.

Health, 825 North Capitol Street, NE., 20002, 671–5000, fax 442–4788.
Director.—Gregg A. Pane, M.D., M.P.A., FACPE.

Housing and Community Development, 801 North Capitol Street, NE., 8th floor, 20002, 442–7200, fax 442–8391.
Director.—Leila Edmonds.

Human Services, 64 New York Avenue, NE, 6th floor, 20002, 671–4200, fax 671–4325.
Director.—Kate Jesberg.

Insurance, Securities and Banking, 810 1st Street, NE., Suite 701, 20002, 727–8000, fax 535–1196.
Commissioner.—Thomas E. Hampton.

Mental Health, 77 P Street, NE., 4th Floor, 20002, phone 673–7440, fax 673–3433.
Director.—Stephen T. Baron, LCSW–C.

Metropolitan Police, 300 Indiana Avenue, NW., 20001, phone 311 or (202) 737–4404 if calling from outside DC, fax 727–9524.

Police Chief.—Cathy L. Lanier.

Motor Vehicles, 301 C Street, NW., 20001, 727–5000, fax 727–4653.
Director.—Lucinda M. Babers.

Parks and Recreation, 3149 16th Street, NW., 20010, 673–7647, fax 673–6694.
Director.—Wanda S. Durden.

Public Works, 2000 14th Street, NW., 6th Floor, 20009, 673–6833, fax 671–0642.
Director.—William O. Howland, Jr.

Small and Local Business Development, 441 4th Street, NW., Suite 970 North, 20001, 727–3900, fax 724–3786.
Director.—Erik A. Moses.

Transportation, 2000 14th Street, NW., 6th Floor, 20009, 673–6813, fax 671–0642.
Director.—Emeka C. Moneme.

Youth Rehabilitation Services, 1000 Mt. Olivet Road, NE., 20002, 576–8175, fax 576–8457.
Director.—Vincent N. Schiraldi.

OFFICES

Administrative Hearings, 825 North Capitol Street, NE., Suite 4150, 20002, 442–9091.
Chief Judge.—Tyrone T. Butler.

Aging, 441 Fourth Street, NW., Suite 900 South, 20001, 724–5622, fax 724–4979.
Director.—Sam A. Gawad.

Asian and Pacific Islander Affairs, 441 4th Street, NW., Suite 805 South, 20001, 727–3120, fax 727–9655.
Executive Director.—Soohyun ''Julie'' Koo.

Attorney General, 1350 Pennsylvania Avenue, NW., Suite 409, 20004, 727–3400, fax 724–6590.
Attorney General.—Linda Singer (acting).

Boards and Commissions, 441 4th Street, NW., Suite 530 South, 20001, 727–1372, fax 727–2359.
Director.—Carla Brailey.

Cable Television and Telecommunications, 3007 Tilden Street, NW., Pod P, 20008, 671–0066, fax 332–7020.
Acting Director.—Eric E. Richardson.

Chief Financial Officer, 1350 Pennsylvania Avenue, NW., Suite 203, 20004, 727–2476, fax 727–1643.
Chief Financial Officer.—Natwar M. Gandhi.

Chief Medical Examiner, 1910 Massachusetts Avenue, SE., Building 27, 20003, 698–9000, fax 698–9100.
Chief Medical Examiner.—Dr. Marie-Lydie Pierre-Louis.

Chief Technology Officer, 441 4th Street, NW., Suite 930 South, 20001, 727–2277, fax 727–6857.
Chief Technology Officer.—Vivek Kundra.

Communications Office, 1350 Pennsylvania Avenue, NW., Suite 533, 20004, 727–5011, fax 727–9561.
Director.—Carrie Brooks.

Community Relations and Services, 1350 Pennsylvania Avenue, NW., Suite 211, 20004, 442–8150, fax 727–5931.
Director.—Merritt Drucker.

Contracting and Procurement, 441 4th Street, NW., Suite 700 South, 20001, 727–0252, fax 727–9385.
Chief Procurement Officer.—Oscar S. Rodriguez.

Emergency Management Agency, 2720 Martin Luther King, Jr. Avenue, SE., 20032, 727–6161, fax 673–2290.
Director.—Barbara Childs-Pair.

Employee Appeals, 717 14th Street, NW., 3rd Floor, 20005, 727–0004, fax 727–5631.

Executive Director.—Warren Cruise, Esq.

Finance and Resource Management, 441 4th Street, NW., Suite 890 North, 20001, 727–0333, fax 727–0659.
Director of Finance Operations.—Mohamed Mohamed.

Human Resources, 441 4th Street, NW., Suite 300 South, 20001, 442–9600, fax 727–6827.
Director.—Brender L. Gregory.

Human Rights, 441 4th Street, NW., Suite 570N, 20001, 727–4559, fax 727–9589.
Director.—Gustavo F. Velasquez.

Labor-Management Programs, 441 4th Street, NW., Suite 1150 North, 20001, 727–4999, fax 724–7713.
Director.—Ronald S. Flowers.

Labor Relations and Collective Bargaining, 441 4th Street, NW., Suite 820 North, 20001, 724–4953, fax 727–6887.
Director.—Natasha Campbell.

Latino Affairs, 2000 14th Street, NW., 2nd Floor, 20009, 671–2825, fax 673–4557.
Director.—Mercedes Lemp.

Lesbian, Gay, Bisexual and Transgender Affairs, 1350 Pennsylvania Avenue, NW., Suite 211, 20004, 442–8150, fax 727–5931.
Director.—Darlene Nipper.

Mayor's Office of Community Relations and Services, 1350 Pennsylvania Avenue, NW., Suite 211, 20004, 442–8150, fax 727–5445.
Director.—Clark Ray.

Motion Picture and Television Development, 441 4th Street, NW., Suite 760 North, 20001, 727–6608, fax 727–3246.
Director.—Crystal Palmer.

Partnerships and Grants Development, 441 4th Street, NW., Suite 1130 North, 20001, 727–8900, fax 727–1652.
Director.—Lafayette Barnes.

Planning, 801 North Capitol Street, NE., Suite 4000, 20002, 442–7600, fax 442–7638.
Director.—Harriet Tregoning.

Policy and Legislative Affairs, 1350 Pennsylvania Avenue, NW., Suite 511, 20004, 727–6979, fax 727–3765.
Deputy Chief of Staff.—JoAnne Ginsberg.

Property Management, 441 4th Street, NW., Suite 1100 South, 20001, 724–4400, fax 727–9877.
Director.—Lars Etzkorn.

Risk Management, 441 4th Street, NW., Suite 800 South, 20001, 727–8600, fax 727–8319.
Director.—Kelly Valentine.

State Education, 441 4th Street, NW., Suite 350 North, 20001, 727–6436, fax 727–2019.
State Education Officer.—Deborah A. Gist.

Unified Communications, 2720 Martin Luther King Jr. Avenue, SE., 20032, 730–0524, fax 730–0513.
Director.—Janice Quintana.

Veterans Affairs, 441 4th Street, NW., Suite 570 South, 20001, 724–5454, fax 727–7117.
Director.—Kerwin E. Miller.

Victim Services, 1350 Pennsylvania Avenue, NW., Suite 407, 20004, 727–3934, fax 727–1617.
Director.—Melissa Hook.

Zoning, 441 4th Street, NW., Suite 210, 20001, 727–6311, fax 727–6072.
Director.—Jerrily R. Kress, FAIA.

INDEPENDENT AGENCIES

Advisory Neighborhood Commissions, 1350 Pennsylvania Avenue, NW., Suite 8, 20004, 727–9945, fax 727–0289.

Executive Director.—Gottlieb Simon.

Alcoholic Beverage Regulation Administration, 941 North Capitol Street, NE., Suite 7200, 20002, 442–4423, fax 727–9685.
Director.—Maria M. Delaney.

Board of Elections and Ethics, 441 4th Street, NW., Suite 250 North, 20001, 727–2525, fax 347–2648.
Chairperson of the Board.—Wilma A. Lewis.

Criminal Justice Coordinating Council, 441 4th Street, NW., Suite 727 North, 20001, 442–9283, fax 442–4922.
Executive Director.—Nancy Ware.

District of Columbia Court of Appeals, 500 Indiana Avenue, NW., Room 6000, 20001, 879–2701, fax 626–8840.
Chief Judge.—Eric T. Washington.

District of Columbia Housing Authority, 1133 North Capitol Street, NE., 20001, 535–1500, fax 535–1740.
Executive Director.—Michael P. Kelly.

District of Columbia Public Defender Service, 633 Indiana Avenue, NW., 20001, 628–1200, fax 824–2378.
Director.—Avis Buchanan.

District of Columbia Public Library, 901 G Street, NW., Suite 400, 20001, 727–1101, fax 727–1129.
Director.—Ginnie Cooper.

District of Columbia Public Schools, 825 North Capitol Street, NW., Suite 9026, 20002, 442–4226, fax 442–5026.
Superintendent.—Dr. Clifford B. Janey.

District of Columbia Retirement Board, 900 7th Street, NW., 2nd Floor, 20001, 343–3200, fax 566–5000.
Executive Director.—Constance Donovan (acting).

District of Columbia Sentencing Commission, 441 4th Street, NW., Suite 830 South, 20001, 727–8822, fax 727–7929.
Executive Director.—Kim S. Hunt.

District of Columbia Sports and Entertainment Commission, 2400 East Capitol Street, SE., 20003, 547–9077, fax 547–7460.
Chief Executive Officer.—Allen Lew.

District Lottery and Charitable Games Control Board, 2101 Martin Luther King Jr. Avenue, SE., 20020, 645–8000, fax 645–7914.
Executive Director.—Jeanette A. Michael.

Housing Finance Agency, 815 Florida Avenue, NW., 20001, 777–1600, fax 986–6705.
Executive Director.—Harry D. Sewell.

Metropolitan Washington Council of Governments, 777 North Capitol Street, NE., 20002, 962–3200, fax 962–3201.
Executive Director.—Dave Robertson.

People's Counsel, 1133 15th Street, NW., Suite 500, 20005, 727–3071, fax 727–1014.
People's Counsel.—Elizabeth A. Noel, Esq.

Police Complaints, 1400 I Street, NW., Suite 700, 20005, 727–3838, fax 727–9182.
Executive Director.—Philip K. Eure.

Public Charter School Board, 1436 U Street, NW., Suite 401, 20009, 328–2660, fax 328–2661.
Executive Director.—Josephine Baker.

Public Employee Relations Board, 717 14th Street, NW., 11th Floor, 20005, 727–1822, fax 727–9116.
Executive Director.—Julio Castillo.

Public Service Commission, 1333 H Street, NW., Suite 200W, 20005, 626–5100, fax 393–1389.
Chairperson.—Agnes A. Yates.

Superior Court of the District of Columbia, H. Carl Moultrie I Courthouse, 500 Indiana Avenue, NW., 20001, 879–1010.

Chief Judge.—Rufus G. King III.

Taxicab Commission, 2041 Martin Luther King Jr. Avenue, SE., Suite 204, 20020, 645–6018, fax 889–3604.
Chairperson.—Doreen Thompson.

Washington Convention Center Authority, 801 Mount Vernon Place, NW., 20001, 249–3012, fax 249–3133.
CEO/General Manager.—Rebecca Pittman Walker.

Washington, DC Convention and Tourism Corporation, 1212 New York Avenue, NW., Suite 600, 20005, 789–7000, fax 789–7037.
President/CEO.—William A. Hanbury.

Water and Sewer Authority, 5000 Overlook Avenue, SW., 20032, 787–2000, fax 787–2210.
Chairperson.—Glenn S. Gerstell.

Workforce Investment Council, 609 H Street, NE., Suite 521, 20002, 698–5826, fax 724–1334.
Chairperson.—Barbara B. Lang.

OTHER

Board of Real Property Assessments and Appeals, 441 4th Street, NW., Suite 430, 20001, 727–6860, fax 727–0392.
Director.—Paul Strauss.

Contract Appeals Board, 717 14th Street, NW., Suite 430, 20005, 727–6597, fax 727–3993.
Chief Administrative Judge.—Jonathan D. Zischkau.

Justice Grants Administration, 1350 Pennsylvania Avenue, NW., Suite 327A, 20004, 727–6239, fax 727–1617.
Director.—John Hallums.

Rehabilitation Services Administration, 810 First Street, NE., 20002, 442–8663, fax 442–8742.
Administrator.—Elizabeth B. Parker.

DISTRICT OF COLUMBIA POST OFFICE LOCATIONS

900 Brentwood Road, NE., 20066–9998, General Information (202) 636–1200

Postmaster.—Delores D. Killett.

CLASSIFIED STATIONS

Station	Phone	Location/Zip Code
Anacostia	523–2119	2650 Naylor Rd., SE., 20020
Ben Franklin	523–2386	1200 Pennsylvania Ave., NW., 20044
B.F. Carriers	636–2289	900 Brentwood Rd., NE., 20004
Benning	523–2391	3937–½ Minnesota Ave., NE., 20019
Bolling AFB	767–4419	Bldg. 10, Brookley Avenue, 20332
Brightwood	726–8119	6323 Georgia Ave., NW., 20
Brookland	523–2126	3401 12th St., NE., 20017
Calvert	523–2908	2336 Wisconsin Ave., NW., 20007
Cleveland Park	523–2396	3430 Connecticut Ave. NW., 20008
Columbia Heights	523–2192	6510 Chillum Pl., NW., 20010
Congress Heights	523–2122	400 Southern Ave., SE., 20032
Customs House	523–2195	3178 Bladensburg Rd., NE., 20018
Dulles	(703) 471–9497	Dulles International Airport, 20041
Farragut	523–2507	1145 19th St., NW., 20033
Fort Davis	842–4964	3843 Pennsylvania Ave., SE., 20020
Fort McNair	523–2144	300 A. St., SW., 20319

CLASSIFIED STATIONS—CONTINUED

Station	Phone	Location / Zip Code
Frederick Douglass	842–4959	Alabama Ave., SE., 20020
Friendship	523–2153 / 2130	4005 Wisconsin Ave., NW., 20016
Georgetown	523–2406	1215 31st St., NW., 20007
Government Mail	523–2138 / 2139	3300 V Street, NE., 20018–9998
Headsville	357–3029	Smithsonian Institute, 20560
Kalorama	523–2906	2300 18th St., NW., 20009
Lamond Riggs	523–2041	6200 North Capitol St., NW., 20
LeDroit Park	483–0973	416 Florida Ave., NW., 20001
L'Enfant Plaza	523–2014	458 L'Enfant Plaza, SW., 20026
Main Office Window	636–2130	Curseen / Morris P & DC, 900 Brentwood Rd., NE., 20066–9998
Martin L. King, Jr	523–2001	1400 L St., NW., 20043
McPherson	523–2394	1750 Pennsylvania Ave., NW, 20038
Mid City	....	Temporarily Closed
NASA	358–0235 / 0199	600 Independence Ave., SW., 20546
National Capitol	523–2368	2 Massachusetts Ave., NE., 20002
Naval Research Lab	767–3426	4565 Overlook Ave., 20390
Navy Annex	(703) 920–0815	1668 D Street, 20335
Northeast	388–5216	1563 Maryland Ave., NE., 20002
Northwest	523–2570	5632 Connecticut Ave., NW., 20015
Palisades	842–2291	5136 MacArthur Blvd., NW., 20016
Pavilion Postique	523–2571	1100 Pennsylvania Ave., NW., 20004
Pentagon	(703) 695–6835	Concourse Pentagon (Army-20301 / 20310; Air Force-20330; Navy-20350)
Petworth	523–2681	4211 9th St., NW., 20
Postal Square	523–2022	2 Massachusetts Ave., NW., 20002
Randle	584–6807	2341 Pennsylvania Ave., SE., 20023
River Terrace	523–2884	3621 Benning Rd., NE., 20019
Southeast	523–2174	327 7th St., SE., 20003
Southwest	523–2597	45 L St., SW., 20024
State Department	523–2574	2201 C St., NW., 20520
T Street	232–6301	1915 14th St., NW., 20009
Tech World	523–2019	800 K St., NW., 20001
Temple Heights	523–2563	1921 Florida Ave., NW., 20009
Twentieth Street	523–2411	2001 M St., NW., 20036
U.S. Naval	433–2216	940 M St., SE., 20374
V Street	636–2272 / 2273	Section 2, Curseen / Morris P & DC, 900 Brentwood Rd., NE., 20002–9998
Walter Reed	782–3768	6800 Georgia Ave., NW., 20012
Ward Place	523–5109	2121 Ward Pl., NW., 20037
Washington Square	523–2632	1050 Connecticut Ave., NW., 20035
Watergate	965–4598	2512 Virginia Ave., NW., 20037
Woodridge	523–2195	2211 Rhode Island Ave., NE., 20018

INTERNATIONAL ORGANIZATIONS

EUROPEAN SPACE AGENCY (E.S.A.)

Headquarters: 8–10 Rue Mario Nikis, 75738 Paris Cedex 15, France
phone 011–33–1–5369–7654, fax 011–33–1–5369–7560

Chairman of the Council.—Per Tegnér.
Director General.—Jean-Jacques Dordain.
Member Countries:

Austria	Greece	Portugal
Belgium	Ireland	Spain
Denmark	Italy	Sweden
Finland	Luxembourg	Switzerland
France	Netherlands	United Kingdom
Germany	Norway	

Cooperative Agreement.—Canada.

European Space Operations Center (E.S.O.C.), Robert-Bosch-Str. 5, D–64293 Darmstadt, Germany, phone 011–49–6151–900, fax 011–49–6151–90495.

European Space Research and Technology Center (E.S.T.E.C.), Keplerlaan 1, NL–2201, AZ Noordwijk, ZH, The Netherlands, phone 011–31–71–565–6565, Telex: 844–39098, fax 011–31–71–565–6040.

European Space Research Institute (E.S.R.I.N.), Via Galileo Galilei, Casella Postale 64, 00044 Frascati, Italy, phone 011–39–6–94–18–01, fax 011–39–6–9418–0280.

Washington Office (E.S.A.), 955 L'Enfant Plaza, SW., Suite 7800, 20024.
Head of Office.—Frederic Nordlund (202) 488–4158, fax 488–4930, *Frederic.Nordlund@esa.int.*

INTER-AMERICAN DEFENSE BOARD

2600 16th Street, NW., 20441, phone (202) 939–6041, fax 387–2880

Chairman.—LTG Jorge Armando de Almeida Ribiero, Army, Brazil.
Vice Chairman.—GB Thomas Pena y Lillo, Army, Bolivia.
Secretary.—CAPT Jaime Navarro, U.S. Navy.
Deputy Secretary for—
Administration.—MAJ Jaime Adames, U.S. Air Force.
Conference.—Cel Heldo F. de Souza, Army, Brazil.
Information Management.—LTC Michael Cobb, U.S. Army.
Protocol.—CAPT William Vivoni, U.S. Air Force.
Staff Vice Director.—COL Ricardo Murillo, Army, Honduras.

CHIEFS OF DELEGATION

Antigua and Barbuda.—COL Trevor Thomas, Army.
Argentina.—Contralmirante Guillermo Oscar Iglesias, Navy.
Barbados.—LTC Atheline Branch, Defense Force.
Bolivia.—GB Gustavo Ardaya Salinas, Army.
Brazil.—Contralmirante Luiz Guilherme Sa de Gusmao, Army.
Canada.—MG Doug Langton, Land Forces.
Chile.—Contralmirante Felipe Carvajal, Navy.
Colombia.—MG Mario Ernesto Corea, Army.
Dominican Republic.—MG Luiz Damian Castro Cruz, Air Force.

Ecuador.—COL Patricio Jorge Mejia, Air Force.
El Salvador.—COL Walter Mauricio Arevalo, Army.
Guyana.—COL Lawrence Paul, Defense Force.
Haiti.—Minister Counselor Leon Charles, Civilian.
Honduras.—COL Aldo Augusto Aldana, Army.
Mexico.—MG Dem. Pedro Felipe Gurrola, Army.
Nicaragua.—COL Elias Guevara, Army.
Paraguay.—GB Antonino Solis Nunez, Army.
Trinidad.—LTC Anthony Phillips-Spencer, Army.
United States.—MG Philip M. Breedlove, Air Force.
Uruguay.—GB Alberto Castillo, Air Force.
Venezuela.—Primer Secretario Carlos Alberto Rodriguez, Interim Representative, Civilian.

INTER-AMERICAN DEFENSE COLLEGE

Director.—MG Keith M. Huber, U.S. Army.
Chief of Studies.—GB Julio Florian, Army, Dominican Republic.

INTER-AMERICAN DEVELOPMENT BANK

1300 New York Avenue, NW., 20577, phone (202) 623–1000

http://www.iadb.org

OFFICERS

President.—Luiz Alberto Moreno (Colombia).
Chief, Office of the President.—Jamal Khokhar.
Executive Vice President.—Daniel M. Zelikow (United States).
Chief Advisor.—Ana Maria Rodriguez-Ortiz.
Private Sector Coordinator.—Juan Ricardo Ortega, a.i.
Director, Office of Evaluation and Oversight.—Stephen A. Quick.
Chief Economist.—Guillermo Calvo.
Auditor General.—Alan N. Siegfried.
External Relations Advisor.—Alfredo Barnechea.
Deputy Advisor.—Chris Sale.
Ombudsperson.—Doris Campos-Infantino.
Manager, Office of:
Budget and Corporate Procurement.—William E. Schuerch.
Development Effectiveness and Strategic Planning Department.—Camille Gaskin-Reyes, a.i.
Finance Department.—John R. Hauge.
General Counsel, Legal Department.—James Spinner.
Human Resources.—Manuel Labrado.
Integration and Regional Programs Department.—Nohra Rey de Marulanda.
Multilateral Investment Fund.—Donald F. Terry.
Private Sector Department.—Hiroshi Toyoda.
Regional Operations Department 1.—Manuel Rapoport.
Regional Operations Department 2.—Màximo Jèria.
Regional Operations Department 3.—Alicia Ritchie.
Sustainable Development Department.—Antonio Vives, a.i.
Secretary.—Carlos Jarque.

BOARD OF EXECUTIVE DIRECTORS

Aregentina and Haiti.—Eugenio Díaz-Bonilla.
Alternate.—Martín Bès.
Austria, Denmark, Finland, France, Norway, Spain, and Sweden.—Michel Planque.
Alternate.—Marta Blanco.
Bahamas, Barbados, Guyana, Jamaica, Trinidad and Tobago.—Jerry Butler.
Alternate.—Winston Cox.
Belgium, Germany, Israel, Italy, The Netherlands, and Switzerland.—Giorgio Leccesi.
Alternate.—Ina-Marlene Ruthenberg.
Belize, Costa Rica, El Salvador, Guatemala, Haiti, Honduras, and Nicaragua.—Hugo Noè Pino.

Alternate.—Nelly Lacayo-Anderson.
Bolivia, Paraguay, and Uruguay.—Hugo R. Càceros.
Alternate.—Marcelo Bisogno.
Brazil, and Suriname.—Rogério Studart.
Alternate.—Arlindo Villaschi.
Canada.—Vinita Watson.
Alternate.—Jill Johnson.
Chile and Peru.—Jaime Quijandria.
Alternate.—Alejandro Foxley.
Colombia and Ecuador.—Luis G. Echeverri.
Croatia, Japan, Portugal, Slovenia, and United Kingdom.—Tsuyoshi Takahashi.
Alternate.—Stewart Mills.
Dominican Republic and Mexico.—Jonathan Davis.
Alternate.—Roberto B. Saladín.
Panama and Venezuela.—Adina Bastidas.
Alternate.—Fernando Eleta Casanovas.
United States.—Héctor E. Morales.

INTER-AMERICAN TROPICAL TUNA COMMISSION

8604 La Jolla Shores Drive, La Jolla, CA 92037–1508

phone (858) 546–7100, fax 546–7133, http://www.iattc.org

Director.—Robin L. Allen.
Commissioners:
Costa Rica.—Asdrubal Vásquez, Ministerio de Agricultura, Ganaderia y Pesca, Apartado 549–7050, San José, Costa Rica (506) 552–1317 or 382–3109, fax 253–4321; email: vazqueza1@ice.co.cr, vasqueza@sardimar.com.
Ecuador:
Juan F. Ballén, COMEXI, Av. Eloy Alfaro y Amazonas Edif.MAG-MICIP 1er Piso, Quito, Ecuador (593–2) 254–3897 or 223–9258, email: jfballen@micip.gov.ec.
Ing. Jorge Kalil Barreiro, Ministerio de Comercio Exterior, Industrialización y Pesca, Av. 9 de Octubre 200 y Pichincha, Edificio Banco Central, 7o.Piso, Guayaquil, Ecuador (593–4) 256–4300, ext. 593, fax 230–6144; email: direc01@subpesca.gov.ec.
Luis Torres, Ministerio de Comercio Exterior, Industrialización, Pesca y Competitividad, Av. 9 de Octubre 200 y Pichincha, Edif. Banco Central, piso 7, Guayaquil, Ecuador (593–4) 256–0993 or 256–4300, fax 256–1489; email: Asesor01@subpesca.gov.ec.
El Salvador:
Manuel Calvo, Luis Calvo Sanz, El Salvador, Avda. Eng. Luis Carlos Berrini 267–7o (Brooklin Novo), Sao Paulo, Brazil 04571–0000 (55–11) 82–77–08–67, fax 55–03–68, email: mane.calvo@grupocalvo.com.sv, mane.calvo@calvo.es.
Manuel F. Oliva, CENDEPESCA, Final 1 Av. Norte Nueva San Salvador, San Salvador, El Salvador (503) 228–0034 or 289–1066, fax 289–6124; email: moliva@mag.gob.sv.
Sonia M. Salaverría, Ministerio de Agricultura y Ganadería, CENDEPESCA, Final 1a. Avenida Norte y Avenida Manuel Gallardo, Santa Tecla, San Salvador, El Salvador (503) 228–0034 or 228–1066, fax 228–0074, email: ssalaverría@mag.gob.sv, ssalaverria24@hotmail.com.
José Emilio Suadi, Ministerio de Agricultura y Ganaderia, Final 1a. Av. Norte y Av. Manuel Gallardo, Santa Tecla, El Salvador (503) 228–9302, fax 228–1938; email: jsuadi@mag.gob.sv.
France:
Rachid Bouabane-Schmitt, Haut Commissariat de la République Française en Polynésie, 43 Avenue Bruat, BP 115, 98713 Papeete, French Polynesias, 689–46–85–17, fax 689–46–86–00; email: rachid.bouabane-schmitt@polynesie-francaise.gouv.fr.
Patrick Brenner, Ministère de l'Outre Mer, 27 Rue OUDINOT, 75007 Paris, France (33–1) 53–69–26–32, fax 53–69–21–97; email: patrick.brenner@outre-mer.gouv.fr.
Marie-Sophie Dufau-Richet, Secretariat d'etat a la Mer, 16 Boulevard Raspail, 75700 Paris, France (33–1) 53–63–41–53, fax (31–1) 53–63–41–7; email: marie.sophie.DUFAU-RICHET@pm.gouv.fr.
Delphine Leguerrier, French Ministry of Agriculture, 3 Place de Fontenoy, 75007 Paris, France (33–1) 49–55–82–36, fax 49–55–82–00; email: delphine.leguerrier@agriculture.gouv.fr.

Guatemala:

Edilberto Ruíz Alvarez, MAGA/Ministerio de Agricultura, Ganadería y Alimentación, Edificio La Ceiba, 3er Nivel Km. 22 Carretera al Pacifico, Guatemala (502) 6630–5839, 6630–5839, fax 5510–3300; email: coor_unipesca@c.net.gt.

Ing. Ricardo Santacruz Rubí, Ministerio de Agricultura, Ganadería y Alimentación, Km. 22 Carretera al Pacifico, Edificio La Ceiba 3er Nivel, Guatemala, Guatemala (502) 6630–5883, fax 6630–3839; email: unipesca@c.net.gt.

Erik Villagran, MAGA / Ministerio de Agricultura, Ganadería y Alimentación, Km. 22 Carretera al Pacifico, Edificio La Ceiba 3er Nivel, Guatemala, Guatemala (502) 2362–4762, fax 6630–5839; email: erick.villagran@gmail.com.

Japan:

Katsuma Hanafusa, Fisheries Agency of Japan, 1–2–1 Chome Kasumigaseki, Chiyoda-ku, 100–8907 Tokyo, Japan (81–3) 3591–1086, fax 3502–0571; email: katsuma_hanafusa@nm.maff.go.jp.

Masahiro Ishikawa, Federation of Japan Tuna Fish Co-operative Associations, 2–3–22 Kudankita Chiyoda-Ku, 102 Tokyo, Japan (81–3) 326–46167 or 326–46161, fax 323–47455; email: section1@intldiv.japantuna.or.jp.

Ryotaro Suzuki, Ministry of Foreign Affairs, 2–11–1 Shibakouen, Minato, 105–8519 Tokyo, Japan (81–3) 3580–3311, fax 6402–2233.

Korea:

Yang-Soo Kim, Ministry of Maritime Affairs and Fisheries, 140–2 Gye-dong, Jongno-gu, 110–793 Seoul, Korea (82–2) 3674–6990, fax 3674–6996; email: kys5196@momaf.go.kr.

Kwang Youl Park, Ministry of Maritime Affairs and Fisheries, 140–2 Gye-dong, Jongno-gu, 110–793 Seoul, Korea, (82–2) 3674–6990, fax 3674–6996; email: icdmomaf@chol.com.

Kyu Jin Seok, Ministry of Maritime Affairs and Fisheries, 140–2 Gye-dong, Jongno-gu, 110–793 Seoul, Korea (82–2) 3673–6994, fax 3674–6996; email: icdmomaf@chol.com.

Mexico:

Miguel A. Cisneros, Instituto Nacional de la Pesca, Pitágoras 1320, Sta Cruz Atoyac, D.F. 03310 México, México (52–55) 5422–3002 or 5688–1469, fax 5604–9169.

Dr. Ramón Corral, CONAPESCA / Comisión Nacional de Acuicultura y Pesca, Av. Camarón-Sabalo S/N Esquina Tiburón, SIN 82100 Mazatlán, México (52–669) 913–0904, fax 913–0904; email: rcorrala@sagarpa.gob.mx.

Michel Dreyfus, Instituto Nacional de la Pesca, Campus CICESE Carretera Tijuana-Ensenada, B.C.N. 22890 Ensenada, México (52–646) 174–5637, fax 174–563; email: dreyfus@cicese.mx.

Panama:

María Patricia Díaz, Apartado 8062 Zona 7, Panamá, Panamá (507) 269–0233, fax 269–2731; email: mpdiaz@robleslaw.com.

Ing. Arnulfo L. Franco, FIPESCA, Clayton 404–A, Panamá, Panamá (507) 677–1000, fax 317–0547; email: afranco@cwpanama.net.

Leika Martinez, Autoridad Marítima de Panamá, Apartado 8062 Zona 7, Panamá, Panamá (507) 232–8570 or 232–6117, fax 232–6477; email: lmartinez@amp.gob.pa.

George Novey, Autoridad Marítima de Panamá, Apartado Postal 8062, Zona 7, Panamá, Panamá (507) 232–8570 or 232–6117, fax 232–6477; email: gnovey@amp.gob.pa.

Peru:

Jorge Vértiz Calderón, Ministerio de Producción (Pesquería), Calle 1 Oeste 60, Urb. Córpac, Lima 27, San Isidro, Perú (51–1) 224–3423, fax 224–2381; email: jvertiz@produce.gob.pe.

Gladys Cárdenas, Instituto del Mar del Perú, Apartado Postal 22, Lima, Callao, Perú (51–1) 429–7630, ext. 2, fax 420–0144; email: gcardenas@imarpe.gob.pe.

Alfonso Miranda, Ministerio de la Producción (Pesqueria), Calle Uno Oeste Nro. 060 Urbanización Corpac, Lima, Perú, Lima 27 (51–1) 224–3334 or 224–3416, fax 616–2222; email: amiranda@minproduce.gob.pe.

Elvira Velásquez, Ministerio de Relaciones Exteriores, Jr. Lampa 545 7mo piso, Lima, Perú, Lima 1 (51–1) 311–2657, fax 311–2659; email: evelasquez@rree.gob.pe.

Liliana Gomez de Weston, Ministerio de Relaciones Exteriores del Perú; email: lgomez@rree.gob.pe.

Spain:

Rafael Centenera, Secretaría General de Relaciones Pesqueras Internacionales, C. Ortega y Gasset, 57, 28006 Madrid, Spain (34–91) 347–6040 or 647–6041, fax 347–6042; email: acuintpm@mpa.es.

Fernando Curcio, Secretaría General de Pesca Marítima, José Ortega y Gasset, 57, 28006 Madrid, Spain (34–91) 347–6030 or 347–6031, fax 347–6032; email: drpesmar@mapya.es.

Samuel Juarez, Embajada de España, 2375 Pennsylvania Avenue, NW., Washington, DC 20037 USA (202) 728–2339, fax 728–2320; email: juarez@mapausa.org.

United States:

Scott Burns, World Wildlife Fund, 1250 24th Street, NW., Washington, DC 20037 USA (202) 778–9547 or 293–4800, fax 887–5293; email: scott.burns@wwfus.org.

Robert C. Fletcher, Sportfishing Association of California, 1084 Bangor Street, San Diego, CA 92106 USA (619) 226–6455, fax 226–0175; email: dart@sacemup.org.

Rodney McInnis, NMFS / National Marine Fisheries Services, 501 West Ocean Boulevard, Suite 4200, Long Beach, CA 90802–4213 USA (562) 980–4001, fax 980–4018; email: rod.mcinnis@noaa.gov.

Patrick Rose, P.O. Box 7242, Rancho Santa Fe, CA 92067 USA (858) 756–2733, fax 756–5850; email: skyline756@aol.com.

Vanuatu:

Moses Amos, Ministry of Agriculture, Quarentine * Inspection Service, Forestry and Fisheries, Private Mail Bag 9045, Port Vila, Vanuatu (678) 23119 or 23621, fax 23641; email: mosesamos@vanuatu.com.vu.

Christophe Emelec, Tuna Fishing (Vanuatu) Limited, P.O. Box 1640 Socapore Area, Lini Highway, Port Vila, Vanuatu (678) 25887, fax 25608; email: tunafishing@vanuatu.com.vu.

Dimitri Malvirlani, Vanuatu Maritime Authority, Maine Quay, P.O. Box 320, Port Vila, Vanuatu (678) 23128, fax 22949; email: vma@vanuatu.com.vu.

Venezuela:

Alvin Delgado, PNOV/FUNDATUN, Edif. San Pablo, P.H., Av. Ppal, El Dique, 6101 Cumaná, Venezuela (58–293) 433–0431, fax 433–0431; email: fundatunpnov@cantv.net, fundatunpnov@yahoo.com.

Luis Felipe Del Moral Oraá, Instituto Nacional de Pesca y Acuacultura, Av. Páez del paraiso, Diagonal a la Plaza Washington Planta Baja, 1010 Caracas Venezuela (58–212) 461–9225 or 509–0384, fax 574–3587; email: presidencia@inapesca.gov.bc.

Nancy Tablante, Instituto Nacional de Pesca y Acuacultura, Torre Este, Piso 10, Parque Central, 1010 Caracas, Venezuela (58–212) 571–4889, fax 571–4889; email: ori@inapesca.gov.ve, heralica@cantv.net.

INTERNATIONAL BOUNDARY AND WATER COMMISSION, UNITED STATES AND MEXICO

UNITED STATES SECTION

The Commons, Building C, Suite 100, 4171 North Mesa, El Paso, TX 79902–1441

phone (915) 832–4100, fax 832–4190, http://www.ibwc.state.gov

Commissioner.—Carlos Marin, 832–4101.
Secretary.—William Harlow, 832–4105.
Principal Engineers: Ken Rakestraw (acting), 832–4160; Steve Smullen (acting), 832–4749.
Human Resources Director.—Kevin Petz, 832–4114.
General Counsel / Legal Advisor.—Susan Daniel, 832–4109.

MEXICAN SECTION

Avenida Universidad, No. 2180, Zona de El Chamizal, A.P. 1612–D, C.P. 32310,

Ciudad Juarez, Chihuahua, Mexico

P.O. Box 10525, El Paso, TX 79995.

phone 011–52–16–13–7311 or 011–52–16–13–7363 (Mexico)

Commissioner.—Arturo Herrera Solis.
Secretary.—Jose de Jesus Luevano Grano.
Principal Engineers: Gilberto Elizalde Hernandez, L. Antonio Rascon Mendoza.

INTERNATIONAL BOUNDARY COMMISSION, UNITED STATES AND CANADA

UNITED STATES SECTION

1250 23rd Street, NW., Suite 100, 20037, phone (202) 736–9100

Commissioner.—Dennis Schornack.
Deputy Commissioner.—Kyle Hipsley.
Administrative Officer.—Tracy Morris.

CANADIAN SECTION

615 Booth Street, Room 555, Ottawa ON, Canada K1A 0E9, phone (613) 995–4341

Commissioner.—Peter Sullivan.
Deputy Commissioner.—Al Arseneault.

INTERNATIONAL COTTON ADVISORY COMMITTEE

Headquarters: 1629 K Street, NW., Suite 702, 20006, secretariat@icac.org
phone (202) 463–6660, fax 463–6950

(Permanent Secretariat of the Organization)

MEMBER COUNTRIES

Argentina
Australia
Belgium
Benin
Brazil
Burkina Faso
Cameroon
Chad
China (Taiwan)
Colombia
Côte d'Ivoire
Egypt
Finland
France
Germany
Greece
India
Iran
Israel
Italy
Kazakhstan
Korea, Republic of
Mali
Netherlands
Nigeria
Pakistan
Paraguay
Philippines
Poland
Russia
South Africa
Spain
Sudan
Switzerland
Syria
Tanzania
Togo
Turkey
Uganda
United Kingdom
United States
Uzbekistan
Zambia
Zimbabwe

Executive Director.—Terry P. Townsend.
Statistician.—Armelle Gruere.
Economists: Carlos Valderrama; Andrei Guitchounts.
Head of Technical Information Section.—M. Rafiq Chaudhry.

INTERNATIONAL JOINT COMMISSION, UNITED STATES AND CANADA

UNITED STATES SECTION

1250 23rd Street, NW., Suite 100, 20440

phone (202) 736–9000, fax 467–0746, http://www.ijc.org

Chairman.—Dennis L. Schornack.
Commissioners: Irene B. Brooks, Allen I. Olson.
Secretary.—Elizabeth C. Bourget.
Legal Adviser.—James G. Chandler.
Engineering Adviser.—Mark Colosimo.
Public Information Officer.—Frank Bevacqua.
Ecologist.—Kay Austin.

CANADIAN SECTION

234 Laurier Avenue West, Ottawa, Ontario Canada K1P 6K6
phone (613) 995–2984, fax 993–5583

Chairman.—Rt. Hon. Herb Gray.
Commissioners: Jack Blaney, Robert Gourd.
Secretary.—Murray Clamen.
Legal Adviser.—Michael Vechsler.
Engineering Adviser.—Paul Pilon.
Senior Environmental Adviser.—Joel Weiner.

GREAT LAKES REGIONAL OFFICE

Eighth Floor, 100 Ouellette Avenue, Windsor, Ontario Canada N9A 6T3
phone (519) 257–6700 (Canada), (313) 226–2170 (U.S.)

Director.—Karen Vigmostad.
Public Affairs Officer.—Bruce Brown.

INTERNATIONAL LABOR ORGANIZATION

Headquarters: Geneva, Switzerland, http://www.ilo.org

Washington Office, 1828 L Street, NW., Suite 600, 20036

phone (202) 653–7652, fax 653–7687, washington@ilo.org

Liaison Office with the United Nations

220 East 42nd Street, Suite 3101, New York, NY 10017–5806

International Labor Office (Permanent Secretariat of the Organization)
Headquarters Geneva:
Director-General.—Juan Somavia.
Washington:
Director.—Armand Pereira.
Special Assistant to the Director.—Jesica Seacor.

INTERNATIONAL MONETARY FUND

700 19th Street, NW., 20431, phone (202) 623–7000

http://www.imf.org

MANAGEMENT AND SENIOR OFFICERS

Managing Director.—Rodrigo de Rato y Figaredo.
First Deputy Managing Director.—John Lipsky.
Deputy Managing Directors: Takatoshi Kato, Murilo Portugal.
Economic Counsellor.—Simon Johnson.
IMF Institute Director.—Leslie Lipschitz.
Legal Department General Counsel.—Sean Hagan.
Departmental Directors:
African.—Abdoulaye Bio-Tchané.
Asia and Pacific.—David Burton.
Budget and Planning.—Barry Potter.
European.—Michael C. Deppler.
External Relations.—Masood Ahmed.
Finance.—Michael Kuhn.
Fiscal Affairs.—Teresa Ter-Minassian.
Internal Audit and Inspection.—Bert Keuppens.
Middle Eastern.—Mohsin S. Khan.
Monetary and Capital Markets.—Jamie Caruana.
Policy Development and Review.—Mark Allen.

Research.—Simon Johnson.
Secretary.—Shailendra J. Anjaria.
Statistics.—Robert W. Edwards.
Technology and General Services.—Frank Harnischfeger.
Western Hemisphere.—Anoop Singh.
Director, Regional Office for Asia and the Pacific.—Akira Ariyoshi.
Director and Special Representative to the United Nations.—Reinhard Munzberg.

EXECUTIVE DIRECTORS AND ALTERNATES

Executive Directors:
Abdallah S. Alazzaz, represents Saudi Arabia.
Alternate.—Ahmed Al Nassar.
Pierre Duquesne, represents France.
Alternate.—Bertrand Dumont.
Tuomas Saarenheimo, represents Denmark, Estonia, Finland, Iceland, Latvia, Lithuania, Norway, Sweden.
Alternate.—Jon Thorvardur Sigurgeirsson.
Roberto Guarnieri, represents Costa Rica, El Salvador, Guatemala, Honduras, Mexico, Nicaragua, Spain, Venezuela (Republica Bolivariana de).
Alternate.—Ramón Guzmán.
Jonathan Fried, represents Antigua and Barbuda, the Bahamas, Barbados, Belize, Canada, Dominica, Grenada, Ireland, Jamaica, St. Kitts and Nevis, St. Lucia, St. Vincent and the Grenadines.
Alternate.—Peter Charleton.
Peter Gakunu, represents Angola, Botswana, Burundi, Eritrea, Ethiopia, Gambia, Kenya, Lesotho, Malawi, Mozambique, Namibia, Nigeria, Sierra Leone, South Africa, Sudan, Swaziland, Tanzania, Uganda, Zambia, Zimbabwe.
Alternate.—Samura Kamara.
Adarsh Kishore, represents Bangladesh, Bhutan, India, Sri Lanka.
Alternate.—Amal Uthum Herat.
Hooi Eng Phang, represents Brunei Darussalam, Cambodia, Fiji, Indonesia, Lao People's Democratic Republic, Malaysia, Myanmar, Nepal, Singapore, Thailand, Tonga, Vietnam.
Alternate.—Chantavarn Sucharitakul.
Thomas Moser, represents Azerbaijan, Kyrgyz Republic, Poland, Switzerland, Tajikistan, Turkmenistan, Uzbekistan, Serbia.
Alternate.—Andrzej Raczko.
Eduardo Loyo, represents Brazil, Colombia, Dominican Republic, Ecuador, Guyana, Haiti, Panama, Suriname, Trinidad and Tobago.
Alternate.—María Ines Agudelo.
Willy Kiekens, represents Austria, Belarus, Belgium, Czech Republic, Hungary, Kazakhstan, Luxembourg, Slovak Republic, Slovenia, Turkey.
Alternate.—Johann Prader.
Laurean W. Rutayisire, represents Benin, Burkina Faso, Cameroon, Cape Verde, Central African Republic, Chad, Comoros, Congo (Democratic Republic of), Congo (Republic of), Côte d'Ivoire, Djibouti, Equatorial Guinea, Gabon, Guinea, Guinea-Bissau, Madagascar, Mali, Mauritania, Mauritius, Niger, Rwanda, São Tomé and Principe, Senegal, Togo.
Alternate.—Kossi Assimaidou.
Arrigo Sadun, represents Albania, Greece, Italy, Malta, Portugal, San Marino.
Alternate.—Miranda Xafa.
Meg Lundsager (Alternate), represents United States.
Alternate.—Meg Lundsager.
Shigeo Kashiwagi, represents Japan.
Alternate.—Michio Kitahara.
Abbas Mirakhor, represents Afghanistan (Islamic State of), Algeria, Ghana, Iran (Islamic Republic of), Morocco, Pakistan, Tunisia.
Alternate.—Mohammed Daïri.
Javier Silva-Ruete, represents Argentina, Bolivia, Chile, Paraguay, Peru, Uruguay.
Alternate.—Héctor R. Torres.
Klaus D. Stein, represents Germany.
Alternate.—Stephan von Stenglin.
A. Shakour Shaalan, represents Bahrain, Egypt, Iraq, Jordan, Kuwait, Lebanon, Libya Arab, Jamahiriya, Maldives, Oman, Qatar, Syrian Arab Republic, United Arab Emirates, Yemen (Republic of).

Alternate.—Samir El-Khouri.
Aleksei V. Mozhin, represents Russian Federation.
Alternate.—Andrei Lushin.
Richard Murray, represents Australia, Kiribati, Korea, Marshall Islands, Micronesia (Federated States of), Mongolia, New Zealand, Palau, Papua New Guinea, Philippines, Samoa, Seychelles, Solomon Islands, Vanuatu.
Alternate.—Wilhelmina C. Mañalac.
Jeroen Kremers, represents Armenia, Bosnia and Herzegovina, Bulgaria, Croatia, Cyprus, Georgia, Israel, Macedonia (former Yugoslav Republic of), Moldova, Montenegro Republic, Netherlands, Romania, Ukraine.
Alternate.—Yuriy G. Yakusha.
G.E. Huayong, represents China.
Alternate.—H.E. Jianxiong.
Tom Scholar, represents United Kingdom.
Alternate.—Jens Larsen.

INTERNATIONAL ORGANIZATION FOR MIGRATION

Headquarters: 17 Route Des Morillons (PO Box 71), CH1211, Geneva 19, Switzerland

Washington Mission: 1752 N Street, NW., Suite 700, 20036, phone (202) 862–1826

New York Mission: 122 East 42nd Street, Suite 1610, New York, NY 10168–1610 phone (212) 681–7000

HEADQUARTERS

Director General.—Brunson McKinley (United States).
Deputy Director General.—Ndioro Ndiaye (Senegal).
Washington Regional Representative.—Richard E. Scott (United States).
New York Chief of Mission.—Michael Gray (United States).
Permanent Observer to the United Nations.—Luca Dall'Oglio (Italy).

MEMBER STATES

Afghanistan
Albania
Algeria
Angola
Argentina
Armenia
Australia
Austria
Azerbaijan
Bahamas
Bangladesh
Belarus
Belgium
Belize
Benin
Bolivia
Bosnia and Herzegovina
Brazil
Bulgaria
Burkina Faso
Cambodia
Cameroon
Canada
Cape Verde
Chile
Colombia
Congo
Costa Rica
Côte d'Ivoire
Croatia
Cyprus
Czech Republic
Democratic Republic of the Congo
Denmark
Dominican Republic
Ecuador
Egypt
El Salvador
Estonia
Finland
France
Gabon
Gambia
Georgia
Germany
Ghana
Greece
Guatemala
Guinea
Guinea-Bissau
Haiti
Honduras
Hungary
Iran, Islamic Republic of
Ireland
Israel
Italy
Jamaica
Japan
Jordan
Kazakhstan
Kenya
Kyrgyzstan
Latvia
Liberia
Libyan Arab Jamahiriya
Lithuania
Luxembourg
Madagascar
Mali
Malta
Mauritania
Mexico
Montenegro
Morocco
Nepal
Netherlands
New Zealand
Nicaragua

Nigeria
Niger (the)
Norway
Pakistan
Panama
Paraguay
Peru
Philippines
Poland
Portugal
Republic of Korea
Republic of Mauritius
Republic of Moldova
Romania
Rwanda
Senegal
Serbia
Sierra Leone
Slovakia
Slovenia
South Africa
Spain
Sri Lanka
Sudan
Sweden
Switzerland
Tajikistan
Thailand
Togo
Tunisia
Turkey
Uganda
Ukraine
United Kingdom of Great Britain and Northern Ireland
United Republic of Tanzania
United States of America
Uruguay
Venezuela, Bolivarian Republic of
Yemen
Zambia
Zimbabwe

STATES WITH OBSERVER STATUS

Belarus
Burundi
China
Cuba
Ethiopia
Guyana
Holy See
India
Indonesia
Mozambique
Namibia
Papua New Guinea
Russian Federation
San Marino
Sao Tomé and Principe
Somalia
Spain
The former Yugoslav Republic of Macedonia
Turkmenistan
Viet Nam

IOM OVERSEAS LIAISON AND OPERATIONAL OFFICES

Afghanistan, Herat, Kabul
Albania, Tirana
Angola, Luanda
Argentina, Buenos Aires *
Armenia, Yerevan
Australia, Canberra *
Austria, Wien *
Azerbaijan, Baku
Bangladesh, Dhaka *
Belarus, Minsk
Belgium / Luxembourg, Bruxelles *
Bolivia, La Paz
Bosnia and Herzegovina, Sarajevo
Bulgaria, Sofia
Cambodia, Phnom Penh
Canada, Ottawa, Ontario
Chile, Santiago de Chile
China, Hong Kong
Colombia, Santafé de Bogotá
Congo, Brazzaville
Congo, (Democratic Republic of), Gombe, Kinshasa
Costa Rica, San José *
Côte D'Ivoire, Abidjan
Croatia, Zagreb
Czech Republic, Praha
Dominican Republic, Santo Domingo
Ecuador, Quito
Egypt, Cairo *
El Salvador, San Salvador
Estonia, Tallinn
Ethiopia, Addis Ababa
Finland, Helsinki *
France, Paris
Gambia, Banjul
Georgia, Tbilisi
Germany, Berlin, Bonn
Ghana, Accra North
Greece, Athens
Guatemala, Ciudad de Guatemala
Guinea, Conakry
Guinea-Bissau, Guinea Bissau
Haita, Port au Prince
Honduras, Tegucigalpa
Hungary, Budapest *
India, Ahmedabad
Indonesia, Jakarta, Kupang
Iran, Tehran
Iraq, Amman
Ireland, Dublin
Italy, Roma *
Jamaica, Kingston
Japan, Tokyo
Jordan, Amman
Kazakhstan, Almaty
Kenya, Nairobi *
Korea (Republic of), Seoul
Kuwait, Kuwait City
Kyrgyzstan, Bishkek City
Latvia, Riga
Liberia, Monrovia
Lithuania, Vilnius
Macedonia, Skopje
Mali, Bamako
Mexico, Mexico DF
Moldova, (Republic of) Chisinau
Morocco, Rabat
Mozambique, Maputo
Namibia, Windhoek
Nauru (Republic of)
Netherlands, Den Haag
Nicaragua, Managua
Nigeria, Abuja
Norway, Oslo
Pakistan, Islamabad *
Papua New Guinea, Manus
Peru, Lima *
Philippines, Metro Manila *
Poland, Warszawa
Portugal, Lisboa
Romania, Bucharest
Russia, Moscow
Saudi Arabia, Riyadh
Senegal, Dakar *
Serbia and Montenegro, Belgrade, Prishtina
Sierra Leone, Freetown
Slovak Republic, Bratislava
Slovenia, Ljubljana
South Africa, Pretoria *
Spain, Madrid
Sri Lanka, Colombo
Sudan, Khartoum
Switzerland, Bern
Syrian Arab Republic, Damascus
Tajikistan, Dushanbe
Tanzania, Dar es Salaam
Thailand, Bangkok *
Timor Leste, Dili
Tunisia, Tunis

Turkey, Ankara
Turkmenistan, Ashgabad
Uganda, Kampala
Ukraine, Kyiv
United Kingdom, London
United States of America, Washington*, New York*, Los Angeles, Miami, Rosemont
Uruguay, Montevideo
Uzbekistan, Tashkent
Venezuela, Caracas
Vietnam, Hanoi, Ho Chi Minh City
Yemen, Yemen
Zambia, Lusaka
Zimbabwe, Harare

INTERNATIONAL PACIFIC HALIBUT COMMISSION, UNITED STATES AND CANADA

Headquarters: University of Washington, Seattle, WA 98195
phone (206) 634–1838, fax 632–2983
Mailing address: PO Box 95009, Seattle WA 98145–2009

American Commissioners:

Ralph G. Hoard, 4019 21st Avenue W., Seattle, WA 98199, (206) 282–0988, fax 281–0329.

Phillip Lestenkof, P.O. Box 288, St. Paul Island, AK 99660, (907) 546–2597.

Dr. Jim Balsiger, National Marine Fisheries Service, PO Box 21668, Juneau, AK 99802, (907) 586–7221, fax 586–7249.

Canadian Commissioners:

Dr. Laura Richards, Pacific Biological Station, 3190 Hammond Bay Road, Nanaimo, B.C., Canada V9T 6N7, (250) 729–8369, fax 756–7053.

Cliff Atleo, 3546 Huff Drive, Port Alberni, BC, Canada V9Y 8B4, (250) 723–0188, fax 723–1393.

Gary Robinson, 7055 Vivian Drive, Vancouver, BC, Canada V5S 2V2 (604) 321–8244, fax 321–8264.

Director and Secretary (ex officio).—Dr. Bruce M. Leaman, PO Box 95009, Seattle, WA 98145–2009.

ORGANIZATION OF AMERICAN STATES

17th Street and Constitution Avenue, NW., 20006
phone (202) 458–3000, fax 458–3967

PERMANENT MISSIONS TO THE OAS

Antigua and Barbuda.—Ambassador Deborah Mae-Lovell, Permanent Representative, 3216 New Mexico Avenue, NW., 20016, phone 362–5122 / 5166 / 5211, fax 362–5225.

Argentina.—Ambassador Rodolfo Gil, Permanent Representative, 1816 Corcoran Street, NW., 20009, phone 387–4142 / 4146 / 4170, fax 328–1591.

The Bahamas.—Ambassador Joshua Sears, Permanent Representative, 2220 Massachusetts Avenue, NW., 20008, phone 319–2660 to 2667, fax 319–2668.

Barbados.—Ambassador Michael I. King, Permanent Representative, 2144 Wyoming Avenue, NW., 20008, phone 939–9200 / 9201 / 9202, fax 332–7467.

Belize.—Ambassador Lisa Shoman, Permanent Representative, 2535 Massachusetts Avenue, NW., 20008–3098, phone 332–9636, ext. 228, fax 332–6888.

Bolivia.—Ambassador Reynaldo Cuadros Anaya, Permanent Representative, 1620 I Street, NW., Suite 703, 20006, phone 785–0218 / 0219 / 0224, fax 296–0563.

Brazil.—Ambassador Osmar Chohfi, Permanent Representative, 2600 Virginia Avenue, NW., Suite 412, 20037, phone 333–4224 / 4225 / 4226, fax 333–6610.

Canada.—Ambassador Graeme C. Clark, Permanent Representative, 501 Pennsylvania Avenue, NW., 20001, phone 682–1768, Ext. 7724, fax 682–7624.

Chile.—Ambassador Pedro Oyarce, Permanent Representative,, 2000 L Street, NW., Suite 720, 20036, phone 887–5475 / 5476 / 5477, fax 775–0713.

Colombia.—Ambassador Camilio Alfonso Ospina, Permanent Representative, 1609 22nd Street, NW., 20008, phone 332–8003 / 8004, fax 234–9781.

Costa Rica.—Ambassador Javier Sancho Bonilla, Permanent Representative, 2112 S Street, NW., Suite 300, 20008, phone 234–9280 / 9281, fax 986–2274.

* Mission with Regional Functions.

Dominica.—Ambassador Swinburne A.S. Lestrade, Permanent Representative, 3216 New Mexico Avenue, NW., 20016, phone 364–6781, fax 364–6791.

Dominican Republic.—Ambassador Roberto Alvarez, Permanent Representative, 1715 22nd Street, NW., 20008, phone 332–9142 / 0616 / 0772, fax 232–5038.

Ecuador.—Gustavo Palacio, Interim Representative, 2535 15th Street, NW., 20009, phone 234–1494 / 1692 / 8053, fax 667–3482.

El Salvador.—Ambassador Abigail Castro de Perez, Permanent Representative, 1400 16tth Street, NW., 20036, phone 595–7546 / 7545, fax 232–4806.

Grenada.—Ambassador Denis G. Antoine, Permanent Representative, 1701 New Hampshire Avenue, NW., 20009, phone 265–2561, fax 265–2468.

Guatemala.—Ambassador Francisco Villagran de León, Permanent Representative, 1507 22nd Street, NW., 20037, phone 833–4015 / 4016 / 4017, fax 833–4011.

Guyana.—Ambassador Bayney R. Karran, Permanent Representative, 2490 Tracy Place, NW., 20008, phone 265–6900 / 6901, fax 232–1297.

Haiti.—Ambassador Duly Brutus, Permanent Representative, 2311 Massachusetts Avenue, NW., 20008, phone 332–4090 / 4096, fax 518–8742.

Honduras.—Ambassador Carlos Sosa Coello, Permanent Representative, 5100 Wisconsin Avenue, NW., Suite 403, 20016, phone 362–9656 / 9657, fax 537–7170.

Jamaica.—Ambassador Gordon Valentine Shirley, Permanent Representative, 1520 New Hampshire Avenue, NW., 20036, phone 986–0121 / 0123 / 452–0660, fax 452–9395.

Mexico.—Ambassador Alejandro Garcia Moreno Elizondo, Permanent Representative, 2440 Massachusetts Avenue, NW., 20008, phone 332–3663 / 3664 / 3984, fax 234–0602.

Nicaragua.—Lila Maria Bolaños Chamoro, Interim Representative, 1627 New Hampshire Avenue, NW., 20009, phone 332–1643 / 1644 / 939–6536, fax 745–0710.

Panama.—Ambassador Aristides Royo, Permanent Representative, 2201 Wisconsin Avenue, NW., Suite C100, 20007, phone 965–4826 / 4819, fax 965–4836.

Paraguay.—Ambassador Manuel Maria Cáceres, Permanent Representative, 2022 Connecticut Avenue, NW., 20008, phone 232–8020 / 8021 / 8022, fax 244–3005.

Peru.—Ambassador Antero Flores-Araoz, Permanent Representative, 1901 Pennsylvania Avenue, NW., Suite 402, 20006, phone 232–2281 / 2282 / 1973, fax 466–3068.

Saint Kitts and Nevis.—Ambassador Dr. Izben C. Williams, Permanent Representative, 3216 New Mexico Avenue, NW., 20016, phone 686–2636, fax 686–5740.

Saint Lucia.—Clenie Greer-Lacascade, Interim Representative, 3216 New Mexico Avenue, NW., 20016, phone 364–6792 to 6795, fax 364–6723.

Saint Vincent and The Grenadines.— Ambassador Ellsworth I.A. John, Permanent Representative, 3216 New Mexico Avenue, NW., 20016, phone 364–6730, fax 364–6736.

Suriname.—Ambassador Jacques R.C. Kross, Permanent Representative, 4301 Connecticut Avenue, NW., Suite 462, 20008, phone 244–7488 / 7590 / 7591 / 7592, fax 244–5878.

Trinidad and Tobago.—Ambassador Marina Valere, Permanent Representative, 1708 Massachusetts Avenue, NW., 20036–1903, phone 467–6490, fax 785–3130.

United States of America.—J. Robert Manzanares, Interim Representative, WHA / USOAS Bureau of Western Hemisphere Affairs, Department of State, Room 5914, 20520–6258, phone 647–9376, fax 647–0911 / 6973.

Uruguay.—Ambassador María del Luján Flores, Permanent Representative, 2801 New Mexico Avenue, NW., Suite 1210, 20007, phone 333–0588 / 0687, fax 337–3758.

Venezuela.—Ambassador Jorge Valero, Permanent Representative, 1099 30th Street, NW., Second Floor, 20007, phone 342–5837 / 5838 / 5839 / 5840 / 5841, fax 625–5657.

GENERAL SECRETARIAT

Secretary General.—José Miguel Insulza, 458–3000.
  Chief of Staff to the Secretary General.—Ricardo Domínguez, 458–3705.
Assistant Secretary General.—Albert R. Ramdin, 458–6046, fax 458–3011.
  Chief of Staff to the Assistant Secretary General.—Sherry Tross, 458–3497.
Executive Secretary for—
  Integral Development.—Alfonso Quiñónez, 458–3510.
  Inter-American Commission on Human Rights.—Santiago A. Canton, 458–6002.
Under Secretary for—
  Administration and Finance.—Frank Almaguer, 458–3436.
  Multidimensional Security.—Alexandre Addor-Neto, 458–6010.
  Political Affairs.—Dante Caputo, 458–3589.
Director, Department of:
  External Relations.—Irene Klinger, 458–6072.
  Legal Services.—Louis G. Ferrand, 458–3415.
  Press and Communications.—Patricia Esquenazi, 458–6829.
Director, Summits Secretariat.—Carmen Marina Gutiérrez, 458–3127.

ORGANIZATION FOR ECONOMIC COOPERATION AND DEVELOPMENT

Headquarters: 2 rue André-Pascal, 75775 Paris CEDEX 16, France
phone (331) 4524–8200, fax 4524–8500

Secretary-General.—Angel Gurria.
Deputy Secretaries General: Mari Amano, Thelma J. Askey, Aart Jan de Geus, Pier Carlo Padoan.

Member Countries:

Australia
Austria
Belgium
Canada
Czech Republic
Denmark
Finland
France
Germany
Greece
Hungary
Iceland
Ireland
Italy
Japan
Korea
Luxembourg
Mexico
Netherlands
New Zealand
Norway
Poland
Portugal
Slovak Republic
Spain
Sweden
Switzerland
Turkey
United Kingdom
United States

OECD WASHINGTON CENTER

2001 L Street, NW., Suite 650, 20036, phone (202) 785–6323, fax 785–0350

http://www.oecdwash.org

Head of Center.—Sandra Wilson.

PAN AMERICAN HEALTH ORGANIZATION (PAHO)
REGIONAL OFFICE OF THE WORLD HEALTH ORGANIZATION

525 23rd Street, NW., 20037, phone (202) 974–3000
fax 974–3663

Director.—Dr. Mirta Roses Periago, 974–3408.
Assistant Director.—Carissa Etienne, 974–3404.
Director of Administration.—Michael A. Boorstein, 974–3412.

PAHO / WHO FIELD OFFICES
OPS / WHO OFICINAS DE LOS REPRESENTANTES EN LOS PAISES

Caribbean Program Coordinator (Antigua and Barbuda, Barbados, Dominica, Grenada, St. Kitts and Nevis, Saint Lucia, St. Vincent and the Grenadines. Eastern Caribbean: Anguilla, British Virgin Islands, Montserrat. French Antilles: Guadaloupe, Martinique, St. Martin and St. Bartholomew, French Guiana).—Dr. Bernadette Theodore-Gandi, P.O. Box 508, Dayralls and Navy Garden Roads, Christ Church, Bridgetown, Barbados, phone (246) 426–3860 / 3865 / 427–9434, fax 436–9779, email: email@cpc.paho.org, http://www.cpc.paho.org.

PAHO / WHO Representatives:

Argentina.—Dr. José Antonio Pagés, Marcelo T. de Alvear 684, 4o. piso, 1058 Buenos Aires, Argentina, phone (54–11) 4319–4200, fax 4319–4201, e-mail: info@ops.org.ar, http://www.ops.org.ar.

Bahamas (Turks and Caicos).—Lynda Rae Campbell, Union Court, Elizabeth Avenue, P.O. Box N 4833, Nassau, Bahamas, phone (242) 326–3390 / 7299 / 325–0121, fax 326–7012, email: email@bah.paho.org.

Belize.—Dr. D. Beverly Barnett, No. 168 Newtown Barracks, P.O. Box 1834, Belize City, Belize, phone (501–2) 448–85 / 52 / 445–36, fax 309–17, e-mail: admin@blz.paho.org, http://www.blz.paho.org.

Bolivia.—Dr. Christian Darras, Calle Víctor Sanjines 2678, Edificio Torre Barcelona, pisos 1, 6 y 7, Zona Sopocachi, Casillas Postales 9790 y 2504, La Paz, Bolivia, phone (591–2) 412–465 / 303 / 313, fax 412–598, e-mail: pwrbol@bol.ops-oms.org, http://www.ops.org.bo.

Brazil.—Diego Victoria, Setor de Embaixadas Norte, Lote 19, 70800–400, Caixa Postal 08–729, Brasilia, D.F., Brasil, phone (55–61) 426–9595 / 9500 / 9550, fax 426–9591, email: email@bra.ops-oms.org, http://www.opas.org.br/.

Chile.—Dr. Juan Manuel Sotelo Figueiredo, Avenida Providencia No. 1017, Piso 4 y 5, Casilla 9459, Santiago, Chile, phone (56–2) 264–9300, fax 264–9311, email: email@chi.ops-oms.org, http://www.chi.ops-oms.org.

Colombia.—Dr. Pier Paolo Balladelli, Carrera 7 No. 74–21, Piso 9, Edificio Seguros Aurora, Apartado Aéreo 253367, Santa Fé de Bogotá, D.C., Colombia, phone (57–1) 314–4141 / 254–7050, fax 254–7070, e-mail: ops-col@latino.net.co, http://www.col.ops-oms.org/.

Costa Rica.—Dr. Carlos Samayoa, Calle 16, Avenida 6 y 8, Distrito Hospital, Apartado 3475, San José, Costa Rica, phone (506) 258–5810 / 257–5930 / 6034, fax 258–5830, email: email@cor.ops-oms.org, http://www.cor.ops-oms.org.

Cuba.—Dra. Lea Guido, Calle 4 No. 407, entre 17 y 19 Vedado, Apartado Postal 68, La Habana, Cuba C.P. 10400, phone (53–7) 831–0245 / 8944 / 855–2526 / 2527 / 853–5808, fax 833–2075 / 866–2075, e-mail: pwr@cub.ops-oms.org or cruzmari@cub.ops-oms.org, http://www.cub.ops-oms.org.

Dominican Republic.—Dr. Ana Cristina Nogueira, Edificio Cruz Roja y OPS / OMS, Calle Pepillo Salcedo—Recta Final, Plaza de la Salud, Ensanche La Fé, Apartado Postal 1464, Santo Domingo, República Dominicana, phone (809) 562–1519 / 544–3241, fax 544–0322, email: email@dor.ops-oms.org, http://www.dor.ops-oms.org.

Ecuador.—Dr. José Luis Prosperi a.i., Av. Amazonas 2889 y Mariana de Jesús, Apartado Postal 17–07–8982, Quito, Ecuador, phone (593–2) 246–0330 / 0332 / 0296 / 0215, fax 246–0325, e-mail: dvictoria@ecu.ops-oms.org, http://www.opsecu.org.ec.

El Salvador.—Dr. Ramon Granados a.i., 73 Avenida Sur No. 135, Colonia Escalón, Apartado Postal 1072, Sucursal Central, San Salvador, El Salvador, phone (503) 298–3491 / 3306 / 0021 / 279–1591 / 4231 / 1650 / 223–8372 / 5582, fax 298–1168, email: email@els.ops-oms.org, http://www.ops.org.sv/.

Guatemala.—Dr. Joaquín Molina, Edificio Etisa, Plaza España, 7a Avenida 12–23, Zona 9, Apartado Postal 383, Guatemala, Guatemala, phone (011–502) 332–2032 / 334–3803 / 331–0583, fax 334–3804, http://www.ops.org.gt.

Guyana.—Dr. Enias Baganizi, a.i., Lot 8 Brickdam Stabroek, P.O. Box 10969, Georgetown, Guyana, phone (592) 225–3000 / 227–5150 / 5158 / 5159 / 6371 / 223–6372, fax 226–6654 / 227–4205, email: email@guy.paho.org.

Haiti.—Paulo F. Piza Teixeira, No. 295 Avenue John Brown, Boite Postale 1330, Port-au-Prince, Haiti, phone (509) 245–4553 / 5315 / 5930 / 8695 / 224–7675 / 7676, fax 245–6917, email: email@hai.ops-oms.org.

Honduras.—Dr. Lilian Reneau-Vernon, Edificio Imperial, 6o.y 7o.piso, Avenida República de Panamá, Frente a la Casa de Naciones Unidas, Apartado Postal 728, Tegucigalpa MDC, Honduras, phone (504) 221–6091 / 6093 / 6094 / 6095 / 6101 / 6102, fax 221–6103, email: email@hon.ops-oms.org, http://www.paho-who.hn.

Jamaica (Bermuda and Cayman).—Dr. Ernest Pate, Old Oceana Building, 7th Floor, 2–4 King St., P.O. Box 384, Cross Roads, Kingston 5, Jamaica, phone (876) 967–4626 / 4691 / 5198 / 922–4630 / 4424, fax 967–5189, email: email@jam.ops-oms.org.

Mexico.—Dr. Gustavo Bergonzoli, Edificio Torre Prisma, Blvd. Manuel Ávila Camacho No. 191, Piso 3, Oficina 305, Colonia Los Morales Polanco, Apartado Postal 10–880 y 37–473, México D.F., 11510, México, phone (52–55) 5089–0860 / 5395–9060, fax 5395–5681, email: email@mex.ops-oms.org, http://www.mex.ops-oms.org.

Nicaragua.—Dr. Soccoro Gross Galiano, Complejo Nacional de Salud, Camino a la Sabana, Apartado Postal 1309, Managua, Nicaragua, phone (505) 289–4200 / 4800, fax 289–4999, email: email@nic.ops-oms.org, http://www.ops.org.ni.

Panama.—Dra. Guadalupe Verdejo, Ministerio de Salud de Panamá, Ancon, Avenida Gorgas, Edificio 261, 2o piso, Apartado Postal 0843–3441, Panamá, Republica de Panamá, phone (507) 262–0030 / 1996, fax 262–4052, email: email@pan.ops-oms.org, http://ops-oms.org.pa.

Paraguay.—Dra. Carmen Rosa Serrano, Edificio ''Faro del Río'' Mcal López 957 Esq. Estados Unidos, Casilla de Correo 839, Asunción, Paraguay, phone (595–21) 450–495 / 496 / 497 / 499 / 499–864, fax 450–498, email: email@par.ops-oms.org, http://www.par.ops-oms.org.

Peru.—Dr. Manuel Peña, Los Cedros 269, San Isidro, Lima 27, Perú Castilla 2117 Lima 100, Perú, phone (51–1) 421–3030 / 442–4471, fax 222–6405, http://www.per.ops.oms.org.

Puerto Rico.—Dr. Raúl Castellanos Bran, P.O. Box 70184, San Juan, Puerto Rico 00936, phone (787) 274–7608, fax 250–6547 / 767–8341.

Suriname.—Dr. Stephen Simon, Burenstraat #33 (PPS Building), P.O. Box 1863, Paramaribo, Suriname, phone (597) 471–676, fax 471–568, email: email@sur.paho.org.

Trinidad and Tobago.—Dr. Carol Boyd-Scobie, 49 Jerningham Avenue, P.O. Box 898, Port-of-Spain, Trinidad, phone (868) 624–7524 / 4376 / 5642 / 5928 / 625–4492, fax 624–5643, email: email@trt.paho.org.

United States–Mexico Border.—Dr. María Teresa Cerqueira, 5400 Suncrest Drive, Suite C–4, El Paso, TX 79912, United States of America, phone (915) 845–5950, fax 845–4361, email: email@fep.paho.org, http://www.fep.paho.org/.

Uruguay.—Dr. José Fernando Dora, Avenida Brasil 2697, Aptos. 5, 6 y 8, 2do. Piso, Casilla de Correo 1821, 11300, Montevideo, Uruguay, phone (598–2) 707–3589 / 3590, fax 707–3530, e-mail: pwr@uru.ops-oms.org, http://www.ops.org.uy/.

Venezuela (Netherlands Antilles).—Dr. Renato d'Affonseca Gusmão, Avenida Sexta entre 5a y 6a, Apartado 6722, Carmelitas, Transversal, Altamira, Caracas 1010, Venezuela, phone (212) 261–6090 / 262–2985 / 0718 / 265–0403 / 267–1622, fax 261–6069 / 262–0718, email: email@ven.ops-oms.org, http://www.ops-oms.org.ve/.

CENTERS

Caribbean Epidemiology Center (CAREC).—Dr. Glenda E. Maynard, 16–18 Jamaica Boulevard, Federation Park, P.O. Box 164, Port-of-Spain, Trinidad, phone (1–868) 622–4261 / 4262 / 3168 / 3277, fax 622–2792, e-mail: email@carec.ops-oms.org.

Caribbean Food and Nutrition Institute (CFNI).—Dr. Fitzroy J. Henry, University of the West Indies, P.O. Box 140–Mona, Kingston 7, Jamaica, phone (1–876), 927–1540 / 1541 / 1927, fax 927–2657, e-mail: e-mail@cfni.paho.org.

Institute of Nutrition of Central America and Panama (INCAP).—Dr. Hernán Delgado, Carretera Roosevelt, Zona 11, Apartado Postal 1188, Guatemala, Guatemala, phone (502) 471–5655 / 472–3762, fax 473–6529, e-mail: email@incap.ops-oms.org, Biblioteca Virtual en Salud: http://www.incap.bvssan.org.gt.

Latin American and Caribbean Center on Health Sciences Information (BIREME).—Abel Laerte Packer, Rua Botucatú 862, Vila Clementino, Caixa Postal 20381, CEP.04023–062, São Paulo, SP, Brasil, phone (55–11) 5576–9800 / 5549–2611, fax 575–8868, e-mail: email@bireme.ops-oms.org.

Latin American Center for Perinatology and Human Development (CLAP).—Dr. Ricardo Fescina, Hospital de Clínicas, Piso 16, Casilla de Correo 627, Montevideo, Uruguay, phone (598–2) 487–2929 / 2930 / 2931 / 2933, fax 487–2593, e-mail: postmaster@clap.ops-oms.org.

Pan American Center for Sanitary Engineering and Environmental Sciences (CEPIS).—Dr. Mauricio Pardón Ojeda, Calle Los Pinos 251, Urbanización Camacho, Casilla Postal 4337, Lima 100, Perú, phone 437–1077 / 7081, fax 437–8289, e-mail: cepis@cepis.ops-oms.org.

Pan American Foot-and-Mouth Disease Center (PANAFTOSA).—Dr. Miguel Ángel Genovese Linares, Avenida Presidente Kennedy 7778, (Antiga Estrada Rio-Petrópolis), São Bento, Duque de Caxias, CEP 25040–000, Caixa Postal 589, 20001 Rio de Janeiro, Brasil, phone (55–21) 3661–9000, fax 3661–9001; email: panaftosa@panaftosa.pos-oms.org.

PERMANENT JOINT BOARD ON DEFENSE, CANADA–UNITED STATES

CANADIAN SECTION

National Defence Headquarters, MG George R. Pearkes Building, Ottawa, ON Canada K1A OK2, phone (613) 992–4423

Members:

CANADACOM.—BG JPPJ Lacroix, Chief of Staff, Canada Command.

Defence Policy.—COL Michael Hachè, Director, Western Hemisphere Policy.

Foreign Affairs.—Dr. Robert McRae, Director, General International Security Bureau.

Military Secretary.—CDR David Peer, Directorate of Western Hemisphere Policy.

Military Policy.—MG Daniel Gosselin, Director, General International Security Policy.

NORAD.—LG Eric Findley, Deputy Commander.

Political Secretary.—Victor Rakmil, Deputy Director, Continental Defence Relations.

Privy Council.—BG Christopher Davis, Directory of Operations Defence / International Security.

Public Safety.—Peter Hill, Director, Emergency Management Policy.

UNITED STATES SECTION

JCS J–5 North America Division, Pentagon, Room 2E773, 20318

phone (703) 695–4477

Members:

DHS.—RDML Dan Lloyd (202) 282–8155.
Joint Staff.—MG Philip Breedlove, Room 2E800 (202) 697–9559.
State Department.—Alex Lee, Room 3917, State Department (202) 647–2273.
OSD.—Stephen Johnson (202) 697–3918.
National Security Council.—Cynthia Pendleton (202) 456–9135.
USNORTHCOM.—MG Mark Volcheff (719) 554–2200.
Military Secretary.—CDR Brian Devany (703) 695–4477.
Political Secretary.—Felix Hernandez, Room 3917, State Department (202) 647–2475.

SECRETARIAT OF THE PACIFIC COMMUNITY

B.P. D5, 98848 Noumea Cedex, New Caledonia, phone (687) 26.20.00, fax 26.38.18
E-mail: spc@spc.int, http://www.spc.int

Director-General.—Lourdes Pangelinan.
Senior Deputy Director General, Suva.—Dr. Jimmie Rodgers.
Deputy Director General, Noumea.—Yves Corbel.
Director of Corporate Services.—Louni Hanipale Mose.
Director of the Marine Resource Division.—Tim Adams.
Head of the Planning Unit.—Richard Mann.

U.S. Contact: Bureau of East Asian and Pacific Affairs, Office of Australia, New Zealand and Pacific Island Affairs, Department of State, Washington, DC 20520, phone (202) 647–9690, fax 647–0118

Countries and Territories Covered by the SPC:

American Samoa
Australia
Cook Islands
Federated States of Micronesia
Fiji
France
French Polynesia
Guam
Kiribati
Marshall Islands
Nauru
New Caledonia
New Zealand
Niue
Northern Mariana Islands
Palau
Papua New Guinea
Pitcairn Islands
Samoa
Solomon Islands
Tokelau
Tonga
Tuvalu
United States
Vanuatu
Wallis and Futuna

UNITED NATIONS

GENERAL ASSEMBLY

The General Assembly is composed of all 191 United Nations Member States.

SECURITY COUNCIL

The Security Council has 15 members. The United Nations Charter designates five States as permanent members, and the General Assembly elects 10 other members for two-year terms. The term of office for each non-permanent member of the Council ends on 31 December of the year indicated in parentheses next to its name.

The five permanent members of the Security Council are China, France, Russian Federation, United Kingdom and the United States.

The 10 non-permanent members of the Council in 2007 are Belgium (2008), Congo (2007), Ghana (2007), Indonesia (2008), Italy (2008), Panama (2008), Peru (2007), Qatar (2007), Solvakia (2007), and South Africa (2008).

ECONOMIC AND SOCIAL COUNCIL

The Economic and Social Council has 54 members, elected for three-year terms by the General Assembly. The term of office for each member expires on 31 December of the year indicated in parentheses next to its name. Voting in the Council is by simple majority; each member has one vote. In 2005, the Council is composed of the following 54 States:

Albania (2007)
Armenia (2006)
Australia (2007)
Azerbaijan (2005)
Bangladesh (2006)
Belgium (2006)
Belize (2006)
Benin (2005)
Brazil (2007)
Canada (2006)
Chad (2007)
China (2007)
Colombia (2006)
Congo (2005)
Costa Rica (2007)
Cuba (2005)
Democratic Republic of the Congo (2007)
Denmark (2007)
Ecuador (2005)
France (2005)
Germany (2005)
Guinea (2007)
Iceland (2007)
India (2007)
Indonesia (2006)
Ireland (2005)
Italy (2006)
Jamaica (2005)
Japan (2005)
Kenya (2005)
Lithuania (2007)
Malaysia (2005)
Mauritius (2006)
Mexico (2007)
Mozambique (2005)
Namibia (2006)
Nicaragua (2005)
Nigeria (2006)
Pakistan (2007)
Panama (2006)
Poland (2006)
Republic of Korea (2006)
Russian Federation (2007)
Saudi Arabia (2005)
Senegal (2005)
South Africa (2007)
Spain (2005)
Thailand (2007)
Tunisia (2006)
Turkey (2005)
United Arab Emirates (2006)
United Kingdom of Great Britain and Northern Ireland (2007)
United Republic of Tanzania (2006)
United States of America (2006)

TRUSTEESHIP COUNCIL

The Trusteeship Council has five members: China, France, Russian Federation, United Kingdom and the United States. With the independence of Palau, the last remaining United Nations trust territory, the Council formerly suspended operation on 1 November 1994. By a resolution adopted on that day, the Council amended its rules of procedure to drop the obligation to meet annually and agreed to meet as occasion required—by its decision or the decision of its President, or at the request of a majority of its members or the General Assembly or the Security Council.

INTERNATIONAL COURT OF JUSTICE

The International Court of Justice has 15 members, elected by both the General Assembly and the Security Council. Judges hold nine-year terms.

The current composition of the court is as follows: President Rosalyn Higgins (United Kingdom); Vice-President Awn Shawkat Al-Khasawneh (Jordan). Judges: Raymond Ranjeva (Madagascar), Shi Jiuyong (China), Abdul G. Koroma (Sierra Leone), Gonzalo Parra-Aranguren (Venezuela), Thomas Buergenthal (United States of America), Hisashi Owada (Japan), Bruno Simma (Germany), Peter Tomka (Slovakia), Ronny Abraham (France), Kenneth Keith (New Zealand), Bernardo Sepúlveda Amor (Mexico), Mohamed Bennouna (Morocco), and Leonid Skotnikov (Russian Federation).

The Registrar of the Court is Mr. Philippe Couvreur (Belgium).

UNITED NATIONS SECRETARIAT

One United Nations Plaza, New York, NY 10017, (212) 963–1234, http://www.un.org

Secretary General.—Ban Ki-moon (Republic of Korea).

Deputy Secretary.—Dr. Asha Rose Migiro (Tanzania).

EXECUTIVE OFFICE OF THE SECRETARY-GENERAL

Chief of Staff.—Vijay Nambiar (India).
Assistant Secretary-General for Policy Planning.—Robert C. Orr (United States).
Spokesman.—Michele Montas.

OFFICE OF INTERNAL OVERSIGHT SERVICES

Under-Secretary-General.—Inga-Britt Ahlenius (Sweden).

OFFICE OF LEGAL AFFAIRS

Under-Secretary-General and Legal Counsel.—Nicholas Michel (Switzerland).
Assistant Secretary General.—Ralph Zacklin (United Kingdom).

DEPARTMENT OF POLITICAL AFFAIRS

Under-Secretary-General.—B. Lynn Pascoe (United States).
Assistant Secretary-General.—Tuliameni Kalomoh (Namibia).
Assistant Secretary-General.—Angela Kane (Germany).

DEPARTMENT FOR DISARMAMENT AFFAIRS

Under-Secretary-General.—Nobunki Tanaka (Japan).

DEPARTMENT OF PEACE-KEEPING OPERATIONS

Under-Secretary-General.—Jean-Marie Guehenno (France).
Assistant Secretary-General.—Hédi Annabi (Tunisia).
Assistant Secretary-General.—Jane Holl Lute (USA).

OFFICE FOR THE COORDINATION OF HUMANITARIAN AFFAIRS

Under-Secretary-General, Emergency Relief Coordinator.—John Holmes (United Kingdom).
Assistant Secretary General/Deputy Emergency Relief Coordinator.—Margaret Wahlstrom (Sierra Leone).
Chief, Humanitarian Emergency Branch/Director, OCHA.—Kasidis Rochanakorn (Geneva).

DEPARTMENT OF ECONOMIC AND SOCIAL AFFAIRS

Under-Secretary-General.—José Antonio Campo (Colombia).
Assistant Secretary-General.—Patricio Civili (Italy).

DEPARTMENT OF GENERAL ASSEMBLY AND CONFERENCE MANAGEMENT

Under-Secretary-General.—Jian Chen (China).
Assistant Secretary-General.—Angela Kane.

DEPARTMENT OF PUBLIC INFORMATION

Under-Secretary-General.—Kiyotaka Akasaka (Japan).

DEPARTMENT OF MANAGEMENT

Under-Secretary-General.—Alicia Barcena.
Assistant Secretary-General, Controller.—Warren Sach (UK).
Officer-in-Charge, Human Resources Management.—Dennis Beissel (USA).
Officer-in-Charge, Central Support Services.—Andrew Toh (Singapore).

OFFICE OF THE SPECIAL REPRESENTATIVE OF THE SECRETARY-GENERAL FOR CHILDREN AND ARMED CONFLICT

Under-Secretary-General.—Radhika Coomaraswamy (Sri Lanka).

UNITED NATIONS FUND FOR INTERNATIONAL PARTNERSHIPS

Executive Director.—Amir A. Dossal (United Kingdom).

UNITED NATIONS AT GENEVA (UNOG)

Palais des Nations, 1211 Geneva 10, Switzerland, phone (41–22) 917–1234.
Director-General of UNOG.—Assistant Secretary-General Sergei A. Ordzhonikidze (Russian Federation).

UNITED NATIONS AT VIENNA (UNOV)

Vienna International Centre, PO Box 500, A–1400 Vienna, Austria, phone (43–1) 21345.
Director-General.—Antonio Maria Costa (Italy).

UNITED NATIONS INFORMATION CENTRE

1775 K Street, NW., Suite 400, Washington, DC 20006

phone: (202) 331–8670, fax: (202) 331–9191, email: unicdc@unicwash.org

http://www.unicwash.org

Director.—William Davis (United States).

REGIONAL ECONOMIC COMMISSIONS

Economic Commission for Africa (ECA), Africa Hall, P.O. Box 3001, Addis Ababa Ethiopia, phone (251–1) 51–72–00, fax (251–1) 51–44–16.
Executive Secretary.—Abdoulie Jannah (Gambia).

Economic Commission for Europe (ECE) Palais des Nations, 1211 Geneva 10, Switzerland, phone (41–22) 917–2893.
Executive Secretary.—Marek Belka (Poland).

Economic Commission for Latin America and the Caribbean (ECLAC), Casilla 179–D, Santiago, Chile, phone (56–2) 210–2000, fax (56–2) 208–0252.
Executive Secretary.—Jose Luis Machinea (Argentina).

Economic and Social Commission for Asia and the Pacific (ESCAP), United Nations Building, Réjdamnern Avenue, Bangkok, Thailand, phone (66–2) 288–1234, fax (66–2) 288–1000.
Executive Secretary.—Hak-Su Kim (Republic of Korea).

Economic and Social Commission for Western Asia (ESCWA), P.O. Box 11–8575, Riad El-Solh Square, Beirut, Lebanon, phone 9611–981301, fax 9611– 981510.
Executive Secretary.—Mervat Tallawy (Egypt).

Regional Commissions, New York Office, (ECE, ESCAP, ECLAC, ECA, ESCWA), fax 963–1500.
Chief.—Sulafa Al-Bassam (Saudi Arabia).
Senior Economic Affairs Officer.—Kazi Rahman (Bangladesh).
Liaison Officer.—Margaret McCaffery (USA).
Documentation.—Maria Baquero (Ecuador).

FUNDS, PROGRAMMES, AND BODIES OF THE UNITED NATIONS

Advisory Committee on Administrative and Budgetary Questions (ACABQ), One United Nations Plaza, New York, NY 10017, phone (212) 963–7456.
Chairman.—Rajat Saha (India).

Office of the High Commissioner for Human Rights, Palais des Nations, 8–14 Avenue de la Paix, 1211 Geneva 10, Switzerland, phone (41–22) 917–1234.
High Commissioner for Human Rights.—Louise Arbour (Canada).

International Civil Service Commission (ICSC), One United Nations Plaza, New York, NY 10017, phone (212) 963–8464.
Chairman.—Kingston Rhodes (Sierra Leone).

Joint Inspection Unit (JIU), Palais des Nations, 1211 Geneva 10, Switzerland, phone (41–22) 917–1234.
Chairman.—Deborah Wynes (United States).

Panel of External Auditors of the UN, Specialized Agencies and International Atomic Energy Agency, One United Nations Plaza, New York, NY 10017, phone (212) 963–1234.
Chairman.—Guillermo Langue (Philippines).

United Nations Human Settlements Programme (UN–HABITAT), UN Office at Nairobi, P.O. Box 30030, Nairobi, Kenya, phone (254–2) 621–1234.
Executive Director: Anna Kajumulo Tibaijuka (UR of Tanzania).

United Nations Children's Fund (UNICEF), UNICEF House, 3 UN Plaza, New York, NY 10017, phone (212) 326–7000.
Executive Director.—Ann Veneman (USA).

United Nations Conference on Trade and Development (UNCTAD), Palais des Nations, 8–14 Avenue de la Paix, 1211 Geneva 10, Switzerland, phone (41–22) 917–1234.
Officer-in-Charge.—Carlos Fortin (Chile).

United Nations Development Fund for Women (UNIFEM), 304 East 45th Street, Sixth Floor, New York, NY 10017, phone (212) 906–6400.
Director.—Noeleen Heyzer (Singapore).

United Nations Development Programme (UNDP), 1 United Nations Plaza, New York, NY 10017, phone (212) 906–5000.
Administrator.—Kemal Dervis (Turkey).

United Nations Development Programme (UNDP), Liaison Office, 1775 K Street, NW., Suite 420, Washington, DC 20006, phone (202) 331–9130.
Director.—Michael Marek (USA).

United Nations Environment Programme (UNEP), P.O. Box 30552, Nairobi, Kenya, phone (254–2) 621–1234.
Executive Director.—Achim Steiner.

United Nations High Commissioner for Refugees (UNHCR), Case Postale 2500, CH–1211 Geneve 2 Depot, Switzerland, phone (41–22) 739–8111.
High Commissioner.—António Guterres (Portugal).

United Nations High Commissioner for Refugees (UNHCR), Regional Office for the United States and the Caribbean, 1775 K Street, NW., Third Floor, Washington, DC 20006, phone (202) 296–5191.
Regional Representative.—Kolude Doherty (Nigeria).

United Nations Institute for Disarmament Research (UNIDIR), Palais des Nations, 1211 Geneva 10, Switzerland, phone (41–22) 917–4292.
Director.—Patricia Lewis (United Kingdom).

United Nations Institute for Training and Research (UNITAR), Palais des Nations, 1211 Geneva 10, Switzerland, phone (41–22) 798–5850.
Executive Director.—Carlos Lopes (Guinea Bissau).

United Nations International Drug Control Programme (UNODC), P.O. Box 500, A–1400 Vienna, Austria, phone (43–1) 21345 ext. 4251.
Executive Director.—Antonio Maria Costa (Italy).

United Nations International Research and Training Institute for the Advancement of Women (INSTRAW), P.O. Box 21747, Santo Domingo, Dominican Republic, phone (1–809) 685–2111.
Director.—Carmen Moreno (Mexico).

United Nations Interregional Crime and Justice Research Institute (UNICRI), Via Giulia 52, 00186 Rome, Italy, phone (39–6) 687–7437.
Director.—Alberto Bradanini (Italy).

United Nations Office for Project Services (UNOPS), Room 1442, 220 East 42nd Street, New York, NY 10017, phone (212) 906–6500.
Executive Director.—Jan Mattson (Sweden).

United Nations Population Fund (UNFPA), 220 East 42nd Street, New York, NY 10017, phone (212) 297–5000.
Executive Director.—Thoraya Ahmed Obaid (Saudi Arabia).

United Nations Relief and Works Agency for Palestine Refugees in the Near East (UNRWA), Vienna International Centre, P.O. Box 700, A–1400 Vienna, Austria, phone (43–1) 21345 ext. 4531.
Commissioner-General.—Karen Konig Abuzayd.

United Nations Research Institute for Social Development (UNRISD), Palais des Nations, 1211 Geneva 10, Switzerland, phone (41–22) 798–8400.
Director.—Thandika Mkandawire (Sweden).

United Nations Volunteers Programme (UNV), Postfach 260111, D–53153 Bonn, Germany, phone (49–228) 815–2000.
Executive Coordinator.—Ad de Raad (Netherlands).

World Food Programme (WFP), 426 Via Cristoforo Colombo, 00145 Rome, Italy, phone (39–6) 552–2821.
Executive Director.—James Morris (USA).

United Nations University (UNU), 53–70, Jingumae 5–Chome, Shibuya-Ku, Tokyo 150, Japan, phone (81–3) 3499–2811.
Rector.—Hans van Ginkel (Netherlands).

SPECIALIZED AGENCIES

Food and Agriculture Organization (FAO), Via delle Terme di Caracalla, 00100 Rome, Italy, phone (39–6) 52251.
Director-General.—Jacques Diouf (Senegal).

Food and Agriculture Organization, Liaison Office for North America, Suite 300, 2175 K Street, NW., Washington, DC 20437, phone (202) 653–2400.
Director.—John Ziolkowski.

International Civil Aviation Organization (ICAO), 1000 Sherbrooke Street West, Montreal, Quebec H3A 2R2 Canada, phone (1–514) 285–8221.
Secretary-General.—Dr. Taïeb Chérif (Algeria).

International Fund for Agricultural Development (IFAD), Via del Serafico 107, 00142 Rome, Italy, phone (39–6) 54591.
President.—Lennart Bage (Sweden).
External Affairs Department, IFAD North American Liaison Office, 1775 K Street, NW., Suite 410, Washington, DC 20006, phone (202) 331–9099.
Representative.—Cheryl Morden (USA).

International Labour Organization (ILO), 4, Routes des Morillons, CH–1211 Geneva 22, Switzerland, phone (41–22) 799–6111.
Director-General.—Juan Somavia (Chile).
ILO Washington Branch Office, 1828 L Street, NW., Suite 801, Washington, DC 20036, phone (202) 653–7652.
Interim Director.—Armand F. Pereria.

International Maritime Organization (IMO), 4 Albert Embankment, London SE1 7SR, England, phone (44–171) 735–7611.
Secretary-General.—Efthimios Mitropoulos (Greece).

International Monetary Fund (IMF), 700 19th Street NW., Washington, DC 20431, phone (202) 623–7000.
Managing Director.—Rodrigo de Rato y Figaredo (Spain).

International Telecommunications Union (ITU), Palais des Nations, 1211 Geneva 20, Switzerland, phone (41–22) 730–5111.
Secretary-General.—Hamadoun Touré (Mali).

United Nations Educational, Scientific and Cultural Organization (UNESCO), 7 Place de Fontenoy, 75732 Paris, 07 SP France, phone (33–1) 4568–1000.

Director-General.—Koichiro Matsuura (Japan).

United Nations Industrial Development Organization (UNIDO), P.O. Box 300, Vienna International Centre, A–1400 Vienna, Austria, phone (43–1) 21131–0.
Director-General.—Kandeh Yumkella (Sierra Leone).

Universal Postal Union (UPU), Weltpoststrasse 4, Case Postale, 3000 Berne 15, Switzerland, phone (41–31) 350–3111.
Director-General.—Edouard Dayan (France).

World Bank Group, 1818 H Street, NW., Washington, DC 20433, phone (202) 477–1234.
President.—Paul Wolfowitz (USA).

World Health Organization (WHO), 20 Avenue Appia, 1211 Geneva 27, Switzerland, phone (41–22) 791–2111.
Director-General.—Margaret Chan (China).
World Health Organization Liaison Office, 1775 K Street, NW., 4th Floor, Washington, DC 20006, phone (202) 331–9081.
Special Adviser to the Director-General.—Thomas Loftus (USA).

World Intellectual Property Organization (WIPO), 34 Chemin des Colombetts, 1211 Geneva 20, Switzerland, phone (41–22) 730–9111.
Director General.—Kamil Idris (Sudan).
World Intellectual Property Organization Coordination Office, 1775 K Street, NW., Washington, DC 20006, phone (202) 454–2460.
Coordinator.—Suzanne Stoll.

World Meteorological Organization (WMO), Case postale No. 2300, CH–1211 Geneva 2, Switzerland, phone (41–22) 730–8111.
Secretary-General.—Michel Jarraud (France).

RELATED BODY

International Atomic Energy Agency (IAEA), P.O. Box 100, Vienna International Centre, A–1400 Vienna, Austria, phone (43–1) 2060–0.
Director General.—Mohamed Elbaradei (Egypt).
(The IAEA is an independent intergovernmental organization under the aegis of the UN).

SPECIAL AND PERSONAL REPRESENTATIVES AND ENVOYS OF THE SECRETARY-GENERAL

AFRICA

African Region:
Special Adviser for Special Assignments.—Legwaila Joseph Legwaila (Botswana).
Special Adviser.—Mohamed Sahnoun (Algeria).

Burundi:
Special Representative.—Youssef Mahmoud (Tunisia).
Principal Deputy Special Representative.—Nureldin Satti (Sudan).
Deputy Special Representative.—Ibrahima Fall (Senegal).

Central African Republic:
Representative.—General Lamine Cissé (Senegal).

Côte d'Ivoire:
Principal Deputy Special Representative.—Abou Moussa (Chad).
Deputy Special Representative.—Abdoulaye Mar Dieye (Senegal).

Democratic Republic of the Congo:
Special Representative.—William Lacy Swing (United States).
Deputy Special Representative.—Ross Mountain (New Zealand).
Special Envoy.—Mustapha Niasse (Senegal).

Ethiopia / Eritrea:
Deputy Special Representative.—Azouz Ennifar.

Great Lakes Region:
Special Representative.—Ibrahima Fall (Senegal).

Guinea-Bissau:
Representative.—Shola Omoregie (Nigeria).

Horn of Africa:
Special Envoy.—Kjell Magne Bondevik (Norway).

Liberia:
Special Representative.—Alan Doss (United States).
Special Representative for Relief, Recovery and Rehabilitation.—Jordan Ryan (United States).

Sierra Leone:
Special Representative.—Victor da Silva Angelo (Portugal).

Somalia:
Representative.—Francois Lonseny Fall (Guinea).

Sudan:
Deputy Special Representatives: Taye-Brook Zerihoun (Ethiopia), Manuel Aranda da Silva (Mozambique).
Special Envoy.—Jan Eliasson (Sweden).

West Africa:
Special Representative.—Ahmedou Ould-Abdallah (Mauritania).

Western Sahara:
Special Representative.—Julian Harston (United Kingdom).

THE AMERICAS

Latin American Region:
Special Adviser.—Diego Cordovez (Ecuador).

Colombia:
Special Adviser.—James LeMoyne (United States).

Haiti:
Special Representative.—Edmund Mulet (Guatemala).
Principal Deputy Special Representative.—Luiz Carlos da Costa (Brazil).
Deputy Special Representative.—Joel Boutroue (France).
Special Adviser.—John Reginald Dumas (Trinidad and Tobago).

ASIA AND THE PACIFIC

Afghanistan:
Special Representative.—Tom Koetigs (Germany).
Principal Deputy Special Representative.—Ameerah Haq (Bangladesh).
Deputy Special Representative.—Filippo Grandi (Italy).

Timor Leste:
Special Representative.—Atul Khure (India).
Deputy Special Representative.—Finn Reske Nielsen (Denmark).

Papua New Guinea:
Observer Mission.—Tor Stenbock (Norway).

Tajikistan:
Representative.—Vladimir Sotirov (Bulgaria).

EUROPE

European Region:
Special Adviser.—Jean-Bernard Merimee (France).

Cyprus:
Special Representative.—Michael Moller (Denmark).

Former Yugoslav Republic of Macedonia-Greece:
Personal Envoy.—Matthew Nimetz (United States).

Georgia:
Special Representative.—Jen Arnault.

Kosovo:
Special Representative.—Joachim Rücker (Germany).
Principal Deputy Special Representative.—Steven Shook (United States).
Deputy Special Representative for Civil Administration.—Patricia Waring-Ripley (Canada).
Deputy Special Representative for Institution Building (OSCE).—Werner Whendt (Germany).

Deputy Special Representative for Reconstruction (European Union).—Paul Acda (United Kingdom).

MIDDLE EAST

Middle East:
Special Envoy for the Implementation of Security Council Resolution 1559.—Terje Roed-Larsen (Norway).

Iraq:
Special Representative.—Ashraf Jehangir Qazi (Pakistan).
Deputy Special Representative.—Michael von der Schulenburg (Germany).

Southern Lebanon:
Personal Representative.—Geir O. Pedersen (Norway).

OTHER HIGH LEVEL APPOINTMENTS

Children and Armed Conflict:
Special Representative.—Radhika Coomaraswamy (Sri Lanka).

Commonwealth of Independent States (CIS):
Special Envoy.—Yuli Vorontsov (Russian Federation).

Conference on Disarmament:
Personal Representative.—Sergei A. Ordzhonikidze (Russian Federation).

Gender Issues and Advancement of Women:
Special Adviser.—Rachel N. Mayanja (Uganda).

Global Compact:
Special Adviser.—Klaus M. Leisinger (United States).

HIV / AIDS in Africa:
Special Envoy.—Stephen Lewis (Canada).

HIV / AIDS in Asia:
Special Envoy.—Nafis Sadik (Pakistan).

HIV / AIDS in the Caribbean Region:
Special Envoy.—George Alleyne (Barbados).

HIV / AIDS in Eastern Europe:
Special Envoy.—Lars O. Kallings (Sweden).

Human Rights:
Special Representative.—Hina Jilani (Pakistan).

Internally Displaced Persons:
Representative.—Walter Kälin (Switzerland).

Least Developed Countries, Landlocked Developing Countries, and Small Island Developing States:
High Representative.—Anwarul K. Chowdhury (Bangladesh).

Millennium Development Goals:
Special Adviser.—Jeffrey D. Sachs (United States).
Executive Coordinator.—Eveline Herfkens (Netherlands).

Prevention of Genocide:
Special Adviser.—Juan E. Méndez (Argentina).
Special Adviser.—Lakhdar Brahimi (Algeria).
Special Adviser.—Maurice Strong (Canada).

Sport for Development and Peace:
Special Adviser.—Adolf Ogi (Switzerland).

United Nations International School (UNIS):
Special Representative.—Silvia Fuhrman (United States).

World Summit on Information Society:
Special Adviser.—Nitin Desai (India).

WORLD BANK GROUP

The World Bank Group comprises five organizations: the International Bank for Reconstruction and Development (IBRD), the International Development Association (IDA), the International Finance Corporation (IFC), the Multilateral Investment Guarantee Agency (MIGA) and the International Centre for the Settlement of Investment Disputes (ICSID).

Headquarters: 1818 H Street, NW., 20433, (202) 473–1000

INTERNATIONAL BANK FOR RECONSTRUCTION AND DEVELOPMENT

President.—Robert Zoellick.
Managing Directors: Graeme Wheeler, Juan Jose Daboub.
Senior Vice President and General Counsel.—Ana Palacio.
Senior Vice President, Development Economics, and Chief Economist.—Francois Bourguignon.
Senior Vice President and Head, Human Development Network.—Joy Phumaphi.
Chief Financial Officer.—Vincenzo La Via.
Vice President and Chief Information Officer and Head, Information Solutions Network.—Guy-Pierre De Poerck.
Vice President and Controller.—Fayezul Choudhury.
Vice President and Corporate Secretary.—W. Paatii Ofusu-Amah.
Vice President and Treasurer.—Kenneth G. Lay.
Vice President of:
Africa.—Obiageli Katryn Ezekwesili.
East Asia and Pacific.—James W. Adams.
Environmentally and Socially Sustainable Development Network.—Katherine Sierra.
Europe (External Affairs).—Cyril Muller.
Europe and Central Asia.—Shigeo Katsu.
External and UN Affairs.—Ian A. Goldin.
Human Resources.—Xavier E. Coll.
Infrastructure.—Katherine Sierra.
Japan (External Affairs).—Lester J. Dally.
Latin America and the Caribbean.—Pamela Cox.
Middle East and North Africa.—Daniela Gressani.
Network, Operational Policy and Country Services.—Jeffrey Gutman.
Poverty Reduction and Economic Management Network.—Danny Leipziger.
Private Sector Development (World Bank and IFC) and Chief Economist (IFC).—Michael U. Klein.
Resource Mobilization and Cofinancing.—Geoffrey B. Lamb.
South Asia.—Praful Patel.
Strategy, Finance and Risk Management.—John Herlihy.
World Bank Institute.—Rakesh Nangia.
Director-General, Operations Evaluation.—Vinod Thomas.
Counselor to the President for U.S. Affairs.—Suzanne Rich Folsom.

OTHER WORLD BANK OFFICES

London: New Zealand House, 15th Floor, Haymarket, London SW1Y 4TE, England.
Geneva: 3, Chemin Louis Dunant, CP 66, CH 1211, Geneva 10, Switzerland.
Paris: 66, Avenue d'Iena, 75116 Paris, France.
Brussels: 10, rue Montoyer, B–1000 Brussels, Belgium.
Tokyo: Fukoku Seimei Building, 10th Floor, 2–2–2 Uchisawai-cho, Chiyoda-Ku, Tokyo 100, Japan.
Sydney: c/o South Pacific Project Facility, 89 York Street, Level 8, GPO Box 1612, Sydney, NSW 2000, Australia.
Frankfurt: Bockenheimer Landstrasse 109, 60325 Frankfurt am Main, Germany.

BOARD OF EXECUTIVE DIRECTORS

Bahrain, Egypt (Arab Republic of), Iraq, Jordan, Kuwait, Lebanon, Libya, Maldives, Oman, Qatar, Syrian Arab Republic, United Arab Emirates, Yemen (Republic of).
Executive Director.—Merza H. Hasan.
Alternate.—Mohamed Kamel Amr.
Saudi Arabia.
Executive Director.—Abdulrahman M. Almofadhi.
Alternate.—Abdulhamid Alkhalifa.

Austria, Belarus, Belgium, Czech Republic, Hungary, Kazakhstan, Luxembourg, Slovak Republic, Slovenia, Turkey.
Executive Director.—Gino Alzetta.
Alternate.—Meliá Nemli.

Australia, Cambodia, Kiribati, Korea (Republic of), Marshall Islands, Micronesia (Federated States of), Mongolia, New Zealand, Palau, Papua New Guinea, Samoa, Solomon Islands, Vanuatu.
Executive Director.—Joong-Kyung Choi.
Alternate.—Terry O'Brien.

Albania, Greece, Italy, Malta, Portugal, San Marino, Timor-Leste.
Executive Director.—Giovanni Majnoni.
Alternate.—Nuno Mota Pinto.

United States.
Executive Director.—E. Whitney Debevoise.

Brazil, Colombia, Dominican Republic, Ecuador, Haiti, Panama, Philippines, Suriname, Trinidad and Tobago.
Executive Director.—Octaviano Canuto.
Alternate.—Jorge Humberto Botero.

Germany.
Executive Director.—Eckhard Deutscher.
Alternate.—Ruediger Von Kleist.

Afghanistan, Algeria, Ghana, Iran (Islamic Republic of), Morocco, Pakistan, Tunisia.
Executive Director.—Shuja Shah.
Alternate.—Sid Ahmed Dib.

France.
Executive Director.—Pierre Duquesne.
Alternate.—Alexis Kohler.

Benin, Burkina Faso, Cameroon, Cape Verde, Central African Republic, Chad, Comoros, Congo (Democratic Republic of), Congo (Republic of), Cote d'lvoire, Djibouti, Equatorial Guinea, Gabon, Guinea, Guinea-Bissau, Madagascar, Mali, Mauritania, Mauritius, Niger, Rwanda, Sao Tome and Principe, Senegal, Togo.
Executive Director.—Louis Philippe Ong Seng.
Alternate.—Agapito Mendes Dias.

Brunei Darussalam, Fiji, Indonesia, Lao People's Democratic Republic, Malaysia, Myanmar, Nepal, Singapore, Thailand, Tonga, Vietnam.
Executive Director.—Mat Aron Deraman.
Alternate.—Chularat Suteethorn.

Denmark, Estonia, Finland, Iceland, Latvia, Lithuania, Norway, Sweden.
Executive Director.—Svein Aass.
Alternate.—Pauli Kariniemi.

Russian Federation.
Executive Director.—Alexey G. Kvasov.
Alternate.—Eugene Miagkov.

Costa Rica, El Salvador, Guatemala, Honduras, Mexico, Nicaragua, Spain, Venezuela (Republica Bolivariana de).
Executive Director.—Jorge Familiar.
Alternate.—Jose Alejandro Rojas Ramirez.

Antigua and Barbuda, Bahamas (The), Barbados, Belize, Canada, Dominica, Grenada, Guyana, Ireland, Jamaica, St. Kitts and Nevis, St. Lucia, St. Vincent and the Grenadines.
Executive Director.—Sammy Watson.
Alternate.—Ishmael Lightbourne.

Armenia, Bosnia and Herzegovina, Bulgaria, Croatia, Cyprus, Georgia, Israel, Macedonia (former Yugoslav Republic of), Moldova, Netherlands, Romania, Ukraine.
Executive Director.—Herman Wjiffels.
Alternate.—Claudis Doltu.

Japan.
Executive Director.—Makato Hosomi.
Alternate.—Masato Kanda.

Argentina, Bolivia, Chile, Paraguay, Peru, Uruguay.
Executive Director.—Felix Alberto Camarasa.
Alternate.—Francisco Bernasconi.

United Kingdom.
Executive Director.—Tom Scholar.
Alternate.—Caroline Sergeant.

Angola, Botswana, Burundi, Eritrea, Ethiopia, Gambia (The), Kenya, Lesotho, Liberia, Malawi, Mozambique, Namibia, Nigeria, Seychelles, Sierra Leone, South Africa, Sudan, Swaziland, Tanzania, Uganda, Zambia, Zimbabwe.

Executive Director.—Mulu Ketsela.
Alternate.—Mathias Sinamenye.
Bangladesh, Bhutan, India, Sri Lanka.
Executive Director.—Dhanendra Kumar.
Alternate.—Zakir Ahmed Khan.
Azerbaijan, Serbia and Montenegro, Kyrgyz Republic, Poland, Switzerland, Tajikistan, Turkmenistan, Uzbekistan, Yugoslavia (Fed. Rep. of).
Executive Director.—Michel Mordasini.
Alternate.—Jakub Karnowski.
China.
Executive Director.—Jianyi Zou.
Alternate.—Jinlin Yang.

INTERNATIONAL DEVELOPMENT ASSOCIATION

[The officers, executive directors, and alternates are the same as those of the International Bank for Reconstruction and Development.]

INTERNATIONAL FINANCE CORPORATION

President.—Robert Zoellick.
Executive Vice President.—Lars Thunell.
Vice President and Corporate Secretary.—W. Paatii Ofusu-Amah.
Vice President:
Finance and Treasurer.—Nina Shapiro.
Human Resources and Administration.—Dorothy H. Berry.
Operations.—Declan Duff.
Portfolio and Risk Management.—Michel G. Maila.
Private Sector Development/Chief Economist.—Michael U. Klein.
Director General, Operations Evaluation.—Vinod Thomas.
Chief Information Officer and Corporate Business Informatics.—William Piatt.
Compliance Advisor/Ombudsman.—Meg Taylor.
General Counsel.—Jennifer A. Sullivan.
Corporate Relations Unit Manager.—Bruce Moats.
Director, Office of:
Agribusiness.—Jean-Paul Pinard.
Controller's and Budgeting.—Christian Grossman.
Corporate Portfolio and Risk Management.—Marc A. Babin.
Credit Review.—Francisco Tourreilles.
Environment and Social Development.—Rachel Kyte.
Financial Operations.—Avil Hofman.
Global Financial Markets.—Jyrki Koskelo.
Global Information and Communications Technologies.—Mohsen A. Khalil.
Global Manufacturing and Services.—Dimitris Tsitsiragos.
Health and Education.—Guy M. Ellena.
Infrastructure.—Rashad-Rudolf Kaldany.
Municipal Fund.—Declan J. Duff.
Oil, Gas, Mining and Chemicals.—Peter van der Veen.
Operations Evaluation Group.—Marvin Taylor-Dormond.
Private Equity and Investment Funds.—Haydee Celaya.
Risk Management and Financial Policy.—Lakashmi Shyam-Sunder.
Special Operations.—Maria Da Graca Domínguez.
Trust Funds.—Mwaghazi Mwachofi.
Central and Eastern Europe.—Jerome Sooklal.
East Asia and Pacific.—Richard Ranken.
Latin America and Caribbean.—Atul Mehta.
Middle East and North Africa.—Michael Essex.
South Asia.—Paolo Martelli.
Southern Europe and Central Asia.—Shabbaz Mavaddat.
Sub-Saharan Africa.—Thierry Tanoh.

MULTILATERAL INVESTMENT GUARANTEE AGENCY

President.—Robert Zoellick.

Vice President and Corporate Secretary.—W. Paatii Ofosu-Amah.

Executive Vice President.—Yukiko Omura.

Vice President and General Counsel, Legal Affairs and Claims Group.—Peter Cleary.

Compliance Advisor/Ombudsman (ICC & MIGA).—Meg Taylor.

Director of:

External Outreach and Partners Group.—Moina Varkie.

Operations Evaluation Unit.—Aysegul Akin-Karasapan.

Operations Group.—Philippe Valahu.

Director and Chief Economist, Economics and Policy Group.—Frank Lysy.

Director and Chief Financial Officer, Finance and Risk Management Group.—Kevin Lu.

FOREIGN DIPLOMATIC OFFICES IN THE UNITED STATES

AFGHANISTAN

Embassy of Afghanistan
2341 Wyoming Avenue, NW., Washington, DC 20008
phone (202) 483–6410, fax 483–6488
His Excellency Said Tayeb Jawad
Ambassador E. and P.
Consular Offices:
- California, Los Angeles
- New York, New York

ALBANIA

Embassy of the Republic of Albania
2100 S Street, NW., Washington, DC 20008
phone (202) 223–4942, fax 628–7342
His Excellency Aleksander Sallabanda
Ambassador E. and P.
Consular Offices:
- Connecticut, Greenwich
- Florida, Ft. Lauderdale
- Georgia, Avondale Estates
- Louisiana, New Orleans
- Michigan, West Bloomfield
- Norrth Carolina, Pinehurst
- Ohio, Cleveland
- Texas, Houston

ALGERIA

Embassy of the Democratic Republic of Algeria
2118 Kalorama Road, NW., Washington, DC 20008
phone (202) 265–2800, fax 667–2174
His Excellency Amine Kherbi
Ambassador E. and P.

ANDORRA

Embassy of Andorra
Two United Nations Plaza, 27th Floor, New York, NY 10017
phone (212) 750–8064, fax 750–6630
Ms. Jelena V. Pia-Comella
Minister-Counselor

ANGOLA

Embassy of the Republic of Angola
2100–2108 16th, Street NW., Washington, DC 20009
phone (202) 785–1156, fax 785–1258
Her Excellency Josefina Pitra Diakité
Ambassador E. and P.
Consular Offices:
- New York, New York
- Texas, Houston

ANTIGUA AND BARBUDA

Embassy of Antigua and Barbuda
3216 New Mexico Avenue, NW., Washington, DC 20016
phone (202) 362–5122, fax 362–5225
Her Excellency Deborah Mae Lovell
Ambassador E. and P. / Consul General
Consular Offices:
- Florida, Miami
- New York, New York

ARGENTINA

Embassy of the Argentine Republic
1600 New Hampshire Avenue, NW., Washington, DC 20009
phone (202) 238–6400, fax 332–3171
His Excellency José Octavio Bordón
Ambassador E. and P.
Consular Offices:
- California, Los Angeles
- Florida, Miami
- Georgia, Atlanta
- Illinois, Chicago
- New York, New York
- Texas, Houston

ARMENIA

Embassy of the Republic of Armenia
2225 R Street, NW., Washington, DC 20008
phone (202) 319–1976, fax 319–2982
His Excellency Tatoul Markarian
Ambassador E. and P.
Consular Office: California, Los Angeles

AUSTRALIA

Embassy of Australia
1601 Massachusetts Avenue, NW., Washington, DC 20036
phone (202) 797–3000, fax 797–3168
His Excellency Dennis James Richardson
Ambassador E. and P.
Consular Offices:
- California:
  - Los Angeles
  - San Francisco
- Colorado, Denver
- Florida, Miami

Georgia, Atlanta
Hawaii, Honolulu
Illinois, Chicago
Massachusetts, Boston
New York, New York
Texas, Houston
Trust Territories of the Pacific Islands:
Kolonia, Micronesia
Pago Pago
Washington, Seattle

AUSTRIA

Embassy of Austria
3524 International Court, NW., Washington, DC 20008–3035
phone (202) 895–6700, fax 895–6750
Her Excellency Dr. Eva Nowotny
Ambassador E. and P.
Consular Offices:
Alaska, Anchorage
Arizona, Scottsdale
California:
Los Angeles
San Francisco
Colorado, Denver
Florida:
Miami
Orlando
Georgia, Atlanta
Hawaii, Honolulu
Illinois, Chicago
Louisiana, New Orleans
Massachusetts, Boston
Michigan, Detroit
Minnesota, St. Paul
Missouri:
Kansas City
St. Louis
Nevada, Las Vegas
New York:
Buffalo
New York
North Carolina, Charlotte
Ohio, Columbus
Oregon, Portland
Pennsylvania, Pittsburgh
Puerto Rico, San Juan
Texas, Houston
Utah, Salt Lake City
Virgin Islands, St. Thomas
Virginia, Richmond
Washington, Seattle
Wisconsin, Milwaukee

AZERBAIJAN

Embassy of the Republic of Azerbaijan
2741 34th Street, NW., Washington, DC 20008
phone (202) 337–3500, fax 337–5911
His Excellency Yashar Aliyev
Ambassador E. and P.
Consular Office: California, Los Angeles

BAHAMAS

Embassy of the Commonwealth of The Bahamas
2220 Massachusetts Avenue, NW., Washington, DC 20008
phone (202) 319–2660, fax 319–2668
Mr. Eugene Torchon Newry
First Secretary
Consular Offices:
Florida, Miami
Georgia, Fairburn
New York, New York

BAHRAIN

Embassy of the Kingdom of Bahrain
3502 International Drive, NW., Washington, DC 20008
phone (202) 342–0741, fax 362–2192
His Excellency Dr. Naser M.Y. Al Belooshi
Ambassador E. and P.
Consular Offices:
California, San Diego
New York, New York

BANGLADESH

Embassy of the People's Republic of Bangladesh
3510 International Drive, NW., Washington, DC 20008
phone (202) 244–0183, fax 244–5366
His Excellency Shamsher M. Chowdhury
Ambassador E. and P.
Consular Offices:
California, Los Angeles
Hawaii, Honolulu
Louisiana, New Orleans
New York, New York
Texas, Houston

BARBADOS

Embassy of Barbados
2144 Wyoming Avenue, NW., Washington, DC 20008
phone (202) 939–9200, fax 332–7467
His Excellency Michael Ian King
Ambassador E. and P.
Consular Offices:
California, San Francisco
Colorado, Denver
Florida, Miami
Georgia, Atlanta
Illinois, Chicago
Kentucky, Louisville
Louisiana, New Orleans
Massachusetts, Boston
Michigan, Detroit
New York, New York

Ohio, Toledo
Oregon, Portland
Texas, Sugar Land

BELARUS

Embassy of the Republic of Belarus
1619 New Hampshire Avenue, NW., Washington, DC 20009
phone (202) 986–1604, fax 986–1805
His Excellency Mikhail Khvostov
Ambassador E. and P.
Consular Office: New York, New York

BELGIUM

Embassy of Belgium
3330 Garfield Street, NW., Washington, DC 20008
phone (202) 333–6900, fax 333–3079
His Excellency Dominique Struye de Swielande
Ambassador E. and P. / Consul General
Consular Offices:
Alaska, Anchorage
Arizona, Phoenix
California:
Los Angeles
San Diego
San Francisco
Colorado, Denver
Florida, Miami
Georgia, Atlanta
Hawaii, Honolulu
Illinois:
Chicago
Moliine
Kansas, Kansas City
Kentucky, Louisville
Louisiana, New Orleans
Maryland, Baltimore
Massachusetts, Boston
Michigan, Bloomfield
Minnesota, St. Paul
Missouri, St. Louis
New York, New York
Ohio, Cincinnati
Oregon, Portland
Pennsylvania, Pittsburgh
Puerto Rico, San Juan
Texas:
Fort Worth
Houston
San Antonio
Utah, Salt Lake City
Virginia, Norfolk
Washington, Seattle
Wisconsin, Milwaukee

BELIZE

Embassy of Belize
2535 Massachusetts Avenue, NW., Washington, DC 20008
phone (202) 332–9636, fax 332–6888
Her Excellency Lisa M. Shoman
Ambassador E. and P.
Consular Offices:
California:
Los Angeles:
San Francisco
Florida, Miami
Illinois:
Belleville
Chicago
Louisiana, New Orleans
Michigan, Detroit
Nevada, Las Vegas
North Carolina, Wilmington
Ohio, Dayton
Puerto Rico, San Juan
Texas:
Dallas
Houston

BENIN

Embassy of the Republic of Benin
2124 Kalorama Road, NW., Washington, DC 20008
phone (202) 232–6656, fax 265–1996
His Excellency Segbe Cyrille Oguin
Ambassador E. and P.
Consular Office: California, Los Angeles

BHUTAN

Consular Office: New York, New York

BOLIVIA

Embassy of the Republic of Bolivia
3014 Massachusetts Avenue, NW., Washington, DC 20008
phone (202) 483–4410, fax 328–3712
His Excellency Gustavo Guzmán Saldaña
Ambassador E. and P.
Consular Offices:
Alabama, Mobile
California:
Los Angeles
San Francisco
Florida, Miami
Georgia, Atlanta
Illinois, Chicago
Massachusetts, Boston
Minnesota, Minneapolis
New York, New York
Oklahoma, Oklahoma City
Puerto Rico, San Juan
Texas:
Dallas
Houston
Washington, Seattle

BOSNIA AND HERZEGOVINA

Embassy of Bosnia and Herzegovina

2109 E Street, NW., Washington, DC 20037
phone (202) 337–1500, fax 337–1502
Her Excellency Dr. Bisera Turkovic
Ambassador E. and P.
Consular Offices:
Illinois, Chicago
New York, New York

BOTSWANA

Embassy of the Republic of Botswana
1531–1533 New Hampshire Avenue, NW., Washington, DC 20036
phone (202) 244–4990, fax 244–4164
His Excellency Lapologang Caesar Lekoa
Ambassador E. and P.
Consular Offices:
California:
Los Angeles
San Francisco
Georgia, Atlanta
Texas, Houston

BRAZIL

Brazilian Embassy
3006 Massachusetts Avenue, NW., Washington, DC 20008
phone (202) 238–2700, fax 238–2827
His Excellency Antonio de Aguiar Patriota
Ambassador E. and P.
Consular Offices:
Alabama, Birmingham
Arizona, Scottsdale
California:
Los Angeles
San Diego
San Francisco
Florida, Miami
Georgia, Atlanta
Hawaii, Honolulu
Illinois, Chicago
Kentucky, Convington
Louisiana, New Orleans
Massachusetts, Boston
New York, New York
Tennessee, Memphis
Trust Territories of the Pacific Islands, Hong Kong
Texas, Houston
Utah, Salt Lake City
Virginia, Norfolk

BRUNEI

Embassy of the State of Brunei Darussalam
3520 International Court, NW., Washington, DC 20008
phone (202) 237–1838, fax 885–0560
His Excellency Pengiran Anak Dato Puteh
Ambassador E. and P.

BULGARIA

Embassy of the Republic of Bulgaria
1621 22nd Street, NW., Washington, DC 20008
phone (202) 387–0174, fax 234–7973
Her Excellency Elena Poptodorova
Ambassador E. and P.
Consular Offices:
California:
Los Angeles
Sacramento
Florida, Boca Raton
Illinois, Chicago
Maryland, Baltimore
Nevada, Las Vegas
New York, New York
Pennsylvania, Media

BURKINA FASO

Embassy of Burkina Faso
2340 Massachusetts Avenue, NW., Washington, DC 20008
phone (202) 332–5577, fax 667–1882
His Excellency Tertius Zongo
Ambassador E. and P.
Consular Offices:
California, Los Angeles
Louisiana, New Orleans

BURUNDI

Embassy of the Republic of Burundi
2233 Wisconsin Avenue, NW., Suite 212, Washington, DC 20007
phone (202) 342–2574, fax 342–2578
His Excellency Celestin Niyongabo
Ambassador E. and P.
Consular Office: California, Los Angeles

CAMBODIA

Royal Embassy of Cambodia
4530 16th Street, NW., Washington, DC 20011
phone (202) 726–7742, fax 726–8381
His Excellency Sereywath Ek
Ambassador E. and P.
Consular Office: Washington, Seattle

CAMEROON

Embassy of the Republic of Cameroon
2349 Massachusetts Avenue, NW., Washington, DC 20008
phone (202) 265–8790, fax 387–3826
His Excellency Jerome Mendouga
Ambassador E. and P.
Consular Offices:
California, San Francisco
Texas, Houston

CANADA

Embassy of Canada

501 Pennsylvania Avenue, NW., Washington, DC 20001
phone (202) 682–1740, fax 682–7726
His Excellency Michael H. Wilson
Ambassador E. and P.
Consular Offices:
Alaska, Anchorage
Arizona:
Phoenix
Tucson
California:
Los Angeles
San Diego
San Francisco
San Jose
Colorado, Denver
Florida:
Miami
Tampa
Georgia, Atlanta
Illinois, Chicago
Louisiana, New Orleans
Maine, Portland
Massachusetts, Boston
Michigan, Detroit
Minnesota, Minneapolis
Montana, Nashua
Nebraska, Omaha
New Jersey, Princeton
New York:
Buffalo
New York
North Carolina:
Huntersville
Raleigh
Ohio, Cleveland
Oregon, Portland
Pennsylvania:
Philadelphia
Pittsburgh
Puerto Rico, San Juan
Tennessee, Memphis
Texas:
Dallas
Houston
San Antonio
Utah, Bountiful
Virginia, Richmond
Washington, Seattle

CAPE VERDE

Embassy of the Republic of Cape Verde
3415 Massachusetts Avenue, NW., Washington, DC 20007
phone (202) 965–6820, fax 965–1207
His Excellency Jose Brito
Ambassador E. and P.
Consular Office: Massachusetts, Boston

CENTRAL AFRICAN REPUBLIC

Embassy of Central African Republic
1618 22nd Street, NW., Washington, DC 20008
phone (202) 483–7800, fax 332–9893
His Excellency Emmanuel Touaboy
Ambassador E. and P.
Consular Offices:
California, Los Angeles
New York, New York

CHAD

Embassy of the Republic of Chad
2002 R Street, NW., Washington, DC 20009
phone (202) 462–4009, fax 265–1937
His Excellency Bechir Mahamoud Adam
Ambassador E. and P.

CHILE

Embassy of the Republic of Chile
1732 Massachusetts Avenue, NW., Washington, DC 20036
phone (202) 785–1746, fax 887–5579
His Excellency Mariano Fernández
Ambassador E. and P.
Consular Offices:
California:
Los Angeles
San Diego
San Francisco
Santa Clara
Florida, Miami
Georgia, Atlanta
Hawaii, Honolulu
Illinois, Chicago
Louisiana, New Orleans
Massachusetts, Boston
Missouri, Kansas City
Nevada, Las Vegas
New York, New York
Pennsylvania, Philadelphia
Puerto Rico, San Juan
South Carolina, Charleston
Texas:
Dallas
Houston
Utah, Provo
Washington, Olympia

CHINA

Embassy of the People's Republic of China
2300 Connecticut Avenue, NW., Washington, DC 20008
phone (202) 328–2500, fax 328–2582
His Excellency Wen Zhong Zhou
Ambassador E. and P.
Consular Offices:
California:
Los Angeles

San Francisco
Illinois, Chicago
New York, New York
Texas, Houston

COLOMBIA

Embassy of Colombia
2118 Leroy Place, NW., Washington, DC 20008
phone (202) 387–8338, fax 232–8643
Her Excellency Maria Carolina Barco Isakson
Ambassador E. and P.
Consular Offices:
California:
Beverly Hills
San Francisco
Florida, Miami
Georgia, Atlanta
Illinois, Chicago
Louisiana, New Orleans
Massachusetts, Boston
New York, New York
Puerto Rico, San Juan
Texas, Houston

COMOROS

Embassy of the Union of Comoros
420 East 50th Street, New York, NY 10022
phone (212) 972–8010, fax 983–4712
[Ambassador departed January 31, 1999]

CONGO, DEMOCRATIC REPUBLIC OF

Embassy of the Democratic Republic of Congo
1726 M Street, NW., Suite 601, Washington, DC 20036
phone (202) 234–7690, fax 234–2609
Her Excellency Faida Mitifu
Ambassador E. and P.
Consular Office: New York, New York

CONGO, REPUBLIC OF

Embassy of the Republic of the Congo
4891 Colorado Avenue, NW., Washington, DC 20011
phone (202) 726–5500, fax 726–1860
His Excellency Serge Mombouli
Ambassador E. and P.
Consular Office: Louisiana, New Orleans

COOK ISLANDS

Consular Offices:
California, Los Angeles
Hawaii, Honolulu

COSTA RICA

Embassy of Costa Rica
2114 S Street, NW., Washington, DC 20008
phone (202) 234–2945, fax 265–4795
His Excellency F. Tomas Duenas
Ambassador E. and P.
Consular Offices:
Arizona, Tucson
California:
Los Angeles
San Francisco
Colorado, Denver
Florida, Miami
Georgia, Atlanta
Illinois, Chicago
Louisiana, New Orleans
Massachusetts, Boston
Minnesota, Minneapolis
New York, New York
Puerto Rico, San Juan
Texas:
Austin
Dallas
Houston

CÔTE D'IVOIRE

Embassy of the Republic of Côte d'Ivoire
2424 Massachusetts Avenue, NW., Washington, DC 20008
phone (202) 797–0300, fax 462–9444
His Excellency Daouda Diabate
Ambassador E. and P.
Consular Offices:
California, San Francisco
Connecticut, Stamford
Florida, Orlando
Michigan, Detroit
Texas, Houston

CROATIA

Embassy of the Republic of Croatia
2343 Massachusetts Avenue, NW., Washington, DC 20008
phone (202) 588–5899, fax 588–8936
His Excellency Neven Jurica
Ambassador E. and P.
Consular Offices:
California, Los Angeles
Illinois, Chicago
Kansas, Kansas City
Louisiana, New Orleans
New York, New York
Pennsylvania, Pittsburgh
Washington, Seattle

CYPRUS

Embassy of the Republic of Cyprus
2211 R Street, NW., Washington, DC 20008
phone (202) 462–5772, fax 483–6710
His Excellency Andreas S. Kakouris
Ambassador E. and P.
Consular Offices:

Arizona, Phoenix
California, Los Angeles
Georgia, Atlanta
Illinois, Chicago
Louisiana, New Orleans
Massachusetts, Boston
Michigan, Detroit
Nebraska, Omaha
New York, New York
North Carolina, Jacksonville
Oregon, Portland
Texas, Houston
Virginia, Virginia Beach
Washington, Seattle

CZECH REPUBLIC

Embassy of the Czech Republic
3900 Spring of Freedom Street, NW., Washington, DC 20008
phone (202) 274–9100, fax 966–8540
His Excellency Petr Kolar
Ambassador E. and P.
Consular Offices:
Alaska, Anchorage
California:
Los Angeles
San Francisco
Florida, Ft. Lauderdale
Georgia, Atlanta
Illinois, Chicago
Louisiana, New Orleans
Massachusetts, Wellesley
Minnesota, St. Paul
Missouri, Kansas City
New York:
Buffalo
New York
Oregon, Portland
Pennsylvania, Philadelphia
Puerto Rico, San Juan
Texas, Houston

DENMARK

Royal Danish Embassy
3200 Whitehaven Street, NW., Washington, DC 20008
phone (202) 234–4300, fax 328–1470
His Excellency Friis Arne Petersen
Ambassador E. and P.
Consular Offices:
Alabama, Mobile
Alaska, Anchorage
Arizona, Scottsdale
California:
San Diego
San Francisco
Studio City
Colorado, Denver
Florida:
Hollywood
Jacksonville
Tampa
Georgia:
Atlanta
Macon
Hawaii, Honolulu
Illinois, Chicago
Indiana, Indianapolis
Iowa, Des Moines
Louisiana, New Orleans
Maryland, Baltimore
Massachusetts, Boston
Michigan, Detroit
Minnesota, Minneapolis
Missouri:
Kansas City
St. Louis
Nebraska, Omaha
New York, New York
Ohio, Cleveland
Oklahoma, Oklahoma City
Oregon, Portland
Pennsylvania:
Philadelphia
Pittsburgh
Puerto Rico, San Juan
South Carolina, Charleston
Tennessee, Nashville
Texas:
Dallas
Houston
Utah, Salt Lake City
Virgin Islands, St. Thomas
Virginia, Norfolk
Washington, Seattle
Wisconsin, Milwaukee

DJIBOUTI

Embassy of the Republic of Djibouti
1156 15th Street, NW., Suite 515, Washington, DC 20005
phone (202) 331–0270, fax 331–0302
His Excellency Roble Olhaye
Ambassador E. and P.

DOMINICA

Embassy of the Commonwealth of Dominica
3216 New Mexico Avenue, NW., Washington, DC 20016
phone (202) 364–6781, fax 364–6791
[Ambassador departed October 12, 2001]
Consular Office: New York, New York

DOMINICAN REPUBLIC

Embassy of the Dominican Republic
1715 22nd Street, NW., Washington, DC 20008

phone (202) 332–6280, fax 265–8057
His Excellency Flavio Dario Espinal
Ambassador E. and P.
Consular Offices:
- California, Sun Valley
- Florida, Miami
- Illinois, Chicago
- Louisiana, New Orleans
- Massachusetts, Boston
- New York, New York
- Puerto Rico:
  - Mayaguez
  - San Juan

EAST TIMOR

Embassy of the Democratic Republic of Timor Leste
4201 Connecticut Avenue, NW., Suite 504, Washington, DC 20008
phone (202) 966–3202, fax 966–3205
Mr. Constancio C. Pinto
Minister-Counselor

ECUADOR

Embassy of Ecuador
2535 15th Street, NW., Washington, DC 20009
phone (202) 234–7200, fax 667–3482
His Excellency Luis Beningo Gallegos Chiriboga
Ambassador E. and P.
Consular Offices:
- California:
  - Los Angeles
  - San Francisco
- Florida:
  - Miami
  - Tampa
- Georgia, Atlanta
- Illinois, Chicago
- Louisiana, New Orleans
- Massachusetts, Boston
- Minnesota, Eden Prairie
- Nevada, Las Vegas
- New Jersey, Newark
- New York, New York
- Puerto Rico, San Juan
- Texas:
  - Dallas
  - Houston

EGYPT

Embassy of the Arab Republic of Egypt
3521 International Court, NW., Washington, DC 20008
phone (202) 895–5400, fax 244–4319
His Excellency M. Nabil Fahmy
Ambassador E. and P.
Consular Offices:
- California, San Francisco
- Illinois, Chicago
- New York, New York
- Texas, Houston

EL SALVADOR

Embassy of El Salvador
1400 16th Street, NW., Suite 100, Washington, DC 20036
phone (202) 265–9671, fax 232–3763
His Excellency René Antonio León
Ambassador E. and P.
Consular Offices:
- Arizona:
  - Nogales
  - Phoenix
- California:
  - Chula Vista
  - Costa Mesa
  - Los Angeles
  - Oakland
  - San Francisco
  - Santa Ana
- Florida, Miami
- Georgia, Duluth
- Illinois, Chicago
- Louisiana, New Orleans
- Massachusetts, Boston
- Missouri:
  - Kansas City
  - St. Louis
- Nevada, Las Vegas
- New Jersey, Elizabeth
- New York, New York
- Pennsylvania, Philadelphia
- Puerto Rico, Bayamon
- Texas:
  - Dallas
  - Houston
- Utah, Salt Lake City
- Virginia, Woodbridge

EQUATORIAL GUINEA

Embassy of the Republic of Equatorial Guinea
2020 16th Street, NW., Washington, DC 20009
phone (202) 518–5700, fax 518–5252
Her Excellency Purificacion Angue Ondo
Ambassador E. and P.

ERITREA

Embassy of the State of Eritrea
1708 New Hampshire Avenue, NW., Washington, DC 20009
phone (202) 319–1991, fax 319–1304
His Excellency Ghirmai Ghebremariam
Appointed Ambassador
Consular Office: California, Oakland

ESTONIA

Embassy of Estonia
2131 Massachusetts Avenue, NW., Washington, DC 20008
phone (202) 588–0101, fax 588–0108
His Excellency Jüri Luik
Ambassador E. and P.
Consular Offices:
California:
Los Angeles
San Francisco
Illinois, Chicago
New Hampshire, Portsmouth
New York, New York

ETHIOPIA

Embassy of Ethiopia
3506 International Drive, NW., Washington, DC 20008
phone (202) 364–1200, fax 686–9551
His Excellency Dr. Samuel Assefa
Ambassador E. and P.
Consular Offices:
California, Los Angeles
New York, New York
Texas, Houston
Washington, Seattle

EUROPEAN UNION

Delegation of the European Commission
2300 M Street, NW., Washington, DC 20037
phone (202) 862–9500, fax 429–1766
His Excellency John Bruton
Ambassador E. and P. (Head of Delegation)

FIJI

Embassy of the Republic of the Fiji Islands
2233 Wisconsin Avenue, NW., Suite 240, Washington, DC 20007
phone (202) 337–8320, fax 337–1996
His Excellency Jesoni Vitusagavulu
Ambassador E. and P.
Consular Offices:
California:
Los Angeles
San Francisco
Oregon, Portland

FINLAND

Embassy of Finland
3301 Massachusetts Avenue, NW., Washington, DC 20008
phone (202) 298–5800, fax 298–6030
His Excellency Pekka Lintu
Ambassador E. and P.
Consular Offices:
Alabama, Birmingham
Alaska, Anchorage
Arizona, Phoenix
California:
Los Angeles
Portola Valley
San Diego
Colorado, Denver
Connecticut, Norwich
Florida:
Lake Worth
Miami
Georgia, Atlanta
Hawaii, Honolulu
Illinois, Chicago
Louisiana, New Orleans
Maryland, Baltimore
Massachusetts, Boston
Michigan:
Detroit
Marquette
Minnesota:
Minneapolis
Virginia
New Jersey, Newark
New Mexico, Albequerque
New York, New York
Oregon, Portland
Puerto Rico, San Juan
Texas, Houston
Virginia, Norfolk
Washington, Seattle

FRANCE

Embassy of France
4101 Reservoir Road, NW., Washington, DC 20007
phone (202) 944–6000, fax 944–6166
His Excellency Jean-David Levitte
Ambassador E. and P.
Consular Offices:
Alabama, Auburn University
Alaska, Anchorage
Arizona, Phoenix
Arkansas, Little Rock
California:
Los Angeles
Sacramento
San Diego
San Francisco
San Jose
Colorado, Denver
Connecticut, Hartford
Florida:
Clearwater
Miami
Orlando
Georgia:
Atlanta
Savannah

Guam, Tamuning
Hawaii, Honolulu
Idaho, Boise
Illinois, Chicago
Indiana, Indianapolis
Iowa, Indianola
Kentucky, Louisville
Louisiana
  Lafayette
  New Orleans
Maine, Portland
Massachusetts, Boston
Minnesota, Minneapolis
Mississippi, Jackson
Missouri:
  Kansas City
  Saint Louis
Montana, Missoula
Nevada, Las Vegas
New Hampshire, Manchester
New Jersey, Princeton
New Mexico, Albequerque
New York:
  Buffalo
  New York
North Carolina, Charlotte
Ohio:
  Cincinnati
  Cleveland
Oklahoma, Oklahoma City
Oregon, Portland
Pennsylvania, Philadelphia
Puerto Rico, San Juan
Rhode Island, Providence
South Carolina, Columbia
Tennessee, Memphis
Texas:
  Austin
  Dallas
  Houston
  San Antonio
Utah, Salt Lake City
Vermont, Essex Junction
Virgin Islands, St. Thomas
Virginia, Norfolk
Washington, Seattle
Wyoming, Dubois

GABON

Embassy of the Gabonese Republic
2034 20th Street, NW., Suite 200, Washington, DC 20009
phone (202) 797–1000, fax 332–0668
His Excellency Jules Marius Ogouebandja
Ambassador E. and P.
Consular Office: New York, New York

GAMBIA

Embassy of The Gambia
1156 15th Street, NW., Suite 905, Washington, DC 20005
phone (202) 785–1379, fax 785–1430
His Excellency Dodou Bammy Jagne
Ambassador E. and P.
Consular Offices:
  California, Los Angeles
  Florida, Miami

GEORGIA, REPUBLIC OF

Embassy of the Republic of Georgia
1101 15th Street, NW., Suite 602, Washington, DC 20005
phone (202) 387–2390, fax 393–4537
His Excellency Vasil Sikharulidze
Ambassador E. and P.
Consular Offices:
  Alabama, Mobile
  California, Orange
  Massachusetts, Boston
  Puerto Rico, San Juan
  Texas, Houston

GERMANY, FEDERAL REPUBLIC OF

Embassy of the Federal Republic of Germany
4645 Reservoir Road, NW., Washington, DC 20007
phone (202) 298–4000, fax 298–4249
His Excellency Dr. Klaus Scharioth
Ambassador E. and P.
Consular Offices:
  Alabama, Birmingham
  Alaska, Anchorage
  Arizona, Phoenix
  California:
    Carlsbad
    Los Angeles
    San Francisco
  Colorado, Denver
  Florida:
    Miami
    Naples
  Georgia, Atlanta
  Illinois, Chicago
  Iowa, Indianola
  Kansas, Kansas City
  Kentucky, Louisville
  Louisiana, New Orleans
  Massachusetts, Boston
  Michigan, Auburn Hills
  Minnesota, Minneapolis
  Mississippi, Jackson
  Missouri, St. Louis
  New Mexico, Albequerque
  New York:
    Buffalo

New York
North Carolina, Charlotte
Ohio:
Cincinnati
Cleveland
Oklahoma, Oklahoma City
Oregon, Portland
Pennsylvania:
Philadelphia
Pittsburgh
South Carolina, Greer
Tennessee, Nashville
Texas:
Corpus Christi
Dallas
Houston
San Antonio
Trust Territories of the Pacific Islands:
Manila, Philippines
Wellington, New Zealand
Utah, Salt Lake City
Virginia, Virginia Beach
Washington, Spokane

GHANA

Embassy of Ghana
3512 International Drive, NW., Washington, DC 20008
phone (202) 686–4520, fax 686–4527
His Excellency Dr. Kwame Bawuah-Edusei
Ambassador E. and P.
Consular Offices:
New York, New York
Texas, Houston

GREAT BRITAIN

See United Kingdom

GREECE

Embassy of Greece
2221 Massachusetts Avenue, NW., Washington, DC 20008
phone (202) 939–1300, fax 939–1324
His Excellency Alexandros P. Mallias
Ambassador E. and P.
Consular Offices:
California:
Los Angeles
San Francisco
Florida, Tampa
Georgia, Atlanta
Illinois, Chicago
Louisiana, New Orleans
Massachusetts, Boston
New York, New York
Texas, Houston

GRENADA

Embassy of Grenada
1701 New Hampshire Avenue, NW., Washington, DC 20009
phone (202) 265–2561, fax 265–2468
His Excellency Dr. Denis G. Antoine
Ambassador E. and P.
Consular Offices:
Florida, Ft. Lauderdale
Illinois, Chicago
Michigan, Northville
New York, New York

GUATEMALA

Embassy of Guatemala
2220 R Street, NW., Washington, DC 20008
phone (202) 745–4952, fax 745–1908
His Excellency Guillermo Castillo
Ambassador E. and P.
Consular Offices:
Alabama, Montgomery
Arizona, Phoenix
California:
Los Angeles
San Diego
San Francisco
Colorado, Denver
Florida:
Ft. Lauderdale
Miami
Georgia, Atlanta
Illinois, Chicago
Louisiana:
Lafayette
New Orleans
Minnesota, Minneapolis
Missouri, Kansas City
Nevada, North Las Vegas
New York, New York
North Carolina, Charlotte
Oregon, Portland
Pennsylvania, Philadelphia
Puerto Rico, San Juan
Rhode Island, Providence
Tennessee, Memphis
Texas:
Houston
San Antonio
Washington, Seattle

GUINEA

Embassy of the Republic of Guinea
2112 Leroy Place, NW., Washington, DC 20008
phone (202) 986–4300, fax 986–3800
Mr. Ibrahim Sory Traore
Counselor
Consular Offices:

Florida, Jacksonville
Ohio, Cleveland
Pennsylvania, Philadelphia

GUINEA-BISSAU

Embassy of the Republic of Guinea-Bissau
P.O. Box 33813, Washington, DC 20033
phone (301) 947–3958
Mr. Henrique Adriano Da Silva
Minister-Counselor

GUYANA

Embassy of Guyana
2490 Tracy Place, NW., Washington, DC 20008
phone (202) 265–6900, fax 232–1297
His Excellency Bayney Karran
Ambassador E. and P.
Consular Offices:
California, Los Angeles
Florida, Miami
New York, New York
Texas, Houston

HAITI

Embassy of the Republic of Haiti
2311 Massachusetts Avenue, NW., Washington, DC 20008
phone (202) 332–4090, fax 745–7215
His Excellency Raymond Alcide Joseph
Ambassador E. and P.
Consular Offices:
California, San Francisco
Colorado, Denver
Florida:
Miami
Orlando
Georgia, Atlanta
Illinois, Chicago
Indiana, Evansville
Louisiana, New Orleans
Massachusetts, Boston
Michigan, Detroit
Missouri, St. Louis
New Jersey, Trenton
New York, New York
Ohio, Cleveland
Pennsylvania, Philadelphia
Puerto Rico, San Juan
Texas, Houston

HOLY SEE

Apostolic Nunciature
3339 Massachusetts Avenue, NW., Washington, DC 20008
phone (202) 333–7121, fax 337–4036
His Excellency Pietro Sambi
Nuncio

HONDURAS

Embassy of Honduras
3007 Tilden Street, NW., Suite 4–M, Washington, DC 20008
phone (202) 966–2604, fax 966–9751
His Excellency Roberto Flores Bermudez
Ambassador E. and P.
Consular Offices:
Arizona, Phoenix
California:
Los Angeles
San Diego
San Francisco
Florida:
Jacksonville
Miami
Georgia, Atlanta
Hawaii, Honolulu
Illinois, Chicago
Louisiana:
Baton Rouge
New Orleans
Maryland, Baltimore
Massachusetts, Boston
Minnesota, Minneapolis
Missouri, St. Louis
Nevada, Reno
New York, New York
Texas, Houston

HUNGARY

Embassy of the Republic of Hungary
3910 Shoemaker Street, NW., Washington, DC 20008
phone (202) 362–6730, fax 966–8135
His Excellency András Simonyi
Ambassador E. and P.
Consular Offices:
California:
Los Angeles
San Francisco
Colorado, Denver
Florida, Miami
Hawaii, Honolulu
Illinois, Chicago
Louisiana, New Orleans
Massachusetts, Boston
Missouri, St. Louis
New York, New York
Ohio, Cleveland
Puerto Rico, Mayaguez
Texas, Houston
Washington, Seattle

ICELAND

Embassy of Iceland
1156 15th Street, NW., Suite 1200, Washington, DC 20005

phone (202) 265–6653, fax 265–6656
His Excellency Albert Jónsson
Ambassador E. and P.
Consular Offices:
- Alaska, Anchorage
- Arizona, Phoenix
- California:
  - Los Angeles
  - San Diego
  - San Francisco
- Colorado, Englewood
- Florida:
  - Hollywood
  - Tallahassee
- Georgia, Atlanta
- Illinois, Chicago
- Kentucky, Louisville
- Louisiana, New Orleans
- Massachusetts, Boston
- Michigan, Detroit
- Minnesota, Minneapolis
- Missouri, Grandview
- New York, New York
- North Dakota, Grand Fork
- Oregon, Portland
- Pennsylvania, Harrisburg
- Puerto Rico, San Juan
- South Carolina, Charleston
- Texas:
  - Dallas
  - Houston
- Utah, Salt Lake City
- Virginia, Norfolk
- Washington, Seattle
- Wisconsin, Madison

INDIA

Embassy of India
2107 Massachusetts Avenue, NW., Washington, DC 20008
phone (202) 939–7000, fax 483–3972
His Excellency Ronen Sen
Ambassador E. and P.
Consular Offices:
- California, San Francisco
- Georgia, Atlanta
- Hawaii, Honolulu
- Illinois, Chicago
- Louisiana, New Orleans
- New York, New York
- Ohio, Cleveland
- Texas, Houston

INDONESIA

Embassy of the Republic of Indonesia
2020 Massachusetts Avenue, NW., Washington, DC 20036
phone (202) 775–5200, fax 775–5365
His Excellency Sudjadnan Parnohadiningrat
Ambassador E. and P.
Consular Offices:
- California:
  - Los Angeles
  - San Francisco
- Hawaii, Honolulu
- Illinois, Chicago
- New York, New York
- Texas, Houston

IRAN

See Pakistan

IRAQ

Embassy of the Republic of Iraq
1801 P Street, NW., Washington, DC 20036
phone (202) 483–7500, fax 462–5066
His Excellency Samir Shakir Mahmood Sumaida'ie
Ambassador E. and P.

IRELAND

Embassy of Ireland
2234 Massachusetts Avenue, NW., Washington, DC 20008
phone (202) 462–3939, fax 232–5993
His Excellency Noel Fahey
Ambassador E. and P.
Consular Offices:
- California:
  - Los Angeles
  - San Francisco
- Florida, Naples
- Georgia, Atlanta
- Illinois, Chicago
- Massachusetts, Boston
- Missouri, St. Louis
- Nevada, Reno
- New York, New York
- Texas, Houston

ISRAEL

Embassy of Israel
3514 International Drive, NW., Washington, DC 20008
phone (202) 364–5500, fax 364–5607
His Excellency Sallai Moshe Meridor
Ambassador E. and P.
Consular Offices:
- California:
  - Los Angeles
  - San Francisco
- Florida, Miami
- Georgia, Atlanta
- Illinois, Chicago
- Massachusetts, Boston
- New York, New York
- Pennsylvania, Philadelphia

Texas, Houston

ITALY

Embassy of Italy
3000 Whitehaven Street, NW., Washington, DC 20008
phone (202) 612–4400, fax 518–2151
His Excellency Giovanni Castellaneta
Ambassador E. and P.
Consular Offices:
Alaska, Anchorage
Arizona, Phoenix
California:
Fresno
Los Angeles
Sacramento
San Francisco
San Jose
Colorado, Denver
Connecticut, Hartford
Florida:
Miami
Orlando
Sarasota
Georgia:
Atlanta
Savannah
Hawaii, Honolulu
Illinois, Chicago
Indiana, Indianapolis
Kansas, Kansas City
Louisiana, New Orleans
Maryland, Baltimore
Massachusetts:
Boston
Worcester
Michigan, Detroit
Minnesota, St. Paul
Missouri, St. Louis
New Jersey:
Newark
Trenton
New York:
Buffalo
Mineola
Mt. Vernon
New York
Rochester
Ohio, Cleveland
Oregon, Portland
Pennsylvania:
Philadelphia
Pittsburgh
Puerto Rico, San Juan
Rhode Island, Providence
South Carolina, Charleston
Texas:
Dallas
Houston
Utah, Salt Lake City
Virginia, Norfolk
Washington, Seattle

IVORY COAST

See Côte d'Ivoire

JAMAICA

Embassy of Jamaica
1520 New Hampshire Avenue, NW., Washington, DC 20036
phone (202) 452–0660, fax 452–0081
His Excellency Gordon Valentine Shirley
Ambassador E. and P.
Consular Offices:
California:
Los Angeles
San Francisco
Florida, Miami
Georgia, Atlanta
Illinois, Chicago
Massachusetts, Boston
New Hampshire, Manchester
New York, New York
Pennsylvania, Philadelphia
Texas:
Dallas
Houston
Virginia, Richmond
Washington, Seattle

JAPAN

Embassy of Japan
2520 Massachusetts Avenue, NW., Washington, DC 20008
phone (202) 238–6700, fax 328–2187
His Excellency Ryozo Kato
Ambassador E. and P.
Consular Offices:
Alabama, Birmingham
Alaska, Anchorage
Arizona, Tempe
California:
Los Angeles
San Diego
San Francisco
Colorado, Denver
Connecticut, Simsbury
Florida, Miami
Georgia, Atlanta
Guam, Agana
Hawaii:
Hilo
Honolulu
Illinois, Chicago

Indiana, Indianapolis
Kansas, Shawnee Mission
Kentucky, Lexington
Louisiana, New Orleans
Massachusetts, Boston
Michigan, Detroit
Minnesota, Minneapolis
Missouri, St. Louis
Nebraska, Omaha
Nevada, Las Vegas
New York:
Buffalo
New York
North Carolina, High Point
Oklahoma, Oklahoma City
Oregon, Portland
Pennsylvania, Philadelphia
Puerto Rico, San Juan
Tennessee, Nashville
Texas:
Dallas
Houston
Trust Territories of the Pacific Islands:
Mariana Islands
Pago Pago
Washington, Seattle
Wyoming, Casper

JORDAN

Embassy of the Hashemite Kingdom of Jordan
3504 International Drive, NW., Washington, DC 20008
phone (202) 966–2664, fax 966–3110
His Excellency Zeid Bin Ra'ad al-Hussein
Ambassador E. and P.
Consular Offices:
California, San Francisco
Illinois, Chicago
Michigan, Detroit

KAZAKHSTAN

Embassy of the Republic of Kazakhstan
1401 16th Street, NW., Washington, DC 20036
phone (202) 232–5488, fax 232–5845
His Excellency Kanat B. Saudabayev
Ambassador E. and P.
Consular Office: New York, New York

KENYA

Embassy of the Republic of Kenya
2249 R Street, NW., Washington, DC 20008
phone (202) 387–6101, fax 462–3829
His Excellency Peter N.R.O. Ogego
Ambassador E. and P.
Consular Offices:
California, Los Angeles
New York, New York

KIRIBATI

Consular Office: Hawaii, Honolulu

KOREA, REPUBLIC OF

Embassy of the Republic of Korea
2450 Massachusetts Avenue, NW., Washington, DC 20008
phone (202) 939–5600, fax 387–0250
His Excellency Tae-sik Lee
Ambassador E. and P.
Consular Offices:
Alaska, Anchorage
California:
Los Angeles
San Francisco
Florida, Miami
Georgia, Atlanta
Guam, Agana
Hawaii, Honolulu
Illinois, Chicago
Louisiana, New Orleans
Massachusetts, Boston
Michigan, Detroit
Minnesota, Minneapolis
Montana, Helena
New York, New York
Oregon, Portland
Puerto Rico, San Juan
South Carolina, Columbia
Texas:
Dallas
Houston
Washington, Seattle

KUWAIT

Embassy of the State of Kuwait
2940 Tilden Street, NW., Washington, DC 20008
phone (202) 966–0702, fax 966–0517
His Excellency Sheikh Salem Abdullah Al Jaber Al-Sabah
Ambassador E. and P.
Consular Office: California, Los Angeles

KYRGYZSTAN

Embassy of the Kyrgyz Republic
1001 Pennsylvania Avenue, NW., Suite 600, Washington, DC 20004
phone (202) 338–5141, fax 338–5139
Her Excellency Zamira Beksultanovna Sydykova
Ambassador E. and P.
Consular Offices:
California:
Buellton
Los Angeles
New York, New York
Texas, Houston
Utah, Orem

LAOS

Embassy of the Lao People's Democratic Republic
2222 S Street, NW., Washington, DC 20008
phone (202) 332–6416, fax 332–4923
His Excellency Phiane Philakone
Ambassador E. and P.

LATVIA

Embassy of Latvia
2306 Massachusetts Avenue, NW., Washington, DC 20008
phone (202) 328–2840, fax 328–2860
Mr. Maris Selga
Charge d'Affaires
Consular Offices:
- California, Los Angeles
- Connecticut, Greenwich
- Florida, Ft. Lauderdale
- New York:
  - Buffalo
  - New York
- Ohio, Cincinnati
- Texas, Houston

LEBANON

Embassy of Lebanon
2560 28th Street, NW., Washington, DC 20008
phone (202) 939–6300, fax 939–6324
His Excellency Dr. Farid Abboud
Ambassador E. and P.
Consular Offices:
- California:
  - Los Angeles
  - San Diego
- Florida, Miami
- Massachusetts, Boston
- Michigan, Detroit
- New York, New York
- North Carolina, Raleigh
- Texas, Houston

LESOTHO

Embassy of the Kingdom of Lesotho
2511 Massachusetts Avenue, NW., Washington, DC 20008
phone (202) 797–5533, fax 234–6815
Her Excellency Molelekeng E. Rapolaki
Ambassador E. and P.
Consular Offices:
- Louisiana, New Orleans
- Texas, Austin

LIBERIA

Embassy of the Republic of Liberia
5201 16th Street, NW., Washington, DC 20011
phone (202) 723–0437, fax 723–0436
His Excellency Charles A. Minor
Ambassador E. and P.
Consular Offices:
- California:
  - Los Angeles
  - San Francisco
- Florida, Tampa
- Georgia, Atlanta
- Illinois, Chicago
- Louisiana, New Orleans
- Michigan, Detroit
- New York, New York
- Pennsylvania, Philadelphia

LIBYA

Embassy of the Libyan Arab Jamahiriya
2600 Virginia Avenue, NW., Suite 705, Washington, DC 20037
phone (202) 944–9601, fax 944–9606
Mr. Ali Suleiman Aujali
Minister

LIECHTENSTEIN

Embassy of the Principality of Liechtenstein
888 17th Street, NW., Suite 1250, Washington, DC 20006
phone (202) 331–0590, fax 331–3221
Her Excellency Claudia Fritsche
Ambassador E. and P.

LITHUANIA

Embassy of the Republic of Lithuania
4590 MacArthur Boulevard, NW., Suite 200, Washington, DC 20007
phone (202) 234–5860, fax 328–0466
His Excellency Audrius Bruzga
Ambassador E. and P.
Consular Offices:
- Arizona, Phoenix
- California:
  - Lafayette
  - Los Angeles
- Florida:
  - Palm Beach
  - St. Petersburg
- Illinois, Chicago
- Michigan:
  - Detroit
  - Lansing
- Minnesota, Stillwater
- New Hampshire, Manchester
- New Jersey, Mendham
- New York:
  - New York
  - Webster
- Ohio, Cleveland
- Oregon, Portland
- Texas, Houston
- Washington, Seattle

LUXEMBOURG

Embassy of Grand Duchy of Luxembourg
2200 Massachusetts Avenue, NW., Washington, DC 20008
phone (202) 265–4171, fax 328–8270
His Excellency Joseph Weyland
Ambassador E. and P.
Consular Offices:
California:
San Francisco
Woodland Hills
Georgia, Atlanta
Illinois, Chicago
Indiana, Indianapolis
Louisiana, New Orleans
Massachusetts, Boston
Michigan, Detroit
Missouri, Kansas City
New York, New York
Ohio, Cleveland
Oregon, Portland
Texas, Ft. Worth
Washington, Seattle

MACEDONIA

Embassy of the Republic of Macedonia
1101 30th Street, NW., Suite 302, Washington, DC 20007
phone (202) 667–0501, fax 667–2131
Mr. Oliver Krliu
Minister-Counselor
Consular Office: Michigan, Southfield

MADAGASCAR

Embassy of the Republic of Madagascar
2374 Massachusetts Avenue, NW., Washington, DC 20008
phone (202) 265–5525, fax 265–3034
His Excellency Rajaonarivony Narisoa
Ambassador E. and P.
Consular Offices:
California, San Diego
New York, New York
Pennsylvania, Philadelphia

MALAWI

Embassy of Malawi
1156 15th Street, NW., Suite 320, Washington, DC 20005
phone (202) 721–0270, fax 721–0288
His Excellency Hawa Olga Ndilowe
Ambassador E. and P.

MALAYSIA

Embassy of Malaysia
3516 International Court, NW., Washington, DC 20008
phone (202) 572–9700, fax 572–9882
Her Excellency Dr. Rajmah Hussein
Ambassador E. and P.
Consular Offices:
California, Los Angeles
Hawaii, Honolulu
New York, New York
Oregon, Portland
Texas, Houston

MALDIVES

Embassy of the Republic of Maldives
800 2nd Avenue, Suite 400E, New York, NY 10017
phone (212) 599–6195, fax 661–6405
His Excellency Dr. Mohamed Latheef
Ambassador E. and P.

MALI

Embassy of the Republic of Mali
2130 R Street, NW., Washington, DC 20008
phone (202) 332–2249, fax 332–6603
His Excellency Abdoulaye Diop
Ambassador E. and P.
Consular Offices:
Florida, Ft. Lauderdale
Louisiana, New Orleans
Massachusetts, Boston
New Mexico, Albuquerque

MALTA

Embassy of Malta
2017 Connecticut Avenue, NW., Washington, DC 20008
phone (202) 462–3611, fax 387–5470
His Excellency John Lowell
Ambassador E. and P.
Consular Offices:
California:
Los Angeles
San Francisco
Florida, Ft. Lauderdale
Louisiana, Metairie
Massachusetts, Bellmont
Michigan, Detroit
Minnesota, St. Paul
New York, New York
Pennsylvania, Philadelphia
Tennessee, Kingsport
Texas:
Austin
Dallas
Houston
Washington, Seattle

MARSHALL ISLANDS

Embassy of the Republic of the Marshall Islands
2433 Massachusetts Avenue, NW., 1st Floor, Washington, DC 20008
phone (202) 234–5414, fax 232–3236
His Excellency Banny de Brum

Ambassador E. and P.
Consular Offices:
- Guam, Agana
- Hawaii, Honolulu

MAURITANIA

Embassy of the Islamic Republic of Mauritania
2129 Leroy Place, NW., Washington, DC 20008
phone (202) 232–5700, fax 319–2623
His Excellency Tijani Ould M.E. Kerim
Ambassador E. and P.

MAURITIUS

Embassy of the Republic of Mauritius
4301 Connecticut Avenue, NW., Suite 441, Washington, DC 20008
phone (202) 244–1491, fax 966–0983
His Excellency Keerteecoomar Ruhee
Ambassador E. and P.
Consular Offices:
- Arizona, Sun City
- California:
  - Los Angeles
  - San Francisco

MEXICO

Embassy of Mexico
1911 Pennsylvania Avenue, NW., Washington, DC 20006
phone (202) 728–1600, fax 728–1698
His Excellency Arturo Sarukhan Casamitjana
Ambassador E. and P.
Consular Offices:
- Alaska, Anchorage
- Arizona:
  - Douglas
  - Nogales
  - Phoenix
  - Tucson
  - Yuma
- Arkansas, Little Rock
- California:
  - Calexico
  - Fresno
  - Los Angeles
  - Oxnard
  - Sacramento
  - Salinas
  - San Bernardino
  - San Diego
  - San Francisco
  - San Jose
  - Santa Ana
- Colorado, Denver
- Florida:
  - Jacksonville
  - Miami
  - Orlando
- Georgia, Atlanta
- Hawaii, Honolulu
- Illinois, Chicago
- Indiana, Indianapolis
- Louisiana, New Orleans
- Massachusetts, Boston
- Michigan, Detroit
- Minnesota, St. Paul
- Missouri, Kansas City
- Nebraska, Omaha
- Nevada, Las Vegas
- New Mexico, Albuquerque
- New York, New York
- North Carolina:
  - Charlotte
  - Raleigh
- Oregon, Portland
- Pennsylvania, Philadelphia
- Puerto Rico, San Juan
- Texas:
  - Austin
  - Brownsville
  - Corpus Christi
  - Dallas
  - Del Rio
  - Eagle Pass
  - El Paso
  - Houston
  - Laredo
  - McAllen
  - Midland
  - San Antonio
- Utah, Salt Lake City
- Virginia, Richmond
- Washington, Seattle
- Wisconsin, Madison

MICRONESIA

Embassy of the Federated States of Micronesia
1725 N Street, NW., Washington, DC 20036
phone (202) 223–4383, fax 223–4391
Mr. James Aviando Naich
Minister
Consular Offices:
- Guam, Tamuning
- Hawaii, Honolulu

MOLDOVA

Embassy of the Republic of Moldova
2101 S Street, NW., Washington, DC 20008
phone (202) 667–1130, fax 667–1204
His Excellency Nicolae Chirtoaca
Ambassador E. and P.
Consular Offices:
- New York, New York
- North Carolina, Hickory
- Pennsylvania, Philadelphia
- Virginia, Norfolk

MONACO

Embassy of Monoco
866 United Nations Plaza, Suite 520, New York, NY 10017
phone (212) 832–0721, fax 832–5358
Ambassador Gilles Alexandre Noghes
Consular Offices:
California:
Los Angeles
San Francisco
Florida, Miami
Illinois, Chicago
Massachusetts, Boston
New York, New York
Texas, Dallas

MONGOLIA

Embassy of Mongolia
2833 M Street, NW., Washington, DC 20007
phone (202) 333–7117, fax 298–9227
His Excellency Ravdan Bold
Ambassador E. and P.
Consular Offices:
California:
Canoga Park
San Francisco
Colorado, Denver
Georgia, Atlanta
Illinois, Chicago
New Jersey, Plainfield
New York, New York
Texas, Houston
Utah, Springfield

MOROCCO

Embassy of the Kingdom of Morocco
1601 21st Street, NW., Washington, DC 20009
phone (202) 462–7980, fax 265–0161
His Excellency Aziz Mekouar
Ambassador E. and P.
Consular Offices:
California, Los Angeles
Hawaii, Honolulu
Kansas, Kansas City
Massachusetts, Cambridge
New York, New York

MOZAMBIQUE

Embassy of the Republic of Mozambique
1990 M Street, NW., Suite 570, Washington, DC 20036
phone (202) 293–7146, fax 835–0245
His Excellency Armando Alexandre Panguene
Ambassador E. and P.

MYANMAR

Embassy of the Union of Myanmar
2300 S Street, NW., Washington, DC 20008
phone (202) 332–3344, fax 332–4351
Minister-Counselor Mr. Myint Lwin
Consular Office: New York, New York

NAMIBIA

Embassy of the Republic of Namibia
1605 New Hampshire Avenue, NW., Washington, DC 20009
phone (202) 986–0540, fax 986–0443
His Excellency Patrick Nandago
Ambassador E. and P.
Consular Office: Michigan, Detroit

NAURU

Embassy of the Republic of Nauru
800 Second Avenue, New York, NY 10017
phone (212) 937–0074, fax 937–0079
Her Excellency Marlene Inemwin Moses
Ambassador E. and P.
Consular Offices:
Guam, Agana
Hawaii, Honolulu
Trust Territories of the Pacific Islands:
Pago Pago

NEPAL

Royal Nepalese Embassy
2131 Leroy Place, NW., Washington, DC 20008
phone (202) 667–4550, fax 667–5534
Mr. Rudra K. Nepal
Minister-Counselor
Consular Offices:
California:
Los Angeles
San Francisco
Illinois, Chicago
Massachusetts, Boston
New York, New York
Ohio, Cleveland

NETHERLANDS

Royal Netherlands Embassy
4200 Linnean Avenue, NW., Washington, DC 20008
phone (202) 244–5300, fax 362–3430
His Excellency Christaan Mark Johan Kröner
Ambassador E. and P.
Consular Offices:
Arizona, Phoenix
California:
Los Angeles
San Francisco
Colorado, Denver
Florida:
Jacksonville
Miami
Georgia, Atlanta
Hawaii, Honolulu
Illinois, Chicago

Louisiana, New Orleans
Massachusetts, Boston
Michigan:
Detroit
Grand Rapids
Minnesota, Minneapolis
Missouri:
Kansas City
St. Louis
New York, New York
North Carolina, Raleigh
Ohio, Cleveland
Oregon, Portland
Pennsylvania, Philadelphia
Puerto Rico, Rio Piedras
Texas, Houston
Trust Territories of the Pacific Islands:
Manila, Phillipines
Utah, Salt Lake City
Washington, Bellevue

NEW ZEALAND

Embassy of New Zealand
37 Observatory Circle, NW., Washington, DC 20008
phone (202) 328–4800, fax 667–5227
His Excellency Roy Neil Ferguson
Ambassador E. and P.
Consular Offices:
California:
Sacramento
San Diego
San Francisco
Santa Monica
Georgia, Atlanta
Guam, Tamuning
Hawaii, Honolulu
Illinois, Chicago
New Hampshire, Boston
New York, New York
Texas, Houston
Trust Territories of the Pacific Islands:
Pago Pago
Utah, Salt Lake City
Washington, Seattle

NICARAGUA

Embassy of the Republic of Nicaragua
1627 New Hampshire Avenue, NW., Washington, DC 20009
phone (202) 939–6570, fax 939–6545
His Excellency Arturo José Cruz Sequeira
Ambassador E. and P.
Consular Offices:
California:
Los Angeles
San Francisco
Florida, Miami
Georgia, Atlanta
Louisiana, Metairie
Massachusetts, Springfield
Missouri, St. Louis
New York, New York
North Carolina, Charlotte
Oklahoma, Tulsa
Pennsylvania:
Philadelphia
Pittsburgh
Puerto Rico, San Juan
Texas, Houston

NIGER

Embassy of the Republic of Niger
2204 R Street, NW., Washington, DC 20008
phone (202) 483–4224, fax 483–3169
Her Excellency Aminata Maiga Djibrilla
Ambassador E. and P.

NIGERIA

Embassy of the Federal Republic of Nigeria
3519 International Court, NW., Washington, DC 20008
phone (202) 986–8400, fax 362–6541
His Excellency Professor George Achulike Obiozor
Ambassador E. and P.
Consular Offices:
Georgia, Atlanta
New York, New York

NORWAY

Royal Norwegian Embassy
2720 34th Street, NW., Washington, DC 20008
phone (202) 333–6000, fax 337–0870
His Excellency Knut Vollebaek
Ambassador E. and P.
Consular Offices:
Alabama, Mobile
Alaska, Anchorage
Arizona, Glendale
California:
Los Angeles
San Diego
San Francisco
Colorado, Denver
Florida:
Jacksonville
Miami
Pensacola
Tampa
Georgia, Atlanta
Hawaii, Honolulu
Illinois, Chicago
Iowa, Des Moines
Louisiana, New Orleans
Massachusetts, Boston
Michigan, Detroit

Minnesota, Minneapolis
Montana, Billings
Nebraska, Omaha
New York, New York
North Dakota, Fargo
Oklahoma, Tulsa
Oregon, Portland
Pennsylvania, Philadelphia
Puerto Rico:
Ponce
San Juan
South Carolina, Charleston
South Dakota, Sioux Falls
Texas:
Dallas
Houston
Utah, Salt Lake City
Virginia, Norfolk
Washington, Seattle
Wisconsin, Madison

OMAN

Embassy of the Sultanate of Oman
2535 Belmont Road, NW., Washington, DC 20008
phone (202) 387–1980, fax 745–4933
Her Excellency Hunaina Sultan Ahmed al-Mughairy
Ambassador E. and P.
Consular Office: California, Los Angeles

PAKISTAN

Embassy of Pakistan
3517 International Court, NW., Washington, DC 20008
phone (202) 243–6500, fax 686–1544
His Excellency Mahmud Ali Durrani
Ambassador E. and P.
Consular Offices:
California:
Los Angeles
Sunnyvale
Illinois, Chicago
Maine, Portland
Massachusetts, Boston
New York, New York
Texas, Houston

Iranian Interests Section

Embassy of Pakistan
2209 Wisconsin Avenue, NW., Washington, DC 20007
phone (202) 965–4990, fax 965–1073

PALAU

Embassy of the Republic of Palau
1700 Pennsylvania Avenue, NW., Suite 400, Washington, DC 20006
phone (202) 452–6814, fax 452–6281
His Excellency Hersey Kyota
Ambassador E. and P.
Consular Offices:
Guam, Tamuning
Hawaii, Honolulu

PANAMA

Embassy of the Republic of Panama
2862 McGill Terrace, NW., Washington, DC 20008
phone (202) 483–1407, fax 483–8416
His Excellency Federico A. Humbert Arias
Ambassador E. and P.
Consular Offices:
California:
San Diego
San Francisco
Florida:
Miami
Tampa
Georgia, Atlanta
Hawaii, Honolulu
Louisiana, New Orleans
New York, New York
Pennsylvania, Philadelphia
Puerto Rico, San Juan
Texas, Houston

PAPUA NEW GUINEA

Embassy of Papua New Guinea
1779 Massachusetts Avenue, NW., Suite 805, Washington, DC 20036
phone (202) 745–3680, fax 745–3679
His Excellency Evan Jeremy Paki
Ambassador E. and P.
Consular Offices:
California, Los Angeles
Texas, Houston

PARAGUAY

Embassy of Paraguay
2400 Massachusetts Avenue, NW., Washington, DC 20008
phone (202) 483–6960, fax 234–4508
His Excellency James Spalding Hellmers
Ambassador E. and P.
Consular Offices:
California, Los Angeles
Florida, Miami
Kansas, Kansas City
Michigan, Detroit
New York, New York
Puerto Rico, San Juan
Texas, Bellaire

PERU

Embassy of Peru
1700 Massachusetts Avenue, NW., Washington, DC 20036
phone (202) 833–9860, fax 659–8124

His Excellency Felipe Ortiz de Zevallos Madueno
Ambassador E. and P.
Consular Offices:
Arizona, Mesa
California:
Los Angeles
Sacramento
San Francisco
Colorado, Denver
Connecticut, Hartford
Florida:
Miami
Tampa
Georgia, Atlanta
Hawaii, Honolulu
Illinois, Chicago
Louisiana, New Orleans
Massachusetts, Boston
Missouri, St. Louis
New Jersey, Paterson
New York, New York
Oklahoma, Tulsa
Puerto Rico, San Juan
Texas, Houston
Washington, Seattle

PHILIPPINES

Embassy of the Republic of the Philippines
1600 Massachusetts Avenue, NW., Washington, DC 20036
phone (202) 467–9300, fax 467–9417
His Excellency Willy C. Gaa
Ambassador E. and P.
Consular Offices:
California:
Los Angeles
San Francisco
Florida, North Miami
Georgia, Atlanta
Guam, Tamuning
Hawaii, Honolulu
Illinois, Chicago
Louisiana, New Orleans
New York, New York
Texas, Houston
Trust Territories of the Pacific Islands:
Mariana Islands

POLAND

Embassy of the Republic of Poland
2640 16th Street, NW., Washington, DC 20009
phone (202) 234–3800, fax 328–6271
His Excellency Janusz Reiter
Ambassador E. and P.
Consular Offices:
Alaska, Anchorage
California, Los Angeles
Colorado, Longmont
Florida, Miami
Hawaii, Honolulu
Illinois, Chicago
Massachusetts, Boston
Missouri, St. Louis
New York, New York
Ohio, Oxford
Oregon, Portland
Puerto Rico, San Juan
Texas, Houston

PORTUGAL

Embassy of Portugal
2012 Massachusetts Avenue, NW., Washington, DC 20036
phone (202) 328–8610, fax 462–3726
His Excellency João de Vallera
Ambassador E. and P.
Consular Offices:
California:
Los Angeles
San Francisco
Tulare
Connecticut, Waterbury
Florida, Miami
Hawaii, Honolulu
Illinois, Chicago
Louisiana, New Orleans
Massachusetts:
Boston
New Bedford
New Jersey, Newark
New York, New York
Puerto Rico, San Juan
Rhode Island, Providence
Texas, Houston

QATAR

Embassy of the State of Qatar
2555 M Street, NW., Suite 200, Washington, DC 20037
phone (202) 274–1600, fax 237–0061
His Excellency Nasser bin Hamad M. Al Khalifa
Ambassador E. and P.
Consular Office: Texas, Houston

ROMANIA

Embassy of Romania
1607 23rd Street, NW., Washington, DC 20008
phone (202) 332–4846, fax 232–4748
Ms. Daniela Anda Grigore Gitman
Minister-Counselor
Consular Offices:
California:
Los Angeles
San Francisco

Florida, Hollywood
Illinois, Chicago
Indiana, Indianapolis
Louisiana, New Orleans
Massachusetts, Boston
Michigan, Detroit
Minnesota, Minneapolis
Nevada, Las Vegas
New York, New York
Ohio, Cleveland
Oklahoma, Norman
Oregon, Portland
Pennsylvania, Philadelphia
Texas:
Dallas
Houston
Utah, Salt Lake City
Virginia, Norfolk

RUSSIA

Embassy of the Russian Federation
2650 Wisconsin Avenue, NW., Washington, DC 20007
phone (202) 298–5700, fax 298–5735
His Excellency Yury V. Ushakov
Ambassador E. and P.
Consular Offices:
Alaska, Anchorage
California, San Francisco
Colorado, Denver
Florida, Pinellas Park
Hawaii, Honolulu
Minnesota, Minneapolis
New York, New York
Puerto Rico, San Juan
Texas, Houston
Utah, Salt Lake City
Washington, Seattle

RWANDA

Embassy of the Republic of Rwanda
1714 New Hampshire Avenue, NW., Washington, DC 20009
phone (202) 232–2882, fax 232–4544
His Excellency Dr. Zac Nsenga
Ambassador E. and P.
Consular Offices:
California, San Francisco
Illinois, Geneva

SAINT KITTS AND NEVIS

Embassy of Saint Kitts and Nevis
3216 New Mexico Avenue, NW., Washington, DC 20016
phone (202) 686–2636, fax 686–5740
His Excellency Dr. Izben Cordinal Williams
Ambassador E. and P.
Consular Offices:
California, Los Angeles
Florida, Miami
Georgia, Atlanta
New York, New York
Texas, Dallas
Virgin Islands, St. Thomas

SAINT LUCIA

Embassy of Saint Lucia
3216 New Mexico Avenue, NW., Washington, DC 20016
phone (202) 364–6792, fax 364–6723
Her Excellency Sonia Merlyn Johnny
Ambassador E. and P.
Consular Offices:
California, Los Angeles
Florida, Miami
New York, New York
Virgin Islands, St. Croix

SAINT VINCENT AND THE GRENADINES

Embassy of Saint Vincent and the Grenadines
3216 New Mexico Avenue, NW., Washington, DC 20016
phone (202) 364–6730, fax 364–6736
His Excellency Ellsworth I.A. John
Ambassador E. and P.
Consular Offices:
California, Los Angeles
Louisiana, New Orleans
New York, New York

SAMOA

Embassy of the Independent State of Samoa
800 2nd Avenue, 4th Floor, New York, NY 10017
phone (212) 599–6196, fax 599–0797
His Excellency Ali'ioaiga Feturi Elisaia
Ambassador E. and P.
Consular Offices:
American Samoa, Pago Pago
California, Torrance

SAN MARINO

Consular Offices:
Hawaii, Honolulu
Michigan, Detroit
New York, New York

SAO TOME AND PRINCIPE

Embassy of Sao Tome and Principe
1211 Connecticut Avenue, NW., Suite 300, Washington, DC 20036
phone (202) 775–2075, fax 775–2077
His Excellency Ovidio Pequeno
Ambassador E. and P.
Consular Offices:
Georgia, Atlanta
Illinois, Chicago

SAUDI ARABIA

Royal Embassy of Saudi Arabia
601 New Hampshire Avenue, NW., Washington, DC 20037
phone (202) 342–3800, fax 944–3113
His Excellency Adel bin Ahmed Al-Jubeir
Ambassador E. and P.
Consular Offices:
- California, Los Angeles
- New York, New York
- Texas, Houston

SENEGAL

Embassy of the Republic of Senegal
2112 Wyoming Avenue, NW., Washington, DC 20008
phone (202) 234–0540, fax 332–6315
His Excellency Dr. Amadou Lamine Ba
Ambassador E. and P.
Consular Offices:
- Florida, Miami
- Georgia, Atlanta
- Louisiana, New Orleans
- Massachusetts, Boston
- New York, New York
- Texas, Houston

SERBIA

Embassy of the Republic of Serbia
2134 Kalorama Road, NW., Washington, DC 20008
phone (202) 332–0333, fax 332–3933
His Excellency Ivan Vujačić
Ambassador E. and P.
Consular Offices:
- Colorado, Denver
- Illinois, Chicago
- Louisiana, Kenner
- New York, New York
- Wyoming, Cheyenne

SEYCHELLES

Embassy of the Republic of Seychelles
800 2nd Avenue, Suite 400C, New York, NY 10017
phone (212) 972–1785, fax 972–1786
His Excellency Emile Patrick Jeremie Bonnelame
Ambassador E. and P.
Consular Offices:
- Alaska, Anchorage
- Washington, Seattle

SIERRA LEONE

Embassy of Sierra Leone
1701 19th Street, NW., Washington, DC 20009
phone (202) 939–9261, fax 483–1793
His Excellency Sulaiman Tejan Jalloh
Ambassador E. and P.

SINGAPORE

Embassy of the Republic of Singapore
3501 International Place, NW., Washington, DC 20008
phone (202) 537–3100, fax 537–0876
Her Excellency Heng Chee Chan
Ambassador E. and P.
Consular Offices:
- California, San Francisco
- Florida, Miami
- Illinois, Chicago
- New York, New York
- Texas, Houston

SLOVAK REPUBLIC

Embassy of the Slovak Republic
3523 International Court, NW., Washington, DC 20008
phone (202) 237–1054, fax 237–6438
His Excellency Rastislav Kacer
Ambassador E. and P.
Consular Offices:
- California:
  - Los Angeles
  - San Francisco
- Colorado, Denver
- Florida, Ft. Lauderdale
- Illinois, Chicago
- Indiana, Indianapolis
- Massachusetts, Weston
- Michigan, Detroit
- Minnesota, Minneapolis
- Missouri, Kansas City
- New York, New York
- Ohio, Cleveland
- Pennsylvania, Pittsburgh
- Washington, Bainbridge Island

SLOVENIA

Embassy of the Republic of Slovenia
1525 New Hampshire Avenue, NW., Washington, DC 20036
phone (202) 332–9332, fax 667–4563
His Excellency Samuel Zbogar
Ambassador E. and P.
Consular Offices:
- Colorado, Denver
- Florida, Palm Beach
- Georgia, Atlanta
- Hawaii, Honolulu
- Kansas, Mission Hills
- New York, New York
- Ohio, Cleveland
- Tennessee, Knoxville
- Texas, Houston

SOLOMON ISLANDS

Embassy of the Solomon Islands
800 2nd Avenue, Suite 400L, New York, NY 10017
phone (212) 599–6192, fax 661–8925

His Excellency Collin D. Beck
Ambassador E. and P.

SOMALIA

Embassy of the Somali Democratic Republic
(Embassy ceased operations May 8, 1991)

SOUTH AFRICA

Embassy of the Republic of South Africa
3051 Massachusetts Avenue, NW., Washington, DC 20008
phone (202) 232–4400, fax 265–1607
Her Excellency Barbara Joyce Mosima Masekela
Ambassador E. and P.
Consular Offices:
- Alabama, Mobile
- California, Los Angeles
- Illinois, Chicago
- New York, New York
- Utah, Salt Lake City

SPAIN

Embassy of Spain
2375 Pennsylvania Avenue, NW., Washington, DC 20037
phone (202) 452–0100, fax 833–5670
His Excellency Carlos Westendorp
Ambassador E. and P.
Consular Offices:
- Alaska, Anchorage
- Arizona, Phoenix
- California:
  - Los Angeles
  - San Diego
  - San Francisco
- Colorado, Denver
- Florida:
  - Miami
  - Orlando
  - Pensacola
  - Saint Augustine
  - Tampa
- Georgia, Atlanta
- Hawaii, Honolulu
- Idaho, Boise
- Illinois, Chicago
- Louisiana, New Orleans
- Massachusetts, Boston
- Minnesota, St. Paul
- Missouri:
  - Kansas City
  - St. Louis
- New Jersey, Newark
- New Mexico, Albuquerque
- New York, New York
- North Carolina, Durham
- Ohio, Cincinnati
- Pennsylvania, Philadelphia
- Puerto Rico, San Juan
- Texas:
  - Corpus Christi
  - Dallas
  - El Paso
  - Houston
  - San Antonio
- Utah, Salt Lake City
- Washington, Seattle

SRI LANKA

Embassy of the Democratic Socialist Republic of Sri Lanka
2148 Wyoming Avenue, NW., Washington, DC 20008
phone (202) 483–4025, fax 232–7181
His Excellency Bernard A.B. Goonetilleke
Ambassador E. and P.
Consular Offices:
- Arizona, Phoenix
- California, Los Angeles
- Georgia, Atlanta
- Hawaii, Honolulu
- Illinois, Chicago
- Louisiana, New Orleans
- Massachusetts, Boston
- New Jersey, Newark
- New Mexico, Santa Fe
- New York, New York

SUDAN

Embassy of the Republic of the Sudan
2210 Massachusetts Avenue, NW., Washington, DC 20008
phone (202) 338–8565, fax 667–2406
Mr. John Ukec Lueth Ukec
Minister

SURINAME

Embassy of the Republic of Suriname
4301 Connecticut Avenue, NW., Suite 460, Washington, DC 20008
phone (202) 244–7488, fax 244–5878
His Excellency Jacques Ruben Constantijn Kross
Ambassador E. and P.
Consular Offices:
- Florida, Miami
- Louisiana, New Orleans

SWAZILAND

Embassy of the Kingdom of Swaziland
1712 New Hampshire Avenue, NW., Washington, DC 20009
phone (202) 234–5002, fax 234–8254
His Excellency Ephraim Mandlenkosi M. Hlophe
Ambassador E. and P.

SWEDEN

Embassy of Sweden
1501 M Street, NW., Suite 900, Washington, DC 20005
phone (202) 467–2600, fax 467–2699
His Excellency Gunnar Wiggo Lund
Ambassador E. and P.
Consular Offices:
Alaska, Anchorage
Arizona, Phoenix
California:
Los Angeles
San Diego
San Francisco
Colorado, Denver
Florida:
Ft. Lauderdale
Tampa
Georgia, Atlanta
Hawaii, Honolulu
Illinois, Chicago
Kansas, Merriam
Louisiana, New Orleans
Massachusetts, Boston
Michigan, Ann Arbor
Minnesota, Minneapolis
Missouri, St. Louis
Nebraska, Omaha
Nevada, Las Vegas
New York:
Jamestown
New York
North Carolina, Raleigh
Ohio, Cleveland
Oregon, Portland
Pennsylvania, Philadelphia
Puerto Rico, San Juan
Texas:
Dallas
Houston
Utah, Salt Lake City
Virgin Islands, St. Thomas
Virginia, Norfolk
Washington, Seattle
Wisconsin, Milwaukee

SWITZERLAND

Embassy of Switzerland
2900 Cathedral Avenue, NW., Washington, DC 20008
phone (202) 745–7900, fax 387–2564
His Excellency Urs Johann Ziswiler
Ambassador E. and P.
Consular Offices:
Arizona, Phoenix
California:
Los Angeles
San Francisco
Colorado, Boulder
Florida:
Miami
Orlando
Georgia, Atlanta
Hawaii, Honolulu
Illinois, Chicago
Indiana, Indianapolis
Louisiana, New Orleans
Massachusetts, Boston
Michigan, Detroit
Minnesota, Minneapollis
Missouri, Kansas City
New York:
New York
Williamsville
North Carolina, Charlotte
Ohio, Cleveland
Pennsylvnaia:
Philadelphia
Pittsburgh
Puerto Rico, San Juan
South Carolina, Spartanburg
Texas:
Dallas
Houston
Trust Territories of the Pacific Islands:
Pago Pago
Utah, Salt Lake City
Washington, Mercer Island

Cuban Interests Section

Embassy of Switzerland
2630 16th Street, NW., Washington, DC 20009
phone (202) 797–8518
Mr. Dagoberto Rodriguez Barrera
Counselor

SYRIA

Embassy of the Syrian Arab Republic
2215 Wyoming Avenue, NW., Washington, DC 20008
phone (202) 232–6313, fax 234–9548
His Excellency Dr. Imad Moustapha
Ambassador E. and P.
Consular Offices:
California, Los Angeles
Michigan, Detroit
Texas, Houston

TAJIKISTAN

Embassy of the Republic of Tajikistan
1005 New Hampshire Avenue, NW., Washington, DC 20037
phone (202) 223–6090, fax 223–6091
His Excellency Abdujabbor Shirinov
Ambassador E. and P.

TANZANIA

Embassy of the United Republic of Tanzania
2139 R Street, NW., Washington, DC 20008
phone (202) 939–6125, fax 797–7408
His Excellency Andrew Mhando Daraja
Ambassador E. and P.
Consular Offices:
- Florida, Boca Raton
- Georgia, Atlanta
- Illinois, St. Louis

THAILAND

Embassy of Thailand
1024 Wisconsin Avenue, NW., Washington, DC 20007
phone (202) 944–3600, fax 944–3611
His Excellency Virasakdi Futrakul
Ambassador E. and P.
Consular Offices:
- Alabama, Montgomery
- California, Los Angeles
- Colorado, Denver
- Florida, Coral Gables
- Georgia, Atlanta
- Hawaii, Honolulu
- Illinois, Chicago
- Louisiana, New Orleans
- Massachusetts, Boston
- Missouri, Kansas City
- New York, New York
- Oklahoma, Broken Arrow
- Oregon, Portland
- Puerto Rico, Hato Rey
- Texas:
  - Dallas
  - El Paso
  - Houston

TOGO

Embassy of the Republic of Togo
2208 Massachusetts Avenue, NW., Washington, DC 20008
phone (202) 234–4212, fax 232–3190
Mrs. B. Mayanendja Nonon Saa Woulu
Minister-Counselor
Consular Offices: Florida, Miami

TONGA

Embassy of the Kingdom of Tonga
250 East 51st Street, New York, NY 10022
phone (917) 369–1025, fax 369–1024
Her Excellency Fekitamoeloa Tupoupai Utoikamanu
Ambassador E. and P.
Consular Offices:
- California, San Francisco
- Hawaii, Honolulu

TRINIDAD AND TOBAGO

Embassy of the Republic of Trinidad and Tobago
1708 Massachusetts Avenue, NW., Washington, DC 20036
phone (202) 467–6490, fax 785–3130
Her Excellency Marina Annette Valere
Ambassador E. and P.
Consular Offices:
- Florida, Miami
- New York, New York
- Puerto Rico, San Juan
- Texas, Houston

TUNISIA

Embassy of Tunisia
1515 Massachusetts Avenue, NW., Washington, DC 20005
phone (202) 862–1850, fax 862–1858
His Excellency Mohamed Nejib Hachana
Ambassador E. and P.
Consular Offices:
- California, San Francisco
- Florida, Miami
- New York, New York
- Texas:
  - Dallas
  - Houston

TURKEY

Embassy of the Republic of Turkey
2525 Massachusetts Avenue, NW., Washington, DC 20008
phone (202) 612–6700, fax 612–6744
His Excellency Nabi Şensoy
Ambassador E. and P.
Consular Offices:
- California:
  - Los Angeles
  - Oakland
- Georgia, Atlanta
- Illinois, Chicago
- Maryland, Baltimore
- Massachusetts, Boston
- Michigan, Farmington
- Mississippi, Jackson
- Missouri, Kansas City
- New York, New York
- Texas, Houston
- Washington, Seattle

TURKMENISTAN

Embassy of Turkmenistan
2207 Massachusetts Avenue, NW., Washington, DC 20008
phone (202) 588–1500, fax 588–0697
His Excellency Meret Bairamovich Orazov
Ambassador E. and P.

UGANDA

Embassy of the Republic of Uganda
5911 16th Street, NW., Washington, DC 20011
phone (202) 726–0416, fax 726–1727
His Excellency Perezi Karukubiro Kamunanwire
Ambassador E. and P.

UKRAINE

Embassy of Ukraine
3350 M Street, NW., Washington, DC 20007
phone (202) 349–2920, fax 333–0817
His Excellency Oleh Shamshur
Ambassador E. and P.
Consular Offices:
California, San Francisco
Illinois, Chicago
Michigan, Detroit
New York, New York
Ohio, Cleveland
Texas, Houston

UNITED ARAB EMIRATES

Embassy of the United Arab Emirates
3522 International Court, NW., Washington, DC 20008
phone (202) 243–2400, fax 243–2432
His Excellency Saqr Ghobash
Ambassador E. and P.

UNITED KINGDOM

British Embassy
3100 Massachusetts Avenue, NW., Washington, DC 20008
phone (202) 588–6500, fax 588–7870
His Excellency Sir David Manning
Ambassador E. and P.
Consular Offices:
Alaska, Anchorage
Arizona, Phoenix
California:
Los Angeles
San Diego
San Francisco
San Jose
Colorado, Denver
Florida:
Miami
Orlando
Georgia, Atlanta
Illinois, Chicago
Indiana, Indianapolis
Kansas, Kansas City
Louisiana, New Orleans
Massachusetts, Boston
Michigan, Detroit
Minnesota, Minneapolis
Nevada, Las Vegas
New York, New York
North Carolina, Charlotte
Ohio, Cleveland
Oklahoma, Tulsa
Oregon, Portland
Pennsylvania:
Philadelphia
Pittsburgh
Puerto Rico, San Juan
Tennessee, Nashville
Texas:
Dallas
Houston
San Antonio
Trust Territories of the Pacific Islands:
Nuku'alofa, Tonga
Utah, Salt Lake City
Washington, Bellevue
Wisconsin, Madison

URUGUAY

Embassy of Uruguay
1913 I Street, NW., Washington, DC 20006
phone (202) 331–1313, fax 331–8142
His Excellency Carlos Alberto Gianelli
Ambassador E. and P.
Consular Offices:
California:
Los Angeles
San Francisco
Florida, Miami
Illinois, Chicago
Louisiana, New Orleans
Nevada, Reno
New York, New York
Puerto Rico, San Juan
Texas, Houston
Utah, Salt Lake City

UZBEKISTAN

Embassy of the Republic of Uzbekistan
1746 Massachusetts Avenue, NW., Washington, DC 20036
phone (202) 293–6803, fax 293–6804
His Excellency Abdulaziz Kamilov
Ambassador E. and P.
Consular Offices:
Colorado, Denver
New York, New York
Washington, Seattle

VANUATU

Consular Office: Northern Mariana Islands, Saipan

VENEZUELA

Embassy of the Bolivarian Republic of Venezuela
1099 30th Street, NW., Washington, DC 20007
phone (202) 342–2214, fax 342–6820
His Excellency Bernardo Alvarez Herrera

Ambassador E. and P.
Consular Offices:
California, San Francisco
Florida, Miami
Illinois, Chicago
Louisiana, New Orleans
Massachusetts, Boston
New York, New York
Puerto Rico, San Juan
Texas, Houston

VIETNAM

Embassy of Vietnam
1233 20th Street, NW., Suite 400, Washington, DC 20036
phone (202) 861–0737, fax 861–0917
His Excellency Chien Tam Nguyen
Ambassador E. and P.
Consular Office: California, San Francisco

YEMEN

Embassy of the Republic of Yemen
2319 Wyoming Avenue, NW., Washington, DC 20008
phone (202) 965–4760, fax 337–2017
His Excellency Abdulwahab A. Al-Hajjri
Ambassador E. and P.
Consular Offices:
California, San Francisco
Michigan, Detroit

ZAMBIA

Embassy of the Republic of Zambia
2419 Massachusetts Avenue, NW., Washington, DC 20008
phone (202) 265–9717, fax 332–0826
Her Excellency Dr. Inonge Mbikusita Lewanika
Ambassador E. and P.

ZIMBABWE

Embassy of the Republic of Zimbabwe
1608 New Hampshire Avenue, NW., Washington, DC 20009
phone (202) 332–7100, fax 483–9326
His Excellency Dr. Machivenyika T. Mapuranga
Ambassador E. and P.

The following is a list of countries with which diplomatic relations have been severed:

After each country, in parenthesis, is the name of the country's protecting power in the United States.

CUBA (Switzerland)
IRAN (Pakistan)

PRESS GALLERIES*

SENATE PRESS GALLERY

The Capitol, Room S–316, phone 224–0241

Director.—S. Joseph Keenan
Deputy Director.—Joan McKinney
Media Coordinators:
Michael Cavaiola
Amy H. Gross
Wendy A. Oscarson
James D. Saris

HOUSE PRESS GALLERY

The Capitol, Room H–315, phone 225–3945

Superintendent.—Jerry L. Gallegos
Deputy Superintendent.—Justin J. Supon
Assistant Superintendents:
Ric Andersen
Molly Cain
Drew Cannon
Laura Reed

STANDING COMMITTEE OF CORRESPONDENTS

Bill Walsh, Times-Picayne, Chair
Thomas Ferraro, Reuters, Secretary
Susan Ferrechio, Congressional Quarterly
Carl Hulse, New York Times
Andrew Taylor, Associated Press

RULES GOVERNING PRESS GALLERIES

1. Administration of the press galleries shall be vested in a Standing Committee of Correspondents elected by accredited members of the galleries. The Committee shall consist of five persons elected to serve for terms of two years. Provided, however, that at the election in January 1951, the three candidates receiving the highest number of votes shall serve for two years and the remaining two for one year. Thereafter, three members shall be elected in odd-numbered years and two in even-numbered years. Elections shall be held in January. The Committee shall elect its own chairman and secretary. Vacancies on the Committee shall be filled by special election to be called by the Standing Committee.

2. Persons desiring admission to the press galleries of Congress shall make application in accordance with Rule VI of the House of Representatives, subject to the direction and control of the Speaker and Rule 33 of the Senate, which rules shall be interpreted and administered by the Standing Committee of Correspondents, subject to the review and an approval by the Senate Committee on Rules and Administration.

3. The Standing Committee of Correspondents shall limit membership in the press galleries to bone fide correspondents of repute in their profession, under such rules as the Standing Committee of Correspondents shall prescribe.

*Information is based on data furnished and edited by each respective gallery.

4. An applicant for press credentials through the Daily Press Galleries must establish to the satisfaction of the Standing Committee of Correspondents that he or she is a full-time, paid correspondent who requires on-site access to congressional members and staff. Correspondents must be employed by a news organization:

(a) with General Publication periodicals mailing privileges under U.S. Postal Service rules, and which publishes daily; or

(b) whose principal business is the daily dissemination of original news and opinion of interest to a broad segment of the public, and which has published continuously for 18 months.

The applicant must reside in the Washington, D.C. area, and must not be engaged in any lobbying or paid advocacy, advertising, publicity or promotion work for any individual, political party, corporation, organization, or agency of the U.S. government, or in prosecuting any claim before Congress or any federal government department, and will not do so while a member of the Daily Press Galleries.

Applicants' publications must be editorially independent of any institution, foundation or interest group that lobbies the federal government, or that is not principally a general news organization.

Failure to provide information to the Standing Committee for this determination, or misrepresenting information, can result in the denial or revocation of credentials.

5. Members of the families of correspondents are not entitled to the privileges of the galleries.

6. The Standing Committee of Correspondents shall propose no changes in the these rules except upon petition in writing signed by not less than 100 accredited members of the galleries. The above rules have been approved by the Committee on Rules and Administration.

NANCY PELOSI,
Speaker of the House of Representatives.

DIANNE FEINSTEIN,
Chair, Senate Committee on Rules and Administration.

MEMBERS ENTITLED TO ADMISSION

PRESS GALLERIES

Abbott, Charles: Reuters
Abrahms, Douglas: Gannett News Service
Abrams, James: Associated Press
Abromowitz, Michael: Washington Post
Abruzzese, Sarah: New York Times
Achenbach, Joel: Washington Post
Ackerman, Andrew: Bond Buyer
Adair, William: St. Petersburg Times
Adams, Christopher: McClatchy Newspapers
Adams, Rebecca: Congressional Quarterly
Adams, Richard: London Guardian
Adcock, Beryl: McClatchy Newspapers
Adler, Joseph: American Banker
Agres, Theodore: Washington Times
Ahearn, David: Defense Daily
Ahlrich, Alan: Congressional Quarterly
Ahmann, Timothy: Reuters
Ahn, Sung Joong: Korea Times
Aitken, Lee: Bloomberg News
Akers, Mary Ann: WashingtonPost.com
Alberts, Sheldon: Canwest News Service
Alconada, Hugo: La Nacion
Alday, Ricardo: Notimex Mexican News Agency
Alexander, Andrew: Cox Newspapers
Alexander, Charles: Reuters
Alexander, Keith: Washington Post
Ali, Syed: Congressional Quarterly
Allen, Amanda: Congressional Quarterly
Allen, JoAnne: Reuters
Allen, Jonathan: Congressional Quarterly
Allen, Ross: Argus Media
Allen, Victoria: Reuters
Allison, Wes: St. Petersburg Times
Alonso-Zaldivar, Ricardo: Los Angeles Times
Alpert, Bruce: New Orleans Times-Picayune
Al-Sowayel, Naila: Saudi Press Agency
Altamirano, Natasha: Washington Times
Anderson, Joanna: Congressional Quarterly
Anderson, Mark: Dow Jones Newswires
Andrews, Edmund: New York Times
Angle, Martha: Congressional Quarterly
Anklam, Jr., Fred: USA Today
Anstey, Chris: Bloomberg News
Anyz, Daniel: Hospodarske Noving Daily
Apfel, Ira: Complinet
Appleby, Julie: USA Today
Apuzzo, Matt: Associated Press
Argetsinger, Amy: Washington Post
Arimoto, Takashi: Sankei Shimbun
Arita, Tsukasa: Kyodo News
Armstrong, Andrew: Congressional Quarterly
Arnold, John Jay: Associated Press
Arnold, Laurence: Bloomberg News
Arthur, William: Bloomberg News
Asher, James: McClatchy Newspapers
Asher, Julie: Catholic News Service
Ashizuka, Tomoko: Nikkei
Asseo, Laurie: Bloomberg News
Aulston, Von: New York Times
Auster, Elizabeth: Cleveland Plain Dealer
Aversa, Jeannine: Associated Press
Azpiazu, Maria: EFE News Services
Babcock, Charles: Bloomberg News
Babington, Charles: Associated Press
Bachelet, Pablo: Miami Herald
Bacon, Jr., Perry: Washington Post
Bai, Matt: New York Times Magazine
Bailey, Anna: CongressDaily
Baker, Peter: Washington Post
Baldor, Lolita: Associated Press
Ball, Michael: Argus Media
Ballard, Lindsay: Asahi Shimbun
Ballard, Tanya: WashingtonPost.com
Balluck, Kyle: WashingtonPost.com
Baltimore, Chris: Reuters
Balz, Daniel: Washington Post
Banales, Jorge: EFE News Services
Banerjee, Neela: New York Times
Bang, June-Oh: Chosun Ilbo
Banks, Adelle: Religion News Service
Baquet, Dean: New York Times
Barakat, Matthew: Associated Press
Bardazzi, Marco: ANSA Italian News Agency
Barker, James: Congressional Quarterly
Barker, Jeffrey: Baltimore Sun
Barnes, Julian: Los Angeles Times
Baron, Kevin: Boston Globe
Barr, Gary: Washington Post
Barrera, Ruben: Notimex Mexican News Agency
Barrett, Barbara: McClatchy Newspapers
Barrett, Devlin: Associated Press
Barrett, Terrence: Bloomberg News
Barringer, Felicity: New York Times
Barry, Theresa: Bloomberg News
Bartash, Jeffry: MarketWatch
Bartolf, Alexandra: Congressional Quarterly
Bartscht, Jill: Washington Post
Bartz, Diane: Reuters
Baschuk, Bryce: Washington Times
Bashir, Mustafa: Saudi Press Agency

MEMBERS ENTITLED TO ADMISSION—Continued

Basken, Paul: Bloomberg News
Bass, Frank: Associated Press
Bater, Jeffrey: Dow Jones Newswires
Batt, Tony: Stephens Media Group
Baygents, Ronald: Kuwait News Agency
Bazar, Emily: USA Today
Bazinet, Kenneth: New York Daily News
Beamish, Rita: Associated Press
Beary, Brian: Europolitics
Beattie, Jeff: Energy Daily
Beaudette, Richard: Newhouse News Service
Beckner; Steven: Market News International
Beech, Eric: Reuters
Behn, Sharon: Washington Times
Behringer, Paul: Kyodo News
Bell, Peter: CongressDaily
Bellantoni, Christina: Washington Times
Bendavid, Naftali: Chicago Tribune
Bender, Bryan: Boston Globe
Benenson, Robert: Congressional Quarterly
Benesova, Dagmar: World Business Press
Benincasa, Robert: Gannett News Service
Benjamin, Matthew: Bloomberg News
Benkelman, Susan: Congressional Quarterly
Berger, Matthew: Congressional Quarterly
Berley, Max: Bloomberg News
Berlin, Stephen: LRP Publications
Berman, Russell: New York Sun
Bernard, Jerome: Agence France-Presse
Berry, Deborah: Gannett News Service
Berry, John: Bloomberg News
Bettelheim, Adriel: Congressional Quarterly
Bicknell, Arwen Adams: Congressional Quarterly
Bicknell, John: Congressional Quarterly
Biddle, Joanna: Agence France-Presse
Bilodeau, Otis: Bloomberg News
Bilski, Christina: Nikkei
Birnbaum, Jeffrey: Washington Post
Bishop, Ian: New York Post
Bishop, Sam: Fairbanks Daily News Miner
Biskupic, Joan: USA Today
Bivins, Larry: Gannett News Service
Bjerga, Alan: Bloomberg News
Blackstone, Brian: Dow Jones Newswires
Bland, Melissa: Reuters
Bliss, Jeffrey: Bloomberg News
Block, Donna: Daily Deal
Block, Robert: Wall Street Journal
Bloedorn, Adam: Congressional Quarterly
Bloom, Rachel: Congressional Quarterly
Blue, Miranda: Congressional Quarterly
Blum, Justin: Bloomberg News
Blumenthal, Les: McClatchy Newspapers
Boessenkool, Antonie: Dow Jones Newswires
Bold, Michael: McClatchy Newspapers
Boles, Gregory: Dow Jones Newswires
Boliek, Brooks: Hollywood Reporter
Bolling, Deborah: LRP Publications
Boorstein, Michelle: Washington Post
Borak, Donna: Associated Press
Borenstein, Seth: Associated Press
Bostick, Romaine: Bloomberg News
Bourge, Christian: CongressDaily
Bouza, Teresa: EFE News Services
Bowen, Joel: Congressional Quarterly
Bowman, Curtis Lee: Scripps Howard News Service
Boyd, Robert: McClatchy Newspapers
Brady, Erik: USA Today
Brady, Jessica: CongressDaily
Bragin, Mikhail: Parlamentskaya Gazeta
Brandmaier, Frank: German Press Agency - DPA
Branson, Louise: USA Today
Brasher, Philip: Des Moines Register
Braun, Stephen: Los Angeles Times
Bravin, Jess: Wall Street Journal
Bremner, Faith: Gannett News Service
Briand, Xavier: Reuters
Bridges, Andrew: Associated Press
Bridis, Ted: Associated Press
Broache, Anne: CNET News.com
Broder, David: Washington Post
Broder, John: New York Times
Broder, Jonathan: Congressional Quarterly
Brodmann, Ronald: Congressional Quarterly
Brogan, Pamela: Gannett News Service
Brooks, David: La Jornada; New York Times
Brosnan, James: Scripps Howard News Service
Brown, Andrew: McClatchy Newspapers
Brown, David: Washington Post
Brown, DeNeen: Washington Post
Brown, Emily: Bloomberg News
Brown, Matthew: Baltimore Sun
Brownstein, Ronald: Los Angeles Times
Brulliard, Nicolas: Dow Jones Newswires
Brune, Thomas: Newsday
Bull, Alister: Reuters
Bumiller, Elisabeth: New York Times
Buncombe, Andrew: London Independent
Bunis, Dena: Orange County Register
Burey, Joe: Congressional Quarterly
Burke, Daniel: Religion News Service
Burns, Judith: Dow Jones Newswires
Burns, Robert: Associated Press
Burns, Susan: Cox Newspapers
Burr, Thomas: Salt Lake Tribune
Burrowes, Philip: Congressional Quarterly
Burt, Andy: Bloomberg News
Buskirk, Howard: Communications Daily
Butler, Desmond: Associated Press
Bzdek, Vincent: Washington Post
Calamur, Krishnadev: United Press International
Callan, Eoin: Financial Times
Calmes, Jackie: Wall Street Journal
Camia, Catalina: USA Today

MEMBERS ENTITLED TO ADMISSION—Continued

Camire, Dennis: Gannett News Service
Campagna, Mary Ann: Agence France-Presse
Canellos, Peter: Boston Globe
Cao, Antonio: El Pais
Capaccio, Anthony: Bloomberg News
Caplan, Abby: Argus Media
Caretto, Ennio: Il Corriere Della Sera
Carey, Mary Agnes: Congressional Quarterly
Carlson, Peter: Washington Post
Carmichael, Kevin: Bloomberg News
Carnevale, MaryLu: Wall Street Journal
Carney, Dan: USA Today
Carney, David: Tech Law Journal
Carney, Michael: USA Today
Carr, LaKiesha: New York Times
Carr, Matthew: Oil Daily
Carr, Rebecca: Cox Newspapers
Carreno, Jose: El Universal
Carrier, Fanny: Agence France-Presse
Carroll, James: Congressional Quarterly
Carter, Thomas: Washington Times
Cartwright, Linda: Congressional Quarterly
Casey, Winter: National Journal's Technology Daily
Caspar, Lucian: Basler Zeitung
Cass, Connie: Associated Press
Cassata, Donna: Associated Press
Casteel, Chris: Oklahoman
Casteneda, Ruben: Washington Post
Cauvin, Henri: Washington Post
Cave, Christine: LRP Publications
Cermak, Christopher: German Press Agency–DPA
Chadbourn, Margaret: Market News International
Chaddock, Gail: Christian Science Monitor
Chaffee, Conrad: Tokyo-Chunichi Shimbun
Chaker, Ann Marie: Wall Street Journal
Chan, Sammie: Gannett News Service
Chandra, Shobhana: Bloomberg News
Chandrasekaran, Rajiv: Washington Post
Chang, Tsung-Chih: United Daily News
Charles, Deborah: Reuters
Chebium, Raju: Gannett News Service
Chen, Cassie: Bloomberg News
Chen, Edwin: Bloomberg News
Chen, Kathy: Wall Street Journal
Chen, Shawn: Associated Press
Chen, Zhigang: Sing Tao Daily
Cheves, John: Lexington Herald-Leader
Chiantaretto, Mariuccia: Il Giornale
Chick, Kristen: Washington Times
Chipman, Kimberly: Bloomberg News
Chmela, Holli: New York Times
Cho, Bock Rae: Yonhap News Agency
Cho, David: Washington Post
Choate, Patricia: Scripps Howard News Service
Choi, Hyung Du: Munwha Ilbo
Choi, Kenneth: Chosun Ilbo
Chong, Christina Young: Korea Times
Christensen, Mike: Congressional Quarterly
Christie, Rebecca: Dow Jones Newswires
Chu, Keith: Western Communications
Chuan, Yang Qing: Xinhua News Agency
Chwallek, Gabriele: German Press Agency–DPA
Cillizza, Chris: Washington Post
Cindemir, Mehmet: Hurriyet
Clark, Evan: Fairchild News Service
Clark, Lesley: Miami Herald
Clarke, David: Congressional Quarterly
Clemetson, Lynette: New York Times
Clerico, Luciano: ANSA Italian News Agency
Cloud, David: New York Times
Cocco, Marie: Washington Post Writer's Group
Cochran, John: Congressional Quarterly
Cochran, Laura Marie: WashingtonPost.com
Codrea, George: Congressional Quarterly
Cohen, Robert: Newark Star-Ledger
Cohen, Sarah: Washington Post
Cohn, Peter: CongressDaily
Coile, Zachary: San Francisco Chronicle
Cole, Justin: Agence France-Presse
Collins, Michael: Scripps Howard News Service
Collinson, Stephen: Agence France-Presse
Condon, Jr., George: Copley News Service
Conkey, Christopher: Wall Street Journal
Conlon, Charles: Congressional Quarterly
Conners, Maureen: Congressional Quarterly
Conrad, Dennis: Associated Press
Conway, Neal: Congressional Quarterly
Cook, David: Christian Science Monitor
Cooke, Anthony: Dow Jones Newswires
Cooney, Jessica Benton: Congressional Quarterly
Cooper, Christopher: Wall Street Journal
Cooper, Helene: New York Times
Cooper, Kent: Political Money Line
Cooper, Richard: Los Angeles Times
Cooper, Sonya: Bloomberg News
Cooperman, Alan: Washington Post
Copeland, Libby: Washington Post
Copeland, Peter: Scripps Howard News Service
Copp, Tara: Austin American-Statesman
Corbett, Rebecca: New York Times
Corbett Dooren, Jennifer: Dow Jones Newswires
Corchado, Alfredo: Dallas Morning News
Cornwell, Rupert: London Independent
Cornwell, Susan: Reuters
Couturier, Greg: Oil Daily
Cowan, Richard: Reuters
Cox, James: USA Today
Craig, Tim: Washington Post
Craik, Euan: Argus Media
Crane, Mark: USA Today
Cranford, John: Congressional Quarterly
Crawford, Craig: Congressional Quarterly
Crawley, James: Media General News Service
Crawley, John: Reuters

MEMBERS ENTITLED TO ADMISSION—Continued

Crewdson, John: Chicago Tribune
Crites, Alice: Washington Post
Crittenden, Michael: Congressional Quarterly
Crutsinger, Martin: Associated Press
Cunningham, Sarah: Reuters
Curl, Joseph: Washington Times
Curran, Timothy: Washington Post
Cushman, Jr., John: New York Times
Czuczka, Anthony: German Press Agency–DPA
DaCosta, Mario Navarro: ABIM News Agency
Dahne, Hans: German Press Agency–DPA
Dalecki, Kenneth: Global D
Dalglish, Arthur: Cox Newspapers
Dally, Chris: Congressional Quarterly
Daly, Corbett: TF News
Daly, Matthew: Associated Press
Daniel, Douglass: Associated Press
Daniels, Alex: Arkansas Democrat-Gazette
Dart, Robert: Cox Newspapers
Davenport, Coral: Congressional Quarterly
Davidson, Julie: LRP Publications
Davidson, Paul: USA Today
Davidz, Elizabeth: Associated Press
Davies, Anne: Sydney Morning Herald
Davies, Frank: San Jose Mercury News
Davis, Crystal: McClatchy Newspapers
Davis, David: Congressional Quarterly
Davis, Julie: Associated Press
Davis, Robert: Wall Street Journal
Day, Kathleen: Washington Post
de Borchgrave, Arnaud: United Press International
De la Cruz, Benedict: WashingtonPost.com
Deans, Jr., Robert: Cox Newspapers
DeBose, Brian: Washington Times
Debusmann, Bernd: Reuters
Decker, Susan: Bloomberg News
DeFrank, Thomas: New York Daily News
Deguchi, Tomohiro: Kyodo News
Del Giudice, Vincent: Bloomberg News
Del Riccio, Cristiano: ANSA Italian News Agency
Delgado, Jose: El Nuevo Dia
Dell'Amore, Christine: United Press International
Delollis, Barbara: USA Today
DeLuce, Daniel: Agence France-Presse
DeMarco, Edward: Bloomberg News
Dennis, Steven: Congressional Quarterly
Deogun, Nikhil: Wall Street Journal
Deparle, Jason: New York Times
Dermann, Philipp: Financial Times
Dermody, William: USA Today
Dermota, Kenneth: Agence France-Presse
DeSenne, Michael: SmartMoney.com
Dessouky, Dean: Saudi Press Agency
Deutsch, Jack: CongressDaily
Diaz, Kevin: McClatchy Newspapers
Diaz-Briseno, Jose: Reforma Newspaper
Dick, Jason: CongressDaily
Dieudonne, David: Agence France-Presse
Dilanian, Ken: USA Today
Dillin, Jr., John: Christian Science Monitor
Dillon, Robert: Oil Daily
DiMascio, Jen: Defense Daily
Dinan, Stephen: Washington Times
Dine, Philip: St. Louis Post-Dispatch
Dineen, John: Congressional Quarterly
Dinesh, Manimoli: Oil Daily
Dinmore, Guy: Financial Times
Dlouhy, Jennifer: Hearst Newspapers
Dobbyn, Timothy: Reuters
Dodge, Catherine: Bloomberg News
Doering, Christopher: Reuters
Doggett, Tom: Reuters
Doherty, Robert: Reuters
Dolan, Christopher: Washington Times
Dolinger, David Allen: Wall Street Journal
Donmoyer, Ryan: Bloomberg News
Donnelly, John: Congressional Quarterly
Dono, Linda: Gannett News Service
Dorell, Oren: USA Today
Dorning, Mike: Chicago Tribune
Doublet, Jean-Louis: Agence France-Presse
Douglas, William: McClatchy Newspapers
Dowd, Maureen: New York Times
Downey, Kirstin: Washington Post
Downing, James: Restructuring Today
Doyle, Michael: McClatchy Newspapers
Drajem, Mark: Bloomberg News
Drawbaugh, Kevin: Reuters
Dreazen, Yochi: Wall Street Journal
Drinkard, Jim: Associated Press
Drobnyk, Josh: Allentown Morning Call
Drogin, Robert: Los Angeles Times
Drummond, Bob: Bloomberg News
Dufour, Jeff: Washington Examiner
Duggan, Loren: Congressional Quarterly
Duggan, Paul: Washington Post
Duin, Julia: Washington Times
Duke, Lynne: Washington Post
Dunbar, John: Associated Press
Dunham, Will: Reuters
Dunphy, Harry: Associated Press
Dvorak, Petula: Washington Post
Dwyer, Paula: New York Times
Dwyer, Timothy: Washington Post
Earle, Geoff: New York Post
Eaton, Sabrina: Cleveland Plain Dealer
Eckert, Paul: Reuters
Eckert, Toby: Congressional Quarterly
Eckstrom, Kevin: Religion News Service
Ecochard, Kristyn: United Press International
Edmonds, Jr., Ronald: Associated Press
Efron, Sonni: Los Angeles Times
Efstathiou, James: Bloomberg News
Eggen, Daniel: Washington Post

MEMBERS ENTITLED TO ADMISSION—Continued

Eichelberger, Cutis: Bloomberg News
Eilperin, Juliet: Washington Post
Eisenberg, Carol: Newsday
Eisenhower, Karl: WashingtonPost.com
Eisler, Peter: USA Today
Eisman, Dale: Virginian-Pilot
El Hamti, Maribel: EFE News Services
El Nasser, Haya: USA Today
Elboghdady, Dina: Washington Post
Ellicott, Val: Gannett News Service
Elliott, Geoff: Australian
Ellis, Kristi: Fairchild News Service
Elsibai, Nadine: Bloomberg News
Emerling, Gary: Washington Times
Endo, Mieko: Kyodo News
Enoch, Daniel: Bloomberg News
Epstein, Edward: San Francisco Chronicle
Espo, David: Associated Press
Estill, Jerry: Associated Press
Evans, Ben: Associated Press
Evans, Donald: Associated Press
Eversley, Melanie: USA Today
Fabbri, Alexis: Washington Internet Daily
Fagan, Amy: Washington Times
Faler, Brian: Bloomberg News
Fang, Tai Ming Bay: Chicago Tribune
Farhi, Paul: Washington Post
Faust, Anthony: Gannett News Service
Fears, Darryl: Washington Post
Feege, Edward: Argus Media
Fehr, Steven: Washington Post
Fein, Geoff: Defense Daily
Feld, Karen: Capital Connections
Feldman, Carole: Associated Press
Feldmann, Linda: Christian Science Monitor
Felker, Edward: SNG Newspapers
Feller, Ben: Associated Press
Felsenthal, Mark: Reuters
Fendrich, Howard: Associated Press
Feng, Shaojie: China Legal Daily
Ferguson, Ellyn: Gannett News Service
Ferrari, Francisco: Agence France-Presse
Ferraro, Thomas: Reuters
Ferrechio, Susan: Congressional Quarterly
Fetterman, Mindy: USA Today
Fialka, John: Wall Street Journal
Fields, Gary: Wall Street Journal
Fields, Robin: Los Angeles Times
Fils, Dyane: Congressional Quarterly
Finkel, David: Washington Post
Fiore, Faye: Los Angeles Times
Fireman, Ken: Bloomberg News
Fischer, Leonard: Gannett News Service
Flaherty, Anne: Associated Press
Flaherty, Mary Pat: Washington Post
Flanders, Gwen: USA Today
Flattau, Edward: Global Horizons Syndicate
Fletcher, Michael: Washington Post
Ford, Matt: Associated Press
Fordney, Jason: Energy Daily
Forsgren Weaver, Heather: Communications Daily
Forsythe, Michael: Bloomberg News
Foss, Brad: Associated Press
Foster-Simeon, Ed: USA Today
Fournier, Ron: Associated Press
Fowler, Maria: Gannett News Service
Fox, Margaret: Reuters
Fram, Alan: Associated Press
Frank, Jacqueline: Reuters
Frank, Thomas: USA Today
Fraze, Barbara: Catholic News Service
Frederick, Don: Los Angeles Times
Freedman, Dan: Hearst Newspapers
Freeman, Alan: Toronto Globe and Mail
Freeman, Sholnn: Washington Post
Freking, Kevin: Associated Press
Friedman, Jeffrey: Congressional Quarterly
Friedman, Lisa: Los Angeles Daily News
Friedman, Robert: Scripps Howard News Service
Frommer, Frederic: Associated Press
Fry, Jamey: Congressional Quarterly
Fu, Norman: China Times
Fuhrig, Frank: German Press Agency–DPA
Fujii, Kazuaki: Nikkei
Furlow, Robert: Associated Press
Galianese, Joseph: Associated Press
Gallagher, Brian: USA Today
Gallen, Claire: Agence France-Presse
Gamboa, Suzanne: Associated Press
Gambrell, Kathy: CongressDaily
Gandarillas, Javier: Gannett News Service
Gaouette, K. Nicole: Los Angeles Times
Garcia Martinez, Adriana: Reuters
Gardett, Peter: Argus Media
Gardiner, Andrew: USA Today
Gardner, Amy: Washington Post
Gaudiano Albright, Nicole: Gannett News Service
Gaul, Gilbert: Washington Post
Gearan, Anne: Associated Press
Gedda, George: Associated Press
Geewax, Marilyn: Cox Newspapers
Gehrke, Robert: Salt Lake Tribune
Gelie, Philippe: Le Figaro
Gensheimer, Lydia: Congressional Quarterly
Gentry, Caroline: Argus Media
George, Elizabeth: Congressional Quarterly
Geracimos, Ann: Washington Times
Gerdts, Jennifer: Tokyo-Chunichi Shimbun
Gerhart, Ann: Washington Post
Gerstenzang, James: Los Angeles Times
Gertz, William: Washington Times
Giacomo, Carol: Reuters
Gibson, William: South Florida Sun-Sentinel
Gienger, Viola: Bloomberg News

MEMBERS ENTITLED TO ADMISSION—Continued

Gilbert, Craig: Milwaukee Journal Sentinel
Gilcrest, Laura: United Press International
Gillman, Todd: Dallas Morning News
Ginsberg, Steven: Washington Post; Reuters
Giroux, Gregory: Congressional Quarterly
Glass, Pamela: Le Mauricien
Glass, Robert: Associated Press
Glod, Maria: Washington Post
Glover, K. Daniel: National Journal's Technology Daily
Goad, Ben: Riverside Press-Enterprise
Godfrey, John: Dow Jones Newswires
Goldbacher, Raymond: USA Today
Goldenberg, Suzanne: London Guardian
Goldfarb, Zachary: Washington Post
Goldman, Julianna: Bloomberg News
Goldstein, Amy: Washington Post
Goldstein, Avram: Bloomberg News
Goldstein, Daniel: Bloomberg News
Goldstein, David: Kansas City Star
Goldstein, Steven: Philadelphia Inquirer
Golle, Vince: Bloomberg News
Goller, Howard Scot: Reuters
Gomez, Alan: USA Today
Gomez, Sergio: El Tiempo
Gomez, Shawn: Associated Press
Goo, Sara: Washington Post
Goode, Darren: CongressDaily
Goodman, Adrianne: New York Times
Gordon, D. Craig: Newsday
Gordon, Greg: McClatchy Newspapers
Gordon, Marcy: Associated Press
Gordon, Michael: New York Times
Gorham, Elizabeth: Canadian Press
Gorman, Siobhan: Baltimore Sun
Gosselin, Peter: Los Angeles Times
Goto, Shihoko: United Press International
Govindarajan, Shweta: Congressional Quarterly
Gowen, Annie: Washington Post
Graham, Bradley: Washington Post
Graham, Jed: Investor's Business Daily
Grangereau, Philippe: Liberation
Grant, Jeremy: Financial Times
Gray, Andrew: Reuters
Green, Mark: Oklahoman
Greenberg, Brigitte: Bloomberg News
Greene, Marcia Slacum: Washington Post
Greene, Robert: Bloomberg News
Greenfield, Heather: National Journal's Technology Daily
Greenhouse, Linda: New York Times
Greiling Keane, Angela: Bloomberg News
Greve, Frank: McClatchy Newspapers
Grier, Peter: Christian Science Monitor
Griffith, Stephanie: Agence France-Presse
Grimaldi, James: Washington Post
Groppe, Maureen: Gannett News Service
Gross, Thomas: Kyodo News
Grudgings, Stuart: Reuters
Gruenwald, Juliana: CongressDaily
Guenther, Markus: Westdeutsche Allgemeine
Guerra, Carlo Daniel: Congressional Quarterly
Guess, Andrew: Inside Higher Ed
Guevara, Tomas: El Diario de Hoy
Guggenheim, Ken: Associated Press
Guha, Krishna: Financial Times
Gulino, Denny: Market News International
Guroian, Rafi: Cox Newspapers
Gutman, Roy: McClatchy Newspapers
Haberkorn, Jennifer: Washington Times
Hackett, Laurel: Scripps Howard News Service
Hagenbaugh, Barbara: USA Today
Hager, George: USA Today
Haggerty, Maryann: Washington Post
Hall, Kevin: McClatchy Newspapers
Hall, Mimi: USA Today
Hallock, Kimberly: Congressional Quarterly
Hallow, Ralph: Washington Times
Halpern-Meekin, Ben: Congressional Quarterly
Hamalainen, Aloysia: St. Louis Post-Dispatch
Hamann, Carlos: Agence France-Presse
Hambrick-Stowe, Thomas: Yomiuri Shimbun
Hamburger, Thomas: Los Angeles Times
Hamrin, Eric: Asahi Shimbun
Han, Yong Kirl: Segye Times
Hananel, Sam: Associated Press
Handley, Paul: Agence France-Presse
Hannett, Thomas: Congressional Quarterly
Hardin, Peter: Richmond Times-Dispatch
Hardy, Karl: Gannett News Service
Hargrove, Thomas: Scripps Howard News Service
Harland, Janis: New York Times
Harnden, Toby: London Daily Telegraph
Harper, Jennifer: Washington Times
Harper, Tim: Toronto Star
Harris, Amanda: Congressional Quarterly
Harris, Charles: Yomiuri Shimbun
Harris, Gardiner: New York Times
Harris, Hamil: Washington Post
Harris, Ronald: St. Louis Post-Dispatch
Hart, Dan: Bloomberg News
Hartnagel, Nancy: Catholic News Service
Hartson, Merrill: Associated Press
Harwood, John: Wall Street Journal
Hasan, Khalid: Lahore Daily Times
Hastings, Maribel: La Opinion
Hatch, David: National Journal's Technology Daily
Havemann, Joel: Los Angeles Times
Hawkings, David: Congressional Quarterly
Hayakawa, Toshiyuki: Sekai Nippo
Haynes, Veryl Dion: Washington Post
He, Yun: Shanghai Wenhui Daily
Healey, James: USA Today
Healy, Patrick: New York Times
Healy, Robert: Congressional Quarterly

MEMBERS ENTITLED TO ADMISSION—Continued

Heaton, Laura: United Press International
Heavey, Susan: Reuters
Hebert, H. Josef: Associated Press
Hedges, Michael: Houston Chronicle
Hedges, Stephen: Chicago Tribune
Hedgpeth, Dana: Washington Post
Hefling, Kimberly: Associated Press
Hegstad, Maria: Washington Examiner
Heilprin, John: Associated Press
Helderman, Rosalind: Washington Post
Heller, Marc: Watertown Daily Times
Heller, Michele: McClatchy Newspapers
Hemingway, Mark: Market News International
Hendel, Caitlin: Congressional Quarterly
Hendel, John: United Press International
Henderson, Celia Nell: Washington Post
Henderson, Diedtra: Boston Globe
Henderson, Gregory: Associated Press
Hendrickx, Frank: Netherlands Press Association
Hendrie, Paul: Congressional Quarterly
Hennessy-Fiske, Marian: Los Angeles Times
Henriksson, Karin: Svenska Dagbladet
Henry, John: Associated Press
Heo, Yongbom: Chosun Ilbo
Herman, Edith: Communications Daily
Herman, Ken: Cox Newspapers
Hernandez, Raymond: New York Times
Herrmann, Frank: Rheinische Post
Hess, David: CongressDaily
Hess, Pamela: United Press International
Higa, Liriel: Congressional Quarterly
Higgins, David: Congressional Quarterly
Higgins, Sean: Investor's Business Daily
Higham, Scott: Washington Post
Higuchi, Takuya: Jiji Press
Hill, Patricia: Washington Times
Hines, Cragg: Houston Chronicle
Hinton, Earl: Associated Press
Hirsch, Claudia: Market News International
Hirsch, Steve: Washington Times
Hisadome, Shinichi: Tokyo-Chunichi Shimbun
Hitt, Greg: Wall Street Journal
Hoeffel, John: Los Angeles Times
Hoffecker, Leslie: Los Angeles Times
Hoffer, Audrey: Milwaukee Journal Sentinel
Hoffman, Lisa: Scripps Howard News Service
Holland, Jesse: Associated Press
Holland, Judy: Hearst Newspapers
Holly, Christopher: Energy Daily
Holly, Derrill: Associated Press
Holmes, Charles: Cox Newspapers
Holzer, Linda: USA Today
Hong, Liu: Xinhua News Agency
Hook, Janet: Los Angeles Times
Hoover, William: Wall Street Journal
Hopkins, Cheyenne: American Banker
Hopkins, Chris: WashingtonPost.com
Horrigan, Marie: Congressional Quarterly
Hortobagyi, Monica: USA Today
Horwich, Lee: USA Today
Horwitz, Sari: Washington Post
Hoskinson, Charles: Congressional Quarterly
Hosler, Karen: Baltimore Sun
Hossain, Farhana: New York Times
Hotakainen, Rob: Minneapolis Star Tribune
House, Billy: Tampa Tribune
Hoy, Anne: Congressional Quarterly
Hsu, Spencer: Washington Post
Hu, Fang: Xinhua News Agency
Hudson, Audrey: Washington Times
Hughes, John: Bloomberg News
Hughes, Siobhan: Dow Jones Newswires
Hughey, Ann: Bloomberg News
Hull, Anne: Washington Post
Hulse, Carl: New York Times
Hultgren, John: Aftenposten
Hultman, Tamela: AllAfrica.com
Hume, Lynn: Bond Buyer
Hunt, Albert: Bloomberg News
Hunt, Kasie: Associated Press
Hunt, Terence: Associated Press
Hunter, Kathleen: Congressional Quarterly
Hurley, Lawrence: Los Angeles Daily Journal
Hurley, Liam: Saudi Press Agency
Hurt, Charles: Washington Examiner; New York Post
Hussein, Sara Ayesha: Saudi Press Agency
Husun, Anita: Washington Post
Hutcheson, Ron: McClatchy Newspapers
Hyde, Justin: Detroit Free Press
Igarashi, Aya: Yomiuri Shimbun
Ikeda, Nestor: Associated Press
Ilustre, Josefina: Malaya
Ip, Gregory: Wall Street Journal
Irwin, Conway: Argus Media
Itkowitz, Colby: Congressional Quarterly
Ivanovich, David: Houston Chronicle
Ives-Halperin, Benton: Dow Jones Newswires
Jackler, Rosalind: USA Today
Jackson, David: USA Today
Jackson, Frankie: Los Angeles Times
Jackson, Herbert: Bergen County Record
Jackson-Randall, Maya: Dow Jones Newswires
Jae Hong, Kim: Yonhap News Agency
Jaffe, Greg: Wall Street Journal
Jakes Jordan, Lara: Associated Press
Jalonick, Mary Clare: Associated Press
James, Frank: Chicago Tribune
James, Michael: USA Today
Jansen, Bart: Portland Press Herald
Jarlenski, Marian: Congressional Quarterly
Jaschik, Scott: Inside Higher Ed
Jaspin, Elliot: Cox Newspapers
Jean-Robert, Alain: Agence France-Presse
Jehl, Douglas: New York Times

MEMBERS ENTITLED TO ADMISSION—Continued

Jelinek, Pauline: Associated Press
Jensen, Kristin: Bloomberg News
Jessen, Kory: Associated Press
Jitsu, Tetsuya: Nikkei
Johnson, Carrie: Washington Post
Johnson, Darragh: Washington Post
Johnson, David: Scripps Howard News Servce
Johnson, Fawn: CongressDaily
Johnson, Kevin: USA Today
Johnson, Matthew: Congressional Quarterly
Johnson, Sandy: Associated Press
Johnson, Toni: Congressional Quarterly
Johnston, David: New York Times
Johnston, Nicholas: Bloomberg News
Jones, Kerry: Congressional Quarterly
Jones, Robert: Scripps Howard News Service
Jordan, Charles: CongressDaily
Joshi, Jitendra: Agence France-Presse
Joy, Patricia: Congressional Quarterly
Joyce, Amy: Washington Post
Joyce, Stacey: Reuters
Junius, Dennis: Associated Press
Justsen, Klaus: Jyllands-Posten
Kady II, Martin: Congressional Quarterly
Kajita, Takehito: Kyodo News
Kamalick, Joseph: ICIS News
Kamazuka, Yumi: Akahata
Kamen, Al: Washington Post
Kammer, Jerry: Copley News Service
Kampeas, Ron: Jewish Telegraphic Agency
Kane, Paul: WashingtonPost.com
Kaper, Stacy Lynn: American Banker
Kaplan, Peter: Reuters
Kapochunas, Rachel: Congressional Quarterly
Karam, Joyce: Al-Hayat
Karey, Gerald: Platts News Service
Karube, Kensuke: Jiji Press
Karush, Sarah: Associated Press
Kasahara, Toshihiko: Mainichi Shimbun
Kastner, Kevin: Market News International
Kato, Hidenaka: Nikkei
Kato, Yoichi: Asahi Shimbun
Keating, Dan: Washington Post
Keefe, Stephen: Nikkei
Keller, Susan: New York Times
Kelley, Matthew: USA Today
Kellman Blazar, Laurie: Associated Press
Kellogg, Sarah: Newhouse News Service
Kelly, Dennis: USA Today
Kelly, Erin: Gannett News Service
Kelly, Ryan: Congressional Quarterly
Kemper, Bob: Atlanta Journal Constitution
Kendall, Brent: Los Angeles Daily Journal
Kercheval, Nancy: Bloomberg News
Kerr, Jennifer: Associated Press
Kerry, Frances: Reuters
Kertes, Noella: Congressional Quarterly
Kessler, Glenn: Washington Post
Kesten, Lou: Associated Press
Kiefer, Francine: Christian Science Monitor
Kiely, Eugene: USA Today
Kiely, Kathy: USA Today
Kilian, Martin: Tages Anzeiger
Kilpatrick, James: Universal Press Syndicate
Kim, Angela: Congressional Quarterly
Kim, Byungsu: Yonhap News Agency
Kim, Eun: Gannett News Service
Kim, Jae Hong: Yonhap News Agency
Kim, Jin Ho: Kyunghyang Shinmun
Kimitch, Rebecca: Congressional Quarterly
Kimura, Jun: Mainichi Shimbun
King, Ledyard: Gannett News Service
King, Llewellyn: Energy Daily
King, Peter: Congressional Quarterly
King, Jr., Neil: Wall Street Journal
Kipling, Bogdan: Kipling News Service
Kirchgaessner, Stephanie: Financial Times
Kirchhoff, Suzanne: USA Today
Kirkland, Michael: United Press International
Kirkman, Joshua: Asahi Shimbun
Kirkpatrick, David: New York Times
Kirsanov, Dmitry: Itar-Tass News Agency
Kiss, Veronique: Agence France-Presse
Kitto, Kris: LRP Publications
Kivlan, Terence: CongressDaily
Klein, Alec: Washington Post
Klein, Allison: Washington Post
Klein, Richard: Boston Globe
Klein Jr., Gilbert: Media General News Service
Klisz, Theresa: Gannett News Service
Kluever, Reymer: Sueddeutsche Zeitung
Klug, Foster: Associated Press
Kniazkov, Maxim: Agence France-Presse
Knox, Noelle: USA Today
Knox, Olivier: Agence France-Presse
Koar, Juergen: Stuttgarter Zeitung
Koch, Wendy: USA Today
Kodjak-Fitzgerald, Alison: Bloomberg News
Koff, Stephen: Cleveland Plain Dealer
Koffler, Keith: CongressDaily
Komori, Yoshihisa: Sankei Shimbun
Komurata, Yoshiyuki: Asahi Shimbun
Kornblut, Anne: Washington Post
Kosseff, Jeffrey: Oregonian
Koszczuk, Jaculine: Congressional Quarterly
Kotake, Hiroyuki: Nikkei
Kralev, Nicholas: Washington Times
Kramer, Reed: AllAfrica.com
Kranish, Michael: Boston Globe
Krawzak, Paul: Copley News Service
Krebs, Brian: WashingtonPost.com
Kreisher, Otto: CongressDaily
Krieger, Hilary Leila: Jerusalem Post
Krieger, Kim: Argus Media

MEMBERS ENTITLED TO ADMISSION—Continued

Krishnaswami, Sridhar: Press Trust of India
Kroepsch, Adrianne: Congressional Quarterly
Kronholz, June: Wall Street Journal
Kuhnhenn, Jim: Associated Press
Kuk, Kiyon: Segye Times
Kumar, Anita: St. Petersburg Times
Kumar, Arun: Indo-Asian News Service
Kumar, Dinesh: Communications Daily
Kunkle, Fredrick: Washington Post
Kuno, Shuko: Jiji Press
La Franchi, Howard: Christian Science Monitor
Labaton, Stephen: New York Times
Labbe, Theola: Washington Post
Labriny, Azeddine: Saudi Press Agency
Lambert, Lisa: Reuters
Lambrecht, William: St. Louis Post-Dispatch
Lambro, Donald: Washington Times
Landay, Jonathan: McClatchy Newspapers
Landers, James: Dallas Morning News
Lando, Ben: United Press International
Landry, Catherine: Platts News Service
Langan, Michael: Agence France-Presse
Lanman, Scott: Bloomberg News
Lanteaume, Sylvie: Agence France-Presse
Larkin, Catherine: Bloomberg News
Lash, Steve: Chicago Daily Law Bulletin
Lawder, David: Reuters
Lawrence, Jill: USA Today
Layton, Lyndsey: Washington Post
Leahy, Michael: Washington Post
Leary, Warren: New York Times
Leavitt, Paul: USA Today
Lebbar, Sabah: Maghreb Arab Press
Lebling, Madonna: Washington Post
Lederman, Douglas: Inside Higher Ed
LeDuc, Daniel: Washington Post
Lee, Byonghan: Korea Times
Lee, Chang-Yul: Korea Times
Lee, Christopher: Washington Post
Lee, Dong Min: Yonhap News Agency
Lee, Jong Kook: Korea Times
Lee, Ki Chang: Yonhap News Agency
Lee, Matthew: Associated Press
Lee, Richard: Media General News Service
Lee, Suevon: New York Times
Lefkow, Chris: Agence France-Presse
LeGras, Gilbert: Reuters
Lehmann, Chris: Congressional Quarterly
Lehmann, Evan: Lowell Sun
Leibovich, Mark: New York Times
Leiby, Richard: Washington Post
Leinwand, Donna: USA Today
Lengel, Allan: Washington Post
Lengell, Sean: Washington Times
Lerman, David: Newport News Daily Press
Lesnes, Corine: Le Monde
Lesparre, Michael: Votes in Congress Newspaper Syndicate
Lester, William: Associated Press
Leubsdorf, Carl: Dallas Morning News
Lever, Robert: Agence France-Presse
Levey, Noam: Los Angeles Times
Levin, Alan: USA Today
Levine, Susan: Washington Post
Levinson, Nathan: Congressional Quarterly
Lewallen, Jonathan: Congressional Quarterly
Lewis, Charles: Hearst Newspapers
Lewis, Finlay: Copley News Service
Lewis, Katherine: Newhouse News Service
Lewis, Neil: New York Times
Li, Zhengxin: China Economic Daily
Lichtblau, Eric: New York Times
Lieberman, Brett: Harrisburg Patriot-News
Lightman, David: Hartford Courant
Lilleston, Thomas: USA Today
Lin, Betty: World Journal
Lindell, Cecile: Daily Deal
Linskey, Regina: Catholic News Service
Lipari, James: Associated Press
Lipman, Laurence: Cox Newspapers
Lipscomb, David: Washington Times
Lipton, Eric: New York Times
Litvan, Laura: Bloomberg News
Liu, Ping: China Times
Lizama, Orlando: EFE News Services
Lloyd-Parry, Roland: Agence France-Presse
Lobe, James: Inter Press Service
Lobsenz, George: Energy Daily
Lochhead, Carolyn: San Francisco Chronicle
Locker, Ray: USA Today
Lopez Zamorano, Jose: Notimex Mexican News Agency
Lorenzetti, Maureen: Reuters
Lorenzo, Aaron: BioWorld Today
Loven, Jennifer: Associated Press
Lovenheim, Sarah: WashingtonPost.com
Lowy, Joan: Associated Press
Lozano, Laurent: Agence France-Presse
Lubold, Gordon: Christian Science Monitor
Luce, Edward: Financial Times
Lueck, Sarah: Wall Street Journal
Lumpkin, Beverley: Associated Press
Luo, Michael: New York Times
Lynch, David: USA Today
Lytle, Tamara: Orlando Sentinel
Macaron, Joe: Kuwait News Agency
Macaskill, Ewen: London Guardian
Mackler, Peter: Agence France-Presse
Madden, Mike: Gannett News Service
Madhani, Aamer: Chicago Tribune
Magner, Mike: CongressDaily
Majano, Rosendo: EFE News Services
Make, Jonathan: Communications Daily
Maler, Sandra: Reuters
Malone, Julia: Cox Newspapers
Mann, Jason: CongressDaily

MEMBERS ENTITLED TO ADMISSION—Continued

Mann, William: Associated Press
Manning, Jason: WashingtonPost.com
Manning, Stephen: Associated Press
Mannion, James: Agence France-Presse
Mantell, Ruth: MarketWatch
Marcus, Aliza: Bloomberg News
Marcus, Ruth: Washington Post
Marech, Rona: Baltimore Sun
Margasak, Lawrence: Associated Press
Margetta, Robert James: Congressional Quarterly
Marimow, Anne: Washington Post
Marino, Marie: Gannett News Service
Mark, Roy: Internetnews.com
Marklein, Mary Beth: USA Today
Marolo, Bruno: L'Unita
Marrero, Diana: Gannett News Service
Marshall, Christa: Denver Post
Marshall, Michael: United Press International
Marshall, Stephen: USA Today
Martin, Gary: San Antonio Express-News
Martinez, Ian: Communications Daily
Martinez, Michael: National Journal's Technology Daily
Marutani, Hiroshi: Nikkei
Mascaro, Lisa: Las Vegas Sun
Mason, Julie: Houston Chronicle
Masumitsu, Hiroshi: Yomiuri Shimbun
Mathews, Anna: Wall Street Journal
Mathewson, Judith: Bloomberg News
Matthews, Mark: Orlando Sentinel
Matthews, Robert Guy: Wall Street Journal
Maynard, Michael: MarketWatch
McAuliff, Michael: New York Daily News
McCaffrey, Raymond: Washington Post
McCarthy, Mike: German Press Agency–DPA
McCaslin, John: Washington Times
McConnell, Alison: Bond Buyer
McConnell, William: Daily Deal
McCutcheon, Chuck: Newhouse News Service
McDonald, Greg: Congressional Quarterly
McFeatters, Dale: Scripps Howard News Service
McGinley, Laurie: Wall Street Journal
McGrane, Victoria: Congressional Quarterly
McKeever, Amy: Mainichi Shimbun
McKenna, Barrie: Toronto Globe and Mail
McKinnon, John: Wall Street Journal
McLaughlin, Seth: Washington Times
McLean, Demian: Bloomberg News
McLoone, Sharon: WashingtonPost.com
McManus, Doyle: Los Angeles Times
McNeil, Margaret: MarketWatch
McQuillan, Mark: Bloomberg News
McQuillen, William: Bloomberg News
Meadows, Clifford: New York Times
Means, Marianne: Hearst Newspapers
Meckler, Laura: Wall Street Journal
Meek, James: New York Daily News
Megali, Brian: Argus Media
Mekay, Emad: Inter Press Service
Melendez, Michele: Newhouse News Service
Memmott, Mark: USA Today
Mercer, Marsha: Media General News Service
Merle, Renae: Washington Post
Merry, Robert: Congressional Quarterly
Meszoly, Robin: Bloomberg News
Metzler, Natasha: Associated Press
Meyer, Joshua: Los Angeles Times
Michaels, Jim: USA Today
Michalski, Patty: USA Today
Middleton, Chris: Market News International
Miga, Andrew: Associated Press
Mihailescu, Andrea: United Press International
Mikes, Zoltan: World Business Press
Mikkelsen, Randall: Reuters
Milbank, Dana: Washington Post
Miller, Alan: Los Angeles Times
Miller, Cheryl: New York Times
Miller, Greg: Los Angeles Times
Miller, Kevin: Bloomberg News
Miller, Leslie: Associated Press
Miller, Richard: Bloomberg News
Miller, Steven: Washington Times
Miller, William: Washington Post
Milligan, Susan: Boston Globe
Millikin, David: Agence France-Presse
Miroff, Nick: Washington Post
Mitchell, Steve: United Press International
Mitoma, Yoshio: Sekai Nippo
Mittelstadt, Michelle: Houston Chronicle
Moffitt, Lawrence: United Press International
Mohammad, Saad: Kuwait News Agency
Mohammed, Arshad: Reuters
Mohr, Patricia: LRP Publications
Molotsky, Irvin: CongressDaily
Monaghan, Elaine: Congressional Quarterly
Monge, Yolanda: El Pais
Montet, Virginie: Agence France-Presse
Montgomery, David: Fort Worth Star-Telegram; Washington Post
Montgomery, Lori: Washington Post
Moore, Pamela: LRP Publications
Morales, Armando: La Razon
Morgan, Dan: Washington Post
Morgan, David: Reuters
Moriarty, Jo Ann: Springfield Republican
Morley, Jefferson: WashingtonPost.com
Morris, Damiko: Associated Press
Morris, David: CongressDaily
Morrison, James: Washington Times
Morrison, Joanne: Reuters
Morse, Dan: Washington Post
Morton, Joseph: Omaha World-Herald
Moscoso, Eunice: Cox Newspapers
Mosk, Matthew: Washington Post
Moss, Daniel: Bloomberg News
Mott, Gregory: Bloomberg News

MEMBERS ENTITLED TO ADMISSION—Continued

Mufson, Steven: Washington Post
Mulkern, Anne: Denver Post
Mulligan, John: Providence Journal
Mullins, Brody: Wall Street Journal
Mundy, Alicia: Seattle Times
Munoz, Cesar: EFE News Services
Murphy, Kathleen: Congressional Quarterly
Murray, Brendan: Bloomberg News
Murray, Frank: Washington Times
Murray, Shailagh: Washington Post
Murray, Shanon: Daily Deal
Murti, Bhattiprolu: Dow Jones Newswires
Mussenden, Sean: Media General News Service
Myers, Jim: Tulsa World
Myers, Laura: Associated Press
Mykkanen, Pekka: Helsingin Sanomat
Naganuma, Aki: Tokyo-Chunichi Shimbun
Nagourney, Adam: New York Times
Nail, Dawson: Communications Daily
Nakamura, David: Washington Post
Nakashima, Ellen: Washington Post
Nather, David: Congressional Quarterly
N'Diaye, Yali: Market News International
Neergaard, Lauran: Associated Press
Neikirk, William: Chicago Tribune
Nesmith, Jeff: Cox Newspapers
Neubauer, Chuck: Los Angeles Times
Neuman, Johanna: Los Angeles Times
Newman, Christopher: Argus Media
Newton Small, Jay: Bloomberg News
Niehaus, Wanita: Scripps Howard News Service
Nielsen, David: Scripps Howard News Service
Niland, Martin: Associated Press
Nippert, Carol: Hearst Newspapers
Nishimura, Takuya: Hokkaido Shimbun
Nishizaki, Kaoru: Asahi Shimbun
Nitkin, David: Baltimore Sun
Niu, Zhen: Shanghai WenHui Daily
Nixon, Ronnie: New York Times
Nkansah, E. Roy: Congressional Quarterly
Noel, Essex: Reuters
Nomiyama, Chizu: Reuters
Norman, Jane: Des Moines Register
Norton, C. JoAnne: Bloomberg News
Novak, Robert: Chicago Sun-Times
Noyes, Andrew: National Journal's Technology Daily
Nutting, Brian: Congressional Quarterly
Nutting, Rex: MarketWatch
Nyitray, Joseph: Congressional Quarterly
O'Brien, Nancy: Catholic News Service
O'Callaghan, John: Reuters
O'Donnell, Jayne: USA Today
O'Keefe, Edward: WashingtonPost.com
O'Neil, Anne: Argus Media
O'Reilly II, Joseph: Bloomberg News
Oguri, Yasuyuki: Tokyo Chunichi Shimbun
Ohji, Tomoko: Mainichi Shimbun
Ohlemacher, Stephen: Associated Press
Ohlsson, Erik: Dagens Nyheter
Okuma, Yoshiaki: Jiji Press
Olchowy, Mark: Associated Press
Oliveri, Frank: Congressional Quarterly
Olmsted, Daniel: United Press International
Olson, Elizabeth: New York Times
Orndorff, Mary: Birmingham News
Orol, Ron: Daily Deal
Orr, J. Scott: Newark Star-Ledger
Osenenko, Derek: Gannett News Service
Ostermann, Dietmar: Frankfurter Rundschau
Ota, Alan: Congressional Quarterly
Otsuka, Ryuichi: Yomiuri Shimbun
Ourlian, Robert: Los Angeles Times
Overberg, Paul: USA Today
Owens, Megan: Associated Press
Ozaeta-Heusel, Cristina: EFE News Services
Pace, David: Associated Press
Pacifici, Sabrina: New York Times
Page, Clarence: Chicago Tribune
Page, Susan: USA Today
Pakhomov, Alexander: Itar-Tass News Agency
Paletta, Damian: Dow Jones Newswires
Paley, Amit: Washington Post
Palmer, Doug: Reuters
Pan, Yunzhao: Xinhua News Agency
Papantoniou, Lambros: Eleftheros Typos
Pappu, Sridhar: Washington Post
Park, Hannah Won: Yonhap News Agency
Park, Jin-Keol: Korea Daily
Park, Ki Chan: Korea Times
Park, Kwang Duk: Korea Times
Parker, Ashley: New York Times
Parker, Laura: USA Today
Parker, Mario: Bloomberg News
Parks, Daniel: Congressional Quarterly
Parnes, Amie: Scripps Howard News Service
Parsons, Christi: Chicago Tribune
Pasternak, Judy: Los Angeles Times
Patterson, Dean: Reuters
Pattison, Mark: Catholic News Service
Patton, Janet: Lexington Herald-Leader
Pear, Robert: New York Times
Peck, Louis: CongressDaily
Pelofsky, Jeremy: Reuters
Pena, Maria: EFE News Services
Perez, Evan: Wall Street Journal
Perine, Keith: Congressional Quarterly
Perkins, Mary: Yomiuri Shimbun
Petersen, Rosemary: Copley News Service
Peterson, Jonathan: Los Angeles Times
Peterson, Molly: Bloomberg News
Pettypiece, Shannon: Bloomberg News
Pfeiffer, Eric: Washington Times
Phelps, Timothy: Newsday
Phillips, Kathleen: New York Times

MEMBERS ENTITLED TO ADMISSION—Continued

Phillips, Lauren: Congressional Quarterly
Phillips, Michael: Wall Street Journal
Philpott, Thomas: Military Update
Pickard-Cambridge, Claire: Argus Media
Pickler, Nedra: Associated Press
Pierce, Olga: United Press International
Pincus, Walter: Washington Post
Pine, Art: CongressDaily
Piotrowski, Matt: Oil Daily
Piper, Greg: Communications Daily
Pitts, Edward Lee: Chattanooga Times Free Press
Pleming, Sue: Reuters
Plocek, Joseph: Market News International
Plungis, Jeff: Bloomberg News
Poirier, John: Reuters
Ponnudurai, Parameswaran: Agence France-Presse
Pope, Charles: Seattle Post-Intelligencer
Pore, Amery: Argus Media
Posner, Michael: CongressDaily
Poulson, Theresa: National Journal's Technology Daily
Povich, Elaine: CongressDaily
Powell, Stewart: Hearst Newspapers
Powelson, Richard: Scripps Howard News Service
Powers, Elia: Inside Higher Ed
Preciphs, Joi: Bloomberg News
Pressley, Sue Ann: Washington Post
Price, Deborah: Detroit News
Price, Elizabeth: Dow Jones Newswires
Price, Marc: Associated Press
Priest, Dana: Washington Post
Puente, Maria: USA Today
Pugh, Anthony: McClatchy Newspapers
Pulizzi, Henry: Dow Jones Newswires
Purce, Melinda: Associated Press
Purger, Tibor: Magyar Szo
Putman, Eileen: Associated Press
Puzzanghera, James: Los Angeles Times
Qianliang, Yu: Xinhua News Agency
Qiu, Jiangbo: China News Service
Quaid, Libby: Associated Press
Raab, Charlotte: Agence France-Presse
Raasch, Charles: Gannett News Service
Rabuffetti, Mauricio: Agence France-Presse
Radelat, Ana: Gannett News Service
Radwan, Ahmed: Kuwait News Agency
Raimon, Marcelo: ANSA Italian News Agency
Rajagopalan, Sethuraman: The Pioneer - India
Raju, Manu: Congressional Quarterly
Ramstack, Thomas: Washington Times
Rankin, Robert: McClatchy Newspapers
Rater, Philippe: Agence France-Presse
Ratnam, Gopal: Bloomberg News
Raum, Thomas: Associated Press
Rauscher, Jr., Carl: Cox Newspapers
Ray, Eric: Congressional Quarterly
Raymond, Anthony: Political Money Line
Reber, Paticia: German Press Agency–DPA
Recio, Maria: Fort Worth Star-Telegram
Redden, Elizabeth: Inside Higher Ed
Reddy, Sudeep: Dallas Morning News
Reeves, Pamela: Scripps Howard News Servce
Rehmann, Marc: Congressional Quarterly
Rehrmann, Laura: Gannett News Service
Reichard, John: Congressional Quarterly
Reilly, Sean: Mobile Register
Rein, Lisa: Washington Post
Reinert-Mason, Patty: Houston Chronicle
Reiss, Cory: New York Times
Remez, Michael: Congressional Quarterly
Retter, Daphne: Congressional Quarterly
Reynolds, Maura: Los Angeles Times
Ricci, Andrea: Reuters
Rich, Eric: Washington Post
Rich, Spencer: CongressDaily
Richardson, Betty: Congressional Quarterly
Richert, Catharine: Congressional Quarterly
Richey, Warren: Christian Science Monitor
Richter, Joseph: Bloomberg News
Richter, Paul: Los Angeles Times
Richwine, Lisa: Reuters
Rickett, Keith: Associated Press
Ricks, Tom: Washington Post
Riechmann-Kepler, Deb: Associated Press
Rief, Norbert: Die Presse
Riley, John: USA Today
Riley, Michael: Congressional Quarterly
Ripley, Neil: Congressional Quarterly
Riskind, Jonathan: Columbus Dispatch
Risser, William: USA Today
Rizzo, Katherine: Congressional Quarterly
Robb, Gregory: MarketWatch
Roberts, Kristin: Reuters
Roberts, Roxanne: Washington Post
Roberts III, William: Bloomberg News
Robertson, Vanessa: London Daily Telegraph
Robinson, Eugene: Washington Post
Robinson, James: Los Angeles Times
Robinson, John: Defense Daily
Roche, Jr., Walter: Los Angeles Times
Rockoff, Jonathan: Baltimore Sun
Rodriguez, Antonio: Agence France-Presse
Rogers, David: Wall Street Journal
Rogin, Joshua: Asahi Shimbun; Congressional Quarterly
Rohner, Mark: Bloomberg News
Roland, Neil: Bloomberg News
Romano, Lois: Washington Post
Roosevelt, Ann: Defense Daily
Rosen, James: McClatchy Newspapers
Rosenberg, Elizabeth: Argus Media
Rosenberg, Eric: Hearst Newspapers
Rosenkrantz, Holly: Bloomberg News
Rosenstein, Bruce: USA Today
Ross, Sonya: Associated Press
Roth, Bennett: Houston Chronicle

MEMBERS ENTITLED TO ADMISSION—Continued

Rowland, Kara: Washington Times
Rowley, James: Bloomberg News
Ruane, Michael: Washington Post
Rubin, James: Bloomberg News
Rubin, Richard: Congressional Quarterly
Rucker, Patrick: Reuters
Ruesch, Andreas: Neue Zuercher Zeitung
Rugaber, Chris: Associated Press
Ruiz, Phillip: Los Angeles Times
Rulon, Malia: Gannett News Service
Runningen, Roger: Bloomberg News
Rutenberg, Jim: New York Times
Ryan, Mary: Reuters
Ryan, Timothy: Reuters
Sadahiro, Takashi: Yomiuri Shimbun
Sadler, Aaron: Stephens Media Group
Sakamoto, Takashi: Yomiuri Shimbun
Salant, Jonathan: Bloomberg News
Salhani, Claude: United Press International
Sanchez, Humberto: Bond Buyer
Sandalow, Marc: San Francisco Chronicle
Sandler, Michael: Congressional Quarterly
Sands, David: Washington Times
Sanner, Ann: Associated Press
Santini, Jean-Louis: Agence France-Presse
Santos, Lori: Reuters
Sanz, Marie: Agence France-Presse
Sato, Nobuyuki: Jiji Press
Savage, Charles: Boston Globe
Savage, David: Los Angeles Times
Sawai, Toshimitsu: Kyodo News
Sawchuk, Stephen: LRP Publications
Saygin, Funda: Argus Media
Scally, William: William Scally Reports
Scannell, Kara: Wall Street Journal
Scarborough, Rowan: Washington Examiner
Schatz, Amy: Wall Street Journal
Scheuble, Kristy: Bloomberg News
Schlesinger, Jacob: Wall Street Journal
Schlisserman, Courtney: Bloomberg News
Schmick, William: Bloomberg News
Schmid, Randolph: Associated Press
Schmid, Sharon: Wall Street Journal
Schmidt, Robert: Bloomberg News
Schmidt, Susan: Washington Post
Schmitt, Eric: New York Times
Schmitt, Richard: Los Angeles Times
Schneider, Andrew: Seatlle Post-Intelligencer
Schneider, Benjamin: CongressDaily
Schneider, Jodi: Congressional Quarterly
Schoeller, Olivia: Berliner Zeitung
Schoof, Renee: McClatchy Newspapers
Schouten, Fredreka: USA Today
Schram, Martin: Scripps Howard News Service
Schroeder, Peter: Bond Buyer
Schroeder, Robert: MarketWatch
Schuler, Kate: CongressDaily
Schwed, Craig: Gannett News Service
Schweid, Barry: Associated Press
Scott, Heather: Market News International
Scott, Katherine: Gannett News Service
Scully, Megan: CongressDaily
Seeley, Tina: Bloomberg News
Sefton, Dru: Newhouse News Service
Seib, Gerald: Wall Street Journal
Seibel, Mark: McClatchy Newspapers
Seim, Sereana: Jiji Press
Semel, Michael: Washington Post
Seper, Jerry: Washington Times
Serrano, Richard: Los Angeles Times
Serrat, Celine: Agence France-Presse
Sevastopulo, Demetri: Financial Times
Shackelford, Lucy: Washington Post
Shaffrey, Mary: Winston-Salem Journal
Shalal-Esa, Andrea: Reuters
Shane, Scott: New York Times
Shanker, Thomas: New York Times
Shapira, Ian: Washington Post
Shaw, John: Market News International
Shea, Patricia: Mainichi Shimbun
Shear, Michael: Washington Post
Shearer, Cody: Shearer and Glen News
Sheehan, Theresa: Market News International
Sheikh, Nezar: Saudi Press Agency
Shelly, Nedra: Cleveland Plain Dealer
Shenon, Philip: New York Times
Shepard, Scott: Cox Newspapers
Shepardson, David: Detroit News
Sheridan, Kerry Colleen: Agence France-Presse
Sheridan, Mary Beth: Washington Post
Sherman, Jerome: Pittsburgh Post-Gazette
Sherman, Mark: Associated Press
Sherzai, Magan: Agence France-Presse
Shesgreen, Deirdre: St. Louis Post-Dispatch
Shields, Gerard: Baton Rouge Advocate
Shipman, Tim: London Daily Telegraph
Shipp, Susan: Congressional Quarterly
Shrader, Katie: Associated Press
Sia, Richard: CongressDaily
Sichelman, Lew: United Media
Siddons, Andrew: Yomiuri Shimbun
Sidorov, Dmitry: Kommersant
Sidoti, Elizabeth: Associated Press
Sieff, Martin: United Press International
Sigurdson, Todd: Associated Press
Silva, Mark: Chicago Tribune
Silvassy, Kathleen: Congressional Quarterly
Silverman, Elissa: Washington Post
Simison, Robert: Bloomberg News
Simon, Richard: Los Angeles Times
Siniff, John: USA Today
Sipress, Alan: Washington Post
Sirak, Michael: Defense Daily
Sisk, Richard: New York Daily News

MEMBERS ENTITLED TO ADMISSION—Continued

Sisto, Carrie: Argus Media
Sitov, Andrei: Itar-Tass News Agency
Skarzenski, Ronald: New York Times
Skiba, Katherine: Milwaukee Journal Sentinel
Skorneck, Carolyn: Associated Press
Slater, James: Agence France-Presse
Slavin, Barbara: USA Today
Sloan, Steven: American Banker
Smith, Donna: Reuters
Smith, Elliot Blair: Bloomberg News
Smith, Jeffrey: Washington Post
Smith, Sylvia: Fort Wayne Journal Gazette
Smith, Veronica: Agence France-Presse
Snider, Michael: USA Today
Sniffen, Michael: Associated Press
Snyder, Charles: Taipei Times
Sobczyk, Joseph: Bloomberg News
Solomon, Deborah: Wall Street Journal
Solomon, John: Washington Post
Solomon, Jonathan: Wall Street Journal
Somerville, Glenn: Reuters
Soraghan, Michael: Denver Post
Soufiya, Hamzaoui: Maghreb Arab Press
Spang, Thomas: US-Report (Germany)
Spangler, Todd: Detroit Free Press
Sparks, Sarah: LRP Publications
Spence, Tony: Catholic News Service
Spencer, George: Restructuring Today
Spencer, Samuel: Restructuring Today
Spencer, Tomoko: Kyodo News
Spetalnick, Matthew: Reuters
Spiegel, Peter: Los Angeles Times
Spieler, Matthew: Congressional Quarterly
Spillius, Alexander: London Daily Telegraph
Spivack, Miranda: Washington Post
Sprengelmeyer, Michael: Scripps Howard News Service
St. Onge, Jeffrey: Bloomberg News
Stables, Eleanor: Congressional Quarterly
Stager, Joshua: Congressional Quarterly
Stanchak, Jesse: Congressional Quarterly
Starks, Tim: Congressional Quarterly
Stearns, Matthew: Kansas City Star
Steiger, Jana: Congressional Quarterly
Stein, Jeff: Congressional Quarterly
Stein, Robert: Washington Post
Steiner, Emil: WashingtonPost.com
Steinman, Jon: Bloomberg News
Stempleman, Neil: Reuters
Stephens, Joe: Washington Post
Stern, Christopher: Bloomberg News
Stern, Marcus: Copley News Service
Stern, Seth: Congressional Quarterly
Sternberg, Steve: USA Today
Sternberg, William: USA Today
Sternstein, Aliya: National Journal's Technology Daily
Stevenson, Richard: New York Times
Stewart, Bruce Scott: Sankei Shimbun
Stewart, Nikita: Washington Post
Stewart, Rhonda: Chicago Tribune
Stockman, Farah: Boston Globe
Stohr, Greg: Bloomberg News
Stolberg, Sheryl: New York Times
Stone, Andrea: USA Today
Storey, David: Reuters
Stoughton, Stephenie: Associated Press
Stout, David: New York Times
Straub, Noelle: Lee Newspapers
Strobel, Warren: McClatchy Newspapers
Strohm, Chris: CongressDaily
Strong, Thomas: Associated Press
Struglinski, Suzanne: Deseret Morning News
Stuever, Hank: Washington Post
Sugita, Hiroki: Kyodo News
Sullivan, Andy: Reuters
Sullivan, Bartholomew: Scripps Howard News Service
Sullivan, Eileen: Congressional Quarterly
Sun, Lena: Washington Post
Supervielle, Ana Baron: Clarin
Superville, Darlene: Associated Press
Surzhanskiy, Andrey: Itar-Tass News Agency
Susami, Fumitaka: Kyodo News
Swann, Christopher: Bloomberg News
Swarns, Rachel: New York Times
Sweeney, Jeanne: LRP Publications
Sweet, Lynn: Chicago Sun-Times
Swindell, Bill: CongressDaily
Szekely, Peter: Reuters
Tachio, Ryoji: Tokyo Chunichi Shimbun
Tackett, R. Michael: Chicago Tribune
Takahashi, Hiroyuki: Jiji Press
Takahashi, Masaya: Kyodo News
Takruri, Lubna: Associated Press
Talbott, Basil: CongressDaily
Talev, Margaret: McClatchy Newspapers
Talhelm, Jennifer: Associated Press
Talley, Ian: Dow Jones Newswires
Tang, Yong: China People's Daily
Tankersley, James: Chicago Tribune
Tanzi, Alex: Bloomberg News
Tatsumi, Tomoji: Kyodo News
Taubman, Philip: New York Times
Tavara, Santiago: Notimex Mexican News Agency
Taylor, Andrew: Associated Press
Taylor, Cynthia: Boston Globe
Taylor, Dan: Washington Times
Taylor, Marisa: McClatchy Newspapers
Teitelbaum, Michael: Congressional Quarterly
Teskrat, Nadia: Agence France-Presse
Tessler, Joelle: Congressional Quarterly
Tetreault, Stephan: Stephens Media Group
Theimer, Sharon: Associated Press
Theobald, William: Gannett News Service
Thibodeaux, Troy: Associated Press

MEMBERS ENTITLED TO ADMISSION—Continued

Thomas, Helen: Hearst Newspapers
Thomas, Ken: Associated Press
Thomas, Richard: Roll Call Report Syndicate
Thomasson, Dan: Scripps Howard News Service
Thomet, Laurent: Agence France-Presse
Thomma, Steven: McClatchy Newspapers
Thompson, Caitlin Ellen: WashingtonPost.com
Thompson, Cheryl: Washington Post
Thompson, Jake: Omaha World-Herald
Thrush, Glenn: Newsday
Tilove, Jonathan: Newhouse News Service
Timmons, Karen: Scripps Howard News Service
Tobe, Hajime: Kyodo News
Tokito, Mineko: Yomiuri Shimbun
Toles, Tom: Washington Post
Tollefson, Jeff: Congressional Quarterly
Tomasky, Michael: London Guardian
Tomkin, Robert: Congressional Quarterly
Tomkins, Richard: United Press International
Tompson, Trevor: Associated Press
Toner, Robin: New York Times
Toppo, Gregory: USA Today
Torres, Carlos: Bloomberg News
Torres, Craig: Bloomberg News
Torry, Jack: Columbus Dispatch
Torry, Saundra: USA Today
Tozier, Carolyn: Restructuring Today
Trankovits, Laszlo: German Press Agency–DPA
Trejos, Nancy: Washington Post
Trescott, Jacqueline: Washington Post
Triplett, William: Daily Variety
Trott, William: Reuters
Trowbridge, Gordon: Detroit News
Tsao, Nadia Y.F.: Liberty Times
Tucker, Boyd Neely: Washington Post
Tumulty, Brian: Gannett News Service
Tunks, Larry: Congressional Quarterly
Turley, Melissa: LRP Publications
Turque, Bill: Washington Post
Tyson, Ann Scott: Washington Post
Tyson, James: Bloomberg News
Ueda, Toshihide: Asahi Shimbun
Uenuma, Francine: WashingtonPost.com
Ukai, Satoshi: Asahi Shimbun
Ullmann, Owen: USA Today
Umehara, Toshiya: Asahi Shimbun
Umemoto, Itsuro: Jiji Press
Urban, Peter: Connecticut Post
Urbina, Ian: New York Times
Usher, Anne: Cox Newspapers
Vadala, Gregory: Congressional Quarterly
Val Mitjavila, Eusebio: La Vanguardia
Valery, Chantal: Agence France-Presse
Van Nostrand, Jim: McClatchy Newspapers
Vanden Brook, Tom: USA Today
Vander Haar, William: Associated Press
Vargas, Jose Antonio: Washington Post
Vaughan, Martin: CongressDaily
Veazey, Walter: Scripps Howard News Service
Vedantam, Shankar: Washington Post
Veigle, Anne: Communications Daily
Vekshin, Alison: Bloomberg News
Vergano, Dan: USA Today
Viccora, Andrew: LRP Publications
Vicini, James: Reuters
Vidal Liy, Macarena: EFE News Services
Vineys, Kevin: Associated Press
Vogel, Stephen: Washington Post
Vogt, Christophe: Agence France-Presse
Volpe, Paul: Congressional Quarterly
Vorman, Julie: Reuters
Wada, Hiroaki: Mainichi Shimbun
Wagman, Robert: Newspaper Enterprise
Wagner, John: Washington Post
Waitz, Nancy: Reuters
Walcott, John: McClatchy Newspapers
Walczak, Leon: Bloomberg News
Wald, Matthew: New York Times
Waldmeir, Patti: Financial Times
Walker, Martin: United Press International
Wallsten, Peter: Los Angeles Times
Walsh, Bill: New Orleans Times-Picayune
Walsh, Brendan: Congressional Quarterly
Walsh, Edmund: Dow Jones Newswires
Walters, Anne: German Press Agency–DPA
Walton-James, Vickie: Chicago Tribune
Wang, Herman: Chattanooga Times Free Press
Ward, Andrew: Financial Times
Ward, Jon: Washington Times
Warminsky, Joseph: Congressional Quarterly
Warner, Judith: New York Times
Warrick, Joby: Washington Post
Watanabe, Hiroo: Sankei Shimbun
Waterman, Shaun: United Press International
Watson, Traci: USA Today
Watters, Susan: Fairchild News Service
Watts, William: MarketWatch
Wayne, Alexander: Congressional Quarterly
Wayne, Leslie: New York Times
Webber, Caitlin: Congressional Quarterly
Webster, Jamie: Argus Media
Weekes Jr., Michael: Reuters
Wegner, Mark: CongressDaily
Wehrman, Jessica: Dayton Daily News
Weil, Martin: Washington Post
Wein, Josh: Communications Daily
Weiner, Mark: Syracuse Post-Standard
Weisman, Jonathan: Washington Post
Weisman, Steven: New York Times
Weiss, Eric: Washington Post
Weiss, Rick: Washington Post
Welch, James: USA Today
Wellisz, Chris: Bloomberg News
Wells, Billie Jean: Gannett News Service

MEMBERS ENTITLED TO ADMISSION—Continued

Wells, Letitia: McClatchy Newspapers
Wells, Robert: Dow Jones Newswires
Welsch, Edward: Dow Jones Newswires
Weng, Xiang: China Youth Daily
Werner, Erica: Associated Press
Wernicke, Christian: Sueddeutsche Zeitung
Wessel, David: Wall Street Journal
West, Elizabeth: Asahi Shimbun
West, Paul: Baltimore Sun
Westbrook, Jesse: Bloomberg News
Westley, Brian: Associated Press
Westphal, David: McClatchy Newspapers
Wetzstein, Cheryl: Washington Times
Wheaton, Sarah: New York Times
Wheeler, Lawrence: Gannett News Service
White, Dina: Chicago Tribune
White, Gordon: Washington Telecommunications Services
White, Josh: Washington Post
White, Keith: CongressDaily
White, Jr., Joseph: Associated Press
Whitesides, John: Reuters
Whitmire, Guy: Congressional Quarterly
Whitney, David: McClatchy Newspapers
Whittle, Richard: Dallas Morning News
Wiessler, David: Reuters
Wilber, Del: Washington Post
Wilke, John: Wall Street Journal
Wilkie, Dana: Copley News Service
Wilkison, David: Associated Press
Williams, Jr., Joseph: Boston Globe
Williamson, Elizabeth: Washington Post
Willing, Richard: USA Today
Willis, Derek: WashingtonPost.com
Willis, Robert: Bloomberg News
Willman, David: Los Angeles Times
Wilson, George: CongressDaily
Wilson, Patricia: Reuters
Winicour, Daniel: Congressional Quarterly
Winski, Joe: Bloomberg News
Winston, Beverly: Gannett News Service
Witcover, Jules: Tribune Media Services
Witkowski, Nancy Benac: Associated Press
Witt, April: Washington Post
Witter, Willis: Washington Times
Wolf, Ariana: Congressional Quarterly
Wolf, Jim: Reuters
Wolf, Richard: USA Today
Wolfe, Kathryn: Congressional Quarterly
Woo, Yee Ling: Congressional Quarterly
Wood, David: Baltimore Sun
Wood, Winston: Wall Street Journal
Woodlee, Yolanda: Washington Post
Woodward, Bob: Washington Post
Wroughton, Lesley: Reuters
Wuetherich, Peter: Agence France-Presse
Wutkowski, Karey: Reuters
Wynn, Randall: Congressional Quarterly
Wysocki, Jr., Bernard: Wall Street Journal
Xiangwen, Ge: Xinhua News Agency
Xiao-Jing, Du: China Press
Xu, Qisheng: Guangming Daily
Xuejiang, Li: China People's Daily
Yada, Toshihiko: Yomiuri Shimbun
Yamamoto, Hideya: Sankei Shimbun
Yamamoto, Rumiko: Nikkei
Yamasaki, Shinji: Akahata
Yamour, Heather: Kuwait News Agency
Yan, Feng: Xinhua News Agency
Yancey, Matthew: Associated Press
Yasunaga, Tatsuro: Kyodo News
Yaukey, John: Gannett News Service
Yen, Hope: Associated Press
Yilmaz, Nuh: Istanbul Star
Yoder, Eric: Washington Post
Yoest, Patrick: Congressional Quarterly
Yoon, Kyongho: Maeil Business Newspaper
Yoshida, Hiroyuki: Mainichi Shimbun
Yost, Pete: Associated Press
Younglai, Rachelle: Reuters
Youssef, Nancy: McClatchy Newspapers
Yu, Donghui: China Press
Yue, Wu: China Press
Zabarenko, Deborah: Reuters
Zablit, Jocelyne: Agence France-Presse
Zacharia, Janine: Bloomberg News
Zagaroli, Lisa: McClatchy Newspapers
Zajac, Andrew: Chicago Tribune
Zakaria, Tabassum: Reuters
Zapor, Patricia: Catholic News Service
Zeleny, Jeff: New York Times
Zeller, Shawn: Congressional Quarterly
Zhang, Jane: Wall Street Journal
Zhang, Zhongxia: Xinhua News Agency
Zibel, Alan: Associated Press
Zimmerman, Carol: Catholic News Service
Zitner, Aaron: Los Angeles Times
Zlodorev, Dmitri: Itar-Tass News Agency
Zongker, Brett: Associated Press
Zoroya, Gregg: USA Today
Zuckerbrod, Nancy: Associated Press
Zuckman, Jill: Chicago Tribune
Zwelling, Michael: Restructuring Today

NEWSPAPERS REPRESENTED IN PRESS GALLERIES

House Gallery 225–3945, 225–6722 Senate Gallery 224–0241

ABIM NEWS AGENCY—(703) 243–2104; 1344 Merrie Ridge Road, McLean, VA 22101: Mario Navarro DaCosta.

AFTENPOSTEN—(202) 812–1443; 2000 M Street, NW., Suite 890, Washington, DC 20036: John Hultgren.

AGENCE FRANCE-PRESSE—(202) 414–0640; 1500 K Street, Suite 600, Washington, DC 20005: Jerome Bernard, Joanna Biddle, Mary Ann Campagna, Fanny Carrier, Justin Cole, Stephen Collinson, Daniel DeLuce, Kenneth Dermota, David Dieudonne, Jean-Louis Doublet, Francisco Ferrari, Claire Gallen, Stephanie Griffith, Carlos Hamann, Paul Handley, Alain Jean-Robert, Jitendra Joshi, Veronique Kiss, Maxim Kniazkov, Olivier Knox, Michael Langan, Sylvie Lanteaume, Chris Lefkow, Robert Lever, Roland Lloyd-Parry, Laurent Lozano, Peter Mackler, James Mannion, David Millikin, Virginie Montet, Parameswaran Ponnudurai, Charlotte Raab, Mauricio Rabuffetti, Philippe Rater, Antonio Rodriguez, Jean-Louis Santini, Marie Sanz, Celine Serrat, Kerry Colleen Sheridan, Magan Sherzai, James Slater, Veronica Smith, Nadia Teskrat, Laurent Thomet, Chantal Valery, Christophe Vogt, Peter Wuetherich, Jocelyne Zablit.

AKAHATA—(202) 393–5238; 978 National Press Building, Washington, DC 20045: Yumi Kamazuka, Shinji Yamasaki.

AL-HAYAT—(202) 783–5544; 1185 National Press Building, Washington, DC 20045: Joyce Karam.

ALLAFRICA.COM—(202) 546–0777; 920 M Street, SE., Washington, DC 20003: Tamela Hultman, Reed Kramer.

ALLENTOWN MORNING CALL—(202) 824–8216; 1025 F Street, NW., Washington, DC 20004: Josh Drobnyk.

AMERICAN BANKER—(202) 434–0310; 1325 G Street, Suite 900, Washington, DC 20005: Joseph Adler, Cheyenne Hopkins, Stacy Lynn Kaper, Steven Sloan.

ANSA ITALIAN NEWS AGENCY—(202) 628–3317; 1285 National Press Building, Washington, DC 20045: Marco Bardazzi, Luciano Clerico, Cristiano Del Riccio, Marcelo Raimon.

ARGUS MEDIA—(202) 349–2878; 1012 14th Street, Suite 1500, Washington, DC 20005: Ross Allen, Michael Ball, Abby Caplan, Euan Craik, Edward Feege, Peter Gardett, Caroline Gentry, Conway Irwin, Kim Krieger, Brian Megali, Christopher Newman, Anne O'Neil, Claire Pickard-Cambridge, Amery Pore, Elizabeth Rosenberg, Funda Saygin, Carrie Sisto, Jamie Webster.

ARKANSAS DEMOCRAT-GAzeTTE—(202) 662–7690; 1190 National Press Building, Washington, DC 20045: Alex Daniels.

ASAHI SHIMBUN—(202) 783–1000; 1022 National Press Building, Washington, DC 20045: Lindsay Ballard, Eric Hamrin, Yoichi Kato, Joshua Kirkman, Yoshiyuki Komurata, Kaoru Nishizaki, Joshua Rogin, Toshihide Ueda, Satoshi Ukai, Toshiya Umehara, Elizabeth West.

ASSOCIATED PRESS—(202) 776–9480; 2021 K Street, NW., 6th Floor, Washington, DC 20006: James Abrams, Matt Apuzzo, John Jay Arnold, Jeannine Aversa, Charles Babington, Lolita Baldor, Matthew Barakat, Devlin Barrett, Frank Bass, Rita Beamish, Donna Borak, Seth Borenstein, Andrew Bridges, Ted Bridis, Robert Burns, Desmond Butler, Connie Cass, Donna Cassata, Shawn Chen, Dennis Conrad, Martin Crutsinger, Matthew Daly, Douglass Daniel, Elizabeth Davidz, Julie Davis, Jim Drinkard, John Dunbar, Harry Dunphy, Ronald Edmonds, Jr., David Espo, Jerry Estill, Ben Evans, Donald Evans, Carole Feldman, Ben Feller, Howard Fendrich, Anne Flaherty, Matt Ford, Brad Foss, Ron Fournier, Alan Fram, Kevin Freking, Frederic Frommer, Robert Furlow, Joseph Galianese, Suzanne Gamboa, Anne Gearan, George Gedda, Robert Glass, Shawn Gomez, Marcy Gordon, Ken Guggenheim, Sam Hananel, Merrill Hartson, H. Josef Hebert, Kimberly Hefling, John Heilprin, Gregory Henderson, John Henry, Earl Hinton, Jesse Holland, Derrill Holly, Kasie Hunt, Terence Hunt, Nestor Ikeda, Lara Jakes Jordan, Mary Clare Jalonick, Pauline Jelinek, Kory Jessen, Sandy Johnson, Dennis Junius, Sarah Karush, Laurie Kellman Blazar, Jennifer Kerr, Lou Kesten, Foster Klug, Jim Kuhnhenn, Matthew Lee, William Lester, James Lipari, Jennifer Loven, Joan Lowy, Beverley Lumpkin, William Mann, Stephen Manning, Lawrence Margasak, Natasha Metzler, Andrew Miga, Leslie Miller, Damiko Morris, Laura Myers, Lauran Neergaard, Martin Niland, Stephen Ohlemacher, Mark Olchowy, Megan Owens, David Pace, Nedra Pickler, Marc Price, Melinda Purce, Eileen Putman, Libby Quaid, Thomas Raum, Keith Rickett, Deb Riechmann-Kepler, Sonya Ross, Chris Rugaber, Ann Sanner, Randolph Schmid, Barry Schweid, Mark Sherman, Katie Shrader, Elizabeth Sidoti, Todd Sigurdson, Carolyn Skorneck, Michael Sniffen, Stephenie Stoughton, Thomas Strong, Darlene Superville, Lubna Takruri, Jennifer Talhelm, Andrew Taylor, Sharon Theimer, Troy Thibodeaux, Ken Thomas, Trevor Tompson, William Vander Haar, Kevin Vineys, Erica Werner, Brian Westley, Brian Westley, Joseph White, Jr., David

NEWSPAPERS REPRESENTED—Continued

Wilkison, Nancy Benac Witkowski, Matthew Yancey, Hope Yen, Pete Yost, Alan Zibel, Brett Zongker, Nancy Zuckerbrod.

ATLANTA JOURNAL CONSTITUTION—(202) 887–8320; 400 N. Capitol Street, Suite 750, Washington, DC 20001: Bob Kemper.

AUSTIN AMERICAN-STATESMAN—(202) 887–8329; 400 N. Capitol Street, Suite 750, Washington, DC 20001: Tara Copp.

AUSTRALIAN—(202) 862–9272; 446 National Press Building, Washington, DC 20045: Geoff Elliott.

BALTIMORE SUN—(410) 332–6771; 1025 F Street, NW., Suite 700 Washington, DC 20006: Jeffrey Barker, Matthew Brown, Siobhan Gorman, Karen Hosler, Rona Marech, David Nitkin, Jonathan Rockoff, Paul West, David Wood.

BASLER ZEITUNG—(202) 986–7542; 1526 Corcoran Street, NW., Washington, DC 20009: Lucian Caspar.

BATON ROUGE ADVOCATE—(202) 554–0458; 12626 Eastbourne Drive, Silver Spring, MD 20905: Gerard Shields.

BERGEN COUNTY RECORD—(202) 249–2160; 4401–A Connecticut Avenue, NW., Washington, DC 20008: Herbert Jackson.

BERLINER ZEITUNG—(202) 388–3450; 1318 Emerald Street, NE., Washington, DC 20002: Olivia Schoeller.

BIOWORLD TODAY—(202) 739–9556; 1725 K Street, Suite 700, Washington, DC 20006: Aaron Lorenzo.

BIRMINGHAM NEWS—(202) 383–7837; 1101 Connecticut Avenue, Suite 300 Washington, DC 20036: Mary Orndorff.

BLOOMBERG NEWS—(202) 654–1227; 1399 New York Avenue, 11th Floor, Washington, DC 20005: Lee Aitken, Chris Anstey, Laurence Arnold, William Arthur, Laurie Asseo, Charles Babcock, Terrence Barrett, Theresa Barry, Paul Basken, Matthew Benjamin, Max Berley, John Berry, Otis Bilodeau, Alan Bjerga, Jeffrey Bliss, Justin Blum, Romaine Bostick, Emily Brown, Andy Burt, Anthony Capaccio, Kevin Carmichael, Shobhana Chandra, Cassie Chen, Edwin Chen, Kimberly Chipman, Sonya Cooper, Susan Decker, Vincent Del Giudice, Edward DeMarco, Catherine Dodge, Ryan Donmoyer, Mark Drajem, Bob Drummond, James Efstathiou, Cutis Eichelberger, Nadine Elsibai, Daniel Enoch, Brian Faler, Ken Fireman, Michael Forsythe, Viola Gienger, Julianna Goldman, Avram Goldstein, Daniel Goldstein, Vince Golle, Brigitte Greenberg, Robert Greene, Angela Greiling Keane, Dan Hart, John Hughes, Ann Hughey, Albert Hunt, Kristin Jensen, Nicholas Johnston, Nancy Kercheval, Alison Kodjak-Fitzgerald, Scott Lanman, Catherine Larkin, Laura Litvan, Aliza Marcus, Judith Mathewson, Demian McLean, Mark McQuillan, William McQuillen, Robin Meszoly, Kevin Miller, Richard Miller, Daniel Moss, Gregory Mott, Brendan Murray, Jay Newton Small, C. JoAnne Norton, Joseph O'Reilly II, Mario Parker, Molly Peterson, Shannon Pettypiece, Jeff Plungis, Joi Preciphs, Gopal Ratnam, Joseph Richter, William Roberts III, Mark Rohner, Neil Roland, Holly Rosenkrantz, James Rowley, James Rubin, Roger Runningen, Jonathan Salant, Kristy Scheuble, Courtney Schlisserman, William Schmick, Robert Schmidt, Tina Seeley, Robert Simison, Elliot Blair Smith, Joseph Sobczyk, Jeffrey St. Onge, Jon Steinman, Christopher Stern, Greg Stohr, Christopher Swann, Alex Tanzi, Carlos Torres, Craig Torres, James Tyson, Alison Vekshin, Leon Walczak, Chris Wellisz, Jesse Westbrook, Robert Willis, Joe Winski, Janine Zacharia.

BOND BUYER—(202) 434–0302; 1325 G Street, Suite 900, Washington, DC 20005: Andrew Ackerman, Lynn Hume, Alison McConnell, Humberto Sanchez, Peter Schroeder.

BOSTON GLOBE—(202) 857–5050; 1130 Connecticut Avenue, Suite 520, Washington, DC 20036: Kevin Baron, Bryan Bender, Peter Canellos, Diedtra Henderson, Richard Klein, Michael Kranish, Susan Milligan, Charles Savage, Farah Stockman, Cynthia Taylor, Cynthia Taylor, Joseph Williams, Jr.

CANADIAN PRESS—(202) 638–3367; 1128 National Press Building, Washington, DC 20045: Elizabeth Gorham.

CANWEST NEWS SERVICE—(202) 662–7576; 1206 National Press Building, Washington, DC 20045: Sheldon Alberts.

CAPITAL CONNECTIONS—(202) 337–2044; 1698 32nd Street, NW., Washington, DC 20007: Karen Feld.

CATHOLIC NEWS SERVICE—(202) 541–3255; 3211 Fourth Street, NE., Washington, DC 20017: Julie Asher, Barbara Fraze, Nancy Hartnagel, Regina Linskey, Nancy O'Brien, Mark Pattison, Tony Spence, Patricia Zapor, Carol Zimmerman.

CHATTANOOGA TIMES FREE PRESS—(202) 662–6751; 1190 National Press Building, Washington, DC 20045: Edward Lee Pitts, Herman Wang.

CHICAGO DAILY LAW BULLETIN—(240) 305–1330; 10 James Spring Court, Rockville, MD 20850: Steve Lash.

CHICAGO SUN-TIMES—(202) 393–4340; 1750 Pennsylvania Avenue, #1203, Washington, DC 20006: Robert Novak, Lynn Sweet.

CHICAGO TRIBUNE—(202) 824–8226; 1025 F Street, NW., Suite 700, Washington, DC 20004: Naftali Bendavid, John Crewdson, Mike Dorning, Tai Ming Bay Fang, Stephen Hedges, Frank James, Aamer Madhani, William Neikirk, Clarence Page, Christi Parsons, Mark Silva, Rhonda Stewart, R. Michael Tackett, James Tankersley, Vickie Walton-James, Dina White, Andrew Zajac, Jill Zuckman.

CHINA ECONOMIC DAILY—(703) 698–8579; 3305 Crest Haven Court, Falls Church, VA 22042: Zhengxin Li.

NEWSPAPERS REPRESENTED—Continued

CHINA LEGAL DAILY—(703) 413–9251; 2111 Jefferson Davis Highway, Apt. 1109, Washington, DC 22202: Shaojie Feng.

CHINA NEWS SERVICE—(703) 527–5887; 1020 North Stafford Street, Apt. 100, Arlington, VA 22201: Jiangbo Qiu.

CHINA PEOPLE'S DAILY—(202) 244–0410; 3707 Massachusetts Avenue, Washington, DC 20016: Yong Tang, Li Xuejiang.

CHINA PRESS—(703) 289–6651; 3207 Allen Street, #301, Falls Church, VA 22042: Du Xiao-Jing, Donghui Yu, Wu Yue.

CHINA TIMES—(202) 347–5670; 952 National Press Building, Washington, DC 20045: Norman Fu, Ping Liu.

CHINA YOUTH DAILY—(703) 534–3378; 251 Gundry Drive, Falls Church, VA 22046: Xiang Weng.

CHOSUN ILBO—(202) 737–4205; 1291 National Press Building, Washington, DC 20045: June-Oh Bang, Kenneth Choi, Yongbom Heo.

CHRISTIAN SCIENCE MONITOR—(202) 481–6642; 910 16th Street, Suite 200, Washington, DC 20006: Gail Chaddock, David Cook, John Dillin, Jr., Linda Feldmann, Peter Grier, Francine Kiefer, Howard La Franchi, Gordon Lubold, Warren Richey.

CLARIN—(202) 737–4850; 1271 National Press Building, Washington, DC 20045: Ana Baron Supervielle.

CLEVELAND PLAIN DEALER—(202) 638–1366; 930 National Press Building, Washington, DC 20045: Elizabeth Auster, Sabrina Eaton, Stephen Koff, Nedra Shelly.

CNET NEWS.COM—(202) 829–5077; 1615 Swann Street, NW., #31, Washington, DC 20009: Anne Broache.

COLUMBUS DISPATCH—(202) 824–6766; 400 North Capitol Street, Suite 850, Washington, DC 20001: Jonathan Riskind, Jack Torry.

COMMUNICATIONS DAILY—(202) 872–9200; 2115 Ward Court, NW., Washington, DC 20037: Howard Buskirk, Heather Forsgren Weaver, Edith Herman, Dinesh Kumar, Jonathan Make, Ian Martinez, Dawson Nail, Greg Piper, Anne Veigle, Josh Wein.

COMPLINET—(301) 320–0309; 7514 Radnor Road, Bethesda, MD 20817: Ira Apfel.

CONGRESSDAILY—(202) 299–4108; 600 New Hampshire Avenue, NW., Washington, DC 20037: Anna Bailey, Peter Bell, Christian Bourge, Jessica Brady, Peter Cohn, Jack Deutsch, Jason Dick, Kathy Gambrell, Darren Goode, Juliana Gruenwald, David Hess, Fawn Johnson, Charles Jordan, Terence Kivlan, Keith Koffler, Otto Kreisher, Mike Magner, Jason Mann, Irvin Molotsky, David Morris, Louis Peck, Art Pine, Michael Posner, Elaine Povich, Spencer Rich, Benjamin Schneider, Kate Schuler, Megan Scully, Richard Sia, Chris Strohm, Bill Swindell, Basil Talbott, Martin Vaughan, Mark Wegner, Keith White, George Wilson.

CONGRESSIONAL QUARTERLY—(202) 419–8654; 1255 22nd Street, Washington, DC 20037: Rebecca Adams, Alan Ahlrich, Syed Ali, Amanda Allen, Jonathan Allen, Joanna Anderson, Martha Angle, Andrew Armstrong, James Barker, Alexandra Bartolf, Robert Benenson, Susan Benkelman, Matthew Berger, Adriel Bettelheim, Arwen Adams Bicknell, John Bicknell, Adam Bloedorn, Rachel Bloom, Miranda Blue, Joel Bowen, Jonathan Broder, Ronald Brodmann, Joe Burey, Philip Burrowes, Mary Agnes Carey, James Carroll, Linda Cartwright, Mike Christensen, David Clarke, John Cochran, George Codrea, Charles Conlon, Maureen Conners, Neal Conway, Jessica Benton Cooney, John Cranford, Craig Crawford, Michael Crittenden, Chris Dally, Coral Davenport, David Davis, Steven Dennis, John Dineen, John Donnelly, Loren Duggan, Toby Eckert, Susan Ferrechio, Dyane Fils, Jeffrey Friedman, Jamey Fry, Lydia Gensheimer, Elizabeth George, Gregory Giroux, Shweta Govindarajan, Carlo Daniel Guerra, Kimberly Hallock, Ben Halpern-Meekin, Thomas Hannett, Amanda Harris, David Hawkings, Robert Healy, Caitlin Hendel, Paul Hendrie, Liriel Higa, David Higgins, Marie Horrigan, Charles Hoskinson, Anne Hoy, Kathleen Hunter, Colby Itkowitz, Marian Jarlenski, Matthew Johnson, Toni Johnson, Kerry Jones, Patricia Joy, Martin Kady II, Rachel Kapochunas, Ryan Kelly, Noella Kertes, Angela Kim, Rebecca Kimitch, Peter King, Jaculine Koszczuk, Adrianne Kroepsch, Chris Lehmann, Nathan Levinson, Jonathan Lewallen, Robert James Margetta, Greg McDonald, Victoria McGrane, Robert Merry, Elaine Monaghan, Kathleen Murphy, David Nather, E. Roy Nkansah, Brian Nutting, Joseph Nyitray, Frank Oliveri, Alan Ota, Daniel Parks, Keith Perine, Lauren Phillips, Manu Raju, Eric Ray, Marc Rehmann, John Reichard, Michael Remez, Daphne Retter, Betty Richardson, Catharine Richert, Michael Riley, Neil Ripley, Katherine Rizzo, Joshua Rogin, Richard Rubin, Michael Sandler, Jodi Schneider, Susan Shipp, Kathleen Silvassy, Matthew Spieler, Eleanor Stables, Joshua Stager, Jesse Stanchak, Tim Starks, Jana Steiger, Jeff Stein, Seth Stern, Eileen Sullivan Michael Teitelbaum, Joelle Tessler, Jeff Tollefson, Robert Tomkin, Larry Tunks, Gregory Vadala, Paul Volpe, Brendan Walsh, Joseph Warminsky, Alexander Wayne, Caitlin Webber, Guy Whitmire, Daniel Winicour, Ariana Wolf, Kathryn Wolfe, Yee Ling Woo, Randall Wynn, Patrick Yoest, Shawn Zeller.

CONNECTICUT POST—(202) 662–8927; 1255 National Press Building, Washington, DC 20045: Peter Urban.

COPLEY NEWS SERVICE—(202) 737–6960; 1100 National Press Building, Washington, DC 20045: George Condon, Jr., Jerry Kammer, Paul Krawzak, Finlay Lewis, Rosemary Petersen, Marcus Stern, Dana Wilkie.

COX NEWSPAPERS—(202) 887–8334; 400 N. Capitol Street, Suite 750, Washington, DC 20001: Andrew Alexander, Susan Burns, Rebecca Carr, Arthur Dalglish, Robert Dart, Robert Deans, Jr., Marilyn

NEWSPAPERS REPRESENTED—Continued

Geewax, Rafi Guroian, Ken Herman, Charles Holmes, Elliot Jaspin, Laurence Lipman, Julia Malone, Eunice Moscoso, Jeff Nesmith, Carl Rauscher, Jr., Scott Shepard, Anne Usher.

DAGENS NYHETER—(202) 429–0134; 1726 M Street, NW., Suite 700, Washington, DC 20036: Erik Ohlsson.

DAILY DEAL—(202) 429–2993; 1775 K Street, Suite 590, Washington, DC 20006: Donna Block, Cecile Lindell, William McConnell, Shanon Murray, Ron Orol.

DAILY VARIETY—(202) 659–3805; 1701 K Street, NW., Suite 510, Washington, DC 20006: William Triplett.

DALLAS MORNING NEWS—(202) 661–8413; 1325 G Street, Suite 250, Washington, DC 20005: Alfredo Corchado, Todd Gillman, James Landers, Carl Leubsdorf, Sudeep Reddy, Richard Whittle.

DAYTON DAILY NEWS—(202) 887–8328; 400 North Capitol Street, NW., Washington, DC 20001: Jessica Wehrman.

DEFENSE DAILY—(202) 662–9729; 1011 Arlington Blvd., Suite 131, Arlington, VA 22209: David Ahearn, Jen DiMascio, Geoff Fein, John Robinson, Ann Roosevelt, Michael Sirak.

DENVER POST—(202) 662–8990; 1255 National Press Building, Washington, DC 20045: Christa Marshall, Anne Mulkern, Michael Soraghan.

DES MOINES REGISTER—(202) 906–8138; 1100 New York Avenue, Washington, DC 20005: Philip Brasher, Jane Norman.

DESERET MORNING NEWS—(202) 737–5311; 960A National Press Building, Washington, DC 20045: Suzanne Struglinski.

DETROIT FREE PRESS—(202) 906–8204; 1100 New York Avenue, Suite 200E, Washington, DC 20005: Justin Hyde, Todd Spangler.

DETROIT NEWS—(202) 906–8205; 1255 National Press Building, Washington, DC 20045: Deborah Price, David Shepardson, Gordon Trowbridge.

DIE PRESSE—(703) 931–9558; 3308 Peace Valley Lane, Falls Church, VA 22044: Norbert Rief.

DOW JONES NEWSWIRES—(202) 862–9230; 1025 Connecticut Avenue, Suite 1100, Washington, DC 20036: Mark Anderson, Jeffrey Bater, Brian Blackstone, Antonie Boessenkool, Gregory Boles, Nicolas Brulliard, Judith Burns, Rebecca Christie, Anthony Cooke, Jennifer Corbett Dooren, John Godfrey, Siobhan Hughes, Benton Ives-Halperin, Maya Jackson-Randall, Bhattiprolu Murti, Damian Paletta, Elizabeth Price, Henry Pulizzi, Ian Talley, Edmund Walsh, Robert Wells, Edward Welsch, Edward Welsch.

EFE NEWS SERVICES—(202) 745–7692; 1252 National Press Building, Washington, DC 20045: Maria Azpiazu, Jorge Banales, Teresa Bouza, Maribel El Hamti, Orlando Lizama, Rosendo Majano, Cesar Munoz, Cristina Ozaeta-Heusel, Maria Pena, Macarena Vidal Liy.

EL DIARIO DE HOY—(571) 278–1321; 603 South Adams Street, Arlington, VA 22204: Tomas Guevara.

EL NUEVO DIA—(202) 662–7360; 1053 National Press Building, Washington, DC 20045: Jose Delgado.

EL PAIS—(202) 638–1533; 1134 National Press Building, Washington, DC 20045: Antonio Caño, Yolanda Monge.

EL TIEMPO—(202) 607–5929; 1102 National Press Building, Washington, DC 20045: Sergio Gomez.

EL UNIVERSAL—(202) 662–7190; 1193 National Press Building, Washington, DC 20045: Jose Carreno.

ELEFTHEROS TYPOS—(202) 675–0697; 1125 6th Street, NE., Washington, DC 20008: Lambros Papantoniou.

ENERGY DAILY—(703) 358–9201; 1011 Arlington Boulvard, Suite 131, Arlington, VA 22209: Jeff Beattie, Jason Fordney, Christopher Holly, Llewellyn King, George Lobsenz.

EUROPOLITICS—(202) 492–2498; 1200 5th Street, #203, Washington, DC 20001: Brian Beary.

FAIRBANKS DAILY NEWS MINER—(202) 662–8721; 1255 National Press Building, Washington, DC 20045: Sam Bishop.

FAIRCHILD NEWS SERVICE—(202) 496–4975; 1050 17th Street, NW, Suite 600, Washington, DC 20036: Evan Clark, Kristi Ellis, Susan Watters.

FINANCIAL TIMES—(202) 253–3278; 1023 15th Street, NW., Suite 700, Washington, DC 20005: Eoin Callan, Philipp Dermann, Guy Dinmore, Jeremy Grant, Krishna Guha, Stephanie Kirchgaessner, Edward Luce, Demetri Sevastopulo, Patti Waldmeir, Andrew Ward.

FORT WAYNE JOURNAL GAZETTE—(202) 879–6710; 551 National Press Building, Washington, DC 20045: Sylvia Smith.

FORT WORTH STAR-TELEGRAM—(202) 383–6016; 700 12th Street, NW., Suite 1000, Washington, DC 20005: David Montgomery, Maria Recio.

FRANKFURTER RUNDSCHAU—(301) 762–9661; 1717 Sunrise Drive, Rockville, MD 20854: Dietmar Ostermann.

GANNETT NEWS SERVICE—(202) 906–8124; 1100 New York Avenue, Washington, DC 20005: Douglas Abrahms, Robert Benincasa, Deborah Berry, Larry Bivins, Faith Bremner, Pamela Brogan, Dennis Camire, Sammie Chan, Raju Chebium, Linda Dono, Val Ellicott, Anthony Faust, Ellyn Ferguson, Leonard Fischer, Maria Fowler, Javier Gandarillas, Nicole Gaudiano Albright, Maureen Groppe, Karl Hardy, Erin Kelly, Eun Kim, Ledyard King, Theresa Klisz, Mike Madden, Marie Marino, Diana Marrero, Derek Osenenko, Charles Raasch, Ana Radelat, Laura Rehrmann, Malia Rulon, Craig Schwed,

NEWSPAPERS REPRESENTED—Continued

Katherine Scott, William Theobald, Brian Tumulty, Billie Jean Wells, Lawrence Wheeler, Beverly Winston, John Yaukey.

GERMAN PRESS AGENCY-DPA—(202) 662–1242; 969 National Press Building, Washington, DC 20045: Frank Brandmaier, Christopher Cermak, Gabriele Chwallek, Anthony Czuczka, Hans Dahne, Frank Fuhrig, Mike McCarthy, Paticia Reber, Laszlo Trankovits, Anne Walters.

GLOBAL D—(301) 680–0592; 12506 Davan Drive, Silver Spring, MD 20904: Kenneth Dalecki.

GLOBAL HORIZONS SYNDICATE—(202) 659–1921; 1330 New Hampshire Avenue, NW., Washington, DC 20036: Edward Flattau.

GUANGMING DAILY—(202) 363–0628; 4816 Butterworth Place, NW., Washington, DC 20016: Qisheng Xu.

HARRISBURG PATRIOT-NEWS—(202) 383–7833; 1101 Connecticut Avenue, Suite 300, Washington, DC 20036: Brett Lieberman.

HARTFORD COURANT—(202) 824–8452; 1325 G Street, Suite 200, Washington, DC 20005: David Lightman.

HEARST NEWSPAPERS—(202) 263–6400; 1850 K Street, NW., Suite 1000 Washington, DC 20006: Jennifer Dlouhy, Dan Freedman, Judy Holland, Charles Lewis, Marianne Means, Carol Nippert, Stewart Powell, Eric Rosenberg, Helen Thomas.

HELSINGIN SANOMAT—(202) 955–7956; 1726 M Street, NW., Suite 700, Washington, DC 20036: Pekka Mykkanen.

HOKKAIDO SHIMBUN—(202) 628–5374; 1012 National Press Building, Washington, DC 20045: Takuya Nishimura.

HOLLYWOOD REPORTER—(202) 833–8845; 910 17th Street, NW., Washington, DC 20006: Brooks Boliek.

HOSPODARSKE NOVING DAILY—(202) 344–7748; 5933 Crescent Street, Bethesda, MD 20816: Daniel Anyz.

HOUSTON CHRONICLE—(202) 263–6500; 1850 K Street, NW., Suite 1000, Washington, DC 20006: Michael Hedges, Cragg Hines, David Ivanovich, Julie Mason, Michelle Mittelstadt, Patty Reinert-Mason, Bennett Roth.

HURRIYET—(301) 564–6691; 16 Grove Ridge Court, Rockville, MD 20852: Mehmet Cindemir.

ICIS NEWS—(202) 776–1352; 1150 18th Street, Suite 600, Washington, DC 20036: Joseph Kamalick.

IL CORRIERE DELLA SERA—(202) 879–6733; 841 National Press Building, Washington, DC 20045: Ennio Caretto.

IL GIORNALE—(202) 237–1019; 2841 Arizona Terrace, Washington, DC 20016: Mariuccia Chiantaretto.

INDO-ASIAN NEWS SERVICE—(301) 412–9234; 4801 Kenmore Avenue, Apt. 910, Alexandria, VA 22304: Arun Kumar.

INSIDE HIGHER ED—(202) 659–9208; 2121 K Street, NW., Suite 630, Washington, DC 20037: Andrew Guess, Scott Jaschik, Douglas Lederman, Elia Powers, Elizabeth Redden.

INTER PRESS SERVICE—(202) 662–7160; 1293 National Press Building, Washington, DC 20045: James Lobe, Emad Mekay.

INTERNETNEWS.COM—(202) 249–8174; 1464 Rhode Island Avenue, NW., Washington, DC 20005: Roy Mark.

INVESTOR'S BUSINESS DAILY—(202) 728–2155; 1001 Connecticut Avenue, Suite 415, Washington, DC 20036: Jed Graham, Sean Higgins.

ISTANBUL STAR—(703) 359–0641; 10400 Fairfax Village Drive, Apt. 1323, Fairfax, VA: Nuh Yilmaz.

ITAR-TASS NEWS AGENCY—(202) 662–7080; 1004 National Press Building, Washington, DC 20045: Dmitry Kirsanov, Alexander Pakhomov, Andrei Sitov, Andrey Surzhanskiy, Dmitri Zlodorev.

JERUSALEM POST—(202) 355–5145; 1706 Q Street, NW., #3, Washington, DC 20009: Hilary Leila Krieger.

JEWISH TELEGRAPHIC AGENCY—(202) 737–0935; 1025 Vermont Avenue, NW., #504, Washington, DC 20005: Ron Kampeas.

JIJI PRESS—(202) 783–4330; 550 National Press Building, Washington, DC 20045: Takuya Higuchi, Kensuke Karube, Shuko Kuno, Yoshiaki Okuma, Nobuyuki Sato, Sereana Seim, Hiroyuki Takahashi, Itsuro Umemoto.

JYLLANDS-POSTEN—(301) 320–9079; 6405 Little Leigh Court, Cabin John, MD 20818: Klaus Justsen.

KANSAS CITY STAR—(202) 383–6105; 700 12th Street, NW., Suite 1000, Washington, DC 20005: David Goldstein, Matthew Stearns.

KIPLING NEWS SERVICE—(301) 929–0760; 12611 Farnell Drive, Silver Spring, MD 20906: Bogdan Kipling.

KOMMERSANT—(202) 248–8191; 3700 Massachusetts Avenue, Suite 317, NW., Washington, DC 20016: Dmitry Sidorov.

KOREA DAILY—(703) 281–9660; 512 Maple Avenue, W. Vienna, VA 22180: Jin-Keol Park.

KOREA TIMES—(703) 941–8002; 7601 Little River Turnpike, Annandale, VA 22003: Sung Joong Ahn, Christina Young Chong, Byonghan Lee, Chang-Yul Lee, Jong Kook Lee, Ki Chan Park, Kwang Duk Park.

NEWSPAPERS REPRESENTED—Continued

KUWAIT NEWS AGENCY—(202) 347–5554; 906 National Press Building, Washington, DC 20045: Ronald Baygents, Joe Macaron, Saad Mohammad, Ahmed Radwan, Heather Yamour.

KYODO NEWS—(202) 347–5767; 400 National Press Building, Washington, DC 20045: Tsukasa Arita, Paul Behringer, Tomohiro Deguchi, Mieko Endo, Thomas Gross, Takehito Kajita, Toshimitsu Sawai, Tomoko Spencer, Tomoko Spencer, Hiroki Sugita, Fumitaka Susami, Masaya Takahashi, Tomoji Tatsumi, Hajime Tobe, Tatsuro Yasunaga.

KYUNGHYANG SHINMUN—(703) 272–3884; 2964 Borge Steet, Oakton, VA 22124: Jin Ho Kim.

LA JORNADA—(202) 547–5852; 132 North Carolina Avenue, SE., Washington, DC 20003: David Brooks.

LA NACION—(202) 744–7737; 1193 National Press Building, Washington, DC 20045: Hugo Alconada.

LA OPINION—(202) 662–1240; 962 National Press Building, Washington, DC 20045: Maribel Hastings.

LA RAZON—(703) 379–0095; 4922 S. Chesterfield Road, Arlington, VA 22206: Armando Morales.

LA VANGUARDIA—(301) 229–1695; 6812 Algonquin Avenue, Bethesda, MD 20817: Eusebio Val Mitjavila.

LAHORE DAILY TIMES—(703) 280–5832; 9019 Bowler Drive, Fairfax, MD 22031: Khalid Hasan.

LAS VEGAS SUN—(202) 662–7436; 1290 National Press Building, Washington, DC 20045: Lisa Mascaro.

LE FIGARO—(202) 342–3199; 1228 30th Street, NW., Washington, DC 20007: Philippe Gelie.

LE MAURICIEN—(301) 424–3884; 1084 Pipestem Place, Potomac, MD 20854: Pamela Glass.

LE MONDE—(202) 248–9075; 1134 National Press Building, Washington, DC 20045: Corine Lesnes.

LEE NEWSPAPERS—(202) 298–6880; 1025 Connecticut Avenue, Suite 1102, Washington, DC 20036: Noelle Straub.

LEXINGTON HERALD-LEADER—(202) 383–6036; 700 12th Street, Suite 1000, Washington, DC 20005: John Cheves, Janet Patton.

LIBERATION—(202) 244–1314; 4330 46th Street, NW., Washington, DC 20016: Philippe Grangereau.

LIBERTY TIMES—(202) 879–6765; 1294 National Press Building, Washington, DC 20045: Nadia Y.F. Tsao.

LONDON DAILY TELEGRAPH—(202) 393–5195; 1310 G Street, NW., Suite 750, Washington, DC 20005: Toby Harnden, Vanessa Robertson, Tim Shipman, Alexander Spillius.

LONDON GUARDIAN—(202) 223–2486; 1730 Rhode Island Avene, #502, Washington, DC 20036: Richard Adams, Suzanne Goldenberg, Ewen Macaskill, Michael Tomasky.

LONDON INDEPENDENT—(202) 467–4460; 1726 M Street, Suite 700, Washington, DC 20008: Andrew Buncombe, Rupert Cornwell.

LOS ANGELES DAILY JOURNAL—(202) 484–8255; 733 15th Street, NW., Suite 917, Washington, DC 20005: Lawrence Hurley, Brent Kendall.

LOS ANGELES DAILY NEWS—(202) 662–8731; 1255 National Press Building, Washington, DC20543: Lisa Friedman.

LOS ANGELES TIMES—(202) 824–8300; 1025 F Street, NW., Suite 700, Washington, DC 20004: Ricardo Alonso-Zaldivar, Julian Barnes, Stephen Braun, Ronald Brownstein, Richard Cooper, Robert Drogin, Sonni Efron, Robin Fields, Faye Fiore, Don Frederick, K. Nicole Gaouette, James Gerstenzang, Peter Gosselin, Thomas Hamburger, Joel Havemann, Marian Hennessy-Fiske, John Hoeffel, Leslie Hoffecker, Janet Hook, Frankie Jackson, Noam Levey, Doyle McManus, Joshua Meyer, Alan Miller, Greg Miller, Chuck Neubauer, Johanna Neuman, Robert Ourlian, Judy Pasternak, Jonathan Peterson, James Puzzanghera, Maura Reynolds, Paul Richter, James Robinson, Walter Roche, Jr., Phillip Ruiz, David Savage, Richard Schmitt, Richard Serrano, Richard Simon, Peter Spiegel, Peter Wallsten, David Willman, Aaron Zitner.

LOWELL SUN—(202) 662–8926; 1255 National Press Building, Washington, DC 20045: Evan Lehmann.

LRP PUBLIC—(703) 516–7002; 1901 North Moore Street, Suite 1106 Arlington, VA 22209: Stephen Berlin, Deborah Bolling, Christine Cave, Julie Davidson, Kris Kitto, Patricia Mohr, Pamela Moore, Stephen Sawchuk, Sarah Sparks, Jeanne Sweeney, Melissa Turley, Andrew Viccora.

L'UNITA—(202) 237–1050; 2841 Arizona Terrace, Washington, DC 20016: Bruno Marolo.

MAEIL BUSINESS NEWSPAPER—(202) 637–0567; 909 National Press Building, Washington, DC 20045: Kyongho Yoon.

MAGHREB ARAB PRESS—(703) 273–7780; 9196 Topaz Street, Fairfax, VA 22031: Sabah Lebbar, Hamzaoui Soufiya.

MAGYAR SZO—(202) 904–4433; 1775 Massachusetts Avenue, Suite 207, Washington, DC 20036: Tibor Purger.

MAINICHI SHIMBUN—(202) 737–2817; 340 National Press Building, Washington, DC 20045: Toshihiko Kasahara, Jun Kimura, Amy McKeever, Tomoko Ohji, Patricia Shea, Hiroaki Wada, Hiroyuki Yoshida.

MALAYA—(703) 685–2665; 841 South Glebe Road, Arlington, VA 22204: Josefina Ilustre.

MARKET NEWS INTERNATIONAL—(202) 371–2121; 552 National Press Building, Washington, DC 20045: Steven Beckner, Margaret Chadbourn, Denny Gulino, Mark Hemingway, Claudia Hirsch, Kevin Kastner, Chris Middleton, Yali N'Diaye, Joseph Plocek, Heather Scott, John Shaw, Theresa Sheehan.

MARKETWATCH—(202) 824–0548; 1240 National Press Building, Washington, DC 20045: Jeffry Bartash, Ruth Mantell, Michael Maynard, Margaret McNeil, Rex Nutting, Gregory Robb, Robert Schroeder, William Watts.

MCCLATCHY NEWSPAPERS—(202) 383–6071; 700 12th Street, NW., Suite 1000, Washington, DC 20005: Christopher Adams, Beryl Adcock, James Asher, Barbara Barrett, Les Blumenthal, Michael

NEWSPAPERS REPRESENTED—Continued

Bold, Robert Boyd, Andrew Brown, Crystal Davis, Kevin Diaz, William Douglas, Michael Doyle, Greg Gordon, Frank Greve, Roy Gutman, Kevin Hall, Michele Heller, Ron Hutcheson, Jonathan Landay, Anthony Pugh, Robert Rankin, James Rosen, Renee Schoof, Mark Seibel, Warren Strobel, Margaret Talev, Marisa Taylor, Steven Thomma, Jim Van Nostrand, John Walcott, Letitia Wells, David Westphal, David Whitney, Nancy Youssef, Lisa Zagaroli.

MEDIA GENERAL NEWS SERVICE—(202) 662–7677; 1214 National Press Building, Washington, DC 20045: James Crawley, Gilbert Klein Jr., Richard Lee, Marsha Mercer, Sean Mussenden.

MIAMI HERALD—(202) 383–6019; 700 12th Street, NW., Suite 1000, Washington, DC 20005: Pablo Bachelet, Lesley Clark.

MILITARY UPDATE—(703) 830–6863; P.O. Box 231111, Centreville, VA 20120: Thomas Philpott.

MILWAUKEE JOURNAL SENTINEL—(202) 662–7290; 940 National Press Building, Washington, DC 20045: Craig Gilbert, Audrey Hoffer, Katherine Skiba.

MINNEAPOLIS STAR TRIBUNE—(202) 383–0009; 700 12th Street, NW., Suite 1000, Washington, DC 20005: Rob Hotakainen.

MOBILE REGISTER—(202) 383–7815; 1101 Connecticut Avenue, Suite 300, Washington, DC 20036: Sean Reilly.

MUNWHA ILBO—(202) 662–7342; 1149 National Press Building, Washington, DC 20045: Hyung Du Choi.

NATIONAL JOURNAL'S TECHNOLOGY DAILY—(202) 261–0353; 600 New Hampshire, NW., Washington, DC 20037: Winter Casey, K. Daniel Glover, Heather Greenfield, David Hatch, Michael Martinez, Andrew Noyes, Theresa Poulson, Aliya Sternstein.

NETHERLANDS PRESS ASSOCIATION—(703) 272–7499; 520 Woodland Court, NW., Vienna, VA 22180: Frank Hendrickx.

NEUE ZUERCHER ZEITUNG—(202) 237–5602; 3808 Woodley Road, NW., Washington, DC 20016: Andreas Ruesch.

NEW ORLEANS TIMES-PICAYUNE—(202) 383–7861; 1101 Connecticut Avenue, Suite 300, Washington, DC 20036: Bruce Alpert, Bill Walsh.

NEW YORK DAILY NEWS—(202) 467–6770; 1050 Thomas Jefferson Street, #3100, Washington, DC 20007: Kenneth Bazinet, Thomas DeFrank, Michael McAuliff, James Meek, Richard Sisk.

NEW YORK POST—(202) 383–1787; 1114 National Press Building, Washington, DC 20045: Ian Bishop, Geoff Earle, Charles Hurt.

NEW YORK SUN—(202) 775–1542; 1101 17th Street, NW., Washington, DC 20036: Russell Berman.

NEW YORK TIMES—(202) 862–0302; 1627 I Street, Suite 700, Washington, DC 20006: Sarah Abruzzese, Edmund Andrews, Von Aulston, Neela Banerjee, Dean Baquet, Felicity Barringer, John Broder, David Brooks, Elisabeth Bumiller, LaKiesha Carr, Holli Chmela, Lynette Clemetson, David Cloud, Helene Cooper, Rebecca Corbett, John Cushman, Jr., Jason Deparle, Maureen Dowd, Paula Dwyer, Adrianne Goodman, Michael Gordon, Linda Greenhouse, Janis Harland, Gardiner Harris, Patrick Healy, Raymond Hernandez, Farhana Hossain, Carl Hulse, Douglas Jehl, David Johnston, Susan Keller, David Kirkpatrick, Stephen Labaton, Warren Leary, Suevon Lee, Mark Leibovich, Neil Lewis, Eric Lichtblau, Eric Lipton, Michael Luo, Clifford Meadows, Cheryl Miller, Adam Nagourney, Ronnie Nixon, Elizabeth Olson, Sabrina Pacifici, Ashley Parker, Robert Pear, Kathleen Phillips, Cory Reiss, Jim Rutenberg, Eric Schmitt, Scott Shane, Thomas Shanker, Philip Shenon, Ronald Skarzenski, Richard Stevenson, Sheryl Stolberg, David Stout, Rachel Swarns, Philip Taubman, Robin Toner, Ian Urbina, Matthew Wald, Judith Warner, Leslie Wayne, Steven Weisman, Sarah Wheaton, Jeff Zeleny.

NEW YORK TIMES MAGAZINE—(202) 237–1218; 3742 Appleton Street, NW., Washington, DC 20016: Matt Bai.

NEWARK STAR-LEDGER—(202) 383–7823; 1101 Connecticut Avenue, Suite 300, Washington, DC 20036: Robert Cohen, J. Scott Orr.

NEWHOUSE NEWS SERVICE—(202) 383–7838; 1101 Connecticut Avenue, Suite 300, Washington, DC 20036: Richard Beaudette, Sarah Kellogg, Katherine Lewis, Chuck McCutcheon, Michele Melendez, Dru Sefton, Jonathan Tilove.

NEWPORT NEWS DAILY PRESS—(202) 824–8224; 1325 G Street, NW., Suite 200, Washington, DC 20005: David Lerman.

NEWSDAY—(202) 393–5630; 1730 Pennsylvania Avenue, NW., #850, Washington, DC 20006: Thomas Brune, Carol Eisenberg, D. Craig Gordon, Timothy Phelps, Glenn Thrush.

NEWSPAPER ENTERPRISE—(301) 320–5559; 6008 Osceola Road, Bethesda, MD 20816: Robert Wagman.

NIKKEI—(202) 393–1388; 815 Connecticut Avenue, Suite 310, Washington, DC 20006: Tomoko Ashizuka, Christina Bilski, Kazuaki Fujii, Tetsuya Jitsu, Hidenaka Kato, Stephen Keefe, Hiroyuki Kotake, Hiroshi Marutani, Rumiko Yamamoto.

NOTIMEX MEXICAN NEWS AGENCY—(202) 347–5227; 975 National Press Building, Washington, DC 20045: Ricardo Alday, Ruben Barrera, Jose Lopez Zamorano, Santiago Tavara.

OIL DAILY—(202) 662–0728; 1411 K Street, Suite 602, Washington, DC 20005: Matthew Carr, Greg Couturier, Robert Dillon, Manimoli Dinesh, Matt Piotrowski.

OKLAHOMAN—(202) 662–7543; 914 National Press Building, Washington, DC 20045: Chris Casteel, Mark Green.

NEWSPAPERS REPRESENTED—Continued

OMAHA WORLD-HERALD—(202) 662–7271; 836 National Press Building, Washington, DC 20045: Joseph Morton, Jake Thompson.

ORANGE COUNTY REGISTER—(202) 628–6381; 1295 National Press Building, Washington, DC 20045: Dena Bunis.

OREGONIAN—(202) 383–7814; 1101 Connecticut Avenue, Suite 300, Washington, DC 20036: Jeffrey Kosseff.

ORLANDO SENTINEL—(202) 824–8255; 1025 F Street, NW., Suite 700, Washington, DC 20004: Tamara Lytle, Mark Matthews.

PARLAMENTSKAYA GAZETA—(202) 249–2562; 2501 Porter Street, NW., #810, Washington, DC 20008: Mikhail Bragin.

PHILADELPHIA INQUIRER—(202) 408–2758; 1090 Vermont Avenue, NW., Suite 1000, Washington, DC 20005: Steven Goldstein.

PITTSBURGH POST-GAZETTE—(202) 631–3417; 955 National Press Building, Washington, DC 20045: Jerome Sherman.

PLATTS NEWS SERVICE—(202) 383–2250; 1200 G Street, Suite 1100, Washington, DC 20005: Gerald Karey, Catherine Landry.

POLITICAL MONEY LINE—(202) 237–2500; 6004 Nevada Avenue, NW., Washington, DC 20015: Kent Cooper, Anthony Raymond.

PORTLAND PRESS HERALD—(202) 488–1119; 1711 Massachusetts Avenue, NW., Washington, DC 20036: Bart Jansen.

PRESS TRUST OF INDIA—(301) 907–2954; 4701 Willard Avenue, #1524, Chevy Chase, MD 20815: Sridhar Krishnaswami.

PROVIDENCE JOURNAL—(202) 681–8423; 1325 G Street, NW., Washington, DC 20005: John Mulligan.

REFORMA NEWSPAPER—(202) 341–3255; 1707 21st Street, NW., Apt. 3, Washington, DC 20009: Jose Diaz-Briseno.

RELIGION NEWS SERVICE—(202) 383–7863; 1101 Connecticut Avenue, Suite 350, Washington, DC 20036: Adelle Banks, Daniel Burke, Kevin Eckstrom.

RESTRUCTURING TODAY—(202) 298–8201; 4418 MacArthur Boulevard, Washington, DC 20007: James Downing, George Spencer, Samuel Spencer, Carolyn Tozier, Michael Zwelling.

REUTERS—(202) 898–8319; 1333 H Street, Suite 410, Washington, DC 20005: Charles Abbott, Timothy Ahmann, Charles Alexander, JoAnne Allen, Victoria Allen, Chris Baltimore, Diane Bartz, Eric Beech, Melissa Bland, Xavier Briand, Alister Bull, Deborah Charles, Susan Cornwell, Richard Cowan, John Crawley, Sarah Cunningham, Bernd Debusmann, Timothy Dobbyn, Christopher Doering, Tom Doggett, Robert Doherty, Kevin Drawbaugh, Will Dunham, Paul Eckert, Mark Felsenthal, Thomas Ferraro, Margaret Fox, Jacqueline Frank, Adriana Garcia Martinez, Carol Giacomo, Steven Ginsburg, Howard Scot Goller, Andrew Gray, Stuart Grudgings, Stuart Grudgings, Susan Heavey, Stacey Joyce, Peter Kaplan, Frances Kerry, Lisa Lambert, David Lawder, Gilbert LeGras, Maureen Lorenzetti, Sandra Maler, Randall Mikkelsen, Arshad Mohammed, David Morgan, Joanne Morrison, Essex Noel, Chizu Nomiyama, John O'Callaghan, Doug Palmer, Dean Patterson, Jeremy Pelofsky, Sue Pleming, John Poirier, Andrea Ricci, Lisa Richwine, Kristin Roberts, Patrick Rucker, Mary Ryan, Timothy Ryan, Lori Santos, Andrea Shalal-Esa, Donna Smith, Glenn Somerville, Matthew Spetalnick, Neil Stempleman, David Storey, Andy Sullivan, Peter Szekely, William Trott, James Vicini, Julie Vorman, Nancy Waitz, Michael Weekes Jr., John Whitesides, David Wiessler, Patricia Wilson, Jim Wolf, Lesley Wroughton, Karey Wutkowski, Rachelle Younglai, Deborah Zabarenko, Tabassum Zakaria.

RHEINISCHE POST—(202) 966–2393; 5810 Chevy Chase Parkway, NW., Washington, DC 20015: Frank Herrmann.

RICHMOND TIMES-DISPATCH—(202) 662–7669; 1214 National Press Building, Washington, DC 20045: Peter Hardin.

RIVERSIDE PRESS-ENTERPRISE—(202) 661–8422; 1325 G Street, Suite 250, Washington, DC 20045: Ben Goad.

ROLL CALL REPORT SYNDICATE—(202) 737–1888; 960A National Press Building, Washington, DC 20045: Richard Thomas.

SALT LAKE TRIBUNE—(202) 662–8732; 1255 National Press Building, Washington, DC 20045: Thomas Burr, Robert Gehrke.

SAN ANTONIO EXPRESS-NEWS—(202) 263–6451; 1850 K Street, NW., Suite 1000, Washington, DC 20006: Gary Martin.

SAN FRANCISCO CHRONICLE—(202) 263–6577; 1850 K Street, NW., Suite 1000, Washington, DC 20006: Zachary Coile, Edward Epstein, Carolyn Lochhead, Marc Sandalow.

SAN JOSE MERCURY NEWS—(202) 662–8921; 1255 National Press Building, Washington, DC 20045: Frank Davies.

SANKEI SHIMBUN—(202) 347–2842; 330 National Press Building, Washington, DC 20045: Takashi Arimoto, Yoshihisa Komori, Bruce Scott Stewart, Hiroo Watanabe, Hideya Yamamoto.

SAUDI PRESS AGENCY—(202) 944–3890; 6012 New Hampshire Avenue, NW., Washington, DC 20037: Naila Al-Sowayel, Mustafa Bashir, Dean Dessouky, Liam Hurley, Sara Ayesha Hussein, Azeddine Labriny, Nezar Sheikh.

NEWSPAPERS REPRESENTED—Continued

SCRIPPS HOWARD NEWS SERVICE—(202) 408–1484; 1090 Vermont Avenue, Suite 1000, Washington, DC 20045: David Johnson, Pamela Reeves, Curtis Lee Bowman, James Brosnan, Patricia Choate, Michael Collins, Peter Copeland, Robert Friedman, Laurel Hackett, Thomas Hargrove, Lisa Hoffman, Robert Jones, Dale McFeatters, Wanita Niehaus, David Nielsen, Amie Parnes, Richard Powelson, Martin Schram, Michael Sprengelmeyer, Bartholomew Sullivan, Dan Thomasson, Karen Timmons, Walter Veazey.

SEATLLE POST-INTELLIGENCER—(202) 422–2313; 1850 K Street, NW., Washington, DC 20006: Andrew Schneider, Charles Pope.

SEATTLE TIMES—(202) 662–7457; 920 National Press Building, Washington, DC 20045: Alicia Mundy.

SEGYE TIMES—(202) 637–0587; 909 National Press Building, Washington, DC 20045: Yong Kirl Han, Kiyon Kuk.

SEKAI NIPPO—(202) 898–8292; 1510 H Street, NW., Washington, DC 20005: Toshiyuki Hayakawa, Yoshio Mitoma.

SHANGHAI WENHUI DAILY—(703) 920–1060; 1600 S. Eads Street, Apt. 814–S, Arlington, VA 22202: Yun He, Zhen Niu.

SHEARER AND GLEN NEWS—(202) 462–6070; 2708 Cathedral Avenue, NW., Washington, DC 20008: Cody Shearer.

SING TAO DAILY—(202) 250–6130; 2201 L Street, NW., Apt. #307, Washington, DC 20037: Zhigang Chen.

SMARTMONEY.COM—(202) 828–3390; 1025 Conneticut Avenue, NW., Suite 1100, Washington, DC 20036: Michael DeSenne.

SNG NEWSPAPERS—(202) 662–7240; 1183 National Press Building, Washington, DC 20045: Edward Felker.

SOUTH FLORIDA SUN-SENTINEL—(202) 824–8256; 1325 G Street, Suite 200, Washington, DC 20005: William Gibson.

SPRINGFIELD REPUBLICAN—(202) 383–7859; 1101 Connecticut Avenue, Suite 300, Washington, DC 20036: Jo Ann Moriarty.

ST. LOUIS POST-DISPATCH—(202) 298–6880; 1025 Connecticut Avenue, Suite 1102, Washington, DC 20036: Philip Dine, Aloysia Hamalainen, Ronald Harris, William Lambrecht, Deirdre Shesgreen.

ST. PETERSBURG TIMES—(202) 463–0575; 1100 Connecticut Avenue, #1300, Washington, DC 20036: William Adair, Wes Allison, Anita Kumar.

STEPHENS MEDIA GROUP—(202) 738–1760; 666 11th Street, Suite 535, Washington, DC 20001: Tony Batt, Aaron Sadler, Stephan Tetreault.

STUTTGARTER ZEITUNG—(301) 983–0735; 11204 Powder Horn Drive, Potomac, MD 20854: Juergen Koar.

SUEDDEUTSCHE ZEITUNG—(202) 965–5245; 4715 Butterworth Place, NW., Washington, DC 20016: Reymer Kluever.

SUEDDEUTSCHE ZEITUNG—(202) 338–1320; 1539 44th Street, NW., Washington, DC 20007: Christian Wernicke.

SVENSKA DAGBLADET—(202) 362–8253; 3601 Connecticut Avenue, #622, Washington, DC 20008: Karin Henriksson.

SYDNEY MORNING HERALD—(202) 737–6360; 1310 G Street, #750, Washington, DC 20005: Anne Davies.

SYRACUSE POST-STANDARD—(202) 383–7818; 1101 Connecticut Avenue, Suite 300, Washington, DC 20036: Mark Weiner.

TAGES ANZEIGER—(202) 332–8575; 2026 16th Street, NW., #5, Washington, DC 20009: Martin Kilian.

TAIPEI TIMES—(301) 942–2442; P.O. Box 571, Garrett Park, MD 20898: Charles Snyder.

TAMPA TRIBUNE—(202) 662–7673; 1214 National Press Building, Washington, DC 20045: Billy House.

TECH LAW JOURNAL—(202) 364–8882; 3034 Newark Street, NW., Washington, DC 20008: David Carney.

TF NEWS—(202) 414–0710; 1015 15th Street, Suite 500, Washington, DC 20005: Corbett Daly.

THE PIONEER-INDIA—(703) 876–6149; 2731 Pleasantdale Road, #203, Vienna, VA 22180: Sethuraman Rajagopalan.

TOKYO CHUNICHI SHIMBUN—(202) 789–9479; 1012 National Press Building, Washington, DC 20045: Yasuyuki Oguri, Ryoji Tachio, Conrad Chaffee, Jennifer Gerdts, Shinichi Hisadome, Aki Naganuma.

TORONTO GLOBE AND MAIL—(202) 662–7165; 2000 M Street, NW., Washington, DC 20036: Alan Freeman, Barrie McKenna.

TORONTO STAR—(202) 662–7390; 982 National Press Building, Washington, DC 20045: Tim Harper.

TRIBUNE MEDIA SERVICES—(202) 298–8359; 3042 Q Street, NW., Washington, DC 20007: Jules Witcover.

TULSA WORLD—(202) 484–1424; 1417 North Inglewood Street, Arlington, VA 22205: Jim Myers.

UNITED DAILY NEWS—(202) 737–6426; 835 National Press Building, Washington, DC 20045: Tsung-Chih Chang.

UNITED MEDIA—(301) 494–0430; 3330 Blue Heron Drive North, Chesapeake Beach, MD 20732: Lew Sichelman.

NEWSPAPERS REPRESENTED—Continued

UNITED PRESS INTERNATIONAL—(202) 898–8238; 1510 H Street, Washington, DC 20005: Krishnadev Calamur, Arnaud de Borchgrave, Christine Dell'Amore, Kristyn Ecochard, Laura Gilcrest, Shihoko Goto, Laura Heaton, John Hendel, Pamela Hess, Michael Kirkland, Ben Lando, Michael Marshall, Andrea Mihailescu, Steve Mitchell, Lawrence Moffitt, Daniel Olmsted, Olga Pierce, Claude Salhani, Martin Sieff, Richard Tomkins, Martin Walker, Shaun Waterman.

UNIVERSAL PRESS SYNDICATE—(202) 243–5301; 2555 Pennsylvania Avenue, NW., Washington, DC 20037: James Kilpatrick.

USA TODAY—(703) 854–5579; 1100 New York Avenue, Washington, DC 20005: Fred Anklam, Jr., Julie Appleby, Emily Bazar, Joan Biskupic, Erik Brady, Louise Branson, Catalina Camia, Dan Carney, Michael Carney, James Cox, Mark Crane Paul Davidson, Barbara Delollis, William Dermody, Ken Dilanian, Oren Dorell, Peter Eisler, Haya El Nasser, Melanie Eversley, Mindy Fetterman, Gwen Flanders, Ed Foster-Simeon, Thomas Frank, Brian Gallagher, Andrew Gardiner, Raymond Goldbacher, Alan Gomez, Barbara Hagenbaugh, George Hager, Mimi Hall, James Healey, Linda Holzer, Monica Hortobagyi, Lee Horwich, Rosalind Jackler, David Jackson, Michael James, Kevin Johnson, Matthew Kelley, Dennis Kelly, Eugene Kiely, Kathy Kiely, Suzanne Kirchhoff, Noelle Knox, Wendy Koch, Jill Lawrence, Paul Leavitt, Donna Leinwand, Alan Levin, Thomas Lilleston, Ray Locker, David Lynch, Mary Beth Marklein, Stephen Marshall, Mark Memmott, Jim Michaels, Patty Michalski, Jayne O'Donnell, Paul Overberg, Susan Page, Laura Parker, Maria Puente, John Riley, William Risser, Bruce Rosenstein, Fredreka Schouten, John Siniff, Barbara Slavin, Michael Snider, Steve Sternberg, William Sternberg, Andrea Stone, Gregory Toppo, Saundra Torry, Owen Ullmann, Tom Vanden Brook, Dan Vergano, Traci Watson, James Welch, Richard Willing, Richard Wolf, Gregg Zoroya.

US-REPORT (Germany)—(301) 299–5777; 1020 Windsor View Drive, Potomac, MD 20854: Thomas Spang.

VIRGINIAN-PILOT—(703) 913–9872; 7802 Glenister Drive, Springfield, VA 22152: Dale Eisman.

VOTES IN CONGRESS NEWSPAPER SYNDICATE—(202) 737–1888; 960A National Press Building, Washington, DC 20045: Michael Lesparre.

WALL STREET JOURNAL—(202) 862–9200; 1025 Connecticut Avenue, Suite 800, Washington, DC 20036: Robert Block, Jess Bravin, Jackie Calmes, MaryLu Carnevale, Ann Marie Chaker, Kathy Chen, Christopher Conkey, Christopher Cooper, Robert Davis, Nikhil Deogun, David Allen Dolinger, Yochi Dreazen, John Fialka, Gary Fields, John Harwood, Greg Hitt, William Hoover, Gregory Ip, Greg Jaffe, Neil King, Jr., June Kronholz, Sarah Lueck, Anna Mathews, Robert Guy Matthews, Laurie McGinley, John McKinnon, Laura Meckler, Brody Mullins, Evan Perez, Michael Phillips, David Rogers, Kara Scannell, Amy Schatz, Jacob Schlesinger, Sharon Schmid, Gerald Seib, Deborah Solomon, Jonathan Solomon, David Wessel, John Wilke, Winston Wood, Bernard Wysocki, Jr., Jane Zhang.

WASHINGTON EXAMINER—(202) 459–4946; 1050 15th Street, Suite 500, Washington, DC 20005: Jeff Dufour, Maria Hegstad, Charles Hurt, Rowan Scarborough.

WASHINGTON INTERNET DAILY—(202) 872–9202; 2115 Ward Court Washington, DC 20037: Alexis Fabbri.

WASHINGTON POST—(202) 334–6050; 1150 15th Street, NW., Washington, DC 20071: Michael Abromowitz, Joel Achenbach, Keith Alexander, Amy Argetsinger, Perry Bacon, Jr., Peter Baker, Daniel Balz, Gary Barr, Jill Bartscht, Jeffrey Birnbaum, Michelle Boorstein, David Broder, David Brown, DeNeen Brown, Vincent Bzdek, Peter Carlson, Ruben Casteneda, Henri Cauvin, Rajiv Chandrasekaran, David Cho, Chris Cillizza, Sarah Cohen, Alan Cooperman, Libby Copeland, Tim Craig, Alice Crites, Timothy Curran, Kathleen Day, Kirstin Downey, Paul Duggan, Lynne Duke, Petula Dvorak, Timothy Dwyer, Daniel Eggen, Juliet Eilperin, Dina Elboghdady, Paul Farhi, Darryl Fears, Steven Fehr, David Finkel, Mary Pat Flaherty, Michael Fletcher, Sholnn Freeman, Amy Gardner, Gilbert Gaul, Ann Gerhart, Steven Ginsberg, Maria Glod, Zachary Goldfarb, Amy Goldstein, Sara Goo, Annie Gowen, Bradley Graham, Marcia Slacum Greene, James Grimaldi, Maryann Haggerty, Hamil Harris, Veryl Dion Haynes, Dana Hedgpeth, Rosalind Helderman, Celia Nell Henderson, Scott Higham, Sari Horwitz, Spencer Hsu, Anne Hull, Anita Husun, Carrie Johnson, Darragh Johnson, Darragh Johnson, Amy Joyce, Al Kamen, Dan Keating, Glenn Kessler, Alec Klein, Allison Klein, Anne Kornblut, Fredrick Kunkle, Theola Labbe, Lyndsey Layton, Michael Leahy, Madonna Lebling, Daniel LeDuc, Christopher Lee, Richard Leiby, Allan Lengel, Susan Levine, Ruth Marcus, Anne Marimow, Raymond McCaffrey, Renae Merle, Dana Milbank, William Miller, Nick Miroff, David Montgomery, Lori Montgomery, Dan Morgan, Dan Morse, Matthew Mosk, Steven Mufson, Shailagh Murray, David Nakamura, Ellen Nakashima, Amit Paley, Sridhar Pappu, Walter Pincus, Sue Ann Pressley, Dana Priest, Lisa Rein, Eric Rich, Tom Ricks, Roxanne Roberts, Eugene Robinson, Lois Romano, Michael Ruane, Susan Schmidt, Michael Semel, Lucy Shackelford, Ian Shapira, Michael Shear, Mary Beth Sheridan, Elissa Silverman, Alan Sipress, Jeffrey Smith, John Solomon, Miranda Spivack, Robert Stein, Joe Stephens, Nikita Stewart, Hank Stuever, Hank Stuever, Lena Sun, Cheryl Thompson, Tom Toles, Nancy Trejos, Jacqueline Trescott, Boyd Neely Tucker, Bill Turque, Ann Scott Tyson, Jose Antonio Vargas, Shankar Vedantam, Stephen Vogel, John Wagner, Joby Warrick, Martin Weil, Jonathan Weisman, Eric Weiss, Rick Weiss, Josh White, Del Wilber, Elizabeth Williamson, April Witt, Yolanda Woodlee, Bob Woodward, Eric Yoder.

NEWSPAPERS REPRESENTED—Continued

WASHINGTON POST WRITER'S GROUP—(703) 916–8315; 3539 Sleepy Hollow Road, Falls Church, VA 22041: Marie Cocco.

WASHINGTON TELECOMMUNICATIONS SERVICES—(804) 776–7947; 1006 Harrison Circle, Alexandria, VA 22304: Gordon White.

WASHINGTON TIMES—(202) 636–3203; 3600 New York Avenue, NE., Washington, DC 20002: Theodore Agres, Natasha Altamirano, Bryce Baschuk, Sharon Behn, Christina Bellantoni, Thomas Carter, Kristen Chick, Joseph Curl, Brian DeBose, Stephen Dinan, Christopher Dolan, Julia Duin, Gary Emerling, Amy Fagan, Ann Geracimos, William Gertz, Jennifer Haberkorn, Ralph Hallow, Jennifer Harper, Patricia Hill, Steve Hirsch, Audrey Hudson, Nicholas Kralev, Donald Lambro, Sean Lengell, David Lipscomb, John McCaslin, Seth McLaughlin, Steven Miller, James Morrison, Frank Murray, Eric Pfeiffer, Thomas Ramstack, Kara Rowland, David Sands, Jerry Seper, Dan Taylor, Jon Ward, Cheryl Wetzstein, Willis Witter.

WASHINGTONPOST.COM—(202) 412–3568; 1515 N. Courthouse Road, Arlington, VA 22201: Mary Ann Akers, Tanya Ballard, Kyle Balluck, Laura Marie Cochran, Benedict De la Cruz, Karl Eisenhower, Chris Hopkins, Paul Kane, Brian Krebs, Sarah Lovenheim, Jason Manning, Sharon McLoone, Jefferson Morley, Edward O'Keefe, Emil Steiner, Caitlin Ellen Thompson, Francine Uenuma, Derek Willis.

WATERTOWN DAILY TIMES—(202) 662–7085; 1001 National Press Building, Washington, DC 20045: Marc Heller.

WESTDEUTSCHE ALLGEMEINE—(202) 363–7791; 4611 47th Street, Washington, DC 20016: Markus Guenther.

WESTERN COMMUNICATIONS—(202) 662–7456; 920 National Press Building, Washington, DC 20045: Keith Chu.

WILLIAM SCALLY REPORTS—(202) 362–2382; 2918 Legation Street, NW., Washington, DC 20015: William Scally.

WINSTON-SALEM JOURNAL—(202) 662–7672; 1214 National Press Club, Washington, DC 20045: Mary Shaffrey.

WORLD BUSINESS PRESS—(646) 784–9776; 4706 Commons Drive, A–303, Annandale, VA 22003: Dagmar Benesova, Zoltan Mikes.

WORLD JOURNAL—(202) 215–1710; 835 National Press Building, Washington, DC 20045: Betty Lin.

XINHUA NEWS AGENCY—(202) 661–8181; 1201 National Press Building, Washington, DC 20045: Yang Qing Chuan, Liu Hong, Fang Hu, Yunzhao Pan, Yu Qianliang, Ge Xiangwen, Feng Yan, Zhongxia Zhang.

YOMIURI SHIMBUN—(202) 783–0363; 802 National Press Building, Washington, DC 20045: Thomas Hambrick-Stowe, Charles Harris, Aya Igarashi, Hiroshi Masumitsu, Ryuichi Otsuka, Mary Perkins, Takashi Sadahiro, Takashi Sakamoto, Andrew Siddons, Mineko Tokito, Toshihiko Yada.

YONHAP NEWS AGENCY—(202) 662–7425; 1299 National Press Building, Washington, DC 20045: Bock Rae Cho, Kim Jae Hong, Byungsu Kim, Jae Hong Kim, Dong Min Lee, Ki Chang Lee, Hannah Won Park.

PRESS PHOTOGRAPHERS' GALLERY*

The Capitol, Room S–317, 224–6548

www.senate.gov/galleries/photo

Director.—Jeffrey S. Kent.
Deputy Director.—Mark A. Abraham.

STANDING COMMITTEE OF PRESS PHOTOGRAPHERS

Scott Applewhite, Associated Press, *Chair*
Dennis Brack, Black Star, *Secretary-Treasurer*
Jim Bourg, Reuters
Khue Bui, Newsweek
Stephen Crowley, New York Times
Chuck Kennedy, McClatchy—Tribune

RULES GOVERNING PRESS PHOTOGRAPHERS' GALLERY

1. (a) Administration of the Press Photographers' Gallery is vested in a Standing Committee of Press Photographers consisting of six persons elected by accredited members of the Gallery. The Committee shall be composed of one member each from Associated Press Photos; Reuters News Pictures or AFP Photos; magazine media; local newspapers; agency or freelance member; and one at-large member. The at-large member may be, but need not be, selected from media otherwise represented on the Committee; however no organization may have more than one representative on the Committee.

(b) Elections shall be held as early as practicable in each year, and in no case later than March 31. A vacancy in the membership of the Committee occurring prior to the expiration of a term shall be filled by a special election called for that purpose by the Committee.

(c) The Standing Committee of the Press Photographers' Gallery shall propose no change or changes in these rules except upon petition in writing signed by not less than 25 accredited members of the gallery.

2. Persons desiring admission to the Press Photographers' Gallery of the Senate shall make application in accordance with Rule 33 of the Senate, which rule shall be interpreted and administered by the Standing Committee of Press Photographers subject to the review and approval of the Senate Committee on Rules and Administration.

3. The Standing Committee of Press photographers shall limit membership in the photographers' gallery to bona fide news photographers of repute in their profession and Heads of Photographic Bureaus under such rules as the Standing Committee of Press Photographers shall prescribe.

4. Provided, however, that the Standing Committee of Press Photographers shall admit to the gallery no person who does not establish to the satisfaction of the Committee all of the following:

(a) That any member is not engaged in paid publicity or promotion work or in prosecuting any claim before Congress or before any department of the Government, and will not become so engaged while a member of the gallery.

---

*Information is based on data furnished and edited by each respective gallery.

(b) That he or she is not engaged in any lobbying activity and will not become so engaged while a member of the gallery.

The above rules have been approved by the Committee on Rules and Administration.

NANCY PELOSI,
Speaker, House of Representatives.

DIANNE FEINSTEIN,
Chair, Senate Committee on Rules and Administration.

MEMBERS ENTITLED FOR ADMISSION

PRESS PHOTOGRAPHERS' GALLERY

Ake, David: Associated Press Photos
Alvarez, Miguel: La Prensa Grafica of El Salvador
Applewhite, J. Scott: Associated Press Photos
Archambault, Charles: U.S. News & World Report
Arrossi, Eddie: Freelance
Ashe, James: Freelance
Ashley, Douglas: Suburban Communications Corp.
Atherton, Jim: Freelance
Augustino, Jocelyn: Freelance
Barouh, Stan: Freelance
Barrett, Steve E.: Freelance
Barrick, Matthew: Freelance
Baughman, Ross J.: Washington Times
Beale, John: Pittsburgh Post Gazette
Beiser, Darr H.: USA/Today
Berg, Lisa: Freelance
Biddle, Susan: Washington Post
Bingham, Mary (Molly): Freelance
Binks, Porter L.: Sports Illustrated
Bivera, Johnny: Freelance
Blass, Eileen M.: USA/Today
Bloom, Richard: National Journal
Bochatey, Terry F.: Reuters News Pictures
Boitano, Stephen J.: Freelance
Boston, Bernard N.: Bryce Mountain Courier
Bourg, Jim: Reuters News Pictures
Bowe, Christy: Image Catcher News
Brack, William D.: Black Star
Brantley, James: Washington Times
Bridges, George S.: McClatchy Tribune
Brier, Joe: Freelance
Brown, Robert A.: Richmond Times Dispatch
Bruce, Andrea: Washington Post
Bui, Khue: Newsweek
Burke, Lauren V.: Freelance
Burnett, David: Contact Press Images
Burns, David S.: Photo Trends, Inc.
Cabe, Brig: The Washington Examiner
Calvert, Mary F.: Washington Times
Cameron, Gary A.: Reuters News Pictures
Carioti, Richard A.: Washington Post
Cavanaugh, Matthew T.: European Pressphoto Agency
Cedeno, Ken: Freelance
Ceneta, Manuel B.: Associated Press Photos
Chikwendu, Jahi: Washington Post
Chung, Andre: The Baltimore Sun
Clark, Bill: Roll Call
Clark, Kevin: Washington Post
Clendenin, Jay: Freelance
Cohen, Marshall H.: Bigmarsh News Photos
Colburn, James E.: Freelance
Connor, Michael: Washington Times
Cook, Dennis: Associated Press Photos
Coppage, Gary R.: Photo Press International
Corcoran, Thomas Michael: Freelance
Council, Andrew: Freelance
Crandall, Bill: Freelance
Crowley, Steve: New York Times
Curtis, Rob: Army Times Publishing
Cutraro, Andrew: Freelance
Davidson, Linda: Washington Post
DeArmas, Adrienne: Freelance
Devorah, Carrie: Freelance
Dharapak, Charles: Associated Press Photos
Dietsch, Kevin: United Press International
Dillon, Timothy P.: USA/Today
DiPasquale, Jill: Fairfax County Times
Donaldson, Kristin: Washington Times
Douliery, Olivier: Abaca USA
Downing, Lawrence: Reuters News Pictures
Drenner, Dennis: Freelance
Du Cille, Michael: Washington Post
Eddins, Jr., Joseph M.: Washington Times
Edmonds, Ronald: Associated Press Photos
Eile, Evan: USA/Today
Ellsworth, Katie: Newsweek
Emanuel, Hector: Freelance
Ernst, Jonathan: Freelance
Etheridge, Susan P.: New York Times
Evans, Sarah: Education Week
Fabiano, Gary: Sipa Press
Falkenberg, Katie: The Washington Times
Ferraro, Beth: Newsweek
Ferrell, Scott: CQ Weekly
Fitz-Patrick, Bill: Freelance
Foster, William H.: Freelance
Foy, Mary Lou: Washington Post
Franko, Jeff: Gannett News Service
Frazza, Luke: Agence France-Presse
Freilich, Jon: Freelance
Frey, Katherine: Washington Post
Fuchs, Christian: Washington Times
Gail, Carl: Washington Post
Gainer, Denny: USA/Today.com
Gamarra, Ruben F.: Notimex
Gandhi, Pareshkumar: Rediff.com/India Abroad Publications
Garcia, Mannie: Freelance
Gatty, Mary Ann: Periodical News Service
Gatty, Michael: Periodical News Service
Geissinger, Michael A.: Freelance

MEMBERS ENTITLED FOR ADMISSION—Continued

Ghanbari, Haraz: Associated Press Photos
Gilbert, Patrice J.: Freelance
Glenn, Alexis: United Press International
Glenn, Larry S.: Freelance
Goulait, Bert V.: Washington Times
Graham, Douglas: Roll Call
Gripas, Yuri: Freelance
Hambach, Eva: Agence France Presse
Haring, Paul: Catholic News Service
Harnik, Andrew: The Washington Examiner
Harrington, John H.: Black Star
Heasley, Shaun: Freelance
Helber, Stephen: Associated Press Photos
Herbert, Gerald: Associated Press Photos
Hershorn, Gary: Reuters News Pictures
Hillian, Vanessa: Washington Post
Hittle, David E.: Freelance
Holt, Victor: Washington Informer
Hutchens, Jeff: Freelance
Jackson, Lawrence: Associated Press Photos
Jenkins, Keith: Washington Post
Jones, Peter: Reuters News Pictures
Jones, Caleb: Freelance
Joseph, Marvin: Washington Post
Juarez, Miguel: Reformer
Kahn, Nikki: Freelance
Kang, Hyungwon: Reuters News Pictures
Kato, Satomi: Kyodo News
Katz, Martin I.: Chesapeake News Service
Kennedy, Chuck: McClatchy Tribune
Kennerly, David H.: Newsweek
Keres, Preston: Washington Post
Kittner, Sam: Freelance
Kleponis, Chris: Freelance
Kossoff, Leslie: Freelance
Kraft, Brooks: Time Magazine
Kuykendal, Stephanie: Freelance
Lamarque, Kevin: Reuters News Pictures
Lamkey, Rod A.: Washington Times
LaVor, Martin L.: Freelance
Lawidjaja, Rudy: Freelance
Lee, James J.: Army Times Publishing
Lee, David Y.: Freelance
Lessig, Alan: Army Times
Lipski, Richard A.: Washington Post
Loeb, Saul: Freelance
LoScalzo, Jim: U.S. News & World Report
Lustig, Raymond J.: Freelance
Lynch, Liz: National Journal
Lynch, M. Patricia: Frontiers News Magazine
MacMillan, Jeffrey G.: U.S. News & World Report
Madrid, Michael: USA/Today
Mahaskey, Michael Scott: Army Times Publishing
Mallin, Jay: Freelance
Maltby, Melissa: Washington Post
Mara, Melina: The Washington Post
Marquette, Joseph C.: Freelance
Martin, Jacquelyn: Associated Press Photos
Martineau, Gerald: Washington Post
Monsivais, Pablo Martinez: Associated Press Photos
Mathieson, Greg E.: MAI Photo Agency
Mattes, Sherilyn: Elsevier
McConigal, Chris: Washington Times
McDonnell, John: Washington Post
McKay, Richard D.: Cox Newspapers
McKee, Staci: Army Times
McNamee, Win: Getty Images
Mellon, Steve: Pittsburg Post-Gazette
Mills, Douglas: New York Times
Morris, Christopher: Time Magazine
Mosley, Leigh H.: The Washington Blade
Murrmann, Mark: Zuma Press
Musi, Vincent J.: Time Magazine
Myers, Benjamin: The Hill
Nelson, Andrew P.: Christian Science Monitor
Newton, Jonathan: Washington Post
Ngan, Mandel: Agence France-Presse
Nipp, Lisa: Freelance
Nisnevitch, Lev: The Weekly Standard
O'Leary, William P: Washington Post
Ommanney, Charles: Newsweek
O'Neill, Anie: Pittsburg Post-Gazette
Otfinowski, Danuta: Freelance
Pajic, Kamenko: Freelance
Palu, Louie: Zuma Press
Panagos, Dimitrios: Greek American News Agency
Parcell, James A.: Washington Post
Pastor, Nancy: Washington Times
Patterson, Kathryn B.: USA/Today
Perkins, Lucien: Washington Post
Petros, Bill: Freelance
Poggi, Jennifer: U.S. News and World Report
Poleski, David: Freelance
Powers, Carol T.: Freelance
Powers, Christopher: Education Week
Purcell, Steven: Freelance
Putnam, Bill: Zuma Press
Raab, Susana A.: Freelance
Radzinschi, Diego: Legal Times
Raimondo, Lois: Washington Post
Rasmussen, Randy L.: Oregonian
Reed, Jason: Reuters News Pictures
Reeder, Robert A.: Politico
Reinhard, Rick: Impact Digitals
Ricardel, Vincent J.: Freelance
Richards, Paul J.: Agence France-Presse
Richardson, Joel M.: Washington Post
Riecken, Astrid: Washington Times
Riley, Molly: Reuters News Pictures
Roberts, Joshua: Freelance
Robinson, Scott: Freelance
Ronay, Vivian: Freelance
Rose, Jamie: Freelance
Rosenbaum, Daniel: Washington Times

MEMBERS ENTITLED FOR ADMISSION—Continued

Ryan, Patrick: The Hill
Salisbury, Barbara L.: Washington Times
Samperton, Kyle: Freelance
Sandys, Toni: Washington Post
Savoia, Stephen: Associated Press Photos
Schaeffer, Sandra L.: MAI Photo Agency
Schwartz, Michael: Gannett
Schwartz, David S.: Freelance
Shell, Mary: Time Magazine
Shelley, Allison: Washington Times
Shimzu, Kenji: Yomiuri Shimbun
Shinkle, John: The Politico
Silverman, Joseph A.: Washington Times
Sisley, Evan: Freelance
Sloan, Timothy: Agence France-Presse
Smialowski, Brendan: Freelance
Somodevilla, Kenneth: Getty Images
Souza, Peter J.: Chicago Tribune
Spillers, Linda J.: Freelance
Spoden, Leonard: Freelance
Starnes, Andy: Pittsburg Post-Gazette
Steele, Rick: Post-Newsweek Media
Stephenson, Al: Freelance
Suau, Anthony: Time Magazine
Sudyatmiko, Karina: Suara Pembaruan
Sweets, Fred: St. Louis American
Sykes, Jack W.: Professional Pilot Magazine
Sypher, Mark F.: Fauquier Times-Democrat
Takeda, Yasushi: Shukan Shincho, Shinchosha Co.
Temchine, Michael: Freelance
Theiler, Michael: Freelance
Thew, Shawn: European Press Association
Thomas, Ricardo: The Detroit News
Thomas, Margaret: Washington Post
Thomas, Ronald W.: Freelance
Thresher, James M.: Washington Post
Tines, Charles: The Detroit News
Trippett, Robert: Sipa Press
Turner, Tyrone: Freelance
Usher, Chris: Freelance
Varias, Stelios A.: Reuters News Pictures
Vemmer, Sheila: Army Times
Vosin, Sarah L.: Washington Post
Voss, Stephen: Freelance
Vucci, Evan: European Press Association
Walker, Diana: Time Magazine
Walker, Harry E.: McClatchy Tribune
Walsh, Susan: Associated Press Photos
Watkins, Frederick L.: Johnson Publishing Co.
Watson, James H.: Agence France-Presse
Wells, Jonathan: Sipa Press
Westcott, Jay: Elsevier
Whitesell, Gregory: The Washington Examiner
Williams, Tom: Roll Call
Williamson, Michael: Washington Post
Wilson, Mark L.: Getty Images
Wines, Heather: Gannett News Service
Wolf, Lloyd: Freelance
Wolf, Kevin: Freelance
Wollenberg, Roger L.: United Press International
Wong, Alex: Getty Images
Woodward, Tracy L.: Washington Post
Yim, Heesoon: HANA
Young, Jim: Reuters
Zaklin, Stefan: Freelance
Ziffer, Steve: Freelance

SERVICES REPRESENTED

(Service and telephone number, office address, and name of representative)

ABACA USA—(212) 224–8460; 28–30 West 36th Street, Suite 1004, New York, NY 10018: Douliery, Olivier.

AGENCE FRANCE PRESSE—(202) 414–0551; 1015 15th Street, NW., Suite 500, Washington, DC 20005: Frazza, Luke; Hambach, Eva; Ngan, Mandel; Pearson, Robert; Richards, Paul; Sloan, Timothy; Watson, James.

ARMY TIMES PUBLISHING—(703) 750–8170; 6883 Commercial Drive, Springfield, VA 22159: Curtis, Rob; Kozak, Richard; Lee, James; Lessig, Alan; Mahaskey, Michael; McKee, Staci; Vemmer, Sheila.

ASSOCIATED PRESS PHOTOS—(202) 776–9510; 2021 K Street, NW., Washington, DC 20006: Ake, David: Associated Press Photos (main contact); Applewhite, Scott J.: Ceneta, Manuel B.; Cook, Dennis; Dharapak, Charles; Edmonds, Ronald; Ghanbari, Haraz; Helber, Stephen; Herbert, Gerald; Jackson, Lawrence; Martin, Jacquelyn; Martinez Monsivais, Pablo; Savoia, Stephen; Walsh, Susan.

BIGMARSH NEWS PHOTOS—(202) 364–8332; 5131 52nd Street, NW., Washington, DC 20016: Cohen, Marshall.

BLACK STAR—(703) 547–1176; 7704 Tauxemont Road, Alexandria, VA 22308: Brack, William; Harrington, John.

BRYCE MOUNTAIN COURIER—(540) 856–3255; P.O. Box 247, 68 Polk Street, Basye, VA 22810: Boston, Bernard.

CHESAPEAKE NEWS SERVICE—(410) 484–3500; P.O. Box 141, Brooklandville, MD 21022: Katz, Martin.

CHICAGO TRIBUNE—(202) 824–8200; 1325 G Street, NW., Suite 200, Washington, DC 20005: Souza, Peter.

CATHOLIC NEWS SERVICE—(202) 541–3250; 3211 Fourth Street, NE., Washington, DC 20017. Haring, Paul.

CHRISTIAN SCIENCE MONITOR—(617) 450–2000; 1 Norway Street, Boston, MA 02115: Nelson, Andrew.

CONSOLIDATED NEWS PICTURES—(202) 543–3203; 10305 Leslie Street, Silver Spring, MD 20902–4857: Sachs, Arnold; Sachs, Ronald.

CONTACT PRESS IMAGES—(212) 695–7750; 341 West 38th Street, 7th Floor, New York, NY 10018: Burnett, David.

COX NEWSPAPERS—(202) 331–0900; 400 North Capitol Street, Suite 750, Washington, DC 20001: McKay, Richard.

CQ WEEKLY—(202) 822–1431; 1414 22nd Street, NW., Washington, DC 20037: Ferrell, Scott.

EDUCATION WEEK—(301) 280–3100; 6935 Arlington Road, Suite 100, Bethesda, MD 20814: Prichard, James; Shelley, Allison.

EUROPEAN PRESS PHOTO—(202) 347–4694; 1252 National Press Building, 529 14th Street, NW., Washington, DC 20045: Cavanaugh, Matthew T.; Thew, Shawn; Vucci, Evan.

ELSEVIER—11830 Westline Industrial Drive, St. Louis, MO 63146: Mattes, Sherilyn; Westcott, Jay.

FAIRFAX COUNTY TIMES—1760 Reston Parkway, Suite 411, Reston, VA 20190: DiPasquale, Jill.

FAUQUIER TIMES DEMOCRAT—39 Culpeper Street, Warrenton, VA 20186: Sypher, Mark.

FRONTIERS NEWS MAGAZINE—(301) 229–0635; P.O. Box 634, Glen Echo, MD 20812: Lynch, M. Patricia.

GANNETT—(703) 854–5800; 7950 Jones Branch Drive, McLean, VA 22107: Schwartz, Michael; Wines, Heather; Franco, Jeff.

GETTY IMAGES—(646) 613–3703; One Hudson Place, 75 Varick Street, New York, NY 10013: Somodevilla, Kenneth; McNamee, Win; Wilson, Mark; Wong, Alex.

GREEK AMERICAN NEWS AGENCY—(202) 332–2727; 107 Frederick Avenue, Babylon, NY 11702: Panagos, Dimitrios.

HANA—(202) 262–4541; 11311 Park Drive, Fairfax, VA 22030: Yim, Heesoon.

IMAGECATCHER NEWS—4911 Hampden Lane, Apt. #3, Bethesda, MD 20814: Bowe, Christy.

IMPACT DIGITALS—(212) 614 8406; 171 Thompson Street, #9, New York, NY 10012: Reinhard, Rick.

JOHNSON PUBLISHING CO—(202) 393–5860; 1750 Pennsylvania Avenue, NW., Washington, DC 20006: Watkins, Jr., Frederick.

KYODO NEWS—(202) 347–5767; 529 14th Street, NW., #400, National Press Building, Washington, DC 20045: Kato, Satomi.

LA PRENSA GRAFICA OF EL SALVADOR—San Salvador, El Salvador: Alvarez, Miguel A.

LEGAL TIMES—(202) 457–0686; 1730 M Street, NW., Suite 802, Washington, DC 20036: Radzinschi, Diego.

SERVICES REPRESENTED—Continued

MAI PHOTO AGENCY—(703) 968–0030; 6601 Ashmere Lane, Centreville, VA 20120: Mathieson, Greg; Schaeffer, Sandra.

McCLATCHY TRIBUNE—(202) 383–6142; 700 12th Street, Suite 1000, Washington, DC 20005: Bridges, George; Kennedy, Chuck; Walker, Harry E.

NATIONAL JOURNAL—(202) 739–8400; 1501 M Street, NW., Suite 300, Washington, DC 20005: Bloom, Richard; Lynch, Liz.

NEWSWEEK— (202) 626–2085; 1750 Pennsylvania Avenue, NW., Suite 1220, Washington, DC 20006: Bui, Khue; Ellsworth, Katie; Ferraro, Beth; Kennerly, David H.; Ommanney, Charles; Steele, Rick.

NOTIMEX—(202) 347–5227; 529 14th Street, NW., Suite 975, Washington, DC 20045: Gamarra, Ruben F.

OREGONIAN—(503) 221–8370; 1320 Southwest Broadway, Portland, OR 97201: Rasmussen, Randy L.

PERIODICAL NEWS SERVICE—9206 Vollmerhausen Road, Jessup, MD 20794: Gatty, Michael; Gatty, Mary Anne.

PHOTO PRESS INTERNATIONAL—(703) 548–7172: Coppage, Gary.

PHOTO TRENDS, INC.—548 8th Avenue, Suite 401, New York, NY 10018: Burns, David.

PITTSBURG POST GAZETTE—34 Boulvard of the Allies, PGH, PA 15222: Beale, John.; Mellon, Steve; O'Neill, Annie; Starnes, Andy.

POLARIS IMAGES—259 West 30th Street, 13th Floor, New York, NY 10001:

PROFESSIONAL PILOT MAGAZINE—3014 Colvin Street, Alexandria, VA 22314: Sykes, Jack.

REDIFF.COM/INDIA ABROAD PUB.—(646) 432–6054; 43 West 24th Street, 2nd Floor, New York, NY 10010: Gandhi, Pareshkumar.

REFORMA—(202) 628–0031; 1126 National Press Building, Washington, DC 20045: Juarez, Miguel.

REUTERS NEWS PICTURES—(202) 898–8333; 1333 H Street, NW., Suite 500, Washington, DC 20005: Bochatey, Terry; Bourg, Jim; Downing, Lawrence; Cameron, Gary A.; Hershorn, Gary; Jones, Peter; Kang, Hyungwon; Lamarque, Kevin; Reed, Jason; Riley, Molly; Varias, Stelios; Young, Jim.

ROLL CALL—(202) 824–6800; 50 F Street, NW., 7th Floor, Washington, DC 20001: Clark, Bill, Graham, Douglas; McGinnis, Lowell; Williams, Tom.

SHUKAN SHINCHO, SHINCHOSHA CO.—(703) 243–1569; 2001 North Adams Street, #715, Arlington, VA 22201: Takeda, Yasushi.

SIPA PRESS—(212) 463–0150; 30 West 21st Street, New York, NY 10010: Fabiano, Gary; Trippett, Robert; Wells, Jonathan.

SPORTS ILLUSTRATED—(212) 522–3325; 1271 Avenue of the Americas, Room 1970, New York, NY 10020: Binks, Porter.

ST. LOUIS AMERICAN—(314) 533–8000; 4242 Lindell, St. Louis, MO 63108: Sweets, Fredric.

SUARA—(703) 534–6014; 1908 Armand Court, Falls Church, VA 22043: Sudyatmiko, Karina.

SUBURBAN COMMUNICATIONS CORP—(810) 645–5164; 872 Dursley Road, Bloomfield Hills, ME 48304: Ashley, Douglas.

THE BALTIMORE SUN—(410) 332–6941; 501 North Calvert Street, Baltimore, MD 21278: Chung, Andre.

THE DETROIT NEWS—(312) 222–2030; 615 West Lafayette Avenue, Photo Dept., Detroit, MI 48226: Tines, Charles; Thomas, Ricardo;

THE HILL—(202) 628–8525; 733 15th Street, Washington, DC 20005: Bandeira, Pedro; Ryan, Patrick.

THE NEW YORK TIMES—(202) 862–0300; 1627 Eye Street, NW., Washington, DC 20006: Crowley, Stephen; Mills, Douglas.

THE OREGONIAN—(503) 221–8370; 1320 Southwest Broadway, Portland, OR 97201: Rasmussen, Randy.

THE POLITICO—(703) 647–7694: 1100 Wilson Boulvard, 6th Floor, Arlington, VA 22209: Reeder, Robert A.; Shinkle, John.

THE RICHMOND TIMES DISPATCH—(804) 649–6486; 300 E Franklin Street, Richmond, VA 23219: Brown, Robert.

THE WASHINGTON BLADE—1408 U Street, NW., 2nd Floor, Washington, DC 20009: Mosley, Leigh.

THE WASHINGTON EXAMINER— 6408 Edsall Road, Alexandria, VA 22312: Cabe, Brig; Harnik, Andrew; Westcott, Jay; Whitsell, Gregory.

THE WASHINGTON INFORMER—(202) 561–4100; 3117 Martin L. King Avenue, SE., Washington, DC 20032: Holt, Victor.

THE WASHINGTON POST—(202) 334–7380; 1150 15th Street, NW., Washington, DC 20071: Biddle, Susan; Bruce, Andrea; Carioti, Richard; Chikwendiu, Jahi; Clark, Kevin; Davidson, Linda; Du Cille, Michel; Foy, Mary Lou; Frey, Katherine; Gail, Carl; Hillian, Vanessa; Jenkins, Keith; Joseph, Marvin; Kahn, Nikki; Keres, Preston; Lipski, Richard; Lustig, Raymond; Maltby, Melissa; Mara, Melina; Martineau, Gerald; McDonnell, John; Morris, Larry; Newton, Jonathan; O'Leary, William; Parcell, James; Perkins, Lucien; Raimondo, Lois; Reeder, Robert; Richardson, Joel; Sandys, Toni; Santoro, Giuliana; Saunders, Ray; Thomas, Margaret; Thresher, James; Voisin, Sarah; Werbeck, Nicole; Williamson, Michael; Woodward, Tracy.

THE WASHINGTON TIMES—(202) 636–3000; 3600 New York Avenue, NE., Washington, DC 20002: Baughman, J. Ross; Brantley, James; Calvert, Mary; Connor, Michael; Donaldson, Kristin; Eddins, Jr., Falkenberg, Katie; Fuchs, Christian; Goulait, Bert; Lamkey, Jr., Rod; Pastor, Nancy; Riecken, Astrid; Rosenbaum, Daniel; Salisbury, Barbra; Silverman, Joseph; McGonigal, Chris.

SERVICES REPRESENTED—Continued

THE WEEKLY STANDARD—1150 17th Street, NW., Suite 505, Washington, DC 20036: Nisnevitch, Lev.

THE YOMIURI SHIMBUN—(212) 582–5827; 50 Rockefeller Plaza, #903, New York, NY 10020: Kon, Toshiyuki.

TIME MAGAZINE—(202) 861–4062; 555 12th Street, NW., Suite 600, Washington, DC 20004: Ellsworth, Katie; Kraft, Brooks; Liss, Steve; Morris, Christopher; Musi, Vincent; Shell, Mary; Walker, Diana.

U.S. NEWS & WORLD REPORT—(202) 955–2210; 1050 Thomas Jefferson Street, NW., Washington, DC 20007: Archambault, Charles; LoScalzo, Jim; MacMillan, Jeffrey; Poggi, Jennifer.

UNITED PRESS INTERNATIONAL—(202) 387–7965; 1510 H Street, NW., Washington, DC 20005: Benic, Patrick; Wollenberg, Roger.

USA/TODAY—(703) 854–5216; 7950 Jones Branch Road, McLean, VA 22107: Beiser, H. Darr; Blass, Eileen; Dillon, Timothy; Eile, Evan; Madrid, Michael; Patterson, Kathryn.

USATODAY.COM—(703) 854–7651; 7950 Jones Branch Drive, McLean, VA 22108: Dukehart, Coburn; Gainer, Denny.

ZUMA PRESS—34189 Pacific Coast Highway, Dana Point, CA 92629: Murrmann, Mark; Palu, Louie; Putnam, Bill.

FREELANCE

Freelancers: Arrossi, Eddie; Ashe, James F.; Atherton, Jim; Augustino, Jocelyn; Barouh, Stan; Barrett, Steve E.; Barrick, Matthew; Berg, Lisa; Bingham, Mary (Molly); Bivera, Johnny; Boitano, Stephen J.; Brier, Joe; Burke, Lauren V.; Cedeno, Ken; Corcoran, Thomas Michael; Colburn, James E.; Clendenin, Jay; Council, Andrew; Crandall, Bill; Cutraro, Andrew; DeArmas, Adrienne; Devorah, Carrie; Drenner, Dennis; Emanuel, Hector; Ernst, Jonathan; Fitz-Patrick, Bill; Foster, William H.; Freilich, Jon; Garcia, Mannie; Geissinger, Michael A.; Gilbert, Patrice J.; Glenn, Larry S.; Gripas, Yuri; Heasley, Shaun; Hittle, David E.; Hutchens, Jeff; Jones, Caleb; Kahn, Nikki; Kittner, Sam; Kleponis, Chris; Kossoff, Leslie; Kuykendal, Stephanie; LaVor, Martin L.; Lawidjaja, Rudy; Lee, David Y.; Loeb, Saul; Lustig, Raymond J.; Mallin, Jay; Marquette, Joseph C.; Nipp, Lisa; Otfinowski, Danuta; Pajic, Kamenko; Petros, Bill; Poleski, David; Powers, Carol T.; Purcell, Steven; Raab, Susana A.; Ricardel, Vincent J.; Roberts, Joshua; Robinson, Scott; Ronay, Vivian; Rose, Jamie; Samperton, Kyle; Schwartz, David S.; Sisley, Evan; Smialowski, Brendan; Spillers, Linda J.; Spoden, Leonard; Stephenson, Al; Temchine, Michael; Theiler, Michael; Thomas, Ronald W.; Turner, Tyrone; Usher, Chris; Voss, Stephen; Wolf, Lloyd; Wolf, Kevin; Zaklin, Stefan; Ziffer, Steve.

WHITE HOUSE NEWS PHOTOGRAPHERS' ASSOCIATION

PO 7119, Washington, DC 20044–7119

www.whnpa.org

OFFICERS

Dennis Brack, Black Star, *President*
Stu Cohen, WashingtonPost.com, *Vice President*
Jamie Rose, Freelance, *Secretary*
Jonathan Elswick, Associated Press, *Treasurer*

EXECUTIVE BOARD

Susan Biddle (Washington Post)
Matthew Cavanaugh (EPA)
Allison Shelley (Washington Times)
Ed Eaves (NBC News)
Pierre Kattar (Washingtonpost.com)
Pete Souza, Contest Chair (Chicago Tribune)
Pege Gilgannon, Contest Chair (WJLA–TV)
Leighton Mark, Education Chair (Associated Press)

MEMBERS REPRESENTED

Abraham, Mark: Freelance
Adlerblum, Robin: CBS News
Ake, J. David: Associated Press
Alberter Jr., William: CNN
Almanza, Armando: Ventana Productions
Andrews, Nancy: Detroit Free Press
Applewhite, J. Scott: Associated Press
Apt Johnson, Roslyn: Freelance
Archambault, Charles: U.S. News & World Report
Arrington, Clyde: ABC News
Ashley, Douglas: Surburban Newspapers & ABC TV
Assaf, Christopher: Baltimore Sun
Atherton, James: Freelance
Auth, William: Freelance
Awdey, Harry: Student
Bacheler, Peter: Freelance
Bahruth, William:
Baker, David: ITN
Ballard, Karen: Freelance
Barrick, Matthew: Caring Magazine
Baughman, J. Ross: Washington Times
Baylen, Elizabeth: Washington Times
Been, Rachel: AOL
Beiser, H. Darr: USA Today
Benic, Patrick: UPI
Bennett, Ronald T.: Executive Branch
Beverly, Ronald: AOL
Biddle, Susan: Washington Post
Binks, Porter: Sports Illustrated
Bivera, Johnny: Freelance
Blair, James: Freelance
Blair, Adam: CTV
Blaylock, Kenneth:
Bodnar, John: CNN
Boston, Bernie: Bryce Mountain Courier
Boswell Jr., Victor: Freelance
Bourg, James: Reuters
Bowe, Christy: ImageCatcher News
Bozick, Peter: Freelance
Brack, Dennis: Black Star
Brandon, Alex: Times-Picayune
Brantley, James: Washington Times
Bridges, George: McClatchy / Tribune
Bridgham, Kenneth:
Brier, Joseph: Freelance
Brookner, Naomi: The Gazette
Brooks, Dudley: Baltimore Sun
Brown, Stephen: Freelance
Brown Sr., Henry: ABC
Bruce, Andrea: Washington Post
Bruneau, Elizabeth: AOL

MEMBERS REPRESENTED—Continued

Bryan, Beverly: WJLA–TV
Bui, Khue: Freelance
Burgess, Robert: Freelance
Burke, Lauren: Freelance
Burnett, David: Contact Press Images
Burns, David: New York Post
Burrows, Alex: Virginian Pilot
Butler, Francis: Freelance
Cain, Stephen: ABC–TV
Calvert, Mary: Washington Times
Carioti, Ricky: Washington Post
Carlson, David: Canon
Carrier, J.: Freelance
Casey, Sean: NBC4
Cassetta, Guido: Freelance
Castner, Edward: Freelance
Castoro, Susan: Associated Press
Cavalletti, Mabel: AOL
Cavanaugh, Matthew: EPA
Cedeno, Ken: Freelance
Ceneta, Manuel: Associated Press
Chang Crandall, Jennifer: Washingtonpost.com
Changuris, Sammy-Zeke: WJLA–TV
Chase, David: Cox Radio
Cheris, Eddie: U.S. State Department/DHS/FEMA
Chikwendiu, Jahi: Washington Post
Chung, Andre: Baltimore Sun
Cirace, Robert: CNN
Clark, Bill: Roll Call
Clark, Kevin: Washington Post
Clarkson, Rich: Rich Clarkson & Associaties
Clendenin, Jay: Freelance
Cobb, Jodi: National Geographic
Cohen, Marshall: Big Marsh News Photos
Cohen, Stuart: Freelance
Colburn, James: Freelance
Collins, Maxine: BBC TV
Collinson, Luke: ITN
Colton, William:
Conger, Dean:
Connor, Michael: Washington Times
Cook, Dennis: Associated Press
Coppage, Gary: GRC Photography & Design
Corder, Chris: AOL
Corporan, Margot: AOL
Costello, Jeff: AOL
Costello II, Thomas: Asbury Park Press
Couig, Carloine: Discovery Communications
Cox Jr., Ernie:
Crane, Arnold: The LaVor Group
Crawford, Walter: WJLA–TV
Crowley, Stephen: The New York Times
Cuong, Pham: CBS
Curran, Patrick: WTTG–TV
Curtis, Rob: Army Times Publishing Co.
Curtiss, Cathaleen: AOL
Dale, Bruce: Freelance
D'Angelo, Rebecca: Freelance
Daniell, Parker: Freelance
Daugherty, Bob: Associated Press
Davidson, Linda: Washington Post
Davis, Amy: Baltimore Sun
de la Cruz, Benedict: Washingtonpost.com
de la Torre, Noemi: AOL
DeArmas, Adrienne: Chris Usher Photography & Associates
Denesha, Julie: Washington Times
Dennehey, Paul:
Desfor, Max:
Deslich, Steve: McClatchy / Tribune Photo Service
Devorah, Carrie: Freelance
Dharapak, Charles: Associated Press
DiBartolo, Melissa: Nikon
Dietsch, Kevin: UPI
Dietz, Jim: AP
Dillon, Tim: USA Today
Doane, Martin: WJLA–TV
Dobkin, Lauren: AOL
Dodson, Richard: NBC
Donaldson, Nancy: WPNI
Douliery, Oliver: Abaca Press
Downing, Larry: Reuters
Drapkin, Arnold: TIME Magazine
Dryden, Valerie: Student
duCille, Michel: Washington Post
Dukehart, Coburn: USAToday.com
Dukehart Jr., Thomas: WUSA–TV
Dunmire, John: WTTG–TV
Eaves, Ed: NBC News
Eddins, Joseph: Washington Times
Edmonds, Ron: Associated Press
Edrington, Michael: American Forces Network Europe
Ehrenberg Jr., Richard: ABC News
Elbert II, Joseph: Washington Post
Elfers, Stephen: Army Times Publishing Co.
Ellsworth, Kathryn: Time
Elswick, Jonathan: Associated Press
Elvington, Glenn: ABC News
Epstein, Linda: McClatchy / Tribune
Ernst, Jonathan: Freelance
Ewan, Julia: Washington Post
Ewing, David: Freelance
Fabiano, Gary: Sipa Press
Fagan, Bill: Noritsu America Corporation
Falk, Steven: Philadelphia Daily News
Falkenberg, Katie: Washington Times
Farmer, Sharon: Freelance
Feld, Ric: Associated Press
Feldman, Roy: Freelance
Feldman, Randy: Viewpoint Communications, Inc.
Ferraro, Beth: Newsweek Magazine
Ferron, Karl: Baltimore Sun
Fiedler Jr., James: AOL
Fielman, Sheldon: NBC News

MEMBERS REPRESENTED—Continued

Figueroa, Noreen: AOL
Fitz-Patrick, Bill: Freelance
Folwell, Frank: USA Today
Fookes, Gary: Freelance
Forrest, Meredith: AOL
Forsythe, Jonathan: WashingtonPost.com
Forte, BJ: WTTG–TV
Foss, Philip: Speed Graphic
Foster, H. William: Freelance
Fox, Lloyd: Baltimore Sun
Fox, Travis: Washingtonpost.com
Fox, Donald:
Foy, Mary Lou: Washington Post
Frame, John: WTTG–TV
Freeman, Barry: ABC News
Freeman, Roland: Freelance
Frey, Katherine: Washington Post
Fridrich, George: Brighter Images Productions LLC
Fuchs, Christian: Washington Times
Fulton, Bradley: CTV
Fuss, Brian: CBS News
Gail, C. Mark: Washington Post
Gainer, Dennis: USA Today
Garcia, Mannie: Freelance
Gardner, Deborah: AOL
Geiger, Ken: National Geographic
Geissinger, Michael: Freelance
Ghanbari, Haraz: Associated Press
Gibson, Craig: Freelance
Gilbert, Kevin: Blue Pixel
Gilgannon, Pege: WJLA
Gilka, Robert:
Ginsburg, Benson: CBS News
Glenn, Alexis: UPI
Gmiter, Bernard: ABC News-Retired-Freelance
Goodman, Jeffrey: NBC/Freelance
Goulait, Bert: Washington Times
Gould-Phillips, Carol: Current Viewpoint
Goulding, David: Emotion Pictures
Goyal, Raghubir: Asia Today & India Globe/ATN News
Grace, Arthur: Freelance
Graham, Douglas: Roll Call
Gray, Monique: AOL
Greenberg, Christopher: Freelance for Bloomberg News, NYT
Grieser Jr., Robert: ATL Picture Text Agency
Gripas, Yuri: Reuters
Guzy, Carol: Washington Post
Hakuta, Michael: Washington Post Newsweek Interactive
Hall, Ellie: Associated Press
Halstead, Dirck: The Digital Journalist
Hamburg, Harry: Retired
Hanka, Roland: ARD German TV
Haring, Paul: Catholic News Service
Harrington, John: Freelance
Harrity, Chick: Whimsy Works
Hartzenbusch, Nanine: Baltimore Sun
Harvey, Alan: NBC
Heffner, Michael: AOL
Heikes, Darryl: Freelance
Heilemann, Tami: Department of Interior
Heiner, Steve: Nikon
Henry, Ashleigh: AOL
Herbert, Gerald: Associated Press
Hershorn, Gary: Reuters
Hicks, David: Washingtonian
Hillian, Vanessa: Washington Post
Hinds, Hugh: WRC/NBC
Hoiland, Harald: WUSA–TV / Retired
Holloway, David: Freelance
Hopkins, Gary: AOL
Hopkins, Brian: WJLA–TV
Horan, Michael: WTTG–TV
Houlihan, Robert: Washington Times
Hoyt, Michael: Catholic Standard
Hutchens, Jeff: Freelance
Imai, Kesaharu: World Photo Press
Ing, Lance: WTTG–TV
Irby, Kenneth: Poynter Institute
Jackson, Lawrence: Associated Press
Jackson, Karen: WJLA–TV Channel 7
Johnson, Fletcher: ABC
Johnson, Kenneth: ABC–TV
Johnston, Frank: Washington Post
Jones, Nelson: WTTG–TV
Joseph, Marvin: Washington Post
Kahn, Nikki: Washington Post
Kang, Hyungwon: Reuters News Pictures
Kapustin, Doug: Baltimore Sun
Kattar, Pierre: Washingtonpost.com
Katz, Marty: Chesapeake News Service
Kawajiri, Chiaki: Baltimore Sun
Kennedy, Charles: McClatchy / Tribune
Kennedy, Thomas: Washington Post Newseek Interactive
Kennerly, David: Eagles Roar Inc.
Kent, Jeffrey: Press Photographers' Gallery
Keres, Preston: Washington Post
Kieffer, Gary: Eurofoto Zurich
Kirschbaum, Jr., Jed: Baltimore Sun
Kittner, Sam: Freelance
Kleber, David:
Kleinfield, Michael: UPI
Koenig III, Paul:
Koppelman, Mitch: Reuters Television
Korab, Alexandra: AOL
Koslow, Jamie: AOL
Kossoff, Leslie: LK Photos
Kottwitz, Kathy: AOL
Kozak, Rick: Military Times
Kraft, Brooks: Time Magazine
Krehnbrink, Mary: WTTG FOX 5
Krieger, Barbara: Freelance/Day Hire
Kuntz Sr., Greg: United States Navy

MEMBERS REPRESENTED—Continued

Kuykendal, Stephanie: Freelance/NYT
Lam, Kenneth: Baltimore Sun
Lamarque, Kevin: Reuters
Lambert, H.M.:
Lamkey Jr., Rod: Washington Times
Larsen, Gregory: Freelance
Lavies, Bianca: Freelance
LaVor, Marty: Freelance
Lawrence, Jeffrey: McClatchy-Tribune
Lee, James: Army Times Publishing Co.
Lee, Erik: WTTG–TV
Lee, Eric: WTTG–TV
Lee, David: Freelance
Lessig, Alan: Army Times Publishing Co.
Levy, Glenn Ann: Freelance
Levy, John:
Lichtenfeld, Sara: AOL
Lipski, Richard: Washington Post
Lizik, Ronald: Associated Press
Lloyd Jr., Raymond: NYANG USAF
Lockhart, June:
Lockley, Peter: Washington Times
Lopossey, Monica: Baltimore Sun
Lorek, Stanley: ABC
LoScalzo, James: U.S. News & World Report
Love, Diane: Tribal Cultures Productions
Lustig, Ray: Retired
Lynaugh, Mike: Freelance
Lyons, Paul: NET
MacDonald, Jim: Canadian TV Network
MacDonald, Charles: National Geographic Channel
MacMillan, Jeffrey: U.S. News & World Report
Maddaloni, Christopher: Roll Call
Madrid, Michael: USA Today
Maggiolo, Vito: CNN
Mahaskey, Michael: Army Times Publishing Co.
Makely, John: Baltimore Sun
Malby, Elizabeth: Baltimore Sun
Malonson, Jacqueline: Freelance AP
Mann, Donna:
Mara, Melina: Washington Post
Mark, Leighton: Associated Press
Marquette, Joseph: Freelance/Bloomberg
Martin, Jacquelin: AP
Martineau, Gerald: Washington Post
Martinez Monsivais, Pablo: Associated Press
Mason, Thomas: WTTG–TV
Mathieson, Greg: MAI Photo News Agency, Inc.
Mawyer, Steve: AOL
Mazariegos, Mark: CBS News
Maze, Stephanie: Maze Productions Inc./Moonstone Press LLC
Mazer Field, Joni: Freelance
Mazzatenta, O.: Freelance
McCarthy III, Edward: Hudson Valley Black Press
McClendon, Jerome: AOL
McDonnell, John: Washington Post
McKay, Richard: Cox Newspapers
McKee, Staci: WashingtonPost.com
McKenna, William: Freelance/BBC
McKiernan, Scott: Zuma Press
McLaughlin, David: National Geographic Channel
McNamee, Wallace: Freelance
McNamee, Win: Getty Images
McNay, James: Brooks Institute of Photography
Mendelsohn, Matthew: Freelance
Milenic, Alexander: Freelance
Mills, Doug: New York Times
Mole, Robert: NBC
Molloy, Michelle: Newsweek
Morris, Peter: CNN
Morris, Larry: Washington Post
Morrisette, Roland: Bloomberg News
Moss, Lisa: AOL
Moulton, Paul:
Murphy, Timothy: Freelance
Murphy, John: Freelance
Murtaugh, Peter: Murtaugh Productions, LLC
Natoli, Sharon: Freelance
Nelson, Andrew: Christian Science Monitor
Newton, Jonathan: Washington Post
Nighswander, Marcia: Ohio University
Nighswander, Larry: Saveur Magazine
Nisselson, Evan: Digital Railroad
Nolan, David: Nolan & Company
Norling, Richard: Freelance
Novak, Jolie: AOL
Oates, Walter:
Ochs, Rochelle: AOL
Ohlson, Kevin: U.S. Air Force
O'Keefe, Dennis: Freelance
O'Leary, William: Washington Post
Ommanney, Charles: Newsweek
O'Regan, Michael: WRC–TV
Ortez, George: Retired since 1980
Owen, Cliff: AOL
Palu, Louie: Zuma Press
Panagos, Dimitrios: Greek American News Photo
Panzer, Chester: NBC–WRC
Parcell, James: Washington Post
Partlow, Wayne: Associated Press
Pastor, Nancy: Washington Times
Patterson, Jay: ABC
Pearson, Robert: AFP
Pekala, Bill: Nikon
Pensinger, Douglas: Getty Images
Perkins, Lucian: Washington Post
Perna, Algerin: AOL
Petros, Bill: Freelance
Philpott, William: AFP
Pinczuk, Murray: Freelance
Pino-Marina, Christina: Washingtonpost.com
Polger, Sarah Beth: AOL
Polich, John: Golden Gate University
Poole, John: Washingtonpost.Newsweek Interactive

MEMBERS REPRESENTED—Continued

Popper, Andrew: Business Week
Potasznik, David: Point of View Production Services, Inc.
Powell Jr., William: NBC/Retired
Powers, Carol: Freelance
Premack, Jay: Washington Post
Proser, Michael: ABC-News
Raab, Susana: Freelance
Rabbage, Mark: BBC TV
Raimondo, Lois: Washington Post
Raker, Lester: ABC News
Reed, Jason: Reuters
Reeder, Robert: Washington Post
Reinstein, Mark: Retired
Rensberger, Scott: Freelance
Rhodes, Charles: Washingtonpost.com
Ribeiro, Luiz: New York Post
Rice, Dorry: BBC News
Richards, Paul: AFP
Richards, Roger: The Digital Filmmaker
Richardson, Joel: Washington Post
Riecken, Astrid: Washington Times
Riley, Molly: Reuters
Rinnert, Bryan: AOL
Rique, Rachel: AOL
Robinson Sr., Clyde:
Robinson-Chavez, Michael: Washington Post
Rogowski, David: AOL
Ronay, Vivian: Freelance
Rose, Jamie: Freelance
Rosenbaum, Daniel: Washington Times
Roth Jr., Johnie: NBC
Sachs, Ronald: Consolidated News Photos
Sachs, Arnie: Consolidated News Photos
Salisbury, Barbara: Washington Times/Insight Magazine
Sandys, Toni: Washington Post
Santoro, Giuliana: Washington Post
Sargent, Michael: Retired
Saunders, Ray: Washington Post
Schaeffer, Sandra: MAI Photo News Agency
Schauble, Justin: Persistent Video Productions
Schlegel, Barry: Team Video Services Inc. CNN
Schmick, Paul: Freelance
Schneider, Jack: NBC–TV
Schwartz, Herb: CBS News
Scicchitano, Carmine: NBC
Scull, David: Freelance
Semiatin, Morris: Morris Semiatin-Photographer
Shannon, Dennis: CBS News
Shelley, Allison: Washington Times
Sheras, Michael: Canon USA, Inc.
Shie, Cassandra: AOL
Shlemon, Christopher: Independent TV News
Shriber, Amy: AOL
Shutt, Charles: Communications Consultant
Sikes, Laura: Freelance
Silverman, Joseph: Washington Times
Singles, Phaedra: MSNBC
Sisco, Paul: Retired
Skeans, Jr., Ronald: BBC
Sladen, Kristin: AOL
Sloan, Tim: AFP
Smialowski, Brendan: Freelance
Smith, Michael: Dispatch Broadcast Group
Smith, Dayna: Washington Post
Smith, Jason: WTTG–TV
Snowden, Thomas: NBC News
Solimano, Guy: AOL
Sommer, Emilie: Freelance
Somodevilla, Kenneth: Freelance
Souza, Peter: Chicago Tribune
Spillers, Linda: Freelance
Squire, Jamie: Getty Images
Stearns, Stan: Freelance
Stein, Norman: RF Central LLC
Stein III, Arthur: Freelance
Stephenson, Al: Freelance
Stewart, Samaruddin: AOL
Stoddard, Mark: Freelance
Suban, Mark: AP
Suddeth, Rick: Freelance
Swain, Bethany Anne: CNN
Swann, Michael: WRC–4
Sweeney Jr., Eugene: Baltimore Sun
Sweetapple, Daniel: Australian Broadcasting Corp.
Swenson, Gordon: ABC
Swiatkowski, Edward:
Sykes, Jack: Professional Pilot Magazine
Tasnadi, Charles: Freelance
Taylor, Barbara: Baltimore Sun
Tefft-Soraghan, Jessica: Freelance
Temchine, Michael: Freelance
Thalman, Mark: Across the Pond Productions
Thew, Shawn: European Pressphoto Agency
Thomas, Ronald: Office of Communication and Public Information DCPS
Thomas, Margaret: Retired
Thresher, James: Washington Post
Tiffen, Steve: The Tiffen Company
Tinsley, Jeff: Smithsonian Institution/Retired
Tolbert IV, George Dalton: Freelance/Retired U.S. Senate
Trikosko, Marion:
Trippett, Robert: World Picture News
Tripplaar, Kristoffer: Corcoran College of Art
Tsuboi, Kazuo: World Photo Press
Usher, Chris: Freelance
Valeri, Charlene: National Geographic
Van Grack, Lee: AOL
Van Riper, Frank: Goodman/Van Riper Photography
Varias, Stelios: Reuters
Vemmer, Shelia: Army Times Publishing Co.
Vennell, Vicki: ABC News
Ventura, Joe: Nikon
Verna, Tressa: NBC-News Dateline

MEMBERS REPRESENTED—Continued

Voisin, Sarah: Washington Post
von Elling, Jennifer: AOL
Vucci, Evan: Associated Press
Wagner, Nikki: AOL
Walker, Diana: Time Magazine
Wallace, Jim: Smithsonian Institution
Walsh, Susan: Associated Press
Walz, Mark: CNN
Ward, Fred: Black Star
Washington, Monica: AOL
Watrud, Donald: WTTG–TV
Watson, James: AFP
Weik, David: ABC Television News
Weller, George: Freelance
Wells, Jim: Freelance
Wiegman Jr., Dave: Retired NBC
Wilkes, Douglas: WTTG–TV
Williams, Adrienne: AOL
Williams, Milton: Freelance
Williams, Robert: NBC News
Williams, Thomas: Roll Call Newspaper
Williamson, Michael: Washington Post
Wilson, Jamal: Freelance
Wilson, Mark: Getty Images
Wilson, Jim: New York Times
Wilson, Woodrow:
Witte, Joel: WTTG–TV
Wolf, Kevin: Freelance
Wollenberg, Roger: United Press International
Wong, Alex: Getty Images
Woodward, Tracy: Washington Post
Wray, Eric: ABC News
Yaqubi, Wajmah: AOL
Yates II, H. William: CBS News Freelance
Yokota, Victoria: Freelance
Young, Bruce: The Evans-McCan Group
Young, Jennifer: The Evans-McCan Group
Young, Jim: Reuters
Zervos, Stratis: Freelance-Zervos Video Productions, LLC
Zlotky, Alan: AOL

RADIO AND TELEVISION CORRESPONDENTS' GALLERIES*

SENATE RADIO AND TELEVISION GALLERY

The Capitol, Room S–325, 224–6421

Director.—Michael Mastrian
Deputy Director.—Jane Ruyle
Senior Media Relations Coordinator.—Michael Lawrence
Media Relations Coordinators: Chris Bois, Erin Yeatman
Assistant Media Relations Coordinator.—Arlen Salazar

HOUSE RADIO AND TELEVISION GALLERY

The Capitol, Room H–321, 225–5214

Director.—Olga Ramirez Kornacki
Deputy Director.—Andy Elias
Administrative Operations Manager.—Gail Davis
Assistant for Technical Operations / Systems Manager.—Gerald Rupert
Assistant Directors: Helen DeBarge, Kimberly Oates

EXECUTIVE COMMITTEE OF THE RADIO AND TELEVISION CORRESPONDENTS' GALLERIES

Steve Chaggaris, CBS News, *Chair*
Heather Dahl, Fox News
Jamie Dupree, Cox Radio
Linda Kenyon, SRN News
Brian Naylor, NPR News
Chad Pergram, Fox News
Deirdre Walsh, CNN News

RULES GOVERNING RADIO AND TELEVISION CORRESPONDENTS' GALLERIES

1. Persons desiring admission to the Radio and Television Galleries of Congress shall make application to the Speaker, as required by Rule 34 of the House of Representatives, as amended, and to the Committee on Rules and Administration of the Senate, as required by Rule 33, as amended, for the regulation of Senate wing of the Capitol. Applicants shall state in writing the names of all radio stations, television stations, systems, or news-gathering organizations by which they are employed and what other occupation or employment they may have, if any. Applicants shall further declare that they are not engaged in the prosecution of claims or the promotion of legislation pending before Congress, the Departments, or the independent agencies, and that they will not become so employed without resigning from the galleries. They shall further declare that they are not employed in any legislative or

*Information is based on data furnished and edited by each respective gallery.

executive department or independent agency of the Government, or by any foreign government or representative thereof; that they are not engaged in any lobbying activities; that they do not and will not, directly or indirectly, furnish special information to any organization, individual, or group of individuals for the influencing of prices on any commodity or stock exchange; that they will not do so during the time they retain membership in the galleries. Holders of visitors' cards who may be allowed temporary admission to the galleries must conform to all the restrictions of this paragraph.

2. It shall be a prerequisite to membership that the radio station, television station, system, or news-gathering agency which the applicant represents shall certify in writing to the Radio and Television Correspondents' Galleries that the applicant conforms to the foregoing regulations.

3. The applications required by the above rule shall be authenticated in a manner that shall be satisfactory to the Executive Committee of the Radio and Television Correspondents' Galleries who shall see that the occupation of the galleries is confined to bona fide news gatherers and/or reporters of reputable standing in their business who represent radio stations, television stations, systems, or news-gathering agencies engaged primarily in serving radio stations, television stations, or systems. It shall be the duty of the Executive Committee of the Radio and Television Correspondents' Galleries to report, at its discretion, violation of the privileges of the galleries to the Speaker or to the Senate Committee on Rules and Administration, and pending action thereon, the offending individual may be suspended.

4. Persons engaged in other occupations, whose chief attention is not given to—or more than one-half of their earned income is not derived from—the gathering or reporting of news for radio stations, television stations, systems, or news-gathering agencies primarily serving radio stations or systems, shall not be entitled to admission to the Radio and Television Galleries. The Radio and Television Correspondents' List in the Congressional Directory shall be a list only of persons whose chief attention is given to or more than one-half of their earned income is derived from the gathering and reporting of news for radio stations, television stations, and systems engaged in the daily dissemination of news, and of representatives of news-gathering agencies engaged in the daily service of news to such radio stations, television stations, or systems.

5. Members of the families of correspondents are not entitled to the privileges of the galleries.

6. The Radio and Television Galleries shall be under the control of the Executive Committee of the Radio and Television Correspondents' Galleries, subject to the approval and supervision of the Speaker of the House of Representatives and the Senate Committee on Rules and Administration.

Approved.

NANCY PELOSI,
Speaker, House of Representatives.

DIANNE FEINSTEIN,
Chair, Senate Committee on Rules and Administration.

MEMBERS ENTITLED TO ADMISSION

RADIO AND TELEVISION CORRESPONDENTS' GALLERIES

Abbott, Stacey: National Public Radio
Abdalla, Hebah: Aljazeera International
Abdallah, Khalil: CNN
Abdalwahab, Yamen: Al Arabiya TV
Abdullah-James, Malik Hassan: BET Nightly News
Abe, Takaaki: Nippon TV Network
Abebe, Addisu: Voice of America
Abed, Nader: Aljazeera Satellite Channel (Peninsula)
Abraha, Zeresnaey: Aljazeera International
Abrams, Mike: Radio One
Abramson, Larry: National Public Radio
Abtar, Rana: Middle East Television Network (Alhurra)
Abuelhawa, Daoud: Al Arabiya TV
Abukasem, Hassan: Radio Free Asia
Abuliak, Larry: Freelance
Aburahma, Eyad: Aljazeera Satellite Channel (Peninsula)
Acharya, Niharika: Voice of America
Ackland, Matt: Freelance
Adams, Doug: Mobile Video Services, LTD
Adams, Douglas A.: NBC News
Adams, James M.: WRC–TV/NBC–4
Adams, Katy: WTTG–Fox Television
Adams, Larry: Native American Television
Adkinson, Jeff: Middle East Television Network (Alhurra)
Adlerblum, Robin: Freelance
Advani, Reena: National Public Radio
Aguayo, Francisco: WZDC–TV
Aguirre, Jose Angel: WMDO–TV Univision
Ahearn, Brian Marshall: East Coast Television
Ahlers, Mike: CNN
Ahmad, Adriana: Voice of America
Ahmed, Lukman: Al Arabiya TV
Ahn, Jaehoon: Radio Free Asia
Aiello, Jr., Augustine ''Bud'': National Public Radio
Aigner-Treworgy, Adam: NBC News
Aischmann, Frank: German Public Radio (ARD)
Aitken, Cynthia: AP–Broadcast
Akassy, Hugues-Denver: Orbite Television Inc.
Alami, Mohammed: Aljazeera Satellite Channel (Peninsula)
Alberter, William: CNN
Albright-Hanna, Kate: CNN
Alcott, Abigail K.: Fox News
Aleemi, Akmal: Voice of America
Alexander, Amy: National Public Radio
Alexander, Clinton N.: CBS News
Alexander, Kenneth: C–SPAN
Alexander, Robert: WJLA–TV/Newschannel 8
Alfa, Nadine: Freelance
Ali, Muhammad: Voice of America
Ali, Shujaat: NBC News
Aliaga, Julio: WZDC–TV
Ali-Haidari, Mohamed: Middle East Television Network (Alhurra)
Aliyarova Horowitz, Dilshad: Voice of America
Allard, John W.: ABC News
Allard, Marc: BBC
Alldredge, Thomas: C–SPAN
Allen, Darrell: Voice of AmErica
Allen, Keith: Reuters Radio & TV
Allison, Lynn Quarles: WETA
Almaguer, Miguel: WRC–TV/NBC–4
Almanza, Armando: Ventana Productions
Almeleh, John: Pacifica Radio
Al-Moajil, Waleed: AP–Broadcast
Alnwick, Melanie: WTTG–Fox Television
Alrawi, Khaldoun: AP–Broadcast
Alvey, Jay: WRC–TV/NBC–4
Amimi, Ali: BBC
Amirault-Michel, Theresa: C–SPAN
Amkas, Karlina: Voice of America
Ammerman, Stuart: Freelance
Anastasi, Patrick: NBC News
Andersen, Kate: Bloomberg Radio & TV
Anderson, Charles: WETA
Anderson, Scott: ABC News
Anderson, Scott: CNN
Andrews, Wyatt: CBS News
Ang, Sarita: Voice of America
Angelini, Mark: Belo Capital Bureau
Angle, James L.: Fox News
Anglim, John: Freelance
Anna, Ubeda: Spanish Public Television (TVE)
Anthony, Karyn: CBS News
Anyse, Alana: Freelance
Aoun, Larissa: Middle East Television Network (Alhurra)
Appelbaum, Lauren: NBC News
Apsell, Natalie: CNN
Apte, Aunshuman: Voice of America
Araia, Asmeret: NBC News
Arbuckle, Andrew: Freelance
Arcega, Milandro: Voice of America
Archer, Nelson: CNN
Archuleta, Eddie: Freelance
Archuleta, John: Freelance
Ardalan, Davar: National Public Radio
Arena, Bruno: Freelance

MEMBERS ENTITLED TO ADMISSION—Continued

Arena, Kelli: CNN
Arenstein, Howard: CBS News
Arent, Lindsey: Bloomberg Radio & TV
Arestad, Anders: C–SPAN
Argentieri, David: National Public Radio
Arioka, Kaori: NHK–Japan Broadcasting Corporation
Arkedis, Robert: The Washington Bureau
Armfield, Robert: Fox News
Armstrong, Patricia M.: Freelance
Armstrong, Phyllis: WUSA–TV
Armstrong, Thomas Ayres: Freelance
Armwood, Adrian: Freelance
Arrasmith, Christine: National Public Radio
Arrington, Percy: Freelance
Artesona, Eva: TV3–Televisio De Catalunya
Aryankalavil, Babu: Middle East Television Network (Alhurra)
Asberg, Stefan: Swedish Broadcasting
Asendio, Jim: Wamu
Asher, Julie: Freelance
Assuras, Thalia: CBS News
Atay, Hande: CNN
Attkisson, Sharyl: CBS News
Aubrey, Allison: National Public Radio
Augenstein, Neal: WTOP Radio
Aung, Ko Ko: Radio Free Asia
Aung, May Pyone: Radio Free Asia
Aung, Win: Voice of America
Aung Lwin, Kyaw: Voice of America
Auster, Bruce: National Public Radio
Austin, Kenneth: NBC News
Austin, Traci Mitchell: Hearst–Argyle Television
Avery-Brown, Verna: Pacifica Radio
Axelrod, Jim: CBS News
Ayoubi, Roula: BBC
Azais, Jean Pascal: Spanish Public Television (TVE)
Azzam, Heni: Aljazeera Satellite Channel (Peninsula)
Baber, Christine: Mobile Video Services, LTD
Babington-Heina, Martin: Freelance
Bach, Stephen: CNN
Bacheler, David: CNN
Bachenheimeri, Stephan: Deutsche Welle TV
Baggott, Marcia: FDCH/E–Media, Inc.
Baghi, Baubak: Aljazeera Satellite Channel (Peninsula)
Bagnall, Thomas: Voice of America
Bagnato, Barry: CBS News
Baier, Bret: Fox News
Bailor, Michelle: C–SPAN
Bain, Ben: Freelance
Baker, Cissy: Tribune Broadcasting
Baker, Dai: Independent Television News (ITN)
Baker, Kieran: Aljazeera International
Baker, Les: Fox News
Baker, Sarah: ABC News
Baktar, Reza James: CNN
Baldwin, Brooke: Freelance
Baldwin, Lorna: The Newshour with Jim Lehrer
Ballard, Carl: Channel One News
Ballenger, Rob: National Public Radio
Ballou, Jeff: Aljazeera International
Balsamo, James: Diversified Communications, Inc. (DCI)
Ban, Hyeonju: Seoul Broadcasting System (SBS)
Banaszak, Brendan: National Public Radio
Banegas, Al: Belo Capital Bureau
Banks, Erik: CNN
Banks, James: Eurovision Americas, Inc.
Banks, Josh: Fox News
Banks, Mark: ABC News
Banks, Morris: CBS News
Bannigan, Michael A.: CNN
Bansal, Monisha: CNSNEWS.COM
Banville, David: CNN
Banville, Lee: The Newshour with Jim Lehrer
Barber, William: WETA
Barbour, Lantz: Freelance
Barnard, Bob: WTTG–Fox Television
Barnes, Audrey: WUSA–TV
Barnes, Christopher: Fox News
Barnett, Christopher: Environment & Energy Publishing, LLC
Barnett, James: CNN
Barocas, Emily: National Public Radio
Baroch, Andy: Voice of America
Barr, Bruce: CBS News
Barreda, Eric: Freelance
Barrett, C. Wesley: Hearst–Argyle Television
Barrett, Gene: ABC News
Barrett, Ted: CNN
Barreyre, Christophe: TF1–French TV
Barry, Caitlin: CNN
Barshak, Valery: Aljazeera International
Bartlett, Scott: Freelance
Bartlett, Stephen: Freelance
Basch, Michelle: Freelance
Bascom, Jon: Bloomberg Radio & TV
Bash, Dana: CNN
Basinger, Stuart: Fox News
Baskerville, Kia: CBS News
Baskin, Roberta: WJLA–TV/Newschannel 8
Bastien, Andrew: Aljazeera International
Bates, Claudia Anke: German TV ZDF
Bates, Glynda: WETA
Bates, Jeff: CNN
Bates, Timothy: Australian Broadcasting Corporation
Batten, Rodney: NBC News
Baumann, Robert: Freelance
Baumel, Susan: Voyage Productions
Bautista, Mark: Freelance
Bawa, Malini: Freelance
Baydyuk, Zorislav: Voice of America
Baysden III, Earl T.: Freelance

MEMBERS ENTITLED TO ADMISSION—Continued

Beahn, James: WTTG–Fox Television
Beale, Jonathan: BBC
Beall, Gary: NBC News
Bearson, Sonya Crawford: ABC News
Beasley, David: Radio Free Asia
Beck, Katie: BBC
Becker, Bruce: Fox News
Becker, Chris: Fox News
Becker, Farrel: CBS News
Beckman, Jennifer: AP–Broadcast
Behnam, Babak: Aljazeera International
Bejarano, Mark: National Public Radio
Belanger, Elizabeth: CNN
Belcher, Christopher: Telesur
Belizaire, Jacquelin: Voice of America
Bell, Anne: The Newshour with Jim Lehrer
Bell, Reginald ''Joey'': NBC News
Bellard, Joseph: Bloomberg Radio & TV
Belmar, Adam: ABC News
Belt, David: The Newshour with Jim Lehrer
Bena, John: CNN
Bender, Bob: ABC News
Bender, Gary: WTTG–Fox Television
Bender, Jason: C–SPAN
Benetato, Michael: NBC News
Benitez, Barbara: Aljazeera International
Benjoar, Jacques: NBC News
Bennett, Julia: WJLA–TV/Newschannel 8
Bennett, Mark R.: CBS News
Bensen, Jackie: WRC–TV/NBC–4
Benson, Miles: Link TV
Benson, Pamela S.: CNN
Bentley, David: Freelance
Bentz, Thomas: CNN
Benz, Kathy: CNN
Beraud, Anyck: Canadian Broadcasting Canada (CBC)
Berbner, Thomas: German TV ARD
Berger, Aaron: Feature Story News
Bergmann, Christina: Deutsche Welle TV
Berman, David: CNN
Bernardini, Laura: CNN
Bernier, Marc: Talk Radio News Service
Berry, Michael P.: Freelance
Berti, Barbara: CNN
Besheer, Margaret: Voice of America
Betsill, Brett: C–SPAN
Bevine, Sue: Freelance
Bey, Latasha: National Public Radio
Beyer, Kevin: Freelance
Beyer, William: WTTG–Fox Television
Bhatia, Varuna: Fox News
Bhungyal, Bhungyal: Radio Free Asia
Biddle, Michael: C–SPAN
Biggs, Mark: Aljazeera International
Bintrim, Tim R.: Freelance
Bistis, George: Voice of America
Bjoergaas, Tove: Norwegian Broadcasting
Black, Phillip M.: ABC News
Blackburn, Regina: NBC News
Blackman, Jay: NBC News
Blackman, John: NBC News
Blackwill, Sarah: NBC News
Blair, Adam Tyler: CTV Canadian TV
Blalock, Sherman: Hearst–Argyle Television
Blanchet, Sharon: BBC
Blanco, Hugo: AP–Broadcast
Blandburg, Victor: Freelance
Blankenship, Anthony: Fednet
Blaszyk, Amy N.: National Public Radio
Blitzer, Wolf: CNN
Block, Deborah: Voice of America
Block, Melissa: National Public Radio
Blooston, Victoria: NBC News
Blount, Jeffrey: NBC News
Blythe, Andrew: Eurovision Americas, Inc.
Bodlander, Gerald: AP–Broadcast
Bodnar, John: CNN
Bohannon, Camille: AP–Broadcast
Bohannon, Joseph: Freelance
Bohn, Kevin: CNN
Bohrman, David: CNN
Bonamigo, Bruno: Canadian Broadcasting Canada (CBC)
Bonny, Jinhee: Radio Free Asia
Bookhultz, Bruce: WUSA–TV
Boone, Dannie: C–SPAN
Borash, Jessica: The Newshour with Jim Lehrer
Borchers, Jens: German Broadcasting Systems–ARD
Borger, Gloria: CBS News
Borniger, Charles: Freelance
Borniger, Herta: German TV ARD
Bosch, Anna: Spanish Public Television (TVE)
Bosch van Rosenthal, Eelco: NOS Dutch Public Radio & TV (VRT)
Bost, Mark: WUSA–TV
Bottorf, Harry: WETA
Boughton, Bryan: Fox News
Bouleau, Gilles: TF1–French TV
Bourar, Hicham: Middle East Television Network (Alhurra)
Bovim, Megan: Fox News
Bowden, Tracy: Australian Broadcasting Corporation
Bowen, Timothy: WETA
Bowman, Michael: Voice of America
Bowman, Tom: National Public Radio
Boyce, Nell: National Public Radio
Boyd, Wayne F.: Freelance
Boysha, Judy: AP–Broadcast
Brablec, Radek: National Public Radio
Bradley, Carlotta L.: AP–Broadcast
Bradley, Tahman: ABC News
Bradley Hagerty, Barbara: National Public Radio
Bragale, Charles: WRC–TV/NBC–4
Bragg, Jennifer: Aljazeera International

MEMBERS ENTITLED TO ADMISSION—Continued

Bramson, Robert E.: ABC News
Brandkamp, Jonathan: Voice of America
Brandt, John: Fox News
Branigan, Patrick: Freelance
Bransford, Fletcher: Fox News
Brasch, Darci: WTOP Radio
Braun, Joshua: CNN
Brawner, Donald: WETA
Brawner, Donte: Freelance
Bream, Shannon D.: WRC–TV/NBC–4
Breisler, Jodi: Capitol News Connection (CNC)
Breiterman, Charles: ABC News
Brennan, William: Freelance
Brevner, Michael: CNN
Brewton, Fashela: Freelance
Bridges, Heidi: CNN
Brieger, Annette: Freelance
Brinberg, Claire: CNN
Brinkley, Danielle: To The Contrary (Persephone Productions)
Briski, Natasa: PRO Plus
Britch, Ray: CNN
Brittain, Becky: CNN
Brock, Alan Matthew: WJLA–TV/Newschannel 8
Brody, David: CBN News
Broffman, Craig A.: CNN
Broleman, Mike: Freelance
Bronson, Jeremy: NBC News
Bronstein, Scott: CNN
Brookes, Adam: BBC
Brooks, Codie: Fox News
Brooks, Kurt: WUSA–TV
Brooks, Sam: ABC News
Brower, Brooke: NBC News
Brown, Daniel: WTTG–Fox Television
Brown, Daryl: WTTG–Fox Television
Brown, Edgar: Fox News
Brown, Henry M.: ABC News
Brown, Jeffrey: The Newshour with Jim Lehrer
Brown, Jim: American Family Radio News
Brown, Kristi: CBS News
Brown, Kristin: Fox News
Brown, Malcolm: Feature Story News
Brown, Pamela: WJLA–TV/Newschannel 8
Brown, Paul: C–SPAN
Brown, Paul: National Public Radio
Brown, Quinn: CNN
Brown, Randall: Freelance
Brown, Tracy Ann: AP–Broadcast
Browne, Kari: BBC
Bruce, Andrea: CBS News
Bruner, Caroline: Fox News
Bruns, Aaron: Fox News
Bruns, David: AP–Broadcast
Bryant, Aubrey: WUSA–TV
Buchanan, Douglas: WUSA–TV
Buck, Melanie: CNN
Buckhorn, Burke: CNN
Buckingham, Joseph: WETA
Buckland, Carol: CNN
Buckley, Julia Redpath: National Public Radio
Buehler, Paul: WTTG–Fox Television
Buel, Meredith: Voice of America
Bugash, Eric: Freelance
Bull, David John G.: ABC News
Bullard, Larry: WRC–TV/NBC–4
Bullard Harmon, Susan: CBS News
Bullock, Peter: Reuters Radio & TV
Bullock, Tom: National Public Radio
Bundock, Susan J.: C–SPAN
Burch, Brian: CNN
Burch, Jennifer: CNN
Burchfiel, Nathan: CNSNEWS.COM
Burchman, Abigail: CNN
Burdick, Leslie: C–SPAN
Burke, James: C–SPAN
Burketh, Ivan: National Public Radio
Burlij, Terence: The Newshour with Jim Lehrer
Burns, Alison: Cox Broadcasting
Burns, Quiana: ABC News
Burrell, Ashley: NBC News
Burton, Daniel: Potomac Television
Buschschluter, Siegfried: Deutscheland Radio
Busher, Jerry: Freelance
Butcher, Robert E: National Public Radio
Butler, Cheryl: Freelance
Butler, Norman: Belo Capital Bureau
Butler, William: Native American Television
Butterworth, David: The Newshour with Jim Lehrer
Byers, Robert Charles: National Public Radio
Byrne, Joseph: Talk Radio News Service
Byrnes, Dennis: National Public Radio
C. W. Hsu, Roger: Voice of America
Cabral, Juan E.: CNN
Cacas, Max: Freelance
Cadoret, Remi: TF1–French TV
Cahill Murphy, Kathy: C–SPAN
Calder, William: CBS News
Caldwell, Leigh: Free Speech Radio News
Caldwell, Traci: Freelance
Calfat, Marcel: Canadian Broadcasting Canada (CBC)
Calo-Christian, Nancy: C–SPAN
Camanducaia, Anna: TV Globo International
Camerini, Michael: Camerini–Robertson, Inc.
Cameron, Carl: Fox News
Camp, Joseph: WETA
Campbell, Christopher: Aljazeera Satellite Channel (Peninsula)
Campbell, Karen: Freelance
Campbell, Meribe: CNN
Cancelleri, Heidi: East Coast Television
Candia, Kirsten: German TV ZDF
Canizales, Cesar A.: NBC Newschannel
Canty, James: Freelance
Cao, Huidong: Radio Free Asia

MEMBERS ENTITLED TO ADMISSION—Continued

Caplan, Craig: C–SPAN
Capra, Anthony: NBC News
Capuchinho, Marcelo: TV Globo International
Capuchinho, Marcio: TV Globo International
Caravello, David: Freelance
Caraway, Chanel: Freelance
Cardon, John Christophe: WETA
Carey, Julie: WRC–TV/NBC–4
Carlson, Brett: Freelance
Carlson, Christopher: ABC News
Carlson, Steve: Fox News
Carlsson, Leif: Swedish Broadcasting
Carlsson, Lisa: Swedish Broadcasting
Carner, John: Eurovision Amerricas, Inc.
Carney, Keith: FEDNET
Caronello, Sophie: Bloomberg Radio & TV
Carpel, Michael: Fox News
Carpio, Erick: WZDC–TV
Carr, Martin: WETA
Carrick, Kenneth: C–SPAN
Carrillo, Silvio: CNN
Carroll, Patricia: CNN
Carroll, Sally: Aljazeera International
Carson, Charles: WTTG–Fox Television
Carter, Brianne: WJLA–TV/Newschannel 8
Carter, Christopher: CNN
Carter, Jr., Walter: Fox News
Cartwright, Robert: WJLA–TV/Newschannel 8
Casanas, Juan: Fox News
Casey, Sean: WRC–TV/NBC–4
Cassano, Joseph Angelo: East Coast Television
Cassidy, David: Belo Capital Bureau
Castellaro, Nick: Aljazeera International
Castiel, Carol: Voice of America
Castner, Edward: German TV ARD
Castrilli, Anthony M.: WUSA–TV
Catanza, Damian: CNN
Cater, Franklyn: National Public Radio
Catrett, David Keith: CNN
Causey, Mike: Federal News Radio AM 1050
Cavin, Anthony: CBS News
Cawley, Kevin: Aljazeera International
Cecil, Brenda: Deutsche Welle TV
Centanni, Steve: Fox News
Cetta, Denise: CBS News
Chaboudez, Patrick: Swiss Broadcasting
Chaggaris, Steven: CBS News
Chalian, David: ABC News
Chamberlain, Richard: Tribune Broadcasting
Champ, Henry: Canadian Broadcasting Canada (CBC)
Chan, Enoch: Voice of America
Chang, Darzen: WETA
Chang, Ellen: WTTG–Fox Television
Chang, Min: New Tang Dynasty TV
Chang, Peggy: Voice of America
Chang, Wen-Hsiang: ETTV
Changuris, Zeke: WJLA–TV/Newschannel 8
Channell, Warren: CNN
Chapman, Irwin: Bloomberg Radio & TV
Chapman, Maria: Aljazeera International
Chappell, Jill: CNN
Charbonneau, Melissa A.: CBN News
Charlip, Lou: Viewpoint Communications
Charner, Flora: AP–Broadcast
Charters, Nadia: Al Arabiya TV
Chase, David: Cox Broadcasting
Chattman, Tanya: C–SPAN
Chaudhry, Humayun: Aljazeera Satellite Channel (Peninsula)
Chavez, Roby: WTTG–Fox Television
Chaytor, David: WUSA–TV
Chen, I-Fang: WTOP Radio
Chen, Joie: CBS News
Chen, Sylvia: Radio Free Asia
Chen, Yi Qiu: Phoenix Satellite Television
Chenevey, Steve: WTTG–Fox Television
Cheng, Yuwen: Voice of America
Chernenkoff, Kelly: Fox News
Cherouny, Robert: Freelance
Cherquis, Gustavo: WZDC–TV
Cheval, Stephanie: France 2 Television
Chevez, Carlos M: National Public Radio
Chiang, Ching-Yi: Public Television Service–Taiwan
Chicca, Trish: CNN
Chick, Jane S.: CBS News
Childress, Jennifer: FDCH/E–Media, Inc.
Childs, Lete: The Newshour with Jim Lehrer
Chimes, Art: Voice of America
Ching, Nike: Broadcasting Corp. of China
Chophel, Lobsang: Radio Free Asia
Chow, Lisa: National Public Radio
Chrisinger, Travis Renee: Freelance
Christian, George: CBS News
Chung, E-Ting: CTI–TV (Taiwan)
Chung, Tina: Formosa TV
Church, James: WJLA–TV/Newschannel 8
Cilberti, David: CNN
Cinque, Vicente: TV Globo International
Claar, Matthew: C–SPAN
Clancy, Martin J.: ABC News
Clapman, Leah: The Newshour with Jim Lehrer
Clark, James: C–SPAN
Clark, Theodore E.: National Public Radio
Clark, Thomas: Freelance
Clark, Tom: CTV Canadian TV
Clarkson, Russ: The Newshour with Jim Lehrer
Clemann, William: WUSA–TV
Clemons, Bobby: CNN
Clogston, Juanita: Freelance
Cloherty, Jack: NBC News
Clow, Julie: Canadian Broadcasting Canada (CBC)
Clugston, Gregory: SRN News (Salem)
Clune, Sarah: The Newshour with Jim Lehrer
Cobetto, Jaqueline: Fox News

MEMBERS ENTITLED TO ADMISSION—Continued

Cochran, John: ABC News
Cockerham, Richard: Fox News
Cocklin, Anne: Freelance
Cocklin, Stephen: Freelance
Codispoti, Alika: To The Contrary (Persephone Productions)
Coffey-Lambert, Claudia: WTTG–Fox Television
Coffman, Mary: Medill News Service
Cofske, Harvey: Irish Radio & TV (RTE)
Cohan, Stacey Lynn: Freelance
Cohen, Stuart: BBC
Colby, Alfred: CBS News
Cole, Bryan: Fox News
Cole, Tom: National Public Radio
Coleman, Korva: National Public Radio
Coleman, Major: NBC News
Coleman, Steven: AP–Broadcast
Coleman, Thomas: Freelance
Coles, David: The Newshour with Jim Lehrer
Colimore, Eric: Fox News
Coll, Dennis: National Public Radio
Collender, Howard: Mobile Video Services, LTD
Collingwood, Eloise: C–SPAN
Collins, Bruce D.: C–SPAN
Collins, Maxine: BBC
Collins, Michael: Voice of America
Collins, Nicole: WJLA–TV/Newschannel 8
Collins, Pat: WRC–TV/NBC–4
Colson, Allison: CNN
Colton, Michael: Canadian Broadcasting Canada (CBC)
Compton, Gregory: Hearst–Argyle Television
Compton, Woodrow: CNN
Conan, Neal: National Public Radio
Conatser, Cynthia: NBC Newschannel
Concaugh Jr., Joseph: Diversified Communications, Inc. (DCI)
Condemaita, Neisa: Azteca America
Coney, Carol: Freelance
Conlin, Sheila: NBC Newschannel
Conner, Cheryl: WJLA–TV/Newschannel 8
Conner, Eric: Fox News
Connolly, Camille: Freelance
Connors, Ben: Aljazeera International
Conover, William: C–SPAN
Conrad, Jacob: National Public Radio
Conrad, Monique: Freelance
Contreras, Felix J.: National Public Radio
Contreras, Glenda: Telemundo Network
Contreras, Jorge: Univision
Cook, James L.: C–SPAN
Cook, Peter: Bloomberg Radio & TV
Cook, Stefanie: FDCH/E–Media, Inc.
Cook, Theresa E.: ABC News
Cooke, David M.: Freelance
Coolidge, Richard L.: ABC News
Coolman, Carla: Voice of America
Coomarasamy, James: BBC
Cooper, Anderson: CNN
Cooper, Caroline: CBS News
Cooper, John: Freelance
Cooper, Rebecca J.: WJLA–TV/Newschannel 8
Coorlim, Leif: WTTG–Fox Television
Copeland, Jeremy: Aljazeera International
Corcoran, Patricia: WTTG–Fox Television
Corke, Kevin: NBC News
Corner, Cleve: C–SPAN
Correa, Lina: Caracol Television
Correa, Pedro: Telemundo Network
Correro, Michael: Aljazeera International
Cortez, William: Freelance
Costantini, Bob: Freelance
Costello, Casey: Channel One News
Costello, Thomas: NBC News
Cote, Timothy: Freelance
Cothren, Timothy: Freelance
Cotterman, Christina: WJLA–TV/Newschannel 8
Coudoux, Sylvain: NHK–Japan Broadcasting Corporation
Coulter, Pam: ABC News
Courbois, Jean Paul: Diversified Communications, Inc. (DCI)
Courson, Paul: CNN
Cowman, Chris: East Coast Television
Cox, Alexis: The Newshour with Jim Lehrer
Cox, Jerry: Freelance
Coyte, Benjamin: CNN
Craca, Thomas: Freelance
Craig, John: Freelance
Cratty, Carol A.: CNN
Cravedi, Dennis: C–SPAN
Craven, William C.: National Public Radio
Crawford, Walter: WJLA–TV/Newschannel 8
Crawford Greenburg, Jan: ABC News
Crawley, Plummer: CNBC
Cremen, Carolyn: WJLA–TV/Newschannel 8
Cridland, Jeffrey: WUSA–TV
Crmaric, Zorz: Voice of America
Crosariol, Paul: Potomac Television
Cross, Tiffany: BET Nightly News
Crowley, Candy: CNN
Crowley, Dennis: United News and Information
Crowson, Rachel Roberts: Metro Networks
Croyle, Erin: Aljazeera International
Crum, John: CBS News
Crutchfield, Curtis: Community TV of PG'S
Crystal, Lester: The Newshour with Jim Lehrer
Cuddy, Matthew: CNBC
Culhane, Max: ABC News
Culhane, Patricia: Freelance
Cullen, Michael: National Public Radio
Cunha, John: CNN
Cuong, Pham Gia: CBS News
Curran, Patrick J.: Freelance
Currier, Liam: C–SPAN
Curry, Thomas: NBC News

MEMBERS ENTITLED TO ADMISSION—Continued

Curtis, Alexander: C–SPAN
Curtis, Jodie: Fox News
Czapliniski, Michael: National Public Radio
Czzowitz, Greg: C–SPAN
Dahl, Heather: Fox News
Dalbah, Mohammad: Aljazeera Satellite Channel (Peninsula)
Dalmasy, Patricia: Voice of America
Daly, John: CBS News
D'Amico, Danny: AP–Broadcast
D'Angelo, Sara: WTOP Radio
Daniels, Brady: NBC News
Daniels, Pete: C–SPAN
Danilko, Derek: Tribune Broadcasting
Dann, Carrie: NBC News
d'Annibale, Thomas J.: ABC News
Dao, Thao: Radio Free Asia
Dargakis, Minas: Voice of America
Darias, Caesar: Tribune Broadcasting
Daschle, Kelly: AP–Broadcast
Date, Jack: ABC News
Daugherty, Jeffery: Voice of America
Davalos-Macdonald, Anna: AP–Broadcast
Davenport, Anne: The Newshour with Jim Lehrer
David, Michael R. M.: CNN
Davie, Bianca: Bloomberg Radio & TV
Davieaud, Helene: TF1–French TV
Davis, Charles: Capitol News Connection (CNC)
Davis, Clinton: Freelance
Davis, Edward ''Teddy'': ABC News
Davis, Jennifer: Freelance
Davis, Marcus: CNN
Davis, Mitch: Fox News
Davis, Patrick A.: CNN
Davis, Rebecca: National Public Radio
Davis, Shoshana: Freelance
Davis O'Keefe, Allison: CBS News
Dawson, Charlie: CBS News
De Chalvron, Alain: France 2 Television
de Guise, Louis: Canadian Broadcasting Canada (CBC)
De Luca, Renee: Channel One News
de Nies, Yunji Elisabeth: ABC News
de Oliveira, Pablo: Hispanic Communications Network
de Schaetzen, Emilie: Eurovision Americas, Inc.
de Vega, Carlos: CNN
Deal, Richard: C–SPAN
Dean, Antoinette: The Newshour with Jim Lehrer
Debre, Guillaume: TF1–French TV
Decker, Jonathan: US Radio Network
DeFrank, Debra: Fox News
DeGray, Clifford E.: ABC News
Delargy, Christine: NBC News
Deluca, Tim: WUSA–TV
DeMar, Brian: National Public Radio
DeMarco, Lauren: WTTG–Fox Television
Demarest, Sarah: NBC News
Demas, William: Diversified Communications, Inc. (DCI)
Demchak, Craig: Sinclair Broadcast Group
Denise, Li: CBS News
Denison, Jeremy: CBN News
Dennert, Mary Pat: Fox News
Densmore, Steven: ABC News
Dentzer, Susan: The Newshour with Jim Lehrer
Deputy, William: National Public Radio
DePuyt, Bruce: WJLA–TV/Newschannel 8
DeSantis, Dominic: ABC News
DeSimone, Bridget: The Newshour with Jim Lehrer
Dessert, Tristan: TF1–French TV
Detrow, Jon: AP–Broadcast
Devereaux, Angela: WJLA–TV/Newschannel 8
DeVito, Andrea: Fox News
Dhindsa, Gurvir: WTTG–Fox Television
Dhue, Stephanie: Nightly Business Report
Dhuy, Hans Peter: Finnish Broadcasting Company (YLE)
Diakides, Anastasia: CNN
Diamond, Aaron: France 2 Television
Diamond, Rebecca: WUSA–TV
Diarra, Fatou: BBC
DiBella, Rick: CNN
Dickerson, Vilinda: CNN
Dietrich, Geoffrey: CNN
Diggs, Bridget: C–SPAN
Diller, Jeremy: Freelance
Dillon, H. Estel: NBC Newschannel
Dimmler, Erika: CNN
Dimsdale, John: Marketplace Radio
Dirner, Elizabeth C.: ABC News
Disselkamp, Henry: ABC News
Dittman, John F.: ABC News
Dittmer, Bryan: Freelance
Diviney, Sue: CNN
Dixon Gumm, Penny: Voice of America
Dixson, Charles H.: CBS News
Djordjevic, Bratislav: Voice of America
Djordjevic, Helena: Voice of America
Doane, Martin C.: WJLA–TV/Newschannel 8
Dobhal, Deepak: Voice of America
Doebele, Constance: C–SPAN
Doell, Michelle: C–SPAN
Doergeloh, Uwe: German TV ZDF
Doherty, Brian: Fox News
Doherty, Peter M.: ABC News
Dolce, Stephen: CNN
Dolma, Dawa: Radio Free Asia
Dolma, Rigdhen: Radio Free Asia
Donaghy, Nina: Fox News
Donald, William: Viewpoint Communications
Donelan, Jennifer: WJLA–TV/Newschannel 8
Donnelly, Julie: Feature Story News
Donovan, Brian: ABC News
Donovan, Christopher: NBC News
Donovan, Pamela: Freelance

MEMBERS ENTITLED TO ADMISSION—Continued

Dooley, Christine: Bloomberg Radio & TV
Dorcil, Cherubin: Voice of America
Dore, Margaret: Freelance
Dorjee, Karma: Radio Free Asia
Dorning, Courtney: National Public Radio
Doshi, Nishith: Tribune Broadcasting
Dougherty, Danny: STATELINE.ORG
Dougherty, Jill: CNN
Dougherty, Mark: WUSA–TV
Dougherty, Martin: CNN
Dougherty, Paul G.: Freelance
Douglas, Dianna: National Public Radio
Downer, Carlton: CNN
Downey, Truval: The Newshour with Jim Lehrer
Doyle, Geoffrey: NBC News
Dozier, Kimberly: CBS News
Drake, Ingrid: Free Speech Radio News
Drosjack, Melissa: Fox News
Drumm, Lawrence L.: ABC News
Dubase, Manelisi: Feature Story News
Dubinsky, Inna: Voice of America
Dubinsky, Vladimir: National Public Radio
Dubroff, Richard: C–SPAN
Duck, Jennifer: ABC News
Dugge, Marc O.: German Broadcasting Systems–ARD
Duitch, David: Belo Capital Bureau
Dumpe, Megan: Fox News
Dunaway, John: CNN
Duncan, Michael J: Potomac Radio News
Duncan, Robert: National Public Radio
Duncan, Victoria: NBC News
Dunlavey, Thomas: CNN
Dunlop, William: Eurovision Americas, Inc.
Dunn, Katia: National Public Radio
Dunn, Lauren: WJLA–TV/Newschannel 8
Dupree, Jamie: Cox Radio
Durham, Deborah: Univision
Durham, Lisa: CNN
Durham, Timothy: Aljazeera International
Durkin, Edward: WRC–TV/NBC–4
Dwyer, George: Voice of America
Dyball, Kenneth: C–SPAN
Eades, Jr, Paul: C–SPAN
Eagle, William: Voice of America
Earnest, Jerry: Voice of America
Eaton, Hugh M.: National Public Radio
Ebitty-Doro, Estelle: AP–Broadcast
Eborn, Katrice: C–SPAN
Echevarria, Pedro L.: C–SPAN
Echols, Jerry: Fox News
Eck, Christina: Deutsche Press Agency
Eckert, Barton: Freelance
Eckert, Jessica: Hearst–Argyle Television
Edmond, Danaj: Freelance
Edmondson, William: Fox News
Edwards, Brian: Freelance
Edwards, Catherine: National Public Radio
Ehrenberg, Richard: ABC News
Eiras, Arlene: Freelance
Eisele, Kitty: National Public Radio
Eisenbarth, Ronald: C–SPAN
El Masry, Faiza: Voice of America
Elbadry, Hanan H.: Egyptian TV
Elders, Sarah: Fox News
Eldridge, James W.: Fox News
Eldridge, Mercedes: FDCH/E–Media, Inc.
Eldridge, Michael: FDCH/E–Media, Inc.
Elfa, Albert: TV3–Televisio De Catalunya
El-Hamalawy, Mahmoud: Aljazeera Satellite Channel (Peninsula)
Elhassani, Camille: Aljazeera International
Elizondo, Gabriel: Aljazeera International
Elkins, Brenda: Aljazeera International
Ellard, Nancy: NBC Newschannel
Ellena, Peter: National Public Radio
Ellenwood, Gary: C–SPAN
Ellerson, Margaret: ABC News
Elliott-Taylor, Debbie: National Public Radio
Elliot-Williams, Ethan: Freelance
Ellis, Neal: National Public Radio
Elmurr, Jessy: Aljazeera Satellite Channel (Peninsula)
Elnour, Waiel: AP–Broadcast
Elsewaify, Mirona Mohamed: Freelance
Elvington, Daniel Glenn: ABC News
Emanuel, Mike: Fox News
Emery, Edie: CNN
Empey, Duane: Freelance
Enciu, Edward: C–SPAN
Engel, Seth: C–SPAN
Engelberg, Matthew: The Newshour with Jim Lehrer
Engvist, Benita: Finnish Broadcasting Company (YLE)
Epatko, Larisa: The Newshour with Jim Lehrer
Epstein, Steve: Freelance
Erbe, Bonnie: To The Contrary (Presephone Productions)
Ernst, Manuel: Freelance
Espinoza, Cholene: Talk Radio News Service
Esquivel, Patricia: C–SPAN
Evans, Kendall A.: ABC News
Evans, Laura: WTTG–Fox Television
Evans, Markham: WJLA–TV/Newschannel 8
Everly, Tom: Freelance
Evstatieva, Monika: National Public Radio
Fabian, Kathleen: CNN
Fabic, Greg: C–SPAN
Facal, Luis: Voice of America
Fagen, Joel: Fox News
Faison, Al: Freelance
Fakhry, Ghida: Aljazeera International
Falls, John: CBS News
Falvella-Garraty, Susan: CNN
Fang, Sabrina: Tribune Broadcasting
Fant, Barbara: NBC News

MEMBERS ENTITLED TO ADMISSION—Continued

Fantacone, John L.: CBS News
Farid, Mahtab: Voice of America
Farkas, Daniel: Middle East Television Network (Alhurra)
Farkas, Mark: C–SPAN
Farley, Jennifer: CNN
Farmer, Scott: Freelance
Farnum, Douglas: NBC News
Farrell, Kathryn: Channel One News
Farzam, Parichehr: Voice of America
Fattahi, Kambiz: BBC
Fauntleroy, Julius Dumarr: WETA
Faure, Sebastien: Swiss Broadcasting
Faw, Robert: NBC News
Fay, Mary Beth: NBC News
Feather, Rich: Ventana Productions
Federico, Hector: Voice of America
Feeney, Susan: National Public Radio
Feist, Sam: CNN
Feldman, Randy: Viewpoint Communications
Fendley, Gail: Religion & Ethics Newsweekly
Fendrick, Anne-Marie: NHK–Japan Broadcasting Corporation
Fennell, Dionne: Aljazeera International
Fenwick, William: Free Speech Radio News
Ferder, Bruce: Voice of America
Feria, Liza: Reuters Radio & TV
Ferrigno, Tony: WJLA–TV/Newschannel 8
Fessehaye, Adanech: Voice of America
Fessler, Pam: National Public Radio
Fetzer, Robert: Diversified Communications, Inc. (DCI)
Fiedler, Maureen: Interfaith Voices
Fiedler, Stephan: German TV ARD
Fiegel, Eric James: CNN
Field, Rebecca: Potomac Television
Fields, Matthew: NBC News
Fielman, Sheldon: NBC News
Fierro, Juan Martinez: Cope Radio (SPAIN)
Figura, John: Freelance
Finamore, Charles: ABC News
Finch, Mark: Fox News
Fincher, Leta Hong: Voice of America
Fingar, Craig: CNN
Fink, Amy: WJLA–TV/Newschannel 8
Finkel, Ben: Viewpoint Communications
Finland, Alexander: Fox News
Finn, Trevor: Bloomberg Radio & TV
Finney, Richard: Radio Free Asia
Fischer, Elizabeth: NBC News
Fishel, Justin: Fox News
Fitzgerald, Tom: WTTG–Fox Television
Fitzmaurice, Frank: WETA
Fitzpatrick, Craig: Voice of America
Flaherty, James: CNN
Flaherty, Linsday: Mobile Video Services, LTD
Flanagan, Danielle: WUSA–TV
Fleeson, Richard: C–SPAN
Fleming, Bon: Nippon TV Network
Fleming, Eileen: AP–Broadcast
Fletcher, Robley: CNN
Flintoff, Corey: National Public Radio
Flood, Randolph: Native American Television
Flores, Cesar: BT Video Productions
Flynn, Liz: CNN
Flynn, Michael: WUSA–TV
Flynn, Michael Francis: WRC–TV/NBC–4
Flynn, Robert: The Newshour with Jim Lehrer
Fogarty, Kevin: Reuters Radio & TV
Fogarty, Patrick: AP–Broadcast
Forcucci, Michael: WJLA–TV/Newschannel 8
Ford, Michael: Freelance
Ford, Sam: WJLA–TV/Newschannel 8
Foreman, Thomas: CNN
Forman, David: NBC News
Forrest, Kerri Lyn: NBC News
Forsyth, Robert: WJLA–TV/Newschannel 8
Forte, B.J.: WTTG–Fox Television
Foster, Carl: C–SPAN
Foster, Scott: NBC News
Foster, Tom: Freelance
Foster Mathewson, Lesli: WUSA–TV
Foty, Tom: Freelance
Foukara, Abderrahim: Aljazeera Satellite Channel (Peninsula)
Fouladvand, Hida: CNN
Foundas, John: WTTG–Fox Television
Fowler, Kathy: WJLA–TV/Newschannel 8
Fowler, Maria: Gannett News Service
Fowler, Tom: Fox News
Fowlin, Joy: To The Contrary (Presephone Productions)
Fox, David: Freelance
Fox, Janet: WUSA–TV
Fox, Jason Erik: Freelance
Fox, Michael: Aljazeera Satellite Channel (Peninsula)
Fox, Peggy: WUSA–TV
Fox, Peter: Reuters Radio & TV
Frado, John: CBS News
Frame, John: WTTG–Fox Television
Francis, Julion: Freelance
Franco, Brian: WUSA–TV
Frank, Angela Kelly: WTTG–Fox Television
Frankel, Bruce: TF1–French TV
Franken, Robert: CNN
Franklin, Deborah: National Public Radio
Fraser, Wilfred: NBC News
Frazier, William: C–SPAN
Freeland, Eric: AP–Broadcast
Frei, Matt: BBC
French, Patrick: Freelance
Friar, David J.: AP–Broadcast
Fridrich, George: Freelance
Frieden, Terry: CNN
Friedman, Dave: Freelance

MEMBERS ENTITLED TO ADMISSION—Continued

Friend-Daniel, Kenya: CNN
Friess, John: Freelance
Frisketti, Anthony: Aljazeera International
Fritz, Mike: NBC News
Frost, Lovisa: Talk Radio News Service
Fry, Jim: Voice of America
Fuchs, Joanne: CNBC
Fullwood, Adrian: AP–Broadcast
Fulton, Bradley: CTV Canadian TV
Furlow, Tony: CBS News
Furman, Hal E.: CBS News
Fuss, Brian: CBS News
Fuss, Robert J.: CBS News
Futrowsky, David: Fox News
Fyanes, Jo Ann Marie: Freelance
Gabala, Rick: C–SPAN
Gabriel, Oscar Wells: AP–Broadcast
Gacka, Monica: Fox News
Gaetano, Lawrence: NBC News
Gaffney, Dennis: Freelance
Gaffney, Matthew: WTTG–Fox Television
Gafner, Randall: Freelance
Gailey, Gretchen: Freelance
Galdabini, Christian: Freelance
Galey, Travis: Tribune Broadcasting
Gallagher, John: C–SPAN
Gallagher, Joseph: Voice of America
Gallasch, Hillery: Deutsche Welle TV
Gallo, Dan: Fox News
Gamble, Hadley: Fox News
Gangel, Jamie: NBC News
Ganz, Jacob: National Public Radio
Garcez, Bruno: BBC
Garcia, Gina: NBC News
Garcia, Guillermo: Reuters Radio & TV
Garcia, Joe: Fox News
Garcia, Jon D.: ABC News
Garcia, Robert G.: ABC News
Gardella, Richard: NBC News
Garg, Maya: Aljazeera International
Garifo, Stephen: WUSA–TV
Garlikov, Lydia: CNN
Garlock, John: C–SPAN
Garner, Jean: Aljazeera International
Garraty, Timothy C.: CNN
Garrett, Major: Fox News
Garske, Jennifer: AP–Broadcast
Garvin, Keith: WRC–TV/NBC–4
Gary, Garney: C–SPAN
Gaskin, Keith: NBC News
Gassman, Mara: CNN
Gato, Pablo: Telemundo Network
Gauss, Martina: Freelance
Gautam, Maurya: Aljazeera International
Gauthier, Arthur R.: ABC News
Gavin, Greg: National Public Radio
Gawad, Atef: Freelance
Gebhardt, William: NBC News
Geimann, Steve: Bloomberg Radio & TV
Geldon, Ben: Bloomberg Radio & TV
Geleschun, Uwe: German TV ARD
Gelles, David: NBC News
Gelman, Micah: AP–Broadcast
Gembara, Deborah: Reuters Radio & TV
Gentilo, Richard: AP–Broadcast
Gentry, Pamela: BET Nightly News
Gentry, Robert: TV ASAHI
George, Maurice: CNN
George, Paviithra: Reuters Radio & TV
Gergely, Valer: Voice of America
Gersh, Darren: Nightly Business Report
Geyelin, Philip: Freelance
Giammetta, Max: WTTG–Fox Television
Gibbons, Gavin: Fox News
Gibbons, Sarah: Eurovision Amerricas, Inc.
Gibson, Charles DeWolf: ABC News
Gibson, Jake: Fox News
Gibson, Jenna: Fox News
Gibson, Sheri Lynn: NBC Newschannel
Giebel, Edward Adam: Freelance
Gilardoni, Diego: Swiss Broadcasting
Gilbert, Sarah: BBC
Gilgannon, Pege: WJLA–TV/Newschannel 8
Gillette, David: WETA
Gilliam, Dirk: Freelance
Gillis, Gary: Fox News
Gilman, Jeff: WTTG–Fox Television
Gilmore, John: CNN
Ginsburg, Benson: CBS News
Giusto, Thomas M.: ABC News
Gjelten, Tom: National Public Radio
Glass, Evan: CNN
Glassman, Matt: WRC–TV/NBC–4
Gleason, Norma: C–SPAN
Gleaton, Oji: WJLA–TV/Newschannel 8
Glennon, John: Freelance
Glover-James, Ian: Independent Television News (ITN)
Glynn, William: NBC Newschannel
Gmiter, Bernard: ABC News
Goddard, Andre: CNN
Goddard, Lisa: CNN
Godoy, Maria: National Public Radio
Godsick, Andrew L.: NBC Newschannel
Gold, Lawrence: AP–Broadcast
Gold, Peter: Fuji TV Japan
Goldberg, Jennifer: ABC News
Goldfein, Michael: Belo Capital Bureau
Goldman, David: Community TV of PG'S
Goldman, Jeff Scott: CBS News
Goler, Wendell: Fox News
Golimowski, Jeff: CNSNEWS.COM
Golloher, Jessica: Wamu
Gombakombra, Caroline: Voice of America
Gomes, Karina: Aljazeera International

MEMBERS ENTITLED TO ADMISSION—Continued

Gomez, Augusto: Freelance
Gomez, Juan Carlos: National Public Radio
Gomez, Serafin: Fox News
Gonsar, Dhondup Namgyal: Radio Free Asia
Gonyea, Don: National Public Radio
Gonzalez, Antonio R.: Freelance
Gonzalez, Carlos: WTTG–Fox Television
Gonzalez, Julio: Hispanic Communications Network
Gonzalez, Liliana: CNN
Goodknight, Charles A: WRC–TV/NBC–4
Goodman, Jeffrey: Freelance
Goodwin, Sue: National Public Radio
Gorbutt, Richard: WUSA–TV
Gordemer, Barry: National Public Radio
Gordon, Herbert: Freelance
Gordon, Stuart: ABC News
Gorman, James W.: AP–Broadcast
Gorsky, Edward: NBC News
Gottlieb, Brian: The Newshour with Jim Lehrer
Gould, Robert: C–SPAN
Gourley, Meghan: C–SPAN
Gousha, Elizabeth: CNN
Gracey, David: CNN
Gradison, Robin: ABC News
Gram, Steffen William: Danish Broadcasting Corporation
Gramlich, John P.: STATELINE.ORG
Granda, Marco: Venezuela TV
Granena, Marc: Eurovision Americas, Inc.
Grant, Neva: National Public Radio
Grasso, Neil: CBS News
Graves, Lindsay: Freelance
Gray, James: CNN
Gray, Melissa: National Public Radio
Graydon, James: CNN
Grayson, Gisele: National Public Radio
Grayson, Tim: National Public Radio
Green, Jessie J.: WTOP Radio
Green, Lauren: Channel One News
Green, Sheila: Reuters Radio & TV
Greenaway, Steve: Potomac Television
Greenback, William: Voice of America
Greenbaum, Adam: NBC Newschannel
Greenberger, Jonathan: ABC News
Greenblatt, Larry: Viewpoint Communications
Greene, David: National Public Radio
Greene, James M.: NBC News
Greene, Thomas: CNN
Greenspon, Dana: Nightly Business Report
Greenwood, John K.: Freelance
Gregory, David: NBC News
Greiner, Nicholas P.: Freelance
Griffin, George: The Newshour with Jim Lehrer
Griffin, Jennifer: Fox News
Grifitts, William: Mobile Video Services, LTD
Grigg, Rex: CNN
Grimes, Sanford: Metro Teleproductions
Groome, Marsha: NBC News
Gross, Andrew F.: NBC News
Gross, David: CBS News
Gross, Josh: CBS News
Gross, Jr., Eddie S.: CNN
Grossman, David: Talk Radio News Service
Groves, Thomas: CNN
Grzech, Cherie: Fox News
Guastadisegni, Richard: WJLA–TV/Newschannel 8
Gudenkauf, Anne: National Public Radio
Guest, Frank: Federal News Service
Guise, Gregory: WUSA–TV
Gural, Kathleen: East Coast Television
Gursky, Gregg L.: Fox News
Guthrie, Savannah: Court TV
Gutmann, Hanna: Washington Radio and Press Service
Gutnikoff, Robert: AP–Broadcast
Guzman, Armando: Azteca America
Guzman, Roberto: Azteca America
Gwadz, Joel: CBS News
Gyal, Palden: Radio Free Asia
Ha, Gwen: Radio Free Asia
Haan, Mike: CNN
Habbick, Alan: Canadian Broadcasting Canada (CBC)
Habermann, Claudette: National Public Radio
Haberstick, Fred: Fox News
Habib, Elias: Al Arabiya TV
Haddad, Tammy: NBC News
Haefeli, Brian: Fox News
Hager, Mary: CBS News
Hager, Nathan: WTOP Radio
Hagerty, Michael E.: WJLA–TV/Newschannel 8
Haggerty, Patrick: This Week in Agribusiness (RFD–TV)
Hahn, Jay: Eurovision Americas, Inc.
Hahn, Stephen: ABC News
Hakel, Peter: WJLA–TV/Newschannel 8
Halkett, Kimberly: Aljazeera International
Hall, Randy: CNSNEWS.COM
Hall, Richard: C–SPAN
Haller, Sylvia: NBC News
Hamberg, Steve: Viewpoint Communications
Hamby, Peter: CNN
Hamilton, Christopher: Middle East Television Network (Alhurra)
Hamilton, Jay: Hamilton Productions, Inc.
Hamilton, Jon: National Public Radio
Hamilton, Valerie: Freelance
Hammons, Cheryl: East Coast Television
Hampton, Cheryl: National Public Radio
Han, Carol: Cox Broadcasting
Handel, Sarah: National Public Radio
Handelsman, Steve: NBC Newschannel
Handleman, Michelle: CBS News
Haning, Evan: WTOP Radio
Hanley, Patricia: Religion & Ethics Newsweekly
Hanneman, Kirk: Federal News Service

MEMBERS ENTITLED TO ADMISSION—Continued

Hanner, Mark: CBS News
Hansen, Eric: C–SPAN
Hansen, Liane: National Public Radio
Hanson, Chris: C–SPAN
Hanson, David: NBC News
Harding, Claus: Freelance
Hardy, Arthur: Freelance
Hardymon, Barrie: National Public Radio
Harkness, Stephen: C–SPAN
Harlan, Jeremy: CNN
Harleston, Robb: C–SPAN
Harmon, Predi-Reko: CBS News
Harmon, Susan: CBS News
Harper, Benjamin: Medill News Service
Harper, Elizabeth: The Newshour with Jim Lehrer
Harper, Steve: Eurovision Amerricas, Inc.
Harris, Lanese: CNN
Harris, Richard: National Public Radio
Harris, Roy: Freelance
Hart, Peter: NBC News
Hartge, John: Freelance
Hartman, Brian Robert: ABC News
Harvey, Alan: NBC News
Harvey, Kinsey: C–SPAN
Harwood, John: CNBC
Haselton, Brennan: WTOP Radio
Hash, James: WUSA–TV
Hass, Thomas: Eurovision Amerricas, Inc.
Hassan, Alegra: CBN News
Hassett, Walter: Freelance
Hastings Wotring, Melanie: WJLA–TV/Newschannel 8
Hatch, William T.: ABC News
Hawk, James: Metro Networks
Hawke, Anne: National Public Radio
Hawkins, Shonty: WUSA–TV
Hayes, Bryan: Capitol News Connection (CNC)
Hayes, Monique: The Newshour with Jim Lehrer
Hayley, Harold ''Pat'': NBC News
Haynes, Mary: Channel One News
Haynes, Maurice: C–SPAN
Hays, Guerin: CNN
Hayward, Jacqueline: WUSA–TV
Haywood, Barry L.: Freelance
Headen, Gregory: Fox News
Healey, Sean: Freelance
Heaney, Vanessa: BBC
Hecht, Barry: Freelance
Heckman, Gary: The Washington Bureau
Heffley, William: C–SPAN
Heiner, Stephen: The Washington Bureau
Heinzman, Elaine: National Public Radio
Helm, Ronald G.: CNN
Helman, Jonathan: Freelance
Helton, Jason Kyle: National Public Radio
Henao, Liliana: WZDC–TV
Henderson, Shelley: FDCH/E–Media, Inc.
Henderson, Susan: AP–Broadcast
Hendin, Robert: CBS News
Hendren, John Edward: ABC News
Hendren, Karen: Freelance
Hendricks, Mark: CBN News
Henn, Stephen: Marketplace Radio
Henneberg, Mary Janne: Fox News
Henrehan, John: WTTG–Fox Television
Henry, Chas: WJLA–TV/Newschannel 8
Henry, Ed: CNN
Henry, Jonelle P.: C–SPAN
Herbas, Francis: Fox News
Heredia, Lourdes: BBC
Herrera, Esequiel: ABC News
Herrera, Ruben: German TV ZDF
Herridge, Catherine: Fox News
Hester, Deirdre: CBS News
Heyman, Leslye: C–SPAN
Hibbitts, Mi Jeong Y.: Voice of America
Hickey, Darby: Free Speech Radio News
Hickman, Stacy: Fox News
Hidaka, Masano: Diversified Communications, Inc. (DCI)
Hidaka, Yoshio: Diversified Communications, Inc. (DCI)
Higgins, Ricardo: Freelance
Higgins, Ricardo: NBC News
Hill, Benjamin F.: CNN
Hill, Dallas: C–SPAN
Hill, Lee: National Public Radio
Hinds, Hugh: Freelance
Hiney, Mark: BBC
Hino, Katsumi: Tokyo Broadcasting System
Hirzel, Conrad: CNN
Ho, King Man: Radio Free Asia
Ho, Stephanie: Voice of America
Hobson, Jeremy: Marketplace Radio
Hochman, Jordana: National Public Radio
Hoder, Shawn: WJLA–TV/Newschannel 8
Hoffman, Brian: AP–Broadcast
Hoffman, Jessica: The Newshour with Jim Lehrer
Hoffmaster, Bob: C–SPAN
Hofstad, Elizabeth H.: FDCH/E–Media, Inc.
Hogan, Kylie A.: ABC News
Holden, Michael: C–SPAN
Holland, Cameron: Fox News
Holland, John: NBC News
Holland, Sarah B.: CNN
Hollenbeck, Paul: BT Video Productions
Hollis, Michael: National Public Radio
Holman, Kwame: The Newshour with Jim Lehrer
Holmes, Horace: WJLA–TV/Newschannel 8
Holtschneider, Joseph: Mobile Video Services, LTD
Holzman, Todd: National Public Radio
Honhadze, Myroslava: Voice of America
Hooley, Gemma: National Public Radio
Hooper, Molly: Fox News
Hoover, Toni: Freelance
Hopkins, Adrienne Moira: Fox News

MEMBERS ENTITLED TO ADMISSION—Continued

Hopkins, Brian: WJLA–TV/Newschannel 8
Hopper, Dave: BBC
Hopper, Douglas: National Public Radio
Hoppock, Julia Kartalia: ABC News
Horan, Michael: WTTG–Fox Television
Horcajuelo, Inigo: Spanish Public Television (TVE)
Horn, Charles: Eye-To-Eye Video
Horne, LaTanya: WJLA–TV/Newschannel 8
Hosford, Matthew Alan: ABC News
Hotep, Amon: ABC News
Houston, Karen Gray: WTTG–Fox Television
Hovell, Bret: ABC News
Hovell, Dean G.: Freelance
Howard, Cory R.: Fox News
Howard, Jim: National Public Radio
Howard, Stephen: WETA
Howe, Martin: Capitol News Connection (CNC)
Howell, George: C–SPAN
Hoye, Matthew: CNN
Hristova, Rozalia: BBC
Hsieh, Yi-Pe: C–SPAN
Hsiung, Yahwa: Voice of America
Hssani, Nasser: Aljazeera Satellite Channel (Peninsula)
Hsu, Andrea: National Public Radio
Htike Oo, Thein: Voice of America
Htun, Kyaw Min: Radio Free Asia
Huang, Laura: Radio Free Asia
Hubert, Aja: WJLA–TV/Newschannel 8
Huckeby, Paul: Fox News
Hudson, Christian: CNN
Huebler, Ryan: WTTG–Fox Television
Huff, Dan: AP–Broadcast
Huff, Priscilla: Feature Story News
Hugel, Dave: CNN
Hughes, D.C.: Freelance
Hughes, James: Freelance
Hughes, Megan: Cox Broadcasting
Hume, Brit: Fox News
Humeau, Thierry: Aljazeera International
Hung, Shirley: CNN
Hunn, Johney Burke: National Public Radio
Hunt, Greg: Fox News
Hunter, Ryan: WUSA–TV
Hurley, Charles: CNN
Hurley, Karina: Hispanic Communications Network
Hurt, James: NBC Newschannel
Hurtado, Eugenia: Aljazeera International
Hussain, Samira: Canadian Broadcasting Canada (CBC)
Hutcherson, Trudy: Freelance
Hutchins, Argin: National Public Radio
Hutchinson, Heather: Freelance
Huyghe, Todd: Freelance
Hyater, John: WETA
Hyatt, George: Freelance
Hylton, Winston: WJLA–TV/Newschannel 8
Ide, Charles: WETA
Ifill, Gwen: The Newshour with Jim Lehrer
II, Tadayoshi: TV Asahi
Iida, Kaori: NHK–Japan Broadcasting Corporation
Iiyama, Laura: Feature Story News
Ikonomi, Ilir: Voice of America
Imaida, Aya: Nippon TV Network
Ing, Lance: WTTG–Fox Television
Ingram, Julian: Community TV of PG'S
Inoue, Hitoshi: TV Asahi
Inoue, Nami: Tokyo Broadcasting System
Inserra, Donna: Freelance
Inskeep, Steve: National Public Radio
Irby, Danyell: National Public Radio
Irvine, John: Independent Television News (ITN)
Irving, Terry: CNN
Irwin, Sarah: Freelance
Isaac, Monique: East Coast Television
Isenberg, Alan: CNN
Iverson, Matthew: Freelance
Jaakson, Uelle-Mall: Austrian Radio & TV (ORF)
Jaber, Bushra: Middle East Television Network (Alhurra)
Jackson, Craig: CNN
Jackson, Katharine: WJLA–TV/Newschannel 8
Jackson, Robert E.: National Public Radio
Jackson, Roberta: C–SPAN
Jackson, Ryan: Cox Broadcasting
Jackson, Samuel: WJLA–TV/Newschannel 8
Jackson, Taryn: C–SPAN
Jacobi, Steve: CBN News
Jacobs, Adia: CNN
Jacobs, Philip H.: WRC–TV/NBC–4
Jacobson, Murrey: The Newshour with Jim Lehrer
Jaconi, Michelle: NBC News
Jacques, Andree-Lyne: TF1–French TV
Jacques, Virg: WTTG–Fox Television
Jaffe, Gary: Voice of America
Jaffe, Matthew: ABC News
Jafri, Syed: Voice of America
Jaje, Joanne: NHK–Japan Broadcasting Corporation
James, Karen: CNBC
James, Thomas: WUSA–TV
Jamison, Dennis: CBS News
Jang, Myeong Hwa: Radio Free Asia
Jansen, Lesa: CNN
Japaridze, NuNu: CNN
Jarboe, Brian: National Public Radio
Jarvis, Julie: NBC Newschannel
Jean-Francois, Edvige: AP–Broadcast
Jeffries, Katherine: C–SPAN
Jenkins, David: CNN
Jenkins, Erin: BET Nightly News
Jenkins, Gene: CBN News
Jenkins, William G.: Fox News
Jennings, Alicia: NBC News
Jennings, Lori: Bloomberg Radio & TV
Jennings, Jr., Edward B.: Freelance
Jensen, Eric: Hearst–Argyle Television

MEMBERS ENTITLED TO ADMISSION—Continued

Jermin, Ede: WRC–TV/NBC–4
Jesenicnik, Vlasta: RTV Slovenija
Jeserich, Mitch: Pacifica Radio
Jessup, John: CBN News
Jibai, Wafaa: Middle East Television Network (Alhurra)
Jillani, Shazeb: BBC
Jimenez, Martin: Freelance
Jing, Hui: New Tang Dynasty TV
Johansson, Bjoem: East Coast Television
Johns, Joseph: CNN
Johnsen, Kyle: CNN
Johnson, Bruce: WUSA–TV
Johnson, Douglas: Voice of America
Johnson, Everett: NBC News
Johnson, Fletcher: ABC News
Johnson, Jennifer: NBC Newschannel
Johnson, Kenneth: ABC News
Johnson, Kevin: Cox Broadcasting
Johnson, Kia: Reuters Radio & TV
Johnson, Leroy: NBC News
Johnson, Paul: Freelance
Johnson, Richard: Fox News
Johnson, Rolanda: Freelance
Johnson, Sasha: CNN
Johnson, Stephanie: WTTG–Fox Television
Johnson, Wendy: National Public Radio
Johnson-McNeely, Helena: National Public Radio
Johnston, Derek Leon: ABC News
Johnston, Jeffrey: CBS News
Joneidi, Majid: BBC
Jones, Dave: Fox News
Jones, Gwyneth: NBC News
Jones, Kimberly: National Public Radio
Jones, Lauren: Fox News
Jones, Lyrone Steven: WTTG–Fox Television
Jones, Morris: Sinclair Broadcast Group
Jones, Nelson: WTTG–Fox Television
Jones, Shawn: Freelance
Jones, Torrance: Fox News
Jones, Victoria: Talk Radio News Service
Jordan, Darrell: Fox News
Joseph, Akilah N.: ABC News
Josipovic, Sasa: Aljazeera International
Jouffriault, Pascal: France 2 Television
Joy, Michael: Freelance
Joy, Richard: Ventana Productions
Joya, Steve E.: ABC News
Joyce, Christopher: National Public Radio
Joyner, Daniel: Freelance
Judge, Michael: CNN
Jung, Mark: Seoul Broadcasting System (SBS)
Kabbas, Abdelhakim: Freelance
Kalashyan, Lusine: Voice of America
Kalbfeld, Brad: AP–Broadcast
Kalbfleisch, Catherine: Aljazeera International
Kanat, Mehmet Omer: Radio Free Asia
Kanawati, Balajia: Al Arabiya TV
Kane, James F.: ABC News
Kanka, James: The Washington Bureau
Kaplan, Bill: Freelance
Kara-Murza, Vladimir: RTVI/ECHO–TV
Kargbo, Judith: Freelance
Karl, Jonathan: ABC News
Karson, Danielle: Wamu
Kastan, Klaus: German Public Radio (ARD)
Katkov, Mark: CBS News
Kato, Atsuchi: NHK–Japan Broadcasting Corporation
Katz, Barry: C–SPAN
Katz, Craig: CBS News
Katz, Jeffrey: National Public Radio
Katz, Nai Chian M.: Phoenix Satellite Television
Kay, Kathy: BBC
Kaye, Matthew: The Berns Bureau, Inc.
Kazama, Shin: Fuji TV Japan
Kearns, Kara: AP–Broadcast
Keator, John C.: National Public Radio
Keedy, Matthew: CBN News
Keeler, Desdemona: TV Asahi
Kehoe, Steven: C–SPAN
Keilar, Brianna: CNN
Kelemen, Michele: National Public Radio
Kelleher, Kristine: AP–Broadcast
Kellerman, Mike: ATN Productions, LTD
Kelley, Alice: German TV ZDF
Kelley, Bridget: National Public Radio
Kelley, Pamela: CNN
Kelly, Carol Anne Clark: National Public Radio
Kelly, Cristina: CNN
Kelly, Mary Louise: National Public Radio
Kelly, Sarah Beyer: National Public Radio
Kelly, Terence: Freelance
Kem, Sos: Radio Free Asia
Kenedy, Katherine: Potomac Television
Kenin, Justine: National Public Radio
Kennedy, Robert: C–SPAN
Kennedy, Suzanne: WJLA–TV/Newschannel 8
Kenny, Christopher: CNN
Kenny, Justin: Reuters Radio & TV
Kenworthy, Zachary: Fox News
Kenyon, Linda: SRN News (Salem)
Kerchner, Eric C.: Freelance
Kerley, David P.: ABC News
Kerpen, Mati: WJLA–TV/Newschannel 8
Kerr, Kristen: WUSA–TV
Kerr, Roxane: C–SPAN
Kessel, Michelle: NBC News
Kessler, Jonathan: Freelance
Kessler, Jonathan L.: Freelance
Kessler (Blumberg), Sarah: Fox News
Kestenbaum, David: National Public Radio
Ketcham, Lew: C–SPAN
Kettlewell, Christian: AP–Broadcast
Keyes, Allison: National Public Radio
Keyes, Charley: CNN

MEMBERS ENTITLED TO ADMISSION—Continued

Khader, Ibrahim: Aljazeera Satellite Channel (Peninsula)
Khalaf, Lina: Aljazeera International
Khalaf, Mysa: Aljazeera Satellite Channel (Peninsula)
Khallash, Affra: ATN Productions, LTD
Khallash, Taleb: ATN Productions, LTD
Khan, Riz: Aljazeera International
Khananayev, Grigory: Fox News
Khanna, Ravi: Voice of America
Kharel, Ram C.: Sagarmatha Television
Khawreen, M. Ayub: Voice of America
Khin, May: Radio Free Asia
Khine, Tin Aung: Radio Free Asia
Kidd, Sally F.: Hearst–Argyle Television
Kiernan, Ryan: NBC News
Kiker, Patrick: CBS News
Kilaru, Vandana: Freelance
Kill, Adrian: Freelance
Killion, Nikole: WJLA–TV/Newschannel 8
Kim, Annabel: MBC–TV Korea (Munhwa)
Kim, Jinkuk: WDCT Radio
Kim, Keunsam: Voice of America
Kim, Naeri: Radio Free Asia
Kim, Yonho: Radio Free Asia
Kim, Young-Kweon: Voice of America
Kimani, Julia: NBC News
Kimmel, Denise: CTV Canadian TV
King, Colleen: NBC News
King, Gregory: WETA
King, John: CNN
King, Kevin: C–SPAN
King, Kevin G.: WUSA–TV
King Lilleston, Kristi: WTOP Radio
Kinlaw, Worth: CNN
Kinney, George P.: CNN
Kinney, Laura: Hearst–Argyle Television
Kinney, Michael: Freelance
Kirk, Beverly: WJLA–TV/Newschannel 8
Kirtz-Garrett, Julie: Fox News
Kitanovska, Lilica: Voice of America
Kiver, Phillip: US Radio Network
Kiyasu, Adilson: CNN
Kizer, James S.: WRC–TV/NBC–4
Klayman, Elliot: Eye-To-Eye Video
Klein, Robert: Freelance
Klenk, Ann: NBC News
Klima, Bojan: Voice of America
Kline, Jeff: Hispanic Communications Network
Knapp, Timothy: Sinclair Broadcast Group
Knell, Yolande: BBC
Knight, Raynel: WJLA–TV/Newschannel 8
Knighton, David: C–SPAN
Knoller, Mark: CBS News
Knott, John: ABC News
Knuckles, Georgette: The Newshour with Jim Lehrer
Kobe, Kathryn: Need To Know News
Koch, Kathleen: CNN
Kodaka, Nami: NHK–Japan Broadcasting Corporation
Kohno, Kenji: NHK–Japan Broadcasting Corporation
Koike, Natsuko: Tokyo Broadcasting System
Kojovic, Predrag: Reuters Radio & TV
Kokufuda, Kaoru: Tokyo Broadcasting System
Kolodziejczak, Thomas: Tribune Broadcasting
Komatsu, Yoshiyaki: TV ASAHI
Konishi, Asuka: Nippon TV Network
Kono, Torao: NHK–Japan Broadcasting Corporation
Koolhof, Vanessa M.: WJLA–TV/Newschannel 8
Koppel, Andrea: CNN
Koprowicz, Tetiana: Voice of America
Korff, Jay: WJLA–TV/Newschannel 8
Kornely, Michael: Belo Capital Bureau
Kornely, Sharon: Medill News Service
Kornreich, Lauren: CNN
Korona, Elizabeth: Channel One News
Kos, Martin: BT Video Productions
Koslow, Marc: NBC News
Kosnar, Michael: NBC News
Koster, Susan: Voice of America
Kotke, Wolfgang: Deutsche Welle TV
Kotuby, Stephanie: CNN
Kovac, Christina: Freelance
Kovach, Robert S.: CNN
Kozel, Sandy: AP–Broadcast
Kraemer-Anderson, Dagmar: German Public Radio (ARD)
Krakower, Gary: CNN
Kreinbihl, Mary: Fox News
Kreindler, Virginia: NBC Newschannel
Kretman, Lester: NBC News
Kreuz, Greta: WJLA–TV/Newschannel 8
Kroll, Donald Eugene: ABC News
Kross, Kathryn: Bloomberg Radio & TV
Krupin, David: Freelance
Kruse, Jan Espen: Norwegian Broadcasting
Kube, Courtney: NBC News
Kubota, Suzanne: Federal News Radio AM 1050
Kuczynski, Ronald: CNN
Kuhar, Ivana: Voice of America
Kuhn, Steve: AP–Broadcast
Kuleta, Gene: Metro Networks
Kulkarni, Rohit: Voice of America
Kulsziski, Peter: Freelance
Kulycky, Maya C.: ABC News
Kumar, Aparna: C–SPAN
Kupper, Carmen: Freelance
Kupperman, Tamara: NBC News
Kurcias, Martin R.: National Public Radio
Kurtz, Judy: WJLA–TV/Newschannel 8
Kwan, Vivian: Radio Free Asia
Kwisnek, Stephanie: Freelance
Kwon, Jai Hong: MBC–TV Korea (Munhwa)
Kyaw, Zaw Moe: Radio Free Asia

MEMBERS ENTITLED TO ADMISSION—Continued

Kyaw Thein, Kyaw: Voice of America
Kyodo, Atsushi: Tokyo Broadcasting System
LaBella, Michael: Nightly Business Report
Labott, Elise: CNN
Laboy, Felix: C–SPAN
Lacey, Donna: Fox News
Lacore, Madeline: WUSA–TV
LaFollette, Marianna: Freelance
Lah, Kyung: CNN
Lamb, Brian: C–SPAN
Lambert, Brandon: Fuji TV Japan
Lambidakis, Stephanie: CBS News
Lamp, Kelly: WJLA–TV/Newschannel 8
Landay, Woodrow: Australian Broadcasting Corporation
Landers, Kim: Australian Broadcasting Corporation
Landphair, Ted: Voice of America
Lane, Christopher: WETA
Lane, Gregory: CNN
Lane, Krista: WJLA–TV/Newschannel 8
Lang, Jessica: Feature Story News
Langfitt, Frank: National Public Radio
Langguth, Dana: Aljazeera International
Langley, Larry: Freelance
Lanier, Peter: CNN
Lanningham, Kyle: Swedish Broadcasting
Lanza, Jessica: Middle East Television Network (Alhurra)
Lanzara, Catherine: WJLA–TV/Newschannel 8
Lapidus, Faith: Voice of America
Larade, Darren: C–SPAN
Larsen, Greg: Freelance
LaSalla, Susan: NBC News
Laslo, Matt: Freelance
Latremoliere, France: Freelance
Laughlin, Ara: Community TV of PG'S
Laughlin, James: Freelance
Laurent, Arthur: National Public Radio
Lavallee, Michael: Tokyo Broadcasting System
Lavietes, Bryan: Court TV
Laville, Molly: C–SPAN
Lawlor, William: WUSA–TV
Lawrence, John: Ventana Productions
Lawrence, Mary: WETA
Lawson, Sam: Freelance
Lawton, Kim: Religion & Ethics Newsweekly
Lazar, Robert: C–SPAN
Lazernik, Ira: WTTG–Fox Television
Lazo, Larry: CNN
Leake, Myron: Freelance
LeCroy, Philip: Fox News
Lee, Daniel N.: Radio Free Asia
Lee, Donald A.: CBS News
Lee, Dong Hyuk: Voice of America
Lee, Edward: WETA
Lee, Erik: WTTG–Fox Television
Lee, Jinsook: MBC–TV Korea (Munhwa)
Lee, Joong Wan: Korean Broadcasting Systems
Lee, Kyu Sang: Radio Free Asia
Leenknegt, Florence: Freelance
Lefebvre, Hilary: ABC News
Lege, Joey: East Coast Television
Legget, Dennis: Aljazeera International
LeGro, Tom: The Newshour with Jim Lehrer
Lehman, Russell: National Public Radio
Lehrer, Jim: The Newshour with Jim Lehrer
Lehrman, Margaret: NBC News
Leidelmeyer, Ronald: WRC–TV/NBC–4
Leiken, Katherine: Freelance
Leiner, Jon: Freelance
Leissner, Janet: CBS News
Leist, Elizabeth: NBC News
Leister, Meaghan: Fox News
LeMay, Gabriel: WJLA–TV/Newschannel 8
Lendzian, Kay: German TV ZDF
Lentz, Rudiger: Deutsche Welle TV
Leone, Amy: WUSA–TV
Leong, Dexter: Freelance
Leong, Ming: WJLA–TV/Newschannel 8
Leshan, Bruce: WUSA–TV
Lessin, Michael: Connectlive
Lester, Paul: WUSA–TV
Levi, Michelle: CBS News
Levin, Al: Diversified Communications, Inc. (DCI)
Levine, Adam: CNN
Levine, Michael: Fox News
Lewine, Frances L.: CNN
Lewinski, George: Feature Story News
Lewis, Aaron: CBS News
Lewis, Edward: Fox News
Lewis, Elliott: Freelance
Lewis, Jerry S.: WETA
Lewis, John B.: WJLA–TV/Newschannel 8
Lewis, Nelson: Fox News
Lewnes, Lisa: Reuters Radio & TV
Lewnes, Pericles: Middle East Television Network (Alhurra)
Li, Bing: Washington Chinese Television
Li, Tian: Radio Free Asia
Li, Wo Tak: Radio Free Asia
Liao, Xiao Qiang: Radio Free Asia
Liasson, Mara: National Public Radio
Libretto, John: NBC News
Licht, Christopher: NBC News
Lielischkies, Udo: German TV ARD
Lien, Arthur: NBC News
Lien, Jonathan: CBS News
Liffiton, Bruce: Freelance
Likowski, Alex: WJLA–TV/Newschannel 8
Lilling, Dave: Metro Teleproductions
Lim, Lister: AP–Broadcast
Lin, Chuan: New Tang Dynasty TV
Lincoln, Diane: The Newshour with Jim Lehrer
Lindblom, Mark: C–SPAN
Linden, Louis: Freelance
Linder, Matthew: Fox News

MEMBERS ENTITLED TO ADMISSION—Continued

Lingner, Tilman: Swiss Broadcasting
Lininger, Christian: Austrian Radio & TV (ORF)
Linker, Ron: NOS Dutch Public Radio & TV (VRT)
Liss, Sharon Kehnemui: Fox News
Lissit, Arleen: Freelance
Little, Craig: WTTG–Fox Television
Little, Jane: BBC
Little, Walter: Bloomberg Radio & TV
Littleton, Philip: CNN
Liu, Shou-lien: Washington Chinese Television
Liu, Ted: Radio Free Asia
Liu, Wei-Ming: Washington Chinese Television
Liu, Zhengzhu: Phoenix Satellite Television
Lively, Lydia: NBC News
Livingston, Abby: NBC News
Livingston, Stephanie: Fox News
Lloyd, Robert: Freelance
LoBreglio, Chris: Freelance
Lobzhanidze, Irakli: Rustavi 2 Broadcasting Company
Lodoe, Kalden: Radio Free Asia
Loebach, Joseph W.: NBC News
Loeschke, Paul: C–SPAN
Loew, Raimund: Austrian Radio & TV (ORF)
Loftus, Kevin: Freelance
Logan, Rebeca: Hispanic Communications Network
Logan, Russell: C–SPAN
Lois, Dyer: CBS News
Lomax, Malik: Freelance
Lombardo, Evelyn: Capitol News Connection (CNC)
Londres, Eduardo: Bloomberg Radio & TV
Long, Culver: Freelance
Long, James V.: NBC News
Longmire, Jennifer: National Public Radio
Loomans, Kathryn: AP–Broadcast
Lopardo, Melissa Anne: ABC News
Loper, Catherine: Fox News
Lopez, Edwing: Azteca America
Lopez, Juan Carlos: CNN
Lopez, Myra B.: AP–Broadcast
Lora, Edwin: CNN
Lora, Willie A.: CNN
Lord, Bill: WJLA–TV/Newschannel 8
Lorek, Stanley: Freelance
Lormand, John: SRN News (Salem)
Losey, Andrew: CNN
Loucks, William: Canadian Broadcasting Canada (CBC)
Lowman, Wayne: Fox News
Lu, Lucy: Radio Free Asia
Lucas, Fred: CNSNEWS.COM
Lucchini, Maria Rosa: WMDO-TV Univision
Ludden, Jennifer: National Public Radio
Ludwig, Robert: WETA
Ludwin, James: AP–Broadcast
Luhn, Laurie: Fox News
Lukas, Jayne: Freelance
Lund, Susan: National Public Radio
Lurch, Jr., David L.: Freelance
Lutt, Howard: CNN
Lutterbeck, Deborah: Reuters Radio & TV
Lutz, Ellsworth M.: ABC News
Luu, Chieu: Aljazeera International
Luzader, Doug: Fox News
Luzquinos, Julio: Freelance
Ly, Sherri: WTTG–Fox Television
Lyles, Brigitte: Fox News
Lynds, Stacia: Fox News
Lynn, Gary: NBC News
Lyon, Daniel: Freelance
Lyon, Michael: Fox News
Lyons, Theodore: East Coast Television
Lyons Sargeant, Nancy: AP–Broadcast
MacAdam, Alison: National Public Radio
MacDonald, James: CTV Canadian TV
MacDonald, Neil: Canadian Broadcasting Canada (CBC)
MacFarlane, Scott: Cox Broadcasting
MacHamer, Lessandra: NBC News
Machin, Carmelo: Spanish Public Television (TVE)
Macholz, Wolfgang: German TV ZDF
Mackamul, David: Aljazeera International
Mackaye, Amanda: Freelance
MacNeil, Lachlan Murdoch: ABC News
MacSpadden, Ian: NBC Newschannel
Maer, Peter: CBS News
Magnuson, Eric: Freelance
Maher, Heather: Radio Free Europe
Majchrowitz, Michael: Fox News
Majeed, Alicia: NBC Newschannel
Makelainen, Mika: Finnish Broadcasting Company (YLE)
Malakoff, David: National Public Radio
Malbon, Joy: CTV Canadian TV
Malloy, Brian: Eurovision Amerricas, Inc.
Malone, Beverly: CNN
Malone, Freddie: Freelance
Malone, James: Voice of America
Malone, Junius: NBC News
Maloney, Erin: Belo Capital Bureau
Maltas, Michael: CNN
Manatt, Dan: Talk Radio News Service
Mandelson, Adam: Eurovision Amerricas, Inc.
Manjardino, Rita: BBC
Mannos, Sofia: AP–Broadcast
Mansour, Fadi: Aljazeera Satellite Channel (Peninsula)
Maranho, Jose: Fox News
Marantz, Michael: WTTG–Fox Television
Marash, Amy: Aljazeera International
Marash, David: Aljazeera International
Marchione, Mark Anthony: CNN
Marchitto, Tom: National Public Radio
Marcus, Michael: Channel One News
Marenco, Julissa: WZDC–TV

MEMBERS ENTITLED TO ADMISSION—Continued

Marks, Simon: Feature Story News
Marlantes, Liz: ABC News
Marno, Joseph: Aljazeera International
Marno, Mike: Aljazeera International
Maroney, Sean: Voice of America
Marquardt, Alexander: Channel One News
Marquardt, Ursula: German TV ZDF
Marriott, Mai: Freelance
Marriott, Marc: Freelance
Marriott, Michael: Freelance
Mars, Harvey: WUSA–TV
Marshall, Mark: Freelance
Marshall, Rudy: Aljazeera International
Marshall, Steve: CBS News
Martens, Jacqueline: BBC
Martin, David: AP–Broadcast
Martin, David: CBS News
Martin, Michel: National Public Radio
Martin, Sam: C–SPAN
Martin, Wisdom: WTTG–Fox Television
Martin Ewing, Samara: WUSA–TV
Martin, Jr., James: ABC News
Martinez, Luis: ABC News
Martinez, Sandra: Aljazeera International
Martinez, Tina Marie: Fox News
Martino, Jeffrey: Freelance
Maskova, Adela: The Newshour with Jim Lehrer
Mason, Cecelia: West Virginia Public Broadcasting
Massey, Yolanda: WJLA–TV/Newschannel 8
Masuda, Tsuyoshi: NHK–Japan Broadcasting Corporation
Mathes, Michael: Voice of America
Mathieu, Joe: Marketwatch
Mattesky, Thomas A.: CBS News
Matthews, Chris: NBC News
Matthews, Claude: Freelance
Matthews, Lisa N.: AP–Broadcast
Matthews, Paul: Freelance
Matthews, Ronald H.: CBS News
Matzka, Jeffrey A.: SRN NEWS (Salem)
Mauro, Craig: Aljazeera International
Mausteller, Elizabeth: WJLA–TV/Newschannel 8
Maxwell, Darraine: ABC News
May, Tim: Fox News
Mayer, Petra: National Public Radio
Mayhew, Linda: Freelance
Mazariegos, Mark: Freelance
McAllister, Ian: WJLA–TV/Newschannel 8
McCabe, Valerie: The Newshour with Jim Lehrer
McCaleb, Ian: Fox News
McCallister, Doreen: National Public Radio
McCann, Michael: C–SPAN
McCann, Sean: C–SPAN
McCarren, Andrea: WJLA–TV/Newschannel 8
McCarthy, Lark: WTTG–Fox Television
McCarty, D. Jay: Freelance
McCarty, D. Page: Freelance
McCash, Douglas: Freelance
McCaughan, Timothy: CNN
McClam, Kevin: Fox News
McCleery, Kathleen: The Newshour with Jim Lehrer
McCloskey, George: Fox News
McClure, Tipp K.: Reuters Radio & TV
McClurkin, Donald: WETA
McConnell, Dave: WTOP Radio
McConnell, Dugald: CNN
McCorkell, Meghan: Sinclair Broadcast Group
McCrary, Scott: CBS News
McCray, Nathan: Al Arabiya TV
McCulloch, Emily: CNN
McCurdy, Nan: Free Speech Radio News
McCutchen, Yolanda: NBC News
McDaniel, Ashley: Freelance
McDermott, Frank: WUSA–TV
McDermott, Michele Marie: ABC News
McDermott, Richard: NBC Newschannel
McDermott, Tara: BBC
McDermott, Todd: WUSA–TV
McDevitt, Rebecca: WJLA–TV/Newschannel 8
McDonald, Mark: Capitol News Connection (CNC)
McDonald, N. Patricia: Freelance
McDonnell, Ellen: National Public Radio
McEachin, Johnny: NBC News
McFadden, Kerith: CNN
McFarland, Patty: Freelance
McGarvy, Sean: WTTG–Fox Television
McGinn, Anne: Fox News
McGinty, Derek: WUSA–TV
McGlinchy, Jim: CBS News
McGrath, Megan: WRC–TV/NBC–4
McGrath, Patrick: WTTG–Fox Television
McGreevy, Allen: BBC
McGriff, Kathryn: WJLA–TV/Newschannel 8
McGuire, Ellen: NBC News
McGuire, Joanna: Freelance
McGuire, Lorna: WTTG–Fox Television
McGuire, Michael: CBS News
McHenry, Jr., Robert: Freelance
McIntosh, Dara: Aljazeera International
McIntosh, Denise: CNN
McIntyre, James: CNN
McIntyre, Kim: Fox News
McKelway, Douglas: WJLA–TV/Newschannel 8
McKenna, William: BBC
McKinley, Karen: NBC News
McKinley, Robert: CBS News
McKinney, Ashley: WJLA–TV/Newschannel 8
McKinney, Richard: Sinclair Broadcast Group
McKnight, William: WUSA–TV
McLaughlin, Ross: WJLA–TV/Newschannel 8
McLellan, Daniel: Freelance
McManamon, Erin T.: Hearst–Argyle Television
McManus, Eleanor Spektor: CNN
McManus, Kevin A.: NBC Newschannel
McManus, Michael: HD News

MEMBERS ENTITLED TO ADMISSION—Continued

McManus, Nicole: NBC Newschannel
McMartin, Philip: Agday
McMichael IV, Samuel J.: CNN
McMinn, Nan Hee: AP–Broadcast
McMullan, Michael: CNN
McNair, Erik T.: ABC News
McNally, Julia: FDCH/E-Media, Inc.
McQuaid, Brendan: C–SPAN
McWhinney, David: Aljazeera International
Means, Jeffrey: Voice of America
Mears, Carroll Ann: NBC News
Mears, William: CNN
Mebane, Ted: National Public Radio
Medenecki, Jason: Bloomberg Radio & TV
Medvee, Dennis: National Public Radio
Meech, James: CNN
Meehan, Brian: Bloomberg Radio & TV
Meghani, Sagar: AP–Broadcast
Mehrpore, Abdu: Voice of America
Meier, Christiane: German TV ARD
Meier, Markus: N–TV News Television
Mejia, Douglas: WZDC–TV
Melendy, David R.: AP–Broadcast
Melhem, Richard: Al Arabiya TV
Melia, Michael: The Newshour with Jim Lehrer
Melia, Natalia: CBS News
Melick, Rob: Fox News
Mellman, Ira: WTOP Radio
Melnyk, Mariana: Canadian Broadcasting Canada (CBC)
Meltzer, Ari: ABC News
Meluza, Lourdes: Univision
Mendelson, Beth: Voice of America
Mengel, Trenton: East Coast Television
Meola, Erin: Freelance
Meraz, Gregorio: Televisa News Network (ECO)
Mergener, Tara: Freelance
Merideth, Lila: Channel One News
Merrill, Robert: NBC News
Merten, Andrew: NBC News
Meserve, Jeanne: CNN
Mesner-Hage, Jesse: Aljazeera International
Mesquita, Christina: AP–Broadcast
Messer, Christopher: Aljazeera Satellite Channel (Peninsula)
Metz, Daniela: German TV ARD
Metzger, Edward: CNN
Metzger, Justin: C–SPAN
Metzger, Rochelle: Community TV of PG'S
Meucci, Jason Robert: CNN
Meyer, Dick: CBS News
Meyer, Kerry: Freelance
Mezick, Byron: NBC News
Michaud, Robert: Aljazeera International
Micklos, Gregg: WJLA–TV/Newschannel 8
Migas, Portia: ABC News
Mihmandarli, Bulut: Voice of America
Miklaszewski, James: NBC News
Mikus, Andrea: SRN News (Salem)
Milenic, Alexander: WTTG–Fox Television
Milford, Robert H.: Mobile Video Services, LTD
Millar, Christopher: NBC News
Miller, Andrew Peter: C–SPAN
Miller, Annette: The Newshour with Jim Lehrer
Miller, Avery: ABC News
Miller, Beth: BBC
Miller, Karen: Free Speech Radio News
Miller, Michael: Fox News
Miller, Mitchell: WTOP Radio
Miller, Paul Keith: CNN
Miller, Sunlen Mari: ABC News
Miller, Tim: Middle East Television Network (Alhurra)
Mills, Jim: Fox News
Mills, Joe: National Public Radio
Mills, Kate: C–SPAN
Mills, Susan: The Newshour with Jim Lehrer
Milne, Claudia: BBC
Min, Kyungwook: Korean Broadcasting Systems
Minner, Richard: NBC News
Minor, Rodney Lee: Fednet
Minoso, Guillermo: National Public Radio
Minott, Gloria: WPFW–FM
Mishkin, Jay: WUSA–TV
Mitchell, Andrea: NBC News
Mitchell, Russell: Voice of America
Mitnick, Steven: Freelance
Miyake, Yuko: TV Tokyo
Mizell, Melinda: Freelance
Mlatisuma, Alen: Voice of America
Mohen, Peter: CNN
Mohyeldin, Ayman: Aljazeera International
Moire, Jennifer: C–SPAN
Molinares-Hess, Ione Indira: Freelance
Molineaux, Diana: Radio Marti
Monack, David: C–SPAN
Monange, Arielle: France 2 Television
Montague, William: Freelance
Monte, John: Freelance
Montenegro, Lori: Telemundo Network
Montenegro, Norma: WMDO–TV Univision
Montgomery, Alica: National Public Radio
Montgomery, Charles: Freelance
Mooar, Brian: NBC Newschannel
Mooney, Kevin: CNSNEWS.COM
Moore, Dennis: Need To Know News
Moore, Garrette: C–SPAN
Moore, Gregg: Freelance
Moore, Karen: CBS News
Moore, Linwood: C–SPAN
Moore, Nathan: Pacifica Radio
Moore, Terrence: Metro Networks
Moore, W. Harrison: Middle East Television Network (Alhurra)
Moorhead, Jeremy: CNN
Moorman, Jeffrey: HD News

MEMBERS ENTITLED TO ADMISSION—Continued

Morales, Olga: Freelance
Morales, Victor: Voice of America
Moreno, Raul: National Public Radio
Morgan, Donald: Freelance
Morgan, Keith B.: ABC News
Morgan, Marcia: National Public Radio
Morgan, Nancy Gerstman: WETA
Morris, Amy: Federal News Radio AM 1050
Morris, Gaven: Aljazeera International
Morris, Holly: WTTG–Fox Television
Morris, Peter: CNN
Morris, Sarah: BBC
Morrisette, Roland: Bloomberg Radio & TV
Morrison, Bridget: C–SPAN
Morrison, Jill: Capitol News Connection (CNC)
Morse, Richard: Fox News
Morton, Dan: C–SPAN
Mortreux, Vincent: TF1–French TV
Moses, Lester: NBC News
Mosettig, Michael: The Newshour with Jim Lehrer
Mosley, Matthew: Fuji TV Japan
Moubray, Virginia: CNN
Moynihan, Mark: AP–Broadcast
Mueller, John: Middle East Television Network (Alhurra)
Muhammad, Alverda: National Scene News
Muhammad, Askia: National Scene News
Muhammad, Seleena M.: Fox News
Muir, Robert: Reuters Radio & TV
Munford, Corey: Radio Free Asia
Munoz, Luis: Middle East Television Network (Alhurra)
Munoz, Luis: Radio Marti
Muratani, Tateki: Fuji TV Japan
Murphy, Fran: Channel One News
Murphy, Frederick: Freelance
Murphy, John: CBS News
Murphy, Richard: WTTG–Fox Television
Murphy, Terry: C–SPAN
Murphy, Thomas: CNN
Murphy, Victor: WUSA–TV
Murray, Mark: NBC News
Murray, Matthew: Freelance
Murray, Timothy K.: Ventana Productions
Mursa, Alexander: Russia Today Television
Mursa, Christina: Russia Today Television
Murtaugh, Peter: BBC
Murugesan, Vidya: Freelance
Musa, Imad: Aljazeera International
Muse, Vince: National Public Radio
Musha, Jilili: Radio Free Asia
Muskat, Steven: NBC Newschannel
Muturi, Muthoni: National Public Radio
Mvunganyi, Jackson: Voice of America
Mwakalyelye, Ndimyake: Voice of America
Myers, Lisa: NBC News
Myo Thet, Khin: Voice of America
Myrick, Yetta: C–SPAN
Nadler, Gary: ABC News
Nagesh, Gautham: Need To Know News
Naidoo, Anand: Aljazeera International
Nakasone, Sarah: Belo Capital Bureau
Namgyal, Tseten: Radio Free Asia
Napier, Joyce: Canadian Broadcasting Canada (CBC)
Napshin, Jeffrey: Freelance
Nardi, William: WRC–TV/NBC–4
Nash, John C.: WETA
Nassar, Mohamedelhussin: Middle East Television Network (Alhurra)
Nathan, Caroline: The Newshour with Jim Lehrer
Nathan, Nancy: NBC News
Nawaz, Amna: NBC News
Naylor, Brian: National Public Radio
Ndiho, Paul: Voice of America
Neal, Jason: NBC News
Neale, Tracey: WUSA–TV
Neapolitan, Michael: Mobile Video Services, LTD
Neel, Joe R.: National Public Radio
Nelson, Christopher: National Public Radio
Nelson, Donna: NBC News
Nelson, Emily Anne: ABC News
Nelson, James: Fox News
Nelson, Joseph: Washington Bureau News Service
Nelson, Marie: National Public Radio
Nelson, Nicole: Freelance
Neubauer, Kristin: Reuters Radio & TV
Neubauer, Sandra: WJLA–TV/Newschannel 8
Neville, Shaun: Hearst–Argyle Television
Nevins, Elizabeth: NBC News
Newberry, Tom: NBC Newschannel
Newman, Scott: National Public Radio
Ngoc, Pham Than: Radio Free Asia
Nguyen, An: Radio Free Asia
Nguyen, Anh: Freelance
Nguyen, Bich-Ha: Radio Free Asia
Nguyen, Dien M.: Radio Free Asia
Nicci, Nicholette: CNN
Nichols, James: WUSA–TV
Nichols, Meka: Channel One News
Nickerson, Dewayne: CBS News
Nicolaidis, Virginia: CNN
Nielsen, John: National Public Radio
Niiler, Eric: Capitol News Connection (CNC)
Nikuradze, David: Rustavi 2 Broadcasting Company
Nishikawa, Yoshio: NHK–Japan Broadcasting Corporation
Nishiumi, Setsu: Fuji TV Japan
Nixon, Adam: Middle East Television Network (Alhurra)
Nixon, Chuck: WETA
Nocciolo, Ernest G.: CNN
Nocciolo, Valorie: CNN
Noce, Julie: Swiss Broadcasting
Noda, Yuiko: TV Tokyo
Noh, Jung Min: Radio Free Asia

MEMBERS ENTITLED TO ADMISSION—Continued

Nolen, John: CBS News
Noonan, Heidi: Fox News
Norborg, Bengt: Swedish Broadcasting
Norins, Jamie: Diversified Communications, Inc. (DCI)
Norland, Dean E.: ABC News
Norling, Richard A.: Freelance
Norris, Donna: C–SPAN
Norris, James: Middle East Television Network (Alhurra)
Norris, Jane: Federal News Radio AM 1050
Norris, Michele: National Public Radio
Northam, Jackie: National Public Radio
Northrop, Rick: Federal News Service
Novy, Michele: Fox News
Nowak, Christopher: CNN
Nunez, Jorge: WMDO-TV Univision
Nurenberg, Gary: Freelance
Nurre, Bridget: NBC News
Nwazota, Kristina: The Newshour with Jim Lehrer
Nyane, Khin Maung: Radio Free Asia
Nyberg, Carina: Federal News Service
Nyi, Nyi: Radio Free Asia
NYROP, SIRI E.: Voice of America
Nyunt Oo, Thar: Voice of America
O'Berry, D. Kerry: Freelance
O'Brien, David: Freelance
O'Brien, Jane: BBC
O'Connell, Benjamin: C–SPAN
O'Connell, Mike: NBC Newschannel
O'Donnell, Emily: ABC News
O'Donnell, Kelly: NBC News
O'Donnell, Norah: NBC News
O'Donnell, Patrick: Eye-To-Eye Video
O'Leary, Lizzie: Bloomberg Radio & TV
O'Regan, Michael: WRC–TV/NBC–4
O'Shea, Jr., Daniel J.: Freelance
O'Toole, Quinn: National Public Radio
Oberti, Ralf: Freelance
Och, Phillip Andrew: Channel One News
Ochsenschlager, Emily: National Public Radio
Odeh, Renee: Aljazeera International
Odom, Quillie: Fox News
Offermann, Claudia: German TV ZDF
Offor, Chinedu: Voice of America
Ogata, Kerry: CNN
Oh, Junghwa: Korean Broadcasting Systems
Ohm-Andress, Jeannie: NBC News
Oinounou, Mosheh: Fox News
Oko, Jennifer Cohen: CBS News
Okorn, Peter: Aljazeera International
Okoshi, Kensuke: NHK–Japan Broadcasting Corporation
Olick, Diana: CNBC
Oliver, LaFontaine: Radio One
Olmsted, Alan: C–SPAN
Ong, Linh: AP–Broadcast
Oo, Win Naing: Radio Free Asia
Oo-Zin, Ma: Voice of America
Orozco Rojas, Nathalia: RCN–TV (Colombia)
Orr, Bob: CBS News
Osinski, Krystyna: AP–Broadcast
Oszancak, Hakan: AP–Broadcast
Otth, John: CNN
Ouafi, Mohamed Said: Freelance
Ouellet, David: Canadian Broadcasting Canada (CBC)
Outen, Gwen: National Public Radio
Overby, Peter: National Public Radio
Owen, Andrea: ABC News
Pace, Julie: AP–Broadcast
Padilla-Cirino, Mercy: Hispanic Communications Network
Pagan, Louis: AP–Broadcast
Page, David: CBN News
Palaruan, Paul: CNN
Palca, Joe: National Public Radio
Panov, Alexander: RTVI/ECHO–TV
Panzer, Chester: WRC–TV/NBC–4
Parenti, Alisa: WJLA–TV/Newschannel 8
Park, Jung-Woo: Radio Free Asia
Park, Sarah Lee: WJLA–TV/Newschannel 8
Parker, Andre: CNN
Parker, Beth: WTTG–Fox Television
Parker, Jennifer L.: ABC News
Parker, Robert Geoffrey: CNN
Parkinson, John R.: ABC News
Parks, Chris: CNN
Parlett, Geoff: Belo Capital Bureau
Parman, John: Interfaith Voices
Parrish, Bryan: Metro Networks
Parsell, Robert: Voice of America
Parshall, Janet: SRN News (Salem)
Passariello (Dodich), Linda: Freelance
Pastre, Dominique: Fox News
Patrick, Michael: WTTG–Fox Television
Patruznick, Michael: C–SPAN
Patsalos, Connie: NBC News
Patsko, Daniel: Freelance
Patterson, Ashley: Belo Capital Bureau
Patterson, Jay E.: ABC News
Pattni, Purvee: BBC
Pauls, Hartmut: Freelance
Paxton, Bradford S.: Fox News
Payne, Aaron C.: CNN
Payne, Nathan: CNN
Payne, Scott: AP–Broadcast
Payton, Strader: TV Tokyo
Paz Vergara, Miguel: CBN News
Peacock, Grant: Freelance
Peaks, Gershon: Reuters Radio & TV
Pearson, Hampton: CNBC
Pearson, John Vincent: National Public Radio
Peltier, Yves: Canadian Broadcasting Canada (CBC)
Pena, Ana Sarai: Telesur
Pena, Celinda: WUSA–TV

MEMBERS ENTITLED TO ADMISSION—Continued

Penaloza, Marisa: National Public Radio
Peppers, Greg: National Public Radio
Perez, Nitza Soledad: ABC News
Pergram, Chad: Fox News
Perkins, Alexis: AP–Broadcast
Perkins, Douglas: Freelance
Perkins, Vernon: C–SPAN
Perlmeter, Alan: WETA
Perron, Marilisa: Freelance
Perry, Andrea: C–SPAN
Perry, Christina: C–SPAN
Perry, Michelle: NBC News
Perry, Jr., Timothy: The Newshour with Jim Lehrer
Peslis, Chris: Fox News
Peters, Ronald: WUSA–TV
Petersen, Hilke: German TV ZDF
Peterson, Gordon: WJLA–TV/Newschannel 8
Peterson, James: Freelance
Peterson, Karen: WUSA–TV
Peterson, Rebecca: CBS News
Peterson, Robert: Freelance
Petraitis, Gerald: AP–Broadcast
Petras, William: NBC News
Pettigrew, Chris: WJLA–TV/Newschannel 8
Pettit, Debra: NBC News
Peyton, Michael: CBS News
Pham, Jacqueline: Fox News
Philippon, Alan: CNN
Phillips, Steven: Reuters Radio & TV
Pickup, Michael: ABC News
Pigott, Bernard: Fox News
Pillon, Annette: ABC News
Piltz, Eberhard: German TV ZDF
Pimble, William: CBS News
Pinczuk, Murray: Freelance
Pinzon, Wingel: Freelance
Piper, Jeff: WRC–TV/NBC–4
Pitocco, Nickolas: C–SPAN
Pittman, Tom: WTTG–Fox Television
Pizarro, Fernando: Univision
Placie, Jordan: CNN
Plaia, Jennifer: WJLA–TV/Newschannel 8
Plante, Gilles: Canadian Broadcasting Canada (CBC)
Plante, William: CBS News
Plater, Christopher: WJLA–TV/Newschannel 8
Pliszak, Richard K.: ABC News
Plotkin, Mark: WTOP Radio
Poch, Reasey: Voice of America
Poduch, Shelby: NBC News
Poley, Michael: CNN
Policastro, Jacqueline: Lilly Broadcasting
Policastro, Jacqueline: AP–Broadcast
Pomerantz, Roni: C–SPAN
Pons, Annie Kate: Aljazeera International
Poole, Michael: Freelance
Pope, Lindsey: Freelance
Popkin, James: NBC News
Popovic, Darko: Voice of America
Popovici, Andrei: RTVI/ECHO–TV
Popp, Chris: CNN
Popp, David: Talk Radio News Service
Porsella, Claude L.: Radio France Internationale
Porter, Almon: C–SPAN
Porter, Christina: C–SPAN
Porteus, Liza: Fox News
Portnoy, Ellen: FDCH/E–Media, Inc.
Portnoy, Steven A.: ABC News
Postovit, David: Hearst–Argyle Television
Potts, Tracie: NBC Newschannel
Poulou, Penelope: Voice of America
Pounds, Michael: Aljazeera International
Powell, Brian William: Radio Free Asia
Powell, Lee: AP–Broadcast
Prah, Pamela M.: STATELINE.ORG
Prann, Elizabeth: Fox News
Pratt, James: WUSA–TV
Pratzel, Ryan: WJLA–TV/Newschannel 8
Preloh, Anne: C–SPAN
Press, Robert: Bloomberg Radio & TV
Preston, Mark: CNN
Presutti, Carolyn: WTTG–Fox Television
Probst, Eva: German TV ARD
Pronko, Tony: C–SPAN
Pryor, Ed: AP–Broadcast
Publicover, Robert: WTOP Radio
Pugliese, Pat: CNBC
Puljic, Ivica: Voice of America
Purbaugh, Michael J.: Freelance
Putic, George: Voice of America
Qadar, Sana: Freelance
Queen, Shegoftah: Voice of America
Quinn, Diana: CBS News
Quinn, John: Voice of America
Quinn, Mary: ABC News
Quinn, Saul: Freelance
Quinnette, John: Freelance
Quinonez, Omar A.: Freelance
Qusaibaty, Olivia: NHK–Japan Broadcasting Corporation
Rabbage, Mark: BBC
Rabin, Carrie: CBS News
Rabin, Mark: Freelance
Rabkin, Job: Independent Television News (ITN)
Rachou, Carol: CNN
Racki, Jason D.: Australian Broadcasting Corporation
Rad, Ali: Freelance
Raddatz, Martha: ABC News
Radia, Kirit M.: ABC News
Raffaele, Robert: Voice of America
Rager, Bryan: Freelance
Raghavan, Malika: Hearst–Argyle Television
Raine, John Patrick: Aljazeera International
Rainey, Brian: Freelance
Ramienski, Dorothy: Federal News Radio AM 1050

MEMBERS ENTITLED TO ADMISSION—Continued

Ramirez, Edwin: Freelance
Ramirez, Fabiana: Religion & Ethics Newsweekly
Ramirez, Roselena: Telesur
Ramos, Raul: Azteca America
Rampy, R. Grant: Tribune Broadcasting
Randev, Sonia: Community TV of PG'S
Randle, Antonia: Sinclair Broadcast Group
Randle, Jim: Voice of America
Randolph, Kimberly: ABC News
Raphel, Paul: WTTG–Fox Television
Rarey, Richard Howell: National Public Radio
Raskin, Molly: The Newshour with Jim Lehrer
Raston, Dina Temple: National Public Radio
Rathner, Jeffrey: WETA
Ratliff, Walter: AP–Broadcast
Ratner, Ellen: Talk Radio News Service
Ratner, Victor: ABC News
Raval, Adi: BBC
Raval, Nikhil: C–SPAN
Ravanello, Chris: CNN
Raviv, Daniel: CBS News
Ray, Alonzo: NBC News
Ray, Douglas: Freelance
Ray, Steven: Aljazeera International
Raz, Guy: National Public Radio
Reagan, Cheryl: Federal News Service
Reals, Gary: WUSA–TV
Reap, Patrick: CNN
Reaux, Richard: Freelance
Redding, William: ABC News
Redman, Justine: CNN
Redmond, Kuren: WJLA–TV/Newschannel 8
Reed, Josephine: Freelance
Reeder, Louis R.: Environment & Energy Publishing, LLC
Reese, Orla: AP–Broadcast
Reeve, Richard: WJLA–TV/Newschannel 8
Reeves, Alea: Aljazeera International
Reeves, Austin: WTTG–Fox Television
Regan, Tom: National Public Radio
Rehman, Fiaz: Voice of America
Reid, Chip: NBC News
Reid, Kaylan: NBC News
Reilly, Robert: C–SPAN
Reinsel, Ed: Freelance
Remillard, Michele: Fox News
Renaud, Jean: CNN
Renken, David: Fox News
Rensberger, Scott: TV2–Denmark
Reuter, Cynthia: C–SPAN
Reyes, Malissa: WJLA–TV/Newschannel 8
Reyes, Victor: Telemundo Network
Reynolds, Andrew: National Public Radio
Reynolds, Catherine C.: Cox Broadcasting
Reynolds, Judy: Religion & Ethics Newsweekly
Reynolds, Robert: Aljazeera International
Rhode, Leslie Cook: WJLA–TV/Newschannel 8
Rhodes, Elizabeth: Fox News
Ricciuti, Leah: ABC News
Rice, Diriki: Freelance
Richard, Sylvain: Canadian Broadcasting Canada (CBC)
Richards, Alison: National Public Radio
Rickard, Michael: WTTG–Fox Television
Riddle, Joel: National Public Radio
Ridgeway, David: CNN
Riess, Steffanie: German TV ZDF
Riggs, James: CNN
Riggs, Tyrone W.: Freelance
Riha, Anne Marie: Fox News
Riner, Corbett: Fox News
Rios, Delia: C–SPAN
Ritchie, Thomas: AP–Broadcast
Rivero, Raul: WUSA–TV
Roach, Amy: C–SPAN
Roan, Ansley: Religion & Ethics Newsweekly
Roane Skehan, Andrea: WUSA–TV
Robbins, Francisco: CBS News
Robbins, Michael: Fox News
Robbins, Sarah: BBC
Robert, Olivier: Freelance
Roberts, Diane: Freelance
Roberts, Eugene W.: Freelance
Roberts, Jean Pierre: Eurovision Amerricas, Inc.
Roberts, John: CNN
Roberts, Nathan: Freelance
Roberts, Susan: CBS News
Robertson, Greg: CNN
Robertson, Laura: CBN News
Robertson, Shari: Camerini–Robertson, Inc.
Robertson, Tamara: Fox News
Robinson, Angela: CNN
Robinson, Daniel: Voice of America
Robinson, David: CNN
Robinson, Douglas: Austrian Radio & TV (ORF)
Robinson, Margaret: The Newshour with Jim Lehrer
Robinson, Querry: NBC News
Robinson, Veronica: WTOP Radio
Roca, Xavier: TV3–Televisio De Catalunya
Rocha, Juan: Ventana Productions
Rocha, Samuel: Freelance
Rockler, Julia: The Washington Bureau
Rockwell, Kelly: Aljazeera International
Rocque, Tiffany: C–SPAN
Rodden, Alison: Hispanic Communications Network
Rodgers, Michelle: WUSA–TV
Rodgers, William: Voice of America
Rodriguez, Janelle: CNN
Rodriguez, Janet: CNN
Rodriguez, Janet: WZDC–TV
Rodriguez, Martine: C–SPAN
Rohrbeck, Douglas: Fox News
Rojas, Carlos A.: ABC News
Rokus, Brian: CNN
Roland, Abu Bakr: Freelance
Roller, Richard L.: ABC News

MEMBERS ENTITLED TO ADMISSION—Continued

Rollins, Bonnie: NBC Newschannel
Romero, Alberto: Freelance
Romilly, George: ABC News
Roof, Peter: Freelance
Rooney, Sarah: Channel One News
Rooney Perkins, Alexis: AP–Broadcast
Root, Sean L.: WUSA–TV
Rose, Francis: Federal News Radio AM 1050
Rose, Raymond: NBC News
Rosefeldt, Sarah: NBC News
Roselli, H. Michael: CNN
Rosen, Amy: Bloomberg Radio & TV
Rosen, James: Fox News
Rosen, Rachel: CNN
Rosenbaum, Jill: CBS News
Rosenberg, Andrew: National Public Radio
Rosenberg, Gary: ABC News
Rosenberg, Howard L.: ABC News
Rosenberg, Jeffrey: National Public Radio
Rosenfelder, Michael: AP–Broadcast
Rosetti, Jeffrey: WUSA–TV
Rosgaard, Jessica: CNN
Ross, Adrienne: Freelance
Ross, Caley: Fox News
Ross, Lee: Fox News
Ross, Mary Katherine: CNN
Rossel, Maria Luisa: W RADIO
Rossetti-Meyer, Misa: Freelance
Roston, Aram: NBC News
Roth, Johnie: NBC News
Roth, Linda: CNN
Roth, Theodore: Freelance
Rovner, Julie: National Public Radio
Rowe, Hildrun: German TV ZDF
Rowe, Tom: Reuters Radio & TV
Rowland, Michael: Australian Broadcasting Corporation
Royce, Lindy: CNN
Roycraft, David: WUSA–TV
Rubin, Joshua: CNN
Ruby, Tracy: C–SPAN
Rudd, Michael: WJLA–TV/Newschannel 8
Rudin, Ken: National Public Radio
Ruff, David: CNN
Ruff, Jennifer: C–SPAN
Ruff, Rivea: Freelance
Ruggiero, Diane: CNN
Rushfield, Stuart: National Public Radio
Rushing, Ian: WJLA–TV/Newschannel 8
Rushing, Joshua: Aljazeera International
Russert, Timothy: NBC News
Russo, Jay R.: ABC News
Rust, Emily: CNN
Rutherford, John: NBC News
Ruttenberg, Roee: Aljazeera International
Ryan, Jason: ABC News
Ryan, Marty: Fox News
Ryan Conley, Jennifer: WUSA–TV
Rydell, Kate: CBS News
Ryntjes, Dan: BBC
Rysak, F. David: WTTG–Fox Television
Saad, Layelle: Aljazeera Satellite Channel (Peninsula)
Sacco, John: CNN
Sachs, Robert: National Public Radio
Sacks, Howard: NBC News
Saffelle, Jeffrey: Global TV Canada
Sagalyn, Daniel: The Newshour with Jim Lehrer
Said Ouafi, Mohamed: ATN Productions, LTD
Sakota, Alija: WUSA–TV
Salam, Najiba: Voice of America
Salan, Jennifer: Aljazeera International
Salkoff, Brooke Hart: NBC Newschannel
Sallstrom, Royce: CBN News
Saloomey, Kristen: Aljazeera International
Saltz, Michael: The Newshour with Jim Lehrer
Salzman, Eric: CBS News
Sam, Borin: Radio Free Asia
Samaniego, Manuel: CNN
Sampaio, Frederico: C–SPAN
Sampy, David: Independent Television News (ITN)
Samuel, Maia: NBC News
Sanchez, George D.: ABC News
Sanchez, Pablo: Univision
Sanders-Smith, Sherry: C–SPAN
Sands, Tiffany: Belo Capital Bureau
Sanfuentes, Jose ''Antoine'': NBC News
Sankey, Jill: CNN
Sano, Jun: Fuji TV Japan
Santer, Sarah: Fox News
Santhuff, Bruce R.: Freelance
Santos, Jose G.: CNN
Sargent, Mark: WTTG–Fox Television
Sargent, Thayer: Freelance
Satchell, David: WUSA–TV
Sato, Keiichi: Nippon TV Network
Satterfield, John T.: Freelance
Savage, Chantell: NBC News
Savage, Craig: Fox News
Savoy, Gregory: Freelance
Scanlan, William: C–SPAN
Scanlon, Jason: Fox News
Scanlon, Mary: C–SPAN
Scarrah, Kathie: Freelance
Schaefer, Robert: National Public Radio
Schaff, Michael: CBN News
Schalch, Kathleen: National Public Radio
Schantz, Douglas N.: CNN
Schantz, Kristine: Channel One News
Scharf, Jason: Eurovision Americas, Inc.
Scherer, David: CNN
Scheuer, John: C–SPAN
Schiavone, Louise: Freelance
Schieffer, Bob: CBS News
Schiff, Brian: Voice of America
Schiffner, Christine: German TV ARD

MEMBERS ENTITLED TO ADMISSION—Continued

Schlachter, Terese: Freelance
Schlegel, Barry C.: CNN
Schleicher, Annie: The Newshour with Jim Lehrer
Schlenker, Aungthu: Radio Free Asia
Schloemer, Peter: Freelance
Schmidt Massey, Emily: WUSA–TV
Schneider, Avie: National Public Radio
Schneider, William: CNN
Schoenholtz, Howard: ABC News
Schoenmann, Donald: Freelance
Scholl, Christopher: NBC News
Schuiten, Jeroen: Eurovision Americas, Inc.
Schule, James: East Coast Television
Schulken, Sonja Deaner: Tribune Broadcasting
Schultze, Franco: WZDC–TV
Schwandt, Kimberly: Hearst–Argyle Television
Schwartz, Sharona: CNN
Schwartz, Steve: ABC News
Schweiger, Ellen: C–SPAN
Schweppe, Michael: National Public Radio
Sciammacco, Sara: Capitol News Connection (CNC)
Scicchitano, Carmine: NBC News
Sckrabulis, David: Sinclair Broadcast Group
Scott, Graham: Austrian Radio & TV (ORF)
Scott, Harry: Radio Free Asia
Scott, Ivan: KGO Radio
Scott, Linda: The Newshour with Jim Lehrer
Scott, Sarah: Freelance
Scritchfield, Andrew: NBC News
Scruggs, Wesley: NBC News
Scully, Steven: C–SPAN
Seabrook, Andrea: National Public Radio
Seabrook, Willliam: WETA
Seaby, Gregory: WJLA–TV/Newschannel 8
Sears, Carl: NBC News
Seddon, Mark: Aljazeera International
Seem, Thomas H.: CBS News
Segraves, Mark: WTOP Radio
Seidel, Stuart: National Public Radio
Seidman, Joel: NBC News
Seium, Michael: Aljazeera International
Selbach, Dunja: Freelance
Seldin, Jeff: Federal News Radio am 1050
Sellers, Bob: WTTG–Fox Television
Selma, Reginald G.: CNN
Sera, Frederick: ABC News
Serensits, Joseph: Freelance
Serper, Noelle: Religion & Ethics Newsweekly
Sesno, Frank: CNN
Seymour, Allison: WTTG–Fox Television
Seymour, Peter: CNN
Shaffir, Gregory: CBS News
Shaffir, Kimberlee: CBS News
Shakhov, Dmytro: RTVI/ECHO–TV
Shalhoup, Joseph: NBC News
Shan, Zijun: Radio Free Asia
Shand, Christina: Fox News
Shand, Susan: German TV ARD
Shannon, Dennis: CBS News
Shapiro, Ari: National Public Radio
Shapiro, Joseph: National Public Radio
Sharp, Meghan: Fox News
Shastri, Namgyal: Voice of America
Shaughnessy, Lawrence: CNN
Shaw, Benjamin: Capitol News Connection (CNC)
Shaw, Cathy: National Public Radio
Shaw, Joseph: Hearst–Argyle Television
Shelton, Steve: Fox News
Shepherd, Sarah: CNN
Shepherd, Shawna: CNN
Sherwood, Tom: WRC–TV/NBC–4
Shi, Wei: New Tang Dynasty TV
Shikaki, Muna: Al Arabiya TV
Shim, Jaegu: MBC–TV Korea (Munhwa)
Shimada, Masaaki: TV Tokyo
Shimizu, Keisuke: NHK–Japan Broadcasting Corporation
Shin, Kyung Youl: Seoul Broadcasting System (SBS)
Shine, Thomas Andrew: ABC News
Shipman, Claire: ABC News
Shively, Caroline: Fox News
Shlemon, Chris: Independent Television News (ITN)
Shoffner, Harry: BBC
Shogren, Elizabeth: National Public Radio
Shon, Robert: WTTG–Fox Television
Shortt, Robert: Irish Radio & TV (RTE)
Shott, Dave: Fox News
Shoup, Anna: The Newshour with Jim Lehrer
Showell, Andre: BET Nightly News
Shriver, Mike: Aljazeera International
Shukhin, Daniel: National Public Radio
Shull, Roger: Reuters Radio & TV
Shuman, Michael: National Public Radio
Shwe, Nyein: Radio Free Asia
Sicuranza (Kelley), Daniela: Fox News
Sides, James: Freelance
Siegel, Robert C.: National Public Radio
Siegfriedt, Anita: Fox News
Siegloch, Klaus-Peter: German TV ZDF
Sierra, Joann: CNN
Sikka, Madhulika: National Public Radio
Silberner, Joanne: National Public Radio
Sills, Cecil John: NBC Newschannel
Silman, III, Jimmie: WUSA–TV
Silva, Juan: CNN
Silva-Pinto, Lauren: Austrian Radio & TV (ORF)
Silva-Pinto, Luis Fernando: TV Globo International
Silver, Darwin: WETA
Silver, David: Freelance
Silver, Diane: The Newshour with Jim Lehrer
Silver, Janet E.: Australian Broadcasting Corporation
Silverberg, Hank: WTOP Radio
Silverman, Art: National Public Radio

MEMBERS ENTITLED TO ADMISSION—Continued

Silverstein, Matthew: Fox News
Silvia, Charpa: German Broadcasting Systems–ARD
Simeone, Nick: Fox News
Simeone, Ronald: NBC News
Simkin, Mark: Australian Broadcasting Corporation
Simmons, Gregory: Fox News
Simmons, Sarah: WTTG–Fox Television
Simms, Jeffery: CNN
Simon, Neil: Fox News
Simon, Scott: National Public Radio
Simons, John: Aljazeera International
Simons, Leigh E.: ABC News
Simpson, Shelley A.: WJLA–TV/Newschannel 8
Sims, Jessica: NBC News
Singer, Lauren: NBC News
Singeri, Sonam Lhamo: Radio Free Asia
Sirait, Sondang: Voice of America
Sit, David: The Newshour with Jim Lehrer
Skeans, Ron: BBC
Skehan, Andrew: East Coast Television
Skehan, Michael: East Coast Television
Skehan, Patrick: East Coast Television
Skinner, Sylvia: East Coast Television
Skirble, Rosanne: Voice of America
Skokowski, Christopher: Fednet
Skomal, Paul: Freelance
Skyrmes, Vanessa: WZDC–TV
Slack, Mary Beth: Need To Know News
Slafka, Kristi: C–SPAN
Slattery, Julie: Bloomberg Radio & TV
Slen, Peter: C–SPAN
Slewka, Stephanie: Freelance
Slie, Charles: Freelance
Sloane, Ward C.: CBS News
Slobogin, Kathy: CNN
Small, Matt: AP–Broadcast
Small, William: Bloomberg Radio & TV
Smith, Alison: Canadian Broadcasting Canada (CBC)
Smith, Anthony: Freelance
Smith, Ashley: Fox News
Smith, Christie: NBC Newschannel
Smith, Cynthia: ABC News
Smith, Graham: National Public Radio
Smith, Hedrick: Hedrick Smith Productions
Smith, James E.: ABC News
Smith, Jason H.: WTTG–Fox Television
Smith, Jill: CNBC
Smith, Mark S.: AP–Broadcast
Smith, Michael J.: Dispatch Broadcast Group
Smith, Phillip: Aljazeera International
Smith, Raeshawn: CNN
Smith, Randolph: Bloomberg Radio & TV
Smith, Sarah: Independent Television News (ITN)
Smith, Sarah Mobley: National Public Radio
Smith, Scott D.: WJLA–TV/Newschannel 8
Smith, Shirley O'Bryan: AP–Broadcast
Smith, Skip: CNN
Smith, William: Belo Capital Bureau
Smith-Spark, Laura: BBC
Sneed, Kimberly: NBC News
Snow, Robbie B.: Washington Bureau News Service
Snyder, Catherine: WUSA–TV
Soe, Khin Maung: Radio Free Asia
Soe Win, Khin: Voice of America
Soh, June: Voice of America
Sohn, Jihun: Voice of America
Sok, Pov: Voice of America
Sokolova, Elena: Russian State TV and Radio (RTR)
Solangi, Murtaza: Voice of America
Solimani-Lezhnev, Andrey: Russian State TV and Radio (RTR)
Solodovnikov, Mikhail: Russian State TV and Radio (RTR)
Solomon, Kifle: Voice of America
Solorzano, Gilbert: Freelance
Som, Sattana: Radio Free Asia
Sorensen, Cali: Channel One News
Sorensen, Eric D.: Global TV Canada
Sorenson, Ben: C–SPAN
Sorenson, Randall: Freelance
Soucy, Peggy: Eurovision Amerricas, Inc.
Southern, Joel: Alaska Public Radio Network
Southworth, Cal R.: National Public Radio
Sozio, George A.: Freelance
Spagnolo, Andrew: Potomac Television
Speck, Alan: C–SPAN
Spector, Teresa: Fox News
Speer, Jack: National Public Radio
Speights, Eric: ABC News
Speiser, Matthew: CNN
Spellman, Jim: CNN
Spence, Patrick: Federal News Radio AM 1050
Spencer, Darcy: WRC–TV/NBC–4
Sperry, Jennifer Businger: CNN
Sperry, Todd: CNN
Spevak, Joe: WTTG–Fox Television
Spiegler, Theodore: Freelance
Spinelli, Paul: Sinclair Broadcast Group
Spire, Richard H.: CBS News
Spiro, David: Freelance
Spoerry, Philip Scott: CNN
Sponder, Myron: Talk Radio News Service
St. James, Gregory: C–SPAN
St. John, Jonathan: CNN
Stafford-Walter, Michael: WUSA–TV
Stahl, Steven: CNN
Stakelbeck, Erick: CBN News
Stamberg, Susan: National Public Radio
Stanford, Dave: CBS News
Stang, Tim: Bloomberg Radio & TV
Stanke, Donald E.: WTTG–Fox Television
Stark, Lisa: ABC News
Starks, Bill: WUSA–TV
Starling, Alison: WJLA–TV/Newschannel 8

MEMBERS ENTITLED TO ADMISSION—Continued

Starling, Guy: NBC News
Staton, Thomas M.: Freelance
Statter, David: WUSA–TV
Stay, Daniel J.: Fox News
Stead, Scott: CNN
Stearns, Scott: Voice of America
Stebbins, William: Aljazeera International
Steele, Andrew: BBC
Stefany, Steve: ABC News
Steib, Aspen: CNN
Steinhauser, Paul: CNN
Stemple, Lexi: Fox News
Stencil, Meredith: CBS News
Stephanopoulos, George: ABC News
Sterling, Vaughn: CNN
Stern, Mitchell: AP–Broadcast
Stevenson, Carrie: CNN
Stevenson, James: Voice of America
Stevenson, Louis: WTTG–Fox Television
Stewart, Andrew: SRN News (Salem)
Stewart, Norman: C–SPAN
Stewart, Robin: Ventana Productions
Stix, Gabriel: CBS News
Stoddard, Mark S.: Freelance
Stoddard, Rick: C–SPAN
Stok, Silvester: RTV Slovenija
Stokes, William: BET Nightly News
Stone, Carolyn: CNN
Stone, Evie: National Public Radio
Stoner, Matt: C–SPAN
Stout, Matthew: Fox News
Strachan, Jason: CNN
Strand, Paul: CBN News
Straub, Matthew: Freelance
Straub, Terry: Diversified Communications, Inc. (DCI)
Streeter, James: NBC News
Streitfeld, Rachel: Freelance
Strickland, Kenneth: NBC News
Strickler, Laura: CBS News
Stringer, Ashley: CNBC
Stuart, Jessica C.: ABC News
Stuart, Matthew: ABC News
Stubblefield, Abraham: WJLA–TV/Newschannel 8
Styles, Julian: CNN
Suarez, Fernando J.: CBS News
Suarez, Rafael: The Newshour with Jim Lehrer
Suddeth, James: Freelance
Suddeth, Rick: Freelance
Sughroue, Jon: NBC News
Sulasma, Olli-Pekka: Finnish Broadcasting Company (YLE)
Sullivan, Laura: National Public Radio
Sullivan, Megan: National Public Radio
Sullivan, Robert: NBC News
Sullivan, Sharon: Ventana Productions
Sullivan, Virginia L.: National Public Radio
Sum, Sok Ry: Radio Free Asia
Summers, Elizabeth: The Newshour with Jim Lehrer
Summers, Patrick: Fox News
Sumrell, John: WTTG–Fox Television
Surbey, Jason: C–SPAN
Sutherland, Leigh: NBC News
Suto, Ena: TV Asahi
Sutton, Todd: NBC Newschannel
Svolopoulos, Christina: Fox News
Swain, Bethany: CNN
Swain, Susan: C–SPAN
Swain, Todd: Mobile Video Services, LTD
Swan, Sean: Independent Television News (ITN)
Swanier, Sherrell: CNN
Swann, Curtis: C–SPAN
Swann, Michael: WRC–TV/NBC–4
Sweeney, Charles: CNN
Sweeney, Robert: WRC–TV/NBC–4
Sweetapple, Dan: Australian Broadcasting Corporation
Sylvester, Lisa: CNN
Syrjanen, Janne: Aljazeera International
Tabaar, Mohammed: BBC
Tait, Ted: BBC
Tallo, Cara: National Public Radio
Tamerlani, George: Reuters Radio & TV
Tang, Yun: Radio Free Asia
Tannen, Elizabeth: National Public Radio
Tapper, Jake: ABC News
Taring, Tenor: Radio Free Asia
Tashi, Yeshi: Radio Free Asia
Tasillo, Mary Ellen: Fox News
Tate, Deborah: Voice of America
Tate, Tiffany: BET Nightly News
Tatton, Abbi: CNN
Tavcar, Erik: Channel One News
Taylor, Allyson Ross: CBS News
Taylor, Dan: CNN
Taylor, Darren: Voice of America
Taylor, Eric S.: ABC News
Taylor, John: WRC–TV/NBC–4
Teboe, Mark: Aljazeera International
Teeples, Joseph: C–SPAN
Tejerina, Pilar: Aljazeera International
Tendencia, Editha: Freelance
Tennent, Gerald W.: National Public Radio
Teply, Marcus: Freelance
Teranishi, Kenji: Nippon TV Network
Teron, Racheel: WJLA–TV/Newschannel 8
Terrell, William B.: ABC News
Terry, David: SRN News (Salem)
Terry, Janet: WUSA–TV
Tevault, Neil David: National Public Radio
Thai, Xuan: CNN
Thalman, Mark: Ventana Productions
Thang, Truong D.: Radio Free Asia
Theall, David J.: CNN
Thery, Samara: The Newshour with Jim Lehrer
Thoman, Eric: C–SPAN

MEMBERS ENTITLED TO ADMISSION—Continued

Thomas, Amy Jo: ABC News
Thomas, Christopher: Community TV of PG'S
Thomas, Evelyn: CBS News
Thomas, Gary: Voice of America
Thomas, Michael: Freelance
Thomas, Pierre G.: ABC News
Thomas, Renu: The Newshour with Jim Lehrer
Thomas, Sharahn: National Public Radio
Thomas, Shari: Freelance
Thomas, Will: WTTG–Fox Television
Thomas III, James B.: CNN
Thompson, James: C–SPAN
Thompson, Jerry: CNN
Thompson, Kelly: Environment & Energy Publishing, LLC
Thompson, Lisa: CNN
Thompson, Nick: NBC News
Thompson, Ron: Radio One
Thompson, Jr., Joseph: Freelance
Thorne, C. Patrick: Washington Bureau News Service
Thornton, Ronald: NBC News
Thuman, Scott: WJLA–TV/Newschannel 8
Till, Morgan: The Newshour with Jim Lehrer
Tiller, Arthur: C–SPAN
Tillery, Richard: The Washington Bureau
Tillette, David: WETA
Tillman, Thomas E.: CBS News
Tilman, Ai: Nippon TV Network
Tilman, Brandon: C–SPAN
Timmermann, Michael: WJLA–TV/Newschannel 8
Tin, Annie: C–SPAN
Tinn, San San: Radio Free Asia
Tipper, William: CNN
Todd, Brian: CNN
Todd, Chuck: NBC News
Todd, Deborah: Freelance
Tofani, Jeff: Voice of America
Tokman, Roman: Russia Today Television
Toman, George: Freelance
Toms, Sarah: BBC
Topgyal, Benpa: Radio Free Asia
Torgerson, Ande: Fox News
Torlone, Lauren: CNN
Torpey, Robert: Fox News
Totenberg, Nina: National Public Radio
Touhey, Emmanuel: C–SPAN
Toulouse, Anne: Radio France Internationale
Tovarek, Steve: CNN
Trainor, Thomas: Eurovision Americas, Inc.
Trammell, Michael: WUSA–TV
Trauzzi, Monica: Environment & Energy Publishing, LLC
Travers, Karen Lynn: ABC News
Traynham, Peter C.: CBS News
Trengrove, James: The Newshour with Jim Lehrer
Triay, Andres P.: CBS News
Truong, Thang Dinh: Radio Free Asia
Trylch, Jeremy: East Çoast Television
Tschida, Stephen: WJLA–TV/Newschannel 8
Tso, Dorjee: Radio Free Asia
Tsou, Chris: Ventana Productions
Tucker, Bill: CNN
Tucker, Danette: The Newshour with Jim Lehrer
Tucker, Elke: German TV ZDF
Tugan, Birusk: Voice of America
Tuggle, Michael D.: Freelance
Tully, Andrew: Radio Free Europe
Tuma, Firas: ATN Productions, LTD
Tuohey, Kenneth: CNN
Tureck, Matthew: NBC Newschannel
Turkevich, Elizabeth: Channel One News
Turner, Al Douglas: Freelance
Turner, Chris: CNN
Turner, Patricia: Fox News
Turner, Renee: Freelance
Turnham, Steve: CNN
Turrell, Elizabeth Ann: ABC News
Tuss, Adam: WTOP Radio
Tutman, Dan D.: CBS News
Twigg, Jonathan: BBC
Tyler, Brett: CNN
Tyler, Thomas: Channel One News
Uchimiya, Ellen: Fox News
Uhl, Kim: CNN
Ulery, Brad: Freelance
Uliano, Richard J.: CNN
Ulloa, Victor: CBS News
Ulmer, Kenya S.: CNN
Umrani, Anthony R.: CNN
Unger, Barry: Voice of America
Urbina, Luis: WRC–TV/NBC–4
Ure, Laurie: CNN
Ureta, Juan E.: Freelance
Usaeva, Nadia: Radio Free Asia
Uyehara, Otto Kenneth: WETA
Vail, Patrick: Washington Bureau News Service
Valdez, Ariel: National Public Radio
Valentine, Vikki: National Public Radio
Van Cleave, Kristopher: WJLA–TV/Newschannel 8
Van de Mark, Ellen: NBC News
van der Laan, Nanette: Freelance
Van Dyk, Peter: BBC
Van Horn, Allan: NBC News
Van Susteren, Greta: Fox News
Van Vleet, Peter: AP–Broadcast
Van Winkle, Saadia: Community TV of PG'S
VanArsdale, Vicki: Bloomberg Radio & TV
Vance, Denise: AP–Broadcast
Vance, Lauren: WUSA–TV
Vanderveen, Paul: Freelance
Vaquer, Veronica: WJLA–TV/Newschannel 8
Vargo, David: AP–Broadcast
Vasa, Sampath: WETA
Vaughan, Vincent: WJLA–TV/Newschannel 8

MEMBERS ENTITLED TO ADMISSION—Continued

Vega, Fernando: Middle East Television Network (Alhurra)
Venkataraman, Nitya K.: ABC News
Vennell, Vicki A.: ABC News
Venuto, Anthony: East Coast Television
Verdugo, Adam: NBC News
Veronelli, Alessio: Swiss Broadcasting
Vestal, Christine: STATELINE.ORG
Vicario, Virginia A.: ABC News
Vicary, Lauren: NBC News
Vidushi, Vidushi: Voice of America
Vigran, Anna: National Public Radio
Vila, Xavier: Catalunya Radio
Villone Garcia, Patricia: Community TV of PG'S
Vinson, Bryce: Fox News
Viqueira, Michael: NBC News
Visioli, Todd: Fox News
Visley, Andrew G.: AP–Broadcast
Vitorovich, Susan: NBC News
Vizcarra, Mario: Univision
Vlahos, Kelley Beaucar: Fox News
Vlamis, Becky: National Public Radio
Vock, Daniel: STATELINE.ORG
Voegeli, Peter: Swiss Broadcasting
Vohar, Den: AP–Broadcast
Volk, Kristin: Potomac Television
Volkov, Dmitri: N-TV News Television
Volskiy, Anton: N-TV News Television
von Goihmann, Nikolai: Freelance
von Trotha, Dorothea: German TV ZDF
Voth, Charles: WETA
Vu, Pauline: STATELINE.ORG
Vu, Tu H.: CNN
Vukmer, David: NBC News
Vurnis, Ambrose: Tribune Broadcasting
Waghorn, Noel: WJLA–TV/Newschannel 8
Wagner, Paul: WTTG–Fox Television
Wahl, Tracy: National Public Radio
Wait, Kevin: National Public Radio
Walch, Jennifer: ABC News
Walde, Thomas: German TV ZDF
Waldon, Michael: AP–Broadcast
Wali, Kurban: Radio Free Asia
Walker, Darius: CNN
Walker, Jackie Lyn: Freelance
Walker, James William: WJLA–TV/Newschannel 8
Walker, Kevin: AP–Broadcast
Walker, Tom: Dispatch Broadcast Group
Walker, William: CBS News
Wallace, Chris: Fox News
Wallace, John L.: Fox News
Wallace, Roger: Belo Capital Bureau
Wallace, Zelda: Cox Broadcasting
Walsh, Carly: CNN
Walsh, Deirdre: CNN
Walsh, Mary: CBS News
Walton, Lindsey: WJLA–TV/Newschannel 8
Walz, Mark: CNN
Wang, Jin: Aljazeera International
Wang, Pei: Radio Free Asia
Wang, Taofeng: Phoenix Satellite Television
Wang, Wendy: Talk Radio News Service
Waqfi, Wajd: Aljazeera Satellite Channel (Peninsula)
Ward, Derrick: Freelance
Warmerdam, Sander: NOS Dutch Public Radio & TV (VRT)
Warner, Craig: CBS News
Warner, Margaret: The Newshour with Jim Lehrer
Warner, Tarik: Freelance
Wasey, Adnaan: The Newshour with Jim Lehrer
Washburn, Kevin: C–SPAN
Washington, Chelsea: Fox News
Washington, Erick: CBS News
Washington, Ervin: Nightly Business Report
Washington Anderson, Robert: WJLA–TV/ Newschannel 8
Wasserman, Amanda: WJLA–TV/Newschannel 8
Waters, Hunter: CNN
Watkins, Duane: WTTG–Fox Television
Watrel, Jane: WRC–TV/NBC–4
Watrud, Don: WTTG–Fox Television
Watson, Carline: National Public Radio
Watson, Walter: National Public Radio
Watts, Andrew M.: National Public Radio
Watts, Michael: CNN
Weakly, David: NBC News
Weaver, David: WJLA–TV/Newschannel 8
Webb, David: WJLA–TV/Newschannel 8
Webb, Justin: BBC
Webster, Aaron: Freelance
Weglarczyk, Izabela: Polish Radio (ESKA)
Wegner, Thomas: German TV ARD
Wehinger, Amy: Fox News
Weidenbosch, Glenn E.: ABC News
Weiner, Eric: Tokyo Broadcasting System
Weiner, Eric: National Public Radio
Weinfeld, Michael: AP–Broadcast
Weinstein, Richard: C–SPAN
Weisbrod, Eric: CNN
Weiss, Brian: Bloomberg Radio & TV
Welch, Joanna: C–SPAN
Weldon, Jody: Sinclair Broadcast Group
Weller, George D.: Freelance
Wells Shott, Courtney: Fox News
Welna, David: National Public Radio
Welsh, Meghan: The Newshour with Jim Lehrer
Werdel, Paul: BBC
Werner, Theresa: AP–Broadcast
Werschkul, Benjamin: The New York Times on the Web
Wertheimer, Linda: National Public Radio
Westhead, James: BBC
Westley, Brian: AP–Broadcast
Whitaker, Morgan: NBC News
White, Douglas: ABC News

MEMBERS ENTITLED TO ADMISSION—Continued

White, Edward: Tribune Broadcasting
White, Katherine: CBS News
White, Kenneth: CNN
White, Mark: Freelance
Whiteside, John P.: Freelance
Whitley, John H.: CBS News
Whitley, Walter: Fox News
Whitney, Michael: Washington Bureau News Service
Whittemore, Megan: Freelance
Whittington, Christopher: NBC News
Widmer, Christopher: CBS News
Wiedenbauer, Heidi: Cox Broadcasting
Wiesen, Stefan: Freelance
Wiggins, Christopher: NBC Newschannel
Wik, Snorre: Aljazeera International
Wilcox, Yuni: Voice of America
Wildman, Jim: National Public Radio
Wilk, Wendy: Hearst–Argyle Television
Wilkes, Douglas H.: WTTG–Fox Television
Wilkins, Tracee: Freelance
Wilkinson, Wendla: NBC News
Williams, Arin: Community TV of PG'S
Williams, Ashton: AP–Broadcast
Williams, Candace: Voice of America
Williams, Clarence: CNN
Williams, Colleen: Fox News
Williams, David: Freelance
Williams, Derek: WTOP Radio
Williams, Jeffrey L.: Cox Broadcasting
Williams, John: Fox News
Williams, John Flawn: National Public Radio
Williams, Juan: National Public Radio
Williams, Keith: WUSA–TV
Williams, Kelia: Aljazeera International
Williams, Kenneth E.: CBS News
Williams, Louis ''Pete'': NBC News
Williams, Robert T.: NBC News
Williamson, Van: National Public Radio
Willingham, Val: Freelance
Willis, Anne Marie: Fox News
Willis, Judith: The Newshour with Jim Lehrer
Wilp, Christian: N–TV News Television
Wilson, Brenda: National Public Radio
Wilson, Brian: Fox News
Wilson, G. Edwin: WJLA–TV/Newschannel 8
Wilson, Mark: Freelance
Wilson, Stephanie: WUSA–TV
Wilson, Toni: ABC News
Wiltermood, James: Potomac Television
Windham, Ronald: Tribune Broadcasting
Winerman, Lea: The Newshour with Jim Lehrer
Winslow, David: AP–Broadcast
Winslow, Linda: The Newshour with Jim Lehrer
Winter, Joerg: Austrian Radio & TV (ORF)
Winterhalter, Ruthann: C–SPAN
Winters, Ronald: Freelance
Wische, Aaron: WTTG–Fox Television
Wisniewski, Walter: Voice of America
Witte, Joel: WTTG–Fox Television
Witten, Robert: NBC News
Wittstock, Melinda: Capitol News Connection (CNC)
Wodele, Greta: C–SPAN
Wolf, Zachary B.: ABC News
Wolfe, Lisa: Federal News Radio AM 1050
Wolfe, Randy: NBC Newschannel
Wolfson, Charles: CBS News
Wolfson, Scott: WTTG–Fox Television
Wolfson-Stevenson, Paula: Voice of America
Won, Il Hee: Seoul Broadcasting System (SBS)
Wood, Audrey: CBS News
Wood, Barry: Voice of America
Wood, Christopher: C–SPAN
Woodruff, Judy: The Newshour with Jim Lehrer
Woodward, Thom J.: National Public Radio
Wordock, Colleen: Bloomberg Radio & TV
Wordock, John: Marketwatch
Wright, Dale: WJLA–TV/Newschannel 8
Wright, James: Aljazeera International
Wright, Kelly: Fox News
Wright, Tracey Marie: Freelance
Wu, Po L.: Freelance
Wu Chung, Eileen: Channel One News
Wulff, John Werner: ABC News
Wygal, Scott: NBC News
Xavier, Wilkins: Aljazeera International
Xia, Amy: New Tang Dynasty TV
Xiang, Dong: New Tang Dynasty TV
Xie, Jiao Christine: Phoenix Satellite Television
Xie, Yanmei: Free Speech Radio News
Xu, Jinglu: New TAng Dynasty TV
Yack, Angie: AP–Broadcast
Yaklyvich, Brian: CNN
Yam, Raymond: Voice of America
Yamada, Mio: NHK–Japan Broadcasting Corporation
Yamada, Nancy M.: WUSA–TV
Yang, Carter: CBS News
Yang, Chunfang: New Tang Dynasty TV
Yang, Eun: Freelance
Yang, John: NBC News
Yang, Lian-Hwa: Freelance
Yang, Sungwon: Radio Free Asia
Yarborough, Rick: WTTG–Fox Television
Yarmuth, Floyd: CNN
Yates, H. William: CBS News
Ydstie, John: National Public Radio
Yee Gaffney, Suzanne: AP–Broadcast
Yeshi, Lobsang: Radio Free Asia
Yeung, Richard: NBC News
Yi, Hyun Joo: Korean Broadcasting Systems
Yianopoulos, Karen: Middle East Television Network (Alhurra)
Yoon, Robert: CNN
Yoon, Yong Chul: MBC–TV Korea (Munhwa)

MEMBERS ENTITLED TO ADMISSION—Continued

Young, Jeremy: Aljazeera International
Young, Melissa A.: ABC News
Young, Robert Latimer: C–SPAN
Young, Saundra: CNN
Young Jr., Jerome: CBN News
Young-Kweon, Kim: Voice of America
Yousef, Dania: Freelance
Yu, Annie: WTTG–Fox Television
Yu, John: New Tang Dynasty TV
Yuille, Jennifer: NBC News
Yun, Jei Choon: Korean Broadcasting Systems
Zaidi, Huma: NBC News
Zairi, Said: ATN Productions, LTD
Zajko, Robert: Diversified Communications, Inc. (DCI)
Zalewski, Anna: Voice of America
Zang, Guohua: CTI–TV (Taiwan)
Zariquiey, Juan Pablo: WZDC–TV
Zarpas, Stephanie: CBS News
Zavarce, Pedro: CNN
Zaw Nyunt, Kyaw: Voice of America
Zayed, Nahedah: Aljazeera International
Zderic, Srdjan: Aljazeera International
Zechar, David: ABC News
Zeffler, Marcus: BBC
Zervos, Stratis: Freelance
Zibel, Eve: Fox News
Ziegler, Albrecht: German Public Radio (ARD)
Zillich, Jose: Aljazeera International
Zin, Min: Radio Free Asia
Zingarelli, Megan: CNN
Zosso, Elizabeth: Middle East Television Network (Alhurra)
Zurkhang, Karma: Radio Free Asia
Zwillich, Todd: Capitol News Connection (CNC)

NETWORKS, STATIONS, AND SERVICES REPRESENTED

Senate Gallery 224–6421 House Gallery 225–5214

ABC NEWS—(202) 222–7700; 1717 DeSales Street, NW., Washington, DC 20036: John W. Allard, Scott Anderson, Sarah Baker, Mark Banks, Gene Barrett, Sonya Crawford Bearson, Adam Belmar, Bob Bender, Phillip M. Black, Tahman Bradley, Robert E. Bramson, Charles Breiterman, Sam Brooks, Henry M. Brown, David John G. Bull, Quiana Burns, Christopher Carlson, David Chalian, Martin J. Clancy, John Cochran, Theresa E. Cook, Richard L. Coolidge, Pam Coulter, Jan Crawford Greenburg, Max Culhane, Thomas J. d'Annibale, Jack Date, Edward Teddy Davis, Yunji Elisabeth de Nies, Clifford E. DeGray, Steven Densmore, Dominic DeSantis, Elizabeth C. Dirner, Henry Disselkamp, John F. Dittman, Peter M. Doherty, Brian Donovan, Lawrence L. Drumm, Jennifer Duck, Richard Ehrenberg, Margaret Ellerson, Daniel Glenn Elvington, Kendall A. Evans, Charles Finamore, Jon D. Garcia, Robert G. Garcia, Arthur R. Gauthier, Charles DeWolf Gibson, Thomas M. Giusto, Bernard Gmiter, Jennifer Goldberg, Stuart Gordon, Robin Gradison, Jonathan Greenberger, Stephen Hahn, Brian Robert Hartman, William T. Hatch, John Edward Hendren, Esequiel Herrera, Kylie A. Hogan, Julia Kartalia Hoppock, Matthew Alan Hosford, Amon Hotep, Bret Hovell, Matthew Jaffe, Fletcher Johnson, Kenneth Johnson, Derek Leon Johnston, Akilah N. Joseph, Steve E. Joya, James F. Kane, Jonathan Karl, David P. Kerley, John Knott, Donald Eugene Kroll, Maya C. Kulycky, Hilary Lefebvre, Melissa Anne Lopardo, Ellsworth M. Lutz, Lachlan Murdoch MacNeil, Liz Marlantes, James Martin, Jr., Luis Martinez, Darraine Maxwell, Michele Marie McDermott, Erik T. McNair, Ari Meltzer, Portia Migas, Avery Miller, Sunlen Mari Miller, Keith B. Morgan, Gary Nadler, Emily Anne Nelson, Dean E. Norland, Emily O'Donnell, Andrea Owen, Jennifer L. Parker, John R. Parkinson, Jay E. Patterson, Nitza Soledad Perez, Michael Pickup, Annette Pillon, Richard K. Pliszak, Steven A. Portnoy, Mary Quinn, Martha Raddatz, Kirit M. Radia, Kimberly Randolph, Victor Ratner, William Redding, Leah Ricciuti, Carlos A. Rojas, Richard L. Roller, George Romilly, Gary Rosenberg, Howard L. Rosenberg, Jay R. Russo, Jason Ryan, George D. Sanchez, Howard Schoenholtz, Steve Schwartz, Frederick Sera, Thomas Andrew Shine, Claire Shipman, Leigh E. Simons, Cynthia Smith, James E. Smith, Eric Speights, Lisa Stark, Steve Stefany, George Stephanopoulos, Jessica C. Stuart, Matthew Stuart, Jake Tapper, Eric S. Taylor, William B. Terrell, Amy Jo Thomas, Pierre G. Thomas, Karen Lynn Travers, Elizabeth Ann Turrell, Nitya K. Venkataraman, Vicki A. Vennell, Virginia A. Vicario, Jennifer Walch, Glenn E. Weidenbosch, Douglas White, Toni Wilson, Zachary B. Wolf, John Werner Wulff, Melissa A. Young, David Zechar.

AGDAY—(574) 631–1313; 54516 Business, U.S. 31 North, South Bend, IN 46637: Philip McMartin.

AL ARABIYA TV—(202) 355–6616; National Press Building, 529 14th Street, NW., Suite 530, Washington, DC 20045: Yamen Abdalwahab, Daoud Abuelhawa, Lukman Ahmed, Nadia Charters, Elias Habib, Balajia Kanawati, Nathan McCray, Richard Melhem, Muna Shikaki.

ALASKA PUBLIC RADIO NETWORK—(907) 277–2776; 810 East Ninth Avenue, Anchorage, AL 99501: Joel Southern.

ALJAZEERA INTERNATIONAL—(202) 496–4500; 1627 K Street, NW., Suite 4006, Washington, DC 20006: Hebah Abdalla, Zeresnaey Abraha, Kieran Baker, Jeff Ballou, Valery Barshak, Andrew Bastien, Babak Behnam, Barbara Benitez, Mark Biggs, Jennifer Bragg, Sally Carroll, Nick Castellaro, Kevin Cawley, Maria Chapman, Ben Connors, Jeremy Copeland, Michael Correro, Erin Croyle, Timothy Durham, Camille Elhassani, Gabriel Elizondo, Brenda Elkins, Ghida Fakhry, Dionne Fennell, Anthony Frisketti, Maya Garg, Jean Garner, Maurya Gautam, Karina Gomes, Kimberly Halkett, Thierry Humeau, Eugenia Hurtado, Sasa Josipovic, Catherine Kalbfleisch, Lina Khalaf, Riz Khan, Dana Langguth, Dennis Legget, Chieu Luu, David Mackamul, Amy Marash, David Marash, Joseph Marno, Mike Marno, Rudy Marshall, Sandra Martinez, Craig Mauro, Dara McIntosh, David McWhinney, Jesse Mesner-Hage, Robert Michaud, Ayman Mohyeldin, Gaven Morris, Imad Musa, Anand Naidoo, Renee Odeh, Peter Okorn, Annie Kate Pons, Michael Pounds, John Patrick Raine, Steven Ray, Alea Reeves, Robert Reynolds, Kelly Rockwell, Joshua Rushing, Roee Ruttenberg, Jennifer Salan, Kristen Saloomey, Mark Seddon, Michael Seium, Mike Shriver, John Simons, Phillip Smith, William Stebbins, Janne Syrjanen, Mark Teboe, Pilar Tejerina, Jin Wang, Snorre Wik, Kelia Williams, James Wright, Wilkins Xavier, Jeremy Young, Nahedah Zayed, Srdjan Zderic, Jose Zillich.

ALJAZEERA SATELLITE CHANNEL—(Peninsula)—(202) 327–8200; 1627 K Street, NW., Suite 200, Washington, DC 20006: Nader Abed, Eyad Aburahma, Mohammed Alami, Heni Azzam, Baubak Baghi, Christopher Campbell, Humayun Chaudhry, Mohammad Dalbah, Mahmoud El-Hamalawy, Jessy Elmurr, Abderrahim Foukara, Michael Fox, Nasser Hssani, Ibrahim Khader, Mysa Khalaf, Fadi Mansour, Christopher Messer, Layelle Saad, Wajd Waqfi.

AMERICAN FAMILY RADIO NEWS P.O. Drawer 3206—107 Parkgate Tupelo, MS 38803: Jim Brown.

NETWORKS, STATIONS, AND SERVICES REPRESENTED—Continued

AP–BROADCAST—(202) 736–1172; 1825 K Street, Washington, DC 20006: Cynthia Aitken, Waleed Al-Moajil, Khaldoun Alrawi, Jennifer Beckman, Hugo Blanco, Gerald Bodlander, Camille Bohannon, Judy Boysha, Carlotta L. Bradley, Tracy Ann Brown, David Bruns, Flora Charner, Steven Coleman, Danny D'Amico, Kelly Daschle, Anna Davalos-Macdonald, Jon Detrow, Estelle Ebitty-Doro, Waiel Elnour, Eileen Fleming, Patrick Fogarty, Eric Freeland, David J. Friar, Adrian Fullwood, Oscar Wells Gabriel, Jennifer Garske, Micah Gelman, Richard Gentilo, Lawrence Gold, James W. Gorman, Robert Gutnikoff, Susan Henderson, Brian Hoffman, Dan Huff, Edvige Jean-Francois, Brad Kalbfeld, Kara Kearns, Kristine Kelleher, Christian Kettlewell, Sandy Kozel, Steve Kuhn, Lister Lim, Kathryn Loomans, Myra B. Lopez, James Ludwin, Nancy Lyons Sargeant, Sofia Mannos, David Martin, Lisa N. Matthews, Nan Hee McMinn, Sagar Meghani, David R. Melendy, Christina Mesquita, Mark Moynihan, Linh Ong, Krystyna Osinski, Hakan Oszancak, Julie Pace, Louis Pagan, Scott Payne, Alexis Perkins, Gerald Petraitis, Jacqueline Policastro, Lee Powell, Ed Pryor, Walter Ratliff, Orla Reese, Thomas Ritchie, Alexis Rooney Perkins, Michael Rosenfelder, Matt Small, Mark S. Smith, Shirley O'Bryan Smith, Mitchell Stern, Peter Van Vleet, Denise Vance, David Vargo, Andrew G. Visley, Den Vohar, Michael Waldon, Kevin Walker, Michael Weinfeld, Theresa Werner, Brian Westley, Ashton Williams, David Winslow, Angie Yack, Suzanne Yee Gaffney.

ATN PRODUCTIONS, LTD.—(202) 898–8270; 1510 H Street, NW., 7th Floor, Washington, DC 20005: Mike Kellerman, Affra Khallash, Taleb Khallash, Mohamed Said Ouafi, Firas Tuma, Said Zairi.

AUSTRALIAN BROADCASTING CORPORATION—(202) 626–5161; 2000 M Street, NW., Suite 660, Washington, DC 20036: Timothy Bates, Tracy Bowden, Woodrow Landay, Kim Landers, Jason D. Racki, Michael Rowland, Janet E. Silver, Mark Simkin, Dan Sweetapple.

AUSTRIAN RADIO & TV (ORF)—(202) 822–9570; 1206 Eton Court, NW., Washington, DC 20007: Uelle-Mall Jaakson, Christian Lininger, Raimund Loew, Douglas Robinson, Graham Scott, Lauren Silva-Pinto, Joerg Winter.

AZTECA AMERICA—(202) 419–6134; 400 North Capitol, NW., Suite 361, Washington, DC 20001: Neisa Condemaita, Armando Guzman, Roberto Guzman, Edwing Lopez, Raul Ramos.

BBC—(202) 223–2050; 2000 M Street, NW., #800, Washington, DC 20009: Marc Allard, Ali Amimi, Roula Ayoubi, Jonathan Beale, Katie Beck, Sharon Blanchet, Adam Brookes, Kari Browne, Stuart Cohen, Maxine Collins, James Coomarasamy, Fatou Diarra, Kambiz Fattahi, Matt Frei, Bruno Garcez, Sarah Gilbert, Vanessa Heaney, Lourdes Heredia, Mark Hiney, Dave Hopper, Rozalia Hristova, Shazeb Jillani, Majid Joneidi, Kathy Kay, Yolande Knell, Jane Little, Rita Manjardino, Jacqueline Martens, Tara McDermott, Allen McGreevy, William McKenna, Beth Miller, Claudia Milne, Sarah Morris, Peter Murtaugh, Jane O'Brien, Purvee Pattni, Mark Rabbage, Adi Raval, Sarah Robbins, Dan Ryntjes, Harry Shoffner, Ron Skeans, Laura Smith-Spark, Andrew Steele, Mohammed Tabaar, Ted Tait, Sarah Toms, Jonathan Twigg, Peter Van Dyk, Justin Webb, Paul Werdel, James Westhead, Marcus Zeffler.

BELO CAPITAL BUREAU—(202) 661–8444; 1325 C Street, NW., Suite 250, Washington, DC 20005: Mark Angelini, Al Banegas, Norman Butler, David Cassidy, David Duitch, Michael Goldfein, Michael Kornely, Erin Maloney, Sarah Nakasone, Geoff Parlett, Ashley Patterson, Tiffany Sands, William Smith, Roger Wallace.

BET NIGHTLY NEWS—(202) 783–0537; 400 N. Capitol Street, NW., Suite 361, Washington, DC 20001: Malik Hassan Abdullah-James, Tiffany Cross, Pamela Gentry, Erin Jenkins, Andre Showell, William Stokes, Tiffany Tate.

BLOOMBERG RADIO & TV—(202) 624–1933; 1399 New York Avenue, NW., 11th Floor, Washington, DC 20005: Kate Andersen, Lindsey Arent, Jon Bascom, Joseph Bellard, Sophie Caronello, Irwin Chapman, Peter Cook, Bianca Davie, Christine Dooley, Trevor Finn, Steve Geimann, Ben Geldon, Lori Jennings, Kathryn Kross, Walter Little, Eduardo Londres, Jason Medenecki, Brian Meehan, Roland Morrisette, Lizzie O'Leary, Robert Press, Amy Rosen, Julie Slattery, William Small, Randolph Smith, Tim Stang, Vicki VanArsdale, Brian Weiss, Colleen Wordock.

BROADCASTING CORP. OF CHINA—(703) 624–8759; 3531 Schuerman House Drive, Fairfax, VA 22031: Nike Ching.

BT VIDEO PRODUCTIONS—(301) 370–0808; 7117 Wolftree Lane Rockville, MD 20852: Cesar Flores, Paul Hollenbeck, Martin Kos.

CAMERINI–ROBERTSON, INC.—(202) 841–4640; Michael Camerini, Shari Robertson.

CANADIAN BROADCASTING CANADA (CBC)—(202) 383–2905; National Press Building, 529 14th Street, NW., Suite 500, Washington, DC 20045: Anyck Beraud, Bruno Bonamigo, Marcel Calfat, Henry Champ, Julie Clow, Michael Colton, Louis de Guise, Alan Habbick, Samira Hussain, William Loucks, Neil MacDonald, Mariana Melnyk, Joyce Napier, David Ouellet, Yves Peltier, Gilles Plante, Sylvain Richard, Alison Smith.

CAPITOL NEWS CONNECTION (CNC)—(202) 498–5483; 110 Maryland Avenue, NE., Washington, DC 20002: Jodi Breisler, Charles Davis, Bryan Hayes, Martin Howe, Evelyn Lombardo, Mark McDonald, Jill Morrison, Eric Niiler, Sara Sciammacco, Benjamin Shaw, Melinda Wittstock, Todd Zwillich.

CARACOL TELEVISION—(202) 504–6300; 529 14th Street, NW., 8th Floor, Washington, DC 20045: Lina Correa.

CATALUNYA RADIO—311 Fallsworth Place, Walkersville, MD 21793: Xavier Vila.

NETWORKS, STATIONS, AND SERVICES REPRESENTED—Continued

CBN NEWS—(202) 833–2707; 1919 M Street, NW., Suite 100, Washington, DC 20036: David Brody, Melissa A. Charbonneau, Jeremy Denison, Alegra Hassan, Mark Hendricks, Steve Jacobi, Gene Jenkins, John Jessup, Matthew Keedy, David Page, Miguel Paz Vergara, Laura Robertson, Royce Sallstrom, Michael Schaff, Erick Stakelbeck, Paul Strand, Jerome Young, Jr.

CBS NEWS—(202) 457–4444; 2020 M Street, NW., Washington, DC 20036: Clinton N. Alexander, Wyatt Andrews, Karyn Anthony, Howard Arenstein, Thalia Assuras, Sharyl Attkisson, Jim Axelrod, Barry Bagnato, Morris Banks, Bruce Barr, Kia Baskerville, Farrel Becker, Mark R. Bennett, Gloria Borger, Kristi Brown, Andrea Bruce, Susan Bullard Harmon, William Calder, Anthony Cavin, Denise Cetta, Steven Chaggaris, Joie Chen, Jane S. Chick, George Christian, Alfred Colby, Caroline Cooper, John Crum, Pham Gia Cuong, John Daly, Allison Davis O'Keefe, Charlie Dawson, Li Denise, Charles H. Dixson, Kimberly Dozier, John Falls, John L. Fantacone, John Frado, Tony Furlow, Hal E. Furman, Brian Fuss, Robert J. Fuss, Benson Ginsburg, Jeff Scott Goldman, Neil Grasso, David Gross, Josh Gross, Joel Gwadz, Mary Hager, Michelle Handleman, Mark Hanner, Predi-Reko Harmon, Susan Harmon, Robert Hendin, Deirdre Hester, Dennis Jamison, Jeffrey Johnston, Mark Katkov, Craig Katz, Patrick Kiker, Mark Knoller, Stephanie Lambidakis, Donald A. Lee, Janet Leissner, Michelle Levi, Aaron Lewis, Jonathan Lien, Dyer Lois, Peter Maer, Steve Marshall, David Martin, Thomas A. Mattesky, Ronald H. Matthews, Scott McCrary, Jim McGlinchy, Michael McGuire, Robert McKinley, Natalia Melia, Dick Meyer, Karen Moore, John Murphy, Dewayne Nickerson, John Nolen, Jennifer Cohen Oko, Bob Orr, Rebecca Peterson, Michael Peyton, William Pimble, William Plante, Diana Quinn, Carrie Rabin, Daniel Raviv, Francisco Robbins, Susan Roberts, Jill Rosenbaum, Kate Rydell, Eric Salzman, Bob Schieffer, Thomas H. Seem, Gregory Shaffir, Kimberlee Shaffir, Dennis Shannon, Ward C. Sloane, Richard H. Spire, Dave Stanford, Meredith Stencil, Gabriel Stix, Laura Strickler, Fernando J. Suarez, Allyson Ross Taylor, Evelyn Thomas, Thomas E. Tillman, Peter C. Traynham, Andres P. Triay, Dan D. Tutman, Victor Ulloa, William Walker, Mary Walsh, Craig Warner, Erick Washington, Katherine White, John H. Whitley, Christopher Widmer, Kenneth E. Williams, Charles Wolfson, Audrey Wood, Carter Yang, H. William Yates, Stephanie Zarpas.

CHANNEL ONE NEWS—(202) 587–4126; 4455 Connecticut Avenue, NW., Suite 225, Washington, DC 20008: Carl Ballard, Casey Costello, Renee De Luca, Kathryn Farrell, Lauren Green, Mary Haynes, Elizabeth Korona, Michael Marcus, Alexander Marquardt, Lila Merideth, Fran Murphy, Meka Nichols, Phillip Andrew Och, Sarah Rooney, Kristine Schantz, Cali Sorensen, Erik Tavcar, Elizabeth Turkevich, Thomas Tyler, Eileen Wu Chung.

CNBC—(202) 467–5400; 1025 Conneticut Avenue, NW., Washington, DC 20836: Plummer Crawley, Matthew Cuddy, Joanne Fuchs, John Harwood, Karen James, Diana Olick, Hampton Pearson, Pat Pugliese, Jill Smith, Ashley Stringer.

CNN—(202) 898–7670; 820 1st Street, NE., Washington, DC 20002: Khalil Abdallah, Mike Ahlers, William Alberter, Kate Albright-Hanna, Scott Anderson, Natalie Apsell, Nelson Archer, Kelli Arena, Hande Atay, Stephen Bach, David Bacheler, Reza James Baktar, Erik Banks, Michael A. Bannigan, David Banville, James Barnett, Ted Barrett, Caitlin Barry, Dana Bash, Jeff Bates, Elizabeth Belanger, John Bena, Pamela S. Benson, Thomas Bentz, Kathy Benz, David Berman, Laura Bernardini, Barbara Berti, Wolf Blitzer, John Bodnar, Kevin Bohn, David Bohrman, Joshua Braun, Michael Brevner, Heidi Bridges, Claire Brinberg, Ray Britch, Becky Brittain, Craig A. Broffman, Scott Bronstein, Quinn Brown, Melanie Buck, Burke Buckhorn, Carol Buckland, Brian Burch, Jennifer Burch, Abigail Burchman, Juan E. Cabral, Meribe Campbell, Silvio Carrillo, Patricia Carroll, Christopher Carter, Damian Catanza, David Keith Catrett, Warren Channell, Jill Chappell, Trish Chicca, David Cilberti, Bobby Clemons, Allison Colson, Woodrow Compton, Anderson Cooper, Paul Courson, Benjamin Coyte, Carol A. Cratty, Candy Crowley, John Cunha, Michael R. M. David, Marcus Davis, Patrick A. Davis, Carlos de Vega, Anastasia Diakides, Rick DiBella, Vilinda Dickerson, Geoffrey Dietrich, Erika Dimmler, Sue Diviney, Stephen Dolce, Jill Dougherty, Martin Dougherty, Carlton Downer, John Dunaway, Thomas Dunlavey, Lisa Durham, Edie Emery, Kathleen Fabian, Susan Falvella-Garraty, Jennifer Farley, Sam Feist, Eric James Fiegel, Craig Fingar, James Flaherty, Robley Fletcher, Liz Flynn, Thomas Foreman, Hida Fouladvand, Robert Franken, Terry Frieden, Kenya Friend-Daniel, Lydia Garlikov, Timothy C. Garraty, Mara Gassman, Maurice George, John Gilmore, Evan Glass, Andre Goddard, Lisa Goddard, Liliana Gonzalez, Elizabeth Gousha, David Gracey, James Gray, James Graydon, Thomas Greene, Rex Grigg, Eddie S. Gross, Jr., Thomas Groves, Mike Haan, Peter Hamby, Jeremy Harlan, Lanese Harris, Guerin Hays, Ronald G. Helm, Ed Henry, Benjamin F. Hill, Conrad Hirzel, Sarah B. Holland, Matthew Hoye, Christian Hudson, Dave Hugel, Shirley Hung, Charles Hurley, Terry Irving, Alan Isenberg, Craig Jackson, Adia Jacobs, Lesa Jansen, NuNu Japaridze, David Jenkins, Joseph Johns, Kyle Johnsen, Sasha Johnson, Michael Judge, Brianna Keilar, Pamela Kelley, Cristina Kelly, Christopher Kenny, Charley Keyes, John King, Worth Kinlaw, George P. Kinney, Adilson Kiyasu, Kathleen Koch, Andrea Koppel, Lauren Kornreich, Stephanie Kotuby, Robert S. Kovach, Gary Krakower, Ronald Kuczynski, Elise Labott, Kyung Lah, Gregory Lane, Peter Lanier, Larry Lazo, Adam Levine, Frances L. Lewine, Philip Littleton, Juan Carlos Lopez, Edwin Lora, Willie A. Lora, Andrew Losey, Howard Lutt, Beverly Malone, Michael Maltas, Mark Anthony Marchione, Timothy McCaughan, Dugald McConnell, Emily McCulloch, Kerith McFadden, Denise McIntosh, James

NETWORKS, STATIONS, AND SERVICES REPRESENTED—Continued

McIntyre, Eleanor Spektor McManus, Samuel J. McMichael IV, Michael McMullan, William Mears, James Meech, Jeanne Meserve, Edward Metzger, Jason Robert Meucci, Paul Keith Miller, Peter Mohen, Jeremy Moorhead, Peter Morris, Virginia Moubray, Thomas Murphy, Nicholette Nicci, Virginia Nicolaidis, Ernest G. Nocciolo, Valorie Nocciolo, Christopher Nowak, Kerry Ogata, John Otth, Paul Palaruan, Andre Parker, Robert Geoffrey Parker, Chris Parks, Aaron C. Payne, Nathan Payne, Alan Philippon, Jordan Placie, Michael Poley, Chris Popp, Mark Preston, Carol Rachou, Chris Ravanello, Patrick Reap, Justine Redman, Jean Renaud, David Ridgeway, James Riggs, John Roberts, Greg Robertson, Angela Robinson, David Robinson, Janelle Rodriguez, Janet Rodriguez, Brian Rokus, H. Michael Roselli, Rachel Rosen, Jessica Rosgaard, Mary Katherine Ross, Linda Roth, Lindy Royce, Joshua Rubin, David Ruff, Diane Ruggiero, Emily Rust, John Sacco, Manuel Samaniego, Jill Sankey, Jose G. Santos, Douglas N. Schantz, David Scherer, Barry C. Schlegel, William Schneider, Sharona Schwartz, Reginald G. Selma, Frank Sesno, Peter Seymour, Lawrence Shaughnessy, Sarah Shepherd, Shawna Shepherd, Joann Sierra, Juan Silva, Jeffery Simms, Kathy Slobogin, Raeshawn Smith, Skip Smith, Matthew Speiser, Jim Spellman, Jennifer Businger Sperry, Todd Sperry, Philip Scott Spoerry, Jonathan St. John, Steven Stahl, Scott Stead, Aspen Steib, Paul Steinhauser, Vaughn Sterling, Carrie Stevenson, Carolyn Stone, Jason Strachan, Julian Styles, Bethany Swain, Sherrell Swanier, Charles Sweeney, Lisa Sylvester, Abbi Tatton, Dan Taylor, Xuan Thai, David J. Theall, James B. Thomas III, Jerry Thompson, Lisa Thompson, William Tipper, Brian Todd, Lauren Torlone, Steve Tovarek, Bill Tucker, Kenneth Tuohey, Chris Turner, Steve Turnham, Brett Tyler, Kim Uhl, Richard J. Uliano, Kenya S. Ulmer, Anthony R. Umrani, Laurie Ure, Tu H. Vu, Darius Walker, Carly Walsh, Deirdre Walsh, Mark Walz, Hunter Waters, Michael Watts, Eric Weisbrod, Kenneth White, Clarence Williams, Brian Yaklyvich, Floyd Yarmuth, Robert Yoon, Saundra Young, Pedro Zavarce, Megan Zingarelli.

CNSNEWS.COM—(703) 683–9733; 325 South Patrick Street, Alexandria, Va 22314: Monisha Bansal, Nathan Burchfiel, Jeff Golimowski, Randy Hall, Fred Lucas, Kevin Mooney.

COMMUNITY TV OF PG'S—(301) 773–0900; 9475 Lottsford Road, Largo, MD 20774: Curtis Crutchfield, David Goldman, Julian Ingram, Ara Laughlin, Rochelle Metzger, Sonia Randev, Christopher Thomas, Saadia Van Winkle, Patricia Villone Garcia, Arin Williams.

CONNECTLIVE—(202) 513–1010; 43720 Trade Center Place, #160, Reston, VA 20190: Michael Lessin.

COPE RADIO (SPAIN)—(202) 686–1982; 4904 Bett Road, NW., Washington, DC 20016: Juan Martinez Fierro.

COURT TV—(202) 828–0366; 400 N. Capitol Street, NW., #366, Washington, DC 20001: Savannah Guthrie.

COURT TV—(202) 828–0366; 400 N. Capitol Street, NW., #366, Washington, DC 20001: Bryan Lavietes.

COX BROADCASTING—(202) 777–7000; 400 N. Capitol Street, NW., #750, Washington, DC 20001: Alison Burns, David Chase, Jamie Dupree, Carol Han, Megan Hughes, Ryan Jackson, Kevin Johnson, Scott MacFarlane, Catherine C. Reynolds, Zelda Wallace, Heidi Wiedenbauer, Jeffrey L. Williams.

C–SPAN—(202) 737–3220; 400 N. Capitol Street, NW., #650, Washington, DC 20001: Kenneth Alexander, Thomas Alldredge, Theresa Amirault-Michel, Anders Arestad, Michelle Bailor, Jason Bender, Brett Betsill, Michael Biddle, Dannie Boone, Paul Brown, Susan J. Bundock, Leslie Burdick, James Burke, Kathy Cahill Murphy, Nancy Calo-Christian, Craig Caplan, Kenneth Carrick, Tanya Chattman, Matthew Claar, James Clark, Eloise Collingwood, Bruce D. Collins, William Conover, James L. Cook, Cleve Corner, Dennis Cravedi, Liam Currier, Alexander Curtis, Greg Czzowitz, Pete Daniels, Richard Deal, Bridget Diggs, Constance Doebele, Michelle Doell, Richard Dubroff, Kenneth Dyball, Paul Eades, Jr., Katrice Eborn, Pedro L. Echevarria, Ronald Eisenbarth, Gary Ellenwood, Edward Enciu, Seth Engel, Patricia Esquivel, Greg Fabic, Mark Farkas, Richard Fleeson, Carl Foster, William Frazier, Rick Gabala, John Gallagher, John Garlock, Garney Gary, Norma Gleason, Robert Gould, Meghan Gourley, Richard Hall, Eric Hansen, Chris Hanson, Stephen Harkness, Robb Harleston, Kinsey Harvey, Maurice Haynes, William Heffley, Jonelle P. Henry, Leslye Heyman, Dallas Hill, Bob Hoffmaster, Michael Holden, George Howell, Yi-Pe Hsieh, Roberta Jackson, Taryn Jackson, Katherine Jeffries, Barry Katz, Steven Kehoe, Robert Kennedy, Roxane Kerr, Lew Ketcham, Kevin King, David Knighton, Aparna Kumar, Felix Laboy, Brian Lamb, Darren Larade, Molly Laville, Robert Lazar, Mark Lindblom, Paul Loeschke, Russell Logan, Sam Martin, Michael McCann, Sean McCann, Brendan McQuaid, Justin Metzger, Andrew Peter Miller, Kate Mills, Jennifer Moire, David Monack, Garrette Moore, Linwood Moore, Bridget Morrison, Dan Morton, Terry Murphy, Yetta Myrick, Donna Norris, Benjamin O'Connell, Alan Olmsted, Michael Patruznick, Vernon Perkins, Andrea Perry, Christina Perry, Nickolas Pitocco, Roni Pomerantz, Almon Porter, Christina Porter, Anne Preloh, Tony Pronko, Nikhil Raval, Robert Reilly, Cynthia Reuter, Delia Rios, Amy Roach, Tiffany Rocque, Martine Rodriguez, Tracy Ruby, Jennifer Ruff, Frederico Sampaio, Sherry Sanders-Smith, William Scanlan, Mary Scanlon, John Scheuer, Ellen Schweiger, Steven Scully, Kristi Slafka, Peter Slen, Ben Sorenson, Alan Speck, Gregory St. James, Norman Stewart, Rick Stoddard, Matt Stoner, Jason Surbey, Susan Swain, Curtis Swann, Joseph Teeples, Eric Thoman, James Thompson, Arthur Tiller, Brandon Tilman, Annie Tin, Emmanuel Touhey, Kevin Washburn, Richard Weinstein, Joanna Welch, Ruthann Winterhalter, Greta Wodele, Christopher Wood, Robert Latimer Young.

NETWORKS, STATIONS, AND SERVICES REPRESENTED—Continued

CTI–TV (TAIWAN)—(202) 331–9110; 1825 K Street, NW., Suite 710, Washington, DC 20006: E-Ting Chung, Guohua Zang.

CTV CANADIAN TV—(202) 466–3595; 2000 M Street, NW., Suite 330, Washington, DC 20036: Adam Tyler Blair, Tom Clark, Bradley Fulton, Denise Kimmel, James MacDonald, Joy Malbon.

DANISH BROADCASTING CORPORATION—(202) 785–1957; 3643 Jenifer Street, NW., Washington, DC 20015: Steffen William Gram.

DEUTSCHE PRESS AGENCY—(202) 662–1220; 969 National Press Building, Washington, DC 20045: Christina Eck.

DEUTSCHE WELLE TV—(703) 931–6644; 2000 M Street, NW., Suite 335, Washington, DC 20036: Stephan Bachenheimeri, Christina Bergmann, Brenda Cecil, Hillery Gallasch, Wolfgang Kotke, Rudiger Lentz.

DEUTSCHELAND RADIO—(703) 917–1561; 7420 Georgetown Court, McLean, VA 22102: Siegfried Buschschluter.

DISPATCH BROADCAST GROUP—(202) 737–4630; 400 N. Capitol Street, Suite 850, Washington, DC 20001: Michael J. Smith, Tom Walker.

DIVERSIFIED COMMUNICATIONS, INC. (DCI)—(202) 775–4300; 2000 M Street, NW., 3rd Floor, Washington, DC 20036: James Balsamo, Joseph Concaugh Jr., Jean Paul Courbois, William Demas, Robert Fetzer, Masano Hidaka, Yoshio Hidaka, Al Levin, Jamie Norins, Terry Straub, Robert Zajko.

EAST COAST TELEVISION—(202) 775–0894; 1919 M. Street, NW., Suite UM, Washington, DC 20036: Brian Marshall Ahearn, Heidi Cancelleri, Joseph Angelo Cassano, Chris Cowman, Kathleen Gural, Cheryl Hammons, Monique Isaac, Bjoem Johansson, Joey Lege, Theodore Lyons, Trenton Mengel, James Schule, Andrew Skehan, Michael Skehan, Patrick Skehan, Sylvia Skinner, Jeremy Trylch, Anthony Venuto.

EGYPTIAN TV—(202) 419–6161; 2000 M Street, NW., #300, Washington, DC 20036: Hanan H. Elbadry.

ENVIRONMENT & ENERGY PUBLISHING, LLC—(202) 628–6500; 122 C Street, NW., Suite 722, Washington, DC 20001: Christopher Barnett, Louis R. Reeder, Kelly Thompson, Monica Trauzzi.

ETTV—(240) 476–5535; 1825 K Street, NW., Washington, DC 20036: Wen-Hsiang Chang.

EUROVISION AMERICAS, INC.—(202) 239–9371; 2000 M Street, NW., Suite 300, Washington, DC 20036: James Banks, Andrew Blythe, John Carner, Emilie de Schaetzen, William Dunlop, Sarah Gibbons, Marc Granena, Jay Hahn, Steve Harper, Thomas Hass, Brian Malloy, Adam Mandelson, Jean Pierre Roberts, Jason Scharf, Jeroen Schuiten, Peggy Soucy, Thomas Trainor.

EYE–TO–EYE VIDEO—(301) 907–7464; 4614 Chevy Chase Boulvard, Chevy Chase, MD 20815: Charles Horn, Elliot Klayman, Patrick O'Donnell.

FDCH/E–MEDIA, INC.—(202) 731–1728; 4200 Forbes Road, Lanham, MD 20912: Marcia Baggott, Jennifer Childress, Stefanie Cook, Mercedes Eldridge, Michael Eldridge, Shelley Henderson, Elizabeth H. Hofstad, Julia McNally, Ellen Portnoy.

FEATURE STORY NEWS—(202) 296–9012; 1730 Rhode Island Avenue, Suite 405, Washington, DC 20036: Aaron Berger, Malcolm Brown, Julie Donnelly, Manelisi Dubase, Priscilla Huff, Laura Iiyama, Jessica Lang, George Lewinski, Simon Marks.

FEDERAL NEWS RADIO AM 1050—(202) 895–5086; Mike Causey, Suzanne Kubota, Amy Morris, Jane Norris, Dorothy Ramienski, Francis Rose, Jeff Seldin, Patrick Spence, Lisa Wolfe.

FEDERAL NEWS SERVICE—(202) 347–1400; 1000 Vermont Avenue, NW., Washington, DC 20005: Frank Guest, Kirk Hanneman, Rick Northrop, Carina Nyberg, Cheryl Reagan.

FEDNET—(202) 393–7300; 50 F Street, NW., Suite 1C, Washington, DC 20001: Anthony Blankenship, Keith Carney, Rodney Lee Minor, Christopher Skokowski.

FINNISH BROADCASTING COMPANY (YLE)—(202) 785–2087; Hans Peter Dhuy, Benita Engvist, Mika Makelainen, Olli-Pekka Sulasma.

FORMOSA TV—(202) 775–8112; 1825 K Street, NW., #17, Washington, DC 20006: Tina Chung.

FOX NEWS—(202) 824–6369; 400 N. Capitol Street, NW., Washington, DC 20001: Abigail K. Alcott, James L. Angle, Robert Armfield, Bret Baier, Les Baker, Josh Banks, Christopher Barnes, Stuart Basinger, Bruce Becker, Chris Becker, Varuna Bhatia, Bryan Boughton, Megan Bovim, John Brandt, Fletcher Bransford, Codie Brooks, Edgar Brown, Kristin Brown, Caroline Bruner, Aaron Bruns, Carl Cameron, Steve Carlson, Michael Carpel, Walter Carter, Jr., Juan Casanas, Steve Centanni, Kelly Chernenkoff, Jaqueline Cobetto, Richard Cockerham, Bryan Cole, Eric Colimore, Eric Conner, Jodie Curtis, Heather Dahl, Mitch Davis, Debra DeFrank, Mary Pat Dennert, Andrea DeVito, Brian Doherty, Nina Donaghy, Melissa Drosjack, Megan Dumpe, Jerry Echols, William Edmondson, Sarah Elders, James W. Eldridge, Mike Emanuel, Joel Fagen, Mark Finch, Alexander Finland, Justin Fishel, Tom Fowler, David Futrowsky, Monica Gacka, Dan Gallo, Hadley Gamble, Joe Garcia, Major Garrett, Gavin Gibbons, Jake Gibson, Jenna Gibson, Gary Gillis, Wendell Goler, Serafin Gomez, Jennifer Griffin, Cherie Grzech, Gregg L. Gursky, Fred Haberstick, Brian Haefeli, Gregory Headen, Mary Janne Henneberg, Francis Herbas, Catherine Herridge, Stacy Hickman, Cameron Holland, Molly Hooper, Adrienne Moira Hopkins, Cory R. Howard, Paul Huckeby, Brit Hume, Greg Hunt, William G. Jenkins, Richard Johnson, Dave Jones, Lauren Jones, Torrance Jones, Darrell Jordan, Zachary Kenworthy, Sarah Kessler—(Blumberg), Grigory Khananayev, Julie Kirtz-Garrett, Mary Kreinbihl, Donna Lacey,

NETWORKS, STATIONS, AND SERVICES REPRESENTED—Continued

Philip LeCroy, Meaghan Leister, Michael Levine, Edward Lewis, Nelson Lewis, Matthew Linder, Sharon Kehnemui Liss, Stephanie Livingston, Catherine Loper, Wayne Lowman, Laurie Luhn, Doug Luzader, Brigitte Lyles, Stacia Lynds, Michael Lyon, Michael Majchrowitz, Jose Maranho, Tina Marie Martinez, Tim May, Ian McCaleb, Kevin McClam, George McCloskey, Anne McGinn, Kim McIntyre, Rob Melick, Michael Miller, Jim Mills, Richard Morse, Seleena M. Muhammad, James Nelson, Heidi Noonan, Michele Novy, Quillie Odom, Mosheh Oinounou, Dominique Pastre, Bradford S. Paxton, Chad Pergram, Chris Peslis, Jacqueline Pham, Bernard Pigott, Liza Porteus, Elizabeth Prann, Michele Remillard, David Renken, Elizabeth Rhodes, Anne Marie Riha, Corbett Riner, Michael Robbins, Tamara Robertson, Douglas Rohrbeck, James Rosen, Caley Ross, Lee Ross, Marty Ryan, Sarah Santer, Craig Savage, Jason Scanlon, Christina Shand, Meghan Sharp, Steve Shelton, Caroline Shively, Dave Shott, Daniela Sicuranza—(Kelley), Anita Siegfriedt, Matthew Silverstein, Nick Simeone, Gregory Simmons, Neil Simon, Ashley Smith, Teresa Spector, Daniel J. Stay, Lexi Stemple, Matthew Stout, Patrick Summers, Christina Svolopoulos, Mary Ellen Tasillo, Ande Torgerson, Robert Torpey, Patricia Turner, Ellen Uchimiya, Greta Van Susteren, Bryce Vinson, Todd Visioli, Kelley Beaucar Vlahos, Chris Wallace, John L. Wallace, Chelsea Washington, Amy Wehinger, Courtney Wells Shott, Walter Whitley, Colleen Williams, John Williams, Anne Marie Willis, Brian Wilson, Kelly Wright, Eve Zibel.

FRANCE 2 TELEVISION—(202) 833–1818; 2000 M Street, NW., Suite 320, Washington, DC 20036: Stephanie Cheval, Alain De Chalvron, Aaron Diamond, Pascal Jouffriault, Arielle Monange, Leigh Caldwell, Ingrid Drake, William Fenwick, Darby Hickey, Nan McCurdy, Karen Miller, Yanmei Xie.

FUJI TV JAPAN—(202) 347–1600; 529 14th Street, NW., Suite 330, Washington, DC 20045: Peter Gold, Shin Kazama, Brandon Lambert, Matthew Mosley, Tateki Muratani, Setsu Nishiumi, Jun Sano.

GANNETT NEWS SERVICE—(202) 906–8125; 1100 New York Avenue, Washington, DC 20005: Maria Fowler.

GERMAN BROADCASTING SYSTEMS–ARD—(202) 298–6535; Jens Borchers, Marc O. Dugge, Charpa Silvia.

GERMAN PUBLIC RADIO–ARD—(202) 362–3889; 3132 M Street, NW., Washington, DC 20007: Frank Aischmann, Klaus Kastan, Dagmar Kraemer-Anderson, Albrecht Ziegler.

GERMAN TV–ARD—(202) 298–6535; 3132 M. Street, NW., Washington, DC 20007: Thomas Berbner, Herta Borniger, Edward Castner, Stephan Fiedler, Uwe Geleschun, Udo Lielischkies, Christiane Meier, Daniela Metz, Eva Probst, Christine Schiffner, Susan Shand, Thomas Wegner.

GERMAN TV–ZDF—(202) 333–3909; 1077 31st Street, NW., Washington, DC 20007: Claudia Anke Bates, Kirsten Candia, Uwe Doergeloh, Ruben Herrera, Alice Kelley, Kay Lendzian, Wolfgang Macholz, Ursula Marquardt, Claudia Offermann, Hilke Petersen, Eberhard Piltz, Steffanie Riess, Hildrun Rowe, Klaus-Peter Siegloch, Elke Tucker, Dorothea von Trotha, Thomas Walde.

GLOBAL TV CANADA—(202) 824–0426; 400 N. Capitol Street, NW., #850, Washington, DC 20001: Jeffrey Saffelle, Eric D. Sorensen.

HAMILTON PRODUCTIONS, INC.—(703) 405–8727; 7732 Georgetown Pike, McLean, VA 22102: Jay Hamilton.

HD NEWS—(202) 470–5137; 2000 M Street, NW., Suite 340, Washington, DC 20036: Michael McManus, Jeffrey Moorman.

HEARST–ARGYLE TELEVISION—(202) 457–0220; 1825 K Street, NW., #720, Washington, DC 20006: Traci Mitchell Austin, C. Wesley Barrett, Sherman Blalock, Gregory Compton, Jessica Eckert, Eric Jensen, Sally F. Kidd, Laura Kinney, Erin T. McManamon, Shaun Neville, David Postovit, Malika Raghavan, Kimberly Schwandt, Joseph Shaw, Wendy Wilk.

HEDRICK SMITH PRODUCTIONS—(301) 654–9848; 6935 Wisconsin Avenue, Suite 208, Chevy Chase, MD 20815: Hedrick Smith.

HISPANIC COMMUNICATIONS NETWORK—(202) 360–4089; 1126 16th Street, NW., 3rd Floor, Washington, DC 20036: Pablo de Oliveira, Julio Gonzalez, Karina Hurley, Jeff Kline, Rebeca Logan, Mercy Padilla-Cirino, Alison Rodden,

INDEPENDENT TELEVISION NEWS (ITN)—(202) 429–9080; 400 N. Capitol Street, NW., #899, Washington, DC 20008: Dai Baker, Ian Glover-James, John Irvine, Job Rabkin, David Sampy, Chris Shlemon, Sarah Smith, Sean Swan.

INTERFAITH VOICES—(202) 699–3443; 3205 Varnum St. Brentwood, MD 20780: Maureen Fiedler, John Parman.

IRISH RADIO & TV (RTE)—(202) 467–5933; 1750 16th Street, NW., #53, Washington, DC 20009: Harvey Cofske, Robert Shortt.

KGO RADIO—(202) 487–7464; P.O. Box 9550, Washington, DC 20016: Ivan Scott.

KOREAN BROADCASTING SYSTEMS—(202) 662–7345; Joong Wan Lee, Kyungwook Min, Junghwa Oh, Hyun Joo Yi, Jei Choon Yun.

LILLY BROADCASTING—(202) 669–6280; 1220 Peach Street, Erie, PA 16501: Jacqueline Policastro.

LINK TV—P.O. Box 2008, San Francisco, CA 94126: Miles Benson.

MARKETPLACE RADIO—(202) 789–5948; 1333 M Street, NW., West Tower #600, Washington, DC 20005: John Dimsdale, Stephen Henn, Jeremy Hobson.

MARKETWATCH—(202) 824–0566; 529 14th Street, NW., #1240, Washington, DC 20045: Joe Mathieu, John Wordock.

NETWORKS, STATIONS, AND SERVICES REPRESENTED—Continued

MBC–TV KOREA—(MUNHWA)—(202) 347–0078; 529 14th Street, NW., #1131, Washington, DC 20045: Annabel Kim, Jai Hong Kwon, Jinsook Lee, Jaegu Shim, Yong Chul Yoon.

MEDILL NEWS SERVICE—(202) 661–0104; 1325 G Street, NW., #730, Washington, DC 20005: Mary Coffman, Benjamin Harper, Sharon Kornely.

METRO NETWORKS—(302) 628–2700; 8403 Colesville Road, #1500, Silver Spring, MD 20910: Rachel Roberts Crowson, James Hawk, Gene Kuleta, Terrence Moore, Bryan Parrish.

METRO TELEPRODUCTIONS—(302) 608–9077; 1400 East West Highway, Suite 628, Silver Spring, MD 20910: Sanford Grimes, Dave Lilling.

MIDDLE EAST TELEVISION NETWORK (ALHURRA)—(703) 852–9338; 7600–D Boston Boulvard, Springfield, VA 22153: Rana Abtar, Jeff Adkinson, Mohamed Ali-Haidari, Larissa Aoun, Babu Aryankalavil, Hicham Bourar, Daniel Farkas, Christopher Hamilton, Bushra Jaber, Wafaa Jibai, Jessica Lanza, Pericles Lewnes, Tim Miller, W. Harrison Moore, John Mueller, Luis Munoz, Mohamedelhussin Nassar, Adam Nixon, James Norris, Fernando Vega, Karen Yianopoulos, Elizabeth Zosso.

MOBILE VIDEO SERVICES, LTD.—(202) 331–8882; 1620 I Street, NW., #1000, Washington, DC 20006: Doug Adams, Christine Baber, Howard Collender, Linsday Flaherty, William Grifitts, Joseph Holtschneider, Robert H. Milford, Michael Neapolitan, Todd Swain.

NATIONAL PUBLIC RADIO—(202) 513–2000; 635 Massachussetts Avenue, NW., Washington, DC 20001: Stacey Abbott, Larry Abramson, Reena Advani, Augustine Bud Aiello, Jr., Amy Alexander, Davar Ardalan, David Argentieri, Christine Arrasmith, Allison Aubrey, Bruce Auster, Rob Ballenger, Brendan Banaszak, Emily Barocas, Mark Bejarano, Latasha Bey, Amy N. Blaszyk, Melissa Block, Tom Bowman, Nell Boyce, Radek Brablec, Barbara Bradley Hagerty, Paul Brown, Julia Redpath Buckley, Tom Bullock, Ivan Burketh, Robert E Butcher, Robert Charles Byers, Dennis Byrnes, Franklyn Cater, Carlos M Chevez, Lisa Chow, Theodore E. Clark, Tom Cole, Korva Coleman, Dennis Coll, Neal Conan, Jacob Conrad, Felix J. Contreras, William C. Craven, Michael Cullen, Michael Czapliniski, Rebecca Davis, Brian DeMar, William Deputy, Courtney Dorning, Dianna Douglas, Vladimir Dubinsky, Robert Duncan, Katia Dunn, Hugh M. Eaton, Catherine Edwards, Kitty Eisele, Peter Ellena, Debbie Elliott-Taylor, Neal Ellis, Monika Evstatieva, Susan Feeney, Pam Fessler, Corey Flintoff, Deborah Franklin, Jacob Ganz, Greg Gavin, Tom Gjelten, Maria Godoy, Juan Carlos Gomez, Don Gonyea, Sue Goodwin, Barry Gordemer, Neva Grant, Melissa Gray, Gisele Grayson, Tim Grayson, David Greene, Anne Gudenkauf, Claudette Habermann, Jon Hamilton, Cheryl Hampton, Sarah Handel, Liane Hansen, Barrie Hardymon, Richard Harris, Anne Hawke, Elaine Heinzman, Jason Kyle Helton, Lee Hill, Jordana Hochman, Michael Hollis, Todd Holzman, Gemma Hooley, Douglas Hopper, Jim Howard, Andrea Hsu, Johney Burke Hunn, Argin Hutchins, Steve Inskeep, Danyell Irby, Robert E. Jackson, Brian Jarboe, Wendy Johnson, Helena Johnson-McNeely, Kimberly Jones, Christopher Joyce, Jeffrey Katz, John C. Keator, Michele Kelemen, Bridget Kelley, Carol Anne Clark Kelly, Mary Louise Kelly, Sarah Beyer Kelly, Justine Kenin, David Kestenbaum, Allison Keyes, Martin R. Kurcias, Frank Langfitt, Arthur Laurent, Russell Lehman, Mara Liasson, Jennifer Longmire, Jennifer Ludden, Susan Lund, Alison MacAdam, David Malakoff, Tom Marchitto, Michel Martin, Petra Mayer, Doreen McCallister, Ellen McDonnell, Ted Mebane, Dennis Medvee, Joe Mills, Guillermo Minoso, Alica Montgomery, Raul Moreno, Marcia Morgan, Vince Muse, Muthoni Muturi, Brian Naylor, Joe R. Neel, Christopher Nelson, Marie Nelson, Scott Newman, John Nielsen, Michele Norris, Jackie Northam, Emily Ochsenschlager, Quinn O'Toole, Gwen Outen, Peter Overby, Joe Palca, John Vincent Pearson, Marisa Penaloza, Greg Peppers, Richard Howell Rarey, Dina Temple Raston, Guy Raz, Tom Regan, Andrew Reynolds, Alison Richards, Joel Riddle, Andrew Rosenberg, Jeffrey Rosenberg, Julie Rovner, Ken Rudin, Stuart Rushfield, Robert Sachs, Robert Schaefer, Kathleen Schalch, Avie Schneider, Michael Schweppe, Andrea Seabrook, Stuart Seidel, Ari Shapiro, Joseph Shapiro, Cathy Shaw, Elizabeth Shogren, Daniel Shukhin, Michael Shuman, Robert C. Siegel, Madhulika Sikka, Joanne Silberner, Art Silverman, Scott Simon, Graham Smith, Sarah Mobley Smith, Cal R. Southworth, Jack Speer, Susan Stamberg, Evie Stone, Laura Sullivan, Megan Sullivan, Virginia L. Sullivan, Cara Tallo, Elizabeth Tannen, Gerald W. Tennent, Neil David Tevault, Sharahn Thomas, Nina Totenberg, Ariel Valdez, Vikki Valentine, Anna Vigran, Becky Vlamis, Tracy Wahl, Kevin Wait, Carline Watson, Walter Watson, Andrew M. Watts, Eric Weiner, David Welna, Linda Wertheimer, Jim Wildman, John Flawn Williams, Juan Williams, Van Williamson, Brenda Wilson, Thom J. Woodward, John Ydstie, Alverda Muhammad, Askia Muhammad.

NATIVE AMERICAN TELEVISION—(202) 347–9713; 444 N. Capitol Street, NW., Suite 524, Washington, DC 20001: Larry Adams, William Butler, Randolph Flood.

NBC NEWS—(202) 885–4200; 4001 Nebraska Avenue, NW., Washington, DC 20016: Douglas A. Adams, Adam Aigner-Treworgy, Shujaat Ali, Patrick Anastasi, Lauren Appelbaum, Asmeret Araia, Kenneth Austin, Rodney Batten, Gary Beall, Reginald Joey Bell, Michael Benetato, Jacques Benjoar, Regina Blackburn, Jay Blackman, John Blackman, Sarah Blackwill, Victoria Blooston, Jeffrey Blount, Jeremy Bronson, Brooke Brower, Ashley Burrell, Anthony Capra, Jack Cloherty, Major Coleman, Kevin Corke, Thomas Costello, Thomas Curry, Brady Daniels, Carrie Dann, Christine Delargy, Sarah Demarest, Christopher Donovan, Geoffrey Doyle, Victoria Duncan, Barbara Fant, Douglas Farnum, Robert Faw, Mary Beth Fay, Matthew Fields, Sheldon Fielman, Elizabeth Fischer, David Forman, Kerri Lyn Forrest,

NETWORKS, STATIONS, AND SERVICES REPRESENTED—Continued

Scott Foster, Wilfred Fraser, Mike Fritz, Lawrence Gaetano, Jamie Gangel, Gina Garcia, Richard Gardella, Keith Gaskin, William Gebhardt, David Gelles, Edward Gorsky, James M. Greene, David Gregory, Marsha Groome, Andrew F. Gross, Tammy Haddad, Sylvia Haller, David Hanson, Peter Hart, Alan Harvey, Harold Pat Hayley, Ricardo Higgins, John Holland, Michelle Jaconi, Alicia Jennings, Everett Johnson, Leroy Johnson, Gwyneth Jones, Michelle Kessel, Ryan Kiernan, Julia Kimani, Colleen King, Ann Klenk, Marc Koslow, Michael Kosnar, Lester Kretman, Courtney Kube, Tamara Kupperman, Susan LaSalla, Margaret Lehrman, Elizabeth Leist, John Libretto, Christopher Licht, Arthur Lien, Lydia Lively, Abby Livingston, Joseph W. Loebach, James V. Long, Gary Lynn, Lessandra MacHamer, Junius Malone, Chris Matthews, Yolanda McCutchen, Johnny McEachin, Ellen McGuire, Karen McKinley, Carroll Ann Mears, Robert Merrill, Andrew Merten, Byron Mezick, James Miklaszewski, Christopher Millar, Richard Minner, Andrea Mitchell, Lester Moses, Mark Murray, Lisa Myers, Nancy Nathan, Amna Nawaz, Jason Neal, Donna Nelson, Elizabeth Nevins, Bridget Nurre, Kelly O'Donnell, Norah O'Donnell, Jeannie Ohm-Andress, Connie Patsalos, Michelle Perry, William Petras, Debra Pettit, Shelby Poduch, James Popkin, Alonzo Ray, Chip Reid, Kaylan Reid, Querry Robinson, Raymond Rose, Sarah Rosefeldt, Aram Roston, Johnie Roth, Timothy Russert, John Rutherford, Howard Sacks, Maia Samuel, Jose Antoine Sanfuentes, Chantell Savage, Christopher Scholl, Carmine Scicchitano, Andrew Scritchfield, Wesley Scruggs, Carl Sears, Joel Seidman, Joseph Shalhoup, Ronald Simeone, Jessica Sims, Lauren Singer, Kimberly Sneed, Guy Starling, James Streeter, Kenneth Strickland, Jon Sughroue, Robert Sullivan, Leigh Sutherland, Nick Thompson, Ronald Thornton, Chuck Todd, Ellen Van de Mark, Allan Van Horn, Adam Verdugo, Lauren Vicary, Michael Viqueira, Susan Vitorovich, David Vukmer, David Weakly, Morgan Whitaker, Christopher Whittington, Wendla Wilkinson, Louis Pete Williams, Robert T. Williams, Robert Witten, Scott Wygal, John Yang, Richard Yeung, Jennifer Yuille, Huma Zaidi.

NBC NEWSCHANNEL—(202) 783–2615; 400 N. Capitol Street, Suite 850, Washington, DC 20001: Cesar A. Canizales, Cynthia Conatser, Sheila Conlin, H. Estel Dillon, Nancy Ellard, Sheri Lynn Gibson, William Glynn, Andrew L. Godsick, Adam Greenbaum, Steve Handelsman, James Hurt, Julie Jarvis, Jennifer Johnson, Virginia Kreindler, Ian MacSpadden, Alicia Majeed, Richard McDermott, Kevin A. McManus, Nicole McManus, Brian Mooar, Steven Muskat, Tom Newberry, Mike O'Connell, Tracie Potts, Bonnie Rollins, Brooke Hart Salkoff, Cecil John Sills, Christie Smith, Todd Sutton, Matthew Tureck, Christopher Wiggins, Randy Wolfe.

NEED TO KNOW NEWS—(202) 297–7751; 440 S. LaSalle Street, #1208, Chicago, IL 60605: Kathryn Kobe, Dennis Moore, Gautham Nagesh, Mary Beth Slack.

NEW TANG DYNASTY TV—(301) 515–5422; 229 W 28th Street, Suite 1200, New York, NY 10001: Min Chang, Hui Jing, Chuan Lin, Wei Shi, Amy Xia, Dong Xiang, Jinglu Xu, Chunfang Yang, John Yu.

NHK–JAPAN BROADCASTING CORPORATION—(202) 828–5180; 2030 M Street, NW., Suite 706, Washington, DC 20036: Kaori Arioka, Sylvain Coudoux, Anne-Marie Fendrick, Kaori Iida, Joanne Jaje, Atsuchi Kato, Nami Kodaka, Kenji Kohno, Torao Kono, Tsuyoshi Masuda, Yoshio Nishikawa, Kensuke Okoshi, Olivia Qusaibaty, Keisuke Shimizu, Mio Yamada.

NIGHTLY BUSINESS REPORT—(202) 682–9029; 1325 G Street, NW., #1005, Washington, DC 20005: Stephanie Dhue, Darren Gersh, Dana Greenspon, Michael LaBella, Ervin Washington.

NIPPON TV NETWORK—(202) 638–0890; 529 14th Street, NW., #1036, Washington, DC 20045: Takaaki Abe, Bon Fleming, Aya Imaida, Asuka Konishi, Keiichi Sato, Kenji Teranishi, Ai Tilman.

NORWEGIAN BROADCASTING—(202) 785–1460; 2000 M Street, NW., #890, Washington, DC 20036: Tove Bjoergaas, Jan Espen Kruse.

NOS DUTCH PUBLIC RADIO & TV (VRT)—(202) 466–8793; 2000 M Street, NW., #365, Washington, DC 20036: Eelco Bosch van Rosenthal, Ron Linker, Sander Warmerdam.

N–TV NEWS TELEVISION—(202) 736–9817; 1825 K Street, NW., Suite 710, Washington, DC 20006: Markus Meier, Dmitri Volkov, Anton Volskiy, Christian Wilp.

ORBITE TELEVISION INC.—(212) 245–5585; P.O. Box 5433 New York, DC 10185: Hugues-Denver Akassy.

PACIFICA RADIO—(202) 588–0999; 2390 Champlain Street, NW., Washington, DC 20009: John Almeleh, Verna Avery-Brown, Mitch Jeserich, Nathan Moore.

PHOENIX SATELLITE TELEVISION—(202) 824–6585; 400 N. Capitol Street, NW., Washington, DC 20001: Yi Qiu Chen, Nai Chian M. Katz, Zhengzhu Liu, Taofeng Wang, Jiao Christine Xie.

POLISH RADIO (ESKA): Izabela Weglarczyk.

POTOMAC RADIO NEWS—(202) 244–2781; P.O. Box 32244, Washington, DC 20007: Michael J Duncan.

POTOMAC TELEVISION—(202) 265–1109; 1510 H Street, NW., Suite 202, Washington, DC 20003: Daniel Burton, Paul Crosariol, Rebecca Field, Steve Greenaway, Katherine Kenedy, Andrew Spagnolo, Kristin Volk, James Wiltermood.

PRO PLUS—(202) 297–0562; 3700 Massachusetts Avenue, NW., #428, Washington, DC 20016: Natasa Briski.

PUBLIC TELEVISION SERVICE–TAIWAN—(202) 460–9789; 1825 K Street, NW., Suite 501, Washington, DC 20006: Ching-Yi Chiang.

NETWORKS, STATIONS, AND SERVICES REPRESENTED—Continued

RADIO FRANCE INTERNATIONALE—(202) 714–9816; 3700 Massachusetts Avenue, NW., #538, Washington, DC 20016: Claude L. Porsella, Anne Toulouse.

RADIO FREE ASIA—(202) 721–7443; 2025 M Street, NW., Suite 300, Washington, DC 20036: Hassan Abukasem, Jaehoon Ahn, Ko Ko Aung, May Pyone Aung, David Beasley, Bhungyal Bhungyal, Jinhee Bonny, Huidong Cao, Sylvia Chen, Lobsang Chophel, Thao Dao, Dawa Dolma, Rigdhen Dolma, Karma Dorjee, Richard Finney, Dhondup Namgyal Gonsar, Palden Gyal, Gwen Ha, King Man Ho, Kyaw Min Htun, Laura Huang, Myeong Hwa Jang, Mehmet Omer Kanat, Sos Kem, May Khin, Tin Aung Khine, Naeri Kim, Yonho Kim, Vivian Kwan, Zaw Moe Kyaw, Daniel N. Lee, Kyu Sang Lee, Tian Li, Wo Tak Li, Xiao Qiang Liao, Ted Liu, Kalden Lodoe, Lucy Lu, Corey Munford, Jilili Musha, Tseten Namgyal, Pham Than Ngoc, An Nguyen, Bich-Ha Nguyen, Dien M. Nguyen, Jung Min Noh, Khin Maung Nyane, Nyi Nyi, Win Naing Oo, Jung-Woo Park, Brian William Powell, Borin Sam, Aungthu Schlenker, Harry Scott, Zijun Shan, Nyein Shwe, Sonam Lhamo Singeri, Khin Maung Soe, Sattana Som, Sok Ry Sum, Yun Tang, Tenor Taring, Yeshi Tashi, Truong D. Thang, San San Tinn, Benpa Topgyal, Thang Dinh Truong, Dorjee Tso, Nadia Usaeva, Kurban Wali, Pei Wang, Sungwon Yang, Lobsang Yeshi, Min Zin, Karma Zurkhang, Heather Maher.

RADIO FREE EUROPE—(202) 457–6950; 1201 Connecticut Avenue, NW., Washington, DC 20036: Andrew Tully.

RADIO MARTI—(305) 437–7178; 4201 Northwest 77th Avenue, Miami, DC 33166: Diana Molineaux, Luis Munoz.

RADIO ONE—(301) 429–2673; 5900 Princess Garden Parkway, 7th Floor, Lanham, MD 20706: Mike Abrams, LaFontaine Oliver, Ron Thompson.

RCN–TV—(COLOMBIA)—(202) 487–0530; 1333 H Street, NW., Washington, DC 20005: Nathalia Orozco Rojas.

RELIGION & ETHICS NEWSWEEKLY—(202) 216–4400; 1333 H Street, NW., 6th Floor, Washington, DC 20005: Gail Fendley, Patricia Hanley, Kim Lawton, Fabiana Ramirez, Judy Reynolds, Ansley Roan, Noelle Serper.

REUTERS RADIO & TV—(202) 310–6475; 1333 H Street, NW., 6th Floor, Washington, DC 20005: Keith Allen, Peter Bullock, Liza Feria, Kevin Fogarty, Peter Fox, Guillermo Garcia, Deborah Gembara, Paviithra George, Sheila Green, Kia Johnson, Justin Kenny, Predrag Kojovic, Lisa Lewnes, Deborah Lutterbeck, Tipp K. McClure, Robert Muir, Kristin Neubauer, Gershon Peaks, Steven Phillips, Tom Rowe, Roger Shull, George Tamerlani.

RTV SLOVENIJA: Vlasta Jesenicnik, Silvester Stok.

RTVI/ECHO–TV—(202) 742–6576; 1001 Pennsylvania Avenue, NW., Suite 6310, Washington, DC 20004: Vladimir Kara-Murza, Alexander Panov, Andrei Popovici, Dmytro Shakhov.

RUSSIA TODAY TELEVISION—(202) 736–9832; 1825 K Street, NW., Suite 710, Washington, DC 20006: Alexander Mursa, Christina Mursa, Roman Tokman.

RUSSIAN STATE TV AND RADIO—(RTR)—(202) 460–6830; 2000 N Street, NW., Suite 810, Washington, DC 20007: Elena Sokolova, Andrey Solimani-Lezhnev, Mikhail Solodovnikov.

RUSTAVI 2 BROADCASTING COMPANY—(703) 867–0381; 6301 Steveson Avenue, #414, Alexandria, VA 22304: Irakli Lobzhanidze, David Nikuradze.

SAGARMATHA TELEVISION—(703) 646–5110; 9655 Hawkshead Drive, Lorton, VA 22079: Ram C. Kharel.

SEOUL BROADCASTING SYSTEM (SBS)—(202) 637–9850; 529 14th Street, NW., #979, Washington, DC 20045: Hyeonju Ban, Mark Jung, Kyung Youl Shin, Il Hee Won.

SINCLAIR BROADCAST GROUP—(202) 293–1092; 1620 I Street, NW., Suite 540, Washington, DC 20006: Craig Demchak, Morris Jones, Timothy Knapp, Meghan McCorkell, Richard McKinney, Antonia Randle, David Sckrabulis, Paul Spinelli, Jody Weldon.

SPANISH PUBLIC TELEVISION (TVE)—(202) 785–1813; 2000 M Street, NW., #325, Washington, DC 20036: Ubeda Anna, Jean Pascal Azais, Anna Bosch, Inigo Horcajuelo, Carmelo Machin.

SRN NEWS—(SALEM)—(703) 528–6213; 1901 N. Moore Street, #201, Arlington, VA 22209: Gregory Clugston, Linda Kenyon, John Lormand, Jeffrey A. Matzka, Andrea Mikus, Janet Parshall, Andrew Stewart, David Terry.

STATELINE.ORG—(202) 419–4464; 1615 L Street, NW., Washington, DC 20016: Danny Dougherty, John P. Gramlich, Pamela M. Prah, Christine Vestal, Daniel Vock, Pauline Vu.

SWEDISH BROADCASTING—(202) 785–1460; 2000 M Street, NW., Suite 890, Washington, DC 20036: Stefan Asberg, Lisa Carlsson, Kyle Lanningham, Bengt Norborg.

SWISS BROADCASTING—(202) 469–9668; 2000 M Street, NW., Suite 370, Washington, DC 20036: Patrick Chaboudez, Sebastien Faure, Diego Gilardoni, Tilman Lingner, Julie Noce, Alessio Veronelli, Peter Voegeli.

TALK RADIO NEWS SERVICE—(202) 337–5322; 2514 Mill Road, NW., Washington, DC 20007: Marc Bernier, Joseph Byrne, Cholene Espinoza, Lovisa Frost, David Grossman, Victoria Jones, Dan Manatt, David Popp, Ellen Ratner, Myron Sponder, Wendy Wang.

TELEMUNDO NETWORK—(202) 737–7830; 400 N. Capitol Street, NW., Suite 850, Washington, DC 20001: Glenda Contreras, Pedro Correa, Pablo Gato, Lori Montenegro, Victor Reyes.

NETWORKS, STATIONS, AND SERVICES REPRESENTED—Continued

TELESUR—(202) 739–1750; 1825 K Street, NW., Suite 710, Washington, DC 20006: Christopher Belcher, Ana Sarai Pena, Roselena Ramirez.

TELEVISA NEWS NETWORK—(ECO)—1825 K Street, NW., Suite 710–G, Washington, DC 20006: Gregorio Meraz.

TF1–FRENCH TV—2000 M Street, NW., Suite 870, Washington, DC 20036: Christophe Barreyre, Gilles Bouleau, Remi Cadoret, Helene Davieaud, Guillaume Debre, Tristan Dessert, Bruce Frankel, Andree-Lyne Jacques, Vincent Mortreux.

THE BERNS BUREAU, INC.—(202) 608–2000: Matthew Kaye.

THE NEW YORK TIMES ON THE WEB—(202) 862–0361; 1627 I Street, NW., #1700, Washington, DC 20006: Benjamin Werschkul.

THE NEWSHOUR WITH JIM LEHRER—(202) 998–2150; 3620 S. 27th Street, Arlington, VA 22206: Lorna Baldwin, Lee Banville, Anne Bell, David Belt, Jessica Borash, Jeffrey Brown, Terence Burlij, David Butterworth, Lete Childs, Leah Clapman, Russ Clarkson, Sarah Clune, David Coles, Alexis Cox, Lester Crystal, Anne Davenport, Antoinette Dean, Susan Dentzer, Bridget DeSimone, Truval Downey, Matthew Engelberg, Larisa Epatko, Robert Flynn, Brian Gottlieb, George Griffin, Elizabeth Harper, Monique Hayes, Jessica Hoffman, Kwame Holman, Gwen Ifill, Murrey Jacobson, Georgette Knuckles, Tom LeGro, Jim Lehrer, Diane Lincoln, Adela Maskova, Valerie McCabe, Kathleen McCleery, Michael Melia, Annette Miller, Susan Mills, Michael Mosettig, Caroline Nathan, Kristina Nwazota, Timothy Perry, Jr., Molly Raskin, Margaret Robinson, Daniel Sagalyn, Michael Saltz, Annie Schleicher, Linda Scott, Anna Shoup, Diane Silver, David Sit, Rafael Suarez, Elizabeth Summers, Samara Thery, Renu Thomas, Morgan Till, James Trengrove, Danette Tucker, Margaret Warner, Adnaan Wasey, Meghan Welsh, Judith Willis, Lea Winerman, Linda Winslow, Judy Woodruff.

THE WASHINGTON BUREAU—(202) 347–6396; 400 N. Capitol, #775, Washington, DC 20001: Robert Arkedis, Gary Heckman, Stephen Heiner, James Kanka, Julia Rockler, Richard Tillery.

THIS WEEK IN AGRIBUSINESS (RFD–TV)—(301) 942–1996; 9915 Hillridge Drive, Kensington, MD 20895: Patrick Haggerty.

TO THE CONTRARY (Persephone Productions)—(202) 973–2066; 1825 K Street, NW., #501, Washington, DC 20006: Danielle Brinkley, Alika Codispoti, Bonnie Erbe, Joy Fowlin.

TOKYO BROADCASTING SYSTEM—(202) 393–3800; 1088 National Press Building, Washington, DC 20045: Katsumi Hino, Nami Inoue, Natsuko Koike, Kaoru Kokufuda, Atsushi Kyodo, Michael Lavallee, Eric Weiner.

TRIBUNE BROADCASTING—(202) 824–8444; 1025 F Street, NW., #700, Washington, DC 20004: Cissy Baker, Richard Chamberlain, Derek Danilko, Caesar Darias, Nishith Doshi, Sabrina Fang, Travis Galey, Thomas Kolodziejczak, R. Grant Rampy, Sonja Deaner Schulken, Ambrose Vurnis, Edward White, Ronald Windham.

TV ASAHI—(202) 347–2933; 529 14th Street, NW., #1280, Washington, DC 20045: Robert Gentry, Tadayoshi II, Hitoshi Inoue, Desdemona Keeler, Yoshiyaki Komatsu, Ena Suto.

TV GLOBO INTERNATIONAL—(202) 429–2525; 2141 Wisconsin Avenue, NW., Suite L, Washington, DC 20007: Anna Camanducaia, Marcelo Capuchinho, Marcio Capuchinho, Vicente Cinque, Luis Fernando Silva-Pinto.

TV TOKYO—(202) 638–0441; 1333 H Street, NW., 5th Floor, Washington, DC 20005: Yuko Miyake, Yuiko Noda, Strader Payton, Masaaki Shimada.

TV2–DENMARK—(202) 828–4555; 2000 M Street, NW., Suite 375, Washington, DC 20036: Scott Rensberger.

TV3–TELEVISIO DE CATALUNYA—(202) 785–0580; 1620 I Street, NW., Suite 150, Washington, DC 20006: Eva Artesona, Albert Elfa, Xavier Roca.

UNITED NEWS AND INFORMATION—(202) 783–2444; 529 14th Street, NW., Suite 1057D, Washington, DC 20045: Dennis Crowley.

UNIVISION—(202) 682–6160; 101 Constitution Avenue, NW., Suite 810E, Washington, DC 20001: Jorge Contreras, Deborah Durham, Lourdes Meluza, Fernando Pizarro, Pablo Sanchez, Mario Vizcarra.

USA RADIO NETWORK—(202) 297–2696; 3101 New Mosaco Avenue, NW., Washington, DC 20016: Jonathan Decker, Phillip Kiver.

VENEZUELA TV Marco Granda.

VENTANA PRODUCTIONS—(202) 785–5112; 1825 K Street, NW., #501 Washington, DC 20006: Armando Almanza, Rich Feather, Richard Joy, John Lawrence, Timothy K. Murray, Juan Rocha, Robin Stewart, Sharon Sullivan, Mark Thalman, Chris Tsou.

VIEWPOINT COMMUNICATIONS—(301) 565–1650; 8607 2nd Avenue, Suite 400, Silver Spring, MD 20910: Lou Charlip, William Donald, Randy Feldman, Ben Finkel, Larry Greenblatt, Steve Hamberg.

VOICE OF AMERICA—(202) 260–0600; 330 Independence Avenue, SW., Washington, DC 20237: Addisu Abebe, Niharika Acharya, Adriana Ahmad, Akmal Aleemi, Muhammad Ali, Dilshad Aliyarova Horowitz, Darrell Allen, Karlina Amkas, Sarita Ang, Aunshuman Apte, Milandro Arcega, Win Aung, Kyaw Aung Lwin, Thomas Bagnall, Andy Baroch, Zorislav Baydyuk, Jacquelin Belizaire, Margaret Besheer, George Bistis, Deborah Block, Michael Bowman, Jonathan Brandkamp, Meredith Buel, Roger C. W. Hsu, Carol Castiel, Enoch Chan, Peggy Chang, Yuwen Cheng, Art Chimes, Michael Collins,

NETWORKS, STATIONS, AND SERVICES REPRESENTED—Continued

Carla Coolman, Zorz Crnaric, Patricia Dalmasy, Minas Dargakis, Jeffery Daugherty, Penny Dixon Gumm, Bratislav Djordjevic, Helena Djordjevic, Deepak Dobhal, Cherubin Dorcil, Inna Dubinsky, George Dwyer, William Eagle, Jerry Earnest, Faiza El Masry, Luis Facal, Mahtab Farid, Parichehr Farzam, Hector Federico, Bruce Ferder, Adanech Fessehaye, Leta Hong Fincher, Craig Fitzpatrick, Jim Fry, Joseph Gallagher, Valer Gergely, Caroline Gombakombra, William Greenback, Mi Jeong Y. Hibbitts, Stephanie Ho, Myroslava Honhadze, Yahwa Hsiung, Thein Htike Oo, Ilir Ikonomi, Gary Jaffe, Syed Jafri, Douglas Johnson, Lusine Kalashyan, Ravi Khanna, M. Ayub Khawreen, Keunsam Kim, Young-Kweon Kim, Lilica Kitanovska, Bojan Klima, Tetiana Koprowicz, Susan Koster, Ivana Kuhar, Rohit Kulkarni, Kyaw Kyaw Thein, Ted Landphair, Faith Lapidus, Dong Hyuk Lee, James Malone, Sean Maroney, Michael Mathes, Jeffrey Means, Abdu Mehrpore, Beth Mendelson, Bulut Mihmandarli, Russell Mitchell, Alen Mlatisuma, Victor Morales, Jackson Mvunganyi, Ndimyake Mwakalyelye, Khin Myo Thet, Paul Ndiho, Siri E. Nyrop, Thar Nyunt Oo, Chinedu Offor, Ma Oo-Zin, Robert Parsell, Reasey Poch, Darko Popovic, Penelope Poulou, Ivica Puljic, George Putic, Shegoftah Queen, John Quinn, Robert Raffaele, Jim Randle, Fiaz Rehman, Daniel Robinson, William Rodgers, Najiba Salam, Brian Schiff, Namgyal Shastri, Sondang Sirait, Rosanne Skirble, Khin Soe Win, June Soh, Jihun Sohn, Pov Sok, Murtaza Solangi, Kifle Solomon, Scott Stearns, James Stevenson, Deborah Tate, Darren Taylor, Gary Thomas, Jeff Tofani, Birusk Tugan, Barry Unger, Vidushi Vidushi, Yuni Wilcox, Candace Williams, Walter Wisniewski, Paula Wolfson-Stevenson, Barry Wood, Raymond Yam, Kim Young-Kweon, Anna Zalewski, Kyaw Zaw Nyunt.

VOYAGE PRODUCTIONS—(202) 296–2389; 1825 K Street, NW., Suite 501, Washington, DC 20006: Susan Baumel.

W RADIO—(202) 404–4092; 4301 Massachussetts Avenue, NW., #A114, Washington, DC 20016: Maria Luisa Rossel.

WAMU—(202) 885–1200; 4000 Brandywine Street, NW., Washington, DC 20016: Jim Asendio, Jessica Golloher, Danielle Karson.

WASHINGTON BUREAU NEWS SERVICE—(202) 255–8685; 7425 Savan Point Way Columbia, MD 21045: Joseph Nelson, Robbie B. Snow, C. Patrick Thorne, Patrick Vail, Michael Whitney.

WASHINGTON CHINESE TELEVISION—(703) 538–1090; 6521 Arlington Blvd. Suite 406 Falls Church, VA 22042: Bing Li, Shou-lien Liu, Wei-Ming Liu.

WASHINGTON RADIO AND PRESS SERVICE—(301) 229–2576; 6702 Pawtucket Rd. Bethesda, MD 20817: Hanna Gutmann.

WDCT RADIO—(703) 273–4000; Fairfax, VA: Jinkuk Kim.

WEST VIRGINIA PUBLIC BROADCASTING—Shepherd University, P.O. Box 3210, Shepherdstown, WV Cecelia Mason.

WETA—(703) 998–2660; 2775 S. Quincy Street, Arlington, VA 22206: Lynn Quarles Allison, Charles Anderson, William Barber, Glynda Bates, Harry Bottorf, Timothy Bowen, Donald Brawner, Joseph Buckingham, Joseph Camp, John Christophe Cardon, Martin Carr, Darzen Chang, Julius Dumarr Fauntleroy, Frank Fitzmaurice, David Gillette, Stephen Howard, John Hyater, Charles Ide, Gregory King, Christopher Lane, Mary Lawrence, Edward Lee, Jerry S. Lewis, Robert Ludwig, Donald McClurkin, Nancy Gerstman Morgan, John C. Nash, Chuck Nixon, Alan Perlmeter, Jeffrey Rathner, Willliam Seabrook, Darwin Silver, David Tillette, Otto Kenneth Uyehara, Sampath Vasa, Charles Voth.

WJLA-TV/NEWSCHANNEL 8—(703) 236–9555; 1100 Wilson Boulvard, Arlington, VA 22209: Robert Alexander, Roberta Baskin, Julia Bennett, Alan Matthew Brock, Pamela Brown, Brianne Carter, Robert Cartwright, Zeke Changuris, James Church, Nicole Collins, Cheryl Conner, Rebecca J. Cooper, Christina Cotterman, Walter Crawford, Carolyn Cremen, Bruce DePuyt, Angela Devereaux, Martin C. Doane, Jennifer Donelan, Lauren Dunn, Markham Evans, Tony Ferrigno, Amy Fink, Michael Forcucci, Sam Ford, Robert Forsyth, Kathy Fowler, Pege Gilgannon, Oji Gleaton, Richard Guastadisegni, Michael E. Hagerty, Peter Hakel, Melanie Hastings Wotring, Chas Henry, Shawn Hoder, Horace Holmes, Brian Hopkins, LaTanya Horne, Aja Hubert, Winston Hylton, Katharine Jackson, Samuel Jackson, Suzanne Kennedy, Mati Kerpen, Nikole Killion, Beverly Kirk, Raynel Knight, Vanessa M. Koolhof, Jay Korff, Greta Kreuz, Judy Kurtz, Kelly Lamp, Krista Lane, Catherine Lanzara, Gabriel LeMay, Ming Leong, John B. Lewis, Alex Likowski, Bill Lord, Yolanda Massey, Elizabeth Mausteller, Ian McAllister, Andrea McCarren, Rebecca McDevitt, Kathryn McGriff, Douglas McKelway, Ashley McKinney, Ross McLaughlin, Gregg Micklos, Sandra Neubauer, Alisa Parenti, Sarah Lee Park, Gordon Peterson, Chris Pettigrew, Jennifer Plaia, Christopher Plater, Ryan Pratzel, Kuren Redmond, Richard Reeve, Malissa Reyes, Leslie Cook Rhode, Michael Rudd, Ian Rushing, Gregory Seaby, Shelley A. Simpson, Scott D. Smith, Alison Starling, Abraham Stubblefield, Racheel Teron, Scott Thuman, Michael Timmermann, Stephen Tschida, Kristopher Van Cleave, Veronica Vaquer, Vincent Vaughan, Noel Waghorn, James William Walker, Lindsey Walton, Robert Washington Anderson, Amanda Wasserman, David Weaver, David Webb, G. Edwin Wilson, Dale Wright.

WMDO-TV UNIVISION—(301) 589–0030; 962 Wayne Avenue, Silver Spring, MD 20910: Jose Angel Aguirre, Maria Rosa Lucchini, Norma Montenegro, Jorge Nunez.

WPFW-FM—(202) 588–0999; 2390 Champlain Street, NW., Washington, DC 20009: Gloria Minott.

NETWORKS, STATIONS, AND SERVICES REPRESENTED—Continued

WRC–TV/NBC-4—(202) 885–4000; 4001 Nebraska Avenue, NW., Suite 6, Washington, DC 20016: James M. Adams, Miguel Almaguer, Jay Alvey, Jackie Bensen, Charles Bragale, Shannon D. Bream, Larry Bullard, Julie Carey, Sean Casey, Pat Collins, Edward Durkin, Michael Francis Flynn, Keith Garvin, Matt Glassman, Charles A Goodknight, Philip H. Jacobs, Ede Jermin, James S. Kizer, Ronald Leidelmeyer, Megan McGrath, William Nardi, Michael O'Regan, Chester Panzer, Jeff Piper, Tom Sherwood, Darcy Spencer, Michael Swann, Robert Sweeney, John Taylor, Luis Urbina, Jane Watrel.

WTOP RADIO—(202) 895–5060; 3400 Idaho Avenue, NW., Washington, DC 20016: Neal Augenstein, Darci Brasch, I-Fang Chen, Sara D'Angelo, Jessie J. Green, Nathan Hager, Evan Haning, Brennan Haselton, Kristi King Lilleston, Dave McConnell, Ira Mellman, Mitchell Miller, Mark Plotkin, Robert Publicover, Veronica Robinson, Mark Segraves, Hank Silverberg, Adam Tuss, Derek Williams.

WTTG–FOX TELEVISION—(202) 895–3000; 5151 Wisconsin Avenue, NW., Washington, DC 20016: Katy Adams, Melanie Alnwick, Bob Barnard, James Beahn, Gary Bender, William Beyer, Daniel Brown, Daryl Brown, Paul Buehler, Charles Carson, Ellen Chang, Roby Chavez, Steve Chenevey, Claudia Coffey-Lambert, Leif Coorlim, Patricia Corcoran, Lauren DeMarco, Gurvir Dhindsa, Laura Evans, Tom Fitzgerald, B.J. Forte, John Foundas, John Frame, Angela Kelly Frank, Matthew Gaffney, Max Giammetta, Jeff Gilman, Carlos Gonzalez, John Henrehan, Michael Horan, Karen Gray Houston, Ryan Huebler, Lance Ing, Virg Jacques, Stephanie Johnson, Lyrone Steven Jones, Nelson Jones, Ira Lazernik, Erik Lee, Craig Little, Sherri Ly, Michael Marantz, Wisdom Martin, Lark McCarthy, Sean McGarvy, Patrick McGrath, Lorna McGuire, Alexander Milenic, Holly Morris, Richard Murphy, Beth Parker, Michael Patrick, Tom Pittman, Carolyn Presutti, Paul Raphel, Austin Reeves, Michael Rickard, F. David Rysak, Mark Sargent, Bob Sellers, Allison Seymour, Robert Shon, Sarah Simmons, Jason H. Smith, Joe Spevak, Donald E. Stanke, Louis Stevenson, John Sumrell, Will Thomas, Paul Wagner, Duane Watkins, Don Watrud, Douglas H. Wilkes, Aaron Wische, Joel Witte, Scott Wolfson, Rick Yarborough, Annie Yu.

WUSA–TV—(202) 895–5700; 4100 Wisconsin Avenue, NW., Washington, DC 20016: Phyllis Armstrong, Audrey Barnes, Bruce Bookhultz, Mark Bost, Kurt Brooks, Aubrey Bryant, Douglas Buchanan, Anthony M. Castrilli, David Chaytor, William Clemann, Jeffrey Cridland, Tim Deluca, Rebecca Diamond, Mark Dougherty, Danielle Flanagan, Michael Flynn, Lesli Foster Mathewson, Janet Fox, Peggy Fox, Brian Franco, Stephen Garifo, Richard Gorbutt, Gregory Guise, James Hash, Shonty Hawkins, Jacqueline Hayward, Ryan Hunter, Thomas James, Bruce Johnson, Kristen Kerr, Kevin G. King, Madeline Lacore, William Lawlor, Amy Leone, Bruce Leshan, Paul Lester, Harvey Mars, Samara Martin Ewing, Frank McDermott, Todd McDermott, Derek McGinty, William McKnight, Jay Mishkin, Victor Murphy, Tracey Neale, James Nichols, Celinda Pena, Ronald Peters, Karen Peterson, James Pratt, Gary Reals, Raul Rivero, Andrea Roane Skehan, Michelle Rodgers, Sean L. Root, Jeffrey Rosetti, David Roycraft, Jennifer Ryan Conley, Alija Sakota, David Satchell, Emily Schmidt Massey, Jimmie Silman III, Catherine Snyder, Michael Stafford-Walter, Bill Starks, David Statter, Janet Terry, Michael Trammell, Lauren Vance, Keith Williams, Stephanie Wilson, Nancy M. Yamada.

WZDC–TV: Francisco Aguayo, Julio Aliaga, Erick Carpio, Gustavo Cherquis, Liliana Henao, Julissa Marenco, Douglas Mejia, Janet Rodriguez, Franco Schultze, Vanessa Skyrmes, Juan Pablo Zariquiey.

FREELANCE

Freelancers: Larry Abuliak, Matt Ackland, Robin Adlerblum, Nadine Alfa, Stuart Ammerman, John Anglim, Alana Anyse, Andrew Arbuckle, Eddie Archuleta, John Archuleta, Bruno Arena, Patricia M. Armstrong, Thomas Ayres Armstrong, Adrian Armwood, Percy Arrington, Julie Asher, Martin Babington-Heina, Ben Bain, Brooke Baldwin, Lantz Barbour, Eric Barreda, Scott Bartlett, Stephen Bartlett, Michelle Basch, Robert Baumann, Mark Bautista, Malini Bawa, Earl T. Baysden III, David Bentley, Michael P. Berry, Sue Bevine, Kevin Beyer, Tim R. Bintrim, Victor Blandburg, Joseph Bohannon, Charles Borniger, Wayne F. Boyd, Patrick Branigan, Donte Brawner, William Brennan, Fashela Brewton, Annette Brieger, Mike Broleman, Randall Brown, Eric Bugash, Jerry Busher, Cheryl Butler, Max Cacas, Traci Caldwell, Karen Campbell, James Canty, David Caravello, Chanel Caraway, Brett Carlson, Robert Cherouny, Travis Renee Chrisinger, Thomas Clark, Juanita Clogston, Anne Cocklin, Stephen Cocklin, Stacey Lynn Cohan, Thomas Coleman, Carol Coney, Camille Connolly, Monique Conrad, David M. Cooke, John Cooper, William Cortez, Bob Costantini, Timothy Cote, Timothy Cothren, Jerry Cox, Thomas Craca, John Craig, Patricia Culhane, Patrick J. Curran, Clinton Davis, Jennifer Davis, Shoshana Davis, Jeremy Diller, Bryan Dittmer, Pamela Donovan, Margaret Dore, Paul G. Dougherty, Barton Eckert, Danaj Edmond, Brian Edwards, Arlene Eiras, Ethan Elliot-Williams, Mirona Mohamed Elsewaify, Duane Empey, Steve Epstein, Manuel Ernst, Tom Everly, Al Faison, Scott Farmer, John Figura, Michael Ford, Tom Foster, Tom Foty, David Fox, Jason Erik Fox, Julion Francis, Patrick French, George Fridrich, Dave Friedman, John Friess, Jo Ann Marie Fyanes, Dennis Gaffney, Randall Gafner, Gretchen Gailey, Christian Galdabini, Martina Gauss, Atef Gawad, Philip Geyelin, Edward Adam Giebel, Dirk Gilliam, John Glennon, Augusto Gomez, Antonio R. Gonzalez, Jeffrey Goodman, Herbert Gordon, Lindsay Graves, John K. Greenwood, Nicholas P. Greiner, Valerie Hamilton, Claus Harding, Arthur Hardy, Roy Harris, John Hartge, Walter Hassett, Barry L. Haywood,

NETWORKS, STATIONS, AND SERVICES REPRESENTED—Continued

Sean Healey, Barry Hecht, Jonathan Helman, Karen Hendren, Ricardo Higgins, Hugh Hinds, Toni Hoover, Dean G. Hovell, D.C. Hughes, James Hughes, Trudy Hutcherson, Heather Hutchinson, Todd Huyghe, George Hyatt, Donna Inserra, Sarah Irwin, Matthew Iverson, Edward B. Jennings, Jr., Martin Jimenez, Paul Johnson, Rolanda Johnson, Shawn Jones, Michael Joy, Daniel Joyner, Abdelhakim Kabbas, Bill Kaplan, Judith Kargbo, Terence Kelly, Eric C. Kerchner, Jonathan Kessler, Jonathan L. Kessler, Vandana Kilaru, Adrian Kill, Michael Kinney, Robert Klein, Christina Kovac, David Krupin, Peter Kulsziski, Carmen Kupper, Stephanie Kwisnek, Marianna LaFollette, Larry Langley, Greg Larsen, Matt Laslo, France Latremoliere, James Laughlin, Sam Lawson, Myron Leake, Florence Leenknegt, Katherine Leiken, Jon Leiner, Dexter Leong, Elliott Lewis, Bruce Liffiton, Louis Linden, Arleen Lissit, Robert Lloyd, Chris LoBreglio, Kevin Loftus, Malik Lomax, Culver Long, Stanley Lorek, Jayne Lukas, David L. Lurch, Jr., Julio Luzquinos, Daniel Lyon, Amanda Mackaye, Eric Magnuson, Freddie Malone, Mai Marriott, Marc Marriott, Michael Marriott, Mark Marshall, Jeffrey Martino, Claude Matthews, Paul Matthews, Linda Mayhew, Mark Mazariegos, D. Jay McCarty, D. Page McCarty, Douglas McCash, Ashley McDaniel, N. Patricia McDonald, Patty McFarland, Joanna McGuire, Robert McHenry, Jr., Daniel McLellan, Erin Meola, Tara Mergener, Kerry Meyer, Steven Mitnick, Melinda Mizell, Ione Indira Molinares-Hess, William Montague, John Monte, Charles Montgomery, Gregg Moore, Olga Morales, Donald Morgan, Frederick Murphy, Matthew Murray, Vidya Murugesan, Jeffrey Napshin, Nicole Nelson, Anh Nguyen, Richard A. Norling, Gary Nurenberg, D. Kerry O'Berry, Ralf Oberti, David O'Brien, Daniel J. O'Shea, Jr., Mohamed Said Ouafi, Linda Passariello (Dodich), Daniel Patsko, Hartmut Pauls, Grant Peacock, Douglas Perkins, Marilisa Perron, James Peterson, Robert Peterson, Murray Pinczuk, Wingel Pinzon, Michael Poole, Lindsey Pope, Michael J. Purbaugh, Sana Qadar, Saul Quinn, John Quinnette, Omar A. Quinonez, Mark Rabin, Ali Rad, Bryan Rager, Brian Rainey, Edwin Ramirez, Douglas Ray, Richard Reaux, Josephine Reed, Ed Reinsel, Diriki Rice, Tyrone W. Riggs, Olivier Robert, Diane Roberts, Eugene W. Roberts, Nathan Roberts, Samuel Rocha, Abu Bakr Roland, Alberto Romero, Peter Roof, Adrienne Ross, Misa Rossetti-Meyer, Theodore Roth, Rivea Ruff, Bruce R. Santhuff, Thayer Sargent, John T. Satterfield, Gregory Savoy, Kathie Scarrah, Louise Schiavone, Terese Schlachter, Peter Schloemer, Donald Schoenmann, Sarah Scott, Dunja Selbach, Joseph Serensits, James Sides, David Silver, Paul Skomal, Stephanie Slewka, Charles Slie, Anthony Smith, Gilbert Solorzano, Randall Sorenson, George A. Sozio, Theodore Spiegler, David Spiro, Thomas M. Staton, Mark S. Stoddard, Matthew Straub, Rachel Streitfeld, James Suddeth, Rick Suddeth, Editha Tendencia, Marcus Teply, Michael Thomas, Shari Thomas, Joseph Thompson, Jr., Deborah Todd, George Toman, Michael D. Tuggle, Al Douglas Turner, Renee Turner, Brad Ulery, Juan E. Ureta, Nanette van der Laan, Paul Vanderveen, Nikolai von Goihmann, Jackie Lyn Walker, Derrick Ward, Tarik Warner, Aaron Webster, George D. Weller, Mark White, John P. Whiteside, Megan Whittemore, Stefan Wiesen, Tracee Wilkins, David Williams, Val Willingham, Mark Wilson, Ronald Winters, Tracey Marie Wright, Po L. Wu, Eun Yang, Lian-Hwa Yang, Dania Yousef, Stratis Zervos.

PERIODICAL PRESS GALLERIES*

HOUSE PERIODICAL PRESS GALLERY

The Capitol, H–304, 225–2941

Director.—Robert M. Zatkowski.
Assistant Directors: Laura L. Eckart, Robert L. Stallings.

SENATE PERIODICAL PRESS GALLERY

The Capitol, S–320, 224–0265

Director.—Edward V. Pesce.
Assistant Directors: Justin Wilson, Shawna Blair.

EXECUTIVE COMMITTEE OF CORRESPONDENTS

Richard E. Cohen, National Journal
Tracy Schmidt, Time Magazine
Ben Pershing, Roll Call
Danielle Knight, U.S. News & World Report
Heather Rothman, BNA News
Eamon Javers, Business Week
Margaret Shreve, Tax Notes

RULES GOVERNING PERIODICAL PRESS GALLERIES

1. Persons eligible for admission to the Periodical Press Galleries must be bona fide resident correspondents of reputable standing, giving their chief attention to the gathering and reporting of news. They shall state in writing the names of their employers and their additional sources of earned income; and they shall declare that, while a member of the Galleries, they will not act as an agent in the prosecution of claims, and will not become engaged or assist, directly or indirectly, in any lobbying, promotion, advertising, or publicity activity intended to influence legislation or any other action of the Congress, nor any matter before any independent agency, or any department or other instrumentality of the Executive branch; and that they will not act as an agent for, or be employed by the Federal, or any State, local or foreign government or representatives thereof; and that they will not, directly or indirectly, furnish special or ''insider'' information intended to influence prices or for the purpose of trading on any commodity or stock exchange; and that they will not become employed, directly or indirectly, by any stock exchange, board of trade or other organization or member thereof, or brokerage house or broker engaged in the buying and selling of any security or commodity. Applications shall be submitted to the Executive Committee of the Periodical Correspondents' Association and shall be authenticated in a manner satisfactory to the Executive Committee.

2. Applicants must be employed by periodicals that regularly publish a substantial volume of news material of either general, economic, industrial, technical, cultural, or trade character. The periodical must require such Washington coverage on a continuing basis and must be owned and operated independently of any government, industry, institution, association, or lobbying organization. Applicants must also be employed by a periodical that is published for profit and is supported chiefly by advertising or by subscription, or by a periodical meeting the conditions in this paragraph but published by a nonprofit organization that, first, operates independently of any government, industry, or institution and, second, does not engage, directly or indirectly, in any lobbying or other activity intended to influence any matter before Congress or before any independent agency or any department or other instrumentality of the Executive branch. House organs are not eligible.

*Information is based on data furnished and edited by each respective gallery.

3. Members of the families of correspondents are not entitled to the privileges of the galleries.

4. The Executive Committee may issue temporary credentials permitting the privileges of the galleries to individuals who meet the rules of eligibility but who may be on short-term assignment or temporarily residing in Washington.

5. Under the authority of rule 6 of the House of Representatives and of rule 33 of the Senate, the Periodical Galleries shall be under the control of the Executive Committee, subject to the approval and supervision of the Speaker of the House of Representatives and the Senate Committee on Rules and Administration. It shall be the duty of the Executive Committee, at its discretion, to report violations of the privileges of the galleries to the Speaker or the Senate Committee on Rules and Administration, and pending action thereon, the offending correspondent may be suspended. The committee shall be elected at the start of each Congress by members of the Periodical Correspondents' Association and shall consist of seven members with no more than one member from any one publishing organization. The committee shall elect its own officers and a majority of the committee may fill vacancies on the committee. The list in the Congressional Directory shall be a list only of members of the Periodical Correspondents' Association.

NANCY PELOSI,
Speaker, House of Representatives.

DIANNE FEINSTEIN,
Chair, Senate Committee on Rules and Administration.

MEMBERS ENTITLED TO ADMISSION

PERIODICAL PRESS GALLERIES

Abramson, Julie L.: National Journal Group, National Journal
Abse, Nathan: Federal Employees News Digest
Ackley, Kate: Roll Call
Acord, David: Food Chemical News
Adhicary, Dave: Tax Notes
Aingst, Martin: Die Zeit
Ainsley, Laura: CD Publications
Alexis, Alexei: BNA News
Ali, Aman A.: The Hill
Allen, James O. ''Jim'': The Hill
Almeras, Jon S.: Tax Notes
Altstadt, David: MII Publications
Amber, Michelle: BNA News
Ambinder, Marc: National Journal Group, The Hotline
Andersen, Ericka L.: Human Events
Anderson, Thomas M.: Kiplinger Washington Editors
Andrews, Catherine: Washingtonian
Anselmo, Joseph: McGraw-Hill Co., Aviation Week
Antonides, David Scott: Tax Notes
Aplin, Donald, G, BNA News
Apokis, Dimitrios: Investor's World
Aquino, John, T, BNA News
Archer, Jeffrey Robert: Education Week
Arnoult, Sandra: Penton Media Inc.
Ash, Katie A.: Education Week
Ashburn, Elyse: Chronicle of Higher Education
Ashton, Jerome C.: BNA News
Ashworth, Jerry: Thompson Publishing Group
Asker, James R.: McGraw-Hill Co., Aviation Week
Assam, Cecelia: BNA News
Astor, April M.: Washington Business Information
Atkins, Pamela S.: BNA News
Atlas, Stephen Terry: U.S. News & World Report
Atwood, John Filar: CCH Inc.
Aulino, Margaret: BNA News
Ault, Alicia: International Medical News Group
Ayayo, Herman P.: Tax Notes
Ayers, Carl Albert: UCG
Babbin, Jed L.: Human Events
Baer, Susan: Washingtonian
Bagley, Moira C.: Roll Call
Bailey, Holly: Newsweek
Bailey, Anna: Inside Washington Publishers, FDA Week
Bain, Ben: Federal Computer Week
Baker, Samuel U.: Inside Washington Publishers
Ballenstedt, Brittany R.: National Journal Group, Government Executive
Bancroft, John: Inside Mortgage Finance
Banner, Valerie: UCG
Barak, Sarah: Thompson Publishing Group
Barbagallo, Paul: Telecommunications Reports
Bardwell, Brian: Tax Notes
Barnes, Fred, W.: Weekly Standard
Barnes, James A.: National Journal Group, National Journal
Barr, Andrew: The Hill
Barrett, Randy: National Journal Group, National Journal
Barry, John A.: Newsweek
Bartholet, Jeffrey I.: Newsweek
Bartlett, Thomas E.: Chronicle of Higher Education
Barton, Robert L.: McGraw-Hill Co.
Basken, Paul A.: Chronicle of Higher Education
Basu, Sandra L.: U.S. Medicine
Baumann, Jeannie: BNA News
Bazelon, Emily: Slate
Beam, Jacob Christopher: Slate
Beaman, William P.: Reader's Digest
Beaven, Lara W.: Inside Washington Publishers
Bedard, Paul: U.S. News & World Report
Beizer, Douglas: 1105 Government Information Group, Washington Technology
Bell, Kevin A.: Tax Notes
Bell, John R.: International Medical News Group
Benjamin, Mark: Salon
Bennett, Alison: BNA News
Bennett, Heather: Tax Notes
Bennett, Brian: Time Inc., Time Magazine
Bennett, John T.: Army Times Publishing Co., Defense News
Benton, Nicholas F.: Falls Church News Press
Ben-Yosef, Andrea, L.: BNA News
Berger, James R.: Washington Trade Daily
Berger, Mary: Washington Trade Daily
Berger, Brian: Space News
Berlin, Joshua L.: FDC Reports
Berman, Dan: Environment & Energy Publishing
Berman, Ari: Nation
Berry, Attila L.: American Lawyer Media, Legal Times
Besser, James David: New York Jewish Week
Best, Frank M.: U.S. Medicine
Bhambhani, Dipka: McGraw-Hill Co.
Bieryla, Doreen: UCG
Billings, Erin P.: Roll Call
Billings, Deborah D.: BNA News
Bivins, Amy: BNA News
Blake, Whitney: Weekly Standard

MEMBERS ENTITLED TO ADMISSION, PERIODICAL PRESS GALLERIES—Continued

Blake, Aaron: The Hill
Blake, JoAnn D.: UCG
Blank, Peter L.: Kiplinger Washington Editors
Block, Jonathan N.: FDC Reports
Blumenstyk, Goldie: Chronicle of Higher Education
Bogardus, Kevin J.: The Hill
Bolen, Cheryl: BNA News
Bollag, Burton: Chronicle of Higher Education
Bolton, Alexander: The Hill
Bolton, Elizabeth: Thompson Publishing Group
Bomster, Mark W.: Education Week
Bond, David: McGraw-Hill Co., Aviation Week
Bontrager, Eric: Environment & Energy Publishing
Borchersen-Keto, Sarah A.: CCH Inc.
Borgia, Kevin C.: Inside Washington Publishers
Borja, Rhea R.: Education Week
Boyd, John D.: Traffic World
Boyle, Katherine V.: Environment & Energy Publishing
Boyles, William R.: Health Market Survey
Bracken, Leonard: BNA News
Brady, Matthew: National Underwriter
Brainard, Jeffrey H.: Chronicle of Higher Education
Brandon, Emily L.: U.S. News & World Report
Braun, Kevin D.: Environment & Energy Publishing
Breier, Ben: Inside Washington Publishers
Brevetti, Rossella E.: BNA News
Brinton, S. Turner: Space News
Briscoe, Daren: Newsweek
Bristow, Melissa S.: Kiplinger Washington Editors
Britt, Angela L.: BNA News
Brodsky, Robert G.: National Journal Group, Government Executive
Brooks, George A.: Inside Mortgage Finance
Brotherton, Elizabeth: Roll Call
Brown, Janet M.: Press Associates
Brown, Jill: Atlantic Information Services
Brown, Steven G.: FDC Reports
Brown, Penelope M.: Traffic World
Brownstein, Andrew D.: Thompson Publishing Group
Bruce, R. Christian: BNA News
Brumfiel, Geoff: Nature
Bruno, Michael: McGraw-Hill Co., Aviation Week
Brush, Silla: U.S. News & World Report
Bryant, Sue: BNA News
Buchta, Cheryl: McGraw-Hill Co.
Buckley, Elizabeth: Food Chemical News
Buhl, John M.: Tax Notes
Bullock, Lorinda M.: International Medical News Group
Bunch, Sonny: Weekly Standard
Buntin, John: Governing
Burkhart, Lori: Public Utilities Fortnightly
Burnham, Michael P.: Environment & Energy Publishing
Buschman, Thomas: Thompson Publishing Group
Butchock, Steve: Medical Devices Report
Butler, Amy: McGraw-Hill Co., Aviation Week
Byerrum, Ellen: BNA News
Byrne, James S.: CD Publications
Byus, Jonathan: 1105 Government Information Group, Government Computer News
Caggiano, Jr., Gabriel R.: Montgomery County Sentinel
Cain, Derrick: BNA News
Calabresi, Massimo T.: Time Inc., Time Magazine
Caldwell, Christopher: Weekly Standard
Cano, Craig: McGraw-Hill Co.
Cardman, Michael: Thompson Publishing Group
Carey, John A.: McGraw-Hill Co., Business Week
Carlile, Amy: Roll Call
Carlile, Nathan: American Lawyer Media, Legal Times
Carlson, Jeffrey E.: CCH Inc.
Carney, Eliza Newlin: National Journal Group, National Journal
Carney, James F.: Time Inc., Time Magazine
Carpenter, Amanda: Human Events
Carr, Jennifer: Tax Notes
Carroll, Conn M.: National Journal Group, The Hotline
Caruso, Lisa: National Journal Group, National Journal
Cash, Catherine: McGraw-Hill Co.
Cassidy, William B.: Traffic World
Castelli, Chistopher: Inside Washington Publishers
Castelli, Elise: Army Times Publishing Co., Federal Times
Cauthen, Carey: Thompson Publishing Group
Cavallaro, Gina: Army Times Publishing Co.
Cavanagh, Sean: Education Week
Cavas, Christopher: Army Times Publishing Co., Defense News
Cecala, Guy David: Inside Mortgage Finance
Cech, Scott J.: Education Week
Censer, Marjorie J.: Inside Washington Publishers
Chan, Wade-Hahn: Federal Computer Week
Chappell, Kevin U.: Jet/Ebony
Chemnick, Jean: McGraw-Hill Co.
Cherkasky, Mara: Thompson Publishing Group
Cherry, Sheila: BNA News
Chibbaro, Jr., Louis M.: Washington Blade
Childress, Rasheeda Crayton: Business Publishers
Chronister, Gregory: Education Week
Cinquegrani, Gayle: BNA News
Clapp, Stephen: Food Chemical News
Clark, Timothy: National Journal Group, Government Executive
Clark, Colin: Space News
Clark, Ben C.: Washingtonian
Clarke, David Paul: Inside Washington Publishers
Clemmitt, Marcia: CQ Researcher
Click, Jennifer S.: BNA News
Clift, Eleanor: Newsweek
Coder, Jeremiah G.: Tax Notes

MEMBERS ENTITLED TO ADMISSION, PERIODICAL PRESS GALLERIES—Continued

Coffin, James B.: Public Lands News
Cohen, Richard E.: National Journal Group, National Journal
Cohen, Janey: BNA News
Cohen, Alan F.: UCG
Cohn, Elizabeth S.: Chronicle of Higher Education
Cole, Torie D.: CCH Inc.
Collins, Brian: National Mortgage News
Collins, Eve: Atlantic Information Services
Collogan, David L.: McGraw-Hill Co., Aviation Week
Comer, John Matthew: Environment & Energy Publishing
Compart, Andrew W.: Travel Weekly
Conant, Eve K.: Newsweek
Conroy, Declan: Setanta Publishing
Continetti, Matthew: Weekly Standard
Cook, Steven: BNA News
Cook, Jr., Charles E.: Cook Political Report
Cooper, Stephen K.: CCH Inc.
Cooper, Rebecca A.: Exchange Monitor Publications
Corbett, Warren: Set-Aside Alert
Corley, Matilda Monroe: BNA News
Corn, David: Nation
Cornibert, Stefan S.: Inside Washington Publishers, Inside EPA
Cottle, M. Michelle: New Republic
Coughlin, Brett G.: Inside Washington Publishers
Couillard, Lauren: BNA News
Cowden, Richard H.: BNA News
Cox, Matthew: Army Times Publishing Co.
Cox, Ana Marie: Time Inc., Time Magazine
Coyle, Marcia: American Lawyer Media, National Law Journal
Coyne, Martin: McGraw-Hill Co.
Crabtree, Susan: The Hill
Craver, Martha L.: Kiplinger Washington Editors
Crawford, Elizabeth: UCG
Crea, Joe: American Lawyer Media, Legal Times
Crider, Richard: Thompson Publishing Group
Crook, Clive: National Journal Group, Nationaljournal.com
Crowley, Michael L.: New Republic
Cruickshank, Paula L.: CCH Inc.
Cruz, Gilbert: Time Magazine
Curran, John: Telecommunications Reports
Currie, Duncan M.: Weekly Standard
Cusack, Robert: The Hill
Dahl, Julia E.: Salon
Daigneau, Elizabeth: Governing
Darcey, Susan: FDC Reports
Davidson, Mark: McGraw-Hill Co.
Davies, Stephen A.: Endangered Species & Wetlands Report
Davis, Steve: Atlantic Information Services
Davis, Susan: Roll Call
Davis, Michelle R.: Education Week
Davis, Molly: Inside Washington Publishers
Davis, Shannon: Inside Washington Publishers
Davis, Jeffrey J.: Transportation Weekly
Davis, Kimberly V.: Thompson Publishing Group
Davis, Bronwyn L.: BNA News
Day, Jeff: BNA News
Deigh, Gloria: BNA News
DeLeon, Carrie: Telecommunications Reports
Dembeck, Chet E.: CD Publications
Dennis, Steven T.: Roll Call
Devernoe, Tanya: BNA News
Diamond, Phyllis: BNA News
Dickerson, John F.: Slate
Diegmueller, Karen: Education Week
Dinnage, Russell: Environment & Energy Publishing
DiSciullo, Joseph: Tax Notes
Dizard, Wilson: 1105 Government Information Group, Government Computer News
Doan, Michael F.: Kiplinger Washington Editors
DoBias, Matthew: Crain Communications
Dobson, Jon: FDC Reports
Doi, Ayako: Japan Digest
Dolley, Steven: McGraw-Hill Co.
Dombroski, Cathy H.: FDC Reports
Donlan, Thomas G.: Barron's
Doolan, Kelley: McGraw-Hill Co.
Doolittle, Amy J.: Army Times Publishing Co., Federal Times
Dorobek, Christopher: Federal Computer Week
Douglass, Linda: National Journal
Doyle, John M.: McGraw-Hill Co., Aviation Week
Doyle, Kenneth P.: BNA News
Doyle, Tim: Forbes
Draper, Robert L.: GQ Magazine
Drew, Elizabeth: New York Review of Books
Dreyfuss, Robert C.: Rolling Stone
Drucker, David M.: Roll Call
Dube, Lawrence E.: BNA News
Dudley, Amy G.: National Journal Group, The Hotline
Duffy, Jennifer: Cook Political Report
Duffy, Michael W.: Time Inc., Time Magazine
Duffy, Thomas Patrick: Inside Washington Publishers
Duncan, Alexander: Exchange Monitor Publications, McGraw-Hill Co.
Dunham, Richard S.: McGraw-Hill Co., Business Week
Duran, Nicole: Roll Call
Eastland, Terry: Weekly Standard
Easton, Nina J.: Time Inc., Fortune Magazine
Eby, Deborah: Business Publishers
Edmondson, Thomas: BNA News
Edmonson, Robert G.: Traffic World
Edney, Hazel Trice: Afro American Newspapers
Edsall, Thomas B.: New Republic
Edwards, Charles J.: Thompson Publishing Group
Edwards, Thomas J.: CD Publications

MEMBERS ENTITLED TO ADMISSION, PERIODICAL PRESS GALLERIES—Continued

Eggerton, John S.: Reed Business Information, Broadcasting & Cable
Eglovitch, Joanne S.: FDC Reports
Eisele, Albert: The Hill
Eisler, Kim: Washingtonian
Elfin, Dana: BNA News
Ellis, Isobel: National Journal Group, National Journal
Elmore, Wesley: Tax Notes
Emeigh, Jr., Geoffrey: BNA News
Engan, Luke: Inside Washington Publishers
Ephron, Dan: Newsweek
Epstein, Keith: McGraw-Hill Co., Business Week
Ericksen, Charles A.: Hispanic Link News Service
Esparza, Eddy Ramirez: U.S. News & World Report
Esquivel, J. Jesus: Proceso
Ethridge, Emily V.: Washington Business Information
Evans, Jeffrey: International Medical News Group
Evans, Larry E.: BNA News
Ezzard, Catherine Sullivan: BNA News
Fabian, Thecla: BNA News
Fabey, Michael: Traffic World
Fain, Paul A.: Chronicle of Higher Education
Fairbanks, Eve R.: New Republic
Fallows, James: National Journal Group, Atlantic Monthly
Fanshel, Fran: UCG
Farrell, Elizabeth: Chronicle of Higher Education
Fauver, Michael: Thompson Publishing Group
Feltman, Peter E.: CCH Inc.
Ferguson, Andrew: Weekly Standard
Ferguson, Brett: BNA News
Fernandez, Lourdes B.: Inside Washington Publishers
Ferris, Nancy B.: Federal Computer Week
Ferullo, Michael: BNA News
Fessenden, Helen: The Hill
Fickling, Amy: McGraw-Hill Co.
Field, Kelly: Chronicle of Higher Education
Field, Christopher: Human Events
Filmore, David: FDC Reports
Finan, Colin: Inside Washington Publishers
Fineman, Howard: Newsweek
Finet, J.P.: BNA News
Fiorino, Frances: McGraw-Hill Co., Aviation Week
Fischer, Karin: Chronicle of Higher Education
Fisher, Elizabeth: National Review
Fitzpatrick, Erika: Congressional Digest
Fleet, Leslie G.: BNA News
Flint, Perry A.: Penton Media Inc.
Flynn, Joan Marie: Thompson Publishing Group
Foer, Franklin L.: New Republic
Forbes, Sean I.: BNA News
Foster, Andrea: Chronicle of Higher Education
Foster, Lawrence D.: McGraw-Hill Co.
Foster, Cassandra P.: Roll Call
Fourney, Susan: National Journal Group, Government Executive
Fowler, Katia P.: FDC Reports
France, Stephen: BNA News
Francis, Laura: BNA News
Frandsen, Jon C.: Kiplinger Washington Editors
Franklin, Mary Beth: Kiplinger Washington Editors
Freda, Diane: BNA News
Freddoso, David: Evans-Novak Political Report, National Review
Freedberg, Jr., Sydney J.: National Journal Group, National Journal
Frick, Robert L.: Kiplinger Washington Editors
Frieden, Joyce: International Medical News Group
Friedman, Daniel: Army Times Publishing Co., Federal Times
Friel, Brian: National Journal Group, National Journal
Fulghum, David: McGraw-Hill Co., Aviation Week
Gallagher, John: Traffic World
Gannon, John: BNA News
Gantz, Rachel: UCG
Garamfalui, Alexia: American Lawyer Media, Legal Times
Garland, Susan B.: Kiplinger Washington Editors
Garner, W. Lynn: BNA News
Gasparello, Linda A.: White House Weekly
Gavant, Kelli L.: Thompson Publishing Group
Gay, Patrice L.: Tax Notes
Gdowski, Jessica C.: UCG
Geisel, Jerome M.: Crain Communications
Geman, Ben: Environment & Energy Publishing
Getter, Lisa: UCG
Gettinger, Steve: National Journal Group, National Journal
Gettlin, Robert H.: National Journal Group, National Journal
Gewertz, Catherine: Education Week
Gibb, Steven K.: Inside Washington Publishers
Gidron, Martin J.: Washington Business Information
Gilbert, Lorraine S.: BNA News
Gilgoff, Daniel: U.S. News & World Report
Gillies, Andrew: Forbes
Gilston, Samuel M.: Gilston-Kalin Communications
Gizzi, John: Human Events
Glazer, Gwen: National Journal Group, Nationaljournal.com
Gleckman, Howard: McGraw-Hill Co., Business Week
Glenn, David G.: Chronicle of Higher Education
Glenn, Heidi: Tax Notes
Glenzer, Michael: Exchange Monitor Publications
Gloger, Katja: Stern
Gnaedinger, Chuck: Tax Notes
Gnezditskaia, Anastasia: Inside Washington Publishers
Go, Alison M.: U.S. News & World Report
Goindi, Geeta: Express India
Goldberg, Kirsten: The Cancer Letter

MEMBERS ENTITLED TO ADMISSION, PERIODICAL PRESS GALLERIES—Continued

Goldberg, Paul: The Cancer Letter
Goldberg, Jeffrey: New Yorker
Goldberg, Jonah: National Review
Goldman, Ted: American Lawyer Media, Legal Times
Goldstein, Peter: Kiplinger Washington Editors
Goldstein, Sid: Letter Publications
Goldwyn, Brant: CCH Inc.
Golub, Barbra: Atlantic Information Services
Gonzales, Nathan: Rothenberg Political Report
Good, Christopher E.: The Hill
Goodin, Emily: National Journal Group, The Hotline
Goodman, Joshua: Governing
Goodwine, Velma: Research Institute of America Group
Gordon, Meryl: Elle
Gordon, Kelly J.: Thompson Publishing Group
Gotsch, Ted: Telecommunications Reports
Goulder, Robert: Tax Notes
Goyal, Raghubir: Asia Today
Graff, Garrett: Washingtonian
Grant, Greg: National Journal Group, Government Executive
Green, Charles A.: National Journal Group, National Journal
Green, Joshua: National Journal Group, Atlantic Monthly
Greenblatt, Alan: Governing
Greenhalgh, Keiron: McGraw-Hill Co.
Gregg, Diana I.: BNA News
Gregorits, Angela: BNA News
Grieve, Timothy: Salon
Greifner, Laura S.: Education Week
Griffith, Cara: Tax Notes
Grilliot, Rebecca S.: UCG
Gross, Grant J.: IDG News Service
Gross-Glaser, Sheryl: Business Publishers
Grover, Elizabeth A.: BNA News
Gruber, Amelia: National Journal Group, Government Executive
Gruenberg, Mark J.: Press Associates
Grupe, Bob C.: CD Publications
Guarino, Douglas: Inside Washington Publishers
Guest, Robert: Economist
Guido, Daniel W.: McGraw-Hill Co.
Gurdon, Hugo: The Hill
Gutierrez, Pedro Ruz: American Lawyer Media
Gutman, James H.: Atlantic Information Services
Gutting, Elizabeth W.: Tax Notes
Hadley, Richard D.: UCG
Hagstrom, Jerry: National Journal Group, National Journal
Hall, Holly: Chronicle of Higher Education
Hall, Barry: Federal Publications, Government Contractor
Halloran, Elizabeth: U.S. News & World Report
Halonen, Douglas J.: Crain Communications
Hamaker, Christian A.: Public Utilities Fortnightly
Hammon, Jamie R.: FDC Reports
Haniffa, Aziz: India Abroad
Hansard, Sara: Crain Communications
Hansen, Brian: McGraw-Hill Co.
Hanson, Melinda: BNA News
Harbrecht, Douglas A.: Kiplinger Washington Editors
Hardin, Angela Y.: McGraw-Hill Co.
Hardy, Michael L.: Washington Technology
Harman, Thomas: CD Publications
Harrington, William: Inside Washington Publishers
Harris, Joann Christine: Tax Notes
Harris, Shane: National Journal Group, National Journal
Harrison, Tom: McGraw-Hill Co.
Harrison, David: BNA News
Hausmann, Helen D.: McGraw-Hill Co.
Hayes, Peter S.: BNA News
Hays, Kimberly: CD Publications
Hearn, Edward T.: Reed Business Information, Multichannel News
Hebel, Sara: Chronicle of Higher Education
Hedges, Joyce: BNA News
Heflin, Jay: Research Institute of America Group
Hegland, Corine: National Journal Group, National Journal
Heil, Emily: Roll Call
Heim, Daniel S.: Roll Call
Hemingway, Mark: National Review
Hemingway, Mollie, Z.: Army Times Publishing Co., Federal Times
Hendrie, Caroline: Education Week
Hennig, Jutta: Inside Washington Publishers
Hernandez, Luis: Thompson Publishing Group
Hess, Ryan E.: MII Publications
Heyd, Cindy Ann: Tax Notes
Hicks, Travis: Thompson Publishing Group
Higgins, John: Business Publishers
Hill, Keith M.: BNA News
Hill, Richard: BNA News
Hill, Jayne A.: Atlantic Information Services
Hipolit, Melissa J.: CQ Researcher
Hiruo, Elaine: McGraw-Hill Co.
Hobbs, M. Nielsen: FDC Reports
Hocking, Bryanna: Roll Call
Hoellwarth, John: Army Times Publishing Co., Marine Corps Times
Hoff, David: Education Week
Hoffman, Donald B.: Thompson Publishing Group
Hoffman, Rebecca E.: BNA News
Hoffman, William: Traffic World
Hofmann, Mark A.: Crain Communications
Holland, William: McGraw-Hill Co.
Hollingsworth, Catherine: BNA News
Hollis, Christopher: Washington Business Information
Holmes, Gwendolyn: BNA News
Holmes, Allan T.: National Journal Group, Government Executive

MEMBERS ENTITLED TO ADMISSION, PERIODICAL PRESS GALLERIES—Continued

Homes, Erik: Army Times Publicshing Co.
Holzer, Jessica: Forbes
Holzer, Jessica: The Hill
Honawar, Vaishali: Education Week
Hoover, Eric: Chronicle of Higher Education
Hoover, Kent: Washington Business Journal
Horner, Daniel: McGraw-Hill Co.
Horowitz, Jay: BNA News
Horwitz, Jeff: American Lawyer Media
Horwood, Rachel Jane: Economist
Hosenball, Mark J.: Newsweek
Houghton, Mary: FDC Reports
Hubbard, Catherine A.: CCH Inc.
Hubler, David: Federal Computer Week
Hughes, Jr., John D.: McGraw-Hill Co., Aviation Week
Humes, James E.: National Journal Group, National Journal
Humphrey, Shonda: Tax Notes
Hunter, Pamela E.: McGraw-Hill Co.
Hurwitz, Amber: CD Publications
Hyland, Terence: BNA News
Hylton, William: GQ Magazine
Ichniowski, Thomas, F.: McGraw-Hill Co.
Idaszak, Jerome: Kiplinger Washington Editors
Iekel, John F.: Thompson Publishing Group
Iroegbu, Osita N.: American Lawyer Media, Legal Times
Isikoff, Michael: Newsweek
Ivey, Brandon: Inside Mortgage Finance
Jackman, Frank: McGraw-Hill Co.
Jackson, Joab: 1105 Government Information Group, Government Computer News
Jackson, Valarie N.: McGraw-Hill Co.
Jackson, William K.: 1105 Government Information Group, Government Computer News
Jacobs, Jeremy P.: The Hill
Jacobson, Todd: Exchange Monitor Publications
Jaffe, Harry S.: Washingtonian
James, Betty: Federal Publications, Interpreter Releases
Javers, Eamon: McGraw-Hill Co., Business Week
Jaworski, Thomas: Tax Notes
Johansen, Alison: BNA News
Johnson, Alisa: BNA News
Johnson, Regina: McGraw-Hill Co.
Johnson, Lyrica: Federal Publications, Government Contractor
Johnson, Wendy: UCG
Johnson, Christopher C.: Inside Washington Publishers
Johnson, Jenny L.: Inside Washington Publishers, Clean Air Report
Johnson, Kimberly E.: Army Times Publishing Co.
Jones, George G.: CCH Inc.
Jones, Joyce: Black Enterprise
Jones, James: Washington City Paper
Jones, Danielle D.: National Journal Group, The Hotline
Jonson, Nick: McGraw-Hill Co.
Jordan, Anne: Governing
Jordan, Bryant: Army Times Publishing Co., Air Force Times
Joseph, Samantha: UCG
Joslyn, Heather: Chronicle of Higher Education
Jost, Kenneth W.: CQ Researcher
Jowers, Karen Grigg: Army Times Publishing Co.
Joyce, Stephen: BNA News
Judis, John B.: New Republic
Jungbaver, Rebecca: FDC Reports
Kafanov, Lucy: Environment & Energy Publishing
Kahn, Debra: Environment & Energy Publishing
Kamarck, Chloe M.: Salon
Kaplan, Hugh B.: BNA News
Kaplan, Jonathan: The Hill
Kaplun, Alex: Environment & Energy Publishing
Karp, Aaron E.: Penton Media Inc.
Karrs, Emily: National Review
Kash, Wyatt: 1105 Government Information Group, Government Computer News
Kass, Marcia: BNA News
Katel, Peter: CQ Researcher
Katz, Marisa: National Journal Group, National Journal
Kauffman, Tim: Army Times Publishing Co., Federal Times
Kaufman, Bruce S.: BNA News
Kaufmann, Carol: Reader's Digest
Kavanagh, Susan: CCH Inc.
Kavruck, Deborah A.: Washington Counseletter
Kavruck, Samuel: Washington Counseletter
Keller, Bess: Education Week
Keller, Gail S.: BNA News
Kelley, Sarah: American Lawyer Media, Legal Times
Kellner, Mark A.: Army Times Publishing Co., Defense News
Kelly, Patrice Wingert: Newsweek
Kelly, Spencer: UCG
Kelly, Catherine A.: FDC Reports
Kennedy, Hugh: UCG
Kennedy, Kelly: Army Times Publishing Co.
Kennedy, Laura W.: Kiplinger Washington Editors
Kenney, Allen: Tax Notes
Kessler, Ronald B.: NewsMax
Kim, Hana: Thompson Publishing Group
Kime, Patricia N.: Army Times Publishing Co., Navy Times
King, Maureen: Telecommunications Reports
Kingsbury, Alex: U.S. News & World Report
Kinney, Jeff: BNA News
Kirby, Paul: Telecommunications Reports
Kirkland, Joel: McGraw-Hill Co.
Kirkland, John R.: BNA News
Kitfield, James: National Journal Group, National Journal
Klein, Alyson: Education Week

MEMBERS ENTITLED TO ADMISSION, PERIODICAL PRESS GALLERIES—Continued

Kleine-Brockhoff, Thomas: Die Zeit
Klimko, Frank: CD Publications
Klumpp, Helena: Tax Notes
Knight, Danielle: U.S. News & World Report
Koch, Kathy: CQ Researcher
Kondracke, Morton, M.: Roll Call
Kopecki, Dawn: McGraw-Hill Co., Business Week
Kosova, Weston: Newsweek
Kosterlitz, Julie A.: National Journal Group, National Journal
Kovski, Alan: McGraw-Hill Co.
Kraft, Scott: UCG
Kramer, David: Science & Government Report
Kriz, Margaret E.: National Journal Group, National Journal
Kubetin, Sally: International Medical News Group
Kubetin W. Randy: BNA News
Kucher, Liane: McGraw-Hill Co.
Kucinich, Jacqueline: The Hill
Kuckro, Rod: McGraw-Hill Co.
Kumar Sen, Ashish: Outlook Magazine
Kurtz, Josh: Roll Call
Kushner, Adam B.: New Republic
LaBrecque, Louis C.: BNA News
Lacey, Anthony: Inside Washington Publishers
Laffler, Mary Jo: FDC Reports
LaGier, Elizabeth: BNA News
Lake, Jessica: FDC Reports
Lally, Rosemarie: Thompson Publishing Group
Lamoreaux, Denise: Thompson Publishing Group
Langer, Emily J.: National Journal Group, National Journal
Lankford, Kimberly: Kiplinger Washington Editors
Larsen, Kathy Carolin: McGraw-Hill Co.
Lash, Jennifer: Roll Call
Lassman, Teresa: International Medical News Group
Last, Jonathan V.: Weekly Standard
Lavelle, Marianne: U.S. News & World Report
Lavin, Abigail J.: Weekly Standard
Learner, Neal: Atlantic Information Services
Leavitt, David I.: Environment & Energy Publishing
Lee, Stephen: UCG
Leeuwenburgh, Todd H.: Atlantic Information Services
Lehr, Katherine V.: National Journal Group, The Hotline
Leitch, Catherine H.: U.S. Medicine
Lening, Carey: BNA News
Leopold, George H.: CMP Media Inc.
Leske, Gisela: Der Spiegel
Levin, Joshua: Slate
Levin, Robin: CD Publications
Levine, Carrie: American Lawyer Media
Lewis, Nicole: Chronicle of Higher Education
Liang, John: Inside Washington Publishers
Lillis, Michael: Inside Washington Publishers
Lim, Nathasha: National Mortgage News
Limpert, John: Washingtonian
Lindeman, Ralph: BNA News
Lindsay, Drew: Washingtonian
Lindsley, Joseph P.: Weekly Standard
Ling, Katherine: Environment & Energy Publishing
Linger, Kristyn: BNA News
Lipowicz, Alice: 1105 Government Information Group, Washington Technology
Lithwick, Dahlia Hannah: Slate
Lizza, Ryan C.: New Republic
Loos, David: Environment & Energy Publishing
Losey, Stephen: Army Times Publishing Co., Federal Times
Loveless, William E.: McGraw-Hill Co.
Lowe, Paul D.: Aviation International News
Lowther, William: Mail on Sunday
Lubell, Jennifer: Crain Communications
Lucey, Eric J.: Thompson Publishing Group
Lumb, Jacquelyn: CCH Inc.
Lund, Brenda M.: Washington Business Information
Lunney, Kellie: National Journal Group, National Journal
Lustig, Joe: Thompson Publishing Group
Lynsen, Joshua J.: Washington Blade
Maas, Angela K.: Atlantic Information Services
MacDonald, Neil A.: Technology Commercialization
Macy, Daniel J.: Thompson Publishing Group
Maggs, John J.: National Journal Group, National Journal
Magill, Barbara: Thompson Publishing Group
Mahoney, Fabia H.: BNA News
Mahtesian, Charles: National Journal Group, National Journal
Maine, Amanda: CCH Inc.
Maixner, Edward: Kiplinger Washington Editors
Malenic, Marina: Inside Washington Publishers
Mandel, Jennifer: Environment & Energy Publishing National Journal Group, Government Executive
Mandell, Dara S.: Jewish Press
Manley, Mary Ann G.: BNA News
Manzo, Kathleen K.: Education Week
Marcucci, Carl: Radio Business Report Inc., Smart Media
Marcum, Karissa: The Hill
Marek, Angela: U.S. News & World Report
Marino, Jonathan: National Journal Group, Government Executive
Marre, Klaus: The Hill
Marris, Emma: Nature
Marron, Jessica: McGraw-Hill Co.
Marson, Brian: FDC Reports
Martin, Sheena: UCG
Martinson, Erica L.: Inside Washington Publishers
Mascolo, Georg Ranier: Der Spiegel
Mattes, Sherilyn: International Medical News Group
Matthews, Martha A.: BNA News
Matthews, Sidney William: Army Times Publishing Co., Defense News

MEMBERS ENTITLED TO ADMISSION, PERIODICAL PRESS GALLERIES—Continued

Mauro, Antony: American Lawyer Media, Legal Times
Maxwell, Lesli A.: Education Week
Mayer, Jane: New Yorker
Maze, Richard: Army Times Publishing Co.
Mazumdar, Anandashankar: BNA News
McAdams, Deborah D.: IMAS Publishing
McAlvanah, Nora J.: National Journal Group, The Hotline
McArdle, John: Roll Call
McBeth Laping, Karen: McGraw-Hill Co.
McCaffery, Gregory: BNA News
McCaney, Kevin: 1105 Government Information Group, Government Computer News
McConnell, Beth Ann: Sedgwick Publishing Co.
McCord, Quinn T.: National Journal Group, The Hotline
McCormack, Richard: Manufacturing & Technology News
McCormack, Kelly: The Hill
McCormally, Kevin: Kiplinger Washington Editors
McCracken, Rebecca P.: BNA News
McDermott, Kevin: Research Institute of America Group
McGeehon, Dale: Thompson Publishing Group
McGoffin, Michael J.: Research Institute of America Group
McGolrick, Susan J.: BNA News
McGowan, Kevin P.: BNA News
McIntosh, Toby: BNA News
McKinney, Amber: BNA News
McLure, Jason: American Lawyer Media, Legal Times
McMichael, William H.: Army Times Publishing Co., Military Times
McMurtrie, Elizabeth: Chronicle of Higher Education
McNeil, Michele: Education Week
McPike, Erin: National Journal Group, Nationaljournal.com
McTague, James: Barron's
McTague, Rachel: BNA News
Medford, Clayton P.: Inside Washington Publishers
Meehan, Chris: Atlantic Information Services
Melillo, Wendy: Adweek Magazine
Melnyk, Yuliya V.: CD Publications
Melvin, Jasmin: Thompson Publishing Group
Memoli, Mike: National Journal Group, The Hotline
Mercurio, John C.: National Journal Group, The Hotline
Merrion, Paul Robert: Crain Communications
Meyer, Cordula: Der Spiegel
Meyers, David B.: Roll Call
Mezo, Ingrid M.J.: FDC Reports
Michels, Jennifer L.: McGraw-Hill Co., Aviation Week
Miller, Jason: 1105 Government Information Group, Government Computer News
Miller, John J.: National Review
Miller, Karla L.: Tax Notes
Miller, Reed J.: FDC Reports
Miller, Tricia L.: National Journal Group, National Journal
Miller, Julie A.: Inside Mortgage Finance
Milligan, Michael: Travel Weekly
Minton-Beddoes, Zanny: Economist
Mitchell, Robert: Business Publishers; FDC Reports
Mitchell, Charles F.: Roll Call
Miyashita, Alex (Shigeki), M.: Hispanic Link News Service
Moan, Rebekah J.: FDC Reports
Mogul, Matthew: Kiplinger Washington Editors
Mokhiber, Russell: Corporate Crime Reporter
Mola, Roger Andrew: Aviation International News
Monastersky, Richard: Chronicle of Higher Education
Moncrief, JoAnne P.: National Journal Group, National Journal
Montwieler, Nancy H.: BNA News
Moore, Miles David: Crain Communications
Moore, Nancy J.: BNA News
Moore, Michael: BNA News
Moorman, Robert W.: Traffic World
Moragne, Lenora: Black Congressional Monitor
Morales, Cecilio: MII Publications
Morello, Lauren: Environment & Energy Publishing
Morgan, Theresa T.: Inside Washington Publishers
Morin, Christopher Scott: Thompson Publishing Group
Morring, Jr., Frank: McGraw-Hill Co., Aviation Week
Morris, Jefferson F.: McGraw-Hill Co., Aviation Week
Morris, Jodie: National Journal Group, National Journal
Morris, Ryan: National Journal Group, National Journal
Morrissey, James A.: Textile World
Morton, Peter: Financial Post
Moscovitch, Ben: Exchange Monitor Publications
Mosquera, Mary: 1105 Government Information Group, Government Computer News
Mpinja, Bora U.: Inside Washington Publishers
Mulligan, Megan: The Hill
Mumford, Christine M.: BNA News
Munoz, German: News Bites
Munoz, Carlo: Inside Washington Publishers
Munro, Neil P.: National Journal Group, National Journal
Muolo, Paul A.: National Mortgage News
Murdoch, Joyce M.: National Journal Group, National Journal
Murray, Matthew: Roll Call
Mutcherson-Ridley, Joyce: CCH Inc.
Myers, Cathleen R.: BNA News
Njuguna, Wangui: BNA News
Nadal, Lisa M.: Tax Notes

MEMBERS ENTITLED TO ADMISSION, PERIODICAL PRESS GALLERIES—Continued

Napoli, Denise E.: International Medical News Group
Nartker, Michael: Exchange Monitor Publications
Natter, Ari: Traffic World
Naylor, Sean D.: Army Times Publishing Co.
Neal, Andrew: BNA News
Neill, Alexander: Army Times Publishing Co.
Nelson, Ryan: FDC Reports
Nelson, Erica L.: Inside Washington Publishers
Neumann, Daniel: Inside Washington Publishers
Newell, Elizabeth: Government Executive
Newkumet, Christopher J.: McGraw-Hill Co.
Newmyer, Arthur: Roll Call
Newton-Small, Jay: Time Magazine
Nicholson, Jonathan: BNA News
Njuguna, Wangui: Business Publishers
Noah, Timothy Robert: Slate
Norman, Brett E.: UCG
Novack, Janet: Forbes
Nutt, Audrey: Tax Notes
O'Beirne, Kate Walsh: National Review
Oberdorfer, Carol: BNA News
Oberle, Sean F.: Oberle Communications, Product Safety Letter
Obey, Douglas: Inside Washington Publishers
O'Brien, Maura E.: National Journal Group, The Hotline
O'Conner, Seamus R.: Army Times Publishing Co., Air Force Times
Oddis, Michelle E.: Human Events
O'Driscoll, Mary: Environment & Energy Publishing
Ognanovich, Nancy: BNA News
Oliphant, James S.: American Lawyer Media, Legal Times
Olsen, Florence: Federal Computer Week
Olsen, Carlene E.: FDC Reports
Olson, Lynn: Education Week
Omestad, Thomas E.: U.S. News & World Report
Onley, Gloria R.: BNA News
Opuiyo, Alafaka: Afro American Newspapers
Orrick, Sarah M.: Congressional Digest
Ostroff, Jim: Kiplinger Washington Editors
O'Toole, Charles: Tax Notes
O'Toole, Thomas: BNA News
Otteman, Scott: Inside Washington Publishers
Ottenhoff, Patrick R.: National Journal Group, The Hotline
Pagans, Christy L.: Thompson Publishing Group
Page, Paul: Traffic World
Pak, Janne Kum Cha: USA Journal
Palazzolo, Johseph: American Lawyer Media
Palmer, Anna: American Lawyer Media, Legal Times, Roll Call
Panepento, Peter V.: Chronicle of Higher Education
Parillo, Jill M.: Exchange Monitor Publications
Parillo, Kristen: Tax Notes
Parker, Susan T.: Natural Gas Intelligence
Parker, Eric: Tax Notes
Parker, Stuart H.: Inside Washington Publishers
Parker, Andrew D.: Professional Pilot Magazine
Parrish, Molly R.: Letter Publications
Paschal, Mack Arthur: BNA News
Patrick, Steven: BNA News
Patterson, James B.: Thompson Publishing Group
Patton, Oliver B.: Heavy Duty Trucking
Patton, Zachary L.: Governing
Payne, January: Atlantic Information Services
Payne, Marisa C.: Exchange Monitor Publications
Pazanowski, Bernard J.: BNA News
Pazanowski, Mary Anne: BNA News
Pearl, Larry: Food Chemical News
Pekow, Charles: Community College Week
Perera, David: National Journal Group, Government Executive
Perlman, Ellen: Governing
Perry, Suzanne: Chronicle of Higher Education
Perry, Elizabeth A.: Washington Blade
Pershing, Benjamin: Roll Call
Peters, Katherine M.: National Journal Group, Government Executive
Petersen, Tina: McGraw-Hill Co.
Peterson, Denise: FDC Reports
Peterson, Zachary M.: Army Times Publishing Co., Navy Times
Pethokoukis, James M.: U.S. News & World Report
Pexton, Patrick: National Journal Group, National Journal
Phelps, Kathryn Ann: FDC Reports
Phelps, Kevin: Federal Publications, Government Contractor
Phillips, Cathleen M.: Tax Notes
Phillips, Lyda: BNA News
Phillips, Zachary: National Journal Group, Government Executive
Piemonte, Philip M.: Federal Employees News Digest
Pierce, Emily: Roll Call
Pilpel, Heidi: Federal Publications, Government Contractor
Pimley, Ward: BNA News
Plank, Kendra Casey: BNA News
Plotz, David: Slate
Pluviose, David: Diverse: Issues in Higher Education
Ponnuru, Ramesh: National Review
Ponnuru, April: National Review
Poppy, Daniel F.: FDC Reports
Postal, Arthur D.: National Underwriter
Powers, Martha C.: Mid-Atlantic Research
Pryde, Joan A.: Kiplinger Washington Editors
Pueschel, Matt: U.S. Medicine
Punj, Shweta: Inside Washington Publishers
Pulliam, Daniel: National Journal Group, Government Executive
Purdum, Todd S.: Vanity Fair

MEMBERS ENTITLED TO ADMISSION, PERIODICAL PRESS GALLERIES—Continued

Putrich, Gayle S.: Army Times Publishing Co., Defense News
Quay, Christopher: Tax Notes
Radford, Bruce W.: Public Utilities Fortnightly
Ragavan, Chitra: U.S. News & World Report
Raju, Manu K.: The Hill
Rash, Wayne: Eweek
Reaves, John P.: UCG
Reed, John R.: Inside Washington Publishers
Rees, John: Mid-Atlantic Research
Reeves, Dawn: Inside Washington Publishers
Reishus, Mark: Thompson Publishing Group
Ressler, Thomas: Inside Mortgage Finance
Richardson, Nathaline: BNA News
Richardson, Zachary: Food Chemical News
Richmond, Linda M.: BNA News
Rickman, Johnathan: Tax Notes
Ripley, Amanda: Time Inc., Time Magazine
Rizzuto, Pat: BNA News
Robelen, Erik: Education Week
Roberts, Edward S.: Credit Union Journal
Roberts, Victoria: BNA News
Robinson, Thomas S.: Mass Transit Lawyer
Robinson-Simmons, Quintin: Tax Notes
Rodriguez, Eva M.: McGraw-Hill Co., Business Week
Roeder, Linda: BNA News
Rogers, Robert L.: American Lawyer Media, Legal Times
Rogers, Benjamin: UCG
Rogin, Joshua: Federal Computer Week
Rohde, Peter: Inside Washington Publishers
Rohrer, S. Scott: National Journal Group, National Journal
Ron, Jane: Nationaljournal.com
Rolfsen, Bruce: Army Times Publishing Co., Air Force Times
Rose, Phil A.: Professional Pilot Magazine
Rosen, Jeffrey M.: New Republic
Rosen, Anne: Thompson Publishing Group
Rosenberg, Alyssa B.: National Journal Group, National Journal
Rothenberg, Stuart: Rothenberg Political Report
Rothman, Heather M.: BNA News
Rothstein, Betsy: The Hill
Roy, Daniel J.: BNA News
Rudd, Jr., Terrence: International Medical News Group
Ruel-Sabatier, Patrick: Le Point
Rummell, Nicholas: UCG; Crain Communications
Russo, Eugene: Nature
Rutherford, Emelie H.: Inside Washington Publishers
Rutzick, Karen: National Journal Group, Government Executive
Ryan, Margaret: McGraw-Hill Co.
Saenz, Cheryl L.: BNA News
Sahd, Timothy J.: National Journal Group, The Hotline
Saiyid, Amena H.: BNA News
Sala, Susan: BNA News
Saletan, William B.: Slate
Salzano, Carlo J.: Waterways Journal
Sami, Tamra: FDC Reports
Sammon, Richard: Kiplinger Washington Editors
Samuels, Christina: Education Week
Samuelsohn, Darren: Environment & Energy Publishing
Samuelson, Robert J.: Newsweek
Sangillo, Gregg Thomas: National Journal Group, National Journal
Sartipzadeh, Saied Ali: BNA News
Sarvana, Adam: Inside Washington Publishers
Savage, Luiza C.: Maclean's
Savoie, Andy: McGraw-Hill Co., Aviation Week
Scales, Sirena J.: Research Institute of America Group
Scheiber, Noam J.: New Republic
Scherer, Michael: Salon
Scherman, Bob: Satellite Business News
Schieken, William: Federal Publications, Government Contractor
Schmidt, Mike: McGraw-Hill Co.
Schmidt, Peter: Chronicle of Higher Education
Schmidt, Tracy S.: Time Inc., Time Magazine
Schneider, Andrew C.: Kiplinger Washington Editors
Schneider, Martin A.: Exchange Monitor Publications
Schoeff, Jr., Mark: Crain Communications
Schoenberg, Tom: American Lawyer Media, Legal Times
Schofield, Adrian: McGraw-Hill Co., Aviation Week
Schomisch, Jeffrey: Thompson Publishing Group
Schor, Elana: The Hill
Schorr, Burt: UCG
Schuff, Sally: Farm Progress News
Schuh, Brian: Atlantic Information Services
Schulte, Bret: U.S. News & World Report
Schwartz, Emma: American Lawyer Media, Legal Times
Schwind, Daniel B.: UCG
Scoblic, J. Peter: New Republic
Scorza, John Forrest: CCH Inc.
Scott, Dean T.: BNA News
Scott, Laura: UCG
Scott Hennaman, Cordia: Tax Notes
Seiden, Daniel I.: BNA News
Selingo, Jeffrey: Chronicle of Higher Education
Sellers, Ivy: Human Events
Serafini, Marilyn Werber: National Journal Group, National Journal
Setze, Karen Jeanne: Tax Notes
Seyler, David P.: Radio Business Report Inc., Smart Media
Sfiligoj, Mark L.: Kiplinger Washington Editors
Shafer, Jack: Slate

MEMBERS ENTITLED TO ADMISSION, PERIODICAL PRESS GALLERIES—Continued

Shannon, Elaine: Time Inc., Time Magazine
Shapiro, Walter: Salon
Shappell, Brian: CD Publications
Sharpe, Kieran: Thompson Publishing Group
Sharpe, Stephanie: McGraw-Hill Co.
Sheedy, Rachel L.: Kiplinger Washington Editors
Sheikh, Fawzia: Inside Washington Publishers
Sheppard, Doug: Tax Notes
Shoop, Thomas J.: National Journal Group, Government Executive
Shreve, Margaret: Tax Notes
Shute, Nancy: U.S. News & World Report
Silva, Jeffrey, S.: Crain Communications
Simendinger, Alexis A.: National Journal Group, National Journal
Simmonds, Susan Jeane: Tax Notes
Simpson, Jason: Inside Washington Publishers
Singer, Paul B.: Roll Call
Skinner, David P.: Weekly Standard
Slaughter, David A.: Thompson Publishing Group
Smaglik, Paul: Nature
Smallen, Jill: National Journal Group, National Journal
Smith, Douglas D.: Tax Notes
Smith, Katie: Roll Call
Smith, Joseph: Business Publishers
Smith, Jennifer C.: Inside Washington Publishers
Smith, Noah J.: BNA News
Snider, Adam: BNA News
Snow, Nicholas J.: Oil & Gas Journal
Snyder, Jim: The Hill
Snyder, Katharine: Mine Safety and Health News
Sobieraj, Sandra: Time Inc., People Magazine
Solomon, Goody L.: News Bites
Soraghan, Mike: The Hill
Southern, E. Richard: Federal Publications, Government Contractor
Spence, Charles F.: General Aviation News
Spencer, Patricia S.: BNA News
Spiering, Charlie: Evans-Novak Political Report
Spicer, Malcolm E.: FDC Reports
Splete, Heidi: International Medical News Group
Spotswood, Stephen: U.S. Medicine
Sprague, John: Budget & Program
Stam, John H.: BNA News
Stamper, Dustin: Tax Notes
Stanton, Lynn: Telecommunications Reports
Stanton, John: Roll Call
Starobin, Paul: National Journal Group, National Journal
Stavros, Richard: Public Utilities Fortnightly
Straus, Brian: Penton Media Inc.
Steele, Zaira: Steele Communications
Steele, Laura: Kiplinger Washington Editors
Steinberg, Julie A.: BNA News
Steinke, Scott A.: FDC Reports
Steis, Ellen Beswick: Natural Gas Intelligence
Steis, Alexander Beswick: Natural Gas Intelligence
Stencel, Mark: Governing
Stevenson, Margaret: FDC Reports
Stevenson, Meredith: Tax Notes
Stewart, William H.: Thompson Publishing Group
Stimson, Leslie P.: IMAS Publishing
Stoddard, Alexandra B.: The Hill
Stoffer, Harry: Crain Communications
Stokeld, Frederick W.: Tax Notes
Stoler, Judith R.: Time Inc., Time Magazine
Stone, Peter H.: National Journal Group, National Journal
Stratton, Sheryl: Tax Notes
Straus, Brian A.: Penton Media Inc.
Strawbridge, James O.: Inside Washington Publishers, Inside U.S. Trade
Sturges, Peyton Mackay: BNA News
Sugarman, Carole: Food Chemical News
Sullivan, John H.: BNA News
Sullivan, Monica C.: National Journal Group, National Journal
Sullivan, William B.: U.S. News & World Report
Sullivan, Martin A.: Tax Notes
Sutter, Susan M.: Scrip World Pharmaceutical News
Sutton, Eileen C.: BNA News
Swanson, Ian B.: The Hill
Sweeney, Ray: CD Publications
Sweeting, Paul: Reed Business Information, Reed Business Information
Swibel, Matthew: Forbes
Swisher, Larry: BNA News
Swope, Christopher: Governing
Tacconelli, Gail: Newsweek
Taft, Chloe: FDC Reports
Tait, Darryl W.: Tax Notes
Tan, Michelle: Army Times Publishing Co.
Tandon, Crystal: Tax Notes
Taulbee, Pamela D.: FDC Reports
Taylor, Dan: Inside Washington Publishers
Taylor, Ronald: BNA News
Taylor, Vincent: UCG
Taylor, Timothy M.: Tax Notes
Taylor II, B.J.: Atlantic Information Services
Taylor, Jr., Stuart: National Journal Group, National Journal
Teinowitz, Ira: Crain Communications
Teske, Steven: BNA News
Thibodeau, Patrick: IDG Communications
Thomas, Richard K.: Newsweek
Thomas, Katherine: FDC Reports
Thompson, Jason: National Journal Group, Nationaljournal.com
Thompson, Mark J.: Time Inc., Time Magazine
Thorn, Judith: BNA News
Thornburg, Linda: Thompson Publishing Group
Thorndike, Joseph: Tax Notes
Thurber, Matthew C.: Aviation International News
Tice, James S.: Army Times Publishing Co.
Tiernan, Tom: McGraw-Hill Co.

MEMBERS ENTITLED TO ADMISSION, PERIODICAL PRESS GALLERIES—Continued

Timmerman, Kenneth R.: NewsMax
Tiron, Roxana: The Hill
Todaro, Jane B.: McGraw-Hill Co., Business Week
Toeplitz, Shira R.: National Journal Group, The Hotline
Tonn, Jessica: Education Week
Torres, Katherine: Penton Media Inc.
Tosh, Dennis A.: Thompson Publishing Group
Triplett, Michael R.: BNA News
Trotter, Andrew: Education Week
Trygstad, Kyle K.: National Journal Group, National Journal
Tsigas, Maria: UCG
Tsikitas, Irene E.: National Journal Group, Nationaljournal.com
Tsui, Amy: BNA News
Tucker, Miriam E.: International Medical News Group
Tumulty, Karen: Time Inc., Time Magazine
Tuttle, Steve: Newsweek
Twachtman, Gregory: FDC Reports
Unni, Adosh: FDC Reports
Unnikrishnan, Madhu: McGraw-Hill Co., Aviation Week
Vaida, Bara: National Journal Group, National Journal
Vail, Bruce H.: BNA News
Vample, Gwendolyn: Thompson Publishing Group
Van Dongen, Rachel A.: Roll Call
Vandegrift, Beth: Thompson Publishing Group
Vanderweide, Emily: Tax Notes
Verespej, Michael: Crain Communications
Verma, Ember M.: Tax Notes
Viadero, Debra: Education Week
Victor, Kirk: National Journal Group, National Journal
Vissat, Melina A.: FDC Reports
Vissiere, Helene: Le Point
Von Zeppelin, Cristina L.: Forbes
Wachter, Kerri: International Medical News Group
Wadman, Meredith: Nature
Wait, Patience: 1105 Government Information Group, Government Computer News
Wakeman, Nick: 1105 Government Information Group, Washington Technology
Walker, Christopher C.: FDC Reports
Walker, Richard W.: Federal Computer Week
Walker, Karen J.: Army Times Publishing Co., Armed Forces Journal
Walker, Chandra: CCH Inc.
Wallace, Charles: Federal Publications, Government Contractor
Walsh, Gertrude: 1105 Government Information Group, Government Computer News
Walsh, Kenneth T.: U.S. News & World Report
Walsh, Mark: Education Week
Walsh, Elsa: New Yorker
Walter, Amy: Cook Political Report
Ware, Patricia: BNA News
Warren, Timothy M.: Inside Mortgage Finance
Wasserbly, Daniel: Inside Washington Publishers
Wasserman, David: Cook Political Report
Wasson, Erik: Inside Washington Publishers
Watkins, Steve: Army Times Publishing Co., Federal Times
Weber, Rick: Inside Washington Publishers
Webster, James C.: Webster Communications
Wechsler, Jill: Pharmaceutical Executive
Weigelt, Matthew: Federal Computer Week
Weil, Jenny: McGraw-Hill Co.
Weiland, Morgan A.: FDC Reports; BNA News
Weiner, Joann M.: Tax Notes
Weisgerber, Marcus: Inside Washington Publishers
Weiss, Jessica: CD Publications
Weisskopf, Michael P.: Time Inc., Time Magazine
Welch, Jake: National Journal Group, National Journal
Wells, Robert J.: Tax Notes
Welsh, William E.: 1105 Government Information Group, Washington Technology
Werner, Karen Leigh: BNA News
Whalen, John M.: BNA News
Whieldon, Esther: McGraw-Hill Co.
White, Rodney A.: McGraw-Hill Co.
White III, Frank: BNA News
Whitelaw, Kevin: U.S. News & World Report
Whitten, Daniel: McGraw-Hill Co.
Whittington, Lauren: Roll Call
Wieser, Eric: McGraw-Hill Co.
Wilczek, Yin: BNA News
Wildstrom, Stephen H.: McGraw-Hill Co., Business Week
Wilkerson, John: Inside Washington Publishers
Willen, Mark: Kiplinger Washington Editors
Willenson, Kim: Japan Digest
Williams, Eileen J.: BNA News
Williams, Grant: Chronicle of Higher Education
Williams, Jeffrey: Satellite Business News
Williams, Risa D.: Tax Notes
Williams, Mark A.: BNA News
Wilson, Stanley E.: Institutional Investor
Winebrenner, Jane A.: BNA News
Wingfield, Brian R.: Forbes
Winn, Patrick O.: Army Times Publishing Co.
Winston, Kate: Inside Washington Publishers
Winter, Allison A.: Environment & Energy Publishing
Witkin, Gordon: U.S. News & World Report
Witt, Elder: Governing
Witze, Alexandra: Nature
Woellert, Lorraine: McGraw-Hill Co., Business Week
Wolfe, Matthew M.: Inside Washington Publishers
Wolffe, Richard: Newsweek
Wolverton, Bradley: Chronicle of Higher Education
Wood, Graeme: Atlantic Information Services
Wooldridge, Adrian: Economist

MEMBERS ENTITLED TO ADMISSION, PERIODICAL PRESS GALLERIES—Continued

Wright, Charlotte: McGraw-Hill Co.
Wright, Karen L.: BNA News
Wright, Jr., James: Afro American Newspapers
Wyand, Michael W.: BNA News
Yachnin, Jennifer: Roll Call
Yaksick, Jr., George L.: CCH Inc.
Yamazaki, Kazutami: Washington Watch
Yeager, Eric: BNA News
Yehle, Emily J.: Roll Call
Yerkey, Gary G.: BNA News
Yingling, Jennifer: The Hill
Yochelson, Mindy: BNA News
Yohannan, Suzanne M.: Inside Washington Publishers
Yordanova-Kline, Milena: McGraw-Hill Co.
York, Byron: National Review
Young, Sam: Tax Notes
Young, Jeffrey: The Hill
Youngman, Sam A.: The Hill
Yuill, Barbara: BNA News
Zagorin, Adam: Time Inc., Time Magazine
Zaneski, Cyril (Cy): Environment & Energy Publishing
Zehr, Mary Ann: Education Week
Zung, Robert Te-Kang: BNA News

PERIODICALS REPRESENTED IN PRESS GALLERIES

House Gallery 225–2941, Senate Gallery 224–0265

ADWEEK MAGAZINE—(202) 833–2551; 910 17th Street, NW., Suite 215, Washington, DC 20005: Wendy Melillo.

AFRO AMERICAN NEWSPAPERS—(202) 332–0080; 1917 Benning Road, NE., Washington, DC 20002: Hazel Trice Edney, Alafaka Opuiyo, James Wright, Jr.

AMERICAN LAWYER MEDIA—(202) 457–0686; 1730 M Street, NW., Suite 800, Washington, DC 20036: Attila Berry, Nathan Carlile, Marcia Coyle, Joe Crea, Alexia Garamfalui, Ted Goldman, Pedro Ruz Gutierrez, Jeff Horwitz, Osita Iroegbu, Carrie Levine, Antony Mauro, Jason McLure, James Oliphant, Joseph Palazzolo, Anna Palmer, Robert Rogers, Tom Schoenberg, Emma Schwartz.

ARMY TIMES PUBLISHING CO.—(703) 750–9000; 6883 Commercial Drive, Springfield, VA 22159: Gina Cavallaro, Matthew Cox, Erik Holmes, Kimberly E. Johnson, Bryant Jordan, Karen Grigg Jowers, Kelly Kennedy, Richard Maze, Sean D. Naylor, Alexander Neill, Seamus R. O'Conner, Bruce Rolfsen, Michelle Tan, James S. Tice, Karen J. Walker, Patrick O. Winn.

ASIA TODAY—(202) 271–1100; 27025 McPhearson Square, Washington, DC 20038: Raghubir Goyal.

ATLANTIC INFORMATION SERVICES—(202) 775–9008; 1100 17th Street, NW., Suite 300, Washington, DC 20036: Jill Brown, Eve Collins, Steve Davis, Barbra Golub, James H. Gutman, Jayne A. Hill, Neal Learner, Todd H. Leeuwenburgh, Angela K. Maas, Chris Meehan, January Payne, Brian Schuh, B.J. Taylor II.

ATLANTIC MONTHLY—(202) 739–8400; 600 New Hampshire Avenue, NW., Washington, DC 20037: James Fallows, Joshua Green, Graeme Wood.

AVIATION INTERNATIONAL NEWS—(203) 798–2400; 5605 Alderbrook Court, #T6, Rockville, MD 20851: Paul D. Lowe, Roger Andrew Mola, Matthew C. Thurber.

AVIATION WEEK—(202) 383–2350; 1200 G Street, NW., Suite 900, Washington, DC 20005: Joseph Anselmo, James R. Asker, David Bond, Michael Bruno, Amy Butler, David L. Collogan, John M. Doyle, Frances Fiorino, David Fulghum, John D. Hughes, Jr., Jennifer L. Michels, Frank Morring, Jr., Jefferson F. Morris, Andy Savoie, Adrian Schofield, Madhu Unnikrishnan.

BNA NEWS—(703) 341–5870; 1801 S. Bell Street, Arlingotn, VA 22202: Alexei Alexis, Michelle Amber, Donald G Aplin, John T Aquino, Jerome C. Ashton, Cecelia Assam, Pamela S. Atkins, Margaret Aulino, Jeannie Baumann, Alison Bennett, Andrea L. Ben-Yosef, Deborah D. Billings, Amy Bivins, Cheryl Bolen, Leonard Bracken, Rossella E. Brevetti, Angela L. Britt, R. Christian Bruce, Sue Bryant, Ellen Byerrum, Derrick Cain, Sheila Cherry, Gayle Cinquegrani, Jennifer S. Click, Janey Cohen, Steven Cook, Matilda Monroe Corley, Lauren Couillard, Richard H. Cowden, Bronwyn L. Davis, Jeff Day, Gloria Deigh, Tanya Devernoe, Phyllis Diamond, Kenneth P. Doyle, Lawrence E. Dube, Thomas Edmondson, Dana Elfin, Geoffrey Emeigh Jr., Larry E. Evans, Catherine Sullivan Ezzard, Thecla Fabian, Brett Ferguson, Michael Ferullo, J.P. Finet, Leslie G. Fleet, Sean I. Forbes, Stephen France, Laura Francis, Diane Freda, John Gannon, W. Lynn Garner, Lorraine S. Gilbert, Diana I. Gregg, Angela Gregorits, Elizabeth A. Grover, Melinda Hanson, David Harrison, Peter S. Hayes, Joyce Hedges, Richard Hill, Keith M. Hill, Rebecca E. Hoffman, Catherine Hollingsworth, Gwendolyn Holmes, Jay Horowitz, Terence Hyland, Alison Johansen, Alisa Johnson, Stephen Joyce, Hugh B. Kaplan, Marcia Kass, Bruce S. Kaufman, Gail S. Keller, Altaf U. Khan, Jeff Kinney, John R. Kirkland, W. Randy Kubetin, Louis C. LaBrecque, Elizabeth LaGier, Carey Lening, Ralph Lindeman, Kristyn Linger, Fabia H. Mahoney, Mary Ann G. Manley, Martha A. Matthews, Anandashankar Mazumdar, Gregory McCaffery, Rebecca P. McCracken, Susan J. McGolrick, Kevin P. McGowan, Toby McIntosh, Amber McKinney, Rachel McTague, Nancy H. Montwieler, Nancy J. Moore, Michael Moore, Christine M. Mumford, Cathleen R. Myers, Andrew Neal, Jonathan Nicholson, Wangui Njuguna, Carol Oberdorfer, Nancy Ognanovich, Gloria R. Onley, Thomas O'Toole, Mack Arthur Paschal, Steven Patrick, Mary Anne Pazanowski, Bernard J. Pazanowski, Lyda Phillips, Ward Pimley, Kendra Casey Plank, Nathaline Richardson, Linda M. Richmond, Pat Rizzuto, Victoria Roberts, Linda Roeder, Heather M. Rothman, Daniel J. Roy, Cheryl L. Saenz, Amena H. Saiyid, Susan Sala, Saied Ali Sartipzadeh, Dean T. Scott, Daniel I. Seiden, Noah J. Smith, Adam Snider, Patricia S. Spencer, John H. Stam, Julie A. Steinberg, Peyton Mackay Sturges, John H. Sullivan, Eileen C. Sutton, Larry Swisher, Ronald Taylor, Steven Teske, Judith Thorn, Michael R. Triplett, Amy Tsui, Bruce H. Vail, Patricia Ware, Morgan Weiland, Karen Leigh Werner, John M. Whalen, Frank White III, Yin Wilczek, Mark A. Williams, Eileen J. Williams, Jane A. Winebrenner, Karen L. Wright, Michael W. Wyand, Eric Yeager, Gary G. Yerkey, Mindy Yochelson, Barbara Yuill, Robert Te-Kang Zung.

BARRON'S—(202) 862–6605; 1025 Connecticut Avenue, NW., Suite 800, Washington, DC 20036: Thomas G. Donlan, James McTague.

BLACK CONGRESSIONAL MONITOR—(202) 488–8879; P.O. Box 75035, Washington, DC 20024: Lenora Moragne.

BLACK ENTERPRISE—(212) 242–8000; 1220 Orren Street, NE., Washington, DC 20002: Joyce Jones.

BROADCASTING & CABLE—(646) 746–6400; 1701 K Street, NW., Suite 510, Washington, DC 20006: John S. Eggerton.

BUDGET & PROGRAM—(202) 628–3860; P.O. Box 6269, Washington, DC 20015: John Sprague.

PERIODICALS REPRESENTED IN PRESS GALLERIES—Continued

BUSINESS WEEK—(202) 383–2100; 1200 G Street, NW., Suite 1100, Washington, DC 20005: John A. Carey, Richard S. Dunham, Keith Epstein, Howard Gleckman, Eamon Javers, Dawn Kopecki, Eva M. Rodriguez, Jane B. Todaro, Stephen H. Wildstrom, Lorraine Woellert.

CCH INC.—(202) 842–7355; 1015 15th Street, NW., Suite 1000, Washington, DC 20005: John Filar Atwood, Sarah A. Borchersen-Keto, Jeffrey E. Carlson, Torie D. Cole, Stephen K. Cooper, Paula L. Cruickshank, Peter E. Feltman, Brant Goldwyn, Catherine A. Hubbard, George G. Jones, Susan Kavanagh, Jacquelyn Lumb, Amanda Maine, Joyce Mutcherson-Ridley, John Forrest Scorza, Chandra Walker, George L. Yaksick, Jr.

CD PUBLICATIONS—(301) 588–6380; 8204 Fenton Street, Silver Spring, MD 20910: Laura Ainsley, James S. Byrne, Chet E. Dembeck, Thomas J. Edwards, Bob C. Grupe, Thomas Harman, Kimberly Hays, Amber Hurwitz, Frank Klimko, Robin Levin, Yuliya V. Melnyk, Brian Shappell, Ray Sweeney, Jessica Weiss.

CMP MEDIA INC.—(202) 746–0611; 1639 York Mills Lane, Reston, VA 20194: George H. Leopold.

CQ RESEARCHER—(202) 729–1800; 1255 22nd Street, NW., Washington, DC 20037: Marcia Clemmitt, Kenneth W. Jost, Pater Katel, Kathy Koch.

CHRONICLE OF HIGHER EDUCATION—(202) 466–1000; 1255 23rd Street, NW., Suite 700, Washington, DC 20037: Elyse Ashburn, Thomas E. Bartlett, Paul A. Basken, Goldie Blumenstyk, Burton Bollag, Jeffrey H. Brainard, Elizabeth S. Cohn, Paul A. Fain, Elizabeth Farrell, Kelly Field, Karin Fischer, Andrea Foster, David G. Glenn, Holly Hall, Sara Hebel, Eric Hoover, Heather Joslyn, Nicole Lewis, Elizabeth McMurtrie, Richard Monastersky, Peter V. Panepento, Suzanne Perry, Peter Schmidt, Jeffrey Selingo, Grant Williams, Bradley Wolverton.

CLEAN AIR REPORT—(703) 416–8516; 1225 South Clark Street, Suite 1400, Arlington VA 22202: Jenny L. Johnson.

COMMUNITY COLLEGE WEEK—(703) 389–1239; 5225 Pooks Hill Road, #1118N, Bethesda, MD 20814: Charles Pekow.

CONGRESSIONAL DIGEST—(301) 634–3114; 4416 East West Highway, Suite 400, Bethesda, MD 20814: Erika Fitzpatrick, Sarah M. Orrick.

COOK POLITICAL REPORT—(202) 739–8525; 600 New Hampshire Avenue, NW., Washington, DC 20037: Charles E. Cook, Jr., Jennifer Duffy, Amy Walter, David Wasserman.

CORPORATE CRIME REPORTER—(202) 737–1680; 1209 National Press Building, Washington, DC 20045: Russell Mokhiber.

CRAIN COMMUNICATIONS—(202) 662–7200; 814 National Press Building, Washington, DC 20045: Matthew DoBias, Jerome M. Geisel, Douglas J. Halonen, Sara Hansard, Mark A. Hofmann, Jennifer Lubell, Paul Robert Merrion, Miles David Moore, Nicholas J. Rummell, Mark Schoeff, Jr., Jeffrey S. Silva, Harry Stoffer, Ira Teinowitz, Michael Verespej.

CREDIT UNION JOURNEL—(888) 832–2929; 1325 G Street, NW., Suite 910, Washington, DC 20005: Edward S. Roberts.

DEFENSE NEWS—(703) 642–7330; 6883 Commercial Drive, Springfield, VA 22159: John T. Bennett, Christopher Cavas, Mark A. Kellner, Sydney William Matthews, Gayle S. Putrich.

DER SPIEGEL—(202) 347–5222; 1202 National Press Building, Washington, DC 20045: Gisela Leske, George Ranier Mascolo, Cordula Meyer.

DIE ZEIT—(202) 223–0165; 4515 44th Street, NW., Washington, DC 20016: Thomas Kleine-Brockhoff, Martin Aingst.

DIVERSE: ISSUES IN HIGHER EDUCATION—(703) 385–2981; 10520 Warwick Avenue, Suite B–8, Fairfax, VA 22030: David Pluviose.

ECONOMIST—(202) 429–0890; 1730 Rhode Island Avenue, NW., Suite 1210, Washington, DC 20036: Robert Guest, Rachel Jane Horwood, Zanny Minton–Beddoes, Adrian Wooldridge.

EDUCATION WEEK—(301) 280–3100; 6935 Arlington Road, Suite 100, Bethesda, MD 20814: Jeffrey Robert Archer, Katie A. Ash, Mark W. Bomster, Rhea R. Borja, Sean Cavanagh, Scott J. Cech, Gregory Chronister, Michelle R. Davis, Karen Diegmueller, Catherine Gewertz, Laura S. Greifner, Caroline Hendrie, David Hoff, Vaishali Honawar, Bess Keller, Alyson Klein, Kathleen K. Manzo, Lesli A. Maxwell, Michele McNeil, Lynn Olson, Erik Robelen, Christina Samuels, Jessica Tonn, Andrew Trotter, Debra Viadero, Mark Walsh, Mary Ann Zehr.

ELLE—(202) 462–2951; 3133 Connecticut Avenue NW., Suite 315, Washington, DC 20008: Meryl Gordon.

ENDANGERED SPECIES & WETLANDS REPORT—(301) 891–3791; 6717 Poplar Avenue, Takoma Park, MD 20912: Stephen A. Davies.

ENVIRONMENT & ENERGY PUBLISHING—(202) 628–6500; 122 C Street, NW., Suite 722, Washington, DC 20001: Dan Berman, Eric Bontrager, Katherine V. Boyle, Kevin D. Braun, Michael P. Burnham, John Matthew Comer, Russell Dinnage, Ben Geman, Lucy Kafanov, Debra Kahn, Alex Kaplun, David I. Leavitt, Katherine Ling, Jennifer Mandel, Lauren Morello, Mary O'Driscoll, Darren Samuelsohn, Allison A. Winter, Cyril (Cy) Zaneski.

EVANS–NOVAK POLITICAL REPORT—(202) 393–4340; 1750 Pennsylvania Avenue, NW., Suite 1203, Washington, DC 20006: David Freddoso, Charlie Spiering.

EWEEK—(703) 425–9231; 11711 Amkin Drive, Clifton, VA 20124: Wayne Rash.

PERIODICALS REPRESENTED IN PRESS GALLERIES—Continued

EXCHANGE MONITOR PUBLICATIONS—(202) 296–2814; 4455 Connecticut Avenue, NW., Suite A700, Washington, DC 20008: Rebecca A. Cooper, Alexander Duncan, Michael Glenzer, Todd Jacobson, Ben Moscovitch, Michael Nartker, Jill M. Parillo, Marissa C. Payne, Martin A. Schneider.

EXPRESS INDIA—(703) 893–5565; 1541 Wellingham Court, Vienna, VA 22182: Geeta Goindi.

FALLS CHURCH NEWS PRESS—(703) 532–3267; 450 West Board Street, Suite 321, Falls Church, VA 22046: Nicholas F. Benton.

FARM PROGRESS NEWS—(952) 930–4346; 520 N Street, SW., Suite 3, Washington, DC 20024: Sally Schuff.

FDA WEEK—(703) 416–8505; 1225 South Clark St., Suite 1400, Arlington, VA 22202: Anna Bailey.

FDC REPORTS—(240) 221–4500; 5635 Fishers Lane, Suite 6000, Rockville, MD 20852: Joshua L. Berlin, Jonathan N. Block, Steven G. Brown, Susan Darcey, Jon Dobson, Cathy H. Dombroski, Joanne S. Eglovitch, David Filmore, Katia P. Fowler, Jamie R. Hammon, M. Nielsen Hobbs, Mary Houghton, Rebecca Jungbaver, Catherine A. Kelly, Mary Jo Laffler, Jessica Lake, Brian Marson, Ingrid M.J. Mezo, Reed J. Miller, Robert W. Mitchell, Rebekah J. Moan, Ryan Nelson, Carlene E. Olsen, Denise Peterson, Kathryn Ann Phelps, Daniel F. Poppy, Tamra S. Sami, Malcolm E. Spicer, Scott A. Steinke, Margaret Stevenson, Chloe Taft, Pamela D. Taulbee, Katherine Thomas, Gregory Twachtman, Adosh Unni, Melina A. Vissat, Christopher C. Walker, Morgan A. Weiland.

FEDERAL COMPUTER WEEK—(703) 876–5100; 3141 Fairview Park Drive, Suite 777, Falls Church, VA 22042: Ben Bain, Wade–Hahn Chan, Christopher Dorobek, Nancy B. Ferris, David Hubler, Florence Olsen, Joshua Rogin, Richard W. Walker, Matthew Weigelt.

FEDERAL EMPLOYEES NEWS DIGEST—(703) 707–1810; 610 Herndon Parkway, Suite 400, Herndon, VA 20170: Nathan Abse, Philip M. Piemonte.

FEDERAL TIMES—(800) 368–5718; 6883 Commercial Drive, Springfield, VA 22159: Elise Castelli, Amy J. Doolittle, Daniel Friedman, Mollie Z. Hemingway, Tim Kauffman, Stephen Losey, Steve Watkins.

FINANCIAL POST—(202) 842–1190; National Press Club, Suite 1206, Washington, DC 20045: Peter Morton.

FOOD CHEMICAL NEWS—(202) 887–6320; 1725 K Street, NW., Suite 506, Washington, DC 20006: David Acord, Elizabeth Buckley, Stephen Clapp, Larry Pearl, Zachary Richardson, Carole Sugarman.

FORBES—(202) 785–1480; 1101 17th Street, NW., Suite 409, Washington, DC 20036: Tim Doyle, Andrew Gillies, Janet Novack, Matthew Swibel, Cristina L. Von Zeppelin, Brian R. Wingfield.

FORTUNE MAGAZINE—(202) 861–4000; 555 12th Street, NW., Suite 600, Washington, DC 20004: Nina J. Easton.

GENERAL AVIATION NEWS—(301) 330–2715; 1915 Windjammer Way, Gaithersburg, MD 20879: Charles F. Spence.

GILSTON-KALIN COMMUNICATIONS—(301) 570–4544; 4816 Sweetbirch Drive, Rockville, MD 20853: Samuel M. Gilston.

GOVERNING—(202) 862–8802; 1100 Connecticut Avenue, NW., Suite 1300, Washington, DC 20036: John Buntin, Elizabeth Daigneau, Joshua Goodman, Alan Greenblatt, Anne Jordan, Zachary L. Patton, Ellen Perlman, Mark Stencel, Christopher Swope, Elder Witt.

GOVERNMENT COMPUTER NEWS—(703) 876–5100; 10 G Street, NE., Suite 500, Washington, DC 20002: Jonathan Byus, Wilson Dizard, Joab Jackson, William K. Jackson, Wyatt Kash, Kevin McCaney, Jason Miller, Mary Mosquera, Patience Wait, Gertrude Walsh.

GOVERNMENT CONTRACTOR—(800) 328–9378; 1100 13th Street, NW., Suite 200, Washington, DC 20005: Barry Hall, Lyrica Johnson, Kevin Phelps, Heidi Pilpel, William Schieken, E. Richard Southern, Charles Wallace.

GOVERNMENT EXECUTIVE—(202) 739–8400; 600 New Hampshire Avenue, NW., Washington, DC 20037: Brittany R. Ballenstedt, Robert G. Brodsky, Timothy Clark, Susan Fourney, Greg Grant, Amelia Gruber, Allan T. Holmes, Jennifer Mandel, Jonathan Marino, Elizabeth Newell, David Perera, Katherine M. Peters, Zachary Phillips, Daniel Pulliam, Karen Rutzick, Thomas J. Shoop.

GQ MAGAZINE—(202) 714–7323; 63 Shifflett Road, Free Union, VA 22940: Robert L. Draper, William Hylton.

HEALTH MARKET SURVEY—(202) 362–5408; 3767 Oliver Street, NW., Wasington, DC 20015: William R. Boyles.

HEAVY DUTY TRUCKING—(703) 683–9935; 320 Mansion Drive, Alexandria, VA 22302: Oliver B. Patton.

HISPANIC LINK NEWS SERVICE—(202) 234–0280; 1420 N Street, NW., Suite 101, Washington, DC 20005: Charles A. Ericksen, Alex (Shigeki) J. Miyashita.

HUMAN EVENTS—(202) 216–0600; One Massachusetts Avenue, NW., Washington, DC 20001: Ericka L. Andersen, Jed Babbin, Amanda Carpenter, Christopher Field, John Gizzi, Michelle E. Oddis, Ivy Sellers.

IDG COMMUNICATIONS—(202) 333–2448; 922 24th Street, NW., Suite 804, Washington, DC 20037: Patrick Thibodeau.

IDG NEWS SERVICE—(301) 604–6250; 906 Phillip Powers Drive, Laurel, MD 20707: Grant J. Gross.

IMAS PUBLISHING—(703) 998–7600; 5827 Columbia Pike, 3rd Floor, Falls Church, VA 22041: Deborah D. McAdams, Leslie P. Stimson.

PERIODICALS REPRESENTED IN PRESS GALLERIES—Continued

INDIA ABROAD—(703) 218–0790; 5026 Huntwood Manor Drive, Fairfax, VA 22030: Aziz Haniffa.

INSIDE EPA—(703) 416–8505; 225 South Clark St., Suite 1400, Arlington, VA 22202: Stefan S. Cornibert.

INSIDE MORTGAGE FINANCE—(301) 951–1240; 7910 Woodmont Avenue, Suite 1000, Bethesda, MD 20814: John Bancroft, George A. Brooks, Guy David Cecala, Brandon Ivey, Julie A. Miller, Thomas Ressler, Timothy M. Warren.

INSIDE U.S. TRADE—(703) 416–8505; 225 South Clark St., Suite 1400, Arlington, VA 22202: James O. Strawbridge.

INSIDE WASHINGTON PUBLISHERS—(703) 416–8500; 1225 South Clark Street, Suite 1400, Arlington, VA 22202: Samuel U. Baker, Lara W. Beaven, Ben Breier, Kevin C. Borgia, Chistopher Castelli, Marjorie J. Censer, David Paul Clarke, Brett G. Coughlin, Molly Davis, Shannon Davis, Thomas Patrick Duffy, Luke Engan, Lourdes B. Fernandez, Colin Finan, Anastasia Gnezditskaia, Douglas Guarino, William Harrignton, Jutta Hennig, Christopher C. Johnson, Anthony Lacey, John Liang, Michael Lillis, Marina Malenic, Erica L. Martinson, Clayton P. Medford, Theresa T. Morgan, Bora U. Mpinja, Carlo Munoz, Erica L. Nelson, Daniel Neumann, Douglas Obey, Scott Otteman, Stuart H. Parker, Shweta Punj, John R. Reed, Dawn Reeves, Peter Rohde, Emelie H. Rutherford, Adam Sarvana, Fawzia Sheikh, Jaosn Simpson, Jennifer C. Smith, Dan Taylor, Daniel Wasserbly, Erik Wasson, Rick Weber, Marcus Weisgerber, John Wilkerson, Kate Winston, Matthew M. Wolfe, Suzanne M. Yohannan.

INSTITUTIONAL INVESTOR—(202) 393–0728; 1319 F Street, NW., Suite 805, Washington, DC 20004: Stanley E. Wilson.

INTERNATIONAL MEDICAL NEWS GROUP—(240) 221–4500; 5635 Fishers Lane, Suite 6100, Rockville, MD 20852: Alicia Ault, John R. Bell, Lorinda M. Bullock, Jeffrey Evans, Joyce Frieden, Sally Kubetin, Teresa Lassman, Sherilyn Mattes, Denise E. Napoli, Terrence Rudd, Jr., Heidi Splete, Miriam E. Tucker, Kerri Wachter.

INTERPRETER RELEASES—(202) 772–8292, 1100 Thirteenth Street, NW., Suite 200 Washington, DC 20005: Betty James.

INVESTOR'S WORLD—(202) 664–2827; 3103 New Mexico Avenue, NW., #1011, Washington, DC 20016; Dimitrios Apokis.

JAPAN DIGEST—(703) 931–2500; 3424 Barger Drive, Falls Church, VA 22044: Ayako Doi, Kim Willenson.

JET / EBONY—(202) 393–5860; 1750 Pennsylvania Avenue, NW., Suite 1201, Washington, DC, 20006: Kevin Chappell.

JEWISH PRESS—(718) 330–1100; 1725 20th Street, NW., #F1, Washington, DC 20009: Dara S. Mandell.

KIPLINGER WASHINGTON EDITORS—(202) 887–6400; 1729 H Street, NW., Washington, DC 20006: Thomas M. Anderson, Peter L. Blank, Melissa S. Bristow, Martha L. Craver, Michael F. Doan, Jon C. Frandsen, Mary Beth Franklin, Robert L. Frick, Susan B. Garland, Peter Goldstein, Douglas A. Harbrecht, Jerome Idaszak, Laura W. Kennedy, Kimberly Lankford, Edward Maixner, Kevin McCormally, Matthew Mogul, Jim Ostroff, Joan A. Pryde, Richard Sammon, Andrew C. Schneider, Mark L. Sfiligoj, Rachel L. Sheedy, Laura Steele, Mark Willen.

LE POINT—(202) 244–6656; 3234 McKinley Street, NW., Washington, DC 20015: Patrick Rupl-Sabatier, Helene Vissiere.

LETTER PUBLICATIONS—(301) 718–1770; 7831 Woodmont Avenue, #386, Bethesda, MD 20814: Sid Goldstein, Molly R. Parrish.

MACLEAN'S—(202) 362–1658; 1111 11th Street, NW., Suite 301, Washington, DC 20001: Luiza C. Savage.

MAIL ON SUNDAY—(202) 547–7980; 510 Constitution Avenue, NE., Washington, DC 20002: William Lowther.

MANUFACTURING & TECHNOLOGY NEWS—(703) 750–2664; P.O. Box 36, Annandale, VA 22003: Richard McCormack.

MARINE CORPS TIMES—(800) 368–5718; 6883 Commercial Drive, Springfield, VA 22159–0500: John Hoellwarth.

MASS TRANSIT LAWYER—(703) 548–5177; P.O. Box 19647, Alexandria, VA 22320: Thomas S. Robinson.

McGRAW–HILL CO.—(212) 382–2000; 1200 G Street, NW., Suite 1000, Washington, DC 20005: Robert L. Barton, Dipka Bhambhani, Cheryl Buchta, Craig Cano, Catherine Cash, Jean Chemnick, Paul G. Ciampoli, Martin Coyne, Mark Davidson, Steven Dolley, Kelley Doolan, Alexander Duncan, Amy Fickling, Lawrence D. Foster, Keiron Greenhalgh, Daniel W. Guido, Brian Hansen, Angela Y. Hardin, Tom Harrison, Helen D. Hausmann, Elaine Hiruo, William Holland, Daniel Horner, Pamela E. Hunter, Thomas F. Ichniowski, Frank Jackman, Valarie N. Jackson, Regina Johnson, Nick Jonson, Joel Kirkland, Alan Kovski, Liane Kucher, Rod Kuckro, Kathy Carolin Larsen, William E. Loveless, Jessica Marron, Karen McBeth Laping, Christopher J. Newkumet, Tina Petersen, Margaret Ryan, Mike Schmidt, Stephanie Sharpe, Tom Tiernan, Jenny Weil, Esther Whieldon, Rodney A. White, Daniel Whitten, Eric Wieser, Charlotte Wright, Milena Yordanova-Kline.

MEDICAL DEVICES REPORT—(703) 361–6472; 7643 Bland Drive, Manassas, VA 20109: Steve Butchock.

MID–ATLANTIC RESEARCH—(800) 227–7140; 2805 St. Paul Street, Baltimore, MD 21218: Martha C. Powers, John Rees.

PERIODICALS REPRESENTED IN PRESS GALLERIES—Continued

MII PUBLICATIONS—(202) 347–4822, 1522 K Street, NW., Suite 1010, Washington, DC 20005: Ryan E. Hess, Cecilio Morales.

MILITARY TIMES—800–368–5718; 6883 Commercial Drive, Springfield, VA 22159–0500: William H. McMichael.

MINE SAFETY & HEALTH NEWS—(703) 524–5692; 5935 4th Street North, Arlington, VA 22203: Katharine Snyder.

MONTGOMERY COUNTY SENTINEL—(301) 838–0788; 30 Courthouse Square, Suite 405, Rockville, MD 20850: Gabriel R. Caggiano, Jr.

MULTICHANNEL NEWS—(202) 659–3874; 1701 K Street, NW., Suite 510, Washington, DC 20006: Edward T. Hearn.

NATION—(202) 546–2239; 110 Maryland Avenue, NE., Suite 308, Washington, DC 20002: Ari Beeman, David Corn.

NATIONAL JOURNAL—(202) 739–8400; 600 New Hampshire Avenue, NW., Washington, DC 20037: Julie L. Abramson, James A. Barnes, Randy Barrett, Eliza Newlin Carney, Lisa Caruso, Richard E. Cohen, Linda Douglass, Isobel Ellis, Sydney J. Freedberg, Jr., Brian Friel, Steve Gettinger, Robert H. Gettlin, Charles A. Green, Jerry Hagstrom, Shane Harris, Corine Hegland, James E. Humes, Marisa S. Katz, James Kitfield, Julie A. Kosterlitz, Margaret E. Kriz, Emily J. Langer, Kellie Lunney, John J. Maggs, Charles Mahtesian, Tricia Miller, JoAnne P. Moncrief, Jodie Morris, Ryan Morris, Neil P. Munro, Joyce M. Murdoch, Patrick Pexton, S. Scott Rohrer, Alyssa B. Rosenberg, Gregg Thomas Sangillo, Marilyn Werber Serafini, Alexis A. Simendinger, Jill Smallen, Paul Starobin, Peter H. Stone, Monica C. Sullivan, Stuart Taylor, Jr., Kyle K. Trygstad, Bara Vaida, Kirk Victor, Jake Welch.

NATIONAL MORTGAGE NEWS—(202) 434–0323, 1325 G Street, NW., Suite 900, Washington, DC 20005: Brian Collins, Nathasha Lim, Paul A. Muolo.

NATIONAL REVIEW—(212) 679–7330; 219 Pennsylvania Avenue, SE., 3rd Floor, Washington, DC 20003: Elizabeth Fisher, David Freddoso, Jonah Goldberg, Mark Hemingway, Emily Karrs, John J. Miller, Kate Walsh O'Beirne, Ramesh Ponnuru, April Ponnuru, Byron York.

NATIONAL UNDERWRITER—(202) 777–1102; National Press Building, Suite 941, Washington, DC 20045: Matthew Brady, Arthur D. Postal.

NATIONALJOURNAL.COM—(202) 739–8400; 600 New Hampshire Avenue, NW., Washington, DC 20037: Clive Crook, Gwen Glazer, Erin McPike, Jane Ron, Jason Thompson, Irene E. Tsikitas.

NATURAL GAS INTELLIGENCE—(703) 318–8848; 22648 Glenn Drive, Suite 305, Sterling, VA 20164: Susan T. Parker, Ellen Beswick Steis, Alexander Beswick Steis.

NATURE—(212) 726–9200; 968 National Press Building, Washington, DC 20045: Geoff Brumfiel, Emma Marris, Eugene I. Russo, Paul Smaglik, Meredith Wadman, Alexandra Witze.

NAVY TIMES—(800) 368–5718; 6883 Commercial Drive, Springfield, VA 22159–0500: Patricia N. Kime, Zachary M. Peterson.

NEW REPUBLIC—(202) 508–4444; 1331 H Street, NW., Suite 700, Washington, DC 20005: M. Michelle Cottle, Michael L. Crowley, Thomas B. Edsall, Eve R. Fairbanks, Franklin L. Foer, John B. Judis, Adam Kushner, Ryan C. Lizza, Jeffrey M. Rosen, Noam J. Scheiber, J. Peter Scoblic.

NEW YORK JEWISH WEEK—(212) 921–7822; 8713 Braeburn Drive, Annandale, VA 22203: James David Besser.

NEW YORK REVIEW OF BOOKS—(212) 757–8070; 5018 Eskridge Terrace, NW., Washington, DC 20016: Elizabeth Drew.

NEW YORKER—(800) 825–2510; 4 Times Square, New York, NY 10036–6592: Jeffrey Goldberg, Jane Mayer, Elsa Walsh.

NEWS BITES—(202) 723–2477; 1712 Taylor Street, NW., Washington, DC 20011: German Munoz, Goody L. Solomon.

NEWSMAX—(301) 279–5818; 2516 Stratton Drive, Potomac, MD 20854; Ronald B. Kessler, Kenneth R. Timmerman.

NEWSWEEK—(202) 626–2000; 1750 Pennsylvania Avenue, NW., Suite 1220, Washington, DC 20006: Holly Bailey, John A. Barry, Jeffrey I. Bartholet, Daren Briscoe, Eleanor Clift, Eve K. Conant, Dan Ephron, Howard Fineman, Mark J. Hosenball, Michael Isikoff, Patrice Wingert Kelly, Weston Kosova, Robert J. Samuelson, Gail Tacconelli, Richard K. Thomas, Steve Tuttle, Richard Wolffe.

OBERLE COMMUNICATIONS—(703) 289–9432; 2573 Holly Manor Drive, Suite 110, Falls Church, VA 22043: Sean F. Oberle.

OIL & GAS JOURNAL—(703) 532–1588; 7013 Jefferson Avenue, Falls Church, VA 22042: Nicholas J. Snow.

OUTLOOK MAGAZINE—(201) 587–8800; 210 Route 4 East, Suite 310, Paramus, NJ 07652: Ashish Kumar Sen.

PENTON MEDIA INC.—(301) 650–2420; 8380 Colesville Road, Suite 700, Silver Spring, MD 20910: Sandra Arnoult, Perry Flint, Aaron Karp, Brian Straus, Katherine Torres.

PEOPLE MAGAZINE—(202) 861–4000; 555 12th Street, NW., Suite 600, Washington, DC 20004: Sandra Sobieraj.

PERIODICALS REPRESENTED IN PRESS GALLERIES—Continued

PHARMACEUTICAL EXECUTIVE—(301) 656–4634; 7715 Rocton Avenue, Chevy Chase, MD 20815: Jill Wechsler.

PRESS ASSOCIATES—(202) 898–4825; 1000 Vermont Avenue, NW., Suite 101, Washington, DC 20005: Janet M. Brown, Mark J. Gruenberg.

PROCESO—(202) 737–1538; 1253 National Press Building, Washington, DC 20045: J. Jesus Esquivel.

PROFESSIONAL PILOT MAGAZINE—(703) 370–0606; 30 South Quaker Lane, Suite 300, Alexandria, VA 22314: Andrew D. Parker, Phil A. Rose.

PUBLIC LANDS NEWS—(703) 533–0552; 133 South Buchanan Street, Arlington, VA 22204: James B. Coffin.

PUBLIC UTILITIES FORTNIGHTLY—(703) 847–7720; 8229 Boone Boulevard, Suite 400, Vienna, VA 22182: Lori Burkhart, Christian A. Hamaker, Bruce W. Radford, Richard Stavros.

RADIO BUSINESS REPORT—(703) 492–8191; 2050 Old Bridge Road B–01, Lake Ridge, VA 22192: Carl Marcucci, David P. Seyler.

READER'S DIGEST—(202) 223–9520; 1730 Rhode Island Avenue, NW., Suite 212, Washington, DC 20036: William P. Beaman, Carol Kaufmann.

REED BUSINESS INFORMATION—(202) 659–3807; 1701 Street, NW., Suite 510, Washington, DC 20006: Paul Sweeting.

RESEARCH INSTITUTE OF AMERICA GROUP—(202) 842–1240; 1275 K Street, NW., Suite 875, Washington, DC 20005: Velma Goodwine, Jay S. Heflin, Kevin McDermott, Michael J. McGoffin, Sirena J. Scales.

ROLL CALL—(202) 824–6800; 50 F Street, NW., Suite 700, Washington, DC 20001: Kate Ackley, Moira C. Bagley, Erin P. Billings, Elizabeth Brotherton, Amy Carlile, Susan Davis, Steven T. Dennis, David M. Drucker, Nicole Duran, Cassandra P. Foster, Emily A., Heil, Daniel S. Heim, Bryanna Hocking, Morton M. Kondracke, Josh Kurtz, Jennifer Lash, John McArdle, David B. Meyers, Charles F. Mitchell, Matthew Murray, Arthur Newmyer, Anna Palmer, Benjamin Pershing, Emily Pierce, Paul B. Singer, Katie Smith, John Stanton, Rachel A. Van Dongen, Lauren Whittington, Jennifer Yachnin, Emily Yehle.

ROLLING STONE—(703) 619–0275; 2200 Lakeshire Drive, Alexandria, VA 22308: Robert Dreyfuss.

ROTHENBERG POLITICAL REPORT—(202) 546–2822; 50 F Street, NW., Suite 700, Washington, DC 20001: Nathan Gonzales, Stuart Rothenberg.

SALON—(202) 333–5695; 3417½ M Street, NW., Washington, DC 20007: Mark Benjamin, Julia E. Dahl, Timothy Grieve, Chloe M. Kamarck, Michael Scherer, Walter Shapiro.

SATELLITE BUSINESS NEWS—(202) 785–0505; 1990 M Street, NW., Suite 510, Washington, DC 20036: Bob Scherman, Jeffrey Williams.

SCIENCE & GOVERNMENT REPORT—(210) 348–1000; P.O. Box 190, Churchton, MD 20733: David Kramer.

SCRIP WORLD PHARMACEUTICAL NEWS—(202) 887–6320 x112; 1725 K Street, NW., Suite 506, Washington, DC 20006: Susan M. Sutter.

SETANTA PUBLISHING—(703) 548–3146; P.O. Box 25277, Alexandria, VA 22313: Declan Conroy.

SEDGWICK PUBLISHING CO.—(202) 337–8066; 5713 Overlea Road, Bethesda, MD 20816: Beth Ann McConnell.

SET–ASIDE ALERT—(301) 229–5561; 7720 Wisconsin Avenue, #213, Bethesda, MD 20814: Warren Corbett.

SLATE—(202) 261–1330; 1350 Connecticut Avenue, Suite 400, Washington, DC 20036: Emily Bazelon, Jacob Christopher Beam, John F. Dickerson, Joshua Levin, Dahlia Hannah Lithwick, Timothy Robert Noah, David Plotz, William B. Saletan, Jack Shafer.

SMART MEDIA—(703) 492–8191; 2050 Old Bridge Road, Suite B–01, Lake Ridge, VA 22192: Carl Marcucci, David P. Seyler.

SPACE NEWS—(703) 658–8400; 6883 Commerce Drive, Springfield, VA 22159: Brian Berger, S. Tuner Brinton, Colin Clark.

STERN—(301) 229–4108; 4829 Fort Sumner Drive, Bethesda, MD 20814: Katja Gloger.

TAX NOTES—(703) 533–4400; 400 S. Maple Avenue, Suite 400, Falls Church, VA 22046: Dave Adhicary, Jon S. Almeras, David Scott Antonides, Herman P. Ayayo, Brian Bardwell, Kevin A. Bell, Heather Bennett, John M. Buhl, Jennifer Carr, Jeremiah G. Coder, Joseph DiSciullo, Wesley Elmore, Patrice L. Gay, Heidi Glenn, Chuck Gnaedinger, Robert Goulder, Cara Griffith, Elizabeth W. Gutting, Joann Christine Harris, Cindy Ann Heyd, Shonda Humphrey, Thomas Jaworski, Allen Kenney, Helena Klumpp, Karla L. Miller, Lisa M. Nadal, Audrey Nutt, Charles O'Toole, Eric Parker, Kristen Pavillo, Cathleen M. Phillips, Christopher Quay, Johnathan Rickman, Quintin Robinson–Simmons, Cordia Scott Hennaman, Karen Jeanne Setze, Andy Sheets, Doug Sheppard, Margaret Shreve, Susan Jeane Simmonds, Douglas D. Smith, Dustin Stamper, Meredith Stevenson, Frederick W. Stokeld, Sheryl Stratton, Martin A. Sullivan, Darryl W. Tait, Crystal Tandon, Timothy M. Taylor, Joseph Thorndike, Emily Vanderweide, Ember M. Verma, Joann M. Weiner, Robert J. Wells, Risa D. Williams, Sam Young.

TECHNOLOGY COMMERCIALIZATION—(703) 522–6648; P.O. Box 100595, Arlington, VA 22210: Neil A. MacDonald.

PERIODICALS REPRESENTED IN PRESS GALLERIES—Continued

TELECOMMUNICATIONS REPORTS—(202) 842–8923; 1015 15th Street, NW., 10th Floor, Washington, DC 20005: Paul Barbagallo, John Curran, Carrie DeLeon, Ted Gotsch, Maureen King, Paul Kirby, Lynn Stanton.

TEXTILE WORLD—(703) 421–5283; 20911 Royal Villa Terrace, Potomac Falls, VA 20165: James A. Morrissey.

THE CANCER LETTER—(800) 513–7042; P.O. Box 9905, Washington, DC 20016: Paul Goldberg, Kirsten Goldberg.

THE HILL—(202) 628–8500; 1625 K Street, NW., Suite 900, Washington, DC 20006: Aman A. Ali, James Jim Allen, Andrew Barr, Aaron Blake, Kevin Bogardus, Alexander Bolton, Susan Crabtree, Robert Cusack, Albert Eisele, Helen Fessenden, Christopher E. Good, Hugo Gurdon, Jessica Holzer, Jeremy P. Jacobs, Jonathan Kaplan, Jacqueline Kucinich, Karissa Marcum, Klaus Marre, Kelly McCormack, Megan Mulligan, Manu K. Raju, Betsy Rothstein, Elana Schor, Jim Snyder, Mike Soraghan, Alexandra B. Stoddard, Ian B. Swanson, Roxana Tiron, Jennifer Yingling, Jeffrey Young, Sam A. Youngman.

THE HOTLINE—(202) 739–8400; 600 New Hampshire Avenue, NW., Washington, DC 20037: Marc Ambinder, Conn M. Carroll, Amy G. Dudley, Emily Goodin, Danielle D. Jones, Katherine V. Lehr, Nora J. McAlvanah, Quinn T. McCord, Mike Memoli, John C. Mercurio, Maura E. O'Brien, Patrick R. Ottenhoff, Timothy J. Sahd, Shira R. Toeplitz.

TIME MAGAZINE—(202) 861–4000; 555 12th Street, NW., Suite 600, Washington, DC 20004: Brian Bennett, Massimo T. Calabresi, James F. Carney, Anna Marie Cox, Gilbert Cruz, Michael W. Duffy, Jay Newton-Small, Amanda Ripley, Tracy S. Schmidt, Elaine Shannon, Judith R. Stoler, Mark J. Thompson, Karen Tumulty, Michael P. Weisskopf, Adam Zagorin.

TRAFFIC WORLD—(202) 355–1150; 1270 National Press Building, Washington, DC 20045: John D. Boyd, Penelope M. Brown, William B. Cassidy, Robert G. Edmonson, Michael Fabey, John Gallagher, William Hoffman, Robert W. Moorman, Ari Natter, Paul Page.

TRANSPORTATION WEEKLY—(703) 842–7420; 2301 N. Stafford Street, Arlington, VA 22207: Jeffrey J. Davis.

TRAVEL WEEKLY—(201) 902–2000; 1625 K Street, NW., Suite 103, Washington, DC 20006: Andrew W. Compart, Michael Milligan.

UCG—(301) 287–2700; 11300 Rockville Pike, Suite 1100, Rockville, MD 20852: Carl Albert Ayers, Valerie Banner, Doreen Bieryla, JoAnn D. Blake, Alan F. Cohen, Elizabeth Crawford, Fran Fanshel, Rachel Gantz, Jessica C. Gdowski, Lisa Getter, Rebecca S. Grilliot, Richard D. Hadley, Wendy Johnson, Samantha Joseph, Spencer Kelly, Hugh Kennedy, Scott Kraft, Stephen Lee, Sheena Martin, Brett E. Norman, John P. Reaves, Benjamin Rogers, Burt Schorr, Daniel B. Schwind, Laura Scott, Vincent Taylor, Maria Tsigas.

U.S. MEDICINE—(202) 463–6000; 2021 L Street, NW., Suite 400, Washington, DC 20036: Sandra L. Basu, Frank M. Best, Catherine H. Leitch, Matt Pueschel, Stephen Spotswood.

U.S. NEWS & WORLD REPORT—(202) 955–2000; 1050 Thomas Jefferson Street, NW., Washington, DC 20007: Stephen Terry Atlas, Paul Bedard, Emily L. Brandon, Silla Brush, Eddy Ramirez Esparza, Daniel Gilgoff, Alison M. Go, Elizabeth Halloran, Alex Kingsbury, Danielle Knight, Marianne Lavelle, Angela Marek, Thomas E. Omestad, James M. Pethokoukis, Chitra Ragavan, Bret Schulte, Nancy Shute, William B. Sullivan, Kenneth T. Walsh, Kevin Whitelaw, Gordon Witkin.

USA JOURNAL—(202) 714–7330; P.O. Box 714, Washington, DC 20044: Janne Kum Cha Pak.

VANITY FAIR—(202) 244–3429; 5146 Klingle Street, NW., Washington, DC 20016: Todd S. Purdum.

WASHINGTON BLADE—(202) 797–7000; 1408 U Street, NW., Second Floor, Washington, DC 20009: Louis M. Chibbaro, Jr., Joshua J. Lynsen, Elizabeth A. Perry.

WASHINGTON BUSINESS INFORMATION—(703) 538–7600; 300 North Washington Street, Suite 200, Falls Church, VA 22046: April M. Astor, Emily V. Ethridge, Martin J. Gidron, Christopher Hollis, Brenda M. Lund.

WASHINGTON BUSINESS JOURNAL—(703) 258–0800; 1555 Wilson Boulevard, Suite 400, Arlington, VA 22209: Kent Hoover.

WASHINGTON CITY PAPER—(202) 332–2100 2390 Champlain Street, NW., Washington, DC 20009: James Jones.

WASHINGTON COUNSELETTER—(800) 622–7284; 5712 26th Street, NW., Washington, DC 20015: Deborah A. Kavruck, Samuel Kavruck.

WASHINGTON TECHNOLOGY—(202) 772–2500; 10 G Street, NE., Suite 500, Washington, DC 20002: Douglas Beizer, Michael L. Hardy, Alice Lipowicz, Nick Wakeman, William E. Welsh.

WASHINGTON TRADE DAILY—(301) 946–0817; P.O. Box 1802, Wheaton, MD 20915: James R. Berger, Mary Berger.

WASHINGTON WATCH—(301) 461–9688; 5923 Onondaga Road, Bethesda, MD 20816: Kazutami Yamazaki.

WASHINGTONIAN—(202) 296–3600; 1828 L Street, NW., Suite 200, Washington, DC 20036: Catherine Andrews, Susan Baer, Ben C. Clark, Kim Eisler, Garrett Graff, Harry S. Jaffe, John Limpert, Drew Lindsay.

PERIODICALS REPRESENTED IN PRESS GALLERIES—Continued

WATERWAYS JOURNAL—(314) 241–7354; 5220 North Carlin Springs Road, Arlington, VA 22203: Carlo J. Salzano.

WEBSTER COMMUNICATIONS—(314) 241–7354; 3835 North 9th Street, Suite 401W, Arlington, VA 22203: James C. Webster.

WEEKLY STANDARD—(202) 293–4900; 1150 17th Street, NW., Suite 505, Washington, DC 20036: Fred W. Barnes, Whitney Blake, Sonny Bunch, Christopher Caldwell, Matthew Continetti, Duncan M. Currie, Terry Eastland, Andrew Ferguson, Jonathan V. Last, Abigail J. Lavin, Joseph P. Lindsley, David Skinner.

WHITE HOUSE WEEKLY—(202) 638–4260; 807 National Press Building, Washington, DC 20045: Linda A. Gasparello.

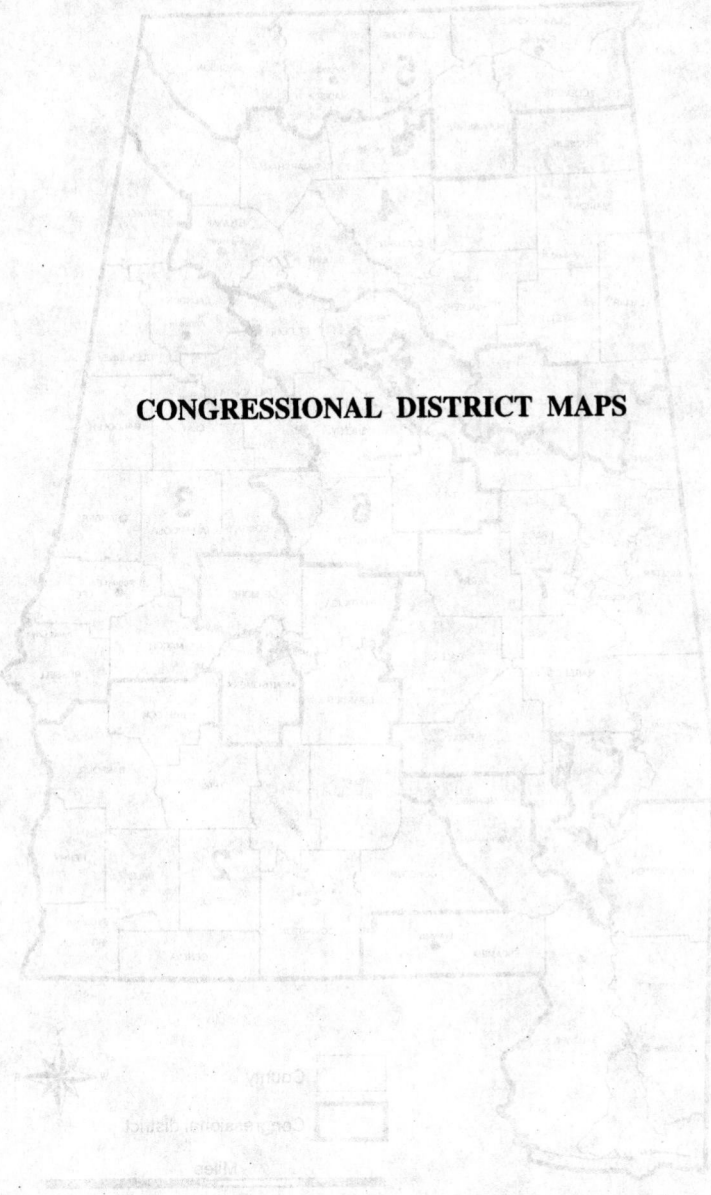

CONGRESSIONAL DISTRICT MAPS

ALABAMA—Congressional Districts—(7 Districts)

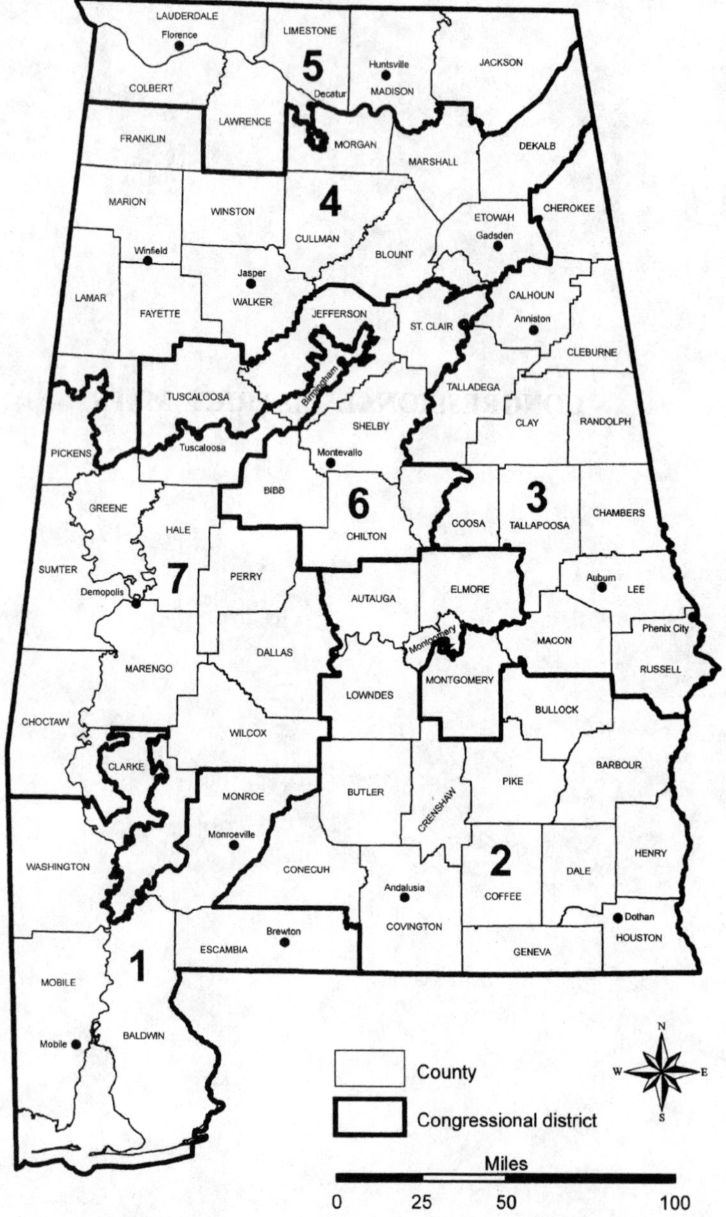

ALASKA—Congressional District—(1 District At Large)

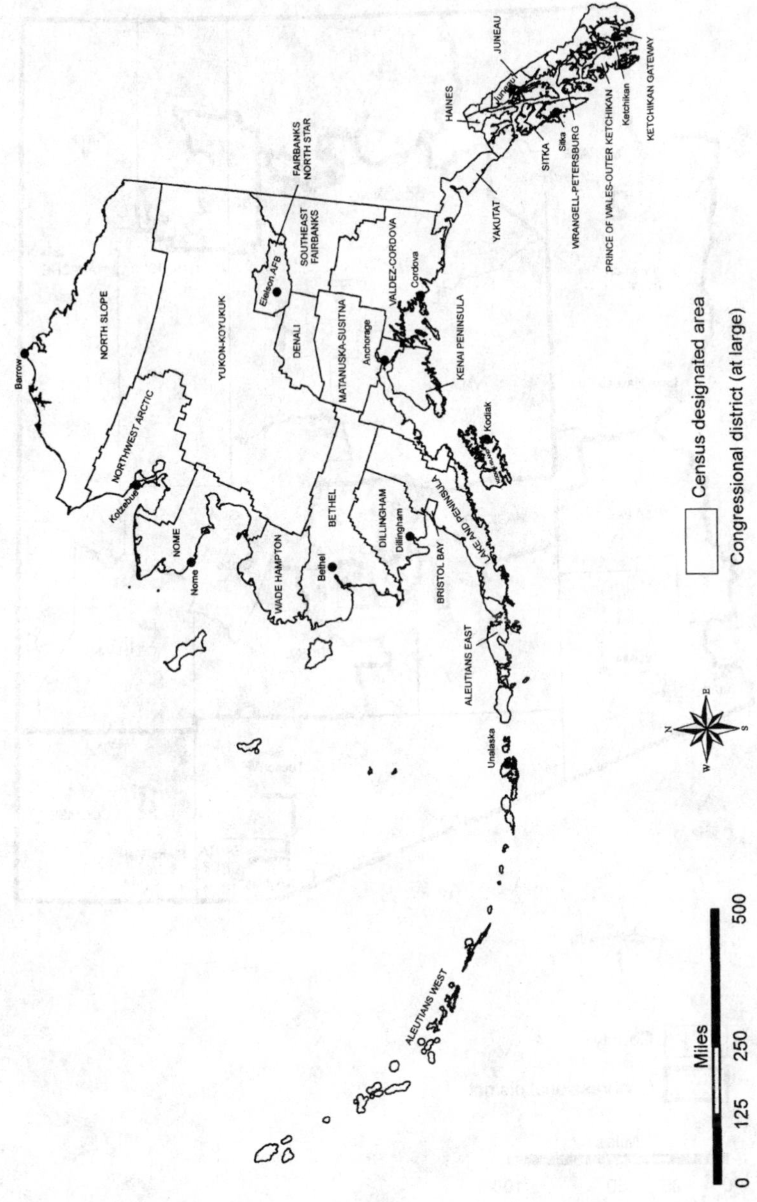

ARIZONA—Congressional Districts—(8 Districts)

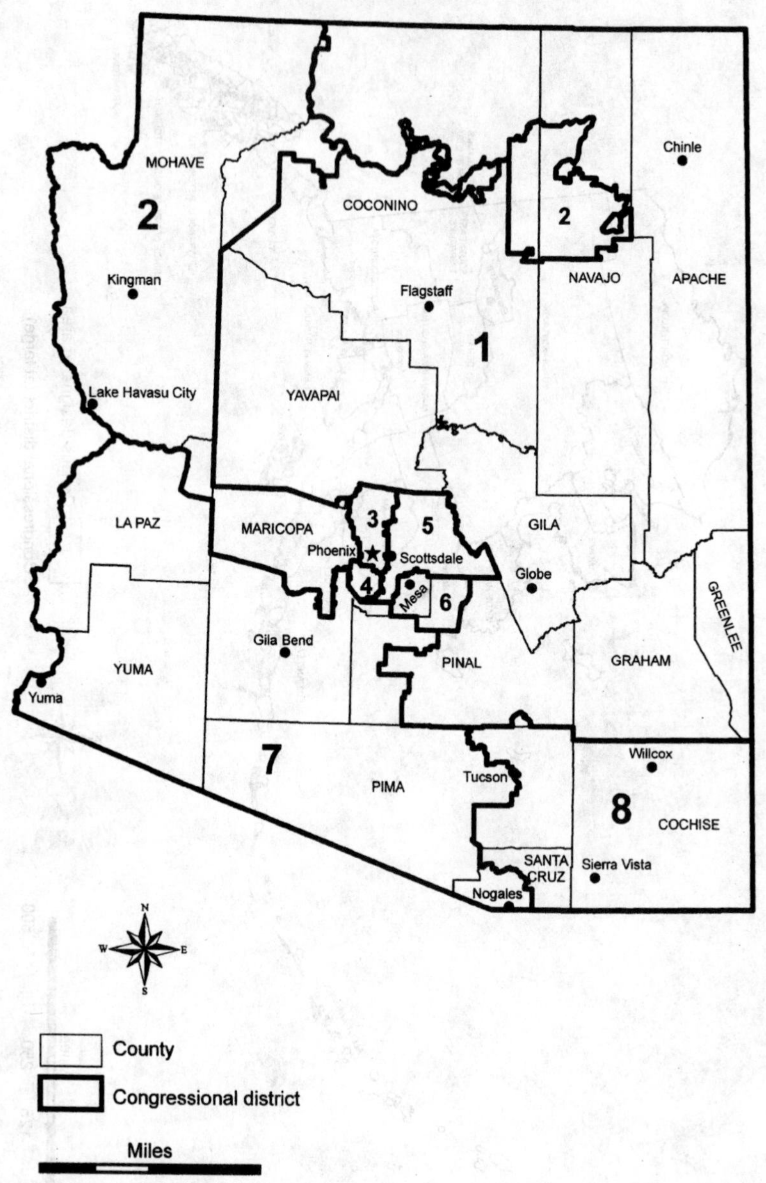

ARKANSAS—Congressional Districts—(4 Districts)

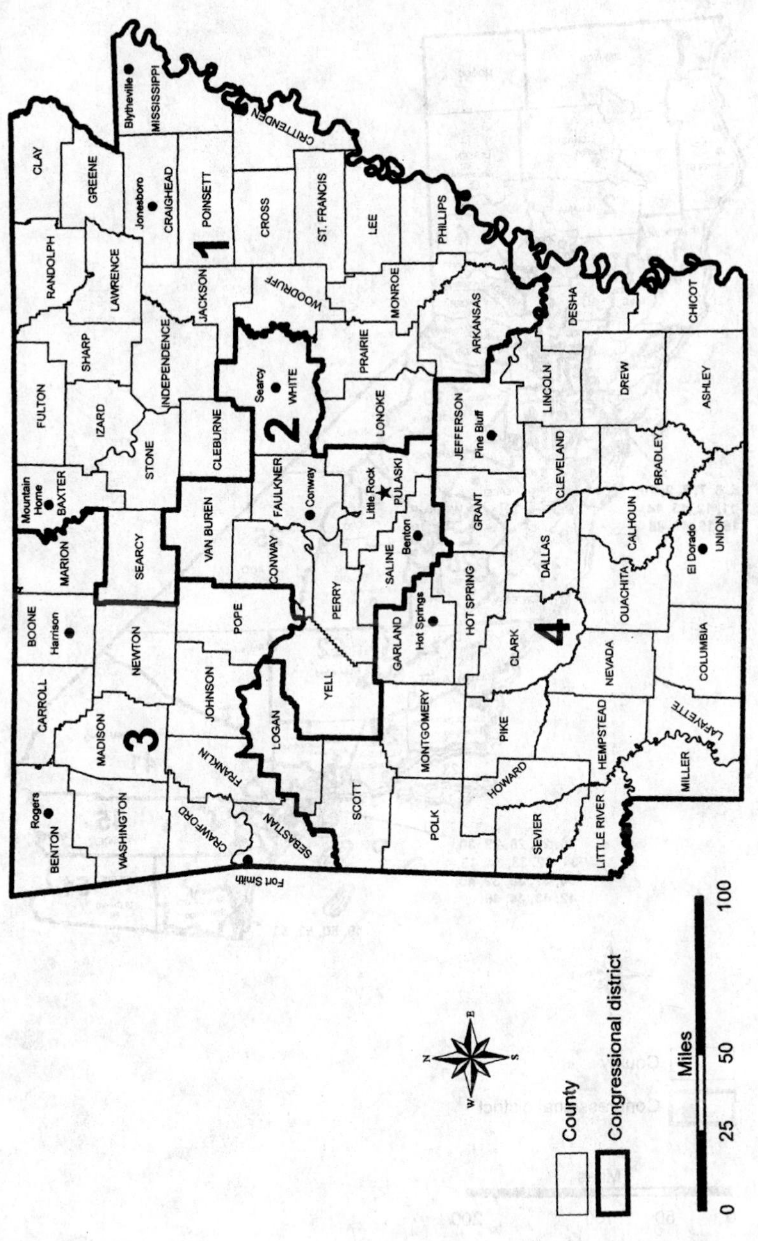

CALIFORNIA—Congressional Districts—(53 Districts)

COLORADO—Congressional Districts—(7 Districts)

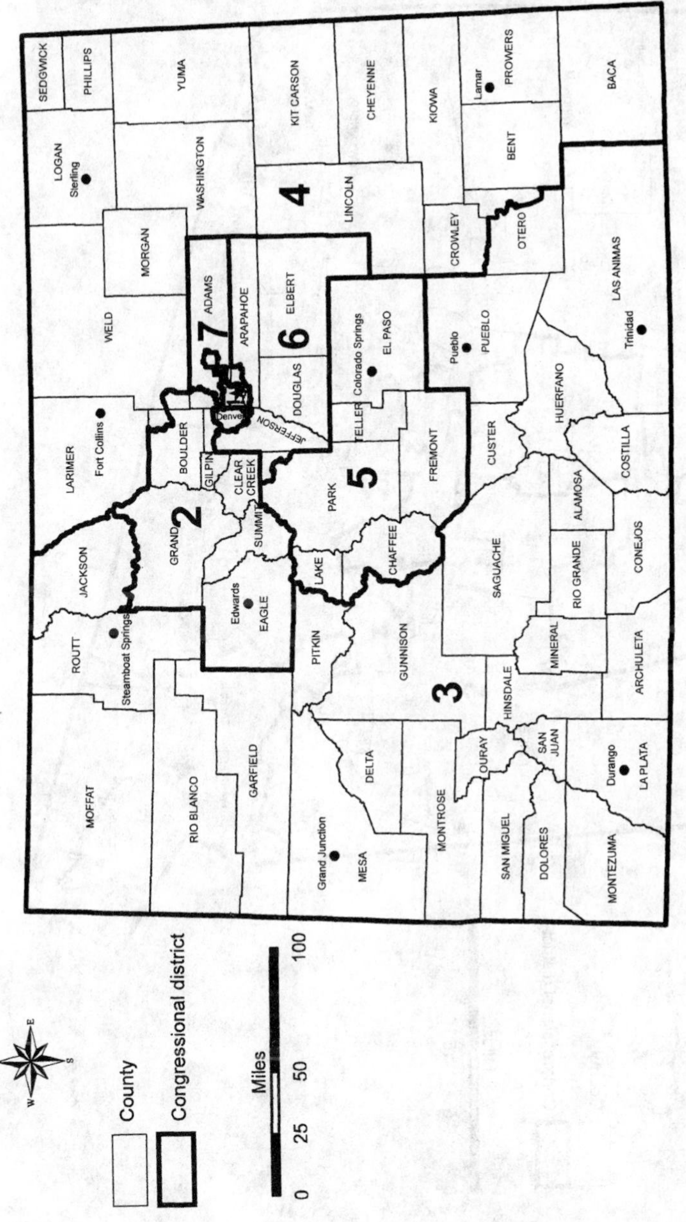

CONNECTICUT—Congressional Districts—(5 Districts)

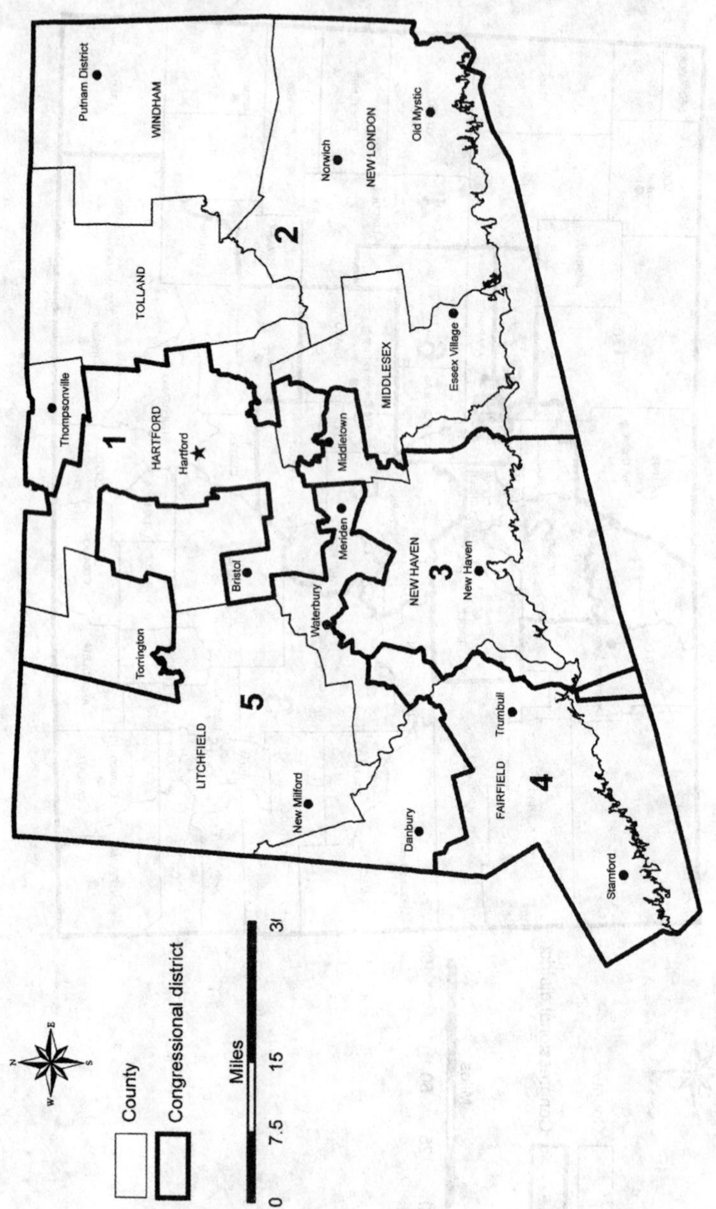

DELAWARE—Congressional District—(1 District At Large)

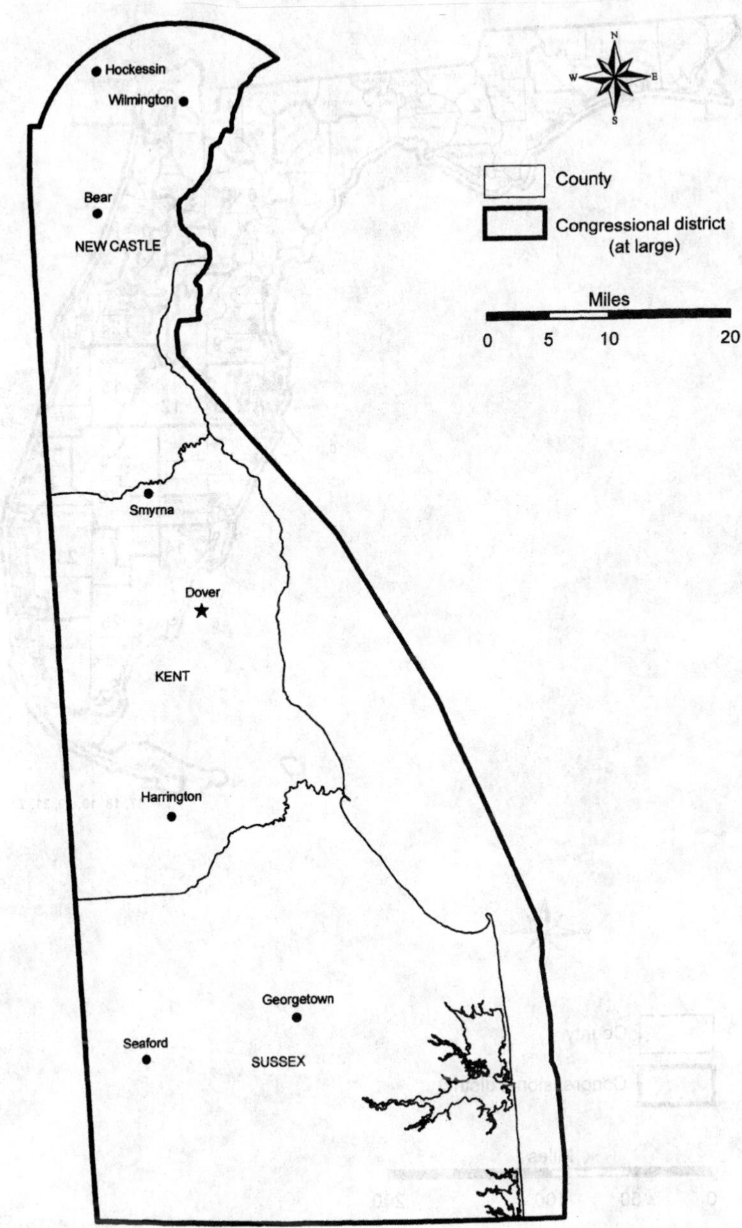

FLORIDA—Congressional Districts—(25 Districts)

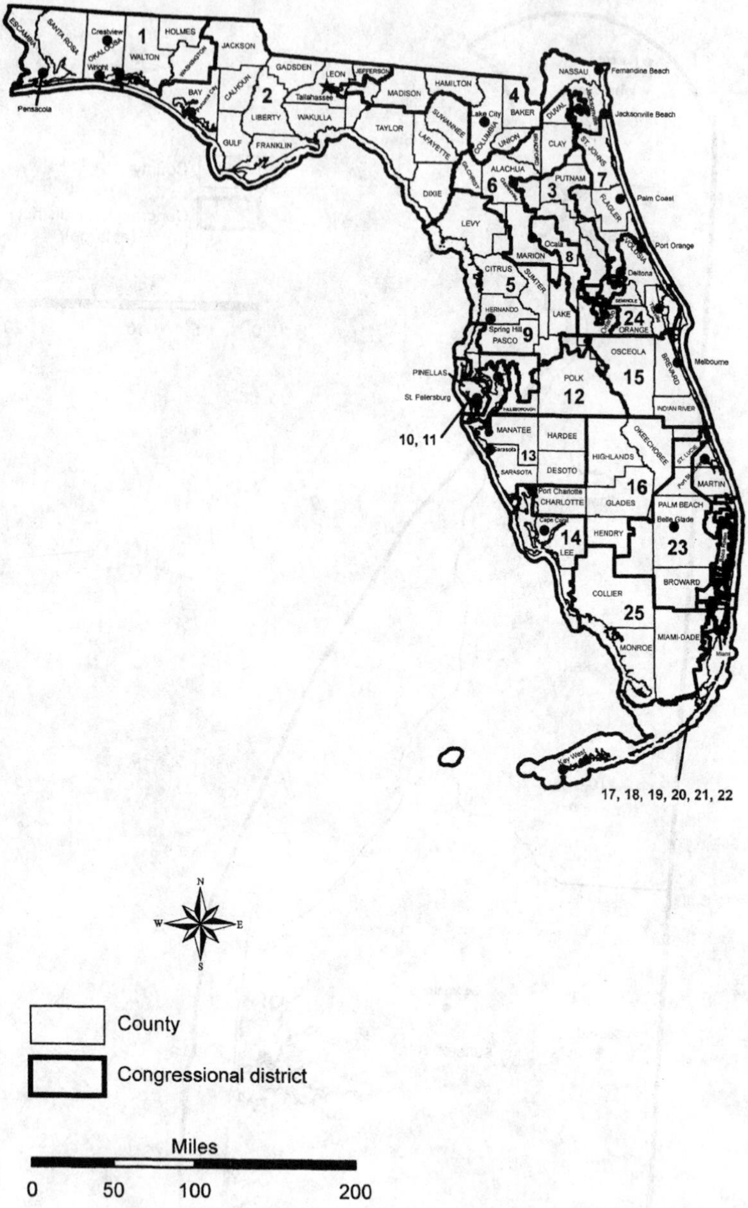

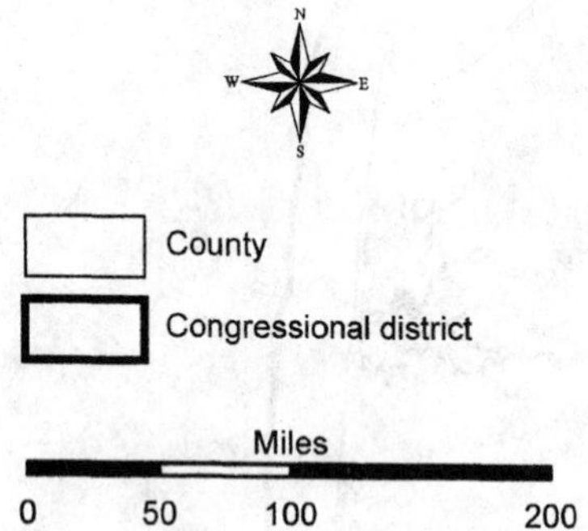

GEORGIA—Congressional Districts—(13 Districts)

HAWAII—Congressional Districts—(2 Districts)

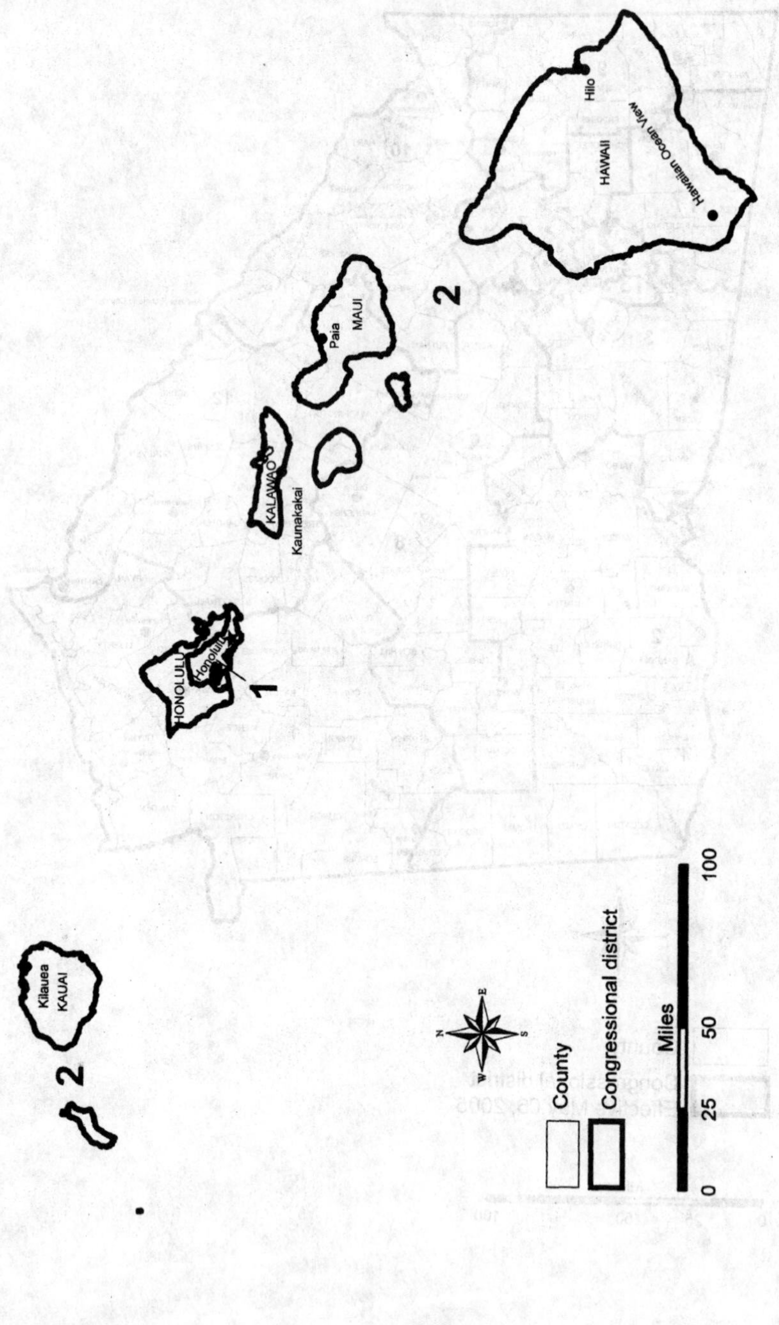

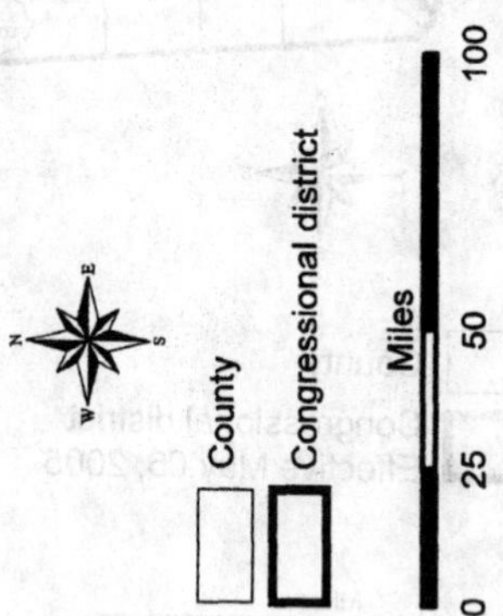

IDAHO—Congressional Districts—(2 Districts)

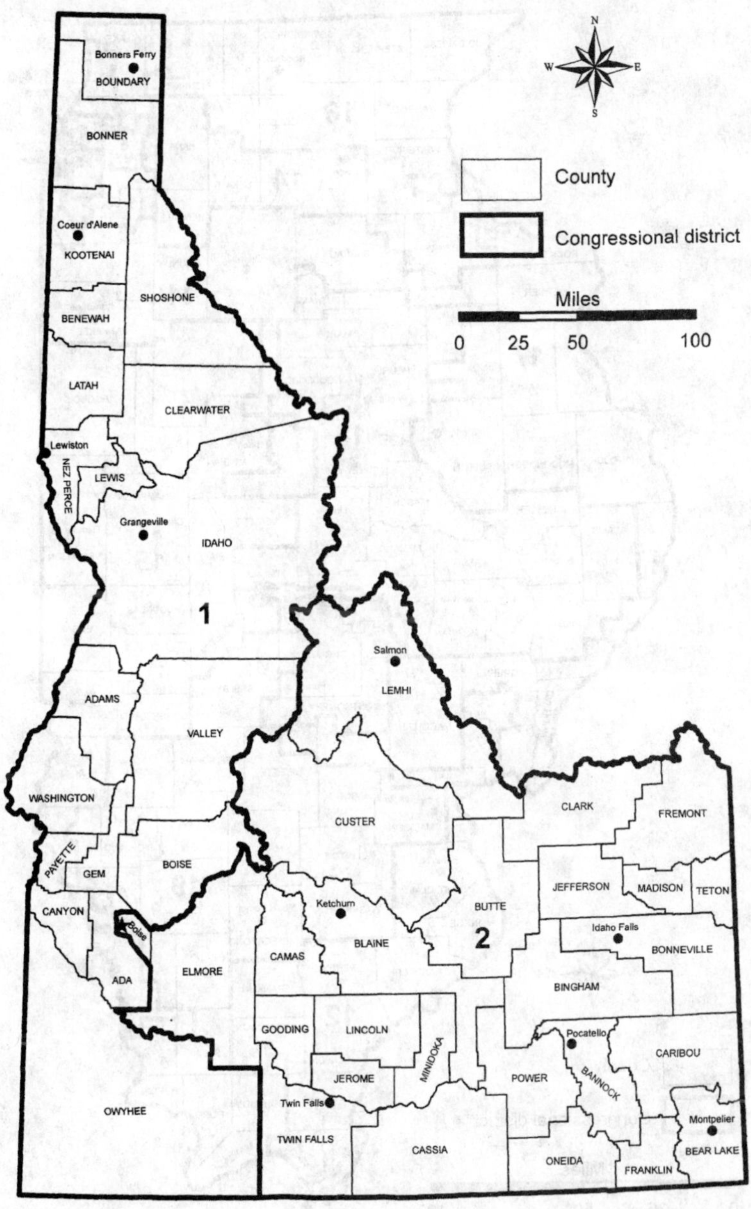

ILLINOIS—Congressional Districts—(19 Districts)

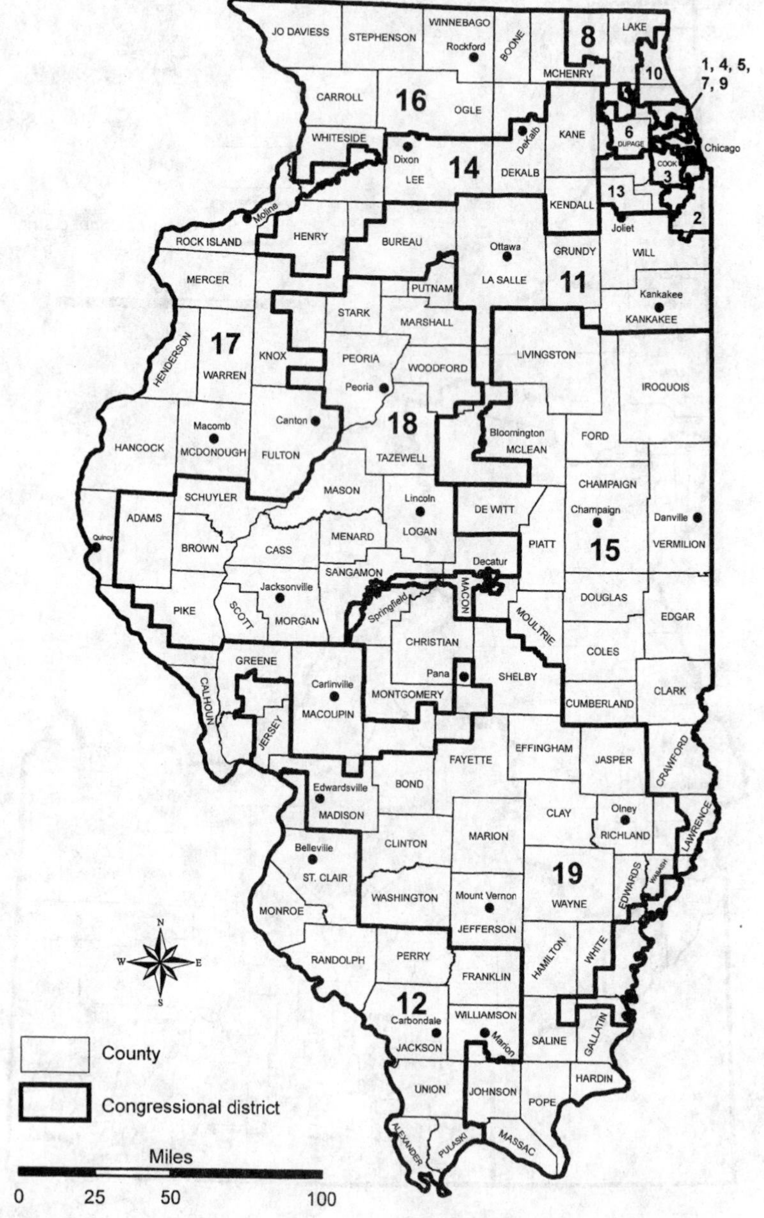

INDIANA—Congressional Districts—(9 Districts)

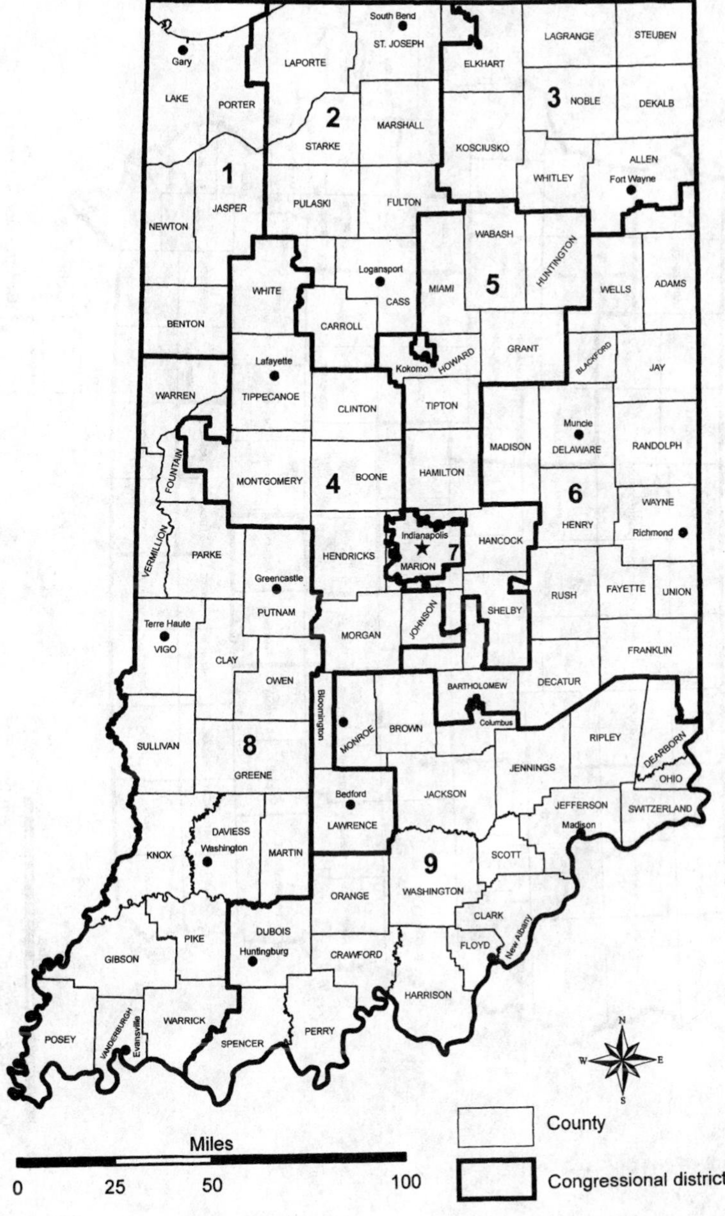

IOWA—Congressional Districts—(5 Districts)

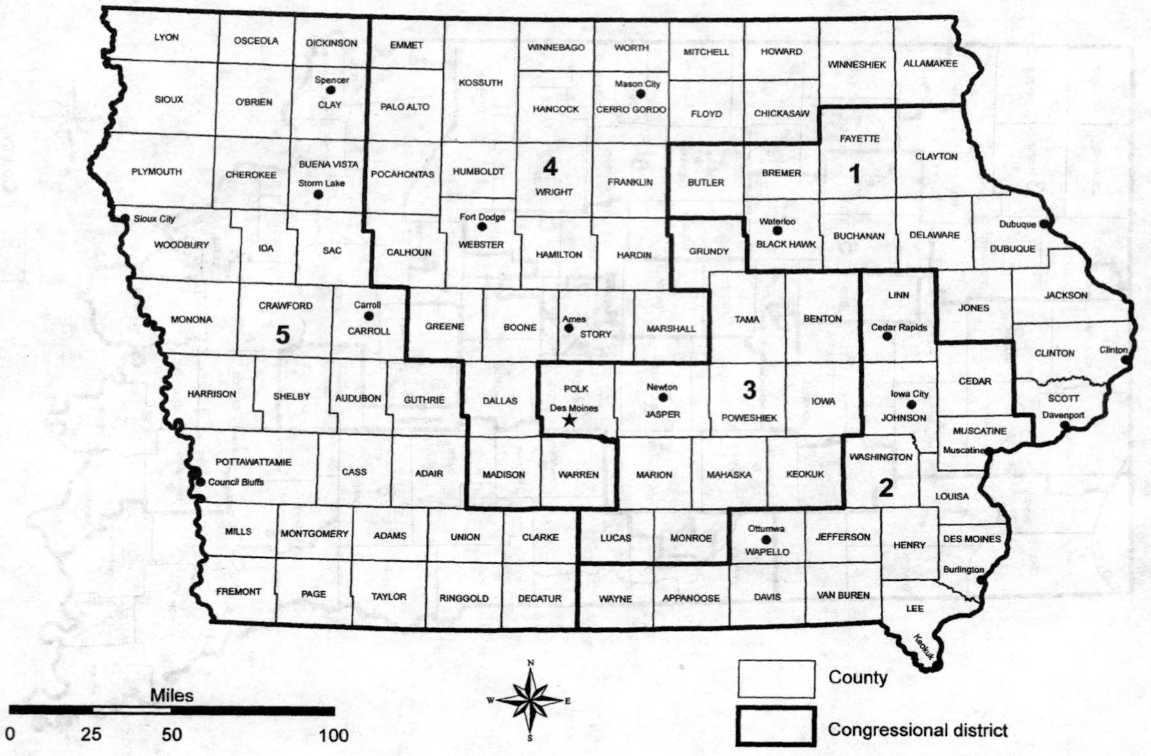

KANSAS—Congressional Districts—(4 Districts)

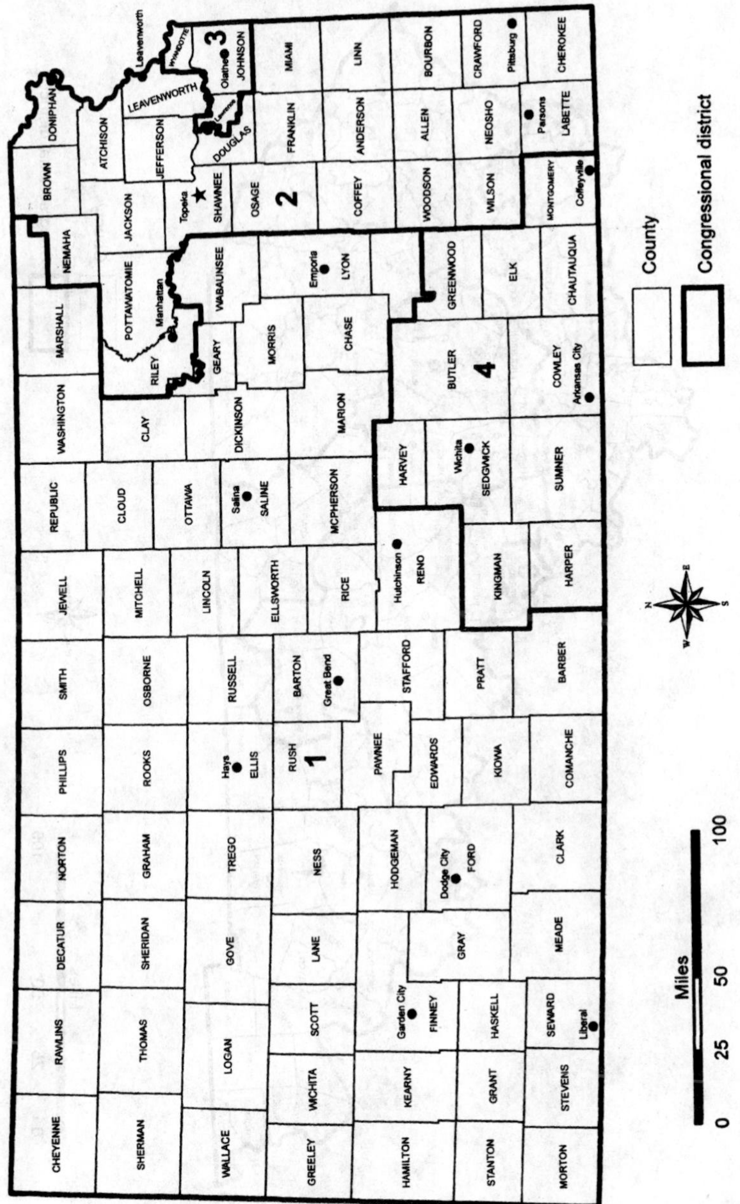

KENTUCKY—Congressional Districts—(6 Districts)

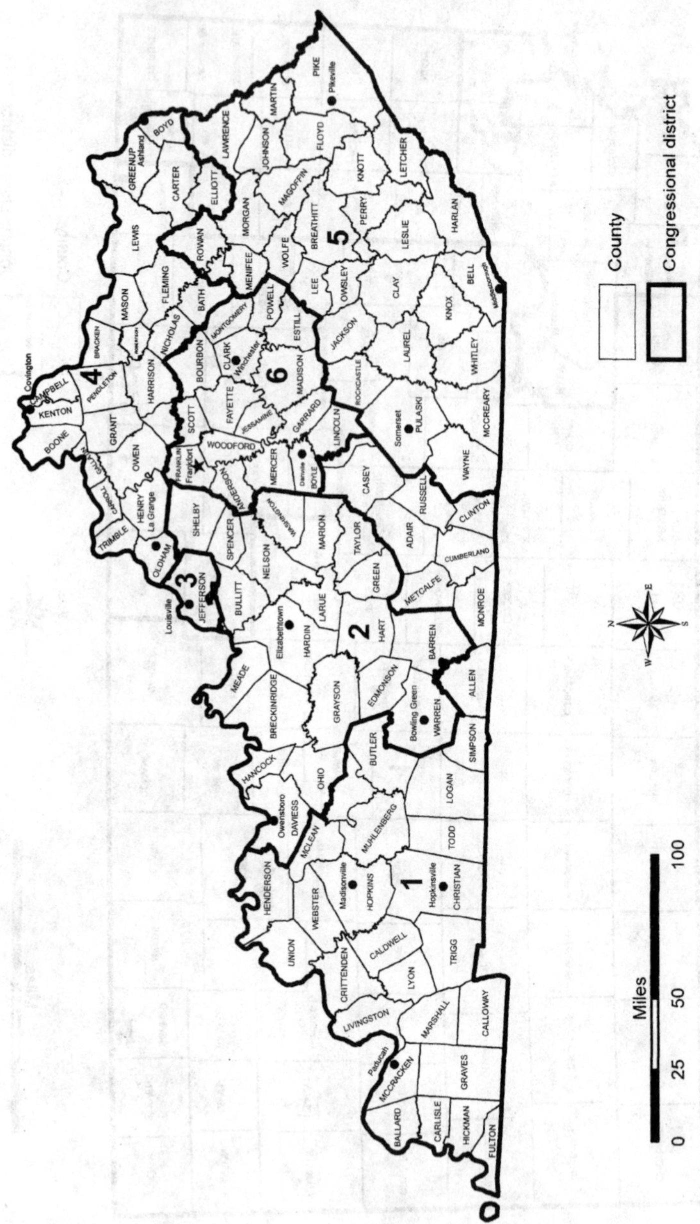

LOUISIANA—Congressional Districts—(7 Districts)

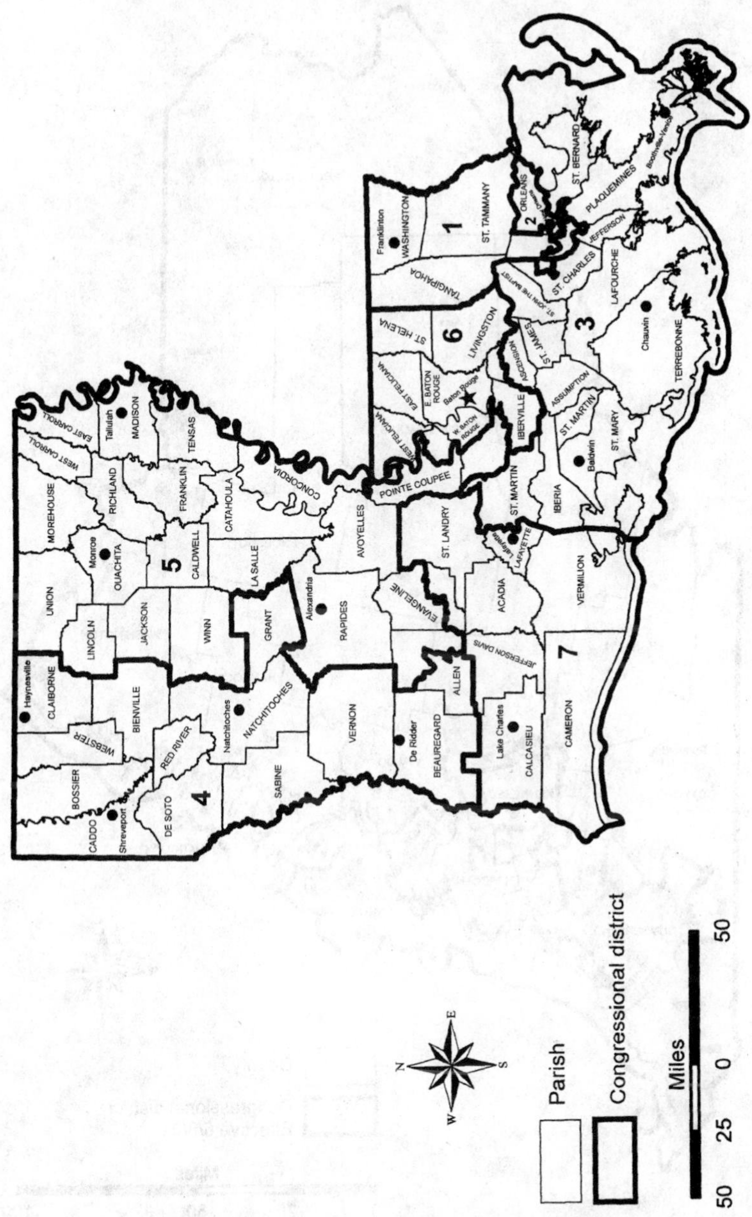

MAINE—Congressional Districts—(2 Districts)

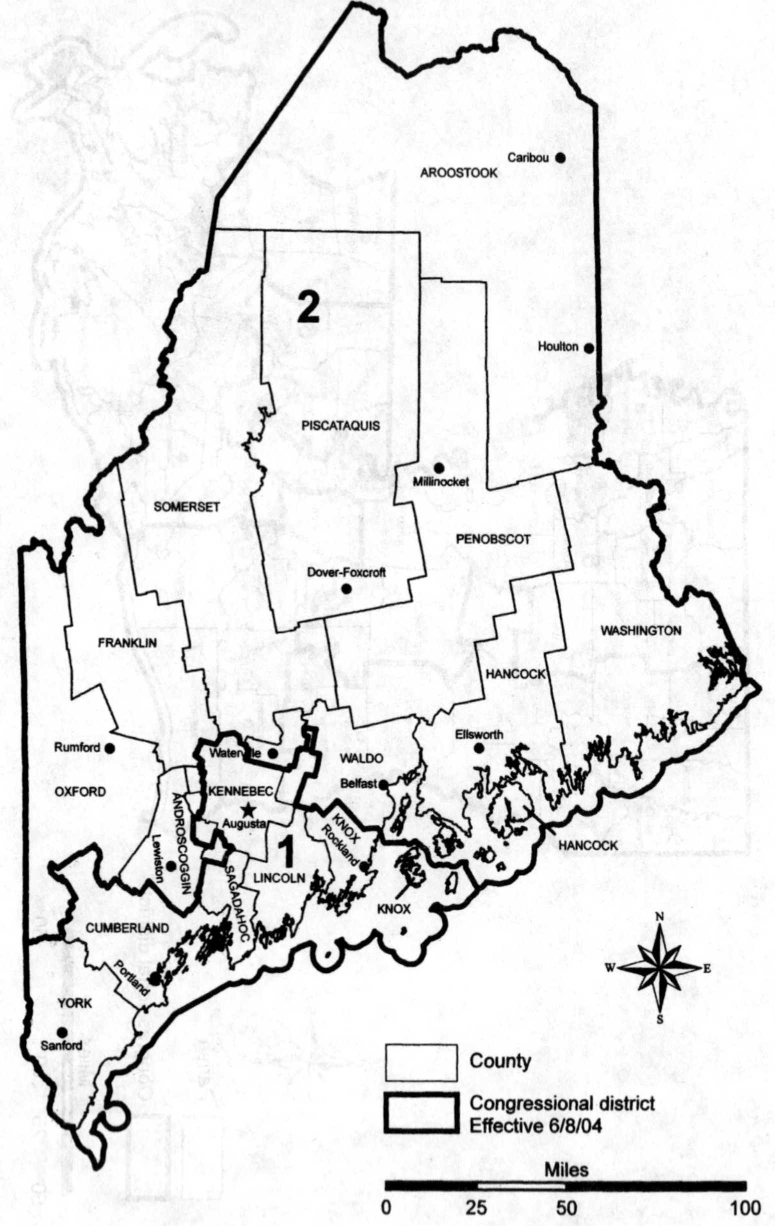

MARYLAND—Congressional Districts—(8 Districts)

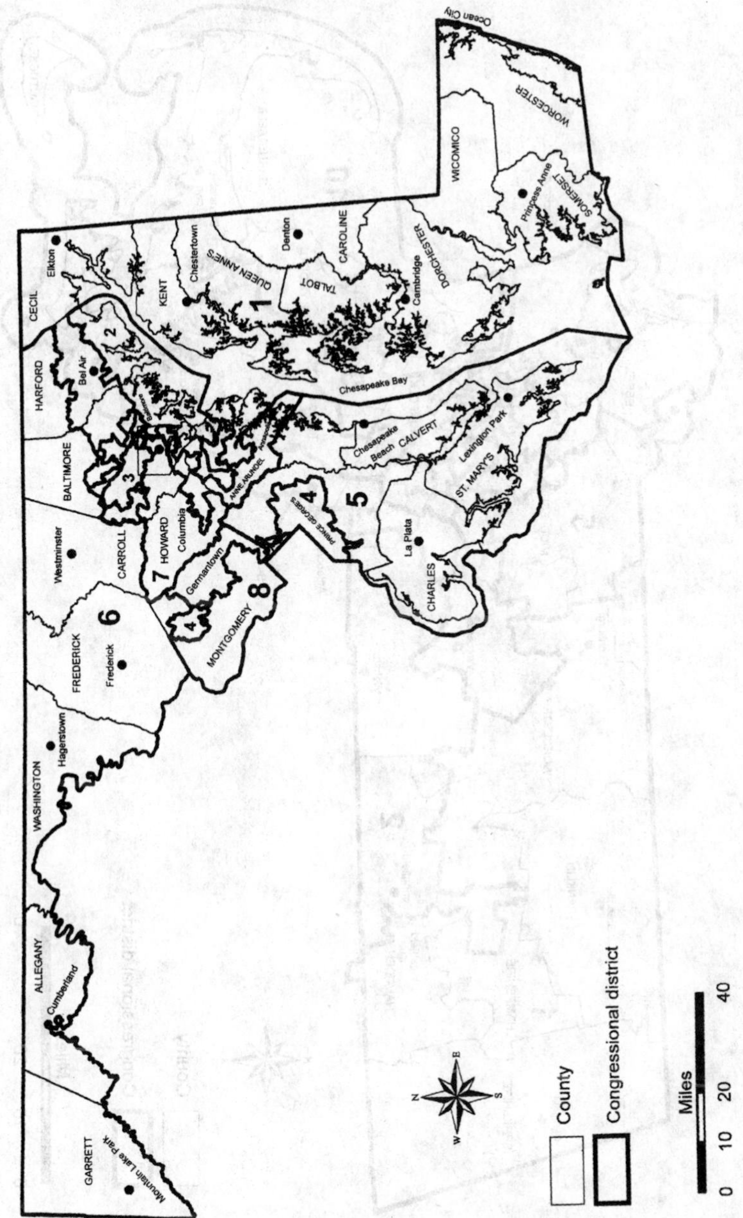

MASSACHUSETTS—Congressional Districts—(10 Districts)

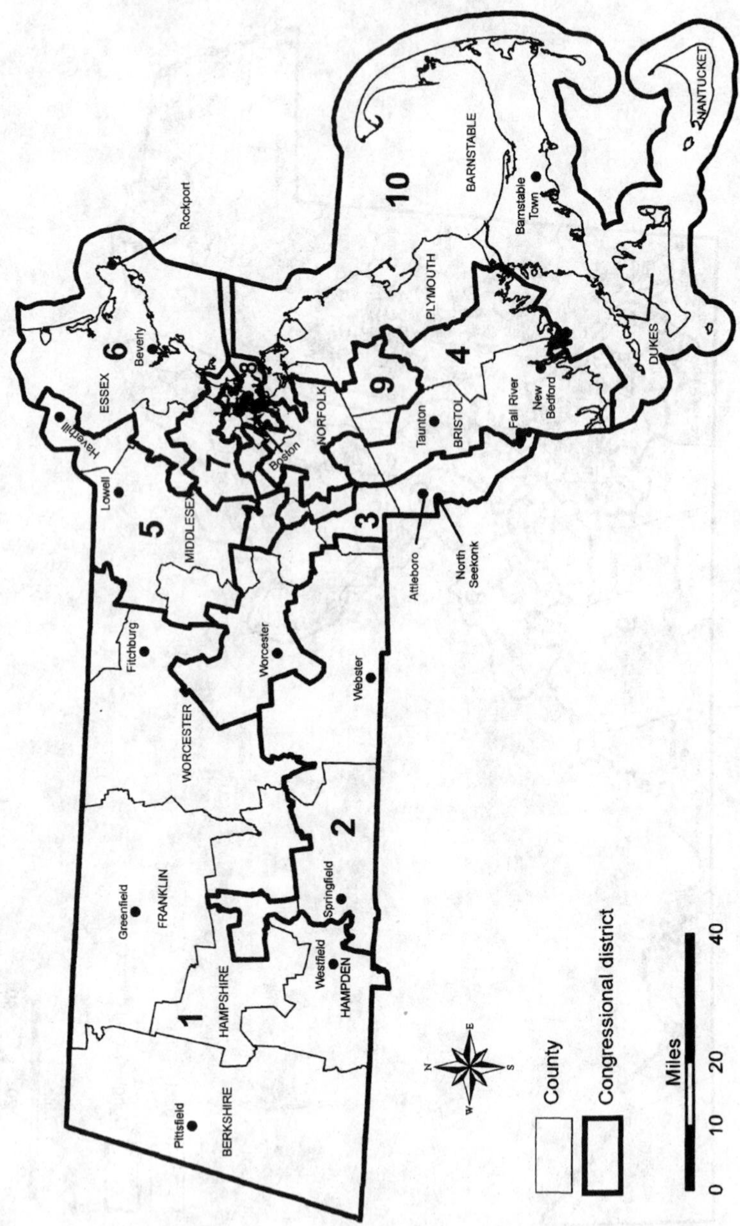

MICHIGAN—Congressional Districts—(15 Districts)

County

Congressional district

Miles

0 25 50 100

MINNESOTA—Congressional Districts—(8 Districts)

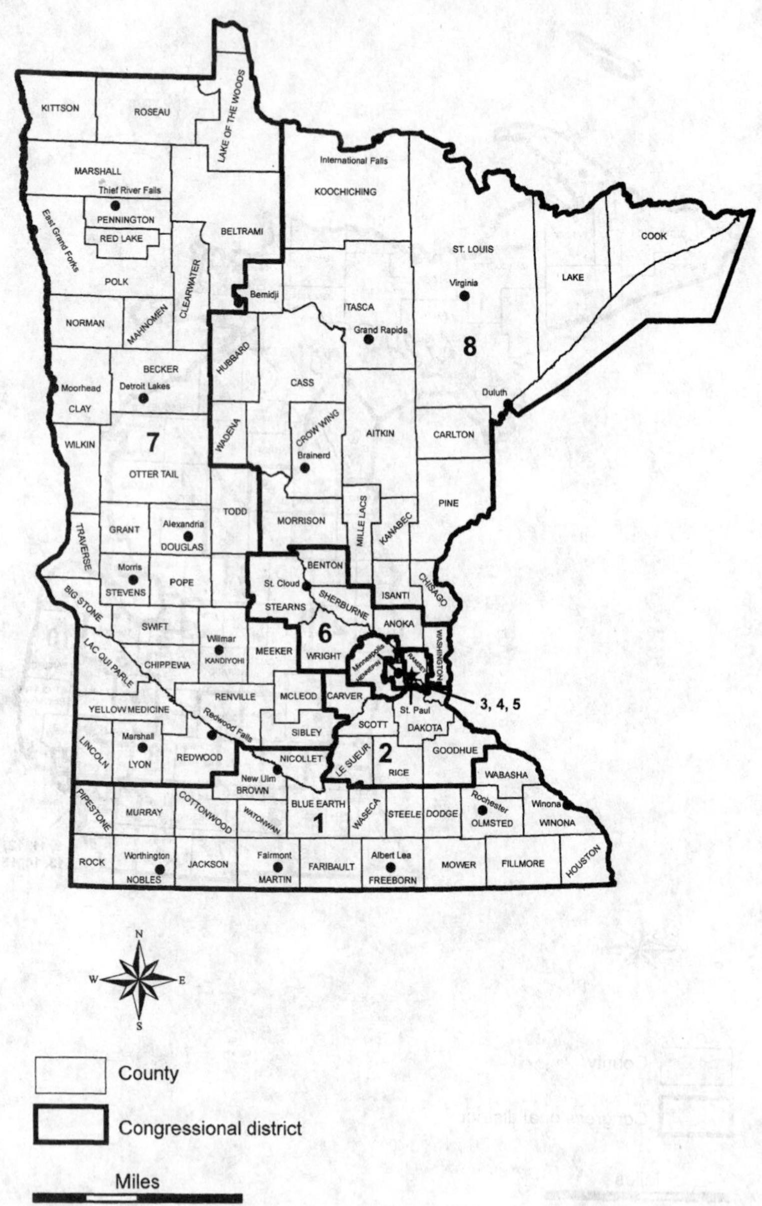

MISSISSIPPI—Congressional Districts—(4 Districts)

MISSOURI—Congressional Districts—(9 Districts)

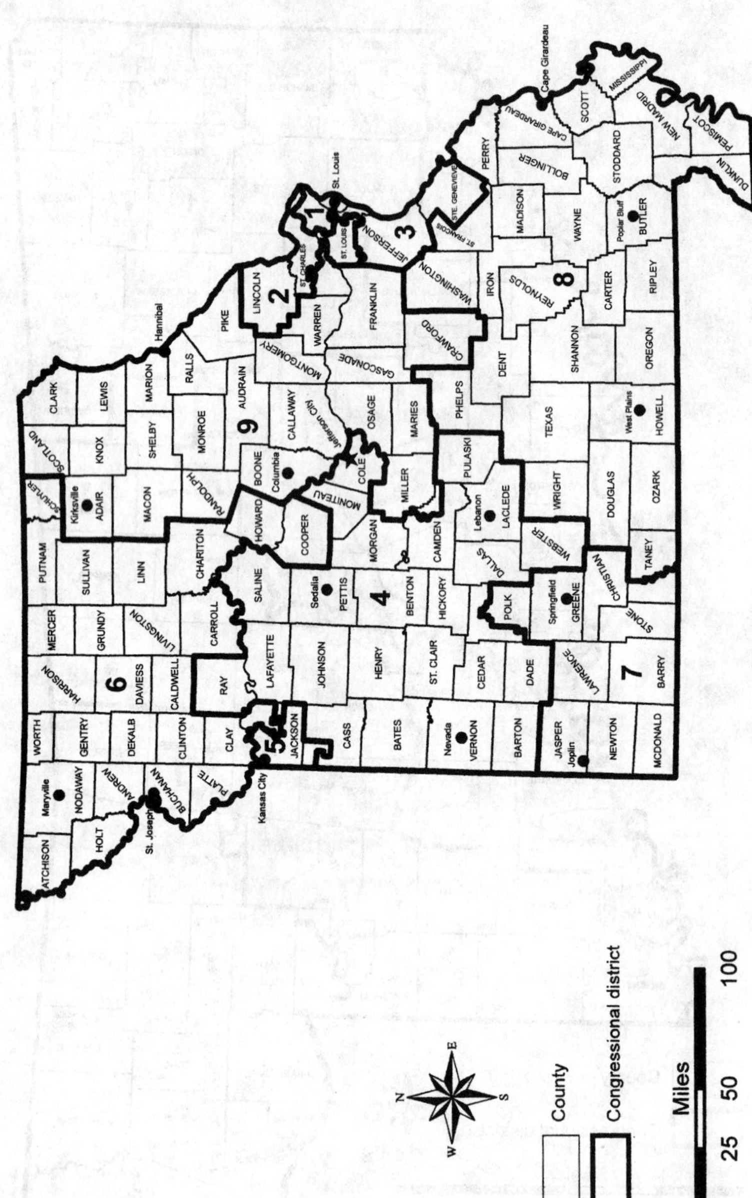

MONTANA—Congressional District—(1 District At Large)

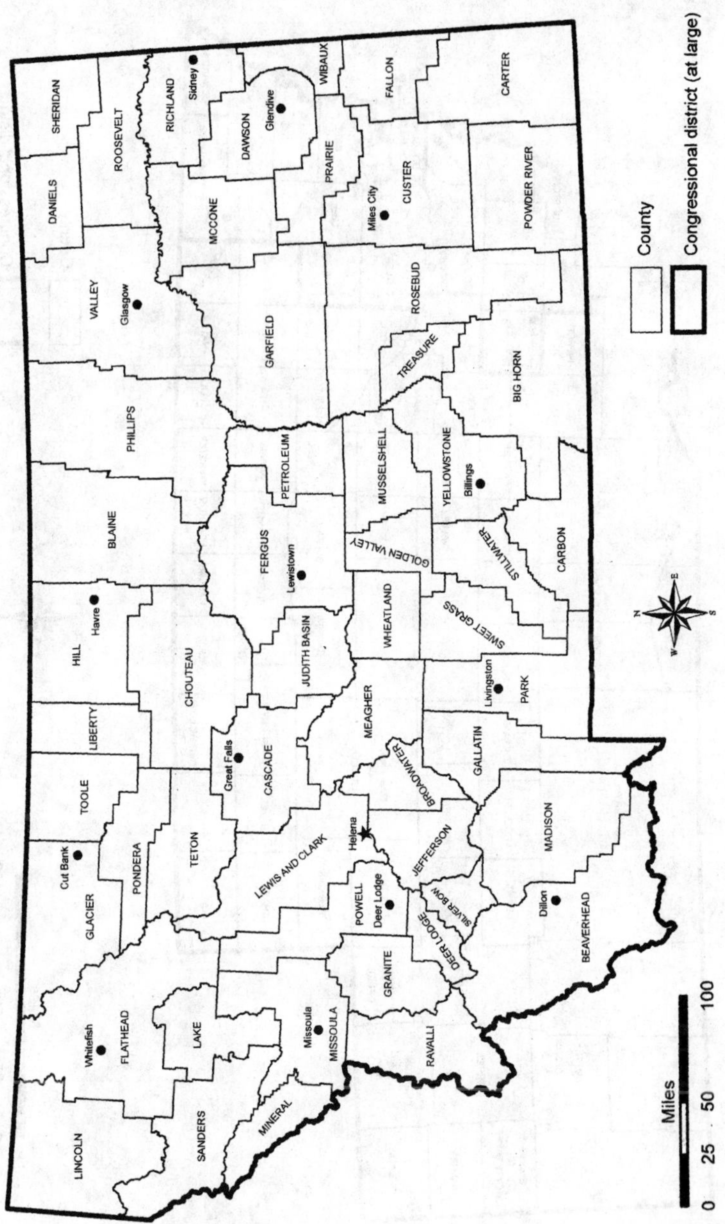

NEBRASKA—Congressional Districts—(3 Districts)

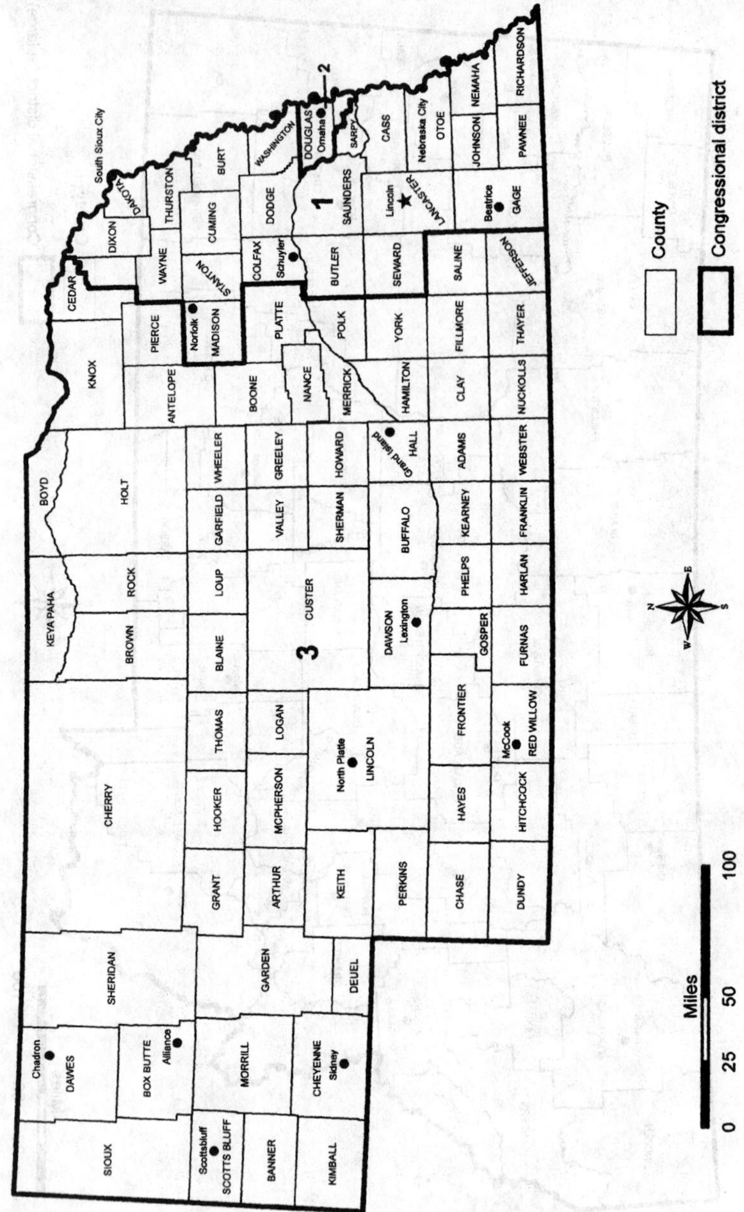

NEVADA—Congressional Districts—(3 Districts)

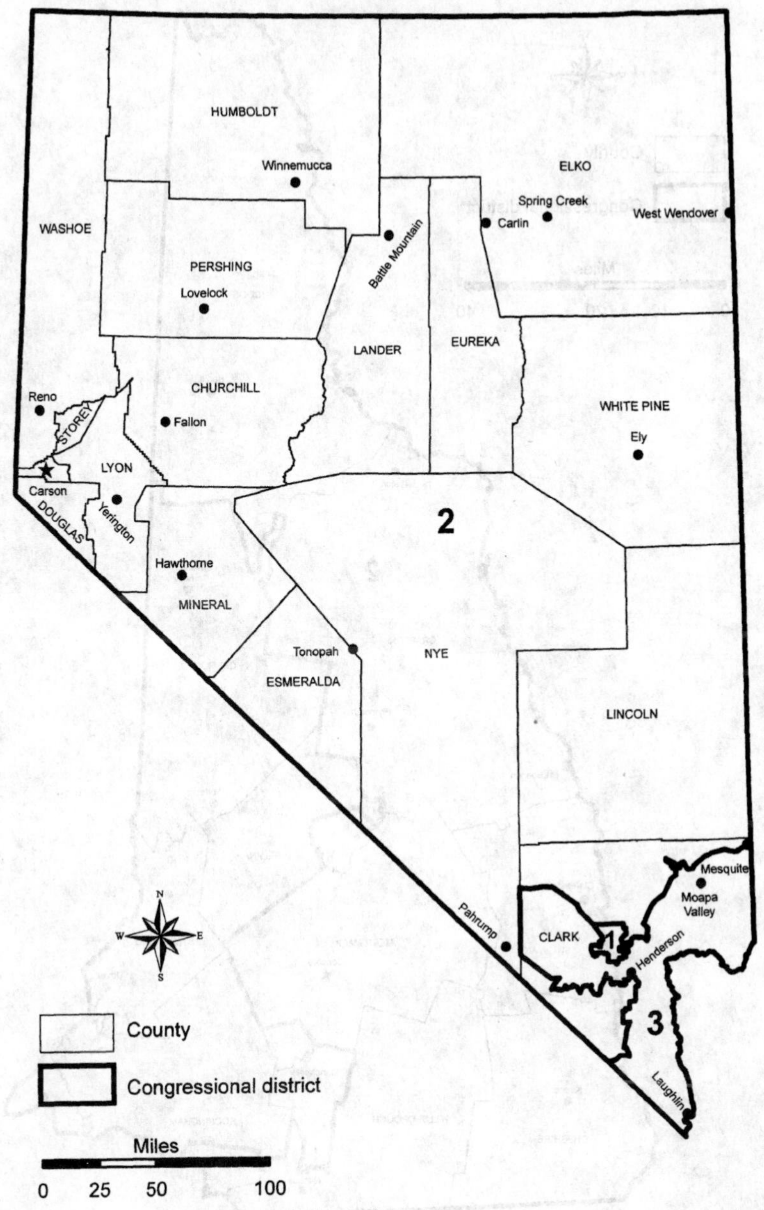

NEW HAMPSHIRE—Congressional Districts—(2 Districts)

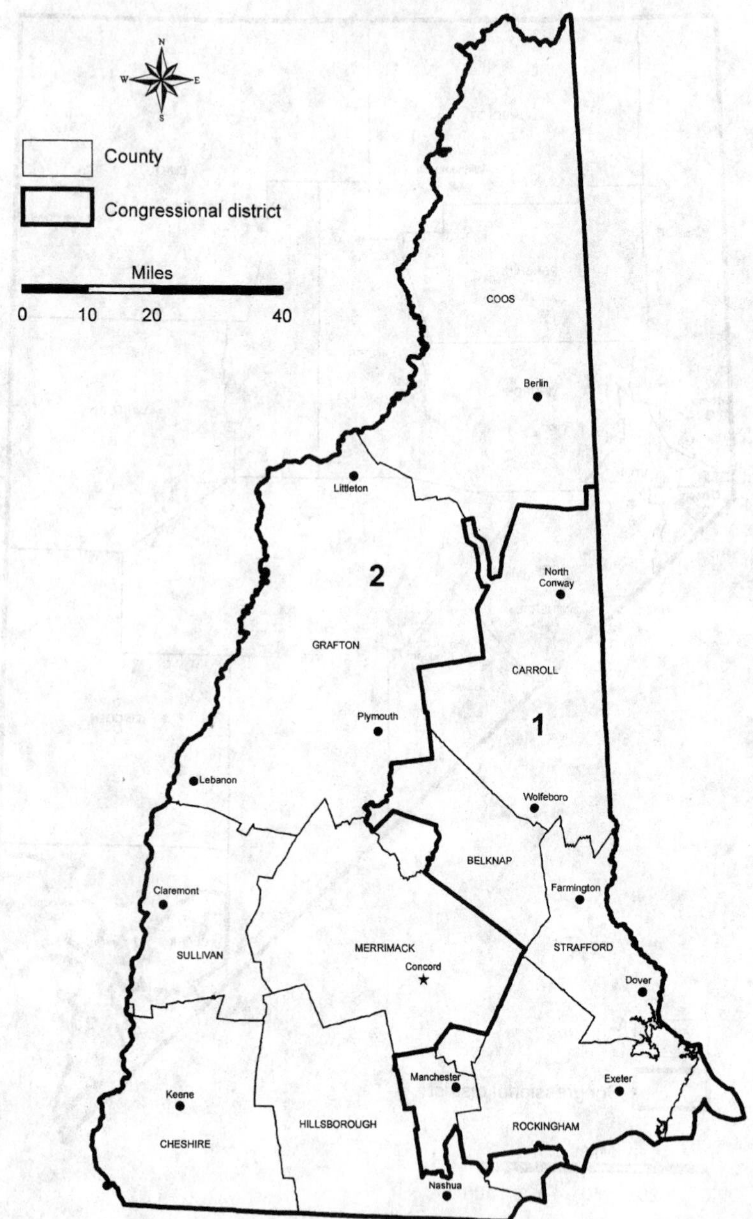

NEW JERSEY—Congressional Districts—(13 Districts)

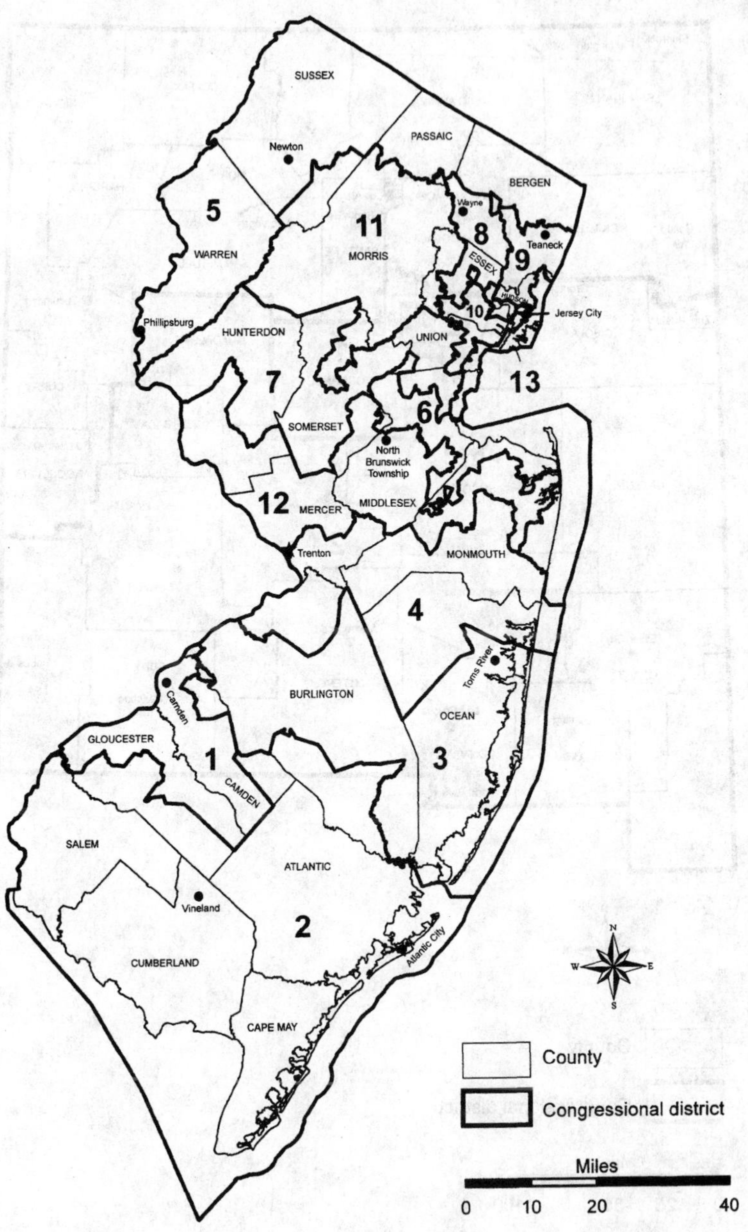

NEW MEXICO—Congressional Districts—(3 Districts)

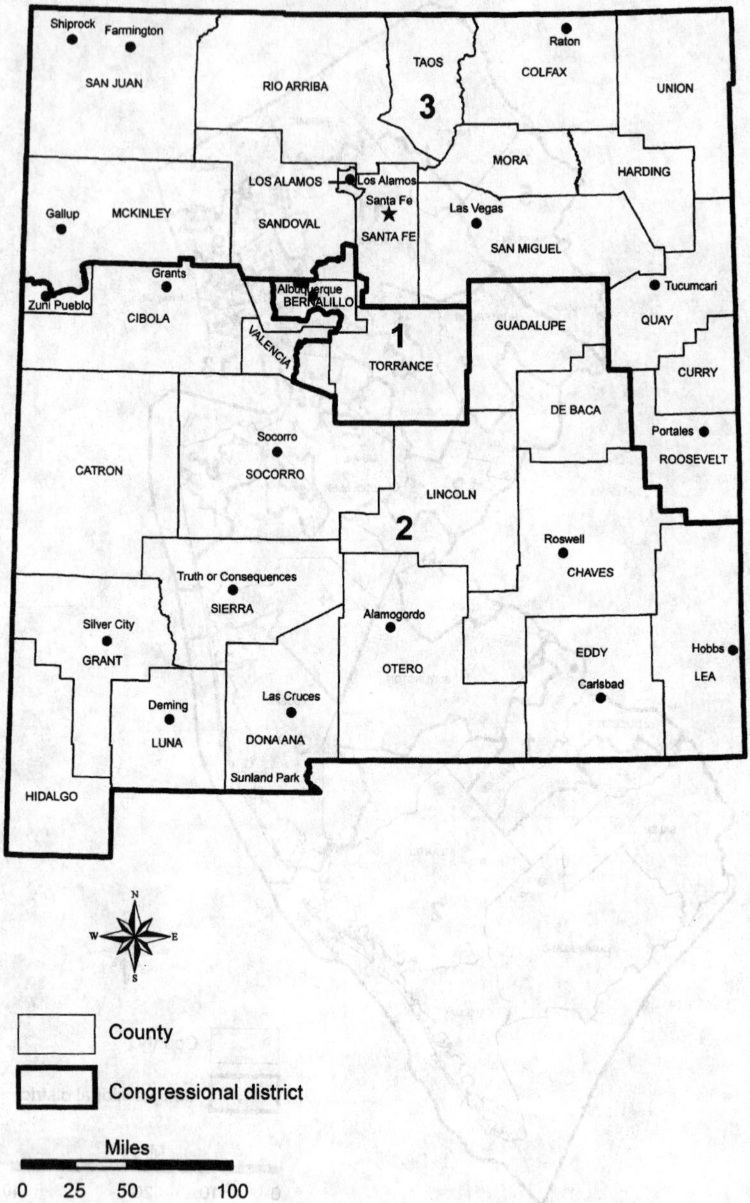

Shiprock
Farmington
SAN JUAN
RIO ARRIBA
TAOS
3
Raton
COLFAX
UNION
MORA
HARDING
LOS ALAMOS
Los Alamos
Santa Fe
SANTA FE
Gallup
MCKINLEY
SANDOVAL
Las Vegas
SAN MIGUEL
Grants
Zuni Pueblo
CIBOLA
Albuquerque
BERNALILLO
VALENCIA
1
TORRANCE
GUADALUPE
Tucumcari
QUAY
CURRY
DE BACA
Portales
ROOSEVELT
CATRON
Socorro
SOCORRO
LINCOLN
2
Roswell
CHAVES
Truth or Consequences
SIERRA
Silver City
GRANT
Alamogordo
OTERO
EDDY
Carlsbad
Hobbs
LEA
Deming
LUNA
Las Cruces
DONA ANA
Sunland Park
HIDALGO
N
W
E
S
County
Congressional district
Miles
0
25
50
100

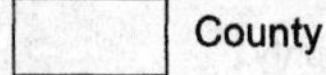

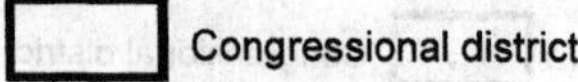

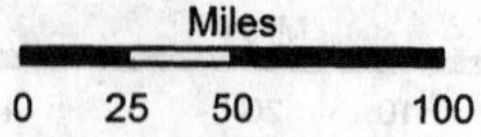

NEW YORK—Congressional Districts—(29 Districts)

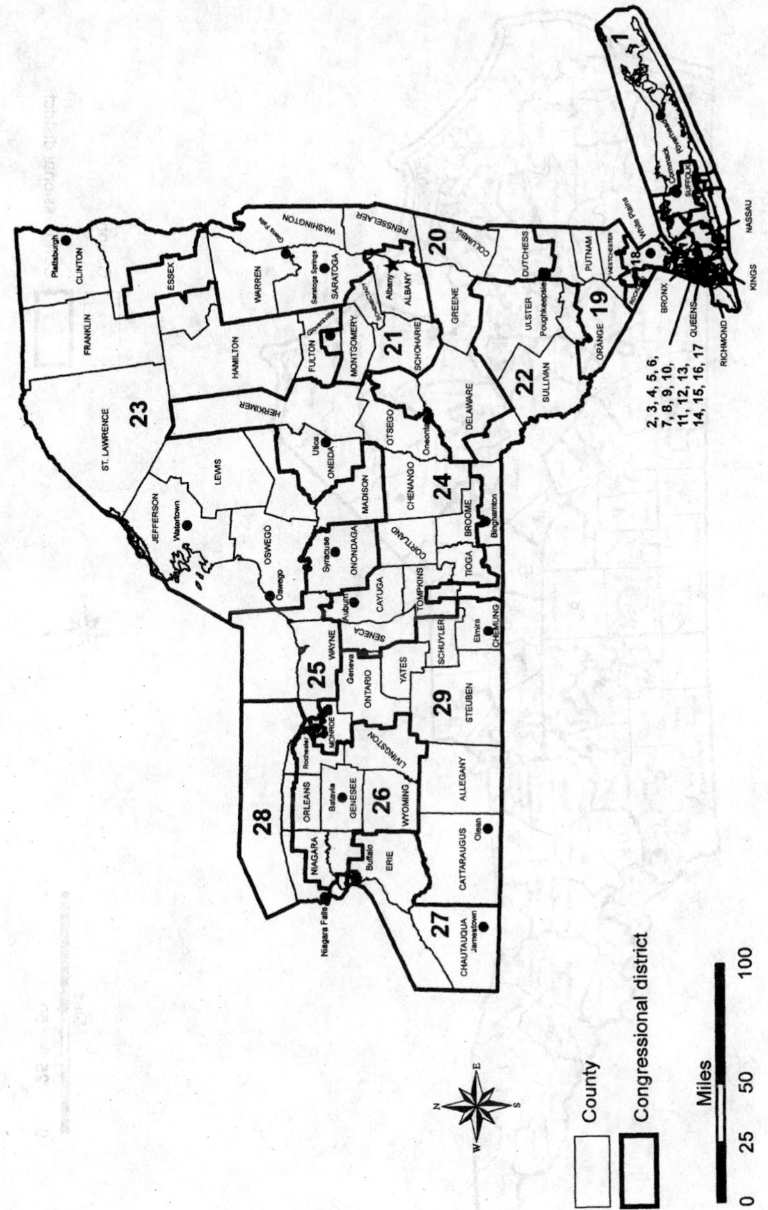

NORTH CAROLINA—Congressional Districts—(13 Districts)

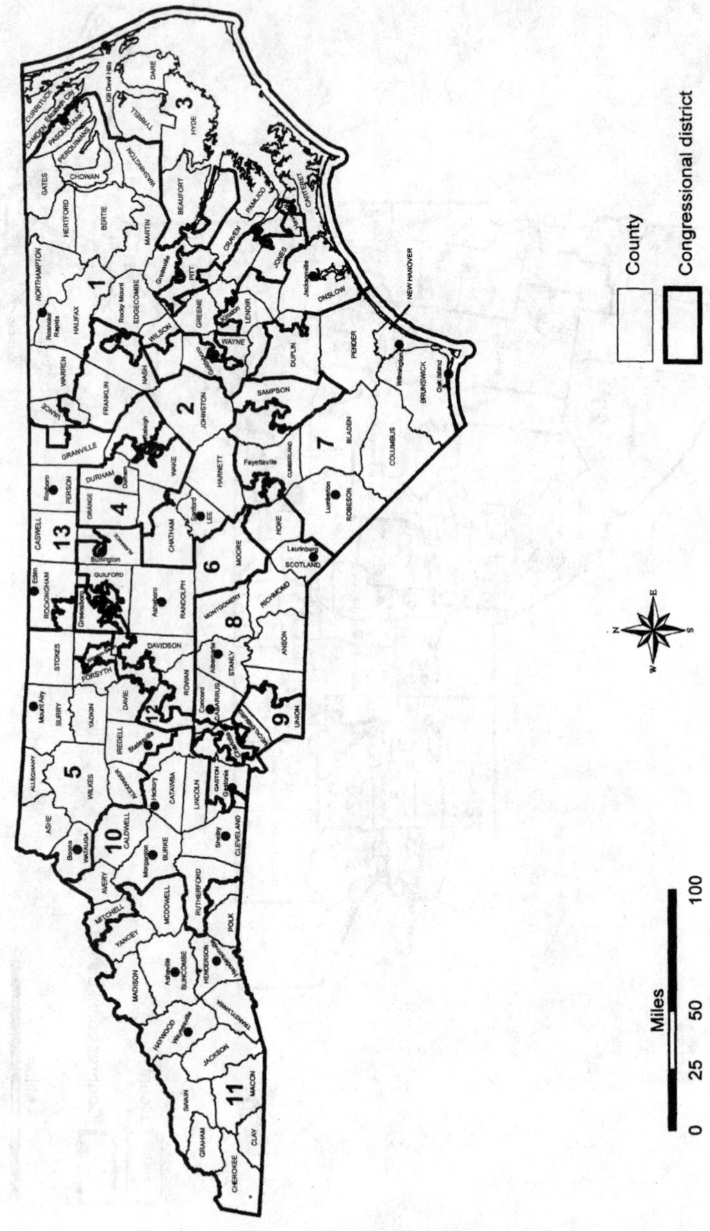

NORTH DAKOTA—Congressional District—(1 District At Large)

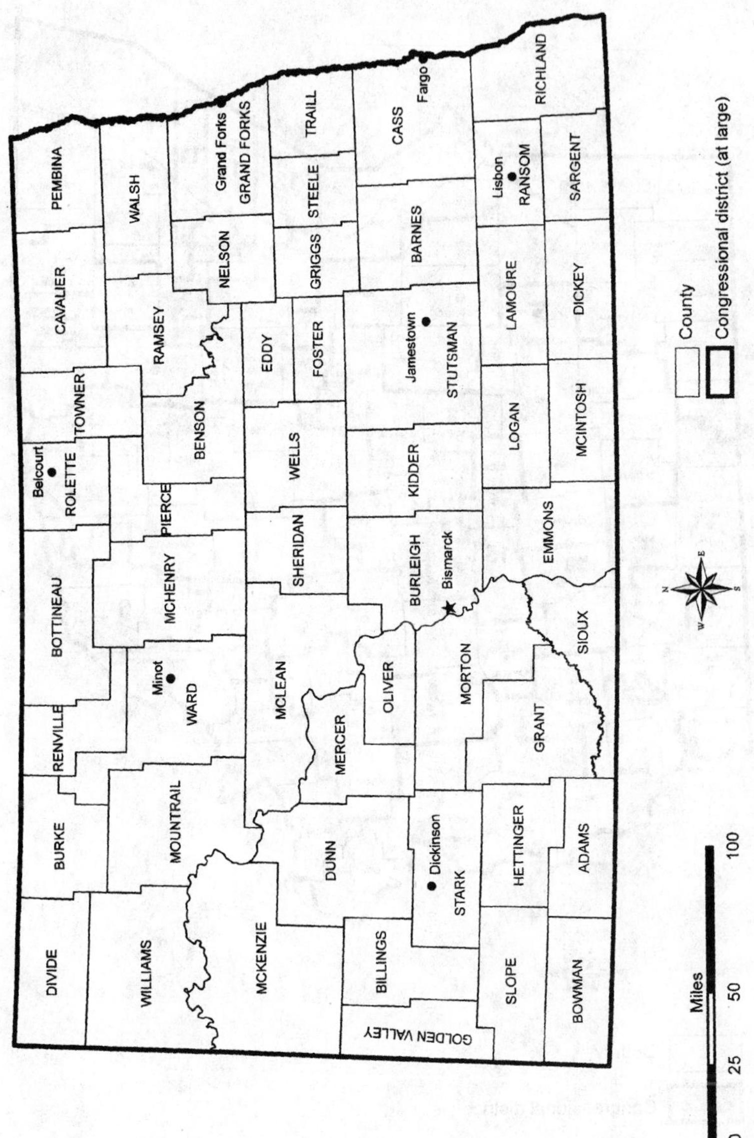

OHIO—Congressional Districts—(18 Districts)

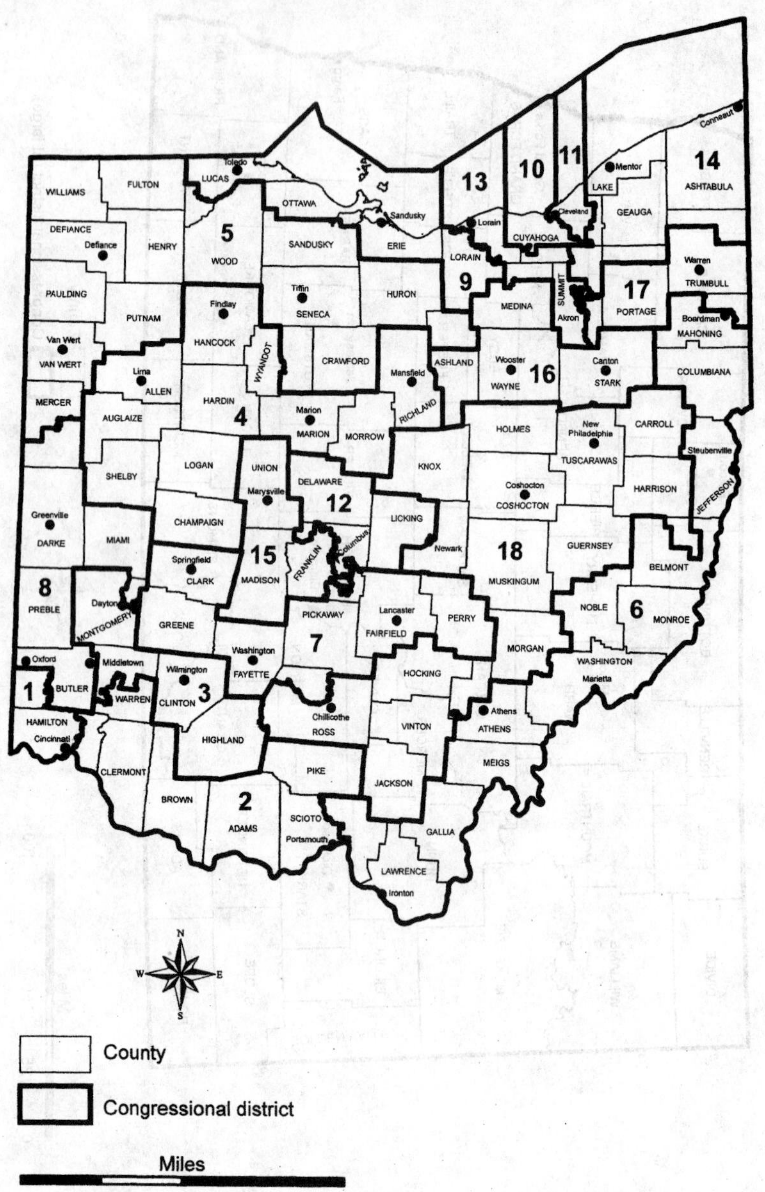

OKLAHOMA—Congressional Districts—(5 Districts)

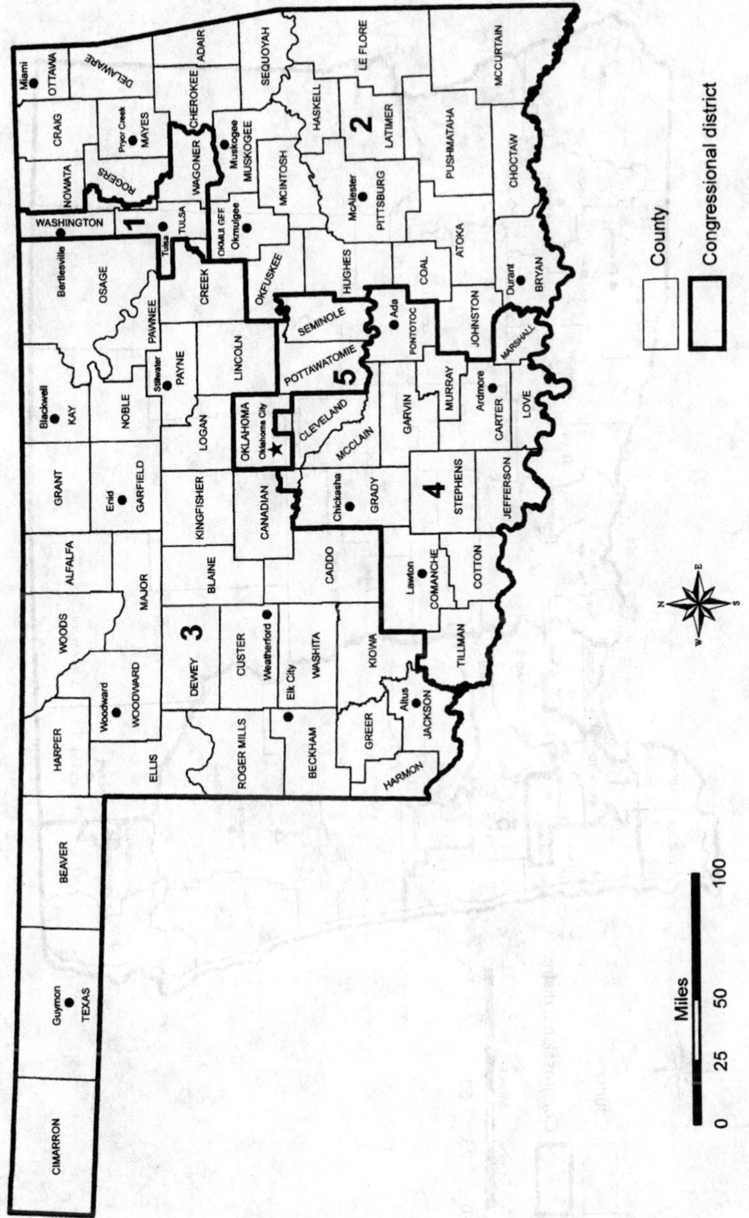

OREGON—Congressional Districts—(5 Districts)

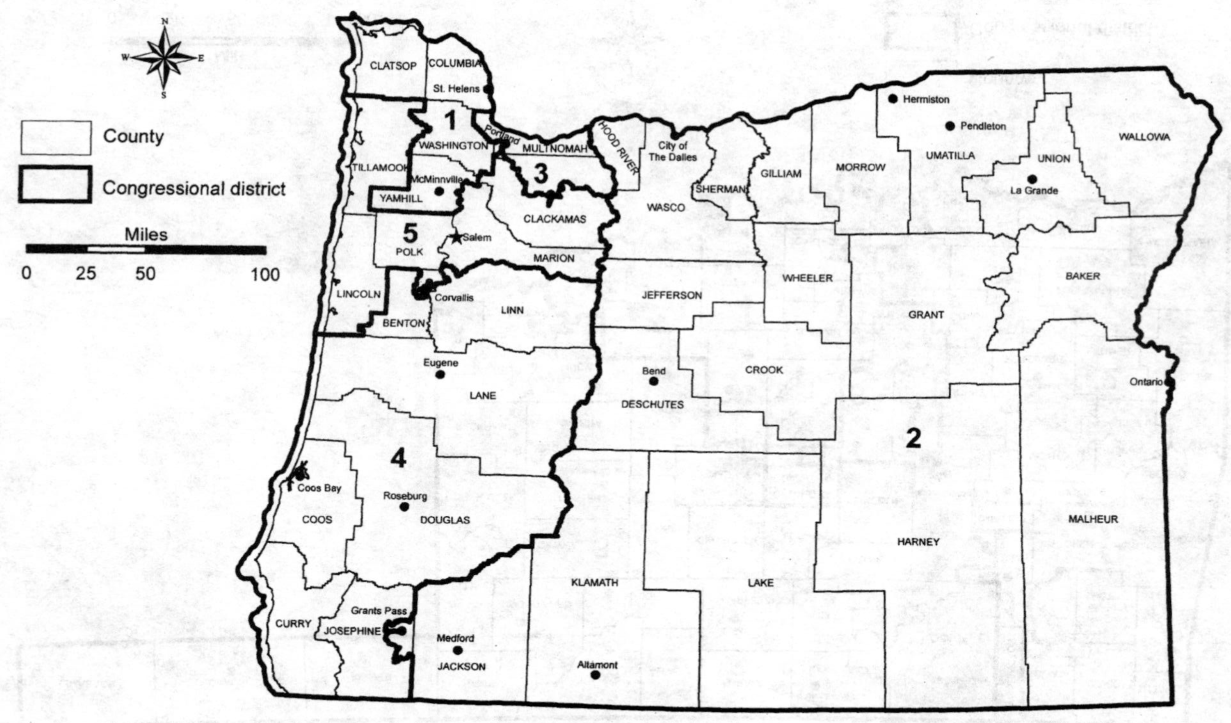

PENNSYLVANIA—Congressional Districts—(19 Districts)

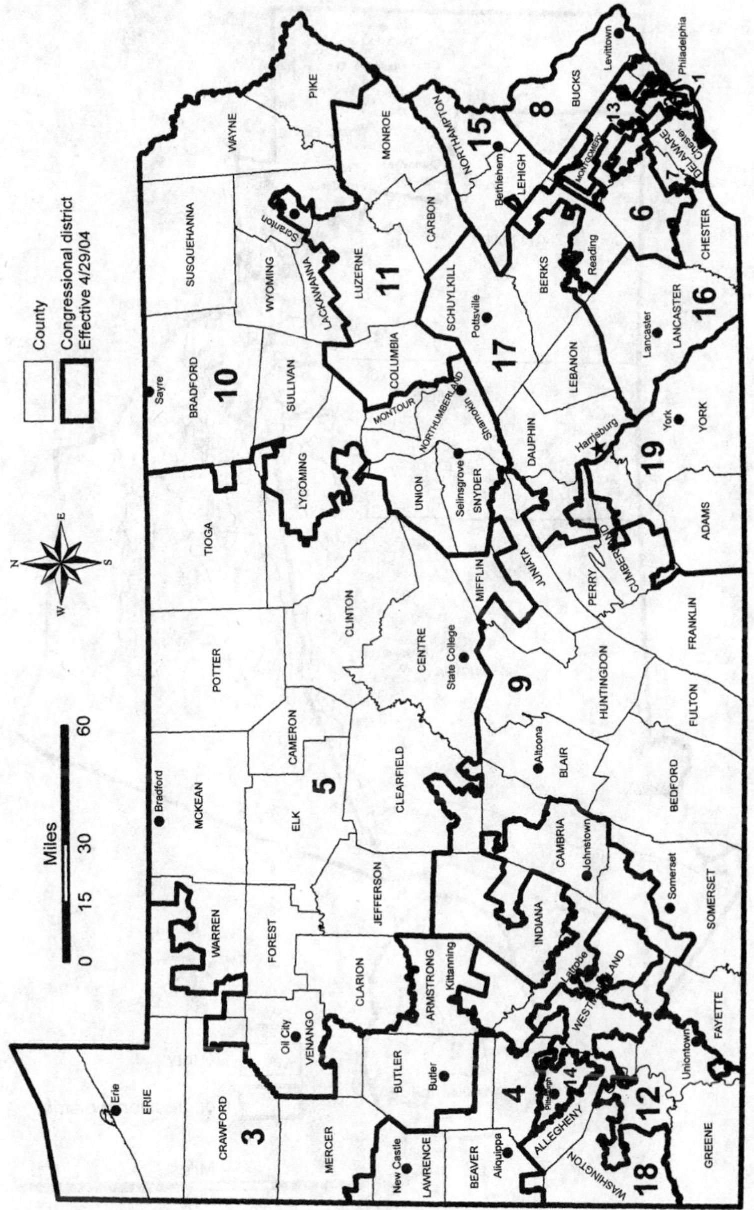

RHODE ISLAND—Congressional Districts—(2 Districts)

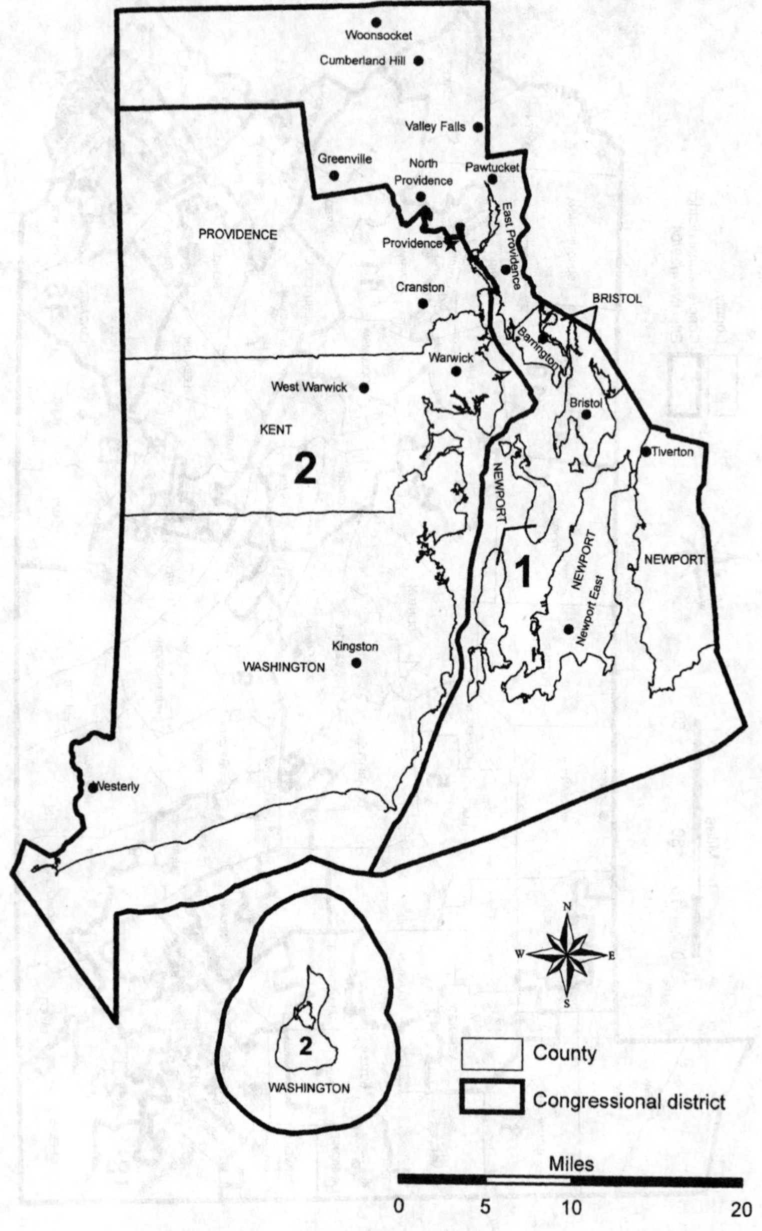

SOUTH CAROLINA—Congressional Districts—(6 Districts)

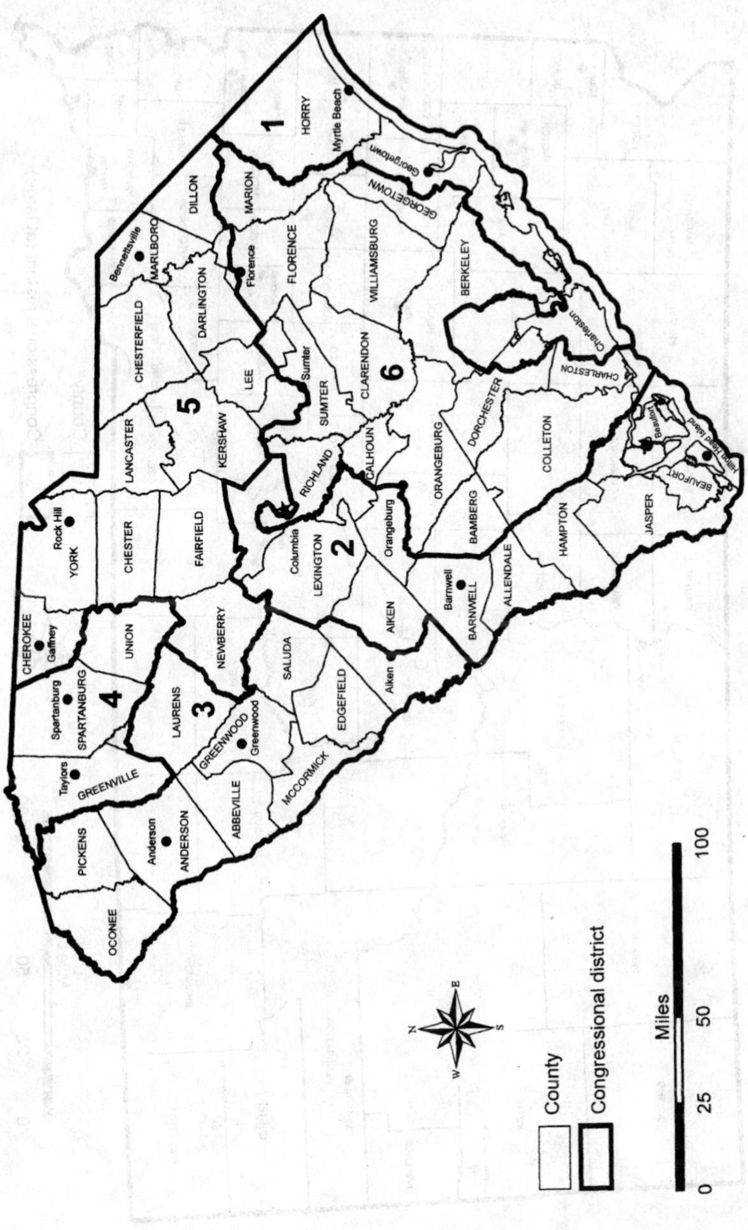

SOUTH DAKOTA—Congressional District—(1 District At Large)

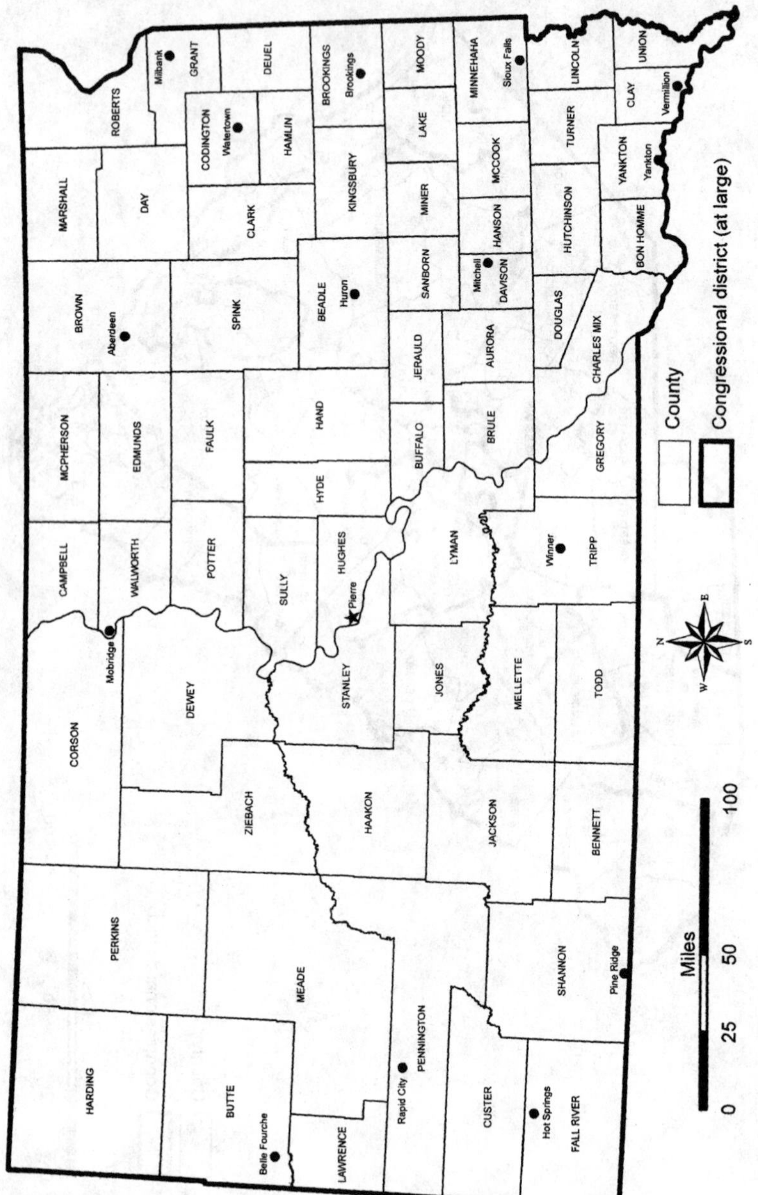

TENNESSEE—Congressional Districts—(9 Districts)

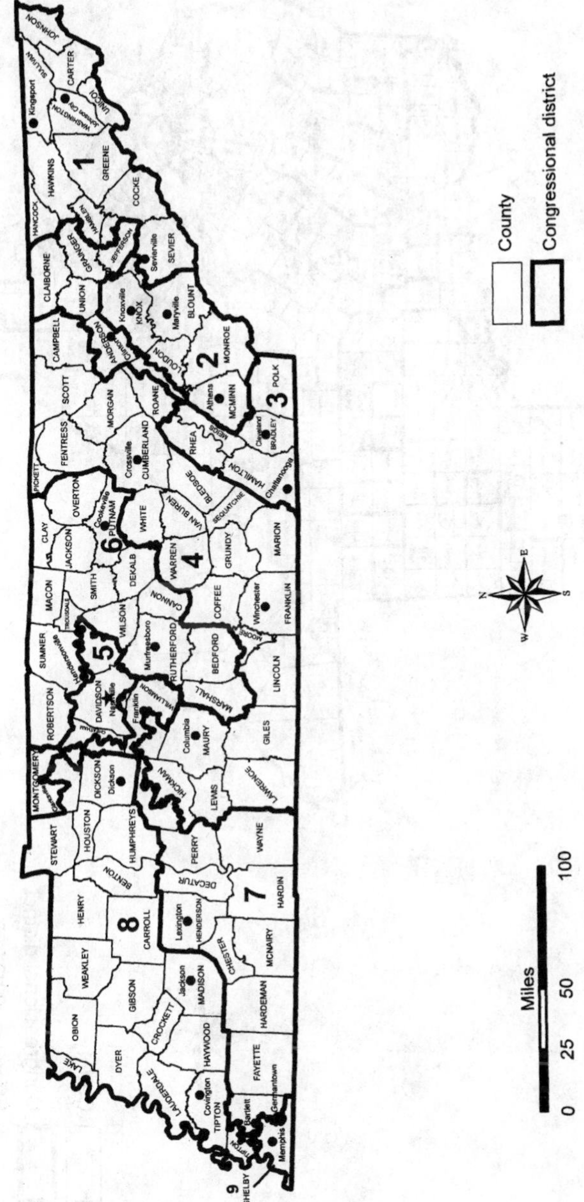

TEXAS—Congressional Districts—(32 Districts)

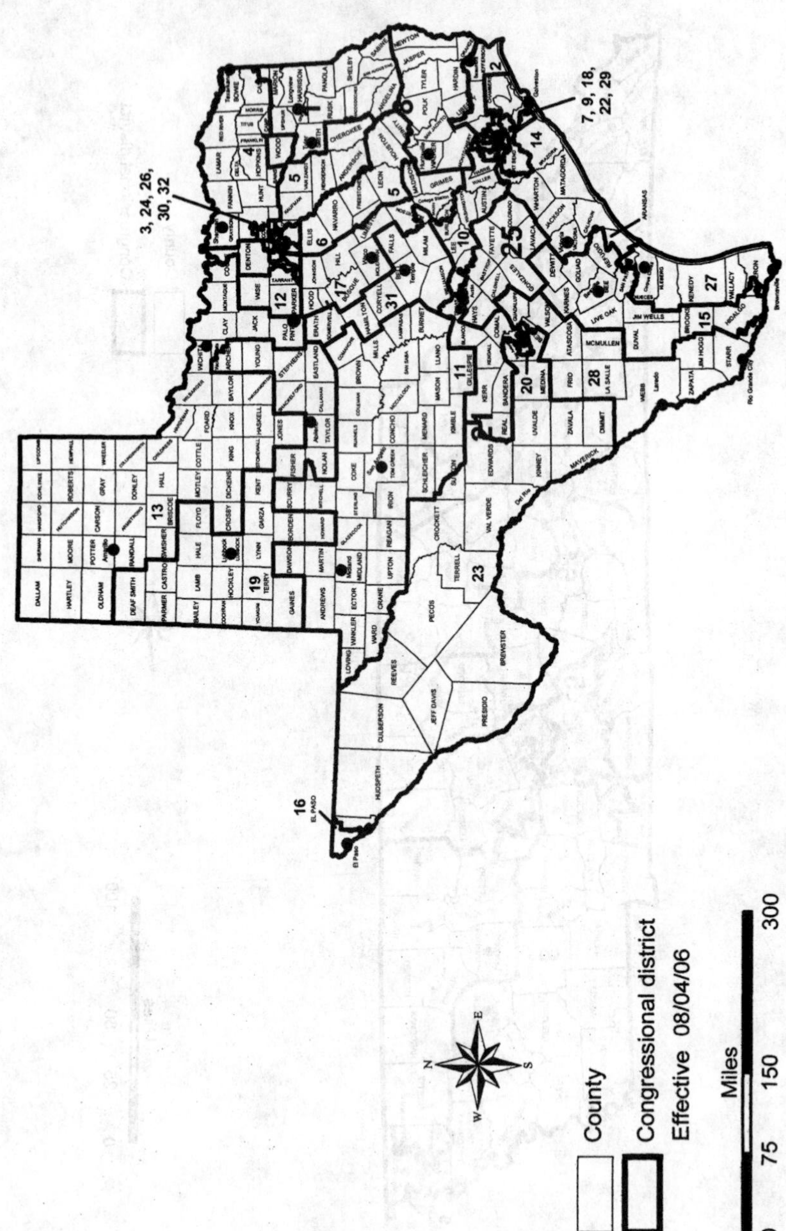

UTAH—Congressional Districts—(3 Districts)

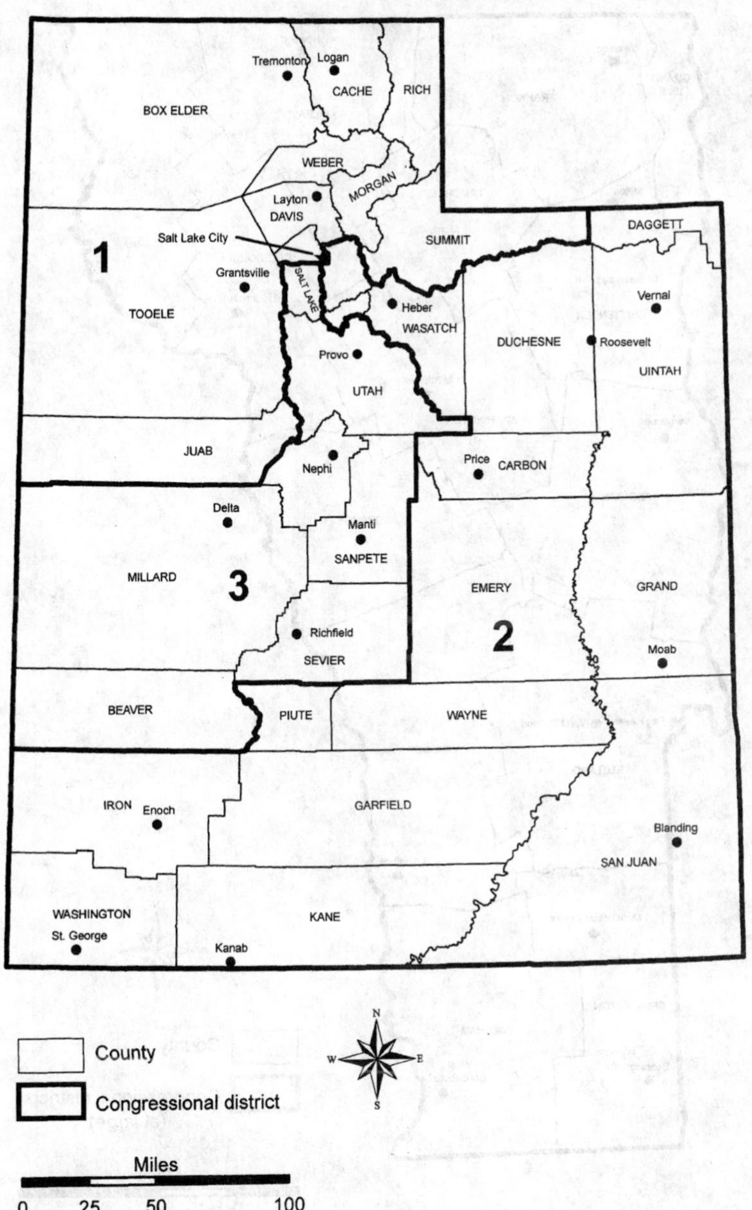

VERMONT—Congressional District—(1 District At Large)

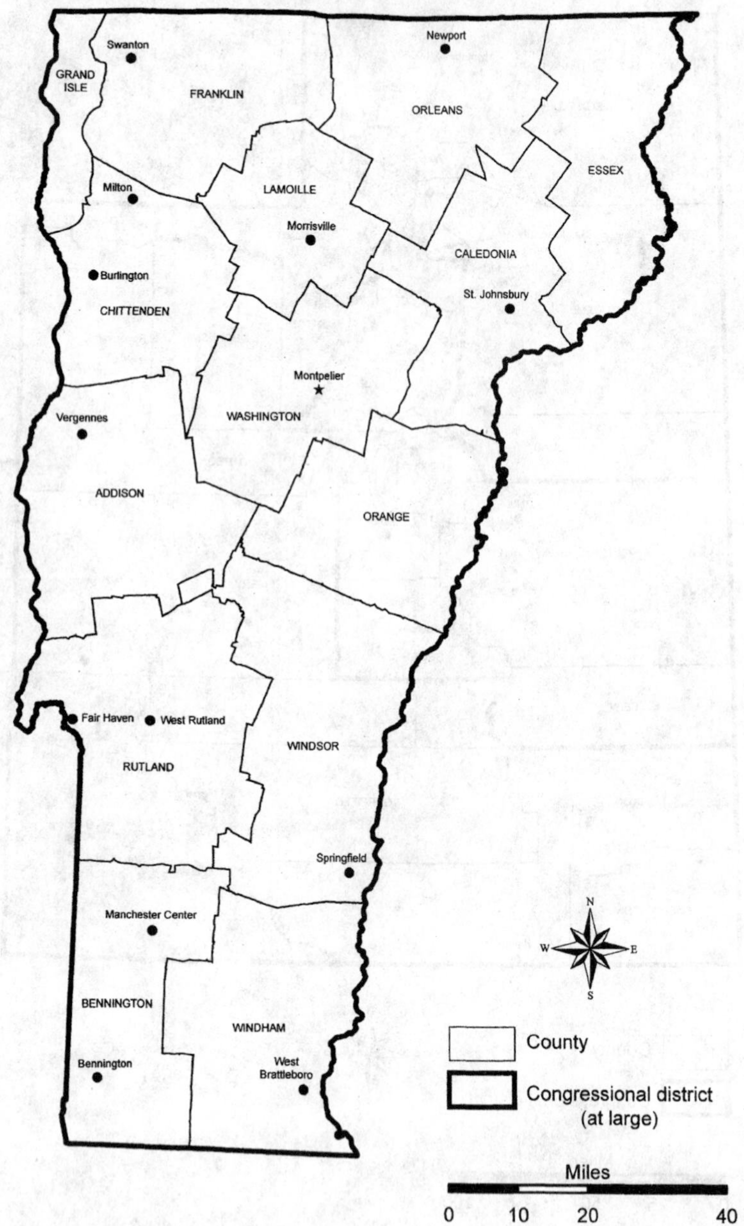

VIRGINIA—Congressional Districts—(11 Districts)

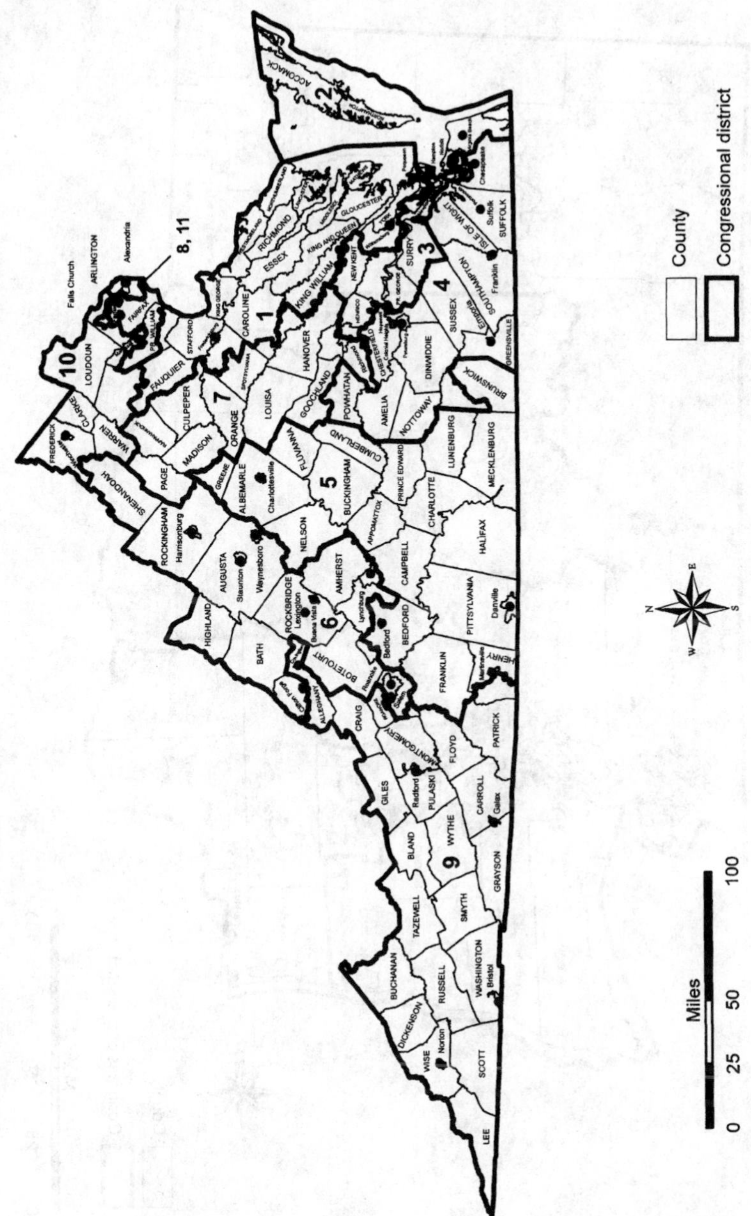

WASHINGTON—Congressional Districts—(9 Districts)

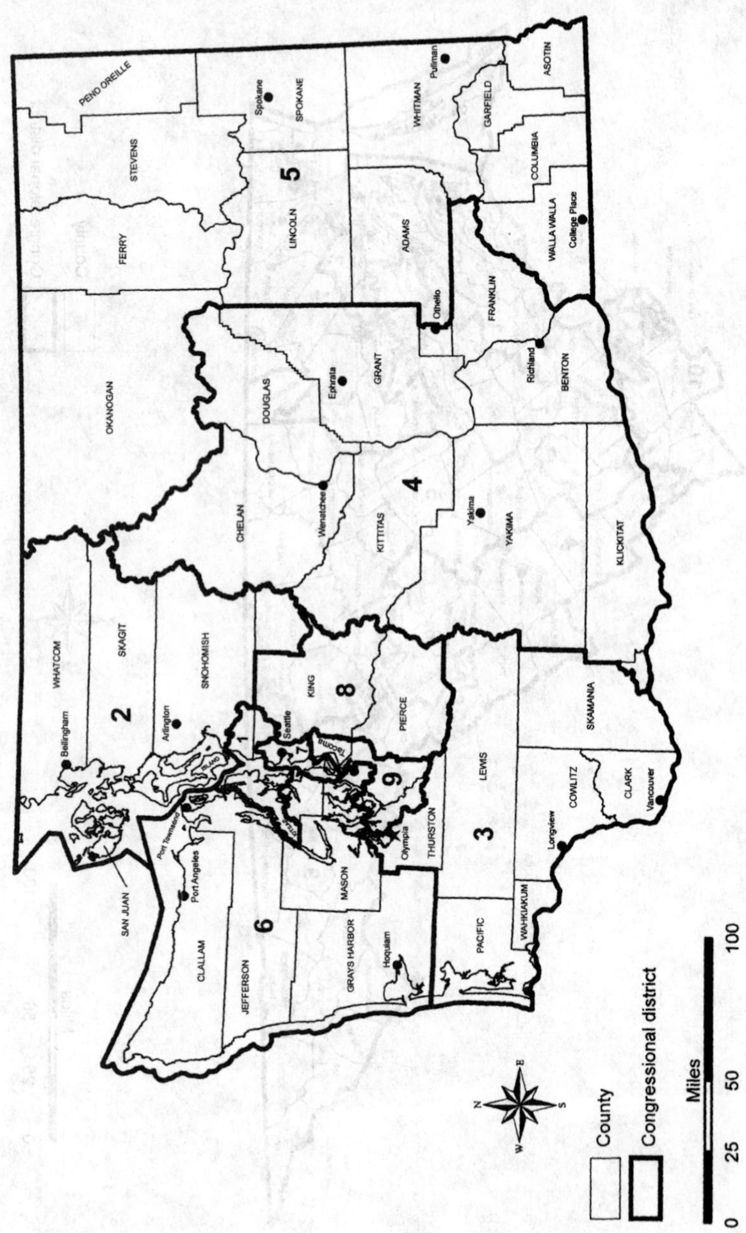

WEST VIRGINIA—Congressional Districts—(3 Districts)

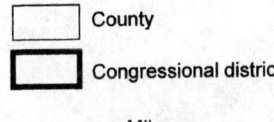

County

Congressional district

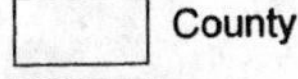

WISCONSIN—Congressional Districts—(8 Districts)

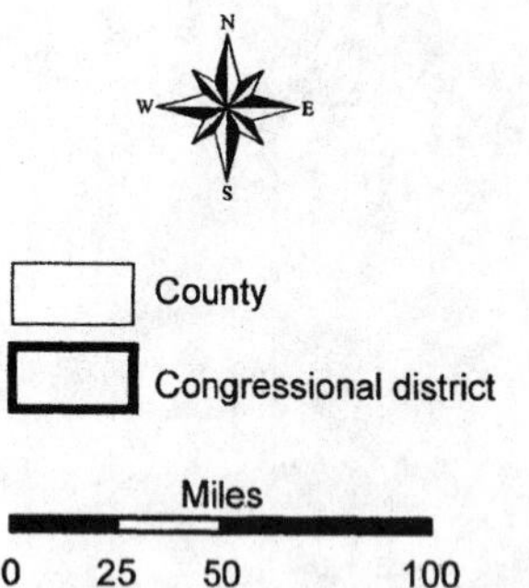

WYOMING—Congressional District—(1 District At Large)

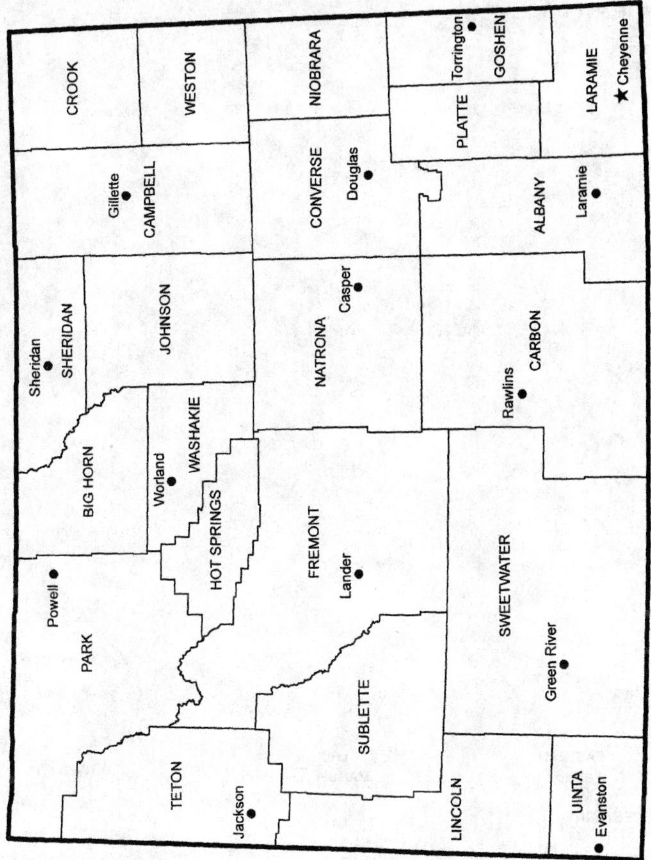

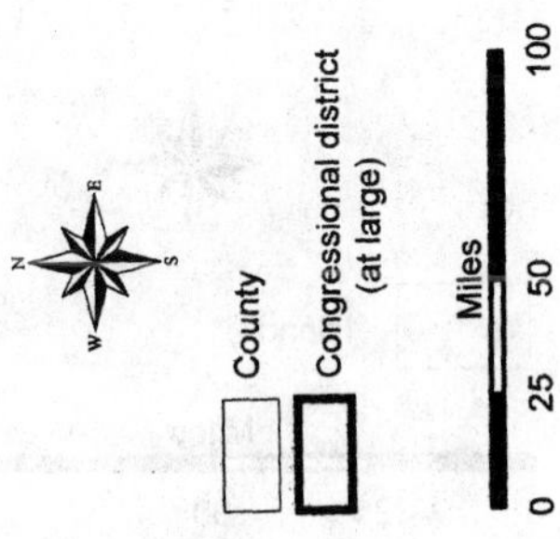

AMERICAN SAMOA—(1 Delegate At Large)

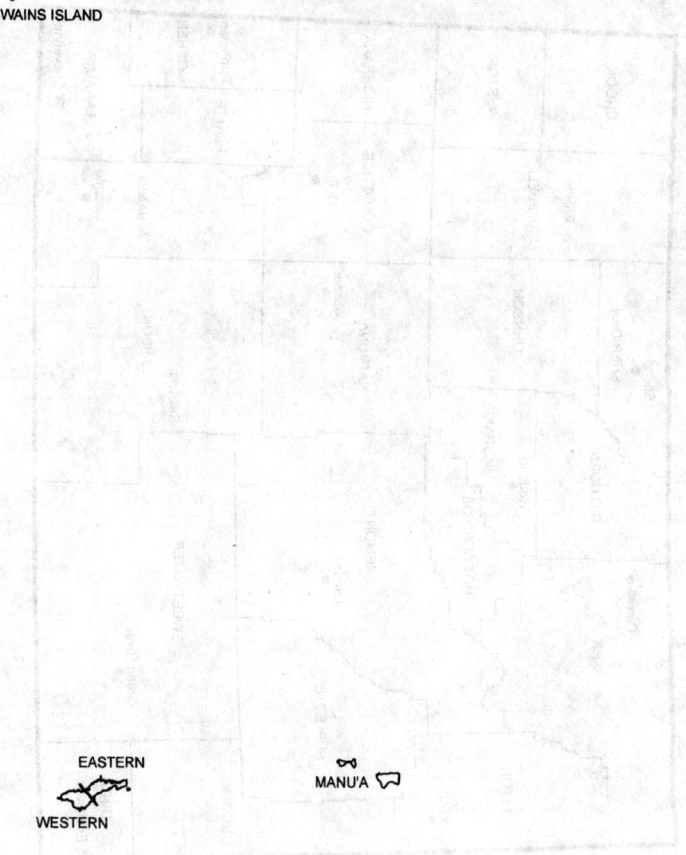

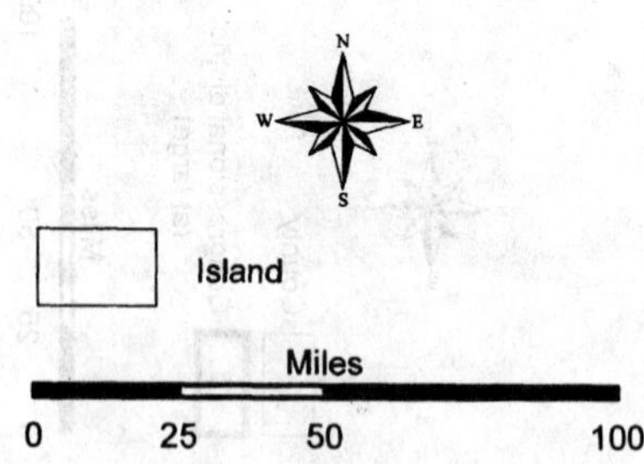

DISTRICT OF COLUMBIA—(1 Delegate At Large)

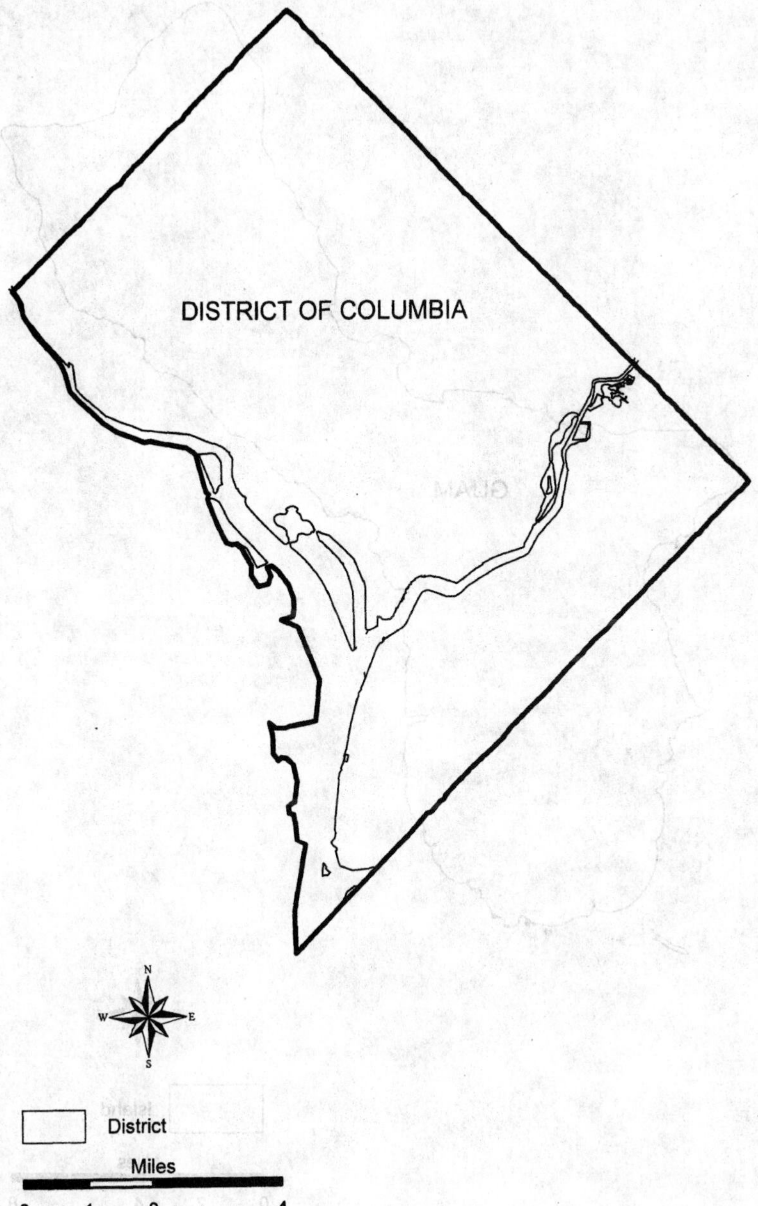

GUAM—(1 Delegate At Large)

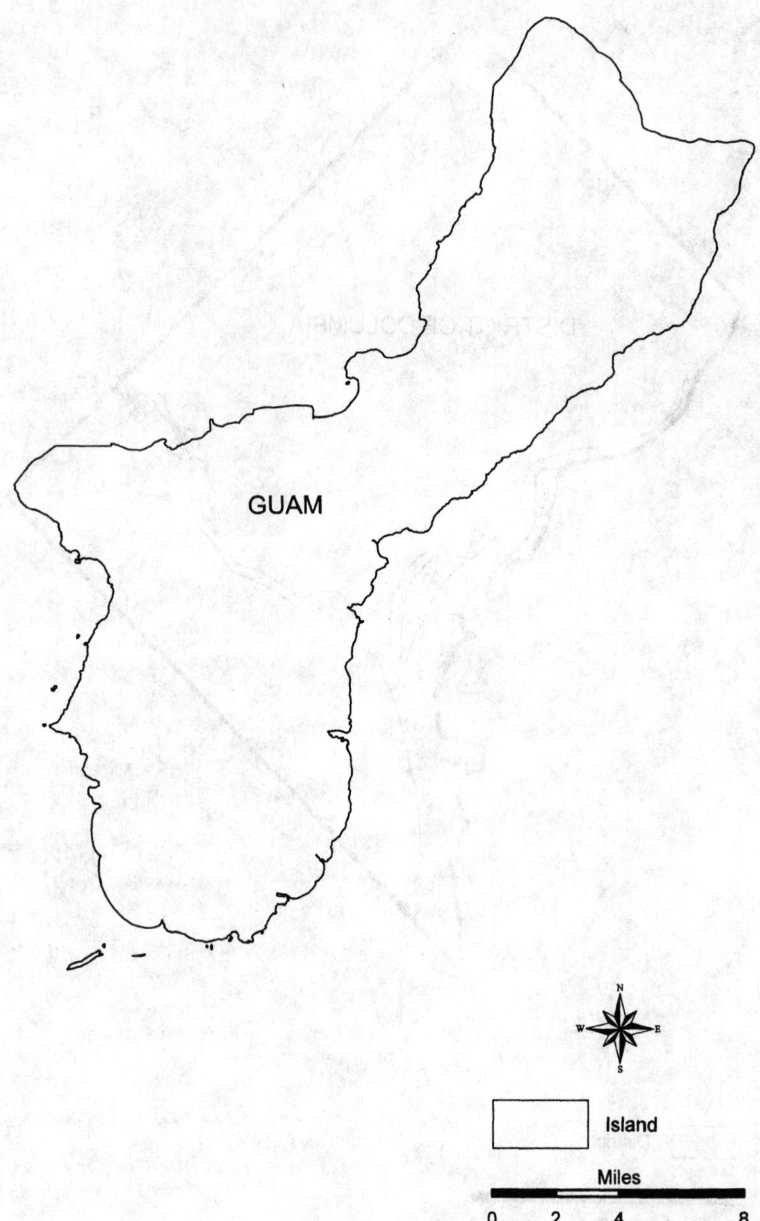

PUERTO RICO—(1 Resident Commissioner At Large)

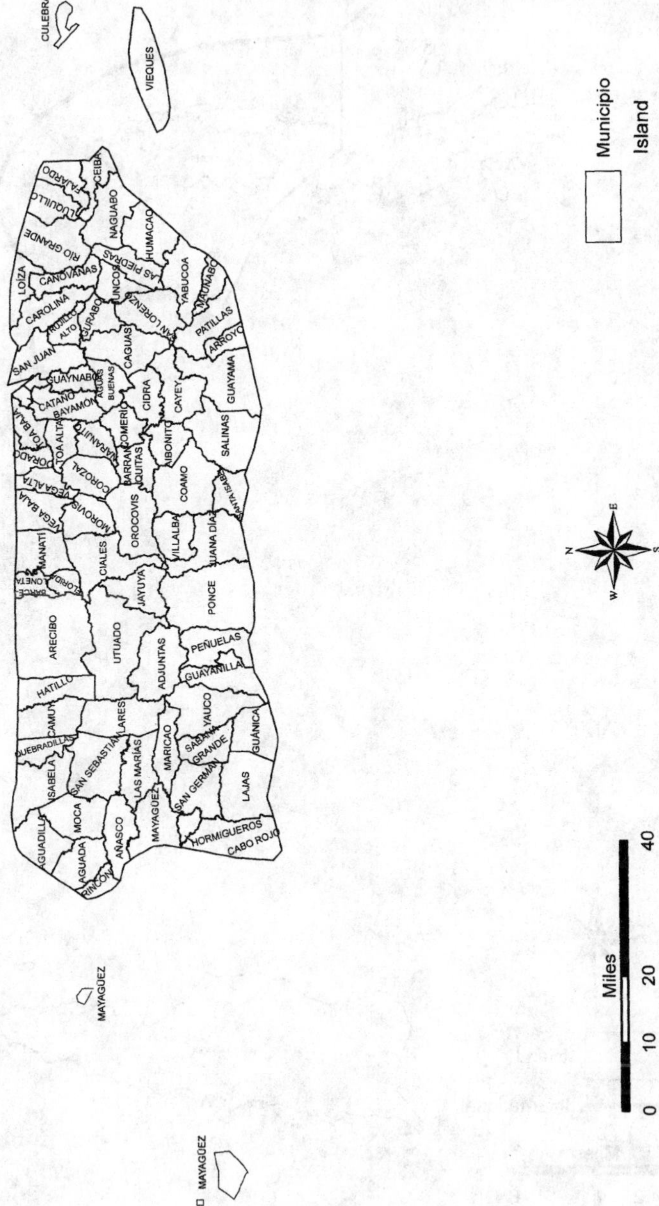

THE VIRGIN ISLANDS OF THE UNITED STATES—(1 Delegate At Large)

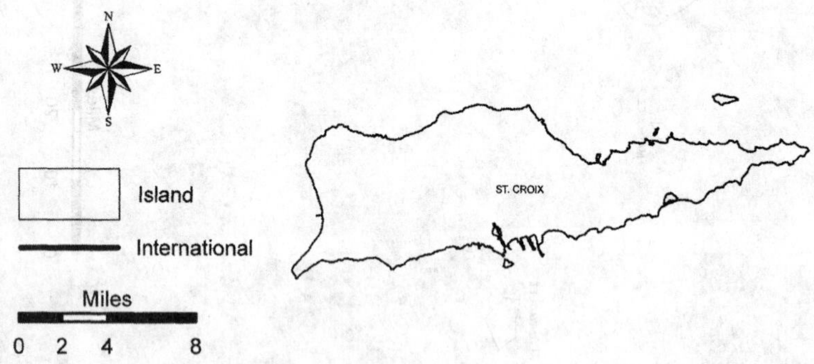

NAME INDEX

H